SYSTEMATIC THEOLOGY

SYSTEMATIC THEOLOGY

A Compendium

DESIGNED FOR THE USE OF THEOLOGICAL STUDENTS

BY

AUGUSTUS HOPKINS STRONG, D. D., LL D.

PRESIDENT AND PROFESSOR OF BIBLICAL THEOLOGY IN THE
ROCHESTER THEOLOGICAL SEMINARY
AUTHOR OF "THE GREAT POETS AND THEIR THEOLOGY"
"CHRIST IN CREATION," "PHILOSOPHY AND RELIGION"
"MISCELLANIES," VOLS. I AND II, ETC.

THREE VOLUMES IN ONE

FLEMING H. REVELL COMPANY
OLD TAPPAN, NEW JERSEY

Thirty-second Printing, 1979

International Standard Book No. 0-8170-0177-8

Printed in U.S.A.

Christo Deo Salvatori.

"THE EYE SEES ONLY THAT WHICH IT BRINGS WITH IT THE POWER OF SEEING."—*Cicero.*

"OPEN THOU MINE EYES, THAT I MAY BEHOLD WONDROUS THINGS OUT OF THY LAW."—*Psalm 119 : 18.*

"FOR WITH THEE IS THE FOUNTAIN OF LIFE : IN THY LIGHT SHALL WE SEE LIGHT."—*Psalm 36 : 9.*

"FOR WE KNOW IN PART, AND WE PROPHESY IN PART; BUT WHEN THAT WHICH IS PERFECT IS COME, THAT WHICH IS IN PART SHALL BE DONE AWAY."—*1 Cor. 13 : 9, 10.*

PREFACE

The present work is a revision and enlargement of my "Systematic Theology," first published in 1886. Of the original work there have been printed seven editions, each edition embodying successive corrections and supposed improvements. During the twenty years which have intervened since its first publication I have accumulated much new material, which I now offer to the reader. My philosophical and critical point of view meantime has also somewhat changed. While I still hold to the old doctrines, I interpret them differently and expound them more clearly, because I seem to myself to have reached a fundamental truth which throws new light upon them all. This truth I have tried to set forth in my book entitled "Christ in Creation," and to that book I refer the reader for further information.

That Christ is the one and only Revealer of God, in nature, in humanity, in history, in science, in Scripture, is in my judgment the key to theology. This view implies a monistic and idealistic conception of the world, together with an evolutionary idea as to its origin and progress. But it is the very antidote to pantheism, in that it recognizes evolution as only the method of the transcendent and personal Christ, who fills all in all, and who makes the universe teleological and moral from its centre to its circumference and from its beginning until now.

Neither evolution nor the higher criticism has any terrors to one who regards them as parts of Christ's creating and educating process. The Christ in whom are hid all the treasures of wisdom and knowledge himself furnishes all the needed safeguards and limitations. It is only because Christ has been forgotten that nature and

law have been personified, that history has been regarded as unpurposed development, that Judaism has been referred to a merely
human origin, that Paul has been thought to have switched the
church off from its proper track even before it had gotten fairly
started on its course, that superstition and illusion have come to
seem the only foundation for the sacrifices of the martyrs and the
triumphs of modern missions. I believe in no such irrational and
atheistic evolution as this. I believe rather in him in whom all
things consist, who is with his people even to the end of the world,
and who has promised to lead them into all the truth.

Philosophy and science are good servants of Christ, but they are
poor guides when they rule out the Son of God. As I reach my
seventieth year and write these words on my birthday, I am thankful for that personal experience of union with Christ which has
enabled me to see in science and philosophy the teaching of my
Lord. But this same personal experience has made me even more
alive to Christ's teaching in Scripture, has made me recognize in
Paul and John a truth profounder than that disclosed by any
secular writers, truth with regard to sin and atonement for sin,
that satisfies the deepest wants of my nature and that is self-
evidencing and divine.

I am distressed by some common theological tendencies of our
time, because I believe them to be false to both science and
religion. How men who have ever felt themselves to be lost sinners and who have once received pardon from their crucified Lord
and Savior can thereafter seek to pare down his attributes, deny
his deity and atonement, tear from his brow the crown of miracle
and sovereignty, relegate him to the place of a merely moral teacher
who influences us only as does Socrates by words spoken across a
stretch of ages, passes my comprehension. Here is my test of
orthodoxy : Do we pray to Jesus ? Do we call upon the name of
Christ, as did Stephen and all the early church ? Is he our living

Lord, omnipresent, omniscient, omnipotent ? Is he divine only in the sense in which we are divine, or is he the only-begotten Son, God manifest in the flesh, in whom is all the fulness of the Godhead bodily ? What think ye of the Christ ? is still the critical question, and none are entitled to the name of Christian who, in the face of the evidence he has furnished us, cannot answer the question aright.

Under the influence of Ritschl and his Kantian relativism, many of our teachers and preachers have swung off into a practical denial of Christ's deity and of his atonement. We seem upon the verge of a second Unitarian defection, that will break up churches and compel secessions, in a worse manner than did that of Channing and Ware a century ago. American Christianity recovered from that disaster only by vigorously asserting the authority of Christ and the inspiration of the Scriptures. We need a new vision of the Savior like that which Paul saw on the way to Damascus and John saw on the isle of Patmos, to convince us that Jesus is lifted above space and time, that his existence antedated creation, that he conducted the march of Hebrew history, that he was born of a virgin, suffered on the cross, rose from the dead, and now lives forevermore, the Lord of the universe, the only God with whom we have to do, our Savior here and our Judge hereafter. Without a revival of this faith our churches will become secularized, mission enterprise will die out, and the candlestick will be removed out of its place as it was with the seven churches of Asia, and as it has been with the apostate churches of New England.

I print this revised and enlarged edition of my " Systematic Theology," in the hope that its publication may do something to stem this fast advancing tide, and to confirm the faith of God's elect. I make no doubt that the vast majority of Christians still hold the faith that was once for all delivered to the saints, and that they will sooner or later separate themselves from those who deny the Lord who bought them. When the enemy comes in like a flood, the Spirit of the Lord will raise up a standard against him. I would do my part in raising up such a standard. I would lead others to avow anew, as I do now, in spite of the supercilious assumptions of modern infidelity, my firm belief, only confirmed by the experience and reflection of a half-century, in the old doctrines of holiness as the fundamental attribute of God, of an original transgression and sin of the whole human race, in a divine preparation in Hebrew history for man's redemption, in the deity, preëxistence, virgin birth, vicarious atonement and bodily resurrection of Jesus Christ our Lord, and in his future coming to judge the quick and the dead. I believe that these are truths of science as well as truths of revelation ; that the supernatural will yet be seen to be most truly natural ; and that not the open-minded theologian but the narrow-minded scientist will be obliged to hide his head at Christ's coming.

The present volume, in its treatment of Ethical Monism, Inspiration, the Attributes of God, and the Trinity, contains an antidote to most of the false doctrine which now threatens the safety of the church. I desire especially to call attention to the section on Perfection, and the Attributes therein involved, because I believe that the recent merging of Holiness in Love, and the practical denial that Righteousness is fundamental in God's nature, are responsible for the utilitarian views of law and the superficial views of sin which now prevail in some systems of theology. There can be no proper doctrine of the atonement and no proper doctrine of retribution, so long as Holiness is refused its preëminence. Love must have a norm or standard, and this norm or standard can be found only in Holiness. The old conviction of sin and the sense of guilt that drove the convicted sinner to the cross are inseparable from a firm belief in the self-affirming attribute of God as logically prior to and as conditioning the self-communicating attribute. The theology of our day needs a new view of the Righteous One. Such a view will make it plain that God must be reconciled before man can be saved, and that the human conscience can be pacified only upon condition that propitiation is made to the divine Righteousness. In this volume I propound what I regard as the true Doctrine of God, because upon it will be based all that follows in the volumes on the Doctrine of Man, and the Doctrine of Salvation.

The universal presence of Christ, the Light that lighteth every man, in heathen as well as in Christian lands, to direct or overrule all movements of the human mind, gives me confidence that the recent attacks upon the Christian faith will fail of their purpose. It becomes evident at last that not only the outworks are assaulted, but the very citadel itself. We are asked to give up all belief in special revelation. Jesus Christ, it is said, has come in the flesh precisely as each one of us has come, and he was before Abraham only in the same sense that we were. Christian experience knows how to characterize such doctrine so soon as it is clearly stated. And the new theology will be of use in enabling even ordinary believers to recognize soul-destroying heresy even under the mask of professed orthodoxy.

I make no apology for the homiletical element in my book. To be either true or useful, theology must be a passion. *Pectus est quod theologum facit*, and no disdainful cries of "Pectoral Theology!" shall prevent me from maintaining that the eyes of the heart must be enlightened in order to perceive the truth of God, and that to know the truth it is needful to do the truth. Theology is a science which can be successfully cultivated only in connection with its practical application. I would therefore, in every discussion of its principles, point out its relations to Christian experience, and its power to awaken Christian emotions and lead to Christian decisions. Abstract theology is not really scientific. Only that theology is scientific which brings the student to the feet of Christ.

I would hasten the day when in the name of Jesus every knee shall bow. I believe that, if any man serve Christ, him the Father will honor, and that to serve Christ means to honor him as I honor the Father. I would not pride myself that I believe so little, but rather that I believe so much. Faith is God's measure of a man. Why should I doubt that God spoke to the fathers through the prophets ? Why should I think it incredible that God should raise the dead ? The things that are impossible with men are possible with God. When the Son of man comes, shall he find faith on the earth ? Let him at least find faith in us who profess to be his followers. In the conviction that the present darkness is but temporary and that it will be banished by a glorious sunrising, I give this new edition of my "Theology" to the public with the prayer that whatever of good seed is in it may bring forth fruit, and that whatever plant the heavenly Father has not planted may be rooted up.

ROCHESTER THEOLOGICAL SEMINARY,

ROCHESTER, N. Y., AUGUST 3, 1906.

TABLE OF CONTENTS.

VOLUME I.

PREFACE, ... vii–xii

TABLE OF CONTENTS, ... xiii–xvii

PART I.—PROLEGOMENA, ... 1–51

CHAPTER I.—IDEA OF THEOLOGY, ... 1–24

  I.—Definition of Theology, ... 1– 2
  II.—Aim of Theology, ... 2
  III.—Possibility of Theology—grounded in, ... 2–15
    1. The existence of a God, ... 3–. 5
    2. Man's capacity for the knowledge of God, ... 5–11
    3. God's revelation of himself to man, ... 11–15
  IV.—Necessity of Theology, ... 15–19
  V.—Relation of Theology to Religion, ... 19–24

CHAPTER II.—MATERIAL OF THEOLOGY, ... 25–37

  I.—Sources of Theology, ... 25–34
    1. Scripture and Nature, ... 26–29
    2. Scripture and Rationalism, ... 29–31
    3. Scripture and Mysticism, ... 31–33
    4. Scripture and Romanism, ... 33–34
  II.—Limitations of Theology, ... 34–36
  III.—Relations of Material to Progress in Theology, ... 36–37

CHAPTER III.—METHOD OF THEOLOGY, ... 38–51

  I.—Requisites to the study of Theology, ... 38–41
  II.—Divisions of Theology, ... 41–44
  III.—History of Systematic Theology, ... 44–49
  IV.—Order of Treatment, ... 49–50
  V.—Text-Books in Theology, ... 50–51

PART II.—THE EXISTENCE OF GOD, ... 52–110

CHAPTER I.—ORIGIN OF OUR IDEA OF GOD'S EXISTENCE, ... 52–70

  I.—First Truths in General, ... 53–56
  II.—The Existence of God a First Truth, ... 56–62
    1. Its universality, ... 56–58
    2. Its necessity, ... 58–59
    3. Its logical independence and priority, ... 59–62
  III.—Other supposed Sources of the Idea, ... 62–67
  IV.—Contents of this Intuition, ... 67–70

CHAPTER II.—CORROBORATIVE EVIDENCES OF GOD'S EXISTENCE, 71–89

I.—The Cosmological Argument,...................... 73–75
II.—The Teleological Argument,....................... 75–80
III.—The Anthropological Argument,.................... 80–85
IV.—The Ontological Argument,...................... 85–89

CHAPTER III.—ERRONEOUS EXPLANATIONS, AND CONCLUSION,.. 90–110

I.—Materialism,.................................... 90– 95
II.—Materialistic Idealism,............................ 95–100
III.—Idealistic Pantheism,............................ 100–105
IV.—Ethical Monism,................................ 105–110

PART III.—THE SCRIPTURES A REVELATION FROM
GOD,... 111–242

CHAPTER I.—PRELIMINARY CONSIDERATIONS,................. 111–144

I.—Reasons *a priori* for expecting a Revelation from God, 111–114
II.—Marks of the Revelation man may expect,.......... 114–117
III.—Miracles as attesting a Divine Revelation,.......... 117–133
    1. Definition of Miracle,........................... 117–120
    2. Possibility of Miracles,.......................... 121–123
    3. Probability of Miracles, ... 124–127
    4. Amount of Testimony necessary to prove a Miracle, 127–128
    5. Evidential Force of Miracles,..................... 128–131
    6. Counterfeit Miracles,............................ 132–133
IV.—Prophecy as attesting a Divine Revelation,.......... 134–141
V.—Principles of Historical Evidence applicable to the
Proof of a Divine Revelation,................... 141–144
    1. As to Documentary Evidence,.................... 141–142
    2. As to Testimony in General,..................... 142–144

CHAPTER II.—POSITIVE PROOFS THAT THE SCRIPTURES ARE A
DIVINE REVELATION,......................... 145–195

I.—Genuineness of the Christian Documents,........... 145–172
    1. Genuineness of the Books of the New Testament,. 146–165
        1st. The Myth-theory of Strauss,............... 155–157
        2d. The Tendency-theory of Baur,............. 157–160
        3d. The Romance-theory of Renan,............ 160–162
        4th. The Development-theory of Harnack,....... 162–165
    2. Genuineness of the Books of the Old Testament,.. 165–172
        The Higher Criticism in General,............... 169–170
        The Authorship of the Pentateuch in particular, 170–172
II.—Credibility of the Writers of the Scriptures,........ 172–175
III.—Supernatural Character of the Scripture Teaching,... 175–190
    1. Scripture Teaching in General,................... 175–177
    2. Moral System of the New Testament,............. 177–186
        Heathen Systems of Morality,.......... 179–186
    3. The Person and Character of Christ,.............. 186–189
    4. The Testimony of Christ to himself,.............. 189–190
IV.—Historical Results of the Propagation of Scripture
Doctrine,..................................... 191–195

CHAPTER III.—INSPIRATION OF THE SCRIPTURES,...... 196–242

  I.—Definition of Inspiration,........................... 196–198

  II.—Proof of Inspiration,.... 198–202

  III.—Theories of Inspiration,........................... 202–212

    1. The Intuition-theory,........................... 202–204

    2. The Illumination-theory,........................ 204–208

    3. The Dictation-theory,....... 208–211

    4. The Dynamical theory,.......................... 211–212

  IV.—The Union of the Divine and Human Elements in

     Inspiration,...................................... 212–222

  V.—Objections to the Doctrine of Inspiration,.......... 222–242

    1. Errors in matters of Science,.................... 223–226

    2. Errors in matters of History,.................... 226–229

    3. Errors in Morality,.............................. 230–232

    4. Errors of Reasoning,............................ 232–233

    5. Errors in Quoting or Interpreting the Old Testament, 234–235

    6. Errors in Prophecy,............................. 235–236

    7. Certain Books unworthy of a Place in inspired Scripture,.. 236–238

    8. Portions of the Scripture Books written by others than the Persons to whom they are ascribed,...... 238–240

    9. Sceptical or Fictitious Narratives,................. 240–242

    10. Acknowledgment of the Non-inspiration of Scripture Teachers and their Writings,................ 242

PART IV.—THE NATURE, DECREES, AND WORKS OF GOD,... 243–370

CHAPTER I.—THE ATTRIBUTES OF GOD,..................... 243–303

  I.—Definition of the term Attributes,.................. 244

  II.—Relation of the Divine Attributes to the Divine Essence, 244–246

  III.—Methods of Determining the Divine Attributes,...... 246–247

  IV.—Classification of the Attributes,.................... 247–249

  V.—Absolute or Immanent Attributes,................... 249–275

    First Division.—Spirituality, and Attributes therein involved,....................................... 249–254

    1. Life, ... 251–252

    2. Personality,.... 252–254

    Second Division.—Infinity and Attributes therein involved,.. 254–260

    1. Self-existence,... 256–257

    2. Immutability,........................... 257–259

    3. Unity,................................. 259–260

    Third Division.—Perfection, and Attributes therein involved,.. 260–275

    1. Truth,... 260–262

    2. Love,.................................. 263–268

    3. Holiness,.............................. 268–275

  VI.—Relative or Transitive Attributes,.................. 275–295

First Division.—Attributes having relation to Time and Space, ... 275–279
   1. Eternity, ... 275–278
   2. Immensity, ... 278–279
Second Division.—Attributes having relation to Creation, ... 279–288
   1. Omnipresence, ... 279–282
   2. Omniscience, ... 282–286
   3. Omnipotence, ... 286–288
Third Division.—Attributes having relation to Moral Beings, ... 288–295
   1. Veracity and Faithfulness, or Transitive Truth, ... 288–289
   2.—Mercy and Goodness, or Transitive Love, .. 289–290
   3. Justice and Righteousness, or Transitive Holiness, ... 290–295
VII.—Rank and Relations of the several Attributes, ... 295–303
   1. Holiness the Fundamental Attribute in God, ... 296–298
   2. The Holiness of God the Ground of Moral Obligation 298–303
CHAPTER II.—DOCTRINE OF THE TRINITY, ... 304–352
I.—In Scripture there are Three who are recognized as God, 305–322
   1. Proofs from the New Testament, ... 305–317
     A. The Father is recognized as God, ... 305
     B. Jesus Christ is recognized as God, ... 305–315
     C. The Holy Spirit is recognized as God, ... 315–317
   2. Intimations of the Old Testament, ... 317–322
     A. Passages which seem to teach Plurality of some sort in the Godhead, ... 317–319
     B. Passages relating to the Angel of Jehovah, ... 319–320
     C. Descriptions of the Divine Wisdom and Word, 320–321
     D. Descriptions of the Messiah, ... 321–322
II.—These Three are so described in Scripture, that we are compelled to conceive them as distinct Persons, ... 322–326
   1. The Father and the Son are Persons distinct from each other, ... 322
   2. The Father and the Son are Persons distinct from the Spirit, ... 322–323
   3. The Holy Spirit is a Person, ... 323–326
III.—This Tripersonality of the Divine Nature is not merely economic and temporal, but is immanent and eternal, 326–330
   1. Scripture Proof that these distinctions of Personality are eternal, ... 326
   2. Errors refuted by the Scripture Passages, ... 327–330
     A. The Sabellian, ... 327–328
     B. The Arian, ... 328–330
IV.—While there are three Persons, there is but one Essence, 330–334
V.—These three Persons are Equal, ... 334–343
   1. These Titles belong to the Persons, ... 334–335

    2. Qualified Sense of these Titles,............... 335–340
    3. Generation and Procession consistent with Equal-
        ity,...................................... 340–343
VI.—The Doctrine of the Trinity inscrutable, yet not self-
    contradictory, but the Key to all other Doctrines, 344–352
    1. The Mode of this Triune Existence is inscrutable, 344–345
    2. The Doctrine of the Trinity is not self-contra-
        dictory,................................... 345–347
    3. The Doctrine of the Trinity has important rela-
        tions to other Doctrines,.................... 347–352
CHAPTER III.—THE DECREES OF GOD,...................... 353–370
I.—Definition of Decrees,............................. 353–355
II.—Proof of the Doctrine of Decrees,....... 355–359
    1. From Scripture,............................. 355–356
    2. From Reason,............................... 356–359
        A. From the Divine Foreknowledge,....... 356–358
        B. From the Divine Wisdom,.............. 358
        C. From the Divine Immutability,......... 358–359
        D. From the Divine Benevolence,.......... 359
III.—Objections to the Doctrine of Decrees,.............. 359–368
    1. That they are inconsistent with the Free Agency
        of Man,............. 359–362
    2. That they take away all Motive for Human Exer-
        tion, ... 363–364
    3. That they make God the Author of Sin,........ 365–368
IV.—Concluding Remarks,............................. 368–370
    1. Practical Uses of the Doctrine of Decrees,...... 368–369
    2. True Method of Preaching the Doctrine........ 369–370

TABLE OF CONTENTS.

VOLUME II.

CHAPTER IV. — THE WORKS OF GOD, OR THE EXECUTION OF THE
    DECREES, ... 371–464
SECTION I. — CREATION, ... 371–410

  I. — Definition of Creation, ... 371–373
  II. — Proof of the Doctrine, ... 374–378
      1. Direct Scripture Statements, ... 374–377
      2. Indirect Evidence from Scripture, ... 377–378
  III. — Theories which oppose Creation, ... 378–391
      1. Dualism, ... 378–383
      2. Emanation, ... 383–386
      3. Creation from Eternity, ... 386–389
      4. Spontaneous Generation, ... 389–391
  IV. — The Mosaic Account of Creation, ... 391–397
      1. Its Twofold Nature, ... 391–393
      2. Its Proper Interpretation, ... 393–397
  V. — God's End in Creation, ... 397–402
      1. The Testimony of Scripture, ... 397–398
      2. The Testimony of Reason, ... 398–402
  VI. — Relation of the Doctrine of Creation to other Doctrines, 402–410
      1. To the Holiness and Benevolence of God, ... 402–403
      2. To the Wisdom and Free Will of God, ... 404–405
      3. To Christ as the Revealer of God, ... 405–407
      4. To Providence and Redemption, ... 407–408
      5. To the Observance of the Sabbath, ... 408–410

SECTION II. — PRESERVATION, ... 410–419

  I. — Definition of Preservation, ... 410–411
  II. — Proof of the Doctrine of Preservation, ... 411–414
      1. From Scripture, ... 411–412
      2. From Reason, ... 412–414
  III. — Theories which virtually deny the Doctrine of Preserva-
    tion, ... 414–418
      1. Deism, ... 414–415
      2. Continuous Creation, ... 415–418
  IV. — Remarks upon the Divine Concurrence, ... 418–419

SECTION III. — PROVIDENCE, ... 419–443

  I. — Definition of Providence, ... 419–420
  II. — Proof of the Doctrine of Providence, ... 421–427
      1. Scriptural Proof, ... 421–425
      2. Rational Proof, ... 425–427

III.—Theories opposing the Doctrine of Providence,....... 427–431
    1. Fatalism,..................................... 427
    2. Casualism,................................... 427–428
    3. Theory of a merely General Providence,........ 428–431
IV.—Relations of the Doctrine of Providence,............. 431–443
    1. To Miracles and Works of Grace,.............. 431–433
    2. To Prayer and its Answer,.................... 433–439
    3. To Christian Activity,....................... 439–441
    4. To the Evil Acts of Free Agents,............. 441–443
Section IV.—Good and Evil Angels..................... 443–464

I.—Scripture Statements and Intimations,.............. 444–459
    1. As to the Nature and Attributes of Angels,...... 444–447
    2. As to their Number and Organization,.......... 447–450
    3. As to their Moral Character,.................. 450–451
    4. As to their Employments,..................... 451–459
        A. The Employments of Good Angels,........ 451–454
        B. The Employments of Evil Angels,......... 454–459
II.—Objections to the Doctrine of Angels,................ 459–462
    1. To the Doctrine of Angels in General,.......... 459–460
    2. To the Doctrine of Evil Angels in Particular,.... 460–462
III.—Practical Uses of the Doctrine of Angels,............. 462–464
    1. Uses of the Doctrine of Good Angels,.......... 462–463
    2. Uses of the Doctrine of Evil Angels,........... 463–464

PART V.—ANTHROPOLOGY, OR THE DOCTRINE OF MAN, 465–664

Chapter I.—Preliminary,............................... 465–513

I.—Man a Creation of God and a Child of God,........ .. 465–476
II.—Unity of the Race,................................ 476 483
    1. Argument from History,...................... 477–478
    2. Argument from Language,.................... 478–479
    3. Argument from Psychology,.................. 479–480
    4. Argument from Physiology,.................. 480–483
III.—Essential Elements of Human Nature,............... 483–488
    1. The Dichotomous Theory,.................... 483–484
    2. The Trichotomous Theory,................... 484–488
IV.—Origin of the Soul,............................... 488–497
    1. The Theory of Preëxistence,.................. 488–491
    2. The Creatian Theory,....................... 491–493
    3. The Traducian Theory,...................... 493–497
V.—The Moral Nature of Man,......................... 497–513
    1. Conscience,................................ 498–504
    2. Will,...................................... 504–513
Chapter II.—The Original State of Man,................ 514–532
I.—Essentials of Man's Original State,.................. 514–523
    1. Natural Likeness to God, or Personality,........ 515–516
    2. Moral Likeness to God, or Holiness,........... 516–523
        A. The Image of God as including only Person-
          ality,...................................... 518–520

B. The Image of God as consisting simply in
Man's Natural Capacity for Religion,..... 520–523

II.—Incidents of Man's Original State,.................. 523–532

   1. Results of Man's Possession of the Divine Image, 523–525

   2. Concomitants of Man's Possession of the Divine
Image,....... 525–527

      1st. The Theory of an Original Condition of
Savagery,............................. 527–531

      2nd. The Theory of Comte as to the Stages of
Human Progress,..................... 531–532

CHAPTER III.—SIN, OR MAN'S STATE OF APOSTASY,........... .. 533–664

SECTION I.—THE LAW OF GOD,......................... 533–549

I.—Law in General,................................... 532–536

II.—The Law of God in Particular,..................... 536–547

   1. Elemental Law,.............................. 536–544

   2. Positive Enactment,.......................... 544–547

III.—Relation of the Law to the Grace of God,............ 547–549

SECTION II.—NATURE OF SIN,............................ 549–573

I.—Definition of Sin,................................. 549–559

   1. Proof,....................................... 552–557

   2. Inferences,.................................. 557–559

II.—The Essential Principle of Sin,..................... 559–573

   1. Sin as Sensuousness,........................ 559–563

   2. Sin as Finiteness,........................... 563–566

   3. Sin as Selfishness, ... 566–573

SECTION III.—UNIVERSALITY OF SIN,..................... 573–582

I.—Every human being who has arrived at moral consciousness has committed acts, or cherished dispositions, contrary to the Divine Law, ... 573–577

II.—Every member of the human race, without exception,
possesses a corrupted nature, which is a source of actual sin, and is itself sin, ... 577–582

SECTION IV.—ORIGIN OF SIN IN THE PERSONAL ACT OF ADAM, 582–593

I.—The Scriptural Account in Genesis,................. 582–585

   1. Its General Character not Mythical or Allegorical,
but Historical,.............................. 582–583

   2. The Course of the Temptation, and the resulting
Fall, ... 584–585

II.—Difficulties connected with the Fall, considered as the
personal Act of Adam,....................... 585–590

   1. How could a holy being fall?................. 585–588

   2. How could God justly permit Satanic Temptation? 588–589

   3. How could a Penalty so great be justly connected
with Disobedience to so slight a Command?... 589–590

III.—Consequences of the Fall—so far as respects Adam,.. 590–593

   1. Death,...................................... 590–592

A. Physical Death or the Separation of the Soul
from the Body, ... 590–591
B. Spiritual Death, or the Separation of the
Soul from God, ... 591–592
2. Positive and formal Exclusion from God's Presence, ... 592–593

SECTION V.—IMPUTATION OF ADAM'S SIN TO HIS POSTERITY,.. 593–637
Scripture Teaching as to Race-sin and Race-responsibility, ... 593–597
I.—Theories of Imputation, ... 597–628
1. The Pelagian Theory, or Theory of Man's Natural
Innocence, ... 597–601
2. The Arminian Theory, or Theory of voluntarily
appropriated Depravity, ... 601–606
3. The New-School Theory, or Theory of uncondemnable Vitiosity, ... 606–612
4. The Federal Theory, or Theory of Condemnation
by Covenant, ... 612–616
5. Theory of Mediate Imputation, or Theory of Condemnation for Depravity, ... 616–619
6. Augustinian Theory, or Theory of Adam's Natural
Headship, ... 619–627
Exposition of Rom. 5 : 12–19, ... 625–627
Tabular View of the various Theories of Imputation, ... 628
II.—Objections to the Augustinian Theory of Imputation,. 629–637
SECTION VI.— CONSEQUENCES OF SIN TO ADAM'S POSTERITY,.. 637–660
I.—Depravity, ... 637–644
1. Depravity Partial or Total ? 637–640
2. Ability or Inability? 640–644
II.—Guilt, ... 644–652
1. Nature of Guilt, ... 644–647
2. Degrees of Guilt, ... 648–652
III.—Penalty, ... 652–660
1. Idea of Penalty, ... 652–656
2. Actual Penalty of Sin, ... 656–660
SECTION VII.— THE SALVATION OF INFANTS, ... 660–664

PART VI.—SOTERIOLOGY, OR THE DOCTRINE OF SAL-
VATION THROUGH THE WORK OF CHRIST
AND OF THE HOLY SPIRIT, ... 665–894

CHAPTER I.—CHRISTOLOGY, OR THE REDEMPTION WROUGHT BY
CHRIST, ... 665–776
SECTION I.— HISTORICAL PREPARATION FOR REDEMPTION, ... 665–668
I.—Negative Preparation, in the History of the Heathen
World, ... 665–666
II.— Positive Preparation, in the History of Israel, ... 666–668

SECTION II.—THE PERSON OF CHRIST, ... 669–700

I.—Historical Survey of Views respecting the Person of
Christ, ... 669–673
  1. The Ebionites, ... 669–670
  2. The Docetæ, ... 670
  3. The Arians, ... 670
  4. The Apollinarians, ... 670–671
  5. The Nestorians, ... 671–672
  6. The Eutychians, ... 672
  7. The Orthodox Doctrine, ... 673
II.—The two Natures of Christ,—their Reality and Integrity, ... 673–683
  1. The Humanity of Christ, ... 673–681
    A. Its Reality, ... 673–675
    B. Its Integrity, ... 675–681
  2. The Deity of Christ, ... 681–683
III.—The Union of the two Natures in one Person, ... 683–700
  1. Proof of this Union, ... 684–686
  2. Modern Misrepresentations of this Union, ... 686–691
    A. The Theory of Gess and Beecher, that the
      Humanity of Christ is a Contracted and
      Metamorphosed Deity, ... 686–688
    B. The Theory of Dorner and Rothe, that the
      Union between the Divine and the Human
      Natures is not completed by the Incarna-
      ting Act, ... 688–691
  3. The Real Nature of this Union, ... 691–700
SECTION III.—THE TWO STATES OF CHRIST, ... 701–710
I.—The State of Humiliation, ... 701–706
  1. The Nature of Christ's Humiliation, ... 701–704
    A. The Theory of Thomasius, Delitzsch, and
      Crosby, that the Humiliation consisted in
      the Surrender of the Relative Attributes, 701–703
    B. The Theory that the Humiliation consisted
      in the Surrender of the Independent Ex-
      ercise of the Divine Attributes, ... 703–704
  2. The Stages of Christ's Humiliation, ... 704–706
    Exposition of Philippians 2 : 5–9, ... 705–706
II.—The State of Exaltation, ... 706–710
  1. The Nature of Christ's Exaltation, ... 706–707
  2. The Stages of Christ's Exaltation, ... 707–710
SECTION IV.—THE OFFICES OF CHRIST, ... 710–776

I. The Prophetic Office of Christ, ... 710–713
  1. The Nature of Christ's Prophetic Work, ... 710–711
  2. The Stages of Christ's Prophetic Work, ... 711–713
II. The Priestly Office of Christ, ... 713–775
  1. Christ's Sacrificial Work, or the Doctrine of the
    Atonement, ... 713–773

General Statement of the Doctrine,.......... 713–716
A. Scriptural Methods of Representing the Atonement, ... 716–722
B. The Institution of Sacrifice, especially as found
in the Mosaic System,.................... 722–728
C. Theories of the Atonement,................ 728–766
    1st. The Socinian, or Example Theory of
the Atonement,.................... 728–733
    2d. The Bushnellian, or Moral-Influence
Theory of the Atonement,.......... 733–740
    3d. The Grotian, or Governmental Theory
of the Atonement,................. 740–744
    4th. The Irvingian Theory, or Theory of
gradually extirpated Depravity,.... 744–747
    5th. The Anselmic, or Commercial Theory
of the Atonement,................. 747–750
    6th. The Ethical Theory of the Atonement, 750–766
First, The Atonement as related to
Holiness in God,........... 751–754
Exposition of Romans 3 : 25, 26,.. 753–754
Secondly, The Atonement as related
to Humanity in Christ,..... 754–766
Exposition of 2 Corinthians 5 : 21, 760–761
D. Objections to the Ethical Theory of the Atone-
ment, ... 766–771
E. The Extent of the Atonement,.............. 771–773
2. Christ's Intercessory Work,.................. 773–775
III.—The Kingly Office of Christ,........ 775–776

VOLUME III.

CHAPTER II.— THE RECONCILIATION OF MAN TO GOD, OF THE
    APPLICATION OF REDEMPTION THROUGH THE
    WORK OF THE HOLY SPIRIT, ... 777-886
SECTION I.— THE APPLICATION OF CHRIST'S REDEMPTION, IN
    ITS PREPARATION, ... 777-793
  I.— Election, ... 779-790
    1. Proof of the Doctrine of Election, ... 779-785
    2. Objections to the Doctrine of Election, ... 785-790
  II.— Calling, ... 790-793
    A. Is God's General Call Sincere ? 791-792
    B. Is God's Special Call Irresistible ? 792-793
SECTION II.— THE APPLICATION OF CHRIST'S REDEMPTION, IN
    ITS ACTUAL BEGINNING, ... 793-868
  I.— Union with Christ, ... 795-809
    1. Scripture Representations of this Union, ... 795-798
    2. Nature of this Union, ... 798-802
    3. Consequences of this Union, ... 802-809
  II.— Regeneration, ... 809-829
    1. Scripture Representations, ... 810-812
    2. Necessity of Regeneration, ... 812-814
    3. The Efficient Cause of Regeneration, ... 814-820
    4. The Instrumentality used in Regeneration, ... 820-823
    5. The Nature of the Change wrought in Regeneration, 823-829
  III.— Conversion, ... 829-849
    1. Repentance, ... 832-836
      Elements of Repentance, ... 832-834
      Explanations of the Scripture Representations, ... 834-836
    2. Faith, ... 836-849
      Elements of Faith, ... 837-840
      Explanations of the Scripture Representations, ... 840-849
  IV.— Justification, ... 846-868
    1. Definition of Justification, ... 849
    2. Proof of the Doctrine of Justification, ... 849-854
    3. Elements of Justification, ... 854-859
    4. Relation of Justification to God's Law and Holiness, 859-861
    5. Relation of Justification to Union with Christ and
      the Work of the Spirit, ... 861-864

6. Relation of Justification to Faith,................... 864–867
7. Advice to Inquirers demanded by a Scriptural View
of Justification,................................. 868
SECTION III.—THE APPLICATION OF CHRIST'S REDEMPTION, IN
ITS CONTINUATION,......................... 868–886
I.—Sanctification,.. 869–881
  1. Definition of Sanctification,...................... 869–870
  2. Explanations and Scripture Proof,................. 870–875
  3. Erroneous Views refuted by the Scripture Passages, 875–881
    A. The Antinomian,............................ 875–877
    B. The Perfectionist,............................ 877–881
II.—Perseverance, ... 881–886
  1. Proof of the Doctrine of Perseverance,............ 882–883
  2. Objections to the Doctrine of Perseverance,........ 883–886
PART VII.—ECCLESIOLOGY, OR THE DOCTRINE OF
THE CHURCH, ... 887–980
CHAPTER I.—THE CONSTITUTION OF THE CHURCH, OR CHURCH
POLITY,.................................. 889–929
I.—Definition of the Church, ... 887–894
  1. The Church, like the Family and the State, is an
Institution of Divine Appointment,.............. 892–893
  2. The Church, unlike the Family and the State, is a
Voluntary Society,............................. 893–894
II.—Organization of the Church,......................... 894–903
  1. The Fact of Organization,........................ 894–897
  2. The Nature of this Organization,................. 897–900
  3. The Genesis of this Organization,................ 900–903
III.—Government of the Church,.......................... 903–926
  1. Nature of this Government in General,............ 903–914
    A. Proof that the Government of the Church is
Democratic or Congregational,.............. 904–908
    B. Erroneous Views as to Church Government,
refuted by the Scripture Passages,.......... 908–914
      (a) The World-church Theory, or the
Romanist View,.................... 908–911
      (b) The National-church Theory, or the
Theory of Provincial or National
Churches,......................... 912–914
  2. Officers of the Church,........................... 914–924
    A. The Number of Offices in the Church is two,... 914–916
    B. The Duties belonging to these Offices,........ 916–918
    C. Ordination of Officers,...................... 918–924
      (a) What is Ordination?................. 918–920
      (b) Who are to Ordain?................. 920–924
  3. Discipline of the Church,......................... 924–926
    A. Kinds of Discipline,......................... 924–925
    B. Relation of the Pastor to Discipline,.......... 925–926
IV.—Relation of Local Churches to one another,........... 926–929

1. The General Nature of this Relation is that of
Fellowship between Equals, ... 926–927
2. This Fellowship involves the Duty of Special Consultation with regard to Matters affecting the
common Interest, ... 927
3. This Fellowship may be broken by manifest Departures from the Faith or Practice of the Scriptures
on the part of any Church, ... 928–929
CHAPTER II. — THE ORDINANCES OF THE CHURCH, ... 930–980
I.— Baptism, ... 931–959
1. Baptism an Ordinance of Christ, ... 931–933
2. The Mode of Baptism, ... 933–940
   A. The Command to Baptize is a Command to
   Immerse, ... 933–938
   B. No Church has the Right to Modify or Dispense
   with this Command of Christ, ... 939–940
3. The Symbolism of Baptism, ... 940–945
   A. Expansion of the Statement as to the Symbolism
   of Baptism, ... 940–942
   B. Inferences from the Passages referred to, ... 942–945
4. The Subjects of Baptism, ... 945–959
   A. Proof that only Persons giving Evidence of
   being Regenerated are proper Subjects of
   Baptism, ... 945–946
   B. Inferences from the Fact that only Persons giv-
   ing Evidence of being Regenerate are proper
   Subjects of Baptism, ... 946–951
   C. Infant Baptism, ... 951–959
      (a) Infant Baptism without Warrant in the
      Scripture, ... 951–952
      (b) Infant Baptism expressly Contradicted
      by Scripture, ... 952–953
      (c) Its Origin in Sacramental Conceptions
      of Christianity, ... 953–954
      (d) The Reasoning by which it is supported
      Unscriptural, Unsound, and Dangerous
      in its Tendency, ... 954–956
      (e) The Lack of Agreement among Pedo-
      baptists, ... 956–957
      (f) The Evil Effects of Infant Baptism, ... 957–959
II.— The Lord's Supper, ... 959–980
1. The Lord's Supper an Ordinance instituted by
Christ, ... 959–960
2. The Mode of Administering the Lord's Supper, ... 960–962
3. The Symbolism of the Lord's Supper, ... 962–965
   A. Expansion of the Statement as to the Symbolism
   of the Lord's Supper, ... 962–964
   B. Inferences from this Statement, ... 964–965
4. Erroneous Views of the Lord's Supper, ... 965–969

    A. The Romanist View, ... 965–968
    B. The Lutheran and High Church View, ... 968–969
  5. Prerequisites to Participation in the Lord's Supper, 969–980
    A. There are Prerequisites, ... 969–970
    B. Laid down by Christ and his Apostles, ... 970
    C. The Prerequisites are Four, ... 970–975
        First, — Regeneration, ... 971
        Secondly, — Baptism, ... 971–973
        Thirdly, — Church Membership, ... 973
        Fourthly, — An Orderly Walk, ... 973–975
    D. The Local Church is the Judge whether these
       Prerequisites are fulfilled, ... 975–977
    E. Special Objections to Open Communion, ... 977–98ı

PART VIII.— ESCHATOLOGY, OR THE DOCTRINE OF
      FINAL THINGS, ... 981–1056
  I.— Physical Death, ... 982–998
    That this is not Annihilation, argued :
    1. Upon Rational Grounds, ... 984–991
    2. Upon Scriptural Grounds, ... 991–998
  II.— The Intermediate State, ... 998–1003
    1. Of the Righteous, ... 998– 999
    2. Of the Wicked, ... 999–1000
    Refutation of the two Errors :
        (a) That the Soul sleeps, between Death
          and the Resurrection, ... 1000
        (b) That the Suffering of the Intermediate
          State is Purgatorial, ... 1000–1002
    Concluding Remark, ... 1002–1003
  III.— The Second Coming of Christ, ... 1003–1015
    1. The Nature of Christ's Coming, ... 1004–1005
    2. The Time of Christ's Coming, ... 1005–1008
    3. The Precursors of Christ's Coming, ... 1008–1010
    4. Relation of Christ's Second Coming to the
       Millennium, ... 1010–1015
  IV.— The Resurrection, ... 1015–1023
    1. The Exegetical Objection, ... 1016–1018
    2. The Scientific Objection, ... 1018–1023
  V.— The Last Judgment, ... 1023–1029
    1. The Nature of the Final Judgment, ... 1024–1025
    2. The Object of the Final Judgment, ... 1025–1027
    3. The Judge in the Final Judgment, ... 1027–1028
    4. The Subjects of the Final Judgment, ... 1028
    5. The Grounds of the Final Judgment, ... 1029
  VI.— The Final States of the Righteous and of the Wicked, .. 1029–1056
    1. Of the Righteous, ... 1029–1033
        A. Is Heaven a Place as well as a State ? 1032
        B. Is this Earth to be the Heaven of the Saints ? 1032–1033
    2. Of the Wicked, ... 1033–1056

TABLE OF CONTENTS.

A. Future Punishment is not Annihilation,..... 1035–1039

B. Punishment after Death excludes new Probation and ultimate Restoration,.......... 1039–1044

C. This Future Punishment is Everlasting,.... . 1044–1046

D. Everlasting Punishment is not inconsistent with God's Justice,...................... 1046–1051

E. Everlasting Punishment is not inconsistent with God's Benevolence,................ 1051–1054

F. Preaching of Everlasting Punishment is not a Hindrance to the Success of the Gospel, 1054–1056

INDEX OF SUBJECTS,............................ .... 1059–111C

INDEX OF AUTHORS,... 1117–1138

INDEX OF SCRIPTURE TEXTS,............................... 1139–1157

INDEX OF APOCRYPHAL TEXTS, ... 1158

INDEX OF GREEK WORDS, ... 1159–1163

INDEX OF HEBREW WORDS,. 1165–1166

SYSTEMATIC THEOLOGY.

VOLUME I.

THE DOCTRINE OF GOD.

PART I.

PROLEGOMENA.

CHAPTER I.

IDEA OF THEOLOGY.

I. DEFINITION.—Theology is the science of God and of the relations between God and the universe.

Though the word "theology" is sometimes employed in dogmatic writings to designate that single department of the science which treats of the divine nature and attributes, prevailing usage, since Abelard (A. D. 1079-1142) entitled his general treatise "Theologia Christiana," has included under that term the whole range of Christian doctrine. Theology, therefore, gives account, not only of God, but of those relations between God and the universe in view of which we speak of Creation, Providence and Redemption.

John the Evangelist is called by the Fathers "the theologian," because he most fully treats of the internal relations of the persons of the Trinity. Gregory Nazianzen (328) received this designation because he defended the deity of Christ against the Arians. For a modern instance of this use of the term "theology" in the narrow sense, see the title of Dr. Hodge's first volume: "Systematic Theology, Vol. I: *Theology.*" But theology is not simply "the science of God," nor even "the science of God and man." It also gives account of the relations between God and the universe.

If the universe were God, theology would be the only science. Since the universe is but a manifestation of God and is distinct from God. there are sciences of nature and of mind. Theology is "the science of the sciences," not in the sense of including all these sciences, but in the sense of using their results and of showing their underlying ground; (see Wardlaw Theology, 1: 1, 2). Physical science is not a part of theology. As a mere physicist, Humboldt did not need to mention the name of God in his "Cosmos" (but see Cosmos, 2: 413, where Humboldt says: "Psalm 104 presents an image of the whole Cosmos"). Bishop of Carlisle: "Science is atheous, and therefore cannot be atheistic."

Only when we consider the relations of finite things to God, does the study of them furnish material for theology. Anthropology is a part of theology, because man's nature is the work of God and because God's dealings with man throw light upon the character of God. God is known through his works and his activities. Theology therefore gives account of these works and activities so far as they come within our knowledge. All other sciences require theology for their complete explanation. Proudhon: "If you go very deeply into politics, you are sure to get into theology." On the definition of theology, see Luthardt, Compendium der Dogmatik, 1: 2; Blunt, Dict. Doct. and Hist. Theol., art.: Theology; H. B. Smith, Introd. to Christ. Theol., 44; cf. Aristotle, Metaph., 10, 7, 4; 11, 6, 4; and Lactantius, De Ira Dei, 11.

II. AIM.—The aim of theology is the ascertainment of the facts respecting God and the relations between God and the universe, and the exhibition of these facts in their rational unity, as connected parts of a formulated and organic system of truth.

In defining theology as a science, we indicate its aim. Science does not create; it discovers. Theology answers to this description of a science. It discovers facts and relations, but it does not create them. Fisher, Nature and Method of Revelation, 141—"Schiller, referring to the ardor of Columbus's faith, says that, if the great discoverer had not found a continent, he would have created one. But faith is not creative. Had Columbus not found the land—had there been no real object answering to his belief—his faith would have been a mere fancy." Because theology deals with objective facts, we refuse to define it as "the science of religion"; *versus* Am. Theol. Rev., 1850: 101-126, and Thornwell, Theology, 1: 139. Both the facts and the relations with which theology has to deal have an existence independent of the subjective mental processes of the theologian.

Science is not only the observing, recording, verifying, and formulating of objective facts; it is also the recognition and explication of the relations between these facts, and the synthesis of both the facts and the rational principles which unite them in a comprehensive, rightly proportioned, and organic system. Scattered bricks and timbers are not a house; severed arms, legs, heads and trunks from a dissecting room are not living men; and facts alone do not constitute science. Science = facts + relations; Whewell, Hist. Inductive Sciences, I, Introd., 43—"There may be facts without science, as in the knowledge of the common quarryman; there may be thought without science, as in the early Greek philosophy." A. MacDonald: "The *a priori* method is related to the *a posteriori* as the sails to the ballast of the boat: the more philosophy the better, provided there are a sufficient number of facts; otherwise, there is danger of upsetting the craft."

President Woodrow Wilson: "'Give us the facts' is the sharp injunction of our age to its historians... But facts of themselves do not constitute the truth. The truth is abstract, not concrete. It is the just idea, the right revelation, of what things mean. It is evoked only by such arrangements and orderings of facts as suggest meanings." Dove, Logic of the Christian Faith, 14—"The pursuit of science is the pursuit of relations." Everett, Science of Thought, 3—"Logy" (*e. g.*, in "theology"), from λόγος, =word + reason, expression + thought, fact + idea; *cf.* John 1: 1—"In the beginning was the Word."

As theology deals with objective facts and their relations, so its arrangement of these facts is not optional, but is determined by the nature of the material with which it deals. A true theology thinks over again God's thoughts and brings them into God's order, as the builders of Solomon's temple took the stones already hewn, and put them into the places for which the architect had designed them; Reginald Heber: "No hammer fell, no ponderous axes rung; Like some tall palm, the mystic fabric sprung." Scientific men have no fear that the data of physics will narrow or cramp their intellects; no more should they fear the objective facts which are the data of theology. We cannot make theology, any more than we can make a law of physical nature. As the natural philosopher is "Naturæ minister et interpres," so the theologian is the servant and interpreter of the objective truth of God. On the Idea of Theology as a System, see H. B. Smith, Faith and Philosophy, 125-166.

III. POSSIBILITY.—The possibility of theology has a threefold ground: 1. In the existence of a God who has relations to the universe; 2. In the capacity of the human mind for knowing God and certain of these relations, and 3. In the provision of means by which God is brought into actual contact with the mind, or in other words, in the provision of a revelation.

Any particular science is possible only when three conditions combine, namely, the actual existence of the object with which the science deals, the subjective capacity of the human mind to know that object, and the provision of definite means by which the object is brought into contact with the mind. We may illustrate the conditions of theology from selenology — the science, not of "lunar politics," which John Stuart Mill thought so vain a pursuit, but of lunar physics. Selenology has three conditions: 1. the objective existence of the moon ; 2. the subjective capacity of the human mind to know the moon ; and 3. the provision of some means (*e. g.*, the eye and the telescope) by which the gulf between man and the moon is bridged over, and by which the mind can come into actual cognizance of the facts with regard to the moon.

1. *In the existence of a God who has relations to the universe.*—It has been objected, indeed, that since God and these relations are objects apprehended only by faith, they are not proper objects of knowledge or subjects for science. We reply :

A. Faith is knowledge, and a higher sort of knowledge.—Physical science also rests upon faith—faith in our own existence, in the existence of a world objective and external to us, and in the existence of other persons than ourselves ; faith in our primitive convictions, such as space, time, cause, substance, design, right ; faith in the trustworthiness of our faculties and in the testimony of our fellow men. But physical science is not thereby invalidated, because this faith, though unlike sense-perception or logical demonstration, is yet a cognitive act of the reason, and may be defined as certitude with respect to matters in which verification is unattainable.

The objection to theology thus mentioned and answered is expressed in the words of Sir William Hamilton, Metaphysics, 44, 531—"Faith—belief—is the organ by which we apprehend what is beyond our knowledge." But science is knowledge, and what is beyond our knowledge cannot be matter for science. Pres. E. G. Robinson says well, that knowledge and faith cannot be severed from one another, like bulkheads in a ship, the first of which may be crushed in, while the second still keeps the vessel afloat. The mind is one,—"it cannot be cut in two with a hatchet." Faith is not antithetical to knowledge,—it is rather a larger and more fundamental sort of knowledge. It is never opposed to reason, but only to sight. Tennyson was wrong when he wrote : "We have but faith : we cannot know ; For knowledge is of things we see" (In Memoriam, Intro- duction). This would make sensuous phenomena the only objects of knowledge. Faith in supersensible realities, on the contrary, is the highest exercise of reason.

Sir William Hamilton consistently declares that the highest achievement of science is the erection of an altar "To the Unknown God." This, however, is not the repre- sentation of Scripture. *Cf*. John 17 : 3 —"this is life eternal, that they should know thee, the only true God "; and Jer. 9 : 24—"let him that glorieth glory in that he hath understanding and knoweth me." For criticism of Hamilton, see H. B. Smith, Faith and Philosophy, 297-336. Fichte : "We are born in faith." Even Goethe called himself a believer in the five senses. Balfour, Defence of Philosophic Doubt, 277-295, shows that intuitive beliefs in space, time, cause, substance, right, are presupposed in the acquisition of all other knowledge. Dove, Logic of the Christian Faith, 14—" If theology is to be overthrown because it starts from some pri- mary terms and propositions, then all other sciences are overthrown with it." Mozley, Miracles, defines faith as "unverified reason." See A. H. Strong, Philosophy and Re- ligion, 19-30.

B. Faith is a knowledge conditioned by holy affection.—The faith which apprehends God's being and working is not opinion or imagination. It is certitude with regard to spiritual realities, upon the testimony of our rational nature and upon the testimony of God. Its only peculiarity as a cog- nitive act of the reason is that it is conditioned by holy affection. As the science of æsthetics is a product of reason as including a power of recog- nizing beauty practically inseparable from a love for beauty, and as the science of ethics is a product of reason as including a power of recognizing the morally right practically inseparable from a love for the morally right, so the science of theology is a product of reason, but of reason as including a power of recognizing God which is practically inseparable from a love for God.

We here use the term "reason" to signify the mind's whole power of knowing. Reason in this sense includes states of the sensibility, so far as they are indispensable to knowledge. We cannot know an orange by the eye alone; to the understanding of it, taste is as necessary as sight. The mathematics of sound cannot give us an understanding of music; we need also a musical ear. Logic alone cannot demonstrate the beauty of a sunset, or of a noble character; love for the beautiful and the right precedes knowledge of the beautiful and the right. Ullman draws attention to the derivation of *sapientia*, wisdom, from *sapere*, to taste. So we cannot know God by intellect alone; the heart must go with the intellect to make knowledge of divine things possible. "Human things," said Pascal, "need only to be known, in order to be loved; but divine things must first be loved, in order to be known." "This [religious] faith of the intellect," said Kant, "is founded on the assumption of moral tempers." If one were utterly indifferent to moral laws, the philosopher continues, even then religious truths "would be supported by strong arguments from analogy, but not by such as an obstinate, sceptical heart might not overcome."

Faith, then, is the highest knowledge, because it is the act of the integral soul, the insight, not of one eye alone, but of the two eyes of the mind, intellect and love to God. With one eye we can see an object as flat, but, if we wish to see around it and get the stereoptic effect, we must use both eyes. It is not the theologian, but the undevout astronomer, whose science is one-eyed and therefore incomplete. The errors of the rationalist are errors of defective vision. Intellect has been divorced from heart, that is, from a right disposition, right affections, right purpose in life. Intellect says: "I cannot know God"; and intellect is right. What intellect says, the Scripture also says: 1 Cor. 2: 14—"the natural man receiveth not the things of the Spirit of God: for they are foolishness unto him; and he cannot know them, because they are spiritually judged"; 1 : 21—"in the wisdom of God the world through its wisdom knew not God."

The Scripture on the other hand declares that "by faith we know" (Heb. 11: 3). By "heart" the Scripture means simply the governing disposition, or the sensibility + the will; and it intimates that the heart is an organ of knowledge: Ex. 35: 25—"the women that were wise-hearted"; Ps. 34: 8 — "O taste and see that Jehovah is good" = a right taste precedes correct sight: Jer. 24: 7—"I will give them a heart to know me"; Mat. 5: 8—"Blessed are the pure in heart; for they shall see God"; Luke 24: 25—"slow of heart to believe"; John 7: 17—"If any man willeth to do his will, he shall know of the teaching, whether it is of God, or whether I speak from myself"; Eph. 1: 18—"having the eyes of your heart enlightened, that ye may know"; 1 John 4: 7, 8—"Every one that loveth is begotten of God, and knoweth God. He that loveth not knoweth not God." See Frank, Christian Certainty, 303–324; Clarke, Christ. Theol., 362; Illingworth, Div. and Hum. Personality, 114–137; R. T. Smith, Man's Knowledge of Man and of God, 6; Fisher, Nat. and Method of Rev., 6; William James, The Will to Believe, 1–31; Geo. T. Ladd, on Lotze's view that love is essential to the knowledge of God, in New World, Sept. 1895: 401–406; Gunsaulus, Transfig. of Christ, 14, 15.

C. **Faith, therefore, can furnish, and only faith can furnish, fit and sufficient material for a scientific theology.**—As an operation of man's higher rational nature, though distinct from ocular vision or from reasoning, faith is not only a kind, but the highest kind, of knowing. It gives us understanding of realities which to sense alone are inaccessible, namely, God's existence, and some at least of the relations between God and his creation.

Philippi, Glaubenslehre, 1 : 50, follows Gerhard in making faith the joint act of intellect and will. Hopkins, Outline Study of Man, 77, 78, speaks not only of "the æsthetic reason" but of "the moral reason." Murphy, Scientific Bases of Faith, 91, 109, 145, 191—"Faith is the certitude concerning matter in which verification is unattainable." Emerson, Essays, 2 : 96—"Belief consists in accepting the affirmations of the soul—unbelief in rejecting them." Morell, Philos. of Religion, 38, 52, 53, quotes Coleridge: "Faith consists in the synthesis of the reason and of the individual will, . . . and by virtue of the former (that is, reason), faith must be a light, a form of knowing, a beholding of truth." Faith, then, is not to be pictured as a blind girl clinging to a cross—faith is not blind—"Else the cross may just as well be a crucifix or an image of Gaudama." "Blind unbelief," not blind faith, "is sure to err, And scan his works in vain." As in conscience we recognize an invisible authority, and know the truth just in proportion to our willingness to "do the truth," so in religion only holiness can understand holiness, and only love can understand love (cf. John 3: 21—"he that doeth the truth cometh to the light").

If a right state of heart be indispensable to faith and so to the knowledge of God, can there be any "theologia irregenitorum," or theology of the unregenerate? Yes, we answer; just as the blind man can have a science of optics. The testimony of others gives it claims upon him; the dim light penetrating the obscuring membrane corroborates this testimony. The unregenerate man can know God as power and justice, and can fear him. But this is not a knowledge of God's inmost character; it furnishes some material for a defective and ill-proportioned theology; but it does not furnish fit or sufficient material for a correct theology. As, in order to make his science of optics satisfactory and complete, the blind man must have the cataract removed from his eyes by some competent oculist, so, in order to any complete or satisfactory theology, the veil must be taken away from the heart by God himself (cf. 2 Cor. 3: 15, 16—"a veil lieth upon their heart. But whensoever it [marg. 'a man'] shall turn to the Lord, the veil is taken away").

Our doctrine that faith is knowledge and the highest knowledge is to be distinguished from that of Ritschl, whose theology is an appeal to the heart to the exclusion of the head—to fiducia without notitia. But fiducia includes notitia, else it is blind, irrational, and unscientific. Robert Browning, in like manner, fell into a deep speculative error, when, in order to substantiate his optimistic faith, he stigmatized human knowledge as merely apparent. The appeal of both Ritschl and Browning from the head to the heart should rather be an appeal from the narrower knowledge of the mere intellect to the larger knowledge conditioned upon right affection. See A. H. Strong, The Great Poets and their Theology, 441. On Ritschl's postulates, see Stearns, Evidence of Christian Experience, 274–280, and Pfleiderer, Die Ritschl'sche Theologie. On the relation of love and will to knowledge, see Kaftan, in Am. Jour. Theology, 1900: 717; Hovey, Manual Christ. Theol., 9; Foundations of our Faith, 12, 13; Shedd, Hist. Doct., 1: 154–164; Presb. Quar., Oct. 1871, Oct. 1872, Oct. 1873; Calderwood, Philos. Infinite, 99, 117; Van Oosterzee, Dogmatics, 2–8; New Englander, July, 1873: 481; Princeton Rev., 1864: 122; Christlieb, Mod. Doubt, 124, 125; Grau, Glaube als höchste Vernunft, in Beweis des Glaubens, 1865: 110; Dorner, Gesch. prot. Theol., 228; Newman, Univ. Sermons, 206; Hinton, Art of Thinking, Introd. by Hodgson, 5.

2. In the capacity of the human mind for knowing God and certain of these relations.—But it has urged that such knowledge is impossible for the following reasons :

A. Because we can know only phenomena. We reply : (a) We know mental as well as physical phenomena. (b) In knowing phenomena, whether mental or physical, we know substance as underlying the phenomena, as manifested through them, and as constituting their ground of unity. (c) Our minds bring to the observation of phenomena not only this knowledge of substance, but also knowledge of time, space, cause, and right, realities which are in no sense phenomenal. Since these objects of knowledge are not phenomenal, the fact that God is not phenomenal cannot prevent us from knowing him.

What substance is, we need not here determine. Whether we are realists or idealists, we are compelled to grant that there cannot be phenomena without noumena, cannot be appearances without something that appears, cannot be qualities without something that is qualified. This something which underlies or stands under appearance or quality we call substance. We are Lotzeans rather than Kantians, in our philosophy. To say that we know, not the self, but only its manifestations in thought, is to confound self with its thinking and to teach psychology without a soul. To say that we know no external world, but only its manifestations in sensations, is to ignore the principle that binds these sensations together; for without a somewhat in which qualities inhere they can have no ground of unity. In like manner, to say that we know nothing

God but his manifestations, is to confound God with the world and practically to den that there is a God.

Stählin, in his work on Kant, Lotze and Ritschl, 186-191, 218, 219, says well that "limitation of knowledge to phenomena involves the elimination from theology of all claim to know the objects of the Christian faith as they are in themselves." This criticism justly classes Ritschl with Kant, rather than with Lotze who maintains that knowing phenomena we know also the noumena manifested in them. While Ritschl professes to follow Lotze, the whole drift of his theology is in the direction of the Kant'an identification of the world with our sensations, mind with our thoughts, and God with such activities of his as we can perceive. A divine nature apart from its activities, a preexistent Christ, an immanent Trinity, are practically denied. Assertions that God is self-conscious love and fatherhood become judgments of merely subjective value. On Ritschl, see the works of Orr, of Garvie, and of Swing; also Minton, in Pres. and Ref. Rev., Jan. 1902: 162-169, and C. W. Hodge, ibid., Apl. 1902: 321-326; Flint, Agnosticism, 590-597; Everett, Essays Theol. and Lit., 92-99.

We grant that we can know God only so far as his activities reveal him, and so far as our minds and hearts are receptive of his revelation. The appropriate faculties must be exercised—not the mathematical, the logical, or the prudential, but the ethical and the religious. It is the merit of Ritschl that he recognizes the practical in distinction from the speculative reason; his error is in not recognizing that, when we do thus use the proper powers of knowing, we gain not merely subjective but also objective truth, and come in contact not simply with God's activities but also with God himself. Normal religious judgments, though dependent upon subjective conditions, are not simply "judgments of worth" or "value-judgments,"—they give us the knowledge of "things in themselves." Edward Caird says of his brother John Caird (Fund. Ideas of Christianity, Introd. cxxi)—"The conviction that God can be known and is known, and that, in the deepest sense, all our knowledge is knowledge of him, was the corner-stone of his theology."

Ritschl's phenomenalism is allied to the positivism of Comte, who regarded all so-called knowledge of other than phenomenal objects as purely negative. The phrase "Positive Philosophy" implies indeed that all knowledge of mind is negative; see Comte, Pos. Philosophy, Martineau's translation, 26, 28, 33—"In order to observe, your intellect must pause from activity—yet it is this very activity you want to observe. If you cannot effect the pause, you cannot observe; if you do effect it, there is nothing to observe." This view is refuted by the two facts: (1) consciousness, and (2) memory; for consciousness is the knowing of the self side by side with the knowing of its thoughts, and memory is the knowing of the self side by side with the knowing of its past; see Martineau, Essays Philos. and Theol., 1: 24-40, 207-212. By phenomena we mean "facts, in distinction from their ground, principle, or law"; "neither phenomena nor qualities, as such, are perceived, but objects, percepts, or beings; and it is by an after-thought or reflex process that these are connected as qualities and are referred to as substances"; see Porter, Human Intellect, 51, 238, 520, 619-637, 640-645.

Phenomena may be internal, e. g., thoughts; in this case the noumenon is the mind, of which these thoughts are the manifestations. Or, phenomena may be external, e. g., color, hardness, shape, size; in this case the noumenon is matter, of which these qualities are the manifestations. But qualities, whether mental or material, imply the existence of a substance to which they belong: they can no more be conceived of as existing apart from substance, than the upper side of a plank can be conceived of as existing without an under side; see Bowne, Review of Herbert Spencer, 47, 207-217; Martineau, Types of Ethical Theory, 1; 455, 456—"Comte's assumption that mind cannot know itself or its states is exactly balanced by Kant's assumption that mind cannot know anything outside of itself. . . . It is precisely because all knowledge is of relations that it is not and cannot be of phenomena alone. The absolute cannot per se be known, because in being known it would ipso facto enter into relations and be absolute no more. But neither can the phenomenal per se be known, i. e., be known as phenomenal, without simultaneous cognition of what is non-phenomenal." McCosh, Intuitions, 138-154, states the characteristics of substance as (1) being, (2) power, (3) permanence. Diman, Theistic Argument, 337, 363—"The theory that disproves God, disproves an external world and the existence of the soul." We know something beyond phenomena, viz.: law, cause, force,—or we can have no science; see Tulloch, on Comte, in Modern Theories, 53-73; see also Bib. Sac., 1874: 211; Alden, Philosophy, 44; Hopkins, Outline Study of Man, 87; Fleming, Vocab. of Philosophy, art.: Phenomena; New Englander. July, 1875: 537-539.

B. Because we can know only that which bears analogy to our own nature or experience. We reply : (*a*) It is not essential to knowledge that there be similarity of nature between the knower and the known. We know by difference as well as by likeness. (*b*) Our past experience, though greatly facilitating new acquisitions, is not the measure of our possible knowledge. Else the first act of knowledge would be inexplicable, and all revelation of higher characters to lower would be precluded, as well as all progress to knowledge which surpasses our present attainments. (*c*) Even if knowledge depended upon similarity of nature and experience, we might still know God, since we are made in God's image, and there are important analogies between the divine nature and our own.

(*a*) The dictum of Empedocles, "Similia similibus percipiuntur," must be supplemented by a second dictum, "Similia dissimilibus percipiuntur." All things are alike, in being objects. But k owing is distinguishing, and there must be contrast between objects to awaken our attention. God knows sin, though it is the antithesis to his holy being. The ego knows the non-ego. We cannot know even self, without objectifying it, distinguishing it from its thoughts, and regarding it as another.

(*b*) *Versus* Herbert Spencer, First Principles, 79-82-"Knowledge is recognition and classification." But we reply that a thing must first be perceived in order to be recognized or compared with something else; and this is as true of the first sensation as of the later and more definite forms of knowledge,—indeed there is no sensation which does not involve, as its complement, an at least incipient perception; see Sir William Hamilton. Metaphysics, 351, 352; Porter, Human Intellect, 206.

(*c*) Porter, Human Intellect, 486—"Induction is possible only upon the assumption that the intellect of man is a reflex of the divine intellect, or that man is made in the image of God." Note, however, that man is made in God's image, not God in man's. The painting is the image of the landscape, not, *vice versa,* the landscape the image of the painting; for there is much in the landscape that has nothing corresponding to it in the painting. Idolatry perversely makes God in the image of man, and so deifies man's weakness and impurity. Trinity in God may have no exact counterpart in man's present constitution, though it may disclose to us the goal of man's future development and the meaning of the increasing differentiation of man's powers. Gore, Incarnation, 116—"If anthropomorphism as applied to God is false, yet theomorphism as applied to man is true; man is made in God's image, and his qualities are, not the measure of the divine, but their counterpart and real expression." See Murphy, Scientific Bases, 122; McCosh, in Internat. Rev., 1875: 105; Bib. Sac., 1867: 624; Martineau, Types of Ethical Theory, 2: 4-8, and Study of Religion, 1: 94.

C. Because we know only that of which we can conceive, in the sense of forming an adequate mental image. We reply : (*a*) It is true that we know only that of which we can conceive, if by the term "conceive" we mean our distinguishing in thought the object known from all other objects. But, (*b*) The objection confounds conception with that which is merely its occasional accompaniment and help, namely, the picturing of the object by the imagination. In this sense, conceivability is not a final test of truth. (*c*) That the formation of a mental image is not essential to conception or knowledge, is plain when we remember that, as a matter of fact, we both conceive and know many things of which we cannot form a mental image of any sort that in the least corresponds to the reality ; for example, force, cause, law, space, our own minds. So we may know God, though we cannot form an adequate mental image of him.

The objection here refuted is expressed most clearly in the words of Herbert Spencer, First Principles, 25-36, 98—"The reality underlying appearances is totally and forever inconceivable by us." Mansel, Prolegomena Logica, 77, 78 (*cf.* 26) suggests the source of this error in a wrong view of the nature of the concept: "The first distinguishing feature of a concept, viz.: that it cannot in itself be depicted to sense or imagination." Porter, Human Intellect, 392 (see also 429, 656)—"The *concept* is not a mental image"—only the *percept* is. Lotze: "Color in general is not representable by any image; it looks neither green nor red, but has no look whatever." The generic horse has no particular color, though the individual horse may be black, white, or bay. So Sir William Hamilton speaks of "the unpicturable notions of the intelligence."

Martineau, Religion and Materialism, 39, 40—"This doctrine of Nescience stands in exactly the same relation to causal power, whether you construe it as Material Force or as Divine Agency. Neither can be *observed;* one or the other must be *assumed.* If you admit to the category of knowledge only what we learn from observation, particular or generalized, then is Force unknown; if you extend the word to what is imported by the intellect itself into our cognitive acts, to make them such, then is God known." Matter, ether, energy, protoplasm, organism, life,—no one of these can be portrayed to the imagination; yet Mr. Spencer deals with them as objects of Science. If these are not inscrutable, why should he regard the Power that gives unity to all things as inscrutable ?

Herbert Spencer is not in fact consistent with himself, for in divers parts of his writings he calls the inscrutable Reality back of phenomena the one, eternal, ubiquitous, infinite, ultimate, absolute Existence, Power and Cause. "It seems," says Father Dalgairns, "that a great deal is known about the Unknowable." Chadwick, Unitarianism, 75—"The beggar phrase 'Unknowable' becomes, after Spencer's repeated designations of it, as rich as Croesus with all saving knowledge." Matheson: "To know that we know nothing is already to have reached a fact of knowledge." If Mr. Spencer intended to exclude God from the realm of Knowledge, he should first have excluded him from the realm of Existence; for to grant that he is, is already to grant that we not only may know him, but that we actually to some extent do know him ; see D. J. Hill, Genetic Philosophy, 22 ; McCosh, Intuitions, 186–189 (Eng. ed., 214); Murphy, Scientific Bases, 133 ; Bowne, Review of Spencer, 30–34 ; New Englander, July, 1875 : 543, 544 ; Oscar Craig, in Presb. Rev., July, 1883 : 594–602.

D. Because we can know truly only that which we know in whole and not in part. We reply : (*a*) The objection confounds partial knowledge with the knowledge of a part. We know the mind in part, but we do not know a part of the mind. (*b*) If the objection were valid, no real knowledge of anything would be possible, since we know no single thing in all its relations. We conclude that, although God is a being not composed of parts, we may yet have a partial knowledge of him, and this knowledge, though not exhaustive, may yet be real, and adequate to the purposes of science.

(*a*) The objection mentioned in the text is urged by Mansel, Limits of Religious Thought, 97, 98, and is answered by Martineau, Essays, 1 : 291. The mind does not exist in space, and it has no parts : we cannot speak of its south-west corner, nor can we divide it into halves. Yet we find the material for mental science in partial knowledge of the mind. So, while we are not "geographers of the divine nature" (Bowne, Review of Spencer, 72), we may say with Paul, not "now know we a part of God," but "now I know [God, in part" (1 Cor. 13: 12). We may know truly what we do not know exhaustively; see Eph. 3: 19—"to know the love of Christ which passeth knowledge." I do not perfectly understand myself, yet I know myself in part ; so I may know God, though I do not perfectly understand him.

(*b*) The same argument that proves God unknowable proves the universe unknowable also. Since every particle of matter in the universe attracts every other, no one particle can be exhaustively explained without taking account of all the rest. Thomas Carlyle : "It is a mathematical fact that the casting of this pebble from my hand alters the centre of gravity of the universe." Tennyson, Higher Pantheism : "Flower in the crannied wall, I pluck you out of the crannies ; Hold you here, root and all, in my hand, Little flower ; but if I could understand What you are, root and all, and all in all, I should know what God and man is." Schurman, Agnosticism, 119—"Partial as it is, this vision of the divine transfigures the life of man on earth." Pfleiderer, Philos. Religion, 1 : 167—"A faint-hearted agnosticism is worse than the arrogant and titanic gnosticism against which it protests."

E. Because all predicates of God are negative, and therefore furnisb no real knowledge. We answer : (a) Predicates derived from our con-sciousness, such as spirit, love, and holiness, are positive. (b) The terme 'infinite" and 'absolute," moreover, express not merely a negative but a positive idea—the idea, in the former case, of the absence of all limit, the idea that the object thus described goes on and on forever ; the idea, in the latter case, of entire self-sufficiency. Since predicates of God, there-fore, are not merely negative, the argument mentioned above furnishes no valid reason why we may not know him.

Versus Sir William Hamilton, Metaphysics, 530—"The absolute and the infinite can each only be conceived as a negation of the thinkable; in other words, of the absolute and infinite we have no conception at all." Hamilton here confounds the infinite, or the absence of all limits, with the indefinite, or the absence of all known limits. Per contra, see Calderwood, Moral Philosophy, 248, and Philosophy of the Infinite, 272— "Negation of one thing is possible only by affirmation of another." Porter, Human Intellect, 652—"If the Sandwich Islanders, for lack of name, had called the ox a not-hog, the use of a negative appellation would not necessarily authorize the inference of a want of definite conceptions or positive knowledge." So with the infinite or not-finite, the unconditioned or not-conditioned, the independent or not-dependent.— these names do not imply that we cannot conceive and know it as something positive. Spencer, First Principles, 92—"Our consciousness of the Absolute, indefinite though it is, is positive, and not negative."

Schurman Agnosticism, 100, speaks of "the farce of nescience playing at omniscience in setting the bounds of science." "The agnostic," he says, "sets up the invisible picture of a Grand Être, formless and colorless in itself, absolutely separated from man and from the world—blank within and void without—its very existence indistinguish-able from its non-existence, and, bowing down before this idolatrous creation, he pours out his soul in lamentations over the incognizableness of such a mysterious and awful non-entity. . . . The truth is that the agnostic's abstraction of a Deity is unknown, only because it is unreal." See McCosh, Intuitions, 194, note ; Mivart, Lessons from Nature, 363. God is not necessarily infinite in every respect. He is infinite only in every excellence. A plane which is unlimited in the one respect of length may be limited in another respect, such as breadth. Our doctrine here is not therefore incon-sistent with what immediately follows.

F. Because to know is to limit or define. Hence the Absolute as unlimited, and the Infinite as undefined, cannot be known. We answer: (a) God is absolute, not as existing in no relation, but as existing in no necessary relation; and (b) God is infinite, not as excluding all coexistence of the finite with himself, but as being the ground of the finite, and so unfettered by it. (c) God is actually limited by the unchangeableness of his own attributes and personal distinctions, as well as by his self-chosen relations to the universe he has created and to humanity in the person of Christ. God is therefore limited and defined in such a sense as to render knowledge of him possible.

Versus Mansel, Limitations of Religious Thought, 75-84, 93-95; cf. Spinoza : "Omnia determinatio est negatio;" hence to define God is to deny him. But we reply that perfection is inseparable from limitation. Man can be other than he is: not so God, at least internally. But this limitation, inherent in his unchangeable attributes and personal distinctions, is God's perfection. Externally, all limitations upon God are self-limitations, and so are consistent with his perfection. That God should not be able thus to limit himself in creation and redemption would render all self-sacrifice in him impossible, and so would subject him to the greatest of limitations. We may say therefore that God's 1. Perfection involves his limitation to (a) personality, (b) trinity, (c) righteousness ; 2. Revelation involves his self-limitation in (a) decree, (b) creation, (c) preservation. (d) government. (e) education of the world ; 3. Redemption involves his infinite self-limitation in the (a) person and (b) work of Jesus Christ; see A. H. Strong, Christ in Creation, 87-101, and in Bap. Quar. Rev., Jan. 1891: 521-532.

Bowne, Philos. of Theism, 135—"The infinite is not the quantitative all; the absolute is not the unrelated . . . Both absolute and infinite mean only the independent ground of things." Julius Müller, Doct. Sin, Introduc., 10—"Religion has to do, not with an Object that must let itself be known because its very existence is contingent upon its being known, but with the Object in relation to whom we are truly subject, dependent upon him, and waiting until he manifest himself." James Martineau, Study of Religion, 1: 346—"We must not confound the infinite with the total. . . . The self-abnegation of infinity is but a form of self-assertion, and the only form . n which it can reveal itself. . . . However instantaneous the omniscient thought, however sure the almighty power, the execution has to be distributed in time, and must have an order of successive steps; on no other terms can the eternal become temporal, and the infinite articulately speak in the finite."

Perfect personality excludes, not self-determination, but determination from without, determination by another. God's self-limitations are the self-limitations of love, and therefore the evidences of his perfection. They are signs, not of weakness but of power. God has limited himself to the method of evolution, gradually unfolding himself in nature and in history. The government of sinners by a holy God involves constant self-repression. The education of the race is a long process of divine forbearance; Herder: "The limitations of the pupil are limitations of the teacher also." In inspiration, God limits himself by the human element through which he works. Above all, in the person and work of Christ, we have infinite self-limitation: Infinity narrows itself down to a point in the incarnation, and holiness endures the agonies of the Cross. God's promises are also self-limitations. Thus both nature and grace are self-imposed restrictions upon God, and these self-limitations are the means by which he reveals himself. See Pfleiderer, Die Religion, 1: 189, 195; Porter, Human Intellect, 653; Murphy, Scientific Bases, 130; Calderwood, Philos. Infinite, 168; McCosh, Intuitions, 186; Hickok, Rational Cosmology, 85; Martineau, Study of Religion, 2: 85, 86, 362; Shedd, Dogmatic Theology, 1: 189-191.

G. Because all knowledge is relative to the knowing agent; that is, what we know, we know, not as it is objectively, but only as it is related to our own senses and faculties. In reply: (a) We grant that we can know only that which has relation to our faculties. But this is simply to say that we know only that which we come into mental contact with, that is, we know only what we know. But, (b) We deny that what we come into mental contact with is known by us as other than it is. So far as it is known at all, it is known as it is. In other words, the laws of our knowing are not merely arbitrary and regulative, but correspond to the nature of things. We conclude that, in theology, we are equally warranted in assuming that the laws of our thought are laws of God's thought, and that the results of normally conducted thinking with regard to God correspond to the objective reality.

Versus Sir Wm. Hamilton, Metaph., 96-116, and Herbert Spencer, First Principles, 68-97. This doctrine of relativity is derived from Kant, Critique of Pure Reason, who holds that a priori judgments are simply "regulative." But we reply that when our primitive beliefs are found to be simply regulative, they will cease to regulate. The forms of thought are also facts of nature. The mind does not, like the glass of a kaleidoscope, itself furnish the forms; it recognizes these as having an existence external to itself. The mind reads its ideas, not into nature, but in nature. Our intuitions are not green goggles, which make all the world seem green: they are the lenses of a microscope, which enable us to see what is objectively real (Royce, Spirit of Mod. Philos., 125). Kant called our understanding "the legislator of nature." But it is so, only as discoverer of nature's laws, not as creator of them. Human reason does impose its laws and forms upon the universe; but, in doing this, it interprets the real meaning of the universe.

Ladd Philos. of Knowledge: "All judgment implies an objective truth according

to which we judge, which constitutes the standard, and with which we have something in common, *i. e.*, our minds are part of an infinite and eternal Mind." French
aphorism: "When you are right, you are more right than you think you are." God
will not put us to permanent intellectual confusion. Kant vainly wrote "No
thoroughfare" over the reason in its highest exercise. Martineau, Study of Religion,
1: 135, 136—"Over against Kant's assumption that the mind cannot know anything outside of itself, we may set Comte's equally unwarrantable assumption that the mind
cannot know itself or its states. We cannot have philosophy without assumptions
You dogmatize if you say that the forms correspond with reality; but you equally
dogmatize if you say that they do not. . . . 79—That our cognitive faculties correspond to things *as they are*, is much less surprising than that they should correspond to
things *as they are not*." W. T. Harris, in Journ. Spec. Philos., 1:22, exposes Herbert
Spencer's self-contradiction: "All knowledge is, not absolute, but relative; our
knowledge of this fact however is, not relative, but absolute."

Ritschl, Justification and Reconciliation, 3: 16–21, sets out with a correct statement
of the nature of knowledge, and gives in his adhesion to the doctrine of Lotze, as distinguished from that of Kant. Ritschl's statement may be summarized as follows:
"We deal, not with the abstract God of metaphysics, but with the God self-limited,
who is revealed in Christ. We do not know either things or God *apart from* their
phenomena or manifestations, as Plato imagined; we do not know phenomena or manifestations *alone*, without knowing either things or God, as Kant supposed; but we do
know both things and God *in* their phenomena or manifestations, as Lotze taught.
We hold to no mystical union with God, back of all experience in religion, as Pietism
does; soul is always and only active, and religion is the activity of the human spirit, in
which feeling, knowing and willing combine in an intelligible order."

But Dr. C. M. Mead, Ritschl's Place in the History of Doctrine, has well shown that
Ritschl has not followed Lotze. His "value-judgments" are simply an application to
theology of the "regulative" principle of Kant. He holds that we can know things
not as they are in themselves, but only as they are for us. We reply that what things
are worth for us depends on what they are in themselves. Ritschl regards the doctrines of Christ's preexistence, divinity and atonement as intrusions of metaphysics
into theology, matters about which we cannot know, and with which we have nothing
to do. There is no propitiation or mystical union with Christ; and Christ is our
Example, but not our atoning Savior. Ritschl does well in recognizing that love in
us gives eyes to the mind, and enables us to see the beauty of Christ and his truth.
But our judgment is not, as he holds, a merely subjective value-judgment,—it is a
coming in contact with objective fact. On the theory of knowledge held by Kant,
Hamilton and Spencer, see Bishop Temple, Bampton Lectures for 1884: 13; H. B.
Smith, Faith and Philosophy, 297–336; J. S. Mill, Examination, 1: 113–134; Herbert,
Modern Realism Examin d; M. B. Anderson, art.: "Hamilton," in Johnson's Encyclopædia; McCosh, Intuitions, 139–146, 340, 341, and Christianity and Positivism, 97–123;
Maurice, What is Revelation? Alden, Intellectual Philosophy, 48–79, esp. 71–79; Por-
ter, Hum. Intellect, 523; Murphy, Scientific Bases, 103; Bib. Sac. April, 1868: 341;
Princeton Rev., 1864: 122; Bowne, Review of Herbert Spencer, 76; Bowen, in Princeton Rev., March, 1878: 445–448; Mind, April, 1878: 257; Carpenter, Mental Physiology,
117; Harris, Philos. Basis of Theism, 109-113; Iverach, in Present Day Tracts, 5: No. 29;
Martineau, Study of Religion, 1: 79, 120, 121, 135, 136.

3. *In God's actual revelation of himself and certain of these relations.*—As we do not in this place attempt a positive proof of God's existence or of man's capacity for the knowledge of God, so we do not now
attempt to prove that God has brought himself into contact with man's
mind by revelation. We shall consider the grounds of this belief hereafter. Our aim at present is simply to show that, granting the fact of
revelation, a scientific theology is possible. This has been denied upon
the following grounds:

A. That revelation, as a making known, is necessarily internal and
subjective—either a mode of intelligence, or a quickening of man's cognitive powers—and hence can furnish no objective facts such as constitute
the proper material for science.

Morell, Philos. Religion, 128-131, 143—"The Bible cannot in strict accuracy of language be called a revelation, since a revelation always implies an actual process of intelligence in a living mind." F. W. Newman, Phases of Faith, 152—"Of our moral and spiritual God we know nothing without—everything within." Theodore Parker: "Verbal revelation can never communicate a simple idea like that of God, Justice, Love, Religion"; see review of Parker in Bib. Sac., 18 : 24-27. James Martineau, Seat of Authority in Religion: "As many minds as there are that know God at first hand, so many revealing acts there have been, and as many as know him at second hand are strangers to revelation"; so, assuming external revelation to be impossible, Martineau subjects all the proofs of such revelation to unfair destructive criticism. Pfleiderer, Philos. Religion, 1 : 185—"As all revelation is originally an *inner* living experience, the springing up of religious truth in the heart, no external event can belong in itself to revelation, no matter whether it be naturally or supernaturally brought about." Professor George M. Forbes: "Nothing can be revealed to us which we do not grasp with our reason. It follows that, so far as reason acts normally, it is a part of revelation." Ritchie, Darwin and Hegel, 30—"The revelation of God is the growth of the idea of God."

In reply to this objection, urged mainly by idealists in philosophy, (*a*) We grant that revelation, to be effective, must be the means of inducing a new mode of intelligence, or in other words, must be understood. We grant that this understanding of divine things is impossible without a quickening of man's cognitive powers. We grant, moreover, that revelation, when originally imparted, was often internal and subjective.

Matheson, Moments on the Mount, 51-53, on Gal. 1 : 16—"to reveal his Son in me": "The revelation on the way to Damascus would not have enlightened Paul, had it been merely a vision to his eye. Nothing can be revealed *to* us which has not been revealed *in* us. The eye does not see the beauty of the landscape, nor the ear hear the beauty of music. So flesh and blood do not reveal Christ to us. Without the teaching of the Spirit, the external facts will be only like the letters of a book to a child that cannot read." We may say with Channing: "I am more sure that my rational nature is from God, than that any book is the expression of his will."

(*b*) But we deny that external revelation is therefore useless or impossible. Even if religious ideas sprang wholly from within, an external revelation might stir up the dormant powers of the mind. Religious ideas, however, do not spring wholly from within. External revelation can impart them. Man can reveal himself to man by external communications, and, if God has equal power with man, God can reveal himself to man in like manner.

Rogers, in his Eclipse of Faith, asks pointedly: "If Messrs. Morell and Newman can teach by a book, cannot God do the same?" Lotze, Microcosmos, 2 : 660 (book 9, chap. 4), speaks of revelation as "either contained in some divine act of historic occurrence, or continually repeated in men's hearts." But in fact there is no alternative here; the strength of the Christian creed is that God's revelation is both external and internal; see Gore, in Lux Mundi, 338. Rainy, in Critical Review, 1 : 1-21, well says that Martineau unwarrantably *isolates* the witness of God to the individual soul. The inward needs to be combined with the outward, in order to make sure that it is not a vagary of the imagination. We need to distinguish God's revelations from our own fancies. Hence, before giving the internal, God commonly gives us the external, as a standard by which to try our impressions. We are finite and sinful, and we need authority. The external revelation commends itself as authoritative to the heart which recognizes its own spiritual needs. External authority evokes the inward witness and gives added clearness to it, but only historical revelation furnishes indubitable proof that God is love, and gives us assurance that our longings after God are not in vain.

/ ,c) Hence God's revelation may be, and, as we shall hereafter see, it is, in great part, an external revelation in works and words. The universe is a revelation of God ; God's works in nature precede God's words in history. We claim, moreover, that, in many cases where truth was originally communicated internally, the same Spirit who communicated it has brought about an external record of it, so that the internal revelation might be handed down to others than those who first received it.

We must not limit revelation to the Scriptures. The eternal Word antedated the written word, and through the eternal Word God is made known in nature and in history. Internal revelation is preceded by, and conditioned upon, external revelation. In point of time earth comes before man, and sensation before perception. Action best expresses character, and historic revelation is more by deeds than by words. Dorner, Hist. Prot. Theol., 1: 231-264—"The Word is not in the Scriptures alone. The whole creation reveals the Word. In nature God shows his power; in incarnation his grace and truth. Scripture testifies of these, but Scripture is not the essential Word. The Scripture is truly apprehended and appropriated when in it and through it we see the living and present Christ. It does not bind men to itself alone, but it points them to the Christ of whom it testifies. Christ is the authority. In the Scriptures he points us to himself and demands our faith in him. This faith, once begotten, leads us to new appropriation of Scripture, but also to new criticism of Scripture. We find Christ more and more in Scripture, and yet we judge Scripture more and more by the standard which we find in Christ."

Newman Smyth, Christian Ethics, 71-82: " There is but one authority— Christ. His Spirit works in many ways, but chiefly in two: first, the inspiration of the Scriptures, and secondly, the leading of the church into the truth. The latter is not to be isolated or separated from the former. Scripture is law to the Christian consciousness, and Christian consciousness in time becomes law to the Scripture—interpreting, criticizing, verifying it. The word and the spirit answer to each other. Scripture and faith are coördinate. Protestantism has exaggerated the first; Romanism the second. Martineau fails to grasp the coördination of Scripture and faith."

(d) With this external record we shall also see that there is given under proper conditions a special influence of God's Spirit, so to quicken our cognitive powers that the external record reproduces in our minds the ideas with which the minds of the writers were at first divinely filled.

We may illustrate the need of internal revelation from Egyptology, which is impossible so long as the external revelation in the hieroglyphics is uninterpreted; from the ticking of the clock in a dark room, where only the lit candle enables us to tell the time; from the landscape spread out around the Rigi in Switzerland, invisible until the first rays of the sun touch the snowy mountain peaks. External revelation ($\phi a\nu \epsilon\rho\omega\sigma\iota s$, Rom. 1:19, 20) must be supplemented by internal revelation ($\dot{a}\pi\sigma\kappa\dot{a}\lambda\upsilon\psi\iota s$, 1 Cor. 2: 10, 12). Christ is the organ of external, the Holy Spirit the organ of internal, revelation. In Christ (2 Cor. 1: 20) are "the yea" and "the Amen"—the objective certainty and the subjective certitude, the reality and the realization.

Objective certainty must become subjective certitude in order to a scientific theology. Before conversion we have the first, the external truth of Christ; only at conversion and after conversion do we have the second, "Christ formed in us" (Gal. 4: 19). We have objective revelation at Sinai (Ex. 20: 22); subjective revelation in Elisha's knowledge of Gehazi (2 K. 5: 26). James Russell Lowell, Winter Evening Hymn to my Fire: "Therefore with thee I love to read Our brave old poets: at thy touch how stirs Life in the withered words! how swift recede Time's shadows! and how glows again Through its dead mass the incandescent verse, As when upon the anvil of the brain It glittering lay, cyclopically wrought By the fast throbbing hammers of the poet's thought!"

(e) Internal revelations thus recorded, and external revelations thus interpreted, both furnish objective facts which may serve as proper material for science. Although revelation in its widest sense may include, and as constituting the ground of the possibility of theology does include, both insight and illumination, it may also be used to denote simply a provision of the external means of knowledge, and theology has to do with inward revelations only as they are expressed in, or as they agree with, this objective standard.

We have here suggested the vast scope and yet the insuperable limitations of theology. So far as God is revealed, whether in nature, history, conscience, or Scripture, theology may find material for its structure. Since Christ is not simply the incarnate Son of God but also the eternal Word, the only Revealer of G od, there is no theology apart from Christ, and all theology is Christian theology. Nature and history are but the dimmer and more general disclosures of the divine Being, of which the Cross is the culmination and the key. God does not intentionally conceal himself. He wishes to be known. He reveals himself at all times just as fully as the capacity of his creatures will permit. The infantile intellect cannot understand God's boundlessness, nor can the perverse disposition understand God's disinterested affection. Yet all truth is in Christ and is open to discovery by the prepared mind and heart.

The Infinite One, so far as he is unrevealed, is certainly unknowable to the finite. But the Infinite One, so far as he manifests himself, is knowable. This suggests the meaning of the declarations: John 1 : 18—"No man hath seen God at any time; the only begotten Son, who is in the bosom of the Father, he hath declared him"; 14: 9—"he that hath seen me hath seen the Father"; 1 Tim. 6: 16 —"whom no man hath seen, nor can see." We therefore approve of the definition of Kaftan, Dogmatik, 1—" Dogmatics is the science of the Christian truth which is believed and acknowledged in the church upon the ground of the divine revelation "—in so far as it limits the scope of theology to truth revealed by God and apprehended by faith. But theology presupposes both God's external and God's internal revelations, and these, as we shall see, include nature, history, conscience and Scripture. On the whole subject, see Kahnis, Dogmatik, 3: 37-43; Nitzsch, System Christ. Doct., 72: Luthardt, Fund. Truths, 193; Auberlen, Div. Rev., Introd., 29; Martineau, Essays, 1: 171, 280; Bib. Sac., 1867: 593, and 1872: 428; Porter, Human Intellect, 373-375; C. M. Mead, in Boston Lectures, 1871: 58.

B.   That many of the truths thus revealed are too indefinite to constitute the material for science, because they belong to the region of the feelings, because they are beyond our full understanding, or because they are destitute of orderly arrangement.

We reply :

(a)   Theology has to do with subjective feelings only as they can be defined, and shown to be effects of objective truth upon the mind.   They are not more obscure than are the facts of morals or of psychology, and the same objection which would exclude such feelings from theology would make these latter sciences impossible.

See Jacobi and Schleiermacher, who regard theology as a mere account of devout Christian feelings, the grounding of which in objective historical facts is a matter of comparative indifference (Hagenbach, Hist. Doctrine, 2: 401-403). Schleiermacher therefore called his system of theology "Der Christliche Glaube," and many since his time have called their systems by the name of "Glaubenslehre." Ritschl's "value-judgments," in like manner, render theology a merely subjective science, if any subjective science is possible. Kaftan improves upon Ritschl, by granting that we know, not only Christian feelings, but also Christian facts. Theology is the science of God, and not simply the science of faith. Allied to the view already mentioned is that of Feuerbach, to whom religion is a matter of subjective fancy; and that of Tyndall, who would remit theology to the region of vague feeling and aspiration, but would exclude it from the realm of science; see Feuerbach, Essence of Christianity, translated by Marian Evans (George Eliot); also Tyndall, Belfast Address.

(b)   Those facts of revelation which are beyond our full understanding may, like the nebular hypothesis in astronomy, the atomic theory in chemistry, or the doctrine of evolution in biology, furnish a principle of union between great classes of other facts otherwise irreconcilable. We may define our concepts of God, and even of the Trinity, at least sufficiently to distinguish them from all other concepts; and whatever difficulty may encumber the putting of them into language only shows the importance of attempting it and the value of even an approximate success.

Horace Bushnell: "Theology can never be a science, on account of the infirmities of language." But this principle would render void both ethical and political science. Fisher, Nat. and Meth. of Revelation, 145—"Hume and Gibbon refer to faith as something too sacred to rest on proof. Thus religious beliefs are made to hang in mid-air, without any support. But the foundation of these beliefs is no less solid for the reason that empirical tests are not applicable to them. The data on which they rest are real, and the inferences from the data are fairly drawn." Hodgson indeed pours contempt on the whole intuitional method by saying: "Whatever you are totally ignorant of, assert to be the explanation of everything else!" Yet he would probably grant that he begins his investigations by assuming his own existence. The doctrine of the Trinity is not wholly comprehensible by us, and we accept it at the first upon the testimony of Scripture; the full proof of it is found in the fact that each successive doctrine of theology is bound up with it, and with it stands or falls. The Trinity is rational because it explains Christian experience as well as Christian doctrine.

(c) Even though there were no orderly arrangement of these facts, either in nature or in Scripture, an accurate systematizing of them by the human mind would not therefore be proved impossible, unless a principle were assumed which would show all physical science to be equally impossible. Astronomy and geology are constructed by putting together multitudinous facts.which at first sight seem to have no order. So with theology. And yet, although revelation does not present to us a dogmatic system ready-made, a dogmatic system is not only implicitly contained therein, but parts of the system are wrought out in the epistles of the New Testament, as for example in Rom. 5 : 12-19; 1 Cor 15 : 3, 4; 8 : 6; 1 Tim. 3 : 16; Heb. 6 1, 2.

We may illustrate the construction of theology from the dissected map, two pieces of which a father puts together, leaving his child to put together the rest. Or we may illustrate from the physical universe, which to the unthinking reveals little of its order. "Nature makes no fences." One thing seems to glide into another. It is man's business to distinguish and classify and combine. Origen: "God gives us truth in single threads, which we must weave into a finished texture." Andrew Fuller said of the doctrines of theology that "they are united together like chain-shot, so that, whichever one enters the heart, the others must certainly follow." George Herbert: "Oh that I knew how all thy lights combine, And the configuration of their glory; Seeing not only how each verse doth shine, But all the constellations of the story!" Scripture hints at the possibilities of combination, in Rom. 5 : 12-19, with its grouping of the facts of sin and salvation about the two persons, Adam and Christ; in Rom. 4 : 24, 25, with its linking of the resurrection of Christ and our justification; in 1 Cor. 8 : 6, with its indication of the relations between the Father and Christ; in 1 Tim. 3 : 16, with its poetical summary of the facts of redemption (see Commentaries of DeWette, Meyer, Fairbairn); in Heb. 6 : 1, 2, with its statement of the first principles of the Christian faith. God's furnishing of concrete facts in theology, which we ourselves are left to systematize, is in complete accordance with his method of procedure with regard to the development of other sciences. See Martineau, Essays, 1 : 29, 40; Am. Theol. Rev., 1859: 101-126 — art. on the Idea, Sources and Uses of Christian Theology.

IV. Necessity.—The necessity of theology has its grounds

(a) *In the organizing instinct of the human mind.* This organizing principle is a part of our constitution. The mind cannot endure confusion or apparent contradiction in known facts. The tendency to harmonize and unify its knowledge appears as soon as the mind becomes reflective.

just in proportion to its endowments and culture does the impulse to systematize and formulate increase. This is true of all departments of human inquiry, but it is peculiarly true of our knowledge of God. Since the truth with regard to God is the most important of all, theology meets the deepest want of man's rational nature. Theology is a rational necessity. If all existing theological systems were destroyed to-day, new systems would rise to-morrow. So inevitable is the operation of this law, that those who most decry theology show nevertheless that they have made a theology for themselves, and often one sufficiently meagre and blundering. Hostility to theology, where it does not originate in mistaken fears for the corruption of God's truth or in a naturally illogical structure of mind, often proceeds from a license of speculation which cannot brook the restraints of a complete Scriptural system.

President E. G. Robinson: "Every man has as much theology as he can hold." Consciously or unconsciously, we philosophize, as naturally as we speak prose. "Se moquer de la philosophie c'est vraiment philosopher." Gore, Incarnation, 21—"Christianity became metaphysical, only because man is rational. This rationality means that he must attempt 'to give account of things,' as Plato said, 'because he was a man, not merely because he was a Greek.'" Men often denounce systematic theology, while they extol the sciences of matter. Has God been left only the facts with regard to himself in so unrelated a state that man cannot put them together? All other sciences are valuable only as they contain or promote the knowledge of God. If it is praiseworthy to classify beetles, one science may be allowed to reason concerning God and the soul. In speaking of Schelling, Royce, Spirit of Modern Philosophy, 173, satirically exhorts us: "Trust your genius; follow your noble heart; change your doctrine whenever your heart changes, and change your heart often,—such is the practical creed of the romanticists." Ritchie, Darwin and Hegel, 3—"Just those persons who disclaim metaphysics are sometimes most apt to be infected with the disease they profess to abhor—and not to know when they have it." See Shedd, Discourses and Essays, 27–52; Murphy, Scientific Bases of Faith, 195-199.

(b) *In the relation of systematic truth to the development of character.* Truth thoroughly digested is essential to the growth of Christian character in the individual and in the church. All knowledge of God has its influence upon character, but most of all the knowledge of spiritual facts in their relations. Theology cannot, as has sometimes been objected, deaden the religious affections, since it only draws out from their sources and puts into rational connection with each other the truths which are best adapted to nourish the religious affections. On the other hand, the strongest Christians are those who have the firmest grasp upon the great doctrines of Christianity; the heroic ages of the church are those which have witnessed most consistently to them; the piety that can be injured by the systematic exhibition of them must be weak, or mystical, or mistaken.

Some knowledge is necessary to conversion—at least, knowledge of sin and knowledge of a Savior; and the putting together of these two great truths is a beginning of theology. All subsequent growth of character is conditioned upon the increase of this knowledge. Col. 1 : 10—αὐξανόμενοι τῇ ἐπιγνώσει τοῦ Θεοῦ [omit ἐν] ="increasing by the knowledge of God"—the instrumental dative represents the knowledge of God as the dew or rain which nurtures the growth of the plant; cf. 2 Pet. 3. 18 — "grow in the grace and knowledge of our Lord and Savior Jesus Christ." For texts which represent truth as nourishment, see Jer. 3 : 15 — "feed you with knowledge and understanding"; Mat. 4 : 4 — "Man shall not live by bread alone, but by every word that proceedeth out of the mouth of God"; 1 Cor. 3 : 1, 2 — "babes in Christ . . . I fed you with milk, not with meat"; Heb. 5 : 14 — "but solid food is for full-grown men." Christian character rests upon Christian truth as its foundation; see 1 Cor. 3 : 10-15 — "I laid a foundation, and another buildeth thereon." See Dorus Clarke, Saying the Catechism; Simon, on Christ Doct. and Life, in Bib. Sac.. July, 1884 : 433–439.

Ignorance is the mother of superstition, not of devotion. Talbot W. Chambers: —"Doctrine without duty is a tree without fruits; duty without doctrine is a tree without roots." Christian morality is a fruit which grows only from the tree of Christian doctrine. We cannot long keep the fruits of faith after we have cut down the tree upon which they have grown. Balfour, Foundations of Belief, 82—"Naturalistic virtue is parasitic, and when the host perishes, the parasite perishes also. Virtue without religion will die." Kidd, Social Evolution, 214—"Because the fruit survives for a time when removed from the tree, and even mellows and ripens, shall we say that it is independent of the tree?" The twelve manner of fruits on the Christmas-tree are only tacked on,—they never grew there, and they can never reproduce their kind. The withered apple swells out under the exhausted receiver, but it will go back again to its former shrunken form; so the self-righteousness of those who get out of the atmosphere of Christ and have no divine ideal with which to compare themselves. W. M. Lisle: "It is the mistake and disaster of the Christian world that effects are sought instead of causes." George A. Gordon, Christ of To-day, 28—"Without the historical Christ and personal love for that Christ, the broad theology of our day will reduce itself to a dream, powerless to rouse a sleeping church."

(c) *In the importance to the preacher of definite and just views of Christian doctrine.* His chief intellectual qualification must be the power clearly and comprehensively to conceive, and accurately and powerfully to express, the truth. He can be the agent of the Holy Spirit in converting and sanctifying men, only as he can wield "the sword of the Spirit, which is the word of God" (Eph. 6 : 17), or, in other language, only as he can impress truth upon the minds and consciences of his hearers. Nothing more certainly nullifies his efforts than confusion and inconsistency in his statements of doctrine. His object is to replace obscure and erroneous conceptions among his hearers by those which are correct and vivid. He cannot do this without knowing the facts with regard to God in their relations — knowing them, in short, as parts of a system. With this truth he is put in trust. To mutilate it or misrepresent it, is not only sin against the Revealer of it,—it may prove the ruin of men's souls. The best safeguard against such mutilation or misrepresentation, is the diligent study of the several doctrines of the faith in their relations to one another, and especially to the central theme of theology, the person and work of Jesus Christ.

The more refined and reflective the age, the more it requires reasons for feeling Imagination, as exercised in poetry and eloquence and as exhibited in politics or war, is not less strong than of old,—it is only more rational. Notice the progress from "Buncombe", in legislative and forensic oratory, to sensible and logical address. Bassanio in Shakespeare's Merchant of Venice, 1 : 1 : 113—"Gratiano speaks an infinite deal of nothing. . . . His reasons are as two grains of wheat hid in two bushels of chaff." So in pulpit oratory, mere Scripture quotation and fervid appeal are no longer sufficient. As well be a howling dervish, as to indulge in windy declamation. Thought is the staple of preaching. Feeling must be roused, but only by bringing men to "the knowledge of the truth" (2 Tim. 2: 25). The preacher must furnish the basis for feeling by producing intelligent conviction. He must instruct before he can move. If the object of the preacher is first to know God, and secondly to make God known, then the study of theology is absolutely necessary to his success.

Shall the physician practice medicine without study of physiology, or the lawyer practice law without study of jurisprudence? Professor Blackie: "One may as well expect to make a great patriot out of a fencing-master, as to make a great orator out of a mere rhetorician." The preacher needs doctrine, to prevent his being a mere barrel-organ, playing over and over the same tunes. John Henry Newman: "The false preacher is one who has to say something; the true preacher is one who has something to say." Spurgeon, Autobiography, 1 : 167—"Constant change of creed is sure loss."

If a tree has to be taken up two or three times a year, you will not need to build a very large loft in which to store the apples. When people are shifting their doctrinal principles, they do not bring forth much fruit. . . . We shall never have great preachers till we have great divines. You cannot build a man of war out of a currant-bush, nor can great soul-moving preachers be formed out of superficial students." Illustrate the harmfulness of ignorant and erroneous preaching, by the mistake in a physician's prescription; by the wrong trail at Lake Placid which led astray those ascending Whiteface; by the sowing of acorns whose crop was gathered only after a hundred years. Slight divergences from correct doctrine on our part may be ruinously exaggerated in those who come after us. Though the moth-miller has no teeth, its offspring has. 2 Tim. 2 : 2—"And the things which thou hast heard from me among many witnesses, the same commit thcu to faithful men, who shall be able to teach others also."

(d) *In the intimate connection between correct doctrine and the safety and aggressive power of the church.* The safety and progress of the church is dependent upon her "holding the pattern of sound words" (2 Tim. 1 : 13), and serving as "pillar and ground of the truth " (1 Tim. 3: 15). Defective understanding of the truth results sooner or later in defects of organization, of operation, and of life. Thorough comprehension of Christian truth as an organized system furnishes, on the other hand, not only an invaluable defense against heresy and immorality, but also an indispensable stimulus and instrument in aggressive labor for the world's conversion.

The creeds of Christendom have not originated in mere speculative curiosity and logical hair-splitting. They are statements of doctrine in which the attacked and imperiled church has sought to express the truth which constitutes her very life. Those who deride the early creeds have small conception of the intellectual acumen and the moral earnestness which went to the making of them. The creeds of the third and fourth centuries embody the results of controversies which exhausted the possibilities of heresy with regard to the Trinity a :d the person of Christ, and which set up bars against false doctrine to the end of time. Mahaffy: "What converted the world was not the example of Christ's life,—it was the dogma of his death." Coleridge: " He who does not withstand, has no standing ground of his own." Mrs. Browning: " Entire intellectual toleration is the mark of those who believe nothing." E. G. Robinson, Christian Theology, 360-362—"A doctrine is but a precept in the style of a proposition ; and a precept is but a doctrine in the form of a command. . . . Theology is God's garden; its trees are trees of his planting; and 'all the trees of the Lord are full of sap ' (Ps. 104:16)."

Bose, Ecumenical Councils: " A creed is not catholic because a council of many or of few bishops decreed it, but because it expresses the common conviction of entire generations of men and women who turned their understanding of the New Testament into those forms of words." Dorner: " The creeds are the precipitate of the religious consciousness of mighty men and times." Foster, Christ. Life and Theol., 162— " It ordinarily requires the shock of some great event to startle men into clear apprehension and crystallization of their substantial belief. Such a shock was given by the rough and coarse doctrine of Arius, upon which the conclusion arrived at in the Council of Nice followed as rapidly as in chilled water the crystals of ice will sometimes form when the containing vessel receiv₂s a blow." Balfour, Foundations of Belief, 287 —"The creeds were not explanations, but rather denials that the Arian and Gnostic explanations were sufficient, and declarations that they irremediably impoverished the idea of the Godhead. They insisted on preserving that idea in all its inexplicable fulness." Denny, Studies in Theology, 192—"Pagan philosophies tried to capture the church for their own ends, and to turn it into a school. In self-defense the church was compelled to become somewhat of a school on its own account. It had to assert its facts: it had to define its ideas; it had to interpret in its own way those facts which men were misinterpreting."

Professor Howard Osgood: "A creed is like a backbone. A man does not need to wear his backbone in front of him; but he must have a backbone, and a straight one, or he will be a flexible if not a humpbacked Christian." Yet we must remember that creeds are *credita*, and not *credenda*; historical statements of what the church has believed. not infallible prescriptions of what the church *must* believe. George Dana

Boardman, The Church, 98—"Creeds are apt to become cages." Schurman, Agnosticism, 151—"The creeds were meant to be defensive fortifications of religion; alas, that they should have sometimes turned their artillery against the citadel itself." T. H. Green: "We are told that we must be loyal to the beliefs of the Fathers. Yes, but who knows what the Fathers believe now?" George A. Gordon, Christ of To-day, 60 —"The assumption that the Holy Spirit is not concerned in the development of theological thought, nor manifest in the intellectual evolution of mankind, is the superlative heresy of our generation. . . . The metaphysics of Jesus are absolutely essential to his ethics. . . . If his thought is a dream, his endeavor for man is a delusion." See Schaff, Creeds of Christendom, 1 : 8, 15, 16; Storrs, Div. Origin of Christianity, 121; Ian Maclaren (John Watson), Cure of Souls, 152; Frederick Harrison, in Fortnightly Rev., Jan. 1889.

(e) *In the direct and indirect injunctions of Scripture.* The Scripture urges upon us the thorough and comprehensive study of the truth (John 5 : 39, marg., — "Search the Scriptures"), the comparing and harmonizing of its different parts (1 Cor. 2 : 13—"comparing spiritual things with spiritual"), the gathering of all about the great central fact of revelation (Col. 1 : 27—"which is Christ in you, the hope of glory"), the preaching of it in its wholeness as well as in its due proportions (2 Tim. 4 : 2— "Preach the word"). The minister of the Gospel is called "a scribe who hath been made a disciple to the kingdom of heaven" (Mat. 13 : 52); the "pastors" of the churches are at the same time to be "teachers" (Eph. 4 : 11); the bishop must be "apt to teach" (1 Tim. 3 : 2), "handling aright the word of truth" (2 Tim. 2 : 15), "holding to the faithful word which is according to the teaching, that he may be able both to exhort in the sound doctrine and to convict the gainsayers" (Tit. 1 : 9).

As a means of instructing the church and of securing progress in his own understanding of Christian truth, it is well for the pastor to preach regularly each month a doctrinal sermon, and to expound in course the principal articles of the faith. The treatment of doctrine in these sermons should be simple enough to be comprehensible by intelligent youth; it should be made vivid and interesting by the help of brief illustrations; and at least one-third of each sermon should be devoted to the practical applications of the doctrine propounded. See Jonathan Edwards's sermon on the Importance of the Knowledge of Divine Truth, in Works, 4 : 1-15. The actual sermons of Edwards, however, are not models of doctrinal preaching for our generation. They are too scholastic in form, too metaphysical for substance; there is too little of Scripture and too little of illustration. The doctrinal preaching of the English Puritans in a similar manner addressed itself almost wholly to adults. The preaching of our Lord on the other hand was adapted also to children. No pastor should count himself faithful, who permits his young people to grow up without regular instruction from the pulpit in the whole circle of Christian doctrine. Shakespeare, K. Henry VI, 2nd part, 4 : 7—"Ignorance is the curse of God; knowledge the wing wherewith we fly to heaven."

V. RELATION TO RELIGION.—Theology and religion are related to each other as effects, in different spheres, of the same cause. As theology is an effect produced in the sphere of systematic thought by the facts respecting God and the universe, so religion is an effect which these same facts produce in the sphere of individual and collective life. With regard to the term 'religion', notice:

1. *Derivation.*

(a) The derivation from *religāre,* 'to bind back' (man to God), is negatived by the authority of Cicero and of the best modern etymologists; by the difficulty, on this hypothesis, of explaining such forms as *religio, religens;* and by the necessity, in that case of presupposing a fuller knowledge of sin and redemption than was common to the ancient world.

(*b*) The more correct derivation is from *relegĕre*, "to go over again," "carefully to ponder." Its original meaning is therefore "reverent observance" (of duties due to the gods).

For advocacy of the derivation of *religio*, as meaning "binding duty," from *religāre*, see Lange, Dogmatik, 1 : 185-196. This derivation was first proposed by Lactantius, Inst. Div., 4 : 28, a Christian writer. To meet the objection that the form *religio* seems derived from a verb of the third conjugation, Lange cites *rebellio*, from *rebellāre*, and *optio*, from *optāre*. But we reply that these verbs of the first conjugation, like many others, are probably derived from obsolete verbs of the third conjugation. For the derivation favored in the text, see Curtius, Griechische Etymologie, 5te Autl., 364; Fick, Vergl. Wörterb. der indoger. Spr., 2 : 227; Vanicek, Gr.-Lat. Etym. Wörterb., 2 : 829; Andrews, Latin Lexicon, *in voce*; Nitzsch, System of Christ. Doctrine, 7; Van Oosterzee, Dogmatics, 75-77; Philippi, Glaubenslehre, 1 : 6; Kahnis, Dogmatik, 3 : 18; Menzies, History of Religion, 11; Max Müller, Natural Religion, lect. 2.

2. *False Conceptions.*

(*a*) Religion is not, as Hegel declared, a kind of knowing; for it would then be only an incomplete form of philosophy, and the measure of knowledge in each case would be the measure of piety.

In a system of idealistic pantheism, like that of Hegel, God is the subject of religion as well as its object. Religion is God's knowing of himself through the human consciousness. Hegel did not utterly ignore other elements in religion. "Feeling, intuition, and faith belong to it," he said, "and mere cognition is one-sided." Yet he was always looking for the movement of *thought* in all forms of life; God and the universe were but developments of the primordial *idea*. "What knowledge is worth knowing," he asked, "if God is unknowable? To know God *is* eternal life, and thinking is also true worship." Hegel's error was in regarding life as a process of thought, rather than in regarding thought as a process of life. Here was the reason for the bitterness between Hegel and Schleiermacher. Hegel rightly considered that feeling must become intelligent before it is truly religious, but he did not recognize the supreme importance of love in a theological system. He gave even less place to the will than he gave to the emotions, and he failed to see that the knowledge of God of which Scripture speaks is a knowing, not of the intellect alone, but of the whole man, including the affectional and voluntary nature.

Goethe: "How can a man come to know himself? Never by thinking, but by doing. Try to do your duty, and you will know at once what you are worth. You cannot play the flute by blowing alone,—you must use your fingers." So we can never come to know God by thinking alone. John 7 : 17—"If any man willeth to do his will, he shall know of the teaching, whether it is of God." The Gnostics, Stapfer, Henry VIII, all show that there may be much theological knowledge without true religion. Chillingworth's maxim, "The Bible only, the religion of Protestants," is inadequate and inaccurate; for the Bible, without faith, love, and obedience, may become a fetich and a snare : John 5 : 39, 40—"Ye search the Scriptures, . . . and ye will not come to me, that ye may have life." See Sterrett, Studies in Hegel's Philosophy of Religion; Porter, Human Intellect, 59, 60, 412, 525-536, 589, 650; Moreli, Hist. Philos., 476, 477; Hamerton, Intel. Life, 214; Bib. Sac., 9 : 374.

(*b*) Religion is not, as Schleiermacher held, the mere feeling of dependence; for such feeling of dependence is not religious, unless exercised toward God and accompanied by moral effort.

In German theology, Schleiermacher constitutes the transition from the old rationalism to the evangelical faith. "Like Lazarus, with the grave clothes of a pantheistic philosophy entangling his steps," yet with a Moravian experience of the life of God in the soul, he based religion upon the inner certainties of Christian feeling But, as Principal Fairbairn remarks, "Emotion is impotent unless it speaks out of conviction; and where conviction is, there will be emotion which is potent to persuade." If Christianity is religious feeling alone, then there is no essential difference between it and other religions, for all alike are products of the religious sentiment. But Christianity is distinguished from other religions by its peculiar religious conceptions. Doctrine precedes life, and Christian doctrine, not mere religious feeling, is the cause of Christianity as a distinctive religion. Though faith begins in feeling, moreover, it does not end there. We see the worthlessness of mere feeling in the transient emotions of theatre-goers, and in the occasional phenomena of revivals.

Sabatier, Philos. Relig., 27, adds to Schleiermacher's passive element of *dependence*, the active element of *prayer*. Kaftan, Dogmatik, 10 — " Schleiermacher regards God as the *Source* of our being, but forgets that he is also our *End*." Fellowship and progress are as important elements in religion as is dependence; and fellowship must come before progress—such fellowship as presupposes pardon and life. Schleiermacher apparently believed in neither a personal God nor his own personal immortality ; see his Life and Letters, 2 : 77-90 ; Martineau, Study of Religion, 2 : 357. Charles Hodge compares him to a ladder in a pit—a good thing for those who wish to get out, but not for those who wish to get in. Dorner: " The Moravian brotherhood was his mother ; Greece was his nurse." On Schleiermacher, see Herzog, Realencyclopädie, *in voce* ; Bib. Sac., 1852: 375 ; 1883: 534 ; Liddon, Elements of Religion, lect. I ; Ebrard, Dogmatik, 1 : 14 ; Julius Müller, Doctrine of Sin, 1: 175 ; Fisher, Supernat. Origin of Christianity, 563-570 ; Caird, Philos. Religion, 160-186.

(c) Religion is not, as Kant maintained, morality or moral action ; for morality is conformity to an abstract law of right, while religion is essentially a relation to a person, from whom the soul receives blessing and to whom it surrenders itself in love and obedience.

Kant, Kritik der praktischen Vernunft, Beschluss: " I know of but two beautiful things, the starry heavens above my head, and the sense of duty within my heart." But the mere sense of duty often distresses. We object to the word " obey " as the imperative of religion, because (1) it makes religion a matter of the will only ; (2) will presupposes affection ; (3) love is not subject to will ; (4) it makes God all law, and no grace ; (5) it makes the Christian a servant only, not a friend ; *cf*. John 15: 15—"No longer do I call you servants .... but I have called you friends "—a relation not of service but of love (Westcott, Bib. Com., *in loco*). The voice that speaks is the voice of love, rather than the voice of law. We object also to Matthew Arnold's definition : " Religion is ethics heightened, enkindled, lit up by feeling ; morality touched with emotion." This leaves out of view the receptive element in religion, as well as its relation to a personal God. A truer statement would be that religion is morality toward God, as morality is religion toward man. Bowne, Philos. of Theism, 251 — " Morality that goes beyond mere conscientiousness must have recourse to religion "; see Lotze, Philos. of Religion, 128-142. Goethe: " Unqualified activity, of whatever kind, leads at last to bankruptcy "; see also Pfleiderer, Philos. Religion, 1 : 65-69 ; Shedd, Sermons to the Natural Man, 244-246 ; Liddon, Elements of Religion, 19.

3. *Essential Idea.* Religion in its essential idea is a life in God, a life lived in recognition of God, in communion with God, and under control of the indwelling Spirit of God. Since it is a life, it cannot be described as consisting solely in the exercise of any one of the powers of intellect, affection, or will. As physical life involves the unity and coöperation of all the organs of the body, so religion, or spiritual life, involves the united working of all the powers of the soul. To feeling, however, we must assign the logical priority, since holy affection toward God, imparted in regeneration, is the condition of truly knowing God and of truly serving him.

See Godet, on the Ultimate Design of Man—" God in man, and man in God "—in Princeton Rev., Nov. 1880 ; Pfleiderer, Die Religion, 5-79, and Religionsphilosophie, 255 —Religion is " Sache des ganzen Geisteslebens "; Crane, Religion of To-morrow, 4—" Religion is the personal influence of the immanent God "; Sterrett, Reason and Authority in Religion, 31, 32—" Religion is the reciprocal relation or communion of God and man, involving (1) revelation, (2) faith "; Dr. J. W. A. Stewart: " Religion is fellowship with God " ; Pascal: " Piety is God sensible to the heart " ; Ritschl, Justif. and Reconcil., 13 —" Christianity is an ellipse with two foci—Christ as Redeemer and Christ as King, Christ for us and Christ in us, redemption and morality, religion and ethics " ; Kaftan, Dogmatik, 8—" The Christian religion is (1) the *kingdom of God* as a goal above the world, to be attained by moral development here, and (2) *reconciliation with God* permitting attainment of this goal in spite of our sins. Christian theology once grounded itself in man's natural knowledge of God; we now start with religion, *i. e.*, that Christian knowledge of God which we call faith."

Herbert Spencer: "Religion is an *a priori* theory of the universe"; Romanes, Thoughts on Religion, 43, adds: "which assumes intelligent personality as the originating cause of the universe, science dealing with the *How*, the phenomenal process, religion dealing with the *Who*, the intelligent Personality who works through the process." Holland, in Lux Mundi, 27—"Natural life is the life in God which has not yet arrived at this recognition"—the recognition of the fact that God is in all things—"it is not yet, as such, religious; ... Religion is the discovery, by the son, of a Father who is in all his works, yet is distinct from them all." Dewey, Psychology, 283—"Feeling finds its absolutely universal expression in religious emotion, which is the finding or realization of self in a completely realized personality which unites in itself truth, or the complete unity of the relations of all objects, beauty or the complete unity of all ideal values, and rightness or the complete unity of all persons. The emotion which accompanies the religious life is that which accompanies the complete activity of ourselves; the self is realized and finds its true life in God." Upton, Hibbert Lectures, 262—"Ethics is simply the growing insight into, and the effort to actualize in society, the sense of fundamental kinship and identity of substance in all men; while religion is the emotion and the devotion which attend the realization in our self-consciousness of an inmost spiritual relationship arising out of that unity of substance which constitutes man the true son of the eternal Father." See Van Oosterzee, Dogmatics, 81–85; Julius Müller, Doct. Sin, 2 : 227; Nitzsch, Syst. of Christ. Doct., 10–28; Luthardt, Fund. Truths, 147; Twesten, Dogmatik, 1 : 12.

4. *Inferences.*

From this definition of religion it follows :

(*a*) That in strictness there is but one religion. Man is a religious being, indeed, as having the capacity for this divine life. He is actually religious, however, only when he enters into this living relation to God. False religions are the caricatures which men given to sin, or the imaginations which men groping after light, form of this life of the soul in God.

Peabody, Christianity the Religion of Nature, 18—"If Christianity be true, it is not *a* religion, but *the* religion. If Judaism be also true, it is so not as distinct from but as coincident with Christianity, the one religion to which it can bear only the relation of a part to the whole. If there be portions of truth in other religious systems, they are not portions of other religions, but portions of the one religion which somehow or other became incorporated with fables and falsities." John Caird, Fund. Ideas of Christianity, 1 : 25 — "You can never get at the true idea or essence of religion merely by trying to find out something that is common to all religions; and it is not the lower religions that explain the higher, but conversely the higher religion explains all the lower religions." George P. Fisher: "The recognition of certain elements of truth in the ethnic religions does not mean that Christianity has defects which are to be repaired by borrowing from them; it only means that the ethnic faiths have in fragments what Christianity has as a whole. Comparative religion does not bring to Christianity new truth; it provides illustrations of how Christian truth meets human needs and aspirations, and gives a full vision of that which the most spiritual and gifted among the heathen only dimly discerned."

Dr. C. H. Parkhurst, sermon on Proverbs 20 : 27—"The spirit of man is the lamp of Jehovah"—"a lamp, but not necessarily lighted; a lamp that can be lit only by the touch of a divine flame" = man has naturally and universally a capacity for religion, but is by no means naturally and universally religious. All false religions have some element of truth; otherwise they could never have gained or kept their hold upon mankind. We need to recognize these elements of truth in dealing with them. There is some silver in a counterfeit dollar, else it would deceive no one; but the thin washing of silver over the lead does not prevent it from being bad money. Clarke, Christian Theology, 8—"See Paul's methods of dealing with heathen religion, in Acts 14 with gross paganism and in Acts 17 with its cultured form. He treats it with sympathy and justice. Christian theology has the advantage of walking in the light of God's self-manifestation in Christ, while heathen

religions grope after God and worship him in ignorance"; *cf.* Acts 14 : 15—"We . . bring you good tidings, that ye should turn from these vain things unto a living God"; 17: 22—"I perceive that ye are more than usually reverent toward the divinities. . . . What therefore ye worship in ignorance, this I set forth unto you."

Matthew Arnold: "Children of men! the unseen Power whose eye Forever doth accompany mankind, Hath looked on no religion scornfully That man did ever find. Which has not taught weak wills how much they can? Which has not fallen on the dry heart like rain? Which has not cried to sunk, self-weary man, Thou must be born again?" Christianity is absolutely exclusive, because it is absolutely inclusive. It is not an amalgamation of other religions, but it has in it all that is best and truest in other religions. It is the white light that contains all the colored rays. God may have made disclosures of truth outside of Judaism, and did so in Balaam and Melchisedek, in Confucius and Socrates. But while other religions have a relative excellence, Christianity is the absolute religion that contains all excellencies. Matheson, Messages of the Old Religions, 328-342 — "Christianity is reconciliation. Christianity includes the aspiration of Egypt; it sees, in this aspiration, God in the soul (Brahmanism); recognizes the evil power of sin with Parseeism; goes back to a pure beginning like China; surrenders itself to human brotherhood like Buddha; gets all things from within like Judaism; makes the present life beautiful like Greece; seeks a universal kingdom like Rome; shows a growth of divine life, like the Teuton. Christianity is the manifold wisdom of God." See also Van Oosterzee, Dogmatics, 88-93, Shakespeare: "There is some soul of goodness in things evil, Would men observingly distill it out."

(*b*) That the content of religion is greater than that of theology. The facts of religion come within the range of theology only so far as they can be definitely conceived, accurately expressed in language, and brought into rational relation to each other.

This principle enables us to define the proper limits of religious fellowship. It should be as wide as is religion itself. But it is important to remember what religion is. Religion is not to be identified with the capacity for religion. Nor can we regard the perversions and caricatures of religion as meriting our fellowship. Otherwise we might be required to have fellowship with devil-worship, polygamy, thuggery, and the inquisition; for all these have been dignified with the name of religion. True religion involves some knowledge, however rudimentary, of the true God, the God of righteousness; some sense of sin as the contrast between human character and the divine standard: some casting of the soul upon divine mercy and a divine way of salvation, in place of self-righteous earning of merit and reliance upon one's works and one's record; some practical effort to realize ethical principle in a pure life and in influence over others. Wherever these marks of true religion appear, even in Unitarians, Romanists, Jews or Buddhists, there we recognize the demand for fellowship. But we also attribute these germs of true religion to the inworking of the omnipresent Christ, "the light which lighteth every man" (John 1: 9), and we see in them incipient repentance and faith, even though the Christ who is their object is yet unknown by name. *Christian* fellowship must have a larger basis in accepted Christian truth, and *Church* fellowship a still larger basis in common acknowledgment of N. T. teaching as to the church. *Religious* fellowship, in the widest sense, rests upon the fact that "God is no respecter of persons: but in every nation he that feareth him and worketh righteousness is acceptable to him" (Acts 10 : 34, 35).

(*c*) That religion is to be distinguished from formal worship, which is simply the outward expression of religion. As such expression, worship is "formal communion between God and his people." In it God speaks to man, and man to God. It therefore properly includes the reading of Scripture and preaching on the side of God, and prayer and song on the side of the people.

Sterrett, Reason and Authority in Religion, 166—"Christian worship is the utterance (outerance) of the spirit." But there is more in true love than can be put into a love-letter, and there is more in true religion than can be expressed either in theology or in worship. Christian worship is communion between God and man. But communion cannot be one-sided. Madame de Staël, whom Heine called "a whirlwind in petticoats," ended one of her brilliant soliloquies by saying: "What a delightful conversation we have had!" We may find a better illustration of the nature of worship in Thomas à Kempis's dialogues between the saint and his Savior, in the Imitation of Christ. Goethe: "Against the great superiority of another there is no remedy but love. . . . To praise a man is to put one's self on his level." If this be the effect of loving and praising man, what must be the effect of loving and praising God! Inscription in Grasmere Church: "Whoever thou art that enterest this church, leave it not without one prayer to God for thyself, for those who minister, and for those who worship here." In James 1: 27—"Pure religion and undefiled before our God and Father is this, to visit the fatherless and widows in their affliction, and to keep oneself unspotted from the world"—"religion," θρησκεία, is *cultus exterior;* and the meaning is that "the external service, the outward garb, the very ritual of Christianity, is a life of purity, love and self-devotion. What its true essence, its inmost spirit may be, the writer does not say, but leaves this to be inferred." On the relation between religion and worship, see Prof. Day, in New Englander, Jan. 1882; **Prof. T.** Harwood Pattison, Public Prayer; Trench, Syn. N. T., 1: sec. 48; Coleridge, **Aids to Reflection,** Introd., Aphorism 23; Lightfoot, Gal., 351, note 2.

CHAPTER II.

I. Sources of Theology.—God himself, in the last analysis, must be the only source of knowledge with regard to his own being and relations. Theology is therefore a summary and explanation of the content of God's self-revelations. These are, first, the revelation of God in nature; secondly and supremely, the revelation of God in the Scriptures.

Ambrose: "To whom shall I give greater credit concerning God than to God himself?" Von Baader: "To know God without God is impossible; there is no knowledge without him who is the prime source of knowledge." C. A. Briggs, Whither, 8 — "God reveals truth in several spheres: in universal nature, in the constitution of mankind, in the history of our race, in the Sacred Scriptures, but above all in the person of Jesus Christ our Lord." F. H. Johnson, What is Reality? 39 — "The teacher intervenes when needed. Revelation *helps* reason and conscience, but is not a *substitute* for them. But Catholicism affirms this substitution for the church, and Protestantism for the Bible. The Bible, like nature, gives many free gifts, but more in the germ. Growing ethical ideals must interpret the Bible." A. J. F. Behrends: "The Bible is only a telescope, not the eye which sees, nor the stars which the telescope brings to view. It is your business and mine to see the stars with our own eyes." Schurman, Agnosticism, 178 — "The Bible is a glass through which to see the living God. But it is useless when you put your eyes out."

We can know God only so far as he has revealed himself. The immanent God is known, but the transcendent God we do not know any more than we know the side of the moon that is turned away from us. A. H. Strong, Christ in Creation, 113 — "The word 'authority' is derived from *auctor*, *augeo*, 'to add.' Authority *adds* something to the truth communicated. The thing added is the personal element of *witness*. This is needed wherever there is ignorance which cannot be removed by our own effort, or unwillingness which results from our own sin. In religion I need to add to my own knowledge that which God imparts. Reason, conscience, church, Scripture, are all delegated and subordinate authorities; the only original and supreme authority is God himself, or Christ, who is only God revealed and made comprehensible by us." Gore, Incarnation, 181 — "All legitimate authority represents the reason of God, educating the reason of man and communicating itself to it..... Man is made in God's image: he is, in his fundamental capacity, a son of God, and he becomes so in fact, and fully, through union with Christ. Therefore in the truth of God, as Christ presents it to him, he can recognize his own better reason, — to use Plato's beautiful expression, he can salute it by force of instinct as something akin to himself, before he can give intellectual account of it."

Balfour, Foundations of Belief, 332-337, holds that there is no such thing as unassisted reason, and that, even if there were, natural religion is not one of its products. Behind all evolution of our own reason, he says, stands the Supreme Reason. "Conscience, ethical ideals, capacity for admiration, sympathy, repentance, righteous indignation, as well as our delight in beauty and truth, are all derived from God." Kaftan, in Am. Jour. Theology, 1900; 718, 719, maintains that there is no other principle for dogmatics than Holy Scripture. Yet he holds that knowledge never comes directly from Scripture, but from faith. The order is not: Scripture, doctrine, faith; but rather, Scripture, faith, doctrine. Scripture is no more a direct authority than is the church. Revelation is addressed to the whole man, that is, to the *will* of the man, and it claims *obedience* from him. Since all Christian knowledge is mediated through faith, it rests on obedience to the authority of revelation, and revelation is self-manifestation on the part of God. Kaftan should have recognized more fully that not simply Scripture, but all knowable truth, is a revelation from God, and that Christ is "the light which lighteth every man" (John 1:9). Revelation is an organic whole, which begins in nature, but finds its climax and key in the historical Christ whom Scripture presents to us. See H. C. Minton's review of Martineau's Seat of Authority, in Presb. and Ref. Rev., Apr. 1900: 203 *sq.*

1. *Scripture and Nature.* By nature we here mean not only physical facts, or facts with regard to the substances, properties, forces, and laws of the material world, but also spiritual facts, or facts with regard to the intellectual and moral constitution of man, and the orderly arrangement of human society and history.

We here use the word "nature" in the ordinary sense, as including man. There is another and more proper use of the word "nature," which makes it simply a complex of forces and beings under the law of cause and effect. To nature in this sense man belongs only as respects his body, while as immaterial and personal he is a supernatural being. F ee will is not under the law of physical and mechanical causation. As Bushnell has said: "Nature and the supernatural together constitute the one system of God." Drummond, Natural Law in the Spiritual World, 232 — "Things are natural or supernatural according to where we stand. Man is supernatural to the mineral; God is supernatural to the man." We shall in subsequent chapters use the term "nature" in the narrow sense. The universal use of the phrase "Natural Theology," however, compels us in this chapter to employ the word "nature" in its broader sense as including man, although we do this under protest, and with this explanation of the more proper meaning of the term. See Hopkins, in Princeton Review, Sept. 1882: 183 *sq.*

E. G. Robinson: "Bushnell separates nature from the supernatural. Nature is a blind train of causes. God has nothing to do with it, except as he steps into it from without. Man is supernatural, because he is outside of nature, having the power of originating an independent train of causes." If this were the proper conception of nature, then we might be compelled to conclude with P. T. Forsyth, in Faith and Criticism, 100 — "There is no revelation in nature. There can be none, because there is no forgiveness. We cannot be sure about her. She is only æsthetic. Her ideal is harmony, not reconciliation. . . . . For the conscience, stricken or strong, she has no word. . . . Nature does not contain her own teleology, and for the moral soul that refuses to be fancy-fed, Christ is the one luminous smile on the dark face of the world." But this is virtually to confine Christ's revelation to Scripture or to the incarnation. As there was an astronomy without the telescope, so there was a theology before the Bible. George Harris, Moral Evolution, 411 — "Nature is both evolution and revelation. As soon as the question *How* is answered, the questions *Whence* and *Why* arise. Nature is to God what speech is to thought." The title of Henry Drummond's book should have been: "Spiritual Law in the Natural World," for nature is but the free though regular activity of God; what we call the supernatural is simply his extraordinary working.

(*a*) Natural theology. — The universe is a source of theology. The Scriptures assert that God has revealed himself in nature. There is not only an outward witness to his existence and character in the constitution and government of the universe (Ps. 19; Acts 14:17; Rom. 1:20), but an inward witness to his existence and character in the heart of every man (Rom. 1:17, 18, 19, 20, 32; 2:15). The systematic exhibition of these facts, whether derived from observation, history or science, constitutes natural theology.

Outward witness: Ps. 19:1-6 — "The heavens declare the glory of God"; Acts 14:17 — "he left not himself without witness, in that he did good, and gave you from heaven rains and fruitful seasons"; Rom. 1:20 — "for the invisible things of him since the creation of the world are clearly seen, being perceived through the things that are made, even his everlasting power and divinity." Inward witness: Rom. 1:19 — τὸ γνωστὸν τοῦ Θεοῦ = "that which is known of God is manifest in them." Compare the ἀποκαλύπτεται of the gospel in verse 17, with the ἀποκαλύπτεται of wrath in verse 18 — two revelations, one of ὀργή, the other of χάρις; see Shedd, Homiletics, 11. Rom. 1:32 — "knowing the ordinance of God"; 2:15 — "they show the work of the law written in their hearts." Therefore even the heathen are "without excuse" (Rom. 1:20). There are two books: Nature and Scripture — one written, the other unwritten: and there is need of studying both. On the passages in Romans, see the Commentary of Hodge.

Spurgeon told of a godly person who, when sailing down the Rhine, closed his eyes, lest the beauty of the scene should divert his mind from spiritual themes. The Puritan turned away from the moss-rose, saying that he would count nothing on earth lovely. But this is to despise God's works. J. H. Barrows: "The Himalayas are the raised letters upon which we blind children put our fingers to spell out the name of God." To despise the works of God is to despise God himself. God is present in nature, and is now speaking. Ps. 19 : 1 — "The heavens declare the glory of God, and the firmament showeth his handiwork" — present tenses. Nature is not so much a *book*, as a *voice*. Hutton, Essays, 2 : 236 — "The direct knowledge of spiritual communion must be supplemented by knowledge of God's ways gained from the study of nature. To neglect the study of the natural mysteries of the universe leads to an arrogant and illicit intrusion of moral and spiritual assumptions into a different world. This is the lesson of the book of Job." Hatch, Hibbert Lectures, 85 — "Man, the servant and interpreter of nature, is also, and is thereby, the servant and interpreter of the living God." Books of science are the record of man's past interpretations of God's works.

(*b*) Natural theology supplemented. — The Christian revelation is the chief source of theology. The Scriptures plainly declare that the revelation of God in nature does not supply all the knowledge which a sinner needs (Acts 17 : 23 ; Eph. 3 : 9). This revelation is therefore supplemented by another, in which divine attributes and merciful provisions only dimly shadowed forth in nature are made known to men. This latter revelation consists of a series of supernatural events and communications, the record of which is presented in the Scriptures.

Acts 17 : 23 — Paul shows that, though the Athenians, in the erection of an altar to an unknown God, "acknowledged a divine existence beyond any which the ordinary rites of their worship recognized, that Being was still unknown to them ; they had no just conception of his nature and perfections" (Hackett, *in loco*). Eph. 3 : 9 — "the mystery which hath been hid in God" — this mystery is in the gospel made known for man's salvation. Hegel, in his Philosophy of Religion, says that Christianity is the only revealed religion, because the Christian God is the only one from whom a revelation can come. We may add that as science is the record of man's progressive interpretation of God's revelation in the realm of nature, so Scripture is the record of man's progressive interpretation of God's revelation in the realm of spirit. The phrase "word of God " does not primarily denote a *record*, — it is the *spoken* word, the *doctrine*, the vitalizing *truth*, disclosed by Christ ; see Mat. 13 : 19 — "heareth the word of the kingdom"; Luke 5 : 1 — "heard the word of God "; Acts 8 : 25 — "spoken the word of the Lord " ; 13 : 48,49 — "glorified the word of God : . . . the word of the Lord was spread abroad " ; 19 : 10, 20 — "heard the word of the Lord, . . . mightily grew the word of the Lord "; 1 Cor. 1 : 18 — "the word of the cross " — all designating not a document, but an unwritten word ; *cf.* Jer. 1 : 4 — "the word of Jehovah came unto me " ; Ez. 1 : 3 — "the word of Jehovah came expressly unto Ezekiel, the priest."

(*c*) The Scriptures the final standard of appeal. — Science and Scripture throw light upon each other. The same divine Spirit who gave both revelations is still present, enabling the believer to interpret the one by the other and thus progressively to come to the knowledge of the truth. Because of our finiteness and sin, the total record in Scripture of God's past communications is a more trustworthy source of theology than are our conclusions from nature or our private impressions of the teaching of the Spirit. Theology therefore looks to the Scripture itself as its chief source of material and its final standard of appeal.

There is an internal work of the divine Spirit by which the outer word is made an inner word, and its truth and power are manifested to the heart. Scripture represents this work of the Spirit, not as a giving of new truth, but as an illumination of the mind to perceive the fulness of meaning which lay wrapped up in the truth already revealed. Christ is "the truth" (John 14:6); "in whom are all the treasures of wisdom and knowledge hidden" (Col. 2:3); the Holy Spirit, Jesus says, "shall take of mine, and shall declare it unto you" (John 16:14). The incarnation and the Cross express the heart of God and the secret of the universe; all discoveries in theology are but the unfolding of truth involved in these facts. The Spirit of Christ enables us to compare nature with Scripture, and Scripture with nature, and to correct mistakes in interpreting the one by light gained from the other. Because the church as a whole, by which we mean the company of true believers in all lands and ages, has the promise that it shall be guided "into all the truth" (John 16:13), we may confidently expect the progress of Christian doctrine.

Christian experience is sometimes regarded as an original source of religious truth. Experience, however, is but a testing and proving of the truth objectively contained in God's revelation. The word "experience" is derived from *experior*, to test, to try. Christian consciousness is not "norma normans," but "norma normata." Light, like life, comes to us through the mediation of others. Yet the first comes from God as really as the last, of which without hesitation we say: "God made me," though we have human parents. As I get through the service pipe in my house the same water which is stored in the reservoir upon the hillside, so in the Scriptures I get the same truth which the Holy Spirit originally communicated to prophets and apostles. Calvin, Institutes, book I, chap. 7—"As nature has an immediate manifestation of God in conscience, a mediate in his works, so revelation has an immediate manifestation of God in the Spirit, a mediate in the Scriptures." "Man's nature," said Spurgeon, "is not an organized lie, yet his inner consciousness has been warped by sin, and though once it was an infallible guide to truth and duty, sin has made it very deceptive. The standard of infallibility is not in man's consciousness, but in the Scriptures. When consciousness in any matter is contrary to the word of God, we must know that it is not God's voice within us, but the devil's." Dr. George A. Gordon says that "Christian history is a revelation of Christ additional to that contained in the New Testament." Should we not say "illustrative," instead of "additional"? On the relation between Christian experience and Scripture, see Stearns, Evidence of Christian Experience, 286–309; Twesten, Dogmatik, 1:344–348; Hodge, Syst. Theol., 1:15.

H. H. Bawden: "God is the ultimate authority, but there are delegated authorities, such as family, state, church; instincts, feelings, conscience; the general experience of the race, traditions, utilities; revelation in nature and in Scripture. But the highest authority available for men in morals and religion is the truth concerning Christ contained in the Christian Scriptures. What the truth concerning Christ *is*, is determined by: (1) the human reason, conditioned by a right attitude of the feelings and the will; (2) in the light of all the truth derived from nature, including man; (3) in the light of the history of Christianity; (4) in the light of the origin and development of the Scriptures themselves. The authority of the generic reason and the authority of the Bible are co-relative, since they both have been developed in the providence of God, and since the latter is in large measure but the reflection of the former. This view enables us to hold a rational conception of the function of the Scripture in religion. This view, further, enables us to rationalize what is called the inspiration of the Bible, the nature and extent of inspiration, the Bible as history—a record of the historic unfolding of revelation; the Bible as literature — a compend of life-principles, rather than a book of rules; the Bible Christocentric—an incarnation of the divine thought and will in human thought and language."

(*d*) The theology of Scripture not unnatural.—Though we speak of the systematized truths of nature as constituting natural theology, we are not to infer that Scriptural theology is unnatural. Since the Scriptures have the same author as nature, the same principles are illustrated in the one as in the other. All the doctrines of the Bible have their reason in that same nature of God which constitutes the basis of all material things. Christianity is a supplementary dispensation, not as contradicting, or correcting errors in, natural theology, but as more perfectly revealing the truth. Christianity is indeed the ground-plan upon which the whole creation is built—the original and eternal truth of which natural theology is but a partial expression. Hence the theology of nature and the theology of Scripture are mutually dependent. Natural theology not only prepares the way for, but it receives stimulus and aid from, Scriptural theology. Natural theology may now be a source of truth, which, before the Scriptures came, it could not furnish.

John Caird, Fund. Ideas of Christianity, 23 — "There is no such thing as a natural religion or religion of reason distinct from revealed religion. Christianity is more profoundly, more comprehensively, rational, more accordant with the deepest principles of human nature and human thought than is natural religion; or, as we may put it, Christianity is natural religion elevated and transmuted into revealed." Peabody, Christianity the Religion of Nature, lecture 2 — "Revelation is the unveiling, uncovering of what previously existed, and it excludes the idea of newness, invention, creation. . . . The revealed religion of earth is the natural religion of heaven." Compare Rev. 13 : 8 — " the Lamb that hath been slain from the foundation of the world " = the coming of Christ was no make-shift ; in a true sense the Cross existed in eternity ; the atonement is a revelation of an eternal fact in the being of God.

Note Plato's illustration of the cave which can be easily threaded by one who has previously entered it with a torch. Nature is the dim light from the cave's mouth; the torch is Scripture. Kant to Jacobi, in Jacobi's Werke, 3 : 523 — " If the gospel had _ot previously taught the universal moral laws, reason would not yet have obtained so perfect an insight into them." Alexander McLaren : " Non-Christian thinkers now talk eloquently about God's love, and even reject the gospel in the name of that love, thus kicking down the ladder by which they have climbed. But it was the Cross that taught the world the love of God, and apart from the death of Christ men may hope that there is a heart at the centre of the universe, but they can never be sure of it." The parrot fancies that he taught men to talk. So Mr. Spencer fancies that he invented ethics. He is only using the twilight, after his sun has gone down. Dorner, Hist. Prot. Theol., 252, 253 — " Faith, at the Reformation, first gave scientific certainty ; it had God sure : hence it proceeded to banish scepticism in philosophy and science." See also Dove, Logic of Christian Faith, 333 ; Bowen, Metaph. and Ethics, 442-463 ; Bib. Sac., 1874 : 436 ; A. H. Strong, Christ in Creation, 226, 227.

2. *Scripture and Rationalism.* Although the Scriptures make known much that is beyond the power of man's unaided reason to discover or fully to comprehend, their teachings, when taken together, in no way contradict a reason conditioned in its activity by a holy affection and enlightened by the Spirit of God. To reason in the large sense, as including the mind's power of cognizing God and moral relations — not in the narrow sense of mere reasoning, or the exercise of the purely logical faculty — the Scriptures continually appeal.

A. The proper office of reason, in this large sense, is : (*a*) To furnish us with those primary ideas of space, time, cause, substance, design, right, and God, which are the conditions of all subsequent knowledge. (*b*) To judge with regard to man's need of a special and supernatural revelation. (*c*) To examine the credentials of communications professing to be, or of documents professing to record, such a revelation. (*d*) To estimate and reduce to system the facts of revelation, when these have been found properly attested. (*e*) To deduce from these facts their natural and logical conclusions. Thus reason itself prepares the way for a revelation above reason, and warrants an implicit trust in such revelation when once given.

Dove, Logic of the Christian Faith, 318 — " Reason terminates in the proposition Look for revelation." Leibnitz : " Revelation is the viceroy who first presents his credentials to the provincial assembly (reason), and then himself presides." Reason can recognize truth after it is made known, as for example in the demonstrations of geometry, although it could never discover that truth for itself. See Calderwood's illustration of the party lost in the woods, who wisely take the course indicated by one at the tree-top with a larger view than their own (Philosophy of the Infinite, 126). The novice does well to trust his guide in the forest, at least till he learns to recognize for himself the marks blazed upon the trees. Luthardt, Fund. Truths, lect. viii—"Reason could never have invented a self-humiliating God, cradled in a manger and dying on a cross." Lessing, Zur Geschichte und Litteratur, 6 : 134—"What is the meaning of a revelation that reveals nothing ?"

Ritschl denies the presuppositions of any theology based on the Bible as the infallible word of God on the one hand, and on the validity of the knowledge of God as obtained by scientific and philosophic processes on the other. Because philosophers, scientists, and even exegetes, are not agreed among themselves, he concludes that no trustworthy results are attainable by human reason. We grant that reason without love will fall into many errors with regard to God, and that faith is therefore the organ by which religious truth is to be apprehended. But we claim that this faith includes reason, and is itself reason in its highest form. Faith criticizes and judges the processes of natural science as well as the contents of Scripture. But it also recognizes in science and Scripture prior workings of that same Spirit of Christ which is the source and authority of the Christian life. Ritschl ignores Christ's world-relations and therefore secularizes and disparages science and philosophy. The faith to which he trusts as the source of theology is unwarrantably sundered from reason. It becomes a subjective and arbitrary standard, to which even the teaching of Scripture must yield precedence. We hold on the contrary, that there are ascertained results in science and in philosophy, as well as in the interpretation of Scripture as a whole, and that these results constitute an authoritative revelation. See Orr, The Theology of Ritschl; Dorner, Hist. Prot. Theol., 1 : 233—"The unreasonable in the empirical reason is taken captive by faith, which is the nascent true reason that despairs of itself and trustfully lays hold of objective Christianity."

B. Rationalism, on the other hand, holds reason to be the ultimate source of all religious truth, while Scripture is authoritative only so far as its revelations agree with previous conclusions of reason, or can be rationally demonstrated. Every form of rationalism, therefore, commits at least one of the following errors : (a) That of confounding reason with mere reasoning, or the exercise of the logical intelligence. (b) That of ignoring the necessity of a holy affection as the condition of all right reason in religious things. (c) That of denying our dependence in our present state of sin upon God's past revelations of himself. (d) That of regarding the unaided reason, even its normal and unbiased state, as capable of discovering, comprehending, and demonstrating all religious truth.

Reason must not be confounded with ratiocination, or mere reasoning. Shall we follow reason ? Yes, but not individual reasoning, against the testimony of those who are better informed than we ; nor by insisting on demonstration, where probable evidence alone is possible ; nor by trusting solely to the evidence of the senses, when spiritual things are in question. Coleridge, in replying to those who argued that all knowledge comes to us from the senses, says : " At any rate we must bring to all facts the light in which we see them." This the Christian does. The light of love reveals much that would otherwise be invisible. Wordsworth, Excursion, book 5 (598) — "The mind's repose On evidence is not to be ensured By act of naked reason. Moral truth Is no mechanic structure, built by rule."

Rationalism is the mathematical theory of knowledge. Spinoza's Ethics is an illustration of it. It would deduce the universe from an axiom. Dr. Hodge very wrongly described rationalism as "an overuse of reason." It is rather the use of an abnormal, perverted, improperly conditioned reason ; see Hodge, Syst. Theol., 1 : 34, 39, 55, and criticism by Miller, in his Fetich in Theology. The phrase " sanctified intellect " means simply intellect accompanied by right affections toward God, and trained to work under their influence. Bishop Butler : " Let reason be kept to, but let not such poor creatures as we are go on objecting to an infinite scheme that we do not see the necessity or usefulness of all its parts, and call that reasoning." Newman Smyth, Death's Place in Evolution, 86—"Unbelief is a shaft sunk down into the darkness of the earth.

Drive the shaft deep enough, and it would come out into the sunlight on the earth's other side." The most unreasonable people in the world are those who depend solely upon reason, in the narrow sense. "The better to exalt reason, they make the world irrational." "The hen that has hatched ducklings walks with them to the water's edge, but there she stops, and she is amazed when they go on. So reason stops and faith goes on, finding its proper element in the invisible. Reason is the feet that stand on solid earth; faith is the wings that enable us to fly; and normal man is a creature with wings." Compare γνῶσις (1 Tim. 6 : 20 — "the knowledge which is falsely so called") with ἐπίγνωσι (2 Pet. 1 : 2 — "the knowledge of God and of Jesus our Lord" = full knowledge, or true knowledge) See Twesten, Dogmatik, 1 : 467-500; Julius Müller, Proof-texts, 4, 5; Mansel, Limits of Religious Thought, 96 ; Dawson, Modern Ideas of Evolution.

3. *Scripture and Mysticism.* As rationalism recognizes too little as coming from God, so mysticism recognizes too much.

A. True mysticism.—We have seen that there is an illumination of the minds of all believers by the Holy Spirit. The Spirit, however, makes no new revelation of truth, but uses for his instrument the truth already revealed by Christ in nature and in the Scriptures. The illuminating work of the Spirit is therefore an opening of men's minds to understand Christ's previous revelations. As one initiated into the mysteries of Christianity, every true believer may be called a mystic. True mysticism is that higher knowledge and fellowship which the Holy Spirit gives through the use of nature and Scripture as subordinate and principal means.

" Mystic " = one initiated, from μύω, "to close the eyes " — probably in order that the soul may have inward vision of truth. But divine truth is a "mystery," not only as something into which one must be initiated, but as ὑπερβάλλουσα τῆς γνώσεως (Eph. 3 : 19) —surpassing full knowledge, even to the believer ; see Meyer on Rom. 11 : 25 — " I would not, brethren, have you ignorant of this mystery." The Germans have *Mystik* with a favorable sense, *Mysticismus* with an unfavorable sense,— corresponding respectively to our true and false mysticism. True mysticism is intimated in John 16 : 13 — "the spirit of truth . . . shall guide you into all the truth "; Eph. 3 : 9 — "dispensation of the mystery " ; 1 Cor. 2 : 10 — "unto us God revealed them through the Spirit." Nitzsch, Syst. of Christ. Doct., 35 — " Whenever true religion revives, there is an outcry against mysticism, *i. e.*, higher knowledge, fellowship, activity through the Spirit of God in the heart." Compare the charge against Paul that he was mad, in Acts 26 : 24, 25, with his self-vindication in 2 Cor. 5 : 13 — "whether we are beside ourselves, it is unto God."

Inge, Christian Mysticism, 21 — " Harnack speaks of mysticism as rationalism applied to a sphere above reason. He should have said reason applied to a sphere above rationalism. Its fundamental doctrine is the unity of all existence. Man can realize his individuality only by transcending it and finding himself in the larger unity of God'. being. Man is a microcosm. He recapitulates the race, the universe, Christ himself." *Ibid.*, 5 — Mysticism is "the attempt to realize in thought and feeling the immanence of the temporal in the eternal, and of the eternal in the temporal. It implies (1) that the soul can see and perceive spiritual truth ; (2) that man, in order to know God, must be a partaker of the divine nature ; (3) that without holiness no man can see the Lord; (4) that the true hierophant of the mysteries of God is love. The 'scala perfectionis' is (a) the purgative life ; (b) the illuminative life; (c) the unitive life." Stevens, Johannine Theology, 239, 240—"The mysticism of John . . . is not a subjective mysticism which absorbs the soul in self-contemplation and revery, but an objective and rational mysticism, which lives in a world of realities, apprehends divinely revealed truth, and bases its experience upon it. It is a mysticism which feeds, not upon its own feelings and fancies, but upon Christ. It involves an acceptance of him, and a life of obedience to him. Its motto is: Abiding in Christ." As the power press cannot dispense with the type, so the Spirit of God does not dispense with Christ's external revelations in nature and in Scripture. E. G. Robinson, Christian Theology, 364 — " The word of God is a form or mould, into which the Holy Spirit delivers us when he creates us anew " ; *cf.* Rom. 6 : 17 — "ye became obedient from the heart to that form of teaching whereunto ye were delivered "

B. False mysticism. — Mysticism, however, as the term is commonly used, errs in holding to the attainment of religious knowledge by direct communication from God, and by passive absorption of the human activities into the divine. It either partially or wholly loses sight of (*a*) the outward organs of revelation, nature and the Scriptures ; (*b*) the activity of the human powers in the reception of all religious knowledge ; (*c*) the personality of man, and, by consequence, the personality of God.

In opposition to false mysticism, we are to remember that the Holy Spirit works through the truth externally revealed in nature and in Scripture (Acts 14 : 17 — " he left not himself without witness "; Rom. 1 : 20 — " the invisible things of him since the creation of the world are clearly seen " ; Acts 7 : 51 — " ye do always resist the Holy Spirit : as your fathers did, so do ye " ; Eph. 6 : 17 — " the sword of the Spirit, which is the word of God "). By this truth already given we are to test all new communications which would contradict or supersede it (1 John 4 : 1 — " believe not every spirit, but prove the spirits, whether they are of God "; Eph. 5 : 10—"proving what is well pleasing unto the Lord "). By these tests we may try Spiritualism, Mormonism, Swedenborgianism. Note the mystical tendency in Francis de Sales, Thomas à Kempis, Madame Guyon, Thomas C. Upham. These writers seem at times to advocate an unwarrantable abnegation of our reason and will, and a "swallowing up of man in God." But Christ does not deprive us of reason and will ; he only takes from us the perverseness of our reason and the selfishness of our will ; so reason and will are restored to their normal clearness and strength. Compare Ps. 16 : 7 — " Jehovah, who hath given me counsel ; yea, my heart instructeth me in the night seasons " = God teaches his people through the exercise of their own faculties.

False mysticism is sometimes present though unrecognized. All expectation of results without the use of means partakes of it. Martineau, Seat of Authority, 288 — "The lazy will would like to have the vision while the eye that apprehends it sleeps." Preaching without preparation is like throwing ourselves down from a pinnacle of the temple and depending on God to send an angel to hold us up. Christian Science would trust to supernatural agencies, while casting aside the natural agencies God has already provided ; as if a drowning man should trust to prayer while refusing to seize the rope. Using Scripture " ad aperturam libri " is like guiding one's actions by a throw of the dice. Allen, Jonathan Edwards, 171, note — "Both Charles and John Wesley were agreed in accepting the Moravian method of solving doubts as to some course of action by opening the Bible at hazard and regarding the passage on which the eye first alighted as a revelation of God's will in the matter " ; *cf.* Wedgwood, Life of Wesley, 193; Southey, Life of Wesley, 1 : 216. J. G. Paton, Life, 2 : 74 — "After many prayers and wrestlings and tears, I went alone before the Lord, and on my knees cast lots, with a solemn appeal to God, and the answer came : ' Go home! ' " He did this only once in his life, in overwhelming perplexity, and finding no light from human counsel. " To whomsoever this faith is given," he says, " let him obey it."

F. B. Meyer, Christian Living, 18 — " It is a mistake to seek a sign from heaven ; to run from counsellor to counsellor ; to cast a lot ; or to trust in some chance coincidence. Not that God may not reveal his will thus ; but because it is hardly the behavior of a child with its Father. There is a more excellent way," — namely, appropriate Christ who is wisdom, and then go forward, sure that we shall be guided, as each new step must be taken, or word spoken, or decision made. Our service is to be "rational service" (Rom. 12 : 1) ; blind and arbitrary action is inconsistent with the spirit of Christianity. Such action makes us victims of temporary feeling and a prey to Satanic deception. In cases of perplexity, waiting for light and waiting upon God will commonly enable us to make an intelligent decision, while "whatsoever is not of faith is sin " (Rom. 14 : 23).

" False mysticism reached its logical result in the Buddhistic theosophy. In that system man becomes most divine in the extinction of his own personality. Nirvana is reached by the eightfold path of right view, aspiration, speech, conduct, livelihood, effort, mindfulness, rapture ; and Nirvana is the loss of ability to say : ' This is I,' and ' This is mine.' Such was Hypatia's attempt, by subjection of self, to be wafted away into the arms of Jove. George Eliot was wrong when she said : ' The happiest woman has no history.' Self-denial is not self-effacement. The cracked bell has no individuality. In Christ we become our complete selves." Col. 2 : 9, 10 — " For in him dwelleth all the fulness of the Godhead bodily, and in him ye are made full."

Royce, World and Individual, 2 : 248, 249 — " Assert the spiritual man ; abnegate the natural man. The fleshly self is the root of all evil ; the spiritual self belongs to a higher realm. But this spiritual self lies at first outside the soul; it becomes ours only by grace. Plato rightly made the eternal Ideas the source of all human truth and goodness. Wisdom comes into a man, like Aristotle's νοῦς." A. H. Bradford, The Inner Light, in making the direct teaching of the Holy Spirit the sufficient if not the sole source of religious knowledge, seems to us to ignore the principle of evolution in religion. God builds upon the past. His revelation to prophets and apostles constitutes the norm and corrective of our individual experience, even while our experience throws new light upon that revelation. On Mysticism, true and false, see Inge, Christian Mysticism, 4, 5, 11; Stearns, Evidence of Christian Experience, 289-294; Dorner, Geschichte d. prot. Theol., 48-59, 243; Herzog, Encycl., art.: Mystik, by Lange; Vaughan, Hours with the Mystics, 1 : 199; Morell, Hist. Philos., 58, 191-215, 556-625, 726; Hodge, Syst. Theol., 1 : 61-69, 97, 104; Fleming, Vocab. Philos., *in voce*; Tholuck, Introd. to Blüthensammlung aus der morgenländischen Mystik; William James, Varieties of Religious Experience, 379-429.

4. *Scripture and Romanism.* While the history of doctrine, as show-ing the progressive apprehension and unfolding by the church of the truth contained in nature and Scripture, is a subordinate source of theology, Protestantism recognizes the Bible as under Christ the primary and final authority.

Romanism, on the other hand, commits the two-fold error (*a*) Of making the church, and not the Scriptures, the immediate and sufficient source of religious knowledge; and (*b*) Of making the relation of the individual to Christ depend upon his relation to the church, instead of making his rela-tion to the church depend upon, follow, and express his relation to Christ.

In Roman Catholicism there is a mystical element. The Scriptures are not the com-plete or final standard of belief and practice. God gives to the world from time to time, through popes and councils, new communications of truth. Cyprian: " He who aas not the church for his mother, has not God for his Father." Augustine: "I would not believe the Scripture, unless the authority of the church also influenced me." Francis of Assisi and Ignatius Loyola both represented the truly obedient person as one dead, moving only as moved by his superior; the true Christian has no life of his own, but is the blind instrument of the church. John Henry Newman, Tracts, Theol· and Eccl., 287--" The Christi·n dogmas were in the church from the time of the apos¹les,—they were ever in their substance what they are now." But this is demon-strably untrue of the immaculate conception of the Virgin Mary; of the treasury of merits to be distributed in indulgences; of the infallibility of the pope (see Gore, Incarnation, 186). In place of the true doctrine, " Ubi Spiritus, ibi ecclesia," Roman-ism substitutes her maxim, "Ubi ecclesia, ibi Spiritus." Luther saw in this the prin-ciple of mysticism, when he said: " Papatus est merus enthusiasmus." See Hodge, Syst. Theol., 1 : 61-69.

In reply to the Romanist argument that the church was before the Bible, and that the same body that gave the truth at the first can make additions to that truth, we say that the unwritten word was before the church and made the church possible. The word of God existed before it was written down, and by that word the first disciples as well as the latest were begotten (1 Pet. 1: 23 — "begotten again . . . through the word of God"). The grain of truth in Roman Catholic doctrine is expressed in 1 Tim. 3: 15 — "the church of the living God, the pillar and ground of the truth " = the church is God's appointed proclaimer of truth; *cf.* Phil. 2: 16 — "holding forth the word of life." But the church can proclaim the truth, only as it is built upon the truth. So we may say that the American Republic is the pillar and ground of liberty in the world; but this is true only so far as the Republic is built upon the principle of liberty as its foundation. When the Romanist asks: "Where was your church before Luther?" the Protestant may reply: "Where yours is not now — in the word of God. Where was your face before it was washed? Where was the fine flour before the wheat went to the mill?" Lady Jane Grey, three days before her execution, February 12, 1554, said: "I ground my faith on God's word, and not upon the church; for, if the church be a good church, the faith of the church must be tried by God's word, and not God's word by the church, nor yet my faith."

The Roman church would keep men in perpetual childhood — coming to her for truth

3

instead of going directly to the Bible; "like the foolish mother who keeps her boy pining in the house lest he stub his toe, and would love best to have him remain a babe forever, that she might mother him still." Martensen, Christian Dogmatics, 30 — "Romanism is so busy in building up a system of guarantees, that she forgets the truth of Christ which she would guarantee." George Herbert: "What wretchedness can give him any room, Whose house is foul while he adores his broom!" It is a semi-parasitic doctrine of safety without intelligence or spirituality. Romanism says: "Man for the machine!" Protestantism: "The machine for man!" Catholicism strangles, Protestantism restores, individuality. Yet the Romanist principle sometimes appears in so-called Protestant churches. The Catechism published by the League of the Holy Cross, in the Anglican Church, contains the following: "It is to the priest only that the child must acknowledge his sins, if he desires that God should forgive him. Do you know why? It is because God, when on earth, gave to his priests and to them alone the power of forgiving sins. Go to the priest, who is the doctor of your soul, and who cures you in the name of God." But this contradicts John 10 : 7 — where Christ says "I am the door"; and 1 Cor. 3 : 11 — "other foundation can no man lay than that which is laid, which is Jesus Christ" = Salvation is attained by immediate access to Christ, and there is no door between the soul and him. See Dorner, Gesch. prot. Theol., 227; Schleiermacher, Glaubenslehre, 1 : 24; Robinson, in Mad. Av. Lectures, 387; Fisher, Nat. and Method of Revelation, 10; Watkins, Bampton Lect. for 1890 : 149; Drummond, Nat. Law in Spir. World, 327.

II. LIMITATIONS OF THEOLOGY. — Although theology derives its material from God's two-fold revelation, it does not profess to give an exhaustive knowledge of God and of the relations between God and the universe. After showing what material we have, we must show what material we have not. We have indicated the sources of theology ; we now examine its limitations. Theology has its limitations :

(a) *In the finiteness of the human understanding.* This gives rise to a class of necessary mysteries, or mysteries connected with the infinity and incomprehensibleness of the divine nature (Job 11 : 7 ; Rom. 11 : 33).

Job 11 : 7 — "Canst thou by searching find out God? Canst thou find out the Almighty to perfection?" Rom. 11: 33 — "how unsearchable are his judgments, and his ways past finding out!" Every doctrine, therefore, has its inexplicable side. Here is the proper meaning of Tertullian's sayings : "Certum est, quia impossible est; quo absurdius, eo verius"; that of Anselm : "Credo, ut intelligam"; and that of Abelard : "Qui credit cito, levis corde est." Drummond, Nat. Law in Spir. World : "A science without mystery is unknown; a religion without mystery is absurd." E. G. Robinson : "A finite being cannot grasp even its own relations to the Infinite." Hovey, Manual of Christ. Theol., 7 — "To infer from the perfection of God that all his works [nature, man, inspiration] will be absolutely and unchangeably perfect; to infer from the perfect love of God that there can be no sin or suffering in the world; to infer from the sovereignty of God that man is not a free moral agent; — all these inferences are rash; they are inferences from the cause to the effect, while the cause is imperfectly known." See Calderwood, Philos. of Infinite, 491; Sir Wm. Hamilton, Discussions, 22.

(b) *In the imperfect state of science, both natural and metaphysical.* This gives rise to a class of accidental mysteries, or mysteries which consist in the apparently irreconcilable nature of truths, which, taken separately, are perfectly comprehensible.

We are the victims of a mental or moral astigmatism, which sees a *single* point of truth as *two*. We see God and man, divine sovereignty and human freedom, Christ's divine nature and Christ's human nature, the natural and the supernatural, respectively, as two disconnected facts, when perhaps deeper insight would see but one. Astronomy has its centripetal and centrifugal forces, yet they are doubtless one force. The child cannot hold two oranges at once in its little hand. Negro preacher : "You can't carry two watermelons under one arm." Shakespeare, Antony and Cleopatra, 1 : 2 — "In nature's infinite book of secresy, A little I can read." Cooke, Credentials of Science, 34 — "Man's progress in knowledge has been so constantly and rapidly accelerated that more has been gained during the lifetime of men still living than during all human history before." And yet we may say with D'Arcy, Idealism and Theology, 248 — "Man's position in the universe is eccentric. God alone is at the centre. To him alone is the orbit of truth completely displayed. . . . There are circumstances in which to us the onward movement of truth may seem a retrogression." William Watson, Collected Poems, 271 — "Think not thy wisdom can illume away The ancient tanglement of night and day. Enough to acknowledge both, and both revere: They see not clearliest who see all things clear."

(c) *In the inadequacy of language.* Since language is the medium through which truth is expressed and formulated, the invention of a proper terminology in theology, as in every other science, is a condition and criterion of its progress. The Scriptures recognize a peculiar difficulty in putting spiritual truths into earthly language (1 Cor. 2 : 13 ; 2 Cor. 3 : 6; 12 : 4).

1 Cor. 2 : 13 — "not in words which man's wisdom teacheth "; 2 Cor. 3 : 6 — "the letter killeth "; 12 : 4 — "unspeakable words." God submits to conditions of revelation; *cf.* John 16 : 12 — "I have yet many things to say unto you, but ye cannot bear them now." Language has to be created. Words have to be taken from a common, and to be put to a larger and more sacred, use, so that they "stagger under their weight of meaning " — *e. g.*, the word "day," in Genesis 1, and the word ἀγάπη in 1 Cor. 13. See Gould, in Amer. Com., on 1 Cor. 13 : 12 — " now we see in a mirror, darkly " — in a metallic mirror whose surface is dim and whose images are obscure = Now we behold Christ, the truth, only as he is reflected in imperfect speech — "but then face to face " = immediately, without the intervention of an imperfect medium. "As fast as we tunnel into the sandbank of thought, the stones of language must be built into walls and arches, to allow further progress into the boundless mine."

(d) *In the incompleteness of our knowledge of the Scriptures.* Since it is not the mere letter of the Scriptures that constitutes the truth, the progress of theology is dependent upon hermeneutics, or the interpretation of the word of God.

Notice the progress in commenting, from homiletical to grammatical, historical, dogmatic, illustrated in Scott, Ellicott, Stanley, Lightfoot. John Robinson : " I am verily persuaded that the Lord hath more truth yet to break forth from his holy word." Recent criticism has shown the necessity of studying each portion of Scripture in the light of its origin and connections. There has been an evolution of Scripture, as truly as there has been an evolution of natural science, and the Spirit of Christ who was in the prophets has brought about a progress from germinal and typical expression to expression that is complete and clear. Yet we still need to offer the prayer of Ps. 119: 18 —"Open thou mine eyes, that I may behold wondrous things out of thy law." On New Testament Interpretation, see A. H. Strong, Philosophy and Religion, 324-336.

(e) *In the silence of written revelation.* For our discipline and probation, much is probably hidden from us, which we might even with our present powers comprehend.

Instance the silence of Scripture with regard to the life and death of Mary the Virgin, the personal appearance of Jesus and his occupations in early life, the origin of evil, the method of the atonement, the state after death. So also as to social and political questions, such as slavery, the liquor traffic, domestic virtues, governmental corruption. " Jesus was in heaven at the revolt of the angels, yet he tells us little about angels or about heaven. He does not discourse about Eden, or Adam, or the fall of man, or death as the result of Adam's sin ; and he says little of departed spirits, whether they are lost or saved." It was better to inculcate principles, and trust his followers to apply them. His gospel is not intended to gratify a vain curiosity. He would not divert men's minds from pursuing the one thing needful; *cf.* Luke 13 : 23, 24 — " Lord, are they few that are saved ? And he said unto them, Strive to enter in by the narrow door : for many, I say unto you, shall seek to enter in, and shall not be able." Paul's silence upon speculative questions which he must have pondered with absorbing interest is a proof of his divine inspiration. John Foster spent his life," gathering questions for eternity "; *cf.* John 13 : 7 — " What I do thou knowest not now ; but thou shalt understand hereafter." The most beautiful thing in a countenance *is* that which a picture can never express. He who would speak well must omit well story: "Of every noble work the silent part is best; Of all expressions that which can not be expressed." *Cf.* 1 Cor. 2: 9 — "Things which eye saw not, and ear heard not, And which entered not into the heart of man, Whatsoever things God prepared for them that love him"; Deut. 29: 29 — "The secret things belong unto Jehovah our God : but the things that are revealed belong unto us and to our children." For Luther's view, see Hagenbach, Hist. Doctrine, 2 : 338. See also B. D. Thomas, The Secret of the Divine Silence.

(*f*) *In the lack of spiritual discernment caused by sin.* Since holy affection is a condition of religious knowledge, all moral imperfection in the individual Christian and in the church serves as a hindrance to the working out of a complete theology.

John 3 : 3 — "Except one be born anew, he cannot see the kingdom of God." The spiritual ages make most progress in theology, — witness the half-century succeeding the Reformation, and the half-century succeeding the great revival in New England in the time of Jonathan Edwards. Ueberweg, Logic (Lindsay's transl.), 514 — "Science is much under the influence of the will; and the truth of knowledge depends upon the purity of the conscience. The will has no power to resist scientific evidence; but scientific evidence is not obtained without the continuous loyalty of the will." Lord Bacon declared that man cannot enter the kingdom of science, any more than he can enter the kingdom of heaven, without becoming a little child. Darwin describes his own mind as having become a kind of machine for grinding general laws out of large collections of facts, with the result of producing "atrophy of that part of the brain on which the higher tastes depend." But a similar abnormal atrophy is possible in the case of the moral and religious faculty (see Gore, Incarnation, 37). Dr. Allen said in his Introductory Lecture at Lane Theological Seminary : "We are very glad to see you if you wish to be students; but the professors' chairs are all filled."

III. RELATIONS OF MATERIAL TO PROGRESS IN THEOLOGY.

(*a*) *A perfect system of theology is impossible.* We do not expect to construct such a system. All science but reflects the present attainment of the human mind. No science is complete or finished. However it may be with the sciences of nature and of man, the science of God will never amount to an exhaustive knowledge. We must not expect to demonstrate all Scripture doctrines upon rational grounds, or even in every case to see the principle of connection between them. Where we cannot do this, we must, as in every other science, set the revealed facts in their places and wait for further light, instead of ignoring or rejecting any of them because we cannot understand them or their relation to other parts of our system.

Three problems left unsolved by the Egyptians have been handed down to our generation: (1) the duplication of the cube; (2) the trisection of the angle; (3) the quadrature of the circle. Dr. Johnson: "Dictionaries are like watches; the worst is better than none; and the best cannot be expected to go quite true." Hood spoke of Dr. Johnson's "Contradictionary," which had both "interiour" and "exterior." Sir William Thompson (Lord Kelvin) at the fiftieth anniversary of his professorship said : "One word characterizes the most strenuous of the efforts for the advancement of science which I have made perseveringly through fifty-five years: that word is *failure*; I know no more of electric and magnetic force, or of the relations between ether, electricity and ponderable matter, or of chemical affinity, than I knew and tried to teach my students of natural philosophy fifty years ago in my first session as professor." Allen, Religious Progress, mentions three tendencies. "The first says: Destroy the new ! The second says: Destroy the old ! The third says: Destroy nothing ! Let the old gradually and quietly grow into the new, as Erasmus wished. We should accept contradictions, whether they can be intellectually reconciled or not. The truth has never prospered by enforcing some 'via media.' Truth lies rather in the union of opposite propositions, as in Christ's divinity and humanity, and in grace and freedom. Blanco White went from Rome to infidelity ; Orestes Brownson from infidelity to Rome ; so the brothers John Henry Newman and Francis W. Newman, and the brothers George Herbert of Bemerton and Lord Herbert of Cherbury. One would secularize the divine, the other would divinize the secular. But if one is true, so is the other. Let us adopt both. All progress is a deeper penetration into the meaning of old truth, and a larger appropriation of it.''

(b) *Theology is nevertheless progressive.* It is progressive in the sense that our subjective understanding of the facts with regard to God, and our consequent expositions of these facts, may and do become more perfect. But theology is not progressive in the sense that its objective facts change, either in their number or their nature. With Martineau we may say : "Religion has been reproached with not being progressive ; it makes amends by being imperishable." Though our knowledge may be imperfect, it will have great value still. Our success in constructing a theology will depend upon the proportion which clearly expressed facts of Scripture bear to mere inferences, and upon the degree in which they all cohere about Christ, the central person and theme.

The progress of theology is progress in apprehension by man, not progress in communication by God. Originality in astronomy is not man's creation of new planets, but man's discovery of planets that were never seen before, or the bringing to light of relations between them that were never before suspected. Robert Kerr Eccles : "Originality is a habit of recurring to origins—the habit of securing personal experience by personal application to original facts. It is not an eduction of novelties either from nature, Scripture, or inner consciousness ; it is rather the habit of resorting to primitive facts, and of securing the personal experiences which arise from contact with these facts." Fisher, Nat. and Meth. of Revelation, 48— "The starry heavens are now what they were of old ; there is no enlargement of the stellar universe, except that which comes through the increased power and use of the telescope." We must not imitate the green sailor who, when set to steer, said he had "sailed *by* that star."

Martineau, Types, 1 : 492, 493 — "Metaphysics, so far as they are true to their work, are stationary, precisely because they have in charge, not what begins and ceases to be, but what always *is*. . . . It is absurd to praise motion for always making way, while disparaging space for still being what it ever was : as if the motion you prefer could be, without the space which you reproach." Newman Smyth, Christian Ethics, 45, 67–70, 79— "True conservatism is progress which takes direction from the past and fulfils its good ; false conservatism is a narrowing and hopeless reversion to the past, which is a betrayal of the promise of the future. So Jesus came not 'to destroy the law or the prophets'; he 'came not to destroy, but to fulfil' (Mat. 5 : 17). . . . The last book on Christian Ethics will not be written before the Judgment Day." John Milton, Areopagitica : "Truth is compared in the Scripture to a streaming fountain ; if her waters flow not in a perpetual progression, they sicken into a muddy pool of conformity and tradition. A man may be a heretic in the truth." Paul in Rom. 2 : 16, and in 2 Tim. 2 : 8— speaks of "my gospel." It is the duty of every Christian to have his own conception of the truth, while he respects the conceptions of others. Tennyson, Locksley Hall : " I that rather held it better men should perish one by one, Than that earth should stand at gaze like Joshua's moon at Ajalon." We do not expect any new worlds, and we need not expect any new Scriptures ; but we may expect progress in the interpretation of both. Facts are final, but interpretation is not.

CHAPTER III.

1. REQUISITES TO THE STUDY. — The requisites to the successful study of theology have already in part been indicated in speaking of its limitations. In spite of some repetition, however, we mention the following:

(*a*) *A disciplined mind.* Only such a mind can patiently collect the facts, hold in its grasp many facts at once, educe by continuous reflection their connecting principles, suspend final judgment until its conclusions are verified by Scripture and experience.

Robert Browning, Ring and Book, 175 (Pope, 228) — "Truth nowhere lies, yet everywhere, in these; Not absolutely in a portion, yet Evolveable from the whole: evolved at last Painfully, held tenaciously by me." Teachers and students may be divided into two classes: (1) those who know enough already; (2) those wish to learn more than they now know. Motto of Winchester School in England: "Disce, aut discede." Butcher, Greek Genius, 213, 230 — "The Sophists fancied that they were imparting education, when they were only imparting results. Aristotle illustrates their method by the example of a shoemaker who, professing to teach the art of making painless shoes, puts into the apprentice's hand a large assortment of shoes ready-made. A witty Frenchman classes together those who would make science popular, metaphysics intelligible, and vice respectable. The word σχόλη, which first meant 'leisure,' then 'philosophical discussion,' and finally 'school,' shows the pure love of learning among the Greeks." Robert G. Ingersoll said that the average provincial clergyman is like the land of the upper Potomac spoken of by Tom Randolph, as almost worthless in its original state, and rendered wholly so by cultivation. Lotze, Metaphysics, 1: 16 — "the constant whetting of the knife is tedious, if it is not proposed to cut anything with it." "To do their duty is their only holiday," is the description of Athenian character given by Thucydides. Chitty asked a father inquiring as to his son's qualifications for the law: "Can your son eat sawdust without any butter?" On opportunities for culture in the Christian ministry, see New Englander, Oct. 1875: 644; A. H. Strong, Philosophy and Religion, 273–275; Christ in Creation, 318–320.

(*b*) *An intuitional as distinguished from a merely logical habit of mind,* — or, trust in the mind's primitive convictions, as well as in its processes of reasoning. The theologian must have insight as well as understanding. He must accustom himself to ponder spiritual facts as well as those which are sensible and material; to see things in their inner relations as well as in their outward forms; to cherish confidence in the reality and the unity of truth.

Vinet, Outlines of Philosophy, 39, 40 — "If I do not feel that good is good, who will ever prove it to me?" Pascal: "Logic, which is an abstraction, may shake everything. A being purely intellectual will be incurably sceptical." Calvin: "Satan is an acute theologian." Some men can see a fly on a barn door a mile away, and yet can never see the door. Zeller, Outlines of Greek Philosophy, 93 — "Gorgias the Sophist was able to show metaphysically that nothing can exist; that what does exist cannot be known by us; and that what is known by us cannot be imparted to others" (quoted by Wenley Socrates and Christ, 28). Aristotle differed from those moderate men who thought it impossible to go over the same river twice, — he held that it could not be done even once (*cf.* Wordsworth, Prelude, 536). Dove, Logic of the Christian Faith, 1-29, and especially 25, gives a demonstration of the impossibility of motion: A thing cannot move in the place where it is; it cannot move in the places where it is not; but the place where it is and the places where it is not are all the places that there are; therefore a thing cannot move ɾ ɞ all. Hazard, Man a Creative First Cause, 109, shows that the bottom of a wheel does not move, since it goes backward as fast as the top goes forward. An instantaneous photograph makes the upper part a confused blur, while the spokes of the lower part are distinctly visible. Abp. Whately: "Weak arguments are often thrust before my path; but, although they are most unsubstantial, it is not easy to destroy them. There is not a more difficult feat known than to cut through a cushion with a sword." *Cf.* 1 Tim. 6: 20 — "oppositions of the knowledge which is falsely so called"; 3: 2 — "the bishop therefore must be . . . sober-minded"— σώφρων = " well balanced." The Scripture speaks of " sound [ὑγιής = healthful] doctrine " (1 Tim 1: 10). Contrast 1 Tim 6: 4 — [νοσῶν = ailing] "diseased about questionings and disputes of words."

(c) *An acquaintance with physical, mental, and moral science.* The method of conceiving and expressing Scripture truth is so affected by our elementary notions of these sciences, and the weapons with which theology is attacked and defended are so commonly drawn from them as arsenals, that the student cannot afford to be ignorant of them.

Goethe explains his own greatness by his avoidance of metaphysics: " Mein Kind, Ich habe es klug gemacht: Ich habe nie über's Denken gedacht "— " I have been wise in never thinking about thinking"; he would have been wiser, had he pondered more deeply the fundamental principles of his philosophy; see A. H. Strong, The Great Poets and their Theology, 296-299, and Philosophy and Religion, 1-18; also in Baptist Quarterly, 2: 393 *sq.* Many a theological system has fallen, like the Campanile at Venice, because its foundations were insecure. Sir William Hamilton: "No difficulty arises in theology which has not first emerged in philosophy." N. W. Taylor: " Give me a young man in metaphysics, and I care not who has him in theology." President Samson Talbot: "I love metaphysics, because they have to do with realities." The maxim "Ubi tres medici, ibi duo athei," witnesses to the truth of Galen's words: ἄριστος ἰατρὸς καὶ φιλόσοφος —" the best physician is also a philosopher." Theology cannot dispense with science, any more than science can dispense with philosophy. E. G. Robinson: "Science has not invalidated any fundamental truth of revelation, though it has modified the statement of many. . . . Physical Science will undoubtedly knock some of our crockery gods on the head, and the sooner the better." There is great advantage to the preacher in taking up, as did Frederick W. Robertson, one science after another. Chemistry entered into his mental structure, as he said, "like iron into the blood."

(d) *A knowledge of the original languages of the Bible.* This is necessary to enable us not only to determine the meaning of the fundamental terms of Scripture, such as holiness, sin, propitiation, justification, but also to interpret statements of doctrine by their connections with the context.

Emerson said that the man who reads a book in a strange tongue, when he can have a good translation, is a fool. Dr. Behrends replied that he is a fool who is satisfied with the substitute. E. G. Robinson: "Language is a great organism, and no study so disciplines the mind as the dissection of an organism." Chrysostom: "This is the cause of all our evils — our not knowing the Scriptures." Yet a modern scholar has said: "The Bible is the most dangerous of all God's gifts to men." It is possible to adore the letter, while we fail to perceive its spirit. A narrow interpretation may contradict its meaning. Much depends upon connecting phrases, as for example, the διὰ τοῦτο and ἐφ' ᾧ, in Rom. 5: 12. Professor Philip Lindsley of Princeton, 1813-1853, said to his pupils: "One of the best preparations for death is a thorough knowledge of the Greek grammar." The youthful Erasmus: "When I get some money, I will get me some Greek books, and, after that, some clothes." The dead languages are the only really living ones — free from danger of misunderstanding from changing usage. Divine Providence has put revelation into fixed forms in the Hebrew and the Greek. Sir William Hamilton, Discussions, 300 — "To be a competent divine is in fact to be a scholar." On the true idea of a Theological Seminary Course, see A. H. Strong, Philos. and Religion, 302-313.

(*e*) *A holy affection toward God.* Only the renewed heart can properly feel its need of divine revelation, or understand that revelation when given.

Ps. 25: 14 — "The secret of Jehovah is with them that fear him"; Rom. 12: 2 — "prove what is the . . . will of God"; *cf.* Ps. 36: 1 — "the transgression of the wicked speaks in his heart like an oracle." "It is the heart and not the brain That to the highest doth attain." To "learn by heart" is something more than to learn by mind, or by head. All heterodoxy is preceded by heteropraxy. In Bunyan's Pilgrim's Progress, Faithful does not go through the Slough of Despond, as Christian did; and it is by getting over the fence to find an easier road, that Christian and Hopeful get into Doubting Castle and the hands of Giant Despair. "Great thoughts come from the heart," said Vauvenargues. The preacher cannot, like Dr. Kane, kindle fire with a lens of ice. Aristotle: "The power of attaining moral truth is dependent upon our acting rightly." Pascal: "We know truth, not only by the reason, but by the heart. . . . The heart has its reasons, which the reason knows nothing of." Hobbes: "Even the axioms of geometry would be disputed, if men's passions were concerned in them." Macaulay: "The law of gravitation would still be controverted, if it interfered with vested interests." Nordau, Degeneracy: "Philosophic systems simply furnish the excuses reason demands for the unconscious impulses of the race during a given period of time."

Lord Bacon: "A tortoise on the right path will beat a racer on the wrong path." Goethe: "As are the inclinations, so also are the opinions. . . . A work of art can be comprehended by the head only with the assistance of the heart. . . . Only law can give us liberty." Fichte: "Our system of thought is very often only the history of our heart. . . . Truth is descended from conscience. . . . Men do not will according to their reason, but they reason according to their will." Neander's motto was: "Pectus est quod theologum facit"—"It is the heart that makes the theologian." John Stirling: "That is a dreadful eye which can be divided from a living human heavenly heart, and still retain its all-penetrating vision,—such was the eye of the Gorgons." But such an eye, we add, is not all-penetrating. E. G. Robinson: "Never study theology in cold blood." W. C. Wilkinson: "The head is a magnetic needle with truth for its pole. But the heart is a hidden mass of magnetic iron. The head is drawn somewhat toward its natural pole, the truth; but more it is drawn by that nearer magnetism." See an affecting instance of Thomas Carlyle's enlightenment, after the death of his wife, as to the meaning of the Lord's Prayer, in Fisher, Nat. and Meth. of Revelation, 165. On the importance of feeling, in association of ideas, see Dewey, Psychology, 106, 107.

(*f*) *The enlightening influence of the Holy Spirit.* As only the Spirit fathoms the things of God, so only he can illuminate our minds to apprehend them.

1 Cor. 2: 11, 12 — "the things of God none knoweth, save the Spirit of God. But we received . . . the Spirit which is from God; that we might know." Cicero, Nat. Deorum, 66 — "Nemo igitur vir magnus sine aliquo adflatu divino unquam fuit." Professor Beck of Tübingen: "For the student, there is no privileged path leading to the truth; the only one which leads to it is also that of the unlearned; it is that of regeneration and of gradual illumination by the Holy Spirit; and without the Holy Spirit, theology is not only a cold stone, it is a deadly poison." As all the truths of the differential and integral calculus are wrapped up in the simplest mathematical axiom, so all theology is wrapped up in the declaration that God is holiness and love, or in the protevangelium uttered at the gates of Eden. But dull minds cannot of themselves evolve the calculus from the axiom, nor can sinful hearts evolve theology from the first prophecy. Teachers are needed to demonstrate geometrical theorems, and the Holy Spirit is needed to show us that the "new commandment" illustrated by the death of Christ is only an "old commandment which ye had from the beginning" (1 John 2: 7). The Principia of Newton is a revelation of Christ, and so are the Scriptures. The Holy Spirit enables us to enter into the meaning of Christ's revelations

in both Scripture and nature; to interpret the one by the other; and so to work out original demonstrations and applications of the truth; Mat. 13 : 52 — "Therefore every scribe who hath been made a disciple of the kingdom of heaven is like unto a man that is a householder, who bringeth forth out of his treasure things new and old." See Adolph Monod's sermons on Christ's Temptation, addressed to the theological students of Montauban, in Select Sermons from the French and German, 117-179.

II. DIVISIONS OF THEOLOGY.—Theology is commonly divided into Biblical, Historical, Systematic, and Practical.

1. *Biblical Theology* aims to arrange and classify the facts of revelation, confining itself to the Scriptures for its material, and treating of doctrine only so far as it was developed at the close of the apostolic age.

Instance DeWette, Biblische Theologie; Hofmann, Schriftbeweis; Nitzsch, System of Christian Doctrine. The last, however, has more of the philosophical element than properly belongs to Biblical Theology. The third volume of Ritschl's Justification and Reconciliation is intended as a system of Biblical Theology, the first and second volumes being little more than an historical introduction. But metaphysics, of a Kantian relativity and phenomenalism, enter so largely into Ritschl's estimates and interpretations, as to render his conclusions both partial and rationalistic. Notice a questionable use of the term Biblical Theology to designate the theology of a part of Scripture severed from the rest, as Steudel's Biblical Theology of the Old Testament: Schmidt's Biblical Theology of the New Testament; and in the common phrases: Biblical Theology of Christ, or of Paul. These phrases are objectionable as intimating that the books of Scripture have only a human origin. Upon the assumption that there is no common divine authorship of Scripture, Biblical Theology is conceived of as a series of fragments, corresponding to the differing teachings of the various prophets and apostles, and the theology of Paul is held to be an unwarranted and incongruous addition to the theology of Jesus. See Reuss, History of Christian Theology in the Apostolic Age.

2. *Historical Theology* traces the development of the Biblical doctrines from the time of the apostles to the present day, and gives account of the results of this development in the life of the church.

By doctrinal development we mean the progressive unfolding and apprehension, by the church, of the truth explicitly or implicitly contained in Scripture. As giving account of the shaping of the Christian faith into doctrinal statements, Historical Theology is called the History of Doctrine. As describing the resulting and accompanying changes in the life of the church, outward and inward, Historical Theology is called Church History. Instance Cunningham's Historical Theology; Hagenbach's and Shedd's Histories of Doctrine; Neander's Church History. There is always a danger that the historian will see his own views too clearly reflected in the history of the church. Shedd's History of Christian Doctrine has been called "The History of Dr. Shedd's Christian Doctrine." But if Dr. Shedd's Augustinianism colors his History, Dr. Sheldon's Arminianism also colors his. G. P. Fisher's History of Christian Doctrine is unusually lucid and impartial. See Neander's Introduction and Shedd's Philosophy of History.

3. *Systematic Theology* takes the material furnished by Biblical and by Historical Theology, and with this material seeks to build up into an organic and consistent whole all our knowledge of God and of the relations between God and the universe, whether this knowledge be originally derived from nature or from the Scriptures.

Systematic Theology is therefore theology proper, of which Biblical and Historical Theology are the incomplete and preparatory stages. Systematic Theology is to be clearly distinguished from Dogmatic Theology. Dogmatic Theology is, in strict usage, the systematizing of the doctrines as expressed in the symbols of the church, together with the grounding of these in the Scriptures, and the exhibition, so far as may be, of their rational necessity. Systematic Theology begins, on the other hand, not with the symbols, but with the Scriptures. It asks first, not what the church has believed, but what is the truth of God's revealed word. It examines that word with all the aids which nature and the Spirit have given it, using Biblical and Historical Theology as its servants and helpers, but not as its masters. Notice here the technical use of the word "symbol," from συμβάλλω, = a brief throwing together, or condensed statement of the essentials of Christian doctrine. Synonyms are : Confession, creed, consensus, declaration, formulary, canons, articles of faith.

Dogmatism argues to foregone conclusions. The word is not, however, derived from "dog," as Douglas Jerrold facetiously suggested, when he said that "dogmatism is puppyism full grown," but from δοκέω, to think, to opine. Dogmatic Theology has two principles : (1) The absolute authority of creeds, as decisions of the church : (2) The application to these creeds of formal logic, for the purpose of demonstrating their truth to the understanding. In the Roman Catholic Church, not the Scripture but the church, and the dogma given by it, is the decisive authority. The Protestant principle, on the contrary, is that Scripture decides, and that dogma is to be judged by it. Following Schleiermacher, Al. Schweizer thinks that the term "Dogmatik" should be discarded as essentially unprotestant, and that "Glaubenslehre" should take its place ; and Harnack, Hist. Dogma, 6, remarks that "dogma has ever, in the progress of history, devoured its own progenitors." While it is true that every new and advanced thinker in theology has been counted a heretic, there has always been a common faith — "the faith which was once for all delivered unto the saints" (Jude 3) — and the study of Systematic Theology has been one of the chief means of preserving this faith in the world. Mat. 15 : 13, 14 — "Every plant which my heavenly Father planted not, shall be rooted up. Let them alone : they are blind guides" = there is truth planted by God, and it has permanent divine life. Human errors have no permanent vitality and they perish of themselves. See Kaftan, Dogmatik, 2, 3.

4. *Practical Theology* is the system of truth considered as a means of renewing and sanctifying men, or, in other words, theology in its publication and enforcement.

To this department of theology belong Homiletics and Pastoral Theology, since these are but scientific presentations of the right methods of unfolding Christian truth, and of bringing it to bear upon men individually and in the church. See Van Oosterzee, Practical Theology ; T. Harwood Pattison, The Making of the Sermon, and Public Prayer ; Yale Lectures on Preaching by H. W. Beecher, R. W. Dale, Phillips Brooks, E. G. Robinson, A. J. F. Behrends, John Watson, and others ; and the work on Pastoral Theology, by Harvey.

It is sometimes asserted that there are other departments of theology not included in those above mentioned. But most of these, if not all, belong to other spheres of research, and cannot properly be classed under theology at all. Moral Theology, so called, or the science of Christian morals, ethics, or theological ethics, is indeed the proper result of theology, but is not to be confounded with it. Speculative theology, so called, respecting, as it does, such truth as is mere matter of opinion, is either extra-scriptural, and so belongs to the province of the philosophy of religion, or is an attempt to explain truth already revealed, and so falls within the province of Systematic Theology. "Speculative theology starts from certain *a priori* principles, and from them undertakes to determine what is and must be. It deduces its scheme of doctrine from the laws of mind or from axioms supposed to be inwrought into its constitution." Bib. Sac., 1852:376 — "Speculative theology tries to show that the dogmas agree with the laws of thought, while the philosophy of religion tries to show that the laws of thought agree with the dogmas." Theological Encyclopædia (the word signifies "instruction in a circle") is a general introduction to all the divisions of Theology, together with an account of the relations between them. Hegel's Encyclopædia was an attempted exhibition of the principles and connections of all the sciences. See Crooks and Hurst, Theological Encyclopædia and Methodology ; Zöckler, Handb. der theol. Wissenschaften, 2:606–769.

The relations of theology to science and philosophy have been variously stated, but by none better than by H. B. Smith, Faith and Philosophy, 18 — "Philosophy is a mode of human knowledge — not the whole of that knowledge, but a mode of it — the knowing of things rationally." Science asks : "What *do* I know ?" Philosophy asks : "What *can* I know ?" William James, Psychology, 1 : 145—"Metaphysics means nothing but an unusually obstinate effort to think clearly." Aristotle: "The particular sciences are toiling workmen, while philosophy is the architect. The workmen are slaves, existing for the free master. So philosophy rules the sciences." With regard to philosophy and science Lord Bacon remarks: "Those who have handled knowledge have been too much either men of mere observation or abstract reasoners. The former are like the ant: they only collect material and put it to immediate use. The abstract reasoners are like spiders, who make cobwebs out of their own substance. But the bee takes a middle course: it gathers its material from the flowers of the garden and the field, while it transforms and digests what it gathers by a power of its own. Not unlike this is the work of the philosopher." Novalis: "Philosophy can bake no bread; but it can give us God, freedom and immortality." Prof. DeWitt of Princeton: "Science, philosophy, and theology are the three great modes of organizing the universe into an intellectual system. Science never goes below second causes; if it does, it is no longer science, — it becomes philosophy. Philosophy views the universe as a unity, and the goal it is always seeking to reach is the source and centre of this unity — the Absolute, the First Cause. This goal of philosophy is the point of departure for theology. What philosophy is striving to find, theology asserts has been found. Theology therefore starts with the Absolute, the First Cause." W. N. Clarke, Christian Theology, 48 — "Science examines and classifies facts; philosophy inquires concerning spiritual meanings. Science seeks to know the universe; philosophy to understand it."

Balfour, Foundations of Belief, 7 — "Natural science has for its subject matter things and events. Philosophy is the systematic exhibition of the grounds of our knowledge. Metaphysics is our knowledge respecting realities which are not phenomenal, e. g., God and the soul." Knight, Essays in Philosophy, 81 — "The aim of the sciences is increase of knowledge, by the discovery of laws within which all phenomena may be embraced and by means of which they may be explained. The aim of philosophy, on the other hand, is to explain the sciences, by at once including and transcending them. Its sphere is substance and essence." Bowne, Theory of Thought and Knowledge, 3-5 — " Philosophy = doctrine of knowledge (is mind passive or active in knowing? — Epistemology) + doctrine of being (is fundamental being mechanical and unintelligent, or purposive and intelligent? — Metaphysics). The systems of Locke, Hume, and Kant are preëminently theories of knowing; the systems of Spinoza and Leibnitz are preëminently theories of being. Historically theories of being come first, because the object is the only determinant for reflective thought. But the instrument of philosophy is thought itself. First then, we must study Logic, or the theory of thought; secondly, Epistemology, or the theory of knowledge; thirdly, Metaphysics, or the theory of being."

Professor George M. Forbes on the New Psychology: " Locke and Kant represent the two tendencies in philosophy — the empirical, physical, scientific, on the one hand, and the rational, metaphysical, logical, on the other. Locke furnishes the basis for the associational schemes of Hartley, the Mills, and Bain; Kant for the idealistic scheme of Fichte, Schelling, and Hegel. The two are not contradictory, but complementary, and the Scotch Reid and Hamilton combine them both, reacting against the extreme empiricism and scepticism of Hume. Hickok, Porter, and McCosh represented the Scotch school in America. It was exclusively analytical; its psychology was the faculty-psychology; it represented the mind as a bundle of faculties. The unitary philosophy of T. H. Green, Edward Caird, in Great Britain, and in America, of W. T. Harris, George S. Morris, and John Dewey, was a reaction against this faculty-psychology, under the influence of Hegel. A second reaction under the influence of the Herbartian doctrine of apperception substituted function for faculty, making all processes phases of apperception. G. F. Stout and J. Mark Baldwin represent this psychology. A third reaction comes from the influence of physical science. All attempts to unify are relegated to a metaphysical Hades. There is nothing but states and processes. The only unity is the laws of their coëxistence and succession. There is nothing a priori. Wundt identifies apperception with will, and regards it as the unitary principle. Külpe and Titchener find no self, or will, or soul, but treat these as inferences little warranted. Their psychology is psychology without a soul. The old psychology was exclusively static, while the new emphasizes the genetic point of view. Growth and development are the leading ideas of Herbert Spencer, Preyer, Tracy and Stanley Hall. William James is explanatory, while George T. Ladd is descriptive. Cattell, Scripture, and Münsterberg apply the methods of Fechner, and the Psychological Review is their organ. Their error is in their negative attitude. The old psychology is needed to supplement the new. It has greater scope and more practical significance." On the relation of theology to philosophy and to science, see Luthardt, Compend. der Dogmatik, 4; Hagenbach, Encyclopädie, 109.

III. History of Systematic Theology.

1. *In the Eastern Church,* Systematic Theology may be said to have had its beginning and end in John of Damascus (700-760).

Ignatius († 115 — Ad Trall., c. 9) gives us "the first distinct statement of the faith drawn up in a series of propositions. This systematizing formed the basis of all later efforts" (Prof. A. H. Newman). Origen of Alexandria (186-254) wrote his Περὶ Ἀρχῶν; Athanasius of Alexandria (300-373) his Treatises on the Trinity and the Deity of Christ; and Gregory of Nyssa in Cappadocia (332-398) his Λόγος κατηχητικὸς ὁ μέγας. Hatch, Hibbert Lectures, 323, regards the "De Principiis" of Origen as the "first complete system of dogma," and speaks of Origen as "the disciple of Clement of Alexandria, the first great teacher of philosophical Christianity." But while the Fathers just mentioned seem to have conceived the plan of expounding the doctrines in order and of showing their relation to one another, it was John of Damascus (700-760) who first actually carried out such a plan. His Ἔκδοσις ἀκριβὴς τῆς ὀρθοδόξου Πίστεως, or Summary of the Orthodox Faith, may be considered the earliest work of Systematic Theology. Neander calls it "the most important doctrinal text-book of the Greek Church." John, like the Greek Church in general, was speculative, theological, semi-pelagian, sacramentarian. The Apostles' Creed, so called, is, in its present form, not earlier than the fifth century; see Schaff, Creeds of Christendom, 1 : 19. Mr. Gladstone suggested that the Apostles' Creed was a development of the baptismal formula. McGiffert, Apostles' Creed, assigns to the meagre original form a date of the third quarter of the second century, and regards the Roman origin of the symbol as proved. It was framed as a baptismal formula, but specifically in opposition to the teachings of Marcion, which were at that time causing much trouble at Rome. Harnack however dates the original Apostles' Creed at 150, and Zahn places it at 120. See also J. C. Long, in Bap. Quar. Rev., Jan. 1892 : 89-101.

2. *In the Western Church,* we may (with Hagenbach) distinguish three periods :

(a) The period of Scholasticism, — introduced by Peter Lombard (1100-1160), and reaching its culmination in Thomas Aquinas (1221-1274) and Duns Scotus (1265-1308).

Though Systematic Theology had its beginning in the Eastern Church, its development has been confined almost wholly to the Western. Augustine (353-430) wrote his "Encheiridion ad Laurentium" and his "De Civitate Dei," and John Scotus Erigena († 850), Roscelin (1092-1122), and Abelard (1079-1142), in their attempts at the rational explanation of the Christian doctrine foreshadowed the works of the great scholastic teachers. Anselm of Canterbury (1034-1109), with his "Proslogion de Dei Existentia" and his "Cur Deus Homo," has sometimes, but wrongly, been called the founder of Scholasticism. Allen, in his Continuity of Christian Thought, represents the transcendence of God as the controlling principle of the Augustinian and of the Western theology. The Eastern Church, he maintains, had founded its theology on God's immanence. Paine, in his Evolution of Trinitarianism, shows that this is erroneous. Augustine was a theistic monist. He declares that "Dei voluntas rerum natura est," and regards God's upholding as a continuous creation. Western theology recognized the immanence of God as well as his transcendence.

Peter Lombard, however, (1100-1160), the "magister sententiarum," was the first great systematizer of the Western Church, and his "Libri Sententiarum Quatuor" was the theological text-book of the Middle Ages. Teachers lectured on the "Sentences" (*Sententia* = sentence, *Satz, locus,* point, article of faith), as they did on the books of Aristotle, who furnished to Scholasticism its impulse and guide. Every doctrine was treated in the order of Aristotle's four causes: the material, the formal, the efficient, the final. ("Cause" here = requisite: (1) matter of which a thing consists, e. g., bricks and mortar; (2) form it assumes, e. g., plan or design; (3) producing agent, e. g., builder; (4) end for which made, e. g., house.) The organization of physical as well as of theological science was due to Aristotle. Dante called him "the master of those who know." James Ten Broeke, Bap. Quar. Rev., Jan. 1892: 1-26 — "The Revival of Learning showed the world that the real Aristotle was much broader than the Scholastic Aristotle — information very unwelcome to the Roman Church." For the influence of Scholasticism, compare the literary methods of Augustine and of Calvin, — the former giving us his materials in disorder, like soldiers bivouacked for the night; the latter arranging them like those same soldiers drawn up in battle array; see A. H. Strong, Philosophy and Religion, 4, and Christ in Creation, 188, 189.

Candlish, art.: Dogmatic, in Encycl. Brit., 7: 340 — "By and by a mighty intellectual force took hold of the whole collected dogmatic material, and reared out of it the great scholastic systems, which have been compared to the grand Gothic cathedrals that were the work of the same ages." Thomas Aquinas (1221-1274), the Dominican, "doctor angelicus," Augustinian and Realist, — and Duns Scotus (1265-1308), the Franciscan, "doctor subtilis," — wrought out the scholastic theology more fully, and left behind them, in their *Summæ*, gigantic monuments of intellectual industry and acumen. Scholasticism aimed at the proof and systematizing of the doctrines of the Church by means of Aristotle's philosophy. It became at last an illimitable morass of useless subtilities and abstractions, and it finally ended in the nominalistic scepticism of William of Occam (1270-1347). See Townsend, The Great Schoolmen of the Middle Ages.

(*b*) The period of Symbolism, — represented by the Lutheran theology of Philip Melanchthon (1497-1560), and the Reformed theology of John Calvin (1509-1564); the former connecting itself with the Analytic theology of Calixtus (1585-1656), and the latter with the Federal theology of Cocceius (1603-1669).

The Lutheran Theology.—Preachers precede theologians, and Luther (1485-1546) was preacher rather than theologian. But Melanchthon (1497-1560), "the preceptor of Germany," as he was called, embodied the theology of the Lutheran church in his "Loci Communes" = points of doctrine common to believers (first edition Augustinian, afterwards substantially Arminian; grew out of lectures on the Epistle to the Romans). He was followed by Chemnitz (1522-1586), "clear and accurate," the most learned of the disciples of Melanchthon. Leonhard Hutter (1563-1616), called "Lutherus redivivus," and John Gerhard (1582-1637) followed Luther rather than Melanchthon. "Fifty years after the death of Melanchthon, Leonhard Hutter, his successor in the chair of theology at Wittenberg, on an occasion when the authority of Melanchthon was appealed to, tore down from the wall the portrait of the great Reformer, and trampled it under foot in the presence of the assemblage" (E. D. Morris, paper at the 60th Anniversary of Lane Seminary). George Calixtus (1586-1656) followed Melanchthon rather than Luther. He taught a theology which recognized the good element in both the Reformed and the Romanist doctrine and which was called "Syncretism." He separated Ethics from Systematic Theology, and applied the analytical method of investigation to the latter, beginning with the end, or final cause, of all things, viz.: blessedness. He was followed in his analytic method by Dannhauer (1603-1666), who treated theology allegorically, Calovius (1612-1686), "the most uncompromising defender of Lutheran orthodoxy and the most drastic polemicist against Calixtus," Quenstedt (1617-1688), whom Hovey calls "learned, comprehensive and logical," and Hollaz (+ 1730). The Lutheran theology aimed to purify the *existing* church, maintaining that what is not against the gospel is for it. It emphasized the material principle of the Reformation, justification by faith; but it retained many Romanist customs not expressly forbidden in Scripture. Kaftan, Am. Jour. Theol., 1900: 716 — "Because the mediæval school-philosophy mainly held sway, the Protestant theology representing the new faith was meanwhile necessarily accommodated to forms of knowledge thereby conditioned, that is, to forms essentially Catholic."

The Reformed Theology. — The word "Reformed" is here used in its technical sense, as designating that phase of the new theology which originated in Switzerland. Zwingle, the Swiss reformer (1484-1531), differing from Luther as to the Lord's Supper and as to Scripture, was more than Luther entitled to the name of systematic theologian. Certain writings of his may be considered the beginning of Reformed theology. But it was left to John Calvin (1509-1564), after the death of Zwingle, to arrange the principles of that theology in systematic form. Calvin dug channels for Zwingle's flood to flow in, as Melanchthon did for Luther's. His Institutes ("Institutio Religionis Christianæ "), is one of the great works in theology (superior as a systematic work to Mel-anchthon's "Loci "). Calvin was followed by Peter Martyr (1500-1562), Chamier (1565-1621), and Theodore Beza (1519-1605). Beza carried Calvin's doctrine of predestination to an extreme supralapsarianism, which is hyper-Calvinistic rather than Calvinistic. Cocceius (1603-1669), and after him Witsius (1626-1708), made theology centre about the idea of the covenants, and founded the Federal theology. Leydecker (1642-1721) treated theology in the order of the persons of the Trinity. Amyraldus (1596-1664) and Placeus of Saumur (1596-1632) modified the Calvinistic doctrine, the latter by his theory of mediate imputation, and the former by advocating the hypothetic universal-ism of divine grace. Turretin (1671-1737), a clear and strong theologian whose work is still a text-book at Princeton, and Pictet (1655-1725), both of them Federalists, showed the influence of the Cartesian philosophy. The Reformed theology aimed to build a *new* church, affirming that what is not derived from the Bible is against it. It emphasized the formal principle of the Reformation, the sole authority of Scripture.

In general, while the line between Catholic and Protestant in Europe runs from west to east, the line between Lutheran and Reformed runs from south to north, the Reformed theology flowing with the current of the Rhine northward from Switzerland to Holland and to England, in which latter country the Thirty-nine Articles represent the Reformed faith, while the Prayer-book of the English Church is substantially Arminian ; see Dorner, Gesch. prot. Theologie, Einleit., 9. On the difference between Lutheran and Reformed doctrine, see Schaff, Germany, its Universities, Theology and Religion, 167-177. On the Reformed Churches of Europe and America, see H. B. Smith, Faith and Philosophy, 87-124.

(c) The period of Criticism and Speculation, — in its three divisions : the Rationalistic, represented by Semler (1725–1791) ; the Transitional, by Schleiermacher (1768–1834) ; the Evangelical, by Nitzsch, Müller, Tholuck and Dorner.

First Division. Rationalistic theologies: Though the Reformation had freed theology in great part from the bonds of scholasticism, other philosophies after a time took its place. The Leibnitz-(1646-1754) Wolffian (1679-1754) exaggeration of the powers of natural religion prepared the way for rationalistic systems of theology. Buddeus (1667-1729) combated the new principles, but Semler's (1725-1791) theology was built upon them, and represented the Scriptures as having a merely local and temporary character. Michaelis (1716-1784) and Doederlein (1714-1789) followed Semler, and the tendency toward rationalism was greatly assisted by the critical philosophy of Kant (1724-1804), to whom "revelation was problematical, and positive religion merely the medium through which the practical truths of reason are communicated " (Hagenbach, Hist. Doct., 2 : 397). Ammon (1766-1850) and Wegscheider (1771-1848) were represent-atives of this philosophy. Daub, Marheinecke and Strauss (1808-1874) were the Hegelian dogmatists. The system of Strauss resembled "Christian theology as a cemetery resem-bles a town." Storr (1746-1805), Reinhard (1753-1812), and Knapp (1753-1825), in the main evangelical, endeavored to reconcile revelation with reason, but were more or less influenced by this rationalizing spirit. Bretschneider (1776-1828) and De Wette (1780-1849) may be said to have held middle ground.

Second Division. Transition to a more Scriptural theology. Herder (1744-1803) and Jacobi (1743-1819), by their more spiritual philosophy, prepared the way for Schleier-macher's (1768-1834) grounding of doctrine in the facts of Christian experience. The writings of Schleiermacher constituted an epoch, and had great influence in delivering Germany from the rationalistic toils into which it had fallen. We may now speak of a

Third Division — and in this division we may put the names of Neander and Tholuck, Twesten and Nitzsch, Müller and Luthardt, Dorner and Philippi, Ebrard and Thomas-ius, Lange and Kahnis, all of them exponents of a far more pure and evangelical the-ology than was common in Germany a century ago. Two new forms of rationalism, however, have appeared in Germany, the one based upon the philosophy of Hegel, and numbering among its adherents Strauss and Baur, Biedermann, Lipsius and Pfleid-erer ; the other based upon the philosophy of Kant, and advocated by Ritschl and his followers, Harnack, Hermann and Kaftan ; the former emphasizing the ideal Christ, the latter emphasizing the historical Christ ; but neither of the two fully recognizing the living Christ present in every believer (see Johnson's Cyclopædia, art.: Theology, by A. H Strong).

3. *Among theologians of views diverse from the prevailing Protestant faith*, may be mentioned :

(*a*) Bellarmine (1542–1621), the Roman Catholic.

Besides Bellarmine, "the best controversial writer of his age" (Bayle), the Roman Catholic Church numbers among its noted modern theologians: — Petavius (1583–1652), whose dogmatic theology Gibbon calls "a work of incredible labor and compass". Melchior Canus (1523–1560), an opponent of the Jesuits and their scholastic method. Bossuet (1627–1704), who idealized Catholicism in his Exposition of Doctrine, and attacked Protestantism in his History of Variations of Protestant Churches; Jansen (1585–1638), who attempted, in opposition to the Jesuits, to reproduce the theology of Augustine, and who had in this the powerful assistance of Pascal (1623–1662). Jansenism, so far as the doctrines of grace are concerned, but not as respects the sacraments, is virtual Protestantism within the Roman Catholic Church. Moehler's Symbolism, Perrone's "Prelectiones Theologicæ," and Hurter's "Compendium Theologiæ Dogmaticæ" are the latest and most approved expositions of Roman Catholic doctrine.

(*b*) Arminius (1560–1609), the opponent of predestination.

Among the followers of Arminius (1560–1609) must be reckoned Episcopius (1583–1643), who carried Arminianism to almost Pelagian extremes; Hugo Grotius (1553–1645), the jurist and statesman, author of the governmental theory of the atonement; and Limborch (1633–1712), the most thorough expositor of the Arminian doctrine.

(*c*) Laelius Socinus (1525–1562), and Faustus Socinus (1539–1604), the leaders of the modern Unitarian movement.

The works of Laelius Socinus (1525–1562) and his nephew, Faustus Socinus (1539–1604) constituted the beginnings of modern Unitarianism. Laelius Socinus was the preacher and reformer, as Faustus Socinus was the theologian; or, as Baumgarten Crusius expresses it : " the former was the spiritual founder of Socinianism, and the latter the founder of the sect." Their writings are collected in the Bibliotheca Fratrum Polonorum. The Racovian Catechism, taking its name from the Polish town Racow, contains the most succinct exposition of their views. In 1660, the Unitarian church of the Socini in Poland was destroyed by persecution, but its Hungarian offshoot has still more than a hundred congregations.

4. *British Theology*, represented by :

(*a*) The Baptists, John Bunyan (1628–1688), John Gill (1697–1771), and Andrew Fuller (1754–1815).

Some of the best British theology is Baptist. Among John Bunyan's works we may mention his "Gospel Truths Opened," though his "Pilgrim's Progress" and "Holy War" are theological treatises in allegorical form. Macaulay calls Milton and Bunyan the two great creative minds of England during the latter part of the 17th century. John Gill's "Body of Practical Divinity" shows much ability, although the Rabbinical learning of the author occasionally displays itself in a curious exegesis, as when on the word "Abba" he remarks: " You see that this word which means ' Father ' reads the same whether we read forward or backward ; which suggests that God is the same whichever way we look at him." Andrew Fuller's "Letters on Systematic Divinity " is a brief compend of theology. His treatises upon special doctrines are marked by sound judgment and clear insight. They were the most influential factor in rescuing the evangelical churches of England from antinomianism. They justify the epithets which Robert Hall, one of the greatest of Baptist preachers, gives him : "sagacious," "luminous," "powerful."

(*b*) The Puritans, John Owen (1616–1683), Richard Baxter (1615–1691), John Howe (1530-1705), and Thomas Ridgeley (1666–1734).

Owen was the most rigid, as Baxter was the most liberal, of the Puritans. The Encyclopædia Britannica remarks: " As a theological thinker and writer, John Owen holds his own distinctly defined place among those titanic intellects with which the age abounded. Surpassed by Baxter in point and pathos, by Howe in imagination and the higher philosophy, he is unrivaled in his power of unfolding the rich meanings of Scripture. In his writings he was preëminently the great theologian." Baxter wrote a "Methodus Theologiæ," and a "Catholic Theology"; John Howe is chiefly known by his "Living Temple"; Thomas Ridgeley by his "Body of Divinity." Charles H. Spurgeon never ceased to urge his students to become familiar with the Puritan Adams, Ambrose, Bowden, Manton and Sibbes.

(c) The Scotch Presbyterians, Thomas Boston (1676–1732), John Dick (1764–1833), and Thomas Chalmers (1780–1847).

Of the Scotch Presbyterians, Boston is the most voluminous, Dick the most calm and fair, Chalmers the most fervid and popular.

(d) The Methodists, John Wesley (1703–1791), and Richard Watson (1781–1833).

Of the Methodists, John Wesley's doctrine is presented in "Christian Theology," collected from his writings by the Rev. Thornley Smith. The great Methodist text-book, however, is the "Institutes" of Watson, who systematized and expounded the Wesleyan theology. Pope, a recent English theologian, follows Watson's modified and improved Arminianism, while Whedon and Raymond, recent American writers, hold rather to a radical and extreme Arminianism.

(e) The Quakers, George Fox (1624–1691), and Robert Barclay (1648–1690).

As Jesus, the preacher and reformer, preceded Paul the theologian; as Luther preceded Melanchthon; as Zwingle preceded Calvin; as Laelius Socinus preceded Faustus Socinus; as Wesley preceded Watson; so Fox preceded Barclay. Barclay wrote an "Apology for the true Christian Divinity," which Dr. E. G. Robinson described as "not a formal treatise of Systematic Theology, but the ablest exposition of the views of the Quakers." George Fox was the reformer, William Penn the social founder, Robert Barclay the theologian, of Quakerism.

(f) The English Churchmen, Richard Hooker (1553–1600), Gilbert Burnet (1643–1715), and John Pearson (1613–1686).

The English church has produced no great systematic theologian (see reasons assigned in Dorner, Gesch. prot. Theologie, 470). The "judicious" Hooker is still its greatest theological writer, although his work is only on "Ecclesiastical Polity." Bishop Burnet is the author of the "Exposition of the XXXIX Articles," and Bishop Pearson of the "Exposition of the Creed." Both these are common English text-books. A recent "Compendium of Dogmatic Theology," by Litton, shows a tendency to return from the usual Arminianism of the Anglican church to the old Augustinianism; so also Bishop Moule's "Outlines of Christian Doctrine," and Mason's "Faith of the Gospel."

5. *American theology*, running in two lines:

(a) The Reformed system of Jonathan Edwards (1703–1758), modified successively by Joseph Bellamy (1719–1790), Samuel Hopkins (1721–1803), Timothy Dwight (1752–1817), Nathanael Emmons (1745–1840), Leonard Woods (1774–1854), Charles G. Finney (1792–1875), Nathaniel W. Taylor (1786–1858), and Horace Bushnell (1802–1876). Calvinism, as thus modified, is often called the New England, or New School, theology.

Jonathan Edwards, one of the greatest of metaphysicians and theologians, was an idealist who held that God is the only real cause, either in the realm of matter or in the realm of mind. He regarded the chief good as happiness—a form of sensibility. Virtue was voluntary choice of this good. Hence union with Adam in acts and exercises was sufficient. This God's will made identity of being with Adam. This led to the exercise-system of Hopkins and Emmons, on the one hand, and to Bellamy's and

Dwight's denial of any imputation of Adam's sin or of inborn depravity, on the other— in which last denial agree many other New England theologians who reject the exercise-scheme, as for example, Strong, Tyler, Smalley, Burton, Woods, and Park. Dr. N. W. Taylor added a more distinctly Arminian element, the power of contrary choice—and with this tenet of the New Haven theology, Charles G. Finney, of Oberlin, substantially agreed. Horace Bushnell held to a practically Sabellian view of the Trinity, and to a moral-influence theory of the atonement. Thus from certain principles admitted by Edwards, who held in the main to an Old School theology, the New School theology has been gradually developed.

Robert Hall called Edwards "the greatest of the sons of men." Dr. Chalmers regarded him as the "greatest of theologians." Dr. Fairbairn says: "He is not only the greatest of all the thinkers that America has produced, but also the highest speculative genius of the eighteenth century. In a far higher degree than Spinoza, he was a 'God-intoxicated man.'" His fundamental notion that there is no causality except the divine was made the basis of a theory of necessity which played into the hands of the deists whom he opposed and was alien not only to Christianity but even to theism. Edwards could not have gotten his idealism from Berkeley; it may have been suggested to him by the writings of Locke or Newton, Cudworth or Descartes, John Norris or Arthur Collier. See Prof. H. N. Gardiner, in Philos. Rev., Nov. 1900 : 573-596; Prof. E. C. Smyth, in Am. Jour. Theol., Oct. 1897 : 956; Allen, Jonathan Edwards, 16, 308-310, and in Atlantic Monthly, Dec. 1891 : 767; Sanborn, in Jour. Spec Philos., Oct. 1883 : 401-420; G. P. Fisher, Edwards on the Trinity, 18, 19.

(b) The older Calvinism, represented by Charles Hodge the father (1797-1878) and A. A. Hodge the son (1823–1886), together with Henry B. Smith (1815–1877), Robert J. Breckinridge (1800–1871), Samuel J. Baird, and William G. T. Shedd (1820-1894). All these, although with minor differences, hold to views of human depravity and divine grace more nearly conformed to the doctrine of Augustine and Calvin, and are for this reason distinguished from the New England theologians and their followers by the popular title of Old School.

Old School theology, in its view of predestination, exalts God; New School theology, by emphasizing the freedom of the will, exalts man. It is yet more important to notice that Old School theology has for its characteristic tenet the guilt of inborn depravity. But among those who hold this view, some are federalists and creatianists, and justify God's condemnation of all men upon the ground that Adam represented his posterity. Such are the Princeton theologians generally, including Charles Hodge, A. A. Hodge, and the brothers Alexander. Among those who hold to the Old School doctrine of the guilt of inborn depravity, however, there are others who are traducians, and who explain the imputation of Adam's sin to his posterity upon the ground of the natural union between him and them. Baird's "Elohim Revealed" and Shedd's essay on "Original Sin" (Sin a Nature and that Nature Guilt) represent this realistic conception of the relation of the race to its first father. R. J. Breckinridge, R. L. Dabney, and J. H. Thornwell assert the fact of inherent corruption and guilt, but refuse to assign any *rationale* for it, though they tend to realism. H. B. Smith holds guardedly to the theory of mediate imputation.

On the history of Systematic Theology in general, see Hagenbach, History of Doctrine (from which many of the facts above given are taken), and Shedd, History of Doctrine; also, Ebrard, Dogmatik, 1 : 44-100; Kahnis, Dogmatik, 1 : 15-128; Hase, Hutterus Redivivus, 24-52. Gretillat, Théologie Systématique, 3 : 24-120, has given an excellent history of theology, brought down to the present time. On the history of New England theology, see Fisher, Discussions and Essays, 285-354.

IV. ORDER OF TREATMENT IN SYSTEMATIC THEOLOGY.

1. *Various methods of arranging the topics of a theological system.*

(a) The Analytical method of Calixtus begins with the assumed end of all things, blessedness, and thence passes to the means by which it is secured. (b) The Trinitarian method of Leydecker and Martensen regards

Christian doctrine as a manifestation successively of the Father, Son and Holy Spirit. (c) The Federal method of Cocceius, Witsius, and Boston treats theology under the two covenants. (d) The Anthropological method of Chalmers and Rothe ; the former beginning with the Disease of Man and passing to the Remedy ; the latter dividing his Dogmatik into the Consciousness of Sin and the Consciousness of Redemption. (e) The Christological method of Hase, Thomasius and Andrew Fuller treats of God, man, and sin, as presuppositions of the person and work of Christ. Mention may also be made of (f) The Historical method, followed by Ursinus, and adopted in Jonathan Edwards's History of Redemption ; and (g) The Allegorical method of Dannhauer, in which man is described as a wanderer, life as a road, the Holy Spirit as a light, the church as a candlestick, God as the end, and heaven as the home ; so Bunyan's Holy War, and Howe's Living Temple.

See Calixtus, Epitome Theologiæ ; Leydecker, De Œconomia trium Personarum in Negotio Salutis humanæ ; Martensen (1808–1884), Christian Dogmatics ; Cocceius, Summa Theologiæ, and Summa Doctrinæ de Fœdere et Testamento Dei, in Works, vol. vi ; Witsius, The Economy of the Covenants ; Boston, A Complete Body of Divinity (in Works, vol. 1 and 2), Questions in Divinity (vol. 6), Human Nature in its Fourfold State (vol. 8) ; Chalmers, Institutes of Theology ; Rothe (1799–1867), Dogmatik, and Theologische Ethik ; Hase (1800–1890), Evangelische Dogmatik ; Thomasius (1802–1875), Christi Person und Werk ; Fuller, Gospel Worthy of all Acceptation (in Works, 2:328–416), and Letters on Systematic Divinity (1:684–711); Ursinus (1534–1583), Loci Theologici (in Works, 1:426–909) ; Dannhauer (1603–1666) Hodosophia Christiana, seu Theologia Positiva in Methodum redacta. Jonathan Edwards's so-called History of Redemption was in reality a system of theology in historical form. It "was to begin and end with eternity, all great events and epochs in time being viewed 'sub specie eternitatis.' The three worlds—heaven, earth and hell—were to be the scenes of this grand drama. It was to include the topics of theology as living factors, each in its own place," and all forming a complete and harmonious whole ; see Allen, Jonathan Edwards, 379, 380.

2. *The Synthetic Method*, which we adopt in this compendium, is both the most common and the most logical method of arranging the topics of theology. This method proceeds from causes to effects, or, in the language of Hagenbach (Hist. Doctrine, 2 :152), "starts from the highest principle, God, and proceeds to man, Christ, redemption, and finally to the end of all things." In such a treatment of theology we may best arrange our topics in the following order :

1st. The existence of God.

2d. The Scriptures a revelation from God.

3d. The nature, decrees and works of God.

4th. Man, in his original likeness to God and subsequent apostasy.

5th. Redemption, through the work of Christ and of the Holy Spirit.

6th. The nature and laws of the Christian church.

7th. The end of the present system of things.

V. TEXT-BOOKS IN THEOLOGY, valuable for reference :—

1. *Confessions :* Schaff, Creeds of Christendom.

2. *Compendiums :* H. B. Smith, System of Christian Theology ; A. A. Hodge, Outlines of Theology ; E. H. Johnson, Outline of Systematic Theology ; Hovey, Manual of Theology and Ethics ; W. N. Clarke, Outline

of Christian Theology ; Hase, Hutterus Redivivus ; Luthardt, Compendium der Dogmatik ; Kurtz, Religionslehre.

3. *Extended Treatises :* Dorner, System of Christian Doctrine ; Shedd, Dogmatic Theology ; Calvin, Institutes ; Charles Hodge, Systematic Theology ; Van Oosterzee, Christian Dogmatics ; Baird, Elohim Revealed ; Luthardt, Fundamental, Saving, and Moral Truths ; Phillippi, Glaubens-lehre ; Thomasius, Christi Person und Werk.

4. *Collected Works :* Jonathan Edwards ; Andrew Fuller.

5. *Histories of Doctrine :* Harnack ; Hagenbach ; Shedd ; Fisher ; Sheldon ; Orr, Progress of Dogma.

6. *Monographs :* Julius Müller, Doctrine of Sin ; Shedd, Discourses and Essays ; Liddon, Our Lord's Divinity ; Dorner, History of the Doctrine of the Person of Christ ; Dale, Atonement ; Strong, Christ in Creation ; Upton, Hibbert Lectures.

7. *Theism :* Martineau, Study of Religion ; Harris, Philosophical Basis of Theism ; Strong, Philosophy and Religion ; Bruce, Apologetics ; Drummond, Ascent of Man ; Griffith-Jones, Ascent through Christ.

8. *Christian Evidences :* Butler, Analogy of Natural and Revealed Religion ; Fisher, Grounds of Theistic and Christian Belief ; Row, Bampton Lectures for 1877 ; Peabody, Evidences of Christianity ; Mair, Christian Evidences ; Fairbairn, Philosophy of the Christian Religion ; Matheson, Spiritual Development of St. Paul.

9. *Intellectual Philosophy :* Stout, Handbook of Psychology ; Bowne, Metaphysics ; Porter, Human Intellect ; Hill, Elements of Psychology ; Dewey, Psychology.

10. *Moral Philosophy:* Robinson, Principles and Practice of Morality ; Smyth, Christian Ethics ; Porter, Elements of Moral Science ; Calderwood, Moral Philosophy ; Alexander, Moral Science ; Robins, Ethics of the Christian Life.

11. *General Science :* Todd, Astronomy ; Wentworth and Hill, Physics ; Remsen, Chemistry ; Brigham, Geology ; Parker, Biology ; Martin, Physiology ; Ward, Fairbanks, or West, Sociology ; Walker, Political Economy.

12. *Theological Encyclopædias :* Schaff-Herzog (English) ; McClintock and Strong ; Herzog (Second German Edition).

13. *Bible Dictionaries :* Hastings ; Davis ; Cheyne ; Smith (edited by Hackett).

14. *Commentaries :* Meyer, on the New Testament ; Philippi, Lange, Shedd, Sanday, on the Epistle to the Romans ; Godet, on John's Gospel ; Lightfoot, on Philippians and Colossians ; Expositor's Bible, on the Old Testament books.

15. *Bibles :* American Revision (standard edition); Revised Greek-English New Testament (published by Harper & Brothers) ; Annotated Paragraph Bible (published by the London Religious Tract Society) Stier and Theile, Polyglotten-Bibel.

An attempt has been made, in the list of text-books given above, to put first in each class the book best worth purchasing by the average theological student, and to arrange the books that follow this first one in the order of their value. German books, however when they are not yet accessible in an English translation, are put last, simply because they are less likely to be used as books of reference by the average student.

PART II.

THE EXISTENCE OF GOD.

CHAPTER I.

ORIGIN OF OUR IDEA OF GOD'S EXISTENCE.

God is the infinite and perfect Spirit in whom all things have their source, support, and end.

On the definition of the term God, see Hodge, Syst. Theol., 1 : 366. Other definitions are those of Calovius: "Essentia spiritualis infinita"; Ebrard: "The eternal source of all that is temporal"; Kahnis: "The infinite Spirit"; John Howe: "An eternal, uncaused, independent, necessary Being, that hath active power, life, wisdom, goodness, and whatsoever other supposable excellency, in the highest perfection, in and of itself"; Westminster Catechism: "A Spirit infinite, eternal and unchangeable in his being, wisdom, power, holiness, justice, goodness and truth"; Andrew Fuller: "The first cause and last end of all things."

The existence of God is a first truth; in other words, the knowledge of God's existence is a rational intuition. Logically, it precedes and conditions all observation and reasoning. Chronologically, only reflection upon the phenomena of nature and of mind occasions its rise in consciousness.

The term intuition means simply direct knowledge. Lowndes (Philos. of Primary Beliefs, 78) and Mansel (Metaphysics, 52) would use the term only of our direct knowledge of substances, as self and body; Porter appli's it by preference to our cognition of first truths, such as have been already mentioned. Harris (Philos. Basis of Theism, 44-151, but esp. 45, 46) makes it include both. He divides intuitions into two classes: 1. *Presentative* intuitions, as self-consciousness (in virtue of which I perceive the existence of spirit and already come in contact with the supernatural), and sense-perception (in virtue of which I perceive the existence of matter, at least in my own organism, and come in contact with nature); 2. *Rational* intuitions, as space, time, substance, cause, final cause, right, absolute being. We may accept this nomenclature, using the terms "first truths" and "rational intuitions" as equivalent to each other, and classifying rational intuitions under the heads of (1) intuitions of relations, as space and time; (2) intuitions of principles, as substance, cause, final cause, right; and (3) intuition of absolute Being, Power, Reason, Perfection, Personality, as God. We hold that, as upon occasion of the senses cognizing (*a*) extended matter, (*b*) succession, (*c*) qualities, (*d*) change, (*e*) order, (*f*) action, respectively, the mind cognizes (*a*) space, (*b*) time, (*c*) substance, (*d*) cause, (*e*) design, (*f*) obligation, so upon occasion of our cognizing our finiteness, dependence and responsibility, the mind directly cognizes the existence of an Infinite and Absolute Authority, Perfection, Personality, upon whom we are dependent and to whom we are responsible.

Bowne, Theory of Thought and Knowledge, 60 — "As we walk in entire ignorance of our muscles, so we often think in entire ignorance of the principles which underlie and determine thinking. But as anatomy reveals that the apparently simple act of walking involves a highly complex muscular activity, so analysis reveals that the apparently simple act of thinking involves a system of mental principles." Dewey, Psychology, 238, 244 — "Perception, memory, imagination, conception — each of these is an act of intuition. . . . Every concrete act of knowledge involves an intuition of God." Martineau, Types, 1: 459 — The attempt to divest experience of either percepts or intuitions is "like the attempt to peel a bubble in search for its colors and contents: in tenuem ex oculis evanuit auram"; Study, 1:199 — "Try with all your might to do something difficult, e. g , to shut a door against a furious wind, and you recognize Self and Nature — causal will, over against external causality"; 201 — "Hence our fellow-feeling with Nature"; 65 — "As Perception gives us Will in the shape of Causality over against us in the non-ego, so Conscience gives us Will in the shape of Authority over against us in the non-ego "; Types, 2: 5 — "In perception it is self and nature, in morals it is self and God, that stand face to face in the subjective and objective antithesis"; Study, 2: 2, 3 — "In volitional experience we meet with objective *causality;* in moral experience we meet with objective *authority,* — both being objects of immediate knowledge, on the same footing of certainty with the apprehension of the external material world. I know of no logical advantage which the belief in finite objects around us can boast over the belief in the infinite and righteous Cause of all"; 51 — "In recognition of God as Cause, we raise the University; in recognition of God as Authority, we raise the Church."

Kant declares that the idea of freedom is the source of our idea of personality,—personality consists in the freedom of the whole soul from the mechanism of nature. Lotze, Metaphysics, §244 — "So far as, and so long as, the soul knows itself as the identical subject of inward experience, it is, and is named simply for that reason, substance." Illingworth, Personality, Human and Divine, 32 — "Our conception of substance is derived, not from the physical, but from the mental world. Substance is first of all that which underlies our *mental* affections and manifestations." James, Will to Believe, 80 — "Substance, as Kant says, means 'das Beharrliche,' the abiding, that which will be as it has been, because its being is essential and eternal." In this sense we have an intuitive belief in an abiding substance which underlies our own thoughts and volitions, and this we call the soul. But we also have an intuitive belief in an abiding substance which underlies all natural phenomena and all the events of history, and this we call God. Among those who hold to this general view of an intuitive knowledge of God may be mentioned the following: — Calvin, Institutes, book I, chap. 3 ; Nitzsch, System of Christian Doctrine, 15-26, 133-140; Julius Müller, Doctrine of Sin, 1 : 78-84; Ulrici, Leib und Seele, 688-725; Porter, Human Intellect, 497 ; Hickok, Rational Cosmology, 58-89; Farrar, Science in Theology, 27-29; Bib. Sac., July, 1872: 533, and January, 1873 : 204; Miller, Fetich in Theology, 110-122; Fisher, Essays, 565-572; Tulloch, Theism, 314-336; Hodge, Systematic Theology, 1 : 191-203; Christlieb, Mod. Doubt and Christian Belief, 75, 76; Raymond, Syst. Theology, 1 : 247-262; Bascom, Science of Mind, 246, 247; Knight, Studies in Philos. and Lit., 155-224; A. H. Strong, Philosophy and Religion, 76-89.

I. FIRST TRUTHS IN GENERAL.

1. *Their nature.*

A. Negatively.—A first truth is not (*a*) Truth written prior to consciousness upon the substance of the soul — for such passive knowledge implies a materialistic view of the soul; (*b*) Actual knowledge of which the soul finds itself in possession at birth — for it cannot be proved that the soul has such knowledge ; (*c*) An idea, undeveloped at birth, but which has the power of self-development apart from observation and experience — for this is contrary to all we know of the laws of mental growth.

Cicero, De Natura Deorum, 1 : 17 — " intelligi necesse est esse deos, quoniam insitas eorum vel potius innatas cogitationes habemus." Origen, Adv. Celsum, 1 : 4 — "Men would not be guilty, if they did not carry in their minds common notions of morality, innate and written in divine letters. Calvin, Institutes, 1 : 3 : 3 — "Those who rightly judge will always agree that there is an indelible sense of divinity engraven upon men's minds." Fleming, Vocab. of Philosophy, art.: "Innate Ideas" — "Descartes is supposed to have taught (and Locke devoted the first book of his Essays to refuting the doctrine) that these ideas are innate or connate with the soul; *i. e.*, the intellect finds itself at birth, or as soon as it wakes to conscious activity, to be possessed of ideas to which it has only to attach the appropriate names, or of judgments which it only needs to express in fit propositions — *i. c.*, prior to any experience of individual objects.''

Royce, Spirit of Modern Philosophy, 77—" In certain families, Descartes teaches, good breeding and the gout are innate. Yet, of course, the children of such families have to be instructed in deportment, and the infants just learning to walk seem happily quite free from gout. Even so geometry is innate in us, but it does not come to our consciousness without much trouble"; 79 — Locke found no innate ideas. He maintained, in reply, that "infants, with their rattles, showed no sign of being aware that things which are equal to the same thing are equal to each other." Schopenhauer said that " Jacobi had the trifling weakness of taking all he had learned and approved before his fifteenth year for inborn ideas of the human mind." Bowne, Principles of Ethics, 5 — " That the rational ideas are conditioned by the sense experience and are sequent to it, is unquestioned by any one; and that experience shows a successive order of manifestation is equally undoubted. But the sensationalist has always shown a curious blindness to the ambiguity of such a fact. He will have it that what comes after must be a modification of what went before; whereas it might be *that, and* it might be a new, though conditioned, manifestation of an immanent nature or law. Chemical affinity is not gravity, although affinity cannot manifest itself until gravity has brought the elements into certain relations."

Pfleiderer, Philosophy of Religion, 1 : 103 — " This principle was not from the beginning in the consciousness of men; for, in order to think ideas, reason must be clearly developed, which in the first of mankind it could just as little be as in children. This however does not exclude the fact that there was from the beginning the unconscious rational impulse which lay at the basis of the formation of the belief in God, however manifold may have been the direct motives which co-operated with it." Self is implied in the simplest act of knowledge. Sensation gives us two things, *e. g.*, black and white; but I cannot compare them without asserting difference *for me*. Different sensations make no *knowledge*, without a *self* to bring them together. Upton, Hibbert Lectures, lecture 2 — " You could as easily prove the existence of an external world to a man who had no senses to perceive it, as you could prove the existence of God to one who had no consciousness of God."

B. Positively.—A first truth is a knowledge which, though developed upon occasion of observation and reflection, is not derived from observation and reflection,—a knowledge on the contrary which has such logical priority that it must be assumed or supposed, in order to make any observation or reflection possible. Such truths are not, therefore, recognized first in order of time ; some of them are assented to somewhat late in the mind's growth ; by the great majority of men they are never consciously formulated at all. Yet they constitute the necessary assumptions upon which all other knowledge rests, and the mind has not only the inborn capacity to evolve them so soon as the proper occasions are presented, but the recognition of them is inevitable so soon as the mind begins to give account to itself of its own knowledge.

Mansel, Metaphysics, 52, 279 — " To describe experience as the cause of the idea of space would be as inaccurate as to speak of the soil in which it was planted as the cause of the oak — though the planting in the soil is the condition which brings into manifestation the latent power of the acorn." Coleridge : " We see before we know that we have eyes; but when once this is known, we perceive that eyes must have preëxisted in order to enable us to see." Coleridge speaks of first truths as "those necessities of mind or forms of thinking, which, though revealed to us by experience, must yet have preëxisted in order to make experience possible." McCosh, Intuitions, 48, 49 — Intuitions are "like flower and fruit, which are in the plant from its embryo, but may not be actually formed till there have been a stalk and branches and leaves." Porter, Human Intellect, 501, 519 — " Such truths cannot be acquired or assented to first of all." Some are reached last of all. The moral intuition is often developed late, and sometimes, even then, only upon occasion of corporal punishment. "Every man is as lazy as circumstances will admit." Our physical laziness is occasional; our mental laziness frequent; our moral laziness incessant. We are too lazy to think, and especially to think of religion. On account of this depravity of human nature we should expect the intuition of God to be developed last of all. Men shrink from contact with God and from the thought of God. In fact, their dislike for the intuition of God leads them not seldom to deny all their other intuitions, even those of freedom and of right. Hence the modern "psychology without a soul."

Schurman, Agnosticism and Religion, 105-115 — "The idea of God . . . is latest to develop into clear consciousness . . . and must be latest, for it is the unity of the difference of the self and the not-self, which are therefore presupposed." But "it has not less validity in itself, it gives no less trustworthy assurance of actuality, than the consciousness of the self, or the consciousness of the not-self. . . . The consciousness of God is the logical *prius* of the consciousness of self and of the world. But not, as already observed, the chronological; for, according to the profound observation of Aristotle, what in the nature of things is first, is in the order of development last. Just because God is the first principle of being and knowing, he is the last to be manifested and known. . . . The finite and the infinite are both known together, and it is as impossible to know one without the other as it is to apprehend an angle without the sides which contain it." For account of the relation of the intuitions to experience, see especially Cousin, True, Beautiful and Good, 39-64, and History of Philosophy, 2 : 199-245. Compare Kant, Critique of Pure Reason, Introd., 1. See also Bascom, in Bib. Sac., 23 : 1-47 ; 27 : 68-90.

2. *Their criteria.* The criteria by which first truths are to be tested are three :

A. Their universality. By this we mean, not that all men assent to them or understand them when propounded in scientific form, but that all men manifest a practical belief in them by their language, actions, and expectations.

B. Their necessity. By this we mean, not that it is impossible to deny these truths, but that the mind is compelled by its very constitution to recognize them upon the occurrence of the proper conditions, and to employ them in its arguments to prove their non-existence.

C. Their logical independence and priority. By this we mean that these truths can be resolved into no others, and proved by no others ; that they are presupposed in the acquisition of all other knowledge, and can therefore be derived from no other source than an original cognitive power of the mind.

Instances of the professed and formal denial of first truths : — the positivist denies causality ; the idealist denies substance ; the pantheist denies personality ; the necessitarian denies freedom ; the nihilist denies his own existence. A man may in like manner argue that there is no necessity for an atmosphere ; but even while he argues, he breathes it. Instance the knock-down argument to demonstrate the freedom of the will. I grant my own existence in the very doubting of it ; for "cogito, ergo sum," as Descartes himself insisted, really means "cogito, scilicet sum" ; H. B. Smith : "The statement is analysis, not proof." Ladd, Philosophy of Knowledge, 59 — "The *cogito*, in barbarous Latin = *cogitans sum*: thinking is self-conscious *being*." Bentham : "The word *ought* is an authoritative imposture, and ought to be banished from the realm of morals." Spinoza and Hegel really deny self-consciousness when they make man a phenomenon of the infinite. Royce likens the denier of personality to the man who goes outside of his own house and declares that no one lives there because, when he looks in at the window, he sees no one inside.

Professor James, in his Psychology, assumes the reality of a brain, but refuses to assume the reality of a soul. This is essentially the position of materialism. But this assumption of a brain is metaphysics, although the author claims to be writing a psychology without metaphysics. Ladd, Philosophy of Mind, 3 — "The materialist believes in causation proper so long as he is explaining the origin of mind from matter, but when he is asked to see in mind the cause of physical change he at once becomes a mere phenomenalist." Royce, Spirit of Modern Philosophy, 400 — " I know that all beings, if only they can count, must find that three and two make five. Perhaps the angels cannot count; but, if they can, this axiom is true for them. If I met an angel who declared that his experience had occasionally shown him a three and two that did *not* make five, I should know at once what sort of an angel he was." On the criteria of first truths, see Porter, Human Intellect, 510, 511. On denial of them, see Shedd, Dogmatic Theology, 1 : 213.

II. The Existence of God a first truth.

1. That *the knowledge of God's existence answers the first criterion of universality,* is evident from the following considerations :

A. It is an acknowledged fact that the vast majority of men have actually recognized the existence of a spiritual being or beings, upon whom they conceived themselves to be dependent.

The Vedas declare: " There is but one Being — no second." Max Müller, Origin and Growth of Religion, 34 — " Not the visible sun, moon and stars are invoked, but something else that cannot be seen." The lowest tribes have conscience, fear death, believe in witches, propitiate or frighten away evil fates. Even the fetich-worshiper, who calls the stone or the tree a god, shows that he has already the idea of a God. We must not measure the ideas of the heathen by their capacity for expression, any more than we should judge the child's belief in the existence of his father by his success in drawing the father's picture. On heathenism, its origin and nature, see Tholuck, in Bib. Repos., 1832 : 86 ; Scholz, Götzendienst und Zauberwesen.

B. Those races and nations which have at first seemed destitute of such knowledge have uniformly, upon further investigation, been found to possess it, so that no tribe of men with which we have thorough acquaintance can be said to be without an object of worship. We may presume that further knowledge will show this to be true of all.

Moffat, who reported that certain African tribes were destitute of religion, was corrected by the testimony of his son-in-law, Livingstone: "The existence of God and of a future life is everywhere recognized in Africa." Where men are most nearly destitute of any formulated knowledge of God, the conditions for the awakening of the idea are most nearly absent. An apple-tree may be so conditioned that it never bears apples. " We do not judge of the oak by the stunted, flowerless specimens on the edge of the Arctic Circle." The presence of an occasional blind, deaf or dumb man does not disprove the definition that man is a seeing, hearing and speaking creature. Bowne, Principles of Ethics, 154 — " We need not tremble for mathematics, even if some tribes should be found without the multiplication-table. . . . Sub-moral and sub-rational existence is always with us in the case of young children; and, if we should find it elsewhere, it would have no greater significance."

Victor Hugo : " Some men deny the Infinite ; some, too, deny the sun ; they are the blind." Gladden, What is Left? 148 — " A man may escape from his shadow by going into the dark ; if he comes under the light of the sun, the shadow is there. A man may be so mentally undisciplined that he does not recognize these ideas ; but let him learn the use of his reason, let him reflect on his own mental processes, and he will know that they are necessary ideas." On an original monotheism, see Diestel, in Jahrbuch für deutsche Theologie, 1860, and vol. 5 : 669 ; Max Müller, Chips, 1 : 337 ; Rawlinson, in Present Day Tracts, No. 11 ; Legge, Religions of China, 8-11 ; Shedd, Dogmatic Theology, 1 : 201-208. *Per contra*, see Asmus, Indogerm. Relig., 2 : 1-8 ; and synopsis in Bib. Sac., Jan. 1877 : 167-172.

C. This conclusion is corroborated by the fact that those individuals, in heathen or in Christian lands, who profess themselves to be without any knowledge of a spiritual power or powers above them, do yet indirectly manifest the existence of such an idea in their minds and its positive influence over them.

Comte said that science would conduct God to the frontier and then bow him out, with thanks for his provisional services. But Herbert Spencer affirms the existence of a "Power to which no limit in time or space is conceivable, of which all phenomena as presented in consciousness are manifestations." The intuition of God, though formally excluded, is implicitly contained in Spencer's system, in the shape of the "irresistible belief" in Absolute Being, which distinguishes his position from that of Comte; see H. Spencer, who says: "One truth must ever grow clearer — the truth that there is an inscrutable existence everywhere manifested, to which we can neither find nor conceive beginning or end — the one absolute certainty that we are ever in the presence of an infinite and eternal energy from which all things proceed." Mr. Spencer assumes unity in the underlying Reality. Frederick Harrison sneeringly asks him : "Why not say 'forces,' instead of 'force'?" While Harrison gives us a supreme moral ideal without a metaphysical ground, Spencer gives us an ultimate metaphysical principle without a final moral purpose. The idea of God is the synthesis of the two, —"They are but broken lights of Thee, And thou, O Lord, art more than they " (Tennyson, In Memoriam).

Solon spoke of ὁ θεός and ι ' τὸ θεῖον, and Sophocles of ὁ μέγας θεός. The term for "God" is identical in all the Indo-European languages, and therefore belonged to the time before those languages separated; see Shedd, Dogm. Theol., 1:201-208. In Virgil's Æneid, Mezentius is an atheist, a despiser of the gods, trusting only in his spear and in his right arm; but, when the corpse of his son is brought to him, his first act is to raise his hands to heaven. Hume was a sceptic, but he said to Ferguson, as they walked on a starry night: "Adam, there is a God!" Voltaire prayed in an Alpine thunderstorm. Shelley wrote his name in the visitors' book of the inn at Montanvert, and added: "Democrat, philanthropist, atheist"; yet he loved to think of a "fine intellectual spirit pervading the universe"; and he also wrote: "The One remains, the many change and pass; Heaven's light forever shines, Earth's shadows fly." Strauss worships the Cosmos, because "order and law, reason and goodness" are the soul of it. Renan trusts in goodness, design, ends. Charles Darwin, Life, 1:274—"In my most extreme fluctuations, I have never been an atheist, in the sense of denying the existence of a God."

D. This agreement among individuals and nations so widely separated in time and place can be most satisfactorily explained by supposing that it has its ground, not in accidental circumstances, but in the nature of man as man. The diverse and imperfectly developed ideas of the supreme Being which prevail among men are best accounted for as misinterpretations and perversions of an intuitive conviction common to all.

Huxley, Lay Sermons, 163 — " There are savages without God, in any proper sense of the word; but there are none without ghosts." Martineau, Study, 2:353, well replies: " Instead of turning other people into ghosts, and then appropriating one to ourselves [and attributing another to God, we may add] by way of imitation, we start from the sense of personal continuity, and then predicate the same of others, under the figures which keep most clear of the physical and perishable." Grant Allen describes the higher religions as "a grotesque fungoid growth," that has gathered about a primitive thread of ancestor-worship. But this is to derive the greater from the less. Sayce, Hibbert Lectures, 358 — " I can find no trace of ancestor-worship in the earliest literature of Babylonia which has survived to us"— this seems fatal to Huxley's and Allen's view that the idea of God is derived from man's prior belief in spirits of the dead. C. M. Tyler, in Am. Jour. Theo., Jan. 1899 : 144 — " It seems impossible to deify a dead man, unless there is embryonic in primitive consciousness a prior concept of Deity."

Renouf, Religion of Ancient Egypt, 93 — "The whole mythology of Egypt . . . turns on the histories of Ra and Osiris. . . . Texts are discovered which identify Osiris and Ra. . . . Other texts are known wherein Ra, Osiris, Amon, and all other gods disappear, except as simple *names*, and the unity of God is asserted in the noblest language of monotheistic religion." These facts are earlier than any known ancestor-worship. "They point to an original idea of divinity above humanity" (see Hill, Genetic Philosophy, 317). We must add the idea of the superhuman, before we can turn any animism or ancestor-worship into a religion. This superhuman element was suggested to early man by all he saw of nature about him, especially by the sight of the heavens above, and by what he knew of causality within. For the evidence of a universal recognition of a superior power, see Flint, Anti-theistic Theories, 250–289, 522–533; Renouf, Hibbert Lectures for 1879: 100; Bib. Sac., Jan. 1884: 132–157; Peschel, Races of Men, 261; Ulrici, Leib und Seele, 688, and Gott und die Natur, 658–670, 758; Tylor, Primitive Culture, 1:377, 381, 418; Alexander, Evidences of Christianity, 22; Calderwood, Philosophy of the Infinite, 512; Liddon, Elements of Religion, 50; Methodist Quar. Rev., Jan. 1875:1; J. F. Clark, Ten Great Religions, 2:17–21.

2. That *the knowledge of God's existence answers the second criterion of necessity,* will be seen by considering:

A. That men, under circumstances fitted to call forth this knowledge, cannot avoid recognizing the existence of God. In contemplating finite existence, there is inevitably suggested the idea of an infinite Being as its correlative. Upon occasion of the mind's perceiving its own finiteness, dependence, responsibility, it immediately and necessarily perceives the existence of an infinite and unconditioned Being upon whom it is dependent and to whom it is responsible.

We could not recognize the finite as finite, except by comparing it with an already existing standard—the Infinite. Mansel, Limits of Religous Thought, lect. 3 — "We are compelled by the constitution of our minds to believe in the existence of an Absolute and Infinite Being—a belief which appears forced upon us as the complement of our consciousness of the relative and finite." Fisher, Journ. Chr. Philos., Jan. 1883: 113 — "Ego and non-ego, each being conditioned by the other, presuppose unconditioned being on which both are dependent. Unconditioned being is the silent presupposition of all our knowing." Perceived dependent being implies an independent; independent being is perfectly self-determining; self-determination is personality; perfect self-determination is infinite Personality. John Watson, in Philos. Rev., Sept. 1893:526 — "There is no consciousness of self apart from the consciousness of other selves and things; and no consciousness of the world apart from the consciousness of the single Reality presupposed in both." E. Caird, Evolution of Religion, 64–68 — In every act of consciousness the primary elements are implied: "the idea of the object, or not-self; the idea of the subject, or self; and the idea of the unity which is presupposed in the difference of the self and not-self, and within which they act and react on each other." See Calderwood, Philos. of Infinite, 46, and Moral Philos., 77; Hopkins, Outline Study of Man, 283–285; Shedd, Dogm. Theol., 1:211.

B. That men, in virtue of their humanity, have a capacity for religion. This recognized capacity for religion is proof that the idea of God is a necessary one. If the mind upon proper occasion did not evolve this idea, there would be nothing in man to which religion could appeal.

"It is the suggestion of the Infinite that makes the line of the far horizon, seen over land or sea, so much more impressive than the beauties of any limited landscape." In times of sudden shock and danger, this rational intuition becomes a presentative intuition,—men become more conscious of God's existence than of the existence of their fellow-men and they instinctively cry to God for help. In the commands and reproaches of the moral nature the soul recognizes a Lawgiver and Judge whose voice conscience merely echoes. Aristotle called man "a political animal"; it is still more true, as Sabatier declares, that "man is incurably religious." St. Bernard: "Noverim me, noverim te." O. P. Gifford: "As milk, from which under proper conditions cream does not rise, is not milk, so the man, who upon proper occasion shows no knowledge of God, is not man, but brute." We must not however expect cream from frozen milk. Proper environment and conditions are needed.

It is the recognition of a divine Personality in nature which constitutes the greatest merit and charm of Wordsworth's poetry. In his Tintern Abbey, he speaks of "A presence that disturbs me with the joy Of elevated thoughts; a sense sublime Of something far more deeply interfused, Whose dwelling is the light of setting suns, And the round ocean and the living air, And the blue sky and in the mind of man: A motion and a spirit that impels All thinking things, all objects of all thought, And rolls through all things." Robert Browning sees God in humanity, as Wordsworth sees God in nature. In his Hohenstiel-Schwangau he writes: "This is the glory, that in all conceived Or felt or known, I recognize a Mind — Not mine, but like mine — for the double joy Making all things for me, and me for Him." John Ruskin held that the foundation of beauty in the world is the presence of God in it. In his youth he tells us that he had "a continual perception of sanctity in the whole of nature, from the slightest thing to the vastest — an instinctive awe mixed with delight, an indefinable thrill such as we sometimes imagine to indicate the presence of a disembodied spirit." But it was not a disembodied, but an embodied, Spirit that he saw. Nitzsch, Christian Doctrine, §7 — "Unless education and culture were preceded by an innate consciousness of God as an operative predisposition, there would be nothing for education and culture to work upon." On Wordsworth's recognition of a divine personality in nature, see Knight, Studies, 282-317, 405-426; Hutton, Essays, 2 : 113.

C. That he who denies God's existence must tacitly assume that existence in his very argument, by employing logical processes whose validity rests upon the fact of God's existence. The full proof of this belongs under the next head.

"I am an atheist, God knows" — was the absurd beginning of an argument to disprove the divine existence. Cutler, Beginnings of Ethics, 22 — "Even the Nihilists, whose first principle is that God and duty are great bugbears to be abolished, assume that God and duty exist, and they are impelled by a sense of duty to abolish them." Mrs. Browning, The Cry of the Human: "'There is no God,' the foolish saith; But none, 'There is no sorrow'; And nature oft the cry of faith In bitter need will borrow : Eyes which the preacher could not school By wayside graves are raised; And lips say, 'God be pitiful,' Who ne'er said, 'God be praised.'" Dr. W. W. Keen, when called to treat an Irishman's aphasia, said: "Well, Dennis, how are you?" "Oh, doctor, I cannot spake!" "But, Dennis, you are speaking." "Oh, doctor, it's many a word I cannot spake!" "Well, Dennis, now I will try you. See if you cannot say, 'Horse.'" "Oh, doctor dear, 'horse' is the very word I cannot spake!" On this whole section, see A. M. Fairbairn, Origin and Development of Idea of God, in Studies in Philos. of Relig. and History; Martineau, Religion and Materialism, 45; Bishop Temple, Bampton Lectures, 1884 : 37-65.

3. That *the knowledge of God's existence answers the third criterion of logical independence and priority,* may be shown as follows :

A. It is presupposed in all other knowledge as its logical condition and foundation. The validity of the simplest mental acts, such as sense-perception, self-consciousness, and memory, depends upon the assumption that a God exists who has so constituted our minds that they give us knowledge of things as they are.

Pfleiderer, Philos. of Religion, 1 : 88 — "The ground of science and of cognition generally is to be found neither in the subject nor in the object *per se*, but only in the divine thinking that combines the two, which, as the common ground of the forms of thinking in all finite minds, and of the forms of being in all things, makes possible the correspondence or agreement between the former and the latter, or in a word makes knowledge of truth possible." 91 — "Religious belief is presupposed in all scientific knowledge as the basis of its possibility." This is the thought of Psalm 36 : 10 — "In thy light shall we see light." A. J. Balfour, Foundations of Belief, 303 — "The uniformity of nature cannot be proved from experience, for it is what makes proof from experience possible. . . . Assume it, and we shall find that facts conform to it. . . . 309 — The uniformity of nature can be established only by the aid of that principle itself, and is necessarily involved in all attempts to prove it. . . . There must be a God, to justify our confidence in innate ideas."

Bowne, Theory of Thought and Knowledge, 276 — "Reflection shows that the community of individual intelligences is possible only through an all-embracing Intelligence, the source and creator of finite minds." Science rests upon the postulate of a world-order. Huxley: "The object of science is the discovery of the rational order which pervades the universe." This rational order presupposes a rational Author. Dubois, in New Englander, Nov. 1890: 468 — "We assume uniformity and continuity, or we can have no science. An intelligent Creative Will is a genuine scientific hypothesis [postulate?], suggested by analogy and confirmed by experience, not contradicting the fundamental law of uniformity but accounting for it." Ritchie, Darwin and Hegel, 18 — "That nature is a system, is the assumption underlying the earliest mythologies: to fill up this conception in the aim of the latest science." Royce, Relig. Aspect of Philosophy, 435 — "There is such a thing as error; but error is inconceivable unless there be such a thing as truth; and truth is inconceivable unless there be a seat of truth, an infinite all-including Thought or Mind; therefore such a Mind exists."

B. The more complex processes of the mind, such as induction and deduction, can be relied on only by presupposing a thinking Deity who has made the various parts of the universe and the various aspects of truth to correspond to each other and to the investigating faculties of man.

We argue from one apple to the others on the tree. Newton argued from the fall of an apple to gravitation in the moon and throughout the solar system. Rowland argued from the chemistry of our world to that of Sirius. In all such argument there is assumed a unifying thought and a thinking Deity. This is Tyndall's "scientific use of the imagination." "Nourished," he says, "by knowledge partially won, and bounded by coöperant reason, imagination is the mightiest instrument of the physical discoverer." What Tyndall calls "imagination", is really insight into the thoughts of God, the great Thinker. It prepares the way for logical reasoning,—it is not the product of mere reasoning. For this reason Goethe called imagination "die Vorschule des Denkens," or "thought's preparatory school."

Peabody, Christianity the Religion of Nature, 23 — "Induction is syllogism, with the immutable attributes of God for a constant term." Porter, Hum. Intellect, 492— "Induction rests upon the assumption, as it demands for its ground, that a personal or thinking Deity exists"; 658 — "It has no meaning or validity unless we assume that the universe is constituted in such a way as to presuppose an absolute and unconditioned originator of its forces and laws"; 662 — "We analyze the several processes of knowledge into their underlying assumptions, and we find that the assumption which underlies them all is that of a self-existent Intelligence who not only can be known by man, but must be known by man in order that man may know anything besides"; see also pages 486, 508, 509, 518, 519, 585, 616. Harris, Philos. Basis of Theism, 81 — "The processes of reflective thought imply that the universe is grounded in, and is the manifestation of, reason"; 560 — "The existence of a personal God is a necessary datum of scientific knowledge." So also, Fisher, Essays on Supernat. Origin of Christianity, 564, and in Journ. Christ. Philos., Jan. 1883: 129, 130.

C. Our primitive belief in final cause, or, in other words, our conviction that all things have their ends, that design pervades the universe, involves a belief in God's existence. In assuming that there is a universe, that the universe is a rational whole, a system of thought-relations, we assume the existence of an absolute Thinker, of whose thought the universe is an expression.

Pfleiderer, Philos. of Religion, 1 : 81 — "The real can only be thinkable if it is realized thought, a thought previously thought, which our thinking has only to think again. Therefore the real, in order to be thinkable for us, must be the realized thought of the creative thinking of an eternal divine Reason which is presented to our cognitive thinking." Royce, World and Individual, 2 : 41 — "Universal teleology constitutes the essence of all facts." A. H. Bradford, The Age of Faith, 142 — "Suffering and sorrow are universal. Either God could prevent them and would not, and therefore he is neither beneficent nor loving ; or else he cannot prevent them and therefore something is greater than God, and therefore there is no God? But here is the use of reason in the individual reasoning. Reasoning in the individual necessitates the absolute or universal reason. If there is the absolute reason, then the universe and history are ordered and administered in harmony with reason; then suffering and sorrow can be neither meaningless nor final, since that would be the contradiction of reason. That cannot be possible in the universal and absolute which contradicts reason in man."

D. Our primitive belief in moral obligation, or, in other words, our conviction that right has universal authority, involves the belief in God's existence. In assuming that the universe is a moral whole, we assume the existence of an absolute Will, of whose righteousness the universe is an expression.

Pfleiderer, Philos. of Religion, 1 : 88 — "The ground of moral obligation is found neither in the subject nor in society, but only in the universal or divine Will that combines both. . . . 103 — The idea of God is the unity of the true and the good, or of the two highest ideas which our reason thinks as theoretical reason, but demands as practical reason. . . . In the idea of God we find the only synthesis of the world that *is* — the world of science, and of the world that *ought to be* — the world of religion." Seth, Ethical Principles, 425 — "This is not a mathematical demonstration. Philosophy never is an exact science. Rather is it offered as the only sufficient foundation of the moral life. . . . The life of goodness . . . is a life based on the conviction that its source and its issues are in the Eternal and the Infinite." As finite truth and goodness are comprehensible only in the light of some absolute principle which furnishes for them an ideal standard, so finite beauty is inexplicable except as there exists a perfect standard with which it may be compared. The beautiful is more than the agreeable or the useful. Proportion, order, harmony, unity in diversity — all these are characteristics of beauty. But they all imply an intellectual and spiritual Being, from whom they proceed and by whom they can be measured. Both physical and moral beauty, in finite things and beings, are symbols and manifestations of Him who is the author and lover of beauty, and who is himself the infinite and absolute Beauty. The beautiful in nature and in art shows that the idea of God's existence is logically independent and prior. See Cousin, The True, the Beautiful, and the Good, 140-153 ; Kant, Metaphysic of Ethics, who holds that belief in God is the necessary presupposition of the belief in duty.

To repeat these four points in another form — the intuition of an Absolute Reason is (*a*) the necessary presupposition of all other knowledge, so that we cannot know anything else to exist except by assuming first of all that God exists ; (*b*) the necessary basis of all logical thought, so that we cannot put confidence in any one of our reasoning processes except by taking for granted that a thinking Deity has constructed our minds with reference to the universe and to truth ; (*c*) the necessary implication of our primitive belief in design, so that we can assume all things to exist for a purpose, only by making the prior assumption that a purposing God exists -— can regard the universe as a thought, only by postulating the existence of an absolute Thinker ; and (*d*) the necessary foundation of our conviction of moral obligation, so that we can believe in the universal authority of right, only by assuming that there exists a God of righteousness who reveals his will both in the individual conscience and in the moral universe at large. We cannot *prove* that God is ; but we can show that, in order to the existence of any knowledge, thought, reason, conscience, in man, man must *assume* that God is.

As Jacobi said of the beautiful : " Es kann gewiesen aber nicht bewiesen werden " — it can be shown, but not proved. Bowne, Metaphysics, 472 — " Our objective knowledge of the finite must rest upon ethical trust in the infinite " ; 480 — " Theism is the absolute postulate of all knowledge, science and philosophy " ; " God is the most certain fact of objective knowledge." Ladd, Bib. Sac., Oct. 1877 : 611-616 — " Cogito, ergo Deus est. We are obliged to postulate a not-ourselves which makes for rationality, as well as for righteousness." W. T. Harris: "Even natural science is impossible, where philosophy has not yet taught that reason made the world, and that nature is a revelation of the rational." Whately, Logic, 270: New Englander, Oct. 1871, art. on Grounds of Confidence in Inductive Reasoning, Bib. Sac., 7 : 415–425; Dorner, Glaubenslehre, 1 : 197; Trendelenburg, Logische Untersuchungen, ch. "Zweck"; Ulrici Gott und die Natur, 540–626; Lachelier, Du Fondement de l'Induction, 78. *Per contra*, see Janet, Final Causes, 174, note, and 457–464, who holds final cause to be, not an intuition, but the result of applying the principle of causality to cases which mechanical laws alone will not explain.

Pascal: "Nature confounds the Pyrrhonist, and Reason confounds the Dogmatist. We have an incapacity of demonstration, which the former cannot overcome; we have a conception of truth which the latter cannot disturb." "There is no Unbelief! Whoever says, 'To-morrow,' 'The Unknown,' 'The Future,' trusts that Power alone, Nor dares disown." Jones, Robert Browning, 314 — "We cannot indeed prove God as the conclusion of a syllogism, for he is the primary hypothesis of all proof." Robert Browning, Hohenstiel-Schwangau : "I know that he is there, as I am here, By the same proof, which seems no proof at all, It so exceeds familiar forms of proof"; Paracelsus, 27 — "To know Rather consists in opening out a way Whence the imprisoned splendor may escape Than in effecting entrance for a light Supposed to be without." Tennyson, Holy Grail: "Let visions of the night or day Come as they will, and many a time they come. . . . In moments when he feels he cannot die, And knows himself no vision to himself, Nor the high God a vision, nor that One Who rose again"; The Ancient Sage, 548 — "Thou canst not prove the Nameless, O my son! Nor canst thou prove the world thou movest in. Thou canst not prove that thou art body alone, Nor canst thou prove that thou art spirit alone, Nor canst thou prove that thou art both in one. Thou canst not prove that thou art immortal, no, Nor yet that thou art mortal. Nay, my son, thou canst not prove that I, who speak with thee, Am not thyself in converse with thyself. For nothing worthy proving can be proven, Nor yet disproven : Wherefore be thou wise, Cleave ever to the sunnier side of doubt, And cling to Faith beyond the forms of Faith."

III. OTHER SUPPOSED SOURCES OF OUR IDEA OF GOD'S EXISTENCE.

Our proof that the idea of God's existence is a rational intuition will not be complete, until we show that attempts to account in other ways for the origin of the idea are insufficient, and require as their presupposition the very intuition which they would supplant or reduce to a secondary place. We claim that it cannot be derived from any other source than an original cognitive power of the mind.

1. Not from external revelation,—whether communicated (*a*) through the Scriptures, or (*b*) through tradition ; for, unless man had from another source a previous knowledge of the existence of a God from whom such a revelation might come, the revelation itself could have no authority for him.

(*a*) See Gillespie, Necessary Existence of God, 10; Ebrard, Dogmatik, 1 : 117; H. B. Smith, Faith and Philosophy, 18 — "A revelation takes for granted that he to whom it is made has some knowledge of God, though it may enlarge and purify that knowledge." We cannot prove God from the authority of the Scriptures, and then also prove the Scriptures from the authority of God. The very idea of Scripture as a revelation presupposes belief in a God who can make it. Newman Smyth, in New Englander, 1878 : 355 — We cannot derive from a sun-dial our knowledge of the existence of a sun. The sun-dial presupposes the sun, and cannot be understood without previous knowledge of the sun. Wuttke, Christian Ethics, 2 : 103 — "The voice of the divine ego does not first come to the consciousness of the individual ego from without; rather does every external revelation presuppose already this inner one ; there must echo out from within man something kindred to the outer revelation, in order to its being recognized and accepted as divine."

Fairbairn, Studies in Philos. of Relig. and Hist., 21, 22 — "If man is dependent on an outer revelation for his idea of God, then he must have what Schelling happily termed 'an original atheism of consciousness.' Religion cannot, in that case, be rooted in the nature of man, — it must be implanted from without." Schurman, Belief in God, 78 — "A primitive revelation of God could only mean that God had endowed man with the capacity of apprehending his divine original. This capacity, like every other, is innate, and like every other, it realizes itself only in the presence of appropriate conditions." Clarke, Christian Theology, 112 — "Revelation cannot demonstrate God's existence, for it must assume it; but it will manifest his existence and character to men, and will serve them as the chief source of certainty concerning him, for it will teach them what they could not know by other means."

(b) Nor does our idea of God come primarily from tradition, for "tradition can perpetuate only what has already been originated" (Patton). If the knowledge thus handed down is the knowledge of a primitive revelation, then the argument just stated applies—that very revelation presupposed in those who first received it, and presupposes in those to whom it is handed down, some knowledge of a Being from whom such a revelation might come. If the knowledge thus handed down is simply knowledge of the results of the reasonings of the race, then the knowledge of God comes originally from reasoning — an explanation which we consider further on. On the traditive theory of religion, see Flint, Theism, 23, 338; Cocker, Christianity and Greek Philosophy, 86–96; Fairbairn, Studies in Philos. of Relig. and Hist., 14, 15; Bowen, Metaph. and Ethics, 453, and in Bib. Sac., Oct. 1876; Pfleiderer, Religionsphilos., 312–322.

Similar answers must be returned to many common explanations of man's belief in God: "Primus in orbe deos fecit timor"; Imagination made religion; Priests invented religion; Religion is a matter of imitation and fashion. But we ask again: What caused the fear? Who made the imagination? What made priests possible? What made imitation and fashion natural? To say that man worships, merely because he sees other men worshiping, is as absurd as to say that a horse eats hay because he sees other horses eating it. There must be a hunger in the soul to be satisfied, or external things would never attract man to worship. Priests could never impose upon men so continuously, unless there was in human nature a universal belief in a God who might commission priests as his representatives. Imagination itself requires some basis of reality, and a larger basis as civilization advances. The fact that belief in God's existence gets a wider hold upon the race with each added century, shows that, instead of fear having caused belief in God, the truth is that belief in God has caused fear; indeed, "the fear of Jehovah is the beginning of wisdom" (Ps. 111 : 10).

2. Not from experience, — whether this mean (a) the sense-perception and reflection of the individual (Locke), (b) the accumulated results of the sensations and associations of past generations of the race (Herbert Spencer), or (c) the actual contact of our sensitive nature with God, the supersensible reality, through the religious feeling (Newman Smyth).

The first form of this theory is inconsistent with the fact that the idea of God is not the idea of a sensible or material object, nor a combination of such ideas. Since the spiritual and infinite are direct opposites of the material and finite, no experience of the latter can account for our idea of the former.

With Locke (Essay on Hum. Understanding, 2 : 1 : 4), experience is the passive reception of ideas by sensation or by reflection. Locke's "tabula rasa" theory mistakes the occasion of our primitive ideas for their cause. To his statement: "Nihil est in intellectu nisi quod ante fuerit in sensu," Leibnitz replied: "Nisi intellectus ipse." Consciousness is sometimes called the source of our knowledge of God. But consciousness, as simply an accompanying knowledge of ourselves and our states, is not properly the source of any other knowledge. The German *Gottesbewusstsein* = not "consciousness of God," but "knowledge of God"; *Bewusstsein* here = not a "conknowing," but a "beknowing"; see Porter, Human Intellect, 86; Cousin, True, Beautiful and Good, 48, 49.

Fraser, Locke, 143–147 — Sensations are the bricks, and association the mortar, of the mental house. Bowne, Theory of Thought and Knowledge, 47 — "Develope language by allowing sounds to associate and evolve meaning for themselves? Yet this is the exact parallel of the philosophy which aims to build intelligence out of sensation.

. . . . 52 — One who does not know how to read would look in vain for meaning in a printed page, and in vain would he seek to help his failure by using strong spectacles." Yet even if the idea of God were a product of experience, we should not be warranted in rejecting it as irrational. See Brooks, Foundations of Zoölogy, 132 — "There is no antagonism between those who attribute knowledge to experience and those who attribute it to our innate reason ; between those who attribute the development of the germ to mechanical conditions and those who attribute it to the inherent potency of the germ itself ; between those who hold that all nature was latent in the cosmic vapor and those who believe that everything in nature is immediately intended rather than predetermined." All these may be methods of the immanent God.

The second form of the theory is open to the objection that the very first experience of the first man, equally with man's latest experience, presupposes this intuition, as well as the other intuitions, and therefore cannot be the cause of it. Moreover, even though this theory of its origin were correct, it would still be impossible to think of the object of the intuition as not existing, and the intuition would still represent to us the highest measure of certitude at present attainable by man. If the evolution of ideas is toward truth instead of falsehood, it is the part of wisdom to act upon the hypothesis that our primitive belief is veracious.

Martineau, Study, 2 : 26 — " Nature is as worthy of trust in her processes, as in her gifts." Bowne, Examination of Spencer, 163, 164 — " Are we to seek truth in the minds of pre-human apes, or in the blind stirrings of some primitive pulp ? In that case we can indeed put away all our science, but we must put away the great doctrine of evolution along with it. The experience-philosophy cannot escape this alternative : either the positive deliverances of our mature consciousness must be accepted as they stand, or all truth must be declared impossible." See also Harris, Philos. Basis Theism, 137-142.

Charles Darwin, in a letter written a year before his death, referring to his doubts as to the existence of God, asks : " Can we trust to the convictions of a monkey's mind ? " We may reply : " Can we trust the conclusions of one who was once a baby ? " Bowne, Ethics, 3 — " The genesis and emergence of an idea are one thing ; its validity is quite another. The logical value of chemistry cannot be decided by reciting its beginnings in alchemy ; and the logical value of astronomy is independent of the fact that it began in astrology. . . . 11 — Even if man came from the ape, we need not tremble for the validity of the multiplication-table or of the Golden Rule. If we have moral insight, it is no matter how we got it ; and if we have no such insight, there is no help in any psychological theory. . . . 159 — We must not appeal to savages and babies to find what is natural to the human mind. . . . In the case of anything that is under the law of development we can find its true nature, not by going back to its crude beginnings, but by studying the finished outcome." Dawson, Mod. Ideas of Evolution, 13 — " If the idea of God be the phantom of an apelike brain, can we trust to reason or conscience in any other matter ? May not science and philosophy themselves be similar phantasies, evolved by mere chance and unreason ? " Even though man came from the ape, there is no explaining his ideas by the ideas of the ape : " A man 's a man for a' that."

We must judge beginnings by endings, not endings by beginnings. It matters not how the development of the eye took place nor how imperfect was the first sense of sight, if the eye now gives us correct information of external objects. So it matters not how the intuitions of right and of God originated, if they now give us knowledge of objective truth. We must take for granted that evolution of ideas is not from sense to nonsense. G. H. Lewes, Study of Psychology, 122 — " We can understand the amoeba and the polyp only by a light reflected from the study of man." Seth, Ethical Principles, 429 — " The oak explains the acorn even more truly than the acorn explains the oak." Sidgwick : " No one appeals from the artist's sense of beauty to the child's. Higher mathematics are no less true, because they can be apprehended only by trained intellect. No strange importance attaches to what was *first* felt or thought." Robert Browning, Paracelsus : " Man, once descried, imprints forever His presence on all lifeless things. . . . A supplementary reflux of light Illustrates all the inferior grades, explains Each back step in the circle." Man, with his higher ideas, shows the meaning and content of all that led up to him. He is the last round of the ascending ladder, and from this highest product and from his ideas we may infer what his Maker is.

Bixby, Crisis in Morals, 162, 245—"Evolution simply gave man such *height* that he could at last discern the stars of moral truth which had previously been below the horizon. This is very different from saying that moral truths are merely transmitted products of the experiences of utility. . . . The germ of the idea of God, as of the idea of right, must have been in man just so soon as he became man, —the brute's gaining it turned him into man. Reason is not simply a register of physical phenomena and of experiences of pleasure and pain: it is creative also. It discerns the oneness of things and the supremacy of God." Sir Charles Lyell: "The presumption is enormous that all our faculties, though liable to err, are true in the main and point to real objects. The religious faculty in man is one of the strongest of all. It existed in the earliest ages, and instead of wearing out before advancing civilization, it grows stronger and stronger, and is to-day more developed among the highest races than it ever was before. I think we may safely trust that it points to a great truth." Fisher, Nat. and Meth. of Rev., 137, quotes Augustine: "Securus judicat orbis terrarum," and tells us that the intellect is assumed to be an organ of knowledge, however the intellect may have been evolved. But if the intellect is worthy of trust, so is the moral nature. George A. Gordon, The Christ of To-day, 103 — "To Herbert Spencer, human history is but an incident of natural history, and force is supreme. To Christianity nature is only the beginning, and man the consummation. Which gives the higher revelation of the life of the tree— the seed, or the fruit?"

The third form of the theory seems to make God a sensuous object, to reverse the proper order of knowing and feeling, to ignore the fact that in all feeling there is at least some knowledge of an object, and to forget that the validity of this very feeling can be maintained only by previously assuming the existence of a rational Deity.

Newman Smyth tells us that feeling comes first ; the idea is secondary. Intuitive ideas are not denied, but they are declared to be direct reflections, in thought, of the feelings. They are the mind's immediate perception of what it feels to exist. Direct knowledge of God by intuition is considered to be idealistic, reaching God by inference is regarded as rationalistic, in its tendency. See Smyth, The Religious Feeling ; reviewed by Harris, in New Englander, Jan., 1878 : reply by Smyth, in New Englander, May, 1878.

We grant that, even in the case of unregenerate men, great peril, great joy, great sin often turn the rational intuition of God into a presentative intuition. The presentative intuition, however, cannot be affirmed to be common to all men. It does not furnish the foundation or explanation of a universal capacity for religion. Without the rational intuition, the presentative would not be possible, since it is only the rational that enables man to receive and to interpret the presentative. The very trust that we put in feeling presupposes an intuitive belief in a true and good God. Tennyson said in 1869 : " Yes, it is true that there are moments when the flesh is nothing to me ; when I know and feel the flesh to be the vision ; God and the spiritual is the real ; it belongs to me more than the hand and the foot. You may tell me that my hand and my foot are only imaginary symbols of my existence, — I could believe you ; but you never, never can convince me that the *I* is not an eternal Reality, and that the spiritual is not the real and true part of me."

3.   Not from reasoning, — because

(*a*)   The actual rise of this knowledge in the great majority of minds is not the result of any conscious process of reasoning. On the other hand, upon occurrence of the proper conditions, it flashes upon the soul with the quickness and force of an immediate revelation.

(*b*)   The strength of men's faith in God's existence is not proportioned to the strength of the reasoning faculty. On the other hand, men of greatest logical power are often inveterate sceptics, while men of unwavering faith are found among those who cannot even understand the arguments for God's existence.

(*c*)   There is more in this knowledge than reasoning could ever have rurnished. Men do not limit their belief in God to the just conclusions of argument. The arguments for the divine existence, valuable as they are for purposes to be shown hereafter, are not sufficient by themselves to warrant our conviction that there exists an infinite and absolute Being. It will appear upon examination that the *a priori* argument is capable of proving only an abstract and ideal proposition, but can never conduct us to the existence of a real Being. It will appear that the *a posteriori* arguments, from merely finite existence, can never demonstrate the existence of the infinite. In the words of Sir Wm. Hamilton (Discussions, 23) — "A demonstration of the absolute from the relative is logically absurd, as in such a syllogism we must collect in the conclusion what is not distributed in the premises " — in short, from finite premises we cannot draw an infinite conclusion.

Whately, Logic, 290–292; Jevons, Lessons in Logic, 81; Thompson, Outline Laws of Thought, sections 82–92; Calderwood, Philos. of Infinite, 60–69, and Moral Philosophy, 238; Turnbull, in Bap. Quarterly, July, 1872:271; Van Oosterzee, Dogmatics, 239; Dove, Logic of Christian Faith, 21. Sir Wm. Hamilton : " Departing from the particular, we admit that we cannot, in our highest generalizations, rise above the finite." Dr. E. G. Robinson : "The human mind turns out larger grists than are ever put in at the hopper." There is more in the idea of God than could have come out so small a knot-hole as human reasoning. A single word, a chance remark, or an attitude of prayer, suggests the idea to a child. Helen Keller told Phillips Brooks that she had always known that there was a God, but that she had not known his name. Ladd, Philosophy of Mind, 119 — " It is a foolish assumption that nothing can be certainly known unless it be reached as the result of a conscious syllogistic process, or that the more complicated and subtle this process is, the more sure is the conclusion. Inferential knowledge is always dependent upon the superior certainty of immediate knowledge." George M. Duncan, in Memorial of Noah Porter, 246 — " All deduction rests either on the previous process of induction, or on the intuitions of time and space which involve the Infinite and Absolute."

(*d*) Neither do men arrive at the knowledge of God's existence by inference; for inference is condensed syllogism, and, as a form of reasoning, is equally open to the objection just mentioned. We have seen, moreover, that all logical processes are based upon the assumption of God's existence. Evidently that which is presupposed in all reasoning cannot itself be proved by reasoning.

By inference, we of course mean mediate inference, for in immediate inference (*e. g.*, " All good rulers are just ; therefore no unjust rulers are good ") there is no reasoning, and no progress in thought. Mediate inference is reasoning — is condensed syllogism ; and what is so condensed may be expanded into regular logical form. Deductive inference : "A negro is a fellow-creature ; therefore he who strikes a negro strikes a fellow-creature." Inductive inference : " The first finger is before the second ; therefore it is before the third." On inference, see Martineau, Essays, 1 : 105-108; Porter, Human Intellect, 444–448; Jevons, Principles of Science, 1 : 14, 136-139, 168, 262.

Flint, in his Theism, 77, and Herbert, in his Mod. Realism Examined, would reach the knowledge of God's existence by inference. The latter says God is not demonstrable, but his existence is inferred, like the existence of our fellow men. But we reply that in this last case we infer only the finite from the finite, while the difficulty in the case of God is in inferring the infinite from the finite. This very process of reasoning, moreover, presupposes the existence of God as the absolute Reason, in the way already indicated.

Substantially the same error is committed by H. B. Smith, Introd. to Chr. Theol., 84–133, and by Diman, Theistic Argument, 316, 364, both of whom grant an intuitive element, but use it only to eke out the insufficiency of reasoning. They consider that the intuition gives us only an abstract idea, which contains in itself no voucher for the existence of an actual being corresponding to the idea, and that we reach real being only by inference from the facts of our own spiritual natures and of the outward world. But we reply, in the words of McCosh, that "the intuitions are primarily directed to individual objects." We know, not the infinite in the abstract, but infinite space and time, and the infinite God. See McCosh, Intuitions, 26, 199, who, however, holds the view here combated.

Schurman, Belief in God, 43 — " I am unable to assign to our belief in God a higher certainty than that possessed by the working hypotheses of science . . . 57 — The nearest approach made by science to our hypothesis of the existence of God lies in the assertion of the universality of law . . . based on the conviction of the unity and systematic connection of all reality . . . 64 — This unity can be found only in self-conscious spirit." The fault of this reasoning is that it gives us nothing necessary or absolute. Instances of working hypotheses are the nebular hypothesis in astronomy, the law of gravitation, the atomic theory in chemistry, the principle of evolution. No one of these is logically independent or prior. Each of them is provisional, and each may be superseded by new discovery. Not so with the idea of God. This idea is presupposed by all the others, as the condition of every mental process and the guarantee of its validity.

IV. CONTENTS OF THIS INTUITION.

1. In this fundamental knowledge *that* God is, it is necessarily implied that to some extent men know intuitively *what* God is, namely, (a) a Reason in which their mental processes are grounded ; (b) a Power above them upon which they are dependent ; (c) a Perfection which imposes law upon their moral natures ; (d) a Personality which they may recognize in prayer and worship.

In maintaining that we have a rational intuition of God, we by no means imply that a presentative intuition of God is impossible. Such a presentative intuition was perhaps characteristic of unfallen man ; it does belong at times to the Christian ; it will be the blessing of heaven (Mat. 5 : 8 — "the pure in heart. . . shall see God"; Rev. 22 : 4 — "they shall see his face"). Men's experiences of face-to-face apprehension of God, in danger and guilt, give some reason to believe that a presentative knowledge of God is the normal condition of humanity. But, as this presentative intuition of God is not in our present state universal, we here claim only that all men have a rational intuition of God.

It is to be remembered, however, that the loss of love to God has greatly obscured even this rational intuition, so that the revelation of nature and the Scriptures is needed to awaken, confirm and enlarge it, and the special work of the Spirit of Christ to make it the knowledge of friendship and communion. Thus from knowing about God, we come to know God (John 17 : 3 — "This is life eternal, that they should know thee"; 2 Tim. 1 : 12 — " I know him whom I have believed").

Plato said, for substance, that there can be no ὅτι οἶδεν without something of the ἅ οἶδεν. Harris, Philosophical Basis of Theism, 208 — " By rational intuition man knows that absolute Being *exists*; his knowledge of *what* it is, is progressive with his progressive knowledge of man and of nature." Hutton, Essays: " A haunting presence besets man behind and before. He cannot evade it. It gives new meanings to his thoughts, new terror to his sins. It becomes intolerable. He is moved to set up some idol, carved out of his own nature, that will take its place — a non-moral God who will not disturb his dream of rest. It is a righteous Life and Will, and not the mere *idea* of righteousness that stirs men so." Porter, Hum. Int., 661 — " The Absolute is a thinking Agent." The intuition does not grow in certainty; what grows is the mind's quickness in applying it and power of expressing it. The intuition is not complex; what is complex is the Being intuitively cognized. See Calderwood. Moral Philosophy, 232; Lowndes, Philos.

of Primary Beliefs, 108–112; Luthardt, Fund. Truths, 157—Latent faculty of speech is called forth by speech of others; the choked-up well flows again when debris is cleared away. Bowen, in Bib. Sac., 33: 740-754; Bowne, Theism, 79.

Knowledge of a person is turned into personal knowledge by actual communication or revelation. First, comes the intuitive knowledge of God possessed by all men—the assumption that there exists a Reason, Power, Perfection, Personality, that makes correct thinking and acting possible. Secondly, comes the knowledge of God's being and attributes which nature and Scripture furnish. Thirdly, comes the personal and presentative knowledge derived from actual reconciliation and intercourse with God, through Christ and the Holy Spirit. Stearns, Evidence of Christian Experience, 108— "Christian experience verifies the claims of doctrine by experiment, — so transforming probable knowledge into real knowledge." Biedermann, quoted by Pfleiderer, Grundriss, 18—"God reveals himself to the human spirit, 1. as its infinite *Ground*, in the reason; 2. as its infinite *Norm*, in the conscience; 3. as its infinite *Strength*, in elevation to religious truth, blessedness, and freedom."

Shall I object to this Christian experience, because only comparatively few have it, and I am not among the number? Because I have not seen the moons of Jupiter, shall I doubt the testimony of the astronomer to their existence? Christian experience, like the sight of the moons of Jupiter, is attainable by all. Clarke, Christian Theology, 113 —"One who will have full proof of the good God's reality must put it to the experimental test. He must take the good God for real, and receive the confirmation that will follow. When faith reaches out after God, it finds him. . . . They who have found him will be the sanest and truest of their kind, and their convictions will be among the safest convictions of man. . . . Those who live in fellowship with the good God will grow in goodness, and will give practical evidence of his existence aside from their oral testimony."

2. The Scriptures, therefore, do not attempt to prove the existence of God, but, on the other hand, both assume and declare that the knowledge that God is, is universal (Rom. 1 : 19–21, 28, 32 ; 2 : 15). God has inlaid the evidence of this fundamental truth in the very nature of man, so that nowhere is he without a witness. The preacher may confidently follow the example of Scripture by assuming it. But he must also explicitly declare it, as the Scripture does. "For the invisible things of him since the creation of the world are clearly seen" (καθορᾶται—spiritually viewed); the organ given for this purpose is the νοῦς (νοούμενα); but then — and this forms the transition to our next division of the subject — they are "perceived through the things that are made" (τοῖς ποιήμασιν, Rom. 1 : 20).

On Rom. 1 : 19–21, see Weiss, Bib. Theol. des N. T., 251, note; also commentaries of Meyer, Alford, Tholuck, and Wordsworth; τὸ γνωστὸν τοῦ θεοῦ = not "that which may be known" (Rev. Vers.) but "that which is known" of God; νοούμενα καθορᾶται = are clearly seen in that they are perceived by the reason — νοούμενα expresses the manner of the καθορᾶται (Meyer); compare John 1 : 9; Acts 17 : 27; Rom. 1 : 28; 2 : 15. On 1 Cor. 15 : 34, see Calderwood, Philos. of Inf., 466 — ἀγνωσίαν Θεοῦ τινὲς ἔχουσι = do not possess the specially exalted knowledge of God which belongs to believers in Christ (cf. 1 Jo. 4 : 7 — "every one that loveth is begotten of God, and knoweth God"). On Eph. 2 : 12, see Pope, Theology, 1 : 240 — ἄθεοι ἐν τῷ κόσμῳ is opposed to being in Christ, and signifies rather forsaken of God, than denying him or entirely ignorant of him. On Scripture passages, see Schmid, Bib. Theol. des N. T., 486; Hofmann, Schriftbeweis, 1 : 62.

E. G. Robinson: "The first statement of the Bible is, not that there is a God, but that 'In the beginning God created the heavens and the earth' (Gen. 1 : 1). The belief in God never was and never can be the result of logical argument, else the Bible would give us proofs." Many texts relied upon as *proofs* of God's existence are simply *explications* of the idea of God, as for example: Ps. 94 : 9, 10 — "He that planted the ear, shall he not hear? He that formed the eye, shall he not see? He that chastiseth the nations, shall not he correct, even he that teacheth man knowledge?" Plato says that God holds the soul by its roots, — he therefore does not need to demonstrate to the soul the fact of his existence. Martineau, Seat of Authority, 308, says well that Scripture and preaching only interpret what is already in the heart which it addresses: "Flinging a warm breath on the inward oracles hid in invisible ink, it renders them articulate and dazzling as the handwriting on the wall. The divine Seer does not convey to you *his* revelation, but qualifies you to receive *your own*. This mutual relation is possible only through the common presence of God in the conscience of mankind." Shedd, Dogmatic Theology, 1 : 195-220 — "The earth and sky make the same sensible impressions on the organs of a brute that they do upon those of a man ; but the brute never discerns the 'invisible things' of God, his 'eternal power and godhood' " (Rom. 1 : 20).

Our subconscious activity, so far as it is normal, is under the guidance of the immanent Reason. Sensation, before it results in thought, has in it logical elements which are furnished by mind — not ours, but that of the Infinite One. Christ, the Revealer of God, reveals God in every man's mental life, and the Holy Spirit may be the principle of self-consciousness in man as in God. Harris, God the Creator, tells us that "man finds the Reason that is eternal and universal revealing itself in the exercise of his own reason." Savage, Life after Death, 268 — " How do you know that your subliminal consciousness does not tap Omniscience, and get at the facts of the universe?" Savage negatives this suggestion, however, and wrongly favors the spirit-theory. For his own experience, see pages 295-329 of his book.

C. M. Barrows, in Proceedings of Soc. for Psychical Research, vol. 12, part 30, pages 34-36 — "There is a subliminal agent. What if this is simply one intelligent Actor, filling the universe with his presence, as the ether fills space ; the common Inspirer of all mankind, a skilled Musician, presiding over many pipes and keys, and playing through each what music he will? The subliminal self is a universal fountain of energy, and each man is an outlet of the stream. Each man's personal self is contained in it, and thus each man is made one with every other man. In that deep Force, the last fact behind which analysis cannot go, all psychical and bodily effects find their common origin." This statement needs to be qualified by the assertion of man's ethical nature and distinct personality; see section of this work on Ethical Monism, in chapter III. But there is truth here like that which Coleridge sought to express in his Æolian Harp : "And what if all of animated Nature Be but organic harps diversely framed, That tremble into thought, as o'er them sweeps, Plastic and vast, one intellectual breeze, At once the soul of each, and God of all ?" See F. W. H. Myers, Human Personality.

Dorner, System of Theology, 1 : 75 — "The consciousness of God is the true fastness of our self-consciousness. . . . Since it is only in the God-conscious man that the innermost personality comes to light, in like manner, by means of the interweaving of that consciousness of God and of the world, the world is viewed in God ('sub specie æternitatis'), and the certainty of the world first obtains its absolute security for the spirit." Royce, Spirit of Mod. Philosophy, synopsis in N. Y. Nation : "The one indubitable fact is the existence of an infinite self, a Logos or World-mind (345). That it exists is clear, I. Because idealism shows that real things are nothing more nor less than ideas, or 'possibilities of experience'; but a mere 'possibility', as such, is nothing, and a world of 'possible' experiences, in so far as it is real, must be a world of actual experience to some self (367). If then there be a real world, it has all the while existed as ideal and mental, even before it became known to the particular mind with which we conceive it as coming into connection (368). II. But there is such a real world; for, when I *think* of an object, when I *mean* it, I do not merely have in mind an idea resembling it, for I aim at the object, I pick it out, I already in some measure possess it. The object is then already present in essence to my hidden self (370). As truth consists in knowledge of the conformity of a cognition to its object, that alone can know a truth which includes within itself both idea and object. This inclusive Knower is the Infinite Self (374). With this I am in essence ident'cal (371); it is my larger self (372): and this larger self alone *is* (379). It includes all reality, and we know other finite minds, because we are one with them in its unity " (409).

The experience of George John Romanes is instructive. For years he could recognize no personal Intelligence controlling the universe. He made four mistakes : 1. *He forgot that only love can see*, that God is not disclosed to the mere intellect, but only to the whole man, to the integral mind, to what the Scripture calls " the eyes of your heart (Eph. 1 : 18). Experience of life taught him at last the weakness of mere reasoning, and led him to depend more upon the affections and intuitions. Then, as one might say, he gave the X-rays of Christianity a chance to photograph God upon his soul. 2. *He began at the wrong end*, with matter rather than with mind, with cause and effect rather than with right and wrong, and so got involved in the mechanical order and tried to interpret the moral realm by it. The result was that instead of recognizing freedom, responsibility, sin, guilt. he threw them out as pretenders. But study of conscience and will set him right. He learned to take what he found instead of trying to turn it into something else, and so came to interpret nature by spirit, instead of interpreting spirit by nature. 3. *He took the Cosmos by bits*, instead of regarding it as a whole. His early thinking insisted on finding design in each particular part, or nowhere. But his more mature thought recognized wisdom and reason in the ordered whole. As he realized that this is a universe, he could not get rid of the idea of an organizing Mind. He came to see that the Universe, as a thought, implies a Thinker. 4. *He fancied that nature excludes God*, instead of being only the method of God's working. When he learned how a thing was done, he at first concluded that God had not done it. His later thought recognized that God and nature are not mutually exclusive. So he came to find no difficulty even in miracles and inspiration ; for the God who is in man and of whose mind and will nature is only the expression, can reveal himself, if need be, in special ways. So George John Romanes came back to prayer, to Christ, to the church.

On the general subject of intuition as connected with our idea of God, see Ladd, in Bib. Sac., 1877 : 1-36, 611-616 ; 1878 : 619; Fisher, on Final Cause an Intuition, in Journ. Christ. Philos., Jan. 1883 : 115-134 ; Patton, on Genesis of Idea of God, in Jour. Christ. Philos., Apl. 1883 : 283-307 ; McCosh, Christianity and Positivism, 124-140 ; Mansel, in Encyc. Brit., 8th ed., vol. 14 : 604 and 615; Robert Hall, sermon on Atheism ; Hutton, on Atheism, in Essays, 1 : 3-37 ; Shairp, in Princeton Rev., March, 1881 : 264.

CHAPTER II.

CORROBORATIVE EVIDENCES OF GOD'S EXISTENCE.

Although the knowledge of God's existence is intuitive, it may be explicated and confirmed by arguments drawn from the actual universe and from the abstract ideas of the human mind.

Remark 1. These arguments are probable, not demonstrative. For this reason they supplement each other, and constitute a series of evidences which is cumulative in its nature. Though, taken singly, none of them can be considered absolutely decisive, they together furnish a corroboration of our primitive conviction of God's existence, which is of great practical value, and is in itself sufficient to bind the moral action of men.

Butler, Analogy, Introd., Bohn's ed., 72 — Probable evidence admits of degrees, from the highest moral certainty to the lowest presumption. Yet probability is the guide of life. In matters of morals and religion, we are not to expect mathematical or demonstrative, but only probable, evidence, and the slightest preponderance of such evidence may be sufficient to bind our moral action. The truth of our religion, like the truth of common matters, is to be judged by the whole evidence taken together; for probable proofs, by being added, not only increase the evidence, but multiply it. Dove, Logic of Christ. Faith, 24—Value of the arguments taken together is much greater than that of any single one. Illustrated from water, air and food, together but not separately, supporting life; value of £1000 note, not in paper, stamp, writing, signature, taken separately. A whole bundle of rods cannot be broken, though each rod in the bundle may be broken separately. The strength of the bundle is the strength of the whole. Lord Bacon, Essay on Atheism: "A little philosophy inclineth man's mind to atheism, but depth in philosophy bringeth men's minds about to religion. For while the mind of man looketh upon second causes scattered, it may sometimes rest in them and go no further, but, when it beholdeth the chain of them confederate and linked together, it must needs fly to Providence and Deity." Murphy, Scientific Bases of Faith, 221-223—"The proof of a God and of a spiritual world which is to satisfy us must consist in a number of different but converging lines of proof."

In a case where only circumstantial evidence is attainable, many lines of proof sometimes converge, and though no one of the lines reaches the mark, the conclusion to which they all point becomes the only rational one. To doubt that there is a London, or that there was a Napoleon, would indicate insanity; yet London and Napoleon are proved by only probable evidence. There is no constraining efficacy in the arguments for God's existence; but the same can be said of all reasoning that is not demonstrative. Another interpretation of the facts is *possible*, but no other conclusion is so *satisfactory*, as that God is; see Fisher, Nature and Method of Revelation, 129. Prof. Rogers: "If in practical affairs we were to hesitate to act until we had absolute and demonstrative certainty, we should never begin to move at all." For this reason an old Indian official advised a young Indian judge "always to give his verdict, but always to avoid giving the grounds of it."

Bowne, Philos. of Theism, 11-14—"Instead of doubting everything that can be doubted, let us rather doubt nothing until we are compelled to doubt. . . . In society we get on better by assuming that men are truthful, and by doubting only for special reasons, than we should if we assumed that all men are liars, and believed them only when compelled. So in all our investigations we make more progress if we assume the truthfulness of the universe and of our own nature than we should if we doubted both. . . . . The first method seems the more rigorous, but it can be applied only to mathematics, which is a purely subjective science. When we come to deal with reality, the method brings thought to a standstill. .... The law the logician lays down is this : Nothing may be believed which is not proved. The law the mind actually follows is this : Whatever the mind demands for the satisfaction of its subjective interests and tendencies may be assumed as real, in default of positive disproof."

Remark 2.   A consideration of these arguments may also serve to expli- cate the contents of an intuition which has remaided obscure and only half conscious for lack of reflection.   The arguments, indeed, are the efforts of the mind that already has a conviction of God's existence to give to itself a formal account of its belief.   An exact estimate of their logical value and of their relation to the intuition which they seek to express in syllogistic form, is essential to any proper refutation of the prevalent atheistic and pantheistic reasoning.

Diman, Theistic Argument, 363 — " Nor have I claimed that the existence, even, of this Being can be demonstrated as we demonstrate the abstract truths of science. I have only claimed that the universe, as a great fact, demands a rational explanation, and that the most rational explanation that can possibly be given is that furnished in the conception of such a Being. In this conclusion reason rests, and refuses to rest in any other." Rückert: " Wer Gott nicht fühlt in sich und allen Lebenskreisen, Dem werdet ihr nicht ihn beweisen mit Beweisen." Harris, Philos. Basis of Theism, 307 — " Theology depends on noetic and empirical science to give the occasion on which the idea of the Absolute Being arises, and to give content to the idea." Andrew Fuller, Part of Syst. of Divin., 4 :283, questions " whether argumentation in favor of the exist- ence of God has not made more sceptics than believers." So far as this true, it is due to an overstatement of the arguments and an exaggerated notion of what is to be expected from them. See Nitzsch, Christian Doctrine, translation, 140 ; Ebrard, Dog- matik, 1 : 119, 120 ; Fisher, Essays on Supernatural Origin of Christianity, 572, 573; Van Oosterzee, 238, 241.

" Evidences of Christianity ? " said Coleridge, " I am weary of the word." The more Christianity was *proved*, the less it was *believed*. The revival of religion under White- field and Wesley did what all the apologists of the eighteenth century could not do,— it quickened men's intuitions into life, and made them practically recognize God. Martineau, Types, 2 :231—Men can " bow the knee to the passing *Zeitgeist*, while turn- ing the back to the consensus of all the ages " ; Seat of Authority, 312 — " Our reason- ings lead to explicit Theism because they start from implicit Theism." Illingworth, Div. and Hum. Personality, 81 — " The proofs are .... attempts to account for and explain and justify something that already exists ; to decompose a highly complex though immediate judgment into its constituent elements, none of which when isolated can have the completeness or the cogency of the original conviction taken as a whole."

Bowne, Philos. of Theism, 31, 32 — " Demonstration is only a makeshift for helping ignorance to insight. . . . When we come to an argument in which the whole nature is addressed, the argument must seem weak or strong, according as the nature is feebly, or fully, developed. The moral argument for theism cannot seem strong to one with- out a conscience. The argument from cognitive interests will be empty when there is no cognitive interest. Little souls find very little that calls for explanation or that excites surprise, and they are satisfied with a correspondingly small view of life and existence. In such a case we cannot hope for universal agreement. We can only proclaim the faith that is in us, in hope that this proclamation may not be without some response in other minds and hearts. .... We have only probable evidence for the uniformity of nature or for the affection of friends. We cannot logically prove either. The deepest convictions are not the certainties of logic, but the certainties of life."

Remark 3.   The arguments for the divine existence may be reduced to four, namely : I. The Cosmological ; II. The Teleological ; III. The Anthropological ; and IV. The Ontological.   We shall examine these in order, seeking first to determine the precise conclusions to which they respectively lead, and then to ascertain in what manner the four may be combined.

I. The Cosmological Argument, or Argument from Change in Nature.

This is not properly an argument from effect to cause; for the proposition that every effect must have a cause is simply identical, and means only that every caused event must have a cause. It is rather an argument from begun existence to a sufficient cause of that beginning, and may be accurately stated as follows:

Everything begun, whether substance or phenomenon, owes its existence to some producing cause. The universe, at least so far as its present form is concerned, is a thing begun, and owes its existence to a cause which is equal to its production. This cause must be indefinitely great.

It is to be noticed that this argument moves wholly in the realm of nature. The argument from man's constitution and beginning upon the planet is treated under another head (see Anthropological Argument). That the present form of the universe is not eternal in the past, but has begun to be, not only personal observation but the testimony of geology assures us. For statements of the argument, see Kant, Critique of Pure Reason (Bohn's transl.), 370; Gillespie, Necessary Existence of God, 8 : 34-44; Bib. Sac., 1849 : 613; 1850 : 613; Porter, Hum. Intellect, 570; Herbert Spencer, First Principles, 93. It has often been claimed, as by Locke, Clarke, and Robert Hall, that this argument is sufficient to conduct the mind to an Eternal and Infinite First Cause. We proceed therefore to mention

1. *The defects of the Cosmological Argument.*

A. It is impossible to show that the universe, so far as its substance is concerned, has had a beginning. The law of causality declares, not that everything has a cause — for then God himself must have a cause — but rather that everything begun has a cause, or in other words, that every event or change has a cause.

Hume, Philos. Works, 2 : 411 *sq.*, urges with reason that we never saw a world made. Many philosophers in Christian lands, as Martineau, Essays, 1 : 206, and the prevailing opinions of ante-Christian times, have held matter to be eternal. Bowne, Metaphysics, 107 — " For being itself, the reflective reason never asks a cause, unless the being show signs of dependence. It is change that first gives rise to the demand for cause." Martineau, Types, 1 : 291 — " It is not existence, as such, that demands a cause, but the coming into existence of what did not exist before. The intellectual law of causality is a law for phenomena, and not for entity." See also McCosh, Intuitions, 225-241; Calderwood, Philos. of Infinite, 61. *Per contra*, see Murphy, Scient. Bases of Faith, 49, 195, and Habit and Intelligence, 1 : 55-67; Knight, Lect. on Metaphysics, lect. ii, p. 19.

B. Granting that the universe, so far as its phenomena are concerned, has had a cause, it is impossible to show that any other cause is required than a cause within itself, such as the pantheist supposes.

Flint, Theism, 65 — " The cosmological argument alone proves only force, and no mere force is God. Intelligence must go with power to make a Being that can be called God." Diman, Theistic Argument: " The cosmological argument alone cannot decide whether the force that causes change is permanent self-existent mind, or permanent self-existent matter." Only intelligence gives the basis for an answer. Only mind in the universe enables us to infer mind in the maker. But the argument from intelligence is not the Cosmological, but the Teleological, and to this last belong all proofs of Deity from order and combination in nature.

Upton, Hibbert Lectures, 201-296 — Science has to do with those changes which one portion of the visible universe causes in another portion. Philosophy and theology deal with the Infinite Cause which brings into existence and sustains the entire series of finite causes. Do we ask the cause of the stars? Science says: Fire-mist, or an infinite regress of causes. Theology says: Granted; but this infinite regress demands for its explanation the belief in God. We must believe both in God, and in an endless series of finite causes. God is the cause of all causes, the soul of all souls: " Centre and soul of every sphere, Yet to each loving heart how near!" We do not need, as mere matter of science, to think of any beginning.

C.   Granting that the universe must have had a cause outside of itself, it is impossible to show that this cause has not itself been caused, *i. e.*, consists of an infinite series of dependent causes.   The principle of causality does not require that everything begun should be traced back to an uncaused cause ; it demands that we should assign a cause, but not that we should assign a first cause.

So with the whole series of causes. The materialist is bound to find a cause for this series, only when the series is shown to have had a beginning. But the very hypothesis of an infinite series of causes excludes the idea of such a beginning. An infinite chain has no topmost link (*versus* Robert Hall); an uncaused and eternal succession does not need a cause (*versus* Clarke and Locke). See Whately, Logic, 276; New Englander, Jan. 1874:75; Alexander, Moral Science, 221; Pfleiderer, Die Religion, 1:160-164; Calderwood, Moral Philos., 225; Herbert Spencer, First Principles, 37 — criticized by Bowne, Review of H. Spencer, 36. Julius Müller, Doct. Sin, 2:128, says that the causal principle is not satisfied till by regress we come to a cause which is not itself an effect — to one who is *causa sui*; Aids to Study of German Theology, 15-17—Even if the universe be eternal, its contingent and relative nature requires us to postulate an eternal Creator; Diman, Theistic Argument, 86 — " While the law of causation does not lead logically up to the conclusion of a first cause, it compels us to affirm it." We reply that it is not the law of causation which compels us to affirm it, for this certainly "does not lead logically up to the conclusion." If we infer an uncaused cause, we do it, not by logical process, but by virtue of the intuitive belief within us. So substantially Secretan, and Whewell, in Indications of a Creator, and in Hist. of Scientific Ideas, 2:321, 322 — "The mind takes refuge, in the assumption of a First Cause, from an employment inconsistent with its own nature"; "we necessarily infer a First Cause, although the palætiological sciences only point toward it, but do not lead us to it."

D.   Granting that the cause of the universe has not itself been caused, it is impossible to show that this cause is not finite, like the universe itself.   The causal principle requires a cause no greater than just sufficient to account for the effect.

We cannot therefore infer an infinite cause, unless the universe is infinite — which cannot be proved, but can only be assumed — and this is assuming an infinite in order to prove an infinite. All we know of the universe is finite. An infinite universe implies infinite number. But no number can be infinite, for to any number, however great, a unit can be added, which shows that it was not infinite before. Here again we see that the most approved forms of the Cosmological Argument are obliged to avail themselves of the intuition of the infinite, to supplement the logical process. *Versus* Martineau, Study, 1:416 — "Though we cannot directly infer the infinitude of God from a limited creation, indirectly we may exclude every other position by resort to its unlimited scene of existence (space)." But this would equally warrant our belief in the infinitude of our fellow men. Or, it is the argument of Clarke and Gillespie (see Ontological Argument below). Schiller, Die Grösse der Welt, seems to hold to a boundless universe. He represents a tired spirit as seeking the last limit of creation. A second pilgrim meets him from the spaces beyond with the words: "Steh! du segelst umsonst, — vor dir Unendlichkeit" — "Hold! thou journeyest in vain,— before thee is only Infinity." On the law of parsimony, see Sir Wm. Hamilton, Discussions, 628.

2.   *The value of the Cosmological Argument,* then, is simply this,— it proves the existence of some cause of the universe indefinitely great. When we go beyond this and ask whether this cause is a cause of being, or merely a cause of change, to the universe ; whether it is a cause apart from the universe, or one with it ; whether it is an eternal cause, or a cause

dependent upon some other cause ; whether it is intelligent or unintelli, gent, infinite or finite, one or many, — this argument cannot assure us.

On the whole argument, see Flint, Theism, 93-130; Mozley, Essays, Hist. and Theol., 2:414-444; Hedge, Ways of the Spirit, 148-154; Studien und Kritiken, 1876:9-31.

II. THE TELEOLOGICAL ARGUMENT, OR ARGUMENT FROM ORDER AND USEFUL COLLOCATION IN NATURE.

This is not properly an argument from design to a designer ; for that design implies a designer is simply an identical proposition. It may be more correctly stated as follows : Order and useful collocation pervading a system respectively imply intelligence and purpose as the cause of that order and collocation. Since order and useful collocation pervade the universe, there must exist an intelligence adequate to the production of this order, and a will adequate to direct this collocation to useful ends.

Etymologically, "teleological argument" = argument to ends or final causes, that is, "causes which, beginning as a thought, work themselves out into a fact as an end or result" (Porter. Hum. Intellect, 592-618); — health, for example, is the final cause of exercise, while exercise is the efficient cause of health. This definition of the argument would be broad enough to cover the proof of a designing intelligence drawn from the constitution of man. This last, however, is treated as a part of the Anthropological Argument, which follows this, and the Teleological Argument covers only the proof of a designing intelligence drawn from nature. Hence Kant, Critique of Pure Reason (Bohn's trans.), 381, calls it the physico-theological argument. On methods of stating the argument, see Bib. Sac., Oct. 1867 : 625. See also Hedge, Ways of the Spirit, 155-185; Mozley, Essays Hist. and Theol., 2 : 365-413.

Hicks, in his Critique of Design-Arguments, 347-389, makes two arguments instead of one : (1) the argument from *order* to *intelligence*, to which he gives the name Eutaxiological ; (2) the argument from *adaptation* to *purpose*, to which he would restrict the name Teleological. He holds that teleology proper cannot prove *intelligence*, because in speaking of "ends" at all, it must assume the very intelligence which it seeks to prove ; that it actually does prove simply the *intentional exercise* of an intelligence whose existence has been previously established. "Circumstances, forces or agencies converging to a definite rational result imply volition — imply that this result is intended — is an end. This is the major premise of this new teleology." He objects to the term "final cause." The end is not a cause at all — it is a motive. The characteristic element of cause is power to produce an effect. Ends have no such power. The will may choose them or set them aside. As already assuming intelligence, ends cannot prove intelligence.

With this in the main we agree, and count it a valuable help to the statement and understanding of the argument. In the very observation of *order*, however, as well as in arguing from it, we are obliged to assume the same all-arranging intelligence. We see no objection therefore to making Eutaxiology the first part of the Teleological Argument, as we do above. See review of Hicks, in Meth. Quar. Rev., July, 1883 : 569-576. We proceed however to certain

1. *Further explanations.*

A. The major premise expresses a primitive conviction. It is not invalidated by the objections : (*a*) that order and useful collocation may exist without being purposed — for we are compelled by our very mental constitution to deny this in all cases where the order and collocation pervade a system : (*b*) that order and useful collocation may result from the mere operation of physical forces and laws — for these very forces and laws imply, instead of excluding, an originating and superintending intelligence and will.

Janet, in his work on Final Causes, 8, denies that finality is a primitive conviction, like causality, and calls it the result of an induction. He therefore proceeds from (1) marks of order and useful collocation to (2) finality in nature, and then to (3) an intelligent cause of this finality or "pre-conformity to future event." So Diman, Theistic Argument, 105, claims simply that, as change requires cause, so orderly change requires intelligent cause. We have shown, however, that induction and argument of every kind presupposes intuitive belief in final cause. Nature does not give us final cause; but no more does she give us efficient cause. Mind gives us both, and gives them as clearly upon one experience as after a thousand. Ladd: "Things have mind in them: else they could not be minded by us." The Duke of Argyll told Darwin that it seemed to him wholly impossible to ascribe the adjustments of nature to any other agency than that of mind. "Well," said Darwin, "that impression has often come upon me with overpowering force. But then, at other times, it all seems—;" and then he passed his hands over his eyes, as if to indicate the passing of a vision out of sight. Darwinism is not a refutation of ends in nature, but only of a particular theory with regard to the way in which ends are realized in the organic world. Darwin would begin with an infinitesimal germ, and make all the subsequent development unteleological; see Schurman, Belief in God, 193.

(a) Illustration of unpurposed order in the single throwing of "double sixes,"—constant throwing of double sixes indicates design. So arrangement of detritus at mouth of river, and warming pans sent to the West Indies,—useful but not purposed. Momerie, Christianity and Evolution, 72—"It is only within narrow limits that seemingly purposeful arrangements are produced by chance. And therefore, as the signs of purpose increase, the presumption in favor of their accidental origin diminishes." Elder, Ideas from Nature, 81, 82—"The uniformity of a boy's marbles shows them to be products of design. A single one might be accidental, but a dozen cannot be. So atomic uniformity indicates manufacture." Illustrations of purposed order, in Beattie's garden, Tillotson's blind men, Kepler's salad. Dr. Carpenter: "The atheist is like a man examining the machinery of a great mill, who, finding that the whole is moved by a shaft proceeding from a brick wall, infers that the shaft is a sufficient explanation of what he sees, and that there is no moving power behind it." Lord Kelvin: "The atheistic idea is nonsensical." J. G. Paton, Life, 2: 191—The sinking of a well on the island of Aniwa convinces the cannibal chief Namakei that Jehovah God exists, the invisible One. See Chauncey Wright, in N. Y. Nation, Jan. 15, 1874; Murphy, Scientific Bases of Faith, 208.

(b) Bowne, Review of Herbert Spencer, 231-247—"Law is *method*, not *cause.* A man cannot offer the very fact to be explained, as its sufficient explanation." Martineau, Essays, 1 : 144—"Patterned damask, made not by the weaver, but by the loom?" Dr. Stevenson: "House requires no architect, because it is built by stone-masons and carpenters?" Joseph Cook: "Natural law without God behind it is no more than a glove without a hand in it, and all that is done by the gloved hand of God in nature is done by the hand and not by the glove. Evolution is a process, not a power; a method of operation, not an operator. A book is not written *by* the laws of spelling and grammar, but *according to* those laws. So the book of the universe is not written by the laws of heat, electricity, gravitation, evolution, but according to those laws." G. F. Wright, Ant. and Orig. of Hum. Race, lecture IX—"It is impossible for evolution to furnish evidence which shall drive design out of nature. It can only drive it back to an earlier point of entrance, thereby increasing our admiration for the power of the Creator to accomplish ulterior designs by unlikely means."

Evolution is only the method of God. It has to do with the *how*, not with the *why*, of phenomena, and therefore is not inconsistent with design, but rather is a new and higher illustration of design. Henry Ward Beecher: "Design by wholesale is greater than design by retail." Frances Power Cobbe: "It is a singular fact that, whenever we find out *how* a thing is done, our first conclusion seems to be that *God* did not do it." Why should we say: "The more law, the less God?" The theist refers the phenomena to a cause that knows itself and what it is doing; the atheist refers them to a power which knows nothing of itself and what it is doing (Bowne). George John Romanes said that, if God be immanent, then all natural causation must appear to be mechanical, and it is no argument against the divine origin of a thing to prove it due to natural causation: "Causes in nature do not obviate the necessity of a cause in nature." Shaler, Interpretation of Nature, 47—Evolution shows that the direction of affairs is under control of something like our own intelligence: "Evolution spells Purpose." Clarke, Christ. Theology, 105—"The modern doctrine of evolution has been awake to the existence of innumerable ends *within* the universe, but not to the one great end *for* the universe itself." Huxley, Critiques and Addresses. 274, 275, 307 —

•"The teleological and mechanical views of the universe are not mutually exclusive."
Sir William Hamilton, Metaphysics: "Intelligence stands first in the order of existence.
Efficient causes are preceded by final causes." See also Thornton, Old Fashioned
Ethics, 199-265; Archbp. Temple, Bampton Lect., 1884: 99-123; Owen, Anat. of Verte-
brates, 3:796; Peirce, Ideality in the Physical Sciences, 1-35; Newman Smyth, Through
Science to Faith, 96; Fisher, Nat. and Meth. of Rev., 135.

B. The minor premise expresses a working-principle of all science,
namely, that all things have their uses, that order pervades the universe, and
that the methods of nature are rational methods. Evidences of this appear
in the correlation of the chemical elements to each other ; in the fitness of
the inanimate world to be the basis and support of life ; in the typical forms
and unity of plan apparent in the organic creation ; in the existence and
coöperation of natural laws ; in cosmical order and compensations.

This minor premise is not invalidated by the objections : (a) That we
frequently misunderstand the end actually subserved by natural events and
objects ; for the principle is, not that we necessarily know the actual end,
but that we necessarily believe that there is some end, in every case of
systematic order and collocation. (b) That the order of the universe is
manifestly imperfect; for this, if granted, would argue, not absence of
contrivance, but some special reason for imperfection, either in the limitations of the contriving intelligence itself, or in the nature of the end sought
(as, for example, correspondence with the moral state and probation of
sinners).

The evidences of order and useful collocation are found both in the indefinitely small
and the indefinitely great. The molecules are manufactured articles; and the compensations of the solar system which provide that a secular flattening of the earth's
orbit shall be made up for by a secular rounding of that same orbit, alike show an
intelligence far transcending our own; see Cooke, Religion and Chemistry, and Credentials of Science, 23 — "Beauty is the harmony of relations which perfect fitness produces; law is the prevailing principle which underlies that harmony. Hence both
beauty and law imply design. From energy, fitness, beauty, order, sacrifice, we argue
might, skill, perfection, law, and love in a Supreme Intelligence. Christianity implies
design, and is the completion of the design argument." Pfleiderer, Philos. Religion,
1:168 — "A good definition of beauty is immanent purposiveness, the teleological ideal
background of reality, the shining of the Idea through phenomena."

Bowne, Philos. Theism, 85 — "Design is never causal. It is only ideal, and it demands
an efficient cause for its realization. If ice is not to sink, and to freeze out life, there
must be some molecular structure which shall make its bulk greater than that of an
equal weight of water." Jackson, Theodore Parker, 355 — "Rudimentary organs are
like the silent letters in many words,—both are witnesses to a past history ; and there
is intelligence in their preservation." Diman, Theistic Argument : "Not only do we
observe in the world the change which is the basis of the Cosmological Argument, but
we perceive that this change proceeds according to a fixed and invariable rule. In inorganic nature, general order, or regularity ; in organic nature, special order or adaptation." Bowne, Review of H. Spencer, 113-115, 224-230: "Inductive science proceeds upon
the postulate that the reasonable and the natural are one." This furnished the guiding
clue to Harvey and Cuvier; see Whewell, Hist. Induct. Sciences, 2: 489-491. Kant:
"The anatomist must assume that nothing in man is in vain." Aristotle: "Nature
makes nothing in vain." On molecules as manufactured articles, see Maxfield, in Nature, Sept. 25, 1873. See also Tulloch, Theism, 116, 120; LeConte, Religion and Science,
lect. 2 and 3; McCosh, Typical Forms, 81, 420; Agassiz, Essay on Classification, 9, 10;
Bib. Sac., 1849 : 626 and 1850 : 613; Hopkins, in Princeton Review, 1882 : 181.

(a) Design, in fact that rivers always run by large towns? that springs are always
found at gambling places? Plants made for man, and man for worms? Voltaire:
"Noses are made for spectacles—let us wear them !" Pope: "While man exclaims
'See all things for my use,' 'See man for mine,' replies the pampered goose." Cher-

ries do not ripen in the cold of winter when they do not taste as well, and grapes do not ripen in the heat of summer when the new wine would turn to vinegar? Nature divides melons into sections for convenience in family eating? Cork-tree made for bottle-stoppers? The child who was asked the cause of salt in the ocean, attributed it to codfish, thus dimly confounding final cause with efficient cause. Teacher: "What are marsupials?" Pupil: "Animals that have pouches in their stomachs." Teacher: "And what do they have pouches for?" Pupil: "To crawl into and conceal themselves in, when they are pursued." Why are the days longer in summer than in winter? Because it is the property of all natural objects to elongate under the influence of heat. A Jena professor held that doctors do not exist because of disease, but that diseases exist precisely in order that there may be doctors. Kepler was an astronomical Don Quixote. He discussed the claims of eleven different damsels to become his second wife, and he likened the planets to huge animals rushing through the sky. Many of the objections to design arise from confounding a part of the creation with the whole, or a structure in the process of development with a structure completed. For illustrations of mistaken ends, see Janet, Final Causes.

(b) Alphonso of Castile took offense at the Ptolemaic System, and intimated that, if he had been consulted at the creation, he could have suggested valuable improvements. Lange, in his History of Materialism, illustrates some of the methods of nature by millions of gun barrels shot in all directions to kill a single hare; by ten thousand keys bought at haphazard to get into a shut room; by building a city in order to obtain a house. Is not the ice a little overdone about the poles? See John Stuart Mill's indictment of nature, in his posthumous Essays on Religion, 29 — "Nature impales men, breaks men as if on a wheel, casts them to be devoured by wild beasts, crushes them with stones like the first Christian martyr, starves them with hunger, freezes them with cold, poisons them with the quick or slow venom of her exhalations, and has hundreds of other hideous deaths in reserve, such as the ingenious cruelty of a Nabis or a Domitian never surpassed." So argue Schopenhauer and Von Hartmann.

The doctrine of evolution answers many of these objections, by showing that order and useful collocation in the system as a whole is necessarily and cheaply purchased by imperfection and suffering in the initial stages of development. The question is: Does the system as a whole imply design? My opinion is of no value as to the usefulness of an intricate machine the purpose of which I do not know. If I stand at the beginning of a road and do not know whither it leads, it is presumptuous in me to point out a more direct way to its destination. Bowne, Philos. of Theism, 20–22 — "In order to counterbalance the impressions which apparent disorder and immorality in nature make upon us, we have to assume that the universe at its root is not only rational, but good. This is faith, but it is an act on which our whole moral life depends." Metaphysics, 165 — "The same argument which would deny mind in nature denies mind in man." Fisher, Nat. and Meth. of Rev., 264 — "Fifty years ago, when the crane stood on top of the tower of unfinished Cologne Cathedral, was there no evidence of design in the whole structure?" Yet we concede that, so long as we cannot with John Stuart Mill explain the imperfections of the universe by any limitations in the Intelligence which contrived it, we are shut up to regarding them as intended to correspond with the moral state and probation of sinners which God foresaw and provided for at the creation. Evil things in the universe are symbols of sin, and helps to its overthrow. See Bowne, Review of H. Spencer, 264, 265; McCosh, Christ. and Positivism, 82 sq.; Martineau, Essays, 1 : 50, and Study, 1 : 351–398; Porter, Hum. Intellect, 599; Mivart, Lessons from Nature, 366–371; Princeton Rev., 1878 : 272–303; Shaw, on Positivism.

2. *Defects of the Teleological Argument.* These attach not to the premises but to the conclusion sought to be drawn therefrom.

A. The argument cannot prove a personal God. The order and useful collocations of the universe may be only the changing phenomena of an impersonal intelligence and will, such as pantheism supposes. The finality may be only immanent finality.

There is such a thing as immanent and unconscious finality. National spirit, without set purpose, constructs language. The bee works unconsciously to ends. Strato of Lampsacus regarded the world as a vast animal. Aristotle, Phys., 2 : 8 — "Plant the ship-builder's skill within the timber itself, and you have the mode in which nature produces." Here we see a dim anticipation of the modern doctrine of development from within instead of creation from without. Neander: "The divine work goes on from within outward." John Fiske: "The argument from the watch has been superseded by the argument from the flower." Iverach, Theism, 91 — "The effect of evolution has been simply to transfer the cause from a mere external influence working from without to an immanent rational principle." Martineau, Study, 1:349, 350 — "Theism is in no way committed to the doctrine of a God external to the world . . . nor does intelligence require, in order to gain an object, to give it externality."

Newman Smyth, Place of Death, 62-80 —"The universe exists in some all-pervasive Intelligence. Suppose we could see a small heap of brick, scraps of metal, and pieces of mortar, gradually shaping themselves into the walls and interior structure of a building, adding needed material as the work advanced, and at last presenting in its completion a factory furnished with varied and finely wrought machinery. Or, a locomotive carrying a process of self-repair to compensate for wear, growing and increasing in size, detaching from itself at intervals pieces of brass or iron endowed with the power of growing up step by step into other locomotives capable of running themselves and of reproducing new locomotives in their turn." So nature in its separate parts may seem mechanical, but as a whole it is rational. Weismann does not "disown a directive power," — only this power is "behind the mechanism as its final cause . . . it must be teleological."

Impressive as are these evidences of intelligence in the universe as a whole, and increased in number as they are by the new light of evolution, we must still hold that nature alone cannot prove that this intelligence is personal. Hopkins, Miscellanies, 18-36 — "So long as there is such a thing as impersonal and adapting intelligence in the brute creation, we cannot necessarily infer from unchanging laws a free and personal God." See Fisher, Supernat. Origin of Christianity, 576-578. Kant shows that the argument does not prove intelligence apart from the world (Critique, 370). We must bring mind to the world, if we would find mind in it. Leave out man, and nature cannot be properly interpreted: the intelligence and will in nature may still be unconscious. But, taking in man, we are bound to get our idea of the intelligence and will in nature from the highest type of intelligence and will we know, and that is man's. "Nullus in microcosmo spiritus, nullus in macrocosmo Deus." "We receive but what we give, And in our life alone does Nature live."

The Teleological Argument therefore needs to be supplemented by the Anthropological Argument, or the argument from the mental and moral constitution of man. By itself, it does not prove a Creator. See Calderwood, Moral Philosophy, 26; Ritter, Hist. Anc. Philos., bk. 9, chap. 6; Foundations of our Faith, 38; Murphy, Scientific Bases, 215; Habit and Intelligence, 2:6, and chap. 27. On immanent finality, see Janet, Final Causes, 345-415; Diman, Theistic Argument, 201-203. Since righteousness belongs only to personality, this argument cannot prove righteousness in God. Flint, Theism, 66 — "Power and Intelligence alone do not constitute God, though they be infinite. A being may have these, and, if lacking righteousness, may be a devil." Here again we see the need of the Anthropological Argument to supplement this.

B. Even if this argument could prove personality in the intelligence and will that originated the order of the universe, it could not prove either the unity, the eternity, or the infinity of God ; not the unity—for the useful collocations of the universe might be the result of oneness of counsel, instead of oneness of essence, in the contriving intelligence ; not the eternity—for a created demiurge might conceivably have designed the universe ; not the infinity — since all marks of order and collocation within our observation are simply finite.

Diman asserts (Theistic Argument, 114) that all the phenomena of the universe must be due to the same source—since all alike are subject to the same method of sequence. e. g., gravitation — and that the evidence points us irresistibly to some *one* explanatory cause. We can regard this assertion only as the utterance of a primitive belief in a first cause, not as the conclusion of logical demonstration, for we know only an infinitesimal part of the universe. From the point of view of the intuition of an Absolute Reason, however, we can cordially assent to the words of F. L. Patton: "When we consider Matthew Arnold's 'stream of tendency,' Spencer's 'unknowable,' Schopenhauer's

wo: rd as will,' and Hartmann's elaborate defence of finality as the product of unconscious intelligence, we may well ask if the theists, with their belief in one personal
God are not in possession of the only hypothesis that can save the language of these
writers from the charge of meaningless and idiotic raving " (Journ. Christ. Philos.,
April, 1883 : 283-307).

The ancient world, which had only the light of nature, believed in many gods.
William James, Will to Believe, 44 — " If there be a divine Spirit of the universe, nature,
such as we know her, cannot possibly be its *ultimate word* to man. Either there is
no spirit revealed in nature, or else it is inadequately revealed there; and (as all
the higher religions have assumed) what we call visible nature, or *this* world, must be
but a veil and surface-show whose full meaning resides in a supplementary unseen, or
other world." Bowne, Theory of Thought and Knowledge, 234 — " But is not intelligence
itself the mystery of mysteries? . . . No doubt, intellect is a great mystery. . . .
But there is a choice in mysteries. Some mysteries leave other things clear, and some
leave things as dark and impenetrable as ever. The former is the case with the mystery of intelligence. It makes possible the comprehension of everything but itself."

3. *The value of the Teleological Argument* is simply this, — it proves
from certain useful collocations and instances of order which have clearly
had a beginning, or in other words, from the present harmony of the universe, that there exists an intelligence and will adequate to its contrivance.
But whether this intelligence and will is personal or impersonal, creator or
only fashioner, one or many, finite or infinite, eternal or owing its being to
another, necessary or free, this argument cannot assure us.

In it, however, we take a step forward. The causative power which we
have proved by the Cosmological Argument has now become an intelligent
and voluntary power.

John Stuart Mill, Three Essays on Theism, 168-170—"In the present state of our
knowledge, the adaptations in nature afford a large balance of probability in favor of
causation by intelligence." Ladd holds that, whenever one being acts upon its like,
each being undergoes changes of state that belong to its own nature under the circumstances. Action of one body on another never consists in transferring the state of
one being to another. Therefore there is no more difficulty in beings that are unlike
acting on one another than in beings that are like. We do not transfer ideas to other
minds, — we only rouse them to develop their own ideas. So force also is positively
not transferable. Bowne, Philos. of Theism, 49, begins with "the conception of things
interacting according to law and forming an intelligible system. Such a system
cannot be construed by thought without the assumption of a unitary being which is
the fundamental reality of the system. 53 — No passage of influences or forces will
avail to bridge the gulf, so long as the things are regarded as independent. 56 — The
system itself cannot explain this interaction, for the system is only the members of it.
There must be some being in them which is their reality, and of which they are in some
sense phases or manifestations. In other words, there must be a basal monism."
All this is substantially the view of Lotze, of whose philosophy see criticism in Stählin's
Kant, Lotze, and Ritschl, 116-156, and especially 123. Falckenberg, Gesch. der neueren
Philosophie, 454, shows as to Lotze's view that his assumption of monistic unity and
continuity does not explain how change of condition in one thing should, as equal-
ization or compensation, follow change of condition in another thing. Lotze explains
this *actuality* by the ethical conception of an all-embracing Person. On the whole argument, see Bib. Sac., 1849 : 634; Murphy, Sci. Bases, 216 ; Flint, Theism, 131-210 ; Pfleiderer,
Die Religion, 1 : 164-174; W. R. Benedict, on Theism and Evolution, in Andover Rev.,
1886 : 307-350, 607-622.

III. The Anthropological Argument, or Argument from Man's
Mental and Moral Nature.

This is an argument from the mental and moral condition of man to
the existence of an Author, Lawgiver, and End. It is sometimes called
the Moral Argument.

The common title "Moral Argument" is much too narrow, for it seems to take account only of conscience in man, whereas the argument which this title so imperfectly designates really proceeds from man's intellectual and emotional, as well as from his moral, nature. In choosing the designation we have adopted, we desire, moreover, to rescue from the mere physicist the term "Anthropology"—a term to which he has attached altogether too limited a signification, and which, in his use of it, implies that man is a mere animal,—to him Anthropology is simply the study of *la bête humaine*. Anthropology means, not simply the science of man's physical nature, origin, and relations, but also the science which treats of his higher spiritual being. Hence, in Theology, the term Anthropology designates that division of the subject which treats of man's spiritual nature and endowments, his original state and his subsequent apostasy. As an argument, therefore, from man's mental and moral nature, we can with perfect propriety call the present argument the Anthropological Argument.

The argument is a complex one, and may be divided into three parts.

1. Man's intellectual and moral nature must have had for its author an intellectual and moral Being. The elements of the proof are as follows:—(a) Man, as an intellectual and moral being, has had a beginning upon the planet. (b) Material and unconscious forces do not afford a sufficient cause for man's reason, conscience, and free will. (c) Man, as an effect, can be referred only to a cause possessing self-consciousness and a moral nature, in other words, personality.

This argument is in part an application to man of the principles of both the Cosmological and the Teleological Arguments. Flint, Theism, 74—"Although causality does not involve design, nor design goodness, yet design involves causality, and goodness both causality and design." Jacobi: "Nature conceals God; man reveals him."

Man is an effect. The history of the geologic ages proves that man has not always existed, and even if the lower creatures were his progenitors, his intellect and freedom are not eternal *a parte ante*. We consider man, not as a physical, but as a spiritual being. Thompson, Christian Theism, 75—"Every true cause must be sufficient to account for the effect." Locke, Essay, book 4, chap. 10—"Cogitable existence cannot be produced out of incogitable." Martineau, Study of Religion, 1 : 258 *sq.*

Even if man had always existed, however, we should not need to abandon the argument. We might start, not from beginning of existence, but from beginning of phenomena. I might see God in the world, just as I see thought, feeling, will, in my fellow men. Fullerton, Plain Argument for God: I do not infer you, as cause of the *existence* of your body : I recognize you as present and *working* through your body. Its changes of gesture and speech reveal a personality behind them. So I do not need to argue back to a Being who once *caused* nature and history ; I recognize a *present* Being, exercising wisdom and power, by signs such as reveal personality in man. Nature is itself the Watchmaker manifesting himself in the very process of making the watch. This is the meaning of the noble Epilogue to Robert Browning's Dramatis Personæ, 252—"That one Face, far from vanish, rather grows, Or decomposes but to recompose, Become my universe that feels and knows." "That Face," said Mr. Browning to Mrs. Orr, "That Face is the face of Christ; that is how I feel him." Nature is an expression of the mind and will of Christ, as my face is an expression of my mind and will. But in both cases, behind and above the face is a personality, of which the face is but the partial and temporary expression.

Bowne, Philos. Theism, 104, 107—"My fellow beings act *as if* they had thought, feeling, and will. So nature looks *as if* thought, feeling, and will were behind it. If we deny mind in nature, we must deny mind in man. If there be no controlling mind in nature, moreover, there can be none in man, for if the basal power is blind and necessary, then all that depends upon it is necessitated also." LeConte, in Royce's Conception of God, 44—"There is only one place in the world where we can get behind physical phenomena, behind the veil of matter, namely, in our own brain, and we find there a self, a person. Is it not reasonable that, if we could get behind the veil of nature, we should find the same, that is, a Person? But if so, we must conclude, an infinite Person, and therefore the only complete Personality that exists. Perfect personality is not only self-conscious, but self-existent. *They* are only imperfect images, and, as it were, separated fragments, of the infinite Personality of God."

Personality = self-consciousness + self-determination in view of moral ends. The brute has intelligence and will, but has neither self-consciousness, conscience, nor free-will. See Julius Müller, Doctrine of Sin, 1 : 76 *sq.* Diman, Theistic Argument, 91, 251 — "Suppose 'the intuitions of the moral faculty are the slowly organized results of experience received from the race'; still, having found that the universe affords evidence of a supremely intelligent cause, we may believe that man's moral nature affords the highest illustration of its mode of working"; 358 — "Shall we explain the lower forms of will by the higher, or the higher by the lower ? "

2. Man's moral nature proves the existence of a holy Lawgiver and Judge. The elements of the proof are :— (*a*) Conscience recognizes the existence of a moral law which has supreme authority. (*b*) Known violations of this moral law are followed by feelings of ill-desert and fears of judgment. (*c*) This moral law, since it is not self-imposed, and these threats of judgment, since they are not self-executing, respectively argue the existence of a holy will that has imposed the law, and of a punitive power that will execute the threats of the moral nature.

See Bishop Butler's Sermons on Human Nature, in Works, Bohn's ed., 385–414. Butler's great discovery was that of the supremacy of conscience in the moral constitution of man : " Had it strength as it has right, had it power as it has manifest authority, it would absolutely govern the world." Conscience = the moral judiciary of the soul — not law, nor sheriff, but judge ; see under Anthropology. Diman, Theistic Argument, 251 — " Conscience does not lay down a law ; it warns us of the existence of a law ; and not only of a law, but of a purpose — not our own, but the purpose of another, which it is our mission to realize." See Murphy, Scientific Bases of Faith, 218 *sq.* It proves personality in the Lawgiver, because its utterances are not abstract, like those of reason, but are in the nature of command ; they are not in the indicative, but in the imperative, mood ; it says, " thou shalt " and " thou shalt not." This argues *will.*

Hutton, Essays, 1 : 11 —" Conscience is an ideal Moses, and thunders from an invisible Sinai " ; " the Atheist regards conscience not as a skylight, opened to let in upon human nature an infinite dawn from above, but as a polished arch or dome, completing and reflecting the whole edifice beneath." But conscience cannot be the mere reflection and expression of nature, for it represses and condemns nature. Tulloch, Theism : " Conscience, like the magnetic needle, indicates the existence of an unknown Power which from afar controls its vibrations and at whose presence it trembles." Nero spends nights of terror in wandering through the halls of his Golden House. Kant holds that faith in duty requires faith in a God who will defend and reward duty — see Critique of Pure Reason, 359–387. See also Porter, Human Intellect, 524.

Kant, in his Metaphysic of Ethics, represents the action of conscience as like " conducting a case before a court," and he adds : " Now that he who is accused before his conscience should be figured to be just the same person as his judge, is an absurd representation of a tribunal ; since, in such an event, the accuser would always lose his suit. Conscience must therefore represent to itself always some other than itself as Judge, unless it is to arrive at a contradiction with itself." See also his Critique of the Practical Reason, Werke, 8 : 214 — " Duty, thou sublime and mighty name, that hast in thee nothing to attract or win, but challengest submission ; and yet dost threaten nothing to sway the will by that which may arouse natural terror or aversion, but merely holdest forth a Law ; a Law which of itself finds entrance into the mind, and even while we disobey, against our will compels our reverence, a Law in presence of which all inclinations grow dumb, even while they secretly rebel ; what origin is there worthy of thee ? Where can we find the root of thy noble descent, which proudly rejects all kinship with the inclinations ? " Archbishop Temple answers, in his Bampton Lectures, 58, 59, " This eternal Law is the Eternal himself, the almighty God." Robert Browning : " The sense within me that I owe a debt Assures me — Somewhere must be Somebody, Ready to take his due. All comes to this : Where due is, there acceptance follows : find Him who accepts the due."

Salter, Ethical Religion, quoted in Pfleiderer's article on Religionless Morality, Am. Jour. Theol., 3 : 237 — " The earth and the stars do not create the law of gravitation which they obey; no more does man, or the united hosts of rational beings in the universe, create the law of duty." The will expressed in the moral imperative is *superior* to ours, for otherwise it would issue no commands. Yet it is *one* with ours as the life of an organism is one with the life of its members. Theonomy is not heteronomy but the highest autonomy, the guarantee of our personal freedom against all servitude of man. Seneca: "Deo parere libertas est." Knight, Essays in Philosophy, 272—"In conscience we see an 'alter ego', in us yet not of us, another Personality behind our own." Martineau, Types, 2 : 105—"Over a person only a person can have authority. . . . A solitary being, with no other sentient nature in the universe, would feel no duty"; Study, 1 : 26—"As Perception gives us Will in the shape of *Causality* over against us in the Non-Ego, so Conscience gives us Will in the shape of *Authority* over against us in the Non-Ego. . . . 2 : 7—We cannot deduce the phenomena of character from an agent who has none." Hutton, Essays, 1 : 41, 42—"When we disobey conscience, the Power which has therein ceased to *move* us has retired only to *observe*—to keep *watch* over us as we mould ourselves." Cardinal Newman, Apologia, 377—"Were it not for the voice speaking so clearly in my conscience and my heart, I should be an atheist, or a pantheist, or a polytheist, when I looked into the world."

3. Man's emotional and voluntary nature proves the existence of a Being who can furnish in himself a satisfying object of human affection and an end which will call forth man's highest activities and ensure his highest progress.

Only a Being of power, wisdom, holiness, and goodness, and all these indefinitely greater than any that we know upon the earth, can meet this demand of the human soul. Such a Being must exist. Otherwise man's greatest need would be unsupplied, and belief in a lie be more productive of virtue than belief in the truth.

Feuerbach calls God "the Brocken-shadow of man himself"; "consciousness of God = self-consciousness"; "religion is a dream of the human soul"; "all theology is anthropology"; "man made God in his own image." But conscience shows that man does not recognize in God simply his like, but also his opposite. Not as Galton: "Piety = conscience + instability." The finest minds are of the leaning type; see Murphy, Scientific Bases, 370; Augustine, Confessions, 1 : 1—"Thou hast made us for thyself, and our heart is restless till it finds rest in thee." On John Stuart Mill—"a mind that could not find God, and a heart that could not do without him"—see his Autobiography, and Browne, in Strivings for the Faith (Christ. Ev. Socy.), 259-287. Comte, in his later days, constructed an object of worship in Universal Humanity, and invented a ritual which Huxley calls "Catholicism *minus* Christianity." See also Tyndall, Belfast Address: "Did I not believe, said a great man to me once, that an Intelligence exists at the heart of things, my life on earth would be intolerable." Martineau, Types of Ethical Theory, 1 : 505, 506.

The last line of Schiller's Pilgrim reads: "Und das Dort ist niemals hier." The finite never satisfies. Tennyson, Two Voices: "'T is life, whereof our nerves are scant, Oh life, not death, for which we pant; More life, and fuller, that I want." Seth, Ethical Principles, 419—"A moral universe, an absolute moral Being, is the indispensable environment of the ethical life, without which it cannot attain to its perfect growth. . . . There is a moral *God*, or this is no *universe*." James, Will to Believe, 116—"A God is the most adequate possible object for minds framed like our own to conceive as lying at the root of the universe. Anything short of God is not a rational object, anything more than God is not possible, if man needs an object of knowledge, feeling, and will."

Romanes, Thoughts on Religion, 41—"To speak of the Religion of the Unknowable, the Religion of Cosmism, the Religion of Humanity, where the personality of the First Cause is not recognized, is as unmeaning as it would be to speak of the love of a triangle or the rationality of the equator." It was said of Comte's system that, "the wine of the real presence being poured out, we are asked to adore the empty cup." "We want an object of devotion, and Comte presents us with a looking-glass" (Martineau). Huxley said he would as soon adore a wilderness of apes as the Positivist's rationalized conception of humanity. It is only the ideal in humanity, the divine element in humanity that can be worshiped. And when we once conceive of this, we cannot be satisfied until we find it somewhere realized, as in Jesus Christ.

Upton, Hibbert Lectures, 265-272 — Huxley believes that Evolution is "a materialized logical process"; that nothing endures save the flow of energy and "the rational order which pervades it." In the earlier part of this process, *nature*, there is no morality or benevolence. But the process ends by producing *man*, who can make progress only by waging moral war against the natural forces which impel him. He must be benevolent and just. Shall we not say, in spite of Mr. Huxley, that this shows what the nature of the system is, and that there must be a benevolent and just Being who ordained it? Martineau, Seat of Authority, 63-68 — "Though the authority of the higher incentive is self-known, it cannot be self-created; for while it is in me, it is above me. . . . This authority to which conscience introduces me, though emerging in consciousness, is yet *objective* to us all, and is necessarily referred to the nature of things, irrespective of the accidents of our mental constitution. It is not dependent on us, but independent. All minds born into the universe are ushered into the presence of a real righteousness, as surely as into a scene of actual space. Perception reveals *another* than ourselves; conscience reveals a *higher* than ourselves."

We must freely grant, however, that this argument from man's aspirations has weight only upon the supposition that a wise, truthful, holy, and benevolent God exists, who has so constituted our minds that their thinking and their affections correspond to truth and to himself. An evil being might have so constituted us that all logic would lead us into error. The argument is therefore the development and expression of our intuitive idea of God. Luthardt, Fundamental Truths: "Nature is like a written document containing only consonants. It is we who must furnish the vowels that shall decipher it. Unless we bring with us the idea of God, we shall find nature but dumb." See also Pfleiderer, Die Religion, 1 : 174.

A. *The defects of the Anthropological Argument are :* (*a*) It cannot prove a creator of the material universe. (*b*) It cannot prove the infinity of God, since man from whom we argue is finite. (*c*) It cannot prove the mercy of God. But,

B. *The value of the Argument* is, that it assures us of the existence of a personal Being, who rules us in righteousness, and who is the proper object of supreme affection and service. But whether this Being is the original creator of all things, or merely the author of our own existence, whether he is infinite or finite, whether he is a Being of simple righteousness or also of mercy, this argument cannot assure us.

Among the arguments for the existence of God, however, we assign to this the chief place, since it adds to the ideas of causative power (which we derived from the Cosmological Argument) and of contriving intelligence (which we derived from the Teleological Argument), the far wider ideas of personality and righteous lordship.

Sir Wm. Hamilton, Works of Reid, 2 : 974, note U; Lect. on Metaph., 1 : 33 — "The only valid arguments for the existence of God and for the immortality of the soul rest upon the ground of man's moral nature"; "theology is wholly dependent upon psychology, for with the proof of the moral nature of man stands or falls the proof of the existence of a Deity." But Diman, Theistic Argument, 244, very properly objects to making this argument from the nature of man the sole proof of Deity: "It should be rather used to show the attributes of the Being whose existence has been already proved from other sources"; "hence the Anthropological Argument is as dependent upon the Cosmological and Teleological Arguments as they are upon it."

Yet the Anthropological Argument is needed to supplement the conclusions of the two others. Those who, like Herbert Spencer, recognize an infinite and absolute Being, Power and Cause, may yet fail to recognize this being as spiritual and personal, simply because they do not recognize themselves as spiritual and personal beings, that is, do not recognize reason, conscience and free-will in man. Agnosticism in philosophy involves agnosticism in religion. R. K. Eccles: "All the most advanced,

.anguages capitalize the word 'God,' and the word 'I.'" See Flint, Theism, 68; Mill, Criticism of Hamilton, 2 : 266; Dove, Logic of Christian Faith, 211-236, 261-299; Martineau, Types, Introd., 3; Cooke, Religion and Chemistry: "God is love; but nature could not prove it, and the Lamb was slain from the foundation of the world in order to attest it."

Everything in philosophy depends on where we begin, whether with nature or with self, whether with the necessary or with the free. In one sense, therefore, we should in practice begin with the Anthropological Argument, and then use the Cosmological and Teleological Arguments as warranting the application to nature of the conclusions which we have drawn from man. As God stands over against man in Conscience, and says to him: "Thou"; so man stands over against God in Nature, and may say to him: "Thou." Mulford, Republic of God, 28—"As the personality of man has its foundation in the personality of God, so the realization by man of his own personality always brings man nearer to God." Robert Browning: "Quoth a young Sadducee: 'Reader of many rolls, Is it so certain we Have, as they tell us, souls?' 'Son, there is no reply!' The Rabbi bit his beard: 'Certain, a soul have I— We may have none,' he sneered. Thus Karshook, the Hiram's Hammer, The Right-hand Temple-column, Taught babes in grace their grammar, And struck the simple, solemn."

It is very common at this place to treat of what are called the Historical and the Biblical Arguments for the existence of God — the former arguing, from the unity of history, the latter arguing, from the unity of the Bible, that this unity must in each case have for its cause and explanation the existence of God. It is a sufficient reason for not discussing these arguments, that, without a previous belief in the existence of God, no one will see unity either in history or in the Bible. Turner, the painter, exhibited a picture which seemed all mist and cloud until he put a dab of scarlet into it. That gave the true point of view, and all the rest became intelligible. So Christ's coming and Christ's blood make intelligible both the Scriptures and human history. He carries in his girdle the key to all mysteries. Schopenhauer, knowing no Christ, admitted no philosophy of history. He regarded history as the mere fortuitous play of individual caprice. Pascal: "Jesus Christ is the centre of everything, and the object of everything, and he that does not know him knows nothing of nature, and nothing of himself."

IV. The Ontological Argument, or Argument from our Abstract and Necessary Ideas.

This argument infers the existence of God from the abstract and necessary ideas of the human mind. It has three forms :

1. That of Samuel Clarke. Space and time are attributes of substance or being. But space and time are respectively infinite and eternal. There must therefore be an infinite and eternal substance or Being to whom these attributes belong.

Gillespie states the argument somewhat differently. Space and time are modes of existence. But space and time are respectively infinite and eternal. There must therefore be an infinite and eternal Being who subsists in these modes. But we reply :

Space and time are neither attributes of substance nor modes of existence. The argument, if valid, would prove that God is not mind but matter, for that could not be mind, but only matter, of which space and time were either attributes or modes.

The Ontological Argument is frequently called the *a priori* argument, that is, the argument from that which is logically prior, or earlier than experience, viz., our intuitive ideas. All the forms of the Ontological Argument are in this sense *a priori*. Space and time are *a priori* ideas. See Samuel Clarke, Works, 2:521; Gillespie, Necessary Existence of God. *Per contra*, see Kant, Critique of Pure Reason, 364: Calderwood, Moral Philosophy, 226—"To begin, as Clarke did, with the proposition that 'something has existed from eternity,' is virtually to propose an argument after having assumed what is to be proved. Gillespie's form of the *a priori* argument, starting with the proposition 'infinity or extension is necessarily existing,' is liable to the same objection, with the additional disadvantage of attributing a property of matter to the Deity.

H. B. Smith says that Brougham misrepresented Clarke: "Clarke's argument is in his sixth proposition, and supposes the existence proved in what goes before. He aims here to establish the infinitude and omnipresence of this First Being. He does not prove *existence* from immensity." But we reply, neither can he prove the *infinity* of God from the immensity of space. Space and time are neither substances nor attributes, but are rather relations; see Calderwood, Philos. of Infinite, 331-335; Cocker, Theistic Conception of the World, 66-96. The doctrine that space and time are attributes or modes of God's existence tends to materialistic pantheism like that of Spinoza, who held that "the one and simple substance" (substantia una et unica) is known to us through the two attributes of thought and extension; mind = God in the mode of thought; matter = God in the mode of extension. Dove, Logic of the Christian Faith, 127, says well that an extended God is a material God ; "space and time are attributes neither of matter nor mind "; " we must carry the moral idea into the natural world, not the natural idea into the moral world." See also, Blunt, Dictionary Doct. and Hist. Theol., 740; Porter, Human Intellect, 567. H. M. Stanley, on Space and Science, in Philos. Rev., Nov. 1898: 615 — "Space is not full of things, but things are spaceful. . . . Space is a form of dynamic appearance." Prof. C. A. Strong: "The world composed of consciousness and other existences is not in space, though it may be in something of which space is the symbol."

2. That of Descartes. We have the idea of an infinite and perfect Being. This idea cannot be derived from imperfect and finite things. There must therefore be an infinite and perfect Being who is its cause.

But we reply that this argument confounds the idea of the infinite with an infinite idea. Man's idea of the infinite is not infinite but finite, and from a finite effect we cannot argue an infinite cause.

This form of the Ontological Argument, while it is *a priori*, as based upon a necessary idea of the human mind, is, unlike the other forms of the same argument, *a posteriori*, as arguing from this idea, as an *effect*, to the existence of a Being who is its *cause*. A *posteriori* argument = from that which is later to that which is earlier, that is, from effect to cause. The Cosmological, Teleological, and Anthropological Arguments are arguments *a posteriori*. Of this sort is the argument of Descartes ; see Descartes, Meditation 3 : Hæc idea quæ in nobis est requirit Deum pro causa ; Deusque proinde existit." The idea in men's minds is the impression of the workman's name stamped indelibly on his work — the shadow cast upon the human soul by that unseen One of whose being and presence it dimly informs us. Blunt, Dict. of Theol., 739; Saisset, Pantheism, 1 : 54 — "Descartes sets out from a fact of consciousness, while Anselm sets out from an abstract conception "; "Descartes's argument might be considered a branch of the Anthropological or Moral Argument, but for the fact that this last proceeds from man's constitution rather than from his abstract ideas." See Bib. Sac., 1849 : 637.

3. That of Anselm. We have the idea of an absolutely perfect Being. But existence is an attribute of perfection. An absolutely perfect Being must therefore exist.

But we reply that this argument confounds ideal existence with real existence. Our ideas are not the measure of external reality.

Anselm, Proslogion, 2 — "Id, quo majus cogitari nequit, non potest esse in intellectu solo." See translation of the Proslogion, in Bib. Sac., 1851 : 529, 699; Kant, Critique, 368. The arguments of Descartes and Anselm, with Kant's reply, are given in their original form by Harris, in Journ. Spec. Philos., 15 : 420-428. The major premise here is not that all perfect ideas imply the existence of the object which they represent, for then, as Kant objects, I might argue from my perfect idea of a $100 bill that I actually possessed the same, which would be far from the fact. So I have a perfect idea of a perfectly evil being, of a centaur, of nothing, — but it does not follow that the evil being, that the centaur, that nothing, exists. The argument is rather from the idea of absolute and perfect Being — of "that, no greater than which can be conceived." There can be but one such being, and there can be but one such idea.

Yet, even thus understood, we cannot argue from the idea to the actual existence of such a being. Case, Physical Realism, 173 — "God is not an idea, and consequently cannot be inferred from mere ideas." Bowne, Philos. Theism, 43 — The Ontological Argument " only points out that the idea of the perfect must include the idea of existence; but there is nothing to show that the self-consistent idea represents an objective reality." I can imagine the Sea-serpent, the Jinn of the Thousand and One Nights, "The Anthropophagi, and men whose heads Do grow beneath their shoulders." The winged horse of Uhland possessed every possible virtue, and only one fault,— it was dead If every perfect idea implied the reality of its object, there might be horses with ten legs, and trees with roots in the air.

"Anselm's argument implies," says Fisher, in Journ. Christ. Philos., Jan. 1883 : 114, "that existence in re is a constituent of the concept. It would conclude the existence of a being from the definition of a word. This inference is justified only on the basis of philosophical realism." Dove, Logic of the Christ. Faith, 141 — "The Ontological Argument is the algebraic formula of the universe, which leads to a valid conclusion with regard to real existence, only when we fill it in with objects with which we become acquainted in the arguments a posteriori." See also Shedd, Hist. Doct., 1 : 331, Dogm. Theol., 1 : 221-241, and in Presb. Rev., April, 1884 : 212-227 (favoring the argument); Fisher, Essays, 574 ; Thompson, Christian Theism, 171 ; H. B. Smith, Introd. to Christ. Theol., 122 ; Pfleiderer, Die Religion, 1 : 181-187 ; Studien und Kritiken, 1875 : 611-655.

Dorner, in his Glaubenslehre, 1 : 197, gives us the best statement of the Ontological Argument : "Reason thinks of God as existing. Reason would not be reason, if it did not think of God as existing. Reason only is, upon the assumption that God is." But this is evidently not argument, but only vivid statement of the necessary assumption of the existence of an absolute Reason which conditions and gives validity to ours.

Although this last must be considered the most perfect form of the Ontological Argument, it is evident that it conducts us only to an ideal conclusion, not to real existence. In common with the two preceding forms of the argument, moreover, it tacitly assumes, as already existing in the human mind, that very knowledge of God's existence which it would derive from logical demonstration. It has value, therefore, simply as showing what God must be, if he exists at all.

But the existence of a Being indefinitely great, a personal Cause, Contriver and Lawgiver, has been proved by the preceding arguments ; for the law of parsimony requires us to apply the conclusions of the first three arguments to one Being, and not to many. To this one Being we may now ascribe the infinity and perfection, the idea of which lies at the basis of the Ontological Argument — ascribe them, not because they are demonstrably his, but because our mental constitution will not allow us to think otherwise. Thus clothing him with all perfections which the human mind can conceive, and these in illimitable fullness, we have one whom we may justly call God.

McCosh, Div. Govt., 12, note — " It is at this place, if we do not mistake, that the idea of the Infinite comes in. The capacity of the human mind to form such an idea, or rather its intuitive belief in an Infinite of which it feels that it cannot form an adequate conception, may be no proof (as Kant maintains) of the existence of an infinite Being ; but it is, we are convinced, the means by which the mind is enabled to invest the Deity, shown on other grounds to exist, with the attributes of infinity, i. e., to look on his being, power, goodness, and all his perfections, as infinite." Even Flint, Theism, 68, who holds that we reach the existence of God by inference, speaks of " necessary conditions of thought and feeling, and ineradicable aspirations, which force on us ideas of absolute existence, infinity, and perfection, and will neither permit us to deny these perfections to God, nor to ascribe them to any other being." Belief in God is not the conclusion of a demonstration, but the solution of a problem. Calderwood, Moral Philosophy, 226 — " Either the whole question is assumed in starting, or the Infinite is not reached in concluding."

Clarke, Christian Theology, 97-114, divides his proof into two parts: I. **Evidence of**
the existence of God from the intellectual starting-point: The discovery of *Mind* in
the universe is made, 1. through the intelligibleness of the universe to us; 2. through
the idea of cause; 3. through the presence of ends in the universe. II. **Evidence of**
the existence of God from the religious starting-point; The discovery of the *good God* is
made, 1. through the religious nature of man; 2. through the great dilemma — God
the best, or the worst; 3. through the spiritual experience of men, especially in Christianity. So far as Dr. Clarke's proof is intended to be a statement, not of a primitive belief,
but of a logical process, we must hold it to be equally defective with the three forms
of proof which we have seen to furnish some corroborative evidence of God's existence. Dr. Clarke therefore does well to add: "Religion was not produced by proof
of God's existence, and will not be destroyed by its insufficiency to some minds. Religion existed before argument; in fact, it is the preciousness of religion that leads to the
seeking for all possible confirmations of the reality of God."

The three forms of proof already mentioned — the Cosmological, the Teleological, and
the Anthropological Arguments — may be likened to the three arches of a bridge over
a wide and rushing river. The bridge has only two defects, but these defects are very
serious. The first is that one cannot get on to the bridge; the end toward the hither
bank is wholly lacking; the bridge of logical argument cannot be entered upon except
by assuming the validity of logical processes; this assumption takes for granted at the
outset the existence of a God who has made our faculties to act correctly; we get on
to the bridge, not by logical process, but only by a leap of intuition, and by assuming
at the beginning the very thing which we set out to prove. The second defect of the
so-called bridge of argument is that when one has once gotten on, he can never get off.
The connection with the further bank is also lacking. All the premises from which
we argue being finite, we are warranted in drawing only a finite conclusion. Argument cannot reach the Infinite, and only an infinite Being is worthy to be called God.
We can get off from our logical bridge, not by logical process, but only by another and
final leap of intuition, and by once more assuming the existence of the infinite Being
whom we had so vainly sought to reach by mere argument. The process seems to be
referred to in Job 11:7 — "Canst thou by searching find out God? Canst thou find out the Almighty unto
perfection?"

As a logical process this is indeed defective, since all logic as well as all
observation depends for its validity upon the presupposed existence of
God, and since this particular process, even granting the validity of logic
in general, does not warrant the conclusion that God exists, except upon a
second assumption that our abstract ideas of infinity and perfection are to
be applied to the Being to whom argument has actually conducted us.

But although both ends of the logical bridge are confessedly wanting, the
process may serve and does serve a more useful purpose than that of mere
demonstration, namely, that of awakening, explicating, and confirming a
conviction which, though the most fundamental of all, may yet have been
partially slumbering for lack of thought.

Morell, Philos. Fragments, 177, 179 — "We can, in fact, no more prove the existence of
a God by a logical argument, than we can prove the existence of an external world; but
none the less may we obtain as strong a *practical* conviction of the one, as the other."
"We arrive at a scientific belief in the existence of God just as we do at any other possible human truth. We *assume* it, as a hypothesis absolutely necessary to account for
the phenomena of the universe; and then evidences from every quarter begin to converge upon it, until, in process of time, the common sense of mankind, cultivated and
enlightened by ever accumulating knowledge, pronounces upon the validity of the
hypothesis with a voice scarcely less decided and universal than it does in the case of
our highest scientific convictions."

Fisher, Supernat. Origin of Christianity, 572 — "What then is the purport and force
of the several arguments for the existence of God? We reply that these proofs are
the different modes in which faith expresses itself and seeks confirmation. In them
faith, or the object of faith, is more exactly conceived and defined, and in them is found
a corroboration, not arbitrary but substantial and valuable, of that faith which springs

from the soul itself. Such proofs, therefore, are neither on the one hand sufficient to create and sustain faith, nor are they on the other hand to be set aside as of no value."
A. J. Barrett: "The arguments are not so much a bridge in themselves, as they are guys, to hold firm the great suspension-bridge of intuition, by which we pass the gulf from man to God. Or, while they are not a ladder by which we may reach heaven, they are the Ossa on Pelion, from whose combined height we may descry heaven."
Anselm: "Negligentia mihi videtur, si postquam confirmati sumus in fide non studemus quod credimus intelligere." Bradley, Appearance and Reality: "Metaphysics is the finding of bad reasons for what we believe upon instinct; but to find these reasons is no less an instinct." Illingworth, Div. and Hum. Personality, lect. III—"Belief in a personal God is an instinctive judgment, progressively justified by reason." Knight, Essays in Philosophy, 241 — The arguments are "historical memorials of the efforts of the human race to vindicate to itself the existence of a reality of which it is conscious, but which it cannot perfectly define." H. Fielding, The Hearts of Men, 313 — "Creeds are the grammar of religion. They are to relig'on what grammar is to speech. Words are the expression of our wants; grammar is the theory formed afterwards. Speech never proceeded from grammar, but the reverse. As speech progresses and changes from unknown causes, grammar must follow." Pascal: "The heart has reasons of its own which the reason does not know." Frances Power Cobbe: "Intuitions are God's tuitions." On the whole subject, see Cudworth, Intel. System, 3 : 42; Calderwood, Philos. of Infinite, 150 sq.; Curtis, Human Element in Inspiration, 242; Peabody, in Andover Rev., July, 1884; Hahn, History of Arguments for Existence of God; Lotze, Philos. of Religion, 8-34; Am. Jour. Theol., Jan. 1906 : 53-71.

Hegel, in his Logic, page 3, speaking of the disposition to regard the proofs of God's existence as the only means of producing faith in God, says: "Such a doctrine would find its parallel, if we said that eating was impossible before we had acquired a knowledge of the chemical, botanical and zoölogical qualities of our food; and that we must delay digestion till we had finished the study of anatomy and physiology." It is a mistake to suppose that there can be no religious *life* without a correct *theory* of life. Must I refuse to drink water or to breathe air, until I can manufacture both for myself? Some things are given to us. Among these things are "grace and truth" (John 1:17; *cf.* 9). But there are ever those who are willing to take nothing as a free gift, and who insist on working out all knowledge, as well as all salvation, by processes of their own. Pelagianism, with its denial of the doctrines of grace, is but the further development of a rationalism which refuses to accept primitive truths unless these can be logically demonstrated. Since the existence of the soul, of the world, and of God cannot be proved in this way, rationalism is led to curtail, or to misinterpret, the deliverances of consciousness, and hence result certain systems now to be mentioned.

CHAPTER III.

Any correct explanation of the universe must postulate an intuitive knowledge of the existence of the external world, of self, and of God. The desire for scientific unity, however, has occasioned attempts to reduce these three factors to one, and according as one or another of the three has been regarded as the all-inclusive principle, the result has been Materialism, Materialistic Idealism, or Idealistic Pantheism. This scientific impulse is better satisfied by a system which we may designate as Ethical Monism.

We may summarize the present chapter as follows: 1. *Materialism:* Universe = Atoms. Reply: Atoms can do nothing without force, and can be nothing (intelligible) without ideas. 2. *Materialistic Idealism:* Universe = Force + Ideas. Reply: Ideas belong to Mind, and Force can be exerted only by Will. 3. *Idealistic Pantheism:* Universe = Immanent and Impersonal Mind and Will. Reply: Spirit in man shows that the Infinite Spirit must be Transcendent and Personal Mind and Will. We are led from these three forms of error to a conclusion which we may denominate 4. *Ethical Monism:* Universe = Finite, partial, graded manifestation of the divine Life; Matter being God's self-limitation under the law of necessity, Humanity being God's self-limitation under the law of freedom, Incarnation and Atonement being God's self-limitations under the law of grace. Metaphysical Monism, or the doctrine of one Substance, Principle, or Ground of Being, is consistent with Psychological Dualism, or the doctrine that the soul is personally distinct from matter on the one hand and from God on the other.

I. MATERIALISM.

Materialism is that method of thought which gives priority to matter, rather than to mind, in its explanations of the universe. Upon this view, material atoms constitute the ultimate and fundamental reality of which all things, rational and irrational, are but combinations and phenomena. Force is regarded as a universal and inseparable property of matter.

The element of truth in materialism is the reality of the external world. Its error is in regarding the external world as having original and independent existence, and in regarding mind as its product.

Materialism regards atoms as the bricks of which the material universe, the house we inhabit, is built. Sir William Thomson (Lord Kelvin) estimates that, if a drop of water were magnified to the size of our earth, the atoms of which it consists would certainly appear larger than boy's marbles, and yet would be smaller than billiard balls. Of these atoms, all things, visible and invisible, are made. Mind, with all its activities, is a combination or phenomenon of atoms. "Man ist was er iszt: ohne Phosphor kein Gedanke"—"One *is* what he *eats:* without phosphorus, no thought." Ethics is a bill of fare; and worship, like heat, is a mode of motion. Agassiz, however, wittily asked: "Are fishermen, then, more intelligent than farmers, because they eat so much fish, and therefore take in more phosphorus?"

It is evident that much is here attributed to atoms which really belongs to force. Deprive atoms of force, and all that remains is extension, which ━ space = zero. Moreover, "if atoms *are* extended, they cannot be ultimate, for extension implies divisibility, and that which is conceivably divisible cannot be a philosophical ultimate.

But, if atoms *are not* extended, then even an infinite multiplication and combination of them could not produce an extended substance. Furthermore, an atom that is neither extended substance nor thinking substance is inconceivable. The real ultimate is force, and this force cannot be exerted by nothing, but, as we shall hereafter see, can be exerted only by a personal Spirit, for this alone possesses the characteristics of reality, namely, definiteness, unity, and activity."

Not only force but also intelligence must be attributed to atoms, before they can explain any operation of nature. Herschel says not only that "the force of gravitation seems like that of a universal will," but that the atoms themselves, in recognizing each other in order to combine, show a great deal of "presence of mind." Ladd, Introd. to Philosophy, 269 — "A distinguished astronomer has said that every body in the solar system is behaving as if it knew precisely how it ought to behave in consistency with its own nature, and with the behavior of every other body in the same system. . . . Each atom has danced countless millions of miles, with countless millions of different partners, many of which required an important modification of its mode of motion, without ever departing from the correct step or the right time." J. P. Cooke, Credentials of Science, 101, 177 suggests that something more than atoms is needed to explain the universe. A correlating Intelligence and Will must be assumed. Atoms by themselves would be like a heap of loose nails which need to be magnetized if they are to hold together. All structures would be resolved, and all forms of matter would disappear, if the Presence which sustains them were withdrawn. The atom, like the monad of Leibnitz, is "parvus in suo genere deus" — "a little god in its nature" — only because it is the expression of the mind and will of an immanent God.

Plato speaks of men who are "dazzled by too near a look at material things." They do not perceive that these very material things, since they can be interpreted only in terms of spirit, must themselves be essentially spiritual. Materialism is the explanation of a world of which we know something — the world of mind — by a world of which we know next to nothing — the world of matter. Upton, Hibbert Lectures, 297, 298 — "How about your material atoms and brain-molecules? They have no real existence save as objects of thought, and therefore the very thought, which you say your atoms produce, turns out to be the essential precondition of their own existence." With this agree the words of Dr. Ladd: "Knowledge of matter involves repeated activities of sensation and reflection, of inductive and deductive inference, of intuitional belief in substance. These are all activities of mind. Only as the mind has a self-conscious life, is any knowledge of what matter is, or can do, to be gained. . . . Everything is real which is the permanent subject of changing states. That which touches, feels, sees, is more real than that which is touched, felt, seen."

H. N. Gardner, Presb. Rev., 1885: 301, 665, 666 — "Mind gives to matter its chief meaning, — hence matter alone can never explain the universe." Gore, Incarnation, 31 — "Mind is not the *product* of nature, but the necessary *constituent* of nature, considered as an ordered knowable system." Fraser, Philos. of Theism: "An immoral act must originate in the immoral agent; a physical effect is not *known* to originate in its physical cause." Matter, inorganic and organic, presupposes mind; but it is not true that mind presupposes matter. LeConte: "If I could remove your brain cap, what would I see? Only physical changes. But you — what do you perceive? Consciousness, thought, emotion, will. Now take external nature, the Cosmos. The observer from the outside sees only physical phenomena. But must there not be in this case also — on the other side — psychical phenomena, a Self, a Person, a Will?"

The impossibility of finding in matter, regarded as mere atoms, any of the attributes of a cause, has led to a general abandonment of this old Materialism of Democritus, Epicurus, Lucretius, Condillac, Holbach, Feuerbach, Büchner; and Materialistic Idealism has taken its place, which instead of regarding force as a property of matter, regards matter as a manifestation of force. From this section we therefore pass to Materialistic Idealism, and inquire whether the universe can be interpreted simply as a system of force and of ideas. A quarter of a century ago, John Tyndall, in his opening address as President of the British Association at Belfast, declared that in matter was to be found the promise and potency of every form of life. But in 1898, Sir William Crookes, in his address as President of that same British Association, reversed the apothegm, and declared that in life he saw the promise and potency of every form of matter. See Lange, History of Materialism; Janet, Materialism; Fabri, Materialismus; Herzog, Encyclopädie, art.: Materialismus; but esp., Stallo, Modern Physics, 148-170.

In addition to the general error indicated above, we object to this system as follows:

1. In knowing matter, the mind necessarily judges itself to be different in kind, and higher in rank, than the matter which it knows.

We here state simply an intuitive conviction. The mind, in using its physical organism and through it bringing external nature into its service, recognizes itself as different from and superior to matter. See Martineau, quoted in Brit. Quar., April, 1882: 173, and the article of President Thomas Hill in the Bibliotheca Sacra, April, 1852: 353 — "All that is really given by the act of sense-perception is the existence of the conscious self, floating in boundless space and boundless time, surrounded and sustained by boundless power. The material moved, which we at first think the great reality, is only the shadow of a real being, which is immaterial." Harris, Philos. Basis of Theism, 317 — "Imagine an infinitesimal being in the brain, watching the action of the molecules, but missing the thought. So science observes the universe, but misses God." Hebberd, in Journ. Spec. Philos., April, 1886: 135.

Robert Browning, "the subtlest assertor of the soul in song," makes the Pope, in The Ring and the Book, say: "Mind is not matter, nor from matter, but above." So President Francis Wayland: "What is mind?" "No matter." "What is matter?" "Never mind." Sully, The Human Mind, 2:369 — "Consciousness is a reality wholly disparate from material processes, and cannot therefore be resolved into these. Materialism makes that which is immediately known (our mental states) subordinate to that which is only indirectly or inferentially known (external things). Moreover, a material entity existing per se out of relation to a cogitant mind is an absurdity.' As materialists work out their theory, their so-called matter grows more and more ethereal, until at last a stage is reached when it cannot be distinguished from what others call spirit. Martineau: "The matter they describe is so exceedingly clever that it is up to anything, even to writing Hamlet and discovering its own evolution. In short, but for the spelling of its name, it does not seem to differ appreciably from our old friends, Mind and God." A. W. Momerie, in Christianity and Evolution, 54 — "A being conscious of his unity cannot possibly be formed out of a number of atoms unconscious of their diversity. Any one who thinks this possible is capable of asserting that half a dozen fools might be compounded into a single wise man."

2. Since the mind's attributes of (a) continuous identity, (b) self-activity, (c) unrelatedness to space, are different in kind and higher in rank than the attributes of matter, it is rational to conclude that mind is itself different in kind from matter and higher in rank than matter.

This is an argument from specific qualities to that which underlies and explains the qualities. (a) Memory proves personal identity. This is not an identity of material atoms, for atoms change. The molecules that come cannot remember those that depart. Some immutable part in the brain? organized or unorganized? Organized decays; unorganized = soul. (b) Inertia shows that matter is not self-moving. It acts only as it is acted upon. A single atom would never move. Two portions are necessary, and these, in order to useful action, require adjustment by a power which does not belong to matter. Evolution of the universe inexplicable, unless matter were first moved by some power outside itself. See Duke of Argyll, Reign of Law, 92. (c) The highest activities of mind are independent of known physical conditions. Mind controls and subdues the body. It does not cease to grow when the growth of the body ceases. When the body nears dissolution, the mind often asserts itself most strikingly.

Kant: "Unity of apprehension is possible on account of the transcendental unity of self-consciousness." I get my idea of unity from the indivisible self. Stout, Manual of Psychology, 53 — "So far as matter exists independently of its presentation to a cognitive subject, it cannot have material properties, such as extension, hardness, color, weight, etc. . . . . The world of material phenomena presupposes a system of immaterial agency. In this immaterial system the individual consciousness originates. This agency, some say, is thought, others will." A. J. Dubois, in Century Magazine, Dec. 1894: 228 — Since each thought involves a molecular movement in the brain, and this moves the whole universe, mind is the secret of the universe, and we should interpret nature as the expression of underlying purpose. Science is mind following the traces of mind. There can oe no mind without antecedent mind. That all human beings have the same menta. modes shows that these modes are not due simply to environment. Bowne: "Things act upon the mind and the mind reacts with knowledge. Knowing is not a passive receiving, but an active construing." Wundt: "We are compelled to admit that the physical development is not the cause, but much more the effect, of psychical development."

Paul Carus, Soul of Man, 52-64, defines soul as "the form of an organism," and memory as "the psychical aspect of the preservation of form in living substance." This seems to give priority to the organism rather than to the soul, regardless of the fact that without soul no organism is conceivable. Clay cannot be the ancestor of the potter, nor stone the ancestor of the mason, nor wood the ancestor of the carpenter. W. N. Clarke, Christian Theology, 99 — "The intelligibleness of the universe to us is strong and ever present evidence that there is an all-pervading rational Mind, from which the universe received its character." We must add to the maxim, "Cogito, ergo sum," the other maxim, "Intelligo, ergo Deus est." Pfleiderer, Philos. Relig., 1:273 — "The whole idealistic philosophy of modern times is in fact only the carrying out and grounding of the conviction that Nature is ordered by Spirit and for Spirit, as a subservient means for its eternal ends; that it is therefore not, as the heathen naturalism thought, the one and all, the last and highest of things, but has the Spirit, and the moral Ends over it, as its Lord and Master." The consciousness by which things are known precedes the things themselves, in the order of logic, and therefore cannot be explained by them or derived from them. See Porter, Human Intellect, 22, 131, 132. McCosh, Christianity and Positivism, chap. on Materialism; Divine Government, 71-94; Intuitions, 140-145. Hopkins, Study of Man, 53-56; Morell, Hist. of Philosophy, 318-334; Hickok, Rational Cosmology, 403; Theol. Eclectic, 6:555; Appleton, Works, 1:151-154; Calderwood, Moral Philos., 235; Ulrici, Leib und Seele, 688-725, and synopsis, in Bap. Quar., July, 1873:380.

3.   Mind rather than matter must therefore be regarded as the original and independent entity, unless it can be scientifically demonstrated that mind is material in its origin and nature. But all attempts to explain the psychical from the physical, or the organic from the inorganic, are acknowledged failures. The most that can be claimed is, that psychical are always accompanied by physical changes, and that the inorganic is the basis and support of the organic. Although the precise connection between the mind and the body is unknown, the fact that the continuity of physical changes is unbroken in times of psychical activity renders it certain that mind is not transformed physical force. If the facts of sensation indicate the dependence of mind upon body, the facts of volition equally indicate the dependence of body upon mind.

The chemist can produce *organic*, but not *organized*, substances. The *life* cannot be produced from matter. Even in living things progress is secured only by plan. Multiplication of desired advantage, in the Darwinian scheme, requires a selecting thought; in other words the natural selection is artificial selection after all. John Fiske, Destiny of the Creature, 109 — "Cerebral physiology tells us that, during the present life, although thought and feeling are always manifested in connection with a peculiar form of matter, yet by no possibility can thought and feeling be in any sense the product of matter. Nothing could be more grossly unscientific than the famous remark of Cabanis, that the brain secretes thought as the liver secretes bile. It is not even correct to say that thought goes on in the brain. What goes on in the brain is an amazingly complex series of molecular movements, with which thought and feeling are in some unknown way correlated, not as effects or as causes, but as concomitants." Leibnitz's "preëstablished harmony" indicates the difficulty of defining the relation between mind and matter. They are like two entirely disconnected clocks, the one of which has a dial and indicates the hour by its hands, while the other without a dial simultaneously indicates the same hour by its striking apparatus. To Leibnitz the world is an aggregate of atomic souls leading absolutely separate lives. There is no real action of one upon another. Everything in the monad is the development of its individual unstimulated activity. Yet there is a preëstablished harmony of them all, arranged from the beginning by the Creator. The internal development of each monad is so adjusted to that of all the other monads, as to produce the false impression that they are mutually influenced by each other (see Johnson, in Andover Rev., Apl. 1890 : 407, 408). Leibnitz's theory involves the complete rejection of the freedom of the human will in the libertarian sense. To escape from this arbitrary connection of mind and matter in Leibnitz's preëstablished harmony, Spinoza rejected the Cartesian doctrine of two God-created substances, and maintained that there is but one fundamental substance, namely, God himself (see Upton, Hibbert Lectures, 172).

There is an increased flow of blood to the head in times of mental activity. Sometimes, in intense heat of literary composition, the blood fairly surges through the brain. No diminution, but further increase, of physical activity accompanies the greatest efforts of mind. Lay a man upon a balance ; fire a pistol shot or inject suddenly a great thought into his mind ; at once he will tip the balance, and tumble upon his head. Romanes, Mind and Motion, 21 — "Consciousness causes physical changes, but not *vice versa*. To say that mind is a function of motion is to say that mind is a function of itself, since motion exists only for mind. Better suppose the physical and the psychical to be only one, as in the violin sound and vibration are one. Volition is a cause in nature because it has cerebration for its obverse and inseparable side. But if there is no motion without mind, then there can be no universe without God." . . . 34 — "Because within the limits of human experience mind is only known as associated with brain, it does not follow that mind cannot exist without brain. Helmholtz's explanation of the effect of one of Beethoven's sonatas on the brain may be perfectly correct, but the explanation of the effect given by a musician may be equally correct within its category."

Herbert Spencer, Principles of Psychology, 1 : § 56 — "Two things, mind and nervous action, exist together, but we cannot imagine how they are related" (see review of Spencer's Psychology, in N. Englander, July, 1873). Tyndall, Fragments of Science, 120 — "The passage from the physics of the brain to the facts of consciousness is unthinkable." Schurman, Agnosticism and Religion, 95 — "The metamorphosis of vibrations into conscious ideas is a miracle, in comparison with which the floating of iron or the turning of water into wine is easily credible." Bain, Mind and Body, 131— There is no break in the physical continuity. See Brit. Quar., Jan. 1874; art. by Herbert, on Mind and the Science of Energy; McCosh, Intuitions, 145; Talbot, in Bap. Quar., Jan. 1871. On Geulincx's "occasional causes" and Descartes's dualism, see Martineau, Types, 144, 145, 156-158, and Study, 2 : 77.

4. The materialistic theory, denying as it does the priority of spirit, can furnish no sufficient cause for the highest features of the existing universe, namely, its personal intelligences, its intuitive ideas, its free-will, its moral progress, its beliefs in God and immortality.

Herbert, Modern Realism Examined : "Materialism has no physical evidence of the existence of consciousness in others. As it declares our fellow men to be destitute of free volition, so it should declare them destitute of consciousness; should call them, as well as brutes, pure automata. If physics are all, there is no God, but there is also no man, existing." Some of the early followers of Descartes used to kick and beat their dogs, laughing meanwhile at their cries and calling them the "creaking of the machine." Huxley, who calls the brutes "conscious automata," believes in the gradual banishment, from all regions of human thought, of what we call spirit and spontaneity : "A spontaneous act is an absurdity ; it is simply an effect that is uncaused."

James, Psychology, 1 : 149 — "The girl in Midshipman Easy could not excuse the illegitimacy of her child by saying that 'it was a very small one.' And consciousness, however small, is an illegitimate birth in any philosophy that starts without it, and yet professes to explain all facts by continued evolution. . . . Materialism denies reality to almost all the impulses which we most cherish. Hence it will fail of universal adoption." Clerk Maxwell, Life, 391 — "The atoms are a very tough lot, and can stand a great deal of knocking about, and it is strange to find a number of them combining to form a man of feeling. . . . 426 — I have looked into most philosophical systems, and I have seen none that will work without a God." President E. B. Andrews : "Mind is the only substantive thing in this universe, and all else is adjective. Matter is not primordial, but is a function of spirit." Theodore Parker : "Man is the highest product of his own history. The discoverer finds nothing so tall or grand as himself, nothing so valuable to him. The greatest star is at the small end of the telescope — the star that is looking, not looked after, nor looked at."

Materialism makes men to be "a serio-comic procession of wax figures or of cunning casts in clay " (Bowne). Man is " the cunningest of clocks." But if there were nothing but matter, there could be no materialism, for a system of thought, like materialism, implies consciousness. Martineau, Types, preface, xii, xiii — " It was the irresistible pleading of the moral consciousness which first drove me to rebel against the limits of the merely scientific conception. It became incredible to me that nothing was possible except the actual. . . . Is there then no *ought to be*, other than *what is?* " Dewey, Psychology, 84 — "A world without ideal elements would be one in which the home would be four walls and a roof to keep out cold and wet; the table a mess for animals; and the grave a hole in the ground." Omar Khayyám, Rubaiyat, stanza 72 — "And that inverted bowl they call the Sky, Whereunder crawling coop'd we live and die, Lift not your hands to It for help — for it As impotently moves as you or I." Victor Hugo : " You say the soul is nothing but the resultant of bodily powers? Why then is my soul more luminous when my bodily powers begin to fail? Winter is on my head, and eternal spring is in my heart. . . . The nearer I approach the end, the plainer I hear the immortal symphonies of the worlds which invite me."

Diman, Theistic Argument, 318 — " Materialism can never explain the fact that matter is always combined with force. Coördinate principles? then dualism, instead of monism. Force cause of matter ? then we preserve unity, but destroy materialism ; for we trace matter to an immaterial source. Behind multiplicity of natural forces we must postulate some single power—which can be nothing but coördinating mind." Mark Hopkins sums up Materialism in Princeton Rev., Nov. 1879:490—"1. Man, who is a person, is made by a thing, *i. e.*, matter. 2. Matter is to be worshiped as man's maker, if anything is to be (Rom. 1:25). 3. Man is to worship himself — his God is his belly." See also Martineau, Religion and Materialism, 25-31, Types, 1 : preface, xii, xiii, and Study, 1 : 248, 250, 345; Christlieb, Modern Doubt and Christian Belief, 145-161; Buchanan, Modern Atheism, 247, 248; McCosh, in International Rev., Jan. 1895 ; Contemp. Rev., Jan. 1875, art.: Man Transcorporeal; Calderwood, Relations of Mind and Brain ; Laycock, Mind and Brain ; Diman, Theistic Argument, 358 ; Wilkinson, in Present Day Tracts, 3 : no. 17 ; Shedd, Dogm. Theol., 1 : 487-499; A. H. Strong, Philos. and Relig., 31-38.

II. Materialistic Idealism.

Idealism proper is that method of thought which regards all knowledge as conversant only with affections of the percipient mind.

Its element of truth is the fact that these affections of the percipient mind are the conditions of our knowledge. Its error is in denying that through these and in these we know that which exists independently of our consciousness.

The idealism of the present day is mainly a materialistic idealism. It defines matter and mind alike in terms of sensation, and regards both as opposite sides or successive manifestations of one underlying and unknowable force.

Modern subjective idealism is the development of a principle found as far back as Locke. Locke derived all our knowledge from sensation ; the mind only combines ideas which sensation furnishes, but gives no material of its own. Berkeley held that externally we can be sure only of sensations,— cannot be sure that any external world exists apart from mind. Berkeley's idealism, however, was objective ; for he maintained that while things do not exist independently of consciousness, they do exist independently of *our* consciousness, namely, in the mind of God, who in a correct philosophy takes the place of a mindless external world as the cause of our ideas. Kant, in like manner, held to existences outside of our own minds, although he regarded these existences as unknown and unknowable. Over against these forms of objective idealism we must put the subjective idealism of Hume, who held that internally also we cannot be sure of anything but mental phenomena ; we know thoughts, feelings and volitions, but we do not know mental substance within, any more than we know material substance without: our ideas are a string of beads, without any string ; we need no cause for these ideas, in an external world, a soul, or God. Mill, Spencer, Bain and Tyndall are Humists, and it is their subjective idealism which we oppose.

All these regard the material atom as a mere centre of force, or a hypothetical cause of sensations. Matter is therefore a manifestation of force, as to the old materialism force was a property of matter. But if matter, mind and God are nothing but sensations, then the body itself is nothing but sensations. There is no *body* to have the sensations, and no *spirit*, either human or divine, to produce them. John Stuart Mill, in his Examination of Sir William Hamilton, 1 : 234-253, makes sensations the only orig· inal sources of knowledge. He defines matter as "a permanent possibility of sensation," and mind as "a series of feelings aware of itself." So Huxley calls matter "only a name for the unknown cause of the states of consciousness"; although he also declares: "If I am compelled to choose between the materialism of a man like Büchner and the Idealism of Berkeley, I would have to agree with Berkeley." He would hold to the priority of matter, and yet regard matter as wholly ideal. Since John Stuart Mill, of all the materialistic idealists, gives the most precise definitions of matter and of mind, we attempt to show the inadequacy of his treatment.

The most complete refutation of subjective idealism is that of Sir William Hamilton, in his Metaphysics, 348-372, and Theories of Sense-perception — the reply to Brown. See condensed statement of Hamilton's view, with estimate and criticism, in Porter, Human Intellect, 236-240, and on Idealism, 129, 132. Porter holds that original perception gives us simply affections of our own sensorium ; as cause of these, we gain knowledge of extended externality. So Sir William Hamilton : "Sensation proper has no object but a subject-object." But both Porter and Hamilton hold that through these sensations we know that which exists independently of our sensations. Hamilton's natural realism, however, was an exaggeration of the truth. Bowne, Introd. to Psych. Theory, 257, 258 — "In Sir William Hamilton's desire to have no go-betweens in perception, he was forced to maintain that every sensation is felt where it seems to be, and hence that the mind fills out the entire body. Likewise he had to affirm that the object in vision is not the thing, but the rays of light, and even the object itself had, at last, to be brought into consciousness. Thus he reached the absurdity that the true object in perception is something of which we are totally unconscious." Surely we cannot be immediately conscious of what is outside of consciousness. James, Psychology, 1 : 11 — "The terminal organs are telephones, and brain-cells are the receivers at which the mind listens." Berkeley's view is to be found in his Principles of Human Knowledge, § 18 *sq.* See also Presb. Rev., Apl. 1885 : 301-315 ; Journ. Spec. Philos., 1884 : 246-260, 383-399 ; Tulloch, Mod. Theories, 360, 361 ; Encyc. Britannica, art. : Berkeley.

There is, however, an idealism which is not open to Hamilton's objections, and to which most recent philosophers give their adhesion. It is the objective idealism of Lotze. It argues that we know nothing of the extended world except through the forces which impress our nervous organism. These forces take the form of vibrations of air or ether, and we interpret them as sound, light, or motion, according as they affect our nerves of hearing, sight, or touch. But the only force which we immediately know is that of our own wills, and we can either not understand matter at all or we must understand it as the product of a will comparable to our own. Things are simply "concreted laws of action," or divine ideas to which permanent reality has been given by divine will. What we perceive in the normal exercise of our faculties has existence not only for us but for all intelligent beings and for God himself : in other words, our idealism is not subjective, but objective. We have seen in the previous section that atoms cannot explain the universe, — they presuppose both ideas and force. We now see that this force presupposes will, and these ideas presuppose mind. But, as it still may be claimed that this mind is not self-conscious mind and that this will is not personal will, we pass in the next section to consider Idealistic Pantheism, of which these claims are characteristic. Materialistic Idealism, in truth, is but a half-way house between Materialism and Pantheism, in which no permanent lodging is to be found by the logical intelligence.

Lotze, Outlines of Metaphysics, 152 — "The objectivity of our cognition consists therefore in this, that it is not a meaningless play of mere seeming ; but it brings before us a world whose coherency is ordered in pursuance of the injunction of the sole Reality in the world, to wit, the Good. Our cognition thus possesses more of truth than if it copied exactly a world that has no value in itself. Although it does not comprehend in what manner all that is phenomenon is presented to the view, still it understands what is the meaning of it all; and is like to a spectator who comprehends the æsthetic significance of that which takes place on the stage of a theatre, and would gain nothing essential if he were to see besides the machinery by means of which the changes are effected on the stage." Professor C. A. Strong: "Perception is a shadow thrown upon the mind by a thing-in-itself. The shadow is the symbol of the thing; and, as shadows are soulless and dead, physical objects may seem soulless and dead, while the reality symbolized is never so soulful and alive. Consciousness is reality. The only existence of which we can conceive is mental in its nature. All existence *for* consciousness is existence *of* consciousness. The horse's shadow accompanies him, but it does not help him to draw the cart. The brain-event is simply the mental state itself regarded from the point of view of the perception."

Aristotle: "Substance is in its nature prior to relation" = there can be no relation without things to be related. Fichte: "Knowledge, just because it is knowledge, is not reality, — it comes not first, but second." Veitch, Knowing and Being, 216, 217, 292, 293 — "Thought can do nothing, except as it is a synonym for Thinker. . . . Neither the finite nor the infinite consciousness, alone or together, can constitute an object external, or explain its existence. The existence of a thing logically precedes the perception of it. Perception is not creation. It is not the thinking that makes the ego, but the ego that makes the thinking." Seth, Hegelianism and Personality: "Divine thoughts presuppose a divine Being. God's thoughts do not constitute the real world. The real force does not lie in them, — it lies in the divine Being, as living, active Will." Here was the fundamental error of Hegel, that he regarded the Universe as mere Idea, and gave little thought to the Love and the Will that constitute it. See John Fiske, Cosmic Philosophy, 1 : 75 ; 2 : 80 ; Contemp. Rev., Oct. 1872 : art. on Huxley; Lowndes, Philos. Primary Beliefs, 115-143 ; Atwater (on Ferrier), in Princeton Rev., 1857 : 258, 280 ; Cousin, Hist. Philosophy, 2 : 239-343 ; Veitch's Hamilton, (Blackwood's Philos. Classics,) 176, 191 ; A. H. Strong, Philosophy and Religion, 58-74.

To this view we make the following objections:

1. Its definition of matter as a "permanent possibility of sensation" contradicts our intuitive judgment that, in knowing the phenomena of matter, we have direct knowledge of substance as underlying phenomena, as distinct from our sensations, and as external to the mind which experiences these sensations.

Bowne, Metaphysics, 432 — "How the possibility of an odor and a flavor can be the cause of the yellow color of an orange is probably unknowable, except to a mind that can see that two and two may make five." See Iverach's Philosophy of Spencer Examined, in Present Day Tracts, 5 : no. 29. Martineau, Study, 1 : 102-112 — "If external impressions are telegraphed to the brain, intelligence must receive the message at the beginning as well as deliver it at the end. . . . It is the external object which gives the possibility, not the possibility which gives the external object. The mind cannot make both its *cognita* and its *cognitio*. It cannot dispense with standing-ground for its own feet, or with atmosphere for its own wings." Professor Charles A. Strong: "Kant held to things-in-themselves back of physical phenomena, as well as to things-in-themselves back of mental phenomena; he thought things-in-themselves back of physical might be identical with things-in-themselves back of mental phenomena. And since mental phenomena, on this theory, are not specimens of reality, and reality manifests itself indifferently through them and through physical phenomena, he naturally concluded that we have no ground for supposing reality to be like either — that we must conceive of it as 'weder Materie noch ein denkend Wesen' — 'neither matter nor a thinking being' — a theory of the Unknowable. Would that it had been also the Unthinkable and the Unmentionable!" Ralph Waldo Emerson was a subjective idealist; but, when called to inspect a farmer's load of wood, he said to his company: "Excuse me a moment, my friends; we have to attend to these matters, just as if they were real." See Mivart, On Truth, 71-141.

2. Its definition of mind as a "series of feelings aware of itself" contradicts our intuitive judgment that, in knowing the phenomena of mind, we have direct knowledge of a spiritual substance of which these phenomena are manifestations, which retains its identity independently of

our consciousness, and which, in its knowing, instead of being the passive recipient of impressions from without, always acts from within by a power of its own.

James, Psychology, 1 : 226 — "It seems as if the elementary psychic fact were not *thought*, or *this thought*, or *that thought*, but *my thought*, every thought being owned. The universal conscious fact is not 'feelings and thoughts exist,' but 'I think,' and 'I feel.'" Professor James is compelled to say this, even though he begins his Psychology without insisting upon the existence of a soul. Hamilton's Reid, 443 —"Shall I think that thought can stand by itself? or that ideas can feel pleasure or pain?" R. T. Smith, Man's Knowledge, 44 — "We say 'my notions and my passions,' and when we use these phrases we imply that our central self is felt to be something different from the notions or passions which belong to it or characterize it for a time." Lichtenberg : "We should say, 'It thinks;' just as we say, 'It lightens,' or 'It rains.' In saying 'Cogito,' the philosopher goes too far if he translates it, 'I think.'" Are the faculties, then, an army without a general, or an engine without a driver? In that case we should not *have* sensations, — we should only *be* sensations.

Professor C. A. Strong : "I have knowledge of *other minds*. This non-empirical knowledge — transcendent knowledge of things-in-themselves, derived neither from experience nor reasoning, and assuming that like consequents (intelligent movements) must have like antecedents (thoughts and feelings), and also assuming instinctively that something exists outside of my own mind — this refutes the post-Kantian phenomenalism. *Perception* and *memory* also involve transcendence. In both I transcend the bounds of experience, as truly as in my knowledge of other minds. In memory I recognize a *past*, as distinguished from the present. In perception I cognize a possibility of *other* experiences like the present, and this alone gives the sense of permanence and reality. Perception and memory refute phenomenalism. Things-in-themselves must be assumed in order to fill the gaps between individual minds, and to give coherence and intelligibility to the universe, and so to avoid pluralism. If matter can influence and even extinguish our minds, it must have some force of its own, some existence in itself. If consciousness is an evolutionary product, it must have arisen from simpler mental facts. But these simpler mental facts are only another name for things-in-themselves. A deep prerational instinct compels us to recognize them, for they cannot be logically demonstrated. We must assume them in order to give continuity and intelligibility to our conceptions of the universe." See, on Bain's Cerebral Psychology, Martineau's Essays, 1 : 265. On the physiological method of mental philosophy, see Talbot, in Bap. Quar., 1871 : 1; Bowen, in Princeton Rev., March, 1878 : 423-450 ; Murray, Psychology, 279-287.

3. In so far as this theory regards mind as the obverse side of matter, or as a later and higher development from matter, the mere reference of both mind and matter to an underlying force does not save the theory from any of the difficulties of pure materialism already mentioned ; since in this case, equally with that, force is regarded as purely physical, and the priority of spirit is denied.

Herbert Spencer, Psychology, quoted by Fiske, Cosmic Philosophy, 2 : 80 —"Mind and nervous action are the subjective and objective faces of the same thing. Yet we remain utterly incapable of seeing, or even of imagining, how the two are related. Mind still continues to us a something without kinship to other things." Owen, Anatomy of Vertebrates, quoted by Talbot, Bap. Quar., Jan. 1871 : 5 — "All that I know of matter and mind in themselves is that the former is an external centre of force, and the latter an internal centre of force." New Englander, Sept. 1883 : 636 — "If the atom be a mere centre of force and not a real thing in itself, then the atom is a supersensual essence, an immaterial being. To make immaterial matter the source of conscious mind is to make matter as wonderful as an immortal soul or a personal Creator." See New Englander, July, 1875 : 532-535 ; Martineau, Study, 102-130, and Relig. and Mod. Materialism, 25 — "If it takes mind to construe the universe, how can the negation of mind constitute it?"

David J. Hill, in his Genetic Philosophy, 200, 201, seems to deny that thought precedes force, or that force precedes thought : "Objects, or things in the external world, may be elements of a thought-process in a cosmic subject, without themselves being conscious. . . . . A true analysis and a rational genesis require the equal recognition of both the objective and the subjective elements of experience, without priority in time, separation in space or disruption of being. So far as our minds can penetrate reality, as disclosed in the activities of thought, we are everywhere confronted with a Dynamic Reason." In Dr. Hill's account of the genesis of the universe, however, the unconscious comes first, and from it the conscious seems to be derived. Consciousness of the object is only the obverse side of the object of consciousness. This is, as Martineau, Study, 1:341, remarks, " to take the sea on board the boat." We greatly prefer the view of Lotze, 2:641 — " Things are acts of the Infinite wrought within minds alone, or states which the Infinite experiences nowhere but in minds. . . . . Things and events are the sum of those actions which the highest Principle performs in all spirits so uniformly and coherently, that to these spirits there must seem to be a world of substantial and efficient things existing in space outside themselves." The data from which we draw our inferences as to the nature of the external world being mental and spiritual, it is more rational to attribute to that world a spiritual reality than a kind of reality of which our experience knows nothing. See also Schurman, Belief in God, 208, 225.

4. In so far as this theory holds the underlying force of which matter and mind are manifestations to be in any sense intelligent or voluntary, it renders necessary the assumption that there is an intelligent and voluntary Being who exerts this force. Sensations and ideas, moreover, are explicable only as manifestations of Mind.

Many recent Christian thinkers, as Murphy, Scientific Bases of Faith, 13-15, 29-36, 42-52, would define mind as a function of matter, matter as a function of force, force as a function of will, and therefore as the power of an omnipresent and personal God. All force, except that of man's free will, is the will of God. So Herschel, Lectures, 460; Argyll, Reign of Law, 121-127; Wallace on Nat. Selection, 363-371; Martineau, Essays, 1:63, 121, 145, 265; Bowen, Metaph. and Ethics, 146-162. These writers are led to their conclusion in large part by the considerations that nothing dead can be a proper cause; that will is the only cause of which we have immediate knowledge; that the forces of nature are intelligible only when they are regarded as exertions of will. Matter, therefore, is simply centres of force — the regular and, as it were, automatic expression of God's mind and will. Second causes in nature are only secondary activities of the great First Cause.

This view is held also by Bowne, in his Metaphysics. He regards only personality as real. Matter is phenomenal, although it is an activity of the divine will outside of us. Bowne's phenomenalism is therefore an objective idealism, greatly preferable to that of Berkeley who held to God's energizing indeed, but only within the soul. This idealism of Bowne is not pantheism, for it holds that, while there are no second causes in nature, man is a second cause, with a personality distinct from that of God, and lifted above nature by his powers of free will. Royce, however, in his Religious Aspect of Philosophy, and in his The World and the Individual, makes man's consciousness a part or aspect of a universal consciousness, and so, instead of making God come to consciousness in man, makes man come to consciousness in God. While this scheme seems, in one view, to save God's personality, it may be doubted whether it equally guarantees man's personality or leaves room for man's freedom, responsibility, sin and guilt. Bowne, Philos. Theism, 175 — "' Universal reason ' is a class-term which denotes no possible existence, and which has reality only in the specific existences from which it is abstracted." Bowne claims that the impersonal finite has only such otherness as a thought or act has to its subject. There is no substantial existence except in persons. Seth, Hegelianism and Personality : "Neo-Kantianism erects into a God the mere form of self-consciousness in general, that is, confounds consciousness *überhaupt* with a *universal* consciousness."

Bowne, Theory of Thought and Knowledge, 318-343, esp. 328 — " Is there anything in existence but myself ? Yes. To escape solipsism I must admit at least other persons. Does the world of apparent objects exist for me only ? No; it exists for others also, so that we live in a common world. Does this common world consist in anything more than a similarity of impressions in finite minds, so that the world apart from these is nothing ? This view cannot be disproved, but it accords so ill with the impression of our total experience that it is practically impossible. Is then the world of things a continuous existence of some kind independent of finite thought and consciousness? This claim cannot be demonstrated, but it is the only view that does not involve insuperable difficulties. What is the nature and where is the place of this cosmic existence? That is the question between Realism and Idealism. Realism views things as existing in a real space, and as true ontological realities. Idealism views both them and the space in which they are supposed to be existing as existing only in and for a cosmic Intelligence, and apart from which they are absurd and contradictory. Things are independent of *our* thought, but not independent of *all* thought, in a lumpish materiality which is the antithesis and negation of consciousness." See also Martineau, Study, 1 : 214-230, 311. For advocacy of the substantive existence of second causes, see Porter, Hum. Intellect, 582-588 ; Hodge, Syst. Theol., 1 : 596 ; Alden, Philosophy, 48-80 ; Hodgson, Time and Space, 149-218 ; A. J. Balfour, in Mind, Oct. 1893 : 430.

III. IDEALISTIC PANTHEISM.

Pantheism is that method of thought which conceives of the universe as the development of one intelligent and voluntary, yet impersonal, substance, which reaches consciousness only in man. It therefore identifies God, not with each individual object in the universe, but with the totality of things. The current Pantheism of our day is idealistic.

The elements of truth in Pantheism are the intelligence and voluntariness of God, and his immanence in the universe ; its error lies in denying God's personality and transcendence.

Pantheism denies the real existence of the finite, at the same time that it deprives the Infinite of self-consciousness and freedom. See Hunt, History of Pantheism ; Manning, Half-truths and the Truth ; Bayne, Christian Life, Social and Individual, 21-53 ; Hutton, on Popular Pantheism, in Essays, 1 : 55-76 — " The pantheist's ' I believe in God ', is a contradiction. He says : ' I perceive the external as different from myself ; but on further reflection, I perceive that this external was itself the percipient agency.' So the worshiped is really the worshiper after all." Harris, Philosophical Basis of Theism, 173 — " Man is a bottle of the ocean's water, in the ocean, temporarily distinguishable by its limitation within the bottle, but lost again in the ocean, so soon as these fragile limits are broken." Martineau, Types, 1 : 23 — Mere immanency excludes Theism ; transcendency leaves it still possible ; 211-225 — Pantheism declares that " there is nothing but God ; he is not only sole cause but entire effect ; he is all in all." Spinoza has been falsely called " the God-intoxicated man." " Spinoza, on the contrary, translated God into the universe ; it was Malebranche who transfigured the universe into God."

The later Brahmanism is pantheistic. Rowland Williams, Christianity and Hinduism, quoted in Mozley on Miracles, 284 — " In the final state personality vanishes. You will not, says the Brahman, accept the term ' void ' as an adequate description of the mysterious nature of the soul, but you will clearly apprehend soul, in the final state, to be unseen and ungrasped being, thought, knowledge, joy — no other than very God." Flint, Theism, 69 — " Where the will is without energy, and rest is longed for as the end of existence, as among the Hindus, there is marked inability to think of God as cause or will, and constant inveterate tendency to pantheism."

Hegel denies God's transcendence : " God is not a spirit beyond the stars ; he is spirit in all spirit " ; which means that God, the impersonal and unconscious Absolute, comes to consciousness only in man. If the eternal system of abstract thoughts were itself conscious, finite consciousness would disappear ; hence the alternative is either *no God*, or *no man*. Stirling : " The Idea, so conceived, is a blind, dumb, invisible idol, and the theory is the most hopeless theory that has ever been presented to humanity." It is practical autolatry, or self-deification. The world is reduced to a mere process of logic ; thought thinks ; there is thought without a thinker. To this doctrine of Hegel we may well oppose the remarks of Lotze : " We cannot make mind the equivalent of the infinitive *to think*,— we feel that it must be that which thinks ; the essence of things cannot be either existence or activity,— it must be that which exists and that which acts. Thinking means nothing, if it is not the thinking of a thinker ; acting and working mean nothing, if we leave out the conception of a subject distinguishable from them and from which they proceed." To Hegel, Being *is* Thought ; to Spinoza, Being *has* Thought + Extension; the truth seems to be that Being *has* Thought + Will, and *may* reveal itself in Extension and Evolution (Creation).

By other philosophers, however, Hegel is otherwise interpreted. Prof. H. Jones, in Mind, July, 1893 : 289-306, claims that Hegel's fundamental Idea is not Thought, but Thinking : "The universe to him was not a system of thoughts, but a thinking reality, manifested most fully in man. . . . . The fundamental reality is the universal intelligence whose operation we should seek to detect in all things. All reality is ultimately explicable as Spirit, or Intelligence,— hence our ontology must be a Logic, and the laws of things must be laws of thinking." Sterrett, in like manner, in his Studies in Hegel's Philosophy of Religion, 17, quotes Hegel's Logic, Wallace's translation, 89, 91, 236: "Spinoza's *Substance* is, as it were, a dark, shapeless abyss, which devours all definite content as utterly null, and produces from itself nothing that has positive subsistence in itself. . . . . God is Substance,— he is, however, no less the Absolute Person." This is essential to religion, but this, says Hegel, Spinoza never perceived : "Everything depends upon the Absolute Truth being perceived, not merely as Substance, but as Subject." God is self-conscious and self-determining Spirit. Necessity is excluded. Man is free and immortal. Men are not mechanical parts of God, nor do they lose their identity, although they *find themselves* truly only in him. With this estimate of Hegel's system, Caird, Erdmann and Mulford substantially agree. This is Tennyson's "Higher Pantheism."

Seth, Ethical Principles, 440 —"Hegel conceived the superiority of his system to Spinozism to lie in the substitution of Subject for Substance. The true Absolute must contain, instead of abolishing, relations ; the true Monism must include, instead of excluding, Pluralism. A One which, like Spinoza's Substance, or the Hegelian Absolute, does not enable us to think the Many, cannot be the true One — the unity of the Manifold. . . . . Since evil exists, Schopenhauer substituted for Hegel's Panlogism, which asserted the identity of the rational and the real, a blind impulse of life,— for absolute Reason he substituted a reasonless Will "—a system of practical pessimism. Alexander, Theories of Will, 5 — "Spinoza recognized no distinction between will and intellectual affirmation or denial." John Caird, Fund. Ideas of Christianity, 1 : 10: — "As there is no reason in the conception of pure space why any figures or forms, lines, surfaces, solids, should arise in it, so there is no reason in the pure colorless abstraction of Infinite Substance why any world of finite things and beings should ever come into existence. It is the grave of all things, the productive source of nothing." Hegel called Schelling's Identity or Absolute "the infinite night in which all cows are black "— an allusion to Goethe's Faust, part 2, act 1, where the words are added: "and cats are gray." Although Hegel's preference of the term Subject, instead of the term Substance, has led many to maintain that he believed in a personality of God distinct from that of man, his over-emphasis of the Idea, and his comparative ignoring of the elements of Love and Will, leave it still doubtful whether his Idea was anything more than unconscious and impersonal intelligence — less materialistic than that of Spinoza indeed, yet open to many of the same objections.

We object to this system as follows :

1. Its idea of God is self-contradictory, since it makes him infinite, yet consisting only of the finite ; absolute, yet existing in necessary relation to the universe ; supreme, yet shut up to a process of self-evolution and dependent for self-consciousness on man ; without self-determination, yet the cause of all that is.

Saisset, Pantheism, 148 — "An imperfect God, yet perfection arising from imperfection." Shedd, Hist. Doctrine, 1 : 13 — "Pantheism applies to God a principle of growth and imperfection, which belongs only to the finite." Calderwood, Moral Philos., 245 — "Its first requisite is moment, or movement, which it assumes, but does not account for." Caro's sarcasm applies here: "Your God is not yet made — he is in process of manufacture." See H. B. Smith, Faith and Philosophy, 25. Pantheism is practical atheism, for impersonal spirit is only blind and necessary force. Angelus Silesius: "Wir beten ' Es gescheh ', mein Herr und Gott, dein Wille'; Und sieh ', Er hat nicht Will',— Er ist ein ew'ge Stille " — which Max Müller translates as follows : "We pray, ' O Lord our God, Do thou thy holy Will'; and see ! God has no will ; He is at peace and still." Angelus Silesius consistently makes God dependent for self-consciousness on man:

"I know that God cannot live An instant without me; He must give up the ghost, If I should cease to be." Seth, Hegelianism and Personality: "Hegelianism destroys both God and man. It reduces man to an object of the universal Thinker, and leaves this universal Thinker without any true personality." Pantheism is a game of solitaire, in which God plays both sides.

2. Its assumed unity of substance is not only without proof, but it directly contradicts our intuitive judgments. These testify that we are not parts and particles of God, but distinct personal subsistences.

Martineau, Essays, 1:158 — "Even for immanency, there must be something wherein to dwell, and for life, something whereon to act." Many systems of monism contradict consciousness; they confound harmony between two with absorption in one. "In Scripture we never find the universe called τὸ πᾶν, for this suggests the idea of a self-contained unity: we have everywhere τὰ πάντα instead." The Bible recognizes the element of truth in pantheism — God is 'through all'; also the element of truth in mysticism — God is 'in you all'; but it adds the element of transcendence which both these fail to recognize—God is 'above all' (Eph. 4: 6). See Fisher, Essays on Supernat. Orig. of Christianity, 539. G. D. B. Pepper: "He who is over all and in all is yet distinct from all. If one is over a thing, he is not that very thing which he is over. If one is in something, he must be distinct from that something. And so the universe, over which and in which God is, must be thought of as something distinct from God. The creation cannot be identical with God, or a mere form of God." We add, however, that it may be a manifestation of God and dependent upon God, as our thoughts and acts are manifestations of our mind and will and dependent upon our mind and will, yet are not themselves our mind and will.

Pope wrote: "All are but parts of one stupendous whole, Whose body nature is and God the soul." But Case, Physical Realism, 193, replies: "Not so. Nature is to God as works are to a man; and as man's works are not his body, so neither is nature the body of God." Matthew Arnold, On Heine's Grave: "What are we all but a mood, A single mood of the life Of the Being in whom we exist, Who alone is all things in one?" Hovey, Studies, 51 — "Scripture recognizes the element of truth in pantheism, but it also teaches the existence of a world of things, animate and inanimate, in distinction from God. It represents men as prone to worship the creature more than the Creator. It describes them as sinners worthy of death . . . moral agents. . . . It no more thinks of men as being literally parts of God, than it thinks of children as being parts of their parents, or subjects as being parts of their king." A. J. F. Behrends: "The true doctrine lies between the two extremes of a crass dualism which makes God and the world two self-contained entities, and a substantial monism in which the universe has only a phenomenal existence. There is no identity of substance nor division of the divine substance. The universe is eternally dependent, the product of the divine Word, not simply manufactured. Creation is primarily a spiritual act." Prof. George M. Forbes: "Matter exists in subordinate dependence upon God; spirit in coördinate dependence upon God. The body of Christ was Christ externalized, made manifest to sense-perception. In apprehending matter, I am apprehending the mind and will of God. This is the highest sort of reality. Neither matter nor finite spirits, then, are mere phenomena."

3. It assigns no sufficient cause for that fact of the universe which is highest in rank, and therefore most needs explanation, namely, the existence of personal intelligences. A substance which is itself unconscious, and under the law of necessity, cannot produce beings who are self-conscious and free.

Gess, Foundations of our Faith, 36 — "Animal instinct, and the spirit of a nation working out its language, might furnish analogies, if they produced personalities as their result, but not otherwise. Nor were these tendencies self-originated, but received from an external source." McCosh, Intuitions, 215, 393, and Christianity and Positivism, 180. Seth, Freedom as an Ethical Postulate, 47 — "If man is an 'imperium in imperio,' not a person, but only an aspect or expression of the universe or God, then he cannot be free. Man may be depersonalized either into nature or into God. Through the conception of our own personality we reach that of God. To resolve our personality into that of God would be to negate the divine greatness itself by invalidating the conception through which it was reached." Bradley, Appearance and Reality, 551, is more ambiguous: "The positive relation of every appearance as an adjective to Reality; and the presence of Reality among its appearances in different degrees and with diverse values; this double truth we have found to be the centre of philosophy." He protests against both "an empty transcendence" and "a shallow pantheism." Hegelian immanence and knowledge, he asserts, identified God and man. But God is more than man or man's thought. He is spirit and life — best understood from the human *self*, with its thoughts, feelings, volitions. Immanence needs to be qualified by transcendence. "God is not God till he has become all-in-all, and a God which is all-in-all is not the God of religion. God is an aspect, and that must mean but an appearance of the Absolute." Bradley's Absolute, therefore, is not so much personal as super-personal; to which we reply with Jackson, James Martineau, 416 — "Higher than personality is lower; beyond it is regression from its height. From the equator we may travel northward, gaining ever higher and higher latitudes; but, if ever the pole is reached, pressing on from thence will be descending into lower latitudes, not gaining higher. . . . Do I say, I am a pantheist? Then, *ipso facto*, I deny pantheism; for, in the very assertion of the Ego, I imply all else as objective to me."

4. It therefore contradicts the affirmations of our moral and religious natures by denying man's freedom and responsibility; by making God to include in himself all evil as well as all good; and by precluding all prayer, worship, and hope of immortality.

Conscience is the eternal witness against pantheism. Conscience witnesses to our freedom and responsibility, and declares that moral distinctions are not illusory. Renouf, Hibbert Lect., 234 — "It is only out of condescension to popular language that pantheistic systems can recognize the notions of right and wrong, of iniquity and sin. If everything really emanates from God, there can be no such thing as sin. And the ablest philosophers who have been led to pantheistic views have vainly endeavored to harmonize these views with what we understand by the notion of sin or moral evil. The great systematic work of Spinoza is entitled 'Ethica'; but for real ethics we might as profitably consult the Elements of Euclid." Hodge, System. Theology, 1 : 299–330 — "Pantheism is fatalistic. On this theory, duty = pleasure; right = might; sin = good in the making. Satan, as well as Gabriel, is a self-development of God. The practical effects of pantheism upon popular morals and life, wherever it has prevailed, as in Buddhist India and China, demonstrate its falsehood." See also Dove, Logic of the Christian Faith, 118; Murphy, Scientific Bases of Faith, 202; Bib. Sac., Oct. 1867: 603–615; Dix, Pantheism, Introd., 12. On the fact of sin as refuting the pantheistic theory, see Bushnell, Nature and the Supernat., 140–164.

Wordsworth: "Look up to heaven! the industrious sun Already half his course hath run; He cannot halt or go astray; But our immortal spirits may." President John H. Harris; "You never ask a cyclone's opinion of the ten commandments." Bowne, Philos. of Theism, 245 — "Pantheism makes man an automaton. But how can an automaton have duties?" Principles of Ethics, 18 — "Ethics is defined as the science of conduct, and the conventions of language are relied upon to cover up the fact that there is no 'conduct' in the case. If man be a proper automaton, we might as well speak of the conduct of the winds as of human conduct; and a treatise on planetary motions is as truly the ethics of the solar system as a treatise on human movements is the ethics of man." For lack of a clear recognition of personality, either human or divine, Hegel's Ethics is devoid of all spiritual nourishment,— his "Rechtsphilosophie" has been called "a repast of bran." Yet Professor Jones, in Mind, July, 1893: 304, tells us that Hegel's task was "to discover what conception of the single principle or fundamental unity which·alone *is*, is adequate to the differences which it carries within it. 'Being,' he found, leaves no room for differences, — it is overpowered by them. . . . He found that the Reality can exist only as absolute Self-consciousness, as a Spirit, who is universal, and who knows himself in all things. In all this he is dealing, not simply with thoughts, but with Reality." Prof. Jones's vindication of Hegel, however, still leaves it undecided whether that philosopher regarded the divine self-consciousness as distinct from that of finite beings, or as simply inclusive of theirs. See John Caird, Fund. Ideas of Christianity, 1 : 109.

5. Our intuitive conviction of the existence of a God of absolute perfection compels us to conceive of God as possessed of every highest quality and attribute of men, and therefore, especially, of that which constitutes the chief dignity of the human spirit, its personality.

Diman, Theistic Argument, 328 — " We have no right to represent the supreme Cause as inferior to ourselves, yet we do this when we describe it under phrases derived from physical causation." Mivart, Lessons from Nature, 351 —" We cannot conceive of anything as impersonal, yet of higher nature than our own, — any being that has not knowledge and will must be indefinitely inferior to one who has them." Lotze holds truly, not that God is *supra*-personal, but that man is *infra*-personal, seeing that in the infinite Being alone is self-subsistence, and therefore perfect personality. Knight, Essays in Philosophy, 224 — " The radical feature of personality is the survival of a permanent self, under all the fleeting or deciduous phases of experience; in other words, the personal identity that is involved in the assertion ' I am.' . . . Is limitation a necessary adjunct of that notion ? " Seth, Hegelianism : " As in us there is more *for ourselves* than *for others*, so in God there is more of thought *for himself* than he manifests *to us*. Hegel's doctrine is that of immanence without transcendence." Heinrich Heine was a pupil and intimate friend of Hegel. He says : " I was young and proud, and it pleased my vain-glory when I learned from Hegel that the true God was not, as my grandmother believed, the God who lived in heaven, but was rather *myself upon the earth*." John Fiske, Idea of God, xvi — " Since our notion of force is purely a generalization from our subjective sensations of overcoming resistance, there is scarcely less anthropomorphism in the phrase ' Infinite Power' than in the phrase ' Infinite Person.' We must symbolize Deity in some form that has meaning to us; we cannot symbolize it as physical ; we are bound to symbolize it as psychical. Hence we may say, God is Spirit. This implies God's personality."

6. Its objection to the divine personality, that over against the Infinite there can be in eternity past no non-ego to call forth self-consciousness, is refuted by considering that even man's cognition of the non-ego logically presupposes knowledge of the ego, from which the non-ego is distinguished ; that, in an absolute mind, self-consciousness cannot be conditioned, as in the case of finite mind, upon contact with a not-self ; and that, if the distinguishing of self from a not-self were an essential condition of divine self-consciousness, the eternal personal distinctions in the divine nature or the eternal states of the divine mind might furnish such a condition.

Pfleiderer, Die Religion, 1 : 163, 190 *sq.* — " Personal self-consciousness is not primarily a distinguishing of the ego from the non-ego, but rather a distinguishing of itself from itself, *i. e.*, of the unity of the self from the plurality of its contents. . . . Before the soul distinguishes self from the not-self, it must know self — else it could not see the distinction. Its development is connected with the knowledge of the non-ego, but this is due, not to the fact of *personality*, but to the fact of *finite* personality. The mature man can live for a long time upon his own resources. God needs no other, to stir him up to mental activity. Finiteness is a hindrance to the development of our personality. Infiniteness is necessary to the highest personality." Lotze, Microcosmos, vol. 3, chapter 4; transl. in N. Eng., March, 1881 : 191-200 — " Finite spirit, not having conditions of existence in itself, can know the ego only upon occasion of knowing the non-ego. The Infinite is not so limited. He alone has an independent existence, neither introduced nor developed through anything not himself, but, in an inward activity without beginning or end, maintains himself in himself." See also Lotze, Philos. of Religion, 55-69 ; H. N. Gardiner on Lotze, in Presb. Rev., 1885 : 669-673; Webb, in Jour. Theol. Studies, 2 : 49-61.

Dorner, Glaubenslehre : " Absolute Personality = perfect consciousness of self, and perfect power over self. We need something external to waken our consciousness -- yet self-consciousness comes [logically] before consciousness of the world. It is the soul's act. Only after it has distinguished self from self, can it consciously distinguish self from another." British Quarterly, Jan. 1874 : 32, note; July, 1884 : 108 — " The ego *is thinkable* only in relation to the non-ego; but the ego is *liveable* long before any such relation." Shedd, Dogm. Theol., 1:185, 186 — In the pantheistic scheme, "God distinguishes himself from the *world*, and thereby finds the object required by the subject; .... in the Christian scheme, God distinguishes himself from *himself*, not from something that is not himself." See Julius Müller, Doctrine of Sin, 2:122-126; Christlieb, Mod. Doubt and Christ. Belief, 161-190; Hanne, Idee der absoluten Persönlichkeit; Eichhorn, Die Persönlichkeit Gottes; Seth, Hegelianism and Personality; Knight, on Personality and the Infinite, in Studies in Philos. and Lit., 70-118.

On the whole subject of Pantheism, see Martineau, Study of Religion, 2:141-194, esp. 192 — "The *personality* of God consists in his voluntary agency as free cause in an unpledged sphere, that is, a sphere transcending that of immanent law. But precisely this also it is that constitutes his *infinity*, extending his sway, after it has filled the actual, over all the possible, and giving command over indefinite alternatives. Though you might deny his infinity without prejudice to his personality, you cannot deny his personality without sacrificing his infinitude : for there is a mode of action — the *preferential*, the very mode which distinguishes rational beings — from which you exclude him "; 341 — "The metaphysicians who, in their impatience of distinction, insist on taking the sea on board the boat, swamp not only it but the thought it holds, and leave an infinitude which, as it can look into no eye and whisper into no ear, they contradict in the very act of affirming." Jean Paul Richter's "Dream": "I wandered to the farthest verge of Creation, and there I saw a *Socket*, where an *Eye* should have been, and I heard the shriek of a Fatherless World " (quoted in David Brown's Memoir of John Duncan, 49-70). Shelley, Beatrice Cenci: "Sweet Heaven, forgive weak thoughts ! If there should be No God, no Heaven, no Earth, in the void world — The wide, grey, lampless, deep, unpeopled world ! "

For the opposite view, see Biedermann, Dogmatik, 638-647 — "Only man, as finite spirit, is personal; God, as absolute spirit, is not personal. Yet in religion the mutual relations of intercourse and communion are always personal. . . . Personality is the only adequate term by which we can represent the theistic conception of God." Bruce, Providential Order, 76 — "Schopenhauer does not level up cosmic force to the human, but levels down human will-force to the cosmic. Spinoza held intellect in God to be no more like man's than the dog-star is like a dog. Hartmann added intellect to Schopenhauer's will, but the intellect is unconscious and knows no moral distinctions." See also Bruce, Apologetics, 71-90; Bowne, Philos. of Theism, 128-134, 171-186; J. M. Whiton, Am. Jour. Theol., Apl. 1901:306 — Pantheism = God consists in all things; Theism= All things consist in God, their ground, not their sum. Spirit in man shows that the infinite Spirit must be personal and transcendent Mind and Will.

IV. ETHICAL MONISM.

Ethical Monism is that method of thought which holds to a single substance, ground, or principle of being, namely, God, but which also holds to the ethical facts of God's transcendence as well as his immanence, and of God's personality as distinct from, and as guaranteeing, the personality of man.

Although we do not here assume the authority of the Bible, reserving our proof of this to the next following division on The Scriptures a Revelation from God, we may yet cite passages which show that our doctrine is not inconsistent with the teachings of holy Writ. The immanence of God is implied in all statements of his omnipresence, as for example: Ps. 139:7 *sq.* — "Whither shall I go from thy spirit? Or whither shall I flee from thy presence?" Jer. 23:23, 24 — "Am I a God at hand, saith Jehovah, and not a God afar off? . . . Do not I fill heaven and earth?" Acts 17:27, 28 — "he is not far from each one of us: for in him we live, and move, and have our being." The transcendence of God is implied in such passages as: 1 Kings 8:27 — "the heaven and the heaven of heavens cannot contain thee"; Ps. 113:5 — "that hath his seat on high"; Is. 57:15 — "the high and lofty One that inhabiteth eternity."

This is the faith of Augustine: "O God, thou hast made us for thyself, and our heart is restless till it find rest in thee. . . . I could not be, O my God, could not be at all, wert thou not in me; rather, were not I in thee, of whom are all things, by whom are all things, in whom are all things." And Anselm, in his Proslogion, says of the divine nature: "It is the essence of the being, the principle of the existence, of all things. . . . Without parts, without differences, without accidents, without changes, it might be said in a certain sense alone to exist, for in respect to it the other things which appear to be have no existence. The unchangeable Spirit is all that is, and it is this without limit, simply, interminably. It is the perfect and absolute Existence. The rest has come from non-entity, and thither returns if not supported by God. It does not exist by itself. In this sense the Creator alone exists; created things do not."

1. While Ethical Monism embraces the one element of truth contained in Pantheism — the truth that God is in all things and that all things are in God — it regards this scientific unity as entirely consistent with the facts of ethics — man's freedom, responsibility, sin, and guilt; in other words, Metaphysical Monism, or the doctrine of one substance, ground, or principle of being, is qualified by Psychological Dualism, or the doctrine that the soul is personally distinct from matter on the one hand, and from God on the other.

Ethical Monism is a monism which holds to the ethical facts of the freedom of man and the transcendence and personality of God; it is the monism of free-will, in which personality, both human and divine, sin and righteousness, God and the world, remain — two in one, and one in two — in their moral antithesis as well as their natural unity. Ladd, Introd. to Philosophy: "Dualism is yielding, in history and in the judgment-halls of reason, to a monistic philosophy. . . . Some form of philosophical monism is indicated by the researches of psycho-physics, and by that philosophy of mind which builds upon the principles ascertained by these researches. Realities correlated as are the body and the mind must have, as it were, a common ground. . . . They have their reality in the ultimate one Reality; they have their interrelated lives as expressions of the one Life which is immanent in the two. . . . Only some form of monism that shall satisfy the facts and truths to which both realism and idealism appeal can occupy the place of the true and final philosophy. . . . Monism must so construct its tenets as to preserve, or at least as not to contradict and destroy, the truths implicated in the distinction between the *me* and the *not-me*, . . . between the morally good and the morally evil. No form of monism can persistently maintain itself which erects its system upon the ruins of fundamentally ethical principles and ideals." . . . Philosophy of Mind, 411 — "Dualism must be dissolved in some ultimate monistic solution. The Being of the world, of which all particular beings are but parts, must be so conceived of as that in it can be found the one ground of all interrelated existences and activities. . . . This one Principle is an Other and an Absolute Mind."

Dorner, Hist. Doct. Person of Christ, II, 3 : 101, 231 — "The unity of essence in God and man is the great discovery of the present age. . . . The characteristic feature of all recent Christologies is the endeavor to point out the essential unity of the divine and human. To the theology of the present day, the divine and human are not mutually exclusive, but are connected magnitudes. . . . Yet faith postulates a difference between the world and God, between whom religion seeks an union. Faith does not wish to be a relation merely to itself, or to its own representations and thoughts; that would be a monologue,—faith desires a dialogue. Therefore it does not consort with a monism which recognizes only God, or only the world; it opposes such a monism as this. Duality is, in fact, a condition of true and vital unity. But duality is not dualism. It has no desire to oppose the rational demand for unity." Professor Small of Chicago: "With rare exceptions on each side, all philosophy to-day is monistic in its ontological presumptions; it is dualistic in its methodological procedures." A. H. Bradford, Age of Faith, 71 — "Men and God are the same in substance, though not identical as individuals." The theology of fifty years ago was merely individualistic, and ignored the complementary truth of solidarity. Similarly we think of the continents and islands of our globe as disjoined from one another. The dissociable sea is regarded as an absolute barrier between them. But if the ocean could be dried, we should see that all the while there had been submarine connections, and the hidden unity of all lands would appear. So the individuality of human beings, real as it is, is not the only reality. There is the profounder fact of a common life. Even the great mountain-peaks of personality are superficial distinctions, compared with the organic oneness in which they are rooted, into which they all dip down, and from which they all, like volcanoes, receive at times quick and overflowing impulses of insight, emotion and energy; see A. H. Strong. Christ in Creation and Ethical Monism, 189, 190.

2. In contrast then with the two errors of Pantheism—the denial of God's transcendence and the denial of God's personality — Ethical Monism holds that the universe, instead of being one with God and conterminous with God, is but a finite, partial and progressive manifestation of the divine Life : Matter being God's self-limitation under the law of Necessity ; Humanity being God's self-limitation under the law of Freedom ; Incarnation and Atonement being God's self-limitations under the law of Grace.

The universe is related to God as my thoughts are related to me, the thinker. I am greater than my thoughts, and my thoughts vary in moral value. Ethical Monism traces the universe back to a beginning, while Pantheism regards the universe as coëternal with God. Ethical Monism asserts God's transcendence, while Pantheism regards God as imprisoned in the universe. Ethical Monism asserts that the heaven of heavens cannot contain him, but that contrariwise the whole universe taken together, with its elements and forces, its suns and systems, is but a light breath from his mouth, or a drop of dew upon the fringe of his garment. Upton, Hibbert Lectures : "The Eternal is present in every finite thing, and is felt and known to be present in every rational soul; but still is not broken up into individualities, but ever remains one and the same eternal substance, one and the same unifying principle, immanently and indivisibly present in every one of that countless plurality of finite individuals into which man's analyzing understanding dissects the Cosmos." James Martineau, in 19th Century, Apl. 1895 : 559 — "What is Nature but the province of God's pledged and habitual causality? And what is Spirit, but the province of his free causality, responding to the needs and affections of his children? . . . God is not a retired architect, who may now and then be called in for repairs. Nature is not self-active, and God's agency is not intrusive." Calvin : Pie hoc potest dici, Deum esse Naturam.

With this doctrine, many poets show their sympathy. "Every fresh and new creation, A divine improvisation, From the heart of God proceeds." Robert Browning asserts God's immanence ; Hohenstiel-Schwangau : "This is the glory that, in all conceived Or felt, or known, I recognize a Mind—Not mine, but like mine — for the double joy, Making all things for me, and me for him "; Ring and Book, Pope : "O thou, as represented to me here In such conception as my soul allows — Under thy measureless, my atom-width ! Man's mind, what is it but a convex glass, Wherein are gathered all the scattered points Picked out of the immensity of sky, To reunite there, be our heaven for earth, Our Known Unknown, our God revealed to man ? " But Browning also asserts God's transcendence : in Death in the Desert, we read : "Man is not God, but hath God's end to serve, A Master to obey, a Cause to take, Somewhat to cast off, somewhat to become "; in Christmas Eve, the poet derides "The important stumble Of adding, he, the sage and humble, Was also one with the Creator "; he tells us that it was God's plan to make man in his image : "To create man, and then leave him Able, his own word saith, to grieve him ; But able to glorify him too, As a mere machine could never do That prayed or praised, all unaware Of its fitness for aught but praise or prayer, Made perfect as a thing of course. . . . God, whose pleasure brought Man into being, stands away, As it were, a hand-breadth off, to give Room for the newly made to live And look at him from a place apart And use his gifts of brain and heart "; "Life's business being just the terrible choice."

So Tennyson's Higher Pantheism : "The sun, the moon, the stars, the seas, the hills, and the plains, Are not these, O soul, the vision of Him who reigns? Dark is the world to thee; thou thyself art the reason why ; For is not He all but thou, that hast power to feel 'I am I'? Speak to him, thou, for he hears, and spirit with spirit can meet; Closer is he than breathing, and nearer than hands and feet. And the ear of man cannot hear, and the eye of man cannot see; But if we could see and hear, this vision — were it not He? " Also Tennyson's Ancient Sage : " But that one ripple on the boundless deep Feels that the deep is boundless, and itself Forever changing form, but evermore One with the boundless motion of the deep "; and In Memoriam : " One God, one law, one element, And one far-off divine event, Toward which the whole creation moves." Emerson : "The day of days, the greatest day in the feast of life, is that in which the inward eye opens to the unity of things "; " In the mud and scum of things Something always, always sings." Mrs. Browning : " Earth is crammed with heaven, And every common bush afire with God ; But only he who sees takes off his shoes." So manhood is itself potentially a divine thing. All life, in all its vast variety, can have but one Source. It is either one God, above all, through all, and in all, or it is no God at all. E. M. Poteat, On Chesapeake Bay : "Night's radiant glory overhead, A softer glory there below, Deep answered unto deep, and said : A kindred fire in us doth glow. For life is one — of sea and stars, Of God and man, of earth and heaven — And by no theologic bars Shall my scant life from God's be riven." See Professor Henry Jones, Robert Browning.

3.   The immanence of God, as the one substance, ground and principle of being, does not destroy, but rather guarantees, the individuality and rights of each portion of the universe, so that there is variety of rank and endowment.   In the case of moral beings, worth is determined by the degree of their voluntary recognition and appropriation of the divine. While God is all, he is also in all ; so making the universe a graded and progressive manifestation of himself, both in his love for righteousness and his opposition to moral evil.

It has been charged that the doctrine of monism necessarily involves moral indifference ; that the divine presence in all things breaks down all distinctions of rank and makes each thing equal to every other ; that the evil as well as the good is legitimated and consecrated. Of pantheistic monism all this is true, – it is not true of ethical monism ; for ethical monism is the monism that recognizes the ethical fact of personal intelligence and will in both God and man, and with these God's purpose in making the universe a varied manifestation of himself. The worship of cats and bulls and crocodiles in ancient Egypt, and the deification of lust in the Brahmanic temples of India, were expressions of a non-ethical monism, which saw in God no moral attributes, and which identified God with his manifestations. As an illustration of the mistakes into which the critics of monism may fall for lack of discrimination between monism that is pantheistic and monism that is ethical, we quote from Emma Marie Caillard : " Integral parts of God are, on monistic premises, liars, sensualists, murderers, evil livers and evil thinkers of every description. Their crimes and their passions enter intrinsically into the divine experience. The infinite Individual in his wholeness may reject them indeed, but none the less are these evil finite individuals constituent parts of him, even as the twigs of a tree, though they are not the tree, and though the tree transcends any or all of them, are yet constituent parts of it. Can he whose universal consciousness includes and defines all finite consciousnesses be other than responsible for all finite actions and motives ? "

To this indictment we may reply in the words of Bowne, The Divine Immanence, 130-133 — " Some weak heads have been so heated by the new wine of immanence as to put all things on the same level, and make men and mice of equal value. But there is nothing in the dependence of all things on God to remove their distinctions of value. One confused talker of this type was led to say that he had no trouble with the notion of a divine man, as he believed in a divine oyster. Others have used the doctrine to cancel moral differences ; for if God be in all things, and if all things represent his will, then whatever is is right. But this too is hasty. Of course even the evil will is not independent of God, but lives and moves and has its being in and through the divine. But through its mysterious power of selfhood and self-determination the evil will is able to assume an attitude of hostility to the divine law, which forthwith vindicates itself by appropriate reactions.

" These reactions are not divine in the highest or ideal sense. They represent nothing which God desires or in which he delights ; but they are divine in the sense that they are things to be done under the circumstances. The divine reaction in the case of the good is distinct from the divine reaction against evil. Both are divine as representing God's action, but only the former is divine in the sense of representing God's approval and sympathy. All things serve, said Spinoza. The good serve, and are furthered by their service. The bad also serve and are used up in the serving. According to Jonathan Edwards, the wicked are useful ' in being acted upon and disposed of.' As ' vessels of dishonor ' they may reveal the majesty of God. There is nothing therefore in the divine immanence, in its only tenable form, to cancel moral distinctions or to minify retribution. The divine reaction against iniquity is even more solemn in this doctrine. The besetting God is the eternal and unescapable environment ; and only as we are in harmony with him can there be any peace. . . . What God thinks of sin, and what his will is concerning it can be plainly seen in the natural consequences which attend it. . . . In law itself we are face to face with God; and natural consequences have a supernatural meaning."

4. Since Christ is the Logos of God, the immanent God, God revealed in Nature, in Humanity, in Redemption, Ethical Monism recognizes the universe as created, upheld, and governed by the same Being who in the course of history was manifest in human form and who made atonement for human sin by his death on Calvary. The secret of the universe and the key to its mysteries are to be found in the Cross.

John 1 : 1–4 (marg.), 14, 18 — "In the beginning was the Word, and the Word was with God, and the Word was God. The same was in the beginning with God. All things were made through him; and without him was not any thing made. That which hath been made was life in him; and the life was the light of men. . . . And the Word became flesh, and dwelt among us. . . . No man hath seen God at any time; the only begotten Son, who is in the bosom of the Father, he hath declared him." Col. 1 : 16, 17 — "for in him were all things created, in the heavens and upon the earth, things visible and things invisible, whether thrones or dominions or principalities or powers; all things have been created through him and unto him; and he is before all things, and in him all things consist." Heb. 1 : 2, 3 — "his Son . . . through whom also he made the worlds . . . upholding all things by the word of his power"; Eph. 1 : 22, 23 — "the church, which is his body, the fulness of him that filleth all in all" — fills all things with all that they contain of truth, beauty, and goodness; Col. 2 : 2, 3, 9 — "the mystery of God, even Christ, in whom are all the treasures of wisdom and knowledge hidden. . . . for in him dwelleth all the fulness of the Godhead bodily."

This view of the relation of the universe to God lays the foundation for a Christian application of recent philosophical doctrine. Matter is no longer blind and dead, but is spiritual in its nature, not in the sense that it *is* spirit, but in the sense that it is the continual *manifestation* of spirit, just as my thoughts are a living and continual manifestation of myself. Yet matter does not consist simply in *ideas*, for ideas, deprived of an external object and of an internal subject, are left suspended in the air. Ideas are the product of Mind. But matter is known only as the operation of force, and force is the product of Will. Since this force works in rational ways, it can be the product only of Spirit. The system of forces which we call the universe is the immediate product of the mind and will of God; and, since Christ is the mind and will of God in exercise, Christ is the Creator and Upholder of the universe. Nature is the omnipresent Christ, manifesting God to creatures.

Christ is the principle of cohesion, attraction, interaction, not only in the physical universe, but in the intellectual and moral universe as well. In all our knowing, the knower and known are "connected by some Being who is their reality," and this being is Christ, "the Light which lighteth every man" (John 1 : 9). We *know* in Christ, just as "in him we live, and move, and have our being" (Acts 17 : 28). As the attraction of gravitation and the principle of evolution are only other names for Christ, so he is the basis of inductive reasoning and the ground of moral unity in the creation. I am bound to lo e my neighbor as myself because he has in him the same life that is in me, the life of God in Christ. The Christ in whom all humanity is created, and in whom all humanity consists, holds together the moral universe, drawing all men to himself and so drawing them to God. Through him God "reconciles all things unto himself . . . whether things upon the earth, or things in the heavens" (Col. 1 : 20).

As Pantheism — exclusive immanence — God imprisoned, so Deism — exclusive transcendence — God banished. Ethical Monism holds to the truth contained in each of these systems, while avoiding their respective errors. It furnishes the basis for a new interpretation of many theological as well as of many philosophical doctrines. It helps our understanding of the Trinity. If within the bounds of God's being there can exist multitudinous finite personalities, it becomes easier to comprehend how within those same bounds there can be three eternal and infinite personalities, — indeed, the integration of plural consciousnesses in an all-embracing divine consciousness may find a valid analogy in the integration of subordinate consciousnesses in the unit-personality of man ; see Baldwin, Handbook of Psychology, Feeling and Will, 53, 54.

Ethical Monism, since it is ethical, leaves room for human wills and for their freedom. While man could never break the natural bond which united him to God, he could break the spiritual bond and introduce into creation a principle of discord and evil. Tie a cord tightly about your finger; you partially isolate the finger, diminish its nutrition, bring about atrophy and disease. So there has been given to each intelligent and moral agent the power, spiritually to isolate himself from God while yet he is naturally joined to God. As humanity is created in Christ and lives only in Christ, man's self-isolation is his moral separation from Christ. Simon, Redemption of Man, 339 — "Rejecting Christ is not so much refusal to *become* one with Christ as it is refusal to *remain* one with him, refusal to let him be our life." All men are naturally one with Christ by physical birth, before they become morally one with him by spiritual birth. They may set themselves against him and may oppose him forever. This our Lord intimates, when he tells us that there are natural branches of Christ, which do not "abide in the vine" or "bear fruit," and so are "cast forth," "withered," and "burned" (John 15 : 4-6).

Ethical Monism, however, since it is Monism, enables us to understand the principle of the Atonement. Though God's holiness binds him to punish sin, the Christ who has joined himself to the sinner must share the sinner's punishment. He who is the life of humanity must take upon his own heart the burden of shame and penalty that belongs to his members. Tie the cord about your finger; not only the finger suffers pain, but also the heart; the life of the whole system rouses itself to put away the evil, to untie the cord, to free the diseased and suffering member. Humanity is bound to Christ, as the finger to the body. Since human nature is one of the "all things" that "consist" or hold together in Christ (Col. 1:17), and man's sin is a self-perversion of a part of Christ's own body, the whole must be injured by the self-inflicted injury of the part, and "it must needs be that Christ should suffer" (Acts 17:3). Simon, Redemption of Man, 321 — "If the Logos is the Mediator of the divine immanence in creation, especially in man; if men are differentiations of the effluent divine energy; and if the Logos is the immanent controlling principle of all differentiation — *i. e.*, the principle of all *form* — must not the self-perversion of these human differentiations react on him who is their constitutive principle?" A more full explanation of the relations of Ethical Monism to other doctrines must be reserved to our separate treatment of the Trinity, Creation, Sin, Atonement, Regeneration. Portions of the subject are treated by Upton, Hibbert Lectures; Le Conte, in Royce's Conception of God, 43-50; Bowne, Theory of Thought and Knowledge, 297-301, 311-317, and Immanence of God, 5-32, 116-153; Ladd, Philos. of Knowledge, 574-590, and Theory of Reality, 525-529; Edward Caird, Evolution of Religion, 2 : 48; Ward, Naturalism and Agnosticism, 2 : 258-283; Göschel, quoted in Dorner, Hist. Doct. Person of Christ, 5 : 170. An attempt has been made to treat the whole subject by A. H. Strong, Christ in Creation and Ethical Monism, 1-86, 141-162, 166-180, 186-208.

PART III.

THE SCRIPTURES A REVELATION FROM GOD.

CHAPTER I.

PRELIMINARY CONSIDERATIONS.

I. REASONS *A PRIORI* FOR EXPECTING A REVELATION FROM GOD.

1. *Needs of man's nature.* Man's intellectual and moral nature requires, in order to preserve it from constant deterioration, and to ensure its moral growth and progress, an authoritative and helpful revelation of religious truth, of a higher and completer sort than any to which, in its present state of sin, it can attain by the use of its unaided powers. The proof of this proposition is partly psychological, and partly historical.

A. Psychological proof.—(*a*) Neither reason nor intuition throws light upon certain questions whose solution is of the utmost importance to us ; for example, Trinity, atonement, pardon, method of worship, personal existence after death. (*b*) Even the truth to which we arrive by our natural powers needs divine confirmation and authority when it addresses minds and wills perverted by sin. (*c*) To break this power of sin, and to furnish encouragement to moral effort, we need a special revelation of the merciful and helpful aspect of the divine nature.

(*a*) Bremen Lectures, 72, 73 ; Plato, Second Alcibiades, 22, 23 ; Phædo, 85 — λόγου θείου τινός. Iamblicus, περὶ τοῦ Πυθαγορικοῦ βίου, chap. 28. Æschylus, in his Agamemnon, shows how completely reason and intuition failed to supply the knowledge of God which man needs : "Renown is loud," he says, "and not to lose one's senses is God's greatest gift. . . . The being praised outrageously Is grave ; for at the eyes of such a one Is launched, from Zeus, the thunder-stone. Therefore do I decide For so much and no more prosperity Than of his envy passes unespied." Though the gods might have favorites, they did not love men as men, but rather, envied and hated them. William James, Is Life Worth Living ? in Internat. Jour. Ethics, Oct. 1895 : 10 — "All we know of good and beauty proceeds from nature, but none the less all we know of evil. . . . To such a harlot we owe no moral allegiance. . . . If there be a divine Spirit of the universe, nature, such as we know her, cannot possibly be its ultimate word to man. Either there is no Spirit revealed in nature, or else it is inadequately revealed there ; and, as all the higher religions have assumed, what we call visible nature, or *this* world, must be but a veil and surface-show whose full meaning resides in a supplementary unseen or *other* world."

(*b*) *Versus* Socrates : Men will do right, if they only know the right. Pfleiderer, Philos. Relig., 1:219 — "In opposition to the opinion of Socrates that badness rests upon ignorance, Aristotle already called the fact to mind that the doing of the good is not always combined with the knowing of it, seeing that it depends also on the passions. If badness consisted only in the want of knowledge, then those who are theoretically most cultivated must also be morally the best, which no one will venture to assert." W. S. Lilly, On Shibboleths: "Ignorance is often held to be the root of all evil. But mere knowledge cannot transform character. It cannot minister to a mind diseased. It cannot convert the will from bad to good. It may turn crime into different channels, and render it less easy to detect. It does not change man's natural propensities or his disposition to gratify them at the expense of others. Knowledge makes the good man more powerful for good, the bad man more powerful for evil. And that is all it can do." Gore, Incarnation, 174—"We must not depreciate the method of argument, for Jesus and Paul occasionally used it in a Socratic fashion, but we must recognize that it is not the basis of the Christian system nor the primary method of Christianity." Martineau, in Nineteenth Century, 1:331, 531, and Types, 1:112—"Plato dissolved the idea of the right into that of the good, and this again was indistinguishably mingled with that of the true and the beautiful." See also Flint, Theism, 305.

(c) *Versus* Thomas Paine: "Natural religion teaches us, without the possibility of being mistaken, all that is necessary or proper to be known." Plato, Laws, 9:854, c, for substance: "Be good; but, if you cannot, then kill yourself." Farrar, Darkness and Dawn, 75—"Plato says that man will never know God until God has revealed himself in the guise of suffering man, and that, when all is on the verge of destruction, God sees the distress of the universe, and, placing himself at the rudder, restores it to order." Prometheus, the type of humanity, can never be delivered "until some god descends for him into the black depths of Tartarus." Seneca in like manner teaches that man cannot save himself. He says: "Do you wonder that men go to the gods? God comes *to* men, yes, *into* men." We are sinful, and God's thoughts are not as our thoughts, nor his ways as our ways. Therefore he must make known his thoughts to us, teach us what we are, what true love is, and what will please him. Shaler, Interpretation of Nature, 227—"The inculcation of moral truths can be successfully effected only in the personal way; . . . it demands the influence of personality; . . . the weight of the impression depends upon the voice and the eye of a teacher." In other words, we need not only the exercise of authority, but also the manifestation of love.

B. Historical proof. — (*a*) The knowledge of moral and religious truth possessed by nations and ages in which special revelation is unknown is grossly and increasingly imperfect. (*b*) Man's actual condition in ante-Christian times, and in modern heathen lands, is that of extreme moral depravity. (*c*) With this depravity is found a general conviction of helplessness, and on the part of some nobler natures, a longing after, and hope of, aid from above.

Pythagoras: "It is not easy to know [duties], except men were taught them by God himself, or by some person who had received them from God, or obtained the knowledge of them through some divine means." Socrates: "Wait with patience, till we know with certainty how we ought to behave ourselves toward God and man." Plato: "We will wait for one, be he a God or an inspired man, to instruct us in our duties and to take away the darkness from our eyes." Disciple of Plato: "Make probability our raft, while we sail through life, unless we could have a more sure and safe conveyance, such as some divine communication would be." Plato thanked God for three things: first, that he was born a rational soul; secondly, that he was born a Greek; and, thirdly, that he lived in the days of Socrates. Yet, with all these advantages, he had only probability for a raft, on which to navigate strange seas of thought far beyond his depth, and he longed for "a more sure word of prophecy" (2 Pet. 1 : 19). See references and quotations in Peabody, Christianity the Religion of Nature, 35, and in Luthardt, Fundamental Truths, 156-172, 335-338 ; Farrar, Seekers after God ; Garbett, Dogmatic Faith, 187.

2. *Presumption of supply.* What we know of God, by nature, affords ground for hope that these wants of our intellectual and moral being will be met by a corresponding supply, in the shape of a special divine revelation. We argue this :

(*a*) From our necessary conviction of God's wisdom. Having made man a spiritual being, for spiritual ends, it may be hoped that he will furnish the means needed to secure these ends. (*b*) From the actual, though incomplete, revelation already given in nature. Since God has actually undertaken to make himself known to men, we may hope that he will finish the work he has begun. (c) From the general connection of want and supply. The higher our needs, the more intricate and ingenious are, in general, the contrivances for meeting them. We may therefore hope that the highest want will be all the more surely met. (d) From analogies of nature and history. Signs of reparative goodness in nature and of forbearance in providential dealings lead us to hope that, while justice is executed, God may still make known some way of restoration for sinners.

(a) There were two stages in Dr. John Duncan's escape from pantheism: 1. when he came first to b lieve in the existence of God, and "danced for joy upon the brig o' Dee"; and 2. when, under Malan's influence, he came also to believe that "God meant that we should know him." In the story in the old Village Reader, the mother broke completely down when she found that her son was likely to grow up stupid, but her tears conquer d him and made him intelligent. Laura Bridgman was blind, deaf and dumb, and had but small sense of taste or smell. When her mother, after long separation, went to her in Boston, the mother's heart was in distress lest the daughter should not recognize her. When at last, by some peculiar mother's sign, she pierced the veil of insensibility, it was a glad time for both. So God, our Father, tries to reveal himself to our blind, deaf and dumb souls. The agony of the Cross is the sign of God's distress over the insensibility of humanity which sin has caused. If he is the Maker of man's being, he will surely seek to fit it for that communion with himself for which it was designed.

(b) Gore, Incarnation, 52, 53 — "Nature is a first volume, in itself incomplete, and demanding a s ond volume, which is Christ." (c) R. T. Smith, Man's Knowledge of Man and of God, 88 — "Mendicants do not ply their calling for years in a desert where there are no givers. Enough of supply has been received to keep the sense of want alive." (d) In the natural arrangements for the healing of bruises in plants and for the mending of broken bones in the animal creation, in the provision of remedial agents for the ure f human diseases, and especially in the delay to inflict punishment upon the transgressor and the space given him for repentance, we have some indications, which, if uncontradicted by other evidence, might lead us to regard the God of nature as a God of forbearance and mercy. Plutarch's treatise "De Sera Numinis Vindicta" is proof that his thought had occurred to the heathen. It may be doubted, indeed, whether a heathen religion could even continue to exist, without embracing in it some element of hope. Yet this very delay in the execution of the divine judgments gave its own occasion for doubting the existence of a God who was both good and just. "Truth forever on the scaffold, Wrong forever on the throne," is a scandal to the divine government which only the sacrifice of Christ can fully remove.

The problem presents itself also in the Old Testament. In Job 21, and in Psalms, 17, 37, 49, 73, there are partial answers; see Job 21: 7 — "Wherefore do the wicked live, Become old, yea, wax mighty in power?" 24: 1 — "Why are not judgment times determined by the Almighty? And they that know him, why see they not his days?" The New Testament intimates the existence of a witness to God's goodness among the heathen, while at the same time it declares that the full knowledge of forgiveness and salvation is brought only by Christ. Compare Acts 14: 17 — "And yet he left not himself without witness, in that he did good, and gave you from heaven rains and fruitful seasons, filling your hearts with food and gladness"; 17: 25-27 — "he himself giveth to all life, and breath, and all things; and he made of one every nation of men . . . that they should seek God, if haply they might feel after him and find him"; Rom. 2: 4 - - "the goodness of God leadeth thee to repentance"; 3: 25 — "the passing over of the sins done aforetime, in the forbearance of God"; Eph. 3: 9 — "to make all men see what is the dispensation of the mystery which for ages hath been hid in God"; 2 Tim. 1: 10 — "our Savior Christ Jesus, who abolished death, and brought life and incorruption to light through the gospel." See Hackett's edition of the treatise of Plutarch, as also Bowen, Metaph. and Ethics, 462-487; Diman, Theistic Argument, 371.

We conclude this section upon the reasons a priori for expecting a revelation from God with the acknowledgment that the facts warrant that degree of expectation which we call hope, rather than that larger degree of expectation which we call assurance: and this, for the reason that, while conscience gives proof that God is a God of holiness, we have not, from the light of nature, equal evidence that God is a God of love. Reason teaches man that, as a sinner, he merits condemnation ; but he cannot, from reason alone, know that God will have mercy upon him and provide salvation. His doubts can be removed only by God's own voice, assuring him of "redemption . . . the forgiveness of . . . trespasses" (Eph. 1 : 7) and revealing to him the way in which that forgiveness has been rendered possible.

Conscience knows no pardon, and no Savior. Hovey, Manual of Christian Theology, 9, seems to us to go too far when he says · " Even natural affection and conscience afford some clue to the goodness and holiness of God, though much more is needed by one who undertakes the study of Christian theology." We grant that natural affection gives some clue to God's goodness, but we regard conscience as reflecting only God's holiness and his hatred of sin. We agree with Alexander McLaren : " Does God's love need to be proved? Yes, as all paganism shows. Gods vicious, gods careless, gods cruel, gods beautiful, there are in abundance ; but where is there a god who loves?"

II. Marks of the Revelation man may expect.

1. *As to its substance.* We may expect this later revelation not to contradict, but to confirm and enlarge, the knowledge of God which we derive from nature, while it remedies the defects of natural religion and throws light upon its problems.

Isaiah's appeal is to God's previous communications of truth : Is. 8 : 20 — "To the law and to the testimony ! if they speak not according to this word, surely there is no morning for them." And Malachi follows the example of Isaiah ; Mal. 4 : 4 — "Remember ye the law of Moses my servant." Our Lord himself based his claims upon the former utterances of God : Luke 24 : 27 — "beginning from Moses and from all the prophets, he interpreted to them in all the scriptures the things concerning himself."

2. *As to its method.* We may expect it to follow God's methods of procedure in other communications of truth.

Bishop Butler (Analogy, part ii, chap. iii) has denied that there is any possibility of judging *a priori* how a divine revelation will be given. " We are in no sort judges beforehand," he says, " by what methods, or in what proportion, it were to be expected that this supernatural light and instruction would be afforded us." But Bishop Butler somewhat later in his great work (part ii, chap. iv) shows that God's progressive plan in revelation has its analogy in the slow, successive steps by which God accomplishes his ends in nature. We maintain that the revelation in nature affords certain presumptions with regard to the revelation of grace, such for example as those mentioned below.

Leslie Stephen, in Nineteenth Century, Feb. 1891 : 189 — " Butler answered the argument of the deists, that the God of Christianity was unjust, by arguing that the God of nature was equally unjust. James Mill, admitting the analogy, refused to believe in either God. Dr. Martineau has said, for similar reasons, that Butler ' wrote one of the most terrible persuasives to atheism ever produced.' So J. H. Newman's ' kill or cure ' argument is essentially that God has either revealed nothing, or has made revelations in some other places than in the Bible. His argument, like Butler's, may be as good a persuasive to scepticism as to belief." To this indictment by Leslie Stephen we reply that it has cogency only so long as we ignore the fact of human sin. Granting this fact, our world becomes a world of discipline, probation and redemption, and both the God of nature and the God of Christianity are cleared from all suspicion of injustice. The analogy between God's methods in the Christian system and his methods in nature becomes an argument in favor of the former.

(*a*) That of continuous historical development,—that it will be given in germ to early ages, and will be more fully unfolded as the race is prepared to receive it.

Instances of continuous development in God's impartations are found in geological history ; in the growth of the sciences ; in the progressive education of the individual and of the race. No other religion but Christianity shows "a steady historical progress of the vision of one infinite Character unfolding itself to man through a period of many centuries." See sermon by Dr. Temple, on the Education of the World, in Essays and Reviews; Rogers, Superhuman Origin of the Bible, 374-384; Walker, Philosophy of the Plan of Salvation. On the gradualness of revelation, see Fisher, Nature and Method of Revelation, 46-86; Arthur H. Hallam, in John Brown's Rab and his Friends, 282—"Revelation is a gradual approximation of the infinite Being to the ways and thoughts of finite humanity." A little fire can kindle a city or a world; but ten times the heat of that little fire, if widely diffused, would not kindle anything.

(*b*) That of original delivery to a single nation, and to single persons in that nation, that it may through them be communicated to mankind.

Each nation represents an idea. As the Greek had a genius for liberty and beauty, and the Roman a genius for organization and law, so the Hebrew nation had a "genius for religion" (Renan); this last, however, would have been useless without special divine aid and superintendence, as witness other productions of this same Semitic race, such as Bel and the Dragon, in the Old Testament Apocrypha; the gospels of the Apocryphal New Testament; and later still, the Talmud and the Koran.

The O. T. Apocrypha relates that, when Daniel was thrown a second time into the lions' den, an angel seized Habbakuk in Judea by the hair of his head and carried him with a bowl of pottage to give to Daniel for his dinner. There were seven lions, and Daniel was among them seven days and nights. Tobias starts from his father's house to secure his inheritance, and his little dog goes with him. On the banks of the great river a great fish threatens to devour him, but he captures and despoils the fish. He finally returns successful to his father's house, and his little dog goes in with him. In the Apocryphal Gospels, Jesus carries water in his mantle when his pitcher is broken; makes clay birds on the Sabbath, and, when rebuked, causes them to fly; strikes a youthful companion with death, and then curses his accusers with blindness; mocks his teachers, and resents control. Later Moslem legends declare that Mohammed caused darkness at noon; whereupon the moon flew to him, went seven times around the Kaâba, bowed, entered his right sleeve, split into two halves after slipping out at the left, and the two halves, after retiring to the extreme east and west, were reunited. These products of the Semitic race show that neither the influence of environment nor a native genius for religion furnishes an adequate explanation of our Scriptures. As the flame on Elijah's altar was caused, not by the dead sticks, but by the fire from heaven, so only the inspiration of the Almighty can explain the unique revelation of the Old and New Testaments.

The Hebrews saw God in conscience. For the most genuine expression of their life we "must look beneath the surface, in the soul, where worship and aspiration and prophetic faith come face to face with God" (Genung, Epic of the Inner Life, 28). But the Hebrew religion needed to be supplemented by the sight of God in reason, and in the beauty of the world. The Greeks had the love of knowledge, and the æsthetic sense. Butcher, Aspects of the Greek Genius, 34—"The Phœnicians taught the Greeks how to write, but it was the Greeks who wrote." Aristotle was the beginner of science, and outside the Aryan race none but the Saracens ever felt the scientific impulse. But the Greek made his problem clear by striking all the unknown quantities out of it. Greek thought would never have gained universal currency and permanence if it had not been for Roman jurisprudence and imperialism. England has contributed her constitutional government, and America her manhood suffrage and her religious freedom. So a definite thought of God is incorporated in each nation, and each nation has a message to every other. Acts 17: 26 — God "made of one every nation of men to dwell on all the face of the earth, having determined their appointed seasons, and the bounds of their habitation "; Rom. 3: 12 — "What advantage then hath the Jew? . . . first of all, that they were entrusted with the oracles of God." God's choice of the Hebrew nation, as the repository and communicator of religious truth, is analogous to his choice of other nations, as the repositories and communicators of æsthetic, scientific, governmental truth.

Hegel: "No nation that has played a weighty and active part in the world's history has ever issued from the simple development of a single race along the unmodified lines of blood-relationship. There must be differences, conflicts, a composition of opposed forces." The conscience of the Hebrew, the thought of the Greek, the organization of the Latin, the personal loyalty of the Teuton, must all be united to form a perfect whole. "While the Greek church was orthodox, the Latin church was Catholic;

while the Greek treated of the two wills in Christ, the Latin treated of the harmony of our wills with God; while the Latin saved through a corporation, the Teuton saved through personal faith." Brereton, in Educational Review, Nov. 1901: 339— "The problem of France is that of the religious orders; that of Germany, the construction of society; that of America, capital and labor." Pfleiderer, Philos. Religion, 1: 183, 184—"Great ideas never come from the masses, but from marked individuals. These ideas, when propounded, however, awaken an echo in the masses, which shows that the ideas had been slumbering unconsciously in the souls of others." The hour strikes, and a Newton appears, who interprets God's will in nature. So the hour strikes, and a Moses or a Paul appears, who interprets God's will in morals and religion. The few grains of wheat found in the clasped hand of the Egyptian mummy would have been utterly lost if one grain had been sown in Europe, a second in Asia, a third in Africa, and a fourth in America; all being planted together in a flower-pot, and their product in a garden-bed, and the still later fruit in a farmer's field, there came at last to be a sufficient crop of new Mediterranean wheat to distribute to all the world. So God followed his ordinary method in giving religious truth first to a single nation and to chosen individuals in that nation, that through them it might be given to all mankind. See British Quarterly, Jan. 1874: art.: Inductive Theology.

(c) That of preservation in written and accessible documents, handed down from those to whom the revelation is first communicated.

Alphabets, writing, books, are our chief dependence for the history of the past; all the great religions of the world are book-religions; the Karens expected their teachers in the new religion to bring to them a book. But notice that false religions have scriptures, but not Scripture; their sacred books lack the principle of unity which is furnished by divine inspiration. H. P. Smith, Biblical Scholarship and Inspiration, 68 —"Mohammed discovered that the Scriptures of the Jews were the source of their religion. He called them a 'book-people,' and endeavored to construct a similar code for his disciples. In it God is the only speaker; all its contents are made known to the prophet by direct revelation; its Arabic style is perfect; its text is incorruptible; it is absolute authority in law, science and history." The Koran is a grotesque human parody of the Bible; its exaggerated pretensions of divinity, indeed, are the best proof that it is of purely human origin. Scripture, on the other hand, makes no such claims for itself, but points to Christ as the sole and final authority. In this sense we may say with Clarke, Christian Theology, 20—"Christianity is not a book-religion, but a life-religion. The Bible does not give us Christ, but Christ gives us the Bible." Still it is true that for our knowledge of Christ we are almost wholly dependent upon Scripture. In giving his revelation to the world, God has followed his ordinary method of communicating and preserving truth by means of written documents. Recent investigations, however, now render it probable that the Karen expectation of a book was the survival of the teaching of the Nestorian missionaries, who as early as the eighth century penetrated the remotest parts of Asia, and left in the wall of the city of Singwadu in Northwestern China a tablet as a monument of their labors. On book-revelation, see Rogers, Eclipse of Faith, 73-96, 281-304.

3. *As to its attestation.* We may expect that this revelation will be accompanied by evidence that its author is the same being whom we have previously recognized as God of nature. This evidence must constitute (a) a manifestation of God himself; (b) in the outward as well as the inward world; (c) such as only God's power or knowledge can make; and (d) such as cannot be counterfeited by the evil, or mistaken by the candid, soul. In short, we may expect God to attest by miracles and by prophecy, the divine mission and authority of those to whom he communicates a revelation. Some such outward sign would seem to be necessary, not only to assure the original recipient that the supposed revelation is not a vagary of his own imagination, but also to render the revelation received by a single individual authoritative to all (compare Judges 6 : 17, 36-40 — Gideon asks a sign, for himself: 1 K. 18: 36-38 — Elijah asks a sign, for others)./

But in order that our positive proof of a divine revelation may not be embarrassed by the suspicion that the miraculous and prophetic elements in the Scripture history create a presumption against its credibility, it will be desirable to take up at this point the general subject of miracles and prophecy.

III. MIRACLES, AS ATTESTING A DIVINE REVELATION.

1. *Definition of Miracle.*

A. Preliminary Definition.—A miracle is an event palpable to the senses, produced for a religious purpose by the immediate agency of God; an event therefore which, though not contravening any law of nature, the laws of nature, if fully known, would not without this agency of God be competent to explain.

This definition corrects several erroneous conceptions of the miracle :—
(*a*) A miracle is not a suspension or violation of natural law; since natural law is in operation at the time of the miracle just as much as before.
(*b*) A miracle is not a sudden product of natural agencies—a product merely foreseen, by him who appears to work it; it is the effect of a will outside of nature. (*c*) A miracle is not an event without a cause; since it has for its cause a direct volition of God. (*d*) A miracle is not an irrational or capricious act of God; but an act of wisdom, performed in accordance with the immutable laws of his being, so that in the same circumstances the same course would be again pursued. (*e*) A miracle is not contrary to experience; since it is not contrary to experience for a new cause to be followed by a new effect. (*f*) A miracle is not a matter of internal experience, like regeneration or illumination; but is an event palpable to the senses, which may serve as an objective proof to all that the worker of it is divinely commissioned as a religious teacher.

For various definitions of miracles, see Alexander, Christ and Christianity, 302. On the whole subject, see Mozley, Miracles; Christlieb, Mod. Doubt and Christ. Belief, 285-339; Fisher, in Princeton Rev., Nov. 1880, and Jan. 1881; A. H. Strong, Philosophy and Religion, 129-147, and in Baptist Review, April, 1879. The definition given above is intended simply as a definition of the miracles of the Bible, or, in other words, of the events which profess to attest a divine revelation in the Scriptures. The New Testament designates these events in a two-fold way, viewing them either subjectively, as producing effects upon men, or objectively, as revealing the power and wisdom of God. In the former aspect they are called τέρατα, 'wonders,' and σημεῖα 'signs,' (John 4: 48; Acts 2: 22). In the latter aspect they are called δυνάμεις, 'powers,' and ἔργα, 'works,' (Mat. 7: 22; John 14: 11). See H. B. Smith, Lect. on Apologetics, 90-116, esp. 94—"σημεῖον, sign, marking the purpose or object, the moral end, placing the event in connection with revelation." The Bible Union Version uniformly and properly renders τέρας by 'wonder, δυνάμις by 'miracle,' ἔργον by 'work,' and σημεῖον by 'sign.' Goethe, Faust: "Alles Vergängliche ist nur ein Gleichniss: Das Unzulängliche wird hier Ereigniss "—"Everything transitory is but a parable; The unattainable appears as solid fact." So the miracles of the New Testament are acted parables,—Christ opens the eyes of the blind to show that he is the Light of the world, multiplies the loaves to show that he is the Bread of Life, and raises the dead to show that he lifts men up from the death of trespasses and sins. See Broadus on Matthew, 175.

A modification of this definition of the miracle, however, is demanded by a large class of Christian physicists, in the supposed interest of natural law. Such a modification is proposed by Babbage, in the Ninth Bridgewater Treatise, chap. viii. Babbage illustrates the miracle by the action of his calculating machine, which would present to the observer in regular succession the series of units from one to ten million, but which would then make a leap and show. not ten million and one, but a hundred million ;

Ephraim Peabody illustrates the miracle from the cathedral clock which strikes only once in a hundred years; yet both these results are due simply to the original construction of the respective machines. Bonnet hold this view; see Dorner, Glaubenslehre, 1: 591, 592; Eng. translation, 2 : 155, 156; so Matthew Arnold, quoted in Bruce, Miraculous Element in Gospels, 52; see also A. H. Strong, Philosophy and Religion, 129-147. Babbage and Peabody would deny that the miracle is due to the direct and immediate agency of God, and would regard it as belonging to a higher order of nature. God is the author of the miracle only in the sense that he instituted the laws of nature at the beginning and provided that at the appropriate time miracle should be their outcome. In favor of this view it has been claimed that it does not dispense with the divine working, but only puts it further back at the origination of the system, while it still holds God's work to be essential, not only to the upholding of the system, but also to the inspiring of the religious teacher or leader with the knowledge needed to predict the unusual working of the system. The wonder is confined to the prophecy, which may equally attest a divine revelation. See Matheson, in Christianity and Evolution, 1-26.

But it is plain that a miracle of this sort lacks to a large degree the element of 'signality' which is needed, if it is to accomplish its purpose. It surrenders the great advantage which miracle, as first defined, possessed over special providence, as an attestation of revelation—the advantage, namely, that while special providence affords *some* warrant that this revelation comes from God, miracle gives *full* warrant that it comes from God. Since man may by natural means possess himself of the knowledge of physical laws, the true miracle which God works, and the pretended miracle which only man works, are upon this theory far less easy to distinguish from each other: Cortez, for example, could deceive Montezuma by predicting an eclipse of the sun. Certain typical miracles, like the resurrection of Lazarus, refuse to be classed as events within the realm of nature, in the sense in which the term nature is ordinarily used. Our Lord, moreover, seems clearly to exclude such a theory as this, when he says : "If I by the finger of God cast out demons " (Luke 11 : 20) ; Mark 1 : 41 — " I will ; be thou made clean." The view of Babbage is inadequate, not only because it fails to recognize any immediate exercise of *will* in the miracle, but because it regards nature as a mere *machine* which can operate apart from God — a purely deistic method of conception. On this view, many of the products of mere natural law might be called miracles. The miracle would be only the occasional manifestation of a higher order of nature, like the comet occasionally invading the solar system. William Elder, Ideas from Nature: "The century-plant which we have seen growing from our childhood may not unfold its blossoms until our old age comes upon us, but the sudden wonder is natural notwithstanding." If, however, we interpret nature dynamically, rather than mechanically, and regard it as the regular working of the divine will instead of the automatic operation of a machine, there is much in this view which we may adopt. Miracle may be both natural and supernatural. We may hold, with Babbage, that it has natural antecedents, while at the same time we hold that it is produced by the immediate agency of God. We proceed therefore to an alternative and preferable definition, which in our judgment combines the merits of both that have been mentioned. On miracles as already defined, see Mozley, Miracles, preface, ix-xxvi, 7, 143-166 ; Bushnell, Nature and Supernatural, 333-336 ; Smith's and Hastings' Dict. of Bible, art.: Miracles; Abp. Temple, Bampton Lectures for 1884 : 193-221 ; Shedd, Dogm. Theology, 1 : 541, 542.

B.   Alternative and Preferable Definition. — A miracle is an event in nature, so extraordinary in itself and so coinciding with the prophecy or command of a religious teacher or leader, as fully to warrant the conviction, on the part of those who witness it, that God has wrought it with the design of certifying that this teacher or leader has been commissioned by him.

This definition has certain marked advantages as compared with the preliminary definition given above : — (a) It recognizes the immanence of God and his immediate agency in nature, instead of assuming an antithesis between the laws of nature and the will of God.   (b) It regards the miracle as simply an extraordinary act of that same God who is already present in all natural operations and who in them is revealing his general plan.

(c) It holds that natural law, as the method of God's regular activity, in no way precludes unique exertions of his power when these will best secure his purpose in creation. (d) It leaves it possible that all miracles may have their natural explanations and may hereafter be traced to natural causes, while both miracles and their natural causes may be only names for the one and self-same will of God. (e) It reconciles the claims of both science and religion : of science, by permitting any possible or probable physical antecedents of the miracle ; of religion, by maintaining that these very antecedents together with the miracle itself are to be interpreted as signs of God's special commission to him under whose teaching or leadership the miracle is wrought.

Augustine, who declares that "Dei voluntas rerum natura est," defines the miracle in De Civitate Dei, 21 : 8 — "Portentum ergo fit non contra naturam, sed contra quam est nota natura." He says also that a birth is more miraculous than a resurrection, because it is more wonderful that something that never was should begin to be, than that something that was and ceased to be should begin again. E. G. Robinson, Christ. Theology, 104 — "The natural is God's work. He originated it. There is no separation between the natural and the supernatural. The natural is supernatural. God works in everything. Every end, even though attained by mechanical means, is God's end as truly as if he wrought by miracle." Shaler, Interpretation of Nature, 141, regards miracle as something exceptional, yet under the control of natural law ; the latent in nature suddenly manifesting itself ; the revolution resulting from the slow accumulation of natural forces. In the Windsor Hotel fire, the heated and charred woodwork suddenly burst into flame. Flame is very different from mere heat, but it may be the result of a regularly rising temperature. Nature may be God's regular action, miracle its unique result. God's regular action may be entirely free, and yet its extraordinary result may be entirely natural. With these qualifications and explanations, we may adopt the statement of Biedermann, Dogmatik, 581-591 — "Everything is miracle, — therefore faith sees God everywhere ; Nothing is miracle, — therefore science sees God nowhere."

Miracles are never considered by the Scripture writers as infractions of law. Bp. Southampton, Place of Miracles, 18 — "The Hebrew historian or prophet regarded miracles as only the emergence into sensible experience of that divine force which was all along, though invisibly, controlling the course of nature." Hastings, Bible Dictionary, 4 : 117 — "The force of a miracle to us, arising from our notion of law, would not be felt by a Hebrew, because he had no notion of natural law." Ps. 77 : 19, 20 — "Thy way was in the sea, And thy paths in the great waters, And thy footsteps were not known " — They knew not, and we know not, by what precise means the deliverance was wrought, or by what precise track the passage through the Red Sea was effected ; all we know is that " Thou leddest thy people like a flock, By the hand of Moses and Aaron." J. M. Whiton, Miracles and Supernatural Religion : "The supernatural is in nature itself, at its very heart, at its very life ; . . . not an outside power interfering with the course of nature, but an inside power vitalizing nature and operating through it." Griffith-Jones, Ascent through Christ, 35 — "Miracle, instead of spelling 'monster', as Emerson said, simply bears witness to some otherwise unknown or unrecognized aspect of the divine character." Shedd, Dogm. Theol., 1 : 533 — "To cause the sun to rise and to cause Lazarus to rise, both demand omnipotence ; but the manner in which omnipotence works in one instance is unlike the manner in the other."

Miracle is an immediate operation of God ; but, since all natural processes are also immediate operations of God, we do not need to deny the use of these natural processes, so far as they will go, in miracle. Such wonders of the Old Testament as the overthrow of Sodom and Gomorrah, the partings of the Red Sea and of the Jordan, the calling down of fire from heaven by Elijah and the destruction of the army of Sennacherib, are none the less works of God when regarded as wrought by the use of natural means. In the New Testament Christ took water to make wine, and took the five loaves to make bread, just as in ten thousand vineyards to-day he is turning the moisture of the earth into the juice of the grape, and in ten thousand fields is turning carbon into corn. The virgin-birth of Christ may be an extreme instance of parthenogenesis, which Professor Loeb of Chicago has just demonstrated to take place in other than the owest forms of life and which he believes to be possible in all. Christ's resurrection may be an illustration of the power of the normal and perfect human spirit to take to itself a proper body, and so may be the type and prophecy of that great change when we too shall lay down our life and take it again. The scientist may yet find that his disbelief is not only disbelief in Christ, but also disbelief in science. All miracle may have its natural side, though we now are not able to discern it; and, if this were true, the Christian argument would not one whit be weakened, for still miracle would evidence the extraordinary working of the immanent God, and the impartation of his knowledge to the prophet or apostle who was his instrument.

This view of the miracle renders entirely unnecessary and irrational the treatment accorded to the Scripture narratives by some modern theologians. There is a credulity of scepticism, which minimizes the miraculous element in the Bible and treats it as mythical or legendary, in spite of clear evidence that it belongs to the realm of actual history. Pfleiderer, Philos. Relig., 1:295 — "Miraculous legends arise in two ways, partly out of the idealizing of the real, and partly out of the realizing of the ideal. . . . Every occurrence may obtain for the religious judgment the significance of a sign or proof of the world-governing power, wisdom, justice or goodness of God. . . . Miraculous histories are a poetic realizing of religious ideas." Pfleiderer quotes Goethe's apothegm : "Miracle is faith's dearest child." Foster, Finality of the Christian Religion, 128-138 — "We most honor biblical miraculous narratives when we seek to understand them as poesies." Ritschl defines miracles as "those striking *natural* occurrences with which the experience of God's special help is connected." He leaves doubtful the bodily resurrection of Christ, and many of his school deny it ; see Mead, Ritschl's Place in the History of Doctrine, 11. We do not need to interpret Christ's resurrection as a mere appearance of his spirit to the disciples. Gladden, Seven Puzzling Books, 202 —" In the hands of perfect and spiritual man, the forces of nature are pliant and tractable as they are not in ours. The resurrection of Christ is only a sign of the superiority of the life of the perfect spirit over external conditions. It may be perfectly in accordance with nature." Myers, Human Personality, 2:288 — "I predict that, in consequence of the new evidence, all reasonable men, a century hence, will believe the resurrection of Christ." We may add that Jesus himself intimates that the working of miracles is hereafter to be a common and natural manifestation of the new life which he imparts : John 14 : 12 — "He that believeth on me, the works that I do shall he do also ; and greater works than these shall he do, because I go unto the Father."

We append a number of opinions, ancient and modern, with regard to miracles, all tending to show the need of so defining them as not to conflict with the just claims of science. Aristotle : "Nature is not full of episodes, like a bad tragedy." Shakespeare, All's Well that Ends Well, 2 : 3 : 1 — "They say miracles are past ; and we have our philosophical persons to make modern and familiar things supernatural and causeless. Hence it is that we make trifles of terrors, ensconsing ourselves into seeming knowledge, when we should submit ourselves to an unknown fear." Keats, Lamia : "There was an awful rainbow once in heaven ; We know her woof, her texture : she is given in the dull catalogue of common things." Hill, Genetic Philosophy, 334 — "Biological and psychological science unite in affirming that every event, organic or psychic, is to be explained in the terms of its immediate antecedents, and that it can be so explained. There is therefore no necessity, there is even no room, for interference. If the existence of a Deity depends upon the evidence of intervention and supernatural agency, faith in the divine seems to be destroyed in the scientific mind." Theodore Parker : "No whim in God, — therefore no miracle in nature." Armour, Atonement and Law, 15-33 — "The miracle of redemption, like all miracles, is by intervention of adequate power, not by suspension of law. Redemption is not 'the great exception.' It is the fullest revelation and vindication of law." Gore, in Lux Mundi, 320 — "Redemption is not natural but supernatural — supernatural, that is, in view of the false nature which man made for himself by excluding God. Otherwise, the work of redemption is only the reconstitution of the nature which God had designed." Abp. Trench : "The world of nature is throughout a witness for the world of spirit, proceeding from the same hand, growing out of the same root, and being constituted for this very end. The characters of nature which everywhere meet the eye are not a common but a sacred writing,— they are the hieroglyphics of God." Pascal : "Nature is the image of grace." President Mark Hopkins : "Christianity and perfect Reason are identical." See Mead, Supernatural Revelation, 97-123 ; art. : Miracle, by Bernard, in Hastings' Dictionary of the Bible. The modern and improved view of the miracle is perhaps best presented by T. H. Wright, The Finger of God ; and by W. N. Rice, Christian Faith in an Age of Science, 336.

2. *Possibility of Miracle.*

An event in nature may be caused by an agent in nature yet above nature. This is evident from the following considerations:

(*a*) Lower forces and laws in nature are frequently counteracted and transcended by the higher (as mechanical forces and laws by chemical, and chemical by vital), while yet the lower forces and laws are not suspended or annihilated, but are merged in the higher, and made to assist in accomplishing purposes to which they are altogether unequal when left to themselves.

By nature we mean nature in the proper sense — not 'everything that is not God,' but everything that is not God or made in the image of God '; see Hopkins, Outline Study of Man, 2,8, 259. Man's will does not belong to nature, but is above nature. On the transcending of lower forces by higher, see Murphy, Habit and Intelligence, 1:88. James Robertson, Early Religion of Israel, 23 — " Is it impossible that there should be unique things in the world? Is it scientific to assert that there are not?" Ladd, Philosophy of Knowledge, 406 — " Why does not the projecting part of the coping-stone fall, in obedience to the law of gravitation, from the top of yonder building? Because, as physics declares, the forces of cohesion, acting under quite different laws, thwart and oppose for the time being the law of gravitation. . . . But now, after a frosty night, the coping-stone actually breaks off and tumbles to the ground; for that unique law which makes water forcibly expand at 32° Fahrenheit has contradicted the laws of cohesion and has restored to the law of gravitation its temporarily suspended rights over this mass of matter." Gore, Incarnation, 48 — " Evolution views nature as a progressive order in which there are new departures, fresh levels won, phenomena unknown before. When organic life appeared, the future did not resemble the past. So when man came. Christ is a new nature — the creative Word made flesh. It is to be expected that, as new nature, he will exhibit new phenomena. New vital energy will radiate from him, controlling the material forces. Miracles are the proper accompaniments of his person." We may add that, as Christ is the immanent God, he is present in nature while at the same time he is above nature, and he whose steady will is the essence of all natural law can transcend all past exertions of that will. The infinite One is not a being of endless monotony. William Elder, Ideas from Nature, 156 — " God is not bound hopelessly to his process, like Ixion to his wheel."

(*b*) The human will acts upon its physical organism, and so upon nature, and produces results which nature left to herself never could accomplish, while yet no law of nature is suspended or violated. Gravitation still operates upon the axe, even while man holds it at the surface of the water — for the axe still has weight (*cf.* 2 K. 6 : 5–7).

Versus Hume, Philos. Works, 4 : 130 — "A miracle is a violation of the laws of nature." Christian apologists have too often needlessly embarrassed their argument by accepting Hume's definition. The stigma is entirely undeserved. If man can support the axe at the surface of the water while gravitation still acts upon it, God can certainly, at the prophet's word, make the iron to swim, while gravitation still acts upon it. But this last is miracle. See Mansel, Essay on Miracles, in Aids to Faith, 26, 27: After the greatest wave of the season has landed its pebble high up on the beach, I can move the pebble a foot further without altering the force of wind or wave or climate in a distant continent. Fisher, Supernat. Origin of Christianity, 471; Hamilton, Autology, 685–690; Bowen, Metaph. and Ethics, 445; Row, Bampton Lectures on Christian Evidences, 54–74; A. A. Hodge: Pulling out a new stop of the organ does not suspend the working or destroy the harmony of the other stops. The pump does not suspend the law of gravitation, nor does our throwing a ball into the air. If gravitation did not act, the upward velocity of the ball would not diminish and the ball would never return. "Gravitation draws iron down. But the magnet overcomes that attraction and draws the iron up. Yet here is no suspension or violation of law, but rather a harmonious working of two laws, each in its sphere. Death and not life is the order of nature. But men live notwithstanding. Life is supernatural. Only as a force additional to mere nature works against nature does life exist. So spiritual life uses and transcends the laws of nature" (Sunday School Times). Gladden, What Is Left? 60 — " Wherever you find thought, choice, love, you find something that is not under the dominion of fixed law. These are the attributes of a free personality." William James: " We need to substitute the *personal* view of life for the *impersonal* and *mechanical* view. Mechanical rationalism is narrowness and partial induction of facts, — it is not *science*."

(c) In all free causation, there is an acting without means. Man acts upon external nature through his physical organism, but, in moving his physical organism, he acts directly upon matter. In other words, the human will can *use* means, only because it has the power of acting initially *without* means.

See Hopkins, on Prayer-gauge, 10, and in Princeton Review, Sept. 1882:188. A. J. Balfour, Foundations of Belief, 311 — " Not Divinity alone intervenes in the world of things. Each living soul, in its measure and degree, does the same." Each soul that acts in any way on its surroundings does so on the principle of the miracle. Phillips Brooks, Life, 2 : 350 — " The making of all events miraculous is no more an abolition of miracle than the flooding of the world with sunshine is an extinction of the sun." George Adam Smith, on Is. 33 : 14 — "devouring fire . . . everlasting burnings": " If we look at a conflagration through smoked glass, we see buildings collapsing, but we see no fire. So science sees results, but not the power which produces them; sees cause and effect, but does not see God." P. S. Henson: " The current in an electric wire is invisible so long as it circulates uniformly. But cut the wire and insert a piece of carbon between the two broken ends, and at once you have an arc-light that drives away the darkness. So miracle is only the momentary interruption in the operation of uniform laws, which thus gives light to the ages," — or, let us say rather, the momentary change in the method of their operation whereby the will of God takes a new form of manifestation. Pfleiderer, Grundriss, 100 — " Spinoza leugnete ihre metaphysische Möglichkeit, Hume ihre geschichtliche Erkennbarkeit, Kant ihre practische Brauchbarkeit, Schleiermacher ihre religiöse Bedeutsamkeit, Hegel ihre geistige Beweiskraft, Fichte ihre wahre Christlichkeit, und die kritische Theologie ihre wahre Geschichtlichkeit."

(d) What the human will, considered as a supernatural force, and what the chemical and vital forces of nature itself, are demonstrably able to accomplish, cannot be regarded as beyond the power of God, so long as God dwells in and controls the universe. If man's will can act directly upon matter in his own physical organism, God's will can work immediately upon the system which he has created and which he sustains. In other words, if there be a God, and if he be a personal being, miracles are possible. The impossibility of miracles can be maintained only upon principles of atheism or pantheism.

See Westcott, Gospel of the Resurrection, 19 ; Cox, Miracles, an Argument and a Challenge: "Anthropomorphism is preferable to hylomorphism." Newman Smyth, Old Faiths in a New Light, ch. 1 — "A miracle is not a sudden blow struck in the face of nature, but a use of nature, according to its inherent capacities, by higher powers." See also Gloatz, Wunder und Naturgesetz, in Studien und Kritiken, 1886 : 403-546; Gunsaulus, Transfiguration of Christ, 18, 19, 26; Andover Review, on " Robert Elsmere," 1888 : 503; W. E. Gladstone, in Nineteenth Century, 1888 : 766-788; Dubois, on Science and Miracle, in New Englander, July, 1889: 1-32 — Three postulates: (1) Every particle attracts every other in the universe; (2) Man's will is free; (2) Every volition is accompanied by corresponding brain-action. Hence every volition of ours causes changes throughout the whole universe; also, in Century Magazine, Dec. 1894:229 — Conditions are never twice the same in nature; all things are the results of will, since we know that the least thought of ours shakes the universe; miracle is simply the action of will in unique conditions; the beginning of life, the origin of consciousness, these are miracles, yet they are strictly natural; prayer and the mind that frames it are conditions which *the Mind* in nature cannot ignore. Cf. Ps. 115 : 3 — "our God is in the heavens: He hath done

whatsoever he pleased ' = his almighty power and freedom do away with all *a priori* objections to miracles. If God is not a mere *force*, but a *person*, then miracles are possible.

(*e*) This possibility of miracles becomes doubly sure to those who see in Christ none other than the immanent God manifested to creatures. The Logos or divine Reason who is the principle of all growth and evolution can make God known only by means of successive new impartations of his energy. Since all progress implies increment, and Christ is the only source of life, the whole history of creation is a witness to the possibility of miracle.

See A. H. Strong, Christ in Creation, 163–166 — "This conception of evolution is that of Lotze. That great philosopher, whose influence is more potent than any other in present thought, does not regard the universe as a *plenum* to which nothing can be added in the way of force. He looks upon the universe rather as a plastic organism to which new impulses can be imparted from him of whose thought and will it is an expression. These impulses, once imparted, abide in the organism and are thereafter subject to its law. Though these impulses come from within, they come not from the finite mechanism but from the immanent God. Robert Browning's phrase, 'All 's love, but all 's law,' must be interpreted as meaning that the very movements of the planets and all the operations of nature are revelations of a personal and present God, but it must not be interpreted as meaning that God runs in a rut, that he is confined to mechanism, that he is incapable of unique and startling manifestations of power.

"The idea that gives to evolution its hold upon thinking minds is the idea of continuity. But absolute continuity is inconsistent with progress. If the future is not simply a reproduction of the past, there must be some new cause of change. In order to progress there must be either a new force, or a new combination of forces, and the new combination of forces can be explained only by some new force that causes the combination. This new force, moreover, must be intelligent force, if the evolution is to be toward the better instead of toward the worse. The continuity must be continuity not of forces but of plan. The forces may increase, nay, they must increase, unless the new is to be a mere repetition of the old. There must be additional energy imparted, the new combination brought about, and all this implies purpose and will. But through all there runs one continuous plan, and upon this plan the rationality of evolution depends.

"A man builds a house. In laying the foundation he uses stone and mortar, but he makes the walls of wood and the roof of tin. In the superstructure he brings into play different laws from those which apply to the foundation. There is continuity, not of material, but of plan. Progress from cellar to garret requires breaks here and there, and the bringing in of new forces; in fact, without the bringing in of these new forces the evolution of the house would be impossible. Now substitute for the foundation and superstructure living things like the chrysalis and the butterfly; imagine the power to work from within and not from without; and you see that true continuity does not exclude but involves new beginnings.

"Evolution, then, depends on increments of force *plus* continuity of plan. New creations are possible because the immanent God has not exhausted himself. Miracle is possible because God is not far away, but is at hand to do whatever the needs of his moral universe may require. Regeneration and answers to prayer are possible for the very reason that these are the objects for which the universe was built. If we were deists, believing in a distant God and a mechanical universe, evolution and Christianity would be irreconcilable. But since we believe in a dynamical universe, of which the personal and living God is the inner source of energy, evolution is but the basis, foundation and background of Christianity, the silent and regular working of him who, in the fulness of time, utters his voice in Christ and the Cross."

Lotze's own statement of his position may be found in his Microcosmos, 2: 479 *sq.* Professor James Ten Broeke has interpreted him as follows: " He makes the possibility of the miracle depend upon the close and intimate action and reaction between the world and the personal Absolute, in consequence of which the movements of the natural world are carried on only *through* the Absolute, with the possibility of a variation in the general course of things, according to existing facts and the purpose of the divine Governor."

3. *Probability of Miracles.*

A. We acknowledge that, so long as we confine our attention to nature, there is a presumption against miracles. Experience testifies to the uniformity of natural law. A general uniformity is needful, in order to make possible a rational calculation of the future, and a proper ordering of life.

See Butler, Analogy, part ii, chap. ii; F. W. Farrar, Witness of History to Christ, 3–45; Modern Scepticism, 1 : 179-227; Chalmers, Christian Revelation, 1 : 47. G. D. B. Pepper : "Where there is no law, no settled order, there can be no miracle. The miracle presupposes the law, and the importance assigned to miracles is the recognition of the reign of law. But the making and launching of a ship may be governed by law, no less than the sailing of the ship after it is launched. So the introduction of a higher spiritual order into a merely natural order constitutes a new and unique event." Some Christian apologists have erred in affirming that the miracle was antecedently as probable as any other event, whereas only its antecedent improbability gives it value as a proof of revelation. Horace : "Nec deus intersit, nisi dignus vindice nodus Inciderit."

B. But we deny that this uniformity of nature is absolute and universal. (*a*) It is not a truth of reason that can have no exceptions, like the axiom that a whole is greater than its parts. (*b*) Experience could not warrant a belief in absolute and universal uniformity, unless experience were identical with absolute and universal knowledge. (*c*) We know, on the contrary, from geology, that there have been breaks in this uniformity, such as the introduction of vegetable, animal and human life, which cannot be accounted for, except by the manifestation in nature of a supernatural power.

(*a*) Compare the probability that the sun will rise to-morrow morning with the certainty that two and two make four. Huxley, Lay Sermons, 158, indignantly denies that there is any 'must' about the uniformity of nature : "No one is entitled to say *a priori* that any given so-called miraculous event is impossible." Ward, Naturalism and Agnosticism, 1 : 84 — "There is no evidence for the statement that the mass of the universe is a definite and unchangeable quantity"; 108, 109 — "Why so confidently assume that a rigid and monotonous uniformity is the only, or the highest, indication of order, the order of an ever living Spirit, above all? How is it that we depreciate machine-made articles, and prefer those in which the artistic impulse, or the fitness of the individual case, is free to shape and to make what is literally manufactured, hand-made? . . . . Dangerous as teleological arguments in general may be, we may at least safely say the world was not designed to make science easy. . . . To call the verses of a poet, the politics of a statesman, or the award of a judge mechanical, implies, as Lotze has pointed out, marked disparagement, although it implies, too, precisely those characteristics — exactness and invariability — in which Maxwell would have us see a token of the divine." Surely then we must not insist that divine wisdom must always run in a rut, must ever repeat itself, must never exhibit itself in unique acts like incarnation and resurrection. See Edward Hitchcock, in Bib. Sac., 20 : 489-561, on "The Law of Nature's Constancy Subordinate to the Higher Law of Change"; Jevons, Principles of Science, 2 : 430-438; Mozley, Miracles, 26.

(*b*) S. T. Coleridge, Table Talk, 18 December, 1831 — "The light which experience gives us is a lantern on the stern of the ship, which shines only on the waves behind us." Hobbes : "Experience concludeth nothing universally." Brooks, Foundations of Zoölogy, 131 — "Evidence can tell us only what has happened, and it can never assure us that the future *must be* like the past; 132 — Proof that all nature is mechanical would not be inconsistent with the belief that everything in nature is immediately sustained by Providence, and that my volition counts for something in determining the course of events." Royce, World and Individual, 2 : 204 — "Uniformity is not absolute. Nature is a vaster realm of life and meaning, of which we men form a part, and of which the final unity is in God's life. The rhythm of the heart-beat has its normal regularity, yet its limited persistence. Nature may be merely the *habits of free will.* Every region of this universally conscious world may be a centre whence issues new conscious life for communication to all the worlds." Principal Fairbairn: "Nature is Spirit." We prefer to say: "Nature is the manifestation of spirit, the regularities of freedom."

(c) Other breaks in the uniformity of nature are the coming of Christ and the regeneration of a human soul. Harnack, What is Christianity, 18, holds that though there are no interruptions to the working of natural law, natural law is not yet fully known. While there are no miracles, there is plenty of the miraculous. The power of mind over matter is beyond our present conceptions. Bowne, Philosophy of Theism, 210 — The effects are no more consequences of the laws than the laws are consequences of the effects — both laws and effects are exercises of divine will. King, Reconstruction in Theology, 56 — We must hold, not to the *uniformity* of law, but to the *universality* of law; for evolution has successive stages with new laws coming in and becoming dominant that had not before appeared. The new and higher stage is practically a miracle from the point of view of the lower. See British Quarterly Review, Oct. 1881: 154; Martineau, Study, 2: 200, 203, 209.

C. Since the inworking of the moral law into the constitution and course of nature shows that nature exists, not for itself, but for the contemplation and use of moral beings, it is probable that the God of nature will produce effects aside from those of natural law, whenever there are sufficiently important moral ends to be served thereby.

Beneath the expectation of uniformity is the intuition of final cause; the former may therefore give way to the latter. See Porter, Human Intellect, 592-615 — Efficient causes and final causes may conflict, and then the efficient give place to the final. This is miracle. See Hutton, in Nineteenth Century, Aug. 1885, and Channing, Evidences of Revealed Religion, quoted in Shedd, Dogm. Theol., 1: 534, 535 — "The order of the universe is a means, not an end, and like all other means must give way when the end can be best promoted without it. It is the mark of a weak mind to make an idol of order and method; to cling to established forms of business when they clog instead of advancing it." Balfour, Foundations of Belief, 357 — "The stability of the heavens is in the sight of God of less importance than the moral growth of the human spirit." This is proved by the Incarnation. The Christian sees in this little earth the scene of God's greatest revelation. The superiority of the spiritual to the physical helps us to see our true dignity in the creation, to rule our bodies, to overcome our sins. Christ's suffering shows us that God is no indifferent spectator of human pain. He subjects himself to our conditions, or rather in this subjection reveals to us God's own eternal suffering for sin. The atonement enables us to solve the problem of sin.

D. The existence of moral disorder consequent upon the free acts of man's will, therefore, changes the presumption against miracles into a presumption in their favor. The non-appearance of miracles, in this case, would be the greatest of wonders.

Stearns, Evidence of Christian Experience, 331-335 — So a man's personal consciousness of sin, and above all his personal experience of regenerating grace, will constitute the best preparation for the study of miracles. "Christianity cannot be proved except to a bad conscience." The dying Vinet said well: "The greatest miracle that I know of is that of my conversion. I was dead, and I live; I was blind, and I see; I was a slave, and I am free; I was an enemy of God, and I love him; prayer, the Bible, the society of Christians, these were to me a source of profound *ennui*; whilst now it is the pleasures of the world that are wearisome to me, and piety is the source of all my joy. Behold the miracle! And if God has been able to work that one, there are none of which he is not capable."

Yet the physical and the moral are not "sundered as with an axe." Nature is but the lower stage or imperfect form of the revelation of God's truth and holiness and love. It prepares the way for the miracle by suggesting, though more dimly, the same essential characteristics of the divine nature. Ignorance and sin necessitate a larger disclosure. G. S. Lee, The Shadow Christ, 54 — "The pillar of cloud was the dim nightlamp that Jehovah kept burning over his infant children, to show them that he was there. They did not know that the night itself was God." Why do we have Christmas presents in Christian homes? Because the parents do not love their children at other times?

No; but because the mind becomes sluggish in the presence of merely regular kindness, and special gifts are needed to wake it to gratitude. So our sluggish and unloving minds need special testimonies of the divine mercy. Shall God alone be shut up to dull uniformities of action? Shall the heavenly Father alone be unable to make special communications of love? Why then are not miracles and revivals of religion constant and uniform? Because uniform blessings would be regarded simply as workings of a machine. See Mozley, Miracles, preface, xxiv; Turner, Wish and Will, 291-315; N. W. Taylor, Moral Government, 2 : 388-423.

E.   As belief in the possibility of miracles rests upon our belief in the existence of a personal God, so belief in the probability of miracles rests upon our belief that God is a moral and benevolent being.   He who has no God but a God of physical order will regard miracles as an impertinent intrusion upon that order.   But he who yields to the testimony of conscience and regards God as a God of holiness, will see that man's unholiness renders God's miraculous interposition most necessary to man and most becoming to God.   Our view of miracles will therefore be determined by our belief in a moral, or in a non-moral, God.

Philo, in his Life of Moses, 1: 88, speaking of the miracles of the quails and of the water from the rock, says that "all these unexpected and extraordinary things are amusements or playthings of God." He believes that there is room for arbitrariness in the divine procedure. Scripture however represents miracle as an extraordinary, rather than as an arbitrary, act. It is "his work, his strange work . . . his act, his strange act" (Is. 28: 21). God's ordinary method is that of regular growth and development. Chadwick, Unitarianism, 72 — "Nature is economical. If she wants an apple, she develops a leaf; if she wants a brain, she develops a vertebra. We always thought well of backbone; and, if Goethe's was a sound suggestion, we think better of it now."

It is commonly, but very erroneously, taken for granted that miracle requires a greater exercise of power than does God's upholding of the ordinary processes of nature. But to an omnipotent Being our measures of power have no application. The question is not a question of power, but of rationality and love. Miracle implies self-restraint, as well as self-unfolding, on the part of him who works it. It is therefore not God's common method of action; it is adopted only when regular methods will not suffice; it often seems accompanied by a sacrifice of feeling on the part of Christ (Mat. 17: 17 — "O faithless and perverse generation, how long shall I be with you? how long shall I bear with you? bring him hither to me"; Mark 7 : 34 — "looking up to heaven, he sighed, and saith unto him, Ephphatha, that is, Be opened"; cf. Mat. 12: 39 — "An evil and adulterous generation seeketh after a sign; and there shall no sign be given to it but the sign of Jonah the prophet."

F.   From the point of view of ethical monism the probability of miracle becomes even greater.   Since God is not merely the intellectual but the moral Reason of the world, the disturbances of the world-order which are due to sin are the matters which most deeply affect him.   Christ, the life of the whole system and of humanity as well, must suffer; and, since we have evidence that he is merciful as well as just, it is probable that he will rectify the evil by extraordinary means, when merely ordinary means do not avail.

Like creation and providence, like inspiration and regeneration, miracle is a work in which God limits himself, by a new and peculiar exercise of his power, — limits himself as part of a process of condescending love and as a means of teaching sense-environed and sin-burdened humanity what it would not learn in any other way. Self-limitation, however, is the very perfection and glory of God, for without it no self-sacrificing love would be possible (see page 9, F.). The probability of miracles is therefore argued not only from God's holiness but also from his love. His desire to save men from their sins must be as infinite as his nature. The incarnation, the atonement, the resurrection, when once made known to us, commend themselves, not only as satisfying our human needs, but as worthy of a God of moral perfection.

An argument for the probability of the miracle might be drawn from the concessions of one of its chief modern opponents, Thomas H. Huxley. He tells us in different places that the object of science is "the discovery of the rational order that pervades the universe," which in spite of his professed agnosticism is an unconscious testimony to Reason and Will at the basis of all things. He tells us again that there is no necessity in the uniformities of nature: "When we change 'will' into 'must,' we introduce an idea of necessity which has no warrant in the observed facts, and has no warranty that I can discover elsewhere." He speaks of "the infinite wickedness that has attended the course of human history." Yet he has no hope in man's power to save himself: "I would as soon adore a wilderness of apes," as the Pantheist's rationalized conception of humanity. He grants that Jesus Christ is "the noblest ideal of humanity which mankind has yet worshiped." Why should he not go further and concede that Jesus Christ most truly represents the infinite Reason at the heart of things, and that his purity and love, demonstrated by suffering and death, make it probable that God will use extraordinary means for man's deliverance? It is doubtful whether Huxley recognized his own personal sinfulness as fully as he recognized the sinfulness of humanity in general. If he had done so, he would have been willing to accept miracle upon even a slight preponderance of historical proof. As a matter of fact, he rejected miracle upon the grounds assigned by Hume, which we now proceed to mention.

4. *The amount of testimony necessary to prove a miracle* is no greater than that which is requisite to prove the occurrence of any other unusual but confessedly possible event.

Hume, indeed, argued that a miracle is so contradictory of all human experience that it is more reasonable to believe any amount of testimony false than to believe a miracle to be true.

The original form of the argument can be found in Hume's Philosophical Works, 4: 124-150. See also Bib. Sac., Oct. 1867:615. For the most recent and plausible statement of it, see Supernatural Religion, 1: 55-94. The argument maintains for substance that things are impossible because improbable. It ridicules the credulity of those who "thrust their fists against the posts, And still insist they see the ghosts," and holds with the German philosopher who declared that he would not believe in a miracle, even if he saw one with his own eyes. Christianity is so miraculous that it takes a miracle to make one believe it.

The argument is fallacious, because

(*a*) It is chargeable with a *petitio principii*, in making our own personal experience the measure of all human experience. The same principle would make the proof of any absolutely new fact impossible. Even though God should work a miracle, he could never prove it.

(*b*) It involves a self-contradiction, since it seeks to overthrow our faith in human testimony by adducing to the contrary the general experience of men, of which we know only from testimony. This general experience, moreover, is merely negative, and cannot neutralize that which is positive, except upon principles which would invalidate all testimony whatever.

(*c*) It requires belief in a greater wonder than those which it would escape. That multitudes of intelligent and honest men should against all their interests unite in deliberate and persistent falsehood, under the circumstances narrated in the New Testament record, involves a change in the sequences of nature far more incredible than the miracles of Christ and his apostles.

(*a*) John Stuart Mill, Essays on Theism, 216-241, grants that, even if a miracle were wrought, it would be impossible to prove it. In this he only echoes Hume, Miracles, 112 — "The ultimate standard by which we determine all disputes that may arise is always derived from experience and observation." But here our own personal exper fence is maoe the standard by which to judge all human experience. Whately, Historic Doubts relative to Napoleon Buonaparte, shows that the same rule would require us to deny the existence of the great Frenchman, since Napoleon's conquests were contrary to all experience, and civilized nations had never before been so subdued. The London Times for June 18, 1888, for the first time in at least a hundred years or in 31,200 issues, was misdated, and certain pages read June 17, although June 17 was Sunday. Yet the paper would have been admitted in a court of justice as evidence of a marriage. The real wonder is, not the break in experience, but the continuity without the break.

(b) Lyman Abbott: "If the Old Testament told the story of a naval engagement between the Jewish people and a pagan people, in which all the ships of the pagan people were absolutely destroyed and not a single man was killed among the Jews, all the sceptics would have scorned the narrative. Every one now believes it, except those who live in Spain." There are people who in a similar way refuse to investigate the phenomena of hypnotism, second sight, clairvoyance, and telepathy, declaring *a priori* that all these things are impossible. Prophecy, in the sense of prediction, is discredited. Upon the same principle wireless telegraphy might be denounced as an imposture. The son of Erin charged with murder defended himself by saying: "Your honor, I can bring fifty people who did not see me do it." Our faith in testimony cannot be due to experience.

(c) On this point, see Chalmers, Christian Revelation, 3 : 70 ; Starkie on Evidence, 739 ; De Quincey, Theological Essays, 1 : 162-188 ; Thornton, Old-fashioned Ethics, 143-153 ; Campbell on Miracles. South's sermon on The Certainty of our Savior's Resurrection had stated and answered this objection long before Hume propounded it.

5. *Evidential force of Miracles.*

(a) Miracles are the natural accompaniments and attestations of new communications from God. The great epochs of miracles — represented by Moses, the prophets, the first and second comings of Christ — are coincident with the great epochs of revelation. Miracles serve to draw attention to new truth, and cease when this truth has gained currency and foothold.

Miracles are not scattered evenly over the whole course of history. Few miracles are recorded during the 2500 years from Adam to Moses. When the N. T. Canon is completed and the internal evidence of Scripture has attained its greatest strength, the external attestations by miracle are either wholly withdrawn or begin to disappear. The spiritual wonders of regeneration remain, and for these the way has been prepared by the long progress from the miracles of power wrought by Moses to the miracles of grace wrought by Christ. Miracles disappeared because newer and higher proofs rendered them unnecessary. Better things than these are now in evidence. Thomas Fuller: "Miracles are the swaddling-clothes of the infant church." John Foster: "Miracles are the great bell of the universe, which draws men to God's sermon." Henry Ward Beecher: "Miracles are the midwives of great moral truths; candles lit before the dawn but put out after the sun has risen." Illingworth, in Lux Mundi, 210 — "When we are told that miracles contradict experience, we point to the daily occurrence of the spiritual miracle of regeneration and ask: 'Which is easier to say, Thy sins are forgiven; or to say, Arise and walk?' (Mat. 9 : 5)."

Miracles and inspiration go together; if the former remain in the church, the latter should remain also; see Marsh, in Bap. Quar. Rev., 1887 : 225-242. On the cessation of miracles in the early church, see Henderson, Inspiration, 443-490; Bückmann, in Zeitsch. f. luth. Theol. u. Kirche, 1878 : 216. On miracles in the second century, see Barnard, Literature of the Second Century, 133-180. A. J. Gordon, Ministry of the Spirit, 167 — "The apostles were commissioned to speak for Christ till the N. T. Scriptures, his authoritative voice, were completed. In the apostolate we have a provisional inspiration; in the N. T. a stereotyped inspiration; the first being endowed with authority *ad interim* to forgive sins, and the second having this authority *in perpetuo*." Dr. Gordon draws an analogy between coal, which is fossil sunlight, and the New Testament, which is fossil inspiration. Sabatier, Philos. Religion, 74 — "The Bible is very free from the senseless prodigies of oriental mythology. The great prophets, Isaiah, Amos, Mican, Jeremiah, John the Baptist, work no miracles. Jesus' temptation in the wilderness is a victory of the moral consciousness over the religion of mere physical prodigy." French says that miracles cluster about the *foundation* of the theocratic kingdom under Moses and Joshua, and about the *restoration* of that kingdom under Elijah and Elisha. In the O. T., miracles confute the gods of Egypt under Moses, the Phœnician Baal under Elijah and Elisha, and the gods of Babylon under Daniel. See Diman, Theistic Argument, 376, and art.: Miracle, by Bernard, in Hastings' Bible Dictionary.

(*b*) Miracles generally certify to the truth of doctrine, not directly, but indirectly ; otherwise a new miracle must needs accompany each new doctrine taught.   Miracles primarily and directly certify to the divine commission and authority of a religious teacher, and therefore warrant acceptance of his doctrines and obedience to his commands as the doctrines and commands of God, whether these be communicated at intervals or all together, orally or in written documents.

The exceptions to the above statement are very few, and are found only in cases where the whole commission and authority of Christ, and not some fragmentary doctrine, are involved. Jesus appeals to his miracles as proof of the truth of his teaching in Mat. 9 : 5, 6 — " Which is easier to say, Thy sins are forgiven; or to say, Arise and walk ? But that ye may know that the Son of man hath authority on earth to forgive sins (then saith he to the sick of the palsy), Arise, and take up thy bed, and go unto thy house " ; 12 : 28 — " if I by the spirit of God cast out demons, then is the kingdom of God come upon you." So Paul in Rom. 1 : 4, says that Jesus " was declared to be the Son of God with power, ... by the resurrection from the dead."   Mair, Christian Evidences, 223, quotes from Natural Religion, 181 — " It is said that the theo-philanthropist Larévellière-Lépeaux once confided to Talleyrand his disappointment at the ill success of his attempt to bring into vogue a sort of improved Christianity, a sort of benevolent rationalism which he had invented to meet the wants of a benevolent age. ' His propaganda made no way,' he said. ' What was he to do ? ' he asked. The ex-bishop Talleyrand politely condoled with him, feared it was a difficult task to found a new religion, more difficult than he had imagined, so difficult that he hardly knew what to advise. ' Still,' — so he went on after a moment's reflection, — ' there is one plan which you might at least try : I should recommend you to be crucified, and to rise again the third day." See also Murphy, Scientific Bases of Faith, 147-167 ; Farrar, Life of Christ, 1 : 168-172.

(*c*) Miracles, therefore, do not stand alone as evidences.   Power alone cannot prove a divine commission. Purity of life and doctrine must go with the miracles to assure us that a religious teacher has come from God. The miracles and the doctrine in this manner mutually support each other, and form parts of one whole. The internal evidence for the Christian system may have greater power over certain minds and over certain ages than the external evidence.

Pascal's aphorism that " doctrines must be judged by miracles, miracles by doctrine," needs to be supplemented by Mozley's statment that " a supernatural fact is the proper proof of a supernatural doctrine, while a supernatural doctrine is not the proper proof of a supernatural fact."   E. G. Robinson, Christian Theology, 107, would " defend miracles, but would not buttress up Christianity by them. . . . No amount of miracles could convince a good man of the divine commission of a known bad man ; nor, on the other hand, could any degree of miraculous power suffice to silence the doubts of an evil-minded man. . . . The miracle is a certification only to him who can perceive its significance. . . . The Christian church has the resurrection written all over it. Its very existence is proof of the resurrection. Twelve men could never have founded the church, if Christ had remained in the tomb. The living church is the burning bush that is not consumed." Gore, Incarnation, 57 — " Jesus did not appear after his resurrection to unbelievers, but to believers only, — which means that this crowning miracle was meant to confirm an existing faith, not to create one where it did not exist."
Christian Union, July 11, 1891 — " If the anticipated resurrection of Joseph Smith were to take place, it would add nothing whatever to the authority of the Mormon religion." Schurman, Agnosticism and Religion, 57 — " Miracles are merely the bells to call primitive peoples to church. Sweet as the music they once made, modern ears find them jangling and out of tune, and their dissonant notes scare away pious souls who would fain enter the temple of worship."   A new definition of miracle which rec-

ognizes their possible classification as extraordinary occurrences in nature, yet sees in all nature the working of the living God, may do much to remove this prejudice. Bishop of Southampton, Place of Miracle, 53 — "Miracles alone could not produce conviction. The Pharisees ascribed them to Beelzebub. Though Jesus had done so many signs, yet they believed not. . . . Though miracles were frequently wrought, they were rarely appealed to as evidence of the truth of the gospel. They are simply signs of God's presence in his world. By itself a miracle had no evidential force. The only test for distinguishing divine from Satanic miracles is that of the moral character and purpose of the worker; and therefore miracles depend for all their force upon a previous appreciation of the character and personality of Christ (79). The earliest apologists make no use of miracles. They are of no value except in connection with prophecy. Miracles *are* the revelation of God, not the *proof* of revelation." *Versus* Supernatural Religion, 1:23, and Stearns, in New Englander, Jan. 1882:80. See Mozley, Miracles, 15; Nicoll, Life of Jesus Christ, 133; Mill, Logic, 374-382; H. B. Smith, Int. to Christ. Theology, 167-169; Fisher, in Journ. Christ. Philos., April, 1883:270-283.

(*d*) Yet the Christian miracles do not lose their value as evidence in the process of ages. The loftier the structure of Christian life and doctrine the greater need that its foundation be secure. The authority of Christ as a teacher of supernatural truth rests upon his miracles, and especially upon the miracle of his resurrection. That one miracle to which the church looks back as the source of her life carries with it irresistibly all the other miracles of the Scripture record ; upon it alone we may safely rest the proof that the Scriptures are an authoritative revelation from God.

The miracles of Christ are simple correlates of the Incarnation — proper insignia of his royalty and divinity. By mere external evidence however we can more easily prove the resurrection than the incarnation. In our arguments with sceptics, we should not begin with the ass that spoke to Balaam, or the fish that swallowed Jonah, but with the resurrection of Christ ; that conceded, all other Biblical miracles will seem only natural preparations, accompaniments, or consequences. G. F. Wright, in Bib. Sac., 1889: 707 — "The difficulties created by the miraculous character of Christianity may be compared to those assumed by a builder when great permanence is desired in the structure erected. It is easier to lay the foundation of a temporary structure than of one which is to endure for the ages." Pressensé : "The empty tomb of Christ has been the cradle of the church, and if in this foundation of her faith the church has been mistaken, she must needs lay herself down by the side of the mortal remains, I say, not of a man, but of a religion."

President Schurman believes the resurrection of Christ to be "an obsolete picture of an eternal truth — the fact of a continued life with God." Harnack, Wesen des Christenthums, 102, thinks no consistent union of the gospel accounts of Christ's resurrection can be attained ; apparently doubts a literal and bodily rising ; yet traces Christianity back to an invincible faith in Christ's conquering of death and his continued life. But why believe the gospels when they speak of the sympathy of Christ, yet disbelieve them when they speak of his miraculous power ? We have no right to trust the narrative when it gives us Christ's words "Weep not" to the widow of Nain, (Luke 7 : 13), and then to distrust it when it tells us of his raising the widow's son. The words "Jesus wept" belong inseparably to a story of which "Lazarus, come forth !" forms a part (John 11 : 35, 43). It is improbable that the disciples should have believed so stupendous a miracle as Christ's resurrection, if they had not previously seen other manifestations of miraculous power on the part of Christ. Christ himself is the great miracle. The conception of him as the risen and glorified Savior can be explained only by the fact that he did so rise. E. G. Robinson, Christ. Theology, 109 — "The Church attests the fact of the resurrection quite as much as the resurrection attests the divine origin of the church. Resurrection, as an evidence, depends on the existence of the church which proclaims it."

(*e*) The resurrection of our Lord Jesus Christ — by which we mean his coming forth from the sepulchre in body as well as in spirit — is demonstrated by evidence as varied and as conclusive as that which proves to us any single fact of ancient history. Without it Christianity itself is inexplicable, as is shown by the failure of all modern rationalistic theories to account for its rise and progress.

In discussing the evidence of Jesus' resurrection, we are confronted with three main rationalistic theories:

I. The *Swoon-theory* of Strauss. This holds that Jesus did not really die. The cold and the spices of the sepulchre revived him. We reply that the blood and water, and the testimony of the centurion (Mark 15: 45), proved actual death (see Bib. Sac., April, 1889 : 228 ; Forrest, Christ of History and Experience, 137-170). The rolling away of the stone, and Jesus' power immediately after, are inconsistent with immediately preceding swoon and suspended animation. How was his life preserved? where did he go? when did he die? His not dying implies deceit on his own part or on that of his disciples.

II. The *Spirit-theory* of Keim. Jesus really died, but only his spirit appeared. The spirit of Jesus gave the disciples a sign of his continued life, a telegram from heaven. But we reply that the telegram was untrue, for it asserted that his body had risen from the tomb. The tomb was empty and the linen cloths showed an orderly departure. Jesus himself denied that he was a bodiless spirit: "a spirit hath not flesh and bones, as ye see me having" (Luke 24: 39). Did "his flesh see corruption" (Acts 2: 31)? Was the penitent thief raised from the dead as much as he? Godet, Lectures in Defence of the Christian Faith, lect. i : A dilemma for those who deny the fact of Christ's resurrection : Either his body remained in the hands of his disciples, or it was given up to the Jews. If the disciples retained it, they were impostors : but this is not maintained by modern rationalists. If the Jews retained it, why did they not produce it as conclusive evidence against the disciples?

III. The *Vision-theory* of Renan. Jesus died, and there was no objective appearance even of his spirit. Mary Magdalene was the victim of subjective hallucination, and her hallucination became contagious. This was natural because the Jews expected that the Messiah would work miracles and would rise from the dead. We reply that the disciples did not expect Jesus' resurrection. The women went to the sepulchre, not to see a risen Redeemer, but to embalm a dead body. Thomas and those at Emmaus had given up all hope. Four hundred years had passed since the days of miracles ; John the Baptist "did no miracle" (John 10: 41) ; the Sadducees said "there is no resurrection" (Mat. 22: 23). There were thirteen different appearances, to : 1. the Magdalen ; 2. other women ; 3. Peter ; 4. Emmaus ; 5. the Twelve ; 6. the Twelve after eight days ; 7. Galilee seashore ; 8. Galilee mountain ; 9. Galilee five hundred ; 10. James ; 11. ascension at Bethany ; 12. Stephen ; 13. Paul on way to Damascus. Paul describes Christ's appearance to him as something objective, and he implies that Christ's previous appearances to others were objective also : "last of all [these bodily appearances], ... he appeared to me also" (1 Cor. 15: 8). Bruce, Apologetics, 396 — "Paul's interest and intention in classing the two together was to level his own vision [of Christ] up to the objectivity of the early Christophanies. He believed that the eleven, that Peter in particular, had seen the risen Christ with the eye of the body, and he meant to claim for himself a vision of the same kind." Paul's was a sane, strong nature. Subjective visions do not transform human lives ; the resurrection moulded the apostles ; they did not create the resurrection (see Gore, Incarnation, 76). These appearances soon ceased, unlike the law of hallucinations, which increase in frequency and intensity. It is impossible to explain the ordinances, the Lord's day, or Christianity itself, if Jesus did not rise from the dead.

The resurrection of our Lord teaches three important lessons : (1) It showed that his work of atonement was completed and was stamped with the divine approval ; (2) It showed him to be Lord of all and gave the one sufficient external proof of Christianity ; (3) It furnished the ground and pledge of our own resurrection, and thus "brought life and immortality to light" (2 Tim. 1 : 10). It must be remembered that the resurrection was the one sign upon which Jesus himself staked his claims — "the sign of Jonah" (Luke 11: 29) ; and that the resurrection is proof, not simply of God's power, but of Christ's own power : John 10 : 18 — "I have power to lay it down, and I have power to take it again" ; 2: 19 — "Destroy this temple, and in three days I will raise it up". .... 21 — "he spake of the temple of his body." See Alexander, Christ and Christianity, 9, 158-224, 302 ; Mill, Theism, 216 ; Auberlen, Div. Revelation, 56 ; Boston Lectures, 203-239 ; Christlieb, Modern Doubt and Christian Belief, 448-503 ; Row, Bampton Lectures, 1887 : 358-423 ; Hutton, Essays, 1 : 119 ; Schaff, in Princton Rev., May, 1880 ; 411-419 Fisher, Christian Evidences, 41-46, 82-85 ; West, in Defence and Conf. of Faith. 80-129 ; also special works on the Resurrection of our Lord, by Milligan, Morrison. Kennedy, J. Baldwin Brown.

6. Counterfeit Miracles.

Since only an act directly wrought by God can properly be called a miracle, it follows that surprising events brought about by evil spirits or by men, through the use of natural agencies beyond our knowledge, are not entitled to this appellation. The Scriptures recognize the existence of such, but denominate them "lying wonders" (2 Thess. 2 : 9).

These counterfeit miracles in various ages argue that the belief in miracles is natural to the race, and that somewhere there must exist the true. They serve to show that not all supernatural occurrences are divine, and to impress upon us the necessity of careful examination before we accept them as divine.

False miracles may commonly be distinguished from the true by (a) their accompaniments of immoral conduct or of doctrine contradictory to truth already revealed—as in modern spiritualism; (b) their internal characteristics of inanity and extravagance—as in the liquefaction of the blood of St. Januarius, or the miracles of the Apocryphal New Testament; (c) the insufficiency of the object which they are designed to further—as in the case of Apollonius of Tyana, or of the miracles said to accompany the publication of the doctrines of the immaculate conception and of the papal infallibility; (d) their lack of substantiating evidence—as in mediæval miracles, so seldom attested by contemporary and disinterested witnesses; (e) their denial or undervaluing of God's previous revelation of himself in nature—as shown by the neglect of ordinary means, in the cases of Faith-cure and of so-called Christian Science.

Only what is valuable is counterfeited. False miracles presuppose the true. Fisher, Nature and Method of Revelation, 283—"The miracles of Jesus originated faith in him, while mediæval miracles follow established faith. The testimony of the apostles was given in the face of incredulous Sadducees. They were ridiculed and maltreated on account of it. It was no time for devout dreams and the invention of romances." The blood of St. Januarius at Naples is said to be contained in a vial, one side of which is of thick glass, while the other side is of thin. A similar miracle was wrought at Hales in Gloucestershire. St. Alban, the first martyr of Britain, after his head is cut off, carries it about in his hand. In Ireland the place is shown where St. Patrick in the fifth century drove all the toads and snakes over a precipice into the nether regions. The legend however did not become current until some hundreds of years after the saint's bones had crumbled to dust at Saul, near Downpatrick (see Hemphill, Literature of the Second Century, 180-182). Compare the story of the book of Tobit (6-8), which relates the expulsion of a demon by smoke from the burning heart and liver of a fish caught in the Tigris, and the story of the Apocryphal New Testament (I, Infancy), which tells of the expulsion of Satan in the form of a mad dog from Judas by the child Jesus. On counterfeit miracles in general, see Mozley, Miracles, 15, 161; F. W. Farrar, Witness of History to Christ, 72; A. S. Farrar, Science and Theology, 208; Tholuck, Vermischte Schriften, 1 : 27 ; Hodge, Syst. Theol., 1 : 630; Presb. Rev., 1881 : 687-719.

Some modern writers have maintained that the gift of miracles still remains in the church. Bengel: "The reason why many miracles are not now wrought is not so much because faith is established, as because unbelief reigns." Christlieb: "It is the want of faith in our age which is the greatest hindrance to the stronger and more marked appearance of that miraculous power which is working here and there in quiet concealment. Unbelief is the final and most important reason for the retrogression of miracles." Edward Irving, Works, 5:464—"Sickness is sin apparent in the body, the presentiment of death, the forerunner of corruption. Now, as Christ came to destroy death, and will yet redeem the body from the bondage of corruption, if the church is to have a first fruits or earnest of this power, it must be by receiving power over diseases that are the first fruits and earnest of death." Dr. A. J. Gordon, in his Ministry of Healing, held to this view. See also Boys, Proofs of the Miraculous in the Experience of the Church; Bushnell, Nature and the Supernatural, 446-492; Review of Gordon, by Vincent, in Presb. Rev., 1883: 475-502; Review of Vincent, in Presb. Rev., 1884: 49-79.

In reply to the advocates of faith-cure in general, we would grant that nature is plastic in God's hand; that he can work miracle when and where it pleases him; and that he has given promises which, with certain Scriptural and rational limitations, encourage believing prayer for healing in cases of sickness. But we incline to the belief that in these later ages God answers such prayer, not by miracle, but by special providence, and by gifts of courage, faith and will, thus acting by his Spirit directly upon the soul and only indirectly upon the body. The laws of nature are generic volitions of God, and to ignore them and disuse means is presumption and disrespect to God himself. The Scripture promise to faith is always expressly or impliedly conditioned upon our use of means: we are to work out our own salvation, for the very reason that it is God who works in us; it is vain for the drowning man to pray, so long as he refuses to lay hold of the rope that is thrown to him. Medicines and physicians are the rope thrown to us by God; we cannot expect miraculous help, while we neglect the help God has already given us; to refuse this help is practically to deny Christ's revelation in nature. Why not live without eating, as well as recover from sickness without medicine? Faith-feeding is quite as rational as faith-healing. To except cases of disease from this general rule as to the use of means has no warrant either in reason or in Scripture. The atonement has purchased complete salvation, and some day salvation shall be ours. But death and depravity still remain, not as penalty, but as chastisement. So disease remains also. Hospitals for Incurables, and the deaths even of advocates of faith-cure, show that they too are compelled to recognize some limit to the application of the New Testament promise.

In view of the preceding discussion we must regard the so-called Christian Science as neither Christian nor scientific. Mrs. Mary Baker G. Eddy denies the authority of all that part of revelation which God has made to man in nature, and holds that the laws of nature may be disregarded with impunity by those who have proper faith; see G. F. Wright, in Bib. Sac., April, 1899: 375. Bishop Lawrence of Massachusetts: "One of the errors of Christian Science is its neglect of accumulated knowledge, of the fund of information stored up for these Christian centuries. That knowledge is just as much God's gift as is the knowledge obtained from direct revelation. In rejecting accu. lated knowledge and professional skill, Christian Science rejects the gift of God." Most of the professed cures of Christian Science are explicable by the influence of the mind upon the body, through hypnosis or suggestion; (see A. A. Bennett, in Watchman, Feb. 13, 1905). Mental disturbance may make the mother's milk a poison to the child; mental excitement is a common cause of indigestion; mental depression induces bowel disorders; depressed mental and moral conditions render a person more susceptible to grippe, pneumonia, typhoid fever. Reading the account of an accident in which the body is torn or maimed, we ourselves feel pain in the same spot; when the child's hand is crushed, the mother's hand, though at a distance, becomes swollen; the mediæval *stigmata* probably resulted from continuous brooding upon the sufferings of Christ (see Carpenter, Mental Physiology, 676-690).

But mental states may help as well as harm the body. Mental expectancy facilitates cure in cases of sickness. The physician helps the patient by inspiring hope and courage. Imagination works wonders, especially in the case of nervous disorders. The diseases said to be cured by Christian Science are commonly of this sort. In every age fakirs, mesmerists, and quacks have availed themselves of these underlying mental forces. By inducing expectancy, imparting courage, rousing the paralyzed will, they have indirectly caused bodily changes which have been mistaken for miracle. Tacitus tell us of the healing of a blind man by the Emperor Vespasian. Undoubted cures have been wrought by the royal touch in England. Since such wonders have been performed by Indian medicine-men, we cannot regard them as having any specific Christian character, and when, as in the present case, we find them used to aid in the spread of false doctrine with regard to sin, Christ, atonement, and the church, we must class them with the "lying wonders" of which we are warned in 2 Thess. 2: 9. See Harris, Philosophical Basis of Theism, 381-386; Buckley, Faith-Healing, and in Century Magazine, June, 1886: 221-236; Bruce, Miraculous Element in Gospels, lecture 8: Andover Review, 1887: 249-264.

IV. PROPHECY AS ATTESTING A DIVINE REVELATION.

We here consider prophecy in its narrow sense of mere prediction, reserving to a subsequent chapter the consideration of prophecy as interpretation of the divine will in general.

1. *Definition.* Prophecy is the foretelling of future events by virtue of direct communication from God — a foretelling, therefore, which, though not contravening any laws of the human mind, those laws, if fully known, would not, without this agency of God, be sufficient to explain.

In discussing the subject of prophecy, we are met at the outset by the contention that there is not, and never has been, any real foretelling of future events beyond that which is possible to natural prescience. This is the view of Kuenen, Prophets and Prophecy in Israel. Pfleiderer, Philos. Relig., 2 : 42, denies any direct prediction. Prophecy in Israel, he intimates, was simply the consciousness of God's righteousness, proclaiming its ideals of the future, and declaring that the will of God is the moral ideal of the good and the law of the world's history, so that the fates of nations are conditioned by their bearing toward this moral purpose of God : "The fundamental error of the vulgar apologetics is that it confounds prophecy with heathen soothsaying — national salvation without character." W. Robertson Smith, in Encyc. Britannica, 19 : 821, tells us that "detailed prediction occupies a very secondary place in the writings of the prophets ; or rather indeed what seem to be predictions in detail are usually only free poetical illustrations of historical principles, which neither received nor demanded exact fulfilment."

As in the case of miracles, our faith in an immanent God, who is none other than the Logos or larger Christ, gives us a point of view from which we may reconcile the contentions of the naturalists and supernaturalists. Prophecy is an immediate act of God ; but, since all natural genius is also due to God's energizing, we do not need to deny the employment of man's natural gifts in prophecy. The instances of telepathy, presentiment, and second sight which the Society for Psychical Research has demonstrated to be facts show that prediction, in the history of divine revelation, may be only an intensification, under the extraordinary impulse of the divine Spirit, of a power that is in some degree latent in all men. The author of every great work of creative imagination knows that a higher power than his own has possessed him. In all human reason there is a natural activity of the divine Reason or Logos, and he is "the light which lighteth every man" (John 1 : 9). So there is a natural activity of the Holy Spirit, and he who completes the circle of the divine consciousness completes also the circle of human consciousness, gives self-hood to every soul, makes available to man the natural as well as the spiritual gifts of Christ ; *cf.* John 16 : 14 — "he shall take of mine, and shall declare it unto you." The same Spirit who in the beginning "brooded over the face of the waters" (Gen. 1 : 2) also broods over humanity, and it is he who, according to Christ's promise, was to "declare unto you the things that are to come" (John 16 : 13). The gift of prophecy may have its natural side, like the gift of miracles, yet may be finally explicable only as the result of an extraordinary working of that Spirit of Christ who to some degree manifests himself in the reason and conscience of every man ; *cf.* 1 Pet. 1 : 11 — "searching what time or what manner of time the Spirit of Christ which was in them did point unto, when it testified beforehand the sufferings of Christ, and the glories that should follow them." See Myers, Human Personality, 2 : 262–292.

A. B. Davidson, in his article on Prophecy and Prophets, in Hastings' Bible Dictionary, 4 : 120, 121, gives little weight to this view that prophecy is based on a natural power of the human mind : "The arguments by which Giesebrecht, Berufsgabung, 13 ff., supports the theory of a 'faculty of presentiment' have little cogency. This faculty is supposed to reveal itself particularly on the approach of death (Gen. 28 and 49). The contemporaries of most great religious personages have attributed to them a prophetic gift. The answer of John Knox to those who credited him with such a gift is worth reading : 'My assurances are not marvels of Merlin, nor yet the dark sentences of profane prophecy. But *first*, the plain truth of God's word ; *second*, the invincible justice of the everlasting God ; and *third*, the ordinary course of his punishments and plagues from the beginning, are my assurances and grounds.'" While Davidson grants the fulfilment of certain specific predictions of Scripture, to be hereafter mentioned, he holds that "such presentiments as we can observe to be authentic are chiefly products of the conscience or moral reason. True prophecy is based on moral grounds. Everywhere the menacing future is connected with the evil past by 'therefore' (Micah 3 : 12 ; Is. 5 : 13 ; Amos 1: 2)." We hold with Davidson to the moral element in prophecy, but we also recognize a power in normal humanity which he would minimize or deny. We claim that the human mind even in its ordinary and secular working gives occasional signs of transcending the limitations of the present. Believing in the continual activity of the divine Reason in the reason of man, we have no need to doubt the possibility of an extraordinary insight into the future, and such insight is needed at the great epochs of religious history. Expositor's Gk. Test., 2: 34—"Savonarola foretold as early as 1496 the capture of Rome, which happened in 1527, and he did this not only in general terms but in detail; his words were realized to the letter when the sacred churches of St. Peter and St. Paul became, as the prophet foretold, stables for the conquerors' horses." On the general subject, see Payne-Smith, Prophecy a Preparation for Christ; Alexander, Christ and Christianity; Farrar, Science and Theology, 106; Newton on Prophecy ; Fairbairn on Prophecy.

2. *Relation of Prophecy to Miracles.* Miracles are attestations of revelation proceeding from divine power ; prophecy is an attestation of revelation proceeding from divine knowledge. Only God can know the contingencies of the future. The possibility and probability of prophecy may be argued upon the same grounds upon which we argue the possibility and probability of miracles. As an evidence of divine revelation, however, prophecy possesses two advantages over miracles, namely : (*a*) The proof, in the case of prophecy, is not derived from ancient testimony, but is under our eyes. (*b*) The evidence of miracles cannot become stronger, whereas every new fulfilment adds to the argument from prophecy.

3. *Requirements in Prophecy, considered as an Evidence of Revelation.* (*a*) The utterance must be distant from the event. (*b*) Nothing must exist to suggest the event to merely natural prescience. (*c*) The utterance must be free from ambiguity. (*d*) Yet it must not be so precise as to secure its own fulfilment. (*e*) It must be followed in due time by the event predicted.

Hume: "All prophecies are real miracles, and only as such can be admitted as proof of any revelation." See Wardlaw, Syst. Theol., 1: 347. (*a*) Hundreds of years intervened between certain of the O. T. predictions and their fulfilment. (*b*) Stanley instances the natural sagacity of Burke, which enabled him to predict the French Revolution. But Burke also predicted in 1793 that France would be partitioned like Poland among a confederacy of hostile powers. Canning predicted that South American colonies would grow up as the United States had grown. D'Israeli predicted that our Southern Confederacy would become an independent nation. Ingersoll predicted that within ten years there would be two theatres for one church. (*c*) Illustrate ambiguous prophecies by the Delphic oracle to Crœsus: "Crossing the river, thou destroyest a great nation " — whether his own or his enemy's the oracle left undetermined. " Ibis et redibis nunquam peribis in bello." (*d*) Strauss held that O. T. prophecy itself determined either the events or the narratives of the gospels. See Greg, Creed of Christendom, chap. 4. (*e*) Cardan, the Italian mathematician, predicted the day and hour of his own death, and committed suicide at the proper time to prove the prediction true. Jehovah makes the fulfilment of his predictions the proof of his deity in the controversy with false gods: Is. 41: 23 — " Declare the things that are to come hereafter, that we may know that ye are gods "; 42: 9 — " Behold, the former things are come to pass and new things do I declare : before they spring forth I tell you of them."

4. *General Features of Prophecy in the Scriptures.* (*a*) Its large amount — occupying a great portion of the Bible, and extending over many hundred years. (*b*) Its ethical and religious nature — the events of the future being regarded as outgrowths and results of men's present attitude

toward God. (c) Its unity in diversity — finding its central point in Christ the true servant of God and deliverer of his people. (d) Its actual fulfilment as regards many of its predictions — while seeming non-fulfilments are explicable from its figurative and conditional nature.

A. B. Davidson, in Hastings' Bible Dictionary, 4: 125, has suggested reasons for the apparent non-fulfilment of certain predictions. Prophecy is poetical and figurative; its details are not to be pressed: they are only drapery, needed for the expression of the idea. In Isa. 13: 16 — "Their infants shall be dashed in pieces . . . and their wives ravished " — the prophet gives an ideal picture of the sack of a city; these things did not actually happen, but Cyrus entered Babylon "in peace." Yet the essential truth remained that the city fell into the enemy's hands. The prediction of Ezekiel with regard to Tyre, Ez. 26: 7-14, is recognized in Ez. 29: 17-20 as having been fulfilled not in its details but in its essence — the actual event having been the breaking of the power of Tyre by Nebuchadnezzar. Is. 17: — "Behold, Damascus is taken away from being a city, and it shall be a ruinous heap " — must be interpreted as predicting the blotting out of its dominion, since Damascus has probably never ceased to be a city. The conditional nature of prophecy explains other seeming non-fulfilments. Predictions were often threats, which might be revoked upon repentance. Jer. 26: 13 — "amend your ways . . . and the Lord will repent him of the evil which he hath pronounced against you." Jonah 3 : 4 — "Yet forty days, and Nineveh shall be overthrown . . . 10 — God saw their works, that they turned from their evil way; and God repented of the evil, which he said he would do unto them; and he did it not"; cf. Jer. 18 : 8; 26 : 19.

Instances of actual fulfilment of prophecy are found, according to Davidson, in Samuel's prediction of some things that would happen to Saul, which the history declares did happen (1 Sam. 1 and 10). Jeremiah predicted the death of Hananiah within the year, which took place (Jer. 28). Micaiah predicted the defeat and death of Ahab at Ramoth-Gilead (1 Kings 22). Isaiah predicted the failure of the northern coalition to subdue Jerusalem (Is. 7); the overthrow in two or three years of Damascus and Northern Israel before the Assyrians (Is. 8 and 17); the failure of Sennacherib to capture Jerusalem, and the melting away of his army (Is. 37:34-37). "And in general, apart from details, the main predictions of the prophets regarding Israel and the nations were verified in history, for example, Amos 1 and 2. The chief predictions of the prophets relate to the imminent downfall of the kingdoms of Israel and Judah; to what lies beyond this, namely, the restoration of the kingdom of God; and to the state of the people in their condition of final felicity." For predictions of the exile and the return of Israel, see especially Amos 9 : 9 — "For, lo, I will command, and I will sift the house of Israel among all the nations, like as grain is sifted in a sieve, yet shall not the least kernel fall upon the earth. . . . 14 — And I will bring again the captivity of my people Israel, and they shall build the waste cities and inhabit them." Even if we accept the theory of composite authorship of the book of Isaiah, we still have a foretelling of the sending back of the Jews from Babylon, and a designation of Cyrus as God's agent, in Is. 44 : 28 — "that saith of Cyrus, He is my shepherd, and shall perform all my pleasure: even saying of Jerusalem, She shall be built; and of the temple, Thy foundation shall be laid "; see George Adam Smith, in Hastings' Bible Dictionary, 2 : 493. Frederick the Great said to his chaplain: "Give me in one word a proof of the divine origin of the Bible"; and the chaplain well replied: "The Jews, your Majesty." In the case of the Jews we have even now the unique phenomena of a people without a land, and a land without a people, — yet both these were predicted centuries before the event.

5. *Messianic Prophecy in general.* (a) Direct predictions of events — as in Old Testament prophecies of Christ's birth, suffering and subsequent glory. (b) General prophecy of the Kingdom in the Old Testament, and of its gradual triumph. (c) Historical types in a nation and in individuals — as Jonah and David. (d) Prefigurations of the future in rites and ordinances — as in sacrifice, circumcision, and the passover.

6. *Special Prophecies uttered by Christ.* (a) As to his own death and resurrection. (b) As to events occurring between his death and the destruction of Jerusalem (multitudes of impostors ; wars and rumors of wars ; famine and pestilence). (c) As to the destruction of Jerusalem

and the Jewish polity (Jerusalem compassed with armies; abomination of desolation in the holy place; flight of Christians; misery; massacre; dispersion). (*d*) As to the world-wide diffusion of his gospel (the Bible already the most widely circulated book in the world).

The most important feature in prophecy is its Messianic element; see Luke 24:27 — "beginning from Moses and from all the prophets, he interpreted to them in all the scriptures the things concerning himself"; Acts 10:43 — "to him bear all the prophets witness"; Rev. 19:10 — "the testimony of Jesus is the spirit of prophecy." Types are intended resemblances, designed prefigurations: for example, Israel is a type of the Christian church; outside nations are types of the hostile world; Jonah and David are types of Christ. The typical nature of Israel rests upon the deeper fact of the community of life. As the life of God the Logos lies at the basis of universal humanity and interpenetrates it in every part, so out of this universal humanity grows Israel in general: out of Israel as a nation springs the spiritual Israel, and out of spiritual Israel Christ according to the flesh, — the upward rising pyramid finds its apex and culmination in him. Hence the predictions with regard to "the servant of Jehovah" (Is. 42:1-7), and "the Messiah" (Is. 61:1; John 1:41), have partial fulfilment in Israel, but perfect fulfilment only in Christ; so Delitzsch, Oehler, and Cheyne on Isaiah, 2:253. Sabatier, Philos. Religion, 59 — "If humanity were not potentially and in some degree Immanuel, God with us, there would never have issued from its bosom he who bore and revealed this blessed name." Gardiner, O. T. and N. T. in their Mutual Relations, 170-194.

In the O. T., Jehovah is the Redeemer of his people. He works through judges, prophets, kings, but he himself remains the Savior; "it is only the Divine in them that saves"; "Salvation is of Jehovah" (Jonah 2:9). Jehovah is manifested in the Davidic King under the monarchy; in Israel, the Servant of the Lord, during the exile; and in the Messiah, or Anointed One, in the post-exilian period. Because of its conscious identification with Jehovah, Israel is always a forward-looking people. Each new judge, king, prophet is regarded as heralding the coming reign of righteousness and peace. These earthly deliverers are saluted with rapturous expectation; the prophets express this expectation in terms that transcend the possibilities of the present; and, when this expectation fails to be fully realized, the Messianic hope is simply transferred to a larger future. Each separate prophecy has its drapery furnished by the prophet's immediate surroundings, and finds its occasion in some event of contemporaneous history. But by degrees it becomes evident that only an ideal and perfect King and Savior can fill out the requirements of prophecy. Only when Christ appears, does the real meaning of the various Old Testament predictions become manifest. Only then are men able to combine the seemingly inconsistent prophecies of a priest who is also a king (Psalm 110), and of a royal but at the same time a suffering Messiah (Isaiah 53). It is not enough for us to ask what the prophet himself meant, or what his earliest hearers understood, by his prophecy. This is to regard prophecy as having only a single, and that a human, author. With the spirit of man coöperated the Spirit of Christ, the Holy Spirit (1 Pet. 1:11 — "the Spirit of Christ which was in them"; 2 Pet. 1:21 — "no prophecy ever came by the will of man; but men spake from God, being moved by the Holy Spirit"). All prophecy has a twofold authorship, human and divine; the same Christ who spoke through the prophets brought about the fulfilment of their words.

It is no wonder that he who through the prophets uttered predictions with regard to himself should, when he became incarnate, be the prophet *par excellence* (Deut. 18:15; Acts 3:22 — "Moses indeed said, A prophet shall the Lord God raise up from among your brethren, like unto me; to him shall ye hearken"). In the predictions of Jesus we find the proper key to the interpretation of prophecy in general, and the evidence that while no one of the three theories — the preterist, the continuist, the futurist — furnishes an exhaustive explanation, each one of these has its element of truth. Our Lord made the fulfilment of the prediction of his own resurrection a test of his divine commission: it was "the sign of Jonah the prophet" (Mat. 12:39). He promised that his disciples should have prophetic gifts: John 15:15 — "No longer do I call you servants; for the servant knoweth not what his lord doeth: but I have called you friends; for all things that I heard from my Father I have made known unto you"; 16:13 — "the Spirit of truth . . . he shall declare unto you the things that are to come." Agabus predicted the famine and Paul's imprisonment (Acts 11:28; 21:10); Paul predicted heresies (Acts 20:29, 30), shipwreck (Acts 27:10, 21-26), "the man of sin" (2 Thess. 2:3), Christ's second coming, and the resurrection of the saints (1 Thess. 4:15-17).

7. *On the double sense of Prophecy.*

(*a*) Certain prophecies apparently contain a fulness of meaning which is not exhausted by the event to which they most obviously and literally refer. A prophecy which had a partial fulfilment at a time not remote from its utterance, may find its chief fulfilment in an event far distant. Since the principles of God's administration find ever recurring and ever enlarging illustration in history, prophecies which have already had a partial fulfilment may have whole cycles of fulfilment yet before them.

In prophecy there is an absence of perspective; as in Japanese pictures the near and the far appear equally distant; as in dissolving views, the immediate future melts into a future immeasurably far away. The candle that shines through a narrow aperture sends out its light through an ever-increasing area; sections of the triangle correspond to each other, but the more distant are far greater than the near. The châlet on the mountain-side may turn out to be only a black cat on the woodpile, or a speck upon the window pane. " A hill which appears to rise close behind another is found on nearer approach to have receded a great way from it." The painter, by foreshortening, brings together things or parts that are relatively distant from each other. The prophet is a painter whose foreshortenings are supernatural; he seems freed from the law of space and time, and, rapt into the timelessness of God, he views the events of history " sub specie eternitatis." Prophecy was the sketching of an outline-map. Even the prophet could not fill up the outline. The absence of perspective in prophecy may account for Paul's being misunderstood by the Thessalonians, and for the necessity of his explanations in 2 Thess. 2 : 1, 2. In Isaiah 10 and 11, the fall of Lebanon (the Assyrian) is immediately connected with the rise of the Branch (Christ); in Jeremiah 51 : 41, the first capture and the complete destruction of Babylon are connected with each other, without notice of the interval of a thousand years between them.

Instances of the double sense of prophecy may be found in Is. 7:14-16; 9:6, 7 — "a virgin shall conceive and bear a son, . . . unto us a son is given " — compared with Mat. 1 : 22, 23, where the prophecy is applied to Christ (see Meyer, *in loco*); Hos. 11 : 1 — "I . . . . called my son out of Egypt " — referring originally to the calling of the nation out of Egypt — is in Mat. 2 : 15 referred to Christ, who embodied and consummated the mission of Israel; Psalm 118 : 22, 23 — " The stone which the builders rejected Is become the head of the corner " — which primarily referred to the Jewish nation, conquered, carried away, and flung aside as of no use, but divinely destined to a future of importance and grandeur, is in Mat. 21 : 42 referred by Jesus to himself, as the true embodiment of Israel. William Arnold Stevens, on The Man of Sin, in Bap. Quar. Rev., July, 1889 : 323–360 — As in Daniel 11 : 36, the great enemy of the faith, who "shall exalt himself, and magnify himself above every god," is the Syrian King, Antiochus Epiphanes, so " the man of lawlessness " described by Paul in 2 Thess. 2:3 is the corrupt and impious Judaism of the apostolic age. This had its seat in the temple of God, but was doomed to destruction when the Lord should come at the fall of Jerusalem. But even this second fulfilment of the prophecy does not preclude a future and final fulfilment. Broadus on Mat., page 480 — In Isaiah 41 : 8 to chapter 53, the predictions with regard to " the servant of Jehovah " make a gradual transition from Israel to the Messiah, the former alone being seen in 41 : 8, the Messiah also appearing in 42 : 1 *sq.*, and Israel quite sinking out of sight in chapter 53.

The most marked illustration of the double sense of prophecy however is to be found in Matthew 24 and 25, especially 24 : 34 and 25 : 31, where Christ's prophecy of the destruction of Jerusalem passes into a prophecy of the end of the world. Adamson, The Mind in Christ, 183 — " To him history was the robe of God, and therefore a constant repetition of positions really similar, kaleidoscopic combining of a few truths, as the facts varied in which they were to be embodied." A. J. Gordon : " Prophecy has no sooner become history, than history in turn becomes prophecy." Lord Bacon : " Divine prophecies have springing and germinant accomplishment through many ages, though the height or fulness of them may refer to some one age." In a similar manner there is a manifoldness of meaning in Dante's Divine Comedy. C. E. Norton, Inferno, xvi — " The narrative of the poet's spiritual journey is so vivid and consistent that it has all the reality of an account of an actual experience; but within and beneath runs a stream of allegory not less consistent and hardly less continuous than the narrative itself." A. H. Strong. The Great Poets and their Theology, 116 — " Dante himself has told us that there are four separate senses which he intends his story to convey. There are the literal, the allegorical, the moral, and the anagogical. In Psalm 114:1 we have the words, ‘When Israel went forth out of Egypt.’ This, says the poet, may be taken literally, of the actual deliverance of God's ancient people; or allegorically, of the redemption of the world through Christ; or morally, of the rescue of the sinner from the bondage of his sin; or anagogically, of the passage of both soul and body from the lower life of earth to the higher life of heaven. So from Scripture Dante illustrates the method of his poem.” See further, our treatment of Eschatology. See also Dr. Arnold of Rugby, Sermons on the Interpretation of Scripture, Appendix A, pages 441-454; Aids to Faith, 449-462; Smith's Bible Dict., 4 : 2727. *Per contra*, see Elliott, Horæ Apocalypticæ, 4 : 662. Gardiner, O. T. and N. T., 262-274, denies double sense, but affirms manifold applications of a single sense. Broadus, on Mat. 24:1, denies double sense, but affirms the use of types.

(*b*) The prophet was not always aware of the meaning of his own prophecies (1 Pet. 1 :11). It is enough to constitute his prophecies a proof of divine revelation, if it can be shown that the correspondences between them and the actual events are such as to indicate divine wisdom and purpose in the giving of them — in other words, it is enough if the inspiring Spirit knew their meaning, even though the inspired prophet did not.

It is not inconsistent with this view, but rather confirms it, that the near event, and not the distant fulfilment, was often chiefly, if not exclusively, in the mind of the prophet when he wrote. Scripture declares that the prophets did not always understand their own predictions: 1 Pet. 1 : 11 — “searching what time or what manner of time the Spirit of Christ which was in them did point unto, when it testified beforehand the sufferings of Christ, and the glories that should follow them.” Emerson: “Himself from God he could not free; He builded better than he knew.” Keble: “As little children lisp and tell of heaven, So thoughts beyond their thoughts to those high bards were given.” Westcott: Preface to Com. on Hebrews, vi — “No one would limit the teaching of a poet's words to that which was definitely present to his mind. Still less can we suppose that he who is inspired to give a message of God to all ages sees himself the completeness of the truth which all life serves to illuminate.” Alexander McLaren: “Peter teaches that Jewish prophets foretold the events of Christ's life and especially his sufferings; that they did so as organs of God's Spirit; that they were so completely organs of a higher voice that they did not understand the significance of their own words, but were wiser than they knew and had to search what were the date and the characteristics of the strange things which they foretold; and that by further revelation they learned that ‘the vision is yet for many days’ (Is. 24:22; Dan. 10 : 14). If Peter was right in his conception of the nature of Messianic prophecy, a good many learned men of to-day are wrong.” Matthew Arnold, Literature and Dogma: “Might not the prophetic ideals be poetic dreams, and the correspondence between them and the life of Jesus, so far as real, only a curious historical phenomenon?” Bruce, Apologetics, 359, replies: “Such scepticism is possible only to those who have no faith in a living God who works out purposes in history.” It is comparable only to the unbelief of the materialist who regards the physical constitution of the universe as explicable by the fortuitous concourse of atoms.

8. *Purpose of Prophecy — so far as it is yet unfulfilled.* (*a*) Not to enable us to map out the details of the future ; but rather (*b*) To give general assurance of God's power and foreseeing wisdom, and of the certainty of his triumph ; and (*c*) To furnish, after fulfilment, the proof that God saw the end from the beginning.

Dan. 12 : 8, 9 — “And I heard, but I understood not ; then said I, O my Lord, what shall be the issue of these things ? And he said, Go thy way, Daniel ; for the words are shut up and sealed till the time of the end ” ; 2 Pet. 1 : 19 — prophecy is “a lamp shining in a dark place, until the day dawn ” = not until day dawns can distant objects be seen ; 20 — “no prophecy of scripture is of private interpretation ” = only God, by the event, can interpret it. Sir Isaac Newton: “God gave the prophecies, not to gratify men's curiosity by enabling them to foreknow things, but that after they were fulfilled they might be interpreted by the event, and his own providence, not the interpreter's, be thereby manifested to the world.” Alexander McLaren: “Great tracts of Scripture are dark to us till life explains them, and then they come on us with the force of a new revelation, like the messages which of old were sent by a strip of parchment coiled upon a bâton and then written upon, and which were unintelligible unless the receiver had a corresponding bâton to wrap them round." A. H. Strong, The Great Poets and their Theology, 23 — "Archilochus, a poet of about 700 B. C., speaks of 'a grievous *scytale*'—the *scytale* being the staff on which a strip of leather for writing purposes was rolled slantwise, so that the message inscribed upon the strip could not be read until the leather was rolled again upon another staff of the same size; since only the writer and the receiver possessed staves of the proper size, the *scytale* answered all the ends of a message in cypher."

Prophecy is like the German sentence, — it can be understood only when we have read its last word. A. J. Gordon, Ministry of the Spirit, 48 — "God's providence is like the Hebrew Bible; we must begin at the end and read backward, in order to understand it." Yet Dr. Gordon seems to assert that such understanding is possible even before fulfilment: "Christ did not know the day of the end when here in his state of humilation; but he does know now. He has shown his knowledge in the Apocalypse, and we have received 'The Revelation of Jesus Christ, which God gave him to show unto his servants, even the things which must shortly come to pass' (Rev. 1: 1)." A study however of the multitudinous and conflicting views of the so-called interpreters of prophecy leads us to prefer to Dr. Gordon's view that of Briggs, Messianic Prophecies, 49 — "The first advent is the resolver of all Old Testament prophecy; . . . the second advent will give the key to New Testament prophecy. It is 'the Lamb that hath been slain' (Rev. 5: 12) . . . who alone opens the sealed book, solves the riddles of time, and resolves the symbols of prophecy."

Nitzsch: "It is the essential condition of prophecy that it should not disturb man's relation to history." In so far as this is forgotten, and it is falsely assumed that the purpose of prophecy is to enable us to map out the precise events of the future before they occur, the study of prophecy ministers to a diseased imagination and diverts attention from practical Christian duty. Calvin: "Aut insanum inveniet aut faciet"; or, as Lord Brougham translated it: "The study of prophecy either finds a man crazy, or it leaves him so." Second Adventists do not often seek conversions. Dr. Cumming warned the women of his flock that they must not study prophecy so much as to neglect their household duties. Paul has such in mind in 2 Thess. 2: 1, 2 — "touching the coming of our Lord Jesus Christ . . . that ye be not quickly shaken from your mind . . . as that the day of the Lord is just at hand"; 3: 11 — "For we hear of some that walk among you disorderly."

9. *Evidential force of Prophecy — so far as it is fulfilled.* Prophecy, like miracles, does not stand alone as evidence of the divine commission of the Scripture writers and teachers. It is simply a corroborative attestation, which unites with miracles to prove that a religious teacher has come from God and speaks with divine authority. We cannot, however, dispense with this portion of the evidences, — for unless the death and resurrection of Christ are events foreknown and foretold by himself, as well as by the ancient prophets, we lose one main proof of his authority as a teacher sent from God.

Stearns, Evidence of Christian Experience, 338 — "The Christian's own life is the progressive fulfilment of the prophecy that whoever accepts Christ's grace shall be born again, sanctified, and saved. Hence the Christian can believe in God's power to predict, and in God's actual predictions." See Stanley Leathes, O. T. Prophecy, xvii — "Unless we have access to the supernatural, we have no access to God." In our discussions of prophecy, we are to remember that before making the truth of Christianity stand or fall with any particular passage that has been regarded as prediction, we must be certain that the passage is meant as prediction, and not as merely figurative description. Gladden, Seven Puzzling Bible Books, 195 — "The book of Daniel is not a prophecy, — it is an apocalypse. . . . The author [of such books] puts his words into the mouth of some historical or traditional writer of eminence. Such are the Book of Enoch, the Assumption of Moses, Baruch, 1 and 2 Esdras, and the Sibylline Oracles. Enigmatic form indicates persons without naming them, and historic events as animal forms or as operations of nature. . . . The book of Daniel is not intended to teach us history. It does not look forward from the sixth century before Christ, but backward from the second century before Christ. It is a kind of story which the Jews called Haggada. It is aimed at Antiochus Epiphanes, who, from his occasional fits of melancholy. was called Epimanes, or Antiochus the Mad."

Whatever may be our conclusion as to the authorship of the book of Daniel, we must recognize in it an element of prediction which has been actually fulfilled. The most radical interpreters do not place its date later than 163 B. C. Our Lord sees in the book clear reference to himself (Mat. 26 : 64 — "the Son of man, sitting at the right hand of Power, and coming on the clouds of heaven"; *cf.* Dan. 7: 13); and he repeats with emphasis certain predictions of the prophet which were yet unfulfilled (Mat. 24 : 15 — "When ye see the abomination of desolation, which was spoken of through Daniel the prophet"; *cf.* Dan. 9 : 27 ; 11: 31; 12 : 11). The book of Daniel must therefore be counted profitable not only for its moral and spiritual lessons, but also for its actual predictions of Christ and of the universal triumph of his kingdom (Dan. 2: 45 — "a stone cut out of the mountain without hands"). See on Daniel, Hastings' Bible Dictionary ; Farrar, in Expositor's Bible. On the general subject see Annotated Paragraph Bible, Introd. to Prophetical Books; Cairns, on Present State of Christian Argument from Prophecy, in Present Day Tracts, 5 : no. 27 ; Edersheim, Prophecy and History ; Briggs, Messianic Prophecy ; Redford, Prophecy, its Nature and Evidence ; Willis J. Beecher, the Prophet and the Promise; Orr, Problem of the O. T., 455–465.

Having thus removed the presumption originally existing against miracles and prophecy, we may now consider the ordinary laws of evidence and determine the rules to be followed in estimating the weight of the Scripture testimony.

V. PRINCIPLES OF HISTORICAL EVIDENCE APPLICABLE TO THE PROOF OF A DIVINE REVELATION (mainly derived from Greenleaf, Testimony of the Evangelists, and from Starkie on Evidence).

1. *As to documentary evidence.*

(*a*) Documents apparently ancient, not bearing upon their face the marks of forgery, and found in proper custody, are presumed to be genuine until sufficient evidence is brought to the contrary. The New Testament documents, since they are found in the custody of the church, their natural and legitimate depository, must by this rule be presumed to be genuine.

The Christian documents were not found, like the Book of Mormon, in a cave, or in the custody of angels. Martineau, Seat of Authority, 322—"The Mormon prophet, who cannot tell God from devil close at hand, is well up with the history of both worlds, and commissioned to get ready the second promised land." Washington Gladden, Who wrote the Bible ?—"An angel appeared to Smith and told him where he would find this book ; he went to the spot designated and found in a stone box a volume six inches thick, composed of thin gold plates, eight inches by seven, held together by three gold rings ; these plates were covered with writing, in the 'Reformed Egyptian tongue' ; with this book were the 'Urim and Thummim', a pair of supernatural spectacles, by means of which he was able to read and translate this 'Reformed Egyptian' language." Sagebeer, The Bible in Court, 113—"If the ledger of a business firm has always been received and regarded as a ledger, its value is not at all impeached if it is impossible to tell which particular clerk kept this ledger. . . . The epistle to the Hebrews would be no less valuable as evidence, if shown not to have been written by Paul.'' See Starkie on Evidence, 480 *sq.* ; Chalmers, Christian Revelation, in Works, 3 : 147-171.

(*b*) Copies of ancient documents, made by those most interested in their faithfulness, are presumed to correspond with the originals, even although those originals no longer exist. Since it was the church's interest to have faithful copies, the burden of proof rests upon the objector to the Christian documents.

Upon the evidence of a copy of its own records, the originals having been lost, the House of Lords decided a claim to the peerage ; see Starkie on Evidence, 51. There is no manuscript of Sophocles earlier than the tenth century, while at least two manuscripts of the N. T. go back to the fourth century. Frederick George Kenyon, Handbook to Textual Criticism of N. T.: "We owe our knowledge of most of the great works of Greek and Latin literature — Æschylus, Sophocles, Thucydides, Horace, Lucretius, Tacitus, and many more — to manuscripts written from 900 to 1500 years after their authors' deaths; while of the N. T. we have two excellent and approximately complete copies at an interval of only 250 years. Again, of the classical writers we have as a rule only a few score of copies (often less), of which one or two stand out as decisively superior to all the rest; but of the N. T. we have more than 3000 copies (besides a very large number of versions), and many of these have distinct and independent value." The mother of Tischendorf named him Lobgott, because her fear that her babe would be born blind had not come true. No man ever had keener sight than he. He spent his life in deciphering old manuscripts which other eyes could not read. The Sinaitic manuscript which he discovered takes us back within three centuries of the time of the apostles.

(c) In determining matters of fact, after the lapse of considerable time, documentary evidence is to be allowed greater weight than oral testimony. Neither memory nor tradition can long be trusted to give absolutely correct accounts of particular facts. The New Testament documents, therefore, are of greater weight in evidence than tradition would be, even if only thirty years had elapsed since the death of the actors in the scenes they relate.

See Starkie on Evidence, 51, 730. The Roman Catholic Church, in its legends of the saints, shows how quickly mere tradition can become corrupt. Abraham Lincoln was assassinated in 1865, yet sermons preached to-day on the anniversary of his birth make him out to be Unitarian, Universalist, or Orthodox, according as the preacher himself believes.

2.   *As to testimony in general.*

(a) In questions as to matters of fact, the proper inquiry is not whether it is possible that the testimony may be false, but whether there is sufficient probability that it is true. It is unfair, therefore, to allow our examination of the Scripture witnesses to be prejudiced by suspicion, merely because their story is a sacred one.

There must be no prejudice against, there must be open-mindedness to, truth; there must be a normal aspiration after the signs of communication from God. Telepathy, forty days fasting, parthenogenesis, all these might once have seemed antecedently incredible. Now we see that it would have been more rational to admit their existence on presentation of appropriate evidence.

(b) A proposition of fact is proved when its truth is established by competent and satisfactory evidence. By competent evidence is meant such evidence as the nature of the thing to be proved admits. By satisfactory evidence is meant that amount of proof which ordinarily satisfies an unprejudiced mind beyond a reasonable doubt. Scripture facts are therefore proved when they are established by that kind and degree of evidence which would in the affairs of ordinary life satisfy the mind and conscience of a common man. When we have this kind and degree of evidence it is unreasonable to require more.

In matters of morals and religion competent evidence need not be mathematical or even logical. The majority of cases in criminal courts are decided upon evidence that is circumstantial. We do not determine our choice of friends or of partners in life by strict processes of reasoning. The heart as well as the head must be permitted a voice, and competent evidence includes considerations arising from the moral needs of the soul. The evidence, moreover, does not require to be demonstrative. Even a slight balance of probability, when nothing more certain is attainable, may suffice to constitute rational proof and to bind our moral action.

(c) In the absence of circumstances which generate suspicion, every witness is to be presumed credible, until the contrary is shown ; the burden of impeaching his testimony lying upon the objector. The principle which leads men to give true witness to facts is stronger than that which leads them to give false witness. It is therefore unjust to compel the Christian to establish the credibility of his witnesses before proceeding to adduce their testimony, and it is equally unjust to allow the uncorroborated testimony of a profane writer to outweigh that of a Christian writer. Christian witnesses should not be considered interested, and therefore untrustworthy ; for they became Christians against their worldly interests, and because they could not resist the force of testimony. Varying accounts among them should be estimated as we estimate the varying accounts of profane writers.

John's account of Jesus differs from that of the synoptic gospels; but in a very similiar manner, and probably for a very similar reason, Plato's account of Socrates differs from that of Xenophon. Each saw and described that side of his subject which he was by nature best fitted to comprehend, — compare the Venice of Canaletto with the Venice of Turner, the former the picture of an expert draughtsman, the latter the vision of a poet who sees the palaces of the Doges glorified by air and mist and distance. In Christ there was a "hiding of his power" (Hab. 3 : 4) ; "how small a whisper do we hear of him ! " (Job 26 : 14); he, rather than Shakespeare, is "the myriad-minded "; no one evangelist can be expected to know or describe him except "in part" (1 Cor. 13 : 12). Frances Power Cobbe, Life, 2 : 402 — "All of us human beings resemble diamonds, in having several distinct facets to our characters; and, as we always turn one of these to one person and another to another, there is generally some fresh side to be seen in a particularly brilliant gem." E. P. Tenney, Coronation, 45 — "The secret and powerful life he [the hero of the story] was leading was like certain solitary streams, deep, wide, and swift, which run unseen through vast and unfrequented forests. So wide and varied was this man's nature, that whole courses of life might thrive in its secret places, — and his neighbors might touch him and know him only on that side on which he was like them."

(d) A slight amount of positive testimony, so long as it is uncontradicted, outweighs a very great amount of testimony that is merely negative. The silence of a second witness, or his testimony that he did not see a certain alleged occurrence, cannot counterbalance the positive testimony of a first witness that he did see it. We should therefore estimate the silence of profane writers with regard to facts narrated in Scripture precisely as we should estimate it if the facts about which they are silent were narrated by other profane writers, instead of being narrated by the writers of Scripture.

Egyptian monuments make no mention of the destruction of Pharaoh and his army: but then, Napoleon's dispatches also make no mention of his defeat at Trafalgar. At the tomb of Napoleon in the Invalides of Paris, the walls are inscribed with names of a multitude of places where his battles were fought, but Waterloo, the scene of his great defeat, is not recorded there. So Sennacherib, in all his monuments, does not refer to the destruction of his army in the time of Hezekiah. Napoleon gathered 450,000 men at Dresden to invade Russia. At Moscow the soft-falling snow conquered him. In one night 20,000 horses perished with cold. Not without reason at Moscow, on the anniversary of the retreat of the French, the exultation of the prophet over the fall of Sennacherib is read in the churches. James Robertson, Early History of Israel, 395, note — "Whately, in his Historic Doubts, draws attention to the fact that the principal Parisian journal in 1814, on the very day on which the allied armies entered Paris as conquerors, makes no mention of any such event. The battle of Poictiers in 732, which effectually checked the spread of Mohammedanism across Europe, is not once referred to in the monastic annals of the period. Sir Thomas Browne lived through the Civil Wars and the Commonwealth, yet there is no syllable in his writings with regard to them. Sale says that circumcision is regarded by Mohammedans as an ancient divine institution, the rite having been in use many years before Mohammed, yet it is not so much as once mentioned in the Koran."

Even though we should grant that Josephus does not mention Jesus, we should have a parallel in Thucydides, who never once mentions Socrates, the most important character of the twenty years embraced in his history. Wieseler, however, in Jahrbuch f. d. Theologie, 23 : 98, maintains the essential genuineness of the commonly rejected passage with regard to Jesus in Josephus, Antiq., 18 : 3 : 3, omitting, however, as interpolations, the phrases : "if it be right to call him man "; "this was the Christ "; " he appeared alive the third day according to prophecy "; for these, if genuine, would prove Josephus a Christian, which he, by all ancient accounts, was not. Josephus lived from A. D. 34 to possibly 114. He does elsewhere speak of Christ; for he records (20 : 9 : 1) that Albinus "assembled the Sanhedrim of judges, and brought before them the brother of Jesus who was called Christ, whose name was James, and some others . . . and delivered them to be stoned." See Niese's new edition of Josephus; also a monograph on the subject by Gustav Adolph Müller, published at Innsbruck, 1890. Rush Rhees, Life of Jesus of Nazareth, 22 — "To mention Jesus more fully would have required some approval of his life and teaching. This would have been a condemnation of his own people whom he desired to commend to Gentile regard, and he seems to have taken the cowardly course of silence concerning a matter more noteworthy, for that generation, than much else of which he writes very fully."

(e) " The credit due to the testimony of witnesses depends upon : first, their ability ; secondly, their honesty ; thirdly, their number and the consistency of their testimony; fourthly, the conformity of their testimony with experience ; and fifthly, the coincidence of their testimony with collateral circumstances." We confidently submit the New Testament witnesses to each and all of these tests.

See Starkie on Evidence, 726.

CHAPTER II.

I. The Genuineness of the Christian Documents, or proof that the books of the Old and New Testaments were written at the age to which they are assigned and by the men or class of men to whom they are ascribed.

Our present discussion comprises the first part, and only the first part, of the doctrine of the Canon (κανών, a measuring-reed; hence, a rule, a standard). It is important to observe that the determination of the Canon, or list of the books of sacred Scripture, is not the work of the church as an organized body. We do not receive these books upon the authority of Fathers or Councils. We receive them, only as the Fathers and Councils received them, because we have evidence that they are the writings of the men, or class of men, whose names they bear, and that they are also credible and inspired. If the previous epistle alluded to in 1 Cor. 5: 9 should be discovered and be universally judged authentic, it could be placed with Paul's other letters and could form part of the Canon, even though it has been lost for 1800 years. Bruce, Apologetics, 321 — "Abstractly the Canon is an open question. It can never be anything else on the principles of Protestantism which forbid us to accept the decisions of church councils, whether ancient or modern, as final. But practically the question of the Canon is closed." The Westminster Confession says that the authority of the word of God "does not rest upon historic evidence; it does not rest upon the authority of Councils; it does not rest upon the consent of the past or the excellence of the matter; but it rests upon the Spirit of God bearing witness to our hearts concerning its divine authority." Clarke, Christian Theology, 24 — "The value of the Scriptures to us does not depend upon our knowing who wrote them. In the O. T. half its pages are of uncertain authorship. New dates mean new authorship. Criticism is a duty, for dates of authorship give means of interpretation. The Scriptures have power because God is in them, and because they describe the entrance of God into the life of man."
Saintine, Picciola, 782 — "Has not a feeble reed provided man with his first arrow, his first pen, his first instrument of music?" Hugh Macmillan: "The idea of stringed instruments was first derived from the twang of the well strung bow, as the archer shot his arrows; the lyre and the harp which discourse the sweetest music of peace were invented by those who first heard this inspiring sound in the excitement of battle. And so there is no music so delightful amid the jarring discord of the world, turning everything to music and harmonizing earth and heaven, as when the heart rises out of the gloom of anger and revenge, and converts its bow into a harp, and sings to it the Lord's song of infinite forgiveness." George Adam Smith, Mod. Criticism and Preaching of O. T., 5 — "The church has never renounced her liberty to revise the Canon. The liberty at the beginning cannot be more than the liberty thereafter. The Holy Spirit has not forsaken the leaders of the church. Apostolic writers nowhere define the limits of the Canon, any more than Jesus did. Indeed, they employed extra-canonical writings. Christ and the apostles nowhere bound the church to believe all the teachings of the O. T. Christ discriminates, and forbids the literal interpretation of its contents. Many of the apostolic interpretations challenge our sense of truth. Much of their exegesis was temporary and false. Their judgment was that much in the O. T. was rudimentary. This opens the question of development in revelation, and justifies the attempt to fix the historic order. The N. T. criticism of the O. T. gives the liberty of criticism, and the need, and the obligation of it. O. T. criticism is not, like Baur's of the N. T., the result of a priori Hegelian reasoning. From the time of Samuel we have real history. The prophets do not appeal to miracles. There is more gospel in the book of Jonah, when

145

ıt is treated as a parable. The O. T. is a gradual ethical revelation of God. Few realize that the church of Christ has a higher warrant for her Canon of the O. T. than she has for her Canon of the N. T. The O. T. was the result of criticism in the widest sense of that word. But what the church thus once achieved, the church may at any time revise."

We reserve to a point somewhat later the proof of the credibility and the inspiration of the Scriptures. We now show their genuineness, as we would show the genuineness of other religious books, like the Koran, or of secular documents, like Cicero's Orations against Catiline. Genuineness, in the sense in which we use the term, does not necessarily imply authenticity (i. e., truthfulness and authority); see Blunt, Dict. Doct. and Hist. Theol., art. : Authenticity. Documents may be genuine which are written in whole or in part by persons other than they whose names they bear, provided these persons belong to the same class. The Epistle to the Hebrews, though not written by Paul, is genuine, because it proceeds from one of the apostolic class. The addition of Deut. 34, after Moses' death, does not invalidate the genuineness of the Pentateuch ; nor would the theory of a later Isaiah, even if it were established, disprove the genuineness of that prophecy ; provided, in both cases, that the additions were made by men of the prophetic class. On the general subject of the genuineness of the Scripture documents, see Alexander, McIlvaine, Chalmers, Dodge, and Peabody, on the Evidences of Christianity ; also Archibald, The Bible Verified.

1. *Genuineness of the Books of the New Testament.*

We do not need to adduce proof of the existence of the books of the New Testament as far back as the third century, for we possess manuscripts of them which are at least fourteen hundred years old, and, since the third century, references to them have been inwoven into all history and literature. We begin our proof, therefore, by showing that these documents not only existed, but were generally accepted as genuine, before the close of the second century.

Origen was born as early as 186 A. D.; yet Tregelles tells us that Origen's works contain citations embracing two-thirds of the New Testament. Hatch, Hibbert Lectures, 12—" The early years of Christianity were in some respects like the early years of our lives. . . . Those early years are the most important in our education. We learn then, we hardly know how, through effort and struggle and innocent mistakes, to use our eyes and ears, to measure distance and direction, by a process which ascends by unconscious steps to the certainty which we feel in our maturity. . . . It was in some such unconscious way that the Christian thought of the early centuries gradually acquired the form which we find when it emerges as it were into the developed manhood of the fourth century."

A. All the books of the New Testament, with the single exception of 2 Peter, were not only received as genuine, but were used in more or less collected form, in the latter half of the second century. These collections of writings, so slowly transcribed and distributed, imply the long continued previous existence of the separate books, and forbid us to fix their origin later than the first half of the second century.

(a) Tertullian (160–230) appeals to the 'New Testament' as made up of the 'Gospels' and 'Apostles.' He vouches for the genuineness of the four gospels, the Acts, 1 Peter, 1 John, thirteen epistles of Paul, and the Apocalypse ; in short, to twenty-one of the twenty-seven books of our Canon.

Sanday, Bampton Lectures for 1893, is confident that the first three gospels took their present shape before the destruction of Jerusalem. Yet he thinks the first and third gospels of composite origin, and probably the second. Not later than 125 A. D. the four gospels of our Canon had gained a recognized and exceptional authority. Andover Professors, Divinity of Jesus Christ, 40—" The oldest of our gospels was written about the year 70. The earlier one, now lost, a great part of which is preserved in Luke and Matthew, was probably written a few years earlier."

(*b*) The Muratorian Canon in the West and the Peshito Version in the East (having a common date of about 160) in their catalogues of the New Testament writings mutually complement each other's slight deficiencies, and together witness to the fact that at that time every book of our present New Testament, with the exception of 2 Peter, was received as genuine.

Hovey, Manual of Christian Theology, 50—"The fragment on the Canon, discovered by Muratori in 1738, was probably written about 170 A. D., in Greek. It begins with the last words of a sentence which must have referred to the Gospel of Mark, and proceeds to speak of the Third Gospel as written by Luke the physician, who did not see the Lord, and then of the Fourth Gospel as written by John, a disciple of the Lord, at the request of his fellow disciples and his elders." Bacon, N. T. Introduction, 50, gives the Muratorian Canon in full; 30—"Theophilus of Antioch (181-190) is the first to cite a gospel by name, quoting John 1:1 as from 'John, one of those who were vessels of the Spirit." On the Muratorian Canon, see Tregelles, Muratorian Canon. On the Peshito Version, see Schaff, Introd. to Rev. Gk.-Eng. N. T., xxxvii; Smith's Bible Dict., pp. 3388, 3389.

(*c*) The Canon of Marcion (140), though rejecting all the gospels but that of Luke, and all the epistles but ten of Paul's, shows, nevertheless, that at that early day "apostolic writings were regarded as a complete original rule of doctrine." Even Marcion, moreover, does not deny the genuineness of those writings which for doctrinal reasons he rejects.

Marcion, the Gnostic, was the enemy of all Judaism, and regarded the God of the O. T. as a restricted divinity, entirely different from the God of the N. T. Marcion was "ipso Paulo paulinior "—"plus loyal que le roi." He held that Christianity was something entirely new, and that it stood in opposition to all that went before it. His Canon consisted of two parts: the "Gospel" (Luke, with its text curtailed by omission of the Hebraistic elements) and the Apostolicon (the epistles of Paul). The epistle to Diognetus by an unknown author, and the epistle of Barnabas, shared the view of Marcion. The name of the Deity was changed from Jehovah to Father, Son, and Holy Ghost. If Marcion's view had prevailed, the Old Testament would have been lost to the Christian Church. God's revelation would have been deprived of its proof from prophecy. Development from the past, and divine conduct of Jewish history, would have been denied. But without the Old Testament, as H. W. Beecher maintained, the New Testament would lack background; our chief source of knowledge with regard to God's natural attributes of power, wisdom, and truth would be removed: the love and mercy revealed in the New Testament would seem characteristics of a weak being, who could not enforce law or inspire respect. A tree has as much breadth below ground as there is above; so the O. T. roots of God's revelation are as extensive and necessary as are its N. T. trunk and branches and leaves. See Allen, Religious Progress, 81, Westcott, Hist. N. T. Canon, and art.: Canon, in Smith's Bible Dictionary. Also Reuss, History of Canon; Mitchell, Critical Handbook, part I.

B. The Christian and Apostolic Fathers who lived in the first half of the second century not only quote from these books and allude to them, but testify that they were written by the apostles themselves. We are therefore compelled to refer their origin still further back, namely, to the first century, when the apostles lived.

(*a*) Irenæus (120–200) mentions and quotes the four gospels by name, and among them the gospel according to John: "Afterwards John, the disciple of the Lord, who also leaned upon his breast, he likewise published a gospel, while he dwelt in Ephesus in Asia." And Irenæus was the disciple and friend of Polycarp (80–166), who was himself a personal acquaintance of the Apostle John. The testimony of Irenæus is virtually the evidence of Polycarp, the contemporary and friend of the Apostle, that each of the gospels was written by the person whose name it bears.

To this testimony it is objected that Irenæus says there are four gospels because there are four quarters of the world and four living creatures in the cherubim. But we reply that Irenæus is here stating, not his own reason for accepting four and only four gospels, but what he conceives to be God's reason for ordaining that there should be four. We are not warranted in supposing that he accepted the four gospels on any other ground than that of testimony that they were the productions of apostolic men.

Chrysostom, in a similar manner, compares the four gospels to a chariot and four: When the King of Glory rides forth in it, he shall receive the triumphal acclamations of all peoples. So Jerome: God rides upon the cherubim, and since there are four cherubim, there must be four gospels. All this however is an early attempt at the philosophy of religion, and not an attempt to demonstrate historical fact. L. L. Paine, Evolution of Trinitarianism, 319-367, presents the radical view of the authorship of the fourth gospel. He holds that John the apostle died A. D. 70, or soon after, and that Irenæus confounded the two Johns whom Papias so clearly distinguished — John the Apostle and John the Elder. With Harnack, Paine supposes the gospel to have been written by John the Elder, a contemporary of Papias. But we reply that the testimony of Irenæus implies a long continued previous tradition. R. W. Dale, Living Christ and Four Gospels, 145 — "Religious veneration such as that with which Irenæus regarded these books is of slow growth. They must have held a great place in the Church as far back as the memory of living men extended." See Hastings' Bible Dictionary, 2: 695.

(b) Justin Martyr (died 148) speaks of 'memoirs (ἀπομνημονεύματα) of Jesus Christ,' and his quotations, though sometimes made from memory, are evidently cited from our gospels.

To this testimony it is objected: (1) That Justin Martyr uses the term 'memoirs' instead of 'gospels.' We reply that he elsewhere uses the term 'gospels' and identifies the 'memoirs' with them: Apol., 1 : 66 — "The apostles, in the memoirs composed by them, which are called gospels," i. e., not memoirs, but gospels, was the proper title of his written records. In writing his Apology to the heathen Emperors, Marcus Aurelius and Marcus Antoninus, he chooses the term 'memoirs', or 'memorabilia', which Xenophon had used as the title of his account of Socrates; simply in order that he may avoid ecclesiastical expressions unfamiliar to his readers and may commend his writing to lovers of classical literature. Notice that Matthew must be added to John, to justify Justin's repeated statement that there were "memoirs" of our Lord "written by apostles," and that Mark and Luke must be added to justify his further statement that these memoirs were compiled by "his apostles and those who followed them." Analogous to Justin's use of the word 'memoirs' is his use of the term 'Sunday', instead of Sabbath: Apol. 1 : 67 — "On the day called Sunday, all who live in cities or in the country gather together to one place, and the memoirs of the apostles or the writings of the prophets are read." Here is the use of our gospels in public worship, as of equal authority with the O. T. Scriptures; in fact, Justin constantly quotes the words and acts of Jesus' life from a written source, using the word γέγραπται. See Morison, Com. on Mat., ix ; Hemphill, Literature of Second Century, 234.

To Justin's testimony it is objected: (2) That in quoting the words spoken from heaven at the Savior's baptism, he makes them to be: "My son, this day have I begotten thee," so quoting Psalm 2: 7, and showing that he was ignorant of our present gospel, Mat. 3: 17. We reply that this was probably a slip of the memory, quite natural in a day when the gospels existed only in the cumbrous form of manuscript rolls. Justin also refers to the Pentateuch for two facts which it does not contain ; but we should not argue from this that he did not possess our present Pentateuch. The plays of Terence are quoted by Cicero and Horace, and we require neither more nor earlier witnesses to their genuineness, — yet Cicero and Horace wrote a hundred years after Terence. It is unfair to refuse similar evidence to the gospels. Justin had a way of combining into one the sayings of the different evangelists — a hint which Tatian, his pupil, probably followed out in composing his Diatessaron. On Justin Martyr's testimony, see Ezra Abbot, Genuineness of the Fourth Gospel, 49, note. B. W. Bacon, Introd. to N. T., speaks of Justin as "writing circa 155 A. D."

(c) Papias (80-164), whom Irenæus calls a 'hearer of John,' testifies that Matthew "wrote in the Hebrew dialect the sacred oracles (τὰ λόγα)," and that "Mark, the interpreter of Peter, wrote after Peter, (ὕστερον Πέτρῳ) [or under Peter's direction], an unsystematic account (οὐ τάξει)" of the same events and discourses.

To this testimony it is objected: (1) That Papias could not have had our gospel of Matthew, for the reason that this is Greek. We reply, either with Bleek, that Papias erroneously supposed a Hebrew translation of Matthew, which he possessed, to be the original; or with Weiss, that the original Matthew was in Hebrew, while our present Matthew is an enlarged version of the same. Palestine, like modern Wales, was bilingual; Matthew, like James, might write both Hebrew and Greek. While B. W. Bacon gives to the writing of Papias a date so late as 145–160 A. D., Lightfoot gives that of 130 A. D. At this latter date Papias could easily remember stories told him so far back as 80 A. D., by men who were youths at the time when our Lord lived, died, rose and ascended. The work of Papias had for its title Λογίων κυριακῶν ἐξήγησις — "Exposition of Oracles relating to the Lord " = Commentaries on the Gospels. Two of these gospels were Matthew and Mark. The view of Weiss mentioned above has been criticized upon the ground that the quotations from the O. T. in Jesus' discourses in Matthew are all taken from the Septuagint and not from the Hebrew. Westcott answers this criticism by suggesting that, in translating his Hebrew gospel into Greek, Matthew substituted for his own oral version of Christ's discourses the version of these already existing in the oral common gospel. There was a common oral basis of true teaching, the "deposit"—τὴν παραθήκην — committed to Timothy (1 Tim. 6: 20; 2 Tim. 1: 12, 14), the same story told many times and getting to be told in the same way. The narratives of Matthew, Mark and Luke are independent versions of this apostolic testimony. First came belief; secondly, oral teaching; thirdly, written gospels. That the original gospel was in Aramaic seems probable from the fact that the Oriental name for "tares," zawân, (Mat. 13: 25) has been transliterated into Greek, ζιζάνια. Morison, Com. on Mat., thinks that Matthew originally wrote in Hebrew a collection of Sayings of Jesus Christ, which the Nazarenes and Ebionites added to, partly from tradition, and partly from translating his full gospel, till the result was the so-called Gospel of the Hebrews; but that Matthew wrote his own gospel in Greek after he had written the Sayings in Hebrew. Professor W. A. Stevens thinks that Papias probably alluded to the original autograph which Matthew wrote in Aramaic, but which he afterwards enlarged and translated into Greek. See Hemphill, Literature of the Second Century, 267.

To the testimony of Papias it is also objected: (2) That Mark is the most systematic of all evangelists, presenting events as a true annalist, in chronological order. We reply that while, so far as chronological order is concerned, Mark is systematic, so far as logical order is concerned he is the most unsystematic of the evangelists, showing little of the power of historical grouping which is so discernible in Matthew. Matthew aimed to portray a life, rather than to record a chronology. He groups Jesus' teachings in chapters 5, 6, and 7; his miracles in chapters 8 and 9; his directions to the apostles in chapter 10; chapters 11 and 12 describe the growing opposition; chapter 13 meets this opposition with his parables; the remainder of the gospel describes our Lord's preparation for his death, his progress to Jerusalem, the consummation of his work in the Cross and in the resurrection. Here is true system, a philosophical arrangement of material, compared with which the method of Mark is eminently unsystematic. Mark is a Froissart, while Matthew has the spirit of J. R. Green. See Bleek, Introd. to N. T., 1: 108, 126; Weiss, Life of Jesus, 1: 27–39.

(d) The Apostolic Fathers, — Clement of Rome (died 101), Ignatius of Antioch (martyred 115), and Polycarp (80–166), — companions and friends of the apostles, have left us in their writings over one hundred quotations from or allusions to the New Testament writings, and among these every book, except four minor epistles (2 Peter, Jude, 2 and 3 John) is represented.

Although these are single testimonies, we must remember that they are the testimonies of the chief men of the churches of their day, and that they express the opinion of the churches themselves. "Like banners of a hidden army, or peaks of a distant mountain range, they represent and are sustained by compact, continuous bodies below." In an article by P. W. Calkins, McClintock and Strong's Encyclopædia, 1: 315–317, quotations from the Apostolic Fathers in great numbers are put side by side with the New Testament passages from which they quote or to which they allude. An examination of these quotations and allusions convinces us that these Fathers were in possession of all the principal books of our New Testament. See Ante-Nicene Library of T. and T. Clark; Thayer, in Boston Lectures for 1871: 324; Nash, Ethics and Revelation, 11—"Ignatius says to Polycarp: 'The times call for thee, as the winds call for the pilot.' So do the times call for reverent, fearless scholarship in the church." Such scholarship, we are persuaded, has already demonstrated the genuineness of the N. T. documents.

(e) In the synoptic gospels, the omission of all mention of the fulfilment of Christ's prophecies with regard to the destruction of Jerusalem is evidence that these gospels were written before the occurrence of that event. In the Acts of the Apostles, universally attributed to Luke, we have an allusion to 'the former treatise', or the gospel by the same author, which must, therefore, have been written before the end of Paul's first imprisonment at Rome, and probably with the help and sanction of that apostle.

Acts 1 : 1 — "The former treatise I made, O Theophilus, concerning all that Jesus began both to do and to teach." If the Acts was written A. D. 63, two years after Paul's arrival at Rome, then "the former treatise," the gospel according to Luke, can hardly be dated later than 60; and since the destruction of Jerusalem took place in 70, Matthew and Mark must have published their gospels at least as early as the year 68, when multitudes of men were still living who had been eye-witnesses of the events of Jesus' life. Fisher, Nature and Method of Revelation, 180—"At any considerably later date [than the capture of Jerusalem] the apparent conjunction of the fall of the city and the temple with the Parousia would have been avoided or explained. . . . Matthew, in its present form, appeared after the beginning of the mortal struggle of the Romans with the Jews, or between 65 and 70. Mark's gospel was still earlier. The language of the passages relative to the Parousia, in Luke, is consistent with the supposition that he wrote after the fall of Jerusalem, but not with the supposition that it was long after." See Norton, Genuineness of the Gospels; Alford, Greek Testament, Prolegomena, 30, 31, 36, 45-47.

C. It is to be presumed that this acceptance of the New Testament documents as genuine, on the part of the Fathers of the churches, was for good and sufficient reasons, both internal and external, and this presumption is corroborated by the following considerations :

(a) There is evidence that the early churches took every care to assure themselves of the genuineness of these writings before they accepted them.

Evidences of care are the following:—Paul, in 2 Thess. 2 : 2, urged the churches to use care, "to the end that ye be not quickly shaken from your mind, nor yet be troubled, either by spirit, or by word, or by epistle as from us"; 1 Cor. 5 : 9—"I wrote unto you in my epistle to have no company with fornicators"; Col. : 16 — "when this epistle hath been read among you, cause that it be read also in the church of the Laodiceans; and that ye also read the epistle from Laodicea." Melito (169), Bishop of Sardis, who wrote a treatise on the Revelation of John, went as far as Palestine to ascertain on the spot the facts relating to the Canon of the O. T., and as a result of his investigations excluded the Apocrypha. Ryle, Canon of O. T., 203 — "Melito, the Bishop of Sardis, sent to a friend a list of the O. T. Scriptures which he professed to have obtained from accurate inquiry, while traveling in the East, in Syria. Its contents agree with those of the Hebrew Canon, save in the omission of Esther." Serapion, Bishop of Antioch (191-213, Abbot), says: "We receive Peter and other apostles as Christ, but as skilful men we reject those writings which are falsely ascribed to them." Geo. H. Ferris, Baptist Congress, 1899 : 94 — "Serapion, after permitting the reading of the Gospel of Peter in public services, finally decided against it, not because he thought there could be no fifth gospel, but because he thought it was not written by Peter." Tertullian (160-230) gives an example of the deposition of a presbyter in Asia Minor for publishing a pretended work of Paul; see Tertullian, De Baptismo, referred to by Godet on John, Introduction; Lardner, Works, 2 : 304, 305; McIlvaine, Evidences, 92.

(b) The style of the New Testament writings, and their complete correspondence with all we know of the lands and times in which they profess to have been written, affords convincing proof that they belong to the apostolic age.

Notice the mingling of Latin and Greek, as in σπεκουλάτωρ (Mark 6:27) and κεντυρίων (Mark 15:39); of Greek and Aramæan, as in πρασιαὶ πρασιαί (Mark 6:40) and βδέλυγμα τῆς ἐρημώσεως (Mat. 24:15); this could hardly have occurred after the first century. Compare the anachronisms of style and description in Thackeray's " Henry Esmond," which, in spite of the author's special studies and his determination to exclude all words and phrases that had originated in his own century, was marred by historical errors that Macaulay in his most remiss moments would hardly have made. James Russell Lowell told Thackeray that "different to" was not a century old. "Hang it, no!" replied Thackeray. In view of this failure, on the part of an author of great literary skill, to construct a story purporting to be written a century before his time and that could stand the test of historical criticism, we may well regard the success of our gospels in standing such tests as a practical demonstration that they were written in, and not after, the apostolic age. See Alexander, Christ and Christianity, 27-37; Blunt, Scriptural Coincidences, 244-354.

(c) The genuineness of the fourth gospel is confirmed by the fact that Tatian (155-170), the Assyrian, a disciple of Justin, repeatedly quoted it without naming the author, and composed a Harmony of our four gospels which he named the Diatessaron ; while Basilides (130) and Valentinus (150), the Gnostics, both quote from it.

The sceptical work entitled "Supernatural Religion " said in 1874: "No one seems to have seen Tatian's Harmony, probably for the very simple reason that there was no such work "; and "There is no evidence whatever connecting Tatian's Gospel with those of our Canon." In 1876, however, there was published in a Latin form in Venice the Commentary of Ephraem Syrus on Tatian, and the commencement of it was: "In the beginning was the Word" (John 1:1). In 1888, the Diatessaron itself was published in Rome in the form of an Arabic translation made in the eleventh century from the Syriac. J. Rendel Harris, in Contemp. Rev., 1893: 800 sq., says that the recovery of Tatian's Diatessaron has indefinitely postponed the literary funeral of St. John. Advanced critics, he intimates, are so called, because they run ahead of the facts they discuss. The gospels must have been well established in the Christian church when Tatian undertook to combine them. Mrs. A. S. Lewis, in S. S. Times, Jan. 23, 1904—"The gospels were translated into Syriac before A. D. 160. It follows that the Greek document from which they were translated was older still, and since the one includes the gospel of St. John, so did the other." Hemphill, Literature of the Second Century, 183-231, gives the birth of Tatian about 120, and the date of his Diatessaron as 172 A. D.

The difference in style between the Revelation and the gospel of John is due to the fact that the Revelation was written during John's exile in Patmos, under Nero, in 67 or 68, soon after John had left Palestine and had taken up his residence at Ephesus. He had hitherto spoken Aramæan, and Greek was comparatively unfamiliar to him. The gospel was written thirty years after, probably about 97, when Greek had become to him like a mother tongue. See Lightfoot on Galatians, 343, 347 ; per contra, see Milligan, Revelation of St. John. Phrases and ideas which indicate a common authorship of the Revelation and the gospel are the following : "the Lamb of God," "the Word of God," "the True " as an epithet applied to Christ, "the Jews " as enemies of God, "manna," "him whom they pierced "; see Elliott, Horæ Apocalypticæ, 1:4, 5. In the fourth gospel we have ἀμνός, in Apoc. ἀρνίον, perhaps better to distinguish "the Lamb " from the diminutive τὸ θηρίον, "the beast." Common to both Gospel and Rev. are ποιεῖν, "to do" [the truth]; περιπατεῖν, of moral conduct; ἀληθινός, "genuine"; διψᾷν, πεινᾷν, of the higher wants of the soul; σκηνοῦν ἐν, ποιμαίνειν, ὁδηγεῖν; also 'overcome,' 'testimony,' 'Bridegooom,' 'Shepherd,' 'Water of life.' In the Revelation there are grammatical solecisms: nominative for genitive, 1:4 — ἀπὸ ὁ ὤν ; nominative for accusative, 7:9 — εἶδον .... ὄχλος πολύς; accusative for nominative, 20:2 -- τὸν δράκοντα ὁ ὄφις. Similarly we have in Rom. 12:5 — τὸ δὲ καθ' εἷς instead of τὸ δὲ καθ' ἕνα, where κατά has lost its regimen — a frequent solecism in later Greek writers; see Godet on John, 1: 269, 270. Emerson reminded Jones Very that the Holy Ghost surely writes good grammar. The Apocalypse seems to show that Emerson was wrong.

The author of the fourth gospel speaks of John in the third person, "and scorned to blot it with a name." But so does Cæsar speak of himself in his Commentaries. Harnack regards both the fourth gospel and the Revelation as the work of John the Pres-byter or Elder, the former written not later than about 110 A. D.; the latter from 93 to 96, but being a revision of one or more underlying Jewish apocalypses. Vischer has expounded this view of the Revelation; and Porter holds substantially the same, in his article on the Book of Revelation in Hastings' Bible Dictionary, 4 : 239-266. "It is the obvious advantage of the Vischer-Harnack hypothesis that it places the original work under Nero and its revised and Christianized edition under Domitian." (Sanday, Inspi-ration, 371, 372, nevertheless dismisses this hypothesis as raising worse difficulties than it removes. He dates the Apocalypse between the death of Nero and the destruction of Jerusalem by Titus.) Martineau, Seat of Authority, 227, presents the moral objections to the apostolic authorship, and regards the Revelation, from chapter 4 : 1 to 22 : 5, as a purely Jewish document of the date 66-70, supplemented and revised by a Christian, and issued not earlier than 136: "How strange that we should ever have thought it possible for a personal attendant upon the ministry of Jesus to write or edit a book mixing up fierce Messianic conflicts, in which, with the sword, the gory garment, the blasting flame, the rod of iron, as his emblems, he leads the war-march, and treads the winepress of the wrath of God until the deluge of blood rises to the horses' bits, with the speculative Christology of the second century, without a memory of his life, a feature of his look, a word from his voice, or a glance back at the hillsides of Galilee, the courts of Jerusalem, the road to Bethany, on which his image must be for-ever seen ! "

The force of this statement, however, is greatly broken if we consider that the apos-tle John, in his earlier days, was one of the "Boanerges, which is, Sons of thunder " (Mark 3 : 17), but became in his later years the apostle of love: 1 John 4 : 7 — "Beloved, let us love one another. for love is of God." The likeness of the fourth gospel to the epistle, which latter was undoubtedly the work of John the apostle, indicates the same authorship for the gos-pel. Thayer remarks that "the discovery of the gospel according to Peter sweeps away half a century of discussion. Brief as is the recovered fragment, it attests indubitably all four of our canonical books." Riddle, in Popular Com., 1 : 25 — "If a forger wrote the fourth gospel, then Beelzebub has been casting out devils for these eighteen hun-dred years." On the genuineness of the fourth gospel, see Bleek, Introd. to N. T., 1 : 250; Fisher, Essays on Supernat. Origin of Christianity, 33, also Beginnings of Chris-tianity, 320-362, and Grounds of Theistic and Christian Belief, 245-309; Sanday, Author-ship of the Fourth Gospel, Gospels in the Second Century, and Criticism of the Fourth Gospel; Ezra Abbott, Genuineness of the Fourth Gospel, 52, 80-87; Row, Bampton Lec-tures on Christian Evidences, 249-287; British Quarterly, Oct. 1872 : 216; Godet, in Pres-ent Day Tracts, 5 : no. 25; Westcott, in Bib. Com. on John's Gospel, Introd., xxviii-xxxii; Watkins, Bampton Lectures for 1890; W. L. Ferguson, in Bib. Sac., 1896 : 1-27.

(d) The epistle to the Hebrews appears to have been accepted during the first century after it was written (so Clement of Rome, Justin Martyr, and the Peshito Version witness). Then for two centuries, especially in the Roman and North African churches, and probably because its internal characteristics were inconsistent with the tradition of a Pauline authorship, its genuineness was doubted (so Tertullian, Cyprian, Irenæus, Muratorian Canon). At the end of the fourth century, Jerome examined the evidence and decided in its favor; Augustine did the same; the third Council of Carthage formally recognized it (397); from that time the Latin churches united with the East in receiving it, and thus the doubt was finally and forever removed.

The Epistle to the Hebrews, the style of which is so unlike that of the Apostle Paul, was possibly written by Apollos, who was an Alexandrian Jew, "a learned man" and "mighty in the Scriptures" (Acts 18 : 24); but it may notwithstanding have been written at the suggestion and under the direction of Paul, and so be essentially Pauline. A. C. Kendrick, in American Commentary on Hebrews, points out that while the style of Paul is prevailingly dialectic, and only in rapt moments becomes rhetorical or poetic, the style of the Epistle to the Hebrews is prevailingly rhetorical, is free from ana-coloutha, and is always dominated by emotion. He holds that these characteristics point to Apollos as its author. Contrast also Paul's method of quoting the O. T.: "it is written" (Rom. 11 : 8; 1 Cor. 1 : 31; Gal. 3 : 10) with that of the Hebrews: "he saith" (8 : 5, 13), "he ḥaḥ said " (4 : 4). Paul quotes the O. T. fifty or sixty times, but never in this latter way. Heb. 2 : 3 — " which having at the first been spoken by the Lord, was confirmed unto us by them that heard " — shows that the writer did not receive the gospel at first hand.   Luther and Calvin rightly saw in this a decisive proof that Paul was not the author, for he always insisted on the primary and independent character of his gospel. Harnack formerly thought the epistle written by Barnabas to Christians at Rome, A. D. 81-96. More recently however he attributes it to Priscilla, the wife of Aquila, or to their joint authorship. The majesty of its diction, seems unfavorable to this view. William T. C. Hanna: " The words of the author . . . are marshalled grandly, and move with the tread of an army, or with the swell of a tidal wave "; see Franklin Johnson, Quotations in N. T. from O. T., xii. Plumptre, Introd. to N. T., 37, and in Expositor, Vol. I, regards the author of this epistle as the same with that of the Apocryphal Wisdom of Solomon, the latter being composed before, the former after the writer's conversion to Christianity. Perhaps our safest conclusion is that of Origen: " God only knows who wrote it."   Harnack however remarks: "The time in which our ancient Christian literature, the N. T. included, was considered as a web of delusions and falsifications, is past. The oldest literature of the church is, in its main points, and in most of its details, true and trustworthy." See articles on Hebrews, in Smith's and in Hastings' Bible Dictionaries.

(e) As to 2 Peter, Jude, and 2 and 3 John, the epistles most frequently held to be spurious, we may say that, although we have no conclusive external evidence earlier than A. D. 160, and in the case of 2 Peter none earlier than A. D. 230–250, we may fairly urge in favor of their genuineness not only their internal characteristics of literary style and moral value, but also the general acceptance of them all since the third century as the actual productions of the men or class of men whose names they bear.

Firmilianus (250), Bishop of Cæsarea in Cappadocia, is the first clear witness to 2 Peter. Origen (230) names it, but, in naming it, admits that its genuineness is questioned. The Council of Laodicea (372) first received it into the Canon. With this very gradual recognition and acceptance of 2 Peter, compare the loss of the later works of Aristotle for a hundred and fifty years after his death, and their recognition as genuine so soon as they were recovered from the cellar of the family of Neleus in Asia; DeWette's first publication of certain letters of Luther after the lapse of three hundred years, yet without occasioning doubt as to their genuineness; or the concealment of Milton's Treatise on Christian Doctrine, among the lumber of the State Paper Office in London, from 1677 to 1823 ; see Mair, Christian Evidences, 95. Sir William Hamilton complained that there were treatises of Cudworth, Berkeley and Collier, still lying unpublished and even unknown to their editors, biographers and fellow metaphysicians, but yet of the highest interest and importance; see Mansel, Letters, Lectures and Reviews, 381; Archibald, The Bible Verified, 27. 2 Peter was probably sent from the East shortly before Peter's martyrdom; distance and persecution may have prevented its rapid circulation in other countries. Sagebeer, The Bible in Court, 114 — "A ledger may have been lost, or its authenticity for a long time doubted, but when once it is discovered and proved, it is as trustworthy as any other part of the res gestæ." See Plumptre, Epistles of Peter, Introd., 73-81; Alford on 2 Peter, 4 : Prolegomena, 157; Westcott, on Canon, in Smith's Bib. Dict., 1 : 370, 373 ; Blunt, Dict. Doct. and Hist. Theol., art. : Canon.

It is urged by those who doubt the genuineness of 2 Peter that the epistle speaks of "your apostles " (3:2), just as Jude 17 speaks of "the apostles," as if the writer did not number himself among them. But 2 Peter begins with "Simon Peter, a servant and apostle of Jesus Christ," and Jude, "brother of James" (verse 1) was a brother of our Lord, but not an apostle. Hovey, Introd. to N. T., xxxi — "The earliest passage manifestly based upon 2 Peter appears to be in the so-called Second Epistle of the Roman Clement, 16 : 3, which however is now understood to be a Christian homily from the middle of the second century."   Origen (born 186) testifies that Peter left one epistle, "and perhaps a second, for that is disputed." He also says: "John wrote the Apocalypse, and an epistle of very few lines; and, it may be, a second and a third; since all do not admit them to be genuine." He quotes also from James and from Jude, adding that their canonicity was doubted.

Harnack regards 1 Peter, 2 Peter, James, and Jude, as written respectively about 160, 170, 130, and 130, but not by the men to whom they are ascribed — the ascriptions to these authors being later additions. Hort remarks: "If I were asked, I should say that the balance of the argument was against 2 Peter, but the moment I had done so I should begin to think I might be in the wrong." Sanday, Oracles of God, 73 note, considers the arguments in favor of 2 Peter unconvincing, but also the arguments against. He cannot get beyond a *non liquet*. He refers to Salmon, Introd. to N. T., 529-559, ed. 4, as expressing his own view. But the later conclusions of Sanday are more radical. In his Bampton Lectures on Inspiration, 348, 399, he says: 2 Peter "is probably at least to this extent a counterfeit, that it appears under a name which is not that of its true author."

Chase, in Hastings' Bib. Dict., 3 : 806-817, says that "the first piece of *certain* evidence as to 2 Peter is the passage from Origen quoted by Eusebius, though it hardly admits of doubt that the Epistle was known to Clement of Alexandria. . . . We find no trace of the epistle in the period when the tradition of apostolic days was still living. . . . It was not the work of the apostle but of the second century . . . put forward without any sinister motive . . . the personation of the apostle an obvious literary device rather than a religious or controversial fraud. The adoption of such a verdict can cause perplexity only when the Lord's promise of guidance to his Church is regarded as a charter of infallibility." Against this verdict we would urge the dignity and spiritual value of 2 Peter — internal evidence which in our judgment causes the balance to incline in favor of its apostolic authorship.

(*f*) Upon no other hypothesis than that of their genuineness can the general acceptance of these four minor epistles since the third century, and of all the other books of the New Testament since the middle of the second century, be satisfactorily accounted for. If they had been mere collections of floating legends, they could not have secured wide circulation as sacred books for which Christians must answer with their blood. If they had been forgeries, the churches at large could neither have been deceived as to their previous non-existence, nor have been induced unanimously to pretend that they were ancient and genuine. Inasmuch, however, as other accounts of their origin, inconsistent with their genuineness, are now current, we proceed to examine more at length the most important of these opposing views.

The genuineness of the New Testament as a whole would still be demonstrable, even if doubt should still attach to one or two of its books. It does not matter that 2nd Alcibiades was not written by Plato, or Pericles by Shakespeare. The Council of Carthage in 397 gave a place in the Canon to the O. T. Apocrypha, but the Reformers tore it out. Zwingli said of the Revelation: "It is not a Biblical book," and Luther spoke slightingly of the Epistle of James. The judgment of Christendom at large is more trustworthy than the private impressions of any single Christian scholar. To hold the books of the N. T. to be written in the second century by other than those whose names they bear is to hold, not simply to forgery, but to a conspiracy of forgery. There must have been several forgers at work, and, since their writings wonderfully agree, there must have been collusion among them. Yet these able men have been forgotten, while the names of far feebler writers of the second century have been preserved.

G. F. Wright, Scientific Aspects of Christian Evidences, 343 — "In civil law there are 'statutes of limitations' which provide that the general acknowledgment of a purported fact for a certain period shall be considered as conclusive evidence of it. If, for example, a man has remained in undisturbed possession of land for a certain number of years, it is presumed that he has a valid claim to it, and no one is allowed to dispute his claim." Mair, Evidences, 99 — "We probably have not a tenth part of the evidence upon which the early churches accepted the N. T. books as the genuine productions of their authors. We have only their verdict." Wynne, in Literature of the Second Century, 58 — "Those who gave up the Scriptures were looked on by their fellow Christians as 'traditores,' traitors, who had basely yielded up what they ought to have treasured as dearer than life. But all their books were not equally sacred. Some were essential, and some were non-essential to the faith. Hence arose the distinction between *canonical* and *non-canonical*. The general consciousness of Christians grew into a distinct registration." Such registration is entitled to the highest respect, and lays the burden of proof upon the objector. See Alexander, Christ and Christianity, Introduction; Hovey, General Introduction to American Commentary on N. T.

D. **Rationalistic Theories as to the origin of the gospels.** These are attempts to eliminate the miraculous element from the New Testament records, and to reconstruct the sacred history upon principles of naturalism.

Against them we urge the general objection that they are unscientific in their principle and method. To set out in an examination of the New Testament documents with the assumption that all history is a mere natural development, and that miracles are therefore impossible, is to make history a matter, not of testimony, but of *a priori* speculation. It indeed renders any history of Christ and his apostles impossible, since the witnesses whose testimony with regard to miracles is discredited can no longer be considered worthy of credence in their account of Christ's life or doctrine.

In Germany, half a century ago, "a man was famous according as he had lifted up axes upon the thick trees" (Ps. 74: 5, A. V.), just as among the American Indians he was not counted a man who could not show his scalps. The critics fortunately scalped each other; see Tyler, Theology of Greek Poets, 79 — on Homer. Nicoll, The Church's One Foundation, 15 — "Like the mummers of old, sceptical critics send one before them with a broom to sweep the stage clear of everything for their drama. If we assume at the threshold of the gospel study that everything of the nature of miracle is impossible, then the specific questions are decided before the criticism begins to operate in earnest." Matthew Arnold: "Our popular religion at present conceives the birth, ministry and death of Christ as altogether steeped in prodigy, brimful of miracle,— and *miracles do not happen.*" This presupposition influences the investigations of Kuenen, and of A. E. Abbott, in his article on the Gospels in the Encyc. Britannica. We give special attention to four of the theories based upon this assumption.

1st. **The Myth-theory of Strauss (1808–1874).**

According to this view, the gospels are crystallizations into story of Messianic ideas which had for several generations filled the minds of imaginative men in Palestine. The myth is a narrative in which such ideas are unconsciously clothed, and from which the element of intentional and deliberate deception is absent.

This early view of Strauss, which has become identified with his name, was exchanged in late years for a more advanced view which extended the meaning of the word 'myths' so as to include all narratives that spring out of a theological idea, and it admitted the existence of 'pious frauds' in the gospels. Baur, he says, first convinced him that the author of the fourth gospel had "not unfrequently composed mere fables, knowing them to be mere fictions." The animating spirit of both the old view and the new is the same. Strauss says: "We know with certainty what Jesus was *not* and what he has *not* done, namely, nothing superhuman and supernatural." "No gospel can claim that degree of historic credibility that would be required in order to make us debase our reason to the point of believing miracles." He calls the resurrection of Christ "ein weltgeschichtlicher Humbug." "If the gospels are really historical documents, we cannot exclude miracle from the life-story of Jesus;" see Strauss, Life of Jesus, 17; New Life of Jesus, 1: preface, xii. Vatke, Einleitung in A. T., 210, 211, distinguishes the myth from the *saga* or legend: The criterion of the pure myth is that the experience is impossible, while the *saga* is a tradition of remote antiquity; the myth has in it the element only of belief, the *saga* has in it an element of history. Sabatier, Philos. Religion, 37 — "A myth is false in appearance only. The divine Spirit can avail himself of the fictions of poetry as well as of logical reasonings. When the heart was pure, the veils of fable always allowed the face of truth to shine through. And does not childhood run on into maturity and old age?"

It is very certain that childlike love of truth was not the animating spirit of Strauss. On the contrary, his spirit was that of remorseless criticism and of uncompromising hostility to the supernatural. It has been well said that he gathered up all the previous objections of sceptics to the gospel narrative and hurled them in one mass, just as if some Sadducee at the time of Jesus' trial had put all the taunts and gibes, all the buffetings and insults, all the shame and spitting, into one blow delivered straight into the face of the Redeemer. An octogenarian and saintly German lady said unsuspectingly that "somehow she never could get interested" in Strauss's Leben Jesu, which her sceptical son had given her for religious reading. The work was almost altogether destructive, only the last chapter suggesting Strauss's own view of what Jesus was.

If Luther's dictum is true that "the heart is the best theologian," Strauss must be regarded as destitute of the main qualification for his task. Encyc. Britannica, 22: 592 — "Strauss's mind was almost exclusively analytical and critical, without depth of religious feeling, or philosophical penetration, or historical sympathy. His work was rarely constructive, and, save when he was dealing with a kindred spirit, he failed as a historian, biographer, and critic, strikingly illustrating Goethe's profoundly true principle that loving sympathy is essential for productive criticism." Pfleiderer, Strauss's Life of Jesus, xix — "Strauss showed that the church formed the mythical traditions about Jesus out of its faith in him as the Messiah; but he did not show how the church came by the faith that Jesus of Nazareth was the Messiah." See Carpenter, Mental Physiology, 362; Grote, Plato, 1: 249.

We object to the Myth-theory of Strauss, that

(a) The time between the death of Christ and the publication of the gospels was far too short for the growth and consolidation of such mythical histories. Myths, on the contrary, as the Indian, Greek, Roman and Scandinavian instances bear witness, are the slow growth of centuries.

(b) The first century was not a century when such formation of myths was possible. Instead of being a credulous and imaginative age, it was an age of historical inquiry and of Sadduceeism in matters of religion.

Horace, in Odes 1: 34 and 3: 6, denounces the neglect and squalor of the heathen temples, and Juvenal, Satire 2 : 150, says that "Esse aliquid manes et subterranea regna Nec pueri credunt." Arnold of Rugby : "The idea of men writing mythic histories between the times of Livy and of Tacitus, and of St. Paul mistaking them for realities!" Pilate's sceptical inquiry, "What is truth?" (John 18 : 38), better represented the age. "The mythical age is past when an idea is presented abstractly — apart from narrative." The Jewish sect of the Sadducees shows that the rationalistic spirit was not confined to Greeks or Romans. The question of John the Baptist, Mat. 11: 3 — "Art thou he that cometh, or look we for another?" and our Lord's answer, Mat. 11 : 4, 5 — "Go and tell John the thing which ye hear and see : the blind receive their sight . . . the dead are raised up," show that the Jews expected miracles to be wrought by the Messiah ; yet John 10 : 41 — "John indeed did no sign" shows also no irresistible inclination to invest popular teachers with miraculous powers ; see E. G. Robinson, Christian Evidences, 22 ; Westcott, Com. on John 10:41 ; Rogers, Superhuman Origin of the Bible, 61 ; Cox, Miracles, 50.

(c) The gospels cannot be a mythical outgrowth of Jewish ideas and expectations, because, in their main features, they run directly counter to these ideas and expectations. The sullen and exclusive nationalism of the Jews could not have given rise to a gospel for all nations, nor could their expectations of a temporal monarch have led to the story of a suffering Messiah.

The O. T. Apocrypha shows how narrow was the outlook of the Jews. 2 Esdras 6: 55, 56 says the Almighty has made the world "for our sakes"; other peoples, though they "also come from Adam," to the Eternal "are nothing, but be like unto spittle." The whole multitude of them are only, before him, "like a single foul drop that oozes out of a cask" (C. Geikie, in S. S. Times). Christ's kingdom differed from that which the Jews expected, both in its *spirituality* and its *universality* (Bruce, Apologetics, 3). There was no missionary impulse in the heathen world; on the other hand, it was blasphemy for an ancient tribesman to make known his god to an outsider (Nash, Ethics and Revelation, 106). The Apocryphal gospels show what sort of myths the N. T. age would have elaborated: Out of a demoniac young woman Satan is said to depart in the form of a young man (Bernard, in Literature of the Second Century, 99-136).

(*d*) The belief and propagation of such myths are inconsistent with what we know of the sober characters and self-sacrificing lives of the apostles.

(*e*) The mythical theory cannot account for the acceptance of the gospels among the Gentiles, who had none of the Jewish ideas and expectations.

(*f*) It cannot explain Christianity itself, with its belief in Christ's crucifixion and resurrection, and the ordinances which commemorate these facts.

(*d*) Witness Thomas's doubting, and Paul's shipwrecks and scourgings. *Cf.* 2 Pet. 1 16 — οὐ γὰρ σεσοφισμένοις μύθοις ἐξακολουθήσαντες = " we have not been on the false track of myths artificially elaborated." See F. W. Farrar, Witness of History to Christ, 49-88. (*e*) See the two books entitled: If the Gospel Narratives are Mythical, — What Then? and, But How, -- if the Gospels are Historic? (*f*) As the existence of the American Republic is proof that there was once a Revolutionary War, so the existence of Christianity is proof of the death of Christ. The change from the seventh day to the first, in Sabbath observance, could never have come about in a nation so Sabbatarian, had not the first day been the celebration of an actual resurrection. Like the Jewish Passover and our own Independence Day, Baptism and the Lord's Supper cannot be accounted for, except as monuments and remembrances of historical facts at the beginning of the Christian church. See Muir, on the Lord's Supper an abiding Witness to the Death of Christ, in Present Day Tracts, 6: no. 36. On Strauss and his theory, see Hackett, in Christian Rev., 48 ; Weiss, Life of Jesus, 155-163 ; Christlieb, Mod. Doubt and Christ. Belief, 379-425 ; Maclear, in Strivings for the Faith, 1-136 ; H. B. Smith, in Faith and Philosophy, 442-468 ; Bayne, Review of Strauss's New Life, in Theol. Eclectic, 4 : 74 ; Row, in Lectures on Modern Scepticism, 305-360 ; Bibliotheca Sacra, Oct. 1871: art. by Prof. W. A. Stevens ; Burgess, Antiquity and Unity of Man, 263, 264 ; Curtis on Inspiration, 62-67 ; Alexander, Christ and Christianity, 92-126 ; A. P. Peabody, in Smith's Bible Dict., 2 : 954-958.

2nd. The Tendency-theory of Baur (1792-1860).

This maintains that the gospels originated in the middle of the second century, and were written under assumed names as a means of reconciling opposing Jewish and Gentile tendencies in the church. "These great national tendencies find their satisfaction, not in events corresponding to them, but in the elaboration of conscious fictions."

Baur dates the fourth gospel at 160-170 A. D.; Matthew at 130; Luke at 150; Mark at 150-160. Baur never inquires who Christ was. He turns his attention from the facts to the documents. If the documents be proved unhistorical, there is no need of examining the facts, for there are no facts to examine. He indicates the presupposition of his investigations, when he says: "The principal argument for the later origin of the gospels must forever remain this, that separately, and still more when taken together, they give an account of the life of Jesus which involves impossibilities "—*i. e.*, miracles. He would therefore' remove their authorship far enough from Jesus' time to permit regarding the miracles as inventions. Baur holds that in Christ were united the universalistic spirit of the new religion, *and* the particularistic form of the Jewish Messianic idea; some of his disciples laid emphasis on the one, some on the other; hence first conflict, but finally reconciliation; see statement of the Tübingen theory and of the way in which Baur was led to it, in Bruce, Apologetics, 360. E. G. Robinson interprets Baur as follows: "Paul — Protestant; Peter — sacramentarian; James — ethical; Paul + Peter + James — Christianity. Protestant preaching should dwell more on the ethical — cases of conscience — and less on mere doctrine, such as regeneration and justification "

Baur was a stranger to the needs of his own soul, and so to the real character of the gospel. One of his friends and advisers wrote, after his death, in terms that were meant to be laudatory: "His was a completely objective nature. No trace of personal needs or struggles is discernible in connection with his investigations of Christianity." The estimate of posterity is probably expressed in the judgment with regard to the Tübingen school by Harnack: "The *possible* picture it sketched was not the *real*, and the key with which it attempted to solve all problems did not suffice for the most simple. . . . The Tübingen views have indeed been compelled to undergo very large modifications. As regards the development of the church in the second century, it may safely be said that the hypotheses of the Tübingen school have proved themselves everywhere inadequate, very erroneous, and are to-day held by only a very few scholars." See Baur, Die kanonischen Evangelien; Canonical Gospels (Eng. transl.), 530; Supernatural Religion, 1 : 212–444 and vol. 2 : Pfleiderer, Hibbert Lectures for 1885. For accounts of Baur's position, see Herzog, Encyclopädie, art.: Baur; Clarke's transl. of Hase's Life of Jesus, 34–36; Farrar, Critical History of Free Thought, 227, 228.

We object to the Tendency-theory of Baur, that

(*a*) The destructive criticism to which it subjects the gospels, if applied to secular documents, would deprive us of any certain knowledge of the past, and render all history impossible.

The assumption of artifice is itself unfavorable to a candid examination of the documents. A perverse acuteness can descry evidences of a hidden *animus* in the most simple and ingenuous literary productions. Instance the philosophical interpretation of "Jack and Jill."

(*b*) The antagonistic doctrinal tendencies which it professes to find in the several gospels are more satisfactorily explained as varied but consistent aspects of the one system of truth held by all the apostles.

Baur exaggerates the doctrinal and official differences between the leading apostles. Peter was not simply a Judaizing Christian, but was the first preacher to the Gentiles, and his doctrine appears to have been subsequently influenced to a considerable extent by Paul's (see Plumptre on 1 Pet., 68–60). Paul was not an exclusively Hellenizing Christian, but invariably addressed the gospel to the Jews before he turned to the Gentiles. The evangelists give pictures of Jesus from different points of view. As the Parisian sculptor constructs his bust with the aid of a dozen photographs of his subject, all taken from different points of view, so from the four portraits furnished us by Matthew, Mark, Luke and John we are to construct the solid and symmetrical life of Christ. The deeper reality which makes reconciliation of the different views possible is the actual historical Christ. Marcus Dods, Expositor's Greek Testament, 1 : 675 — "They are not two Christs, but one, which the four Gospels depict: diverse as the profile and front face, but one another's complement rather than contradiction."

Godet, Introd. to Gospel Collection, 272 — Matthew shows the greatness of Jesus — his full-length portrait; Mark his indefatigable activity; Luke his beneficent compassion; John his essential divinity. Matthew first wrote Aramæan Logia. This was translated into Greek and completed by a narrative of the ministry of Jesus for the Greek churches founded by Paul. This translation was not made by Matthew and did not make use of Mark (217-224). E. D. Burton: Matthew — fulfilment of past prophecy; Mark — manifestation of present power. Matthew is argument from prophecy; Mark is argument from miracle. Matthew, as prophecy, made most impression on Jewish readers; Mark, as power, was best adapted to Gentiles. Prof. Burton holds Mark to be based upon oral tradition alone; Matthew upon his Logia (his real earlier Gospel) and other fragmentary notes; while Luke has a fuller origin in manuscripts and in Mark. See Aids to the Study of German Theology, 148-155; F. W. Farrar, Witness of History to Christ, 61.

(*c*) It is incredible that productions of such literary power and lofty religious teaching as the gospels should have sprung up in the middle of the second century, or that, so springing up, they should have been published under assumed names and for covert ends.

The general character of the literature of the second century is illustrated by Igna-tius's fanatical desire for martyrdom, the value ascribed by Hermas to ascetic rigor, the insipid allegories of Barnabas, Clement of Rome's belief in the phœnix, and the absurdities of the Apocryphal Gospels. The author of the fourth gospel among the writers of the second century would have been a mountain among mole-hills. Wynne, Literature of the Second Century, 60—"The apostolic and the sub-apostolic writers dif fer from each other as a nugget of pure gold differs from a block of quartz with veins of the precious metal gleaming through it." Dorner, Hist. Doct. Person Christ, 1:1:92 —"Instead of the writers of the second century marking an advance on the apostolic age, or developing the germ given them by the apostles, the second century shows great retrogression,—its writers were not able to retain or comprehend all that had been given them." Martineau, Seat of Authority, 291—"Writers not only barbarous in speech and rude in art, but too often puerile in conception, passionate in temper, and credulous in belief. The legends of Papias, the visions of Hermas, the imbecility of Irenæus, the fury of Tertullian, the rancor and indelicacy of Jerome, the stormy intoler-ance of Augustine, cannot fail to startle and repel the student; and, if he turns to the milder Hippolytus, he is introduced to a brood of thirty heresies which sadly dissipate his dream of the unity of the church." We can apply to the writers of the second century the question of R. G. Ingersoll in the Shakespeare-Bacon controversy: "Is it possible that Bacon left the best children of his brain on Shakespeare's doorstep, and kept only the deformed ones at home?" On the Apocryphal Gospels, see Cowper, in Strivings for the Faith, 73–108.

(d) The theory requires us to believe in a moral anomaly, namely, that a faithful disciple of Christ in the second century could be guilty of fabri-cating a life of his master, and of claiming authority for it on the ground that the author had been a companion of Christ or his apostles.

"A genial set of Jesuitical religionists"—with mind and heart enough to write the gospel according to John, and who at the same time have cold-blooded sagacity enough to keep out of their writings every trace of the developments of church authority belonging to the second century. The newly discovered "Teaching of the Twelve Apostles," if dating from the early part of that century, shows that such a combi-nation is impossible. The critical theories assume that one who knew Christ as a man could not possibly also regard him as God. Lowrie, Doctrine of St. John, 12—"If St. John wrote, it is not possible to say that the genius of St. Paul foisted upon the church a conception which was strange to the original apostles." Fairbairn has well shown that if Christianity had been simply the ethical teaching of the human Jesus, it would have vanished from the earth like the sects of the Pharisees and of the Sadducees; if on the other hand it had been simply the Logos-doctrine, the doctrine of a divine Christ, it would have passed away like the speculations of Plato or Aristotle; because Christianity unites the idea of the eternal Son of God with that of the incarnate Son of man, it is fitted to be and it has become an universal religion; see Fairbairn, Philos-ophy of the Christian Religion, 4, 15—"Without the personal charm of the historical Jesus, the œcumenical creeds would never have been either formulated or tolerated, and without the metaphysical conception of Christ the Christian religion would long ago have ceased to live. . . . It is not Jesus of Nazareth who has so powerfully entered into history; it is the deified Christ who has been believed, loved and obeyed as the Savior of the world. . . . The two parts of Christian doctrine are combined in the one name ' Jesus Christ.' "

(e) This theory cannot account for the universal acceptance of the gos-pels at the end of the second century, among widely separated communi-ties where reverence for writings of the apostles was a mark of orthodoxy, and where the Gnostic heresies would have made new documents instantly liable to suspicion and searching examination.

Abbot, Genuineness of the Fourth Gospel, 52, 80, 88, 89. The Johannine doctrine of the Logos, if first propounded in the middle of the second century, would have ensured the instant rejection of that gospel by the Gnostics, who ascribed creation, not to the Logos, but to successive " Æons." How did the Gnostics, without " peep or mutter," come to accept as genuine what had only in their own time been first sprung upon the churches? While Basilides (130) and Valentinus (150), the Gnostics, both quote from the fourth gospel, they do not dispute its genuineness or suggest that it was of recent origin. Bruce, in his Apologetics, says of Baur "He believed in the all-sufficiency of the Hegelian theory of development through antagonism. He saw tendency everywhere. Anything additional, putting more contents into the person and teaching of Jesus than suits the initial stage of development, must be reckoned spurious. If we find Jesus in any of the gospels claiming to be a supernatural being, such texts can with the utmost confidence be set aside as spurious, for such a thought could not belong to the initial stage of Christianity." But such a conception certainly existed in the second century, and it directly antagonized the speculations of the Gnostics. F. W. Farrar, on Hebrews 1 2—"The word æon was used by the later Gnostics to describe the various emanations by which they tried at once to widen and to bridge over the gulf between the human and the divine. Over that imaginary chasm John threw the arch of the Incarnation, when he wrote : 'The Word became flesh' (John 1 : 14)." A document which so contradicted the Gnostic teachings could not in the second century have been quoted by the Gnostics themselves without dispute as to its genuineness, if it had not been long recognized in the churches as a work of the apostle John.

(*f*) The acknowledgment by Baur that the epistles to the Romans, Galatians and Corinthians were written by Paul in the first century is fatal to his theory, since these epistles testify not only to miracles at the period at which they were written, but to the main events of Jesus' life and to the miracle of his resurrection, as facts already long acknowledged in the Christian church.

Baur, Paulus der Apostel, 276—"There never has been the slightest suspicion of unauthenticity cast on these epistles (Gal., 1 and 2 Cor., Rom.), and they bear so incontestably the character of Pauline originality, that there is no conceivable ground for the assertion of critical doubts in their case." Baur, in discussing the appearance of Christ to Paul on the way to Damascus, explains the outward from the inward : Paul translated intense and sudden conviction of the truth of the Christian religion into an outward scene. But this cannot explain the hearing of the outward sound by Paul's companions. On the evidential value of the epistles here mentioned, see Lorimer, in Strivings for the Faith, 109–144 ; Howson, in Present Day Tracts, 4 : no. 24; Row, Bampton Lectures for 1877: 289–356. On Baur and his theory in general, see Weiss, Life of Jesus, 1: 157 sq.; Christlieb, Mod. Doubt and Christ. Belief, 504–549 ; Hutton, Essays, 1: 176–215; Theol. Eclectic, 5 : 1–42; Auberlen, Div. Revelation; Bib. Sac., 19: 75; Answers to Supernatural Religion, in Westcott, Hist. N. T. Canon, 4th ed., Introd.; Lightfoot, in Contemporary Rev., Dec. 1874, and Jan. 1875; Salmon, Introd. to N. T., 6–31; A. B. Bruce, in Present Day Tracts, 7 : no. 38.

3d. The Romance-theory of Renan (1823–1892).

This theory admits a basis of truth in the gospels and holds that they all belong to the century following Jesus' death. "According to" Matthew, Mark, etc., however, means only that Matthew, Mark, etc., wrote these gospels in substance. Renan claims that the facts of Jesus' life were so sublimated by enthusiasm, and so overlaid with pious fraud, that the gospels in their present form cannot be accepted as genuine,—in short, the gospels are to be regarded as historical romances which have only a foundation in fact.

The *animus* of this theory is plainly shown in Renan's Life of Jesus, preface to 13th ed.—"If miracles and the inspiration of certain books are realities, my method is detestable. If miracles and the inspiration of books are beliefs without reality, my method is a good one. But the question of the supernatural is decided for us with perfect certainty by the single consideration that there is no room for believing in a thing of which the world offers no experimental trace." "On the whole," says Renan, "I admit as authentic the four canonical gospels. All, in my opinion, date from the first century, and the authors are, generally speaking, those to whom they are attributed." He regards Gal., 1 and 2 Cor., and Rom., as "indisputable and undisputed." He speaks of them as " being texts of an absolute authenticity, of complete sincerity, and without legends " (Les Apôtres, xxix ; Les Évangiles, xi). Yet he denies to Jesus "sincerity with himself "; attributes to him "innocent artifice " and the toleration of pious fraud, as for example in the case of the stories of Lazarus and of his own resurrection. " To conceive the good is not sufficient : it must be made to succeed; to accomplish this, less pure paths must be followed. . . . Not by any fault of his own, his conscience lost somewhat of its original purity, — his mission overwhelmed him. . . . Did he regret his too lofty nature, and, victim of his own greatness, mourn that he had not remained a simple artizan ? " So Renan " pictures Christ's later life as a misery and a lie, yet he requests us to bow before this sinner and before his superior, Sakya-Mouni, as demi-gods " (see Nicoll, The Church's One Foundation, 62, 63). Of the highly wrought imagi-nation of Mary Magdalene, he says: " O divine power of love ! sacred moments, in which the passion of one whose senses were deceived gives us a resuscitated God ! " See Renan, Life of Jesus, 21.

To this Romance-theory of Renan, we object that

(a) It involves an arbitrary and partial treatment of the Christian doc-uments. The claim that one writer not only borrowed from others, but interpolated *ad libitum*, is contradicted by the essential agreement of the manuscripts as quoted by the Fathers, and as now extant.

Renan, according to Mair, Christian Evidences, 153, dates Matthew at 84 A. D.; Mark at 76; Luke at 94; John at 125. These dates mark a considerable retreat from the advanced positions taken by Baur. Mair, in his chapter on Recent Reverses in Nega-tive Criticism, attributes this result to the late discoveries with regard to the Epistle of Barnabas, Hippolytus's Refutation of all Heresies, the Clementine Homilies, and Tatian's Diatessaron : " According to Baur and his immediate followers, we have less than one quarter of the N. T. belonging to the first century. According to Hilgenfeld, the present head of the Baur school, we have somewhat less than three quarters belong-ing to the first century, while substantially the same thing may be said with regard to Holzmann. According to Renan, we have distinctly more than three quarters of the N. T. falling within the first century, and therefore within the apostolic age. This surely indicates a very decided and extraordinary retreat since the time of Baur's grand assault, that is, within the last fifty years." We may add that the concession of author-ship within the apostolic age renders nugatory Renan's hypothesis that the N. T. docu-ments have been so enlarged by pious fraud that they cannot be accepted as trustworthy accounts of such events as miracles. The oral tradition itself had attained so fixed a form that the many manuscripts used by the Fathers were in substantial agreement in respect to these very events, and oral tradition in the East hands down without serious alteration much longer narratives than those of our gospels. The Pundita Ramabai can repeat after the lapse of twenty years portions of the Hindu sacred books exceed-ing in amount the whole contents of our Old Testament. Many cultivated men in Athens knew by heart all the Iliad and the Odyssey of Homer. Memory and reverence alike kept the gospel narratives free from the corruption which Renan supposes.

(b) It attributes to Christ and to the apostles an alternate fervor of romantic enthusiasm and a false pretense of miraculous power which are utterly irreconcilable with the manifest sobriety and holiness of their lives and teachings. If Jesus did not work miracles, he was an impostor.

On Ernest Renan, His Life and the Life of Jesus, see A. H. Strong, Christ in Creation, 332–363, especially 356 — " Renan attributes the origin of Christianity to the predomi-nance in Palestine of a constitutional susceptibility to mystic excitements. Christ is to him the incarnation of sympathy and tears, a being of tender impulses and passionate ardors, whose native genius it was to play upon the hearts of men. Truth or falsehood made little difference to him ; anything that would comfort the poor, or touch the finer feelings of humanity, he availed himself of; ecstasies, visions, melting moods, these were the secrets of his power. Religion was a beneficent superstition, a sweet delusion — excellent as a balm and solace for the ignorant crowd, who never could be philoso-phers if they tried. And so the gospel river, as one has said, is traced back to a foun-tain of weeping men and women whose brains had oozed out at their eyes, and the per-fection of spirituality is made to be a sort of maudlin monasticism. . . . How different from the strong and holy love of Christ, which would save men only by bringing them to the truth, and which claims men's imitation only because, without love for God and for the soul, a man is without truth.   How inexplicable from this view the fact that a pure Christianity has everywhere quickened the intellect of the nations, and that every revival of it, as at the Reformation, has been followed by mighty forward leaps of civilization.   Was Paul a man carried away by mystic dreams and irrational enthusiasms?   Let the keen dialectic skill of his epistles and his profound grasp of the great matters of revelation answer.   Has the Christian church been a company of puling sentimentalists?   Let the heroic deaths for the truth suffered by the martyrs witness.   Nay.   he must have a low idea of his kind, and a yet lower idea of the God who made them, who can believe that the noblest spirits of the race have risen to greatness by abnegating will and reason, and have gained influence over all ages by resigning themselves to semi-idiocy.''

(c) It fails to account for the power and progress of the gospel, as a system directly opposed to men's natural tastes and prepossessions — a system which substitutes truth for romance and law for impulse.

A. H. Strong, Christ in Creation, 358 — "And if the later triumphs of Christianity are inexplicable upon the theory of Renan, how can we explain its founding? The sweet swain of Galilee, beloved by women for his beauty, fascinating the unlettered crowd by his gentle speech and his poetic ideals, giving comfort to the sorrowing and hope to the poor, credited with supernatural power which at first he thinks it not worth while to deny and finally gratifies the multitude by pretending to exercise, roused by opposition to polemics and invective until the delightful young rabbi becomes a gloomy giant, an intractable fanatic, a fierce revolutionist, whose denunciation of the powers that be brings him to the Cross,— what is there in *him* to account for the moral wonder which we call Christianity and the beginnings of its empire in the world?   Neither delicious pastorals like those of Jesus' first period, nor apocalyptic fevers like those of his second period, according to Renan's gospel, furnish any rational explanation of that mighty movement which has swept through the earth and has revolutionized the faith of mankind.''

Berdoe, Browning, 47 — "If Christ were not God, his life at that stage of the world's history could by no possibility have had the vitalizing force and love-compelling power that Renan's pages everywhere disclose.   Renan has strengthened faith in Christ's deity while laboring to destroy it.''

Renan, in discussing Christ's appearance to Paul on the way to Damascus, explains the inward from the outward. thus precisely reversing the conclusion of Baur.   A sudden storm, a flash of lightning, a sudden attack of ophthalmic fever, Paul took as an appearance from heaven.   But we reply that so keen an observer and reasoner could not have been thus deceived.   Nothing could have made him the apostle to the Gentiles but a sight of the glorified Christ and the accompanying revelation of the holiness of God, his own sin, the sacrifice of the Son of God, its universal efficacy, the obligation laid upon him to proclaim it to the ends of the earth.   For reviews of Renan, see Hutton, Essays, 261-281, and Contemp. Thought and Thinkers, 1 : 227-234; H. B. Smith, Faith and Philosophy, 401-441; Christlieb, Mod. Doubt, 425-447; Pressensé, in Theol. Eclectic. 1 : 190; Uhlhorn, Mod. Representations of Life of Jesus, 1-33; Bib. Sac., 22 : 207; 23 : 353 529; Present Day Tracts, 3 : no. 16, and 4 : no. 21; E. G. Robinson, Christian Evidences 43-48; A. H. Strong, Sermon before Baptist World Congress, 1905.

4th.   The Development-theory of Harnack (born 1851).

This holds Christianity to be a historical development from germs which were devoid of both dogma and miracle.   Jesus was a teacher of ethics, and the original gospel is most clearly represented by the Sermon on the Mount.   Greek influence, and especially that of the Alexandrian philosophy, added to this gospel a theological and supernatural element, and so changed Christianity from a life into a doctrine.

Harnack dates Matthew at 70-75; Mark at 65-70: Luke at 78-93; the fourth gospel at 80-110. He regards both the fourth gospel and the book of Revelation as the works, not of John the Apostle, but of John the Presbyter. He separates the prologue of the fourth gospel from the gospel itself, and considers the prologue as a preface added after its original composition in order to enable the Hellenistic reader to understand it. "The gospel itself," says Harnack, "contains no Logos-idea; it d d not develop out of a Logos-idea, such as flourished at Alexandria; it only connects itself with such an idea. The gospel itself is based upon the historic Christ; he is the subject of all its statements. This historical trait can in no way be dissolved by any kind of speculation. The memory of what was actually historical was still too powerful to admit at this point any Gnostic influences. The Logos-idea of the prologue is the Logos of Alexandrine Judaism, the Logos of Philo, and it is derived ultimately from the 'Son of man' in the book of Daniel. . . . The fourth gospel, which does not proceed from the Apostle John and does not so claim, cannot be used as a historical source in the ordinary sense of that word. . . . The author has managed with sovereign freedom; has transposed occurrences and has put them in a light that is foreign to them; has of his own accord composed the discourses, and has illustrated lofty thoughts by inventing situations for them. Difficult as it is to recognize, an actual tradition in his work is not wholly lacking. For the history of Jesus, however, it can hardly anywhere be taken into account; only little can be taken from it, and that with caution. . . . On the other hand it is a source of the first rank for the answer of the question what living views of the person of Jesus, what light and what warmth, the gospel has brought into being." See Harnack's article in Zeitschrift für Theol. u. Kirche, 2:189–231, and his Wesen des Christenthums, 13. Kaftan also, who belongs to the same Ritschlian school with Harnack, tells us in his Truth of the Christian Religion, 1:97, that as the result of the Logos-speculation, "the centre of gravity, instead of being placed in the historical Christ who founded the kingdom of God, is placed in the Christ who as eternal Logos of God was the mediator in the creation of the world." This view is elaborated by Hatch in his Hibbert Lectures for 1888, on the Influence of Greek Ideas and Usages upon the Christian Church.

We object to the Development-theory of Harnack, that

(a) The Sermon on the Mount is not the sum of the gospel, nor its original form. Mark is the most original of the gospels, yet Mark omits the Sermon on the Mount, and Mark is preëminently the gospel of the miracle-worker.

(b) All four gospels lay the emphasis, not on Jesus' life and ethical teaching, but on his death and resurrection. Matthew implies Christ's deity when it asserts his absolute knowledge of the Father (11 : 27), his universal judgeship (25 : 32), his supreme authority (28 : 18), and his omnipresence (28 : 20), while the phrase "Son of man" implies that he is also "Son of God."

Mat. 11 : 27 — "All things have been delivered unto me of my Father: and no one knoweth the Son, save the Father; neither doth any know the Father, save the Son, and he to whomsoever the Son willeth to reveal him ": 25 : 32 — "and before him shall be gathered all the nations: and he shall separate them one from another, as the shepherd separateth the sheep from the goats"; 28 : 18 — "All authority hath been given unto me in heaven and on earth "; 28 : 20 — "lo, I am with you always, even unto the end of the world." These sayings of Jesus in Matthew's gospel show that the conception of Christ's greatness was not peculiar to John : "I am" transcends time; "with you" transcends space. Jesus speaks "sub specie eternitatis"; his utterance is equivalent to that of John 8:58 — "Before Abraham was born, I am," and to that of Hebrews 13:8 — "Jesus Christ is the same yesterday and to-day, yea and for ever." He is, as Paul declares in Eph. 1:23, one "that filleth all in all," that is, who is omnipresent.

A. H. Strong, Philos. and Religion, 206 — The phrase "Son of man" intimates that Christ was more than man: "Suppose I were to go about proclaiming myself 'Son of man.' Who does not see that it would be mere impertinence, unless I claimed to be something more. 'Son of Man? But what of that? Cannot every human being call himself the same?' When one takes the title 'Son of man' for his characteristic designation, as Jesus did, he implies that there is something strange in his being Son of man; that this is not his original condition and dignity; that it is condescension on his part to be Son of man. In short, when Christ calls himself Son of man, it implies that he has come from a higher level of being to inhabit this low earth of ours. And so, when we are asked 'What think ye of the Christ? whose son is he?' we must answer, not simply, He is Son of man, but also, He is Son of God." On Son of man, see Driver; on Son of God, see Sanday; both in Hastings' Dictionary of the Bible. Sanday: "The Son is so called primarily as incarnate. But that which is the essence of the Incarnation must needs be also larger than the Incarnation. It must needs have its roots in the eternity of Godhead." Gore, Incarnation, 65, 73 — "Christ, the final Judge, of the synoptics, is not dissociable from the divine, eternal Being, of the fourth gospel."

(c) The preëxistence and atonement of Christ cannot be regarded as accretions upon the original gospel, since these find expression in Paul who wrote before any of our evangelists, and in his epistles anticipated the Logos-doctrine of John.

(d) We may grant that Greek influence, through the Alexandrian philosophy, helped the New Testament writers to discern what was already present in the life and work and teaching of Jesus ; but, like the microscope which discovers but does not create, it added nothing to the substance of the faith.

Gore, Incarnation, 62 — "The divinity, incarnation, resurrection of Christ were not an accretion upon the original belief of the apostles and their first disciples, for these are all recognized as uncontroverted matters of faith in the four great epistles of Paul, written at a date when the greater part of those who had seen the risen Christ were still alive." The Alexandrian philosophy was not the source of apostolic doctrine, but only the form in which that doctrine was cast, the light thrown upon it which brought out its meaning. A. H. Strong, Christ in Creation, 146 — " When we come to John's gospel, therefore, we find in it the mere unfolding of truth that for substance had been in the world for at least sixty years. . . . If the Platonizing philosophy of Alexandria assisted in this genuine development of Christian doctrine, then the Alexandrian philosophy was a providential help to inspiration. The microscope does not invent; it only discovers. Paul and John did not add to the truth of Christ; their philosophical equipment was only a microscope which brought into clear view the truth that was there already."

Pfleiderer, Philos. Religion, 1 : 126 — "The metaphysical conception of the Logos, as immanent in the world and ordering it according to law, was filled with religious and moral contents. In Jesus the cosmical principle of nature became a religious principle of salvation." See Kilpatrick's article on Philosophy, in Hastings' Bible Dictionary. Kilpatrick holds that Harnack ignores the self-consciousness of Jesus; does not fairly interpret the Acts in its mention of the early worship of Jesus by the church before Greek philosophy had influenced it; refers to the intellectual peculiarities of the N. T. writers conceptions which Paul insists are simply the faith of all Christian people as such; forgets that the Christian idea of union with God secured through the atoning and reconciling work of a personal Redeemer utterly transcended Greek thought, and furnished the solution of the problem after which Greek philosophy was vainly groping.

(e) Though Mark says nothing of the virgin-birth because his story is limited to what the apostles had witnessed of Jesus' deeds, Matthew apparently gives us Joseph's story and Luke gives Mary's story — both stories naturally published only after Jesus' resurrection.

(f) The larger understanding of doctrine after Jesus' death was itself predicted by our Lord (John 16 : 12). The Holy Spirit was to bring his teachings to remembrance, and to guide into all the truth (16 : 13), and the apostles were to continue the work of teaching which he had begun (Acts 1 : 1).

John 16 : 12, 13 — "I have yet many things to say unto you, but ye cannot bear them now. Howbeit, when he, the Spirit of truth, is come, he shall guide you into all the truth "; Acts 1 : 1 — "The former treatise I made, O Theophilus, concerning all that Jesus began to do and to teach." A. H. Strong, Christ in Creation, 146 — "That the beloved disciple, after a half century of meditation upon what he had seen and heard of God manifest in the flesh, should have penetrated more deeply into the meaning of that wonderful revelation is not only not surprising, — it is precisely what Jesus nimself foretold. Our Lord had many things to say to his disciples, but then they could not bear them. He promised that the Holy Spirit should bring to their remembrance both himself and his words, and should lead them into all the truth. And this is the whole secret of what are called accretions to original Christianity. So far as they are contained in Scripture, they are inspired discoveries and unfoldings, not mere speculations and inventions. They are not additions, but elucidations, not vain imaginings, but correct interpretations. . . . When the later theology, then, throws out the supernatural and dogmatic, as coming not from Jesus but from Paul's epistles and from the fourth gospel, our claim is that Paul and John are only inspired and authoritative interpreters of Jesus, seeing themselves and making us see the fulness of the Godhead that dwelt in him."

While Harnack, in our judgment, errs in his view that Paul contributed to the gospel elements which it did not originally possess, he shows us very clearly many of the elements in that gospel which he was the first to recognize. In his Wesen des Christenthums, 111, he tells us that a few years ago a celebrated Protestant theologian declared that Paul, with his Rabbinical theology, was the destroyer of the Christian religion. Others have regarded him as the founder of that religion. But the majority have seen in him the apostle who best understood his Lord and did most to continue his work. Paul, as Harnack maintains, first comprehended the gospel definitely: (1) as an accomplished redemption and a present salvation — the crucified and risen Christ as giving access to God and righteousness and peace therewith; (2) as something new, which does away with the religion of the law; (3) as meant for all, and therefore for Gentiles also, indeed, as superseding Judaism; (4) as expressed in terms which are not simply Greek but also human, — Paul made the gospel comprehensible to the world. Islam, rising in Arabia, is an Arabian religion still. Buddhism remains an Indian religion. Christianity is at home in all lands. Paul put new life into the Roman empire, and inaugurated the Christian culture of the West. He turned a local into a universal religion. His influence however, according to Harnack, tended to the undue exaltation of organization and dogma and O. T. inspiration — points in which, in our judgment, Paul took sober middle ground and saved Christian truth for the world.

2. *Genuineness of the Books of the Old Testament.*

Since nearly one half of the Old Testament is of anonymous authorship and certain of its books may be attributed to definite historic characters only by way of convenient classification or of literary personification, we here mean by genuineness honesty of purpose and freedom from anything counterfeit or intentionally deceptive so far as respects the age or the authorship of the documents.

We show the genuineness of the Old Testament books :

(*a*) From the witness of the New Testament, in which all but six books of the Old Testament are either quoted or alluded to as genuine.

The N. T. shows coincidences of language with the O. T. Apocryphal books, but it contains only one direct quotation from them; while, with the exception of Judges, Ecclesiastes, Canticles, Esther, Ezra, and Nehemiah, every book in the Hebrew canon. is used either for illustration or proof. The single Apocryphal quotation is found in Jude 14 and is in all probability taken from the book of Enoch. Although Volkmar puts the date of this book at 132 A. D., and although some critics hold that Jude quoted only the same primitive tradition of which the author of the book of Enoch afterwards made use, the weight of modern scholarship inclines to the opinion that the book itself was written as early as 170-70 B. C., and that Jude quoted from it; see Hastings' Bible Dictionary : Book of Enoch; Sanday, Bampton Lect. on Inspiration, 95. "If Paul could quote from Gentile poets (Acts 17 : 28 ; Titus 1 : 12), it is hard to understand why Jude could not cite a work which was certainly in high standing among the faithful"; see Schodde, Book of Enoch, 41, with the Introd. by Ezra Abbot. While Jude 14 gives us the only direct and express quotation from an Apocryphal book, Jude 6 and 9 contain allusions to the Book of Enoch and to the Assumption of Moses; see Charles, Assumption of Moses, 62. In Hebrews 1: 3, we have words taken from Wisdom 7 : 26 ; and Hebrews 11 : 34-38 is a reminiscence of 1 Maccabees.

(*b*)   From the testimony of Jewish authorities, ancient and modern, who declare the same books to be sacred, and only the same books, that are now comprised in our Old Testament Scriptures.

Josephus enumerates twenty-two of these books " which are justly accredited " (omit θεῖα — Niese, and Hastings' Dict., 3 : 607). Our present Hebrew Bible makes twenty-four, by separating Ruth from Judges, and Lamentations from Jeremiah. See Josephus, Against Apion, 1 : 8 ; Smith's Bible Dictionary, article on the Canon, 1 : 359, 360. Philo (born 20 B. C.) never quotes an Apocryphal book, although he does quote from nearly all the books of the O. T.; see Ryle, Philo and Holy Scripture. George Adam Smith, Modern Criticism and Preaching, 7 — " The theory which ascribed the Canon of the O. T. to a single decision of the Jewish church in the days of its inspiration is not a theory supported by facts. The growth of the O. T. Canon was very gradual. Virtually it began in 621 B. C., with the acceptance by all Judah of Deuteronomy, and the adoption of the whole Law, or first five books of the O. T., under Nehemiah in 445 B. C. Then came the prophets before 200 B. C., and the Hagiographa from a century to two centuries later. The strict definition of the last division was not complete by the time of Christ. Christ seems to testify to the Law, the Prophets, and the Psalms ; yet neither Christ nor his apostles make any quotation from Ezra, Nehemiah, Esther, Canticles, or Ecclesiastes, the last of which books were not yet recognized by all the Jewish schools. But while Christ is the chief authority for the O. T., he was also its first critic. He rejected some parts of the Law and was indifferent to many others. He enlarged the sixth and seventh commandments, and reversed the eye for an eye, and the permission of divorce ; touched the leper, and reckoned all foods lawful ; broke away from literal observance of the Sabbath-day ; left no commands about sacrifice, temple-worship, circumcision, but, by institution of the New Covenant, abrogated these sacraments of the Old. The apostles appealed to extra-canonical writings." Gladden, Seven Puzzling Bible Books, 68–96 — " Doubts were entertained in our Lord's day as to the canonicity of several parts of the O. T., especially Proverbs, Ecclesiastes, Song of Solomon, Esther."

(*c*)   From the testimony of the Septuagint translation, dating from the first half of the third century, or from 280 to 180 B. C.

MSS. of the Septuagint contain, indeed, the O. T. Apocrypha, but the writers of the latter do not recognize their own work as on a level with the canonical Scriptures, which they regard as distinct from all other books (Ecclesiasticus, prologue, and 48 : 24 ; also 24 : 23 27 ; 1 Mac. 12 : 9 ; 2 Mac. 6 : 23 ; 1 Esd. 1 : 28 ; 6 : 1 ; Baruch 2 : 21). So both ancient and modern Jews. See Bissell, in Lange's Commentary on the Apocrypha, Introduction, 44. In the prologue to the apocryphal book of Ecclesiasticus, we read of " the Law and the Prophets and the rest of the books," which shows that as early as 130 B. C., the probable date of Ecclesiasticus, a threefold division of the Jewish sacred books was recognized. That the author, however, did not conceive of these books as constituting a completed canon seems evident from his assertion in this connection that his grandfather Jesus also wrote. 1 Mac. 12 : 9 (80–90 B. C.) speaks of " the sacred books which are now in our hands." Hastings, Bible Dictionary, 3 : 611 — " The O. T. was the result of a gradual process which began with the sanction of the Hexateuch by Ezra and Nehemiah, and practically closed with the decisions of the Council of Jamnia " — Jamnia is the ancient Jabneh, 7 miles south by west of Tiberias, where met a council of rabbins at some time between 90 to 118 A. D. This Council decided in favor of Canticles and Ecclesiastes. and closed the O. T. Canon.

The Greek version of the Pentateuch which forms a part of the Septuagint is said by Josephus to have been made in the reign and by the order of Ptolemy Philadelphus, King of Egypt, about 270 or 280 B. C. " The legend is that it was made by seventy-two persons in seventy-two days. It is supposed, however, by modern critics that this version of the several books is the work not only of different hands but of separate times. It is probable that at first only the Pentateuch was translated, and the remaining books gradually ; but the translation is believed to have been completed by the second century B. C." (Century Dictionary, *in voce*). It therefore furnishes an important witness to the genuineness of our O. T. documents. Driver, Introd. to O. T. Lit., xxxi — " For the opinion, often met with in modern books, that the Canon of the O. T. was closed by Ezra, or in Ezra's time, there is no foundation in antiquity whatever. . . . All that can reasonably be treated as historical in [the accounts of Ezra's literary labors is limited to the **Law**."

(*d*) From indications that soon after the exile, and so early as the times of Ezra and Nehemiah (500–450 B. C.), the Pentateuch together with the book of Joshua was not only in existence but was regarded as authoritative.

2 Mac. 2: 13-15 intimates that Nehemiah founded a library, and there is a tradition that a "Great Synagogue" was gathered in his time to determine the Canon. But Hastings' Dictionary, 4: 644, asserts that "the Great Synagogue was originally a meeting, and not an institution. It met once for all, and all that is told about it, except what we read in Nehemiah, is pure fable of the later Jews." In like manner no dependence is to be placed upon the tradition that Ezra miraculously restored the ancient Scriptures that had been lost during the exile. Clement of Alexandria says: "Since the Scriptures perished in the Captivity of Nebuchadnezzar, Esdras (the Greek form of Ezra) the Levite, the priest, in the time of Artaxerxes, King of the Persians, having become inspired in the exercise of prophecy, restored again the whole of the ancient Scriptures." But the work now divided into 1 and 2 Chronicles, Ezra and Nehemiah, mentions Darius Codomannus (Neh. 12 : 22), whose date is 336 B.C. The utmost the tradition proves is that about 300 B. C. the Pentateuch was in some sense attributed to Moses; see Bacon, Genesis of Genesis, 35 ; Bib. Sac., 1863 : 381, 660, 799 ; Smith, Bible Dict., art.: Pentateuch ; Theological Eclectic, 6 : 215 ; Bissell, Hist. Origin of the Bible, 398–403. On the Men of the Great Synagogue, see Wright, Ecclesiastes, 5–12, 475–477.

(*e*) From the testimony of the Samaritan Pentateuch, dating from the time of Ezra and Nehemiah (500–450 B. C.).

The Samaritans had been brought by the king of Assyria from "Babylon, and from Cuthah and from Avva, and from Hamath and Sepharvaim " (2 K. 17 : 6, 24, 26), to take the place of the people of Israel whom the king had carried away captive to his own land. The colonists had brought their heathen gods with them, and the incursions of wild beasts which the intermission of tillage occasioned gave rise to the belief that the God of Israel was against them. One of the captive Jewish priests was therefore sent to teach them "the law of the god of the land " and he "taught them how they should fear Jehovah " (2 K. 17 : 27, 28). The result was that they adopted the Jewish ritual, but combined the worship of Jehovah with that of their graven images (verse 33). When the Jews returned from Babylon and began to rebuild the walls of Jerusalem, the Samaritans offered their aid, but this aid was indignantly refused (Ezra 4 and Nehemiah 4). Hostility arose between Jews and Samaritans — a hostility which continued not only to the time of Christ (John 4 : 9), but even to the present day. Since the Samaritan Pentateuch substantially coincides with the Hebrew Pentateuch, it furnishes us with a definite past date at which it certainly existed in nearly its present form. It witnesses to the existence of our Pentateuch in essentially its present form as far back as the time of Ezra and Nehemiah.

Green, Higher Criticism of the Pentateuch, 44, 45 — "After being repulsed by the Jews, the Samaritans, to substantiate their claim of being sprung from ancient Israel, eagerly accepted the Pentateuch which was brought them by a renegade priest." W. Robertson Smith, in Encyc. Brit., 21 : 244 — "The priestly law, which is throughout based on the practice of the priests of Jerusalem before the captivity, was reduced to form after the exile, and was first published by Ezra as the law of the rebuilt temple of Zion. The Samaritans must therefore have derived their Pentateuch from the Jews after Ezra's reforms, *i. e.*, after 444 B. C. Before that time Samaritanism cannot have existed in a form at all similar to that which we know ; but there must have been a community ready to accept the Pentateuch." See Smith's Bible Dictionary, art.: Samaritan Pentateuch ; Hastings, Bible Dictionary, art.: Samaria ; Stanley Leathes, Structure of the O. T., 1–41.

(*f*) From the finding of "the book of the law" in the temple, in the eighteenth year of King Josiah, or in 621 B. C.

2 K. 22: 8 — "And Hilkiah the high priest said unto Shaphan the scribe, I have found the book of the law in the house of Jehovah." 23 : 2 — "The book of the covenant" was read before the people by the king and proclaimed to be the law of the land. Curtis, in Hastings' Bible Dict., 3 : 596 — "The earliest written law or book of divine instruction of whose introduction or enactment an authentic account is given, was Deuteronomy or its main portion, represented as found in the temple in the 18th year of king Josiah (B. C. 621) and

proclaimed by the king as the law of the land. From that time forward Israel had a written law which the pious believer was commanded to ponder day and night (Joshua 1 : 8; Ps. 1 : 2); and thus the Torah, as sacred literature, formally commenced in Israel. This law aimed at a right application of Mosaic principles." Ryle, in Hastings' Bible Dict., 1 : 602 — "The law of Deuteronomy represents an expansion and development of the ancient code contained in Exodus 20-23, and precedes the final formulation of the priestly ritual, which only received its ultimate form in the last period of revising the structure of the Pentateuch."

Andrew Harper, on Deuteronomy, in Expositor's Bible : "Deuteronomy does not claim to have been written by Moses. He is spoken of in the third person in the introduction and historical framework, while the speeches of Moses are in the first person. In portions where the author speaks for himself, the phrase 'beyond Jordan' means east of Jordan ; in the speeches of Moses the phrase 'beyond Jordan' means west of Jordan ; and the only exception is Deut. 3 : 8, which cannot originally have been part of the speech of Moses. But the style of both parts is the same, and if the 3rd person parts are by a later author, the 1st person parts are by a later author also. Both differ from other speeches of Moses in the Pentateuch. Can the author be a contemporary writer who gives Moses' words, as John gave the words of Jesus? No, for Deuteronomy covers only the book of the Covenant, Exodus 20-23. It uses JE but not P, with which JE is interwoven. But JE appears in Joshua and contributes to it an account of Joshua's death. JE speaks of kings in Israel (Gen. 36 : 31-39). Deuteronomy plainly belongs to the early centuries of the Kingdom, or to the middle of it."

Bacon, Genesis of Genesis, 43-49 — "The Deuteronomic law was so short that Shaphan could read it aloud before the king (2 K. 22 : 10) and the king could read "the whole of it" before the people (23 : 2); compare the reading of the Pentateuch for a whole week (Neh. 8 : 2-18). It was in the form of a covenant; it was distinguished by curses; it was an expansion and modification, fully within the legitimate province of the prophet, of a Torah of Moses codified from the traditional form of at least a century before. Such a Torah existed, was attributed to Moses, and is now incorporated as 'the book of the covenant' in Exodus 20 to 24. The year 620 is therefore the *terminus a quo* of Deuteronomy. The date of the priestly code is 444 B. C." Sanday, Bampton Lectures for 1893, grants " (1) the presence in the Pentateuch of a considerable element which in its present shape is held by many to be not earlier than the captivity ; (2) the composition of the book of Deuteronomy, not long, or at least not very long, before its promulgation by king Josiah in the year 621, which thus becomes a pivot-date in the history of Hebrew literature."

(*g*) From references in the prophets Hosea (B. C. 743-737) and Amos (759-745) to a course of divine teaching and revelation extending far back of their day.

Hosea 8 : 12 — "I wrote for him the ten thousand things of my law"; here is asserted the existence prior to the time of the prophet, not only of a law, but of a written law. All critics admit the book of Hosea to be a genuine production of the prophet, dating from the eighth century B. C. ; see Green, in Presb. Rev., 1886 : 585-608. Amos 2 : 4 — "they have rejected the law of Jehovah, and have not kept his statutes"; here is proof that, more than a century before the finding of Deuteronomy in the temple, Israel was acquainted with God's law. Fisher, Nature and Method of Revelation, 26, 27 — "The lofty plane reached by the prophets was not reached at a single bound. . . . There must have been a tap-root extending far down into the earth." Kurtz remarks that "the later books of the O. T. would be a tree without roots, if the composition of the Pentateuch were transferred to a later period of Hebrew history." If we substitute for the word 'Pentateuch' the words 'Book of the covenant,' we may assent to this dictum of Kurtz. There is sufficient evidence that, before the times of Hosea and Amos, Israel possessed a written law — the law embraced in Exodus 20-24 — but the Pentateuch as we now have it, including Leviticus, seems to date no further back than the time of Jeremiah, 445 B. C. The Levitical law however was only the codification of statutes and customs whose origin lay far back in the past and which were believed to be only the natural expansion of the principles of Mosaic legislation.

Leathes, Structure of O. T., 54 — "Zeal for the restoration of the temple after the exile implied that it had long before been the centre of the national polity, that there had been a ritual and a law before the exile." Present Day Tracts, 3 : 52 — Levitical institutions could not have been first established by David. It is inconceivable that he "could have taken a whole tribe, and no trace remain of so revolutionary a measure as the dispossessing them of their property to make them ministers of religion." James Robertson, Early History of Israel: "The varied literature of 850-750 B. C. implies the existence of reading and writing for some time before. Amos and Hosea hold, for the period succeeding Moses, the same scheme of history which modern critics pronounce late and unhistorical. The eighth century B. C. was a time of broad historic day, when Israel had a definite account to give of itself and of its history. The critics appeal to the prophets, but they reject the prophets when these tell us that other teachers taught the same truth before them, and when they declare that their nation had been taught a better religion and had declined from it, in other words, that there had been law long before their day. The kings did not *give law*. The priests *presupposed* it. There must have been a formal system of law much earlier than the critics admit, and also an earlier reference in their worship to the great events which made them a separate people." And Dillman goes yet further back and declares that the entire work of Moses presupposes "a preparatory stage of higher religion in Abraham."

(*h*) From the repeated assertions of Scripture that Moses himself wrote a law for his people, confirmed as these are by evidence of literary and legislative activity in other nations far antedating his time.

Ex. 24 : 4 — "And Moses wrote all the words of Jehovah "; 34 : 27 — "And Jehovah said unto Moses, Write thou these words: for after the tenor of these words I have made a covenant with thee and with Israel"; Num. 33 : 2 — "And Moses wrote their goings out according to their journeys by the commandment of Jehovah "; Deut. 31 : 9 — "And Moses wrote this law, and delivered it unto the priests the sons of Levi, that bare the ark of the covenant of Jehovah, and unto all the elders of Israel "; 22 — "So Moses wrote this song the same day, and taught it the children of Israel"; 24-26 — "And it came to pass, when Moses had made an end of writing the words of this law in a book, until they were finished, that Moses commanded the Levites, that bare the ark of the covenant of Jehovah, saying, Take this book of the law, and put it by the side of the ark of the covenant of Jehovah your God, that it may be there for a witness against thee." The law here mentioned may possibly be only 'the book of the covenant" (Ex. 20-24), and the speeches of Moses in Deuteronomy may have been orally handed down. But the fact that Moses was "instructed in all the wisdom of the Egyptians " (Acts 7:22), together with the fact that the art of writing was known in Egypt for many hundred years before his time, make it more probable that a larger portion of the Pentateuch was of his own composition.

Kenyon, in Hastings' Dict., art.: Writing, dates the Proverbs of Ptah-hotep, the first recorded literary composition in Egypt, at 3580-3536 B. C., and asserts the free use of writing among the Sumerian inhabitants of Babylonia as early as 4000 B. C. The statutes of Hammurabi king of Babylon compare for extent with those of Leviticus, yet they date back to the time of Abraham, 2200 B. C., — indeed Hammurabi is now regarded by many as the Amraphel of Gen. 14:1. Yet these statutes antedate Moses by 700 years. It is interesting to observe that Hammurabi professes to have received his statutes directly from the Sun-god of Sippar, his capital city. See translation by Winckler, in Der alte Orient, 97; Johns, The Oldest Code of Laws; Kelso, in Princeton Theol. Rev., July, 1905: 399-412 — Facts "authenticate the traditional date of the Book of the Covenant, overthrow the formula Prophets and Law, restore the old order Law and Prophets, and put into historical perspective the tradition that Moses was the author of the Sinaitic legislation."

As the controversy with regard to the genuineness of the Old Testament books has turned of late upon the claims of the Higher Criticism in general, and upon the claims of the Pentateuch in particular, we subjoin separate notes upon these subjects.

The Higher Criticism in general. Higher Criticism does not mean criticism in any invidious sense, any more than Kant's Critique of Pure Reason was an unfavorable or destructive examination. It is merely a dispassionate investigation of the authorship, date and purpose of Scripture books, in the light of their composition, style and internal characteristics. As the Lower Criticism is a text-critique, the Higher Criticism is a structure-critique. A bright Frenchman described a literary critic as one who rips open the doll to get at the sawdust there is in it. This can be done with a sceptical and hostile spirit, and there can be little doubt that some of the higher critics of the Old Testament have begun their studies with prepossessions against the supernatural, which have vitiated all their conclusions. These presuppositions are often unconscious, but none the less influential. When Bishop Colenso examined the Pentateuch and Joshua, he disclaimed any intention of assailing the miraculous narratives as such; as if he had said : " My dear little fish, you need not fear me ; I do not wish to catch you ; I only intend to drain the pond in which you live." To many scholars the waters at present seem very low in the Hexateuch and indeed throughout the whole Old Testament.

Shakespeare made over and incorporated many old Chronicles of Plutarch and Holinshed, and many Italian tales and early tragedies of other writers; but Pericles and Titus Andronicus still pass current under the name of Shakespeare. We speak even now of " Gesenius' Hebrew Grammar," although of its twenty-seven editions the last fourteen have been published since his death, and more of it has been written by other editors than Gesenius ever wrote himself. We speak of " Webster's Dictionary," though there are in the " Unabridged " thousands of words and definitions that Webster never saw. Francis Brown : " A modern writer masters older records and writes a wholly new book. Not so with eastern historians. The latest comer, as Renan says, ' absorbs his predecessors without assimilating them, so that the most recent has in its belly the fragments of the previous works in a raw state.' The Diatessaron of Tatian is a parallel to the composite structure of the O. T. books. One passage yields the following : Mat. 21 : 12 a ; John 2 : 14 a ; Mat. 21 : 12 b ; John 2 : 14 b, 15 ; Mat. 21 : 12 c, 13 ; John 2 : 16 ; Mark 11 : 16 ; John 2 : 17–22 ; all succeeding each other without a break." Gore, Lux Mundi, 353 —" There is nothing materially untruthful, though there is something uncritical, in attributing the whole legislation to Moses acting under the divine command. It would be only of a piece with the attribution of the collection of Psalms to David, and of Proverbs to Solomon."

The opponents of the Higher Criticism have much to say in reply. Sayce, Early History of the Hebrews, holds that the early chapters of Genesis were copied from Babylonian sources, but he insists upon a Mosaic or pre-Mosaic date for the copying. Hilprecht however declares that the monotheistic faith of Israel could never have proceeded "from the Babylonian mountain of gods —'that charnel-house full of corruption and dead men's bones." Bissell, Genesis Printed in Colors, Introd., iv —" It is improbable that so many documentary histories existed so early, or if existing that the compiler should have attempted to combine them. Strange that the earlier should be J and should use the word ' Jehovah,' while the later P should use the word ' Elohim,' when ' Jehovah ' would have far better suited the Priests' Code. . . . xiii — The Babylonian tablets contain in a continuous narrative the more prominent facts of both the alleged Elohistic and Jehovistic sections of Genesis, and present them mainly in the Biblical order. Several hundred years before Moses what the critics call *two* were already *one*. It is absurd to say that the unity was due to a redactor at the period of the exile, 444 B. C. He who believes that God revealed himself to primitive man as one God, will see in the Akkadian story a polytheistic corruption of the original monotheistic account." We must not estimate the antiquity of a pair of boots by the last patch which the cobbler has added; nor must we estimate the antiquity of a Scripture book by the glosses and explanations added by later editors. As the London Spectator remarks on the Homeric problem : " It is as impossible that a first-rate poem or work of art should be produced without a great master-mind which first conceives the whole, as that a fine living bull should be developed out of beef-sausages." As we shall proceed to show, however, these utterances overestimate the unity of the Pentateuch and ignore some striking evidences of its gradual growth and composite structure.

The Authorship of the Pentateuch in particular. Recent critics, especially Kuenen and Robertson Smith, have maintained that the Pentateuch is Mosaic only in the sense of being a gradually growing body of traditional law, which was codified as late as the time of Ezekiel, and, as the development of the spirit and teachings of the great lawgiver, was called by a legal fiction after the name of Moses and was attributed to him. The actual order of composition is therefore : (1) Book of the Covenant (Exodus 20-23); (2) Deuteronomy ; (3) Leviticus. Among the reasons assigned for this view are the facts (a) that Deuteronomy ends with an account of Moses' death, and therefore could not have been written by Moses ; (b) that in Leviticus Levites are mere servants to the priests, while in Deuteronomy the priests are officiating Levites, or, in other words, all the Levites are priests ; (c) that the books of Judges and of 1 Samuel, with their record of sacrifices offered in many places, give no evidence that either Samuel or the nation of Israel had any knowledge of a law confining worship to a local sanctuary. See

Kuenen, Prophets and Prophecy in Israel ; Wellhausen, Geschichte Israels, Band 1 ; and art.: Israel, in Encyc. Brit., 13 : 398, 399, 415 ; W. Robertson Smith, O. T. in Jewish Church, 306, 386, and Prophets of Israel ; Hastings, Bible Dict., arts. : Deuteronomy, Hexateuch, and Canon of the O. T.

It has been urged in reply, (1) that Moses may have written, not autographically, but through a scribe (perhaps Joshua), and that this scribe may have completed the history in Deuteronomy with the account of Moses' death ; (2) that Ezra or subsequent prophets may have subjected the whole Pentateuch to recension, and may have added explanatory notes ; (3) that documents of previous ages may have been incorporated, in course of its composition by Moses, or subsequently by his successors ; (4) that the apparent lack of distinction between the different classes of Levites in Deuteronomy may be explained by the fact that, while Leviticus was written with exact detail for the priests, Deuteronomy is the record of a brief general and oral summary of the law, addressed to the people at large and therefore naturally mentioning the clergy as a whole ; (5) that the silence of the book of Judges as to the Mosaic ritual may be explained by the design of the book to describe only general history, and by the probability that at the tabernacle a ritual was observed of which the people in general were ignorant. Sacrifices in other places only accompanied special divine manifestations which made the recipient temporarily a priest. Even if it were proved that the law with regard to a central sanctuary was not observed, it would not show that the law did not exist, any more than violation of the second commandment by Solomon proves his ignorance of the decalogue, or the mediæval neglect of the N. T. by the Roman church proves that the N. T. did not then exist. We cannot argue that "where there was transgression, there was no law" (Watts, New Apologetic, 83, and The Newer Criticism).

In the light of recent research, however, we cannot regard these replies as satisfactory. Woods, in his article on the Hexateuch, Hastings' Dictionary, 2 : 365, presents a moderate statement of the results of the higher criticism which commends itself to us as more trustworthy. He calls it a theory of stratification, and holds that "certain more or less independent documents, dealing largely with the same series of events, were composed at different periods, or, at any rate, under different auspices, and were afterwards combined, so that our present Hexateuch, which means our Pentateuch with the addition of Joshua, contains these several different literary strata. . . . The main grounds for accepting this hypothesis of stratification are (1) that the various literary pieces, with very few exceptions, will be found on examination to arrange themselves by common characteristics into comparatively few groups ; (2) that an original consecution of narrative may be frequently traced between what in their present form are isolated fragments.

"This will be better understood by the following illustration. Let us suppose a problem of this kind : Given a patchwork quilt, explain the character of the original pieces out of which the bits of stuff composing the quilt were cut. First, we notice that, however well the colors may blend, however nice and complete the whole may look, many of the adjoining pieces do not agree in material, texture, pattern, color, or the like. Ergo, they have been made up out of very different pieces of stuff. . . . But suppose we further discover that many of the bits, though now separated, are like one another in material, texture, etc., we may conjecture that these have been cut out of one piece. But we shall prove this beyond reasonable doubt if we find that several bits when unpicked fit together, so that the pattern of one is continued in the other; and, moreover, that if all of like character are sorted out, they form, say, four groups, each of which was evidently once a single piece of stuff, though parts of each are found missing, because, no doubt, they have not been required to make the whole. But we make the analogy of the Hexateuch even closer, if we further suppose that in certain parts of the quilt the bits belonging to, say, two of these groups are so combined as to form a subsidiary pattern within the larger pattern of the whole quilt, and had evidently been sewed together before being connected with other parts of the quilt; and we may make it even closer still, if we suppose that, besides the more important bits of stuff, smaller embellishments, borderings, and the like, had been added so as to improve the general effect of the whole."

The author of this article goes on to point out three main portions of the Hexateuch which essentially differ from each other. There are three distinct codes: the Covenant code (C = Ex. 20 : 22 to 23 : 33, and 24 : 3-8), the Deuteronomic code (D), and the Priestly code (P). These codes have peculiar relations to the narrative portions of the

Hexateuch. In Genesis, for example, "the greater part of the book is divided into groups of longer or shorter pieces, generally paragraphs or chapters, distinguished respectively by the almost exclusive use of Elohim or Jehovah as the name of God." Let us call these portions J and E. But we find such close affinities between C and JE, that we may regard them as substantially one. " We shall find that the larger part of the narratives, as distinct from the laws, of Exodus and Numbers belong to JE; whereas, with special exceptions, the legal portions belong to P. In the last chapters of Deuteronomy and in the whole of Joshua we find elements of JE. In the latter book we also find elements which connect it with D.

"It should be observed that not only do we find here and there *separate pieces* in the Hexateuch, shown by their characters to belong to these three sources, JE, D, and P, but the pieces will often be found connected together by an obvious continuity of subject when pieced together, like the bits of patchwork in the illustration with which we started. For example, if we read continuously Gen. 11:27-32; 12:4 b, 5; 13:6 a, 11 b, 12 c; 16 : 1 a, 3, 15, 16; 17; 19 : 29; 21 : 1 a, 2 b -5; 23; 25 : 7-11 a — passages mainly, on other grounds, attributed to P, we get an almost continuous and complete, though very concise, account of Abraham's life." We may concede the substantial correctness of the view thus propounded. It simply shows God's actual method in making up the record of his revelation. We may add that any scholar who grants that Moses did not himself write the account of his own death and burial in the last chapter of Deuteronomy, or who recognizes two differing accounts of creation in Genesis 1 and 2, has already begun an analysis of the Pentateuch and has accepted the essential principles of the higher criticism.

In addition to the literature already referred to mention may also be made of Driver's Introd. to O. T., 118-150, and Deuteronomy, Introd.; W. R. Harper, in Hebraica, Oct.-Dec. 1888, and W. H. Green's reply in Hebraica, Jan.-Apl. 1889; also Green, The Unity of the Book of Genesis, Moses and the Prophets, Hebrew Feasts, and Higher Criticism of the Pentateuch; with articles by Green in Presb. Rev., Jan. 1882 and Oct. 1886; Howard Osgood, in Essays on Pentateuchal Criticism, and in Bib. Sac., Oct. 1888, and July, 1893; Watts, The Newer Criticism, and New Apologetic, 83; Presb. Rev., arts. by H. P. Smith, April, 1882, and by F. L. Patton, 1883 : 341-410; Bib. Sac., April, 1882 : 291-344, and by G. F. Wright, July, 1898 : 515-525; Brit. Quar., July, 1881 : 123; Jan. 1884 : 138-143; Mead, Supernatural Revelation, 373-385; Stebbins, A Study in the Pentateuch; Bissell, Historic Origin of the Bible, 277-342, and The Pentateuch, its Authorship and Structure; Bartlett, Sources of History in the Pentateuch, 180-216, and The Veracity of the Hexateuch; Murray, Origin and Growth of the Psalms, 58; Payne-Smith, in Present Day Tracts, 3 : no. 15; Edersheim, Prophecy and History; Kurtz, Hist. Old Covenant, 1 : 46; Perowne, in Contemp. Rev., Jan. and Feb. 1888; Chambers, Moses and his Recent Critics; Terry, Moses and the Prophets; Davis, Dictionary of the Bible, art.: Pentateuch; Willis J. Beecher, The Prophets and the Promise; Orr, Problem of the O. T., 326-329.

II. CREDIBILITY OF THE WRITERS OF THE SCRIPTURES.

We shall attempt to prove this only of the writers of the gospels ; for if they are credible witnesses, the credibility of the Old Testament, to which they bore testimony, follows as a matter of course.

1. *They are capable or competent witnesses,* — that is, they possessed actual knowledge with regard to the facts they professed to relate. (*a*) They had opportunities of observation and inquiry. (*b*) They were men of sobriety and discernment, and could not have been themselves deceived. (*c*) Their circumstances were such as to impress deeply upon their minds the events of which they were witnesses.

2. *They are honest witnesses.* This is evident when we consider that: (*a*) Their testimony imperiled all their worldly interests. (*b*) The moral elevation of their writings, and their manifest reverence for truth and constant inculcation of it, show that they were not wilful deceivers, but good

men. (c) There are minor indications of the honesty of these writers in the circumstantiality of their story, in the absence of any expectation that their narratives would be questioned, in their freedom from all disposition to screen themselves or the apostles from censure.

Lessing says that Homer never calls Helen beautiful, but he gives the reader an impression of her surpassing loveliness by portraying the effect produced by her presence. So the evangelists do not describe Jesus' appearance or character, but lead us to conceive the cause that could produce such effects. Gore, Incarnation, 77 — "Pilate, Caiaphas, Herod, Judas, are not abused,— they are photographed. The sin of a Judas and a Peter is told with equal simplicity. Such fairness, wherever you find it, belongs to a trustworthy witness."

3. *The writings of the evangelists mutually support each other.* We argue their credibility upon the ground of their number and of the consistency of their testimony. While there is enough of discrepancy to show that there has been no collusion between them, there is concurrence enough to make the falsehood of them all infinitely improbable. Four points under this head deserve mention : (a) The evangelists are independent witnesses. This is sufficiently shown by the futility of the attempts to prove that any one of them has abridged or transcribed another. (b) The discrepancies between them are none of them irreconcilable with the truth of the recorded facts, but only present those facts in new lights or with additional detail. (c) That these witnesses were friends of Christ does not lessen the value of their united testimony, since they followed Christ only because they were convinced that these facts were true. (d) While one witness to the facts of Christianity might establish its truth, the combined evidence of four witnesses gives us a warrant for faith in the facts of the gospel such as we possess for no other facts in ancient history whatsoever. The same rule which would refuse belief in the events recorded in the gospels "would throw doubt on any event in history."

No man does or can write his own signature twice precisely alike. When two signatures, therefore, purporting to be written by the same person, are precisely alike, it is safe to conclude that one of them is a forgery. Compare the combined testimony of the evangelists with the combined testimony of our five senses. "Let us assume," says Dr. C. E. Rider, "that the chances of deception are as one to ten when we use our eyes alone, one to twenty when we use our ears alone, and one to forty when we use our sense of touch alone ; what are the chances of mistake when we use all these senses simultaneously ? The true result is obtained by multiplying these proportions together. This gives one to eight thousand."

4. *The conformity of the gospel testimony with experience.* We have already shown that, granting the fact of sin and the need of an attested revelation from God, miracles can furnish no presumption against the testimony of those who record such a revelation, but, as essentially belonging to such a revelation, miracles may be proved by the same kind and degree of evidence as is required in proof of any other extraordinary facts. We may assert, then, that in the New Testament histories there is no record of facts contrary to experience, but only a record of facts not witnessed in ordinary experience — of facts, therefore, in which we may believe, if the evidence in other respects is sufficient.

5. *Coincidence of this testimony with collateral facts and circumstances.* Under this head we may refer to (a) the numberless correspon-

dences between the narratives of the evangelists and contemporary history; (*b*) the failure of every attempt thus far to show that the sacred history is contradicted by any single fact derived from other trustworthy sources; (*c*) the infinite improbability that this minute and complete harmony should ever have been secured in fictitious narratives.

6. *Conclusion from the argument for the credibility of the writers of the gospels.* These writers having been proved to be credible witnesses, their narratives, including the accounts of the miracles and prophecies of Christ and his apostles, must be accepted as true. But God would not work miracles or reveal the future to attest the claims of false teachers. Christ and his apostles must, therefore, have been what they claimed to be, teachers sent from God, and their doctrine must be what they claimed it to be, a revelation from God to men.

On the whole subject, see Ebrard, Wissensch. Kritik der evang. Geschichte; Greenleaf, Testimony of the Evangelists, 30, 31; Starkie on Evidence, 734; Whately, Historic Doubts as to Napoleon Buonaparte; Haley, Examination of Alleged Discrepancies; Smith's Voyage and Shipwreck of St. Paul; Paley, Horæ Paulinæ; Birks, in Strivings for the Faith, 37-72 — "Discrepancies are like the slight diversities of the different pictures of the stereoscope." Renan calls the land of Palestine a fifth gospel. Weiss contrasts the Apocryphal Gospels, where there is no historical setting and all is in the air, with the evangelists, where time and place are always stated.

No modern apologist has stated the argument for the credibility of the New Testament with greater clearness and force than Paley,— Evidences, chapters 8 and 10 —" No historical fact is more certain than that the original propagators of the gospel voluntarily subjected themselves to lives of fatigue, danger, and suffering, in the prosecution of their undertaking. The nature of the undertaking, the character of the persons employed in it, the opposition of their tenets to the fixed expectations of the country in which they at first advanced them, their undissembled condemnation of the religion of all other countries, their total want of power, authority, or force, render it in the highest degree *probable* that this must have been the case.

" The probability is increased by what we know of the fate of the Founder of the institution, who was put to death for his attempt, and by what we also know of the cruel treatment of the converts to the institution within thirty years after its commencement — both which points are attested by heathen writers, and, being once admitted, leave it very incredible that the primitive emissaries of the religion who exercised their ministry first amongst the people who had destroyed their Master, and afterwards amongst those who persecuted their converts, should themselves escape with impunity or pursue their purpose in ease and safety.

"This probability, thus sustained by foreign testimony, is advanced, I think, to historical certainty by the evidence of our own books, by the accounts of a writer who was the companion of the persons whose sufferings he relates, by the letters of the persons themselves, by predictions of persecutions, ascribed to the Founder of the religion, which predictions would not have been inserted in this history, much less, studiously dwelt upon, if they had not accorded with the event, and which, even if falsely ascribed to him, could only have been so ascribed because the event suggested them ; lastly, by incessant exhortations to fortitude and patience, and by an earnestness, repetition and urgency upon the subject which were unlikely to have appeared, if there had not been, at the time, some extraordinary call for the exercise of such virtues. It is also made out, I think, with sufficient evidence, that both the teachers and converts of the religion, in consequence of their new profession, took up a new course of life and conduct.

" The next great question is, what they did this *for*. It was for a miraculous story of some kind, since for the proof that Jesus of Nazareth ought to be received as the Messiah, or as a messenger for God, they neither had nor could have anything but miracles to stand upon. . . . If this be so, the religion must be true. These men could not be deceivers. By only not bearing testimony, they might have avoided all these sufferings and lived quietly. Would men in such circumstances pretend to have seen what they never saw, assert facts which they had no knowledge of, go about lying to 'teach virtue, and though not only convinced of Christ's being an impostor, but having seen the success of his imposture in his crucifixion, yet persist in carrying it on, and so persist as to bring upon themselves, for nothing, and with a full knowledge of the consequences, enmity and hatred, danger and death?"

Those who maintain this, moreover, require us to believe that the Scripture writers were "villains for no end but to teach honesty, and martyrs without the least prospect of honor or advantage." Imposture must have a motive. The self-devotion of the apostles is the strongest evidence of their truth, for even Hume declares that "we cannot make use of a more convincing argument in proof of honesty than to prove that the actions ascribed to any persons are contrary to the course of nature, and that no human motives, in such circumstances, could ever induce them to such conduct."

III. The Supernatural Character of the Scripture Teaching.

1. *Scripture teaching in general.*

A. The Bible is the work of one mind.

(*a*) In spite of its variety of authorship and the vast separation of its writers from one another in point of time, there is a unity of subject, spirit, and aim throughout the whole.

We here begin a new department of Christian evidences. We have thus far only adduced external evidence. We now turn our attention to internal evidence. The relation of external to internal evidence seems to be suggested in Christ's two questions in Mark 8: 27, 29 — "Who do *men* say that I am? . . . who say *ye* that I am?" The unity in variety displayed in Scripture is one of the chief internal evidences. This unity is indicated in our word "Bible," in the singular number. Yet the original word was "Biblia," a plural number. The world has come to see a unity in what were once scattered fragments: the many "Biblia" have become one "Bible." In one sense R. W. Emerson's contention is true: "The Bible is not a book, — it is a literature." But we may also say, and with equal truth: "The Bible is not simply a collection of books, — it is a book." The Bible is made up of sixty-six books, by forty writers, of all ranks, — shepherds, fishermen, priests, warriors, statesmen, kings, — composing their works at intervals through a period of seventeen centuries. Evidently no collusion between them is possible. Scepticism tends ever to ascribe to the Scriptures greater variety of authorship and date, but all this only increases the wonder of the Bible's unity. If unity in a half dozen writers is remarkable, in forty it is astounding. "The many diverse instruments of this orchestra play one perfect tune: hence we feel that they are led by one master and composer." Yet it takes the same Spirit who inspired the Bible to teach its unity. The union is not an external or superficial one, but one that is internal and spiritual.

(*b*) Not one moral or religious utterance of all these writers has been contradicted or superseded by the utterances of those who have come later, but all together constitute a consistent system.

Here we must distinguish between the external form and the moral and religious substance. Jesus declares in Mat. 5: 21, 22, 27, 28, 33, 34, 38, 39, 43, 44, "Ye have heard that it was said to them of old time . . . but I say unto you," and then he seems at first sight to abrogate certain original commands. But he also declares in this connection, Mat. 5: 17, 18 — "Think not I am come to destroy the law or the prophets: I came not to destroy but to fulfil. For verily I say unto you, Till heaven and earth pass away, one jot or one tittle shall in no wise pass away from the law, till all things be accomplished." Christ's new commandments only bring out the inner meaning of the old. He fulfils them not in their literal form but in their essential spirit. So the New Testament completes the revelation of the Old Testament and makes the Bible a perfect unity. In this unity the Bible stands alone. Hindu, Persian, and Chinese religious books contain no consistent system of faith. There is progress in revelation from the earlier to the later books of the Bible, but this is not progress through successive steps of falsehood; it is rather progress from a less to a more clear and full unfolding of the truth. The whole truth lay germinally in the *protevangelium* uttered to our first parents (Gen. 3:15 — the seed of the woman should bruise the serpent's head).

(*c*) Each of these writings, whether early or late, has represented moral and religious ideas greatly in advance of the age in which it has appeared, and these ideas still lead the world.

All our ideas of progress, with all the forward-looking spirit of modern Christendom, are due to Scripture. The classic nations had no such ideas and no such spirit, except as they caught them from the Hebrews. Virgil's prophecy, in his fourth Eclogue, of a coming virgin and of the reign of Saturn and of the return of the golden age, was only the echo of the Sibylline books and of the hope of a Redeemer with which the Jews had leavened the whole Roman world; see A. H. Strong, The Great Poets and their Theology, 94-96.

(*d*) It is impossible to account for this unity without supposing such a supernatural suggestion and control that the Bible, while in its various parts written by human agents, is yet equally the work of a superhuman intelligence.

We may contrast with the harmony between the different Scripture writers the contradictions and refutations which follow merely human philosophies — *e. g.*, the Hegelian idealism and the Spencerian materialism. Hegel is "a name to swear at, as well as to swear by." Dr. Stirling, in his Secret of Hegel, "kept all the secret to himself, if he ever knew it." A certain Frenchman once asked Hegel if he could not gather up and express his philosophy in one sentence for him. "No," Hegel replied, "at least not in French." If Talleyrand's maxim be true that whatever is not intelligible is not French, Hegel's answer was a correct one. Hegel said of his disciples: "There is only one man living who understands me, and he does not."

Goeschel, Gabler, Daub, Marheinecke, Erdmann, are Hegel's right wing, or orthodox representatives and followers in theology; see Sterrett, Hegel's Philosophy of Religion. Hegel is followed by Alexander and Bradley in England, but is opposed by Seth and Schiller. Upton, Hibbert Lectures, 279-300, gives a valuable estimate of his position and influence: Hegel is all thought and no will. Prayer has no effect on God,— it is a purely psychological phenomenon. There is no free-will, and man's sin as much as man's holiness is a manifestation of the Eternal. Evolution is a fact, but it is only fatalistic evolution. Hegel notwithstanding did great service by substituting knowledge of reality for the oppressive Kantian relativity, and by banishing the old notion of matter as a mysterious substance wholly unlike and incompatible with the properties of mind. He did great service also by showing that the interactions of matter and mind are explicable only by the presence of the Absolute Whole in every part, though he erred greatly by carrying that idea of the unity of God and man beyond its proper limits, and by denying that God has given to the will of man any power to put itself into antagonism to His Will. Hegel did great service by showing that we cannot know even the part without knowing the whole, but he erred in teaching, as T. H. Green did, that the *relations* constitute the *reality* of the thing. He deprives both physical and psychical existences of that degree of selfhood or independent reality which is essential to both science and religion. We want real force, and not the mere idea of force; real will, and not mere thought.

B. This one mind that made the Bible is the same mind that made the soul, for the Bible is divinely adapted to the soul.

(*a*) It shows complete acquaintance with the soul.

The Bible addresses all parts of man's nature. There are Law and Epistles for man's reason; Psalms and Gospels for his affections; Prophets and Revelations for his imagination. Hence the popularity of the Scriptures. Their variety holds men. The Bible has become interwoven into modern life. Law, literature, art, all show its moulding influence.

(*b*) It judges the soul — contradicting its passions, revealing its guilt, and humbling its pride.

No product of mere human nature could thus look down upon human nature and condemn it. The Bible speaks to us from a higher level. The Samaritan woman's words apply to the whole compass of divine revelation; it tells us all things that ever we did (John 4: 29). The Brahmin declared that Romans 1, with its description of heathen vices, must have been forged after the missionaries came to India.

(*c*) It meets the deepest needs of the soul — by solutions of its problems, disclosures of God's character, presentations of the way of pardon, consolations and promises for life and death.

Neither Socrates nor Seneca sets forth the nature, origin and consequences of sin as committed against the holiness of God, nor do they point out the way of pardon and renewal. The Bible teaches us what nature cannot, viz.: God's creatorship, the origin of evil, the method of restoration, the certainty of a future state, and the principle of rewards and punishments there.

(*d*) Yet it is silent upon many questions for which writings of merely human origin seek first to provide solutions.

Compare the account of Christ's infancy in the gospels with the fables of the Apocryphal New Testament; compare the scant utterances of Scripture with regard to the future state with Mohammed's and Swedenborg's revelations of Paradise. See Alexander McLaren's sermon on The Silence of Scripture, in his book entitled: Christ in the Heart, 131-141.

(*e*) There are infinite depths and inexhaustible reaches of meaning in Scripture, which difference it from all other books, and which compel us to believe that its author must be divine.

Sir Walter Scott, on his death bed : " Bring me the Book! " " What book? " said Lockhart, his son-in-law. " There is but one book ! " said the dying man. Réville concludes an Essay in the Revue des deux Mondes (1864): " One day the question was started, in an assembly, what book a man condemned to lifelong imprisonment, and to whom but one book would be permitted, had better take into his cell with him. The company consisted of Catholics, Protestants, philosophers and even materialists, but all agreed that their choice would fall only on the Bible."
On the whole subject, see Garbett, God's Word Written, 3-56; Luthardt, Saving Truths, 210; Rogers, Superhuman Origin of Bible, 155-181; W. L. Alexander, Connection and Harmony of O. T. and N. T.; Stanley Leathes, Structure of the O. T.; Bernard, Progress of Doctrine in the N. T.; Rainy, Delivery and Development of Doctrine; Titcomb, in Strivings for the Faith; Immer, Hermeneutics, 91; Present Day Tracts, 4: no. 23; 5: no. 28; 6: no. 31; Lee on Inspiration, 26-32.

2. *Moral System of the New Testament.*

The perfection of this system is generally conceded. All will admit that it greatly surpasses any other system known among men. Among its distinguishing characteristics may be mentioned :

(*a*) Its comprehensiveness, — including all human duties in its code, even the most generally misunderstood and neglected, while it permits no vice whatsoever.

Buddhism regards family life as sinful. Suicide was commended by many ancient philosophers. Among the Spartans to steal was praiseworthy, — only to be caught stealing was criminal. Classic times despised humility. Thomas Paine said that Christianity cultivated " the spirit of a spaniel," and John Stuart Mill asserted that Christ ignored duty to the state. Yet Peter urges Christians to add to their faith manliness, courage, heroism (2 Pet. 1 : 5 — "in your faith supply virtue "), and Paul declares the state to be God's ordinance (Rom. 13 : 1 — " Let every soul be in subjection to the higher powers: for there is no power but of God; and the powers that be are ordained of God "). Patriotic defence of a nation's unity and freedom has always found its chief incitement and ground in these injunctions of Scripture. E. G. Robinson: "Christian ethics do not contain a particle of chaff, — all is pure wheat."

(*b*) Its spirituality, — accepting no merely external conformity to right precepts, but judging all action by the thoughts and motives from which it springs.

The superficiality of heathen morals is well illustrated by the treatment of the corpse of a priest in Siam : the body is covered with gold leaf, and then is left to rot and shine. Heathenism divorces religion from ethics. External and ceremonial observances take the place of purity of heart. The Sermon on the Mount on the other hand pronounces blessing only upon inward states of the soul. Ps. 51:6 — "Behold, thou desirest truth in the inward parts, and in the hidden part thou wilt make me to know wisdom"; Micah 6:8 — "what doth Jehovah require of thee, but to do justly, and to love kindness, and to walk humbly with thy God?"

(c) Its simplicity, — inculcating principles rather than imposing rules; reducing these principles to an organic system ; and connecting this system with religion by summing up all human duty in the one command of love to God and man.

Christianity presents no extensive code of rules, like that of the Pharisees or of the Jesuits. Such codes break down of their own weight. The laws of the State of New York alone constitute a library of themselves, which only the trained lawyer can master. It is said that Mohammedanism has recorded sixty-five thousand special instances in which the reader is directed to do right. It is the merit of Jesus' system that all its requisitions are reduced to unity. Mark 12:29-31 — " Hear, O Israel; The Lord our God, the Lord is one : and thou shalt love the Lord thy God with all thy heart, and with all thy soul, and with all thy mind, and with all thy strength. The second is this : Thou shalt love thy neighbor as thyself. There is none other commandment greater than these." Wendt, Teaching of Jesus, 2:384-814, calls attention to the inner unity of Jesus' teaching. The doctrine that God is a loving Father is applied with unswerving consistency. Jesus confirmed whatever was true in the O. T., and he set aside the unworthy. He taught not so much about God, as about the kingdom of God, and about the ideal fellowship between God and men. Morality was the necessary and natural expression of religion. In Christ teaching and life were perfectly blended. He was the representative of the religion which he taught.

(d) Its practicality, — exemplifying its precepts in the life of Jesus Christ; and, while it declares man's depravity and inability in his own strength to keep the law, furnishing motives to obedience, and the divine aid of the Holy Spirit to make this obedience possible.

Revelation has two sides: Moral law, and provision for fulfilling the moral law that has been broken. Heathen systems can incite to temporary reformations, and they can terrify with fears of retribution. But only God's regenerating grace can make the tree good, in such a way that its fruit will be good also (Mat. 12:33). There is a difference between touching the pendulum of the clock and winding it up, — the former may set it temporarily swinging, but only the latter secures its regular and permanent motion. The moral system of the N. T. is not simply law, — it is also grace: John 1:17 — " the law was given through Moses; grace and truth came through Jesus Christ." Dr. William Ashmore's tract represents a Chinaman in a pit. Confucius looks into the pit and says: "If you had done as I told you, you would never have gotten in." Buddha looks into the pit and says: "If you were up here I would show you what to do." So both Confucius and Buddha pass on. But Jesus leaps down into the pit and helps the poor Chinaman out.

At the Parliament of Religions in Chicago there were many ideals of life propounded, but no religion except Christianity attempted to show that there was any power given to realize these ideals. When Joseph Cook challenged the priests of the ancient religions to answer Lady Macbeth's question: "How cleanse this red right hand?" the priests were dumb. But Christianity declares that "the blood of Jesus his Son cleanseth us from all sin" (1 John 1:7). E. G. Robinson: Christianity differs from all other religions in being (1) a historical religion; (2) in turning abstract law into a person to be loved; (3) in furnishing a demonstration of God's love in Christ; (4) in providing atonement for sin and forgiveness for the sinner; (5) in giving a power to fulfil the law and sanctify the life. Bowne, Philos. of Theism, 249 — "Christianity, by making the moral law the expression of a holy Will, brought that law out of its impersonal abstraction, and assured its ultimate triumph. Moral principles may be what they were before, but moral practice is forever different. Even the earth itself has another look, now that it has heaven above it." Frances Power Cobbe, Life, 92 — "The achievement of Christianity was not the inculcation of a new, still less of a systematic, morality; but the introduction of a new spirit into morality; as Christ himself said, a leaven into the lump."

We may justly argue that a moral system so pure and perfect, since it surpasses all human powers of invention and runs counter to men's natural tastes and passions, must have had a supernatural, and if a supernatural, then a divine, origin.

Heathen systems of morality are in general defective, in that they furnish for man's moral action no sufficient example, rule, motive, or end. They cannot do this, for the reason that they practically identify God with nature, and know of no clear revelation of his holy will. Man is left to the law of his own being, and since he is not conceived of as wholly responsible and free, the lower impulses are allowed sway as well as the higher, and selfishness is not regarded as sin. As heathendom does not recognize man's depravity, so it does not recognize his dependence upon divine grace, and its virtue is self-righteousness. Heathenism is man's vain effort to lift himself to God ; Christianity is God's coming down to man to save him ; see Gunsaulus, Transfig. of Christ, 11, 12. Martineau, 1 : 15, 16, calls attention to the difference between the physiological ethics of heathendom and the psychological ethics of Christianity. Physiological ethics begins with nature ; and, finding in nature the uniform rule of necessity and the operation of cause and effect, it comes at last to man and applies the same rule to him, thus extinguishing all faith in personality, freedom, responsibility, sin and guilt. Psychological ethics, on the contrary, wisely begins with what we know best, with man ; and finding in him free-will and a moral purpose, it proceeds outward to nature and interprets nature as the manifestation of the mind and will of God.

"Psychological ethics are altogether peculiar to Christendom. . . . Other systems begin outside and regard the soul as a homogeneous part of the *universe*, applying to the soul the principle of necessity that prevails outside of it. . . . In the Christian religion, on the other hand, the interest, the mystery of the world are concentrated in *human nature*. . . . The sense of sin—a sentiment that left no trace in Athens—involves a consciousness of personal alienation from the Supreme Goodness ; the aspiration after holiness directs itself to a union of affection and will with the source of all Perfection ; the agency for transforming men from their old estrangement to new reconciliation is a Person, in whom the divine and human historically blend ; and the sanctifying Spirit by which they are sustained at the height of their purer life is a living link of communion between their minds and the Soul of souls. . . . So Nature, to the Christian consciousness, sank into the accidental and the neutral." Measuring ourselves by human standards, we nourish pride ; measuring ourselves by divine standards, we nourish humility. Heathen nations, identifying God with nature or with man, are unprogressive. The flat architecture of the Parthenon, with its lines parallel to the earth, is the type of heathen religion ; the aspiring arches of the Gothic cathedral symbolize Christianity.

Sterrett, Studies in Hegel, 33, says that Hegel characterized the Chinese religion as that of Measure, or temperate conduct ; Brahmanism as that of Phantasy, or inebriate dream-life ; Buddhism as that of Self-involvement ; that of Egypt as the imbruted religion of Enigma, symbolized by the Sphynx ; that of Greece, as the religion of Beauty ; the Jewish as that of Sublimity ; and Christianity as the Absolute religion, the fully revealed religion of truth and freedom. In all this Hegel entirely fails to grasp the elements of Will, Holiness, Love, Life, which characterize Judaism and Christianity, and distinguish them from all other religions. R. H. Hutton : "Judaism taught us that Nature must be interpreted by our knowledge of God, not God by our knowledge of Nature." Lyman Abbott : "Christianity is not a new *life*, but a new *power* ; not a *summons* to a new life, but an *offer* of new life ; not a reënactment of the old law, but a power of God unto salvation ; not love to God and man, but Christ's message that God loves us, and will help us to the life of love."

Beyschlag, N. T. Theology, 5, 6—" Christianity postulates an opening of the heart of the eternal God to the heart of man coming to meet him. Heathendom shows us the heart of man blunderingly grasping the hem of God's garment, and mistaking Nature, his majestic raiment, for himself. Only in the Bible does man press beyond God's external manifestations to God himself." See Wuttke, Christian Ethics, 1 : 37-173 ; Porter, in Present Day Tracts, 4 : no. 19, pp. 33-64 ; Blackie, Four Phases of Morals ; Faiths of the World (St. Giles Lectures, second series) ; J. F. Clarke, Ten Great Religions, 2 : 280-317 ; Garbett, Dogmatic Faith ; Farrar, Witness of History to Christ, 134, and Seekers after God, 181, 182, 320 ; Curtis on Inspiration, 288. For denial of the all-comprehensive character of Christian Morality, see John Stuart Mill, on Liberty ; *per contra*, see Review of Mill, in Theol. Eclectic, 6 : 508-512 ; Row, in Strivings for the Faith, pub. by Christian Evidence Society, 181-226 ; also, Bampton Lectures, 1877 : 130-176 ; Fisher, Beginnings of Christianity, 28-38, 174.

In contrast with the Christian system of morality the defects of heathen systems are so marked and fundamental, that they constitute a strong corroborative evidence of the divine origin of the Scripture revelation. We therefore append certain facts and references with regard to particular heathen systems.

1. CONFUCIANISM. Confucius (*Kung-fu-tse*), B. C. 551-478, contemporary with Pythagoras and Buddha. Socrates was born ten years after Confucius died. Mencius (371-278) was a disciple of Confucius. Matheson, in Faiths of the World (St. Giles Lectures), 73-108, claims that Confucianism was "an attempt to substitute a morality for theology." Legge, however, in Present Day Tracts, 3: no. 18, shows that this is a mistake. Confucius simply left religion where he found it. God, or Heaven, is worshiped in China, but only by the Emperor. Chinese religion is apparently a survival of the worship of the patriarchal family. The father of the family was its only head and priest. In China, though the family widened into the tribe, and the tribe into the nation, the father still retained his sole authority, and, as the father of his people, the Emperor alone officially offered sacrifice to God. Between God and the people the gulf has so widened that the people may be said to have no practical knowledge of God or communication with him. Dr. W. A. P. Martin : "Confucianism has degenerated into a pantheistic medley, and renders worship to an impersonal 'anima mundi,' under the leading forms of visible nature."

Dr. William Ashmore, private letter: "The common people of China have: (1) Ancestor-worship, and the worship of deified heroes: (2) Geomancy, or belief in the controlling power of the elements of nature ; but back of these, and antedating them, is (3) the worship of Heaven and Earth, or Father and Mother, a very ancient dualism ; this belongs to the common people also, though once a year the Emperor, as a sort of high-priest of his people, offers sacrifice on the altar of Heaven ; in this he acts alone. 'Joss' is not a Chinese word at all. It is the corrupted form of the Portuguese word 'Deos.' The word 'pidgin' is similarly an attempt to say 'business' (big-i-ness or bidgin). 'Joss-pidgin' therefore means simply 'divine service,' or service offered to Heaven and Earth, or to spirits of any kind, good or bad. There are many gods, a Queen of Heaven, King of Hades, God of War, god of literature, gods of the hills, valleys, streams, a goddess of small-pox, of child-bearing, and all the various trades have their gods. The most lofty expression the Chinese have is 'Heaven,' or 'Supreme Heaven,' or 'Azure Heaven.' This is the surviving indication that in the most remote times they had knowledge of one supreme, intelligent and personal Power who ruled over all." Mr. Yugoro Chiba has shown that the Chinese classics permit sacrifice by all the people. But it still remains true that sacrifice to "Supreme Heaven" is practically confined to the Emperor, who like the Jewish high-priest offers for his people once a year.

Confucius did nothing to put morality upon a religious basis. In practice, the relations between man and man are the only relations considered. Benevolence, righteousness, propriety, wisdom, sincerity, are enjoined, but not a word is said with regard to man's relations to God. Love to God is not only not commanded — it is not thought of as possible. Though man's being is theoretically an ordinance of God, man is practically a law to himself. The first commandment of Confucius is that of filial piety. But this includes worship of dead ancestors, and is so exaggerated as to bury from sight the related duties of husband to wife and of parent to child. Confucius made it the duty of a son to slay his father's murderer, just as Moses insisted on a strictly retaliatory penalty for bloodshed; see J. A. Farrer, Primitive Manners and Customs, 80. He treated invisible and superior beings with respect, but held them at a distance. He recognized the "Heaven" of tradition; but, instead of adding to our knowledge of it, he stifled inquiry. Dr. Legge: "I have been reading Chinese books for more than forty years, and any general requirement to love God, or the mention of any one as actually loving him, has yet to come for the first time under my eye."

Ezra Abbot asserts that Confucius gave the golden rule in positive as well as negative form ; see Harris, Philos. Basis of Theism, 222. This however seems to be denied by Dr. Legge, Religions of China, 1-58. Wu Ting Fang, former Chinese minister to Washington, assents to the statement that Confucius gave the golden rule only in its negative form, and he says this difference is the difference between a passive and an aggressive civilization, which last is therefore dominant. The golden rule, as Confucius gives it, is : "Do not unto others that which you would not they should do unto you." Compare with this, Isocrates: "Be to your parents what you would have your children be to you. ... Do not to others the things which make you angry when others do them to you"; Herodotus: "What I punish in another man, I will myself, as far as I can, refrain from"; Aristotle: "We should behave toward our friends as we should wish them to behave toward us"; Tobit, 4 : 15—"What thou hatest, do to no one"; Philo: "What one hates to endure, let him not do", Seneca bids us "give as we wish to receive"; Rabbi Hillel: "Whatsoever is hateful to you, do not to another; this is the whole law, and all the rest is explanation."

Broadus, in Am. Com. on Matthew, 161—"The sayings of Confucius, Isocrates, and the three Jewish teachers, are merely negative; that of Seneca is confined to giving, and that of Aristotle to the treatment of friends. Christ lays down a rule for positive action, and that toward all men." He teaches that I am bound to do to others all that they could rightly desire me to do to them. The golden rule therefore requires a supplement, to show what others can rightly desire, namely, God's glory first, and their good as second and incidental thereto. Christianity furnishes this divine and perfect standard; Confucianism is defective in that it has no standard higher than human convention. While Confucianism excludes polytheism, idolatry, and deification of vice, it is a shallow and tantalizing system, because it does not recognize the hereditary corruption of human nature, or furnish any remedy for moral evil except the "doctrines of the sages." "The heart of man," it says, "is naturally perfectly upright and correct." Sin is simply "a disease, to be cured by self-discipline; a debt, to be canceled by meritorious acts; an ignorance, to be removed by study and contemplation." See Bib. Sac., 1883 : 292, 293; N. Englander, 1883:565; Marcus Dods, in Erasmus and other Essays, 239.

2. THE INDIAN SYSTEMS. *Brahmanism*, as expressed in the Vedas, dates back to 1000–1500 B. C. As Caird (in Faiths of the World, St. Giles Lectures, lecture i) has shown, it originated in the contemplation of the power in nature apart from the moral Personality that works in and through nature. Indeed we may say that all heathenism is man's choice of a non-moral in place of a moral God. Brahamanism is a system of pantheism, "a false or illegitimate consecration of the finite." All things are a manifestation of Brahma. Hence evil is deified as well as good. And many thousand gods are worshiped as partial representations of the living principle which moves through all. "How many gods have the Hindus?" asked Dr. Duff of his class. Henry Drummond thought there were about twenty-five. "Twenty-five?" responded the indignant professor; "twenty-five millions of millions!" While the early Vedas present a comparatively pure nature-worship, later Brahmanism becomes a worship of the vicious and the vile, of the unnatural and the cruel. Juggernaut and the suttee did not belong to original Hindu religion.

Bruce, Apologetics, 15—"Pantheism in theory always means polytheism in practice." The early Vedas are hopeful in spirit; later Brahmanism is a religion of disappointment. Caste is fixed and consecrated as a manifestation of God. Originally intended to express, in its four divisions of priest, soldier, agriculturist, slave, the different degree of unworldliness and divine indwelling, it becomes an iron fetter to prevent all aspiration and progress. Indian religion sought to exalt receptivity, the unity of existence, and rest from self-determination and its struggles. Hence it ascribed to its gods the same character as nature-forces. God was the common source of good and of evil. Its ethics is an ethics of moral indifference. Its charity is a charity for sin, and the temperance it desires is a temperance that will let the intemperate alone. Mozoomdar, for example, is ready to welcome everything in Christianity but its reproof of sin and its demand for righteousness. Brahmanism degrades woman, but it deifies the cow.

Buddhism, beginning with Buddha, 600 B. C., "recalls the mind to its elevation above the finite," from which Brahmanism had fallen away. Buddha was in certain respects a reformer. He protested against caste, and proclaimed that truth and morality are for all. Hence Buddhism, through its possession of this one grain of truth, appealed to the human heart, and became, next to Christianity, the greatest missionary religion. Notice then, first, its *universalism*. But notice also that this is a false universalism, for it ignores individualism and leads to universal stagnation and slavery. While Christianity is a religion of history, of will, of optimism, Buddhism is a religion of illusion, of quietism, of pessimism; see Nash, Ethics and Revelation, 107–109. In characterizing Buddhism as a missionary religion, we must notice, secondly, its element of *altruism*. But this altruism is one which destroys the self, instead of preserving it. The future Buddha, out of compassion for a famished tiger, permits the tiger to devour him. "Incarnated as a hare, he jumps into the fire to cook himself for a meal for a beggar.

—having previously shaken himself three times, so that none of the insects in his fur should perish with him"; see William James, Varieties of Religious Experience, 283. Buddha would deliver man, not by philosophy, nor by asceticism, but by self-renunciation. All isolation and personality are sin, the guilt of which rests, however, not on man, but on existence in general.

While Brahmanism is pantheistic, Buddhism is atheistic in its spirit. Pfleiderer, Philos. Religion, 1 : 285 — "The Brahmanic Akosmism, that had explained the world as mere seeming, led to the Buddhistic Atheism." Finiteness and separateness are evil, and the only way to purity and rest is by ceasing to exist. This is essential pessimism. The highest morality is to endure that which must be, and to escape from reality and from personal existence as soon as possible. Hence the doctrine of *Nirvana*. Rhys Davids, in his Hibbert Lectures, claims that early Buddhism meant by *Nirvana*, not annihilation, but the extinction of the self-life, and that this was attainable during man's present mortal existence. But the term *Nirvana* now means, to the great mass of those who use it, the loss of all personality and consciousness, and absorption into the general life of the universe. Originally the term denoted only freedom from individual desire, and those who had entered into *Nirvana* might again come out of it; see Ireland, Blot on the Brain, 238. But even in its original form, *Nirvana* was sought only from a selfish motive. Self-renunciation and absorption in the whole was not the enthusiasm of benevolence, — it was the refuge of despair. It is a religion without god or sacrifice. Instead of communion with a personal God, Buddhism has in prospect only an extinction of personality, as reward for untold ages of lonely self-conquest, extending through many transmigrations. Of Buddha it has been truly said "That all the all he had for needy man Was nothing, and his best of being was But not to be." Wilkinson, Epic of Paul, 296 — "He by his own act dying all the time, In ceaseless effort utterly to cease, Will willing not to will, desire desiring To be desire no more, until at last The fugitive go free, emancipate But by becoming naught." Of Christ Bruce well says: "What a contrast this Healer of disease and Preacher of pardon to the worst, to Buddha, with his religion of despair!"

Buddhism is also fatalistic. It inculcates submission and compassion — merely negative virtues. But it knows nothing of manly freedom, or of active love — the positive virtues of Christianity. It leads men to spare others, but not to help them. Its morality revolves around self, not around God. It has in it no organizing principle, for it recognizes no God, no inspiration, no soul, no salvation, no personal immortality. Buddhism would save men only by inducing them to flee from existence. To the Hindu, family life involves sin. The perfect man must forsake wife and children. All gratification of natural appetites and passions is evil. Salvation is not from sin, but from desire, and from this men can be saved only by escaping from life itself. Christianity buries sin, but saves the man; Buddha would save the man by killing him. Christianity symbolizes the convert's entrance upon a new life by raising him from the baptismal waters; the baptism of Buddhism should be immersion without emersion. The fundamental idea of Brahmanism, extinction of personality, remains the same in Buddhism; the only difference being that the result is secured by active atonement in the former, by passive contemplation in the latter. Virtue, and the knowledge that everything earthly is a vanishing spark of the original light, delivers man from existence and from misery.

Prof. G. H. Palmer, of Harvard, in The Outlook, June 19, 1897 — "Buddhism is unlike Christianity in that it abolishes misery by abolishing desire; denies personality instead of asserting it; has many gods, but no one God who is living and conscious; makes a shortening of existence rather than a lengthening of it to be the reward of righteousness. Buddhism makes no provision for family, church, state, science, or art. It give us a religion that is little, when we want one that is large." Dr. E. Benjamin Andrews: "Schopenhauer and Spencer are merely teachers of Buddhism. They regard the central source of all as unknowable force, instead of regarding it as a Spirit, living and holy. This takes away all impulse to scientific investigation. We need to start from a Person, and not from a thing."

For comparison of the sage of India, Sakya Muni, more commonly called Buddha (properly "the Buddha" = the enlightened; but who, in spite of Edwin Arnold's "Light of Asia," is represented as not pure from carnal pleasures before he began his work), with Jesus Christ, see Bib. Sac., July, 1882: 458-498; W. C. Wilkinson, Edwin Arnold, Poetizer and Paganizer; Kellogg, The Light of Asia and the Light of the World. Buddhism and Christianity are compared in Presb. Rev., July, 1883 : 505-548; Wuttke, Christian Ethics, 1 : 47-54; Mitchell, in Present Day Tracts, 6 : no. 33. See also

Oldenberg, Buddha; Lillie, Popular Life of Buddha; Beal, Catena of Buddhist Scriptures, 153 — " Buddhism declares itself ignorant of any mode of personal existence compatible with the idea of spiritual perfection, and so far it is ignorant of God"; 157 — "The earliest idea of *Nirvana* seems to have included in it no more than the enjoyment of a state of rest consequent on the extinction of all causes of sorrow." The impossibility of satisfying the human heart with a system of atheism is shown by the fact that the Buddha himself has been apotheosized to furnish an object of worship. Thus Buddhism has reverted to Brahmanism.

Monier Williams: "Mohammed has as much claim to be 'the Light of Asia' as Buddha has. What light from Buddha? Not about the heart's depravity, or the origin of sin, or the goodness, justice, holiness, fatherhood of God, or the remedy for sin, but only the ridding self from suffering by ridding self from life — a doctrine of merit, of self-trust, of pessimism, and annihilation of personality." Christ, himself personal, loving and holy, shows that God is a person of holiness and love. Robert Browning: "He that created love, shall not he love?" Only because Jesus is God, have we a gospel for the world. The claim that Buddha is "the Light of Asia" reminds one of the man who declared the moon to be of greater value than the sun, because it gives light in the darkness when it is needed, while the sun gives light in the daytime when it is not needed.

3. THE GREEK SYSTEMS. *Pythagoras* (584-504) based morality upon the principle of numbers. "Moral good was identified with unity; evil with multiplicity; virtue was harmony of the soul and its likeness to God. The aim of life was to make it represent the beautiful order of the Universe. The whole practical tendency of Pythagoreanism was ascetic, and included a strict self-control and an earnest culture." Here already we seem to see the defect of Greek morality in confounding the good with the beautiful, and in making morality a mere self-development. Matheson, Messages of the Old Religions: Greece reveals the intensity of the hour, the value of the present life, the beauty of the world that now is. Its religion is the religion of beautiful humanity. It anticipates the new heaven and the new earth. Rome on the other hand stood for union, incorporation, a universal kingdom. But its religion deified only the Emperor, not all humanity. It was the religion, not of love, but of power, and it identified the church with the state.

Socrates (469-400) made knowledge to be virtue. Morality consisted in subordinating irrational desires to rational knowledge. Although here we rise above a subjectively determined good as the goal of moral effort, we have no proper sense of sin. Knowledge, and not love, is the motive. If men know the right, they will do the right. This is a great overvaluing of knowledge. With Socrates, teaching is a sort of midwifery — not depositing information in the mind, but drawing out the contents of our own inner consciousness. Lewis Morris describes it as the life-work of Socrates to "doubt our doubts away." Socrates holds it right to injure one's enemies. He shows proud self-praise in his dying address. He warns against pederasty, yet compromises with it. He does not insist upon the same purity of family life which Homer describes in Ulysses and Penelope. Charles Kingsley, in Alton Locke, remarks that the spirit of the Greek tragedy was 'man mastered by circumstance'; that of modern tragedy is 'man mastering circumstance.' But the Greek tragedians, while showing man thus mastered, do still represent him as inwardly free, as in the case of Prometheus, and this sense of human freedom and responsibility appears to some extent in Socrates.

Plato (430-348) held that morality is pleasure in the good, as the truly beautiful, and that knowledge produces virtue. The good is likeness to God, — here we have glimpses of an extra-human goal and model. The body, like all matter, being inherently evil, is a hindrance to the soul, — here we have a glimpse of hereditary depravity. But Plato "reduced moral evil to the category of natural evil." He failed to recognize God as creator and master of matter; failed to recognize man's depravity as due to his own apostasy from God; failed to found morality on the divine will rather than on man's own consciousness. He knew nothing of a common humanity, and regarded virtue as only for the few. As there was no common sin, so there was no common redemption. Plato thought to reach God by intellect alone, when only conscience and heart could lead to him. He believed in a freedom of the soul in a preëxistent state where a choice was made between good and evil, but he believed that, after that antemundane decision had been made, the fates determined men's acts and lives irreversibly. Reason drives two horses, appetite and emotion, but their course has been predetermined.

Man acts as reason prompts. All sin is ignorance. There is nothing in this life but determinism. Martineau, Types, 13, 18, 49, 78, 88 — Plato in general has no proper notion of responsibility ; he reduces moral evil to the catagory of natural evil. His Ideas with one exception are not causes. Cause is mind, and mind is the Good. The Good is the apex and crown of Ideas. The Good is the highest Idea, and this highest Idea is a Cause. Plato has a feeble conception of personality, whether in God or in man. Yet God is a person in whatever sense man is a person, and man's personality is reflective self-consciousness. Will in God or man is not so clear. The Right is dissolved into the Good. Plato advocated infanticide and the killing off of the old and the helpless.

Aristotle (384–322) leaves out of view even the element of God-likeness and antemundane evil which Plato so dimly recognized, and makes morality the fruit of mere rational self-consciousness. He grants evil proclivities, but he refuses to call them immoral. He advocates a certain freedom of will, and he recognizes inborn tendencies which war against this freedom, but how these tendencies originated he cannot say, nor how men may be delivered from them. Not all can be moral ; the majority must be restrained by fear. He finds in God no motive, and love to God is not so much as mentioned as the source of moral action. A proud, composed, self-centered, and self-contained man is his ideal character. See Nicomachean Ethics, 7: 6, and 10: 10; Wuttke, Christian Ethics, 1 : 92–126. Alexander, Theories of Will, 39–54 — Aristotle held that desire and reason are the springs of action. Yet he did not hold that knowledge of itself would make men virtuous. He was a determinist. Actions are free only in the sense of being devoid of external compulsion. He viewed slavery as both rational and right. Butcher, Aspects of Greek Genius, 76 — " While Aristotle attributed to the State a more complete personality than it really possessed, he did not grasp the depth and mear ug of the personality of the individual." A. H. Strong, Christ in Creation, 289 — Aristotle had no conception of the unity of humanity. His doctrine of unity did not extend beyond the State. " He said that ' the whole is before the parts,' but he meant by ' the whole ' only the pan-Hellenic world, the commonwealth of Greeks; he never thought of humanity, and the word ' mankind ' never fell from his lips. He could not understand the unity of humanity, because he knew nothing of Christ, its organizing principle." On Aristotle's conception of God, see James Ten Broeke, in Bap. Quar. Rev., Jan. 1892 — God is recognized as personal, yet he is only the Greek Reason, and not the living, loving, providential Father of the Hebrew revelation. Aristotle substitutes the logical for the dynamical in his dealing with the divine causality. God is thought, not power.

Epicurus (342–270) regarded happiness, the subjective feeling of pleasure, as the highest criterion of truth and good. A prudent calculating for prolonged pleasure is the highest wisdom. He regards only this life. Concern for retribution and for a future existence is folly. If there are gods, they have no concern for men. " Epicurus, on pretense of consulting for their ease, complimented the gods, and bowed them out of existence." Death is the falling apart of material atoms and the eternal cessation of consciousness. The miseries of this life are due to imperfection in the fortuitously constructed universe. The more numerous these undeserved miseries, the greater our right to seek pleasure. Alexander, Theories of the Will, 55–75 — The Epicureans held that the soul is composed of atoms, yet that the will is free. The atoms of the soul are excepted from the law of cause and effect. An atom may decline or deviate in the universal descent, and this is the Epicurean idea of freedom. This indeterminism was held by all the Greek sceptics, materialists though they were.

Zeno, the founder of the Stoic philosophy (340–264), regarded virtue as the only good. Thought is to subdue nature. The free spirit is self-legislating, self-dependent, self-sufficient. Thinking, not feeling, is the criterion of the true and the good. Pleasure is the consequence, not the end of moral action. There is an irreconcilable antagonism of existence. Man cannot reform the world, but he can make himself perfect. Hence an unbounded pride in virtue. The sage never repents. There is not the least recognition of the moral corruption of mankind. There is no objective divine ideal, or revealed divine will. The Stoic discovers moral law only within, and never suspects his own moral perversion. Hence he shows self-control and justice, but never humility or love. He needs no compassion or forgiveness, and he grants none to others. Virtue is not an actively outworking character, but a passive resistance to irrational reality. Man may retreat into himself. The Stoic is indifferent to pleasure and pain, not because he believes in a divine government, or in a divine love for mankind, but as a proud defiance of the irrational world. He has no need of God or of redemption. As the Epicurean gives himself to enjoyment of the world, the Stoic gives himself to contempt of the world. In all afflictions, each can say, "The door is open." To the Epicurean, the refuge is intoxication; to the Stoic, the refuge is suicide: "If the house smokes, quit it." Wuttke, Christian Ethics, 1: 62-161, from whom much of this account of the Greeks systems is condensed, describes Epicureanism and Stoicism as alike making morality subjective, although Epicureanism regarded spirit as determined by nature, while Stoicism regarded nature as determined by spirit.

The Stoics were materialists and pantheists. Though they speak of a personal God, this is a figure of speech. False opinion is at the root of all vice. Chrysippus denied what we now call the liberty of indifference, saying that there could not be an effect without a cause. Man is enslaved to passion. The Stoics could not explain how a vicious man could become virtuous. The result is apathy. Men act only according to character. and this a doctrine of fate. The Stoic indifference or apathy in misfortune is not a bearing of it at all, but rather a cowardly retreat from it. It is in the actual suffering of evil that Christianity finds "the soul of good." The office of misfortune is disciplinary and purifying; see Seth, Ethical Principles, 417. "The shadow of the sage's self, projected on vacancy, was called God, and, as the sage had long since abandoned interest in practical life, he expected his Divinity to do the same."

The Stoic reverenced God just because of his unapproachable majesty. Christianity sees in God a Father, a Redeemer, a carer for our minute wants, a deliverer from our sin. It teaches us to see in Christ the humanity of the divine, affinity with God, God's supreme interest in his handiwork. For the least of his creatures Christ died. Kinship with God gives dignity to man. The individuality that Stoicism lost in the whole, Christianity makes the end of the creation. The State exists to develop and promote it. Paul took up and infused new meaning into certain phrases of the Stoic philosophy about the freedom and royalty of the wise man, just as John adopted and glorified certain phrases of Alexandrian philosophy about the Word. Stoicism was lonely and pessimistic. The Stoics said that the best thing was not to be born; the next best thing was to die. Because Stoicism had no God of helpfulness and sympathy, its virtue was mere conformity to nature, majestic egoism and self-complacency. In the Roman *Epictetus* (89), *Seneca* (†65), and *Marcus Aurelius* (121-180), the religious element comes more into the foreground, and virtue appears once more as God-likeness; but it is possible that this later Stoicism was influenced by Christianity. On Marcus Aurelius, see New Englander, July, 1881: 415-431; Capes, Stoicism.

4. SYSTEMS OF WESTERN ASIA. *Zoroaster* (1000 B. C. ?), the founder of the Parsees, was a dualist, at least so far as to explain the existence of evil and of good by the original presence in the author of all things of two opposing principles. Here is evidently a limit put upon the sovereignty and holiness of God. Man is not perfectly dependent upon him, nor is God's will an unconditional law for his creatures. As opposed to the Indian systems, Zoroaster's insistence upon the divine personality furnished a far better basis for a vigorous and manly morality. Virtue was to be won by hard struggle of free beings against evil. But then, on the other hand, this evil was conceived as originally due, not to finite beings themselves, but either to an evil deity who warred against the good, or to an evil principle in the one deity himself. The burden of guilt is therefore shifted from man to his maker. Morality becomes subjective and unsettle .. Not love to God or imitation of God, but rather self-love and self-development. furnish the motive and aim of morality. No fatherhood or love is recognized in the deity, and other things besides God (e. g., fire) are worshiped. There can be no depth to the consciousness of sin, and no hope of divine deliverance.

It is the one merit of Parseeism that it recognizes the moral conflict of the world : its error is that it carries this moral conflict into the very nature of God. We can apply to Parseeism the words of the Conference of Foreign Mission Boards to the Buddhists of Japan : " All religions are expressions of man's sense of dependence, but only one provides fellowship with God. All religions speak of a higher truth, but only one speaks of that truth as found in a loving personal God, our Father. All religions show man's helplessness, but only one tells of a divine Savior, who offers to man forgiveness of sin, and salvation through his death, and who is now a living person, working in and with all who believe in him, to make them holy and righteous and pure." Matheson, Messages of Old Religions, says that Parseeism recognize an obstructive element in the nature of God himself. Moral evil is reality; but there is no reconciliation, nor is it shown that all things work together for good. See Wuttke. Christian Ethics, 1: 47-54; Faiths of the World (St. Giles Lectures), 109-144; Mitchell, in Present Day Tracts, 3: no. 25; Whitney on the Avesta, in Oriental and Linguistic Studies.

Mohammed (570–632 A. D.), the founder of Islam, gives us in the Koran a system containing four dogmas of fundamental immorality, namely, polygamy, slavery, persecution, and suppression of private judgement. Mohammedanism is heathenism in monotheistic form. Its good points are its conscientiousness and its relation to God. It has prospered because it has preached the unity of God, and because it is a book-religion. But both these it got from Judaism and Christianity. It has appropriated the Old Testament saints and even Jesus. But it denies the death of Christ and sees no need of atonement. The power of sin is not recognized. The idea of sin, in Moslems, is emptied of all positive content. Sin is simply a falling short, accounted for by the weakness and shortsightedness of man, inevitable in the fatalistic universe, or not remembered in wrath by the indulgent and merciful Father. Forgiveness is indulgence, and the conception of God is emptied of the quality of justice. Evil belongs only to the individual, not to the race. Man attains the favor of God by good works, based on prophetic teaching. Morality is not a fruit of salvation, but a means. There is no penitence or humility, but only self-righteousness; and this self-righteousness is consistent with great sensuality, unlimited divorce, and with absolute despotism in family, civil and religious affairs. There is no knowledge of the fatherhood of God or of the brotherhood of man. In all the Koran, there is no such declaration as that "God so loved the world" (John 3 : 16).

The submission of Islam is submission to an arbitrary will, not to a God of love. There is no basing of morality in love. The highest good is the sensuous happiness of the individual. God and man are external to one another. Mohammed is a teacher but not a priest. Mozley, Miracles, 140, 141 — "Mohammed had no faith in human nature. There were two things which he thought men could do, and would do, for the glory of God — transact religious *forms*, and *fight*, and upon these two points he was severe; but within the sphere of common practical life, where man's great trial lies, his code exhibits the disdainful laxity of a legislator who accomodates his rule to the recipient, and shows his estimate of the recipient by the accommodation which he adopts. . . . ' Human nature is weak,' said he." Lord Houghton : The Koran is all wisdom, all law, all religion, for all time. Dead men bow before a dead God. "Though the world rolls on from change to change, And realms of thought expand, The letter stands without expanse or range, Stiff as a dead man's hand." Wherever Mohammedanism has gone, it has either found a desert or made one. Fairbairn, in Contemp. Rev., Dec. 1882 : 866 —"The Koran has frozen Mohammedan thought; to obey is to abandon progress." Muir, in Present Day Tracts, 3 : no. 14 —"Mohammedanism reduces men to a dead level of social depression, despotism, and semi-barbarism. Islam is the work of man; Christianity of God." See also Faiths of the World (St. Giles Lectures, Second Series), 361–396 ; J. F. Clarke, Ten Great Religions, 1 : 448–488 ; 280–317 ; Great Religions of the World, published by the Harpers ; Zwemer, Moslem Doctrine of God.

3.   *The person and character of Christ.*

A.   The conception of Christ's person as presenting deity and humanity indissolubly united, and the conception of Christ's character, with its faultless and all-comprehending excellence, cannot be accounted for upon any other hypothesis than that they were historical realities.

The stylobate of the Parthenon at Athens rises about three inches in the middle of the 101 feet of the front, and four inches in the middle of the 228 feet of the flanks. A nearly parallel line is found in the entablature. The axes of the columns lean inward nearly three inches in their height of 34 feet, thus giving a sort of pyramidal character to the structure. Thus the architect overcame the apparent sagging of horizontal lines, and at the same time increased the apparent height of the edifice ; see Murray, Handbook of Greece, 5th ed., 1834, 1 : 308, 309 ; Ferguson, Handbook of Architecture, 268–270. The neglect to counteract this optical illusion has rendered the Madeleine in Paris a stiff and ineffective copy of the Parthenon. The Galilean peasant who should minutely describe these peculiarities of the Parthenon would prove, not only that the edifice was a historical reality, but that he had actually seen it. Bruce, Apologetics, 343—"In reading the memoirs of the evangelists, you feel as one sometimes feels in a picture-gallery. Your eye alights on the portrait of a person whom you do not know. You look at it intently for a few moments and then remark to a companion : ' That must ne like the original. — it is so life-like.' " Theodore Parker : "It would take a Jesus to forge a Jesus." See Row, Bampton Lectures, 1877 : 178-219, and in Present Day Tracts, 4 : no. 22 ; F. W. Farrar, Witness of History to Christ ; Barry, Boyle Lecture on Manifold Witness for Christ.

(*a*) No source can be assigned from which the evangelists could have derived such a conception. The Hindu avatars were only temporary unions of deity with humanity. The Greeks had men half-deified, but no unions of God and man. The monotheism of the Jews found the person of Christ a perpetual stumbling-block. The Essenes were in principle more opposed to Christianity than the Rabbinists.

Herbert Spencer, Data of Ethics, 279 — "The coëxistence of a perfect man and an imperfect society is impossible ; and could the two coëxist, the resulting conduct would not furnish the ethical standard sought." We must conclude that the perfect manhood of Christ is a miracle, and the greatest of miracles. Bruce, Apologetics, 346, 351 — "When Jesus asks : ' Why callest thou me good ? ' he means : ' Learn first what goodness is, and call no man good till you are sure that he deserves it.' Jesus' goodness was entirely free from religious scrupulosity ; it was distinguished by humanity ; it was full of modesty and lowliness. . . . Buddhism has flourished 2000 years, though little is known of its founder. Christianity might have been so perpetuated, but it is not so. I want to be sure that the ideal has been embodied in an actual life. Otherwise it is only poetry, and the obligation to conform to it ceases." For comparison of Christ's incarnation with Hindu, Greek, Jewish, and Essene ideas, see Dorner, Hist. Doct. Person of Christ, Introduction. On the Essenes, see Herzog, Encyclop., art.: Essener ; Pressensé, Jesus Christ, Life, Times and Work, 84-87 ; Lightfoot on Colossians, 349-419 ; Godet, Lectures in Defence of the Christian Faith.

(*b*) No mere human genius, and much less the genius of Jewish fishermen, could have originated this conception. Bad men invent only such characters as they sympathize with. But Christ's character condemns badness. Such a portrait could not have been drawn without supernatural aid. But such aid would not have been given to fabrication. The conception can be explained only by granting that Christ's person and character were historical realities.

Between Pilate and Titus 30,000 Jews are said to have been crucified around the walls of Jerusalem. Many of these were young men. What makes one of them stand out on the pages of history? There are two answers : The character of Jesus was a perfect character, and, He was God as well as man. Gore, Incarnation, 63 — "The Christ of the gospels, if he be not true to history, represents a combined effort of the creative imagination without parallel in literature. But the literary characteristics of Palestine in the first century make the hypothesis of such an effort morally impossible." The Apocryphal gospels show us what mere imagination was capable of producing. That the portrait of Christ is not puerile, inane, hysterical, selfishly assertive, and self-contradictory, can be due only to the fact that it is the photograph from real life.

For a remarkable exhibition of the argument from the character of Jesus, see Bushnell, Nature and the Supernatural, 276-332. Bushnell mentions the originality and vastness of Christ's plan, yet its simplicity and practical adaptation ; his moral traits of independence, compassion, meekness, wisdom, zeal, humility, patience ; the combination in him of seemingly opposite qualities. With all his greatness, he was condescending and simple : he was unworldly, yet not austere ; he had strong feelings, yet was self-possessed ; he had indignation toward sin, yet compassion toward the sinner ; he showed devotion to his work, yet calmness under opposition ; universal philanthropy, yet susceptibility to private attachments ; the authority of a Savior and Judge, yet the gratitude and the tenderness of a son ; the most elevated devotion, yet a life of activity and exertion. See chapter on The Moral Miracle, in Bruce, Miraculous Element of the Gospels, 43-78.

B. The acceptance and belief in the New Testament descriptions of Jesus Christ cannot be accounted for except upon the ground that the person and character described had an actual existence.

(*a*) If these descriptions were false, there were witnesses still living who had known Christ and who would have contradicted them. (*b*) There was no motive to induce acceptance of such false accounts, but every motive to the contrary. (*c*) The success of such falsehoods could be explained only by supernatural aid, but God would never have thus aided falsehood. This person and character, therefore, must have been not fictitious but real; and if real, then Christ's words ai true, and the system of which his person and character are a part is a revelation from God.

"The counterfeit may for a season Deceive the wide earth; But the lie waxing great comes to labor, And truth has its birth." Matthew Arnold, The Better Part: "Was Christ a man like us? Ah, let us see, If we then too can be Such men as he!" When the blatant sceptic declared: "I do not believe that such a man as Jesus Christ ever .ived," George Warren merely replied: "I wish I were like him!" Dwight L. Moody was called a hypocrite, but the stalwart evangelist answered: "Well, suppose I am. How does that make your case any better? I know some pretty mean things about myself; but you cannot say anything against my Master." Goethe: "Let the culture of the spirit advance forever; let the human spirit broaden itself as it will; yet it will never go beyond the neight and moral culture of Christianity, as it glitters and shines in the gospels."

Renan, Life of Jesus: "Jesus founded the absolute religion, excluding nothing, determining nothing, save its essence. . . . The foundation of the true religion is indeed his work. After him, there is nothing left but to develop and fructify." And a Christian scholar has remarked: "It is an astonishing proof of the divine guidance vouchsafed to the evangelists that no man, of their time or since, has been able to touch the picture of Christ without debasing it." We may find an illustration of this in the words of Chadwick, Old and New Unitarianism, 207 — "Jesus' doctrine of marriage was ascetic, his doctrine of property was communistic, his doctrine of charity was sentimental, his doctrine of non-resistance was such as commends itself to Tolstoi, but not to many others of our time. With the example of Jesus, it is the same as with his teachings. Followed unreservedly, would it not justify those who say : 'The hope of the race is in its extinction'; and bring all our joys and sorrows to a sudden end?" To this we may answer in the words of Huxley, who declares that Jesus Christ is "the noblest ideal of humanity which mankind has yet worshiped." Gordon, Christ of To-Day, 179 — "The question is not whether Christ is good enough to represent the Supreme Being, but whether the Supreme Being is good enough to have Christ for his representative. John Stuart Mill looks upon the Christian religion as the worship of Christ, rather than the worship of God, and in this way he explains the beneficence of its influence."

John Stuart Mill, Essays on Religion, 254 — "The most valuable part of the effect on the character which Christianity has produced, by holding up in a divine person a standard of excellence and a model for imitation, is available even to the absolute unbeliever, and can never more be lost to humanity. For it is Christ rather than God whom Christianity has held up to believers as the pattern of perfection for humanity. It is the God incarnate, more than the God of the Jews or of nature, who, being idealized, has taken so great and salutary hold on the modern mind. And whatever else may be taken away from us by rational criticism, Christ is still left: a unique figure, not more unlike all his precursors than all his followers, even those who had the direct benefit of his personal preaching. . . . Who among his disciples, or among their proselytes, was capable of inventing the sayings ascribed to Jesus, or of imagining the life and character revealed in the Gospels? . . . About the life and sayings of Jesus there is a stamp of personal originality combined with profundity of insight which, if we abandon the idle expectation of finding scientific precision where something very different was aimed at, must place the Prophet of Nazareth, even in the estimation of those who have no belief in his inspiration, in the very first rank of the men of sublime genius of whom our species can boast. When this preëminent genius is combined with the qualities of probably the greatest moral reformer and martyr to that mission who ever existed upon earth, religion cannot be said to have made a bad choice in pitching on this man as the ideal representative and guide of humanity; nor even now would it be easy, even for an unbeliever, to find a better translation of the rule of virtue from the abstract into the concrete than the endeavor so to live that Christ would approve our life.

Woen to this we add that, to the conception of the rational sceptic, it remains a possibility that Christ actually was . . . a man charged with a special, express and unique commission from God to lead mankind to truth and virtue, we may well conclude that the influences of religion on the character, which will remain after rational criticism has done its utmost against the evidences of religion, are well worth preserving, and that what they lack in direct strength as compared with those of a firmer belief is more than compensated by the greater truth and rectitude of the morality they sanction." See also Ullmann, Sinlessness of Jesus; Alexander, Christ and Christianity, 129-157; Schaff, Person of Christ; Young, The Christ in History; George Dana Boardman, The Problem of Jesus.

4. *The testimony of Christ to himself*—as being a messenger from God and as being one with God.

Only one personage in history has claimed to teach absolute truth, to be one with God, and to attest his divine mission by works such as only God could perform.

A. This testimony cannot be accounted for upon the hypothesis that Jesus was an intentional deceiver : for (*a*) the perfectly consistent holiness of his life; (*b*) the unwavering confidence with which he challenged investigation of his claims and staked all upon the result ; (*c*) the vast improbability of a lifelong lie in the avowed interests of truth; and (*d*) the impossibility that deception should have wrought such blessing to the world, — all show that Jesus was no conscious impostor.

Fisher, Essays on the Supernat. Origin of Christianity, 515-538 — Christ knew how vast his claims were, yet he staked all upon them. Though others doubted, he never doubted himself. Though persecuted unto death, he never ceased his consistent testimony. Yet he lays claim to humility: Mat. 11:29 — "I am meek and lowly in heart." How can we reconcile with humility his constant self-assertion? We answer that Jesus' self-assertion was absolutely essential to his mission, for he and the truth were one : he could not assert the truth without asserting himself, and he could not assert himself without asserting the truth. Since he was the truth, he needed to say so, for men's sake and for the truth's sake, and he could be meek and lowly in heart in saying so. Humility is not self-depreciation, but only the judging of ourselves according to God's perfect standard. 'Humility' is derived from '*humus*'. It is the coming down from airy and vain self-exploitation to the solid ground, the hard-pan, of actual fact.

God requires of us only so much humility as is consistent with truth. The self-glorification of the egotist is nauseating, because it indicates gross ignorance or misrepresentation of self. But it is a duty to be self-asserting, just so far as we represent the truth and righteousness of God. There is a noble self-assertion which is perfectly consistent with humility. Job must stand for his integrity. Paul's humility was not of the Uriah Heep variety. When occasion required, he could assert his manhood and his rights, as at Philippi and at the Castle of Antonia. So the Christian should frankly say out the truth that is in him. Each Christian has an experience of his own, and should tell it to others. In testifying to the truth he is only following the example of "Christ Jesus, who before Pontius Pilate witnessed the good confession" (1 Tim. 6:13).

B. Nor can Jesus' testimony to himself be explained upon the hypothesis that he was self-deceived : for this would argue (*a*) a weakness and folly amounting to positive insanity. But his whole character and life exhibit a calmness, dignity, equipoise, insight, self-mastery, utterly inconsistent with such a theory. Or it would argue (*b*) a self-ignorance and self-exaggeration which could spring only from the deepest moral perversion. But the absolute purity of his conscience, the humility of his spirit, the self-denying beneficence of his life, show this hypothesis to be incredible.

Rogers, Superhuman Origin of the Bible, 39 — If he were man, then to demand that all the world should bow down to him would be worthy of scorn like that which we feel for some straw-crowned monarch of Bedlam. Forrest, The Christ of History and of

Experience, 22, 76 — Christ never united with his disciples in prayer. He went up into the mountain to pray, but not to pray *with them :* Luke 9 :18 — "as he was *alone* praying, his disciples were with him." The consciousness of preëxistence is the indispensable precondition of the total demand which he makes in the Synoptics. Adamson, The Mind in Christ, 81, 82 — We value the testimony of Christians to their communion with God. Much more should we value the testimony of Christ. Only one who, first being divine, also knew that he was divine, could reveal heavenly things with the clearness and certainty that belong to the utterances of Jesus. In him we have something very different from the momentary flashes of insight which leave us in all the greater darkness.

Nash, Ethics and Revelation, 5 — " Self-respect is bottomed upon the ability to become what one desires to be ; and, if the ability steadily falls short of the task, the springs of self-respect dry up ; the motives of happy and heroic action wither. Science, art, generous civic life, and especially religion, come to man's rescue," — showing him his true greatness and breadth of being in God. The State is the individual's larger self. Humanity, and even the universe, are parts of him. It is the duty of man to enable all men to be men. It is possible for men not only truthfully but also rationally to assert themselves, even in earthly affairs. Chatham to the Duke of Devonshire : "My Lord, I believe I can save this country, and that no one else can." Leonardo da Vinci, in his thirtieth year, to the Duke of Milan : "I can carry through every kind of work in sculpture, in clay, marble, and bronze ; also in painting I can execute everything that can be demanded, as well as any one whosoever."

Horace : " Exegi monumentum ære perennius." Savage, Life beyond Death, 209 — A famous old minister said once, when a young and zealous enthusiast tried to get him to talk, and failing, burst out with, " Have you no religion at all ? " "None *to speak of,*" was the reply. When Jesus perceived a tendency in his disciples to self-glorification, he urged silence ; but when he saw the tendency to introspection and inertness, he bade them proclaim what he had done for them (Mat. 8 : 4 ; Mark 5 : 19). It is never right for the Christian to proclaim himself ; but, if Christ had not proclaimed himself, the world could never have been saved. Rush Rhees, Life of Jesus of Nazareth, 235-237 — " In the teaching of Jesus, two topics have the leading place — the Kingdom of God, and himself. He sought to be Lord, rather than Teacher only. Yet the Kingdom is not one of power, national and external, but one of fatherly love and of mutual brotherhood."

Did Jesus do anything for effect, or as a mere example ? Not so. His baptism had meaning for him as a consecration of himself to death for the sins of the world, and his washing of the disciples' feet was the fit beginning of the paschal supper and the symbol of his laying aside his heavenly glory to purify us for the marriage supper of the Lamb. Thomas à Kempis : " Thou art none the holier because thou art praised, and none the worse because thou art censured. What thou art, that thou art, and it avails thee naught to be called any better than thou art in the sight of God." Jesus' consciousness of his absolute sinlessness and of his perfect communion with God is the strongest of testimonies to his divine nature and mission. See Theological Eclectic, 4 : 37 ; Liddon, Our Lord's Divinity, 153 ; J. S. Mill, Essays on Religion, 253 ; Young, Christ of History ; Divinity of Jesus Christ, by Andover Professors, 37-62.

If Jesus, then, cannot be charged with either mental or moral unsoundness, his testimony must be true, and he himself must be one with God and the revealer of God to men.

Neither Confucius nor Buddha claimed to be divine, or the organs of divine revelation, though both were moral teachers and reformers. Zoroaster and Pythagoras apparently believed themselves charged with a divine mission, though their earliest biographers wrote centuries after their death. Socrates claimed nothing for himself which was beyond the power of others. Mohammed believed his extraordinary states of body and soul to be due to the action of celestial beings ; he gave forth the Koran as " a warning to all creatures," and sent a summons to the King of Persia and the Emperor of Constantinople, as well as to other potentates, to accept the religion of Islam ; yet he mourned when he died that he could not have opportunity to correct the mistakes of the Koran and of his own life. For Confucius or Buddha, Zoroaster or Pythagoras, Socrates or Mohammed to claim all power in heaven and earth, would show insanity or moral perversion. But this is precisely what Jesus claimed. He was either mentally or morally unsound, or his testimony is true. See Baldensperger, Selbstbewusstsein Jesu ; E. Ballentine, Christ his own Witness.

IV. The Historical Results of the Propagation of Scripture Doctrine.

1. *The rapid progress of the gospel in the first centuries of our era shows its divine origin.*

A. That Paganism should have been in three centuries supplanted by Christianity, is an acknowledged wonder of history.

The conversion of the Roman Empire to Christianity was the most astonishing revolution of faith and worship ever known. Fifty years after the death of Christ, there were churches in all the principal cities of the Roman Empire. Nero (37-68) found (as Tacitus declares) an "ingens multitudo" of Christians to persecute. Pliny writes to Trajan (52-117) that they "pervaded not merely the cities but the villages and country places, so that the temples were nearly deserted." Tertullian (160-230) writes: "We are but of yesterday, and yet we have filled all your places, your cities, your islands, your castles, your towns, your council-houses, even your camps, your tribes, your senate, your forum. We have left you nothing but your temples." In the time of the emperor Valerian (253-268), the Christians constituted half the population of Rome. The conversion of the emperor Constantine (272-337) brought the whole empire, only 300 years after Jesus' death, under the acknowledged sway of the gospel. See McIlvaine and Alexander, Evidences of Christianity.

B. The wonder is the greater when we consider the obstacles to the progress of Christianity :

(*a*) The scepticism of the cultivated classes; (*b*) the prejudice and hatred of the common people ; and (*c*) the persecutions set on foot by government.

(*a*) Missionaries even now find it difficult to get a hearing among the cultivated classes of the heathen. But the gospel appeared in the most enlightened age of antiquity — the Augustan age of literature and historical inquiry. Tacitus called the religion of Christ " exitiabilis superstitio " — " quos per flagitia invisos vulgus Christianos appellabat." Pliny : " Nihil aliud inveni quam superstitionem pravam et immodicam." If the gospel had been false, its preachers would not have ventured into the centres of civilization and refinement; or if they had, they would have been detected. (*b*) Consider the interweaving of heathen religions with all the relations of life. Christians often had to meet the furious zeal and blind rage of the mob, — as at Lystra and Ephesus. (*c*) Rawlinson, in his Historical Evidences, claims that the Catacombs of Rome comprised nine hundred miles of streets and seven millions of graves within a period of four hundred years — a far greater number than could have died a natural death — and that vast multitudes of these must have been massacred for their faith. The Encyclopædia Britannica, however, calls the estimate of De Marchi, which Rawlinson appears to have taken as authority, a great exaggeration. Instead of nine hundred miles of streets, Northcote has three hundred fifty. The number of interments to correspond would be less than three millions. The Catacombs began to be deserted by the time of Jerome. The times when they were universally used by Christians could have been hardly more than two hundred years. They did not begin in sand-pits. There were three sorts of tufa : (1) rocky, used for quarrying and too hard for Christian purposes ; (2) sandy, used for sand-pits, too soft to permit construction of galleries and tombs; (3) granular, that used by Christians. The existence of the Catacombs must have been well known to the heathen. After Pope Damasus the exaggerated reverence for them began. They were decorated and improved. Hence many paintings are of later date than 400, and testify to papal polity, not to that of early Christianity. The bottles contain, not blood, but wine of the eucharist celebrated at the funeral.

Fisher, Nature and Method of Revelation, 256-258, calls attention to Matthew Arnold's description of the needs of the heathen world, yet his blindness to the true remedy: " On that hard pagan world disgust And secret loathing fell ; Deep weariness and sated lust Made human life a hell. In his cool hall, with haggard eyes, The Roman noble lay ; He drove abroad, in furious guise, Along the Appian Way : He made a feast, drank fierce and fast, And crowned his hair with flowers, — No easier nor no quicker passed The impracticable hours." Yet with mingled pride and sadness, Mr. Arnold fastidiously rejects more heavenly nutriment. Of Christ he says: "Now he is dead! Far hence ne lies, In the lorn Syrian town, And on his grave, with shining eyes, The Syrian stars look down." He sees that the millions " Have such need of joy, And joy whose grounds are true, And joy that should all hearts employ As when the past was new!" The want of the world is: "One mighty wave of thought and joy, Lifting mankind amain." But the poet sees no ground of hope: "Fools! that so often here, Happiness mocked our prayer, I think might make us fear A like event elsewhere, — Make us not fly to dreams, But moderate desire." He sings of the time when Christianity was young: "Oh, had I lived in that great day, How had its glory new Filled earth and heaven, and caught away My ravished spirit too!" But desolation of spirit does not bring with it any lowering of self-esteem, much less the humility which deplores the presence and power of evil in the soul, and sighs for deliverance. "They that are whole have no need of a physician, but they that are sick" (Mat. 9: 12). Rejecting Christ, Matthew Arnold embodies in his verse "the sweetness, the gravity, the strength, the beauty, and the languor of death" (Hutton, Essays, 302).

C. The wonder becomes yet greater when we consider the natural insufficiency of the means used to secure this progress.

(a) The proclaimers of the gospel were in general unlearned men, belonging to a despised nation. (b) The gospel which they proclaimed was a gospel of salvation through faith in a Jew who had been put to an ignominious death. (c) This gospel was one which excited natural repugnance, by humbling men's pride, striking at the root of their sins, and demanding a life of labor and self-sacrifice. (d) The gospel, moreover, was an exclusive one, suffering no rival and declaring itself to be the universal and only religion.

(a) The early Christians were more unlikely to make converts than modern Jews are to make proselytes, in vast numbers, in the principal cities of Europe and America. Celsus called Christianity "a religion of the rabble." (b) The cross was the Roman gallows — the punishment of slaves. Cicero calls it "servitutis extremum summumque supplicium." (c) There were many bad religions · why should the mild Roman Empire have persecuted the only good one? The answer is in part: Persecution did not originate with the official classes; it proceeded really from the people at large. Tacitus called Christians "haters of the human race." Man recognized in Christianity a foe to all their previous motives, ideals, and aims. Altruism would break up the old society, for every effort that centered in self or in the present life was stigmatized by the gospel as unworthy. (d) Heathenism, being without creed or principle, did not care to propagate itself. "A man must be very weak," said Celsus, "to imagine that Greeks and barbarians, in Asia, Europe, and Libya, can ever unite under the same system of religion." So the Roman government would allow no religion which did not participate in the worship of the State. "Keep yourselves from idols," "We worship no other God," was the Christian's answer. Gibbon, Hist. Decline and Fall, 1: chap. 15, mentions as secondary causes: (1) the zeal of the Jews; (2) the doctrine of immortality; (3) miraculous powers; (4) virtues of early Christians; (5) privilege of parcipation in church government. But these causes were only secondary, and all would have been insufficient without an invincible persuasion of the truth of Christianity. For answer to Gibbon, see Perrone, Prelectiones Theologicæ, 1 : 133.

Persecution destroys falsehood by leading its advocates to investigate the grounds of their belief; but it strengthens and multiplies truth by leading its advocates to see more clearly the foundations of their faith. There have been many conscientious persecutors: John 16 : 2 — "They shall put you out of the synagogues: yea, the hour cometh, that whosoever killeth you shall think that he offereth service unto God." The Decretal of Pope Urban II reads: "For we do not count them to be homicides, to whom it may have happened, through their burning zeal against the excommunicated, to put any of them to death." St. Louis, King of France, urged his officers "not to argue with the infidel, but to subdue unbelievers by thrusting the sword into them as far as it will go." Of the use of the rack in England on a certain occasion, it was said that it was used with all the tenderness which the nature of the instrument would allow. This reminds us of Isaak Walton's instruction as to the use of the frog: "Put the hook through his mouth and out at his gills; and, in so doing, use him as though you loved him."

Robert Browning, in his Easter Day, 275-288, gives us what purports to be A Martyr's Epitaph, inscribed upon a wall of the Catacombs, which furnishes a valuable contrast to the sceptical and pessimistic strain of Matthew Arnold: "I was born sickly, poor and mean, A slave: no misery could screen The holders of the pearl of price From Cæsar's envy: therefore twice I fought with beasts, and three times saw My children suffer by his law; At length my own release was earned: I was some time in being burned, But at the close a Hand came through The fire above my head, and drew My soul to Christ, whom now I see. Sergius, a brother, writes for me This testimony on the wall — For me, I have forgot it all."

The progress of a religion so unprepossessing and uncompromising to outward acceptance and dominion, within the space of three hundred years, cannot be explained without supposing that divine power attended its promulgation, and therefore that the gospel is a revelation from God.

Stanley, Life and Letters, 1 : 527 — "In the Kremlin Cathedral, whenever the Metropolitan advanced from the altar to give his blessing, there was always thrown under his feet a carpet embroidered with the eagle of old Pagan Rome, to indicate that the Christian Church and Empire of Constantinople had succeeded and triumphed over it." On this whole section, see F. W. Farrar, Witness of History to Christ, 91; McIlvaine, Wisdom of Holy Scripture. 139.

2. *The beneficent influence of the Scripture doctrines and precepts, wherever they have had sway, shows their divine origin.* Notice :

A. Their influence on civilization in general, securing a recognition of principles which heathenism ignored, such as Garbett mentions : (*a*) the importance of the individual ; (*b*) the law of mutual love ; (*c*) the sacredness of human life ; (*d*) the doctrine of internal holiness ; (*e*) the sanctity of home ; (*f*) monogamy, and the religious equality of the sexes ; (*g*) identification of belief and practice.

The continued corruption of heathen lands shows that this change is not due to any laws of merely natural progress. The confessions of ancient writers show that it is not due to philosophy. Its only explanation is that the gospel is the power of God.

Garbett, Dogmatic Faith, 177-186; F. W. Farrar, Witness of History to Christ, chap. on Christianity and the Individual; Brace, Gesta Christi, preface, vi — "Practices and principles implanted, stimulated or supported by Christianity, such as regard for the personality of the weakest and poorest; respect for woman; duty of each member of the fortunate classes to raise up the unfortunate; humanity to the child, the prisoner, the stranger, the needy, and even to the brute; unceasing opposition to all forms of cruelty, oppression and slavery; the duty of personal purity, and the sacredness of marriage; the necessity of temperance; obligation of a more equitable division of the profits of labor, and of greater coöperation between employers and employed; the right of every human being to have the utmost opportunity of developing his faculties, and of all persons to enjoy equal political and social privileges; the principle that the injury of one nation is the injury of all, and the expediency and duty of unrestricted trade and intercourse between all countries; and finally, a profound opposition to war, a determination to limit its evils when existing, and to prevent its arising by means of international arbitration."

Max Müller: "The concept of humanity is the gift of Christ." Guizot, History of Civilization, 1: Introd., tells us that in ancient times the individual existed for the sake of the State; in modern times the State exists for the sake of the individual. "The individual is a discovery of Christ." On the relations between Christianity and Political Economy, see A. H. Strong, Philosophy and Religion, pages 443-460; on the cause of the changed view with regard to the relation of the individual to the State, see page 207 — "What has wrought the change? Nothing but the death of the Son of God. When it was seen that the smallest child and the lowest slave had a soul of such worth that Christ left his throne and gave up his life to save it, the world's estimate or values changed, and modern history began." Lucian, the Greek satirist and humorist, 160 A. D., said of the Christians: "Their first legislator [Jesus] has put it into their heads that they are all brothers."

It is this spirit of common brotherhood which has led in most countries to the abolition of cannibalism, infanticide, widow-burning, and slavery. Prince Bismarck: "For social well-being I ask nothing more than Christianity without phrases" — which means the religion of the deed rather than of the creed. Yet it is only faith in the historic revelation of God in Christ which has made Christian deeds possible. Shaler, Interpretation of Nature, 232-278 — Aristotle, if he could look over society to-day, would think modern man a new species, in his going out in sympathy to distant peoples. This cannot be the result of natural selection, for self-sacrifice is not profitable to the individual. Altruistic emotions owe their existence to God. Worship of God has flowed back upon man's emotions and has made them more sympathetic. Self-consciousness and sympathy, coming into conflict with brute emotions, originate the sense of sin. Then begins the war of the natural and the spiritual. Love of nature and absorption in others is the true *Nirvana*. Not physical science, but the humanities, are most needed in education.

H. E. Hersey, Introd. to Browning's Christmas Eve, 19 — "Sidney Lanier tells us that the last twenty centuries have spent their best power upon the development of personality. Literature, education, government, and religion, have learned to recognize the individual as the unit of force. Browning goes a step further. He declares that so powerful is a complete personality that its very touch gives life and courage and potency. He turns to history for the inspiration of enduring virtue and the stimulus for sustained effort, and he finds both in Jesus Christ." J. P. Cooke, Credentials of Science, 43 — The change from the ancient philosopher to the modern investigator is the change from self-assertion to self-devotion, and the great revolution can be traced to the influence of Christianity and to the spirit of humility exhibited and inculcated by Christ. Lewes, Hist. Philos., 1 : 408 — Greek morality never embraced any conception of humanity ; no Greek ever attained to the sublimity of such a point of view.

Kidd, Social Evolution, 165, 287—It is not intellect that has pushed forward the world of modern times : it is the altruistic feeling that originated in the cross and sacrifice of Christ. The French Revolution was made possible by the fact that humanitarian ideas had undermined the upper classes themselves, and effective resistance was impossible. Socialism would abolish the struggle for existence on the part of individuals. What security would be left for social progress ? Removing all restrictions upon population ensures progressive deterioration. A non-socialist community would outstrip a socialist community where all the main wants of life were secure. The real tendency of society is to bring all the people into *rivalry*, not only on a footing of political equality, but on conditions of equal social opportunities. The State in future will interfere and control, in order to preserve or secure free competition, rather than to suspend it. The goal is not socialism or State management, but competition in which all shall have equal advantages. The evolution of human society is not primarily intellectual but religious. The winning races are the religious races. The Greeks had more intellect, but we have more civilization and progress. The Athenians were as far above us as we are above the negro race. Gladstone said that we are intellectually weaker than the men of the middle ages. When the intellectual development of any section of the race has for the time being outrun its ethical development, natural selection has apparently weeded it out, like any other unsuitable product. Evolution is developing *reverence*, with its allied qualities, mental energy, resolution, enterprise, prolonged and concentrated application, simple minded and single minded devotion to duty. Only religion can overpower selfishness and individualism and ensure social progress.

B.   Their influence upon individual character and happiness, wherever they have been tested in practice. This influence is seen (*a*) in the moral transformations they have wrought--as in the case of Paul the apostle, and of persons in every Christian community; (*b*) in the self-denying labors for human welfare to which they have led — as in the case of Wilberforce and Judson; (*c*) in the hopes they have inspired in times of sorrow and death.

These beneficent fruits cannot have their source in merely natural causes, apart from the truth and divinity of the Scriptures; for in that case the contrary beliefs would be accompanied by the same blessings. But since we find these blessings only in connection with Christian teaching, we may justly consider this as their cause. This teaching, then, must be true, and the Scriptures must be a divine revelation. Else God has made a lie to be the greatest blessing to the race.

The first Moravian missionaries to the West Indies walked six hundred miles to take ship, worked their passage, and then sold themselves as slaves, in order to get the privilege of preaching to the negroes. . . . The father of John G. Paton was a stocking-weaver. The whole family, with the exception of the very small children, worked from 6 a. m. to 10 p. m., with one hour for dinner at noon and a half hour each for breakfast and supper. Yet family prayer was regularly held twice a day. In these breathing-spells for daily meals John G. Paton took part of his time to study the Latin Grammar, that he might prepare himself for missionary work. When told by an uncle that, if he went to the New Hebrides, the cannibals would eat him, he replied: "You yourself will soon be dead and buried, and I had as lief be eaten by cannibals as by worms." The Aneityumese raised arrow-root for fifteen years and sold it to pay the £1200 required for printing the Bible in their own language. Universal church-attendance and Bible-study make those South Sea Islands the most heavenly place on earth on the Sabbath-day.

In 1839, twenty thousand negroes in Jamaica gathered to begin a life of freedom. Into a coffin were put the handcuffs and shackles of slavery, relics of the whipping-post and the scourge. As the clock struck twelve at night, a preacher cried with the first stroke: "The monster is dying!" and so with every stroke until the last, when he cried: "The monster is dead!" Then all rose from their knees and sang: "Praise God from whom all blessings flow!" . . . "What do you do that for?" said the sick China-man whom the medical missionary was tucking up in bed with a care which the patient had never received since he was a baby. The missionary took the opportunity to tell him of the love of Christ. . . . The aged Australian mother, when told that her two daughters, missionaries in China, had both of them been murdered by a heathen mob, only replied: "This decides me; I will go to China now myself, and try to teach those poor creatures what the love of Jesus means." . . . Dr. William Ashmore: "Let one missionary die, and ten come to his funeral." A shoemaker, teaching neglected boys and girls while he worked at his cobbler's bench, gave the impulse to Thomas Guthrie's life of faith.

We must judge religions not by their ideals, but by their performances. Omar Khay-yam and Mozoomdar give us beautiful thoughts, but the former is not Persia, nor is the latter India. "When the microscopic search of scepticism, which has hunted the heavens and sounded the seas to disprove the existence of a Creator, has turned its attention to human society and has found on this planet a place ten miles square where a decent man can live in decency, comfort, and security, supporting and educating his children, unspoiled and unpolluted; a place where age is reverenced, infancy protected, manhood respected, womanhood honored, and human life held in due regard — when sceptics can find such a place ten miles square on this globe, where the gospel of Christ has not gone and cleared the way and laid the foundations and made decency and security possible, it will then be in order for the sceptical literati to move thither and to ventilate their views. But so long as these very men are dependent upon the very religion they discard for every privilege they enjoy, they may well hesitate before they rob the Christian of his hope and humanity of its faith in that Savior who alone has given that hope of eternal life which makes life tolerable and society possible, and robs death of its terrors and the grave of its gloom." On the beneficent influence of the gospel, see Schmidt, Social Results of Early Christianity; D. J. Hill, The Social Influence of Christianity.

CHAPTER III.

I. DEFINITION OF INSPIRATION.

Inspiration is that influence of the Spirit of God upon the minds of the Scripture writers which made their writings the record of a progressive divine revelation, sufficient, when taken together and interpreted by the same Spirit who inspired them, to lead every honest inquirer to Christ and to salvation.

Notice the significance of each part of this definition : 1. Inspiration is an influence of the Spirit of God. It is not a merely naturalistic phenomenon or psychological vagary, but is rather the effect of the inworking of the personal divine Spirit. 2. Yet inspiration is an influence upon the mind, and not upon the body. God secures his end by awakening man's rational powers, and not by an external or mechanical communication. 3. The writings of inspired men are the record of a revelation. They are not themselves the revelation. 4. The revelation and the record are both progressive. Neither one is complete at the beginning. 5. The Scripture writings must be taken together. Each part must be viewed in connection with what precedes and with what follows. 6. The same Holy Spirit who made the original revelations must interpret to us the record of them, if we are to come to the knowledge of the truth. 7. So used and so interpreted, these writings are sufficient, both in quantity and in quality, for their religious purpose. 8. That purpose is, not to furnish us with a model history or with the facts of science, but to lead us to Christ and to salvation.

(a) Inspiration is therefore to be defined, not by its method, but by its result. It is a general term including all those kinds and degrees of the Holy Spirit's influence which were brought to bear upon the minds of the Scripture writers, in order to secure the putting into permanent and written form of the truth best adapted to man's moral and religious needs.

(b) Inspiration may often include revelation, or the direct communication from God of truth to which man could not attain by his unaided powers. It may include illumination, or the quickening of man's cognitive powers to understand truth already revealed. Inspiration, however, does not necessarily and always include either revelation or illumination. It is simply the divine influence which secures a transmission of needed truth to the future, and, according to the nature of the truth to be transmitted, it may be only an inspiration of superintendence, or it may be also and at the same time an inspiration of illumination or revelation.

(c) It is not denied, but affirmed, that inspiration may qualify for oral utterance of truth, or for wise leadership and daring deeds. Men may be inspired to render external service to God's kingdom, as in the cases of Bezalel and Samson ; even though this service is rendered unwillingly or unconsciously, as in the cases of Balaam and Cyrus. All human intelligence, indeed, is due to the inbreathing of that same Spirit who created man at the beginning. We are now concerned with inspiration, however, only as it pertains to the authorship of Scripture.

Gen. 2 : 7 — "And Jehovah God formed man of the dust of the ground, and breathed into his nostrils the breath of life; and man became a living soul"; Ex. 31 : 2, 3 — "I have called by name Bezalel . . . and I have filled him with the Spirit of God . . . in all manner of workmanship"; Judges 13 : 24, 25 — "called his name Samson: and the child grew, and Jehovah blessed him   And the Spirit of Jehovah began to move him"; Num. 23 : 5 — "And Jehovah put a word in Balaam's mouth, and said, Return unto Balak, and thus shalt thou speak"; 2 Chron. 36 : 22 — "Jehovah stirred up the spirit of Cyrus"; Is. 44 : 28 — "that saith of Cyrus, He is my shepherd"; 45 : 5 — "I will gird thee, though thou hast not known me"; Job 32 : 8 — "there is a spirit in man, and the breath of the Almighty giveth them understanding." These passages show the true meaning of 2 Tim. 3 : 16 — "Every scripture inspired of God." The word θεόπνευστος is to be understood as alluding, not to the flute-player's breathing into his instrument, but to God's original inbreathing of life. The flute is passive, but man's soul is active. The flute gives out only what it receives, but the inspired man under the divine influence is a conscious and free originator of thought and expression. Although the inspiration of which we are to treat is simply the inspiration of the Scripture writings, we can best understand this narrower use of the term by remembering that all real knowledge has in it a divine element, and that we are possessed of complete consciousness only as we live, move, and have our being in God. Since Christ, the divine Logos or Reason, is "the light which lighteth every man" (John 1 : 9), a special influence of "the spirit of Christ which was in them" (1 Pet. 1 : 11) rationally accounts for the fact that "men spake from God, being moved by the Holy Spirit" (2 Pet. 1 : 21).

It may help our understanding of terms above employed if we adduce instances of
(1) Inspiration without revelation, as in Luke or Acts, Luke 1 : 1-3;
(2) Inspiration including revelation, as in the Apocalypse, Rev. 1 : 1, 11;
(3) Inspiration without illumination, as in the prophets, 1 Pet. 1 : 11;
(4) Inspiration including illumination, as in the case of Paul, 1 Cor. 2 : 12;
(5) Revelation without inspiration, as in God's words from Sinai, Ex. 20 : 1, 22;
(6) Illumination without inspiration, as in modern preachers, Eph. 2 : 20.

Other definitions are those of Park: "Inspiration is such an influence over the writers of the Bible that all their teachings which have a religious character are trustworthy"; of Wilkinson: "Inspiration is help from God to keep the report of divine revelation free from error. Help to whom? No matter to whom, so the result is secured. The final result, viz.: the record or report of revelation, this must be free from error. Inspiration may affect one or all of the agents employed"; of Hovey: "Inspiration was an influence of the Spirit of God on those powers of men which are concerned in the reception, retention and expression of religious truth — an influence so pervading and powerful that the teaching of inspired men was according to the mind of God. Their teaching did not in any instance embrace all truth in respect to God, or man, or the way of life; but it comprised just so much of the truth on any particular subject as could be received in faith by the inspired teacher and made useful to those whom he addressed. In this sense the teaching of the original documents composing our Bible may be pronounced free from error"; of G. B. Foster: "Revelation is the action of God in the soul of his child, resulting in divine self-expression then: Inspiration is the action of God in the soul of his child, resulting in apprehension and appropriation of the divine expression. Revelation has logical but not chronological priority"; of Horton, Inspiration and the Bible, 10-13 — "We mean by Inspiration exactly those qualities or characteristics which are the marks or notes of the Bible . . . We call our Bible inspired; by which we mean that by reading and studying it we find our way to God, we find his will for us, and we find how we can conform ourselves to his will."

Fairbairn, Christ in Modern Theology, 496, while nobly setting forth the naturalness of revelation, has misconceived the relation of inspiration to revelation by giving priority to the former: "The idea of a written revelation may be said to be logically involved in the notion of a living God. Speech is natural to spirit; and if God is by nature spirit, it will be to him a matter of nature to reveal himself. But if he speaks to man, it will be through men; and those who hear best will be most possessed of God. This possession is termed 'inspiration.' God inspires, man reveals: revelation is the mode or form — word, character, or institution — in which man embodies what he has received. The terms, though not equivalent, are co-extensive, the one denoting the process on its inner side, the other on its outer." This statement, although approved by Sanday, Inspiration, 124, 125, seems to us almost precisely to reverse the right meaning of the words. We prefer the view of Evans, Bib. Scholarship and Inspiration, 54 — "God has first revealed himself and then has inspired men to interpret, record and apply this revelation. In redemption, inspiration is the formal factor, as revelation is the material factor. The men are inspired, as Prof. Stowe said. The thoughts are inspired, as Prof. Briggs said. The words are inspired, as Prof. Hodge said. The warp and woof of the Bible is πνεῦμα: "the words that I have spoken unto you are spirit" (John 6 : 63). Its fringes run off, as was inevitable, into the secular, the material, the psychic.' Phillips Brooks, Life, 2 : 351—"If the true revelation of God is in Christ, the Bible is not properly a revelation, but the history of a revelation. This is not only a fact but a necessity, for a person cannot be revealed in a book, but must find revelation, if at all, in a person. The centre and core of the Bible must therefore be the gospels, as the story of Jesus."

Some, like Priestley, have held that the gospels are authentic but not inspired. We therefore add to the proof of the genuineness and credibility of Scripture, the proof of its inspiration. Chadwick, Old and New Unitarianism, 11—"Priestley's belief in supernatural revelation was intense. He had an absolute distrust of reason as qualified to furnish an adequate knowledge of religious things, and at the same time a perfect confidence in reason as qualified to prove that negative and to determine the contents of the revelation." We might claim the historical truth of the gospels, even if we did not call them inspired. Gore, in Lux Mundi, 341—"Christianity brings with it a doctrine of the inspiration of the Holy Scriptures, but is not based upon it." Warfield and Hodge, Inspiration, 8—"While the inspiration of the Scriptures is true, and being true is fundamental to the adequate interpretation of Scripture, it nevertheless is not, in the first instance, a principle fundamental to the truth of the Christian religion."

On the idea of Revelation, see Ladd, in Journ. Christ. Philos., Jan. 1883 : 156-178; on Inspiration, ibid., Apr. 1883: 225-248. See Henderson on Inspiration (2nd ed.), 58, 205, 249, 303, 310. For other works on the general subject of Inspiration, see Lee, Bannerman, Jamieson, Macnaught; Garbett, God's Word Written; Aids to Faith, essay on Inspiration. Also, Philippi, Glaubenslehre, 1 : 205; Westcott, Introd. to Study of the Gospels, 27-65; Bib. Sac., 1 : 97; 4 : 154; 12 : 217; 15 : 29, 314; 25 : 192-198; Dr. Barrows, in Bib. Sac., 1867 : 593; 1872 : 428; Farrar, Science in Theology, 208; Hodge and Warfield, in Presb. Rev., Apr. 1881 : 225-261; Manly, The Bible Doctrine of Inspiration; Watts, Inspiration; Mead, Supernatural Revelation, 350; Whiton, Gloria Patri, 136; Hastings, Bible Dict., 1 : 296-299; Sanday, Bampton Lectures on Inspiration.

II. Proof of Inspiration.

1. Since we have shown that God has made a revelation of himself to man, we may reasonably presume that he will not trust this revelation wholly to human tradition and misrepresentation, but will also provide a record of it essentially trustworthy and sufficient; in other words, that the same Spirit who originally communicated the truth will preside over its publication, so far as is needed to accomplish its religious purpose.

Since all natural intelligence, as we have seen, presupposes God's indwelling, and since in Scripture the all-prevailing atmosphere, with its constant pressure and effort to enter every cranny and corner of the world, is used as an illustration of the impulse of God's omnipotent Spirit to vivify and energize every human soul (Gen. 2 : 7; Job 32 : 8), we may infer that, but for sin, all men would be morally and spiritually inspired (Num. 11 : 29—"Would that all Jehovah's people were prophets, that Jehovah would put his Spirit upon them!" Is. 59 : 2—"your iniquities have separated between you and your God"). We have also seen that God's method of communicating his truth in matters of religion is presumably analogous to his method of communicating secular truth, such as that of astronomy or history. There is an original delivery to a single nation, and to single persons in that nation, that it may through them be given to mankind. Sanday, Inspiration, 140—"There is a 'purpose of God according to selection' (Rom. 9 : 11); there is an 'election' or 'selection of grace'; and the object of that selection was Israel and those who take their name from Israel's Messiah. If a tower is built in ascending tiers, those who stand upon the lower tiers are yet raised above the ground, and some may be raised higher than others, but the full and unimpeded view is reserved for those who mount upward to the top. And that is the place destined for us if we will take it."

If we follow the analogy of God's working in other communications of knowledge, we shall reasonably presume that he will preserve the record of his revelations in written and accessible documents, handed down from those to whom these revelations were first communicated, and we may expect that these documents will be kept surficiently correct and trustworthy to accomplish their religious purpose, namely, that of furnishing to the honest inquirer a guide to Christ and to salvation. The physician commits his prescriptions to writing ; the Clerk of Congress records its proceedings; the State Department of our government instructs our foreign ambassadors, not orally, but by dispatches. There is yet greater need that revelation should be recorded, since it is to be transmitted to distant ages ; it contains long discourses ; it embraces mysterious doctrines. Jesus did not write himself ; for he was the subject, not the mere channel, of revelation. His unconcern about the apostles' immediately committing to writing what they saw and heard is inexplicable, if he did not expect that inspiration would assist them.

We come to the discussion of Inspiration with a presumption quite unlike that of Kuenen and Wellhausen, who write in the interest of almost avowed naturalism. Kuenen, in the opening sentences of his Religion of Israel, does indeed assert the rule of God in the world. But Sanday, Inspiration, 117, says well that " Kuenen keeps this idea very much in the background. He expended a whole volume of 593 large octavo pages (Prophets and Prophecy in Israel, London, 1877) in proving that the prophets were *not* moved to speak by God, but that their utterances were all their own." The following extract, says Sanday, indicates the position which Dr. Kuenen really held : " We do not allow ourselves to be deprived of God's presence in history. In the fortunes and development of nations, and not least clearly in those of Israel, we see Him, the holy and all-wise Instructor of his human children. But the old *contrasts* must be altogether set aside. So long as we derive a separate part of Israel's religious life directly from God, and allow the supernatural or immediate revelation to intervene in even one single point, so long also our view of the whole continues to be incorrect, and we see ourselves here and there necessitated to do violence to the well-authenticated contents of the historical documents. It is the supposition of a natural development alone which accounts for all the phenomena" (Kuenen, Prophets and Prophecy in Israel, 585).

2. Jesus, who has been proved to be not only a credible witness, but a messenger from God, vouches for the inspiration of the Old Testament, by quoting it with the formula : " It is written " ; by declaring that " one jot or one tittle " of it " shall in no wise pass away," and that " the Scripture cannot be broken."

Jesus quotes from four out of the five books of Moses, and from the Psalms, Isaiah, Malachi, and Zechariah, with the formula, "it is written " ; see Mat. 4 : 4, 6, 7 ; 11 : 10 ; Mark 14 : 27 ; Luke 4 : 4–12. This formula among the Jews indicated that the quotation was from a sacred book and was divinely inspired. Jesus certainly regarded the Old Testament with as much reverence as the Jews of his day. He declared that " one jot or one tittle shall in no wise pass away from the law " (Mat. 5 : 18). He said that " the scripture cannot be broken " (John 10 : 35) = " the normative and judicial authority of the Scripture cannot be set aside ; notice here [in the singular, ἡ γραφή] the idea of the unity of Scripture" (Meyer). And yet our Lord's use of O. T. Scripture was wholly free from the superstitious literalism which prevailed among the Jews of his day. The phrases " word of God " (John 10 : 35 ; Mark 7 : 13), " wisdom of God " (Luke 11 : 49) and " oracles of God " (Rom. 3 : 2) probably designate the original revelations of God and not the record of these in Scripture ; *cf.* 1 Sam. 9 : 27; 1 Chron. 17 : 3 ; Is. 40 : 8 ; Mat. 13 : 19 ; Luke 3 : 2 ; Acts 8 : 25. Jesus refuses assent to the O. T. law respecting the Sabbath (Mark 2 : 27 *sq.*), external defilements (Mark 7 : 15), divorce (Mark 10 : 2 *sq.*). He " came not to destroy but to fulfil " (Mat. 5 : 17) ; yet he fulfilled the law by bringing out its inner spirit in his perfect life, rather than by formal and minute obedience to its precepts ; see Wendt, Teaching of Jesus, 2 : 5–35.

The apostles quote the O. T. as the utterance of God (Eph. 4 : 8 — διὸ λέγει, *sc*. θεός). Paul's insistence upon the form of even a single word, as in Gal. 3 : 16, and his use of the O. T. for purposes of allegory, as in Gal. 4 : 21–31, show that in his view the O. T. text was sacred. Philo, Josephus and the Talmud, in their interpretations of the O. T., fall continually into a " narrow and unhappy literalism." " The N. T. does not indeed escape Rabbinical methods, but even where these are most prominent they seem to affect the form far more than the substance. And through the temporary and local form the writer constantly penetrates to the very heart of the O. T. teaching ; " see Sanday, Bampton Lectures on Inspiration, 87 ; Henderson, Inspiration, 254.

3. Jesus commissioned his apostles as teachers and gave them promises of a supernatural aid of the Holy Spirit in their teaching, like the promises made to the Old Testament prophets.

Mat. 28: 19, 20 — "Go ye . . . teaching . . . and lo, I am with you." Compare promises to Moses (Ex. 3 : 12), Jeremiah (Jer. 1: 5–8), Ezekiel (Ezek. 2 and 3). See also Is. 44: 3 and Joel 2: 28 — "I will pour my Spirit upon thy seed" · Mat. 10: 7 — "as ye go, preach"; 19 — "be not anxious how or what ye shall speak "; John 14 : 26 — "the Holy Spirit . . . shall teach you all things"; 15: 26, 27 — "the Spirit of truth . . . shall bear witness of me: and ye also bear witness" = the Spirit shall witness in and through you; 16: 13 — "he shall guide you into all the truth " = (1) limitation — all *the* truth of Christ, *i. e.*, not of philosophy or science, but of religion; (2) comprehension — *all* the truth within this limited range, *i. e.*, sufficiency of Scripture as rule of faith and practice (Hovey); 17: 8 — "the words which thou gavest me I have given unto them"; Acts 1: 4 — "he charged them . . . to wait for the promise of the Father"; John 20 : 22 — "he breathed on them, and saith unto them, Receive ye the Holy Spirit." Here was both promise and communication of the personal Holy Spirit. Compare Mat. 10 : 19, 20 — "it shall be given you in that hour what ye shall speak. For it is not ye that speak, but the Spirit of your Father that speaketh in you." See Henderson, Inspiration, 247, 248.

Jesus' testimony here is the testimony of God. In Deut. 18: 18, it is said that God will put his words into the mouth of the great Prophet. In John 12: 49, 50, Jesus says: "I spake not from myself, but the Father that sent me, he hath given me a commandment, what I should say, and what I should speak. And I know that his commandment is life eternal; the things therefore which I speak, even as the Father hath said unto me, so I speak." John 17: 7, 8 — "all things whatsoever thou hast given me are from thee: for the words which thou gavest me I have given unto them." John 8 : 40 — "a man that hath told you the truth, which I heard from God."

4.   The apostles claim to have received this promised Spirit, and under his influence to speak with divine authority, putting their writings upon a level with the Old Testament Scriptures. We have not only direct statements that both the matter and the form of their teaching were supervised by the Holy Spirit, but we have indirect evidence that this was the case in the tone of authority which pervades their addresses and epistles.

Statements : – 1 Cor. 2: 10, 13 — "unto us God revealed them through the Spirit. . . . Which things also we speak, not in words which man's wisdom teacheth, but which the Spirit teacheth"; 11: 23 — "I received of the Lord that which also I delivered unto you "; 12: 8, 28 — the λόγος σοφίας was apparently a gift peculiar to the apostles ; 14: 37, 38 — "the things which I write unto you . . . they are the commandment of the Lord "; Gal. 1 : 12 — "neither did I receive it from man, nor was I taught it, but it came to me through revelation of Jesus Christ"; 1 Thess. 4 : 2, 8 — "ye know what charge we gave you through the Lord Jesus. . . . Therefore he that rejecteth, rejecteth not man, but God, who giveth his Holy Spirit unto you." The following passages put the teaching of the apostles on the same level with O. T. Scripture : 1 Pet. 1: 11, 12 — "Spirit of Christ which was in them " [O. T. prophets] ; — [N. T. preachers] "preached the gospel unto you by the Holy Spirit "; 2 Pet. 1: 21 — O. T. prophets "spake from God, being moved by the Holy Spirit "; 3: 2 — "remember the words which were spoken before by the holy prophets" [O. T.], "and the commandment of the Lord and Savior through your apostles" [N. T.]; 16 — "wrest [Paul's Epistles], as they do also the *other scriptures*, unto their own destruction." *Cf.* Ex. 4 : 14–16; 7 : 1.

Implications : – 2 Tim. 3 : 16 — "Every scripture inspired of God is also profitable" — a clear implication of inspiration, though not a direct statement of it = *there is a divinely inspired Scripture.* In 1 Cor. 5 : 3–5, Paul, commanding the Corinthian church with regard to the incestuous person, was arrogant if not inspired. There are more imperatives in the Epistles than in any other writings of the same extent. Notice the continual asseveration of authority, as in Gal. 1: 1, 2, and the declaration that disbelief of the record is sin, as in 1 John 5 : 10, 11. Jude 3 — "the faith which was once for all (ἅπαξ) delivered unto the saints." See Kahnis, Dogmatik, 3 : 122 ; Henderson, Inspiration (2nd ed.), 34, 234 ; Conant, Genesis, Introd., xiii, note ; Charteris, New Testament Scriptures : They claim truth, unity, authority.

The passages quoted above show that inspired men distinguished inspiration from their own unaided thinking. These inspired men claim that their inspiration is the same with that of the prophets. Rev. 22: 6 — "the Lord, the God of the spirits of the prophets, sent his angel to show unto his servants the things which must shortly come to pass " = inspiration gave them supernatural knowledge of the future. As inspiration in the O. T. was the work of the pre-incarnate Christ, so inspiration in the N. T. is the work of the ascended and glorified Christ by his Holy Spirit. On the Relative Authority of the Gospels, see Gerhardt, in Am. Journ. Theol., Apl. 1899: 275–294, who shows that not the words of Jesus in the gospels are the final revelation, but rather the teaching of the risen and glorified Christ in the Acts and the Epistles. The Epistles are the posthumous works of Christ. Pattison, Making of the Sermon, 23 — "The apostles, believing themselves to be inspired teachers, often preached without texts; and the fact that their successors did not follow their example shows that for themselves they made no such claim. Inspiration ceased, and henceforth authority was found in the use of the words of the now complete Scriptures."

5. The apostolic writers of the New Testament, unlike professedly inspired heathen sages and poets, gave attestation by miracles or prophecy that they were inspired by God, and there is reason to believe that the productions of those who were not apostles, such as Mark, Luke, Hebrews, James, and Jude, were recommended to the churches as inspired, by apostolic sanction and authority.

The twelve wrought miracles (Mat. 10 : 1). Paul's "signs of an apostle" (2 Cor. 13 : 12) = miracles. Internal evidence confirms the tradition that Mark was the "interpreter of Peter," and that Luke's gospel and the Acts had the sanction of Paul. Since the purpose of the Spirit's bestowment was to qualify those who were to be the teachers and founders of the new religion, it is only fair to assume that Christ's promise of the Spirit was valid not simply to the twelve but to all who stood in their places, and to these not simply as speakers, but, since in this respect they had a still greater need of divine guidance, to them as writers also.

The epistle to the Hebrews, with the letters of James and Jude, appeared in the lifetime of some of the twelve, and passed unchallenged; and the fact that they all, with the possible exception of 2 Peter, were very early accepted by the churches founded and watched over by the apostles, is sufficient evidence that the apostles regarded them as inspired productions. As evidences that the writers regarded their writings as of universal authority, see 1 Cor. 1 : 2 — "unto the church of God which is at Corinth . . . with all that call upon the name of our Lord Jesus Christ in every place," etc. ; 7 : 17 — "so ordain I in all the churches" ; Col. 4 : 16 —" And when this epistle hath been read among you, cause that it be read also in the church of the Laodiceans" ; 2 Pet. 3 : 15, 16 — "our beloved brother Paul also, according to the wisdom given to him, wrote unto you." See Bartlett, in Princeton Rev., Jan. 1880 : 23-57 ; Bib. Sac., Jan. 1884 : 204, 205.

Johnson, Systematic Theology, 40 — "Miraculous gifts were bestowed at Pentecost on many besides apostles. Prophecy was not an uncommon gift during the apostolic period." There is no antecedent improbability that inspiration should extend to others than to the principal leaders of the church, and since we have express instances of such inspiration in oral utterances (Acts 11 : 28 ; 21 : 9, 10) it seems natural that there should have been instances of inspiration in written utterances also. In some cases this appears to have been only an inspiration of superintendence. Clement of Alexandria says only that Peter neither forbade nor encouraged Mark in his plan of writing the gospel. Irenæus tells us that Mark's gospel was written after the death of Peter. Papias says that Mark wrote down what he remembered to have heard from Peter. Luke does not seem to have been aware of any miraculous aid in his writing, and his methods appear to have been those of the ordinary historian.

6. The chief proof of inspiration, however, must always be found in the internal characteristics of the Scriptures themselves, as these are disclosed to the sincere inquirer by the Holy Spirit. The testimony of the Holy Spirit combines with the teaching of the Bible to convince the earnest reader that this teaching is as a whole and in all essentials beyond the power of man to communicate, and that it must therefore have been put into permanent and written form by special inspiration of God.

Foster, Christian Life and Theology, 105 — "The testimony of the Spirit is an argument from identity of effects — the doctrines of experience and the doctrines of the Bible — to identity of cause. . . . . God-wrought experience proves a God-wrought Bible. . . . . This covers the Bible as a whole, if not the whole of the Bible. It is true so far as I can test it. It is to be believed still further if there is no other evidence." Lyman Abbott, in his Theology of an Evolutionist, 105, calls the Bible "a record of man's laboratory work in the spiritual realm, a history of the dawning of the consciousness of God and of the divine life in the soul of man." This seems to us unduly subjective. We prefer to say that the Bible is also God's witness to us of his presence and working in human hearts and in human history — a witness which proves its divine origin by awakening in us experiences similar to those which it describes, and which are beyond the power of man to originate.

G. P. Fisher, in Mag. of Christ. Lit., Dec. 1892: 239 — "Is the Bible infallible? Not in the sense that all its statements extending even to minutiæ in matters of history and science are strictly accurate. Not in the sense that every doctrinal and ethical statement in all these books is incapable of amendment. The whole must sit in judgment on the parts. Revelation is progressive. There is a human factor as well as a divine. The treasure is in earthen vessels. But the Bible is infallible in the sense that whoever surrenders himself in a docile spirit to its teaching will fall into no hurtful error in matters of faith and charity. Best of all, he will find in it the secret of a new, holy and blessed life, 'hidden with Christ in God' (Col. 3 : 3). The Scriptures are the witness to Christ. . . . . Through the Scriptures he is truly and adequately made known to us." Denney, Death of Christ, 314 — "The unity of the Bible and its inspiration are correlative terms. If we can discern a real unity in it — and I believe we can when we see that it converges upon and culminates in a divine love bearing the sin of the world — then that unity and its inspiration are one and the same thing. And it is not only inspired as a whole, it is the only book that is inspired. It is the only book in the world to which God sets his seal in our hearts when we read in search of an answer to the question, How shall a sinful man be righteous with God? . . . . The conclusion of our study on inspiration should be the conviction that the Bible gives us a body of doctrine — a 'faith which was once for all delivered unto the saints' (Jude 3)."

III. THEORIES OF INSPIRATION.

1. *The Intuition-theory.*

This holds that inspiration is but a higher development of that natural insight into truth which all men possess to some degree; a mode of intelligence in matters of morals and religion which gives rise to sacred books, as a corresponding mode of intelligence in matters of secular truth gives rise to great works of philosophy or art. This mode of intelligence is regarded as the product of man's own powers, either without special divine influence or with only the inworking of an impersonal God.

This theory naturally connects itself with Pelagian and rationalistic views of man's independence of God, or with pantheistic conceptions of man as being himself the highest manifestation of an all-pervading but unconscious intelligence. Morell and F. W. Newman in England, and Theodore Parker in America, are representatives of this theory. See Morell, Philos. of Religion, 127–179 — "Inspiration is only a higher potency of what every man possesses in some degree." See also Francis W. Newman (brother of John Henry Newman), Phases of Faith (= phases of unbelief); Theodore Parker, Discourses of Religion, and Experiences as a Minister: "God is infinite; therefore he is immanent in nature, yet transcending it ; immanent in spirit, yet transcending that. He must fill each point of spirit, as of space ; matter must unconsciously obey; man, conscious and free, has power to a certain extent to disobey, but obeying, the immanent God acts in man as much as in nature " — quoted in Chadwick, Theodore Parker, 271. Hence Parker's view of Inspiration: If the conditions are fulfilled, inspiration comes in proportion to man's gifts and to his use of those gifts. Chadwick himself, in his Old and New Unitarianism, 68, says that " the Scriptures are inspired just so far as they are inspiring, and no more. "

W. C. Gannett, Life of Ezra Stiles Gannett, 196 — "Parker's spiritualism affirmed, as the grand truth of religion, the immanence of an infinitely perfect God in matter and mind, and his activity in both spheres." Martineau, Study of Religion, 2 : 178–180 — "Theodore Parker treats the regular results of the human faculties as an immediate working of God, and regards the Principia of Newton as inspired. . . . . What then becomes of the human personality? He calls God not only omnipresent, but omniactive. Is then Shakespeare only by courtesy author of Macbeth? . . . . If this were more than rhetorical, it would be unconditional pantheism." Both nature and man are other names for God. Martineau is willing to grant that our intuitions and ideals are expressions of the Deity in us, but our personal reasoning and striving, he thinks, can not be attributed to God. The word νοῦς has no plural: intellect, in whatever subject manifested, being all one, just as a . . . . . one and the same, in however many persons' consciousness it may present itself; see Martineau, Seat of Authority, 408. Palmer, Studies in Theological Definition, 27 — "We can draw no sharp distinction between the human mind discovering truth, and the divine mind imparting revelation." Kuenen belongs to this school.

With regard to this theory we remark:

(*a*)   Man has, indeed, a certain natural insight into truth, and we grant that inspiration uses this, so far as it will go, and makes it an instrument in discovering and recording facts of nature or history.

In the investigation, for example, of purely historical matters, such as Luke records, merely natural insight may at times have been sufficient. When this was the case, Luke may have been left to the exercise of his own faculties, inspiration only inciting and supervising the work. George Harris, Moral Evolution, 413 — "God could not reveal himself *to* man, unless he first revealed himself *in* man. If it should be written in letters on the sky: 'God is good,' — the words would have no meaning, unless goodness had been made known already in human volitions. Revelation is not by an occasional stroke, but by a continuous process. It is not superimposed, but inherent. . . . . Genius is inspired; for the mind which perceives truth must be responsive to the Mind that made things the vehicles of thought." Sanday, Bampton Lectures on Inspiration: "In claiming for the Bible inspiration, we do not exclude the possibility of other lower or more partial degrees of inspiration in other literatures. The Spirit of God has doubtless touched other hearts and other minds . . . . in such a way as to give insight into truth, besides those which could claim descent from Abraham." Philo thought the LXX translators, the Greek philosophers, and at times even himself, to be inspired. Plato he regards as " most sacred " ($\iota \epsilon \rho \omega \tau a \tau o s$), but all good men are in various degrees inspired. Yet Philo never quotes as authoritative any but the Canonical Books. He attributes to them an authority unique in its kind.

(*b.*)   In all matters of morals and religion, however, man's insight into truth is vitiated by wrong affections, and, unless a supernatural wisdom can guide him, he is certain to err himself, and to lead others into error.

1 Cor. 2 : 14 — " Now the natural man receiveth not the things of the Spirit of God : for they are foolishness unto him ; and he cannot know them, because they are spiritually judged "; 10 — " But unto us God revealed them through the Spirit : for the Spirit searcheth all things, yea, the deep things of God. " See quotation from Coleridge, in Shairp, Culture and Religion, 114 — "Water cannot rise higher than its source; neither can human reasoning "; Emerson, Prose Works, 1 : 474; 2 : 468 — " 'T is curious we only believe as deep as we live "; Ullmann, Sinlessness of Jesus, 183, 184. For this reason we hold to a communication of religious truth, at least at times, more direct and objective than is granted by George Adam Smith, Com. on Isaiah, 1 : 372 — " To Isaiah inspiration was nothing more nor less than the possession of certain strong moral and religious convictions, which he felt he owed to the communication of the Spirit of God, and according to which he interpreted, and even dared to foretell, the history of his people and of the world. Our study completely dispels, on the evidence of the Bible itself, that view of inspiration and prediction so long held in the church." If this is meant as a denial of any communication of truth other than the internal and subjective, we set over against it Num. 12 : 6-8 — "if there be a prophet among you, I the Lord will make myself known unto him in a vision, I will speak with him in a dream. My servant Moses is not so; he is faithful in all my house: with him will I speak mouth to mouth, even manifestly, and not in dark speeches; and the form of Jehovah shall he behold."

(*c*)   The theory in question, holding as it does that natural insight is the only source of religious truth, involves a self-contradiction; — if the theory be true, then one man is inspired to utter what a second is inspired to pronounce false. The Vedas, the Koran and the Bible cannot be inspired to contradict each other.

The Vedas permit thieving, and the Koran teaches salvation by works; these cannot be inspired and the Bible also. Paul cannot be inspired to write his epistles, and Swedenborg also inspired to reject them. The Bible does not admit that pagan teachings have the same divine endorsement with its own. Among the Spartans to steal was praiseworthy; only to be caught stealing was criminal. On the religious consciousness with regard to the personality of God, the divine goodness, the future life, the utility of prayer, in all of which Miss Cobbe, Mr. Greg and Mr. Parker disagree with each other. see Bruce, Apologetics, 143, 144. With Matheson we may grant that the leading idea of inspiration is "the growth of the divine through the capacities of the human," while yet we deny that inspiration confines itself to this subjective enlightenment of the human faculties, and also we exclude from the divine working all those perverse and erroneous utterances which are the results of human sin.

(*d*) It makes moral and religious truth to be a purely subjective thing — a matter of private opinion — having no objective reality independently of men's opinions regarding it.

On this system truth is what men 'trow'; things are what men 'think' — words representing only the subjective. "Better the Greek ἀλήθεια = 'the unconcealed' (objective truth)"— Harris, Philos. Basis of Theism, 182. If there be no absolute truth, Lessing's 'search for truth' is the only thing left to us. But who will search, if there is no truth to be found? Even a wise cat will not eternally chase its own tail. The exercise within certain limits is doubtless useful, but the cat gives it up so soon as it becomes convinced that the tail cannot be caught. Sir Richard Burton became a Roman Catholic, a Brahmin, and a Mohammedan, successively, apparently holding with Hamlet that "there is nothing either good or bad, but thinking makes it so." This same scepticism as to the existence of objective truth appears in the sayings: " Your religion is good for you, and mine for me "; " One man is born an Augustinian, and another a Pelagian." See Dix, Pantheism, Introd., 12. Richter: " It is not the goal, but the course, that makes us happy."

(*e*) It logically involves the denial of a personal God who is truth and reveals truth, and so makes man to be the highest intelligence in the universe. This is to explain inspiration by denying its existence; since, if there be no personal God, inspiration is but a figure of speech for a purely natural fact.

The *animus* of this theory is denial of the supernatural. Like the denial of miracles, it can be maintained only upon grounds of atheism or pantheism. The view in question, as Hutton in his Essays remarks, would permit us to say that the word of the Lord came to Gibbon, amid the ruins of the Coliseum, saying: " Go, write the history of the Decline and Fall!" But, replies Hutton: Such a view is pantheistic. Inspiration is the voice of a living friend, in distinction from the voice of a dead friend, *i. e.*, the influence of his memory. The inward impulse of genius, Shakespeare's for example, is not properly denominated inspiration. See Row, Bampton Lectures for 1877: 428-474; Rogers, Eclipse of Faith, 73 *sq.* and 283 *sq.*; Henderson, Inspiration (2nd ed.), 443-469, 481-490. The view of Martineau, Seat of Authority, 302, is substantially this. See criticism of Martineau, by Rainy, in Critical Rev., 1: 5-20.

2. *The Illumination Theory.*

This regards inspiration as merely an intensifying and elevating of the religious perceptions of the Christian, the same in kind, though greater in degree, with the illumination of every believer by the Holy Spirit. It holds, not that the Bible is, but that it contains, the word of God, and that not the writings, but only the writers, were inspired. The illumination given by the Holy Spirit, however, puts the inspired writer only in full possession of his normal powers, but does not communicate objective truth beyond his ability to discover or understand.

This theory naturally connects itself with Arminian views of mere coöperation with God. It differs from the Intuition-theory by containing several distinctively Christian elements: (1) the influence of a personal God; (2) an extraordinary work of the Holy Spirit; (3) the Christological character of the Scriptures, putting into form a revelation of which Christ is the centre (Rev. 19:10). But while it grants that the Scripture writers were "moved by the Holy Spirit" ($\phi\epsilon\rho\acute{o}\mu\epsilon\nu o\iota$ — 2 Pet. 1 : 21), it ignores the complementary fact that the Scripture itself is "inspired of God" ($\vartheta\epsilon\acute{o}\pi\nu\epsilon\upsilon\sigma\tau o\varsigma$ — 2 Tim. 3 : 16). Luther's view resembles this; see Dorner, Gesch. prot. Theol., 236, 237. Schleiermacher, with the more orthodox Neander, Tholuck and Cremer, holds it; see Essays by Tholuck, in Herzog, Encyclopädie, and in Noyes, Theological Essays; Cremer, Lexicon N. T., $\vartheta\epsilon\acute{o}\pi\nu\epsilon\upsilon\sigma$-$\tau o\varsigma$, and in Herzog and Hauck, Realencyc., 9 : 183-203. In France, Sabatier, Philos. Religion, 90, remarks : " Prophetic inspiration is piety raised to the second power "—it differs from the piety of common men only in intensity and energy. See also Godet, in Revue Chrétienne, Jan. 1878.

In England Coleridge propounded this view in his Confessions of an Inquiring Spirit (Works, 5 : 669)—" Whatever *finds me* bears witness that it has proceeded from a Holy Spirit; in the Bible there is more that *finds me* than I have experienced in all other books put together." [Shall we then call Baxter's " Saints' Rest " inspired, while the Books of Chronicles are not?] See also F. W. Robertson, Sermon I ; Life and Letters, letter 53, vol. 1 : 270 ; 2 : 143-150—" The *other* way, some twenty or thirty men in the world's history have had special communication, miraculous and from God; in *this* way, all may have it, and by devout and earnest cultivation of the mind and heart may have it illimitably increased." Frederick W. H. Myers, Catholic Thoughts on the Bible and Theology, 10-20, emphasizes the idea that the Scriptures are, in their earlier parts, not merely inadequate, but partially untrue, and subsequently superseded by fuller revelations. The leading thought is that of *accommodation ;* the record of revelation is not necessarily infallible. Allen, Religious Progress, 44, quotes Bishop Thirlwall : " If that Spirit by which every man spoke of old is a living and present Spirit, its later lessons may well transcend its earlier "; — Pascal's ' colossal man ' is the race ; the first men represented only infancy ; *we* are ' the ancients', and we are wiser than our fathers. See also Farrar, Critical History of Free Trought, 473, note 50 ; Martineau, Studies in Christianity : " One Gospel in Many Dialects."

Of American writers who favor this view, see J. F. Clarke, Orthodoxy, its Truths and Errors, 74 ; Curtis, Human Element in Inspiration ; Whiton, in N. Eng., Jan. 1882 : 63-72 ; Ladd, in Andover Review, July, 1885, in What is the Bible? and in Doctrine of Sacred Scripture, 1 : 759 —" a large proportion of its writings inspired "; 2 : 178, 275, 497 — " that fundamental misconception which identifies the Bible and the word of God "; 2 : 488 — " Inspiration, as the subjective condition of Biblical revelation and the predicate of the word of God, is *specifically* the same illumining. quickening, elevating and purifying work of the Holy Spirit as that which goes on in the persons of the entire believing community." Professor Ladd therefore pares down all predictive prophecy, and regards Isaiah 53, not as directly and solely, but only as typically, Messianic. Clarke, Christian Theology, 35-44 —" Inspiration is exaltation, quickening of ability, stimulation of spiritual power ; it is uplifting and enlargement of capacity for perception, comprehension and utterance ; and all under the influence of a thought, a truth, or an ideal that has taken possession of the soul. . . . Inspiration to write was not different in kind from the common influence of God upon his people. . . . Inequality in the Scriptures is plain. . . . Even if we were convinced that some book would better have been omitted from the Canon, our confidence in the Scriptures would not thereby be shaken. The Canon did not make Scripture, but Scripture made the Canon. The inspiration of the Bible does not prove its excellence, but its excellence proves its inspiration. The Spirit brought the Scriptures to help Christ's work, but not to take his place. Scripture says with Paul : 'Not that we have lordship over your faith, but are helpers of your joy : for in faith ye stand fast' (2 Cor. 1 : 24)."

E. G. Robinson : "The office of the Spirit in inspiration is not different from that which he performed for Christians at the time the gospels were written. . . . When the prophets say : 'Thus saith the Lord,' they mean simply that they have divine authority for what they utter." Calvin E. Stowe, History of Books of Bible, 19—" It is not the words of the Bible that were inspired. It is not the thoughts of the Bible that were inspired. It was the men who wrote the Bible who were inspired." Thayer, Changed Attitude toward the Bible, 63—" It was not before the polemic spirit became rife in the controversies which followed the Reformation that the fundamental distinction between the word of God and the record of that word became obliterated, and the pestilent tenet gained currency that the Bible is absolutely free from every error of every sort." Principal Cave, in Homiletical Review, Feb. 1892, admitting errors but none serious in the Bible, proposes a mediating statement for the present controversy, namely, that Revelation implies inerrancy, but that Inspiration does not. Whatever God reveals must be true, but many have become inspired without being rendered infallible. See also Mead. Supernatural Revelation, 291 *sq.*

With regard to this theory we remark :

(*a*) There is unquestionably an illumination of the mind of every believer by the Holy Spirit, and we grant that there may have been instances in which the influence of the Spirit, in inspiration, amounted only to illumination.

Certain applications and interpretations of Old Testament Scripture, as for example, John the Baptist's application to Jesus of Isaiah's prophecy (John 1 : 29 —"Behold, the Lamb of God, that taketh away [marg. 'beareth'] the sin of the world "), and Peter's interpretation of David's words (Acts 2 : 27 — "thou wilt not leave my soul unto Hades, Neither wilt thou give thy Holy One to see corruption "), may have required only the illuminating influence of the Holy Spirit. There is a sense in which we may say that the Scriptures are inspired only to those who are themselves inspired. The Holy Spirit must show us Christ before we recognize the work of the Spirit in Scripture. The doctrines of atonement and of justification perhaps did not need to be newly revealed to the N. T. writers ; illumination as to earlier revelations may have sufficed. But that Christ existed before his incarnation, and that there are personal distinctions in the Godhead, probably required revelation. Edison says that "inspiration is simply perspiration." Genius has been defined as "unlimited power to take pains." But it is more — the power to do spontaneously and without effort what the ordinary man does by the hardest. Every great genius recognizes that this power is due to the inflowing into him of a Spirit greater than his own — the Spirit of divine wisdom and energy. The Scripture writers attribute their understanding of divine things to the Holy Spirit ; see next paragraph. On genius, as due to "subliminal uprush," see F. W. H. Myers, Human Personality, 1 : 70–120.

(*b*) But we deny that this was the constant method of inspiration, or that such an influence can account for the revelation of new truth to the prophets and apostles. The illumination of the Holy Spirit gives no new truth, but only a vivid apprehension of the truth already revealed. Any original communication of truth must have required a work of the Spirit different, not in degree, but in kind.

The Scriptures clearly distinguish between revelation, or the communication of new truth, and illumination, or the quickening of man's cognitive powers to perceive truth already revealed. No increase in the power of the eye or the telescope will do more than to bring into clear view what is already within its range. Illumination will not lift the veil that hides what is beyond. Revelation, on the other hand, is an 'unveiling '— the raising of a curtain, or the bringing within our range of what was hidden before. Such a special operation of God is described in 2 Sam. 23 : 2, 3 — "The Spirit of Jehovah spake by me, And his word was upon my tongue. The God of Israel said, The Rock of Israel spake to me " ; Mat. 10 : 20 —"For it is not ye that speak, but the Spirit of your Father that speaketh in you " ; 1 Cor. 2 : 9-13 —"Things which eye saw not, and ear heard not, And which entered not into the heart of man, Whatsoever things God prepared for them that love him. But unto us God revealed them through the Spirit : for the Spirit searcheth all things, yea, the deep things of God. For who among men knoweth the things of a man, save the spirit of the man, which is in him ? even so the things of God none knoweth, save the Spirit of God. But we received, not the spirit of the world, but the spirit which is from God ; that we might know the things that were freely given to us of God."

Clairvoyance and second sight, of which along with many cases of imposition and exaggeration there seems to be a small residuum of proved fact, show that there may be extraordinary operations of our natural powers. But, as in the case of miracle, the inspiration of Scripture necessitated an exaltation of these natural powers such as only the special influence of the Holy Spirit can explain. That the product is inexplicable as due to mere illumination seems plain when we remember that revelation sometimes *excluded* illumination as to the meaning of that which was communicated, for the prophets are represented in 1 Pet. 1 : 11 as "searching what time or what manner of time the Spirit of Christ which was in them did point unto, when it testified beforehand the sufferings of Christ, and the glories that should follow them." Since no degree of illumination can account for the prediction of "things that are to come" (John 16 : 13), this theory tends to the denial of any immediate revelation in prophecy so-called, and the denial easily extends to any immediate revelation of doctrine

(c) Mere illumination could not secure the Scripture writers from frequent and grievous error. The spiritual perception of the Christian is always rendered to some extent imperfect and deceptive by remaining depravity. The subjective element so predominates in this theory, that no certainty remains even with regard to the trustworthiness of the Scriptures as a whole.

While we admit imperfections of detail in matters not essential to the moral and religious teaching of Scripture, we claim that the Bible furnishes a sufficient guide to Christ and to salvation. The theory we are considering, however, by making the measure of holiness to be the measure of inspiration, renders even the collective testimony of the Scripture writers an uncertain guide to truth. We point out therefore that inspiration is not absolutely limited by the moral condition of those who are inspired. Knowledge, in the Christian, may go beyond conduct. Balaam and Caiaphas were not holy men, yet they were inspired (Num. 23 : 5 ; John 11 : 49-52). The promise of Christ assured at least the essential trustworthiness of his witnesses (Mat. 10 : 7, 19, 20 ; John 14 : 26 ; 15 : 26, 27 ; 16 : 13 ; 17 : 8). This theory that inspiration is a wholly subjective communication of truth leads to the practical rejection of important parts of Scripture, in fact to the rejection of all Scripture that professes to convey truth beyond the power of man to discover or to understand. Notice the progress from Thomas Arnold (Sermons, 2 : 185) to Matthew Arnold (Literature and Dogma, 134, 137). Notice also Swedenborg's rejection of nearly one half the Bible (Ruth, Chronicles, Ezra, Nehemiah, Esther, Job, Proverbs, Ecclesiastes, Song of Solomon, and the whole of the N. T. except the Gospels and the Apocalypse), connected with the claim of divine authority for his new revelation. "His interlocutors all Swedenborgize " (R. W. Emerson). On Swedenborg, see Hours with the Mystics, 2 : 230 ; Moehler, Symbolism, 436-466 ; New Englander, Jan. 1874 : 195 ; Baptist Review, 1883 : 143-157 ; Pond, Swedenborgianism ; Ireland, The Blot on the Brain, 1-129.

(d) The theory is logically indefensible, as intimating that illumination with regard to truth can be imparted without imparting truth itself, whereas God must first furnish objective truth to be perceived before he can illuminate the mind to perceive the meaning of that truth.

The theory is analogous to the views that preservation is a continued creation: knowledge is recognition ; regeneration is increase of light. In order to preservation, something must first be created which can be preserved ; in order to recognition, something must be known which can be recognized or known again ; in order to make increase of light of any use, there must first be the power to see. In like manner, inspiration cannot be mere illumination, because the external necessarily precedes the internal, the objective precedes the subjective, the truth revealed precedes the apprehension of that truth. In the case of all truth that surpasses the normal powers of man to perceive or evolve, there must be special communication from God ; revelation must go before inspiration : inspiration alone is not revelation. It matters not whether this communication of truth be from without or from within. As in creation, God can work from within, yet the new result is not explicable as mere reproduction of the past. The eye can see only as it receives and uses the external light furnished by the sun, even though it be equally true that without the eye the light of the sun would be nothing worth.

Pfleiderer, Grundriss, 17-19, says that to Schleiermacher revelation is the original appearance of a proper religious life, which life is derived neither from external communication nor from invention and reflection, but from a divine impartation, which impartation can be regarded, not merely as an instructive influence upon man as an intellectual being, but as an endowment determining his whole personal existence — an endowment analogous to the higher conditions of poetic and heroic exaltation. Pfleiderer himself would give the name "revelation" to "every original experience in which man becomes aware of, and is seized by, supersensible truth, truth which does not come from external impartation nor from purposed reflection, but from the unconscious and undivided transcendental ground of the soul, and so is received as an impartation from God through the medium of the soul's human activity." Kaftan, Dogmatik, 51 sq. — "We must put the conception of revelation in place of inspiration.

Scripture is the record of divine revelation. We do not propose a new doctrine of inspiration, in place of the old. We need only revelation, and, here and there, providence. The testimony of the Holy Spirit is given, not to inspiration, but to revelation — the truths that touch the human spirit and have been historically revealed."

Allen, Jonathan Edwards, 182 — Edwards held that spiritual life in the soul is given by God only to his favorites and dear children, while inspiration may be thrown out, as it were, to dogs and swine — a Balaam, Saul, and Judas. The greatest privilege of apostles and prophets was, not their inspiration, but their holiness. Better to have grace in the heart, than to be the mother of Christ (Luke 11 : 27, 28). Maltbie D. Babcock, in S. S. Times, 1901 : 590 — "The man who mourns because infallibility cannot be had in a church, or a guide, or a set of standards, does not know when he is well off. How could God develop our minds, our power of moral judgment, if there were no 'spirit to be tried' (1 John 4 : 1), no necessity for discrimination, no discipline of search and challenge and choice? To give the right answer to a problem is to put him on the side of infallibility so far as that answer is concerned, but it is to do him an ineffable wrong touching his real education. The blessing of life's schooling is not in knowing the right answer in advance, but in developing power through struggle."

Why did John Henry Newman surrender to the Church of Rome? Because he assumed that an external authority is absolutely essential to religion, and, when such an assumption is followed, Rome is the only logical terminus. "Dogma was," he says, "the fundamental principle of my religion." Modern ritualism is a return to this mediæval notion. "Dogmatic Christianity," says Harnack, "is Catholic. It needs an inerrant Bible, and an infallible church to interpret that Bible. The dogmatic Protestant is of the same camp with the sacramental and infallible Catholic." Lyman Abbott: "The new Reformation denies the infallibility of the Bible, as the Protestant Reformation denied the infallibility of the Church. There is no infallible authority. Infallible authority is undesirable. . . . God has given us something far better, — life. . . . The Bible is the record of the gradual manifestation of God to man in human experience, in moral laws and their applications, and in the life of Him who was God manifest in the flesh."

Leighton Williams: "There is no inspiration apart from experience. Baptists are not sacramental, nor creedal, but experimental Christians" — not Romanists, nor Protestants, but believers in an inner light. "Life, as it develops, awakens into self-consciousness. That self-consciousness becomes the most reliable witness as to the nature of the life of which it is the development. Within the limits of its own sphere, its authority is supreme. Prophecy is the utterance of the soul in moments of deep religious experience. The inspiration of Scripture writers is not a peculiar thing,— it was given that the same inspiration might be perfected in those who read their writings." Christ is the only ultimate authority, and he reveals himself in three ways, through Scripture, the Reason, and the Church. Only Life saves, and the Way leads through the Truth to the Life. Baptists stand nearer to the Episcopal system of life than to the Presbyterian system of creed. Whiton, Gloria Patri, 136 — "The mistake is in looking to the Father above the world, rather than to the Son and the Spirit within the world, as the immediate source of revelation. . . . Revelation is the unfolding of the life and thought of God within the world. One should not be troubled by finding errors in the Scriptures, any more than by finding imperfections in any physical work of God, as in the human eye."

3. *The Dictation-theory.*

This theory holds that inspiration consisted in such a possession of the minds and bodies of the Scripture writers by the Holy Spirit, that they became passive instruments or amanuenses — pens, not penmen, of God.

This theory naturally connects itself with that view of miracles which regards them as suspensions or violations of natural law. Dorner, Glaubenslehre, 1 : 624 (transl. 2 : 186-189), calls it a "docetic view of inspiration. It holds to the abolition of second causes, and to the perfect passivity of the human instrument; denies any inspiration of persons, and maintains inspiration of writings only. This exaggeration of the divine element led to the hypothesis of a multiform divine sense in Scripture, and, in assigning the spiritual meaning, a rationalizing spirit led the way." Representatives of this view are Quenstedt, Theol. Didact., 1 : 76 — "The Holy Ghost inspired his amanuenses with those expressions which they would have employed, had they been left to themseives"; Hooker, Works, 2; 383 — "They neither spake nor wrote any word of their own, but uttered syllable by syllable as the Spirit put it into their mouths"; Gaussen, Theopneusty. 61 — "The Bible is not a book which God charged men already enlightened to make under his protection; it is a book which God dictated to them"; Cunningham, Theol. Lectures, 349 — "The verbal inspiration of the Scriptures [which he advocates] implies in general that the words of Scripture were suggested or dictated by the Holy Spirit, as well as the substance of the matter, and this, not only in some portion of the Scriptures, but through the whole." This reminds us of the old theory that God created fossils in the rocks, as they would be had ancient seas existed.

Sanday, Bamp. Lect. on Inspiration, 74, quotes Philo as saying: "A prophet gives forth nothing at all of his own, but acts as interpreter at the prompting of another in all his utterances, and as long as he is under inspiration he is in ignorance, his reason departing from its place and yielding up the citadel of the soul, when the divine Spirit enters into it and dwells in it and strikes at the mechanism of the voice, sounding through it to the clear declaration of that which he prophesieth"; in Gen. 15: 12 — "About the setting of the sun a trance came upon Abram" — the sun is the light of human reason which sets and gives place to the Spirit of God. Sanday, 78, says also: "Josephus holds that even historical narratives, such as those at the beginning of the Pentateuch which were not written down by contemporary prophets, were obtained by direct inspiration from God. The Jews from their birth regard their Scripture as 'the decrees of God,' which they strictly observe, and for which if need be they are ready to die." The Rabbis said that "Moses did not write one word out of his own knowledge."

The Reformers held to a much freer view than this. Luther said: "What does not carry Christ with it, is not apostolic, even though St. Peter or St. Paul taught it. If our adversaries fall back on the Scripture against Christ, we fall back on Christ against the Scripture." Luther refused canonical authority to books not actually written by apostles or composed, like Mark and Luke, under their direction. So he rejected from the rank of canonical authority Hebrews, James, Jude, 2 Peter and Revelation. Even Calvin doubted the Petrine authorship of 2 Peter, excluded the book of Revelation from the Scripture on which he wrote Commentaries, and also thus ignored the second and third epistles of John; see Prof. R. E. Thompson, in S. S. Times, Dec. 3, 1898: 803, 804. The dictation-theory is post-Reformation. H. P. Smith, Bib. Scholarship and Inspiration, 85 — "After the Council of Trent, the Roman Catholic polemic became sharper. It became the endeavor of that party to show the necessity of tradition and the untrustworthiness of Scripture alone. This led the Protestants to defend the Bible more tenaciously than before." The Swiss Formula of Consensus in 1675 not only called the Scriptures "the very word of God," but declared the Hebrew vowel-points to be inspired, and some theologians traced them back to Adam. John Owen held to the inspiration of the vowel-points; see Horton, Inspiration and Bible, 8. Of the age which produced the Protestant dogmatic theology, Charles Beard, in the Hibbert Lectures for 1883, says: "I know no epoch of Christianity to which I could more confidently point in illustration of the fact that where there is most theology, there is often least religion."

Of this view we may remark :

(a) We grant that there are instances when God's communications were uttered in an audible voice and took a definite form of words, and that this was sometimes accompanied with the command to commit the words to writing.

For examples, see Ex. 3: 4 — "God called unto him out of the midst of the bush, and said, Moses, Moses"; 20: 22 — "Ye yourselves have seen that I have talked with you from heaven"; cf. Heb. 12:19 — "the voice of words; which voice they that heard entreated that no word more should be spoken unto them"; Numbers 7:89 — "And when Moses went into the tent of meeting to speak with him, then he heard the Voice speaking unto him from above the mercy-seat that was upon the ark of the testimony, from between the two cherubim: and he spake unto him"; 8 1 — "And Jehovah spake unto Moses, saying," etc.; Dan. 4:31 — "While the word was in the king's mouth, there fell a voice from heaven, saying, O king Nebuchadnezzar, to thee it is spoken: The kingdom is departed from thee"; Acts 9: 5 — "And he said, Who art thou, Lord? And he said, I am Jesus whom thou persecutest"; Rev. 19: 9 — "And he saith unto me, Write, Blessed are they that are bidden to the marriage supper of the Lamb"; 21:5 — "And he that sitteth on the throne said, Behold, I make all things new"; cf. 1:10, 11 — "and I heard behind me a great voice, as of a trumpet saying, What thou seest, write in a book and send it to the seven churches." So the voice from heaven at the baptism, and at the transfiguration, of Jesus (Mat. 3:17, and 17:5; see Broadus, Amer. Com., on these passages).

14

(*b*) The theory in question, however, rests upon a partial induction of Scripture facts, — unwarrantably assuming that such occasional instances of direct dictation reveal the invariable method of God's communications of truth to the writers of the Bible.

Scripture nowhere declares that this immediate communication of the words was universal. On 1 Cor. 2:13 — οὐκ ἐν διδακτοῖς ἀνθρωπίνης σοφίας λόγοις, ἀλλ' ἐν διδακτοῖς πνεύματος, the text usually cited as proof of invariable dictation — Meyer says : "There is no dictation here ; διδακτοῖς excludes everything mechanical." Henderson, Inspiration (2nd ed.), 333, 349 — "As human wisdom did not dictate word for word, so the Spirit did not." Paul claims for Scripture simply a general style of plainness which is due to the influence of the Spirit. Manly : "Dictation to an amanuensis is not *teaching*." Our Revised Version properly translates the remainder of the verse, 1 Cor. 2:13 — "combining spiritual things with spiritual words."

(*c*) It cannot account for the manifestly human element in the Scriptures. There are peculiarities of style which distinguish the productions of each writer from those of every other, and there are variations in accounts of the same transaction which are inconsistent with the theory of a solely divine authorship.

Notice Paul's anacoloutha and his bursts of grief and indignation (Rom. 5 : 12 *sq.*, 2 Cor 11:1 *sq.*), and his ignorance of the precise number whom he had baptized (1 Cor. 1 : 16). One beggar or two (Mat. 20 : 30 ; *cf.* Luke 18 : 35) ; "about five and twenty or thirty furlongs" (John 6 : 19) ; "shed for many" (Mat. 26 : 28 has περί, Mark 14 : 24 and Luke 22 : 20 have ὑπέρ). Dictation of words which were immediately to be lost by imperfect transcription? Clarke, Christian Theology, 33-37 — "We are under no obligation to maintain the complete inerrancy of the Scriptures. In them we have the freedom of life, rather than extraordinary precision of statement or accuracy of detail. We have become Christians in spite of differences between the evangelists. The Scriptures are various, progressive, free. There is no authority in Scripture for applying the word 'inspired' to our present Bible as a whole, and theology is not bound to employ this word in defining the Scriptures. Christianity is founded in history, and will stand whether the Scriptures are inspired or not. If special inspiration were wholly disproved, Christ would still be the Savior of the world. But the divine element in the Scriptures will never be disproved."

(*d*) It is inconsistent with a wise economy of means, to suppose that the Scripture writers should have had dictated to them what they knew already, or what they could inform themselves of by the use of their natural powers.

Why employ eye-witnesses at all? Why not dictate the gospels to Gentiles living a thousand years before? God respects the instruments he has called into being, and he uses them according to their constitutional gifts. George Eliot represents Stradivarius as saying : — "If my hand slacked, I should rob God — since he is fullest good — Leaving a blank instead of violins. God cannot make Antonio Stradivari s violins, Without Antonio." Mark 11 : 3 — "The Lord hath need of him," may apply to man as well as beast.

(*e*) It contradicts what we know of the law of God's working in the soul. The higher and nobler God's communications, the more fully is man in possession and use of his own faculties. We cannot suppose that this highest work of man under the influence of the Spirit was purely mechanical.

Joseph receives communication by vision (Mat. 1 : 20); Mary, by words of an angel spoken in her waking moments (Luke 1 : 28). The more advanced the recipient, the more conscious the communication. These four theories might almost be called the Pelagian, the Arminian, the Docetic, and the Dynamical. Sabatier, Philos. Religion, 41, 42, 87 — "In the Gospel of the Hebrews, the Father says at the baptism to Jesus : ' My Son, in all the prophets I was waiting for thee, that thou mightest come, and that I might rest in thee. For thou art my Rest.' Inspiration becomes more and more internal, until in Christ it is continuous and complete. Upon the opposite Docetic view, the most perfect inspiration should have been that of Balaam's ass." Semler represents the Pelagian or Ebionitic view, as Quenstedt represents this Docetic view. Semler localizes and temporalizes the contents of Scripture. Yet, though he carried this to the extreme of excluding any divine authorship, he did good service in leading the way to the historical study of the Bible.

4. *The Dynamical Theory.*

The true view holds, in opposition to the first of these theories, that inspiration is not simply a natural but also a supernatural fact, and that it is the immediate work of a personal God in the soul of man.

It holds, in opposition to the second, that inspiration belongs, not only to the men who wrote the Scriptures, but to the Scriptures which they wrote, so that these Scriptures, when taken together, constitute a trustworthy and sufficient record of divine revelation.

It holds, in opposition to the third theory, that the Scriptures contain a human as well as a divine element, so that while they present a body of divinely revealed truth, this truth is shaped in human moulds and adapted to ordinary human intelligence.

In short, inspiration is characteristically neither natural, partial, nor mechanical, but supernatural, plenary, and dynamical. Further explanations will be grouped under the head of The Union of the Divine and Human Elements in Inspiration, in the section which immediately follows.

If the small circle be taken as symbol of the human element in inspiration, and the large circle as symbol of the divine, then the Intuition-theory would be represented by the small circle alone ; the Dictation-theory by the large circle alone ; the Illumination-theory by the small circle external to the large, and touching it at only a single point ; the Dynamical-theory by two concentric circles, the small included in the large. Even when inspiration is but the exaltation and intensification of man's natural powers, it must be considered the work of God as well as of man. God can work from within as well as from without. As creation and regeneration are works of the immanent rather than of the transcendent God, so inspiration is in general a work within man's soul, rather than a communication to him from without. Prophecy may be natural to perfect humanity. Revelation is an unveiling, and the Röntgen rays enable us to see through a veil. But the insight of the Scripture writers into truth so far beyond their mental and moral powers is inexplicable except by a supernatural influence upon their minds ; in other words, except as they were lifted up into the divine Reason and endowed with the wisdom of God.

Although we propose this Dynamical-theory as one which best explains the Scripture facts, we do not regard this or any other theory as of essential importance. No theory of inspiration is necessary to Christian faith. Revelation precedes inspiration. There was religion before the Old Testament, and an oral gospel before the New Testament. God might reveal without recording ; might permit record without inspiration ; might inspire without vouching for anything more than religious teaching and for the history, only so far as was necessary to that religious teaching. Whatever theory of inspiration we frame, should be the result of a strict induction of the Scripture facts, and not an *a priori* scheme to which Scripture must be conformed. The fault of many past discussions of the subject is the assumption that God must adopt some particular method of inspiration, or secure an absolute perfection of detail in matters not essential to the religious teaching of Scripture. Perhaps the best theory of inspiration is to have no theory.

Warfield and Hodge, Inspiration, 8 — "Very many religious and historical truths must be established before we come to the question of inspiration, as for instance the being and moral government of God, the fallen condition of man, the fact of a redemptive scheme, the general historical truth of the Scriptures, and the validity and authority of the revelation of God's will which they contain, *i. e.*, the general truth of Christianity and of its doctrines. Hence it follows that while the inspiration of the Scriptures is true, and being true is a principle fundamental to the adequate interpretation of Scripture, it nevertheless is not, in the first instance, a principle fundamental to the truth of the Christian religion." Warfield, in Presb. and Ref. Rev., April, 1893: 208 — " We do not found the whole Christian system on the doctrine of inspiration. . . . . Were there no such thing as inspiration, Christianity would be true, and all its essential doctrines would be credibly witnessed to us"—in the gospels and in the living church. F. L. Patton, Inspiration, 22 — " I must take exception to the disposition of some to stake the fortunes of Christianity on the doctrine of inspiration. Not that I yield to any one in profound conviction of the truth and importance of the doctrine. But it is proper for us to bear in mind the immense argumentative advantage which Christianity has, aside altogether from the inspiration of the documents on which it rests." So argue also Sanday, Oracles of God, and Dale, The Living Christ.

IV. The Union of the Divine and Human Elements in Inspiration.

1. The Scriptures are the production equally of God and of man, and are therefore never to be regarded as merely human or merely divine.

The mystery of inspiration consists in neither of these terms separately, but in the union of the two.   Of this, however, there are analogies in the interpenetration of human powers by the divine efficiency in regeneration and sanctification, and in the union of the divine and human natures in the person of Jesus Christ.

According to " Dalton's law," each gas is as a vacuum to every other : " Gases are mutually passive, and pass into each other as into vacua." Each interpenetrates the other. But this does not furnish a perfect illustration of our subject. The atom of oxygen and the atom of nitrogen, in common air, remain side by side but they do not unite. In inspiration the human and the divine elements do unite. The Lutheran maxim, " Mens humana capax divinæ," is one of the most important principles of a true theology. " The Lutherans think of humanity as a thing made by God for himself and to receive himself. The Reformed think of the Deity as ever preserving himself from any confusion with the creature. They fear pantheism and idolatry " (Bp. of Salisbury, quoted in Swayne, Our Lord's Knowledge, xx).

Sabatier, Philos. Religion, 66 — " That initial mystery, the relation in our conscious-ness between the individual and the universal element, between the finite and the infinite, between God and man, -- how can we comprehend their coëxistence and their union, and yet how can we doubt it? Where is the thoughtful man to-day who has not broken the thin crust of his daily life, and caught a glimpse of those profound and obscure waters on which floats our consciousness? Who has not felt within himself a veiled presence, and a force much greater than his own? What worker in a lofty cause has not perceived within his own personal activity, and saluted with a feeling of veneration, the mysterious activity of a universal and eternal Power? ' In Deo vivimus, movemur, et sumus.' . . . . This mystery cannot be dissipated, for without it religion itself would no longer exist." Quackenbos, in Harper's Magazine, July, 1900 : 264, says that "hypnotic suggestion is but inspiration." The analogy of human influence thus communicated may at least help us to some understanding of the divine.

2. This union of the divine and human agencies in inspiration is not to be conceived of as one of external impartation and reception.

On the other hand, those whom God raised up and providentially qualified to do this work, spoke and wrote the words of God, when inspired, not as from without, but as from within, and that not passively, but in the most conscious possession and the most exalted exercise of their own powers of intellect, emotion, and will.

The Holy Spirit does not dwell in man as water in a vessel. We may rather illustrate the experience of the Scripture writers by the experience of the preacher who under the influence of God's Spirit is carried beyond himself, and is conscious of a clearer appre-hension of truth and of a greater ability to utter it than belong to his unaided nature, yet knows himself to be no passive vehicle of a divine communication, but to be as never before in possession and exercise of his own powers. The inspiration of the Scripture writers, however, goes far beyond the illumination granted to the preacher, in that it qualifies them to put the truth, without error, into permanent and written form. This inspiration, moreover, is more than providential preparation. Like miracles, inspiration may use man's natural powers, but man's natural powers do not explain it. Moses, David, Paul, and John were providentially endowed and educated for their work of writing Scripture, but this endowment and education were not inspiration itself, but only the preparation for it.

Beyschlag : " With John, remembrance and exposition had become inseparable." E. G. Robinson ; " Novelists do not *create* characters,—they reproduce with modifications material presented to their memories. So the apostles reproduced their impressions of Christ." Hutton, Essays, 2 : 231 — " The Psalmists vacillate between the first person and the third, when they deliver the purposes of God. As they warm with their spiritual inspiration, they lose themselves in the person of Him who inspires them, and then they are again recalled to themselves." Stanley, Life and Letters, 1 : 380 — " Revelation is not resolved into a mere human process because we are able to distinguish the natural agencies through which it was communicated"; 2:102 — " You seem to me to transfer too much to these ancient prophets and writers and chiefs our modern notions of *divine origin*. . . . Our notion, or rather, the modern Puritanical notion of divine origin, is of a preternatural force or voice, putting aside secondary agencies, and separated from those agencies by an impassable gulf. The ancient, Oriental, Biblical notion was of a supreme Will acting through those agencies, or rather, being inseparable from them. *Our* notions of inspiration and divine communications insist on absolute perfection of fact, morals, doctrine. The Biblical notion was that inspiration was compatible with weakness, infirmity, contradiction." Ladd, Philosophy of Mind, 182 — " In inspiration the thoughts, feelings, purposes are organized into another One than the self in which they were themselves born. That other One is *in themselves*. They enter into communication with Him. Yet this may be supernatural, even though natural psychological means are used. Inspiration which is external is not inspiration at all." This last sentence, however, seems to us a needless exaggeration of the true principle. Though God originally inspires from within, he may also communicate truth from without.

3. Inspiration, therefore, did not remove, but rather pressed into its own service, all the personal peculiarities of the writers, together with their defects of culture and literary style.

Every imperfection not inconsistent with truth in a human composition may exist in inspired Scripture. The Bible is God's word, in the sense that it presents to us divine truth in human forms, and is a revelation not for a select class but for the common mind. Rightly understood, this very humanity of the Bible is a proof of its divinity.

Locke : " When God made the prophet, he did not unmake the man." Prof. Day : " The bush in which God appeared to Moses remained a bush, while yet burning with the brightness of God and uttering forth the majesty of the mind of God." The paragraphs of the Koran are called *ayat*, or "sign," from their supposed supernatural elegance. But elegant literary productions do not touch the heart. The Bible is not merely the word of God; it is also the word made flesh. The Holy Spirit hides himself, that he may show forth Christ (John 3 : 8) ; he is known only by his effects — a pattern for preachers, who are ministers of the Spirit (2 Cor. 3 : 6). See Conant on Genesis, 65.

The Moslem declares that every word of the Koran came by the agency of Gabriel from the seventh heaven, and that its very pronunciation is inspired. Better the doctrine of Martineau, Seat of Authority, 289 — " Though the pattern be divine, the web that bears it must still be human." Jackson, James Martineau, 255 — " Paul's metaphor of the ' treasure in earthen vessels ' (2 Cor. 4 : 7) you cannot allow to give you guidance ; you want, not the treasure only, but the casket too, to come from above, and be of the crystal of the sky. You want the record to be divine, not only in its spirit, but also in its letter." Charles Hodge, Syst. Theol., 1 : 157 — " When God ordains praise out of the mouths of babes, they must speak as babes, or the whole power and beauty of the tribute will be lost."

Evans, Bib. Scholarship and Inspiration, 16, 25 — " The πνεῦμα of a dead wind is never changed, as the Rabbis of old thought, into the πνεῦμα of a living spirit. The raven that fed Elijah was nothing more than a bird. Nor does man, when supernaturally influenced, cease to be a man. An inspired man is not God, nor a divinely manipulated automaton"; "In Scripture there may be as much imperfection as, in the parts of any organism, would be consistent with the perfect adaptation of that organism to its destined end. Scripture then, taken together, is a statement of moral and religious truth sufficient for men's salvation, or an infallible and sufficient rule of *faith and practice*." J. S. Wrightnour: "Inspire means to breathe in, as a flute-player breathes into his instrument. As different flutes may have their own shapes, peculiarities, and what might seem like defects, so here; yet all are breathed into by one Spirit. The same Spirit who inspired them selected those instruments which were best for his purpose, as the Savior selected his apostles. In these writings therefore is given us, in the precise way that is best for us, the spiritual instruction and food that we need. Food for the body is not always given in the most concentrated form, but in the form that is best adapted for digestion. So God gives gold, not in coin ready stamped, but in the quartz of the mine whence it has to be dug and smelted." Remains of Arthur H. Hallam, in John Brown's Rab and his Friends, 274 — "I see that the Bible fits in to every fold of the human heart. I am a man, and I believe it is God's book, because it is man's book."

4.   In inspiration God may use all right and normal methods of literary composition.

As we recognize in literature the proper function of history, poetry, and fiction ; of prophecy, parable, and drama ; of personification and proverb ; of allegory and dogmatic instruction ; and even of myth and legend ; we cannot deny the possibility that God may use any one of these methods of communicating truth, leaving it to us to determine in any single case which of these methods he has adopted.

In inspiration, as in regeneration and sanctification, God works "in divers manners" (Heb. 1:1). The Scriptures, like the books of secular literature, must be interpreted in the light of their purpose. Poetry must not be treated as prose, and parable must not be made to "go on all fours," when it was meant to walk erect and to tell one simple story. Drama is not history, nor is personification to be regarded as biography. There is a rhetorical overstatement which is intended only as a vivid emphasizing of important truth. Allegory is a popular mode of illustration. Even myth and legend may convey great lessons not otherwise apprehensible to infantile or untrained minds. A literary sense is needed in our judgments of Scripture, and much hostile criticism is lacking in this literary sense.

Denney, Studies in Theology, 218 — "There is a stage in which the whole contents of the mind, as yet incapable of science or history, may be called mythological. And what criticism shows us, in its treatment of the early chapters of Genesis, is that God does not disdain to speak to the mind, nor through it, even when it is at this lowly stage. Even the myth, in which the beginnings of human life, lying beyond human research, are represented to itself by the child-mind of the race, may be made the medium of revelation. . . . But that does not make the first chapter of Genesis science, nor the third chapter history. And what is of authority in these chapters is not the quasi-scientific or quasi-historical form, but the message, which through them comes to the heart, of God's creative wisdom and power." Gore, in Lux Mundi, 356 — "The various sorts of mental or literary activity develop in their different lines out of an earlier condition in which they lie fused and undifferentiated. This we can vaguely call the mythical stage of mental evolution. A myth is not a falsehood; it is a product of mental activity, as instructive and rich as any later product, but its characteristic is that it is not yet distinguished into history and poetry and philosophy." So Grote calls the Greek myths the whole intellectual stock of the age to which they belonged — the common root of all the history, poetry, philosophy, theology, which afterwards diverged and proceeded from it. So the early part of Genesis may be of the nature of myth in which we cannot distinguish the historical germ, though we do not deny that it exists. Robert Browning's Clive and Andrea del Sarto are essentially correct representations of historical characters, though the details in each poem are imaginary.

5.   The inspiring Spirit has given the Scriptures to the world by a process of gradual evolution.

As in communicating the truths of natural science, God has communicated the truths of religion by successive steps, germinally at first, more fully as men have been able to comprehend them. The education of the race is analogous to the education of the child. First came pictures, object-lessons, external rites, predictions ; then the key to these in Christ, and their didactic exposition in the Epistles.

There have been " divers portions," as well as " divers manners" (Heb. 1:1). The early prophecies like that of Gen. 3 : 15 — the seed of the woman bruising the serpent's head — were but faint glimmerings of the dawn. Men had to be raised up who were capable of receiving and transmitting the divine communications. Moses, David, Isaiah mark successive advances in recipiency and transparency to the heavenly light. Inspiration has employed men of various degrees of ability, culture and religious insight. As all the truths of the calculus lie germinally in the simplest mathematical axiom, so all the truths of salvation may be wrapped up in the statement that God is holiness and love. But not every scholar can evolve the calculus from the axiom. The teacher may dictate propositions which the pupil does not understand : he may demonstrate in such a way that the pupil participates in the process; or, best of all, he may incite the pupil to work out the demonstration for himself. God seems to have used all these methods. But while there are instances of dictation and illumination, and inspiration sometimes includes these, the general method seems to have been such a divine quickening of man's powers that he discovers and expresses the truth for himself.

A. J. Balfour, Foundations of Belief, 339 — " Inspiration is that, seen from its divine side, which we call discovery when seen from the human side. . . . Every addition to knowledge, whether in the individual or the community, whether scientific, ethical or theological, is due to a coöperation between the human soul which assimilates and the divine power which inspires. Neither acts, or could act, in independent isolation. For ' unassisted reason ' is a fiction, and pure receptivity it is impossible to conceive. Even the emptiest vessel must limit the quantity and determine the configuration of any liquid with which it may be filled. . . . Inspiration is limited to no age, to no country, to no people." The early Semites had it, and the great Oriental reformers. There can be no gathering of grapes from thorns, or of figs from thistles. Whatever of true or of good is found in human history has come from God. On the Progressiveness of Revelation, see Orr, Problem of the O. T., 431–478.

6. Inspiration did not guarantee inerrancy in things not essential to the main purpose of Scripture.

Inspiration went no further than to secure a trustworthy transmission by the sacred writers of the truth they were commissioned to deliver. It was not omniscience. It was a bestowal of various kinds and degrees of knowledge and aid, according to need; sometimes suggesting new truth, sometimes presiding over the collection of preëxisting material and guarding from essential error in the final elaboration. As inspiration was not omniscience, so it was not complete sanctification. It involved neither personal infallibility, nor entire freedom from sin.

God can use imperfect means. As the imperfection of the eye does not disprove its divine authorship, and as God reveals himself in nature and history in spite of their shortcomings, so inspiration can accomplish its purpose through both writers and writings in some respects imperfect. God is, in the Bible as he was in Hebrew history, leading his people onward to Christ, but only by a progressive unfolding of the truth. The Scripture writers were not perfect men. Paul at Antioch resisted Peter, " because he stood condemned " (Gal. 2 : 11). But Peter differed from Paul, not in public utterances, nor in written words, but in following his own teachings (cf. Acts 15 : 6-11); versus Norman Fox, in Bap. Rev., 1885 : 469–482. Personal defects do not invalidate an ambassador, though they may hinder the reception of his message. So with the apostles' ignorance of the time of Christ's second coming. It was only gradually that they came to understand Christian doctrines ; they did not teach the truth all at once; their final utterances supplemented and completed the earlier ; and all together furnished only that measure of knowledge which God saw needful for the moral and religious teaching of mankind. Many things are yet unrevealed, and many things which inspired men uttered, they did not, when they uttered them, fully understand.

Pfleiderer, Grundriss, 53, 54 — "The word is divine-human in the sense that it has for its contents divine truth in human, historical, and individually conditioned form. The Holy Scripture contains the word of God in a way plain, and entirely sufficient to beget saving faith." Frances Power Cobbe, Life, 87 — " Inspiration is not a miraculous and therefore incredible thing, but normal and in accordance with the natural relations of the infinite and finite spirit, a divine inflowing of *mental* light precisely analogous to that *moral* influence which divines call grace. As every devout and obedient soul may expect to share in divine grace, so the devout and obedient souls of all the ages have shared, as Parker taught, in divine inspiration. And, as the reception of grace even in large measure does not render us *impeccable*, so neither does the reception of inspiration render us *infallible*." We may concede to Miss Cobbe that inspiration consists with imperfection, while yet we grant to the Scripture writers an authority higher than our own.

7.   Inspiration did not always, or even generally, involve a direct communication to the Scripture writers of the words they wrote.

Thought is possible without words, and in the order of nature precedes words.   The Scripture writers appear to have been so influenced by the Holy Spirit that they perceived and felt even the new truths they were to publish, as discoveries of their own minds, and were left to the action of their own minds in the expression of these truths, with the single exception that they were supernaturally held back from the selection of wrong words, and when needful were provided with right ones.   Inspiration is therefore not verbal, while yet we claim that no form of words which taken in its connections would teach essential error has been admitted into Scripture.

Before expression there must be something to be expressed. Thought is possible without language. The concept may exist without words. See experiences of deaf-mutes, in Princeton Rev., Jan. 1881 : 104-128. The prompter interrupts only when the speaker's memory fails. The writing-master guides the pupil's hand only when it would otherwise go wrong. The father suffers the child to walk alone, except when it is in danger of stumbling. If knowledge be rendered certain, it is as good as direct revelation. But whenever the mere communication of ideas or the direction to proper material would not suffice to secure a correct utterance, the sacred writers were guided in the very selection of their words. Minute criticism proves more and more conclusively the suitableness of the verbal dress to the thoughts expressed ; all Biblical exegesis is based, indeed, upon the assumption that divine wisdom has made the outward form a trustworthy vehicle of the inward substance of revelation. See Henderson, Inspiration (2nd ed.), 102, 114 ; Bib. Sac., 1872 : 428, 640 ; William James, Psychology, 1 : 266 *sq.*

Watts, New Apologetic, 40, 111, holds to a verbal inspiration : "The bottles are not the wine, but if the bottles perish the wine is sure to be spilled"; the inspiring Spirit certainly gave language to Peter and others at Pentecost, for the apostles spoke with other tongues ; holy men of old not only thought, but "spake from God, being moved by the Holy Spirit" (2 Pet. 1 : 21). So Gordon, Ministry of the Spirit, 171 — " Why the minute study of the *words* of Scripture, carried on by all expositors, their search after the precise shade of verbal significance, their attention to the minutest details of language, and to all the delicate coloring of mood and tense and accent ? " Liberal scholars, Dr. Gordon thinks, thus affirm the very doctrine which they deny. Rothe, Dogmatics, 238, speaks of " a language of the Holy Ghost." Oetinger : " It is the style of the heavenly court." But Broadus, an almost equally conservative scholar, in his Com. on Mat. 3 :17, says that the difference between "This is my beloved Son," and Luke 3 : 22 — "Thou art my beloved Son," should make us cautious in theorizing about verbal inspiration, and he intimates that in some cases that hypothesis is unwarranted. The theory of verbal inspiration is refuted by the two facts : 1. that the N. T. quotations from the O. T., in 99 cases, differ both from the Hebrew and from the LXX ; 2. that Jesus' own words are reported with variations by the different evangelists ; see Marcus Dods, The Bible, its Origin and Nature, chapter on Inspiration.

Helen Keller told Phillips Brooks that she had always known that there was a God, but she had not known his name. Dr. Z. F. Westervelt, of the Deaf Mute Institute, had under his charge four children of different mothers. All of these children were dumb, though there was no defect of hearing and the organs of speech were perfect. But their mothers had never loved them and had never talked to them in the loving way that provoked imitation. The children heard scolding and harshness, but this did not attract. So the older members of the church in private and in the meetings for prayer should teach the younger to talk. But harsh and contentious talk will not accomplish the result, — it must be the talk of Christian love. William D. Whitney, in his review of Max Müller's Science of Language, 26–31, combats the view of Müller that thought and language are identical. Major Bliss Taylor's reply to Santa Anna : " General Taylor never surrenders ! " was a substantially correct, though a diplomatic and euphemistic, version of the General's actual profane words. Each Scripture writer uttered old truth in the new forms with which his own experience had clothed it. David reached his greatness by leaving off the mere repetition of Moses, and by speaking out of his own heart. Paul reached his greatness by giving up the mere teaching of what he had been taught, and by telling what God's plan of mercy was to all. Augustine : " Scriptura est sensus Scripturæ " — " Scripture *is* what Scripture *means*." Among the theological writers who admit the errancy of Scripture writers as to some matters unessential to their moral and spiritual teaching, are Luther, Calvin, Cocceius, Tholuck, Neander, Lange, Stier, Van Oosterzee, John Howe, Richard Baxter, Conybeare, Alford, Mead.

8. Yet, notwithstanding the ever-present human element, the all-pervading inspiration of the Scriptures constitutes these various writings an organic whole.

Since the Bible is in all its parts the work of God, each part is to be judged, not by itself alone, but in its connection with every other part. The Scriptures are not to be interpreted as so many merely human productions by different authors, but as also the work of one divine mind. Seemingly trivial things are to be explained from their connection with the whole. One history is to be built up from the several accounts of the life of Christ. One doctrine must supplement another. The Old Testament is part of a progressive system, whose culmination and key are to be found in the New. The central subject and thought which binds all parts of the Bible together, and in the light of which they are to be interpreted, is the person and work of Jesus Christ.

The Bible says : " There is no God " (*Ps.* 14: 1); but then, this is to be taken with the context: " The fool hath said in his heart." Satan's " it is written," (Mat. 4: 6) is supplemented by Christ's " It is written again" (Mat. 4: 7). Trivialities are like the hair and nails of the body — they have their place as parts of a complete and organic whole , see Ebrard, Dogmatik, 1 : 40. The verse which mentions Paul's cloak at Troas (2 Tim. 4: 13) is (1) a sign of genuineness — a forger would not invent it ; (2) an evidence of temporal need endured for the gospel ; (3) an indication of the limits of inspiration, — even Paul must have books and parchments. Col. 2: 21 — " Handle not, nor taste, nor touch "—is to be interpreted by the context in verse 20 — " why . . . do ye subject yourselves to ordinances ? ", and by verse 22 — "after the precepts and doctrines of men." Hodge, Syst. Theol., 1 : 164 — " The difference between John's gospel and the book of Chronicles is like that between man's brain and the hair of his head ; nevertheless the life of the body is as truly in the hair as in the brain." Like railway coupons, Scripture texts are " Not good if detached."

Crooker, The New Bible and its New Uses, 137–144, utterly denies the unity of the Bible. Prof. A. B. Davidson of Edinburgh says that " A theology of the O. T. is really an impossibility, because the O. T. is not a homogeneous whole." These denials proceed from an insufficient recognition of the principle of evolution in O. T. history and doctrine. Doctrines in early Scripture are like rivers at their source; they are not yet fully expanded ; many affluents are yet to come. See Bp. Bull's Sermon, in Works, xv: 183 ; and Bruce, Apologetics, 323 — " The literature of the early stages of revelation must share the defects of the revelation which it records and interprets. . . . The final revelation enables us to see the defects of the earlier. . . . We should find Christ in the O. T. as we find the butterfly in the caterpiller, and man the crown of the universe in the fiery cloud." Crane, Religion of To-morrow, 224 — Every part is to be modified b / every other part. No verse is true *out of* the Book, but the whole Book taken together is true. Gore, in Lux Mundi, 350 — "To recognize the inspiration of the Scriptures is to put ourselves to school in every part of them." Robert Browning, Ring and Book, 175 (Pope, 228) — " Truth nowhere lies, yet everywhere, in these ; Not absolutely in a portion, yet Evolvable from the whole ; evolved at last Painfully, held tenaciously by me." On the Organic Unity of the O. T., see Orr, Problem of the O. T., 27–51.

9. When the unity of the Scripture is fully recognized, the Bible, in spite of imperfections in matters non-essential to its religious purpose, furnishes a safe and sufficient guide to truth and to salvation.

The recognition of the Holy Spirit's agency makes it rational and natural to believe in the organic unity of Scripture. When the earlier parts are taken in connection with the later, and when each part is interpreted by the whole, most of the difficulties connected with inspiration disappear. Taken together, with Christ as its culmination and explanation, the Bible furnishes the Christian rule of faith and practice.

The Bible answers two questions : What has God done to save me ? and What must I do to be saved ? The propositions of Euclid are not invalidated by the fact that he believed the earth to be flat. The ethics of Plato would not be disproved by his mistakes with regard to the solar system. So religious authority is independent of merely secular knowledge.— Sir Joshua Reynolds was a great painter, and a great teacher of his art. His lectures on painting laid down principles which have been accepted as authority for generations. But Joshua Reynolds illustrates his subject from history and science. It was a day when both history and science were young. In some unimportant matters of this sort, which do not in the least affect his conclusions, Sir Joshua Reynolds makes an occasional slip ; his statements are inaccurate. Does he, therefore, cease to be an authority in matters of his art ?— The Duke of Wellington said once that no human being knew at what time of day the battle of Waterloo began. One historian gets his story from one combatant, and he puts the hour at eleven in the morning. Another historian gets his information from another combatant, and he puts it at noon. Shall we say that this discrepancy argues error in the whole account, and that we have no longer any certainty that the battle of Waterloo was ever fought at all ?

Such slight imperfections are to be freely admitted, while at the same time we insist that the Bible, taken as a whole, is incomparably superior to all other books, and is "able to make thee wise unto salvation "(2 Tim. 3: 15). Hooker, Eccl. Polity : " Whatsoever is spoken of God or things pertaining to God otherwise than truth is, though it seem an honor, it is an injury. And as incredible praises given unto men do often abate and impair the credit of their deserved commendation, so we must likewise take great heed lest, in attributing to Scripture more than it can have, the incredibility of that do cause even those things which it hath more abundantly to be less reverently esteemed." Baxter, Works, 21 : 349 — " Those men who think that these human imperfections of the writers do extend further, and may appear in some passages of chronologies or history which are no part of the rule of faith and life, do not hereby destroy the Christian cause. For God might enable his apostles to an infallible recording and preaching of the gospel, even all things necessary to salvation, though he had not made them infallible in every by-passage and circumstance, any more than they were indefectible in life."

The Bible, says Beet, " contains possible errors in small details or allusions, but it gives us with absolute certainty the great facts of Christianity, and upon these great facts, and upon these only, our faith is based." Evans, Bib. Scholarship and Inspiration, 15, 18, 65 — " Teach that the shell is part of the kernel and men who find that they cannot keep the shell will throw away shell and kernel together. . . . This overstatement of inspiration made Renan, Bradlaugh and Ingersoll sceptics. . . . If in creation God can work out a perfect result through imperfection why cannot he do the like in inspiration ? If in Christ God can appear in human weakness and ignorance, why not in the *written* word ? "

We therefore take exception to the view of Watts, New Apologetic, 71 — " Let the theory of historical errors and scientific errors be adopted, and Christianity must share the fate of Hinduism. If its inspired writers err when they tell us of earthly things, none will believe when they tell of heavenly things." Watts adduces instances of

Spinoza's giving up the form while claiming to hold the substance, and in this way reducing revelation to a phenomenon of naturalistic pantheism. We reply that no *a priori* theory of perfection in divine inspiration must blind us to the evidence of actual imperfection in Scripture. As in creation and in Christ, so in Scripture, God humbles himself to adopt human and imperfect methods of self-revelation. See Jonathan Edwards, Diary: " I observe that old men seldom have any advantage of new discoveries, because they are beside the way to which they have been so long used. *Resolved,* if ever I live to years, that I will be impartial to hear the reasons of all pretended discoveries, and receive them if rational, however long soever I have been used to another way of thinking."

Bowne, The Immanence of God, 109, 110 — " Those who would find the source of certainty and the seat of authority in the Scriptures alone, or in the church alone, or reason and conscience alone, rather than in the complex and indivisible coworking of all these factors, should be reminded of the history of religious thought. The stiffest doctrine of Scripture inerrancy has not prevented warring interpretations; and those who would place the seat of authority in reason and conscience are forced to admit that outside illumination may do much for both. In some sense the religion of the spirit is a very important fact, but when it sets up in opposition to the religion of a book, the light that is in it is apt to turn to darkness."

10. While inspiration constitutes Scripture an authority more trustworthy than are individual reason or the creeds of the church, the only ultimate authority is Christ himself.

Christ has not so constructed Scripture as to dispense with his personal presence and teaching by his Spirit. The Scripture is the imperfect mirror of Christ. It is defective, yet it reflects him and leads to him. Authority resides not in it, but in him, and his Spirit enables the individual Christian and the collective church progressively to distinguish the essential from the non-essential, and so to perceive the truth as it is in Jesus. In thus judging Scripture and interpreting Scripture, we are not rationalists, but are rather believers in him who promised to be with us alway even unto the end of the world and to lead us by his Spirit into all the truth.

James speaks of the law as a mirror (James 1 : 23-25 — "like unto a man beholding his natural face in a mirror . . . looketh into the perfect law"); the law convicts of sin because it reflects Christ. Paul speaks of the gospel as a mirror (2 Cor. 3 :18 — "we all, beholding as in a mirror the glory of the Lord"); the gospel transforms us because it reflects Christ. Yet both law and gospel are imperfect; they are like mirrors of polished metal, whose surface is often dim, and whose images are obscure ; (1 Cor. 13 : 12 — "For now we see in a mirror, darkly ; but then face to face ") ; even inspired men know only in part, and prophesy only in part. Scripture itself is the conception and utterance of a child, to be done away when that which is perfect is come, and we see Christ as he is.

Authority is the right to impose beliefs or to command obedience. The only ultimate authority is God, for he is truth, justice and love. But he can impose beliefs and command obedience only as he is known. Authority belongs therefore only to God revealed, and because Christ is God revealed he can say : "All authority hath been given unto me in heaven and on earth " (Mat. 28 :18). The final authority in religion is Jesus Christ. Every one of his revelations of God is authoritative. Both nature and human nature are such revelations. He exercises his authority through delegated and subordinate authorities, such as parents and civil government. These rightfully claim obedience so long as they hold to their own respective spheres and recognize their relation of dependence upon him. "The powers that be are ordained of God " (Rom. 13 :1), even though they are imperfect manifestations of his wisdom and righteousness. The decisions of the Supreme Court are authoritative even though the judges are fallible and come short of establishing absolute justice. Authority is not infallibility, in the government either of the family or of the state.

The church of the middle ages was regarded as possessed of absolute authority. But the Protestant Reformation showed how vain were these pretensions. The church is an authority only as it recognizes and expresses the supreme authority of Christ. The Reformers felt the need of some external authority in place of the church. They substituted the Scripture. The phrase "the word of God," which designates the truth orally uttered or affecting the minds of men, came to signify only a book. Supreme authority was ascribed to it. It often usurped the place of Christ. While we vindicate the proper authority of Scripture, we would show that its authority is not immediate and absolute, but mediate and relative, through human and imperfect records, and needing a supplementary and divine teaching to interpret them. The authority of Scripture is not apart from Christ or above Christ, but only in subordination to him and to his Spirit. He who inspired Scripture must enable us to interpret Scripture. This is not a doctrine of rationalism, for it holds to man's absolute dependence upon the enlightening Spirit of Christ. It is not a doctrine of mysticism, for it holds that Christ teaches us only by opening to us the meaning of his past revelations. We do not expect any new worlds in our astronomy, nor do we expect any new Scriptures in our theology. But we do expect that the same Christ who gave the Scriptures will give us new insight into their meaning and will enable us to make new applications of their teachings.

The right and duty of private judgment with regard to Scripture belong to no ecclesiastical caste, but are inalienable liberties of the whole church of Christ and of each individual member of that church. And yet this judgment is, from another point of view, no private judgment. It is not the judgment of arbitrariness or caprice. It does not make the Christian consciousness supreme, if we mean by this term the consciousness of Christians apart from the indwelling Christ. When once we come to Christ, he joins us to himself, he seats us with him upon his throne, he imparts to us his Spirit, he bids us use our reason in his service. In judging Scripture, we make not ourselves but Christ supreme, and recognize him as the only ultimate and infallible authority in matters of religion. We can believe that the total revelation of Christ in Scripture is an authority superior to individual reason or to any single affirmation of the church, while yet we believe that this very authority of Scripture has its limitation, and that Christ himself must teach us what this total revelation is. So the judgment which Scripture encourages us to pass upon its own limitations only induces a final and more implicit reliance upon the living and personal Son of God. He has never intended that Scripture should be a substitute for his own presence, and it is only his Spirit that is promised to lead us into all the truth.

On the authority of Scripture, see A. H. Strong, Christ in Creation, 113-136 — "The source of all authority is not Scripture, but Christ. . . Nowhere are we told that the Scripture of itself is able to convince the sinner or to bring him to God. It is a glittering sword, but it is 'the sword of the Spirit' (Eph. 6 :17); and unless the Spirit use it, it will never pierce the heart. It is a heavy hammer, but only the Spirit can wield it so that it breaks in pieces the flinty rock. It is the type locked in the form, but the paper will never receive an impression until the Spirit shall apply the power. No mere instrument shall have the glory that belongs to God. Every soul shall feel its entire dependence upon him. Only the Holy Spirit can turn the outer word into an inner word. And the Holy Spirit is the Spirit of Christ. Christ comes into direct contact with the soul. He himself gives his witness to the truth. He bears testimony to Scripture, even more than Scripture bears testimony to him."

11. The preceding discussion enables us at least to lay down three cardinal principles and to answer three common questions with regard to inspiration.

Principles : (a) The human mind can be inhabited and energized by God while yet attaining and retaining its own highest intelligence and freedom. (b) The Scriptures being the work of the one God, as well as of the men in whom God moved and dwelt, constitute an articulated and organic unity. (c) The unity and authority of Scripture as a whole are entirely consistent with its gradual evolution and with great imperfection in its non-essential parts.

Questions : (a) Is any part of Scripture uninspired? Answer : Every part of Scripture is inspired in its connection and relation with every other part. (b) Are there degrees of inspiration? Answer : There are degrees of value, but not of inspiration. Each part in its connection with the rest is made completely true, and completeness has no degrees. (c) How may we know what parts are of most value and what is the teaching of the whole ? Answer : The same Spirit of Christ who inspired the Bible is promised to take of the things of Christ, and, by showing them to us, to lead us progressively into all the truth.

Notice the value of the Old Testament, revealing as it does the natural attributes of God, as a basis and background for the revelation of mercy in the New Testament. Revelation was in many parts (πολυμερῶς — Heb. 1:1) as well as in many ways. "Each individual oracle, taken by itself, was partial and incomplete " (Robertson Smith, O. T. in Jewish Ch., 21). But the person and the words of Christ sum up and complete the revelation, so that, taken together and in their connection with him, the various parts of Scripture constitute an infallible and sufficient rule of faith and practice. See Browne, Inspiration of the N. T.; Bernard, Progress of Doctrine in the N. T.; Stanley Leathes, Structure of the O. T.; Rainy, Delivery and Development of Doctrine. See A. H. Strong, on Method of Inspiration, in Philosophy and Religion, 148-155.

The divine influence upon the minds of post-biblical writers, leading to the composition of such allegories as Pilgrim's Progress, and such dramas as Macbeth, is to be denominated illumination rather than inspiration, for the reasons that these writings contain error as well as truth in matters of religion and morals ; that they add nothing essential to what the Scriptures give us ; and that, even in their expression of truth previously made known, they are not worthy of a place in the sacred canon. W. H. P. Faunce : " How far is Bunyan's Pilgrim's Progress true to present Christian experience ? It is untrue : 1. In its despair of this world. The Pilgrim has to leave this world in order to be saved. Modern experience longs to do God's will *here*, and to save others instead of forsaking them. 2. In its agony over sin and frightful conflict. Bunyan illustrates modern experience better by Christiana and her children who go through the Valley and the Shadow of Death in the daytime, and without conflict with Apollyon. 3. In the constant uncertainty of the issue of the Pilgrim's fight. Christian enters Doubting Castle and meets Giant Despair, even after he has won most of his victories. In modern experience, "at evening time there shall be light " — (Zech. 14 : 7). 4. In the constant conviction of an absent Christ. Bunyan's Christ is never met this side of the Celestial City. The Cross at which the burden dropped is the symbol of a sacrificial act, but it is not the Savior himself. Modern experience has Christ living in us and with us alway, and not simply a Christ whom we hope to see at the end of the journey."

Beyschlag, N. T. Theol., 2 : 18 — " Paul declares his own prophecy and inspiration to be essentially imperfect (1 Cor. 13 : 9, 10, 12 ; *cf.* 1 Cor. 12 : 10 ; 1 Thess. 5 : 19-21). This admission justifies a Christian criticism even of his views. He can pronounce an anathema on those who preach 'a different gospel' (Gal. 1 : 8, 9), for what belongs to simple faith, the facts of salvation, are absolutely certain. But where prophetic thought and speech go beyond these facts of salvation, wood and straw may be mingled with the gold, silver and precious stones upon the one foundation. So he distinguishes his own modest γνώμη from the ἐπιταγὴ κυρίου (1 Cor. 7 : 25, 40)." Clarke, Christian Theology, 44 — " The authority of Scripture is not one that binds, but one that sets free. Paul is writing of Scripture when he says : 'Not that we have lordship over your faith, but are helpers of your joy : for in faith ye stand fast' (2 Cor. 1 : 24)."

Cremer, in Herzog, Realencyc., 183-203 — " The church doctrine is *that* the Scriptures are inspired, but it has never been determined by the church *how* they are inspired." Butler, Analogy, part II, chap. III — " The only question concerning the truth of Christianity is, whether it be a real revelation, not whether it be attended with every circumstance which we should have looked for ; and concerning the authority of Scripture, whether it be what it claims to be, not whether it be a book of such sort, and so promulgated, as weak men are apt to fancy a book containing a divine revelation should. And therefore, neither obscurity, nor seeming inaccuracy of style, nor various readings, nor early disputes about the authors of particular parts, nor any other things of the like kind, though they had been much more considerable than they are, could overthrow the authority of the Scripture ; unless the prophets, apostles, or our Lord had promised that the book containing the divine revelation should be secure from these things." W. Robertson Smith : " If I am asked why I receive the Scriptures as the word of God and as the only perfect rule of faith and life, I answer with all the Fathers of the Protestant church : ' Because the Bible is the only record of the redeeming love of God ; because in the Bible alone I find God drawing nigh to men in Jesus

Christ, and declaring his will for our salvation. And the record I know to be true by the witness of his Spirit in my heart, whereby I am assured that none other than God himself is able to speak such words to my soul." The gospel of Jesus Christ is the ἅπαξ λεγόμενον of the Almighty. See Marcus Dods, The Bible, its Origin and Nature; Bowne, The Immanence of God, 66-115.

V. Objections to the Doctrine of Inspiration.

In connection with a divine-human work like the Bible, insoluble difficulties may be expected to present themselves. So long, however, as its inspiration is sustained by competent and sufficient evidence, these difficulties cannot justly prevent our full acceptance of the doctrine, any more than disorder and mystery in nature warrant us in setting aside the proofs of its divine authorship. These difficulties are lessened with time ; some have already disappeared ; many may be due to ignorance, and may be removed hereafter ; those which are permanent may be intended to stimulate inquiry and to discipline faith.

It is noticeable that the common objections to inspiration are urged, not so much against the religious teaching of the Scriptures, as against certain errors in secular matters which are supposed to be interwoven with it. But if these are proved to be errors indeed, it will not necessarily overthrow the doctrine of inspiration ; it will only compel us to give a larger place to the human element in the composition of the Scriptures, and to regard them more exclusively as a text-book of religion. As a rule of religious faith and practice, they will still be the infallible word of God. The Bible is to be judged as a book whose one aim is man's rescue from sin and reconciliation to God, and in these respects it will still be found a record of substantial truth. This will appear more fully as we examine the objections one by one.

"The Scriptures are given to teach us, not how the heavens go, but how to go to heaven." Their aim is certainly not to teach science or history, except so far as science or history is essential to their moral and religious purpose. Certain of their doctrines, like the virgin-birth of Christ and his bodily resurrection, are historical facts, and certain facts, like that of creation, are also doctrines. With regard to these great facts, we claim that inspiration has given us accounts that are essentially trustworthy, whatever may be their imperfections in detail. To undermine the scientific trustworthiness of the Indian Vedas is to undermine the religion which they teach. But this only because their scientific doctrine is an essential part of their religious teaching. In the Bible, religion is not dependent upon physical science. The Scriptures aim only to declare the creatorship and lordship of the personal God. The method of his working may be described pictorially without affecting this substantial truth. The Indian cosmogonies, on the other hand, polytheistic or pantheistic as they are, teach essential untruth, by describing the origin of things as due to a series of senseless transformations without basis of will or wisdom.

So long as the difficulties of Scripture are difficulties of form rather than substance, of its incidental features rather than its main doctrine, we may say of its obscurities as Isocrates said of the work of Heraclitus: "What I understand of it is so excellent that I can draw conclusions from it concerning what I do not understand." "If Bengel finds things in the Bible too hard for his critical faculty, he finds nothing too hard for his believing faculty." With John Smyth, who died at Amsterdam in 1612, we may say: "I profess I have changed, and shall be ready still to change, for the better"; and with John Robinson, in his farewell address to the Pilgrim Fathers: "I am verily persuaded that the Lord hath more truth yet to break forth from his holy word." See Luthardt, Saving Truths, 205 ; Philippi, Glaubenslehre, 205 sq. ; Bap. Rev., April, 1881; art. by O. P. Eaches ; Cardinal Newman. in 19th Century, Feb. 1884.

1. *Errors in matters of Science.*

Upon this objection we remark :

(*a*) We do not admit the existence of scientific error in the Scripture. What is charged as such is simply truth presented in popular and impres·sive forms.

The common mind receives a more correct idea of unfamiliar facts when these are narrated in phenomenal language and in summary form than when they are described in the abstract terms and in the exact detail of science.

The Scripture writers unconsciously observe Herbert Spencer's principle of style: Economy of the reader's or hearer's attention,—the more energy is expended upon the form the less there remains to grapple with the substance (Essays, 1-47). Wendt, Teaching of Jesus, 1 : 130, brings out the principle of Jesus' style: "The greatest clearness in the smallest compass." Hence Scripture uses the phrases of common life rather than scientific terminology. Thus the language of appearance is probably used in Gen. 7:19—"all the high mountains that were under the whole heaven were covered"—such would be the appearance, even if the deluge were local instead of universal ; in Josh. 10 : 12, 13 — "and the sun stood still"—such would be the appearance, even if the sun's rays were merely refracted so as preternaturally to lengthen the day; in Ps. 93:1 — "The world also is established, that it cannot be moved"—such is the appearance, even though the earth turns on its axis and moves round the sun. In narrative, to substitute for "sunset" some scientific description would divert attention from the main subject. Would it be preferable, in the O. T., if we should read : "When the revolution of the earth upon its axis caused the rays of the solar luminary to impinge horizontally upon the retina, Isaac went out to meditate" (Gen. 24 : 63)? "Le secret d'ennuyer est de tout dire." Charles Dickens, in his American Notes, 72, describes a prairie sunset: "The decline of day here was very gorgeous, tinging the firmament deeply with red and gold, up to the very keystone of the arch above us" (quoted by Hovey, Manual of Christian Theology, 97). Did Dickens therefore believe the firmament to be a piece of solid masonry ?

Canon Driver rejects the Bible story of creation because the distinctions made by modern science cannot be found in the primitive Hebrew. He thinks the fluid state of the earth's substance should have been called "surging chaos," instead of "waters" (Gen. 1:2). "An admirable phrase for modern and cultivated minds," replies Mr. Gladstone, "but a phrase that would have left the pupils of the Mosaic writer in exactly the condition out of which it was his purpose to bring them, namely, a state of utter ignorance and darkness, with possibly a little ripple of bewilderment to boot " ; see Sunday School Times, April 26, 1890. The fallacy of holding that Scripture gives in detail all the facts connected with a historical narrative has led to many curious arguments. The Gregorian Calendar which makes the year begin in January was opposed by representing that Eve was tempted at the outset by an apple, which was possible only in case the year began in September ; see Thayer, Change of Attitude towards the Bible, 46.

(*b*) It is not necessary to a proper view of inspiration to suppose that the human authors of Scripture had in mind the proper scientific interpretation of the natural events they recorded.

It is enough that this was in the mind of the inspiring Spirit. Through the comparatively narrow conceptions and inadequate language of the Scripture writers, the Spirit of inspiration may have secured the expression of the truth in such germinal form as to be intelligible to the times in which it was first published, and yet capable of indefinite expansion as science should advance. In the miniature picture of creation in the first chapter of Genesis, and in its power of adjusting itself to every advance of scientific investigation, we have a strong proof of inspiration.

The word "day" in Genesis 1 is an instance of this general mode of expression. It would be absurd to teach early races, that deal only in small numbers, about the myriads of years of creation. The child's object-lesson, with its graphic summary, conveys to his mind more of truth than elaborate and exact statement would convey. Conant (Genesis 2 : 10) says of the description of Eden and its rivers: " Of course the author's object is not a minute topographical description, but a general and impressive conception as a whole." Yet the progress of science only shows that these accounts are not less but more true than was supposed by those who first received them. Neither the Hindu Shasters nor any heathen cosmogony can bear such comparison with the results of science. Why change our interpretations of Scripture so often ? Answer : We do not assume to be original teachers of science, but only to interpret Scripture with the new lights we have. See Dana, Manual of Geology, 741-746 ; Guyot, in Bib. Sac., 1855 : 324 ; Dawson, Story of Earth and Man, 32.

This conception of early Scripture teaching as elementary and suited to the childhood of the race would make it possible, if the facts so required, to interpret the early chapters of Genesis as mythical or legendary. God might condescend to " Kindergarten formulas." Goethe said that " We should deal with children as God deals with us : we are happiest under the influence of innocent delusions." Longfellow : " How beautiful is youth ! how bright it gleams, With its illusions, aspirations, dreams! Book of beginnings, story without end, Each maid a heroine, and each man a friend ! " We might hold with Goethe and with Longfellow, if we only excluded from God's teaching all essential error. The narratives of Scripture might be addressed to the imagination, and so might take mythical or legendary form, while yet they conveyed substantial truth that could in no other way be so well apprehended by early man ; see Robert Browning's poem, " Development," in Asolando. The Koran, on the other hand, leaves no room for imagination, but fixes the number of the stars and declares the firmament to be solid. Henry Drummond : " Evolution has given us a new Bible. . . . The Bible is not a book which has been made, — it has grown."

Bagehot tells us that " One of the most remarkable of Father Newman's Oxford sermons explains how science teaches that the earth goes round the sun, and how Scripture teaches that the sun goes round the earth ; and it ends by advising the discreet believer to accept both." This is mental bookkeeping by double entry ; see Mackintosh, in Am. Jour. Theology, Jan. 1899 : 41. Lenormant, in Contemp. Rev., Nov. 1879 — " While the tradition of the deluge holds so considerable a place in the legendary memories of all branches of the Aryan race, the monuments and original texts of Egypt, with their many cosmogonic speculations, have not afforded any, even distant, allusion to this cataclysm." Lenormant here wrongly assumed that the language of Scripture is scientific language. If it is the language of appearance, then the deluge may be a local and not a universal catastrophe. G. F. Wright, Ice Age in North America, suggests that the numerous traditions of the deluge may have had their origin in the enormous floods of the receding glacier. In South-western Queensland, the standard guage at the Meteorological Office registered 10¼, 20, 35½, 10¼ inches of rainfall, in all 77¼ inches, in four successive days.

(c) It may be safely said that science has not yet shown any fairly interpreted passage of Scripture to be untrue.

With regard to the antiquity of the race, we may say that owing to the differences of reading between the Septuagint and the Hebrew there is room for doubt whether either of the received chronologies has the sanction of inspiration. Although science has made probable the existence of man upon the earth at a period preceding the dates assigned in these chronologies, no statement of inspired Scripture is thereby proved false.

Usher's scheme of chronology, on the basis of the Hebrew, puts the creation 4004 years before Christ. Hales's, on the basis of the Septuagint, puts it 5411 B. C. The Fathers followed the LXX. But the genealogies before and after the flood may present us only with the names of " leading and representative men." Some of these names seem to stand, not for individuals, but for tribes, e. g.: Gen. 10 : 16 — where Canaan is said to have begotten the Jebusite and the Amorite ; 29 — Joktan begot Ophir and Havilah. In Gen. 10 : 6, we read that Mizraim belonged to the sons of Ham. But Mizraim is a dual, coined to designate the two parts, Upper and Lower Egypt. Hence a son of Ham could not bear the name of Mizraim. Gen. 10 : 13 reads : "And Mizraim begat Ludim." But Ludim is a plural form. The word signifies a whole nation, and "begat" is not employed in a literal sense. So in verses 15, 16 : "Canaan begat . . . the Jebusite," a tribe ; the ancestors of which would have been called Jebus. Abraham, Isaac and Jacob, however, are names, not of tribes or nations, but of individuals ; see Prof. Edward König, of Bonn, in S. S. Times, Dec. 14, 1901. E. G. Robinson : " We may pretty safely go back to the time of Abraham, but no further." Bib. Sac., 1899 : 403 — " The lists in Genesis may relate to families and not to individuals."

G. F. Wright, Ant. and Origin of Human Race, lect. II — " When in David's time it is said that 'Shebuel, the son of Gershom, the son of Moses, was ruler over the treasures' (1 Chron. 23 : 16; 26 : 24), Gershom was the immediate son of Moses, but Shebuel was separated by many generations from Gershom. So when Seth is said to have begotten Enosh when he was 105 years old (Gen. 5 : 6), it is, according to Hebrew usage, capable of meaning that Enosh was descended from the branch of Seth's line which set off at the 105th year, with any number of intermediate links omitted." The appearance of completeness in the text may be due to alteration of the text in the course of centuries ; see Bib. Com., 1 : 30. In the phrase " Jesus Christ, the son of David, the son of Abraham " (Mat. 1 : 1) thirty-eight to forty generations are omitted. It may be so in some of the Old Testament genealogies. There is room for a hundred thousand years, if necessary (Conant). W. H. Green, in Bib. Sac., April, 1890 : 303, and in Independent, June 18, 1891 — " The Scriptures furnish us with no data for a chronological computation prior to the life of Abraham. The Mosaic records do not fix, and were not intended to fix, the precise date of the Flood or of the Creation . . . They give a series of specimen lives, with appropriate numbers attached, to show by selected examples what was the original term of human life. To make them a complete and continuous record, and to deduce from them the antiquity of the race, is to put them to a use they were never intended to serve."

Comparison with secular history also shows that no such length of time as 100.000 years for man's existence upon earth seems necessary. Rawlinson, in Jour. Christ. Philosophy, 1883 : 339–364, dates the beginning of the Chaldean monarchy at 2400 B. C. Lenormant puts the entrance of the Sanskritic Indians into Hindustan at 2500 B. C. The earliest Vedas are between 1200 and 1000 B. C. (Max Müller). Call of Abraham, probably 1945 B. C. Chinese history possibly began as early as 2356 B. C. (Legge). The old Empire in Egypt possibly began as early as 2650 B. C. Rawlinson puts the flood at 3600 B. C., and adds 2000 years between the deluge and the creation, making the age of the world 1886 + 3600 + 2000 = 7486. S. R. Pattison, in Present Day Tracts, 3 : no. 13, concludes that " a term of about 8000 years is warranted by deductions from history, geology, and Scripture." See also Duke of Argyll, Primeval Man, 76–128; Cowles on Genesis, 49–80; Dawson, Fossil Men, 246; Hicks, in Bap. Rev., July, 1884 (15000 years) Zöckler, Urgeschichte der Erde und des Menschen, 137–163. On the critical side, see Crooker, The New Bible and its Uses, 80–102.

Evidence of a geological nature seems to be accumulating, which tends to prove man's advent upon earth at least ten thousand years ago. An arrowhead of tempered copper and a number of human bones were found in the Rocky Point mines, near Gilman, Colorado, 460 feet beneath the surface of the earth, embedded in a vein of silver-bearing ore. More than a hundred dollars worth of ore clung to the bones when they were removed from the mine. On the age of the earth and the antiquity of man, see G. F. Wright, Man and the Glacial Epoch, lectures IV and X, and in McClure's Magazine, June, 1901. and Bib. Sac., 1903 : 31 — " Charles Darwin first talked about 300 million years as a mere trifle of geologic time. His son George limits it to 50 or 100 million ; Croll and Young to 60 or 70 million ; Wallace to 28 million ; Lord Kelvin to 24 million ; Thompson and Newcomb to only 10 million." Sir Archibald Geikie, at the British Association at Dover in 1899, said that 100 million years sufficed for that small portion of the earth's history which is registered in the stratified rocks of the crust.

Shaler, Interpretation of Nature, 122, considers vegetable life to have existed on the planet for at least 100 million years. Warren Upham, in Pop. Science Monthly, Dec. 1893 : 153 — " How old is the earth? 100 million years." D. G. Brinton, in Forum, Dec. 1893 : 454, puts the minimum limit of man's existence on earth at 50,000 years. G. F. Wright does not doubt that man's presence on this continent was preglacial, say eleven or twelve thousand years ago. He asserts that there has been a subsidence of Central Asia and Southern Russia since man's advent, and that Arctic seals are still found in Lake Baikal in Siberia. While he grants that Egyptian civilization may go back to 5000 B. C., he holds that no more than 6000 or 7000 years before this are needed as preparation for history. Le Conte, Elements of Geology, 613 — " Men saw the great glaciers of the second glacial epoch, but there is no reliable evidence of their existence before the first glacial epoch. Deltas, implements, lake shores, waterfalls, indicate only 7000 to

15

10,000 years.   Recent calculations of Prof. Prestwich, the most eminent living geologist of Great Britain, tend to bring the close of the glacial epoch down to within 10,000 or 15,000 years.

(*d*) Even if error in matters of science were found in Scripture, it would not disprove inspiration, since inspiration concerns itself with science only so far as correct scientific views are necessary to morals and religion.

Great harm results from identifying Christian doctrine with specific theories of the universe. The Roman church held that the revolution of the sun around the earth was taught in Scripture, and that Christian faith required the condemnation of Galileo; John Wesley thought Christianity to be inseparable from a belief in witchcraft; opposers of the higher criticism regard the Mosaic authorship of the Pentateuch as "articulus stantis vel cadentis ecclesiæ." We mistake greatly when we link inspiration with scientific doctrine. The purpose of Scripture is not to teach science, but to teach religion, and, with the exception of God's creatorship and preserving agency in the universe, no scientific truth is essential to the system of Christian doctrine. Inspiration might leave the Scripture writers in possession of the scientific ideas of their time, while yet they were empowered correctly to declare both ethical and religious truth. A right spirit indeed gains some insight into the meaning of nature, and so the Scripture writers seem to be preserved from incorporating into their productions much of the scientific error of their day. But entire freedom from such error must not be regarded as a necessary accompaniment of inspiration.

2.   *Errors in matters of History.*

To this objection we reply :

(*a*) What are charged as such are often mere mistakes in transcription, and have no force as arguments against inspiration, unless it can first be shown that inspired documents are by the very fact of their inspiration exempt from the operation of those laws which affect the transmission of other ancient documents.

We have no right to expect that the inspiration of the original writer will be followed by a miracle in the case of every copyist. Why believe in infallible copyists, more than in infallible printers? God educates us to care for his word, and for its correct transmission. Reverence has kept the Scriptures more free from various readings than are other ancient manuscripts. None of the existing variations endanger any important article of faith. Yet some mistakes in transcription there probably are. In 1 Chron. 22 : 14, instead of 100,000 talents of gold and 1,000,000 talents of silver (= $3,750,000,000), Josephus divides the sum by ten. Dr. Howard Osgood : "A French writer, Revillout, has accounted for the differing numbers in Kings and Chronicles, just as he accounts for the same differences in Egyptian and Assyrian later accounts, by the change in the value of money and debasement of issues. He shows the change all over Western Asia." *Per contra*, see Bacon, Genesis of Genesis, 45.

In 2 Chron. 13 : 3, 17, where the numbers of men in the armies of little Palestine are stated as 400,000 and 800,000, and 500,000 are said to have been slain in a single battle, "some ancient copies of the Vulgate and Latin translations of Josephus have 40,000, 80,000, and 50,000 "; see Annotated Paragraph Bible, *in loco*. In 2 Chron. 17 : 14-19, Jehoshaphat's army aggregates 1,160,000, besides the garrisons of his fortresses. It is possible that by errors in transcription these numbers have been multiplied by ten. Another explanation however, and perhaps a more probable one, is given under (*d*) below. Similarly, compare 1 Sam. 6 : 19, where 50,070 are slain, with the 70 of Josephus; 2 Sam. 8 : 4 — "1,700 horsemen," with 1 Chron. 18 : 4 — "7,000 horsemen"; Esther 9 : 16 — 75,000 slain by the Jews, with LXX — 15,000. In Mat. 27 : 9, we have "Jeremiah" for "Zechariah" — this Calvin allows to be a mistake ; and, if a mistake, then one made by the first copyist, for it appears in all the uncials, all the manuscripts and all the versions except the Syriac Peshito where it is omitted, evidently on the authority of the individual transcriber and translator. In Acts 7 : 16 — "the tomb that Abraham bought " — Hackett regards "Abraham" as a clerical error for "Jacob" (compare Gen. 33 : 18, 19). See Bible Com., 3 : 165, 249, 251, 217.

(*b*) Other so-called errors are to be explained as a permissible use of round numbers, which cannot be denied to the sacred writers except upon the principle that mathematical accuracy was more important than the general impression to be secured by the narrative.

In Numbers 25 : 9, we read that there fell in the plague 24,000 ; 1 Cor. 10 : 8 says 23,000. The actual number was possibly somewhere between the two. Upon a similar principle, we do not scruple to celebrate the Landing of the Pilgrims on December 22nd and the birth of Christ on December 25th. We speak of the battle of Bunker Hill, although at Bunker Hill no battle was really fought. In Ex. 12 : 40, 41, the sojourn of the Israelites in Egypt is declared to be 430 years. Yet Paul, in Gal. 3 : 17, says that the giving of the law through Moses was 430 years after the call of Abraham, whereas the call of Abraham took place 215 years before Jacob and his sons went down into Egypt, and Paul should have said 645 years instead of 430. Franz Delitzsch : "The Hebrew Bible counts four centuries of Egyptian sojourn (Gen. 15 : 13-16), more accurately, 430 years (Ex. 12 : 40); but according to the LXX (Ex. 12 : 40) this number comprehends the sojourn in Canaan and Egypt, so that 215 years come to the pilgrimage in Canaan, and 215 to the servitude in Egypt. This kind of calculation is not exclusively Hellenistic ; it is also found in the oldest Palestinian Midrash. Paul stands on this side in Gal. 3 : 17, making, not the immigration into Egypt, but the covenant with Abraham the *terminus a quo* of the 430 years which end in the Exodus from Egypt and in the legislation " ; see also Hovey, Com. on Gal. 3 : 17. It was not Paul's purpose to write chronology,— so he may follow the LXX, and call the time between the promise to Abraham and the giving of the law to Moses 430 years, rather than the actual 600. If he had given one larger number, it might have led to perplexity and discussion about a matter which had nothing to do with the vital question in hand. Inspiration may have employed current though inaccurate statements as to matters of history, because they were the best available means of impressing upon men's minds truth of a more important sort. In Gen. 15 : 13 the 430 years is called in round numbers 400 years, and so in Acts 7 : 6.

(*c*) Diversities of statement in accounts of the same event, so long as they touch no substantial truth, may be due to the meagreness of the narrative, and might be fully explained if some single fact, now unrecorded, were only known. To explain these apparent discrepancies would not only be beside the purpose of the record, but would destroy one valuable evidence of the independence of the several writers or witnesses.

On the Stokes trial, the judge spoke of two apparently conflicting testimonies as neither of them necessarily false. On the difference between Matthew and Luke as to the scene of the Sermon on the Mount (Mat. 5 : 1 ; *cf.* Luke 6 : 17) see Stanley, Sinai and Palestine, 360. As to one blind man or two (Mat. 20 : 30 ; *cf.* Luke 18 : 35) see Bliss, Com. on Luke, 275, and Gardiner, in Bib. Sac., July, 1879 : 513, 514 ; Jesus may have healed the blind men during a day's excursion from Jericho, and it might be described as " when they went out," or " as they drew nigh to Jericho." Prof. M. B. Riddle : " Luke 18 : 35 describes the general movement towards Jerusalem and not the precise detail preceding the miracle ; Mat. 20 : 30 intimates that the miracle occurred during an excursion from the city,— Luke afterwards telling of the final departure " ; Calvin holds to two meetings ; Godet to two cities ; if Jesus healed two blind men, he certainly healed one, and Luke did not need to mention more than one, even if he knew of both ; see Broadus on Mat. 20 : 30. In Mat. 8 : 28, where Matthew has two demoniacs at Gadara and Luke has only one at Gerasa, Broadus supposes that the village of Gerasa belonged to the territory of the city of Gadara, a few miles to the Southeast of the lake, and he quotes the case of Lafayette : " In the year 1824 Lafayette visited the United States and was welcomed with honors and pageants. Some historians will mention only Lafayette, but others will relate the same visit as made and the same honors as enjoyed by two persons, namely, Lafayette and his son. Will not both be right ? " On Christ's last Passover, see Robinson, Harmony, 212 ; E. H. Sears, Fourth Gospel, Appendix A ; Edersheim, Life and Times of the Messiah, 2 : 507. Augustine : " Locutiones variæ, sed non contrariæ : diversæ, sed non adversæ."

Bartlett, in Princeton Rev., Jan. 1880 : 46, 47, gives the following modern illustrations : Winslow's Journal (of Plymouth Plantation) speaks of a ship sent out " by Master Thomas Weston." But Bradford in his far briefer narrative of the matter, mentions it as sent "by Mr. Weston and another." John Adams, in his letters, tells the story of the daughter of Otis about her father's destruction of his own manuscripts. At one time he makes her say: "In one of his unhappy moments he committed them all to the flames"; yet, in the second letter, she is made to say that "he was several days in doing it." One newspaper says: President Hayes attended the Bennington centennial; another newspaper says: the President and Mrs. Hayes; a third: the President and his Cabinet; a fourth: the President, Mrs. Hayes and a majority of his Cabinet. Archibald Forbes, in his account of Napoleon III at Sedan, points out an agreement of narratives as to the salient points, combined with "the hopeless and bewildering discrepancies as to details," even as these are reported by eye-witnesses, including himself, Bismarck, and General Sheridan who was on the ground, as well as others.

Thayer, Change of Attitude, 52, speaks of Luke's "plump anachronism in the matter of Theudas"— Acts 5 : 36 — "For before those days rose up Theudas." Josephus, Antiquities, 20 : 5 : 1, mentions an insurrectionary Theudas, but the date and other incidents do not agree with those of Luke. Josephus however may have mistaken the date as easily as Luke, or he may refer to another man of the same name. The inscription on the Cross is given in Mark 15 : 26, as "The King of the Jews"; in Luke 23 : 38, as "This is the King of the Jews"; in Mat. 27 : 37, as "This is Jesus the King of the Jews"; and in John 19 : 19, as "Jesus of Nazareth the King of the Jews." The entire superscription, in Hebrew, Greek and Latin, may have contained every word given by the several evangelists combined, and may have read "This is Jesus of Nazareth, the King of the Jews," and each separate report may be entirely correct so far as it goes. See, on the general subject, Haley, Alleged Discrepancies; Fisher, Beginnings of Christianity, 406-412.

(d) While historical and archæological discovery in many important particulars goes to sustain the general correctness of the Scripture narratives, and no statement essential to the moral and religious teaching of Scripture has been invalidated, inspiration is still consistent with much imperfection in historical detail and its narratives "do not seem to be exempted from possibilities of error."

The words last quoted are those of Sanday. In his Bampton Lectures on Inspiration, 400, he remarks that "Inspiration belongs to the historical books rather as conveying a religious lesson, than as histories; rather as interpreting, than as narrating plain matter of fact. The crucial issue is that in these last respects they do not seem to be exempted from possibilities of error." R. V. Foster, Systematic Theology, (Cumberland Presbyterian): The Scripture writers "were not inspired to do otherwise than to take these statements as they found them." Inerrancy is not freedom from misstatements, but from error defined as "that which misleads in any serious or important sense." When we compare the accounts of 1 and 2 Chronicles with those of 1 and 2 Kings we find in the former an exaggeration of numbers, a suppression of material unfavorable to the writer's purpose, and an emphasis upon that which is favorable, that contrasts strongly with the method of the latter. These characteristics are so continuous that the theory of mistakes in transcription does not seem sufficient to account for the facts. The author's aim was to draw out the religious lessons of the story, and historical details are to him of comparative unimportance.

H. P. Smith, Bib. Scholarship and Inspiration, 108 — "Inspiration did not correct the Chronicler's historical point of view, more than it corrected his scientific point of view, which no doubt made the earth the centre of the solar system. It therefore left him open to receive documents, and to use them, which idealized the history of the past, and described David and Solomon according to the ideas of later times and the priestly class. David's sins are omitted, and numbers are multiplied, to give greater dignity to the earlier kingdom." As Tennyson's Idylls of the King give a nobler picture of King Arthur, and a more definite aspect to his history, than actual records justify, yet the picture teaches great moral and religious lessons, so the Chronicler seems to have manipulated his material in the interest of religion. Matters of arithmetic were minor matters. "Majoribus intentus est."

E. G. Robinson: "The numbers of the Bible are characteristic of a semi-barbarous age. The writers took care to guess enough. The tendency of such an age is always to exaggerate." Two Formosan savages divide five pieces between them by taking two apiece and throwing one away. The lowest tribes can count only with the fingers of their hands: when they use their toes as well, it marks an advance in civilization. To tne modern child a hundred is just as great a number as a million. So the early Scriptures seem to use numbers with a childlike ignorance as to their meaning. Hundreds of thousands can be substituted for tens of thousands, and the substitution seems only a proper tribute to the dignity of the subject. Gore, in Lux Mundi, 353 — "This was not conscious perversion, but unconscious idealizing of history, the reading back into past records of a ritual development which was really later. Inspiration excludes conscious deception, but it appears to be quite consistent with this sort of idealizing; always supposing that the result read back into the earlier history does represent the real purpose of God and only anticipates the realization."

There are some who contend that these historical imperfections are due to transcription and that they did not belong to the original documents. Watts, New Apologetic, 71, 111, when asked what is gained by contending for infallible original autographs if they have been since corrupted, replies: "Just what we gain by contending for the original perfection of human nature, though man has since corrupted it. We must believe God's own testimony about his own work. God may permit others to do what, as a holy righteous God, he cannot do himself." When the objector declares it a matter of little consequence whether a pair of trousers were or were not originally perfect, so long as they are badly rent just now, Watts replies: "The tailor who made them would probably prefer to have it understood that the trousers did not leave his shop in their present forlorn condition. God drops no stitches and sends out no imperfect work." Watts however seems dominated by an *a priori* theory of inspiration, which blinds him to the actual facts of the Bible.

Evans, Bib. Scholarship and Inspiration, 40 — "Does the *present* error destroy the inspiration of the Bible as we have it? No. Then why should the *original* error destroy the inspiration of the Bible, as it was first given? There are spots on yonder sun; do they stop its being the sun? Why, the sun is all the more a sun for the spots. So the Bible." Inspiration seems to have permitted the gathering of such material as was at hand, very much as a modern editor might construct his account of an army movement from the reports of a number of observers; or as a modern historian might combine the records of a past age with all their imperfections of detail. In the case of the Scripture writers, however, we maintain that inspiration has permitted no sacrifice of moral and religious truth in the completed Scripture, but has woven its historical material together into an organic whole which teaches all the facts essential to the knowledge of Christ and of salvation.

When we come to examine in detail what purport to be historical narratives, we must be neither credulous nor sceptical, but simply candid and open-minded. With regard for example to the great age of the Old Testament patriarchs, we are no more warranted in rejecting the Scripture accounts upon the ground that life in later times is so much shorter, than we are to reject the testimony of botanists as to trees of the Sequoia family between four and five hundred feet high, or the testimony of geologists as to Saurians a hundred feet long, upon the ground that the trees and reptiles with which we are acquainted are so much smaller. Every species at its introduction seems to exhibit the maximum of size and vitality. Weismann, Heredity, 6, 30 — "Whales live some hundreds of years; elephants two hundred — their gestation taking two years. Giants prove that the plan upon which man is constructed can also be carried out on a scale far larger than the normal one." E. Ray Lankester, Adv. of Science, 205-237, 2 6 — agrees with Weismann in his general theory. Sir George Cornewall Lewis long denied centenarism, but at last had to admit it.

Charles Dudley Warner, in Harper's Magazine, Jan. 1895, gives instances of men 137, 140, and 192 years old. The German Haller asserts that "the ultimate limit of human life does not exceed two centuries: to fix the exact number of years is exceedingly difficult." J. Norman Lockyer, in Nature, regards the years of the patriarchs as lunar years. In Egypt, the sun being used, the unit of time was a year; but in Chaldea, the unit of time was a month, for the reason that the standard of time was the moon. Divide the numbers by twelve, and the lives of the patriarchs come out very much the same length with lives at the present day. We may ask, however, how this theory would work in shortening the lives between Noah and Moses. On the genealogies in Matthew and Luke, see Lord Harvey, Genealogies of our Lord, and his art. in Smith's Bible Dictionary; *per contra*, see Andrews, Life of Christ, 55 *sq*. On Quirinius and the enrollment for taxation (Luke 2: 2), see Pres. Woolsey, in New Englander, 1869. On the general subject, see Rawlinson, Historical Evidences, and essay in Modern Scepticism, published by Christian Evidence Society, 1: 265; Crooker, New Bible and New Uses, 102-126.

3. *Errors in Morality.*

(*a*) What are charged as such are sometimes evil acts and words of good men — words and acts not sanctioned by God. These are narrated by the inspired writers as simple matter of history, and subsequent results, or the story itself, is left to point the moral of the tale.

Instances of this sort are Noah's drunkenness (Gen. 9 : 20–27); Lot's incest (Gen. 19 : 30–38); Jacob's falsehood (Gen. 27 : 19–24); David's adultery (2 Sam. 11 : 1–4); Peter's denial (Mat. 26 : 69–75). See Lee, Inspiration, 265, note. Esther's vindictiveness is not commended, nor are the characters of the Book of Esther said to have acted in obedience to a divine command. Crane, Religion of To-morrow, 241 — " In law and psalm and prophecy we behold the influence of Jehovah working as leaven among a primitive and barbarous people. Contemplating the Old Scriptures in this light, they become luminous with divinity, and we are furnished with the principle by which to discriminate between the divine and the human in the book. Particularly in David do we see a rugged, half-civilized, kingly man, full of gross errors, fleshly and impetuous, yet permeated with a divine Spirit that lifts him, struggling, weeping, and warring, up to some of the lofti-est conceptions of Deity which the mind of man has conceived. As an angelic being, David is a caricature ; as a man of God, as an example of God moving upon and raising up a most human man, he is a splendid example. The proof that the church is of God, is not its impeccability, but its progress."

(*b*) Where evil acts appear at first sight to be sanctioned, it is frequently some right intent or accompanying virtue, rather than the act itself, upon which commendation is bestowed.

As Rahab's faith, not her duplicity (Josh. 2 : 1–24 ; *cf.* Heb. 11 : 31 and James 2 : 25); Jael's patriotism, not her treachery (Judges 4 : 17–22 ; *cf.* 5 : 24). Or did they cast in their lot with Israel and use the common stratagems of war (see next paragraph)? Herder: " The limitations of the pupil are also limitations of the teacher." While Dean Stanley praises Solomon for tolerating idolatry, James Martineau, Study, 2 : 137, remarks: " It would be a ridiculous pedantry to apply the Protestant pleas of private judgment to such communities as ancient Egypt and Assyria. . . . It is the survival of coercion, after conscience has been born to supersede it, that shocks and revolts us in persecu-tion."

(*c*) Certain commands and deeds are sanctioned as relatively just — expressions of justice such as the age could comprehend, and are to be judged as parts of a progressively unfolding system of morality whose key and culmination we have in Jesus Christ.

Ex. 20 : 25 — " I gave them statutes that were not good " — as Moses' permission of divorce and retaliation (Deut. 24 : 1 ; *cf.* Mat. 5 : 31, 32 ; 19 : 7-9. Ex. 21 : 24 ; *cf.* Mat. 5 : 38, 39). Compare Elijah's calling down fire from heaven (2 K. 1 : 10–12) with Jesus' refusal to do the same, and his intimation that the spirit of Elijah was not the spirit of Christ (Luke 9 : 52–56) ; *cf.* Mattheson, Moments on the Mount, 253–255, on Mat. 17 : 8 — " Jesus only " : " The strength of Elias paled before him. To shed the blood of enemies requires less strength than to shed one's own blood, and to conquer by fire is easier than to conquer by love." Hovey : " In divine revelation, it is first starlight, then dawn, finally day." George Washing-ton once gave directions for the transportation to the West Indies and the sale there of a refractory negro who had given him trouble. This was not at variance with the best morality of his time, but it would not suit the improved ethical standards of to-day. The use of force rather than moral suasion is sometimes needed by children and by barbarians. We may illustrate by the Sunday School scholar's unruliness which was cured by his classmates during the week. " What did you say to him ? " asked the teacher. " We did n't say nothing ; we just punched his head for him." This was Old Testament righteousness. The appeal in the O. T. to the hope of earthly rewards was suitable to a stage of development not yet instructed as to heaven and hell by the com-ing and work of Christ ; compare Ex. 20 : 12 with Mat. 5 : 10 ; 25 : 46. The Old Testament aimed to fix in the mind of a selected people the idea of the unity and holiness of God ; in order to exterminate idolatry, much other teaching was postponed. See Peabody,

Religion of Nature, 45; Mozley, Ruling Ideas of Early Ages; Green, in Presb. Quar., April, 1877: 221-252; McIlvaine, Wisdom of Holy Scripture, 328-368; Brit. and For. Evang. Rev., Jan. 1878: 1-32; Martineau, Study, 2: 137.

When therefore we find in the inspired song of Deborah, the prophetess (Judges 5: 30), an allusion to the common spoils of war — "a damsel, two demsels to every man" or in Prov. 31: 6, 7 — "Give strong drink unto him that is ready to perish, and wine unto the bitter in soul. Let him drink, and forget his poverty, and remember his misery no more" — we do not need to maintain that these passages furnish standards for our modern conduct. Dr. Fisher calls the latter "the worst advice to a person in affliction, or dispirited by the loss of property." They mark past stages in God's providential leading of mankind. A higher stage indeed is already intimated in Prov. 31: 4— "it is not for kings to drink wine, Nor for princes to say, Where is strong drink?" We see that God could use very imperfect instruments and could inspire very imperfect men. Many things were permitted for men's "hardness of heart" (Mat. 19: 8). The Sermon on the Mount is a great advance on the law of Moses (Mat. 5: 21 — "Ye have heard that it was said to them of old time"; cf. 22 — "But I say unto you").

Robert G. Ingersoll would have lost his stock in trade if Christians had generally recognized that revelation is gradual, and is completed only in Christ. This gradualness of revelation is conceded in the common phrase: "the new dispensation." Abraham Lincoln showed his wisdom by never going far ahead of the common sense of the people. God similarly adapted his legislation to the capacities of each successive age. The command to Abraham to sacrifice his son (Gen. 22: 1-19) was a proper test of Abraham's faith in a day when human sacrifice violated no common ethical standard because the Hebrew, like the Roman, "patria potestas" did not regard the child as having a separate individuality, but included the child in the parent and made the child equally responsible for the parent's sin. But that very command was given *only* as a test of faith, and with the intent to make the intended obedience the occasion of revealing God's provision of a substitute and so of doing away with human sacrifice for all future time. We may well imitate the gradualness of divine revelation in our treatment of dancing and of the liquor traffic.

(d) God's righteous sovereignty affords the key to other events. He has the right to do what he will with his own, and to punish the transgressor when and where he will; and he may justly make men the foretellers or executors of his purposes.

Foretellers, as in the imprecatory Psalms (137: 9; cf. Is. 13: 16-18 and Jer. 50: 16, 29) executors, as in the destruction of the Canaanites (Deut. 7: 2, 16). In the former case the Psalm was not the ebullition of personal anger, but the expression of judicial indignation against the enemies of God. We must distinguish the substance from the form. The substance was the denunciation of God's righteous judgments; the form was taken from the ordinary customs of war in the Psalmist's time. See Park, in Bib. Sac., 1862: 165; Cowles, Com. on Ps. 137; Perowne on Psalms, Introd., 61; Presb. and Ref. Rev., 1897: 490-505; cf. 2 Tim. 4: 14 — "the Lord will render to him according to his works" = a prophecy, not a curse, ἀποδώσει, not ἀποδῴη, as in A. V. In the latter case, an exterminating war was only the benevolent surgery that amputated the putrid limb, and so saved the religious life of the Hebrew nation and of the after-world. See Dr. Thomas Arnold, Essay on the Right Interpretation of Scripture; Fisher, Beginnings of Christianity, 11-24.

Another interpretation of these events has been proposed, which would make them illustrations of the principle indicated in (c) above: E. G. Robinson, Christian Theology, 45 — "It was not the imprecations of the Psalm that were inspired of God, but his purposes and ideas of which these were by the times the necessary vehicle; just as the adultery of David was not by divine command, though through it the purpose of God as to Christ's descent was accomplished." John Watson (Ian Maclaren), Cure of Souls, 143 — "When the massacre of the Canaanites and certain proceedings of David are flung in the face of Christians, it is no longer necessary to fall back on evasions or special pleading. It can now be frankly admitted that, from our standpoint in this year of grace, such deeds were atrocious, and that they never could have been according to the mind of God, but that they must be judged by their date, and considered the defects of elementary moral processes. The Bible is vindicated, because it is, on the whole, a steady ascent, and because it culminates in Christ."

Lyman Abbott, Theology of an Evolutionist. 56 — ' Abraham mistook the voice of conscience, calling on him to consecrate his only son to God, and interpreted it as command to slay his son as a burnt offering. Israel misinterpreted his righteous indignation at the cruel and lustful rites of the Canaanitish religion as a divine summons to destroy the worship by putting the worshipers to death; a people undeveloped in moral judgment could not distinguish between formal regulations respecting camp-life and eternal principles of righteousness, such as, Thou shalt love thy neighbor as thyself, but embodied them in the same code, and seemed to regard them as of equal authority." Wilkinson, Epic of Paul, 281 — "If so be such man, so placed . . . did in some part That utterance make his own, profaning it, To be his vehicle for sense not meant By the august supreme inspiring Will" — i. e., putting some of his own sinful anger into God's calm predictions of judgment. Compare the stern last words of "Zechariah, the son of Jehoiada, the priest" when stoned to death in the temple court: "Jehovah look upon it and require it" (2 Chron. 24 : 20-22), with the last words of Jesus: "Father, forgive them, for they know not what they do" (Luke 23 : 34) and of Stephen : "Lord, lay not this sin to their charge " (Acts 7 : 60).

(e) Other apparent immoralities are due to unwarranted interpretations. Symbol is sometimes taken for literal fact ; the language of irony is understood as sober affirmation ; the glow and freedom of Oriental description are judged by the unimpassioned style of Western literature ; appeal to lower motives is taken to exclude, instead of preparing for, the higher.

In Hosea 1 : 2, 3, the command to the prophet to marry a harlot was probably received and executed in vision, and was intended only as symbolic: compare Jer. 25 : 15-18 — "Take this cup . . . . and cause all the nations . . . . to drink." Literal obedience would have made the prophet contemptible to those whom he would instruct, and would require so long a time as to weaken, if not destroy, the designed effect; see Ann. Par. Bible, in loco. In 2 K. 6 : 19, Elisha's deception, so called, was probably only ironical and benevolent; the enemy dared not resist, because they were completely in his power. In the Song of Solomon, we have, as Jewish writers have always held, a highly-wrought dramatic description of the union between Jehovah and his people, which we must judge by Eastern and not by Western literary standards.

Francis W. Newman, in his Phases of Faith, accused even the New Testament of presenting low motives for human obedience. It is true that all right motives are appealed to, and some of these motives are of a higher sort than are others. Hope of heaven and fear of hell are not the highest motives, but they may be employed as preliminary incitements to action, even though only love for God and for holiness will ensure salvation. Such motives are urged both by Christ and by his apostles : Mat. 6 : 20 — "lay up for yourselves treasures in heaven"; 10 : 28 — "fear him who is able to destroy both soul and body in hell"; Jude 23 — "some save with fear, snatching them out of the fire." In this respect the N. T. does not differ from the O. T. George Adam Smith has pointed out that the royalists got their texts, "the powers that be" (Rom. 13 : 1) and "the king as supreme" (1 Pet. 2 : 13), from the N. T., while the O. T. furnished texts for the defenders of liberty. While the O. T. deals with national life, and the discharge of social and political functions, the N. T. deals in the main with individuals and with their relations to God. On the whole subject, see Hessey, Moral Difficulties of the Bible; Jellett, Moral Difficulties of the O. T.; Faith and Free Thought (Lect. by Christ. Ev. Soc.), 2 : 173 ; Rogers, Eclipse of Faith ; Butler, Analogy, part ii, chap. iii ; Orr, Problem of the O. T., 465-483.

4. *Errors of Reasoning.*

(a) What are charged as such are generally to be explained as valid argument expressed in highly condensed form. The appearance of error may be due to the suppression of one or more links in the reasoning.

In Mat. 22 : 32, Christ's argument for the resurrection, drawn from the fact that God is the God of Abraham, Isaac, and Jacob, is perfectly and obviously valid, the moment we put in the suppressed premise that the living relation to God which is here implied cannot properly be conceived as something merely spiritual, but necessarily requires a new and restored life of the body. If God is the God of the living, then Abraham, Isaac, and Jacob shall rise from the dead. See more full exposition, under Eschatology. Some of the Scripture arguments are enthymemes, and an enthymeme, according to Arbuthnot and Pope, is "a syllogism in which the major is married to the minor, and the marriage is kept secret."

(*b*) Where we cannot see the propriety of the conclusions drawn from given premises, there is greater reason to attribute our failure to ignorance of divine logic on our part, than to accommodation or *ad hominem* argu ments on the part of the Scripture writers.

By divine logic we mean simply a logic whose elements and processes are correct, though not understood by us. In Heb. 7 : 9, 10 (Levi's pay ag tithes in Abraham), there is probably a recognition of the organic unity of the family, which in miniature illustrates the organic unity of the race. In Gal. 3 : 20 — "a mediator is not a mediator of one; but God is one" — the law, with its two contracting parties, is contrasted with the promise, which proceeds from the sole fiat of God and is therefore unchangeable. Paul's argument here rests on Christ's divinity as its foundation — otherwise Christ would have been a mediator in the same sense in which Moses was a mediator (see Lightfoot, *in loco*). In Gal. 4 : 21-31, Hagar and Ishmael on the one hand, and Sarah and Isaac on the other, illustrate the exclusion of the bondmen of the law from the privileges of the spiritual seed of Abraham. Abraham's two wives, and the two classes of people in the two sons, represent the two covenants (so Calvin). In John 10 : 34 — "I said, Ye are gods," the implication is that Judaism was not a system of mere monotheism, but of theism tending to theanthropism, a real union of God and man (Westcott, Bib. Com., *in loco*). Godet well remarks that he who doubts Paul's logic will do well first to suspect his own.

(*c*) The adoption of Jewish methods of reasoning, where it could be proved, would not indicate error on the part of the Scripture writers, but rather an inspired sanction of the method as applied to that particular case.

In Gal. 3 : 16 — "He saith not, And to seeds, as of many; but as of one, And to thy seed, which is Christ." Here it, is intimated that the very form of the expression in Gen. 22 : 18, which denotes unity, was selected by the Holy Spirit as significant of that one person, Christ, who was the true seed of Abraham and in whom all nations were to be blessed. Argument from the form of a single word is in this case correct, although the Rabbins often made more of single words than the Holy Spirit ever intended. Watts, New Apologetic, 69 — " F. W. Farrar asserts that the plural of the Hebrew or Greek terms for 'seed' is never used by Hebrew or Greek writers as a designation of human offspring. But see Sophocles, Œdipus at Colonus, 599, 600 — γῆς ἐμῆς ἀπηλάθην πρὸς τῶν ἐμαυτοῦ σπερμάτων — ' I was driven away from my own country by my own offspring.' " In 1 Cor. 10 : 1-6 — "and the rock was Christ" — the Rabbinic tradition that the smitten rock followed the Israelites in their wanderings is declared to be only the absurd literalizing of a spiritual fact — the continual presence of Christ, as preëxistent Logos, with his ancient people. *Per contra*, see Row, Rev. and Mod. Theories, 98–128.

(*d*) If it should appear however upon further investigation that Rabbinical methods have been wrongly employed by the apostles in their argumentation, we might still distinguish between the truth they are seeking to convey and the arguments by which they support it. Inspiration may conceivably make known the truth, yet leave the expression of the truth to human dialectic as well as to human rhetoric.

Johnson, Quotations of the N. T. from the O. T., 137, 138 — " In the utter absence of all evidence to the contrary, we ought to suppose that the allegories of the N. T. are like the allegories of literature in general, merely luminous embodiments of the truth. . . . . If these allegories are not presented by their writers as evidences, they are none the less precious, since they illuminate the truth otherwise evinced, and thus render it at once clear to the apprehension and attractive to the taste." If however the purpose of the writers was to use these allegories for proof, we may still see shining through the rifts of their traditional logic the truth which they were striving to set forth. Inspiration may have put them in possession of this truth without altering their ordinary scholastic methods of demonstration and expression. Horton, Inspiration, 108 — " Discrepancies and illogical reasonings were but inequalities or cracks in the mirrors, which did not materially distort or hide the Person " whose glory they sought to reflect. Luther went even further than this when he said that a certain argument in the epistle was " good enough for the Galatians."

5. *Errors in quoting or interpreting the Old Testament.*

(*a*) What are charged as such are commonly interpretations of the meaning of the original Scripture by the same Spirit who first inspired it.

In Eph. 5:14, "arise from the dead, and Christ shall shine upon thee" is an inspired interpretation of Is. 60:1 — "Arise, shine; for thy light is come." Ps. 68:18 — "Thou hast received gifts among men" — is quoted in Eph. 4:8 as "gave gifts to men." The words in Hebrew are probably a concise expression for "thou hast taken spoil which thou mayest distribute as gifts to men." Eph. 4:8 agrees exactly with the sense, though not with the words, of the Psalm. In Heb. 11:21, "Jacob .... worshipped, leaning upon the top of his staff" (LXX); Gen. 47:31 has "bowed himself upon the bed's head." The meaning is the same, for the staff of the chief and the spear of the warrior were set at the bed's head. Jacob, too feeble to rise, prayed in his bed. Here Calvin says that "the apostle does not hesitate to accommodate to his own purpose what was commonly received, — they were not so scrupulous" as to details. Even Gordon, Ministry of the Spirit, 177, speaks of "a reshaping of his own words by the Author of them." We prefer, with Calvin, to see in these quotations evidence that the sacred writers were insistent upon the substance of the truth rather than upon the form, the spirit rather than the letter.

(*b*) Where an apparently false translation is quoted from the Septuagint, the sanction of inspiration is given to it, as expressing a part at least of the fulness of meaning contained in the divine original — a fulness of meaning which two varying translations do not in some cases exhaust.

Ps. 4:4 — Heb.: "Tremble, and sin not" (= no longer); LXX: "Be ye angry, and sin not." Eph. 4:26 quotes the LXX. The words may originally have been addressed to David's comrades, exhorting them to keep their anger within bounds. Both translations together are needed to bring out the meaning of the original. Ps. 40:6-8 — "Mine ears hast thou opened" is translated in Heb. 10:5-7 — "a body didst thou prepare for me." Here the Epistle quotes from the LXX. But the Hebrew means literally: "Mine ears hast thou bored" — an allusion to the custom of pinning a slave to the doorpost of his master by an awl driven through his ear, in token of his complete subjection. The sense of the verse is therefore given in the Epistle: "Thou hast made me thine in body and soul—lo, I come to do thy will." A. C. Kendrick: "David, just entering upon his kingdom after persecution, is a type of Christ entering on his earthly mission. Hence David's words are put into the mouth of Christ. For 'ears,' the organs with which we hear and obey and which David conceived to be hollowed out for him by God, the author of the Hebrews substitutes the word 'body,' as the *general* instrument of doing God's will" (Com. on Heb. 10:5-7).

(*c*) The freedom of these inspired interpretations, however, does not warrant us in like freedom of interpretation in the case of other passages whose meaning has not been authoritatively made known.

We have no reason to believe that the scarlet thread of Rahab (Josh. 2:18) was a designed prefiguration of the blood of Christ, nor that the three measures of meal in which the woman hid her leaven (Mat. 13:33) symbolized Shem, Ham and Japheth, the three divisions of the human race. C. H. M., in his notes on the tabernacle in Exodus, tells us that "the loops of blue = heavenly grace; the taches of gold = the divine energy of Christ; the rams' skins dyed red = Christ's consecration and devotedness; the badgers' skins — his holy vigilance against temptation"! The tabernacle was indeed a type of Christ (John 1:14 — ἐσκήνωσεν. 2:19, 21 — "in three days I will raise it up .... but he spake of the temple of his body"); yet it does not follow that every detail of the structure was significant. So each parable teaches some one main lesson, — the particulars may be mere drapery; and while we may use the parables for illustration, we should never ascribe divine authority to our private impressions of their meaning.

Mat. 25:1-13 — the parable of the five wise and the five foolish virgins — has been made to teach that the number of the saved precisely equals the number of the lost. Augustine defended persecution from the words in Luke 14:23 — "constrain them to come in." The Inquisition was justified by Mat. 13:30 — "bind them in bundles to burn them." Innocent III denied the Scriptures to the laity, quoting Heb. 12:20 — "If even a beast touch the mountain, it shall be stoned." A Plymouth Brother held that he would be safe on an evangelizing journey because he read in John 19:36 — "A bone of him shall not be broken." Mat. 17:8 — "they saw no one, save Jesus only"—has been held to mean that we should trust only Jesus. The Epistle of Barnabas discovered in Abraham's 318 servants a prediction of the crucified Jesus, and others have seen in Abraham's three days' journey to Mount Moriah the three stages in the development of the soul. Clement of Alexandria finds the four natural elements in the four colors of the Jewish Tabernacle. All this is to make a parable "run on all fours." While we call a hero a lion, we do not need to find in the man something to correspond to the lion's mane and claws. See Toy, Quotations in the N. T.; Franklin Johnson, Quotations of the N. T. from the O. T.; Crooker, The New Bible and its New Uses, 126–136.

(*d*) While we do not grant that the New Testament writers in any proper sense misquoted or misinterpreted the Old Testament, we do not regard absolute correctness in these respects as essential to their inspiration. The inspiring Spirit may have communicated truth, and may have secured in the Scriptures as a whole a record of that truth sufficient for men's moral and religious needs, without imparting perfect gifts of scholarship or exegesis.

In answer to Toy, Quotations in the N. T., who takes a generally unfavorable view of the correctness of the N. T. writers, Johnson, Quotations of the N. T. from the O. T., maintains their correctness. On pages x, xi, of his Introduction, Johnson remarks : " I think it just to regard the writers of the Bible as the creators of a great literature, and to judge and interpret them by the laws of literature. They have produced all the chief forms of literature, as history, biography, anecdote, proverb, oratory, allegory, poetry, fiction. They have needed therefore all the resources of human speech, its sobriety and scientific precision on one page, its rainbow hues of fancy and imagination on another, its fires of passion on yet another. They could not have moved and guided men in the best manner had they denied themselves the utmost force and freedom of language; had they refused to employ its wide range of expressions, whether exact or poetic; had they not borrowed without stint its many forms of reason, of terror, of rapture, of hope, of joy, of peace. So also, they have needed the usual freedom of literary allusion and citation, in order to commend the gospel to the judgment, the tastes, and the feelings of their readers."

6. *Errors in Prophecy.*

(*a*) What are charged as such may frequently be explained by remembering that much of prophecy is yet unfulfilled.

It is sometimes taken for granted that the book of Revelation, for example, refers entirely to events already past. Moses Stuart, in his Commentary, and Warren's Parousia, represent this preterist interpretation. Thus judged, however, many of the predictions of the book might seem to have failed.

(*b*) The personal surmises of the prophets as to the meaning of the prophecies they recorded may have been incorrect, while yet the prophecies themselves are inspired.

In 1 Pet. 1:10, 11, the apostle declares that the prophets searched "what time or what manner of time the Spirit of Christ which was in them did point unto, when it testified beforehand the sufferings of Christ and the glories that should follow them." So Paul, although he does not announce it as certain, seems to have had some hope that he might live to witness Christ's second coming. See 2 Cor. 5:4 — "not for that we would be unclothed, but that we would be clothed upon " (ἐπενδύσασθαι—put on the spiritual body, as over the present one, without the intervention of death); 1 Thess. 4:15, 17 — "we that are alive, that are left unto the coming of the Lord." So Mat. 2:15 quotes from Hosea 11:1 — "Out of Egypt did I call my son," and applies the prophecy to Christ, although Hosea was doubtless thinking only of the exodus of the people of Israel.

(*c*) The prophet's earlier utterances are not to be severed from the later utterances which elucidate them, nor from the whole revelation of which they form a part. It is unjust to forbid the prophet to explain his own meaning.

2 Thessalonians was written expressly to correct wrong inferences as to the apostle's teaching drawn from his peculiar mode of speaking in the first epistle. In 2 Thess. 2:2-5 he removes the impression "that the day of the Lord is now present" or "just at hand"; declares that "it will not be, except the falling away come first, and the man of sin be revealed"; reminds the Thessalonians: "when I was yet with you, I told you these things." Yet still, in verse 1, he speaks of "the coming of our Lord Jesus Christ, and *our* gathering together unto him."

These passages, taken together, show: (1) that the two epistles are one in their teaching; (2) that in neither epistle is there any prediction of the immediate coming of the Lord; (3) that in the second epistle great events are foretold as intervening before that coming; (4) that while Paul never taught that Christ would come during his own lifetime, he hoped at least during the earlier part of his life that it might be so—a hope that seems to have been dissipated in his later years. (See 2 Tim. 4:6—"I am already being offered, and the time of my departure is come.") We must remember, however, that there was a "coming of the Lord" in the destruction of Jerusalem within three or four years of Paul's death. Henry Van Dyke: "The point of Paul's teaching in 1 and 2 Thess. is not that Christ is coming to-morrow, but that he is surely coming." The absence of perspective in prophecy may explain Paul's not at first defining the precise time of the end, and so leaving it to be misunderstood.

The second Epistle to the Thessalonians, therefore, only makes more plain the meaning of the first, and adds new items of prediction. It is important to recognize in Paul's epistles a progress in prophecy, in doctrine, in church polity. The full statement of the truth was gradually drawn out, under the influence of the Spirit, upon occasion of successive outward demands and inward experiences. Much is to be learned by studying the chronological order of Paul's epistles, as well as of the other N. T. books. For evidence of similar progress in the epistles of Peter, compare 1 Pet. 4:7 with 2 Pet. 3:4 *sq.*

(*d*) The character of prophecy as a rough general sketch of the future, in highly figurative language, and without historical perspective, renders it peculiarly probable that what at first sight seem to be errors are due to a misinterpretation on our part, which confounds the drapery with the substance, or applies its language to events to which it had no reference.

James 5:9 and Phil 4:5 are instances of that large prophetic speech which regards the distant future as near at hand, because so certain to the faith and hope of the church. Sanday, Inspiration, 376-378 — "No doubt the Christians of the Apostolic age did live in immediate expectation of the Second Coming, and that expectation culminated at the crisis in which the Apocalypse was written. In the Apocalypse, as in every predictive prophecy, there is a double element, one part derived from the circumstances of the present and another pointing forwards to the future. . . . All these things, in an exact and literal sense have fallen through with the postponement of that great event in which they centre. From the first they were but meant as the imaginative pictorial and symbolical clothing of that event. What measure of real fulfilment the Apocalypse may yet be destined to receive we cannot tell. But in predictive prophecy, even when most closely verified, the essence lies less in the prediction than in the eternal laws of moral and religious truth which the fact predicted reveals or exemplifies." Thus we recognize both the divinity and the freedom of prophecy, and reject the rationalistic theory which would relate the fall of the Beaconsfield government in Matthew's way: "That it might be fulfilled which was spoken by Cromwell, saying: 'Get you gone, and make room for honest men!'" See the more full statement of the nature of prophecy, on pages 132-141. Also Bernard, Progress of Doctrine in the N. T.

7. *Certain books unworthy of a place in inspired Scripture.*

(*a*) This charge may be shown, in each single case, to rest upon a misapprehension of the aim and method of the book, and its connection with the remainder of the Bible, together with a narrowness of nature or of doctrinal view, which prevents the critic from appreciating the wants of the peculiar class of men to which the book is especially serviceable.

Luther called James "a right strawy epistle." His constant pondering of the doctrine of justification by faith alone made it difficult for him to grasp the complementary truth that we are justified only by such faith as brings forth good works, or to perceive the essential agreement of James and Paul. Prof. R. E. Thompson, in S. S. Times, Dec. 3, 1898 : 803, 804 — " Luther refused canonical authority to books not actually written by apostles or composed (as Mark and Luke) under their direction. So he rejected from the rank of canonical authority Hebrews, James, Jude, 2 Peter, Revelation. Even Calvin doubted the Petrine authorship of 2 Peter, excluded the book of Revelation from the Scripture on which he wrote Commentaries, and also thus ignored 2 and 3 John." G. P. Fisher in S. S. Times, Aug. 29, 1891 — " Luther, in his preface to the N. T. (Edition of 1522), gives a list of what he considers as the principal books of the N. T. These are John's Gospel and First Epistle, Paul's Epistles, especially Romans and Galatians, and Peter's First Epistle. Then he adds that 'St. James' Epistle is a right strawy Epistle *compared with them* ' — ' *ein recht strohern Epistel gegen sie*,' thus characterizing it not absolutely but only relatively." Zwingle even said of the Apocalypse: " It is not a Biblical book." So Thomas Arnold, with his exaggerated love for historical accuracy and definite outline, found the Oriental imagery and sweeping visions of the book of Revelation so bizarre and distasteful that he doubted their divine authority.

(*b*) The testimony of church history and general Christian experience to the profitableness and divinity of the disputed books is of greater weight than the personal impressions of the few who criticize them.

Instance the testimonies of the ages of persecution to the worth of the prophecies, which assure God's people that his cause shall surely triumph. Denney, Studies in Theology, 226 — " It is at least as likely that the individual should be insensible to the divine message in a book, as that the church should have judged it to contain such a message if it did not do so." Milton, Areopagitica : " The Bible brings in holiest men passionately murmuring against Providence through all the arguments of Epicurus." Bruce, Apologetics, 329 — " O. T. religion was querulous, vindictive, philolevitical, hostile toward foreigners, morbidly self-conscious, and tending to self-righteousness. Ecclesiastes shows us how we ought *not* to feel. To go about crying *Vanitas!* is to miss the lesson it was meant to teach, namely, that the Old Covenant was vanity — proved to be vanity by allowing a son of the Covenant to get into so despairing a mood." Chadwick says that Ecclesiastes got into the Canon only after it had received an orthodox postscript.

Pfleiderer, Philos. Religion, 1 : 193 — " Slavish fear and self-righteous reckoning with God are the unlovely features of this Jewish religion of law to which the ethical idealism of the prophets had degenerated, and these traits strike us most visibly in Pharsiaism. . . . It was this side of the O. T. religion to which Christianity took a critical and destroying attitude, while it revealed a new and higher knowledge of God. For, says Paul, ' ye received not the spirit of bondage again unto fear; but ye received the spirit of adoption ' (Rom. 8 : 15). In unity with God man does not lose his soul but preserves it. God not only commands but gives." Ian Maclaren (John Watson), Cure of Souls, 144 — " When the book of Ecclesiastes is referred to the days of the third century B. C., then its note is caught, and any man who has been wronged and embittered by political tyranny and social corruption has his bitter cry included in the book of God."

(*c*) Such testimony can be adduced in favor of the value of each one of the books to which exception is taken, such as Esther, Job, Song of Solomon, Ecclesiastes, Jonah, James, Revelation.

Esther is the book, next to the Pentateuch, held in highest reverence by the Jews. " Job was the discoverer of infinity, and the first to see the bearing of infinity on righteousness. It was the return of religion to nature. Job heard the voice beyond the Sinai-voice " (Shadow-Cross, 89). Inge, Christian Mysticism, 43 — " As to the Song of Solomon, its influence upon Christian Mysticism has been simply deplorable. A graceful romance in honor of true love has been distorted into a precedent and sanction for giving way to hysterical emotions in which sexual imagery has been freely used to symbolize the relation between the soul and its Lord." Chadwick says that the Song of Solomon got into the Canon only after it had received an allegorical interpretation. Gladden, Seven Puzzling Bible Books, 165, thinks it impossible that " the addition of one more inmate to the harem of that royal rake, King Solomon, should have been made the type of the spiritual affection between Christ and his church. Instead of this, the book is a glorification of pure love. The Shulamite, transported to the court of Solomon, remains faithful to her shepherd lover, and is restored to him."

Bruce, Apologetics, 321 — "The Song of Solomon, literally interpreted as a story of true love, proof against the blandishments of the royal harem, is rightfully in the Canon as a buttress to the true religion; for whatever made for purity in the relations of the sexes made for the worship of Jehovah — Baal worship and impurity being closely associated." Rutherford, McCheyne, and Spurgeon have taken more texts from the Song of Solomon than from any other portion of Scripture of like extent. Charles G. Finney, Autobiography, 378 — "At this time it seemed as if my soul was wedded to Christ in a sense which I never had any thought or conception of before. The language of the Song of Solomon was as natural to me as my breath. I thought I could understand well the state he was in when he wrote that Song, and concluded then, as I have ever thought since, that that Song was written by him after he had been reclaimed from his great backsliding. I not only had all the fulness of my first love, but a vast accession to it. Indeed, the Lord lifted me up so much above anything that I had experienced before, and taught me so much of the meaning of the Bible, of Christ's relations and power and willingness, that I found myself saying to him : I had not known or conceived that any such thing was true." On Jonah, see R. W. Dale, in Expositor, July, 1892, advocating the non-historical and allegorical character of the book. Bib. Sac., 10:757-764 — "Jonah represents the nation of Israel as emerging through a miracle from the exile, in order to carry out its mission to the world at large. It teaches that God is the God of the whole earth; that the Ninevites as well as the Israelites are dear to him ; that his threatenings of penalty are conditional."

8.   *Portions of the Scripture books written by others than the persons to whom they are ascribed.*

The objection rests upon a misunderstanding of the nature and object of inspiration.   It may be removed by considering that

(*a*) In the case of books made up from preëxisting documents, inspiration simply preserved the compilers of them from selecting inadequate or improper material.   The fact of such compilation does not impugn their value as records of a divine revelation, since these books supplement each other's deficiencies and together are sufficient for man's religious needs.

Luke distinctly informs us that he secured the materials for his gospel from the reports of others who were eye-witnesses of the events he recorded (Luke 1:1-4). The book of Genesis bears marks of having incorporated documents of earlier times. The account of creation which begins with Gen. 2:4 is evidently written by a different hand from that which penned 1 : 1-31 and 2 : 1-3.   Instances of the same sort may be found in the books of Chronicles.   In like manner, Marshall's Life of Washington incorporates documents by other writers.   By thus incorporating them, Marshall vouches for their truth.   See Bible Com., 1 : 2, 22.

Dorner, Hist. Prot. Theology, 1 : 243 — "Luther ascribes to faith critical authority with reference to the Canon.   He denies the canonicity of James, without regarding it as spurious.   So of Hebrews and Revelation, though later, in 1545, he passed a more favorable judgment upon the latter.   He even says of a proof adduced by Paul in Galatians that it is too weak to hold.   He allows that in external matters not only Stephen but even the sacred authors contain inaccuracies.   The authority of the O. T. does not seem to him invalidated by the admission that several of its writings have passed through revising hands.   What would it matter, he asks, if Moses did not write the Pentateuch? The prophets studied Moses and one another.   If they built in much wood, hay and stubble along with the rest, still the foundation abides; the fire of the great day shall consume the former; for in this manner do we treat the writings of Augustine and others.   Kings is far more to be believed than Chronicles.   Ecclesiastes is forged and cannot come from Solomon.   Esther is not canonical.   The church may have erred in adopting a book into the Canon.   Faith first requires proof.   Hence he ejects the Apocryphal books of the O. T. from the Canon.   So some parts of the N. T. receive only a secondary, deuterocanonical position.   There is a difference between the word of God and the holy Scriptures, not merely in reference to the form, but also in reference to the subject matter."

H. P. Smith, Bib. Scholarship and Inspiration, 94 — "The Editor of the Minor Prophets united in one roll the prophetic fragments which were in circulation in his time.

Finding a fragment without an author's name he inserted it in the series. It would not have been distinguished from the work of the author immediately preceding. So Zech. 9:1-4 came to go under the name of Zechariah, and Is. 40-66 under the name of Isaiah. Reuss called these 'anatomical studies.'" On the authorship of the book of Daniel, see W. C. Wilkinson, in Homiletical Review, March, 1902 : 208, and Oct. 1902 : 305; on Paul, see Hom. Rev., June, 1902 : 501; on 110th Psalm, Hom. Rev., April, 1902 : 309.

(b) In the case of additions to Scripture books by later writers, it is reasonable to suppose that the additions, as well as the originals, were made by inspiration, and no essential truth is sacrificed by allowing the whole to go under the name of the chief author.

Mark 16:9-20 appears to have been added by a later hand (see English Revised Version). The Eng. Rev. Vers. also brackets or segregates a part of verse 3 and the whole of verse 4 in John 5 (the moving of the water by the angel), and the whole passage John 7 : 53 — 8 : 11 (the woman taken in adultery). Westcott and Hort regard the latter passage as an interpolation, probably " Western " in its origin (so also Mark 16 : 9-20). Others regard it as authentic, though not written by John. The closing chapter of Deuteronomy was apparently added after Moses' death — perhaps by Joshua. If criticism should prove other portions of the Pentateuch to have been composed after Moses' time, the inspiration of the Pentateuch would not be invalidated, so long as Moses was its chief author or even the original source and founder of its legislation (John 5 : 46 — " he wrote of me "). Gore, in Lux Mundi, 355 — " Deuteronomy may be a republication of the law, in the spirit and power of Moses, and put dramatically into 'is mouth."

At a spot near the Pool of Siloam, Manasseh is said to have ordered that Isaiah should be sawn asunder with a wooden saw. The prophet is again sawn asunder by the recent criticism. But his prophecy opens (Is. 1:1) with the statement that it was composed during a period which covered the reigns of four kings — Uzziah, Jotham, Ahaz and Hezekiah — nearly forty years. In so long a time the style of a writer greatly changes. Chapters 40-66 may have been written in Isaiah's later age, after he had retired from public life. Compare the change in the style of Zechariah, John and Paul, with that in Thomas Carlyle and George William Curtis. On Isaiah, see Smyth, Prophecy a Preparation for Christ; Bib. Sac., Apr. 1881 : 230-253; also July, 1881; Stanley, Jewish Ch., 2 : 646, 647 ; Nägelsbach, Int. to Lange's Isaiah.

For the view that there were two Isaiahs, see George Adam Smith, Com. on Isaiah, 2 : 1-25: Isaiah flourished B. C. 740-700. The last 27 chapters deal with the captivity (598-538) and with Cyrus (550), whom they name. The book is not one continuous prophecy, but a number of separate orations. Some or these claim to be Isaiah's own, and have titles, such as " The vision of Isaiah the son of Amoz " (1 : 1); " The word that Isaiah the son of Amoz saw " (2 : 1). But such titles describe only the individual prophecies they head. Other portions of the book, on other subjects and in different styles, have no titles at all Chapters 40-66 do not claim to be his. There are nine citations in the N. T. from the disputed chapters, but none by our Lord. None of these citations were given in answer to the question : Did Isaiah write chapters 44-66 ? Isaiah's name is mentioned only for the sake of reference. Chapters 44-66 set forth the exile and captivity as already having taken place. Israel is addressed as ready for deliverance. Cyrus is named as deliverer. There is no grammar of the future like Jeremiah's. Cyrus is pointed out as proof that former prophecies of deliverance are at last coming to pass. He is not presented as a prediction, but as a proof that prediction is being fulfilled. The prophet could not have referred the heathen to Cyrus as proof that prophecy had been fulfilled, had he not been visible to them in all his weight of war. Babylon has still to fall before the exiles can go free. But chapters 40-66 speak of the coming of Cyrus as past, and of the fall of Babylon as yet to come. Why not use the prophetic perfect of both, if both were yet future ? Local color, language and thought are all consistent with exilic authorship. All suits the exile, but all is foreign to the subjects and methods of Isaiah, for example, the use of the terms *righteous* and *righteousness*. Calvin admits exilic authorship (on Is. 55 : 3). The passage 56 : 9-57, however, is an exception and is preëxilic. 40-48 are certainly by one hand, and may be dated 555-538. 2nd Isaiah is not a unity, but consists of a number of pieces written before, during, and after the exile, to comfort the people of God.

(*c*) It is unjust to deny to inspired Scripture the right exercised by all historians of introducing certain documents and sayings as simply historical, while their complete truthfulness is neither vouched for nor denied.

An instance in point is the letter of Claudius Lysias in Acts 23 : 26-30—a letter which represents his conduct in a more favorable light than the facts would justify—for he had not learned that Paul was a Roman when he rescued him in the temple (Acts 21 : 31-33 ; 22 : 26-29). An incorrect statement may be correctly reported. A set of pamphlets printed in the time of the French Revolution might be made an appendix to some history of France without implying that the historian vouched for their truth. The sacred historians may similarly have been inspired to use only the material within their reach, leaving their readers by comparison with other Scriptures to judge of its truthfulness and value. This seems to have been the method adopted by the compiler of 1 and 2 Chronicles. The moral and religious lessons of the history are patent, even though there is inaccuracy in reporting some of the facts. So the assertions of the authors of the Psalms cannot be taken for absolute truth. The authors were not sinless models for the Christian,— only Christ is that. But the Psalms present us with a record of the actual experience of believers in the past. It has its human weakness, but we can profit by it, even though it expresses itself at times in imprecations. Jeremiah 20 : 7 — " O Lord, thou hast deceived me "—may possibly be thus explained.

2.   *Sceptical or fictitious Narratives.*

(*a*) Descriptions of human experience may be embraced in Scripture, not as models for imitation, but as illustrations of the doubts, struggles, and needs of the soul. In these cases inspiration may vouch, not for the correctness of the views expressed by those who thus describe their mental history, but only for the correspondence of the description with actual fact, and for its usefulness as indirectly teaching important moral lessons.

The book of Ecclesiastes, for example, is the record of the mental struggles of a soul seeking satisfaction without God. If written by Solomon during the time of his religious declension, or near the close of it, it would constitute a most valuable commentary upon the inspired history. Yet it might be equally valuable, though composed by some later writer under divine direction and inspiration. H. P. Smith, Bib. Scholarship and Inspiration, 97 — " To suppose Solomon the author of Ecclesiastes is like supposing Spenser to have written In Memoriam." Luther, Keil, Delitzsch, Ginsburg, Hengstenberg all declare it to be a production of later times (330 B. C.). The book shows experience of misgovernment. An earlier writer cannot write in the style of a later one, though the later can imitate the earlier. The early Latin and Greek Fathers quoted the Apocryphal Wisdom of Solomon as by Solomon ; see Plumptre, Introd. to Ecclesiastes, in Cambridge Bible. Gore, in Lux Mundi, 355— " Ecclesiastes, though like the book of Wisdom purporting to be by Solomon, may be by another author. . . . ' A pious fraud ' cannot be inspired ; an idealizing personification, as a normal type of literature, can be inspired." Yet Bernhard Schäfer, Das Buch Koheleth, ably maintains the Solomonic authorship.

(*b*) Moral truth may be put by Scripture writers into parabolic or dramatic form, and the sayings of Satan and of perverse men may form parts of such a production. In such cases, inspiration may vouch, not for the historical truth, much less for the moral truth of each separate statement, but only for the correspondence of the whole with ideal fact ; in other words, inspiration may guarantee that the story is true to nature, and is valuable as conveying divine instruction.

It is not necessary to suppose that the poetical speeches of Job's friends were actually delivered in the words that have come down to us. Though Job never had had a historical existence, the book would still be of the utmost value, and would convey to us a vast amount of true teaching with regard to the dealings of God and the problem of evil. Fact is local ; truth is universal. Some novels contain more truth than can be found in some histories. Other books of Scripture, however, assure us that Job was an actual historical character (Ez. 14:14; James 5:11). Nor is it necessary to suppose that our Lord, in telling the parable of the Prodigal Son (Luke 15:11-32) or that of the Unjust Steward (16:1-8), had in mind actual persons of whom each parable was an exact description.

Fiction is not an unworthy vehicle of spiritual truth. Parable, and even fable, may convey valuable lessons. In Judges 9:14, 15, the trees, the vine, the bramble, all talk. If truth can be transmitted in myth and legend, surely God may make use of these methods of communicating it, and even though Gen. 1-3 were mythical it might still be inspired. Aristotle said that poetry is truer than history. The latter only tells us that certain things happened. Poetry presents to us the permanent passions, aspirations and deeds of men which are behind all history and which make it what it is; see Dewey, Psychology, 197. Though Job were a drama and Jonah an apologue, both might be inspired. David Copperfield, the Apology of Socrates, Fra Lippo Lippi, were not the authors of the productions which bear their names, but Dickens, Plato and Browning, rather. Impersonation is a proper method in literature. The speeches of Herodotus and Thucydides might be analogues to those in Deuteronomy and in the Acts, and yet these last might be inspired.

The book of Job could not have been written in patriarchal times. Walled cities, kings, courts, lawsuits, prisons, stocks, mining enterprises, are found in it. Judges are bribed by the rich to decide against the poor. All this belongs to the latter years of the Jewish Kingdom. Is then the book of Job all a lie? No more than Bunyan's Pilgrim's Progress and the parable of the Good Samaritan are all a lie. The book of Job is a dramatic poem. Like Macbeth or the Ring and the Book, it is founded in fact. H. P. Smith. Biblical Scholarship and Inspiration, 101 — "The value of the book of Job lies in the spectacle of a human soul in its direst affliction working through its doubts, and at last humbly confessing its weakness and sinfulness in the presence of its Maker. The inerrancy is not in Job's words or in those of his friends, but in the truth of the picture presented. If Jehovah's words at the end of the book are true, then the first thirty-five chapters are not infallible teaching."

Gore, in Lux Mundi, 355, suggests in a similar manner that the books of Jonah and of Daniel may be dramatic compositions worked up upon a basis of history. George Adam Smith, in the Expositors' Bible, tells us that Jonah flourished 780 B. C., in the reign of Jeroboam II. Nineveh fell in 606. The book implies that it was written after this (3:3 — "Nineveh *was* an exceeding great city"). The book does not claim to be written by Jonah, by an eye-witness, or by a contemporary. The language has Aramaic forms. The date is probably 300 B. C. There is an absence of precise data, such as the sin of Nineveh, the journey of the prophet thither, the place where he was cast out on land, the name of the Assyrian king. The book illustrates God's mission of prophecy to the Gentiles, his care for them, their susceptibility to his word. Israel flies from duty, but is delivered to carry salvation to the heathen. Jeremiah had represented Israel as swallowed up and cast out (Jer. 51:34, 44 *sq*. — "Nebuchadnezzar the king of Babylon hath devoured me. . . . he hath, like a monster, swallowed me up, he hath filled his maw with my delicacies; he hath cast me out. . . . I will bring forth out of his mouth that which he hath swallowed up." Some tradition of Jonah's proclaiming doom to Nineveh may have furnished the basis of the apologue. Our Lord uses the story as a mere illustration, like the homiletic use of Shakespeare's dramas. "As Macbeth did," "As Hamlet said," do not commit us to the historical reality of Macbeth or of Hamlet. Jesus may say as to questions of criticism: "Man, who made me a judge or a divider over you?" "I came not to judge the world, but to save the world" (Luke 12:14; John 12:47). He had no thought of confirming, or of not confirming, the historic character of the story. It is hard to conceive the compilation of a psalm by a man in Jonah's position. It is not the prayer of one inside the fish, but of one already saved. More than forty years ago President Woolsey of Yale conceded that the book of Jonah was probably an apologue.

(c) In none of these cases ought the difficulty of distinguishing man's words from God's words, or ideal truth from actual truth, to prevent our acceptance of the fact of inspiration ; for in this very variety of the Bible, combined with the stimulus it gives to inquiry and the general plainness of its lessons, we have the very characteristics we should expect in a book whose authorship was divine.

The Scripture is a stream in which " the lamb may wade and the elephant may swim." There is need both of literary sense and of spiritual insight to interpret it. This sense and this insight can be given only by the Spirit of Christ, the Holy Spirit, who inspired the various writings to witness of him in various ways, and who is present in the world to take of the things of Christ and show them to us (Mat. 28 : 20 ; John 16 : 13, 14). In a subordinate sense the Holy Spirit inspires us to recognize inspiration in the Bible. In the sense here suggested we may assent to the words of Dr. Charles H. Parkhurst at the inauguration of William Adams Brown as Professor of Systematic Theology in the Union Theological Seminary, November 1, 1898 — " Unfortunately we have condemned the word ' inspiration ' to a particular and isolated field of divine operation, and it is a trespass upon current usage to employ it in the full urgency of its Scriptural intent in connection with work like your own or mine. But the word voices a reality that lies so close to the heart of the entire Christian matter that we can ill afford to relegate it to any single or technical function. Just as much to-day as back at the first beginnings of Christianity, those who would *declare* the truths of God must be inspired to *behold* the truths of God. . . . The only irresistible persuasiveness is that which is born of vision, and it is *not* vision to be able merely to describe what some seer has seen, though it were Moses or Paul that was the seer."

10. *Acknowledgment of the non-inspiration of Scripture teachers and their writings.*

This charge rests mainly upon the misinterpretation of two particular passages :

(*a*) Acts 23 : 5 (" I wist not, brethren, that he was the high priest ") may be explained either as the language of indignant irony : " I would not recognize such a man as high priest " ; or, more naturally, an actual confession of personal ignorance and fallibility, which does not affect the inspiration of any of Paul's final teachings or writings.

Of a more reprehensible sort was Peter's dissimulation at Antioch, or practical disavowal of his convictions by separating or withdrawing himself from the Gentile Christians (Gal. 2 : 11-13). Here was no public teaching, but the influence of private example. But neither in this case, nor in that mentioned above, did God suffer the error to be a final one. Through the agency of Paul, the Holy Spirit set the matter right.

(*b*) 1 Cor. 7 : 12, 10 (" I, not the Lord " ; " not I, but the Lord "). Here the contrast is not between the apostle inspired and the apostle uninspired, but between the apostle's words and an actual saying of our Lord, as in Mat. 5 : 32 ; 19 : 3-10 ; Mark 10 : 11 ; Luke 16 : 18 (Stanley on Corinthians). The expressions may be paraphrased :— " With regard to this matter no express command was given by Christ before his ascension. As one inspired by Christ, however, I give you my command."

Meyer on 1 Cor. 7 : 10 — " Paul distinguishes, therefore, here and in verses 12, 25, not between his *own* and *inspired* commands, but between those which proceeded from his own (God-inspired) subjectivity and those which Christ himself supplied by his objective word." " Paul knew from the living voice of tradition what commands Christ had given concerning divorce." Or if it should be maintained that Paul here disclaims inspiration,— a supposition contradicted by the following δοκῶ — " I think that I also have the Spirit of God" (verse 40),— it only proves a single exception to his inspiration, and since it is expressly mentioned, and mentioned only once, it implies the inspiration of all the rest of his writings. We might illustrate Paul's method, if this were the case, by the course of the New York Herald when it was first published. Other journals had stood by their own mistakes and had never been willing to acknowledge error. The Herald gained the confidence of the public by correcting every mistake of its reporters. The result was that, when there was no confession of error, the paper was regarded as absolutely trustworthy. So Paul's one acknowledgment of non-inspiration might imply that in all other cases his words had divine authority. On Authority in Religion, see Wilfred Ward, in Hibbert Journal, July, 1903 : 677-692.

PART IV.

THE NATURE, DECREES, AND WORKS OF GOD.

CHAPTER I.

THE ATTRIBUTES OF GOD.

In contemplating the words and acts of God, as in contemplating the words and acts of individual men, we are compelled to assign uniform and permanent effects to uniform and permanent causes. Holy acts and words, we argue, must have their source in a principle of holiness; truthful acts and words, in a settled proclivity to truth; benevolent acts and words, in a benevolent disposition.

Moreover, these permanent and uniform sources of expression and action to which we have applied the terms principle, proclivity, disposition, since they exist harmoniously in the same person, must themselves inhere, and find their unity, in an underlying spiritual substance or reality of which they are the inseparable characteristics and partial manifestations.

Thus we are led naturally from the works to the attributes, and from the attributes to the essence, of God.

For all practical purposes we may use the words essence, substance, being, nature, as synonymous with each other. So, too, we may speak of attribute, quality, characteristic, principle, proclivity, disposition, as practically one. As, in cognizing matter, we pass from its effects in sensation to the qualities which produce the sensations, and then to the material substance to which the qualities belong; and as, in cognizing mind, we pass from its phenomena in thought and action to the faculties and dispositions which give rise to these phenomena, and then to the mental substance to which these faculties and dispositions belong; so, in cognizing God, we pass from his words and acts to his qualities or attributes, and then to the substance or essence to which these qualities or attributes belong.

The teacher in a Young Ladies' Seminary described substance as a cushion, into which the attributes as pins are stuck. But pins and cushion alike are substance,— neither one is quality. The opposite error is illustrated from the experience of Abraham Lincoln on the Ohio River. "What is this transcendentalism that we hear so much about?" asked Mr. Lincoln. The answer came: "You see those swallows digging holes in yonder bank? Well, take away the bank from around those holes, and what is left is transcendentalism." Substance is often represented as being thus transcendental. If such representations were correct, metaphysics would indeed be "that, of which those who listen understand nothing, and which he who speaks does not himself understand," and the metaphysician would be the fox who ran into the hole and then pulled in the hole after him. Substance and attributes are correlates,— neither one is possible without the other. There is no quality that does not qualify something; and there is no thing, either material or spiritual, that can be known or can exist without qualities to differentiate it from other things. In applying the categories of substance and attribute to God, we indulge in no merely curious speculation, but rather yield to the necessities of rational thought and show how we must think of God if we think at all. See Shedd, History of Doctrine, 1:240; Kahnis, Dogmatik, 3:172-188.

I. DEFINITION OF THE TERM ATTRIBUTES.

The attributes of God are those distinguishing characteristics of the divine nature which are inseparable from the idea of God and which constitute the basis and ground for his various manifestations to his creatures.

We call them attributes, because we are compelled to attribute them to God as fundamental qualities or powers of his being, in order to give rational account of certain constant facts in God's self-revelations.

II. RELATION OF THE DIVINE ATTRIBUTES TO THE DIVINE ESSENCE.

1. *The attributes have an objective existence.* They are not mere names for human conceptions of God — conceptions which have their only ground in the imperfection of the finite mind. They are qualities objectively distinguishable from the divine essence and from each other.

The nominalistic notion that God is a being of absolute simplicity, and that in his nature there is no internal distinction of qualities or powers, tends directly to pantheism; denies all reality of the divine perfections; or, if these in any sense still exist, precludes all knowledge of them on the part of finite beings. To say that knowledge and power, eternity and holiness, are identical with the essence of God and with each other, is to deny that we know God at all.

The Scripture declarations of the possibility of knowing God, together with the manifestation of the distinct attributes of his nature, are conclusive against this false notion of the divine simplicity.

Aristotle says well that there is no such thing as a science of the unique, of that which has no analogies or relations. Knowing is distinguishing; what we cannot distinguish from other things we cannot know. Yet a false tendency to regard God as a being of absolute simplicity has come down from mediæval scholasticism, has infected much of the post-reformation theology, and is found even so recently as in Schleiermacher, Rothe, Olshausen, and Ritschl. E. G. Robinson defines the attributes as " our methods of conceiving of God." But this definition is influenced by the Kantian doctrine of relativity and implies that we cannot know God's essence, that is, the thing-in-itself, God's real being. Bowne, Philosophy of Theism, 141 — "This notion of the divine simplicity reduces God to a rigid and lifeless stare. . . . The One is manifold without being many."

The divine simplicity is the starting-point of Philo: God is a being absolutely bare of quality. All quality in finite beings has limitation, and no limitation can be predicated of God who is eternal, unchangeable, simple substance, free, self-sufficient, better than the good and the beautiful. To predicate any quality of God would reduce him to the sphere of finite existence. Of him we can only say *that* he is, not *what* he is; see art. by Schürer, in Encyc. Brit., 18:761.

Illustrations of this tendency are found in Scotus Erigena: " Deus nescit se quid est, quia non est quid "; and in Occam: The divine attributes are distinguished neither substantially nor logically from each other or from the divine essence; the only distinction is that of names; so Gerhard and Quenstedt. Charnock, the Puritan writer, identifies both knowledge and will with the simple essence of God. Schleiermacher makes all the attributes to be modifications of power or causality; in his system God and world = the "natura naturans" and "natura naturata" of Spinoza. There is no distinction of attributes and no succession of acts in God, and therefore no real personality or even spiritual being; see Pfleiderer, Prot. Theol. seit Kant, 110. Schleiermacher said: " My God is the Universe." God is causative force. Eternity, omniscience and holiness are simply aspects of causality. Rothe, on the other hand, makes omniscience to be the all-comprehending principle of the divine nature; and Olshausen, on John 1:1, in a similar manner attempts to prove that the Word of God must have objective and substantial being, by assuming that knowing = willing; whence it would seem to follow that, since God wills all that he knows, he must will moral evil

Bushnell and others identify righteousness in God with benevolence, and therefore cannot see that any atonement needs to be made to God. Ritschl also holds that love is the fundamental divine attribute, and that omnipotence and even personality are simply modifications of love; see Mead, Ritschl's place in the History of Doctrine, 8. Herbert Spencer only carries the principle further when he concludes God to be simple unknowable force.

But to call God everything is the same as to call him nothing. With Dorner, we say that "definition is no limitation." As we rise in the scale of creation from the mere jelly-sac to man, the homogeneous becomes the heterogeneous, there is differentiation of functions, complexity increases. We infer that God, the highest of all, instead of being simple force, is 'infinitely complex, that he has an infinite variety of attributes and powers. Tennyson, Palace of Art (lines omitted in the later editions): "All nature widens upward: evermore The simpler essence lower lies: More complex is more perfect, owning more Discourse, more widely wise."

Jer. 10:10 — God is "the living God"; John 5:26 — he "hath life in himself" — unsearchable riches of positive attributes; John 17:23 — "thou lovedst me" — manifoldness in unity. This complexity in God is the ground of blessedness for him and of progress for us: 1 Tim. 1:11 — "the blessed God"; Jer. 9:23, 24 — "let him glory in this, that he knoweth me." The complex nature of God permits anger at the sinner and compassion for him at the same moment: Ps. 7:11 — "a God that hath indignation every day"; John 3:16 — "God so loved the world"; Ps. 85:10, 11 — "mercy and truth are met together." See Julius Müller, Doct. Sin, 2:116 sq.; Schweizer, Glaubenslehre, 1:229–235; Thomasius, Christi Person und Werk, 1:43, 50; Martensen, Dogmatics, 91 — "If God were the simple One, τὸ ἁπλῶς ἕν, the mystic abyss in which every form of determination were extinguished, there would be nothing in the Unity to be known." Hence "nominalism is incompatible with the idea of revelation. We teach, with realism, that the attributes of God are objective determinations in his revelation and as such are rooted in his inmost essence."

2. *The attributes inhere in the divine essence.* They are not separate existences. They are attributes of God.

While we oppose the nominalistic view which holds them to be mere names with which, by the necessity of our thinking, we clothe the one simple divine essence, we need equally to avoid the opposite realistic extreme of making them separate parts of a composite God.

We cannot conceive of attributes except as belonging to an underlying essence which furnishes their ground of unity. In representing God as a compound of attributes, realism endangers the living unity of the Godhead.

Notice the analogous necessity of attributing the properties of matter to an underlying substance, and the phenomena of thought to an underlying spiritual essence; else matter is reduced to mere force, and mind, to mere sensation,— in short, all things are swallowed up in a vast idealism. The purely realistic explanation of the attributes tends to low and polytheistic conceptions of God. The mythology of Greece was the result of personifying the divine attributes. The *nomina* were turned into *numina*, as Max Müller says; see Taylor, Nature on the Basis of Realism, 293. Instance also Christmas Evans's sermon describing a Council in the Godhead, in which the attributes of Justice, Mercy, Wisdom, and Power argue with one another. Robert Hall called Christmas Evans "the one-eyed orator of Anglesey," but added that his one eye could "light an army through a wilderness"; see Joseph Cross, Life and Sermons of Christmas Evans. 112–116: David Rhys Stephen, Memoirs of Christmas Evans, 168–176. We must remember that "Realism may so exalt the attributes that no personal subject is left to constitute the ground of unity. Looking upon Personality as anthropomorphism, it falls into a worse personification, that of omnipotence, holiness, benevolence, which are mere blind thoughts, unless there is one who is the Omnipotent, the Holy, the Good." See Luthardt, Compendium der Dogmatik, 70.

3. *The attributes belong to the divine essence as such.* They are to be distinguished from those other powers or relations which do not appertain to the divine essence universally.

The personal distinctions (*proprietates*) in the nature of the one God are not to be denominated attributes ; for each of these personal distinctions belongs not to the divine essence as such and universally, but only to the particular person of the Trinity who bears its name, while on the contrary all of the attributes belong to each of the persons.

The relations which God sustains to the world (*predicata*), moreover, such as creation, preservation, government, are not to be denominated attributes ; for these are accidental, not necessary or inseparable from the idea of God. God would be God, if he had never created.

To make creation eternal and necessary is to dethrone God and to enthrone a fatalistic development. It follows that the nature of the attributes is to be illustrated, not alone or chiefly from wisdom and holiness in man, which are not inseparable from man's nature, but rather from intellect and will in man, without which he would cease to be man altogether. Only that is an attribute, of which it can be safely said that he who possesses it would, if deprived of it, cease to be God. Shedd, Dogm. Theol., 1 : 335 — "The attribute is the whole essence acting in a certain way. The centre of unity is not in any one attribute, but in the essence. . . . The difference between the divine attribute and the divine person is, that the person is a mode of the *existence* of the essence, while the attribute is a mode either of the *relation*, or of the *operation*, of the essence."

4. *The attributes manifest the divine essence.* The essence is revealed only through the attributes. Apart from its attributes it is unknown and unknowable.

But though we can know God only as he reveals to us his attributes, we do, notwithstanding, in knowing these attributes, know the being to whom these attributes belong. That this knowledge is partial does not prevent its corresponding, so far as it goes, to objective reality in the nature of God.

All God's revelations are, therefore, revelations of himself in and through his attributes. Our aim must be to determine from God's works and words what qualities, dispositions, determinations, powers of his otherwise unseen and unsearchable essence he has actually made known to us; or in other words, what are the revealed attributes of God.

John 1 : 18 — "No man hath seen God at any time ; the only begotten Son, who is in the bosom of the Father, he hath declared him " ; 1 Tim. 6 : 16 — " whom no man hath seen, nor can see " ; Mat. 5 : 8 — " Blessed are the pure in heart : for they shall see God " ; 11 : 27 — " neither doth any man know the Father, save the Son, and he to whomsoever the Son willeth to reveal him." C. A. Strong : " Kant, not content with knowing the reality *in* the phenomena, was trying to know the reality *apart from* the phenomena ; he was seeking to know, without fulfilling the conditions of knowledge ; in short, he wished to know without knowing." So Agnosticism perversely regards God as concealed by his own manifestation. On the contrary, in knowing the phenomena we know the object itself. J. C. C. Clarke, Self and the Father, 6 — " In language, as in nature, there are no verbs without subjects, but we are always hunting for the noun that has no adjective, and the verb that has no subject, and the subject that has no verb. Consciousness is necessarily a consciousness of self. Idealism and monism would like to see all verbs solid with their subjects, and to write ' I do ' or ' I feel ' in the mazes of a monogram, but consciousness refuses, and before it says ' Do ' or ' Feel,' it finishes saying ' I.' " J. G. Holland's Katrina, to her lover : " God is not worshiped in his attributes. I do not love your attributes, but you. Your attributes all meet me otherwhere, Blended in other personalities, Nor do I love nor do I worship them, Nor those who bear them. E'en the spotted pard Will dare a danger which will make you pale ; But shall his courage steal my heart from you ? You cheat your conscience, for you know That I may like your attributes, Yet love not you."

III. Methods of determining the divine Attributes.

We have seen that the existence of God is a first truth. It is presupposed in all human thinking, and is more or less consciously recognized by all men. This intuitive knowledge of God we have seen to be corroborated and explicated by arguments drawn from nature and from mind. Reason leads us to a causative and personal Intelligence upon whom we depend. This Being of indefinite greatness we clothe, by a necessity of our thinking, with all the attibutes of perfection. The two great methods of determining what these attributes are, are the Rational and the Biblical.

1. *The Rational method.* This is threefold :—(*a*) the *via negationis*, or the way of negation, which consists in denying to God all imperfections observed in created beings; (*b*) the *via eminentiæ*, or the way of climax, which consists in attributing to God in infinite degree all the perfections found in creatures; and (*c*) the *via causalitatis*, or the way of causality, which consists in predicating of God those attributes which are required in him to explain the world of nature and of mind.

This rational method explains God's nature from that of his creation, whereas the creation itself can be fully explained only from the nature of God. Though the method is valuable, it has insuperable limitations, and its place is a subordinate one. While we use it continually to confirm and supplement results otherwise obtained, our chief means of determining the divine attributes must be

2. *The Biblical method.* This is simply the inductive method, applied to the facts with regard to God revealed in the Scriptures. Now that we have proved the Scriptures to be a revelation from God, inspired in every part, we may properly look to them as decisive authority with regard to God's attributes.

The rational method of determining the attributes of God is sometimes said to have been originated by Dionysius the Areopagite, reputed to have been a judge at Athens at the time of Paul and to have died A. D. 95. It is more probably eclectic, combining the results attained by many theologians, and applying the intuitions of perfection and causality which lie at the basis of all religious thinking. It is evident from our previous study of the arguments for God's existence, that from nature we cannot learn either the Trinity or the mercy of God, and that these deficiencies in our rational conclusions with respect to God must be supplied, if at all, by revelation. Spurgeon, Autobiography, 166 — "The old saying is 'Go from Nature up to Nature's God.' But it is hard work going up hill. The best thing is to go from Nature's God down to Nature; and, if you once get to Nature's God and believe him and love him, it is surprising how easy it is to hear music in the waves, and songs in the wild whisperings of the winds, and to see God everywhere." See also Kahnis, Dogmatik, 3 : 181.

IV. CLASSIFICATION OF THE ATTRIBUTES.

The attributes may be divided into two great classes : Absolute or Immanent, and Relative or Transitive.

By Absolute or Immanent Attributes, we mean attributes which respect the inner being of God, which are involved in God's relations to himself, and which belong to his nature independently of his connection with the universe.

By Relative or Transitive Attributes, we mean attributes which respect the outward revelation of God's being, which are involved in God's relations to the creation, and which are exercised in consequence of the existence of the universe and its dependence upon him.

Under the head of Absolute or Immanent Attributes, we make a three-fold division into Spirituality, with the attributes therein involved, namely, Life and Personality; Infinity, with the attributes therein involved, namely, Self-existence, Immutability, and Unity; and Perfection, with the attributes therein involved, namely, Truth, Love, and Holiness.

Under the head of Relative or Transitive Attributes, we make a three-fold division, according to the order of their revelation, into Attributes having relation to Time and Space, as Eternity and Immensity; Attributes having relation to Creation, as Omnipresence, Omniscience, and Omnipotence; and Attributes having relation to Moral Beings, as Veracity and Faithfulness, or Transitive Truth; Mercy and Goodness, or Transitive Love; and Justice and Righteousness, or Transitive Holiness.

This classification may be better understood from the following schedule:

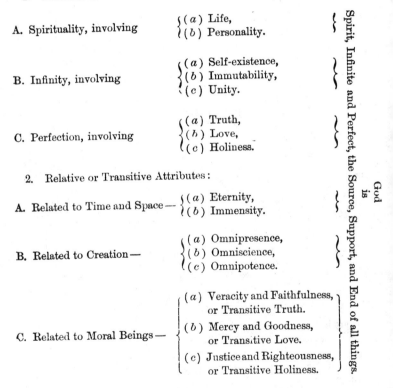

1. Absolute or Immanent Attributes:

A. Spirituality, involving — (a) Life, (b) Personality.

B. Infinity, involving — (a) Self-existence, (b) Immutability, (c) Unity.

C. Perfection, involving — (a) Truth, (b) Love, (c) Holiness.

2. Relative or Transitive Attributes:

A. Related to Time and Space — (a) Eternity, (b) Immensity.

B. Related to Creation — (a) Omnipresence, (b) Omniscience, (c) Omnipotence.

C. Related to Moral Beings — (a) Veracity and Faithfulness, or Transitive Truth. (b) Mercy and Goodness, or Transitive Love. (c) Justice and Righteousness, or Transitive Holiness.

God is Spirit, Infinite and Perfect, the Source, Support, and End of all things.

It will be observed, upon examination of the preceding schedule, that our classification presents God first as Spirit, then as the infinite Spirit, and finally as the perfect Spirit. This accords with our definition of the term God (see page 52). It also corresponds with the order in which the attributes commonly present themselves to the human mind. Our first thought of God is that of mere Spirit, mysterious and undefined, over against our own spirits. Our next thought is that of God's greatness; the quantitative element suggests itself; his natural attributes rise before us; we recognize him as the infinite One. Finally comes the qualitative element; our moral natures recognize a moral God; over against our error, selfishness and impurity, we perceive his absolute perfection.

It should also be observed that this moral perfection, as it is an immanent attribute, involves relation of God to himself. Truth, love and holiness, as they respectively imply an exercise in God of intellect, affection and will, may be conceived of as God's self-knowing, God's self-loving, and God's self-willing. The significance of this will appear more fully in the discussion of the separate attributes.

Notice the distinction between absolute and relative, between immanent and transitive, attributes. Absolute = existing in no necessary relation to things outside of God. Relative = existing in such relation. Immanent = "remaining within, limited to, God's own nature in their activity and effect, inherent and indwelling, internal and subjective — opposed to emanent or transitive." Transitive = having an object outside of God himself. We speak of transitive verbs, and we mean verbs that are followed by an object. God's transitive attributes are so called, because they respect and affect things and beings outside of God.

The aim of this classification into Absolute and Relative Attributes is to make plain the divine self-sufficiency. Creation is not a necessity, for there is a πλήρωμα in God (Col. 1:19), even before he makes the world or becomes incarnate. And πλήρωμα is not "the filling material," nor "the vessel filled," but "that which is complete in itself," or, in other words, "plenitude," "fulness," "totality," "abundance." The whole universe is but a drop of dew upon the fringe of God's garment, or a breath exhaled from his mouth. He could create a universe a hundred times as great. Nature is but the symbol of God. The tides of life that ebb and flow on the far shores of the universe are only faint expressions of his life. The Immanent Attributes show us how completely matters of grace are Creation and Redemption, and how unspeakable is the condescension of him who took our humanity and humbled himself to the death of the Cross. Ps. 8:3, 4 — "When I consider thy heavens . . . . what is man that thou art mindful of him?" 113:5, 6 — "Who is like unto Jehovah our God, that hath his seat on high, that humbleth himself?" Phil. 2:6, 7 — "Who, existing in the form of God, ... emptied himself, taking the form of a servant."

Ladd, Theory of Reality, 69 — "I know that I am, because, as the basis of all discriminations as to what I am, and as the core of all such self-knowledge, I immediately know myself as will." So as to the non-ego, "that things actually are is a factor in my knowledge of them which springs from the root of an experience with myself as a will, at once active and inhibited, as an agent and yet opposed by another." The ego and the non-ego as well are fundamentally and essentially will. "Matter must be, per se. Force. But this is . . . to be a Will" (439). We know nothing of the atom apart from its force (442). Ladd quotes from G. E. Bailey: "The life-principle, varying only in degree, is omnipresent. There is but one indivisible and absolute Omniscience and Intelligence, and this thrills through every atom of the whole Cosmos" (446). "Science has only made the Substrate of material things more and more completely self-like" (449). Spirit is the true and essential Being of what is called Nature (472). "The ultimate Being of the world is a self-conscious Mind and Will, which is the Ground of all objects made known in human experience" (550).

On classification of attributes, see Luthardt, Compendium, 71; Rothe, Dogmatik, 71: Kahnis, Dogmatik, 3:162; Thomasius, Christi Person und Werk, 1:47, 52, 136. On the general subject, see Charnock, Attributes; Bruce, Eigenschaftslehre.

V. Absolute or Immanent Attributes.

First division. —Spirituality, and attributes therein involved.

In calling spirituality an attribute of God, we mean, not that we are justified in applying to the divine nature the adjective "spiritual," but that the substantive "Spirit" describes that nature (John 4:24, marg.—"God is spirit"; Rom. 1:20 — "the invisible things of him"; 1 Tim. 1:17 — "incorruptible, invisible"; Col. 1:15 — "the invisible God"). This implies, negatively, that (a) God is not matter. Spirit is not a refined form of matter but an immaterial substance, invisible, uncompounded, indestructible. (b) God is not dependent upon matter. It cannot be shown that the human mind, in any other state than the present, is dependent for consciousness upon its connection with a physical organism Much less is it true that God is dependent upon the material universe as his sensorium. God is not only spirit, but he is pure spirit. He is not only not matter, but he has no necessary connection with matter (Luke 24 : 39 — "A spirit hath not flesh and bones, as ye behold me having").

John gives us the three characteristic attributes of God when he says that God is "spirit," "light," "love" (John 4 : 24 ; 1 John 1 : 5 ; 4 : 8),—not *a* spirit, *a* light, *a* love. Le Conte, in Royce's Conception of God, 45 — "God is spirit, for spirit is essential Life and essential Energy, and essential Love, and essential Thought ; in a word, essential Person." Biedermann, Dogmatik, 631 — "Das Wesen des Geistes als des reinen Gegensatzes zur Materie, ist das *reine Sein*, das *in sich ist*, aber *nicht da ist*." Martineau, Study, 2 : 366 — "The subjective Ego is always *here*, as opposed to all else, which is variously *there*. . . . . Without local relations, therefore, the soul is inaccessible." But, Martineau continues, "if matter be but centres of force, all the soul needs may be centres from which to act." Romanes, Mind and Motion, 34 — "Because within the limits of human experience mind is only known as associated with brain, it does not follow that mind cannot exist in any other mode." La Place swept the heavens with his telescope, but could not find anywhere a God. "He might just as well," says President Sawyer, "have swept his kitchen with a broom." Since God is not a material being, he cannot be apprehended by any physical means.

Those passages of Scripture which seem to ascribe to God the possession of bodily parts and organs, as eyes and hands, are to be regarded as anthropomorphic and symbolic. When God is spoken of as appearing to the patriarchs and walking with them, the passages are to be explained as referring to God's temporary manifestations of himself in human form — manifestations which prefigured the final tabernacling of the Son of God in human flesh. Side by side with these anthropomorphic expressions and manifestations, moreover, are specific declarations which repress any materializing conceptions of God ; as, for example, that heaven is his throne and the earth his footstool (Is. 66 : 1), and that the heaven of heavens cannot contain him (1 K. 8 : 27).

Ex. 33 : 18-20 declares that man cannot see God and live ; 1 Cor. 2 : 7-16 intimates that without the teaching of God's Spirit we cannot know God ; all this teaches that God is above sensuous perception, in other words, that he is not a material being. The second command of the decalogue does not condemn sculpture and painting, but only the making of images of *God*. It forbids our conceiving God after the likeness of a *thing*, but it does not forbid our conceiving God after the likeness of our inward *self*, *i. e.*, as *personal*. This again shows that God is a spiritual being. Imagination can be used in religion, and great help can be derived from it. Yet we do not know God by imagination, — imagination only helps us vividly to realize the presence of the God whom we already know. We may almost say that some men have not imagination enough to be religious. But imagination must not lose its wings. In its representations of God, it must not be confined to a picture, or a form, or a place. Humanity tends too much to rest in the material and the sensuous, and we must avoid all representations of God which would identify the Being who is worshiped with the helps used in order to realize his presence ; John 4 : 24 — "they that worship him must worship in spirit and truth."

An Egyptian Hymn to the Nile, dating from the 19th dynasty (14th century B. C.), contains these words : "His abode is not known ; no shrine is found with painted figures ; there is no building that can contain him" (Cheyne, Isaiah, 2 : 120). The repudiation of images among the ancient Persians (Herod. 1 : 131), as among the Japanese Shintos, indicates the remains of a primitive spiritual religion. The representation of Jehovah with body or form degrades him to the level of heathen gods. Pictures of the Almighty over the chancels of Romanist cathedrals confine the mind and degrade the conception of the worshiper. We may use imagination in prayer, picturing God as a benignant form holding out arms of mercy, but we should regard such pictures only as scaffolding for the building of our edifice of worship, while we recognize, with the Scripture, that the reality worshiped is immaterial and spiritual. Otherwise our idea of

God is brought down to the low level of man's material being. Even man's spiritual nature may be misrepresented by physical images, as when mediæval artists pictured death, by painting a doll-like figure leaving the body at the mouth of the person dying.

The longing for a tangible, incarnate God meets its satisfaction in Jesus Christ. Yet even pictures of Christ soon lose their power. Luther said: "If I have a picture of Christ in my heart, why not one upon canvas?" We answer: Because the picture in the heart is capable of change and improvement, as we ourselves change and improve; the picture upon canvas is fixed, and holds to old conceptions which we should outgrow. Thomas Carlyle: "Men never think of painting the face of Christ, till they lose the impression of him upon their hearts." Swedenborg, in modern times, represents the view that God exists in the shape of a man — an anthropomorphism of which the making of idols is only a grosser and more barbarous form; see H. B. Smith, System of Theology, 9, 10. This is also the doctrine of Mormonism; see Spencer, Catechism of Latter Day Saints. The Mormons teach that God is a man; that he has numerous wives by whom he peoples space with an infinite number of spirits. Christ was a favorite son by a favorite wife, but birth as man was the only way he could come into the enjoyment of real life. These spirits are all the sons of God, but they can realize and enjoy their sonship only through birth. They are about every one of us pleading to be born. Hence, polygamy.

We come now to consider the positive import of the term Spirit. The spirituality of God involves the two attributes of Life and Personality.

1. Life.

The Scriptures represent God as the living God.

Jer. 10 : 10 — "He is the living God"; 1 Thess. 1 : 9 — "turned unto God from idols, to serve a living and true God"; John 5 : 26 — "hath life in himself"; *cf.* 14 : 6 — "I am . . . the life," and Heb. 7 : 16 — "the power of an endless life"; Rev. 11 : 11 — "the Spirit of life."

Life is a simple idea, and is incapable of real definition. We know it, however, in ourselves, and we can perceive the insufficiency or inconsistency of certain current definitions of it. We cannot regard life in God as

(*a*) Mere *process*, without a subject; for we cannot conceive of a divine life without a God to live it.

Versus Lewes, Problems of Life and Mind, 1 : 10 — "Life and mind are processes; neither is a substance; neither is a force; . . . the name given to the whole group of phenomena becomes the personification of the phenomena, and the product is supposed to have been the producer." Here we have a product without any producer — a series of phenomena without any substance of which they are manifestations. In a similar manner we read in Dewey, Psychology, 247 — "Self is an *activity*. It is not something which *acts*; it is activity. . . . It is constituted by activities. . . . Through its activity the soul *is*." Here it does not appear how there can be activity, without any subject or being that is active. The inconsistency of this view is manifest when Dewey goes on to say: "The activity may further or develop the self," and when he speaks of "the organic activity of the self." So Dr. Burdon Sanderson: "Life is a state of ceaseless change,— a state of change with permanence; living matter ever changes while it is ever the same." "Plus ça change, plus c'est la même chose." But this permanent thing in the midst of change is the subject, the self, the being, that *has* life.

Nor can we regard life as

(*b*) Mere *correspondence* with outward condition and environment; for this would render impossible a life of God before the existence of the universe.

Versus Herbert Spencer, Biology, 1 : 59-71 — "Life is the definite combination of heterogeneous changes, both simultaneous and successive, in correspondence with external coëxistences and sequences." Here we have, at best, a definition of physical and finite life; and even this is insufficient, because the definition recognizes no original source of activity within, but only a power of reaction in response to stimulus from without. We might as well say that the boiling tea-kettle is alive (Mark Hopkins). We find this defect also in Robert Browning's lines in The Ring and the Book (The Pope, 1307): " O Thou — as represented here to me In such conception as my soul allows — Under thy measureless, my atom-width ! — Man's mind, what is it but a convex glass Wherein are gathered all the scattered points Picked out of the immensity of sky, To reunite there, be our heaven for earth, Our known Unknown, our God revealed to man ? " Life is something more than a passive receptivity.

(c) Life is rather *mental energy*, or energy of intellect, affection, and will. God is the living God, as having in his own being a source of being and activity, both for himself and others.

Life means energy, activity, movement. Aristotle: "Life is energy of mind." Wordsworth, Excursion, book 5 : 602 — " Life is love and immortality, The Being one, and one the element. . . . Life, I repeat, is energy of love Divine or human." Prof. C. L. Herrick, on Critics of Ethical Monism, in Denison Quarterly, Dec. 1896 : 248 — " Force is energy under resistance, or self-limited energy, for all parts of the universe are derived from the energy. Energy manifesting itself under self-conditioning or differential forms is force. The change of pure energy into force is creation." Prof. Herrick quotes from S. T. Coleridge, Anima Poetæ : " Space is the name for God ; it is the most perfect image of soul — pure soul being to us nothing but unresisted action. Whenever action is resisted, limitation begins — and limitation is the first constituent of body ; the more omnipresent it is in a given space, the more that space is body or matter ; and thus all body presupposes soul, inasmuch as all resistance presupposes action." Schelling : " Life is the tendency to individualism."

If spirit in man implies life, spirit in God implies endless and inexhaustible life. The total life of the universe is only a faint image of that moving energy which we call the life of God. Dewey, Psychology, 253 — " The sense of being alive is much more vivid in childhood than afterwards. Leigh Hunt says that, when he was a child, the sight of certain palings painted red gave him keener pleasure than any experience of manhood." Matthew Arnold : " Bliss was it in that dawn to be alive, But to be young was very heaven." The child's delight in country scenes, and our intensified perceptions in brain fever, show us by contrast how shallow and turbid is the stream of our ordinary life. Tennyson, Two Voices : " 'T is life, whereof our nerves are scant, Oh life, not death, for which we pant ; More life, and fuller, that we want." That life the needy human spirit finds only in the infinite God. Instead of Tyndall's : " Matter has in it the promise and potency of every form of life," we accept Sir William Crookes's dictum : " Life has in it the promise and potency of every form of matter." See A. H. Strong, on The Living God, in Philos. and Religion, 180–187.

2. Personality.

The Scriptures represent God as a personal being. By personality we mean the power of self-consciousness and of self-determination. By way of further explanation we remark :

(a) Self-consciousness is more than consciousness. This last the brute may be supposed to possess, since the brute is not an automaton. Man is distinguished from the brute by his power to objectify self. Man is not only conscious of his own acts and states, but by abstraction and reflection he recognizes the self which is the subject of these acts and states. (b) Self-determination is more than determination. The brute shows determination, but his determination is the result of influences from without; there is no inner spontaneity. Man, by virtue of his free-will, determines his action from within. He determines self in view of motives, but his determination is not caused by motives ; he himself is the cause.

God, as personal, is in the highest degree self-conscious and self-determining. The rise in our own minds of the idea of God, as personal, depends largely upon our recognition of personality in ourselves. Those who deny spirit in man place a bar in the way of the recognition of this attribute of God.

Ex. 3 : 14—"And God said unto Moses, I AM THAT I AM: and he said, Thus shalt thou say unto the children of Israel, I A M hath sent me unto you." God is not the everlasting "IT IS," or "I WAS," but the everlasting "I AM" (Morris, Philosophy and Christianity, 128); "I AM" implies both personality and presence. 1 Cor. 2 : 11 — "the things of God none knoweth, save the Spirit of God"; Eph. 1 : 9 —"good pleasure which he purposed"; 11 —"the counsel of his will." Definitions of personality are the following: Boethius—"Persona est animæ rationalis individua substantia" (quoted in Dorner, Glaubenslehre, 2 : 415). F. W. Robertson, Genesis 3 — "Personality = self-consciousness, will, character." Porter, Human Intellect, 626 — "Distinct subsistence, either actually or latently self-conscious and self-determining." Harris, Philos. Basis of Theism : Person = "being, conscious of self, subsisting in individuality and identity, and endowed with intuitive reason, rational sensibility, and free-will." See Harris, 98, 99, quotation from Mansel — "The freedom of the will is so far from being, as it is generally considered, a controvertible question in philosophy, that it is the fundamental postulate without which all action and all speculation, philosophy in all its branches and human consciousness itself, would be impossible."

One of the most astounding announcements in all literature is that of Matthew Arnold, in his "Literature and Dogma," that the Hebrew Scriptures recognize in God only "the power, not ourselves, that makes for righteousness" = the God of pantheism. The "I AM" of Ex. 3 : 14 could hardly have been so misunderstood, if Matthew Arnold had not lost the sense of his own personality and responsibility. From free-will in man we rise to freedom in God — "That living Will that shall endure, When all that seems shall suffer shock." Observe that personality needs to be accompanied by life — the power of self-consciousness and self-determination needs to be accompanied by activity — in order to make up our total idea of God as Spirit. Only this personality of God gives proper meaning to his punishments or to his forgiveness. See Bib. Sac., April, 1884 : 217–233; Eichhorn, die Persönlichkeit Gottes.

Illingworth, Divine and Human Personality, 1 : 25, shows that the sense of personality has had a gradual growth; that its pre-Christian recognition was imperfect; that its final definition has been due to Christianity. In 29–53, he notes the characteristics of personality as reason, love, will. The brute *perceives*; only the man *apperceives, i. e.*, recognizes his perception as belonging to himself. In the German story, Dreiäuglein, the three-eyed child, had besides her natural pair of eyes one other to see what the pair did, and besides her natural will had an additional will to set the first to going right. On consciousness and self-consciousness, see Shedd, Dogm. Theol., 1 : 179-189 — "In consciousness the object is another substance than the subject; but in self-consciousness the object is the same substance as the subject." Tennyson, in his Palace of Art, speaks of "the abysmal depths of personality." We do not fully know ourselves, nor yet our relation to God. But the divine consciousness embraces the whole divine content of being: "the Spirit searcheth all things, yea, the deep things of God" (1 Cor. 2 : 10).

We are not fully masters of ourselves. Our self-determination is as limited as is our self-consciousness. But the divine will is absolutely without hindrance; God's activity is constant, intense, infinite; Job 23 : 13 —"What his soul desireth, even that he doeth"; John 5 : 17—"My Father worketh even until now, and I work." Self-knowledge and self-mastery are the dignity of man; they are also the dignity of God; Tennyson: "Self-reverence, self-knowledge, self-control, These three lead life to sovereign power." Robert Browning, The Last Ride Together: "What act proved all its thought had been? What will but felt the fleshly screen?" Moberly, Atonement and Personality, 6, 161, 216–255 — "Perhaps the root of personality is capacity for affection." . . . . Our personality is incomplete; we reason truly only with God helping; our love in higher Love endures; we will rightly, only as God works in us to will and to do; to make us truly ourselves we need an infinite Personality to supplement and energize our own; we are complete only in Christ (Col. 2 : 9, 10 —"In him dwelleth all the fulness of the Godhead bodily, and in him ye are made full."

Webb, on the Idea of Personality as applied to God, in Jour. Theol. Studies, 2 : 50 — "Self knows itself and what is not itself as two, just because both alike are embraced within the unity of its experience, stand out against this background, the apprehension of which is the very essence of that rationality or personality which distinguishes us from the lower animals. We find that background, God, present in us, or rather, we find ourselves present in it. But if I find myself present in it, then it, as more complete, is simply more personal than I. Our not-self is outside of us, so that we are finite and lonely, but God's not-self is within him, so that there is a mutual inwardness of love and insight of which the most perfect communion among men is only a faint symbol. We are 'hermit-spirits,' as Keble says, and we come to union with others only by realizing our union with God. Personality is not impenetrable in man, for 'in him we live, and move, and have our being' (Acts 17 : 28), and 'that which hath been made is life in him (John 1 : 3, 4)." Palmer, Theologic Definition, 39 — "That which has its cause without itself is a thing, while that which has its cause within itself is a person."

Second Division.—Infinity, and attributes therein involved.

By infinity we mean, not that the divine nature has no known limits or bounds, but that it has no limits or bounds. That which has simply no known limits is the indefinite. The infinity of God implies that he is in no way limited by the universe or confined to the universe ; he is transcendent as well as immanent. Transcendence, however, must not be conceived as freedom from merely spatial restrictions, but rather as unlimited resource, of which God's glory is the expression.

Ps. 145 : 3 —"his greatness is unsearchable"; Job 11 : 7-9 — "high as heaven . . . deeper than Sheol "; Is. 66 : 1— " Heaven is my throne, and the earth is my footstool "; 1 K. 8 : 27 — " Heaven and the heaven of heavens cannot contain thee "; Rom. 11 : 33 — "how unsearchable are his judgments, and his ways past finding out." There can be no infinite number, since to any assignable number a unit can be added, which shows that this number was not infinite before. There can be no infinite universe, because an infinite universe is conceivable only as an infinite number of worlds or of minds. God himself is the only real Infinite, and the universe is but the finite expression or symbol of his greatness.

We therefore object to the statement of Lotze, Microcosm, 1 : 446 — "The complete system, grasped in its totality, offers an expression of the whole nature of the One. . . . . The Cause makes actual existence its complete manifestation." In a similar way Schurman, Belief in God, 26, 173-178, grants infinity, but denies transcendence : "The infinite Spirit may include the finite, as the idea of a single organism embraces within a single life a plurality of members and functions. . . . The world is the expression of an ever active and inexhaustible will. That the external manifestation is as boundless as the life it expresses, science makes exceedingly probable. In any event, we have not the slightest reason to contrast the finitude of the world with the infinity of God. . . . . If the natural order is eternal and infinite, as there seems no reason to doubt, it will be difficult to find a meaning for 'beyond' or 'before.' Of this illimitable, ever-existing universe, God is the inner ground or substance. There is no evidence, neither does any religious need require us to believe, that the divine Being manifest in the universe has any actual or possible existence elsewhere, in some transcendent sphere. . . . . The divine will can express itself only as it does, because no other expression would reveal what it is. Of such a will, the universe is the eternal expression."

In explanation of the term infinity, we may notice :

(a) That infinity can belong to but one Being, and therefore cannot be shared with the universe. Infinity is not a negative but a positive idea. It does not take its rise from an impotence of thought, but is an intuitive conviction which constitutes the basis of all other knowledge.

See Porter, Human Intellect, 651, 652, and this Compendium, pages 59-62. Versus Mansel, Proleg. Logica, chap. 1 — "Such negative notions . . . imply at once an attempt to think, and a failure in that attempt." On the contrary, the conception of the Infinite is perfectly distinguishable from that of the finite, and is both necessary and logically prior to that of the finite. This is not true of our idea of the universe, of which all we know is finite and dependent. We therefore regard such utterances as those of Lotze and Schurman above, and those of Chamberlin and Caird below, as pantheistic in tendency, although the belief of these writers in divine and human personality saves them from falling into other errors of pantheism.

Prof. T. C. Chamberlin, of the University of Chicago : "It is not sufficient to the modern scientific thought to think of a Ruler outside of the universe, nor of a universe with the Ruler outside. A supreme Being who does not embrace all the activities and possibilities and potencies of the universe seems something less than the supremest Being, and a universe with a Ruler outside seems something less than a universe. And therefore the thought is growing on the minds of scientific thinkers that the supreme Being is the universal Being, embracing and comprehending all things."

Caird, Evolution of Religion, 2:62 — "Religion, if it would continue to exist, must combine the monotheistic idea with that which it has often regarded as its greatest enemy, the spirit of pantheism." We grant in reply that religion must appropriate the element of truth in pantheism, namely, that God is the only substance, ground and principle of being, but we regard it as fatal to religion to side with pantheism in its denials of God's transcendence and of God's personality.

(b) That the infinity of God does not involve his identity with 'the all,' or the sum of existence, nor prevent the coëxistence of derived and finite beings to which he bears relation. Infinity implies simply that God exists in no necessary relation to finite things or beings, and that whatever limitation of the divine nature results from their existence is, on the part of God, a self-limitation.

Ps. 113 : 5, 6 — "that humbleth himself to behold the things that are in heaven and in the earth." It is involved in God's infinity that there should be no barriers to his self-limitation in creation and redemption (see page 9, F.). Jacob Boehme said : "God is infinite, for God is all." But this is to make God all imperfection, as well as all perfection. Harris, Philos. Basis Theism : "The relation of the absolute to the finite is not the mathematical relation of a total to its parts, but it is a dynamical and rational relation." Shedd, Dogm. Theol., 1 : 189-191 — "The infinite is not the total ; 'the all' is a pseudo-infinite, and to assert that it is greater than the simple infinite is the same error that is committed in mathematics when it is asserted that an infinite number plus a vast finite number is greater than the simple infinite." Fullerton, Conception of the Infinite, 90 — "The Infinite, though it involves unlimited possibility of quantity, is not itself a quantitative but rather a qualitative conception." Hovey, Studies of Ethics and Religion, 39-47 — "Any number of finite beings, minds, loves, wills, cannot reveal fully an infinite Being, Mind, Love, Will. God must be transcendent as well as immanent in the universe, or he is neither infinite nor an object of supreme worship."

Clarke, Christian Theology, 117 — "Great as the universe is, God is not limited to it, wholly absorbed by what he is doing in it, and capable of doing nothing more. God in the universe is not like the life of the tree in the tree, which does all that it is capable of in making the tree what it is. God in the universe is rather like the spirit of a man in his body, which is greater than his body, able to direct his body, and capable of activities in which his body has no share. God is a free spirit, personal, self-directing, unexhausted by his present activities." The Persian poet said truly : "The world is a bud from his bower of beauty ; the sun is a spark from the light of his wisdom ; the sky is a bubble on the sea of his power." Faber : "For greatness which is infinite makes room For all things in its lap to lie. We should be crushed by a magnificence Short of infinity. We share in what is infinite ; 't is ours, For we and it alike are Thine. What I enjoy, great God, by right of Thee, Is more than doubly mine."

(c) That the infinity of God is to be conceived of as intensive, rather than as extensive. We do not attribute to God infinite extension, but rather infinite energy of spiritual life. That which acts up to the measure of its power is simply natural and physical force. Man rises above nature by virtue of his reserves of power. But in God the reserve is infinite. There is a transcendent element in him, which no self-revelation exhausts, whether creation or redemption, whether law or promise.

Transcendence is not mere outsideness, — it is rather boundless supply within. God is not infinite by virtue of existing "extra flammantia mœnia mundi" (Lucretius) or of filling a space outside of space, — he is rather infinite by being the pure and perfect Mind that passes b- yond all phenomena and constitutes the ground of them. The former conception of infinity is simply supra-cosmic, the latter alone is properly transcendent ; see Hatch, Hibbert Lectures, 244. "God is the living God, and has not yet spoken his last word on any subject " (G. W. Northrup). God's life "operates unspent." There is "ever more to follow." The legend stamped with the Pillars of Hercules upon the old coins of Spain was Ne plus ultra — "Nothing beyond," but when Columbus discovered America the legend was fitly changed to Plus ultra — " More beyond." So the motto of the University of Rochester is Meliora — "Better things."

Since God's infinite resources are pledged to aid us, we may, as Emerson bids us, "hitch our wagon to a star," and believe in progress. Tennyson, Locksley Hall: "Men, my brothers, men the workers, ever reaping something new, That which they have done but earnest of the things that they shall do." Millet's L'Angelus is a witness to man's need of God's transcendence. Millet's aim was to paint, not *air* but *prayer*. We need a God who is not confined to nature. As Moses at the beginning of his ministry cried, "Show me, I pray thee, thy glory" (Ex. 33:18), so we need marked experiences at the beginning of the Christian life, in order that we may be living witnesses to the supernatural. And our Lord promises such manifestations of himself: John 14:21 — "I will love him, and will manifest myself unto him."

Ps. 71:15 — "My mouth shall tell of thy righteousness, And of thy salvation all the day; For I know not the numbers thereof" = it is infinite. Ps. 89:2 — "Mercy shall be built up forever" = ever growing manifestations and cycles of fulfilment — first literal, then spiritual. Ps. 113:4–6 — "Jehovah is high above all nations, And his glory above the heavens. Who is like unto Jehovah our God, That hath his seat on high, That humbleth himself [stoopeth down] to behold The things that are in heaven and in the earth?" Mal. 2:15 — "did he not make one, although he had the residue of the Spirit?" = he might have created many wives for Adam, though he did actually create but one. In this "residue of the Spirit," says Caldwell, Cities of our Faith, 300, "there yet lies latent — as winds lie calm in the air of a summer noon, as heat immense lies cold and hidden in the mountains of coal — the blessing and the life of nations, the infinite enlargement of Zion."

Is. 52:10 —"Jehovah hath made bare his holy arm" = nature does not exhaust or entomb God; nature is the mantle in which he commonly reveals himself; but he is not fettered by the robe he wears — he can thrust it aside, and make bare his arm in providential interpositions for earthly deliverance, and in mighty movements of history for the salvation of the sinner and for the setting up of his own kingdom. See also John 1:16 — "of his fulness we all received, and grace for grace" = "Each blessing appropriated became the foundation of a greater blessing. To have realized and used one measure of grace was to have gained a larger measure in exchange for it χάριν ἀντὶ χάριτος"; so Westcott, in Bib. Com., *in loco*. Christ can ever say to the believer, as he said to Nathanael (John 1:50): "thou shalt see greater things than these."

Because God is infinite, he can love each believer as much as if that single soul were the only one for whom he had to care. Both in providence and in redemption the whole heart of God is busy with plans for the interest and happiness of the single Christian. Threatenings do not half reveal God, nor his promises half express the "eternal weight of glory" (2 Cor. 4:17). Dante, Paradiso, 19:40-63 — God "Could not upon the universe so write The impress of his power, but that his word Must still be left in distance infinite." To "limit the Holy One of Israel" (Ps. 78:41 — marg.) is falsehood as well as sin.

This attribute of infinity, or of transcendence, qualifies all the other attributes, and so is the foundation for the representations of majesty and glory as belonging to God (see Ex. 33:18; Ps. 19:1; Is. 6:3; Mat. 6:13; Acts 7:2; Rom. 1:23; 9:23; Heb. 1:3; 1 Pet. 4:14; Rev. 21:23). Glory is not itself a divine attribute; it is rather a result — an objective result — of the exercise of the divine attributes. This glory exists irrespective of the revelation and recognition of it in the creation (John 17:5). Only God can worthily perceive and reverence his own glory. He does all for his own glory. All religion is founded on the glory of God. All worship is the result of this immanent quality of the divine nature. Kedney, Christian Doctrine, 1:360-373, 2:354, apparently conceives of the divine glory as an eternal material environment of God, from which the universe is fashioned. This seems to contradict both the spirituality and the infinity of God. God's infinity implies absolute completeness apart from anything external to himself. We proceed therefore to consider the attributes involved in infinity.

Of the attributes involved in Infinity, we mention:

1. Self-existence.

By self-existence we mean

(a) That God is "*causa sui*," having the ground of his existence in himself. Every being must have the ground of its existence either in or out of itself. We have the ground of our existence outside of us. God is not thus dependent. He is *a se;* hence we speak of the aseity of God

God's self-existence is implied in the name "Jehovah" (Ex. 6:3) and in the declaration "I AM THAT I AM" (Ex. 3:14), both of which signify that it is God's nature to be. Self-existence is certainly incomprehensible to us, yet a self-existent person is no greater mystery than a self-existent thing, such as Herbert Spencer supposes the universe to be; indeed it is not so great a mystery, for it is easier to derive matter from mind than to derive mind from matter. See Porter, Human Intellect, 661. Joh. Angelus Silesius: "Gott ist das was Er ist; Ich was Ich durch Ihn bin; Doch kennst du Einen wohl, So kennst du mich und Ihn." Martineau, Types, 1:302 — "A *cause* may be eternal, but nothing that is *caused* can be so." He protests against the phrase "*causa sui.*" So Shedd, Dogm. Theol., 1:338, objects to the phrase "God is his own cause," because God is the uncaused Being. But when we speak of God as "*causa sui*," we do not attribute to him beginning of existence. The phrase means rather that the ground of his existence is not outside of himself, but that he himself is the living spring of all energy and of all being.

But lest this should be be misconstrued, we add

(*b*) That God exists by the necessity of his own being. It is his nature to be. Hence the existence of God is not a contingent but a necessary existence. It is grounded, not in his volitions, but in his nature.

Julius Müller, Doctrine of Sin, 2:126, 130, 170, seems to hold that God is primarily will, so that the essence of God is his act: "God's essence does not precede his freedom"; "if the essence of God were for him something given, something already present, the question 'from whence it was given?' could not be evaded; God's essence must in this case have its origin in something apart from him, and thus the true conception of God would be entirely swept away." But this implies that truth, reason, love, holiness, equally with God's essence, are all products of will. If God's essence moreover, were his act, it would be in the power of God to annihilate himself. Act presupposes essence; else there is no God to act. The will by which God exists, and in virtue of which he is *causa sui*, is therefore not will in the sense of volition, but will in the sense of the whole movement of his active being. With Müller's view Thomasius and Delitzsch are agreed. For refutation of it, see Philippi, Glaubenslehre, 2:63.

God's essence is not his act, not only because this would imply that he could destroy himself, but also because before willing there must be being. Those who hold God's essence to be simple activity are impelled to this view by the fear of postulating some dead thing in God which precedes all exercise of faculty. So Miller, Evolution of Love, 43 — "Perfect action, conscious and volitional, is the highest generalization, the ultimate unit, the unconditioned nature, of infinite Being"; *i. e.*, God's nature is subjective action, while external nature is his objective action. A better statement, however, is that of Bowne, Philos. of Theism, 170 — "While there is a necessity in the soul, it becomes controlling only through freedom; and we may say that everyone must constitute himself a rational soul. . . . This is absolutely true of God."

2. Immutability.

By this we mean that the nature, attributes, and will of God are exempt from all change. Reason teaches us that no change is possible in God, whether of increase or decrease, progress or deterioration, contraction or development. All change must be to better or to worse. But God is absolute perfection, and no change to better is possible. Change to worse would be equally inconsistent with perfection. No cause for such change exists, either outside of God or in God himself.

Psalm 102:27 — "thou art the same"; Mal. 3:6 — "I, Jehovah, change not"; James 1:17 — "with whom can be no variation, neither shadow that is cast by turning." Spenser, Faerie Queen, Cantos of Mutability, 8:2 — "Then 'gin I think on that which nature sayde, Of that same time when no more change shall be, But steadfast rest of all things, firmly stayed Upon the pillours of eternity; For all that moveth doth in change delight, But henceforth all shall rest eternally With him that is the God of Sabaoth hight; Oh thou great Sabaoth God, grant me that Sabbath's sight!" Bowne, Philos. of Theism, 146, defines immutability as "the constancy and continuity of the divine nature which exists through all the divine acts as their law and source."

The passages of Scripture which seem at first sight to ascribe change to God are to be explained in one of three ways :

(*a*) As illustrations of the varied methods in which God manifests his immutable truth and wisdom in creation.

Mathematical principles receive new application with each successive stage of creation. The law of cohesion gives place to chemical law, and chemistry yields to vital forces, but through all these changes there is a divine truth and wisdom which is unchanging, and which reduces all to rational order. John Caird, Fund. Ideas of Christianity, 2 : 140 — "Immutability is not stereotyped sameness, but impossibility of deviation by one hair's breadth from the course which is best. A man of great force of character is continually finding new occasions for the manifestation and application of moral principle. In God infinite consistency is united with infinite flexibility. There is no iron-bound impassibility, but rather an infinite originality in him."

(*b*) As anthropomorphic representations of the revelation of God's unchanging attributes in the changing circumstances and varying moral conditions of creatures.

Gen. 6 : 6 — "it repented Jehovah that he had made man" — is to be interpreted in the light of Num. 23 : 19 — "God is not a man, that he should lie : neither the son of man, that he should repent." So *cf.* 1 Sam. 15 : 11 with 15 : 29. God's unchanging holiness requires him to treat the wicked differently from the righteous. When the righteous become wicked, his treatment of them must change. The sun is not fickle or partial because it melts the wax but hardens the clay, — the change is not in the sun but in the objects it shines upon. The change in God's treatment of men is described anthropomorphically, as if it were a change in God himself,—other passages in close conjunction with the first being given to correct any possible misapprehension. Threats not fulfilled, as in Jonah 3 : 4, 10, are to be explained by their conditional nature. Hence God's immutability itself renders it certain that his love will adapt itself to every varying mood and condition of his children, so as to guide their steps, sympathize with their sorrows, answer their prayers. God responds to us more quickly than the mother's face to the changing moods of her babe. Godet, in The Atonement, 338 —"God is of all beings the most delicately and infinitely sensitive."

God's immutability is not that of the stone, that has no internal experience, but rather that of the column of mercury, that rises and falls with every change in the temperature of the surrounding atmosphere. When a man bicycling against the wind turns about and goes with the wind instead of going against it, the wind seems to change, though it is blowing just as it was before. The sinner struggles against the wind of prevenient grace until he seems to strike against a stone wall. Regeneration is God's conquest of our wills by his power, and conversion is our beginning to turn round and to work with God rather than against God. Now we move without effort, because we have God at our back; Phil. 2 : 12, 13 — "work out your own salvation . . . for it is God who worketh in you." God has not changed, but we have changed; John 3 : 8 — "The wind bloweth where it will . . . so is every one that is born of the Spirit." Jacob's first wrestling with the Angel was the picture of his lifelong self-will, opposing God; his subsequent wrestling in prayer was the picture of a consecrated will, working with God (Gen. 32 : 24-28). We seem to conquer God, but he really conquers us. He seems to change, but it is we who change after all.

(*c*) As describing executions, in time, of purposes eternally existing in the mind of God. Immutability must not be confounded with immobility. This would deny all those imperative volitions of God by which he enters into history, The Scriptures assure us that creation, miracles, incarnation, regeneration, are immediate acts of God. Immutability is consistent with constant activity and perfect freedom.

The abolition of the Mosaic dispensation indicates no change in God's plan; it is rather the execution of his plan. Christ's coming and work were no sudden makeshift, to remedy unforeseen defects in the Old Testament scheme : Christ came rather in "the fulness of the time" (Gal. 4 : 4), to fulfill the "counsel" of God (Acts 2 : 23). Gen. 8 : 1 — "God remembered Noah" — interposed by special act for Noah's deliverance, showed that he remembered Noah. While we change, God does not. There is no fickleness or inconstancy in him. Where we once found him, there we may find him still, as Jacob did at Bethel (Gen. 35 : 1, 6, 9). Immutability is a consolation to the faithful, but a terror to God's enemies (Mal. 3 : 6 — " I, Jehovah, change not; therefore ye, O sons of Jacob, are not consumed " ; Ps. 7 : 11 — " a God that hath indignation every day "). It is consistent with constant activity in nature and in grace (John 5 : 17 — "My Father worketh even until now, and I work " ; Job 23 :13, 14 — "he is in one mind, and who can turn him ? . . . For he performeth that which is appointed for me : and many such things are with him "). If God's immutability were immobility, we could not worship him, any more than the ancient Greeks were able to worship Fate. Arthur Hugh Clough : " It fortifies my soul to know, That, though I perish, Truth is so : That, howsoe'er I stray and range, Whate'er I do, Thou dost not change. I steadier step when I recall That, if I slip, Thou dost not fall." On this attribute see Charnock, Attributes, 1 : 310-362 ; Dorner, Gesammelte Schriften, 188-377 ; translated in Bib. Sac., 1879 : 28-59, 209-223.

3. Unity.

By this we mean (a) that the divine nature is undivided and indivisible (unus) ; and (b) that there is but one infinite and perfect Spirit (unicus).

Deut. 6 : 4 — "Hear, O Israel: Jehovah our God is one Jehovah " ; Is. 44 : 6 — "besides me there is no God " ; John 5 : 44 — "the only God " ; 17 : 3 — "the only true God " ; 1 Cor. 8 : 4 —"no God but one "; 1 Tim. 1 : 17 — "the only God " ; 6 : 15 —"the blessed and only Potentate " ; Eph. 4 : 5, 6 — " one Lord, one faith, one baptism, one God and Father of all, who is over all, and through all, and in all." When we read in Mason, Faith of the Gospel, 25 — " The unity of God is not numerical, denying the existence of a second ; it is integral, denying the possibility of division," we reply that the unity of God is both,— it includes both the numerical and the integral elements.

Humboldt, in his Cosmos, has pointed out that the unity and creative agency of the heavenly Father have given unity to the order of nature, and so have furnished the impulse to modern physical science. Our faith in a "universe " rests historically upon the demonstration of God's unity which has been given by the incarnation and death of Christ. Tennyson, In Memoriam : "That God who ever lives and loves, One God, one law, one element, And one far off divine event To which the whole creation moves." See A. H. Strong, Christ in Creation, 184-187. Alexander McLaren : "The heathen have many gods because they have no one that satisfies hungry hearts or corresponds to their unconscious ideals. Completeness is not reached by piecing together many fragments. The wise merchantman will gladly barter a sack full of ' goodly pearls ' for the one of great price. Happy they who turn away from the many to embrace the One ! "

Against polytheism, tritheism, or dualism, we may urge that the notion of two or more Gods is self-contradictory ; since each limits the other and destroys his godhood. In the nature of things, infinity and absolute perfection are possible only to one. It is unphilosophical, moreover, to assume the existence of two or more Gods, when one will explain all the facts. The unity of God is, however, in no way inconsistent with the doctrine of the Trinity ; for, while this doctrine holds to the existence of hypostatical, or personal, distinctions in the divine nature, it also holds that this divine nature is numerically and eternally one.

Polytheism is man's attempt to rid himself of the notion of responsibility to one moral Lawgiver and Judge by dividing up his manifestations, and attributing them to separate wills. So Force, in the terminology of some modern theorizers, is only God with his moral attributes left out. " Henotheism " (says Max Müller, Origin and Growth of Religion, 285) " conceives of each individual god as unlimited by the power of other gods. Each is felt, at the time, as supreme and absolute, notwithstanding the limitations which to our minds must arise from his power being conditioned by the power of all the gods."

Even polytheism cannot rest in the doctrine of many gods, as an exclusive and all comprehending explanation of the universe. The Greeks believed in one supreme Fate that ruled both gods and men. Aristotle : "God, though he is one, has many names, because he is called according to states into which he is ever entering anew." The doctrine of God's unity should teach men to give up hope of any other God, to reveal himself to them or to save them. They are in the hands of the one and only God, and therefore there is but one law, one gospel, one salvation; one doctrine, one duty, one destiny. We cannot rid ourselves of responsibility by calling ourselves mere congeries of impressions or mere victims of circumstance. As God is one, so the soul made in God's image is one also. On the origin of polytheism, see articles by Tholuck, in Bib. Repos., 2:84, 246, 441, and Max Müller, Science of Religion, 124.

Moberly, Atonement and Personality, 83 — "The Alpha and Omega, the beginning and end and sum and meaning of Being, is but One. We who believe in a personal God do not believe in a limited God. We do not mean one more, a bigger specimen of existences, amongst existences. Rather, we mean that the reality of existence itself is personal: that Power, that Law, that Life, that Thought, that Love, are ultimately, in their very reality, identified in one supreme, and that necessarily a personal Existence. Now such supreme Being cannot be multiplied : it is incapable of a plural : it cannot be a generic term. There cannot be more than one all-inclusive, more than one ultimate, more than one God. Nor has Christian thought, at any point, for any moment, dared or endured the least approach to such a thought or phrase as 'two Gods.' If the Father is God, and the Son God, they are both the same God wholly, unreservedly. God is a particular, an unique, not a general, term. Each is not only God, but is the very same 'singularis unicus et totus Deus.' They are not both *generically* God, as though 'God' could be an attribute or predicate; but both *identically* God, the God, the one all-inclusive, indivisible, God. . . . If the thought that wishes to be orthodox had less tendency to become tritheistic, the thought that claims to be free would be less Unitarian."

Third Division. — Perfection, and attributes therein involved.

By perfection we mean, not mere quantitative completeness, but qualitative excellence. The attributes involved in perfection are moral attributes. Right action among men presupposes a perfect moral organization, a normal state of intellect, affection and will. So God's activity presupposes a principle of intelligence, of affection, of volition, in his inmost being, and the existence of a worthy object for each of these powers of his nature. But in eternity past there is nothing existing outside or apart from God. He must find, and he does find, the sufficient object of intellect, affection, and will, in himself. There is a self-knowing, a self-loving, a self-willing, which constitute his absolute perfection. The consideration of the immanent attributes is, therefore, properly concluded with an account of that truth, love, and holiness, which render God entirely sufficient to himself.

Mat. 5:48 — "Ye therefore shall be perfect, as your heavenly Father is perfect"; Rom. 12:2 — "perfect will of God"; Col. 1:28 — "perfect in Christ"; *cf.* Deut. 32:4 — "The Rock, his work is perfect"; Ps. 18:30 — "As for God, his way is perfect."

1. Truth.

By truth we mean that attribute of the divine nature in virtue of which God's being and God's knowledge eternally conform to each other.

In further explanation we remark :

A. Negatively :

(a) The immanent truth of God is not to be confounded with that veracity and faithfulness which partially manifest it to creatures. These are transitive truth, and they presuppose the absolute and immanent attribute.

Deut. 32:4 — "A God of faithfulness and without iniquity, Just and right is he "; John 17:3 — "the only true God " (ἀληθινόν); 1 John 5:20 — " we know him that is true " (τὸν ἀληθινόν). In both these passages ἀληθινός describes God as the genuine, the real, as distinguished from ἀληθής, the veracious (compare John 6:32 — "the true bread "; Heb. 8:2 — "the true tabernacle "). John 14:6 — "I am the truth." As "I am . . . the life" signifies, not "I am the living one," but rather "I am he who is life and the source of life," so "I am . . . the truth" signifies, not "I am the truthful one," but "I am he who is truth and the source of truth"—in other words, truth of being, not merely truth of expression. So 1 John 5:7—"the Spirit is the truth." *Cf.* 1 Esdras 1:38—"The truth abideth and is forever strong, and it liveth and ruleth forever" = personal truth? See Godet on John 1:18; Shedd, Dogm. Theol., 1:181.

Truth is God perfectly revealed and known. It may be likened to the electric current which manifests and measures the power of the dynamo. There is no realm of truth apart from the world-ground, just as there is no law of nature that is independent of the Author of nature. While we know ourselves only partially, God knows himself fully. John Caird, Fund. Ideas of Christianity, 1:192—"In the life of God there are no unrealized possibilities. The presupposition of all our knowledge and activity is that absolute and eternal unity of knowing and being which is only another expression for the nature of God. In one sense, he is all reality, and the only reality, whilst all finite existence is but a *becoming*, which never *is*." Lowrie, Doctrine of St. John, 57-63—"Truth is reality revealed. Jesus is the Truth, because in him the sum of the qualities hidden in God is presented and revealed to the world, God's nature in terms of an active force and in relation to his rational creation." This definition however ignores the fact that God is truth, apart from and before all creation. As an immanent attribute, truth implies a conformity of God's knowledge to God's being, which antedates the universe; see B. (*b*) below.

(*b*) Truth in God is not a merely active attribute of the divine nature. God is truth, not only in the sense that he is the being who truly knows, but also in the sense that he is the truth that is known. The passive precedes the active ; truth of being precedes truth of knowing.

Plato: "Truth is his (God's) body, and light his shadow." Hollaz (quoted in Thomasius, Christi Person und Werk, 1:137) says that "truth is the conformity of the divine essence with the divine intellect." See Gerhard, loc. ii:152; Kahnis, Dogmatik, 2:272, 279; 3:193—"Distinguish in God the personal self-consciousness [spirituality, personality—see pages 252, 253] from the unfolding of this in the divine knowledge, which can have no other object but God himself. So far, now, as self-knowing in God is absolutely identical with his being is he the absolutely true. For truth is the knowledge which answers to the being, and the being which answers to the knowledge."

Royce, World and Individual, 1:270—"Truth either may mean that about which we judge, *or* it may mean the correspondence between our ideas and their objects." God's truth is both object of his knowledge and knowledge of his object. Miss Clara French, The Dramatic Action and Motive of King John: "You spell Truth with a capital, and make it an independent existence to be sought for and absorbed; but, unless truth is God, what can it do for man? It is only a personality that can touch a personality." So we assent to the poet's declaration that "Truth, crushed to earth, shall rise again," only because Truth is personal. Christ, the Revealer of God, is the Truth. He is not simply the medium but also the object of all knowledge; Eph. 4:20—"ye did not so learn Christ" = ye knew more than the doctrine about Christ,—ye knew Christ himself; John 17:3—"this is life eternal, that they should know thee the only true God, and him whom thou didst send, even Jesus Christ."

B. Positively :

(*a*) All truth among men, whether mathematical, logical, moral, or religious, is to be regarded as having its foundation in this immanent truth of the divine nature and as disclosing facts in the being of God.

There is a higher Mind than our mind. No apostle can say "I am the truth," though each of them can say "I speak the truth." Truth is not a scientific or moral, but a substantial, thing—"nicht Schulsache, sondern Lebenssache." Here is the dignity of education, that knowledge of truth is knowledge of God. The laws of mathematics are disclosures to us, not of the divine reason merely, for this would imply truth outside of and before God, but of the divine nature. J. W. A. Stewart: "Science is possible because God is scientific." Plato: "God geometrizes." Bowne: "The heavens are crystalized mathematics." The statement that two and two make four, or that virtue is commendable and vice condemnable, expresses an everlasting principle in the being of God. Separate statements of truth are inexplicable apart from the total revelation of truth, and this total revelation is inexplicable apart from One who is truth and who is thus revealed. The separate electric lights in our streets are inexplicable apart from the electric current which throbs through the wires, and this electric current is itself inexplicable apart from the hidden dynamo whose power it exactly expresses and measures. The separate lights of truth are due to the realizing agency of the Holy Spirit; the one unifying current which they partially reveal is the outgoing work of Christ, the divine Logos; Christ is the one and only Revealer of him who dwells "in light unapproachable; whom no man hath seen, nor can see" (1 Tim. 6:16).

Prof. H. E. Webster began his lectures " by assuming the Lord Jesus Christ *and* the multiplication-table." But this was tautology, because the Lord Jesus Christ, the Truth, the only revealer of God, includes the multiplication-table. So Wendt, Teaching of Jesus, 1:257; 2:202, unduly narrows the scope of Christ's revelation when he maintains that with Jesus truth is not the truth which corresponds to reality but rather the right conduct which corresponds to the duty prescribed by God. " Grace and truth " (John 1:17) then means the favor of God and the righteousness which God approves. To understand Jesus is impossible without being ethically like him. He is king of truth, in that he reveals this righteousness, and finds obedience for it among men. This ethical aspect of the truth, we would reply, important as it is, does not exclude but rather requires for its complement and presupposition that other aspect of the truth as the reality to which all being must conform and the conformity of all being to that reality. Since Christ is the truth of God, we are successful in our search for truth only as we recognize him. Whether all roads lead to Rome depends upon which way your face is turned. Follow a point of land out into the sea, and you find only ocean. With the back turned upon Jesus Christ all following after truth leads only into mist and darkness. Aristotle's ideal man was "a hunter after truth." But truth can never be found disjoined from love, nor can the loveless seeker discern it. " For the loving worm within its clod Were diviner than a loveless God " (Robert Browning). Hence Christ can say : John 18:37 — "Every one that is of the truth heareth my voice."

(*b*) This attribute therefore constitutes the principle and guarantee of all revelation, while it shows the possibility of an eternal divine self-contemplation apart from and before all creation. It is to be understood only in the light of the doctrine of the Trinity.

To all this doctrine, however, a great school of philosophers have opposed themselves. Duns Scotus held that God's will made truth as well as right. Descartes said that God could have made it untrue that the radii of a circle are all equal. Lord Bacon said that Adam's sin consisted in seeking a good in itself, instead of being content with the merely empirical good. Whedon, On the Will, 316 — " Infinite wisdom and infinite holiness consist in, and result from, God's volitions eternally." We reply that, to make truth and good matters of mere will, instead of regarding them as characteristics of God's being, is to deny that anything is true or good in itself. If God can make truth to be falsehood, and injustice to be justice, then God is indifferent to truth or falsehood, to good or evil, and he ceases thereby to be God. Truth is not arbitrary,— it is matter of being — the being of God. There are no regulative principles of knowledge which are not transcendental also. God knows and wills truth, because he is truth. Robert Browning, A Soul's Tragedy, 214 — " Were 't not for God, I mean, what hope of truth — Speaking truth, hearing truth — would stay with Man ? " God's will does not make truth, but truth rather makes God's will. God's perfect knowledge in eternity past has an object. That object must be himself. He is the truth Known, as well as the truthful Knower. But a perfect objective must be personal. The doctrine of the Trinity is the necessary complement to the doctrine of the Attributes. Shedd, Dogm. Theol., i:183 — " The pillar of cloud becomes a pillar of fire." See A. H. Strong, Christ in Creation, 102-112.

On the question whether it is ever right to deceive, see Paine, Ethnic Trinities, 300-339. Plato said that the use of such medicines should be restricted to physicians. The rulers of the state may lie for the public good, but private people not: " officiosum mendacium." It is better to say 'hat deception is justifiable only where the person deceived has, like a wild beast or a criminal or an enemy in war, put himself out of human society and deprived himself of the right to truth. Even then deception is a sad necessity which witnesses to an abnormal condition of human affairs. With James Martineau, when asked what answer he would give to an intending murderer when truth would mean death, we may say: "I suppose I should tell an untruth, and then should be sorry for it forever after." On truth as an attribute of God, see Bib. Sac., Oct. 1877 : 735; Finney, Syst. Theol., 661: Janet. Final Causes. 416.

2. Love.

By love we mean that attribute of the divine nature in virtue of which God is eternally moved to self-communication.

1 Johns 4 : 8 — "God is love"; 3 : 36 — "hereby know we love, because he laid down his life for us"; John 17 : 24 — "thou lovedst me before the foundation of the world"; Rom. 15 : 30 — "the love of the Spirit."

In further explanation we remark :

A. Negatively :

(a) The immanent love of God is not to be confounded with mercy and goodness toward creatures. These are its manifestations, and are to be denominated transitive love.

Thomasius, Christi Person und Werk, 1 : 138, 139 — " God's regard for the happiness of his creatures flows from this self-communicating attribute of his nature. Love, in the true sense of the word, is living good-will, with impulses to impartation and union ; self-communication (bonum communicativum sui); devotion, merging of the *ego* in another, in order to penetrate, fill, bless this other with itself, and in this other, as in another self, to possess itself, without giving up itself or losing itself. Love is therefore possible only between persons, and always presupposes personality. Only as Trinity has God love, absolute love ; because as Father, Son, and Holy Ghost he stands in perfect self-impartation, self-devotion, and communion with himself." Julius Müller, Doct. Sin, 2 : 136 — " God has in himself the eternal and wholly adequate object of his love, independently of his relation to the world."

In the Greek mythology, Eros was one of the oldest and yet one of the youngest of the gods. So Dante makes the oldest angel to be the youngest, because nearest to God the fountain of life. In 1 John 2 : 7, 8, " the old commandment " of love is evermore " a new commandment," because it reflects this eternal attribute of God. " There is a love unstained by selfishness, Th' outpouring tide of self-abandonment, That loves to love, and deems its preciousness Repaid in loving, though no sentiment Of love returned reward its sacrament ; Nor stays to question what the loved one will, But hymns its overture with blessings immanent ; Rapt and sublimed by love's exalting thrill, Loves on, through frown or smile, divine, immortal still." Clara Elizabeth Ward : " If I could gather every look of love, That ever any human creature wore, And all the looks that joy is mother of, All looks of grief that mortals ever bore, And mingle all with God-begotten grace, Methinks that I should see the Savior's face."

(b) Love is not the all-inclusive ethical attribute of God. It does not include truth, nor does it include holiness.

Ladd, Philosophy of Conduct, 352, very properly denies that benevolence is the all-inclusive virtue. Justness and Truth, he remarks, are not reducible to benevolence. In a review of Ladd's work in Bib. Sac., Jan. 1903 : 185, C. M. Mead adds : " He comes to the conclusion that it is impossible to resolve all the virtues into the generic one of love or benevolence without either giving a definition of benevolence which is unwarranted and virtually nullifies the end aimed at, or failing to recognize certain virtues which are as genuinely virtues as benevolence itself. Particularly is it argued that the virtues of the will (courage, constancy, temperance), and the virtues of judgment (wisdom, justness, trueness), get no recognition in this attempt to subsume all virtues under the one virtue of love. ' The unity of the virtues is due to the unity of a personality, in active and varied relations with other persons ' (361). If benevolence means wishing *happiness* to all men, then happiness is made the ultimate good, and eudæmonism is accepted as the true ethical philosophy. But if, on the other hand, in order to avoid this conclusion, benevolence is made to mean wishing the highest *welfare* to all men, and the highest welfare is conceived as a life of virtue, then we come to the rather inane conclusion that the essence of virtue is to wish that men may be virtuous." See also art. by Vos, in Presb. and Ref. Rev., Jan. 1892 : 1–37.

(c) Nor is God's love a mere regard for being in general, irrespective of its moral quality.

Jonathan Edwards, in his treatise On the Nature of Virtue, defines virtue as regard for being in general. He considers that God's love is first of all directed toward himself as having the greatest quantity of being, and only secondarily directed toward his creatures whose quantity of being is infinitesimal as compared with his. But we reply that being in general is far too abstract a thing to elicit or justify love. Charles Hodge said truly that, if obligation is primarily due to being in general, then there is no more virtue in loving God than there is in loving Satan. Virtue, we hold, must consist, not in love for being in general, but in love for good being, that is, in love for God as holy. Love has no moral value except as it is placed upon a right object and is proportioned to the worth of that object. "Love of being in general" makes virtue an irrational thing, because it has no standard of conduct. Virtue is rather the love of God as right and as the source of right.

G. S. Lee, The Shadow-cross, 38 — "God is love, and law is the way he loves us. But it is also true that God is law, and love is the way he rules us." Clarke, Christian Theology, 88 — "Love is God's desire to impart himself, and so all good, to other persons, and to possess them for his own spiritual fellowship." The intent to communicate himself is the intent to communicate holiness, and this is the "terminus ad quem" of God's administration. Drummond, in his Ascent of Man, shows that Love began with the first cell of life. Evolution is not a tale of battle, but a love-story. We gradually pass from selfism to otherism. Evolution is the object of nature, and altruism is the object of evolution. Man = nutrition, looking to his own things; Woman = reproduction, looking to the things of others. But the greatest of these is love. The mammalia = the mothers, last and highest, care for others. As the mother gives love, so the father gives righteousness. Law, once a latent thing, now becomes active. The father makes a sort of conscience for those beneath him. Nature, like Raphael, is producing a Holy Family."

Jacob Boehme: "Throw open and throw out thy heart. For unless thou dost exercise thy heart, and the love of thy heart, upon every man in the world, thy self-love, thy pride, thy envy, thy distaste, thy dislike, will still have dominion over thee. . . . . In the name and in the strength of God, love all men. Love thy neighbor as thyself, and do to thy neighbor as thou doest to thyself. And do it now. For now is the accepted time, and now is the day of salvation." These expressions are scriptural and valuable, if they are interpreted ethically, and are understood to inculcate the supreme duty of loving the Holy One, of being holy as he is holy, and of seeking to bring all intelligent beings into conformity with his holiness.

(*d*) God's love is not a merely emotional affection, proceeding from sense or impulse, nor is it prompted by utilitarian considerations.

Of the two words for love in the N. T., φιλέω designates an emotional affection, which is not and cannot be commanded (John 11:36 — "Behold how he loved him !"), while ἀγαπάω expresses a rational and benevolent affection which springs from deliberate choice (John 3:16 — "God so loved the world"; Mat. 19:19 — "Thou shall love thy neighbor as thyself"; 5:44 — "Love your enemies"). Thayer, N. T. Lex., 653 — 'Aγαπᾶν "properly denotes a love founded in admiration, veneration, esteem, like the Lat. *diligere*, to be kindly disposed to one, to wish one well; but φιλεῖν denotes an inclination prompted by sense and emotion, Lat. *amare*. . . . Hence men are said ἀγαπᾶν God, not φιλεῖν." In this word ἀγάπη, when used of God, it is already implied that God loves, not for what he can get, but for what he can give. The rationality of his love involves moreover a subordination of the emotional element to a higher law than itself, namely, that of holiness. Even God's self-love must have a reason and norm in the perfections of his own being.

B.   Positively :

(*a*)   The immanent love of God is a rational and voluntary affection, grounded in perfect reason and deliberate choice.

Ritschl, Justification and Reconciliation, 3:277 — "Love is will, aiming either at the appropriation of an object, or at the enrichment of its existence, because moved by a feeling of its worth. . . . Love is to persons; it is a constant will; it aims at the promotion of the other's personal end, whether known or conjectured; it takes up the other's personal end and makes it part of his own. Will, as love, does not give itself up for the other's sake; it aims at closest fellowship with the other for a common end." A. H. Strong, Christ in Creation, 388-405 — "Love is not rightfully independent of the other faculties, but is subject to regulation and control. . . . We sometimes say that religion consists in love. . . . It would be more strictly true to say that religion consists in a new direction of our love, a turning of the current toward God which once flowed toward self. . . . . Christianity rectifies the affections, before excessive, impulsive, lawless, — gives them worthy and immortal objects, regulates their intensity in some due proportion to the value of the things they rest upon, and teaches the true methods of their manifestation. In true religion love forms a copartnership with reason. . . . God's love is no arbitrary, wild, passionate torrent of emotion. . . . and we become like God by bringing our emotions, sympathies, affections, under the dominion of reason and conscience."

(b) Since God's love is rational, it involves a subordination of the emotional element to a higher law than itself, namely, that of truth and holiness.

Phil. 1 : 9 — "And this I pray, that your love may abound yet more and more in knowledge and all discernment." True love among men illustrates God's love. It merges self in another instead of making that other an appendage to self. It seeks the other's true good, not merely his present enjoyment or advantage. Its aim is to realize the divine idea in that other, and therefore it is exercised for God's sake and in the strength which God supplies. Hence it is a love for holiness, and is under law to holiness. So God's love takes into account the highest interests, and makes infinite sacrifice to secure them. For the sake of saving a world of sinners, God "spared not his own Son, but deliverered him up for us all" (Rom. 8 : 32), and "Jehovah hath laid on him the iniquity of us all " (Is. 53 : 6). Love requires a rule or standard for its regulation. This rule or standard is the holiness of God. So once more we see that love cannot include holiness, because it is subject to the law of holiness. Love desires only the *best* for its object, and the best is *God*. The golden rule does not bid us give what others desire, but what they need : Rom. 15 : 2 — "Let each one of us please his neighbor for that which is good, unto edifying."

(c) The immanent love of God therefore requires and finds a perfect standard in his own holiness, and a personal object in the image of his own infinite perfections. It is to be understood only in the light of the doctrine of the Trinity.

As there is a higher Mind than our mind, so there is a greater Heart than our heart. God is not simply the loving One — he is also the Love that is loved. There is an infinite life of sensibility and affection in God. God has feeling, and in an infinite degree. But feeling alone is not love. Love implies not merely receiving but giving, not merely emotion but impartation. So the love of God is shown in his eternal giving. James 1 : 5 — "God, who giveth," or "the giving God" (τοῦ διδόντος Θεοῦ) = giving is not an episode in his being — it is his nature to give. And not only to *give*, but to give *himself*. This he does eternally in the self-communications of the Trinity ; this he does transitively and temporally in his giving of himself for us in Christ, and to us in the Holy Spirit.

Jonathan Edwards, Essay on Trinity (ed. G. P. Fisher), 79 — "That in John God is love shows that there are more persons than one in the Deity, for it shows love to be essential and necessary to the Deity, so that his nature consists in it, and this supposes that there is an eternal and necessary object, because all love respects another that is the beloved. By love here the apostle certainly means something beside that which is commonly called self-love : that is very improperly called love, and is a thing of an exceeding diverse nature from the affection or virtue of love the apostle is speaking of." When Newman Smyth, Christian Ethics, 226–239, makes the first characteristic of love to be self-affirmation, and when Dorner, Christian Ethics, 73, makes self-assertion an essential part of love, they violate linguistic usage by including under love what properly belongs to holiness.

(d) The immanent love of God constitutes a ground of the divine blessedness. Since there is an infinite and perfect object of love, as well as of knowledge and will, in God's own nature, the existence of the universe is not necessary to his serenity and joy.

Blessedness is not itself a divine attribute ; it is rather a result of the exercise of the divine attributes. It is a subjective result of this exercise, as glory is an objective result. Perfect faculties, with perfect objects for their exercise, ensure God's blessedness. But love is especially its source. Acts 20 : 35 — "It is more blessed to give than to receive." Happiness (hap, happen) is grounded in circumstances ; blessedness, in character.

Love precedes creation and is the ground of creation. Its object therefore cannot be the universe, for that does not exist, and, if it did exist, could not be a proper object of love for the infinite God. The only sufficient object of his love is the image of his own perfections, for that alone is equal to himself. Upton, Hibbert Lectures, 264 — "Man most truly realizes his own nature, when he is ruled by rational, self-forgetful love. He cannot help inferring that the highest thing in the individual consciousness is the dominant thing in the universe at large." Here we may assent, if we remember that not the love itself but that which is loved must be the dominant thing, and we shall see that to be not love but holiness.

Jones, Robert Browning, 219 — "Love is for Browning the highest, richest conception man can form. It is our idea of that which is perfect; we cannot even imagine anything better. And the idea of evolution necessarily explains the world as the return of the highest to itself. The universe is homeward bound. . . . All things are potentially spirit, and all the phenomena of the world are manifestations of love. . . . Man's reason is not, but man's love is, a direct emanation from the inmost being of God" (345). Browning should have applied to truth and holiness the same principle which he recognized with regard to love. But we gratefully accept his dicta : " He that created love, shall not he love? . . . God! thou art Love! I build my faith on that."

(e) The love of God involves also the possibility of divine suffering, and the suffering on account of sin which holiness necessitates on the part of God is itself the atonement.

Christ is "the Lamb that hath been slain from the foundation of the world " (Rev. 13 : 8); 1 Pet. 1 : 19, 20 — "precious blood, as of a lamb without blemish and without spot, even the blood of Christ : who was foreknown indeed before the foundation of the world." While holiness requires atonement, love provides it. The blessedness of God is consistent with sorrow for human misery and sin. God is passible, or capable of suffering. The permission of moral evil in the decree of creation was at cost to God. Scripture attributes to him emotions of grief and anger at human sin (Gen. 6 : 6 — "it grieved him at his heart"; Rom. 1 : 18 — "wrath of God" ; Eph. 4 : 30 — "grieve not the Holy Spirit of God "); painful sacrifice in the gift of Christ (Rom. 8 : 32 — "spared not his own son "; cf. Gen. 22 : 16—"hast not withheld thy son ") and participation in the suffering of his people (Is. 63 : 9 — "in all their affliction he was afflicted "); Jesus Christ in his sorrow and sympathy, his tears and agony, is the revealer of God's feelings toward the race, and we are urged to follow in his steps, that we may be perfect, as our Father in heaven is perfect. We cannot, indeed, conceive of love without self-sacrifice, nor of self-sacrifice without suffering. It would seem, then, that as immutability is consistent with imperative volitions in human history, so the blessedness of God may be consistent with emotions of sorrow.

But does God feel in proportion to his greatness, as the mother suffers more than the sick child whom she tends? Does God suffer infinitely in every suffering of his creatures? We must remember that God is infinitely greater than his creation, and that he sees all human sin and woe as part of his great plan. We are entitled to attribute to him only such passibleness as is consistent with infinite perfection. In combining passibleness with blessedness, then, we must allow blessedness to be the controlling element, for our fundamental idea of God is that of absolute perfection. Martensen, Dogmatics, 101 — "This limitation is swallowed up in the inner life of perfection which God lives, in total independence of his creation, and in triumphant prospect of the fulfilment of his great designs. We may therefore say with the old theosophic writers : ' In the outer chambers is sadness, but in the inner ones is unmixed joy.'" Christ was "anointed . . . with the oil of gladness above his fellows," and "for the joy that was set before him endured the cross " (Heb. 1 : 9; 12 : 2). Love rejoices even in pain, when this brings good to those beloved. "Though round its base the rolling clouds are spread, Eternal sunshine settles on its head."

In George Adam Smith's Life of Henry Drummond, 11, Drummond cries out after hearing the confessions of men who came to him : " I am sick of the sins of these men ! How can God bear it ? " Simon, Reconciliation, 338–343, shows that before the incarnation, the Logos was a sufferer from the sins of men. This suffering however was kept in check and counterbalanced by his consciousness as a factor in the Godhead, and by the clear knowledge that men were themselves the causes of this suffering. After he became incarnate he suffered without knowing whence all the suffering came. He had a subconscious life into which were interwoven elements due to the sinful conduct of the race whose energy was drawn from himself and with which in addition he had organically united himself. If this is limitation, it is also self-limitation which

Christ could have avoided by not creating, preserving, and redeeming mankind. We rejoice in giving away a daughter in marriage, even though it costs pain. The highest blessedness in the Christian is coincident with agony for the souls of others. We partake of Christ's joy only when we know the fellowship of his sufferings. Joy and sorrow can coëxist, like Greek fire, that burns under water.

Abbé Gratry, La Morale et la Loi de l'Histoire, 165, 166—" What! Do you really suppose that the personal God, free and intelligent, loving and good, who knows every detail of human torture, and hears every sigh—this God who sees, who loves as we do, and more than we do—do you believe that he is present and looks pitilessly on what breaks your heart, and what to him must be the spectacle of Satan reveling in the blood of humanity? History teaches us that men so feel for sufferers that they have been drawn to die with them, so that their own executioners have become the next martyrs. And yet you represent God, the absolute goodness, as alone impassible? It is here that our evangelical faith comes in. Our God was made man to suffer and to die ! Yes, here is the true God. He has suffered from the beginning in all who have suffered. He has been hungry in all who have hungered. He has been immolated in all and with all who have offered up their lives. He is the Lamb slain from the foundation of the world." Similarly Alexander Vinet, Vital Christianity, 240, remarks that " The suffering God is not simply the teaching of modern divines. It is a New Testament thought, and it is one that answers all the doubts that arise at the sight of human suffering. To know that God is suffering with it makes that suffering more awful, but it gives strength and life and hope, for we know that, if God is in it, suffering is the road to victory. If he shares our suffering we shall share his crown," and we can say with the Psalmist, 68 : 19 —" Blessed be God, who daily beareth our burden, even the God who is our salvation," and with Isaiah 63 : 9 — "In all their affliction he was afflicted, and the angel of his presence saved them."

Borden P. Bowne, Atonement: "Something like this work of grace was a moral necessity with God. It was an awful responsibility that was taken when our human race was launched with its fearful possibilities of good and evil. God thereby put himself under infinite obligation to care for his human family ; and reflections on his position as Creator and Ruler, instead of removing, only make more manifest this obligation. So long as we conceive God as sitting apart in supreme ease and self-satisfaction, he is not *love* at all, but only a reflection of our selfishness and vulgarity. So long as we conceive him as bestowing blessing upon us out of his infinite fulness, but at no real cost to himself, he sinks below the moral heroes of our race. There is ever a higher thought possible, until we see God taking the world upon his heart, entering into the fellowship of our sorrow, and becoming the supreme burden bearer and leader in self-sacrifice. Then only are the possibilities of grace and condescension and love and moral heroism filled up, so that nothing higher remains. And the work of Christ, so far as it was a historical event, must be viewed not merely as a piece of history, but also as a manifestation of that cross which was hidden in the divine love from the foundation of the world, and which is involved in the existence of the human world at all."

Royce, Spirit of Modern Philosophy, 264 — "The eternal resolution that, if the world *will* be tragic, it *shall* still, in Satan's despite, be spiritual, is the very essence of the eternal joy of that World-Spirit of whose wisdom ours is but a fragmentary reflection. . . . . When you suffer, your sufferings are God's sufferings,—not his external work nor his external penalty, nor the fruit of his neglect, but identically his own personal woe. In you God himself suffers, precisely as you do, and has all your reason for overcoming this grief." Henry N. Dodge, Christus Victor: "O Thou, that from eternity Upon thy wounded heart hast borne Each pang and cry of misery Wherewith our human hearts are torn, Thy love upon the grievous cross Doth glow, the beacon-light of time, Forever sharing pain and loss With every man in every clime. How vast, how vast Thy sacrifice, As ages come and ages go, Still waiting till it shall suffice To draw the last cold heart and slow ! "

On the question, Is God passible? see Bennett Tyler, Sufferings of Christ; A Layman, Sufferings of Christ ; Woods, Works, 1 : 299-317 ; Bib. Sac., 11 : 744 ; 17 : 422-424 ; Emmons, Works, 4 : 201-208 ; Fairbairn, Place of Christ, 483-487 ; Bushnell, Vic. Sacrifice, 59-93 ; Kedney, Christ. Doctrine Harmonized, 1 : 185-245 ; Edward Beecher, Concord of Ages, 61-20⅓, Young, Life and Light of Men, 20-43, 147-150 ; Schaff, Hist. Christ. Church, 1 : 197, Crawford, Fatherhood of God, 43, 44 ; Anselm, Prosiogion, cap. 8 ; Upton, Hibbert Lectures, 268 ; John Caird, Fund. Ideas of Christianity, 2 : 117, 118, 137-142. *Per contra*, see Shedd, Essays and Addresses, 277, 279 note; Woods, in Lit. and Theol. Rev., 1834 : 43–61; Harris, God the Creator and Lord of All, 1 : 201. On the Biblical conception of Love in general, see article by James Orr, in Hastings' Bible Dictionary.

3. Holiness.

Holiness is self-affirming purity. In virtue of this attribute of his nature, God eternally wills and maintains his own moral excellence. In this definition are contained three elements : first, purity ; secondly, purity willing ; thirdly, purity willing itself.

Ex. 15 : 11 — " glorious in holiness "; 19 : 10–16 — the people of Israel must purify themselves before they come into the presence of God ; Is. 6 : 3 — " Holy, holy, holy, is Jehovah of hosts " — notice the contrast with the unclean lips, that must be purged with a coal from the altar (verses 5–7); 2 Cor. 7 : 1 — " cleanse ourselves from all defilement of flesh and spirit, perfecting holiness in the fear of God "); 1 Thess. 3 : 13 — " unblamable in holiness "; 4 : 7 — " God called us not for uncleanness, but in sanctification "; Heb. 12 : 29 — " our God is a consuming fire " — to all iniquity. These passages show that holiness is the opposite to impurity, that it is itself purity.

The development of the conception of holiness in Hebrew history was doubtless a gradual one. At first it may have included little more than the idea of separation from all that is common, small and mean. Physical cleanliness and hatred of moral evil were additional elements which in time became dominant. We must remember however that the proper meaning of a term is to be determined not by the earliest but by the latest usage. Human nature is ethical from the start, and seeks to express the thought of a rule or standard of obligation, and of a righteous Being who imposes that rule or standard. With the very first conceptions of majesty and separation which attach to the apprehension of divinity in the childhood of the race there mingles at least some sense of the contrast between God's purity and human sin. The least developed man has a conscience which condemns some forms of wrong doing, and causes a feeling of separation from the power or powers above. Physical defilement becomes the natural symbol of moral evil. Places and vessels and rites are invested with dignity as associated with or consecrated to the Deity.

That the conception of holiness clears itself of extraneous and unessential elements only gradually, and receives its full expression only in the New Testament revelation and especially in the life and work of Christ, should not blind us to the fact that the germs of the idea lie far back in the very beginnings of man's existence upon earth. Even then the sense of wrong within had for its correlate a dimly recognized righteousness without. So soon as man knows himself as a sinner he knows something of the holiness of that God whom he has offended. We must take exception therefore to the remark of Schurman, Belief in God, 231 — " The first gods were probably non-moral beings," for Schurman himself had just said : " A God without moral character is no God at all." Dillmann, in his O. T. Theology, very properly makes the fundamental thought of O. T. religion, not the unity or the majesty of God, but his holiness. This alone forms the ethical basis for freedom and law. E. G. Robinson, Christian Theology — " The one aim of Christianity is personal holiness. But personal holiness will be the one absorbing and attainable aim of man, only as he recognizes it to be the one preëminent attribute of God. Hence everything divine is holy — the temple. the Scriptures, the Spirit." See articles on Holiness in O. T., by J. Skinner, and on Holiness in N. T., by G. B. Stevens, in Hastings' Bible Dictionary.

The development of the idea of holiness as well as the idea of love was prepared for before the advent of man. A. H. Strong, Education and Optimism : " There was a time when the past history of life upon the planet seemed one of heartless and cruel slaughter. The survival of the fittest had for its obverse side the destruction of myriads. Nature was ' red in tooth and claw with ravine.' But further thought has shown that this gloomy view results from a partial induction of facts. Paleontological life was marked not only by a struggle for life, but by a struggle for the life of others. The beginnings of altruism are to be seen in the instinct of reproduction, and in the care of offspring. In every lion's den and tiger's lair, in every mother eagle's feeding of her young, there is a self-sacrifice which faintly shadows forth man's subordination of personal interests to the interests of others. But in the ages before man can be found incipient justice as well as incipient love. The struggle for one's own life has its moral side as well as the struggle for the life of others. The instinct of self-preservation is the beginning of right, righteousness, justice, and law, on earth. Every creature owes it to God to preserve its own being. So we can find an adumbration of morality even in the predatory and internecine warfare of the geologic ages. The immanent God was even then preparing the way for the rights, the dignity, the freedom of humanity.' And, we may add. was preparing the way for the understanding by men of his own fundamental attribute of holiness. See Henry Drummond, Ascent of Man, Griffith-Jones, Ascent through Christ.

In further explanation we remark :

A. Negatively, that holiness is not

(a) Justice, or purity demanding purity from creatures. Justice, the relative or transitive attribute, is indeed the manifestation and expression of the immanent attribute of holiness, but it is not to be confounded with it.

Quenstedt, Theol., 8:1:34, defines holiness as "summa omnisque labis expers in Deo puritas, puritatem debitam exigens a creaturis "— a definition of transitive holiness, or justice, rather than of the immanent attribute. Is. 5:16 — "Jehovah of hosts is exalted in justice, and God the Holy One is sanctified in righteousness " = Justice is simply God's holiness in its judicial activity. Though holiness is commonly a term of separation and expresses the inherent opposition of God to all that is sinful, it is also used as a term of union, as in Lev. 11:44 — "be ye holy ; for I am holy." When Jesus turned from the young ruler (Mark 10 · 23 ' he illustrated the first ; John 8:29 illustrates the second : "he that sent me is with me." Lowrie, Doctrine of St. John, 51–57 — " 'God is light' (1 John 1:5) indicates the character of God, moral purity as revealed, as producing joy and life, as contrasted with doing ill, walking in darkness, being in a state of perdition."

Universal human conscience is itself a revelation of the holiness of God, and the joining everywhere of suffering with sin is the revelation of God's justice. The wrath, anger, jealousy of God show that this reaction of God's nature is necessary. God's nature is itself holy, just, and good. Holiness is not replaced by love, as Ritschl holds, since there is no self-impartation without self-affirmation. Holiness not simply *demands* in law, but *imparts* in the Holy Spirit ; see Pfleiderer, Grundriss, 79—*versus* Ritschl's doctrine that holiness is God's exaltation, and that it includes love ; see also Pfleiderer, Die Ritschl'sche Theologie, 53–63. Santayana, Sense of Beauty, 69—"If perfection is the ultimate justification of being, we may understand the ground of the moral dignity of beauty. Beauty is a pledge of the possible conformity between the soul and nature, and consequently a ground of faith in the supremacy of the good." We would regard nature however as merely the symbol and expression of God, and so would regard beauty as a ground of faith in his supremacy. What Santayana says of beauty is even more true of holiness. Wherever we see it, we recognize in it a pledge of the possible conformity between the soul and God, and consequently a ground of faith in the supremacy of God.

(b) Holiness is not a complex term designating the aggregate of the divine perfections. On the other hand, the notion of holiness is, both in Scripture and in Christian experience, perfectly simple, and perfectly distinct from that of other attributes.

Dick, Theol., 1:275— Holiness = venerableness, *i. e.*, "no particular attribute, but the general character of God as resulting from his moral attributes." Wardlaw calls holiness the union of all the attributes, as pure white light is the union of all the colored rays of the spectrum (Theology, 1:618-634). So Nitzsch, System of Christ. Doct., 166 ; H. W. Beecher : "Holiness = wholeness." Approaching this conception is the definition of W. N. Clarke, Christian Theology, 83 — "Holiness is the glorious fulness of the goodness of God, consistently held as the principle of his own action, and the standard for his creatures." This implies, according to Dr. Clarke, 1. An inward character of perfect goodness ; 2. That character as the consistent principle of his own action ; 3. The goodness which is the principle of his own action is also the standard for theirs." In other words, holiness is 1. character ; 2. self-consistency ; 3. requirement. We object to this definition that it fails to define. We are not told what is essential to this character ; the definition includes in holiness that which properly belongs to love : it omits all mention of the most important elements in holiness, namely purity and right.

A similar lack of clear definition appears in the statement of Mark Hopkins, Law of Love, 105 — "It is this double aspect of love, revealing the whole moral nature, and turning every way like the flaming sword that kept the way of the tree of life, that is termed holiness." As has been shown above, holiness is contrasted in Scripture, not with mere finiteness or littleness or misfortune or poverty or even unreality, but only with uncleanness and sinfulness. E. G. Robinson, Christ. Theology, 80 — "Holiness in man is the image of God's. But it is clear that holiness in man is not in proportion to the other perfections of his being — to his power, his knowledge, his wisdom, though it is in proportion to his rectitude of will — and therefore cannot be the sum of all perfections. . . . To identify holiness with the sum of all perfections is to make it mean mere completeness of character."

(c) Holiness is not God's self-love, in the sense of supreme regard for his own interest and happiness. There is no utilitarian element in holiness.

Buddeus, Theol. Dogmat., 2:1:36, defines holiness as God's self-love. But God loves and affirms self, not as self, but as the holiest. There is no self-seeking in God. Not the seeking of God's interests, but love for God as holy, is the principle and source of holiness in man. To call holiness God's self-love is to say that God is holy because of what he can make by it, i. e., to deny that holiness has any independent existence. See Thomasius, Christi Person und Werk, 1:155.

We would not deny, but would rather maintain, that there is a proper self-love which is not selfishness. This proper self-love, however, is not love at all. It is rather self-respect, self-preservation, self-vindication, and it constitutes an important characteristic of holiness. But to define holiness as merely God's love for himself, is to leave out of the definition the reason for this love in the purity and righteousness of the divine nature. God's self-respect implies that God respects himself for something in his own being. What is that something? Is holiness God's "moral excellence" (Hopkins), or God's " perfect goodness " (Clarke)? But what is this moral excellence or perfect goodness? We have here the method and the end described, but not the motive and ground. God does not love himself for his love, but he loves himself for his holiness. Those who maintain that love is self-affirming as well as self-communicating, and therefore that holiness is God's love for himself, must still admit that this self-affirming love which is holiness conditions and furnishes the standard for the self-communicating love which is benevolence.

G. B. Stevens, Johannine Theology, 364, tells us that "God's righteousness is the self-respect of perfect love." Miller, Evolution of Love, 53 — " Self-love is that kind of action which in a perfect being actualizes, in a finite being seeks to actualize, a perfect or ideal self." In other words, love is self-affirmation. But we object that self-love is not love at all, because there is in it no self-communicating. If holiness is in any sense a form or manifestation of love — a question which we have yet to consider — it is certainly not a unitarian and utilitarian self-love, which would be identical with selfishness, but rather an affection which implies trinitarian otherness and the maintenance of self as an ideal object. This appears to be the meaning of Jonathan Edwards, in his Essay on the Trinity (ed. Fisher), 79 — " All love respects another that is the beloved. By love the apostle certainly means something beside that which is commonly called self-love : that is very improperly called love, and is a thing of an exceeding diverse nature from the affection or virtue of love the apostle is speaking of." Yet we shall see that while Jonathan Edwards denies holiness to be a unitarian and utilitarian self-love, he regards its very essence to be God's trinitarian love for himself as a being of perfect moral excellence.

Ritschl's lack of trinitarian conviction makes it impossible for him to furnish any proper ground for either love or holiness in the nature of God. Ritschl holds that Christ as a person is an end in himself ; he realized his own ideal ; he developed his own personality ; he reached his own perfection in his work for man ; he is not merely a means toward the end of man's salvation. But when Ritschl comes to his doctrine of God, he is strangely inconsistent with all this, for he fails to represent God as having any end in himself, and deals with him simply as a means toward the kingdom of God as an end. Garvie, Ritschlian Theology, 256, 278, 279, well points out that personality means self-possession as well as self-communication, distinction from others as well as union with others. Ritschl does not see that God's love is primarily directed towards his Son, and only secondarily directed toward the Christian community. So he ignores the immanent Trinity. Before self-communication there must be self-maintenance. Otherwise God gives up his independence and makes created existence necessary.

(*d*) Holiness is not identical with, or a manifestation of, love. Since self-maintenance must precede self-impartation, and since benevolence has its object, motive, standard and limit in righteousness, holiness the self-affirming attribute can in no way be resolved into love the self-communicating.

That holiness is a form of love is the doctrine of Jonathan Edwards, Essay on the Trinity (ed. Fisher), 97 — " 'T is in God's infinite love to himself that his holiness consists. As all creature holiness is to be resolved into love, as the Scripture teaches us, so doth the holiness of God himself consist in infinite love to himself. God's holiness is the infinite beauty and excellence of his nature, and God's excellency consists in his love to himself." In his treatise on The Nature of Virtue, Jonathan Edwards defines virtue as regard for being in general. He considers that God's love is first of all directed toward himself as having the greatest quantity of being, and only secondarily directed towards his creatures whose quantity of being is infinitesimal as compared with his. God therefore finds his chief end in himself, and God's self-love is his holiness. This principle has permeated and dominated subsequent New England theology, from Samuel Hopkins, Works, 2 : 9–66, who maintains that holiness — love of being in general, to Horace Bushnell, Vicarious Sacrifice, who declares : "Righteousness, transferred into a word of the affections, is love ; and love, translated back into a word of the conscience, is righteousness ; the eternal law of right is only another conception of the law of love ; the two principles, right and love, appear exactly to measure each other." So Park, Discourses, 155-180.

Similar doctrine is taught by Dorner, Christian Ethics, 73, 93, 184 — "Love unites existence for self with existence for others, self-assertion and self-impartation. . . . Self-love in God is not selfishness, because he is the original and necessary seat of good in general, universal good. God guards his honor even in giving himself to others. . . . Love is the power and desire to be one's self while in another, and while one's self to be in another who is taken into the heart as an end. . . . I am to love my neighbor only as myself. . . . Virtue however requires not only good will, but the willing of the right thing." So Newman Smyth, Christian Ethics, 226-239, holds that 1. Love is self-affirmation. Hence he maintains that holiness or self-respect is involved in love. Righteousness is not an independent excellence to be contrasted with or put in opposition to benevolence ; it is an essential part of love. 2. Love is self-impartation. The only limit is ethical. Here is an ever deepening immanence, yet always some transcendence of God, for God cannot deny himself. 3. Love is self-finding in another. Vicariousness belongs to love. We reply to both Dorner and Smyth that their acknowledgment that love has its condition, limit, motive, object and standard, shows that there is a principle higher than love, and which regulates love. This principle is recognized as ethical. It is identical with the right. God cannot deny himself because he is fundamentally the right. This self-affirmation is holiness, and holiness cannot be a part of love, or a form of love, because it conditions and dominates love. To call it benevolence is to ignore its majestic distinctness and to imperil its legitimate supremacy.

God must first maintain his own being before he can give to another, and this self-maintenance must have its reason and motive in the worth of that which is maintained. Holiness cannot be love, because love is irrational and capricious except as it has a standard by which it is regulated, and this standard cannot be itself love, but must be holiness. We agree with Clarke, Christian Theology, 92, that "love is the desire to impart holiness." Love is a means to holiness, and holiness is therefore the supreme good and something higher than mere love. It is not true, *vice versa*, that holiness is the desire to impart love, or that holiness is a means to love. Instead then of saying, with Clarke, that " holiness is central in God, but love is central in holiness," we should prefer to say : "Love is central in God, but holiness is central in love," though in this case we should use the term love as including self-love. It is still better not to use the word love at all as referring to God's regard for himself. In ordinary usage, love means only regard for another and self-communication to that other. To embrace in it God's self-affirmation is to misinterpret holiness and to regard it as a means to an end, instead of making it what it really is, the superior object, and the regulative principle, of love.

That which lays down the norm or standard for love must be the superior of love. When we forget that "Righteousness and justice are the foundation of his throne" (Ps. 97:2), we lose one of the chief landmarks of Christian doctrine and involve ourselves in a mist of error. Rev. 4:3 — "there was a rainbow round about the throne" — in the midst of the rainbow of pardon and peace there is a throne of holiness and judgment. In Mat. 6:9, 10, "Thy kingdom come" is not the first petition, but rather, "Hallowed be thy name." It is a false idea of the divine simplicity which would reduce the attributes to one. Self-assertion is not a form of self-impartation. Not sentiency, a state of the sensibility, even though it be the purest benevolence, is the fundamental thing, but rather activity of will and a right direction of that will. Hodge, Essays, 133-136, 262-273, shows well that holy love is a love controlled by holiness. Holiness is not a mere means to happiness. To be happy is not the ultimate reason for being holy. Right and wrong are not matters of profit and loss. To be told that God is only benevolence, and that he punishes only when the happiness of the universe requires it, destroys our whole allegiance to God and does violence to the constitution of our nature.

That God is only love has been called " the doctrine of the papahood of God." God is " a summer ocean of kindliness, never agitated by storms " (Dale, Ephesians, 59). But Jesus gives us the best idea of God, and in him we find, not only pity, but at times moral indignation. John 17:11 — "Holy Father" — more than love. Love can be exercised by God only when it is right love. Holiness is the track on which the engine of love must run. The track cannot be the engine. If either includes the other, then it is holiness that includes love, since holiness is the maintenance of God's perfection, and perfection involves love. He that is holy affirms himself also as the perfect love. If love were fundamental, there would be nothing to give, and so love would be vain and worthless. There can be no giving of self, without a previous self-affirming. God is not holy because he loves, but he loves because he is holy. Love cannot direct itself ; it is under bonds to holiness. Justice is not dependent on love for its right to be. Stephen G. Barnes : " Mere good will is not the sole content of the law ; it is insufficient in times of fiery trial ; it is inadequate as a basis for retribution. Love needs justice, and justice needs love ; both are commanded in God's law and are perfectly revealed in God's character."

There may be a friction between a man's two hands, and there may be a conflict between a man's conscience and his will, between his intellect and his affection. Force is God's energy under resistance, the resistance as well as the energy being his. So, upon occasion of man's sin, holiness and love in God become opposite poles or forces. The first and most serious effect of sin is not its effect upon man, but its effect upon God. Holiness necessarily requires suffering, and love endures it. This eternal suffering of God on account of sin is the atonement, and the incarnate Christ only shows what has been in the heart of God from the beginning. To make holiness a form of love is really to deny its existence, and with this to deny that any atonement is necessary for man's salvation. If holiness is the same as love, how is it that the classic world, that knew of God's holiness, did not also know of his love? The ethics here reminds one of Abraham Lincoln's meat broth that was made of the shadow of a pigeon that died of starvation. Holiness that is only good will is not holiness at all, for it lacks the essential elements of purity and righteousness.

At the railway switching grounds east of Rochester, there is a man whose duty it is to move a bar of iron two or three inches to the left or to the right. So he determines whether a train shall go toward New York or toward Washington, toward New Orleans or San Francisco. Our conclusion at this point in our theology will similarly determine what our future system will be. The principle that holiness is a manifestation of love, or a form of benevolence, leads to the conclusions that happiness is the only good, and the only end ; that law is a mere expedient for the securing of happiness ; that penalty is simply deterrent or reformatory in its aim ; that no atonement needs to be offered to God for human sin ; that eternal retribution cannot be vindicated, since there is no hope of reform. This view ignores the testimony of conscience and of Scripture that sin is intrinsically ill-deserving, and must be punished on that account, not because punishment will work good to the universe,— indeed, it could not work good to the universe, unless it were just and right in itself. It ignores the fact that mercy is optional with God, while holiness is invariable ; that punishment is many times traced to God's holiness, but never to God's love ; that God is not simply love but light — moral light — and therefore is "a consuming fire" (Heb. 12 : 29) to all iniquity. Love chastens (Heb. 12 : 6), but only holiness punishes (Jer. 10 : 24 — "correct me, but in measure; not in thine anger"; Ez. 28 : 22 — "I shall have executed judgments in her, and shall be sanctified in her"; 36 : 21, 22 —

in judgment "I do not this for your sake, but for my holy name"; 1 John 1 : 5 — "God is light, and in him is no darkness" — moral darkness; Rev. 15 : 4, 4 — "the wrath of God . . . thou only art holy . . . thy righteous acts have been made manifest"; 16 : 5 — "righteous art thou . . . . because thou didst thus judge"; 19 : 2 — "true and righteous are his judgments; for he hath judged the great harlot"). See Hovey, God with Us, 187-221; Philippi, Glaubenslehre, 2 : 80-82; Thomasius, Christi Person und Werk, 154, 155, 346-353; Lange, Pos. Dogmatik, 203.

B. Positively, that holiness is

(*a*) Purity of substance.—In God's moral nature, as necessarily acting, there are indeed the two elements of willing and being. But the passive logically precedes the active; being comes before willing; God *is* pure before he *wills* purity. Since purity, however, in ordinary usage is a negative term and means only freedom from stain or wrong, we must include in it also the positive idea of moral rightness. God is holy in that he is the source and standard of the right.

E. G. Robinson, Christian Theology, 80 — "Holiness is moral purity, not only in the sense of absence of all moral stain, but of complacency in all moral good." Shedd, Dogm. Theology, 1 : 362 — "Holiness in God is conformity to his own perfect nature. The only rule for the divine will is the divine reason; and the divine reason prescribes everything that is befitting an infinite Being to do. God is not under law, nor above law. He *is* law. He is righteous by nature and necessity. . . . . God is the source and author of law for all moral beings." We may better Shedd's definition by saying that holiness is that attribute in virtue of which God's being and God's will eternally conform to each other. In thus maintaining that holy being logically precedes holy willing, we differ from the view of Lotze, Philos. of Religion. 139 — "Such will of God no more follows from his nature as secondary to it, or precedes it as primary to it than, in motion, direction can be antecedent or subsequent to velocity." Bowne, Philos. of Theism, 16 — "God's nature = a fixed law of activity or mode of manifestation. . . . . But laws of thought are no limitation, because they are simply modes of thought-activity. They do not *rule* intellect, but only express what intellect *is*."

In spite of these utterances of Lotze and of Bowne, we must maintain that, as truth of being logically precedes truth of knowing, and as a loving nature precedes loving emotions, so purity of substance precedes purity of will. The opposite doctrine leads to such utterances as that of Whedon (On the Will, 316): "God is holy, in that he freely chooses to make his own happiness in eternal right. Whether he could not make himself equally happy in wrong is more than we can say. . . . . Infinite wisdom and infinite holiness consist in, and result from, God's volitions eternally." Whedon therefore believes, not in God's *unchangeableness*, but in God's *unchangingness*. He cannot say whether motives may not at some time prove strongest for divine apostasy to evil. The essential holiness of God affords no basis for certainty. Here we have to rely on our faith, more than on the object of faith; see H. B. Smith, Review of Whedon, in Faith and Philosophy, 355-399. As we said with regard to truth, so here we say with regard to holiness, that to make holiness a matter of mere will, instead of regarding it as a characteristic of God's being, is to deny that anything is holy in itself. If God can make impurity to be purity, then God in himself is indifferent to purity or impurity, and he ceases therefore to be God. Robert Browning, A Soul's Tragedy, 223 — "I trust in God — the Right shall be the Right And other than the Wrong, while He endures." P. S. Moxom: "Revelation is a disclosure of the divine righteousness. We do not add to the thought when we say that it is also a disclosure of the divine love, for love is a manifestation or realization of that rightness of relations which righteousness is." H. B. Smith, System, 223-231 — "Virtue = love for both happiness and holiness, yet holiness as ultimate, — love to the highest Person and to his ends and objects."

(*b*) Energy of will.—This purity is not simply a passive and dead quality; it is the attribute of a personal being; it is penetrated and pervaded by will. Holiness is the free moral movement of the Godhead.

As there is a higher Mind than our mind, and a greater Heart than our heart, so there is a grander Will than our will. Holiness contains this element of will, although it is a will which expresses nature, instead of causing nature. It is not a still and moveless purity, like the whiteness of the new-fallen snow, or the stainless blue of the summer

18

sky. It is the most tremendous of energies, in unsleeping movement. It is "a glassy sea "
(Rev. 15 : 2), but "a glassy sea mingled with fire." A. J. Gordon: "Holiness is not a dead-white
purity, the perfection of the faultless marble statue. Life, as well as purity, enters
into the idea of holiness. They who are 'without fault before the throne' are they
who 'follow the Lamb whithersoever he goeth' — holy activity attending and expressing their holy state." Martensen, Christian Ethics, 62, 63 — "God is the perfect unity
of the ethically necessary and the ethically free"; "God cannot do otherwise than will
his own essential nature." See Thomasius, Christi Person und Werk, 141; and on the
Holiness of Christ, see Godet, Defence of the Christian Faith, 203–241.

The centre of personality is will. Knowing has its end in feeling, and feeling has its
end in willing. Hence I must make feeling subordinate to willing, and happiness to
righteousness. I must will with God and for God, and must use all my influence over
others to make them like God in holiness. William James, Will to Believe, 123 — "Mind
must first get its impression from the object; then define what that object is and what
active measures its presence demands; and finally react. . . . . All faiths and philosophies, moods and systems, subserve and pass into a third stage, the stage of action."
What is true of man is even more true of God. All the wills of men combined, aye,
even the whole moving energy of humanity in all climes and ages, is as nothing compared with the extent and intensity of God's willing. The whole momentum of God's
being is behind moral law. That law is his self-expression. His beneficent yet also
his terrible arm is ever defending and enforcing it. God must maintain his holiness,
for this is his very Godhead. If he did not maintain it, love would have nothing to
give away, or to make others partakers of.

Does God will the good because it is the good, or is the good good because God wills
it? In the former case, there would seem to be a good above God; in the latter case,
good is something arbitrary and changeable. Kaftan, Dogmatik, 186, 187, says that
neither of these is true; he holds that there is no *a priori* good before the willing of it,
and he also holds that will without direction is not will; the good is good for God, not
before, but *in*, his self-determination. Dorner, System Doctrine, 1 : 432, holds on the
contrary that both these are true, because God has no mere simple form of being,
whether necessary or free, but rather a manifoldly diverse being, absolutely correlated
however, and reciprocally conditioning itself, — that is, a trinitarian being, both necessary and free. We side with Dorner here, and claim that the belief that God's will is
the executive of God's being is necessary to a correct ethics and to a correct theology.
Celsus justified polytheism by holding that whatever is a part of God reveals God,
serves God, and therefore may rationally be worshiped. Christianity he excepted
from this wide toleration, because it worshiped a jealous God who was not content
to be one of many. But this jealousy really signifies that God is a Being to whom
moral distinctions are real. The God of Celsus, the God of pantheism, is not jealous,
because he is not the Holy One, but simply the Absolute. The category of the ethical is
merged in the category of being; see Bruce, Apologetics, 16. The great lack of modern
theology is precisely this ethical lack; holiness is merged in benevolence; there is no
proper recognition of God's righteousness. John 17 : 25 — "O righteous Father, the world knew thee
not" — is a text as true to-day as in Jesus' time. See Issel, Begriff der Heiligkeit in N. T.,
41, 84, who defines holiness in God as "the ethical perfection of God in its exaltation
above all that is sinful," and holiness in men as "the condition corresponding to that
of God, in which man keeps himself pure from sin."

(c) Self-affirmation.—Holiness is God's self-willing. His own purity is
the supreme object of his regard and maintenance. God is holy, in that
his infinite moral excellence affirms and asserts itself as the highest possible motive and end. Like truth and love, this attribute can be understood only in the light of the doctrine of the Trinity.

Holiness is purity willing itself. We have an analogy in man's duty of self-preservation, self-respect, self-assertion. Virtue is bound to maintain and defend itself, as in
the case of Job. In his best moments, the Christian feels that purity is not simply the
negation of sin, but the affirmation of an inward and divine principle of righteousness.
Thomasius, Christi Person und Werk, 1 : 137 — "Holiness is the perfect agreement of
the divine willing with the divine being; for as the personal creature is holy when it
wills and determines itself as God wills, so is God the holy one because he wills himself
as what he is (or, to be what he is). In virtue of this attribute, God excludes from
himself everything that contradicts his nature, and affirms himself in his absolutely

good being—his being like himself." Tholuck on Romans, 5th ed., 151—"The term holiness should be used to indicate a relation of God to himself. That is holy which, undisturbed from without, is wholly like itself." Dorner, System of Doctrine, 1:456 — "It is the part of goodness to protect goodness." We shall see, when we consider the doctrine of the Trinity, that that doctrine has close relations to the doctrine of the immanent attributes. It is in the Son that God has a perfect object of will, as well as of knowledge and love.

The object of God's willing in eternity past can be nothing outside of himself. It must be the highest of all things. We see what it must be, only when we remember that the right is the unconditional imperative of our moral nature. Since we are made in his image we must conclude that God eternally wills righteousness. Not all God's acts are acts of love, but all are acts of holiness. The self-respect, self-preservation, self-affirmation, self-assertion, self-vindication, which we call God's holiness, is only faintly reflected in such utterances as Job 27:5, 6—"Till I die I will not put away mine integrity from me. My righteousness I hold fast, and will not let it go"; 31:37—"I would declare unto him the number of my steps; as a prince would I go near unto him." The fact that the Spirit of God is denominated the Holy Spirit should teach us what is God's essential nature, and the requisition that we should be holy as he is holy should teach us what is the true standard of human duty and object of human ambition. God's holiness moreover since it is self-affirmation, furnishes the guarantee that God's love will not fail to secure its end, and that all things will serve his purpose. Rom. 11:36 — "For of him, and through him, and unto him, are all things. To him be the glory for ever. Amen." On the whole subject of Holiness, as an attribute of God, see A. H. Strong, Philosophy and Religion, 188-200, and Christ in Creation, 388-405; Delitzsch, art. Heiligkeit, in Herzog, Realencyclop.; Baudissin, Begriff der Heiligkeit im A. T.,—synopsis in Studien und Kritiken, 1880:169; Robertson Smith, Prophets of Israel, 224-234; E. B. Coe, in Presb. and Ref. Rev., Jan. 1890:42-47; and articles on Holiness in O. T., and Holiness in N. T., in Hastings' Bible Dictionary.

VI. Relative or Transitive Attributes.

First Division.—Attributes having relation to Time and Space.

1. Eternity.

By this we mean that God's nature (*a*) is without beginning or end ; (*b*) is free from all succession of time ; and (*c*) contains in itself the cause of time.

Deut. 32:40 — "For I lift up my hand to heaven, And say, As I live forever . . . ."; Ps. 90:2—"Before the mountains . . . . from everlasting . . . . thou art God"; 102:27— "thy years shall have no end"; Is. 41:4—"I Jehovah, the first, and with the last"; 1 Cor. 2:7— πρὸ τῶν αἰώνων—"before the worlds" or "ages"=πρὸ καταβολῆς κόσμου—"before the foundation of the world" (Eph. 1·4). 1 Tim. 1:17— Βασιλεῖ τῶν αἰώνων — "King of the ages" (so also Rev. 15:8). 1 Tim. 6:16—"who only hath immortality." Rev. 1:8 — "the Alpha and the Omega." Dorner: "We must not make Kronos (time) and Uranos (space) earlier divinities before God." They are among the "all things" that were "made by him" (John 1:3). Yet time and space are not *substances;* neither are they *attributes* (qualities of substance); they are rather *relations* of finite existence. (Porter, Human Intellect, 568, prefers to call time and space "*correlates* to beings and events.") With finite existence they come into being; they are not mere regulative conceptions of our minds; they exist objectively, whether we perceive them or not. Ladd: "Time is the mental presupposition of the duration of events and of objects. Time is not an entity, or it would be necessary to suppose some other time in which it endures. We think of space and time as unconditional, because they furnish the conditions of our knowledge. The age of a son is conditioned on the age of his father. The conditions themselves cannot be conditioned. Space and time are mental forms, but not only that. There is an extramental something in the case of space and time, as in the case of sound."

Ex. 3:14—"I am"—involves eternity. Ps. 102:12-14 — "But thou, O Jehovah, wilt abide forever . . . . Thou wilt arise, and have mercy upon Zion; for it is time to have pity upon her . . . . For thy servants . . . . . have p ty upon her dust"= because God is eternal, he will have compassion upon Zion: he will do this, for even we, her children, love her very dust. Jude 25 — "glory, majesty, dominion and power, before all time, and now, and for evermore." Pfleiderer, Philos. Religion, 1:165—"God is 'King of the æons' (1 Tim. 1:17), because he distinguishes, in his thinking, his eternal inner essence from his changeable working in the world. He is not merged in the process." Edwards the younger describes timelessness as "the immediate and invariable possession of the whole unlimited life together and at once." Tyler, Greek Poets, 148 — "The heathen gods had only existence without end. The Greeks seem never to have conceived of existence without beginning." On precognition as connected with the so-called future already existing, and on apparent time progression as a subjective human sensation and not inherent in the universe as it exists in an infinite Mind, see Myers, Human Personality, 2:262 sq. Tennyson, Life, 1:322 — "For was and is and will be are but is: And all creation is one act at once, The birth of light; but we that are not all, As parts, can see but parts, now this, now that, And live perforce from thought to thought, and make The act a phantom of succession: there Our weakness somehow shapes the shadow, Time."

Augustine: "Mundus non in tempore, sed cum tempore, factus est." There is no meaning to the question: Why did creation take place when it did rather than earlier? or the question: What was God doing before creation? These questions presuppose an independent time in which God created — a time before time. On the other hand, creation did not take place at any time, but God gave both the world and time their existence. Royce, World and Individual, 2:111-115 — "Time is the form of the will, as space is the form of the intellect (cf. 124, 133). Time runs only in one direction (unlike space), toward fulfilment of striving or expectation. In pursuing its goals, the self lives in time. Every now is also a succession, as is illustrated in any melody. To God the universe is 'totum simul', as to us any succession is one whole. 233 — Death is a change in the time-span — the minimum of time in which a succession can appear as a completed whole. To God "a thousand years" are "as one day" (2 Pet. 3:8). 419 — God, in his totality as the Absolute Being, is conscious not, in time, but of time, and of all that infinite time contains. In time there follow, in their sequence, the chords of his endless symphony. For him is this whole symphony of life at once. . . . . You unite present, past and future in a single consciousness whenever you hear any three successive words, for one is past, another is present, at the same time that a third is future. So God unites in timeless perception the whole succession of finite events. . . . The single notes are not lost in the melody. You are in God, but you are not lost in God." Mozart, quoted in Wm. James, Principles of Psychology, 1:255 — "All the inventing and making goes on in me as in a beautiful strong dream. But the best of all is *the hearing of it all at once*."

Eternity is infinity in its relation to time. It implies that God's nature is not subject to the law of time. God is not in time. It is more correct to say that time is in God. Although there is logical succession in God's thoughts, there is no chronological succession.

Time is duration measured by successions. Duration without succession would still be duration, though it would be immeasurable. Reid, Intellectual Powers, essay 3, chap. 5 — "We may measure duration by the succession of thoughts in the mind, as we measure length by inches or feet, but the notion or idea of duration must be antecedent to the mensuration of it, as the notion of length is antecedent to its being measured." God is not under the law of time. Solly, The Will, 254 — "God looks through time as we look through space." Murphy, Scientific Bases, 90 — "Eternity is not, as men believe, Before and after us, an endless line. No, 't is a circle, infinitely great — All the circumference with creations thronged: God at the centre dwells, beholding all. And as we move in this eternal round, The finite portion which alone we see Behind us, is the past; what lies before We call the future. But to him who dwells Far at the centre, equally remote From every point of the circumference, Both are alike, the future and the past." Vaughan (1655): "I saw Eternity the other night, Like a great ring of pure and endless light, And calm as it was bright; and round beneath it Time in hours, days, years, Driven by the spheres, Like a vast shadow moved, in which the world And all her train were hurled."

We cannot have derived from experience our idea of eternal duration in the past, for experience gives us only duration that has had beginning. The idea of duration as without beginning must therefore be given us by intuition. Case, Physical Realism, 379, 380 — "Time is the continuance, or continual duration, of the universe." Bradley, Appearance and Reality, 39 — Consider time as a stream — under a spatial form: "If you take time as a relation between units without duration, then the whole time has no duration, and is not time at all. But if you give duration to the whole time, then a, once the units themselves are found to possess it, and they cease to be units." The *now* is not time, unless it turns past into future, and this is a process. The now then consists of nows, and these nows are undiscoverable. The unit is nothing but its own relation to something beyond, something not discoverable. Time therefore is not real, but is appearance.

John Caird, Fund. Ideas, 1 : 185 — " That which grasps and correlates objects in space cannot itself be one of the things of space ; that which apprehends and connects events as succeeding each other in time must itself stand above the succession or stream of events. In being able to measure them, it cannot be flowing with them. There could not be for self-consciousness any such thing as time, if it were not, in one aspect of it, above time, if it did not belong to an order which is or has in it an element which is eternal. . . . . As taken up into thought, succession is not successive." A. H. Strong, Historical Discourse, May 9, 1900 — " God is above space and time, and we are in God. We mark the passage of time, and we write our histories. But we can do this, only because in our highest being we do not belong to space and time, but have in us a bit of eternity. John Caird tells us that we could not perceive the flowing of the stream if we were ourselves a part of the current ; only as we have our feet planted on solid rock, can we observe that the water rushes by. We belong to God ; we are akin to God ; and while the world passes away and the lust thereof, he that doeth the will of God abideth forever." J. Estlin Carpenter and P. H. Wicksteed, Studies in Theology, 10 — " Dante speaks of God as him in whom 'every *where* and every *when* are focused in a point', that is, to whom every season is *now* and every place is *here*."

Amiel's Journal : " Time is the supreme illusion. It is the inner prism by which we decompose being and life, the mode by which we perceive successively what is simultaneous in idea. . . . . Time is the successive dispersion of being, just as speech is the successive analysis of an intuition, or of an act of the will. In itself it is relative and negative, and it disappears within the absolute Being. . . . . Time and space are fragments of the Infinite for the use of finite creatures. God permits them that he may not be alone. They are the mode under which creatures are possible and conceivable. . . . . . If the universe subsists, it is because the eternal Mind loves to perceive its own content, in all its wealth and expression, especially in its stages of preparation. . . . . . The radiations of our mind are imperfect reflections from the great show of fireworks set in motion by Brahma, and great art is great only because of its conformities with the divine order — with that which is."

Yet we are far from saying that time, now that it exists, has no objective reality to God. To him, past, present, and future are " one eternal now," not in the sense that there is no distinction between them, but only in the sense that he sees past and future as vividly as he sees the present. With creation time began, and since the successions of history are veritable successions, he who sees according to truth must recognize them.

Thomas Carlyle calls God " the Eternal Now." Mason, Faith of the Gospel, 30—" God is not contemptuous of time. . . . One day is with the Lord as a thousand years. He values the infinitesimal in time, even as he does in space. Hence the patience, the long-suffering, the expectation, of God." We are reminded of the inscription on the sun-dial, in which it is said of the hours: " Pereunt et imputantur " — " They pass by, and they are charged to our account." A certain preacher remarked on the wisdom of God which has so arranged that the moments of time come successively and not simultaneously, and thus prevent infinite confusion ! Shedd, Dogm. Theol., 1 : 344, illustrates God's eternity by the two ways in which a person may see a procession : first from a doorway in the street through which the procession is passing ; and secondly, from the top of a steeple which commands a view of the whole procession at the same instant.

S. E. Meze, quoted in Royce, Conception of God, 40 — " As if all of us were cylinders, with their ends removed, moving through the waters of some placid lake. To the cylinders the waters seem to move. What has passed is a memory, what is to come is doubtful. But the lake knows that all the water is equally real, and that it is quiet, immovable, unruffled. Speaking technically, time is no reality. Things *seem* past and future, and, in a sense, non-existent to us, but, in fact, they are just as genuinely real as the present is." Yet even here there is an order. You cannot play a symphony backward and have music. This qualification at least must be put upon the words of Berkeley ; " A succession of ideas I take to *constitute* time, and not to be only the sensible measure thereof, as Mr. Locke and others think."

Finney, quoted in Bib. Sac., Oct. 1877:722 — "Eternity to us means all past, present, and future duration. But to God it means only now. Duration and space, as they respect his existence, mean infinitely different things from what they do when they respect our existence. God's existence and his acts, as they respect finite existence, have relation to time and space. But as they respect his own existence, everything is *here* and *now*. With respect to all finite existences, God can say : I was, I am, I shall be, I will do ; but with respect to his own existence, all that he can say is : I am, I do."

Edwards the younger, Works, 1 : 386, 387—" There is no succession in the divine mind ; therefore no new operations take place. All the divine acts are from eternity, nor is there any time with God. The *effects* of these divine acts do indeed all take place in time and in a succession. If it should be said that on this supposition the effects take place not till long after the acts by which they are produced, I answer that they do so in our view, but not in the view of God. With him there is no time ; no before or after with respect to time : nor has time any existence in the divine mind, or in the nature of things independently of the minds and perceptions of creatures ; but it depends on the succession of those perceptions." We must qualify this statement of the younger Edwards by the following from Julius Müller : " If God's working can have no relation to time, then all bonds of union between God and the world are snapped asunder."

It is an interesting question whether the human spirit is capable of timeless existence, and whether the conception of time is purely physical. In dreams we seem to lose sight of succession ; in extreme pain an age is compressed into a minute. Does this throw light upon the nature of prophecy ? Is the soul of the prophet rapt into God's timeless existence and vision ? It is doubtful whether Rev. 10 : 6 — " there shall be time no longer " can be relied upon to prove the affirmative ; for the Rev. Vers. marg. and the American Revisers translate " there shall be delay no longer." Julius Müller, Doct. Sin, 2 : 147 — "All self-consciousness is a victory over time." So with memory ; see Dorner, Glaubenslehre, 1 : 471. On " the death-vision of one's whole existence," see Frances Kemble Butler's experience in Shedd, Dogm. Theol., 1 : 351—" Here there is succession and series, only so exceedingly rapid as to seem simultaneous." This rapidity however is so great as to show that each man can at the last be judged in an instant. On space and time as unlimited, see Porter, Hum. Intellect, 564-566. On the conception of eternity, see Mansel, Lectures, Essays and Reviews, 111-126, and Modern Spiritualism, 255-292 ; New Englander, April, 1875 : art. on the Metaphysical Idea of Eternity. For practical lessons from the Eternity of God, see Park, Discourses, 137-154 ; Westcott, Some Lessons of the Rev. Vers., (Pott, N. Y., 1897), 187 — with comments on αἰῶνες in Eph. 3 : 21, Heb. 11 : 3, Rev. 4 ; 10, 11 — " the universe under the aspect of time."

2. Immensity.

By this we mean that God's nature (*a*) is without extension ; (*b*) is subject to no limitations of space ; and (*c*) contains in itself the cause of space.

1 Kings 8 : 27 — " behold, heaven and the heaven of heavens cannot contain thee." Space is a creation of God ; Rom. 8 : 39 — " nor height, nor depth, nor any other creature." Zahn, Bib. Dogmatik, 149 — " Scripture does not teach the immanence of God in the world, but the immanence of the world in God." Dante does not put God, but Satan at the centre ; and Satan, being at the centre, is crushed with the whole weight of the universe. God is the Being who encompasses all. All things exist in him. E. G. Robinson : " Space is a relation ; God is the author of relations and of our modes of thought ; therefore God is the author of space. Space conditions our thought, but it does not condition God's thought."

Jonathan Edwards : " Place itself is mental, and within and without are mental conceptions. . . . When I say the material universe exists only in the mind, I mean that it is absolutely dependent on the conception of the mind for its existence, and does not exist as spirits do, whose existence does not consist in, nor in dependence on, the conception of other minds." H. M. Stanley, on Space and Science, in Philosophical Rev., Nov. 1898 : 615 — " Space is not full of things, but things are spaceful. . . . Space is a form of dynamic appearance." Bradley carries the ideality of space to an extreme, when, in his Appearance and Reality, 35-38, he tells us : Space is not a mere relation, for it has parts, and what can be the parts of a relation ? But space is nothing but a relation, for it is lengths of lengths of — nothing that we can find. We can find no terms either inside or outside. Space, to be space, must have space outside itself. Bradley therefore concludes that space is not reality but only appearance.

Immensity is infinity in its relation to space. God's nature is not subject to the law of space. God is not in space. It is more correct to say that space is in God. Yet space has an objective reality to God. With creation space began to be, and since God sees according to truth, he recognizes relations of space in his creation.

Many of the remarks made in explanation of time apply equally to space. Space is not a substance nor an attribute, but a relation. It exists so soon as extended matter exists, and exists as its necessary condition, whether our minds perceive it or not. Reid, Intellectual Powers, essay 2, chap. 9 — "Space is not so properly an object of sense, as a necessary concomitant of the objects of sight and touch." When we see or touch body, we get the idea of space in which the body exists, but the idea of space is not furnished by the sense; it is an *a priori* cognition of the reason. Experience furnishes the occasion of its evolution, but the mind evolves the conception by its own native energy.

Anselm, Proslogion, 19 — "Nothing contains thee, but thou containest all things." Yet it is not precisely accurate to say that space is in God, for this expression seems to intimate that God is a greater space which somehow includes the less. God is rather unspatial and is the Lord of space. The notion that space and the divine immensity are identical leads to a materialistic conception of God. Space is not an attribute of God, as Clarke maintained, and no argument for the divine existence can be constructed from this premise (see pages 85, 86). Martineau, Types, 1 : 138, 139, 170 — "Malebranche said that God is the place of all spirits, as space is the place of all bodies. . . . Descartes held that there is no such thing as empty space. *Nothing* cannot possibly have extension. Wherever extension is, there must be *something* extended. Hence the doctrine of a *plenum*, A *vacuum* is inconceivable." Lotze, Outlines of Metaphysics, 87— "According to the ordinary view . . . space *exists*, and things exist *in it;* according to our view, only things exist, and *between them* nothing exists, but space exists *in them.*"

Case, Physical Realism, 379, 380 — "Space is the continuity, or continuous extension, of the universe as one substance." Ladd: "Is space extended? Then it must be extended in some other space. That other space is the space we are talking about. Space then is not an entity, but a mental presupposition of the existence of extended substance. Space and time are neither finite nor infinite. Space has neither circumference nor centre,—its centre would be everywhere. We cannot *imagine* space at all. It is simply a precondition of mind enabling us to perceive things." In Bib. Sac., 1890 : 415-444, art.: Is Space a Reality? Prof. Mead opposes the doctrine that space is purely subjective, as taught by Bowne; also the doctrine that space is a certain order of relations among realities; that space is nothing apart from things; but that things, when they exist, exist in certain relations, and that the sum, or system, of these relations constitutes space.

We prefer the view of Bowne, Metaphysics, 127, 137, 143, that "Space is the form of objective experience, and is nothing in abstraction from that experience. . . . It is a form of intuition, and not a mode of existence. According to this view, things are not in space and space-relations, but appear to be. In themselves they are essentially non-spatial; but by their interactions with one another, and with the mind, they give rise to the appearance of a world of extended things in a common space. Space predicates, then, belong to phenomena only, and not to things-in-themselves. . . . Apparent reality exists spatially; but proper ontological reality exists spacelessly and without spatial predicates." For the view that space is relative, see also Cocker, Theistic Conception of the World, 66-96; Calderwood, Philos. of the Infinite, 331-335. *Per contra*, see Porter, Human Intellect, 662; Hazard, Letters on Causation in Willing, appendix; Bib. Sac., Oct. 1877 : 726; Gear, in Bap. Rev., July, 1880 : 434; Lowndes, Philos. of Primary Beliefs, 144-161.

Second Division.—Attributes having relation to Creation.

1. Omnipresence.

By this we mean that God, in the totality of his essence, without diffusion or expansion, multiplication or division, penetrates and fills the universe in all its parts.

Ps. 139 : 7 sq. — " Whither shall I go from thy Spirit? Or whither shall I flee from thy presence ? " Jer. 23 : 23, 24 — " Am I a God at hand, saith Jehovah, and not a God afar off ? . . . . Do not I fill heaven and earth ? " Acts 17 : 27, 28 — " he is not far from each one of us : for in him we live, and move, and have our being." Faber : " For God is never so far off As even to be near. He is within. Our spirit is The home he holds most dear. To think of him as by our side Is almost as untrue As to remove his shrine beyond Those skies of starry blue. So all the while I thought myself Homeless, forlorn and weary, Missing my joy, I walked the earth Myself God's sanctuary." Henri Amiel : " From every point on earth we are equally near to heaven and the infinite." Tennyson, The Higher Pantheism : " Speak to him then, for he hears, and spirit with spirit can meet ; Closer is he than breathing, and nearer than hands and feet." " As full, as perfect, in a hair as heart."

The atheist wrote : " God is nowhere," but his little daughter read it : " God is now here," and it converted him. The child however sometimes asks : " if God is everywhere, how is there any room for us ? " and the only answer is that God is not a material but a spiritual being, whose presence does not exclude finite existence but rather makes such existence possible. This universal presence of God had to be learned gradually. It required great faith in Abraham to go out from Ur of the Chaldees, and yet to hold that God would be with him in a distant land (Heb. 11 : 8). Jacob learned that the heavenly ladder followed him wherever he went (Gen. 28 : 15). Jesus taught that " neither in this mountain, nor in Jerusalem, shall ye worship the Father " (John 4 : 21). Our Lord's mysterious comings and goings after his resurrection were intended to teach his disciples that he was with them " always, even unto the end of the world " (Mat. 28 : 20). The omnipresence of Jesus demonstrates, a fortiori, the omnipresence of God.

In explanation of this attribute we may say :

(a) God's omnipresence is not potential but essential.—We reject the Socinian representation that God's essence is in heaven, only his power on earth. When God is said to " dwell in the heavens," we are to understand the language either as a symbolic expression of exaltation above earthly things, or as a declaration that his most special and glorious self-manifestations are to the spirits of heaven.

Ps. 123 : 1 — " 0 thou that sittest in the heavens " ; 113 : 5 — " That hath his seat on high " ; Is. 57 : 15 — " the high and lofty One that inhabiteth eternity." Mere potential omnipresence is Deistic as well as Socinian. Like birds in the air or fish in the sea, " at home, abroad, We are surrounded still with God." We do not need to go up to heaven to call him down, or into the abyss to call him up (Rom. 10 : 6, 7). The best illustration is found in the presence of the soul in every part of the body. Mind seems not confined to the brain. Natural realism in philosophy, as distinguished from idealism, requires that the mind should be at the point of contact with the outer world, instead of having reports and ideas brought to it in the brain ; see Porter, Human Intellect, 149. All believers in a soul regard the soul as at least present in all parts of the brain, and this is a relative omnipresence no less difficult in principle than its presence in all parts of the body. An animal's brain may be frozen into a piece solid as ice, yet, after thawing, it will act as before : although freezing of the whole body will cause death. If the immaterial principle were confined to the brain we should expect freezing of the brain to cause death. But if the soul may be omnipresent in the body or even in the brain, the divine Spirit may be omnipresent in the universe. Bowne, Metaphysics, 136 — " If finite things are modes of the infinite, each thing must be a mode of the entire infinite ; and the infinite must be present in its unity and completeness in every finite thing, just as the entire soul is present in all its acts." This idealistic conception of the entire mind as present in all its thoughts must be regarded as the best analogue to God's omnipresence in the universe. We object to the view that this omnipresence is merely potential, as we find it in Clarke, Christian Theology, 74 — " We know, and only know, that God is able to put forth all his power of action, without regard to place. . . . Omnipresence is an element in the immanence of God. . . . A local God would be no real God. If he is not everywhere, he is not true God anywhere. Omnipresence is implied in all providence, in all prayer, in all communion with God and reliance on God."

So long as it is conceded that consciousness is not confined to a single point in the brain, the question whether other portions of the brain or of the body are also the seat of consciousness may be regarded as a purely academic one, and the answer need not affect our present argument. The principle of omnipresence is granted when once we hold that the soul is conscious at more than one point of the physical organism. Yet the question suggested above is an interesting one and with regard to it psychologists are divided. Paulsen, Einleitung in die Philosophie (1892), 133–159, holds that consciousness is correlated with the sum-total of bodily processes, and with him agree Fechner and Wundt. "Pflüger and Lewes say that as the hemispheres of the brain owe their intelligence to the consciousness which we know to be there, so the intelligence of the spinal cord's acts must really be due to the invisible presence of a consciousness lower in degree." Professor Brewer's rattlesnake, after several hours of decapitation, still struck at him with its bloody neck, when he attempted to seize it by the tail. From the reaction of the frog's leg after decapitation may we not infer a certain consciousness? "Robin, on tickling the breast of a criminal an hour after decapitation, saw the arm and hand move toward the spot." Hudson, Demonstration of a Future Life, 239–249, quotes from Hammond, Treatise on Insanity, chapter 2, to prove that the brain is not the sole organ of the mind. Instinct does not reside exclusively in the brain; it is seated in the *medulla oblongata*, or in the spinal cord, or in both these organs. Objective mind, as Hudson thinks, is the function of the physical brain, and it ceases when the brain loses its vitality. Instinctive acts are performed by animals after excision of the brain, and by human beings born without brain. Johnson, in Andover Rev., April, 1890:421 — " The brain is not the only seat of consciousness. The same evidence that points to the brain as the *principal* seat of consciousness points to the nerve-centres situated in the spinal cord or elsewhere as the seat of a more or less *subordinate* consciousness or intelligence." Ireland, Blot on the Brain, 26 — " I do not take it for proved that consciousness is entirely confined to the brain."

In spite of these opinions, however, we must grant that the general consensus among psychologists is upon the other side. Dewey, Psychology, 349 — " The sensory and motor nerves have points of meeting in the spinal cord. When a stimulus is transferred from a sensory nerve to a motor without the conscious intervention of the mind, we have reflex action. . . . If something approaches the eye, the stimulus is transferred to the spinal cord, and instead of being continued to the brain and giving rise to a sensation, it is discharged into a motor nerve and the eye is immediately closed. . . . The reflex action in itself involves no consciousness." William James, Psychology, 1:16, 66, 134, 214 — " The cortex of the brain is the sole organ of consciousness in man. . . . If there be any consciousness pertaining to the lower centres, it is a consciousness of which the self knows nothing. . . . In lower animals this may not be so much the case. . . . The seat of the mind, so far as its dynamical relations are concerned, is somewhere in the cortex of the brain." See also C. A. Strong, Why the Mind has a Body, 40–50.

(*b*) God's omnipresence is not the presence of a part but of the whole of God in every place.—This follows from the conception of God as incorporeal. We reject the materialistic representation that God is composed of material elements which can be divided or sundered. There is no multiplication or diffusion of his substance to correspond with the parts of his dominions. The one essence of God is present at the same moment in all.

1 Kings 8 : 27 — "the heaven and the heaven of heavens cannot contain (circumscribe) thee." God must be present in all his essence and all his attributes in every place. He is "totus in omni parte." Alger, Poetry of the Orient: "Though God extends beyond Creation's rim, Each smallest atom holds the whole of him." From this it follows that the whole Logos can be united to and be present in the man Christ Jesus, while at the same time he fills and governs the whole universe ; and so the whole Christ can be united to, and can be present in, the single believer, as fully as if that believer were the only one to receive of his fulness.

A. J. Gordon: "In mathematics the whole is equal to the sum of its parts. But we know of the Spirit that every part is equal to the whole. Every church, every true body of Jesus Christ, has just as much of Christ as every other, and each has the whole Christ." Mat. 13 : 20 — "where two or three are gathered together in my name, there am I in the midst of them." "The parish priest of austerity Climbed up in a high church steeple, To be nearer God so that he might Hand his word down to the people. And in sermon script he daily wrote What he thought was sent from heaven, And he dropt it down on the people's heads Two times one day in seven. In his age God said, ' Come down and die,' And he cried out from the steeple, ' Where art thou, Lord ? ' And the Lord replied, ' Down here among my people.' "

(c) God's omnipresence is not necessary but free.—We reject the pantheistic notion that God is bound to the universe as the universe is bound to God. God is immanent in the universe, not by compulsion, but by the free act of his own will, and this immanence is qualified by his transcendence.

God might at will cease to be omnipresent, for he could destroy the universe; but while the universe exists, he is and must be in all its parts. God is the life and law of the universe,—this is the truth in pantheism. But he is also personal and free,—this pantheism denies. Christianity holds to a free, as well as to an essential, omnipresence—qualified and supplemented, however, by God's transcendence. The boasted truth in pantheism is an elementary principle of Christianity, and is only the stepping-stone to a nobler truth—God's personal presence with his church. The Talmud contrasts the worship of an idol and the worship of Jehovah: " The idol seems so near, but is so far, Jehovah seems so far, but is so near!" God's omnipresence assures us that he is present with us to hear, and present in every heart and in the ends of the earth to answer, prayer. See Rogers, Superhuman Origin of the Bible, 10; Bowne, Metaphysics, 136; Charnock, Attributes, 1 : 363–405.

The Puritan turned from the moss-rose bud, saying: " I have learned to call nothing on earth lovely." But this is to despise not only the workmanship but the presence of the Almighty. The least thing in nature is worthy of study because it is the revelation of a present God. The uniformity of nature and the reign of law are nothing but the steady will of the omnipresent God. Gravitation is God's omnipresence in space, as evolution is God's omnipresence in time. Dorner, System of Doctrine, 1 : 73—" God being omnipresent, contact with him may be sought at any moment in prayer and contemplation; indeed, it will always be true that we live and move and have our being in him, as the perennial and omnipresent source of our existence." Rom. 10 : 6–8— " Say not in thy heart, Who shall ascend into heaven ? (that is, to bring Christ down :) or, Who shall descend into the abyss ? (that is, to bring Christ up from the dead.) But what saith it ? The word is nigh thee, in thy mouth, and in thy heart." Lotze, Metaphysics, § 256, quoted in Illingworth, Divine Immanence, 135, 136. Sunday-school scholar: " Is God in my pocket ?" " Certainly." " No, he is n't, for I have n't any pocket." God is omnipresent so long as there is a universe, but he ceases to be omnipresent when the universe ceases to be.

2. Omniscience.

By this we mean God's perfect and eternal knowledge of all things which are objects of knowledge, whether they be actual or possible, past, present, or future.

God knows his inanimate creation : Ps. 147 : 4 —"counteth the number of the stars ; He calleth them all by their names." He has knowledge of brute creatures : Mat. 10 · 29 —sparrows—"not one of them shall fall on the ground without your Father." Of men and their works : Ps. 33 : 13-15—"beholdeth all the sons of men . . . . considereth all their works." Of hearts of men and their thoughts : Acts 15 : 8 — ' God, who knoweth the heart;" Ps. 139 : 2 —"understandest my thought afar off." Of our wants : Mat. 6 : 8— "knoweth what things ye have need of." Of the least things : Mat. 10 : 30 —"the very hairs of your head are all numbered." Of the past : Mal. 2 : 16 — "book of remembrance." Of the future : Is. 46 . 9, 10 — "declaring the end from the beginning." Of men's future free acts : Is. 44 : 28 — "that saith of Cyrus, He is my shepherd and shall perform all my pleasure." Of men's future evil acts : Acts 2 : 23 — " him, being delivered up by the determinate counsel and foreknowledge of God." Of the ideally possible : 1 Sam. 23 : 12 — "Will the men of Keilah deliver up me and my men into the hands of Saul ? And Jehovah said, They will deliver thee up " (sc. if thou remainest) ; Mat. 11 : 23 — "if the mighty works had been done in Sodom which were done in thee, it would have remained." From eternity : Acts 15 : 18 — " the Lord, who maketh these things known from of old." Incomprehensible : Ps. 139 : 6 — "Such knowledge is too wonderful for me"; Rom. 11 : 33 — "O the depth of the riches both of the wisdom and the knowledge of God." Related to wisdom : Ps. 104 : 24 — "In wisdom hast thou made them all " ; Eph. 3 · 10 — "manifold wisdom of God."

Job 7 : 20 — "O thou watcher of men "; Ps. 56 : 8 — "Thou numberest my wanderings " = my whole life has been one continuous exile ; " Put thou my tears into thy bottle " = the skin bottle of the east,— there are tears enough to fill one ; " Are they not in thy book?" = no tear has fallen to the ground unnoted,— God has gathered them all. Paul Gerhardt : "Du zählst wie oft ein Christe wein', Und was sein Kummer sei ; Kein stilles Thränlein ist so klein, Du hebst und legst es bei." Heb. 4 : 13 — "there is no creature that is not manifest in his sight : but all things are naked and laid open before the eyes of him with whom we have to do" — τετραχηλισμένα — with head bent back and neck laid bare, as animals slaughtered in sacrifice, or seized by the throat and thrown on the back, so that the priest might discover whether there was any blemish. Japanese proverb: "God has forgotten to forget."

(a) The omniscience of God may be argued from his omnipresence, as well as from his truth or self-knowledge, in which the plan of creation has its eternal ground, and from prophecy, which expresses God's omniscience.

It is to be remembered that omniscience, as the designation of a relative and transitive attribute, does not include God's self-knowledge. The term is used in the technical sense of God's knowledge of all things that pertain to the universe of his creation. H. A. Gordon: "Light travels faster than sound. You can see the flash of fire from the cannon's mouth, a mile away, considerably before the noise of the discharge reaches the ear. God flashed the light of prediction upon the pages of his word, and we see it. Wait a little and we see the event itself."

Royce, The Conception of God, 9 — "An omniscient being would be one who simply found presented to him, not by virtue of fragmentary and gradually completed processes of inquiry, but by virtue of an all-embracing, direct and transparent insight into his own truth — who found thus presented to him, I say, the complete, the fulfilled answer to every genuinely rational question."

Browning, Ferishtah's Fancies, Plot-culture : "How will it fare shouldst thou impress on me That certainly an Eye is over all And each, to make the minute's deed, word, thought As worthy of reward and punishment? Shall I permit my sense an Eye-viewed shame, Broad daylight perpetration,—so to speak,—I had not dared to breathe within the Ear, With black night's help around me ? "

(b) Since it is free from all imperfection, God's knowledge is immediate, as distinguished from the knowledge that comes through sense or imagination ; simultaneous, as not acquired by successive observations, or built up by processes of reasoning ; distinct, as free from all vagueness or confusion ; true, as perfectly corresponding to the reality of things ; eternal, as comprehended in one timeless act of the divine mind.

An infinite mind must always act, and must always act in an absolutely perfect manner. There is in God no sense, symbol, memory, abstraction, growth, reflection, reasoning,— his knowledge is all direct and without intermediaries. God was properly represented by the ancient Egyptians, not as having eye, but as being eye. His thoughts toward us are "more than can be numbered " (Ps. 40 : 5), not because there is succession in them, now a remembering and now a forgetting, but because there is never a moment of our existence in which we are out of his mind ; he is always thinking of us. See Charnock, Attributes, 1 : 406-497. Gen. 16 : 13 — "Thou art a God that seeth." Mivart, Lessons from Nature, 374 — "Every creature of every order of existence, while its existence is sustained, is so complacently contemplated by God, that the intense and concentrated attention of all men of science together upon it could but form an utterly inadequate symbol of such divine contemplation." So God's scrutiny of every deed of darkness is more searching than the gaze of a whole Coliseum of spectators, and his eye is more watchful over the good than would be the united care of all his hosts in heaven and earth.

Armstrong, God and the Soul: "God's energy is concentrated attention, attention concentrated everywhere. We can attend to two or three things at once ; the pianist plays and talks at the same time ; the magician does one thing while he seems to do another. God attends to all things, does all things, at once." Marie Corelli, Master Christian, 104 — "The biograph is a hint that every scene of human life is reflected in a ceaseless moving panorama some where, for the beholding of some one." Wireless telegraphy is a stupendous warning that from God no secrets are hid, that "there is not ing covered that shall not be revealed ; and hid, that shall not be known " (Mat. 10 : 26). The Röntgen rays, which take photographs of our insides, right through our clothes, and even in the darkness of midnight, show that to God "the night shineth as the day " (Ps. 139 : 12).

Professor Mitchel's equatorial telescope, slowly moving by clockwork, toward sunset, suddenly touched the horizon and disclosed a boy in a tree stealing apples, but the boy was all unconscious that he was under the gaze of the astronomer. Nothing was so fearful to the prisoner in the French *cachot* as the eye of the guard that never ceased to watch him in perfect silence through the loophole in the door. As in the Roman empire the whole world was to a malefactor one great prison, and in his flight to the most distant lands the emperor could track him, so under the government of God no sinner can escape **the eye of** his Judge. But omnipresence is protective as well as detective. The text Gen. 16:13 — "Thou, God, seest me" — has been used as a restraint from evil more than as a stimulus to good. To the child of the devil it should certainly be the former. But to the child of God it should as certainly be the latter. God should not be regarded as an exacting overseer or a standing threat, but rather as one who understands us, loves us, and helps us. Ps. 139:17, 18 — "How precious also are thy thoughts unto me, O God! How great is the sum of them! If I should count them, they are more in number than the sand: When I awake, I am still with thee."

(*c*) Since God knows things as they are, he knows the necessary sequences of his creation as necessary, the free acts of his creatures as free, the ideally possible as ideally possible.

God knows what would have taken place under circumstances not now present; knows what the universe would have been, had he chosen a different plan of creation; knows what our lives would have been, had we made different decisions in the past (Is. 48:18 — "Oh that thou hadst hearkened . . . . then had thy peace been as a river "). Clarke, Christian Theology, 77 — " God has a double knowledge of his universe. He knows it as it exists eternally in his mind, as his own idea; and he knows it as actually existing in time and space, a moving, changing, growing universe, with perpetual process of succession. In his own idea, he knows it all at once; but he is also aware of its perpetual becoming, and with reference to events as they occur he has foreknowledge, present knowledge, and knowledge afterwards. . . . He conceives of all things simultaneously, but observes all things in their succession."

Royce, World and Individual, 2:374 — holds that God does not temporally foreknow anything except as he is expressed in finite beings, but yet that the Absolute possesses a perfect knowledge at one glance of the whole of the temporal order, present, past and future. This, he says, is not foreknowledge, but eternal knowledge. Priestley denied that any contingent event could be an object of knowledge. But Reid says the denial that any free action can be foreseen involves the denial of God's own free agency, since God's future actions can be foreseen by men; also that while God foresees his own free actions, this does not determine those actions necessarily. Tennyson, In Memoriam, 26 —"And if that eye which watches guilt And goodness, and hath power to see Within the green the mouldered tree, And towers fallen as soon as built—Oh, if indeed that eye foresee Or see (in Him is no before) In more of life true life no more And Love the indifference to be, Then might I find, ere yet the morn Breaks hither over Indian seas, That Shadow waiting with the keys, To shroud me from my proper scorn."

(*d*) The fact that there is nothing in the present condition of things from which the future actions of free creatures necessarily follow by natural law does not prevent God from foreseeing such actions, since his knowledge is not mediate, but immediate. He not only foreknows the motives which will occasion men's acts, but he directly foreknows the acts themselves. The possibility of such direct knowledge without assignable grounds of knowledge is apparent if we admit that time is a form of finite thought to which the divine mind is not subject.

Aristotle maintained that there is no certain knowledge of contingent future events. Socinus, in like manner, while he admitted that God knows all things that are knowable, abridged the objects of the divine knowledge by withdrawing from the number those objects whose future existence he considered as uncertain, such as the determinations of free agents. These, he held, cannot be certainly foreknown, because there is nothing in the present condition of things from which they will necessarily follow by natural law. The man who makes a clock can tell when it will strike. But free-will, not being subject to mechanical laws, cannot have its acts predicted or foreknown. God knows things only in their causes — future events only in their antecedents. John Milton seems also to deny God's foreknowledge of free acts: " So, without least impulse or shadow of fate, Or aught by me immutably foreseen, They trespass."

With this Socinian doctrine some Arminians agree, as McCabe, in his Foreknowledge of God, and in his Divine Nescience of Future Contingencies a Necessity. McCabe, however, sacrifices the principle of free will, in defence of which he makes this surrender of God's foreknowledge, by saying that in cases of fulfilled prophecy, like Peter's denial and Judas's betrayal, God brought special influences to bear to secure the result, — so that Peter's and Judas's wills acted irresponsibly under the law of cause and effect. He quotes Dr. Daniel Curry as declaring that "the denial of absolute divine foreknowledge is the essential complement of the Methodist theology, without which its philosophical incompleteness is defenceless against the logical consistency of Calvinism." See also article by McCabe in Methodist Review, Sept. 1892 : 760-773. Also Simon, Reconciliation, 287 — "God has constituted a creature, the actions of which he can only know as such when they are performed. In presence of man, to a certain extent, even the great God condescends to wait ; nay more, has himself so ordained things that he must wait, inquiring, 'What will he do?'"

So Dugald Stewart: "Shall we venture to affirm that it exceeds the power of God to permit such a train of contingent events to take place as his own foreknowledge shall not extend to?" Martensen holds this view, and Rothe, Theologische Ethik, 1 : 212-234, who declares that the free choices of men are continually increasing the knowledge of God. So also Martineau, Study of Religion, 2 : 279 — "The belief in the divine foreknowledge of our future has no basis in philosophy. We no longer deem it true that even God knows the moment of my moral life that is coming next. Even he does not know whether I shall yield to the secret temptation at midday. To him life is a drama of which he knows not the conclusion." Then, says Dr. A. J. Gordon, there is nothing so dreary and dreadful as to be living under the direction of such a God. The universe is rushing on like an express-train in the darkness without headlight or engineer ; at any moment we may be plunged into the abyss. Lotze does not deny God's foreknowledge of free human actions, but he regards as insoluble by the intellect the problem of the relation of time to God, and such foreknowledge as "one of those postulates as to which we know not how they can be fulfilled." Bowne, Philosophy of Theism, 159 — "Foreknowledge of a free act is a knowledge without assignable grounds of knowing. On the assumption of a real time, it is hard to find a way out of this difficulty. . . . The doctrine of the ideality of time helps us by suggesting the possibility of an all-embracing present, or an eternal now, for God. In that case the problem vanishes with time, its condition."

Against the doctrine of the divine nescience we urge not only our fundamental conviction of God's perfection, but the constant testimony of Scripture. In Is. 41 : 21, 22, God makes his foreknowledge the test of his Godhead in the controversy with idols. If God cannot foreknow free human acts, then "the Lamb that hath been slain from the foundation of the world" (Rev. 13 : 8) was only a sacrifice to be offered in case Adam should fall, God not knowing whether he would or not, and in case Judas should betray Christ, God not knowing whether he would or not. Indeed, since the course of nature is changed by man's will when he burns towns and fells forests, God cannot on this theory predict even the course of nature. All prophecy is therefore a protest against this view.

How God foreknows free human decisions we may not be able to say, but then the method of God's knowledge in many other respects is unknown to us. The following explanations have been proposed. God may foreknow free acts :—

1. *Mediately*, by foreknowing the motives of these acts, and this either because these motives induce the acts, (1) necessarily, or (2) certainly. This last "certainly" is to be accepted, if either : since motives are never *causes*, but are only *occasions*, of action. The cause is the will, or the man himself. But it may be said that foreknowing acts through their motives is not foreknowing at all, but is reasoning or inference rather. Moreover, although intelligent beings commonly act according to motives previously dominant, they also at critical epochs, as at the fall of Satan and of Adam, choose between motives, and in such cases knowledge of the motives which have hitherto actuated them gives no clue to their next decisions. Another statement is therefore proposed to meet these difficulties, namely, that God may foreknow free acts :—

2. *Immediately*, by pure intuition, inexplicable to us. Julius Müller, Doctrine of Sin, 2 : 203, 225 — "If God can know a future event as certain only by a calculation of causes, it must be allowed that he cannot with certainty foreknow any free act of man ; for his foreknowledge would then be proof that the act in question was the necessary consequence of certain causes, and was not in itself free. If, on the contrary, the divine knowledge be regarded as *intuitive*, we see that it stands in the same immediate relation to the act itself as to its antecedents, and thus the difficulty is removed." Even

upon this view there still remains the difficulty of perceiving how there can be in God's mind a subjective certitude with regard to acts in respect to which there is no assignable objective ground of certainty. Yet, in spite of this difficulty, we feel bound both by Scripture and by our fundamental idea of God's perfection to maintain God's perfect knowledge of the future free acts of his creatures. With President Pepper we say : "Knowledge of contingency is not necessarily contingent knowledge." With Whedon : "It is not calculation, but pure knowledge." See Dorner, System of Doct., 1 : 332–337; 2 : 58–62; Jahrbuch für deutsche Theologie. 1858 : 601–605 ; Charnock, Attributes, 1 : 429–446 ; Solly, The Will, 240–254. For a valuable article on the whole subject, though advocating the view that God foreknows acts by foreknowing motives, see Bib. Sac., Oct. 1883 : 655–694. See also Hill, Divinity, 517.

(e) Prescience is not itself causative. It is not to be confounded with the predetermining will of God. Free actions do not take place because they are foreseen, but they are foreseen because they are to take place.

Seeing a thing in the future does not cause it to be, more than seeing a thing in the past causes it to be. As to future events, we may say with Whedon : "Knowledge *takes* them, not *makes* them." Foreknowledge may, and does, presuppose predetermination, but it is not itself predetermination. Thomas Aquinas, in his Summa, 1 : 38 : 1 : 1, says that "the knowledge of God is the cause of things "; but he is obliged to add : "God is not the cause of all things that are known by God, since evil things that are known by God are not from him." John Milton, Paradise Lost, book 3 — "Foreknowledge had no influence on their fault, Which had no less proved certain unforeknown."

(f) Omniscience embraces the actual and the possible, but it does not embrace the self-contradictory and the impossible, because these are not objects of knowledge.

God does not know what the result would be if two and two made five, nor does he know "whether a chimæra ruminating in a vacuum devoureth second intentions"; and that, simply for the reason that he cannot know self-contradiction and nonsense. These things are not objects of knowledge. Clarke, Christian Theology, 80 — "Can God make an old man in a minute? Could he make it well with the wicked while they remained wicked? Could he create a world in which $2 + 2 = 5$?" Royce, Spirit of Modern Philosophy, 366 — "Does God know the whole number that is the square root of 65? or what adjacent hills there are that have no valleys between them? Does God know round squares, and sugar salt-lumps, and Snarks and Boojums and Abracadabras?"

(g) Omniscience, as qualified by holy will, is in Scripture denominated "wisdom." In virtue of his wisdom God chooses the highest ends and uses the fittest means to accomplish them.

Wisdom is not simply "estimating all things at their proper value" (Olmstead) ; it has in it also the element of counsel and purpose. It has been defined as "the talent of using one's talents." It implies two things : first, choice of the highest end ; secondly, choice of the best means to secure this end. J. C. C. Clarke, Self and the Father, 39 — "Wisdom is not invented conceptions, or harmony of theories with theories; but is humble obedience of mind to the reception of facts that are found in things." Thus man's wisdom, obedience, faith, are all names for different aspects of the same thing. And wisdom in God is the moral choice which makes truth and holiness supreme. Bowne, Principles of Ethics, 261 — "Socialism pursues a laudable end by unwise or destructive means. It is not enough to mean well. Our methods must take some account of the nature of things, if they are to succeed. We cannot produce well-being by law. No legislation can remove inequalities of nature and constitution. Society cannot produce equality, any more than it can enable a rhinoceros to sing, or legislate a cat into a lion."

3. Omnipotence.

By this we mean the power of God to do all things which are objects of power, whether with or without the use of means.

Gen. 17 : 1 — "I am God Almighty." He performs natural wonders : Gen. 1 : 1–3—"Let there be Light"; Is. 44 : 24 — "stretcheth forth the heavens alone " ; Heb. 1 : 3 — "upholding all things by the word of his power." Spiritual wonders : 2 Cor. 4 : 6 — " God, that said, Light shall shine out of darkness, who shined in our hearts ";

Eph. 1 : 19 — "exceeding greatness of his power to us-ward who believe " ; Eph. 3 : 20 — "able to do exceeding abund-antly." Power to create new things : Mat. 3 : 9—"able of these stones to raise up children unto Abraham " Rom. 4 : 17 — "giveth life to the dead, and calleth the things that are not, as though they were." After his own pleasure : Ps. 115 : 3 — "He hath done whatsoever he hath pleased" ; Eph. 1 : 11 — "worketh all things after the counsel of his will." Nothing impossible : Gen. 18 : 14 — "Is anything too hard for Jehovah ?" Mat. 19 : 26 — "with God all things are possible." E. G. Robinson, Christian Theology, 73 — "If all power in the universe is dependent on his creative will for its existence, it is impossible to con-ceive any limit to his power except that laid on it by his own will. But this is only negative proof; absolute omnipotence is not logically demonstrable, though readily enough recognized as a just conception of the infinite God, when propounded on the authority of a positive revelation."

The omnipotence of God is illustrated by the work of the Holy Spirit, which in Script-ure is compared to wind, water and fire. The ordinary manifestations of these ele-ments afford no criterion of the effects they are able to produce. The rushing mighty wind at Pentecost was the analogue of the wind-Spirit who bore everything before him on the first day of creation (Gen. 1 : 2 ; John 3 : 8 ; Acts 2 : 2). The pouring out of the Spirit is likened to the flood of Noah when the windows of heaven were opened and there was not room enough to receive that which fell (Mal. 3 : 10). And the baptism of the Holy Spirit is like the fire that shall destroy all impurity at the end of the world (Mat. 3 : 11 ; 2 Pet. 3 : 7-13). See A. H. Strong, Christ in Creation, 307-310.

(a) Omnipotence does not imply power to do that which is not an object of power ; as, for example, that which is self-contradictory or contradictory to the nature of God.

Self-contradictory things : "facere factum infectum "— the making of a past event to have not occurred (hence the uselessness of praying : "May it be that much good was done "); drawing a shorter than a straight line between two given points ; putting two separate mountains together without a valley between them. Things contradictory to the nature of God : for God to lie, to sin, to die. To do such things would not imply power, but impotence. God has all the power that is consistent with infinite per-fection — all power to do what is worthy of himself. So no greater thing can be said by man than this: "I dare do all that may become a man; Who dares do more is none." Even God cannot make wrong to be right, nor hatred of himself to be blessed. Some have held that the prevention of sin in a moral system is not an object of power, and therefore that God cannot prevent sin in a moral system. We hold the contrary; see this Compendium : Objections to the Doctrine of Decrees.

Dryden, Imitation of Horace, 3 : 29 : 71 — "Over the past not heaven itself has power ; What has been has, and I have had my hour "— words applied by Lord John Russell to his own career. Emerson, The Past : "All is now secure and fast, Not the gods can shake the Past." Sunday-school scholar : "Say, teacher, can God make a rock so big that he can't lift it ?" Seminary Professor : "Can God tell a lie ? " Seminary student : "With God all things are possible."

(b) Omnipotence does not imply the exercise of all his power on the part of God. He has power over his power ; in other words, his power is under the control of wise and holy will. God can do all he will, but he will not do all he can. Else his power is mere force acting necessarily, and God is the slave of his own omnipotence.

Schleiermacher held that nature not only is grounded in the divine causality, but fully expresses that causality ; there is no causative power in God for anything that is not real and actual. This doctrine does not essentially differ from Spinoza's *natura naturans* and *natura naturata*. See Philippi, Glaubenslehre, 2 : 62-66. But omnipo-tence is not instinctive ; it is a power used according to God's pleasure. God is by no means encompassed by the laws of nature, or shut up to a necessary evolution of his own being, as pantheism supposes. As Rothe has shown, God has a will-power over his nature-power, and is not compelled to do all that he can do. He is able from the stones of the street to "raise up children unto Abraham," but he has not done it In God are unopened treasures, an inexhaustible fountain of new beginnings, new creations, new revelations. To suppose that in creation he has expended all the inner possibilities of his being is to deny his omnipotence. So Job 26 : 14 — "Lo, these are but the outskirts of his ways: And how small a whisper do we hear of him! But the thunder of his power who can understand?" See Rogers, Superhuman Origin of the Bible, 10; Hodgson, Time and Space, 579, 580.

1 Pet. 5 : 6—"Humble yourselves therefore under the mighty hand of God"—his mighty hand of providence, salvation, blessing —"that he may exalt you in due time; casting all your anxiety upon him, because he careth for you." "The mighty powers held under mighty control" — this is the greatest exhibition of power. Unrestraint is not the highest freedom. Young men must learn that self-restraint is the true power. Prov.16:32—"He that is slow to anger is better than the mighty; And he that ruleth his spirit, than he that taketh a city." Shakespeare, Coriolanus, 2:3— "We have power in ourselves to do it, but it is a power that we have no power to do." When dynamite goes off, it all goes off: there is no reserve. God uses as much of his power as he pleases: the remainder of wrath in himself, as well as in others, he restrains

(c) Omnipotence in God does not exclude, but implies, the power of self-limitation. Since all such self-limitation is free, proceeding from neither external nor internal compulsion, it is the act and manifestation of God's power. Human freedom is not rendered impossible by the divine omnipotence, but exists by virtue of it. It is an act of omnipotence when God humbles himself to the taking of human flesh in the person of Jesus Christ.

Thomasius: "If God is to be over all and in all, he cannot himself be all." Ps. 113: 5, 6 —"Who is like unto Jehovah our God . . . . That humbleth himself to behold The things that are in heaven and in the earth?" Phil. 2 : 7, 8— "emptied himself . . . . humbled himself." See Charnock, Attributes, 2: 5-107. President Woolsey showed true power when he controlled his indignation and let an offending student go free. Of Christ on the cross, says Moberly, Atonement and Personality, 116—"It was the power [to retain his life, to escape suffering], with the will to hold it unused, which proved him to be what he was, the obedient and perfect man." We are likest the omnipotent One when we limit ourselves for love's sake. The attribute of omnipotence is the ground of trust, as well as of fear, on the part of God's creatures. Isaac Watts: "His every word of grace is strong As that which built the skies; The voice that rolls the stars along Speaks all the promises."

Third Division.—Attributes having relation to Moral Beings.

1. Veracity and Faithfulness, or Transitive Truth.

By veracity and faithfulness we mean the transitive truth of God, in its twofold relation to his creatures in general and to his redeemed people in particular.

Ps. 138:2 — "I will . . . . give thanks unto thy name for thy lovingkindness and for thy truth: For thou hast magnified thy word above all thy name"; John 3 : 33 — "hath set his seal to this, that God is true"; Rom. 3 : 4 — "let God be found true, but every man a liar"; Rom. 1 : 25—"the truth of God"; John 14:17—"the Spirit of truth"; 1 John 5 : 7—"the Spirit is the truth"; 1 Cor. 1 : 9 — "God is faithful"; 1 Thess. 5 : 24 — "faithful is he that calleth you"; 1 Pet. 4 : 19—"a faithful Creator"; 2 Cor. 1 : 20—"how many soever be the promises of God, in him is the yea"; Num. 23 : 19—"God is not a man that he should lie"; Tit. 1 : 2 —"God, who cannot lie, promised"; Heb. 6 : 18 — "in which it is impossible for God to lie."

(a) In virtue of his veracity, all his revelations to creatures consist with his essential being and with each other.

In God's veracity we have the guarantee that our faculties in their normal exercise do not deceive us; that the laws of thought are also laws of things; that the external world, and second causes in it, have objective existence; that the same causes will always produce the same effects; that the threats of the moral nature will be executed upon the unrepentant transgressor; that man's moral nature is made in the image of God's; and that we may draw just conclusions from what conscience is in us to what holiness is in him. We may therefore expect that all past revelations, whether in nature or in his word, will not only not be contradicted by our future knowledge, but will rather prove to have in them more of truth than we ever dreamed. Man's word may pass away, but God's word abides forever (Mat. 5 : 18—"one jot or one tittle shall in no wise pass away from the law"; Is. 40 : 8 —"the word of God shall stand forever").

Mat. 6 : 16—"be not as the hypocrites." In God the outer expression and the inward reality always correspond. Assyrian wills were written on a small tablet encased in another upon which the same thing was written over again. Breakage, or falsification, of the outer envelope could be corrected by reference to the inner. So our outer life should conform to the heart within, and the heart within to the outer life. On the duty of speaking the truth, and the limitations of the duty, see Newman Smyth, Christian Ethics, 386–403 — "Give the truth always to those who in the bonds of humanity have a right to the truth ; conceal it, or falsify it, only when the human right to the truth has been forfeited, or is held in abeyance, by sickness, weakness, or some criminal intent."

(*b*) In virtue of his faithfulness, he fulfills all his promises to his people, whether expressed in words or implied in the constitution he has given them.

In God's faithfulness we have the sure ground of confidence that he will perform what his love has led him to promise to those who obey the gospel. Since his promises are based, not upon what we are or have done, but upon what Christ is and has done, our defects and errors do not invalidate them, so long as we are truly penitent and believing : 1 John 1 : 9 —"faithful and righteous to forgive us our sins"= faithful to his promise, and righteous to Christ. God's faithfulness also ensures a supply for all the real wants of our being, both here and hereafter, since these wants are implicit promises of him who made us : Ps. 84 : 11—"No good thing will he withold from them that walk uprightly" ; 91 : 4 —"His truth is a shield and a buckler" ; Mat. 6 : 33 —"all these things shall be added unto you" ; 1 Cor. 2 : 9 —"Things which eye saw not, and ear heard not, And which entered not into the heart of man, Whatsoever things God prepared for them that love him."

Regulus goes back to Carthage to die rather than break his promise to his enemies. George William Curtis economizes for years, and gives up all hope of being himself a rich man, in order that he may pay the debts of his deceased father. When General Grant sold all the presents made to him by the crowned heads of Europe, and paid the obligations in which his insolvent son had involved him, he said : " Better poverty and honor, than wealth and disgrace." Many a business man would rather die than fail to fulfil his promise and let his note go to protest. " Maxwelton braes are bonnie, Where early falls the dew, And 't was there that Annie Laurie Gave me her promise true ; Which ne'er forget will I ; And for bonnie Annie Laurie I 'd lay me down and dee." Betray the man she loves ? Not " Till a' the seas gang dry, my dear, And the rocks melt wi' the sun." God's truth will not be less than that of mortal man. God's veracity is the natural correlate to our faith.

2. Mercy and Goodness, or Transitive Love.

By mercy and goodness we mean the transitive love of God in its two-fold relation to the disobedient and to the obedient portions of his creatures.

Titus 3 : 4 —"his love toward man" ; Rom. 2 : 4 —"goodness of God" ; Mat. 5 : 44, 45 —"love your enemies . . . that ye may be sons of your Father" ; John 3 : 16 —"God so loved the world" ; 2 Pet. 1 : 3 —"granted unto us all things that pertain unto life and godliness" ; Rom. 8 : 32 —"freely give us all things" ; John 4 : 10 — "Herein is love, not that we loved God, but that he loved us, and sent his Son to be the propitiation for our sins."

(*a*) Mercy is that eternal principle of God's nature which leads him to seek the temporal good and eternal salvation of those who have opposed themselves to his will, even at the cost of infinite self-sacrifice.

Martensen : " Viewed in relation to sin, eternal love is compassionate grace." God's continued impartation of natural life is a foreshadowing, in a lower sphere, of what he desires to do for his creatures in the higher sphere — the communication of spiritual and eternal life through Jesus Christ. When he bids us love our enemies, he only bids us follow his own example. Shakespeare, Titus Andronicus, 2 : 2 — " Wilt thou draw near the nature of the gods ? Draw near them, then, in being merciful." Twelfth Night, 3 : 4 —" In nature there's no blemish but the mind ; None can be called deformed but the unkind. Virtue is beauty."

(*b*) Goodness is the eternal principle of God's nature which leads him to communicate of his own life and blessedness to those who are like him in moral character. Goodness, therefore, is nearly identical with the love of complacency ; mercy, with the love of benevolence.

Notice, however, that transitive love is but an outward manifestation of immanent love. The eternal and perfect object of God's love is in his own nature. Men become subordinate objects of that love only as they become connected and identified with its principal object, the image of God's perfections in Christ. Only in the Son do men become sons of God. To this is requisite an acceptance of Christ on the part of man. Thus it can he said that God imparts himself to men just so far as men are willing to receive him. And as God gives himself to men, in all his moral attributes, to answer for them and to renew them in character, there is truth in the statement of Nordell (Examiner, Jan. 17, 1884) that "the maintenance of holiness is the function of divine justice; the diffusion of holiness is the function of divine love." We may grant this as substantially true, while yet we deny that love is a mere form or manifestation of holiness. Self-impartation is different from self-affirmation. The attribute which moves God to pour out is not identical with the attribute which moves him to maintain The two ideas of holiness and of love are as distinct as the idea of integrity on the one hand and of generosity on the other. Park: "God loves Satan, in a certain sense, and we ought to." Shedd: "This same love of compassion God feels toward the non-elect; but the expression of that compassion is forbidden for reasons which are sufficient for God, but are entirely unknown to the creature." The goodness of God is the basis of reward, under God's government. Faithfulness leads God to keep his promises; goodness leads him to make them.

Edwards, Nature of Virtue, in Works, 2:263—Love of benevolence does not presuppose beauty in its object. Love of complacence does presuppose beauty. Virtue is not love to an object for its beauty. The beauty of intelligent beings does not consist in love for beauty, or virtue in love for virtue. Virtue is love for being in general, exercised in a general good will. This is the doctrine of Edwards. We prefer to say that virtue is love, not for being in general, but for good being, and so for God, the holy One. The love of compassion is perfectly compatible with hatred of evil and with indignation against one who commits it. Love does not necessarily imply approval, but it does imply desire that all creatures should fulfil the purpose of their existence by being morally conformed to the holy One; see Godet, in The Atonement, 339.

Rom. 5:8—"God commendeth his own love toward us, in that, while we were yet sinners, Christ died for us." We ought to love our enemies, and Satan is our worst enemy. We ought to will the good of Satan, or cherish toward him the love of benevolence, though not the love of complacence. This does not involve a condoning of his sin, or an ignoring of his moral depravity, as seems implied in the verses of Wm. C. Gannett: "The poem hangs on the berry-bush When comes the poet's eye; The street begins to masquerade When Shakespeare passes by. The Christ sees white in Judas' heart And loves his traitor well; The God, to angel his new heaven, Explores his deepest hell."

3.   Justice and Righteousness, or Transitive Holiness.

By justice and righteousness we mean the transitive holiness of God, in virtue of which his treatment of his creatures conforms to the purity of his nature,— righteousness demanding from all moral beings conformity to the moral perfection of God, and justice visiting non-conformity to that perfection with penal loss or suffering.

Gen. 18:25—"shall not the Judge of all the earth do right?" Deut. 32:4—"All his ways are justice; A God of faithfulness and without iniquity, Just and right is he"; Ps. 5:5—"Thou hatest all workers of iniquity"; 7:9-12 —"the righteous God trieth the hearts .... saveth the upright .... is a righteous judge, Yea, a God that hath indignation every day"; 18:24-26—"Jehovah recompensed me according to my righteousness .... With the merciful, thou wilt show thyself merciful .... with the perverse thou wilt show thyself froward"; Mat. 5:48—"Ye therefore shall be perfect, as your heavenly Father is perfect"; Rom. 2:6—"will render to every man according to his works"; 1 Pet. 1:16—"Ye shall be holy; for I am holy." These passages show that God loves the same persons whom he hates. It is not true that he hates the sin, but loves the sinner; he both hates and loves the sinner himself, hates him as he is a living and wilful antagonist of truth and holiness, loves him as he is a creature capable of good and ruined by his transgression.

There is no abstract sin that can be hated apart from the persons in whom that sin is represented and embodied. Thomas Fuller found it difficult to starve the profaneness but to feed the person of the impudent beggar who applied to him for food. Mr.

Finney declared that he would kill the slave-catcher, but would love him with all his heart. In our civil war Dr. Kirk said : " God knows that we love the rebels, but God also knows that we will kill them if they do not lay down their arms." The complex nature of God not only permits but necessitates this same double treatment of the sinner, and the earthly father experiences the same conflict of emotions when his heart yearns over the corrupt son whom he is compelled to banish from the household. Moberly, Atonement and Personality, 7—" It is the sinner who is punished, not the sin."

(a) Since justice and righteousness are simply transitive holiness— righteousness designating this holiness chiefly in its mandatory, justice chiefly in its punitive, aspect,—they are not mere manifestations of benevolence, or of God's disposition to secure the highest happiness of his creatures, nor are they grounded in the nature of things as something apart from or above God.

Cremer, N. T. Lexicon : δίκαιος = " the perfect coincidence existing between God's nature, which is the standard for all, and his acts." Justice and righteousness are simply holiness exercised toward creatures. The same holiness which exists in God in eternity past manifests itself as justice and righteousness, so soon as intelligent creatures come into being. Much that was said under Holiness as an immanent attribute of God is equally applicable here. The modern tendency to confound holiness with love shows itself in the merging of justice and righteousness in mere benevolence. Instances of this tendency are the following : Ritschl, Unterricht, § 16—" The righteousness of God denotes the manner in which God carries out his loving will in the redemption alike of humanity as a whole and of individual men; hence his righteousness is indistinguishable from his grace "; see also Ritschl, Rechtf. und Versöhnung, 2 : 113; 3 : 296. Prof. George M. Forbes : " Only right makes love moral : only love makes right moral." Jones, Robert Browning, 70 — " Is it not beneficence that places death at the heart of sin? Carlyle forgot this. God is not simply a great taskmaster. The power that imposes law is not an alien power." D'Arcy, Idealism and Theology, 237-240 — " How can self-realization be the realization of others? Why must the true good be always the common good? Why is the end of each the end of all? . . . . We need a concrete universal which will unify all persons."

So also, Harris, Kingdom of Christ on Earth, 39-42; God the Creator, 287, 299, 302 — " Love, as required and regulated by reason, may be called righteousness. Love is universal good will or benevolence, regulated in its exercise by righteousness. Love is the choice of God and man as the objects of trust and service. This choice involves the determination of the will to seek universal well-being, and in this aspect it is benevolence. It also involves the consent of the will to the reason, and the determination to regulate all action in seeking well-being by its truths, laws, and ideals; and in this aspect it is righteousness. . . . Justice is the consent of the will to the law of love, in its authority, its requirements, and its sanctions. God's wrath is the necessary reaction of this law of love in the constitution and order of the universe against the wilful violator of it, and Christ's sufferings atone for sin by asserting and maintaining the authority, universality, and inviolability of God's law of love in his redemption of men and his forgiveness of their sins. . . . . Righteousness cannot be the whole of love, for this would shut us up to the merely formal principle of the law without telling us what the law requires. Benevolence cannot be the whole of love, for this would shut us up to hedonism, in the form of utilitarianism, excluding righteousness from the character of God and man."

Newman Smyth also, in his Christian Ethics, 227-231, tells us that " love, as self-affirming, is righteousness; as self-imparting, is benevolence; as self-finding in others, is sympathy. Righteousness, as subjective regard for our own moral being, is holiness; as objective regard for the persons of others, is justice. Holiness is involved in love as its essential respect to itself ; the heavenly Father is the holy Father (John 17 : 11). Love contains in its unity a trinity of virtue. Love affirms its own worthiness, imparts to others its good, and finds its life again in the well-being of others. The ethical limit of self-impartation is found in self-affirmation. Love in self-bestowal cannot become suicidal. The benevolence of love has its moral bounds in the holiness of love. True love in God maintains its transcendence, and excludes pantheism."

The above doctrine, quoted for substance from Newman Smyth, seems to us unwar rantably to include in love what properly belongs to holiness. It virtually denies that holiness has any independent existence as an attribute of God. To make holiness a manifestation of love seems to us as irrational as to say that self-affirmation is a form of self-impartation. The concession that holiness regulates and limits love shows that holiness cannot itself be love, but must be an independent and superior attribute. Right furnishes the rule and law for love, but it is not true that love furnishes the rule and law for right. There is no such double sovereignty as this theory would imply. The one attribute that is independent and supreme is holiness, and love is simply the impulse to communicate this holiness.

William Ashmore: "Dr. Clarke lays great emphasis on the character of 'a good God.' . . . But he is more than a merely *good* God ; he is a just God, and a righteous God, and a holy God—a God who is 'angry with the wicked,' even while ready to forgive them, if they are willing to repent in his way, and not in their own. He is the God who brought in a flood upon the world of the ungodly ; who rained down fire and brimstone from heaven ; and who is to come in ' flaming fire, taking vengence on them that know not God' and obey not the gospel of his son. . . . . Paul reasoned about both the 'goodness' and the 'severity' of God."

(*b*) Transitive holiness, as righteousness, imposes law in conscience and Scripture, and may be called legislative holiness. As justice, it executes the penalties of law, and may be called distributive or judicial holiness. In righteousness God reveals chiefly his love of holiness ; in justice, chiefly his hatred of sin.

The self-affirming purity of God demands a like purity in those who have been made in his image. As God wills and maintains his own moral excellence, so all creatures must will and maintain the moral excellence of God. There can be only one centre in the solar system, — the sun is its own centre and the centre for all the planets also. So God's purity is the object of his own will,—it must be the object of all the wills of all his creatures also. Bixby, Crisis in Morals, 282—"It is not rational or safe for the hand to separate itself from the heart. This is a *universe*, and God is the heart of the great system. Altruism is not the result of society, but society is the result of altruism. It begins in creatures far below man. The animals which know how to combine have the greatest chance of survival. The unsociable animal dies out. The most perfect organism is the most sociable. Right is the debt which the part owes to the whole." This seems to us but a partial expression of the truth. Right is more than a debt to others,—it is a debt to one's self, and the self-affirming, self-preserving, self-respecting element constitutes the limit and standard of all outgoing activity. The sentiment of loyalty is largely a reverence for this principle of order and stability in government. Ps. 145 : 5 — " Of the glorious majesty of thine honor, And of thy wondrous works, will I meditate " ; 97 : 2 —" Clouds and darkness are round about him : Righteousness and justice are the foundation of his throne."

John Milton, Eikonoklastes : "Truth and justice are all one ; for truth is but justice in our knowledge, and justice is but truth in our practice. . . . . For truth is properly no more than contemplation, and her utmost efficiency is but teaching ; but justice in her very essence is all strength and activity, and hath a sword put into her hand to use against all violence and oppression on the earth. She it is who accepts no person, and exempts none from the severity of her stroke." A. J. Balfour, Foundations of Belief, 326—"Even the poet has not dared to represent Jupiter torturing Prometheus without the dim figure of Avenging Fate waiting silently in the background. . . . Evolution working out a nobler and nobler justice is proof that God is just. Here is 'preferential action '." S. S. Times, June 9, 1900—"The natural man is born with a wrong personal astronomy. Man should give up the conceit of being the centre of all things. He should accept the Copernican theory, and content himself with a place on the edge of things—the place he has always really had. We all laugh at John Jasper and his thesis that ' the sun do move.' The Copernican theory is leaking down into human relations, as appears from the current phrase : ' There are others'."

(*c*) Neither justice nor righteousness, therefore, is a matter of arbitrary will. They are revelations of the inmost nature of God, the one in the form of moral requirement, the other in the form of judicial sanction. As

God cannot but demand of his creatures that they be like him in moral character, so he cannot but enforce the law which he imposes upon them. Justice just as much binds God to punish as it binds the sinner to be punished.

All arbitrariness is excluded here. God is what he is — infinite purity. He cannot change. If creatures are to attain the end of their being, they must be like God in moral purity. Justice is nothing but the recognition and enforcement of this natural necessity. Law is only the transcript of God's nature. Justice does not make law,— it only reveals law. Penalty is only the reaction of God's holiness against that which is its opposite. Since righteousness and justice are only legislative and retributive holiness, God can cease to demand purity and to punish sin only when he ceases to be holy, that is, only when he ceases to be God. "Judex damnatur cum nocens absolvitur."

Simon, Reconciliation, 141 — "To claim the performance of duty is as truly obligatory as it is obligatory to perform the duty which is prescribed." E. H. Johnson, Systematic Theology, 84 — " Benevolence intends what is well for the creature ; justice insists on what is fit. But the well-for-us and the fit-for-us precisely coincide. The only thing that is well for us is our normal employment and development; but to provide for this is precisely what is fitting and therefore due to us. In the divine nature the distinction between justice and benevolence is one of form." We criticize this utterance as not sufficiently taking into account the nature of the right. The right is not merely the fit. Fitness is only general adaptation which may have in it no ethical element, whereas right is solely and exclusively ethical. The right therefore regulates the fit and constitutes its standard. The well-for-us is to be determined by the right-for-us, but not *vice versa*. George W. Northrup : " God is not bound to bestow the same endowments upon creatures, nor to keep all in a state of holiness forever, nor to redeem the fallen, nor to secure the greatest happiness of the universe. But he is bound to purpose and to do what his absolute holiness requires. He has no attribute, no will, no sovereignty, above this law of his being. He cannot lie, he cannot deny himself, he cannot look upon sin with complacency, he cannot acquit the guilty without an atonement."

(*d*) Neither justice nor righteousness bestows rewards. This follows from the fact that obedience is due to God, instead of being optional or a gratuity. No creature can claim anything for his obedience. If God rewards, he rewards in virtue of his goodness and faithfulness, not in virtue of his justice or his righteousness. What the creature cannot claim, however, Christ *can* claim, and the rewards which are goodness to the creature are righteousness to Christ. God rewards Christ's work *for* us and *in* us.

Bruch, Eigenschaftslehre, 280-282, and John Austin, Province of Jurisprudence, 1: 88-93, 220-223, both deny, and rightly deny, that justice bestows rewards. Justice simply punishes infractions of law. In Mat. 25 : 34 — "inherit the kingdom" — inheritance implies no merit; 46 — the wicked are adjudged to eternal punishment; the righteous, not to eternal reward, but to eternal life. Luke 17 : 7-10 — "when ye shall have done all the things that are commanded you, say, We are unprofitable servants; we have done that which it was our duty to do." Rom. 6 : 23 — punishment is the " wages of sin ": but salvation is "the gift of God "; 2 : 6 — God rewards, not *on account of* man's work but "according to his works." Reward is thus seen to be in Scripture a matter of grace to the creature; only to the Christ who works for us in atonement, and in us in regeneration and sanctification, is reward a matter of debt (see also John 6 : 27 and 2 John 8). Martineau, Types, 2 : 86, 244, 249 — "Merit is toward man; virtue toward God."

All mere service is unprofitable, because it furnishes only an equivalent to duty, and there is no margin. Works of supererogation are impossible, because our all is due to God. He would have us rise into the region of friendship, realize that he has been treating us not as Master but as Father, enter into a relation of uncalculating love. With this proviso that rewards are matters of grace, not of debt, we may assent to the maxim of Solon : " A republic walks upon two feet — just punishment for the unworthy and due reward for the worthy." George Harris, Moral Evolution, 139 — "Love seeks righteousness, and is satisfied with nothing other than that." But when Harris adopts the words of the poet: "The very wrath from pity grew, From love of men the hate of wrong," he seems to us virtually to deny that God hates evil for any other reason than because of its utilitarian disadvantages, and to imply that good has no independent existence in his nature. Bowne, Ethics, 171 — "Merit is desert of reward, or better, desert of moral approval." Tennyson: "For merit lives from man to man, And not from man, O Lord, to thee." Baxter: "*Desert* is written over the gate of hell ; but over the gate of heaven only, *The Gift of God*."

(*e*)   Justice in God, as the revelation of his holiness, is devoid of all passion or caprice.   There is in God no selfish anger.   The penalties he inflicts upon transgression are not vindictive but vindicative.   They express the revulsion of God's nature from moral evil, the judicial indignation of purity against impurity, the self-assertion of infinite holiness against its antagonist and would-be destroyer.   But because its decisions are calm, they are irreversible.

Anger, within certain limits, is a duty of man. Ps. 97:10 — "ye that love Jehovah, hate evil" ; Eph. 4 : 26 — "Be ye angry, and sin not." The calm indignation of the judge, who pronounces sentence with tears, is the true image of the holy anger of God against sin. Weber, Zorn Gottes, 28, makes wrath only the jealousy of love. It is more truly the jealousy of holiness. Prof. W. A. Stevens, Com. on 1 Thess. 2 :10 — "Holily and righteously are terms that describe the same conduct in two aspects ; the former, as conformed to God's character in itself ; the latter, as conformed to his law ; both are positive." Lillie, on 2 Thess. 1:6 — "Judgment is 'a righteous thing with God.' Divine justice requires it for its own satisfaction." See Shedd, Dogm. Theol., 1 : 175-178, 365-385 ; Trench, Syn. N. T., 1 : 180, 181.

Of Gaston de Foix, the old chronicler admirably wrote: "He loved what ought to be loved, and hated what ought to be hated, and never had miscreant with him." Compare Ps. 101 : 5, 6 — "Him that hath a high look and a proud heart will I not suffer. Mine eyes shall be upon the faithful of the land, that they may dwell with me." Even Horace Bushnell spoke of the "wrath-principle" in God. 1 K. 11 : 9 — "And Jehovah was angry with Solomon" because of his polygamy. Jesus' anger was no less noble than his love. The love of the right involved hatred of the wrong. Those may hate who hate evil for its hatefulness and for the sake of God. Hate sin in yourself first, and then you may hate it in itself and in the world. Be angry only in Christ and with the wrath of God. W. C. Wilkinson, Epic of Paul, 264 — "But we must purge ourselves of self-regard, Or we are sinful in abhorring sin." Instance Judge Harris's pity, as he sentenced the murderer ; see A. H. Strong, Philosophy and Religion, 192, 193.

Horace's "Ira furor brevis est "— "Anger is a temporary madness "— is true only of selfish and sinful anger. Hence the man who is angry is popularly called "mad." But anger, though apt to become sinful, is not necessarily so. Just anger is neither madness, nor is it brief. Instance the judicial anger of the church of Corinth in inflicting excommunication : 2 Cor. 7 : 11 — "what indignation, yea what fear, yea what longing, yea what zeal, yea what avenging !" The only revenge permissible to the Christian church is that in which it pursues and exterminates sin. To be incapable of moral indignation against wrong is to lack real love for the right. Dr. Arnold of Rugby was never sure of a boy who only loved good ; till the boy also began to hate evil, Dr. Arnold did not feel that he was safe. Herbert Spencer said that good nature with Americans became a crime. Lecky, Democracy and Liberty : "There is one thing worse than corruption, and that is acquiescence in corruption."

Colestock, Changing Viewpoint, 139 — "Xenophon intends to say a very commendable thing of Cyrus the Younger, when he writes of him that no one had done more good to his friends or more harm to his enemies." Luther said to a monkish antagonist: "I will break in pieces your heart of brass and pulverize your iron brains." Shedd, Dogmatic Theology, 1 : 175-178 — "Human character is worthless in proportion as abhorrence of sin is lacking in it. It is related of Charles II that 'he felt no gratitude for benefits, and no resentment for wrongs ; he did not love anyone, and he did not hate any one.' He was indifferent toward right and wrong, and the only feeling he had was contempt." But see the death-bed scene of the "merry monarch," as portrayed in Bp. Burnet, Evelyn's Memoirs, or the Life of Bp. Ken. Truly "The end of mirth is heaviness" (Prov 14 : 13).

Stout, Manual of Psychology, 2—"Charles Lamb tells us that his friend George Dyer could never be brought to say anything in condemnation of the most atrocious crimes, except that the criminal must have been very eccentric." Professor Seeley: "No heart is pure that is not passionate." D. W. Simon, Redemption of Man, 249, 250, says that God's resentment "is a resentment of an essentially altruistic character." If this means that it is perfectly consistent with love for the sinner, we can accept the statement; if it means that love is the only source of the resentment, we regard the statement as a misinterpretation of God's justice, which is but the manifestation of his holiness and is not an mere expression of his love. See a similar statement of Lidgett, Spiritual Principle of the Atonement, 251—"Because God is love, his love coëxists with his wrath against sinners, is the very life of that wrath, and is so persistent that it uses wrath as its instrument, while at the same time it seeks and supplies a propitiation." This statement ignores the fact that punishment is never in Scripture regarded as an expression of God's love, but always of God's holiness. When we say that we love God, let us make sure that it is the true God, the God of holiness, that we love, for only this love will make us like him.

The moral indignation of a whole universe of holy beings against moral evil, added to the agonizing self-condemnations of awakened conscience in all the unholy, is only a faint and small reflection of the awful revulsion of God's infinite justice from the impurity and selfishness of his creatures, and of the intense, organic, necessary, and eternal reaction of his moral being in self-vindication and the punishment of sin; see Jer. 44 : 4 — "Oh, do not this abominable thing that I hate!" Num. 32 : 23 — "be sure your sin will find you out" ; Heb. 10 : 30, 31 — "For we know him that said, Vengeance belongeth unto me, I will recompense. And again, The Lord shall judge his people. It is a fearful thing to fall into the hands of the living God." On justice as an attribute of a moral governor, see N. W. Taylor, Moral Government, 2 : 253–293 ; Owen, Dissertation on Divine Justice, in Works, 10 : 483–624.

VII. RANK AND RELATIONS OF THE SEVERAL ATTRIBUTES.

The attributes have relations to each other. Like intellect, affection and will in man, no one of them is to be conceived of as exercised separately from the rest. Each of the attributes is qualified by all the others. God's love is immutable, wise, holy. Infinity belongs to God's knowledge, power, justice. Yet this is not to say that one attribute is of as high rank as another. The moral attributes of truth, love, holiness, are worthy of higher reverence from men, and they are more jealously guarded by God, than the natural attributes of omnipresence, omniscience, and omnipotence. And yet even among the moral attributes one stands as supreme. Of this and of its supremacy we now proceed to speak.

Water is not water unless composed of oxygen and hydrogen. Oxygen cannot be resolved into hydrogen, nor hydrogen into oxygen. Oxygen has its own character, though only in combination with hydrogen does it appear in water. Will in man never acts without intellect and sensibility, yet will, more than intellect or sensibility, is the manifestation of the man. So when God acts, he manifests not one attribute alone, but his total moral excellence. Yet holiness, as an attribute of God, has rights peculiar to itself; it determines the attitude of the affections; it more than any other faculty constitutes God's moral being.

Clarke, Christian Theology, 83, 92 — "God would not be holy if he were not love, and could not be love if he were not holy. Love is an element in holiness. If this were lacking, there would be no perfect character as principle of his own action or as standard for us. On the other hand only the perfect being can be love. God must be free from all taint of selfishness in order to be love. Holiness requires God to act as love, for holiness is God's self-consistency. Love is the desire to impart holiness. Holiness makes God's character the standard for his creatures; but love, desiring to impart the best good, does the same. All work of love is work of holiness, and all work of holiness is work of love. Conflict of attributes is impossible, because holiness always includes love, and love always expresses holiness. They never need reconciliation with each other."

The general correctness of the foregoing statement is impaired by the vagueness of its conception of holiness. The Scriptures do not regard holiness as including love, or make all the acts of holiness to be acts of love. Self-affirmation does not include self-impartation, and sin necessitates an exercise of holiness which is not also an exercise of love. But for the Cross, and God's suffering for sin of which the Cross is the expression, there would be conflict between holiness and love. The wisdom of God is most shown, not in reconciling man and God, but in reconciling the holy God with the loving God.

1. *Holiness the fundamental attribute in God.*

That holiness is the fundamental attribute in God, is evident:

(*a*) From Scripture,— in which God's holiness is not only most constantly and powerfully impressed upon the attention of man, but is declared to be the chief subject of rejoicing and adoration in heaven.

It is God's attribute of holiness that first and most prominently presents itself to the mind of the sinner, and conscience only follows the method of Scripture : 1 Pet. 1 : 16 — "Ye shall be holy ; for I am holy " ; Heb. 12 : 14 — "the sanctification without which no man shall see the Lord " ; *cf.* Luke 5 : 8 —"Depart from me ; for I am a sinful man, O Lord." Yet this constant insistence upon holiness cannot be due simply to man's present state of sin, for in heaven, where there is no sin, there is the same reiteration : Is. 6 : 3 — "Holy, holy, holy, is Jehovah of hosts " ; Rev. 4 : 8 — "Holy, holy, holy is the Lord God, the Almighty." Of no other attribute is it said that God's throne rests upon it : Ps. 97 : 2 — "Righteousness and justice are the foundation of his throne " ; 99 : 4, 5, 9 — "The king's strength also loveth justice. . . . Exalt ye Jehovah our God. . . . holy is he." We would substitute the word holiness for the word love in the statement of Newman Smyth, Christian Ethics, 45 — " We assume that love is lord in the divine will, not that the will of God is sovereign over his love. God's omnipotence, as Dorner would say, exists for his love."

(*b*) From our own moral constitution,— in which conscience asserts its supremacy over every other impulse and affection of our nature. As we may be kind, but must be righteous, so God, in whose image we are made, may be merciful, but must be holy.

See Bishop Butler's Sermons upon Human Nature, Bohn's ed., 385-414, showing " the supremacy of conscience in the moral constitution of man." We must be just, before we are generous. So with God, justice must be done always ; mercy is optional with him. He was not under obligation to provide a redemption for sinners : 2 Pet. 2 : 4 —" God spared not angels when they sinned, but cast them down to hell." Salvation is a matter of grace, not of debt. Shedd, Discourses and Essays, 277-298 —" The quality of justice is necessary exaction ; but 'the quality of mercy is not (con) strained ' " [*cf.* Denham : " His mirth is forced and strained "]. God can apply the salvation, after he has wrought it out, to whomsoever he will : Rom. 9 : 18 —" he hath mercy on whom he will." Young, Night-Thoughts. 4 : 233 —" A God all mercy is a God unjust." Emerson : " Your goodness must have some edge to it ; else it is none." Martineau, Study, 2 : 100 —" No one can be just without subordinating Pity to the sense of Right."

We may learn of God's holiness *a priori.* Even the heathen could say " Fiat justitia, ruat cœlum," or " pereat mundus." But, for our knowledge of God's mercy, we are dependent upon special revelation. Mercy, like omnipotence, may exist in God without being exercised. Mercy is not grace but debt, if God owes the exercise of it either to the sinner or to himself ; *versus* G. B. Stevens, in New Eng., 1888 : 421-443. " But justice is an attribute which not only *exists* of necessity, but must be *exercised* of necessity ; because not to exercise it would be injustice " ; see Shedd, Dogm. Theol., 1 : 218, 219, 389, 390 ; 2 : 402, and Sermons to Nat. Man, 366. If it be said that, by parity of reasoning, for God not to exercise mercy is to show himself unmerciful, — we reply that this is not true so long as higher interests require that exercise to be withheld. I am not unmerciful when I refuse to give the poor the money needed to pay an honest debt ; nor is the Governor unmerciful when he refuses to pardon the condemned and unrepentant criminal. Mercy has its conditions, as we proceed to show, and it does not cease to *be* when these conditions do not permit it to *be exercised.* Not so with justice : justice must always be exercised ; when it ceases to *be exercised*, it also ceases to *be.*

The story of the prodigal shows a love that ever reaches out after the son in the far country, but which is ever conditioned by the father's holiness and restrained from acting until the son has voluntarily forsaken his riotous living. A just father may banish a corrupt son from the household. yet may love him so tenderly that his banishment causes exquisite pain. E. G. Robinson: "God, Christ and the Holy Spirit have a conscience, that is, they distinguish between right and wrong." E. H. Johnson, Syst. Theology, 85, 86 — "Holiness is primary as respects benevolence; for (*a*) Holiness is itself moral excellence, while the moral excellence of benevolence can be explained. (*b*) Holiness is an attribute of being, while benevolence is an attribute of action; but action presupposes and is controlled by being. (*c*) Benevolence must take counsel of holiness, since for a being to desire aught contrary to holiness would be to wish him harm, while that which holiness leads God to seek, benevolence finds best for the creature. (*d*) The Mosaic dispensation elaborately symbolized, and the Christian dispensation makes provision to meet, the requirements of holiness as supreme; James 3 : 17 — 'First pure, then [by consequence] peaceable.' "

We are "to do justly," as well as "to love kindness, and to walk humbly with" our God (Micah 6 : 8) Dr. Samuel Johnson: "It is surprising to find how much more kindness than justice society contains." There is a sinful mercy. A School Commissioner finds it terrible work to listen to the pleas of incompetent teachers begging that they may not be dismissed, and he can nerve himself for it only by remembering the children whose education may be affected by his refusal to do justice. Love and pity are not the whole of Christian duty, nor are they the ruling attributes of God.

(*c*) From the actual dealings of God,—in which holiness conditions and limits the exercise of other attributes. Thus, for example, in Christ's redeeming work, though love makes the atonement, it is violated holiness that requires it; and in the eternal punishment of the wicked, the demand of holiness for self-vindication overbears the pleading of love for the sufferers.

Love cannot be the fundamental attribute of God, because love always requires a norm or standard, and this norm or standard is found only in holiness; Phil. 1 : 9 — "And th s I pray, that your love may abound yet more in knowledge and all discernment"; see A. H. Strong, Christ in Creation, 388-405. That which conditions all is highest of all. Holiness shows itself higher than love, in that it conditions love. Hence God's mercy does not consist in outraging his own law of holiness, but in enduring the penal affliction by which that law of holiness is satisfied. Conscience in man is but the reflex of holiness in God. Conscience demands either retribution or atonement. This demand Christ meets by his substituted suffering. His sacrifice assuages the thirst of conscience in man, as well as the demand of holiness in God: John 6 : 55 — "For my flesh is meat indeed, and my blood is drink indeed." See Shedd, Discourses and Essays, 280, 291, 292 ; Dogmatic Theology, 1 . 377, 378 — " The sovereignty and freedom of God in respect to justice relates not to the *abolition*, nor to the *relaxation*, but to the *substitution*, of punishment. It does not consist in any power to violate or waive legal claims. The exercise of the other attributes of God is regulated and conditioned by that of justice. . . . Where then is the mercy of God, in case justice is strictly satisfied by a vicarious person? There is mercy in *permitting* another person to do for the sinner what the sinner is bound to do for himself; and greater mercy in *providing* that person; and still greater mercy in *becoming* that person."

Enthusiasm, like fire, must not only burn, but must be controlled. Man invented chimneys to keep in the heat but to let out the smoke. We need the walls of discretion and self-control to guide the flaming of our love. The holiness of God is the regulating principle of his nature. The ocean of his mercy is bounded by the shores of his justice. Even if holiness be God's self-love, in the sense of God's self-respect or self-preservation, still this self-love must condition love to creatures. Only as God maintains himself in his holiness, can he have anything of worth to give; love indeed is nothing but the self-communication of holiness. And if we say, with J. M. Whiton, that self-affirmation in a universe in which God is immanent is itself a form of self-impartation, still this form of self-impartation must condition and limit that other form of self-impartation which we call love to creatures. See Thomasius, Christi Person und Werk, 1 : 137-155, 346-353; Patton, art. on Retribution and the Divine Goodness, in Princeton Rev., Jan. 1878 : 8-16; Owen, Dissertation on the Divine Justice, in Works, 10 : 483-624.

(*d*) From God's eternal purpose of salvation, —in which justice and mercy are reconciled only through the foreseen and predetermined sacrifice of Christ. The declaration that Christ is "the Lamb . . . slain from the foundation of the world" implies the existence of a principle in the divine nature which requires satisfaction, before God can enter upon the work of redemption. That principle can be none other than holiness.

Since both mercy and justice are exercised toward sinners of the human race, the otherwise inevitable antagonism between them is removed only by the atoning death of the God-man. Their opposing claims do not impair the divine blessedness, because the reconciliation exists in the eternal counsels of God. This is intimated in Rev. 13:8 — "the Lamb that hath been slain from the foundation of the world." This same reconciliation is alluded to in Ps. 85:10 — "Mercy and truth are met together; Righteousness and peace have kissed each other"; and in Rom. 3:26 — "that he might himself be just, and the justifier of him that hath faith in Jesus." The atonement, then, if man was to be saved, was necessary, not primarily on man's account, but on God's account. Shedd, Discourses and Essays, 279 — The sacrifice of Christ was an "atonement ab intra, a self-oblation on the part of Deity himself, by which to satisfy those immanent and eternal imperatives of the divine nature which without it must find their satisfaction in the punishment of the transgressor, or else be outraged." Thus God's word of redemption, as well as his word of creation, is forever "settled in heaven" (Ps. 119:89). Its execution on the cross was "according to the pattern" on high. The Mosaic sacrifice prefigured the sacrifice of Christ; but the sacrifice of Christ was but the temporal disclosure of an eternal fact in the nature of God. See Kreibig, Versöhnung, 155, 156.

God requires satisfaction because he is holiness, but he makes satisfaction because he is love. The Judge himself, with all his hatred of transgression, still loves the transgressor, and comes down from the bench to take the criminal's place and bear his penalty. But this is an eternal provision and an eternal sacrifice. Heb. 9:14 — "the blood of Christ, who through the eternal Spirit offered himself without blemish unto God." Matheson, Voices of the Spirit, 215, 216 — "Christ's sacrifice was offered through the Spirit. It was not wrung from a reluctant soul through obedience to outward law; it came from the inner heart, from the impulse of undying love. It was a completed offering before Calvary began; it was seen by the Father before it was seen by the world. It was finished in the Spirit, ere it began in the flesh, finished in the hour when Christ exclaimed: 'not as I will, but as thou wilt' (Mat. 26:39)."

Lang, Homer, 506 — "Apollo is the bringer of pestilence and the averter of pestilence, in accordance with the well-known rule that the two opposite attributes should be combined in the same deity." Lord Bacon, Confession of Faith: "Neither angel, man nor world, could stand or can stand one moment in God's sight without beholding the same in the face of a Mediator; and therefore before him, with whom all things are present, the Lamb of God was slain before all worlds; without which eternal counsel of his, it was impossible for him to have descended to any work of creation." Orr, Christian View of God and the World, 319 — "Creation is built on redemption lines" — which is to say that incarnation and atonement were included in God's original design of the world.

2. The holiness of God the ground of moral obligation.

A. Erroneous Views. The ground of moral obligation is not

(a) In power, — whether of civil law (Hobbes, Gassendi), or of divine will (Occam, Descartes). We are not bound to obey either of these, except upon the ground that they are right. This theory assumes that nothing is good or right in itself, and that morality is mere prudence.

Civil law: See Hobbes, Leviathan, part i, chap. 6 and 13: part ii, chap. 30 ; Gassendi, Opera, 6:120. Upon this view, might makes right; the laws of Nero are always binding; a man may break his promise when civil law permits; there is no obligation to obey a father, a civil governor, or God himself, when once it is certain that the disobedience will be hidden, or when the offender is willing to incur the punishment. Martineau, Seat of Authority, 67 — "Mere magnitude of scale carries no moral quality; nor could a whole population of devils by unanimous ballot confer righteousness upon their will, or make it binding upon a single Abdiel." Robert Browning, Christmas Eve, xvii — "Justice, good, and truth were still Divine if, by some demon's will, Hatred and wrong had been proclaimed Law through the world, and right misnamed."

Divine will: See Occam, lib. 2, quæs. 19 (quoted in Porter, Moral Science, 125); Descartes (referred to in Hickok, Moral Science, 27, 28); Martineau, Types, 148—"Descartes held that the will of God is not the revealer but the inventor of moral distinctions. God could have made Euclid a farrago of lies, and Satan a model of moral perfection." Upon this view, right and wrong are variable quantities. Duns Scotus held that God's will makes not only truth but right. God can make lying to be virtuous and purity to be wrong. If Satan were God, we should be bound to obey him. God is essentially indifferent to right and wrong, good and evil. We reply that behind the divine will is the divine nature, and that in the moral perfection of that nature lies the only ground of moral obligation. God pours forth his love and exerts his power in accordance with some determining principle in his own nature. That principle is not happiness. Finney, Syst. Theology, 936, 937 — "Could God's command make it obligatory upon us to will evil to him? If not, then his will is not the ground of moral obligation. The thing that is most valuable, namely, the highest good of God and of the universe must be both the end and the ground. It is the divine reason and not the divine will that perceives and affirms the law of conduct. The divine will publishes, but does not originate the rule. God's will could not make vice to be virtuous."

As between power or utility on the one hand, and right on the other hand, we must regard right as the more fundamental. We do not, however, as will be seen further on, place the ground of moral obligation even in right, considered as an abstract principle; but place it rather in the moral excellence of him who is the personal Right and therefore the source of right. Character obliges, and the master often bows in his heart to the servant, when this latter is the nobler man.

(*b*) Nor in utility, — whether our own happiness or advantage present or eternal (Paley), for supreme regard for our own interest is not virtuous ; or the greatest happiness or advantage to being in general (Edwards), for we judge conduct to be useful because it is right, not right because it is useful. This theory would compel us to believe that in eternity past God was holy only because of the good he got from it, — that is, there was no such thing as holiness in itself, and no such thing as moral character in God.

Our own happiness: Paley, Mor. and Pol. Philos., book i, chap. vii — "Virtue is the doing good to mankind, in obedience to the will of God, and for the sake of everlasting happiness." This unites (*a*) and (*b*). John Stuart Mill and Dr. N. W. Taylor held that our own happiness is the supreme end. These writers indeed regard the highest happiness as attained only by living for others (Mill's altruism), but they can assign no reason why one who knows no other happiness than the pleasures of sense should not adopt the maxim of Epicurus, who, according to Lucretius, taught that "ducit quemque voluptas." This theory renders virtue impossible; for a virtue which is mere regard to our own interest is not virtue but prudence. "We have a sense of right and wrong independently of all considerations of happiness or its loss." James Mill held that the utility is not the criterion of the morality but itself constitutes the morality. G. B. Foster well replies that virtue is not mere egoistic sagacity, and the moral act is not simply a clever business enterprise. All languages distinguish between virtue and prudence. To say that the virtues are great utilities is to confound the effect with the cause. Carlyle says that a man can do without happiness. Browning, Red Cotton Nightcap Country : "Thick heads ought to recognize The devil, that old stager, at his trick Of general utility, who leads Downward perhaps, but fiddles all the way." This is the morality of Mother Goose : "He put in his thumb, And pulled out a plum, And said, 'What a good boy am I!'"

E. G. Robinson, Principles and Practice of Morality, 160 — "Utility has nothing ultimate in itself, and therefore can furnish no ground of obligation. Utility is mere fitness of one thing to minister to something else." To say that things are right because they are useful, is like saying that things are beautiful because they are pleasing. Martineau, Types of Ethical Theory, 2 : 170, 511. 556 — "The moment the appetites pass into the self-conscious state, and become ends instead of impulses, they draw to themselves terms of censure. . . . So intellectual conscientiousness, or strict submission of the mind to evidence, has its inspiration in pure love of truth, and would not survive an hour, if entrusted to the keeping either of providence or of social affection. . . . Instincts, which provide for they know not what, are proof that *want* is the original impulse to action, instead of pleasure being the end." On the happiness theory, appeals to self-interest on behalf of religion ought to be effective, — as a matter of fact few are moved by them.

Dewey, Psychology, 300, 362 — " Emotion turned inward eats up itself. Live on feelings rather than on the things to which feelings belong, and you defeat your own end, exhaust your power of feeling, commit emotional suicide. Hence arise cynicism, the *nil admirari* spirit, restless searching for the latest sensation. The only remedy is to get outside of self, to devote self to some worthy object, not for feeling's sake but for the sake of the object. . . . We do not desire an object because it gives us pleasure, but it gives us pleasure because it satisfies the impulse which, in connection with the idea of the object, constitutes the desire. . . . Pleasure is the accompaniment of the activity or development of the *self*."

Salter, First Steps in Philosophy, 150 — " It is right to aim at happiness. Happiness is *an* end. Utilitarianism errs in making happiness the only and the highest end. It exalts a state of feeling into the supremely desirable thing. Intuitionalism gives the same place to a state of will. The truth includes both. The true end is the highest development of being, self and others, the realization of the divine idea, God in man."

Bowne, Principles of Ethics, 96 — " The standard of appeal is not the actual happiness of the actual man but the normal happiness of the normal man. . . . Happiness must have a law. But then also the law must lead to happiness. . . . The true ethical aim is to realize the good. But then the contents of this good have to be determined in accordance with an inborn ideal of human worth and dignity. . . . Not all good, but the true good, not the things which please, but the things which should please, are to be the aim of action."

Bixby, Crisis of Morals, 223 — " The Utilitarian is really asking about the wisest method of embodying the ideal. He belongs to that second stage in which the moral artist considers through what material and in what form and color he may best realize his thought. What the ideal is, and why it is the highest, he does not tell us. Morality begins. not in feeling, but in reason. And reason is impersonal. It discerns the moral equality of personalities." Genung, Epic of the Inner Life, 20 — Job speaks out his character like one of Robert Browning's heroes. He teaches that " there is a service of God which is not work for reward : it is a heart-loyalty, a hunger after God's presence, which survives loss and chastisement ; which in spite of contradictory seeming cleaves to what is godlike as the needle seeks the pole ; and which reaches up out of the darkness and hardness of this life into the light and love beyond."

Greatest good of being : Not only Edwards, but Priestley, Bentham, Dwight, Finney, Hopkins, Fairchild, hold this view. See Edwards, Works, 2 : 261-304 — " Virtue is benevolence toward being in general " ; Dwight, Theology, 3 : 150-162 — " Utility the foundation of Virtue " ; Hopkins, Law of Love, 7-28 ; Fairchild, Moral Philosophy ; Finney, Syst. Theol., 42-135. This theory regards good as a mere state of the sensibility, instead of consisting in purity of being. It forgets that in eternity past " love for being in general " = simply God's self-love, or God's regard for his own happiness. This implies that God is holy only for a purpose ; he is bound to be unholy, if greater good would result ; that is, holiness has no independent existence in his nature. We grant that a thing is often known to be right by the fact that it is useful ; but this is very different from saying that its usefulness makes it right. " Utility is only the setting of the diamond, which *marks*, but does not *make*, its value." " If utility be a criterion of rectitude, it is only because it is a revelation of the divine nature." See British Quarterly, July, 1877, on Matthew Arnold and Bishop Butler. Bp. Butler, Nature of Virtue, in Works, Bohn's ed., 334 — " Benevolence is the true self-love." Love and holiness are obligatory in themselves, and not because they promote the general good. Cicero well said that they who confounded the *honestum* with the *utile* deserved to be banished from society. See criticism on Porter's Moral Science, in Lutheran Quarterly, Apr. 1885 : 325-331 ; also F. L. Patton, on Metaphysics of Oughtness, in Presb. Rev., 1886 : 127-150.

Encyc. Britannica, 7 : 690, on Jonathan Edwards — " Being in general, being without any qualities, is too abstract a thing to be the primary cause of love. The feeling which Edwards refers to is not love, but awe or reverence, and moreover necessarily a blind awe. Properly stated therefore, true virtue, according to Edwards, would consist in a blind awe of being in general, — only this would be inconsistent with his definition of virtue as existing in God. In reality, as he makes virtue merely the second object of love, his theory becomes identical with that utilitarian theory with which the names of Hume, Bentham and Mill are associated." Hodge, Essays, 275 — " If obligation is due primarily to being in general, then there is no more virtue in loving God—

willing his good — than there is in loving Satan. But love to Christ differs in its nature from benevolence toward the devil." Plainly virtue consists, not in love for mere being, but in love for good being, or in other words, in love for the holy God. Not the greatest good of being, but the holiness of God, is the ground of moral obligation.

Dr. E. A. Park interprets the Edwardean theory as holding that virtue is love to all beings according to their value, love of the greater therefore more than the less, "love to particular beings in a proportion compounded of the degree of being and the degree of virtue or benevolence to being which they have." Love is choice. Happiness, says Park, is not the sole good, much less the happiness of creatures. The *greatest* good is holiness, though the *last* good aimed at is happiness. Holiness is disinterested love — free choice of the general above the private good. But we reply that this gives us no reason or standard for virtue. It does not tell us what is good nor why we should choose it. Martineau, Types, 2: 70, 77, 471, 484 — "Why should I promote the general well-being? Why should I sacrifice myself for others? Only because this is godlike. It would never have been prudent to do right, had it not been something infinitely more. . . . It is not fitness that makes an act moral, but it is its morality that makes it fit."

Herbert Spencer must be classed as a utilitarian. He says that justice requires that "every man be free to do as he wills provided he infringes not the equal freedom of every other man." But, since this would permit injury to another by one willing to submit to injury in return, Mr. Spencer limits the freedom to "such actions as subserve life." This is practically equivalent to saying that the greatest sum of happiness is the ultimate end. On Jonathan Edwards, see Robert Hall, Works, 1:43 *sq.* ; Alexander, Moral Science, 194-198 ; Bib. Repertory (Princeton Review), 25:22; Bib. Sacra, 9: 176, 197; 10:403, 705.

(*c*) Nor in the nature of things (Price),—whether by this we mean their fitness (Clarke), truth (Wollaston), order (Jouffroy), relations (Wayland), worthiness (Hickok), sympathy (Adam Smith), or abstract right (Haven and Alexander); for this nature of things is not ultimate, but has its ground in the nature of God. We are bound to worship the highest; if anything exists beyond and above God, we are bound to worship that,—that indeed is God.

See Wayland, Moral Science, 33-48; Hickok, Moral Science, 27-34; Haven, Moral Philosophy, 27-50; Alexander, Moral Science, 159-198. In opposition to all the forms of this theory, we urge that nothing exists independently of or above God. "If the ground of morals exist independently of God, either it has ultimately no authority, or it usurps the throne of the Almighty. Any rational being who kept the law would be perfect without God, and the moral centre of all intelligences would be outside of God" (Talbot). God is not a Jupiter controlled by Fate. He is subject to no law but the law of his own nature. *Noblesse oblige,* — character rules, — purity is the highest. And therefore to holiness all creatures, voluntarily or involuntarily, are constrained to bow. Hopkins, Law of Love, 77 — "Right and wrong have nothing to do with things, but only with actions; nothing to do with any nature of things existing necessarily, but only with the nature of persons." Another has said : "The idea of right cannot be original, since right means conformity to some standard or rule." This standard or rule is not an abstraction, but an existing being — the infinitely perfect God.

Faber: "For right is right, since God is God ; And right the day must win ; To doubt would be disloyalty, To falter would be sin." Tennyson : "And because right is right, to follow right Were wisdom in the scorn of consequence." Right is right, and I should will the right, not because God *wills* it, but because God *is* it. E. G. Robinson, Principles and Practice of Morality, 178-180 — "Utility and relations simply reveal the constitution of things and so represent God. Moral law was not made for purposes of utility, nor do relations constitute the reason for obligation. They only show what the nature of God is who made the universe and revealed himself in it. In his nature is found the *reason* for morality." S. S. Times, Oct. 17, 1891 — "Only that is level which conforms to the curvature of the earth's surface. A straight line tangent to the earth's curve would at its ends be much further from the earth's centre than at its middle. Now equity means levelness. The standard of equity is not an impersonal thing, a 'nature of things' outside of God. Equity or righteousness is no more to be conceived independently of the divine centre of the moral world than is levelness comprehensible apart from the earth's centre."

Since God finds the rule and limitation of his action solely in his own being, and his love is conditioned by his holiness, we must differ from such views as that of Moxom : "Whether we define God's nature as perfect holiness or perfect love is immaterial, since his nature is manifested only through his action, that is, through his relation to other beings. Most of our reasoning on the divine standard of righteousness, or the ultimate ground of moral obligation, is reasoning in a circle, since we must always go back to God for the principle of his action ; which principle we can know only by means of his action. God, the perfectly righteous Being, is the ideal standard of human righteousness. Righteousness in man therefore is conformity to the nature of God. God, in agreement with his perfect nature, always wills the perfectly good toward man. His righteousness is an expression of his love ; his love is a manifestation of his righteousness."

So Newman Smyth : "Righteousness is the eternal genuineness of the divine love. It is not therefore an independent excellence, to be contrasted with, or even put in opposition to, benevolence ; it is an essential part of love." In reply to which we urge as before that that which is the object of love, that which limits and conditions love, that which furnishes the norm and reason for love, cannot itself be love, nor hold merely equal rank with love. A double standard is as irrational in ethics as in commerce, and it leads in ethics to the same debasement of the higher values, and the same unsettling of relations, as has resulted in our currency from the attempt to make silver regulate gold at the same time that gold regulates silver.

B. The Scriptural View.—According to the Scriptures, the ground of moral obligation is the holiness of God, or the moral perfection of the divine nature, conformity to which is the law of our moral being (Robinson, Chalmers, Calderwood, Gregory, Wuttke). We show this :

(a) From the commands : "Ye shall be holy," where the ground of obligation assigned is simply and only : "for I am holy" (1 Pet. 1 : 16) : and "Ye therefore shall be perfect," where the standard laid down is : "as your heavenly Father is perfect" (Mat. 5 : 48). Here we have an ultimate reason and ground for being and doing right, namely, that God is right, or, in other words, that holiness is his nature.

(b) From the nature of the love in which the whole law is summed up (Mat. 22 : 37 —"Thou shalt love the Lord thy God" ; Rom. 13 : 10 — "love therefore is the fulfilment of the law ") . This love is not regard for abstract right or for the happiness of being, much less for one's own interest, but it is regard for God as the fountain and standard of moral excellence, or in other words, love for God as holy. Hence this love is the principle and source of holiness in man.

(c) From the example of Christ, whose life was essentially an exhibition of supreme regard for God, and of supreme devotion to his holy will. As Christ saw nothing good but what was in God (Mark 10 : 18 —"none is good save one, even God") , and did only what he saw the Father do (John 5 : 19 ; see also 30 —"I seek not mine own will, but the will of him that sent me ") , so for us, to be like God is the sum of all duty, and God's infinite moral excellence is the supreme reason why we should be like him.

For statements of the correct view of the ground of moral obligation, see E. G. Robinson, Principles and Practice of Morality, 138–180 ; Chalmers, Moral Philosophy, 412–420 ; Calderwood, Moral Philosophy ; Gregory, Christian Ethics, 112–122 ; Wuttke, Christian Ethics, 2 : 80–107 ; Talbot, Ethical Prolegomena, in Bap. Quar., July, 1877 : 257–274 —"The ground of all moral law is the nature of God, or the ethical nature of God in relation to the like nature in man, or the imperativeness of the divine nature." Plato : "The divine will is the fountain of all efficiency ; the divine reason is the fountain of all law ; the divine nature is the fountain of all virtue." If it be said that God is love as well as holiness, we ask: Love to what? And the only answer is: Love to the right, or to holiness. To ask why right is a good, is no more sensible than to ask why happiness is a good. There must be something ultimate. Schiller said there are people who want to know why ten is not twelve. We cannot study character apart from conduct, nor conduct apart from character. But this does not prevent us from recognizing that character is the fundamental thing and that conduct is only the expression of it.

The moral perfection of the divine nature includes truth and love, but since it is holiness that conditions the exercise of every other attribute, we must conclude that holiness is the ground of moral obligation. Infinity also unites with holiness to make it the perfect ground, but since the determining element is holiness, we call this, and not infinity, the ground of obligation. J. H. Harris, Baccalaureate Sermon, Bucknell University, 1890 — "As holiness is the fundamental attribute of God, so holiness is the supreme good of man. Aristotle perceived this when he declared the chief good of man to be energizing according to virtue. Christianity supplies the Holy Spirit and makes this energizing possible." Holiness is the goal of man's spiritual career; see 1 Thess. 3 : 13 — "to the end he may establish your hearts unblamable in holiness before our God and Father."

Arthur H. Hallam, in John Brown's Rab and his Friends, 272 — " Holiness and happiness are two notions of one thing. . . . . Unless therefore the heart of a created being is at one with the heart of God, it cannot but be miserable." It is more true to say that holiness and happiness are, as cause and effect, inseparably bound together. Martineau, Types, 1 : xvi ; 2 : 70–77 —"Two classes of facts it is indispensable for us to know : what are the springs of voluntary conduct, and what are its effects"; Study, 1 : 26 —" Ethics must either perfect themselves in Religion, or disintegrate themselves into Hedonism." William Law remarks : " Ethics are not external but internal. The essence of a moral act does not lie in its result, but in the motive from which it springs. And that again is good or bad, according as it conforms to the character of God." For further discussion of the subject see our chapter on The Law of God. See also Thornwell, Theology, 1 : 36'-373; Hinton, Art of Thinking, 47-62; Goldwin Smith, in Contemporary Review, March, 1882, and Jan. 1884; H. B. Smith, System of Theology, 195-231, esp. 223.

CHAPTER II.

DOCTRINE OF THE TRINITY.

In the nature of the one God there are three eternal distinctions which are represented to us under the figure of persons, and these three are equal. This tripersonality of the Godhead is exclusively a truth of revelation. It is clearly, though not formally, made known in the New Testament, and intimations of it may be found in the Old.

The doctrine of the Trinity may be expressed in the six following statements : 1. In Scripture there are three who are recognized as God. 2. These three are so described in Scripture that we are compelled to conceive of them as distinct persons. 3. This tripersonality of the divine nature is not merely economic and temporal, but is immanent and eternal. 4. This tripersonality is not tritheism ; for while there are three persons, there is but one essence. 5. The three persons, Father, Son and Holy Spirit, are equal. 6. Inscrutable yet not self-contradictory, this doctrine furnishes the key to all other doctrines.—These statements we proceed now to prove and to elucidate.

Reason shows us the Unity of God ; only revelation shows us the Trinity of God, thus filling out the indefinite outlines of this Unity and vivifying it. The term 'Trinity' is not found in Scripture, although the conception it expresses is Scriptural. The invention of the term is ascribed to Tertullian. The Montanists first defined the personality of the Spirit, and first formulated the doctrine of the Trinity. The term 'Trinity' is not a metaphysical one. It is only a designation of four facts: (1) the Father is God; (2) the Son is God; (3) the Spirit is God; (4) there is but one God.

Park : "The doctrine of the Trinity does not on the one hand assert that three persons are united in one person, or three beings in one being, or three Gods in one God (tritheism); nor on the other hand that God merely manifests himself in three different ways (modal trinity, or trinity of manifestations); but rather that there are three eternal distinctions in the substance of God." Smyth, preface to Edwards, Observations on the Trinity : "The church doctrine of the Trinity affirms that there are in the Godhead three distinct hypostases or subsistences—the Father, the Son and the Holy Spirit — each possessing one and the same divine nature, though in a different manner. The essential points are (1) the unity of essence; (2) the reality of immanent or ontological distinctions." See Park on Edwards's View of the Trinity, in Bib. Sac., April, 1881 : 333. Princeton Essays, 1 : 28 —"There is one God; Father, Son, and Holy Spirit are this one God; there is such a distinction between Father, Son and Holy Spirit as to lay a sufficient ground for the reciprocal use of the personal pronouns." Joseph Cook : "(1) The Father, the Son. and the Holy Ghost are one God; (2) each has a peculiarity incommunicable to the others; (3) neither is God without the others; (4) each, with the others, is God."

We regard the doctrine of the Trinity as implicitly held by the apostles and as involved in the New Testament declarations with regard to Father, Son and Holy Spirit, while we concede that the doctrine had not by the New Testament writers been formulated. They held it, as it were in solution ; only time, reflection, and the shock of controversy and opposition, caused it to crystalize into definite and dogmatic form. Chadwick, Old and New Unitarianism, 59, 60, claims that the Jewish origin of Christianity shows that the Jewish Messiah could not originally have been conceived of as divine. If Jesus had claimed this, he would not have been taken before Pilate,— the Jews would have dispatched him. The doctrine of the Trinity, says Chadwick, was not developed until the Council of Nice, 325. E. G. Robinson : "There was no doctrine of

304

the Trinity in the Patristic period, as there was no doctrine of the Atonement before Anselm." The Outlook, Notes and Queries, March 30, 1901—"The doctrine of the Trinity cannot be said to have taken final shape before the appearance of the so-called Athanasian Creed in the 8th or 9th century. The Nicene Creed, formulated in the 4th century, is termed by Dr. Schaff, from the orthodox point of view, 'semi-trinitarian.' The earliest time known at which Jesus was deified was, after the New Testament writers, in the letters of Ignatius, at the beginning of the second century."

Gore, Incarnation, 179—"The doctrine of the Trinity is not so much heard, as over-heard, in the statements of Scripture." George P. Fisher quotes some able and pious friend of his as saying: "What meets us in the New Testament is the *disjecta membra* of the Trinity." G. B. Foster: "The doctrine of the Trinity is the Christian attempt to make intelligible the personality of God without dependence upon the world." Charles Kingsley said that, whether the doctrine of the Trinity is in the Bible or no, it ought to be there, because our spiritual nature cries out for it. Shedd, Dogmatic Theology, 1:259—"Though the doctrine of the Trinity is not discoverable by human reason, it is susceptible of a rational defense, when revealed." On New England Trinitarianism, see New World, June, 1896: 272-295—art. by Levi L. Paine. He says that the last phase of it is represented by Phillips Brooks, James M. Whiton and George A. Gordon. These hold to the essential divineness of humanity and preëminently of Christ, the unique representative of mankind, who was, in this sense, a true incarnation of Deity. See also, L. L. Paine, Evolution of Trinitarianism, 141, 287.

Neander declared that the Trinity is not a fundamental doctrine of Christianity. He was speaking however of the speculative, metaphysical form which the doctrine has assumed in theology. But he speaks very differently of the devotional and practical form in which the Scriptures present it, as in the baptismal formula and in the apostolic benediction. In regard to this he says: "We recognize therein the essential contents of Christianity summed up in brief." Whiton, Gloria Patri, 10, 11, 55, 91, 92—"God transcendent, the Father, is revealed by God immanent, the Son. This one nature belongs equally to God, to Christ, and to mankind, and in this fact is grounded the immutableness of moral distinctions and the possibility of moral progress. . . . . The-immanent life of the universe is one with the transcendent Power; the filial stream is one with its paternal Fount. To Christ supremely belongs the name of Son, which includes all that life that is begotten of God. In Christ the before unconscious Sonship of the world awakes to consciousness of the Father. The Father is the Life transcendent, above all; the Son is Life immanent, through all; the Holy Spirit is the Life individualized, in all. In Christ we have collectivism; in the Holy Spirit we have individualism; as Bunsen says: 'The chief power in the world is personality.'"

For treatment of the whole doctrine, see Dorner, System of Doctrine, 1:344-465; Twesten, Dogmatik, and translation in Bib. Sac., 3:502; Ebrard, Dogmatik, 1:145-199; Thomasius, Christi Person und Werk, 1:57-135; Kahnis, Dogmatik, 3:203-229; Shedd, Dogm. Theol., 1:248-333, and History of Doctrine, 1:246-385; Farrar, Science and Theology, 138; Schaff, Nicene Doctrine of the Holy Trinity, in Theol. Eclectic, 4:209. For the Unitarian view, see Norton, Statement of Reasons, and J. F. Clarke, Truths and Errors of Orthodoxy.

I. In Scripture there are Three who are recognized as God.

1. *Proofs from the New Testament*

A. The Father is recognized as God,—and that in so great a number of passages (such as John 6:27—"him the Father, even God, hath sealed," and 1 Pet. i:2—"foreknowledge of God the Father") that we need not delay to adduce extended proof.

B. Jesus Christ is recognized as God.

(*a*) He is expressly called God.

In John 1:1—Θεὸς ἦν ὁ λόγος—the absence of the article shows Θεός to be the predicate (*cf.* 4:24—πνεῦμα ὁ Θεός). This predicate precedes the verb by way of emphasis, to indicate progress in the thought = 'the Logos was not only with God, but was God' (see Meyer and Luthardt, Comm. *in loco*). " Only ὁ λόγος can be the subject, for in the whole Introduction the question is, not who God is, but who the Logos is " (Godet).

Westcott in Bible Commentary, *in loco* — " The predicate stands emphatically first. It is necessarily without the article, inasmuch as it describes the nature of the Word and does not identify his person. It would be pure Sabellianism to say : 'The Word was ὁ Θεός.' Thus in verse 1 we have set forth the Word in his absolute eternal being, (*a*) his existence : beyond time ; (*b*) his personal existence : in active communion with God ; (*c*) his nature : God in essence." Marcus Dods, in Expositor's Greek Testament, *in loco* : " The Word is distinguishable from God, yet Θεὸς ἦν ὁ λόγος — the word was God, of divine nature ; not ' a God,' which to a Jewish ear would have been abominable, nor yet identical with all that can be called God, for then the article would have been inserted (*cf*. 1 John 3 : 4)."

In John 1 : 18, μονογενὴς Θεός — 'the only begotten God'—must be regarded as the correct reading, and as a plain ascription of absolute Deity to Christ. He is not simply the only revealer of God, but he is himself God revealed.

John 1 : 18 — "No man hath seen God at any time ; the only begotten God, who is in the bosom of the Father, he hath declared him." In this passage, although Tischendorf (8th ed.) has μονογενὴς υἱός, Westcott and Hort (with א*BC*L Pesh. Syr.) read μονογενὴς Θεός, and the Rev. Vers. puts " the only begotten God " in the margin, though it retains " the only begotten Son " in the text. Harnack says the reading μονογενὴς Θεός is " established beyond contradiction " ; see Westcott, Bib. Com. on John, pages 32, 33. Here then we have a new and unmistakable assertion of the deity of Christ. Meyer says that the apostles actually call Christ God only in John 1 : 1 and 20 : 28, and that Paul never so recognizes him. But Meyer is able to maintain his position only by calling the doxologies to Christ, in 2 Tim. 4 : 18, Heb. 13 : 21 and 2 Pet. 3 : 18, post-apostolic. See Thayer, N. T. Lexicon, on Θεός, and on μονογενής.

In John 20 : 28, the address of Thomas Ὁ κύριός μου καὶ ὁ θεός μου, — ' My Lord and my God '—since it was unrebuked by Christ, is equivalent to an assertion on his own part of his claim to Deity.

John 20 : 28 — " Thomas answered and said unto him, My Lord and my God." This address cannot be interpreted as a sudden appeal to God in surprise and admiration, without charging the apostle with profanity. Nor can it be considered a mere exhibition of overwrought enthusiasm, since it was accepted by Christ. Contrast the conduct of Paul and Barnabas when the heathen at Lystra were bringing sacrifice to them as Jupiter and Mercury (Acts 14 : 11-18). The words of Thomas, as addressed directly to Christ and as accepted by Christ, can be regarded only as a just acknowledgment on the part of Thomas that Christ was his Lord and his God. Alford, Commentary, *in loco* : " The Socinian view that these words are merely an exclamation is refuted (1) by the fact that no such exclamations were in use among the Jews ; (2) by the εἶπεν αὐτῷ ; (3) by the impossibility of referring the ὁ κύριός μου to another than Jesus : see verse 13 ; (4) by the N. T. usage of expressing the vocative by the nominative with an article ; (5) by the psychological absurdity of such a supposition : that one just convinced of the presence of him whom he dearly loved should, instead of addressing him, break out into an irrelevant cry ; (6) by the further absurdity of supposing that, if such were the case, the Apostle John, who of all the sacred writers most constantly keeps in mind the object for which he is writing, should have recorded anything so beside that object ; (7) by the intimate conjunction of πεπίστευκας." *Cf*. Mat. 5 : 34 — " Swear not . . . by the heaven "—swearing by Jehovah is not mentioned, because no Jew did so swear. This exclamation of Thomas, the greatest doubter among the twelve, is the natural conclusion of John's gospel. The thesis " the Word was God " (John 1 : 1) has now become part of the life and consciousness of the apostles. Chapter 21 is only an Epilogue, or Appendix, written later by John, to correct the error that he was not to die ; see Westcott, Bible Com. *in loco*. The Deity of Christ is the subject of the apostle who best understood his Master. Lyman Beecher : " Jesus Christ is the acting Deity of the universe."

In Rom. 9 : 5, the clause ὁ ὢν ἐπὶ πάντων Θεὸς εὐλογητός cannot be translated 'blessed be the God over all,' for ὢν is superfluous if the clause is a doxology ; " εὐλογητός precedes the name of God in a doxology, but follows it, as here, in a description" (Hovey). The clause can therefore justly be interpreted only as a description of the higher nature of the Christ who had just been said, τὸ κατὰ σάρκα, or according to his lower nature, to have had his origin from Israel (see Tholuck, Com. *in loco*).

Sanday, Com. on Rom. 9 : 5 — "The words would naturally refer to Christ, unless 'God' is so definitely a proper name that it would imply a contrast in itself. We have seen that this is not so." Hence Sanday translates : "of whom is the Christ as concerning the flesh, who is over all, God blessed forever." See President T. Dwight, in Jour. Soc. Bib. Exegesis, 1881 : 22-55 ; per contra, Ezra Abbot, in the same journal, 1881 : 1-19, and Denney, in Expositor's Gk. T'st., *in loco*.

In Titus 2 : 13, ἐπιφάνειαν τῆς δόξης τοῦ μεγάλου Θεοῦ καὶ σωτῆρος ἡμῶν 'Ιησοῦ Χριστοῦ we regard (with Ellicott) as "a direct, definite, and even studied declaration of Christ's divinity " = "the . . . appearing of the glory of our great God and Savior Jesus Christ" (so English Revised Version). 'Επιφάνεια is a term applied specially to the Son and never to the Father, and μεγάλου is uncalled for if used of the Father, but peculiarly appropriate if used of Christ. Upon the same principles we must interpret the similar text 2 Pet. 1 : 1 (see Huther, in Meyer's Com. : "The close juxtaposition indicates the author's certainty of the oneness of God and Jesus Christ ").

Titus 2 : 13 — "Looking for the blessed hope and appearing of the glory of our great God and Savior, Jesus Christ "— so the English Revised Version. The American Revisers however translate : "the glory of the great God and Savior " ; and Westcott and Hort bracket the word ἡμῶν. These consider- ations somewhat lessen the cogency of this passage as a proof-text, yet upon the whole the balance of argument seems to us still to incline in favor of Ellicott's interpretation as given above.

In Heb. 1 : 8, πρὸς δὲ τὸν υἱόν · ὁ θρόνος σου, ὁ Θεὸς, εἰς τὸν αἰῶνα is quoted as an address to Christ, and verse 10 which follows — "Thou, Lord, in the beginning hast laid the foundation of the earth "— by applying to Christ an Old Testament ascription to Jehovah, shows that ὁ Θεός, in verse 8, is used in the sense of absolute Godhead.

It is sometimes objected that the ascription of the name God to Christ proves noth- ing as to his absolute deity, since angels and even human judges are called gods, as representing God's authority and executing his will. But we reply that, while it is true that the name is sometimes so applied, it is always with adjuncts and in connec- tions which leave no doubt of its figurative and secondary meaning. When, however, the name is applied to Christ, it is, on the contrary, with adjuncts and in connections which leave no doubt that it signifies absolute Godhead. See Ex. 4 : 16 — "thou shalt be to him as God " ; 7 : 1 — "See, I have made thee as God to Pharaoh " ; 22 : 28 — "Thou shalt not revile God, [marg., the judges], nor curse a ruler of thy people " ; Ps. 82 : 1 — "God standeth in the congregation of God ; He judgeth among the gods " [among the mighty] ; 6 — "I said, Ye are gods, And all of you sons of the Most High " ; 7 — "Nevertheless ye shall die like men, And fall like one of the princes." Cf. John 10 : 34-36 — "If he called them gods, unto whom the word of God came" (who were God's commissioned and appointed represent- atives), how much more proper for him who is one with the Father to call himself God.

As in Ps. 82 · 7 those who had been called gods are represented as dying, so in Ps. 97 : 7 — "Worship him, all ye gods " — they are bidden to fall down before Jehovah. Ann. Par. Bible : "Although the deities of the heathen have no positive existence, they are often described in Scripture as if they had, and are represented as bowing down before the majesty of Jehovah." This verse is quoted in Heb. 1 : 6 — "let all the angels of God worship him "— i. e., Christ. Here Christ is identified with Jehovah. The quotation is made from the Septuagint, which has "angels" for "gods." "Its use here is in accordance with the spirit of the Hebrew word, which includes all that human error might regard as objects of worship." Those who are figuratively and rhetorically called "gods" are bidden to fall down in worship before him who is the true God, Jesus Christ. See Dick, Lectures on Theology, 1 : 314 ; Liddon, Our Lord's Divinity, 10.

In 1 John 5 : 20— ἐσμὲν ἐν τῷ ἀληθινῷ, ἐν τῷ υἱῷ αὐτοῦ Ἰησοῦ Χριστῷ. οὖτός ἐστιν ὁ ἀληθινὸς Θεός — "it would be a flat repetition, after the Father had been twice called ὁ ἀληθινός, to say now again : 'this is ὁ ἀληθινὸς Θεός.' Our being in God has its basis in Christ his Son, and this also makes it more natural that οὖτος should be referred to υἱῷ. But ought not ὁ ἀληθινός then to be without the article (as in John 1 : 1— Θεός ἦν ὁ λόγος) ? No, for it is John's purpose in 1 John 5 : 20 to say, not *what* Christ is, but *who* he is. In declaring *what* one is, the predicate must have no article ; in declaring *who* one is, the predicate must have the article. St. John here says that this Son, on whom our being in the true God rests, is this true God himself" (see Ebrard, Com. *in loco*).

Other passages might be here adduced, as Col. 2 : 9 — "in him dwelleth all the fulness of the Godhead bodily "; Phil. 2 : 6 — "existing in the form of God"; but we prefer to consider these under other heads as indirectly proving Christ's divinity. Still other passages once relied upon as direct statements of the doctrine must be given up for textual reasons. Such are Acts 20 : 28, where the correct reading is in all probability not ἐκκλησίαν τοῦ Θεοῦ, but ἐκκλησίαν τοῦ Κυρίου (so ACDE Tregelles and Tischendorf; B and אֻ, however, have τοῦ Θεοῦ. The Rev. Vers. continues to read "church of God"; Amer. Revisers, however, read "church of the Lord"—see Ezra Abbot's investigation in Bib. Sac., 1876 : 313–352); and 1 Tim. 3 : 16, where ὅς is unquestionably to be substituted for Θεός, though even here ἐφανερώθη intimates preëxistence.

Rev. George E. Ellis, D. D., before the Unitarian Club, Boston, November, 1882 — " Fifty years of study, thought and reading given largely to the Bible and to the literature which peculiarly relates to it, have brought me to this conclusion, that the book — taken with the especial divine quality and character claimed for it, and so extensively assigned to it, as inspired and infallible as a whole, and in all its contents— is an Orthodox book. It yields what is called the Orthodox creed. The vast majority of its readers, following its letter, its obvious sense, its natural meaning, and yielding to the impression which some of its emphatic texts make upon them, find in it Orthodoxy. Only that kind of ingenious, special, discriminative, and in candor I must add, forced treatment, which it receives from us liberals can make the book teach anything but Orthodoxy. The evangelical sects, so called, are clearly right in maintaining that their view of Scripture and of its doctrines draws a deep and wide division of creed between them and ourselves. In that earnest controversy by pamphlet warfare between Drs. Channing and Ware on the one side, and Drs. Worcester and Woods and Professor Stuart on the other — a controversy which wrought up the people of our community sixty years ago more than did our recent political campaign — I am fully convinced that the liberal contestants were worsted. Scripture exegesis, logic and argument were clearly on the side of the Orthodox contestants. And this was so, mainly because the liberal party put themselves on the same plane with the Orthodox in their way of regarding and dealing with Scripture texts in their bearing upon the controversy. Liberalism cannot vanquish Orthodoxy, if it yields to the latter in its own way of regarding and treating the whole Bible. Martin Luther said that the Papists burned the Bible because it was not on their side. Now I am not about to attack the Bible because it is not on my side ; but I am about to object as emphatically as I can against a character and quality assigned to the Bible, which it does not claim for itself, which cannot be certified for it; and the origin and growth and intensity of the fond and superstitious influences resulting in that view we can trace distinctly to agencies accounting for, but not warranting, the current belief. Orthodoxy cannot readjust its creeds till it readjusts its estimate of the Scriptures. The only relief which one who professes the Orthodox creed can find is either by forcing his ingenuity into the proof-texts or indulging his liberty outside of them."

With this confession of a noted Unitarian it is interesting to compare the opinion of the so-called Trinitarian, Dr. Lyman Abbott, who says that the New Testament nowhere calls Christ God, but everywhere calls him man, as in 1 Tim. 2 : 5 — " For there is one God, one mediator also between God and man, himself man, Christ Jesus." On this passage Prof. L. L. Paine remarks in the New World, Dec. 1894 — " That Paul ever confounded Christ with God himself, or regarded him as in any way the Supreme Divinity, is a position invalidated not only by direct statements, but also by the whole drift of his epistles."

(*b*) Old Testament descriptions of God are applied to him.

This application to Christ of titles and names exclusively appropriated to God is inexplicable, if Christ was not regarded as being himself God. The peculiar awe with which the term 'Jehovah' was set apart by a nation of strenuous monotheists as the sacred and incommunicable name of the one self-existent and covenant-keeping God forbids the belief that the Scripture writers could have used it as the designation of a subordinate and created being.

Mat. 3 : 3 —"Make ye ready the way of the Lord "—is a quotation from Is. 40 : 3 —"Prepare ye . . . . the way of Jehovah." John 12 : 41 —"These things said Isaiah, because he saw his glory; and he spake of him" [*i. e.,* Christ] — refers to Is. 6 : 1 —"In the year that King Uzziah died I saw the Lord sitting upon a throne." So in Eph. 4 : 7, 8 —"measure of the gift of Christ . . . . led captivity captive "—is an application to Christ of what is said of Jehovah in Ps. 68 : 18. In 1 Pet. 3 : 15, moreover, we read, with all the great uncials, several of the Fathers, and all the best versions: "sanctify in your hearts Christ as Lord "; here the apostle borrows his language from Is. 8 : 13, where we read : "Jehovah of hosts, him shall ye sanctify." When we remember that, with the Jews, God's covenant-title was so sacred that for the Kethib (= "writtten ") *Jehovah* there was always substituted the Keri (= "read "—imperative) *Adonai,* in order to avoid pronunciation of the great Name, it seems the more remarkable that the Greek equivalent of ' Jehovah' should have been so constantly used of Christ. *Cf.* Rom. 10 : 9 —"confess . . . . Jesus as Lord "; 1 Cor. 12 : 3 —"no man can say, Jesus is Lord, but in the Holy Spirit." We must remember also the indignation of the Jews at Christ's assertion of his equality and oneness with the Father. Compare Goethe's, " Wer darf ihn nennen ? " with Carlyle's, " the awful Unnameable of this Universe." The Jews, it has been said, have always vibrated between monotheism and moneytheism. Yet James, the strongest of Hebrews, in his Epistle uses the word ' Lord , freely and alternately of God the Father and of Christ the Son. This would have been impossible if James had not believed in the community of essence between the Son and the Father.

It is interesting to note that 1 Maccabees does not once use the word Θεός, or κύριος, or any other direct designation of God unless it be οὐρανός (*cf.* "swear . . . . by the heaven' — Mat. 5 : 34). So the book of Esther contains no mention of the name of God, though the apocryphal additions to Esther, which are found only in Greek, contain the name of God in the first verse, and mention it in all eight times. See Bissell, Apocrypha, in Lange's Commentary ; Liddon, Our Lord's Divinity, 93 ; Max Müller on Semitic Monotheism, in Chips from a German Workshop, 1 : 337.

(*c*) He possesses the attributes of God.

Among these are life, self-existence, immutability, truth, love, holiness, eternity, omnipresence, omniscience, omnipotence. All these attributes are ascribed to Christ in connections which show that the terms are used in no secondary sense, nor in any sense predicable of a creature.

Life : John 1 : 4 — " In him was life "; 14 : 6 —"I am . . . . the life." *Self-existence :* John 5 : 26 —"have life in himself "; Heb. 7 : 16 —"power of an endless life." *Immutability :* Heb. 13 : 8 —"Jesus Christ is the same yesterday and to-day, yea and forever." *Truth :* John 14 : 6 —"I am . . . . the truth "; Rev. 3 : 7 —"he that is true." *Love :* 1 John 3 : 16 —"Hereby know we love " (τὴν ἀγάπην = the personal Love, as the personal Truth) " because he laid down his life for us." *Holiness :* Luke 1 : 35 —"that which is to be born shall be called holy, the Son of God "; John 6 : 69 —"thou art the Holy One of God "; Heb. 7 : 26 —"holy, guileless, undefiled, separated from sinners."

Eternity : John 1 : 1 —"In the beginning was the Word." Godet says ἐν ἀρχῇ = not 'in eternity,' but ' in the beginning of the creation '; the eternity of the Word being an inference from the ἦν — the Word *was,* when the world was *created : cf.* Gen. 1 : 1 — " In the beginning God created." But Meyer says, ἐν ἀρχῇ here rises above the historical conception of "in the beginning" in Genesis (which includes the beginning of time itself) to the absolute conception of anteriority to time ; the creation is something subsequent. He finds a parallel in Prov. 8 : 23 —ἐν ἀρχῇ πρὸ τοῦ τὴν γῆν ποιῆσαι. The interpretation ' in the beginning of the gospel ' is entirely unexegetical ; so Meyer. So John 17 : 5 —"glory which I had with thee before the world was "; Eph. 1 : 4 —"chose us in him before the foundation of the world." Dorner also says that ἐν ἀρχῇ in John 1 : 1 is not 'the beginning of the world,' but designates the point back cf which it is impossible to go, *i. e.*, eternity ; the world is first spoken of in verse 3. John 8 : 58 —" Before Abraham was born, I am " ; *cf.* 1 : 15 ; Col. 1 : 17 —" he is before all things " ; Heb. 1 : 11 — the heavens " shall perish ; but thou continuest " ; Rev. 21 : 6 —" I am the Alpha and the Omega, the beginning and the end." *Omnipresence :* Mat. 28 : 20 —" I am with you always " ; Eph. 1 : 23 —" the fulness of him that filleth all in all." *Omniscience :* Mat. 9 : 4 —" Jesus knowing their thoughts " ; John 2 : 24, 25 —" knew all men . . . . knew what was in man " ; 16 : 30 —"knowest all things " ; Acts 1 : 24 —"Thou, Lord, who knowest the hearts of all men "— a prayer offered before the day of Pentecost and showing the attitude of the disciples toward their Master ; 1 Cor. 4 : 5 — " until the Lord come, who will both bring to light the hidden th.ngs of darkness, and make manifest the counsels of the hearts " ; Col. 2 : 3 —" in whom are all the treasures of wisdom and knowledge hidden." *Omnipotence :* Mat. 27 : 18 —" All authority hath been given unto me in heaven and on earth " ; Rev. 1 : 8 —" the Lord God, which is and which was and which is to come, the Almighty."

Beyschlag, N. T. Theology, 1 : 249–260, holds that Jesus' preëxistence is simply the concrete form given to an ideal conception. Jesus traces himself back, as everything else holy and divine was traced back in the conceptions of his time, to a heavenly original in which it preëxisted before its earthly appearance ; *e. g.* : the tabernacle, in Heb. 8 : 5 ; Jerusalem, in Gal. 4 : 25 and Rev. 21 : 10 ; the kingdom of God, in Mat. 13 : 24 ; much more the Messiah, in John 6 : 62 —" ascending where he was before " ; 8 : 58 — " Before Abraham was born, I am " ; 17 : 4, 5 — " glory which I had with thee before the world was " 17 : 24 — " thou lovedst me before the foundation of the world." This view that Jesus existed before creation only ideally in the divine mind, means simply that God foreknew him and his coming. The view is refuted by the multiplied intimations of a personal, in distinction from an ideal, preëxistence.

Lowrie, Doctrine of St. John, 115 — " The words ' In the beginning ' (John 1 : 1) suggest that the author is about to write a second book of Genesis, an account of a new creation." As creation presupposes a Creator, the preëxistence of the personal Word is assigned as the explanation of the being of the universe. The ἦν indicates absolute existence, which is a loftier idea than that of mere preëxistence, although it includes this. While John the Baptist and Abraham are said to have arisen, appeared, come into being, it is said that the Logos *was*, and that the Logos was *God*. This implies coëternity with the Father. But, if the view we are combating were correct, John the Baptist and Abraham preëxisted, equally with Christ. This is certainly not the meaning of Jesus in John 8 · 58 — " Before Abraham was born, I am" ; *cf.* Col. 1 : 17 — " he *is* before all things " — " αὐτός emphasizes the personality, while ἔστιν declares that the preëxistence is absolute existence" (Lightfoot) ; John 1 : 15 — " He that cometh after me is become before me : for he was before me " = not that Jesus was *born* earlier than John the Baptist, for he was born six months later, but that he *existed* earlier. He stands before John in rank, because he existed long before John in time ; 6 : 62 — " the Son of man ascending where he was before " ; 16 : 28 — " I came out from the Father, and am come into the world." So Is. 9 : 6, 7, calls Christ " Everlasting Father " = eternity is an attribute of the Messiah. T. W. Chambers, in Jour. Soc. Bib. Exegesis, 1881 : 169–171 — " Christ is the Everlasting One, ' whose goings forth have been from of old, even from the days of eternity ' (Micah 5 : 2). ' Of the increase of his government . . . . . there shall be no end,' just because of his existence there has been no beginning."

(*d*) The works of God are ascribed to him.

We do not here speak of miracles, which may be wrought by communicated power, but of such works as the creation of the world, the upholding of all things, the final raising of the dead, and the judging of all men. Power to perform these works cannot be delegated, for they are characteristic of omnipotence.

Creation : John 1 : 3 —" All things were made through him " ; 1 Cor. 8 : 6 —" one Lord, Jesus Christ, through whom are all things " ; Col. 1 . 16 —" all things have been created through him, and unto him " ; Heb. 1 : 10 — " Thou, Lord, in the beginning didst lay the foundation of the earth, And the heavens are the works of thy hands " ; 3 : 3, 4 — " he that built all things is God " = Christ, the builder of the house of Israel,¯is the God who made all things ; Rev. 3 : 14 — " the beginning of the creation of God " (*cf.* Plato : " Mind is the ἀρχή of motion "). *Upholding :* Col. 1 : 17 — " in him all things consist " (marg. " hold together ") ; Heb. 1 : 3 — " upholding all things by the word of his power." *Raising the dead and judging the world :* John 5 : 27–29 — " authority to execute judgment . . . . all that are in the tombs shall hear his voice, and shall come forth " ; Mat. 25 : 3i, 32 — " sit on the throne of his glory ; and before him shall be gathered all the nations." If our argument were addressed wholly to believers, we might also urge Christ's work in the world as Revealer of God and Redeemer from sin, as a proof of his deity. On the works of Christ, see Liddon, Our Lord's Divinity. 153 ; *ver contra*, see Examination of Liddon's Bampton Lectures. 72.

Statements of Christ's creative and of his upholding activity are combined in John 1 : 3, 4 — Πάντα δι' αὐτοῦ ἐγένετο, καὶ χωρὶς αὐτοῦ ἐγένετο οὐδὲ ἕν.   ὃ γέγονεν ἐν αὐτῷ ζωὴ ἦν — "All things were made through him ; and without him was not anything made. That which hath been made was life in him " (marg.). Westcott : " It would be difficult to find a more complete consent of ancient authorities in favor of any reading than that which supports this punctuation." Westcott therefore adopts it. The passage shows that the universe 1. exists within the bounds of Christ's being ; 2. is not dead, but living ; 3. derives its life from him ; see Inge, Christian Mysticism, 46. Creation requires the divine presence, as well as the divine agency. God creates through Christ. All things were made, not ὑπὸ αὐτοῦ — " by him," but δι' αὐτοῦ — " through him." Christian believers " Behind creation's throbbing screen Catch movements of the great Unseen."

Van Oosterzee, Christian Dogmatics, lv, lvi — " That which many a philosopher dimly conjectured, namely, that God did not produce the world in an absolute, immediate manner, but in some way or other, mediately, here presents itself to us with the lustre of revelation, and exalts so much the more the claim of the Son of God to our deep and reverential homage." Would that such scientific men as Tyndall and Huxley might see Christ in nature, and, doing his will, might learn of the doctrine and be led to the Father ! The humblest Christian who sees Christ's hand in the physical universe and in human history knows more of the secret of the universe than all the mere scientists put together.

Col. 1 : 17 — " In him all things consist," or " hold together," means nothing less than that Christ is the principle of cohesion in the universe, making it a cosmos instead of a chaos. Tyndall said that the attraction of the sun upon the earth was as inconceivable as if a horse should draw a cart without traces. Sir Isaac Newton : " Gravitation must be caused by an agent acting constantly according to certain laws." Lightfoot : " Gravitation is an expression of the mind of Christ." Evolution also is a method of his operation. The laws of nature are the habits of Christ, and nature itself is but his steady and constant will. He binds together man and nature in one organic whole, so that we can speak of a ' universe.' Without him there would be no intellectual bond, no uniformity of law, no unity of truth. He is the principle of induction, that enables us to argue from one thing to another. The medium of interaction between things is also the medium of intercommunication between minds. It is fitting that he who draws and holds together the physical and intellectual, should also draw and hold together the moral universe, drawing all men to himself (John 12 : 32) and so to God, and reconciling all things in heaven and earth (Col. 1 : 20). In Christ " the law appears, Drawn out in living characters," because he is the ground and source of all law, both in nature and in humanity. See A. H. Strong, Christ in Creation, 6-12.

(e) He receives honor and worship due only to God.

In addition to the address of Thomas, in John 20 : 28, which we have already cited among the proofs that Jesus is expressly called God, and in which divine honor is paid to him, we may refer to the prayer and worship offered by the apostolic and post-apostolic church.

John 5 : 23 — " that all may honor the Son, even as they honor the Father " ; 14 : 14 — " If ye shall ask me [so א B and Tisch. 8th ed.] anything in my name, that will I do " ; Acts 7 : 59 — "Stephen, calling upon the Lord, and saying, Lord Jesus, receive my spirit " (cf. Luke 23 : 46 — Jesus' words : " Father, into thy hands I commend my spirit ") ; Rom. 10 : 9 — " confess with thy mouth Jesus as Lord " ; 13 — " whosoever shall call upon the name of the Lord shall be saved " (cf. Gen. 4 : 26 — " Then began men to call upon the name of Jehovah ") ; 1 Cor. 11 : 24, 25 — " this do in remembrance of me " = worship of Christ ; Heb. 1 : 6 — " let all the angels of God worship him " ; Phil. 2 : 10, 11 — " in the name of Jesus every knee should bow . . . . every tongue should confess that Jesus Christ is Lord " ; Rev. 5 : 12-14 — " Worthy is the Lamb that hath been slain to receive the power . . . . " ; 2 Pet. 3 : 18 — " Lord and Savior Jesus Christ. To him be the glory " ; 2 Tim. 4 : 18 and Heb. 13 : 21 — " to whom be the glory for ever and ever " — these ascriptions of eternal glory to Christ imply his deity. See also 1 Pet. 3 : 15 — " Sanctify in your hearts Christ as Lord," and Eph. 5 : 21 — " subjecting yourselves one to another in the fear of Christ." Here is enjoined an attitude of mind towards Christ which would be idolatrous if Christ were not God. See Liddon, Our Lord's Divinity, 266, 366.

Foster, Christian Life and Theology, 154 — " In the eucharistic liturgy of the ' Teaching ' we read : ' Hosanna to the God of David ' ; Ignatius styles him repeatedly God ' begotten and unbegotten, come in the flesh ' ; speaking once of ' the blood of God ', in evident allusion to Acts 20 : 28 ; the epistle to Diognetus takes up the Pauline words and calls him the ' architect and world-builder by whom [God] created the heavens '. and names him God (chap. vii); Hermas speaks of him as 'the holy preëxistent Spirit, that created every creature', which style of expression is followed by Justin, who calls him God, as also all the later great writers. In the second epistle of Clement (130–160, Harnack), we read : ' Brethren, it is fitting that you should think of Jesus Christ as of God — as the Judge of the living and the dead.' And Ignatius describes him as ' begotten and unbegotten, passible and impassible, . . . who was before the eternities with the Father.' "

These testimonies only give evidence that the Church Fathers saw in Scripture divine honor ascribed to Christ. They were but the precursors of a host of later interpreters. In a lull of the awful massacre of Armenian Christians at Sassouan, one of the Kurdish savages was heard to ask : " Who was that ' Lord Jesus ' that they were calling to ? " In their death agonies, the Christians, like Stephen of old, called upon the name of the Lord. Robert Browning quoted, in a letter to a lady in her last illness, the words of Charles Lamb, when " in a gay fancy with some friends as to how he and they would feel if the greatest of the dead were to appear suddenly in flesh and blood once more — on the first suggestion, ' And if Christ entered this room ? ' changed his tone at once and stuttered out as his manner was when moved : ' You see — if Shakespere entered, we should all rise ; if He appeared, we must kneel.' " On prayer to Jesus, see Liddon, Bampton Lectures, note F ; Bernard, in Hastings' Bib. Dict., 4 : 44 ; Zahn, Skizzen aus dem Leben der alten Kirche, 9, 288.

(*f*) His name is associated with that of God upon a footing of equality.

We do not here allude to 1 John 5 : 7 (the three heavenly witnesses), for the latter part of this verse is unquestionably spurious ; but to the formula of baptism, to the apostolic benedictions, and to those passages in which eternal life is said to be dependent equally upon Christ and upon God, or in which spiritual gifts are attributed to Christ equally with the Father.

The formula of baptism : Mat. 28 : 19 — " baptizing them into the name of the Father and of the Son and of the Holy Spirit " ; *cf.* Acts 2 : 38 —" be baptized every one of you in the name of Jesus Christ " ; Rom. 6 : 3 —" baptized into Christ Jesus." " In the common baptismal formula the Son and the Spirit are coördinated with the Father, and εἰς ὄνομα has religious significance." It would be both absurd and profane to speak of baptizing into the name of the Father and of Moses.

The apostolic benedictions : 1 Cor. 1 : 3 — " Grace to you and peace from God our Father and the Lord Jesus Christ " ; 2 Cor. 13 : 14 —" The grace of the Lord Jesus Christ, and the love of God, and the communion of the Holy Spirit, be with you all." " In the benedictions grace is something divine, and Christ has power to impart it. But why do we find ' God,' instead of simply ' the Father,' as in the baptismal formula ? Because it is only the Father who does not become man or have a historical existence. Elsewhere he is specially called ' God the Father,' to distinguish him from God the Son and God the Holy Spirit (Gal. 1 : 3 ; Eph. 3 : 14 ; 6 : 23)."

Other passages : John 5 : 23 -- " that all may honor the Son, even as they honor the Father " ; John 14 : 1 — " believe in God, believe also in me " — double imperative (so Westcott, Bible Com., *in loco*); 17 : 3 — " this is life eternal, that they should know thee the only true God, and him whom thou didst send, even Jesus Christ " ; Mat. 11 : 27 — " no one knoweth the Son, save the Father ; neither doth any know the Father, save the Son, and he to whomsoever the Son willeth to reveal him " ; 1 Cor. 12 : 4-6 —" the same Spirit . . . . the same Lord [Christ] . . . . the same God " [the Father] bestow spiritual gifts, *e. g.*, faith : Rom. 10 : 17 — " belief cometh of hearing, and hearing by the word of Christ " ; peace : Col. 3 : 15 —" let the peace of Christ rule in your hearts." 2 Thess. 2 : 16, 17 — " now our Lord Jesus Christ himself, and God our Father . . . . comfort your hearts " — two names with a verb in the singular intimate the oneness of the Father and the Son (Lillie). Eph. 6 : 5 — " kingdom of Christ and God " ; Col. 3 : 1 — " Christ . . . . seated on the right hand of God "= participation in the sovereignty of the universe, — the Eastern divan held not only the monarch but his son ; Rev. 20 : 6 — " priests of God and of Christ " ; 22 : 3 — " the throne of God and of the Lamb " ; 16 — " the root and the offspring of David "= both the Lord of David and his son. Hackett : " As the dying Savior said to the Father, ' Into thy hands I commend my spirit ' (Luke 23 : 46), so the dying Stephen said to the Savior, ' receive my spirit ' (Acts 7 : 59)."

(*g*) Equality with God is expressly claimed.

Here we may refer to Jesus' testimony to himself, already treated of among the proofs of the supernatural character of the Scripture teaching (see pages 189, 190). Equality with God is not only claimed for himself by Jesus, but it is claimed for him by his apostles.

John 5 : 18 — " called God his own Father, making himself equal with God " ; Phil. 2 : 6 —" who, existing in the form of God, counted not the being on an equality with God a thing to be grasped " = counted not his equality with God a thing to be forcibly retained. Christ made and left upon his contemporaries the impression that he claimed to be God. The New Testament has left, upon the great mass of those who have read it, the impression that Jesus Christ claims to be God. If he is not God, he is a deceiver or is self-deceived, and, in either case, *Christus, si non Deus, non bonus.* See Nicoll, Life of Jesus Christ, 187.

(*h*) Further proof of Christ's deity may be found in the application to him of the phrases : ' Son of God,' ' Image of God ' ; in the declarations of his oneness with God ; in the attribution to him of the fulness of the Godhead.

Mat. 26 : 63, 64 — "I adjure thee by the living God, that thou tell us whether thou art the Christ, the Son of God. Jesus saith unto him, Thou hast said " — it is for this testimony that Christ dies. Col. 1 : 15 — "the image of the invisible God " ; Heb. 1 : 3 — "the effulgence of his [the Father's] glory, and the very image of his substance "; John 10 : 30 —"I and the Father are one " ; 14 : 9 —"he that hath seen me hath seen the Father "; 17 : 11, 22 — "that they may be one, even as we are " — ἕν, not εἷς ; *unum,* not *unus ;* one substance, not one person. " *Unum* is antidote to the Arian, *sumus* to the Sabellian heresy." Col. 2 : 9 — "in him dwelleth all the fulness of the Godhead bodily "; *cf.* 1 : 19 — "for it was the pleasure of the Father that in him should all the fulness dwell ;" or (marg.) "for the whole fulness of God was pleased to dwell in him." John 16 : 15 — "all things whatsoever the Father hath are mine " ; 17 : 10 — "all things that are mine are thine, and thine are mine."

Meyer on John 10 : 30 — "I and the Father are one " — " Here the Arian understanding of a mere ethical harmony as taught in the words 'are one ' is unsatisfactory, because irrelevant to the exercise of power. Oneness of essence, though not contained in the words themselves, is, by the necessities of the argument, presupposed in them." Dalman, The Words of Jesus : " Nowhere do we find that Jesus called himself the Son of God in such a sense as to suggest a merely religious and ethical relation to God — a relation which others also possessed and which they were capable of attaining or were destined to acquire." We may add that while in the lower sense there are many ' sons of God,' there is but one ' only begotten Son.'

(*i*) These proofs of Christ's deity from the New Testament are corroborated by Christian experience.

Christian experience recognizes Christ as an absolutely perfect Savior, perfectly revealing the Godhead and worthy of unlimited worship and adoration ; that is, it practically recognizes him as Deity. But Christian experience also recognizes that through Christ it has introduction and reconciliation to God as one distinct from Jesus Christ, as one who was alienated from the soul by its sin, but who is now reconciled through Jesus's death. In other words, while recognizing Jesus as God, we are also compelled to recognize a distinction between the Father and the Son through whom we come to the Father.

Although this experience cannot be regarded as an independent witness to Jesus' claims, since it only tests the truth already made known in the Bible, still the irresistible impulse of every person whom Christ has saved to lift his Redeemer to the highest place, and bow before him in the lowliest worship, is strong evidence that only that interpretation of Scripture can be true which recognizes Christ's absolute Godhead. It is the church's consciousness of her Lord's divinity, indeed, and not mere speculation upon the relations of Father, Son, and Holy Ghost, that has compelled the formulation of the Scripture doctrine of the Trinity.

In the letter of Pliny to Trajan, it is said of the early Christians " quod essent soliti carmen Christo quasi Deo dicere invicem." The prayers and hymns of the church show what the church has believed Scripture to teach. Dwight Moody is said to have received his first conviction of the truth of the gospel from hearing the concluding words of a prayer, " For Christ's sake, Amen," when awakened from physical slumber in Dr. Kirk's church, Boston. These words, wherever uttered, imply man's dependence and Christ's deity. See New Englander, 1878 : 432. In Eph. 4 : 32, the Revised Version substitutes "in Christ" for " for Christ's sake." The exact phrase "for Christ's sake" is not found in the N. T. in connection with prayer, although the O. T. phrase " for my name's sake " (Ps. 25 : 11) passes into the N. T. The phrase " in the name of Jesus" (Phil. 2 : 10); cf. Ps. 72 : 15 — " men shall pray for him continually " = the words of the hymn : " For him shall endless prayer be made, And endless blessings crown his head." All this is proof that the idea of prayer for Christ's sake is in Scripture, though the phrase is absent.

A caricature scratched on the wall of the Palatine palace in Rome, and dating back to the third century, represents a human figure with an ass's head, hanging upon a cross, while a man stands before it in the attitude of worship. Under the effigy is this ill-spelled inscription : " Alexamenos adores his God."

This appeal to the testimony of Christian consciousness was first made by Schleiermacher. William E. Gladstone: " All I write, and all I think, and all I hope, is based upon the divinity of our Lord, the one central hope of our poor, wayward race." E. G. Robinson : " When you preach salvation by faith in Christ, you preach the Trinity." W. G. T. Shedd : " The construction of the doctrine of the Trinity started, not from the consideration of the three persons, but from belief in the deity of one of them." On the worship of Christ in the authorized services of the Anglican church, see Stanley, Church and State, 333-335; Liddon, Divinity of our Lord, 514.

In contemplating passages apparently inconsistent with those now cited, in that they impute to Christ weakness and ignorance, limitation and subjection, we are to remember, first, that our Lord was truly man, as well as truly God, and that this ignorance and weakness may be predicated of him as the God-man in whom deity and humanity are united ; secondly, that the divine nature itself was in some way limited and humbled during our Savior's earthly life, and that these passages may describe him as he was in his estate of humiliation, rather than in his original and present glory ; and, thirdly, that there is an order of office and operation which is consistent with essential oneness and equality, but which permits the Father to be spoken of as first and the Son as second. These statements will be further elucidated in the treatment of the present doctrine and in subsequent examination of the doctrine of the Person of Christ.

There are certain things of which Christ was ignorant : Mark 13 : 32 — "of that day or that hour knoweth no one, not even the angels in heaven, neither the Son, but the Father." He was subject to physical fatigue : John 4 : 6 — "Jesus therefore, being wearied with his journey, sat thus by the well." There was a limitation connected with Christ's taking of human flesh : Phil. 2 : 7 — "emptied himself, taking the form of a servant, being made in the likeness of men" ; John 14 : 28 — "the Father is greater than I." There is a subjection, as respects order of office and operation, which is yet consistent with equality of essence and oneness with God ; 1 Cor. 15 : 28 — "then shall the Son also himself be subjected to him that did subject all things unto him, that God may be all in all." This must be interpreted consistently with John 17 : 5 — "glorify thou me with thine own self with the glory which I had with thee before the world was," and with Phil. 2 : 6, where this glory is described as being "the form of God" and "equalty with God."

Even in his humiliation, Christ was the Essential Truth, and ignorance in him never involved error or false teaching. Ignorance on his part might make his teaching at times incomplete, — it never in the smallest particular made his teaching false. Yet here we must distinguish between what he intended to teach and what was merely incidental to his teaching. When he said : Moses " wrote of me " (John 5 : 46) and " David in the Spirit called him Lord " (Mat. 22 : 43), if his purpose was to teach the authorship of the Pentateuch and of the 110th Psalm, we should regard his words as absolutely authoritative. But it is possible that he intended only to locate the passages referred to, and if so, his words cannot be used to exclude critical conclusions as to their authorship. Adamson, The Mind in Christ, 136 — " If he spoke of Moses or David, it was only to identify the passage. The authority of the earlier dispensation did not rest upon its record being due to Moses, nor did the appropriateness of the Psalm lie in its being uttered by David.

There is no evidence that the question of authorship ever came before him." Adamson rather more precariously suggests that " there may have been a lapse of memory in Jesus' mention of 'Zacharias, son of Barachiah ' (Mat. 23:35), since this was a matter of no spiritual import."

For assertions of Jesus' knowledge, see John 2 : 24, 25 — " he knew all men . . . he needed not that any one should bear witness concerning man ; for he himself knew what was in man ; " 6 : 64 — " Jesus knew from the beginning who they were that believed not, and who it was that should betray him " ; 12 : 33 — " this he said, signifying by what manner of death he should die " ; 21 : 19 — " Now this he spake, signifying by what manner of death he [Peter] should glorify God " ; 13 : 1 — " knowing that his hour was come that he should depart " ; Mat. 25 : 31 — " when the Son of man shall come in his glory, and all the angels with him, then shall he sit on the throne of his glory " = he knew that he was to act as final judge of the human race. Other instances are mentioned by Adamson, The Mind in Christ, 24-49: 1. Jesus' knowledge of Peter (John 1 : 42) ; 2. his finding Philip (1 : 43) ; 3. his recognition of Nathanael (1 : 47-50) ; 4. of the woman of Samaria (4 : 17-19, 39) ; 5. miraculous draughts of fishes (Luke 5 : 6-9; John 21 : 6) ; 6. death of Lazarus (John 11 : 14) ; 7. the ass's colt (Mat. 21 : 2) ; 8. of the upper room (Mark 14 : 15) ; 9. of Peter's denial (Mat. 26 : 34) ; 10. of the manner of his own death (John 12 · 33 ; 18 : 32) ; 11. of the manner of Peter's death (John 21 : 19) ; 12. of the fall of Jerusalem (Mat. 24 : 2).

On the other hand there are assertions and implications of Jesus' ignorance : he did not know the day of the end (Mark 13 : 32), though even here he intimates his superiority to angels; 5 : 30-34 — "Who touched my garments ? " though even here power had gone forth from him to heal; John 11 : 34 — " Where have ye laid him ? " though here he is about to raise Lazarus from the dead ; Mark 11 : 13 — "seeing a fig tree afar off having leaves, he came, if haply he might find anything thereon " = he did not know that it had no fruit, yet he had power to curse it. With these evidences of the limitations of Jesus' knowledge, we must assent to the judgment of Bacon, Genesis of Genesis, 33 — " We must decline to stake the authority of Jesus on a question of literary criticism "; and of Gore, Incarnation, 195 — " That the use by our Lord of such a phrase as ' Moses wrote of me' binds us to the Mosaic authorship of the Pentateuch as a whole, I do not think we need to yield." See our section on The Person of Christ; also Rush Rhees, Life of Jesus, 243, 244. Per contra, see Swayne, Our Lord's Knowledge as Man ; and Crooker, The New Bible, who very unwisely claims that belief in a Kenosis involves the surrender of Christ's authority and atonement.

It is inconceivable that any mere creature should say, " God is greater than I am." Or should be spoken of as ultimately and in a mysterious way becoming " subject to God." In his state of humiliation Christ was subject to the Spirit (Acts 1 : 2 — " after that he had given commandment through the Holy Spirit "; 10 : 38 — "God anointed him with the Holy Spirit . . . . for God was with him " ; Heb. 9 : 14 — " through the eternal Spirit offered himself without blemish unto God "), but in his state of exaltation Christ is Lord of the Spirit (κυρίου πνεύματος — 2 Cor. 3 : 18 — Meyer), giving the Spirit and working through the Spirit. Heb. 2 : 7, marg.—"Thou madest him for a little while lower than the angels." On the whole subject, see Shedd, Hist. Doctrine, 262, 351; Thomasius, Christi Person und Werk, 1 : 61-64; Liddon, Our Lord's Divinity, 127, 207, 458; per contra, see Examination of Liddon, 252, 294; Professors of Andover Seminary, Divinity of Christ.

C. The Holy Spirit is recognized as God.

(a) He is spoken of as God ; (b) the attributes of God are ascribed to him, such as life, truth, love, holiness, eternity, omnipresence, omniscience, omnipotence ; (c) he does the works of God, such as creation, regeneration, resurrection ; (d) he receives honor due only to God ; (e) he is associated with God on a footing of equality, both in the formula of baptism and in the apostolic benedictions.

(a) Spoken of as God. Acts 5 : 3, 4 — "lie to the Holy Spirit . . . . not lied unto man, but unto God" ; 1 Cor. 3 : 16 — "ye are a temple of God . . . . the Spirit of God dwelleth in you " ; 6 : 19 — "your body is a temple of the Holy Spirit " ; 12 : 4-6 "same Spirit . . . . same Lord . . . . same God, who worketh all things in all " — " The divine Trinity is here indicated in an ascending climax, in such a way that we pass from the Spirit who bestows the gifts to the Lord [Christ] who is served by means of them, and finally to God, who as the absolute first cause and possessor of all Christian powers works the entire sum of all charismatic gifts in all who are gifted " (Meyer in loco).

(b) *Attributes of God.* Life: Rom. 8 : 2 — "Spirit of life." Truth : John 16 : 13 "Spirit of truth." Love : Rom. 15 : 30 — "love of the Spirit." Holiness : Eph. 4 : 30 — "the Holy Spirit of God." Eternity : Heb. 9 : 14 — "the eternal Spirit." Omnipresence : Ps. 139 : 7 — "Whither shall I go from thy Spirit ?" Omniscience : 1 Cor. 12 : 11 — "all these [including gifts of healings and miracles] worketh the one and the same Spirit, dividing to each one severally even as he will."

(c) *Works of God.* Creation : Gen. 1 : 2, marg.—"Spirit of God was brooding upon the face of the waters." Casting out of demons : Mat. 12 : 28 — "But if I by the Spirit of God cast out demons." Conviction of sin : John 16 : 8 — "convict the world in respect of sin." Regeneration : John 3 : 8 — "born of the Spirit" ; Tit. 3 . 5 — "renewing of the Holy Spirit." Resurrection : Rom. 8 : 11 — "give life also to your mortal bodies through his Spirit" ; 1 Cor. 15 : 45 — "The last Adam became a life-giving spirit."

(d) *Honor due to God.* 1 Cor. 3 : 16 — "ye are a temple of God . . . . the Spirit of God dwelleth in you"— he who inhabits the temple is the object of worship there. See also the next item.

(e) *Associated with God.* Formula of baptism : Mat. 28 : 19 — "baptizing them into the name of the Father and of the Son and of the Holy Spirit." If the baptismal formula is worship, then we have here worship paid to the Spirit. Apostolic benedictions : 2 Cor. 13 : 14 — "The grace of the Lord Jesus Christ, and the love of God, and the communion of the Holy Spirit, be with you all." If the apostolic benedictions are prayers, then we have here a prayer to the Spirit. 1 Pet. 1 : 2 — "foreknowledge of God the Father . . . sanctification of the Spirit . . . sprinkling of the blood of Jesus Christ."

On Heb. 9 : 14, Kendrick, Com. *in loco,* interprets : "Offers himself by virtue of an eternal spirit which dwells within him and imparts to his sacrifice a spiritual and an eternal efficacy. The 'spirit' here spoken of was not, then, the ' Holy Spirit' ; it was not his purely divine nature ; it was that blending of his divine nature with his human personality which forms the mystery of his being, that 'spirit of holiness' by virtue of which he was declared ' the Son of God with power,' on account of his resurrection from the dead." Hovey adds a note to Kendrick's Commentary, *in loco,* as follows : " This adjective 'eternal' naturally suggests that the word 'Spirit' refers to the higher and divine nature of Christ. His truly human nature, on its spiritual side, was indeed eternal as to the future, but so also is the spirit of every man. The unique and superlative value of Christ's self-sacrifice seems to have been due to the impulse of the divine side of his nature." The phrase 'eternal spirit' would then mean his divinity. To both these interpretations we prefer that which makes the passage refer to the Holy Spirit, and we cite in support of this view Acts 1 : 2 — "he had given commandment through the Holy Spirit unto the apostles" ; 10 : 38 — "God anointed him with the Holy Spirit." On 1 Cor. 2 : 10, Mason, Faith of the Gospel, 63, remarks : " The Spirit of God finds nothing even in God which baffles his scrutiny. His 'search' is not a seeking for knowledge yet beyond him. . . . Nothing but God could search the depths of God."

As spirit is nothing less than the inmost principle of life, and the spirit of man is man himself, so the spirit of God must be God (see 1 Cor. 2 : 11 — Meyer). Christian experience, moreover, expressed as it is in the prayers and hymns of the church, furnishes an argument for the deity of the Holy Spirit similar to that for the deity of Jesus Christ. When our eyes are opened to see Christ as a Savior, we are compelled to recognize the work in us of a divine Spirit who has taken of the things of Christ and has shown them to us ; and this divine Spirit we necessarily distinguish both from the Father and from the Son. Christian experience, however, is not an original and independent witness to the deity of the Holy Spirit : it simply shows what the church has held to be the natural and unforced interpretation of the Scriptures, and so confirms the Scripture argument already adduced.

The Holy Spirit is God himself personally present in the believer. E. G. Robinson : "If 'Spirit of God' no more implies deity than does 'angel of God,' why is not the Holy Spirit called simply the angel or messenger, of God ? " Walker, The Spirit and the Incarnation, 337 — "The Holy Spirit is God in his innermost being or essence, the principle of life of both the Father and the S on ; that in which God, both as Father and Son, does everything, and in which he comes to us and is in us increasingly through his manifestations. Through the working and indwelling of this Holy Spirit, God in his person of Son was fully incarnate in Christ." Gould, Am. Com. on 1 Cor. 2 : 11 — "For who among men knoweth the things of a man, save the spirit of the man, which is in him ? even so the things of

God none knoweth, save the Spirit of God" — " The analogy must not be pushed too far, as if the Spirit of God and God were coëxtensive terms, as the corresponding terms are, substantially, in man. The point of the analogy is evidently *self-knowledge*, and in both cases the contrast is between the spirit within and anything outside." Andrew Murray, Spirit of Christ, 140— " We must not expect always to feel the power of the Spirit when it works. Scripture links power and weakness in a wonderful way, not as succeeding each other but as existing together. 'I was with you in weakness . . . my preaching was in power' (1 Cor. 2 : 3); 'when I am weak then am I strong' (2 Cor. 12 : 10). The power is the power of God given to faith, and faith grows strong in the dark. . . . He who would command nature must first and most absolutely obey her. . . . We want to get possession of the Power, and use it. God wants the Power to get possession of us, and use us."

This proof of the deity of the Holy Spirit is not invalidated by the limitations of his work under the Old Testament dispensation. John 7 : 39 — " for the Holy Spirit was not yet " — means simply that the Holy Spirit could not fulfill his peculiar office as Revealer of Christ until the atoning work of Christ should be accomplished.

John 7 : 39 is to be interpreted in the light of other Scriptures which assert the agency of the Holy Spirit under the old dispensation (Ps. 51 : 11 — " take not thy holy Spirit from me ") and which describe his peculiar office under the new dispensation (John 16 : 14, 15 — " he shall take of mine, and shall declare it unto you"). Limitation in the *manner* of the Spirit's work in the O. T. involved a limitation in the *extent* and *power* of it also. Pentecost was the flowing forth of a tide of spiritual influence which had hitherto been dammed up. Henceforth the Holy Spirit was the Spirit of Jesus Christ, taking of the things of Christ and showing them, applying his finished work to human hearts, and rendering the hitherto localized Savior omnipresent with his scattered followers to the end of time.

Under the conditions of his humiliation, Christ was a servant. All authority in heaven and earth was given him only after his resurrection. Hence he could not send the Holy Spirit until he ascended. The mother can show off her son only when he is fully grown. The Holy Spirit could reveal Christ only when there was a complete Christ to reveal. The Holy Spirit could fully sanctify, only after the example and motive of holiness were furnished in Christ's life and death. Archer Butler: "The divine Artist could not fitly descend to make the copy, before the original had been provided."

And yet the Holy Spirit is " the eternal Spirit " (Heb. 9 : 14), and he not only existed, but also wrought, in Old Testament times. 2 Pet. 1 : 21 — " men spake from God, being moved by the Holy Spirit " —seems to fix the meaning of the phrase " the Holy Spirit," where it appears in the O. T. Before Christ " the Holy Spirit was not yet " (John 7 : 39), just as before Edison electricity was not yet. There was just as much electricity in the world before Edison as there is now. Edison has only taught us its existence and how to use it. Still we can say that, before Edison, electricity, as a means of lighting, warming and transporting people, had no existence. So until Pentecost, the Holy Spirit, as the revealer of Christ, " was not yet.' Augustine calls Pentecost the *dies natalis*, or birthday, of the Holy Spirit ; and for the same reason that we call the day when Mary brought forth her firstborn son the birthday of Jesus Christ, though before Abraham was born, Christ was. The Holy Spirit had been engaged in the creation, and had inspired the prophets, but *officially*, as Mediator between men and Christ, " the Holy Spirit was not yet." He could not show the things of Christ until the things of Christ were ready to be shown. See Gordon, Ministry of the Spirit, 19-25; Prof. J. S. Gubelmann, Person and Work of the Holy Spirit in O. T. Times. For proofs of the deity of the Holy Spirit, see Walker, Doctrine of the Holy Spirit ; Hare, Mission of the Comforter ; Parker, The Paraclete ; Cardinal Manning, Temporal Mission of the Holy Ghost ; Dick, Lectures on Theology, 1 : 341-350. Further references will be given in connection with the proof of the Holy Spirit's personality.

2. *Intimations of the Old Testament.*

The passages which seem to show that even in the Old Testament there are three who are implicitly recognized as God may be classed under four heads :

A. Passages which seem to teach plurality of some sort in the Godhead.

(a) The plural noun אֱלֹהִים is employed, and that with a plural verb — a use remarkable, when we consider that the singular אֵל was also in existence ; (b) God uses plural pronouns in speaking of himself ; (c) Jehovah distinguishes himself from Jehovah ; (d) a Son is ascribed to Jehovah ; (e) the Spirit of God is distinguished from God ; (f) there are a threefold ascription and a threefold benediction.

(a) Gen. 20 : 13 — "God caused [plural] me to wander from my father's house " ; 35 : 7 —" built there an altar, and called the place El-Beth-el ; because there God was revealed [plural] unto him." (b) Gen. 1 : 26 — " Let us make man in our image, after our likeness " ; 3 : 22 — "Behold, the man is become as one of us " ; 11 : 7 — "Come, let us go down, and there confound their language " ; Is. 6 : 8 —" Whom shall I send, and who will go for us ?" (c) Gen. 19 : 24 — "Then Jehovah rained upon Sodom and upon Gomorrah brimstone and fire from Jehovah out of heaven " ; Hos. 1 : 7 — "I will have mercy upon the house of Judah, and will save them by Jehovah, their God" ; cf. 2 Tim. 1 : 18 — "The Lord grant unto him to find mercy of the Lord in that day " — though Ellicott here decides adversely to the Trinitarian reference. (d) Ps. 2 : 7 — "Thou art my son ; this day have I begotten thee " ; Prov. 30 : 4 — " Who hath established all the ends of the earth ? What is his name, and what is his son's name, if thou knowest ?" (e) Gen. 1 : 1 and 2, marg. — "God created . . . . the Spirit of God was brooding " ; Ps. 33 : 6 — " By the word of Jehovah were the heavens made, And all the host of them by the breath [spirit] of his mouth " ; Is. 48 : 16 — "the Lord Jehovah hath sent me, and his Spirit " ; 63 : 7, 10 —" loving kindnesses of Jehovah . . . . grieved his holy Spirit." (f) Is. 6 : 3 — the trisagion : "Holy, holy, holy "; Num. 6 : 24–26 — " Jehovah bless thee, and keep thee : Jehovah make his face to shine upon thee, and be gracious unto thee : Jehovah lift up his countenance upon thee, and give thee peace."

It has been suggested that as Baal was worshiped in different places and under different names, as Baal-Berith, Baal-hanan, Baal-peor, Baal-zeebub, and his priests could call upon any one of these as possessing certain personified attributes of Baal, while yet the whole was called by the plural term ' Baalim,' and Elijah could say : " Call ye upon your Gods," so ' Elohim' may be the collective designation of the God who was worshiped in different localities ; see Robertson Smith, Old Testament in the Jewish Church, 229. But this ignores the fact that Baal is always addressed in the singular, never in the plural, while the plural ' Elohim ' is the term commonly used in addresses to God. This seems to show that ' Baalim' is a collective term, while ' Elohim ' is not. So when Ewald, Lehre von Gott, 2 : 333, distinguishes five names of God, corresponding to five great periods of the history of Israel, viz., the "Almighty " of the Patriarchs, the " Jehovah " of the Covenant, the " God of Hosts " of the Monarchy, the " Holy One " of the Deuteronomist and the later prophetic age, and the " Our Lord " of Judaism, he ignores the fact that these designations are none of them confined to the times to which they are attributed, though they may have been predominantly used in those times.

The fact that אֱלֹהִים is sometimes used in a narrower sense, as applicable to the Son (Ps. 45 : 6 ; cf. Heb. 1 : 8), need not prevent us from believing that the term was originally chosen as containing an allusion to a certain plurality in the divine nature. Nor is it sufficient to call this plural a simple pluralis majestaticus; since it is easier to derive this common figure from divine usage than to derive the divine usage from this common figure — especially when we consider the constant tendency of Israel to polytheism.

Ps. 45 : 6 ; cf. Heb. 1 : 8 — " of the Son he saith, Thy throne, O God, is for ever and ever." Here it is God who calls Christ " God " or " Elohim." The term Elohim has here acquired the significance of a singular. It was once thought that the royal style of speech was a custom of a later date than the time of Moses. Pharaoh does not use it. In Gen. 41 : 41-44, he says : " I have set thee over all the land of Egypt. . . . I am Pharaoh." But later investigations seem to prove that the plural for God was used by the Canaanites before the Hebrew occupation. The one Pharaoh is called ' my gods ' or ' my god,' indifferently. The word ' master ' is usually found in the plural in the O. T. (cf. Gen. 24 : 9, 51 ; 39 : 19 ; 40 : 1). The plural gives utterance to the sense of awe. It signifies magnitude or completeness. (See The Bible Student, Aug. 1900 : 67.)

This ancient Hebrew application of the plural to God is often explained as a mere plural of dignity, = one who combines in himself many reasons for adoration (אֱלֹהִים from אָלַהּ to fear, to adore). Oehler, O. T. Theology, 1 : 128-130, calls it a " quantitative plural," signifying unlimited greatness. The Hebrews had many plural forms, where we should use the singular, as 'heavens' instead of 'heaven,' 'waters' instead of 'water.' We too speak of ' news,' ' wages,' and say ' you' instead of 'thou'; see F. W. Robertson, on Genesis, 12. But the Church Fathers, such as Barnabas, Justin Martyr, Irenæus, Theophilus, Epiphanius, and Theodoret, saw in this plural an allusion to the Trinity, and we are inclined to follow them. When finite things were pluralized to express man's reverence, it would be far more natural to pluralize the name of God. And God's purpose in securing this pluralization may have been more far-reaching and intelligent than man's. The Holy Spirit who presided over the development of revelation may well have directed the use of the plural in general, and even the adoption of the plural name Elohim in particular, with a view to the future unfolding of truth with regard to the Trinity.

We therefore dissent from the view of Hill, Genetic Philosophy, 323, 330 — "The Hebrew religion, even much later than the time of Moses, as it existed in the popular mind, was, according to the prophetic writings, far removed from a real monotheism, and consisted in the wavering acceptance of the preëminence of a tribal God, with a strong inclination towards a general polytheism. It is impossible therefore to suppose that anything approaching the philosophical monotheism of modern theology could have been elaborated or even entertained by primitive man. . . . 'Thou shalt have no other gods before me ' (Ex. 20 : 3), the first precept of Hebrew monotheism, was not understood at first as a denial of the hereditary polytheistic faith, but merely as an exclusive claim to worship and obedience." E. G. Robinson says, in a similar strain, that "we can explain the idolatrous tendencies of the Jews only on the supposition that they had lurking notions that their God was a merely national god. Moses seems to have understood the doctrine of the divine unity, but the Jews did not."

To the views of both Hill and Robinson we reply that the primitive intuition of God is not that of many, but that of One. Paul tells us that polytheism is a later and retrogressive stage of development, due to man's sin (Rom. 1 : 19-23). We prefer the statement of McLaren : "The plural Elohim is not a survival from a polytheistic stage, but expresses the divine nature in the manifoldness of its fulnesses and perfections, rather than in the abstract unity of its being "—and, we may add, expresses the divine nature in its essential fulness, as a complex of personalities. See Conant, Gesenius' Hebrew Grammar, 198; Green, Hebrew Grammar, 306; Girdlestone, O. T. Synonyms, 38, 53; Alexander on Psalm 11 : 7; 29 : 1; 58 : 11.

B. Passages relating to the Angel of Jehovah.

(a) The angel of Jehovah identifies himself with Jehovah ; (b) he is identified with Jehovah by others ; (c) he accepts worship due only to God. Though the phrase 'angel of Jehovah' is sometimes used in the later Scriptures to denote a merely human messenger or created angel, it seems in the Old Testament, with hardly more than a single exception, to designate the pre-incarnate Logos, whose manifestations in angelic or human form foreshadowed his final coming in the flesh.

(a) Gen. 22 : 11, 16 — "the angel of Jehovah called unto him [Abraham, when about to sacrifice Isaac] . . . . By myself have I sworn, saith Jehovah "; 31 : 11, 13 — "the angel of God said unto me [Jacob] . . . . I am the God of Beth-el." (b) Gen. 16 : 9, 13 — "angel of Jehovah said unto her . . . . and she called the name of Jehovah that spake unto her, Thou art a God that seeth " ; 48 : 15, 16 — "the God who hath fed me . . . . the angel who hath redeemed me." (c) Ex. 3 : 2, 4, 5 — "the angel of Jehovah appeared unto him . . . . God called unto him out of the midst of the bush . . . . put off thy shoes from off thy feet "; Judges 13 : 20-22 — " angel of Jehovah ascended. . . . Manoah and his wife . . . . fell on their faces . . . . Manoah said . . . . We shall surely die, because we have seen God."

The " angel of the Lord " appears to be a human messenger in Haggai 1 : 13 —" Haggai, Jehovah's messenger "; a created angel in Mat. 1 : 20 — "an angel of the Lord [called Gabriel] appeared unto " Joseph ; in Acts 8 : 26 — "an angel of the Lord spake unto Philip "; and in 12 : 7 —"an angel of the Lord stood by him " (Peter). But commonly, in the O. T., the "angel of Jehovah" is a theophany, a self-manifestation of God. The only distinction is that between Jehovah in himself and Jehovah in manifestation. The appearances of "the angel of Jehovah" seem to be preliminary manifestations of the divine Logos, as in Gen. 18 : 2, 13 — "three men stood over against him [Abraham] . . . And Jehovah said unto Abraham"; Dan. 3 : 25, 28— "the aspect of the fourth is like a son of the gods. . . . Blessed be the God . . . . who hath sent his angel." The N. T. "angel of the Lord" does not permit, the O. T. "angel of the Lord" requires, worship (Rev. 22 : 8, 9 — "See thou do it not "; cf. Ex. 3 : 5 — " put off thy shoes "). As supporting this interpretation, see Hengstenberg, Christology, 1 : 107-123 ; J. Pye Smith,

Scripture Testimony to the Messiah. As opposing it, see Hofmann, Schriftbeweis, 1: 329, 378; Kurtz, History of Old Covenant, 1: 181. On the whole subject, see Bib. Sac., 1879: 593-615.

C. Descriptions of the divine Wisdom and Word.

(*a*) Wisdom is represented as distinct from God, and as eternally existing with God ; (*b*) the Word of God is distinguished from God, as executor of his will from everlasting.

(*a*) Prov. 8 : 1 — " Doth not wisdom cry ? "   *Cf.* Mat. 11 : 19 — " wisdom is justified by her works " ; Luke 7 : 35 — " wisdom is justified of all her children " ; 11 : 49 — " Therefore also said the wisdom of God, I will send unto them prophets and apostles " ; Prov. 8 : 22, 30, 31 — " Jehovah possessed me in the beginning of his way, Before his works of old. . . . I was by him, as a master workman : And I was daily his delight. . . . And my delight was with the sons of men " ; *cf.* 3 : 19 — " Jehovah by wisdom founded the earth," and Heb. 1 : 2 — " his Son . . . . through whom . . . . he made the worlds."   (*b*) Ps. 107 : 20 — " He sendeth his word, and healeth them " ; 119 : 89 — " For ever, 0 Jehovah, Thy word is settled in heaven " ; 147 : 15-18 — " He sendeth out his commandment. . . . He sendeth out his word."

In the Apocryphal book entitled Wisdom, 7 : 26, 28, wisdom is described as "the brightness of the eternal light," "the unspotted mirror of God's majesty," and "the image of his goodness "— reminding us of Heb. 1 : 3 — "the effulgence of his glory, and the very image of his substance."   In Wisdom, 9 : 9, 10, wisdom is represented as being present with God when he made the world, and the author of the book prays that wisdom may be sent to him out of God's holy heavens and from the throne of his glory. In 1 Esdras 4 : 35-38, Truth in a similar way is spoken of as personal: "Great is the Truth and stronger than all things. All the earth calleth upon the Truth, and the heaven blesseth it; all works shake and tremble at it, and with it is no unrighteous thing. As for the Truth, it endureth and is always strong; it liveth and conquereth forevermore."

It must be acknowledged that in none of these descriptions is the idea of personality clearly developed. Still less is it true that John the apostle derived his doctrine of the Logos from the interpretations of these descriptions in Philo Judæus. John's doctrine (John 1 : 1-18) is radically different from the Alexandrian Logos-idea of Philo. This last is a Platonizing speculation upon the mediating principle between God and the world. Philo seems at times to verge towards a recognition of personality in the Logos, though his monotheistic scruples lead him at other times to take back what he has given, and to describe the Logos either as the thought of God or as its expression in the world. But John is the first to present to us a consistent view of this personality, to identify the Logos with the Messiah, and to distinguish the Word from the Spirit of God.

Dorner, in his History of the Doctrine of the Person of Christ, 1 : 13-45, and in his System of Doctrine, 1 : 348, 349, gives the best account of Philo's doctrine of the Logos. He says that Philo calls the Logos ἀρχάγγελος, ἀρχιερεύς, δεύτερος θεός. Whether this is anything more than personification is doubtful, for Philo also calls the Logos the κόσμος νοητός. Certainly, so far as he makes the Logos a distinct personality, he makes him also a subordinate being. It is charged that the doctrine of the Trinity owes its origin to the Platonic philosophy in its Alexandrian union with Jewish theology. But Platonism had no Trinity. The truth is that by the doctrine of the Trinity Christianity secured itself against false heathen ideas of God's multiplicity and immanence, as well as against false Jewish ideas of God's unity and transcendence. It owes nothing to foreign sources.

We need not assign to John's gospel a later origin, in order to account for its doctrine of the Logos, any more than we need to assign a later origin to the Synoptics in order to account for their doctrine of a suffering Messiah. Both doctrines were equally unknown to Philo. Philo's Logos does not and cannot become man. So says Dorner. Westcott, in Bible Commentary on John, Introd., xv-xviii, and on John 1 : 1 — " The theological use of the term [in John's gospel] appears to be derived directly from the Palestinian *Memra*, and not from the Alexandrian *Logos*."   Instead of Philo's doctrine being a stepping-stone from Judaism to Christianity, it was a stumbling-stone. It had no doctrine of the Messiah or of the atonement. Bennett and Adeny, Bib. Introd., 340 —" The difference between Philo and John may be stated thus: Philo's Logos is Reason, while John's is Word; Philo's is impersonal, while John's is personal; Philo's is not incarnate, while John's is incarnate; Philo's is not the Messiah, while John's is the Messiah."

Philo lived from B. C. 10 or 20 to certainly A. D. 40, when he went at the head of a Jewish embassy to Rome, to persuade the Emperor to abstain from claiming divine honor from the Jews. In his De Opifice Mundi he says: "The Word is nothing else but the intelligible world." He calls the Word the "chainband," "pilot," "steersman," of all things. Gore, Incarnation, 69 — "Logos in Philo must be translated 'Reason.' But in the Targums, or early Jewish paraphrases of the O. T., the ' Word ' of Jehovah (*Memra, Devra*) is constantly spoken of as the efficient instrument of the divine action, in cases where the O. T. speaks of Jehovah himself. ' The Word of God ' had come to be used personally, as almost equivalent to God manifesting himself, or God in action." George H. Gilbert, in Biblical World, Jan. 1899 : 44 — " John's use of the term Logos was suggested by Greek philosophy, while at the same time the content of the word is Jewish."

Hatch, Hibbert Lectures, 174–208 — "The Stoics invested the Logos with personality. They were Monists and they made λόγος and ὕλη the active and the passive forms of the one principle. Some made God a mode of matter — *natura naturata*; others made matter a mode of God — *natura naturans* — the world a self-evolution of God. The Platonic forms, as manifold expressions of a single λόγος, were expressed by a singular term, Logos, rather than the Logoi, of God. From this Logos proceed all forms of mind or reason. So held Philo: 'The mind is an offshoot from the divine and happy soul (of God), an offshoot not separated from him, for nothing divine is cut off and disjoined, but only extended.' Philo's Logos is not only form but force — God's creative energy — the eldest-born of the ' I am,' which robes itself with the world as with a vesture, the high priest's robe, embroidered with all the forces of the seen and unseen worlds."

Wendt, Teaching of Jesus, 1 : 53 —" Philo carries the transcendence of God to its logical conclusions. The Jewish doctrine of angels is expanded in his doctrine of the Logos. The Alexandrian philosophers afterwards represented Christianity as a spiritualized Judaism. But a philosophical system dominated by the idea of the divine transcendence never could have furnished a motive for missionary labors like those of Paul. Philo's belief in transcendence abated his redemptive hopes. But, conversely, the redemptive hopes of orthodox Judaism saved it from some of the errors of exclusive transcendence." See a quotation from Siegfried, in Schürer's History of the Jewish People, article on Philo: " Philo's doctrine grew out of God's distinction and distance from the world. It was dualistic. Hence the need of mediating principles, some being less than God and more than creature. The cosmical significance of Christ bridged the gulf between Christianity and contemporary Greek thought. Christianity stands for a God who is revealed. But a Logos-doctrine like that of Philo may reveal less than it conceals. Instead of God incarnate for our salvation, we may have merely a mediating principle between God and the world, as in Arianism."

The preceding statement is furnished in substance by Prof. William Adams Brown. With it we agree, adding only the remark that the Alexandrian philosophy gave to Christianity, not the substance of its doctrine, but only the terminology for its expression. The truth which Philo groped after, the Apostle John seized and published, as only he could, who had heard, seen, and handled "the Word of life " (1 John 1 : 1). "The Christian doctrine of the Logos was perhaps before anything else an effort to express how Jesus Christ was God (Θεός), and yet in another sense was not God (ὁ θεός); that is to say, was not the whole Godhead " (quoted in Marcus Dods, Expositors' Bible, on John 1 : 1). See also Kendrick, in Christian Review, 26 : 369–399; Gloag, in Presb. and Ref. Rev., 1891 : 45–57; Réville, Doctrine of the Logos in John and Philo ; Godet on John, Germ. transl., 13, 135; Cudworth, Intellectual System, 2 : 320–333; Pressensé, Life of Jesus Christ, 83; Hagenbach, Hist. Doct., 1 : 114–117; Liddon, Our Lord's Divinity, 59–71 . Conant on Proverbs, 53.

D. Descriptions of the Messiah.

(*a*) He is one with Jehovah ; (*b*) yet he is in some sense distinct from Jehovah.

(*a*) Is. 9 : 6 — "unto us a child is born, unto us a son is given . . . and his name shall be called Wonderful Counselor, Mighty God, Everlasting Father, Prince of Peace " ; Micah 5 : 2 — "thou Betalehem . . . which art little . . . out of thee shall one come forth unto me that is to be ruler in Israel ; whose goings forth are from of old, from everlasting." (*b*) Ps. 45 : 3, 7 — "Thy throne, O God, is for ever and ever. . . . Therefore God, thy God, hath anointed thee " ; Mal. 3 : 1 — "I send my messenger, and he shall prepare the way before me : and the Lord, whom ye seek, will suddenly come to his temple ; and the messenger of the covenant, whom ye desire." Henderson, in his Commentary on this passage, points out that the Messiah is here called "the Lord" or "the Sovereign"—a title nowhere given in this form (with the article) to any but Jehovah ; that he is predicted as coming to the temple as its proprietor ; and that he is identified with the angel of the covenant, elsewhere shown to be one with Jehovah himself.

It is to be remembered, in considering this, as well as other classes of passages previously cited, that no Jewish writer before Christ's coming had succeeded in constructing from them a doctrine of the Trinity. Only to those who bring to them the light of New Testament revelation do they show their real meaning.

Our general conclusion with regard to the Old Testament intimations must therefore be that, while they do not by themselves furnish a sufficient basis for the doctrine of the Trinity, they contain the germ of it, and may be used in confirmation of it when its truth is substantially proved from the New Testament.

That the doctrine of the Trinity is not plainly taught in the Hebrew Scriptures is evident from the fact that Jews unite with Mohammedans in accusing trinitarians of polytheism. It should not surprise us that the Old Testament teaching on this subject is undeveloped and obscure. The first necessity was that the Unity of God should be insisted on. Until the danger of idolatry was past, a clear revelation of the Trinity might have been a hindrance to religious progress. The child now, like the race then, must learn the unity of God before it can profitably be taught the Trinity,—else it will fall into tritheism ; see Gardiner, O. T. and N. T., 49. We should not therefore begin our proof of the Trinity with a reference to passages in the Old Testament. We should speak of these passages, indeed, as furnishing intimations of the doctrine rather than proof of it. Yet, after having found proof of the doctrine in the New Testament, we may expect to find traces of it in the Old which will corroborate our conclusions. As a matter of fact, we shall see that traces of the idea of a Trinity are found not only in the Hebrew Scriptures but in some of the heathen religions as well. E. G. Robinson : "The doctrine of the Trinity underlay the O. T., unperceived by its writers, was first recognized in the economic revelation of Christianity, and was first clearly enunciated in the necessary evolution of Christian doctrine."

II.   THESE THREE ARE SO DESCRIBED IN SCRIPTURE THAT WE ARE COMPELLED TO CONCEIVE OF THEM AS DISTINCT PERSONS.

1.   *The Father and the Son are persons distinct from each other.*

(*a*) Christ distinguishes the Father from himself as 'another' ; (*b*) the Father and the Son are distinguished as the begetter and the begotten ; (*c*) the Father and the Son are distinguished as the sender and the sent.

(*a*) John 5 : 32, 37 — "It is another that beareth witness of me . . . the Father that sent me, he hath borne witness of me." (*b*) Ps. 2 : 7 — "Thou art my Son ; this day have I begotten thee " · John 1 : 14 — "the only begotten from the Father" ; 18 — "the only begotten Son" ; 3 : 16 — "gave his only begotten Son." (*c*) John 10 : 36 —"say ye of him, whom the Father sanctified and sent into the world, Thou blasphemest ; because I said, I am the Son of God ?" Gal. 4 : 4 — "when the fulness of the time came, God sent forth his Son." In these passages the Father is represented as objective to the Son, the Son to the Father, and both the Father and Son to the Spirit.

2.   *The Father and the Son are persons distinct from the Spirit.*

(*a*) Jesus distinguishes the Spirit from himself and from the Father ; (*b*) the Spirit proceeds from the Father ; (*c*) the Spirit is sent by the Father and by the Son.

(*a*) John 14 : 16, 17 — "I will pray the Father, and he shall give you another Comforter, that he may be with you for ever, even the Spirit of truth "— or "Spirit of the truth," = he whose work it is to reveal and apply the truth, and especially to make manifest him who is the truth. Jesus had been their Comforter: he now promises them another Comforter. If he himself was a person, then the Spirit is a person. (*b*) John 15 : 26 — "the Spirit of truth which proceedeth from the Father." (*c*) John 14 : 26 — "the Comforter, even the Holy Spirit, whom the Father will send in my name "; 15 : 26 — "when the Comforter is come, whom I will send unto you from the Father"; Gal. 4 : 6 — "God sent forth the Spirit of his Son into our hearts." The Greek church holds that the Spirit proceeds from the Father only ; the Latin church, that the Spirit proceeds both from the Father and from the Son. The true formula is : The Spirit proceeds from the Father *through* or *by* (not 'and') the Son. See Hagenbach, History of Doctrine, 1 : 262, 263. Moberly, Atonement and Personality, 195 — " The *Filioque* is a valuable defence of the truth that the Holy Spirit is not simply the abstract second Person of the Trinity, but rather the Spirit of the incarnate Christ, reproducing Christ in human hearts, and revealing in them the meaning of true manhood."

3. *The Holy Spirit is a person.*

A. Designations proper to personality are given him.

(*a*) The masculine pronoun ἐκεῖνος, though πνεῦμα is neuter ; (*b*) the name παράκλητος, which cannot be translated by 'comfort', or be taken as the name of any abstract influence. The Comforter, Instructor, Patron, Guide, Advocate, whom this term brings before us, must be a person. This is evident from its application to Christ in 1 John 2 : 1 — "we have an Advocate — παράκλητον — with the Father, Jesus Christ the righteous."

(*a*) John 16 : 14 — "He (ἐκεῖνος) shall glorify me " ; in Eph. 1 : 14 also, some of the best authorities, including Tischendorf (8th ed.), read ὅς, the masculine pronoun : " who is an earnest of our inheritance." But in John 14 : 16-18, παράκλητος is followed by the neuters ὸ and αὐτό, because πνεῦμα had intervened. Grammatical and not theological considerations controlled the writer. See G. B. Stevens, Johannine Theology, 189–217, especially on the distinction between Christ and the Holy Spirit. The Holy Spirit is another person than Christ, in spite of Christ's saying of the coming of the Holy Spirit : "I come unto you." (*b*) John 16 : 7 — "if I go not away, the Comforter will not come unto you." The word παράκλητος, as appears from 1 John 2 : 1, quoted above, is a term of broader meaning than merely "Comforter." The Holy Spirit is, indeed, as has been said, " the mother-principle in the Godhead," and "as one whom his mother comforteth " so God by his Spirit comforts his children (Is. 66 : 13). But the Holy Spirit is also an Advocate of God's claims in the soul, and of the soul's interests in prayer (Rom. 8 : 26 — "maketh intercession for us "). He comforts not only by being our advocate, but by being our instructor, patron, and guide ; and all these ideas are found attaching to the word παράκλητος in good Greek usage. The word indeed is a verbal adjective, signifying 'called to one's aid,' hence a 'helper' ; the idea of encouragement is included in it, as well as those of comfort and of advocacy. See Westcott, Bible Com., on John 14 : 16; Cremer, Lexicon of N. T. Greek, *in voce.*

T. Dwight, in S. S. Times, on John 14 : 16 — " The fundamental meaning of the word παράκλητος, which is a verbal adjective, is ' called to one's aid,' and thus, when used as a noun, it conveys the idea of ' helper.' This more general sense probably attaches to its use in John's Gospel, while in the Epistle (1 John 2 : 1, 2) it conveys the idea of Jesus acting as advocate on our behalf before God as a Judge." So the Latin *advocatus* signifies one ' called to '— *i. e..* called in to aid, counsel, plead. In this connection Jesus says : "I will not leave you orphans " (John 14 : 18). Cumming, Through the Eternal Spirit, 228 — " As the orphaned family, in the day of the parent's death, need some friend who shall lighten their sense of loss by his own presence with them, so the Holy Spirit is ' called in ' to supply the present love and help which the Twelve are losing in the death of Jesus." A. A. Hodge, Pop. Lectures, 237 — " The Roman ' client,' the poor and dependent man, called in his ' patron ' to help him in all his needs. The patron thought for, advised, directed, supported, defended, supplied, restored, comforted his client in all his complications. The client, though weak, with a powerful patron, was socially and politically secure forever."

B. His name is mentioned in immediate connection with other persons, and in such a way as to imply his own personality.

(*a*) In connection with Christians ; (*b*) in connection with Christ ; (*c*) in connection with the Father and the Son. If the Father and the Son are persons, the Spirit must be a person also.

(*a*) Acts 15 : 28 — "it seemed good to the Holy Spirit, and to us." (*b*) John 16 : 14 — "He shall glorify me : for he shall take of mine, and shall declare it unto you " ; *cf*. 17 : 4 — "I glorified thee on the earth." (*c*) Mat. 28 : 29 —"baptizing them into the name of the Father and of the Son and of the Holy Spirit " ; 2 Cor. 13 : 14 — "the grace of the Lord Jesus Christ, and the love of God, and the communion of the Holy Spirit, be with you all"; Jude 21 — "praying in the Holy Spirit, keep yourselves in the love of God, looking for the mercy of our Lord Jesus Christ." 1 Pet. 1 : 1, 2 — "elect . . . according to the fcreknowledge of God the Father, in sanctification of the Spirit, unto obedience and sprinkling of the blood of Jesus Christ." Yet it is noticeable in all these passages that there is no obtrusion of the Holy Spirit's personality, as if he desired to draw attention to himself. The Holy Spirit shows, not himself, but Christ. Like John the Baptist, he is a mere voice, and so is an example to Christian preachers, who are themselves "made . . . sufficient as ministers . . . of the Spirit " (2 Cor. 3 : 6). His leading is therefore often unperceived ; he so joins himself to us that we infer his presence only from the new and holy exercises of our own minds ; he continues to work in us even when his presence is ignored and his purity is outraged by our sins.

C.   He performs acts proper to personality.

That which searches, knows, speaks, testifies, reveals, convinces, commands, strives, moves, helps, guides, creates, recreates, sanctifies, inspires, makes intercession, orders the affairs of the church, performs miracles, raises the dead — cannot be a mere power, influence, efflux, or attribute of God, but must be a person.

Gen. 1 : 2, marg.—"the Spirit of God was brooding upon the face of the waters"; 6 : 3 —"My Spirit shalt not strive with man for ever " ; Luke 12 : 12 — "the Holy Spirit shall teach you in that very hour what ye ought to say " ; John 3 : 8 — "born of the Spirit " — here Bengel translates : "the Spirit breathes where he wills, and thou hearest his voice" — see also Gordon, Ministry of the Spirit, 166 ; 16 : 8 —"convict the world in respect of sin, and of righteousness, and of judgment"; Acts 2 : 4 — "the Spirit gave them utterance"; 8 : 29 — "the Spirit said unto Philip, Go near " ; 10 : 19, 20 — "the Spirit said unto him [Peter], Behold, three men seek thee . . . go with them . . . for I have sent them " ; 13 : 2 — "the Holy Spirit said, Separate me Barnabas and Saul "; 16 : 6, 7 —"forbidden of the Holy Spirit . . . Spirit of Jesus suffered them not " ; Rom. 8 : 11 — "give life also to your mortal bodies through his Spirit "; 26 — "the Spirit also helpeth our infirmity . . . maketh intercession for us " ; 15 : 19 — "in the power of signs and wonders, in the power of the Holy Spirit"; 1 Cor. 2 : 10, 11 — "the Spirit searcheth all things . . . things of God none knoweth, save the Spirit of God"; 12 : 8–11 — distributes spiritual gifts "to each one severally even as he will" — here Meyer calls attention to the words "as he will," as proving the personality of the Spirit ; 2 Pet. 1 : 21 — "men spake from God, being moved by the Holy Spirit" ; 1 Pet. 1 : 2 — "sanctification of the Spirit." How can a person be given in various measures ? We answer, by being permitted to work in our behalf with various degrees of power. Dorner : "To be power does not belong to the impersonal."

D.   He is affected as a person by the acts of others.

That which can be resisted, grieved, vexed, blasphemed, must be a person ; for only a person can perceive insult and be offended. The blasphemy against the Holy Ghost cannot be merely blasphemy against a power or attribute of God, since in that case blasphemy against God would be a less crime than blasphemy against his power. That against which the unpardonable sin can be committed must be a person.

Is. 63 : 10 — "they rebelled and grieved his holy Spirit" ; Mat. 12 : 31 — "Every sin and blasphemy shall be forgiven unto men; but the blasphemy against the Spirit shall not be forgiven "; Acts 5 : 3, 4, 9 — "lie to the Holy Ghost . . . thou hast not lied unto men but unto God . . . agreed together to try the Spirit of the Lord "; 7 : 51 — "ye do always resist the Holy Spirit"; Eph. 4 : 30 — "grieve not the Holy Spirit of God." Satan cannot be 'grieved.' Selfishness can be angered, but only love can be grieved. Blaspheming the Holy Spirit is like blaspheming one's own mother. The passages just quoted show the Spirit's possession of an emotional nature. Hence we read of "the love of the Spirit" (Rom. 15 : 30). The unutterable sighings of the Christian in intercessory prayer (Rom. 8 : 26, 27) reveal the mind of the Spirit, and show the infinite depths of feeling which are awakened in God's heart by the sins and needs of men. These deep desires and emotions which are only partially communicated to us, and which only God can understand, are conclusive proof that the Holy Spirit is a person. They are only the overflow into us of the infinite fountain of divine love to which the Holy Spirit unites us.

As Christ in the garden "began to be sorrowful and sore troubled" (Mat. 26 : 37), so the Holy Spirit is sorrowful and sore troubled at the ignoring, despising, resisting of his work, on the part of those whom he is trying to rescue from sin and to lead out into the freedom and joy of the Christian life. Luthardt, in S. S. Times, May 26, 1888 — " Every sin can be forgiven — even the sin against the Son of man — except the sin against the Holy Spirit. The sin against the Son of man can be forgiven because he can be misconceived. For he did not appear as that which he really was. Essence and appearance, truth and reality, contradicted each other." Hence Jesus could pray : "Father, forgive them, for they know not what they do " (Luke 23 : 34). The office of the Holy Spirit, however, is to show to men the nature of their conduct, and to sin against him is to sin against light and without excuse. See A. H. Strong, Christ in Creation, 297-313. Salmond, in Expositor's Greek Testament, on Eph. 4 : 30 —" What love is in us points truly, though tremulously, to what love is in God. But in us love, in proportion as it is true and sovereign, has both its *wrath-side* and its *grief-side ;* and so must it be with God, however difficult for us to think it out."

E. He manifests himself in visible form as distinct from the Father and the Son, yet in direct connection with personal acts performed by them.

Mat. 3 : 16, 17 — " Jesus, when he was baptized, went up straightway from the water : and lo, the heavens were opened unto him, and he saw the Spirit of God descending as a dove, and coming upon him ; and lo, a voice out of the heavens, saying, This is my beloved Son, in whom I am well pleased " ; Luke 3 : 21, 22 — " Jesus also having been baptized, and praying, the heaven was opened, and the Holy Spirit descended in a bodily form, as a dove, upon him, and a voice came out of heaven, Thou art my beloved Son ; in thee I am well pleased." Here are the prayer of Jesus, the approving voice of the Father, and the Holy Spirit descending in visible form to anoint the Son of God for his work. " I ad Jordanem, et videbis Trinitatem."

F. This ascription to the Spirit of a personal subsistence distinct from that of the Father and of the Son cannot be explained as personification ; for :

(a) This would be to interpret sober prose by the canons of poetry. Such sustained personification is contrary to the genius of even Hebrew poetry, in which Wisdom itself is most naturally interpreted as designating a personal existence. (b) Such an interpretation would render a multitude of passages either tautological, meaningless, or absurd, — as can be easily seen by substituting for the name Holy Spirit the terms which are wrongly held to be its equivalents ; such as the power, or influence, or efflux, or attribute of God. (c) It is contradicted, moreover, by all those passages in which the Holy Spirit is distinguished from his own gifts.

(a) The Bible is not primarily a book of poetry, although there is poetry in it. It is more properly a book of history and law. Even if the methous of allegory were used by the Psalmists and the Prophets, we should not expect them largely to characterize the Gospels and Epistles ; 1 Cor. 13 : 4 — "Love suffereth long, and is kind "— is a rare instance in which Paul's style takes on the form of poetry. Yet it is the Gospels and Epistles which most constantly represent the Holy Spirit as a person. (b) Acts 10 : 38 — " God anointed him [Jesus] with the Holy Spirit and with power "= anointed him with power and with power ? Rom. 15 : 13 — " abound in hope, in the power of the Holy Spirit " = in the power of the power of God ? 19 — "in the power of signs and wonders, in the power of the Holy Spirit" = in the power of the power of God ? 1 Cor. 2 : 4 — "demonstration of the Spirit and of power " = demonstration of power and of power? (c) Luke 1 : 35 — " the Holy Spirit shall come upon thee, and the power of the Most High shall overshadow thee " ; 4 : 14 — "Jesus returned in the power of the Spirit into Galilee " ; 1 Cor. 12 : 4, 8, 11 — after mention of the gifts of the Spirit, such as wisdom, knowledge, faith, healings, miracles, prophecy, discerning of spirits, tongues, interpretation of tongues, all these are traced to the Spirit who bestows them : "all these worketh the one and the same Spirit, dividing to each one severally even as he will." Here is not only giving, but giving discreetly, in the exercise of an independent will such as belongs only to a person. Rom. 8 : 26 — " the Spirit himself maketh intercession for us " — must be interpreted, if the Holy Spirit is not a person distinct from the Father, as meaning that the Holy Spirit intercedes with himself.

"The personality of the Holy Spirit was virtually rejected by the Arians, as it has since been by Schleiermacher, and it has been positively denied by the Socinians" (E. G. Robinson). Gould, Bib. Theol. N. T., 83, 96 —" The Twelve represent the Spirit as sent by the Son, who has been exalted that he may send this new power out of the heavens. Paul represents the Spirit as bringing to us the Christ. In the Spirit Christ dwells in us. The Spirit is the historic Jesus translated into terms of universal Spirit. Through the Spirit we are in Christ and Christ in us. The divine Indweller is to Paul alternately Christ and the Spirit. The Spirit is the divine principle incarnate in Jesus and explaining his preëxistence (2 Cor. 3 : 17, 18). Jesus was an incarnation of the Spirit of God."

This seeming identification of the Spirit with Christ is to be explained upon the ground that the divine essence is common to both and permits the Father to dwell in and to work through the Son, and the Son to dwell in and to work through the Spirit. It should not blind us to the equally patent Scriptural fact that there are personal relations between Christ and the Holy Spirit, and work done by the latter in which Christ is the object and not the subject ; John 16 : 14 — " He shall glorify me : for he shall take of mine, and shall declare it unto you." The Holy Spirit is not some *thing*, but some *one* ; not αὐτό, but Αὐτός ; Christ's *alter ego*, or other self. We should therefore make vivid our belief in the personality of Christ and of the Holy Spirit by addressing each of them frequently in the prayers we offer and in such hymns as " Jesus, lover of my soul," and " Come, Holy Spirit, heavenly Dove ! " On the personality of the Holy Spirit, see John Owen, in Works, 3 : 64-92 ; Dick, Lectures on Theology, 1 : 341-350.

III. This Tripersonality of the Divine Nature is not merely Economic and Temporal, but is Immanent and Eternal.

1. *Scripture proof that these distinctions of personality are eternal.*

We prove this (*a*) from those passages which speak of the existence of the Word from eternity with the Father ; (*b*) from passages asserting or implying Christ's preëxistence ; (*c*) from passages implying intercourse between the Father and the Son before the foundation of the world ; (*d*) from passages asserting the creation of the world by Christ ; (*e*) from passages asserting or implying the eternity of the Holy Spirit.

(*a*) John 1 : 1, 2 — "In the beginning was the Word, and the Word was with God, and the Word was God " ; *cf.* Gen. 1 : 1 — "In the beginning God created the heavens and the earth " ; Phil. 2 : 6 — "existing in the form of God . . . on an equality with God." (*b*) John 8 : 58 — " before Abraham was born, I am " ; 1 : 18 — "the only begotten Son, who is in the bosom of the Father " (R. V.) ; Col. 1 : 15-17 — "firstborn of all creation" or " before every creature . . . he is before all things." In these passages "am" and "is" indicate an eternal fact ; the present tense expresses permanent being. Rev. 22 : 13, 14 — "I am the Alpha and the Omega, the first and the last, the beginning and the end." (*c*) John 17 : 5 —"Father, glorify thou me with thine own self with the glory which I had with thee before the world was " ; 24 — " Thou lovedst me before the foundation of the world." (*d*) John 1 : 3 — "All things were made through him " ; 1 Cor. 8 . 6 — " one Lord, Jesus Christ, through whom are all things " ; Col. 1 : 16 — " all things have been created through him and unto him " ; Heb. 1 : 2 —" through whom also he made the worlds " ; 10 — "Thou, Lord, in the beginning didst lay the foundation of the earth, and the heavens are the works of thy hands." (*e*) Gen. 1 : 2 —"the Spirit of God was brooding " — existed therefore before creation ; Ps. 33 : 6 — "by the word of Jehovah were the heavens made ; and all the host of them by the breath [Spirit] of his mouth " ; Heb. 9 : 14 — "through the eternal Spirit."

With these passages before us, we must dissent from the statement of Dr. E. G. Robinson : " About the ontologic Trinity we know absolutely nothing. The Trinity we can contemplate is simply a revealed one, one of economic manifestations. We may suppose that the ontologic underlies the economic." Scripture compels us, in our judgment, to go further than this, and to maintain that there are personal relations between the Father, the Son, and the Holy Spirit, independently of creation and of time ; in other words we maintain that Scripture reveals to us a social Trinity and an intercourse of love apart from and before the existence of the universe. Love before time implies distinctions of personality before time. There are three eternal consciousnesses and three eternal wills in the divine nature. We here state only the fact, — the explanation of it, and its reconciliation with the fundamental unity of God is treated in our next section. We now proceed to show that the two varying systems which ignore this tripersonality are unscriptural and at the same time exposed to philosophical objection.

2. *Errors refuted by the foregoing passages.*

A. The Sabellian.

Sabellius (of Ptolemais in Pentapolis, 250) held that Father, Son, and Holy Spirit are mere developments or revelations to creatures, in time, of the otherwise concealed Godhead — developments which, since creatures will always exist, are not transitory, but which at the same time are not eternal *a parte ante.* God as united to the creation is Father ; God as united to Jesus Christ is Son ; God as united to the church is Holy Spirit. The Trinity of Sabellius is therefore an economic and not an immanent Trinity — a Trinity of forms or manifestations, but not a necessary and eternal Trinity in the divine nature.

Some have interpreted Sabellius as denying that the Trinity is eternal *a parte post,* as well as *a parte ante,* and as holding that, when the purpose of these temporary manifestations is accomplished, the Triad is resolved into the Monad. This view easily merges in another, which makes the persons of the Trinity mere names for the ever shifting phases of the divine activity.

The best statement of the Sabellian doctrine, according to the interpretation first mentioned, is that of Schleiermacher, translated with comments by Moses Stuart, in Biblical Repository, 6 : 1-16. The one unchanging God is differently reflected from the world on account of the world's different receptivities. Praxeas of Rome (200) Noetus of Smyrna (230), and Beryl of Arabia (250) advocated substantially the same views. They were called Monarchians (μόνη ἀρχή), because they believed not in the Triaa, but only in the Monad. They were called Patripassians, because they held that, as Christ is only God in human form, and this God suffers, therefore the Father suffers. Knight, Colloquia Peripatetica, xlii, suggests a connection between Sabellianism and Emanationism. See this Compendium, on Theories which oppose Creation.

A view similar to that of Sabellius was held by Horace Bushnell, in his God in Christ, 113-115, 130 sq., 172-175, and Christ in Theology, 119, 120 — " Father, Son and Holy Spirit, being incidental to the revelation of God, may be and probably are from eternity to eternity, inasmuch as God may have revealed himself from eternity, and certainly will reveal himself so long as there are minds to know him. It may be, in fact, the nature of God to reveal himself, as truly as it is of the sun to shine or of living mind to think." He does not deny the immanent Trinity, but simply says we know nothing about it. Yet a Trinity of Persons in the divine essence itself he called plain tritheism. He prefers " instrumental Trinity " to " modal Trinity " as a designation of his doctrine. The difference between Bushnell on the one hand, and Sabellius and Schleiermacher on the other, seems then to be the following : Sabellius and Schleiermacher hold that the One *becomes* three in the process of revelation, and the three are only *media* or *modes* of revelation. Father, Son, and Spirit are mere names applied to these modes of the divine action, there being no internal distinctions in the divine nature. This is modalism, or a modal Trinity. Bushnell stands by the Trinity of revelation alone, and protests against any constructive reasonings with regard to the immanent Trinity. Yet in his later writings he reverts to Athanasius and speaks of God as eternally " threeing himself " ; see Fisher, Edwards on the Trinity, 73.

Lyman Abbott, in The Outlook, proposes as illustration of the Trinity, 1. the artist working on his pictures ; 2. the same man teaching pupils how to paint ; 3. the same man entertaining his friends at home. He has not taken on these types of conduct. They are not masks (*personæ*), nor offices, which he takes up and lays down. There is a threefold *nature* in him : he is artist, teacher, friend. God is complex, and not simple. I do not know him, till I know him in all these relations. Yet it is evident that Dr. Abbott's view provides no basis for love or for society within the divine nature. The three persons are but three successive aspects or activities of the one God. General Grant, when in office, was but one person, even though he was a father, a President, and a commander in chief of the army and navy of the United States.

It is evident that this theory, in whatever form it may be held, is far from satisfying the demands of Scripture. Scripture speaks of the second person of the Trinity as existing and acting before the birth of Jesus Christ, and of the Holy Spirit as existing and acting before the formation of the church. Both have a personal existence, eternal in the past as well as in the future — which this theory expressly denies.

A revelation that is not a self-revelation of God is not honest. Stuart: Since God is revealed as three, he must be essentially or immanently three, back of revelation; else the revelation would not be true. Dorner: A Trinity of revelation is a misrepresentation, if there is not behind it a Trinity of nature. Twesten properly arrives at the threeness by considering, not so much what is involved in the revelation of God to us, as what is involved in the revelation of God to himself. The unscripturalness of the Sabellian doctrine is plain, if we remember that upon this view the Three cannot exist at once: when the Father says "Thou art my beloved Son" (Luke 3 : 22), he is simply speaking to himself; when Christ sends the Holy Spirit, he only sends himself. John 1 : 1 — "In the beginning was the Word, and the Word was with God, and the Word was God" — " sets aside the false notion that the Word become *personal* first at the time of creation, or at the incarnation " (Westcott, Bib. Com. *in loco*).

Mason, Faith of the Gospel, 50, 51 — " Sabellius claimed that the Unity became a Trinity by expansion. Fatherhood began with the world. God is not eternally Father, nor does he love eternally. We have only an impersonal, unintelligible God, who has played upon us and confused our understanding by showing himself to us under three disguises. Before creation there is no Fatherhood, even in germ."

According to Pfleiderer, Philos. Religion, 2 : 269, Origen held that the Godhead might be represented by three concentric circles; the widest, embracing the whole being, is that of the Father; the next, that of the Son, which extends to the rational creation; and the narrowest is that of the Spirit, who rules in the holy men of the church. King, Reconstruction of Theology, 192, 194 — " To affirm social relations in the Godhead is to assert absolute Tritheism. . . . Unitarianism emphasizes the humanity of Christ, to preserve the unity of God; the true view emphasizes the divinity of Christ, to preserve the unity."

L. L. Paine, Evolution of Trinitarianism, 141, 287, says that New England Trinitarianism is characterized by three things: 1. Sabellian Patripassianism; Christ is all the Father there is, and the Holy Spirit is Christ's continued life; 2. Consubstantiality, or community of essence, of God and man; unlike the essential difference between the created and the uncreated which Platonic dualism maintained, this theory turns *moral* likeness into *essential* likeness; 3. Philosophical monism, matter itself being but an evolution of Spirit. . . . In the next form of the scientific doctrine of evolution, the divineness of man becomes a vital truth, and out of it arises a Christology that removes Jesus of Nazareth indeed out of the order of absolute Deity, but at the same time exalts him to a place of moral eminence that is secure and supreme."

Against this danger of regarding Christ as a merely economic and temporary manifestation of God we can guard only by maintaining the Scriptural doctrine of an immanent Trinity. Moberly, Atonement and Personality, 86, 165 — " We cannot incur any Sabellian peril while we maintain — what is fatal to Sabellianism — that that which is revealed within the divine Unity is not only a distinction of aspects or of names, but a real reciprocity of mutual relation. One 'aspect' cannot contemplate, or be loved by, another. . . . Sabellianism degrades the persons of Deity into aspects. But there can be no mutual relation between aspects. The heat and the light of flame cannot severally contemplate and be in love with one another." See Bushnell's doctrine reviewed by Hodge, Essays and Reviews, 433–473. On the whole subject, see Dorner, Hist. Doct. Person of Christ, 2 : 152–169; Shedd, Hist. Doctrine, 1 : 259; Baur, Lehre von der Dreieinigkeit, 1 : 256–305; Thomasius, Christi Person und Werk 1 : 83.

B. The Arian.

Arius (of Alexandria ; condemned by Council of Nice, 325) held that the Father is the only divine being absolutely without beginning; the Son and the Holy Spirit, through whom God creates and recreates, having been themselves created out of nothing before the world was ; and Christ being called God, because he is next in rank to God, and is endowed by God with divine power to create.

The followers of Arius have differed as to the precise rank and claims of Christ. While Socinus held with Arius that worship of Christ was obligatory, the later Unitarians have perceived the impropriety of worshiping even the highest of created beings, and have constantly tended to a view of the Redeemer which regards him as a mere man, standing in a peculiarly intimate relation to God.

For statement of the Arian doctrine, see J. Freeman Clarke, Orthodoxy, Its Truths and Errors. Per contra, see Schäffer, in Bib. Sac., 21 : 1, article on Athanasius and the Arian controversy. The so-called Athanasian Creed, which Athanasius never wrote, is more properly designated as the Symbolum Quicumque. It has also been called, though facetiously, 'the Anathemasian Creed.' Yet no error in doctrine can be more perilous or worthy of condemnation than the error of Arius (1 Cor. 16:22 — "If any man loveth not the Lord, let him be anathema "; 1 John 2 : 23 — "Whosoever denieth the Son, the same hath not the Father"; 4 : 3 — "every spirit that confesseth not Jesus is not of God : and this is the spirit of the antichrist "). It regards Christ as called God only by courtesy, much as we give to a Lieutenant Governor the title of Governor. Before the creation of the Son, the love of God, if there could be love, was expended on himself. Gwatkin, Studies of Arianism : "The Arian Christ is nothing but a heathen idol, invented to maintain a heathenish Supreme in heathen isolation from the world. The nearer the Son is pulled down towards man by the attenuation of his Godhead, the more remote from man becomes the unshared Godhead of the Father. You have an Être Suprême who is practically unapproachable, a mere One-and-all, destitute of personality."

Gore, Incarnation, 90, 91, 110, shows the immense importance of the controversy with regard to ὁμοούσιον and ὁμοιούσιον. Carlyle once sneered that "the Christian world was torn in pieces over a diphthong." But Carlyle afterwards came to see that Christianity itself was at stake, and that it would have dwindled away to a legend, if the Arians had won. Arius appealed chiefly to logic, not to Scripture. He claimed that a Son must be younger than his Father. But he was asserting the principle of heathenism and idolatry, in demanding worship for a creature. The Goths were easily converted to Arianism. Christ was to them a hero-god, a demigod, and the later Goths would worship Christ and heathen idols impartially.

It is evident that the theory of Arius does not satisfy the demands of Scripture. A created God, a God whose existence had a beginning and therefore may come to an end, a God made of a substance which once was not, and therefore a substance different from that of the Father, is not God, but a finite creature. But the Scripture speaks of Christ as being in the beginning God, with God, and equal with God.

Luther, alluding to John 1:1, says : " 'The Word was God' is against Arius; 'the Word was with God' is against Sabellius." The Racovian Catechism, Quaes. 183, 184, 211, 236, 237, 245, 246, teaches that Christ is to be truly worshiped, and they are denied to be Christians who refuse to adore him. Davidis was persecuted and died in prison for refusing to worship Christ; and Socinus was charged, though probably unjustly, with having caused his imprisonment. Bartholomew Legate, an Essexman and an Arian, was burned to death at Smithfield, March 13, 1613. King James I asked him whether he did not pray to Christ. Legate's answer was that "indeed he had prayed to Christ in the days of his ignorance, but not for these last seven years"; which so shocked James that "he spurned at him with his foot." At the stake Legate still refused to recant, and so was burned to ashes amid a vast conflux of people. The very next month another Arian named Whiteman was burned at Burton-on-Trent.

It required courage, even a generation later, for John Milton, in his Christian Doctrine, to declare himself a high Arian. In that treatise he teaches that "the Son of God did not exist from all eternity, is not coëval or coëssential or coëqual with the Father, but came into existence by the will of God to be the next being to himself, the first-born and best beloved, the Logos or Word through whom all creation should take its begin.

nings." So Milton regards the Holy Spirit as a created being, inferior to the Son and possibly confined to our heavens and earth. Milton's Arianism, however, is characteristic of his later, rather than his earlier, writings ; compare the Ode on Christ's Nativity with Paradise Lost, 3 : 383–391 ; and see Masson's Life of Milton, 1 : 39 ; 6 : 823, 824 ; A. H. Strong, Great Poets and their Theology, 260–262.

Dr. Samuel Clarke, when asked whether the Father who had created could not also destroy the Son, said that he had not considered the question. Ralph Waldo Emerson broke with his church and left the ministry because he could not celebrate the Lord's Supper, — it implied a profounder reverence for Jesus than he could give him. He wrote : "It seemed to me at church to-day, that the Communion Service, as it is now and here celebrated, is a document of the dullness of the race. How these, my good neighbors, the bending deacons, with their cups and plates, would have straightened themselves to sturdiness, if the proposition came before them to honor thus a fellow-man" ; see Cabot's Memoir, 314. Yet Dr. Leonard Bacon said of the Unitarians that "it seemed as if their exclusive contemplation of Jesus Christ in his human character as the example for our imitation had wrought in them an exceptional beauty and Christlikeness of living."

Chadwick, Old and New Unitarian Belief, 20, speaks of Arianism as exalting Christ to a degree of inappreciable difference from God, while Socinus looked upon him only as a miraculously endowed man, and believed in an infallible book. The term " Unitarians," he claims, is derived from the " Uniti," a society in Transylvania, in support of mutual toleration between Calvinists, Romanists, and Socinians. The name stuck to the advocates of the divine Unity, because they were its most active members. B. W. Lockhart: " Trinity guarantees God's knowableness. Arius taught that Jesus was neither human nor divine, but created in some grade of being between the two, essentially unknown to man. An absentee God made Jesus his messenger, God himself not touching the world directly at any point, and unknown and unknowable to it. Athanasius on the contrary asserted that God did not send a messenger in Christ, but came himself, so that to know Christ is really to know God who is essentially revealed in him. This gave the Church the doctrine of God immanent, or Immanuel, God knowable and actually known by men, because actually present." Chapman, Jesus Christ and the Present Age, 14 — " The world was never further from Unitarianism than it is to-day ; we may add that Unitarianism was never further from itself." On the doctrines of the early Socinians, see Princeton Essays, 1 : 195. On the whole subject, see Blunt, Dict. of Heretical Sects, art. : Arius ; Guericke, Hist. Doctrine, 1 : 313, 319. See also a further account of Arianism in the chapter of this Compendium on the Person of Christ.

IV. THIS TRIPERSONALITY IS NOT TRITHEISM ; FOR, WHILE THERE ARE THREE PERSONS, THERE IS BUT ONE ESSENCE.

(a) The term 'person' only approximately represents the truth. Although this word, more nearly than any other single word, expresses the conception which the Scriptures give us of the relation between the Father, the Son, and the Holy Spirit, it is not itself used in this connection in Scripture, and we employ it in a qualified sense, not in the ordinary sense in which we apply the word 'person' to Peter, Paul, and John.

The word ' person ' is only the imperfect and inadequate expression of a fact that transcends our experience and comprehension. Bunyan : " My dark and cloudy words, they do but hold The truth, as cabinets encase the gold." Three Gods, limiting each other, would deprive each other of Deity. While we show that the unity is articulated by the persons, it is equally important to remember that the persons are limited by the unity. With us personality implies entire separation from all others — distinct individuality. But in the one God there can be no such separation. The personal distinctions in him must be such as are consistent with essential unity. This is the merit of the statement in the *Symbolum Quicumque* (or Athanasian Creed, wrongly so called) : " The Father is God, the Son is God, the Holy Ghost is God ; and yet there are not three Gods but one God. So likewise the Father is Lord, the Son is Lord, the Holy Ghost is Lord ; yet there are not three Lords but one Lord. For as we are compelled by Christian truth to acknowledge each person by himself to be God and Lord, so we are forbidden by the same truth to say that there are three Gods or three Lords." See

Hagenbach, History of Doctrine, 1:270. We add that the personality of the Godhead as a whole is separate and distinct from all others, and in this respect is more fully analogous to man's personality than is the personality of the Father or of the Son.

The church of Alexandria in the second century chanted together: "One only is holy, the Father; One only is holy, the Son; One only is holy, the Spirit." Moberly, Atonement and Personality, 154, 167, 168 — "The three persons are neither three Gods, nor three parts of God. Rather are they God threefoldly, tri-personally. . . . The personal distinction in Godhead is a distinction within, and of, Unity: not a distinction which qualifies Unity, or usurps the place of it, or destroys it. It is not a relation of mutual exclusiveness, but of mutual inclusiveness. No one person is or can be without the others. . . . The personality of the supreme or absolute Being cannot be without self-contained mutuality of relations such as Will and Love. But the mutuality would not be real, unless the subject which becomes object, and the object which becomes subject, were on each side alike and equally Personal. . . . . The Unity of all-comprehending inclusiveness is a higher mode of unity than the unity of singular distinctiveness. . . . The disciples are not to have the presence of the Spirit instead of the Son, but to have the Spirit is to have the Son. We mean by the Personal God not a limited alternative to unlimited abstracts, such as Law, Holiness, Love, but the transcendent and inclusive completeness of them all. The terms Father and Son are certainly terms which rise more immediately out of the temporal facts of the incarnation than out of the eternal relations of the divine Being. They are metaphors, however, which mean far more in the spiritual than they do in the material sphere. Spiritual hunger is more intense than physical hunger. So sin, judgment, grace, are metaphors. But in John 1:1-18 'Son' is not used, but 'Word.' "

(*b*) The necessary qualification is that, while three persons among men have only a *specific* unity of nature or essence — that is, have the same *species* of nature or essence,— the persons of the Godhead have a *numerical* unity of nature or essence — that is, have the *same* nature or essence. The undivided essence of the Godhead belongs equally to each of the persons; Father, Son, and Holy Spirit, each possesses all the substance and all the attributes of Deity. The plurality of the Godhead is therefore not a plurality of essence, but a plurality of hypostatical, or personal, distinctions. God is not three and one, but three in one. The one indivisible essence has three modes of subsistence.

The Trinity is not simply a partnership, in which each member can sign the name of the firm ; for this is unity of council and operation only, not of essence. God's nature is not an abstract but an organic unity. God, as living, cannot be a mere Monad. Trinity is the organism of the Deity. The one divine Being exists in three modes. The life of the vine makes itself known in the life of the branches, and this union between vine and branches Christ uses to illustrate the union between the Father and himself. (See John 15:10 — "If ye keep my commandments, ye shall abide in my love ; even as I have kept my Father's commandments, and abide in his love" ; *cf.* verse 5 — "I am the vine, ye are the branches; he that abideth in me, and I in him, the same beareth much fruit" ; 17:22, 23 — "That they may be one, even as we are one ; I in them, and thou in me.") So, in the organism of the body, the arm has its own life, a different life from that of the head or the foot, yet has this only by partaking of the life of the whole. See Dorner, System of Doctrine, 1:450-453 — "The one divine personality is so present in each of the distinctions, that these, which singly and by themselves would not be personal, yet do participate in the one divine personality, each in its own manner. This one divine personality is the unity of the three modes of subsistence which participate in itself. Neither is personal without the others. In each, in its manner, is the whole Godhead."

The human body is a complex rather than a simple organism, a unity which embraces an indefinite number of subsidiary and dependent organisms. The one life of the body manifests itself in the life of the nervous system, the life of the circulatory system, and the life of the digestive system. The complete destruction of either one of these systems destroys the other two. Psychology as well as physiology reveals to us the possibility of a three-fold life within the bounds of a single being. In the individual man there is sometimes a double and even a triple consciousness. Herbert Spencer, Autobiography, 1:459: 2:204 —"Most active minds have, I presume, more or less frequent experiences of double consciousness — one consciousness seeming to take note of what the other is about, and to applaud or blame." He mentions an instance in his own experience, "May there not be possible a bi-cerebral thinking, as there is a binocular vision ? . . . In these cases it seems as though there were going on, quite apart from the consciousness which seemed to constitute myself, some process of elaborating coherent thoughts — as though one part of myself was an independent originator over whose sayings and doings I had no control, and which were nevertheless in great measure consistent; while the other part of myself was a passive spectator or listener, quite unprepared for many of the things that the first part said, and which were nevertheless, though unexpected, not illogical." This fact that there can be more than one consciousness in the same personality among men should make us slow to deny that there can be three consciousnesses in the one God.

Humanity at large is also an organism, and this fact lends new confirmation to the Pauline statement of organic interdependence. Modern sociology is the doctrine of one life constituted by the union of many. " Unus homo, nullus homo" is a principle of ethics as well as of sociology. No man can have a conscience to himself. The moral life of one results from and is interpenetrated by the moral life of all. All men moreover live, move and have their being in God. Within the bounds of the one universal and divine consciousness there are multitudinous *finite* consciousnesses. Why then should it be thought incredible that in the nature of this one God there should be three *infinite* consciousnesses? Baldwin, Psychology, 53, 54—" The integration of finite consciousnesses in an all-embracing divine consciousness may find a valid analogy in the integration of subordinate consciousnesses in the unit-personality of man. In the hypnotic state, multiple consciousnesses may be induced in the same nervous organism. In insanity there is a secondary consciousness at war with that which normally dominates." Schurman, Belief in God, 26, 161 — " The infinite Spirit may include the finite, as the idea of a single organism embraces within a single life a plurality of members and functions. . . . All souls are parts or functions of the eternal life of God, who is above all, and through all, and in all, and in whom we live, and move, and have our being." We would draw the conclusion that, as in the body and soul of man, both as an individual and as a race, there is diversity in unity, so in the God in whose image man is made, there is diversity in unity, and a triple consciousness and will are consistent with, and even find their perfection in, a single essence.

By the personality of God we mean more than we mean when we speak of the personality of the Son and the personality of the Spirit. The personality of the Godhead is distinct and separate from all others, and is, in this respect, like that of man. Hence Shedd, Dogm. Theol., 1 .394, says " it is preferable to speak of the *personality* of the essence rather than of the *person* of the essence; because the essence is not one person, but three persons. . . . The divine essence cannot be at once three persons and one person, if ' person ' is employed in one signification; but it can be at once three persons and one personal Being." While we speak of the one God as having a personality in which there are three persons, we would not call this personality a superpersonality, if this latter term is intended to intimate that God's personality is less than the personality of man. The personality of the Godhead is inclusive rather than exclusive.

With this qualification we may assent to the words of D'Arcy, Idealism and Theology, 93, 94, 218, 230, 236, 254 — " The innermost truth of things, God, must be conceived as personal; but the ultimate Unity, which is his, must be believed to be superpersonal. It is a unity of persons, not a personal unity. For us personality is the ultimate form of unity. It is not so in him. For in him all persons live and move and have their being. . . . God is personal and also superpersonal. In him there is a transcendent unity that can embrace a personal multiplicity. . . . There is in God an ultimate superpersonal unity in which all persons are one — [all human persons and the three divine persons]. . . . Substance is more real than quality, and subject is more real than substance. The most real of all is the concrete totality, the all-inclusive Universal. . . . What human love strives to accomplish — the overcoming of the opposition of person to person — is perfectly attained in the divine Unity. . . . The presupposition on which philosophy is driven back — [that persons have an underlying ground of unity] is identical with that which underlies Christian theology." See Pfleiderer and Lotze on personality, in this Compendium, p. 104.

(c) This oneness of essence explains the fact that, while Father, Son, and Holy Spirit, as respects their personality, are distinct subsistences, there is an intercommunion of persons and an immanence of one divine person in another which permits the peculiar work of one to be ascribed, with a single limitation, to either of the others, and the manifestation of one to be recognized in the manifestation of another. The limitation is simply this, that although the Son was sent by the Father, and the Spirit by the Father and the Son, it cannot be said *vice versa* that the Father is sent either by the Son, or by the Spirit. The Scripture representations of this intercommunion prevent us from conceiving of the distinctions called Father, Son, and Holy Spirit as involving separation between them.

Dorner adds that " in one is each of the others." This is true with the limitation mentioned in the text above. Whatever Christ does, God the Father can be said to do; for God acts only in and through Christ the Revealer. Whatever the Holy Spirit does, Christ can be said to do; for the Holy Spirit is the Spirit of Christ. The Spirit is the omnipresent Jesus, and Bengel's dictum is true: " Ubi Spiritus, ibi Christus." Passages illustrating this intercommunion are the following: Gen. 1 : 1 — " God created"; *cf.* Heb. 1 : 2 — "through whom [the Son] also he made the worlds"; John 5 : 17, 19 — " My Father worketh even until now, and I work. . . . The Son can do nothing of himself, but what he seeth the Father doing; for what things soever he doeth, these the Son also doeth in like manner"; 14 : 9 — " he that hath seen me hath seen the Father"; 11 — " I am in the Father and the Father in me"; 18 — " I will not leave you desolate: I come unto you" (by the Holy Spirit); 15 : 26 — " when the Comforter is come, whom I will send unto you from the Father, even the Spirit of truth"; 17 : 21 — " that they may all be one; even as thou, Father, art in me, and I in thee"; 2 Cor. 5 : 19 — " God was in Christ reconciling"; Titus 2 : 10 — " God our Savior "; Heb. 12 : 23 — " God the Judge of all "; *cf.* John 5 : 22 — " neither doth the Father judge any man, but he hath given all judgment unto the Son"; Acts 17 : 31 — " judge the world in righteousness by the man whom he hath ordained."

It is this intercommunion, together with the order of personality and operation to be mentioned hereafter, which explains the occasional use of the term ' Father ' ior the whole Godhead; as in Eph. 4 : 6 — " one God and Father of all, who is over all and through all [in Christ], and in you all " [by the Spirit]. This intercommunion also explains the designation of Christ as " the Spirit," and of the Spirit as " the Spirit of Christ," as in 1 Cor. 15 : 45 — " the last Adam became a life-giving Spirit"; 2 Cor. 3 : 17 — " Now the Lord is the Spirit"; Gal. 4 : 6 — " sent forth the Spirit of his Son "; Phil. 1 : 19 — " supply of the Spirit of Jesus Christ" (see Alford and Lange on 2 Cor. 3 : 17, 18). So the Lamb, in Rev. 5 : 6, has " seven horns and seven eyes, which are the seven Spirits of God, sent forth into all the earth"= the Holy Spirit, with his manifold powers, is the Spirit of the omnipotent, omniscient, and omnipresent Christ. Theologians have designated this intercommunion by the terms περιχώρησις, *circumincessio, intercommunicatio, circulatio, inexistentia.* The word οὐσία was used to denote essence, substance, nature, being; and the words πρόσωπον and ὑπόστασις for person, distinction, mode of subsistence. On the changing uses of the words πρόσωπον and ὑπόστασις, see Dorner, Glaubenslehre, 2 : 321, note 2. On the meaning of the word ' person ' in connection with the Trinity, see John Howe, Calm Discourse of the Trinity; Jonathan Edwards, Observations on the Trinity; Shedd, Dogm. Theol., 1 : 194, 267-275, 299, 300.

The Holy Spirit is Christ's *alter ego,* or other self. When Jesus went away, it was an exchange of his presence for his omnipresence; an exchange of limited for unlimited power; an exchange of companionship for indwelling. Since Christ comes to men in the Holy Spirit, he speaks through the apostles as authoritatively as if his own lips uttered the words. Each believer, in having the Holy Spirit, has the whole Christ for his own; see A. J. Gordon, Ministry of the Spirit. Gore, Incarnation, 218 — " The persons of the Holy Trinity are not separable individuals. Each involves the others; the coming of each is the coming of the others. Thus the coming of the Spirit must have involved the coming of the Son. But the specialty of the Pentecostal gift appears to be the coming of the Holy Spirit out of the uplifted and glorified *manhood* of the incarnate Son. The Spirit is the life-giver, but the life with which he works in the church is the life of the *Incarnate,* the life of Jesus."

Moberly, Atonement and Personality, 85 — " For centuries upon centuries, the essential unity of God had been burnt and branded in upon the consciousness of Israel. It had to be completely established first, as a basal element of thought, indispensable, unalterable, before there could begin the disclosure to man of the reality of the eternal relations within the one indivisible being of God. And when the disclosure came, it came not as modifying, but as further interpreting and illumining, that unity which it absolutely presupposed." E. G. Robinson. Christian Theology, 238 —"There is extreme difficulty in giving any statement of a triunity that shall not verge upon tritheism on the one hand, or upon mere modalism on the other. It was very natural that Calvin should be charged with Sabellianism, and John Howe with tritheism."

V. The Three Persons, Father, Son, and Holy Spirit, are equal.

In explanation, notice that :

1. *These titles belong to the Persons.*

(*a*) The Father is not God as such ; for God is not only Father, but also Son and Holy Spirit. The term 'Father' designates that hypostatical distinction in the divine nature in virtue of which God is related to the Son, and through the Son and the Spirit to the church and the world. As author of the believer's spiritual as well as natural life, God is doubly his Father ; but this relation which God sustains to creatures is not the ground of the title. God is Father primarily in virtue of the relation which he sustains to the eternal Son ; only as we are spiritually united to Jesus Christ do we become children of God.

(*b*) The Son is not God as such ; for God is not only Son, but also Father and Holy Spirit. 'The Son' designates that distinction in virtue of which God is related to the Father, is sent by the Father to redeem the world, and with the Father sends the Holy Spirit.

(*c*) The Holy Spirit is not God as such ; for God is not only Holy Spirit, but also Father and Son. 'The Holy Spirit' designates that distinction in virtue of which God is related to the Father and the Son, and is sent by them to accomplish the work of renewing the ungodly and of sanctifying the church.

Neither of these names designates the Monad as such. Each designates rather that personal distinction which forms the eternal basis and ground for a particular self-revelation. In the sense of being the Author and Provider of men's natural life, God is the Father of all. But even this natural sonship is mediated by Jesus Christ ; see 1 Cor. 8 : 6 — "one Lord, Jesus Christ, through whom are all things, and we through him." The phrase "Our Father," however, can be used with the highest truth only by the regenerate, who have been newly born of God by being united to Christ through the power of the Holy Spirit. See Gal. 3 : 26 — "For ye are all sons of God, through faith, in Jesus Christ " ; 4 : 4-6 — "God sent forth his Son . . . . that we might receive the adoption of sons . . . sent forth the Spirit of his Son into our hearts, crying, Abba, Father " ; Eph. 1 : 5 — "foreordained us unto adoption as sons through Jesus Christ." God's love for Christ is the measure of his love for those who are one with Christ. Human nature in Christ is lifted up into the life and communion of the eternal Trinity. Shedd, Dogm. Theol., 1 : 306-310.

Human fatherhood is a reflection of the divine, not, *vice versa*, the divine a reflection of the human ; *cf.* Eph. 3 : 14, 15 — "the Father, from whom every fatherhood ($\pi\alpha\tau\rho\iota\dot{\alpha}$) in heaven and on earth is named." Chadwick, Unitarianism, 77-83, makes the name 'Father' only a symbol for the great Cause of organic evolution, the Author of all being. But we may reply with Stearns, Evidence of Christian Experience, 177 — "to know God outside of the sphere of redemption is not to know him in the deeper meaning of the term 'Father'. It is only through the Son that we know the Father: Mat. 11 : 27 —'Neither doth any know the Father, save the Son, and he to whomsoever the Son willeth to reveal him.'"

Whiton, Gloria Patri, 38 —"The Unseen can be known only by the seen which comes forth from it. The all-generating or Paternal Life which is hidden from us can be known only by the generated or Filial Life in which it reveals itself. The goodness and righteousness which inhabits eternity can be known only by the goodness and righteousness which issues from it in the successive births of time. God above the world is made known only by God in the world. God transcendent, the Father, is revealed by God immanent, the Son." Faber: "O marvellous, O worshipful! No song or sound is heard, But everywhere and every hour, In love, in wisdom and in power.

the Father speaks his dear eternal Word." We may interpret this as meaning that self-expression is a necessity of nature to an infinite Mind. The Word is therefore eternal. Christ is the mirror from which are flashed upon us the rays of the hidden Luminary. So Principal Fairbairn says : " Theology must be on its historical side Christocentric, but on its doctrinal side Theocentric."

Salmond, Expositor's Greek Testament, on Eph. 1 : 5 — " By 'adoption ' Paul does not mean the bestowal of the full privileges of the family on those who are sons by nature, but the acceptance into the family of those who are not sons originally and by right in the relation proper of those who are sons by birth. Hence υἱοθεσία is never affirmed of Christ, for he alone is Son of God by nature. So Paul regards our sonship, not as lying in the natural relation in which men stand to God as his children, but as implying a new relation of grace, founded on a covenant relation of God and on the work of Christ (Gal. 4 : 5 sq.)."

2. *Qualified sense of these titles.*

Like the word ' person ', the names Father, Son, and Holy Spirit are not to be confined within the precise limitations of meaning which would be required if they were applied to men.

(*a*) The Scriptures enlarge our conceptions of Christ's Sonship by giving to him in his preëxistent state the names of the Logos, the Image, and the Effulgence of God.—The term 'Logos' combines in itself the two ideas of thought and word, of reason and expression. While the Logos as divine thought or reason is one with God, the Logos as divine word or expression is distinguishable from God. Words are the means by which personal beings express or reveal themselves. Since Jesus Christ was "the Word " before there were any creatures to whom revelations could be made, it would seem to be only a necessary inference from this title that in Christ God must be from eternity expressed or revealed to himself ; in other words, that the Logos is the principle of truth, or self-consciousness, in God.—The term ' Image ' suggests the ideas of copy or counterpart. Man is the image of God only relatively and derivatively. Christ is the Image of God absolutely and archetypally. As the perfect representation of the Father's perfections, the Son would seem to be the object and principle of love in the Godhead.— The term ' Effulgence,' finally, is an allusion to the sun and its radiance. As the effulgence of the sun manifests the sun's nature, which otherwise would be unrevealed, yet is inseparable from the sun and ever one with it, so Christ reveals God, but is eternally one with God. Here is a principle of movement, of will, which seems to connect itself with the holiness, or self-asserting purity, of the divine nature.

Smyth, Introd. to Edwards' Observations on the Trinity : "The ontological relations of the persons of the Trinity are not a mere blank to human thought." John 1 : 1 —"In the beginning was the Word "— means more than "in the beginning was the *x*, or the zero." Godet indeed says that Logos = ' reason' only in philosophical writings, but never in the Scriptures. He calls this a Hegelian notion. But both Plato and Philo had made this signification a common one. On λόγος as = reason + speech, see Lightfoot on Colossians, 143, 144. Meyer interprets it as " personal subsistence, the self-revelation of the divine essence, before all time immanent in God." Neander, Planting and Training, 369 — Logos = " the eternal Revealer of the divine essence." Bushnell : " Mirror of creative imagination " ; " form of God."

Word = 1. Expression ; 2. Definite expression ; 3. Ordered expression ; 4. Complete expression. We make thought definite by putting it into language. So God's wealth of ideas is in the Word formed into an ordered Kingdom, a true Cosmos ; see Mason, Faith of the Gospel, 76. Max Müller : "A word is simply a spoken thought made audible as sound. Take away from a word the sound, and what is left is simply the thought of it." Whiton, Gloria Patri, 72, 73—"The Greek saw in the word the abiding thought behind the passing form. The Word was God and yet finite— finite only as to form. infinite as to what the form suggests or expresses. By Word some form must be meant, and any form is finite. The Word is the form taken by the infinite Intelligence which transcends all forms." We regard this identification of the Word with the finite manifestation of the Word as contradicted by John 1 : 1, where the Word is represented as being with God before creation, and by Phil. 2 : 6, where the Word is represented as existing in the form of God before his self-limitation in human nature. Scripture requires us to believe in an objectification of God to himself in the person of the Word prior to any finite manifestation of God to men. Christ existed as the Word, and the Word was with God, before the Word was made flesh and before the world came into being ; in other words, the Logos was the eternal principle of truth or self-consciousness in the nature of God.

Passages representing Christ as the Image of God are Col. 1 : 15 — " who is the image of the invisible God " ; 2 Cor. 4 : 4 — " Christ, who is the image of God " (εἰκών) ; Heb. 1 : 3 — " the very image of his substance '' (χαρακτὴρ τῆς ὑποστάσεως αὐτοῦ) ; here χαρακτήρ means 'impress,' ' counterpart.' Christ is the perfect image of God, as men are not. He therefore has consciousness and will. He possesses all the attributes and powers of God. The word ' Image ' suggests the perfect equality with God which the title ' Son ' might at first seem to deny. The living Image of God which is equal to himself and is the object of his infinite love can be nothing less than personal. As the bachelor can never satisfy his longing for companionship by lining his room with mirrors which furnish only a lifeless reflection of himself, so God requires for his love a personal as well as an infinite object. The Image is not precisely the *repetition* of the original. The stamp from the seal is not precisely the *reproduction* of the seal. The letters on the seal run backwards and can be easily read only when the impression is before us. So Christ is the only interpretation and revelation of the hidden Godhead. As only in love do we come to know the depths of our own being, so it is only in the Son that " God is love " (1 John 4 : 8).

Christ is spoken of as the Effulgence of God in Heb. 1 : 3 — " who being the effulgence of his glory " (ἀπαύγασμα τῆς δόξης) ; *cf.* 2 Cor. 4 : 6 — " shined in our hearts, to give the light of the knowledge of the glory of God in the face of Jesus Christ." Notice that the radiance of the sun is as old as the sun itself, and without it the sun would not be sun. So Christ is coëqual and coëternal with the Father. Ps. 84 : 11 — " Jehovah God is a sun." But we cannot see the sun except by the sunlight. Christ is the sunlight which streams forth from the Sun and which makes the Sun visible. If there be an eternal Sun, there must be also an eternal Sunlight, and Christ must be eternal. Westcott on Hebrews 1 : 3 — " The use of the absolute timeless term ὤν, 'being ', guards against the thought that the Lord's sonship was by adoption, and not by nature. ἀπαύγασμα does not express personality, and χαρακτήρ does not express coëssentiality. The two words are related exactly as ὁμοούσιος and μονογενής, and like those must be combined to give the fulness of the truth. The truth expressed thus antithetically holds good absolutely. . . . In Christ the essence of God is made distinct ; in Christ the revelation of God's character is seen." On Edwards's view of the Trinity, together with his quotations from Ramsey's Philosophical Principles, from which he seems to have derived important suggestions, see Allen, Jonathan Edwards, 338–376 ; G. P. Fisher, Edwards's Essay on the Trinity, 110–116.

(*b*) The names thus given to the second person of the Trinity, if they have *any* significance, bring him before our minds in the general aspect of Revealer, and suggest a relation of the doctrine of the Trinity to God's immanent attributes of truth, love, and holiness. The prepositions used to describe the internal relations of the second person to the first are not prepositions of rest, but prepositions of direction and movement. The Trinity, as the organism of Deity, secures a life-movement of the Godhead, a process in which God evermore objectifies himself and in the Son gives forth of his fulness. Christ represents the centrifugal action of the deity. But there must be centripetal action also. In the Holy Spirit the movement is completed, and the divine activity and thought returns into itself. True religion, in reuniting us to God, reproduces in us, in our limited measure, this eternal process of the divine mind. Christian experience witnesses that

God in himself is unknown; Christ is the organ of external revelation; the Holy Spirit is the organ of internal revelation — only he can give us an inward apprehension or realization of the truth. It is "through the eternal Spirit" that Christ "offered himself without blemish unto God," and it is only through the Holy Spirit that the church has access to the Father, or fallen creatures can return to God.

Here we see that God is Life, self-sufficient Life, infinite Life, of which the life of the universe is but a faint reflection, a rill from the fountain, a drop from the ocean. Since Christ is the only Revealer, the only outgoing principle in the Godhead, it is he in whom the whole creation comes to be and holds together. He is the Life of nature: all natural beauty and grandeur, all forces molecular and molar, all laws of gravitation and evolution, are the work and manifestation of the omnipresent Christ. He is the Life of humanity: the intellectual and moral impulses of man, so far as they are normal and uplifting, are due to Christ; he is the principle of progress and improvement in history. He is the Life of the church: the one and only Redeemer and spiritual Head of the race is also its Teacher and Lord.

All objective revelation of God is the work of Christ. But all subjective manifestation of God is the work of the Holy Spirit. As Christ is the principle of outgoing, so the Holy Spirit is the principle of return to God. God would take up finite creatures into himself, would breath into them his breath, would teach them to launch their little boats upon the infinite current of his life. Our electric cars can go up hill at great speed so long as they grip the cable. Faith is the grip which connects us with the moving energy of God. "The universe is homeward bound," because the Holy Spirit is ever turning objective revelation into subjective revelation, and is leading men consciously or unconsciously to appropriate the thought and love and purpose of Him in whom all things find their object and end; "for of him, and through him, and unto him, are all things" (Rom. 11 : 36), — here there is allusion to the Father as the source, the Son as the medium, and the Spirit as the perfecting and completing agent, in God's operations. But all these external processes are only signs and finite reflections of a life-process internal to the nature of God.

Meyer on John 1 : 1 — "the Word was with God": "πρὸς τὸν θεόν does not = παρὰ τῷ θεῷ, but expresses the existence of the Logos in God in respect of intercourse. The moral essence of this essential fellowship is love, which excludes any merely modalistic conception." Marcus Dods, Expositor's Greek Testament, in loco: "This preposition implies intercourse and therefore separate personality."

Mason, Faith of the Gospel, 62 — "And the Word was toward God "= his face is not outwards, as if he were merely revealing, or waiting to reveal, God to the creation. His face is turned inwards. His whole Person is directed toward God, motion corresponding to motion, thought to thought. . . . In him God stands revealed to himself. Contrast the attitude of fallen Adam, with his face averted from God. Godet, on John 1 : 1 — "Πρὸς τὸν θεόν intimates not only personality but movement. . . . . The tendency of the Logos ad extra rests upon an anterior and essential relation ad intra. To reveal God, one must know him; to project him outwardly, one must have plunged into his bosom." Compare John 1 : 18 — "the only begotten Son, who is in the bosom of the Father " (R. V.) where we find, not ἐν τῷ κόλπῳ, but εἰς τὸν κόλπον. As ἦν εἰς τὴν πόλιν means ' went into the city and was there,' so the use of these prepositions indicates in the Godhead movement as well as rest. Dorner, System of Doctrine, 3 : 193, translates πρός by ' hingewandt zu,' or ' turned toward.' The preposition would then imply that the Revealer, who existed in the beginning, was ever over against God, in the life-process of the Trinity, as the perfect objectification of himself. "Das Aussichselbstsein kraft des Durchsichselbstsein mit dem Fürsichselbstsein zusammenschliesst." Dorner speaks of "das Aussensichoderineinemandernsein; Sichgeltendmachen des Ausgeschlossenen; Sichnichtsogesetzthaben; Stehenbleibenwollen."

There is in all human intelligence a threefoldness which points toward a trinitarian life in God. We can distinguish a Wissen, a Bewusstsein, a Selbstbewusstsein. In complete self-consciousness there are the three elements: 1. We are ourselves; 2. We form a picture of ourselves; 3. We recognize this picture as the picture of ourselves. The little child speaks of himself in the third person: "Baby did it." The objective comes before the subject; "me" comes first, and "I" is a later development; "himself" still holds its place, rather than "heself." But this duality belongs only to undeveloped intelligence; it is characteristic of the animal creation; we revert to it in our

22

dreams; the insane are permanent victims of it; and since sin is moral insanity, the sinner has no hope until, like the prodigal, he "comes to himself". (Luke 15 : 17). The insane person is *mente alienatus*, and we call physicians for the insane by the name of *alienists*. Mere duality gives us only the notion of separation. Perfect self-consciousness whether in man or in God requires a third unifying element. And in God mediation between the "I" and the "Thou" must be the work of a Person also, and the Person who mediates between the two must be in all respects the equal of either, or he could not adequately interpret the one to the other; see Mason, Faith of the Gospel, 57-59.

Shedd, Dogm. Theol., 1 : 179-189, 276-283 — "It is one of the effects of conviction by the Holy Spirit to convert consciousness into self-consciousness. . . . Conviction of sin is the consciousness of self as the guilty author of sin. Self-consciousness is trinal, while mere consciousness is dual. . . . One and the same human spirit subsists in two modes or distinctions — subject and object. . . . The three hypostatical consciousnesses in their combination and unity constitute the one consciousness of God . . . . as the three persons make one essence."

Dorner considers the internal relations of the Trinity (System, 1 : 412 *sq.*) in three aspects: 1. Physical. God is *causa sui*. But effect that equals cause must itself be causative. Here would be duality, were it not for a third principle of unity. Trinitas dualitatem ad unitatem reducit. 2. Logical. Self-consciousness sets self over against self, Yet the thinker must not regard self as one of many, and call himself 'he,' as children do; for the thinker would then be, not *self*-conscious, but *mente alienatus*, 'beside himself.' He therefore 'comes to himself' in a third, as the brute cannot. 3. Ethical. God=self-willing right. But right based on arbitrary will is not right. Right based on passive nature is not right either. Right as *being* = Father. Right as *willing* = Son. Without the latter principle of freedom, we have a dead ethic, a dead God, an enthroned necessity. The unity of necessity and freedom is found by God, as by the Christian, in the Holy Spirit. The Father — I; the Son — Me; the Spirit the unity of the two; see C. C. Everett, Essays, Theological and Literary, 32. There must be not only Sun and Sunlight, but an Eye to behold the Light. William James, in his Psychology, distinguishes the *Me*, the self as known, from the *I*, the self as knower.

But we need still further to distinguish a third principle, a subject-object, from both subject and object. The subject cannot recognize the object as one with itself except through a unifying principle which can be distinguished from both. We may therefore regard the Holy Spirit as the principle of self-consciousness in man as well as in God. As there was a natural union of Christ with humanity prior to his redeeming work, so there is a natural union of the Holy Spirit with all men prior to his regenerating work : Job 32 : 18 — "there is a spirit in man, And the breath of the Almighty giveth them understanding." Kuyper, Work of the Holy Spirit, teaches that the Holy Spirit constitutes the principle of life in all living things, and animates all rational beings, as well as regenerates and sanctifies the elect of God. Matheson, Voices of the Spirit, 75, remarks on Job 34 : 14, 15 — "If he gather unto himself his Spirit and his breath; all flesh shall perish together" — that the Spirit is not only necessary to man's salvation, but also to keep up even man's natural life.

Ebrard, Dogmatik, 1 : 172, speaks of the Son as the centrifugal, while the Holy Spirit is the centripetal movement of the Godhead. God apart from Christ is unrevealed (John 1 : 18 — "No man hath seen God at any time"); Christ is the organ of external revelation (18 — "the only begotten Son, who is in the bosom of the Father, he hath declared him"); the Holy Spirit is the organ of internal revelation (1 Cor. 2 : 10 — "unto us Christ revealed them through the Spirit"). That the Holy Spirit is the principle of all movement towards God appears from Heb. 9 : 14 — Christ "through the eternal Spirit offered himself without blemish unto God"; Eph. 2 : 28 — "access in one Spirit unto the Father"; Rom. 8 : 26 — "the Spirit also helpeth our infirmity . . . . the Spirit himself maketh intercession for us"; John 4 : 24 — "God is a Spirit: and they that worship him must worship in spirit"; 16 : 8-11 — "convict the world in respect of sin, and of righteousness, and of judgment." See Twesten, Dogmatik, on the Trinity; also Thomasius, Christi Person und Werk, 1 : 111. Mason, Faith of the Gospel, 68 — "It is the joy of the Son to receive, his gladness to welcome most those wishes of the Father which will cost most to himself. The Spirit also has his joy in making known, — in perfecting fellowship and keeping the eternal love alive by that incessant sounding of the deeps which makes the heart of the Father known to the Son, and the heart of the Son known to the Father." We may add that the Holy Spirit is the organ of internal revelation even to the Father and to the Son.

(c) In the light of what has been said, we may understand somewhat more fully the characteristic differences between the work of Christ and that of the Holy Spirit. We may sum them up in the four statements that, first, all outgoing seems to be the work of Christ, all return to God the work of the Spirit; secondly, Christ is the organ of external revelation, the Holy Spirit the organ of internal revelation; thirdly, Christ is our advocate in heaven, the Holy Spirit is our advocate in the soul; fourthly, in the work of Christ we are passive, in the work of the Spirit we are active. Of the work of Christ we shall treat more fully hereafter, in speaking of his Offices as Prophet, Priest, and King. The work of the Holy Spirit will be treated when we come to speak of the Application of Redemption in Regeneration and Sanctification. Here it is sufficient to say that the Holy Spirit is represented in the Scriptures as the author of life — in creation, in the conception of Christ, in regeneration, in resurrection; and as the giver of light — in the inspiration of Scripture writers, in the conviction of sinners, in the illumination and sanctification of Christians.

Gen. 1:2 — "The Spirit of God was brooding"; Luke 1:35 — to Mary: "The Holy Spirit shall come upon thee". John 3:8 — "born of the Spirit"; Ez. 37:9, 14 — "Come from the four winds, 0 breath . . . . I will put my Spirit in you, and ye shall live"; Rom. 8:11 — "give life also to your mortal bodies through his Spirit." 1 John 2:1 — "an advocate (παράκλητον) with the Father, Jesus Christ the righteous"; John 14:16, 17 — "another Comforter (παράκλητον), that he may be with you for ever, even the Spirit of truth"; Rom. 8:26 — "the Spirit himself maketh intercession for us." 2 Pet. 1:21 — "men spake from God, being moved by the Holy Spirit"; John 16:8 — "convict the world in respect of sin"; 13 — "when he, the Spirit of truth, is come, he shall guide you into all the truth"; Rom. 8:14 — "as many as are led by the Spirit of God, these are sons of God."

McCosh: The works of the Spirit are Conviction, Conversion, Sanctification, Comfort. Donovan: The Spirit is the Spirit of conviction, enlightenment, quickening, in the sinner; and of revelation, remembrance, witness, sanctification, consolation, to the saint. The Spirit enlightens the sinner, as the flash of lightning lights the traveler stumbling on the edge of a precipice at night; enlightens the Christian, as the rising sun reveals a landscape which was all there before, but which was hidden from sight until the great luminary made it visible. "The morning light did not create The lovely prospect it revealed; It only showed the real state Of what the darkness had concealed." Christ's advocacy before the throne is like that of legal counsel pleading in our stead; the Holy Spirit's advocacy in the heart is like the mother's teaching her child to pray for himself.

J. W. A. Stewart: "Without the work of the Holy Spirit redemption would have been impossible, as impossible as that fuel should warm without being lighted, or that bread should nourish without being eaten. Christ is God entering into human history, but without the Spirit Christianity would be only history. The Holy Spirit is God entering into human hearts. The Holy Spirit turns creed into life. Christ is the physician who leaves the remedy and then departs. The Holy Spirit is the nurse who applies and administers the remedy, and who remains with the patient until the cure is completed." Matheson, Voices of the Spirit, 78 — "It is in vain that the mirror exists in the room, if it is lying on its face; the sunbeams cannot reach it till its face is upturned to them. Heaven lies about thee not only in thine infancy but at all times. But it is not enough that a place is prepared for thee; thou must be prepared for the place. It is not enough that thy light has come; thou thyself must arise and shine. No outward shining can reveal, unless thou art thyself a reflector of its glory. The Spirit must set thee on thy feet, that thou mayest hear him that speaks to thee (Ez. 2:2)."

The Holy Spirit reveals not himself but Christ. John 16:14 — "He shall glorify me: for he shall take of mine, and shall declare it unto you." So should the servants of the Spirit hide themselves while they make known Christ. E. H. Johnson, The Holy Spirit, 40 — "Some years ago a large steam engine all of glass was exhibited about the country. When it was at work one would see the piston and the valves go; but no one could see what made them go. When steam is hot enough to be a continuous elastic vapor, it is invisible." So we perceive the presence of the Holy Spirit, not by visions or voices, but by the effect he produces within us in the shape of new knowledge, new love, and new energy of our own powers. Denney, Studies in Theology, 161 — "No man can bear witness to Christ and to himself at the same time. Esprit is fatal to unction; no man can give the impression that he himself is clever and also that Christ is mighty to save. The power of the Holy Spirit is felt only when the witness is unconscious of self, and when others remain unconscious of him." Moule, Veni Creator, 8 — "The Holy Spirit, as Tertullian says, is the vicar of Christ. The night before the Cross, the Holy Spirit was present to the mind of Christ as a person."

Gore, in Lux Mundi, 318 — "It was a point in the charge against Origen that his language seemed to involve an exclusion of the Holy Spirit from nature, and a limitation of his activity to the church. The whole of life is certainly his. And yet, because his special attribute is holiness, it is in rational natures, which alone are capable of holiness, that he exerts his special influence. A special inbreathing of the divine Spirit gave to man his proper being." See Gen. 2 : 7 — "Jehovah God . . . breathed into his nostrils the breath of life ; and man become a living soul" ; John 3 : 8 — "The Spirit breatheth where it will . . . so is every one that is born of the Spirit." E. H. Johnson, on The Offices of the Holy Spirit, in Bib. Sac., July, 1892: 361-382 — "Why is he specially called the Holy, when Father and Son are also holy, unless because he produces holiness, i. e., makes the holiness of God to be ours individually ? Christ is the principle of collectivism, the Holy Spirit the principle of individualism. The Holy Spirit shows man the Christ in him. God above all = Father ; God through all = Son ; God in all = Holy Spirit (Eph. 4 : 6)."

The doctrine of the Holy Spirit has never yet been scientifically unfolded. No treatise on it has appeared comparable to Julius Müller's Doctrine of Sin, or to I. A. Dorner's History of the Doctrine of the Person of Christ. The progress of doctrine in the past has been marked by successive stages. Athanasius treated of the Trinity ; Augustine of sin ; Anselm of the atonement ; Luther of justification ; Wesley of regeneration ; and each of these unfoldings of doctrine has been accompanied by religious awakening. We still wait for a complete discussion of the doctrine of the Holy Spirit, and believe that widespread revivals will follow the recognition of the omnipotent Agent in revivals. On the relations of the Holy Spirit to Christ, see Owen in Works, 3 : 152-159 ; on the Holy Spirit's nature and work, see works by Faber, Smeaton, Tophel, G. Campbell Morgan, J. D. Robertson, Biederwolf ; also C. E. Smith, The Baptism of Fire J. D. Thompson, The Holy Comforter ; Bushnell, Forgiveness and Law, last chapter Bp. Andrews, Works, 3 : 107-400 ; James S. Candlish, Work of the Holy Spirit ; Redford, Vox Dei ; Andrew Murray, The Spirit of Christ ; A. J. Gordon, Ministry of the Spirit ; Kuyper, Work of the Holy Spirit ; J. E. Cumming, Through the Eternal Spirit ; Lechler, Lehre vom Heiligen Geiste ; Arthur, Tongue of Fire ; A. H. Strong, Philosophy and Religion, 250-258, and Christ in Creation, 297-313.

3. *Generation and procession consistent with equality.*

That the Sonship of Christ is eternal, is intimated in Psalm 2 : 7. "This day have I begotten thee" is most naturally interpreted as the declaration of an eternal fact in the divine nature. Neither the incarnation, the baptism, the transfiguration, nor the resurrection marks the beginning of Christ's Sonship, or constitutes him Son of God. These are but recognitions or manifestations of a preëxisting Sonship, inseparable from his Godhood. He is "born before every creature" (while yet no created thing existed — see Meyer on Col. 1 : 15) and "by the resurrection of the dead" is not *made* to be, but only "*declared* to be," "according to the Spirit of holiness" (= according to his divine nature) "the Son of God with power" (see Philippi and Alford on Rom. 1 : 3, 4). This Sonship is unique — not predicable of, or shared with, any creature. The Scriptures intimate, not only an eternal generation of the Son, but an eternal procession of the Spirit.

Psalm 2 : 7 — "I will tell of the decree : Jehovah said unto me, Thou art my Son ; This day I have begotten thee" see Alexander, Com. *in loc* ; also Com. on Acts 13 : 33 — "'To-day' refers to the date of the decree itself ; but this, as a divine act, was eternal, — and so must be the Sonship which it affirms." Philo says that "to-day" with God means "forever." This begetting of which the Psalm speaks is not the resurrection, for while Paul in Acts 13 : 33 refers to this Psalm to establish the fact of Jesus' Sonship, he refers in Acts 13 : 34, 35 to another Psalm, the sixteenth, to establish the fact that this Son of God was to rise from the dead. Christ is shown to be Son of God by his incarnation (Heb. 1 : 5, 6 — "when he again bringeth in the firstborn into the world he saith, And let all the angels of God worship him "), his baptism (Mat. 3 : 17 — "This is my beloved Son "), his transfiguration (Mat. 17 : 5 — "This is my beloved Son "), his resurrection (Acts 13 : 34, 35 — " as concerning that he raised him up from the dead . . . he saith also in another psalm, Thou wilt not give thy Holy One to see corruption "). Col. 1 : 15 — "the firstborn of all creation " — πρωτότοκος πάσης κτίσεως = " begotten first before all creation " (Julius Müller, Proof-texts, 14) ; or " first-born before every creature, *i. e.*, begotten, and that antecedently to everything that was created " (Ellicott, Com. *in loco*). " Herein " (says Luthardt, Compend. Dogmatik, 81, on Col. 1 : 15) " is indicated an antemundane origin from God — a relation internal to the divine nature." Lightfoot, on Col. 1 : 15, says that in Rabbi Bechai God is called the " *primogenitus mundi*."

On Rom. 1 : 4 (ὁρισθέντος = " manifested to be the mighty Son of God ") see Lange's Com., notes by Schaff on pages 56 and 61. Bruce, Apologetics, 404 — " The resurrection was the actual introduction of Christ into the full possession of divine Sonship so far as thereto belonged, not only the *inner* of a holy spiritual essence, but also the *outer* of an existence in power and heavenly glory."   Allen, Jonathan Edwards, 353, 354 — " Calvin waves aside eternal generation as an 'absurd fiction.' But to maintain the deity of Christ merely on the ground that it is essential to his making an adequate atonement for sin, is to involve the rejection of his deity if ever the doctrine of atonement becomes obnoxious. . . . Such was the process by which, in the mind of the last century, the doctrine of the Trinity was undermined. Not to ground the distinctions of the divine essence by some immanent eternal necessity was to make easy the denial of what has been called the ontological Trinity, and then the rejection of the economical Trinity was not difficult or far away."

If Westcott and Hort's reading ὁ μονογενὴς Θεός, "the only begotten God," in John 1 : 18, is correct, we have a new proof of Christ's eternal Sonship. Meyer explains ἑαυτοῦ in Rom. 8 : 3 — "God, sending his own Son," as an allusion to the metaphysical Sonship. That this Sonship is unique, is plain from John 1 : 14, 18 — "the only begotten from the Father . . . the only begotten Son who is in the bosom of the Father " ; Rom. 8 : 32 — "his own Son " ; Gal. 4 · 4 — "sent forth his Son " ; *cf.* Prov. 8 : 22-31 — "When he marked out the foundations of the earth ; Then I was by him as a master workman " ; 30 : 4 — "Who hath established all the ends of the earth ? What is his name, and what is his son's name, if thou knowest ? " The eternal procession of the Spirit seems to be implied in John 15 : 26 — "the Spirit of truth which proceedeth from the Father " — see Westcott, Bib. Com., *in loco* ; Heb. 9 : 14 — "the eternal Spirit." Westcott here says that παρά (not ἐξ) shows that the reference is to the temporal mission of the Holy Spirit, not to the eternal procession. At the same time he maintains that the temporal corresponds to the eternal.

The Scripture terms ' generation ' and ' procession,' as applied to the Son and to the Holy Spirit, are but approximate expressions of the truth, and we are to correct by other declarations of Scripture any imperfect impressions which we might derive solely from them. We use these terms in a special sense, which we explicitly state and define as excluding all notion of inequality between the persons of the Trinity. The eternal generation of the Son to which we hold is

(*a*) Not creation, but the Father's communication of himself to the Son. Since the names, Father, Son, and Holy Spirit are not applicable to the divine essence, but are only applicable to its hypostatical distinctions, they imply no derivation of the essence of the Son from the essence of the Father.

The error of the Nicene Fathers was that of explaining Sonship as derivation of essence. The Father cannot impart his essence to the Son and yet retain it. The Father is *fons trinitatis*, not *fons deitatis*. See Shedd, Hist. Doct., 1 : 308-311, and Dogm. Theol., 1 : 287-299 ; *per contra*, see Bib. Sac., 41 : 698-760.

(*b*) Not a commencement of existence, but an eternal relation to the Father, — there never having been a time when the Son began to be, or when the Son did not exist as God with the Father.

If there had been an eternal sun, it is evident that there must have been an eternal sunlight also. Yet an eternal sunlight must have evermore proceeded from the sun.

When Cyril was asked whether the Son existed before generation, he answered: "The generation of the Son did not precede his existence, but he always existed, and that by generation."

(c) Not an act of the Father's will, but an internal necessity of the divine nature,—so that the Son is no more dependent upon the Father than the Father is dependent upon the Son, and so that, if it be consistent with deity to be Father, it is equally consistent with deity to be Son.

The sun is as dependent upon the sunlight as the sunlight is upon the sun ; for without sunlight the sun is no true sun. So God the Father is as dependent upon God the Son, as God the Son is dependent upon God the Father; for without Son the Father would be no true Father. To say that aseity belongs only to the Father is logically Arianism and Subordinationism proper, for it implies a subordination of the essence of the Son to the Father. Essential subordination would be inconsistent with equality. See Thomasius, Christi Person und Werk, 1 : 115. Palmer, Theol. Definitions, 66, 67, says that Father = independent life ; Son begotten = independent life voluntarily brought under limitations ; Spirit = necessary consequence of existence of the other two. . . . The words and actions whereby we design to affect others are " begotten." The atmosphere of unconscious influence is not " begotten," but " proceeding."

(d) Not a relation in any way analogous to physical derivation, but a life-movement of the divine nature, in virtue of which Father, Son, and Holy Spirit, while equal in essence and dignity, stand to each other in an order of personality, office, and operation, and in virtue of which the Father works through the Son, and the Father and the Son through the Spirit.

The subordination of the *person* of the Son to the *person* of the Father, or in other words an order of personality, office, and operation which permits the Father to be officially first, the Son second, and the Spirit third, is perfectly consistent with equality. Priority is not necessarily superiority. The possibility of an order, which yet involves no inequality, may be illustrated by the relation between man and woman. In office man is first and woman second, but woman's soul is worth as much as man's ; see 1 Cor. 11 : 3 — "the head of every man is Christ; and the head of the woman is the man : and the head of Christ is God." On John 14 : 28 — "the Father is greater than I " — see Westcott, Bib. Com., *in loco*.

Edwards, Observations on the Trinity (edited by Smyth), 22 — " In the Son the whole deity and glory of the Father is as it were repeated or duplicated. Everything in the Father is repeated or expressed again, and that fully, so that there is properly no inferiority." Edwards, Essay on the Trinity (edited by Fisher), 110-116 — " The Father is the Deity subsisting in the prime, unoriginated, and most absolute manner, or the Deity in its direct existence. The Son is the Deity generated by God's understanding, or having an Idea of himself and subsisting in that Idea. The Holy Ghost is the Deity subsisting in act, or the divine essence flowing out and breathed forth in God's infinite love to and delight in himself. And I believe the whole divine essence does truly and distinctly subsist both in the divine Idea and in the divine Love, and each of them are properly distinct persons. . . . We find no other attributes of which it is said in Scripture that they are God, or that God is they, but λόγος and ἀγάπη, the Reason and the Love of God, Light not being different from Reason. . . . Understanding may be predicated of this Love. . . . It is not a blind Love. . . . The Father has Wisdom or Reason by the Son's being in him. . . . Understanding is in the Holy Spirit, because the Son is in him." Yet Dr. Edwards A. Park declared eternal generation to be "eternal nonsense," and is thought to have hid Edwards's unpublished Essay on the Trinity for many years because it taught this doctrine.

The New Testament calls Christ Θεός, but not ὁ Θεός. We frankly recognize an eternal subordination of Christ to the Father, but we maintain at the same time that this subordination is a subordination of order, office, and operation, not a subordination of essence. " Non de essentia dicitur, sed de ministeriis." E. G. Robinson : "An eternal generation is necessarily an eternal subordination and dependence. This seems to be fully admitted even by the most orthodox of the Anglican writers, such as Pearson and Hooker. Christ's subordination to the Father is merely official, not essential." Whiton, Gloria Patri, 42, 96 — "The early Trinitarians by eternal Sonship meant, first, that it is of the very nature of Deity to issue forth into visible expression. Thus next, that this outward expression of God is not something other than God, but God himself, in a self-expression as divine as the hidden Deity. Thus they answered Philip's cry, 'show us the Father, and it sufficeth us ' (John 14 : 8), and thus they affirmed Jesus' declaration, they secured Paul's faith that God has never left himself without witness. They meant, ' he that hath seen me hath seen the Father ' (John 14 : 9). . . . The Father is the Life transcendent, the divine Source, 'above all'; the Son is the Life immanent, the divine Stream, 'through all ', the Holy Spirit is the Life individualized, 'in all ' (Eph. 4 : 6). The Holy Spirit has been called ' the executive of the Godhead.' " Whiton is here speaking of the economic Trinity; but all this is even more true of the immanent Trinity. On the Eternal Sonship, see Weiss, Bib. Theol. N. T., 424, note; Treffrey, Eternal Sonship of our Lord ; Princeton Essays, 1 : 30-56; Watson, Institutes, 1 : 530-577 ; Bib. Sac., 27 : 263. On the procession of the Spirit, see Shedd, Dogm. Theol., 1 : 300-304, and History of Doctrine, 1 : 387 ; Dick, Lectures on Theology, 1 : 347-350.

The same principles upon which we interpret the declaration of Christ's eternal Sonship apply to the procession of the Holy Spirit from the Father through the Son, and show this to be not inconsistent with the Spirit's equal dignity and glory.

We therefore only formulate truth which is concretely expressed in Scripture, and which is recognized by all ages of the church in hymns and prayers addressed to Father, Son, and Holy Spirit, when we assert that in the nature of the one God there are three eternal distinctions, which are best described as persons, and each of which is the proper and equal object of Christian worship.

We are also warranted in declaring that, in virtue of these personal distinctions or modes of subsistence, God exists in the relations, respectively, first, of Source, Origin, Authority, and in this relation is the Father ; secondly, of Expression, Medium, Revelation, and in this relation is the Son ; thirdly, of Apprehension, Accomplishment, Realization, and in this relation is the Holy Spirit.

John Owen, Works, 3 : 64-92 — "The office of the Holy Spirit is that of concluding, completing, perfecting. To the Father we assign *opera naturæ ;* to the Son, *opera gratiæ procuratæ ;* to the Spirit, *opera gratiæ applicatæ.*" All God's revelations are through the Son or the Spirit, and the latter includes the former. Kuyper, Work of the Holy Spirit, designates the three offices respectively as those of Causation, Construction, Consummation ; the Father brings forth, the Son arranges, the Spirit perfects. Allen, Jonathan Edwards, 365-373 — "God is Life, Light, Love. As the Fathers regarded Reason both in God and man as the personal, omnipresent second Person of the Trinity, so Jonathan Edwards regarded Love both in God and in man as the personal, omnipresent third Person of the Trinity. Hence the Father is never said to love the Spirit as he is said to love the Son — for this love *is* the Spirit. The Father and the Son are said to love men, but the Holy Spirit is never said to love them, for love *is* the Holy Spirit. But why could not Edwards also hold that the Logos or divine Reason also dwelt in humanity, so that manhood was constituted in Christ and shared with him in the consubstantial image of the Father ? Outward nature reflects God's light and has Christ in it,— why not universal humanity ? "

Moberly, Atonement and Personality, 136, 202, speaks of "1. God, the Eternal, the Infinite, in his infinity, as himself ; 2. God, as self-expressed within the nature and faculties of man — body, soul, and spirit — the consummation and interpretation and revelation of what true manhood means and is, in its very truth, in its relation to God ; 3. God, as Spirit of Beauty and Holiness, which are himself present in things created, animate and inanimate, and constituting in them their divine response to God ; constituting above all in created personalities the full reality of their personal response. Or again : 1. What a man is invisibly in himself ; 2. his outward material projection or expression as body ; and 3. the response which that which he is through his bodily utterance or operation makes to him, as the true echo or expression of himself." Moberly seeks thus to find in man's nature an analogy to the inner processes of the divine.

VI. INSCRUTABLE, YET NOT SELF-CONTRADICTORY, THIS DOCTRINE FURNISHES THE KEY TO ALL OTHER DOCTRINES.

1. *The mode of this triune existence is inscrutable.*

It is inscrutable because there are no analogies to it in our finite experience. For this reason all attempts are vain adequately to represent it :

(*a*) From inanimate things — as the fountain, the stream, and the rivulet trickling from it (Athanasius); the cloud, the rain, and the rising mist (Boardman); color, shape, and size (F. W. Robertson); the actinic, luminiferous, and calorific principles in the ray of light (Solar Hieroglyphics, 34).

Luther : " When logic objects to this doctrine that it does not square with her rules, we must say : ' Mulier taceat in ecclesia.' " Luther called the Trinity a flower, in which might be distinguished its form, its fragrance, and its medicinal efficacy ; see Dorner, Gesch. prot. Theol., 189. In Bap. Rev., July, 1880 : 434, Geer finds an illustration of the Trinity in infinite space with its three dimensions. For analogy of the cloud, rain, mist, see W. E. Boardman, Higher Christian Life. Solar Hieroglyphics, 34 (reviewed in New Englander, Oct. 1874 : 789) — " The Godhead is a tripersonal unity, and the light is a trinity. Being immaterial and homogeneous, and thus essentially one in its nature, the light includes a plurality of constituents, or in other words is essentially three in its constitution, its constituent principles being the actinic, the luminiferous, and the calorific ; and in glorious manifestation the light is one, and is the created, constituted, and ordained emblem of the tripersonal God " — of whom it is said that "God is light, and in him is no darkness at all " (1 John 1 : 5). The actinic rays are in themselves invisible ; only as the luminiferous manifest them, are they seen ; only as the calorific accompany them, are they felt.

Joseph Cook : " Sunlight, rainbow, heat — one solar radiance ; Father, Son, Holy Spirit, one God. As the rainbow shows what light is when unfolded, so Christ reveals the nature of God. As the rainbow is unraveled light, so Christ is unraveled God, and the Holy Spirit, figured by heat, is Christ's continued life." Ruder illustrations are those of Oom Paul Krüger : the fat, the wick, the flame, in the candle ; and of Augustine : the root, trunk, branches, all of one wood, in the tree. In Geer's illustration, mentioned above, from the three dimensions of space, we cannot demonstrate that there is not a fourth, but besides length, breadth, and thickness, we cannot conceive of its existence. As these three exhaust, so far as we know, all possible modes of material being, so we cannot conceive of any fourth person in the Godhead.

(*b*) From the constitution or processes of our own minds — as the psychological unity of intellect, affection, and will (substantially held by Augustine); the logical unity of thesis, antithesis, and synthesis (Hegel); the metaphysical unity of subject, object, and subject-object (Melanchthon, Olshausen, Shedd).

Augustine : "Mens meminit sui, intelligit se, diligit se ; si hoc cernimus, Trinitatem cernimus." . . . I exist, I am conscious, I will ; I exist as conscious and willing, I am conscious of existing and willing, I will to exist and be conscious ; and these three functions, though distinct, are inseparable and form one life, one mind, one essence. . . . "Amor autem alicujus amantis est, et amore aliquid amatur. Ecce tria sunt, amans, et quod amatur, et amor. Quid est ergo amor, nisi quædam vita duo aliqua copulans, vel copulare appetans, amantem scilicet et quod amatur." Calvin speaks of Augustine's view as "a speculation far from solid." But Augustine himself had said : "If asked to define the Trinity, we can only say that it is not this or that." John of Damascus : " All we know of the divine nature is that it is not to be known." By this, however, both Augustine and John of Damascus meant only that the precise *mode* of God's triune existence is unrevealed and inscrutable.

Hegel, Philos. Relig., transl., 3 : 99, 100 — " God is, but is at the same time the Other, the self-differentiating, the Other in the sense that this Other is God himself and has potentially the Divine nature in it, and that the abolishing of this difference, of this otherness, this return, this love, is Spirit." Hegel calls God "the absolute Idea, the unity of Life and Cognition, the Universal that thinks itself and thinkingly recognizes itself in an infinite Actuality, from which, as its Immediacy, it no less distinguishes itself again"; see Schwegler, History of Philosophy, 321, 331. Hegel's general doctrine is that the highest unity is to be reached only through the fullest development and reconciliation of the deepest and widest antagonism. Pure being is pure nothing; we must die to live. Light is thesis, Darkness is antithesis, Shadow is synthesis, or union of both. Faith is thesis, Unbelief is antithesis, Doubt is synthesis, or union of both. *Zweifel* comes from *Zwei*, as doubt from δύο. Hegel called Napoleon "ein Weltgeist zu Pferde"—"a world-spirit on horseback." Ladd, Introd. to Philosophy, 202, speaks of "the monotonous tit-tat-too of the Hegelian logic." Ruskin speaks of it as "pure, definite, and highly finished no sense." On the Hegelian principle good and evil cannot be contradictory to each other; without evil there could be no good. Stirling well entitled his exposition of the Hegelian Philosophy "The Secret of Hegel," and his readers have often remarked that, if Stirling discovered the secret, he never made it known.

Lord Coleridge told Robert Browning that he could not understand all his poetry. "Ah, well," replied the poet, "if a reader of your calibre understands ten per cent. of what I write, he ought to be content." When Wordsworth was told that Mr. Browning had married Miss Barrett, he said: "It is a good thing that these two understand each other, for no one else understands them." A pupil once brought to Hegel a passage in the latter's writings and asked for an interpretation. The philosopher examined it and replied: "When that passage was written, there were two who knew its meaning—God and myself. Now, alas! there is but one, and that is God." Heinrich Heine, speaking of the effect of Hegelianism upon the religious life of Berlin, says: "I could accommodate myself to the very enlightened Christianity, filtrated from all superstition, which could then be had in the churches, and which was free from the divinity of Christ, like turtle soup without turtle." When German systems of philosophy die, their ghosts take up their abode in Oxford. But if I see a ghost sitting in a chair and then sit down boldly in the chair, the ghost will take offence and go away. Hegel's doctrine of God as the only begotten Son is translated in the Journ. Spec. Philos., 15:395-404.

The most satisfactory exposition of the analogy of subject, object, and subject-object is to be found in Shedd, History of Doctrine, 1:365, note 2. See also Olshausen on John 1:1; H.N. Day, Doctrine of Trinity in Light of Recent Psychology, in Princeton Rev., Sept. 1882: 156-179; Morris, Philosophy and Christianity, 122-163. Moberly, Atonement and Personality, 174, has a similar analogy: 1. A man's invisible self; 2. the visible expression of himself in a picture or poem; 3. the response of this picture or poem to himself. The analogy of the family is held to be even better, because no man's personality is complete in itself; husband, wife, and child are all needed to make perfect unity. Allen, Jonathan Edwards, 372, says that in the early church the Trinity was a doctrine of reason; in the Middle Ages it was a mystery; in the 18th century it was a meaningless or irrational dogma; again in the 19th century it becomes a doctrine of the reason, a truth essential to the nature of God. To Allen's characterization of the stages in the history of the doctrine we would add that even in our day we cannot say that a complete exposition of the Trinity is possible. Trinity is a unique fact, different aspects of which may be illustrated, while, as a whole, it has no analogies. The most we can say is that human nature, in its processes and powers, points towards something higher than itself, and that Trinity in God is needed in order to constitute that perfection of being which man seeks as an object of love, worship and service.

No one of these furnishes any proper analogue of the Trinity, since in no one of them is there found the essential element of tripersonality. Such illustrations may sometimes be used to disarm objection, but they furnish no positive explanation of the mystery of the Trinity, and, unless carefully guarded, may lead to grievous error.

2. *The Doctrine of the Trinity is not self-contradictory.*

This it would be, only if it declared God to be three in the same numerical sense in which he is said to be one. This we do not assert. We assert simply that the same God who is one with respect to his essence is three with respect to the internal distinctions of that essence, or with respect to the modes of his being. The possibility of this cannot be denied, except by assuming that the human mind is in all respects the measure of the divine.

The fact that the ascending scale of life is marked by increasing differentiation of faculty and function should rather lead us to expect in the highest of all beings a nature more complex than our own. In man many faculties are united in one intelligent being, and the more intelligent man is, the more distinct from each other these faculties become; until intellect and affection, conscience and will assume a relative independence, and there arises even the possibility of conflict between them. There is nothing irrational or self-contradictory in the doctrine that in God the leading functions are yet more markedly differentiated, so that they become personal, while at the same time these personalities are united by the fact that they each and equally manifest the one indivisible essence.

Unity is as essential to the Godhead as threeness. The same God who in one respect is three, in another respect is one. We do not say that one God is three Gods, nor that one person is three persons, nor that three Gods are one God, but only that there is one God with three distinctions in his being. We do not refer to the faculties of man as furnishing any proper analogy to the persons of the Godhead; we rather deny that man's nature furnishes any such analogy. Intellect, affection, and will in man are not distinct personalities. If they were personalized, they might furnish such an analogy F. W. Robertson, Sermons, 3 : 58, speaks of the Father, Son, and Holy Spirit as best conceived under the figure of personalized intellect, affection and will. With this agrees the saying of Socrates, who called thought the soul's conversation with itself. See D. W. Simon, in Bib. Sac., Jan. 1887.

Ps. 86 : 11 — " Unite my heart to fear thy name " — intimates a complexity of powers in man, and a possible disorganization due to sin. Only the fear and love of God can reduce our faculties to order and give us peace, purity, and power. When William after a long courtship proposed marriage, Mary said that she " unanimously consented." " Thou shalt love the Lord thy God with all thy heart, and with all thy soul, and with all thy strength, and with all thy mind" (Luke 10 : 27). Man must not lead a dual life, a double life, like that of Dr. Jekyll and Mr. Hyde. The good life is the unified life. H. H. Bawden: " Theoretically, symmetrical development is the complete criterion. This is the old Greek conception of the perfect life. The term which we translate ' temperance ' or ' self-control ' is better expressed by ' whole-mindedness.' "

Illingworth, Personality Divine and Human, 54–80 — " Our sense of divine personality culminates in the doctrine of the Trinity. Man's personality is essentially triune, because it consists of a subject, an object, and their relation. What is potential and unrealized triunity in man is complete in God. . . . Our own personality is triune, but it is a potential unrealized triunity, which is incomplete in itself and must go beyond itself for completion, as for example in the family. . . . But God's personality has nothing potential or unrealized about it. . . . Trinity is the most intelligible mode of conceiving of God as personal."

John Caird, Fundamental Ideas of Christianity, 1 : 59, 80 — " The parts of a stone are all precisely alike; the parts of a skilful mechanism are all different from one another. In which of the two cases is the unity more real — in that in which there is an absence of distinction, or in that in which there is essential difference of form and function, each separate part having an individuality and activity of its own ? The highest unities are not simple but complex." Gordon, Christ of To-day, 106 — "All things and persons are modes of one infinite consciousness. Then it is not incredible that there should be three consciousnesses in God. Over against the multitudinous finite personalities are three infinite personalities. This socialism in Deity may be the ground of human society."

The phenomena of double and even of triple consciousness in one and the same individual confirm this view. This fact of more than one consciousness in a finite creature points towards the possibility of a threefold consciousness in the nature of God. Romanes, Mind and Motion, 102, intimates that the social organism, if it attained the highest level of psychical perfection, might be endowed with personality, and that it now has something resembling it — phenomena of thought and conduct which compel us to conceive of families and communities and nations as having a sort of moral personality which implies responsibility and accountability. "The *Zeitgeist*," he says, "is the product of a kind of collective psychology, which is something other than the sum of all the individual minds of a generation." We do not maintain that any one of these fragmentary or collective consciousnesses attains personality in man, at least in the present life. We only maintain that they indicate that a larger and more complex life is possible than that of which we have common experience, and that there is no necessary contradiction in the doctrine that in the nature of the one and perfect God there are three personal distinctions. R. H. Hutton: "A voluntary self-revelation of the divine mind may be expected to reveal even deeper complexities of spiritual relations in his eternal nature and essence than are found to exist in our humanity — the simplicity of a harmonized complexity, not the simplicity of absolute unity."

3. *The doctrine of the Trinity has important relations to other doctrines.*

A. It is essential to any proper theism.

Neither God's independence nor God's blessedness can be maintained upon grounds of absolute unity. Anti-trinitarianism almost necessarily makes creation indispensable to God's perfection, tends to a belief in the eternity of matter, and ultimately leads, as in Mohammedanism, and in modern Judaism and Unitarianism, to Pantheism. "Love is an impossible exercise to a solitary being." Without Trinity we cannot hold to a living Unity in the Godhead.

Brit. and For. Evang. Rev., Jan. 1882: 35–63 — "The problem is to find a *perfect objective*, congruous and fitting, for a perfect intelligence, and the answer is: '*a perfect intelligence.*'" The author of this article quotes James Martineau, the Unitarian philosopher, as follows: "There is only one resource left for completing the needful objectivity for God, viz., to admit in some form the coëval existence of matter, as the condition or medium of the divine agency or manifestation. Failing the proof [of the absolute origination of matter] we are left with the *divine cause*, and the *material condition* of all nature, in eternal co-presence and relation, as supreme object and rudimentary object." See also Martineau, Study, 1 : 405 — "In denying that a plurality of self-existences is possible, I mean to speak only of self-existent *causes*. A self-existence which is *not* a cause is by no means excluded, so far as I can see, by a self-existence which *is* a cause; nay, is even required for the exercise of its causality." Here we see that Martineau's Unitarianism logically drove him into Dualism. But God's blessedness, upon this principle, requires not merely an eternal universe but an infinite universe, for nothing less will afford fit object for an infinite mind. Yet a God who is necessarily bound to the universe, or by whose side a universe, which is not himself, eternally exists, is not infinite, independent, or free. The only exit from this difficulty is in denying God's self-consciousness and self-determination, or in other words, exchanging our theism for dualism, and our dualism for pantheism.

E. H. Johnson, in Bib. Sac., July, 1892: 379, quotes from Oxenham's Catholic Doctrine of the Atonement, 108, 109 — "Forty years ago James Martineau wrote to George Macdonald : 'Neither my intellectual preference nor my moral admiration goes heartily with the Unitarian heroes, sects or productions, of any age. Ebionites, Arians, Socinians, all seem to me to contrast unfavorably with their opponents, and so exhibit a type of thought far less worthy, on the whole, of the true genius of Christianity.' In his paper entitled A Way out of the Unitarian Controversy, Martineau says that the Unitarian worships the Father ; the Trinitarian worships the Son: 'But he who is the Son in one creed is the Father in the other. . . . The two creeds are agreed in that which constitutes the pith and kernel of both. The Father is God in his primeval essence. But God, as manifested, is the Son.'" Dr. Johnson adds: "So Martineau, after a lifelong service in a Unitarian pulpit and professorship, at length publicly accepts for truth the substance of that doctrine which, in common with the church, he has found so profitable, and tells Unitarians that they and we alike worship the Son, because all that we know of

God was revealed by act of the Son." After he had reached his eightieth year, Martineau withdrew from the Unitarian body, though he never formally united with any Trinitarian church.

H. C. Minton, in Princeton Rev., 1903 : 655–659, has quoted some of Martineau's most significant utterances, such as the following : "The great strength of the orthodox doctrine lies, no doubt, in the appeal it makes to the inward 'sense of sin,'—that sad weight whose burden oppresses every serious soul. And the great weakness of Unitarianism has been its insensibility to this abiding sorrow of the human consciousness. But the orthodox remedy is surely the most terrible of all mistakes, *viz.*, *to get rid* of the burden, by throwing it on Christ or permitting him to take it. . . . For myself I own that the literature to which I turn for the nurture and inspiration of Faith, Hope and Love is almost exclusively the product of orthodox versions of the Christian religion. The Hymns of the Wesleys, the Prayers of the Friends, the Meditations of Law and Tauler, have a quickening and elevating power which I rarely feel in the books on our Unitarian shelves. . . . Yet I can less than ever appropriate, or even intellectually excuse, any distinctive article of the Trinitarian scheme of salvation."

Whiton, Gloria Patri, 23–26, seeks to reconcile the two forms of belief by asserting that " both Trinitarians and Unitarians are coming to regard human nature as essentially one with the divine. The Nicene Fathers builded better than they knew, when they declared Christ *homoousios* with the Father. We assert the same of mankind." But here Whiton goes beyond the warrant of Scripture. Of none but the only begotten Son can it be said that before Abraham was born he was, and that in him dwelleth all the fulness of the Godhead bodily (John 8 : 57; Col. 2 : 9).

Unitarianism has repeatedly demonstrated its logical insufficiency by this " facilis descensus Averno," this lapse from theism into pantheism. In New England the high Arianism of Channing degenerated into the half-fledged pantheism of Theodore Parker, and the full-fledged pantheism of Ralph Waldo Emerson. Modern Judaism is pantheistic in its philosophy, and such also was the later Arabic philosophy of Mohammedanism. Single personality is felt to be insufficient to the mind's conception of Absolute Perfection. We shrink from the thought of an eternally lonely God. " We take refuge in the term 'Godhead.' The literati find relief in speaking of 'the gods.' " Twesten (translated in Bib. Sac., 3 : 502) — " There may be in polytheism an element of truth, though disfigured and misunderstood. John of Damascus boasted that the Christian Trinity stood midway between the abstract monotheism of the Jews and the idolatrous polytheism of the Greeks." Twesten, quoted in Shedd, Dogm. Theology, 1 : 255 — " There is a $\pi\lambda\acute{\eta}\rho\omega\mu\alpha$ in God. Trinity does not contradict Unity, but only that solitariness which is inconsistent with the living plenitude and blessedness ascribed to God in Scripture, and which God possesses in himself and independently of the finite." Shedd himself remarks : " The attempt of the Deist and the Socinian to construct the doctrine of divine *Unity* is a failure, because it fails to construct the doctrine of the divine *Personality*. It contends by implication that God can be self-knowing as a single subject merely, without an object ; without the distinctions involved in the subject contemplating, the object contemplated, and the perception of the identity of both."

Mason, Faith of the Gospel, 75 — " God is no sterile and motionless unit." Bp. Phillips Brooks : " Unitarianism has got the notion of God as tight and individual as it is possible to make it, and is dying of its meagre Deity." Unitarianism is not the doctrine of one God — for the Trinitarian holds to this ; it is rather the unipersonality of this one God. The divine nature demands either an eternal Christ or an eternal creation. Dr. Calthorp, the Unitarian, of Syracuse, therefore consistently declares that " Nature and God are the same." It is the old worship of Baal and Ashtaroth — the deification of power and pleasure. For " Nature" includes everything — all bad impulses as well as good. When a man discovers gravity, he has not discovered God, but only one of the manifestations of God.

Gordon, Christ of To-day, 112 — " The supreme divinity of Jesus Christ is but the sovereign expression in human history of the great law of difference in identity that runs through the entire universe and that has its home in the heart of the Godhead." Even James Freeman Clarke, in his Orthodoxy, its Truths and Errors, 436, admits that " there is an essential truth hidden in the idea of the Trinity. While the church doctrine, in every form which it has taken, has failed to satisfy the human intellect, the human heart has clung to the substance contained in them all." William Adams Brown : " If God is by nature love, he must be by nature social. Fatherhood and Sonship must be immanent in him. In him the limitations of finite personality are removed." But Dr. Brown wrongly adds : " Not the mysteries of God's being, as he is fn himself, but as he is revealed, are opened to us in this doctrine." Similarly P. S. Moxom : " I do not know how it is possible to predicate any moral quality of a person who is absolutely out of relation to other persons. If God were conceived of as solitary in the universe, he could not be characterized as righteous." But Dr. Moxom erroneously thinks that these other moral personalities must be outside of God. We maintain that righteousness, like love, requires only plurality of persons within the God-head. See Thomasius, Christi Person und Werk, 1 : 105, 156. For the pantheistic view, see Strauss, Glaubenslehre, 1 : 462-524.

W. L. Walker, Christian Theism, 317, quotes Dr. Paul Carus, Primer of Philosophy, 101 — " We cannot even conceive of God without attributing trinity to him. An absolute unity would be non-existence. God, if thought of as real and active, involves an antithesis, which may be formulated as God and World, or *natura naturans* and *natura naturata*, or in some other way. This antithesis implies already the trinity-conception. When we think of God, not only as that which is eternal and immutable in existence, but also as that which changes, grows, and evolves, we cannot escape the result and we must progress to a triune God-idea. The conception of a God-man, of a Savior, of God revealed in evolution, brings out the antithesis of God Father and God Son, and the very conception of this relation implies God the Spirit that proceeds from both." This confession of an economic Trinity is a rational one only as it implies a Trinity immanent and eternal.

B. It is essential to any proper revelation.

If there be no Trinity, Christ is not God, and cannot perfectly know or reveal God. Christianity is no longer the one, all-inclusive, and final revelation, but only one of many conflicting and competing systems, each of which has its portion of truth, but also its portion of error. So too with the Holy Spirit. " As God can be revealed only through God, so also can he be appropriated only through God. If the Holy Spirit be not God, then the love and self-communication of God to the human soul are not a reality." In other words, without the doctrine of the Trinity we go back to mere natural religion and the far-off God of deism, — and this is ultimately exchanged for pantheism in the way already mentioned.

Martensen, Dogmatics, 104 ; Thomasius, Christi Person und Werk, 156. If Christ be not God, he cannot perfectly know himself, and his testimony to himself has no independent authority. In prayer the Christian has practical evidence of the Trinity, and can see the value of the doctrine ; for he comes to God the Father, pleading the name of Christ, and taught how to pray aright by the Holy Spirit. It is impossible to identify the Father with either the Son or the Spirit. See Rom. 8 : 27 — "he that searcheth the hearts [*i. e.*, God] knoweth what is the mind of the Spirit, because he maketh intercession for the saints according to the will of God." See also Godet on John 1 : 18 — "No man hath seen God at any time ; the only begotten Son, who is in the bosom of the Father, he hath declared him " ; notice here the relation between ὁ ὢν and ἐξηγήσατο. Napoleon I : " Christianity says with simplicity, ' No man hath seen God, except God.' " John 16 : 15 — " All things whatsoever the Father hath are mine : therefore said I, that he taketh of mine, and shall declare it unto you " ; here Christ claims for himself all that belongs to God, and then declares that the Holy Spirit shall reveal him. Only a divine Spirit can do this, even as only a divine Christ can put out an unpresumptuous hand to take all that belongs to the Father. See also Westcott, on John 14 : 9 — "he that hath seen me hath seen the Father ; how sayest thou, Show us the Father ? "

The agnostic is perfectly correct in his conclusions, if there be no Christ, no medium of communication, no principle of revelation in the Godhead. Only the Son has revealed the Father. Even Royce, in his Spirit of Modern Philosophy, speaks of the existence of an infinite Self, or Logos, or World-mind, of which all individual minds are parts or bits, and of whose timeless choice we partake. Some such principle in the divine nature must be assumed, if Christianity is the complete and sufficient revelation of God's will to men. The Unitarian view regards the religion of Christ as only " one of the day's works of humanity "— an evanescent moment in the ceaseless advance of the race. The Christian on the other hand regards Christ as the only Revealer of God, the only God with whom we have to do, the final authority in religion, the source of all truth and the judge of all mankind. "Heaven and earth shall pass away, but my words shall not pass away " (Mat. 24:35). The resurrection of just and unjust shall be his work (John 5:28), and future retribution shall be " the wrath of the Lamb " (Rev. 6:16). Since God never thinks, says, or does any thing, except through Christ, and since Christ does his work in human hearts only through the Holy Spirit, we may conclude that the doctrine of the Trinity is essential to any proper revelation.

C. It is essential to any proper redemption.

If God be absolutely and simply one, there can be no mediation or atonement, since between God and the most exalted creature the gulf is infinite. Christ cannot bring us nearer to God than he is himself. Only one who is God can reconcile us to God. So, too, only one who is God can purify our souls. A God who is only unity, but in whom is no plurality, may be our Judge, but, so far as we can see, cannot be our Savior or our Sanctifier.

"God is the way to himself." " Nothing human holds good before God, and nothing but God himself can satisfy God." The best method of arguing with Unitarians, therefore, is to rouse the sense of sin ; for the soul that has any proper conviction of its sins feels that only an infinite Redeemer can ever save it. On the other hand, a slight estimate of sin is logically connected with a low view of the dignity of Christ. Twesten, translated in Bib. Sac., 3:510 — "It would seem to be not a mere accident that Pelagianism, when logically carried out, as for example among the Socinians, has also always led to Unitarianism." In the reverse order, too, it is manifest that rejection of the deity of Christ must tend to render more superficial men's views of the sin and guilt and punishment from which Christ came to save them, and with this to deaden religious feeling and to cut the sinews of all evangelistic and missionary effort (John 12:44; Heb. 10:26). See Arthur, on the Divinity of our Lord in relation to his work of Atonement, in Present Day Tracts, 6 : no. 35; Ellis, quoted by Watson, Theol. Inst., 23; Gunsaulus, Transfig. of Christ, 13 — " We have tried to see God in the light of nature, while he said : 'In thy light shall we see light' (Ps. 36:9)." We should see nature in the light of Christ. Eternal life is attained only through the knowledge of God in Christ (John 16:9). Hence to accept Christ is to accept God ; to reject Christ is to turn one's back on God : John 12:44 — " He that believeth on me, believeth not on me, but on him that sent me " : Heb. 10 : 26, 29 — "there remaineth no more a sacrifice for sin . . . . [for him] who hath trodden under foot the Son of God."

In The Heart of Midlothian, Jeanie Deans goes to London to secure pardon for her sister. She cannot in her peasant attire go direct to the King, for he will not receive her. She goes to a Scotch housekeeper in London ; through him to the Duke of Argyle ; through him to the Queen ; through the Queen she gets pardon from the King, whom she never sees. This was mediæval mediatorship. But now we come directly to Christ, and this suffices us, because he is himself God (The Outlook). A man once went into the cell of a convicted murderer, at the request of the murderer's wife and pleaded with him to confess his crime and accept Christ, but the murderer refused. The seeming clergyman was the Governor, with a pardon which he had designed to bestow in case he found the murderer penitent. A. H. Strong, Christ in Creation, 86 — "I have heard that, during our Civil War, a swaggering, drunken, blaspheming officer insulted and almost drove from the dock at Alexandria, a plain unoffending man in citizen's dress ; but I have also heard that that same officer turned pale, fell on his knees, and begged for mercy, when the plain man demanded his sword, put him under arrest and made himself known as General Grant. So we may abuse and reject the Lord Jesus Christ, and fancy that we can ignore his claims and disobey his commands with impunity ; but it will seem a more serious thing when we find at the last that he whom we have abused and rejected is none other than the living God before whose judgment bar we are to stand."

Henry B. Smith began life under Unitarian influences, and had strong prejudices against evangelical doctrine, especially the doctrines of human depravity and of the divinity of Christ. In his Senior year in College he was converted. Cyrus Hamlin says: " I regard Smith's conversion as the most remarkable event in College in my day." Doubts of depravity vanished with one glimpse into his own heart ; and doubts about Christ's divinity could not hold their own against the confession : " Of one thing I feel assured : I need an infinite Savior." Here is the ultimate strength of Trinitarian doctrine. When the Holy Spirit convinces a man of his sin, and brings him face to face with the outraged holiness and love of God, he is moved to cry from the depths of his soul : " None but an infinite Savior can ever save me !" Only in a divine Christ—

Christ *for* us upon the Cross, and Christ *in* us by his Spirit — can the convicted soul find peace and rest. And so every revival of true religion gives a new impulse to the Trinitarian doctrine. Henry B. Smith wrote in his later life: "When the doctrine of the Trinity was abandoned, other articles of the faith, such as the atonement and regeneration, have almost always followed, by logical necessity, as, when one draws the wire from a necklace of gems, the gems all fall asunder."

D. It is essential to any proper model for human life.

If there be no Trinity immanent in the divine nature, then Fatherhood in God has had a beginning and it may have an end ; Sonship, moreover, is no longer a perfection, but an imperfection, ordained for a temporary purpose. But if fatherly giving and filial receiving are eternal in God, then the law of love requires of us conformity to God in both these respects as the highest dignity of our being.

See Hutton, Essays, 1 : 232 — "The Trinity tells us something of God's absolute and essential nature ; not simply what he is *to us*, but what he is *in himself*. If Christ is the eternal Son of the Father, God is indeed and in essence a Father ; the social nature, the spring of love is of the very essence of the eternal Being ; the communication of life, the reciprocation of affection dates from beyond time, belongs to the very being of God. The Unitarian idea of a solitary God profoundly affects our conception of God, reduces it to mere power, identifies God with abstract cause and thought. Love is grounded in power, not power in love. The Father is merged in the omniscient and omnipotent genius of the universe." Hence 1 John 2 : 23 — "Whosoever denieth the Son, the same hath not the Father." D'Arcy, Idealism and Theology, 204 — "If God be simply one great person, then we have to think of him as waiting until the whole process of creation has been accomplished before his love can find an object upon which to bestow itself. His love belongs, in that case, not to his inmost essence, but to his relation to some of his creatures. The words ' God is love ' (1 John 4 : 8) become a rhetorical exaggeration, rather than the expression of a truth about the divine nature."

Hutton, Essays, 1 : 239 — "We need also the inspiration and help of a perfect filial will. We cannot conceive of the Father as sharing in that dependent attitude of spirit which is our chief spiritual want. It is a Father's perfection to originate — a Son's to receive. We need sympathy and aid in this *receptive* life ; hence, the help of the true Son. Humility, self-sacrifice, submission, are heavenly, eternal, divine. Christ's filial life is the root of all filial life in us. See Gal. 2 : 19, 20 — "it is no longer I that live, but Christ liveth in me : and that life which I now live in the flesh I live in faith, the faith which is in the Son of God, who loved me, and gave himself up for me." Thomas Erskine of Linlathen, The Spiritual Order, 233 — "There is nothing degrading in this dependence, for we share it with the eternal Son." Gore, Incarnation, 162 — "God can limit himself by the conditions of manhood, because the Godhead contains in itself eternally the prototype of human self-sacrifice and self-limitation, for God is love." On the practical lessons and uses of the doctrine of the Trinity, see Presb. and Ref. Rev., Oct. 1902 : 524–550 — art. by R. M. Edgar ; also sermon by Ganse, in South Church Lectures, 300–310. On the doctrine in general, see Robie, in Bib. Sac., 27 : 262–289 ; Pease, Philosophy of Trinitarian Doctrine ; N. W. Taylor, Revealed Theology, 1 : 133 ; Schultz, Lehre von der Gottheit Christi.

On heathen trinities, see Bib. Repos., 6 : 116 ; Christlieb, Mod. Doubt and Christian Belief, 266, 267 — "Lao-tse says, 600 B. C., 'Tao, the intelligent principle of all being, is by nature one ; the first begat the second ; both together begat the third ; these three made all things.' " The Egyptian triad of Abydos was Osiris, Isis his wife, and Horus their Son. But these were no true persons ; for not only did the Son proceed from the Father, but the Father proceeded from the Son ; the Egyptian trinity was pantheistic in its meaning. See Renouf, Hibbert Lectures, 29 ; Rawlinson, Religions of the Ancient World, 46, 47. The Trinity of the Vedas was Dyaus, Indra, Agni. Derived from the three dimensions of space ? Or from the family — father, mother, son ? Man creates God in his own image, and sees family life in the Godhead ?

The Brahman Trimurti or Trinity, to the members of which are given the names Brahma, Vishnu, Siva — source, supporter, end — is a personification of the pantheistic All, which dwells equally in good and evil, in god and man. The three are represented in the three mystic letters of the syllable *Om*, or *Aum*, and by the image at Elephanta of three heads and one body ; see Hardwick, Christ and Other Masters, 1 : 276. The places of the three are interchangeable. Williams: " In the three persons the one God is shown ; Each first in place, each last, not one alone ; Of Siva, Vishnu, Brahma, each may be, First, second, third, among the blessed three." There are ten incarnations of Vishnu for men's salvation in various times of need ; and the one Spirit which temporarily invests itself with the qualities of matter is reduced to its original essence at the end of the æon (Kalpa). This is only a grosser form of Sabellianism, or of a modal Trinity. According to Renouf it is not older than A. D. 1400. Buddhism in later times had its triad. Buddha, or Intelligence, the first principle, associated with Dharma, or Law, the principle of matter, through the combining influence of Sangha, or Order, the mediating principle. See Kellogg, The Light of Asia and the Light of the World, 184, 355. It is probably from a Christian source.

The Greek trinity was composed of Zeus, Athena, and Apollo. Apollo or Loxias (λόγος) utters the decisions of Zeus. "These three surpass all the other gods in moral character and in providential care over the universe. They sustain such intimate and endearing relations to each other, that they may be said to 'agree in one'"; see Tyler, Theol. of Greek Poets, 170, 171 ; Gladstone, Studies of Homer, vol. 2, sec. 2. Yet the Greek trinity, while it gives us three persons, does not give us oneness of essence. It is a system of tritheism. Plotinus, 300 A. D., gives us a philosophical Trinity in his τὸ ἕν, ὁ νοῦς, ἡ ψυχή.

Watts, New Apologetic, 195 — The heathen trinities are " residuary fragments of the lost knowledge of God, not different stages in a process of theological evolution, but evidence of a moral and spiritual degradation." John Caird, Fund. Ideas of Christianity, 92 — " In the Vedas the various individual divinities are separated by no hard and fast distinction from each other. They are only names for one indivisible whole, of which the particular divinity invoked at any one time is the type or representative. There is a latent recognition of a unity beneath all the multiplicity of the objects of adoration. The personal or anthropomorphic element is never employed as it is in the Greek and Roman mythology. The personality ascribed to Mitra or Varuna or Indra or Agni is scarcely more real than our modern smiling heaven or whispering breeze or sullen moaning restless sea. 'There is but one,' they say, 'though the poets call him by different names.' The all-embracing heaven, mighty nature, is the reality behind each of these partial manifestations. The pantheistic element which was implicit in the Vedic phase of Indian religion becomes explicit in Brahmanism, and in particular in the so-called Indian systems of philosophy and in the great Indian epic poems. They seek to find in the flux and variety of things the permanent underlying essence. That is Brahma. So Spinoza sought rest in the one eternal substance, and he wished to look at all things 'under the form of eternity.' All things and beings are forms of one whole, of the infinite substance which we call God." See also L. L. Paine, Ethnic Trinities.

The gropings of the heathen religions after a trinity in God, together with their inability to construct a consistent scheme of it, are evidence of a rational want in human nature which only the Christian doctrine is able to supply. This power to satisfy the inmost needs of the believer is proof of its truth. We close our treatment with the words of Jeremy Taylor: " He who goes about to speak of the mystery of the Trinity, and does it by words and names of man's invention, talking of essence and existences, hypostases and personalities, priority in coëquality, and unity in pluralities, may amuse himself and build a tabernacle in his head, and talk something — he knows not what ; but the renewed man, that feels the power of the Father, to whom the Son is become wisdom, sanctification, and redemption, in whose heart the love of the Spirit of God is shed abroad — this man, though he understand nothing of what is unintelligible, yet he alone truly understands the Christian doctrine of the Trinity."

CHAPTER III.

THE DECREES OF GOD.

I. Definition of Decrees.

By the decrees of God we mean that eternal plan by which God has rendered certain all the events of the universe, past, present, and future. Notice in explanation that:

(*a*) The decrees are many only to our finite comprehension ; in their own nature they are but one plan, which embraces not only effects but also causes, not only the ends to be secured but also the means needful to secure them.

In Rom. 8 : 28 — "called according to his purpose" — the many decrees for the salvation of many individuals are represented as forming but one purpose of God. Eph. 1 : 11 — "foreordained according to the purpose of him who worketh all things after the counsel of his will" — notice again the word "purpose," in the singular. Eph. 3 : 11 — "according to the eternal purpose which he purposed in Christ Jesus our Lord." This one purpose or plan of God includes both means and ends, prayer and its answer, labor and its fruit. Tyrolese proverb : "God has his plan for every man." Every man, as well as Jean Paul, is "der Einzige" — the unique. There is a single plan which embraces all things; "we use the word 'decree' when we think of it partitively" (Pepper). See Hodge, Outlines of Theology, 1st ed., 165 ; 2d ed., 200 — "In fact, no event is isolated — to determine one involves determination of the whole concatenation of causes and effects which constitutes the universe." The word "plan" is preferable to the word "decrees," because "plan" excludes the ideas of (1) plurality, (2) short-sightedness, (3) arbitrariness, (4) compulsion.

(*b*) The decrees, as the eternal act of an infinitely perfect will, though they have logical relations to each other, have no chronological relation. They are not therefore the result of deliberation, in any sense that implies short-sightedness or hesitancy.

Logically, in God's decree the sun precedes the sunlight, and the decree to bring into being a father precedes the decree that there shall be a son. God decrees man before he decrees man's act ; he decrees the creation of man before he decrees man's existence. But there is no chronological succession. "Counsel" in Eph. 1 : 11 — "the counsel of his will " — means, not deliberation, but wisdom.

(*c*) Since the will in which the decrees have their origin is a free will, the decrees are not a merely instinctive or necessary exercise of the divine intelligence or volition, such as pantheism supposes.

It belongs to the perfection of God that he have a plan, and the best possible plan. Here is no necessity, but only the certainty that infinite wisdom will act wisely. God's decrees are not God ; they are not identical with his essence ; they do not flow from his being in the same necessary way in which the eternal Son proceeds from the eternal Father. There is free will in God, which acts with infinite certainty, yet without necessity. To call even the decree of salvation necessary is to deny grace, and to make an unfree God. See Dick, Lectures on Theology, 1 : 355 ; lect. 34.

(*d*) The decrees have reference to things outside of God. God does not decree to be holy, nor to exist as three persons in one essence.

Decrees are the preparation for external events — the embracing of certain things and acts in a plan. They do not include those processes and operations within the Godhead which have no reference to the universe.

(*e*) The decrees primarily respect the acts of God himself, in Creation, Providence, and Grace ; secondarily, the acts of free creatures, which he foresees will result therefrom.

While we deny the assertion of Whedon, that " the divine plan embraces *only* divine actions," we grant that God's plan has reference *primarily* to his own actions, and that the sinful acts of men, in particular, are the objects, not of a decree that God will efficiently produce them, but of a decree that God will permit men, in the exercise of their own free will, to produce them.

(*f*) The decree to act is not the act. The decrees are an internal exercise and manifestation of the divine attributes, and are not to be confounded with Creation, Providence, and Redemption, which are the execution of the decrees.

The decrees are the first operation of the attributes, and the first manifestation of personality of which we have any knowledge within the Godhead. They presuppose those essential acts or movements within the divine nature which we call generation and procession. They involve by way of consequence that execution of the decrees which we call Creation, Providence, and Redemption, but they are not to be confounded with either of these.

(*g*) The decrees are therefore not addressed to creatures ; are not of the nature of statute law ; and lay neither compulsion nor obligation upon the wills of men.

So ordering the universe that men *will* pursue a given course of action is a very different thing from declaring, ordering, or commanding that they *shall*. " Our acts are in accordance with the decrees, but not *necessarily* so — we *can* do otherwise and often *should*" (Park). The Frenchman who fell into the water and cried: " I will drown, — no one shall help me ! " was very naturally permitted to drown; if he had said : "I shall drown, — no one will help me ! " he might perchance have called some friendly person to his aid.

(*h*) All human acts, whether evil or good, enter into the divine plan and so are objects of God's decrees, although God's actual agency with regard to the evil is only a permissive agency.

No decree of God reads: " You shall sin." For (1) no decree is addressed to *you*; (2) no decree with respect to you says *shall*; (3) God cannot cause *sin*, or decree to cause it. He simply decrees to create, and himself to act, in such a way that you will, of your own free choice, commit sin. God determines upon his own acts, foreseeing what the results will be in the free acts of his creatures, and so he determines those results. This permissive decree is the only decree of God with respect to sin. Man of himself is capable of producing sin. Of himself he is not capable of producing holiness. In the production of holiness two powers must concur, God's will and man's will, and God's will must act first. The decree of good, therefore, is not simply a permissive decree, as in the case of evil. God's decree, in the former case, is a decree to bring to bear positive agencies for its production, such as circumstances, motives, influences of his Spirit. But, in the case of evil, God's decrees are simply his arrangement that man may do as he pleases, God all the while foreseeing the result.

Permissive agency should not be confounded with conditional agency, nor permissive decree with conditional decree. God foreordained sin only indirectly. The machine is constructed not for the sake of the friction, but in spite of it. In the parable Mat. 13 : 24-30, the question "Whence then hath it tares ?" is answered, not by saying, " I decreed the tares," but by saying : "An enemy hath done this." Yet we must take exception to Principal Fairbairn, Place of Christ in Theology, 456, when he says : "God did not *permit* sin to be ; it is, in its essence, the transgression of his law, and so his only attitude toward it is one of opposition. It *is*, because man has contradicted and resisted his will." Here the truth of God's opposition to sin is stated so sharply as almost to deny the decree of sin in any sense. We maintain that God does decree sin in the sense of embracing in his plan the foreseen transgressions of men, while at the same time we maintain that these foreseen transgressions are chargeable wholly to men and not at all to God.

(*i*) While God's total plan with regard to creatures is called predestination, or foreordination, his purpose so to act that certain will believe and be saved is called election, and his purpose so to act that certain will refuse to believe and be lost is called reprobation. We discuss election and reprobation, in a later chapter, as a part of the Application of Redemption.

God's decrees may be divided into decrees with respect to nature, and decrees with respect to moral beings. These last we call foreordination, or predestination ; and of these decrees with respect to moral beings there are two kinds, the decree of election, and the decree of reprobation ; see our treatment of the doctrine of Election. George Herbert : " We all acknowledge both thy power and love To be exact, transcendent, and divine ; Who dost so strongly and so sweetly move, While all things have their will — yet none but thine. For either thy *command* or thy *permission* Lays hands on all ; they are thy right and left. The first puts on with speed and expedition ; The other curbs sin's stealing pace and theft. Nothing escapes them both ; all must appear And be disposed and dressed and tuned by thee Who sweetly temperest all. If we could hear Thy skill and art, what music it would be ! " On the whole doctrine, see Shedd, Presb. and Ref. Rev., Jan. 1890 : 1-25.

II. Proof of the doctrine of Decrees.

1. *From Scripture.*

A. The Scriptures declare that all things are included in the divine decrees. B. They declare that special things and events are decreed ; as, for example, (*a*) the stability of the physical universe ; (*b*) the outward circumstances of nations ; (*c*) the length of human life ; (*d*) the mode of our death ; (*e*) the free acts of men, both good acts and evil acts. C. They declare that God has decreed (*a*) the salvation of believers ; (*b*) the establishment of Christ's kingdom ; (*c*) the work of Christ and of his people in establishing it.

A. Is. 14 : 26, 27 — "This is the purpose that is purposed upon the whole earth ; and this is the hand that is stretched out upon all the nations ; for Jehovah of hosts hath purposed . . . and his hand is stretched out, and who shall turn it back ? " 46 : 10, 11 — "declaring the end from the beginning, and from ancient times the things that are not yet done, saying, My counsel shall stand, and I will do all my pleasure . . . yea, I have spoken, I will also bring it to pass ; I have purposed, I will also do it." Dan. 4 : 35 — "doeth according to his will in the army of heaven, and among the inhabitants of the earth ; and none can stay his hand, or say unto him, What doest thou ? " Eph. 1 : 11 — "the purpose of him who worketh all things after the counsel of his will."

B. (*a*) Ps. 119 : 89-91 — "For ever, O Jehovah, thy word is settled in heaven. Thy faithfulness is unto all generations: Thou hast established the earth and it abideth. They abide this day according to thine ordinances ; For all things are thy servants." (*b*) Acts 17 : 26 — "he made of one every nation of men to dwell on all the face of the earth, having determined their appointed seasons, and the bounds of their habitation " ; *cf.* Zech. 5 : 1 — "came four chariots out from between two mountains ; and the mountains were mountains of brass " = the fixed decrees from which proceed God's providential dealings ? (*c*) Job 14 : 5 — "Seeing his days are determined, The number of his months is with thee, And thou hast determined his bounds that he cannot pass." (*d*) John 21 : 19 — "this he spake, signifying by what manner of death he should glorify God." (*e*) Good acts : Is. 44 : 28 — "that saith of Cyrus, He is my shepherd and shall perform all my pleasure, even saying of Jerusalem, She shall be built ; and of the temple, Thy foundation shall be laid " ; Eph. 2 : 10 — "For we are his workmanship, created in Christ Jesus for good works, which God afore prepared that we should walk in them." Evil acts : Gen. 50 : 20 — "as for you, ye meant evil against me ; but God meant it for good, to bring to pass, as it is this day, to save much people alive " ; 1 K. 12 : 15 — "So the king hearkened not unto the people, for it was a thing brought about of Jehovah " ; 24 — "for this thing is of me " ; Luke 22 : 22 — "For the Son of man indeed goeth, as it hath been determined : but woe unto that man through whom he is betrayed " ; Acts 2 : 23 — "him, being delivered up by the determinate counsel and foreknowledge of God, ye by the hand of lawless men did crucify and slay " ; 4 : 27, 28 — "of a truth in this city against thy holy Servant Jesus, whom thou didst anoint, both Herod and Pontius Pilate, with the Gentiles and the people of Israel, were gathered together, to do whatsoever thy hand and thy counsel foreordained to come to pass " ; Rom. 9 : 17 — "For the scripture saith unto Pharaoh, For this very purpose did I raise thee up, that I might show in thee my power " ; 1 Pet. 2 : 8 — "They stumble at the word, being disobedient : whereunto also they were appointed " ; Rev. 17 : 17 — "For God did put in their hearts to do his mind, and to come to one mind, and to give their kingdom unto the beast, until the words of God should be accomplished."

C. (a) Cor. 2 : 7 — "the wisdom which hath been hidden, which God foreordained before the worlds unto our glory " ; Eph. 3 : 10, 11 — "manifold wisdom of God, according to the eternal purpose which he purposed in Christ Jesus our Lord." Ephesians 1 is a pæan in praise of God's decrees. (b) The greatest decree of all is the decree to give the world to Christ. Ps. 2 : 7, 8 — "I will tell of the decree : . . . I will give thee the nations for thine inheritance " ; cf. verse 6 — "I have set my king Upon my holy hill of Zion " ; 1 Cor. 15 : 25 — "he must reign, till he hath put all his enemies under his feet." (c) This decree we are to convert into our decree ; God's will is to be executed through our wills. Phil. 2 : 12, 13 — "work out your own salvation with fear and trembling ; for it is God who worketh in you both to will and to work, for his good pleasure." Rev. 5 : 1, 7 — "I saw in the right hand of him that sat on the throne a book written within and on the back, close sealed with seven seals. . . . And he [the Lamb] came, and he taketh it out of the right hand of him that sat on the throne " ; verse 9 — " Worthy art thou to take the book, and to open the seals thereof" — Christ alone has the omniscience to know, and the omnipotence to execute, the divine decrees. When John weeps because there is none in heaven or earth to loose the seals and to read the book of God's decrees, the Lion of the tribe of Judah prevails to open it. Only Christ conducts the course of history to its appointed end. See A. H. Strong, Christ in Creation, 268–283, on The Decree of God as the Great Encouragement to Missions.

2. *From Reason.*

(a) From the divine foreknowledge.

Foreknowledge implies fixity, and fixity implies decree. — From eternity God foresaw all the events of the universe as fixed and certain. This fixity and certainty could not have had its ground either in blind fate or in the variable wills of men, since neither of these had an existence. It could have had its ground in nothing outside the divine mind, for in eternity nothing existed besides the divine mind. But for this fixity there must have been a cause ; if anything in the future was fixed, something must have fixed it. This fixity could have had its ground only in the plan and purpose of God. In fine, if God foresaw the future as certain, it must have been because there was something in himself which made it certain ; or, in other words, because he had decreed it.

We object therefore to the statement of E. G. Robinson, Christian Theology, 74 — "God's knowledge and God's purposes both being eternal, one cannot be conceived as the ground of the other, nor can either be predicated to the exclusion of the other as the cause of things, but, correlative and eternal, they must be coëqual quantities in thought." We reply that while decree does not chronologically precede, it does logically precede, foreknowledge. Foreknowledge is not of possible events, but of what is certain to be. The certainty of future events which God foreknew could have had its ground only in his decree, since he alone existed to be the ground and explanation of this certainty. Events were fixed only because God had fixed them. Shedd, Dogm. Theol., 1 : 397 — "An event must be *made* certain, before it can be *known* as a certain event." Turretin, Inst. Theol., loc. 3, quaes. 12, 18 — "Præcipuum fundamentum scientiæ divinæ circa futura contingentia est decretum solum."

Decreeing creation implies decreeing the foreseen results of creation. — To meet the objection that God might have foreseen the events of the universe, not because he had decreed each one, but only because he had decreed to create the universe and institute its laws, we may put the argument in another form. In eternity there could have been no cause of the future existence of the universe, outside of God himself, since no being existed but God himself. In eternity God foresaw that the creation of the world and the institution of its laws would make certain its actual history even to the most insignificant details. But God decreed to create and to institute these laws. In so decreeing he necessarily decreed all that was to come. In fine, God foresaw the future events of the universe as certain, because he had decreed to create ; but this determination to create involved also a determination of all the actual results of that creation ; or, in other words, God decreed those results.

E. G. Robinson, Christian Theology, 84 — " The existence of divine decrees may be inferred from the existence of natural law." Law — certainty — God's will. Positivists express great contempt for the doctrine of the eternal purpose of God, yet they consign us to the iron necessity of physical forces and natural laws. Dr. Robinson also points out that decrees are " implied in the prophecies. We cannot conceive that all events should have converged toward the one great event — the death of Christ — without the intervention of an eternal purpose." E. H. Johnson, Outline Syst. Theol., 2d ed., 251, note—" Reason is confronted by the paradox that the divine decrees are at once absolute and conditional ; the resolution of the paradox is that God absolutely decreed a conditional system — a system, however, the workings of which he thoroughly foreknows." The rough unhewn stone and the statue into which it will be transformed are both and equally included in the plan of the sculptor.

No undecreed event can be foreseen.— We grant that God decrees primarily and directly his own acts of creation, providence, and grace ; but we claim that this involves also a secondary and indirect decreeing of the acts of free creatures which he foresees will result therefrom. There is therefore no such thing in God as *scientia media,* or knowledge of an event that is to be, though it does not enter into the divine plan ; for to say that God foresees an undecreed event, is to say that he views as future an event that is merely possible ; or, in other words, that he views an event not as it is.

We recognize only two kinds of knowledge : (1) Knowledge of undecreed possibles, and (2) foreknowledge of decreed actuals. *Scientia media* is a supposed intermediate knowledge between these two, namely (3) foreknowledge of undecreed actuals. See further explanations below. We deny the existence of this third sort of knowledge. We hold that sin is decreed in the sense of being *rendered certain* by God's determining upon a system in which it was foreseen that sin would exist. The sin of man can be foreknown, while yet God is not the immediate cause of it. God knows possibilities, without having decreed them at all. But God cannot foreknow actualities unless he has by his decree made them to be certainties of the future. He cannot foreknow that which is not there to be foreknown. Royce, World and Individual, 2 : 374, maintains that God has, not *fore*knowledge, but only *eternal* knowledge, of temporal things. But we reply that to foreknow how a moral being *will* act is no more impossible than to know how a moral being in given circumstances *would* act.

Only knowledge of that which is decreed is foreknowledge.— Knowledge of a plan as ideal or possible may precede decree ; but knowledge of a plan as actual or fixed must follow decree. Only the latter knowledge is properly *fore*knowledge. God therefore foresees creation, causes, laws, events, consequences, because he has decreed creation, causes, laws, events, consequences ; that is, because he has embraced all these in his plan. The denial of decrees logically involves the denial of God's foreknowledge of free human actions ; and to this Socinians, and some Arminians, are actually led.

An Arminian example of this denial is found in McCabe, Foreknowledge of God, and Divine Nescience of Future Contingencies a Necessity. *Per contra,* see notes on God's foreknowledge, in this Compendium, pages 283-286. Pepper : " Divine volition stands logically between two divisions and kinds of divine knowledge." God knew free human actions as *possible, before* he decreed them ; he knew them as *future, because* he decreed them. Logically, though not chronologically, decree comes before foreknowledge. When I say, " I know what I will do," it is evident that I have determined already, and that my knowledge does not precede determination, but follows it and is based upon it. It is therefore not correct to say that God foreknows his decrees. It is more true to say that he decrees his foreknowledge. He foreknows the future which he has decreed, and he foreknows it because he has decreed it. His decrees are eternal, and nothing that is eternal can be the object of foreknowledge. G. F. Wright, in Bib.

Sac., 1877 : 723 — "The *knowledge* of God comprehended the details and incidents of every possible plan. The *choice* of a plan made his knowledge determinate as *foreknowledge*."

There are therefore two kinds of divine knowledge : (1) knowledge of what may be — of the possible (*scientia simplicis intelligentiæ*); and (2) knowledge of what is, and is to be, because God has decreed it (*scientia visionis*). Between these two Molina, the Spanish Jesuit, wrongly conceived that there was (3) a middle knowledge of things which were to be, although God had not decreed them (*scientia media*). This would of course be a knowledge which God derived, not from himself, but from his creatures ! See Dick, Theology, 1 : 351. A. S. Carman : "It is difficult to see how God's knowledge can be caused from eternity by something that has no existence until a definite point of time." If it be said that what is to be will be "in the nature of things," we reply that there is no "nature of things" apart from God, and that the ground of the objective certainty, as well as of the subjective certitude corresponding to it, is to be found only in God himself.

But God's decreeing to create, when he foresees that certain free acts of men will follow, is a decreeing of those free acts, in the only sense in which we use the word decreeing, *viz.*, a rendering certain, or embracing in his plan. No Arminian who believes in God's foreknowledge of free human acts has good reason for denying God's decrees as thus explained. Surely God did not foreknow that Adam would exist and sin, whether God determined to create him or not. Omniscience, then, becomes *foreknowledge* only on condition of God's decree. That God's foreknowledge of free acts is intuitive does not affect this conclusion. We grant that, while man can predict free action only so far as it is rational (*i. e.*, in the line of previously dominant motive), God can predict free action whether it is rational or not. But even God cannot predict what is not certain to be. God can have intuitive foreknowledge of free human acts only upon condition of his own decree to create; and this decree to create, in foresight of all that will follow, is a decree of what follows. For the Arminian view, see Watson, Institutes, 2 : 375–398, 422–448. *Per contra*, see Hill, Divinity, 512–532; Fiske, in Bib. Sac., April, 1862; Bennett Tyler, Memoir and Lectures, 214–254; Edwards the younger, 1 : 398– 420 ; A. H. Strong, Philosophy and Religion, 98–101.

(*b*) From the divine wisdom.

It is the part of wisdom to proceed in every undertaking according to a plan. The greater the undertaking, the more needful a plan. Wisdom, moreover, shows itself in a careful provision for all possible circumstances and emergencies that can arise in the execution of its plan. That many such circumstances and emergencies are uncontemplated and unprovided for in the plans of men, is due only to the limitations of human wisdom. It belongs to infinite wisdom, therefore, not only to have a plan, but to embrace all, even the minutest details, in the plan of the universe.

No architect would attempt to build a Cologne cathedral without a plan ; he would rather, if possible, have a design for every stone. The great painter does not study out his picture as he goes along ; the plan is in his mind from the start ; preparations for the last effects have to be made from the beginning. So in God's work every detail is foreseen and provided for; sin and Christ entered into the original plan of the universe. Raymond, Syst. Theol., 2 ; 156, says this implies that God cannot govern the world unless all things be reduced to the condition of machinery; and that it cannot be true, for the reason that God's government is a government of persons and not of things. But we reply that the wise statesman governs persons and not things, yet just in proportion to his wisdom he conducts his administration according to a preconceived plan. God's power might, but God's wisdom would not, govern the universe without embracing all things, even the least human action, in his plan.

(*c*) From the divine immutability.

What God does, he always purposed to do. Since with him there is no increase of knowledge or power, such as characterizes finite beings, it follows that what under any given circumstances he permits or does, he must have eternally decreed to permit or do.   To suppose that God has a multitude of plans, and that he changes his plan with the exigencies of the situation, is to make him infinitely dependent upon the varying wills of his creatures, and to deny to him one necessary element of perfection, namely, immutability.

God has been very unworthily compared to a chess-player, who will checkmate his opponent whatever moves he may make (George Harris). So Napoleon is said to have had a number of plans before each battle, and to have betaken himself from one to another as fortune demanded. Not so with God. Job 23 : 13 — "he is in one mind, and who can turn him?" James 1 : 17 — "the Father of lights, with whom can be no variation, neither shadow that is cast by turning." Contrast with this Scripture McCabe's statement in his Foreknowledge of God, 62 — "This new factor, the godlike liberty of the human will, is capable of thwarting, and in uncounted instances does thwart, the divine will, and compel the great I Am to modify his actions, his purposes, and his plans, in the treatment of individuals and of communities."

(*d*)   From the divine benevolence.

The events of the universe, if not determined by the divine decrees, must be determined either by chance or by the wills of creatures.   It is contrary to any proper conception of the divine benevolence to suppose that God permits the course of nature and of history, and the ends to which both these are moving, to be determined for myriads of sentient beings by any other force or will than his own.   Both reason and revelation, therefore, compel us to accept the doctrine of the Westminster Confession, that " God did from all eternity, by the most just and holy counsel of his own will, freely and unchangeably ordain whatsoever comes to pass."

It would not be benevolent for God to put out of his own power that which was so essential to the happiness of the universe. Tyler, Memoir and Lectures, 231-243 — " The denial of decrees involves denial of the essential attributes of God, such as omnipotence, omniscience, benevolence; exhibits him as a disappointed and unhappy being; implies denial of his universal providence; leads to a denial of the greater part of our own duty of submission; weakens the obligations of gratitude." We give thanks to God for blessings which come to us through the free acts of others; but unless God has purposed these blessings, we owe our thanks to these others and not to God. Dr. A. J. Gordon said well that a universe without decrees would be as irrational and appalling as would be an express-train driving on in the darkness without headlight or engineer, and with no certainty that the next moment it might not plunge into the abyss. And even Martineau, Study, 2 : 108, in spite of his denial of God's foreknowledge of man's free acts, is compelled to say: "It cannot be left to mere created natures to play unconditionally with the helm of even a single world and steer it uncontrolled into the haven or on to the reefs; and some security must be taken for keeping the deflections within tolerable bounds." See also Emmons, Works, 4 : 273-401; and Princeton Essays, 1 : 57-73.

III.   OBJECTIONS TO THE DOCTRINE OF DECREES.

1.   *That they are inconsistent with the free agency of man.*

To this we reply that :

A.   The objection confounds the decrees with the execution of the decrees.   The decrees are, like foreknowledge, an act eternal to the divine nature, and are no more inconsistent with free agency than foreknowledge is.   Even foreknowledge of events implies that those events are fixed.   If this absolute fixity and foreknowledge is not inconsistent with free agency, much less can that which is more remote from man's action, namely, the hidden cause of this fixity and foreknowledge — God's decrees — be inconsistent with free agency. If anything be inconsistent with man's free agency, it must be, not the decrees themselves, but the execution of the decrees in creation and providence.

On this objection, see Tyler, Memoir and Lectures, 244-249 ; Forbes, Predestination and Free Will, 3 — "All things are *predestinated* by God, both good and evil, but not *prenecessitated*, that is, causally preördained by him — unless we would make God the author of sin. Predestination is thus an indifferent word, in so far as the originating author or anything is concerned; God being the originator of good, but the creature, of evil. Predestination therefore means that God included in his plan of the world every act of every creature, good or bad. Some acts he predestined causally, others permissively. The certainty of the fulfilment of all God's purposes ought to be distinguished from their necessity." This means simply that God's decree is not the *cause* of any act or event. God's decrees may be executed by the causal efficiency of his creatures, or they may be executed by his own efficiency. In either case it is, if anything, the execution, and not the decree, that is inconsistent with human freedom.

B.   The objection rests upon a false theory of free agency—namely, that free agency implies indeterminateness or uncertainty ; in other words, that free agency cannot coëxist with certainty as to the results of its exercise. But it is necessity, not certainty, with which free agency is inconsistent. Free agency is the power of self-determination in view of motives, or man's power (*a*) to chose between motives, and (*b*) to direct his subsequent activity according to the motive thus chosen.   Motives are never a cause, but only an occasion ; they influence, but never compel ; the man is the cause, and herein is his freedom.   But it is also true that man is never in a state of indeterminateness ; never acts without motive, or contrary to all motives ; there is always a reason why he acts, and herein is his rationality. Now, so far as man acts according to previously dominant motive — see (*b*) above — we may by knowing his motive predict his action, and our certainty what that action will be in no way affects his freedom.   We may even bring motives to bear upon others, the influence of which we foresee, yet those who act upon them may act in perfect freedom.   But if man, influenced by man, may still be free, then man, influenced by divinely foreseen motives, may still be free, and the divine decrees, which simply render certain man's actions, may also be perfectly consistent with man's freedom.

We must not assume that decreed ends can be secured only by compulsion.   Eternal purposes do not necessitate efficient causation on the part of the purposer.   Freedom may be the very means of fulfilling the purpose.   E. G. Robinson, Christian Theology, 74 — "Absolute certainty of events, which is all that omniscience determines respecting them, is not identical with their necessitation."   John Milton, Christian Doctrine : "Future events which God has foreseen will happen certainly, but not of necessity. They will happen certainly, because the divine prescience will not be deceived; but they will not happen necessarily, because prescience can have no influence on the object foreknown, inasmuch as it is only an intransitive action."

There is, however, a smaller class of human actions by which character is changed, rather than expressed, and in which the man acts according to a motive different from that which has previously been dominant—see (*a*) above.   These actions also are foreknown by God, although they cannot be predicted by man.   Man's freedom in them would be inconsistent with God's decrees, if the previous certainty of their occurrence were, not certainty, but necessity ; or, in other words, if God's decrees were in all cases decrees efficiently to produce the acts of his creatures.   But this is not the case. God's decrees may be executed by man's free causation, as easily as by God's ; and God's decreeing this free causation, in decreeing to create a universe of which he foresees that this causation will be a part, in no way interferes with the freedom of such causation, but rather secures and establishes it. Both consciousness and conscience witness that God's decrees are not executed by laying compulsion upon the free wills of men.

The farmer who, after hearing a sermon on God's decrees, took the break-neck road instead of the safe one to his home and broke his wagon in consequence, concluded before the end of his journey that he at any rate had been predestinated to be a fool, and that he had made his calling and election sure. Ladd, Philosophy of Conduct, 146, 187, shows that the will is free, first, by man's consciousness of ability, and, secondly, by man's consciousness of imputability. By nature, he is *potentially* self-determining; as matter of fact, he often *becomes* self-determining.

Allen, Religious Progress, 110 — " The coming church must embrace the sovereignty of God and the freedom of the will ; total depravity and the divinity of human nature ; the unity of God and the triune distinctions in the Godhead ; gnosticism and agnosticism ; the humanity of Christ and his incarnate deity ; the freedom of the Christian man and the authority of the church ; individualism and solidarity ; reason and faith ; science and theology ; miracle and uniformity of law ; culture and piety ; the authority of the Bible as the word of God with absolute freedom of Biblical criticism ; the gift of administration as in the historic episcopate and the gift of prophecy as the highest sanction of the ministerial commission ; the apostolic succession but also the direct and immediate call which knows only the succession of the Holy Ghost." Without assenting to these latter clauses we may commend the comprehensive spirit of this utterance, especially with reference to the vexed question of the relation of divine sovereignty to human freedom.

It may aid us, in estimating the force of this objection, to note the four senses in which the term 'freedom' may be used. It may be used as equivalent to (1) *physical* freedom, or absence of outward constraint ; (2) *formal* freedom, or a state of moral indeterminateness ; (3) *moral* freedom, or self-determinateness in view of motives ; (4) *real* freedom, or ability to conform to the divine standard. With the first of these we are not now concerned, since all agree that the decrees lay no outward constraint upon men. Freedom in the second sense has no existence, since all men have character. Free agency, or freedom in the third sense, has just been shown to be consistent with the decrees. Freedom in the fourth sense, or real freedom, is the special gift of God, and is not to be confounded with free agency. The objection mentioned above rests wholly upon the second of these definitions of free agency. This we have shown to be false, and with this the objection itself falls to the ground.

Ritschl, Justification and Reconciliation, 133-188, gives a good definition of this fourth kind of freedom : " Freedom is self-determination by universal ideals. Limiting our ends to those of family or country is a refined or idealized selfishness. Freedom is self-determination by universal love for man or by the kingdom of God. But the free man must then be dependent on God in everything, because the kingdom of God is a revelation of God." John Caird, Fundamental Ideas of Christianity, 1 : 133 — " In being determined by God we are self-determined ; *i. e.*, determined by nothing alien to us, but by our noblest, truest self. The universal life lives in us. The eternal consciousness becomes our own ; for 'he that abideth in love abideth in God and God abideth in him ' " (1 John 4 : 16).

Moberly, Atonement and Personality, 226—" Free will is not the independence of the creature, but is rather his self-realization in perfect dependence. Freedom is self-identity with goodness. Both goodness and freedom are, in their perfectness, in God Goodness in a creature is not distinction from, but correspondence with, the goodness of God. Freedom in a creature is correspondence with God's own self-identity with goodness. It is to realize and to find *himself*, his *true* self. in Christ, so that God's love in us has become a divine response, adequate to, because truly mirroring, God.' G. S. Lee, The Shadow Christ, 32—"The ten commandments could not be chanted. The Israelites sang about Jehovah and what he had done, but they did not sing about what he told them to do, and that is why they never did it. The conception of duty that cannot sing must weep until it learns to sing. This is Hebrew history."

"There is a liberty, unsung By poets and by senators unpraised, Which monarchs cannot grant nor all the powers Of earth and hell confederate take away; A liberty which persecution, fraud, Oppressions, prisons, have no power to bind; Which whoso tastes can be enslaved no more. 'T is liberty of heart, derived from heaven, Bought with his blood who gave it to mankind, And sealed with the same token." Robert Herrick: "Stone walls do not a prison make, Nor iron bars a cage; Minds innocent and quiet take That for a hermitage. If I have freedom in my love, And in my soul am free, Angels alone that soar above Enjoy such liberty."

A more full discussion of the doctrine of the Will is given under Anthropology, Vol. II. It is sufficient here to say that the Arminian objections to the decrees arise almost wholly from erroneously conceiving of freedom as the will's power to decide, in any given case, against its own character and all the motives brought to bear upon it. As we shall hereafter see, this is practically to deny that man has character, or that the will by its right or wrong moral action gives to itself, as well as to the intellect and affections, a permanent bent or predisposition to good or evil. It is to extend the power of contrary choice, a power which belongs to the sphere of transient volition, over all those permanent states of intellect, affection, and will which we call the moral character, and to say that we can change directly by a single volition that which, as a matter of fact, we can change only indirectly through process and means. Yet even this exaggerated view of freedom would seem not to exclude God's decrees, or prevent a practical reconciliation of the Arminian and Calvinistic views, so long as the Arminian grants God's foreknowledge of free human acts, and the Calvinist grants that God's decree of these acts is not necessarily a decree that God will efficiently produce them. For a close approximation of the two views, see articles by Raymond and by A. A. Hodge, respectively, on the Arminian and the Calvinistic Doctrines of the Will, in McClintock and Strong's Cyclopædia, 10 : 989, 992.

We therefore hold to the certainty of human action, and so part company with the Arminian. We cannot with Whedon (On the Will), and Hazard (Man a Creative First Cause), attribute to the will the freedom of indifference, or the power to act without motive. We hold with Calderwood, Moral Philosophy, 183, that action without motive, or an act of pure will, is unknown in consciousness (see, however, an inconsistent statement of Calderwood on page 188 of the same work). Every future human act will not only be performed with a motive, but will certainly be one thing rather than another; and God knows what it will be. Whatever may be the method of God's foreknowledge, and whether it be derived from motives or be intuitive, that foreknowledge presupposes God's decree to create, and so presupposes the making certain of the free acts that follow creation.

But this certainty is not necessity. In reconciling God's decrees with human freedom, we must not go to the other extreme, and reduce human freedom to mere determinism, or the power of the agent to act out his character in the circumstances which environ him. Human action is not simply the expression of previously dominant affections; else neither Satan nor Adam could have fallen, nor could the Christian ever sin. We therefore part company with Jonathan Edwards and his Treatise on the Freedom of the Will, as well as with the younger Edwards (Works, 1 : 420), Alexander (Moral Science, 107), and Charles Hodge (Syst. Theology, 2 : 278), all of whom follow Jonathan Edwards in identifying sensibility with the will, in regarding affections as the causes of volitions, and in speaking of the connection between motive and action as a necessary one. We hold, on the contrary, that sensibility and will are two distinct powers, that affections are occasions but never causes of volitions, and that, while motives may infallibly persuade, they never compel the will. The power to make the decision other than it is resides in the will, though it may never be exercised. With Charnock, the Puritan (Attributes, 1 : 448-450), we say that "man hath a power to do otherwise than that which God foreknows he will do." Since, then, God's decrees are not executed by laying compulsion upon human wills, they are not inconsistent with man's freedom. See Martineau, Study, 2 : 237, 249, 258, 261; also article by A. H. Strong, on Modified Calvinism, or Remainders of Freedom in Man, in Baptist Review, 1883 : 219-243; reprinted in the author's Philosophy and Religion, 114-128.

2. *That they take away all motive for human exertion.*

To this we reply that:

(*a*) They cannot thus influence men, since they are not addressed to men, are not the rule of human action, and become known only after the event. This objection is therefore the mere excuse of indolence and disobedience.

Men rarely make this excuse in any enterprise in which their hopes and their interests are enlisted. It is mainly in matters of religion that men use the divine decrees as an apology for their sloth and inaction. The passengers on an ocean steamer do not deny their ability to walk to starboard or to larboard, upon the plea that they are being carried to their destination by forces beyond their control. Such a plea would be still more irrational in a case where the passengers' inaction, as in case of fire, might result in destruction to the ship.

(*b*) The objection confounds the decrees of God with fate. But it is to be observed that fate is unintelligent, while the decrees are framed by a personal God in infinite wisdom ; fate is indistinguishable from material causation and leaves no room for human freedom, while the decrees exclude all notion of physical necessity ; fate embraces no moral ideas or ends, while the decrees make these controlling in the universe.

North British Rev., April, 1870—"Determinism and predestination spring from premises which lie in quite separate regions of thought. The predestinarian is obliged by his theology to admit the existence of a free will in God, and, as a matter of fact, he does admit it in the devil. But the final consideration which puts a great gulf between the determinist and the predestinarian is this, that the latter asserts the reality of the vulgar notion of moral desert. Even if he were not obliged by his interpretation of Scripture to assert this, he would be obliged to assert it in order to help out his doctrine of eternal reprobation."

Hawthorne expressed his belief in human freedom when he said that destiny itself had often been worsted in the attempt to get him out to dinner. Benjamin Franklin, in his Autobiography, quotes the Indian's excuse for getting drunk: "The Great Spirit made all things for some use, and whatsoever use they were made for, to that use they must be put. The Great Spirit made rum for Indians to get drunk with, and so it must be." Martha, in Isabel Carnaby, excuses her breaking of dishes by saying: "It seems as if it was to be. It is the thin edge of the wedge that in time will turn again and rend you." Seminary professor: "Did a man ever die before his time?" Seminary student: "I never knew of such a case." The decrees of God, considered as God's all-embracing plan, leave room for human freedom.

(*c*) The objection ignores the logical relation between the decree of the end and the decree of the means to secure it. The decrees of God not only ensure the end to be obtained, but they ensure free human action as logically prior thereto. All conflict between the decrees and human exertion must therefore be apparent and not real. Since consciousness and Scripture assure us that free agency exists, it must exist by divine decree ; and though we may be ignorant of the method in which the decrees are executed, we have no right to doubt either the decrees or the freedom. They must be held to be consistent, until one of them is proved to be a delusion.

The man who carries a vase of gold-fish does not prevent the fish from moving unrestrainedly within the vase. The double track of a railway enables a formidable approaching train to slip by without colliding with our own. Our globe takes us with it, as it rushes around the sun, yet we do our ordinary work without interruption. The two movements which at first sight seem inconsistent with each other are really parts of one whole. God's plan and man's effort are equally in harmony. Myers, Human Personality, 2:272, speaks of "molecular motion amid molar calm."

Dr. Duryea: "The way of life has two fences. There is an Arminian fence to keep us out of Fatalism; and there is a Calvinistic fence to keep us out of Pelagianism. Some good brethren like to walk on the fences. But it is hard in that way to keep one's balance. And it is needless, for there is plenty of room between the fences. For my part I prefer to walk in the road." Archibald Alexander's statement is yet better: "Calvinism is the broadest of systems. It regards the divine sovereignty and the freedom of the human will as the two sides of a roof which come together at a ridge-pole above the clouds. Calvinism accepts both truths. A system which denies either one of the two has only half a roof over its head."

Spurgeon, Autobiography, 1:176, and The Best Bread, 109—"The system of truth revealed in the Scriptures is not simply one straight line but two, and no man will ever get a right view of the gospel until he knows how to look at the two lines at once. . . . . These two facts [of divine sovereignty and of human freedom] are parallel lines; I cannot make them unite, but you cannot make them cross each other." John A. Broadus: "You can see only two sides of a building at once; if you go around it, you see two different sides, but the first two are hidden. This is true if you are on the ground. But if you get up upon the roof or in a balloon, you can see that there are four sides, and you can see them all together. So our finite minds can take in sovereignty and freedom alternately, but not simultaneously. God from above can see them both, and from heaven we too may be able to look down and see."

(*d*) Since the decrees connect means and ends together, and ends are decreed only as the result of means, they encourage effort instead of discouraging it. Belief in God's plan that success shall reward toil, incites to courageous and persevering effort. Upon the very ground of God's decree, the Scripture urges us to the diligent use of means.

God has decreed the harvest only as the result of man's labor in sowing and reaping; God decrees wealth to the man who works and saves; so answers are decreed to prayer, and salvation to faith. Compare Paul's declaration of God's purpose (Acts 27:22, 24—"there shall be no loss of life among you . . . . God hath granted thee all them that sail with thee") with his warning to the centurion and sailors to use the means of safety (verse 31—"Except these abide in the ship, ye cannot be saved"). See also Phil. 2:12, 13 —"work out your own salvation with fear and trembling, for it is God who worketh in you both to will and to work, for his good pleasure"; Eph. 2:10 —"we are his workmanship, created in Christ Jesus for good works, which God afore prepared that we should walk in them"; Deut. 29:29—"the secret things belong unto Jehovah our God: but the things that are revealed belong unto us and to our children for ever, that we may do all the words of this law." See Bennet Tyler, Memoir and Lectures, 252–254.

Ps. 59:10 (A. V.)—"The God of my mercy shall prevent me"— shall anticipate, or go before, me; Is. 65:24 —"before they call, I will answer; and while they are yet speaking, I will hear"; Ps. 23:2 —"He leadeth me"; John 10:3 — "calleth his own sheep by name, and leadeth them out." These texts describe prevenient grace in prayer, in conversion, and in Christian work. Plato called reason and sensibility a mismatched pair, one of which was always getting ahead of the other. Decrees and freedom *seem* to be mismatched, but they are not so. Even Jonathan Edwards, with his deterministic theory of the will, could, in his sermon on Pressing into the Kingdom, insist on the use of means, and could appeal to men as if they had the power to choose between the motives of self and of God. God's sovereignty and human freedom are like the positive and the negative poles of the magnet,— they are inseparable from one another, and are both indispensable elements in the attraction of the gospel.

Peter Damiani, the great monk-cardinal, said that the sin he found it hardest to uproot was his disposition to laughter. The homage paid to asceticism is the homage paid to the conqueror. But not all conquests are worthy of homage. Better the words of Luther: "If our God may make excellent large pike and good Rhenish wine, I may very well venture to eat and drink. Thou mayest enjoy every pleasure in the world that is not sinful; thy God forbids thee not, but rather wills it. And it is pleasing to the dear God whenever thou rejoicest or laughest from the bottom of thy heart." But our freedom has its limits. Martha Baker Dunn: "A man fishing for pickerel baits his hook with a live minnow and throws him into the water. The little minnow seems to be swimming gaily at his own free will, but just the moment he attempts to move out of his appointed course he begins to realize that there is a hook in his back. That is what we find out when we try to swim against the stream of God's decrees."

3. *That they make God the author of sin.*

To this we reply :

(*a*) They make God, not the author of sin, but the author of free beings who are themselves the authors of sin. God does not decree efficiently to work evil desires or choices in men. He decrees sin only in the sense of decreeing to create and preserve those who will sin ; in other words, he decrees to create and preserve human wills which, in their own self-chosen courses, will be and do evil. In all this, man attributes sin to himself and not to God, and God hates, denounces, and punishes sin.

Joseph's brethren were none the less wicked for the fact that God meant their conduct to result in good (Gen. 50:20). Pope Leo X and his indulgences brought on the Reformation, but he was none the less guilty. Slaveholders would have been no more excusable, even if they had been able to prove that the negro race was cursed in the curse of Canaan (Gen. 9 : 25 — "Cursed be Canaan ; a servant of servants shall he be unto his brethren "). Fitch, in Christian Spectator, 3 : 601 — " There can be and is a purpose of God which is not an *efficient* purpose. It embraces the voluntary acts of moral beings, without creating those acts by divine efficiency." See Martineau, Study, 2 : 107, 136.

Mat. 26 : 24 — "The Son of man goeth even as it is written of him ; but woe unto that man through whom the Son of man is betrayed ! good were it for that man if he had not been born." It was appointed that Christ should suffer, but that did not make men less free agents, nor diminish the guilt of their treachery and injustice. Robert G. Ingersoll asked : " Why did God create the devil ? " We reply that God did not create the devil,—it was the devil who made the devil. God made a holy and free spirit who abused his liberty, himself created sin, and so made himself a devil.

Pfleiderer, Philos. Religion, 1 : 299 — " Evil has been referred to 1. an extra-divine principle — to one or many evil spirits, or to fate, or to matter — at all events to a principle limiting the divine power ; 2. a want or defect in the Deity himself, either his imperfect wisdom or his imperfect goodness ; 3. human culpability, either a universal imperfection of human nature, or particular transgressions of the first men." The third of these explanations is the true one : the first is irrational ; the second is blasphemous. Yet this second is the explanation of Omar Khayyám, Rubáiyat, stanzas 80, 81 — " Oh Thou, who didst with pitfall and with gin Beset the road I was to wander in, Thou wilt not with predestined evil round Enmesh, and then impute my fall to sin. Oh Thou, who man of baser earth didst make, And ev'n with Paradise devise the snake : For all the sin wherewith the face of man Is blackened — man's forgiveness give — and take ! " And David Harum similarly says : " If I've done anything to be sorry for, I'm willing to be forgiven."

(*b*) The decree to permit sin is therefore not an efficient but a permissive decree, or a decree to permit, in distinction from a decree to produce by his own efficiency. No difficulty attaches to such a decree to permit sin, which does not attach to the actual permission of it. But God does actually permit sin, and it must be right for him to permit it. It must therefore be right for him to decree to permit it. If God's holiness and wisdom and power are not impugned by the actual existence of moral evil, they are not impugned by the original decree that it should exist.

Jonathan Edwards, Works, 2 : 100 — " The sun is not the *cause* of the darkness that follows its setting, but only the *occasion* " ; 254 — " If by the author of sin be meant the sinner, the agent, or the actor of sin, or the doer of a wicked thing — so it would be a reproach and blasphemy to suppose God to be the author of sin. . . . . But if by author of sin is meant the permitter or non-hinderer of sin, and at the same time a disposer of the state of events in such a manner, for wise, holy, and most excellent ends and purposes, *that sin*, if it be permitted and not hindered, *will most certainly follow*, I do not deny that God is the author of sin ; it is no reproach to the Most High to be *thus* the author of sin." On the objection that the doctrine of decrees imputes to God two wills, and that he has foreordained what he has forbidden, see Bennet Tyler, Memoir and Lectures. 250–252 — " A ruler may forbid treason ; but his command does not oblige him to do all in his power to prevent disobedience to it. It may promote the good of his king-dom to suffer the treason to be committed, and the traitor to be punished according to law. That in view of this resulting good he chooses not to prevent the treason, does not imply any contradiction or opposition of will in the monarch."

An ungodly editor excused his vicious journalism by saying that he was not ashamed to describe anything which Providence had permitted to happen. But "permitted" here had an implication of causation. He laid the blame of the evil upon Providence. He was ashamed to describe many things that were good and which God actually caused, while he was not ashamed to describe the immoral things which God did not cause, but only permitted men to cause. In this sense we may assent to Jonathan Edwards's words: "The divine Being is not the author of sin, but only disposes things in such a manner that sin will certainly ensue." These words are found in his treatise on Original Sin. In his Essay on Freedom of the Will, he adds a doctrine of causation which we must repudiate: "The essence of virtue and vice, as they exist in the dis-position of the heart, and are manifested in the acts of the will, lies not in their *Cause* but in their *Nature.*" We reply that sin could not be condemnable in its nature, if God and not man were its cause.

Robert Browning, Mihrab Shah: "Wherefore should any evil hap to man — From ache of flesh to agony of soul — Since God's All-mercy mates All-potency? Nay, why permits he evil to him. elf — man's sin, accounted such? Suppose a world purged of all pain, with fit inhabitant — Man pure of evil in thought, word and deed—were it not w ·l? Then, wherefore otherwise?" Fairbairn answers the question, as follows, in his Christ in Modern Theology, 456 — "Evil once intended may be vanquished by being allowed; but were it hindered by an act of annihilation, then the victory would rest with he evil which had compelled the Creator to retrace his steps. And, to carry the prevention backward another stage, if the possibility of evil had hindered the creative action of God, then he would have been, as it were, overcome by its very shadow. But why did he create a being capable of sinning? Only so could he create a being capable of obey-ing. The ability to do good implies the capability of doing evil. The engine can neither obey nor disobey, and the creature who was without this double ability might be a machine, but could be no child. Moral perfection can be attained, but cannot be cre-ated; God can make a being capable of moral action, but not a being with all the fruits of moral action garnered within him."

(c) The difficulty is therefore one which in substance clings to all theis-tic systems alike — the question why moral evil is permitted under the government of a God infinitely holy, wise, powerful, and good. This problem is, to our finite powers, incapable of full solution, and must remain to a great degree shrouded in mystery. With regard to it we can only say :

Negatively, — that God does not permit moral evil because he is not unal-terably opposed to sin ; nor because moral evil was unforeseen and inde-pendent of his will ; nor because he could not have prevented it in a moral system. Both observation and experience, which testify to multiplied instances of deliverance from sin without violation of the laws of man's being, forbid us to limit the power of God.

Positively, — we seem constrained to say that God permits moral evil because moral evil, though in itself abhorrent to his nature, is yet the inci-dent of a system adapted to his purpose of self-revelation ; and further, because it is his wise and sovereign will to institute and maintain this sys-tem of which moral evil is an incident, rather than to withhold his self-revelation or to reveal himself through another system in which moral evil should be continually prevented by the exercise of divine power.

There are four questions which neither Scripture nor reason enables us completely to solve and to which we may safely say that only the higher knowledge of the future state will furnish the answers. These questions are, first, how can a holy God permit moral evil? secondly, how could a being created pure ever fall? thirdly, how can we be responsible for inborn depravity? fourthly, how could Christ justly suffer? The first of these questions now confronts us. A complete theodicy (Θεός, God, and δίκη, justice) would be a vindication of the justice of God in permitting the natural and moral evil that exists under his government. While a complete theodicy is beyond our powers, we throw some light upon God's permission of moral evil by considering (1) that freedom of will is necessary to virtue ; (2) that God suffers from sin more than does the sinner ; (3) that, with the permission of sin, God provided a redemption ; and, (4) that God will eventually overrule all evil for good.

It is possible that the elect angels belong to a moral system in which sin is prevented by constraining motives. We cannot deny that God could prevent sin in *a* moral system. But it is very doubtful whether God could prevent sin in the *best* moral system. The most perfect freedom is indispensable to the attainment of the highest virtue. Spurgeon : " There could have been no moral government without permission to sin. God could have created blameless puppets, but they could have had no virtue." Behrends : " If moral beings were incapable of perversion, man would have had all the virtue of a planet, — that is, no virtue at all." Sin was permitted, then, only because it could be overruled for the greatest good. This greatest good, we may add, is not simply the highest nobility and virtue of the creature, but also the revelation of the Creator. But for sin, God's justice and God's mercy alike would have been unintelligible to the universe. E. G. Robinson : " God could not have revealed his character so well without moral evil as with moral evil."

Robert Browning, Christmas Eve, tells us that it was God's plan to make man in his own image : " To create man, and then leave him Able, his own word saith, to grieve him ; But able to glorify him too, As a mere machine could never do, That prayed or praised, all unaware Of its fitness for aught but praise or prayer, Made perfect as a thing of course." Upton, Hibbert Lectures, 268–270, 324, holds that sin and wickedness is an absolute evil, but an evil permitted to exist because the effacement of it would mean the effacement at the same time both for God and man, of the possibility of reaching the highest spiritual good. See also Martineau, Study of Religion, 2 : 108 ; Momerie, Origin of Evil ; St. Clair, Evil Physical and Moral ; Vovsey, Mystery of Pain, Death and Sin.

C. G. Finney, Skeletons of a Course of Theological Studies, 26, 27 — " Infinite goodness, knowledge and power imply only that, if a universe were made, it would be the best that was naturally possible." To say that God could not be the author of a universe in which there is so much of evil, he says, " assumes that a better universe, upon the whole, was a natural possibility. It assumes that a universe of moral beings could, under a moral government administered in the wisest and best manner, be wholly restrained from sin ; but this needs proof, and never can be proved. . . . The best possible universe may not be the best conceivable universe. Apply the legal maxim, ' The defendant is to have the benefit of the doubt, and that in proportion to the established character of his reputation.' There is so much clearly indicating the benevolence of God, that we may *believe* in his benevolence, where we cannot *see* it."

For advocacy of the view that God cannot prevent evil in a moral system, see Birks, Difficulties of Belief, 17 ; Young, The Mystery, or Evil not from God ; Bledsoe, Theodicy ; N. W. Taylor, Moral Government, 1 : 283–349 ; 2 : 327–356. According to Dr. Taylor's view, God has not a complete control over the moral universe ; moral agents can do wrong under every possible influence to prevent it ; God prefers, all things considered, that all his creatures should be holy and happy, and does all in his power to make them so ; the existence of sin is not on the whole for the best ; sin exists because God cannot prevent it in a moral system ; the blessedness of God is actually impaired by the disobedience of his creatures. For criticism of these views, see Tyler, Letters on the New Haven Theology, 120, 219. Tyler argues that election and non-election imply power in God to prevent sin ; that *permitting* is not mere *submitting* to something which he could not possibly prevent. We would add that as a matter of fact God has preserved holy angels, and that there are "just men" who have been "made perfect" (Heb. 12 : 23) without violating the laws of moral agency. We infer that God could have so preserved Adam. The history of the church leads us to believe that there is no sinner so stubborn that God cannot renew his heart, — even a Saul can be turned into a Paul. We hesitate therefore to ascribe limits to God's power. While Dr. Taylor held that God could not prevent sin in *a* moral system, that is, in *any* moral system, Dr. Park is understood to hold the greatly preferable view that God cannot prevent sin in the *best* moral system. Flint, Christ's Kingdom upon Earth, 59 — " The alternative is, not evil or no evil, but evil or the miraculous **prevention** of evil." See Shedd, Dogm. Theol., 1 : 406–422.

But even granting that the present is the best moral system, and that in such a system evil cannot be prevented consistently with God's wisdom and goodness, the question still remains how the decree to initiate such a system can consist with God's fundamental attribute of holiness. Of this insoluble mystery we must say as Dr. John Brown, in Spare Hours, 273, says of Arthur H. Hallam's Theodicæa Novissima: "As was to be expected, the tremendous subject remains where he found it. His glowing love and genius cast a gleam here and there across its gloom, but it is as brief as the lightning in the collied night — the jaws of darkness do devour it up — this secret belongs to God. Across its deep and dazzling darkness, and from out its abyss of thick cloud, 'all dark, dark, irrecoverably dark,' no steady ray has ever or will ever come; over its face its own darkness must brood, till he to whom alone the darkness and the light are both alike, to whom the night shineth as the day, says 'Let there be light!'"

We must remember, however, that the decree of redemption is as old as the decree of the apostasy. The provision of salvation in Christ shows at how great a cost to God was permitted the fall of the race in Adam. He who ordained sin ordained also an atonement for sin and a way of escape from it. Shedd, Dogm. Theol., 1:388 — "The permission of sin has cost God more than it has man. No sacrifice and suffering on account of sin has been undergone by any man, equal to that which has been endured by an incarnate God. This shows that God is not acting selfishly in permitting it." On the permission of moral evil, see Butler, Analogy, Bohn's ed., 177, 232 — "The Government of God, and Christianity, as Schemes imperfectly Comprehended"; Hill, System of Divinity, 528-559; Ulrici, art.: Theodicée, in Herzog's Encyclopädie; Cunningham, Historical Theology, 2:416-489; Patton, on Retribution and the Divine Purpose, in Princeton Rev., 1878:16-23; Bib. Sac., 20:471-488; Wood, The Witness of Sin.

IV. CONCLUDING REMARKS.

1. *Practical uses of the doctrine of decrees.*

(*a*) It inspires humility by its representation of God's unsearchable counsels and absolute sovereignty. (*b*) It teaches confidence in him who has wisely ordered our birth, our death, and our surroundings, even to the minutest particulars, and has made all things work together for the triumph of his kingdom and the good of those who love him; (*c*) It shows the enemies of God that, as their sins have been foreseen and provided for in God's plan, so they can never, while remaining in their sins, hope to escape their decreed and threatened penalty. (*d*) It urges the sinner to avail himself of the appointed means of grace, if he would be counted among the number of those for whom God has decreed salvation.

This doctrine is one of those advanced teachings of Scripture which requires for its understanding a matured mind and a deep experience. The beginner in the Christian life may not see its value or even its truth, but with increasing years it will become a staff to lean upon. In times of affliction, obloquy, and persecution, the church has found in the decrees of God, and in the prophecies in which these decrees are published, her strong consolation. It is only upon the basis of the decrees that we can believe that "all things work together for good" (Rom. 8:28) or pray "Thy will be done" (Mat. 6:10).

It is a striking evidence of the truth of the doctrine that even Arminians pray and sing like Calvinists. Charles Wesley, the Arminian, can write: "He wills that I should holy be — What can withstand his will? The counsel of his grace in me He surely will fulfill." On the Arminian theory, prayer that God will soften hard hearts is out of place, — the prayer should be offered to the sinner; for it is his will, not God's, that is in the way of his salvation. And yet this doctrine of Decrees, which at first sight might seem to discourage effort, is the greatest, in fact is the only effectual, incentive to effort. For this reason Calvinists have been the most strenuous advocates of civil liberty. Those who submit themselves most unreservedly to the sovereignty of God are most delivered from the fear of man. Whitefield the Calvinist, and not Wesley the Arminian, originated the great religious movement in which the Methodist church was born (see McFetridge, Calvinism in History, 153), and Spurgeon's ministry has been as fruitful in conversions as Finney's. See Froude, Essay on Calvinism; Andrew Fuller, Calvinism and Socinianism compared in their Practical Effects; Atwater, Calvinism in Doctrine and Life, in Princeton Review. 1876:73: J. A. Smith, Historical Lectures.

Calvinism logically requires the separation of Church and State: though Calvin did not see this, the Calvinist Roger Williams did. Calvinism logically requires a republican form of government: Calvin introduced laymen into the government of the church, and the same principle requires civil liberty as its correlate. Calvinism holds to individualism and the direct responsibility of the individual to God. In the Netherlands, in Scotland, in England, in America, Calvinism has powerfully influenced the development of civil liberty. Ranke: "John Calvin was virtually the founder of America." Motley: "To the Calvinists more than to any other class of men, the political liberties of Holland, England and America are due." John Fiske, The Beginnings of New England: "Perhaps not one of the mediæval popes was more despotic than Calvin; but it is not the less true that the promulgation of his theology was one of the longest steps that mankind have taken towards personal freedom. . . . It was a religion fit to inspire men who were to be called to fight for freedom, whether in the marshes of the Netherlands or on the moors of Scotland."

Æsop, when asked what was the occupation of Zeus, replied: "To humble the exalted and to exalt the humble." "I accept the universe," said Margaret Fuller. Some one reported this remark to Thomas Carlyle. "Gad! she'd better!" he replied. Dr. John Watson (Ian McLaren): "The greatest reinforcement religion could have in our time would be a return to the ancient belief in the sovereignty of God." Whittier: "All is of God that is and is to be, And God is good. Let this suffice us still Resting in childlike trust upon his will Who moves to his great ends unthwarted by the ill." Every true minister preaches Arminianism and prays Calvinism. This means simply that there is more, in God's love and in God's purposes, than man can state or comprehend. Beecher called Spurgeon a camel with one hump — Calvinism. Spurgeon called Beecher a camel without any hump: "He does not know what he believes, and you never know where to find him."

Arminians sing: "Other refuge have I none; Hangs my helpless soul on thee"; yet John Wesley wrote to the Calvinist Toplady, the author of the hymn: "Your God is my devil." Calvinists replied that it was better to have the throne of the universe vacant than to have it filled by such a pitiful nonentity as the Arminians worshiped. It was said of Lord Byron that all his life he believed in Calvinism, and hated it. Oliver Wendell Holmes similarly, in all his novels except Elsie Venner, makes the orthodox thinblooded and weakkneed, while his heretics are all strong in body. Dale, Ephesians, 52 — "Of the two extremes, the suppression of man which was the offence of Calvinism, and the suppression of God which was the offence against which Calvinism so fiercely protested, the fault and error of Calvinism was the nobler and grander. . . . The most heroic forms of human courage, strength and righteousness have been found in men who in their theology seemed to deny the possibility of human virtue and made the will of God the only real force in the universe."

2. *True method of preaching the doctrine.*

(*a*) We should most carefully avoid exaggeration or unnecessarily obnoxious statement. (*b*) We should emphasize the fact that the decrees are not grounded in arbitrary will, but in infinite wisdom. (*c*) We should make it plain that whatever God does or will do, he must from eternity have purposed to do. (*d*) We should illustrate the doctrine so far as possible by instances of completeness and far-sightedness in human plans of great enterprises. (*e*) We may then make extended application of the truth to the encouragement of the Christian and the admonition of the unbeliever.

For illustrations of foresight, instance Louis Napoleon's planning the Suez Canal, and declaring his policy as Emperor, long before he ascended the throne of France. For instances of practical treatment of the theme in preaching, see Bushnell, Sermon on Every Man's Life a Plan of God, in Sermons for the New Life; Nehemiah Adams, Evenings with the Doctrines, 243; Spurgeon's Sermon on Ps. 44 : 3 — "Because thou hadst a favor unto them." Robert Browning, Rabbi Ben Ezra: "Grow old along with me! The best is yet to be, The last of life, for which the first was made: Our times are in his hand Who saith 'A whole I planned, Youth shows but half; trust God: See all nor be afraid!'"

Shakespeare, King Lear, 1 : 2 — "This is the excellent foppery of the world that when we are sick in fortune (often the surfeit of our own behavior) we make guilty of our disasters the sun, the moon and the stars, as if we were villains by necessity, fools by heavenly compulsion, and all that we are evil in by a divine thrusting on ; an admirable evasion of man to lay his disposition to the charge of a star!" All's Well: " Our remedies oft in ourselves do lie Which we ascribe to heaven : the fated sky Gives us free scope; only doth backward pull Our slow designs, when we ourselves are dull.' Julius Cæsar, 1 : 2 — " Men at some time are masters of their fates : The fault, dear Brutus, is not in our stars, But in ourselves, that we are underlings.''

SYSTEMATIC THEOLOGY.
VOLUME II.

CHAPTER IV.

THE WORKS OF GOD; OR THE EXECUTION OF THE DECREES.

SECTION I.—CREATION.

I. DEFINITION OF CREATION.

By creation we mean that free act of the triune God by which in the beginning for his own glory he made, without the use of preëxisting materials, the whole visible and invisible universe.

Creation is designed origination, by a transcendent and personal God, of that which itself is not God. The universe is related to God as our own volitions are related to ourselves. They are not ourselves, and we are greater than they. Creation is not simply the idea of God, or even the plan of God, but it is the idea externalized, the plan executed; in other words, it implies an exercise, not only of intellect, but also of will, and this will is not an instinctive and unconscious will, but a will that is personal and free. Such exercise of will seems to involve, not self-development, but self-limitation, on the part of God; the transformation of energy into force, and so a beginning of time, with its finite successions. But, whatever the relation of creation to time, creation makes the universe wholly dependent upon God, as its originator.

F. H. Johnson, in Andover Rev., March, 1891 : 280, and What is Reality, 285—" Creation is designed origination. . . . Men never could have thought of God as the Creator of the world, were it not that they had first known themselves as creators." We agree with the doctrine of Hazard, Man a Creative First Cause. Man creates ideas and volitions, without use of preëxisting material. He also indirectly, through these ideas and volitions, creates brain-modifications. This creation, as Johnson has shown, is without hands, yet elaborate, selective, progressive. Schopenhauer: "Matter is nothing more than causation; its true being is its action."

Prof. C. L. Herrick, Denison Quarterly, 1896 : 248, and Psychological Review, March, 1899, advocates what he calls *dynamism*, which he regards as the only alternative to a materialistic dualism which posits matter, and a God above and distinct from matter. He claims that the predicate of reality can apply only to energy. To speak of energy as *residing in* something is to introduce an entirely incongruous concept, for it continues our guest *ad infinitum*. "Force," he says, "is energy under resistance, or self-limited energy, for all parts of the universe are derived from the energy. Energy manifesting itself under self-conditioning or differential forms is force. The change of pure energy into force is creation—the introduction of resistance. The progressive complication of this interference is evolution—a form of orderly resolution of energy. Substance is pure spontaneous energy. God's substance is his energy—the infinite and inexhaustible store of spontaneity which makes up his being. The form which self-limitation impresses upon substance, in revealing it in force, is not God, because it no longer possesses the attributes of spontaneity and universality, though it emanates from him. When we speak of energy as self-limited, we simply imply that spontaneity is intelligent. The sum of God's acts is his being. There is no *causa posterior* or *extranea*, which spurs him on. We must recognize in the source what appears in the outcome. We can speak of *absolute*, but not of *infinite* or *immutable*, substance. The Universe is but the partial expression of an infinite God."

Our view of creation is so nearly that of Lotze, that we here condense Ten Broeke's statement of his philosophy : " Things are concreted laws of action. If the idea of being must include permanence as well as activity, we must say that only the personal truly is. All else is flow and process. We can interpret ontology only from the side of personality. Possibility of interaction requires the dependence of the mutually related many of the system upon an all-embracing, coördinating One. The finite is a mode or phenomenon of the One Being. Mere things are only modes of energizing of the One. Self-conscious personalities are created, posited, and depend on the One in a different way. Interaction of things is immanent action of the One, which the perceiving mind interprets as causal. Real interaction is possible only between the Infinite and the created finite, *i. e.*, self-conscious persons. The finite is not a part of the Infinite, nor does it partly exhaust the stuff of the Infinite. The One, by an act of freedom, posits the many, and the many have their ground and unity in the Will and Thought of the One. Both the finite and the Infinite are free and intelligent.

" Space is not an extra-mental reality, *sui generis*, nor an order of relations among realities, but a form of dynamic appearance, the ground of which is the fixed orderly changes in reality. So time is the form of change, the subjective interpretation of timeless yet successive changes in reality. So far as God is the ground of the world-process, he is in time. So far as he transcends the world-process in his self-conscious personality, he is not in time. Motion too is the subjective interpretation of changes in things, which changes are determined by the demands of the world-system and the purpose being realized in it. Not atomism, but dynamism, is the truth. Physical phenomena are referable to the activity of the Infinite, which activity is given a substantive character because we think under the form of substance and attribute. Mechanism is compatible with teleology. Mechanism is universal and is necessary to all system. But it is limited by purpose, and by the possible appearance of any new law, force, or act of freedom.

" The soul is not a function of material activities, but is a true reality. The system is such that it can admit new factors, and the soul is one of these possible new factors. The soul is created as substantial reality, in contrast with other elements of the system, which are only phenomenal manifestations of the One Reality. The relation between soul and body is that of interaction between the soul and the universe, the body being that part of the universe which stands in closest relation with the soul (*versus* Bradley, who holds that 'body and soul alike are phenomenal arrangements, neither one of which has any title to fact which is not owned by the other'). Thought is a knowledge of reality. We must assume an adjustment between subject and object. This assumption is founded on the postulate of a morally perfect God." To Lotze, then, the only real creation is that of finite personalities, — matter being only a mode of the divine activity. See Lotze, Microcosmos, and Philosophy of Religion. Bowne, in his Metaphysics and his Philosophy of Theism, is the best expositor of Lotze's system.

In further explanation of our definition we remark that

(*a*) Creation is not "production out of nothing," as if "nothing" were a substance out of which "something" could be formed.

We do not regard the doctrine of Creation as bound to the use of the phrase "creation out of nothing," and as standing or failing with it. The phrase is a philosophical one, for which we have no Scriptural warrant, and it is objectionable as intimating that "nothing" can itself be an object of thought and a source of being. The germ of truth intended to be conveyed in it can better be expressed in the phrase "without use of preëxisting materials."

(*b*) Creation is not a fashioning of preëxisting materials, nor an emanation from the substance of Deity, but is a making of that to exist which once did not exist, either in form or substance.

There is nothing divine in creation but the origination of substance. Fashioning is competent to the creature also. Gassendi said to Descartes that God's creation, if he is the author of forms but not of substances, is only that of the tailor who clothes a man with his apparel. But substance is not necessarily material. We are to conceive of it rather after the analogy of our own ideas and volitions, and as a manifestation of spirit. Creation is not simply the thought of God, nor even the plan of God, but rather the externalization of that thought and the execution of that plan. Nature is "a great sheet let down from God out of heaven," and containing "nothing that is common or unclean;" but nature is not God nor a part of God, any more than our ideas and volitions are ourselves or a part of ourselves. Nature is a partial manifestation of God, but it does not exhaust God.

(c) Creation is not an instinctive or necessary process of the divine nature, but is the free act of a rational will, put forth for a definite and sufficient end.

Creation is different in kind from that eternal process of the divine nature in virtue of which we speak of generation and procession. The Son is begotten of the Father, and is of the same essence ; the world is created without preëxisting material, is different from God, and is made by God. Begetting is a necessary act; creation is the act of God's free grace. Begetting is eternal, out of time; creation is in time, or with time.

Studia Biblica, 4:148 —" Creation is the voluntary limitation which God has imposed on himself. . . . It can only be regarded as a creation of free spirits. . . . It is a form of almighty power to submit to limitation. Creation is not a development of God, but a circumscription of God. . . . The world is not the expression of God, or an emanation from God, but rather his self-limitation."

(d) Creation is the act of the triune God, in the sense that all the persons of the Trinity, themselves uncreated, have a part in it — the Father as the originating, the Son as the mediating, the Spirit as the realizing cause.

That all of God's creative activity is exercised through Christ has been sufficiently proved in our treatment of the Trinity and of Christ's deity as an element of that doctrine (see pages 310, 311). We may here refer to the texts which have been previously considered, namely, John 1 : 3, 4 — "All things were made through him, and without him was not anything made. That which hath been made was life in him"; 1 Cor. 8 : 6 —"one Lord, Jesus Christ, through whom are all things"; Col. 1 : 16 — "all things have been created through him, and unto him"; Heb. 1 : 10 —"Thou, Lord, in the beginning hast laid the foundation of the earth, and the heavens are the works of thy hands."

The work of the Holy Spirit seems to be that of completing, bringing to perfection. We can understand this only by remembering that our Christian knowledge and love are brought to their consummation by the Holy Spirit, and that he is also the principle of our natural self-consciousness, uniting subject and object in a subject-object. If matter is conceived of as a manifestation of spirit, after the idealistic philosophy, then the Holy Spirit may be regarded as the perfecting and realizing agent in the externalization of the divine ideas. While it was the Word though whom all things were made, the Holy Spirit was the author of life, order, and adornment. Creation is not a mere manufacturing,—it is a spiritual act.

John Caird, Fundamental Ideas of Christianity, 1 : 120 —" The creation of the world cannot be by a Being who is external. Power presupposes an object on which it is exerted. 129 — There is in the very nature of God a reason why he should reveal himself in, and communicate himself to, a world of finite existences, or fulfil and realize himself in the being and life of nature and man. His nature would not be what it is if such a world did not exist; something would be lacking to the completeness of the divine being without it. 144 — Even with respect to human thought or intelligence, it is mind or spirit which creates the world. It is not a ready-made world on which we look ; in perceiving our world we make it. 152-154 — We make progress as we cease to think our own thoughts and become media of the universal Intelligence." While we accept Caird's idealistic interpretation of creation, we dissent from his intimation that creation is a necessity to God. The trinitarian being of God renders him sufficient to himself, even without creation. Yet those very trinitarian relations throw light upon the method of creation. since they disclose to us the order of all the divine activity. On the definition of Creation, see Shedd, History of Doctrine, 1 : 11.

II. Proof of the Doctrine of Creation.

Creation is a truth of which mere science or reason cannot fully assure us. Physical science can observe and record changes, but it knows nothing of origins. Reason cannot absolutely disprove the eternity of matter. For proof of the doctrine of Creation, therefore, we rely wholly upon Scripture. Scripture supplements science, and renders its explanation of the universe complete.

Drummond, in his Natural Law in the Spiritual World, claims that atoms, as "manufactured articles," and the dissipation of energy, prove the creation of the visible from the invisible. See the same doctrine propounded in "The Unseen Universe." But Sir Charles Lyell tells us: "Geology is the autobiography of the earth,— but like all autobiographies, it does not go back to the beginning." Hopkins, Yale Lectures on the Scriptural View of Man: "There is nothing *a priori* against the eternity of matter." Wardlaw, Syst. Theol., 2:65 — "We cannot form any distinct conception of creation out of nothing. The very idea of it might never have occurred to the mind of man, had it not been traditionally handed down as a part of the original revelation to the parents of the race."

Hartmann, the German philosopher, goes back to the original elements of the universe, and then says that science stands petrified before the question of their origin, as before a Medusa's head. But in the presence of problems, says Dorner, the duty of science is not petrifaction, but solution. This is peculiarly true, if science is, as Hartmann thinks, a complete explanation of the universe. Since science, by her own acknowledgment, furnishes no such explanation of the origin of things, the Scripture revelation with regard to creation meets a demand of human reason, by adding the one fact without which science must forever be devoid of the highest unity and rationality. For advocacy of the eternity of matter, see Martineau, Essays, 1:157-169.

E. H. Johnson, in Andover Review, Nov. 1891:505 *sq.*, and Dec. 1891:592 *sq.*, remarks that evolution can be traced backward to more and more simple elements, to matter without motion and with no quality but being. Now make it still more simple by divesting it of existence, and you get back to the necessity of a Creator. An infinite number of past stages is impossible. There is no infinite number. Somewhere there must be a beginning. We grant to Dr. Johnson that the only alternative to creation is a materialistic dualism, or an eternal matter which is the product of the divine mind and will. The theories of dualism and of creation from eternity we shall discuss hereafter.

1. *Direct Scripture Statements.*

A. Genesis 1 : 1 —"In the beginning God created the heaven and the earth." To this it has been objected that the verb בָּרָא does not necessarily denote production without the use of preëxisting materials (see Gen. 1 : 27 —"God created man in his own image"; *cf.* 2 : 7 —"the Lord God formed man of the dust of the ground"; also Ps. 51 : 10—"Create in me a clean heart").

"In the first two chapters of Genesis בָּרָא is used (1) of the creation of the universe (1:1); (2) of the creation of the great sea monsters (1:21); (3) of the creation of man (1:27). Everywhere else we read of God's *making*, as from an already created substance, the firmament (1:7), the sun, moon and stars (1:16), the brute creation (1:25); or of his *forming* the beasts of the field out of the ground (2:19); or, lastly, of his *building up* into a woman the rib he had taken from man (2:22, margin)"— quoted from Bible Com., 1:31. Guyot, Creation, 30 — "*Bara* is thus reserved for marking the first introduction of each of the three great spheres of existence — the world of matter, the world of life, and the spiritual world represented by man."

We grant, in reply, that the argument for absolute creation derived from the mere word בָּרָא is not entirely conclusive. Other considerations in connection with the use of this word, however, seem to render this inter-

pretation of Gen. 1 : 1 the most plausible.   Some of these considerations
we proceed to mention.

(*a*) While we acknowledge that the verb בָּרָא " does not necessarily or
invariably denote production without the use of preëxisting materials, we
still maintain that it signifies the production of an effect for which no natural antecedent existed before, and which can be only the result of divine
agency." For this reason, in the Kal species it is used only of God, and is
never accompanied by any accusative denoting material.

No accusative denoting material follows *bara*, in the passages indicated, for the reason
that all thought of material was absent. See Dillmann, Genesis, 18; Oehler, Theol.
O. T., 1 : 177. The quotation in the text above is from Green, Hebrew Chrestomathy,
87. But E. G. Robinson, Christian Theology, 88, remarks: " Whether the Scriptures
teach the absolute origination of matter — its creation out of nothing — is an open
question. . . . No decisive evidence is furnished by the Hebrew word *bara*."

A moderate and scholarly statement of the facts is furnished by Professor W. J.
Beecher, in S. S. Times, Dec. 23, 1893 : 807 — " To create is to originate divinely. . . . Creation, in the sense in which the Bible uses the word, does not exclude the use of materials previously existing; for man was taken from the ground (Gen. 2 : 7), and woman
was builded from the rib of a man (2 : 22). Ordinarily God brings things into existence
through the operation of second causes. But it is possible, in our thinking, to withdraw attention from the second causes, and to think of anything as originating simply
from God, apart from second causes. To think of a thing thus is to think of it as
created. The Bible speaks of Israel as created, of the promised prosperity of Jerusalem
as created, of the Ammonite people and the king of Tyre as created, of persons of any
date in history as created (Is. 43 : 1-15; 65 : 18; Ez. 21 : 30; 28 : 13, 15; Ps. 102 : 18; Eccl. 12 : 1; Mal. 2 : 10).
Miracles and the ultimate beginnings of second causes are necessarily thought of as
creative acts; all other originating of things may be thought of, according to the purpose we have in mind, either as creation or as effected by second causes."

(*b*) In the account of the creation, כָּרָא seems to be distinguished from
עָשָׂה, " to make" either with or without the use of already existing material
(בָּרָא לַעֲשׂוֹת, " created in making" or "made by creation," in 2 : 3 ; and
וַיַּעַשׂ, of the firmament, in 1 : 7), and from יָצַר, " to form " out of such material. (See וַיִּבְרָא, of man regarded as a spiritual being, in 1 : 27 ; but וַיִּיצֶר,
of man regarded as a physical being, in 2 : 7.)

See Conant, Genesis, 1; Bible Com., 1 : 37 — "' created to make ' (in Gen. 2 : 3) = created
out of nothing, in order that he might make out of it all the works recorded in the six
days." Over against these texts, however, we must set others in which there appears
no accurate distinguishing of these words from one another. *Bara* is used in Gen. 1 : 1,
asah in Gen. 2 : 4, of the creation of the heaven and earth. Of earth, both *yatzar* and
asah are used in Is. 45 : 18. In regard to man, in Gen. 1 : 27 we find *bara* ; in Gen. 1 : 26 and 9 ;
6, *asah* ; and in Gen. 2 : 7, *yatzar*. In Is. 43 : 7, all three are found in the same verse : "whom
I have *bara* for my glory, I have *yatzar*, yea, I have *asah* him." In Is. 45 : 12, " *asah* the earth, and *bara*
man upon it"; but in Gen. 1 : 1 we read: "God *bara* the earth," and in 9 : 6 " *asah* man." Is. 44 : 2 —
"the Lord that *asah* thee (*i. e.*, man) and *yatzar* thee"; but in Gen. 1 : 27, God " *bara* man." Gen. 5 : 2
— "male and female *bara* he them." Gen. 2 : 22 — "the rib *asah* he a woman "; Gen. 2 : 7 — "he *yatzar* man ";
i. e., *bara* male and female, yet *asah* the woman and *yatzar* the man. *Asah* is not
always used for *transform :* Is. 41 : 20 — "fir-tree, pine, box-tree" in nature — *bara* ; Ps. 51 : 10 —
"*bara* in me a clean heart"; Is. 65 : 18 — God " *bara* Jerusalem into a rejoicing."

(*c*) The context shows that the meaning here is a making without the
use of preëxisting materials. Since the earth in its rude, unformed, chaotic
condition is still called "the earth" in verse 2, the word בָּרָא in verse 1
cannot refer to any shaping or fashioning of the elements, but must signify
the calling of them into being.

Oehler, Theology of O. T., 1:177 — "By the absolute *berashith*, 'in the beginning,' the divine creation is fixed as an absolute beginning, not as a working on something that already existed." Verse 2 cannot be the beginning of a history, for it begins with 'and.' Delitzsch says of the expression 'the earth was without form and void': "From this it is evident that the void and formless state of the earth was not uncreated or without a beginning. . . . It is evident that 'the heaven and earth' as God created them in the beginning were not the well-ordered universe, but the world in its elementary form."

(*d*) The fact that בָּרָא may have had an original signification of "cutting," "forming," and that it retains this meaning in the Piel conjugation, need not prejudice the conclusion thus reached, since terms expressive of the most spiritual processes are derived from sensuous roots. If בָּרָא does not signify absolute creation, no word exists in the Hebrew language that can express this idea.

(*e*) But this idea of production without the use of preëxisting materials unquestionably existed among the Hebrews. The later Scriptures show that it had become natural to the Hebrew mind. The possession of this idea by the Hebrews, while it is either not found at all or is very dimly and ambiguously expressed in the sacred books of the heathen, can be best explained by supposing that it was derived from this early revelation in Genesis.

E. H. Johnson, Outline of Syst. Theol., 94 — "Rom. 4:17 tells us that the faith of Abraham, to whom God had promised a son, grasped the fact that God calls into existence 'the things that are not.' This may be accepted as Paul's interpretation of the first verse of the Bible." It is possible that the heathen had occasional glimpses of this truth, though with no such clearness as that with which it was held in Israel. Perhaps we may say that through the perversions of later nature-worship something of the original revelation of absolute creation shines, as the first writing of a palimpsest appears faintly through the subsequent script with which it has been overlaid. If the doctrine of absolute creation is found at all among the heathen, it is greatly blurred and obscured. No one of the heathen books teaches it as do the sacred Scriptures of the Hebrews. Yet it seems as if this "One accent of the Holy Ghost The heedless world has never lost."

Bib. Com., 1 : 31 — "Perhaps no other ancient language, however refined and philosophical, could have so clearly distinguished the different acts of the Maker of all things [as the Hebrew did with its four different words], and that because all heathen philosophy esteemed matter to be eternal and uncreated." Prof. E. D. Burton: "Brahmanism, and the original religion of which Zoroastrianism was a reformation, were Eastern and Western divisions of a primitive Aryan, and probably monotheistic, religion. The Vedas, which represented the Brahmanism, leave it a question whence the world came, whether from God by emanation, or by the shaping of material eternally existent. Later Brahmanism is pantheistic, and Buddhism, the Reformation of Brahmanism, is atheistic." See Shedd, Dogm. Theol., 1:471, and Mosheim's references in Cudworth's Intellectual System, 3 : 140.

We are inclined still to hold that the doctrine of absolute creation was known to no other ancient nation besides the Hebrews. Recent investigations, however, render this somewhat more doubtful than it once seemed to be. Sayce, Hibbert Lectures, 142, 143, finds creation among the early Babylonians. In his Religions of Ancient Egypt and Babylonia, 372–397, he says : "The elements of Hebrew cosmology are all Babylonian ; even the creative word itself was a Babylonian conception ; but the spirit which inspires the cosmology is the antithesis to that which inspired the cosmology of Babylonia. Between the polytheism of Babylonia and the monotheism of Israel a gulf is fixed which cannot be spanned. So soon as we have a clear monotheism, absolute creation is a corollary. As the monotheistic idea is corrupted, creation gives place to pantheistic transformation."

It is now claimed by others that Zoroastrianism, the Vedas, and the religion of the ancient Egyptians had the idea of absolute creation. On creation in the Zoroastrian system, see our treatment of Dualism, page 382. Vedic hymn in Rig Veda, 10 : 9, quoted by J. F. Clarke, Ten Great Religions, 2 : 205 — "Originally this universe was soul only ; nothing else whatsoever existed, active or inactive. He thought : 'I will create worlds' ; thus he created these various worlds: earth, light, mortal being, and the waters." Renouf, Hibbert Lectures, 216-222, speaks of a papyrus on the staircase of the British Museum, which reads: "The great God, the Lord of heaven and earth, who made all things which are . . . the almighty God, self-existent, who made heaven and earth ; . . . the heaven was yet uncreated, uncreated was the earth ; thou hast put together the earth ; . . . who made all things, but was not made."

But the Egyptian religion in its later development, as well as Brahmanism, was pantheistic, and it is possible that all the expressions we have quoted are to be interpreted, not as indicating a belief in creation out of nothing, but as asserting emanation, or the taking on by deity of new forms and modes of existence. On creation in heathen systems, see Pierret, Mythologie, and answer to it by Maspero; Hymn to Amen-Rha, in "Records of the Past"; G. C. Müller, Literature of Greece, 87, 88; George Smith, Chaldean Genesis, chapters 1, 3, 5 and 6; Dillmann, Com. on Genesis, 6th edition, Introd., 5-10; LeNormant. Hist. Ancienne de l' Orient, 1 : 17-26; 5 : 238; Otto Zöckler, art. : Schöpfung, in Herzog and Plitt, Encyclop.; S. B. Gould, Origin and Devel. of Relig. Beliefs, 281-292.

B. Hebrews 11 : 3 — "By faith we understand that the worlds have been framed by the word of God, so that what is seen hath not been made out of things which appear " = the world was not made out of sensible and preëxisting material, but by the direct fiat of omnipotence (see Alford, and Lünemann, Meyer's Com. *in loco*).

Compare 2 Maccabees 7 : 28 — ἐξ οὐκ ὄντων ἐποίησεν αὐτὰ ὁ Θεός. This the Vulgate translated by "quia ex nihilo fecit illa Deus," and from the Vulgate the phrase " creation out of nothing " is derived. Hedge, Ways of the Spirit, points out that Wisdom 11 : 17 has ἐξ ἀμόρφου ὕλης, interprets by this the ἐξ οὐκ ὄντων in 2 Maccabees, and denies that this last refers to creation out of nothing. But we must remember that the later Apocryphal writings were composed under the influence of the Platonic philosophy; that the passage in Wisdom may be a rationalistic interpretation of that in Maccabees; and that even if it were independent, we are not to assume a harmony of view in the Apocrypha. 2 Maccabees 7 : 28 must stand by itself as a testimony to Jewish belief in creation without use of preëxisting material,—belief which can be traced to no other source than the Old Testament Scriptures. Compare Ex. 34 : 10 — "I will do marvels such as have not been wrought [marg. ' created '] in all the earth "; Num. 16 : 30 — "if Jehovah make a new thing " [marg. ' create a creation"]; Is. 4 : 5 — "Jehovah will create . . . a cloud and smoke "; 41 : 20 — "the Holy One of Israel hath created it "; 45 : 7, 8 — "I form the light, and create darkness "; 57 : 19 — "I create the fruit of the lips "; 65 : 17 — "I create new heavens and a new earth "; Jer. 31 : 22 — "Jehovah hath created a new thing."

Rom. 4 : 17 — "God, who giveth life to the dead, and calleth the things that are not, as though they were "; 1 Cor. 1 : 28 — "things that are not" [did God choose] "that he might bring to naught the things that are "; 2 Cor. 4 : 6 — "God, that said, Light shall shine out of darkness" = created light without preëxisting material,— for darkness is no material ; Col. 1 : 16, 17 — "in him were all things created . . . . and he is before all things "; so also Ps. 33 : 9 — "he spake, and it was done "; 148 : 5 — "he commanded, and they were created." See Philo, Creation of the World, chap. 1-7, and Life of Moses, book 3, chap. 36 — "He produced the most perfect work, the Cosmos, out of non-existence (τοῦ μὴ ὄντος) into being (εἰς τὸ εἶναι)." E. H. Johnson, Syst. Theol., 94 — "We have no reason to believe that the Hebrew mind had the idea of creation out of *invisible* materials. But creation out of *visible* materials is in Hebrews 11 : 3 expressly denied. This text is therefore equivalent to an assertion that the universe was made without the use of *any* preëxisting materials."

2. *Indirect evidence from Scripture.*

(*a*) The past duration of the world is limited ; (*b*) before the world began to be, each of the persons of the Godhead already existed ; (*c*) the origin of the universe is ascribed to God, and to each of the persons of the Godhead. These representations of Scripture are not only most consistent with the view that the universe was created by God without use of preëxisting material, but they are inexplicable upon any other hypothesis.

(*a*) Mark 13 : 19 — "from the beginning of the creation which God created until now"; John 17 : 5 — "before the world was"; Eph. 1 : 4 — "before the foundation of the world." (*b*) Ps. 90 : 2 — "Before the mountains were brough⸺ forth, Or ever thou hadst formed the earth and the world, Even from everlasting to everlasting thou art God"; Prov. 8 : 23 — "I was set up from everlast ng, from the beginning, Before the earth was"; John 1 : 1 — "In the beginning was the Word"; Col. 1 : 17 — "he is before all things"; Heb. 9 : 14 — "the eternal Spirit" (see Tholuck, Com. *in loco*). (*c*) Eph. 3 : 9 — "God who created all things"; Rom. 11 : 36 — "of him . . . . are all things"; 1 Cor. 8 : 6 — "one God, the Father, of whom are all things . . . one Lord, Jesus Christ, through whom are all things"; John 1 : 3 — "all things were made through him"; Col. 1 : 16 — "in him were all things created . . . all things have been created through him, and unto him"; Heb. 1 : 2 — "through whom also he made the worlds"; Gen. 1 : 2 — "and the Spirit of God moved [marg. 'was brooding '] upon the face of the waters." From these passages we may also infer that (1) all things are absolutely dependent upon God; (2) God exercises supreme control over all things; (3) God is the only infinite Being; (4) God alone is eternal; (5) there is no substance out of which God creates; (6) things do not proceed from God by necessary emanation; the universe has its source and originator in God's transcendent and personal will. See, on this indirect proof of creation, Philippi, Glaubenslehre, 2 : 231. Since other views, however, have been held to be more rational, we proceed to the examination of

III. Theories which oppose Creation.

1. *Dualism.*

Of dualism there are two forms :

A. That which holds to two self-existent principles, God and matter. These are distinct from and coëternal with each other. Matter, however, is an unconscious, negative, and imperfect substance, which is subordinate to God and is made the instrument of his will. This was the underlying principle of the Alexandrian Gnostics. It was essentially an attempt to combine with Christianity the Platonic or Aristotelian conception of the ὕλη. In this way it was thought to account for the existence of evil, and to escape the difficulty of imagining a production without use of preëxisting material. Basilides (flourished 125) and Valentinus (died 160), the representatives of this view, were influenced also by Hindu philosophy, and their dualism is almost indistinguishable from pantheism. A similar view has been held in modern times by John Stuart Mill and apparently by Frederick W. Robertson.

Dualism seeks to show how the One becomes the many, how the Absolute gives birth to the relative, how the Good can consist with evil. The ὕλη of Plato seems to have meant nothing but empty space, whose not-being, or merely negative existence, prevented the full realization of the divine ideas. Aristotle regarded the ὕλη as a more positive cause of imperfection,— it was like the hard material which hampers the sculptor in expressing his thought. The real problem for both Plato and Aristotle was to explain the passage from pure spiritual existence to that which is phenomenal and imperfect, from the absolute and unlimited to that which exists in space and time. Finiteness, instead of being created, was regarded as having eternal existence and as limiting all divine manifestations. The ὕλη, from being a mere abstraction, became either a negative or a positive source of evil. The Alexandrian Jews, under the influence of Hellenic culture, sought to make this dualism explain the doctrine of creation.

Basilides and Valentinus, however, were also under the influence of a pantheistic philosophy brought in from the remote East — the philosophy of Buddhism, which taught that the original Source of all was a nameless Being, devoid of all qualities, and so, indistinguishable from Nothing. From this Being, which is Not-being, all existing things proceed. Aristotle and Hegel similarly taught that pure Being = Nothing. But inasmuch as the object of the Alexandrian philosophers was to show how something could be originated, they were obliged to conceive of the primitive Nothing as capable of such originating. They, moreover, in the absence of any conception of absolute creation, were compelled to conceive of a material which could be fashioned. Hence the Void, the Abyss, is made to take the place of matter. If it be said that they did not conceive of the Void or the Abyss as substance, we reply that they gave it just as substantial existence as they gave to the first Cause of things, which, in spite of their negative descriptions of it, involved Will and Design. And although they do not attribute to this secondary substance a positive influence for evil, they notwithstanding see in it the unconscious hinderer of all good.

Principal Tulloch, in Encyc. Brit., 10 : 704 — "In the Alexandrian Gnosis . . . . . the stream of being in its ever outward flow at length comes in contact with dead matter which thus receives animation and becomes a living source of evil." Windelband, Hist. Philosophy, 129, 144, 239 — " With Valentinus, side by side with the Deity poured forth into the Pleroma or Fulness of spiritual forms, appears the Void, likewise original and from eternity ; beside Form appears matter ; beside the good appears the evil." Mansel, Gnostic Heresies, 139 —"The Platonic theory of an inert, semi-existent matter, ... was adopted by the Gnosis of Egypt . . . . . 187 — Valentinus does not content himself, like Plato, ... with assuming as the germ of the natural world an unformed matter existing from all eternity. . . . . The whole theory may be described as a development, in allegorical language, of the pantheistic hypothesis which in its outline had been previously adopted by Basilides." A. H. Newman, Ch. History, 1 : 181-192, calls the philosophy of Basilides "fundamentally pantheistic." " Valentinus," he says, " was not so careful to insist on the original non-existence of God and everything." We reply that even to Basilides the Non-existent One is endued with power ; and this power accomplishes nothing until it comes in contact with things non-existent, and out of them fashions the seed of the world. The things non-existent are as substantial as is the Fashioner, and they imply both objectivity and limitation.

Lightfoot, Com. on Colossians, 76-113, esp. 82, has traced a connection between the Gnostic doctrine, the earlier Colossian heresy, and the still earlier teaching of the Essenes of Palestine. All these were characterized by (1) the spirit of caste or intellectual exclusiveness ; (2) peculiar tenets as to creation and as to evil ; (3) practical asceticism. Matter is evil and separates man from God ; hence intermediate beings between man and God as objects of worship ; hence also mortification of the body as a means of purifying man from sin. Paul's antidote for both errors was simply the person of Christ, the true and only Mediator and Sanctifier. See Guericke, Church History, 1 : 161.

Harnack, Hist. Dogma, 1 : 128 — "The majority of Gnostic undertakings may be viewed as attempts to transform Christianity into a theosophy. . . . In Gnosticism the Hellenic spirit desired to make itself master of Christianity, or more correctly, of the Christian communities." . . . 232 — Harnack represents one of the fundamental philosophic doctrines of Gnosticism to be that of the Cosmos as a mixture of matter with divine sparks, which has arisen from a descent of the latter into the former [Alexandrian Gnosticism], or, as some say, from the perverse, or at least merely permitted undertaking of a subordinate spirit [Syrian Gnosticism]. We may compare the Hebrew Sadducee with the Greek Epicurean ; the Pharisee with the Stoic ; the Essene with the Pythagorean. The Pharisees overdid the idea of God's transcendence. Angels must come in between God and the world. Gnostic intermediaries were the logical outcome. External works of obedience were alone valid. Christ preached, instead of this, a religion of the heart. Wendt, Teaching of Jesus, 1 : 52 — " The rejection of animal sacrifices and consequent abstaining from temple-worship on the part of the Essenes, which seems out of harmony with the rest of their legal obedience, is most simply explained as the consequence of their idea that to bring to God a bloody animal offering was derogatory to his transcendental character. Therefore they interpreted the O. T. command in an allegorizing way."

Lyman Abbott: "The Oriental dreams ; the Greek defines ; the Hebrew acts. All these influences met and intermingled at Alexandria. Emanations were mediations between the absolute, unknowable, all-containing God, and the personal, revealed and holy God of Scripture. Asceticism was one result : matter is undivine, therefore get rid of it. License was another result : matter is undivine, therefore disregard it — there is no disease and there is no sin — the modern doctrine of Christian Science." Kedney, Christian Doctrine, 1 : 360-373 ; 2 : 354, conceives of the divine glory as an eternal material environment of God, out of which the universe is fashioned.

The author of " The Unseen Universe " (page 17) wrongly calls John Stuart Mill a Manichæan. But Mill disclaims belief in the *personality* of this principle that resists and limits God,— see his posthumous Essays on Religion, 176-195. F. W. Robertson, Lectures on Genesis, 4-16 — " Before the creation of the world all was chaos . . . but with the creation, order began. . . . God did not cease from creation, for creation is going on every day. Nature is God at work. Only after surprising changes, as in spring-time, do we say figuratively, 'God rests.'" See also Frothingham, Christian Philosophy.

With regard to this view we remark :

(*a*) The maxim *ex nihilo nihil fit*, upon which it rests, is true only in so far as it asserts that no event takes place without a cause. It is false, if it mean that nothing can ever be made except out of material previously existing. The maxim is therefore applicable only to the realm of second causes, and does not bar the creative power of the great first Cause. The doctrine of creation does not dispense with a cause ; on the other hand, it assigns to the universe a sufficient cause in God.

Lucretius : "Nihil posse creari De nihilo, neque quod genitum est ad nihil revocari." Persius : "Gigni De nihilo nihil, in nihilum nil posse reverti." Martensen, Dogmatics, 116 — "The nothing, out of which God creates the world, is the eternal possibilities of his will, which are the sources of all the actualities of the world." Lewes, Problems of Life and Mind, 2 : 292 — "When therefore it is argued that the creation of something from nothing is unthinkable and is therefore peremptorily to be rejected, the argument seems to me to be defective. The process is thinkable, but not imaginable, conceivable but not probable." See Cudworth, Intellectual System, 3 : 81 *sq.* Lipsius, Dogmatik, 288, remarks that the theory of dualism is quite as difficult as that of absolute creation. It holds to a point of time when God began to fashion preëxisting material, and can give no reason why God did not do it before, since there must always have been in him an impulse toward this fashioning.

(*b*) Although creation without the use of preëxisting material is inconceivable, in the sense of being unpicturable to the imagination, yet the eternity of matter is equally inconceivable. For creation without preexisting material, moreover, we find remote analogies in our own creation of ideas and volitions, a fact as inexplicable as God's bringing of new substances into being.

Mivart, Lessons from Nature, 371, 372 — "We have to a certain extent an aid to the thought of absolute creation in our own free volition, which, as absolutely originating and determining, may be taken as the type to us of the creative act." We speak of ' the creative faculty ' of the artist or poet. We cannot give reality to the products of our imaginations, as God can to his. But if thought were only substance, the analogy would be complete. Shedd, Dogm. Theol., 1 : 467 — "Our thoughts and volitions are created *ex nihilo*, in the sense that one thought is not made out of another thought, nor one volition out of another volition." So created substance may be only the mind and will of God in exercise, automatically in matter, freely in the case of free beings (see pages 90, 105-110, 383, and in our treatment of Preservation.

Beddoes : " I have a bit of *Fiat* in my soul, And can myself create my little world." Mark Hopkins : " Man is an image of God as a creator. . . . He can purposely create, or cause to be, a future that, but for him, would not have been." E. C. Stedman, Nature of Poetry, 223 — " So far as the Poet, the artist, is creative, he becomes a sharer of the divine imagination and power, and even of the divine responsibility." Wordsworth calls the poet a "serene creator of immortal things." Imagination, he says, is but another name for " clearest insight, amplitude of mind, And reason in her most exalted mood." "If we are 'gods' (Ps. 82 : 6), that part of the Infinite which is embodied in us must partake to a limited extent of his power to create." Veitch, Knowing and Being, 289 — " Will, the expression of personality, both as originating resolutions and moulding existing material into form, is the nearest approach in thought which we can make to divine creation."

Creation is not simply the thought of God, — it is also the will of God — thought in expression, reason externalized. Will is creation out of nothing, in the sense that there is no use of preëxisting material. In man's exercise of the creative imagination there is will, as well as intellect. Royce, Studies of Good and Evil, 256, points out that we can be original in (1) the style or form of our work ; (2) in the selection of the objects we imitate ; (3) in the invention of relatively novel combinations of material. Style, subject, combination, then, comprise the methods of our originality. Our new conceptions of nature as the expression of the divine mind and will bring creation more within our comprehension than did the old conception of the world as substance capable of existing apart from God. Hudson, Law of Psychic Phenomena, 294, thinks that we have power to create visible phantasms, or embodied thoughts, that can be subjectively perceived by others. See also Hudson's Scientific Demonstration of Future Life, 153. He defines genius as the result of the synchronous action of the objective and subjective faculties. Jesus of Nazareth, in his judgment, was a wonderful psychic. Intuitive perception and objective reason were with him always in the ascendant. His miracles were misinterpreted psychic phenomena. Jesus never claimed that his works were outside of natural law. All men have the same intuitional power, though in differing degrees.

We may add that the begetting of a child by man is the giving of substantial existence to another. Christ's creation of man may be like his own begetting by the Father. Behrends: "The relation between God and the universe is more intimate and organic than that between an artist and his work. The marble figure is independent of the sculptor the moment it is completed. It remains, though he die. But the universe would vanish in the withdrawal of the divine presence and indwelling. If I were to use any figure, it would be that of generation. The immanence of God is the secret of natural permanence and uniformity. Creation is primarily a spiritual act. The universe is not what we see and handle. The real universe is an empire of energies, a hierarchy of correlated forces, whose reality and unity are rooted in the rational will of God perpetually active in preservation. But there is no identity of substance, nor is there any division of the divine substance."

Bowne, Theory of Thought and Knowledge, 36—"A mind is conceivable which should create its objects outright by pure self-activity and without dependence on anything beyond itself. Such is our conception of the Creator's relation to his objects. But this is not the case with us except to a very slight extent. Our mental life itself begins, and we come only gradually to a knowledge of things and of ourselves. In some sense our objects are given; that is, we cannot have objects at will or vary their properties at our pleasure. In this sense we are passive in knowledge, and no idealism can remove this fact. But in some sense also our objects are our own products: for an existing object becomes an object for us only as we think it, and thus make it our object. In this sense, knowledge is an active process, and not a passive reception of readymade information from without." Clarke, Self and the Father, 38—"Are we humiliated by having data for our imaginations to work upon? by being unable to create material? Not unless it be a shame to be second to the Creator." Causation is as mysterious as Creation. Balzac lived with his characters as actual beings. On the Creative Principle, see N. R. Wood, The Witness of Sin, 114-135.

(c) It is unphilosophical to postulate two eternal substances, when one self-existent Cause of all things will account for the facts. (d) It contradicts our fundamental notion of God as absolute sovereign to suppose the existence of any other substance to be independent of his will. (e) This second substance with which God must of necessity work, since it is, according to the theory, inherently evil and the source of evil, not only limits God's power, but destroys his blessedness. (f) This theory does not answer its purpose of accounting for moral evil, unless it be also assumed that spirit is material,—in which case dualism gives place to materialism.

Martensen, Dogmatics, 121 —" God becomes a mere demiurge, if nature existed befor spirit. That spirit only who in a perfect sense is able to commence his work of crea tion can have power to complete it." If God does not create, he must use what mate rial he finds, and this working with intractable material must be his perpetual sorrow Such limitation in the power of the deity seemed to John Stuart Mill the best explana tion of the existing imperfections of the universe.

The other form of dualism is :

B. That which holds to the eternal existence of two antagonistic spirits, one evil and the other good. In this view, matter is not a negative and imperfect substance which nevertheless has self-existence, but is either the work or the instrument of a personal and positively malignant intelligence, who wages war against all good. This was the view of the Manichæans. Manichæanism is a compound of Christianity and the Persian doctrine of two eternal and opposite intelligences. Zoroaster, however, held matter to be pure, and to be the creation of the good Being. Mani apparently regarded matter as captive to the evil spirit, if not absolutely his creation.

The old story of Mani's travels in Greece is wholly a mistake. Guericke, Church History, 1 : 185-187, maintains that Manichæanism contains no mixture of Platonic philosophy, has no connection with Judaism, and as a sect came into no direct relations with the Catholic church. Harnoch, Wegweiser, 22, calls Manichæanism a compound of Gnosticism and Parseeism. Herzog, Encyclopädie, art.: Mani und die Manichäer, regards Manichæanism as the fruit, acme, and completion of Gnosticism. Gnosticism was a heresy in the church; Manichæanism, like New Platonism, was an anti-church. J. P. Lange: "These opposing theories represent various pagan conceptions of the world, which, after the manner of palimpsests, show through Christianity." Isaac Taylor speaks of "the creator of the carnivora"; and some modern Christians practically regard Satan as a second and equal God.

On the Religion of Zoroaster, see Haug, Essays on Parsees, 139-161, 302-309; also our quotations on pp. 347-349; Monier Williams, in 19th Century, Jan. 1881 : 155-177 — Ahura Mazda was the creator of the universe. Matter was created by him, and was neither identified with him nor an emanation from him. In the divine nature there were two opposite, but not opposing, principles or forces, called "twins" — the one constructive, the other destructive; the one beneficent, the other maleficent. Zoroaster called these "twins" also by the name of "spirits," and declared that "these two spirits created, the one the reality, the other the non-reality." Williams says that these two principles were conflicting only in name. The only antagonism was between the resulting good and evil brought about by the free agent, man. See Jackson, Zoroaster.

We may add that in later times this personification of principles in the deity seems to have become a definite belief in two opposing personal spirits, and that Mani, Manes, or Manichæus adopted this feature of Parseeism, with the addition of certain Christian elements. Hagenbach, History of Doctrine, 1 : 470 — "The doctrine of the Manichæans was that creation was the work of Satan." See also Gieseler, Church History, 1 : 203; Neander, Church History, 1 : 478-505; Blunt, Dict. Doct. and Hist. Theology, art.: Dualism; and especially Baur, Das manichäische Religionssystem. A. H. Newman, Ch. History, 1 : 194 — "Manichæism is Gnosticism, with its Christian elements reduced to a minimum, and the Zoroastrian, old Babylonian, and other Oriental elements raised to the maximum. Manichæism is Oriental dualism under Christian names, the Christian names employed retaining scarcely a trace of their proper meaning. The most fundamental thing in Manichæism is its absolute dualism. The kingdom of light and the kingdom of darkness with their rulers stand eternally opposed to each other."

Of this view we need only say that it is refuted (a) by all the arguments for the unity, omnipotence, sovereignty, and blessedness of God ; (b) by the Scripture representations of the prince of evil as the creature of God and as subject to God's control.

Scripture passages showing that Satan is God's creature or subject are the following : Col. 1 : 16 — "for in him were all things created. in the heavens and upon the earth, things visible and things invisible, whether thrones or dominions or principalities or powers"; cf. Eph. 6 : 12 — "our wrestling is not against flesh and blood, but against the principalities, against the powers, against the world-rulers of this darkness, against the spiritual hosts of wickedness in the heavenly places"; 2 Pet. 2 : 4 — "God spared not the angels when they sinned, but cast them down to hell, and committed them to pits of darkness, to be reserved unto judgment"; Rev. 20 : 2 — "laid hold on the dragon, the old serpent, which is the Devil and Satan "; 10 — "and the devil that deceived them was cast into the lake of fire and brimstone."

The closest analogy to Manichæan dualism is found in the popular conception of the devil held by the mediæval Roman church. It is a question whether he was regarded as a rival or as a servant of God. Matheson, Messages of Old Religions, says that Parseeism recognizes an obstructive element in the nature of God himself. Moral evil is reality. and there is that element of truth in Parseeism. But there is no reconcilia' tion, nor is it shown that all things work together for good. E. H. Johnson: "This theory sets up matter as a sort of deity, a senseless idol endowed with the truly divine attribute of self-existence. But we can acknowledge but one God. To erect matter into an eternal Thing, independent of the Almighty but forever beside him, is the most revolting of all theories." Tennyson, Unpublished Poem (Life, 1 : 514) — "Oh me ! for why is all around us here As if some lesser God had made the world, But had not force to shape it as he would Till the high God behold it from beyond, And enter it and make it beautiful ? "

E. G. Robinson: "Evil is not eternal; if it were, we should be paying our respects to it. . . . There is much Manichæism in modern piety. We would influence soul through the body. Hence sacramentarianism and penance. Puritanism is theological Manichæanism. Christ recommended fasting because it belonged to his age. Christianity came from Judaism. Churchism comes largely from reproducing what Christ did. Christianity is not perfunctory in its practices. We are to fast only when there is good reason for it." L. H. Mills, New World, March, 1895 : 51, suggests that Phariseeism may be the same with Farseeism, which is but another name for Parseeism. He thinks that Resurrection, Immortality, Paradise, Satan, Judgment, Hell, came from Persian sources, and gradually drove out the old Sadduceean simplicity. Pfleiderer, Philos. Religion, 1 : 206 — "According to the Persian legend, the first human pair was a good creation of the all-wise Spirit, Ahura, who had breathed into them his own breath. But soon the primeval men allowed themselves to be seduced by the hostile Spirit Angromainyu into lying and idolatry, whereby the evil spirits obtained power over them and the earth and spoiled the good creation."

Disselhoff, Die klassische Poesie und die göttliche Offenbarung, 13-25 — " The Gathas of Zoroaster are the first poems of humanity. In them man rouses himself to assert his superiority to nature and the spirituality of God. God is not identified with nature. The impersonal nature-gods are vain idols and are causes of corruption. Their worshipers are servants of falsehood. Ahura-Mazda (living-wise) is a moral and spiritual personality. Ahriman is equally eternal but not equally powerful. Good has not complete victory over evil. Dualism is admitted and unity is lost. The conflict of faiths leads to separation. While one portion of the race remains in the Iranian highlands to maintain man's freedom and independence of nature, another portion goes South-East to the luxuriant banks of the Ganges to serve the deified forces of nature. The East stands for unity, as the West for duality. Yet Zoroaster in the Gathas is almost deified; and his religion, which begins by giving predominance to the good Spirit, ends by being honey-combed with nature-worship."

2. *Emanation.*

This theory holds that the universe is of the same substance with God, and is the product of successive evolutions from his being. This was the view of the Syrian Gnostics. Their system was an attempt to interpret Christianity in the forms of Oriental theosophy. A similar doctrine was taught, in the last century, by Swedenborg.

We object to it on the following grounds : (a) It virtually denies the infinity and transcendence of God, — by applying to him a principle of evolution, growth, and progress which belongs only to the finite and imperfect. (b) It contradicts the divine holiness, — since man, who by the theory is of the substance of God, is nevertheless morally evil. (c) It leads logically to pantheism, — since the claim that human personality is illusory cannot be maintained without also surrendering belief in the personality of God.

Saturninus of Antioch, Bardesanes of Edessa, Tatian of Assyria, Marcion of Sinope, all of the second century, were representatives of this view. Blunt, Dict. of Doct. and Hist. Theology, art.: Emanation : "The divine operation was symbolized by the image of the rays of light proceeding from the sun, which were most intense when nearest to the luminous substance of the body of which they formed a part, but which decreased in intensity as they receded from their source, until at last they disappeared altogether in darkness. So the spiritual effulgence of the Supreme Mind formed a world of spirit.

the intensity of which varied inversely with its distance from its source, until at length it vanished in matter. Hence there is a chain of ever expanding Æons which are increasing attenuations of his substance and the sum of which constitutes his fulness, *i. e.*, the complete revelation of his hidden being." Emanation, from *e*, and *manare*, to flow forth. Guericke, Church History, 1 : 160 — "many flames from one light . . . . the direct contrary to the doctrine of creation from nothing." Neander, Church History, 1 : 372-374. The doctrine of emanation is distinctly materialistic. We hold, on the contrary, that the universe is an expression of God, but not an emanation from God.

On the difference between Oriental emanation and eternal generation, see Shedd, Dogm. Theol., 1 : 470, and History Doctrine, 1 : 11-13, 318, note — "1. That which is eternally generated is infinite, not finite ; it is a divine and eternal person who is not the world or any portion of it. In the Oriental schemes, emanation is a mode of accounting for the origin of the finite. But eternal generation still leaves the finite to be originated. The begetting of the Son is the generation of an infinite person who afterwards creates the finite universe *de nihilo*. 2. Eternal generation has for its result a subsistence or personal hypostasis totally distinct from the world ; but emanation in relation to the deity yields only an impersonal or at most a personified energy or effluence which is one of the powers or principles of nature — a mere *anima mundi*." The truths of which emanation was the perversion and caricature were therefore the generation of the Son and the procession of the Spirit.

Principal Tulloch, in Encyc. Brit., 10 : 704 — " All the Gnostics agree in regarding this world as not proceeding immediately from the Supreme Being. . . . The Supreme Being is regarded as wholly inconceivable and indescribable — as the unfathomable Abyss (Valentinus) — the Unnameable (Basilides). From this transcendent source existence springs by emanation in a series of spiritual powers. . . . The passage from the higher spiritual world to the lower material one is, on the one hand, apprehended as a mere continued degeneracy from the Source of Life, at length terminating in the kingdom of darkness and death — the bordering chaos surrounding the kingdom of light. On the other hand the passage is apprehended in a more precisely dualistic form, as a positive invasion of the kingdom of light by a self-existent kingdom of darkness. According as Gnosticism adopted one or other of these modes of explaining the existence of the present world, it fell into the two great divisions which, from their places of origin, have received the respective names of the Alexandrian and Syrian Gnosis. The one, as we have seen, presents more a Western, the other more an Eastern type of speculation. The dualistic element in the one case scarcely appears beneath the pantheistic, and bears resemblance to the Platonic notion of the ὕλη, a mere blank necessity, a limitless void. In the other case, the dualistic element is clear and prominent, corresponding to the Zarathustrian doctrine of an active principle of evil as well as of good — of a kingdom of Ahriman, as well as a kingdom of Ormuzd. In the Syrian Gnosis . . . there appears from the first a hostile principle of evil in collision with the good."

We must remember that dualism is an attempt to substitute for the doctrine of absolute creation, a theory that matter and evil are due to something negative or positive outside of God. Dualism is a theory of origins, not of results. Keeping this in mind, we may call the Alexandrian Gnostics dualists, while we regard emanation as the characteristic teaching of the Syrian Gnostics. These latter made matter to be only an efflux from God and evil only a degenerate form of good. If the Syrians held the world to be independent of God, this independence was conceived of only as a later result or product, not as an original fact. Some like Saturninus and Bardesanes verged toward Manichæan doctrine ; others like Tatian and Marcion toward Egyptian dualism ; but all held to emanation as the philosophical explanation of what the Scriptures call creation. These remarks will serve as qualification and criticism of the opinions which we proceed to quote.

Sheldon, Ch. Hist., 1 : 206 — "The Syrians were in general more dualistic than the Alexandrians. Some, after the fashion of the Hindu pantheists, regarded the material realm as the region of emptiness and illusion, the void opposite of the Pleroma, that world of spiritual reality and fulness ; others assigned a more positive nature to the material, and regarded it as capable of an evil aggressiveness even apart from any quickening by the incoming of life from above." Mansel, Gnostic Heresies, 139 — "Like Saturninus, Bardesanes is said to have combined the doctrine of the malignity of matter with that of an active principle of evil ; and he connected together these two usually antagonistic theories by maintaining that the inert matter was co-eternal with God, while Satan as the active principle of evil was produced from matter (or, according to another statement, co-eternal with it), and acted in conjunction with it. 142 —

The feature which is usually selected as characteristic of the Syrian Gnosis is the doctrine of dualism, that is to say, the assumption of the existence of two active and independent principles, the one of good, the other of evil. This assumption was distinctly held by Saturninus and Bardesanes . . . in contradistinction to the Platonic theory of an inert semi-existent matter, which was adopted by the Gnosis of Egypt. The former principle found its logical development in the next century in Mani cheism; the latter leads with almost equal certainty to Pantheism."

A. H. Newman, Ch. History, 1 : 192 — " Marcion did not speculate as to the origin of evil. The Demiurge and his kingdom are apparently regarded as existing from eternity. Matter he regarded as intrinsically evil, and he practised a rigid asceticism." Mansel, Gnostic Heresies, 210 — " Marcion did not, with the majority of the Gnostics, regard the Demiurge as a derived and dependent being, whose imperfection is due to his remoteness from the highest Cause; nor yet, according to the Persian doctrine, did he assume an eternal principle of pure malignity. His second principle is independent of and co-eternal with, the first; opposed to it however, not as evil to good, but as imperfection to perfection, or, as Marcion expressed it, as a just to a good being. 218 — Non-recognition of any principle of pure evil. Three principles only : the Supreme God, the Demiurge, and the eternal Matter, the two latter being imperfect but not necessarily evil. Some of the Marcionites seem to have added an evil spirit as a fourth principle. . . . 31 — The Indian influence may be seen in Egypt, the Persian in Syria. . . . 32 — To Platonism, modified by Judaism, Gnosticism owed much of its philosophical form and tendencies. To the dualism of the Persian religion it owed one form at least of its speculations on the origin and remedy of evil, and many of the details of its doctrine of emanations. To the Buddhism of India, modified again probably by Platonism, it was indebted for the doctrines of the antagonism between spirit and matter and the unreality of derived existence (the germ of the Gnostic Docetism), and in part at least for the theory which regards the universe as a series of successive emanations from the absolute Unity."

Emanation holds that some stuff has proceeded from the nature of God, and that God has formed this stuff into the universe. But matter is not composed of stuff at all. It is merely an activity of God. Origen held that ψυχή etymologically denotes a being which, struck off from God the central source of light and warmth, has cooled in its love for the good, but still has the possibility of returning to its spiritual origin. Pfleiderer, Philosophy of Religion, 2 : 271, thus describes Origen's view : " As our body, while consisting of many members, is yet an organism which is held together by one soul, so the universe is to be thought of as an immense living being, which is held together by one soul, the power and the Logos of God." Palmer, Theol. Definition, 63, note —" The evil of Emanationism is seen in the history of Gnosticism. An emanation is a portion of the divine essence regarded as separated from it and sent forth as independent. Having no perpetual bond of connection with the divine, it either sinks into degradation, as Basilides taught, or becomes actively hostile to the divine, as the Ophites believed. . . . . In like manner the Deists of a later time came to regard the laws of nature as having an independent existence, i. e., as emanations."

John Milton, Christian Doctrine, holds this view. Matter is an efflux from God himself, not intrinsically bad, and incapable of annihilation. Finite existence is an emanation from God's substance. and God has loosened his hold on those living portions or centres of finite existence which he has endowed with free will, so that these independent beings may originate actions not morally referable to himself. This doctrine of free will relieves Milton from the charge of pantheism ; see Masson, Life of Milton, 6 : 824–826. Lotze, Philos. Religion, xlviii, li, distinguishes creation from emanation by saying that creation necessitates a divine Will, while emanation flows by natural consequence from the being of God. God's motive in creation is love, which urges him to communicate his holiness to other beings. God creates individual finite spirits, and then permits the thought, which at first was only his, to become the thought of these other spirits. This transference of his thought by will is the creation of the world. F. W. Farrar, on Heb. 1 : 2 — " The word Æon was used by the Gnostics to describe the various emanations by which they tried at once to widen and to bridge over the gulf between the human and the divine. Over that imaginary chasm John threw the arch of the Incarnation, when he wrote : ' The Word became flesh ' (John 1 : 14)."

Upton, Hibbert Lectures, chap. 2 — " In the very making of souls of his own essence and substance, and in the vacating of his own causality in order that men may be free, God already dies in order that they may live. God withdraws himself from our wills, so as to make possible free choice and even possible opposition to himself. Individual

25

ism admits dualism but not complete division. Our dualism holds still to underground connections of life between man and man, man and nature, man and God. Even the physical creation is ethical at heart: each thing is dependent on other things, and must serve them, or lose its own life and beauty. The branch must abide in the vine, or it withers and is cut off and burned " (275).

Swedenborg held to emanation, — see Divine Love and Wisdom, 283, 363, 305 — "Every one who thinks from clear reason sees that the universe is not created from nothing. . . . . All things were created out of a substance. . . . . As God alone is substance in itself and therefore the real *esse*, it is evidence that the existence of things is from no other source. . . . Yet the created universe is not God, because God is not in time and space. . . . There is a creation of the universe, and of all things therein, by continual mediations from the First. . . . . In the substances and matters of which the earths consist, there is nothing of the Divine in itself, but they are deprived of all that is divine in itself. . . . . Still they have brought with them by continuation from the substance of the spiritual sum that which was there from the Divine." Swedenborgianism is "materialism driven deep and clinched on the inside." This system reverses the Lord's prayer; it should read : " As on earth, so in heaven." He disliked certain sects, and he found that all who belonged to those sects were in the hells, condemned to everlasting punishment. The truth is not materialistic emanation, as Swedenborg imagined, but rather divine energizing in space and time. The universe is God's system of graded self-limitation, from matter up to mind. It has had a beginning, and God has instituted it. It is a finite and partial manifestation of the infinite Spirit. Matter is an expression of spirit, but not an emanation from spirit, any more than our thoughts and volitions are. Finite spirits, on the other hand, are differentiations within the being of God himself, and so are not emanations from him.

Napoleon asked Goethe what mattter was. " *Esprit gelé* — frozen spirit" was the answer Schelling wished Goethe had given him. But neither is matter spirit, nor are matter and spirit together mere natural effluxes from God's substance. A divine institution of them is requisite (quoted substantially from Dorner, System of Doctrine, 2 : 40). Schlegel in a similar manner called architecture " frozen music," and another writer calls music "dissolved architecture." There is a " psychical automatism," as Ladd says, in his Philosophy of Mind, 169 ; and Hegel calls nature "the corpse of the understanding — spirit in alienation from itself." But spirit is the Adam, of which nature is the Eve ; and man says to nature : "This is bone of my bones, and flesh of my flesh," as Adam did in Gen. 2 : 23.

3.   *Creation from eternity.*

This theory regards creation as an act of God in eternity past. It was propounded by Origen, and has been held in recent times by Martensen, Martineau, John Caird, Knight, and Pfleiderer. The necessity of supposing such creation from eternity has been argued from God's omnipotence, God's timelessness, God's immutability, and God's love. We consider each of these arguments in their order.

Origen held that God was from eternity the creator of the world of spirits. Martensen, in his Dogmatics, 114, shows favor to the maxims : " Without the world God is not God. . . . . God created the world to satisfy a want in himself. . . . . He cannot but constitute himself the Father of spirits." Schiller, Die Freundschaft, last stanza, gives the following popular expression to this view : " Freundlos war der grosse Weltenmeister ; Fühlte Mangel, darum schuf er Geister, Sel'ge Spiegel seiner Seligkeit. Fand das höchste Wesen schon kein Gleiches; Aus dem Kelch des ganzen Geisterreiches Schäumt ihm die Unendlichkeit." The poet's thought was perhaps suggested by Goethe's Sorrows of Werther : " The flight of a bird above my head inspired me with the desire of being transported to the shores of the immeasurable waters, there to quaff the pleasures of life from the foaming goblet of the infinite." Robert Browning, Rabbi Ben Ezra, 31 — " But I need now as then, Thee, God, who mouldest men. And since, not even when the whirl was worst, Did I — to the wheel of life With shapes and colors rife, Bound dizzily — mistake my end, To slake thy thirst." But this regards the Creator as dependent upon, and in bondage to, his own world.

Pythagoras held that nature's substances and laws are eternal. Martineau, Study of Religion, 1 : 144 ; 2 : 250, seems to make the creation of the world an eternal process.

conceiving of it as a self-sundering of the Deity, in whom in some way the world was always contained (Schurman, Belief in God, 140). Knight, Studies in Philos. and Lit., 94, quotes from Byron's Cain, I : 1—"Let him Sit on his vast and solitary throne, Creating worlds, to make eternity Less burdensome to his immense existence And unparticipated solitude. . . . . He, so wretched in his height, So restless in his wretchedness, must still Create and recreate." Byron puts these words into the mouth of Lucifer. Yet Knight, in his Essays in Philosophy, 143, 247, regards the universe as the everlasting effect of an eternal Cause. Dualism, he thinks, is involved in the very notion of a search for God.

W. N. Clarke, Christian Theology, 117 — "God is the source of the universe. Whether by immediate production at some point of time, so that after he had existed alone there came by his act to be a universe, *or* by perpetual production from his own spiritual being, so that his eternal existence was always accompanied by a universe in some stage of being, God has brought the universe into existence. . . . . Any method in which the independent God could produce a universe which without him could have had no existence, is accordant with the teachings of Scripture. Many find it easier philosophically to hold that God has eternally brought forth creation from himself, so that there has never been a time when there was not a universe in some stage of existence, than to think of an instantaneous creation of all existing things when there had been nothing but God before. Between these two views theology is not compelled to decide, provided we believe that God is a free Spirit greater than the universe." We dissent from this conclusion of Dr. Clarke, and hold that Scripture requires us to trace the universe back to a beginning, while reason itself is better satisfied with this view than it can be with the theory of creation from eternity.

(*a*) Creation from eternity is not necessitated by God's omnipotence. Omnipotence does not necessarily imply actual creation ; it implies only power to create. Creation, moreover, is in the nature of the case a thing begun. Creation from eternity is a contradiction in terms, and that which is self-contradictory is not an object of power.

The argument rests upon a misconception of eternity, regarding it as a prolongation of time into the endless past. We have seen in our discussion of eternity as an attribute of God, that eternity is not endless time, or time without beginning, but rather superiority to the law of time. Since eternity is no more past than it is present, the idea of creation from eternity is an irrational one. We must distinguish *creation in eternity past* (= God and the world coëternal, yet God the cause of the world, as he is the begetter of the Son) from *continuous creation* (which is an explanation of preservation, but not of creation at all). It is this latter, not the former, to which Rothe holds (see under the doctrine of Preservation, pages 415, 416). Birks, Difficulties of Belief, 81, 82 — "Creation is not from eternity, since past eternity cannot be actually traversed any more than we can reach the bound of an eternity to come. There was no *time* before creation, because there was no *succession*."

Birks, Scripture Doctrine of Creation, 78–105 —"The first verse of Genesis excludes five speculative falsehoods : 1. that there is nothing but uncreated matter ; 2. that there is no God distinct from his creatures ; 3. that creation is a series of acts without a beginning ; 4. that there is no real universe ; 5. that nothing can be known of God or the origin of things." Veitch, Knowing and Being, 22 —"The ideas of creation and creative energy are emptied of meaning, and for them is substituted the conception or fiction of an eternally related or double-sided world, not of what has been, but of what always is. It is another form of the see-saw philosophy. The eternal Self only is, if the eternal manifold is ; the eternal manifold is, if the eternal Self is. The one, in being the other, is or makes itself the one ; the other, in being the one, is or makes itself the other. This may be called a unity ; it is rather, if we might invent a term suited to the new and marvellous conception, an unparalleled and unbegotten twinity."

(*b*) Creation from eternity is not necessitated by God's timelessness. Because God is free from the law of time it does not follow that creation is free from that law. Rather is it true that no eternal creation is conceivable, since this involves an infinite number. Time must have had a beginning, and since the universe and time are coëxistent, creation could not have been from eternity.

Jude 25 — "Before all time" — implies that time had a beginning, and Eph. 1 : 4 — "before the foundation of the world" — implies that creation itself had a beginning. Is creation infinite? No, says Dorner, Glaubenslehre, 1 : 459, because to a perfect creation unity is as necessary as multiplicity. The universe is an organism, and there can be no organism without a definite number of parts. For a similar reason Dorner, System Doctrine, 2 : 28, denies that the universe can be eternal. Granting on the one hand that the world though eternal might be dependent upon God and as soon as the plan was evolved there might be no reason why the execution should be delayed, yet on the other hand the absolutely limitless is the imperfect and no universe with an infinite number of parts is conceivable or possible. So Julius Müller, Doctrine of Sin, 1 : 220–225 — "What has a goal or end must have a beginning ; history, as teleological, implies creation."

Lotze, Philos. Religion, 74 — "The world, with respect to its existence as well as its content, is completely dependent on the will of God, and not as a mere involuntary development of his nature. . . . The word 'creation' ought not to be used to designate a deed of God so much as the absolute dependence of the world on his will." So Schurman, Belief in God, 146, 156, 225 — "Creation is the eternal dependence of the world on God. . . . . Nature is the externalization of spirit. . . . . Material things exist simply as modes of the divine activity ; they have no existence for themselves." On this view that God is the Ground but not the Creator of the world, see Hovey, Studies in Ethics and Religion, 23–56 — "Creation is no more of a mystery than is the causal action" in which both Lotze and Schurman believe. "To deny that divine power can originate real being — can add to the sum total of existence — is much like saying that such power is finite." No one can prove that "it is of the essence of spirit to reveal itself," or if so, that it must do this by means of an organism or externalization. Eternal succession of changes in nature is no more comprehensible than are a creating God and a universe originating in time."

(c) Creation from eternity is not necessitated by God's immutability. His immutability requires, not an eternal creation, but only an eternal plan of creation. The opposite principle would compel us to deny the possibility of miracles, incarnation, and regeneration. Like creation, these too would need to be eternal.

We distinguish between idea and plan, between plan and execution. Much of God's plan is not yet executed. The beginning of its execution is as easy to conceive as is the continuation of its execution. But the beginning of the execution of God's plan is creation. Active will is an element in creation. God's will is not always active. He waits for "the fulness of the time" (Gal. 4 : 4) before he sends forth his Son. As we can trace back Christ's earthly life to a beginning, so we can trace back the life of the universe to a beginning. Those who hold to creation from eternity usually interpret Gen. 1 : 1 — "In the beginning God created the heavens and the earth," and John 1 : 1 — "In the beginning was the Word," as both and alike meaning "in eternity." But neither of these texts has this meaning. In each we are simply carried back to the beginning of the creation, and it is asserted that God was its author and that the Word already was.

(d) Creation from eternity is not necessitated by God's love. Creation is finite and cannot furnish perfect satisfaction to the infinite love of God. God has moreover from eternity an object of love infinitely superior to any possible creation, in the person of his Son.

Since all things are created in Christ, the eternal Word, Reason, and Power of God, God can "reconcile all things to himself" in Christ (Col. 1 : 20). Athanasius called God κτίστης, ού τεχνίτης — Creator, not Artisan. By this he meant that God is immanent, and not the God of deism. But the moment we conceive of God as revealing himself in Christ, the idea of creation as an eternal satisfaction of his love vanishes. God can have a plan without executing his plan. Decree can precede creation. Ideas of the universe may exist in the divine mind before they are realized by the divine will. There are purposes of salvation in Christ which antedate the world (Eph. 1 : 4). The doctrine of the Trinity, once firmly grasped, enables us to see the fallacy of such views as that of Pfleiderer, Philos. Religion, 1 : 286 — "A beginning and ending in time of the creating of God are not thinkable. That would be to suppose a change of creating and resting in God, which would equalize God's being with the changeable course of human life. Nor could it be conceived what should have hindered God from creating the world up to the beginning of his creating. . . . We say rather, with Scotus Erigena, that the divine creating is equally eternal with God's being."

(*e*) Creation from eternity, moreover, is inconsistent with the divine independence and personality. Since God's power and love are infinite, a creation that satisfied them must be infinite in extent as well as eternal in past duration — in other words, a creation equal to God. But a God thus dependent upon external creation is neither free nor sovereign. A God existing in necessary relations to the universe, if different in substance from the universe, must be the God of dualism : if of the same substance with the universe, must be the God of pantheism.

Gore, Incarnation, 136, 137 —"Christian theology is the harmony of pantheism and deism. . . . It enjoys all the riches of pantheism without its inherent weakness on the moral side, without making God dependent on the world, as the world is dependent on God. On the other hand, Christianity converts an unintelligible deism into a rational theism. It can explain how God became a creator in time, because it knows how creation has its eternal analogue in the uncreated nature ; it was God's nature eternally to produce, to communicate itself, to live." In other words, it can explain how God can be eternally alive, independent, self-sufficient, since he is Trinity. Creation from eternity is a natural and logical outgrowth of Unitarian tendencies in theology. It is of a piece with the Stoic monism of which we read in Hatch, Hibbert Lectures, 177 — "Stoic monism conceived of the world as a self-evolution of God. Into such a conception the idea of a beginning does not necessarily enter. It is consistent with the idea of an eternal process of differentiation. That which is always has been under changed and changing forms. The theory is cosmological rather than cosmogonical. It rather explains the world as it is, than gives an account of its origin."

4. *Spontaneous generation.*

This theory holds that creation is but the name for a natural process still going on, — matter itself having in it the power, under proper conditions, of taking on new functions, and of developing into organic forms. This view is held by Owen and Bastian. We object that

(*a*) It is a pure hypothesis, not only unverified, but contrary to all known facts. No credible instance of the production of living forms from inorganic material has yet been adduced. So far as science can at present teach us, the law of nature is " omne vivum e vivo," or " ex ovo. "

Owen, Comparative Anatomy of the Vertebrates, 3 : 814–818 — on Monogeny or Thaumatogeny ; quoted in Argyle, Reign of Law, 281 — " We discern no evidence of a pause or intromission in the creation or coming-to-be of new plants and animals." So Bastian, Modes or Origin of Lowest Organisms, Beginnings of Life, and articles on Heterogeneous Evolution of Living Things, in Nature, 2 : 170, 193, 219, 410, 431. See Huxley's Address before the British Association, and Reply to Bastian, in Nature, 2 : 400, 473 ; also Origin of Species, 69–79, and Physical Basis of Life, in Lay Sermons, 142. Answers to this last by Stirling, in Half-hours with Modern Scientists, and by Beale, Protoplasm or Life, Matter, and Mind, 73–75.

In favor of Redi's maxim, "omne vivum e vivo," see Huxley, in Encyc. Britannica, art.: Biology, 689 —"At the present moment there is not a shadow of trustworthy direct evidence that abiogenesis does take place or has taken place within the period during which the existence of the earth is recorded " ; Flint, Physiology of Man, 1 : 263–265 — "As the only true philosophic view to take of the question, we shall assume in common with nearly all the modern writers on physiology that there is no such thing as spontaneous generation. — admitting that the exact mode of production of the infusoria lowest in the scale of life is not understood." On the Philosophy of Evolution, see A. H. Strong, Philosophy and Religion, 39–57.

(*b*) If such instances could be authenticated, they would prove nothing as against a proper doctrine of creation, — for there would still exist an impossibility of accounting for these vivific properties of matter, except upon the Scriptural view of an intelligent Contriver and Originator of matter and its laws. In short, evolution implies previous involution, — if anything comes out of matter, it must first have been put in.

Sully: " Every doctrine of evolution must assume some definite initial arrangement which is supposed to contain the possibilities of the order which we find to be evolved and no other possibility." Bixby, Crisis of Morals, 258 — "If no creative fiat can be believed to create something out of nothing, still less is evolution able to perform such a contradiction." As we can get morality only out of a moral germ, so we can get vitality only out of a vital germ. Martineau, Seat of Authority, 14 — "By brooding long enough on an egg that is next to nothing, you can in this way hatch any universe actual or possible. Is it not evident that this is a mere trick of imagination, concealing its thefts of causation by committing them little by little, and taking the heap from the divine storehouse grain by grain ? "

Hens come before eggs. Perfect organic forms are antecedent to all life-cells, whether animal or vegetable. " Omnis cellula e cellula, sed primaria cellula ex organismo." God created first the tree, and its seed was in it when created (Gen. 1 : 12). Protoplasm is not *proton*, but *deuteron* ; the elements are antecedent to it. It is not true that man was never made at all but only " growed " like Topsy ; see Watts, New Apologetic, xvi, 312. Royce, Spirit of Modern Philosophy, 273 — " Evolution is the attempt to comprehend the world of experience in terms of the fundamental idealistic postulates : (1) without ideas, there is no reality ; (2) rational order requires a rational Being to introduce it ; (1) beneath our conscious self there must be an infinite Self. The question is : Has the world a meaning ? It is not enough to refer ideas to mechanism. Evolution, from the nebula to man, is only the unfolding of the life of a divine Self."

(*c*) This theory, therefore, if true, only supplements the doctrine of original, absolute, immediate creation, with another doctrine of mediate and derivative creation, or the development of the materials and forces originated at the beginning. This development, however, cannot proceed to any valuable end without guidance of the same intelligence which initiated it. The Scriptures, although they do not sanction the doctrine of spontaneous generation, do recognize processes of development as supplementing the divine fiat which first called the elements into being.

There is such a thing as free will, and free will does not, like the deterministic will, run in a groove. If there be free will in man, then much more is there free will in God, and God's will does not run in a groove. God is not bound by law or to law. Wisdom does not imply monotony or uniformity. God can do a thing once that is never done again. Circumstances are never twice alike. Here is the basis not only of creation but of new creation, including miracle, incarnation, resurrection, regeneration, redemption. Though will both in God and in man is for the most part automatic and acts according to law, yet the power of new beginnings, of creative action, resides in will, wherever it is free, and this free will chiefly makes God to be God and man to be man. Without it life would be hardly worth the living, for it would be only the life of the brute. All schemes of evolution which ignore this freedom of God are pantheistic in their tendencies, for they practically deny both God's transcendence and his personality.

Leibnitz declined to accept the Newtonian theory of gravitation because it seemed to him to substitute natural forces for God. In our own day many still refuse to accept the Darwinian theory of evolution because it seems to them to substitute natural forces for God ; see John Fiske, Idea of God, 97–102. But law is only a method ; it presupposes a lawgiver and requires an agent. Gravitation and evolution are but the habitual operations of God. If spontaneous generation should be proved true, it would be only God's way of originating life. E. G. Robinson, Christian Theology, 91 — "Spontaneous generation does not preclude the idea of a creative will working by natural law and secondary causes. . . . Of beginnings of life physical science knows nothing. . . . Of the processes of nature science is competent to speak and against its teachings respecting these there is no need that theology should set itself in hostility. . . . Even if man were derived from the lower animals, it would not prove that God did not create and order the forces employed. It may be that God bestowed upon animal life a plastic power."

Ward, Naturalism and Agnosticism, 1 : 180 — " It is far truer to say that the universe is a life, than to say that it is a mechanism. . . . . We can never get to God through a mere mechanism. . . . With Leibnitz I would argue that absolute passivity or inertness is not a reality but a limit. 269 — Mr. Spencer grants that to interpret spirit in terms of matter is impossible. 302 — Natural selection without teleological factors is not adequate to account for biological evolution, and such teleological factors imply a psychical something endowed with feelings and will, *i. e.*, Life and Mind. 2 : 130-135 — Conation is more fundamental than cognition. 149-151 — Things and events precede space and time. There is no empty space or time. 252-257 — Our assimilation of nature is the greeting of spirit by spirit. 259-267 — Either nature is itself intelligent, or there is intelligence beyond it. 274-276 — Appearances do not veil reality. 274 — The truth is not God *and* mechanism, but God *only* and no mechanism. 283 — Naturalism and Agnosticism, in spite of themselves, lead us to a world of Spiritualistic Monism." Newman Smyth, Christian Ethics, 36 — "Spontaneous generation is a fiction in ethics, as it is in psychology and biology. The moral cannot be derived from the non-moral, any more than consciousness can be derived from the unconscious, or life from the azoic rocks."

IV. THE MOSAIC ACCOUNT OF CREATION.

1. *Its twofold nature,* — as uniting the ideas of creation and of develop. ment.

(*a*) Creation is asserted. — The Mosaic narrative avoids the error of making the universe eternal or the result of an eternal process. The cosmogony of Genesis, unlike the cosmogonies of the heathen, is prefaced by the originating act of God, and is supplemented by successive manifestations of creative power in the introduction of brute and of human life.

All nature-worship, whether it take the form of ancient polytheism or modern materialism, looks upon the universe only as a birth or growth. This view has a basis of truth, inasmuch as it regards natural forces as having a real existence. It is false in regarding these forces as needing no originator or upholder. Hesiod taught that in the beginning was formless matter. Genesis does not begin thus. God is not a demiurge, working on eternal matter. God antedates matter. He is the creator of matter at the first (Gen. 1 : 1 — *bara*) and he subsequently created animal life (Gen. 1 : 21 — "and God created " — *bara*) and the life of man (Gen. 1 : 27 — "and God created man " — *bara* again).

Many statements of the doctrine of evolution err by regarding it as an eternal or self-originated process. But the process requires an originator, and the forces require an upholder. Each forward step implies increment of energy, and progress toward a rational end implies intelligence and foresight in the governing power. Schurman says well that Darwinism explains the *survival* of the fittest, but cannot explain the *arrival* of the fittest. Schurman, Agnosticism and Religion, 34 — "A primitive chaos of star-dust which held in its womb not only the cosmos that fills space, not only the living creatures that teem upon it, but also the intellect that interprets it, the will that confronts it, and the conscience that transfigures it, must as certainly have God at the centre, as a universe mechanically arranged and periodically adjusted must have him at the circumference. . . . There is no real antagonism between creation and evolution. 59 — Natural causation is the expression of a supernatural Mind in nature, and man — a being at once of sensibility and of rational and moral self-activity — is a signal and ever-present example of the interfusion of the natural with the supernatural in that part of universal existence nearest and best known to us."

Seebohm, quoted in J. J. Murphy, Nat. Selection and Spir. Freedom, 76 — " When we admit that Darwin's argument in favor of the theory of evolution proves its truth, we doubt whether natural selection can be in any sense the *cause* of the origin of species. It has probably played an important part in the history of evolution ; its rôle has been that of increasing the rapidity with which the process of development has proceeded. Of itself it has probably been powerless to originate a species ; the machinery by which species have been evolved has been completely independent of natural selection and could have produced all the results which we call the evolution of species without its aid ; though the process would have been slow had there been no struggle of life to increase its pace." New World, June, 1896 : 237–262, art. by Howison on the Limits of Evolution, finds limits in (1) the noumenal Reality ; (2) the break between the organic and the inorganic ; (3) break between physiological and logical genesis ; (4) inability to explain the great fact on which its own movement rests ; (5) the *a priori* self-consciousness which is the essential being and true person of the mind.

Evolution, according to Herbert Spencer, is "an integration of matter and concomitant dissipation of motion, during which the matter passes from an indefinite incoherent homogeneity to a definite coherent heterogeneity, and during which the retained motion goes through a parallel transformation." D. W. Simon criticizes this definition as defective "because (1) it omits all mention both of energy and its differentiations ; and (2) because it introduces into the definition of the process one of the phenomena thereof, namely, motion. As a matter of fact, both energy and force, and law, are subsequently and illicitly introduced as distinct factors of the process : they ought therefore to have found recognition in the definition or description." Mark Hopkins, Life, 189 — " God : what need of him ? Have we not force, uniform force, and do not all things continue as they were from the beginning of the creation, if it ever had a beginning ? Have we not the τὸ πᾶν, the universal All, the Soul of the universe, working itself up from unconsciousness through molecules and maggots and mice and marmots and monkeys to its highest culmination in man ? "

(*b*) Development is recognized.—The Mosaic account represents the present order of things as the result, not simply of original creation, but also of subsequent arrangement and development. A fashioning of inorganic materials is described, and also a use of these materials in providing the conditions of organized existence. Life is described as reproducing itself, after its first introduction, according to its own laws and by virtue of its own inner energy.

Martensen wrongly asserts that " Judaism represented the world exclusively as *creatura*, not *natura* ; as κτίσις, not φύσις." This is not true. Creation is represented as the bringing forth, not of something dead, but of something living and capable of self-development. Creation lays the foundation for cosmogony. Not only is there a fashioning and arrangement of the material which the original creative act has brought into being (see Gen. 1 : 2, 4, 6, 7, 9, 16, 17 ; 2 : 2, 6, 7, 8 — Spirit brooding ; dividing light from darkness, and waters from waters ; dry land appearing ; setting apart of sun, moon, and stars ; mist watering ; forming man's body ; planting garden) but there is also an imparting and using of the productive powers of the things and beings created (Gen. 1 : 12, 22, 24, 28 — earth brought forth grass ; trees yielding fruit whose seed was in itself ; earth brought forth the living creatures ; man commanded to be fruitful and multiply).

The tendency at present among men of science is to regard the whole history of life upon the planet as the result of evolution, thus excluding creation, both at the beginning of the history and along its course. On the progress from the Orohippus, the lowest member of the equine series, an animal with four toes, to Anchitherium with three, then to Hipparion, and finally to our common horse, see Huxley, in Nature for May 11, 1873 : 33, 34. He argues that, if a complicated animal like the horse has arisen by gradual modification of a lower and less specialized form, there is no reason to think that other animals have arisen in a different way. Clarence King, Address at Yale College, 1877, regards American geology as teaching the doctrine of sudden yet natural modification of species. " When catastrophic change burst in upon the ages of uniformity and sounded in the ear of every living thing the words : ' Change or die ! ' plasticity became the sole principle of action." Nature proceeded then by leaps, and corresponding to the leaps of geology we find leaps of biology.

We grant the probability that the great majority of what we call species were produced in some such ways. If science should render it certain that all the present species of living creatures were derived by natural descent from a few original germs, and that these germs were themselves an evolution of inorganic forces and materials, we should not therefore regard the Mosaic account as proved untrue. We should only be required to revise our interpretation of the word *bara* in Gen. 1 : 21, 27, and to give it there the meaning of mediate creation, or creation by law. Such a meaning might almost seem to be favored by Gen. 1 : 11 — " let the earth put forth grass" ; 20 — "let the waters bring forth abundantly the moving creature that hath life " ; 2 : 7 — " the Lord God formed man of the dust " ; 9 — " out of the ground made the Lord God to grow every tree " ; *cf.* Mark 4 : 28 — αὐτομάτη ἡ γῆ καρποφορεῖ — " the earth brings forth fruit automatically." Goethe, Sprüche in Reimen : " Was wär ein Gott der nur von aussen stiesse, Im Kreis das All am Finger laufen liesse? Ihm ziemt's die Welt im Innern zu bewegen, Sich in Natur, Natur in sich zu hegen, So dass, was in Ihm lebt und webt und ist, Nie seine Kraft, nie seinen Geist vermisst "—" No, such a God my worship may not win, Who lets the world about his finger spin, A thing eternal ; God must dwell within."

All the growth of a tree takes place in from four to six weeks in May, June and July. The addition of woody fibre between the bark and the trunk results, not by impartation into it of a new force from without, but by the awakening of the life within. Environment changes and growth begins. We may even speak of an immanent transcendence of God — an unexhausted vitality which at times makes great movements forward. This is what the ancients were trying to express when they said that trees were inhabited by dryads and so groaned and bled when wounded. God's life is in all. In evolution we cannot say, with LeConte, that the higher form of energy is " derived from the lower." Rather let us say that both the higher and the lower are constantly dependent for their being on the will of God. The lower is only God's preparation for his higher self-manifestation ; see Upton, Hibbert Lectures, 165, 166.

Even Haeckel, Hist. Creation, 1 : 38, can say that in the Mosaic narrative " two great and fundamental ideas meet us — the idea of separation or differentiation, and the idea of progressive development or perfecting. We can bestow our just and sincere admiration on the Jewish lawgiver's grand insight into nature, and his simple and natural hypothesis of creation, without discovering in it a divine revelation." Henry Drummond, whose first book, Natural Law in the Spiritual World, he himself in his later days regretted as tending in a deterministic and materialistic direction, came to believe rather in " spiritual law in the natural world." His Ascent of Man regards evolution and law as only the methods of a present Deity. Darwinism seemed at first to show that the past history of life upon the planet was a history of heartless and cruel slaughter. The survival of the fittest had for its obverse side the destruction of myriads. Nature was " red in tooth and claw with ravine." But further thought has shown that this gloomy view results from a partial induction of facts. Palæontological life was not only a struggle for life, but a struggle for the life of others. The beginnings of altruism are to be seen in the instinct of reproduction and in the care of offspring. In every lion's den and tiger's lair, in every mother-eagle's feeding of her young, there is a self-sacrifice which faintly shadows forth man's subordination of personal interests to the interests of others.

Dr. George Harris, in his Moral Evolution, has added to Drummond's doctrine the further consideration that the struggle for one's own life has its moral side as well as the struggle for the life of others. The instinct of self-preservation is the beginning of right, righteousness, justice and law upon earth. Every creature owes it to God to preserve its own being. So we can find an adumbration of morality even in the predatory and internecine warfare of the geologic ages. The immanent God was even then preparing the way for the rights, the dignity, the freedom of humanity. B. P. Bowne, in the Independent, April 19, 1900 —" The Copernican system made men dizzy for a time, and they held on to the Ptolemaic system to escape vertigo. In like manner the conception of God, as revealing himself in a great historic movement and process, in the consciences and lives of holy men, in the unfolding life of the church, makes dizzy the believer in a dictated book, and he longs for some fixed word that shall be sure and stedfast." God is not limited to creating from without : he can also create from within ; and development is as much a part of creation as is the origination of the elements. For further discussion of man's origin, see section on Man a Creation of God, in our treatment of Anthropology.

2. *Its proper interpretation.*

We adopt neither (*a*) the allegorical, or mythical, (*b*) the hyperliteral, nor (*c*) the hyperscientific interpretation of the Mosaic narrative ; but rather (*d*) the pictorial-summary interpretation, — which holds that the account is a rough sketch of the history of creation, true in all its essential features, but presented in a graphic form suited to the common mind and to earlier as well as to later ages. While conveying to primitive man as accurate an idea of God's work as man was able to comprehend, the revelation was yet given in pregnant language, so that it could expand to all the ascertained results of subsequent physical research. This general correspondence of the narrative with the teachings of science, and its power to adapt itself to every advance in human knowledge, differences it from every other cosmogony current among men.

(a) The *allegorical*, or *mythical interpretation* represents the Mosaic account as embodying, like the Indian and Greek cosmogonies, the poetic speculations of an early race as to the origin of the present system. We object to this interpretation upon the ground that the narrative of creation is inseparably connected with the succeeding history, and is therefore most naturally regarded as itself historical. This connection of the narrative of creation with the subsequent history, moreover, prevents us from believing it to be the description of a vision granted to Moses. It is more probably the record of an original revelation to the first man, handed down to Moses' time, and used by Moses as a proper introduction to his history.

We object also to the view of some higher critics that the book of Genesis contains two inconsistent stories. Marcus Dods, Book of Genesis, 2 — "The compiler of this book ... lays side by side two accounts of man's creation which no ingenuity can reconcile." Charles A. Briggs: "The doctrine of creation in Genesis 1 is altogether different from that taught in Genesis 2." W. N. Clarke, Christian Theology, 199-201 — "It has been commonly assumed that the two are parallel, and tell one and the same story; but examination shows that this is not the case. ... We have here the record of a tradition, rather than a revelation. ... It cannot be taken as literal history, and it does not tell by divine authority how man was created." To these utterances we reply that the two accounts are not inconsistent but complementary, the first chapter of Genesis describing man's creation as the crown of God's general work, the second describing man's creation with greater particularity as the beginning of human history.

Canon Rawlinson, in Aids to Faith, 275, compares the Mosaic account with the cosmogony of Berosus, the Chaldean. Pfleiderer, Philos. of Religion, 1 : 267-272, gives an account of heathen theories of the origin of the universe. Anaxagoras was the first who represented the chaotic first matter as formed through the ordering understanding (νοῦς) of God, and Aristotle for that reason called him "the first sober one among many drunken." Schurman, Belief in God, 138 — "In these cosmogonies the world and the gods grow up together; cosmogony is, at the same time, theogony." Dr. E. G. Robinson: "The Bible writers believed and intended to state that the world was made in three literal days. But, on the principle that God may have meant more than they did, the doctrine of periods may not be inconsistent with their account." For comparison of the Biblical with heathen cosmogonies, see Blackie in Theol. Eclectic, 1 : 77-87; Guyot, Creation, 58-63; Pope, Theology, 1 : 401, 402; Bible Commentary, 1 : 36,48; McIlvaine, Wisdom of Holy Scripture, 1-54; J. F. Clarke, Ten Great Religions, 2 : 193-221. For the theory of 'prophetic vision,' see Kurtz, Hist. of Old Covenant, Introd., i-xxxvii, civ-cxxx; and Hugh Miller, Testimony of the Rocks, 179-210; Hastings, Dict. Bible, art.: Cosmogony; Sayce, Religions of Ancient Egypt and Babylonia, 372-397.

(b) The *hyperliteral interpretation* would withdraw the narrative from all comparison with the conclusions of science, by putting the ages of geological history between the first and second verses of Gen. 1, and by making the remainder of the chapter an account of the fitting up of the earth, or of some limited portion of it, in six days of twenty-four hours each. Among the advocates of this view, now generally discarded, are Chalmers, Natural Theology, Works, 1 : 228-258, and John Pye Smith, Mosaic Account of Creation, and Scripture and Geology. To this view we object that there is no indication, in the Mosaic narrative, of so vast an interval between the first and the second verses; that there is no indication, in the geological history, of any such break between the ages of preparation and the present time (see Hugh Miller, Testimony of the Rocks, 141-178); and that there are indications in the Mosaic record itself that the word "day" is not used in its literal sense; while the other Scriptures unquestionably employ it to designate a period of indefinite duration (Gen. 1 : 5 — "God called the light Day" — a day before there was a sun; 8 — "there was evening and there was morning, a second day"; 2 : 2 — God "rested on the seventh day"; cf. Heb. 4 : 3-10 — where God's day of rest seems to continue, and his people are exhorted to enter into it; Gen. 2 : 4 — "the day that Jehovah made earth and heaven" — "day" here covers all the seven days; cf. Is. 2 : 12 — "a day of Jehovah of hosts"; Zech. 14 : 7 — "it shall be one day which is known unto Jehovah; not day, and not night"; 2 Pet. 3 : 8 — "one day is with the Lord as a thousand years, and a thousand years as one day "). Guyot, Creation, 34, objects also to this interpretation, that the narrative purports to give a history of the making of the heavens as well as of the earth (Gen. 2 : 4 — "these are the generations of the heaven and of the earth "), whereas this interpretation confines the history to the earth. On the meaning of the word "day," as a period of indefinite duration, see Dana, Manual of Geology, 744; LeConte, Religion and Science, 262.

(c) The *hyperscientific interpretation* would find in the narrative a minute and precise correspondence with the geological record. This is not to be expected, since it is foreign to the purpose of revelation to teach science. Although a general concord between the Mosaic and geological histories may be pointed out, it is a needless embarrassment to compel ourselves to find in every detail of the former an accurate statement of some scientific fact. Far more probable we hold to be

(d) The *pictorial-summary interpretation.* Before explaining this in detail, we would premise that we do not hold this or any future scheme of reconciling Genesis and geology to be a finality. Such a settlement of all the questions involved would presuppose not only a perfected science of the physical universe, but also a perfected science of hermeneutics. It is enough if we can offer tentative solutions which represent the present state of thought upon the subject. Remembering, then, that any such scheme of reconciliation may speedily be outgrown without prejudice to the truth of the Scripture narrative, we present the following as an approximate account of the coincidences between the Mosaic and the geological records. The scheme here given is a combination of the conclusions of Dana and Guyot, and assumes the substantial truth of the nebular hypothesis. It is interesting to observe that Augustine, who knew nothing of modern science, should have reached, by simple study of the text, some of the same results. See his Confessions, 12 : 8 — "First God created a chaotic matter which was *next* to *nothing.* This chaotic matter was made from nothing, before all days. Then this chaotic, amorphous matter was subsequently arranged, in the succeeding six days "; De Genes. ad Lit., 4 : 27 — "The length of these days is not to be determined by the length of our week-days. There is a series in both cases, and that is all." We proceed now to the scheme :

1. The earth, if originally in the condition of a gaseous fluid, must have been void and formless as described in Genesis 1 : 2. Here the earth is not yet separated from the condensing nebula, and its fluid condition is indicated by the term "waters."

2. The beginning of activity in matter would manifest itself by the production of light, since light is a resultant of molecular activity. This corresponds to the statement in verse 3. As the result of condensation, the nebula becomes luminous, and this process from darkness to light is described as follows: "there was evening and there was morning, one day." Here we have a day without a sun — a feature in the narrative quite consistent with two facts of science : first, that the nebula would naturally be self-luminous, and, secondly, that the earth proper, which reached its present form before the sun, would, when it was thrown off, be itself a self-luminous and molten mass. The day was therefore continuous — day without night.

3. The development of the earth into an independent sphere and its separation from the fluid around it answers to the dividing of "the waters under the firmament from the waters above," in verse 7. Here the word "waters" is used to designate the "primordial cosmic material" (Guyot, Creation, 35-37), or the molten mass of earth and sun united, from which the earth is thrown off. The term "waters" is the best which the Hebrew language affords to express this idea of a fluid mass. Ps. 148 seems to have this meaning, where it speaks of the "waters that are above the heavens" (verse 4) — waters which are distinguished from the "deeps" below (verse 7), and the "vapor" above (verse 8).

4. The production of the earth's physical features by the partial condensation of the vapors which enveloped the igneous sphere, and by the consequent outlining of the continents and oceans, is next described in verse 9 as the gathering of the waters into one place and the appearing of the dry land.

5. The expression of the idea of life in the lowest plants, since it was in type and effect the creation of the vegetable kingdom, is next described in verse 11 as a bringing into existence of the characteristic forms of that kingdom. This precedes all mention of animal life, since the vegetable kingdom is the natural basis of the animal. If it be said that our earliest fossils are animal, we reply that the earliest vegetable forms, the *algœ,* were easily dissolved, and might as easily disappear; that graphite and bog-iron ore, appearing lower down than any animal remains, are the result of preceding vegetation; that animal forms, whenever and wherever existing, must subsist upon and presuppose the vegetable. The Eozoön is of necessity preceded by the Eophyte. If it

be said that fruit-trees could not have been created on the third day, we reply that since the creation of the vegetable kingdom was to be described at one stroke and no mention of it was to be made subsequently, this is the proper place to introduce it and to mention its main characteristic forms.   See Bible Commentary, 1 : 36; LeConte, Elements of Geology, 136, 285.

6.   The vapors which have hitherto shrouded the planet are now cleared away as preliminary to the introduction of life in its higher animal forms.   The consequent appearance of solar light is described in verses 16 and 17 as a making of the sun, moon, and stars, and a giving of them as luminaries to the earth. Compare Gen. 9 : 13 — "I do set my bow in the cloud." As the rainbow had existed in nature before, but was now appointed to serve a peculiar purpose, so in the record of creation sun, moon and stars, which existed before, were appointed as visible lights for the earth, — and that for the reason that the earth was no longer self-luminous, and the light of the sun struggling through the earth's encompassing clouds was not sufficient for the higher forms of life which were to come.

7.   The exhibition of the four grand types of the animal kingdom (radiate, molluscan, articulate, vertebrate), which characterizes the next stage of geological progress, is represented in verses 20 and 21 as a creation of the lower animals — those that swarm in the waters, and the creeping and flying species of the land. Huxley, in his American Addresses, objects to this assigning of the origin of birds to the fifth day, and declares that terrestrial animals exist in lower strata than any form of bird, — birds appearing only in the Oölitic, or New Red Sandstone. But we reply that the fifth day is devoted to sea-productions, while land-productions belong to the sixth. Birds, according to the latest science, are sea-productions, not land-productions. They originated from Saurians, and were, at the first, flying lizards. There being but one mention of sea-productions, all these, birds included, are crowded into the fifth day. Thus Genesis anticipates the latest science. On the ancestry of birds, see Pop. Science Monthly, March, 1884 : 606; Baptist Magazine, 1877 : 505.

8.   The introduction of mammals — viviparous species, which are eminent above all other vertebrates for a quality prophetic of a high moral purpose, that of suckling their young — is indicated in verses 24 and 25 by the creation, on the sixth day, of cattle and beasts of prey.

9.   Man, the first being of moral and intellectual qualities, and the first in whom the unity of the great design has full expression, forms in both the Mosaic and geologic record the last step of progress in creation (see verses 26–31). With Prof. Dana, we may say that " in this succession we observe not merely an order of events like that deduced from science ; there is a system in the arrangement, and a far-reaching prophecy, to which philosophy could not have attained, however instructed." See Dana, Manual of Geology, 741-746, and Bib. Sac., April, 1885 : 201-224.   Richard Owen : " Man from the beginning of organisms was ideally present upon the earth" ; see Owen, Anatomy of Vertebrates, 3 : 796; Louis Agassiz : " Man is the purpose toward which the whole animal creation tends from the first appearance of the first palæozoic fish."

Prof. John M. Taylor : " Man is not merely a mortal but a moral being. If he sinks below this plane of life he misses the path marked out for him by all his past development. In order to progress, the higher vertebrate had to subordinate everything to mental development. In order to become human it had to develop the rational intelligence. In order to become higher man, present man must subordinate everything to moral development. This is the great law of animal and human development clearly revealed in the sequence of physical and psychical functions." W. E. Gladstone in S. S. Times, April 26, 1890, calls the Mosaic days " chapters in the history of creation." He objects to calling them epochs or periods, because they are not of equal length, and they sometimes overlap. But he defends the general correspondence of the Mosaic narrative with the latest conclusions of science, and remarks: "Any man whose labor and duty for several scores of years has included as their central point the study of the means of making himself intelligible to the mass of men, is in a far better position to judge what would be the forms and methods of speech proper for the Mosaic writer to adopt, than the most perfect Hebraist as such, or the most consummate votary of physical science as such."

On the whole subject, see Guyot, Creation ; Review of Guyot, in N. Eng., July, 1884 : 591-594 ; Tayler Lewis, Six Days of Creation ; Thompson, Man in Genesis and in Geology; Agassiz, in Atlantic Monthly, Jan. 1874 ; Dawson, Story of the Earth and Man, 32, and in Expositor, Apl. 1886 ; LeConte, Science and Religion, 264 ; Hill, in Bib. Sac., April, 1875 ; Peirce, Ideality in the Physical Sciences, 38-72 ; Boardman, The Creative Week:

Godet, Bib. Studies of O. T., 65-138; Bell, in Nature, Nov. 24 and Dec. 1, 1882; W. E Gladstone, in Nineteenth Century, Nov. 1885: 685-707, Jan. 1886: 1, 176; reply by Huxley, in Nineteenth Century, Dec. 1885, and Feb. 1886; Schmid, Theories of Darwin; Bartlett, Sources of History in the Pentateuch, 1-35; Cotterill, Does Science Aid Faith in Regard to Creation? Cox, Miracles, 1-39 — chapter i, on the Original Miracle — that of Creation; Zöckler, Theologie und Naturwissenschaft, and Urgeschichte, 1-77; Reusch, Bib. Schöpfungsgeschichte. On difficulties of the nebular hypothesis, see Stallo, Modern Physics, 277-293.

V. GOD'S END IN CREATION.

Infinite wisdom must, in creating, propose to itself the most comprehensive and the most valuable of ends, — the end most worthy of God, and the end most fruitful in good. Only in the light of the end proposed can we properly judge of God's work, or of God's character as revealed therein.

It would seem that Scripture should give us an answer to the question: Why did God create? The great Architect can best tell his own design. Ambrose: "To whom shall I give greater credit concerning God than to God himself?" George A. Gordon, New Epoch for Faith, 15 — "God is necessarily a being of ends. Teleology is the warp and woof of humanity; it must be in the warp and woof of Deity. Evolutionary science has but strengthened this view. Natural science is but a mean disguise for ignorance if it does not imply cosmical purpose. The movement of life from lower to higher is a movement upon ends. Will is the last account of the universe, and will is the faculty for ends. The moment one concludes that God is, it appears certain that he is a being of ends. The universe is alive with desire and movement. Fundamentally it is throughout an expression of will. And it follows, that the ultimate end of God in human history must be worthy of himself."

In determining this end, we turn first to:

1. *The testimony of Scripture.*

This may be summed up in four statements. God finds his end (*a*) in himself; (*b*) in his own will and pleasure; (*c*) in his own glory; (*d*) in the making known of his power, his wisdom, his holy name. All these statements may be combined in the following, namely, that God's supreme end in creation is nothing outside of himself, but is his own glory — in the revelation, in and through creatures, of the infinite perfection of his own being.

(*a*) Rom. 11:36 — "unto him are all things"; Col. 1:16 — "all things have been created .... unto him" (Christ); compare Is. 48:11 — "for mine own sake, for mine own sake, will I do it .... and my glory will I not give to another"; and 1 Cor. 15:28 — "subject all things unto him, that God may be all in all." Proverbs 16:4 = not "The Lord hath made all things for himself" (A. V.) but "Jehovah hath made everything for its own end" (Rev. Vers.).

(*b*) Eph. 1:5, 6, 9 — "having foreordained us .... according to the good pleasure of his will, to the praise of the glory of his grace .... mystery of his will, according to his good pleasure which he purposed in him"; Rev. 4:11 — "thou didst create all things, and because of thy will they were, and were created."

(*c*) Is. 43:7 — "whom I have created for my glory"; 60:21 and 61:3 — the righteousness and blessedness of the redeemed are secured, that "he may be glorified"; Luke 2:14 — the angels' song at the birth of Christ expressed the design of the work of salvation: "Glory to God in the highest," and only through, and for its sake, "on earth peace among men in whom he is well pleased."

(*d*) Ps. 143:11 — "In thy righteousness bring my soul out of trouble"; Ez. 36:21, 22 — "I do not this for your sake .... but for mine holy name"; 39:7 — "my holy name will I make known"; Rom. 9:17 — to Pharaoh: "For this very purpose did I raise thee up, that I might show in thee my power, and that my name might be published abroad in all the earth"; 22, 23 — "riches of his glory" made known in vessels of wrath, and in vessels of mercy; Eph. 3:9, 10 — "created all things; to the intent that now unto the principalities and the powers in the heavenly places might be made known through the church the manifold wisdom of God." See Godet, on Ultimate Design of Man; "God in man and man in God," in Princeton Rev., Nov 1880; Hodge, Syst. Theol., 1:436, 535, 565, 568. *Per contra*, see Miller, Fetich in Theology 19, 39-45, 88-98, 143-146.

Since holiness is the fundamental attribute in God, to make himself, his own pleasure, his own glory, his own manifestation, to be his end in creation, is to find his chief end in his own holiness, its maintenance, expression, and communication. To make this his chief end, however, is not to exclude certain subordinate ends, such as the revelation of his wisdom, power, and love, and the consequent happiness of innumerable creatures to whom this revelation is made.

God's glory is that which makes him glorious. It is not something without, like the praise and esteem of men, but something within, like the dignity and value of his own attributes. To a noble man, praise is very distasteful unless he is conscious of something in himself that justifies it. We must be like God to be self-respecting. Pythagoras said well: "Man's end is to be like God." And so God must look within, and find his honor and his end in himself. Robert Browning, Hohenstiel-Schwangau: "This is the glory, that in all conceived Or felt or known, I recognize a Mind, Not mine but like mine,—for the double joy Making all things for me, and me for Him." Schurman, Belief in God, 214-216 — "God glorifies himself in communicating himself." The object of his love is the exercise of his holiness. Self-affirmation conditions self-communication.

E. G. Robinson, Christian Theology, 94, 196 — "Law and gospel are only two sides of the one object, the highest glory of God in the highest good of man . . . . Nor is it unworthy of God to make himself his own end: (a) It is both unworthy and criminal for a finite being to make himself his own end, because it is an end that can be reached only by degrading self and wronging others; but (b) For an infinite Creator not to make himself his own end would be to dishonor himself and wrong his creatures; since, thereby, (c) he must either act without an end, which is irrational, or from an end which is impossible without wronging his creatures; because (d) the highest welfare of his creatures, and consequently their happiness, is impossible except through the subordination and conformity of their wills to that of their infinitely perfect Ruler; and (e) without this highest welfare and happiness of his creatures God's own end itself becomes impossible, for he is glorified only as his character is reflected in, and recognized by, his intelligent creatures." Creation can add nothing to the essential wealth or worthiness of God. If the end were outside himself, it would make him dependent and a servant. The old theologians therefore spoke of God's "declarative glory," rather than God's "essential glory," as resulting from man's obedience and salvation.

2. *The testimony of reason.*

That his own glory, in the sense just mentioned, is God's supreme end in creation, is evident from the following considerations :

(a) God's own glory is the only end actually and perfectly attained in the universe. Wisdom and omnipotence cannot choose an end which is destined to be forever unattained ; for "what his soul desireth, even that he doeth " (Job 23 : 13). God's supreme end cannot be the happiness of creatures, since many are miserable here and will be miserable forever. God's supreme end cannot be the holiness of creatures, for many are unholy here and will be unholy forever. But while neither the holiness nor the happiness of creatures is actually and perfectly attained, God's glory is made known and will be made known in both the saved and the lost. This then must be God's supreme end in creation.

This doctrine teaches us that none can frustrate God's plan. God will get glory out of every human life. Man may glorify God voluntarily by love and obedience, but if he will not do this he will be compelled to glorify God by his rejection and punishment. Better be the molten iron that runs freely into the mold prepared by the great Designer, than be the hard and cold iron that must be hammered into shape. Cleanthes, quoted by Seneca: "Ducunt volentem fata, nolentem trahunt." W. C. Wilkinson, Epic of Saul, 271 — "But some are tools, and others ministers, Of God, who works his holy will with all." Christ baptizes "in the Holy Spirit and in fire" (Mat. 3 : 11). Alexander

McLaren: " There are two fires, to one or other of which we must be delivered. Either we shall gladly accept the purifying fire of the Spirit which burns sin out of us, or we shall have to meet the punitive fire which burns up us and our sins together. To be cleansed by the one or to be consumed by the other is the choice before each one of us." Hare, Mission of the Comforter, on John 16:8, shows that the Holy Spirit either *convinces* those who yield to his influence, or *convicts* those who resist — the word ἐλέγχω having this double significance.

(*b*) God's glory is the end intrinsically most valuable. The good of creatures is of insignificant importance compared with this. Wisdom dictates that the greater interest should have precedence of the less. Because God can choose no greater end, he must choose for his end himself. But this is to choose his holiness, and his glory in the manifestation of that holiness.

Is. 40:15, 16 — "Behold, the nations are as a drop of a bucket, and are counted as the small dust of the balance " — like the drop that falls unobserved from the bucket, like the fine dust of the scales which the tradesman takes no notice of in weighing, so are all the combined millions of earth and heaven before God. He created, and he can in an instant destroy. The universe is but a drop of dew upon the fringe of his garment. It is more important that God should be glorified than that the universe should be happy. As we read in Heb. 6:13 — "since he could swear by none greater, he sware by himself" — so here we may say: Because he could choose no greater end in creating, he chose himself. But to swear by himself is to swear by his holiness (Ps. 89:35). We infer that to find his end in himself is to find that end in his holiness. See Martineau on Malebranche, in Types, 177.

The stick or the stone does not exist for itself, but for some consciousness. The soul of man exists in part for itself. But it is conscious that in a more important sense it exists for God. "Modern thought," it is said, " worships and serves the creature more than the Creator ; indeed, the chief end of the Creator seems to be to glorify man and to enjoy him forever." So the small boy said his Catechism : " Man's chief end is to glorify God and to annoy him forever." Prof. Clifford: "The kingdom of God is obsolete; the kingdom of man has now come." All this is the insanity of sin. *Per contra*, see Allen, Jonathan Edwards, 329, 330 — "Two things are plain in Edwards's doctrine: first, that God cannot love anything other than himself: he is so great, so preponderating an amount of being, that what is left is hardly worth considering; secondly, so far as God has any love for the creature, it is because he is himself diffused therein : the fulness of his own essence has overflowed into an outer world, and that which he loves in created beings is his essence imparted to them." But we would add that Edwards does not say they are themselves of the essence of God; see his Works, 2:210, 211.

(*c*) His own glory is the only end which consists with God's independence and sovereignty. Every being is dependent upon whomsoever or whatsoever he makes his ultimate end. If anything in the creature is the last end of God, God is dependent upon the creature. But since God is dependent only on himself, he must find in himself his end.

To create is not to increase his blessedness, but only to reveal it. There is no need or deficiency which creation supplies. The creatures who derive all from him can add nothing to him. All our worship is only the rendering back to him of that which is his own. He notices us only for his own sake and not because our little rivulets of praise add anything to the ocean-like fulness of his joy. For his own sake, and not because of our misery or our prayers, he redeems and exalts us. To make our pleasure and welfare his ultimate end would be to abdicate his throne. He creates, therefore, only for his own sake and for the sake of his glory. To this reasoning the London Spectator replies: "The glory of God is the splendor of a manifestation, not the intrinsic splendor manifested. The splendor of a manifestation, however, consists in the effect of the manifestation on those to whom it is given. Precisely because the manifestation of God's goodness can be useful to us and cannot be useful to him, must its manifestation be intended for our sake and not for his sake. We gain everything by it — he nothing. except so far as it is his own will that we should gain what he desires to bestow upon us." In this last clause we find the acknowledgment of weakness in the theory that God's supreme end is the good of his creatures. God does gain the fulfilment of his plan, the doing of his will, the manifestation of himself. The great painter loves his picture less than he loves his ideal. He paints in order to express himself. God loves each soul which he creates, but he loves yet more the expression of his own perfections in it. And this self expression is his end. Robert Browning, Paracelsus, 54 — " God is the perfect Poet, Who in creation acts his own conceptions." Shedd, Dogm. Theol., 1 : 557, 358; Shairp, Province of Poetry, 11, 12.

God's love makes him a self-expressing being. Self-expression is an inborn impulse in his creatures. All genius partakes of this characteristic of God. Sin substitutes concealment for outflow, and stops this self-communication which would make the good of each the good of all. Yet even sin cannot completely prevent it. The wicked man is impelled to confess. By natural law the secrets of all hearts will be made manifest at the judgment. Regeneration restores the freedom and joy of self-manifestation. Christianity and confession of Christ are inseparable. The preacher is simply a Christian further advanced in this divine privilege. We need utterance. Prayer is the most complete self-expression, and God's presence is the only land of perfectly free speech.

The great poet comes nearest, in the realm of secular things, to realizing this privilege of the Christian. No great poet ever wrote his best work for money, or for fame, or even for the sake of doing good. Hawthorne was half-humorous and only partially sincere, when he said he would never have written a page except for pay. The hope of pay may have set his pen a-going, but only love for his work could have made that work what it is. Motley more truly declared that it was all up with a writer when he began to consider the money he was to receive. But Hawthorne needed the money to live on, while Motley had a rich father and uncle to back him. The great writer certainly absorbs himself in his work. With him necessity and freedom combine. He sings as the bird sings, without dogmatic intent. Yet he is great in proportion as he is moral and religious at heart. " Arma virumque cano " is the only first person singular in the Æneid in which the author himself speaks, yet the whole Æneid is a revelation of Virgil. So we know little of Shakespeare's life, but much of Shakespeare's genius.

Nothing is added to the tree when it blossoms and bears fruit; it only reveals its own inner nature. But we must distinguish in man his true nature from his false nature. Not his private peculiarities, but that in him which is permanent and universal, is the real treasure upon which the great poet draws. Longfellow : " He is the greatest artist then, Whether of pencil or of pen, Who follows nature. Never man, as artist or as artizan, Pursuing his own fantasies, Can touch the human heart or please, Or satisfy our nobler needs." Tennyson, after observing the subaqueous life of a brook, exclaimed : " What an imagination God has ! " Caird, Philos. Religion, 215 — " The world of finite intelligences, though distinct from God, is still in its ideal nature one with him. That which God creates, and by which he reveals the hidden treasures of his wisdom and love, is still not foreign to his own infinite life, but one with it. In the knowledge of the minds that know him, in the self-surrender of the hearts that love him, it is no paradox to affirm that he knows and loves himself."

(d) His own glory is an end which comprehends and secures, as a subordinate end, every interest of the universe. The interests of the universe are bound up in the interests of God. There is no holiness or happiness for creatures except as God is absolute sovereign, and is recognized as such. It is therefore not selfishness, but benevolence, for God to make his own glory the supreme object of creation. Glory is not vain-glory, and in expressing his ideal, that is, in expressing himself, in his creation, he communicates to his creatures the utmost possible good.

This self-expression is not selfishness but benevolence. As the true poet forgets himself in his work, so God does not manifest himself for the sake of what he can make by it. Self-manifestation is an end in itself. But God's self-manifestation comprises all good to his creatures. We are bound to love ourselves and our own interests just in proportion to the value of those interests. The monarch of a realm or the general of an army must be careful of his life, because the sacrifice of it may involve the loss of thousands of lives of soldiers or subjects. So God is the heart of the great system. Only by being tributary to the heart can the members be supplied with streams of holiness and happiness. And so for only one Being in the universe is it safe to live for himself. Man should not live for himself, because there is a higher end. But there is no higher end for God. "Only one being in the universe is excepted from the duty of subordination. Man must be subject to the 'higher powers' (Rom. 13:1). But there are no higher powers to God." See Park, Discourses, 181-209.

Bismarck's motto: "Ohne Kaiser, kein Reich"—"Without an emperor, there can be no empire"—applies to God, as Von Moltke's motto: "Erst wägen, dann wagen"—"First weigh, then dare"—applies to man. Edwards, Works, 2:215—"Selfishness is no otherwise vicious or unbecoming than as one is less than a multitude. The public weal is of greater value than his particular interest. It is fit and suitable that God should value himself infinitely more than his creatures." Shakespeare, Hamlet, 3:3—"The single and peculiar life is bound With all the strength and armor of the mind To keep itself from noyance; but much more That spirit upon whose weal depends and rests The lives of many. The cease of majesty Dies not alone, but like a gulf doth draw What's near it with it: it is a massy wheel Fixed on the summit of the highest mount, To whose huge spokes ten thousand lesser things Are mortis'd and adjoined; which when it falls, Each small annexment, petty consequence, Attends the boisterous ruin. Never alone did the king sigh, But with a general groan."

(*e*) God's glory is the end which in a right moral system is proposed to creatures. This must therefore be the end which he in whose image they are made proposes to himself. He who constitutes the centre and end of all his creatures must find his centre and end in himself. This principle of moral philosophy, and the conclusion drawn from it, are both explicitly and implicitly taught in Scripture.

The beginning of all religion is the choosing of God's end as our end — the giving up of our preference of happiness, and the entrance upon a life devoted to God. That happiness is not the ground of moral obligation, is plain from the fact that there is no happiness in seeking happiness. That the holiness of God is the ground of moral obligation, is plain from the fact that the search after holiness is not only successful in itself, but brings happiness also in its train. Archbishop Leighton, Works, 635—"It is a wonderful instance of wisdom and goodness that God has so connected his own glory with our happiness, that we cannot properly intend the one, but that the other must follow as a matter of course, and our own felicity is at last resolved into his eternal glory." That God will certainly secure the end for which he created, his own glory, and that his end is our end, is the true source of comfort in affliction, of strength in labor, of encouragement in prayer. See Psalm 25:11—"For thy name's sake.... Pardon mine iniquity for it is great"; 115:1—"Not unto us, O Jehovah, not unto us, But unto thy name give glory"; Mat. 6:33—"Seek ye first his kingdom, and his righteousness; and all these things shall be added unto you"; 1 Cor. 10:31—"Whether ye eat, or drink, or whatsoever ye do, do all to the glory of God"; 1 Pet. 2:9—"ye are an elect race .... that ye may show forth the excellencies of him who called you out of darkness into his marvelous light"; 4:11—speaking, ministering, "that in all things God may be glorified through Jesus Christ, whose is the glory and the dominion for ever and ever. Amen." On the whole subject, see Edwards, Works, 2:193-257; Janet, Final Causes, 443-455; Princeton Theol. Essays, 2:15-32; Murphy, Scientific Bases of Faith, 358-362.

It is a duty to make the most of ourselves, but only for God's sake. Jer. 45:5—"seekest thou great things for thyself? seek them not!" But it is nowhere forbidden us to seek great things for God. Rather we are to "desire earnestly the greater gifts" (1 Cor. 12:31). Self-realization as well as self-expression is native to humanity. Kant: "Man, and with him every rational creature, is an end in himself." But this seeking of his own good is to be subordinated to the higher motive of God's glory. The difference between the regenerate and the unregenerate may consist wholly in motive. The latter lives for self, the former for God. Illustrate by the young man in Yale College who began to learn his lessons for God instead of for self, leaving his salvation in Christ's hands. God requires self-renunciation, taking up the cross, and following Christ, because the first need of the sinner is to change his centre. To be self-centered is to be a savage. The struggle for the life of others is better. But there is something higher still. Life has dignity according to the worth of the object we install in place of self. Follow Christ. make God the center of your life,—so shall you achieve the best; see Colestock, Changing Viewpoint, 113-123.

26

George A. Gordon, The New Epoch for Faith, 11-13 — "The ultimate view of the universe is the religious view. Its worth is ultimately worth for the supreme Being. Here is the note of permanent value in Edwards's great essay on The End of Creation. The final value of creation is its value for God. . . . . Men are men in and through society — here is the truth which Aristotle teaches — but Aristotle fails to see that society attains its end only in and through God." Hovey, Studies, 65 — "To manifest the glory or perfection of God is therefore the chief end of our existence. To live in such a manner that his life is reflected in ours; that his character shall reappear, at least faintly, in ours; that his holiness and love shall be recognized and declared by us, is to do that for which we are made. And so, in requiring us to glorify himself, God simply requires us to do what is absolutely right, and what is at the same time indispensable to our highest welfare. Any lower aim could not have been placed before us, without making us content with a character unlike that of the First Good and the First Fair." See statement and criticism of Edwards's view in Allen, Jonathan Edwards, 227-238.

VI. Relation of the Doctrine of Creation to other Doctrines.

1. *To the holiness and benevolence of God.*

Creation, as the work of God, manifests of necessity God's moral attributes. But the existence of physical and moral evil in the universe appears, at first sight, to impugn these attributes, and to contradict the Scripture declaration that the work of God's hand was "very good" (Gen. 1 : 31). This difficulty may be in great part removed by considering that :

(*a*) At its first creation, the world was good in two senses : first, as free from moral evil, — sin being a later addition, the work, not of God, but of created spirits ; secondly, as adapted to beneficent ends, — for example, the revelation of God's perfection, and the probation and happiness of intelligent and obedient creatures.

(*b*) Physical pain and imperfection, so far as they existed before the introduction of moral evil, are to be regarded : first, as congruous parts of a system of which sin was foreseen to be an incident ; and secondly, as constituting, in part, the means of future discipline and redemption for the fallen.

The coprolites of Saurians contain the scales and bones of fish which they have devoured. Rom. 8 : 20-22 — "For the creation was subjected to vanity, not of its own will, but by reason of him who subjected it, in hope that the creation itself also shall be delivered from the bondage of corruption into the liberty of the glory of the children of God. For we know that the whole creation [the irrational creation] groaneth and travaileth in pain together until now " ; 23 — our mortal body, as a part of nature, participates in the same groaning. 2 Cor. 4 : 17 — "our light affliction, which is for the moment, worketh for us more and more exceedingly an eternal weight of glory." Bowne, Philosophy of Theism, 224-240 — "How explain our rather shabby universe? Pessimism assumes that perfect wisdom is compatible only with a perfect work, and that we know the universe to be truly worthless and insignificant." John Stuart Mill, Essays on Religion, 29, brings in a fearful indictment of nature, her storms, lightnings, earthquakes, blight, decay, and death. Christianity however regards these as due to man, not to God ; as incidents of sin : as the groans of creation, crying out for relief and liberty. Man's body, as a part of nature, waits for the adoption, and resurrection of the body is to accompany the renewal of the world.

It was Darwin's judgment that in the world of nature and of man, on the whole, "happiness decidedly prevails." Wallace, Darwinism, 36-40 — "Animals enjoy all the happiness of which they are capable." Drummond, Ascent of Man, 203 *sq.* — "In the struggle for life there is no hate — only hunger." Martineau, Study, 1 : 330 — "Waste of life is simply nature's exuberance." Newman Smyth, Place of Death in Evolution, 44-56 — "Death simply buries the useless waste. Death has entered for life's sake." These utterances, however, come far short of a proper estimate of the evils of the world, and they ignore the Scriptural teaching with regard to the connection between death and sin. A future world into which sin and death do not enter shows that the present world is abnormal, and that morality is the only cure for mortality. Nor can the imperfections of the univrse be explained by saying that they furnish opportunity for struggle and for virtue. Robert Browning, Ring and Book, Pope, 1375 — "I can believe this dread machinery Of sin and sorrow, would confound me else, Devised,— all pain, at most expenditure Of pain by Who devised pain,— to evolve, By new machinery in counterpart, The moral qualities of man — how else ? — To make him love in turn and be beloved, Creative and self-sacrificing too, And thus eventually godlike." This seems like doing evil that good may come. We can explain mortality only by immorality, and that not in God but in man. Fairbairn : "Suffering is God's protest against sin."

Wallace's theory of the survival of the fittest was suggested by the prodigal destructiveness of nature. Tennyson : "Finding that of fifty seeds She often brings but one to bear." William James : "Our dogs are *in* our human life, but not *of* it. The dog, under the knife of vivisection, cannot understand the purpose of his suffering. For him it is only pain. So we may lie soaking in a spiritual atmosphere, a dimension of Being which we have at present no organ for apprehending. If we knew the purpose of our life, all that is heroic in us would religiously acquiesce." Mason, Faith of the Gospel, 72 — "Love is prepared to take deeper and sterner measures than benevolence, which is by itself a shallow thing." The Lakes of Killarny in Ireland show what a paradise this world might be if war had not desolated it, and if man had properly cared for it. Our moral sense cannot justify the evil in creation except upon the hypothesis that this has some cause and reason in the misconduct of man.

This is not a perfect world. It was not perfect even when originally constituted. Its imperfection is due to sin. God made it with reference to the Fall,— the stage was arranged for the great drama of sin and redemption which was to be enacted thereon. We accept Bushnell's idea of "anticipative consequences," and would illustrate it by the building of a hospital-room while yet no member of the family is sick, and by the salvation of the patriarchs through a Christ yet to come. If the earliest vertebrates of geological history were types of man and preparations for his coming, then pain and death among those same vertebrates may equally have been a type of man's sin and its results of misery. If sin had not been an incident, foreseen and provided for, the world might have been a paradise. As a matter of fact, it will become a paradise only at the completion of the redemptive work of Christ. Kreibig, Versöhnung, 369 — "The death of Christ was accompanied by startling occurrences in the outward world, to show that the effects of his sacrifice reached even into nature." Perowne refers Ps. 96 : 10 — "Tho world also is established that it cannot be moved " — to the restoration of the inanimate creation ; *cf.* Heb. 12 : 27 — "And this word, Yet once more, signifieth the removing of those things that are shaken, as of things that have been made, that those things which are not shaken may remain "; Rev. 21 : 1, 5 — "a new heaven and a new earth . . . Behold, I make all things new."

Much sport has been made of this doctrine of anticipative consequences. James D. Dana : "It is funny that the sin of Adam should have killed those old trilobites ! The blunderbuss must have kicked back into time at a tremendous rate to have hit those poor innocents ! " Yet *every* insurance policy, *every* taking out of an umbrella, *every* buying of a wedding ring, is an anticipative consequence. To deny that God made the world what it is in view of the events that were to take place in it, is to concede to him less wisdom than we attribute to our fellow-man. The most rational explanation of physical evil in the universe is that of Rom. 8 : 20, 21 — "the creation was subjected to vanity . . . . by reason of him who subjected it" — *i. e.*, by reason of the first man's sin — "in hope that the creation itself also shall be delivered."

Martineau, Types, 2 : 151 — "What meaning could Pity have in a world where suffering was not meant to be ? " Hicks, Critique of Design Arguments, 386 — "The very badness of the world convinces us that God is good." And Sir Henry Taylor's words : "Pain in man Bears the high mission of the flail and fan ; In brutes 't is surely piteous " — receive their answer : The brute is but an appendage to man, and like inanimate nature it suffers from man's fall — suffers not wholly in vain, for even pain in brutes serves to illustrate the malign influence of sin and to suggest motives for resisting it. Pascal : "Whatever virtue can be bought with pain is cheaply bought." The pain and imperfection of the world are God's frown upon sin and his warning against it. See Bushnell, chapter on Anticipative Consequences, in Nature and the Supernatural, 194–219. Also McCosh, Divine Government, 26–35, 249–261 : Farrar, Science and Theology, 82–105 ; Johnson, in Bap. Rev., 6 : 141–154 : Fairbairn. Philos. Christ. Religion, 94–168.

2. *To the wisdom and free-will of God.*

No plan whatever of a finite creation can fully express the infinite perfection of God. Since God, however, is immutable, he must always have had a plan of the universe; since he is perfect, be must have had the best possible plan. As wise, God cannot choose a plan less good, instead of one more good. As rational, he cannot choose between plans equally good make a merely arbitrary choice. Here is no necessity, but only the certainty that infinite wisdom will act wisely. As no compulsion from without, so no necessity from within, moves God to create the actual universe. Creation is both wise and free.

As God is both rational and wise, his having a plan of the universe must be better than his not having a plan would be. But the universe once was not; yet without a universe God was blessed and sufficient to himself. God's perfection therefore requires, not that he have a universe, but that he have a plan of the universe. Again, since God is both rational and wise, his actual creation cannot be the worst possible, nor one arbitrarily chosen from two or more equally good. It must be, all things considered, the best possible. We are optimists rather than pessimists.

But we reject that form of optimism which regards evil as the indispensable condition of the good, and sin as the direct product of God's will. We hold that other form of optimism which regards sin as naturally destructive, but as made, in spite of itself, by an overruling providence, to contribute to the highest good. For the optimism which makes evil the necessary condition of finite being, see Leibnitz, Opera Philosophica, 168, 624; Hedge, Ways of the Spirit, 241; and Pope's Essay on Man. For the better form of optimism, see Herzog, Encyclopädie, art.: Schöpfung, 13 : 651-653; Chalmers, Works, 2 : 286; Mark Hopkins, in Andover Rev., March, 1885 : 197-210; Luthardt, Lehre des freien Willens, 9, 10—"Calvin's *Quia voluit* is not the last answer. We could have no heart for such a God, for he would himself have no heart. Formal will alone has no heart. In God real freedom controls formal, as in fallen man, formal controls real."

Janet, in his Final Causes, 429 *sq.* and 490-503, claims that optimism subjects God to fate. We have shown that this objection mistakes the certainty which is consistent with freedom for the necessity which is inconsistent with freedom. The opposite doctrine attributes an irrational arbitrariness to God. We are warranted in saying that the universe at present existing, considered as a partial realization of God's developing plan, is the best possible for this particular point of time,— in short, that all is for the best,— see Rom. 8 : 28—"to them that love God all things work together for good"; 1 Cor. 3 : 21—"all things are yours."

For denial of optimism in any form, see Watson, Theol. Institutes, 1 : 419; Hovey, God with Us, 206-208; Hodge, Syst. Theol., 1 : 419, 432, 566, and 2 : 145; Lipsius, Dogmatik, 234-255; Flint, Theism, 227-256; Baird, Elohim Revealed, 397-409, and esp. 405—"A wisdom the resources of which have been so expended that it cannot equal its past achievements is a finite capacity, and not the boundless depth of the infinite God." But we reply that a wisdom which does not do that which is best is not wisdom. The limit is not in God's abstract power, but in his other attributes of truth, love, and holiness. Hence God can say in Is. 5 : 4—"what could have been done more to my vineyard, that I have not done in it?"

The perfect antithesis to an ethical and theistic optimism is found in the non-moral and atheistic pessimism of Schopenhauer (Die Welt als Wille und Vorstellung) and Hartmann (Philosophie des Unbewussten). "All life is summed up in effort, and effort is painful; therefore life is pain." But we might retort: "Life is active, and action is always accompanied with pleasure; therefore life is pleasure." See Frances Power Cobbe, Peak in Darien, 95-134, for a graphic account of Schopenhauer's heartlessness, cowardice and arrogance. Pessimism is natural to a mind soured by disappointment and forgetful of God: Eccl. 2 : 11—"all was vanity and a striving after wind." Homer: "There is nothing whatever more wretched than man." Seneca praises death as the best invention of nature. Byron: "Count o'er the joys thine hours have seen, Count o'er thy days from anguish free, And know, whatever thou hast been, 'T is something better not to be." But it has been left to Schopenhauer and Hartmann to define will as unsatisfied yearning, to regard life itself as a huge blunder, and to urge upon the human race, as the only measure of permanent relief, a united and universal act of suicide.

G. H. Beard, in Andover Rev., March, 1892—"Schopenhauer utters one New Testament truth: the utter delusiveness of self-indulgence. Life which is dominated by the desires, and devoted to mere getting, is a pendulum swinging between pain and ennui." Bowne, Philos. of Theism, 124—" For Schopenhauer the world-ground is pure will, without intellect or personality. But pure will is nothing. Will itself, except as a function of a conscious and intelligent spirit, is nothing." Royce, Spirit of Mod. Philos., 253-260—" Schopenhauer united Kant's thought, ' The inmost life of all things is one,' with the Hindoo insight, 'The life of all these things, That art Thou.' To him music shows best what the will is : passionate, struggling, wandering, restless, ever returning to itself, full of longing, vigor, majesty, caprice. Schopenhauer condemns individual suicide, and counsels resignation. That I must ever desire yet never fully attain, leads Hegel to the conception of the absolutely active and triumphant spirit. Schopenhauer finds in it proof of the totally evil nature of things. Thus while Hegel is an optimist, Schopenhauer is a pessimist."

Winwood Reade, in the title of his book, The Martyrdom of Man, intends to describe human history. O. W. Holmes says that Bunyan's Pilgrim's Progress " represents the universe as a trap which catches most of the human vermin that have its bait dangled before them." Strauss: "If the prophets of pessimism prove that man had better never have lived, they thereby prove that themselves had better never have prophesied." Hawthorne, Note-book : " Curious to imagine what mournings and discontent would be excited, if any of the great so-called calamities of human beings were to be abolished,—as, for instance, death."

On both the optimism of Leibnitz and the pessimism of Schopenhauer, see Bowen, Modern Philosophy ; Tulloch, Modern Theories, 169-221 ; Thompson, on Modern Pessimism, in Present Day Tracts, 6 : no. 34 ; Wright, on Ecclesiastes, 141-216 ; Barlow, Ultimatum of Pessimism : Culture tends to misery ; God is the most miserable of beings: creation is a plaster for the sore. See also Mark Hopkins, in Princeton Review, Sept. 1882 : 197—" Disorder and misery are so mingled with order and beneficence, that both optimism and pessimism are possible." Yet it is evident that there must be more construction than destruction, or the world would not be existing. Buddhism, with its Nirvana-refuge, is essentially pessimistic.

3. *To Christ as the Revealer of God.*

Since Christ is the Revealer of God in creation as well as in redemption, the remedy for pessimism is (1) the recognition of God's transcendence — the universe at present not fully expressing his power, his holiness or his love, and nature being a scheme of progressive evolution which we imperfectly comprehend and in which there is much to follow ; (2) the recognition of sin as the free act of the creature, by which all sorrow and pain have been caused, so that God is in no proper sense its author ; (3) the recognition of Christ *for* us on the Cross and Christ *in* us by his Spirit, as revealing the age-long sorrow and suffering of God's heart on account of human transgression, and as manifested, in self-sacrificing love, to deliver men from the manifold evils in which their sins have involved them ; and (4) the recognition of present probation and future judgment, so that provision is made for removing the scandal now resting upon the divine government and for justifying the ways of God to men.

Christ's Cross is the proof that God suffers more than man from human sin, and Christ's judgment will show that the wicked cannot always prosper. In Christ alone we find the key to the dark problems of history and the guarantee of human progress. Rom. 3 25 — "whom God set forth to be a propitiation, through faith, in his blood, to show his righteousness because of the passing over of the sins done aforetime in the forbearance of God " ; 8 : 32 —"He that spared not his own Son, but delivered him up for us all, how shall he not also with him freely give us all things ? " Heb. 2 : 8, 9 —"we see not yet all things subjected to him. But we behold . . . . Jesus . . . . crowned with glory and honor"; Acts 17 : 31 — "he hath appointed a day in which he will judge the earth in righteousness by the man whom he hath ordained." See Hill, Psychology, 283; Bradford, Heredity and Christian Problems, 240, 241; Bruce, Providential Order, 71-88 ; J. M. Whiton, in Am. Jour. Theology, April, 1901 : 318.

G. A. Gordon, New Epoch of Faith, 199—" The book of Job is called by Huxley the classic of pessimism." Dean Swift, on the successive anniversaries of his own birth, was accustomed to read the third chapter of Job, which begins with the terrible "Let the day perish wherein I was born" (3 : 3). But predestination and election are not arbitrary. Wisdom has chosen the best possible plan, has ordained the salvation of all who could wisely have been saved, has permitted the least evil that it was wise to permit. Rev. 4 : 11—"Thou didst create all things, and because of thy will they were, and were created." Mason, Faith of the Gospel, 79 — "All things were present to God's mind because of his will, and then, when it pleased him, had being given to them." Pfleiderer, Grundriss, 36, advocates a realistic idealism. Christianity, he says, is not abstract optimism, for it recognizes the evil of the actual and regards conflict with it as the task of the world's history ; it is not pessimism, for it regards the evil as not unconquerable, but regards the good as the end and the power of the world.

Jones, Robert Browning, 109, 311 — "Pantheistic optimism asserts that all things *are* good ; Christian optimism asserts that all things are *working together* for good. Reverie in Asolando : ' From the first Power was — I knew, Life has made clear to me That, strive but for closer view, Love were as plain to see.' Balaustion's Adventure : ' Gladness be with thee, Helper of the world ! I think this is the authentic sign and seal Of Godship, that it ever waxes glad, And more glad, until gladness blossoms, bursts Into a rage to suffer for mankind And recommence at sorrow.' Browning endeavored to find God in man, and still to leave man free. His optimistic faith sought reconciliation with morality. He abhorred the doctrine that the evils of the world are due to merely arbitrary sovereignty, and this doctrine he has satirized in the monologue of Caliban on Setebos : ' Loving not, hating not, just choosing so.' Pippa Passes : ' God 's in his heaven —All 's right with the world.' But how is this consistent with the guilt of the sinner ? Browning does not say. He leaves the antinomy unsolved, only striving to hold both truths in their fulness. Love demands distinction between God and man, yet love unites God and man. Saul : 'All 's love, but all 's law.' Carlyle forms a striking contrast to Browning. Carlyle was a pessimist. He would renounce happiness for duty, and as a means to this end would suppress, not idle speech alone, but thought itself. The battle is fought moreover in a foreign cause. God's cause is not ours. Duty is a menace, like the duty of a slave. The moral law is not a beneficent revelation, reconciling God and man. All is fear, and there is no love." Carlyle took Emerson through the London slums at midnight and asked him : " Do you believe in a devil now ? " But Emerson replied : " I am more and more convinced of the greatness and goodness of the English people." On Browning and Carlyle, see A. H. Strong, Great Poets and their Theology, 373-447.

Henry Ward Beecher, when asked whether life was worth living, replied that that depended very much upon the liver. Optimism and pessimism are largely matters of digestion. President Mark Hopkins asked a bright student if he did not believe this the best possible system. When the student replied in the negative, the President asked him how he could improve upon it. He answered : " I would kill off all the bed-bugs, mosquitoes and fleas, and make oranges and bananas grow further north." The lady who was bitten by a mosquito asked whether it would be proper to speak of the creature as " a depraved little insect." She was told that this would be improper, because depravity always implies a previous state of innocence, whereas the mosquito has always been as bad as he now is. Dr. Lyman Beecher, however, seems to have held the contrary view. When he had captured the mosquito who had bitten him, he crushed the insect, saying : " There ! I 'll show you that there is a God in Israel ! " He identified the mosquito with all the corporate evil of the world. Allen, Religious Progress, 22 — " Wordsworth hoped still, although the French Revolution depressed him ; Macaulay, after reading Ranke's History of the Popes, denied all religious progress." On Huxley's account of evil, see Upton, Hibbert Lectures, 265 *sq.*

Pfleiderer, Philos. Religion, 1 : 301, 302—" The Greeks of Homer's time had a naïve and youthful optimism. But they changed from an optimistic to a pessimistic view. This change resulted from their increasing contemplation of the moral disorder of the world. " On the melancholy of the Greeks, see Butcher, Aspects of Greek Genius, 130-165. Butcher holds that the great difference between Greeks and Hebrews was that the former had no hope or ideal of progress. A. H. Bradford, Age of Faith, 74-102 — " The voluptuous poets are pessimistic, because sensual pleasure quickly passes, and leaves lassitude and enervation behind. Pessimism is the basis of Stoicism also. It is inevitable where there is no faith in God and in a future life. The life of a seed underground is not inspiring, except in prospect of sun and flowers and fruit." Bradley, Appearance and Reality, xiv, sums up the optimistic view as follows : "The world is the best of all possible worlds, and everything in it is a necessary evil." He should have added that pain is the exception in the world, and finite free will is the cause of the trouble. Pain is made the means of developing character, and, when it has accomplished its purpose, pain will pass away.

Jackson, James Martineau, 390—"All is well, says an American preacher, for if there is anything that is not well, it is well that it is not well. It is well that falsity and hate are not well, that malice and envy and cruelty are not well. What hope for the world or what trust in God, if they were well?" *Live* spells *Evil*, only when we read it the wrong way. James Russell Lowell, Letters, 2:51—"The more I learn . . . . the more my confidence in the general good sense and honest intentions of mankind increases. . . . . The signs of the times cease to alarm me, and seem as natural as to a mother the teething of her seventh baby. I take great comfort in God. I think that he is considerably amused with us sometimes, and that he likes us on the whole, and would not let us get at the matchbox so carelessly as he does, unless he knew that the frame of his universe was fireproof."

Compare with all this the hopeless pessimism of Omar Khayyám, Rubáiyát, stanza 99 — "Ah Love! could you and I with Him conspire To grasp this sorry scheme of things entire, Would not we shatter it to bits—and then Remould it nearer to the heart's desire?" Royce, Studies of Good and Evil, 14, in discussing the Problem of Job, suggests the following solution: "When you suffer, your sufferings are God's sufferings, not his external work, not his external penalty, not the fruit of his neglect, but identically his own personal woe. In you God himself suffers, precisely as you do, and has all your concern in overcoming this grief." F. H. Johnson, What is Reality, 349, 505—"The Christian ideal is not maintainable, if we assume that God could as easily develop his creation without conflict. . . . . Happiness is only one of his ends; the evolution of moral character is another." A. E. Waffle, Uses of Moral Evil: "(1) It aids development of holy character by opposition; (2) affords opportunity for ministering; (3) makes known to us some of the chief attributes of God; (4) enhances the blessedness of heaven."

4. *To Providence and Redemption.*

Christianity is essentially a scheme of supernatural love and power. It conceives of God as above the world, as well as in it, — able to manifest himself, and actually manifesting himself, in ways unknown to mere nature.

But this absolute sovereignty and transcendence, which are manifested in providence and redemption, are inseparable from creatorship. If the world be eternal, like God, it must be an efflux from the substance of God and must be absolutely equal with God. Only a proper doctrine of creation can secure God's absolute distinctness from the world and his sovereignty over it.

The logical alternative of creation is therefore a system of pantheism, in which God is an impersonal and necessary force. Hence the pantheistic *dicta* of Fichte: "The assumption of a creation is the fundamental error of all false metaphysics and false theology"; of Hegel: "God evolves the world out of himself, in order to take it back into himself again in the Spirit"; and of Strauss: "Trinity and creation, speculatively viewed, are one and the same, — only the one is viewed absolutely, the other empirically."

Starrett, Studies, 155, 156—"Hegel held that it belongs to God's nature to create. Creation is God's positing an *other* which is not an *other*. The creation is *his*, belongs to his being or essence. This involves the finite as his own self-posited object and self-revelation. It is necessary for God to create. Love, Hegel says, is only another expression of the eternally Triune God. Love must create and love *another*. But in loving this *other*, God is only loving himself." We have already, in our discussion of the theory of creation from eternity, shown the insufficiency of creation to satisfy either the love or the power of God. A proper doctrine of the Trinity renders the hypothesis of an eternal creation unnecessary and irrational. That hypothesis is pantheistic in tendency

Luthardt, Compendium der Dogmatik, 97 — " Dualism might be called a **logical alterna.** tive of creation, but for the fact that its notion of two gods in self-contradictory, and leads to the lowering of the idea of the Godhead, so that the impersonal god of pantheism takes its place. " Dorner, System of Doctrine, 2·11 — " The world cannot be necessitated in order to satisfy either want or over-fulness 1 God. . . . . The doctrine of absolute creation prevents the *confounding* of God with the world. The declaration that the Spirit brooded over the formless elements, and that life was developed under the continuous operation of God's laws and presence, prevents the *separation* of God from the world. Thus pantheism and deism are both avoided." See Kant and Spinoza contrasted in Shedd, Dogm. Theol., 1:468, 469. The unusually full treatment of the doctrine of creation in this chapter is due to a conviction that the doctrine constitutes an antidote to most of the false philosophy of our time.

5. *To the Observance of the Sabbath.*

We perceive from this point of view, moreover, the importance and value of the Sabbath, as commemorating God's act of creation, and thus God's personality, sovereignty, and transcendence.

(*a*) The Sabbath is of perpetual obligation as God's appointed memorial of his creating activity. The Sabbath requisition antedates the decalogue and forms a part of the moral law. Made at the creation, it applies to man as man, everywhere and always, in his present state of being.

Gen. 2 : 3 — " And God blessed the seventh day, and hallowed it; because that in it he rested from all his work which God had created and made. " Our rest is to be a miniature representation of God's rest. As God worked six divine days and rested one divine day, so are we in imitation of him to work six human days and to rest one human day. In the Old Testament there are indications of an observance of the Sabbath day before the Mosaic legislation : Gen. 4 : 3 — " And in process of time [lit. 'at the end of days '] it came to pass that Cain brought of the fruit of the ground an offering unto Jehovah "; Gen. 8 : 10, 12 — Noah twice waited seven days before sending forth the dove from the ark ; Gen. 29 : 27, 28 — " fulfil the week "; *cf.* Judges 14 : 12 — " the seven days of the feast " ; Ex. 16 : 5 — double portion of manna promised on the sixth day, that none be gathered on the Sabbath (*cf*. verses 20, 30). This division of days into weeks is best explained by the original institution of the Sabbath at man's creation. Moses in the fourth commandment therefore speaks of it as already known and observed : Ex. 20 : 8 — " Remember the Sabbath day to keep it holy."

The Sabbath is recognized in Assyrian accounts of the Creation ; see Trans. Soc. Bib. Arch., 5 : 427, 428 ; Schrader, Keilinschriften, ed. 1883 : 18-22. Professor Sayce : " Seven was a sacred number descended to the Semites from their Accadian predecessors. Seven by seven had the magic knots to be tied by the witch ; seven times had the body of the sick man to be anointed by the purifying oil. As the Sabbath of rest fell on each seventh day of the week, so the planets, like the demon-messengers of Anu, were seven in number, and the gods of the number seven received a particular honor." But now the discovery of a calendar tablet in Mesopotamia shows us the week of seven days and the Sabbath in full sway in ancient Babylon long before the days of Moses. In this tablet the seventh, the fourteenth, the twenty-first and the twenty-eighth days are called Sabbaths, the very word used by Moses, and following it are the words : ' A day of rest. ' The restrictions are quite as rigid in this tablet as those in the law of Moses. This institution must have gone back to the Accadian period, before the days of Abraham. In one of the recent discoveries this day is called ' the day of rest for the heart,' but of the gods, on account of the propitiation offered on that day, their heart being put at rest. See Jastrow, in Am. Jour. Theol., April, 1898.

S. S. Times, Jan. 1892, art. by Dr. Jensen of the University of Strassburg on the Biblical and Babylonian Week : *Subattu* in Babylonia means day of propitiation, implying a religious purpose. A week of seven days is implied in the Babylonian Flood-Story, the rain continuing six days and ceasing on the seventh, and another period of seven days intervening between the cessation of the storm and the disembarking of Noah, the dove, swallow and raven being sent out again on the seventh day. Sabbaths are called days of rest for the heart, days of the completion of labor." Hutton, **Essays.** 2 : 229 — " Because there is in God's mind a spring of eternal rest as well as of **creative energy,** we are enjoined to respect the law of rest as well as the law of **labor." We** may question, indeed, whether this doctrine of God's rest does not of itself refute the theory of eternal, continuous, and necessary creation.

(*b*) Neither our Lord nor his apostles abrogated the Sabbath of the decalogue. The new dispensation does away with the Mosaic prescriptions as to the method of keeping the Sabbath, but at the same time declares its observance to be of divine origin and to be a necessity of human nature.

Not everything in the Mosaic law is abrogated in Christ. Worship and reverence, regard for life and purity and property, are binding still. Christ did not nail to his cross every commandment of the decalogue. Jesus does not defend himself from the charge of Sabbath-breaking by saying that the Sabbath is abrogated, but by asserting the true idea of the Sabbath as fulfilling a fundamental human need. Mark 2:27 — "The Sabbath was made [by God] for man, and not man for the Sabbath." The Puritan restrictions are not essential to the Sabbath, nor do they correspond even with the methods of later Old Testament observance. The Jewish Sabbath was more like the New England Thanksgiving than like the New England Fast-day. Nehemiah 8:12, 18 — "And all the people went their way to eat, and to drink, and to send portions, and to make great mirth. . . . And they kept the feast seven days; and on the eighth day was a solemn assembly, according unto the ordinance "—seems to include the Sabbath day as a day of gladness.

Origen, in Homily 23 on Numbers (Migne, II : 358): "Leaving therefore the Jewish observances of the Sabbath, let us see what ought to be for a Christian the observance of the Sabbath. On the Sabbath day nothing of all the actions of the world ought to be done." Christ walks through the cornfield, heals a paralytic, and dines with a Pharisee, all on the Sabbath day. John Milton, in his Christian Doctrine, is an extreme anti-sabbatarian, maintaining that the decalogue was abolished with the Mosaic law. He thinks it uncertain whether "the Lord's day" was weekly or annual. The observance of the Sabbath, to his mind, is a matter not of authority, but of convenience. Archbishop Paley : "In my opinion St. Paul considered the Sabbath a sort of Jewish ritual, and not obligatory on Christians. A cessation on that day from labor beyond the time of attending public worship is not intimated in any part of the New Testament. The notion that Jesus and his apostles meant to retain the Jewish Sabbath, only shifting the day from the seventh to the first, prevails without sufficient reason."

According to Guizot, Calvin was so pleased with a play to be acted in Geneva on Sunday, that he not only attended but deferred his sermon so that his congregation might attend. When John Knox visited Calvin, he found him playing a game of bowls on Sunday. Martin Luther said : "Keep the day holy for its use's sake, both to body and soul. But if anywhere the day is made holy for the mere day's sake, if any one set up its observance on a Jewish foundation, then I order you to work on it, to ride on it, to dance on it, to do anything that shall reprove this encroachment on the Christian spirit and liberty." But the most liberal and even radical writers of our time recognize the economic and patriotic uses of the Sabbath. R. W. Emerson said that its observance is "the core of our civilization." Charles Sumner : "If we would perpetuate our Republic, we must sanctify it as well as fortify it, and make it at once a temple and a citadel." Oliver Wendell Holmes : "He who ordained the Sabbath loved the poor." In Pennsylvania they bring up from the mines every Sunday the mules that have been working the whole week in darkness,—otherwise they would become blind. So men's spiritual sight will fail them if they do not weekly come up into God's light.

(*c*) The Sabbath law binds us to set apart a seventh portion of our time for rest and worship. It does not enjoin the simultaneous observance by all the world of a fixed portion of absolute time, nor is such observance possible. Christ's example and apostolic sanction have transferred the Sabbath from the seventh day to the first, for the reason that this last is the day of Christ's resurrection, and so the day when God's spiritual creation became in Christ complete.

No exact portion of absolute time can be simultaneously observed by men in different longitudes. The day in Berlin begins six hours before the day in New York, so that a whole quarter of what is Sunday in Berlin is still Saturday in New York. Crossing the 180th degree of longitude from West to East we gain a day, and a seventh-day

Sabbatarian who circumnavigated the globe might thus return to his starting point observing the same Sabbath with his fellow Christians. A. S. Carman, in the Examiner Jan. 4, 1894, asserts that Heb. 4:5-9 alludes to the change of day from the seventh to the first, in the references to "a Sabbath rest" that "remaineth," and to "another day" taking the place of the original promised day of rest. Teaching of the Twelve Apostles: "On the Lord's Day assemble ye together, and give thanks, and break bread."

The change from the seventh day to the first seems to have been due to the resurrection of Christ upon "the first day of the week" (Mat. 28:1), to his meeting with the disciples upon that day and upon the succeeding Sunday (John 20:26), and to the pouring out of the Spirit upon the Pentecostal Sunday seven weeks after (Acts 2:1—see Bap. Quar. Rev., 185:229-232). Thus by Christ's own example and by apostolic sanction the first day became "the Lord's day" (Rev. 1:10), on which believers met regularly each week with their Lord (Acts 20:7—"the first day of the week, when we were gathered together to break bread") and brought together their benevolent contributions (1 Cor. 16:1, 2—"Now concerning the collection for the saints . . . Upon the first day of the week let each one of you lay by him in store, as he may prosper, that no collections be made when I come"). Eusebius, Com. on Ps. 92 (Migne, V:1191, C): "Wherefore those things [the Levitical regulations] having been already rejected, the Logos through the new Covenant transferred and changed the festival of the Sabbath to the rising of the sun . . . the Lord's day . . . holy and spiritual Sabbaths."

Justin Martyr, First Apology: "On the day called Sunday all who live in city or country gather together in one place, and the memoirs of the apostles or the writings of the prophets are read. . . . Sunday is the day on which we all hold our common assembly, because it is the first day on which God made the world and Jesus our Savior on the same day rose from the dead. For he was crucified on the day before, that of Saturn (Saturday); and on the day after that of Saturn, which is the day of the Sun (Sunday), having appeared to his apostles and disciples he taught them these things which we have submitted to you for your consideration." This seems to intimate that Jesus between his resurrection and ascension gave command respecting the observance of the first day of the week. He was "received up" only after "he had given commandment through the Holy Spirit unto the apostles whom he had chosen" (Acts 1:2).

The Christian Sabbath, then, is the day of Christ's resurrection. The Jewish Sabbath commemorated only the beginning of the world; the Christian Sabbath commemorates also the new creation of the world in Christ, in which God's work in humanity first becomes complete. C. H. M. on Gen. 2: "If I celebrate the seventh day it marks me as an earthly man, inasmuch as that day is clearly the rest of earth — creation-rest; if I intelligently celebrate the first day of the week, I am marked as a heavenly man, believing in the new creation in Christ." (Gal. 4:10, 11—"Ye observe days, and months, and seasons, and years. I am afraid of you, least by any means I have bestowed labor upon you in vain"; Col. 2:16, 17—"Let no man therefore judge you in meat, or in drink, or in respect of a feast day or a new moon or a sabbath day : which are a shadow of the things to come; but the body is Christ's.') See George S. Gray, Eight Studies on the Lord's Day; Hessey, Bampton Lectures on the Sunday; Gilfillan, The Sabbath; Wood, Sabbath Essays; Bacon, Sabbath Observance; Hadley, Essays Philological and Critical, 325-345; Hodge, Syst. Theol., 3:321-348: Lotz, Quæstiones de Historia Sabbati; Maurice, Sermons on the Sabbath; Prize Essays on the Sabbath; Crafts, The Sabbath for Man; A. E. Waffle, The Lord's Day; Alvah Hovey, Studies in Ethics and Religion, 271-320; Guirey, The Hallowed Day; Gamble, Sunday and the Sabbath; Driver, art.: Sabbath, in Hastings' Bible Dictionary; Broadus, Am. Com. on Mat. 12:3. For the seventh-day view, see T. B. Brown, The Sabbath; J. N. Andrews, History of the Sabbath. *Per contra*, see Prof. A. Rauschenbusch, Saturday or Sunday?

SECTION II.— PRESERVATION.

1. DEFINITION OF PRESERVATION.

Preservation is that continuous agency of God by which he maintains in existence the things he has created, together with the properties and powers with which he has endowed them. As the doctrine of creation is our attempt to explain the existence of the universe, so the doctrine of Preservation is our attempt to explain its continuance.

In explanation we remark :

(*a*) Preservation is not creation, for preservation presupposes creation. That which is preserved must already exist, and must have come into existence by the creative act of God.

(*b*) Preservation is not a mere negation of action, or a refraining to destroy, on the part of God. It is a positive agency by which, at every moment, he sustains the persons and the forces of the universe.

(*c*) Preservation implies a natural concurrence of God in all operations of matter and of mind. Though personal beings exist and God's will is not the sole force, it is still true that, without his concurrence, no person or force can continue to exist or to act.

Dorner, System of Doctrine, 2: 40-42 — " Creation and preservation cannot be the same thing, for then man would be only the product of natural forces supervised by God, — whereas, man is above nature and is inexplicable from nature. Nature is not the whole of the universe, but only the preliminary basis of it. . . . The *rest* of God is not cessation of activity, but is a new exercise of power." Nor is God " the soul of the universe." This phrase is pantheistic, and implies that God is the only agent.

It is a wonder that physical life continues. The pumping of blood through the heart, whether we sleep or wake, requires an expenditure of energy far beyond our ordinary estimates. The muscle of the heart never rests except between the beats. All the blood in the body passes through the heart in each half-minute. The grip of the heart is greater than that of the fist. The two ventricles of the heart hold on the average ten ounces or five-eighths of a pound, and this amount is pumped out at each beat. At 72 per minute, this is 45 pounds per minute, 2,700 pounds per hour, and 64,800 pounds or 32 and four tenths tons per day. Encyclopædia Britannica, 11 : 554 — " The heart does about one-fifth of the whole mechanical work of the body — a work equivalent to raising its own weight over 13,000 feet an hour. It takes its rest only in short snatches, as it were, its action as a whole being continuous. It must necessarily be the earliest sufferer from any improvidence as regards nutrition, mental emotion being in this respect quite as potential a cause of constitutional bankruptcy as the most violent muscular exertion."

Before the days of the guillotine in France, when the criminal to be executed sat in a chair and was decapitated by one blow of the sharp sword, an observer declared that the blood spouted up several feet into the air. Yet this great force is exerted by the heart so noiselessly that we are for the most part unconscious of it. The power at work is the power of God, and we call that exercise of power by the name of preservation. Crane, Religion of To-morrow, 130 — " We do not get bread because God instituted certain laws of growing wheat or of baking dough, he leaving these laws to run of themselves. But God, personally present in the wheat, makes it grow, and in the dough turns it into bread. He does not make gravitation or cohesion, but these are phases of his present action. Spirit is the reality, matter and law are the modes of its expression. So in redemption it is not by the working of some perfect plan that God saves. He is the immanent God, and all of his benefits are but phases of his person and immediate influence."

II. PROOF OF THE DOCTRINE OF PRESERVATION.

1. *From Scripture.*

In a number of Scripture passages, preservation is expressly distinguished from creation. Though God rested from his work of creation and established an order of natural forces, a special and continuous divine activity is declared to be put forth in the upholding of the universe and its powers. This divine activity, moreover, is declared to be the activity of Christ ; as he is the mediating agent in creation, so he is the mediating agent in preservation.

Nehemiah 9 : 6 — "Thou art Jehovah, even thou alone ; thou hast made heaven, the heaven of heavens, with all their host, the earth and all things that are thereon, the seas and all that is in them, and thou preservest them all" ; Job 7 : 20 — "O thou watcher [marg. 'preserver'] of men !" Ps. 36 : 6 — "thou preservest man and beast" ; 104 : 29, 30 — "Thou takest away their breath, they die, And return to their dust.   Thou sendest forth thy Spirit, they are created, And thou renewest the face of the ground." See Perowne on Ps. 104 — "A psalm to the God who is in and with nature for good. " Humboldt, Cosmos, 2 : 413 — "Psalm 104 presents an image of the whole Cosmos." Acts 17 : 28 — "in him we live, and move, and have our being" ; Col. 1 : 17 — "in him all things consist" ; Heb. 1 : 2, 3 — "upholding all things by the word of his power." John 5 : 17 — "My Father worketh even until now, and I work" — refers most naturally to preservation, since creation is a work completed ; compare Gen. 2 : ? — "on the seventh day God finished his work which he had made ; and he rested on the seventh day from all his work which he had made." God is the upholder of physical life ; see Ps. 66 : 8, 9 — "O bless our God . . . . who holdeth our soul in life." God is also the upholder of spiritual life ; see 1 Tim. 6 : 13 — "I charge thee in the sight of God who preserveth all things alive" (ζωογονοῦντος τὰ πάντα) — the great Preserver enables us to persist in our Christian course. Mat. 4 : 4 — "Man shall not live by bread alone, but by every word that proceedeth out of the mouth of God" — though originally referring to physical nourishment is equally true of spiritual sustentation. In Ps. 104 : 26 — "There go the ships," Dawson, Mod. Ideas of Evolution, thinks the reference is not to man's works but to God's, as the parallelism : "There is leviathan" would indicate, and that by "ships" are meant "floaters" like the nautilus, which is a "little ship." The 104th Psalm is a long hymn to the preserving power of God, who keeps alive all the creatures of the deep, both small and great.

2. *From Reason.*

We may argue the preserving agency of God from the following considerations :

(*a*) Matter and mind are not self-existent. Since they have not the cause of their being in themselves, their continuance as well as their origin must be due to a superior power.

Dorner, Glaubenslehre : "Were the world self-existent, it would be God, not world, and no religion would be possible. . . . The world has receptivity for new creations ; but these, once introduced, are subject, like the rest, to the law of preservation" — *i. e.*, are dependent for their continued existence upon God.

(*b*) Force implies a will of which it is the direct or indirect expression. We know of force only through the exercise of our own wills. Since will is the only cause of which we have direct knowledge, second causes in nature may be regarded as only secondary, regular, and automatic workings of the great first Cause.

For modern theories identifying force with divine will, see Herschel, Popular Lectures on Scientific Subjects, 460 ; Murphy, Scientific Bases, 13-15, 29-36, 42-52 ; Duke of Argyll, Reign of Law, 121-127 ; Wallace, Natural Selection, 363-371 ; Bowen, Metaphysics and Ethics, 146-162 ; Martineau, Essays, 1 : 63, 265, and Study, 1 : 244 — "Second causes in nature bear the same relation to the First Cause as the automatic movement of the muscles in walking bears to the first decision of the will that initiated the walk." It is often objected that we cannot thus identify force with will, because in many cases the effort of our will is fruitless for the reason that nervous and muscular force is lacking. But this proves only that force cannot be identified with human will, not that it cannot be identified with the divine will. To the divine will no force is lacking ; in God will and force are one.

We therefore adopt the view of Maine de Biran, that causation pertains only to spirit Porter, Human Intellect, 582-588, objects to this view as follows: "This implies, first, that the conception of a material cause is self-contradictory. But the mind recognizes in itself spiritual energies that are not voluntary ; because we derive our notion of cause from will. it does not follow that the causal relation always involves will; it would follow that the universe, so far as it is not intelligent, is impossible. It implies, secondly, that there is but one agent in the universe, and that the phenomena of matter and mind are but manifestations of one single force — the Creator's." We reply to this reasoning by asserting that no dead thing can act, and that what we call involuntary spiritual energies are really unconscious or unremembered activities of the will.

From our present point of view we would also criticize Hodge, Systematic Theology, 1 : 596 — "Because we get our idea of force from mind, it does not follow that mind is the only force. That mind is a cause is no proof that electricity may not be a cause. If matter is force and nothing but force, then matter is nothing, and the external world is simply God. In spite of such argument, men will believe that the external world is a reality — that matter is, and that it is the cause of the effects we attribute to its agency." New Englander, Sept. 1883 : 552 — "Man in early time used second causes, i. e., machines, very little to accomplish his purposes. His usual mode of action was by the direct use of his hands, or his voice, and he naturally ascribed to the gods the same method as his own. His own use of second causes has led man to higher conceptions of the divine action." Dorner: "If the world had no independence, it would not reflect God, nor would creation mean anything." But this independence is not absolute. Even man lives, moves and has his being in God (Acts 17 : 28), and whatever has come into being, whether material or spiritual, has life only in Christ (John 1 : 3, 4, marginal reading).

Preservation is God's continuous willing. Bowne, Introd. to Psych. Theory, 305, speaks of "a kind of wholesale willing." Augustine: "Dei voluntas est rerum natura." Principal Fairbairn: "Nature is spirit." Tennyson, The Ancient Sage: "Force is from the heights." Lord Gifford, quoted in Max Müller, Anthropological Religion, 392 — "The human soul is neither self-derived nor self-subsisting. It would vanish if it had not a substance, and its substance is God." Upton, Hibbert Lectures, 284, 285 — "Matter is simply spirit in its lowest form of manifestation. The absolute Cause must be that deeper Self which we find at the heart of our own self-consciousness. By self-differentiation God creates both matter and mind."

(c) God's sovereignty requires a belief in his special preserving agency ; since this sovereignty would not be absolute, if anything occurred or existed independent of his will.

James Martineau, Seat of Authority, 29, 30 — "All cosmic force is will. . . . This iden tification of nature with God's will *would* be pantheistic only *if* we turned the proposition round and identified God with *no more* than the life of the universe. But we do not deny transcendency. Natural forces are God's will, but God's will is more than they. He is not the equivalent of the All, but its directing Mind. God is not the rage of the wild beast, nor the sin of man. There are things and beings objective to him. . . . He puts his power into that which is *other than himself*, and he parts with *other use of it* by preëngagement to an end. Yet he is the continuous source and supply of power to the system."

Natural forces are generic volitions of God. But human wills, with their power of alternative, are the product of God's self-limitation, even more than nature is, for human wills do not always obey the divine will, — they may even oppose it. Nothing finite is only finite. In it is the Infinite, not only as immanent, but also as transcendent, and in the case of sin, as opposing the sinner and as punishing him. This continuous willing of God has its analogy in our own subconscious willing. J. M. Whiton, in Am. Jour. Theol., Apl. 1901 : 320 — "Our own will, when we walk, does not put forth a separate volition for every step, but depends on the automatic action of the lower nerve-centres, which it both sets in motion and keeps to their work. So the divine Will does not work in innumerable separate acts of volition." A. R. Wallace: "The whole universe is not merely dependent on, but actually *is*, the will of higher intelligences or of one supreme Intelligence. . . . Man's free will is only a larger artery for the controlling current of the universal Will, whose time-long evolutionary flow constitutes the self-revelation of the Infinite One." This latter statement of Wallace merges the finite will far too completely in the will of God. It is true of nature and of all holy beings, but it is untrue of the wicked. These are indeed upheld by God in their being, but opposed by God in their conduct. Preservation leaves room for human freedom, responsibility, sin, and guilt.

All natural forces and all personal beings therefore give testimony to the will of God which originated them and which continually sustains them. The physical universe, indeed, is in no sense independent of God, for its forces are only the constant willing of God, and its laws are only the habits of God. Only in the free will of intelligent beings has God disjoined from himself any portion of force and made it capable of contradicting his holy will. But even in free agents God does not cease to uphold. The being that sins can maintain its existence only through the preserving agency of God. The doctrine of preservation therefore holds a middle ground between two extremes. It holds that finite personal beings have a real existence and a relative independence. On the other hand it holds that these persons retain their being and their powers only as they are upheld by God.

God is the soul, but not the sum, of things. Christianity holds to God's transcendence as well as to God's immanence. Immanence alone is God imprisoned, as transcendence alone is God banished. Gore, Incarnation, 136 *sq.*—" Christian theology is the harmony of pantheism and deism." It maintains transcendence, and so has all the good of pantheism without its limitations. It maintains immanence, and so has all the good of deism without its inability to show how God could be blessed without creation. Diman, Theistic Argument, 367 — " The dynamical theory of nature as a plastic organism, pervaded by a system of forces uniting at last in one supreme Force, is altogether more in harmony with the spirit and teaching of the Gospel than the mechanical conceptions which prevailed a century ago, which insisted on viewing nature as an intricate machine, fashioned by a great Artificer who stood wholly apart from it." On the persistency of force, *super cuncta, subter cuncta*, see Bib. Sac., Jan. 1881 : 1-24 ; Cocker, Theistic Conception of the World, 172-243, esp. 236. The doctrine of preservation therefore holds to a God both in nature and beyond nature. According as the one or the other of these elements is exclusively regarded, we have the error of Deism, or the error of Continuous Creation — theories which we now proceed to consider.

III.   THEORIES WHICH VIRTUALLY DENY THE DOCTRINE OF PRESERVATION.

1. *Deism.*

This view represents the universe as a self-sustained mechanism, from which God withdrew as soon as he had created it, and which he left to a process of self-development. It was held in the seventeenth and eighteenth centuries by the English Herbert, Collins, Tindal, and Bolingbroke.

Lord Herbert of Cherbury was one of the first who formed deism into a system. His book *De Veritate* was published in 1624. He argues against the probability of God's revealing his will to only a portion of the earth. This he calls " particular religion." Yet he sought, and according to his own account he received, a revelation from heaven to encourage the publication of his work in disproof of revelation. He " asked for a sign," and was answered by a " loud though gentle noise from the heavens." He had the vanity to think his book of such importance to the cause of truth as to extort a declaration of the divine will, when the interests of half mankind could not secure any revelation at all ; what God would not do for a nation, he would do for an individual. See Leslie and Leland, Method with the Deists. Deism is the exaggeration of the truth of God's transcendence. See Christlieb, Modern Doubt and Christian Belief, 190-209. Melanchthon illustrates by the shipbuilder : " Ut faber discedit a navi exstructa et relinquit eam nautis." God is the maker, not the keeper, of the watch. In Sartor Resartus, Carlyle makes Teufelsdröckh speak of "An absentee God, sitting idle ever since the first Sabbath at the outside of the universe, and seeing it go." Blunt, Dict. Doct. and Hist. Theology, art. : Deism.

" Deism emphasized the inviolability of natural law, and held to a mechanical view of the world " (Ten Broeke). Its God is a sort of Hindu Brahma, " as idle as a painted ship upon a painted ocean "— mere being, without content or movement. Bruce, Apologetics, 115-131 —" God made the world so good at the first that the best he can do is to let it alone. Prayer is inadmissible. Deism implies a Pelagian view of human nature. Death redeems us by separating us from the body. There is natural immortality, but no resurrection. Lord Herbert of Cherbury, the brother of the poet George Herbert of Bemerton, represents the rise of Deism ; Lord Bolingbroke its decline. Blount assailed the divine Person of the founder of the faith ; Collins its foundation in prophecy ; Woolston its miraculous attestation ; Toland its canonical literature. Tindal took more general ground, and sought to show that a special revelation was unnecessary, impossible, unverifiable, the religion of nature being sufficient and superior to all religions of positive institution."

We object to this view that :

(*a*) It rests upon a false analogy. — Man is able to construct a self-moving watch only because he employs preëxisting forces, such as gravity, elasticity, cohesion. But in a theory which likens the universe to a machine, these forces are the very things to be accounted for.

Deism regards the universe as a " perpetual motion." Modern views of the dissipation of energy have served to discredit it. Will is the only explanation of the forces in nature. But according to deism, God builds a house, shuts himself out, locks the door, and then ties his own hands in order to make sure of never using the key. John Caird, Fund. Ideas of Christianity, 114–138 — " A made mind, a spiritual nature created by an external omnipotence, is an impossible and self-contradictory notion. . . . The human contriver or artist deals with materials prepared to his hand. Deism reduces God to a finite anthropomorphic personality, as pantheism annuls the finite world or absorbs it in the Infinite." Hence Spinoza, the pantheist, was the great antagonist of 16th century deism. See Woods, Works, 2 : 40.

(*b*) It is a system of anthropomorphism, while it professes to exclude anthropomorphism.— Because the upholding of all things would involve a multiplicity of minute cares if man were the agent, it conceives of the upholding of the universe as involving such burdens in the case of God. Thus it saves the dignity of God by virtually denying his omnipresence, omniscience, and omnipotence.

The infinity of God turns into sources of delight all that would seem care to man. To God's inexhaustible fulness of life there are no burdens involved in the upholding of the universe he has created. Since God, moreover, is a perpetual observer, we may alter the poet's verse and say : " There 's not a flower that 's born to blush unseen And waste its sweetness on the desert air." God does not expose his children as soon as they are born. They are not only his offspring ; they also live, move and have their being in him, and are partakers of his divine nature. Gordon, Christ of To-day, 200 — "The worst person in all history is something to God, if he be nothing to the world." See Chalmers, Astronomical Discourses, in Works, 7 : 68. Kurtz, The Bible and Astronomy, in Introd. to History of Old Covenant, lxxxii — xcviii.

(*c*) It cannot be maintained without denying all providential interference, in the history of creation and the subsequent history of the world.— But the introduction of life, the creation of man, incarnation, regeneration, the communion of intelligent creatures with a present God, and interpositions of God in secular history, are matters of fact.

Deism therefore continually tends to atheism. Upton, Hibbert Lectures, 287 — "The defect of deism is that, on the human side, it treats all men as isolated individuals, forgetful of the immanent divine nature which interrelates them and in a measure unifies them ; and that, on the divine side, it separates men from God and makes the relation between them a purely external one." Ruskin : " The divine mind is as visible in its full energy of operation on every lowly bank and mouldering stone as in the lifting of the pillars of heaven and settling the foundations of the earth ; and to the rightly perceiving mind there is the same majesty, the same power, the same unity, and the same perfection manifested in the casting of the clay as in the scattering of the cloud, in the mouldering of dust as in the kindling of the day-star." See Pearson, Infidelity, 87 ; Hanne, Idee der absoluten Persönlichkeit, 76.

2. *Continuous Creation.*

This view regards the universe as from moment to moment the result of a new creation. It was held by the New England theologians Edwards, Hopkins, and Emmons, and more recently in Germany by Rothe

Edwards, Works, 2 : 486–490, quotes and defends Dr. Taylor's utterance : "God is the original of all being, and the only cause of all natural effects." Edwards himself says : "God's upholding created substance, or causing its existence in each successive moment, is altogether equivalent to an immediate production out of nothing at each moment." He argues that the past existence of a thing cannot be the cause of its present existence, because a thing cannot act at a time and place where it is not. "This is equivalent to saying that God cannot produce an effect which shall last for one moment beyond the direct exercise of his creative power. What man can do, God, it seems, cannot" (A. S. Carman). Hopkins, Works, 1 : 164–167 — Preservation "is really continued creation." Emmons, Works, 4 : 363–389, esp. 381 — "Since all men are dependent agents, all their motions, exercises, or actions must originate in a divine efficiency." 2 : 683 — "There is but one true and satisfactory answer to the question which has been agitated for centuries : 'Whence came evil?' and that is : It came from the first great Cause of all things. . . . It is as consistent with the moral rectitude of the Deity to produce sinful as holy exercises in the minds of men. He puts forth a positive influence to make moral agents act, in every instance of their conduct, as he pleases." God therefore creates all the volitions of the soul, as he effects by his almighty power all the changes of the material world. Rothe also held this view. To his mind external expression is necessary to God. His maxim was : "Kein Gott ohne Welt"—"There can be no God without an accompanying world." See Rothe, Dogmatik, 1 : 126–160, esp. 150, and Theol. Ethik, 1 : 186–190 ; also in Bib. Sac., Jan. 1875 : 144. See also Lotze, Philos. of Religion, 81–94.

The element of truth in Continuous Creation is its assumption that all force is will. Its error is in maintaining that all force is *divine* will, and divine will in *direct* exercise. But the human will is a force as well as the divine will, and the forces of nature are secondary and automatic, not primary and immediate, workings of God. These remarks may enable us to estimate the grain of truth in the following utterances which need important qualification and limitation. Bowne, Philosophy of Theism, 202, likens the universe to the musical note, which exists only on condition of being incessantly reproduced. Herbert Spencer says that "ideas are like the successive chords and cadences brought out from a piano, which successively die away as others are produced." Maudsley, Physiology of Mind, quotes this passage, but asks quite pertinently : "What about the performer, in the case of the piano and in the case of the brain, respectively? Where in the brain is the equivalent of the harmonic conceptions in the performer's mind?" Professor Fitzgerald : "All nature is living thought — the language of One in whom we live and move and have our being." Dr. Oliver Lodge, to the British Association in 1891 : "The barrier between matter and mind may melt away, as so many others have done."

To this we object, upon the following grounds :

(*a*) It contradicts the testimony of consciousness that regular and executive activity is not the mere repetition of an initial decision, but is an exercise of the will entirely different in kind.

Ladd, in his Philosophy of Mind, 144, indicates the error in Continuous Creation as follows : "The whole world of things is momently quenched and then replaced by a similar world of actually new realities." The words of the poet would then be literally true : "Every fresh and new creation, A divine improvisation, From the heart of God proceeds." Ovid, Metaph., 1 : 16 — "Instabilis tellus, innabilis unda." Seth, Hegelianism and Personality, 60, says that, to Fichte, "the world was thus perpetually created anew in each finite spirit, — revelation to intelligence being the only admissible meaning of that much abused term, creation." A. L. Moore, Science and the Faith, 184, 185 — "A theory of occasional intervention implies, as its correlate, a theory of ordinary absence. . . . For Christians the facts of nature are the acts of God. Religion relates these facts to God as their author ; science relates them to one another as parts of a visible order. Religion does not tell of this interrelation ; science cannot tell of their relation to God."

Continuous creation is an erroneous theory because it applies to human wills a principle which is true only of irrational nature and which is only partially true of that. I know that I am not God acting. My will is proof that not all force is divine will. Even on the monistic view, moreover, we may speak of second causes in nature, since God's regular and habitual action is a second and subsequent thing, while his act of initiation and organization is the first. Neither the universe nor any part of it is to be identified with God, any more than my thoughts and acts are to be identified with me. Martineau, in Nineteenth Century, April, 1895 : 559 — "What is *nature*, but the promise of God : pledged and habitual causality ? And what is *spirit*, but the province of his free causality responding to needs and affections of his free children ? . . . God is not a retired architect who may now and then be called in for repairs. Nature is not self-active, and God's agency is not intrusive." William Watson, Poems, 88 — "If nature be a phantasm, as thou say'st, A splendid fiction and prodigious dream, To reach the real and true I'll make no haste, More than content with worlds that only seem."

(*b*) It exaggerates God's power only by sacrificing his truth, love, and holiness ; — for if finite personalities are not what they seem — namely, objective existences — God's veracity is impugned ; if the human soul has no real freedom and life, God's love has made no self-communication to creatures ; if God's will is the only force in the universe, God's holiness can no longer be asserted, for the divine will must in that case be regarded as the author of human sin.

Upon this view personal identity is inexplicable. Edwards bases identity upon the arbitrary decree of God. God can therefore, by so decreeing, make Adam's posterity one with their first father and responsible for his sin. Edwards's theory of continuous creation, indeed, was devised as an explanation of the problem of original sin. The divinely appointed union of acts and exercises with Adam was held sufficient, without union of substance, or natural generation from him, to explain our being born corrupt and guilty. This view would have been impossible, if Edwards had not been an idealist, making far too much of acts and exercises and far too little of substance.

It is difficult to explain the origin of Jonathan Edwards's idealism. It has sometimes been attributed to the reading of Berkeley. Dr. Samuel Johnson, afterwards President of King's College in New York City, a personal friend of Bishop Berkeley and an ardent follower of his teaching, was a tutor in Yale College while Edwards was a student. But Edwards was in Weathersfield while Johnson remained in New Haven, and was among those disaffected towards Johnson as a tutor. Yet Edwards, Original Sin, 479, seems to allude to the Berkeleyan philosophy when he says: "The course of nature is demonstrated by recent improvements in philosophy to be indeed . . . . nothing but the established order and operation of the Author of nature " (see Allen, Jonathan Edwards, 16, 308, 309). President McCracken, in Philos. Rev., Jan. 1892 : 26-42, holds that Arthur Collier's Clavis Universalis is the source of Edwards's idealism. It is more probable that his idealism was the result of his own independent thinking, occasioned perhaps by mere hints from Locke, Newton, Cudworth, and Norris, with whose writings he certainly was acquainted. See E. C. Smyth, in Am. Jour. Theol., Oct. 1897 : 956 ; Prof. Gardiner, in Philos. Rev., Nov. 1900 : 573-596.

How thorough-going this idealism of Edwards may be learned from Noah Porter's Discourse on Bishop George Berkeley, 71, and quotations from Edwards, in Journ. Spec. Philos., Oct. 1883 : 401-420 — "Nothing else has a proper being but spirits, and bodies are but the shadow of being. . . . Seeing the brain exists only mentally, I therefore acknowledge that I speak improperly when I say that the soul is in the brain only, as to its operations. For, to speak yet more strictly and abstractedly, 't is nothing but the connection of the soul with these and those modes of its own ideas, or those mental acts of the Deity, seeing the brain exists only in idea. . . . That which truly is the substance of all bodies is the infinitely exact and precise and perfectly stable idea in God's mind, together with his stable will that the same shall be gradually communicated to us and to other minds according to certain fixed and established methods and laws ; or, in somewhat different language, the infinitely exact and precise divine idea, together with an answerable, perfectly exact, precise, and stable will, with respect to correspondent communications to created minds and effects on those minds." It is easy to see how, from this view of Edwards, the "Exercise-system " of Hopkins and Emmons naturally developed itself. On Edwards's Idealism, see Frazer's Berkeley (Blackwood's Philos. Classics), 139, 140. On personal identity, see Bp. Butler, Works (Bohn's ed.), 327-334.

(*c*) As deism tends to atheism, so the doctrine of continuous creation tends to pantheism. — Arguing that, because we get our notion of force from the action of our own wills, therefore all force must be will, and divine will, it is compelled to merge the human will in this all-comprehending will of God. Mind and matter alike become phenomena of one force, which has the attributes of both ; and, with the distinct existence and personality of the human soul, we lose the distinct existence and personality of God, as well as the freedom and accountability of man.

Lotze tries to escape from *material* causes and yet hold to *second* causes, by intimating that these second causes may be spirits. But though we can see how there can be a sort of spirit in the brute and in the vegetable, it is hard to see how what we call insensate matter can have spirit in it. It must be a very peculiar sort of spirit—a deaf and dumb spirit, if any—and such a one does not help our thinking. On this theory the body of a dog would need to be much more highly endowed than its soul. James Seth, in Philos. Rev., Jan. 1894:73—" This principle of unity is a veritable lion's den,—all the footprints are in one direction. Either it is a bare unity—the One annuls the many ; or it is simply the All,—the ununified totality of existence." Dorner well remarks that " Preservation is empowering of the creature and maintenance of its activity, not new bringing it into being." On the whole subject, see Julius Müller, Doctrine of Sin, 1 : 220–225 ; Philippi, Glaubenslehre, 2 : 258–272 ; Baird, Elohim Revealed, 50 ; Hodge, Syst. Theol., 1 : 577–581, 595 ; Dabney, Theology, 338, 339.

IV. REMARKS UPON THE DIVINE CONCURRENCE.

(*a*) The divine efficiency interpenetrates that of man without destroying or absorbing it. The influx of God's sustaining energy is such that men retain their natural faculties and powers. God does not work all, but all in all.

Preservation, then, is midway between the two errors of denying the first cause (deism or atheism) and denying the second causes (continuous creation or pantheism). 1 Cor. 12 : 6—" there are diversities of workings, but the same God, who worketh all things in all" ; *cf.* Eph. 1 : 23— the church, " which is his body, the fulness of him that filleth all in all." God's action is no *actio in distans*, or action where he is not. It is rather action in and through free agents, in the case of intelligent and moral beings, while it is his own continuous willing in the case of nature. Men are second causes in a sense in which nature is not. God works through these human second causes, but he does not supersede them. We cannot see the line between the two—the action of the first cause and the action of second causes ; yet both are real, and each is distinct from the other, though the method of God's concurrence is inscrutable. As the pen and the hand together produce the writing, so God's working causes natural powers to work with him. The natural growth indicated by the words " wherein is the seed thereof" (Gen. 1 : 11) has its counterpart in the spiritual growth described in the words " his seed abideth in him" (1 John 3 : 9). Paul considers himself a reproductive agency in the hands of God : he begets children in the gospel (1 Cor. 4 : 15) ; yet the New Testament speaks of this begetting as the work of God (1 Pet. 1 : 3). We are bidden to work out our own salvation with fear and trembling, upon the very ground that it is God who works in us both to will and to work (Phil. 2 : 12, 13).

(*b*) Though God preserves mind and body in their working, we are ever to remember that God concurs with the evil acts of his creatures only as they are natural acts, and not as they are evil.

In holy action God gives the natural powers, and by his word and Spirit influences the soul to use these powers aright. But in evil action God gives only the natural powers ; the evil direction of these powers is caused only by man. Jer. 44 : 4—"Oh, do not this abominable thing that I hate" ; Hab. 1 : 13—"Thou that art of purer eyes than to behold evil, and that canst not look on perverseness, wherefore lookest thou upon them that deal treacherously, and holdest thy peace when the wicked swalloweth up the man that is more righteous than he ?" James 1 : 13, 14—"Let no man say when he is tempted, I am tempted of God ; for God cannot be tempted with evil, and he himself tempteth no man : but each man is tempted, when he is drawn away by his own lust, and enticed." Aaron excused himself for making an Egyptian idol by saying that the fire did it ; he asked the people for gold ; "so they gave it me ; and I cast it into the fire, and there came out this calf" (Ex. 32 : 24). Aaron leaves out one important point

— his own personal agency in it all. In like manner we lay the blame of our sins upon nature and upon God. Pym said of Strafford that God had given him great talents, of which the devil had given the application. But it is more true to say of the wicked man that he himself gives the application of his God-given powers. We are electric cars for which God furnishes the motive-power, but to which we the conductors give the direction. We are organs; the wind or breath of the organ is God's; but the fingering of the keys is ours. Since the maker of the organ is also present at every moment as its preserver, the shameful abuse of his instrument and the dreadful music that is played are a continual grief and suffering to his soul. Since it is Christ who upholds all things by the word of his power, preservation involves the suffering of Christ, and this suffering is his atonement, of which the culmination and demonstration are seen in the cross of Calvary (Heb. 1:3). On the importance of the idea of preservation in Christian doctrine, see Calvin, Institutes, 1:182 (chapter 16).

SECTION III.—PROVIDENCE.

I. DEFINITION OF PROVIDENCE.

Providence is that continuous agency of God by which he makes all the events of the physical and moral universe fulfill the original design with which he created it.

As Creation explains the existence of the universe, and as Preservation explains its continuance, so Providence explains its evolution and progress.

In explanation notice :

(*a*) Providence is not to be taken merely in its etymological sense of *fore*seeing. It is *for*seeing also, or a positive agency in connection with all the events of history.

(*b*) Providence is to be distinguished from preservation. While preservation is a maintenance of the existence and powers of created things, providence is an actual care and control of them.

(*c*) Since the original plan of God is all-comprehending, the providence which executes the plan is all-comprehending also, embracing within its scope things small and great, and exercising care over individuals as well as over classes.

(*d*) In respect to the good acts of men, providence embraces all those natural influences of birth and surroundings which prepare men for the operation of God's word and Spirit, and which constitute motives to obedience.

(*e*) In respect to the evil acts of men, providence is never the efficient cause of sin, but is by turns preventive, permissive, directive, and determinative.

(*f*) Since Christ is the only revealer of God, and he is the medium of every divine activity, providence is to be regarded as the work of Christ; see 1 Cor. 8:6 — "one Lord, Jesus Christ, through whom are all things"; *cf.* John 5:17 — "My Father worketh even until now, and I work."

The Germans have the word *Fürsehung*, foreseeing, looking out for, as well as the word *Vorsehung*, foreseeing, seeing beforehand. Our word 'providence' embraces the meanings of both these words. On the general subject of providence, see Philippi,

Glaubenslehre, 2:272-284; Calvin, Institutes, 1:182-219; Dick, Theology, 1:416-446; Hodge, Syst. Theol., 1:581-616; Bib. Sac., 12:179; 21:584; 26:315; 30:593; N. W. Taylor, Moral Government, 2:294-326.

Providence is God's attention concentrated everywhere. His care is microscopic as well as telescopic. Robert Browning, Pippa Passes, *ad finem:* "All service is the same with God — With God, whose puppets, best and worst, Are we: there is no last nor first." Canon Farrar: "In one chapter of the Koran is the story how Gabriel, as he waited by the gates of gold, was sent by God to earth to do two things. One was to prevent king Solomon from the sin of forgetting the hour of prayer in exultation over his royal steeds; the other to help a little yellow ant on the slope of Ararat, which had grown weary in getting food for its nest, and which would otherwise perish in the rain. To Gabriel the one behest seemed just as kingly as the other, since God had ordered it. 'Silently he left The Presence, and prevented the king's sin, And help the little ant at entering in.' 'Nothing is too high or low, Too mean or mighty, if God wills it so.'" Yet a preacher began his sermon on Mat. 10:30 — "The very hairs of your head are all numbered" — by saying: "Why, some of you, my hearers, do not believe that even your heads are all numbered!"

A modern prophet of unbelief in God's providence is William Watson. In his poem entitled The Unknown God, we read: "When overarched by gorgeous night, I wave my trivial self away; When all I was to all men's sight Shares the erasure of the day; Then do I cast my cumbering load, Then do I gain a sense of God." Then he likens the God of the Old Testament to Odin and Zeus, and continues: "O streaming worlds, O crowded sky, O life, and mine own soul's abyss, Myself am scarce so small that I Should bow to Deity like this! This my Begetter? This was what Man in his violent youth begot. The God I know of I shall ne'er Know, though he dwells exceeding nigh. Raise thou the stone and find me there, Cleave thou the wood and there am I. Yea, in my flesh his Spirit doth flow, Too near, too far, for me to know. Whate'er my deeds, I am not sure That I can pleasure him or vex: I, that must use a speech so poor It narrows the Supreme with sex. Notes he the good or ill in man? To hope he cares is all I can. I hope with fear. For did I trust This vision granted me at birth, The sire of heaven would seem less just Than many a faulty son of earth. And so he seems indeed! But then, I trust it not, this bounded ken. And dreaming much, I never dare To dream that in my prisoned soul The flutter of a trembling prayer Can move the Mind that is the Whole. Though kneeling nations watch and yearn, Does the primeval Purpose turn? Best by remembering God, say some, We keep our high imperial lot. Fortune, I fear, hath oftenest come When we forgot — when we forgot! A lovelier faith their happier crown, But history laughs and weeps it down: Know they not well how seven times seven, Wronging our mighty arms with rust, We dared not do the work of heaven, Lest heaven should hurl us in the dust? The work of heaven! 'T is waiting still The sanction of the heavenly will. Unmeet to be profaned by praise Is he whose coils the world enfold; The God on whom I ever gaze, The God I never once behold: Above the cloud, above the clod, The unknown God, the unknown God."

In pleasing contrast to William Watson's Unknown God, is the God of Rudyard Kipling's Recessional: "God of our fathers, known of old — Lord of our far-flung battle-line — Beneath whose awful hand we hold Dominion over palm and pine — Lord God of hosts, be with us yet, Lest we forget — lest we forget! The tumult and the shouting dies — The captains and the kings depart — Still stands thine ancient Sacrifice, An humble and a contrite heart. Lord God of hosts, be with us yet, Lest we forget — lest we forget! Far-called our navies melt away — On dune and headland sinks the fire — So, all our pomp of yesterday Is one with Nineveh and Tyre! Judge of the nations, spare us yet, Lest we forget — lest we forget! If, drunk with sight of power, we loose Wild tongues that have not thee in awe — Such boasting as the Gentiles use, Or lesser breeds without the Law — Lord God of hosts, be with us yet, Lest we forget — lest we forget! For heathen heart that puts her trust In reeking tube and iron shard — All valiant dust that builds on dust, And guarding calls not thee to guard — For frantic boast and foolish word, Thy mercy on thy people, Lord!"

These problems of God's providential dealings are intelligible only when we consider that Christ is the revealer of God, and that his suffering for sin opens to us the heart of God. All history is the progressive manifestation of Christ's holiness and love, and in the cross we have the key that unlocks the secret of the universe. With the cross in view, we can believe that Love rules over all, and that "all things work together for good to them that love God" (Rom. 8:?

II. Proof of the Doctrine of Providence.

1. *Scriptural Proof.*

The Scripture witnesses to

A. A general providential government and control (*a*) over the universe at large ; (*b*) over the physical world ; (*c*) over the brute creation ; (*d*) over the affairs of nations ; (*e*) over man's birth and lot in life ; (*f*) over the outward successes and failures of men's lives ; (*g*) over things seemingly accidental or insignificant ; (*h*) in the protection of the righteous ; (*i*) in the supply of the wants of God's people ; (*j*) in the arrangement of answers to prayer ; (*k*) in the exposure and punishment of the wicked.

(*a*) Ps. 103 : 19 — " his kingdom ruleth over all " ; Dan. 4 : 35 — " doeth according to his will in the army of heaven, and among the inhabitants of the earth " ; Eph. 1 : 11 — " worketh all things after the counsel of his will."

(*b*) Job 37 : 5, 10 — " God thundereth . . . . By the brea h of God ice is given " ; Ps. 104 : 14 — " causeth the grass to grow for the cattle " ; 135 : 6, 7 — " Whatsoever Jehovah pleased, that hath he done, In heaven and in earth, in the seas and in all deeps . . . . vapors . . . . lightnings . . . . wind " ; Mat. 5 : 45 — " maketh his sun to rise . . . . sendeth rain " ; Ps. 104 : 16 — " The trees of Jehovah are filled " — are planted and tended by God as carefully as those which come under human cultivation ; *cf.* Mat. 6 : 30 — " if God so clothe the grass of the field."

(*c*) Ps. 104 : 21, 28 — " young lions roar . . . . seek their food from God . . . . that thou givest them they gather " Mat. 6 : 26 — " birds of the heaven . . . . your heavenly Father feedeth them " ; 10 : 29 — " two sparrows . . . . not one of them shall fall on the ground without your Father."

(*d*) Job 12 : 23 — " He increaseth the nations, and he destroyeth them : He enlargeth the nations, and he leadeth them captive " ; Ps. 22 : 28 — " the kingdom is Jehovah's ; And he is the ruler over the nations " ; 66 : 7 — " He ruleth by his might for ever ; His eyes observe the nations " ; Acts 17 : 26 — " made of one every nation of men to dwell on all the face of the earth, having determined their appointed seasons, and the bounds of their habitation " (instance Palestine, Greece, England).

(*e*) 1 Sam. 16 : 1 — " fill thy horn with oil, and go : I will send thee to Jesse the Bethlehemite ; for I have provided me a king among his sons " ; Ps. 139 : 16 — " Thine eyes did see mine unformed substance, And in thy book were all my members written " ; Is. 45 : 5 — " I will gird thee, though thou hast not known me " ; Jer. 1 : 5 — " Before I formed thee in the belly I knew thee . . . . sanctified thee . . . . appointed thee " ; Gal. 1 : 15, 16 — " God, who separated me, even from my mother's womb, and called me through his grace, to reveal his Son in me, that I might preach him among the Gentiles."

(*f*) Ps. 75 : 6, 7 — " neither from the east, nor from the west, Nor yet from the south cometh lifting up. But God is the judge , He putteth down one, and lifteth up another " ; Luke 1 : 52 — " He hath put down princes from their thrones, And hath exalted them of low degree. "

(*g*) Prov. 16 : 33 — " The lot is cast into the lap ; But the whole disposing thereof is of Jehovah " ; Mat. 10 : 30 — " the very hairs of your head are all numbered."

(*h*) Ps. 4 : 8 — " In peace will I both lay me down and sleep ; For thou, Jehovah, alone makest me dwell in safety " ; 5 : 12 — " thou wilt compass him with favor as with a shield " ; 63 : 8 — " Thy right hand upholdeth me " ; 121 : 3 — " He that keepeth thee will not slumber " ; Rom. 8 : 28 — " to them that love God all things work together for good."

(*i*) Gen. 22 : 8, 14 — " God will provide himself the lamb . . . . Jehovah-jireh " (marg.: that is, ' Jehovah will see, ' or ' provide ') ; Deut. 8 : 3 — " man doth not live by bread only, but by every thing that proceedeth out of the mouth of Jehovah doth man live " ; Phil. 4 : 19 — " my God shall supply every need of yours."

(*j*) Ps. 68 : 10 — " Thou, O God, didst prepare of thy goodness for the poor " ; Is. 64 : 4 — " neither hath the eye seen a God besides thee, who worketh for him that waiteth for him " ; Mat. 6 : 8 — " your Father knoweth what things ye have need of, before ye ask him " ; 32, 33 — " all these things shall be added unto you."

(*k*) Ps. 7 : 12, 13 — " If a man turn not, he will whet his sword ; He hath bent his bow and made it ready ; He hath also prepared for him the instruments of death ; He maketh his arrows fiery shafts " ; 11 : 6 — " Upon the wicked he will rain snares ; Fire and brimstone and burning wind shall be the portion of their cup."

The statements of Scripture with regard to God's providence are strikingly confirmed by recent studies in physiography. In the early stages of human development man was almost wholly subject to nature, and environment was a determining factor in his progress. This is the element of truth in Buckle's view. But Buckle ignored the fact that, as civilization advanced, ideas, at least at times, played a greater part than environment. Thermopylæ cannot be explained by climate. In the later stages of human development, nature is largely subject to man, and environment counts for comparatively little. " There shall be no Alps ! " says Napoleon. Charles Kingsley

"The spirit of ancient tragedy was man conquered by circumstance; the spirit of modern tragedy is man conquering circumstance." Yet many national characteristics can be attributed to physical surroundings, and so far as this is the case they are due to the ordering of God's providence. Man's need of fresh water leads him to rivers,— hence the original location of London. Commerce requires seaports, — hence New York. The need of defense leads man to bluffs and hills, — hence Jerusalem, Athens, Rome, Edinburgh. These places of defense became also places of worship and of appeal to God.

Goldwin Smith, in his Lectures and Essays, maintains that national characteristics are not congenital, but are the result of environment. The greatness of Rome and the greatness of England have been due to position. The Romans owed their successes to being at first less warlike than their neighbors. They were traders in the centre of the Italian seacoast, and had to depend on discipline to make headway against marauders on the surrounding hills. Only when drawn into foreign conquest did the ascendency of the military spirit become complete, and then the military spirit brought despotism as its natural penalty. Brought into contact with varied races, Rome was led to the founding of colonies. She adopted and assimilated the nations which she conquered, and in governing them learned organization and law. *Parcere subjectis* was her rule, as well as *debellare superbos*. In a similiar manner Goldwin Smith maintains that the greatness of England is due to position. Britain being an island, only a bold and enterprising race could settle it. Maritime migration strengthened freedom. Insular position gave freedom from invasion. Isolation however gave rise to arrogance and self-assertion. The island became a natural centre of commerce. There is a steadiness of political progress which would have been impossible upon the continent. Yet consolidation was tardy, owing to the fact that Great Britain consists of *several* islands. Scotland was always liberal, and Ireland foredoomed to subjection.

Isaac Taylor, Spirit of Hebrew Poetry, has a valuable chapter on Palestine as the providential theatre of divine revelation. A little land, yet a sample-land of all lands, and a thoroughfare between the greatest lands of antiquity, it was fitted by God to receive and to communicate his truth. George Adam Smith's Historical Geography of the Holy Land is a repertory of information on this subject. Stanley, Life and Letters, 1: 269–271, treats of Greek landscape and history. Shaler, Interpretation of Nature, sees such difference between Greek curiosity and search for causes on the one hand, and Roman indifference to scientific explanation of facts on the other, that he cannot think of the Greeks and the Romans as cognate peoples. He believes that Italy was first peopled by Etrurians, a Semitic race from Africa, and that from them the Romans descended. The Romans had as little of the spirit of the naturalist as had the Hebrews. The Jews and the Romans originated and propagated Christianity, but they had no interest in science.

On God's pre-arrangement of the physical conditions of national life, striking suggestions may be found in Shaler, Nature and Man in America. Instance the settlement of Massachusetts Bay between 1629 and 1639, the only decade in which such men as John Winthrop could be found and the only one in which they actually emigrated from England. After 1639 there was too much to do at home, and with Charles II the spirit which animated the Pilgrims no longer existed in England. The colonists builded better than they knew, for though they sought a place to worship God themselves, they had no idea of giving this same religious liberty to others. R. E. Thompson, The Hand of God in American History, holds that the American Republic would long since have broken in pieces by its own weight and bulk, if the invention of steamboat in 1807, railroad locomotive in 1829, telegraph in 1837, and telephone in 1877, had not bound the remote parts of the country together. A woman invented the reaper by combining the action of a row of scissors in cutting. This was as early as 1835. Only in 1855 the competition on the Emperor's farm at Compiègne gave supremacy to the reaper. Without it farming would have been impossible during our civil war, when our men were in the field and women and boys had to gather in the crops.

B. A government and control extending to the free actions of men — (*a*) to men's free acts in general ; (*b*) to the sinful acts of men also.

(*a*) Ex. 12 : 36 — "Jehovah gave the people favor in the sight of the Egyptians, so that they let them have what they asked. And they despoiled the Egyptians" ; 1 Sam. 24 : 18 — "Jehovah had delivered me up into thy hand (Saul to David) ; Ps. 33 : 14, 15 — "He looketh forth Upon all the inhabitants of the earth, He that fashioneth the hearts of them all " (*i. e.*, equally, one as well as another) ; Prov. 16 : 1 — "The plans of the heart belong to man ; But the answer of the tongue is from Jehovah " ; 19 : 21 — "There are many devices in a man's heart: But the counsel of Jehovah,

that shall stand"; 20: 24—"A man's goings are of Jehovah; How then can man understand his way?" 21: 1—"The king's heart is in the hand of Jehovah as the watercourses: He turneth it whithersoever he will" (*i. e.*, as easily as the rivulets of the eastern fields are turned by the slightest motion of the hand or the foot of the husbandman) ; Jer. 10: 23 — "O Jehovah, I know that the way of man is not in himself; it is not in man that walketh to direct his steps"; Phil. 2: 13 — "it is God who worketh in you both to will and to work, for his good pleasure"; Eph. 2: 10 — "we are his workmanship, created in Christ Jesus for good works, which God afore prepared that we should walk in them"; James 4: 13-15 — "If the Lord will, we shall both live, and do this or that."

(*b*) 2 Sam. 16: 10 — "because Jehovah hath said unto him [Shimei]: Curse David"; 24: 1 — "the anger of Jehovah was kindled against Israel, and he moved David against them, saying, Go, number Israel and Judah"; Rom. 11: 32 — "God hath shut up all unto disobedience, that he might have mercy upon all"; 2 Thess. 2: 11, 12 — "God sendeth them a working of error, that they should believe a lie: that they all might be judged who believed not the truth, but had pleasure in unrighteousness."

Henry Ward Beecher : "There seems to be no order in the movements of the bees of a hive, but the honey-comb shows that there was a plan in them all." John Hunter compared his own brain to a hive in which there was a great deal of buzzing and apparent disorder, while yet a real order underlay it all. "As bees gather their stores of sweets against a time of need, but are colonized by man's superior intelligence for his own purposes, so men plan and work yet are overruled by infinite Wisdom for his own glory." Dr. Deems: "The world is wide In Time and Tide, And God is guide: Then do not hurry. That man is blest Who does his best And leaves the rest: Then do not worry." See Bruce, Providential Order, 183 *sq.*; Providence in the Individual Life, 231 *sq.*

God's providence with respect to men's evil acts is described in Scripture as of four sorts :

(*a*) Preventive,— God by his providence prevents sin which would otherwise be committed. That he thus prevents sin is to be regarded as matter, not of obligation, but of grace.

Gen. 20: 6 — Of Abimelech: "I also withheld thee from sinning against me"; 31: 24 —"And God came to Laban the Syrian in a dream of the night, and said unto him, Take heed to thyself that thou speak not to Jacob either good or bad"; Psalm 19: 13 —"Keep back thy servant also from presumptuous sins; Let them not have dominion over me"; Hosea 2: 6 — "Behold, I will hedge up thy way with thorns, and I will build a wall against her, that she shall not find her paths" — here the "thorns" and the "wall" may represent the restraints and sufferings by which God mercifully checks the fatal pursuit of sin (see Annotated Par. Bible *in loco*). Parents, government, church, traditions, customs, laws, age, disease, death, are all of them preventive influences. Man sometimes finds himself on the brink of a precipice of sin, and strong temptation hurries him on to make the fatal leap. Suddenly every nerve relaxes, all desire for the evil thing is gone, and he recoils from the fearful brink over which he was just now going to plunge. God has interfered by the voice of conscience and the Spirit. This too is a part of his preventive providence. Men at sixty years of age are eight times less likely to commit crime than at the age of twenty-five. Passion has subsided ; fear of punishment has increased. The manager of a great department store, when asked what could prevent its absorbing all the trade of the city, replied : "Death!" Death certainly limits aggregations of property, and so constitutes a means of God's preventive providence. In the life of John G. Paton, the rain sent by God prevented the natives from murdering him and taking his goods.

(*b*) Permissive,—God permits men to cherish and to manifest the evil dispositions of their hearts. God's permissive providence is simply the negative act of withholding impediments from the path of the sinner, instead of preventing his sin by the exercise of divine power. It implies no ignorance, passivity, or indulgence, but consists with hatred of the sin and determination to punish it.

2 Chron. 32: 31 —"God left him [Hezekiah], to try him, that he might know all that was in his heart"; *cf.* Deut. 8: 2 — "that he might humble thee, to prove thee, to know what was in thine heart." Ps. 17: 13, 14 — "Deliver my soul from the wicked, who is thy sword, from men who are thy hand, O Jehovah"; Ps. 81: 12, 13 —"So I let them go after the stubbornness of their heart, That they might walk in their own counsels. Oh that my people would hearken unto me!" Is. 53 · · 4º — "Surely he hath borne our griefs. . . . Yet it pleased Jehovah to bruise him." Hosea 4

17 — "Ephraim is joined to idols; let him alone"; Acts 14 : 16 — "who in the generations gone by suffered all the nations to walk in their own ways"; Rom. 1 : 24, 28 — "God gave them up in the lusts of their hearts unto uncleanness. . . . God gave them up unto a reprobate mind, to do those things which are not fitting"; 3 : 25 — "to show his righteousness, because of the passing over of the sins done aforetime, in the forbearance of God." To this head of permissive providence is possibly to be referred 1 Sam. 18 : 10 — "an evil spirit from God came mightily upon Saul." As the Hebrew writers saw in second causes the operation of the great first Cause, and said: "The God of glory thundereth" (Ps. 29 : 3), so, because even the acts of the wicked entered into God's plan, the Hebrew writers sometimes represented God as doing what he merely permitted finite spirits to do. In 2 Sam. 24 : 1, God moves David to number Israel, but in 1 Chron. 21 : 1 the same thing is referred to Satan. God's providence in these cases, however, may be directive as well as permissive.

Tennyson, The Higher Pantheism: "God is law, say the wise; O Soul, and let us rejoice, For if he thunder by law the thunder is yet his voice." Fisher, Nature and Method of Revelation, 56 — "The clear separation of God's efficiency from God's permissive act was reserved to a later day. All emphasis was in the Old Testament laid upon the sovereign power of God." Coleridge, in his Confessions of an Inquiring Spirit, letter II, speaks of "the habit, universal with the Hebrew doctors, of referring all excellent or extraordinary things to the great first Cause, without mention of the proximate and instrumental causes — a striking illustration of which may be found by comparing the narratives of the same events in the Psalms and in the historical books. . . . The distinction between the providential and the miraculous did not enter into their forms of thinking — at any rate, not into their mode of conveying their thoughts." The woman who had been slandered rebelled when told that God had permitted it for her good; she maintained that Satan had inspired her accuser; she needed to learn that God had permitted the work of Satan.

(c) Directive, — God directs the evil acts of men to ends unforeseen and unintended by the agents. When evil is in the heart and will certainly come out, God orders its flow in one direction rather than in another, so that its course can be best controlled and least harm may result. This is sometimes called overruling providence.

Gen. 50 : 20 — "as for you, ye meant evil against me; but God meant it for good, to bring to pass, as it is this day, to save much people alive"; Ps. 76 : 10 — "the wrath of man shall praise thee: The res due of wrath shalt thou gird upon thee" = put on as an ornament — clothe thyself with it for thine own glory; Is. 10 : 5 — "Ho Assyrian, the rod of mine anger, and the staff in whose hand is mine indignation"; John 13 : 27 — "What thou doest, do quickly" = do in a particular way what is actually being done (Westcott, Bib. Com., *in loco*; Acts 4 : 27, 28 — "against thy holy Servant Jesus, whom thou didst anoint, both Herod and Pontius Pilate, with the Gentiles and the peoples of Israel, were gathered together, to do whatsoever thy hand and thy counsel foreordained to come to pass."

To this head of directive providence should probably be referred the passages with regard to Pharaoh in Ex. 4 : 21 — "I will harden his heart, and he will not let the people go"; 7 : 13 — "and Pharaoh's heart was hardened"; 8 : 15 — "he hardened his heart" — i. e., Pharaoh hardened his own heart. Here the controlling agency of God did not interfere with the liberty of Pharaoh or oblige him to sin; but in judgment for his previous cruelty and impiety God withdrew the external restraints which had hitherto kept his sin within bounds, and placed him in circumstances which would have influenced to right action a well-disposed mind, but which God foresaw would lead a disposition like Pharaoh's to the peculiar course of wickedness which he actually pursued.

God hardened Pharaoh's heart, then, first, by permitting him to harden his own heart, God being the author of his sin only in the sense that he is the author of a free being who is himself the direct author of his sin; secondly, by giving to him the means of enlightenment, Pharaoh's very opportunities being perverted by him into occasions of more virulent wickedness, and good resisted being thus made to result in greater evil; thirdly, by judicially forsaking Pharaoh, when it became manifest that he would not do God's will, and thus making it morally certain, though not necessary, that he would do evil; and fourthly, by so directing Pharaoh's surroundings that his sin would manifest itself in one way rather than in another. Sin is like the lava of the volcano, which will certainly come out, but which God directs in its course down the mountain-side so that it will do least harm. The gravitation downward is due to man's evil will; the direction to this side or to that is due to God's providence. See Rom. 9 : 17, 18 — "For this very purpose did I raise thee up, that I might show in thee my power, and that my name might be published abroad in all the earth. So then he hath mercy on whom he will and whom he will he hardeneth" Thus the very passions which excite men to rebel against God are made completely subservient to his purposes; see Annotated Paragraph Bible, on Ps. 76 : 10.

God hardens Pharaoh's heart only after all the earlier plagues have been sent. Pharaoh had hardened his own heart before. God hardens no man's heart who has not first hardened it himself. Crane, Religion of To-morrow, 140—"Jehovah is never said to harden the heart of a good man, or of one who is set to do righteousness. It is always those who are bent on evil whom God hardens. Pharaoh hardens his own heart before the Lord is said to harden it. Nature is God, and it is the nature of human beings to harden when they resist softening influences." The Watchman, Dec. 5, 1901 : 11—"God decreed to Pharaoh what Pharaoh had chosen for himself. Persistence in certain inclinations and volitions awakens within the body and soul forces which are not under the control of the will, and which drive the man on in the way he has chosen. After a time nature hardens the hearts of men to do evil."

(*d*) Determinative,—God determines the bounds reached by the evil passions of his creatures, and the measure of their effects. Since moral evil is a germ capable of indefinite expansion, God's determining the measure of its growth does not alter its character or involve God's complicity with the perverse wills which cherish it.

Job 1 : 12—"And Jehovah said unto Satan, Behold, all that he hath is in thy power ; only upon himself put not forth thy hand "; 2 : 6—"Behold, he is in thy hand ; only spare his life "; Ps. 124 : 2—" If it had not been Jehovah who was on our side, when men rose up against us ; Then had they swallowed us up alive "; 1 Cor. 10 : 13—"will not suffer you to be tempted above that ye are able ; but will with the temptation make also the way of escape, that ye may be able to endure it "; 2 Thess. 2 : 7—" For the mystery of lawlessness doth already work ; only there is one that restraineth now, until he be taken out of the way "; Rev. 20 : 2, 3—" And he laid hold on the dragon, the old serpent, which is the Devil and Satan, and bound him for a thousand years."

Pepper, Outlines of Syst. Theol., 76—The union of God's will and man's will is "such that, while in one view all can be ascribed to God, in another all can be ascribed to the creature. But how God and the creature are united in operation is doubtless known and knowable only to God. A very dim analogy is furnished in the union of the soul and body in men. The hand retains its own physical laws, yet is obedient to the human will. This theory recognizes the veracity of consciousness in its witness to personal freedom, and yet the completeness of God's control of both the bad and the good. Free beings are ruled, but are ruled as free and in their freedom. The freedom is not sacrificed to the control. The two coëxist, each in its integrity. Any doctrine which does not allow this is false to Scripture and destructive of religion."

2. *Rational proof.*

A. Arguments *a priori* from the divine attributes. (*a*) From the immutability of God. This makes it certain that he will execute his eternal plan of the universe and its history. But the execution of this plan involves not only creation and preservation, but also providence. (*b*) From the benevolence of God. This renders it certain that he will care for the intelligent universe he has created. What it was worth his while to create, it is worth his while to care for. But this care is providence. (*c*) From the justice of God. As the source of moral law, God must assure the vindication of law by administering justice in the universe and punishing the rebellious. But this administration of justice is providence.

For heathen ideas of providence, see Cicero, De Natura Deorum, 11 : 30, where Balbus speaks of the existence of the gods as that, "quo concesso, confitendum est eorum consilio mundum administrari." Epictetus, sec. 41—"The principal and most important duty in religion is to possess your mind with just and becoming notions of the gods—to believe that there are such supreme beings, and that they govern and dispose of all the affairs of the world with a just and good providence." Marcus Antoninus : "If there are no gods, or if they have no regard for human affairs, why should I desire to live in a world without gods and without a providence ? But gods undoubtedly there are, and they regard human affairs." See also Bib. Sac., 16 : 374. As we shall see, however, many of the heathen writers believed in a general, rather than in a particular providence.

On the argument for providence derived from God's benevolence, see Appleton, Works, 1 : 146—"Is indolence more consistent with God's majesty than action would be? The happiness of creatures is a good. Does it honor God to say that he is indifferent to that which he knows to be good and valuable? Even if the world had come into exist- ence without his agency, it would become God's moral character to pay some attention to creatures so numerous and so susceptible to pleasure and pain, especially when he might have so great and favorable an influence on their moral condition." John 5: 17 — " My Father worketh even until now, and I work "— is as applicable to providence as to preservation.

The complexity of God's providential arrangements may be illustrated by Tyndall's explanation of the fact that heartsease does not grow in the neighborhood of English villages : 1. In English villages dogs run loose. 2. Where dogs run loose, cats must stay at home. 3. Where cats stay at home, field mice abound. 4. Where field mice abound, the nests of bumble-bees are destroyed. 5. Where bumble-bees' nests are destroyed, there is no fertilization of pollen. Therefore, where dogs go loose, no hearts- ease grows.

B. Arguments *a posteriori* from the facts of nature and of history. (*a*) The outward lot of individuals and nations is not wholly in their own hands, but is in many acknowledged respects subject to the disposal of a higher power. (*b*) The observed moral order of the world, although imperfect, cannot be accounted for without recognition of a divine provi- dence. Vice is discouraged and virtue rewarded, in ways which are beyond the power of mere nature. There must be a governing mind and will, and this mind and will must be the mind and will of God.

The birthplace of individuals and of nations, the natural powers with which they are endowed, the opportunities and immunities they enjoy, are beyond their own control. A man's destiny for time and for eternity may be practically decided for him by his birth in a Christian home, rather than in a tenement-house at the Five Points, or in a kraal of the Hottentots. Progress largely depends upon " variety of environment " (H. Spencer). But this variety of environment is in great part independent of our own efforts.

" There 's a Divinity that shapes our ends, Rough hew them how we will." Shakes- peare here expounds human consciousness. " Man proposes and God disposes " has become a proverb. Experience teaches that success and failure are not wholly due to us. Men often labor and lose ; they consult and nothing ensues ; they " embattle and are broken." Providence is not always on the side of the heaviest batallions. Not arms but ideas have decided the fate of the world — as Xerxes found at Thermopylæ, and Napoleon at Waterloo. Great movements are generally begun without consciousness of their greatness. *Cf.* Is. 42 : 16 — "I will bring the blind by a way that they know not " ; 1 Cor. 5 : 37, 38 — "thou sowest . . . a bare grain . . . but God giveth it a body even as it pleased him."

The deed returns to the doer, and character shapes destiny. This is true in the long run. Eternity will show the truth of the maxim. But here in time a sufficient number of apparent exceptions are permitted to render possible a moral probation. If evil were always immediately followed by penalty, righteousness would have a compelling power upon the will and the highest virtue would be impossible. Job's friends accuse Job of acting upon this principle. The Hebrew children deny its truth, when they say : " But if not " —even if God does not deliver us — " we will not serve thy gods, nor worship the golden Image which thou hast set up " (Dan. 3 : 18).

Martineau, Seat of Authority, 298 — " Through some misdirection or infirmity, most of the larger agencies in history have failed to reach their own ideal, yet have accom- plished revolutions greater and more beneficent ; the conquests of Alexander, the empire of Rome, the Crusades, the ecclesiastical persecutions, the monastic asceti- cisms, the missionary zeal of Christendom, have all played a momentous part in the drama of the world, yet a part which is a surprise to each. All this shows the control- ling presence of a Reason and a Will transcendent and divine." Kidd, Social Evolution, 90, declares that the progress of the race has taken place only under conditions which have had no sanction from the reason of the great proportion of the individuals who submit to them. He concludes that a rational religion is a scientific impossibility, and that the function of religion is to provide a super-rational sanction for social progress. We prefer to say that Providence pushes the race forward even against its will.

James Russell Lowell, Letters, 2 : 51, suggests that God's calm control of the forces of the universe, both physical and mental, should give us confidence when evil seems impending: "How many times have I seen the fire-engines of church and state clanging and lumbering along to put out — a false alarm! And when the heavens are cloudy, what a glare can be cast by a burning shanty!" See Sermon on Providence in Political Revolutions, in Farrar's Science and Theology, 228. On the moral order of the world, notwithstanding its imperfections, see Butler, Analogy, Bohn's ed., 98; King, in Baptist Review, 1884: 202-222. •

III. THEORIES OPPOSING THE DOCTRINE OF PROVIDENCE.

1. *Fatalism.*

Fatalism maintains the certainty, but denies the freedom, of human self-determination, — thus substituting fate for providence.

To this view we object that (*a*) it contradicts consciousness, which testifies that we are free ; (*b*) it exalts the divine power at the expense of God's truth, wisdom, holiness, love ; (*c*) it destroys all evidence of the personality and freedom of God ; (*d*) it practically makes necessity the only God, and leaves the imperatives of our moral nature without present validity or future vindication.

The Mohammedans have frequently been called fatalists, and the practical effect of the teachings of the Koran upon the masses is to make them so. The ordinary Mohammedan will have no physician or medicine, because everything happens as God has before appointed. Smith, however, in his Mohammed and Mohammedanism, denies that fatalism is essential to the system. *Islam* = "submission," and the participle *Moslem* = "submitted," *i. e.*, to God. Turkish proverb: "A man cannot escape what is written on his forehead." The Mohammedan thinks of God's dominant attribute as being greatness rather than righteousness, power rather than purity. God is the personification of arbitrary will, not the God and Father of our Lord Jesus Christ. But there is in the system an absence of sacerdotalism, a jealousy for the honor of God, a brotherhood of believers, a reverence for what is considered the word of God, and a bold and habitual devotion of its adherents to their faith.

Stanley, Life and Letters, 1 : 489, refers to the Mussulman tradition existing in Egypt that the fate of Islam requires that it should at last be superseded by Christianity. F. W. Sanders "denies that the Koran is peculiarly *sensual.* The Christian and Jewish religions," he says, "have their paradise also. The Koran makes this the reward, but not the ideal, of conduct; ' Grace from thy Lord — that is the grand bliss.' The emphasis of the Koran is upon right living. The Koran does not teach the propagation of religion by *force.* It declares that there shall be no compulsion in religion. The practice of converting by the sword is to be distinguished from the teaching of Mohammed, just as the Inquisition and the slave-trade in Christendom do not prove that Jesus taught them. The Koran did not institute *polygamy.* It found unlimited polygamy, divorce, and infanticide. The last it prohibited ; the two former it restricted and ameliorated, just as Moses found polygamy, but brought it within bounds. The Kofan is not hostile to *secular learning.* Learning flourished under the Bagdad and Spanish Caliphates. When Moslems oppose learning, they do so without authority from the Koran. The Roman Catholic church has opposed schools, but we do not attribute this to the gospel." See Zwemer, Moslem Doctrine of God.

Calvinists can assert freedom, since man's will finds its highest freedom only in submission to God. Islam also cultivates submission, but it is the submission not of love but of fear. The essential difference between Mohammedanism and Christianity is found in the revelation which the latter gives of the love of God in Christ — a revelation which secures from free moral agents the submission of love ; see page 186. On fatalism, see McCosh, Intuitions, 266 ; Kant, Metaphysic of Ethics, 52-74, 93-108 ; Mill, Autobiography, 168-170, and System of Logic, 521-526 ; Hamilton, Metaphysics, 692 ; Stewart, Active and Moral Powers of Man, ed. Walker, 268-324.

2. *Casualism.*

Casualism transfers the freedom of mind to nature, as fatalism transfers the fixity of nature to mind. It thus exchanges providence for chance.

Upon this view we remark :

(*a*) If chance be only another name for human ignorance, a name for the fact that there are trivial occurrences in life which have no meaning or relation to us, — we may acknowledge this, and still hold that providence arranges every so-called chance, for purposes beyond our knowledge. Chance, in this sense, is providential coincidence which we cannot understand, and do not need to trouble ourselves about.

Not all chances are of equal importance. The casual meeting of a stranger in the street need not bring God's providence before me, although I know that God arranges it. Yet I can conceive of that meeting as leading to religious conversation and to the stranger's conversion. When we are prepared for them, we shall see many opportunities which are now as unmeaning to us as the gold in the river-beds was to the early Indians in California. I should be an ingrate, if I escaped a lightning-stroke, and did not thank God ; yet Dr. Arnold's saying that every school boy should put on his hat for God's glory, and with a high moral purpose, seems morbid. There is a certain room for the play of arbitrariness. We must not afflict ourselves or the church of God by requiring a Pharisaic punctiliousness in minutiæ. Life is too short to debate the question which shoe we shall put on first. " Love God and do what you will," said Augustine ; that is, Love God, and act out that love in a simple and natural way. Be free in your service, yet be always on the watch for indications of God's will.

(*b*) If chance be taken in the sense of utter absence of all causal connections in the phenomena of matter and mind, — we oppose to this notion the fact that the causal judgment is formed in accordance with a fundamental and necessary law of human thought, and that no science or knowledge is possible without the assumption of its validity.

In Luke 10 : 31, our Savior says: "By chance a certain priest was going down that way." Janet : " Chance is not a cause, but a coincidence of causes." Bowne, Theory of Thought and Knowledge, 197 — " By chance is not meant lack of causation, but the coincidence in an event of mutually independent series of causation. Thus the unpurposed meeting of two persons is spoken of as a chance one, when the movement of neither implies that of the other. Here the antithesis of chance is purpose."

(*c*) If chance be used in the sense of undesigning cause, — it is evidently insufficient to explain the regular and uniform sequences of nature, or the moral progress of the human race. These things argue a superintending and designing mind — in other words, a providence. Since reason demands not only a cause, but a sufficient cause, for the order of the physical and moral world, casualism must be ruled out.

The observer at the signal station was asked what was the climate of Rochester. "Climate ? " he replied ; " Rochester has no climate, — only weather ! " So Chauncey Wright spoke of the ups and downs of human affairs as simply " cosmical weather." But our intuition of design compels us to see mind and purpose in individual and national history, as well as in the physical universe. The same argument which proves the existence of God proves also the existence of a providence. See Farrar, Life of Christ, 1 : 155, note.

3. *Theory of a merely general providence.*

Many who acknowledge God's control over the movements of planets and the destinies of nations deny any divine arrangement of particular events. Most of the arguments against deism are equally valid against the theory of a merely general providence. This view is indeed only a form of deism, which holds that God has not wholly withdrawn himself from the universe, but that his activity within it is limited to the maintenance of general laws.

This appears to have been the view of most of the heathen philosophers. Cicero: "Magna dii curant; parva negligunt." "Even in kingdoms among men," he says, "kings do not trouble themselves with insignificant affairs." Fullerton, Conceptions of the Infinite, 9 — "Plutarch thought there could not be an infinity of worlds, — Providence could not possibly take charge of so many. 'Troublesome and boundless infinity' could be grasped by no consciousness." The ancient Cretans made an image of Jove without ears, for they said: "It is a shame to believe that God would hear the talk of men." So Jerome, the church Father, thought it absurd that God should know just how many gnats and cockroaches there were in the world. David Harum is wiser when he expresses the belief that there is nothing wholly bad or useless in the world: "A reasonable amount of fleas is good for a dog, — they keep him from broodin' on bein' a dog." This has been paraphrased: "A reasonable number of beaux are good for a girl, — they keep her from brooding over her being a girl."

In addition to the arguments above alluded to, we may urge against this theory that:

(a) General control over the course of nature and of history is impossible without control over the smallest particulars which affect the course of nature and of history. Incidents so slight as well-nigh to escape observation at the time of their occurrence are frequently found to determine the whole future of a human life, and through that life the fortunes of a whole empire and of a whole age.

"Nothing great has great beginnings." "Take care of the pence, and the pounds will take care of themselves." "Care for the chain is care for the links of the chain." Instances in point are the sleeplessness of King Ahasuerus (Esther 6:1), and the seeming chance that led to the reading of the record of Mordecai's service and to the salvation of the Jews in Persia; the spider's web spun across the entrance to the cave in which Mohammed had taken refuge, which so deceived his pursuers that they passed on in a bootless chase, leaving to the world the religion and the empire of the Moslems; the preaching of Peter the Hermit, which occasioned the first Crusade; the chance shot of an archer, which pierced the right eye of Harold, the last of the purely English kings, gained the battle of Hastings for William the Conqueror, and secured the throne of England for the Normans; the flight of pigeons to the south-west, which changed the course of Columbus, hitherto directed towards Virginia, to the West Indies, and so prevented the dominion of Spain over North America; the storm that dispersed the Spanish Armada and saved England from the Papacy, and the storm that dispersed the French fleet gathered for the conquest of New England — the latter on a day of fasting and prayer appointed by the Puritans to avert the calamity; the settling of New England by the Puritans, rather than by French Jesuits; the order of Council restraining Cromwell and his friends from sailing to America; Major André's lack of self-possession in presence of his captors, which led him to ask an improper question instead of showing his passport, and which saved the American cause; the unusually early commencement of cold weather, which frustrated the plans of Napoleon and destroyed his army in Russia; the fatal shot at Fort Sumter, which precipitated the war of secession and resulted in the abolition of American slavery. Nature is linked to history; the breeze warps the course of the bullet; the worm perforates the plank of the ship. God must care for the least, or he cannot care for the greatest.

"Large doors swing on small hinges." The barking of a dog determined F. W. Robertson to be a preacher rather than a soldier. Robert Browning, Mr. Sludge the Medium: "We find great things are made of little things, And little things go lessening till at last Comes God behind them." E. G. Robinson: "We cannot suppose only a general outline to have been in the mind of God, while the filling-up is left to be done in some other way. The general includes the special." Dr. Lloyd, one of the Oxford Professors, said to Pusey, "I wish you would learn something about those German critics." "In the obedient spirit of those times," writes Pusey, "I set myself at once to learn German, and I went to Göttingen, to study at once the language and the theology. My life turned on that hint of Dr. Lloyd's."

Goldwin Smith: "Had a bullet entered the brain of Cromwell or of William III in his first battle, or had Gustavus not fallen at Lützen, the course of history apparently would have been changed. The course even of science would have been changed, if there had not been a Newton and a Darwin." The annexation of Corsica to France gave to France a Napoleon, and to Europe a conqueror. Martineau, Seat of Authority, 101 — "Had the monastery at Erfurt deputed another than young Luther on its errand to paganized Rome, or had Leo X sent a less scandalous agent than Tetzel on his business to Germany, the seeds of the Reformation might have fallen by the wayside where they had no deepness of earth, and the Western revolt of the human mind might have taken another date and another form." See Appleton, Works, 1 : 149 sq.; Lecky, Eng. and in the Eighteenth Century, chap. I.

(b) The love of God which prompts a general care for the universe must also prompt a particular care for the smallest events which affect the happiness of his creatures. It belongs to love to regard nothing as trifling or beneath its notice which has to do with the interests of the object of its affection. Infinite love may therefore be expected to provide for all, even the minutest things in the creation. Without belief in this particular care, men cannot long believe in God's general care. Faith in a particular providence is indispensable to the very existence of practical religion ; for men will not worship or recognize a God who has no direct relation to them.

Man's care for his own body involves care for the least important members of it. A lover's devotion is known by his interest in the minutest concerns of his beloved. So all our affairs are matters of interest to God. Pope's Essay on Man: "All nature is but art unknown to thee ; All chance, direction which thou canst not see ; All discord, harmony not understood; All partial evil, universal good." If harvests may be labored for and lost without any agency of God ; if rain or sun may act like fate, sweeping away the results of years, and God have no hand in it all ; if wind and storm may wreck the ship and drown our dearest friends, and God not care for us or for our loss, then all possibility of general trust in God will disappear also.

God's care is shown in the least things as well as in the greatest. In Gethsemane Christ says : "Let these go their way : that the word might be fulfilled which he spake, Of those whom thou hast given me I lost not one" (John 18 : 8, 9). It is the same spirit as that of his intercessory prayer : "I guarded them, and not one of them perished, but the son of perdition" (John 17 : 12). Christ gives himself as a prisoner that his disciples may go free, even as he redeems us from the curse of the law by being made a curse for us (Gal. 3 : 13). The dewdrop is moulded by the same law that rounds the planets into spheres. Gen. Grant said he had never but once sought a place for himself, and in that place he was a comparative failure; he had been an instrument in God's hand for the accomplishing of God's purposes, apart from any plan or thought or hope of his own.

Of his journey through the dark continent in search of David Livingstone, Henry M. Stanley wrote in Scribner's Monthly for June, 1890 : "Constrained at the darkest hour humbly to confess that without God's help I was helpless, I vowed a vow in the forest solitudes that I would confess his aid before men. Silence as of death was around me ; it was midnight ; I was weakened by illness, prostrated with fatigue, and wan with anxiety for my white and black companions, whose fate was a mystery. In this physical and mental distress I besought God to give me back my people. Nine hours later we were exulting with a rapturous joy. In full view of all was the crimson flag with the crescent, and beneath its waving folds was the long-lost rear column. . . . . My own designs were frustrated constantly by unhappy circumstances. I endeavored to steer my course as direct as possible, but there was an unaccountable influence at the helm. . . . . I have been conscious that the issues of every effort were in other hands. . . . . Divinity seems to have hedged us while we journeyed, impelling us whither it would, effecting its own will, but constantly guiding and protecting us." He refuses to believe that it is all the result of 'luck', and he closes with a doxology which we should expect from Livingston but not from him : "Thanks be to God, forever and ever !"

(c) In times of personal danger, and in remarkable conjunctures of public affairs, men instinctively attribute to God a control of the events which take place around them. The prayers which such startling emergencies force from men's lips are proof that God is present and active in human affairs. This testimony of our mental constitution must be regarded as virtually the testimony of him who framed this constitution.

No advance of science can rid us of this conviction, since it comes from a deeper source than mere reasoning. The intuition of design is awakened by the connection of events in our daily life, as much as by the useful adaptations which we see in nature. Ps. 107 : 23-28 — " They that go down to the sea in ships . . . . . mount up to the heavens, they go down again to the depths . . . . And are at their wits' end. Then they cry unto Jehovah in their trouble." A narrow escape from death shows us a present God and Deliverer. Instance the general feeling throughout the land, expressed by the press as well as by the pulpit, at the breaking out of our rebellion and at the President's subsequent Proclamation of Emancipation.

" Est deus in nobis ; agitante calescimus illo." For contrast between Nansen's ignoring of God in his polar journey and Dr. Jacob Chamberlain's calling upon God in his strait in India, see Missionary Review, May, 1898. Sunday School Times, March 4, 1893—" Benjamin Franklin became a deist at the age of fifteen. Before the Revolutionary War he was merely a shrewd and pushing business man. He had public spirit, and he made one happy discovery in science. But ' Poor Richard's ' sayings express his mind at that time. The perils and anxieties of the great war gave him a deeper insight. He and others entered upon it ' with a rope around their necks.' As he told the Constitutional Convention of 1787, when he proposed that its daily sessions be opened with prayer, the experiences of that war showed him that ' God verily rules in the affairs of men.' And when the designs for an American coinage were under discussion, Franklin proposed to stamp on them, not ' A Penny Saved is a Penny Earned,' or any other piece of worldly prudence, but ' The Fear of the Lord is the Beginning of Wisdom.' "

(*d*) Christian experience confirms the declarations of Scripture that particular events are brought about by God with special reference to the good or ill of the individual. Such events occur at times in such direct connection with the Christian's prayers that no doubt remains with regard to the providential arrangement of them. The possibility of such divine agency in natural events cannot be questioned by one who, like the Christian, has had experience of the greater wonders of regeneration and daily intercourse with God, and who believes in the reality of creation, incarnation, and miracles.

Providence prepares the way for men's conversion, sometimes by their own partial reformation, sometimes by the sudden death of others near them. Instance Luther and Judson. The Christian learns that the same Providence that led him before his conversion is busy after his conversion in directing his steps and in supplying his wants. Daniel Defoe : " I have been fed more by miracle than Elijah when the angels were his purveyors." In Psalm 32, David celebrates not only God's pardoning mercy but his subsequent providential leading : "I will counsel thee with mine eye upon thee " (verse 8). It may be objected that we often mistake the meaning of events. We answer that, as in nature, so in providence, we are compelled to believe, not that we *know* the design, but that there *is* a design. Instance Shelley's drowning, and Jacob Knapp's prayer that his opponent might be stricken dumb. Lyman Beecher's attributing the burning of the Unitarian church to God's judgment upon false doctrine was invalidated a little later by the burning of his own church.

Job 23 : 10 — " He knoweth the way that is mine," or " the way that is with me," *i. e.*, my inmost way, life, character ; " When he hath tried me, I shall come forth as gold." 1 Cor. 10 : 4 — " and the rock was Christ "== Christ was the ever present source of their refreshment and life, both physical and spiritual. God's providence is all exercised through Christ. 2 Cor. 2 : 14 — " But thanks be unto God, who always leadeth us in triumph in Christ "; not, as in A. V., " causeth us to triumph." Paul glories, not in conquering, but in being conquered. Let Christ triumph, not Paul. " Great King of grace, my heart subdue ; I would be led in triumph too, A willing captive to my Lord, To own the conquests of his word." Therefore Paul can call himself " the prisoner of Christ Jesus " (Eph. 3 : 1). It was Christ who had shut him up two years in Cæsarea, and then two succeeding years in Rome.

IV. RELATIONS OF THE DOCTRINE OF PROVIDENCE.

1. *To miracles and works of grace.*

Particular providence is the agency of God in what seem to us the minor affairs of nature and human life. Special providence is only an instance of God's particular providence which has special relation to us or makes peculiar impression upon us. It is special, not as respects the means which God makes use of, but as respects the effect produced upon us. In special providence we have only a more impressive manifestation of God's universal control.

Miracles and works of grace like regeneration are not to be regarded as belonging to a different order of things from God's special providences. They too, like special providences, may have their natural connections and antecedents, although they more readily suggest their divine authorship. Nature and God are not mutually exclusive,—nature is rather God's method of working. Since nature is only the manifestation of God, special providence, miracle, and regeneration are simply different degrees of extraordinary nature. Certain of the wonders of Scripture, such as the destruction of Sennacherib's army and the dividing of the Red Sea, the plagues of Egypt, the flight of quails, and the draught of fishes, can be counted as exaggerations of natural forces, while at the same time they are operations of the wonder-working God.

The falling of snow from a roof is an example of ordinary (or particular) providence. But if a man is killed by it, it becomes a special providence to him and to others who are thereby taught the insecurity of life. So the providing of coal for fuel in the geologic ages may be regarded by different persons in the light either of a general or of a special providence. In all the operations of nature and all the events of life God's providence is exhibited. That providence becomes special, when it manifestly suggests some care of God for us or some duty of ours to God. Savage, Life beyond Death, 285 — " Mary A. Livermore's life was saved during her travels in the West by her hearing and instantly obeying what seemed to her a voice. She did not know where it came from ; but she leaped, as the voice ordered, from one side of a car to the other, and instantly the side where she had been sitting was crushed in and utterly demolished." In a similiar way, the life of Dr. Oncken was saved in the railroad disaster at Norwalk.

Trench gives the name of "providential miracles" to those Scripture wonders which may be explained as wrought through the agency of natural laws (see Trench, Miracles, 29). Mozley also (Miracles, 117-120) calls these wonders miracles, because of the predictive word of God which accompanied them. He says that the difference in effect between miracles and special providences is that the latter give some warrant, while the former give full warrant, for believing that they are wrought by God. He calls special providences "invisible miracles." Bp. of Southampton, Place of Miracles, 12, 13 — " The art of Bezaleel in constructing the tabernacle, and the plans of generals like Moses and Joshua, Gideon, Barak, and David, are in the Old Testament ascribed to the direct inspiration of God. A less religious writer would have ascribed them to the instinct of military skill. No miracle is necessarily involved, when, in devising the system of ceremonial law it is said : 'Jehovah spake unto Moses' (Num. 5 : 1). God is everywhere present in the history of Israel, but miracles are strikingly rare." We prefer to say that the line between the natural and the supernatural, between special providence and miracle, is an arbitrary one, and that the same event may often be regarded either as special providence or as miracle, according as we look at it from the point of view of its relation to other events or from the point of view of its relation to God.

E. G. Robinson : " If Vesuvius should send up ashes and lava, and a strong wind should scatter them, it could be said to rain fire and brimstone, as at Sodom and Gomorrha." There is abundant evident of volcanic action at the Dead Sea. See article on the Physical Preparation for Israel in Palestine, by G. Frederick Wright, in Bib. Sac., April, 1901 : 364. The three great miracles—the destruction of Sodom and Gomorrha, the parting of the waters of the Jordan, the falling down of the walls of Jericho — are described as effect of volcanic eruption, elevation of the bed of the river by a landslide, and earthquake-shock overthrowing the walls. Salt slime thrown up may have enveloped Lot's wife and turned her into "a mound of salt" (Gen. 19 : 26). In like manner, some of Jesus' works of healing, as for instance those wrought upon paralytics and epileptics, may be susceptible of natural explanation, while yet they show that Christ is absolute Lord of nature. For the naturalistic view, see Tyndall on Miracles and Special Providences, in Fragments of Science, 45, 418. *Per contra*, see Farrar, on Divine Providence and General Laws, in Science and Theology, 54–80; Row, Bampton Lect. on Christian Evidences, 109–115; Godet, Defence of Christian Faith, Chap. 2; Bowne, The Immanence of God, 56–65.

2. *To prayer and its answer.*

What has been said with regard to God's connection with nature suggests the question, how God can answer prayer consistently with the fixity of natural law.

Tyndall (see reference above), while repelling the charge of denying that God can answer prayer at all, yet docs deny that he can answer it without a miracle. He says expressly "that without a disturbance of natural law quite as serious as the stoppage of an eclipse, or the rolling of the St. Lawrence up the falls of Niagara, no act of humilation, individual or national, could call one shower from heaven or deflect toward us a single beam of the sun." In reply we would remark:

A. Negatively, that the true solution is not to be reached :

(*a*) By making the sole effect of prayer to be its reflex influence upon the petitioner. — Prayer presupposes a God who hears and answers. It will not be offered, unless it is believed to accomplish objective as well as subjective results.

According to the first view mentioned above, prayer is a mere spiritual gymnastics — an effort to lift ourselves from the ground by tugging at our own boot-straps. David Hume said well, after hearing a sermon by Dr. Leechman: "We can make use of no expression or even thought in prayers and entreaties which does not imply that these prayers have an influence." See Tyndall on Prayer and Natural Law, in Fragments of Science, 35. Will men pray to a God who is both deaf and dumb? Will the sailor on the bowsprit whistle to the wind for the sake of improving his voice? Horace Bushnell called this perversion of prayer a "mere dumb-bell exercise." Baron Munchausen pulled himself out of the bog in China by tugging away at his own pigtail.

Hyde, God's Education of Man, 154, 155 — "Prayer is not the reflex action of my will upon itself, but rather the communion of two wills, in which the finite comes into connection with the Infinite, and, like the trolley, appropriates its purpose and power." Harnack, Wesen des Christenthums, 42, apparently follows Schleiermacher in unduly limiting prayer to general petitions which receive only a subjective answer. He tells us that "Jesus taught his disciples the Lord's Prayer in response to a request for directions how to pray. Yet we look in vain therein for requests for special gifts of grace, or for particular good things, even though they are spiritual. The name, the will, the kingdom of God — these are the things which are the objects of petition." Harnack forgets that the same Christ said also : "All things whatsoever ye pray and ask for, believe that ye receive them, and ye shall have them" (Mark 11 : 24).

(*b*) Nor by holding that God answers prayer simply by spiritual means, such as the action of the Holy Spirit upon the spirit of man. — The realm of spirit is no less subject to law than the realm of matter. Scripture and experience, moreover, alike testify that in answer to prayer events take place in the outward world which would not have taken place if prayer had not gone before.

According to this second theory, God feeds the starving Elijah, not by a distinct message from heaven but by giving a compassionate disposition to the widow of Zarephath so that she is moved to help the prophet. 1 K. 17 : 9 — "behold, I have commanded a widow there to sustain thee." But God could also feed Elijah by the ravens and the angel (1 K. 17 : 4; 19 : 15), and the pouring rain that followed Elijah's prayer (1 K. 18 : 42–45) cannot be explained as a subjective spiritual phenomenon. Diman, Theistic Argument, 268 — "Our charts map out not only the solid shore but the windings of the ocean currents, and we look into the morning papers to ascertain the gathering of storms on the slopes of the Rocky Mountains." But law rules in the realm of spirit as well as in the realm of nature. See Baden Powell, in Essays and Reviews, 106–162; Knight, Studies in Philosophy and Literature, 340–404; George I. Chace, discourse before the Porter Rhet. Soc. of Andover, August, 1854. Governor Rice in Washington is moved to send money to a starving family in New York, and to secure employment for them. Though he has had no information with regard to their need, they have knelt in prayer for help just before the coming of the aid.

(c) Nor by maintaining that God suspends or breaks in upon the order of nature, in answering every prayer that is offered. — This view does not take account of natural laws as having objective existence, and as revealing the order of God's being. Omnipotence might thus suspend natural law, but wisdom, so far as we can see, would not.

This third theory might well be held by those who see in nature no force but the all-working will of God. But the properties and powers of matter are revelations of the divine will, and the human will has only a relative independence in the universe. To desire that God would answer all our prayers is to desire omnipotence without omniscience. All true prayer is therefore an expression of the one petition : "Thy will be done " (Mat. 6 : 10). E. G. Robinson : "It takes much common sense to pray, and many prayers are destitute of this quality. Man needs to pray audibly even in his private prayers, to get the full benefit of them. One of the chief benefits of the English liturgy is that the individual minister is lost sight of. Protestantism makes you work ; in Romanism the church will do it all for you. "

(d) Nor by considering prayer as a physical force, linked in each case to its answer, as physical cause is linked to physical effect. — Prayer is not a force acting directly upon nature ; else there would be no discretion as to its answer. It can accomplish results in nature, only as it influences God.

We educate our children in two ways : first, by training them to do for themselves what they can do ; and, secondly, by encouraging them to seek our help in matters beyond their power. So God educates us, first, by impersonal law, and, secondly, by personal dependence. He teaches us both to work and to ask. Notice the "perfect unwisdom of modern scientists who place themselves under the training of impersonal law, to the exclusion of that higher and better training which is under personality " (Hopkins, Sermon on Prayer-gauge, 16).

It seems more in accordance with both Scripture and reason to say that:

B. God may answer prayer, even when that answer involves changes in the sequences of nature,—

(a) By new combinations of natural forces, in regions withdrawn from our observation, so that effects are produced which these same forces left to themselves would never have accomplished. As man combines the laws of chemical attraction and of combustion, to fire the gunpowder and split the rock asunder, so God may combine the laws of nature to bring about answers to prayer. In all this there may be no suspension or violation of law, but a use of law unknown to us.

Hopkins, Sermon on the Prayer-gauge : " Nature is uniform in her processes but not in her results. Do you say that water cannot run uphill? Yes, it can and does. When-ever man constructs a milldam the water runs up the environing hills till it reaches the top of the milldam. Man can make a spark of electricity do his bidding ; why can-not God use a bolt of electricity? Laws are not our masters, but our servants. They do our bidding all the better because they are uniform. And our servants are not God's masters." Kendall Brooks : "The master of a musical instrument can vary without limit the combination of sounds and the melodies which these combinations can produce. The laws of the instrument are not changed, but in their unchanging steadfastness produce an infinite variety of tunes. It is necessary that they should be

unchanging in order to secure a desired result. So nature, which exercises the infinite skill of the divine Master, is governed by unvarying laws; but he, by these laws, produces an infinite variety of results."

Hodge, Popular Lectures, 45, 99 — "The system of natural laws is far more flexible in God's hands than it is in ours. We act on second causes externally; God acts on them internally. We act upon them at only a few isolated points; God acts upon every point of the system at the same time. The whole of nature may be as plastic to his will as the air in the organs of the great singer who articulates it into a fit expression of every thought and passion of his soaring soul." Upton, Hibbert Lectures, 155 — "If all the chemical elements of our solar system preëxisted in the fiery cosmic mist, there must have been a time when quite suddenly the attractions between these elements overcame the degree of caloric force which held them apart, and the rush of elements into chemical union must have been consummated with inconceivable rapidity. Uniformitarianism is not universal."

Shaler, Interpretation of Nature, chap. 2 — "By a little increase of centrifugal force the elliptical orbit is changed into a parabola, and the planet becomes a comet. By a little reduction in temperature water becomes solid and loses many of its powers. So unexpected results are brought about and surprises as revolutionary as if a Supreme Power immediately intervened." William James, Address before Soc. for Psych. Research: "Thought-transference may involve a critical point, as the physicists call it, which is passed only when certain psychic conditions are realized, and otherwise not reached at all — just as a big conflagration will break out at a certain temperature, below which no conflagration whatever, whether big or little, can occur." Tennyson, Life, 1 : 324 — "Prayer is like opening a sluice between the great ocean and our little channels, when the great sea gathers itself together and flows in at full tide."

Since prayer is nothing more nor less than appeal to a personal and present God, whose granting or withholding of the requested blessing is believed to be determined by the prayer itself, we must conclude that prayer moves God, or, in other words, induces the putting forth on his part of an imperative volition.

The view that in answering prayer God combines natural forces is elaborated by Chalmers, Works, 2 : 314, and 7 : 234. See Diman, Theistic Argument, 111 — "When laws are conceived of, not as single, but as combined, instead of being immutable in their operation, they are the agencies of ceaseless change. Phenomena are governed, not by invariable forces, but by *endlessly varying combinations of invariable forces*." Diman seems to have followed Argyll, Reign of Law, 100.

Janet, Final Causes, 219 — "I kindle a fire in my grate. I only intervene to produce and combine together the different agents whose natural action behooves to produce the effect I have need of; but the first step once taken, all the phenomena constituting combustion engender each other, conformably to their laws, without a new intervention of the agent; so that an observer who should study the series of these phenomena, without perceiving the first hand that had prepared all, could not seize that hand in any special act, and yet there is a preconceived plan and combination."

Hopkins, Sermon on Prayer-gauge: Man, by sprinkling plaster on his field, may cause the corn to grow more luxuriantly; by kindling great fires and by firing cannon, he may cause rain; and God can surely, in answer to prayer, do as much as man can. Lewes says that the fundamental character of all theological philosophy is conceiving of phenomena as subject to supernatural volition, and consequently as eminently and irregularly variable. This notion, he says, is refuted, first, by exact and rational prevision of phenomena, and, secondly, by the possibility of our modifying these phenomena so as to promote our own advantage. But we ask in reply: If we can modify them, cannot God? But, lest this should seem to imply mutability in God or inconsistency in nature, we remark, in addition, that:

(*b*) God may have so preärranged the laws of the material universe and the events of history that, while the answer to prayer is an expression of his will, it is granted through the working of natural agencies, and in perfect accordance with the general principle that results, both temporal and spiritual, are to be attained by intelligent creatures through the use of the appropriate and appointed means.

J. P. Cooke, Credentials of Science, 194—"The Jacquard loom of itself would weave a perfectly uniform plain fabric; the perforated cards determine a selection of the threads, and through a combination of these variable conditions, so complex that the observer cannot follow their intricate workings, the predesigned pattern appears." E. G. Robinson: "The most formidable objection to this theory is the apparent countenance it lends to the doctrine of necessitarianism. But if it presupposes that free actions have been taken into account, it cannot easily be shown to be false." The bishop who was asked by his curate to sanction prayers for rain was unduly sceptical when he replied: "First consult the barometer." Phillips Brooks: "Prayer is not the conquering of God's reluctance, but the taking hold of God's willingness."

The Pilgrims at Plymouth, somewhere about 1628, prayed for rain. They met at 9 A. M., and continued in prayer for eight or nine hours. While they were assembled clouds gathered, and the next morning began rains which, with some intervals, lasted fourteen days. John Easter was many years ago an evangelist in Virginia. A large out-door meeting was being held. Many thousands had assembled, when heavy storm clouds began to gather. There was no shelter to which the multitudes could retreat. The rain had already reached the adjoining fields when John Easter cried: "Brethren, be still, while I call upon God to stay the storm till the gospel is preached to this multitude!" Then he knelt and prayed that the audience might be spared the rain, and that after they had gone to their homes there might be refreshing showers. Behold, the clouds parted as they came near, and passed to either side of the crowd and then closed again, leaving the place dry where the audience had assembled, and the next day the postponed showers came down upon the ground that had been the day before omitted.

Since God is immanent in nature, an answer to prayer, coming about through the intervention of natural law, may be as real a revelation of God's personal care as if the laws of nature were suspended, and God interposed by an exercise of his creative power. Prayer and its answer, though having God's immediate volition as their connecting bond, may yet be provided for in the original plan of the universe.

The universe does not exist for itself, but for moral ends and moral beings, to reveal God and to furnish facilities of intercourse between God and intelligent creatures. Bishop Berkeley: "The universe is God's ceaseless conversation with his creatures." The universe certainly subserves moral ends—the discouragement of vice and the reward of virtue; why not spiritual ends also? When we remember that there is no true prayer which God does not inspire; that every true prayer is part of the plan of the universe linked in with all the rest and provided for at the beginning; that God is in nature and in mind, supervising all their movements and making all fulfill his will and reveal his personal care; that God can adjust the forces of nature to each other far more skilfully than can man when man produces effects which nature of herself could never accomplish; that God is not confined to nature or her forces, but can work by his creative and omnipotent will where other means are not sufficient,—we need have no fear, either that natural law will bar God's answers to prayer, or that these answers will cause a shock or jar in the system of the universe.

Matheson, Messages of the Old Religions, 321, 322—"Hebrew poetry never deals with outward nature for its own sake. The eye never rests on beauty for itself alone. The heavens are the work of God's hands, the earth is God's footstool, the winds are God's ministers, the stars are God's host, the thunder is God's voice. What we call Nature the Jew called God." Miss Heloise E. Hersey: "Plato in the Phædrus sets forth in a splendid myth the means by which the gods refresh themselves. Once a year, in a mighty host, they drive their chariots up the steep to the topmost vault of heaven. Thence they may behold all the wonders and the secrets of the universe; and, quickened by the sight of the great plain of truth, they return home replenished and made glad by the celestial vision." Abp. Trench, Poems, 134—"Lord, what a change within us one short hour Spent in thy presence will prevail to make—What heavy burdens from our bosoms take, What parched grounds refresh as with a shower! We kneel, and all around us seems to lower; We rise, and all, the distant and the near, Stands forth in sunny outline, brave and clear; We kneel how weak, we rise how full of power! Why, therefore, should we do ourselves this wrong, Or others—that we are not always strong; That we are ever overborne with care: That we should ever weak or heartless be, Anxious or troubled, when with us is prayer, And joy and strength and courage are with thee?" See Calderwood, Science and Religion, 299–309; McCosh, Divine Government, 215; Liddon, Elements of Religion, 178–203; Hamilton, Autology, 690–694. See also Jellett, Donnellan Lectures on the Efficacy of Prayer; Butterworth, Story of Notable Prayers; Patton, Prayer and its Answers; Monrad, World of Prayer; Prime, Power of Prayer; Phelps, The Still Hour; Haven, and Bickersteth, on Prayer; Prayer for Colleges; Cox, in Expositor, 1877 : chap. 3; Faunce, Prayer as a Theory and a Fact; Trumbull, Prayer, Its Nature and Scope.

C. If asked whether this relation between prayer and its providential answer can be scientifically tested, we reply that it may be tested just as a father's love may be tested by a dutiful son.

(a) There is a general proof of it in the past experience of the Christian and in the past history of the church.

Ps. 116 : 1-8—"I love Jehovah because he heareth my voice and my supplications." Luther prays for the dying Melanchthon, and he recovers. George Müller trusts to prayer, and builds his great orphan-houses. For a multitude of instances, see Prime, Answers to Prayer. Charles H. Spurgeon : " If there is any fact that is proved, it is that God hears prayer. If there is any scientific statement that is capable of mathematical proof, this is." Mr. Spurgeon's language is rhetorical : he means simply that God's answers to prayer remove all reasonable doubt. Adoniram Judson : " I never was deeply interested in any object, I never prayed sincerely and earnestly for anything, but it came ; at some time — no matter at how distant a day — somehow, in some shape, probably the last I should have devised — it came. And yet I have always had so little faith ! May God forgive me, and while he condescends to use me as his instrument, wipe the sin of unbelief from my heart ! "

(b) In condescension to human blindness, God may sometimes submit to a formal test of his faithfulness and power,— as in the case of Elijah and the priests of Baal.

Is. 7 : 10-13 — Ahaz is rebuked for not asking a sign, — in him it indicated unbelief. 1 K. 18 : 36-38 — Elijah said, " let it be known this day that thou art God in Israel. . . . Then the fire of Jehovah fell, and consumed the burnt offering." Romaine speaks of " a year famous for believing." Mat. 21 : 21, 22 — " even if ye shall say unto this mountain, Be thou taken up and cast into the sea, it shall be done. And all things, whatsoever ye shall ask in prayer, believing, ye shall receive." " Impossible ? " said Napoleon ; " then it shall be done ! " Arthur Hallam, quoted in Tennyson's Life, 1 : 44 — " With respect to prayer, you ask how I am to distinguish the operations of God in me from the motions of my own heart. Why should you distinguish them, or how do you know that there is any distinction ? Is God less God because he acts by general laws when he deals with the common elements of nature? " " Watch in prayer to see what cometh. Foolish boys that knock at a door in wantonness, will not stay till somebody open to them; but a man that hath business will knock, and knock again, till he gets his answer."

Martineau, Seat of Authority, 102, 103 — " God is not beyond nature simply,— he is within it. In nature and in mind we must find the action of his power. There is no need of his being a third factor over and above the life of nature and the life of man." Hartley Coleridge : " Be not afraid to pray,— to pray is right. Pray if thou canst with hope, but ever pray, Though hope be weak, or sick with long delay ; Pray in the darkness, if there be no light. Far is the time, remote from human sight, When war and discord on the earth shall cease ; Yet every prayer for universal peace Avails the blessed time to expedite. Whate'er is good to wish, ask that of heaven, Though it be what thou canst not hope to see ; Pray to be perfect, though the material leaven Forbid the spirit so on earth to be ; But if for any wish thou dar'st not pray, Then pray to God to cast that wish away."

(c) When proof sufficient to convince the candid inquirer has been already given, it may not consist with the divine majesty to abide a test imposed by mere curiosity or scepticism,— as in the case of the Jews who sought a sign from heaven.

Mat. 12 : 39 —"An evil and adulterous generation seeketh after a sign; and there shall no sign be given to it but the sign of Jonah the prophet." Tyndall's prayer-gauge would ensure a conflict of prayers. Since our present life is a moral probation, delay in the answer to our prayers, and even the denial of specific things for which we pray, may be only signs of God's faithfulness and love. George Müller : " I myself have been bringing certain requests before God now for seventeen years and six months, and never a day has passed without my praying concerning them all this time ; yet the full answer has not come up to the present. But I look for it; I confidently expect it." Christ's prayer, " let this cup pass away from me " (Mat. 26 : 39), and Paul's prayer that the "thorn in the flesh " might depart from him (2 Cor. 12 : 7, 8), were not answered in the precise way requested. No more are our prayers always answered in the way we expect. Christ's prayer was not answered by the literal removing of the cup, because the drinking of the cup was really his glory ; and Paul's prayer was not answered by the literal removal of the thorn, because the thorn was needful for his own perfecting. In the case of both Jesus and Paul, there were larger interests to be consulted than their own freedom from suffering.

(d) Since God's will is the link between prayer and its answer, there can be no such thing as a physical demonstration of its efficacy in any proposed case. Physical tests have no application to things into which free will enters as a constitutive element. But there are moral tests, and moral tests are as scientific as physical tests can be.

Diman, Theistic Argument, 576, alludes to Goldwin Smith's denial that any scientific method can be applied to history because it would make man a necessary link in a chain of cause and effect and so would deny his free will. But Diman says this is no more impossible than the development of the individual according to a fixed law of growth, while yet free will is sedulously respected. Froude says history is not a science, because no science could foretell Mohammedanism or Buddhism ; and Goldwin Smith says that "prediction is the crown of all science." But, as Diman remarks: "geometry, geology, physiology, are sciences, yet they do not predict." Buckle brought history into contempt by asserting that it could be analyzed and referred solely to intellectual laws and forces. To all this we reply that there may be scientific tests which are not physical, or even intellectual, but only moral. Such a test God urges his people to use, in Mal. 3 : 10 —"Bring ye the whole tithe into the storehouse . . . . and prove me now herewith, if I will not open you the windows of heaven, and pour you out a blessing, that there shall not be room enough to receive it." All such prayer is a reflection of Christ's words — some fragment of his teaching transformed into a supplication (John 15 : 7 ; see Westcott, Bib. Com., in loco) ; all such prayer is moreover the work of the Spirit of God (Rom. 8 : 26, 27). It is therefore sure of an answer.

But the test of prayer proposed by Tyndall is not applicable to the thing to be tested by it. Hopkins, Prayer and the Prayer-gauge, 22 sq. — " We cannot measure wheat by the yard, or the weight of a discourse with a pair of scales. . . . . God's wisdom might see that it was not best for the petitioners, nor for the objects of their petition, to grant their request. Christians therefore could not, without special divine authorization, rest their faith upon the results of such a test. . . . Why may we not ask for great changes in nature ? For the same reason that a well-informed child does not ask for the moon as a plaything. . . . There are two limitations upon prayer. First, except by special direction of God, we cannot ask for a miracle, for the same reason that a child could not ask his father to burn the house down. Nature is the house we live in. Secondly, we cannot ask for anything under the laws of nature which would contravene the object of those laws. Whatever we can do for ourselves under these laws, God expects us to do. If the child is cold, let him go near the fire, — not beg his father to carry him."

Herbert Spencer's Sociology is only social physics. He denies freedom, and declares anyone who will affix D. V. to the announcement of the Mildmay Conference to be incapable of understanding sociology. Prevision excludes divine or human will. But Mr. Spencer intimates that the evils of natural selection may be modified by artificial selection. What is this but the interference of will ? And if man can interfere, cannot God do the same ? Yet the wise child will not expect the father to give everything he asks for. Nor will the father who loves his child give him the razor to play with, or stuff him with unwholesome sweets, simply because the child asks these things. If the engineer of the ocean steamer should give me permission to press the lever that sets all the machinery in motion, I should decline to use my power and should prefer to leave such matters to him, unless he first suggested it and showed me how. So the Holy Spirit " helpeth our infirmity; for we know not how to pray as we ought ; but the Spirit himself maketh intercession for us with groanings which cannot be uttered " (Rom. 8 : 26). And we ought not to talk of "submitting" to perfect Wisdom, or of "being resigned" to perfect Love. Shakespeare, Antony and Cleopatra, 2 : 1 — "What they [the gods] do delay, they do not deny. . . . We, ignorant of ourselves, Beg often our own harms, which the wise powers Deny us for our good ; so find we profit By losing of our prayers." See Thornton, Old-Fashioned Ethics, 286–297. *Per contra*, see Galton, Inquiries into Human Faculty, 277–294.

3. *To Christian activity.*

Here the truth lies between the two extremes of quietism and naturalism.

(*a*) In opposition to the false abnegation of human reason and will which quietism demands, we hold that God guides us, not by continual miracle, but by his natural providence and the energizing of our faculties by his Spirit, so that we rationally and freely do our own work, and work out our own salvation.

Upham, Interior Life, 356, defines quietism as "cessation of wandering thoughts and discursive imaginations, rest from irregular desires and affections, and perfect submission of the will." Its advocates, however, have often spoken of it as a giving up of our will and reason, and a swallowing up of these in the wisdom and will of God. This phraseology is misleading, and savors of a pantheistic merging of man in God. Dorner : "Quietism makes God a monarch without living subjects." Certain English quietists, like the Mohammedans, will not employ physicians in sickness. They quote 2 Chron. 16 : 12, 13 — Asa "sought not to Jehovah, but to the physicians. And Asa slept with his fathers." They forget that the "physicians" alluded to in Chronicles were probably heathen necromancers. Cromwell to his Ironsides : "Trust God, and keep your powder dry ! "

Providence does not exclude. but rather implies the operation of natural law, by which we mean God's regular way of working. It leaves no excuse for the sarcasm of Robert Browning's Mr. Sludge the Medium, 233 — "Saved your precious self from what befell The thirty-three whom Providence forgot." Schurman, Belief in God, 213 — "The temples were hung with the votive offerings of those only who had *escaped* drowning." "So like Provvy ! " Bentham used to say, when anything particularly unseemly occurred in the way of natural catastrophe. God reveals himself in natural law. Physicians and medicine are his methods, as well as the impartation of faith and courage to the patient. The advocates of faith-cure should provide by faith that no believing Christian should die. With the apostolic miracles should go inspiration, as Edward Irving declared. " Every man is as lazy as circumstances will admit." We throw upon the shoulders of Providence the burdens which belong to us to bear. "Work out your own salvation with fear and trembling ; for it is God who worketh in you both to will and to work, for his good pleasure " (Phil. 2 : 12, 13).

Prayer without the use of means is an insult to God. "If God has decreed that you should live, what is the use of your eating or drinking ? " Can a drowning man refuse to swim, or even to lay hold of the rope that is thrown to him, and yet ask God to save him on account of his faith ? "Tie your camel," said Mohammed, "and commit it to God." Frederick Douglas used to say that when in slavery he often prayed for freedom, but his prayer was never answered till he prayed with his feet — and ran away. Whitney, Integrity of Christian Science, 68 — "The existence of the dynamo at the power-house does not make unnecessary the trolley line, nor the secondary motor, nor the conductor's application of the power. True quietism is a resting in the Lord after we have done our part." Ps. 37 : 7 — "Rest in Jehovah, and wait patiently for him " ; Is. 57 : 2 — "He entereth into peace ; they rest in their beds, each one that walketh in his uprightness." Ian Maclaren, Cure of Souls, 147 — "Religion has three places of abode : in the reason, which is theology ; in the conscience, which is ethics ; and in the heart, which is quietism." On the self-guidance of Christ, see Adamson, The Mind in Christ, 202–232.

George Müller, writing about ascertaining the will of God, says : "I seek at the beginning to get my heart into such a state that it has no will of its own in regard to a given matter. Nine tenths of the difficulties are overcome when our hearts are ready to do the Lord's will, whatever it may be. Having done this, I do not leave the result to feeling or simple impression. If I do so, I make myself liable to a great delusion. I seek the will of the Spirit of God through, or in connection with, the Word of God. The Spirit and the Word must be combined. If I look to the Spirit alone, with, out the Word, I lay myself open to great delusions also. If the Holy Ghost guides us at all, he will do it according to the Scriptures, and never contrary to them. Next I take into account providential circumstances. These often plainly indicate God's will in connection with his Word and his Spirit. I ask God in prayer to reveal to me his will aright. Thus through prayer to God, the study of the Word, and reflection, I come to a deliberate judgment according to the best of my knowledge and ability, and, if my mind is thus at peace, I proceed accordingly."

We must not confound rational piety with false enthusiasm. See Isaac Taylor, Natural History of Enthusiasm. "Not quiescence, but acquiescence, is demanded of us." As God feeds "the birds of the heaven" (Mat. 6:26), not by dropping food from heaven into their mouths, but by stimulating them to seek food for themselves, so God provides for his rational creatures by giving them a sanctified common sense and by leading them to use it. In a true sense Christianity gives us more will than ever. The Holy Spirit emancipates the will, sets it upon proper objects, and fills it with new energy. We are therefore not to surrender ourselves passively to whatever professes to be a divine suggestion; 1 John 4:1 — "believe not every spirit, but prove the spirits, whether they are of God." The test is the revealed word of God : Is. 8:20 — "To the law and to the testimony! if they speak not according to this word, surely there is no morning for them." See remarks on false Mysticism, pages 32, 33.

(b) In opposition to naturalism, we hold that God is continually near the human spirit by his providential working, and that this providential working is so adjusted to the Christian's nature and necessities as to furnish instruction with regard to duty, discipline of religious character, and needed help and comfort in trial.

In interpreting God's providences, as in interpreting Scripture, we are dependent upon the Holy Spirit. The work of the Spirit is, indeed, in great part an application of Scripture truth to present circumstances. While we never allow ourselves to act blindly and irrationally, but accustom ourselves to weigh evidence with regard to duty, we are to expect, as the gift of the Spirit, an understanding of circumstances—a fine sense of God's providential purposes with regard to us, which will make our true course plain to ourselves, although we may not always be able to explain it to others.

The Christian may have a continual divine guidance. Unlike the unfaithful and unbelieving, of whom it is said, in Ps. 106:13, "They waited not for his counsel," the true believer has wisdom given him from above. Ps. 32:8 — "I will instruct thee and teach thee in the way which thou shalt go"; Prov. 3:6 — "In all thy ways acknowledge him, And he will direct thy paths"; Phil. 1:9 — "And this I pray, that your love may abound yet more and more in knowledge and all discernment " (αἰσθήσει = spiritual discernment) ; James 1:5 — "if any of you lacketh wisdom, let him ask of God, who giveth (τοῦ διδόντος Θεοῦ) to all liberally and upbraideth not " ; John 15:15 — "No longer do I call you servants; for the servant knoweth not what his lord doeth : but I have called you friends " ; Col. 1:9, 10 — "that ye may be filled with the knowledge of his will in all spiritual wisdom and understanding, to walk worthily of the Lord unto all pleasing."

God's Spirit makes Providence as well as the Bible personal to us. From every page of nature, as well as of the Bible, the living God speaks to us. Tholuck: "The more we recognize in every daily occurrence God's secret inspiration, guiding and controlling us, the more will all which to others wears a common and every-day aspect prove to us a sign and a wondrous work." Hutton, Essays: "Animals that are blind slaves of impulse, driven about by forces from within, have so to say fewer valves in their moral constitution for the entrance of divine guidance. But minds alive to every word of God give constant opportunity for his interference with suggestions that may alter the course of their lives. The higher the mind, the more it glides into the region of providential control. God turns the good by the slightest breath of thought." So the Christian hymn, "Guide me, O thou great Jehovah!" likens God's leading of the believer to that of Israel by the pillar of fire and cloud ; and Paul in his dungeon calls himself "the prisoner of Christ Jesus" (Eph. 3:1). Affliction is the discipline of God's providence. Greek proverb: "He who does not get thrashed, does not get educated." On God's Leadings see A. H. Strong, Philosophy and Religion, 560-562.

Abraham "went out, not knowing whither he went" (Heb. 11:8). Not till he reached Canaan did he know the place of his destination. Like a child he placed his hand in the hand of his unseen Father, to be led whither he himself knew not. We often have guidance without discernment of that guidance. Is. 42:16 — "I will bring the blind by a way that they know not; in paths that they know not will I lead them." So we act more wisely than we ourselves understand, and afterwards look back with astonishment to see what we have been able to accomplish. Emerson: "Himself from God he could not free; He builded better than he knew." Disappointments? Ah, you make a mistake in the spelling; the D should be an H: His appointments. Melanchthon: "Quem poetæ fortunam, nos Deum appellamus." Chinese proverb: "The good God never smites with both hands." "Tact is a sort of psychical automatism" (Ladd). There is a Christian tact which is rarely at fault, because its possessor is "led by the Spirit of God" (Rom. 8:14). Yet we must always make allowance, as Oliver Cromwell used to say, "for the possibility of being mistaken.'

When Luther's friends wrote despairingly of the negotiations at the Diet of Worms, he replied from Coburg that he had been looking up at the night sky, spangled and studded with stars, and had found no pillars to hold them up. And yet they did not fall. God needs no props for his stars and planets. He hangs them on nothing. So, in the working of God's providence, the unseen is prop enough for the seen. Henry Drummond, Life, 127 — "To find out God's will: 1. Pray. 2. Think. 3. Talk to wise people, but do not regard their decision as final. 4. Beware of the bias of your own will, but do not be too much afraid of it (God never unnecessarily thwarts a man's nature and likings, and it is a mistake to think that his will is always in the line of the disagreeable). 5. Meantime, do the next thing (for doing God's will in small things is the best preparation for knowing it in great things). 6. When decision and action are necessary, go ahead. 7. Never reconsider the decision when it is finally acted on; and 8. You will probably not find out until afterwards, perhaps long afterwards, that you have been led at all."

Amiel lamented that everything was left to his own responsibility and declared: "It is this thought that disgusts me with the government of my own life. To win true peace, a man needs to feel himself directed, pardoned and sustained by a supreme Power, to feel himself in the right road, at the point where God would have him be, — in harmony with God and the universe. This faith gives strength and calm. I have not got it. All that is seems to me arbitrary and fortuitous." How much better is Wordsworth's faith, Excursion, book 4:581 — "One adequate support For the calamities of mortal life Exists, one only: an assured belief That the procession of our fate, howe'er Sad or disturbed, is ordered by a Being Of infinite benevolence and power, Whose everlasting purposes embrace All accidents, converting them to good." Mrs. Browning, De Profundis, stanza xxiii — "I praise thee while my days go on; I love thee while my days go on! Through dark and dearth, through fire and frost, With emptied arms and treasure lost, I thank thee while my days go on!"

4. *To the evil acts of free agents.*

(*a*) Here we must distinguish between the natural agency and the moral agency of God, or between acts of permissive providence and acts of efficient causation. We are ever to remember that God neither works evil, nor causes his creatures to work evil. All sin is chargeable to the self-will and perversity of the creature; to declare God the author of it is the greatest of blasphemies.

Bp. Wordsworth: "God *foresees* evil deeds, but never *forces* them." "God does not cause sin, any more than the rider of a limping horse causes the limping." Nor can it be said that Satan is the author of man's sin. Man's powers are his own. Not Satan, but the man himself, gives the wrong application to these powers. Not the cause, but the occasion, of sin is in the tempter; the cause is in the evil will which yields to his persuasions.

(*b*) But while man makes up his evil decision independently of God, God does, by his natural agency, order the method in which this inward evil shall express itself, by limiting it in time, place, and measure, or by guiding it to the end which his wisdom and love, and not man's intent, has set. In all this, however, God only allows sin to develop itself after its own nature, so that it may be known, abhorred, and if possible overcome and forsaken.

Philippi, Glaubenslehre, 2: 272-284 — "Judas's treachery works the reconciliation of the world, and Israel's apostasy the salvation of the Gentiles. . . . . God smooths the path of the sinner, and gives him chance for the outbreak of the evil, like a wise physician who draws to the surface of the body the disease that has been raging within, in order that it may be cured, if possible, by mild means, or, if not, may be removed by the knife."

Christianity rises in spite of, nay, in consequence of opposition, like a kite against the wind. When Christ has used the sword with which he has girded himself, as he used Cyrus and the Assyrian, he breaks it and throws it away. He turns the world upside down that he may get it right side up. He makes use of every member of society, as the locomotive uses every cog. The sufferings of the martyrs add to the number of the church; the worship of relics stimulates the Crusades; the worship of the saints leads to miracle plays and to the modern drama; the worship of images helps modern art; monasticism, scholasticism, the Papacy, even sceptical and destructive criticism stir up defenders of the faith. Shakespeare, Richard III, 5:1 — "Thus doth he force the swords of wicked men To turn their own points on their masters' bosoms"; Hamlet, 1:2 — "Foul deeds will rise, though all the earth o'erwhelm them, to men's eyes"; Macbeth, 1:7 — "Even handed justice Commends the ingredients of the poisoned chalice To our own lips."

The Emperor of Germany went to Paris incognito and returned, thinking that no one had known of his absence. But at every step, going and coming, he was surrounded by detectives who saw that no harm came to him. The swallow drove again and again at the little struggling moth, but there was a plate glass window between them which neither one of them knew. Charles Darwin put his cheek against the plate glass of the cobra's cage, but could not keep himself from starting when the cobra struck. Tacitus, Annales, 14:5 — "Noctem sideribus illustrem, quasi convincendum ad scelus, dii praebuere" — "a night brilliant with stars, as if for the purpose of proving the crime, was granted by the gods." See F. A. Noble, Our Redemption, 59-76, on the self-registry and self-disclosure of sin, with quotation from Daniel Webster's speech in the case of Knapp at Salem: "It must be confessed. It will be confessed. There is no refuge from confession but suicide, and suicide is confession."

(c) In cases of persistent iniquity, God's providence still compels the sinner to accomplish the design with which he and all things have been created, namely, the manifestation of God's holiness. Even though he struggle against God's plan, yet he must by his very resistance serve it. His sin is made its own detector, judge, and tormentor. His character and doom are made a warning to others. Refusing to glorify God in his salvation, he is made to glorify God in his destruction.

Is. 10:5, 7 — "Ho Assyrian, the rod of mine anger, the staff in whose hand is mine indignation! . . . Howbeit, he meaneth not so." Charles Kingsley, Two Years Ago: "He [Treluddra] is one of those base natures, whom fact only lashes into greater fury, — a Pharaoh, whose heart the Lord himself can only harden" — here we would add the qualification: 'consistently with the limits which he has set to the operations of his grace.' Pharaoh's ordering the destruction of the Israelitish children (Ex. 1:16) was made the means of putting Moses under royal protection, of training him for his future work, and finally of rescuing the whole nation whose sons Pharaoh sought to destroy. So God brings good out of evil; see Tyler, Theology of Greek Poets, 28-35. Emerson: "My will fulfilled shall be, For in daylight as in dark My thunderbolt has eyes to see His way home to the mark." See also Edwards, Works, 4:300-312.

Col. 2:15 — "having stripped off from himself the principalities and the powers" — the hosts of evil spirits that swarmed upon him in their final onset — "he made a show of them openly, triumphing over them in it," i. e., in the cross, thus turning their evil into a means of good. Royce, Spirit of Modern Philosophy, 443, — "Love, seeking for absolute evil, is like an electric light engaged in searching for a shadow, — when Love gets there, the shadow has disappeared." But this means, not that all things are good, but that "all things work together r good " (Rom. 8 : 28) — God overruling for good that which in itself is only evil. John Wesley : "God buries his workmen, but carries on his work. " Sermon on " The Devil's Mistakes " : Satan thought he could overcome Christ in the wilderness, in the garden, on the cross. He triumphed when he cast Paul into prison. But the cross was to Christ a lifting up, that should draw all men to him (John 12 : 32), and Paul's imprisonment furnished his epistles to the New Testament.

"It is one of the wonders of divine love that even our blemishes and sins God will take when we truly repent of them and give them into his hands, and will in some way make them to be blessings. A friend once showed Ruskin a costly handkerchief on which a blot of ink had been made. 'Nothing can be done with that,' the friend said, thinking the handkerchief worthless and ruined now. Ruskin carried it away with him, and after a time sent it back to his friend. In a most skilful and artistic way, he had made a fine design in India ink, using the blot as its basis. Instead of being ruined, the handkerchief was made far more beautiful and valuable. So God takes the blots and stains upon our lives, the disfiguring blemishes, when we commit them to him, and by his marvellous grace changes them into marks of beauty. David's grievous sin was not only forgiven, but was made a transforming power in his life. Peter's pitiful fall became a step upward through his Lord's forgiveness and gentle dealing." So "men may rise on stepping stones Of their dead selves to higher things " (Tennyson, In Memoriam, I).

SECTION IV.—GOOD AND EVIL ANGELS.

As ministers of divine providence there is a class of finite beings, greater in intelligence and power than man in his present state, some of whom positively serve God's purpose by holiness and voluntary execution of his will, some negatively, by giving examples to the universe of defeated and punished rebellion, and by illustrating God's distinguishing grace in man's salvation.

The scholastic subtleties which encumbered this doctrine in the Middle Ages, and the exaggerated representations of the power of evil spirits which then prevailed, have led, by a natural reaction, to an undue depreciation of it in more recent times.

For scholastic discussions, see Thomas Aquinas, Summa (ed. Migne), 1 : 833–993. The scholastics debated the questions, how many angels could stand at once on the point of a needle (relation of angels to space) ; whether an angel could be in two places at the same time ; how great was the interval between the creation of angels and their fall ; whether the sin of the first angel caused the sin of the rest ; whether as many retained their integrity as fell ; whether our atmosphere is the place of punishment for fallen angels ; whether guardian-angels have charge of children from baptism, from birth, or while the infant is yet in the womb of the mother ; even the excrements of angels were subjects of discussion, for if there was "angels' food " (Ps. 78 : 25), and if angels ate (Gen. 18 : 8), it was argued that we must take the logical consequences.

Dante makes the creation of angels simultaneous with that of the universe at large. "The fall of the rebel angels he considers to have taken place within twenty seconds of their creation, and to have originated in the pride which made Lucifer unwilling to await the time prefixed by his Maker for enlightening him with perfect knowledge " — see Rossetti, Shadow of Dante, 14, 15. Milton, unlike Dante, puts the creation of angels ages before the creation of man. He tells us that Satan's first name in heaven is now lost. The sublime associations with which Milton surrounds the adversary diminish our abhorrence of the evil one. Satan has been called the hero of the Paradise Lost. Dante's representation is much more true to Scripture. But we must not go to the extreme of giving ludicrous designations to the devil. This indicates and causes scepticism as to his existence.

In mediæval times men's minds were weighed down by the terror of the spirit of evil. It was thought possible to sell one's soul to Satan, and such compacts were written with blood. Goethe represents Mephistopheles as saying to Faust: "I to thy service here agree to bind me, To run and never rest at call of thee; When *over yonder* thou shalt find me, Then thou shalt do as much for me." The cathedrals cultivated and perpetuated this superstition, by the figures of malignant demons which grinned from the gargoyles of their roofs and the capitals of their columns, and popular preaching exalted Satan to the rank of a rival god — a god more feared than was the true and living God. Satan was pictured as having horns and hoofs — an image of the sensual and bestial — which led Cuvier to remark that the adversary could not devour, because horns and hoofs indicated not a carnivorous but a ruminant quadruped.

But there is certainly a possibility that the ascending scale of created intelligences does not reach its topmost point in man. As the distance between man and the lowest forms of life is filled in with numberless gradations of being, so it is possible that between man and God there exist creatures of higher than human intelligence. This possibility is turned to certainty by the express declarations of Scripture. The doctrine is interwoven with the later as well as with the earlier books of revelation.

Quenstedt (Theol., 1:629) regards the existence of angels as antecedently probable, because there are no gaps in creation; nature does not proceed *per saltum.* As we have (1) beings purely corporeal, as stones; (2) beings partly corporeal and partly spiritual, as men: so we should expect in creation (3) beings wholly spiritual, as angels. Godet, in his Biblical Studies of the O. T., 1–29, suggests another series of gradations. As we have (1) vegetables = species without individuality; (2) animals = individuality in bondage to species; and (3) men = species overpowered by individuality: so we may expect (4) angels = individuality without species.

If souls live after death, there is certainly a class of disembodied spirits. It is not impossible that God may have *created* spirits without bodies. E. G. Robinson, Christian Theology, 110 — "The existence of lesser deities in all heathen mythologies, and the disposition of man everywhere to believe in beings superior to himself and inferior to the supreme God, is a presumptive argument in favor of their existence." Locke: "That there should be more species of intelligent creatures above us than there are of sensible and material below us, is probable to me from hence, that in all the visible and corporeal world we see no chasms and gaps." Foster, Christian Life and Theology, 193 — "A man may certainly believe in the existence of angels upon the testimony of one who claims to have come from the heavenly world, if he can believe in the Ornithorhyncus upon the testimony of travelers." Tennyson, Two Voices: "This truth within thy mind rehearse, That in a boundless universe Is boundless better, boundless worse. Think you this world of hopes and fears Could find no statelier than his peers In yonder hundred million spheres?"

The doctrine of angels affords a barrier against the false conception of this world as including the whole spiritual universe. Earth is only part of a larger organism. As Christianity has united Jew and Gentile, so hereafter will it blend our own and other orders of creation : Col. 2:10 — "who is the head of all principality and power " = Christ is the head of angels as well as of men ; Eph. 1:10 — "to sum up all things in Christ, the things in the heavens, and the things upon the earth." On Christ and Angels, see Robertson Smith in The Expositor, second series, vols. 1, 2, 3. On the general subject of angels, see also Whately, Good and Evil Angels; Twesten, transl. in Bib. Sac., 1:768, and 2:108; Philippi, Glaubenslehre, 2: 282-437, and 3:251-354; Birks, Difficulties of Belief, 78 *sq.* ; Scott, Existence of Evil Spirits; Herzog, Encyclopädie, arts.: Engel, Teufel; Jewett, Diabolology,—the Person and Kingdom of Satan ; Alexander, Demonic Possession.

I. SCRIPTURE STATEMENTS AND INTIMATIONS.

1. *As to the nature and attributes of angels.*

(a) They are created beings.

Ps. 148:2-5 — "Praise ye him, all his angels .... For he commanded, and they were created "; Col. 1:16 — "for in him were all things created .... whether thrones or dominions or principalities or powers"; *cf.* 1 Pet. 3:32 — "angels and authorities and powers." God alone is uncreated and eternal. This is implied in 1 Tim. 6:16 — "who only hath immortality"

(b) They are incorporeal beings.

In Heb. 1:14, where a single word is used to designate angels, they are described as "spirits" — "are they not all ministering spirits?" Men, with their twofold nature, material as well as immaterial, could not well be designated as "spirits." That their being characteristically "spirits" forbids us to regard angels as having a bodily organism, seems implied in Eph. 6:12 — "for our wrestling is not against flesh and blood, but against . . . . the spiritual hosts [or 'things'] of wickedness in the heavenly places"; cf. Eph. 1:3; 2:6. In Gen. 6:2, "sons of God" =, not angels, but descendants of Seth and worshipers of the true God (see Murphy, Com., in loco). In Ps. 78:25 (A. V.), "angels' food" = manna coming from heaven where angels dwell; better, however, read with Rev. Vers.: "bread of the mighty" — probably meaning angels, though the word "mighty" is nowhere else applied to them; possibly = "bread of princes or nobles," i. e., the finest, most delicate bread. Mat. 22:30 — "neither marry, nor are given in marriage, but are as angels in heaven" — and Luke 20:36 — "neither can they die any more: for they are equal unto the angels" — imply only that angels are without distinctions of sex. Saints are to be like angels, not as being incorporeal, but as not having the same sexual relations which they have here.

There are no "souls of angels," as there are "souls of men" (Rev. 18:13), and we may infer that angels have no bodies for souls to inhabit; see under Essential Elements of Human Nature. Nevius, Demon-Possession, 258, attributes to evil spirits an instinct or longing for a body to possess, even though it be the body of an inferior animal: "So in Scripture we have spirits represented as wandering about to seek rest in bodies, and asking permission to enter into swine" (Mat. 12:43; 8:31). Angels therefore, since they have no bodies, know nothing of growth, age, or death. Martensen, Christian Dogmatics, 133 — "It is precisely because the angels are only spirits, but not souls, that they cannot possess the same rich existence as man, whose soul is the point of union in which spirit and nature meet."

(c) They are personal — that is, intelligent and voluntary — agents.

2 Sam. 14:20 — "wise, according to the wisdom of an angel of God"; Luke 4:34 — "I know thee who thou art, the Holy One of God"; 2 Tim. 2:26 — "snare of the devil . . . . taken captive by him unto his will"; Rev. 22:9 — "See thou do it not" = exercise of will; Rev. 12:12 — "The devil is gone down unto you, having great wrath" = set purpose of evil.

(d) They are possessed of superhuman intelligence and power, yet an intelligence and power that has its fixed limits.

Mat. 24:36 — "of that day and hour knoweth no one, not even the angels of heaven" = their knowledge, though superhuman, is yet finite. 1 Pet. 1:12 — "which things angels desire to look into"; Ps. 103:20 — "angels . . . . mighty in strength"; 2 Thess. 1:7 — "the angels of his power"; 2 Pet. 2:11 — "angels, though greater [than men] in might and power"; Rev. 20:2, 10 — "laid hold on the dragon . . . . and bound him . . . . cast into the lake of fire." Compare Ps. 72:18 — "God . . . . Who only doeth wondrous things" = only God can perform miracles. Angels are imperfect compared with God (Job 4:18; 15:15; 25:5).

Power, rather than beauty or intelligence, is their striking characteristic. They are "principalities and powers" (Col. 1:16). They terrify those who behold them (Mat. 28:4). The rolling away of the stone from the sepulchre took strength. A wheel of granite, eight feet in diameter and one foot thick, rolling in a groove, would weigh more than four tons. Mason, Faith of the Gospel, 86 — "The spiritual might and burning indignation in the face of Stephen reminded the guilty Sanhedrin of an angelic vision." Even in their tenderest ministrations they strengthen (Luke 22:43; cf. Dan. 10:19). In 1 Tim. 6:15 — "King of kings and Lord of lords" — the words "kings" and "lords" (βασιλευόντων and κυριευόντων) may refer to angels. In the case of evil spirits especially, power seems the chief thing in mind, e. g., "the prince of this world," "the strong man armed," "the power of darkness," "rulers of the darkness of this world," "the great dragon," "all the power of the enemy," "all these things will I give thee," "deliver us from the evil one."

(e) They are an order of intelligences distinct from man and older than man.

Angels are distinct from man. 1 Cor. 6:3 — "we shall judge angels"; Heb. 1:14 — "Are they not all ministering spirits, sent forth to do service for the sake of them that shall inherit salvation?" They are not glorified human spirits; see Heb. 2:16 — "for verily not to angels doth he give help, but he giveth help to the seed of Abraham ", also 12 : 22, 24, where "the innumerable hosts of angels " are distinguished from "the church of the firstborn " and "the spirits of just men made perfect." In Rev. 22 : 9 — "I am a fellow-servant with thee " — "fellow-servant " intimates likeness to men, not in nature, but in service and subordination to God, the proper object of worship. Sunday School Times, Mch. 15, 1902 : 146 — "Angels are spoken of as greater in power and might than man, but that could be said of many a lower animal, or even of whirlwind and fire. Angels are never spoken of as a superior order of spiritual beings. We are to 'judge angels' (1 Cor. 6 : 3), and inferiors are not to judge superiors."

Angels are an order of intelligences older than man. The Fathers made the creation of angels simultaneous with the original calling into being of the elements, perhaps basing their opinion on the apocryphal Ecclesiasticus, 18 : 1 — "he that liveth eternally created all things together." In Job 38 : 7, the Hebrews parallelism makes "morning stars " = "sons of God," so that angels are spoken of as present at certain stages of God's creative work. The mention of "the serpent" in Gen. 3 : 1 implies the fall of Satan before the fall of man. We may infer that the creation of angels took place before the creation of man — the lower before the higher. In Gen. 2 : 1, "all the host of them," which God had created, may be intended to include angels. Man was the crowning work of creation, created after angels were created. Mason, Faith of the Gospel, 81 — " Angels were perhaps created before the material heavens and earth — a spiritual substratum in which the material things were planted, a preparatory creation to receive what was to follow. In the vision of Jacob they ascend first and descend after; their natural place is in the world below."

The constant representation of angels as personal beings in Scripture cannot be explained as a personification of abstract good and evil, in accommodation to Jewish superstitions, without wresting many narrative passages from their obvious sense ; implying on the part of Christ either dissimulation or ignorance as to an important point of doctrine ; and surrendering belief in the inspiration of the Old Testament from which these Jewish views of angelic beings were derived.

Jesus accommodated himself to the popular belief in respect at least to "Abraham's bosom " (Luke 16 : 22), and he confessed ignorance with regard to the time of the end (Mark 13 : 32); see Rush Rhees, Life of Jesus of Nazareth, 245-248. But in the former case his hearers probably understood him to speak figuratively and rhetorically, while in the latter case there was no teaching of the false but only limitation of knowledge with regard to the true. Our Lord did not hesitate to contradict Pharisaic belief in the efficacy of ceremonies, and Sadducean denial of resurrection and future life. The doctrine of angels had even stronger hold upon the popular mind than had these errors of the Pharisees and Sadducees. That Jesus did not correct or deny the general belief, but rather himself expressed and confirmed it, implies that the belief was rational and Scriptural. For one of the best statements of the argument for the existence of evil spirits, see Broadus, Com. on Mat. 8 : 28.

Eph. 3 : 10 — "to the intent that now unto the principalities and the powers in the heavenly places might be made known through the church the manifold wisdom of God " — excludes the hypothesis that angels are simply abstract conceptions of good or evil. We speak of "moon-struck" people (lunatics), only when we know that nobody supposes us to believe in the power of the moon to cause madness. But Christ's contemporaries *did* suppose him to believe in angelic spirits, good and evil. If this belief was an error, it was by no means a harmless one, and the benevolence as well as the veracity of Christ would have led him to correct it. So too, if Paul had known that there were no such beings as angels, he could not honestly have contented himself with forbidding the Colossians to worship them (Col. 2 : 18). but would have denied their existence, as he denied the existence of heathen gods (1 Cor. 8 : 4).

Theodore Parker said it was very evident that Jesus Christ believed in a personal devil. Harnack, Wesen des Christenthums, 35 — " There can be no doubt that Jesus shared with his contemporaries the representation of two kingdoms, the kingdom of God and the kingdom of the devil." Wendt, Teaching of Jesus, 1 : 164 — Jesus "makes it appear as if Satan was the immediate tempter. I am far from thinking that he does so in a merely figurative way. Beyond all doubt Jesus accepted the contemporary ideas as to the real existence of Satan, and accordingly, in the particular cases of disease referred to, he supposes a real Satanic temptation." Maurice, Theological Essays,

82, 34 —" The acknowledgment of an evil spirit is characteristic of Christianity." H. B. Smith, System, 261 —"It would appear that the power of Satan in the world reached its culminating point at the time of Christ, and has been less ever since."

The same remark applies to the view which regards Satan as but a collective term for all evil beings, human or superhuman. The Scripture representations of the progressive rage of the great adversary, from his first assault on human virtue in Genesis to his final overthrow in Revelation, join with the testimony of Christ just mentioned, to forbid any other conclusion than this, that there is a personal being of great power, who carries on organized opposition to the divine government.

Crane, The Religion of To-morrow, 299 *sq.*— " We well say ' personal devil,' for there is no devil but personality." We cannot deny the personality of Satan except upon principles which would compel us to deny the existence of good angels, the personality of the Holy Spirit, and the personality of God the Father, — we may add, even the personality of the human soul. Says Nigel Penruddock in Lord Beaconsfield's " Endym. ion ": " Give me a single argument against his [Satan's] personality, which is not applicable to the personality of the Deity." One of the most ingenious devices of Satan is that of persuading men that he has no existence. Next to this is the device of substituting for belief in a personal devil the belief in a merely impersonal spirit of evil. Such a substitution we find in Pfleiderer, Philosophy of Religion, 1 : 311 — "The idea of the devil was a welcome expedient for the need of advanced religious reflection, to put God out of relation to the evil and badness of the world." Pfleiderer tells us that the early optimism of the Hebrews, like that of the Greeks, gave place in later times to pessimism and despair. But the Hebrews still had hope of deliverance by the Messiah and an apocalyptic reign of good.

For the view that Satan is merely a collective term for all evil beings, see Bushnell, Nature and the Supernatural, 134-137. Bushnell, holding moral evil to be a necessary " condition privative " of all finite beings as such, believes that "good angels have all been passed through and helped up out of a fall, as the redeemed of mankind will be." "Elect angels" (1 Tim. 5 : 21) then would mean those saved *after* falling, not those saved *from* falling ; and "Satan" would be, not the name of a particular person, but the all or total of all bad minds and powers. *Per contra*, see Smith's Bible Dictionary, arts.: Angels, Demons, Demoniacs, Satan ; Trench, Studies in the Gospels, 16-26. For a comparison of Satan in the Book of Job, with Milton's Satan in " Paradise Lost," and Goethe's Mephistopheles in " Faust," see Masson, The Three Devils. We may add to this list Dante's Satan (or Dis) in the "Divine Comedy," Byron's Lucifer in " Cain," and Mrs. Browning's Lucifer in her " Drama of Exile"; see Gregory, Christian Ethics, 219.

2. *As to their number and organization.*

(*a*) They are of great multitude.

Deut. 33 : 2 — "Jehovah .... came from the ten thousands of holy ones " ; Ps. 68 : 17 — "The chariots of God are twenty thousand, even thousands upon thousands " ; Dan. 7 : 10 — "thousands of thousands ministered unto him, and ten thousand times ten thousand stood before him " ; Rev. 5 : 11 — "I heard a voice of many angels . . . . and the number of them was ten thousand times ten thousand, and thousands of thousands." Anselm thought that the number of lost angels was filled up by the number of elect men. Savage, Life after Death, 61 — The Pharisees held very exaggerated notions of the number of angelic spirits. They " said that a man, if he threw a stone over his shoulder or cast away a broken piece of pottery, asked pardon of any spirit that he might possibly have hit in so doing." So in W. H. H. Murray's time it was said to be dangerous in the Adirondack to fire a gun, — you might hit a man.

(*b*) They constitute a company, as distinguished from a race.

Mat. 22 : 30 — "they neither marry, nor are given in marriage, but are as angels in heaven " ; Luke 20 : 36 — " neither can they die any more : for they are equal unto the angels ; and are sons of God." We are called " sons of men," but angels are never called "sons of angels," but only "sons of God." They are not developed from one original stock, and no such common nature binds them together as binds together the race of man. They have no common character and history. Each was created separately, and each apostate angel fell by himself. Humanity fell all at once in its first father. Cut down a tree, and you cut down its branches. But angels were so many separate trees. Some lapsed into sin, but some remained holy. See Godet. Bib. Studies O. T., 1–29. This may be one reason why salvation was provided for fallen man, but not for fallen angels. Christ could join himself to humanity by taking the common nature of all. There was no common nature of angels which he could take. See Heb. 2:16—"not to angels doth he give help." The angels are "sons of God," as having no earthly parentage and no parentage at all except the divine. Eph. 3:14, 15—"the Father, of whom every fatherhood in heaven and on earth is named,"—not "every family," as in R. V., for there are no families among the angels. The marginal rendering "fatherhood" is better than "family,"—all the πατριαί are named from the πατήρ. Dodge, Christian Theology, 172—"The bond between angels is simply a mental and moral one. They can gain nothing by inheritance, nothing through domestic and family life, nothing through a society held together by a bond of blood. . . . Belonging to two worlds and not simply to one, the human soul has in it the springs of a deeper and wider experience than angels can have. . . . God comes nearer to man than to his angels." Newman Smyth, Through Science to Faith, 191— "In the resurrection life of man, the species has died; man the individual lives on. Sex shall be no more needed for the sake of life; they shall no more marry, but men and women, the children of marriage, shall be as the angels. Through the death of the human species shall be gained, as the consummation of all, the immortality of the individuals."

(c) They are of various ranks and endowments.

Col. 1:16—"thrones or dominions or principalities or powers"; 1 Thess. 4:16—"the voice of the archangel"; Jude 9—"Michael the archangel." Michael (= who is like God?) is the only one expressly called an archangel in Scripture, although Gabriel (= God's hero) has been called an archangel by Milton. In Scripture, Michael seems the messenger of law and judgment; Gabriel, the messenger of mercy and promise. The fact that Scripture has but one archangel is proof that its doctrine of angels was not, as has sometimes been charged, derived from Babylonian and Persian sources; for there we find seven archangels instead of one. There, moreover, we find the evil spirit enthroned as a god, while in Scripture he is represented as a trembling slave.

Wendt, Teaching of Jesus, 1:51—"The devout and trustful consciousness of the immediate nearness of God, which is expressed in so many beautiful utterances of the Psalmist, appears to be supplanted in later Judaism by a belief in angels, which is closely analogous to the superstitious belief in the saints on the part of the Romish church. It is very significant that the Jews in the time of Jesus could no longer conceive of the promulgation of the law on Sinai, which was to them the foundation of their whole religion, as an immediate revelation of Jehovah to Moses, except as instituted through the mediation of angels (Acts 7:38, 53; Gal. 3:19; Heb. 2:2; Josephus, Ant.′ 15:5, 3).

(d) They have an organization.

1 Sam. 1:11—"Jehovah of hosts"; 1 K. 22:19—"Jehovah sitting on his throne, and all the host of heaven standing by him on his right hand and on his left"; Mat. 26:53—"twelve legions of angels"—suggests the organization of the Roman army; 25:41—"the devil and his angels"; Eph. 2:2—"the prince of the powers in the air"; Rev. 2:13—"Satan's throne" (not "seat"); 16:10—"throne of the beast"—"a hellish parody of the heavenly kingdom" (Trench). The phrase "host of heaven," in Deut. 4:19; 17:3; Acts 7:42, probably = the stars; but in Gen. 32:2, "God's host" = angels, for when Jacob saw the angels he said "This is God's host." In general the phrases "God of hosts", "Lord of hosts" seem to mean "God of angels", "Lord of angels": compare 2 Chron. 18:18; Luke 2:13; Rev. 19:14 —"the armies which are in heaven." Yet in Neh. 9:6 and Ps. 33:6 the word "host" seems to include both angels and stars.

Satan is "the ape of God." He has a throne. He is "the prince of the world" (John 14:30; 16:11), "the prince of the powers of the air" (Eph. 2:2). There is a cosmos and order of evil, as well as a cosmos and order of good, though Christ is stronger than the strong man armed (Luke 11:21) and rules even over Satan. On Satan in the Old Testament, see art. by T. W. Chambers, in Presb. and Ref. Rev., Jan. 1892:22–34. The first mention of Satan is in the account of the Fall in Gen. 3:1–15; the second in Lev. 16:8, where one of the two goats on the day of atonement is said to be "for Azazel," or Satan; the third where Satan moved David to number Israel (1 Chron. 21:1); the fourth in the book of Job 1:6–12; the fifth in Zech. 3:1–3, where Satan stands as the adversary of Joshua the high priest, but Jehovah addresses Satan and rebukes him. Cheyne, Com. on Isaiah, vol. 1, p. 11, thinks that the stars were first called the hosts of God, with the notion that they were animated creatures. In later times the belief in angels threw into the background the belief in the stars as animated beings; the angels however were connected very closely with the stars. Marlowe, in his Tamburlaine, says: "The moon, the planets, and the meteors light, These angels in their crystal armor fight A doubtful battle."

With regard to the 'cherubim' of Genesis, Exodus, and Ezekiel, — with which the 'seraphim' of Isaiah and the 'living creatures' of the book of Revelation are to be identified, — the most probable interpretation is that which regards them, not as actual beings of higher rank than man, but as symbolic appearances, intended to represent redeemed humanity, endowed with all the creature perfections lost by the Fall, and made to be the dwelling-place of God.

Some have held that the cherubim are symbols of the divine attributes, or of God's government over nature; see Smith's Bib. Dict., art.: Cherub; Alford, Com. on Rev. 4: 6–8, and Hulsean Lectures, 1841: vol. 1, Lect. 2; Ebrard, Dogmatik, 1:278. But whatever of truth belongs to this view may be included in the doctrine stated above. The cherubim are indeed symbols of nature pervaded by the divine energy and subordinated to the divine purposes, but they are symbols of nature only because they are symbols of man in his twofold capacity of *image of God* and *priest of nature*. Man, as having a body, is a part of nature; as having a soul, he emerges from nature and gives to nature a voice. Through man, nature, otherwise blind and dead, is able to appreciate and to express the Creator's glory.

The doctrine of the cherubim embraces the following points: 1. The cherubim are not personal beings, but are artificial, temporary, symbolic figures. 2. While they are not themselves personal existences, they are symbols of personal existence — symbols not of divine or angelic perfections but of human nature (Ex. 1: 5 — "they had the likeness of a man"; Rev. 5: 9 — A. V. — "thou hast redeemed us to God by thy blood" — so read א, B, and Tregelles, the Eng. and Am. Rev. Vers., however, follow A and Tischendorf, and omit the word "us"). 3. They are emblems of human nature, not in its present stage of development, but possessed of all its original perfections; for this reason the most perfect animal forms — the kinglike courage of the lion, the patient service of the ox, the soaring insight of the eagle — are combined with that of man (Ez. 1 and 10; Rev. 4: 6–8). 4. These cherubic forms represent, not merely material or earthly perfections, but human nature spiritualized and sanctified. They are "living creatures" and their life is a holy life of obedience to the divine will (Ez. 1: 12 — "whither the spirit was to go, they went"). 5. They symbolize a human nature exalted to be the dwelling-place of God. Hence the inner curtains of the tabernacle were inwoven with cherubic figures, and God's glory was manifested on the mercy-seat between the cherubim (Ex. 37: 6–9). While the flaming sword at the gates of Eden was the symbol of justice, the cherubim were symbols of mercy — keeping the "way of the tree of life" for man, until by sacrifice and renewal Paradise should be regained (Gen. 3: 24).

In corroboration of this general view, note that angels and cherubim never go together; and that in the closing visions of the book of Revelation these symbolic forms are seen no longer. When redeemed humanity has entered heaven, the figures which typified that humanity, having served their purpose, finally disappear. For fuller elaboration, see A. H. Strong, The Nature and Purpose of the Cherubim, in Philosophy and Religion, 391–399: Fairbairn, Typology, 1: 185–208; Elliott, Horæ Apocalypticæ, 1: 87: Bib. Sac., 1876: 32–51; Bib. Com., 1: 49–52 — "The winged lions, eagles, and bulls, that guard the entrances of the palace of Nineveh, are worshipers rather than divinities." It has lately been shown that the winged bull of Assyria was called "Kerub" almost as far back as the time of Moses. The word appears in its Hebrew form 500 years before the Jews had any contact with the Persian dominion. The Jews did not derive it from any Aryan race. It belonged to their own language.

The variable form of the cherubim seems to prove that they are symbolic appearances rather than real beings. A parallel may be found in classical literature. In Horace, Carmina, 3: 11, 15, Cerberus has three heads; in 2: 13, 34, he has a hundred. Bréal Semantics suggests that the three heads may be dog-heads, while the hundred heads may be snake-heads. But Cerberus is also represented in Greece as having only one head. Cerberus must therefore be a symbol rather than an actually existing creature. M. W Congdon of Wyoming N. Y., held, however, that the cherubim are symbols of

God's life in the universe as a whole. Ez. 28 : 14-19 — "the anointed cherub that covereth" — the power of the King of Tyre was so all-pervading throughout his dominion, his sovereignty so absolute, and his decrees so instantly obeyed, that his rule resembled the divine government over the world. Mr. Congdon regarded the cherubim as a proof of monism. See Margoliouth, The Lord's Prayer, 159-180. On animal characteristics in man, see Hopkins, Scriptural Idea of Man, 105.

3. *As to their moral character.*

(a) They were all created holy.

Gen. 1 : 31 — "God saw everything that he had made, and, behold, it was very good"; Jude 6 — "angels that kept not their own beginning" — ἀρχήν seems here to mean their beginning in holy character, rather than their original lordship and dominion.

(b) They had a probation.

This we infer from 1 Tim. 5 : 21 — "the elect angels"; *cf.* 1 Pet. 1 : 1, 2 — "elect . . . . unto obedience." It certain angels, like certain men, are "elect . . . . unto obedience," it would seem to follow that there was a period of probation, during which their obedience or disobedience determined their future destiny; see Ellicott on 1 Tim. 5 : 21. Mason, Faith of the Gospel, 106-108 — " Gen. 3 : 14 — 'Because thou hast done this, cursed art thou ' — in the sentence on the serpent, seems to imply that Satan's day of grace was ended when he seduced man. Thenceforth he was driven to live on dust, to triumph only in sin, to pick up a living out of man, to possess man's body or soul, to tempt from the good."

(c) Some preserved their integrity.

Ps. 89 : 7 — "the council of the holy ones" — a designation of angels; Mark 8 : 38 — "the holy angels." Shakespeare, Macbeth, 4 : 3 — " Angels are bright still, though the brightest fell."

(d) Some fell from their state of innocence.

John 8 : 44 — "He was a murderer from the beginning, and standeth not in the truth, because there is no truth in him "; 2 Pet. 2 : 4 — "angels when they sinned "; Jude 6 — "angels who kept not their own beginning, but left their proper habitation." Shakespeare, Henry VIII, 3 : 2 — "Cromwell, I charge thee, fling away ambition; By that sin fell the angels; how can man then, The image of his Maker, hope to win by it? . . . . How wretched Is that poor man that hangs on princes' favors ! . . . . When he falls, he falls like Lucifer, Never to hope again."

(e) The good are confirmed in good.

Mat. 6 : 10 — "Thy will be done, as in heaven, so on earth "; 18 : 10 — "in heaven their angels do always behold the face of my Father who is in heaven "; 2 Cor. 11 : 14 — "an angel of light."

(f) The evil are confirmed in evil.

Mat. 13 : 19 — "the evil one "; 1 John 5 : 18, 19 — "the evil one toucheth him not . . . . the whole world lieth in the evil one "; *cf.* John 8 : 44 — "Ye are of your father the devil . . . . When he speaketh a lie, he speaketh of his own: or he is a liar, and the father thereof"; Mat. 6 : 13 — "deliver us from the evil one."

From these Scriptural statements we infer that all free creatures pass through a period of probation; that probation does not necessarily involve a fall; that there is possible a sinless development of moral beings. Other Scriptures seem to intimate that the revelation of God in Christ is an object of interest and wonder to other orders of intelligence than our own; that they are drawn in Christ more closely to God and to us; in short, that they are confirmed in their integrity by the cross. See 1 Pet. 1 : 12 — "which things angels desire to look into"; Eph. 3 : 10 — "that now unto the principalities and the powers in the heavenly places might be made known through the church the manifold wisdom of God "; Col. 1 : 20 — "through him to reconcile all things unto himself . . . . whether things upon the earth, or things in the heavens "; Eph. 1 : 10 — "to sum up all things in Christ, the things in the heavens, and the things upon the earth "=" the unification of the whole universe in Christ as the divine centre. . . . . The great system is a harp all whose strings are in tune but one, and that one jarring string makes discord throughout the whole. The whole universe shall feel the influence, and shall be reduced to harmony, when that one string, the world in which we live, shall be put in tune by the hand of love and mercy" — freely quoted from Leitch, God's Glory in the Heavens, 327-330.

It is not impossible that God is using this earth as a breeding-ground from which to populate the universe. Mark Hopkins, Life, 317 — " While there shall be gathered at last and preserved, as Paul says, a holy church, and every man shall be perfect and the church shall be spotless, ... there will be other forms of perfection in other departments of the universe. And when the great day of restitution shall come and God shall vindicate his government, there may be seen to be coming in from other departments of the universe a long procession of angelic forms, great white legions from Sirius, from Arcturus and the chambers of the South, gathering around the throne of God and that centre around which the universe revolves."

4. *As to their employments.*

A. The employments of good angels.

(*a*) They stand in the presence of God and worship him.

Ps. 29 : 1, 2 — "Ascribe unto Jehovah, O ye sons of the mighty, Ascribe unto Jehovah glory and strength. Ascribe unto Jehovah the glory due unto his name. Worship Jehovah in holy array " — Perowne: "Heaven being thought of as one great temple, and all the worshipers therein as clothed in priestly vestments." Ps. 89 : 7 — "a God very terrible in the council of the holy ones, " *i. e.*, angels — Perowne: "Angels are called an assembly or congregation, as the church above, which like the church below worships and praises God." Mat. 18 : 10 — "in heaven their angels do always behold the face of my Father who is in heaven." In apparent allusion to this text, Dante represents the saints as dwelling in the presence of God yet at the same time rendering humble service to their fellow men here upon the earth. Just in proportion to their nearness to God and the light they receive from him, is the influence they are able to exert over others.

(*b*) They rejoice in God's works.

Job 38 : 7 — "all the sons of God shouted for joy"; Luke 15 : 10 — "there is joy in the presence of the angels of God over one sinner that repenteth"; *cf.* 2 Tim. 2 : 25 — "if peradventure God may give them repentance." Dante represents the angels that are nearest to God, the infinite source of life, as ever advancing toward the spring-time of youth, so that the oldest angels are the youngest.

(*c*) They execute God's will, — by working in nature;

Ps. 103 : 20 — " Ye his angels . . . that fulfil his word, Hearkening unto the voice of his word;" 104 : 4 marg — "Who maketh his angels winds; His ministers a flaming fire," *i. e.*, lightnings. See Alford on Heb. 1 : 7 — "The order of the Hebrew words here [in Ps. 104 : 4] is not the same as in the former verses (see especially v. 3), where we have : ' Who maketh the clouds his chariot.' For this transposition, those who insist that the passage means 'he maketh winds his messengers can give no reason." Farrar on Heb. 1 : 7 — "He maketh his angels winds": "The Rabbis often refer to the fact that God makes his angels assume any form he pleases, whether man (Gen. 18 : 2) or woman (Zech 5 : 9 — "two women, and the wind was in their wings"), or wind or flame (Ex. 3 : 2 — "angel . . . in a flame of fire"; 2 K 6 : 17). But that untenable and fleeting form of existence which is the glory of the angels would be an inferiority in the Son. He could not be clothed, as they are at God's will, in the fleeting robes of material phenomena." John Henry Newman, in his Apologia, sees an angel in every flower. Mason, Faith of the Gospel, 82 — "Origen thought not a blade of grass nor a fly was without its angel. Rev. 14 : 18 — an angel 'that hath power over fire'; John 5 : 4 — intermittent spring under charge of an angel; Mat. 28 : 2 — descent of an angel caused earthquake on the morning of Christ's resurrection; Luke 13 : 11 — control of diseases is ascribed to angels."

(*d*) by guiding the affairs of nations;

Dan. 10 : 12, 13, 21 — "I come for thy words' sake. But the prince of the kingdom of Persia withstood me . . . Michael, one of the chief princes, came to help me . . . Michael your prince"; 11 : 1 — " And as for me, in the first year of Darius the Mede, I stood up to confirm and strengthen him "; 12 : 1 — " at that time shall Michael stand up, the great prince who standeth for the children of thy people." Mason, Faith of the Gospel, 87, suggests the question whether "the spirit of the age" or "the national character " in any particular case may not be due to the unseen "principalities" under which men live. Paul certainly recognizes, in Eph. 2 : 2, "the prince of the powers of the air, . . . the spirit that now worketh in the sons of disobedience." May not good angels be entrusted with influence over nations' affairs to counteract the evil and help the good?

(e) by watching over the interests of particular churches ;

1 Cor. 11 : 10 — " for this cause ought the women to have a sign of authority [*i. e.*, a veil] on her head, because of the angels " — who watch over the church and have care for its order.   Matheson, Spiritual Development of St. Paul, 242 — " Man's covering is woman's power.   Ministration *is* her power and it allies her with a greater than man — the angel.   Christianity is a feminine strength.   Judaism had made woman only a means to an end — the multiplication of the race.   So it had degraded her.   Paul will restore woman to her original and equal dignity."   Col. 2 : 18 — " Let no man rob you of your prize by a voluntary humility and worshiping of the angels " — a false worship which would be very natural if angels were present to guard the meetings of the saints.   1 Tim. 5 : 21 — " I charge thee in the sight of God, and Christ Jesus, and the elect angels, that thou observe these things " — the public duties of the Christian minister.

Alford regards " the angels of the seven churches " (Rev. 1 : 20) as superhuman beings appointed to represent and guard the churches, and that upon the grounds : (1) that the word is used elsewhere in the book of Revelation only in this sense ; and (2) that nothing in the book is addressed to a teacher individually, but all to some one who reflects the complexion and fortunes of the church as no human person could.   We prefer, however, to regard " the angels of the seven churches " as meaning simply the pastors of the seven churches.   The word " angel" means simply " messenger," and may be used of human as well as of superhuman beings — see Hag. 1 : 13 — " Haggai, Jehovah's messenger " — literally, " the angel of Jehovah."   The use of the word in this figurative sense would not be incongruous with the mystical character of the book of Revelation (see Bib. Sac. 12 : 339).   John Lightfoot, Heb. and Talmud. Exerc., 2 : 90, says that " angel " was a term designating officer or elder of a synagogue.   See also Bp. Lightfoot, Com. on Philippians, 187, 180 ; Jacobs, Eccl. Polity, 100 and note.   In the Irvingite church, accordingly, " angels " constitute an official class.

(*f*) by assisting and protecting individual believers ;

1 K. 19 : 5 — " an angel touched him [Elijah], and said unto him, Arise and eat " ; Ps. 91 : 11 — " he will give his angels charge over thee, To keep thee in all thy ways.   They shall bear thee up in their hands, Lest thou dash thy foot against a stone " ; Dan. 6 : 22 — " My God hath sent his angel, and hath shut the lions' mouths, and they have not hurt me " ; Mat. 4 : 11 —" angels came and ministered unto him " — Jesus was the type of all believers ; 18 : 10 — " despise not one of these little ones, for I say unto you, that in heaven their angels do always behold the face of my Father " ; compare verse 6 — " one of these little ones that believe on me " ; see Meyer, Com. *in loco*, who regards these passages as proving the doctrine of guardian angels.   Luke 16 : 22 — " the beggar died, and . . . . was carried away by the angels into Abraham's bosom " ; Heb. 1 : 14 — " Are they not all ministering spirits, sent forth to do service for the sake of them that shall inherit salvation ? "   Compare Acts 12 : 15 — " And they said, It is his angel " — of Peter standing knocking ; see Hackett, Com. *in loco* : the utterance " expresses a popular belief prevalent among the Jews, which is neither affirmed nor denied."   Shakespeare, Henry IV, 2nd part, 2 : 2 — " For the boy — there is a good angel about him."   *Per contra*, see Broadus, Com. on Mat. 18 : 10 — " It is simply said of believers as a class that there are angels which are ' their angels ' ; but there is nothing here or elsewhere to show that one angel has special charge of one believer."

(*g*) by punishing God's enemies.

2 K. 19 : 35 — " it came to pass that night, that the angel of Jehovah went forth. and smote in the camp of the Assyrians an hundred fourscore and five thousand " ; Acts 12 : 23 —" And immediately an angel of the Lord smote him, because he gave not God the glory : and he was eaten of worms, and gave up the ghost. "

A general survey of this Scripture testimony as to the employments of good angels leads us to the following conclusions :

First, — that good angels are not to be considered as the mediating agents of God's regular and common providence, but as the ministers of his special providence in the affairs of his church.   He ' maketh his angels winds ' and ' a flaming fire,' not in his ordinary procedure, but in connection with special displays of his power for moral ends (Deut. 33 : 2 ; Acts 7 : 53 ; Gal. 3 : 19 ; Heb. 2 : 2).   Their intervention is apparently occasional and exceptional — not at their own option, but only as it is permitted or commanded by God.   Hence we are not to conceive of angels as coming

between us and God, nor are we, without special revelation of the fact, to
attribute to them in any particular case the effects which the Scriptures
generally ascribe to divine providence.   Like miracles, therefore, angelic
appearances generally mark God's entrance upon new epochs in the unfolding of his plans.   Hence we read of angels at the completion of creation
(Job 38 : 7) ; at the giving of the law (Gal. 3 : 19) ; at the birth of Christ
(Luke 2 : 13) ; at the two temptations in the wilderness and in Gethsemane
(Mat. 4 : 11, Luke 22 : 43) ; at the resurrection (Mat. 28 : 2) ; at the ascen
sion (Acts 1 : 10) ; at the final judgment (Mat. 25 : 31).

The substance of these remarks may be found in Hodge, Systematic Theology, 1 : 637-
645. Milton tells us that "Millions of spiritual creatures walk the earth Unseen, both
when we wake and when we sleep." Whether this be true or not, it is a question of
interest why such angelic beings as have to do with human affairs are not at present
seen by men. Paul's admonition against the "worshiping of the angels" (Col. 2 : 18) seems to
suggest the reason. If men have not abstained from worshiping their fellow-men,
when these latter have been priests or media of divine communications, the danger of
idolatry would be much greater if we came into close and constant contact with angels;
see Rev. 22 : 8, 9 — "I fell down to worship before the feet of the angel which showed me these things. And he saith
unto me, See thou do it not."

The fact that we do not in our day see angels should not make us sceptical as to their
existence any more than the fact that we do not in our day see miracles should make
us doubt the reality of the New Testament miracles. As evil spirits were permitted to
work most actively when Christianity began its appeal to men, so good angels were then
most frequently recognized as executing the divine purposes. Nevius, Demon-Possession, 278, thinks that evil spirits are still at work where Christianity comes in conflict
with heathenism, and that they retire into the background as Christianity triumphs.
This may be true also of good angels. Otherwise we might be in danger of overestimat-
ing their greatness and authority. Father Taylor was right when he said : " Folks are
better than angels." It is vain to sing : "I want to be an angel." We never shall be
angels. Victor Hugo is wrong when he says: "I am the tadpole of an archangel."
John Smith is not an angel, and he never will be. But he may be far greater than an
angel, because Christ took, not the nature of angels, but the nature of man (Heb. 2 : 16).

As intimated above, there is no reason to believe that even the invisible presence of
angels is a constant one. Doddridge's dream of accident prevented by angelic interposition seems to embody the essential truth. We append the passages referred to in the
text. Job 38 : 7 — " When the morning stars sang together, And all the sons of God shouted for joy " ; Deut. 33 : 2 —
" Jehovah came from Sinai . . . . he came from the ten thousands of holy ones : At his right hand was a fiery law
for them " ; Gal. 3 : 19 — "it [the law] was ordained through angels by the hand of a mediator"; Heb. 2 : 2 —
" the word spoken through angels"; Acts 7 : 53 — "who received the law as it was ordained'by angels "; Luke 2 : 13 —
" suddenly there was with the angel a multitude of the heavenly host" ; Mat. 4 : 11 — "Then the devil leaveth him; and
behold, angels came and ministered unto him" ; Luke 22 : 43 — "And there appeared unto him an angel from heaven,
strengthening him" ; Mat. 28 : 2 — "an angel of the Lord descended from heaven, and came and rolled away the stone,
and sat upon it"; Acts 1 : 10 — "And while they were looking steadfastly into heaven as he went, behold, two men
stood by them in white apparel" ; Mat. 25 : 31 — "when the Son of man shall come in his glory, and all the angels with
him, then shall he sit on the throne of his glory."

Secondly, — that their power, as being in its nature dependent and derived,
is exercised in accordance with the laws of the spiritual and natural world.
They cannot, like God, create, perform miracles, act without means, search
the heart. Unlike the Holy Spirit, who can influence the human mind
directly, they can influence men only in ways analogous to those by which
men influence each other. As evil angels may tempt men to sin, so it is
probable that good angels may attract men to holiness.

Recent psychical researches disclose almost unlimited possibilities of influencing
other minds by suggestion. Slight physical phenomena, as the odor of a violet or the
sight in a book of a crumpled roseleaf, may start trains of thought which change the
whole course of a life. A word or a look may have great power over us. Fisher, Nature

and Method of Revelation, 276 — "The facts of hypnotism illustrate the possibility of one mind falling into a strange thraldom under another." If other men can so powerfully influence us, it is quite possible that spirits which are not subject to limitations of the flesh may influence us yet more.

Binet, in his Alterations of Personality, says that experiments on hysterical patients have produced in his mind the conviction that, in them at least, "a plurality of persons exists. . . . We have established almost with certainty that in such patients, side by side with the principal personality, there is a secondary personality, which is unknown by the first, which sees, hears, reflects, reasons and acts "; see Andover Review, April, 1890 : 422. Hudson, Law of Psychic Phenomena, 81–143, claims that we have two minds, the objective and conscious, and the subjective and unconscious. The latter works automatically upon suggestion from the objective or from other minds. In view of the facts referred to by Binet and Hudson, we claim that the influence of angelic spirits is no more incredible than is the influence of suggestion from living men. There is no need of attributing the phenomena of hypnotism to spirits of the dead. Our human nature is larger and more susceptible to spiritual influence than we have commonly believed. These psychical phenomena indeed furnish us with a corroboration of our Ethical Monism, for if in one human being there may be two or more consciousnesses, then in the one God there may be not only three infinite personalities but also multitudinous finite personalities. See T. H. Wright, The Finger of God, 124–133.

B.   The employments of evil angels.

(*a*) They oppose God and strive to defeat his will. This is indicated in the names applied to their chief. The word "Satan" means "adversary " — primarily to God, secondarily to men ; the term "devil" signifies "slanderer" — of God to men, and of men to God. It is indicated also in the description of the "man of sin" as "he that opposeth and exalteth himself against all that is called God."

Job 1 : 6 — Satan appears among "the sons of God"; Zech. 3 : 1 — "Joshua the high priest . . . . and Satan standing at his right hand to be his adversary "; Mat. 13 : 39 — "the enemy that sowed them is the devil"; 1 Pet. 5 : 8 — "your adversary the devil." Satan slanders God to men, in Gen. 3 : 4, 4 — "Yea, hath God said ? . . . . Ye shall not surely die "; men to God, in Job 1 : 9, 11 — "Doth Job fear God for naught ? . . . . put forth thy hand now, and touch all that he hath, and he will renounce thee to thy face "; 2 : 4, 5 — "Skin for skin, yea, all that a man hath will he give for his life. But put forth thine hand now, and touch his bone and his flesh, and he will renounce thee to thy face "; Rev. 12 : 10 — "the accuser of our brethren is cast down, who accuseth them before our God night and day."

Notice how, over against the evil spirit who thus accuses God to man and man to God, stands the Holy Spirit, the Advocate, who pleads God's cause with man and man's cause with God : John 16 : 8 — "he, when he is come, will convict the world in respect of sin, and of righteousness, and of judgment "; Rom. 8 : 26 — "the Spirit also helpeth our infirmity : for we know not how to pray as we ought ; but the Spirit himself maketh intercession for us with groanings which cannot be uttered." Hence Balaam can say : Num. 23 : 21, "He hath not beheld iniquity in Jacob, Neither hath he seen perverseness in Israel "; and the Lord can say to Satan as he resists Joshua : "Jehovah rebuke thee, O Satan ; yea, Jehovah that hath chosen Jerusalem rebuke thee " (Zech. 3 : 2). "Thus he puts himself between his people and every tongue that would accuse them " (C. H. M.). For the description of the "man of sin," see 2 Thess. 2 : 3, 4 — "he that opposeth "; *cf*. verse 9 — "whose coming is according to the working of Satan." On the "man of sin," see Wm. Arnold Stevens, in Bap. Quar. Rev., July, 1889 : 328–360. As in Daniel 11 : 36, the great enemy of the faith, he who "shall exalt himself, and magnify himself above every God", is the Syrian King, Antiochus Epiphanes, so the man of lawlessness described by Paul in 2 Thess. 2 : 3, 4 was "the corrupt and impious Judaism of the apostolic age." This only had its seat in the temple of God. It was doomed to destruction when the Lord should come at the fall of Jerusalem. But this fulfilment does not preclude a future and final fulfilment of the prophecy.

Contrasts between the Holy Spirit and the spirit of evil : 1. The dove, and the serpent : 2. the father of lies, and the Spirit of truth ; 3. men possessed by dumb spirits, and men given wonderful utterance in diverse tongues ; 4. the murderer from the beginning, and the life-giving Spirit, who regenerates the soul and quickens our mortal bodies ; 5. the adversary, and the Helper ; 6. the slanderer, and the Advocate ; 7. Satan's sifting, and the Master's winnowing ; 8. the organizing intelligence and malignity of the evil one, and the Holy Spirit's combination of all the forces of matter and mind to build up the kingdom of God; 9. the strong man fully armed, and a stronger than he; 10. the evil one who works only evil, and the holy One who is the author of holiness in the hearts of men. The opposition of evil angels, at first and ever since their fall, may be a reason why they are incapable of redemption.

(*b*) They hinder man's temporal and eternal welfare, — sometimes by exercising a certain control over natural phenomena, but more commonly by subjecting man's soul to temptation. Possession of man's being, either physical or spiritual, by demons, is also recognized in Scripture.

Control of natural phenomena is ascribed to evil spirits in Job 1 : 12, 16, 19 and 2 : 7 — " all that he hath is in thy power " — and Satan uses lightning, whirlwind, disease, for his purposes; Luke 13 : 11, 16 — " a woman that had a spirit of infirmity . . . . whom Satan had bound, lo, these eighteen years " . Acts 10 : 38 — " healing all that were oppressed of the devil "; 2 Cor. 12 : 7 — " a thorn in the flesh, a messenger of Satan to buffet me "; 1 Thess. 2 : 18 — " we would fain have come unto you, I Paul once and again; and Satan hindered us "; Heb. 2 : 14 — " him that had the power of death, that is, the devil." Temptation is ascribed to evil spirits in Gen. 3 : 1 *sq.* — " Now the serpent was more subtle "; *cf.* Rev. 20 : 2 — " the old serpent, which is the Devil and Satan "; Mat. 4 : 3 — " the tempter came "; John 13 : 27 — " after the sop, then entered Satan into him "; Acts 5 : 3 — " why hath Satan filled thy heart to lie to the Holy Spirit ? " Eph. 2 : 2 — " the spirit that now worketh in the sons of disobedience "; 1 Thess. 3 : 5 — " lest by any means the tempter had tempted you "; 1 Pet. 5 : 8 — " your adversary the devil, as a roaring lion, walketh about, seeking whom he may devour."

At the time of Christ, popular belief undoubtedly exaggerated the influence of evil spirits. Savage, Life after Death, 113 — " While God was at a distance, the demons were very, very near. The air about the earth was full of these evil tempting spirits. They caused shipwreck at sea, and sudden death on land; they blighted the crops; they smote and blasted in the tempests; they took possession of the bodies and the souls of men. They entered into compacts, and took mortgages on men's souls." If some good end has been attained in spite of them they feel that " Their labor must be to pervert that end, And out of good still to find means of evil." In Goethe's Faust, Margaret detects the evil in Mephistopheles : " You see that he with no soul sympathizes. 'T is written on his face — he never loved. . . . . Whenever he comes near, I cannot pray." Mephistopheles describes himself as " Ein Theil von jener Kraft Die stäts das Böse will Und stäts das Gute schafft " — " Part of that power not understood, which always wills the bad, and always works the good " — through the overruling Providence of God. " The devil says his prayers backwards." " He tried to learn the Basque language, but had to give it up, having learned only three words in two years." Walter Scott tells us that a certain sulphur spring in Scotland was reputed to owe its quality to an ancient compulsory immersion of Satan in it.

Satan's temptations are represented as both negative and positive, — he takes away the seed sown, and he sows tares. He controls many subordinate evil spirits; there is only one devil, but there are many angels or demons, and through their agency Satan may accomplish his purposes.

Satan's negative agency is shown in Mark 4 : 15 — " when they have heard, straightway cometh Satan, and taketh away the word which hath been sown in them "; his positive agency in Mat. 13 : 38, 39 — " the tares are the sons of the evil one; and the enemy that sowed them is the devil." One devil, but many angels : see Mat. 25 : 41 — " the devil and his angels "; Mark 5 : 9 — " My name is Legion, for we are many "; Eph. 2 : 2 — " the prince of the powers of the air "; 6 : 12 — " principalities . . . . powers . . . . world-rulers of this darkness . . . . spiritual hosts of wickedness." The mode of Satan's access to the human mind we do not know. It may be that by moving upon our physical organism he produces subtle signs of thought and so reaches the understanding and desires. He certainly has the power to present in captivating forms the objects of appetite and selfish ambition, as he did to Christ in the wilderness (Mat. 4 : 3, 6, 9), and to appeal to our love for independence by saying to us, as he did to our first parents — " ye shall be as God " (Gen. 3 : 5).

C. C. Everett, Essays Theol. and Lit., 186–218, on The Devil : " If the supernatural powers would only hold themselves aloof and not interfere with the natural processes of the world, there would be no sickness, no death, no sorrow. . . . . This shows a real, though perhaps unconscious, faith in the goodness and trustworthiness of nature. The world in itself is a source only of good. Here is the germ of a positive religion, though this religion when it appears, may adopt the form of supernaturalism." If there was no Satan, then Christ's temptations came from within, and showed a predisposition to evil on his own part.

Possession is distinguished from bodily or mental disease, though such disease often accompanies possession or results from it. — The demons speak in their own persons, with supernatural knowledge, and they are directly addressed by Christ. Jesus recognizes Satanic agency in these cases of possession, and he rejoices in the casting out of demons, as a sign of Satan's downfall. These facts render it impossible to interpret the narratives of demoniac possession as popular descriptions of abnormal physical or mental conditions.

Possession may apparently be either physical, as in the case of the Gerasene demoniacs (Mark 5 : 2-4), or spiritual, as in the case of the "maid having a spirit of divination " (Act 16 : 16), where the body does not seem to have been affected. It is distinguished from bodily disease : see Mat. 17 : 15, 18 —"epileptic . . . . the demon went out from him : and the boy was cured " ; Mark 9 : 25 —"Thou dumb and deaf spirit" ; 3 : 11, 12 — " the unclean spirits . . . . cried, saying, Thou art the Son of God. And he charged them much that they should not make him known" ; Luke 8 : 30, 31 — " And Jesus asked him, What is thy name ? And he said, Legion ; for many demons were entered unto him. And they entreated him that he would not command them to depart into the abyss " ; 10 : 17, 18 — " And the seventy returned with joy, saying, Lord, even the demons are subject unto us in thy name. And he said unto them, I beheld Satan fallen as lightning from heaven."

These descriptions of personal intercourse between Christ and the demons cannot be interpreted as metaphorical. " In the temptation of Christ and in the possession of the swine, imagination could have no place. Christ was *above* its delusions ; the brutes were *below* them." Farrar (Life of Christ, 1 : 337-341, and 2 : excursus vii), while he admits the existence and agency of good angels, very inconsistently gives a metaphorical interpretation to the Scriptural accounts of evil angels. We find corroborative evidence of the Scripture doctrine in the domination which one wicked man frequently exercises over others ; in the opinion of some modern physicians in charge of the insane, that certain phenomena in their patients' experience are best explained by supposing an actual subjection of the will to a foreign power ; and, finally, in the influence of the Holy Spirit upon the human heart. See Trench, Miracles, 125-136 ; Smith's Bible Dictionary, 1 : 586 — " Possession is distinguished from mere temptation by the complete or incomplete loss of the sufferer's reason or power of will : his actions, words, and almost his thoughts, are mastered by the evil spirit, till his personality seems to be destroyed, or at least so overborne as to produce the consciousness of a twofold will within him like that in a dream. In the ordinary assaults and temptations of Satan, the will itself yields consciously, and by yielding gradually assumes, without losing its apparent freedom of action, the characteristics of the Satanic nature. It is solicited, urged, and persuaded against the strivings of grace, but it is not overborne."

T. H. Wright, The Finger of God, argues that Jesus, in his mention of demoniacs, accommodated himself to the beliefs of his time. Fisher, Nature and Method of Revelation, 274, with reference to Weiss's Meyer on Mat. 4 : 24, gives Meyer's arguments against demoniacal possession as follows : 1. the absence of references to demoniacal possession in the Old Testament, and the fact that so-called demoniacs were cured by exorcists : 2. that no clear case of possession occurs at present ; 3. that there is no notice of demoniacal possession in John's Gospel, though the overcoming of Satan is there made a part of the Messiah's work and Satan is said to enter into a man's mind and take control there (John 13 : 27) ; 4. and that the so-called demoniacs are not, as would be expected, of a diabolic temper and filled with malignant feelings toward Christ. Harnack, Wesen des Christenthums, 38 — " The popular belief in demon-possession gave form to the conceptions of those who had nervous diseases, so that they expressed themselves in language proper only to those who were actually possessed. Jesus is no believer in Christian Science : he calls sickness sickness and health health ; but he regards all disease as a proof and effect of the working of the evil one."

On Mark 1 : 21-34, see Maclaren in S. S. Times, Jan. 23, 1904 — " We are told by some that this demoniac was an epileptic. Possibly ; but, if the epilepsy was not the result of possession, why should it take the shape of violent hatred of Jesus ? And what is there in epilepsy to give discernment of his character and the purpose of his mission ? " Not Jesus' exorcism of demons as a fact, but his casting them out by a word, was our Lord's wonderful characteristic. Nevius, Demon-Possession, 240 — " May not demon-possession be only a different, a more advanced, form of hypnotism ? . . . . It is possible that these evil spirits are familiar with the organism of the nervous system, and are capable of acting upon and influencing mankind in accordance with physical and psychological laws. . . . . The hypnotic trance may be effected, without the use of physical organs, by the mere force of will-power, spirit acting upon spirit." Nevius quotes F. W. A. Myers, Fortnightly Rev., Nov. 1885 — "One such discovery, that of telepathy, or the transference of thought and sensation from mind to mind without the agency of the recognized organs of sense, has, as I hold, been already achieved." See Bennet, Diseases of the Bible; Kedney, Diabolology; and references in Pool's Synopsis, 1:343; also Bramwell, Hypnotism, 358–398.

(c) Yet, in spite of themselves, they execute God's plans of punishing the ungodly, of chastening the good, and of illustrating the nature and fate of moral evil.

Punishing the ungodly : Ps. 78 : 49 — "He cast upon them the fierceness of his anger, Wrath and indignation and trouble, A band of angels of evil "; 1 K. 22 : 23 — "Jehovah hath put a lying spirit in the mouth of all these thy prophets ; and Jehovah hath spoken evil concerning thee." In Luke 22 : 31, Satan's sifting accomplishes the opposite of the sifter's intention, and the same as the Master's winnowing (Maclaren).

Chastening the good : see Job, chapters 1 and 2 ; 1 Cor. 5 : 5 — "deliver such a one unto Satan for the destruction of the flesh, that the spirit may be saved in the day of the Lord Jesus "; *cf.* 1 Tim. 1 : 20 — "Hymenæus and Alexander; whom I delivered unto Satan, that they might be taught not to blaspheme." This delivering to Satan for the destruction of the flesh seems to have involved four things: (1) excommunication from the church; (2) authoritative infliction of bodily disease or death : (3) loss of all protection from good angels, who minister only to saints; (4) subjection to the buffetings and tormentings of the great accuser. Gould, in Am. Com. on 1 Cor. 5 :5, regards "delivering to Satan " as merely putting a man out of the church by excommunication. This of itself was equivalent to banishing him into "the world," of which Satan was the ruler.

Evil spirits illustrate the nature and fate of moral evil: see Mat. 8 : 29 — "art thou come hither to torment us before the time ? " 25 : 41 — "eternal fire which is prepared for the devil and his angels "; 2 Thess 2 : 8 — "then shall be revealed the lawless one "; James 2 : 19 — "the demons also believe, and shudder "; Rev. 12 : 9, 12 — "the Devil and Satan, the deceiver of the whole world . . . . the devil is gone down unto you, having great wrath, knowing that he hath but a short time "; 20 : 10 — "cast into the lake of fire . . . . tormented day and night for ever and ever."

It is an interesting question whether Scripture recognizes any special connection of evil spirits with the systems of idolatry, witchcraft, and spiritualism which burden the world. 1 Cor. 10 : 20 — "the things which the Gentiles sacrifice, they sacrifice to demons, and not to God "; 2 Thess. 2 : 9 — "the working of Satan with all power and signs of lying wonders " — would seem to favor an affirmative answer. But 1 Cor. 8 : 4 — "concerning therefore the eating of things sacrificed to idols, we know that no idol is anything in the world" — seems to favor a negative answer. This last may, however, mean that "the beings whom the idols are designed to *represent* have no existence, although it is afterwards shown (10 :20) that there are *other* beings connected with false worship " (Ann. Par. Bible, *in loco*). "Heathenism is the reign of the devil " (Meyer), and while the heathen think themselves to be sacrificing to Jupiter or Venus, they are really "sacrificing to demons," and are thus furthering the plans of a malignant spirit who uses these forms of false religion as a means of enslaving their souls. In like manner, the network of influences which support the papacy, spiritualism, modern unbelief, is difficult of explanation, unless we believe in a superhuman intelligence which organizes these forces against God. In these, as well as in heathen religions, there are facts inexplicable upon merely natural principles of disease and delusion.

Nevius, Demon-Possession, 294 — "Paul teaches that the gods mentioned under different names are imaginary and non-existent; but that, behind and in connection with these gods, there are demons who make use of idolatry to draw men away from God ; and it is to these that the heathen are unconsciously rendering obedience and service. . . . It is most reasonable to believe that the sufferings of people bewitched were caused by the devil, not by the so-called witches. Let us substitute ' devilcraft' for ' witchcraft.' . . . Had the courts in Salem proceeded on the Scriptural presumption that the testimony of those under the control of evil spirits would, in the nature of the case, be false, such a thing as the Salem tragedy would never have been known."

A survey of the Scripture testimony with regard to the employments of evil spirits leads to the following general conclusions :

First, — the power of evil spirits over men is not independent of the human will. This power cannot be exercised without at least the original consent of the human will, and may be resisted and shaken off through prayer and faith in God.

Luke 22 : 31, 40 — "Satan asked to have you, that he might sift you as wheat . . . . Pray that ye enter not into temptation"; Eph. 6 : 11 — "Put on the whole armor of God, that ye may be able to stand against the wiles of the devil"; 16 — "the shield of faith, wherewith ye shall be able to quench all the fiery darts of the evil one"; James 4 : 7 — "resist the devil, and he will flee from you"; 1 Pet. 5 : 9 — "whom withstand stedfast in your faith." The coals are already in the human heart, in the shape of corrupt inclinations; Satan only blows them into flame. The double source of sin is illustrated in Acts 5 : 3, 4 — "Why hath Satan filled thy heart? . . . How is it that thou hast conceived this thing in thine heart?" The Satanic impulse could have been resisted, and "after it was" suggested, it was still "in his own power," as was the land that he had sold (Maclaren).

The soul is a castle into which even the king of evil spirits cannot enter without receiving permission from within. Bp. Wordsworth: "The devil may *tempt* us to fall, but he cannot *make* us fall; he may persuade us to cast *ourselves* down, but he cannot *cast* us down." E. G. Robinson: "It is left to us whether the devil shall get control of us. We pack off on the devil's shoulders much of our own wrong doing, just as Adam had the impertinence to tell God that the woman did the mischief." Both God and Satan stand at the door and knock, but neither heaven nor hell can come in unless we will. "We cannot prevent the birds from flying over our heads, but we can prevent them from making their nests in our hair." Mat. 12 : 43-45 — "The unclean spirit, when he is gone out of a man" — suggests that the man who gets rid of one vice but does not occupy his mind with better things is ready to be repossessed. "Seven other spirits more evil than himself" implies that some demons are more wicked than others and so are harder to cast out (Mark 9 : 29). The Jews had cast out idolatry, but other and worse sins had taken possession of them.

Hudson, Law of Psychic Phenomena, 129 — "The hypnotic subject cannot be controlled so far as to make him do what he knows to be wrong, unless he himself voluntarily assents." A. S. Hart: "Unless one is willing to be hypnotized, no one can put him under the influence. The more intelligent one is, the more susceptible. Hypnotism requires the subject to do two-thirds of the work, while the instructor does only one-third — that of telling the subject what to do. It is not an inherent influence, nor a gift, but can be learned by any one who can read. It is impossible to compel a person to do wrong while under the influence, for the subject retains a consciousness of the difference between right and wrong."

Höffding, Outlines of Psychology, 330-335 — "Some persons have the power of intentionally calling up hallucinations; but it often happens to them as to Goethe's Zauberlehrling, or apprentice-magician, that the phantoms gain power over them and will not be again dispersed. Goethe's Fischer — 'Half she drew him down and half he sank' — repeats the duality in the second term; for to sink is to let one's self sink." Manton, the Puritan: "A stranger cannot call off a dog from the flock, but the Shepherd can do so with a word; so the Lord can easily rebuke Satan when he finds him most violent." Spurgeon, the modern Puritan, remarks on the above: "O Lord, when I am worried by my great enemy, call him off, I pray thee! Let me hear a voice saying: 'Jehovah rebuke thee, O Satan; even Jehovah that hath chosen Jerusalem rebuke thee!' (Zech. 3 : 2). By thine election of me, rebuke him, I pray thee, and deliver me from 'the power of the dog'! (Ps. 22 : 20)."

Secondly,— their power is limited, both in time and in extent, by the permissive will of God. Evil spirits are neither omnipotent, omniscient, nor omnipresent. We are to attribute disease and natural calamity to their agency, only when this is matter of special revelation. Opposed to God as evil spirits are, God compels them to serve his purposes. Their power for harm lasts but for a season, and ultimate judgment and punishment will vindicate God's permission of their evil agency.

1 Cor. 10 : 13 — "God is faithful, who will not suffer you to be tempted above that ye are able; but will with the temptation make also the way of escape, that you may be able to endure it"; Jude 6 — "angels which kept not their own beginning, but left their proper habitation, he hath kept in everlasting bonds under darkness unto the judgment of the great day."

Luther saw Satan nearer to man than his coat, or his shirt, or even his skin. In all misfortune he saw the devil's work. Was there a conflagration in the town? By looking closely you might see a demon blowing upon the flame. Pestilence and storm he attributed to Satan. All this was a relic of the mediæval exaggerations of Satan's power. It was then supposed that men might make covenants with the evil one, in which supernatural power was purchased at the price of final perdition (see Goethe's Faust).

Scripture furnishes no warrant for such representations. There seems to have been permitted a special activity of Satan in temptation and possession during our Savior's ministry, in order that Christ's power might be demonstrated. By his death Jesus brought "to naught him that had the power of death, that is, the devil" (Heb. 2 : 14) and "having despoiled the principalities and the powers, he made a show of them openly, triumphing over them in it," *i. e.*, in the Cross (Col. 2 : 15). 1 John 3 : 8 — "To this end was the Son of God manifested, that he might destroy the works of the devil." Evil spirits now exist and act only upon sufferance. McLeod, Temptation of our Lord, 24 —"Satan's power is limited, (1) by the fact that he is a creature; (2) by the fact of God's providence; (3) by the fact of his own wickedness."

Genung, Epic of the Inner Life, 136 — "Having neither fixed principle in himself nor connection with the source of order outside, Satan has not prophetic ability. He can appeal to chance, but he cannot foresee. So Goethe's Mephistopheles insolently boasts that he can lead Faust astray: 'What will you bet? There's still a chance to gain him, If unto me full leave you give Gently upon *my* road to train him !' And in Job 1 : 11; 2 : 5, Satan wagers: 'He will renounce thee to thy face.'" William Ashmore: "Is Satan omnipresent? No, but he is very spry. Is he bound? Yes, but with a rather loose rope." In the Persian story, God scattered seed. The devil buried it, and sent the rain to rot it. But soon it sprang up, and the wilderness blossomed as the rose.

II. OBJECTIONS TO THE DOCTRINE OF ANGELS.

1. *To the doctrine of angels in general.* It is objected:

(*a*) That it is opposed to the modern scientific view of the world, as a system of definite forces and laws.—We reply that, whatever truth there may be in this modern view, it does not exclude the play of divine or human free agency. It does not, therefore, exclude the possibility of angelic agency.

Ladd, Philosophy of Knowledge, 332 —"It is easier to believe in angels than in ether; in God rather than atoms; and in the history of his kingdom as a divine self-revelation rather than in the physicist's or the biologist's purely mechanical process of evolution."

(*b*) That it is opposed to the modern doctrine of infinite space above and beneath us — a space peopled with worlds. With the surrender of the old conception of the firmament, as a boundary separating this world from the regions beyond, it is claimed that we must give up all belief in a heaven of the angels.—We reply that the notions of an infinite universe, of heaven as a definite place, and of spirits as confined to fixed locality, are without certain warrant either in reason or in Scripture. We know nothing of the modes of existence of pure spirits.

What we know of the universe is certainly finite. Angels are apparently incorporeal beings, and as such are free from all laws of matter and space. Heaven and hell are essentially conditions, corresponding to character — conditions in which the body and the surroundings of the soul express and reflect its inward state. The main thing to be insisted on is therefore the state; place is merely incidental. The fact that Christ ascended to heaven with a human body, and that the saints are to possess glorified bodies, would seem to imply that heaven is a place. Christ's declaration with regard to him who is " able to destroy both soul and body in hell " (Mat. 10 : 28) affords some reason for believing that hell is also a place.

Where heaven and hell are, is not revealed to us. But it is not necessary to suppose that they are in some remote part of the universe; for aught we know, they may be right about us, so that if our eyes were opened, like those of the prophet's servant (2 Kings 6 : 17), we ourselves should behold them. Upon ground of Eph. 2 : 2 — "prince of the

powers of the air" — and 3 : 10 — "the principalities and the powers in the heavenly places " — some have assigned the atmosphere of the earth as the abode of angelic spirits, both good and evil. But the expressions "air" and "heavenly places" may be merely metaphorical designations of their spiritual method of existence.

The idealistic philosophy, which regards time and space as merely subjective forms of our human thinking and as not conditioning the thought of God, may possibly afford some additional aid in the consideration of this problem. If matter be only the expression of God's mind and will, having no existence apart from his intelligence and volition, the question of place ceases to have significance. Heaven is in that case simply the state in which God manifests himself in his grace, and hell is the state in which a moral being finds himself in opposition to God, and God in opposition to him. Christ can manifest himself to his followers in all parts of the earth and to all the inhabitants of heaven at one and the same time (John 14 : 21 ; Mat. 28 : 20 ; Rev. 1 : 7). Angels in like manner, being purely spiritual beings, may be free from the laws of space and time, and may not be limited to any fixed locality.

We prefer therefore to leave the question of place undecided, and to accept the existence and working of angels both good and evil as a matter of faith, without professing to understand their relations to space. For the rationalistic view, see Strauss, Glaubenslehre, 1 : 670–675. *Per contra*, see Van Oosterzee, Christian Dogmatics, 1 : 308-317; Martensen, Christian Dogmatics, 127-136.

2. *To the doctrine of evil angels in particular.* It is objected that :

(*a*) The idea of the fall of angels is self-contradictory, since a fall determined by pride presupposes pride — that is, a fall before the fall. — We reply that the objection confounds the occasion of sin with the sin itself. The outward motive to disobedience is not disobedience. The fall took place only when that outward motive was chosen by free will. When the motive of independence was selfishly adopted, only then did the innocent desire for knowledge and power become pride and sin. How an evil volition could originate in spirits created pure is an insoluble problem. Our faith in God's holiness, however, compels us to attribute the origin of this evil volition, not to the Creator, but to the creature.

There can be no sinful propensity before there is sin. The reason of the *first* sin can not be sin itself. This would be to make sin a necessary development; to deny the holiness of God the Creator; to leave the ground of theism for pantheism.

(*b*) It is irrational to suppose that Satan should have been able to change his whole nature by a single act, so that he thenceforth willed only evil. — But we reply that the circumstances of that decision are unknown to us; while the power of single acts permanently to change character is matter of observation among men.

Instance the effect, upon character and life, of a single act of falsehood or embezzlement. The first glass of intoxicating drink, and the first yielding to impure suggestion, often establish nerve-tracts in the brain and associations in the mind which are not reversed and overcome for a whole lifetime. "Sow an act, and you reap a habit; sow a habit, and you reap a character; sow a character, and you reap a destiny." And what is true of men, may be also true of angels.

(*c*) It is impossible that so wise a being should enter upon a hopeless rebellion. — We answer that no amount of mere knowledge ensures right moral action. If men gratify present passion, in spite of their knowledge that the sin involves present misery and future perdition, it is not impossible that Satan may have done the same.

Scherer, Essays on English Literature, 139, puts this objection as follows: "The idea of Satan is a contradictory idea : for it is contradictory to know God and yet attempt rivalry with him." But we must remember that understanding is the servant of will.

and is darkened by will. Many clever men fail to see what belongs to their peace. It is the very madness of sin, that it persists in iniquity, even when it sees and fears the approaching judgment of God. Jonathan Edwards: "Although the devil be exceedingly crafty and subtle, yet he is one of the greatest fools and blockheads in the world, as the subtlest of wicked men are. Sin is of such a nature that it strangely infatuates and stultifies the mind." One of Ben Jonson's plays has for its title: "The Devil is an Ass."

Schleiermacher, Die Christliche Glaube, 1:210, urges that continual wickedness must have weakened Satan's understanding, so that he could be no longer feared, and he adds: "Nothing is easier than to contend against emotional evil." On the other hand, there seems evidence in Scripture of a progressive rage and devastating activity in the case of the evil one, beginning in Genesis and culminating in the Revelation. With this increasing malignity there is also abundant evidence of his unwisdom. We may instance the devil's mistakes in misrepresenting 1. God to man (Gen. 3:1 — "hath God said?"). 2. Man to himself (Gen. 3:4 — "Ye shall not surely die"). 3. Man to God (Job 1:9 — "Doth Job fear God for naught?"). 4. God to himself (Mat. 4:3 — "If thou art the Son of God"). 5. Himself to man (2 Cor. 11:14 — "Satan fashioneth himself into an angel of light"). 6. Himself to himself (Rev. 12:12 — "the devil is gone down unto you, having great wrath" — thinking he could successfully oppose God or destroy man).

(*d*) It is inconsistent with the benevolence of God to create and uphold spirits, who he knows will be and do evil. — We reply that this is no more inconsistent with God's benevolence than the creation and preservation of men, whose action God overrules for the furtherance of his purposes, and whose iniquity he finally brings to light and punishes.

Seduction of the pure by the impure, piracy, slavery, and war, have all been permitted among men. It is no more inconsistent with God's benevolence to permit them among angelic spirits. Caroline Fox tells of Emerson and Carlyle that the latter once led his friend, the serene philosopher, through the abominations of the streets of London at midnight, asking him with grim humor at every few steps: "Do you believe in the devil now?" Emerson replied that the more he saw of the English people, the greater and better he thought them. It must have been because with such depths beneath them they could notwithstanding reach such heights of civilization. Even vice and misery can be overruled for good, and the fate of evil angels may be made a warning to the universe.

(*e*) The notion of organization among evil spirits is self-contradictory, since the nature of evil is to sunder and divide. — We reply that such organization of evil spirits is no more impossible than the organization of wicked men, for the purpose of furthering their selfish ends. Common hatred to God may constitute a principle of union among them, as among men.

Wicked men succeed in their plans only by adhering in some way to the good. Even a robber-horde must have laws, and there is a sort of "honor among thieves." Else the world would be a pandemonium, and society would be what Hobbes called it: "bellum omnium contra omnes." See art. on Satan, by Whitehouse, in Hastings, Dictionary of the Bible: "Some personalities are ganglionic centres of a nervous system, incarnations of evil influence. The Bible teaches that Satan is such a centre." But the organizing power of Satan has its limitations. Nevius, Demon-Possession, 279 — "Satan is not omniscient, and it is not certain that all demons are perfectly subject to his control. Want of vigilance on his part, and personal ambition in them, may obstruct and delay the execution of his plans, as among men." An English parliamentarian comforted himself by saying: "If the fleas were all of one mind, they would have us out of bed." Plato, Lysis, 214 — "The good are like one another, and friends to one another, and the bad are never at unity with one another or with themselves; for they are passionate and restless, and anything which is at variance and enmity with itself is not likely to be in union or harmony with any other thing."

(*f*) The doctrine is morally pernicious, as transferring the blame of human sin to the being or beings who tempt men thereto. — We reply that neither conscience nor Scripture allows temptation to be an excuse for sin, or regards Satan as having power to compel the human will. The objection, moreover, contradicts our observation,—for only where the personal existence of Satan is recognized, do we find sin recognized in its true nature.

The diabolic character of sin makes it more guilty and abhorred. The immorality lies, not in the maintenance, but in the denial, of the doctrine. Giving up the doctrine of Satan is connected with laxity in the administration of criminal justice. Penalty comes to be regarded as only deterrent or reformatory.

(*g*) The doctrine degrades man, by representing him as the tool and slave of Satan. — We reply that it does indeed show his actual state to be degraded, but only with the result of exalting our idea of his original dignity, and of his possible glory in Christ. The fact that man's sin was suggested from without, and not from within, may be the one mitigating circumstance which renders possible his redemption.

It rather puts a stigma upon human nature to say that it is *not* fallen — that its present condition is its original and normal state. Nor is it worth while to attribute to man a dignity he does not possess, if thereby we deprive him of the dignity that may be his. Satan's sin was, in its essence, sin against the Holy Ghost, for which there can be no " Father, forgive them, for they know not what they do " (Luke 23 : 34), since it was choosing evil with the *mala gaudia mentis*, or the clearest intuition that it was evil. If there be no devil, then man himself is devil. It has been said of Voltaire, that without believing in a devil, he saw him everywhere—even where he was not. Christian, in Bunyan's Pilgrim's Progress, takes comfort when he finds that the blasphemous suggestions which came to him in the dark valley were suggestions from the fiend that pursued him. If all temptation is from within, our case would seem hopeless. But if "an enemy hath done this " (Mat. 13 : 28), then there is hope. And so we may accept the maxim : " Nullus diabolus, nullus Redemptor." Unitarians have no Captain of their Salvation, and so have no Adversary against whom to contend. See Trench, Studies in the Gospels, 17 ; Birks, Difficulties of Belief, 78-100; Ebrard, Dogmatik, 1 : 291-293. Many of the objections and answers mentioned above have been taken from Philippi, Glaubenslehre, 3 : 251-284, where a fuller statement of them may be found.

III. Practical uses of the Doctrine of Angels.

A. *Uses of the doctrine of good angels.*

(*a*) It gives us a new sense of the greatness of the divine resources, and of God's grace in our creation, to think of the multitude of unfallen intelligences who executed the divine purposes before man appeared.

(*b*) It strengthens our faith in God's providential care, to know that spirits of so high rank are deputed to minister to creatures who are environed with temptations and are conscious of sin.

(*c*) It teaches us humility, that beings of so much greater knowledge and power than ours should gladly perform these unnoticed services, in behalf of those whose only claim upon them is that they are children of the same common Father.

(*d*) It helps us in the struggle against sin, to learn that these messengers of God are near, to mark our wrong doing if we fall, and to sustain us if we resist temptation.

(*e*) It enlarges our conceptions of the dignity of our own being, and of the boundless possibilities of our future existence, to remember these forms of typical innocence and love, that praise and serve God unceasingly in heaven.

Instance the appearance of angels in Jacob's life at Bethel (Gen. 28 : 12 — Jacob's conversion ?) and at Mahanaim (Gen. 32 : 1, 2 — two camps, of angels, on the right hand and on the left; *cf*. Ps. 34 : 7 — "The angel of Jehovah encampeth round about them that fear him, And delivereth them "); so too the Angel at Penuel that struggled with Jacob at his entering the promised land (Gen. 32 : 24; *cf*. Hos. 12 : 3, 4 — "in his manhood he had power with God : yea, he had power over the angel, and prevailed "), and " the angel who hath redeemed me from all evil " (Gen. 48 : 16) to whom Jacob refers on his dying bed. Edmund Spenser, The Faerie Queene: "And is there care in heaven ? and is there love In heavenly spirits to these creatures base That may compassion of their evils move? There is; else much more wretched were the case Of men than beasts. But O, th' exceeding grace Of highest God that loves his creatures so. And all his works with mercy doth embrace, That blessed angels he sends to and fro To serve to wicked man, to serve his wicked foe! How oft do they their silver bowers leave And come to succor us who succor want! How oft do they with golden pinions cleave The flitting skies like flying pursuivant, Against foul fiends to aid us militant! They for us fight; they watch and duly ward, And their bright squadrons round about us plant; And all for love, and nothing for reward. Oh, why should heavenly God for men have such regard!"

It shows us that sin is not mere finiteness, to see these finite intelligences that maintained their integrity. Shakespeare, Henry VIII, 2 : 2 — "He counsels a divorce — a loss of her That, like a jewel, has hung twenty years About his neck, yet never lost her lustre; Of her that loves him with that excellence That angels love good men with; even of her That, when the greatest stroke of fortune falls, Will bless the king." Measure for Measure, 2 : 2 — "Man, proud man, Plays such fantastic tricks before high heaven, As makes the angels weep."

B. *Uses of the doctrine of evil angels.*

(*a*) It illustrates the real nature of sin, and the depth of the ruin to which it may bring the soul, to reflect upon the present moral condition and eternal wretchedness to which these spirits, so highly endowed, have brought themselves by their rebellion against God.

(*b*) It inspires a salutary fear and hatred of the first subtle approaches of evil from within or from without, to remember that these may be the covert advances of a personal and malignant being, who seeks to overcome our virtue and to involve us in his own apostasy and destruction.

(*c*) It shuts us up to Christ, as the only Being who is able to deliver us or others from the enemy of all good.

(*d*) It teaches us that our salvation is wholly of grace, since for such multitudes of rebellious spirits no atonement and no renewal were provided — simple justice having its way, with no mercy to interpose or save.

Philippi, in his Glaubenslehre, 3 : 151–284, suggests the following relations of the doctrine of Satan to the doctrine of sin : 1. Since Satan is a fallen *angel*, who once was pure, evil is not self-existent or necessary. Sin does not belong to the substance which God created, but is a later addition. 2. Since Satan is a purely *spiritual* creature, sin cannot have its origin in mere sensuousness, or in the mere possession of a physical nature. 3. Since Satan is not a *weak* and *poorly endowed* creature, sin is not a necessary result of weakness and limitation. 4. Since Satan is *confirmed in evil*, sin is not necessarily a transient or remediable act of will. 5. Since in Satan sin *does not come to an end*, sin is not a step of creaturely development, or a stage of progress to something higher and better. On the uses of the doctrine, see also Van Oosterzee, Christian Dogmatics, 1 : 316; Robert Hall, Works, 3 : 35–51; Brooks, Satan and his Devices.

"They never sank so low, They are not raised so high; They never knew such depths of woe, Such heights of majesty. The Savior did not join Their nature to his own; For them he shed no blood divine, Nor heaved a single groan." If no redemption has been provided for them, it may be because : 1. sin originated with them ; 2. the sin which they committed was "an eternal sin" (*cf*. Mark 3 : 29); 3. they sinned with clearer intellect and fuller knowledge than ours (*cf*. Luke 23 : 34); 4. their incorporeal being aggravated their sin and made it analogous to our sinning against the Holy

Spirit (*cf.* Mat. 12 :31, 32) ; 5. this incorporeal being gave no opportunity for Christ to objectify his grace and visibly to join himself to them (*cf.* Heb. 2 : 16) ; 6. their persistence in evil, in spite of their growing knowledge of the character of God as exhibited in human history, has resulted in a hardening of heart which is not susceptible of salvation.

Yet angels were created in Christ (Col. 1 :16) ; they consist in him (Col. 1 :17) ; he must suffer in their sin ; God would save them, if he consistently could. Dr. G. W. Samson held that the Logos became an angel before he became man, and that this explains his appearances as " the angel of Jehovah " in the Old Testament (Gen. 22 : 11). It is not asserted that *all* fallen angels shall be eternally tormented (Rev. 14 :10). In terms equally strong (Mat. 25 : 41 ; Rev. 20 : 10) the existence of a place of eternal punishment for wicked men is declared, but nevertheless we do not believe that all men will go there, in spite of the fact that all men are wicked. The silence of Scripture with regard to a provision of salvation for fallen angels does not prove that there is no such provision. 2 Pet. 2 : 4 shows that evil angels have not received *final* judgment, but are in a temporary state of existence, and their final state is yet to be revealed. If God has not already provided, may he not yet provide redemption for them, and the " elect angels " (1 Tim. 5 : 21) be those whom God has predestinated to stand this future probation and be saved, while only those who persist in their rebellion will be consigned to the lake of fire and brimstone (Rev. 20 : 10) ?

The keeper of a young tigress patted her head and she licked his hand. But when she grew older she seized his hand with her teeth and began to craunch it. He pulled away his hand in shreds. He learned not to fondle a tigress. Let us learn not to fondle Satan. Let us not be " ignorant of his devices " (2 Cor. 2 :11). It is not well to keep loaded firearms in the chimney corner. " They who fear the adder's sting will not come near her hissing." Talmage : " O Lord, help us to hear the serpent's rattle before we feel its fangs." Ian Maclaren, Cure of Souls, 215 — The pastor trembles for a soul, " when he sees the destroyer hovering over it like a hawk poised in midair, and would have it gathered beneath Christ's wing."

Thomas K. Beecher : " Suppose I lived on Broadway where the crowd was surging past in both directions all the time. Would I leave my doors and windows open, saying to the crowd of strangers : ' Enter my door, pass through my hall, come into my parlor, make yourselves at home in my dining-room, go up into my bedchambers ' ? No ! I would have my windows and doors barred and locked against intruders, to be opened only to me and mine and those I would have as companions. Yet here we see foolish men and women stretching out their arms and saying to the spirits of the vasty deep : ' Come in, and take possession of me. Write with my hands, think with my brain, speak with my lips, walk with my feet, use me as a medium for whatever you will .' God respects the sanctity of man's spirit. Even Christ stands at the door and knocks. Holy Spirit. fill me, so that there shall be room for no other ! " (Rev. 3 :20. Eph. 5 : 18.)

PART V.

ANTHROPOLOGY, OR THE DOCTRINE OF MAN.

CHAPTER I.

PRELIMINARY.

1. Man a Creation of God and a Child of God.

The fact of man's creation is declared in Gen. 1 : 27 — "And God created man in his own image, in the image of God created he him"; 2 : 7 — "And Jehovah God formed man of the dust of the ground, and breathed into his nostrils the breath of life ; and man became a living soul."

(*a*) The Scriptures, on the one hand, negative the idea that man is the mere product of unreasoning natural forces. They refer his existence to a cause different from mere nature, namely, the creative act of God.

Compare Hebrews 12 : 9 — "the Father of spirits" ; Num. 16 : 22 — "the God of the spirits of all flesh" ; 27 : 16 — "Jehovah, the God of the spirits of all flesh"; Rev. 22 : 6 — "the God of the spirits of the prophets." Bruce, The Providential Order, 25 — "Faith in God may remain intact, though we concede that man in all his characteristics, physical and psychical, is no exception to the universal law of growth, no breach in the continuity of the evolutionary process." By "*mere* nature" we mean nature apart from God. Our previous treatment of the doctrine of creation in general has shown that the laws of nature are only the regular methods of God, and that the conception of a nature apart from God is an irrational one. If the evolution of the lower creation cannot be explained without taking into account the originating agency of God, much less can the coming into being of man, the crown of all created things. Hudson, Divine Pedigree of Man: "Spirit in man is linked with, because derived from, God, who is spirit."

(*b*) But, on the other hand, the Scriptures do not disclose the method of man's creation. Whether man's physical system is or is not derived, by natural descent, from the lower animals, the record of creation does not inform us. As the command "Let the earth bring forth living creatures" (Gen. 1 : 24) does not exclude the idea of mediate creation, through natural generation, so the forming of man "of the dust of the ground" (Gen. 2 : 7) does not in itself determine whether the creation of man's body was mediate or immediate.

We may believe that man sustained to the highest preceding brute the same relation which the multiplied bread and fish sustained to the five loaves and two fishes (Mat. 14 : 19), or which the wine sustained to the water which was transformed at Cana (John 2 : 7-10), or which the multiplied oil sustained to the original oil in the O. T. miracle (2 K. 4 : 1-7). The "dust," before the breathing of the spirit into it, may have been animated dust. Natural means may have been used, so far as they would go. Sterrett, Reason and Authority in Religion, 39 — "Our heredity is from God, even though it be from lower forms of life, and our goal is also God, even though it be through imperfect manhood."

Evolution does not make the idea of a Creator superfluous, because evolution is only the method of God. It is perfectly consistent with a Scriptural doctrine of Creation that man should emerge at the proper time, governed by different laws from the brute creation yet growing out of the brute, just as the foundation of a house built of stone is perfectly consistent with the wooden structure built upon it. All depends upon the plan. An atheistic and undesigning evolution cannot include man without excluding what Christianity regards as essential to man; see Griffith-Jones, Ascent through Christ, 43–73. But a theistic evolution can recognize the whole process of man's creation a equally the work of nature and the work of God.

Schurman, Agnosticism and Religion, 42 — "You are not what you have come from, but what you have become." Huxley said of the brutes: "Whether *from* them or not, man is assuredly not *of* them." Pfleiderer, Philos. Religion, 1 : 289 — "The religious dignity of man rests after all upon what he *is*, not upon the mode and manner in which he has *become* what he is." Because he came *from* a beast, it does not follow that he *is* a beast. Nor does the fact that man's existence can be traced back to a brute ancestry furnish any proper reason why the brute should become man. Here is a teleology which requires a divine Creatorship.

J. M. Bronson : "The theist must accept evolution if he would keep his argument for the existence of God from the unity of design in nature. Unless man is an *end*, he is an *anomaly*. The gr-atest argument for God is the fact that all animate nature is one vast and connected unity. Man has developed not *from* the ape, but *away from* the ape. He was never anything but potential man. He did not, as man, come into being until he became a conscious moral agent." This conscious moral nature, which we call personality, requires a divine Author, because it surpasses all the powers which can be found in the animal creation. Romanes, Mental Evolution in Animals, tells us that: 1. Mollusca learn by experience; 2. Insects and spiders recognize offspring; 3. Fishes make mental association of objects by their similarity ; 4. Reptiles recognize persons ; 5. Hymenoptera, as bees and ants, communicate ideas; 6. Birds recognize pictorial representations and understand words; 7. Rodents, as rats and foxes, understand mechanisms ; 8. Monkeys and elephants learn to use tools; 9. Anthropoid apes and dogs have indefinite morality.

But it is definite and not indefinite morality which differences man from the brute. Drummond, in his Ascent of Man, concedes that man passed through a period when he resembled the ape more than any known animal, but at the same time declares that no anthropoid ap could develop into a man. The brute can be defined in terms of man, but man cannot be defined in terms of the brute. It is significant that in insanity the higher endowments of man disappear in an order precisely the reverse of that in which, according to the development theory, they have been acquired. The highest part of man totters first. The last added is first to suffer. Man moreover can transmit his own acquisitions to his posterity, as the brute cannot. Weismann, Heredity, 2 : 69 — "The evolution of music does not depend upon any increase of the musical faculty or any alteration in the inherent physical nature of man, but solely upon the power of transmitting the intellectual achievements of each generation to those which follow. This, more than anything, is the cause of the superiority of men over animals — this, and not merely human faculty, although it may be admitted that this latter is much higher than in animals." To this utterance of Weismann we would add that human progress depends quite as much upon man's power of reception as upon man's power of transmission. Interpretation must equal expression ; and, in this interpretation of the past, man has a guarantee of the future which the brute does not possess.

(c) Psychology, however, comes in to help our interpretation of Scripture. The radical differences between man's soul and the principle of intelligence in the lower animals, especially man's possession of self-consciousness, general ideas, the moral sense, and the power of self-determination, show that that which chiefly constitutes him man could not have been derived, by any natural process of development, from the inferior creatures. We are compelled, then, to believe that God's "breathing into man's nostrils the breath of life" (Gen. 2 : 7), though it was a mediate creation as presupposing existing material in the shape of animal forms, was yet an immediate creation in the sense that only a divine reinforcement of the process of life turned the animal into man. In other words, man came not *from* the brute, but *through* the brute, and the same immanent God who had previously created the brute created also the man.

Tennyson, In Memoriam, XLV — "The baby new to earth and sky, What time his tender palm is pressed Against the circle of the breast, Has never thought that 'this is I': But as he grows he gathers much, And learns the use of 'I' and 'me,' And finds 'I am not what I see, And other than the things I touch.' So rounds he to a separate mind From whence clear memory may begin, As thro' the frame that binds him in His isolation grows defined." Fichte called that the birthday of his child, when the child awoke to self-consciousness and said "I." Memory goes back no further than language. Knowledge of the ego is objective, before it is subjective. The child at first speaks of himself in the third person: "Henry did so and so." Hence most men do not remember what happened before their third year, though Samuel Miles Hopkins, Memoir, 20, remembered what must have happened when he was only 23 months old. Only a conscious person remembers, and he remembers only as his will exerts itself in attention.

Jean Paul Richter, quoted in Ladd, Philosophy of Mind, 110—"Never shall I forget the phenomenon in myself, never till now recited, when I stood by the birth of my own self-consciousness, the place and time of which are distinct in my memory. On a certain forenoon, I stood, a very young child, within the house-door, and was looking out toward the wood-pile, as in an instant the inner revelation 'I am I,' like lightning from heaven, flashed and stood brightly before me ; in that moment I had seen myself as I, for the first time and forever."

Höffding, Outlines of Psychology, 3—"The beginning of conscious life is to be placed probably before birth. . . . Sensations only faintly and dimly distinguished from the general feeling of vegetative comfort and discomfort. Still the experiences undergone before birth perhaps suffice to form the foundation of the consciousness of an external world." Hill, Genetic Philosophy, 282, suggests that this early state, in which the child speaks of self in the third person and is devoid of *self*-consciousness, corresponds to the brute condition of the race, before it had reached self-consciousness, attained language, and become man. In the race, however, there was no heredity to predetermine self-consciousness — it was a new acquisition, marking transition to a superior order of being.

Connecting these remarks with our present subject, we assert that no brute ever yet said, or thought, "I." With this, then, we may begin a series of simple distinctions between man and the brute, so far as the immaterial principle in each is concerned. These are mainly compiled from writers hereafter mentioned.

1. The brute is conscious, but man is self-conscious. The brute does not objectify self. "If the pig could once say, 'I am a pig,' it would at once and thereby cease to be a pig." The brute does not distinguish itself from its sensations. The brute has perception, but only the man has apperception, *i. e.*, perception accompanied by reference of it to the self to which it belongs.

2. The brute has only percepts; man has also concepts. The brute knows white things, but not whiteness. It remembers things, but not thoughts. Man alone has the power of abstraction, *i. e.*, the power of deriving abstract ideas from particular things or experiences.

3. Hence the brute has no language. "Language is the expression of general notions by symbols" (Harris). Words are the symbols of concepts. Where there are no concepts there can be no words. The parrot utters cries ; but "no parrot ever yet spoke a true word." Since language is a sign, it presupposes the existence of an intellect capable of understanding the sign,—in short, language is the effect of mind, not the cause of mind. See Mivart, in Brit. Quar., Oct. 1881:154-172. "The ape's tongue is eloquent in his own dispraise." James, Psychology, 2:356—"The notion of a sign as such, and the general purpose to apply it to everything, is the distinctive characteristic of man." Why do not animals speak ? Because they have nothing to say, *i. e.*, have no general ideas which words might express.

4. The brute forms no judgments, e. g., that *this* is like *that*, accompanied with belief. Hence there is no sense of the ridiculous, and no laughter. James, Psychology, 2:360 —"The brute does not associate ideas by similarity . . . . Genius in man is the possession of this power of association in an extreme degree."

5. The brute has no reasoning — no sense that *this* follows from *that*, accompanied by a feeling that the sequence is necessary. Association of ideas without judgment is the

typical process of the brute mind, though not that of the mind of man. See Mind 5:402–409, 575–581. Man's dream-life is the best analogue to the mental life of the brute.

6. The brute has no general ideas or intuitions, as of space, time, substance, cause, right. Hence there is no generalizing, and no proper experience or progress. There is no capacity for improvement in animals. The brute cannot be trained, except in certain inferior matters of association, where independent judgment is not required. No animal makes tools, uses clothes, cooks food, breeds other animals for food. No hunter's dog, however long its observation of its master, ever learned to put wood on a fire to keep itself from freezing. Even the rudest stone implements show a break in continuity and mark the introduction of man; see J. P. Cook, Credentials of Science, 14. "The dog can see the printed page as well as a man can, but no dog was ever taught to read a book. The animal cannot create in its own mind the thoughts of the writer. The physical in man, on the contrary, is only an aid to the spiritual. Education is a trained capacity to discern the inner meaning and deeper relations of things. So the universe is but a symbol and expression of spirit, a garment in which an invisible Power has robed his majesty and glory"; see S. S. Times, April 7, 1900. In man, mind first became supreme.

7. The brute has determination, but not self-determination. There is no freedom of choice, no conscious forming of a purpose, and no self-movement toward a predetermined end. The donkey is determined, but not self-determined; he is the victim of heredity and environment; he acts only as he is acted upon. Harris, Philos. Basis of Theism, 537–554 — "Man, though implicated in nature through his bodily organization, is in his personality supernatural; the brute is wholly submerged in nature. . . . Man is like a ship in the sea — in it, yet above it — guiding his course, by observing the heavens, even against wind and current. A brute has no such power; it is in nature like a balloon, wholly immersed in air, and driven about by its currents, with no power of steering." Calderwood, Philosophy of Evolution, chapter on Right and Wrong: "The grand distinction of human life is self-control in the field of action — control over all the animal impulses, so that these do not spontaneously and of themselves determine activity" [as they do in the brute]. By what Mivart calls a process of "inverse anthropomorphism," we clothe the brute with the attributes of freedom; but it does not really possess them. Just as we do not transfer to God all our human imperfections, so we ought not to transfer all our human perfections to the brute, "reading our full selves in life of lower forms." The brute has no power to choose between motives; it simply obeys motive. The necessitarian philosophy, therefore, is a correct and excellent philosophy for the brute. But man's power of initiative — in short, man's free will — renders it impossible to explain his higher nature as a mere natural development from the inferior creatures. Even Huxley has said that, taking mind into the account, there is between man and the highest beasts an "enormous gulf," a "divergence immeasurable" and "practically infinite."

8. The brute has no conscience and no religious nature. No dog ever brought back to the butcher the meat it had stolen. "The aspen trembles without fear, and dogs skulk without guilt." The dog mentioned by Darwin, whose behavior in presence of a newspaper moved by the wind seemed to testify to 'a sense of the supernatural,' was merely exhibiting the irritation due to the sense of an unknown future; see James, Will to Believe, 79. The bearing of flogged curs does not throw light upon the nature of conscience. If ethics is not hedonism, if moral obligation is not a refined utilitarianism, if the right is something distinct from the good we get out of it, then there must be a flaw in the theory that man's conscience is simply a development of brute instincts; and a reinforcement of brute life from the divine source of life must be postulated in order to account for the appearance of man. Upton, Hibbert Lectures, 165–167 — "Is the spirit of man derived from the soul of the animal? No, for neither one of these has self-existence. Both are self-differentiations of God. The latter is simply God's preparation for the former." Calderwood, Evolution and Man's Place in Nature, 337, speaks of "the impossibility of tracing the origin of man's rational life to evolution from a lower life. . . . . There are no physical forces discoverable in nature sufficient to account for the appearance of this life." Shaler, Interpretation of Nature, 186 — "Man's place has been won by an entire change in the limitations of his psychic development. . . . . The old bondage of the mind to the body is swept away. . . . . In this new freedom we find the one dominant characteristic of man, the feature which entitles us to class him as an entirely new class of animal."

John Burroughs, Ways of Nature : " Animal life parallels human life at many points, but it is in another plane. Something guides the lower animals, but it is not thought; something restrains them, but it is not judgment; they are provident without prudence ; they are active without industry ; they are skilful without practice ; they are wise without knowledge ; they are rational without reason ; they are deceptive without guile. . . . . When they are joyful, they sing or they play ; when they are distressed, they moan or they cry ; . . . . and yet I do not suppose they experience the emotion of joy or sorrow, or anger or love, as we do, because these feelings in them do not involve reflection, memory, and what we call the higher nature, as with us." Their instinct is intelligence directed outward, never inward, as in man. They share with man the emotions of his animal nature, but not of his moral or æsthetic nature ; they know no altruism, no moral code." Mr. Burroughs maintains that we have no proof that animals in a state of nature can reflect, form abstract ideas, associate cause and effect. Animals, for instance, that store up food for the winter simply follow a provident instinct but do not take thought for the future, any more than does the tree that forms new buds for the coming season. He sums up his position as follows : "To attribute human motives and faculties to the animals is to caricature them ; but to put us in such relation to them that we feel their kinship, that we see their lives embosomed in the same iron necessity as our own, that we see in their minds a humbler manifestation of the same psychic power and intelligence that culminates and is conscious of itself in man — that, I take it, is the true humanization." We assent to all this except the ascription to human life of the same iron necessity that rules the animal creation. Man is man, because his free will transcends the limitations of the brute.

While we grant, then, that man is the last stage in the development of life and that he has a brute ancestry, we regard him also as the offspring of God. The same God who was the author of the brute became in due time the creator of man. Though man came *through* the brute, he did not come *from* the brute, but from God, the Father of spirits and the author of all life. Œdipus' terrific oracle : "Mayst thou ne'er know the truth of what thou art ! " might well be uttered to those who believe only in the brute origin of man. Pascal says it is dangerous to let man see too clearly that he is on a level with the animals unless at the same time we show him his greatness. The doctrine that the brute is imperfect man is logically connected with the doctrine that man is a perfect brute. Thomas Carlyle : "If this brute philosophy is true, then man should go on all fours, and not lay claim to the dignity of being moral." G. F. Wright, Ant. and Origin of Human Race, lecture IX — " One or other of the lower animals may exhibit all the faculties used by a child of fifteen months. The difference may seem very little, but what there is is very important. It is like the difference in direction in the early stages of two separating curves, which go on forever diverging. . . . . The probability is that both in his bodily and in his mental development man appeared as a *sport* in nature, and leaped at once in some single pair from the plane of irrational being to the possession of the higher powers that have ever since characterized him and dominated both his development and his history."

Scripture seems to teach the doctrine that man's nature is the creation of God. Gen. 2 : 7 — "Jehovah God formed man of the dust of the ground, and breathed into his nostrils the breath of life ; and man became a living soul " — appears, says Hovey (State of the Impen. Dead, 14), " to distinguish the vital informing principle of human nature from its material part, pronouncing the former to be more directly from God, and more akin to him, than the latter." So in Zech. 12 : 1 — "Jehovah, who stretcheth forth the heavens, and layeth the foundation of the earth, and formeth the spirit of man within him" — the soul is recognized as distinct in nature from the body, and of a dignity and value far beyond those of any material organism. Job 32 : 8 — "there is a spirit in man, and the breath of the Almighty giveth them understanding " ; Eccl. 12 : 7 — "the dust returneth to the earth as it was, and the spirit returneth unto God who gave it." A sober view of the similarities and differences between man and the lower animals may be found in Lloyd Morgan, Animal Life and Intelligence. See also Martineau, Types, 2 : 65, 140, and Study, 1 : 180 ; 2 : 9, 13, 184, 350 ; Hopkins, Outline Study of Man, 8 : 23 ; Chadbourne, Instinct, 187–211 ; Porter, Hum. Intellect, 384, 386, 397 ; Bascom, Science of Mind, 295–305 ; Mansel, Metaphysics, 49, 50 ; Princeton Rev., Jan. 1881 : 104–128 ; Henslow, in Nature, May 1, 1879 : 21, 22 ; Ferrier, Remains, 2 : 39 ; Argyll, Unity of Nature, 117–119 ; Bib. Sac., 29 : 275–282 ; Max Müller, Lectures on Philos. of Language, no. 1, 2, 3 ; F. W. Robertson, Lectures on Genesis, 21. Le Conte, in Princeton Rev., May, 1884 : 236–261 ; Lindsay, Mind in Lower Animals; Romanes, Mental Evolution in Animals ; Fiske, The Destiny of Man.

(*d*) Comparative physiology, moreover, has, up to the present time, done nothing to forbid the extension of this doctrine to man's body. No single instance has yet been adduced of the transformation of one animal species into another, either by natural or artificial selection ; much less has it been demonstrated that the body of the brute has ever been developed into that of man. All evolution implies progress and reinforcement of life, and is unintelligible except as the immanent God gives new impulses to the process. Apart from the direct agency of God, the view that man's physical system is descended by natural generation from some ancestral simian form can be regarded only as an irrational hypothesis. Since the soul, then, is an immediate creation of God, and the forming of man's body is mentioned by the Scripture writer in direct connection with this creation of the spirit, man's body was in this sense an immediate creation also.

For the theory of natural selection, see Darwin, Origin of Species, 398–424, and Descent of Man, 2 : 368–387 ; Huxley, Critiques and Addresses, 241–269, Man's Place in Nature, 71–138, Lay Sermons, 323, and art. : Biology, in Encyc. Britannica, 9th ed. ; Romanes, Scientific Evidences of Organic Evolution. The theory holds that, in the struggle for existence, the varieties best adapted to their surroundings succeed in maintaining and reproducing themselves, while the rest die out. Thus, by gradual change and improvement of lower into higher forms of life, man has been evolved. We grant that Darwin has disclosed one of the important features of God's method. We concede the partial truth of his theory. We find it supported by the vertebrate structure and nervous organization which man has in common with the lower animals ; by the facts of embryonic development ; of rudimentary organs ; of common diseases and remedies ; and of reversion to former types. But we refuse to regard natural selection as a complete explanation of the history of life, and that for the following reasons :

1. It gives no account of the origin of substance, nor of the origin of variations. Darwinism simply says that " round stones will roll down hill further than flat ones " (Gray, Natural Science and Religion). It accounts for the selection, not for the creation, of forms. " Natural selection originates nothing. It is a destructive, not a creative, principle. If we must idealize it as a positive force, we must think of it, not as the preserver of the fittest, but as the destroyer, that follows ever in the wake of creation and devours the failures ; the scavenger of creation, that takes out of the way forms which are not fit to live and reproduce themselves " (Johnson, on Theistic Evolution, in Andover Review, April, 1884 : 363–381). Natural selection is only unintelligent repression. Darwin's Origin of Species is in fact " not the Genesis, but the Exodus, of living forms." Schurman : " The *survival* of the fittest does nothing to explain the *arrival* of the fittest " ; see also DeVries, Species and Varieties, *ad finem.* Darwin himself acknowledged that " Our ignorance of the laws of variation is profound. . . . The cause of each slight variation and of each monstrosity lies much more in the nature or constitution of the organism than in the nature of the surrounding conditions " (quoted by Mivart, Lessons from Nature, 280–301). Weismann has therefore modified the Darwinian theory by asserting that there would be no development unless there were a spontaneous, innate tendency to variation. In this innate tendency we see, not mere nature, but the work of an originating and superintending God. E. M. Caillard in Contemp. Rev., Dec. 1893 : 873–881 — " Spirit was the moulding power, from the beginning, of those lower forms which would ultimately become man. Instead of the physical derivation of the soul, we propose the spiritual derivation of the body."

2. Some of the most important forms appear suddenly in the geological record, without connecting links to unite them with the past. The first fishes are the Ganoid, large in size and advanced in type. There are no intermediate gradations between the ape and man. Huxley, in Man's Place in Nature, 94, tells us that the lowest gorilla has a skull capacity of 24 cubic inches, whereas the highest gorilla has 34½. Over against this, the lowest man has a skull capacity of 62 ; though men with less than 65 are invariably idiotic ; the highest man has 114. Professor Burt G. Wilder of Cornell University : " The largest ape-brain is only half as large as the smallest normal human." Wallace, Darwinism, 458 — " The average human brain weighs 48 or 49 ounces ; the average ape's brain is only 18 ounces." The brain of Daniel Webster weighed 53 ounces ; but Dr.

Bastian tells of an imbecile whose intellectual deficiency was congenital, yet whose brain weighed 55 ounces. Large heads do not always indicate great intellect. Professor Virchow points out that the Greeks, one of the most intellectual of nations, are also one of the smallest-headed of all. Bain: " While the size of the brain increases in arithmetical proportion, intellectual range increases in geometrical proportion."

Respecting the Enghis and Neanderthal crania, Huxley says: "The fossil remains of man hitherto discovered do not seem to me to take us appreciably nearer to that lower pithecoid form by the modification of which he has probably become what he is. . . . In vain have the links which should bind man to the monkey been sought: not a single one is there to show. The so-called *Protanthropos* who should exhibit this link has not been found. . . . None have been found that stood nearer the monkey than the men of to-day." Huxley argues that the difference between man and the gorilla is smaller than that between the gorilla and some apes; if the gorilla and the apes constitute one family and have a common origin, may not man and the gorilla have a common ancestry also? We reply that the space between the lowest ape and the highest gorilla is filled in with numberless intermediate gradations. The space between the lowest man and the highest man is also filled in with many types that shade off one into the other. But the space between the highest gorilla and the lowest man is absolutely vacant; there are no intermediate types; no connecting links between the ape and man have yet been found.

Professor Virchow has also very recently expressed his belief that no relics of any predecessor of man have yet been discovered. He said: "In my judgment, no skull hitherto discovered can be regarded as that of a predecessor of man. In the course of the last fifteen years we have had opportunities of examining skulls of all the various races of mankind—even of the most savage tribes; and among them all no group has been observed differing in its essential characters from the general human type. . . . Out of all the skulls found in the lake-dwellings there is not one that lies outside the boundaries of our present population." Dr. Eugene Dubois has discovered in the Post-pliocene deposits of the island of Java the remains of a preeminently hominine anthropoid which he calls *Pithecanthropus erectus*. Its cranial capacity approaches the physiological minimum in man, and is double that of the gorilla. The thigh bone is in form and dimensions the absolute analogue of that of man, and gives evidence of having supported a habitually erect body. Dr. Dubois unhesitatingly places this extinct Javan ape as the intermediate form between man and the true anthropoid apes. Haeckel (in The Nation, Sept. 15, 1898) and Keane (in Man Past and Present, 3), regard the *Pithecanthropus* as a "missing link." But "Nature" regards it as the remains of a human microcephalous idiot. In addition to all this, it deserves to be noticed that man does not degenerate as we travel back in time. "The Enghis skull, the contemporary of the mammoth and the cave-bear, is as large as the average of to-day, and might have belonged to a philosopher." The monkey nearest to man in physical form is no more intelligent than the elephant or the bee.

3. There are certain facts which mere heredity cannot explain, such for example as the origin of the working-bee from the queen and the drone, neither of which produces honey. The working-bee, moreover, does not transmit the honey-making instinct to its posterity; for it is sterile and childless. If man had descended from the conscience-less brute, we should expect him, when degraded, to revert to his primitive type. On the contrary, he does not revert to the brute, but dies out instead. The theory can give no explanation of beauty in the lowest forms of life, such as molluscs and diatoms. Darwin grants that this beauty must be of use to its possessor, in order to be consistent with its origination through natural selection. But no such use has yet been shown; for the creatures which possess the beauty often live in the dark, or have no eyes to see. So, too, the large brain of the savage is beyond his needs, and is inconsistent with the principle of natural selection which teaches that no organ can permanently attain a size unrequired by its needs and its environment. See Wallace, Natural Selection, 338–360. G. F. Wright, Man and the Glacial Epoch, 242–301—"That man's bodily organization is in some way a development from some extinct member of the animal kingdom allied to the anthropoid apes is scarcely any longer susceptible of doubt. . . . But he is certainly not descended from any *existing* species of anthropoid apes. . . . When once *mind* became supreme, the bodily adjustment must have been rapid, if indeed it is not necessary to suppose that the bodily preparation for the highest mental faculties was instantaneous, or by what is called in nature a *sport*." With this statement of Dr. Wright we substantially agree, and therefore differ from

Shedd when he says that there is just as much reason for supposing that monkeys are degenerate men, as that men are improved monkeys. Shakespeare, Timon of Athens, 1 : 1 : 249, seems to have hinted the view of Dr. Shedd : " The strain of man's bred out into baboon and monkey." Bishop Wilberforce asked Huxley whether he was related to an ape on his grandfather's or grandmother's side. Huxley replied that he should prefer such a relationship to having for an ancestor a man who used his position as a minister of religion to ridicule truth which he did not comprehend. "Mamma, am I descended from a monkey?" "I do not know, William, I never met any of your father's people."

4. No species is yet known to have been produced either by artificial or by natural selection. Huxley, Lay Sermons, 323 — " It is not absolutely proven that a group of animals having all the characters exhibited by species in nature has ever been originated by selection, whether artificial or natural"; Man's Place in Nature, 107 — " Our acceptance of the Darwinian hypothesis must be provisional, so long as one link in the chain of evidence is wanting ; and so long as all the animals and plants certainly produced by selective breeding from a common stock are fertile with one another, that link will be wanting." Huxley has more recently declared that the missing proof has been found in the descent of the modern horse with one toe, from Hipparion with two toes, Anchitherium with three, and Orohippus with four. Even if this were demonstrated, we should still maintain that the only proper analogue was to be found in that artificial selection by which man produces new varieties, and that natural selection can bring about no useful results and show no progress, unless it be the method and revelation of a wise and designing mind. In other words, selection implies intelligence and will, and therefore cannot be exclusively natural. Mivart, Man and Apes, 192 — " If it is inconceivable and impossible for man's body to be developed or to exist without his informing soul, we conclude that, as no natural process accounts for the different kind of soul — one capable of articulately expressing general conceptions, — so no merely natural process can account for the origin of the body informed by it — a body to which such an intellectual faculty was so essentially and intimately related." Thus Mivart, who once considered that evolution could account for man's body, now holds instead that it can account neither for man's body nor for his soul, and calls natural selection " a puerile hypothesis " (Lessons from Nature, 300; Essays and Criticisms, 2 : 289-314).

(e)   While we concede, then, that man has a brute ancestry, we make two claims by way of qualification and explanation : first, that the laws of organic development which have been followed in man's origin are only the methods of God and proofs of his creatorship ; secondly, that man, when he appears upon the scene, is no longer brute, but a self-conscious and self-determining being, made in the image of his Creator and capable of free moral decision between good and evil.

Both man's original creation and his new creation in regeneration are creations from within, rather than from without. In both cases. God builds the new upon the basis of the old. Man is not a product of blind forces, but is rather an emanation from that same divine life of which the brute was a lower manifestation. The fact that God used preëxisting material does not prevent his authorship of the result. The wine in the miracle was not water because water had been used in the making of it, nor is man a brute because the brute has made some contributions to his creation. Professor John H. Strong : " Some who freely allow the presence and power of God in the age-long process seem nevertheless not clearly to see that, in the final result of finished man, God successfully revealed himself. God's work was never really or fully done ; man was a compound of brute and man ; and a compound of two such elements could not be said to possess the qualities of either. God did not really succeed in bringing moral personality to birth. The evolution was incomplete ; man is still on all fours ; he cannot sin, because he was begotten of the brute ; no fall, and no regeneration, is conceivable. We assert, on the contrary, that, though man came through the brute, he did not come from the brute. He came from God, whose immanent life he reveals, whose image he reflects in a finished moral personality. Because God succeeded, a fall was possible. We can believe in the age-long creation of evolution, provided only that this evolution completed itself. With that proviso. sin remains and the fall." See also A. H. Strong, Christ in Creation, 163-180.

An atheistic and unteleological evolution is a reversion to the savage view of animals as brethren, and to the heathen idea of a sphynx-man growing out of the brute. Darwin himself did not deny God's authorship. He closes his first great book with the declaration that life, with all its potencies, was originally breathed "by the Creator into the first forms of organic being. And in his letters he refers with evident satisfaction to Charles Kingsley's finding nothing in the theory which was inconsistent with an earnest Christian faith. It was not Darwin, but disciples like Haeckel, who put forward the theory as making the hypothesis of a Creator superfluous. We grant the principle of evolution, but we regard it as only the method of the divine intelligence, and must moreover consider it as preceded by an original creative act, introducing vegetable and animal life, and as supplemented by other creative acts at the introduction of man and at the incarnation of Christ. Chadwick, Old and New Unitarianism, 33 — "What seemed to wreck our faith in human nature [its origin from the brute] has been its grandest confirmation. For nothing argues the essential dignity of man more clearly than his triumph over the limitations of his brute inheritance, while the long way that he has come is prophecy of the moral heights undreamed of that await his tireless feet." All this is true if we regard human nature, not as an undesigned result of atheistic evolution, but as the efflux and reflection of the divine personality. R. E. Thompson, in S. S. Times, Dec. 29, 1906 — "The greatest fact in heredity is our descent from God, and the greatest fact in environment is his presence in human life at every point."

The atheistic conception of evolution is well satirized in the verse: "There was an ape in days that were earlier; Centuries passed and his hair became curlier; Centuries more and his thumb gave a twist, And he was a man and a Positivist." That this conception is not a necessary conclusion of modern science, is clear from the statements of Wallace, the author with Darwin of the theory of natural selection. Wallace believes that man's body was developed from the brute, but he thinks there have been three breaks in continuity: 1. the appearance of life; 2. the appearance of sensation and consciousness; and 3. the appearance of spirit. These seem to correspond to 1. vegetable; 2. animal; and 3. human life. He thinks natural selection may account for man's place *in* nature, but not for man's place *above* nature, as a spiritual being. See Wallace, Darwinism, 445-478 — "I fully accept Mr. Darwin's conclusion as to the essential identity of man's bodily structure with that of the higher mammalia, and his descent from some ancestral form common to man and the anthropoid apes." But the conclusion that man's higher faculties have also been derived from the lower animals "appears to me not to be supported by adequate evidence, and to be directly opposed to many well-ascertained facts" (461). . . . The mathematical, the artistic and musical faculties, are results, not causes, of advancement, — they do not help in the struggle for existence and could not have been developed by natural selection. The introduction of life (vegetable), of consciousness (animal), of higher faculty (human). point clearly to a world of spirit, to which the world of matter is subordinate (474-476) . . . . Man's intellectual and moral faculties could not have been developed from the animal, but must have had another origin; and for this origin we can find an adequate cause only in the world of spirit."

Wallace, Natural Selection, 338 — "The average cranial capacity of the lowest savage is probably not less than five-sixths of that of the highest civilized races, while the brain of the anthropoid apes scarcely amounts to one-third of that of man, in both cases taking the average; or the proportions may be represented by the following figures: anthropoid apes, 10; savages, 26; civilized man, 32." *Ibid.*, 360 — "The inference I would draw from this class of phenomena is, that a superior intelligence has guided the development of man in a definite direction and for a special purpose, just as man guides the development of many animal and vegetable forms. . . . The controlling action of a higher intelligence is a necessary part of the laws of nature, just as the action of all surrounding organisms is one of the agencies in organic development, — else the laws which govern the material universe are insufficient for the production of man." Sir Wm. Thompson: "That man could be evolved out of inferior animals is the wildest dream of materialism, a pure assumption which offends me alike by its folly and by its arrogance." Hartmann, in his Anthropoid Apes, 302-306, while not despairing of "the possibility of discovering the true link between the world of man and mammals," declares that "that purely hypothetical being, the common ancestor of man and apes, is still to be found," and that "man cannot have descended from any of the fossil species which have hitherto come to our notice, nor yet from any of the species of apes now extant." See Dana, Amer. Journ. Science and Arts, 1876 · 251, and Geology, 603,

604; Lotze, Mikrokosmos, vol. I, bk. 3, chap. 1 ; Mivart, Genesis of Species, 202-222, 259-307, Man and Apes, 88, 149-192, Lessons from Nature, 128-242, 280-301, The Cat, and Encyclop. Britannica, art. : Apes ; Quatrefages, Natural History of Man, 64-87; Bp. Temple, Bampton Lect., 1884:161-189 ; Dawson, Story of the Earth and Man, 321-329; Duke of Argyll, Primeval Man, 38-75; Asa Gray, Natural Science and Religion ; Schmid, Theories of Darwin, 115-140; Carpenter, Mental Physiology, 59; McIlvaine, Wisdom of Holy Scripture, 55-86; Bible Commentary, 1 : 43; Martensen, Dogmatics, 136 ; Le Conte, in Princeton Rev., Nov. 1878 : 776-803; Zöckler Urgeschichte, 81-105; Shedd, Dogm. Theol., 1 : 499-515. Also, see this Compendium, pages 392, 393.

(*f*) The truth that man is the offspring of God implies the correlative truth of a common divine Fatherhood. God is Father of all men, in that he originates and sustains them as personal beings like in nature to himself. Even toward sinners God holds this natural relation of Father. It is his fatherly love, indeed, which provides the atonement. Thus the demands of holiness are met and the prodigal is restored to the privileges of sonship which have been forfeited by transgression. This natural Fatherhood, therefore, does not exclude, but prepares the way for, God's special Fatherhood toward those who have been regenerated by his Spirit and who have believed on his Son ; indeed, since all God's creations take place in and through Christ, there is a natural and physical sonship of all men, by virtue of their relation to Christ, the eternal Son, which antedates and prepares the way for the spiritual sonship of those who join themselves to him by faith. Man's natural sonship underlies the history of the fall, and qualifies the doctrine of Sin.

Texts referring to God's natural and common Fatherhood are : Mal. 2 : 10 — "Have we not all one father [Abraham]? hath not one God created us?" Luke 3 : 38 — "Adam, the son of God "; 15 : 11-32 — the parable of the prodigal son, in which the father is father even before the prodigal returns ; John 3 : 16 — "God so loved the world, that he gave his only begotten Son"; John 15 : 6 — "If a man abide not in me, he is cast forth as a branch, and is withered; and they gather them, and cast them into the fire, and they are burned "; — these words imply a natural union of all men with Christ, — otherwise they would teach that those who are spiritually united to him can perish everlastingly. Acts 17 : 28 — "For we are also his offspring"— words addressed by Paul to a heathen audience ; Col. 1 : 16, 17— "in him were all things created . . . . and in him all things consist ;" Heb. 12 : 9 —"the Father of spirits." Fatherhood, in this larger sense, implies: 1. Origination ; 2. Impartation of life; 3. Sustentation; 4. Likeness in faculties and powers; 5. Government; 6. Care; 7. Love. In all these respects God is the Father of all men, and his fatherly love is both preserving and atoning. God's natural fatherhood is mediated by Christ, through whom all things were made, and in whom all things, even humanity, consist. We are naturally children of God, as we were *created* in Christ ; we are spiritually sons of God, as we have been *created anew* in Christ Jesus. G. W. Northrop: "God never *becomes* Father to any men or class of men ; he only becomes a *reconciled* and *complacent* Father to those who become ethically like him. Men are not sons in the full ideal sense until they comport themselves as sons of God." Chapman, Jesus Christ and the Present Age, 39— " While God is the Father of all men, all men are not the children of God : in other words, God always realizes completely the idea of Father to every man ; but the majority of men realize only partially the idea of sonship."

Texts referring to the special Fatherhood of grace are: John 1 : 12, 13 — "as many as received him, to them gave he the right to become children of God, even to them that believe on his name; who were born, not of l ood, nor of the will of the flesh, nor of the will of man, but of God "; Rom. 8 : 14 —"for as many as are led by the Spirit of God, these are sons of God "; 15 — "ye received the spirit of adoption, whereby we cry, Abba, Father "; 2 Cor. 6 : 17 — "Come ye out from among them, and be ye separate, saith the Lord, and touch no unclean thing, and I will receive you, and will be to you a Father, and ye shall be to me sons and daughters, saith the Lord Almighty "; Eph. 1 : 5, 6 — "having foreordained us unto adoption as sons through Jesus Christ unto himself"; 3 : 14, 15 — "the Father, from whom every family [marg. 'fatherhood'] in heaven and on earth is named " (= every race among angels or men— so Meyer, Romans. 158, 159); Gal. 3 : 26 — "for ye are all sons of God, through faith, in Christ Jesus " ; 4 : 6 — "And because ye are sons, God sent forth the Spirit of his Son into our hearts, crying, Abba, Father "; 1 John 3 : 2 ² — "Behold what manner of love the Father hath bestowed upon us, that we should be called children of God:

and such we are. . . . Beloved, now are we children of God." The sonship of the race is only rudiment-ary. The actual realization of sonship is possible only through Christ. Gal. 4 : 1-7 inti-mates a universal sonship, but a sonship in which the child "differeth noth ng from a bondservant though he is lord of all," and needs still to "receive the adoption of sons." Simon, Reconciliation, 81 — "It is one thing to be a father ; another to discharge all the fatherly functions. Human fathers sometimes fail to behave like fathers for reasons lying solely in themselves ; sometimes because of hindrances in the conduct or character of their children. No father can normally discharge his fatherly functions toward children who are unchild-like. So even the rebellious son is a son, but he does not act like a son." Because all men are naturally sons of God, it does not follow that all men will be saved. Many who are naturally sons of God are not spiritually sons of God ; they are only "servants" who "abide not in the house forever" (John 8 : 35). God is their Father, but they have yet to "become" his children (Mat. 5 : 45).

The controversy between those who maintain and those who deny that God is the Father of all men is a mere logomachy. God is physically and naturally the Father of all men ; he is morally and spiritually the Father only of those who have been renewed by his Spirit. All men are sons of God in a lower sense by virtue of their natural union with Christ ; only those are sons of God in the higher sense who have joined themselves by faith to Christ in a spiritual union. We can therefore assent to much that is said by those who deny the universal divine fatherhood, as, for example, C. M. Mead, in Am. Jour. Theology, July, 1897 : 577–600, who maintains that sonship consists in spiritual kinship with God, and who quotes, in support of this view, John 8 : 41-44 — "If God were your Father, ye would love me. . . . Ye are of your father, the devil " = the Fatherhood of God is not uni-versal ; Mat. 5 : 44, 45 — "Love your enemies . . . in order that ye may become sons of your Father who is in heaven " ; John 1 : 12 — "as many as received him, to them gave he the right to become children of God, even to them that believe on his name." Gordon, Ministry of the Spirit, 103 — "That God has created all men does not constitute them his sons in the evangelical sense of the word. The sonship on which the N. T. dwells so constantly is based solely on the experience of the new birth, while the doctrine of universal sonship rests either on a daring denial or a daring assumption — the denial of the universal fall of man through sin, or the assump-tion of the universal regeneration of man through the Spirit. In either case the teaching belongs to 'another gospel' (Gal. 1 : 7), the recompense of whose preaching is not a beatitude, but an anathema' (Gal. 1 : 8)."

But we can also agree with much that is urged by the opposite party, as for example, Wendt, Teaching of Jesus, 1 : 193 — "God does not become the Father, but is the heavenly Father, even of those who become his sons. . . . This Fatherhood of God, instead of the kingship which was the dominant idea of the Jews, Jesus made the primary doc-trine. The relation is ethical, not the Fatherhood of mere origination, and therefore only those who live aright are true sons of God. . . . 209 — Mere kingship, or exalta-tion above the world, led to Pharisaic legal servitude and external ceremony and to Alexandrian philosophical speculation. The Fatherhood apprehended and announced by Jesus was essentially a relation of love and holiness." A. H. Bradford, Age of Faith, 116-120 — "There is something sacred in humanity. But systems of theology once began with the essential and natural worthlessness of man. . . . If there is no Fatherhood, then selfishness is logical. But Fatherhood carries with it identity of nature between the parent and the child. Therefore every laborer is of the nature of God, and he who has the nature of God cannot be treated like the products of factory and field. . . . All the children of God are by nature partakers of the life of God. They are called 'children of wrath' (Eph. 2 : 3), or 'of perdition' (John 17 : 12), only to indicate that their proper relations and duties have been violated. . . . Love for man is dependent on something worthy of love, and that is found in man's essential divinity." We object to this last statement, as attributing to man at the beginning what can come to him only through grace. Man was indeed created in Christ (Col. 1 : 16) and was a son of God by virtue of his union with Christ (Luke 3 : 38 ; John 15 : 6). But since man has sinned and has renounced his sonship, it can be restored and realized, in a moral and spiritual sense, only through the atoning work of Christ and the regenerating work of the Holy Spirit (Eph. 2 : 10 — "created in Christ Jesus for good works " ; 2 Pet. 1 : 4 — "his precious and exceeding great prom-ises ; that through these ye may become partakers of the divine nature ").

Many who deny the universal Fatherhood of God refuse to carry their doctrine to its logical extreme. To be consistent they should forbid the unconverted to offer the Lord's Prayer or even to pray at all. A mother who did not believe God to be the Father of all actually said : "My children are not converted, and if I were to teach them the Lord's Prayer, I must teach them to say : 'Our father who art in hell '; for they are only children of the devil." Papers on the question: Is God the Father of all Men? are to be found in the Proceedings of the Baptist Congress, 1896:106-136. Among these the essay of F. H. Rowley asserts God's universal Fatherhood upon the grounds: 1. Man is created in the image of God; 2. God's fatherly treatment of man, especially in the life of Christ among men; 3. God's universal claim on man for his filial love and trust; 4. Only God's Fatherhood makes incarnation possible, for this implies oneness of nature between God and man. To these we may add: 5. The atoning death of Christ could be efficacious only upon the ground of a common nature in Christ and in humanity; and 6. The regenerating work of the Holy Spirit is intelligible only as the restoration of a filial relation which was native to man, but which his sin had put into abeyance. For denial that God is Father to any but the regenerate, see Candlish, Fatherhood of God; Wright, Fatherhood of God. For advocacy of the universal Fatherhood, see Crawford, Fatherhood of God; Lidgett, Fatherhood of God.

II. Unity of the Human Race.

(a) The Scriptures teach that the whole human race is descended from a single pair.

Gen. 1:27, 28 — "And God created man in his own image, in the image of God created he him; male and female created he them. And God blessed them: and God said unto them, Be fruitful, and multiply, and replenish the earth, and subdue it"; 2:7—"And Jehovah God formed man of the dust of the ground, and breathed into his nostrils the breath of life; and man became a living soul"; 22 — "and the rib, which Jehovah God had taken from the man, made he a woman, and brought her unto the man"; 3:20 — "And the man called his wife's name Eve; because she was the mother of all living" = even Eve is traced back to Adam; 9:19 — "These three were the sons of Noah; and of these was the whole earth overspread." Mason, Faith of the Gospel, 110—"Logically, it seems easier to account for the divergence of what was at first one, than for the union of what was at first heterogeneous."

(b) This truth lies at the foundation of Paul's doctrine of the organic unity of mankind in the first transgression, and of the provision of salvation for the race in Christ.

Rom. 5:12 — "Therefore, as through one man sin entered into the world, and death through sin; and so death passed unto all men, for that all sinned"; 19 — "For as through the one man's disobedience the many were made sinners, even so through the obedience of the one shall the many be made righteous"; 1 Cor. 15:21, 22 — "For since by man came death, by man came also the resurrection of the dead. For as in Adam all die, so also in Christ shall all be made alive"; Heb. 2:16 — "For verily not of angels doth he take hold, but he taketh hold of the seed of Abraham." One of the most eminent ethnologists and anthropologists, Prof. D. G. Brinton, said not long before his death that all scientific research and teaching tended to the conviction that mankind has descended from one pair.

(c) This descent of humanity from a single pair also constitutes the ground of man's obligation of natural brotherhood to every member of the race.

Acts 17:26 — "he made of one every nation of men to dwell on all the face of the earth" — here the Rev. Vers. omits the word "blood" ("made of one blood"— Auth. Vers.). The word to be supplied is possibly "father," but more probably "body"; cf. Heb. 2:11 — "for both he that sanctifieth and they that are sanctified are all of one [father or body]: for which cause he is not ashamed to call them brethren, saying, I will declare thy name unto my brethren, In the midst of the congregation will I sing thy praise."

Winchell, in his Preadamites, has recently revived the theory broached in 1655 by Peyrerius, that there were men before Adam : "Adam is descended from a black race — not the black races from Adam." Adam is simply "the remotest ancestor to whom the Jews could trace their lineage. . . . The derivation of Adam from an older human stock is essentially the creation of Adam." Winchell does not deny the unity of the race, nor the retroactive effect of the atonement upon those who lived before Adam; he simply denies that Adam was the first man. 297 — He "regards the Adamic stock as derived from an older and humbler human type," originally as low in the scale as the present Australian savages.

Although this theory furnishes a plausible explanation of certain Biblical facts, such as the marriage of Cain (Gen. 4:17), Cain's fear that men would slay him (Gen. 4:14), and the distinction between "the sons of God" and "the daughters of men" (Gen. 6:1, 2), it treats the

Mosaic narrative as legendary rather than historical. Shem, Ham, and Japheth, it is intimated, may have lived hundreds of years apart from one another (409). Upon this view, Eve could not be "the mother of all living" (Gen. 3:20), nor could the transgression of Adam be the cause and beginning of condemnation to the whole race (Rom. 5:12, 19). As to Cain's fear of other families who might take vengeance upon him, we must remember that we do not know how many children were born to Adam between Cain and Abel, nor what the age of Cain and Abel was, nor whether Cain feared only those that were then living. As to Cain's marriage, we must remember that even if Cain married into another family, his wife, upon any hypothesis of the unity of the race, must have been descended from some other original Cain that married his sister.

See Keil and Delitzsch, Com. on Pentateuch, 1:116—"The marriage of brothers and sisters was inevitable in the case of children of the first man, in case the human race was actually to descend from a single pair, and may therefore be justified, in the face of the Mosaic prohibition of such marriages, on the ground that the sons and daughters of Adam represented not merely the family but the genus, and that it was not till after the rise of several families that the bonds of fraternal and conjugal love became distinct from one another and assumed fixed and mutually exclusive forms, the violation of which is sin." Prof. W. H. Green: "Gen. 20·12 shows that Sarah was Abraham's half, sister; . . . . the regulations subsequently ordained in the Mosaic law were not then in force." G. H. Darwin, son of Charles Darwin, has shown that marriage between cousins is harmless where there is difference of temperament between the parties. Modern palæontology makes it probable that at the beginning of the race there was greater differentiation of brothers and sisters in the same family than obtains in later times. See Ebrard, Dogmatik, 1:275. For criticism of the doctrine that there were men before Adam, see Methodist Quar. Rev., April, 1881:205-231; Presb. Rev., 1881:440-444.

The Scripture statements are corroborated by considerations drawn from history and science. Four arguments may be briefly mentioned:

1. The argument from history.

So far as the history of nations and tribes in both hemispheres can be traced, the evidence points to a common origin and ancestry in central Asia.

The European nations are acknowledged to have come, in successive waves of migration, from Asia. Modern ethnologists generally agree that the Indian races of America are derived from Mongoloid sources in Eastern Asia, either through Polynesia or by way of the Aleutian Islands. Bunsen, Philos. of Universal History, 2:112—the Asiatic origin of all the North American Indians " is as fully proved as the unity of family among themselves." Mason, Origins of Invention, 361—"Before the time of Columbus, the Polynesians made canoe voyages from Tahiti to Hawaii, a distance of 2300 miles." Keane, Man Past and Present, 1-15, 349-440, treats of the American Aborigines under two primitive types: Longheads from Europe and Roundheads from Asia. The human race, he claims, originated in Indomalaysia and spread thence by migration over the globe. The world was peopled from one center by Pleistocene man. The primary groups were evolved each in its special habitat, but all sprang from a Pleiocene precursor 100,000 years ago. W. T. Lopp, missionary to the Eskimos, at Port Clarence, Alaska, on the American side of Bering Strait, writes under date of August 31, 1892: "No thaws during the winter, and ice blocked in the Strait. This has always been doubted by whalers. Eskimos have told them that they sometimes crossed the Strait on ice, but they have never believed them. Last February and March our Eskimos had a tobacco famine. Two parties (five men) went with dogsleds to East Cape, on the Siberian coast, and traded some beaver, otter and marten skins for Russian tobacco, and returned safely. It is only during an occasional winter that they can do this. But every summer they make several trips in their big wolf-skin boats — forty feet long. These observations may throw some light upon the origin of the prehistoric races of America."

Tylor, Primitive Culture, 1:48—"The semi-civilized nations of Java and Sumatra are found in possession of a civilization which at first glance shows itself to have been borrowed from Hindu and Moslem sources." See also Sir Henry Rawlinson, quoted in Burgess, Antiquity and Unity of the Race, 156, 157; Smyth, Unity of Human Races 223-236; Pickering, Races of Man, Introd., synopsis, and page 316; Guyot, Earth and Man, 298-334; Quatrefages, Natural History of Man, and Unité de l'Espèce Humaine,

Godron, Unité de l'Espèce Humaine, 2:412 *sq. Per contra*, however, see Prof. **A. H.** Sayce: " The evidence is now all tending to show that the districts in the neighborhood of the Baltic were those from which the Aryan languages first radiated, and where the race or races who spoke them originally dwelt. The Aryan invaders of Northwestern India could only have been a late and distant offshoot of the primitive stock, speedily absorbed into the earlier population of the country as they advanced southward; and to speak of ' our Indian brethren ' is as absurd and false as to claim relationship with the negroes of the United States because they now use an Aryan language." Scribner, Where Did Life Begin ? has lately adduced arguments to prove that life on the earth originated at the North Pole, and Prof. Asa Gray favors this view ; see his Darwiniana, 205, and Scientific Papers, 2:152; so also Warren, Paradise Found; and Wieland, in Am. Journal of Science, Dec. 1903: 401-430. Dr. J. L. Wortman, in Yale Alumni Weekly, Jan. 14, 1903: 129 — " The appearance of all these primates in North America was very abrupt at the beginning of the second stage of the Eocene. And it is a striking coincidence that approximately the same forms appear in beds of exactly corresponding age in Europe. Nor does this synchronism stop with the apes. It applies to nearly all the other types of Eocene mammalia in the Northern Hemisphere, and to the accompanying flora as well. These facts can be explained only on the hypothesis that there was a common centre from which these plants and animals were distributed. Considering further that the present continental masses were essentially the same in the Eocene time as now, and that the North Polar region then enjoyed a subtropical climate, as is abundantly proved by fossil plants, we are forced to the conclusion that this common centre of dispersion lay approximately within the Arctic Circle. . . . . The origin of the human species did not take place on the Western Hemisphere."

2.   The argument from language.

Comparative philology points to a common origin of all the more important languages, and furnishes no evidence that the less important are not also so derived.

On Sanskrit as a connecting link between the Indo-Germanic languages, see Max Müller, Science of Language, 1:146-165, 326-342, who claims that all languages pass through the three stages: monosyllabic, agglutinative, inflectional; and that nothing necessitates the admission of different independent beginnings for either the material or the formal elements of the Turanian, Semitic, and Aryan branches of speech. The changes of language are often rapid. Latin becomes the Romance languages, and Saxon and Norman are united into English, in three centuries. The Chinese may have departed from their primitive abodes while their language was yet monosyllabic.

G. J. Romanes, Life and Letters, 195 — " Children are the constructors of all *languages*, as distinguished from *language*." Instance Helen Keller's sudden acquisition of language, uttering publicly a long piece only three weeks after she first began to imitate the motions of the lips. G. F. Wright, Man and the Glacial Period, 242-301 — " Recent investigations show that children, when from any cause isolated at an early age, will often produce at once a language *de novo*. Thus it would appear by no means improbable that various languages in America, and perhaps the earliest languages of the world, may have arisen in a short time where conditions were such that a family of small children could have maintained existence when for any cause deprived of parental and other fostering care. . . . . Two or three thousand years of prehistoric time is perhaps all that would be required to produce the diversification of languages which appears at the dawn of history. . . . The prehistoric stage of Europe ended less than a thousand years before the Christian Era." In a people whose speech has not been fixed by being committed to writing, baby-talk is a great source of linguistic corruption, and the changes are exceedingly rapid. Humboldt took down the vocabulary of a South American tribe, and after fifteen years of absence found their speech so changed as to seem a different language.

Zöckler, in Jahrbuch für deutsche Theologie, 8:68 *sq.*, denies the progress from lower methods of speech to higher, and declares the most highly developed inflectional languages to be the oldest and most widespread. Inferior languages are a degeneration from a higher state of culture. In the development of the Indo-Germanic languages (such as the French and the English), we have instances of change from more full and luxuriant expression to that which is monosyllabic or agglutinative. The theory of Max Müller is also opposed by Pott, Die Verschiedenheiten der menschlichen Rassen,

202, 242. Pott calls attention to the fact that the Australian languages show unmistakable similarity to the languages of Eastern and Southern Asia, although the physical characteristics of these tribes are far different from the Asiatic.

On the old Egyptian language as a connecting link between the Indo-European and the Semitic tongues, see Bunsen, Egypt's Place, 1 : preface, 10; also see Farrar, Origin of Language, 213. Like the old Egyptian, the Berber and the Touareg are Semitic in parts of their vocabulary, while yet they are Aryan in grammar. So the Tibetan and Burmese stand between the Indo-European languages, on the one hand, and the monosyllabic languages, as of China, on the other. A French philologist claims now to have interpreted the *Yh-King*, the oldest and most unintelligible monumental writing of the Chinese, by regarding it as a corruption of the old Assyrian or Accadian cuneiform characters, and as resembling the syllabaries, vocabularies, and bilingual tablets in the ruined libraries of Assyria and Babylon; see Terrien de Lacouperie, The Oldest Book of the Chinese and its Authors, and The Languages of China before the Chinese, 11, note; he holds to "the non-indigenousness of the Chinese civilization and its derivation from the old Chaldæo-Babylonian focus of culture by the medium of Susiana." See also Sayce, in Contemp. Rev., Jan. 1884 : 934-936; also, The Monist, Oct. 1906 : 562-596, on The Ideograms of the Chinese and the Central American Calendars. The evidence goes to show that the Chinese came into China from Susiana in the 23d century before Christ. Initial G wears down in time into a Y sound. Many words which begin with Y in Chinese are found in Accadian beginning with G, as Chinese Ye, 'night,' is in Accadian Ge, 'night.' The order of development seems to be: 1. picture writing; 2. syllabic writing; 3. alphabetic writing.

In a similar manner, there is evidence that the Pharaonic Egyptians were immigrants from another land, namely, Babylonia. Hommel derives the hieroglyphs of the Egyptians from the pictures out of which the cuneiform characters developed, and he shows that the elements of the Egyptian language itself are contained in that mixed speech of Babylonia which originated in the fusion of Sumerians and Semites. The Osiris of Egypt is the Asari of the Sumerians. Burial in brick tombs in the first two Egyptian dynasties is a survival from Babylonia, as are also the seal-cylinders impressed on clay. On the relations between Aryan and Semitic languages, see Renouf, Hibbert Lectures, 55–61; Murray, Origin and Growth of the Psalms, 7; Bib. Sac., 1870 : 162; 1876 : 352-380: 1879 : 674–706. See also Pezzi, Aryan Philology, 125; Sayce, Principles of Comp. Philology, 132–174; Whitney, art. on Comp. Philology in Encyc. Britannica, also Life and Growth of Language, 269, and Study of Language, 307, 308 — "Language affords certain indications of doubtful value, which, taken along with certain other ethnological considerations, also of questionable pertinency, furnish ground for suspecting an ultimate relationship. . . . That more thorough comprehension of the history of Semitic speech will enable us to determine this ultimate relationship, may perhaps be looked for with hope, though it is not to be expected with confidence." See also Smyth, Unity of Human Races, 199–222; Smith's Bib. Dict., art.: Confusion of Tongues.

We regard the facts as, on the whole, favoring an opposite conclusion from that in Hastings's Bible Dictionary, art.: Flood: "The diversity of the human race and of language alike makes it improbable that men were derived from a single pair." E. G. Robinson: "The only trustworthy argument for the unity of the race is derived from comparative philology. If it should be established that one of the three families of speech was more ancient than the others, and the source of the others, the argument would be unanswerable. Coloration of the skin seems to lie back of climatic influences. We believe in the unity of the race because in this there are the fewest difficulties. We would not know how else to interpret Paul in Romans 5." Max Müller has said that the fountain head of modern philology as of modern freedom and international law is the change wrought by Christianity, superseding the narrow national conception of patriotism by the recognition of all the nations and races as members of one great human family.

3. The argument from psychology.

The existence, among all families of mankind, of common mental and moral characteristics, as evinced in common maxims, tendencies and capacities, in the prevalence of similar traditions, and in the universal applicability of one philosophy and religion, is most easily explained upon the theory of a common origin.

Among the widely prevalent traditions may be mentioned the tradition of the fash-ioning of the world and man, of a primeval garden, of an original innocence and happi-ness, of a tree of knowledge, of a serpent, of a temptation and fall, of a division of time into weeks, of a flood, of sacrifice. It is possible, if not probable, that certain myths, common to many nations, may have been handed down from a time when the families of the race had not yet separated. See Zöckler, in Jahrbuch für deutsche Theologie, 8 : 71-90 ; Max Müller, Science of Language, 2 : 444-455 ; Prichard, Nat. Hist. of Man, 2 : 657-714 ; Smyth, Unity of Human Races, 236-240 ; Hodge, Syst. Theol., 2 : 77-91 ; Gladstone, Juventus Mundi.

4.   The argument from physiology.

A.   It is the common judgment of comparative physiologists that man constitutes but a single species.   The differences which exist between the various families of mankind are to be regarded as varieties of this species. In proof of these statements we urge :   (a) The numberless intermediate gradations which connect the so-called races with each other.   (b) The essential identity of all races in cranial, osteological, and dental character-istics.   (c) The fertility of unions between individuals of the most diverse types, and the continuous fertility of the offspring of such unions.

Huxley, Critiques and Addresses, 163 — " It may be safely affirmed that, even if the differences between men are specific, they are so small that the assumption of more than one primitive stock for all is altogether superfluous. We may admit that Negroes and Australians are distinct species, yet be the strictest monogenists, and even believe in Adam and Eve as the primeval parents of mankind, i. e., on Darwin's hypothesis "; Origin of Species, 113 — " I am one of those who believe that at present there is no evidence whatever for saying that mankind sprang originally from more than a single pair ; I must say that I cannot see any good ground whatever, or any tenable evidence, for believing that there is more than one species of man." Owen, quoted by Burgess, Ant. and Unity of Race, 185 — " Man forms but one species, and differences are but indications of varieties. These variations merge into each other by easy gradations." Alex. von Humboldt : " The different races of men are forms of one sole species, — they are not different species of a genus."

Quatrefages, in Revue d. deux Mondes, Dec. 1860 : 814 — " If one places himself exclu-sively upon the plane of the natural sciences, it is impossible not to conclude in favor of the monogenist doctrine." Wagner, quoted in Bib. Sac., 19 : 607 — " Species = the collective total of individuals which are capable of producing one with another an uninterruptedly fertile progeny." Pickering, Races of Man, 316 — " There is no middle ground between the admission of eleven distinct species in the human family and their reduction to one. The latter opinion implies a central point of origin."

There is an impossibility of deciding how many races there are, if we once allow that there are more than one. While Pickering would say eleven, Agassiz says eight, Morton twenty-two, and Burke sixty-five. Modern science all tends to the derivation of each family from a single germ. Other common characteristics of all races of men, in addition to those mentioned in the text, are the duration of pregnancy, the normal temperature of the body, the mean frequency of the pulse, the liability to the same diseases. Meehan, State Botanist of Pennsylvania, maintains that hybrid vegetable products are no more sterile than are ordinary plants (Independent, Aug. 21, 1884).

E. B. Tylor, art.: Anthropology, in Encyc. Britannica : " On the whole it may be asserted that the doctrine of the unity of mankind now stands on a firmer basis than in previous ages." Darwin, Animals and Plants under Domestication, 1 : 39 — " From the resemblance in several countries of the half-domesticated dogs to the wild species still living there, from the facility with which they can be crossed together, from even half tamed animals being so much valued by savages, and from the other circumstances previously remarked on which favor domestication, it is highly probable that the domestic dogs of the world have descended from two good species of wolf (viz., Canis lupus and Canis latrans), and from two or three other doubtful species of wolves (namely, the European, Indian and North American forms); from at least one or two South American canine species ; from several races or species of the jackal : and perhaps from one or more extinct species." Dr. E. M. Moore tried unsuccessfully to produce offspring by pairing a Newfoundland dog and a wolf-like dog from Canada. He only proved anew the repugnance of even slightly separated species toward one another.

B. Unity of species is presumptive evidence of unity of origin. Oneness of origin furnishes the simplest explanation of specific uniformity, if indeed the very conception of species does not imply the repetition and reproduction of a primordial type-idea impressed at its creation upon an individual empowered to transmit this type-idea to its successors.

Dana, quoted in Burgess, Antiq. and Unity of Race, 185, 186 — "In the ascending scale of animals, the number of species in any genus diminishes as we rise, and should by analogy be smallest at the head of the series. Among mammals, the higher genera have few species, and the highest group next to man, the orang-outang, has only eight, and these constitute but two genera. Analogy requires that man should have preëminence and should constitute only one." 194 — "A species corresponds to a specific amount or condition of concentrated force defined in the act or law of creation. . . . . The species in any particular case began its existence when the first germ-cell or individual was created. When individuals multiply from generation to generation, it is but a repetition of the primordial type-idea. . . . . The specific is based on a numerical unity, the species being nothing else than an enlargement of the individual." For full statement of Dana's view, see Bib. Sac., Oct. 1857 : 862-866. On the idea of species, see also Shedd, Dogm. Theol., 2 : 63-74.

(a) To this view is opposed the theory, propounded by Agassiz, of different centres of creation, and of different types of humanity corresponding to the varying fauna and flora of each. But this theory makes the plural origin of man an exception in creation. Science points rather to a single origin of each species, whether vegetable or animal. If man be, as this theory grants, a single species, he should be, by the same rule, restricted to one continent in his origin. This theory, moreover, applies an unproved hypothesis with regard to the distribution of organized beings in general to the very being whose whole nature and history show conclusively that he is an exception to such a general rule, if one exists. Since man can adapt himself to all climes and conditions, the theory of separate centres of creation is, in his case, gratuitous and unnecessary.

Agassiz's view was first published in an essay on the Provinces of the Animal World. in Nott and Gliddon's Types of Mankind, a book gotten up in the interest of slavery. Agassiz held to eight distinct centres of creation, and to eight corresponding types of humanity — the Arctic, the Mongolian, the European, the American, the Negro, the Hottentot, the Malay, the Australian. Agassiz regarded Adam as the ancestor only of the white race, yet like Peyrerius and Winchell he held that man in all his various races constitutes but one species.

The whole tendency of recent science, however, has been adverse to the doctrine of separate centres of creation, even in the case of animal and vegetable life. In temperate North America there are two hundred and seven species of quadrupeds, of which only eight, and these polar animals, are found in the north of Europe or Asia. If North America be an instance of a separate centre of creation for its peculiar species, why should God create the same species of man in eight different localities ? This would make man an exception in creation. There is, moreover, no need of creating man in many separate localities ; for, unlike the polar bears and the Norwegian firs, which cannot live at the equator, man can adapt himself to the most varied climates and conditions. For replies to Agassiz, see Bib. Sac., 19 : 607-632 ; Princeton Rev., 1862 : 435-464.

(b) It is objected, moreover, that the diversities of size, color, and physical conformation, among the various families of mankind, are inconsistent with the theory of a common origin. But we reply that these diversities are of a superficial character, and can be accounted for by cor-

31

responding diversities of condition and environment. Changes which have been observed and recorded within historic times show that the differences alluded to may be the result of slowly accumulated divergences from one and the same original and ancestral type. The difficulty in the case, moreover, is greatly relieved when we remember (1) that the period during which these divergences have arisen is by no means limited to six thousand years (see note on the antiquity of the race, pages 224–226); and (2) that, since species in general exhibit their greatest power of divergence into varieties immediately after their first introduction, all the varieties of the human species may have presented themselves in man's earliest history.

Instances of physiological change as the result of new conditions: The Irish driven by the English two centuries ago from Armagh and the south of Down, have become prognathous like the Australians. The inhabitants of New England have descended from the English, yet they have already a physical type of their own. The Indians of North America, or at least certain tribes of them, have permanently altered the shape of the skull by bandaging the head in infancy. The Sikhs of India, since the establishment of Bába Nának's religion (1500 A. D.) and their consequent advance in civilization, have changed to a longer head and more regular features, so that they are now distinguished greatly from their neighbors, the Afghans, Tibetans, Hindus. The Ostiak savages have become the Magyar nobility of Hungary. The Turks in Europe are, in cranial shape, greatly in advance of the Turks in Asia from whom they descended. The Jews are confessedly of one ancestry; yet we have among them the light-haired Jews of Poland, the dark Jews of Spain, and the Ethiopian Jews of the Nile Valley. The Portuguese who settled in the East Indies in the 16th century are now as dark in complexion as the Hindus themselves. Africans become lighter in complexion as they go up from the alluvial river-banks to higher land, or from the coast; and on the contrary the coast tribes which drive out the negroes of the interior and take their territory end by becoming negroes themselves. See, for many of the above facts, Burgess, Antiquity and Unity of the Race, 195–202.

The law of originally greater plasticity, mentioned in the text, was first hinted by Hall, the palæontologist of New York. It is accepted and defined by Dawson, Story of the Earth and Man, 360 — " A new law is coming into view : that species when first introduced have an innate power of expansion, which enables them rapidly to extend themselves to the limit of their geographical range, and also to reach the limit of their divergence into races. This limit once reached, these races run on in parallel lines until they one by one run out and disappear. According to this law the most aberrant races of men might be developed in a few centuries, after which divergence would cease, and the several lines of variation would remain permanent, at least so long as the conditions under which they originated remained." See the similar view of Von Baer in Schmid, Theories of Darwin, 55, note. Joseph Cook: Variability is a lessening quantity ; the tendency to change is greatest at the first, but, like the rate of motion of a stone thrown upward, it lessens every moment after. Ruskin, Seven Lamps, 125 — "The life of a nation is usually, like the flow of a lava-stream, first bright and fierce, then languid and covered, at last advancing only by the tumbling over and over of its frozen blocks." Renouf, Hibbert Lectures, 54 — "The further back we go into antiquity, the more closely does the Egyptian type approach the European." Rawlinson says that negroes are not represented in the Egyptian monuments before 1500 B. C. The influence of climate is very great, especially in the savage state.

In May, 1891, there died in San Francisco the son of an interpreter at the Merchants' Exchange. He was 21 years of age. Three years before his death his clear skin was his chief claim to manly beauty. He was attacked by "Addison's disease," a gradual darkening of the color of the surface of the body. At the time of his death his skin was as dark as that of a full-blooded negro. His name was George L. Sturtevant. Ratzel, History of Mankind, 1 : 9, 10 — As there is only one species of man, "the reunion into one real whole of the parts which have diverged after the fashion of sports" is said to be "the unconscious ultimate aim of all the movements" which have taken place since man began his wanderings. "With Humboldt we can only hold fast to the external unity of the race." See Sir Wm. Hunter, The Indian Empire, 223, 410; Encyc. Britannica, 12 : 808; 20 : 110; Zöckler, Urgeschichte, 109–132, and in Jahrbuch für deutsche

Theologie, 8 : 51–71 ; Prichard, Researches, 5 : 547–552, and Nat. Hist. of Man, 2 : 644–656 ; Duke of Argyll, Primeval Man, 96–108 ; Smith, Unity of Human Races, 255–283 ; Morris Conflict of Science and Religion, 325–385 ; Rawlinson, in Journ. Christ. Philosophy. April, 1883 : 359.

III. Essential Elements of Human Nature.

I. *The Dichotomous Theory.*

Man has a two-fold nature, — on the one hand material, on the other hand immaterial. He consists of body, and of spirit, or soul. That there are two, and only two, elements in man's being, is a fact to which consciousness testifies. This testimony is confirmed by Scripture, in which the prevailing representation of man's constitution is that of dichotomy.

Dichotomous, from δίχα, ' in two,' and τέμνω, ' to cut,' = composed of two parts. Man is as conscious that his immaterial part is a unity, as that his body is a unity. He knows two, and only two, parts of his being — body and soul. So man is the true Janus (Martensen), Mr. Facing-both-ways (Bunyan). That the Scriptures favor dichotomy will appear by considering :

(*a*) The record of man's creation (Gen. 2 : 7), in which, as a result of the inbreathing of the divine Spirit, the body becomes possessed and vitalized by a single principle — the living soul.

Gen. 2 : 7 — " And Jehovah God formed man of the dust of the ground, and breathed into his nostrils the breath of life ; and man became a living soul " — here it is not said that man was first a living soul, and that then God breathed into him a spirit ; but that God inbreathed spirit, and man became a living soul = God's life took possession of clay, and as a result, man had a soul.   *Cf.* Job 27 : 3 —" For my life is yet whole in me, And the spirit of God is in my nostrils " ; 32 : 8 —" there is a spirit in man, And the breath of the Almighty giveth them understanding " ; 33 : 4 — " The Spirit of God hath made me, And the breath of the Almighty giveth me life."

(*b*) Passages in which the human soul, or spirit, is distinguished, both from the divine Spirit from whom it proceeded, and from the body which it inhabits.

Num. 16 : 22 — " O God, the God of the spirits of all flesh " ; Zech. 12 : 1 — " Jehovah, who . . . . formeth the spirit of man within him " ; 1 Cor. 2 : 11 — " the spirit of the man which is in him . . . . the Spirit of God " ; Heb. 12 : 9 — " the Father of spirits." The passages just mentioned distinguish the spirit of man from the Spirit of God. The following distinguish the soul, or spirit, of man from the body which it inhabits : Gen. 35 : 18 — " it came to pass, as her soul was departing (for she d ed) " ; 1 K. 17 : 21 — " O Jehovah my God, I pray thee, let this child's soul come into him again " ; Eccl. 12 : 7 — " the dust returneth to the earth as it was, and the spirit returneth unto God who gave it " ; James 2 : 26 — " the body apart from the spirit is dead." The first class of passages refutes pantheism ; the second refutes materialism.

(*c*) The interchangeable use of the terms ' soul ' and ' spirit. '

Gen. 41 : 8 — " his spirit was troubled " ; *cf.* Ps. 42 : 6 — " my soul is cast down within me."   John 12 : 27 — " Now is my soul troubled " ; *cf.* 13 : 21 — " he was troubled in the spirit." Mat. 20 : 28 — " to g ve his life (ψυχήν) a ransom for many " ; *cf.* 27 : 50 — " yielded up his spirit (πνεῦμα)." Heb. 12 : 23 — " spirits of just men made perfect " ; *cf.* Rev. 6 : 9 — " I saw underneath the altar the souls of them that had been slain for the word of God."   In these passages " spirit " and " soul " seem to be used interchangeably.

(*d*) The mention of body and soul (or spirit) as together constituting the whole man.

Mat. 10 : 28 — " able to destroy both soul and body in hell " ; 1 Cor. 5 : 3 — " absent in body but present in spirit " ; 3 John 2 — " I pray that thou mayest prosper and be in health, even as thy soul prospereth." These texts imply that body and soul (or spirit) together constitute the whole man.

For advocacy of the dichotomous theory, see Goodwin, in Journ. Society Bib. Exegesis, 1881 : 73–86 ; Godet, Bib. Studies of the O. T., 32 ; Oehler, Theology of the O. T., 1 : 219 ; Hahn, Bib. Theol. N. T., 390 *sq.*; Schmid, Bib. Theology N. T., 503 ; Weiss, Bib. Theology N. T., 214 ; Luthardt, Compendium der Dogmatik, 112, 113 ; Hofmann, Schrift-

beweis, 1:294–298 ; Kahnis, Dogmatik, 1:549 ; 3:249 ; Harless, Com. on Eph., 4:23, and Christian Ethics, 22 ; Thomasius, Christi Person und Werk, 1:164–168 ; Hodge, in Princeton Review, 1865:116, and Systematic Theol., 2:47–51 ; Ebrard, Dogmatik, 1:261–263 ; Wm. H. Hodge, in Presb. and Ref. Rev., Apl. 1897.

2. *The Trichotomous Theory.*

Side by side with this common representation of human nature as consisting of two parts, are found passages which at first sight appear to favor trichotomy. It must be acknowledged that πνεῦμα (spirit) and ψυχή (soul), although often used interchangeably, and always designating the same indivisible substance, are sometimes employed as contrasted terms.

In this more accurate use, ψυχή denotes man's immaterial part in its inferior powers and activities ;—as ψυχή, man is a conscious individual, and, in common with the brute creation, has an animal life, together with appetite, imagination, memory, understanding. Πνεῦμα, on the other hand, denotes man's immaterial part in its higher capacities and faculties ;—as πνεῦμα, man is a being related to God, and possessing powers of reason, conscience, and free will, which difference him from the brute creation and constitute him responsible and immortal.

In the following texts, spirit and soul are distinguished from each other : 1 Thess. 5 : 23 — " And the God of peace himself sanctify you wholly ; and may your spirit and soul and body be preserved entire, without blame at the coming of our Lord Jesus Christ " ; Heb. 4 : 12 — " For the word of God is living, and active, and sharper than any two-edged sword, and piercing even to the dividing of soul and spirit, of both joints and marrow, and quick to discern the thoughts and intents of the heart." Compare 1 Cor. 2 : 14 — "Now the natural [Gr. 'psychical'] man receiveth not the things of the Spirit of God " ; 15 : 44 — " It is sown a natural [Gr. 'psychical'] body ; it is raised a spiritual body. If there is a natural [Gr. 'psychical'] body, there is also a spiritual body " ; Eph. 4 : 23 — " that ye be renewed in the spirit of your mind " ; Jude 19 — "sensual [Gr. 'psychical'], having not the Spirit."

For the proper interpretation of these texts, see note on the next page. Among those who cite them as proofs of the trichotomous theory (trichotomous, from τρίχα, 'in three parts,' and τέμνω, 'to cut,' = composed of three parts, *i. e.*, spirit, soul, and body) may be mentioned Olshausen, Opuscula, 134, and Com. on 1 Thess, 5 : 23 ; Beck, Biblische Seelenlehre, 31 ; Delitzsch, Biblical Psychology, 117, 118 ; Göschel in Herzog, Realencyclopädie, art. : Seele ; also, art. by Auberlen : Geist des Menschen ; Cremer, N. T. Lexicon, on πνεῦμα and ψυχή ; Usteri, Paulin. Lehrbegriff, 384 *sq.* ; Neander, Planting and Training, 394 ; Van Oosterzee, Christian Dogmatics, 365, 366 ; Boardman, in Bap. Quarterly, 1 : 177, 325, 428 ; Heard, Tripartite Nature of Man, 62–114 ; Ellicott, Destiny of the Creature, 106–125.

The element of truth in trichotomy is simply this, that man has a triplicity of endowment, in virtue of which the single soul has relations to matter, to self, and to God. The trichotomous theory, however, as it is ordinarily defined, endangers the unity and immateriality of our higher nature, by holding that man consists of three *substances*, or three component *parts*— body, soul, and spirit—and that soul and spirit are as distinct from each other as are soul and body.

The advocates of this view differ among themselves as to the nature of the ψυχή and its relation to the other elements of our being ; some (as Delitzsch) holding that the ψυχή is an efflux of the πνεῦμα, distinct in substance, but not in essence, even as the divine Word is distinct from God, while yet he is God ; others (as Göschel) regarding the ψυχή, not as a distinct substance, but as a resultant of the union of the πνεῦμα and the σῶμα. Still others (as Cremer) hold the ψυχή to be the subject of the personal life whose principle is the πνεῦμα. Heard, Tripartite Nature of Man, 103 — " God is the Creator *ex traduce* of the animal and intellectual part of every man. . . . . Not so with the spirit. . . . It proceeds from God, not by creation, but by emanation."

We regard the trichotomous theory as untenable, not only for the reasons already urged in proof of the dichotomous theory, but from the following additional considerations:

(*a*) Πνεῦμα, as well as ψυχή, is used of the brute creation.

Eccl. 3 : 21 — "Who knoweth the spirit of man, whether it goeth [marg. 'that goeth'] upward, and the spirit of the beast, whether it goeth [marg. 'that goeth'] downward to the earth?" Rev. 16 : 3 — "And the second poured out his bowl into the sea; and it became blood, as of a dead man; and every living soul died, even the things that were in the sea" = the fish.

(*b*) Ψυχή is ascribed to Jehovah.

Amos 6 : 8 — "The Lord Jehovah hath sworn by himself" (lit. 'by his soul,' LXX ἑαυτόν); Is. 42 : 1 — "my chosen in whom my soul delighteth"; Jer. 9 : 9 — "Shall I not visit them for these things? saith Jehovah; shall not my soul be avenged?" Heb. 10 : 38 — "my righteous one shall live by faith: And if he shrink back, my soul hath no pleasure in him."

(*c*) The disembodied dead are called ψυχαί.

Rev. 6 : 9 — "I saw underneath the altar the souls of them that had been slain for the word of God"; *cf.* 20 : 4 — "souls of them that had been beheaded."

(*d*) The highest exercises of religion are attributed to the ψυχή.

Mark 12: 30 — "thou shalt love the Lord thy God . . . . with all thy soul"; Luke 1 : 46 — "My soul doth magnify the Lord"; Heb. 6 : 18, 19 — " the hope set before us : which we have as an anchor of the soul"; James 1 : 21 — "the implanted word, which is able to save your souls."

(*e*) To lose this ψυχή is to lose all.

Mark 8 : 36, 37 — "For what doth it profit a man, to gain the whole world, and forfeit his life [or 'soul,' ψυχή]? For what should a man give in exchange for his life [or 'soul,' ψυχή]?"

(*f*) The passages chiefly relied upon as supporting trichotomy may be better explained upon the view already indicated, that soul and spirit are not two distinct substances or parts, but that they designate the immaterial principle from different points of view.

1 Thess. 5 : 23 — "may your spirit and soul and body be preserved entire" = not a scientific enumeration of the constituent parts of human nature, but a comprehensive sketch of that nature in its chief relations; compare Mark 12: 30 — "thou shalt love the Lord thy God with all thy heart, and with all thy soul, and with all thy mind, and with all thy strength" — where none would think of finding proof of a fourfold division of human nature. On 1 Thess. 5 : 23, see Riggenbach (in Lange's Com.), and Commentary of Prof. W. A. Stevens. Heb. 4 : 12 — "piercing even to the dividing of soul and spirit, of both joints and marrow" = not the dividing of soul *from* spirit, or of joints *from* marrow, but rather the piercing of the soul and of the spirit, even to their very joints and marrow; *i. e.*, to the very depths of the spiritual nature. On Heb. 4 : 12, see Ebrard (in Olshausen's Com.), and Lünemann (in Meyer's Com.); also Tholuck, Com. *in loco.* Jude 19 — "sensual, having not the Spirit" (ψυχικοί, πνεῦμα μὴ ἔχοντες) — even though πνεῦμα = the human spirit, need not mean that there is no spirit existing, but only that the spirit is torpid and inoperative — as we say of a weak man: ' he has no mind,' or of an unprincipled man : ' he has no conscience'; so Alford; see Nitzsch, Christian Doctrine, 102. But πνεῦμα here probably = the divine πνεῦμα. Meyer takes this view, and the Revised Version capitalizes the word "Spirit." See Goodwin, Soc. Bib. Exegesis, 1881: 85 — "The distinction between ψυχή and πνεῦμα is a *functional*, and not a *substantial*, distinction." Moule, Outlines of Christian Doctrine, 161, 162 — " Soul = spirit organized, inseparably linked with the body; spirit = man's inner being considered as God's gift, Soul = man's inner being viewed as his own; spirit = man's inner being viewed as from God. They are not separate elements." See Lightfoot, Essay on St. Paul and Seneca, appended to his Com. on Philippians, on the influence of the ethical language of Stoicism on the N. T. writers. Martineau, Seat of Authority, 39 — "The difference between man and his companion creatures on this earth is not that his instinctive life is less than theirs, for in truth it goes far beyond them; but that in him it acts in the presence and under the eye of other powers which transform it, and by giving to it vision as well as light take its blindness away. He is let into his own secrets."

We conclude that the immaterial part of man, viewed as an individual and conscious life, capable of possessing and animating a physical organism, is called ψυχή; viewed as a rational and moral agent, susceptible of divine influence and indwelling, this same immaterial part is called πνεῦμα. The πνεῦμα, then, is man's nature looking Godward, and capable of receiving and manifesting the Πνεῦμα ἅγιον; the ψυχή is man's nature looking earthward, and touching the world of sense. The πνεῦμα is man's higher part, as related to spiritual realities or as capable of such relation; the ψυχή is man's higher part, as related to the body, or as capable of such relation. Man's being is therefore not trichotomous but dichotomous, and his immaterial part, while possessing duality of powers, has unity of substance.

Man's nature is not a three-storied house, but a two-storied house, with windows in the upper story looking in two directions— toward earth and toward heaven. The lower story is the physical part of us — the body. But man's "upper story" has two aspects; there is an outlook toward things below, and a skylight through which to see the stars. " Soul," says Hovey, " is spirit as modified by union with the body." Is man then the same in kind with the brute, but different in degree? No, man is different in kind, though possessed of certain powers which the brute has. The frog is not a magnified sensitive-plant, though his nerves automatically respond to irritation. The animal is different in kind from the vegetable, though he has some of the same powers which the vegetable has. God's powers include man's; but man is not of the same substance with God, nor could man be enlarged or developed into God. So man's powers include those of the brute, but the brute is not of the same substance with man, nor could he be enlarged or developed into man. _

Porter, Human Intellect, 39 — " The spirit of man, in addition to its higher endowments, may also possess the lower powers which vitalize dead matter into a human body." It does not follow that the soul of the animal or plant is capable of man's higher functions or developments, or that the subjection of man's spirit to body, in the present life, disproves his immortality. Porter continues: "That the soul begins to exist as a vital force, does not require that it should always exist as such a force or in connection with a material body. Should it require another such body, it may have the power to create it for itself, as it has formed the one it first inhabited; or it may have already formed it, and may hold it ready for occupation and use as soon as it sloughs off the one which connects it with the earth."

Harris, Philos. Basis of Theism, 547 — " Brutes may have organic life and sensitivity, and yet remain submerged in nature. It is not life and sensitivity that lift man above nature, but it is the distinctive characteristic of personality." Parkhurst, The Pattern in the Mount, 17-30, on Prov. 20 : 27 — "The spirit of man is the lamp of Jehovah" — not necessarily lighted, but capable of being lighted, and intended to be lighted, by the touch of the divine flame. Cf. Mat. 6 : 22, 23 — "The lamp of the body . . . . If therefore the light that is in thee be darkness, how great is the darkness."

Schleiermacher, Christliche Glaube, 2 : 487 — " We think of the spirit as soul, only when in the body, so that we cannot speak of an immortality of the soul, in the proper sense, without bodily life." The doctrine of the spiritual body is therefore the complement to the doctrine of the immortality of the soul. A. A. Hodge, Pop. Lectures, 221 — " By soul we mean only one thing, i. e., an incarnate spirit, a spirit with a body. Thus we never speak of the souls of angels. They are pure spirits, having no bodies." Lisle, Evolution of Spiritual Man, 72 — " The animal is the foundation of the spiritual; it is what the cellar is to the house; it is the base of supplies." Ladd, Philosophy of Mind, 371-378 — "Trichotomy is absolutely untenable on grounds of psychological science. Man's reason, or the spirit that is in man, is not to be regarded as a sort of Mansard roof, built on to one building in a block, all the dwellings in which are otherwise substantially alike. . . . On the contrary, in every set of characteristics, from those called lowest to those pronounced highest, the soul of man differences itself from the soul of any species of animals. . . . The highest has also the lowest. All must be assigned to one subject."

This view of the soul and spirit as different aspects of the same spiritual principle furnishes a refutation of six important errors :

(a) That of the Gnostics, who held that the πνεῦμα is part of the divine essence, and therefore incapable of sin.

(b) That of the Apollinarians, who taught that Christ's humanity embraced only σῶμα and ψυχή, while his divine nature furnished the νπεῦμα.

(c) That of the Semi-Pelagians, who excepted the human πνεῦμα from the dominion of original sin.

(d) That of Placeus, who held that only the πνεῦμα was directly created by God (see our section on Theories of Imputation).

(e) That of Julius Müller, who held that the ψυχή comes to us from Adam, but that our πνεῦμα was corrupted in a previous state of being (see page 490).

(f) That of the Annihilationists, who hold that man at his creation had a divine element breathed into him, which he lost by sin, and which he recovers only in regeneration ; so that only when he has this πνεῦμα restored by virtue of his union with Christ does man become immortal, death being to the sinner a complete extinction of being.

Tacitus might almost be understood to be a trichotomist when he writes : " Si ut sapientibus placuit, non extinguuntur cum corpore magnæ animæ." Trichotomy allies itself readily with materialism. Many trichotomists hold that man can exist without a πνεῦμα, but that the σῶμα and the ψυχή by themselves are mere matter, and are incapable of eternal existence. Trichotomy, however, when it speaks of the πνεῦμα as the divine principle in man, seems to savor of emanation or of pantheism. A modern English poet describes the glad and winsome child as "A silver stream, Breaking with laughter from the lake divine, Whence all things flow." Another poet, Robert Browning, in his Death in the Desert, 107, describes body, soul, and spirit, as "What does, what knows, what is — three souls, one man."

The Eastern church generally held to trichotomy, and is best represented by John of Damascus (ii : 12) who speaks of the soul as the sensuous life-principle which takes up the spirit — the spirit being an efflux from God. The Western church, on the other hand, generally held to dichotomy, and is best represented by Anselm : " Constat homo ex duabus naturis, ex natura animæ et ex natura carnis."

Luther has been quoted upon both sides of the controversy : by Delitzsch, Bib. Psych., 460–462, as trichotomous, and as making the Mosaic tabernacle with its three divisions an image of the tripartite man. " The first division," he says, " was called the holy of holies, since God dwelt there, and there was no light therein. The next was denominated the holy place, for within it stood a candlestick with seven branches and lamps. The third was called the atrium or court ; this was under the broad heaven, and was open to the light of the sun. A regenerate man is depicted in this figure. His spirit is the holy of holies, God's dwelling-place, in the darkness of faith, without a light, for he believes what he neither sees, nor feels, nor comprehends. The *psyche* of that man is the holy place, whose seven lights represent the various powers of understanding, the perception and knowledge of material and visible things. His body is the atrium or court, which is open to everybody, so that all can see how he acts and lives."

Thomasius, however, in his Christi Person und Werk, 1 : 164–168, quotes from Luther the following statement, which is clearly dichotomous : " The first part, the spirit, is the highest, deepest, noblest part of man. By it he is fitted to comprehend eternal things, and it is, in short, the house in which dwell faith and the word of God. The other, the soul, is this same spirit, according to nature, but yet in another sort of activity, namely, in this, that it animates the body and works through it ; and it is its method not to grasp things incomprehensible, but only what reason can search out, know, and measure." Thomasius himself says : " Trichotomy, I hold with Meyer, is not Scripturally sustained." Neander, sometimes spoken of as a trichotomist, says that spirit is soul in its elevated and normal relation to God and divine things ; ψυχή is that same soul in its relation to the sensuous and perhaps sinful things of this world. Godet, Bib. Studies of O. T., 32 — " Spirit — the breath of God, considered as independent of the body : soul — that same breath, in so far as it gives life to the body."

The doctrine we have advocated, moreover, in contrast with the heathen view, puts honor upon man's body, as proceeding from the hand of God and as therefore originally pure (Gen. 1 : 31 — "And God saw everything that he had made, and, behold, it was very good ") ; as intended to be the dwelling place of the divine Spirit (1 Cor. 6 : 19 — "know ye not that your body is a temple of the Holy Spirit which is in you, which ye have from God ? "); and as containing the germ of the heavenly body (1 Cor. 15 : 44 — "it is sown a natural body ; it is raised a spiritual body " ; Rom. 8 : 11 — "shall give life also to your mortal bodies through his Spirit that dwelleth in you " — here many ancient authorities read " because of his Spirit that dwelleth in you " — διά τὸ ἐνοικοῦν αὐτοῦ πνεῦμα). Birks, in his Difficulties of Belief, suggests that man, unlike angels, may have been provided with a fleshly body, (1) to objectify sin, and (2) to enable Christ to unite himself to the race, in order to save it.

IV. ORIGIN OF THE SOUL.

Three theories with regard to this subject have divided opinion :

1. The Theory of Preëxistence.

This view was held by Plato, Philo, and Origen ; by the first, in order to explain the soul's possession of ideas not derived from sense; by the second, to account for its imprisonment in the body ; by the third, to justify the disparity of conditions in which men enter the world. We concern ourselves, however, only with the forms which the view has assumed in modern times. Kant and Julius Müller in Germany, and Edward Beecher in America, have advocated it, upon the ground that the inborn depravity of the human will can be explained only by supposing a personal act of self-determination in a previous, or timeless, state of being.

The truth at the basis of the theory of preëxistence is simply the ideal existence of the soul, before birth, in the mind of God — that is, God's foreknowledge of it. The intuitive ideas of which the soul finds itself in possession, such as space, time, cause, substance, right, God, are evolved from itself; in other words, man is so constituted that he perceives these truths upon proper occasions or conditions. The apparent recollection that we have seen at some past time a landscape which we know to be now for the first time before us, is an illusory putting together of fragmentary concepts or a mistaking of a part for the whole; we have seen something like a part of the landscape,— we fancy that we have seen this landscape, and the whole of it. Our recollection of a past event or scene is one whole, but this one idea may have an indefinite number of subordinate ideas existing within it. The sight of something which is similar to one of these parts suggests the past whole. Coleridge: "The great law of the imagination that likeness in part tends to become likeness of the whole." Augustine hinted that this illusion of memory may have played an important part in developing the belief in metempsychosis.

Other explanations are those of William James, in his Psychology: The brain tracts excited by the event proper, and those excited in its recall, are different; Baldwin, Psychology, 263, 264: We may remember what we have seen in a dream, or there may be a revival of ancestral or race experiences. Still others suggest that the two hemispheres of the brain act asynchronously; self-consciousness or apperception is distinguished from perception ; divorce, from fatigue, of the processes of sensation and perception, causes paramnesia. Sully, Illusions, 280, speaks of an organic or atavistic memory : "May it not happen that by the law of hereditary transmission . . . ancient experiences will now and then reflect themselves in our mental life, and so give rise to apparently personal recollections?" Letson, The Crowd, believes that the mob is atavistic and that it bases its action upon inherited impulses: "The inherited reflexes are atavistic memories" (quoted in Colegrove, Memory, 204).

Plato held that intuitive ideas are reminiscences of things learned in a previous state of being; he regarded the body as the grave of the soul; and urged the fact that the soul had knowledge before it entered the body, as proof that the soul would have knowledge after it left the body, that is, would be immortal. See Plato, Meno, 82-85, Phædo, 72-75, Phædrus, 245-250, Republic, 5 : 460 and 10 : 614. Alexander, Theories of the Will, 36, 37 — " Plato represents preëxistent souls as having set before them a choice of virtue. The choice is free, but it will determine the destiny of each soul. Not God, but he who chooses, is responsible for his choice. After making their choice, the souls go to the fates, who spin the threads of their destiny, and it is thenceforth irreversible. As Christian theology teaches that man was free but lost his freedom by the fall of Adam, so Plato affirms that the preëxistent soul is free until it has chosen its lot in life." See Introductions to the above mentioned works of Plato in Jowett's translation. Philo held that all souls are emanations from God, and that those who allowed themselves, unlike the angels, to be attracted by matter, are punished for this fall by imprisonment in the body, which corrupts them, and from which they must break loose. See Philo, De Gigantibus, Pfeiffer's ed., 2 : 360–364. Origen accounted for disparity of conditions at birth by the differences in the conduct of these same souls in a previous state. God's justice at the first made all souls equal; condition here corresponds to the degree of previous guilt; Mat. 20 : 3 — "others standing in the market place idle " = souls not yet brought into the world. The Talmudists regarded all souls as created at once in the beginning, and as kept like grains of corn in God's granary, until the time should come for joining each to its appointed body. See Origen, De Anima, 7 ; περὶ ἀρχῶν, ii : 9 : 6; cf. i : 1 : 2, 4, 18 ; 4 : 36. Origen's view was condemned at the Synod of Constantinople, 538. Many of the preceding facts and references are taken from Bruch, Lehre der Präexistenz, translated in Bib. Sac., 20 : 681–733.

For modern advocates of the theory, see Kant, Critique of Pure Reason, sec. 15; Religion in. d. Grenzen d. bl. Vernunft, 26, 27 ; Julius Müller, Doctrine of Sin, 2 : 357–401; Edward Beecher, Conflict of Ages. The idea of preëxistence has appeared to a notable extent in modern poetry. See Vaughan, The Retreate (1621); Wordsworth, Intimations of Immortality in Early Childhood ; Tennyson, Two Voices, stanzas 105–119, and Early Sonnets, 25 — " As when with downcast eyes we muse and brood, And ebb into a former life, or seem To lapse far back in some confused dream To states of mystical similitude ; If one but speaks or hems or stirs his chair, Ever the wonder waxeth more and more, So that we say ' All this hath been before, All this hath been, I know not when or where.' So, friend, when first I looked upon your face, Our thought gave answer each to each, so true — Opposed mirrors each reflecting each — That though I knew not in what time or place, Methought that I had often met with you, And either lived in either's heart and speech." Robert Browning, La Saisiaz, and Christina : "Ages past the soul existed ; Here an age 't is resting merely, And hence fleets again for ages." Rossetti, House of Life : " I have been here before, But when or how I cannot tell ; I know the grass beyond the door, The sweet, keen smell, The sighing sound, the lights along the shore. You have been mine before, How long ago I may not know ; But just when, at that swallow's soar, Your neck turned so, Some veil did fall — I knew it all of yore " ; quoted in Colegrove, Memory, 103–106, who holds the phenomenon due to false induction and interpretation.

Briggs, School, College and Character, 95 — " Some of us remember the days when we were on earth for the first time ; "—which reminds us of the boy who remembered sitting in a corner before he was born and crying for fear he would be a girl. A more notable illustration is that found in the Life of Sir Walter Scott, by Lockhart, his son-in-law, 8 : 274 — " Yesterday, at dinner time, I was strangely haunted by what I would call the sense of preëxistence — viz., a confused idea that nothing that passed was said for the first time — that the same topics had been discussed and the same persons had started the same opinions on them. It is true there might have been some ground for recollections, considering that three at least of the company were old friends and had kept much company together. . . . . But the sensation was so strong as to resemble what is called a mirage in the desert, or a calenture on board of ship, when lakes are seen in the desert and sylvan landscapes in the sea. It was very distressing yesterday and brought to mind the fancies of Bishop Berkeley about an ideal world. There was a vile sense of want of reality in all I did and said. . . . . I drank several glasses of wine, but these only aggravated the disorder. I did not find the in vino veritas of the philosophers."

To the theory of preëxistence we urge the following objections :

(a) It is not only wholly without support from Scripture, but it directly contradicts the Mosaic account of man's creation in the image of God, and Paul's description of all evil and death in the human race as the result of Adam's sin.

Gen. 1:27 — "And God created man in his own image, in the image of God created he him"; 31 — "And God saw every thing that he had made, and, behold, it was very good." Rom. 5:12 —"Therefore, as through one man sin entered into the world, and death through sin; and so death passed unto all men, for that all sinned." The theory of preëxistence would still leave it doubtful whether all men are sinners, or whether God assembles only sinners upon the earth.

(*b*) If the soul in this preëxistent state was conscious and personal, it is inexplicable that we should have no remembrance of such preëxistence, and of so important a decision in that previous condition of being ;—if the soul was yet unconscious and impersonal, the theory fails to show how a moral act involving consequences so vast could have been performed at all.

Christ remembered his preëxistent state; why should not we? There is every reason to believe that in the future state we shall remember our present existence; why should we not now remember the past state from which we came? It may be objected that Augustinians hold to a sin of the race in Adam — a sin which none of Adam's descendants can remember. But we reply that no Augustinian holds to a personal existence of each member of the race in Adam, and therefore no Augustinian needs to account for lack of memory of Adam's sin. The advocate of preëxistence, however, does hold to a personal existence of each soul in a previous state, and therefore needs to account for our lack of memory of it.

(*c*) The view sheds no light either upon the origin of sin, or upon God's justice in dealing with it, since it throws back the first transgression to a state of being in which there was no flesh to tempt, and then represents God as putting the fallen into sensuous conditions in the highest degree unfavorable to their restoration.

This theory only increases the difficulty of explaining the origin of sin, by pushing back its beginning to a state of which we know less than we do of the present. To say that the soul in that previous state was only potentially conscious and personal, is to deny any real probation, and to throw the blame of sin on God the Creator. Pfleiderer, Philos. of Religion, 1:228 — "In modern times, the philosophers Kant, Schelling and Schopenhauer have explained the bad from an intelligible act of freedom, which (according to Schelling and Schopenhauer) also at the same time effectuates the temporal existence and condition of the individual soul. But what are we to think of as meant by such a mystical deed or act through which the subject of it first comes into existence? Is it not this, that perhaps under this singular disguise there is concealed the simple thought that the origin of the bad lies not so much in a *doing* of the individual freedom as rather in the *rise* of it,— that is to say, in the process of development through which the natural man becomes a moral man, and the merely potentially rational man becomes an actually rational man?"

(*d*) While this theory accounts for inborn spiritual sin, such as pride and enmity to God, it gives no explanation of inherited sensual sin, which it holds to have come from Adam, and the guilt of which must logically be denied.

While certain forms of the preëxistence theory are exposed to the last objection indicated in the text, Julius Müller claims that his own view escapes it; see Doctrine of Sin, 2:393. His theory, he says, "would contradict holy Scripture if it derived inborn sinfulness *solely* from this extra-temporal act of the individual, without recognizing in this sinfulness the element of hereditary depravity in the sphere of the natural life, and its connection with the sin of our first parents." Müller, whose trichotomy here determines his whole subsequent scheme, holds only the πνεῦμα to have thus fallen in a preëxistent state. The ψυχή comes, with the body, from Adam. The tempter only brought man's latent perversity of will into open transgression. Sinfulness, as hereditary, does not involve guilt, but the hereditary principle is the "medium through which the transcendent self-perversion of the spiritual nature of man is transmitted to his whole temporal mode of being." While man is born guilty as to his πνεῦμα, for the reason that this πνεῦμα sinned in a preëxistent state, he is also born guilty as to his ψυχή, because this was one with the first man in his transgression.

Even upon the most favorable statement of Müller's view, we fail to see how it can consist with the organic unity of the race; for in that which chiefly constitutes us men — the πνεῦμα — we are as distinct and separate creations as are the angels. We also fail to see how, upon this view, Christ can be said to take our nature; or, if he takes it, how it can be without sin. See Ernesti, Ursprung der Sünde, 2:1-247; Frohschammer, Ursprung der Seele, 11-17: Philippi, Glaubenslehre, 3:92-122; Bruch, Lehre der Präexistenz, translated in Bib. Sac., 20:681-733. Also Bib. Sac., 11:186-191; 12:156; 17:419-427; 20:447; Kahnis, Dogmatik, 3:250 — "This doctrine is inconsistent with the indisputable fact that the souls of children are like those of the parents; and it ignores the connection of the individual with the race."

2. *The Creatian Theory.*

This view was held by Aristotle, Jerome, and Pelagius, and in modern times has been advocated by most of the Roman Catholic and Reformed theologians. It regards the soul of each human being as immediately created by God and joined to the body either at conception, at birth, or at some time between these two. The advocates of the theory urge in its favor certain texts of Scripture, referring to God as the Creator of the human spirit, together with the fact that there is a marked individuality in the child, which cannot be explained as a mere reproduction of the qualities existing in the parents.

Creatianism, as ordinarily held, regards only the body as propagated from past generations. Creatianists who hold to trichotomy would say, however, that the animal soul, the ψυχή, is propagated with the body, while the highest part of man, the πνεῦμα, is in each case a direct creation of God,— the πνεῦμα not being created, as the advocates of preëxistence believe, ages before the body, but rather at the time that the body assumes its distinct individuality.

Aristotle (De Anima) first gives definite expression to this view. Jerome speaks of God as "making souls daily." The scholastics followed Aristotle, and through the influence of the Reformed church, creatianism has been the prevailing opinion for the last two hundred years. Among its best representatives are Turretin, Inst., 5:13 (vol. 1:425); Hodge, Syst. Theol., 2; 65-76; Martensen, Dogmatics, 141-148; Liddon, Elements of Religion, 99-106. Certain Reformed theologians have defined very exactly God's method of creation. Polanus (5:31:1) says that God breathes the soul into boys, forty days, and into girls, eighty days, after conception. Göschel (in Herzog, Encyclop., art.: Seele) holds that while dichotomy leads to traducianism, trichotomy allies itself to that form of creatianism which regards the πνεῦμα as a direct creation of God, but the ψυχή as propagated with the body. To the latter answers the family name; to the former the Christian name. Shall we count George Macdonald as a believer in Preëxistence or in Creatianism, when he writes in his Baby's Catechism : "Where did you come from, baby dear? Out of the everywhere into here. Where did you get your eyes so blue? Out of the sky, as I came through. Where did you get that little tear? I found it waiting when I got here. Where did you get that pearly ear? God spoke, and it came out to hear. How did they all just come to be you? God thought about me, and so I grew."

Creatianism is untenable for the following reasons :

(a) The passages adduced in its support may with equal propriety be regarded as expressing God's mediate agency in the origination of human souls ; while the general tenor of Scripture, as well as its representations of God as the author of man's body, favor this latter interpretation.

Passages commonly relied upon by creatianists are the following: Eccl. 12:7 — "the spirit returneth unto God who gave it"; Is. 57:16 — "the souls that I have made"; Zech. 12:1 — "Jehovah . . . . who formeth the spirit of man within him"; Heb. 12:9 — "the Father of spirits." But God is with equal clearness declared to be the former of man's body: see Ps. 139:13, 14 — "thou didst form my inward parts: Thou didst cover me [marg. 'knit me together'] in my mother's womb. I will give thanks unto thee; for I am fearfully and wonderfully made: Wonderful are thy works"; Jer. 1:5 — "I formed thee in the belly." Yet we do not hesitate to interpret these latter passages as expressive of mediate, not immediate, creatorship,— God works through natural laws of generation and development so far as the production of man's body is concerned. None of the passages first mentioned forbid us to suppose that he works through these same natural laws in the production of the soul. The truth in creatianism is the presence and operation of God in all natural processes. A transcendent God manifests himself in all physical begetting. Shakespeare: "There's a divinity that shapes our ends, Rough hew them how we will." Pfleiderer, Grundriss, 112 — "Creatianism, which emphasizes the divine origin of man, is entirely compatible with Traducianism, which emphasizes the mediation of natural agencies. So for the race as a whole, its origin in a creative activity of God is quite consistent with its being a product of natural evolution."

(*b*) Creatianism regards the earthly father as begetting only the body **of** his child — certainly as not the father of the child's highest part. This makes the beast to possess nobler powers of propagation than man ; for the beast multiplies himself after his own image.

The new physiology properly views soul, not as something added from without, but as the animating principle of the body from the beginning and as having a determining influence upon its whole development. That children are like their parents, in intellectual and spiritual as well as in physical respects, is a fact of which the creatian theory gives no proper explanation. Mason, Faith of the Gospel, 115 — "The love of parents to children and of children to parents protests against the doctrine that only the body is propagated." Aubrey Moore, Science and the Faith, 207, — quoted in Contemp. Rev., Dec. 1893 : 876 — "Instead of the physical derivation of the soul, we stand for the spiritual derivation of the body." We would amend this statement by saying that we stand for the spiritual derivation of both soul and body, natural law being only the operation of spirit, human and divine.

(*c*) The individuality of the child, even in the most extreme cases, as in the sudden rise from obscure families and surroundings of marked men like Luther, may be better explained by supposing a law of variation impressed upon the species at its beginning — a law whose operation is foreseen and supervised by God.

The differences of the child from the parent are often exaggerated; men are generally more the product of their ancestry and of their time than we are accustomed to think. Dickens made angelic children to be born of depraved parents, and to grow up in the slums. But this writing belongs to a past generation, when the facts of heredity were unrecognized. George Eliot's school is nearer the truth; although she exaggerates the doctrine of heredity in turn, until all idea of free will and all hope of escaping our fate vanish. Shaler, Interpretation of Nature, 78, 90 — "Separate motives, handed down from generation to generation, sometimes remaining latent for great periods, to become suddenly manifested under conditions the nature of which is not discernible. . . . . Conflict of inheritances [from different ancestors] may lead to the institution of variety."

Sometimes, in spite of George Eliot, a lily grows out of a stagnant pool — how shall we explain the fact ? We must remember that the paternal and the maternal elements are themselves unlike; the union of the two may well produce a third in some respects unlike either ; as, when two chemical elements unite, the product differs from either of the constituents. We must remember also that *nature* is one factor ; *nurture* is another; and that the latter is often as potent as the former (see Galton, Inquiries into Human Faculty, 77-81). Environment determines to a large extent both the fact and the degree of development. Genius is often another name for Providence. Yet before all and beyond all we must recognize a manifold wisdom of God, which in the very organization of species impresses upon it a law of variation, so that at proper times and under proper conditions the old is modified in the line of progress and advance to something higher. Dante, Purgatory, canto vii — "Rarely into the branches of the tree Doth human worth mount up ; and so ordains He that bestows it, that as his free gift It may be called." Pompilia, the noblest character in Robert Browning's Ring and the Book, came of "a bad lot." Geo. A. Gordon, Christ of To-day, 123-126 — "It is mockery to account for Abraham Lincoln and Robert Burns and William Shakespeare upon naked principles of heredity and environment. . . . . All intelligence and all high character are transcendent, and have their source in the mind and heart of God. It is in the range of Christ's transcendence of his earthly conditions that we note the complete uniqueness of his person."

(*d*) This theory, if it allows that the soul is originally possessed of depraved tendencies, makes God the direct author of moral evil ; if it holds the soul to have been created pure, it makes God indirectly the author of moral evil, by teaching that he puts this pure soul into a body which will inevitably corrupt it.

The decisive argument againt creatianism is this one, that it makes God the author of moral evil. See Kahnis, Dogmatik, 3 : 250 — " Creatianism rests upon a justly anti-quated dualism between soul and body, and is irreconcilable with the sinful condition of the human soul. The truth in the doctrine is just this only, that generation can bring forth an immortal human life only according to the power imparted by God's word, and with the special coöperation of God himself." The difficulty of supposing that God immediately creates a pure soul, only to put it into a body that will infallibly corrupt it — " sicut vinum in vase acetoso " — has led many of the most thoughtful Reformed theologians to modify the creatian doctrine by combining it with traducianism.

Rothe, Dogmatik, 1 : 249-251, holds to creatianism in a wider sense — a union of the paternal and maternal elements under the express and determining efficiency of God. Ebrard, Dogmatik, 1 : 327-332, regards the soul as new-created, yet by a process of mediate creation according to law, which he calls ' metaphysical generation.' Dorner, System of Doctrine, 3 : 56, says that the individual is not simply a manifestation of the species ; God applies to the origination of every single man a special creative thought and act of will ; yet he does this through the species, so that it is creation by law, — else the child would be, not a continuation of the old species, but the establishment of a new one. So in speaking of the human soul of Christ, Dorner says (3 : 340-349) that the soul itself does not owe its origin to Mary nor to the species, but to the creative act of God. This soul appropriates to itself from Mary's body the elements of a human form. purifying them in the process so far as is consistent with the beginning of a life yet subject to development and human weakness.

Bowne, Metaphysics, 500 — " The laws of heredity must be viewed simply as descrip-tions of a fact and never as its explanation. Not as if ancestors passed on something to posterity, but solely because of the inner consistency of the divine action " are children like their parents. We cannot regard either of these mediating views as self-consistent or intelligible. We pass on therefore to consider the traducian theory which we believe more fully to meet the requirements of Scripture and of reason. For fur-ther discussion of creatianism, see Frohschammer, Ursprung der Seele, 18-58 ; Alger, Doctrine of a Future Life, 1-17.

3. *The Traducian Theory.*

This view was propounded by Tertullian, and was implicitly held by Augustine. In modern times it has been the prevailing opinion of the Lutheran Church. It holds that the human race was immediately created in Adam, and, as respects both body and soul, was propagated from him by natural generation — all souls since Adam being only mediately created by God, as the upholder of the laws of propagation which were originally established by him.

Tertullian, De Anima : " Tradux peccati, tradux animæ." Gregory of Nyssa : " Man being one, consisting of soul and body, the common beginning of his constitution must be supposed also one ; so that he may not be both older and younger than himself — that in him which is bodily being first, and the other coming after " (quoted in Crippen, Hist. of Christ. Doct., 80). Augustine, De Pec. Mer. et Rem., 3 : 7 — " In Adam all sinned, at the time when in his nature all were still that one man " ; De Civ. Dei, 13 : 14 — " For we all were in that one man, when we all were that one man. . . . . The form in which we each should live was not as yet individually created and distributed to us, but there already existed the seminal nature from which we were propagated."

Augustine, indeed, wavered in his statements with regard to the origin of the soul, apparently fearing that an explicit and pronounced traducianism might involve materialistic consequences; yet, as logically lying at the basis of his doctrine of original sin, traducianism came to be the ruling view of the Lutheran reformers. In his Table Talk, Luther says: "The reproduction of mankind is a great marvel and mystery. Had God consulted me in the matter, I should have advised him to continue the generation of the species by fashioning them out of clay, in the way Adam was fashioned; as I should have counseled him also to let the sun remain always suspended over the earth, like a great lamp, maintaining perpetual light and heat."

Traducianism holds that man, as a species, was created in Adam. In Adam, the substance of humanity was yet undistributed. We derive our immaterial as well as our material being, by natural laws of propagation, from Adam, — each individual man after Adam possessing a part of the substance that was originated in him. Sexual reproduction has for its purpose the keeping of variations within limit. Every marriage tends to bring back the individual type to that of the species. The offspring represents not one of the parents but both. And, as each of these parents represents two grandparents, the offspring really represents the whole race. Without this conjugation the individual peculiarities would reproduce themselves in divergent lines like the shot from a shot-gun. Fission needs to be supplemented by conjugation. The use of sexual reproduction is to preserve the average individual in the face of a progressive tendency to variation. In asexual reproduction the offspring start on deviating lines and never mix their qualities with those of their mates. Sexual reproduction makes the individual the type of the species and gives solidarity to the race. See Maupas, quoted by Newman Smith, Place of Death in Evolution, 19–22.

John Milton, in his Christian Doctrine, is a Traducian. He has no faith in the notion of a soul separate from and inhabiting the body. He believes in a certain corporeity of the soul. Mind and thought are rooted in the bodily organism. Soul was not inbreathed after the body was formed. The breathing of God into man's nostrils was only the quickening impulse to that which already had life. God does not create souls every day. Man is a body-and-soul, or a soul-body, and he transmits himself as such. Harris, Moral Evolution, 171 — The individual man has a great number of ancestors as well as a great number of descendants. He is the central point of an hour-glass, or a strait between two seas which widen out behind and before. How then shall we escape the conclusion that the human race was most numerous at the beginning? We must remember that other children have the same great-grandparents with ourselves; that there have been inter-marriages; and that, after all, the generations run on in parallel lines, that the lines spread a little in some countries and periods, and narrow a little in other countries and periods. It is like a wall covered with paper in diamond pattern. The lines diverge and converge, but the figures are parallel. See Shedd, Dogm. Theol., 2:7–94, Hist. Doctrine, 2:1–26, Discourses and Essays, 259; Baird, Elohim Revealed, 137–151, 335–384; Edwards, Works, 2:483; Hopkins, Works, 1:289; Birks, Difficulties of Belief, 161; Delitzsch, Bib. Psych., 128–142; Frohschammer, Ursprung der Seele, 59–224.

With regard to this view we remark:

(*a*) It seems best to accord with Scripture, which represents God as creating the species in Adam (Gen. 1 : 27), and as increasing and perpetuating it through secondary agencies (1 : 28 ; *cf.* 22). Only once is breathed into man's nostrils the breath of life (2 : 7, *cf.* 22 ; 1 Cor. 11 : 8. Gen. 4 : 1 ; 5 : 3 ; 46 : 26 ; *cf.* Acts 17 : 21–26 ; Heb. 7 : 10), and after man's formation God ceases from his work of creation (Gen. 2 : 2).

Gen. 1 : 27 — "And God created man in his own image, in the image of God created he him: male and female created he them"; 28 — "And God blessed them: and God said unto them, Be fruitful, and multiply, and replenish the earth"; *cf.* 22 — of the brute creation: "And God blessed them, saying, Be fruitful, and multiply, and fill the waters in the seas, and let birds multiply on the earth." Gen. 2 : 7 -- "And Jehovah God formed man of the dust of the ground, and breathed into his nostrils the breath of life; and man became a living soul"; *cf.* 22 — "and the rib which Jehovah God had taken from the man, made he a woman, and brought her unto the man"; 1 Cor. 11 : 8 — "For the man is not of the woman; but the woman of the man" (ἐξ ἀνδρός). Gen. 4 : 1 — "Eve . . . . bare Cain"; 5 : 3 — "Adam . . . . begat a son . . . . Seth"; 46 : 26 — "All the souls that came with Jacob into Egypt, that came out of his loins"; Acts 17 : 26 — "he made of one ['father' or 'body'] every nation of men"; Heb. 7 : 10 — Levi "was yet in the loins of his father, when Melchisedek met him"; Gen. 2 : 2 — "And on the seventh day God finished his work which he had made;

and he rested on the seventh day from all his work which he had made." Shedd, Dogm. Theol., 2 : 19–29, adduces also John 1 : 13; 3 : 6; Rom. 1 : 13; 5 : 12; 1 Cor. 15 : 22; Eph. 2 : 3; Heb. 12 : 9; Ps. 139 : 15, 16. Only Adam had the right to be a creatianist. Westcott, Com. on Hebrews, 114 — "Levi paying tithes in Abraham implies that descendants are included in the ancestor so far that his acts have force for them. Physically, at least, the dead so rule the living. The individual is not a completely self-centred being. He is member in a body. So far traducianism is true. But, if this were all, man would be a mere result of the past, and would have no individual responsibility. There is an element not derived from birth, though it may follow upon it. Recognition of individuality is the truth in creatianism. Power of vision follows upon preparation of an organ of vision, modified by the latter but not created by it. So we have the social unity of the race, *plus* the personal responsibility of the individual, the influence of common thoughts *plus* the power of great men, the foundation of hope *plus* the condition of judgment."

(*b*) It is favored by the analogy of vegetable and animal life, in which increase of numbers is secured, not by a multiplicity of immediate creations, but by the natural derivation of new individuals from a parent stock. A derivation of the human soul from its parents no more implies a materialistic view of the soul and its endless division and subdivision, than the similar derivation of the brute proves the principle of intelligence in the lower animals to be wholly material.

God's method is not the method of endless miracle. God works in nature through second causes. God does not create a new vital principle at the beginning of existence of each separate apple, and of each separate dog. Each of these is the result of a self-multiplying force, implanted once for all in the first of its race. To say, with Moxom (Baptist Review, 1881 : 278), that God is the immediate author of each new individual, is to deny second causes, and to merge nature in God. The whole tendency of modern science is in the opposite direction. Nor is there any good reason for making the origin of the individual human soul an exception to the general rule. Augustine wavered in his traducianism because he feared the inference that the soul is divided and subdivided,— that is, that it is composed of parts, and is therefore material in its nature. But it does not follow that all separation is material separation. We do not, indeed, know how the soul is propagated. But we know that animal life is propagated, and still that it is not material, nor composed of parts. The fact that the soul is not material, nor composed of parts, is no reason why it may not be propagated also.

It is well to remember that *substance* does not necessarily imply either *extension* or *figure*. *Substantia* is simply that which stands under, underlies, supports, or in other words that which is the *ground* of phenomena. The propagation of mind therefore does not involve any dividing up, or splitting off, as if the mind were a material mass. Flame is propagated, but not by division and subdivision. Professor Ladd is a creatianist, together with Lotze, whom he quotes, but he repudiates the idea that the mind is susceptible of division ; see Ladd, Philosophy of Mind, 206, 359–366 — "The mind comes from nowhere, for it never was, as mind, in space, is not now in space, and cannot be conceived of as coming and going in space. . . . . Mind is a growth. . . . . Parents do not transmit their minds to their offspring. The child's mind does not exist before it acts. Its activities *are* its existence." So we might say that flame has no existence before it acts. Yet it may owe its existence to a preceding flame. The Indian proverb is: "No lotus without a stem." Hall Caine, in his novel The Manxman, tells us that the Deemster of the Isle of Man had two sons. These two sons were as unlike each other as are the inside and the outside of a bowl. But the bowl was old Deemster himself. Hartley Coleridge inherited his father's imperious desire for stimulants and with it his inability to resist their temptation.

(*c*) The observed transmission not merely of physical, but of mental and spiritual, characteristics in families and races, and especially the uniformly evil moral tendencies and dispositions which all men possess from their birth, are proof that in soul, as well as in body, we derive our being from our human ancestry.

Galton, in his Hereditary Genius, and Inquiries into Human Faculty, furnishes abundant proof of the transmission of mental and spiritual characteristics from father to son. Illustrations, in the case of families, are the American Adamses, the English Georges, the French Bourbons, the German Bachs. Illustrations, in the case of races, are the Indians, the Negroes, the Chinese, the Jews. Hawthorne represented the intro-spection and the conscience of Puritan New England. Emerson had a minister among his ancestry, either on the paternal or the maternal side, for eight generations back. Every man is "a chip of the old block." "A man is an omnibus, in which all his ances-tors are seated" (O. W. Holmes). Variation is one of the properties of living things, —the other is transmission. "On a dissecting table, in the membranes of a new-born infant's body, can be seen 'the drunkard's tinge.' The blotches on his grand-child's cheeks furnish a mirror to the old debauchee. Heredity is God's visiting of sin to the third and fourth generations." On heredity and depravity, see Phelps, in Bib. Sac., Apr. 1884 : 254—" When every molecule in the paternal brain bears the shape of a point of interrogation, it would border on the miraculous if we should find the exclamation-sign of faith in the brain-cells of the child."

Robert G. Ingersoll said that most great men have great mothers, and that most great women have great fathers. Most of the great are like mountains, with the valley of ancestors on one side and the depression of posterity on the other. Haw-thorne's House of the Seven Gables illustrates the principle of heredity. But in his Marble Faun and Transformation, Hawthorne unwisely intimates that sin is a necessity to virtue, a background or condition of good. Dryden, Absalom and Ahithophel, 1 : 156 —"Great wits are sure to madness near allied, And thin partititions do their bounds divide." Lombroso, The Man of Genius, maintains that genius is a mental disease allied to epileptiform mania or the dementia of cranks. If this were so, we should inter that civilization is the result of insanity, and that, so soon as Napoleons, Dantes and Newtons manifest themselves, they should be confined in Genius Asylums. Robert Browning, Hohenstiel-Schwangau, comes nearer the truth: "A solitary great man's worth the world. God takes the business into his own hands At such time: Who creates the novel flower Contrives to guard and give it breathing-room. . . . . . 'T is the great Gardener grafts the excellence On wildlings, where he will."

(*d*) The traducian doctrine embraces and acknowledges the element of truth which gives plausibility to the creatian view. Traducianism, properly defined, admits a divine concurrence throughout the whole development of the human species, and allows, under the guidance of a superintending Providence, special improvements in type at the birth of marked men, similar to those which we may suppose to have occurred in the introduction of new varieties in the animal creation.

Page-Roberts, Oxford University Sermons: "It is no more unjust that man should inherit evil tendencies, than that he should inherit good. To make the former impos-sible is to make the latter impossible. To object to the law of heredity, is to object to God's ordinance of society, and to say that God should have made men, like the angels, a company, and not a race." The common moral characteristics of the race can only be accounted for upon the Scriptural view that "that which is born of the flesh is flesh " (John 3 : 6). Since propagation is a propagation of soul, as well as body, we see that to beget children under improper conditions is a crime, and that fœticide is murder. Haeckel, Evolu-tion of Man, 2 : 3 — "The human embryo passes through the whole course of its devel-opment in forty weeks. Each man is really older by this period than is usually assumed. When, for example, a child is said to be nine and a quarter years old, he is really ten years old." Is this the reason why Hebrews call a child a year old at birth? President Edwards prayed for his children and his children's children to the end of time, and President Woolsey congratulated himself that he was one of the inheritors of those prayers. R. W. Emerson: "How can a man get away from his ancestors?" Men of genius should select their ancestors with great care. When begin the instruc-tion of a child? A hundred years before he is born. A lady whose children were noisy and troublesome said to a Quaker relative that she wished she could get a good Quaker governess for them, to teach them the quiet ways of the Society of Friends. "It would not do them that service," was the reply ; "they should have been rocked in a Quaker cradle, if they were to learn Quakerly ways."

Galton, Natural Inheritance, 104 —" The child inherits partly from his parents, partly from his ancestry. In every population that intermarries freely, when the genealogy of any man is traced far backwards, his ancestry will be found to consist of such varied elements that they are indistinguishable from the sample taken at haphazard from the general population. Galton speaks of the tendency of peculiarities to revert to the general type, and says that a man's brother is twice as nearly related to him as his father is, and nine times as nearly as his cousin. The mean stature of any particular class of men will be the same as that of the race; in other words, it will be mediocre. This tells heavily against the full hereditary transmission of any rare and valuable gift, as only a few of the many children would resemble their parents." We may add to these thoughts of Galton that Christ himself, as respects his merely human ancestry, was not so much son of Mary, as he was Son of man.

Brooks, Foundations of Zoölogy, 144-167 — In an investigated case, "in seven and a half generations the maximum ancestry for one person is 382, or for three persons 1146. The names of 452 of them, or nearly half, are recorded, and these 452 named ancestors are not 452 distinct persons, but only 149, many of them, in the remote generations, being common ancestors of all three in many lines. If the lines of descent from the unrecorded ancestors were interrelated in the same way, as they would surely be in an old and stable community, the total ancestry of these three persons for seven and a half generations would be 378 persons instead of 1146. The descendants of many die out. All the members of a species descend from a few ancestors in a remote generation, and these few are the common ancestors of all. Extinction of family names is very common. We must seek in the modern world and not in the remote past for an explanation of that diversity among individuals which passes under the name of variation. The genealogy of a species is not a tree, but a slender thread of very few strands, a little frayed at the near end, but of immeasurable length. A fringe of loose ends all along the thread may represent the animals which having no descendants are now as if they had never been. Each of the strands at the near end is important as a possible line of union between the thread of the past and that of the distant future."

Weismann, Heredity, 270, 272, 380, 384, denies Brooks's theory that the male element represents the principle of variation. He finds the cause of variation in the union of elements from the two parents. Each child unites the hereditary tendencies of two parents, and so must be different from either. The third generation is a compromise between four different hereditary tendencies. Brooks finds the cause of variation in sexual reproduction, but he bases his theory upon the transmission of acquired characters. This transmission is denied by Weismann, who says that the male germ-cell does not play a different part from that of the female in the construction of the embryo. Children inherit quite as much from the father as from the mother. Like twins are derived from the same egg-cell. No two germ-cells contain exactly the same combinations of hereditary tendencies. Changes in environment and organism affect posterity, not directly, but only through other changes produced in its germinal matter. Hence efforts to reach high food cannot directly produce the giraffe. See Dawson, Modern Ideas of Evolution, 235-239; Bradford, Heredity and Christian Problems; Ribot, Heredity; Woods, Heredity in Royalty. On organic unity in connection with realism, see Hodge, in Princeton Rev., Jan. 1865 : 125-135; Dabney, Theology, 317-321.

V. The Moral Nature of Man.

By the moral nature of man we mean those powers which fit him for right or wrong action. These powers are intellect, sensibility, and will, together with that peculiar power of discrimination and impulsion, which we call conscience. In order to moral action, man has intellect or reason, to discern the difference between right and wrong; sensibility, to be moved by each of these; free will, to do the one or the other. Intellect, sensibility, and will, are man's three faculties. But in connection with these faculties there is a sort of activity which involves them all, and without which there can be no moral action, namely, the activity of conscience. Conscience applies the moral law to particular cases in our personal experience, and proclaims that law as binding upon us. Only a rational and sentient being can be truly moral; yet it does not come within our province to treat of man's intellect or sensibility in general. We speak here only of Conscience and of Will.

1. *Conscience.*

A. Conscience an accompanying knowledge. — As already intimated, conscience is not a separate faculty, like intellect, sensibility, and will, but rather a mode in which these faculties act. Like consciousness, conscience is an accompanying knowledge. Conscience is a knowing of self (including our acts and states) in connection with a moral standard, or law. Adding now the element of feeling, we may say that conscience is man's consciousness of his own moral relations, together with a peculiar feeling in view of them. It thus involves the combined action of the intellect and of the sensibility, and that in view of a certain class of objects, viz.: right and wrong.

There is no separate ethical faculty any more than there is a separate æsthetic faculty. Conscience is like taste: it has to do with moral being and relations, as taste has to do with æsthetic being and relations. But the ethical judgment and impulse are, like the æsthetic judgment and impulse, the mode in which intellect, sensibility and will act with reference to a certain class of objects. Conscience deals with the right, as taste deals with the beautiful. As consciousness (*con* and *scio*) is a con-knowing, a knowing of our thoughts, desires and volitions in connection with a knowing of the self that has these thoughts, desires and volitions; so conscience is a con-knowing, a knowing of our moral acts and states in connection with a knowing of some moral standard or law which is conceived of as our true self, and therefore as having authority over us. Ladd, Philosophy of Mind, 183–185 — " The condemnation of self involves self-diremption, double consciousness. Without it Kant's categorical imperative is impossible. The one self lays down the law to the other self, judges it, threatens it. This is what is meant, when the apostle says : 'It is no more I that do it, but sin that dwelleth in me ' (Rom. 7 : 17)."

B. Conscience discriminative and impulsive. — But we need to define more narrowly both the intellectual and the emotional elements in conscience. As respects the intellectual element, we may say that conscience is a power of judgment, — it declares our acts or states to conform, or not to conform, to law; it declares the acts or states which conform to be obligatory, — those which do not conform, to be forbidden. In other words, conscience judges : (1) This is right (or, wrong); (2) I ought (or, I ought not). In connection with this latter judgment, there comes into view the emotional element of conscience, — we feel the claim of duty; there is an inner sense that the wrong must not be done. Thus conscience is (1) discriminative, and (2) impulsive.

Robinson, Principles and Practice of Morality, 173 — " The one distinctive function of conscience is that of authoritative self-judgments in the conscious presence of a supreme Personality to whom we as persons feel ourselves accountable. It is this twofold personal element in every judgment of conscience, *viz.,* the conscious self-judgment in the presence of the all-judging Deity, which has led such writers as Bain and Spencer and Stephen to attempt the explanation of the origin and authority of conscience as the product of parental training and social environment. . . . Conscience is not prudential nor advisory nor executive, but solely judicial. Conscience is the moral reason, pronouncing upon moral actions. Consciousness furnishes law; conscience pronounces judgments; it says : Thou shalt, Thou shalt not. Every man must obey his conscience; if it is not enlightened, that is his look-out. The callousing of conscience in this life is already a penal infliction." S. S. Times, Apl. 5, 1902 : 185 — " Doing as well as we know how is not enough, unless we know just what is right and then do that. God never tells us merely to do our best, or according to our knowledge. It is our duty to know what is right, and then to do it. Ignorantia legis neminem excusat. We have responsibility for knowing preliminary to doing."

C. Conscience distinguished from other mental processes. — The nature and office of conscience will be still more clearly perceived if we distinguish it from other processes and operations with which it is too often confounded. The term conscience has been used by various writers to designate either one or all of the following : 1. *Moral intuition* — the intuitive perception of the difference between right and wrong, as opposite moral categories. 2. *Accepted law* — the application of the intuitive idea to general classes of actions, and the declaration that these classes of actions are right or wrong, apart from our individual relation to them. This accepted law is the complex product of (*a*) the intuitive idea, (*b*) the logical intelligence, (*c*) experiences of utility, (*d*) influences of society and education, and (*e*) positive divine revelation. 3. *Judgment* — applying this accepted law to individual and concrete cases in our own experience, and pronouncing our own acts or states either past, present, or prospective, to be right or wrong. 4. *Command* — authoritative declaration of obligation to do the right, or forbear the wrong, together with an impulse of the sensibility away from the one, and toward the other. 5. *Remorse* or *approval* — moral senti- ments either of approbation or disapprobation, in view of past acts or states, regarded as wrong or right. 6. *Fear* or *hope* — instinctive disposition of disobedience to expect punishment, and of obedience to expect reward.

Ladd, Philos. of Conduct, 70 —"The feeling of the ought is primary, essential, unique ; the judgments as to what one ought are the results of environment, education and reflection." The sentiment of justice is not an inheritance of civilized man alone. No Indian was ever robbed of his lands or had his government allowance stolen from him who was not as keenly conscious of the wrong as in like circumstances we could con ceive that a philosopher would be. The *oughtness* of the ought is certainly intuitive, the *whyness* of the ought (conformity to God) is possibly intuitive also ; the *whatness* of the ought is less certainly intuitive. Cutler, Beginnings of Ethics, 163, 164 — "Intuition tells us *that* we are obliged ; *why* we are obliged, and *what* we are obliged to, we must learn elsewhere." *Obligation* = that which is binding on a man ; *ought* is something owed ; *duty* is something due. The intuitive notion of duty (intellect) is matched by the sense of obligation (feeling).

Bixby, Crisis in Morals, 203, 270 — "All men have a sense of right,— of right to life, and contemporaneously perhaps, but certainly afterwards, of right to personal property. And my right implies duty in my neighbor to respect it. Then the sense of right becomes objective and impersonal. My neighbor's duty to me implies my duty to him. I put myself in his place." Bowne, Principles of Ethics, 156, 188 — " First, the feeling of obligation, the idea of a right and a wrong with corresponding duties, is uni- versal. . . . Secondly, there is a very general agreement in the formal principles of action, and largely in the virtues also, such as benevolence, justice, gratitude. . . . . Whether we owe anything to our neighbor has never been a real question. The prac- tical trouble has always lain in the other question : Who is my neighbor ? Thirdly, the specific contents of the moral ideal are not fixed, but the direction in which the ideal lies is generally discernible. . . . We have in ethics the same fact as in intellect — a potentially infallible standard, with manifold errors in its apprehension and appli- cation. Lucretius held that degradation and paralysis of the moral nature result from religion. Many claim on the other hand that without religion morals would disappear from the earth."

Robinson, Princ. and Prac. of Morality, 173 — " Fear of an omnipotent will is very different from remorse in view of the nature of the supreme Being whose law we have violated." A duty is to be settled in accordance with the standard of absolute right, not as public sentiment would dictate. A man must be ready to do right in spite of what everybody thinks. Just as the decisions of a judge are for the time binding on all good citizens, so the decisions of conscience, as relatively binding, must always be obeyed. They are presumptively right and they are the only present guide of action. Yet man's present state of sin makes it quite possible that the decisions which are relatively right may be absolutely wrong. It is not enough to take one's time from the watch; the watch may go wrong; there is a prior duty of regulating the watch by astronomical standards. Bishop Gore: "Man's first duty is, not to *follow* his conscience, but to *enlighten* his conscience." Lowell says that the Scythians used to eat their grandfathers out of humanity. Paine, Ethnic Trinities, 300 —"Nothing is so stubborn or so fanatical as a wrongly instructed conscience, as Paul showed in his own case by his own confession" (Acts 26 : 9 — "I verily thought with myself that I ought to do many things contrary to the name of Jesus of Nazareth").

D. Conscience the moral judiciary of the soul.— From what has been previously said, it is evident that only 3. and 4. are properly included under the term conscience. Conscience is the moral judiciary of the soul —the power within of judgment and command. Conscience must judge according to the law given to it, and therefore, since the moral standard accepted by the reason may be imperfect, its decisions, while relatively just, may be absolutely unjust. — 1. and 2. belong to the *moral reason*, but not to conscience proper. Hence the duty of enlightening and cultivating the moral reason, so that conscience may have a proper standard of judgment.— 5. and 6. belong to the sphere of *moral sentiment*, and not to conscience proper. The office of conscience is to "bear witness" (Rom. 2 : 15).

In Rom. 2 : 15 — "they show the work of the law written in their hearts, their conscience bearing witness therewith, and their thoughts one with another accusing or else excusing them" — we have conscience clearly distinguished both from the law and the perception of law on the one hand, and from the moral sentiments of approbation and disapprobation on the other. Conscience does not furnish the law, but it bears witness with the law which is furnished by other sources. It is not "that power of mind by which moral law is discovered to each individual" (Calderwood, Moral Philosophy, 77), nor can we speak of "Conscience, the Law" (as Whewell does in his Elements of Morality, 1 : 259-266). Conscience is not the law-book, in the court room, but it is the judge,— whose business is, not to make law, but to decide cases according to the law given to him.

As conscience is not legislative, so it is not retributive; as it is not the law-book, so it is not the sheriff. We say, indeed, in popular language, that conscience scourges or chastises, but it is only in the sense in which we say that the judge punishes,— *i. e.*, through the sheriff. The moral sentiments are the sheriff,— they carry out the decisions of conscience, the judge; but they are not themselves conscience, any more than the sheriff is the judge.

Only this doctrine, that conscience does not discover law, can explain on the one hand the fact that men are bound to follow their consciences, and on the other hand the fact that their consciences so greatly differ as to what is right or wrong in particular cases. The truth is, that conscience is uniform and infallible, in the sense that it always decides rightly according to the law given it. Men's decisions vary, only because the moral reason has presented to the conscience different standards by which to judge.

Conscience can be educated only in the sense of acquiring greater facility and quickness in making its decisions. Education has its chief effect, not upon the conscience, but upon the moral reason, in rectifying its erroneous or imperfect standards of judgment. Give conscience a right law by which to judge, and its decisions will be uniform, and absolutely as well as relatively just. We are bound, not only to "follow our conscience," but to have a right conscience to follow,— and to follow it, not as one follows the beast he drives, but as the soldier follows his commander. Robert J. Burdette: "Following conscience as a guide is like following one's nose. It is important to get the nose pointed right before it is safe to follow it. A man can keep the approval of his own conscience in very much the same way that he can keep directly behind his nose, and go wrong all the time."

Conscience is the con-knowing of a particular act or state, as coming under the law accepted by the reason as to right and wrong; and the judgment of conscience subsumes this act or state under that general standard. Conscience cannot *include* the law — cannot itself *be* the law,—because reason only knows, never *con*-knows. Reason says *scio*; only judgment says *conscia*.

This view enables us to reconcile the intuitional and the empirical theories of morals. Each has its element of truth. The original sense of right and wrong is intuitive, — no education could ever impart the idea of the difference between right and wrong to one who had it not. But what classes of things *are* right or wrong, we learn by the exercise of our logical intelligence, in connection with experiences of utility, influences of society and tradition, and positive divine revelation. Thus our moral reason, through a combination of intuition and education, of internal and external information as to general principles of right and wrong, furnishes the standard according to which conscience may judge the particular cases which come before it.

This moral reason may become depraved by sin, so that the light becomes darkness (Mat. 6:22, 23) and conscience has only a perverse standard by which to judge. The "weak" conscience (1 Cor. 8:12) is one whose standard of judgment is yet imperfect; the conscience "branded" (Rev. Vers.) or "seared" (A. V.) "as with a hot iron" (1 Tim. 4:2) is one whose standard has been wholly perverted by practical disobedience. The word and the Spirit of God are the chief agencies in rectifying our standards of judgment, and so of enabling conscience to make absolutely right decisions. God can so unite the soul to Christ, that it becomes partaker on the one hand of his satisfaction to justice and is thus "sprinkled from an evil conscience" (Heb. 10:22), and on the other hand of his sanctifying power and is thus enabled in certain respects to obey God's command and to speak of a "good conscience" (1 Pet. 3:16 — of single act; 3:21 — of state) instead of an "evil conscience" (Heb. 10:22) or a conscience "defiled" (Tit. 1:15) by sin. Here the "good conscience" is the conscience which has been obeyed by the will, and the "evil conscience" the conscience which has been disobeyed; with the result, in the first case, of approval from the moral sentiments, and, in the second case, of disapproval.

E. Conscience in its relation to God as law-giver. — Since conscience, in the proper sense, gives uniform and infallible judgment that the right is supremely obligatory, and that the wrong must be forborne at every cost, it can be called an echo of God's voice, and an indication in man of that which his own true being requires.

Conscience has sometimes been described as the voice of God in the soul, or as the personal presence and influence of God himself. But we must not identify conscience with God. D. W. Faunce: "Conscience is not God, — it is only a part of one's self. To build up a religion about one's own conscience, as if it were God, is only a refined selfishness — a worship of one part of one's self by another part of one's self." In The Excursion, Wordsworth speaks of conscience as "God's most intimate presence in the soul And his most perfect image in the world." But in his Ode to Duty he more discreetly writes: "Stern daughter of the voice of God! O Duty! if that name thou love, Who art a light to guide, a rod To check the erring, and reprove, Thou who art victory and law When empty terrors overawe, From vain temptations dost set free And calmst the weary strife of frail humanity!" Here is an allusion to the Hebrew Bath Kol. "The Jews say that the Holy Spirit spoke during the Tabernacle by Urim and Thummim, under the first Temple by the Prophets, and under the second Temple by the Bath Kol — a divine intimation as inferior to the oracular voice proceeding from the mercy seat as a daughter is supposed to be inferior to her mother. It is also used in the sense of an approving conscience. In this case it is the echo of the voice of God in those who by obeying hear" (Hershon's Talmudic Miscellany, 2, note). This phrase, "the echo of God's voice," is a correct description of conscience, and Wordsworth probably had it in mind when he spoke of duty as "the daughter of the voice of God." Robert Browning describes conscience as "the great beacon-light God sets in all. . . . . The worst man upon earth . . . . knows in his conscience more Of what right is, than arrives at birth In the best man's acts that we bow before." Jackson, James Martineau, 154 — The sense of obligation is "a piercing ray of the great Orb of souls." On Wordsworth's conception of conscience, see A. H. Strong, Great Poets, 365–368.

Since the activity of the immanent God reveals itself in the normal operations of our own faculties, conscience might be also regarded as man's true self over against the false self which we have set up against it. Theodore Parker defines conscience as "our consciousness of the conscience of God." In his fourth year, says Chadwick, his biographer (pages 12, 13, 185), young Theodore saw a little spotted tortoise and lifted his hand to strike. All at once something checked his arm, and a voice within said clear and loud: "It is wrong." He asked his mother what it was that told him it was wrong.

She wiped a tear from her eye with her apron, and taking him in her arms said : " Some men call it conscience, but I prefer to call it the voice of God in the soul of man. If you listen and obey it, then it will speak clearer and clearer, and will always guide you right ; but if you turn a deaf ear and disobey, then it will fade out little by little, and will leave you all in the dark and without a guide. Your life depends on your hearing this little voice." R. T. Smith, Man's Knowledge of Man and of God, 87, 171 — " Man has conscience, as he has talents. Conscience, no more than talent, makes him good. He is good, only as he follows conscience and uses talent. . . . . The relation between the terms consciousness and conscience, which are in fact but forms of the same word, testifies to the fact that it is in the action of conscience that man's consciousness of himself is chiefly experienced."

The conscience of the regenerate man may have such right standards, and its decisions may be followed by such uniformly right action, that its voice, though it is not itself God's voice, is yet the very echo of God's voice. The renewed conscience may take up into itself, and may express, the witness of the Holy Spirit (Rom. 9 : 1 — " I say the truth in Christ, I lie not, my conscience bearing witness with me in the Holy Spirit " ; cf. 8 : 16 — " the Spirit himself beareth witness with our spirit, that we are children of God "). But even when conscience judges according to imperfect standards, and is imperfectly obeyed by the will, there is a spontaneity in its utterances and a sovereignty in its commands. It declares that whatever is right must be done. The imperative of conscience is a " categorical imperative " (Kant). It is independent of the human will. Even when disobeyed, it still asserts its authority. Before conscience, every other impulse and affection of man's nature is called to bow.

F. Conscience in its relation to God as holy.— Conscience is not an original authority. It points to something higher than itself. The "authority of conscience" is simply the authority of the moral law, or rather, the authority of the personal God, of whose nature the law is but a transcript. Conscience, therefore, with its continual and supreme demand that the right should be done, furnishes the best witness to man of the existence of a personal God, and of the supremacy of holiness in him in whose image we are made.

In knowing self in connection with moral law, man not only gets his best knowledge of self, but his best knowledge of that other self opposite to him, namely, God. Gordon, Christ of To-day, 236 — " The conscience is the true Jacob's ladder, set in the heart of the individual and reaching unto heaven ; and upon it the angels of self-reproach and self-approval ascend and descend." This is of course true if we confine our thoughts to the mandatory element in revelation. There is a higher knowledge of God which is given only in grace. Jacob's ladder symbolizes the Christ who publishes not only the gospel but the law, and not only the law but the gospel. Dewey, Psychology, 344 — " Conscience is intuitive, not in the sense that it enunciates universal laws and principles, for it lays down no laws. Conscience is a name for the experience of personality that any given act is in harmony or in discord with a truly realized personality." Because obedience to the dictates of conscience is always relatively right, Kant could say that "an erring conscience is a chimæra." But because the law accepted by conscience may be absolutely wrong, conscience may in its decisions greatly err from the truth. S. S. Times : " Saul before his conversion was a conscientious wrong doer. His spirit and character was commendable, while his conduct was reprehensible." We prefer to say that Saul's zeal for the law was a zeal to make the law subservient to his own pride and honor.

Horace Bushnell said that the first requirement of a great ministry is a great conscience. He did not mean the punitive, inhibitory conscience merely, but rather the discovering, arousing, inspiring conscience, that sees at once the great things to be done, and moves toward them with a shout and a song. This unbiased and pure conscience is inseparable from the sense of its relation to God and to God's holiness. Shakespeare, Henry VI, 2d Part, 3 : 2 — " What stronger breastplate than a heart untainted ? Thrice is he armed that hath his quarrel just ; And he but naked, though locked up in steel, Whose conscience with injustice is corrupted." Huxley, in his lecture at Oxford in 1893, admits and even insists that ethical practice must be and should be in opposition to evolution ; that the methods of evolution do not account for ethical man and his ethical progress. Morality is not a product of the same methods by which lower orders have advanced in perfection of organization, namely, by the struggle for existence and survival of the fittest. Human progress is moral, is in freedom, is under the law of love, is different in kind from physical evolution. James Russell Lowell: " In vain we call old notions fudge, And bend our conscience to our dealing: The ten commandments will not budge, And stealing will continue stealing."

R. T. Smith, Man's Knowledge of Man and of God, 161 — " Conscience lives in human nature like a rightful king, whose claim can never be forgotten by his people, even though they dethrone and misuse him, and whose presence on the seat of judgment can alone make the nation to be at peace with itself." Seth, Ethical Principles, 424 — " The Kantian theory of autonomy does not tell the whole story of the moral life. Its unyielding Ought, its categorical Imperative, issues not merely from the depths of our own nature, but from the heart of the universe itself. We are self-legislative; but we reënact the law already enacted by God; we recognize, rather than constitute, the law of our own being. The moral law is an echo, within our own souls, of the voice of the Eternal, 'whose offspring we are' (Acts 17 : 28)."

Schenkel, Christliche Dogmatik, 1 : 135-155 — " The conscience is the organ by which the human spirit finds God in itself and so becomes aware of itself in him. Only in conscience is man conscious of himself as eternal, as distinct from God, yet as normally bound to be determined wholly by God. When we subject ourselves wholly to God, conscience gives us peace. When we surrender to the world the allegiance due only to God, conscience brings remorse. In this latter case we become aware that while God is in us, we are no longer in God. Religion is exchanged for ethics, the relation of communion for the relation of separation. In conscience alone man distinguishes himself absolutely from the brute. Man does not make conscience, but conscience makes man. Conscience feels every separation from God as an injury to self. Faith is the relating of the self-consciousness to the God-consciousness, the becoming sure of our own personality, in the absolute personality of God. Only in faith does conscience come to itself. But by sin this faith-consciousness may be turned into law-consciousness. Faith affirms God *in* us; Law affirms God *outside* of us." Schenkel differs from Schleiermacher in holding that religion is not feeling but conscience, and that it is not a sense of dependence on the world, but a sense of dependence on God. Conscience recognizes a God distinct from the universe, a moral God and so makes an unmoral religion impossible.

Hopkins, Outline Study of Man, 283-285, Moral Science, 49, Law of Love, 41 — " Conscience is the moral consciousness of man in view of his own actions as related to moral law. It is a double knowledge of self and of the law. Conscience is not the whole of the moral nature. It presupposes the moral reason, which recognizes the moral law and affirms its universal obligation for all moral beings. It is the office of conscience to bring man into personal relation to this law. It sets up a tribunal within him by which his own actions are judged. Not conscience, but the moral reason, judges of the conduct of others. This last is *science*, but not *conscience*."

Peabody, Moral Philos., 41-60 — " Conscience not a source, but a means, of knowledge. Analogous to consciousness. A judicial faculty. Judges according to the law before it. Verdict (verum dictum) always relatively right, although, by the absolute standard of right, it may be wrong. Like all perceptive faculties, educated by use (not by increase of knowledge only, for man may act worse, the more knowledge he has). For absolutely right decisions, conscience is dependent upon knowledge. To recognize conscience as *legislator* (as well as judge), is to fail to recognize any objective standard of right." The Two Consciences, 46, 47 — " Conscience the Law, and Conscience the Witness. The latter is the true and proper Conscience."

H. B. Smith, System of Christ. Theology, 178-191 — " The unity of conscience is not in its being one faculty or in its performing one function, but in its having one *object*, its relation to one idea, viz., *right*. . . . The term 'conscience' no more designates a special faculty than the term 'religion' does (or than the 'æsthetic sense'). . . . . The existence of conscience proves a moral law above us; it leads logically to a Moral Governor; . . . . it implies an essential distinction between right and wrong, an immutable morality; . . . . yet needs to be enlightened; . . . men may be conscientious in iniquity; . . . conscience is not righteousness; . . . this may only show the greatness of the depravity, having conscience, and yet ever disobeying it."

On the New Testament passages with regard to conscience, see Hofmann, Lehre von dem Gewissen, 30-38; Kähler, Das Gewissen, 225-293. For the view that conscience is primarily the cognitive or intuitional power of the soul, see Calderwood, Moral Philosophy, 77; Alexander, Moral Science, 20; McCosh, Div. Govt., 297-312; Talbot, Ethical

Prolegomena, in Bap. Quar., July, 1877 : 257-274 ; Park, Discourses, 260-296 ; **Whewell,** Elements of Morality, 1 : 259-266. On the whole subject of conscience, see Mansel, Metaphysics, 158-170 ; Martineau, Religion and Materialism, 45 — "The discovery of duty is as distinctly relative to an objective Righteousness as the perception of form to an external space " ; also Types, 2 : 27-30 — " We first judge ourselves ; then others " ; 53, 54, 74, 103 — "Subjective morals are as absurd as subjective mathematics." The best brief treatment of the whole subject is that of E. G. Robinson, Principles and Practice of Morality, 26-78. See also Wayland, Moral Science, 49 ; Harless, Christian Ethics, 45, 60 ; H. N. Day, Science of Ethics, 17 ; Janet, Theory of Morals, 264, 348 ; Kant, Metaphysic of Ethics, 62 ; *cf.* Schwegler, Hist. Philosophy, 233 ; Haven, Mor. Philos., 41 ; Fairchild, Mor. Philos., 75 ; Gregory, Christian Ethics, 71 ; Passavant, Das Gewissen ; Wm. Schmid, Das Gewissen.

2. *Will.*

A. Will defined.—Will is the soul's power to choose between motives and to direct its subsequent activity according to the motive thus chosen,— in other words, the soul's power to choose both an end and the means to attain it. The choice of an ultimate end we call immanent preference ; the choice of means we call executive volition.

In this definition we part company with Jonathan Edwards, Freedom of the Will, in Works, vol. 2. He regards the will as the soul's power to act according to motive, *i. e.,* to act out its nature, but he denies the soul's power to choose between motives, *i. e.,* to initiate a course of action contrary to the motive which has been previously dominant. Hence he is unable to explain how a holy being, like Satan or Adam, could ever fall. If man has no power to change motives, to break with the past, to begin a new course of action, he has no more freedom than the brute. The younger Edwards (Works, 1 : 483) shows what his father's doctrine of the will implies, when he says : " Beasts therefore, according to the measure of their intelligence, are as free as men. Intelligence, and not liberty, is the only thing wanting to constitute them moral agents." Yet Jonathan Edwards, determinist as he was, in his sermon on Pressing into the Kingdom of God (Works, 4 : 381), urges the use of means, and appeals to the sinner as if he had the power of choosing between the motives of self and of God. He was unconsciously making a powerful appeal to the will, and the human will responded in prolonged and mighty efforts ; see Allen, Jonathan Edwards, 109.

For references, and additional statements with regard to the will and its freedom, see chapter on Decrees, pages 361, 362, and article by A. H. Strong, in Baptist Review, 1883 : 219-242, and reprinted in Philosophy and Religion, 114-128. In the remarks upon the Decrees, we have intimated our rejection of the Arminian liberty of indifference, or the doctrine that the will can act without motive. See this doctrine advocated in Peabody, Moral Philosophy, 1-9. But we also reject the theory of determinism propounded by Jonathan Edwards (Freedom of the Will, in Works, vol. 2), which, as we have before remarked, identifies sensibility with the will, regards affections as the efficient causes of volitions, and speaks of the connection between motive and action as a necessary one. Hazard, Man a Creative First Cause, and The Will, 407 — " Edwards gives to the controlling cause of volition in the past the name of motive. He treats the inclination as a motive, but he also makes inclination synonymous with choice and will, which would make will to be only the soul willing — and therefore the cause of its own act." For objections to the Arminian theory, see H. B. Smith, Review of Whedon, in Faith and Philosophy, 359-399 ; McCosh, Divine Government, 263-318, esp. 312 ; E. G. Robinson, Principles and Practice of Morality, 109-137 ; Shedd, Dogm. Theol., 2 : 115-147.

James, Psychology, 1 : 139 — " Consciousness is primarily a selecting agency." 2 : 393 —" Man possesses all the instincts of animals, and a great many more besides. Reason, *per se,* can inhibit no impulses ; the only thing that can neutralize an impulse is an impulse the other way. Reason may however make an inference which will excite the imagination to let loose the impulse the other way." 549 — " Ideal or moral action is action in the line of the greatest resistance." 562 — " Effort of attention is the essential phenomenon of will." 567 — " The terminus of the psychological process is volition ; the point to which the will is directly applied is always an idea." 568 — " Though attention is the first thing in volition, express consent to the reality of what is attended to is an additional and distinct phenomenon. We say not only : It is a reallty ; but we also say : 'Let it be a reality.'" 571 — "Are the duration and intensity of this effort fixed functions of the object, or are they not? We answer, *No*, and so we maintain freedom of the will." 584 — "The soul presents nothing, creates nothing, is at the mercy of material forces for all possibilities, and, by reinforcing one and checking others, it figures not as an *epiphenomenon*, but as something from which the play gets moral support." Alexander, Theories of the Will, 201-214, finds in Reid's Active Powers of the Human Mind the most adequate empirical defense of indeterminism.

B. **Will and other faculties.** — (*a*) We accept the threefold division of human faculties into intellect, sensibility, and will. (*b*) Intellect is the soul knowing ; sensibility is the soul feeling (desires, affections) ; will is the soul choosing (end or means). (*c*) In every act of the soul, all the faculties act. Knowing involves feeling and willing ; feeling involves knowing and willing ; willing involves knowing and feeling. (*d*) Logically, each latter faculty involves the preceding action of the former ; the the soul must know before feeling ; must know and feel before willing. (*e*) Yet since knowing and feeling are activities, neither of these is possible without willing.

Socrates to Theætetus : " It would be a singular thing, my lad, if each of us was, as it were, a wooden horse, and within us were seated many separate senses. For manifestly these senses unite into one nature, call it the soul or what you will. And it is with this central form, through the organs of sense, that we perceive sensible objects." Lewey, Psychology, 21 — " Knowledge and feeling are partial aspects of the self, and hence more or less abstract, while will is complete, comprehending both aspects. . . . While the universal element is knowledge, the individual element is feeling, and the relation which connects them into one concrete content is will." 364 — "There is conflict of desires or motives. Deliberation is the comparison of desires ; choice is the decision in favor of one. This desire is then the strongest because the whole force of the self is thrown into it." 411 — "The man determines himself by setting up either good or evil as a motive to himself, and he sets up either, as he will have himself be. There is no thought without will, for thought implies inhibition." Ribot, Diseases of the Will, 73, cites the case of Coleridge, and his lack of power to inhibit scattering and useless ideas ; 114 — " Volition plunges its roots into the profoundest depths of the individual, and beyond the individual, into the species and into all species."

As God is not mere nature but originating force, so man is chiefly will. Every other act of the soul has will as an element. Wundt : " Jedes Denken ist ein Wollen." There is no perception, and there is no thought, without attention, and attention is an act of the will. Hegelians and absolute idealists like Bradley, (see Mind, July, 1886), deny that attention is an active function of the self. They regard it as a necessary consequence of the more interesting character of preceding ideas. Thus all power to alter character is denied to the agent. This is an exact reversal of the facts of consciousness, and it would leave no will in God or man. T. H. Green says that the self makes the motives by identifying itself with one solicitation of desire rather than another, but that the self has no power of alternative choice in thus identifying itself with one solicitation of desire rather than another ; see Upton, Hibbert Lectures, 310. James Seth, Freedom of Ethical Postulate : " The only hope of finding a place for real free will is in another than the Humian, empirical or psychological account of the moral person or self. Hegel and Green bring will again under the law of necessity. But personality is ultimate. Absolute uniformity is entirely unproved. We contend for a power of free and incalculable initiation in the self, and this it is necessary to maintain in the interests of morality." Without will to attend to pertinent material and to reject the impertinent, we can have no *science* ; without will to select and combine the elements of imagination, we can have no *art* ; without will to choose between evil and good, we can have no *morality*. Ælfric, A. D. 900 : "The verb 'to will' has no imperative, for that the will must be always free."

C. **Will and permanent states.** — (*a*) Though every act of the soul involves the action of all the faculties, yet in any particular action one faculty may be more prominent than the others. So we speak of acts of

intellect, of affection, of will. (*b*) This predominant action of any single
faculty produces effects upon the other faculties associated with it. The
action of will gives a direction to the intellect and to the affections, as well
as a permanent bent to the will itself. (*c*) Each faculty, therefore, has its
permanent states as well as its transient acts, and the will may originate
these states. Hence we speak of voluntary affections, and may with equal
propriety speak of voluntary opinions. These permanent voluntary states
we denominate character.

I "make up." my mind. Ladd, Philosophy of Conduct, 152 — " I will the influential
ideas, feelings and desires, rather than allow these ideas, feelings and desires to influence
— not to say, determine me." All men can say with Robert Browning's Paracelsus: " I
have subdued my life to the one purpose Whereto I ordained it." " Sow an act, and
you reap a habit ; sow a habit, and you reap a character ; sow a character, and you reap
a destiny." Tito, in George Eliot's Romola, and Markheim in R. L. Stevenson's story
of that name, are instances of the gradual and almost imperceptible fixation in evil
ways which results from seemingly slight original decisions of the will; see art. on Tito
Melema, by Julia H. Gulliver, in New World, Dec. 1895 : 688 — " Sin lies in the choice of
the ideas that shall frequent the moral life, rather than of the actions that shall
form the outward life. . . . . The pivotal point of the moral life is the intent involved
in attention. . . . . Sin consists, not only in the motive, but in the making of the
motive." By every decision of the will in which we turn our thought either toward or
away from an object of desire, we set nerve-tracts in operation, upon which thought
may hereafter more or less easily travel. " Nothing makes an inroad, without making
a road." By slight efforts of attention to truth which we know ought to influence us,
we may " make level in the desert a highway for our God " (Is. 40 : 3), or render the soul a hard trodden
ground impervious to " the word of the kingdom " (Mat. 13 : 19).

The word "character" meant originally the mark of the engraver's tool upon the
metal or the stone. It came then to signify the collective result of the engraver's work.
The use of the word in morals implies that every thought and act is chiseling itself
into the imperishable substance of the soul. J. S. Mill : " A character is a completely
fashioned will." We may talk therefore of a "generic volition " (Dewey). There is
a permanent bent of the will toward good or toward evil. Reputation is man's shadow,
sometimes longer, sometimes shorter, than himself. Character, on the other hand, is
the man's true self — " what a man is in the dark " (Dwight L. Moody). In this sense,
" purpose is the autograph of mind." Duke of Wellington : " Habit a second nature?
Habit is ten times nature !" When Macbeth says: " If 't were done when 't is done, Then
't were well 't were done quickly," the trouble is that when 't is done, it is only begun.
Robert Dale Owen gives us the fundamental principle of socialism in the maxim : " A
man's character is made for him, not by him." Hence he would change man's diet or
his environment, as a means of forming man's character. But Jesus teaches that what
defiles comes not from without but from within (Mat. 15 : 18). Because character is the
result of will, the maxim of Heraclitus is true : ἦθος ἀνθρώπῳ δαίμων = man's character
is his destiny. On habit, see James, Psychology, 1 : 122–127.

D. Will and motives. — (*a*) The permanent states just mentioned, when
they have been once determined, also influence the will. Internal views and
dispositions, and not simply external presentations, constitute the strength
of motives. (*b*) These motives often conflict, and though the soul never
acts without motive, it does notwithstanding choose between motives, and
so determines the end toward which it will direct its activities. (*c*)
Motives are not *causes*, which compel the will, but *influences*, which persuade it. The power of these motives, however, is proportioned to the
strength of will which has entered into them and has made them what
they are.

"Incentives comes from the soul's self : the rest avail not." The same wind may
drive two ships in opposite directions, according as they set their sails. The same
external presentation may result in George Washington's refusing, and Benedict

Arnold's accepting, the bribe to betray his country. Richard Lovelace of Canterbury: "Stone walls do not a prison make, Nor iron bars a cage; Minds innocent and quiet take That for a hermitage." Jonathan Edwards made motives to be *efficient* causes, when they are only *final* causes. We must not interpret motive as if it were locomotive. It is always a man's fault when he becomes a drunkard: drink never takes to a man; the man takes to drink. Men who deny demerit are ready enough to claim merit. They hold others responsible, if not themselves. Bowne: "Pure arbitrariness and pure necessity are alike incompatible with reason. There must be a law of reason in the mind with which volition cannot tamper, and there must also be the power to determine ourselves accordingly." Bowne, Principles of Ethics, 135—"If necessity is a universal thing, then the belief in freedom is also necessary. All grant freedom of thought, so that it is only executive freedom that is denied." Bowne, Theory of Thought and Knowledge, 239-244—"Every system of philosophy must invoke freedom for the solution of the problem of error, or make shipwreck of reason itself. . . . Our faculties are made for truth, but they may be carelessly used, or wilfully misused, and thus error is born. . . . . We need not only laws of thought, but self-control in accordance with them."

The will, in choosing *between* motives, chooses *with* a motive, namely, the motive chosen. Fairbairn, Philos. Christian Religion, 76—"While motives may be necessary, they need not necessitate. The will selects motives; motives do not select the will. Heredity and environment do not cancel freedom, they only condition it. Thought is transcendence as regards the phenomena of space; will is transcendence as regards the phenomena of time; this double transcendence involves the complete supernatural character of man." New World, 1892:152—"It is not the character, but the self that has the character, to which the ultimate moral decision is due." William Ernest Henly, Poems, 119—"It matters not how strait the gate, How charged with punishments the scroll, I am the master of my fate, I am the captain of my soul."

Julius Müller, Doctrine of Sin, 2:54—"A being is free, in so far as the inner centre of its life, from which it acts, is conditioned by self-determination. It is not enough that the deciding agent in an act be the man himself, his own nature, his distinctive character. In order to accountability, we must have more than this; we must prove that this, his distinctive nature and character, springs from his own volition, and that it is itself the product of freedom in moral development. Matt. 12:33—"make the tree good, and its fruit good"—combines both. Acts depend upon nature; but nature again depends upon the primary decisions of the will ("make the tree good"). Some determinism is not denied; but it is partly limited [by the will's remaining power of choice] and partly traced back to a former self-determining." *Ibid.*, 67—"If freedom be the self-determining of the will from that which is undetermined, Determinism is found wanting,—because in its most spiritual form, though it grants a self-determination of the will, it is only such a one as springs from a determinateness already present; and Indifferentism is found wanting too, because while it maintains indeterminateness as presupposed in every act of will, it does not recognize an actual self-determining on the part of the will, which, though it be a self-determining, yet begets determinateness of ·character. . . . . We must, therefore, hold the doctrine of a *conditional* and *limited* freedom."

E. Will and contrary choice. — (*a*) Though no act of pure will is possible, the soul may put forth single volitions in a direction opposed to its previous ruling purpose, and thus far man has the power of a contrary choice (Rom. 7 : 18— "to will is present with me"). (*b*) But in so far as will has entered into and revealed itself in permanent states of intellect and sensibility and in a settled bent of the will itself, man cannot by a single act reverse his moral state, and in this respect has not the power of a contrary choice. (*c*) In this latter case he can change his character only indirectly, by turning his attention to considerations fitted to awaken opposite dispositions, and by thus summoning up motives to an opposite course.

There is no such thing as an act of pure will. Peters, Willenswelt, 126—"Jedes Wollen ist ein Etwas wollen"—"all willing is a willing of some thing"; it has an object which the mind conceives, which awakens the sensibility, and which the will strives

to realize. Cause without alternative is not true cause. J. F. Watts: " We know causality only as we know will, *i. e.*, where of two possibles it makes one actual. A cause
may therefore have more than one certain effect. In the external material world we
cannot find *cause*, but only *antecedent.* To construct a theory of the will from a study
of the material universe is to seek the living among the dead. Will is power to *make* a
decision, not to *be made* by decisions, to decide between motives, and not to be determined by motives. Who conducts the trial between motives ? Only the self." While
we agree with the above in its assertion of the certainty of nature's sequences, we
object to its attribution even to nature of anything like necessity. Since nature's laws
are merely the habits of God, God's causality in nature is the regularity, not of necessity, but of freedom. We too are free at the strategic points. Automatic as most of
our action is, there are times when we know ourselves to have power of initiative ;
when we put under our feet the motives which have dominated us in the past ; when
we mark out new courses of action. In these critical times we assert our manhood :
but for them we would be no better than the beasts that perish. " Unless above himself he can erect himself, How mean a thing is man ! "

Will, with no remaining power of contrary choice, may be brute will, but it is not
free will. We therefore deny the relevancy of Herbert Spencer's argument, in his
Data of Ethics, and in his Psychology, 2 : 503 — "Psychical changes either conform to
law, or they do not. If they do not conform to law, no science of Psychology is possible. If they do conform to law, there cannot be any such thing as free will." Spinoza
also, in his Ethics, holds that the stone, as it falls, would if it were conscious think itself free, and with as much justice as man ; for it is doing that to which its constitution
leads it ; but no more can be said for him. Fisher, Nature and Method of Revelation,
xiii — " To try to collect the 'data of ethics' when there is no recognition of man as a
personal agent, capable of freely originating the conduct and the states of will for
which he is morally responsible, is labor lost." Fisher, chapter on the Personality of
God, in Grounds of Theistic and Christian Belief — "Self-determination, as the very
term signifies, is attended with an irresistible conviction that the direction of the will is
self-imparted. . . . . That the will is free, that is, not constrained by causes exterior,
which is *fatalism* — and not a mere spontaneity, confined to one path by a force acting
from within, which is *determinism* — is immediately evident to every unsophisticated
mind. We can initiate action by an efficiency which is neither irresistibly controlled
by motives, nor determined, without any capacity of alternative action, by a proneness
inherent in its nature. . . . . Motives have an *influence*, but influence is not to be confounded with *causal* efficiency."

Talbot, on Will and Free Will, Bap. Rev., July, 1882 — " Will is neither a power of
unconditioned self-determination — which is not freedom, but an aimless, irrational,
fatalistic power ; nor pure spontaneity — which excludes from will all law but its own ;
but it is rather a power of originating action — a power which is limited however by
inborn dispositions, by acquired habits and convictions, by feelings and social relations."
Ernest Naville, in Rev. Chrétienne, Jan. 1878 : 7 — " Our liberty does not consist in producing an action of which it is the only source. It consists in choosing between two
preëxistent impulses. It is *choice*, not *creation*, that is our destiny — a drop of water
that can choose whether it will go into the Rhine or the Rhone. Gravity carries it
down, — it chooses only its direction. Impulses do not come from the will, but from the
sensibility ; but free will chooses between these impulses." Bowne, Metaphysics, 169 —
" Freedom is not a power of acting without, or apart from, motives, but simply a power
of choosing an end or law, and of governing one's self accordingly." Porter, Moral
Science, 77-111 — Will is "not a power to choose without motive." It "does not exclude
motives to the contrary." Volition "supposes two or more objects between which
election is made. It is an act of preference, and to prefer implies that one motive is
chosen to the exclusion of another. . . . . To the conception and the act two motives at
least are required." Lyall, Intellect, Emotions, and Moral Nature, 581, 592 — " The will
follows reasons, inducements — but it is not *caused*. It obeys or acts under inducement,
but it does so sovereignly. It exhibits the phenomena of activity, in relation to the
very motive it obeys. It obeys it, rather than another. It determines, in reference to
it, that this is the very motive it will obey. There is undoubtedly this phenomenon
exhibited : the will obeying — but elective, active, in its obedience. If it be asked how
this is possible — how the will can be under the influence of motive, and yet possess an
intellectual activity — we reply that this is one of those ultimate phenomena which
must be admitted, while they cannot be explained."

F. Will and responsibility.—(*a*) By repeated acts of will put forth in a given moral direction, the affections may become so confirmed in evil or in good as to make previously certain, though not necessary, the future good or evil action of the man. Thus, while the will is free, the man may be the "bondservant of sin" (John 8 : 31-36) or the "servant of righteousness " (Rom. 6 : 15-23 ; *cf.* Heb. 12-23 — "spirits of just men made perfect "). (*b*) Man is responsible for all effects of will, as well as for will itself ; for voluntary affections, as well as for voluntary acts ; for the intellectual views into which will has entered, as well as for the acts of will by which these views have been formed in the past or are maintained in the present (2 Pet. 3 : 5 — "wilfully forget ").

Ladd, Philosophy of Knowledge, 415 — "The self stands between the two laws of Nature and of Conscience, and, under perpetual limitations from both, exercises its choice. Thus it becomes more and more enslaved by the one, or more and more free by habitually choosing to follow the other. Our conception of causality according to the laws of nature, and our conception of the other causality of freedom, are both derived from one and the same experience of the self. There arises a seeming antinomy only when we hypostatize each severally and apart from the other." R. T. Smith, Man's Knowledge of Man and of God, 69 — "Making a *will* is significant. Here the action of will is limited by conditions : the amount of the testator's property, the number of his relatives, the nature of the objects of bounty within his knowledge."

Harris, Philos. Basis of Theism, 349-407 — "Action without motives, or contrary to all motives, would be irrational action. Instead of being free, it would be like the convulsions of epilepsy. Motives = sensibilities. Motive is not *cause ;* does not determine ; is only influence. Yet determination is always made under the influence of motives. Uniformity of action is not to be explained by any law of uniform influence of motives, but by *character* in the will. By its choice, will forms in itself a character ; by action in accordance with this choice, it confirms and develops the character. Choice modifies sensibilities, and so modifies motives. Volitional action expresses character, but also forms and modifies it. Man may change his choice ; yet intellect, sensibility, motive, habit, remain. Evil choice, having formed intellect and sensibility into accord with itself, must be a powerful hindrance to fundamental change by new and contrary choice ; and gives small ground to expect that man left to himself ever will make the change. After will has acquired character by choices, its determinations are not transitions from complete indeterminateness or indifference, but are more or less expressions of character already formed. The theory that indifference is essential to freedom implies that will never acquires character ; that voluntary action is atomistic ; that every act is disintegrated from every other ; that character, if acquired, would be incompatible with freedom. Character is a choice, yet a choice which persists, which modifies sensibility and intellect, and which influences subsequent determinations."

My freedom then is freedom within limitations. Heredity and environment, and above all the settled dispositions which are the product of past acts of will, render a large part of human action practically automatic. The deterministic theory is valid for perhaps nine-tenths of human activity. Mason, Faith of the Gospel, 118, 119 — " We naturally will with a bias toward evil. To act according to the perfection of nature would be true freedom. And this man has lost. He recognizes that he is not his true self. It is only with difficulty that he works toward his true self again. By the fall of Adam, the will, which before was conditioned but free, is now not only conditioned but enslaved. Nothing but the action of grace can free it." Tennyson, In Memoriam, Introduction: " Our wills are ours, we know not how ; Our wills are ours, to make them thine." Studying the action of the sinful will alone, one might conclude that there is no such thing as freedom. Christian ethics, in distinction from naturalistic ethics, reveals most clearly the degradation of our nature, at the same time that it discloses the remedy in Christ : "If therefore the Son shall make you free, ye shall be free indeed " (John 8 : 36).

Mind, Oct. 1882 : 567 — "Kant seems to be in quest of the phantasmal freedom which is supposed to consist in the absence of determination by motives. The error of the determinists from which this idea is the recoil, involves an equal abstraction of the man from his thoughts, and interprets the relation between the two as an instance of the mechanical causality which exists between two things in nature. The point to be grasped in the controversy is that a man and his motives are one, and that consequently he is in every instance self-determined. . . . . Indeterminism is tenable only if an ego can be found which is not an ego already determinate; but such an ego, though it may be logically distinguished and verbally expressed, is not a factor in psychology." Morell, Mental Philosophy, 390 — "Motives determine the will, and *so far* the will is not free; but the man governs the motives, allowing them a less or a greater power of influencing his life, and *so far* the man is a free agent." Santayana: "A free man, because he is free, may make himself a slave; but once a slave, because he is a slave, he cannot make himself free." Sidgwick, Method of Ethics, 51, 65 — "This almost overwhelming cumulative proof [of necessity] seems, however, more than balanced by a single argument on the other side: the immediate affirmation of consciousness in the moment of deliberate volition. It is impossible for me to think, at each moment, that my volition is completely determined by my formed character and the motives acting upon it. The opposite conviction is so strong as to be absolutely unshaken by the evidence brought against it. I cannot believe it to be illusory."

G. Inferences from this view of the will. — (*a*) We can be responsible for the voluntary evil affections with which we are born, and for the will's inherited preference of selfishness, only upon the hypothesis that we originated these states of the affections and will, or had a part in originating them. Scripture furnishes this explanation, in its doctrine of Original Sin, or the doctrine of a common apostasy of the race in its first father, and our derivation of a corrupted nature by natural generation from him. (*b*) While there remains to man, even in his present condition, a natural power of will by which he may put forth transient volitions externally conformed to the divine law and so may to a limited extent modify his character, it still remains true that the sinful bent of his affections is not directly under his control; and this bent constitutes a motive to evil so constant, inveterate, and powerful, that it actually influences every member of the race to reäffirm his evil choice, and renders necessary a special working of God's Spirit upon his heart to ensure his salvation. Hence the Scripture doctrine of Regeneration.

There is such a thing as "psychical automatism" (Ladd, Philos. Mind, 169). Mother: "Oscar, why can't you be good?" "Mamma, it makes me so tired!" The wayward four-year-old is a type of universal humanity. Men are born morally tired, though they have energy enough of other sorts. The man who sins may lose all freedom, so that his soul becomes a seething mass of eructant evil. T. C. Chamberlain: "Conditions may make choices run rigidly in one direction and give as fixed uniformity as in physical phenomena. Put before a million typical Americans the choice between a quarter and a dime, and rigid uniformity of results can be safely predicted." Yet Dr. Chamberlain not only grants but claims liberty of choice. Romanes, Mind and Motion, 155-160 — "Though volitions are largely determined by other and external causes, it does not follow that they are determined *necessarily*, and this makes all the difference between the theories of will as bond or free. Their intrinsic character as first causes protects them from being coerced by these causes and therefore from becoming only the mere effects of them. The condition to the effective operation of a *motive* — as distinguished from a *motor* — is the acquiescence of the first cause upon whom that motive is operating." Fichte: "If any one adopting the dogma of necessity should remain virtuous, we must seek the cause of his goodness elsewhere than in the innocuousness of his doctrine. Upon the supposition of free will alone can duty, virtue, and morality have any existence." Lessing: "Kein Mensch muss müssen." Delitzsch: 'Der Mensch, wie er jetzt ist, ist wahlfrei, aber nicht machtfrei."

Kant regarded freedom as an exception to the law of natural causality. But this freedom is not phenomenal but noumenal, for causality is not a category of noumen. From this freedom we get our whole idea of personality, for personality is freedom of the whole soul from the mechanism of nature. Kant treated scornfully the determinism of Leibnitz. He said it was the freedom of a turnspit, which when once wound up directed its own movements, *i. e.*, was merely automatic. Compare with this the view of Baldwin, Psychology, Feeling and Will, 373 — "Free choice is a synthesis, the outcome of which is in every case conditioned upon its elements, but in no case caused by them. A logical inference is conditioned upon its premises, but it is not caused by them. Both inference and choice express the nature of the conscious principle and the unique method of its life. . . . The motives do not grow into volitions, nor does the volition stand apart from the motives. The motives are partial expressions, the volition is a total expression, of the same existence. . . . . Freedom is the expression of one's self conditioned by past choices and present environment." Shakespeare, Hamlet, 3 : 4 — "Refrain to-night, And that shall lend a kind of easiness To the next abstinence: the next more easy: For use can almost change the stamp of nature, And either curb the devil or throw him out With wondrous potency." 3 : 2 — "Purpose is but the slave to memory; Of violent birth but poor validity." 4 : 7 — "That we would do, We should do when we would; for this *would* changes And hath abatements and delays as many As there are tongues, are hands, are accidents." Goethe: "Von der Gewalt die alle Wesen bindet, Befreit der Mensch sich der sich überwindet."

Scotus Novanticus (Prof. Laurie of Edinburgh), Ethica, 287 — "The chief good is fulness of life achieved through law by the action of will as reason on sensibility. . . . Immorality is the letting loose of feeling, in opposition to the idea and the law in it; it is individuality in opposition to personality. . . . . In immorality, will is defeated, the personality overcome, and the subject volitionizes just as a dog volitionizes. The subject takes possession of the personality and uses it for its natural desires." Maudsley, Physiology of Mind, 456, quotes Ribot, Diseases of the Will, 133 — "Will is not the cause of anything. It is like the verdict of a jury, which is an effect, without being a cause. It is the highest force which nature has yet developed — the last consummate blossom of all her marvellous works." Yet Maudsley argues that the mind itself has power to prevent insanity. This implies that there is an owner of the instrument endowed with power and responsibility to keep it in order. Man can do much, but God can do more.

H. Special objections to the deterministic theory of the will. — Determinism holds that man's actions are uniformly determined by motives acting upon his character, and that he has no power to change these motives or to act contrary to them. This denial that the will is free has serious and pernicious consequences in theology. On the one hand, it weakens even if it does not destroy man's conviction with regard to responsibility, sin, guilt and retribution, and so obscures the need of atonement; on the other hand, it weakens if it does not destroy man's faith in his own power as well as in God's power of initiating action, and so obscures the possibility of atonement.

Determinism is exemplified in Omar Khayyám's Rubáiyat: "With earth's first clay they did the last man knead, And there of the last harvest sowed the seed; And the first morning of creation wrote What the last dawn of reckoning shall read." William James, Will to Believe, 145-183, shows that determinism involves pessimism or subjectivism — good and evil are merely means of increasing knowledge. The result of subjectivism is in theology antinomianism; in literature romanticism; in practical life sensuality or sensualism, as in Rousseau, Renan and Zola. Hutton, review of Clifford in Contemp. Thoughts and Thinkers, 1 : 254 — "The determinist says there would be no moral quality in actions that did not express previous tendency, *i. e.*, a man is responsible only for what he cannot help doing. No effort against the grain will be made by him who believes that his interior mechanism settles for him whether he shall make it or no." Royce, World and Individual, 2 : 342 — "Your unique voices in the divine symphony are no more the voices of moral agents than are the stones of a mosaic." The French monarch announced that all his subjects should be free to choose their own religion, but he added that nobody should choose a different religion from the king's. "Johnny, did you give your little sister the choice between those two apples?" "Yes, Mamma; I told her she could have the little one or none, and she chose the little one." Hobson's choice was always the choice of the last horse in the row. The bartender with revolver in hand met all criticisms upon the quality of his liquor with the remark: " You 'll drink that whisky, and you 'll like it too ! "

Balfour, Foundations of Belief, 22 — " There must be implicitly present to primitive man the sense of freedom, since his fetichism largely consists in attributing to inanimate objects the spontaneity which he finds in himself." Freedom does not contradict conservation of energy. Professor Lodge, in Nature, March 26, 1891 — " Although expenditure of energy is needed to increase the speed of matter, none is needed to alter its direction. . . . The rails that guide a train do not propel it, nor do they retard it : they have no essential effect upon its energy but a guiding effect." J. J. Murphy, Nat. Selection and Spir. Freedom, 170-203 — " Will does not create force but directs it. A very small force is able to guide the action of a great one, as in the steering of a modern steamship." James Seth, in Philos. Rev., 3 : 285, 286 — " As life is not energy but a determiner of the paths of energy, so the will is a cause, in the sense that it controls and directs the channels which activity shall take." See also James Seth, Ethical Principles, 345-388, and Freedom as Ethical Postulate, 9 — " The philosophical proof of freedom must be the demonstration of the inadequacy of the categories of science : its philosophical disproof must be the demonstration of the adequacy of such scientific categories." Shadworth Hodgson : " Either liberty is true, and then the categories are insufficient, or the categories are sufficient, and then liberty is a delusion." Wagner is the composer of determinism ; there is no freedom or guilt ; action is the result of influence and environment ; a mysterious fate rules all. Life : " The views upon heredity Of scientists remind one That, shape one's conduct as one may, One's future is behind one."

We trace willing in God back, not to motives and antecedents, but to his infinite personality. If man is made in God's image, why we may not trace man's willing also back, not to motives and antecedents, but to his finite personality ? We speak of God's fiat, but we may speak of man's fiat also. Napoleon : " There shall be no Alps ! " Dutch William III : " I may fall, but shall fight every ditch, and die in the last one ! " When God energizes the will, it becomes indomitable. Phil. 4 : 13 — " I can do all things in him that strengtheneth me." Dr. E. G. Robinson was theoretically a determinist, and wrongly held that the highest conceivable freedom is to act out one's own nature. He regarded the will as only the nature in movement. Will is self-determining, not in the sense that will determines the self, but in the sense that self determines the will. The will cannot be compelled, for unless self-determined it is no longer will. Observation, history and logic, he thought, lead to necessitarianism. But consciousness, he conceded, testifies to freedom. Consciousness must be trusted, though we cannot reconcile the two. The will is as great a mystery as is the doctrine of the Trinity. Single volitions, he says, are often directly in the face of the current of a man's life. Yet he held that we have no consciousness of the power of a contrary choice. Consciousness can testify only to what springs out of the moral nature, not to the moral nature itself.

Lotze, Religionsphilosophie, section 61 — "An indeterminate choice is of course incomprehensible and inexplicable, for if it were comprehensible and explicable by the human intellect, if, that is, it could be seen to follow necessarily from the preëxisting conditions, it from the nature of the case could not be a morally free choice at all. . . . But we cannot comprehend any more how the mind can move the muscles, nor how a moving stone can set another stone in motion, nor how the Absolute calls into existence our individual selves." Upton, Hibbert Lectures, 308-327, gives an able exposé of the deterministic fallacies. He cites Martineau and Balfour in England, Renouvier and Fonsegrive in France, Edward Zeller, Kuno Fischer and Saarschmidt in Germany, and William James in America, as recent advocates of free will.

Martineau, Study, 2 : 227 — " Is there not a Causal Self, over and above the Caused Self, or rather the Caused State and contents of the self left as a deposit from previous behavior ? Absolute idealism, like Green's, will not recognize the existence of this Causal Self " ; Study of Religion, 2 : 195-324, and especially 240 — " Where two or more rival preconceptions enter the field together, they cannot compare themselves *inter se* : they need and meet a superior : it rests with the mind itself to decide. The decision will not be *unmotived*, for it will have its reasons. It will not be unconformable to the characteristics of the mind, for it will express its preferences. But none the less is it issued by a free cause that elects among the conditions, and is not elected by them." 241 — " So far from admitting that different effects cannot come from the same cause. I even venture on the paradox that nothing is a proper cause which is limited to one effect." 309 — " Freedom, in the sense of option, and will, as the power of deciding an alternative, have no place in the doctrines of the German schools." 311 — " The whole illusion of Necessity springs from the attempt to fling out, for contemplation in the field of Nature, the creative new beginnings centered in personal subjects that transcend it."

See also H. B. Smith, System of Christ. Theol., 236-251 ; Mansel, Proleg. Log., 113-155, 270-278, and Metaphysics, 366 ; Gregory, Christian Ethics, 60 ; Abp. Manning, in Contem. Rev., Jan. 1871 : 468 ; Ward, Philos. of Theism, 1 : 287-352 ; 2 : 1-79, 274-349 ; Bp. Temple, Bampton Lect., 1884 : 69-96 ; Row, Man not a Machine, in Present Day Tracts, 5 : no. 30 ; Richards, Lectures on Theology, 97-153 ; Solly, The Will, 167-203 ; William James. The Dilemma of Determinism, in Unitarian Review, Sept. 1884, and in The Will to Believe, 145-183 ; T. H. Green, Prolegomena to Ethics, 90-159 ; Upton, Hibbert Lectures, 310 ; Bradley, in Mind, July, 1886 ; Bradford, Heredity and Christian Problems, 70-101 ; Illingworth, Divine Immanence, 229-254 ; Ladd, Philos. of Conduct, 133-188. For Lotze's view of the Will, see his Philos. of Religion, 95-106, and his Practical Philosophy, 35-50.

CHAPTER II.

THE ORIGINAL STATE OF MAN.

In determining man's original state, we are wholly dependent upon Scripture. This represents human nature as coming from God's hand, and therefore "very good" (Gen. 1 : 31). It moreover draws a parallel between man's first state and that of his restoration (Col. 3 : 10 ; Eph. 4 : 24). In interpreting these passages, however, we are to remember the twofold danger, on the one hand of putting man so high that no progress is conceivable, on the other hand of putting him so low that he could not fall. We shall the more easily avoid these dangers by distinguishing between the essentials and the incidents of man's original state.

Gen. 1 : 31 — "And God saw everything that he had made, and, behold, it was very good " ; Col. 3 : 10 — " the new man, that is being renewed unto knowledge after the image of him that created him " ; Eph. 4 : 24 — " the new man that after God hath been created in righteousness and holiness of truth."

Philippi, Glaubenslehre, 2 : 337-399 — " The original state must be (1) a contrast to sin ; (2) a parallel to the state of restoration. Difficulties in the way of understanding it : (1) What lives in regeneration is something foreign to our present nature ("it is no longer I that live, but Christ liveth in me " — Gal. 2 : 20); but the original state was something native (2) It was a state of childhood. We cannot fully enter into childhood, though we see it about us, and have ourselves been through it. The original state is yet more difficult to reproduce than reason. (3) Man's external circumstances and his organization have suffered great changes, so that the present is no sign of the past. We must recur to the Scriptures, therefore, as well-nigh our only guide." John Caird, Fund. Ideas of Christianity, 1 : 164-195, points out that ideal perfection is to be looked for, not at the outset, but at the final stage of the spiritual life. If man were wholly finite, he would not know his finitude.

Lord Bacon: "The sparkle of the purity of man's first estate." Calvin: "It was monstrous impiety that a son of the earth should not be satisfied with being made after the similitude of God, unless he could also be equal with him." Prof. Hastings: " The truly natural is not the real, but the ideal. Made in the image of God — between that beginning and the end stands God made in the image of man." On the general subject of man's original state, see Zöckler, 3 : 283-290; Thomasius, Christi Person und Werk, 1 : 215-243 ; Ebrard, Dogmatik, 1 : 267-276 ; Van Oosterzee, Dogmatics, 374-375; Hodge, Syst. Theol., 2 : 92-116.

I. ESSENTIALS OF MAN'S ORIGINAL STATE.

These are summed up in the phrase " the image of God." In God's image man is said to have been created (Gen. 1 : 26, 27). In what did this image of God consist? We reply that it consisted in 1. Natural likeness to God, or personality ; 2. Moral likeness to God, or holiness.

Gen. 1 : 26, 27 — "And God said, Let us make man in our image, after our likeness. . . . . And God created man in his own image, in the image of God created he him." It is of great importance to distinguish clearly between the two elements embraced in this image of God, the natural and the moral. By virtue of the first, man possessed certain *faculties* (intellect, affection, will); by virtue of the second, he had *right tendencies* (bent, proclivity, disposition). By virtue of the first, he was invested with certain *powers;* by virtue of the second, a certain *direction* was imparted to these powers. As created in the natural image of God, man had a moral *nature;* as created in the moral image of God, man had a holy *character.* The first gave him *natural* ability ; the second gave him *moral* ability. The Greek

Fathers emphasized the first element, or *personality*; the Latin Fathers emphasized the second element, or *holiness*. See Orr, God's Image in Man.

As the Logos, or divine Reason, Christ Jesus, dwells in humanity and constitutes the principle of its being, humanity shares with Christ in the image of God. That image is never wholly lost. It is completely restored in sinners when the Spirit of Christ gains control of their wills and they merge their life in his. To those who accused Jesus of blasphemy, he replied by quoting the words of Psalm 82 : 6 — "I said, Ye are gods"— words spoken of imperfect earthly rulers. Thus, in John 10 : 34-36, Jesus, who constitutes the very essence of humanity, justifies his own claim to divinity by showing that even men who represent God are also in a minor sense "partakers of the divine nature" (2 Pet. 1 : 4). Hence the many legends, in heathen religions, of the divine descent of man. 1 Cor. 11 : 3 — "the head of every man is Christ." In every man, even the most degraded, there is an image of God to be brought out, as Michael Angelo saw the angel in the rough block of marble. This natural *worth* does not imply *worthiness*; it implies only capacity for redemption. "The abysmal depths of personality," which Tennyson speaks of, are sounded, as man goes down in thought successively from individual sins to sin of the heart and to race-sin. But "the deeper depth is out of reach To all, O God, but thee." From this deeper depth, where man is rooted and grounded in God, rise aspirations for a better life. These are not due to the man himself, but to Christ, the immanent God, who ever works within him. Fanny J. Crosby: "Rescue the perishing, Care for the dying. . . . Down in the human heart, crushed by the tempter, Feelings lie buried that grace can restore; Touched by a loving heart, wakened by kindness, Chords that were broken will vibrate once more."

1. *Natural likeness to God, or personality.*

Man was created a personal being, and was by this personality distinguished from the brute. By personality we mean the twofold power to know self as related to the world and to God, and to determine self in view of moral ends. By virtue of this personality, man could at his creation choose which of the objects of his knowledge — self, the world, or God — should be the norm and centre of his development. This natural likeness to God is inalienable, and as constituting a capacity for redemption gives value to the life even of the unregenerate (Gen. 9 : 6 ; 1 Cor. 11 : 7 ; James 3 : 9).

For definitions of personality, see notes on the Anthropological Argument, page 82 ; on Pantheism, pages 104, 105 ; on the Attributes, pages 252-254 ; and on the Person of Christ, in Part VI. Here we may content ourselves with the formula : Personality = self-consciousness + self-determination. *Self*-consciousness and *self*-determination, as distinguished from the consciousness and determination of the brute, involve all the higher mental and moral powers which constitute us men. Conscience is but a mode of their activity. Notice that the term 'image' does not, in man, imply *perfect* representation. Only Christ is the "very image" of God (Heb. 1 : 3), the "image of the invisible God" (Col. 1 : 15 — on which see Lightfoot). Christ is the image of God absolutely and archetypally ; man, only relatively and derivatively. But notice also that, since God is Spirit, man made in God's image cannot be a material thing. By virtue of his possession of this first element of the image of God, namely, personality, materialism is excluded.

This first element of the divine image man can never lose until he ceases to be man. Even insanity can only obscure this natural image,— it cannot destroy it. St. Bernard well said that it could not be burned out, even in hell. The lost piece of money (Luke 15 : 8) still bore the image and superscription of the king, even though it did not know it, and did not even know that it was lost. Human nature is therefore to be reverenced, and he who destroys human life is to be put to death : Gen. 9 : 6 — "for in the image of God made he man" ; 1 Cor. 11 : 7 — "a man indeed ought not to have his head veiled, forasmuch as he is the image and glory of God" ; James 3 : 9 — even men whom we curse "are made after the likeness of God" ; *cf.* Ps. 8 : 5 — "thou hast made him but little lower than God" ; 1 Pet. 2 : 17 — "Honor all men." In the being of every man are continents which no Columbus has ever yet discovered, depths of possible joy or sorrow which no plummet has ever yet sounded. A whole heaven, a whole hell, may lie within the compass of his single soul. If we could see the meanest real Christian as he will be in the great hereafter, we should bow before him as John bowed before the angel in the Apocalypse, for we should not be able to distinguish him from God (Rev. 22 : 8, 9).

Sir William Hamilton: "On earth there is nothing great but man; In man there is nothing great but mind." We accept this dictum only if "mind" can be understood to include man's moral powers together with the right direction of those powers. Shakespeare, Hamlet, 2 : 2 — "What a piece of work is man! how noble in reason! how infinite in faculty! in form and moving how express and admirable! in action how like an angel! in apprehension how like a god!" Pascal: "Man is greater than the universe; the universe may crush him, but it does not know that it crushes him." Whiton, Gloria Patri, 94 — "God is not only the Giver but the Sharer of my life. My natural powers are that part of God's power which is lodged with me in trust to keep and use." Man can be an *instrument* of God, without being an *agent* of God. "Each man has his place and value as a reflection of God and of Christ. Like a letter in a word, or a word in a sentence, he gets his meaning from his context; but the sentence is meaningless without him; rays from the whole universe converge in him." John Howe's Living Temple shows the greatness of human nature in its first construction and even in its ruin. Only a noble ship could make so great a wreck. Aristotle, Problem, sec. 30 — "No excellent soul is exempt from a mixture of madness." Seneca, De Tranquillitate Animi, 15 — "There is no great genius without a tincture of madness."

Kant: "So act as to treat humanity, whether in thine own person or in that of any other, in every case as an *end*, and never as a *means* only." If there is a divine element in every man, then we have no right to *use* a human being merely for our own pleasure or profit. In receiving him we receive Christ, and in receiving Christ we receive him who sent Christ (Mat. 10 : 40). Christ is the vine and all men are his natural branches, cutting themselves off only when they refuse to bear fruit, and condemning themselves to the burning only because they destroy, so far as they can destroy, God's image in them, all that makes them worth preserving (John 15 : 1–6). Cicero: "Homo mortalis deus." This possession of natural likeness to God, or personality, involves boundless possibilities of good or ill, and it constitutes the natural foundation of the love for man which is required of us by the law. Indeed it constitutes the reason why Christ should die. Man was worth redeeming. The woman whose ring slipped from her finger and fell into the heap of mud in the gutter, bared her white arm and thrust her hand into the slimy mass until she found her ring; but she would not have done this if the ring had not contained a costly diamond. The lost piece of money, the lost sheep, the lost son, were worth effort to seek and to save (Luke 15). But, on the other hand, it is folly when man, made in the image of God, "blinds himself with clay." The man on shipboard, who playfully tossed up the diamond ring which contained his whole fortune, at last to his distress tossed it overboard. There is a "merchandise of souls" (Rev. 18 : 13) and we must not juggle with them.

Christ's death for man, by showing the worth of humanity, has recreated ethics. "Plato defended infanticide as under certain circumstances permissible. Aristotle viewed slavery as founded in the nature of things. The reason assigned was the essential inferiority of nature on the part of the enslaved." But the divine image in man makes these barbarities no longer possible to us. Christ sometimes looked upon men with anger, but he never looked upon them with contempt. He taught the woman, he blessed the child, he cleansed the leper, he raised the dead. His own death revealed the infinite worth of the meanest human soul, and taught us to count all men as brethren for whose salvation we may well lay down our lives. George Washington answered the salute of his slave. Abraham Lincoln took off his hat to a negro who gave him his blessing as he entered Richmond; but a lady who had been brought up under the old regime looked from a window upon the scene with unspeakable horror. Robert Burns, walking with a nobleman in Edinburgh, met an old townsfellow from Ayr and stopped to talk with him. The nobleman, kept waiting, grew restive, and afterward reproved Burns for talking to a man with so bad a coat. Burns replied: "I was not talking to the coat,—I was talking to the man." Jean Ingelow: "The street and market place Grow holy ground: each face -- Pale faces marked with care, Dark, toilworn brows — grows fair. King's children are all these, though want and sin Have marred their beauty, glorious within. We may not pass them but with reverent eye." See Porter, Human Intellect, 393, 394, 401 ; Wuttke, Christian Ethics, 2 : 42; Philippi, Glaubenslehre, 2 : 343

2. *Moral likeness to God, or holiness.*

In addition to the powers of self-consciousness and self-determination just mentioned, man was created with such a direction of the affections and the will, as constituted God the supreme end of man's being, and constituted man a finite reflection of God's moral attributes. Since holiness is the fundamental attribute of God, this must of necessity be the chief attribute of his image in the moral beings whom he creates. That original righteousness was essential to this image, is also distinctly taught in Scripture (Eccl. 7:29 ; Eph. 4 : 24 ; Col. 3 : 10).

Besides the possession of natural powers, the image of God involves the possession of right moral tendencies. It is not enough to say that man was created in a state of innocence. The Scripture asserts that man had a righteousness like God's: Eccl. 7:29 — "God made man upright"; Eph. 4 : 24 — "the new man, that after God hath been created in righteousness and holiness of truth" — here Meyer says: " κατὰ Θεόν, 'after God,' i. e., ad exemplum Dei, after the pattern of God (Gal. 4:28 — κατὰ Ἰσαάκ, 'after Isaac' = as Isaac was). This phrase makes the creation of the new man a parallel to that of our first parents, who were created after God's image; they too, before sin came into existence through Adam, were sinless — 'in righteousness and holiness of truth.'" On N. T. " truth " = rectitude, see Wendt, Teaching of Jesus, 1 : 257-260.

Meyer refers also, as a parallel passage, to Col. 3 : 10 — "the new man, that is being renewed unto knowledge after the image of him that created him." Here the "knowledge" referred to is that knowledge of God which is the source of all virtue, and which is inseparable from holiness of heart. " Holiness has two sides or phases : (1) it is perception and knowledge ; (2) it is inclination and feeling " (Shedd, Dogm. Theol., 2 : 97). On Eph. 4:24 and Col. 3:10, the classical passages with regard to man's original state, see also the Commentaries of DeWette, Rückert, Ellicott, and compare Gen. 5 : 3 — "And Adam lived an hundred and thirty years, and begat a son in his own likeness, after his image," i. e., in his own sinful likeness, which is evidently contrasted with the "likeness of God " (verse 1) in which he himself had been created (An. Par. Bible). 2 Cor. 4:4 — "Christ, who is the image of God " — where the phrase "image of God" is not simply the natural, but also the moral, image. Since Christ is the image of God primarily in his holiness, man's creation in the image of God must have involved a holiness like Christ's, so far as such holiness could belong to a being yet untried, that is, so far as respects man's tastes and dispositions prior to moral action.

" Couldst thou in vision see Thyself the man God meant, Thou nevermore couldst be The man thou art — content." Newly created man had right moral tendencies, as well as freedom from actual fault. Otherwise the communion with God described in Genesis would not have been possible. Goethe: "Unless the eye were sunlike, how could it see the sun?" Because a holy disposition accompanied man's innocence, he was capable of obedience, and was guilty when he sinned. The loss of this moral likeness to God was the chief calamity of the Fall. Man is now " the glory and the scandal of the universe." He has defaced the image of God in his nature, even though that image, in its natural aspect, is ineffaceable (E. H. Johnson).

The dignity of human nature consists, not so much in what man is, as in what God meant him to be, and in what God means him yet to become, when the lost image of God is restored by the union of man's soul with Christ. Because of his future possibilities, the meanest of mankind is sacred. The great sin of the second table of the decalogue is the sin of despising our fellow man. To cherish contempt for others can have its root only in idolatry of self and rebellion against God. Abraham Lincoln said well that " God must have liked common people,— else he would not have made so many of them." Regard for the image of God in man leads also to kind and reverent treatment even of those lower animals in which so many human characteristics are foreshadowed. Bradford, Heredity and Christian Problems, 166 — " The current philosophy says : The fittest will survive; let the rest die. The religion of Christ says: That maxim as applied to men is just, only as regards their characteristics, of which indeed only the fittest should survive. It does not and cannot apply to the men themselves, since all men, being children of God, are supremely fit. The very fact that a human being is sick, weak, poor, an outcast, and a vagabond, is the strongest possible appeal for eff ¢ toward his salvation. Let individuals look upon humanity from the point of view of Christ, and they will not be long in finding ways in which environment can be caused to work for righteousness."

This original righteousness, in which the image of God chiefly consisted, is to be viewed :

(*a*) Not as constituting the substance or essence of human nature, — for in this case human nature would have ceased to exist as soon as man sinned.

Men every day change their tastes and loves, without changing the essence or substance of their being. When sin is called a "nature," therefore (as by Shedd, in his Essay on "Sin a Nature, and that Nature Guilt"), it is only in the sense of being something inborn (*natura*, from *nascor*). Hereditary tastes may just as properly be denominated a "nature" as may the substance of one's being. Moehler, the greatest modern Roman Catholic critic of Protestant doctrine, in his Symbolism, 58, 59, absurdly holds Luther to have taught that by the Fall man lost his essential nature, and that another essence was substituted in its room. Luther, however, is only rhetorical when he says: "It is the nature of man to sin; sin constitutes the essence of man; the nature of man since the Fall has become quite changed; original sin is that very thing which is born of father and mother; the clay out of which we are formed is damnable; the fœtus in the maternal womb is sin; man as born of his father and mother, together with his whole essence and nature, is not only a sinner but sin itself."

(*b*) Nor as a gift from without, foreign to human nature, and added to it after man's creation, —for man is said to have possessed the divine image by the fact of creation, and not by subsequent bestowal.

As men, since Adam, are born with a sinful nature, that is, with tendencies away from God, so Adam was created with a holy nature, that is, with tendencies toward God. Moehler says: "God cannot give a man actions." We reply: "No, but God can give man dispositions; and he does this at the first creation, as well as at the new creation (regeneration)."

(*c*) But rather, as an original direction or tendency of man's affections and will, still accompanied by the power of evil choice, and so, differing from the perfected holiness of the saints, as instinctive affection and child-like innocence differ from the holiness that has ·been developed and confirmed by experience of temptation.

Man's original righteousness was not immutable or indefectible; there was still the possibility of sinning. Though the first man was fundamentally good, he still had the power of choosing evil. There was a bent of the affections and will toward God, but man was not yet confirmed in holiness. Man's love for God was like the germinal filial affection in the child, not developed, yet sincere — "caritas puerilis, non virilis."

(*d*) As a moral disposition, moreover, which was propagable to Adam's descendants, if it continued, and which, though lost to him and to them, if Adam sinned, would still leave man possessed of a natural likeness to God which made him susceptible of God's redeeming grace.

Hooker (Works, ed. Keble, 2:683) distinguishes between aptness and ableness. The latter, men have lost; the former, they retain,— else grace could not work in us, more than in the brutes. Hase: "Only enough likeness to God remained to remind man of what he had lost, and enable him to feel the hell of God's forsaking." The moral likeness to God can be restored, but only by God himself. God secures this to men by making "the light of the gospel of the glory of Christ, who is the image of God, ... dawn upon them" (2 Cor. 4:4). Pusey made Ps. 72:6 — "He will come down like rain upon the mown grass" — the image of a world hopelessly dead, but with a hidden capacity for receiving life. Dr. Daggett: "Man is a 'son of the morning' (Is. 14:12), fallen, yet arrested midway between heaven and hell, a prize between the powers of light and darkness." See Edwards, Works, 2:19, 20, 381–390; Hopkins, Works, 1:162; Shedd, Hist. Doctrine, 2:50–66; Augustine, De Civitate Dei 14:11.

In the light of the preceding investigation, we may properly estimate two theories of man's original state which claim to be more Scriptural and reasonable :

A.   The image of God as including only personality.

This theory denies that any positive determination to virtue inhered originally in man's nature, and regards man at the beginning as simply possessed of spiritual powers, perfectly adjusted to each other. This is the view of Schleiermacher, who is followed by Nitzsch, Julius Müller, and Hofmann.

For the view here combated, see Schleiermacher, Christl. Glaube, sec. 60; Nitzsch, System of Christian Doctrine, 201; Julius Müller, Doct. of Sin, 2 : 113-133, 350-357; Hofmann, Schriftbeweis, 1 : 287-291; Bib. Sac., 7 : 409-425. Julius Müller's theory of the Fall in a preëxistent state makes it impossible for him to hold here that Adam was possessed of moral likeness to God. The origin of his view of the image of God renders it liable to suspicion. Pfleiderer, Grundriss, 113—" The original state of man was that of childlike innocence or morally indifferent naturalness, which had in itself indeed the possibility (*Anlage*) of ideal development, but in such a way that its realization could be reached only by struggle with its natural opposite. The image of God was already present in the original state, but only as the possibility (*Anlage*) of real likeness to God — the endowment of reason which belonged to human personality. The *reality* of a spirit like that of God has appeared first in the *second* Adam, and has become the principle of the kingdom of God."

Raymond (Theology, 2 : 43, 132) is an American representative of the view that the image of God consists in mere personality: "The image of God in which man was created did not consist in an inclination and determination of the will to holiness." This is maintained upon the ground that such a moral likeness to God would have rendered it impossible for man to fall, — to which we reply that Adam's righteousness was not immutable, and the bias of his will toward God did not render it impossible for him to sin. Motives do not compel the will, and Adam at least had a certain power of contrary choice. E. G. Robinson, Christ. Theology, 119-122, also maintains that the image of God signified only that personality which distinguished man from the brute. Christ, he says, carries forward human nature to a higher point, instead of merely restoring what is lost. "Very good" (Gen. 1 : 31) does not imply moral perfection,—this cannot be the result of creation, but only of discipline and will. Man's original state was only one of untried innocence. Dr. Robinson is combating the view that the first man was at his creation possessed of a developed character. He distinguishes between character and the germs of character. These germs he grants that man possessed. And so he defines the image of God as a constitutional predisposition toward a course of right conduct. This is all the perfection which we claim for the first man. We hold that this predisposition toward the good can properly be called character, since it is the germ from which all holy action springs.

In addition to what has already been said in support of the opposite view, we may urge against this theory the following objections :

(*a*) It is contrary to analogy, in making man the author of his own holiness; our sinful condition is not the product of our individual wills, nor is our subsequent condition of holiness the product of anything but God's regenerating power.

To hold that Adam was created undecided, would make man, as Philippi says, in the highest sense his own creator. But morally, as well as physically, man is God's creature. In regeneration it is not sufficient for God to give *power* to decide for good ; God must give new *love* also. If this be so in the new creation, God could give love in the first creation also. Holiness therefore is creatable. " *Underived* holiness is possible only in God; in its origin, it is *given* both to angels and men." Therefore we pray : "Create in me a clean heart" (Ps. 51 : 10); "Incline my heart unto thy testimonies " (Ps. 119 : 36). See Edwards, Eff. Grace, sec. 43-51; Kaftan, Dogmatik, 290 — "If Adam's perfection was not a moral perfection, then his sin was no real moral corruption." The *animus* of the theory we are combating seems to be an unwillingness to grant that man, either in his first creation or in his new creation, owes his holiness to God.

(*b*) The knowledge of God in which man was originally created logically presupposes a direction toward God of man's affections and will, since only the holy heart can have any proper understanding of the God of holiness.

" Ubi caritas, ibi claritas." Man's heart was originally filled with divine love, and out of this came the knowledge of God. We know God only as we love him, and this love comes not from our own single volition. No one loves by command, because no one can give himself love. In Adam love was an inborn impulse, which he could affirm or deny. Compare 1 Cor. 8 : 3 — "if any man loveth God, the same [God] is known by him "; 1 John 4 : 8 — "He that loveth not knoweth not God." See other Scripture references on pages 3, 4.

(c) A likeness to God in mere personality, such as Satan also possesses, comes far short of answering the demands of the Scripture, in which the ethical conception of the divine nature so overshadows the merely natural. The image of God must be, not simply ability to be like God, but actual likeness.

God could never create an intelligent being evenly balanced between good and evil — "on the razor's edge"—"on the fence." The preacher who took for his text "Adam, where art thou?" had for his first head: "It is every man's business to be somewhere;" for his second: "Some of you are where you ought not to be;" and for his third: "Get where you ought to be, as soon as possible." A simple capacity for good or evil is, as Augustine says, already sinful. A man who is neutral between good and evil is already a violator of that law, which requires likeness to God in the bent of his nature. Delitzsch, Bib. Psychol., 45-84—"Personality is only the basis of the divine image,— it is not the image itself." Bledsoe says there can be no created virtue or viciousness. Whedon (On the Will, 388) objects to this, and says rather: "There can be no created moral desert, good or evil. Adam's nature as created was pure and excellent, but there was nothing meritorious until he had freely and rightly exercised his will with full power to the contrary." We add: There was nothing meritorious even then. For substance of these objections, see Philippi, Glaubenslehre, 2 : 346. Lessing said that the character of the Germans was to have no character. Goethe partook of this cosmopolitan characterlessness (Prof. Seely). Tennyson had Goethe in view when he wrote in The Palace of Art : "I sit apart, holding no form of creed, but contemplating all." And Goethe is probably still alluded to in the words: " A glorious devil, large in heart and brain, That did love beauty only, Or if good, good only for its beauty"; see A. H. Strong, The Great Poets and their Theology, 331; Robert Browning, Christmas Eve: "The truth in God's breast Lies trace for trace upon ours impressed: Though he is so bright, and we so dim, We are made in his image to witness him."

B. The image of God as consisting simply in man's natural capacity for religion.

This view, first elaborated by the scholastics, is the doctrine of the Roman Catholic Church. It distinguishes between the image and the likeness of God. The former (צֶלֶם — Gen. 1 : 26) alone belonged to man's nature at its creation. The latter (דְּמוּת) was the product of his own acts of obedience. In order that this obedience might be made easier and the consequent likeness to God more sure, a third element was added — an element not belonging to man's nature — namely, a supernatural gift of special grace, which acted as a curb upon the sensuous impulses, and brought them under the control of reason. Original righteousness was therefore not a natural endowment, but a joint product of man's obedience and of God's supernatural grace.

Roman Catholicism holds that the white paper of man's soul received two impressions instead of one. Protestantism sees no reason why both impressions should not have been given at the beginning. Kaftan, in Am. Jour. Theology, 4 : 708, gives a good statement of the Roman Catholic view. It holds that the supreme good transcends the finite mind and its powers of comprehension. Even at the first it was beyond man's created nature. The *donum superadditum* did not inwardly and personally belong to him. Now that he has lost it, he is entirely dependent on the church for truth and grace. He does not receive the truth because it is this and no other, but because the church tells him that it is the truth.

The Roman Catholic doctrine may be roughly and pictorially stated as follows: As created, man was morally naked, or devoid of positive righteousness (*pura naturalia*, or *in puris naturalibus*). By obedience he obtained as a reward from God (*donum supernaturale*, or *superadditum*) a suit of clothes or robe of righteousness to protect him, so that he became clothed (*vestitus*). This suit of clothes, however, was a sort of magic spell of which he could be divested. The adversary attacked him and stripped him of his suit. After his sin he was one despoiled (*spoliatus*). But his condition after differed from his condition before this attack, only as a stripped man differs from a naked man (*spoliatus a nudo*). He was now only in the same state in which he was created, with the single exception of the weakness he might feel as the result of losing his customary clothing. He could still earn himself another suit,—in fact, he could earn two or more, so as to sell, or give away, what he did not need for himself. The phrase *in puris naturalibus* describes the original state, as the phrase *spoliatus a nudo* describes the difference resulting from man's sin.

Many of the considerations already adduced apply equally as arguments against this view. We may say, however, with reference to certain features peculiar to the theory :

(*a*) No such distinction can justly be drawn between the words צֶלֶם and דְּמוּת. The addition of the synonym simply strengthens the expression, and both together signify "the very image."

(*b*) Whatever is denoted by either or both of these words was bestowed upon man in and by the fact of creation, and the additional hypothesis of a supernatural gift not originally belonging to man's nature, but subsequently conferred, has no foundation either here or elsewhere in Scripture. Man is said to have been created in the image and likeness of God, not to have been afterwards endowed with either of them.

(*c*) The concreated opposition between sense and reason which this theory supposes is inconsistent with the Scripture declaration that the work of God's hands "was very good" (Gen. 1:31), and transfers the blame of temptation and sin from man to God. To hold to a merely negative innocence, in which evil desire was only slumbering, is to make God author of sin by making him author of the constitution which rendered sin inevitable.

(*d*) This theory directly contradicts Scripture by making the effect of the first sin to have been a weakening but not a perversion of human nature, and the work of regeneration to be not a renewal of the affections but merely a strengthening of the natural powers. The theory regards that first sin as simply despoiling man of a special gift of grace and as putting him where he was when first created — still able to obey God and to coöperate with God for his own salvation,—whereas the Scripture represents man since the fall as "dead through . . . trespasses and sins" (Eph. 2 : 1), as incapable of true obedience (Rom. 8 : 7— "not subject to the law of God, neither indeed can it be"), and as needing to be "created in Christ Jesus for good works" (Eph. 2 :10).

At few points in Christian doctrine do we see more clearly than here the large results of error which may ultimately spring from what might at first sight seem to be only a slight divergence from the truth. Augustine had rightly taught that in Adam the *posse non peccare* was accompanied by a *posse peccare*, and that for this reason man's holy disposition needed the help of divine grace to preserve its integrity. But the scholastics wrongly added that this original disposition to righteousness was not the outflow of man's nature as originally created, but was the gift of grace. As this later teaching, however, was by some disputed, the Council of Trent (sess. 5, cap. 1) left the matter more indefinite, simply declaring man: "Sanctitatem et justitiam in qua *constitutus fuerat*, amisisse." The Roman Catechism, however (1:2:19), explained the phrase "constitutus fuerat" by the words: "Tum originalis justitiæ admirabile donum *addidit*." And Bellarmine (De Gratia, 2) says plainly: "Imago, quæ est ipsa natura mentis et voluntatis, a solo Deo fieri potuit; similitudo autem, quæ in virtute et probitate consistit, *a nobis quoque* Deo adjuvante perficitur." .... (5) "Integritas illa ... non fuit naturalis ejus conditio, sed supernaturalis evectio. .... Addidisse homini donum quoddam insigne, justitiam videlicet originalem, qua veluti aureo quodam fræno pars inferior parti superiori subjecta contineretur."

Moehler (Symbolism, 21-35) holds that the religious faculty—the "image of God"; the pious exertion of this faculty—the "likeness of God." He seems to favor the view that Adam received "this supernatural gift of a holy and blessed communion with God at a later period than his creation, *i. e.*, only when he had prepared himself for its reception and by his own efforts had rendered himself worthy of it." He was created "just" and acceptable to God, even without communion with God or help from God. He became "holy" and enjoyed communion with God, only when God rewarded his obedience and bestowed the *supernaturale donum*. Although Moehler favors this view and claims that it is permitted by the standards, he also says that it is not definitely taught. The quotations from Bellarmine and the Roman Catechism above make it clear that it is the prevailing doctrine of the Roman Catholic church.

So, to quote the words of Shedd, "the Tridentine theology starts with Pelagianism and ends with Augustinianism. Created without character, God subsequently endows man with character. .... The Papal idea of creation differs from the Augustinian in that it involves imperfection. There is a disease and languor which require a subsequent and supernatural act to remedy." The Augustinian and Protestant conception of man's original state is far nobler than this. The ethical element is not a later addition, but is man's true nature—essential to God's idea of him. The normal and original condition of man (*pura naturalia*) is one of grace and of the Spirit's indwelling—hence, of direction toward God.

From this original difference between Roman Catholic and Protestant doctrine with regard to man's original state result diverging views as to sin and as to regeneration. The Protestant holds that, as man was possessed by creation of moral likeness to God, or holiness, so his sin robbed his nature of its integrity, deprived it of essential and concreated advantages and powers, and substituted for these a positive corruption and tendency to evil. Unpremeditated evil desire, or concupiscence, is original sin; as concreated love for God constituted man's original righteousness. No man since the fall has original righteousness, and it is man's sin that he has it not. Since without love to God no act, emotion, or thought of man can answer the demands of God's law, the Scripture denies to fallen man all power of himself to know, think, feel, or do aright. His nature therefore needs a new-creation, a resurrection from death, such as God only, by his mighty Spirit, can work; and to this work of God man can contribute nothing, except as power is first given him by God himself.

According to the Roman Catholic view, however, since the image of God in which man was created included only man's religious faculty, his sin can rob him only of what became subsequently and adventitiously his. Fallen man differs from unfallen only as *spoliatus a nudo*. He loses only a sort of magic spell, which leaves him still in possession of all his essential powers. Unpremeditated evil desire, or concupiscence, is not sin; for this belonged to his nature even before he fell. His sin has therefore only put him back into the natural state of conflict and concupiscence, ordered by God in the concreated opposition of sense and reason. The sole qualification is this, that, having made an evil decision, his will is weakened. "Man does not need resurrection from death, but rather a crutch to help his lameness, a tonic to reinforce his feebleness, a medicine to cure his sickness." He is still able to turn to God; and in regeneration the Holy Spirit simply awakens and strengthens the natural ability slumbering in the natural man. But even here, man must yield to the influence of the Holy Spirit; and regeneration is effected by uniting his power to the divine. In baptism the guilt of original sin is remitted, and everything called sin is taken away. No baptized person has any further process of regeneration to undergo. Man has not only strength to coöperate with God for his own salvation, but he may even go beyond the demands of the law and perform works of supererogation. And the whole sacramental system of the Roman Catholic Church, with its salvation by works, its purgatorial fires, and its invocation of the saints, connects itself logically with this erroneous theory of man's original state.

See Dorner's Augustinus, 116; Perrone, Prælectiones Theologicæ, 1 : 737-748; Winer, Confessions, 19, 80; Dorner, History Protestant Theology, 38, 39, and Glaubenslehre, 1 : 51; Van Oosterzee, Dogmatics, 376; Cunningham, Historical Theology, 1 : 516-586; Shedd, Hist. Doctrine, 2 : 140-149.

II. INCIDENTS OF MAN'S ORIGINAL STATE.

1. *Results of man's possession of the divine image.*

(*a*) Reflection of this divine image in man's physical form.— Even in man's body were typified those higher attributes which chiefly constituted his likeness to God. A gross perversion of this truth, however, is the view which holds, upon the ground of Gen. 2 : 7, and 3 : 8, that the image of God consists in bodily resemblance to the Creator. In the first of these passages, it is not the divine image, but the body, that is formed of dust, and into this body the soul that possesses the divine image is breathed. The second of these passages is to be interpreted by those other portions of the Pentateuch in which God is represented as free from all limitations of matter (Gen. 11 : 5 ; 18 : 15).

The spirit presents the divine image immediately : the body, mediately. The scholastics called the soul the image of God *proprie;* the body they called the image of God *significative.* Soul is the direct reflection of God ; body is the reflection of that reflection. The *os sublime* manifests the dignity of the endowments within. Hence 'he word 'upright,' as applied to moral condition ; one of the first impulses of the renewed man is to physical purity. Compare Ovid, Metaph., bk. 1, Dryden's transl. : " Thus while the mute creation downward bend Their sight, and to their earthly mother tend, Man looks aloft, and with erected eyes Beholds his own hereditary skies." ('Ανθρωπος, from ἀνά, ἀνω, suffix *tra*, and ὡψ, with reference to the upright posture.) Milton speaks of "the human face divine." S. S. Times, July 28, 1900 — " Man is the only erect being among living creatures. He alone looks up naturally and without effort. He foregoes his birthright when he looks only at what is on a level with his eyes and occupies himself only with what lies in the plane of his own existence."

Bretschneider (Dogmatik, 1 : 682) regards the Scripture as teaching that the image of God consists in bodily resemblance to the Creator, but considers this as only the imperfect method of representation belonging to an early age. So Strauss, Glaubenslehre, 1 : 687. They refer to Gen. 2 : 7—"And Jehovah God formed man of the dust of the ground " ; 3 : 8—"And Jehovah God walking in the garden." But see Gen. 11 : 5—"And Jehovah came down to see the city and the tower, which the children of men builded " ; Is. 66 : 1—"Heaven is my throne, and the earth is my footstool " ; 1 K. 8 : 27—"behold, heaven and the heaven of heavens cannot contain thee." On the Anthropomorphites, see Hagenbach, Hist. Doct., 1 : 103, 308, 491. For answers to Bretschneider and Strauss, see Philippi, Glaubenslehre, 2 : 364.

(*b*) Subjection of the sensuous impulses to the control of the spirit.— Here we are to hold a middle ground between two extremes. On the one hand, the first man possessed a body and a spirit so fitted to each other that no conflict was felt between their several claims. On the other hand, this physical perfection was not final and absolute, but relative and provisional. There was still room for progress to a higher state of being (Gen. 3 : 22).

Sir Henry Watton's Happy Life: " That man was free from servile bands Of hope to rise or fear to fall, Lord of himself if not of lands, And having nothing yet had all." Here we hold to the *æquale temperamentum.* There was no disease, but rather the joy of abounding health. Labor was only a happy activity. God's infinite creatorship and fountainhead of being was typified in man's powers of generation. But there was no concreated opposition of sense and reason, nor an imperfect physical nature with whose impulses reason was at war. With this moderate Scriptural doctrine, contrast the exaggerations of the Fathers and of the scholastics. Augustine says that Adam's reason was to ours what the bird's is to that of the tortoise; propagation in the unfallen state would have been without concupiscence, and the new-born child would have attained perfection at birth. Albertus Magnus thought the first man would have felt no pain, even though he had been stoned with heavy stones. Scotus Erigena held that the male and female elements were yet undistinguished. Others called sexuality the first sin. Jacob Boehme regarded the intestinal canal, and all connected with it, as the consequence of the Fall; he had the fancy that the earth was transparent at the first and cast no shadow,— sin, he thought, had made it opaque and dark; redemption would restore it to its first estate and make night a thing of the past. South, Sermons, 1 : 24, 25 — " Man came into the world a philosopher. . . . . . Aristotle was but the rubbish of an Adam." Lyman Abbott tells us of a minister who assured his congregation that Adam was acquainted with the telephone. But God educates his children, as chemists educate their pupils, by putting them into the laboratory and letting them work. Scripture does not represent Adam as a walking encyclopædia, but as a being yet inexperienced; see Gen. 3 : 22 — "Behold, the man is become as one of us, to know good and evil"; 1 Cor. 15 : 46 — "that is not first which is spiritual, but that which is natural; then that which is spiritual." On this last text, see Expositor's Greek Testament.

(c) **Dominion over the lower creation.**—Adam possessed an insight into nature analogous to that of susceptible childhood, and therefore was able to name and to rule the brute creation (Gen. 2 : 19). Yet this native insight was capable of development into the higher knowledge of culture and science. From Gen. 1 : 26 (cf. Ps. 8 : 5–8), it has been erroneously inferred that the image of God in man consists in dominion over the brute creation and the natural world. But, in this verse, the words "let them have dominion" do not define the image of God, but indicate the result of possessing that image. To make the image of God consist in this dominion, would imply that only the divine omnipotence was shadowed forth in man.

Gen. 2 : 19 —" Jehovah God formed every beast of the field, and every bird of the heavens; and brought them unto the man to see what he would call them "; 20 —" And the man gave names to all cattle "; Gen. 1 : 26 — "Let us make man in our image, after our likeness: and let them have dominion over the fish of the sea, and over the birds of the heavens, and over the cattle "; cf. Ps. 8 : 5-8 — "thou hast made him but little lower than God, And crownest him with glory and nonor. Thou makest him to have dominion over the works of thy hands; Thou hast put all things under his feet: All sheep and oxen, Yea, and the beasts of the field." Adam's naming the animals implied insight into their nature; see Porter, Hum. Intellect, 393, 394, 401. On man's original dominion over (1) self, (2) nature, (3) fellow-man, see Hopkins, Scriptural Idea of Man, 105.

Courage and a good conscience have a power over the brute creation, and unfallen man can well be supposed to have dominated creatures which had no experience of human cruelty. Rarey tamed the wildest horses by his steadfast and fearless eye. In Paris a young woman was hypnotized and put into a den of lions. She had no fear of the lions and the lions paid not the slightest attention to her. The little daughter of an English officer in South Africa wandered away from camp and spent the night among lions. "Katrina," her father said when he found her, " were you not afraid to be alone here?" "No, papa," she replied, "the big dogs played with me and one of them lay here and kept me warm." MacLaren, in S. S. Times, Dec. 23, 1893 — "The dominion over all creatures results from likeness to God. It is not then a mere right to use them for one's own material advantage, but a viceroy's authority, which the holder is bound to employ for the honor of the true King." This principle gives the warrant and the limit to vivisection and to the killing of the lower animals for food (Gen. 9 : 2. 3).

Socinian writers generally hold the view that the image of God consisted simply in this dominion. Holding a low view of the nature of sin, they are naturally disinclined to believe that the fall has wrought any profound change in human nature. See their view stated in the Racovian Catechism, 21. It is held also by the Arminian Limborch. Theol. Christ., ii, 24 : 2, 3, 11. Upon the basis of this interpretation of Scripture, the Encratites held, with Peter Martyr, that women do not possess the divine image at all.

(d) **Communion with God.**—Our first parents enjoyed the divine presence and teaching (Gen. 2 : 16). It would seem that God manifested himself to them in visible form (Gen. 3 : 8). This companionship was both in kind and degree suited to their spiritual capacity, and by no means necessarily involved that perfected vision of God which is possible to beings of confirmed and unchangeable holiness (Mat. 5 : 8 ; 1 John 3 : 2).

Gen. 2 : 16 — "And Jehovah God commanded the man " ; 3 : 8 — " And they heard the voice of Jehovah God walking in the garden in the cool of the day " ; Mat. 5 : 8 —"Blessed are the pure in heart: for they shall see God " ; 1 John 3 : 2 — ' We know that, if he shall be manifested, we shall be like him; for we shall see him even as he is " ; Rev. 22 : 4—"and they shall see his face."

2. *Concomitants of man's possession of the divine image.*

(*a*) Surroundings and society fitted to yield happiness and to assist a holy development of human nature (Eden and Eve). We append some recent theories with regard to the creation of Eve and the nature of Eden.

Eden = pleasure, delight. Tennyson : " When high in Paradise By the four rivers the first roses blew." Streams were necessary to the very existence of an oriental garden. Hopkins, Script. Idea of Man, 107 — " Man includes woman. Creation of *a* man without a woman would not have been the creation of man. Adam called her name Eve but God called their name Adam." Mat. Henry : " Not out of his head to top him, nor out of his feet to be trampled on by him; but out of his side to be equal with him, under his arm to be protected by him, and near his heart to be beloved." Robert Burns says of nature : " Her 'prentice hand she tried on man, And then she made the lasses, O ! " Stevens, Pauline Theology, 329 — " In the natural relations of the sexes there is a certain reciprocal dependence, since it is not only true that woman was made from man, but that man is born of woman (1 Cor. 11 : 11, 12)." Of the Elgin marbles Boswell asked : " Don't you think them indecent ? " Dr. Johnson replied : " No, sir; but your question is." Man, who in the adult state possesses twelve pairs of ribs, is found in the embryonic state to have thirteen or fourteen. Dawson, Modern Ideas of Evolution, 148 — " Why does not the male man lack one rib ? Because only the individual skeleton of Adam was affected by the taking of the rib. . . . The unfinished vertebral arches of the skin-fibrous layer may have produced a new individual by a process of budding or gemmation."

H. H. Bawden suggests that the account of Eve's creation may be the " pictorial summary " of an actual phylogenetic evolutionary process by which the sexes were separated or isolated from a common hermaphroditic ancestor or ancestry. The mesodermic portion of the organism in which the urinogenital system has its origin develops later than the ectodermic or the endodermic portions. The word "rib " may designate this mesodermic portion. Bayard Taylor, John Godfrey's Fortunes, 392, suggests that a genius is hermaphroditic, adding a male element to the woman, and a female element to the man. Professor Loeb, Am. Journ. Physiology, Vol. III, no. 3, has found that in certain chemical solutions prepared in the laboratory, approximately the concentration of sea-water, the unfertilized eggs of the sea-urchin will mature without the intervention of the spermatozoön. Perfect embryos and normal individuals are produced under these conditions. He thinks it probable that similar parthenogenesis may be produced in higher types of being. In 1900 he achieved successful results on Annelids, though it is doubtful whether he produced anything more than normal *larvæ*. These results have been criticized by a European investigator who is also a Roman priest. Prof. Loeb wrote a rejoinder in which he expressed surprise that a representative of the Roman church did not heartily endorse his conclusions, since they afford a vindication of the doctrine of the immaculate conception.

H. H. Bawden has reviewed Prof. Loeb's work in the Psychological Review, Jan. 1900. Janósik has found segmentation in the unfertilized eggs of mammalians. Prof. Loeb considers it possible that only the ions of the blood prevent the parthenogenetic origin of embryos in mammals, and thinks it not improbable that by a transitory change in these ions it will be possible to produce complete parthenogenesis in these higher types. Dr. Bawden goes on to say that "both parent and child are dependent upon a common source of energy. The universe is one great organism, and there is no inorganic or non-organic matter, but differences only in degrees of organization. Sex is designed only secondarily for the perpetuation of species ; primarily it is the bond or medium for the connection and interaction of the various parts of this great organism, for maintaining that degree of heterogeneity which is the prerequisite of a high degree of organization. By means of the growth of a lifetime I have become an essential part in a great organic system. What I call my individual personality represents simply the focusing, the flowering of the universe at one finite concrete point or centre. Must not then my personality continue as long as that universal system continues? And is immortality conceivable if the soul is something shut up within itself, unshareable and unique? Are not the many foci mutually interdependent, instead of mutually exclusive? We must not then conceive of an immortality which means the continued existence of an individual cut off from that social context which is really essential to his very nature."

J. H. Richardson suggests in the Standard, Sept. 10, 1901, that the first chapter of Genesis describes the creation of the spiritual part of man only — that part which was made in the image of God — while the second chapter describes the creation of man's body, the animal part which may have been originated by a process of evolution. S. W. Howland, in Bib. Sac., Jan. 1903: 121-128, supposes Adam and Eve to have been twins, joined by the ensiform cartilage or breast-bone, as were the Siamese Chang and Eng. By violence or accident this cartilage was broken before it hardened into bone, and the two were separated until puberty. Then Adam saw Eve coming to him with a bone projecting from her side corresponding to the hollow in his own side, and said: "She is bone of my bone; she must have been taken from my side when I slept." This tradition was handed down to his posterity. The Jews have a tradition that Adam was created double-sexed, and that the two sexes were afterwards separated. The Hindus say that man was at first of both sexes and divided himself in order to people the earth. In the Zodiac of Dendera, Castor and Pollux appear as man and woman, and these twins, some say, were called Adam and Eve. The Coptic name for this sign is *Pi Mahi*, "the United." Darwin, in the postscript to a letter to Lyell, written as early as July, 1850, tells his friend that he has "a pleasant genealogy for mankind," and describes our remotest ancestor as "an animal which breathed water, had a swim-bladder, a great swimming tail, an imperfect skull, and was undoubtedly a hermaphrodite."

Matthew Arnold speaks of "the freshness of the early world." Novalis says that "all philosophy begins in homesickness." Shelley, Skylark: "We look before and after, And pine for what is not; Our sincerest laughter With some pain is fraught; Our sweetest songs are those That tell of saddest thought." — "The golden conception of a Paradise is the poet's guiding thought." There is a universal feeling that we are not now in our natural state; that we are far away from home; that we are exiles from our true habitation. Keble, Groans of Nature: "Such thoughts, the wreck of Paradise, Through many a dreary age, Upbore whate'er of good or wise Yet lived in bard or sage." Poetry and music echo the longing for some possession lost. Jessica in Shakespeare's Merchant of Venice: "I am never merry when I hear sweet music." All true poetry is forward-looking or backward-looking prophecy, as sculpture sets before us the original or the resurrection body. See Isaac Taylor, Hebrew Poetry, 94-101; Tyler, Theol. of Greek Poets, 225, 226.

Wellhausen, on the legend of a golden age, says: "It is the yearning song which goes through all the peoples: having attained the historical civilization, they feel the worth of the goods which they have sacrificed for it." He regards the golden age as only an ideal image, like the millennial kingdom at the end. Man differs from the beast in this power to form ideals. His destination *to* God shows his descent *from* God. Hegel in a similar manner claimed that the Paradisaic condition is only an ideal conception underlying human development. But may not the traditions of the gardens of Brahma and of the Hesperides embody the world's recollection of an historical fact, when man was free from external evil and possessed all that could minister to innocent joy? The "golden age" of the heathen was connected with the hope of restoration. So the use of the doctrine of man's original state is to convince men of the high ideal once realized, properly belonging to man, now lost, and recoverable, not by man's own powers, but only through God's provision in Christ. For references in classic writers to a golden age, see Luthardt, Compendium, 115. He mentions the following: Hesiod, Works and Days, 109-208; Aratus, Phenom., 100-184; Plato, Tim., 233; Vergil, Ec., 4, Georgics, 1: 135, Æneid, 8: 314.

(*b*) Provisions for the trying of man's virtue. — Since man was not yet in a state of confirmed holiness, but rather of simple childlike innocence, he could be made perfect only through temptation. Hence the "tree of the knowledge of good and evil" (Gen. 2 : 9). The one slight command best tested the spirit of obedience. Temptation did not necessitate a fall

If resisted, it would strengthen virtue. In that case, the *posse non peccare* would have become the *non posse peccare.*

Thomasius: "That evil is a necessary transition-point to good, is Satan's doctrine and philosophy." The tree was mainly a tree of probation, It is right for a father to make his son's title to his estate depend upon the performance of some filial duty, as Thaddeus Stevens made his son's possession of property conditional upon his keeping the temperance-pledge. Whether, besides this, the tree of knowledge was naturally hurtful or poisonous, we do not know.

(*c*) Opportunity of securing physical immortality. —The body of the first man was in itself mortal (1 Cor. 15 : 45). Science shows that physical life involves decay and loss. But means were apparently provided for checking this decay and preserving the body's youth. This means was the "tree of life" (Gen. 2 : 9). If Adam had maintained his integrity, the body might have been developed and transfigured, without intervention of death. In other words, the *posse non mori* might have become a *non posse mori.*

The tree of life was symbolic of communion with God and of man's dependence upon him. But this, only because it had a physical efficacy. It was sacramental and memorial to the soul, because it sustained the life of the body. Natural immortality without holiness would have been unending misery. Sinful man was therefore shut out from the tree of life, till he could be prepared for it by God's righteousness. Redemption and resurrection not only restore that which was lost, but give what man was originally created to attain : 1 Cor. 15 : 45 — "The first man Adam became a living soul. The last man Adam became a life-giving spirit"; Rev. 22 : 14 — "Blessed are they that wash their robes, that they may have the right to come to the tree of life."

The conclusions we have thus reached with regard to the incidents of man's original state are combated upon two distinct grounds :

1st. The facts bearing upon man's prehistoric condition point to a development from primitive savagery to civilization. Among these facts may be mentioned the succession of implements and weapons from stone to bronze and iron ; the polyandry and communal marriage systems of the lowest tribes ; the relics of barbarous customs still prevailing among the most civilized.

For the theory of an originally savage condition of man, see Sir John Lubbock, Prehistoric Times, and Origin of Civilization: "The primitive condition of mankind was one of utter barbarism"; but especially L. H. Morgan, Ancient Society, who divides human progress into three great periods, the savage, the barbarian, and the civilized. Each of the two former has three states, as follows: I. Savage: 1. Lowest state, marked by attainment of speech and subsistence upon roots. 2. Middle state, marked by fish-food and fire. 3. Upper state, marked by use of the bow and hunting. II. Barbarian: 1. Lower state, marked by invention and use of pottery. 2. Middle state, marked by use of domestic animals, maize, and building stone. 3. Upper state, marked by invention and use of iron tools. III. Civilized man next appears, with the introduction of the phonetic alphabet and writing. J. S. Stuart-Glennie, Contemp. Rev., Dec. 1892 : 844, defines civilization as "enforced social organization, with written records, and hence intellectual development and social progress."

With regard to this view we remark :

(*a*) It is based upon an insufficient induction of facts.—History shows a law of degeneration supplementing and often counteracting the tendency to development. In the earliest times of which we have any record, we find nations in a high state of civilization ; but in the case of every nation whose history runs back of the Christian era — as for example, the Romans, the Greeks, the Egyptians — the subsequent progress has been downward, and no nation is known to have recovered from barbarism except as the result of influence from without.

Lubbock seems to admit that cannibalism was not primeval; yet he shows a general tendency to take every brutal custom as a sample of man's first state. And this, in spite of the fact that many such customs have been the result of corruption. Bride-catching, for example, could not possibly have been primeval, in the strict sense of that term. Tylor, Primitive Culture, 1 : 48, presents a far more moderate view. He favors a theory of development, but with degeneration "as a secondary action largely and deeply affecting the development of civilization." So the Duke of Argyll, Unity of Nature: "Civilization and savagery are both the results of evolutionary development; but the one is a development in the upward, the latter in the downward direction; and for this reason, neither civilization nor savagery can rationally be looked upon as the primitive condition of man." Shedd, Dogm. Theol., 1 : 467 — "As plausible an argument might be constructed out of the deterioration and degradation of some of the human family to prove that man may have evolved downward into an anthropoid ape, as that which has been constructed to prove that he has been evolved upward from one."

Modern nations fall far short of the old Greek perception and expression of beauty. Modern Egyptians, Bushmen, Australians, are unquestionably degenerate races. See Lankester, Degeneration. The same is true of Italians and Spaniards, as well as of Turks. Abyssinians are now polygamists, though their ancestors were Christians and monogamists. The physical degeneration of portions of the population of Ireland is well known. See Mivart, Lessons from Nature, 146-160, who applies to the savage-theory the tests of language, morals, and religion, and who quotes Herbert Spencer as saying : "Probably most of them [savages], if not all of them, had ancestors in higher states, and among their beliefs remain some which were evolved during those higher states . . . . It is quite possible, and I believe highly probable, that retrogression has been as frequent as progression." Spencer, however, denies that savagery is always caused by lapse from civilization.

Bib. Sac., 6 : 715 ; 29 : 282 — "Man as a moral being does not tend to rise but to fall, and that with a geometric progress, except he be elevated and sustained by some force from without and above himself. While man once civilized may advance, yet moral ideas are apparently never developed from within." Had savagery been man's primitive condition, he never could have emerged. See Whately, Origin of Civilization, who maintains that man needed not only a divine Creator, but a divine Instructor. Seelye, Introd. to A Century of Dishonor, 3 — "The first missionaries to the Indians in Canada took with them skilled laborers to teach the savages how to till their fields, to provide them with comfortable homes, clothing, and food. But the Indians preferred their wigwams, skins, raw flesh, and filth. Only as Christian influences taught the Indian his inner need, and how this was to be supplied, was he led to wish and work for the improvement of his outward condition and habits. Civilization does not reproduce itself. It must first be kindled, and it can then be kept alive only by a power genuinely Christian." So Wallace, in Nature, Sept. 7, 1876, vol. 14 : 408-412.

Griffith-Jones, Ascent through Christ, 149-168, shows that evolution does not necessarily involve development as regards particular races. There is degeneration in all the organic orders. As regards man, he may be evolving in some directions, while in others he has degenerated. Lidgett, Spir. Principle of the Atonement, 245, speaks of "Prof. Clifford as pointing to the history of human progress and declaring that mankind is a risen and not a fallen race. There is no real contradiction between these two views. God has not let man go because man has rebelled against him. Where sin abounded, grace did much more abound." The humanity which was created in Christ and which is upheld by his power has ever received reinforcements of its physical and mental life, in spite of its moral and spiritual deterioration. "Some shrimps, by the adjustment of their bodily parts, go onward to the higher structure of the lobsters and crabs; while others, taking up the habit of dwelling in the gills of fishes, sink downward into a state closely resembling that of the worms." Drummond, Ascent of Man : "When a boy's kite comes down in our garden, we do not hold that it originally came from the clouds. So nations went up, before they came down. There is a national gravitation. The stick age preceded the stone age, but has been lost." Tennyson : "Evolution ever climbing after some ideal good, And Reversion ever dragging Evolution in the mud." Evolution often becomes devolution, if not devilution. A. J. Gordon, Ministry of the Spirit, 104 — "The Jordan is the fitting symbol of our natural life, rising in a lofty elevation, and from pure springs, but plunging steadily down till it pours itself into that Dead Sea from which there is no ouriet."

(*b*) Later investigations have rendered it probable that the stone age of some localities was contemporaneous with the bronze and iron ages of others, while certain tribes and nations, instead of making progress from one to the other, were never, so far back as we can trace them, without the knowledge and use of the metals. It is to be observed, moreover, that even without such knowledge and use man is not necessarily a barbarian, though he may be a child.

On the question whether the arts of civilization can be lost, see Arthur Mitchell, Past in the Present, 219: Rude art is often the debasement of a higher, instead of being the earlier; the rudest art in a nation may coëxist with the highest; cave-life may accompany high civilization. Illustrations from modern Scotland, where burial of a cock for epilepsy, and sacrifice of a bull, were until very recently extant. Certain arts have unquestionably been lost, as glass-making and iron-working in Assyria (see Mivart, referred to above). The most ancient men do not appear to have been inferior to the latest, either physically or intellectually. Rawlinson: "The explorers who have dug deep into the Mesopotamian mounds, and have ransacked the tombs of Egypt, have come upon no certain traces of savage man in those regions which a wide-spread tradition makes the cradle of the human race." The Tyrolese peasants show that a rude people may be moral, and a very simple people may be highly intelligent. See Southall, Recent Origin of Man, 386–449; Schliemann, Troy and her Remains, 274.

Mason, Origins of Invention, 110, 124, 128 — "There is no evidence that a stone age ever existed in some regions. In Africa, Canada, and perhaps Michigan, the metal age was as old as the stone age." An illustration of the mathematical powers of the savage is given by Rev. A. E. Hunt in an account of the native arithmetic of Murray Islands, Torres Straits. "Netat" (one) and "neis" (two) are the only numerals, higher numbers being described by combinations of these, as "neis-netat" for three, "neis-i-neis" for four, etc., or by reference to one of the fingers, elbows or other parts of the body. A total of thirty-one could be counted by the latter method. Beyond this all numbers were "many," as this was the limit reached in counting before the introduction of English numerals, now in general use in the islands.

Shaler, Interpretation of Nature, 171 — "It is commonly supposed that the direction of the movement [in the variation of species] is ever upward. The fact is on the contrary that in a large number of cases, perhaps in the aggregate in more than half, the change gives rise to a form which, by all the canons by which we determine relative rank, is to be regarded as regressive or degradational. . . . . Species, genera, families, and orders have all, like the individuals of which they are composed, a period of decay in which the gain won by infinite toil and pains is altogether lost in the old age of the group." Shaler goes on to say that in the matter of variation successes are to failures as 1 to 100,000, and if man be counted the solitary distinguished success, then the proportion is something like 1 to 100,000,000. No species that passes away is ever reinstated. If man were now to disappear, there is no reason to believe that by any process of change a similar creature would be evolved, however long the animal kingdom continued to exist. The use of these successive chances to produce man is inexplicable except upon the hypothesis of an infinite designing Wisdom.

(*c*) The barbarous customs to which this view looks for support may better be explained as marks of broken-down civilization than as relics of a primitive and universal savagery. Even if they indicated a former state of barbarism, that state might have been itself preceded by a condition of comparative culture.

Mark Hopkins, in Princeton Rev. Sept., 1882: 194 — "There is no cruel treatment of females among animals. If man came from the lower animals, then he cannot have been originally savage; for you find the most of this cruel treatment among savages." Tylor instances "street Arabs." He compares street Arabs to a ruined house, but savage tribes to a builder's yard. See Duke of Argyll, Primeval Man, 129, 133; Bush-nell, Nature and the Supernatural, 223; McLennan, Studies in Ancient History. Gulick, in Bib. Sac., July, 1892 : 517 — " Cannibalism and infanticide are unknown among the anthropoid apes. These must be the results of degradation. Pirates and slavetraders are not men of low and abortive intelligence, but men of education who deliberately throw off all restraint, and who use their powers for the destruction of society."

Keane, Man, Past and Present, 40, quotes Sir H. H. Johnston, an administrator who has had a wider experience of the natives of Africa than any man living, as saying that " the tendency of the negro for several centuries past has been an actual retrograde one — return toward the savage and even the brute. If he had been cut off from the immigration of the Arab and the European, the purely Negroid races, left to them-selves, so far from advancing towards a higher type of humanity, might have actually reverted by degrees to a type no longer human." Ratzel's History of Mankind: "We assign no great antiquity to Polynesian civilization. In New Zealand it is a matter of only some centuries back. In newly occupied territories, the development of the population began upon a higher level and then fell off. The Maoris' decadence resulted in the rapid impoverishment of culture, and the character of the people became more savage and cruel. Captain Cook found objects of art worshiped by the descendants of those who produced them."

Recent researches have entirely discredited L. H. Morgan's theory of an original brutal promiscuity of the human race. Ritchie, Darwin and Hegel, 6, note — " The theory of an original promiscuity is rendered extremely doubtful by the habits of many of the higher animals." E. B. Tylor, in 19th Century, July, 1906 — "A sort of family life, lasting for the sake of the young, beyond a single pairing season, exists among the higher manlike apes. The male gorilla keeps watch and ward over his progeny. He is the antetype of the house-father. The matriarchal system is a later device for politi-cal reasons, to bind together in peace and alliance tribes that would otherwise be hos-tile. But it is an artificial system introduced as a substitute for and in opposition to the natural paternal system. When the social pressure is removed, the maternalized husband emancipates himself, and paternalism begins." Westermarck, History of Human Marriage : " Marriage and the family are thus intimately connected with one another; it is for the benefit of the young that male and female continue to live together. Marriage is therefore rooted in the family, rather than the family in marriage. . . . . There is not a shred of genuine evidence for the notion that promiscuity ever formed a general stage in the social history of mankind. The hypothesis of promiscuity, instead of belonging to the class of hypotheses which are scientifically permissible, has no real foundation, and is essentially unscientific." Howard, History of Matrimonial Institutions: " Marriage or pairing between one man and one woman, though the union be often transitory and the rule often violated, is the typical form of sexual union from the infancy of the human race."

(*d*) The well-nigh universal tradition of a golden age of virtue and happiness may be most easily explained upon the Scripture view of an actual creation of the race in holiness and its subsequent apostasy.

For references in classic writers to a golden age, see Luthardt, Compendium der Dogmatik, 115; Pfleiderer, Philos. Religion, 1 : 205 — " In Hesiod we have the legend of a golden age under the lordship of Chronos, when man was free from cares and toils, in untroubled youth and cheerfulness, with a superabundance of the gifts which the earth furnished of itself ; the race was indeed not immortal, but it experienced death even as a soft sleep." We may add that capacity for religious truth depends upon moral conditions. Very early races therefore have a purer faith than the later ones. Increasing depravity makes it harder for the later generations to exercise faith. The wisdom-literature may have been very early instead of very late, just as monothe-istic ideas are clearer the further we go back. Bixby, Crisis in Morals, 171 — " Precisely because such tribes [Australian and African savages] have been deficient in average moral quality, have they failed to march upward on the road of civilization with the rest of mankind, and have fallen into these bog holes of savage degradation." On petrified civilizations, see Henry George, Progress and Poverty, 433-439 — " The law of human progress, what is it but the moral law ?" On retrogressive development in nature, see Weismann, Heredity, 2 : 1-30. But see also Mary E. Case, " Did the Romans Degenerate?" in Internat. Journ. Ethics, Jan. 1893 : 165-182, in which it is maintained that the Romans made constant advances rather. Henry Sumner Maine calls the Bible the most important single document in the history of sociology, because it exhibits authentically the early development of society from the family, through the tribe, into the nation,—a progress learned only by glimpses, intervals, and survivals of old usages in the literature of other nations.

2nd. That the religious history of mankind warrants us in inferring a necessary and universal law of progress, in accordance with which man passes from fetichism to polytheism and monotheism,—this first theological stage, of which fetichism, polytheism, and monotheism are parts, being succeeded by the metaphysical stage, and that in turn by the positive.

This theory is propounded by Comte, in his Positive Philosophy, English transl., 25, 26, 515–636 — "Each branch of our knowledge passes successively through three different theoretical conditions: the Theological, or fictitious; the Metaphysical, or abstract; and the Scientific, or positive. . . . . The first is the necessary point of departure of the human understanding; and the third is its fixed and definite state. The second is merely a state of transition. In the theological state, the human mind, seeking the essential nature of beings, the first and final causes, the origin and purpose, of all effects — in short, absolute knowledge — supposes all phenomena to be produced by the immediate action of supernatural beings. In the metaphysical state, which is only a modification of the first, the mind supposes, instead of supernatural beings, abstract forces, veritable entities, that is, personified abstractions, inherent in all beings, and capable of producing all phenomena. What is called the explanation of phenomena is, in this stage, a mere reference of each to its proper entity. In the final, the positive state, the mind has given over the vain search after absolute notions, the origin and destination of the universe, and the causes of phenomena, and applies itself to the study of their laws — that is, their invariable relations of succession and resemblance. . . . . The theological system arrived at its highest perfection when it substituted the providential action of a single Being for the varied operations of numerous divinities. In the last stage of the metaphysical system, men substituted one great entity, Nature, as the cause of all phenomena, instead of the multitude of entities at first supposed. In the same way the ultimate perfection of the positive system would be to represent all phenomena as particular aspects of a single general fact — such as Gravitation, for instance."

This assumed law of progress, however, is contradicted by the following facts :

(*a*) Not only did the monotheism of the Hebrews precede the great polytheistic systems of antiquity, but even these heathen religions are purer from polytheistic elements, the further back we trace them ; so that the facts point to an original monotheistic basis for them all.

The gradual deterioration of all religions, apart from special revelation and influence from God, is proof that the purely evolutionary theory is defective. The most natural supposition is that of a primitive revelation, which little by little receded from human memory. In Japan, Shinto was originally the worship of Heaven. The worship of the dead, the deification of the Mikado, etc., were a corruption and aftergrowth. The Mikado's ancestors, instead of coming from heaven, came from Korea. Shinto was originally a form of monotheism. Not one of the first emperors was deified after death. Apotheosis of the Mikados dated from the corruption of Shinto through the importation of Buddhism. Andrew Lang, in his Making of Religion, advocates primitive monotheism. T. G. Pinches, of the British Museum, 1894, declares that, as in the earliest Egyptian, so in the early Babylonian records, there is evidence of a primitive monotheism. Nevins, Demon-Possession, 170–173, quotes W. A. P. Martin, President of the Peking University, as follows: "China, India, Egypt and Greece all agree in the monotheistic type of their early religion. The Orphic Hymns, long before the advent of the popular divinities, celebrated the *Pantheos*, the universal God. The odes compiled by Confucius testify to the early worship of Shangte, the Supreme Ruler. The Vedas speak of 'one unknown true Being, all-present, all-powerful, the Creator, Preserver and Destroyer of the Universe.' And in Egypt, as late as the time of Plutarch, there were still vestiges of a monotheistic worship."

On the evidences of an original monotheism, see Max Müller, Chips, 1 : 337 ; Rawlinson, in Present Day Tracts. 2 : no. 11 ; Legge, Religions of China, 8, 11 ; Diestel, in Jahrbuch für deutsche Theologie, 1860, and vol. 5 : 669 ; Philip Smith, Anc. Hist. of East, 65, 195; Warren, on the Earliest Creed of Mankind, in the Meth. Quar. Rev., Jan. 1884.

(*b*) "There is no proof that the Indo-Germanic or Semitic stocks ever practiced fetich worship, or were ever enslaved by the lowest types of mythological religion, or ascended from them to somewhat higher " (Fisher).

See Fisher, Essays on Supernat. Origin of Christianity, 545 ; Bartlett, Sources of History in the Pentateuch, 36-115. Herbert Spencer once held that fetichism was primordial. But he afterwards changed his mind, and said that the facts proved to be exactly the opposite when he had become better acquainted with the ideas of savages ; see his Principles of Sociology, 1 : 343. Mr. Spencer finally traced the beginnings of religion to the worship of ancestors. But in China no ancestor has ever become a god ; see Hill, Genetic Philosophy, 304-313. And unless man had an inborn sense of divinity, he could deify neither ancestors nor ghosts. Professor Hilprecht of Philadelphia says: " As the attempt has recently been made to trace the pure monotheism of Israel to Babylonian sources, I am bound to declare this an absolute impossibility, on the basis of my fourteen years' researches in Babylonian cuneiform inscriptions. The faith of Israel's chosen people is : ' Hear, O Israel: the Lord our God is one Lord.' And this faith could never have proceeded from the Babylonian mountain of gods, that charnelhouse full of corruption and dead men's bones."

(*c*) Some of the earliest remains of man yet found show, by the burial of food and weapons with the dead, that there already existed the idea of spiritual beings and of a future state, and therefore a religion of a higher sort than fetichism.

Idolatry proper regards the idol as the symbol and representative of a spiritual being who exists apart from the material object, though he manifests himself through it. Fetichism, however, identifies the divinity with the material thing, and worships the stock or stone ; spirit is not conceived of as existing apart from body. Belief in spiritual beings and a future state is therefore proof of a religion higher in kind than fetichism. See Lyell, Antiquity of Man, quoted in Dawson, Story of Earth and Man, 384 ; see also 368, 372, 386 — " Man's capacities for degradation are commensurate with his capacities for improvement " (Dawson). Lyell, in his last edition, however, admits the evidence from the Aurignac cave to be doubtful. See art. by Dawkins, in Nature, 4 : 208.

(*d*) The theory in question, in making theological thought a merely transient stage of mental evolution, ignores the fact that religion has its root in the intuitions and yearnings of the human soul, and that therefore no philosophical or scientific progress can ever abolish it. While the terms theological, metaphysical, and positive may properly mark the order in which the ideas of the individual and the race are acquired, positivism errs in holding that these three phases of thought are mutually exclusive, and that upon the rise of the later the earlier must of necessity become extinct.

John Stuart Mill suggests that " personifying " would be a much better term than "theological " to designate the earliest efforts to explain physical phenomena. On the fundamental principles of Positivism, see New Englander, 1873 : 323-386 ; Diman, Theistic Argument, 338 — " Three coëxistent states are here confounded with three successive stages of human thought; three aspects of things with three epochs of time. Theology, metaphysics, and science must always exist side by side, for all positive science rests on metaphysical principles, and theology lies behind both. All are as permanent as human reason itself." Martineau, Types, 1 : 487 — " Comte sets up mediæval Christianity as the typical example of evolved monotheism, and develops it out of the Greek and Roman polytheism which it overthrew and dissipated. But the religion of modern Europe notoriously does not descend from the same source as its civilization and is no continuation of the ancient culture," — it comes rather from Hebrew sources ; Essays, Philos. and Theol., 1 : 24, 62 — " The Jews were always a disobliging people ; what business had they to be up so early in the morning, disturbing the house ever so long before M. Comte's bell rang to prayers ? " See also Gillett, God in Human Thought, 1 : 17-23 ; Rawlinson, in Journ. Christ. Philos., April, 1883 : 353 ; Nineteenth Century, Oct. 1886 : 4 :3-490.

CHAPTER III.

SIN, OR MAN'S STATE OF APOSTASY.

SECTION I.— THE LAW OF GOD.

As preliminary to a treatment of man's state of apostasy, it becomes necessary to consider the nature of that law of God, the transgression of which is sin. We may best approach the subject by inquiring what is the true conception of

I. LAW IN GENERAL.

1. Law is an expression of *will*.

The essential idea of law is that of a general expression of will enforced by power. It implies : (*a*) A lawgiver, or authoritative will. (*b*) Subjects, or beings upon whom this will terminates. (*c*) A general command, or expression of this will. (*d*) A power, enforcing the command.

These elements are found even in what we call natural law. The phrase 'law of nature' involves a self-contradiction, when used to denote a mode of action or an order of sequence behind which there is conceived to be no intelligent and ordaining will. Physics derives the term 'law' from jurisprudence, instead of jurisprudence deriving it from physics. It is first used of the relations of voluntary agents. Causation in our own wills enables us to see something besides mere antecedence and consequence in the world about us. Physical science, in her very use of the word 'law,' implicitly confesses that a supreme Will has set general rules which control the processes of the universe.

Wayland, Moral Science, 1, unwisely defines law as " a mode of existence or order of sequence," thus leaving out of his definition all reference to an ordaining will. He subsequently says that law presupposes an establisher, but in his definition there is nothing to indicate this. We insist, on the other hand, that the term 'law' itself includes the idea of force and cause. The word 'law' is from 'lay' (German *legen*), = something laid down ; German *Gesetz*, from *setzen*, = something set or established ; Greek νόμος, from νέμω, = something assigned or apportioned ; Latin *lex*, from *lego*, = something said or spoken.

All these derivations show that man's original conception of law is that of something proceeding from volition. Lewes, in his Problems of Life and Mind, says that the term 'law' is so suggestive of a giver and impresser of law, that it ought to be dropped, and the word 'method' substituted. The merit of Austin's treatment of the subject is that he "rigorously limits the term 'law' to the commands of a superior "; see John Austin, Province of Jurisprudence, 1 : 88-93, 220-223. The defects of his treatment we shall note further on.

J. S. Mill : " It is the custom, wherever they [scientific men] can trace regularity of any kind, to call the general proposition which expresses the nature of that regularity, a law ; as when in mathematics we speak of the law of the successive terms of a converging series. But the expression 'law of nature' is generally employed by scientific men with a sort of tacit reference to the original sense of the word 'law,' namely, the expression of the will of a superior — the superior in this case being the Ruler of the universe." Paley, Nat. Theology, chap. 1—"It is a perversion of language to assign any *law* as the efficient operative cause of anything. A law presupposes an agent; this is only the mode according to which an agent proceeds; it implies a power, for it is the order according to which that power acts. Without this agent, without this power, which are both distinct from itself, the law does nothing." "Quis custodiet ipsos custodes?" "Rules do not fulfill themselves, any more than a statute-book can quell a riot" (Martineau, Types, 1 : 367).

Charles Darwin got the suggestion of natural selection, not from the study of lower plants and animals, but from Malthus on Population; see his Life and Letters, Vol. I, autobiographical chapter. Ward, Naturalism and Agnosticism, 2 : 248-252 — "The conception of natural law rests upon the analogy of civil law." Ladd, Philosophy of Knowledge, 333 — "Laws are only the more or less frequently repeated and uniform modes of the behavior of things"; Philosophy of Mind, 122 — "To be, to stand in relation, to be self-active, to act upon other being, to obey law, to be a cause, to be a permanent subject of states, to be the same to-day as yesterday, to be identical, to be one, — all these and all similar conceptions, together with the proofs that they are valid for real beings, are affirmed of physical realities, or projected into them, only on a basis of self-knowledge, envisaging and affirming the reality of mind. Without psychological insight and philosophical training, such terms or their equivalents are meaningless in physics. And because writers on physics do not in general have this insight and this training, in spite of their utmost endeavors to treat physics as an empirical science without metaphysics, they flounder and blunder and contradict themselves hopelessly whenever they touch upon fundamental matters." See President McGarvey's Criticism on James Lane Allen's Reign of Law: "It is not in the nature of law to reign. To reign is an act which can be literally affirmed only of persons. A man may reign; a God may reign; a devil may reign; but a law cannot reign. If a law could reign, we should have no gambling in New York and no open saloons on Sunday. There would be no false swearing in courts of justice, and no dishonesty in politics. It is men who reign in these matters—the judges, the grand jury, the sheriff and the police. They may reign according to law. Law cannot reign even over those who are appointed to execute the law."

2. Law is a *general* expression of will.

The characteristic of law is generality. It is addressed to substances or persons in classes. Special legislation is contrary to the true theory of law.

When the Sultan of Zanzibar orders his barber to be beheaded because the latter has cut his master, this order is not properly a law. To be a law it must read: "Every barber who cuts his majesty shall thereupon be decapitated." *Einmal ist keinmal =* "Once is no custom." Dr. Schurman suggests that the word *meal* (Mahl) means originally *time (mal in einmal)*. The measurement of time among ourselves is astronomical; among our earliest ancestors it was gastronomical, and the reduplication *mealtime* — the ding-dong of the dinner bell. The Shah of Persia once asked the Prince of Wales to have a man put to death in order that he might see the English method of execution. When the Prince told him that this was beyond his power, tne Shah wished to know what was the use of being a king if he could not kill people at his pleasure. Peter the Great suggested a way out of the difficulty. He desired to see keelhauling. When informed that there was no sailor liable to that penalty, he replied: "That does not matter,—take one of my suite." Amos, Science of Law, 33, 34—"Law eminently deals in general rules." It knows not persons or personality. It must apply to more than one case. "The characteristic of law is generality, as that of morality is individual application." Special legislation is the bane of good government; it does not properly fall within the province of the law-making power; it savors of the caprice of despotism, which gives commands to each subject at will. Hence our more advanced political constitutions check lobby influence and bribery, by prohibiting special legislation in all cases where general laws already exist.

3. Law implies *power to enforce.*

It is essential to the existence of law, that there be power to enforce. Otherwise law becomes the expression of mere wish or advice. Since physical substances and forces have no intelligence and no power to resist, the four elements already mentioned exhaust the implications of the term 'law' as applied to nature. In the case of rational and free agents, however, law implies in addition : (e) Duty or obligation to obey ; and (f) Sanctions, or pains and penalties for disobedience.

"Law that has no penalty is not law but advice, and the government in which infliction does not follow transgression is the reign of rogues or demons." On the question whether any of the punishments of civil law are legal sanctions, except the punishment of death, see N. W. Taylor, Moral Govt., 2:367-387. Rewards are motives, but they are not sanctions. Since public opinion may be conceived of as inflicting penalties for violation of her will, we speak figuratively of the laws of society, of fashion, of etiquette, of honor. Only so far as the community of nations can and does by sanctions compel obedience, can we with propriety assert the existence of international law. Even among nations, however, there may be moral as well as physical sanctions. The decision of an international tribunal has the same sanction as a treaty, and if the former is impotent, the latter also is. Fines and imprisonment do not deter decent people from violations of law half so effectively as do the social penalties of ostracism and disgrace, and it will be the same with the findings of an international tribunal. Diplomacy without ships and armies has been said to be law without penalty. But exclusion from civilized society is penalty. "In the unquestioning obedience to fashion's decrees, to which we all quietly submit, we are simply yielding to the pressure of the persons about us. No one adopts a style of dress because it is reasonable, for the styles are often most unreasonable ; but we meekly yield to the most absurd of them rather than resist this force and be called eccentric. So what we call public opinion is the most mighty power to-day known, whether in society or in politics."

4. Law expresses and demands *nature*.

The will which thus binds its subjects by commands and penalties is an expression of the nature of the governing power, and reveals the normal relations of the subjects to that power. Finally, therefore, law (g) Is an expression of the nature of the lawgiver ; and (h) Sets forth the condition or conduct in the subjects which is requisite for harmony with that nature. Any so-called law which fails to represent the nature of the governing power soon becomes obsolete. All law that is permanent is a transcript of the facts of being, a discovery of what is and must be, in order to harmony between the governing and the governed ; in short, positive law is just and lasting only as it is an expression and republication of the law of nature.

Diman, Theistic Argument, 106, 107 : John Austin, although he "rigorously limited the term law to the commands of a superior," yet "rejected Ulpian's explanation of the law of nature, and ridiculed as fustian the celebrated description in Hooker." This we conceive to be the radical defect of Austin's conception. The Will from which natural law proceeds is conceived of after a deistic fashion, instead of being immanent in the universe. Lightwood, in his Nature of Positive Law, 78-90, criticizes Austin's definition of law as command, and substitutes the idea of law as custom. Sir Henry Maine's Ancient Law has shown us that the early village communities had customs which only gradually took form as definite laws. But we reply that custom is not the ultimate source of anything. Repeated acts of will are necessary to constitute custom. The first customs are due to the commanding will of the father in the patriarchal family. So Austin's definition is justified. Collective morals (mores) come from individual duty (due) ; law originates in will ; Martineau, Types, 2:18, 19. Behind this will, however, is something which Austin does not take account of, namely, the nature of things as constituted by God, as revealing the universal Reason, and as furnishing the standard to which all positive law, if it would be permanent, must conform.

See Montesquieu, Spirit of Laws, book 1, sec. 14 — "Laws are the necessary relations arising from the nature of things. . . . . There is a primitive Reason, and laws are the relations subsisting between it and different beings, and the relations of these to one another. . . . These rules are a fixed and invariable relation. . . . Particular intelligent beings may have laws of their own making, but they have some likewise that they never made. . . . . To say that there is nothing just or unjust but **what is commanded or forbidden by positive laws, is the same as saying** that before the describing of a circle all the radii were not equal. We must therefore acknowledge relations antecedent to the positive law by which they were established." Kant, Metaphysic of Ethics, 169–172—" By the science of law is meant systematic knowledge of the principles of the law of nature—from which positive law takes its rise—which is forever the same, and carries its sure and unchanging obligations over all nations and throughout all ages."

It is true even of a despot's law, that it reveals his nature, and shows what is requisite in the subject to constitute him in harmony with that nature. A law which does not represent the nature of things, or the real relations of the governor and the governed, has only a nominal existence, and cannot be permanent. On the definition and nature of law, see also Pomeroy, in Johnson's Encyclopædia, art.: Law; Ahrens, Cours de Droit Naturel, book 1, sec. 14; Lorimer, Institutes of Law, 256, who quotes from Burke: "All human laws are, properly speaking, only declaratory. They may alter the mode and application, but have no power over the substance of original justice"; Lord Bacon: "Regula enim legem (ut acus nautica polos) indicat, non statuit." Duke of Argyll, Reign of Law, 64; H. C. Carey, Unity of Law.

Fairbairn, in Contemp. Rev., Apl. 1895: 473—"The Roman jurists draw a distinction between *jus naturale* and *jus civile*, and they used the former to affect the latter. The *jus civile* was statutory, established and fixed law, as it were, the actual legal environment; the *jus naturale* was ideal, the principle of justice and equity immanent in man, yet with the progress of his ethical culture growing ever more articulate." We add the fact that *jus* in Latin and *Recht* in German have ceased to mean merely abstract right, and have come to denote the legal system in which that abstract right is embodied and expressed. Here we have a proof that Christ is gradually moralizing the world and translating law into life. E. G. Robinson: "Never a government on earth made its own laws. Even constitutions simply declare laws already and actually existing. Where society falls into anarchy, the *lex talioni* becomes the prevailing principle."

II. The Law of God in Particular.

The law of God is a general expression of the divine will enforced by power. It has two forms: Elemental Law and Positive Enactment.

1. *Elemental Law*, or law inwrought into the elements, substances, and forces of the rational and irrational creation. This is twofold:

A. The expression of the divine will in the constitution of the material universe;—this we call physical, or natural law. Physical law is not necessary. Another order of things is conceivable. Physical order is not an end in itself; it exists for the sake of moral order. Physical order has therefore only a relative constancy, and God supplements it at times by miracle.

Bowne, Theory of Thought and Knowledge, 210—"The laws of nature represent no necessity, but are only the orderly forms of procedure of some Being back of them. . . . . Cosmic uniformities are God's methods in freedom." Philos. of Theism, 73—"Any of the cosmic laws, from gravitation on, might conceivably have been lacking or altogether different. . . . . No trace of necessity can be found in the Cosmos or in its laws." Seth, Hegelianism and Personality: "Nature is not necessary. Why put an island where it is, and not a mile east or west? Why connect the smell and shape of the rose, or the taste and color of the orange? Why do H_2O form water? No one knows." William James: "The parts seem shot at us out of a pistol." Rather, we would say, out of a shotgun. Martineau, Seat of Authority, 33—"Why undulations in one medium should produce sound, and in another light; why one speed of vibration should give red color, and another blue, can be explained by no reason of necessity. Here is selecting will."

Brooks, Foundations of Zoölogy, 126—"So far as the philosophy of evolution involves belief that nature is determinate, or due to a necessary law of universal progress or evolution, it seems to me to be utterly unsupported by evidence and totally unscientific." There is no power to deduce anything whatever from homogeneity. Press the button and law does the rest? Yes, but what presses the button? The solution crys-

tallzes when shaken? Yes, but what shakes it? Ladd, Philos. of Knowledge, 310 —
" The directions and velocities of the stars fall under no common principles that
astronomy can discover. One of the stars — ' 1830 Groombridge ' — is flying through
space at a rate many times as great as it could attain if it had fallen through infinite
space through all eternity toward the entire physical universe. . . . . Fluids contract
when cooled and expand when heated, — yet there is the well known exception of
water at the degree of freezing." 263 — " Things do not appear to be mathematical all
the way through. The system of things may be a Life, changing its modes of manifestation according to immanent ideas, rather than a collection of rigid entities, blindly
subject in a mechanical way to unchanging laws."

Augustine : " Dei voluntas rerum natura est." Joseph Cook : " The laws of nature
are the habits of God." But Campbell, Atonement, Introd., xxvi, says there is this
difference between the laws of the moral universe and those of the physical, namely,
that we do not trace the existence of the former to an act of will, as we do the latter.
" To say that God has given existence to goodness, as he has to the laws of nature, would
be equivalent to saying that he has given existence to himself." Pepper, Outlines of
Syst. Theol., 91 — " Moral law, unlike natural law, is a standard of action to be adopted
or rejected in the exercise of rational freedom, *i. e.*, of moral agency." See also Shedd,
Dogm. Theol., 1 : 531.

Mark Hopkins, in Princeton Rev., Sept. 1882 : 190 — " In moral law there is enforcement
by punishment only — never by power, for this would confound moral law with physical, and obedience can never be produced or secured by power. In physical law, on the
contrary, enforcement is wholly by power, and punishment is impossible. So far as man
is free, he is not subject to law at all, in its physical sense. Our wills are free *from* law
as enforced by *power*; but are free *under* law, as enforced by *punishment*. Where law
prevails in the same sense as in the material world, there can be no freedom. Law does
not prevail when we reach the region of choice. We hold to a power in the mind of
man originating a free choice. Two objects or courses of action, between which choice
is to be made, are presupposed : (1) A uniformity or set of uniformities implying a
force by which the uniformity is produced [physical or natural law] ; (2) A command,
addressed to free and intelligent beings, that can be obeyed or disobeyed, and that has
connected with it rewards or punishments " [moral law]. See also Wm. Arthur Difference between Physical and Moral Law.

B.   The expression of the divine will in the constitution of rational and
free agents ; — this we call moral law.   This elemental law of our moral
nature, with which only we are now concerned, has all the characteristics
mentioned as belonging to law in general.   It implies : (*a*) A divine Lawgiver, or ordaining Will.   (*b*) Subjects, or moral beings upon whom the
law terminates.   (*c*) General command, or expression of this will in the
moral constitution of the subjects.   (*d*) Power, enforcing the command.
(*e*) Duty, or obligation to obey.   (*f*) Sanctions, or pains and penalties
for disobedience.

All these are of a loftier sort than are found in human law.   But we need
especially to emphasize the fact that this law (*g*) Is an expression of the
moral nature of God, and therefore of God's holiness, the fundamental
attribute of that nature ; and that it (*h*) Sets forth absolute conformity to
that holiness, as the normal condition of man.   This law is inwrought into
man's rational and moral being.   Man fulfills it, only when in his moral as
well as his rational being he is the image of God.

Although the will from which the moral law springs is an expression of the nature
of God, and a necessary expression of that nature in view of the existence of moral
beings, it is none the less a personal will. We should be careful not to attribute to law
a personality of its own. When Plutarch says : " Law is king both of mortal and
immortal beings," and when we say : " The law will take hold of you," " The criminal
is in danger of the law," we are simply substituting the name of the agent for that of
the principal. God is not subject to law ; God is the source of law ; and we may say
" If Jehovah be God, worship him ; but if Law, worship it."

Since moral law merely reflects God, it is not a thing *made*. Men *discover* laws, but they do not *make* them, any more than the chemist makes the laws by which the elements combine. Instance the solidification of hydrogen at Geneva. Utility does not constitute law, although we test law by utility; see Murphy, Scientific Bases of Faith, 53–71. The true nature of the moral law is set forth in the noble though rhetorical description of Hooker (Eccl. Pol., 1 : 19½)—" Of law there can be no less acknowledged than that her seat is in the bosom of God; her voice the harmony of the world; all things in heaven and earth do her homage, the very least as feeling her care, and the greatest as not exempted from her power; both angels and men, and creatures of what condition soever, though each in a different sort and manner, yet all with uniform consent admiring her as the mother of their peace and joy." See also Martineau, Types, 2 : 119, and Study, 1 : 35.

Curtis, Primitive Semitic Religions, 66, 101—" The Oriental believes that God makes right by edict. Saladin demonstrated to Henry of Champagne the loyalty of his Assassins, by commanding two of them to throw themselves down from a lofty tower to certain and violent death." H. B. Smith, System, 192 — " Will implies personality, and personality adds to abstract truth and duty the element of authority. Law therefore has the force that a person has over and above that of an idea." Human law forbids only those offences which constitute a breach of public order or of private right. God's law forbids all that is an offence against the divine order, that is, all that is unlike God. The whole law may be summed up in the words: " Be like God." Salter, First Steps in Philosophy, 101–126 — " The realization of the nature of each being is the end to be striven for. Self-realization is an ideal end, not of one being, but of each being, with due regard to the value of each in the proper scale of worth. The beast can be sacrificed for man. All men are sacred as capable of unlimited progress. It is our duty to realize the capacities of our nature so far as they are consistent with one another and go to make up one whole." This means that man fulfills the law only as he realizes the divine idea in his character and life, or, in other words, as he becomes a finite image of God's infinite perfections.

Bixby, Crisis in Morals, 191, 201, 285, 286 — " Morality is rooted in the nature of things. There is a universe. We are all parts of an infinite organism. Man is inseparably bound to man [and to God]. All rights and duties arise out of this common life. In the solidarity of social life lies the ground of Kant's law : So will, that the maxim of thy conduct may apply to all. The planet cannot safely fly away from the sun, and the hand cannot safely separate itself from the heart. It is from the fundamental unity of life that our duties flow. . . . The infinite world-organism is the body and manifestation of God. And when we recognize the solidarity of our vital being with this divine life and embodiment, we begin to see into the heart of the mystery, the unquestionable authority and supreme sanction of duty. Our moral intuitions are simply the unchanging laws of the universe that have emerged to consciousness in the human heart. . . . The inherent principles of the universal Reason reflect themselves in the mirror of the moral nature. . . . The enlightened conscience is the expression in the human soul of the divine Consciousness. . . . Morality is the victory of the divine Life in us. . . . Solidarity of our life with the universal Life gives it unconditional sacredness and transcendental authority. . . . . The microcosm must bring itself *en rapport* with the Macrocosm. Man must bring his spirit into resemblance to the World-essence, and into union with it."

The law of God, then, is simply an expression of the nature of God in the form of moral requirement, and a necessary expression of that nature in view of the existence of moral beings (Ps. 19 : 7 ; *cf.* 1). To the existence of this law all men bear witness. The consciences even of the heathen testify to it (Rom. 2 : 14, 15). Those who have the written law recognize this elemental law as of greater compass and penetration (Rom. 7 : 14; 8 : 4). The perfect embodiment and fulfillment of this law is seen only in Christ (Rom. 10 : 4 ; Phil. 3 : 8, 9).

Ps. 19 : 7 —"The law of Jehovah is perfect, restoring the soul"; *cf.* verse 1 —"The heavens declare the glory of God" = two revelations of God — one in nature, the other in the moral law. Rom. 2 : 14, 15 —"for when Gentiles that have not the law do by nature the things of the law, these, not having the law, are the law unto themselves; in that they show the work of the law written in their hearts, their conscience bearing witness therewith, and their thoughts one with another accusing or else excusing them " —here the "work of the law" =, not the ten commandments, for of these the heathen were ignorant, but rather the work corresponding to them, *i. e.*, the substance of them. Rom. 7: 14 — "For we know that the law is spiritual" — this, says Meyer, is equivalent to saying " its essence is divine, of like nature with the Holy Spirit who gave it, a holy self-revelation of God." Rom. 8: 4 — "that the ordinance of the law might be fulfilled in us, who walk not after the flesh, but after the Spirit"; 10: 4 — "For Christ is the end of the law unto righteousness to every one that believeth"; Phil. 3: 8, 9 — "that I may gain Christ, and be found in him, not having a righteousness of mine own, even that which is of the law, but that which is through faith in Christ, the righteousness which is from God by faith"; Heb. 10: 9 — "Lo, I am come to do thy will." In Christ "the law appears Drawn out in living characters." Just such as he was and is, we feel that we ought to be. Hence the character of Christ convicts us of sin, as does no other manifestation of God. See, on the passages from Romans, the Commentary of Philippi.

Fleming, Vocab. Philos., 286 — " Moral laws are derived from the nature and will of God, *and* the character and condition of man." God's nature is reflected in the laws of our nature. Since law is inwrought into man's nature, man is a law unto himself. To conform to his own nature, in which conscience is supreme, is to conform to the nature of God. The law is only the revelation of the constitutive principles of being, the declaration of what must be, so long as man is man and God is God. It says in effect: " Be like God, or you cannot be truly man." So moral law is not simply a test of obedience, but is also a revelation of eternal reality. Man cannot be lost to God, without being lost to himself. "The 'hands of the living God' (Heb. 10 : 31) into which we fall, are the laws of nature." In the spiritual world "the same wheels revolve, only there is no iron" (Drummond, Natural Law in the Spiritual World, 27). Wuttke, Christian Ethics, 2: 82-92 — " The totality of created being is to be in harmony with God and with itself. The idea of this harmony, as active in God under the form of will, is God's law." A manuscript of the U. S. Constitution was so written that when held at a little distance the shading of the letters and their position showed the countenance of George Washington. So the law of God is only God's face disclosed to human sight.

R. W. Emerson, Woodnotes, 57 — " Conscious Law is King of kings." Two centuries ago John Norton wrote a book entitled The Orthodox Evangelist, "designed for the begetting and establishing of the faith which is in Jesus," in which we find the following : "God doth not will things because they are just, but things are therefore just because God so willeth them. What reasonable man but will yield that the being of the moral law hath no necessary connection with the being of God ? That the actions of men not conformable to this law should be sin, that death should be the punishment of sin, these are the constitutions of God, proceeding from him not by way of necessity of nature, but freely, as effects and products of his eternal good pleasure." This is to make God an arbitrary despot. We should not say that God *makes* law, nor on the other hand that God *is subject to* law, but rather that God *is* law and *the source* of law.

Bowne, Philos. of Theism, 161 —" God's law is organic — inwrought into the constitution of men and things. The chart however does not make the channel. . . . A law of nature is never the antecedent but the consequence of reality. What right has this consequence of reality to be personalized and made the ruler and source of reality ? Law is only the fixed mode in which reality works. Law therefore can explain nothing. Only God, from whom reality springs, can explain reality." In other words, law is never an agent but always a method — the method of God, or rather of Christ who is the only Revealer of God. Christ's life in the flesh is the clearest manifestation of him who is the principle of law in the physical and moral universe. Christ is the Reason of God in expression. It was he who gave the law on Mount Sinai at well as in the Sermon on the Mount. For fuller treatment of the subject, see Bowen, Metaph. and Ethics, 321-344; Talbot, Ethical Prolegomena, in Bap. Quar., July, 1877 : 257-274; Whewell, Elements of Morality, 2 : 35; and especially E. G. Robinson, Principles and Practice of Morality, 79-108.

Each of the two last-mentioned characteristics of God's law is important in its implications. We treat of these in their order.

First, the law of God as a transcript of the divine nature.—If this be the nature of the law, then certain common misconceptions of it are excluded. The law of God is

(*a*) Not arbitrary, or the product of arbitrary will. Since the will from which the law springs is a revelation of God's nature, there can be no rashness or unwisdom in the law itself.

E. G. Robinson, Christ. Theology, 193 — "No law of God seems ever to have been arbitrarily enacted, or simply with a view to certain ends to be accomplished; it always represented some reality of life which it was inexorably necessary that those who were to be regulated should carefully observe." The theory that law originates in arbitrary will results in an effeminate type of piety, just as the theory that legislation has for its sole end the greatest happiness results in all manner of compromises of justice. Jones, Robert Browning, 43 — "He who cheats his neighbor believes in tortuosity, and, as Carlyle says, has the supreme Quack for his god."

(b) Not temporary, or ordained simply to meet an exigency. The law is a manifestation, not of temporary moods or desires, but of the essential nature of God.

The great speech of Sophocles' Antigone gives us this conception of law: "The ordinances of the gods are unwritten, but sure. Not one of them is for to-day or for yesterday alone, but they live forever." Moses might break the tables of stone upon which the law was inscribed, and Jehoiakim might cut up the scroll and cast it into the fire (Ex. 32:19; Jer. 36:23), but the law remained eternal as before in the nature of God and in the constitution of man. Prof. Walter Rauschenbusch: "The moral laws are just as stable as the law of gravitation. Every fuzzy human chicken that is hatched into this world tries to fool with those laws. Some grow wiser in the process and some do not. We talk about breaking God's laws. But after those laws have been broken several billion times since Adam first tried to play with them, those laws are still intact and no seam or fracture is visible in them, — not even a scratch on the enamel. But the lawbreakers — that is another story. If you want to find their fragments, go to the ruins of Egypt, of Babylon, of Jerusalem; study statistics; read faces; keep your eyes open; visit Blackwell's Island; walk through the graveyard and read the invisible inscriptions left by the Angel of Judgment, for instance: 'Here lie the fragments of John Smith, who contradicted his Maker, played football with the ten commandments, and departed this life at the age of thirty-five. His mother and wife weep for him. Nobody else does. May he rest in peace!'"

(c) Not merely negative, or a law of mere prohibition, — since positive conformity to God is the inmost requisition of law.

The negative form of the commandments in the decalogue merely takes for granted the evil inclination in men's hearts and practically opposes its gratification. In the case of each commandment a whole province of the moral life is taken into the account, although the act expressly forbidden is the acme of evil in that one province. So the decalogue makes itself intelligible: it crosses man's path just where he most feels inclined to wander. But back of the negative and specific expression in each case lies the whole mass of moral requirement: the thin edge of the wedge has the positive demand of holiness behind it, without obedience to which even the prohibition cannot in spirit be obeyed. Thus "the law is spiritual" (Rom. 7:14), and requires likeness in character and life to the spiritual God; John 4:24 — "God is spirit, and they that worship him must worship in spirit and truth."

(d) Not partial, or addressed to one part only of man's being, — since likeness to God requires purity of substance in man's soul and body, as well as purity in all the thoughts and acts that proceed therefrom. As law proceeds from the nature of God, so it requires conformity to that nature in the nature of man.

Whatever God gave to man at the beginning he requires of man with interest; cf. Mat. 25:27 — "thou oughtest therefore to have put my money to the bankers, and at my coming I should have received back mine own with interest." Whatever comes short of perfect purity in soul or perfect health in body is non-conformity to God and contradicts his law, it being understood that only that perfection is demanded which answers to the creature's stage of growth and progress, so that of the child there is required only the perfection of the child, of the youth only the perfection of the youth, of the man only the perfection of the man. See Julius Müller, Doctrine of Sin, chapter 1.

(e) Not outwardly published, — since all positive enactment is only the imperfect expression of this underlying and unwritten law of being.

Much misunderstanding of God's law results from confounding it with published enactment. Paul takes the larger view that the law is independent of such expression. see Rom. 2:14,15 — "for when Gentiles that have not the law do by nature the things of the law, these, not having the law, are the law unto themselves ; in that they show the work of the law written in their hearts, their conscience bearing witness therewith, and their thoughts one with another accusing or else excusing them:" see Expositor's Greek Testament, *in loco:* "'written on their hearts,' when contrasted with the law written on the tables of stone, is equal to 'unwritten'; the Apostle refers to what the Greeks called ἄγραφος νόμος."

(*f*) Not inwardly conscious, or limited in its scope by men's consciousness of it. Like the laws of our physical being, the moral law exists whether we recognize it or not.

Overeating brings its penalty in dyspepsia, whether we are conscious of our fault or not. We cannot by ignorance or by vote repeal the laws of our physical system. Self-will does not secure independence, any more than the stars can by combination abolish gravitation. Man cannot get rid of God's dominion by denying its existence, nor by refusing submission to it. Psalm 2:1-4 — "Why do the nations rage . . . . against Jehovah . . . . saying, Let us break their bonds asunder . . . . He that sitteth in the heavens will laugh." Salter, First Steps in Philosophy, 94 — "The fact that one is not aware of obligation no more affects its reality than ignorance of what is at the centre of the earth affects the nature of what is really discoverable there. We discover obligation, and do not create it by thinking of it, any more than we create the sensible world by thinking of it."

(*g*) Not local, or confined to place, — since no moral creature can escape from God, from his own being, or from the natural necessity that unlikeness to God should involve misery and ruin.

"The Dutch auction" was the public offer of property at a price beyond its value, followed by the lowering of the price until some one accepted it as a purchaser. There is no such local exception to the full validity of God's demands. The moral law has even more necessary and universal sway than the law of gravitation in the physical universe. It is inwrought into the very constitution of man, and of every other moral being. The man who offended the Roman Emperor found the whole empire a prison.

(*h*) Not changeable, or capable of modification. Since law represents the unchangeable nature of God, it is not a sliding scale of requirements which adapts itself to the ability of the subjects. God himself cannot change it without ceasing to be God.

The law, then, has a deeper foundation than that God merely "said so." God's word and God's will are revelations of his inmost being; every transgression of the law is a stab at the heart of God. Simon, Reconciliation, 141, 142 — "God continues to demand loyalty even after man has proved disloyal. Sin changes man, and man's change involves a change in God. Man now regards God as a ruler and exactor, and God must regard man as a defaulter and a rebel." God's requirement is not lessened because man is unable to meet it. This inability is itself non-conformity to law, and is no excuse for sin ; see Dr. Bushnell's sermon on "Duty not measured by Ability." The man with the withered hand would not have been justified in refusing to stretch it forth at Jesus' command (Mat. 12:10-13).

The obligation to obey this law and to be conformed to God's perfect moral character is based upon man's original ability and the gifts which God bestowed upon him at the beginning. Created in the image of God, it is man's duty to render back to God that which God first gave, enlarged and improved by growth and culture (Luke 19:23 — "wherefore gavest thou not my money into the bank, and I at my coming should have required it with interest"). This obligation is not impaired by sin and the weakening of man's powers. To let down the standard would be to misrepresent God. Adolphe Monod would not save himself from shame and remorse by lowering the claims of the law : "Save first the holy law of my God," he says, " after that you shall save me! "

Even salvation is not through violation of law. The moral law is immutable, because it is a transcript of the nature of the immutable God. Shall nature conform to me, or I to nature? If I attempt to resist even physical laws, I am crushed. I can use nature only by obeying her laws. Lord Bacon: "Natura enim non nisi parendo vincitur." Sc in the moral realm. We cannot buy off nor escape the moral law of God. God will not, and God can not, change his law by one hair's breadth, even to save a universe of sinners. Omar Kháyyám, in his Rubáiyat, begs his god to "reconcile the law to my desires." Marie Corelli says well: "As if a gnat should seek to build a cathedral, and should ask to have the laws of architecture altered to suit its gnat-like capacity." See Martineau, Types, 2:120.

Secondly, the law of God as the ideal of human nature.—A law thus identical with the eternal and necessary relations of the creature to the Creator, and demanding of the creature nothing less than perfect holiness, as the condition of harmony with the infinite holiness of God, is adapted to man's finite nature, as needing law ; to man's free nature, as needing moral law ; and to man's progressive nature, as needing ideal law.

Man, as finite, needs law, just as railway cars need a track to guide them—to leap the track is to find, not freedom, but ruin. Railway President: "Our rules are written in blood." Goethe, Was Wir Bringen, 19 Auftritt: "In vain shall spirits that are all unbound To the pure heights of perfectness aspire; In limitation first the Master shines, And law alone can give us liberty."—Man, as a free being, needs moral law. He is not an automaton, a creature of necessity, governed only by physical influences. With conscience to command the right, and will to choose or reject it, his true dignity and calling are that he should freely realize the right.—Man, as a progressive being, needs nothing less than an ideal and infinite standard of attainment, a goal which he can never overpass, an end which shall ever attract and urge him forward. This he finds in the holiness of God.

The law is a *fence*, not only for ownership, but for care. God not only demands, but he protects. Law is the transcript of love as well as of holiness. We may reverse the well-known couplet and say: "I slept, and dreamed that life was Duty; I woke and found that life was Beauty." "Cui servire regnare est." Butcher, Aspects of Greek Genius, 56—"In Plato's Crito, the Laws are made to present themselves in person to Socrates in prison, not only as the guardians of his liberty, but as his lifelong friends, his well-wishers, his equals, with whom he had of his own free will entered into binding compact." It does not harm the scholar to have before him the ideal of perfect scholarship ; nor the teacher to have before him the ideal of a perfect school ; nor the legislator to have before him the ideal of perfect law. Gordon, The Christ of To-day, 134—"The moral goal must be a flying goal; the standard to which we are to grow must be ever rising ; the type to which we are to be conformed must have in it inexhaustible fulness."

John Caird, Fund. Ideas of Christianity, 2:119—"It is just the best, purest, noblest human souls, who are least satisfied with themselves and their own spiritual attainments ; and the reason is that the human is not a nature essentially different from the divine, but a nature which, just because it is in essential affinity with God, can be satisfied with nothing less than a divine perfection." J. M. Whiton, The Divine Satisfaction: "Law requires being, character, likeness to God. It is automatic, self-operating. Penalty is untransferable. It cannot admit of any other satisfaction than the reëstablishment of the normal relation which it requires. Punishment proclaims that the law has not been satisfied. There is no cancelling of the curse except through the growing up of the normal relation. Blessing and curse ensue upon what we are, not upon what we were. Reparation is within the spirit itself. The atonement is educational, not governmental." We reply that the atonement is both governmental and educational, and that reparation must first be made to the holiness of God before conscience, the mirror of God's holiness, can reflect that reparation and be at peace.

The law of God is therefore characterized by :

(a) All-comprehensiveness.—It is over us at all times ; it respects our past, our present, our future. It forbids every conceivable sin ; it requires every conceivable virtue ; omissions as well as commissions are condemned by it.

Ps. 119:96 — "I have seen an end of all perfection . . . . thy commandment is exceeding broad"; Rom. 3:23 — "all have sinned, and fall short of the glory of God"; James 4:17 — 'To him therefore that knoweth to do good, and

doeth it not, to him it is sin." Gravitation holds the mote as well as the world. God's law detects and denounces the least sin, so that without atonement it cannot be pardoned. The law of gravitation may be suspended or abrogated, for it has no necessary ground in God's being; but God's moral law cannot be suspended or abrogated, for that would contradict God's holiness. "About right" is not "all right." "The giant hexagonal pillars of basalt in the Scottish Staffa are identical in form with the microscopic crystals of the same mineral." So God is our pattern, and goodness is our likeness to him.

(*b*) Spirituality.— It demands not only right acts and words, but also right dispositions and states. Perfect obedience requires not only the intense and unremitting reign of love toward God and man, but conformity of the whole inward and outward nature of man to the holiness of God.

Mat. 5 : 22, 28 — the angry word is murder; the sinful look is adultery. Mark 12 : 30, 31 — "thou shalt love the Lord thy God with all thy heart, and with all thy soul, and with all thy mind, and with all thy strength . . . . Thou shalt love thy neighbor as thyself"; 2 Cor. 10 : 5 — "bringing every thought into captivity to the obedience of Christ"; Eph. 5 : 1 — "Be ye therefore imitators of God, as beloved children"; 1 Pet. 1 : 16 — "Ye shall be holy; for I am holy." As the brightest electric light, seen through a smoked glass against the sun, appears like a black spot, so the brightest unregenerate character is dark, when compared with the holiness of God. Matheson, Moments on the Mount, 235, remarks on Gal. 6 : 4 — "let each man prove his own work, and then shall he have his glorying in regard of himself alone, and not of his neighbor" — "I have a small candle and I compare it with my brother's taper and come away rejoicing. Why not compare it with the sun ? Then I shall lose my pride and uncharitableness." The distance to the sun from the top of an ant-hill and from the top of Mount Everest is nearly the same. The African princess praised for her beauty had no way to verify the compliments paid her but by looking in the glassy surface of the pool. But the trader came and sold her a mirror. Then she was so shocked at her own ugliness that she broke the mirror in pieces. So we look into the mirror of God's law, compare ourselves with the Christ who is reflected there, and hate the mirror which reveals us to ourselves (James 1 : 23, 24).

(*c*) Solidarity.— It exhibits in all its parts the nature of the one Lawgiver, and it expresses, in its least command, the one requirement of harmony with him.

Mat. 5 : 48 — " Ye therefore shall be perfect, as your heavenly Father is perfect"; Mark 12 : 29, 30 — "The Lord our God, the Lord is one : and thou shalt love the Lord thy God "; James 2 : 10 — "For whosoever shall keep the whole law, and yet stumble in one point, he is become guilty of all "; 4 : 12 — "One only is the lawgiver and judge." Even little rattlesnakes are snakes. One link broken in the chain, and the bucket falls into the well. The least sin separates us from God. The least sin renders us guilty of the whole law, because it shows us to lack the love which is required in all the commandments. Those who send us to the Sermon on the Mount for salvation send us to a tribunal that damns us. The Sermon on the Mount is but a republication of the law given on Sinai, but now in more spiritual and penetrating form. Thunders and lightnings proceed from the N. T., as from the O. T., mount. The Sermon on the Mount is only the introductory lecture of Jesus' theological course, as John 14-17 is the closing lecture. In it is announced the law, which prepares the way for the gospel. Those who would degrade doctrine by exalting precept will find that they have left men without the motive or the power to keep the precept. Æschylus, Agamemnon : "For there's no bulwark in man's wealth to him Who, through a surfeit, kicks—into the dim And disappearing— Right's great altar."

Only to the first man, then, was the law proposed as a method of salvation. With the first sin, all hope of obtaining the divine favor by perfect obedience is lost. To sinners the law remains as a means of discovering and developing sin in its true nature, and of compelling a recourse to the mercy provided in Jesus Christ.

2 Chron. 34 : 19 — "And it came to pass, when the king had heard the words of the law, that he rent his clothes "; Job 42 : 5, 6 — "I had heard of thee by the hearing of the ear; But now mine eye seeth thee; Wherefore I abhor myself, And repent in dust and ashes." The revelation of God in Is. 6 : 3, 5 — "Holy, holy, holy, is Jehovah of hosts " — causes the prophet to cry like the leper : "Woe is me ! for I am undone; because I am a man of unclean lips." Rom. 3 : 20 — "by the works of the law shall no flesh be justified in his sight; for through the law cometh the

knowledge of sin " ; 5 : 20 — " the law came in besides, that the trespass might abound " ; 7 : 7, 8 — " I had not known sin, except through the law : for I had not known coveting, except the law had said, Thou shalt not covet : but sin, finding occasion, wrought in me through the commandment all manner of coveting : for apart from the law sin is dead " ; Gal. 3 : 24 — " So that the law is become our tutor," or attendant-slave, " to bring us unto Christ, that we might be justified by faith " = the law trains our wayward boyhood and leads it to Christ the Master, as in old times the slave accompanied children to school. Stevens, Pauline Theology, 177, 178 — " The law increases sin by increasing the knowledge of sin and by increasing the activity of sin. The law does not add to the inherent energy of the sinful principle which pervades human nature, but it does cause this principle to reveal itself more energetically in sinful act." The law inspires fear, but it leads to love. The Rabbins said that, if Israel repented but for one day, the Messiah would appear.

No man ever yet drew a straight line or a perfect curve ; yet he would be a poor architect who contented himself with anything less. Since men never come up to their ideals, he who aims to live only an *average* moral life will inevitably fall *below* the average. The law, then, leads to Christ. He who is the *ideal* is also the *way* to attain the ideal. He who is himself the Word and the Law embodied, is also the Spirit of life that makes obedience possible to us (John 14 : 6 — " I am the way, and the truth, and the life "; Rom. 8 : 2 —" For the law of the Spirit of life in Christ Jesus made me free from the law of sin and of death "). Mrs. Browning, Aurora Leigh: "The Christ himself had been no Lawgiver, Unless he had given the Life too with the Law." Christ *for* us upon the Cross, and Christ *in* us by his Spirit, is the only deliverance from the curse of the law ; Gal. 3 : 13 — " Christ redeemed us from the curse of the law, having become a curse for us." We must see the claims of the law satisfied and the law itself written on our hearts. We are "reconciled to God through the death of his Son," but we are also "saved by his life " (Rom. 5 : 10).

Robert Browning, in The Ring and the Book, represents Caponsacchi as comparing himself at his best with the new ideal of " perfect as Father in heaven is perfect " suggested by Pompilia's purity, and as breaking out into the cry : " O great, just, good God! Miserable me ! " In the Interpreter's House of Pilgrim's Progress, Law only stirred up the dust in the foul room, — the Gospel had to sprinkle water on the floor before it could be cleansed. E. G. Robinson: "It is necessary to smoke a man out, before you can bring a higher motive to bear upon him." Barnabas said that Christ was the answer to the riddle of the law. Rom. 10 : 4 —"Christ is the end of the law unto righteousness to every one that believeth." The railroad track opposite Detroit on the St. Clair River runs to the edge of the dock and seems intended to plunge the train into the abyss. But when the ferry boat comes up, rails are seen upon its deck, and the boat is the end of the track, to carry passengers over to Detroit. So the law, which by itself would bring only destruction, finds its end in Christ who ensures our passage to the celestial city.

Law, then, with its picture of spotless innocence, simply reminds man of the heights from which he has fallen. " It is a mirror which reveals derangement, but does not create or remove it." With its demand of absolute perfection, up to the measure of man's original endowments and possibilities, it drives us, in despair of ourselves, to Christ as our only righteousness and our only Savior (Rom. 8 : 3, 4 — "For what the law could not do, in that it was weak through the flesh, God, sending his own Son in the likeness of sinful flesh and for sin, condemned sin in the flesh: that the ordinance of the law might be fulfilled in us, who walk not after the flesh, but after the Spirit " ; Phil. 3 : 8, 9 — " that I may gain Christ, and be found in him, not having a righteousness of mine own, even that which is of the law, but that which is through faith in Christ, the righteousness which is from God by faith "). Thus law must prepare the way for grace, and John the Baptist must precede Christ.

When Sarah Bernhardt was solicited to add an eleventh commandment, she declined upon the ground there were already ten too many. It was an expression of pagan contempt of law. In heathendom, sin and insensibility to sin increased together. In Judaism and Christianity, on the contrary, there has been a growing sense of sin's guilt and condemnableness. McLaren, in S. S. Times, Sept. 23, 1893 : 600 —"Among the Jews there was a far profounder sense of sin than in any other ancient nation. The law written on men's hearts evoked a lower consciousness of sin, and there are prayers on the Assyrian and Babylonian tablets which may almost stand beside the 51st Psalm. But, on the whole, the deep sense of sin was the product of the revealed law." See Fairbairn, Revelation of Law and Scripture ; Baird, Elohim Revealed, 187–242; Hovey, God with Us, 187–210 ; Julius Müller, Doctrine of Sin, 1 : 45–50 ; Murphy, Scientific Bases of Faith, 53–71 ; Martineau, Types, 2 : 120–125.

2. *Positive Enactment,* or the expression of the will of God in published ordinances. This is also two-fold :

A. General moral precepts.— These are written summaries of the elemental law (Mat. 5 : 48 ; 22 : 37–40), or authorized applications of it to special human conditions (Ex. 20 : 1–17 ; Mat. chap. 5- 8).

Mat. 5 : 48 —" Ye therefore shall be perfect, as your heavenly Father is perfect "; 22 : 37–40 —"Thou shalt love the Lord thy God . . . . Thou shalt love thy neighbor as thyself. On these two commandments the whole law hangeth and the prophets "; Ex. 20 : 1–17 — the Ten Commandments ; Mat., chap. 5–8 — the Sermon on the Mount. *Cf.* Augustine, on Ps. 57 : 1.

Solly, On the Will, 162, gives two illustrations of the fact that positive precepts are merely applications of elemental law or the law of nature : " ' *Thou shalt not steal,*' is a moral law which may be stated thus : *thou shalt not take that for thy own property, which is the property of another.* The contradictory of this proposition would be : *thou mayest take that for thy own property which is the property of another.* But this is a contradiction in terms ; for it is the very conception of property, that the owner stands in a peculiar relation to its subject matter ; and what is every man's property is no man's property, as it is *proper* to no man. Hence the contradictory of the commandment contains a simple contradiction directly it is made a rule universal ; and the command ment itself is established as one of the principles for the harmony of individual wills.

" ' *Thou shalt not tell a lie,*' as a rule of morality, may be expressed generally : *thou shalt not by thy outward act make another to believe thy thought to be other than it is.* The contradictory made universal is : *every man may by his outward act make another to believe his thought to be other than it is.* Now this maxim also contains a contradiction, and is self-destructive. It conveys a permission to do that which is rendered impossible by the permission itself. Absolute and universal indifference to truth, or the entire mutual independence of the thought and symbol, makes the symbol cease to be a symbol, and the conveyance of thought by its means, an impossibility."

Kant, Metaphysic of Ethics, 48, 90 — " Fundamental law of reason : So act, that thy maxims of will might become laws in a system of universal moral legislation." This is Kant's categorical imperative. He expresses it in yet another form : "Act from maxims fit to be regarded as universal laws of nature." For expositions of the Decalogue which bring out its spiritual meaning, see Kurtz, Religionslehre, 9–72 ; Dick, Theology, 2:513– 554 ; Dwight, Theology, 3 : 163–560 ; Hodge, Syst. Theol., 3 : 259–465.

B. Ceremonial or special injunctions.— These are illustrations of the elemental law, or approximate revelations of it, suited to lower degrees of capacity and to earlier stages of spiritual training (Ez. 20 : 25 ; Mat. 19 : 8 ; Mark 10 : 5). Though temporary, only God can say when they cease to be binding upon us in their outward form.

All positive enactments, therefore, whether they be moral or ceremonial, are republications of elemental law. Their forms may change, but the substance is eternal. Certain modes of expression, like the Mosaic system, may be abolished, but the essential demands are unchanging (Mat. 5 : 17, 18 ; *cf.* Eph. 2 : 15). From the imperfection of human language, no positive enactments are able to express in themselves the whole content and meaning of the elemental law. " It is not the purpose of revelation to disclose the whole of our duties." Scripture is not a complete code of rules for practical action, but an enunciation of principles, with occasional precepts by way of illustration. Hence we must supplement the positive enactment by the law of being — the moral ideal found in the nature of God,

Ez. 20 : 25 — " Moreover also I gave them statutes that were not good, and ordinances wherein they should not live ". Mat. 19 : 8 — " Moses for your hardness of heart suffered you to put away your wives "; Mark 10 : 5 — " For your hard ness of heart he wrote you this commandment "; Mat. 5 : 17, 18 —" Think not that I came to destroy the law or the proph ets : I came not to destroy, but to fulfil. For verily I say unto you, Till heaven and earth pass away, one jot or one tittle shall in no wise pass away from the law, till all things be accomplished "; *cf.* Eph. 2 : 15 — "having abolished in his flesh the enmity, even the law of commandments contained in ordinances "; Heb. 8 : 7 — " if that first covenant had been faultless, then would no place have been sought for a second." Fisher, Nature and Method of Revela- lation, 90 — " After the coming of the new covenant, the keeping up of the old was as needless a burden as winter garments in the mild air of summer, or as the attempt of an adult to wear the clothes of a child."

Wendt, Teaching of Jesus, 2 : 5-35 — " Jesus repudiates for himself and for his disciples absolute subjection to O. T. Sabbath law (Mark 2 : 27 sq.); to O. T. law as to external defilements (Mark 7 : 15); to O. T. divorce law (Mark 10 : 2 sq.). He would 'fulfil' law and prophets by complete practical performance of the revealed will of God. He would bring out their inner meaning, not by literal and slavish obedience to every minute requirement of the Mosaic law, but by revealing in himself the perfect life and work toward which they tended. He would perfect the O. T. conceptions of God — not keep them intact in their literal form, but in their essential spirit. Not by quantitative extension, but by qualitative renewal, he would fulfil the law and the prophets. He would bring the imperfect expression in the O. T. to perfection, not by servile letter-worship or allegorizing, but through grasp of the divine idea."

Scripture is not a series of minute injunctions and prohibitions such as the Pharisees and the Jesuits laid down. The Koran showed its immeasurable inferiority to the Bible by establishing the letter instead of the spirit, by giving permanent, definite, and specific rules of conduct, instead of leaving room for the growth of the free spirit and for the education of conscience. This is not true either of O. T. or of N. T. law. In Miss Fowler's novel The Farringdons, Mrs. Herbert wishes " that the Bible had been written on the principle of that dreadful little book called 'Don't,' which gives a list of the solecisms you should avoid; she would have understood it so much better than the present system." Our Savior's words about giving to him that asketh, and turning the cheek to the smiter (Mat. 5 : 39-42) must be interpreted by the principle of love that lies at the foundation of the law. Giving to every tramp and yielding to every marauder is not pleasing our neighbor "for that which is good unto edifying " (Rom. 15 : 2). Only by confounding the divine law with Scripture prohibition could one write as in N. Amer. Rev., Feb. 1890 : 275 — " Sin is the transgression of a divine law; but there is no divine law against suicide; therefore suicide is not sin."

The written law was imperfect because God could, at the time, give no higher to an unenlightened people. " But to say that the *scope* and *design* were imperfectly moral, is contradicted by the whole course of the history. We must ask what is the moral standard in which this course of education issues." And this we find in the life and precepts of Christ. Even the law of repentance and faith does not take the place of the old law of being, but applies the latter to the special conditions of sin. Under the Levitical law, the prohibition of the touching of the dry bone (Num. 19 : 16), equally with the purifications and sacrifices, the separations and penalties of the Mosaic code, expressed God's holiness and his repelling from him all that savored of sin or death. The laws with regard to leprosy were symbolic, as well as sanitary. So church polity and the ordinances are not arbitrary requirements, but they publish to dull sense-environed consciences, better than abstract propositions could have done, the fundamental truths of the Christian scheme. Hence they are not to be abrogated "till he come " (1 Cor. 11 : 26).

The Puritans, however, in reënacting the Mosaic code, made the mistake of confounding the eternal law of God with a partial, temporary, and obsolete expression of it. So we are not to rest in external precepts respecting woman's hair and dress and speech, but to find the underlying principle of modesty and subordination which alone is of universal and eternal validity. Robert Browning, The Ring and the Book, 1 : 255 — " God breathes, not speaks, his verdicts, felt not heard — Passed on successively to each court I call Man's conscience, custom, manners, all that make More and more effort to promulgate, mark God's verdict in determinable words, Till last come human jurists — solidify Fluid results, — what's fixable lies forged, Statute, — the residue escapes in fume, Yet hangs aloft a cloud, as palpable To the finer sense as word the legist welds. Justinian's Pandects only make precise What simply sparkled in men's eyes before, Twitched in their brow or quivered on their lip, Waited the speech they called, but would not come." See Mozley, Ruling Ideas in Early Ages, 104; Tulloch, Doctrine of Sin, 141-144; Finney, Syst. Theol., 1-40, 135-319; Mansel, Metaphysics, 378, 379; H. B. Smith, System of Theology, 191-195.

Paul's injunction to women to keep silence in the churches (1 Cor. 14 : 35; 1 Tim. 2 : 11, 12) is to be interpreted by the larger law of gospel equality and privilege (Col. 3 : 11). Modesty and subordination once required a seclusion of the female sex which is no longer obligatory. Christianity has emancipated woman and has restored her to the dignity which belonged to her at the beginning. " In the old dispensation Miriam and Deborah and Huldah were recognized as leaders of God's people, and Anna was a notable prophetess in the temple courts at the time of the coming of Christ. Elizabeth and Mary spoke songs of praise for all generations. A prophecy of Joel 2:28 was that the daughters of the Lord's people should prophesy, under the guidance of the Spirit, in the new dispensation. Philip the evangelist had 'four virgin daughters, who prophesied' (Acts 21:9), and Paul cautioned Christian women to have their heads covered when they prayed or prophesied in public (1 Cor. 11:5), but had no words against the work of such women. He brought Priscilla with him to Ephesus, where she aided in training Apollos into better preaching power (Acts 18:26). He welcomed and was grateful for the work of those women who labored with him in the gospel at Philippi (Phil. 4:3). And it is certainly an inference from the spirit and teachings of Paul that we should rejoice in the efficient service and sound words of Christian women to-day in the Sunday School and in the missionary field." The command "And he that heareth let him say, Come" (Rev. 22:17) is addressed to women also. See Ellen Batelle Dietrick, Women in the Early Christian Ministry; per contra, see G. F. Wilkin, Prophesying of Women, 183-193.

III. RELATION OF THE LAW TO THE GRACE OF GOD.

In human government, while law is an expression of the will of the governing power, and so of the nature lying behind the will, it is by no means an exhaustive expression of that will and nature, since it consists only of general ordinances, and leaves room for particular acts of command through the executive, as well as for "the institution of equity, the faculty of discretionary punishment, and the prerogative of pardon."

Amos, Science of Law, 29-46, shows how "the institution of equity, the faculty of discretionary punishment, and the prerogative of pardon" all involve expressions of will above and beyond what is contained in mere statute. Century Dictionary, on Equity : " English law had once to do only with property in goods, houses and lands. A man who had none of these might have an interest in a salary, a patent, a contract, a copyright, a security, but a creditor could not at common law levy upon these. When the creditor applied to the crown for redress, a chancellor or keeper of the king's conscience was appointed, who determined what and how the debtor should pay. Often the debtor was required to put his intangible property into the hands of a receiver and could regain possession of it only when the claim against it was satisfied. These chancellors' courts were called courts of equity, and redressed wrongs which the common law did not provide for. In later times law and equity are administered for the most part by the same courts. The same court sits at one time as a court of law, and at another time as a court of equity." " Summa lex, summa injuria," is sometimes true.

Applying now to the divine law this illustration drawn from human law, we remark :

(a) The law of God is a *general* expression of God's will, applicable to all moral beings. It therefore does not exclude the possibility of special injunctions to individuals, and special acts of wisdom and power in creation and providence. The very specialty of these latter expressions of will prevents us from classing them under the category of law.

Lord Bacon, Confession of Faith : " The soul of man was not produced by heaven or earth, but was breathed immediately from God ; so the ways and dealings of God with spirits are not included in nature, that is, in the laws of heaven and earth, but are reserved to the law of his secret will and grace."

(b) The law of God, accordingly, is a *partial*, not an exhaustive, expression of God's nature. It constitutes, indeed, a manifestation of that attribute of holiness which is fundamental in God, and which man must possess in order to be in harmony with God. But it does not fully express God's nature in its aspects of personality, sovereignty, helpfulness, mercy.

The chief error of all pantheistic theology is the assumption that law is an exhaustive expression of God : Strauss, Glaubenslehre, 1:31—"If nature, as the self-realization of the divine essence. is equal to this divine essence, then it is infinite, and there can be nothing above and beyond it." This is a denial of the transcendence of God (see notes on Pantheism, pages 100-105). Mere law is illustrated by the Buddhist proverb: "As the cartwheel follows the tread of the ox, so punishment follows sin." Denovan: "Apart from Christ, even if we have never yet broken the law, it s only by steady and perfect obedience for the entire future that we can remain justified. If we have sinned, we can be justified [without Christ] only by suffering and exhausting the whole penalty of the law."

(c) Mere law, therefore, leaves God's nature in these aspects of personality, sovereignty, helpfulness, mercy, to be expressed toward sinners in another way, namely, through the atoning, regenerating, pardoning, sanctifying work of the gospel of Christ. As creation does not exclude miracles, so law does not exclude grace (Rom. 8 : 3 — "what the law could not do . . . . . God" did).

Murpay, Scientific Bases, 303-327, esp. 315—"To impersonal law, it is indifferent whether its subjects obey or not. But God desires, not the punishment, but the destruction, of sin." Campbell, Atonement, Introd., 28 — "There are two regions of the divine self-manifestation, one the reign of law, the other the kingdom of God." C. H. M.: "Law is the transcript of the mind of God as to what man ought to be. But God is not merely law, but love. There is more in his heart than could be wrapped up in the 'ten words.' Not the law, but only Christ, is the perfect image of God" (John 1 : 17 — "For the law was given through Moses; grace and truth came through Jesus Christ"). So there is more in man's heart toward God than exact fulfilment of requirement. The mother who sacrifices herself for her sick child does it, not because she must, but because she loves. To say that we are saved by grace, is to say ᵗhat we are saved both without merit on our own part, and without necessity on the part of God. Grace is made known in proclamation, offer, command ; but in all these it is gospel, or glad-tidings.

(d) Grace is to be regarded, however, not as abrogating law, but as republishing and enforcing it (Rom. 3 : 31—"we establish the law "). By removing obstacles to pardon in the mind of God, and by enabling man to obey, grace secures the perfect fulfilment of law (Rom. 8 : 4 — "that the ordinance of the law might be fulfilled in us "). Even grace has its law (Rom. 8 : 2 — "the law of the Spirit of life ") ; another higher law of grace, the operation of individualizing mercy, overbears the "law of sin and of death," — this last, as in the case of the miracle, not being suspended, annulled, or violated, but being merged in, while it is transcended by, the exertion of personal divine will.

Hooker, Eccl. Polity, 1 : 155, 185, 194 — " Man, having utterly disabled his nature unto those [natural] means, hath had other revealed by God, and hath received from heaven a law to teach him how that which is desired naturally, must now be supernaturally attained. Finally, we see that, because those latter exclude not the former as unnecessary. therefore the law of grace teaches and includes natural duties also, such as are hard to ascertain by the law of nature." The truth is midway between the Pelagian view, that there is no obstacle to the forgiveness of sins, and the modern rationalistic view, that since law fully expresses God, there can be no forgiveness of sins at all. Greg, Creed of Christendom, 2 : 217-228 — " God is the only being who cannot forgive sins. ... Punishment is not the execution of a sentence, but the occurrence of an effect." Robertson, Lect. on Genesis, 100 — " Deeds are irrevocable,—their consequences are knit up with them irrevocably." So Baden Powell, Law and Gospel, in Noyes' Theological Essays, 27. All this is true if God be regarded as merely the source of law. But there is such a thing as grace, and grace is more than law. There is no forgiveness in nature, but grace is above and beyond nature.

Bradford, Heredity, 233, quotes from Huxley the terrible utterance : " Nature always checkmates, without haste and without remorse, never overlooking a mistake, or naking the slightest allowance for ignorance." Bradford then remarks: "This is Calvinism with God left out. Christianity does not deny or minimize the law of retri bution, but it discloses a Person who is able to deliver in spite of it. There is grace, but grace brings salvation to those who accept the terms of salvation — terms strictly in accord with the laws revealed by science." God revealed himself, we add, not only in law but in life; see Deut. 1 : 6, 7 — "Ye have dwelt long enough in this mountain" — the mountain of the law; "turn you and take your journey" — *i. e.*, see how God's law is to be applied to life.

(*e*) Thus the revelation of grace, while it takes up and includes in itself the revelation of law, adds something different in kind, namely, the manifestation of the personal love of the Lawgiver. Without grace, law has only a demanding aspect. Only in connection with grace does it become "the perfect law, the law of liberty" (James 1 : 25). In fine, grace is that larger and completer manifestation of the divine nature, of which law constitutes the necessary but preparatory stage.

Law reveals God's love and mercy, but only in their mandatory aspect; it requires in men conformity to the love and mercy of God; and as love and mercy in God are conditioned by holiness, so law requires that love and mercy should be conditioned by holiness in men. Law is therefore chiefly a revelation of holiness: it is in grace that we find the chief revelation of love; though even love does not save by ignoring holiness, but rather by vicariously satisfying its demands. Robert Browning, Saul: "I spoke as I saw. I report as man may of God's work — All 's Love, yet all 's Law."

Dorner, Person of Christ, 1 : 64, 78 — "The law was a word (λόγος), but it was not a λόγος τέλειος, a plastic word, like the words of God that brought forth the world, for it was only imperative, and there was no reality nor willing corresponding to the command (*dem Sollen fehlte das Seyn, das Wollen*). The Christian λόγος is λόγος ἀληθείας — νόμος τέλειος τῆς ἐλευθερίας — an operative and effective word, as that of creation." Chaucer, The Persones Tale: "For sothly the lawe of God is the love of God." S. S. Times, Sept. 14, 1901 : 595 — "Until a man ceases to be an outsider to the kingdom and knows the liberty of the sons of God, he is apt to think of God as the great Exacter, the great Forbidder, who reaps where he has not sown and gathers where he has not strewn." Burton, in Bap. Rev., July, 1879 : 261–273, art. : Law and Divine Intervention; Farrar, Science and Theology, 184; Salmon, Reign of Law; Philippi, Glaubenslehre, 1 : 31.

SECTION II.—NATURE OF SIN.

I. DEFINITION OF SIN.

Sin is lack of conformity to the moral law of God, either in act, disposition, or state.

In explanation, we remark that (*a*) This definition regards sin as predicable only of rational and voluntary agents. (*b*) It assumes, however, that man has a rational nature below consciousness, and a voluntary nature apart from actual volition. (*c*) It holds that the divine law requires moral likeness to God in the affections and tendencies of the nature, as well as in its outward activities. (*d*) It therefore considers lack of conformity to the divine holiness in disposition or state as a violation of law, equally with the outward act of transgression.

In our discussion of the Will (pages 504–513), we noticed that there are permanent states of the will, as well as of the intellect and of the sensibilities. It is evident, moreover, that these permanent states, unlike man's deliberate acts, are always very imperfectly conscious, and in many cases are not conscious at all. Yet it is in these very states that man is most unlike God, and so, as law only reflects God (see pages 537–544), most lacking in conformity to God's law.

One main difference between Old School and New School views of sin is that the latter constantly tends to limit sin to mere act, while the former finds sin in the states of the soul. We propose what we think to be a valid and proper compromise between the two.

We make sin coextensive, not with act, but with activity. The Old School and the New School are not so far apart, when we remember that the New School "choice" is *elective preference*, exercised so soon as the child is born (Park) and reasserting itself in all the subordinate choices of life; while the Old School "state" is not a dead, passive, mechanical thing, but is a *state of active movement*, or of tendency to move, toward evil. As God's holiness is not passive purity but purity willing (pages 268-275), so the opposite to this, sin, is not passive impurity but is impurity willing.

The soul may not always be conscious, but it may always be active. At his creation man "became a living soul" (Gen. 2:7), and it may be doubted whether the human spirit ever ceases its activity, any more than the divine Spirit in whose image it is made. There is some reason to believe that even in the deepest sleep the body rests rather than the mind. And when we consider how large a portion of our activity is automatic and continuous, we see the impossibility of limiting the term 'sin' to the sphere of momentary act, whether conscious or unconscious.

E. G. Robinson: "Sin is not mere act—something foreign to the being. It is a quality of being. There is no such thing as a sin apart from a sinner, or an act apart from an actor. God punishes sinners, not sins. Sin is a mode of being; as an entity by itself it never existed. God punishes sin as a state, not as an act. Man is not responsible for the consequences of his crimes, nor for the acts themselves, except as they are symptomatic of his personal states." Dorner, Hist. Doct. Person Christ, 5:162—"The knowledge of sin has justly been termed the β and ψ of philosophy."

Our treatment of Holiness, as belonging to the nature of God (pages 268-275); of Will, as not only the faculty of volitions, but also a permanent state of the soul (pages 504-513); and of Law as requiring the conformity of man's nature to God's holiness (pages 537-544); has prepared us for the definition of sin as a state. The chief psychological defect of New School theology, next to its making holiness to be a mere form of love, is its ignoring of the unconscious and subconscious elements in human character. To help our understanding of sin as an underlying and permanent state of the soul, we subjoin references to recent writers of note upon psychology and its relations to theology.

We may preface our quotations by remarking that mind is always greater than its conscious operations. The man is more than his acts. Only the smallest part of the self is manifested in the thoughts, feelings, and volitions. In counting, to put myself to sleep, I find, when my attention has been diverted by other thoughts, that the counting has gone on all the same. Ladd, Philosophy of Mind, 176, speaks of the "dramatic sundering of the ego." There are dream-conversations. Dr. Johnson was once greatly vexed at being worsted by his opponent in an argument in a dream. M. Maury in a dream corrected the bad English of his real self by the good English of his other unreal self. Spurgeon preached a sermon in his sleep after vainly trying to excogitate one when awake, and his wife gave him the substance of it after he woke. Hegel said that "Life is divided into two realms—a night-life of genius, and a day-life of consciousness."

Du Prel, Philosophy of Mysticism, propounds the thesis: "The ego is not wholly embraced in self-consciousness," and claims that there is much of psychical activity within us of which our common waking conception of ourselves takes no account. Thus when 'dream dramatizes'—when we engage in a dream-conversation in which our interlocutor's answer comes to us with a shock of surprise—if our own mind is assumed to have furnished that answer, it has done so by a process of unconscious activity. Dwinell, in Bib. Sac., July, 1890:369-389—"The soul is only imperfectly in possession of its organs, and is able to report only a small part of its activities in consciousness." Thoughts come to us like foundlings laid at our door. We slip in a question to the librarian, Memory, and after leaving it there awhile the answer appears on the bulletin board. Delbœuf, Le Sommeil et les Rêves, 91—"The dreamer is a momentary and involuntary dupe of his own imagination, as the poet is the momentary and voluntary dupe, and the insane man is the permanent and involuntary dupe." If we are the organs not only of our own past thinking, but, as Herbert Spencer suggests, also the organs of the past thinking of the race, his doctrine may give additional, though unintended, confirmation to a Scriptural view of sin.

William James, Will to Believe, 316, quotes from F. W. H. Myers, in Jour. Psych. Research, who likens our ordinary consciousness to the visible part of the solar spectrum ; the total consciousness is like that spectrum prolonged by the inclusion of the ultra-red and the ultra-violet rays = 1 to 12 and 96. "Each of us," he says, "is an abiding psychical entity far more extensive than he knows — an individuality which can never express itself completely through any corporeal manifestation. The self manifests itself through the organism ; but there is always some part of the self unmanifested, and always, as it seems, some power of organic expression in abeyance or reserve." William James himself, in Scribner's Monthly, March, 1890 : 361-373, sketches the hypnotic investigations of Janet and Binet. There is a secondary, subconscious self. Hysteria is the lack of synthetising power, and consequent disintegration of the field of consciousness into mutually exclusive parts. According to Janet, the secondary and the primary consciousnesses, added together, can never exceed the normally total consciousness of the individual. But Prof. James says : "There are trances which obey another type. I know a non-hysterical woman, who in her trances knows facts which altogether transcend her possible normal consciousness, facts about the lives of people whom she never saw or heard of before."

Our affections are deeper and stronger than we know. We learn how deep and strong they are, when their current is resisted by affliction or dammed up by death. We know how powerful evil passions are, only when we try to subdue them. Our dreams show us our naked selves. On the morality of dreams, the London Spectator remarks : "Our conscience and power of self-control act as a sort of watchdog over our worse selves during the day, but when the watchdog is off duty, the primitive or natural man is at liberty to act as he pleases ; our 'soul' has left us at the mercy of our own evil nature, and in our dreams we become what, except for the grace of God, we would always be."

Both in conscience and in will there is a self-diremption. Kant's categorical imperative is only one self laying down the law to the other self. The whole Kantian system of ethics is based on this doctrine of double consciousness. Ladd, in his Philosophy of Mind, 169 sq., speaks of "psychical automatism." Yet this automatism is possible only to self-conscious and cognitively remembering minds. It is always the "I" that puts itself into "that other." We could not conceive of the other self except under the figure of the "I." All our mental operations are ours, and we are responsible for them, because the subconscious and even the unconscious self is the product of past self-conscious thoughts and volitions. The present settled state of our wills is the result of former decisions. The will is a storage battery, charged by past acts, full of latent power, ready to manifest its energy so soon as the force which confines it is withdrawn. On unconscious mental action, see Carpenter, Mental Physiology, 139, 515-543, and criticism of Carpenter, in Ireland, Blot on the Brain, 226-238 ; Bramwell, Hypnotism, its History, Practice and Theory, 358-398 ; Porter, Human Intellect, 333, 334 ; versus Sir Wm. Hamilton, who adopts the maxim : "Non sentimus, nisi sentiamus nos sentire" (Philosophy, ed. Wight, 171). Observe also that sin may infect the body, as well as the soul, and may bring it into a state of non-conformity to God's law (see H. B. Smith, Syst. Theol., 267).

In adducing our Scriptural and rational proof of the definition of sin as a state, we desire to obviate the objection that this view leaves the soul wholly given over to the power of evil. While we maintain that this is true of man apart from God, we also insist that side by side with the evil bent of the human will there is always an immanent divine power which greatly counteracts the force of evil, and if not resisted leads the individual soul — even when resisted leads the race at large — toward truth and salvation. This immanent divine power is none other than Christ, the eternal Word, the Light which lighteth every man ; see John 1 : 4, 9.

John 1 : 4, 9 — "In him was life, and the life was the light of men. . . . There was the true light, even the light which lighteth every man." See a further statement in A. H. Strong, Cleveland Sermon, May, 1904, with regard to the old and the new view as to sin : — "Our fathers believed in total depravity, and we agree with them that man naturally is devoid of love to God and that every faculty is weakened, disordered, and corrupted by the selfish bent of his will. They held to original sin. The selfish bent of man's will can be traced back to the apostacy of our first parents ; and, on account of that departure of the race from God, all men are by nature children of wrath. And all this is true, if it is regarded as a statement of the facts, apart from their relation to Christ. But our fathers did not see, as we do, that man's relation to Christ antedated the Fall and constituted an underlying and modifying condition of man's life. Humanity was naturally in Christ, in whom all things were created and in whom they all consist. Even man's sin did not prevent Christ from still working in him to counteract the evil and to suggest the good. There was an internal, as well as an external, preparation for man's redemption. In this sense, of a divine principle in man striving against the selfish and godless will, there was a total redemption, over against man's total depravity; and an original grace, that was even more powerful than original sin.

"We have become conscious that total depravity alone is not a sufficient or proper expression of the truth; and the phrase has been outgrown. It has been felt that the old view of sin did not take account of the generous and noble aspirations, the unselfish efforts, the strivings after God, of even unregenerate men. For this reason there has been less preaching about sin, and less conviction as to its guilt and condemnation. The good impulses of men outside the Christian pale have been often credited to human nature, when they should have been credited to the indwelling Spirit of Christ. I make no doubt that one of our radical weaknesses at this present time is our more superficial view of sin. Without some sense of sin's guilt and condemnation, we cannot feel our need of redemption. John the Baptist must go before Christ; the law must prepare the way for the gospel.

" My belief is that the new apprehension of Christ's relation to the race will enable us to declare, as never before, the lost condition of the sinner; while at the same time we show him that Christ is with him and in him to save. This presence in every man of a power not his own that works for righteousness is a very different doctrine from that ' divinity of man ' which is so often preached. The divinity is not the divinity of man, but the divinity of Christ. And the power that works for righteousness is not the power of man, but the power of Christ. It is a power whose warning, inviting, persuading influence renders only more marked and dreadful the evil will which hampers and resists it. Depravity is all the worse, when we recognize in it the constant antagonist of an ever-present, all-holy, and all-loving Redeemer."

1.   *Proof.*

As it is readily admitted that the outward act of transgression is properly denominated sin, we here attempt to show only that lack of conformity to the law of God in disposition or state is also and equally to be so denominated.

A.   From Scripture.

(*a*) The words ordinarily translated ' sin,' or used as synonyms for it, are as applicable to dispositions and states as to acts (חָטָאָה and ἁμαρτία = a missing, failure, coming short [*sc.* of God's will]).

See Num. 15 : 28 — " sinneth unwittingly " ; Ps. 51 : 2 — " cleanse me from my sin " ; 5 — " Behold, I was brought forth in iniquity ; And in sin did my mother conceive me "; Rom. 7 : 17 — " sin which dwelleth in me "; compare Judges 20 : 16, where the literal meaning of the word appears : " sling stones at a hair-breadth, and not miss " (חָטָא). In a similar manner, פֶּשַׁע [LXX ἀσέβεια] = separation from, rebellion against [*sc.* God]; see Lev. 16 : 16, 21 ; *cf.* Delitzsch on Ps. 32 : 1. עָוֹן [LXX ἀδικία] = bending, perversion [*sc.* of what is right], iniquity ; see Lev. 5 : 17; *cf.* John 7 : 18. See also the Hebrew רַע, רֶשַׁע, [= ruin, confusion], and the Greek ἀποστασία, ἐπιθυμία, ἔχθρα, κακία, πονηρία, σάρξ. None of these designations of sin limits it to mere act,— most of them more naturally suggest disposition or state. 'Αμαρτία implies that man in sin does not reach what he seeks therein ; sin is a state of delusion and deception (Julius Müller). On the words mentioned, see Girdlestone, O. T. Synonyms ; Cremer, Lexicon N. T. Greek ; Present Day Tracts, 5 : no. 28, pp. 43-47; Trench, N. T. Synonyms, part 2 : 61, 73.

(*b*) The New Testament descriptions of sin bring more distinctly to view the states and dispositions than the outward acts of the soul (1 John 3 : 4 — ἡ ἁμαρτία ἐστὶν ἡ ἀνομία, where ἀνομία = , not " transgression of the law," but, as both context and etymology show, " lack of conformity to law " or " lawlessness "— Rev. Vers.).

See 1 John 5 : 17 — "All unrighteousness is sin " ; Rom. 14 : 23 — " whatsoever is not of faith is sin " ; James 4 : 17 — "To him therefore that knoweth to do good, and doeth it not, to him it is sin." Where the sin is that of *not doing*, sin cannot be said to consist in *act*. It must then at least be a *state*.

(c) Moral evil is ascribed not only to the thoughts and affections, but to the heart from which they spring (we read of the " evil thoughts " and of the " evil heart "— Mat. 15 : 19 and Heb. 3 : 12).

See also Mat. 5 : 22 — anger in the heart is murder ; 28 — impure desire is adultery. Luke 6 : 45 — "the evil man out of the evil treasure [of his heart] bringeth forth that which is evil." Heb. 3 : 12 — "an evil heart of unbelief " ; *cf.* Is. 1 : 5 — " the whole head is sick, and the whole heart faint " ; Jer. 17 : 9 — " The heart is deceitful above all things, and it is exceedingly corrupt : who can know it ?"— here the sin that cannot be known is not sin of act, but sin of the heart. " Below the surface stream, shallow and light, Of what we *say* we feel ; below the stream, As light, of what we *think* we feel, there flows, With silent current, strong, obscure and deep, The central stream of what we feel *indeed*."

(d) The state or condition of the soul which gives rise to wrong desires and acts is expressly called sin (Rom. 7 : 8—"Sin . . . wrought in me . . . all manner of coveting ").

John 8 : 34 — " Every one that committeth sin is the bondservant of sin " ; Rom. 7 : 11, 13, 14, 17, 20 — "sin . . . . beguiled me . . . . working death to me . . . . I am carnal, sold under sin . . . . sin which dwelleth in me." These representations of sin as a principle or state of the soul are incompatible with the definition of it as a mere act. John Byrom, 1691–1763 : " Think and be careful what thou art within, For there is sin in the desire of sin. Think and be thankful in a different case, For there is grace in the desire of grace."

Alexander, Theories of the Will, 85 — " In the person of Paul is represented the man who has been already justified by faith and who is at peace with God. In the 6th chapter of Romans, the question is discussed whether such a man is obliged to keep the moral law. But in the 7th chapter the question is not, *must* man keep the moral law ? but why is he so *incapable* of keeping the moral law ? The struggle is thus, not in the soul of the unregenerate man who is dead in sin, but in the soul of the regenerate man who has been pardoned and is endeavoring to keep the law. . . . In a state of sin the will is determined toward the bad ; in a state of grace the will is determined toward righteousness ; but not wholly so, for the flesh is not at once subdued, and there is a war between the good and bad principles of action in the soul of him who has been pardoned."

(e) Sin is represented as existing in the soul, prior to the consciousness of it, and as only discovered and awakened by the law (Rom. 7 : 9, 10 — " when the commandment came, sin revived, and I died "— if sin "revived," it must have had previous existence and life, even though it did not manifest itself in acts of conscious transgression).

Rom. 7 : 8 — " apart from the law sin is dead " — here is sin which is not yet sin of act. Dead or unconscious sin is still sin. The fire in a cave discovers reptiles and stirs them, but they were there before ; the light and heat do not create them. Let a beam of light, says Jean Paul Richter, through your window-shutter into a darkened room, and you reveal a thousand motes floating in the air whose existence was before unsuspected. So the law of God reveals our "hidden faults " (Ps. 19 : 12) — infirmities, imperfections, evil tendencies and desires — which also cannot all be classed as *acts* of transgression.

(f) The allusions to sin as a permanent power or reigning principle, not only in the individual but in humanity at large, forbid us to define it as a momentary act, and compel us to regard it as being primarily a settled depravity of nature, of which individual sins or acts of transgression are the workings and fruits (Rom. 5 : 21 — " sin reigned in death " ; 6 : 12 — "let not therefore sin reign in your mortal body ").

In Rom. 5 : 21, the reign of sin is compared to the reign of grace. As grace is not an act but a principle, so sin is not an act but a principle. As the poisonous exhalations from a well indicate that there is corruption and death at the bottom, so the ever-recurring thoughts and acts of sin are evidence that there is a principle of sin in the heart,—in other words, that sin exists as a permanent disposition or state. A momentary act cannot "reign" nor "dwell"; a disposition or state can. Maudsley, Sleep, its Psychology, makes the damaging confession: "If we were held responsible for our dreams, there is no living man who would not deserve to be hanged."

(*g*) The Mosaic sacrifices for sins of ignorance and of omission, and especially for general sinfulness, are evidence that sin is not to be limited to mere act, but that it includes something deeper and more permanent in the heart and the life (Lev. 1 : 3 ; 5 : 11 ; 12 : 8 ; *cf.* Luke 2 : 24).

The sin-offering for sins of ignorance (Lev. 4: 14, 20, 31), the trespass-offering for sins of omission (Lev. 5 : 5, 6), and the burnt offering to expiate general sinfulness (Lev. 1 : 3 ; *cf.* Luke 2 : 22–24), all witness that sin is not confined to mere act. John 1 : 29 — "the Lamb of God, who taketh away the sin," not the sins, "of the world." See Oehler, O. T. Theology, 1 : 233 ; Schmid, Bib. Theol. N. T., 194, 381, 442, 448, 492, 604 ; Philippi, Glaubenslehre, 3 : 210–217 ; Julius Müller, Doctrine of Sin, 2 : 259–306 ; Edwards, Works, 3 : 16–18. For the New School definition of sin, see Fitch, Nature of Sin, and Park, in Bib. Sac., 7 : 551.

B. From the common judgment of mankind.

(*a*) Men universally attribute vice as well as virtue not only to conscious and deliberate acts, but also to dispositions and states. Belief in something more permanently evil than acts of transgression is indicated in the common phrases, "hateful temper," "wicked pride," "bad character."

As the beatitudes (Mat. 5 : 1–12) are pronounced, not upon acts, but upon dispositions of the soul, so the curses of the law are uttered not so much against single acts of transgression as against the evil affections from which they spring. Compare the "works of the flesh" (Gal. 5 : 19) with the "fruit of the Spirit " (5 : 22). In both, dispositions and states predominate.

(*b*) Outward acts, indeed, are condemned only when they are regarded as originating in, and as symptomatic of, evil dispositions. Civil law proceeds upon this principle in holding crime to consist, not alone in the external act, but also in the evil motive or intent with which it is performed.

The *mens rea* is essential to the idea of crime. The "idle word" (Mat. 12 : 36) shall be brought into the judgment, not because it is so important in itself, but because it is a floating straw that indicates the direction of the whole current of the heart and life. Murder differs from homicide, not in any outward respect, but simply because of the motive that prompts it,— and that motive is always, in the last analysis, an evil disposition or state.

(*c*) The stronger an evil disposition, or in other words, the more it connects itself with, or resolves itself into, a settled state or condition of the soul, the more blameworthy is it felt to be. This is shown by the distinction drawn between crimes of passion and crimes of deliberation.

Edwards: " Guilt consists in having one's heart wrong, and in doing wrong from the heart." There is guilt in evil desires, even when the will combats them. But there is greater guilt when the will consents. The outward act may be in each case the same, but the guilt of it is proportioned to the extent to which the evil disposition is settled and strong.

(*d*) This condemning sentence remains the same, even although the origin of the evil disposition or state cannot be traced back to any conscious act of the individual. Neither the general sense of mankind, nor the civil law in which this general sense is expressed, goes behind the fact of an existing evil will. Whether this evil will is the result of personal transgression or is a hereditary bias derived from generations passed, this evil will is the man himself, and upon him terminates the blame. We do not excuse arrogance or sensuality upon the ground that they are family traits.

The young murderer in Boston was not excused upon the ground of a congenitally cruel disposition. We repent in later years of sins of boyhood, which we only now see to be sins; and converted cannibals repent, after becoming Christians, of the sins of heathendom which they once committed without a thought of their wickedness. The peacock cannot escape from his feet by flying, nor can we absolve ourselves from blame for an evil state of will by tracing its origin to a remote ancestry. We are responsible for what we are. How this can be, when we have not personally and consciously originated it, is the problem of original sin, which we have yet to discuss.

(*e*) When any evil disposition has such strength in itself, or is so combined with others, as to indicate a settled moral corruption in which no power to do good remains, this state is regarded with the deepest disapprobation of all. Sin weakens man's power of obedience, but the can-not is a will-not, and is therefore condemnable. The opposite principle would lead to the conclusion that, the more a man weakened his powers by transgression, the less guilty he would be, until absolute depravity became absolute innocence.

The boy who hates his father cannot change his hatred into love by a single act of will; but he is not therefore innocent. Spontaneous and uncontrollable profanity is the worst profanity of all. It is a sign that the whole will, like a subterranean Kentucky river, is moving away from God, and that no recuperative power is left in the soul which can reach into the depths to reverse its course. See Dorner, Glaubenslehre, 2 : 110-114; Shedd, Hist. Doct., 2 : 79-92, 152-157; Richards, Lectures on Theology, 256-301; Edwards, Works, 2 : 134; Baird, Elohim Revealed, 243-262; Princeton Essays, 2 : 224-239; Van Oosterzee, Dogmatics, 394.

C. From the experience of the Christian.

Christian experience is a testing of Scripture truth, and therefore is not an independent source of knowledge. It may, however, corroborate conclusions drawn from the word of God. Since the judgment of the Christian is formed under the influence of the Holy Spirit, we may trust this more implicitly than the general sense of the world. We affirm, then, that just in proportion to his spiritual enlightenment and self-knowledge, the Christian

(*a*) Regards his outward deviations from God's law, and his evil inclinations and desires, as outgrowths and revelations of a depravity of nature which lies below his consciousness; and

(*b*) Repents more deeply for this depravity of nature, which constitutes his inmost character and is inseparable from himself, than for what he merely feels or does.

In proof of these statements we appeal to the biographies and writings of those in all ages who have been by general consent regarded as most advanced in spiritual culture and discernment.

"Intelligentia prima est, ut te noris peccatorem." Compare David's experience, Ps. 51 : 6 — "Behold, thou desirest truth in the inward parts: And in the hidden part thou wilt make me to know wisdom" — with Paul's experience in Rom. 7 : 24 — "Wretched man that I am! who shall deliver me out of the body of this death?" — with Isaiah's experience (6 : 5), when in the presence of God's glory he uses the words of the leper (Lev. 13 : 45) and calls himself "unclean," and with Peter's experience (Luke 5 : 8) when at the manifestation of Christ's miraculous power he "fell down at Jesus' knees, saying, Depart from me; for I am a sinful man, O Lord." So the publican cries: "God, be thou merciful to me the sinner" (Luke 18:13), and Paul calls himself the "chief" of sinners (1 Tim. 1:15). It is evident that in none of these cases were there merely single acts of transgression in view; the humiliation and self-abhorrence were in view of permanent states of depravity. Van Oosterzee: "What we do outwardly is only the revelation of our inner nature." The outcropping and visible rock is but small in extent compared with the rock that is underlying and invisible. The iceberg has eight-ninths of its mass below the surface of the sea, yet icebergs have been seen near Cape Horn from 700 to 800 feet high above the water.

It may be doubted whether any repentance is genuine which is not repentance for *sin* rather than for *sins;* compare John 16:8 — the Holy Spirit "will convict the world in respect of sin." On the difference between conviction of sins and conviction of sin, see Hare, Mission of the Comforter. Dr. A. J. Gordon, just before his death, desired to be left alone. He was then overheard confessing his sins in such seemingly extravagant terms as to excite fear that he was in delirium. Martensen, Dogmatics, 389 — Luther during his early experience "often wrote to Staupitz: 'Oh, my sins, my sins!' and yet in the confessional he could name no sins in particular which he had to confess; so that it was clearly a sense of the general depravity of his nature which filled his soul with deep sorrow and pain." Luther's conscience would not accept the comfort that he *wished* to be without sin, and therefore *had* no real sin. When he thought himself too great a sinner to be saved, Staupitz replied: "Would you have the semblance of a sinner and the semblance of a Savior?"

After twenty years of religious experience, Jonathan Edwards wrote (Works 1:22, 23; also 3:16-18): "Often since I have lived in this town I have had very affecting views of my own sinfulness and vileness, very frequently to such a degree as to hold me in a kind of loud weeping, sometimes for a considerable time together, so that I have been often obliged to shut myself up. I have had a vastly greater sense of my own wickedness and the badness of my heart than ever I had before my conversion. It has often appeared to me that if God should mark iniquity against me, I should appear the very worst of all mankind, of all that have been since the beginning of the world to this time; and that I should have by far the lowest place in hell. When others that have come to talk with me about their soul's concerns have expressed the sense they have had of their own wickedness, by saying that it seemed to them they were as bad as the devil himself; I thought their expressions seemed exceeding faint and feeble to represent my wickedness."

Edwards continues: "My wickedness, as I am in myself, has long appeared to me perfectly ineffable and swallowing up all thought and imagination — like an infinite deluge, or mountains over my head. I know not how to express better what my sins appear to me to be, than by heaping infinite on infinite and multiplying infinite by infinite. Very often for these many years, these expressions are in my mind and in my mouth: 'Infinite upon infinite — infinite upon infinite!' When I look into my heart and take a view of my wickedness, it looks like an abyss infinitely deeper than hell. And it appears to me that were it not for free grace, exalted and raised up to the infinite height of all the fulness and glory of the great Jehovah, and the arm of his power and grace stretched forth in all the majesty of his power and in all the glory of his sovereignty, I should appear sunk down in my sins below hell itself, far beyond the sight of everything but the eye of sovereign grace that can pierce even down to such a depth. And yet it seems to me that my conviction of sin is exceeding small and faint; it is enough to amaze me that I have no more sense of my sin. I know certainly that I have very little sense of my sinfulness. When I have had turns of weeping for my sins, I thought I knew at the time that my repentance was nothing to my sin. . . . . It is affecting to think how ignorant I was, when a young Christian, of the bottomless, infinite depths of wickedness, pride, hypocrisy, and deceit left in my heart."

Jonathan Edwards was not an ungodly man, but the holiest man of his time. He was not an enthusiast, but a man of acute, philosophic mind. He was not a man who indulged in exaggerated or random statements, for with his power of introspection and analysis he combined a faculty and habit of exact expression unsurpassed among the sons of men. If the maxim "cuique in arte sua credendum est" is of any value, Edwards's statements in a matter of religious experience are to be taken as correct interpretations of the facts. H. B. Smith (System. Theol., 275) quotes Thomasius as saying: "It is a striking fact in Scripture that statements of the depth and power of sin are chiefly from the regenerate." Another has said that "a serpent is never seen at its whole length until it is dead." Thomas à Kempis (ed. Gould and Lincoln, 142) — "De not think that thou hast made any progress toward perfection, till thou feelest that thou art less than the least of all human beings." Young's Night Thoughts: "Heaven's Sovereign saves all beings but himself That hideous sight — a naked human heart.

Law's Serious Call to a Devout and Holy Life: "You may justly condemn yourself for being the greatest sinner that you know, 1. Because you know more of the folly of your own heart than of other people's, and can charge yourself with various sins which you know only of yourself and cannot be sure that others are guilty of them. 2. The greatness of our guilt arises from the greatness of God's goodness to us. You know more of these aggravations of your sins than you do of the sins of other people. Hence the greatest saints have in all ages condemned themselves as the greatest sinners." We may add : 3. That, since each man is a peculiar being, each man is guilty of peculiar sins, and in certain particulars and aspects may constitute an example of the enormity and hatefulness of sin, such as neither earth nor hell can elsewhere show.

Of Cromwell, as a representative of the Puritans, Green says (Short History of the English People, 454): "The vivid sense of the divine Purity close to such men, made the life of common men seem sin." Dr. Arnold of Rugby (Life and Corresp., App. D.): "In a deep sense of moral evil, more perhaps than anything else, abides a saving knowledge of God." Augustine, on his death-bed, had the 32d Psalm written over against him on the wall. For his expressions with regard to sin, see his Confessions, book 10. See also Shedd, Discourses and Essays, 284, note.

2. *Inferences.*

In the light of the preceding discussion, we may properly estimate the elements of truth and of error in the common definition of sin as 'the voluntary transgression of known law.'

(*a*) Not all sin is voluntary as being a distinct and conscious volition ; for evil disposition and state often precede and occasion evil volition, and evil disposition and state are themselves sin. All sin, however, is voluntary as springing either directly from will, or indirectly from those perverse affections and desires which have themselves originated in will. 'Voluntary' is a term broader than 'volitional,' and includes all those permanent states of intellect and affection which the will has made what they are. Will, moreover, is not to be regarded as simply the faculty of volitions, but as primarily the underlying determination of the being to a supreme end.

Will, as we have seen, includes preference (θέλημα, *voluntas, Wille*) as well as volition (βουλή, *arbitrium, Willkür*). We do not, with Edwards and Hodge, regard the sensibilities as states of the will. They are, however, in their character and their objects determined by the will, and so they may be called voluntary. The permanent state of the will (New School "elective preference") is to be distinguished from the permanent state of the sensibilities (dispositions, or desires). But both are voluntary because both are due to past decisions of the will, and "whatever springs from will we are responsible for" (Shedd, Discourses and Essays, 243). Julius Müller, 2:51 — "We speak of self-consciousness and reason as something which the ego *has,* but we identify the will *with* the ego. No one would say, 'my will has decided this or that,' although we do say, 'my reason, my conscience teaches me this or that.' The will is the very man himself, as Augustine says: 'Voluntas est in omnibus ; imo omnes nihil aliud quam voluntates sunt.' "

For other statements of the relation of disposition to will, see Alexander, Moral Science, 151 — "In regard to dispositions, we say that they are in a sense voluntary. They properly belong to the will, taking the word in a large sense. In judging of the morality of voluntary acts, the principle from which they proceed is always included in our view and comes in for a large part of the blame"; see also pages 201, 207, 208, Edwards on the Affections, 3:1–22; on the Will, 3:4 — "The affections are only certain modes of the exercise of the will." A. A. Hodge, Outlines of Theology, 234 — "All sin is voluntary, in the sense that all sin has its root in the perverted dispositions, desires, and affections which constitute the depraved state of the will." But to Alexander, Edwards, and Hodge, we reply that the first sin was not voluntary in this sense, for there was no such depraved state of the will from which it could spring. We are responsible for dispositions, not upon the ground that they are a part of the will, but upon the ground that they are effects of will, in other words, that past decisions of the will have made them what they are. See pages 504-513.

(*b*) Deliberate intention to sin is an aggravation of transgression, but it is not essential to constitute any given act or feeling a sin. Those evil inclinations and impulses which rise unbidden and master the soul before it is well aware of their nature, are themselves violations of the divine law, and indications of an inward depravity which in the case of each descendant of Adam is the chief and fontal transgression.

Joseph Cook : " Only the surface-water of the sea is penetrated with light. Beneath is a half-lit region. Still further down is absolute darkness. We are greater than we know." Weismann, Heredity, 2 : 8 — " At the depth of 170 meters, or 552 feet, there is about as much light as that of a starlight night when there is no moon. Light penetrates as far as 400 meters, or 1,300 feet, but animal life exists at a depth of 4,000 meters, or 13,000 feet. Below 1,300 feet, all animals are blind." *Cf.* Ps. 51 : 6 ; 19 : 12 — "the inward parts . . . the hidden parts . . . . hidden faults "—hidden not only from others, but even from ourselves. The light of consciousness plays only on the surface of the waters of man's soul.

(*c*) Knowledge of the sinfulness of an act or feeling is also an aggravation of transgression, but it is not essential to constitute it a sin. Moral blindness is the effect of transgression, and, as inseparable from corrupt affections and desires, is itself condemned by the divine law.

It is our duty to do better than we know. Our duty of knowing is as real as our duty of doing. Sin is an opiate. Some of the most deadly diseases do not reveal themselves in the patient's countenance, nor has the patient any adequate understanding of his malady. There is an ignorance which is indolence. Men are often unwilling to take the trouble of rectifying their standards of judgment. There is also an ignorance which is intention. Instance many students' ignorance of College laws.

We cannot excuse disobedience by saying : " I forgot." God's commandment is : "Remember " — as in Ex. 20 : 8 ; *cf.* 2 Pet. 3 : 5 — " For this they wilfully forget." " Ignorantia legis neminem excusat." Rom. 2 : 12 — " as many as have sinned without the law shall also perish without the law "· Luke 12 : 48 — " he that knew not, and did things worthy of stripes, shall be beaten [though] with few stripes." The aim of revelation and of preaching is to bring man " to himself" (*cf.* Luke 15 : 17) — to show him what he has been doing and what he is. Goethe: " We are never deceived : we deceive ourselves." Royce, World and Individual, 2 : 359 — " The sole possible free moral action is then a freedom that relates to the present fixing of attention upon the ideas of the Ought which are already present. To sin is *consciously to choose to forget*, through a narrowing of the field of attention, an Ought that one already recognizes."

(*d*) Ability to fulfill the law is not essential to constitute the non-fulfilment sin. Inability to fulfill the law is a result of transgression, and, as consisting not in an original deficiency of faculty but in a settled state of the affections and will, it is itself condemnable. Since the law presents the holiness of God as the only standard for the creature, ability to obey can never be the measure of obligation or the test of sin.

Not power to the contrary, in the sense of ability to change all our permanent states by mere volition, is the basis of obligation and responsibility ; for surely Satan's responsibility does not depend upon his power at any moment to turn to God and be holy.

Definitions of sin — Melanchthon : Defectus vel inclinatio vel actio pugnans cum lege Dei. Calvin : Illegalitas, seu difformitas a lege. Hollaz : Aberratio a lege divina. Hollaz adds : " Voluntariness does not enter into the definition of sin, generically considered. Sin may be called voluntary, either in respect to its cause, as it inheres in the will, or in respect to the act, as it procedes from deliberate volition. Here is the antithesis to the Roman Catholics and to the Socinians, the latter of whom define sin as a voluntary [*i. e.*, a volitional] transgression of law "—a view, says Hase (Hutterus Redivivus, 11th ed., 162-164), " which is derived from the necessary methods of civil tribunals, and which is incompatible with the orthodox doctrine of original sin."

On the New School definition of sin, see Fairchild, Nature of Sin, in Bib. Sac., 25 : 30-48; Whedon, in Bib. Sac., 19 : 251, and On the Will, 328. *Per contra*, see Hodge, Syst. Theol., 2 : 180-190; Lawrence, Old School in N. E. Theol., in Bib. Sac., 20 : 317-328; Julius Müller, Doc. Sin, 1 : 40-72; Nitzsch, Christ. Doct., 216; Luthardt, Compendium der Dogmatik, 124-126.

II. THE ESSENTIAL PRINCIPLE OF SIN.

The definition of sin as lack of conformity to the divine law does not exclude, but rather necessitates, an inquiry into the characterizing motive or impelling power which explains its existence and constitutes its guilt. Only three views require extended examination. Of these the first two constitute the most common excuses for sin, although not propounded for this purpose by their authors : Sin is due (1) to the human body, or (2) to finite weakness. The third, which we regard as the Scriptural view, considers sin as (3) the supreme choice of self, or selfishness.

In the preceding section on the Definition of Sin, we showed that sin is a *state*, and a state of the *will*. We now ask : What is the nature of this state? and we expect to show that it is essentially a *selfish* state of the will.

1. *Sin as Sensuousness.*

This view regards sin as the necessary product of man's sensuous nature —a result of the soul's connection with a physical organism. This is the view of Schleiermacher and of Rothe. More recent writers, with John Fiske, regard moral evil as man's inheritance from a brute ancestry.

For statement of the view here opposed, see Schleiermacher, Der Christliche Glaube, 1 : 361-364 — "Sin is a prevention of the determining power of the spirit, caused by the independence (Selbständigkeit) of the sensuous functions." The child lives at first a life of sense, in which the bodily appetites are supreme. The senses are the avenues of all temptation, the physical domineers over the spiritual, and the soul never shakes off the body. Sin is, therefore, a malarious exhalation from the low grounds of human nature, or, to use the words of Schleiermacher, "a positive opposition of the flesh to the spirit." Pfleiderer, Prot. Theol. seit Kant, 113, — says that Schleiermacher here repeats Spinoza's "inability of the spirit to control the sensuous affections." Pfleiderer, Philos. Religion, 1 : 230 — "In the development of man out of naturality, the lower impulses have already won a power of self-assertion and resistance, before the reason could yet come to its valid position and authority. As this propensity of the self-will is grounded in the specific nature of man, it may be designated as inborn, hereditary, or *original* sinfulness."

Rothe's view of sin may be found in his Dogmatik, 1 : 300-302; notice the connection of Rothe's view of sin with his doctrine of continuous creation (see page 416 of this Compendium). Encyclopædia Britannica, 21 : 2 — "Rothe was a thorough going evolutionist who regarded the natural man as the consummation of the development of physical nature, and regarded spirit as the personal attainment, with divine help, of those beings in whom the further creative process of moral development is carried on. This process of development necessarily takes an abnormal form and passes through the phase of sin. This abnormal condition necessitates a fresh creative act, that of salvation, which was however from the very first a part of the divine plan of development. Rothe, notwithstanding his evolutionary doctrine, believed in the supernatural birth of Christ."

John Fiske, Destiny of Man, 103 — "Original sin is neither more nor less than the brute inheritance which every man carries with him, and the process of evolution is an advance toward true salvation." Thus man is a sphynx in whom the human has not yet escaped from the animal. So Bowne, Atonement, 69, declares that sin is "a relic of the animal not yet outgrown, a resultant of the mechanism of appetite and impulse and reflex action for which the proper inhibitions are not yet developed. Only slowly does it grow into a consciousness of itself as evil. . . . . It would be hysteria to regard the common life of men as rooting in a conscious choice of unrighteousness."

In refutation of this view, it will be sufficient to urge the following considerations :

(*a*) It involves an assumption of the inherent evil of matter, at least so
far as regards the substance of man's body. But this is either a form of
dualism, and may be met with the objections already brought against that
system, or it implies that God, in being the author of man's physical
organism, is also the responsible originator of human sin.

This has been called the " caged-eagle theory " of man's existence ; it holds that the
body is a prison only, or, as Plato expressed it, " the tomb of the soul," so that the soul
can be pure only by escaping from the body. But matter is not eternal. God made it,
and made it pure. The body was made to be the servant of the spirit. We must not
throw the blame of sin upon the senses, but upon the spirit that used the senses so
wickedly. To attribute sin to the body is to make God, the author of the body, to be
also the author of sin,—which is the greatest of blasphemies. Men cannot "justly
accuse Their Maker, or their making, or their fate " (Milton, Paradise Lost, 3 :112). Sin
is a contradiction within the spirit itself, and not simply between the spirit and the
flesh. Sensuous activities are not themselves sinful—this is essential Manichæanism.
Robert Burns was wrong when he laid the blame for his delinquencies upon " the passions wild and strong." And Samuel Johnson was wrong when he said that "Every
man is a rascal so soon as he is sick." The normal soul has power to rise above both
passion and sickness and to make them serve its moral development. On the development of the body, as the organ of sin, see Straffen's Hulsean Lectures on Sin, 33-50.
The essential error of this view is its identification of the moral with the physical. If
it were true, then Jesus, who came in human flesh, must needs be a sinner.

(*b*) In explaining sin as an inheritance from the brute, this theory
ignores the fact that man, even though derived from a brute ancestry, is no
longer brute, but man, with power to recognize and to realize moral ideals,
and under no necessity to violate the law of his being.

See A. H. Strong, Christ in Creation, 163-180, on The Fall and the Redemption of Man,
in the Light of Evolution : " Evolution has been thought to be incompatible with any
proper doctrine of a fall. It has been assumed by many that man's immoral course
and conduct are simply survivals of his brute inheritance, inevitable remnants of his
old animal propensities, yieldings of the weak will to fleshly appetites and passions.
This is to deny that sin is truly sin, but it is also to deny that man is truly man. . . . .
Sin must be referred to freedom, or it is not sin. To explain it as the natural result of
weak will overmastered by lower impulses is to make the animal nature, and not the
will, the cause of transgression. And that is to say that man at the beginning is not
man, but brute." See also D. W. Simon, in Bib. Sac., Jan. 1897 : 1-20 — " The key to the
strange and dark contrast between man and his animal ancestry is to be found in the
fact of the Fall. Other species live normally. No remnant of the reptile hinders the
bird. The bird is a true bird. Only man fails to live normally and is a true man only
after ages of time and misery." Marlowe very properly makes his Faustus to be tempted
by sensual baits only after he has sold himself to Satan for power.

To regard vanity, deceitfulness, malice, and revenge as inherited from brute ancestors
is to deny man's original innocence and the creatorship of God. B. W. Lockhart : " The
animal mind knows not God, is not subject to his law, neither indeed can be, just
because it is animal, and as such is incapable of right or wrong. . . . . If man were an
animal and nothing more, he could not sin. It is by virtue of being something more,
that he becomes capable of sin. Sin is the yielding of the known higher to the known
lower. It is the soul's abdication of its being to the brute. . . . Hence the need of
spiritual forces from the spiritual world of divine revelation, to heal and build and
discipline the soul within itself, giving it the victory over the animal passions which
constitute the body and over the kingdom of blind desire which constitutes the world.
The final purpose of man is growth of the soul into liberty, truth, love, likeness to
God. Education is the word that covers the movement, and probation is incident to
education." We add that reparation for past sin and renewing power from above must
follow probation, in order to make education possible.

Some recent writers hold to a real fall of man, and yet regard that fall as necessary to his moral development. Emma Marie Caillard, in Contemp. Rev., Dec. 1893:879 — "Man passed out of a state of innocence — unconscious of his own imperfection — into a state of consciousness of it. The will became slave instead of master. The result would have been the complete stoppage of his evolution but for redemption, which restored his will and made the continuance of his evolution possible. Incarnation was the method of redemption. But even apart from the fall, this incarnation would have been necessary to reveal to man the goal of his evolution and so to secure his coöperation in it." Lisle, Evolution of Spiritual Man, 39, and in Bib. Sac., July, 1892:431–452 — "Evolution by catastrophe in the natural world has a striking analogue in the spiritual world. . . . . Sin is primarily not so much a fall from a higher to a lower, as a failure to rise from a lower to a higher; not so much eating of the forbidden tree, as failure to partake of the tree of life. The latter represented communion and correspondence with God, and had innocent man continued to reach out for this, he would not have fallen. Man's refusal to choose the higher preceded and conditioned his fall to the lower, and the essence of sin is therefore in this refusal, whatever may cause the will to make it. . . . Man chose the lower of his own free will. Then his centripetal force was gone. His development was swiftly and endlessly away from God. He reverted to his original type of savage animalism; and yet, as a self-conscious and free-acting being, he retained a sense of responsibility that filled him with fear and suffering."

On the development-theory of sin, see W. W. McLane, in New Englander, 1891:180–188; A. B. Bruce, Apologetics, 60–62; Lyman Abbott, Evolution of Christianity, 203–208; Le Conte, Evolution, 330, 365–375: Henry Drummond, Ascent of Man, 1–13, 329, 342; Salem Wilder, Life, its Nature, 266–273; Wm. Graham, Creed of Science, 38–44; Frank H. Foster, Evolution and the Evangelical System; Chandler, The Spirit of Man, 45–47.

(c) It rests upon an incomplete induction of facts, taking account of sin solely in its aspect of self-degradation, but ignoring the worst aspect of it as self-exaltation. Avarice, envy, pride, ambition, malice, cruelty, revenge, self-righteousness, unbelief, enmity to God, are none of them fleshly sins, and upon this principle are incapable of explanation.

Two historical examples may suffice to show the insufficiency of the sensuous theory of sin. Goethe was not a markedly sensual man; yet the spiritual vivisection which he practised on Friederike Brion, his perfidious misrepresentation of his relations with Kestner's wife in the "Sorrows of Werther," and his flattery of Napoleon, when a patriot would have scorned the advances of the invader of his country, show Goethe to have been a very incarnation of heartlessness and selfishness. The patriot Boerne said of him: "Not once has he ever advanced a poor solitary word in his country's cause — he who from the lofty height he has attained might speak out what none other but himself would dare pronounce." It has been said that Goethe's first commandment to genius was: "Thou shalt love thy neighbor and thy neighbor's wife." His biographers count up sixteen women to whom he made love and who reciprocated his affection, though it is doubtful whether he contented himself with the doctrine of 16 to 1. As Sainte-Beuve said of Châteaubriand's attachments: "They are like the stars in the sky, — the longer you look, the more of them you discover." Christiane Vulpius, after being for seventeen years his mistress, became at last his wife. But the wife was so slighted that she was driven to intemperance, and Goethe's only son inherited her passion and died of drink. Goethe was the great heathen of modern Christendom, deriding self-denial, extolling self-confidence, attention to the present, the seeking of enjoyment, and the submission of one's self to the decrees of fate. Hutton calls Goethe "a Narcissus in love with himself." Like George Eliot's "Dinah," in Adam Bede, Goethe's "Confessions of a Beautiful Soul," in Wilhelm Meister, are the purely artistic delineation of a character with which he had no inner sympathy. On Goethe, see Hutton, Essays, 2:1–79; Shedd, Dogm. Theology, 1:490; A. H. Strong, Great Poets, 279–331; Principal Shairp, Culture and Religion, 16 — "Goethe, the high priest of culture, loathes Luther, the preacher of righteousness"; S. Law Wilson, Theology of Modern Litera-ture, 149–156.

Napoleon was not a markedly sensual man, but "his self-sufficiency surpassed the self-sufficiency of common men as the great Sahara desert surpasses an ordinary sand patch." He wantonly divulged his amours to Josephine, with all the details of his ill-conduct, and when she revolted from them, he only replied: "I have the right to meet all your complaints with an eternal I." When his wars had left almost no able-bodied men in France, he called for the boys, saying: "A boy can stop a bullet as well as a man," and so the French nation lost two inches of stature. Before the battle of Leipzig, when there was prospect of unexampled slaughter, he exclaimed: "What are the lives of a million of men, to carry out the will of a man like me?" His most truthful epitaph was: "The little butchers of Ghent to Napoleon the Great" [butcher]. Heine represents Napoleon as saying to the world: "Thou shalt have no other gods before me." Memoirs of Madame de Rémusat, 1:225 — "At a fête given by the city of Paris to the Emperor, the repertory of inscriptions being exhausted, a brilliant device was resorted to. Over the throne which he was to occupy, were placed, in letters of gold, the following words from the Holy Scriptures: 'I am the I am.' And no one seemed to be scandalized." Iago, in Shakespeare's Othello, is the greatest villain of all literature; but Coleridge, Works, 4:180, calls attention to his passionless character. His sin is, like that of Goethe and of Napoleon, sin not of the flesh but of the intellect and will.

(*d*) It leads to absurd conclusions,—as, for example, that asceticism, by weakening the power of sense, must weaken the power of sin ; that man becomes less sinful as his senses fail with age ; that disembodied spirits are necessarily holy ; that death is the only Redeemer.

Asceticism only turns the current of sin in other directions. Spiritual pride and tyranny take the place of fleshly desires. The miser clutches his gold more closely as he nears death. Satan has no physical organism, yet he is the prince of evil. Not our own death, but Christ's death, saves us. But when Rousseau's Émile comes to die, he calmly declares: "I am delivered from the trammels of the body, and am myself without contradiction." At the age of seventy-five Goethe wrote to Eckermann: "I have ever been esteemed one of fortune's favorites, nor can I complain of the course my life has taken. Yet truly there has been nothing but care and toil, and I may say that I have never had four weeks of genuine pleasure." Shedd, Dogm. Theology, 2:743 — "When the authoritative demand of Jesus Christ, to confess sin and beg remission through atoning blood, is made to David Hume, or David Strauss, or John Stuart Mill, none of whom were sensualists, it wakens intense mental hostility."

(*e*) It interprets Scripture erroneously. In passages like Rom. 7 : 18— οὐκ οἰκεῖ ἐν ἐμοί, τοῦτ' ἔστιν ἐν τῇ σαρκί μου, ἀγαθόν — σάρξ, or flesh, signifies, not man's body, but man's whole being when destitute of the Spirit of God. The Scriptures distinctly recognize the seat of sin as being in the soul itself, not in its physical organism. God does not tempt man, nor has he made man's nature to tempt him (James 1 : 13, 14).

In the use of the term "flesh," Scripture puts a stigma upon sin, and intimates that human nature without God is as corruptible and perishable as the body would be without the soul to inhabit it. The "carnal mind," or "mind of the flesh" (Rom. 8 : 7), accordingly means, not the sensual mind, but the mind which is not under the control of the Holy Spirit, its true life. See Meyer, on 1 Cor. 1 : 26 — σάρξ = "the purely human element in man, as opposed to the divine principle"; Pope, Theology, 2 : 65 — σάρξ = "the whole being of man, body, soul, and spirit, separated from God and subjected to the creature"; Julius Müller, Proof-texts, 19 — σάρξ = "human nature as living in and for itself, sundered from God and opposed to him." The earliest and best statement of this view of the term σάρξ is that of Julius Müller, Doctrine of Sin, 1 : 295-333, especially 321. See also Dickson, St. Paul's Use of the Terms Flesh and Spirit, 270-271 — σάρξ = "human nature without the πνεῦμα . . . . man standing by himself, or left to himself, over against God . . . . the natural man, conceived as not having yet received grace, or as not yet wholly under its influence."

James 1 : 14, 15 — "desire, when it hath conceived, beareth sin" = innocent desire — for it comes in before the sin — innocent constitutional propensity, not yet of the nature of depravity, is only the *occasion* of sin. The love of freedom is a part of our nature ; sin arises only when the will determines to indulge this impulse without regard to the restraints of the divine law. Luther, Preface to Romans: "Thou must not understand 'flesh' as though that only were 'flesh' which is connected with unchastity. St. Paul uses 'flesh' of the whole man, body and soul, reason and all his faculties included, because all that is in him longs and strives after the 'flesh'." Melanchthon : "Note that 'flesh' signifies the entire nature of man, sense and reason, without the Holy Spirit." Gould

Bib. Theol. N. T., 76 — "The σάρξ of Paul corresponds to the κόσμος of John. Paul sees the divine economy; John the divine nature. That Paul did not hold sin to consist in the possession of a body appears from his doctrine of a bodily resurrection (1 Cor. 15:38-49). This resurrection of the body is an integral part of immortality." On σάρξ, see Thayer, N. T. Lexicon, 571; Kaftan, Dogmatik, 319.

(*f*) Instead of explaining sin, this theory virtually denies its existence, — for if sin arises from the original constitution of our being, reason may recognize it as misfortune, but conscience cannot attribute to it guilt.

Sin which in its ultimate origin is a necessary thing is no longer sin. On the whole theory of the sensuous origin of sin, see Neander, Planting and Training, 386, 428; Ernesti, Ursprung der Sünde, 1:29-274; Philippi, Glaubenslehre, 2:132-147; Tulloch, Doctrine of Sin, 144 — "That which is an inherent and necessary power in the creation cannot be a contradiction of its highest law." This theory confounds sin with the mere consciousness of sin. On Schleiermacher, see Julius Müller, Doctrine of Sin, 1:341-349. On the sense-theory of sin in general, see John Caird, Fund. Ideas of Christianity, 2:26-52; N. R. Wood, The Witness of Sin, 79-87.

2. *Sin as Finiteness.*

This view explains sin as a necessary result of the limitations of man's finite being. As an incident of imperfect development, the fruit of ignorance and impotence, sin is not absolutely but only relatively evil — an element in human education and a means of progress. This is the view of Leibnitz and of Spinoza. Modern writers, as Schurman and Royce, have maintained that moral evil is the necessary background and condition of moral good.

The theory of Leibnitz may be found in his Théodicée, part 1, sections 20 and 31; that of Spinoza in his Ethics, part 4, proposition 20. Upon this view sin is the blundering of inexperience, the thoughtlessness that takes evil for good, the ignorance that puts its fingers into the fire, the stumbling without which one cannot learn to walk. It is a fruit which is sour and bitter simply because it is immature. It is a means of discipline and training for something better,— it is holiness in the germ, good in the making —"Erhebung des Menschen zur freien Vernunft." The Fall was a fall up, and not down.

John Fiske, in addition to his sense-theory of sin already mentioned, seems to hold this theory also. In his Mystery of Evil, he says: "Its impress upon the human soul is the indispensable background against which shall be set hereafter the eternal joys of heaven"; in other words, sin is necessary to holiness, as darkness is the indispensable contrast and background to light; without black, we should never be able to know white. Schurman, Belief in God, 251 *sq.*— "The possibility of sin is the correlative of the free initiative God has vacated on man's behalf. . . . The essence of sin is the enthronement of self. . . . Yet, without such self-absorption, there could be no sense of union with God. For consciousness is possible only through opposition. To know A, we must know it through not-A. Alienation from God is the necessary condition of communion with God. And this is the meaning of the Scripture that ' where sin abounded, grace shall much more abound.' . . . . Modern culture protests against the Puritan enthronement of goodness above truth. . . . For the decalogue it would substitute the wider new commandment of Goethe: ' Live resolutely in the Whole, in the Good, in the Beautiful.' The highest religion can be content with nothing short of the synthesis demanded by Goethe. . . . God is the universal life in which individual activities are included as movements of a single organism."

Royce, World and Individual, 2:364-384 — "Evil is a discord necessary to perfect harmony. In itself it is evil, but in relation to the whole it has value by showing us its own finiteness and imperfection. It is a sorrow to God as much as to us; indeed, all our sorrow is his sorrow. The evil serves the good only by being overcome, thwarted, overruled. Every evil deed must somewhere and at some time be atoned for, by some other than the agent, if not by the agent himself. . . . All finite life is a struggle with evil. Yet from the final point of view the Whole is good. The temporal order contains at no moment anything that can satisfy. Yet the eternal order is perfect. We have all sinned and come short of the glory of God. Yet in just our life, viewed in its entirety, the glory of God is completely manifest. These hard sayings are the deepest expressions of the essence of true religion. They are also the most inevitable outcome of philosophy. . . . Were there no longing in time, there would be no peace in eternity. The prayer that God's will may be done on earth as it is in heaven is identical with what philosophy regards as simple fact."

We object to this theory that

(a) It rests upon a pantheistic basis, as the sense-theory rests upon dualism. The moral is confounded with the physical ; might is identified with right. Since sin is a necessary incident of finiteness, and creatures can never be infinite, it follows that sin must be everlasting, not only in the universe, but in each individual soul.

Goethe, Carlyle, and Emerson are representatives of this view in literature. Goethe spoke of the "idleness of wishing to jump off from one's own shadow." He was a disciple of Spinoza, who believed in one substance with contradictory attributes of thought and extension. Goethe took the pantheistic view of God with the personal view of man. He ignored the fact of sin. Hutton calls him "the wisest man the world has seen who was without humility and faith, and who lacked the wisdom of a child." Speaking of Goethe's Faust, Hutton says: "The great drama is radically false in its fundamental philosophy. Its primary notion is that even a spirit of pure evil is an exceedingly useful being, because he stirs into activity those whom he leads into sin, and so prevents them from rusting away in pure indolence. There are other and better means of stimulating the positive affections of men than by tempting them to sin." On Goethe, see Hutton, Essays, 2 : 1–79; Shedd, Dogm. Theol., 1 : 490; A. H. Strong, Great Poets and their Theology, 279–331.

Carlyle was a Scotch Presbyterian *minus* Christianity. At the age of twenty-five, he rejected miraculous and historical religion, and thenceforth had no God but natural Law. His worship of objective truth became a worship of subjective sincerity, and his worship of personal will became a worship of impersonal force. He preached truth, service, sacrifice, but all in a mandatory and pessimistic way. He saw in England and Wales "twenty-nine millions — mostly fools." He had no love, no remedy, no hope. In our civil war, he was upon the side of the slaveholder. He claimed that his philosophy made right to be might, but in practice he made might to be right. Confounding all moral distinctions, as he did in his later writings, he was fit to wear the title which he invented for another : "President of the Heaven-and-Hell-Amalgamation Society." Froude calls him "a Calvinist without the theology"—a believer in predestination without grace. On Carlyle, see S. Law Wilson, Theology of Modern Literature, 131–178.

Emerson also is the worshiper of successful force. His pantheism is most manifest in his poems "Cupido" and "Brahma," and in his Essays on "Spirit" and on "The Over-soul." Cupido: "The solid, solid universe Is pervious to Love ; With bandaged eyes he never errs, Around, below, above. His blinding light He flingeth white On God's and Satan's brood, And reconciles by mystic wiles The evil and the good." Brahma: "If the red slayer thinks he slays, Or if the slain think he is slain, They know not well the subtle ways I keep, and pass, and turn again. Far or forgot to me is near ; Shadow and sunlight are the same ; The vanished gods to me appear ; And one to me are shame or fame. They reckon ill who leave me out ; When me they fly, I am the wings ; I am the doubter and the doubt, And I the hymn the Brahmin sings. The strong gods pine for my abode, And pine in vain the sacred Seven ; But thou, meek lover of the good, Find me, and turn thy back on heaven."

Emerson taught that man's imperfection is not sin, and that the cure for it lies in education. "He lets God evaporate into abstract Ideality. Not a Deity in the concrete, nor a superhuman Person, but rather the immanent divinity in things, the essentially spiritual structure of the universe, is the object of the transcendental cult." His view of Jesus is found in his Essays, 2 : 263 — "Jesus would absorb the race ; but Tom Paine, or the coarsest blasphemer, helps humanity by resisting this exuberance of power." In his Divinity School Address, he banished the person of Jesus from genuine religion. He thought "one could not be a man if he must subordinate his nature to Christ's nature." He failed to see that Jesus not only absorbs but transforms, and that we grow only by the impact of nobler souls than our own. Emerson's essay style is devoid of clear and precise theological statement, and in this vagueness lies its harmfulness. Fisher, Nature and Method of Revelation, xii — "Emerson's pantheism is not hardened into a consistent creed, for to the end he clung to the belief in personal immortality, and he pronounced the acceptance of this belief ' the test of mental sanity.' " On Emerson, see S. L. Wilson, Theology of Modern Literature, 97-128.

We may call this theory the "green-apple theory" of sin. Sin is a green apple, which needs only time and sunshine and growth to bring it to ripeness and beauty and usefulness. But we answer that sin is not a green apple, but an apple with a worm at its heart. The evil of it can never be cured by growth. The fall can never be anything else than downward. Upon this theory, sin is an inseparable factor in the nature of finite things. The highest archangel cannot be without it. Man in moral character is " the asymptote of God, "— forever learning, but never able to come to the knowledge of the truth. The throne of iniquity is set up forever in the universe. If this theory were true. Jesus, in virtue of his partaking of our finite humanity, must needs be a sinner. His perfect development, without sin, shows that sin was not a necessity of finite progress. Matthews, in Christianity and Evolution, 137 — " It was not necessary for the prodigal to go into the far country and become a swineherd, in order to find out the father's love." E. H. Johnson, Syst. Theol., 141 — " It is not the privilege of the Infinite alone to be good." Dorner, System, 1 : 119, speaks of the moral career which this theory describes, as "a *progressus in infinitum*, where the constant approach to the goal has as its reverse side an eternal separation from the goal." In his "Transformation," Hawthorne hints, though rather hesitatingly, that without sin the higher humanity of man could not be taken up at all, and that sin may be essential to the first conscious awakening of moral freedom and to the possibility of progress; see Hutton, Essays, 2 : 381.

(b) So far as this theory regards moral evil as a necessary presupposition and condition of moral good, it commits the serious error of confounding the possible with the actual. What is necessary to goodness is not the actuality of evil, but only the possibility of evil.

Since we cannot know white except in contrast to black, it is claimed that without knowing actual evil we could never know actual good. George A. Gordon, New Epoch for Faith, 49, 50, has well shown that in that case the elimination of evil would imply the elimination of good. Sin would need to have place in God's being in order that he might be holy, and thus he would be divinity and devil in one person. Jesus too must needs be evil as well as good. Not only would it be true, as intimated above that Christ, since his humanity is finite, must be a sinner, but also that we ourselves who must always be finite, must always be sinners. We grant that holiness, in either God or man, must involve the abstract possibility of its opposite. But we maintain that, as this possibility in God is only abstract and never realized, so in man it should be only abstract and never realized. Man has power to reject this possible evil. His sin is a turning of the merely possible evil, by the decision of his will, into actual evil. Robert Browning is not free from the error above mentioned ; see S. Law Wilson, Theology of Modern Literature, 207-210 ; A. H. Strong, Great Poets and their Theology, 433-444.

This theory of sin dates back to Hegel. To him there is no real sin and cannot be. Imperfection there is and must always be, because the relative can never become the absolute. Redemption is only an evolutionary process, indefinitely prolonged, and evil must remain an eternal condition. All finite thought is an element in the infinite thought, and all finite will an element in the infinite will. As good cannot exist without evil as its antithesis, infinite righteousness should have for its counterpart an infinite wickedness. Hegel's guiding principle was that "What is rational is real, and what is real is rational." Seth, Hegelianism and Personality, remarks that this principle ignores "the riddle of the painful earth." The disciples of Hegel thought that nothing remained for history to accomplish, now that the World-spirit had come to know himself in Hegel's philosophy.

Biedermann's Dogmatik is based upon the Hegelian philosophy. At page 649 we read : " Evil is the finiteness of the world-being which clings to all individual existences by virtue of their belonging to the immanent world-order. Evil is therefore a necessary element in the divinely willed being of the world." Bradley follows Hegel in making sin to be no reality, but only a relative appearance. There is no free will, and no antagonism between the will of God and the will of man. Darkness is an evil, a destroying agent. But it is not a positive force, as light is. It cannot be attacked and overcome as an entity. Bring light, and darkness disappears. So evil is not a positive force, as good is. Bring good, and evil disappears. Herbert Spencer's Evolutionary Ethics is at one with such a system, for he says: "A perfect man in an imperfect race is impossible." On Hegel's view of sin, a view which denies holiness even to Christ, see J. Müller, Doct. Sin, 1 : 390–407 ; Dorner, Hist. Doct. Person of Christ, B. 3 : 131–162 ; Stearns, Evidence of Christ. Experience, 92–96 ; John Caird, Fund. Ideas, 2 : 1–25 ; Forrest, Authority of Christ, 13–16.

(c) It is inconsistent with known facts,— as for example, the following : Not all sins are negative sins of ignorance and infirmity ; there are acts of positive malignity, conscious transgressions, wilful and presumptuous choices of evil. Increased knowledge of the nature of sin does not of itself give strength to overcome it ; but, on the contrary, repeated acts of conscious transgression harden the heart in evil. Men of greatest mental powers are not of necessity the greatest saints, nor are the greatest sinners men of least strength of will and understanding.

Not the weak but the strong are the greatest sinners. We do not pity Nero and Cæsar Borgia for their weakness; we abhor them for their crimes. Judas was an able man, a practical administrator ; and Satan is a being of great natural endowments. Sin is not simply a weakness,— it is also a power. A pantheistic philosophy should worship Satan most of all ; for he is the truest type of godless intellect and selfish strength.

John 12 : 6 — Judas, "having the bag, made away with what was put therein." Judas was set by Christ to do the work he was best fitted for, and that was best fitted to interest and save him. Some men may be put into the ministry, because that is the only work that will prevent their destruction. Pastors should find for their members work suited to the aptitudes of each. Judas was tempted, or tried, as all men are, according to his native propensity. While his motive in objecting to Mary's generosity was really avarice, his pretext was charity, or regard for the poor. Each one of the apostles had his own peculiar gift, and was chosen because of it. The sin of Judas was not a sin of weakness, or ignorance, or infirmity. It was a sin of disappointed ambition, of malice, of hatred for Christ's self-sacrificing purity.

E. H. Johnson: "Sins are not men's limitations, but the active expressions of a perverse nature." M. F. H. Round, Sec. of Nat. Prison Association, on examining the record of a thousand criminals, found that one quarter of them had an exceptionally fine basis of physical life and strength, while the other three quarters fell only a little below the average of ordinary humanity ; see The Forum, Sept. 1893. The theory that sin is only holiness in the making reminds us of the view that the most objectionable refuse can by ingenious processes be converted into butter or at least into oleomargarine. It is not true that "tout comprendre est tout pardonner." Such doctrine obliterates all moral distinctions. Gilbert, Bab Ballads, "My Dream" : "I dreamt that somehow I had come To dwell in Topsy-Turvydom, Where vice is virtue, virtue vice; Where nice is nasty, nasty nice ; Where right is wrong, and wrong is right; Where white is black and black is white."

(d) Like the sense-theory of sin, it contradicts both conscience and Scripture by denying human responsibility and by transferring the blame of sin from the creature to the Creator. This is to explain sin, again, by denying its existence.

Œdipus said that his evil deeds had been suffered, not done. Agamemnon, in the Iliad, says the blame belongs, not to himself, but to Jupiter and to fate. So sin blames everything and everybody but self. Gen. 3 : 12 — "The woman whom thou gavest to be with me, she gave me of the tree, and I did eat." But self-vindicating is God-accusing. Made imperfect at the start, man cannot help his sin. By the very fact of his creation he is cut loose from God. That cannot be sin which is a necessary outgrowth of human nature, which is not our act but our fate. To all this, the one answer is found in Conscience. Conscience testifies that sin is not "das Gewordene," but "das Gemachte," and that it was his own act when man by transgression fell. The Scriptures refer man's sin, not to the limitations of his being, but to the free will of man-himself. On the theory here combated, see Müller, Doct. Sin, 1 : 271–295 ; Philippi, Glaubenslehre, 3 : 123–131 ; N. R. Wood, The Witness of Sin, 20–42.

3. *Sin as Selfishness.*

We hold the essential principle of sin to be selfishness. By selfishness we mean not simply the exaggerated self-love which constitutes the antithesis of benevolence, but that choice of self as the supreme end which constitutes the antithesis of supreme love to God. That selfishness is the essence of sin may be shown as follows :

A. Love to God is the essence of all virtue. The opposite to this, the choice of self as the supreme end, must therefore be the essence of sin.

We are to remember, however, that the love to God in which virtue consists is love for that which is most characteristic and fundamental in God, namely, his holiness. It is not to be confounded with supreme regard for God's interests or for the good of being in general. Not mere benevolence, but love for God as holy, is the principle and source of holiness in man. Since the love of God required by the law is of this sort, it not only does not imply that love, in the sense of benevolence, is the essence of holiness in God,— it implies rather that holiness, or self-loving and self-affirming purity, is fundamental in the divine nature. From this self-loving and self-affirming purity, love properly so-called, or the self-communicating attribute, is to be carefully distinguished (see vol. 1, pages 271-275).

Bossuet, describing heathendom, says: "Every thing was God but God himself." Sin goes further than this, and says: "I am myself all things,"—not simply as Louis XVI : "I am the state," but : "I am the world, the universe, God." Heinrich Heine : "I am no child. I do not want a heavenly Father any more." A French critic of Fichte's philosophy said that it was a flight toward the infinite which began with the ego, and never got beyond it. Kidd, Social Evolution, 75—"In Calderon's tragic story, the unknown figure, which throughout life is everywhere in conflict with the individual whom it haunts, lifts the mask at last to disclose to the opponent his own features." Caird, Evolution of Religion, 1 : 78—"Every self, once awakened, is naturally a despot. and 'bears, like the Turk, no brother near the throne.'" Every one has, as Hobbes said, "an infinite desire for gain or glory," and can be satisfied with nothing but a whole universe for himself. Selfishness = "homo homini lupus." James Martineau : "We ask Comte to lift the veil from the holy of holies and show us the all-perfect object of worship,— he produces a looking-glass and shows us ourselves." Comte's religion is a "synthetic idealization of our existence"—a worship, not of God, but of humanity ; and "the festival of humanity" among Positivists = Walt Whitman's "I celebrate myself." On Comte, see Martineau, Types, 1 : 499. The most thorough discussion of the essential principle of sin is that of Julius Müller, Doct. Sin, 1 : 147-182. He defines sin as "a turning away from the love of God to self-seeking."

N. W. Taylor holds that self-love is the primary cause of all moral action ; that selfishness is a different thing, and consists not in making our own happiness our ultimate end, which we must do if we are moral beings, but in love of the world, and in preferring the world to God as our portion or chief good (see N. W. Taylor, Moral Govt., 1 : 24-26 ; 2 :20-24, and Rev. Theol., 134-162; Tyler, Letters on the New Haven Theology, 72). We claim, on the contrary, that to make our own happiness our ultimate aim is itself sin, and the essence of sin. As God makes his holiness the central thing, so we are to live for that, loving self only in God and for God's sake. This love for God as holy is the essence of virtue. The opposite to this, or supreme love for self, is sin. As Richard Lovelace writes: "I could not love thee, dear, so much, Loved I not honor more," so Christian friends can say : "Our loves in higher love endure." The sinner raises some lower object of instinct or desire to supremacy, regardless of God and his law, and this he does for no other reason than to gratify self. On the distinction between mere benevolence and the love required by God's law, see Hovey, God With Us, 187-200 ; Hopkins, Works, 1 : 235; F. W. Robertson, Sermon I. Emerson: "Your goodness must have some edge to it, else it is none." See Newman Smyth, Christian Ethics, 327-370, on duties toward self as a moral end.

Love to God is the essence of all virtue. We are to love God with all the heart. But what God? Surely, not the false God, the God who is indifferent to mora. distinctions and who treats the wicked as he treats the righteous. The love which the law requires is love for the true God, the God of holiness. Such love aims at the reproduction of God's holiness in ourselves and in others. We are to love ourselves only for God's sake and for the sake of realizing the divine idea in us. We are to love others only for God's sake and for the sake of realizing the divine idea in them. In our moral progress we, first, love self for our own sake; secondly, God for our own sake; thirdly, God for his own sake; fourthly, ourselves for God's sake. The first is our state by nature; the second requires prevenient grace; the third, regenerating grace; and the fourth, sanctifying grace. Only the last is reasonable self-love. Balfour, Foundations of Belief, 27 — "Reasonable self-love is a virtue wholly incompatible with what is commonly called selfishness. Society suffers, not from having too much of it, but from having too little." Altruism is not the whole of duty. Self-realization is equally important. But to care only for self, like Goethe, is to miss the true self-realization, which love to God ensures.

Love desires only *the best* for its object, and the best is *God.* The golden rule bids us give, not what others desire, but what they need. Rom. 15 : 2 — "Let each one of us please his neighbor for that which is good, unto edifying." Deutsche Liebe: "Nicht Liebe die fragt: Willst du mein sein? Sondern Liebe die sagt: Ich muss dein sein." Sin consists in taking for one's self alone and apart from God that in one's self and in others to which one has a right only in God and for God's sake. Mrs. Humphrey Ward, David Grieve, 403 — "How dare a man pluck from the Lord's hand, for his wild and reckless use, a soul and body for which he died? How dare he, the Lord's bondsman, steal his joy, carrying it off by himself into the wilderness, like an animal his prey, instead of asking it at the hands and under the blessing of the Master? How dare he, a member of the Lord's body, forget the whole, in his greed for the one — eternity in his thirst for the present?" Wordsworth, Prelude, 546 — "Delight how pitiable, Unless this love by a still higher love Be hallowed, love that breathes not without awe; Love that adores, but on the knees of prayer, By heaven inspired. . . . . This spiritual love acts not nor can exist Without imagination, which in truth Is but another name for absolute power, And clearest insight, amplitude of mind, And reason in her most exalted mood."

Aristotle says that the wicked have no right to love themselves, but that the good may. So, from a Christian point of view, we may say: No unregenerate man can properly respect himself. Self-respect belongs only to the man who lives in God and who has God's image restored to him thereby. True self-love is not love for the *happiness* of the self, but for the *worth* of the self in God's sight, and this self-love is the condition of all genuine and worthy love for others. But true self-love is in turn conditioned by love to God as holy, and it seeks primarily, not the happiness, but the holiness, of others. Asquith, Christian Conception of Holiness, 98, 145, 154, 207 — "Benevolence or love is not the same with altruism. Altruism is instinctive, and has not its origin in the moral reason. It has utility, and it may even furnish material for reflection on the part of the moral reason. But so far as it is not deliberate, not indulged for the sake of the end, but only for the gratification of the instinct of the moment, it is not moral. . . . Holiness is dedication to God, the Good, not as an external Ruler, but as an internal controller and transformer of character. . . . God is a being whose every thought is love, of whose thoughts not one is for himself, save so far as himself is not himself, that is, so far as there is a distinction of persons in the Godhead. Creation is one great unselfish thought — the bringing into being of creatures who can know the happiness that God knows. . . . To the spiritual man holiness and love are one. Salvation is deliverance from selfishness." Kaftan, Dogmatik, 319, 320, regards the essence of sin as consisting, not in selfishness, but in turning away from God and so from the love which would cause man to grow in knowledge and likeness to God. But this seems to be nothing else than choosing self instead of God as our object and end.

B. All the different forms of sin can be shown to have their root in selfishness, while selfishness itself, considered as the choice of self as a supreme end, cannot be resolved into any simpler elements.

(*a*) Selfishness may reveal itself in the elevation to supreme dominion of any one of man's natural appetites, desires, or affections. Sensuality is selfishness in the form of inordinate appetite. Selfish desire takes the forms respectively of avarice, ambition, vanity, pride, according as it is set upon property, power, esteem, independence. Selfish affection is falsehood or malice, according as it hopes to make others its voluntary servants, or regards them as standing in its way; it is unbelief or enmity to God, according as it simply turns away from the truth and love of God, or conceives of God's holiness as positively resisting and punishing it.

Augustine and Aquinas held the essence of sin to be pride; Luther and Calvin regarded its essence to be unbelief. Kreibig (Versöhnungslehre) regards it as "world-love"; still others consider it as enmity to God. In opposing the view that sensuality is the essence of sin, Julius Müller says: "Wherever we find sensuality, there we find selfishness, but we do not find that, where there is selfishness, there is always sensuality. Selfishness may embody itself in fleshly lust or inordinate desire for the creature, but this last cannot bring forth spiritual sins which have no element of sensuality in them."

Covetousness or avarice makes, not sensual gratification itself, but the things that may minister thereto, the object of pursuit, and in this last chase often loses sight of its original aim. Ambition is selfish love of power; vanity is selfish love of esteem. Pride is but the self-complacency, self-sufficiency, and self-isolation of a selfish spirit that desires nothing so much as unrestrained independence. Falsehood originates in selfishness, first as self-deception, and then, since man by sin isolates himself and yet in a thousand ways needs the fellowship of his brethren, as deception of others. Malice, the perversion of natural resentment (together with hatred and revenge), is the reaction of selfishness against those who stand, or are imagined to stand, in its way. Unbelief and enmity to God are effects of sin, rather than its essence; selfishness leads us first to doubt, and then to hate, the Lawgiver and Judge. Tacitus: "Humani generis proprium est odisse quem læseris." In sin, self-affirmation and self-surrender are not coördinate elements, as Dorner holds, but the former conditions the latter.

As love to God is love to God's holiness, so love to man is love for holiness in man and desire to impart it. In other words, true love for man is the longing to make man like God. Over against this normal desire which should fill the heart and inspire the life, there stands a hierarchy of lower desires which may be utilized and sanctified by the higher love, but which may assert their independence and may thus be the occasions of sin. Physical gratification, money, esteem, power, knowledge, family, virtue, are proper objects of regard, so long as these are sought for God's sake and within the limitations of his will. Sin consists in turning our backs on God and in seeking any one of these objects for its own sake; or, which is the same thing, for our own sake. Appetite gratified without regard to God's law is lust; the love of money becomes avarice; the desire for esteem becomes vanity; the longing for power becomes ambition; the love for knowledge becomes a selfish thirst for intellectual satisfaction; parental affection degenerates into indulgence and nepotism; the seeking of virtue becomes self-righteousness and self-sufficiency. Kaftan, Dogmatik, 323— "Jesus grants that even the heathen and sinners love those who love them. But family love becomes family pride; patriotism comes to stand for country right or wrong; happiness in one's calling leads to class distinctions."

Dante, in his Divine Comedy, divides the Inferno into three great sections: those in which are punished, respectively, incontinence, bestiality, and malice. Incontinence = sin of the heart, the emotions, the affections. Lower down is found bestiality = sin of the head, the thoughts, the mind, as infidelity and heresy. Lowest of all is malice = sin of the will, deliberate rebellion, fraud and treachery. So we are taught that the heart carries the intellect with it, and that the sin of unbelief gradually deepens into the intensity of malice. See A. H. Strong, Great Poets and their Theology, 133— "Dante teaches us that sin is the self-perversion of the will. If there is any thought fundamental to his system, it is the thought of freedom. Man is not a waif swept irresistibly downward on the current; he is a being endowed with power to resist, and therefore guilty if he yields. Sin is not misfortune, or disease, or natural necessity; it is wilfulness, and crime, and self-destruction. The Divine Comedy is, beyond all other poems, the poem of conscience; and this could not be, if it did not recognize man as a free agent, the responsible cause of his own evil acts and his own evil state." See also Harris, in Jour. Spec. Philos., 21 : 350–451; Dinsmore, Atonement in Literature and Life, 69–86.

In Greek tragedy, says Prof. Wm. Arnold Stevens, the one sin which the gods hated and would not pardon was ὕβρις — obstinate self-assertion of mind or will, absence of reverence and humility — of which we have an illustration in Ajax. George MacDonald: "A man may be possessed of himself, as of a devil." Shakespeare depicts this insolence of infatuation in Shylock, Macbeth, and Richard III. Troilus and Cres-

sida, 4:4 — " Something may be done that we will not ; And sometimes we are devils to
ourselves, When we will tempt the frailty of our powers, Presuming on their changeful potency." Yet Robert G. Ingersoll said that Shakespeare holds crime to be the
mistake of ignorance! N. P. Willis, Parrhasius: "How like a mounting devil in the
heart Rules unrestrained ambition!"

(*b*) Even in the nobler forms of unregenerate life, the principle of selfishness is to be regarded as manifesting itself in the preference of lower
ends to that of God's proposing.   Others are loved with idolatrous affection
because these others are regarded as a part of self.   That the selfish element is present even here, is evident upon considering that such affection
does not seek the highest interest of its object, that it often ceases when
unreturned, and that it sacrifices to its own gratification the claims of God
and his law.

Even in the mother's idolatry of her child, the explorer's devotion to science, the
sailor's risk of his life to save another's, the gratification sought may be that of a lower
instinct or desire, and any substitution of a lower for the highest object is non-conformity to law, and therefore sin.   H. B. Smith, System Theology, 277 — "Some lower
affection is supreme."   And the underlying motive which leads to this substitution is
self-gratification.   There is no such thing as disinterested sin, for " every one that loveth is
begotten of God " (1 John 4:7).   Thomas Hughes, The Manliness of Christ : Much of the heroism
of battle is simply " resolution in the actors to have their way, contempt for ease,
animal courage which we share with the bulldog and the weasel, intense assertion of
individual will and force, avowal of the rough-handed man that he has that in him
which enables him to defy pain and danger and death."

Mozley on Blanco White, in Essays, 2:143: Truth may be sought in order to absorb
truth in self, not for the sake of absorbing self in truth.   So Blanco White, in spite of
the pain of separating from old views and friends, lived for the selfish pleasure of
new discovery, till all his early faith vanished, and even immortality seemed a dream.
He falsely thought that the pain he suffered in giving up old beliefs was evidence of
self-sacrifice with which God must be pleased, whereas it was the inevitable pain which
attends the victory of selfishness.   Robert Browning, Paracelsus, 81 — "I still must
hoard, and heap, and class all truths With one ulterior purpose : I must know ! Would
God translate me to his throne, believe That I should only listen to his words To further
my own ends."   F. W. Robertson on Genesis, 57 — " He who sacrifices his sense of right,
his conscience, for another, sacrifices the God within him; he is not sacrificing self.
. . . . He who prefers his dearest friend or his beloved child to the call of duty, will soon
show that he prefers himself to his dearest friend, and would not sacrifice himself for
his child."   *Ib.*, 91 — " In those who love little, love [for finite beings] is a primary
affection, — a secondary, in those who love much. . . . . The only true affection is that
which is subordinate to a higher."   True love is love for the soul and its highest, its
eternal, interests ; love that seeks to make it holy ; love for the sake of God and for the
accomplishment of God's idea in his creation.

Although we cannot, with Augustine, call the virtues of the heathen "splendid
vices" — for they were relatively good and useful, — they still, except in possible
instances where God's Spirit wrought upon the heart, were illustrations of a morality
divorced from love to God, were lacking in the most essential element demanded by the
law, were therefore infected with sin.   Since the law judges all action by the heart from
which it springs, no action of the unregenerate can be other than sin.   The ebony-tree
is white in its outer circles of woody fibre; at heart it is black as ink.   There is no
unselfishness in the unregenerate heart, apart from the divine enlightenment and
energizing.   Self-sacrifice for the sake of self is selfishness after all.   Professional burg-
lars and bank-robbers are often carefully abstemious in their personal habits, and they
deny themselves the use of liquor and tobacco while in the active practice of their
trade.   Herron, The Larger Christ, 47 — "It is as truly immoral to seek truth out of
mere love of knowing it, as it is to seek money out of love to gain.   Truth sought for
truth's sake is an intellectual vice : it is spiritual covetousness.   It is an idolatry, setting up the worship of abstractions and generalities in place of the living God."

(*c*) It must be remembered, however, that side by side with the selfish
will, and striving against it, is the power of Christ, the immanent God,

imparting aspirations and impulses foreign to unregenerate humanity, and preparing the way for the soul's surrender to truth and righteousness.

Rom. 8 : 7 — "the mind of the flesh is enmity against God"; Acts 17 : 27, 28 — "he is not far from each one of us; for in him we live, and move, and have our being "; Rom. 2 : 4 — "the goodness of God leadeth thee to repentance "; John 1 : 9 — "the light which lighteth every man." Many generous traits and acts of self-sacrifice in the unregenerate must be ascribed to the prevenient grace of God and to the enlightening influence of the Spirit of Christ. A mother, during the Russian famine, gave to her children all the little supply of food that came to her in the distribution, and died that they might live. In her decision to sacrifice herself for her offspring she may have found her probation and may have surrendered herself to God. The impulse to make the sacrifice may have been due to the Holy Spirit, and her yielding may have been essentially an act of saving faith. In Mark 10 : 21, 22 — "And Jesus looking upon him loved him . . . he went away sorrowful " — our Lord apparently loved the young man, not only for his gifts, his efforts, and his possibilities, but also for the manifest working in him of the divine Spirit, even while in his natural character he was without God and without love, self-ignorant, self-righteous, and self-seeking.

Paul, in like manner, before his conversion, loved and desired righteousness, provided only that this righteousness might be the product and achievement of his own will and might reflect honor on himself; in short, provided only that self might still be uppermost. To be dependent for righteousness upon another was abhorrent to him. And yet this very impulse toward righteousness may have been due to the divine Spirit within him. On Paul's experience before conversion, see E. D. Burton, Bib. World, Jan. 1893. Peter objected to the washing of his feet by Jesus (John 13 : 8), not because it humbled the Master too much in the eyes of the disciple, but because it humbled the disciple too much in his own eyes. Pfleiderer, Philos. Religion, 1 : 218 — " Sin is the violation of the God-willed moral order of the world by the self-will of the individual." Tophel on the Holy Spirit, 17 — " You would deeply wound him [the average sinner] if you told him that his heart, full of sin, is an object of horror to the holiness of God." The impulse to repentance, as well as the impulse to righteousness, is the product, not of man's own nature, but of the Christ within him who is moving him to seek salvation.

Elizabeth Barrett wrote to Robert Browning after she had accepted his proposal of marriage : " Henceforth I am yours for everything but to do you harm." George Harris, Moral Evolution, 138 — " Love seeks the true good of the person loved. It will not minister in an unworthy way to afford a temporary pleasure. It will not approve or tolerate that which is wrong. It will not encourage the coarse, base passions of the one loved. It condemns impurity, falsehood, selfishness. A parent does not really love his child if he tolerates the self-indulgence, and does not correct or punish the faults, of the child." Hutton : " You might as well say that it is a fit subject for art to paint the morbid exstasy of cannibals over their horrid feasts, as to paint lust without love. If you are to delineate man at all, you must delineate him with his human nature, and therefore you can never omit from any worthy picture that conscience which is its crown."

Tennyson, in In Memoriam, speaks of " Fantastic beauty such as lurks In some wild poet when he works Without a conscience or an aim." Such work may be due to mere human nature. But the lofty work of true creative genius, and the still loftier acts of men still unregenerate but conscientious and self-sacrificing, must be explained by the working in them of the immanent Christ, the life and light of men. James Martineau, Study, 1 : 20 — " Conscience may act as human, before it is discovered to be divine." See J. D. Stoops, in Jour. Philos., Psych., and Sci. Meth., 2 : 512 — " If there is a divine life over and above the separate streams of individual lives, the welling up of this larger life in the experience of the individual is precisely the point of contact between the individual person and God." Caird, Fund. Ideas of Christianity, 2 : 122 — " It is this divine element in man, this relationship to God, which gives to sin its darkest and direst complexion. For such a life is the turning of a light brighter than the sun into darkness, the squandering or bartering away of a boundless wealth, the suicidal abasement, to the things that perish, of a nature destined by its very constitution and structure for participation in the very being and blessedness of God."

On the various forms of sin as manifestations of selfishness, see Julius Müller, Doct. Sin, 1 : 147-182; Jonathan Edwards, Works, 2 : 266, 269; Philippi, Glaubenslehre, 3 : 5, 6; Baird, Elohim Revealed, 243-262; Stewart, Active and Moral Powers, 11-91; Hopkins, Moral Science, 86-156. On the Roman Catholic " Seven Deadly Sins" (Pride, Envy

Anger, Sloth, Avarice, Gluttony, Lust), see Wetzer und Welte, Kirchenlexikon, and Orby Shipley, Theory about Sin, preface, xvi-xviii.

C.   This view accords best with Scripture.

(a) The law requires love to God as its all-embracing requirement. (b) The holiness of Christ consisted in this, that he sought not his own will or glory, but made God his supreme end. (c) The Christian is one who has ceased to live for self.   (d) The tempter's promise is a promise of selfish independence. (e) The prodigal separates himself from his father, and seeks his own interest and pleasure.   (f) The "man of sin" illustrates the nature of sin, in "opposing and exalting himself against all that is called God."

(a) Mat. 22 : 37-39 — the command of love to God and man ; Rom. 13 : 8-10 — "love therefore is the fulfilment of the law" ; Gal. 5 : 14 — "the whole law is fulfilled in one word, even in this: Thou shalt love thy neighbor as thyself" ; James 2 : 8 — "the royal law." (b) John 5 : 30 — "my judgment is righteous; because I seek not mine own will, but the will of him that sent me" ; 7 : 18 — "He that speaketh from himself seeketh his own glory : but he that seeketh the glory of him that sent him, the same is true, and no unrighteousness is in him "; Rom. 15 : 3 - — "Christ also pleased not himself." (c) Rom. 14 : 7 —"none of us liveth to himself, and none dieth to himself" ; 2 Cor. 5 : 15 — "he died for all, that they that live should no longer live unto themselves, but unto him who for their sakes died and rose again" ; Gal. 2 : 20 — "I have been crucified with Christ; and it is no longer I that live, but Christ liveth in me." Contrast 2 Tim. 3 : 2 —"lovers of self." (d) Gen. 3 : 5 —"ye shall be as God, knowing good and evil." (e) Luke 15 : 12, 13 — "give me the portion of thy substance . . . . gathered all together and took his journey into a far country." (f) 2 Thess. 2 : 3, 4 — "the man of sin . . . . the son of perdition, he that opposeth and exalteth himself against all that is called God or that is worshipped ; so that he sitteth in the temple of God, setting himself forth as God."

Contrast "the man of sin" who "exalteth himself" (2 Thess. 2 : 3, 4) with the Son of God who "emptied himself" (Phil. 2 : 7). On "the man of sin", see Wm. Arnold Stevens, in Bap. Quar. Rev., July, 1889 : 328-360. Ritchie, Darwin, and Hegel, 24 — "We are conscious of sin, because we know that our true self is God, from whom we are severed. No ethics is possible unless we recognize an ideal for all human effort in the presence of the eternal Self which any account of conduct presupposes." John Caird, Fund. Ideas of Christianity, 2 : 53-73 — "Here, as in all organic life, the individual member or organ has no independent or exclusive life, and the attempt to attain to it is fatal to itself." Milton describes man as "affecting Godhead, and so losing all." Of the sinner, we may say with Shakespeare, Coriolanus, 5 : 4 — "He wants nothing of a god but eternity and a heaven to throne in. . . . . There is no more mercy in him than there is milk in a male tiger." No one of us, then, can sign too early "the declaration of dependence." Both Old School and New School theologians agree that sin is selfishness ; see Bellamy, Hopkins, Emmons, the younger Edwards, Finney, Taylor. See also A. H. Strong, Christ in Creation, 287-292.

Sin, therefore, is not merely a negative thing, or an absence of love to God.   It is a fundamental and positive choice or preference of self instead of God, as the object of affection and the supreme end of being.   Instead of making God the centre of his life, surrendering himself unconditionally to God and possessing himself only in subordination to God's will, the sinner makes self the centre of his life, sets himself directly against God, and constitutes his own interest the supreme motive and his own will the supreme rule.

We may follow Dr. E. G. Robinson in saying that, while sin as a state is unlikeness to God, as a principle is opposition to God, and as an act is transgression of God's law, the essence of it always and everywhere is selfishness.   It is therefore not something external, or the result of compulsion from without ; it is a depravity of the affections and a perversion of the will, which constitutes man's inmost character.

See Harris, in Bib. Sac.. 18 : 148 — "Sin is essentially egoism or selfism, putting self in God's place. It has four principal characteristics or manifestations: (1) self-sufficiency, instead of faith : (2) self-will, instead of submission ; (3) self-seeking instead of benevolence ; (4) self-righteousness, instead of humility and reverence." All sin is either explicit or implicit "enmity against God " (Rom. 8 : 7). All true confessions are like David's (Ps. 51 : 4) — "Against thee, thee only, have I sinned, And done that which is evil in thy sight." Of all sinners it might be said that they "Fight neither with small nor great, save only with the king of Israel " (1 K. 22 : 31).

Not every sinner is conscious of this enmity. Sin is a principle in course of development. It is not yet "full-grown " (James 1 : 15 — "the sin, when it is full-grown, bringeth forth death "). Even now, as James Martineau has said : " If it could be known that God was dead, the news would cause but little excitement in the streets of London and Paris." But this indifference easily grows, in the presence of threatening and penalty, into violent hatred to God and positive defiance of his law. If the sin which is now hidden in the sinner's heart were but permitted to develop itself according to its own nature, it would hurl the Almighty from his throne, and would set up its own kingdom upon the ruins of the moral universe. Sin is world-destroying, as well as God-destroying, for it is inconsistent with the conditions which make being as a whole possible ; see Royce, World and Individual, 2 : 366 ; Dwight, Works, sermon 80.

SECTION III.—UNIVERSALITY OF SIN.

We have shown that sin is a state, a state of the will, a selfish state of the will. We now proceed to show that this selfish state of the will is universal. We divide our proof into two parts. In the first, we regard sin in its aspect as conscious violation of law ; in the second, in its aspect as a bias of the nature to evil, prior to or underlying consciousness.

I. EVERY HUMAN BEING WHO HAS ARRIVED AT MORAL CONSCIOUSNESS HAS COMMITTED ACTS, OR CHERISHED DISPOSITIONS, CONTRARY TO THE DIVINE LAW.

1. *Proof from Scripture.*

The universality of transgression is :

(*a*) Set forth in direct statements of Scripture.

1 K. 8 : 46 — " there is no man that sinneth not" ; Ps. 143 : 2 — "enter not into judgment with thy servant ; For in thy sight no man living is righteous " ; Prov. 20 : 9 — "Who can say, I have made my heart clean, I am pure from my sin ? " Eccl. 7 : 20 —"Surely there is not a righteous man upon earth, that doeth good, and sinneth not " ; Luke 11 : 13 — "If ye, then, being evil " ; Rom. 3 : 10, 12 — "There is none righteous, no, not one . . . . There is none that doeth good, no, not so much as one " ; 19, 20 — "that every mouth may be stopped, and all the world may be brought under the judgment of God : because by the works of the law shall no flesh be justified in his sight ; for through the law cometh the knowledge of sin " ; 23 — "for all have sinned, and fall short of the glory of God " ; Gal. 3 : 22 — "the scripture shut up all things under sin " ; James 3 : 2 —"For in many things we all stumble " ; 1 John 1 : 8 —"If we say that we have no sin, we deceive ourselves, and the truth is not in us." Compare Mat. 6 : 12 —"forgive us our debts "—given as a prayer for all men ; 14 —"if ye forgive men their trespasses "—the condition of our own forgiveness.

(*b*) Implied in declarations of the universal need of atonement, regeneration, and repentance.

Universal need of atonement : Mark 16 : 16 — " He that believeth and is baptized shall be saved " (Mark 16 : 9–20, though probably not written by Mark, is nevertheless of canonical authority) ; John 3 : 16 — "God so loved the world, that he gave his only begotten Son, that whosoever believeth on him should not perish " ; 6 : 50 — "This is the bread which cometh down out of heaven, that a man may eat thereof, and not die " ; 12 : 47 — "I came not to judge the world, but to save the world " ; Acts 4 : 12 — "in none other is there salvation : for neither is there any other name under heaven, that is given among men, wherein we must be saved." Universal need of regeneration : John 3 : 3, 5 — "Except one be born anew, he cannot see the kingdom of God. . . . . Except one be born of water and the Spirit, he cannot enter into the kingdom of God." Universal need of repentance : Acts 17 : 30 — "commandeth men that they should all everywhere repent." Yet Mrs. Mary Baker G. Eddy, in her "Unity of Good," speaks of "the illusion which calls sin real and man a sinner needing a Savior."

(c) Shown from the condemnation resting upon all who do not **accept Christ.**

John 3 : 18 — "he that believeth not hath been judged already, because he hath not believed on the name of the only begotten Son of God"; 36 — "he that obeyeth not the Son shall not see life, but the wrath of God abideth on him"; Compare 1 John 5 : 19 — "the whole world lieth in [i. e., in union with] the evil one"; see Annotated Paragraph Bible, in loco. Kaftan, Dogmatik, 318 — "Law requires love to God. This implies love to our neighbor, not only abstaining from all injury to him, but righteousness in all our relations, forgiving instead of requiting, help to enemies as well as friends in all salutary ways, self-discipline, avoidance of all sensuous immoderation, subjection of all sensuous activity as means for spiritual ends in the kingdom of God, and all this, not as a matter of outward conduct merely, but from the heart and as the satisfaction of one's own will and desire. This is the will of God respecting us, which Jesus has revealed and of which he is the example in his life. Instead of this, man universally seeks to promote his own life, pleasure, and honor."

(d) Consistent with those passages which at first sight seem to ascribe to certain men a goodness which renders them acceptable to God, where a closer examination will show that in each case the goodness supposed is a merely imperfect and fancied goodness, a goodness of mere aspiration and impulse due to preliminary workings of God's Spirit, or a goodness resulting from the trust of a conscious sinner in God's method of salvation.

In Mat. 9 : 12 — "They that are whole have no need of a physician, but they that are sick"— Jesus means those who in their own esteem are whole; cf. 13 — "I came not to call the righteous, but sinners" = "if any were truly righteous, they would not need my salvation; if they think themselves so, they will not care to seek it" (An. Par. Bib.). In Luke 10 : 30-37 — the parable of the good Samaritan — Jesus intimates, not that the good Samaritan was not a sinner, but that there were saved sinners outside of the bounds of Israel. In Acts 10 : 35 — "in every nation he that feareth him, and worketh righteousness, is acceptable to him"— Peter declares, not that Cornelius was not a sinner, but that God had accepted him through Christ; Cornelius was already justified, but he needed to know (1) that he was saved, and (2) how he was saved; and Peter was sent to tell him of the fact, and of the method, of his salvation in Christ. In Rom. 2 : 14 — "for when Gentiles that have not the law do by nature the things of the law, these, not having the law, are a law unto themselves" — it is only said that in certain respects the obedience of these Gentiles shows that they have an unwritten law in their hearts; it is not said that they perfectly obey the law and therefore have no sin — for Paul says immediately after (Rom. 3 : 9) — "we before laid to the charge both of Jews and Greeks, that they are all under sin."

So with regard to the words "perfect" and "upright," as applied to godly men. We shall see, when we come to consider the doctrine of Sanctification, that the word "perfect," as applied to spiritual conditions already attained, signifies only a relative perfection, equivalent to sincere piety or maturity of Christian judgment, in other words, the perfection of a sinner who has long trusted in Christ, and in whom Christ has overcome his chief defects of character. See 1 Cor. 2 : 6 — "we speak wisdom among the perfect" (Am. Rev.: "among them that are full-grown"); Phil. 3 : 15 — "Let us therefore, as many as are perfect, be thus minded " — i.e., to press toward the goal—a goal expressly said by the apostles to be not yet attained (v. 12-14).

"Est deus in nobis; agitante calescimus illo." God is the "spark that fires our clay." S. S. Times, Sept. 21, 1901 : 609 —" Humanity is better and worse than men have painted it. There has been a kind of theological pessimism in denouncing human sinfulness, which has been blind to the abounding love and patience and courage and fidelity to duty among men." A. H. Strong, Christ in Creation, 287-290 — "There is a natural life of Christ, and that life pulses and throbs in all men everywhere. All men are created in Christ, before they are recreated in him. The whole race lives, moves, and has its being in him, for he is the soul of its soul and the life of its life." To Christ then, and not to unaided human nature, we attribute the noble impulses of unregenerate men. These impulses are drawings of his Spirit, moving men to repentance. But they are influences of his grace which, if resisted, leave the soul in more than its original darkness.

2. *Proof from history, observation, and the common judgment of mankind.*

(a) History witnesses to the universality of sin, in its accounts of the universal prevalence of priesthood and sacrifice.

See references in Luthardt, Fund. Truths, 161-172, 335-339. Baptist Review, 1882:343 — "Plutarch speaks of the tear-stained eyes, the pallid and woe-begone countenances which he sees at the public altars, men rolling themselves in the mire and confessing their sins. Among the common people the dull feeling of guilt was too real to be shaken off or laughed away."

(b) Every man knows himself to have come short of moral perfection, and, in proportion to his experience of the world, recognizes the fact that every other man has come short of it also.

Chinese proverb : "There are but two good men ; one is dead, and the other is not yet born." Idaho proverb: "The only good Indian is a dead Indian." But the proverb applies to the white man also. Dr. Jacob Chamberlain, the missionary, said : "I never but once in India heard a man deny that he was a sinner. But once a Brahmin interrupted me and said : 'I deny your premisses. I am not a sinner. I do not need to do better.' For a moment I was abashed. Then I said : 'But what do your neighbors say?' Thereupon one cried out: 'He cheated me in trading horses'; another: 'He defrauded a widow of her inheritance.' The Brahmin went out of the house, and I never saw him again." A great nephew of Richard Brinsley Sheridan, Joseph Sheridan Le Fanu, when a child, wrote in a few lines an " Essay on the Life of Man," which ran as follows: " A man's life naturally divides itself into three distinct parts: the first when he is contriving and planning all kinds of villainy and rascality, — that is the period of youth and innocence. In the second, he is found putting in practice all the villainy and rascality he has contrived,— that is the flower of mankind and prime of life. The third and last period is that when he is making his soul and preparing for another world,— that is the period of dotage."

(c) The common judgment of mankind declares that there is an element of selfishness in every human heart, and that every man is prone to some form of sin. This common judgment is expressed in the maxims : "No man is perfect" ; "Every man has his weak side", or "his price" ; and every great name in literature has attested its truth.

Seneca, De Ira, 3:26 — " We are all wicked. What one blames in another he will find in his own bosom. We live among the wicked, ourselves being wicked " ; Ep., 22 — " No one has strength of himself to emerge [from this wickedness]; some one must needs hold forth a hand; some one must draw us out." Ovid, Met., 7 : 19 — " I see the things that are better and I approve them, yet I follow the worse . . . . We strive even after that which is forbidden, and we desire the things that are denied." Cicero : "Nature has given us faint sparks of knowledge; we extinguish them by our immoralities." Shakespeare, Othello, 3 : 3 — " Where's that palace whereinto foul things Sometimes intrude not? Who has a breast so pure, But some uncleanly apprehensions keep leets [meetings in court] and law-days, and in sessions sit With meditations lawful?" Henry VI., II : 3 : 3 — " Forbear to judge, for we are sinners all." Hamlet, 2 : 2, compares God's influence to the sun which "breeds maggots in a dead dog, Kissing carrion,"— that is, God is no more responsible for the corruption in man's heart and the evil that comes from it, than the sun is responsible for the maggots which its heat breeds in a dead dog ; 3 : 1 — " We are arrant knaves all." Timon of Athens, 1 : 2 — " Who lives that 's not depraved or depraves ? " Goethe : "I see no fault committed which I too might not have committed." Dr. Johnson : " Every man knows that of himself which he dare not tell to his dearest friend." Thackeray showed himself a master in fiction by having no heroes ; the paragons of virtue belonged to a cruder age of romance. So George Eliot represents life correctly by setting before us no perfect characters ; all act from mixed motives. Carlyle, hero-worshiper as he was inclined to be, is said to have become disgusted with each of his heroes before he finished his biography. Emerson said that to understand any crime, he had only to look into his own heart. Robert Burns : " God knows I 'm no thing I would be, Nor am I even the thing I could be." Huxley : " The best men of the best epochs are simply those who make the fewest blunders and commit the fewest sins." And he speaks of "the infinite wickedness" which has attended the course of human history. Matthew Arnold : " What mortal, when he saw, Life's voyage done, his heavenly Friend, Could ever yet dare tell him fearlessly :— I have kept uninfringed my nature's law: The inly written chart thou gavest me, to guide me, I have kept by to the end?" Walter Besant, Children of Gibeon: "The men of ability do not desire a system in which they shall not be able to do good to themselves first." "Ready to offer praise and prayer on Sunday, if on Monday they may go into the market place to skin their fellows and sell their hides." Yet Confucius declares that "man is born good." He confounds conscience with will — the *sense* of right with the *love* of right. Dean Swift's worthy sought many years for a method of extracting sunbeams from cucumbers. Human nature of itself is as little able to bear the fruits of God.

Every man will grant (1) that he is not perfect in moral character; (2) that love to God has not been the constant motive of his actions, *i. e.*, that he has been to some degree selfish; (3) that he has committed at least one known violation of conscience. Shedd, Sermons to the Natural Man, 86, 87 — "Those theorists who reject revealed religion, and remand man to the first principles of ethics and morality as the only religion that he needs, send him to a tribunal that damns him"; for it is simple fact that "no human creature, in any country or grade of civilization, has ever glorified God to the extent of his knowledge of God."

3.   *Proof from Christian experience.*

(*a*) In proportion to his spiritual progress does the Christian recognize evil dispositions within him, which but for divine grace might germinate and bring forth the most various forms of outward transgression.

See Goodwin's experience, in Baird, Elohim Revealed, 409; Goodwin, member of the Westminster Assembly of Divines, speaking of his conversion, says: "An abundant discovery was made to me of my inward lusts and concupiscence, and I was amazed to see with what greediness I had sought the gratification of every sin." Töllner's experience, in Martensen's Dogmatics: Töllner, though inclined to Pelagianism, says: "I look into my own heart and I see with penitent sorrow that I must in God's sight accuse myself of all the offences I have named," — and he had named only deliberate transgressions; — "he who does not allow that he is similarly guilty, let him look deep into his own heart." John Newton sees the murderer led to execution, and says: "There, but for the grace of God, goes John Newton." Count de Maistre: "I do not know what the heart of a villain may be — I only know that of a virtuous man, and that is frightful." Tholuck, on the fiftieth anniversary of his professorship at Halle, said to his students: "In review of God's manifold blessings, the thing I seem most to thank him for is the conviction of sin."

Roger Ascham: "By experience we find out a short way, by a long wandering." Luke 15:25-32 is sometimes referred to as indicating that there are some of God's children who never wander from the Father's house. But there were two prodigals in that family. The elder was a servant in spirit as well as the younger. J. J. Murphy, Nat. Selection and Spir. Freedom, 41, 42 — "In the wish of the elder son that he might sometimes feast with his own friends apart from his father, was contained the germ of that desire to escape the wholesome restraints of home which, in its full development, had brought his brother first to riotous living, and afterwards to the service of the stranger and the herding of swine. This root of sin is in us all, but in him it was not so full-grown as to bring death. Yet he says: 'Lo, these many years do I serve thee' (δουλεύω — as a bondservant), 'and I never transgressed a commandment of thine.' Are the father's commandments grievous? Is service true and sincere, without love from the heart? The elder brother was calculating toward his father and unsympathetic toward his brother." Sir J. R. Seelye, Ecce Homo: "No virtue can be safe, unless it is enthusiastic." Wordsworth: "Heaven rejects the love Of nicely calculated less or more."

(*b*) Since those most enlightened by the Holy Spirit recognize themselves as guilty of unnumbered violations of the divine law, the absence of any consciousness of sin on the part of unregenerate men must be regarded as proof that they are blinded by persistent transgression.

It is a remarkable fact that, while those who are enlightened by the Holy Spirit and who are actually overcoming their sins see more and more of the evil of their hearts and lives, those who are the slaves of sin see less and less of that evil, and often deny that they are sinners at all. Rousseau, in his Confessions, confesses sin in a spirit which itself needs to be confessed. He glosses over his vices, and magnifies his virtues. "No man,' he says, "can come to the throne of God and say: 'I am a better man than Rousseau.' . . . . Let the trumpet of the last judgment sound when it will: I will present myself before the Sovereign Judge with this book in my hand, and I will say aloud: 'Here is what I did, what I thought, and what I was.'" "Ah," said he, just before he expired, "how happy a thing it is to die, when one has no reason for remorse or self-reproach!" And then, addressing himself to the Almighty, he said: "Eternal Being, the soul that I am going to give thee back is as pure at this moment as it was when it proceeded from thee; render it a partaker of thy felicity!" Yet, in his boyhood, Rousseau was a petty thief. In his writings, he advocated adultery and suicide. He lived for more than twenty years in practical licentiousness. His children, most of whom, if not all, were illegitimate, he sent off to the foundling hospital as soon as they were born, thus casting them upon the charity of strangers, yet he inflamed the mothers of France with his eloquent appeals to them to nurse their own babies. He was mean, vacillating, treacherous, hypocritical, and blasphemous. And in his Confessions, he rehearses the exciting scenes of his life in the spirit of the bold adventurer. See N. M Williams, in Bap. Review, art.: Rousseau, from which the substance of the above is taken.

Edwin Forrest, when accused of being converted in a religious revival, wrote an indignant denial to the public press, saying that he had nothing to regret; his sins were those of omission rather than commission; he had always acted upon the principle of loving his friends and hating his enemies; and trusting in the justice as well as the mercy of God, he hoped, when he left this earthly sphere, to 'wrap the drapery of his couch about him, and lie down to pleasant dreams.' And yet no man of his time was more arrogant, self-sufficient, licentious, revengeful. John Y. McCane, when sentenced to Sing Sing prison for six years for violating the election laws by the most highhanded bribery and ballot-stuffing, declared that he had never done anything wrong in his life. He was a Sunday School Superintendent, moreover. A lady who lived to the age of 92, protested that, if she had her whole life to live over again, she would not alter a single thing. Lord Nelson, after he had received his death wound at Trafalgar, said: "I have never been a great sinner." Yet at that very time he was living in open adultery. Tennyson, Sea Dreams: "With all his conscience and one eye askew, So false, he partly took himself for true." Contrast the utterance of the apostle Paul: 1 Tim. 1:15 — "Christ Jesus came into the world to save sinners; of whom I am chief." It has been well said that "the greatest of sins is to be conscious of none." Rowland Hill: "The devil makes little of sin, that he may retain the sinner."

The following reasons may be suggested for men's unconsciousness of their sins: 1. We never know the force of any evil passion or principle within us, until we begin to resist it. 2. God's providential restraints upon sin have hitherto prevented its full development. 3. God's judgments against sin have not yet been made manifest. 4. Sin itself has a blinding influence upon the mind. 5. Only he who has been saved from the penalty of sin is willing to look into the abyss from which he has been rescued. — That a man is unconscious of any sin is therefore only proof that he is a great and hardened transgressor. This is also the most hopeless feature of his case, since for one who never realizes his sin there is no salvation. In the light of this truth, we see the amazing grace of God, not only in the gift of Christ to die for sinners, but in the gift of the Holy Spirit to convince men of their sins and to lead them to accept the Savior. Ps. 90:8 — "Thou hast set . . . Our secret sins in the light of thy countenance" = man's inner sinfulness is hidden from himself, until it is contrasted with the holiness of God. Light = a luminary or sun, which shines down into the depths of the heart and brings out its hidden evil into painful relief. See Julius Müller, Doctrine of Sin, 2:248-259; Edwards, Works, 2:326; John Caird, Reasons for Men's Unconsciousness of their Sins, in Sermons, 33.

II. Every member of the human race, without exception, posses-ses a corrupted nature, which is a source of actual sin, and is itself sin.

1. *Proof from Scripture.*

A. The sinful acts and dispositions of men are referred to, and explained by, a corrupt nature.

By 'nature' we mean that which is *born* in a man, that which he has by birth. That there is an inborn corrupt state, from which sinful acts and dispositions flow, is evident from Luke 6 : 43–45 — "there is no good tree that bringeth forth corrupt fruit. . . . . the evil man out of the evil treasure [of his heart] bringeth forth that which is evil "; Mat. 12 : 34 — " Ye offspring of vipers, how can ye, being evil, speak good things ?" Ps. 58 : 3 — "The wicked are estranged from the womb : They go astray as soon as they are born, speaking lies."

This corrupt nature (a) belongs to man from the first moment of his being ; (b) underlies man's consciousness ; (c) cannot be changed by man's own power ; (d) first constitutes him a sinner before God ; (e) is the common heritage of the race.

(a) Ps. 51 : 5 — " Behold, I was brought forth in iniquity ; And in sin did my mother conceive me " — here David is confessing, not his mother's sin, but his own sin ; and he declares that this sin goes back to the very moment of his conception. Tholuck, quoted by H. B. Smith, System, 281 — " David confesses that sin begins with the life of man ; that not only his works, but the man himself, is guilty before God." Shedd, Dogm. Theol., 2 : 94 — " David mentions the fact that he was born sinful, as an aggravation of his particular act of adultery, and not as an excuse for it." (b) Ps. 19 : 12 — " Who can discern his errors ? Clear thou me from hidden faults " ; 51 : 6, 7 — " Behold, thou desirest truth in the inward parts ; And in the hidden part thou wilt make me to know wisdom. Purify me with hyssop, and I shall be clean : Wash me, and I shall be whiter than snow." (c) Jer. 13 : 23 — " Can the Ethiopian change his skin, or the leopard his spots ? then may ye also do good, that are accustomed to do evil " ; Rom. 7 : 24 — " Wretched man that I am ! who shall deliver me out of the body of this death ? " (d) Ps. 51 : 6 — " Behold, thou desirest truth in the inward parts " ; Jer. 17 : 9 — " The heart is deceitful above all things and it is exceedingly corrupt : who can know it ? I, Jehovah, search the mind, I try the heart," — only God can fully know the native and incurable depravity of the human heart ; see Annotated Paragraph Bible, in loco. (e) Job 14 : 4 — " Who can bring a clean thing out of an unclean ? not one " ; John 3 : 6 — " That which is born of the flesh is flesh," i. e., human nature sundered from God. Pope, Theology, 2 : 53 — " Christ, who knew what was in man, says : 'If ye then, being evil' (Mat. 7 : 11), and ' That which is born of the flesh is flesh ' (John 3 : 6), that is — putting the two together — ' men are evil, because they are born evil.' "

Nathaniel Hawthorne's story of The Minister's Black Veil portrays the isolation of every man's deepest life, and the awe which any visible assertion of that isolation inspires. C. P. Cranch : " We are spirits clad in veils ; Man by man was never seen ; All our deep communing fails To remove the shadowy screen." In the heart of every one of us is that fearful " black drop," which the Koran says the angel showed to Mohammed. Sin is like the taint of scrofula in the blood, which shows itself in tumors, in consumption, in cancer, in manifold forms, but is everywhere the same organic evil. Byron spoke truly of " This ineradicable taint of sin, this boundless Upas, this all-blasting tree."

E. G. Robinson, Christ. Theol., 161, 162 — " The objection that conscience brings no charge of guilt against inborn depravity, however true it may be of the nature in its passive state, is seen, when the nature is roused to activity, to be unfounded. This faculty, on the contrary, lends support to the doctrine it is supposed to overthrow. When the conscience holds intelligent inquisition upon single acts, it soon discovers that these are mere accessories to crime, while the principal is hidden away beyond the reach of consciousness. In following up its inquisition, it in due time extorts the exclamation of David : Ps. 51 : 5 — ' Behold, I was brought forth in iniquity ; And in sin did my mother conceive me.' Conscience traces guilt to its seat in the inherited nature."

B. All men are declared to be by nature children of wrath (Eph. 2 : 3). Here ' nature ' signifies something inborn and original, as distinguished from that which is subsequently acquired. The text implies that : (a) Sin is a nature, in the sense of a congenital depravity of the will. (b) This nature is guilty and condemnable, — since God's wrath rests only upon that which deserves it. (c) All men participate in this nature and in this consequent guilt and condemnation.

Eph. 2 : 3 — "were by nature children of wrath, even as the rest." Shedd : " Nature here is not substance created by God, but corruption of that substance, which corruption is created by man." ' Nature ' (from nascor) may denote anything inborn, and the term may just as properly designate inborn evil tendencies and state, as inborn faculties or substance. " By nature " therefore = " by birth " ; compare Gal. 2 : 15 — " Jews by nature." E. G. Robinson : " Nature = not οὐσία, or essence, but only qualification of essence, as something born in us. There is just as much difference in babes, from the beginning of their existence, as there is in adults. If sin is defined as 'voluntary transgression of known law,' the definition of course disposes of original sin." But if sin is a selfish state of the will, such a state is demonstrably inborn. Aristotle speaks of some men as born to be savages (φύσει βάρβαροι), and of others as destined by nature to be slaves (φύσει δοῦλοι). Here evidently is a congenital aptitude and disposition. Similarily we can interpret Paul's words as declaring nothing less than that men are possessed at birth of an aptitude and disposition which is the object of God's just displeasure.

The opposite view can be found in Stevens, Pauline Theology, 152–157. Principal Fairbairn also says that inherited sinfulness " is *not* transgression, and is *without* guilt." Ritschl, Just. and Recon., 344—" The predicate ' children of wrath ' refers to the former actual transgression of those who now as Christians have the right to apply to themselves that divine purpose of grace which is the antithesis of wrath." Meyer interprets the verse : " We *become* children of wrath by following a natural propensity." He claims the doctrine of the apostle to be, that man incurs the divine wrath by his *actual* sin, when he submits his will to the inborn sin principle. So N. W. Taylor, Concic ad Clerum, quoted in H. B. Smith, System, 281 —" We were by nature such that we became through our own act children of wrath." " But," says Smith, " if the apostle had meant this, he could have said so ; there is a proper Greek word for 'became '; the word which is used can only be rendered 'were.'" So 1 Cor. 7 : 14 — " else were your children unclean "— implies that, apart from the operations of grace, all men are defiled in virtue of their very birth from a corrupt stock. Cloth is first died in the wool, and then dye' again after the weaving. Man is a " double-dyed villain." He is corrupted by nature and afterwards by practice. The colored physician in New Orleans advertised that his method was " first to remove the disease, and then to eradicate the system." The New School method of treating this text is of a similar sort. Beginning with a definition of sin which excludes from that category all inborn states of the will, it proceeds to vacate of their meaning the positive statements of Scripture.

For the proper interpretation of Eph. 2 : 3, see Julius Müller, Doct. of Sin, 2 : 278, and Commentaries of Harless and Olshausen. See also Philippi, Glaubenslehre, 3 : 212 *sq.*; Thomasius, Christi Person und Werk, 1 : 289 ; and an excellent note in the Expositor's Greek N. T., *in loco. Per contra*, see Reuss, Christ. Theol. in Apost. Age, 2 : 29, 79–84 ; Weiss, Bib. Theol. N. T., 239.

C. Death, the penalty of sin, is visited even upon those who have never exercised a personal and conscious choice (Rom. 5 : 12–14). This text implies that (*a*) Sin exists in the case of infants prior to moral consciousness, and therefore in the nature, as distinguished from the personal activity. (*b*) Since infants die, this visitation of the penalty of sin upon them marks the ill-desert of that nature which contains in itself, though undeveloped, the germs of actual transgression. (*c*) It is therefore certain that a sinful, guilty, and condemnable nature belongs to all mankind.

Rom. 5 : 12–14 — "Therefore, as through one man sin entered into the world, and death through sin ; and so death passed unto all men, for that all sinned : — for until the law sin was in the world ; but sin is not imputed when there is no law. Nevertheless death reigned from Adam until Moses, even over them that had not sinned after the likeness of Adam's transgression" — that is, over those who, like infants, had never personally and consciously sinned. See a more full treatment of these last words in connection with an exegesis of the whole passage — Rom. 5 : 12–19 — under Imputation of Sin, pages 625–627.

N. W. Taylor maintained that infants, prior to moral agency, are not subjects of the moral government of God, any more than are animals. In this he disagreed with Edwards, Bellamy, Hopkins, Dwight, Smalley, Griffin. See Tyler, Letters on N. E. Theol., 8, 132–142 — " To say that animals die, and therefore death can be no proof of sin in infants, is to take infidel ground. The infidel has just as good a right to say : Because animals die without being sinners, therefore adults may. If death may reign to such an alarming extent over the human race and yet be no proof of sin, then you adopt the principle that death may reign to any extent over the universe, yet never can be made a proof of sin in any case." We reserve our full proof that physical death is the penalty of sin to the section on Penalty as one of the Consequences of Sin.

2. *Proof from Reason.*

Three facts demand explanation : (*a*) The universal existence of sinful dispositions in every mind, and of sinful acts in every life. (*b*) The preponderating tendencies to evil, which necessitate the constant education of good impulses, while the bad grow of themselves. (*c*) The yielding of the will to temptation, and the actual violation of the divine law, in the case of every human being so soon as he reaches moral consciousness.

The fundamental selfishness of man is seen in childhood, when human nature acts itself out spontaneously. It is difficult to develop courtesy in children. There can be no true courtesy without regard for man as man and willingness to accord to each man his place and right as a son of God equal with ourselves. But children wish to please themselves without regard to others. The mother asks the child: "Why don't you do right instead of doing wrong?" and the child answers: "Because it makes me so tired," or "Because I do wrong without trying." Nothing runs itself, unless it is going down hill. "No other animal does things habitually that will injure and destroy it, and does them from the love of it. But man does this, and he is born to do it, he does it from birth. As the seedlings of the peach-tree are all peaches, not apples, and those of thorns are all thorns, not grapes, so all the descendants of man are born with evil in their natures. That sin continually comes back to us, like a dog or cat that has been driven away, proves that our hearts are its home."

Mrs. Humphrey Ward's novel, Robert Elsmere, represents the milk-and-water school of philanthropists. "Give man a chance," they say; "give him good example and favorable environment and he will turn out well. He is more sinned against than sinning. It is the outward presence of evil that drives men to evil courses." But God's indictment is found in Rom. 8:7 — "the mind of the flesh is enmity against God." G. P. Fisher: "Of the ideas of natural religion, Plato, Plutarch and Cicero found in the fact that they are in man's *reason*, but not obeyed and realized in man's *will*, the most convincing evidence that humanity is at schism with itself, and therefore depraved, fallen, and unable to deliver itself. The reason why many moralists fail and grow bitter and hateful is that they do not take account of this state of sin."

Reason seeks an underlying principle which will reduce these multitudinous phenomena to unity. As we are compelled to refer common physical and intellectual phenomena to a common physical and intellectual nature, so we are compelled to refer these common moral phenomena to a common moral nature, and to find in it the cause of this universal, spontaneous, and all-controlling opposition to God and his law. The only possible solution of the problem is this, that the common nature of mankind is corrupt, or, in other words, that the human will, prior to the single volitions of the individual, is turned away from God and supremely set upon self-gratification. This unconscious and fundamental direction of the will, as the source of actual sin, must itself be sin; and of this sin all mankind are partakers.

The greatest thinkers of the world have certified to the correctness of this conclusion. See Aristotle's doctrine of "the slope," described in Chase's Introduction to Aristotle's Ethics, xxxv and 32 — "In regard to moral virtue, man stands on a slope. His appetites and passions gravitate downward; his reason attracts him upward. Conflict occurs. A step upward, and reason gains what passion has lost; but the reverse is the case if he steps downward. The tendency in the former case is to the entire subjection of passion; in the latter case, to the entire suppression of reason. The slope will terminate upwards in a level summit where men's steps will be secure, or downwards in an irretrievable plunge over the precipice. Continual self-control leads to absolute self-mastery; continual failure, to the utter absence of self-control. But *all we can see is the slope*. No man is ever at the ἠρεμία or the summit, nor can we say that a man has irretrievably fallen into the abyss. How it is that men constantly act against their own convictions of what is right, and their previous determinations to follow right, is a mystery which Aristotle discusses, but leaves unexplained.

"Compare the passage in the Ethics, 1:11 — 'Clearly there is in them [men], besides the Reason, some other inborn principle (πεφυκός) which fights with and strains against the Reason .... There is in the soul also somewhat besides the Reason which is opposed to this and goes against it.'—Compare this passage with Paul, in Rom. 7:23—'I see a different law in my members, warring against the law of my mind, and bringing me into captivity under the law of sin which is in my members.' But as Aristotle does not explain the cause, so he suggests no cure. Revelation alone can account for the disease, or point out the remedy."

Wuttke, Christian Ethics, 1 : 102—"Aristotle makes the significant and almost surprising observation, that the character which has become evil by guilt can just as little be thrown off again at mere volition, as the person who has made himself sick by his own fault can become well again at mere volition ; once become evil or sick, it stands no longer within his discretion to cease to be so ; a stone, when once cast, cannot be caught back from its flight ; and so is it with the character that has become evil." He does not tell "how a reformation in character is possible,—moreover, he does not concede to evil any other than an individual effect,—knows nothing of any natural solidarity of evil in self-propagating, morally degenerated races" (Nic. Eth., 3 : 6, 7 ; 5 : 12 ; 7 : 2, 3 : 10 : 10). The good nature, he says, "is evidently not within our power, but is by some kind of divine causality conferred upon the truly happy."

Plato speaks of "that blind, many-headed wild beast of all that is evil within thee." He repudiates the idea that men are naturally good, and says that, if this were true, all that would be needed to make them holy would be to shut them up, from their earliest years, so that they might not be corrupted by others. Republic, 4 (Jowett's translation, 11 : 276)—" There is a rising up of part of the soul against the whole of the soul." Meno, 89—" The cause of corruption is from our parents, so that we never relinquish their evil way, or escape the blemish of their evil habit." Horace, Ep., 1 : 10—" Naturam expellas furca, tamen usque recurret." Latin proverb: "Nemo repente fuit turpissimus." Pascal : " We are born unrighteous ; for each one tends to himself, and the bent toward self is the beginning of all disorder." Kant, in his Metaphysical Principles of Human Morals, speaks of "the indwelling of an evil principle side by side with the good one, or the radical evil of human nature," and of " the contest between the good and the evil principles for the control of man." " Hegel, pantheist as he was, declared that original sin is the nature of every man,—every man begins with it" (H. B. Smith).

Shakespeare, Timon of Athens, 4 : 3—" All is oblique : There's nothing level in our cursed natures, But direct villainy." All's Well, 4 : 3—" As we are in ourselves, how weak we are ! Merely our own traitors." Measure for Measure, 1 : 2—" Orr natures do pursue, Like rats that ravin down their proper bane, A thirsty evil, and when we drink, we die." Hamlet, 3 : 1—" Virtue cannot so inoculate our old stock, but we shall relish of it." Love's Labor Lost, 1 : 1—" Every man with his affects is born, Not by might mastered, but by special grace." Winter's Tale, 1 : 2—" We should have answered Heaven boldly, Not guilty ; the imposition cleared Hereditary ours "—that is, provided our hereditary connection with Adam had not made us guilty. On the theology of Shakespeare, see A. H. Strong, Great Poets, 195-211—" If any think it irrational to believe in man's depravity, guilt, and need of supernatural redemption, they must also be prepared to say that Shakespeare did not understand human nature."

S. T. Coleridge, Omniana, at the end : "It is a fundamental article of Christianity that I am a fallen creature . . . . that an evil ground existed in my will, previously to any act or assignable moment of time in my consciousness ; I am born a child of wrath. This fearful mystery I pretend not to understand. I cannot even conceive the possibility of it ; but I know that it is so, ... and what is real must be possible." A sceptic who gave his children no religious training, with the view of letting them each in mature years choose a faith for himself, reproved Coleridge for letting his garden run to weeds ; but Coleridge replied, that he did not think it right to prejudice the soil in favor of roses and strawberries. Van Oosterzee : Rain and sunshine make weeds grow more quickly, but could not draw them out of the soil if the seeds did not lie there already ; so evil education and example draw out sin, but do not implant it. Tennyson, Two Voices : " He finds a baseness in his blood, At such strange war with what is good, He cannot do the thing he would." Robert Browning, Gold Hair : a Legend of Pornic : " The faith that launched point-blank her dart At the head of a lie—taught Original Sin, The corruption of Man's Heart." Taine, Ancien Régime : " Savage, brigand and madman each of us harbors, in repose or manacled, but always living, in the recesses of his own heart." Alexander Maclaren : " A great mass of knotted weeds growing in a stagnant pool is dragged toward you as you drag one filament." Draw out one sin, and it brings with it the whole matted nature of sin.

Chief Justice Thompson, of Pennsylvania : "If those who preach had been lawyers previous to entering the ministry, they would know and say far more about the depravity of the human heart than they do. The old doctrine of total depravity is the only thing that can explain the falsehoods, the dishonesties, the licentiousness, and the murders which are so rife in the world. Education, refinement, and even a high order of talent, cannot overcome the inclination to evil which exists in the heart, and has taken possession of the very fibres of our nature." See Edwards, Original Sin, in Works, 2 : 309-510; Julius Müller, Doct. Sin, 2 : 259-307; Hodge, Syst. Theol., 2 : 231-238; Shedd, Discourses and Essays, 226-236.

SECTION IV. — ORIGIN OF SIN IN THE PERSONAL ACT OF ADAM.

With regard to the origin of this sinful nature which is common to the race, and which is the occasion of all actual transgressions, reason affords no light. The Scriptures, however, refer the origin of this nature to that free act of our first parents by which they turned away from God, corrupted themselves, and brought themselves under the penalties of the law.

Chandler, Spirit of Man. 76 — "It is vain to attempt to sever the moral life of Christianity from the historical fact in which it is rooted. We may cordially assent to the assertion that the whole value of historical events is in their ideal significance. But in many cases, part of that which the idea signifies is the fact that it has been exhibited in history. The value and interest of the conquest of Greece over Persia lie in the significant idea of freedom and intelligence triumphing over despotic force; but surely a part, and a very important part, of the idea, is the fact that this triumph was won in a historical past, and the encouragement for the present which rests upon that fact. So too, the value of Christ's resurrection lies in its immense moral significance as a principle of life; but an essential part of that very significance is the fact that the principle was actually realized by One in whom mankind was summed up and expressed, and by whom, therefore, the power of realizing it is conferred on all who receive him."

As it is important for us to know that redemption is not only ideal but actual, so it is important for us to know that sin is not an inevitable accompaniment of human nature, but that it had a historical beginning. Yet no a priori theory should prejudice our examination of the facts. We would preface our consideration of the Scriptural account, therefore, by stating that our view of inspiration would permit us to regard that account as inspired, even if it were mythical or allegorical. As God can use all methods of literary composition, so he can use all methods of instructing mankind that are consistent with essential truth. George Adam Smith observes that the myths and legends of primitive folk-lore are the intellectual equivalents of later philosophies and theories of the universe, and that "at no time has revelation refused to employ such human conceptions for the investiture and conveyance of the higher spiritual truths." Sylvester Burnham: "Fiction and myth have not yet lost their value for the moral and religious teacher. What a knowledge of his own nature has shown man to be good for his own use, God surely may also have found to be good for his use. Nor would it of necessity affect the value of the Bible if the writer, in using for his purpose myth or fiction, supposed that he was using history. Only when the value of the truth of the teaching depends upon the historicity of the alleged fact, does it become impossible to use myth or fiction for the purpose of teaching." See vol. 1, page 241 of this work, with quotations from Denney, Studies in Theology, 218, and Gore, in Lux Mundi, 356. Euripides: "Thou God of all! infuse light into the souls of men, whereby they may be enabled to know what is the root from which all their evils spring, and by what means they may avoid them!"

I. THE SCRIPTURAL ACCOUNT OF THE TEMPTATION AND FALL IN GENESIS 3 : 1-7.

1. *Its general character not mythical or allegorical, but historical.*

We adopt this view for the following reasons : — (a) There is no intimation in the account itself that it is not historical. (b) As a part of a historical book, the presumption is that it is itself historical. (c) The later Scripture writers refer to it as a veritable history even in its details. (d) Particular features of the narrative, such as the placing of our first parents in a garden and the speaking of the tempter through a serpent-form, are incidents suitable to man's condition of innocent but untried childhood. (e) This view that the narrative is historical does not forbid our assuming that the trees of life and of knowledge were symbols of spiritual truths, while at the same time they were outward realities.

See John 8 : 44 — "Ye are of your father the devil, and the lusts of your father it is your will to do. He was a murderer from the beginning, and standeth not in the truth, because there is no truth in him. When he speaketh a lie, he speaketh of his own : for he is a liar and the father thereof"; 2 Cor. 11 : 3 — "the serpent beguiled Eve in his craftiness"; Rev. 20 : 2 — "the dragon, the old serpent, which is the Devil and Satan." H. B. Smith, System, 261 — "If Christ's temptation and victory over Satan were historical events, there seems to be no ground for supposing that the first temptation was not a historical event." We believe in the unity and sufficiency of Scripture. We moreover regard the testimony of Christ and the apostles as conclusive with regard to the historicity of the account in Genesis. We assume a divine superintendence in the choice of material by its author, and the fulfilment to the apostles of Christ's promise that they should be guided into the truth. Paul's doctrine of sin is so manifestly based upon the historical character of the Genesis story, that the denial of the one must naturally lead to the denial of the other. John Milton writes, in his Areopagitica: "It was from out of the rind of one apple tasted that the knowledge of good and evil, as two twins cleaving together, leaped forth into the world. And perhaps this is that doom which Adam fell into, that is to say, of knowing good by evil." He should have learned to know evil as God knows it — as a thing possible, hateful, and forever rejected. He actually learned to know evil as Satan knows it — by making it actual and matter of bitter experience.

Infantile and innocent man found his fit place and work in a garden. The language of appearances is doubtless used. Satan might enter into a brute-form, and might appear to speak through it. In all languages, the stories of brutes speaking show that such a temptation is congruous with the condition of early man. Asiatic myths agree in representing the serpent as the emblem of the spirit of evil. The tree of the knowledge of good and evil was the symbol of God's right of eminent domain, and indicated that all belonged to him. It is not necessary to suppose that it was known by this name before the Fall. By means of it man came to know good, by the loss of it; to know evil, by bitter experience; C. H. M.: "To know good, without the power to do it; to know evil, without the power to avoid it." Bible Com., 1 : 40 — The tree of life was symbol of the fact that "life is to be sought, not from within, from himself, in his own powers or faculties; but from that which is without him, even from him who hath life in himself."

As the water of baptism and the bread of the Lord's supper, though themselves common things, are symbolic of the greatest truths, so the tree of knowledge and the tree of life were sacramental. McIlvaine, Wisdom of Holy Scripture, 99–141 — "The two trees represented good and evil. The prohibition of the latter was a declaration that man of himself could not distinguish between good and evil, and must trust divine guidance. Satan urged man to discern between good and evil by his own wisdom, and so become independent of God. Sin is the attempt of the creature to exercise God's attribute of discerning and choosing between good and evil by his own wisdom. It is therefore self-conceit, self-trust, self-assertion, the preference of his own wisdom and will to the wisdom and will of God." McIlvaine refers to Lord Bacon, Works, 1 : 82, 162. See also Pope, Theology, 2 : 10, 11 ; Boston Lectures for 1871 : 80, 81.

Griffith-Jones, Ascent through Christ, 142, on the tree of the knowledge of good and evil — "When for the first time man stood face to face with definite conscious temptation to do that which he knew to be wrong, he held in his hand the fruit of that tree, and his destiny as a moral being hung trembling in the balance. And when for the first time he succumbed to temptation and faint dawnings of remorse visited his heart, at that moment he was banished from the Eden of innocence, in which his nature had hitherto dwelt, and he was driven forth from the presence of the Lord." With the first sin was started another and a downward course of development. For the mythical or allegorical explanation of the narrative, see also Hase, Hutterus Redivivus, 164, 165, and Nitzsch, Christian Doctrine, 218.

2. *The course of the temptation, and the resulting fall.*

The stages of the temptation appear to have been as follows :

(a) An appeal on the part of Satan to innocent appetites, together with an implied suggestion that God was arbitrarily withholding the means of their gratification (Gen. 3 : 1). The first sin was in Eve's isolating herself and choosing to seek her own pleasure without regard to God's will. This initial selfishness it was, which led her to listen to the tempter instead of rebuking him or flying from him, and to exaggerate the divine command in her response (Gen. 3 : 3).

Gen. 3 : 1 — "Yea, hath God said, Ye shall not eat of any tree of the garden?" Satan emphasizes the *limitation*, but is silent with regard to the generous *permission* — "Of every tree of the garden [but one] thou mayest freely eat" (2 : 16). C. H. M., *in loco:* "To admit the question 'hath God said?' is already positive infidelity. To add to God's word is as bad as to take from it. 'Hath God said?' is quickly followed by 'Ye shall not surely die.' Questioning whether God has spoken, results in open contradiction of what God has said. Eve suffered God's word to be contradicted by a creature, only because she had abjured its authority over her conscience and heart." The command was simply : "thou shalt not eat of it" (Gen. 2 : 17). In her rising dislike to the authority she had renounced, she exaggerates the command into : "Ye shall not eat of it, neither shall ye touch it" (Gen. 3 : 3). Here is already self-isolation, instead of love. Matheson, Messages of the Old Religions, 318 —" Ere ever the human soul disobeyed, it had learned to distrust. . . . Before it violated the existing law, it had come to think of the Lawgiver as one who was jealous of his creatures." Dr. C. H. Parkhurst: "The first question ever asked in human history was asked by the devil, and the interrogation point still has in it the trail of the serpent."

(b) A denial of the veracity of God, on the part of the tempter, with a charge against the Almighty of jealousy and fraud in keeping his creatures in a position of ignorance and dependence (Gen. 3 : 4, 5). This was followed, on the part of the woman, by positive unbelief, and by a conscious and presumptuous cherishing of desire for the forbidden fruit, as a means of independence and knowledge. Thus unbelief, pride, and lust all sprang from the self-isolating, self-seeking spirit, and fastened upon the means of gratifying it (Gen. 3 : 6).

Gen. 3 : 4, 5 — "And the serpent said unto the woman, Ye shall not surely die: for God doth know that in the day ye eat thereof, then your eyes shall be opened, and ye shall be as God, knowing good and evil " ; 3 : 6 — "And when the woman saw that the tree was good for food, and that it was a delight to the eyes, and that the tree was to be desired to make one wise, she took of the fruit thereof, and did eat ; and she gave also unto her husband with her, and he did eat" — so " taking the word of a Professor of Lying, that he does not lie" (John Henry Newman). Hooker, Eccl. Polity, book I — " To live by one man's will became the cause of all men's misery." Godet on John 1 : 4 —" In the words 'life' and 'light' it is natural to see an allusion to the tree of life and to that of knowledge. After having eaten of the former, man would have been called to feed on the second. John initiates us into the real essence of these primordial and mysterious facts and gives us in this verse, as it were, the philosophy of Paradise." Obedience is the way to knowledge, and the sin of Paradise was the seeking of light without life ; cf. John 7 : 17 — "If any man willeth to do his will, he shall know of the teaching, whether it is of God, or whether I speak from myself."

(c) The tempter needed no longer to urge his suit. Having poisoned the fountain, the stream would naturally be evil. Since the heart and its desires had become corrupt, the inward dispositition manifested itself in act (Gen. 3 : 6 — 'did eat ; and she gave also unto her husband with her'= who had been with her, and had shared her choice and longing). Thus man fell inwardly, before the outward act of eating the forbidden fruit,—fell in that one fundamental determination whereby he made supreme choice of self instead of God. This sin of the inmost nature gave rise to sins of the desires, and sins of the desires led to the outward act of transgression (James 1 : 15).

James 1: 15 — "Then the lust, whea it hath conceived, beareth sin." Bairú, Elohim Revealed, 388 — "The law of God had already been violated; man was fallen before the fruit had been plucked, or the rebellion had been thus signalized. The law required not only outward obedience but fealty of the heart, and this was withdrawn before any outward token indicated the change." Would he part company with God, or with his wife? When the Indian asked the missionary where his ancestors were, and was told that they were in hell, he replied that he would go with his ancestors. He preferred hell with his tribe to heaven with God. Sapphira, in like manner, had opportunity given her to part company with her husband, but she preferred him to God; Acts 5 : 7-11.

Philippi, Glaubenslehre: "So man became like God, a setter of law to himself. Man's self-elevation to godhood was his fall. God's self-humiliation to manhood was man's restoration and elevation. . . . Gen. 3 : 22 — 'The man has become as one of us' in his condition of self-centered activity,—thereby losing all real likeness to God, which consists in having the same aim with God himself. *De te fabula nar atur*; it is the condition, not of one alone, but of all the race." Sin once brought into being is self-propagating; its seed is in itself: the centuries of misery and crime that have followed have only shown what endless possibilities of evil were wrapped up in that single sin. Keble: "'T was but a little drop of sin We saw this morning enter in, And lo, at eventide a world is drowned!" Farrar, Fall of Man: "The guilty wish of one woman has swollen into the irremediable corruption of a world." See Oehler, O. T. Theology, 1 : 231; Müller, Doct. Sin, 2 : 381-385; Edwards, on Original Sin, part 4, chap. 2; Shedd, Dogm. Theol., 2 : 168-180.

II. DIFFICULTIES CONNECTED WITH THE FALL CONSIDERED AS THE PERSONAL ACT OF ADAM.

1. *How could a holy being fall?*

Here we must acknowledge that we cannot understand how the first unholy emotion could have found lodgment in a mind that was set supremely upon God, nor how temptation could have overcome a soul in which there were no unholy propensities to which it could appeal. The mere power of choice does not explain the fact of an unholy choice. The fact of natural desire for sensuous and intellectual gratification does not explain how this desire came to be inordinate. Nor does it throw light upon the matter, to resolve this fall into a deception of our first parents by Satan. Their yielding to such deception presupposes distrust of God and alienation from him. Satan's fall, moreover, since it must have been uncaused by temptation from without, is more difficult to explain than Adam's fall.

We may distinguish six incorrect explanations of the origin of sin: 1. Emmons: Sin is due to God's efficiency — God wrought the sin in man's heart. This is the "exercise system," and is essentially pantheistic. 2. Edwards: Sin is due to God's providence — God caused the sin indirectly by presenting motives. This explanation has all the difficulties of determinism. 3. Augustine: Sin is the result of God's withdrawal from man's soul. But inevitable sin is not sin, and the blame of it rests on God who withdrew the grace needed for obedience. 4. Pfleiderer: The fall results from man's already existing sinfulness. The fault then belongs, not to man, but to God who made man sinful. 5. Hadley: Sin is due to man's moral insanity. But such concreated ethical defect would render sin impossible. Insanity is the effect of sin, but not its cause. 6. Newman: Sin is due to man's weakness. It is a negative, not a positive, thing, an incident of finiteness. But conscience and Scripture testify that it is positive as well as negative, opposition to God as well as non-conformity to God.

Emmons was really a pantheist: "Since God," he says, "works in all men both to will and to do of his good pleasure, it is as easy to account for the first offence of Adam as for any other sin. . . . . There is no difficulty respecting the fall of Adam from his original state of perfection and purity into a state of sin and guilt, which is in any way peculiar. . . . . It is as consistent with the moral rectitude of the Deity to produce sinful as holy exercises in the minds of men. He puts forth a positive influence to make moral agents act, in every instance of their conduct, as he pleases. . . . . There is but one satisfactory answer to the question *Whence came evil?* and that is : It came from the great first Cause of all things " ; see Nathaniel Emmons, Works, 2 : 683.

Jonathan Edwards also denied power to the contrary even in Adam's first sin. God did not immediately cause that sin. But God was active in the region of motives though his action was not seen. Freedom of the Will, 161 — " It was fitting that the transaction should so take place that it might not appear to be from God as the apparent fountain." Yet " God may actually in his providence so dispose and permit things that the event may be certainly and infallibly connected with such disposal and permission "; see Allen, Jonathan Edwards, 304. Encyc. Britannica, 7 : 690 — " According to Edwards, Adam had two principles, — natural and supernatural. When Adam sinned, the super-natural or divine principle was withdrawn from him, and thus his nature became cor-rupt without God infusing any evil thing into it. His posterity came into being entirely under the government of natural and inferior principles. But this solves the difficulty of making God the author of sin only at the expense of denying to sin any real existence, and also destroys Edwards's essential distinction between natural and moral ability." Edwards on Trinity, Fisher's edition, 44 — " The sun does not cause darkness and cold, when these follow infallibly upon the withdrawal of his beams. God's disposing the result is not a positive exertion on his part." Shedd, Dogm. Theol., 2 : 50 — " God did not withdraw the common supporting grace of his Spirit from Adam until after transgression." To us Adam's act was irrational, but not impossible ; to a determinist like Edwards, who held that men simply act out their characters, Adam's act should have been not only irrational, but impossible. Edwards nowhere shows how, according to his principles, a holy being could possibly fall.

Pfleiderer, Grundriss, 123 — " The account of the fall is the first appearance of an already existing sinfulness, and a typical example of the way in which every individual becomes sinful. Original sin is simply the universality and originality of sin. There is no such thing as indeterminism. The will can lift itself from natural unfreedom, the unfreedom of the natural impulses, to real spiritual freedom, only by distinguishing itself from the law which sets before it its true end of being. The opposition of nature to the law reveals an original nature power which precedes all free self-determination. Sin is the evil bent of lawless self-willed selfishness." Pfleiderer appears to make this sinfulness concreated, and guiltless, because proceeding from God. Hill, Genetic Philosophy, 288 — " The wide discrepancy between precept and practice gives rise to the theological conception of *sin*, which, in low types of religion, is as often a violation of some trivial prescription as it is of an ethical principle. The presence of sin, contrasted with a state of innocence, occasions the idea of a fall, or lapse from a sinless condition. This is not incompatible with man's derivation from an animal ancestry, which prior to the rise of self-consciousness may be regarded as having been in a state of moral *innocence*, the sense and reality of sin being impossible to the animal. . . . . The exist-ence of sin, both as an inherent disposition, and as a perverted form of action, may be explained as a survival of animal propensity in human life. . . . . Sin is the disturbance of higher life by the intrusion of lower."

Professor James Hadley : " Every man is more or less insane." We prefer to say : Every man, so far as he is apart from God, is morally insane. But we must not make sin the result of insanity. Insanity is the result of sin. Insanity, moreover, is a physical disease, — sin is a perversion of the will. John Henry Newman, Idea of a University, 60 — " Evil has no substance of its own, but is only the defect, excess, perversion or corruption of that which has substance." Augustine seems at times to favor this view. He maintains that evil has no origin, inasmuch as it is negative, not positive ; that it is merely defect or failure. He illustrates it by the damaged state of a discordant harp ; see Moule, Outlines of Theology, 171. So too A. A. Hodge, Popular Lectures, 190, tells us that Adam's will was like a violin in tune, which through mere inattention and neglect got out of tune at last. But here, too, we must say with E. G. Robinson, Christ. Theology, 124 — " Sin explained is sin defended." All these explanations fail to explain, and throw the blame of sin upon God, as directly or indirectly its cause.

But sin is an existing fact. God cannot be its author, either by creating man's nature so that sin was a necessary incident of its development, or by withdrawing a supernatural grace which was necessary to keep man holy.

Reason, therefore, has no other recourse than to accept the Scripture doctrine that sin originated in man's free act of revolt from God — the act of a will which, though inclined toward God, was not yet confirmed in virtue and was still capable of a contrary choice. The original possession of such power to the contrary seems to be the necessary condition of probation and moral development. Yet the exercise of this power in a sinful direction can never be explained upon grounds of reason, since sin is essentially unreason. It is an act of wicked arbitrariness, the only motive of which is the desire to depart from God and to render self supreme.

Sin is a "mystery of lawlessness" (2 Thess. 2 : 7), at the beginning, as well as at the end. Neander, Planting and Training, 388 — " Whoever explains sin nullifies it." Man's power at the beginning to choose evil does not prove that, now that he has fallen, he has equal power of himself permanently to choose good. Because man has power to cast himself from the top of a precipice to the bottom, it does not follow that he has equal power to transport himself from the bottom to the top.

Man fell by wilful resistance to the inworking God. Christ is in all men as he was in Adam, and all good impulses are due to him. Since the Holy Spirit is the Christ within, all men are the subjects of his striving. He does not withdraw from them except upon, and in consequence of, their withdrawing from him. John Milton makes the Almighty say of Adam's sin: " Whose fault? Whose but his own? Ingrate, he had of me All he could have ; I made him just and right, Sufficient to have stood, though free to fall. Such I created all the Etherial Powers, And Spirits, both them who stood and them who failed ; Freely they stood who stood, and fell who failed." The word " cussedness " has become an apt word here. The Standard Dictionary defines it as " 1. Cursedness, meanness, perverseness ; 2. resolute courage, endurance: ' Jim Bludsoe's voice was heard, And they all had trust in his cussedness And knowed he would keep his word.' " (John Hay, Jim Bludsoe, stanza 6). Not the last, but the first, of these definitions best describes the first sin. The most thorough and satisfactory treatment of the fall of man ·in connection with the doctrine of evolution is found in Griffith-Jones, Ascent through Christ, 73–240.

Hodge, Essays and Reviews, 30 —" There is a broad difference between the commencement of holiness and the commencement of sin, and more is necessary for the former than for the latter. An act of obedience, if it is performed under the mere impulse of self-love, is virtually no act of obedience. It is not performed with any intention to obey, for that is holy, and cannot, according to the theory, precede the act. But an act of disobedience, performed from the desire of happiness, is rebellion. The cases are surely different. If, to please myself, I do what God commands, it is not holiness ; but if, to please myself, I do what he forbids, it is sin. Besides, no creature is immutable. Though created holy, the taste for holy enjoyments may be overcome by a temptation sufficiently insidious and powerful, and a selfish motive or feeling excited in the mind. Neither is a sinful character immutable. By the power of the Holy Spirit, the truth may be clearly presented and so effectually applied as to produce that change which is called regeneration ; that is, to call into existence a taste for holiness, so that it is chosen for its own sake, and not as a means of happiness."

H. B. Smith, System, 262 — " The state of the case, as far as we can enter into Adam's experience, is this: Before the command, there was the state of love without the thought of the opposite : a knowledge of good only, a yet unconscious goodness : there was also the knowledge that the eating of the fruit was against the divine command. The temptation aroused pride; the yielding to that was the sin. The change was there. The change was not in the choice as an executive act, nor in the result of that act — the eating ; but in the choice of supreme love to the world and self, rather than supreme devotion to God. It, was an immanent preference of the world, —not a love of the world following the choice, but a love of the world which is the choice itself."

263 —" We cannot account for Adam's fall, psychologically. In saying this we mean ; It is inexplicable by anything outside itself. We must receive the fact as ultimate, and rest there. Of course we do not mean that it was not in accordance with the laws of moral agency — that it was a violation of those laws: but only that we do not see the mode, that we cannot construct it for ourselves in a rational way. It differs from all other similar cases of ultimate preference which we know ; viz., the sinner's immanent preference of the world, where we know there is an antecedent ground in the bias to

sin, and the Christian's regeneration, or immanent preference of God, where we know there is an influence from without, the working of the Holy Spirit." 264 — " We must leave the whole question with the immanent preference standing forth as the ultimate fact in the case, which is not to be constructed philosophically, as far as the processes of Adam's soul are concerned: we must regard that immanent preference as both a choice and an affection, not an affection the result of a choice, not a choice which is the consequence of an affection, but both together."

In one particular, however, we must differ with H. B. Smith: Since the power of voluntary internal movement is the power of the will, we must regard the change from good to evil as primarily a choice, and only secondarily a state of affection caused thereby. Only by postulating a free and conscious act of transgression on the part of Adam, an act which bears to evil affection the relation not of effect but of cause, do we reach, at the beginning of human development, a proper basis for the responsibility and guilt of Adam and the race. See Shedd, Dogm. Theol., 2:148–167.

2. *How could God justly permit Satanic temptation?*

We see in this permission not justice but benevolence.

(*a*) Since Satan fell without external temptation, it is probable that man's trial would have been substantially the same, even though there had been no Satan to tempt him.

Angels had no animal nature to obscure the vision; they could not be influenced through sense; yet they were tempted and they fell. As Satan and Adam sinned under the best possible circumstances, we may conclude that the human race would have sinned with equal certainty. The only question at the time of their creation, therefore, was how to modify the conditions so as best to pave the way for repentance and pardon. These conditions are: 1. a material body — which means confinement, limitation, need of self-restraint; 2. infancy — which means development, deliberation, with no memory of the first sin; 3. the parental relation — repressing the wilfulness of the child, and teaching submission to authority.

(*b*) In this case, however, man's fall would perhaps have been without what now constitutes its single mitigating circumstance. Self-originated sin would have made man himself a Satan.

Mat. 13:28 — "An enemy hath done this." "God permitted Satan to divide the guilt with man, so that man might be saved from despair." See Trench, Studies in the Gospels, 16–29. Mason, Faith of the Gospel, 103 — "Why was not the tree made outwardly repulsive? Because only the abuse of that which was positively good and desirable could have attractiveness for Adam or could constitute a real temptation."

(*c*) As, in the conflict with temptation, it is an advantage to objectify evil under the image of corruptible flesh, so it is an advantage to meet it as embodied in a personal and seducing spirit.

Man's body, corruptible and perishable as it is, furnishes him with an illustration and reminder of the condition of soul to which sin has reduced him. The flesh, with its burdens and pains, is thus, under God, a help to the distinct recognition and overcoming of sin. So it was an advantage to man to have temptation confined to a single external voice. We may say of the influence of the tempter, as Birks, in his Difficulties of Belief, 101, says of the tree of the knowledge of good and evil: "Temptation did not depend upon the tree. Temptation was certain in any event. The tree was a type into which God contracted the possibilities of evil, so as to strip them of delusive vastness, and connect them with definite and palpable warning,— to show man that it was only one of the many possible activities of his spirit which was forbidden, that God had right to all and could forbid all." The originality of sin was the most fascinating element in it. It afforded boundless range for the imagination. Luther did well to throw his inkstand at the devil. It was an advantage to localize him. The concentration of the human powers upon a definite offer of evil helps our understanding of the evil and increases our disposition to resist it.

(*b*) Such temptation has in itself no tendency to lead the soul astray. If the soul be holy, temptation may only confirm it in virtue. Only the evil will, self-determined against God, can turn temptation into an occasion of ruin.

As the sun's heat has no tendency to wither the plant rooted in deep and moist soil, but only causes it to send down its roots the deeper and to fasten itself the more strongly, so temptation has in itself no tendency to pervert the soul. It was only the seeds that "fell upon the rocky places, where they had not much earth" (Mat. 13:5, 6), that "were scorched" when "the sun was risen"; and our Lord attributes their failure, not to the sun, but to their lack of root and of soil: "because they had no root," "because they had no deepness of earth." The same temptation which occasions the ruin of the false disciple stimulates to sturdy growth the virtue of the true Christian. Contrast with the temptation of Adam the temptation of Christ. Adam had everything to plead for God, the garden and its delights, while Christ had everything to plead against him, the wilderness and its privations. But Adam had confidence in Satan, while Christ had confidence in God; and the result was in the former case defeat, in the latter victory. See Baird, Elohim Revealed, 385-396.

C. H. Spurgeon: "All the sea outside a ship can do it no damage till the water enters and fills the hold. Hence, it is clear, our greatest danger is within. All the devils in hell and tempters on earth could do us no injury, if there were no corruption in our own natures. The sparks will fly harmlessly, if there is no tinder. Alas, our heart is our greatest enemy; this is the little home-born thief. Lord, save me from that evil man, myself!"

Lyman Abbott: "The scorn of goody-goody is justified; for goody-goody is innocence, not virtue; and the boy who never does anything wrong because he never does anything at all is of no use in the world. . . . . Sin is not a help in development; it is a hindrance. But temptation is a help; it is an indispensable means." E. G. Robinson, Christ. Theology, 123 — "Temptation in the bad sense and a fall from innocence were no more necessary to the perfection of the first man, than a marring of any one's character is now necessary to its completeness." John Milton, Areopagitica: "Many there be that complain of divine providence for suffering Adam to transgress. Foolish tongues! When God gave him reason, he gave him freedom to choose, for reason is but choosing; he had been else a mere artificial Adam, such an Adam as he is in the motions" (puppet shows). Robert Browning, Ring and the Book, 204 (Pope, 1183)— "Temptation sharp? Thank God a second time! Why comes temptation but for man to meet And master and make crouch beneath his foot, And so be pedestaled in triumph? Pray 'Lead us into no such temptations, Lord'? Yea, but, O thou whose servants are the bold, Lead such temptations by the head and hair, Reluctant dragons, up to who dares fight, That so he may do battle and have praise!"

3. *How could a penalty so great be justly connected with disobedience to so slight a command?*

To this question we may reply:

(*a*) So slight a command presented the best test of the spirit of obedience.

Cicero: "Parva res est, at magna culpa." The child's persistent disobedience in one single respect to the mother's command shows that in all his other acts of seeming obedience he does nothing for his mother's sake, but all for his own,—shows, in other words, that he does not possess the spirit of of obedience in a single act. S. S. Times: "Trifles are trifles only to triflers. Awake to the significance of the insignificant! for you are in a world that belongs not alone to the God of the infinite, but also to the God of the infinitesimal."

(*b*) The external command was not arbitrary or insignificant in its substance. It was a concrete presentation to the human will of God's claim to eminent domain or absolute ownership.

John Hall, Lectures on the Religious Use of Property, 10 — "It sometimes happens that owners of land, meaning to give the use of it to others, without alienating it, impose a nominal rent — a quit-rent, the passing of which acknowledges the recipient as owner and the occupier as tenant. This is understood in all lands. In many an old English deed, 'three barley-corns,' 'a fat capon,' or 'a shilling,' is the consideration which permanently recognizes the rights of lordship. God taught men by the forbidden tree that he was owner, that man was occupier. He selected the matter of property to be the test of man's obedience, the outward and sensible sign of a right state of heart toward God; and when man put forth his hand and did eat, he denied God's ownership and asserted his own. Nothing remained but to eject him."

(c) The sanction attached to the command shows that man was not left ignorant of its meaning or importance.

Gen. 2:17 — "in the day that thou eatest thereof thou shalt surely die." Cf. Gen. 3:3 — "the tree which is in the midst of the garden"; and see Dodge, Christian Theology, 206, 207 —"The tree was central, as the commandment was central. The choice was between the tree of life and the tree of death, — between self and God. Taking the one was rejecting the other."

(d) The act of disobedience was therefore the revelation of a will thoroughly corrupted and alienated from God — a will given over to ingratitude. unbelief, ambition, and rebellion.

The motive to disobedience was not appetite, but the ambition to be as God. The outward act of eating the forbidden fruit was only the thin edge of the wedge, behind which lay the whole mass — the fundamental determination to isolate self and to seek personal pleasure regardless of God and his law. So the man under conviction for sin commonly clings to some single passion or plan, only half-conscious of the fact that opposition to God in one thing is opposition in all.

III. CONSEQUENCES OF THE FALL, SO FAR AS RESPECTS ADAM.

1. *Death.* — This death was twofold. It was partly :

A. Physical death, or the separation of the soul from the body. — The seeds of death, naturally implanted in man's constitution, began to develop themselves the moment that access to the tree of life was denied him. Man from that moment was a dying creature.

In a true sense death began at once. To it belonged the pains which both man and woman should suffer in their appointed callings. The fact that man's earthly existence did not at once end, was due to God's counsel of redemption. "The law of the Spirit of life" (Rom. 8:2) began to work even then, and grace began to counteract the effects of the Fall. Christ has now "abolished death" (2 Tim. 1:10) by taking its terrors away, and by turning it into the portal of heaven. He will destroy it utterly (1 Cor. 15:26) when by resurrection from the dead, the bodies of the saints shall be made immortal. Dr. William A. Hammond, following a French scientist, declares that there is no reason in a normal physical system why man should not live forever.

That death is not a physical necessity is evident if we once remember that life is, not fuel, but fire. Weismann, Heredity, 8, 24, 72, 159—"The organism must not be looked upon as a heap of combustible material, which is completely reduced to ashes in a certain time, the length of which is determined by its size and by the rate at which it burns; but it should be compared to a fire, to which fresh fuel can be continually added, and which, whether it burns quickly or slowly, can be kept burning as long as necessity demands. . . . . Death is not a primary necessity, but it has been acquired secondarily, as an adaptation. . . . . Unicellular organisms, increasing by means of fission, in a certain sense possess immortality. No Amœba has ever lost an ancestor by death. . . . . Each individual now living is far older than mankind, and is almost as old as life itself. . . . . Death is not an essential attribute of living matter."

If we regard man as primarily spirit, the possibility of life without death is plain. God lives on eternally, and the future physical organism of the righteous will have in it no seed of death. Man might have been created without being mortal. That he is mortal is due to anticipated sin. Regard body as simply the constant energizing of God, and we see that there is no inherent necessity of death. Denney, Studies in Theology, 98 — "Man, it is said, must die because he is a natural being, and what belongs to nature belongs to him. But we assert, on the contrary, that he was created a supernatural being, with a primacy over nature, so related to God as to be immortal. Death is an intrusion. and it is finally to be abolished." Chandler, The Spirit of Man, 45-47 — "T first stage in the fall was the disintegration of spirit into body and mind; and the second was the enslavement of mind to body."

Some recent writers, however, deny that death is a consequence of the Fall, except in the sense that man's fear of death results from his sin. Newman Smyth, Place of Death in Evolution, 19-22, indeed, asserts the value and propriety of death as an element of the normal universe. He would oppose to the doctrine of Weismann the conclusions of Maupas, the French biologist, who has followed infusoria through 600 generations. Fission, says Maupas, reproduces for many generations, but the unicellular germ ultimately weakens and dies out. The asexual reproduction must be supplemented by a higher conjugation, the meeting and partial blending of the contents of two cells. This is only occasional, but it is necessary to the permanence of the species. Isolation is ultimate death. Newman Smyth adds that death and sex appear together. When sex enters to enrich and diversify life, all that will not take advantage of it dies out. Survival of the fittest is accompanied by death of that which will not improve. Death is a secondary thing — a consequence of life. A living form acquired the power of giving up its life for another. It died in order that its offspring might survive in a higher form. Death helps life on and up. It does not put a stop to life. It became an advantage to life as a whole that certain primitive forms should be left by the way to perish. We owe our human birth to death in nature. The earth before us has died that we might live. We are the living children of a world that has died for us. Death is a means of life, of increasing specialization of function. Some cells are born to give up their life sacrificially for the organism to which they belong.

While we regard Newman Smyth's view as an ingenious and valuable explanation of the incidental results of death, we do not regard it as an explanation of death's origin. God has overruled death for good, and we can assent to much of Dr. Smyth's exposition. But that this good could be gained only by death seems to us wholly unproved and unprovable. Biology shows us that other methods of reproduction are possible, and that death is an incident and not a primary requisite to development. We regard Dr. Smyth's theory as incompatible with the Scripture representations of death as the consequence of sin, as the sign of God's displeasure, as a means of discipline for the fallen, as destined to complete abolition when sin itself has been done away. We reserve, however, the full proof that physical death is part of the penalty of sin until we discuss the Consequences of Sin to Adam's Posterity.

But this death was also, and chiefly,

B. **Spiritual death, or the separation of the soul from God.** — In this are included : (*a*) Negatively, the loss of man's moral likeness to God, or that underlying tendency of his whole nature toward God which constituted his original righteousness. (*b*) Positively, the depraving of all those powers which, in their united action with reference to moral and religious truth, we call man's moral and religious nature ; or, in other words, the blinding of his intellect, the corruption of his affections, and the enslavement of his will.

Seeking to be a god, man became a slave ; seeking independence, he ceased to be master of himself. Once his intellect was pure, — he was supremely conscious of God, and saw all things else in God's light. Now he was supremely conscious of self, and saw all things as they affected self. This self-consciousness — how unlike the objective life of the first apostles, of Christ, and of every loving soul ! Once man's affections were pure, — he loved God supremely, and other things in subordination to God's will. Now he loved self supremely, and was ruled by inordinate affections toward the creatures which could minister to his selfish gratification. Now man could do nothing pleasing to God, because he lacked the love which is necessary to all true obedience.

G. F. Wilkin, Control in Evolution, shows that the will may initiate a counter-evolution which shall reverse the normal course of man's development. First comes an act, then a habit, of surrender to animalism ; then subversion of faith in the true and the good ; then active championship of evil ; then transmission of evil disposition and tendencies to posterity. This subversion of the rational will by an evil choice took place very early, indeed in the first man. All human history has been a conflict between these two antagonistic evolutions, the upward and the downward. Biological rather than moral phenomena predominate. No human being escapes transgressing the law of his evolutionary nature. There is a moral deadness and torpor resulting. The rational will must be restored before man can go right again. Man must commit himself to a true life; then to the restoration of other men to that same life; then there must be coöperation of society; this work must extend to the limits of the human species. But this will be practicable and rational only as it is shown that the unfolding plan of the universe has destined the righteous to a future incomparably more desirable than that of the wicked; in other words, immortality is necessary to evolution.

"If immortality be necessary to evolution, then immortality becomes scientific. Jesus has the authority and omnipresence of the power behind evolution. He imposes upon his followers the same normal evolutionary mission that sent him into the world. He organizes them into churches. He teaches a moral evolution of society through the united voluntary efforts of his followers. They are 'the good seed .... the sons of the kingdom' (Mat. 13:38). Theism makes a definite attempt to counteract the evil of the counter-evolution, and the attempt justifies itself by its results. Christianity is scientific (1) in that it satisfies the conditions of knowledge: the persisting and comprehensive harmony of phenomena, and the interpretation of all the facts: (2) in its aim, the moral regeneration of the world; (3) in its methods, adapting itself to man as an ethical being, capable of endless progress; (4) in its conception of normal society, as of sinners uniting together to help one another to depend on God and conquer self, so recognizing the ethical bond as the most essential. This doctrine harmonizes science and religion, revealing the new species of control which marks the highest stage of evolution; shows that the religion of the N. T. is essentially scientific and its truths capable of practical verification; that Christianity is not any particular church, but the teachings of the Bible; that Christianity is the true system of ethics, and should be taught in public institutions; that cosmic evolution comes at last to depend on the wisdom and will of man, the immanent God working in finite and redeemed humanity."

In fine, man no longer made God the end of his life, but chose self instead. While he retained the power of self-determination in subordinate things, he lost that freedom which consisted in the power of choosing God as his ultimate aim, and became fettered by a fundamental inclination of his will toward evil. The intuitions of the reason were abnormally obscured, since these intuitions, so far as they are concerned with moral and religious truth, are conditioned upon a right state of the affections; and — as a necessary result of this obscuring of reason — conscience, which, as the normal judiciary of the soul, decides upon the basis of the law given to it by reason, became perverse in its deliverances. Yet this inability to judge or act aright, since it was a moral inability springing ultimately from will, was itself hateful and condemnable.

See Philippi, Glaubenslehre, 3 : 61–73; Shedd, Sermons to the Natural Man, 202–230, esp. 205 — "Whatsoever springs from will we are responsible for. Man's inability to love God supremely results from his intense self-will and self-love, and therefore his impotence is a part and element of his sin, and not an excuse for it." And yet the question "Adam, where art thou?" (Gen. 3:9), says C. J. Baldwin, "was, (1) a question, not as to Adam's physical locality, but as to his moral condition; (2) a question, not of justice threatening, but of love inviting to repentance and return; (3) a question, not to Adam as an individual only, but to the whole humanity of which he was the representative."

Dale, Ephesians, 40 — "Christ is the eternal Son of God; and it was the first, the primeval purpose of the divine grace that his life and sonship should be shared by all mankind; that through Christ all men should rise to a loftier rank than that which belonged to them by their creation; should be 'partakers of the divine nature' (2 Pet. 1:4), and share the divine righteousness and joy. Or rather, the race was actually created in Christ; and it was created that the whole race might in Christ inherit the life and glory of God. The divine purpose has been thwarted and obstructed and partially defeated by human sin. But it is being fulfilled in all who are 'in Christ' (Eph. 1:3)."

2. *Positive and formal exclusion from God's presence.* — This included:

(a) The cessation of man's former familiar intercourse with God, and the setting up of outward barriers between man and his Maker (cherubim and sacrifice).

"In die Welt hinausgestossen, Steht der Mensch verlassen da." Though God punished Adam and Eve, he did not curse them as he did the serpent. Their exclusion from the tree of life was a matter of benevolence as well as of justice, for it prevented the immortality of sin.

(b) Banishment from the garden, where God had specially manifested his presence. — Eden was perhaps a spot reserved, as Adam's body had been, to show what a sinless world would be. This positive exclusion from God's presence, with the sorrow and pain which it involved, may have been intended to illustrate to man the nature of that eternal death from which he now needed to seek deliverance.

At the gates of Eden, there seems to have been a manifestation of God's presence, in the cherubim, which constituted the place a sanctuary. Both Cain and Abel brought offerings "unto the Lord" (Gen. 4:3, 4), and when Cain fled, he is said to have gone out "from the presence of the Lord" (Gen. 4:16). On the consequences of the Fall to Adam, see Edwards, Works, 2:390-405; Hopkins, Works, 1:206-246; Dwight, Theology, 1:393-434; Watson, Institutes, 2:19-42; Martensen, Dogmatics, 155-173; Van Oosterzee, Dogmatics, 402-412.

SECTION V. — IMPUTATION OF ADAM'S SIN TO HIS POSTERITY.

We have seen that all mankind are sinners ; that all men are by nature depraved, guilty, and condemnable ; and that the transgression of our first parents, so far as respects the human race, was the first sin. We have still to consider the connection between Adam's sin and the depravity, guilt, and condemnation of the race.

(a) The Scriptures teach that the transgression of our first parents constituted their posterity sinners (Rom. 5 : 19 — " through the one man's disobedience the many were made sinners "), so that Adam's sin is imputed, reckoned, or charged to every member of the race of which he was the germ and head (Rom. 5 : 16 — " the judgment came of one [offence] unto condemnation "). It is because of Adam's sin that we are born depraved and subject to God's penal inflictions (Rom. 5 : 12 — " through one man sin entered into the world, and death through sin " ; Eph. 2 : 3 — "by nature children of wrath "). Two questions demand answer, — first, how we can be responsible for a depraved nature which we did not personally and consciously originate ; and, secondly, how God can justly charge to our account the sin of the first father of the race. These questions are substantially the same, and the Scriptures intimate the true answer to the problem when they declare that " in Adam all die " (1 Cor. 15 : 22) and " that death passed unto all men, for that all sinned " when " through one man sin entered into the world " (Rom. 5 : 12). In other words, Adam's sin is the cause and ground of the depravity, guilt, and condemnation of all his posterity, simply because Adam and his posterity are one, and, by virtue of their organic unity, the sin of Adam is the sin of the race.

Amiel says that " the best measure of the profundity of any religious doctrine is given by its conception of sin and of the cure of sin." We have seen that sin is a state ; a state of the will ; a selfish state of the will ; a selfish state of the will inborn and universal ; a selfish state of the will inborn and universal by reason of man's free act.

Connecting the present discussion with the preceding doctrines of theology, the steps of our treatment thus far are as follows: 1. God's holiness is purity of nature. 2. God's law demands purity of nature. 3. Sin is impure nature. 4. All men have this impure nature. 5. Adam originated this impure nature. In the present section we expect to add: 6. Adam and we are one; and, in the succeeding section, to complete the doctrine with: 7. The guilt and penalty of Adam's sin are ours.

(b) According as we regard this twofold problem from the point of view of the abnormal human condition, or of the divine treatment of it, we may call it the problem of original sin, or the problem of imputation. Neither of these terms is objectionable when its meaning is defined. By imputation of sin we mean, not the arbitrary and mechanical charging to a man of that for which he is not naturally responsible, but the reckoning to a man of a guilt which is properly his own, whether by virtue of his individual acts, or by virtue of his connection with the race. By original sin we mean that participation in the common sin of the race with which God charges us, in virtue of our descent from Adam, its first father and head.

We should not permit our use of the term 'imputation' to be hindered or prejudiced by the fact that certain schools of theology, notably the Federal school, have attached to it an arbitrary, external, and mechanical meaning — holding that God imputes sin to men, not because they are sinners, but upon the ground of a legal fiction whereby Adam, without their consent, was made their representative. We shall see, on the contrary, that (1) in the case of Adam's sin imputed to us, (2) in the case of our sins imputed to Christ, and (3) in the case of Christ's righteousness imputed to the believer, there is always a realistic basis for the imputation, namely, a real union, (1) between Adam and his descendants, (2) between Christ and the race, and (3) between believers and Christ, such as gives in each case community of life, and enables us to say that God imputes to no man what does not properly belong to him.

Dr. E. G. Robinson used to say that "imputed righteousness and imputed sin are as absurd as any notion that ever took possession of human nature." He had in mind, however, only that constructive guilt and merit which was advocated by Princeton theologians. He did not mean to deny the imputation to men of that which is their own. He recognized the fact that all men are sinners by inheritance as well as by voluntary act, and he found this taught in Scripture, both in the O. T. and in the N. T.; e. g., Neh. 1:6 — "I confess the sins of the children of Israel, which we have sinned against thee. Yea, I and my father's house have sinned"; Jer. 3:25 — "Let us lie down in our shame, and let our confusion cover us; for we have sinned against Jehovah our God, we and our fathers"; 14:20 — "We acknowledge, O Jehovah, our wickedness, and the iniquity of our fathers; for we have sinned against thee." The word "imputed" is itself found in the N. T.; e. g., 2 Tim. 4:16 — "At my first defence no one took my part: may it not be laid to their account," or "imputed to them" — μὴ αὐτοῖς λογισθείη. Rom. 5:13 — "sin is not imputed when there is no law" — οὐκ ἐλλογᾶται.

Not only the saints of Scripture times, but modern saints also, have imputed to themselves the sins of others, of their people, of their times, of the whole world. Jonathan Edwards, Resolutions, quoted by Allen, 28 — "I will take it for granted that no one is so evil as myself; I will identify myself with all men and act as if their evil were my own, as if I had committed the same sins and had the same infirmities, so that the knowledge of their failings will promote in me nothing but a sense of shame." Frederick Denison Maurice: "I wish to confess the sins of the time as my own." Moberly, Atonement and Personality, 87 — "The phrase 'solidarity of humanity' is growing every day in depth and significance. Whatever we do, we do not for ourselves alone. It is not as an individual alone that I can be measured or judged." Royce, World and Individual, 2:404 — "The problem of evil indeed demands the presence of free will in the world; while, on the other hand, it is equally true that no moral world whatever can be made consistent with the realistic thesis according to which free will agents are, in fortune and in penalty, independent of the deeds of other moral agents. It follows that, in our moral world, the righteous can suffer without individually deserving their suffering, just because their lives have no independent being, but are linked with all life — God himself also sharing in their suffering."

The above quotations illustrate the belief in a human responsibility that goes beyond the bounds of personal sins. What this responsibility is, and what its limits are, we have yet to define. The problem is stated, but not solved, by A. H. Bradford, Heredity,

198, and The Age of Faith, 235 —" Stephen prays : 'Lord, lay not this sin to their charge' (Acts 7 : 60). To whose charge then ? We all have a share in one another's sins. We too stood by and consented, as Paul did. ' My sins gave sharpness to the nails, And pointed every thorn ' that pierced the brow of Jesus. . . . . Yet in England and Wales the severer forms of this teaching [with regard to sin] have almost disappeared; not because of more thorough study of the Scripture, but because the awful congestion of population, with its attendant miseries, has convinced the majority of Christian thinkers that the old interpretations were too small for the near and terrible facts of human life, such as women with babies in their arms at the London gin-shops giving the infants sips of liquor out of their glasses, and a tavern keeper setting his four or five year old boy upon the counter to drink and swear and fight in imitation of his elders."

(c) There are two fundamental principles which the Scriptures already cited seem clearly to substantiate, and which other Scriptures corroborate. The first is that man's relations to moral law extend beyond the sphere of conscious and actual transgression, and embrace those moral tendencies and qualities of his being which he has in common with every other member of the race. The second is, that God's moral government is a government which not only takes account of persons and personal acts, but also recognizes race responsibilities and inflicts race-penalties ; or, in other words, judges mankind, not simply as a collection of separate individuals, but also as an organic whole, which can collectively revolt from God and incur the curse of the violated law.

On race-responsibility, see H. B. Smith, System of Theology, 288–302 —" No one can apprehend the doctrine of original sin, nor the doctrine of redemption, who insists that the whole moral government of God has respect only to individual desert, who does not allow that the moral government of God, *as* moral, has a wider scope and larger relations, so that God may dispense suffering and happiness (in his all-wise and inscrutable providence) on other grounds than that of personal merit and demerit. The dilemma here is : the facts connected with native depravity and with the redemption through Christ either belong to the moral government of God, or not. If they do, then that government has to do with other considerations than those of personal merit and demerit (since our disabilities in consequence of sin and the grace offered in Christ are not in any sense the result of our personal choice, though we do choose in our relations to both). If they do not belong to the moral government of God, where shall we assign them ? To the physical ? That certainly can not be. To the divine sovereignty ? But that does not relieve any difficulty ; for the question still remains, Is that sovereignty, as thus exercised, just or unjust ? We must take one or the other of these. The whole (of sin and grace) is either a mystery of sovereignty — of mere omnipotence — or a proceeding of moral government. The question will arise with respect to grace as well as to sin : How can the theory that all moral government has respect only to the merit or demerit of personal acts be applied to our justification ? If all sin is in sinning, with a personal desert of everlasting death, by parity of reasoning all holiness must consist in a holy choice with personal merit of eternal life. We say then, generally, that all definitions of sin which mean *a* sin are irrelevant here." Dr. Smith quotes Edwards, 2 : 309 —" Original sin, the innate sinful depravity of the heart, includes not only the depravity of nature but the imputation of Adam's first sin, or, in other words, the liableness or exposedness of Adam's posterity, in the divine judgment, to partake of the punishment of that sin."

The watchword of a large class of theologians — popularly called " New School " — is that " all sin consists in sinning," — that is, all sin is sin of act. But we have seen that the dispositions and states in which a man is unlike God and his purity are also sin according to the meaning of the law. We have now to add that each man is responsible also for that sin of our first father in which the human race apostatized from God. In other words, we recognize the guilt of race-sin as well as of personal sin. We desire to say at the outset, however, that our view, and, as we believe, the Scriptural view, requires us also to hold to certain qualifications of the doctrine which to some extent alleviate its harshness and furnish its proper explanation. These qualifications we now proceed to mention.

(d) In recognizing the guilt of race-sin, we are to bear in mind: (1) that actual sin, in which the personal agent reaffirms the underlying determination of his will, is more guilty than original sin alone; (2) that no human being is finally condemned solely on account of original sin; but that all who, like infants, do not commit personal transgressions, are saved through the application of Christ's atonement; (3) that our responsibility for inborn evil dispositions, or for the depravity common to the race, can be maintained only upon the ground that this depravity was caused by an original and conscious act of free will, when the race revolted from God in Adam; (4) that the doctrine of original sin is only the ethical interpretation of biological facts — the facts of heredity and of universal congenital ills, which demand an ethical ground and explanation; and (5) that the idea of original sin has for its correlate the idea of original grace, or the abiding presence and operation of Christ, the immanent God, in every member of the race, in spite of his sin, to counteract the evil and to prepare the way, so far as man will permit, for individual and collective salvation.

Over against the maxim: "All sin consists in sinning," we put the more correct statement: Personal sin consists in sinning, but in Adam's first sinning the race also sinned, so that "in Adam all die" (1 Cor. 15: 22). Denney, Studies in Theology, 86 — "Sin is not only personal but social; not only social but organic; character and all that is involved in character are capable of being attributed not only to individuals but to societies, and eventually to the human race itself; in short, there are not only isolated sins and individual sinners, but what has been called a kingdom of sin upon earth." Leslie Stephen: "Man not dependent on a race is as meaningless a phrase as an apple that does not grow on a tree." "Yet Aaron Burr and Abraham Lincoln show how a man may throw away every advantage of the best heredity and environment, while another can triumph over the worst. Man does not take his character from external causes, but shapes it by his own willing submission to influences from beneath or from above."

Wm. Adams Brown: "The idea of inherited guilt can be accepted only if paralleled by the idea of inherited good. The consequences of sin have often been regarded as social, while the consequences of good have been regarded as only individual. But heredity transmits both good and evil." Mrs. Lydia Avery Coonley Ward: "Why bowest thou, O soul of mine, Crushed by ancestral sin? Thou hast a noble heritage, That bids thee victory win. The tainted past may bring forth flowers, As blossomed Aaron's rod: No legacy of sin annuls Heredity from God." For further statements with regard to race-responsibility, see Dorner, Glaubenslehre, 2:29-39 (System Doctrine, 2:324-333). For the modern view of the Fall, and its reconciliation with the doctrine of evolution, see J. H. Bernard, art.: The Fall, in Hastings' Dict. of Bible; A. H. Strong, Christ in Creation, 163-180; Griffith-Jones, Ascent through Christ.

(e) There is a race-sin, therefore, as well as a personal sin; and that race-sin was committed by the first father of the race, when he comprised the whole race in himself. All mankind since that time have been born in the state into which he fell — a state of depravity, guilt, and condemnation. To vindicate God's justice in imputing to us the sin of our first father, many theories have been devised, a part of which must be regarded as only attempts to evade the problem by denying the facts set before us in the Scriptures. Among these attempted explanations of the Scripture statements, we proceed to examine the six theories which seem most worthy of attention.

The first three of the theories which we discuss may be said to be evasions of the problem of original sin; all, in one form or another, deny that God imputes to all men Adam's sin, in such a sense that all are guilty for it. These theories are the Pelagian, the Arminian, and the New School. The last three of the theories which we are about to treat, namely, the Federal theory, the theory of Mediate Imputation, and the theory of Adam's Natural Headship, are all Old School theories, and have for their common characteristic that they assert the guilt of inborn depravity. All three, moreover, hold that we are in some way responsible for Adam's sin, though they differ as to the precise way in which we are related to Adam. We must grant that no one, even of these latter theories, is wholly satisfactory. We hope, however, to show that the last of them — the Augustinian theory, the theory of Adam's natural headship, the theory that Adam and his descendants are naturally and organically one — explains the largest number of facts, is least open to objection, and is most accordant with Scripture.

I. Theories of Imputation.

1. *The Pelagian Theory, or Theory of Man's natural Innocence.*

Pelagius, a British monk, propounded his doctrines at Rome, 409. They were condemned by the Council of Carthage, 418. Pelagianism, however, as opposed to Augustinianism, designates a complete scheme of doctrine with regard to sin, of which Pelagius was the most thorough representative, although every feature of it cannot be ascribed to his authorship. Socinians and Unitarians are the more modern advocates of this general scheme.

According to this theory, every human soul is immediately created by God, and created as innocent, as free from depraved tendencies, and as perfectly able to obey God, as Adam was at his creation. The only effect of Adam's sin upon his posterity is the effect of evil example ; it has in no way corrupted human nature ; the only corruption of human nature is that habit of sinning which each individual contracts by persistent transgression of known law.

Adam's sin therefore injured only himself ; the sin of Adam is imputed only to Adam, — it is imputed in no sense to his descendants ; God imputes to each of Adam's descendants only those acts of sin which he has personally and consciously committed. Men can be saved by the law as well as by the gospel ; and some have actually obeyed God perfectly, and have thus been saved. Physical death is therefore not the penalty of sin, but an original law of nature ; Adam would have died whether he had sinned or not ; in Rom. 5 : 12, "death passed unto all men, for that all sinned," signifies : "all incurred eternal death by sinning after Adam's example."

Wiggers, Augustinism and Pelagianism, 59, states the seven points of the Pelagian doctrine as follows : (1) Adam was created mortal, so that he would have died even if he had not sinned ; (2) Adam's sin injured, not the human race, but only himself ; (3) new-born infants are in the same condition as Adam before the Fall ; (4) the whole human race neither dies on account of Adam's sin, nor rises on account of Christ's resurrection ; (5) infants, even though not baptized, attain eternal life ; (6) the law is as good a means of salvation as the gospel ; (7) even before Christ some men lived who did not commit sin.

In Pelagius' Com. on Rom. 5 : 12, published in Jerome's Works, vol. xi, we learn who these sinless men were, namely, Abel, Enoch, Joseph, Job, and, among the heathen, Socrates, Aristides, Numa. The virtues of the heathen entitle them to reward. Their worthies were not indeed without evil thoughts and inclinations ; but, on the view of Pelagius that all sin consists in act, these evil thoughts and inclinations were not sin, "Non pleni nascimur" : we are born, not full, but vacant, of character. Holiness Pelagius thought, could not be concreated. Adam's descendants are not weaker, but stronger, than he ; since they have fulfilled many commands, while he did not fulfil so much as one. In every man there is a natural conscience ; he has an ideal of life ; he forms right resolves ; he recognizes the claims of law ; he accuses himself when he sins, — all these things Pelagius regards as indications of a certain holiness in all men, and misinterpretation of these facts gives rise to his system ; he ought to have seen in them evidences of a divine influence opposing man's bent to evil and leading him to repent.

ance. Grace, on the Pelagian theory, is simply the grace of *creation*—God's originally endowing man with his high powers of reason and will. While Augustinianism regards human nature as *dead*, and Semi-Pelagianism regards it as *sick*, Pelagianism proper declares it to be *well*.

Dorner, Glaubenslehre, 2 : 43 (Syst. Doct., 2 : 338)—" Neither the body, man's surroundings, nor the inward operation of God, have any determining influence upon the will. God reaches man only through external means, such as Christ's doctrine, example, and promise. This clears God of the charge of evil, but also takes from him the authorship of good. It is Deism, applied to man's nature. God cannot enter man's being if he would, and he would not if he could. Free will is everything." *Ib.*, 1 : 626 (Syst. Doct., 2 : 188, 189)—" Pelagianism at one time counts it too great an honor that man should be directly moved upon by God, and at another, too great a dishonor that man should not be able to do without God. In this inconsistent reasoning, it shows its desire to be rid of God as much as possible. The true conception of God requires a living relation to man, as well as to the external universe. The true conception of man requires satisfaction of his longings and powers by reception of impulses and strength from God. Pelagianism, in seeking for man a development only like that of nature, shows that its high estimate of man is only a delusive one; it really degrades him, by ignoring his true dignity and destiny." See *Ib.*, 1 : 124, 125 (Syst. Doct., 1 : 136, 137); 2 : 43-45 (Syst. Doct., 2 : 338, 339); 2 : 148 (Syst. Doct., 3 : 44). Also Schaff, Church History, 2 : 783-856; Doctrines of the Early Socinians, in Princeton Essays, 1 : 194-211; Wörter, Pelagianismus. For substantially Pelagian statements, see Sheldon, Sin and Redemption; Ellis, Half Century of Unitarian Controversy, 76.

Of the Pelagian theory of sin, we may say :

A. It has never been recognized as Scriptural, nor has it been formulated in confessions, by any branch of the Christian church. Held only sporadically and by individuals, it has ever been regarded by the church at large as heresy. This constitutes at least a presumption against its truth.

As slavery was " the sum of all villainy," so the Pelagian doctrine may be called the sum of all false doctrine. Pelagianism is a survival of paganism, in its majestic egoism and self-complacency. " Cicero, in his Natura Deorum, says that men thank the gods for external advantages, but no man ever thanks the gods for his virtues—that he is honest or pure or merciful. Pelagius was first roused to opposition by hearing a bishop in the public services of the church quote Augustine's prayer : ' Da quod jubes, et jube quod vis '—' Give what thou commandest, and command what thou wilt.' From this he was led to formulate the gospel according to St. Cicero, so perfectly does the Pelagian doctrine reproduce the Pagan teaching." The impulse of the Christian, on the other hand, is to refer all gifts and graces to a divine source in Christ and in the Holy Spirit. Eph. 2 : 10 —" For we are his workmanship, created in Christ Jesus for good works, which God afore prepared that we should walk in them "; John 15 : 16 —" Ye did not choose me, but I chose you "; 1 : 13 —" who were born, not of blood, nor of the will of the flesh, nor of the will of man, but of God." H. Auber : " And every virtue we possess, And every victory won, And every thought of holiness, Are his alone."

Augustine had said that " Man is most free when controlled by God alone"— "[Deo] solo dominante, liberrimus " (De Mor. Eccl., xxi). Gore, in Lux Mundi, 320— " In Christ humanity is perfect, because in him it retains no part of that false independence which, in all its manifold forms, is the secret of sin." Pelagianism, on the contrary, is man's declaration of independence. Harnack, Hist. Dogma, 5 : 200 —" The essence of Pelagianism, the key to its whole mode of thought, lies in this proposition of Julian : ' Homo libero arbitrio emancipatus a Deo '—man, created free, is in his whole being independent of God. He has no longer to do with God, but with himself alone. God reënters man's life only at the end, at the judgment,—a doctrine of the orphanage of humanity."

B. It contradicts Scripture in denying : (*a*) that evil disposition and state, as well as evil acts, are sin ; (*b*) that such evil disposition and state are inborn in all mankind ; (*c*) that men universally are guilty of overt transgression so soon as they come to moral consciousness ; (*d*) that no man is able without divine help to fulfil the law ; (*e*) that all men, without exception, are dependent for salvation upon God's atoning, regenerat-ing, sanctifying grace; (*f*) that man's present state of corruption, condemnation, and death, is the direct effect of Adam's transgression.

The Westminster Confession, ch. vi, ? 4, declares that "we are utterly indisposed, disabled, and made opposite to all good, and wholly inclined to all evil." To Pelagius, on the contrary, sin is a mere incident. He knows only of *sins*, not of *sin*. He holds the atomic, or atomistic, theory of sin, which regards it as consisting in isolated voli-tions. Pelagianism, holding, as it does, that virtue and vice consist only in single decis-ions, does not account for *character* at all. There is no such thing as a state of sin, or a self-propagating power of sin. And yet upon these the Scriptures lay greater emphasis than upon mere acts of transgression. John 3 : 6 — "That which is born of the flesh is flesh "—" that which comes of a sinful and guilty stock is itself, from the very beginning, sinful and guilty " (Dorner). Witness the tendency to degradation in families and nations.

Amiel says that the great defect of liberal Christianity is its superficial conception of sin. The tendency dates far back : Tertullian spoke of the soul as naturally Christian — "anima naturaliter Christiana." The tendency has come down to modern times : Crane, The Religion of To-morrow, 246 — "It is only when children grow up, and begin to absorb their environment, that they lose their artless loveliness." A Rochester Unitar-ian preacher publicly declared it to be as much a duty to believe in the natural purity of man, as to believe in the natural purity of God. Dr. Lyman Abbott speaks of "the shadow which the Manichæan theology of Augustine, borrowed by Calvin, cast upon all children, in declaring them born to an inheritance of wrath as a viper's brood." Dr. Abbott forgets that Augustine was the greatest opponent of Manichæanism, and that his doctrine of inherited guilt may be supplemented by a doctrine of inherited divine influences tending to salvation.

Prof. G. A. Coe tells us that "all children are within the household of God"; that "they are already members of his kingdom "; that "the adolescent change" is "a step not *into* the Christian life, but *within* the Christian life." We are taught that salvation is by education. But education is only a way of presenting truth. It still remains needful that the soul should accept the truth. Pelagianism ignores or denies the pres-ence in every child of a congenital selfishness which hinders acceptance of the truth, and which, without the working of the divine Spirit, will absolutely counteract the influence of the truth. Augustine was taught his guilt and helplessness by transgres-sion, while Pelagius remained ignorant of the evil of his own heart. Pelagius might have said with Wordsworth, Prelude, 534 — "I had approached, like other youths, the shield Of human nature from the golden side; And would have fought, even unto the death, to attest The quality of the metal which I saw."

Schaff, on the Pelagian controversy, in Bib. Sac., 5 : 205-243 — The controversy "resolves itself into the question whether redemption and sanctification are the work of man or of God. Pelagianism in its whole mode of thinking starts from man and seeks to work itself upward gradually, by means of an imaginary good-will, to holiness and communion with God. Augustinianism pursues the opposite way, deriving from God's unconditioned and all-working grace a new life and all power of working good. The first is led from freedom into a legal, self-righteous piety; the other rises from the slavery of sin to the glorious liberty of the children of God. For the first, revelation is of force only as an outward help, or the power of a high example; for the last, it is the inmost life, the very marrow and blood of the new man. The first involves an Ebion-itic view of Christ, as noble man, not high-priest or king; the second finds in him one in whom dwells all the fulness of the Godhead bodily. The first makes conversion a process of gradual moral purification on the ground of original nature; with the last, it is a total change, in which the old passes away and all becomes new. . . . Rationalism is simply the form in which Pelagianism becomes theoretically complete. The high opinion which the Pelagian holds of the natural will is transferred with equal right by the Rationalist to the natural reason. The one does without grace, as the other does without revelation. Pelagian divinity is rationalistic. Rationalistic morality is Pelagian." See this Compendium, page 89.

Allen, Religious Progress, 98-100 — "Most of the mischief of religious controversy springs from the desire and determination to impute to one's opponent positions which he does not hold, or to draw inferences from his principles, insisting that he shall be held responsible for them, even though he declares that he does not teach them. We say that he ought to accept them ; that he is bound logically to do so ; that they are necessary deductions from his system : that the tendency of his teaching is in these directions; and then we denounce and condemn him for what he disowns. It was in this way that Augustine filled out for Pelagius the gaps in his scheme, which he thought it necessary to do, in order to make Pelagius's teaching consistent and complete; and Pelagius, in his turn, drew inferences from the Augustinian theology, about which Augustine would have preferred to maintain a discreet silence. Neither Augustine nor Calvin was anxious to make prominent the doctrine of the reprobation of the wicked to damnation, but preferred to dwell on the more attractive, more rational tenet of the elect to salvation, as subjects of the divine choice and approbation; substituting for the obnoxious word reprobation the milder, euphemistic word preterition. It was their opponents who were bent on forcing them out of their reserve, pushing them into what seemed the consistent sequence of their attitude, and then holding it up before the world for execration. And the same remark would apply to almost every theological contention that has embittered the church's experience."

C. It rests upon false philosophical principles; as, for example: (*a*) that the human will is simply the faculty of volitions; whereas it is also, and chiefly, the faculty of self-determination to an ultimate end; (*b*) that the power of a contrary choice is essential to the existence of will; whereas the will fundamentally determined to self-gratification has this power only with respect to subordinate choices, and cannot by a single volition reverse its moral state; (*c*) that ability is the measure of obligation,—a principle which would diminish the sinner's responsibility, just in proportion to his progress in sin; (*d*) that law consists only in positive enactment; whereas it is the demand of perfect harmony with God, inwrought into man's moral nature; (*e*) that each human soul is immediately created by God, and holds no other relations to moral law than those which are individual; whereas all human souls are organically connected with each other, and together have a corporate relation to God's law, by virtue of their derivation from one common stock.

(*a*) Neander, Church History, 2 : 564–625, holds one of the fundamental principles of Pelagianism to be "the ability to choose, equally and at any moment, between good and evil." There is no recognition of the law by which acts produce states; the power which repeated acts of evil possess to give a definite character and tendency to the will itself.—"Volition is an everlasting 'tick,' 'tick,' and swinging of the pendulum, but no moving forward of the hands of the clock follows." "There is no continuity of moral life—no *character*, in man, angel, devil, or God."—(*b*) See art. on Power of Contrary Choice, in Princeton Essays, 1 : 212–233 : Pelagianism holds that no confirmation in holiness is possible. Thornwell, Theology : "The sinner is as free as the saint; the devil as the angel." Harris, Philos. Basis of Theism, 399 — "The theory that indifference is essential to freedom implies that will never acquires character; that voluntary action is atomistic, every act disintegrated from every other; that character, if acquired, would be incompatible with freedom." "By mere volition the soul now a *plenum* can become a *vacuum*, or now a *vacuum* can become a *plenum*." On the Pelagian view of freedom, see Julius Müller, Doctrine of Sin, 37–44.

(*e*) Ps. 79 : 8 — "Remember not against us the iniquities of our forefathers"; 106 : 6 — "We have sinned with our fathers." Notice the analogy of individuals who suffer from the effects of parental mistakes or of national transgression. Julius Müller, Doct. Sin, 2 : 316, 317 — "Neither the *atomistic* nor the *organic* view of human nature is the complete truth." Each must be complemented by the other. For statement of race-responsibility, see Dorner, Glaubenslehre, 2 : 30–39, 51–64, 161, 162 (System of Doctrine, 2 : 324–334, 345–359; 3 : 50–54) —"Among the Scripture proofs of the moral connection of the individual with the race are the visiting of the sins of the fathers upon the children; the obligation of the people to punish the sin of the individual, that the whole land may not incur guilt; the offering of sacrifice for a murder, the perpetrator of which is unknown. Achan's crime is charged to the whole people. The Jewish race is the better for its parentage, and other nations are the worse for theirs. The Hebrew people become a legal personality.

"Is it said that none are punished for the sins of their fathers unless they are like their fathers? But to be unlike their fathers requires a new heart. They who are not held accountable for the sins of their fathers are those who have recognized their responsibility for them, and have repented for their likeness to their ancestors. Only the self-isolating spirit says: 'Am I my brother's keeper?' (Gen. 4:9), and thinks to construct a constant equation between individual misfortune and individual sin. The calamities of the righteous led to an ethical conception of the relation of the individual to the community. Such sufferings show that men can love God disinterestedly, that the good has unselfish friends. These sufferings are substitutionary, when borne as belonging to the sufferer, not foreign to him, the guilt of others attaching to him by virtue of his national or race-relation to them. So Moses in Ex. 34:9, David in Ps. 51:6, Isaiah in Is. 59:9-16, recognize the connection between personal sin and race-sin.

"Christ restores the bond between man and his fellows, turns the hearts of the fathers to the children. He is the creator of a new race-consciousness. In him as the head we see ourselves bound to, and responsible for, others. Love finds it morally impossible to isolate itself. It restores the consciousness of unity and the recognition of common guilt. Does every man stand for himself in the N. T.? This would be so, only if each man became a sinner solely by free and conscious personal decision, either in the present, or in a past state of existence. But this is not Scriptural. Something comes before personal transgression: 'That which is born of the flesh is flesh' (John 3:6). Personality is the stronger for recognizing the race-sin. We have common joy in the victories of the good; so in shameful lapses we have sorrow. These are not our worst moments, but our best,— there is something great in them. Original sin must be displeasing to God; for it perverts the reason, destroys likeness to God, excludes from communion with God, makes redemption necessary, leads to actual sin, influences future generations. But to complain of God for permitting its propagation is to complain of his not destroying the race,— that is, to complain of one's own existence." See Shedd, Hist. Doctrine, 2:93-110; Hagenbach, Hist. Doctrine, 1:287, 296-310; Martensen, Dogmatics, 354-362; Princeton Essays, 1:74-97; Dabney, Theology, 296-302, 314, 315.

2. *The Arminian Theory, or Theory of voluntarily appropriated Depravity.*

Arminius (1560-1609), professor in the University of Leyden, in South Holland, while formally accepting the doctrine of the Adamic unity of the race propounded both by Luther and Calvin, gave a very different interpretation to it—an interpretation which verged toward Semi-Pelagianism and the anthropology of the Greek Church. The Methodist body is the modern representative of this view.

According to this theory, all men, as a divinely appointed sequence of Adam's transgression, are naturally destitute of original righteousness, and are exposed to misery and death. By virtue of the infirmity propagated from Adam to all his descendants, mankind are wholly unable without divine help perfectly to obey God or to attain eternal life. This inability, however, is physical and intellectual, but not voluntary. As matter of justice, therefore, God bestows upon each individual from the first dawn of consciousness a special influence of the Holy Spirit, which is sufficient to counteract the effect of the inherited depravity and to make obedience possible, provided the human will coöperates, which it still has power to do.

The evil tendency and state may be called sin; but they do not in themselves involve guilt or punishment; still less are mankind accounted guilty of Adam's sin. God imputes to each man his inborn tendencies to evil, only when he consciously and voluntarily appropriates and ratifies these in spite of the power to the contrary, which, in justice to man, God has specially communicated. In Rom. 5:12, "death passed unto all men, for that all sinned," signifies that physical and spiritual death is inflicted upon all men, not as the penalty of a common sin in Adam, but because, by divine decree, all suffer the consequences of that sin, and because all personally consent to their inborn sinfulness by acts of transgression.

See Arminius, Works, 1 : 252-254, 317-324, 325-327, 523-531, 575-583. The description given above is a description of Arminianism proper. The expressions of Arminius himself are so guarded that Moses Stuart (Bib. Repos., 1831) found it possible to construct an argument to prove that Arminius was not an Arminian. But it is plain that by inherited sin Arminius meant only inherited evil, and that it was not of a sort to justify God's condemnation. He denied any inbeing in Adam, such as made us justly chargeable with Adam's sin, except in the sense that we are obliged to endure certain consequences of it. This Shedd has shown in his History of Doctrine, 2 : 178-196. The system of Arminius was more fully expounded by Limborch and Episcopius. See Limborch, Theol. Christ., 3 : 4 : 6 (p. 189). The sin with which we are born " does not inhere in the soul, for this [soul] is immediately created by God, and therefore, if it were infected with sin, that sin would be from God." Many so-called Arminians, such as Whitby and John Taylor, were rather Pelagians.

John Wesley, however, greatly modified and improved the Arminian doctrine. Hodge, Syst. Theol., 2 : 329, 330 —" Wesleyanism (1) admits entire moral depravity ; (2) denies that men in this state have any power to coöperate with the grace of God ; (3) asserts that the guilt of all through Adam was removed by the justification of all through Christ; (4) ability to coöperate is of the Holy Spirit, through the universal influence of the redemption of Christ. The order of the decrees is (1) to permit the fall of man ; (2) to send the Son to be a full satisfaction for the sins of the whole world ; (3) on that ground to remit all original sin, and to give such grace as would enable all to attain eternal life ; (4) those who improve that grace and persevere to the end are ordained to be saved." We may add that Wesley made the bestowal upon our depraved nature of ability to coöperate with God to be a matter of grace, while Arminius regarded it as a matter of justice, man without it not being accountable.

Wesleyanism was systematized by Watson, who, in his Institutes, 2 : 53-55, 59, 77, although denying the imputation of Adam's sin in any proper sense, yet declares that " Limborch and others materially departed from the tenets of Arminius in denying inward lusts and tendencies to be sinful till complied with and augmented by the will. But men universally choose to ratify these tendencies ; therefore they are corrupt in heart. If there be a universal depravity of will previous to the actual choice, then it inevitably follows that though infants do not commit actual sin, yet that theirs is a sinful nature. . . . . As to infants, they are not indeed born justified and regenerate ; so that to say original sin is taken away, as to infants, by Christ, is not the correct view of the case, for the reasons before given ; but they are all born under ' the free gift,' the effects of the ' righteousness ' of one, which is extended to all men ; and this free gift is bestowed on them in order to justification of life, the adjudging of the condemned to live. . . . . Justification in adults is connected with repentance and faith ; in infants, we do not know how. The Holy Spirit may be given to children. Divine and effectual influence may be exerted on them, to cure the spiritual death and corrupt tendency of their nature."

It will be observed that Watson's Wesleyanism is much more near to Scripture than what we have described, and properly described, as Arminianism proper. Pope, in his Theology, follows Wesley and Watson, and (2 : 70-86) gives a valuable synopsis of the differences between Arminius and Wesley. Whedon and Raymond, in America, better represent original Arminianism. They hold that God was under *obligation* to restore man's ability, and yet they inconsistently speak of this ability as a *gracious* ability. Two passages from Raymond's Theology show the inconsistency of calling that " grace," which God is bound in justice to bestow, in order to make man responsible : 2 : 84-86 — " The race came into existence under grace. Existence and justification are secured for it only through Christ ; for, apart from Christ, punishment and destruction would have followed the first sin. So all gifts of the Spirit necessary to qualify him for the putting forth of free moral choices are secured for him through Christ. The Spirit of God is not a bystander, but a quickening power. So man is by grace, not by his fallen nature, a moral being capable of knowing, loving, obeying, and enjoying God. Such he ever will be, if he does not frustrate the grace of God. Not till the Spirit takes his final flight is he in a condition of total depravity."

Compare with this the following passage of the same work in which this " grace " is called a debt : 2 : 317 — " The relations of the posterity of Adam to God are substantially those of newly created beings. Each individual person is obligated to God, and

God to him, precisely the same as if God had created him such as he is. Ability must equal obligation. God was not obligated to provide a Redeemer for the first transgressors, but having provided Redemption for them, and through it having permitted them to propagate a degenerate race, an adequate compensation is due. The gracious influences of the Spirit are then a debt due to man—a compensation for the disabilities of inherited depravity." McClintock and Strong (Cyclopædia, art.: Arminius) endorse Whedon's art. in the Bib. Sac., 19 : 241, as an exhibition of Arminianism, and Whedon himself claims it to be such. See Hagenbach, Hist. Doct., 2 : 214-216.

With regard to the Arminian theory we remark :

A. We grant that there is a universal gift of the Holy Spirit, if by the Holy Spirit is meant the natural light of reason and conscience, and the manifold impulses to good which struggle against the evil of man's nature. But we regard as wholly unscriptural the assumptions : (*a*) that this gift of the Holy Spirit of itself removes the depravity or condemnation derived from Adam's fall ; (*b*) that without this gift man would not be responsible for being morally imperfect ; and (*c*) that at the beginning of moral life men consciously appropriate their inborn tendencies to evil.

John Wesley adduced in proof of universal grace the text : John 1 : 9 — "the light which lighteth every man " —which refers to the natural light of reason and conscience which the preincarnate Logos bestowed on all men, though in different degrees, before his coming in the flesh. This light can be called the Holy Spirit, because it was "the Spirit of Christ " (1 Pet. 1 : 11). The Arminian view has a large element of truth in its recognition of an influence of Christ, the immanent God, which mitigates the effects of the Fall and strives to prepare men for salvation. But Arminianism does not fully recognize the evil to be removed, and it therefore exaggerates the effect of this divine working. Universal grace does not remove man's depravity or man's condemnation ; as is evident from a proper interpretation of Rom. 5 : 12-19 and of Eph. 2 : 3 ; it only puts side by side with that depravity and condemnation influences and impulses which counteract the evil and urge the sinner to repentance : John 1 : 5 — "the light shineth in the darkness ; and the darkness apprehended it not." John Wesley also referred to Rom. 5 : 18 — "through one act of righteousness the free gift came unto all men to justification of life " —but here the "all men " is conterminous with "the many " who are "made righteous " in verse 19, and with the "all" who are "made alive " in 1 Cor. 15 : 22 ; in other words, the "all " in this case is "all believers " : else the passage teaches, not universal gift of the Spirit, but universal salvation.

Arminianism holds to inherited sin, in the sense of infirmity and evil tendency, but not to inherited guilt. John Wesley, however, by holding also that the giving of ability is a matter of grace and not of justice, seems to imply that there is a common guilt as well as a common sin, before consciousness. American Arminians are more logical, but less Scriptural. Sheldon, Syst. Christian Doctrine, 321, tells us that "guilt cannot possibly be a matter of inheritance, and consequently original sin can be affirmed of the posterity of Adam only in the sense of hereditary corruption, which first becomes an occasion of guilt when it is embraced by the will of the individual." How little the Arminian means by "sin," can be inferred from the saying of Bishop Simpson that "Christ inherited sin." He meant of course only physical and intellectual infirmity, without a tinge of guilt. "A child inherits its parent's nature," it is said, "not as a punishment, but by natural law." But we reply that this natural law is itself an expression of God's moral nature, and the inheritance of evil can be justified only upon the ground of a common non-conformity to God in both the parent and the child, or a participation of each member in the common guilt of the race.

In the light of our preceding treatment, we can estimate the element of good and the element of evil in Pfleiderer, Philos. Religion, 1 : 232 — "It is an exaggeration when original sin is considered as personally imputable guilt ; and it is going too far when it is held to be the whole state of the natural man, and yet the actually present good, the ' original grace,' is overlooked. . . . We may say, with Schleiermacher, that original sin is the common deed and common guilt of the human race. But the individual always participates in this collective guilt in the measure in which he takes part with his personal doing in the collective act that is directed to the furtherance of the bad." Dabney, Theology, 315, 316 —" Arminianism is orthodox as to the legal consequences of Adam's sin to his posterity ; but what it gives with one hand, it takes back with the other, attributing to grace the restoration of this natural ability lost by the Fall. If the effects of Adam's Fall on his posterity are such that they would have been unjust if not repaired by a redeeming plan that was to follow it, then God's act in providing a Redeemer was not an act of pure grace. He was under obligation to do some such thing,— salvation is not grace, but debt." A. J. Gordon, Ministry of the Spirit, 187 sq., denies the universal gift of the Spirit, quoting John 14 : 17 — " whom the world cannot receive; for it beholdeth him not, neither knoweth him " ; 16 : 7 — " if I go, I will send him unto you " ; i. e., Christ's disciples were to be the recipients and distributers of the Holy Spirit, and his church the mediator between the Spirit and the world. Therefore Mark 16 : 15 — " Go ye into all the world, and preach," implies that the Spirit shall go only with them. Conviction of the Spirit does not go beyond the church's evangelizing. But we reply that Gen. 6 : 3 implies a wider striving of the Holy Spirit.

B. It contradicts Scripture in maintaining : (*a*) that inherited moral evil does not involve guilt ; (*b*) that the gift of the Spirit, and the regeneration of infants, are matters of justice ; (*c*) that the effect of grace is simply to restore man's natural ability, instead of disposing him to use that ability aright ; (*d*) that election is God's choice of certain men to be saved upon the ground of their foreseen faith, instead of being God's choice to make certain men believers ; (*e*) that physical death is not the just penalty of sin, but is a matter of arbitrary decree.

(*a*) See Dorner, Glaubenslehre, 2 : 58 (System of Doctrine, 2 : 352-359) —" With Arminius, original sin is original *evil* only, not *guilt*. He explained the problem of original sin by denying the fact, and turning the native sinfulness into a morally indifferent thing. No sin without consent ; no consent at the beginning of human development ; therefore, no guilt in evil desire. This is the same as the Romanist doctrine of concupiscence, and like that leads to blaming God for an originally bad constitution of our nature. . . . Original sin is merely an enticement to evil addressed to the free will. All internal disorder and vitiosity is morally indifferent, and becomes sin only through appropriation by free will. But involuntary, loveless, proud thoughts are recognized in Scripture as sin ; yet they spring from the heart without our conscious consent. Undeliberate and deliberate sins run into each other, so that it is impossible to draw a line between them. The doctrine that there is no sin without consent implies power to withhold consent. But this contradicts the universal need of redemption and our observation that none have ever thus entirely withheld consent from sin."

(*b*) H. B. Smith's Review of Whedon on the Will, in Faith and Philosophy, 359-399 — "A child, upon the old view, needs only growth to make him guilty of actual sin ; whereas, upon this view, he needs growth and grace too." See Bib. Sac., 20 : 327, 328. According to Whedon, Com. on Rom. 5 : 12, " the condition of an infant apart from Christ is that of a sinner, *as one sure to sin*, yet never actually condemned before personal apostasy. This *would be* its condition, rather, for in Christ the infant is regenerate and justified and endowed with the Holy Spirit. Hence all actual sinners are apostates from a state of grace." But we ask : 1. Why then do infants die before they have committed actual sin ? Surely not on account of Adam's sin, for they are delivered from all the evils of that, through Christ. It must be because they are still somehow sinners. 2. How can we account for all infants sinning so soon as they begin morally to act, if, before they sin, they are in a state of grace and sanctification ? It must be because they were still somehow sinners. In other words, the universal regeneration and justification of infants contradict Scripture and observation.

(*c*) Notice that this " gracious " ability does not involve saving grace to the recipient, because it is given equally to all men. Nor is it more than a restoring to man of his natural ability lost by Adam's sin. It is not sufficient to explain why one man who has the gracious ability chooses God, while another who has the same gracious ability chooses self. 1 Cor. 4 : 7 — " who maketh thee to differ ? " Not God, but thyself. Over against this doctrine of Arminians, who hold to universal, resistible grace, restoring natural ability, Calvinists and Augustinians hold to particular, irresistible grace, giving moral ability, or, in other words, bestowing the disposition to use natural ability aright. " Grace " is a word much used by Arminians. Methodist Doctrine and Discipline, Articles of Religion, viii —" The condition of man after the fall of Adam is such that he cannot turn and prepare himself, by his own natural strength and works, to faith, and calling upon God : wherefore we have no power to do good works, pleasant and acceptable to God, without the grace of God by Christ preventing us, that we may have a good will, and working with us, when we have that good will." It is important to understand that, in Arminian usage, grace is simply the restoration of man's natural ability to act for himself: it never actually saves him, but only enables him to save himself—if he will. Arminian grace is evenly bestowed grace of spiritual endowment, as Pelagian grace is evenly bestowed grace of creation. It regards redemption as a compensation for innate and consequently irresponsible depravity.

(d) In the Arminian system, the order of salvation is, (1) faith—by an unrenewed but convicted man ; (2) justification ; (3) regeneration, or a holy heart. God decrees not to *originate* faith, but to *reward* it. Hence Wesleyans make faith a work, and regard election as God's ordaining those who, he foresees, will of their own accord believe. The Augustinian order, on the contrary, is (1) regeneration ; (2) faith ; (3) justification. Memoir of Adolph Saphir, 255 — " My objection to the Arminian or semi-Arminian is not that they make the entrance very wide ; but that they do not give you anything definite, safe and real, when you have entered. . . . Do not believe the devil's gospel, which is a *chance* of salvation : chance of salvation is chance of damnation." Grace is not a *reward* for good deeds done, but a *power* enabling us to do them. Francis Rous of Truro, in the Parliament of 1629, spoke as a man nearly frantic with horror at the increase of that "error of Arminianism which makes the grace of God lackey it after the will of man " ; see Masson, Life of Milton, 1 : 277. Arminian converts say : " I gave my heart to the Lord " ; Augustinian converts say : "The Holy Spirit convicted me of sin and renewed my heart." Arminianism tends to self-sufficiency ; Augustinianism promotes dependence upon God.

C. It rests upon false philosophical principles, as for example : (*a*) That the will is simply the faculty of volitions. (*b*) That the power of contrary choice, in the sense of power by a single act to reverse one's moral state, is essential to will. (*c*) That previous certainty of any given moral act is incompatible with its freedom. (*d*) That ability is the measure of obligation. (*e*) That law condemns only volitional transgression. (*f*) That man has no organic moral connection with the race.

(*b*) Raymond says : " Man is responsible for character, but only so far as that character is self-imposed. We are not responsible for character irrespective of its origin. Freedom *from* an act is as essential to responsibility as freedom *to* it. If power to the contrary is impossible, then freedom does not exist in God or man. Sin was a necessity, and God was the author of it." But this is a denial that there is any such thing as character ; that the will can give itself a bent which no single volition can change ; that the wicked man can become the slave of sin ; that Satan, though without power now in himself to turn to God, is yet responsible for his sin. The power of contrary choice which Adam had exists no longer in its entirety ; it is narrowed down to a power to the contrary in temporary and subordinate choices ; it no longer is equal to the work of changing the fundamental determination of the being to selfishness as an ultimate end. Yet for this very inability, because originated by will, man is responsible.

Julius Müller, Doctrine of Sin, 2 : 28 — " Formal freedom leads the way to real freedom. The starting-point is a freedom which does not yet involve an inner necessity, but the possibility of something else ; the goal is the freedom which is identical with necessity. The first is a means to the last. When the will has fully and truly chosen, the power of acting otherwise may still be said to exist in a metaphysical sense ; but morally, *i. e.*, with reference to the contrast of good and evil, it is entirely done away. Formal freedom is freedom of choice, in the sense of volition with the express consciousness of other possibilities." Real freedom is freedom to choose the good only, with no remaining possibility that evil will exert a counter attraction. But as the will can reach a "moral necessity " of good, so it can through sin reach a "moral necessity " of evil.

(*c*) Park : " The great philosophical objection to Arminianism is its denial of the *certainty* of human action — the idea that a man may act either way without certainty how he will act — power of a contrary choice in the sense of a moral indifference which can choose without motive, or contrary to the strongest motive. The New School view is better than this, for that holds to the certainty of wrong choice, while yet the soul has power to make a right one. . . . The Arminians believe that it is objectively uncertain whether a man shall act in this way or in that, right or wrong. There is nothing, antecedently to choice, to decide the choice. It was the whole aim of Edwards to refute the idea that man would not *certainly* sin. The old Calvinists believe that ante cedently to the Fall Adam was in this state of objective uncertainty, but that after the Fall it was certain he would sin, and his probation therefore was closed. Edwards affirms that no such objective uncertainty or power to the contrary ever existed, and that man now has all the liberty he ever had or could have. The truth in 'power to the contrary' is simply the power of the will to act contrary to the way it does act. President Edwards believed in this, though he is commonly understood as reasoning to the contrary. The false 'power to the contrary' is *uncertainty* how one will act, or a willingness to act otherwise than one does act. This is the Arminian power to the contrary, and it is this that Edwards opposes."

(*e*) Whedon, On the Will, 338-360, 388-395—" Prior to free volition, man may be unconformed to law, yet not a subject of retribution. The law has two offices, one judicatory and critical, the other retributive and penal. Hereditary evil may not be visited with retribution, as Adam's concreated purity was not meritorious. Passive, prevolitional holiness is moral rectitude, but not moral desert. Passive, prevolitional impurity needs concurrence of active will to make it condemnable."

D. It renders uncertain either the universality of sin or man's responsibility for it. If man has full power to refuse consent to inborn depravity, then the universality of sin and the universal need of a Savior are merely hypothetical. If sin, however, be universal, there must have been an absence of free consent ; and the objective certainty of man's sinning, according to the theory, destroys his responsibility.

Raymond, Syst. Theol., 2 : 86-89, holds it "theoretically possible that a child may be so trained and educated in the nurture and admonition of the Lord, as that he will never knowingly and willingly transgress the law of God; in which case he will certainly grow up into regeneration and final salvation. But it is grace that preserves him from sin — [common grace ?]. We do not know, either from experience or Scripture, that none have been free from known and wilful transgressions." J. J. Murphy, Nat. Selection and Spir. Freedom, 26-33— "It is possible to walk from the cradle to the grave, not indeed altogether without sin, but without any period of alienation from God, and with the heavenly life developing along with the earthly, as it did in Christ, from the first." But, since grace merely restores ability without giving the disposition to use that ability aright, Arminianism does not logically provide for the certain salvation of any infant. Calvinism can provide for the salvation of all dying in infancy, for it knows of a divine power to renew the will, but Arminianism knows of no such power, and so is furthest from a solution of the problem of infant salvation. See Julius Müller, Doct. Sin, 2 : 320-326 : Baird, Elohim Revealed, 479-494; Bib. Sac., 23 : 206; 28 : 279; Philippi, Glaubenslehre, 3 : 56 *sq.*

3. *The New School Theory, or Theory of uncondemnable Vitiosity.*

This theory is called New School, because of its recession from the old Puritan anthropology of which Edwards and Bellamy in the last century were the expounders. The New School theory is a general scheme built up by the successive labors of Hopkins, Emmons, Dwight, Taylor, and Finney. It is held at present by New School Presbyterians, and by the larger part of the Congregational body.

According to this theory, all men are born with a physical and moral constitution which predisposes them to sin, and all men do actually sin so soon as they come to moral consciousness. This vitiosity of nature may be called sinful, because it uniformly leads to sin ; but it is not itself sin, since nothing is to be properly denominated sin but the voluntary act of transgressing known law.

God imputes to men only their own acts of personal transgression ; he does not impute to them Adam's sin ; neither original vitiosity nor physical death are penal inflictions; they are simply consequences which God has in his sovereignty ordained to mark his displeasure at Adam's transgression, and subject to which evils God immediately creates each human soul. In Rom. 5 : 12, "death passed unto all men, for that all sinned," signifies: "spiritual death passed on all men, because all men have actually and personally sinned."

Edwards held that God imputes Adam's sin to his posterity by arbitrarily identifying them with him, — identity, on the theory of continuous creation (see pages 415-418), being only what God appoints. Since this did not furnish sufficient ground for imputation, Edwards joined the Placean doctrine to the other, and showed the justice of the condemnation by the fact that man is depraved. He adds, moreover, the consideration that man ratifies this depravity by his own act. So Edwards tried to combine three views. But all were vitiated by his doctrine of continuous creation, which logically made God the only cause in the universe, and left no freedom, guilt, or responsibility to man. He held that preservation is a continuous series of new divine volitions, personal identity consisting in consciousness or rather memory, with no necessity for identity of substance. He maintained that God could give to an absolutely new creation the consciousness of one just annihilated, and thereby the two would be identical. He maintained this not only as a possibility, but as the actual fact. See Lutheran Quarterly, April, 1901 : 149-169; and H. N. Gardiner, in Philos. Rev., Nov. 1900 : 573-596.

The idealistic philosophy of Edwards enables us to understand his conception of the relation of the race to Adam. He believed in "a real union between the root and the branches of the world of mankind, established by the author of the whole system of the universe . . . . the full consent of the hearts of Adam's posterity to the first apostasy . . . . and therefore the sin of the apostasy is not theirs merely because God imputes it to them, but it is truly and properly theirs, and *on that ground* God imputes it to them." Hagenbach, Hist. Doct., 2 : 435-448, esp. 436, quotes from Edwards: "The guilt a man has upon his soul at his first existence is one and simple, *viz.*: the guilt of the original apostasy, the guilt of the sin by which the species first rebelled against God." Interpret this by other words of Edwards: "The child and the acorn, which come into existence in the course of nature, are truly immediately created by God " — *i. e.*, continuously created (quoted by Dodge, Christian Theology, 188). Allen, Jonathan Edwards, 310 — "It required but a step from the principle that each individual has an identity of consciousness with Adam, to reach the conclusion that each individual *is* Adam and repeats his experience. Of every man it might be said that like Adam he comes into the world attended by the divine nature, and like him sins and falls. In this sense the sin of every man becomes original sin." Adam becomes not the head of humanity but its generic type. Hence arises the New School doctrine of exclusively individual sin and guilt.

Shedd, Hist. Doctrine, 2 : 25, claims Edwards as a Traducianist. But Fisher, Discussions, 240, shows that he was not. As we have seen (Prolegomena, pages 48, 49), Edwards thought too little of *nature*. He tended to Berkeleyanism as applied to mind. Hence the chief good was in happiness — a form of *sensibility*. Virtue is voluntary *choice* of this good. Hence union of *acts* and *exercises* with Adam was sufficient. This God's will might make identity of *being* with him. Baird, Elohim Revealed, 250 *sq.*, says well, that "Edwards's idea that the character of an act was to be sought somewhere else than in its cause involves the fallacious assumption that acts have a subsistence and moral agency of their own apart from that of the actor." This divergence from the truth led to the Exercise-system of Hopkins and Emmons, who not only denied moral character prior to individual choices (*i. e.*, denied sin of nature), but attributed all human acts and exercises to the direct efficiency of God. Hopkins declared that Adam's act, in eating the forbidden fruit, was not the act of his posterity; therefore they did not sin at the same time that he did. The sinfulness of that act could not be transferred to them afterwards; because the sinfulness of an act can no more be transferred from one person to another than an act itself. Therefore, though men became sinners by Adam, according to divine constitution, yet they have, and are accountable for, no sins but personal. See Woods, History of Andover Theological Seminary, 33. So the doctrine of continuous creation led to the Exercise-system, and the Exercise-system led to the theology of acts. On Emmons, see Works, 4 : 502-597, and Bib. Sac., 7 : 479; 20 : 317; also H. B. Smith, in Faith and Philosophy, 215-263.

N. W. Taylor, of New Haven, agreed with Hopkins and Emmons that there is no imputation of Adam's sin or of inborn depravity. He called that depravity physical, not moral. But he repudiated the doctrine of divine efficiency in the production of man's acts and exercises, and made all sin to be personal. He held to the power of contrary choice. Adam had it, and contrary to the belief of Augustinians, he never lost it. Man "not only can if he will, but he can if he won't." He can, but, without the Spirit, will not. He said: "Man can, whatever the Holy Spirit does or does not do"; but also: "Man will not, unless the Holy Spirit helps"; "If I were as eloquent as the Holy Ghost, I could convert sinners as fast as he." Yet he did not hold to the Arminian liberty of indifference or contingence. He believed in the certainty of wrong action, yet in power to the contrary. See Moral Government, 2 : 132—"The error of Pelagius was not in asserting that man *can* obey God without grace, but in saying that man does *actually* obey God without grace." There is a part of the sinner's nature to which the motives of the gospel may appeal—a part of his nature which is neither holy nor unholy, viz., self-love, or innocent desire for happiness. Greatest happiness is the ground of obligation. Under the influence of motives appealing to happiness, the sinner can suspend his choice of the world as his chief good, and can give his heart to God. He can do this, whatever the Holy Spirit does, or does not do; but the *moral* inability can be overcome only by the Holy Spirit, who moves the soul, without coercing, by means of the truth. On Dr. Taylor's system, and its connection with prior New England theology, see Fisher, Discussions, 285–354.

This form of New School doctrine suggests the following questions: 1. Can the sinner suspend his selfishness before he is subdued by divine grace? 2. Can his choice of God from mere self-love be a holy choice? 3. Since God demands love in every choice, must it not be a positively unholy choice? 4. If it is not itself a holy choice, how can it be a beginning of holiness? 5. If the sinner can become regenerate by preferring God on the ground of self-interest, where is the necessity of the Holy Spirit to renew the heart? 6. Does not this asserted ability of the sinner to turn to God contradict consciousness and Scripture? For Taylor's views, see his Revealed Theology, 134–309. For criticism of them, see Hodge, in Princeton Rev., Jan. 1868 : 63 *sq.*, and 368–398 ; also, Tyler, Letters on the New Haven Theology. Neither Hopkins and Emmons on the one hand, nor Taylor on the other, represent most fully the general course of New England theology. Smalley, Dwight, Woods, all held to more conservative views than Taylor, or than Finney, whose system had much resemblance to Taylor's. All three of these denied the power of contrary choice which Dr. Taylor so strenuously maintained, although all agreed with him in denying the imputation of Adam's sin or of our hereditary depravity. These are not sinful, except in the sense of being occasions of actual sin.

Dr. Park, of Andover, was understood to teach that the disordered state of the sensibilities and faculties with which we are born is the *immediate* occasion of sin, while Adam's transgression is the *remote* occasion of sin. The will, though influenced by an evil tendency, is still free ; the evil tendency itself is not free, and therefore is not sin. The statement of New School doctrine given in the text is intended to represent the common New England doctrine, as taught by Smalley, Dwight, Woods and Park ; although the historical tendency, even among these theologians, has been to emphasize less and less the depraved tendencies prior to actual sin, and to maintain that moral character begins only with individual choice, most of them, however, holding that this individual choice begins at birth. See Bib. Sac., 7 : 552, 567 ; 8 : 607–647 ; 20 : 462–471, 576–593 ; Van Oosterzee, Christian Dogmatics, 407–412 ; Foster, Hist. N. E. Theology.

Both Ritschl and Pfleiderer lean toward the New School interpretation of sin. Ritschl, Unterricht, 25—"Universal death was the consequence of the sin of the first man, and the death of his posterity proved that they too had sinned." Thus death is universal, not because of natural generation from Adam, but because of the individual sins of Adam's posterity. Pfleiderer, Grundriss, 122—"Sin is a direction of the will which contradicts the moral Idea. As preceding personal acts of the will, it is not personal guilt but imperfection or evil. When it persists in spite of awaking moral consciousness, and by indulgence become habit, it is guilty abnormity."

To the New School theory we object as follows :

A. It contradicts Scripture in maintaining or implying : (*a*) That sin consists solely in acts, and in the dispositions caused in each case by man's individual acts, and that the state which predisposes to acts of sin is not itself sin. (*b*) That the vitiosity which predisposes to sin is a part of each man's nature as it proceeds from the creative hand of God. (*c*) That physical death in the human race is not a penal consequence of Adam's transgression. (*d*) That infants, before moral consciousness, do not need Christ's sacrifice to save them. Since they are innocent, no penalty rests upon them, and none needs to be removed. (*e*) That we are neither condemned upon the ground of actual inbeing in Adam, nor justified upon the ground of actual inbeing in Christ.

If a child may not be unholy before he voluntarily transgresses, then, by parity of reasoning, Adam could not have been holy before he obeyed the law, nor can a change of heart precede Christian action. New School principles would compel us to assert that right action precedes change of heart, and that obedience in Adam must have preceded his holiness. Emmons held that, if children die before they become moral agents, it is most rational to conclude that they are annihilated. They are mere animals. The common New School doctrine would regard them as saved either on account of their innocence, or because the atonement of Christ avails to remove the *consequences* as well as the *penalty* of sin.

But to say that infants are pure contradicts Rom. 5 : 12 —"all sinned " ; 1 Cor. 7 : 14 — " else were your children unclean " ; Eph. 2 : 3 — " by nature children of wrath." That Christ's atonement removes natural consequences of sin is nowhere asserted or implied in Scripture. See, *per contra*, H. B. Smith, System, 271, where, however, it is only maintained that Christ saves from all the *just* consequences of sin. But all *just* consequences are penalty, and should be so called. The exigencies of New School doctrine compel it to put the beginning of sin in the infant at the very first moment of its separate existence,— in order not to contradict those Scriptures which speak of sin as being universal, and of the atonement as being needed by all. Dr. Park held that infants sin so soon as they are born. He was obliged to hold this, or else to say that some members of the human race exist who are not sinners. But by putting sin thus early in human experience, all meaning is taken out of the New School definition of sin as the " voluntary transgression of known law." It is difficult to say, upon this theory, what sort of a *choice* the infant makes of sin, or what sort of a *known law* it violates.

The first need in a theory of sin is that of satisfying the statements of Scripture. The second need is that it should point out an act of man which will justify the infliction of pain, suffering, and death upon the whole human race. Our moral sense refuses to accept the conclusion that all this is a matter of arbitrary sovereignty. We cannot find the act in each man's conscious transgression, nor in sin committed at birth. We do find such a voluntary transgression of known law in Adam ; and we claim that the New School definition of sin is much more consistent with this last explanation of sin's origin than is the theory of a multitude of individual transgressions.

The final test of every theory, however, is its conformity to Scripture. We claim that a false philosophy prevents the advocates of New School doctrine from understanding the utterances of Paul. Their philosophy is a modified survival of atomistic Pelagianism. They ignore nature in both God and man, and resolve character into transient acts. The unconscious or subconscious state of the will they take little or no account of, and the possibility of another and higher life interpenetrating and transforming our own life is seldom present to their minds. They have no proper idea of the union of the believer with Christ, and so they have no proper idea of the union of the race with Adam. They need to learn that, as all the spiritual life of the race was in Christ, the second Adam, so all the natural life of the race was in the first Adam ; as we derive righteousness from the former, so we derive corruption from the latter. Because Christ's life is in them, Paul can say that all believers rose in Christ's resurrection ; because Adam's life is in them, he can say that in Adam all die. We should prefer to say with Pfleiderer that Paul teaches this doctrine but that Paul is no authority for us, rather than to profess acceptance of Paul's teaching while we ingeniously evade the force of his argument. We agree with Stevens, Pauline Theology, 135, 136, that all men "sinned in the same sense in which believers were crucified to the world and died unto sin when Christ died upon the cross." But we protest that to make Christ's death the mere *occasion* of the death of the believer, and Adam's sin the mere *occasion* of the sins of men, is to ignore the central truths of Paul's teaching — the *vital union* of the believer with Christ, and the *vital union* of the race with Adam.

B. It rests upon false philosophical principles, as for example : (*a*) That the soul is immediately created by God. (*b*) That the law of God consists wholly in outward command. (c) That present natural ability to obey the law is the measure of obligation. (d) That man's relations to moral law are exclusively individual. (e) That the will is merely the faculty of individual and personal choices. (f) That the will, at man's birth, has no moral state or character.

See Baird, Elohim Revealed, 250 *sq.*—" Personality is inseparable from nature. The one duty is love. Unless any given duty is performed through the activity of a principle of love springing up in the nature, it is not performed at all. *The law addresses the nature.* The efficient cause of moral action is the proper subject of moral law. It is only in the perversity of unscriptural theology that we find the absurdity of separating the moral character from the substance of the soul, and tying it to the vanishing deeds of life. The idea that responsibility and sin are predicable of actions merely is only consistent with an utter denial that man's nature as such owes anything to God, or has an office to perform in showing forth his glory. It ignores the fact that actions are empty phenomena, which in themselves have no possible value. It is the heart, soul, might, mind, strength, with which we are to love. Christ conformed to the law, by being 'that holy thing' (Luke 1:35, marg.)."

Erroneous philosophical principles lie at the basis of New School interpretations of Scripture. The solidarity of the race is ignored, and all moral action is held to be individual. In our discussion of the Augustinian theory of sin, we shall hope to show that underlying Paul's doctrine there is quite another philosophy. Such a philosophy together with a deeper Christian experience would have corrected the following statement of Paul's view of sin, by Orello Cone, in Am. Jour. Theology, April, 1898 : 241-267. On the phrase Rom. 5:12 — "for that all sinned," he remarks: "If under the new order men do not become righteous simply because of the righteousness of Christ and without their choice, neither under the old order did Paul think them to be subject to death without their own acts of sin. Each representative head is conceived only as the occasion of the results of his work, on the one hand in the tragic order of death, and on the other hand in the blessed order of life—the occasion indispensable to all that follows in either order. . . . It may be questioned whether Pfleiderer does not state the case too strongly when he says that the sin of Adam's posterity is regarded as 'the necessary consequence' of the sin of Adam. It does not follow from the employment of the aorist ἥμαρτον that the sinning of all is contained in that of Adam, although this sense must be considered as grammatically possible. It is not however the only grammatically defensible sense. In Rom. 3:23, ἥμαρτον certainly does not denote such a definite past act filling only one point of time." But we reply that the context determines that in Rom. 5:12, ἥμαρτον *does* denote such a definite past act; see our interpretation of the whole passage, under the Augustinian Theory, pages 625-627.

C. It impugns the justice of God :

(a) By regarding him as the direct creator of a vicious nature which infallibly leads every human being into actual transgression. To maintain that, in consequence of Adam's act, God brings it about that all men become sinners, and this, not by virtue of inherent laws of propagation, but by the direct creation in each case of a vicious nature, is to make God indirectly the author of sin.

(b) By representing him as the inflicter of suffering and death upon millions of human beings who in the present life do not come to moral consciousness, and who are therefore, according to the theory, perfectly innocent. This is to make him visit Adam's sin on his posterity, while at the same time it denies that moral connection between Adam and his posterity which alone could make such visitation just.

(c) By holding that the probation which God appoints to men is a separate probation of each soul, when it first comes to moral consciousness and is least qualified to decide aright. It is much more consonant with our ideas of the divine justice that the decision should have been made by the whole race, in one whose nature was pure and who perfectly understood God's law, than that heaven and hell should have been determined for each of us by a decision made in our own inexperienced childhood, under the influence of a vitiated nature.

On this theory, God determines, in his mere sovereignty, that because one man sinned, all men should be called into existence depraved, under a constitution which secures the certainty of their sinning. But we claim that it is unjust that any should suffer without ill-desert. To say that God thus marks his sense of the guilt of Adam's sin is to contradict the main principle of the theory, namely, that men are held responsible only for their own sins. We prefer to justify God by holding that there is a reason for this infliction, and that this reason is the connection of the infant with Adam. If mere tendency to sin is innocent, then Christ might have taken it, when he took our nature. But if he had taken it, it would not explain the fact of the atonement, for upon this theory it would not need to be atoned for. To say that the child inherits a sinful nature, not as penalty, but by natural law, is to ignore the fact that this natural law is simply the regular action of God, the expression of his moral nature, and so is itself penalty.

"Man kills a snake," says Raymond, "because it is a snake, and not because it is to blame for being a snake,"—which seems to us a new proof that the advocates of innocent depravity regard infants, not as moral beings, but as mere animals. "We must distinguish automatic excellence or badness," says Raymond again, "from moral desert, whether good or ill." This seems to us a doctrine of punishment without guilt. Princeton Essays, 1 : 138, quote Coleridge : "It is an outrage on common sense to affirm that it is no evil for men to be placed on their probation under such circumstances that not one of ten thousand millions ever escapes sin and condemnation to eternal death. There is evil inflicted on us, as a consequence of Adam's sin, antecedent to our personal transgressions. It matters not what this evil is, whether temporal death, corruption of nature, certainty of sin, or death in its more extended sense ; if the ground of the evil's coming on us is Adam's sin, the principle is the same." Baird, Elohim Revealed, 488 — So, it seems, "if a creature is punished, it implies that some one has sinned, but does not necessarily intimate the sufferer to be the sinner ! But this is wholly contrary to the argument of the apostle in Rom. 5 : 12–19, which is based upon the opposite doctrine, and it is also contrary to the justice of God, who punishes only those who deserve it." See Julius Müller, Doct. Sin, 2 : 67–74.

D. Its limitation of responsibility to the evil choices of the individual and the dispositions caused thereby is inconsistent with the following facts :

(*a*) The first moral choice of each individual is so undeliberate as not to be remembered. Put forth at birth, as the chief advocates of the New School theory maintain, it does not answer to their definition of sin as a voluntary transgression of known law. Responsibility for such choice does not differ from responsibility for the inborn evil state of the will which manifests itself in that choice.

(*b*) The uniformity of sinful action among men cannot be explained by the existence of a mere faculty of choices. That men should uniformly choose may be thus explained ; but that men should uniformly choose evil requires us to postulate an evil tendency or state of the will itself, prior to these separate acts of choice. This evil tendency or inborn determination to evil, since it is the real cause of actual sins, must itself be sin, and as such must be guilty and condemnable.

(*c*) Power in the will to prevent the inborn vitiosity from developing itself is upon this theory a necessary condition of responsibility for actual sins. But the absolute uniformity of actual transgression is evidence that the will is practically impotent. If responsibility diminishes as the difficulties in the way of free decision increase, the fact that these difficulties are insuperable shows that there can be no responsibility at all. To deny the guilt of inborn sin is therefore virtually to deny the guilt of the actual sin which springs therefrom.

The aim of all the theories is to find a decision of the will which will justify God in condemning men. Where shall we find such a decision? At the age of fifteen, ten, five? Then all who die before this age are not sinners, cannot justly be punished with death, do not need a Savior. Is it at birth? But decision at such a time is not such a conscious decision against God as, according to this theory, would make it the proper determiner of our future destiny. We claim that the theory of Augustine — that of a sin of the race in Adam — is the only one that shows a conscious transgression fit to be the cause and ground of man's guilt and condemnation.

Wm. Adams Brown: " Who can tell how far his own acts are caused by his own will, and how far by the nature he has inherited? Men do feel guilty for acts which are largely due to their inherited natures, which inherited corruption is guilt, deserving of punishment and certain to receive it." H. B. Smith, System, 350, note—" It has been said, in the way of a taunt against the older theology, that men are very willing to speculate about sinning in Adam, so as to have their attention diverted from the sense of personal guilt. But the whole history of theology bears witness that those who have believed most fully in our native and strictly moral corruption — as Augustine, Calvin, and Edwards — have ever had the deepest sense of their personal demerit. We know the full evil of sin only when we know its roots as well as its fruits." " Causa causæ est causa causati." Inborn depravity is the cause of the first actual sin. The cause of inborn depravity is the sin of Adam. If there be no guilt in original sin, then the actual sin that springs therefrom cannot be guilty. There are subsequent presumptuous sins in which the personal element overbears the element of race and heredity. But this cannot be said of the first acts which make man a sinner. These are so naturally and uniformly the result of the inborn determination of the will, that they cannot be guilty, unless that inborn determination is also guilty. In short, not all sin is personal. There must be a sin of nature — a race-sin — or the beginnings of actual sin cannot be accounted for or regarded as objects of God's condemnation. Julius Müller, Doctrine of Sin, 2 : 320-328, 341 — " If the deep-rooted depravity which we bring with us into the world be not our sin, it at once becomes an excuse for our actual sins." Princeton Essays, 1 : 138, 139 — Alternative: 1. May a man by his own power prevent the development of this hereditary depravity? Then we do not know that all men are sinners, or that Christ's salvation is needed by all. 2. Is actual sin a necessary consequence of hereditary depravity? Then it is, on this theory, a free act no longer, and is not guilty, since guilt is predicable only of voluntary transgression of known law. See Baird, Elohim Revealed, 256 sq.; Hodge, Essays, 571-633; Philippi, Glaubenslehre, 2 : 61-73; Edwards on the Will, part iii, sec. 4; Bib. Sac., 20 : 317-320.

4. The Federal Theory, or Theory of Condemnation by Covenant.

The Federal theory, or theory of the Covenants, had its origin with Cocceius (1603–1669), professor at Leyden, but was more fully elaborated by Turretin (1623–1687). It has become a tenet of the Reformed as distinguished from the Lutheran church, and in this country it has its main advocates in the Princeton school of theologians, of whom Dr. Charles Hodge was the representative.

According to this view, Adam was constituted by God's sovereign appointment the representative of the whole human race. With Adam as their representative, God entered into covenant, agreeing to bestow upon them eternal life on condition of his obedience, but making the penalty of his disobedience to be the corruption and death of all his posterity. In accordance with the terms of this covenant, since Adam sinned, God accounts all his descendants as sinners, and condemns them because of Adam's transgression.

In execution of this sentence of condemnation, God immediately creates each soul of Adam's posterity with a corrupt and depraved nature, which infallibly leads to sin, and which is itself sin. The theory is therefore a theory of the immediate imputation of Adam's sin to his posterity, their corruption of nature not being the cause of that imputation, but the effect of it. In Rom. 5 : 12, " death passed unto all men, for that all sinned," signifies : "physical, spiritual, and eternal death came to all, because all were regarded and treated as sinners."

Fisher, Discussions, 355-409, compares the Augustinian and Federal theories of Original Sin. His account of the Federal theory and its origin is substantially as follows : The Federal theory is a theory of the covenants (*fœdus*, a covenant). 1. The covenant is a sovereign constitution imposed by God. 2. Federal union is the legal ground of imputation, though kinship to Adam is the reason why Adam and not another war selected as our representative. 3. Our guilt for Adam's sin is simply a legal responsibility. 4. That imputed sin is punished by inborn depravity, and that inborn depravity by eternal death. Augustine could not reconcile inherent depravity with the justice of God ; hence he held that we sinned in Adam.

So Anselm says : " Because the whole human nature was in them (Adam and Eve), and outside of them there was nothing of it, the whole was weakened and corrupted." After the first sin " this nature was propagated just as it had made itself by sinning." All sin belongs to the will ; but this is a part of our inheritance. The descendants of Adam were not in him as individuals ; yet what he did as a person, he did not do *sine natura*, and this nature is ours as well as his. So Peter Lombard. Sins of our immediate ancestors, because they are qualities which are purely personal, are not propagated. After Adam's first sin, the actual qualities of the first parent or of other later parents do not corrupt the nature as concerns *its* qualities, but only as concerns the qualities of the *person*.

Calvin maintained two propositions : 1. We are not condemned for Adam's sin apart from our own inherent depravity which is derived from him. The sin for which we are condemned is our own sin. 2. This sin is ours, for the reason that our nature is vitiated in Adam, and we receive it in the condition in which it was put by the first transgression. Melanchthon also held to an imputation of the first sin conditioned upon our innate depravity. The impulse to Federalism was given by the difficulty, on the pure Augustinian theory, of accounting for the non-imputation of Adam's subsequent sins, and those of his posterity.

Cocceius (Dutch, Coch : English, Cook), the author of the covenant-theory, conceived that he had solved this difficulty by making Adam's sin to be imputed to us upon the ground of a covenant between God and Adam, according to which Adam was to stand as the representative of his posterity. In Cocceius's use of the term, however, the only difference between covenant and command is found in the promise attached to the keeping of it. Fisher remarks on the mistake, in modern defenders of imputation, of ignoring the capital fact of a true and real participation in Adam's sin. The great body of Calvinistic theologians in the 17th century were Augustinians as well as Federalists. So Owen and the Westminster Confession. Turretin, however, almost merged the natural relation to Adam in the federal.

Edwards fell back on the old doctrine of Aquinas and Augustine. He tried to make out a real participation in the first sin. The first rising of sinful inclination, by a divinely constituted identity, *is* this participation. But Hopkins and Emmons regarded the sinful inclination, not as a *real* participation, but only as a *constructive* consent to Adam's first sin. Hence the New School theology, in which the imputation of Adam's sin was given up. On the contrary, Calvinists of the Princeton school planted themselves on the Federal theory, and taking Turretin as their text book, waged war on New England views, not wholly sparing Edwards himself. After this review of the origin of the theory, for which we are mainly indebted to Fisher, it can be easily seen how little show of truth there is in the assumption of the Princeton theologians that the Federal theory is " the immemorial doctrine of the church of God."

Statements of the theory are found in Cocceius, Summa Doctrinæ de Fœdere, cap. 1, 5 ; Turretin, Inst., loc. 9, quæs. 9 ; Princeton Essays, 1 : 98-185, esp. 120 — " In imputation there is, first, an ascription of something to those concerned ; secondly, a determination to deal with them accordingly." The ground for this imputation is " the union between Adam and his posterity, which is twofold,— a natural union, as between father and children, and the union of representation, *which is the main idea here insisted on*." 128 —"As in Christ we are constituted righteous by the imputation of righteousness, so in Adam we are made sinners by the imputation of his sin. . . . . Guilt is liability or exposedness to punishment; it does not in theological usage imply moral turpitude or criminality." 162—Turretin is quoted: "The foundation, therefore, of imputation is not merely the *natural* connection which exists between us and Adam — for, were this the case, all his sins would be imputed to us, but principally the *moral* and *federal*, on the ground of which God entered into covenant with him as our head. Hence in that sin Adam acted not as a private but a public person and representative." The oneness results from contract; the natural union is frequently not mentioned at all. Marck: All men sinned in Adam, "*eos representante.*" The acts of Adam and of Christ are ours "*jure representationis.*"

G. W. Northrup makes the order of the Federal theory to be: "(1) imputation of Adam's guilt; (2) condemnation on the ground of this imputed guilt; (3) corruption of nature consequent upon treatment as condemned. So judicial imputation of Adam's sin is the cause and ground of innate corruption. . . . . All the acts, with the single exception of the sin of Adam, are divine acts: the appointment of Adam, the creation of his descendants, the imputation of his guilt, the condemnation of his posterity, their consequent corruption. Here we have guilt without sin, exposure to divine wrath without ill-desert, God regarding men as being what they are not, punishing them on the ground of a sin committed before they existed, and visiting them with gratuitous condemnation and gratuitous reprobation. Here are arbitrary representation, fictitious imputation, constructive guilt, limited atonement." The Presb. Rev., Jan. 1882 : 30, claims that Kloppenburg (1642) preceded Cocceius (1648) in holding to the theory of the Covenants, as did also the Canons of Dort. For additional statements of Federalism, see Hodge, Essays, 49–86, and Syst. Theol., 2 : 192–204; Bib. Sac., 21 : 95–107; Cunningham, Historical Theology.

To the Federal theory we object :

A. It is extra-Scriptural, there being no mention of such a covenant with Adam in the account of man's trial. The assumed allusion to Adam's apostasy in Hosea 6 : 7, where the word " covenant " is used, is too precarious and too obviously metaphorical to afford the basis for a scheme of imputation (see Henderson, Com. on Minor Prophets, *in loco*). In Heb. 8 : 8 — "new covenant"—there is suggested a contrast, not with an Adamic, but with the Mosaic, covenant (*cf.* verse 9).

In Hosea 6 : 7 — "they like Adam [marg. 'men'] have trangressed the covenant" (Rev. Ver.) — the correct translation is given by Henderson, Minor Prophets : "But they, like men that break a covenant, there they proved false to me." LXX ; αὐτοὶ δέ εἰσιν ὡς ἄνθρωπος παραβαίνων διαθήκην. De Wette : "Aber sie übertreten den Bund nach Menschenart; daselbst sind sie mir treulos." Here the word *adam*, translated "man," either means "a man," or "man," *i. e.*, generic man. "Israel had as little regard to their covenants with God as men of unprincipled character have for ordinary contracts." "Like a man " = as men do. Compare Ps. 82 : 7 — "ye shall die like men "; Hosea 8 : 1, 2 — "they have transgressed my covenant " — an allusion to the Abrahamic or Mosaic covenant. Heb. 8 : 9 — "Behold, the days come, saith the Lord, that I will make a new covenant with the house of Israel and with the house of Judah ; Not according to the covenant that I made with their fathers In the day that I took them by the hand to lead them forth out of the land of Egypt."

B. It contradicts Scripture, in making the first result of Adam's sin to be God's *regarding and treating* the race as sinners. The Scripture, on the contrary, declares that Adam's offense *constituted* us sinners (Rom. 5 : 19). We are not sinners simply because God regards and treats us as such, but God regards us as sinners because we are sinners. Death is said to have " passed unto all men," not because all were regarded and treated as sinners, but "because all sinned " (Rom. 5 : 12).

For a full exegesis of the passage Rom. 5 : 12–19, see note to the discussion of the Theory of Adam's Natural Headship, pages 625–627. Dr. Park gave great offence by saying that the so-called " covenants " of law and of grace, referred in the Westminster Confession as made by God with Adam and Christ respectively, were really " made in Holland." The word *fœdus*, in such a connection, could properly mean nothing more than "ordinance"; see Vergil, Georgics, 1 : 60-63 — "eterna fœdera." E. G. Robinson, Christ. Theol., 185 — "God's 'covenant' with men is simply his method of dealing with then according to their knowledge and opportunities."

C. It impugns the justice of God by implying:

(*a*) That God holds men responsible for the violation of a covenant which they had no part in establishing. The assumed covenant is only a sovereign decree; the assumed justice, only arbitrary will.

We not only never authorized Adam to make such a covenant, but there is no evidence that he ever made one at all. It is not even certain that Adam knew he should have posterity. In the case of the imputation of our sins to Christ, Christ covenanted voluntarily to bear them, and joined himself to our nature that he might bear them. In the case of the imputation of Christ's righteousness to us, we first become one with Christ, and upon the ground of our union with him are justified. But upon the Federal theory, we are condemned upon the ground of a covenant which we neither instituted, nor participated in, nor assented to.

(*b*) That upon the basis of this covenant God accounts men as sinners who are not sinners. But God judges according to truth. His condemnations do not proceed upon a basis of legal fiction. He can regard as responsible for Adam's transgression only those who in some real sense have been concerned, and have had part, in that transgression.

See Baird, Elohim Revealed, 544 — "Here is a sin, which is no crime, but a mere condition of being regarded and treated as sinners; and a guilt, which is devoid of sinfulness, and which does not imply moral demerit or turpitude,"— that is, a sin which is no sin, and a guilt which is no guilt. Why might not God as justly reckon Adam's sin to the account of the fallen angels, and punish them for it? Dorner, System Doct., 2 : 351; 3 : 53, 54 — "Hollaz held that God treats men in accordance with what he foresaw all would do, if they were in Adam's place" (*scientia media* and *imputatio metaphysica*). Birks, Difficulties of Belief, 141 — "Immediate imputation is as unjust as *imputatio metaphysica*, i. e., God's condemning us for what he knew we would have done in Adam's place. On such a theory there is no need of a trial at all. God might condemn half the race at once to hell without probation, on the ground that they would ultimately sin and come thither at any rate." Justification can be gratuitous, but not condemnation. "Like the social-compact theory of government, the covenant-theory of sin is a mere legal fiction. It explains, only to belittle. The theory of New England theology, which attributes to mere sovereignty God's making us sinners in consequence of Adam's sin, is more reasonable than the Federal theory" (Fisher).

Professor Moses Stuart characterized this theory as one of "fictitious guilt, but veritable damnation." The divine economy admits of no fictitious substitutions nor forensic evasions. No legal quibbles can modify eternal justice. Federalism reverses the proper order, and puts the effect before the cause, as is the case with the social-compact theory of government. Ritchie, Darwin and Hegel, 27 — "It is illogical to say that society originated in a contract; for contract presupposes society." Unus homo, nullus homo = without society, no persons. T. H. Green, Prolegomena to Ethics, 351 — "No individual can make a conscience for himself. He always needs a society to make it for him. . . . 200 — Only through society is personality actualized." Royce, Spirit of Modern Philosophy, 209, note — "Organic interrelationship of individuals is the condition even of their relatively independent selfhood." We are "members one of another" (Rom, 12 : 15). Schurman, Agnosticism, 176 — "The individual could never have developed into a personality but for his training through society and under law." Imagine a theory that the family originated in a compact! We must not define the state by its first crude beginnings, any more than we define the oak by the acorn. On the theory of a social-compact, see Lowell, Essays on Government, 136-188.

(*c*) That, after accounting men to be sinners who are not sinners, God makes them sinners by immediately creating each human soul with a corrupt nature such as will correspond to his decree. This is not only to assume a false view of the origin of the soul, but also to make God directly the author of sin. Imputation of sin cannot precede and account for corruption ; on the contrary, corruption must precede and account for imputation.

By God's act we became depraved, as a penal consequence of Adam's act imputed to us solely as *peccatum alienum*. Dabney, Theology, 342, says the theory regards the soul as originally pure until imputation. See Hodge on Rom. 5:13; Syst. Theol., 2 : 203, 210 ; Thornwell, Theology, 1 : 346-349; Chalmers, Institutes, 1 : 485, 487. The Federal theory " makes sin in us to be the penalty of another's sin, instead of being the penalty of our own sin, as on the Augustinian scheme, which regards depravity in us as the punishment of our own sin in Adam. . . . It holds to a sin which does not bring eternal punishment, but for which we are legally responsible as truly as Adam." It only remains to say that Dr. Hodge always persistently refused to admit the one added element which might have made his view less arbitrary and mechanical, namely, the traducian theory of the origin of the soul. He was a creatianist, and to the end maintained that God immediately created the soul, and created it depraved. Acceptance of the traducian theory would have compelled him to exchange his Federalism for Augustinianism. Creatianism was the one remaining element of Pelagian atomism in an otherwise Scriptural theory. Yet Dr. Hodge regarded this as an essential part of Biblical teaching. His unwavering confidence was like that of Fichte, whom Caroline Schelling represented as saying : "Zweifle an der Sonne Klarheit, Zweifle an der Sterne Licht, Leser, nur an meiner Wahrheit Und an deiner Dummheit, nicht."

As a corrective to the atomistic spirit of Federalism we may quote a view which seems to us far more tenable, though it perhaps goes to the opposite extreme. Dr. H. H. Bawden writes: "The self is the product of a social environment. An ascetic self is so far forth not a self. Selfhood and consciousness are essentially social. We are members one of another. The biological view of selfhood regards it as a function, activity, process, inseparable from the social matrix out of which it has arisen. Consciousness is simply the name for the functioning of an organism. Not that the soul is a secretion of the brain, as bile is a secretion of the liver ; not that the mind is a function of the body in any such materialistic sense. But that mind or consciousness is only the growing of an organism, while, on the other hand, the organism is just that which grows. The psychical is not a second, subtle, parallel form of energy causally interactive with the physical ; much less is it a concomitant series, as the parallelists hold. Consciousness is not an order of existence or a thing, but rather a function. It is the organization of reality, the universe coming to a focus, flowering, so to speak, in a finite centre. Society is an organism in the same sense as the human body. The separation of the units of society is no greater than the separation of the unit factors of the body, — in the microscope the molecules are far apart. Society is a great sphere with many smaller spheres within it.

" Each self is not impervious to other selves. Selves are not water-tight compartments, each one of which might remain complete in itself, even if all the others were destroyed. But there are open sluiceways between all the compartments. Society is a vast plexus of interweaving personalities. We are members one of another. What affects my neighbor affects me, and what affects me ultimately affects my neighbor. The individual is not an impenetrable atomic unit. . . . The self is simply the social whole coming to consciousness at some particular point. Every self is rooted in the social organism of which it is but a local and individual expression. A self is a mere cipher apart from its social relations. As the old Greek adage has it: ' He who lives quite alone is either a beast or a god.'" While we regard this exposition of Dr. Bawden as throwing light upon the origin of consciousness and so helping our contention against the Federal theory of sin, we do not regard it as proving that consciousness, once developed, may not become relatively independent and immortal. Back of society, as well as back of the individual, lies the consciousness and will of God, in whom alone is the guarantee of persistence. For objections to the Federal theory, see Fisher, Discussions, 401 *sq.* ; Bib. Sac., 20 : 455-462, 577 ; New Englander, 1868 : 551-603 ; Baird, Elohim Revealed, 305-334, 435-450; Julius Müller, Doct. Sin, 2 : 336 ; Dabney, Theology, 341-351.

5. *Theory of Mediate Imputation, or Theory of Condemnation for Depravity.*

This theory was first maintained by Placeus (1606-1655), professor of

Theology at Saumur in France. Placeus originally denied that Adam's sin was in any sense imputed to his posterity, but after his doctrine was condemned by the Synod of the French Reformed Church at Charenton in 1644, he published the view which now bears his name.

According to this view, all men are born physically and morally depraved ; this native depravity is the source of all actual sin, and is itself sin ; in strictness of speech, it is this native depravity, and this only, which God imputes to men. So far as man's physical nature is concerned, this inborn sinfulness has descended by natural laws of propagation from Adam to all his posterity. The soul is immediately created by God, but it becomes actively corrupt so soon as it is united to the body. Inborn sinfulness is the consequence, though not the penalty, of Adam's transgression.

There is a sense, therefore, in which Adam's sin may be said to be imputed to his descendants,— it is imputed, not immediately, as if they had been in Adam or were so represented in him that it could be charged directly to them, corruption not intervening,— but it is imputed mediately, through and on account of the intervening corruption which resulted from Adam's sin. As on the Federal theory imputation is the cause of depravity, so on this theory depravity is the cause of imputation. In Rom. 5 : 12, " death passed unto all men, for that all sinned," signifies : "death physical, spiritual, and eternal passed upon all men, because all sinned by possessing a depraved nature."

See Placeus, De Imputatione Primi Peccati Adami, in Opera, 1 : 709 — " The sensitive soul is produced from the parent ; the intellectual or rational soul is directly created. The soul, on entering the corrupted physical nature, is not passively corrupted, but becomes corrupt actively, accommodating itself to the other part of human nature in character." 710— So this soul " contracts from the vitiosity of the dispositions of the body a corresponding vitiosity, not so much by the action of the body upon the soul, as by that essential appetite of the soul by which it unites itself to the body in a way accommodated to the dispositions of the body, as liquid put into a bowl accommodates itself to the figure of a bowl — sicut vinum in vase accesso. God was therefore neither the author of Adam's fall, nor of the propagation of sin."

Herzog, Encyclopædie, art. : Placeus — " In the title of his works we read ' Placæus ' ; he himself, however, wrote ' Placeus,' which is the more correct Latin form [of the French ' de la Place ']. In Adam's first sin, Placeus distinguish d between the actual sinning and the first habitual sin (corrupted disposition). The former was transient ; the latter clung to his person, and was propagated to all. It is truly sin, and it is imputed to all, since it makes all condemnable. Placeus believes in the imputation of this corrupted disposition, but not in the imputation of the first act of Adam, except mediately, through the imputation of the inherited depravity " Fisher, Discussions, 389 — " Mere native corruption is the whole of original sin. Placeus justifies his use of the term ' imputation ' by Rom. 2 : 26 — ' If therefore the uncircumcision keep the ordinances of the law, shall not his uncircumcision be reckoned [imputed] for circumcision ? ' Our own depravity is the necessary condition of the imputation of Adam's sin, just as our own faith is the necessary condition of the imputation of Christ's righteousness."

Advocates of Mediate Imputation are, in Great Britain, G. Payne, in his book entitled : Original Sin ; John Caird, Fund. Ideas of Christianity, 1 : 196-232 ; and James S. Candlish, Biblical Doctrine of Sin, 111-122 ; in America, H. B. Smith, in his System of Christian Doctrine, 169, 284, 285, 314-323 ; and E. G. Robinson, Christian Theology. The editor of Dr. Smith's work says : " On the whole, he favored the theory of Mediate Imputation. There is a note which reads thus : ' Neither Mediate nor Immediate Imputation is wholly satisfactory.' Understand by ' Mediate Imputation ' a full statement of the facts in the case, and the author accepted it ; understand by it a theory professing to give the final explanation of the facts, and it was ' not wholly satisfactory.' " Dr. Smith himself says, 316 — " Original sin is a doctrine respecting the moral conditions of human nature as from Adam -- generic : and it is not a doctrine respecting personal liabilities and desert. For the latter, we need more and other circumstances. Strictly speaking, it is not sin, which is ill-deserving, but only the sinner. The ultimate distinction is here : There is a well-grounded difference to be made between personal desert, strictly personal character and liabilities (of each individual under the divine law, as applied specifically, *e. g.*, in the last adjudication), and a generic moral condition — the antecedent ground of such personal character.

"The distinction, however, is not between what has moral quality and what has not, but between the moral state of each as a member of the race, and his personal liabilities and desert as an individual. This original sin would wear to us only the character of evil, and not of sinfulness, were it not for *the fact* that we feel guilty in view of our corruption when it becomes known to us in our own acts. Then there is involved in it not merely a sense of evil and misery, but also a sense of guilt ; moreover, redemption is also necessary to remove it, which shows that it is a moral state. Here is the point of junction between the two extreme positions, that we sinned in Adam, and that all sin consists in sinning. The guilt of Adam's sin is — this exposure, this liability on account of such native corruption, our having the same nature in the same moral bias. The guilt of Adam's sin is *not to be separated* from the existence of this evil disposition. And this guilt is what is imputed to us." See art. on H. B. Smith, in Presb. Rev., 1881 : "He did not fully acquiesce in Placeus's view, which makes the corrupt nature by descent the only ground of imputation."

The theory of Mediate Imputation is exposed to the following objections :

A. It gives no explanation of man's responsibility for his inborn depravity. No explanation of this is possible, which does not regard man's depravity as having had its origin in a free personal act, either of the individual, or of collective human nature in its first father and head. But this participation of all men in Adam's sin the theory expressly denies.

The theory holds that we are responsible for the effect, but not for the cause —" post Adamum, non propter Adamum." But, says Julius Müller, Doct. Sin, 2 : 209, 331 — "If this sinful tendency be in us solely through the act of others, and not through our own deed, they, and not we, are responsible for it, — it is not our guilt, but our misfortune. And even as to actual sins which spring from this inherent sinful tendency, these are not strictly our own, but the acts of our first parents through us. Why impute them to us as actual sins, for which we are to be condemned ? Thus, if we deny the existence of guilt, we destroy the reality of sin, and *vice versa*." Thornwell, Theology, 1 : 348, 349 — This theory " does not explain the sense of guilt, as connected with depravity of nature,— how the feeling of ill-desert can arise in relation to a state of mind of which we have been only passive recipients. The child does not reproach himself for the afflictions which a father's follies have brought upon him. But our inward corruption we do feel to be our own fault,— it is our crime as well as our shame."

B. Since the origination of this corrupt nature cannot be charged to the account of man, man's inheritance of it must be regarded in the light of an arbitrary divine infliction — a conclusion which reflects upon the justice of God. Man is not only condemned for a sinfulness of which God is the author, but is condemned without any real probation, either individual or collective.

Dr. Hovey, Outlines of Theology, objects to the theory of Mediate Imputation, because : " 1. It casts so faint a light on the justice of God in the imputation of Adam's sin to adults who do as he did. 2. It casts no light on the justice of God in bringing into existence a race inclined to sin by the fall of Adam. The inherited bias is still unexplained, and the imputation of it is a riddle, or a wrong, to the natural understanding." It is unjust to hold us guilty of the effect, if we be not first guilty of the cause.

C. It contradicts those passages of Scripture which refer the origin of human condemnation, as well as of human depravity, to the sin of our first parents, and which represent universal death, not as a matter of divine sovereignty, but as a judicial infliction of penalty upon all men for the sin of the race in Adam (Rom. 5 : 16, 18). It moreover does violence to the Scripture in its unnatural interpretation of "all sinned," in Rom. 5 : 12 — words which imply the oneness of the race with Adam, and the causative relation of Adam's sin to our guilt.

Certain passages which Dr. H. B. Smith, System, 317, quotes from Edwards, as favoring the theory of Mediate Imputation, seem to us to favor quite a different view. See Edwards, 2 : 482 *sq.*—" The first existing of a corrupt disposition in their hearts is not to be looked upon as sin belonging to them distinct from their participation in Adam's first sin ; it is, as it were, the extended pollution of that sin through the whole tree, by virtue of the constituted union of the branches with the root. . . . . I am humbly of the opinion that, if any have supposed the children of Adam to come into the world with a double guilt, one the guilt of Adam's sin, another the guilt arising from their having a corrupt heart, they have not so well considered the matter." And afterwards " Derivation of evil disposition (or rather co-existence) is in consequence of the union,' — but "not properly a consequence of the imputation of his sin ; nay, rather anteceden'' to it, as it was in Adam himself. The first depravity of heart, and the imputation o ' that sin, are both the consequences of that established union ; but yet in such order that the evil disposition is first, and the charge of guilt consequent, as it was in the case of Adam himself."

Edwards quotes Stapfer : " The Reformed divines do not hold immediate and mediate imputation *separately,* but always together." And still further, 2 : 493 —" And therefore the sin of the apostasy is not theirs, merely because God imputes it to them ; but it is truly and properly theirs, and on that ground God imputes it to them." It seems to us that Dr. Smith mistakes the drift of these passages from Edwards, and that in making the identification with Adam primary, and imputation of his sin secondary, they favor the theory of Adam's Natural Headship rather than the theory of Mediate Imputation. Edwards regards the order as (1) apostasy ; (2) depravity : (3) guilt ; — but in all three, Adam and we are, by divine constitution, one. To be guilty of the depravity, therefore, we must first be guilty of the apostasy.

For the reasons above mentioned we regard the theory of Mediate Imputation as a half-way house where there is no permanent lodgment. The logical mind can find no satisfaction therein, but is driven either forward, to the Augustinian doctrine which we are next to consider, or backward, to the New School doctrine with its atomistic conception of man and its arbitrary sovereignty of God. On the theory of Mediate Imputation, see Cunningham, Historical Theology, 1 : 496–639; Princeton Essays, 1 : 129, 154, 168; Hodge, Syst. Theology, 2 : 205–214; Shedd, History of Doctrine, 2 : 158; Baird, Elohim Revealed, 46, 47, 474–479, 504–507.

6. *The Augustinian Theory, or Theory of Adam's Natural Headship.*

This theory was first elaborated by Augustine (354–430), the great opponent of Pelagius ; although its central feature appears in the writings of Tertullian (died about 220), Hilary (350), and Ambrose (374). It is frequently designated as the Augustinian view of sin. It was the view held by the Reformers, Zwingle excepted. Its principal advocates in this country are Dr. Shedd and Dr. Baird.

It holds that God imputes the sin of Adam immediately to all his posterity, in virtue of that organic unity of mankind by which the whole race at the time of Adam's transgression existed, not individually, but seminally, in him as its head. The total life of humanity was then in Adam ; the race as yet had its being only in him. Its essence was not yet individualized ; its forces were not yet distributed ; the powers which now exist in separate men were then unified and localized in Adam ; Adam's will was yet the will of the species. In Adam's free act, the will of the race revolted from God and the nature of the race corrupted itself. The nature which we now possess is the same nature that corrupted itself in Adam — " not the same in kind merely, but the same as flowing to us continuously from him."

Adam's sin is imputed to us immediately, therefore, not as something foreign to us, but because it is ours — we and all other men having existed as one moral person or one moral whole, in him, and, as the result of that transgression, possessing a nature destitute of love to God and prone to evil. In Rom. 5 : 12 — "death passed unto all men, for that all sinned," signifies: "death physical, spiritual, and eternal passed unto all men, because all sinned in Adam their natural head."

Milton, Par. Lost, 9:414 — "Where likeliest he [Satan] might find The only two of mankind, but in them The whole included race, his purpos'd prey." Augustine, De Pec. Mer. et Rem., 3:7 — "In Adamo omnes tunc peccaverunt, quando in ejus natura adhuc omnes ille unus fuerunt"; De Civ. Dei, 13, 14 — "Omnes enim fuimus in illo uno, quando omnes fuimus ille unus. . . . . Nondum erat nobis singillatim creata et distributa forma in qua singuli viveremus, sed jam natura erat seminalis ex qua propagaremur." On Augustine's view, see Dorner, Glaubenslehre, 2; 43-45 (System Doct., 2 : 338, 339) — In opposition to Pelagius who made sin to consist in single acts, "Augustine emphasized the sinful state. This was a deprivation of original righteousness + inordinate love. Tertullian, Cyprian, Hilarius, Ambrose had advocated traducianism, according to which, without their personal participation, the sinfulness of all is grounded in Adam's free act. They incur its consequences as an evil which is, at the same time, punishment of the inherited fault. But Irenæus, Athanasius, Gregory of Nyssa, say Adam was not simply a single individual, but the universal man. We were comprehended in him, so that in him we sinned. On the first view, the posterity were passive; on the second, they were active, in Adam's sin. Augustine represents both views, desiring to unite the universal sinfulness involved in traducianism with the universal will and guilt involved in coöperation with Adam's sin. Adam, therefore, to him, is a double conception, and = individual + race."

Mozley on Predestination, 402 — "In Augustine, some passages refer all wickedness to original sin ; some account for different degrees of evil by different degrees of original sin (Op. imp. cont. Julianum, 4 : 128 —' Malitia naturalis . . . . in aliis minor, in aliis major est'); in some, the individual seems to add to original sin (De Correp. et Gratia, c. 13 —' Per liberum arbitrium alia insuper addiderunt, alii majus, alii minus, sed omnes mali.' De Grat. et Lib. Arbit., 2 : 1 —' Added to the sin of their birth sins of their own commission'; 2 : 4 — 'Neither denies our liberty of will, whether to choose an evil or a good life, nor attributes to it so much power that it can avail anything without God's grace, or that it can change itself from evil to good')." These passages seem to show that, side by side with the race-sin and its development, Augustine recognized a domain of free personal decision, by which each man could to some extent modify his character, and make himself more or less depraved.

The theory of Augustine was not the mere result of Augustine's temperament or of Augustine's sins. Many men have sinned like Augustine, but their intellects have only been benumbed and have been led into all manner of unbelief. It was the Holy Spirit who took possession of the temperament, and so overruled the sin as to make it a glass through which Augustine saw the depths of his nature. Nor was his doctrine one of exclusive divine transcendence, which left man a helpless worm at enmity with infinite justice. He was also a passionate believer in the immanence of God. He writes: "I could not be, O my God, could not be at all, wert not thou in me ; rather, were not I in thee, of whom are all things, by whom are all things, in whom are are all things. . . . O God, thou hast made us for thyself, and our heart is restless, till it find rest in thee. . . . The will of God is the very nature of things — Dei voluntas rerum natura est."

Allen, Continuity of Christian Thought, Introduction, very erroneously declares that "the Augustinian theology rests upon the transcendence of Deity as its controlling principle, and at every point appears as an inferior rendering of the earlier interpretation of the Christian faith." On the other hand, L. L. Paine, Evolution of Trinitarianism, 69, 368-397, shows that, while Athanasius held to a dualistic transcendence, Augustine held to a theistic immanence: "Thus the Stoic, Neo-Platonic immanence, with Augustine, supplants the Platonico-Aristotelian and Athanasian transcendence." Alexander, Theories of the Will, 90 — "The theories of the early Fathers were indeterministic, and the pronounced Augustinianism of Augustine was the result of the rise into prominence of the doctrine of original sin. . . . The early Fathers thought of the origin of sin in angels and in Adam as due to free will. Augustine thought of the origin of sin in Adam's posterity as due to inherited evil will." Harnack, Wesen des Christen-thums. 161 — "To this day in Catholicism inward and living piety and the expression of it is in essence wholly Augustinian."

Calvin was essentially Augustinian and realistic; see his Institutes, book 2, chap. 1-3; Hagenbach, Hist. Doct., 1 : 505, 506, with the quotations and references. Zwingle was not an Augustinian. He held that native vitiosity, although it is the uniform occasion of sin, is not itself sin: "It is not a crime, but a condition and a disease." See Hagen-bach, Hist. Doct. 2 : 256, with references. Zwingle taught that every new-born child — thanks to Christ's making alive of all those who had died in Adam — is as free from any taint of sin as Adam was before the fall. The Reformers, however, with the single exception of Zwingle, were Augustinians, and accounted for the hereditary guilt of mankind, not by the fact that all men were represented in Adam, but that all men par-ticipated in Adam's sin. This is still the doctrine of the Lutheran church.

The theory of Adam's Natural Headship regards humanity at large as the outgrowth of one germ. Though the leaves of a tree appear as disconnected units when we look down upon them from above, a view from beneath will discern the common connection with the twigs, branches, trunk, and will finally trace their life to the root, and to the seed from which it originally sprang. The race of man is one because it sprang from one head. Its members are not to be regarded atomistically, as segregated individuals; the deeper truth is the truth of organic unity. Yet we are not philosophical realists; we do not believe in the separate existence of universals. We hold, not to *universalia ante rem*, which is extreme realism; nor to *universalia post rem*, which is nominalism; but to *universalia in re*, which is moderate realism. Extreme realism cannot see the trees for the wood; nominalism cannot see the wood for the trees; moderate realism sees the wood in the trees. We hold to "*universalia in re*, but insist that the universals must be recognized as *realities*, as truly as the individuals are" (H. B. Smith, System, 319, note). Three acorns have a common life, as three spools have not. Moderate realism is true of organic things; nominalism is true only of proper names. God has not created any new tree nature since he created the first tree; nor has he created any new human nature since he created the first man. I am but a branch and outgrowth of the tree of humanity.

Our realism then only asserts the real historical connection of each member of the race with its first father and head, and such a derivation of each from him as makes us partakers of the character which he formed. Adam was once the race; and when he fell, the race fell. Shedd: "We all existed in Adam in our elementary invisible substance. The *Seyn* of all was there, though the *Daseyn* was not; the *noumenon*, though not the *phenomenon*, was in existence." On realism, see Koehler, Realismus und Nominalismus; Neander, Ch. Hist., 4 : 356; Dorner, Person Christ, 2 : 377; Hase, Anselm, 2 : 77; F. E. Abbott, Scientific Theism, Introd., 1-29, and in Mind, Oct. 1882 : 476, 477; Raymond, Theology, 2 : 30-33; Shedd, Dogm. Theol., 2 : 69-74; Bowne, Theory of Thought and Knowledge, 129-132; Ten Broeke, in Baptist Quar. Rev., Jan. 1892 : 1-26; Baldwin, Psychol-ogy, 280, 281; D. J. Hill, Genetic Philosophy, 186; Hours with the Mystics, 1 : 213; Case, Physical Realism, 17-19; Fullerton, Samenesss and Identity, 88, 89, and Concept of the Infinite, 95-114.

The new conceptions of the reign of law and of the principle of heredity which pre-vail in modern science are working to the advantage of Christian theology. The doc-trine of Adam's Natural Headship is only a doctrine of the hereditary transmission of character from the first father of the race to his descendants. Hence we use the word "imputation" in its proper sense — that of a reckoning or charging to us of that which is truly and properly ours. See Julius Müller, Doctrine of Sin, 2 : 259-357, esp. 328 — "The problem is : We must allow that the depravity, which all Adam's descendants inherit by natural generation, nevertheless involves personal guilt; and yet this depravity, so far as it is natural, wants the very conditions on which guilt depends. The only satisfactory explanation of this difficulty is the Christian doctrine of original sin. Here alone, if its inner possibility can be maintained, can the apparently contra-dictory principles be harmonized, viz.: the universal and deep-seated depravity of human nature, as the source of actual sin, and individual responsibility and guilt." These words, though written by one who advocates a different theory, are nevertheless a valuable argument in corroboration of the theory of Adam's Natural Headship.

Thornwell, Theology, 1 : 343 — "We must contradict every Scripture text and every Scripture doctrine which makes hereditary impurity hateful to God and punishable in his sight, or we must maintain that we sinned in Adam in his first transgression." Sec-retan, in his Work on Liberty, held to a *collective* life of the race in Adam. He was answered by Naville, Problem of Evil: "We existed in Adam, not individually, but seminally. Each of us, as an individual, is responsible only for his personal acts, or, to speak more exactly, for the personal part of his acts. But each of us, as he is man, is jointly and severally (*solidairement*) responsible for the fall of the human race." Bersier, The Oneness of the Race, in its Fall and in its Future: "If we are commanded to love our neighbor as ourselves, it is because our neighbor is ourself."

See Edwards, Original Sin, part 4, chap. 3; Shedd, on Original Sin, in Discourses and Essays, 218-271, and references, 261-263, also Dogm. Theol., 2:181-195; Baird, Elohim Revealed, 410-435, 451-460, 494; Schaff, in Bib. Sac., 5:220, and in Lange's Com., on Rom. 5:12; Auberlen, Div. Revelation, 175-180; Philippi, Glaubenslehre, 3:28-38, 204-236; Thomasius, Christi Person und Werk, 1:269-400; Martensen, Dogmatics, 173-183; Murphy, Scientific Bases, 262 *sq.*, *cf.* 101; Birks, Difficulties of Belief, 135; Bp. Reynolds, Sinfulness of Sin, in Works, 1:102-350; Mozley on Original Sin, in Lectures, 136-152; Kendall, on Natural Heirship, or All the World Akin, in Nineteenth Century, Oct. 1885:614-626. *Per contra*, see Hodge, Syst. Theol., 2:157-164, 227-257; Haven, in Bib. Sac., 20:451-455; Criticism of Baird's doctrine, in Princeton Rev., Apr. 1860:335-376; of Schaff's doctrine, in Princeton Rev., Apr. 1870:239-262.

We regard this theory of the Natural Headship of Adam as the most satisfactory of the theories mentioned, and as furnishing the most important help towards the understanding of the great problem of original sin. In its favor may be urged the following considerations:

A. It puts the most natural interpretation upon Rom. 5 : 12-21. In verse 12 of this passage — "death passed unto all men, for that all sinned" — the great majority of commentators regard the word "sinned" as describing a common transgression of the race in Adam. The death spoken of is, as the whole context shows, mainly though not exclusively physical. It has passed upon all — even upon those who have committed no conscious and personal transgression whereby to explain its infliction (verse 14). The legal phraseology of the passage shows that this infliction is not a matter of sovereign decree, but of judicial penalty (verses 13, 14, 15, 16, 18 — "law," "transgression," "trespass," "judgment . . . . of one unto condemnation," "act of righteousness," "justification"). As the explanation of this universal subjection to penalty, we are referred to Adam's sin. By that one act ("so," verse 12) — the "trespass of the one" man (v. 15, 17), the "one trespass" (v. 18) — death came to all men, because all [not 'have sinned', but] sinned ($\pi\acute{a}\nu\tau\epsilon\varsigma\ \mathring{\eta}\mu\alpha\rho\tau\upsilon\nu$ — aorist of instantaneous past action) — that is, all sinned in "the one trespass" of "the one" man. Compare 1 Cor. 15 : 22 — "As in Adam all die" — where the contrast with physical resurrection shows that physical death is meant; 2 Cor. 5 : 14 — "one died for all, therefore all died." See Commentaries of Meyer, Bengel, Olshausen, Philippi, Wordsworth, Lange, Godet, Shedd. This is also recognized as the correct interpretation of Paul's words by Beyschlag, Ritschl, and Pfleiderer, although no one of these three accepts Paul's doctrine as authoritative.

Beyschlag, N. T. Theology, 2:58-60 — "To understand the apostle's view, we must follow the exposition of Bengel (which is favored also by Meyer and Pfleiderer): 'Because they — viz., in Adam — all have sinned'; they all, namely, who were included in Adam according to the O. T. view which sees the whole race in its founder, acted in his action." Ritschl: "Certainly Paul treated the universal destiny of death as due to the sin of Adam. Nevertheless it is not yet suited for a theological rule just for the reason that the apostle has formed this idea;" in other words, Paul's teaching it does not make it binding upon our faith. Philippi, Com. on Rom., 168 — Interpret Rom. 5:12 — "one sinned for all, therefore all sinned," by 2 Cor. 5:15 — "one died for all, therefore all died." Evans, in Presb. Rev., 1883:294 — "by the trespass of the one the many died," "by the trespass of the one, death reigned through the one," "through the one man's disobedience"—all these phrases, and the phrases with respect to salvation which correspond to them, indicate that the fallen race and the redeemed race are each regarded as a multitude, a totality. So οἱ πάντες in 2 Cor. 5 : 14 indicates a corresponding conception of the organic unity of the race.

Prof. George B. Stevens, Pauline Theology, 32–40, 129–139, denies that Paul taught the sinning of all men in Adam: "They sinned in the same sense in which believers were crucified to the world and died unto sin when Christ died upon the cross. The believer's renewal is conceived as wrought in advance by those acts and experiences of Christ in which it has its ground. As the consequences of his vicarious sufferings are traced back to their cause, so are the consequences which flowed from the beginning of sin in Adam traced back to that original fount of evil and identified with it; but the latter statement should no more be treated as a rigid logical formula than the former, its counterpart. . . . . There is a mystical identification of the procuring cause with its effect,—both in the case of Adam and of Christ."

In our treatment of the New School theory of sin we have pointed out that the inability to understand the vital union of the believer with Christ incapacitates the New School theologian from understanding the organic union of the race with Adam. Paul's phrase "in Christ" meant more than that Christ is the type and beginner of salvation, and sinning in Adam meant more to Paul than following the example or acting in the spirit of our first father. In 2 Cor. 5 : 14 the argument is that since Christ died, all believers died to sin and death in him. Their resurrection-life is the same life that died and rose again in his death and resurrection. So Adam's sin is ours because the same life which transgressed and became corrupt in him has come down to us and is our possession. In Rom. 5 : 14, the individual and conscious sins to which the New School theory attaches the condemning sentence are expressly excluded, and in verses 15–19 the judgment is declared to be "of one trespass." Prof. Wm. Arnold Stevens, of Rochester, says well: "Paul teaches that Adam's sin is ours, not potentially, but actually." Of ἥμαρτον, he says : "This might conceivably be: (1) the historical aorist proper, used in its momentary sense; (2) the comprehensive or collective aorist, as in διῆλθεν in the same verse; (3) the aorist used in the sense of the English perfect, as in Rom. 3 : 23 — πάντες γὰρ ἥμαρτον καὶ ὑστεροῦνται. In 5 : 12, the context determines with great probability that the aorist is used in the first of these senses." We may add that interpreters are not wanting who so take ἥμαρτον in 3 : 23; see also margin of Rev. Version. But since the passage Rom. 5 : 12-19 is so important, we reserve to the close of this section a treatment of it in greater detail.

B. It permits whatever of truth there may be in the Federal theory and in the theory of Mediate Imputation to be combined with it, while neither of these latter theories can be justified to reason unless they are regarded as corollaries or accessories of the truth of Adam's Natural Headship. Only on this supposition of Natural Headship could God justly constitute Adam our representative, or hold us responsible for the depraved nature we have received from him. It moreover justifies God's ways, in postulating a real and a fair probation of our common nature as preliminary to imputation of sin — a truth which the theories just mentioned, in common with that of the New School, virtually deny,—while it rests upon correct philosophical principles with regard to will, ability, law, and accepts the Scriptural representations of the nature of sin, the penal character of death, the origin of the soul, and the oneness of the race in the transgression.

John Caird, Fund. Ideas of Christianity, 1 : 196–232, favors the view that sin consists simply in an inherited bias of our nature to evil, and that we are guilty from birth because we are sinful from birth. But he recognizes in Augustinianism the truth of the organic unity of the race and the implication of every member in its past history. He tells us that we must not regard man simply as an abstract or isolated individual. The atomistic theory regards society as having no existence other than that of the individuals who compose it. But it is nearer the truth to say that it is society which creates the individual, rather than that the individual creates society. Man does not come into existence a blank tablet on which external agencies may write whatever record they will. The individual is steeped in influences which are due to the past history of his kind. The individualistic theory runs counter to the most obvious facts of observation and experience. As a philosophy of life, Augustinianism has a depth and significance which the individualistic theory cannot claim."

Alvah Hovey, Manual of Christian Theology, 175 (2d ed.) — "Every child of Adam is accountable for the degree of sympathy which he has for the whole system of evil in the world, and with the primal act of disobedience among men. If that sympathy is full, whether expressed by deed or thought, if the whole force of his being is arrayed against heaven and on the side of hell, it is difficult to limit his responsibility." Schleiermacher held that the guilt of original sin attached, not to the individual as an individual, but as a member of the race, so that the consciousness of race-union carried with it the consciousness of race-guilt. He held all men to be equally sinful and to differ only in their different reception of or attitude toward grace, sin being the universal *malum metaphysicum* of Spinoza; see Pfleiderer, Prot. Theol. seit Kant, 113.

C. While its fundamental presupposition — a determination of the will of each member of the race prior to his individual consciousness — is an hypothesis difficult in itself, it is an hypothesis which furnishes the key to many more difficulties than it suggests. Once allow that the race was one in its first ancestor and fell in him, and light is thrown on a problem otherwise insoluble — the problem of our accountability for a sinful nature which we have not personally and consciously originated. Since we cannot, with the three theories first mentioned, deny either of the terms of this problem — inborn depravity or accountability for it, — we accept this solution as the best attainable.

Sterrett, Reason and Authority in Religion, 20 — "The whole swing of the pendulum of thought of to-day is away from the individual and towards the social point of view. Theories of society are supplementing theories of the individual. The solidarity of man is the regnant thought in both the scientific and the historical study of man. It is even running into the extreme of a determinism that annihilates the individual." Chapman, Jesus Christ and the Present Age, 43 — "It was never less possible to deny the truth to which theology gives expression in its doctrine of original sin than in the present age. It is only one form of the universally recognized fact of heredity. There is a collective evil, for which the responsibility rests on the whole race of man. Of this common evil each man inherits his share; it is organized in his nature; it is established in his environment." E. G. Robinson : "The tendency of modern theology [in the last generation] was to individualization, to make each man 'a little Almighty.' But the human race is one in kind, and in a sense is numerically one. The race lay potentially in Adam. The entire developing force of the race was in him. There is no carrying the race up, except from the starting-point of a fallen and guilty humanity." Goethe said that while humanity ever advances, individual man remains the same.

The true test of a theory is, not that it can itself be explained, but that it is capable of explaining. The atomic theory in chemistry, the theory of the ether in physics, the theory of gravitation, the theory of evolution, are all in themselves indemonstrable hypotheses, provisionally accepted simply because, if granted, they unify great aggregations of facts. Coleridge said that original sin is the one mystery that makes all other things clear. In this mystery, however, there is nothing self-contradictory or arbitrary. Gladden, What is Left? 131 — "Heredity is God working in us, and environment is God working around us." Whether we adopt the theory of Augustine or not, the facts of universal moral obliquity and universal human suffering confront us. We are compelled to reconcile these facts with our faith in the righteousness and goodness of God. Augustine gives us a unifying principle which, better than any other, explains these facts and justifies them. On the solidarity of the race, see Bruce, The Providential Order, 280–310, and art. on Sin, by Bernard, in Hastings' Bible Dictionary.

D. This theory finds support in the conclusions of modern science : with regard to the moral law, as requiring right states as well as right acts ; with regard to the human will, as including subconscious and unconscious bent and determination ; with regard to heredity, and the transmission of evil character ; with regard to the unity and solidarity of the human race.

The Augustinian theory may therefore be called an ethical or theological interpretation of certain incontestable and acknowledged biological facts.

Ribot, Heredity, 1—" Heredity is that biological law by which all beings endowed with life tend to repeat themselves in their descendants; it is for the species what personal identity is for the individual. By it a groundwork remains unchanged amid incessant variations. By it nature ever copies and imitates herself." Griffith-Jones, Ascent through Christ, 202-218—" In man's moral condition we find arrested development; reversion to a savage type; hypocritical and self-protective mimicry of virtue; parasitism; physical and moral abnormality; deep-seated perversion of faculty." Simon, Reconciliation, 154 sq.—"The organism was affected before the individuals which are its successive differentiations and products were affected. . . . . Humanity as an organism received an injury from sin. It received that injury at the very beginning. . . . . At the moment when the seed began to germinate disease entered and it was smitten with death on account of sin."

Bowne, Theory of Thought and Knowledge, 134—" A general notion has no actual or possible metaphysical existence. All real existence is necessarily singular and individual. The only way to give the notion any metaphysical significance is to turn it into a law inherent in reality, and this attempt will fail unless we finally conceive this law as a rule according to which a basal intelligence proceeds in positing individuals." Sheldon, in the Methodist Review, March, 1901 : 214-227, applies this explanation to the doctrine of original sin. Men have a common nature, he says, only in the sense that they are resembling personalities. If we literally died in Adam, we also literally died in Christ. There is no all-inclusive Christ, any more than there is an all-inclusive Adam. We regard this argument as proving the precise opposite of its intended conclusion. There is an all-inclusive Christ, and the fundamental error of most of those who oppose Augustinianism is that they misconceive the union of the believer with Christ. " A basal intelligence" here "posits individuals." And so with the relation of men to Adam. Here too there is " a law inherent in reality "—the regular working of the divine will, according to which like produces like, and a sinful germ reproduces itself.

E. We are to remember, however, that while this theory of the method of our union with Adam is merely a valuable hypothesis, the problem which it seeks to explain is, in both its terms, presented to us both by conscience and by Scripture. In connection with this problem a central fact is announced in Scripture, which we feel compelled to believe upon divine testimony, even though every attempted explanation should prove unsatisfactory. That central fact, which constitutes the substance of the Scripture doctrine of original sin, is simply this: that the sin of Adam is the immediate cause and ground of inborn depravity, guilt and condemnation to the whole human race.

Three things must be received on Scripture testimony : (1) inborn depravity ; (2) guilt and condemnation therefor ; (3) Adam's sin the cause and ground of both. From these three positions of Scripture it seems not only natural, but inevitable, to draw the inference that we "all sinned" in Adam. The Augustinian theory simply puts in a link of connection between two sets of facts which otherwise would be difficult to reconcile. But, in putting in that link of connection, it claims that it is merely bringing out into clear light an underlying but implicit assumption of Paul's reasoning, and this it seeks to prove by showing that upon no other assumption can Paul's reasoning be understood at all. Since the passage in Rom. 5 : 12-19 is so important, we proceed to examine it in greater detail. Our treatment is mainly a reproduction of the substance of Shedd's Commentary, although we have combined with it remarks from Meyer, Schaff, Moule, and others.

Exposition of Rom. 5 : 12-19.—*Parallel between the salvation in Christ and the ruin that has come through Adam*, in each case through no personal act of our own, neither by our earning salvation in the case of the life received through Christ, nor by our individually sinning in the case of the death received through Adam. The statement of the parallel is begun in

Verse 12 : "as through one man sin entered into the world, and death through sin, and so death passed unto all men, for that all sinned," so (as we may complete the interrupted sentence) by one man rig·t-eousness entered into the world, and life by righteousness, and so life passed upon all men, because all became partakers of this righteousness. Both physical and spiritual death is meant. That it is physical, is shown (1) from verse 14; (2) from the allusion to Gen. 3:19; (3) from the universal Jewish and Christian assumption that physical death was the result of Adam's sin. See Wisdom 2 : 23, 24 ; Sirach 25 : 24 ; 3 Esdras 3 : 7, 21 ; 7 : 11, 46, 48, 118 ; 9 : 19 ; John 8 : 44 ; 1 Cor. 15 : 21. That it is spiritual, is evident from Rom. 5 : 18, 21, where ζωή is the opposite of θάνατος, and from 2 Tim. 1 : 10, where the same contrast occurs. The οὕτως in verse 12 shows the *mode* in which historically death has come to all, namely, that the *one* sinned, and thereby brought death to all ; in other words, death is the effect, of which the sin of the one is the cause. By Adam's act, physical and spiritual death passed upon all men, because all sinned. ἐφ' ᾧ = because, on the ground of the fact that, for the reason that, all sinned. πάντες = all, without exception, infants included, as verse 14 teaches.

" Ἥμαρτον mentions the particular reason why all men died, *viz.*, because all men sinned. It is the aorist of momentary past action — sinned when, through the one, sin entered into the world. It is as much as to say, " because, when Adam sinned, all men sinned in and with him." This is proved by the succeeding explanatory context (verses 15-19), in which it is reiterated five times in succession that one and only one sin is the cause of the death that befalls all men. Compare 1 Cor. 15 : 22. The senses " all were sinful," " all became sinful," are inadmissible, for ἁμαρτάνειν is not ἁμαρτωλὸν γίγνεσθαι or εἶναι. The sense " death passed upon all men, because all have consciously and personally sinned," is contradicted (1) by verse 14, in which it is asserted that certain persons who are a part of πάντες, the subject of ἥμαρτον, and who suffer the death which is the penalty of sin, did not commit sins resembling Adam's first sin, *i. e.*, individual and conscious transgressions ; and (2) by verses 15-19, in which it is asserted repeatedly that only one sin, and not millions of transgressions, is the cause of the death of all men. This sense would seem to require ἐφ' ᾧ πάντες ἁμαρτάνουσιν. Neither can ἥμαρτον have the sense " were accounted and treated as sinners " ; for (1) there is no other instance in Scripture where this active verb has a passive signification ; and (2) the passive makes ἥμαρτον to denote God's action, and not man's. This would not furnish the justification of the infliction of death, which Paul is seeking.

Verse 13 begins a demonstration of the proposition, in verse 12, that death comes to all, because all men sinned the one sin of the one man. The argument is as follows : Before the law sin existed ; for there was death, the penalty of sin. But this sin was not sin committed against the *Mosaic* law, because that law was not yet in existence. The death in the world prior to that law proves that there must have been some other law, against which sin had been committed.

Verse 14. Nor could it have been personal and conscious violation of an *unwritten* law, for which death was inflicted ; for death passed upon multitudes, such as infants and idiots, who did not sin in their own persons, as Adam did, by violating some known commandment. Infants are not specifically named here, because the intention is to include others who, though mature in years, have not reached moral consciousness. But since death is everywhere and always the penalty of sin, the death of all must have been the penalty of the common sin of the race, when πάντες ἥμαρτον in Adam. The law which they violated was the Eden statute, Gen. 2 : 17. The relation between their sin and Adam's is not that of *resemblance*, but of *identity*. Had the sin by which death came upon them been one *like* Adam's, there would have been as many sins, to be the cause of death and to account for it, as there were individuals. Death would have come into the world through millions of men, and not "through one man " (verse 12), and judgment would have come upon all men to condemnation through millions of trespasses, and not "through one trespass " (v. 18). The object, then, of the parenthetical digression in verses 13 and 14 is to prevent the reader from supposing, from the statement that "all men sinned," that the individual transgressions of all men are meant, and to make it clear that only the one first sin of the one first man is intended. Those who died before Moses must have violated some law. The Mosaic law, and the law of conscience, have been ruled out of the case. These persons must, therefore, have sinned against the commandment in Eden, the probationary statute ; and their sin was not *similar* (ὁμοίως) to Adam's, but Adam's *identical* sin, the very same sin numerically of the "one man." They did not, in their own persons and consciously, sin as Adam did ; yet in Adam, and in the nature common to him and them, they sinned and fell (*versus* Current Discussions in Theology, 5 : 277, 278). They did not sin *like* Adam, but they "sinned *in* him, and fell *with* him, in that first transgression " (Westminster Larger Catechism, 22).

Verses 15-17 show how the work of grace differs from, and surpasses, the work of sin.

Over against God's exact justice in punishing all for the first sin which all committed in Adam, is set the gratuitous justification of all who are in Christ. Adam's sin is the act of Adam and his posterity together; hence the imputation to the posterity is just, and merited. Christ's obedience is the work of Christ alone; hence the imputation of it to the elect is gracious and unmerited. Here τοὺς πολλούς is not of equal extent with οἱ πολλοί in the first clause, because other passages teach that "the many" who die in Adam are not conterminous with "the many" who live in Christ; see 1 Cor. 15:22; Mat. 25:46; also, see note on verse 18, below. Τοὺς πολλούς here refers to the same persons who, in verse 17, are said to "receive the abundance of grace and of the gift of righteousness." Verse 16 notices a numerical difference between the condemnation and the justification. Condemnation results from *one* offense; justification delivers from *many* offences. Verse 17 enforces and explains verse 16. If the union with Adam in his sin was certain to bring destruction, the union with Christ in his righteousness is yet more certain to bring salvation.

Verse 18 resumes the parallel between Adam and Christ which was commenced in verse 12, but was interrupted by the explanatory parenthesis in verses 13-17. "As through one trespass . . . . . . unto all men to condemnation ; even so through one act of righteousness . . . . unto all men unto justification of [necessary to] life." Here the "all men to condemnation " = the οἱ πολλοί in verse 15 ; and the "all men unto justification of life " = the τοὺς πολλούς in verse 15. There is a totality in each case; but, in the former case, it is the "all men" who derive their physical life from Adam,— in the latter case, it is the "all men" who derive their spiritual life from Christ (compare 1 Cor. 15:22 — "For as in Adam all die, so also in Christ shall all be made alive " — in which last clause Paul is speaking, as the context shows, not of the resurrection of all men, both saints and sinners, but only of the blessed resurrection of the righteous; in other words, of the resurrection of those who are one with Christ).

Verse 19. "For as through the one man's disobedience the many were constituted sinners, even so through the obedience of the one shall the many be constituted righteous." The many were constituted sinners because. according to verse 12, they sinned in and with Adam in his fall. The verb presupposes the fact of natural union between those to whom it relates. All men are declared to be sinners on the ground of that "one trespass," because, when that one trespass was committed, all men were one man — that is, were one common nature in the first human pair. Sin is imputed, because it is committed. All men are punished with death, because they literally sinned in Adam, and not because they are metaphorically reputed to have done so, but in fact did not. Οἱ πολλοί is used in contrast with the one forefather, and the atonement of Christ is designated as ὑπακοή, in order to contrast it with the παρακοή of Adam.

Κατασταθήσονται has the same signification as in the first part of the verse. Δίκαιοι κατασταθήσονται means simply " shall be justified," and is used instead of δικαιωθήσονται, in order to make the antithesis of ἁμαρτωλοὶ κατεστάθησαν more perfect. This being " constituted righteous " presupposes the fact of a union between ὁ εἷς and οἱ πολλοί, *i. e.*, between Christ and believers, just as the being " constituted sinners " presupposed the fact of a union between ὁ εἷς and οἱ πολλοί, *i. e.*, between all men and Adam. The future κατασταθήσονται refers to the succession of believers; the justification of all was, ideally, complete already, but actually, it would await the times of individual believing. "The many" who shall be "constituted righteous" = not all mankind, but only "the many" to whom, in verse 15, grace abounded, and who are described, in verse 17, as "they that receive abundance of grace and of the gift of righteousness."

" But this union differs in several important particulars from that between Adam and his posterity. It is not natural and substantial, but moral and spiritual; not generic and universal, but individual and by election; not caused by the creative act of God, but by his regenerating act. All men, without exception, are one with Adam; only believing men are one with Christ. The imputation of Adam's sin is not an arbitrary act in the sense that, if God so pleased, he could reckon it to the account of any beings in the universe, by a volition. The sin of Adam could not be imputed to the fallen angels, for example, and punished in them, because they never were one with Adam by unity of substance and nature. The fact that they have committed actual transgression of their own will not justify the imputation of Adam's sin to them, any more than the fact that the posterity of Adam have committed actual transgressions of their own would be a sufficient reason for imputing the first sin of Adam to them. Nothing but a real union of nature and being can justify the imputation of Adam's sin; and, similarly, the obedience of Christ could no more be imputed to an unbelieving man than to a lost angel, because neither of these is morally and spiritually one with Christ" (Shedd). For a different interpretation (ἥμαρτον = sinned personally and individually), see Kendrick, in Bap. Rev., 1885 : 48-72.

TABULAR VIEW OF THE VARIOUS THEORIES OF IMPUTATION.

	NO CONDEMNATION INHERITED.			CONDEMNATION INHERITED.		
	PELAGIAN.	ARMINIAN.	NEW SCHOOL.	FEDERAL.	PLACEAN.	AUGUSTINIAN.
I. Origin of the soul.	Immediate creation.	Immediate creation.	Immediate creation.	Immediate creation.	Immediate creation.	Mediate creation.
II. Man's state at birth.	Innocent, and able to obey God.	Depraved, but still able to co-operate with the Spirit.	Depraved and vicious, but this not sin.	Depraved, unable, and condemnable.	Depraved, unable, and condemnable.	Depraved, unable, and condemnable.
III. Effects of Adam's sin.	Only upon himself.	To corrupt his posterity physically and intellectually. No guilt of Adam's sin imputed.	To communicate vitiosity to the whole race.	To insure condemnation of his fellows in covenant, and their creation as depraved.	Natural connection of depravity in all his descendants.	Guilt of Adam's sin, corruption, and death.
IV. How did all sin?	By following Adam's example.	By consciously ratifying Adam's own deed, in spite of the Spirit's aid.	By voluntary transgression of known law.	By being accounted sinners in Adam's sin.	By possessing a depraved nature.	By having part in the sin of Adam, as seminal head of the race.
V. What is corruption?	Only of evil habit, in each case.	Evil tendencies kept in spite of the Spirit.	Uncondemnable, but evil tendencies.	Condemnable, evil disposition and state.	Condemnable, evil disposition and state.	Condemnable, evil disposition and state.
VI. What is imputed?	Every man's own sins.	Only man's own sins and ratifying of this nature.	Man's individual acts of transgression.	Adam's sin, man's own corruption, and man's own sins.	Only depraved nature and man's own sins.	Adam's sin, our depravity, and our own sins.
VII. What is the death incurred?	Spiritual and eternal.	Physical and spiritual death by decree.	Spiritual and eternal death only.	Physical, spiritual, and eternal.	Physical, spiritual, and eternal.	Physical, spiritual, and eternal.
VIII. How are men saved?	By following Christ's example.	By co-operating with the Spirit given to all	By accepting Christ under the influences of truth presented by the Spirit.	By being accounted righteous through the act of Christ.	By becoming possessors of a new nature in Christ.	By Christ's work, with whom we are one.

II.—Objections to the Augustinian Doctrine of Imputation.

The doctrine of Imputation, to which we have thus arrived, is met by its opponents with the following objections. In discussing them, we are to remember that a truth revealed in Scripture may have claims to our belief, in spite of difficulties to us insoluble. Yet it is hoped that examination will show the objections in question to rest either upon false philosophical principles or upon misconception of the doctrine assailed.

A. That there can be no sin apart from and prior to consciousness.

This we deny. The larger part of men's evil dispositions and acts are imperfectly conscious, and of many such dispositions and acts the evil quality is not discerned at all. The objection rests upon the assumption that law is confined to published statutes or to standards formally recognized by its subjects. A profounder view of law as identical with the constituent principles of being, as binding the nature to conformity with the nature of God, as demanding right volitions only because these are manifestations of a right state, as having claims upon men in their corporate capacity, deprives this objection of all its force.

If our aim is to find a conscious act of transgression upon which to base God's charge of guilt and man's condemnation, we can find this more easily in Adam's sin than at the beginning of each man's personal history; for no human being can remember his first sin. The main question at issue is therefore this: Is all sin personal? We claim that both Scripture and reason answer this question in the negative. There is such a thing as race-sin and race-responsibility.

B. That man cannot be responsible for a sinful nature which he did not personally originate.

We reply that the objection ignores the testimony of conscience and of Scripture. These assert that we are responsible for what we are. The sinful nature is not something external to us, but is our inmost selves. If man's original righteousness and the new affection implanted in regeneration have moral character, then the inborn tendency to evil has moral character; as the former are commendable, so the latter is condemnable.

If it be said that sin is the act of a person, and not of a nature, we reply that in Adam the whole human nature once subsisted in the form of a single personality, and the act of the person could be at the same time the act of the nature. That which could not be at any subsequent point of time, could be and was, at that time. Human nature could fall in Adam, though that fall could not be repeated in the case of any one of his descendants. Hovey, Outlines, 129—"Shall we say that *will* is the cause of sin in holy beings, while *wrong desire* is the cause of sin in unholy beings? Augustine held this." Pepper, Outlines, 112—"We do not fall each one by himself. We were so on probation in Adam, that his fall was our fall."

C. That Adam's sin cannot be imputed to us, since we cannot repent of it.

The objection has plausibility only so long as we fail to distinguish between Adam's sin as the inward apostasy of the nature from God, and Adam's sin as the outward act of transgression which followed and manifested that apostasy. We cannot indeed repent of Adam's sin as our personal act or as Adam's personal act, but regarding his sin as the apostasy of our common nature—an apostasy which manifests itself in our personal transgressions as it did in his, we can repent of it and do repent of it. In truth it is this nature, as self-corrupted and averse to God, for which the Christian most deeply repents.

God, we know, has not made our nature as we find it. We are conscious of our depravity and apostasy from God. We know that God cannot be responsible for this; we know that our nature is responsible. But this it could not be, unless its corruption were self-corruption. For this self-corrupted nature we should repent, and do repent. Anselm, De Concep. Virg., 23—"Adam sinned in one point of view as a person, in another as man (*i. e.*, as human nature which at that time existed in him alone). But since Adam and humanity could not be separated, the sin of the person necessarily affected the *nature*. This nature is what Adam transmitted to his posterity, and transmitted it such as his sin had made it, burdened with a debt which it could not pay, robbed of the righteousness with which God had originally invested it; and in every one of his descendants this impaired nature makes the *persons* sinners. Yet not in the same degree sinners as Adam was, for the latter sinned both as human nature and as a person, while new-born infants sin only as they possess the nature,"—more briefly, in Adam a person made nature sinful; in his posterity, nature makes persons sinful.

D. That, if we be responsible for Adam's first sin, we must also be responsible not only for every other sin of Adam, but for the sins of our immediate ancestors.

We reply that the apostasy of human nature could occur but once. It occurred in Adam before the eating of the forbidden fruit, and revealed itself in that eating. The subsequent sins of Adam and of our immediate ancestors are no longer acts which determine or change the nature, —they only show what the nature is. Here is the truth and the limitation of the Scripture declaration that "the son shall not bear the iniquity of the father" (Ez. 18 : 20 ; *cf.* Luke 13 : 2, 3 ; John 9 : 2, 3). Man is not responsible for the specifically evil tendencies communicated to him from his immediate ancestors, as distinct from the nature he possesses ; nor is he responsible for the sins of those ancestors which originated these tendencies. But he is responsible for that original apostasy which constituted the one and final revolt of the race from God, and for the personal depravity and disobedience which in his own case has resulted therefrom.

Augustine, Encheiridion, 46, 47, leans toward an imputing of the sins of immediate ancestors, but intimates that, as a matter of grace, this may be limited to "the third and fourth generation " (Ex. 20:5). Aquinas thinks this last is said by God, because fathers live to see the third and fourth generation of their descendants, and influence them by their example to become voluntarily like themselves. Burgesse, Original Sin, 397, adds the covenant-idea to that of natural generation, in order to prevent imputation of the sins of immediate ancestors as well as those of Adam. So also Shedd. But Baird, Elohim Revealed, 508, gives a better explanation, when he distinguishes between the first sin of nature when it apostatized, and those subsequent personal actions which merely manifest the nature but do not change it. Imagine Adam to have remained innocent, but one of his posterity to have fallen. Then the descendants of that one would have been guilty for the change of nature in him, but not guilty for the sins of ancestors intervening between him and them.

We add that man may direct the course of a lava-stream, already flowing downward, into some particular channel, and may even dig a new channel for it down the mountain. But the stream is constant in its quantity and quality, and is under the same influence of gravitation in all stages of its progress. I am responsible for the downward tendency which my nature gave itself at the beginning ; but I am not responsible for inherited and specifically evil tendencies as something apart from the nature,— for they are not apart from it,— they are forms or manifestations of it. These tendencies run out after a time,— not so with sin of nature. The declaration of Ezekiel (18 : 20), "the son shall not bear the iniquity of the father," like Christ's denial that blindness was due to the blind man's individual sins or those of his parents (John 9 : 2, 3), simply shows that God does not impute to us the sins of our immediate ancestors; it is not inconsistent with the doctrine that all the physical and moral evil of the world is the result of a sin of Adam with which the whole race is chargeable.

Peculiar tendencies to avarice or sensuality inherited from one's immediate ancestry are merely wrinkles in native depravity which add nothing to its amount or its guilt. Shedd, Dogm. Theol., 2 : 88–94 — "To inherit a temperament is to inherit a secondary trait." H. B. Smith, System, 296 —"Ezekiel 18 does not deny that descendants are involved in the evil results of ancestral sins, under God's moral government; but simply shows that there is opportunity for extrication, in personal repentance and obedience." Mozley on Predestination, 179 — "Augustine says that Ezekiel's declarations that the son shall not bear the iniquity of the father are not a universal law of the divine dealings, but only a special prophetical one, as alluding to the divine mercy under the gospel dispensation and the covenant of grace, under which the effect of original sin and the punishment of mankind for the sin of their first parent was removed." See also Dorner, Glaubenslehre, 2 : 31 (Syst. Doct., 2 : 326, 327), where God's visiting the sins of the fathers upon the children (Ex. 20 : 5) is explained by the fact that the children repeat the sins of the parents. German proverb : "The apple does not fall far from the tree."

E.   That if Adam's sin and condemnation can be ours by propagation, the righteousness and faith of the believer should be propagable also.

We reply that no merely personal qualities, whether of sin or righteousness, are communicated by propagation. Ordinary generation does not transmit *personal* guilt, but only that guilt which belongs to the whole *species.* So personal faith and righteousness are not propagable. "Original sin is the consequent of man's *nature,* whereas the parents' grace is a *personal* excellence, and cannot be transmitted " (Burgesse).

Thornwell, Selected Writings, 1 : 543, says the Augustinian doctrine would imply that Adam, penitent and believing, must have begotten penitent and believing children, seeing that the nature as it is in the parent always flows from parent to child. But see Fisher, Discussions, 370, where Aquinas holds that no quality or guilt that is *personal* is propagated (Thomas Aquinas, 2 : 629). Anselm (De Concept. Virg. et Origin. Peccato, 98) will not decide the question. "The original nature of the tree is propagated — not the nature of the graft "—when seed from the graft is planted. Burgesse: "Learned parents do not convey learning to their children, but they are born in ignorance as others." Augustine: "A Jew that was circumcised begat children not circumcised, but uncircumcised ; and the seed that was sown without husks, yet produced corn with husks."

The recent modification of Darwinism by Weismann has confirmed the doctrine of the text. Lamarck's view was that development of each race has taken place through the *effort* of the individuals, — the giraffe has a long neck because successive giraffes have reached for food on high trees. Darwin held that development has taken place not because of effort, but because of *environment*, which kills the unfit and permits the fit to survive, — the giraffe has a long neck because among the children of giraffes only the long-necked ones could reach the fruit, and of successive generations of giraffes only the long-necked ones lived to propagate. But Weismann now tells us that even then there would be no development unless there were a spontaneous *innate tendency* in giraffes to become long-necked,— nothing is of avail after the giraffe is born ; all depends upon the germs in the parents. Darwin held to the transmission of acquired characters, so that individual men are *affluents* of the stream of humanity ; Weismann holds, on the contrary, that acquired characters are not transmitted, and that individual men are only *effluents* of the stream of humanity : the stream gives its characteristics to the individuals, but the individuals do not give their characteristics to the stream : see Howard Ernest Cushman, in The Outlook, Jan. 10, 1897.

Weismann, Heredity, 2 : 14, 266–270, 482 — "Characters only acquired by the operation of external circumstances, acting during the life of the individual, cannot be transmitted. . . . The loss of a finger is not inherited ; increase of an organ by exercise is a purely personal acquirement and is not transmitted ; no child of reading parents ever read without being taught ; children do not even learn to speak untaught." Horses with docked tails, Chinese women with cramped feet, do not transmit their peculiarities. The rupture of the hymen in women is not transmitted. Weismann cut off the tails of 66 white mice in five successive generations, but of 901 offspring none were tailless. G. J. Romanes, Life and Letters, 300 — "Three additional cases of cats which have lost their tails having tailless kittens afterwards." In his Weismannism, Romanes writes: "The truly scientific attitude of mind with regard to the problem of heredity is to say with Galton: 'We might almost reserve our belief that the structural cells can react on the sexual elements at all, and we may be confident that at most they do so in a very faint degree; in other words, that acquired modifications are barely if at all *inherited*, in the correct sense of that word.'" This seems to class both Romanes and Galton on the side of Weismann in the controversy. Burbank, however, says that "acquired characters are transmitted, or I know nothing of plant life."

A. H. Bradford, Heredity, 19, 20, illustrates the opposing views: "Human life is not a clear stream flowing from the mountains, receiving in its varied course something from a thousand rills and rivulets on the surface and in the soil, so that it is no longer pure as at the first. To this view of Darwin and Spencer, Weismann and Haeckel oppose the view that human life is rather a stream flowing underground from the mountains to the sea, and rising now and then in fountains, some of which are saline, some sulphuric, and some tinctured with iron; and that the differences are due entirely to the soil passed through in breaking forth to the surface, the mother-stream down and beneath all the salt, sulphur and iron, flowing on toward the sea substantially unchanged. If Darwin is correct, then we must change individuals in order to change their posterity. If Weismann is correct, then we must change environment in order that better individuals may be born. That which is born of the Spirit is spirit; but that which is born of spirit tainted by corruptions of the flesh is still tainted."

The conclusion best warranted by science seems to be that of Wallace, in the Forum, August, 1890, namely, that there is always a *tendency* to transmit acquired characters, but that only those which affect the blood and nervous system, like drunkenness and syphilis, overcome the fixed habit of the organism and make themselves permanent. Applying this principle now to the connection of Adam with the race, we regard the sin of Adam as a radical one, comparable only to the act of faith which merges the soul in Christ. It was a turning away of the whole being from the light and love of God, and a setting of the face toward darkness and death. Every subsequent act was an act in the same direction, but an act which manifested, not altered, the nature. This first act of sin deprived the nature of all moral sustenance and growth, except so far as the still immanent God counteracted the inherent tendencies to evil. Adam's posterity inherited his corrupt nature, but they do not inherit any subsequently acquired characters, either those of their first father or of their immediate ancestors.

Bascom, Comparative Psychology, chap. VII—"Modifications, however great, like artificial disablement, that do not work into physiological structure, do not transmit themselves. The more conscious and voluntary our acquisitions are, the less are they transmitted by inheritance." Shaler, Interpretation of Nature, 88—"Heredity and individual action may combine their forces and so intensify one or more of the inherited motives that the form is affected by it and the effect may be transmitted to the offspring. So conflict of inheritances may lead to the institution of variety. Accumulation of impulses may lead to sudden revolution, and the species may be changed, not by environment, but by contest between the host of inheritances." Visiting the sins of the fathers upon the children was thought to be outrageous doctrine, so long as it was taught only in Scripture. It is now vigorously applauded, since it takes the name of heredity. Dale, Ephesians, 189—"When we were young, we fought with certain sins and killed them; they trouble us no more; but their ghosts seem to rise from their graves in the distant years and to clothe themselves in the flesh and blood of our children." See A. M. Marshall, Biological Lectures, 273; Mivart, in Harper's Magazine, March, 1895: 682; Bixby, Crisis in Morals, 176.

F.   That, if all moral consequences are properly penalties, sin, considered as a sinful nature, must be the punishment of sin, considered as the act of our first parents.

But we reply that the impropriety of punishing sin with sin vanishes when we consider that the sin which is punished is our own, equally with the sin with which we are punished. The objection is valid as against the Federal theory or the theory of Mediate Imputation, but not as against the theory of Adam's Natural Headship. To deny that God, through the operation of second causes, may punish the act of transgression by the habit and tendency which result from it, is to ignore the facts of every-day life, as well as the statements of Scripture in which sin is represented as ever reproducing itself, and with each reproduction increasing its guilt and punishment (Rom. 6 : 19 ; James 1 : 15.)

Rom. 6:19 — "as ye presented your members as servants to uncleanness and to iniquity *unto iniquity*, even so now present your members as servants to righteousness *unto sanctification*" ; Eph. 4: 22 — "waxeth corrupt after the lusts of deceit" ; James 1 : 15 — "Then the lust, when it hath conceived, beareth sin: and the sin, when it is full-grown, bringeth forth death" ; 2 Tim. 3 : 13 — "evil men and impostors shall wax worse and worse, deceiving and being deceived." See Meyer on Rom. 1 : 24 — "Wherefore God gave them up in the lusts of their hearts unto uncleanness." All effects become in their turn causes. Schiller : "This is the very curse or evil deed, That of new evil it becomes the seed." Tennyson, Vision of Sin : " Behold it was a crime Of sense, avenged by sense that wore with time. Another said : The crime of sense became The crime of malice, and is equal blame." Whiton, Is Eternal Punishment Endless, 52 — "The punishment of sin essentially consists in the wider spread and stronger hold of the malady of the soul. Prov. 5 : 22 — 'His own iniquities shall take the wicked.' The habit of sinning holds the wicked 'with the cords of his sin.' Sin is self-perpetuating. The sinner gravitates from worse to worse, in an ever-deepening fall." The least of our sins has in it a power of infinite expansion,— left to itself it would flood a world with misery and destruction.

Wisdom, 11 : 16 —" Wherewithal a man sinneth, by the same also he shall be punished." Shakespeare, Richard II, 5 : 5 — "J wasted time, and now doth time waste me" ; Richard III, 4 : 2 —"I am in so far in blood, that sin will pluck on sin " ; Pericles, 1 : 1 —" One sin I know another doth provoke ; Murder 's as near to lust as flame to smoke ;" King Lear, 5 : 3 — "The gods are just, and of our pleasant vices Make instruments to scourge us." " Marlowe's Faustus typifies the continuous degradation of a soul that has renounced its ideal, and the drawing on of one vice by another, for they go hand in hand like the Hours " (James Russell Lowell). Mrs. Humphrey Ward, David Grieve, 410 — " After all, there 's not much hope when the craving returns on a man of his age, especially after some years' interval."

G.   That the doctrine excludes all separate probation of individuals since Adam, by making their moral life a mere manifestation of tendencies received from him.

We reply that the objection takes into view only our connection with the race, and ignores the complementary and equally important fact of each man's personal will. That personal will does more than simply express the nature ; it may to a certain extent curb the nature, or it may, on the other hand, add a sinful character and influence of its own. There is, in other words, a remainder of freedom, which leaves room for personal probation, in addition to the race-probation in Adam.

Kreibig, Versöhnungslehre, objects to the Augustianian view that if personal sin proceeds from original, the only thing men are guilty for is Adam's sin ; all subsequent sin is a spontaneous development ; the individual will can only manifest its inborn character.   But we reply that this is a misrepresentation of Augustine. He does not thus lose sight of the remainders of freedom in man (see references on page 620, in the statement of Augustine's view, and in the section following this, on Ability, 640-644). He says that the corrupt tree may produce the wild fruit of morality, though not the divine fruit of grace. It is not true that the will is absolutely as the character.   Though character is the surest index as to what the decisions of the will may be, it is not an infallible one. Adam's first sin, and the sins of men after regeneration, prove this. Irregular, spontaneous, exceptional though these decisions are, they are still acts of the will, and they show that the agent is not *bound* by motives nor by character.

Here is our answer to the question whether it be not a sin to propagate the race and produce offspring. Each child has a personal will which may have a probation of its own and a chance for deliverance. Denney, Studies in Theology, 87-99 — " What we inherit may be said to fix our trial, but not our fate. We belong to God as well as to the past." "All souls are mine" (Ez. 18 : 4) ; "Every one that is of the truth heareth my voice" (John 18 : 37). Thomas Fuller : "1. Roboam begat Abia ; that is, a bad father begat a bad son ; 2. Abia begat Asa; that is, a bad father begat a good son; 3. Asa begat Josaphat; that is, a good father a good son; 4. Josaphat begat Joram; that is, a good father a bad son. 1 see, Lord, from hence, that my father's piety cannot be entailed; that is bad news for me. But I see that actual impiety is not always hereditary; that is good news for my son." Butcher, Aspects of Greek Genius, 121 — Among the Greeks, "The popular view was that guilt is inherited; that is, that the children are punished for their fathers' sins. The view of Æschylus, and of Sophocles also, was that a tendency towards guilt was inherited, but that this tendency does not annihilate man's free will. If therefore the children are punished, they are punished for their own sins. But Sophocles saw the further truth that innocent children may suffer for their fathers' sins."

Julius Müller, Doc. Sin, 2 : 316 — "The merely organic theory of sin leads to naturalism, which endangers not only the doctrine of a final judgment, but that of personal immortality generally." In preaching, therefore, we should begin with the known and acknowledged sins of men. We should lay the same stress upon our connection with Adam that the Scripture does, to explain the problem of universal and inveterate sinful tendencies, to enforce our need of salvation from this common ruin, and to illustrate our connection with Christ. Scripture does not, and we need not, make our responsibility for Adam's sin the great theme of preaching. See A. H. Strong, on Christian Individualism, and on The New Theology, in Philosophy and Religion, 156–163, 164–179.

H. That the organic unity of the race in the transgression is a thing so remote from common experience that the preaching of it neutralizes all appeals to the conscience.

But whatever of truth there is in this objection is due to the self-isolating nature of sin. Men feel the unity of the family, the profession, the nation to which they belong, and, just in proportion to the breadth of their sympathies and their experience of divine grace, do they enter into Christ's feeling of unity with the race (cf. Is. 6 : 5 ; Lam. 3 : 39–45 ; Ezra 9 : 6 ; Neh. 1 : 6). The fact that the self-contained and self-seeking recognize themselves as responsible only for their personal acts should not prevent our pressing upon men's attention the more searching standards of the Scriptures. Only thus can the Christian find a solution for the dark problem of a corruption which is inborn yet condemnable ; only thus can the unregenerate man be led to a full knowledge of the depth of his ruin and of his absolute dependence upon God for salvation.

Identification of the individual with the nation or the race: Is. 6 : 5 — "Woe is me! for I am undone; because I am a man of unclean lips, and I dwell in the midst of a people of unclean lips"; Lam. 3 : 42 — "We have transgressed and have rebelled"; Ezra 9 : 6 — "I am ashamed and blush to lift up my face to thee, my God; for our iniquities are increased over our head"; Neh. 1 : 6 — "I confess the sins of the children of Israel . . . . Yea, I and my father's house have sinned." So God punishes all Israel for David's sin of pride; so the sins of Reuben, Canaan, Achan, Gehazi, are visited on their children or descendants.

H. B. Smith, System, 296, 297 — "Under the moral government of God one man may justly suffer on account of the sins of another. An organic relation of men is regarded in the great judgment of God in history. . . . . There is evil which comes upon individuals, not as punishment for their personal sins, but still as suffering which comes under a moral government. . . . . Jer. 32 : 18 reasserts the declaration of the second commandment, that God visits the iniquity of the fathers upon their children. It may be said that all these are merely ' consequences ' of family or tribal or national or race relations, — ' Evil becomes cosmical by reason of fastening on relations which were originally adapted to making good cosmical:' but then God's plan must be in the consequences — a plan administered by a moral being, over moral beings, according to moral considerations, and for moral ends; and, if that be fully taken into view, the dispute as to 'consequences' or 'punishment' becomes a merely verbal one."

There is a common conscience over and above the private conscience, and it controls individuals, as appears in great crises like those at which the fall of Fort Sumter summoned men to defend the Union and the Proclamation of Emancipation sounded the death-knell of slavery. Coleridge said that original sin is the one mystery that makes all things clear; see Fisher, Nature and Method of Revelation, 151-157. Bradford, Heredity, 34, quotes from Elam, A Physician's Problems, 5 — "An acquired and habitual vice will rarely fail to leave its trace upon one or more of the offspring, either in its original form, or one closely allied. The habit of the parent becomes the all but irresistible impulse of the child ; . . . . the organic tendency is excited to the uttermost, and the power of will and of conscience is proportionally weakened. . . . . So the sins of the parents are visited upon the children."

Pascal : " It is astonishing that the mystery which is furthest removed from our knowledge — I mean the transmission of original sin — should be that without which we have no true knowledge of ourselves. It is in this abyss that the clue to our condition takes its turnings and windings, insomuch that man is more incomprehensible without the mystery than this mystery is incomprehensible to man." Yet Pascal's perplexity was largely due to his holding the Augustinian position that inherited sin is damning and brings eternal death, while not holding to the coördinate Augustinian position of a primary existence and act of the species in Adam ; see Shedd, Dogm. Theol., 2 : 18. Atomism is egotistic. The purest and noblest feel most strongly that humanity is not like a heap of sand-grains or a row of bricks set on end, but that it is an organic unity. So the Christian feels for the family and for the church. So Christ, in Gethsemane, felt for the race. If it be said that the tendency of the Augustinian view is to diminish the sense of guilt for personal sins, we reply that only those who recognize *sins* as rooted in *sin* can properly recognize the evil of them. To such they are *symptoms* of an apostasy from God so deep-seated and universal that nothing but infinite grace can deliver us from it.

I. That a constitution by which the sin of one individual involves in guilt and condemnation the nature of all men who descend from him is contrary to God's justice.

We acknowledge that no human theory can fully solve the mystery of imputation. But we prefer to attribute God's dealings to justice rather than to sovereignty. The following considerations, though partly hypothetical, may throw light upon the subject : (*a*) A probation of our common nature in Adam, sinless as he was and with full knowledge of God's law, is more consistent with divine justice than a separate probation of each individual, with inexperience, inborn depravity, and evil example, all favoring a decision against God. (*b*) A constitution which made a common fall possible may have been indispensable to any provision of a common salvation. (*c*) Our chance for salvation as sinners under grace may be better than it would have been as sinless Adams under law. (*d*) A constitution which permitted oneness with the first Adam in the transgression cannot be unjust, since a like principle of oneness with Christ, the second Adam, secures our salvation. (*e*) There is also a *physical and natural* union with Christ which antedates the fall and which is incident to man's creation. The immanence of Christ in humanity guarantees a continuous divine effort to remedy the disaster caused by man's free will, and to restore the *moral* union with God which the race has lost by the fall.

Thus our ruin and our redemption were alike wrought out without personal act of ours. As all the natural life of humanity was in Adam, so all the spiritual life of humanity was in Christ. As our old nature was corrupted in Adam and propagated to us by physical generation, so our new nature was restored in Christ and communicated to us by the regenerating work of the Holy Spirit. If then we are justified upon the ground of our inbeing in Christ, we may in like manner be condemned on the ground of our inbeing in Adam.

Stearns, in N. Eng., Jan. 1882 : 95 — " The silence of Scripture respecting the precise connection between the first great sin and the sins of the millions of individuals who have lived since then is a silence that neither science nor philosophy has been, or is, able to break with a satisfactory explanation. Separate the twofold nature of man, corporate and individual. Recognize in the one the region of necessity; in the other the region of freedom. The scientific law of heredity has brought into new currency the doctrine which the old theologians sought to express under the name of original sin,—a term which had a meaning as it was at first used by Augustine, but which is an awkward misnomer if we accept any other theory but his."

Dr. Hovey claims that the Augustinian view breaks down when applied to the connection between the justification of believers and the righteousness of Christ: for believers were not in Christ, as to the substance of their souls, when he wrought out redemption for them. But we reply that the life of Christ which makes us Christians is the same life which made atonement upon the cross and which rose from the grave for our justification. The parallel between Adam and Christ is of the nature of analogy, not of identity. With Adam, we have a connection of physical life; with Christ, a connection of spiritual life.

Stahl, Philosophie des Rechts, quoted in Olshausen's Com. on Rom. 5:12-21 — " Adam is the original *matter* of humanity; Christ is its original *idea* in God; both personally living. Mankind is one in them. Therefore Adam's sin became the sin of all; Christ's sacrifice the atonement for all. Every leaf of a tree may be green or wither by itself; but each suffers by the disease of the root, and recovers only by its healing. The shallower the man, so much more isolated will everything appear to him; for upon the surface all lies apart. He will see in mankind, in the nation, nay, even in the family, mere individuals, where the act of the one has no connection with that of the other. The profounder the man, the more do these inward relations of unity, proceeding from the very centre, force themselves upon him. Yea, the love of our neighbor is itself nothing but the deep feeling of this unity; for we love him only, with whom we feel and acknowledge ourselves to be one. What the Christian love of our neighbor is for the heart, that unity of race is for the understanding. If sin through one, and redemption through one, is not possible, the command to love our neighbor is also unintelligible. Christian ethics and Christian faith are therefore in truth indissolubly united. Christianity effects in history an advance like that from the animal kingdom to man by its revealing the essential unity of men, the consciousness of which in the ancient world had vanished when the nations were separated."

If the sins of the parents were not visited upon the children, neither could their virtues be; the possibility of the one involves the possibility of the other. If the guilt of our first father could not be transmitted to all who derive their life from him, then the justification of Christ could not be transmitted to all who derive their life from him. We do not, however, see any Scripture warrant for the theory that all men are justified from original sin by virtue of their natural connection with Christ. He who is the life of all men bestows manifold temporal blessings upon the ground of his atonement. But justification from sin is conditioned upon conscious surrender of the human will and trust in the divine mercy. The immanent Christ is ever urging man individually and collectively toward such decision. But the acceptance or rejection of the offered grace is left to man's free will. This principle enables us properly to estimate the view of Dr. Henry E. Robins which follows.

H. E. Robins, Harmony of Ethics with Theology, 51—"All men born of Adam stand in such a relation to Christ that salvation is their birthright under promise—a birthright which can only be forfeited by their intelligent, personal, moral action, as was Esau's." Dr. Robins holds to an inchoate justification of all—a justification which becomes actual and complete only when the soul closes with Christ's offer to the sinner. We prefer to say that humanity in Christ is ideally justified because Christ himself is justified, but that individual men are justified only when they consciously appropriate his offered grace or surrender themselves to his renewing Spirit. Allen, Jonathan Edwards, 312—"The grace of God is as organic in its relation to man as is the evil in his nature. Grace also reigns wherever justice reigns." William Ashmore, on the New Trial of the Sinner, in Christian Review, 26:245-264—"There is a gospel of nature commensurate with the law of nature; Rom. 3:22— 'unto all, and upon all them that believe'; the first 'all' is unlimited; the second 'all' is limited to those who believe."

R. W. Dale, Ephesians, 180—"Our fortunes were identified with the fortunes of Christ; in the divine thought and purpose we were inseparable from him. Had we been true and loyal to the divine idea, the energy of Christ's righteousness would have drawn us upward to height after height of goodness and joy, until we ascended from this earthly life to the larger powers and loftier services and richer delights of other and diviner worlds; and still, through one golden age of intellectual and ethical and spiritual growth after another, we should have continued to rise towards Christ's transcendent and infinite perfection. But we sinned; and as the union between Christ and us could not be broken without the final and irrevocable defeat of the divine purpose, Christ was drawn down from the serene heavens to the confused and troubled life of our race, to pain, to temptation, to anguish, to the cross and to the grave, and so the mystery of his atonement for our sin was consummated."

For replies to the foregoing and other objections, see Schaff, in Bib. Sac., 5 : 230; Shedd, Sermons to the Nat. Man, 266–284; Baird, Elohim Revealed, 507–509, 529–544; Birks, Difficulties of Belief, 134–188; Edwards, Original Sin, in Works, 2 : 473–510; Atwater, on Calvinism in Doctrine and Life, in Princeton Review, 1875 : 73; Stearns, Evidence of Christian Experience, 96–100. *Per contra*, see Moxom, in Bap. Rev., 1881 : 273–287; Park Discourses, 210–233; Bradford, Heredity, 237.

SECTION VI.—CONSEQUENCES OF SIN TO ADAM'S POSTERITY.

As the result of Adam's transgression, all his posterity are born in the same state into which he fell. But since law is the all-comprehending demand of harmony with God, all moral consequences flowing from transgression are to be regarded as sanctions of law, or expressions of the divine displeasure through the constitution of things which he has established. Certain of these consequences, however, are earlier recognized than others and are of minor scope; it will therefore be useful to consider them under the three aspects of depravity, guilt, and penalty.

I. DEPRAVITY.

By this we mean, on the one hand, the lack of original righteousness or of holy affection toward God, and, on the other hand, the corruption of the moral nature, or bias toward evil. That such depravity exists has been abundantly shown, both from Scripture and from reason, in our consideration of the universality of sin.

Salvation is twofold: deliverance from the evil—the penalty and the power of sin: and accomplishment of the good—likeness to God and realization of the true idea of humanity. It includes all these for the race as well as for the individual: removal of the barriers that keep men from each other; and the perfecting of society in communion with God; or, in other words, the kingdom of God on earth. It was the nature of man, when he first came from the hand of God, to fear, love, and trust God above all things. This tendency toward God has been lost; sin has altered and corrupted man's innermost nature. In place of this bent toward God there is a fearful bent toward evil. Depravity is both negative—absence of love and of moral likeness to God—and positive—presence of manifold tendencies to evil. Two questions only need detain us:

1. Depravity partial or total?

The Scriptures represent human nature as totally depraved. The phrase "total depravity," however, is liable to misinterpretation, and should not be used without explanation. By the total depravity of universal humanity we mean:

A. Negatively,—not that every sinner is: (*a*) Destitute of conscience, —for the existence of strong impulses to right, and of remorse for wrongdoing, show that conscience is often keen; (*b*) devoid of all qualities pleasing to men, and useful when judged by a human standard,—for the existence of such qualities is recognized by Christ; (c) prone to every form of sin, —for certain forms of sin exclude certain others ; (d) intense as he can be in his selfishness and opposition to God,—for he becomes worse every day.

(a) John 8 : 9 — "And they, when they heard it, went out one by one, beginning from the eldest, even unto the last " (John 7 : 53 — 8 : 11, though not written by John, is a perfectly true narrative, descended from the apostolic age). The muscles of a dead frog's leg will contract when a current of electricity is sent into them. So the dead soul will thrill at touch of the divine law. Natural conscience, combined with the principle of self-love, may even prompt choice of the good, though no love for God is in the choice. Bengel : " We have lost our likeness to God ; but there remains notwithstanding an indelible nobility which we ought to revere both in ourselves and in others. We still have remained men, to be conformed to that likeness, through the divine blessing to which man's will should subscribe. This they forget who speak evil of human nature. Absalom fell out of his father's favor ; but the people, for all that, recognized in him the son of the king."

(b) Mark 10 : 21 — "And Jesus looking upon him loved him." These very qualities, however, may show that their possessors are sinning against great light and are the more guilty; cf. Mal. 1 : 6 — "A son honoreth his father, and a servant his master : if then I am a father, where is mine honor ? and if I am a master, where is my fear?" John Caird, Fund. Ideas of Christianity, 2 : 75 —"The assertor of the total depravity of human nature, of its absolute blindness and incapacity, presupposes in himself and in others the presence of a criterion or principle of good, in virtue of which he discerns himself to be wholly evil; yet the very proposition that human nature is wholly evil would be unintelligible unless it were false. . . . Consciousness of sin is a negative sign of the possibility of restoration. But it is not in itself proof that the possibility will become actuality." A ruined temple may have beautiful fragments of fluted columns, but it is no proper habitation for the god for whose worship it was built.

(c) Mat. 23 : 23 — "ye tithe mint and anise and cummin, and have left undone the weightier matters of the law, justice and mercy, and faith : but these ye ought to have done, and not to have left the other undone"; Rom. 2 : 14 — "when Gentiles that have not the law do by nature the things of the law, these, not having the law, are the law unto themselves ; in that they show the work of the law written in their hearts, their conscience bearing witness therewith." The sin of miserliness may exclude the sin of luxury ; the sin of pride may exclude the sin of sensuality. Shakespeare, Othello, 2 : 3 — " It hath pleased the devil Drunkenness to give place to the devil Wrath." Franklin Carter, Life of Mark Hopkins, 321–323 — Dr. Hopkins did not think that the sons of God should describe themselves as once worms or swine or vipers. Yet he held that man could sink to a degradation below the brute : " No brute is any more capable of rebelling against God than of serving him ; is any more capable of sinking below the level of its own nature than of rising to the level of man. No brute can be either a fool or a fiend. . . . In the way that sin and corruption came into the spiritual realm we find one of those analogies to what takes place in the lower forms of being that show the unity of the system throughout. All disintegration and corruption of matter is from the domination of a lower over a higher law. The body begins to return to its original elements as the lower chemical and physical forces begin to gain ascendency over the higher force of life. In the same way all sin and corruption in man is from his yielding to a lower law or principle of action in opposition to the demands of one that is higher."

(d) Gen. 15 : 16 — "the iniquity of the Amorite is not yet full " ; 2 Tim. 3 : 13 — "evil men and impostors shall wax worse and worse." Depravity is not simply being deprived of good. Depravation (de, and pravus, crooked, perverse) is more than deprivation. Left to himself man tends downward, and his sin increases day by day. But there is a divine influence within which quickens conscience and kindles aspiration for better things. The immanent Christ is 'the light which lighteth every man " (John 1 : 9). Prof. Wm. Adams Brown : "In so far as God's Spirit is at work among men and they receive 'the Light which lighteth every man,' we must qualify our statement of total depravity. Depravity is not so much a state as a tendency. With growing complexity of life, sin becomes more complex. Adam's sin was not the worst. 'It shall be more tolerable for the land of Sodom in the day of judgment, than for thee ' (Mat. 11 : 24)."

Men are not yet in the condition of demons. Only here and there have they attained to "a disinterested love of evil." Such men are few, and they were not born so. There are degrees in depravity. E. G. Robinson : "There is a good streak left in the devil yet." Even Satan will become worse than he now is. The phrase "total depravity" has respect only to relations to God, and it means incapability of doing anything which in the sight of God is a good act. No act is perfectly good that does not proceed from a true heart and constitute an expression of that heart. Yet we have no right to say that every act of an unregenerate man is displeasing to God. Right acts from right motives are good, whether performed by a Christian or by one who is unrenewed in heart. Such acts, however, are always prompted by God, and thanks for them are due to God and not to him who performed them.

B. Positively, — that every sinner is: (*a*) totally destitute of that love to God which constitutes the fundamental and all-inclusive demand of the law ; (*b*) chargeable with elevating some lower affection or desire above regard for God and his law ; (*c*) supremely determined, in his whole inward and outward life, by a preference of self to God ; (*d*) possessed of an aversion to God which, though sometimes latent, becomes active enmity, so soon as God's will comes into manifest conflict with his own ; (*e*) disordered and corrupted in every faculty, through this substitution of selfishness for supreme affection toward God; (*f*) credited with no thought, emotion, or act of which divine holiness can fully approve ; (*g*) subject to a law of constant progress in depravity, which he has no recuperative energy to enable him successfully to resist.

(*a*) John 5 : 42 — "But I know you, that ye have not the love of God in yourselves." (*b*) 2 Tim. 3 : 4 — "lovers of pleasure rather than lovers of God "; *cf*. Mal. 1 : 6 — "A son honoreth his father, and a servant his master: if then I am a father, where is mine honor ? and if I am a master, where is my fear ? " (*c*) 2 Tim. 3 : 2 — "lovers of self"; (*d*) Rom. 8 : 7 — "the mind of the flesh is enmity against God." (*e*) Eph. 4 : 18 — "darkened in their understanding . . . . hardening of their heart " ; Tit. 1 : 15 — "both their mind and their conscience are defiled " ; 2 Cor. 7 : 1 — "defilement of flesh and spirit " ; Heb. 3 : 12 — "an evil heart of unbelief" ; (*f*) Rom. 3 : 9 — "they are all under sin "; 7 : 18 — "in me, that is, in my flesh, dwelleth no good thing." (*g*) Rom. 7 : 18 — "to will is present with me, but to do that which is good is not " ; 23 — "law in my members, warring against the law of my mind, and bringing me into captivity under the law of sin which is in my members."

Every sinner would prefer a milder law and a different administration. But whoever does not love God's law does not truly love God. The sinner seeks to secure his own interests rather than God's. Even so-called religious acts he performs with preference of his own good to God's glory. He disobeys, and always has disobeyed, the fundamental law of love. He is like a railway train on a down grade, and the brakes must be applied by God or destruction is sure. There are latent passions in every heart which if let loose would curse the world. Many a man who escaped from the burning Iroquois Theatre in Chicago, proved himself a brute and a demon, by trampling down fugitives who cried for mercy. Denney, Studies in Theology, 83 — "The depravity which sin has produced in human nature extends to the whole of it. There is no part of man's nature which is unaffected by it. Man's nature is all of a piece, and what affects it at all affects it altogether. When the conscience is violated by disobedience to the will of God, the moral understanding is darkened, and the will is enfeebled. We are not constructed in water-tight compartments, one of which might be ruined while the others remained intact." Yet over against total depravity, we must set total redemption ; over against original sin, original grace. Christ is in every human heart mitigating the affects of sin, urging to repentance, and "able to save to the uttermost them that draw near unto God through him " (Heb. 7 : 25). Even the unregenerate heathen may "put away . . . . the old man " and "put on the new man " (Eph. 4 : 22, 24), being delivered "out of the body of this death . . . . through Jesus Christ our Lord " (Rom. 7 : 24, 25).

H. B. Smith, System, 277 — "By total depravity is never meant that men are as bad as they can be ; nor that they have not, in their natural condition, certain amiable qualities; nor that they may not have virtues in a limited sense (*justitia civilis*). But it is meant (1) that depravity, or the sinful condition of man, infects the whole man : intellect, feeling, heart and will ; (2) that in each unrenewed person some lower affection is supreme ; and (3) that each such is destitute of love to God. On these positions : as to (1) the power of depravity over the *whole* man, we have given proof from Scripture ; as to (2) the fact that in every unrenewed man some lower affection is supreme, experience may be always appealed to ; men know that their supreme affection is fixed on some lower good — intellect, heart, and will going together in it ; or that some form of selfishness is predominant — using selfish in a general sense —

self seeks its happiness in some inferior object, giving to that its supreme affection; as to (3) that every unrenewed person is without supreme love to God, it is the point which is of greatest force, and is to be urged with the strongest effect, in setting forth the depth and 'totality' of man's sinfulness: unrenewed men have not that supreme love of God which is the substance of the first and great command." See also Shedd, Discourses and Essays, 248; Baird, Elohim Revealed, 510–522; Chalmers, Institutes, 1:519–542; Cunningham, Hist. Theology, 1:516–531; Princeton Review, 1877:470.

2. *Ability or inability?*

In opposition to the plenary ability taught by the Pelagians, the gracious ability of the Arminians, and the natural ability of the New School theologians, the Scriptures declare the total inability of the sinner to turn himself to God or to do that which is truly good in God's sight (see Scripture proof below). A proper conception also of the law, as reflecting the holiness of God and as expressing the ideal of human nature, leads us to the conclusion that no man whose powers are weakened by either original or actual sin can of himself come up to that perfect standard. Yet there is a certain remnant of freedom left to man. The sinner *can* (*a*) avoid the sin against the Holy Ghost ; (*b*) choose the less sin rather than the greater ; (*c*) refuse altogether to yield to certain temptations ; (*d*) do outwardly good acts, though with imperfect motives; (*e*) seek God from motives of self-interest.

But on the other hand the sinner *cannot* (*a*) by a single volition bring his character and life into complete conformity to God's law; (*b*) change his fundamental preference for self and sin to supreme love for God ; nor (*c*) do any act, however insignificant, which shall meet with God's approval or answer fully to the demands of law.

So long, then, as there are states of intellect, affection and will which man cannot, by any power of volition or of contrary choice remaining to him, bring into subjection to God, it cannot be said that he possesses any sufficient ability of himself to do God's will; and if a basis for man's responsibility and guilt be sought, it must be found, if at all, not in his plenary ability, his gracious ability, or his natural ability, but in his *original* ability, when he came, in Adam, from the hands of his Maker.

Man's present inability is natural, in the sense of being inborn,— it is not acquired by our personal act, but is congenital. It is not natural, however, as resulting from the original limitations of human nature, or from the subsequent loss of any essential faculty of that nature. Human nature, at its first creation, was endowed with ability perfectly to keep the law of God. Man has not, even by his sin, lost his essential faculties of intellect, affection, or will. He has weakened those faculties, however, so that they are now unable to work up to the normal measure of their powers. But more especially has man given to every faculty a bent away from God which renders him morally unable to render spiritual obedience. The inability to good which now characterizes human nature is an inability that results from sin, and is itself sin.

We hold, therefore, to an inability which is both natural and moral,— moral, as having its source in the self-corruption of man's moral nature and the fundamental aversion of his will to God;—natural, as being inborn, and as affecting with partial paralysis all his natural powers of intellect, affection, conscience, and will. For his inability, in both these aspects of it, man is responsible.

The sinner can do one very important thing, *viz.*: give attention to divine truth. Ps. 119:59 — "I thought on my ways, And turned my feet unto thy testimonies." G. W. Northrup: "The sinner can seek God from: (*a*) self-love, regard for his own interest; (*b*) feeling of duty, sense of obligation, awakened conscience; (*c*) gratitude for blessings already received; (*d*) aspiration after the infinite and satisfying." Denney, Studies in Theology, 85 — "A witty French moralist has said that God does not need to grudge to his enemies even what they call their virtues; and neither do God's ministers. . . . But there is *one* thing which man cannot do *alone*, — he cannot bring his state into harmony with his nature. When a man has been discovered who has been able, without Christ, to reconcile himself to God and to obtain dominion over the world and over sin, *then* the doctrine of inability, or of the bondage due to sin, may be denied; *then*, but *not till then*." The Free Church of Scotland, in the Declaratory Act of 1892, says "that, in holding and teaching, according to the Confession of Faith, the corruption of man's whole nature as fallen, this church also maintains that there remain tokens of his greatness as created in the image of God; that he possesses a knowledge of God and of duty; that he is responsible for compliance with the moral law and with the gospel; and that, although unable without the aid of the Holy Spirit to return to God, he is yet capable of affections and actions which in themselves are virtuous and praiseworthy.'

To the use of the term "natural ability" to designate merely the sinner's possession of all the constituent faculties of human nature, we object upon the following grounds :

A. **Quantitative lack.**— The phrase "natural ability" is misleading, since it seems to imply that the existence of the mere powers of intellect, affection, and will is a sufficient quantitative qualification for obedience to God's law, whereas these powers have been weakened by sin, and are naturally unable, instead of naturally able, to render back to God with interest the talent first bestowed. Even if the moral direction of man's faculties were a normal one, the effect of hereditary and of personal sin would render naturally impossible that large likeness to God which the law of absolute perfection demands. Man has not therefore the natural ability perfectly to obey God. He had it once, but he lost it with the first sin.

When Jean Paul Richter says of himself : "I have made of myself all that could be made out of the stuff," he evinces a self-complacency which is due to self-ignorance and lack of moral insight. When a man realizes the extent of the law's demands, he sees that without divine help obedience is impossible. John B. Gough represented the confirmed drunkard's efforts at reformation as a man's walking up Mount Etna knee-deep in burning lava, or as one's rowing against the rapids of Niagara.

B. **Qualitative lack.**— Since the law of God requires of men not so much right single volitions as conformity to God in the whole inward state of the affections and will, the power of contrary choice in single volitions does not constitute a natural ability to obey God, unless man can by those single volitions change the underlying state of the affections and will. But this power man does not possess. Since God judges all moral action in connection with the general state of the heart and life, natural ability to good involves not only a full complement of faculties but also a bias of the affections and will toward God. Without this bias there is no possibility of right moral action, and where there is no such possibility, there can be no ability either natural or moral.

Wilkinson, Epic of Paul, 21 — "Hatred is like love Herein, that it, by only being, grows, Until at last usurping quite the man, It overgrows him like a polypus." John Caird, Fund. Ideas, 1:53 — "The ideal is the revelation in me of a power that is mightier than my own. The supreme command 'Thou oughtest' is the utterance, only different in form, of the same voice in my spirit which says 'Thou canst'; and my highest spiritual attainments are achieved, not by self-assertion, but by self-renunciation and self-surrender to the infinite life of truth and righteousness that is living and reigning within me." This conscious inability in one's self, together with reception of "the strength which God supplieth" (1 Pet. 4:11), is the secret of Paul's courage; 2 Cor. 12:10 — "when I am weak, then am I strong"; Phil. 2:12, 13 — "work out your own salvation with fear and trembling; for it is God who worketh in you both to will and to work, for his good pleasure."

C. **No such ability known.** — In addition to the psychological argument just mentioned, we may urge another from experience and observa tion. These testify that man is cognizant of no such ability. Since no man has ever yet, by the exercise of his natural powers, turned himself to God or done an act truly good in God's sight, the existence of a natural ability to do good is a pure assumption. There is no scientific warrant for inferring the existence of an ability which has never manifested itself in a single instance since history began.

"Solomon could not keep the Proverbs, —so he wrote them." The book of Proverbs needs for its complement the New Testament explanation of helplessness and offer of help : John 15 : 5 — "apart from me ye can do nothing "; 6 : 37 — "him that cometh to me I will in no wise cast out." The palsied man's inability to walk is very different from his indisposition to accept a remedy. The paralytic cannot climb the cliff, but by a rope let down to him he may be lifted up, provided he will permit himself to be tied to it. Darling, in Presb. and Ref. Rev., July, 1901 : 505—"If bidden, we can stretch out a withered arm ; but God does not require this of one born armless. We may 'hear the voice of the Son of God' and 'live' (John 5 : 25), but we shall not bring out of the tomb faculties not possessed before death."

D.   Practical evil of the belief.— The practical evil attending the preaching of natural ability furnishes a strong argument against it. The Scriptures, in their declarations of the sinner's inability and helplessness, aim to shut him up to sole dependence upon God for salvation. The doctrine of natural ability, assuring him that he is able at once to repent and turn to God, encourages delay by putting salvation at all times within his reach. If a single volition will secure it, he may be saved as easily to-morrow as to-day. The doctrine of inability presses men to immediate acceptance of God's offers, lest the day of grace for them pass by.

Those who care most for self are those in whom self becomes thoroughly subjected and enslaved to external influences. Mat. 16 : 25 —"whosoever would save his life shall lose it." The selfish man is a straw on the surface of a rushing stream. He becomes more and more a victim of circumstance, until at last he has no more freedom than the brute. Ps. 49 : 20 —"Man that is in honor, and understandeth not, Is like the beasts that perish ;" see R. T. Smith, Man's Knowledge of Man and of God, 121. Robert Browning, unpublished poem : " ' Would a man 'scape the rod ? ' Rabbi Ben Karshook saith, ' See that he turn to God The day before his death.' ' Aye, could a man inquire When it shall come ? ' I say. The Rabbi's eye shoots fire — ' Then let him turn to-day.' "

Let us repeat, however, that the denial to man of all ability, whether natural or moral, to turn himself to God or to do that which is truly good in God's sight, does not imply a denial of man's power to order his external life in many particulars conformably to moral rules, or even to attain the praise of men for virtue. Man has still a range of freedom in acting out his nature, and he may to a certain limited extent act down upon that nature, and modify it, by isolated volitions externally conformed to God's law. He may choose higher or lower forms of selfish action, and may pursue these chosen courses with various degrees of selfish energy. Freedom of choice, within this limit, is by no means incompatible with complete bondage of the will in spiritual things.

John 1 : 13 — " born, not of blood, nor of the will of the flesh, nor of the will of man, but of God "; 3 : 5 — "Except one be born of water and the Spirit, he cannot enter into the kingdom of God "; 6 : 44 — "No man can come to me, except the Father that sent me draw him " ; 8 : 34 —"Every one that committeth sin is the bondservant of sin " ; 15 : 4, 5 — " the branch cannot bear fruit of itself . . . . apart from me ye can do nothing "; Rom. 7 : 18 — "in me, that is, in my flesh, dwelleth no good thing ; for to will is present with me, but to do that which is good is not " ; 24 — " Wretched man that I am ! who shall deliver me out of the body of this death ? " 8 : 7, 8 — "the mind of the flesh is enmity against God ; for it is not subject to the law of God, neither indeed can it be : and they that are in the flesh cannot please God "; 1 Cor. 2 : 14 — "the natural man receiveth not the things of the Spirit of God : for they are foolishness unto him.

and he cannot know them, because they are spiritually judged"; 2 Cor. 3 : 5 — "not that we are sufficient of ourselves to account anything as from ourselves"; Eph. 2 : 1 — "dead through your trespasses and sins"; 8–10 — "by grace have ye been saved through faith; and that not of yourselves, it is the gift of God; not of works, that no man should glory. For we are his workmanship, created in Christ Jesus for good works"; Heb. 11 : 6 — "without faith it is impossible to be well-pleasing unto him."

Kant's "I ought, therefore I can" is the relic of man's original consciousness of freedom — the freedom with which man was endowed at his creation — a freedom, now, alas! destroyed by sin. Or it may be the courage of the soul in which God is working anew by his Spirit. For Kant's "Ich soll, also Ich kann," Julius Müller would substitute: "Ich sollte freilich können, aber Ich kann nicht"—"I ought indeed to be able, but I am not able." Man truly repents only when he learns that his sin has made him unable to repent without the renewing grace of God. Emerson, in his poem entitled "Voluntariness," says: "So near is grandeur to our dust, So near is God to man, When duty whispers low, *Thou must*, The youth replies, *I can*." But, apart from special grace, all the ability which man at present possesses comes far short of fulfilling the spiritual demands of God's law. Parental and civil law implies a certain kind of power. Puritan theology called man *"free among the dead"* (Ps. 88 : 5, A. V.). There was a range of freedom inside of slavery, — the will was "a drop of water imprisoned in a solid crystal" (Oliver Wendell Holmes). The man who kills himself is as dead as if he had been killed by another (Shedd, Dogm. Theol., 2 : 106).

Westminster Confession, 9 : 3 — "Man by his fall into a state of sin hath wholly lost all ability of will to any spiritual good accompanying salvation; so, as a natural man, being altogether averse from that good and dead in sin, he is not able by his own strength to convert himself, or to prepare himself thereunto." Hopkins, Works, 1 : 233 -235 — "So long as the sinner's opposition of heart and will continues, he cannot come to Christ. It is impossible, and will continue so, until his unwillingness and opposition be removed by a change and renovation of his heart by divine grace, and he be made willing in the day of God's power." Hopkins speaks of "utter inability to obey the law of God, yea, utter impossibility."

Hodge, Syst. Theol., 2 : 257–277 — "Inability consists, not in the loss of any faculty of the soul, nor in the loss of free agency, for the sinner determines his own acts, nor in mere disinclination to what is good. It arises from want of spiritual discernment, and hence want of proper affections. Inability belongs only to the things of the Spirit. What man cannot do is to repent, believe, regenerate himself. He cannot put forth any act which merits the approbation of God. Sin cleaves to all he does, and from its dominion he cannot free himself. The distinction between natural and moral ability is of no value. Shall we say that the uneducated man can understand and appreciate the Iliad, because he has all the faculties that the scholar has? Shall we say that man can love God, if he will? This is false, if will means volition. It is a truism, if will means affection. The Scriptures never thus address men and tell them that they have power to do all that God requires. It is dangerous to teach a man this, for until a man feels that he can do nothing, God never saves him. Inability is involved in the doctrine of original sin; in the necessity of the Spirit's influence in regeneration. Inability is consistent with obligation, when inability arises from sin and is removed by the removal of sin."

Shedd, Dogm. Theol., 2 : 213–257, and in South Church Sermons, 33–59 — "The origin of this helplessness lies, not in creation, but in sin. God can command the ten talents or the five which he originally committed to us, together with a diligent and faithful improvement of them. Because the servant has lost the talents, is he discharged from obligation to return them with interest? Sin contains in itself the element of servitude. In the very act of transgressing the law of God, there is a reflex action of the human will upon itself, whereby it becomes less able than before to keep that law. Sin is the suicidal action of the human will. To do wrong destroys the power to do right. Total depravity carries with it total impotence. The voluntary faculty may be ruined from within; may be made impotent to holiness, by its own action; may surrender itself to appetite and selfishness with such an intensity and earnestness, that it becomes unable to convert itself and overcome its wrong inclination." See Stevenson, Dr. Jekyll and Mr. Hyde, — noticed in Andover Rev., June, 1886 : 664. We can merge ourselves in the life of another — either bad or good; can almost transform ourselves into Satan or into Christ, so as to say with Paul, in Gal. 2 : 20 — "it is no longer I that live, but Christ liveth in me"; or be minions of "the spirit that now worketh in the sons of disobedience" (Eph. 2 : 2). But if we yield ourselves to the influence of Satan, the recovery of our true personality becomes increasingly difficult, and at last impossible.

There is nothing in literature sadder or more significant than the self-bewailing of Charles Lamb, the gentle Elia, who writes in his Last Essays, 214 — " Could the youth to whom the flavor of the first wine is delicious as the opening scenes of life or the entering of some newly discovered paradise, look into my desolation, and be made to understand what a dreary thing it is when he shall feel himself going down a precipice with open eyes and a passive will; to see his destruction, and have no power to stop it; to see all goodness emptied out of him, and yet not be able to forget a time when it was otherwise; to bear about the piteous spectacle of his own ruin, — could he see my fevered eye, fevered with the last night's drinking, and feverishly looking for to-night's repetition of the folly; could he but feel the body of this death out of which I cry hourly, with feebler outcry, to be delivered, it were enough to make him dash the sparkling beverage to the earth, in all the pride of its mantling temptation."

For the Arminian ' gracious ability,' see Raymond, Syst. Theol., 2:130; McClintock & Strong, Cyclopædia, 10:990. *Per contra*, see Calvin, Institutes, bk. 2, chap. 2 (1:282); Edwards, Works, 2:464 (Orig. Sin, 3:1); Bennet Tyler, Works, 73; Baird, Elohim Revealed, 523–528; Cunningham, Hist. Theology, 1:567–639; Turretin, 10:4:19; A. A. Hodge, Outlines of Theology, 260–269; Thornwell, Theology, 1:394–399; Alexander, Moral Science, 89–208; Princeton Essays, 1:224–239; Richards, Lectures on Theology. On real as distinguished from formal freedom, see Julius Müller, Doct. Sin, 2:1–225. On Augustine's *lineamenta extrema* (of the divine image in man), see Wiggers, Augustinism and Pelagianism, 119, note. See also art. by A. H. Strong, on Modified Calvinism, or Remainders of Freedom in Man, in Bap. Rev., 1883:219–242; and reprinted in the author's Philosophy and Religion, 114–128.

II. GUILT.

1. *Nature of guilt.*

By guilt we mean desert of punishment, or obligation to render satisfaction to God's justice for self-determined violation of law. There is a reaction of holiness against sin, which the Scripture denominates "the wrath of God" (Rom. 1 : 18). Sin is in us, either as act or state; God's punitive righteousness is over against the sinner, as something to be feared; guilt is a relation of the sinner to that righteousness, namely, the sinner's desert of punishment.

Guilt is related to sin as the burnt spot to the blaze. Schiller, Die Braut von Messina: "Das Leben ist der Güter höchstes nicht; Der Uebel grösstes aber ist die Schuld" — "Life is not the highest of possessions; the greatest of ills, however, is guilt." Delitzsch: "Die Schamröthe ist die Abendröthe der untergegangenen Sonne der ursprünglichen Gerechtigkeit"—"The blush of shame is the evening red after the sun of original righteousness has gone down." E. G. Robinson: "Pangs of conscience do not arise from the fear of penalty, — they are the penalty itself." See chapter on Fig-leaves, in McIlvaine, Wisdom of Holy Scripture, 142–154 — "Spiritual shame for sin sought an outward symbol, and found it in the nakedness of the lower parts of the body."

The following remarks may serve both for proof and for explanation :

A. Guilt is incurred only through self-determined transgression either on the part of man's nature or person. We are guilty only of that sin which we have originated or have had part in originating. Guilt is not, therefore, mere liability to punishment, without participation in the transgression for which the punishment is inflicted, — in other words, there is no such thing as constructive guilt under the divine government. We are accounted guilty only for what we have done, either personally or in our first parents, and for what we are, in consequence of such doing.

Ez. 18 : 20 — "the son shall not bear the iniquity of the father" =, as Calvin says (Com. *in loco*): "The son shall not bear the father's iniquity, since he shall receive the reward due to himself, and shall bear his own burden. . . . All are guilty through their own fault. . . . Every one perishes through his own iniquity." In other words, the whole race fell in Adam, and is punished for its own sin in him, not for the sins of immediate ancestors, nor for the sin of Adam as a person foreign to us. John 9 : 3 — "Neither did this man sin, nor his parents " (that he should be born blind) — Do not attribute to any special later sin what is a consequence of the sin of the race — the first sin which " brought death into the world, and all our woe." Shedd, Dogm. Theol., 2 : 195–213.

B. **Guilt is an objective result of sin, and is not to be confounded with subjective pollution, or depravity.** Every sin, whether of nature or person, is an offense against God (Ps. 51 : 4–6), an act or state of opposition to his will, which has for its effect God's personal wrath (Ps. 7 : 11 ; John 3 : 18, 36), and which must be expiated either by punishment or by atonement (Heb. 9 : 22). Not only does sin, as unlikeness to the divine purity, involve *pollution,* — it also, as antagonism to God's holy will, involves *guilt.* This guilt, or obligation to satisfy the outraged holiness of God, is explained in the New Testament by the terms " debtor" and "debt " (Mat. 6 : 12 ; Luke 13 : 4 ; Mat. 5 : 21 ; Rom. 3 : 19 ; 6 : 23 ; Eph. 2 : 3). Since guilt, the objective result of sin, is entirely distinct from depravity, the subjective result, human nature may, as in Christ, have the guilt without the depravity (2 Cor. 5 : 21), or may, as in the Christian, have the depravity without the guilt (1 John 1 : 7, 8).

Ps. 51 : 4–6 — "Against thee, thee only, have I sinned, And done that which is evil in thy sight; That thou mayest be justified when thou speakest, And be clear when thou judgest " ; 7 : 11 — "God is a righteous judge, Yea, a God that hath indignation every day " ; John 3 : 18 — "he that believeth not hath been judged already "; 36 — " he that obeyeth not the Son shall not see life, but the wrath of God abideth on him " ; Heb. 9 : 22 — "apart from shedding of blood there is no remission " ; Mat. 6 : 12 — "debts " ; Luke 13 : 4 — "offenders " (marg. "debtors ") ; Mat. 5 : 21 — "shall be in danger of [exposed to] the judgment " ; Rom. 3 : 19 — "that . . . . all the world may be brought under the judgment of God " ; 6 : 23 — "the wages of sin is death " = death is sin's desert ; Eph. 2 : 3 — "by nature children of wrath " ; 2 Cor. 5 : 21 — "Him who knew no sin he made to be sin on our behalf "; 1 John 1 : 7, 8 — "the blood of Jesus his Son cleanseth us from all sin. [Yet] If we say that we have no sin, we deceive ourselves, and the truth is not in us."

Sin brings in its train not only depravity but guilt, not only *macula* but *reatus.* Scripture sets forth the *pollution* of sin by its similies of " a cage of unclean birds " and of " wounds, bruises, and putrefying sores "; by leprosy and Levitical uncleanness, under the old dispensation ; by death and the corruption of the grave, under both the old and the new. But Scripture sets forth the *guilt* of sin, with equal vividness, in the fear of Cain and in the remorse of Judas. The revulsion of God's holiness from sin, and its demand for satisfaction, are reflected in the shame and remorse of every awakened conscience. There is an instinctive feeling in the sinner's heart that sin will be punished, and ought to be punished. But the Holy Spirit makes this need of reparation so deeply felt that the soul has no rest until its debt is paid. The offending church member who is truly penitent loves the law and the church which excludes him, and would not think it faithful if it did not. So Jesus, when laden with the guilt of the race, pressed forward to the cross, saying : "I have a baptism to be baptized with ; and how am I straitened till it be accomplished ! " (Luke 12 : 50 ; Mark 10 : 32).

All sin involves guilt, and the sinful soul itself demands penalty, so that all will ultimately go where they most desire to be. All the great masters in literature have recognized this. The inextinguishable thirst for reparation constitutes the very essence of tragedy. The Greek tragedians are full of it, and Shakespeare is its most impressive teacher : Measure for Measure, 5 : 1 — " I am sorry that such sorrow I procure, And so deep sticks it in my penitent heart That I crave death more willingly than mercy ; 'T is my deserving, and I do entreat it " ; Cymbeline, 5 : 4 — "and so, great Powers, If you will take this audit, take this life, And cancel these cold bonds ! . . . . Desired, more than constrained, to satisfy, ... take No stricter render of me than my all " ; that is, settle the account with me by taking my life, for nothing less than that will pay my debt. And later writers follow Shakespeare. Marguerite, in Goethe's Faust, fainting in the great cathedral under the solemn reverberations of the Dies Iræ ; Dimmesdale, in Hawthorne's Scarlet Letter, putting himself side by side with Hester Prynne, his victim, in her place of obloquy ; Bulwer's Eugene Aram, coming forward, though unsuspected, to confess the murder he had committed, all these are illustrations of the inner impulse that moves even a sinful soul to satisfy the claims of justice upon it. See A. H. Strong, Philosophy and Religion, 215, 216. On Hawthorne, see Hutton, Essays, 2 : 370-416 — "In the Scarlet Letter, the minister gains fresh reverence and popularity as the very fruit of the passionate anguish with which his heart is consumed. Frantic with the stings of unacknowledged guilt, he is yet taught by these very stings to understand the hearts and stir the consciences of others." See also Dinsmore, Atonement in Literature and Life.

Nor are such scenes confined to the pages of romance. In a recent trial at Syracuse, Earl, the wife-murderer, thanked the jury that had convicted him; declared the verdict just; begged that no one would interfere to stay the course of justice; said that the greatest blessing that could be conferred on him would be to let him suffer the penalty of his crime. In Plattsburg, at the close of another trial in which the accused was a life-convict who had struck down a fellow-convict with an axe, the jury, after being out two hours, came in to ask the Judge to explain the difference between murder in the first and second degree. Suddenly the prisoner rose and said : "This was not a murder in the second degree. It was a deliberate and premeditated murder. I know that I have done wrong, that I ought to confess the truth, and that I ought to be hanged." This left the jury nothing to do but render their verdict, and the Judge sentenced the murderer to be hanged, as he confessed he deserved to be. In 1891, Lars Ostendahl, the most famous preacher of Norway, startled his hearers by publicly confessing that he had been guilty of immorality, and that he could no longer retain his pastorate. He begged his people for the sake of Christ to forgive him and not to desert the poor in his asylums. He was not only preacher, but also head of a great philanthropic work.

Such is the movement and demand of the enlightened conscience. The lack of conviction that crime ought to be punished is one of the most certain signs of moral decay in either the individual or the nation (Ps. 97 : 10 — "Ye that love the Lord, hate evil"; 149 : 6 — "Let the high praises of God be in their mouth, And a two-edged sword in their hand" — to execute God's judgment upon iniquity).

This relation of sin to God shows us how Christ is "made sin on our behalf" (2 Cor. 5 : 21). Since Christ is the immanent God, he is also essential humanity, the universal man, the life of the race. All the nerves and sensibilities of humanity meet in him. He is the central brain to which and through which all ideas must pass. He is the central heart to which and through which all pains must be communicated. You cannot telephone to your friend across the town without first ringing up the central office. You cannot injure your neighbor without first injuring Christ. Each one of us can say of him : "Against thee, thee only, have I sinned" (Ps. 51 : 4). Because of his central and all-inclusive humanity, Christ can feel all the pangs of shame and suffering which rightfully belong to sinners, but which they cannot feel, because their sin has stupefied and deadened them. The Messiah, if he be truly man, must be a suffering Messiah. For the very reason of his humanity he must bear in his own person all the guilt of humanity and must be "the Lamb of God who" takes, and so "takes away, the sin of the world" (John 1 : 29).

Guilt and depravity are not only distinguishable in thought, — they are also separable in fact. The convicted murderer might repent and become pure, yet he might still be under obligation to suffer the punishment of his crime. The Christian is freed from guilt (Rom. 8 : 1), but he is not yet freed from depravity (Rom. 7 : 23). Christ, on the other hand, was under obligation to suffer (Luke 24 : 26; Acts 3 : 18; 26 : 23), while yet he was without sin (Heb. 7 : 26). In the book entitled Modern Religious Thought, 3–29, R. J. Campbell has an essay on The Atonement, with which, apart from its view as to the origin of moral evil in God, we are in substantial agreement. He holds that "to relieve men from their sense of guilt, objective atonement is necessary," — we would say : to relieve men from guilt itself — the obligation to suffer. "If Christ be the eternal Son of God, that side of the divine nature which has gone forth in creation, if he contains humanity and is present in every article and act of human experience, then he is associated with the existence of the primordial evil. . . . He and only he can sever the entail between man and his responsibility for personal sin. Christ has not *sinned* in man, but he takes responsibility for that experience of evil into which humanity is born, and the yielding to which constitutes sin. He goes forth to suffer, and actually does suffer, in man. The eternal Son in whom humanity is contained is therefore a sufferer since creation began. This mysterious passion of Deity must continue until redemption is consummated and humanity restored to God. Thus every consequence of human ill is felt in the experience of Christ. Thus Christ not only assumes the guilt but bears the punishment of every human soul." We claim however that the necessity of this suffering lies, not in the needs of man, but in the holiness of God.

C. Guilt, moreover, as an objective result of sin, is not to be confounded with the subjective consciousness of guilt (Lev. 5 : 17). In the condemnation of conscience, God's condemnation partially and prophetically manifests itself (1 John 3 : 20). But guilt is primarily a relation to God, and only secondarily a relation to conscience. Progress in sin is marked by diminished sensitiveness of moral insight and feeling. As "the greatest of sins is to be conscious of none," so guilt may be great, just in proportion to the absence of consciousness of it (Ps. 19 : 12 ; 51 : 6 ; Eph. 4 : 18, 19 — ἀπηλγηκότες). There is no evidence, however, that the voice of conscience can be completely or finally silenced. The time for repentance may pass, but not the time for remorse. Progress in holiness, on the other hand, is marked by increasing apprehension of the depth and extent of our sinfulness, while with this apprehension is combined, in a normal Christian experience, the assurance that the guilt of our sin has been taken, and taken away, by Christ (John 1 : 29).

Lev. 5 :17 — "And if any one sin, and do any of the things which Jehovah hath commanded not to be done; though he knew it not, yet is he guilty, and shall bear his iniquity"; 1 John 3 : 20 — "because if our heart condemn us, God is greater than our heart, and knoweth all things"; Ps. 19 : 12 — "Who can discern his errors? Clear thou me from hidden faults"; 51 : 6 — "Behold, thou desirest truth in the inward parts; And in the hidden part thou wilt make me to know wisdom"; Eph. 4 : 18, 19 — "darkened in their understanding . . . . being past feeling"; John 1 : 29 — "Behold, the Lamb of God, that taketh away [marg. 'beareth '] the sin of the world."

Plato, Republic, 1 : 330 — "When death approaches, cares and alarms awake, especially the fear of hell and its punishments." Cicero, De Divin., 1 : 30 — "Then comes remorse for evil deeds." Persius, Satire 3 — "His vice benumbs him; his fibre has become fat; he is conscious of no fault; he knows not the loss he suffers; he is so far sunk, that there is not even a bubble on the surface of the deep." Shakespeare, Hamlet, 3 : 1 — "Thus conscience doth make cowards of us all"; 4 : 5 — "To my sick soul, as sin's true nature is, Each toy seems prologue to some great amiss; So full of artless jealousy is guilt, It spills itself in fearing to be spilt"; Richard III, 5 : 3 — "O coward conscience, how thou dost afflict me! . . . My conscience hath a thousand several tongues, and every tongue brings in a several tale, And every tale condemns me for a villain"; Tempest, 3 : 3 — "All three of them are desperate; their great guilt, Like poison given to work a great time after, Now 'gins to bite the spirits"; Ant. and Cleop., 3 : 9 — "When we in our viciousness grow hard (O misery on 't!) the wise gods seel our eyes; In our own filth drop our clear judgments; make us Adore our errors; laugh at us, while we strut To our confusion."

Dr. Shedd said once to a graduating class of young theologians : "Would that upon the naked, palpitating heart of each one of you might be laid one redhot coal of God Almighty's wrath!" Yes, we add, if only that redhot coal might be quenched by one red drop of Christ's atoning blood. Dr. H. E. Robins : "To the convicted sinner a merely external hell would be a cooling flame, compared with the agony of his remorse." John Milton represents Satan as saying: "Which way I fly is hell; myself am hell." James Martineau, Life by Jackson, 190 — "It is of the essence of guilty declension to administer its own anæsthetics." But this deadening of conscience cannot last always. Conscience is a mirror of God's holiness. We may cover the mirror with the veil of this world's diversions and deceits. When the veil is removed, and conscience again reflects the sunlike purity of God's demands, we are visited with self-loathing and self-contempt. John Caird, Fund. Ideas, 2 : 25 — "Though it may cast off every other vestige of its divine origin, our nature retains at least this one terrible prerogative of it, the capacity of preying on itself." Lyttelton in Lux Mundi, 277 — "The common fallacy that a self-indulgent sinner is no one's enemy but his own would, were it true, involve the further inference that such a sinner would not feel himself guilty." If any dislike the doctrine of guilt, let them remember that without wrath there is no pardon, without guilt no forgiveness. See, on the nature of guilt, Julius Müller, Doct. Sin, 1 : 193–267 ; Martensen, Christian Dogmatics, 203–209 ; Thomasius, Christi Person und Werk, 1 : 346 ; Baird, Elohim Revealed, 461–473 ; Delitzsch, Bib. Psychologie, 121–148 ; Thornwell, Theology, 1 : 400–424.

2. *Degrees of guilt.*

The Scriptures recognize different degrees of guilt as attaching to different kinds of sin. The variety of sacrifices under the Mosaic law, and the variety of awards in the judgment, are to be explained upon this principle.

Luke 12 : 47, 48 — "shall be beaten with many stripes . . . shall be beaten with few stripes "; Rom. 2 : 6 — "who will render to every man according to his works." See also John 19 : 11 — "he that delivered me unto thee hath greater sin "; Heb. 2 : 2, 3 — if "every transgression . . . . received a just recompense of reward; how shall we escape, if we neglect so great a salvation ? " 10 : 28, 29 — "A man that hath set at nought Moses' law dieth without compassion on the word of two or three witnesses : of how much sorer punishment, think ye, shall he be judged worthy, who hath trodden under foot the Son of God ? "

Casuistry, however, has drawn many distinctions which lack Scriptural foundation. Such is the distinction between venial sins and mortal sins in the Roman Catholic Church, — every sin unpardoned being mortal, and all sins being venial, since Christ has died for all. Nor is the common distinction between sins of omission and sins of commission more valid, since the very omission is an act of commission.

Mat. 25 : 45 — "Inasmuch as ye did it not unto one of these least "; James 4 : 17 — " To him therefore that knoweth to do good, and doeth it not, to him it is sin." John Ruskin : " The condemnation given from the Judgment Throne — most solemnly described — is for all the 'undones' and not the 'dones.' People are perpetually afraid of doing wrong ; but unless they are doing its reverse energetically, they *do it all day long,* and the degree does not matter." The Roman Catholic Church proceeds upon the supposition that she can determine the precise malignity of every offence, and assign its proper penance at the confessional. Thornwell, Theology, 1 : 424–441, says that "all sins are venial but one — for there is a sin against the Holy Ghost," yet "not one is venial in itself — for the least proceeds from an apostate state and nature." We shall see, however, that the hindrance to pardon, in the case of the sin against the Holy Spirit, is subjective rather than objective.

J. Spencer Kennard : " Roman Catholicism in Italy presents the spectacle of the authoritative representatives and teachers of morals and religion themselves living in all forms of deceit, corruption, and tyranny ; and, on the other hand, discriminating between venial and mortal sin, classing as venial sins lying, fraud, fornication, marital infidelity, and even murder, all of which may be atoned for and forgiven or even permitted by the mere payment of money ; and at the same time classing as mortal sins disrespect and disobedience to the church."

The following distinctions are indicated in Scripture as involving different degrees of guilt :

A. Sin of nature, and personal transgression.

Sin of nature involves guilt, yet there is greater guilt when this sin of nature reässerts itself in personal transgression ; for, while this latter includes in itself the former, it also adds to the former a new element, namely, the conscious exercise of the individual and personal will, by virtue of which a new decision is made against God, special evil habit is induced, and the total condition of the soul is made more depraved. Although we have emphasized the guilt of inborn sin, because this truth is most contested, it is to be remembered that men reach a conviction of their native depravity only through a conviction of their personal transgressions. For this reason, by far the larger part of our preaching upon sin should consist in applications of the law of God to the acts and dispositions of men's lives.

Mat. 19 : 14 — "to such belongeth the kingdom of heaven " == relative innocence of childhood ; 23 : 32 — 'Fill ye up then the measure of your fathers " == personal transgression added to inherited depravity. In preaching, we should first treat individual transgressions, and thence proceed to heart-sin, and race-sin. Man is not wholly a spontaneous development of inborn tendencies, a manifestation of original sin. Motives do not *determine* but they *persuade* the will, and every man is guilty of conscious personal transgressions which may, with the help of the Holy Spirit, be brought under the condemning judgment of conscience. Birks, Difficulties of Belief, 169-174 — "Original sin does not do away with the significance of personal transgression. Adam was pardoned; but some of his descendants are unpardonable. The second death is referred, in Scripture, to our own personal guilt."

This is not to say that original sin does not involve as great sin as that of Adam in the first transgression, for original sin *is* the sin of the first transgression; it is only to say that personal transgression is original sin *plus* the conscious ratification of Adam's act by the individual. "We are guilty for what we *are*, as much as for what we *do*. Our *sin* is not simply the sum total of all our *sins*. There is a *sinfulness* which is the common denominator of all our sins." It is customary to speak lightly of original sin, as if personal sins were all for which man is accountable. But it is only in the light of original sin that personal sins can be explained. Prov. 14 : 9, marg. —"Fools make a mock at sin." Simon, Reconciliation, 122 — "The sinfulness of individual men varies; the sinfulness of humanity is a constant quantity." Robert Browning, Ferishtah's Fancies: "Man lumps his kind i' the mass. God singles thence unit by unit. Thou and God exist— So think! for certain: Think the mass — mankind — Disparts, disperses, leaves thyself alone! Ask thy lone soul what laws are plain to thee,— Thou and no other. stand or fall by them! That is the part for thee."

B. Sins of ignorance, and sins of knowledge.

Here guilt is measured by the degree of light possessed, or in other words, by the opportunities of knowledge men have enjoyed, and the powers with which they have been naturally endowed. Genius and privilege increase responsibility. The heathen are guilty, but those to whom the oracles of God have been committed are more guilty than they.

Mat. 10 : 15 — "more tolerable for the land of Sodom and Gomorrah in the day of judgment, than for that city"; Luke 12 : 47, 48 — "that servant, who knew his Lord's will . . . . shall be beaten with many stripes; but he that knew not . . . . shall be beaten with few stripes"; 23 : 34 — "Father, forgive them; for they know not what they do" — complete knowledge would put them beyond the reach of forgiveness. John 19 : 11 — "he that delivered me unto thee hath greater sin"; Acts 17 : 30 — "The times of ignorance therefore God overlooked"; Rom. 1 : 32 — "who, knowing the ordinance of God, that they that practise such things are worthy of death, not only do the same, but also consent with them that practise them"; 2 : 12 — "For as many as have sinned without the law shall also perish without the law: and as many as have sinned under the law shall be judged by the law"; 1 Tim. 1 : 13, 15, 16 — "I obtained mercy, because I did it ignorantly in unbelief."

Is. 42 : 19 — "Who is blind . . . . as Jehovah's servant?" It was the Pharisees whom Jesus warned of the sin against the Holy Spirit. The guilt of the crucifixion rested on Jews rather than on Gentiles. Apostate Israel was more guilty than the pagans. The greatest sinners of the present day may be in Christendom, not in heathendom. Satan was an archangel; Judas was an apostle; Alexander Borgia was a pope. Jackson, Jame Martineau, 362 — "Corruptio optimi pessima est, as seen in a drunken Webster, a treacherous Bacon, a licentious Goethe." Sir Roger de Coverley observed that none but men of fine parts deserve to be hanged. Kaftan, Dogmatik, 317 — "The greater sin often involves the lesser guilt; the lesser sin the greater guilt." Robert Browning, The Ring and the Book, 227 (Pope, 1975) —"There's a new tribunal now Higher than God's, — the educated man's! Nice sense of honor in the human breast Supersedes here the old coarse oracle!" Dr. H. E. Robins holds that "palliation of guilt according to light is not possible under a system of pure law, and is possible only because the probation of the sinner is a probation of grace."

C. Sins of infirmity, and sins of presumption.

Here the guilt is measured by the energy of the evil will. Sin may be known to be sin, yet may be committed in haste or weakness. Though haste and weakness constitute a palliation of the offence which springs therefrom, yet they are themselves sins, as revealing an unbelieving and disordered heart. But of far greater guilt are those presumptuous choices of evil in which not weakness, but strength of will, is manifest.

Ps. 19:12, 13 —"Clear thou me from hidden faults. Keep back thy servant also from presumptuous sins"; Is. 5:18 —"Woe unto them that draw iniquity with cords of falsehood, and sin as it were with a cart-rope " = not led away insensibly by sin, but earnestly, perseveringly, and wilfully working away at it; Gal. 6:1 —"overtaken in any trespass "; 1 Tim. 5:24 — "Some men's sins are evident, going before unto judgment; and some men also they follow after " = some men's sins are so open, that they act as officers to bring to justice those who commit them; whilst others require after-proof (An. Par. Bible). Luther represents one of the former class as saying to himself: "Esto peccator, et pecca fortiter." On sins of passion and of reflection, see Bittinger, in Princeton Rev., 1873 : 219.

Micah 7 : 3, marg.—"Both hands are put forth for evil, to do it diligently." So we ought to do good. "My art is my life," said Grisi, the prima donna of the opera, "I save myself all day for that one bound upon the stage." H. Bonar: "Sin worketh,—Let me work too. Busy as sin, my work I ply, Till I rest in the rest of eternity." German criminal law distinguishes between intentional homicide without deliberation, and intentional homicide with deliberation. There are three grades of sin : 1. Sins of ignorance, like Paul's persecuting ; 2. sins of infirmity, like Peter's denial; 3. sins of presumption, like David's murder of Uriah. Sins of presumption were unpardonable under the Jewish law; they are not unpardonable under Christ.

D. Sin of incomplete, and sin of final, obduracy.

Here the guilt is measured, not by the objective sufficiency or insufficiency of divine grace, but by the degree of unreceptiveness into which sin has brought the soul. As the only sin unto death which is described in Scripture is the sin against the Holy Spirit, we here consider the nature of that sin.

Mat. 12 : 31 — "Every sin and blasphemy shall be forgiven unto men ; but the blasphemy against the Spirit shall not be forgiven " ; 32 —"And whosoever shall speak a word against the Son of man, it shall be forgiven him ; but whosoever shall speak against the Holy Spirit, it shall not be forgiven him, neither in this world, nor in that which is to come " ; Mark 3 : 29 —"whosoever shall blaspheme against the Holy Spirit hath never forgiveness, but is guilty of an eternal sin " ; 1 John 5 : 16, 17 — "If any man see his brother sinning a sin not unto death, he shall ask, and God will give him life for them that sin not unto death. There is a sin unto death : not concerning this do I say that he should make request. All unrighteousness is sin : and there is a sin not unto death "; Heb. 10 : 26 — "if we sin wilfully after that we have received the knowledge of the truth, there remaineth no more a sacrifice for sins, but a certain fearful expectation of judgment, and a fierceness of fire which shall devour the adversaries."

Ritschl holds all sin that comes short of definitive rejection of Christ to be ignorance rather than sin, and to be the object of no condemning sentence. This is to make the sin against the Holy Spirit the only real sin. Conscience and Scripture alike contradict this view. There is much incipient hardening of the heart that precedes the sin of final obduracy. See Denney, Studies in Theology, 80. The composure of the criminal is not always a sign of innocence. S. S. Times, April 12, 1902 : 200 —"Sensitiveness of conscience and of feeling, and responsiveness of countenance and bearing, are to be retained by purity of life and freedom from transgression. On the other hand composure of countenance and calmness under suspicion and accusation are likely to be a result of continuance in wrong doing, with consequent hardening of the whole moral nature."

Weismann, Heredity, 2 : 8 — "As soon as any organ falls into disuse, it degenerates, and finally is lost altogether. . . . . In parasites the organs of sense degenerate." Marconi's wireless telegraphy requires an attuned "receiver." The "transmitter" sends out countless rays into space : only one capable of corresponding vibrations can understand them. The sinner may so destroy his receptivity, that the whole universe may be uttering God's truth, yet he be unable to hear a word of it. The Outlook: "If a man should put out his eyes, he could not see — nothing could make him see. So if a man should by obstinate wickedness destroy his power to believe in God's forgiveness, he would be in a hopeless state. Though God would still be gracious, the man could not see it, and so could not take God's forgiveness to himself."

The sin against the Holy Spirit is not to be regarded simply as an isolated act, but also as the external symptom of a heart so radically and finally set against God that no power which God can consistently use will ever save it. This sin, therefore, can be only the culmination of a long course of self-hardening and self-depraving. He who has committed it must be either profoundly indifferent to his own condition, or actively and bitterly hostile to God ; so that anxiety or fear on account of one's condition is evidence that it has not been committed. The sin against the Holy Spirit cannot be forgiven, simply because the soul that has committed it has ceased to be receptive of divine influences, even when those influences are exerted in the utmost strength which God has seen fit to employ in his spiritual administration.

The commission of this sin is marked by a loss of spiritual sight ; the blind fish of the Mammoth Cave left light for darkness, and so in time lost their eyes. It is marked by a loss of religious sensibility ; the sensitive-plant loses its sensitiveness, in proportion to the frequency with which it is touched. It is marked by a loss of power to will the good ; "the lava hardens after it has broken from the crater, and in that state cannot return to its source " (Van Oosterzee). The same writer also remarks (Dogmatics, 2:428): " Herod Antipas, after earlier doubt and slavishness, reached such deadness as to be able to mock the Savior, at the mention of whose name he had not long before trembled." Julius Müller, Doctrine of Sin, 2:425 — " It is not that divine grace is absolutely refused to any one who in true penitence asks forgiveness of this sin ; but he who commits it never fulfills the subjective conditions upon which forgiveness is possible, because the aggravation of sin to this ultimatum destroys in him all susceptibility of repentance. The way of return to God is closed against no one who does not close it against himself." Drummond, Natural Law in the Spiritual World, 97-120, illustrates the downward progress of the sinner by the law of degeneration in the vegetable and animal world: pigeons, roses, strawberries, all tend to revert to the primitive and wild type. "How shall we escape, if we neglect so great a salvation ?" (Heb. 2:3).

Shakespeare, Macbeth, 3:5 — "You all know security Is mortals' chiefest enemy." Moulton, Shakespeare as a Dramatic Artist, 90-124 — " Richard III is the ideal villain. Villainy has become an end in itself. Richard is an artist in villainy. He lacks the emotions naturally attending crime. He regards villainy with the intellectual enthusiasm of the artist. His villainy is ideal in its success. There is a fascination of irresistibility in him. He is imperturbable in his crime. There is no effort, but rather humor, in it ; a recklessness which suggests boundless resources ; an inspiration which excludes calculation. Shakespeare relieves the representation from the charge of monstrosity by turning all this villainous history into the unconscious development of Nemesis." See also A. H. Strong, Great Poets, 188-193. Robert Browning's Guido, in The Ring and the Book, is an example of pure hatred of the good. Guido hates Pompilia for her goodness, and declares that, if he catches her in the next world, he will murder her there, as he murdered her here.

Alexander VI, the father of Cæsar and Lucrezia Borgia, the pope of cruelty and lust, wore yet to the day of his death the look of unfailing joyousness and geniality, yes, of even retiring sensitiveness and modesty. No fear or reproach of conscience seemed to throw gloom over his life, as in the cases of Tiberius and Louis XI. He believed himself under the special protection of the Virgin, although he had her painted with the features of his paramour, Julia Farnese. He never scrupled at false witness, adultery, or murder. See Gregorovius, Lucrezia Borgia, 294, 295. Jeremy Taylor thus describes the progress of sin in the sinner : " First it startles him, then it becomes pleasing, then delightful, then frequent, then habitual, then confirmed ; then the man is impenitent, then obstinate, then resolved never to repent, then damned."

There is a state of utter insensibility to emotions of love or fear, and man by his sin may reach that state. The act of blasphemy is only the expression of a hardened or a hateful heart. B. H. Payne : "The calcium flame will char the steel wire so that it is no longer affected by the magnet. . . . . As the blazing cinders and black curling smoke which the volcano spews from its rumbling throat are the accumulation of months and years, so the sin against the Holy Spirit is not a thoughtless expression in a moment of passion or rage, but the giving vent to a state of heart and mind abounding in the accumulations of weeks and months of opposition to the gospel."

Dr. J. P. Thompson : "The unpardonable sin is the knowing, wilful, persistent, contemptuous, malignant spurning of divine truth and grace, as manifested to the soul by the convincing and illuminating power of the Holy Ghost." Dorner says that " therefore this sin does not belong to Old Testament times, or to the mere revelation of law. It implies the full revelation of the grace in Christ, and the conscious rejection of it by a soul to which the Spirit has made it manifest (Acts 17 : 30 — "The times of ignorance, therefore God overlooked " ; Rom. 3 : 25 — " the passing over of the sins done aforetime ")." But was it not under the Old Testament that God said : " My Spirit shall not strive with man forever " (Gen. 6 : 3), and "Ephraim is joined to idols; let him alone " (Hosea 4 : 17)? The sin against the Holy Ghost is a sin against grace, but it does not appear to be limited to New Testament times.

It is still true that the unpardonable sin is a sin committed against the Holy Spirit rather than against Christ : Mat. 12 : 32 — "whosoever shall speak a word against the Son of man, it shall be forgiven him ; but whosoever shall speak against the Holy Spirit, it shall not be forgiven him, neither in this world, nor in that which is to come." Jesus warns the Jews against it, — he does not say they had already committed it. They would seem to have committed it when, after Pentecost, they added to their rejection of Christ the rejection of the Holy Spirit's witness to Christ's resurrection. See Schaff, Sin against the Holy Ghost ; Lemme, Sünde wider den Heiligen Geist ; Davis, in Bap. Rev., 1882 : 317–326 ; Nitzsch, Christian Doctrine, 283–289. On the general subject of kinds of sin and degrees of guilt, see Kahnis, Dogmatik, 3 : 284, 298.

III. Penalty.

1. *Idea of penalty.*

By penalty, we mean that pain or loss which is directly or indirectly inflicted by the Lawgiver, in vindication of his justice outraged by the violation of law.

Turretin, 1 : 213 — " Justice necessarily demands that all sin be punished, but it does not equally demand that it be punished in the very person that sinned, or in just such time and degree." So far as this statement of the great Federal theologian is intended to explain our guilt in Adam and our justification in Christ, we can assent to his words ; but we must add that the reason, in each case, why we suffer the penalty of Adam's sin, and Christ suffers the penalty of our sins, is not to be found in any covenant-relation, but rather in the fact that the sinner is one with Adam, and Christ is one with the believer, — in other words, not covenant-unity, but life-unity. The word ' penalty,' like ' pain,' is derived from *pœna*, ποινή, and it implies the correlative notion of desert. As under the divine government there can be no constructive *guilt*, so there can be no *penalty* inflicted by legal fiction. Christ's sufferings were penalty, not arbitrarily inflicted, nor yet borne to expiate personal guilt, but as the just due of the human nature with which he had united himself, and a part of which he was. Prof. Wm. Adams Brown : "Loss, not suffering, is the supreme penalty for Christians. The real penalty is separation from God. If such separation involves suffering, that is a sign of God's mercy, for where there is life, there is hope. Suffering is always to be interpreted as an appeal from God to man."

In this definition it is implied that :

A.   The natural consequences of transgression, although they constitute a part of the penalty of sin, do not exhaust that penalty. In all penalty there is a personal element — the holy wrath of the Lawgiver, — which natural consequences but partially express.

We do not deny, but rather assert, that the natural consequences of transgression are a part of the penalty of sin. Sensual sins are punished, in the deterioration and corruption of the body ; mental and spiritual sins, in the deterioration and corruption of the soul. Prov. 5 : 22 — "His own iniquities shall take the wicked, And he shall be holden with the cords of his sin " — as the hunter is caught in the toils which he has devised for the wild beast. Sin is self-detecting and self-tormenting. But this is only half the truth. Those who would confine all penalty to the reaction of natural laws are in danger of forgetting that God is not simply immanent in the universe, but is also transcendent, and that "to fall into the hands of the living God" (Heb. 10 : 31) is to fall into the hands, not simply of the law, but also of the Lawgiver. Natural law is only the regular expression of God's mind and will. We abhor a person who is foul in body and in speech. There is no penalty of sin more dreadful than its being an object of abhorrence to God. Jer. 44 : 4 — "Oh, do not this abominable thing that I hate ! " Add to this the law of continuity which makes sin reproduce itself, and the law of conscience which makes sin its own detecter, judge, and tormentor, and we have sufficient evidence of God's wrath against it, apart from any external inflictions.

The divine feeling toward sin is seen in Jesus' scourging the traffickers in the temple, his denunciation of the Pharisees, his weeping over Jerusalem, his agony in Gethsemane. Imagine the feeling of a father toward his daughter's betrayer, and God's feeling toward sin may be faintly understood.

The deed returns to the doer, and character determines destiny — this law is a revelation of the righteousness of God. Penalty will vindicate the divine character in the long run, though not always in time. This is recognized in all religions. Buddhist priest in Japan: "The evil doer weaves a web around himself, as the silkworm weaves its cocoon." Socrates made Circe's turning of men into swine a mere parable of the self-brutalizing influence of sin. In Dante's Inferno, the punishments are all of them the sins themselves; hence men are in hell before they die. Hegel: "Penalty is the other half of crime." R. W. Emerson: "Punishment not follows, but accompanies, crime." Sagebeer, The Bible in Court, 59 — "Corruption is destruction, and the sinner is a suicide; penalty corresponds with transgression and is the outcome of it; sin is death in the making; death is sin in the final infliction." J. B. Thomas, Baptist Congress, 1901 : 110 — "What matters it whether I wait by night for the poacher and deliberately shoot him, or whether I set the pistol so that he shall be shot by it when he commits the depredation ?" Tennyson, Sea Dreams: "His gain is loss; for he that wrongs his friend Wrongs himself more, and ever bears about A silent court of justice in his breast, Himself the judge and jury, and himself The prisoner at the bar, ever condemn'd : And that drags down his life : then comes what comes Hereafter."

B.   The object of penalty is not the reformation of the offender or the ensuring of social or governmental safety.   These ends may be incidentally secured through its infliction, but the great end of penalty is the vindication of the character of the Lawgiver.   Penalty is essentially a necessary reaction of the divine holiness against sin.   Inasmuch, however, as wrong views of the object of penalty have so important a bearing upon our future studies of doctrine, we make fuller mention of the two erroneous theories which have greatest currency.

(a)   Penalty is not essentially reformatory. — By this we mean that the reformation of the offender is not its primary design, — as penalty, it is not intended to reform.   Penalty, in itself, proceeds not from the love and mercy of the Lawgiver, but from his justice.   Whatever reforming influences may in any given instance be connected with it are not parts of the penalty, but are mitigations of it, and they are added not in justice but in grace.   If reformation follows the infliction of penalty, it is not the effect of the penalty, but the effect of certain benevolent agencies which have been provided to turn into a means of good what naturally would be to the offender only a source of harm.

That the object of penalty is not reformation appears from Scripture, where punishment is often referred to God's justice, but never to God's love ; from the intrinsic ill-desert of sin, to which penalty is correlative ; from the fact that punishment must be vindicative, in order to be disciplinary, and just, in order to be reformatory ; from the fact that upon this theory punishment would not be just when the sinner was already reformed or could not be reformed, so that the greater the sin the less the punishment must be.

Punishment is essentially different from chastisement.   The latter proceeds from love (Jer. 10 : 24 — "correct me, but in measure ; not in thine anger " ; Heb. 12 : 6 — "whom the Lord loveth he chasteneth "). Punishment proceeds not from love but from justice — see Ez. 28 : 22 — "I shall have executed judgments in her, and shall be sanctified in her" ; 36 : 21, 22 — in judgment, "I do not this for your sake, but for my holy name " ; Heb. 12 : 29 — "our God is a consuming fire " ; Rev. 15 : 1, 4 — "wrath of God . . . . thou only art holy . . . . thy righteous acts have been made manifest" ; 16 : 5 — "Righteous art thou . . . . thou Holy One, because thou didst thus judge " ; 19 : 2 — "true and righteous are his judgments ; for he hath judged the great harlot." So untrue is the saying of Sir Thomas More's Utopia: "The end of all punishment is the destruction of vice, and the saving of men." Luther: "God has two rods: one of mercy and goodness; another of anger and fury." Chastisement is the former; penalty the latter.

If the reform-theory of penalty is correct, then to punish crime, without asking about reformation, makes the state the transgressor; its punishments should be proportioned, not to the greatness of the crime, but to the sinner's state; the death-penalty should be abolished, upon the ground that it will preclude all hope of reformation. But the same theory would abolish any final judgment, or eternal punishment; for, when the soul becomes so wicked that there is no more hope of reform, there is no longer any justice in punishing it. The greater the sin, the less the punishment; and Satan, the greatest sinner, should have no punishment at all.

Modern denunciations of capital punishment are often based upon wrong conceptions of the object of penalty. Opposition to the doctrine of future punishment would give way, if the opposers realized what penalty is ordained to secure. Harris, God the Creator, 2: 447, 451 — "Punishment is not primarily reformatory; it educates conscience and vindicates the authority of law." R. W. Dale: "It is not necessary to prove that hanging is beneficial to the person hanged. The theory that society has no right to send a man to jail, to feed him on bread and water, to make him pick hemp or work a treadmill, except to reform him, is utterly rotten. He must deserve to be punished, or else the law has no right to punish him." A House of Refuge or a State Industrial School is primarily a penal institution, for it deprives persons of their liberty and compels them against their will to labor. This loss and deprivation on their part cannot be justified except upon the ground that it is the desert of their wrong doing. Whatever gracious and philanthropic influences may accompany this confinement and compulsion, they cannot of themselves explain the penal element in the institution. If they could, a *habeas corpus* decree could be sought, and obtained, from any competent court.

God's treatment of men in this world also combines the elements of penalty and of chastisement. Suffering is first of all deserved, and this justifies its infliction. But it is at the beginning accompanied with all manner of alleviating influences which tend to draw men back to God. As these gracious influences are resisted, the punitive element becomes preponderating, and penalty reflects God's holiness rather than his love. Moberly, Atonement and Personality, 1-25 — "Pain is not the immediate object of punishment. It must be a means to an end, a moral end, namely, penitence. But where the depraved man becomes a human tiger, there punishment must reach its culmination. There is a punishment which is not restorative. According to the spirit in which punishment is received, it may be internal or external. All punishment begins as discipline. It tends to repentance. Its triumph would be the triumph within. It becomes retributive only as the sinner refuses to repent. Punishment is only the development of sin. The ideal penitent condemns himself, identifies himself with righteousness by accepting penalty. In proportion as penalty fails in its purpose to produce penitence, it acquires more and more a retributive character, whose climax is not Calvary but Hell."

Alexander, Moral Order and Progress, 327-333 (quoted in Ritchie, Darwin, and Hegel, 67) — "Punishment has three characters: It is retributive, in so far as it falls under the general law that resistance to the dominant type recoils on the guilty or resistant creature; it is preventive, in so far as, being a statutory enactment, it aims at securing the maintenance of the law irrespective of the individual's character. But this latter characteristic is secondary, and the former is comprehended in the third idea, that of reformation, which is the superior form in which retribution appears when the type is a mental ideal and is affected by conscious persons." Hyslop on Freedom, Responsibility, and Punishment, in Mind, April, 1894: 167-189 — "In the Elmira Reformatory, out of 2295 persons paroled between 1876 and 1889, 1907 or 83 per cent. represent a probably complete reformation. Determinists say that this class of persons cannot do otherwise. Something is wrong with their theory. We conclude that 1. Causal responsibility justifies preventive punishment; 2. Potential moral responsibility justifies corrective punishment; 3. Actual moral responsibility justifies retributive punishment." Here we need only to point out the incorrect use of the word "punishment," which belongs only to the last class. In the two former cases the word "chastisement" should have been used. See Julius Müller, Lehre von der Sünde, 1: 334; Thornton, Old Fashioned Ethics, 70-73; Dorner, Glaubenslehre, 2: 238, 239 (Syst. Doct., 3: 134, 135); Robertson's

Sermons, 4th Series, no. 18 (Harper's ed., 752); see also this Compendium, references on Holiness, A. (d), page 273.

(b) Penalty is not essentially deterrent and preventive.— By this we mean that its primary design is not to protect society, by deterring men from the commission of like offences. We grant that this end is often secured in connection with punishment, both in family and civil government and under the government of God. But we claim that this is a merely incidental result, which God's wisdom and goodness have connected with the infliction of penalty, — it cannot be the reason and ground for penalty itself. Some of the objections to the preceding theory apply also to this. But in addition to what has been said, we urge :

Penalty cannot be primarily designed to secure social and governmental safety, for the reason that it is never right to punish the individual simply for the good of society. No punishment, moreover, will or can do good to others that is not just and right in itself. Punishment does good, only when the person punished deserves punishment ; and that *desert* of punishment, and not the good effects that will follow it, must be the ground and reason why it is inflicted. The contrary theory would imply that the criminal might go free but for the effect of his punishment on others, and that man might rightly commit crime if only he were willing to bear the penalty.

Kant, Praktische Vernunft, 151 (ed. Rosenkranz) — " The notion of ill-desert and punishableness is necessarily implied in the idea of voluntary transgression ; and the idea of punishment excludes that of happiness in all its forms. For though he who inflicts punishment may, it is true, also have a benevolent purpose to produce by the punishment some good effect upon the criminal, yet the punishment must be justified first of all as pure and simple requital and retribution. . . . . In every punishment as such, justice is the very first thing and constitutes the essence of it. A benevolent purpose, it is true, may be conjoined with punishment ; but the criminal cannot claim this as his due, and he has no right to reckon on it." These utterances of Kant apply to the deterrent theory as well as to the reformatory theory of penalty. The element of desert or retribution is the basis of the other elements in punishment. See James Seth, Ethical Principles, 333-338 ; Shedd, Dogm. Theology, 2 : 717 ; Hodge, Essays, 133.

A certain English judge, in sentencing a criminal, said that he punished him, not for stealing sheep, but that sheep might not be stolen. But it is the greatest injustice to punish a man for the mere sake of example. Society cannot be benefited by such injustice. The theory can give no reason why one should be punished rather than another, nor why a second offence should be punished more heavily than the first. On this theory, moreover, if there were but one creature in the universe, and none existed beside himself to be affected by his suffering, he could not justly be punished, however great might be his sin. The only principle that can explain punishment is the principle of *desert*. See Martineau, Types of Ethical Theory, 2 : 348.

" Crime is most prevented by the conviction that crime deserves punishment ; the greatest deterrent agency is conscience." So in the government of God " there is no hint that future punishment works good to the lost or to the universe. The integrity of the redeemed is not to be maintained by subjecting the lost to a punishment they do not deserve. The wrong merits punishment, and God is bound to punish it, whether good comes of it or not. Sin is intrinsically ill-deserving. Impurity must be banished from God. God must vindicate himself, or cease to be holy " (see art. on the Philosophy of Punishment, by F. L. Patton, in Brit. and For. Evang. Rev., Jan. 1878 : 126-139).

Bowne, Principles of Ethics, 186, 274 — Those who maintain punishment to be essentially deterrent and preventive " ignore the metaphysics of responsibility and treat the problem ' positively and objectively ' on the basis of physiology, sociology, etc., and in the interests of public safety. The question of guilt or innocence is as irrelevant as the question concerning the guilt or innocence of wasps and hornets. An ancient holder of this view set forth the opinion that " it was expedient that one man should die for the people "

(John 18 : 14), and so Jesus was put to death. . . . A mob in eastern Europe might be persuaded that a Jew had slaughtered a Christian child as a sacrifice. The authorities might be perfectly sure of the man's innocence, and yet proceed to punish him because of the mob's clamor, and the danger of an outbreak.'' Men high up in the French government thought it was better that Dreyfus should suffer for the sake of France, than that a scandal affecting the honor of the French army should be made public. In perfect consistency with this principle, McKim, Heredity and Human Progress, 192, advocates infliction of painless death upon idiots, imbeciles, epileptics, habitual drunkards, insane criminals, murderers, nocturnal house breakers, and all dangerous and incorrigible persons. He would change the place of slaughter from our streets and homes to our penal institutions ; in other words, he would abandon punishment, but protect society.

Failure to recognize holiness as the fundamental attribute of God, and the affirmation of that holiness as conditioning the exercise of love, vitiates the discussion of penalty by A. H. Bradford, Age of Faith, 243–250 — " What is penal suffering designed to accomplish? Is it to manifest the holiness of God? Is it to express the sanctity of the moral law? Is it simply a natural consequence? Does it manifest the divine Fatherhood? God does not inflict penalty simply to satisfy himself or to manifest his holiness, any more than an earthly father inflicts suffering on his child to show his wrath against the wrongdoer or to manifest his own goodness. The idea of punishment is essentially barbaric and foreign to all that is known of the Deity. Penalty that is not reformatory or protective is barbarism. In the home, punishment is always discipline. Its object is the welfare of the child and the family. Punishment as an expression of wrath or enmity, with no remedial purpose beyond, is a relic of barbarism. It carries with it the content of vengeance. It is the expression of anger, of passion, or at best of cold justice. Penal suffering is undoubtedly the divine holiness expressing its hatred of sin. But, if it stops with such expression, it is not holiness, but selfishness. If on the other hand that expression of holiness is used or permitted in order that the sinner may be made to hate his sin, then it is no more punishment, but chastisement. On any other hypothesis, penal suffering has no justification except the arbitrary will of the Almighty, and such a hypothesis is an impeachment both of his justice and his love." This view seems to us to ignore the necessary reaction of divine holiness against sin ; to make holiness a mere form of love ; a means to an end and that end utilitarian ; and so to deny to holiness any independent, or even real, existence in the divine nature.

The wrath of God is calm and judicial, devoid of all passion or caprice, but it is the expression of eternal and unchangeable righteousness. It is vindicative but not vindictive. Without it there could be no government, and God would not be God. F. W. Robertson : " Does not the element of vengeance exist in all punishment, and does not the feeling exist, not as a sinful, but as an essential, part of human nature? If so, there must be wrath in God." Lord Bacon : " Revenge is a wild sort of justice." Stephen : " Criminal law provides legitimate satisfaction of the passions of revenge." Dorner, Glaubenslehre, 1 : 287. *Per contra*, see Bib. Sac., Apr. 1881 : 286-302 ; H. B. Smith, System of Theology, 46, 47 ; Chitty's ed. of Blackstone's Commentaries. 4 : 7 ; Wharton, Criminal Law, vol. 1, bk. 1, chap. 1.

2. *The actual penalty of sin.*

The one word in Scripture which designates the total penalty of sin is "death." Death, however, is twofold :

A. Physical death,— or the separation of the soul from the body, including all those temporal evils and sufferings which result from disturbance of the original harmony between body and soul, and which are the working of death in us. That physical death is a part of the penalty of sin, appears :

(*a*) From Scripture.

This is the most obvious import of the threatening in Gen. 2 : 17 —" thou shalt surely die " ; *cf.* 3 : 19 —" unto dust shalt thou return." Allusions to this threat in the O. T. confirm this interpretation : Num. 16 : 29 —" visited after the visitation of all men," where פָּקַד = judicial visitation, or punishment; 27 : 3 (LXX. — δι' ἁμαρτίαν αὐτοῦ). The prayer of Moses in Ps. 90 : 7-9, 11, and the prayer of Hezekiah in Is. 38 : 17, 18, recognize plainly the penal nature of death. The same doctrine is taught in the N. T., as for example, John 8 : 44; Rom. 5 : 12, 14, 16, 17, where the judicial phraseology is to be noted (cf. 1 : 32) ; see 6 : 23 also. In 1 Pet. 4 : 6, physical death is spoken of as God's judgment against sin. In 1 Cor. 15 : 21, 22, the bodily resurrection of all believers, in Christ, is contrasted with the bodily death of all men, in Adam. Rom. 4 : 24, 25 ; 6 : 9, 10 ; 8 : 3, 10, 11 ; Gal. 3 : 13, show that Christ submitted to physical death as the penalty of sin, and by his resurrection from the grave gave proof that the penalty of sin was exhausted and that humanity in him was justified. "As the resurrection of the body is a part of the redemption, so the death of the body is a part of the penalty."

Ps. 90 : 7, 9 — " we are consumed in thine anger . . . . all our days are passed away in thy wrath "; Is. 38 : 17, 18 — "thou hast in love to my soul delivered it from the pit . . . . thou hast cast all my sins behind thy back. For Sheol cannot praise thee "; John 8 : 44 — "He [Satan] was a murderer from the beginning "; 11 : 33 — Jesus "groaned in the spirit " = was moved with indignation at what sin had wrought; Rom. 5 : 12, 14, 16, 17 — " death through sin . . . . death passed unto all men, for that all sinned . . . . death reigned . . . . even over them that had not sinned after the likeness of Adam's transgression . . . . the judgment came of one [trespass] unto condemnation . . . . by the trespass of the one, death reigned through the one " ; cf. the legal phraseology in 1 : 32 — "who, knowing the ordinance of God, that they that practise such things are worthy of death." Rom. 6 : 23 — "the wages of sin is death " = death is sin's just due. 1 Pet. 4 : 6 — "that they might be judged indeed according to men in the flesh "= that they might suffer physical death, which to men in general is the penalty of sin. 1 Cor. 15 : 21, 22 — "as in Adam all die, so also in Christ shall all be made alive "; Rom. 4 : 24, 25 — "raised Jesus our Lord from the dead, who was delivered up for our trespasses, and was raised for our justification "; 6 : 9, 10 — "Christ being raised from the dead dieth no more; death no more hath dominion over him. For the death that he died, he died unto sin once : but the life that he liveth, he liveth unto God " ; 8 : 3, 10, 11 — " God, sending his own Son in the likeness of sinful flesh and for sin, condemned sin in the flesh . . . . the body is dead because of sin" (= a corpse, on account of sin — Meyer; so Julius Müller, Doct. Sin, 2 : 291) . . . . "he that raised up Christ Jesus from the dead shall give life also to your mortal bodies "; Gal. 3 : 13 — " Christ redeemed us from the curse of the law, having become a curse for us ; for it is written, Cursed is every one that hangeth on a tree."

On the relation between death and sin. see Griffith-Jones, Ascent through Christ, 169-185 — " They are not antagonistic, but complementary to each other — the one spiritual and the other biological. The natural fact is fitted to a moral use." Savage, Life after Death, 33 — " Men did not at first believe in natural death. If a man died, it was because some one had killed him. No ethical reason was desired or needed. At last however they sought some moral explanation, and came to look upon death as a punishment for human sin." If this has been the course of human evolution, we should conclude that the later belief represents the truth rather than the earlier. Scripture certainly affirms the doctrine that death itself, and not the mere accompaniments of death, is the consequence and penalty of sin. For this reason we cannot accept the very attractive and plausible theory which we have now to mention :

Newman Smyth, Place of Death in Evolution, holds that as the bow in the cloud was appointed for a moral use, so death, which before had been simply the natural law of the creation, was on occasion of man's sin appointed for a moral use. It is this *acquired* moral character of death with which Biblical Genesis has to do. Death becomes a curse, by being a fear and a torment. Animals have not this fear. But in man death stirs up conscience. Redemption takes away the fear, and death drops back into its natural aspect, or even becomes a gateway to life. Death is a curse to no animal but man. The retributive element in death is the effect of sin. When man has become perfected, death will cease to be of use, and will, as the last enemy, be destroyed. Death here is Nature's method of securing always fresh, young, thrifty life, and the greatest possible exuberance and joy of it. It is God's way of securing the greatest possible number and variety of immortal beings. There are many schoolrooms for eternity in God's universe, and a ceaseless succession of scholars through them. There are many folds, but one flock. The reaper Death keeps making room. Four or five generations are as many as we can individually love, and get moral stimulus from.

Methuselahs too many would hold back the new generations. Bagehot says that civilization needs first to form a cake of custom, and secondly to break it up. Death, says Martineau, Study, 1 : 372-374, is the provision for taking us abroad, before we have stayed too long at home to lose our receptivity. Death is the liberator of souls. The death of successive generations gives variety to heaven. Death perfects love, reveals it to itself, unites as life could not. As for Christ, so for us, it is expedient that we should go away.

While we welcome this reasoning as showing how God has overruled evil for good, we regard the explanation as unscriptural and unsatisfactory, for the reason that it takes no account of the ethics of natural law. The law of death is an expression of the nature of God, and specially of his holy wrath against sin. Other methods of propagating the race and reinforcing its life could have been adopted than that which involves pain and suffering and death. These do not exist in the future life, — they would not exist here, if it were not for the fact of sin. Dr. Smyth shows how the evil of death has been overruled, — he has not shown the reason for the original existence of the evil. The Scriptures explain this as the penalty and stigma which God has attached to sin: Psalm 90 : 7, 8 makes this plain : "For we are consumed in thine anger, And in thy wrath are we troubled. Thou hast set our iniquities before thee, Our secret sins in the light of thy countenance." The whole psalm has or its theme : Death as the wages of sin. And this is the teaching of Paul, in Rom. 5 : 2— "through one man sin entered into the world, and death through sin."

(b)   From reason.

The universal prevalence of suffering and death among rational cr .tures cannot be reconciled with the divine justice, except upon the supposition that it is a judicial infliction on account of a common sinfulness of nature belonging even to those who have not reached moral consciousness.

The objection that death existed in the animal creation before the Fall may be answered by saying that, but for the fact of man's sin, it would not have existed. We may believe that God arranged even the geologic history to correspond with the foreseen fact of human apostasy (cf. Rom. 8 : 20-23 — where the creation is said to have been made subject to vanity by reason of man's sin).

On Rom. 8 : 20-23 — "the creation was subjected to vanity, not of its own will" — see Meyer's Com., and Bap. Quar., 1 : 143 ; also Gen. 3 : 17-19 — "cursed is the ground for thy sake." See also note on the Relation of Creation to the Holiness and Benevolence of God, and references, pages 402, 403. As the vertebral structure of the first fish was an " anticipative consequence " of man, so the suffering and death of fish pursued and devoured by other fish were an " anticipative consequence " of man's foreseen war with God and with himself.

The translation of Enoch and Elijah, and of the saints that remain at Christ's second coming, seems intended to teach us that death is not a necessary law of organized being, and to show what would have happened to Adam if he had been obedient. He was created a "natural," " earthly " body, but might have attained a higher being, the " spiritual," "heavenly " body, without the intervention of death. Sin, however, has turned the normal condition of things into the rare exception (cf. 1 Cor. 15 : 42-50). Since Christ endured death as the penalty of sin, death to the Christian becomes the gateway through which he enters into full communion with his Lord (see references below).

Through physical death all Christians will pass, except those few who like Enoch and Elijah were translated, and those many who shall be alive at Christ's second coming. Enoch and Elijah were possible types of those surviving saints. On 1 Cor. 15 : 51 — " We shall not all sleep, but we shall all be changed," see Edward Irving, Works, 5 : 135. The apocryphal Assumption of Moses, verse 9, tells us that Joshua, being carried in vision to the spot at the moment of Moses' decease, beheld a double Moses, one dropped into the grave as belonging to the earth, the other mingling with the angels. The belief in Moses

Immortality was not conditioned upon any resuscitation of the earthly corpse; see Martineau, Seat of Authority, 364. When Paul was caught up to the third heaven, it may have been a temporary translation of the disembodied spirit. Set free for a brief space from the prison house which confined it, it may have passed within the veil and have seen and heard what mortal tongue could not describe; see Luckock, Intermediate State, 4. So Lazarus probably could not tell what he saw: "He told it not; or something sealed The lips of that Evangelist"; see Tennyson, In Memoriam, xxxi.

Nicoll, Life of Christ: "We have every one of us to face the last enemy, death. Ever since the world began, all who have entered it sooner or later have had this struggle, and the battle has always ended in one way. Two indeed escaped, but they did not escape by meeting and mastering their foe; they escaped by being taken away from the battle." But this physical death, for the Christian, has been turned by Christ into a blessing. A pardoned prisoner may be still kept in prison, as the best possible benefit to an exhausted body; so the external fact of physical death may remain, although it has ceased to be penalty. Macaulay: "The aged prisoner's chains are needed to support him; the darkness that has weakened his sight is necessary to preserve it." So spiritual death is not wholly removed from the Christian; a part of it, namely, depravity, still remains; yet it has ceased to be punishment,— it is only chastisement. When the finger unties the ligature that bound it, the body which previously had only chastised begins to cure the trouble. There is still pain, but the pain is no longer punitive, — it is now remedial. In the midst of the whipping, when the boy repents, his punishment is changed to chastisement.

John 14 : 3 — "And if I go and prepare a place for you, I come again, and will receive you unto myself; that where I am, there ye may be also"; 1 Cor. 15 : 54-57 —"Death is swallowed up in victory . . . . O death, where is thy sting? The sting of death is sin; and the power of sin is the law"— *i. e.*, the law's condemnation, its penal infliction; 2 Cor. 5 : 1-9 —"For we know that if the earthly house of our tabernacle be dissolved we have a building from God . . . . we are of good courage, I say, and are willing rather to be absent from the body, and to be at home with the Lord "; Phil. 1 : 21, 23 — "to die is gain . . . . having the desire to depart and be with Christ; for it is very far better." In Christ and his bearing the penalty of sin, the Christian has broken through the circle of natural race-connection, and is saved from corporate evil so far as it is punishment. The Christian may be chastised, but he is never punished: Rom. 8 : 1 — "There is therefore now no condemnation to them that are in Christ Jesus." At the house of Jairus Jesus said: "Why make ye a tumult, and weep?" and having reproved the doleful clamorists, "he put them all forth" (Mark 5 : 39, 40). The wakes and requiems and masses and vigils of the churches of Rome and of Russia are all heathen relics, entirely foreign to Christianity.

Palmer, Theological Definition, 57 —"Death feared and fought against is terrible; but a welcome to death is the death of death and the way to life." The idea that punishment yet remains for the Christian is "the bridge to the papal doctrine of purgatorial fires." Browning's words, in The Ring and the Book, 2 : 60 —"In His face is light, but in his shadow healing too," are applicable to God's fatherly chastenings, but not to his penal retributions. On Acts 7 : 60 — "he fell asleep" — Arnot remarks: "When death becomes the property of the believer, it receives a new name, and is called sleep." Another has said: "Christ did not send, but came himself to save; The ransom-price he did not lend, but gave; Christ *died*, the shepherd for the sheep; We only *fall asleep.*" *Per contra*, see Kreibig, Versöhnungslehre, 375, and Hengstenberg, Ev. K.-Z., 1864 : 1063 —"All suffering is punishment."

B. Spiritual death,— or the separation of the soul from God, including all that pain of conscience, loss of peace, and sorrow of spirit, which result from disturbance of the normal relation between the soul and God.

(*a*) Although physical death is a part of the penalty of sin, it is by no means the chief part. The term 'death' is frequently used in Scripture in a moral and spiritual sense, as denoting the absence of that which constitutes the true life of the soul, namely, the presence and favor of God.

Mat. 8 : 22 — "Follow me; and leave the [spiritually] dead to bury their own [physically] dead "; Luke 15 : 32 — "this thy brother was dead, and is alive again "; John 5 : 24 —"He that heareth my word, and believeth him that sent me, hath eternal life, and cometh not into judgment, but hath passed out of death into life "; 8 : 51—"If a man keep my word, he shall never see death "; Rom. 8 : 13 — "if ye live after the flesh ye must die; but if by the Spirit ye put to death the deeds of the body, ye shall live "; Eph. 2 : 1 — "when ye were dead through your trespasses and sins "; 5 : 14 — "Awake, thou that sleepest, and arise from the dead "; 1 Tim. 5 : 6 — "she that giveth herself to pleasure is dead while she liveth"; James 5 : 20 — "he who converteth a sinner from the error of his way shall save a soul from death"; 1 John 3 : 14 — "He that loveth not abideth in death"; Rev. 3 : 1 — "thou hast a name that thou livest, and thou art dead."

(*b*) It cannot be doubted that the penalty denounced in the garden and fallen upon the race is primarily and mainly that death of the soul which consists in its separation from God. In this sense only, death was fully visited upon Adam in the day on which he ate the forbidden fruit (Gen. 2 : 17). In this sense only, death is escaped by the Christian (John 11 : 26). For this reason, in the parallel between Adam and Christ (Rom. 5 : 12–21), the apostle passes from the thought of mere physical death in the early part of the passage to that of both physical and spiritual death at its close (verse 21 — " as sin reigned in death, even so might grace reign through righteousness unto eternal life through Jesus Christ our Lord "— where "eternal life " is more than endless physical existence, and " death " is more than death of the body).

Gen. 2 : 17 — "in the day that thou eatest thereof thou shalt surely die"; John 11 : 26 — "whosoever liveth and believeth on me shall never die"; Rom. 5 : 14, 18, 21 — "justification of life .... eternal life"; con.trast these with "death reigned .... sin reigned in death."

(*c*) Eternal death may be regarded as the culmination and completion of spiritual death, and as essentially consisting in the correspondence of the outward condition with the inward state of the evil soul (Acts 1 : 25). It would seem to be inaugurated by some peculiar repellent energy of the divine holiness (Mat. 25 : 41 ; 2 Thess. 1 : 9), and to involve positive retribution visited by a personal God upon both the body and the soul of the evil-doer (Mat. 10 : 28 ; Heb. 10 : 31 ; Rev. 14 : 11).

Acts 1 : 25 — "Judas fell away, that he might go to his own place"; Mat. 25 : 41 — "Depart from me, ye cursed, into the eternal fire which is prepared for the devil and his angels"; 2 Thess. 1 : 9 —"who shall suffer punishment, even eternal destruction from the face of the Lord and from the glory of his might"; Mat 10 : 28 — "fear him who is able to destroy both soul and body in hell"; Heb. 10 : 31 — "It is a fearful thing to fall into the hands of the living God"; Rev. 14 : 11 — "the smoke of their torment goeth up for ever and ever."

Kurtz, Religionslehre, 67 — " So long as God is holy, he must maintain the order of the world, and where this is destroyed, restore it. This however can happen in no other way than this : the injury by which the sinner has destroyed the order of the world falls back upon himself,— and this is penalty. Sin is the negation of the law. Penalty is the negation of that negation, that is, the reëstablishment of the law. Sin is a thrust of the sinner against the law. Penalty is the adverse thrust of the elastic because living law, which encounters the sinner."

Plato, Gorgias, 472 E ; 509 B ; 511 A ; 515 B — " Impunity is a more dreadful curse than any punishment, and nothing so good can befall the criminal as his retribution, the failure of which would make a double disorder in the universe. The offender himself may spend his arts in devices of escape and think himself happy if he is not found out. But all this plotting is but part of the delusion of his sin ; and when he comes to himself and sees his transgression as it really is, he will yield himself up the prisoner of eternal justice and know that it is good for him to be afflicted, and so for the first time to be set at one with truth."

On the general subject of the penalty of sin, see Julius Müller, Doct. Sin, 1 : 245 *sq.* ; 2 : 286–397 ; Baird ; Elohim Revealed, 263–279 ; Bushnell, Nature and the Supernatural, 194–219 ; Krabbe, Lehre von der Sünde und vom Tode ; Weisse, in Studien und Kritiken, 1836 : 371 ; S. R. Mason, Truth Unfolded, 369–384 ; Bartlett, in New Englander, Oct. 1871 : 677, 678.

SECTION VII.—THE SALVATION OF INFANTS.

The views which have been presented with regard to inborn depravity and the reaction of divine holiness against it suggest the question whether infants dying before arriving at moral consciousness are saved, and if so, in what way. To this question we reply as follows :

(a) Infants are in a state of sin, need to be regenerated, and can be saved only through Christ.

Job 14 : 4 — "Who can bring a clean thing out of an unclean ? not one " ; Ps. 51 : 5 — "Behold, I was brought forth in iniquity ; And in sin did my mother conceive me " ; John 3 : 6 — "That which is born of the flesh is flesh " ; Rom. 5 : 14 — "Nevertheless death reigned from Adam until Moses, even over them that had not sinned after the likeness of Adam's transgression " ; Eph. 2 : 3 — "by nature children of wrath " ; 1 Cor. 7 : 14 — "else were your children unclean " — clearly intimate the naturally impure state of infants ; and Mat. 19 : 14 — "Suffer the little children, and forbid them not, to come unto me " — is not only consistent with this doctrine, but strongly confirms it ; for the meaning is : "forbid them not to come unto me " — whom they need as a Savior. "Coming to Christ " is always the coming of a sinner, to him who is the sacrifice for sin ; cf. Mat. 11 : 28 — "Come unto me, all ye that labor."

(b) Yet as compared with those who have personally transgressed, they are recognized as possessed of a relative innocence, and of a submissiveness and trustfulness, which may serve to illustrate the graces of Christian character.

Deut. 1 : 39 — "your little ones . . . . and your children, that this day have no knowledge of good or evil " ; Jonah 4 : 11 — "sixscore thousand persons that cannot discern between their right hand and their left hand " ; Rom. 9 : 11 — "for the children being not yet born, neither having done anything good or bad " ; Mat. 18 : 3, 4 — "Except ye turn, and become as little children, ye shall in no wise enter into the kingdom of heaven. Whosoever therefore shall humble himself as this little child, the same is the greatest in the kingdom of heaven. " See Julius Müller, Doct. Sin, 2 : 265. Wendt, Teaching of Jesus, 2 : 50 — "Unpretentious receptivity, ... not the reception of the kingdom of God at a childlike age, but in a childlike character . . . . . is the condition of entering ; . . . . not blamelessness, but receptivity itself, on the part of those who do not regard themselves as too good or too bad for the offered gift, but receive it with hearty desire. Children have this unpretentious receptivity for the kingdom of God which is characteristic of them generally, since they have not yet other possessions on which they pride themselves."

(c) For this reason, they are the objects of special divine compassion and care, and through the grace of Christ are certain of salvation.

Mat. 18 : 5, 6, 10, 14 — "whoso shall receive one such little child in my name receiveth me : but whoso shall cause one of these little ones that believe on me to stumble, it is profitable for him that a great millstone should be hanged about his neck, and that he should be sunk in the depth of the sea. . . . . See that ye despise not one of these little ones : for I say unto you, that in heaven their angels do always behold the face of my Father who is in heaven. . . . . Even so it is not the will of your Father who is in heaven, that one of these little ones should perish " ; 19 : 14 — "Suffer the little children, and forbid them not, to come unto me : for to such belongeth the kingdom of heaven " — not God's kingdom of nature, but his kingdom of grace, the kingdom of saved sinners. "Such' means, not children as children, but childlike believers. Meyer, on Mat. 19 : 14, refers the passage to spiritual infants only : "Not little children," he says, "but men of a childlike disposition." Geikie : "Let the little children come unto me, and do not forbid them, for the kingdom of heaven is given only to such as have a childlike spirit and nature like theirs." The Savior's words do not intimate that little children are either (1) sinless creatures, or (2) subjects for baptism ; but only that their (1) humble teachableness, (2) intense eagerness, and (3) artless trust, illustrate the traits necessary for admission into the divine kingdom. On the passages in Matthew, see Commentaries of Bengel, De Wette, Lange ; also Neander, Planting and Training (ed. Robinson), 407.

We therefore substantially agree with Dr. A. C. Kendrick, in his article in the Sunday School Times : "To infants and children, as such, the language cannot apply. It must be taken figuratively, and must refer to those qualities in childhood, its dependence, its trustfulness, its tender affection, its loving obedience, which are typical of the essential Christian graces. . . . . If asked after the logic of our Savior's words — how he could assign, as a reason for allowing literal little children to be brought to him, that spiritual little children have a claim to the kingdom of heaven — I reply : the persons that thus, as a class, typify the subjects of God's spiritual kingdom cannot be in themselves objects of indifference to him, or be regarded otherwise than with intense interest. . . . . The class that in its very nature thus shadows forth the brightest features of Christian excellence must be subjects of God's special concern and care."

To these remarks of Dr. Kendrick we would add, that Jesus' words seem to us to intimate more than special concern and care. While these words seem intended to exclude all idea that infants are saved by their natural holiness, or without application to them of the blessings of his atonement, they also seem to us to include infants among the number of those who have the right to these blessings; in other words, Christ's concern and care go so far as to choose infants to eternal life, and to make them subjects of the kingdom of heaven. *Cf.* Mat. 18 : 14 — "it is not the will of your Father who is in heaven, that one of those little ones should perish" = those whom Christ has received here, he will not reject hereafter. Of course this is said to infants, as infants. To those, therefore, who die before coming to moral consciousness, Christ's words assure salvation. Personal transgression, however, involves the necessity, before death, of a personal repentance and faith, in order to salvation.

(*d*) The descriptions of God's merciful provision as coëxtensive with the ruin of the Fall also lead us to believe that those who die in infancy receive salvation through Christ as certainly as they inherit sin from Adam.

John 3 : 16 — "For God so loved the world" — includes infants. Rom. 5 : 14 — "death reigned from Adam until Moses, even over them that had not sinned after the likeness of Adam's transgression, who is a figure of him that was to come" = there is an application to infants of the life in Christ, as there was an application to them of the death in Adam ; 19–21 — "For as through the one man's disobedience the many were made sinners, even so through the obedience of the one shall the many be made righteous. And the law came in besides, that the trespass might abound; but where sin abounded, grace did abound more exceedingly : that, as sin reigned in death, even so might grace reign through righteousness unto eternal life through Jesus Christ our Lord" = as without personal act of theirs infants inherited corruption from Adam, so without personal act of theirs salvation is provided for them in Christ.

Hovey, Bib. Eschatology, 170, 171 — "Though the sacred writers say nothing in respect to the future condition of those who die in infancy, one can scarcely err in deriving from this silence a favorable conclusion. That no prophet or apostle, that no devout father or mother, should have expressed any solicitude as to those who die before they are able to discern good from evil is surprising, unless such solicitude was prevented by the Spirit of God. There are no instances of prayer for children taken away in infancy. The Savior nowhere teaches that they are in danger of being lost. We therefore heartily and confidently believe that they are redeemed by the blood of Christ and sanctified by his Spirit, so that when they enter the unseen world they will be found with the saints." David ceased to fast and weep when his child died, for he said : "I shall go to him, but he will not return to me" (2 Sam. 12 : 23).

(*e*) The condition of salvation for adults is personal faith. Infants are incapable of fulfilling this condition. Since Christ has died for all, we have reason to believe that provision is made for their reception of Christ in some other way.

2 Cor. 5 : 15 — "he died for all"; Mark 16 : 16 — "He that believeth and is baptized shall be saved; but he that disbelieveth shall be condemned" (verses 9–20 are of canonical authority, though probably not written by Mark). Dr. G. W. Northrop held that, as death to the Christian has ceased to be penalty, so death to all infants is no longer penalty, Christ having atoned for and removed the guilt of original sin for all men, infants included. But we reply that there is no evidence that there is any guilt taken away except for those who come into vital union with Christ. E. G. Robinson, Christian Theology, 166 — "The curse falls alike on every one by birth, but may be alleviated or intensified by every one who comes to years of responsibility, according as his nature which brings the curse rules, or is ruled by, his reason and conscience. So the blessings of salvation are procured for all alike, but may be lost or secured according to the attitude of everyone toward Christ who alone procures them. To infants, as the curse comes without their election, so in like manner comes its removal."

(*f*) At the final judgment, personal conduct is made the test of character. But infants are incapable of personal transgression. We have reason, therefore, to believe that they will be among the saved, since this rule of decision will not apply to them.

Mat. 25 : 45, 46 — "Inasmuch as ye did it not unto one of these least, ye did it not unto me. And these shall go away into eternal punishment" : Rom. 2 : 5, 6 — "the day of wrath and revelation of the righteous judgment of God; who will render to every man according to his works." Norman Fox, The Unfolding of Baptist Doctrine, 24 — " Not only the Roman Catholics believed in the damnation of infants. The Lutherans, in the Augsburg Confession, condemn the Baptists for affirming that children are saved without baptism —'damnant Anabaptistas qui . . . affirmant pueros sine baptismo salvos fieri ' — and the favorite poet of Presbyterian Scotland, in his Tam O'Shanter, names among objects from hell ' Twa span-lang, wee, unchristened bairns.' The Westminster Confession, in declaring that ' elect infants dying in infancy' are saved, implies that non-elect infants dying in infancy are lost. This was certainly taught by some of the framers of that creed."

Yet John Calvin did not believe in the damnation of infants, as he has been charged with believing. In the Amsterdam edition of his works, 8 : 522, we read : "I do not doubt that the infants whom the Lord gathers together from this life are regenerated by a secret operation of the Holy Spirit." In his Institutes, book 4, chap. 16, p. 335, he speaks of the exemption of infants from the grace of salvation "as an idea not free from execrable blasphemy." The Presb. and Ref. Rev., Oct. 1890 : 634-651, quotes Calvin as follows : "I everywhere teach that no one can be justly condemned and perish except on account of actual sin ; and to say that the countless mortals taken from life while yet infants are precipitated from their mothers' arms into eternal death is a blasphemy to be universally detested." So also John Owen, Works, 8 : 522 — "There are two ways by which God saveth infants. First, by interesting them in the covenant, if their immediate or remote parents have been believers ; . . . . Secondly, by his grace of election, which is most free and not tied to any conditions ; by which I make no doubt but God taketh unto him in Christ many whose parents never knew, or were despisers of, the gospel."

(*g*) Since there is no evidence that children dying in infancy are regenerated prior to death, either with or without the use of external means, it seems most probable that the work of regeneration may be performed by the Spirit in connection with the infant soul's first view of Christ in the other world. As the remains of natural depravity in the Christian are eradicated, not by death, but at death, through the sight of Christ and union with him, so the first moment of consciousness for the infant may be coincident with a view of Christ the Savior which accomplishes the entire sanctification of its nature.

2 Cor. 3 : 18 — "But we all, beholding as in a mirror the glory of the Lord, are transformed into the same image from glory to glory, even as from the Lord the Spirit " ; 1 John 3 : 2 — "We know that, if he shall be manifested, we shall be like him ; for we shall see him as he is." If asked why more is not said upon the subject in Scripture, we reply : It is according to the analogy of God's general method to hide things that are not of immediate practical value. In some past ages, moreover, knowledge of the fact that all children dying in infancy are saved might have seemed to make infanticide a virtue.

While we agree with the following writers as to the salvation of all infants who die before the age of conscious and wilful transgression, we dissent from the seemingly Arminian tendency of the explanation which they suggest. H. E. Robins, Harmony of Ethics with Theology : "The judicial declaration of acquittal on the ground of the death of Christ which comes upon all men, into the benefits of which they are introduced by natural birth, is inchoate justification, and will become perfected justification through the new birth of the Holy Spirit, unless the working of this divine agent is resisted by the personal moral action of those who are lost." So William Ashmore, in Caristian Review, 26 : 245-264. F. O. Dickey : " As infants are members of the race, and as they are justified from the penalty against inherited sin by the mediatorial work of Christ, so the race itself is justified from the same penalty and to the same extent as are they, and were the race to die in infancy it would be saved." The truth in the above utterances seems to us to be that Christ's union with the race secures the objective reconciliation of the race to God. But subjective and personal reconciliation depends upon a moral union with Christ which can be accomplished for the infant only by his own appropriation of Christ at death.

While, in the nature of things and by the express declarations of Script-ure, we are precluded from extending this doctrine of regeneration at death to any who have committed personal sins, we are nevertheless warranted in the conclusion that, certain and great as is the guilt of original sin, no human soul is eternally condemned solely for this sin of nature, but that, on the other hand, all who have not consciously and wilfully transgressed are made partakers of Christ's salvation.

The advocates of a second probation, on the other hand, should logically hold that infants in the next world are in a state of sin, and that at death they only enter upon a period of probation in which they may, or may not, accept Christ, — a doctrine much less comforting than that propounded above. See Prentiss, in Presb. Rev., July, 1883 : 548–580 — "Lyman Beecher and Charles Hodge first made current in this country the doctrine of the salvation of all who die in infancy. If this doctrine be accepted, then it follows : (1) that these partakers of original sin must be saved wholly through divine grace and power ; (2) that in the child unborn there is the promise and potency of complete spiritual manhood ; (3) that salvation is possible entirely apart from the visible church and the means of grace ; (4) that to a full half of the race this life is not in any way a period of probation ; (5) that heathen may be saved who have never even heard of the gospel ; (6) that the providence of God includes in its scope both infants and heathen."

" Children exert a redeeming and reclaiming influence upon us, their casual acts and words and simple trust recalling our world-hardened and wayward hearts again to the feet of God. Silas Marner, the old weaver of Raveloe, so pathetically and vividly described in George Eliot's novel, was a hard, desolate, godless old miser, but after little Eppie strayed into his miserable cottage that memorable winter night, he began again to believe. ' I think now,' he said at last, ' I can trusten God until I die.' An incident in a Southern hospital illustrates the power of children to call men to repentance. A little girl was to undergo a dangerous operation. When she mounted the table, and the doctor was about to etherize her, he said : ' Before we can make you well, we must put you to sleep.' ' Oh then, if you are going to put me to sleep,' she sweetly said, ' I must say my prayers first.' Then, getting down on her knees, and folding her hands, she repeated that lovely prayer learned at every true mother's feet : ' Now I lay me down to sleep, I pray the Lord my soul to keep.' Just for a moment there were moist eyes in that group, for deep chords were touched, and the surgeon afterwards said : ' I prayed that night for the first time in thirty years.' " The child that is old enough to sin against God is old enough to trust in Christ as the Savior of sinners. See Van Dyke, Christ and Little Children ; Whitsitt and Warfield, Infant Baptism and Infant Salvation ; Hodge, Syst. Theol., 1 : 26, 27 ; Ridgeley, Body of Div., 1 : 422–425 ; Calvin, Institutes, II, i, 8 ; Westminster Larger Catechism, x, 3 ; Krauth, Infant Salvation in the Calvinistic System ; Candlish on Atonement, part ii, chap. 1 ; Geo. P. Fisher, in New Englander, Apr. 1868 : 338 ; J. F. Clarke, Truths and Errors of Orthodoxy, 360.

PART VI.

SOTERIOLOGY, OR THE DOCTRINE OF SALVATION THROUGH
THE WORK OF CHRIST AND OF THE HOLY SPIRIT.

CHAPTER I.

CHRISTOLOGY, OR THE REDEMPTION WROUGHT BY CHRIST.

SECTION I. — HISTORICAL PREPARATION FOR REDEMPTION.

Since God had from eternity determined to redeem mankind, the history
of the race from the time of the Fall to the coming of Christ was providentially arranged to prepare the way for this redemption. The preparation
was two-fold:

I. NEGATIVE PREPARATION, — in the history of the heathen world.

This showed (1) the true nature of sin, and the depth of spiritual ignorance and of moral depravity to which the race, left to itself, must fall ; and
(2) the powerlessness of human nature to preserve or regain an adequate
knowledge of God, or to deliver itself from sin by philosophy or art.

Why could not Eve have been the mother of the chosen seed, as she doubtless at the
first supposed that she was? (Gen. 4 : 1 — "and she conceived, and bare Cain [*i. e.*, 'gotten', or
'acquired'], and said, I have gotten a man, even Jehovah "). Why was not the cross set up at the
gates of Eden? Scripture intimates that a preparation was needful (Gal. 4 : 4 — " but when
the fulness of the time came, God sent forth his Son "). Of the two agencies made use of, we have
called heathenism the negative preparation. But it was not wholly negative; it was
partly positive also. Justin Martyr spoke of a Λόγος σπερματικός among the heathen.
Clement of Alexandria called Plato a Μωσῆς ἀττικίζων — a Greek-speaking Moses. Notice
the priestly attitude of Pythagoras, Socrates, Plato, Pindar, Sophocles. The Bible
recognizes Job, Balaam, Melchisedek, as instances of priesthood, or divine communication, outside the bounds of the chosen people. Heathen religions either were not
religions, or God had a part in them. Confucius, Buddha, Zoroaster, were at least
reformers, raised up in God's providence. Gal. 4 : 3 classes Judaism with the 'rudiments of
the world,' and Rom. 5 : 20 tells us that 'the law came in beside,' as a force coöperating with
other human factors, primitive revelation, sin, *etc.*"

The positive preparation in heathenism receives greater attention when we conceive
of Christ as the immanent God, revealing himself in conscience and in history. This
was the real meaning of Justin Martyr, Apol. 1 : 46; 2 : 10, 13 — " The whole race of men
partook of the Logos, and those who lived according to reason (λόγου), were Christians,
even though they were accounted atheists. Such among the Greeks were Socrates and
Heracleitus, and those who resembled them. . . . Christ was known in part even to
Socrates. . . . The teachings of Plato are not alien to those of Christ, though not in all
respects similar. For all the writers of antiquity were able to have a dim vision
of realities by means of the indwelling seed of the implanted Word (λόγου)." Justin
Martyr claimed inspiration for Socrates. Tertullian spoke of Socrates as " pæne nos-

ter"—"almost one of us." Paul speaks of the Cretans as having "a prophet of their own" (Tit. 1 : 12)—probably Epimenides (596 B. C.) whom Plato calls a θεῖος ἀνήρ — "a man of God," and whom Cicero couples with Bacis and the Erythræan Sibyl. Clement of Alexandria, Stromata, 1 : 19 ; 6 : 5—"The same God who furnished both the covenants was the giver of the Greek philosophy to the Greeks, by which the Almighty is glorified among the Greeks." Augustine : "Plato made me know the true God ; Jesus Christ showed me the way to him."

Bruce, Apologetics, 207 —"God gave to the Gentiles at least the starlight of religious knowledge. The Jews were elected for the sake of the Gentiles. There was some light even for pagans, though heathenism on the whole was a failure. But its very failure was a prepartion for receiving the true religion." Hatch, Hibbert Lectures, 133, 238 — "Neo-Platonism, that splendid vision of incomparable and irrecoverable cloudland in which the sun of Greek philosophy set. . . . On its ethical side Christianity had large elements in common with reformed Stoicism ; on its theological side it moved in harmony with the new movements of Platonism." E. G. Robinson : "The idea that all religions but the Christian are the direct work of the devil is a Jewish idea, and is now abandoned. On the contrary, God has revealed himself to the race just so far as they have been capable of knowing him. . . . Any religion is better than none, for all religion implies restraint."

John 1 : 9 — "There was the true light, even the light which lighteth every man, coming into the world"—has its Old Testament equivalent in Ps. 94 : 10 — "He that chastiseth the nations, shall not he correct, Even he that teacheth man knowledge ? " Christ is the great educator of the race. The preincarnate Word exerted an influence upon the consciences of the heathen. He alone makes it true that "anima naturaliter Christiana est." Sabatier, Philos. Religion, 138-140 — "Religion is union between God and the soul. That experience was first perfectly realized in Christ. Here are the ideal fact and the historical fact united and blended. Origen's and Tertullian's rationalism and orthodoxy each has its truth. The religious consciousness of Christ is the fountain head from which Christianity has flowed. He was a beginning of life to men. He had the spirit of sonship—God in man, and man in God. ' Quid interius Deo ? ' He showed us insistence on the moral ideal, yet the preaching of mercy to the sinner. The gospel was the acorn, and Christianity is the oak that has sprung from it. In the acorn, as in the tree, are some Hebraic elements that are temporary. Paganism is the materializing of religion ; Judaism is the legalizing of religion. ' In me,' says Charles Secretan, ' lives some one greater than I.' "

But the positive element in heathenism was slight. Her altars and sacrifices, her philosophy and art, roused cravings which she was powerless to satisfy. Her religious systems became sources of deeper corruption. There was no hope, and no progress. "The Sphynx's moveless calm symbolizes the monotony of Egyptian civilization." Classical nations became more despairing, as they became more cultivated. To the best minds, truth seemed impossible of attainment, and all hope of general well-being seemed a dream. The Jews were the only forward-looking people ; and all our modern confidence in destiny and development comes from them. They, in their turn, drew their hopefulness solely from prophecy. Not their "genius for religion," but special revelation from God, made them what they were.

Although God was in heathen history, yet so exceptional were the advantages of the Jews, that we can almost assent to the doctrine of the New Englander, Sept. 1883 : 576 —"The Bible does not recognize other revelations. It speaks of the 'face of the covering that covereth all peoples, and the veil that is spread over all nations' (Is. 25 : 7) ; Acts 14 : 16, 17 — ' who in the generations gone by suffered all the nations to walk in their own ways. And yet he left not himself without witness' = not an internal revelation in the hearts of sages, but an external revelation in nature, 'in that he did good and gave you from heaven rains and fruitful seasons, filling your hearts with food and gladness.' The convictions of heathen reformers with regard to divine inspiration were dim and intangible, compared with the consciousness of prophets and apostles that God was speaking through them to his people."

On heathenism as a preparation for Christ, see Tholuck, Nature and Moral Influence of Heathenism, in Bib. Repos., 1832 : 80, 246, 441 ; Döllinger, Gentile and Jew ; Pressensé, Religions before Christ ; Max Müller, Science of Religion, 1-128 ; Cocker, Christianity and Greek Philosophy ; Ackerman, Christian Element in Plato ; Farrar, Seekers after God ; Renan, on Rome and Christianity, in Hibbert Lectures for 1880.

II. Positive Preparation,—in the history of Israel.

A single people was separated from all others, from the time of Abraham, and was educated in three great truths : (1) the majesty of God, in his unity, omnipotence, and holiness; (2) the sinfulness of man, and his moral helplessness; (3) the certainty of a coming salvation. This education from the time of Moses was conducted by the use of three principal agencies:

A. Law.—The Mosaic legislation, (a) by its theophanies and miracles, cultivated faith in a personal and almighty God and Judge; (b) by its commands and threatenings, wakened the sense of sin; (c) by its priestly and sacrificial system, inspired hope of some way of pardon and access to God.

The education of the Jews was first of all an education by Law. In the history of the world, as in the history of the individual, law must precede gospel, John the Baptist must go before Christ, knowledge of sin must prepare a welcome entrance for knowledge of a Savior. While the heathen were studying God's works, the chosen people were studying God. Men teach by words as well as by works,—so does God. And words reveal heart to heart, as works never can. "The Jews were made to know, on behalf of all mankind, the guilt and shame of sin. Yet just when the disease was at its height, the physicians were beneath contempt." Wrightnour: "As if to teach all subsequent ages that no outward cleansing would furnish a remedy, the great deluge, which washed away the whole sinful antediluvian world with the exception of one comparatively pure family, had not cleansed the world from sin."

With this gradual growth in the sense of sin there was also a widening and deepening faith. Kuyper, Work of the Holy Spirit, 67—"Abel, Abraham, Moses = the individual, the family, the nation. By faith Abel obtained witness; by faith Abraham received the son of the promise; and by faith Moses led Israel through the Red Sea." Kurtz, Religionslehre, speaks of the relation between law and gospel as "Ein fliessender Gegensatz"—"a flowing antithesis"—like that between flower and fruit. A. B. Davidson, Expositor, 6:163—"The course of revelation is like a river, which cannot be cut up into sections." E. G. Robinson: "The two fundamental ideas of Judaism were: 1. theological—the unity of God; 2. philosophical—the distinctness of God from the material world. Judaism went to seed. Jesus, with the sledge-hammer of truth, broke up the dead forms, and the Jews thought he was destroying the Law." On methods pursued with humanity by God, see Simon, Reconciliation, 232-251.

B. Prophecy. — This was of two kinds: (a) verbal, — beginning with the protevangelium in the garden, and extending to within four hundred years of the coming of Christ; (b) typical, — in persons, as Adam, Melchisedek, Joseph, Moses, Joshua, David, Solomon, Jonah; and in acts, as Isaac's sacrifice, and Moses' lifting up the serpent in the wilderness.

The relation of law to gospel was like that of a sketch to the finished picture, or of David's plan for the temple to Solomon's execution of it. When all other nations were sunk in pessimism and despair, the light of hope burned brightly among the Hebrews. The nation was forward-bound. Faith was its very life. The O. T. saints saw all the troubles of the present "sub specie eternitatis," and believed that "Light is sown for the righteous, And gladness for the upright in heart" (Ps. 97 : 11). The hope of Job was the hope of the chosen people: "I know that my Redeemer liveth, And at last he will stand up upon the earth" (Job 19 : 25). Hutton, Essays, 2 : 237 — "Hebrew supernaturalism has transmuted forever the pure naturalism of Greek poetry. And now no modern poet can ever become really great who does not feel and reproduce in his writings the difference between the natural and the supernatural."

Christ was the reality, to which the types and ceremonies of Judaism pointed; and these latter disappeared when Christ had come, just as the petals of the blossom drop away when the fruit appears. Many promises to the O. T. saints which seemed to them promises of temporal blessing, were fulfilled in a better, because a more spiritual, way than they expected. Thus God cultivated in them a boundless trust—a trust which was essentially the same thing with the faith of the new dispensation, because it was the absolute reliance of a consciously helpless sinner upon God's method of salvation, and so was implicitly, though not explicitly, a faith in Christ.

The protevangelium (Gen. 3 : 15) said "it [this promised seed] shall bruise thy head." The "it" was rendered in some Latin manuscripts "*ipsa.*" Hence Roman Catholic divines attributed the victory to the Virgin. Notice that Satan was cursed, but not Adam and Eve; for they were candidates for restoration. The promise of the Messiah narrowed itself down as the race grew older, from Abraham to Judah, David, Bethlehem, and the Virgin. Prophecy spoke of "the sceptre" and of "the seventy weeks." Haggai and Malachi foretold that the Lord should suddenly come to the second temple. Christ was to be true man and true God; prophet, priest, and king; humbled and exalted. When prophecy had become complete, a brief interval elapsed, and then he, of whom Moses in the law, and the prophets, did write, actually came.

All these preparations for Christ's coming, however, through the perversity of man became most formidable obstacles to the progress of the gospel. The Roman Empire put Christ to death. Philosophy rejected Christ as foolishness. Jewish ritualism, the mere shadow, usurped the place of worship and faith, the substance of religion. God's last method of preparation in the case of Israel was that of

C. Judgment.—Repeated divine chastisements for idolatry culminated in the overthrow of the kingdom, and the captivity of the Jews. The exile had two principal effects : (*a*) religious,—in giving monotheism firm root in the heart of the people, and in leading to the establishment of the synagogue-system, by which monotheism was thereafter preserved and propagated; (*b*) civil,—in converting the Jews from an agricultural to a trading people, scattering them among all nations, and finally imbuing them with the spirit of Roman law and organization.

Thus a people was made ready to receive the gospel and to propagate it throughout the world, at the very time when the world had become conscious of its needs, and, through its greatest philosophers and poets, was expressing its longings for deliverance.

At the junction of Europe, Asia, and Africa, there lay a little land through which passed all the caravan-routes from the East to the West. Palestine was "the eye of the world." The Hebrews throughout the Roman world were "the greater Palestine of the Dispersion." The scattering of the Jews through all lands had prepared a monotheistic starting point for the gospel in every heathen city. Jewish synagogues had prepared places of assembly for the hearing of the gospel. The Greek language—the universal literary language of the world—had prepared a medium in which that gospel could be spoken. "Cæsar had unified the Latin West, as Alexander the Greek East"; and universal peace, together with Roman roads and Roman law, made it possible for that gospel, when once it had got a foothold, to spread itself to the ends of the earth. The first dawn of missionary enterprise appears among the proselyting Jews before Christ's time. Christianity laid hold of this proselyting spirit, and sanctified it, to conquer the world to the faith of Christ.

Beyschlag, N. T. Theology, 2:9, 10—"In his great expedition across the Hellespont, Paul reversed the course which Alexander took, and carried the gospel into Europe to the centres of the old Greek culture." In all these preparations we see many lines converging to one result, in a manner inexplicable, unless we take them as proofs of the wisdom and power of God preparing the way for the kingdom of his Son; and all this in spite of the fact that "a hardening in part hath befallen Israel, until the fulness of the Gentiles be come in" (Rom. 11:25). James Robertson, Early Religion of Israel, 15—"Israel now instructs the world in the worship of Mammon, after having once taught it the knowledge of God."

On Judaism, as a preparation for Christ, see Döllinger, Gentile and Jew, 2:291-419; Martensen, Dogmatics, 224-236; Hengstenberg, Christology of the O. T.; Smith, Prophecy a Preparation for Christ; Van Oosterzee, Dogmatics, 458-485; Fairbairn, Typology; MacWhorter, Jahveh Christ; Kurtz, Christliche Religionslehre, 114; Edwards' History of Redemption, in Works, 1:297-395; Walker, Philosophy of the Plan of Salvation; Conybeare and Howson, Life and Epistles of St. Paul, 1:1-37; Luthardt, Fundamental Truths, 257-281; Schaff, Hist. Christian Ch., 1:32-49; Butler's Analogy, Bohn's ed., 228-238; Bushnell, Vicarious Sac., 65-66; Max Müller, Science of Language, 2:443; Thomasius, Christi Person und Werk, 1:463-485; Fisher, Beginnings of Christianity, 47-75.

SECTION II.—THE PERSON OF CHRIST.

The redemption of mankind from sin was to be effected through a Mediator who should unite in himself both the human nature and the divine, in order that he might reconcile God to man and man to God. To facilitate an understanding of the Scriptural doctrine under consideration, it will be desirable at the outset to present a brief historical survey of views respecting the Person of Christ.

In the history of doctrine, as we have seen, beliefs held in solution at the beginning are only gradually precipitated and crystallized into definite formulas. The first question which Christians naturally asked themselves was "What think ye of the Christ" (Mat. 22:42); then his relation to the Father; then, in due succession, the nature of sin, of atonement, of justification, of regeneration. Connecting these questions with the names of the great leaders who sought respectively to answer them, we have: 1. the Person of Christ, treated by Gregory Nazianzen (328); 2. the Trinity, by Athanasius (325–373); 3. Sin, by Augustine (353–430); 4. Atonement, by Anselm (1033–1109); 5. Justification by faith, by Luther (1485–1560); 6. Regeneration, by John Wesley (1703–1791); — six weekdays of theology, leaving only a seventh, for the doctrine of the Holy Spirit, which may be the work of our age. John 10:36 — "him whom the Father sanctified and sent into the world" — hints at some mysterious process by which the Son was prepared for his mission. Athanasius: "If the Word of God is in the *world*, as in a body, what is there strange in affirming that he has also entered into *humanity?*" This is the natural end of evolution from lower to higher. See Medd, Bampton Lectures for 1882, on The One Mediator: The Operation of the Son of God in Nature and in Grace; Orr, God's Image in Man.

I. HISTORICAL SURVEY OF VIEWS RESPECTING THE PERSON OF CHRIST.

1. *The Ebionites* (אֶבְיוֹן = 'poor'; A. D. 107 ?) denied the reality of Christ's divine nature, and held him to be merely man, whether naturally or supernaturally conceived. This man, however, held a peculiar relation to God, in that, from the time of his baptism, an unmeasured fulness of the divine Spirit rested upon him. Ebionism was simply Judaism within the pale of the Christian church, and its denial of Christ's godhood was occasioned by the apparent incompatibility of this doctrine with monotheism.

Fürst (Heb. Lexicon) derives the name 'Ebionite' from the word signifying 'poor'; see Is. 25:4 — "thou hast been a stronghold to the poor"; Mat. 5:3 — "Blessed are the poor in spirit." It means "oppressed, pious souls." Epiphanius traces them back to the Christians who took refuge, A. D. 66, at Pella, just before the destruction of Jerusalem. They lasted down to the fourth century. Dorner can assign no age for the formation of the sect, nor any historically ascertained person as its head. It was not Judaic Christianity, but only a fraction of this. There were two divisions of the Ebionites:

(*a*) The Nazarenes, who held to the supernatural birth of Christ, while they would not go to the length of admitting the preëxisting hypostasis of the Son. They are said to have had the gospel of Matthew, in Hebrew.

(*b*) The Cerinthian Ebionites, who put the baptism of Christ in place of his supernatural birth, and made the ethical sonship the cause of the physical. It seemed to them a heathenish fable that the Son of God should be born of the Virgin. There was no personal union between the divine and human in Christ. Christ, as distinct from Jesus, was not a merely impersonal power descending upon Jesus, but a preëxisting hypostasis above the world-creating powers. The Cerinthian Ebionites, who on the whole best represent the spirit of Ebionism, approximated to Pharisaic Judaism, and were hostile to the writings of Paul. The Epistle to the Hebrews, in fact, is intended to counteract an Ebionitic tendency to overstrain law and to underrate Christ. In a complete view, however, should also be mentioned:

(*c*) The Gnostic Ebionism of the pseudo-Clementines, which in order to destroy the deity of Christ and save the pure monotheism, so-called, of primitive religion, gave up even the best part of the Old Testament. In all its forms, Ebionism conceives of God and man as external to each other. God could not become man. Christ was no more than a prophet or teacher, who, as the reward of his virtue, was from the time of his baptism specially endowed with the Spirit. After his death he was exalted to kingship. But that would not justify the worship which the church paid him. A merely creaturely mediator would separate us from God, instead of uniting us to him. See Dorner, Glaubenslehre, 2 : 305-307 (Syst. Doct., 3 : 201-204), and Hist. Doct. Person Christ, A. 1 : 187-217; Reuss, Hist. Christ. Theol., 1 : 100-107; Schaff, Ch. Hist., 1 : 212-215.

2. *The Docetæ* (δοκέω —' to seem,' ' to appear '; A. D. 70-170), like most of the Gnostics in the second century and the Manichees in the third, denied the reality of Christ's human body. This view was the logical sequence of their assumption of the inherent evil of matter. If matter is evil and Christ was pure, then Christ's human body must have been merely phantasmal. Docetism was simply pagan philosophy introduced into the church.

The Gnostic Basilides held to a real human Christ, with whom the divine νοῦς became united at the baptism; but the followers of Basilides became Docetæ. To them, the body of Christ was merely a seeming one. There was no real life or death. Valentinus made the Æon, Christ, with a body purely pneumatic and worthy of himself, pass through the body of the Virgin, as water through a reed, taking up into himself nothing of the human nature through which he passed; or as a ray of light through colored glass which only imparts to the light a portion of its own darkness. Christ's life was simply a theophany. The Patripassians and Sabellians, who are only sects of the Docetæ, denied all real humanity to Christ. Mason, Faith of the Gospel, 141 — " He treads the thorns of death and shame ' like a triumphal path,' of which he never felt the sharpness. There was development only externally and in appearance. No ignorance can be ascribed to him amidst the omniscience of the Godhead." Shelley : " A mortal shape to him Was as the vapor dim Which the orient planet animates with light." The strong argument against Docetism was found in Heb. 2 : 14 — "Since then the children are sharers in flesh and blood, he also himself in like manner partook of the same."

That Docetism appeared so early, shows that the impression Christ made was that of a superhuman being. Among many of the Gnostics, the philosophy which lay at the basis of their Docetism was a pantheistic apotheosis of the world. God did not need to become man, for man was essentially divine. This view, and the opposite error of Judaism, already mentioned, both showed their insufficiency by attempts to combine with each other, as in the Alexandrian philosophy. See Dorner, Hist. Doct. Person Christ, A. 1 : 218-252, and Glaubenslehre, 2 : 307-310 (Syst. Doct., 3 : 204-206); Neander, Ch. Hist., 1 : 387.

3. *The Arians* (Arius, condemned at Nice, 325) denied the integrity of the divine nature in Christ. They regarded the Logos who united himself to humanity in Jesus Christ, not as possessed of absolute godhood, but as the first and highest of created beings. This view originated in a misinterpretation of the Scriptural accounts of Christ's state of humiliation, and in mistaking temporary subordination for original and permanent inequality.

Arianism is called by Dorner a reaction from Sabellianism. Sabellius had reduced the incarnation of Christ to a temporary phenomenon. Arius thought to lay stress on the hypostasis of the Son, and to give it fixity and substance. But, to his mind, the reality of Sonship seemed to require subordination to the Father. Origen had taught the subordination of the Son to the Father, in connection with his doctrine of eternal generation. Arius held to the subordination, and also to the generation, but this last, he declared, could not be eternal, but must be in time. See Dorner, Person Christ, A. 2 : 227-244, and Glaubenslehre, 2 : 307, 312, 313 (Syst. Doct., 3 : 203, 207-210) ; Herzog, Encyclopädie, art. : Arianismus. See also this Compendium, Vol. I : 328-330.

4. *The Apollinarians* (Apollinaris, condemned at Constantinople, 381) denied the integrity of Christ's human nature. According to this view, Christ had no human νοῦς or πνεῦμα, other than that which was furnished by

the divine nature. Christ had only the human σῶμα and ψυχή; the place of the human νοῦς or πνεῦμα was filled by the divine Logos. Apollinarism is an attempt to construe the doctrine of Christ's person in the forms of the Platonic trichotomy.

Lest divinity should seem a foreign element, when added to this curtailed manhood. Apollinaris said that there was an eternal tendency to the human in the Logos himself: that in God was the true manhood; that the Logos is the eternal, archetypal man. But here is no *becoming* man — only a manifestation in flesh of what the Logos already *was*. So we have a Christ of great head and dwarfed body. Justin Martyr preceded Apollinaris in this view. In opposing it, the church Fathers said that " what the Son of God has not taken to himself, he has not sanctified " — τὸ ἀπρόσληπτον καὶ ἀθεράπευτον. See Dorner, Jahrbuch f. d. Theol., 1 : 397-408 — " The impossibility, on the Arian theory, of making two finite souls into one, finally led to the [Apollinarian] denial of any human soul in Christ "; see also, Dorner, Person Christ, A. 2 : 352-399, and Glaubenslehre, 2 : 310 (Syst. Doct., 3 : 206, 207); Shedd, Hist. Doctrine, 1 : 394.

Apollinaris taught that the eternal Word took into union with himself, not a complete human nature, but an irrational human animal. Simon, Reconciliation, 329, comes near to being an Apollinarian, when he maintains that the incarnate Logos was human, but was not *a* man. He is the constituter of man, self-limited, in order that he may save that to which he has given life. Gore, Incarnation, 93 — "Apollinaris suggested that the archetype of manhood exists in God, who made man in his own image. so that man's nature in some sense preëxisted in God. The Son of God was eternally human, and he could fill the place of the human mind in Christ without his ceasing to be in some sense divine. . . . This the church negatived, — man is not God, nor God man. The first principle of theism is that manhood at the bottom is not the same thing as Godhead. This is a principle intimately bound up with man's responsibility and the reality of sin. The interests of theism were at stake."

5. *The Nestorians* (Nestorius, removed from the Patriarchate of Constantinople, 431) denied the real union between the divine and the human natures in Christ, making it rather a moral than an organic one. They refused therefore to attribute to the resultant unity the attributes of each nature, and regarded Christ as a man in very near relation to God. Thus they virtually held to two natures and two persons, instead of two natures in one person.

Nestorius disliked the phrase : " Mary, mother of God." The Chalcedon statement asserted its truth, with the significant addition : " as to his humanity." Nestorius made Christ a peculiar temple of God. He believed in συνάφεια, not ἕνωσις, — junction and indwelling, but not absolute union. He made too much of the analogy of the union of the believer with Christ, and separated as much as possible the divine and the human. The two natures were, in his view, ἄλλος καὶ ἄλλος, instead of being ἄλλο καὶ ἄλλο, which together constitute εἷς — one personality. The union which he accepted was a moral union, which makes Christ simply God and man, instead of the God-man.

John of Damascus compared the passion of Christ to the felling of a tree on which the sun shines. The axe fells the tree, but does no harm to the sunbeams. So the blows which struck Christ's humanity caused no harm to his deity ; while the flesh suffered, the deity remained impassible. This leaves, however, no divine efficacy of the human sufferings, and no personal union of the human with the divine. The error of Nestorius arose from a philosophic nominalism, which refused to conceive of nature without personality. He believed in nothing more than a local or moral union, like the marriage union, in which two become one ; or like the state, which is sometimes called a moral person, because having a unity composed of many persons. See Dorner, Person Christ, B. 1 : 53-79, and Glaubenslehre, 2 : 315, 316 (Syst. Doct., 3 : 211-213); Philippi, Glaubenslehre, 4 : 210; Wilberforce, Incarnation, 152-154.

"There was no need here of the virgin-birth, — to secure a sinless father as well as mother would have been enough. Nestorianism holds to no real incarnation — only to an alliance between God and man. After the fashion of the Siamese twins, Chang and Eng, man and God are joined together. But the incarnation is not merely a higher degree of the mystical union." Gore, Incarnation, 94 — " Nestorius adopted and popularized the doctrine of the famous commentator, Theodore of Mopsuestia. But the Christ of Nestorius was simply a deified man, not God incarnate, — he was from below, not from above. If he was exalted to union with the divine essence, his exaltation was only that of one individual man."

6. *The Eutychians* (condemned at Chalcedon, 451) denied the distinction and coëxistence of the two natures, and held to a mingling of both into one, which constituted a *tertium quid*, or third nature. Since in this case the divine must overpower the human, it follows that the human was really absorbed into or transmuted into the divine, although the divine was not in all respects the same, after the union, that it was before. Hence the Eutychians were often called Monophysites, because they virtually reduced the two natures to one.

They were an Alexandrian school, which included monks of Constantinople and Egypt. They used the words σύγχυσις, μεταβολή — confounding, transformation — to describe the union of the two natures in Christ. Humanity joined to deity was as a drop of honey mingled with the ocean. There was a change in either element, but as when a stone attracts the earth, or a meteorite the sun, or when a small boat pulls a ship, all the movement was virtually on the part of the smaller object. Humanity was so absorbed in deity, as to be altogether lost. The union was illustrated by electron, a metal compounded of silver and gold. A more modern illustration would be that of the chemical union of an acid and an alkali, to form a salt unlike either of the constituents.

In effect this theory denied the human element, and, with this, the possibility of atonement, on the part of human nature, as well as of real union of man with God. Such a magical union of the two natures as Eutyches described is inconsistent with any real *becoming man* on the part of the Logos, — the manhood is well-nigh as illusory as upon the theory of the Docetæ. Mason, Faith of the Gospel, 140 — "This turns not the Godhead only but the manhood also into something foreign — into some nameless nature, betwixt and between — the fabulous nature of a semi-human demigod," like the Centaur.

The author of "The German Theology" says that "Christ's human nature was utterly bereft of self, and was nothing else but a house and habitation of God." The Mystics would have human personality so completely the organ of the divine that "we may be to God what man's hand is to a man," and that "I" and "mine" may cease to have any meaning. Both these views savor of Eutychianism. On the other hand, the Unitarian says that Christ was "a mere man." But there cannot be such a thing as a mere man, exclusive of aught above and beyond him, self-centered and self-moved. The Trinitarian sometimes declares himself as believing that Christ is God *and* man, thus implying the existence of two substances. Better say that Christ is the God-man, who manifests all the divine powers and qualities of which all men and all nature are partial embodiments. See Dorner, Person of Christ, B. 1:83-93, and Glaubenslehre, 2:318, 319 (Syst. Doct., 3:214-216); Guericke, Ch. History, 1:356-360.

The foregoing survey would seem to show that history had exhausted the possibilities of heresy, and that the future denials of the doctrine of Christ's person must be, in essence, forms of the views already mentioned. All controversies with regard to the person of Christ must, of necessity, hinge upon one of three points : first, the reality of the two natures ; secondly, the integrity of the two natures ; thirdly, the union of the two natures in one person. Of these points, Ebionism and Docetism deny the reality of the natures ; Arianism and Apollinarianism deny their integrity ; while Nestorianism and Eutychianism deny their proper union. In opposition to all these errors, the orthodox doctrine held its ground and maintains it to this day.

We may apply to this subject what Dr. A. P. Peabody said in a different connection : ' The canon of infidelity was closed almost as soon as that of the Scriptures " — modern unbelievers having, for the most part, repeated the objections of their ancient predecessors. Brooks, Foundations of Zoölogy, 126 — "As a shell which has failed to burst is picked up on some old battle-field, by some one on whom experience is thrown away, and is exploded by him in the bosom of his approving family, with disastrous results, so one of these abandoned beliefs may be dug up by the head of some intellectual family, to the confusion of those who follow him as their leader."

7. *The Orthodox doctrine* (promulgated at Chalcedon, 451) holds that in the one person Jesus Christ there are two natures, a human nature and a divine nature, each in its completeness and integrity, and that these two natures are organically and indissolubly united, yet so that no third nature is formed thereby. In brief, to use the antiquated dictum, orthodox doctrine forbids us either to divide the person or to confound the natures.

That this doctrine is Scriptural and rational, we have yet to show. We may most easily arrange our proofs by reducing the three points mentioned to two, namely : first, the reality and integrity of the two natures ; secondly, the union of the two natures in one person.

The formula of Chalcedon is negative, with the exception of its assertion of a ἕνωσις ὑποστατική. It proceeds from the natures, and regards the result of the union to be the person. Each of the two natures is regarded as in movement toward the other. The symbol says nothing of an ἀνυποστασία of the human nature, nor does it say that the Logos furnishes the ego in the personality. John of Damascus, however, pushed forward to these conclusions, and his work, translated into Latin, was used by Peter Lombard, and determined the views of the Western church of the Middle Ages. Dorner regards this as having given rise to the Mariolatry, saint-invocation, and transubstantiation of the Roman Catholic Church. See Philippi, Glaubenslehre, 4 : 189 *sq.* ; Dorner, Person Christ, B. 1 : 93-119, and Glaubenslehre, 2 : 320 528 (Syst. Doct., 3 : 216-223), in which last passage may be found valuable matter with regard to the changing uses of the words πρόσωπον, ὑπόστασις, οὐσία, *etc.*

Gore, Incarnation, 96, 101 — "These decisions simply express in a new form, without substantial addition, the apostolic teaching as it is represented in the New Testament. They express it in a new form for protective purposes, as a legal enactment protects a moral principle. They are developments only in the sense that they represent the apostolic teaching worked out into formulas by the aid of a terminology which was supplied by Greek dialectics. . . . . What the church borrowed from Greek thought was her terminology, not the substance of her creed. Even in regard to her terminology we must make one important reservation ; for Christianity laid all stress on the personality of God and man, of which Hellenism had thought but little."

II. The Two Natures of Christ, — their Reality and Integrity.

1. *The Humanity of Christ.*

A. Its Reality. — This may be shown as follows :

(*a*) He expressly called himself, and was called, "man."

John 8 : 40 — "ye seek to kill me, a man that hath told you the truth "; Acts 2 : 22 — "Jesus of Nazareth, a man approved of God unto you"; Rom. 5 : 15 — "the one man, Jesus Christ"; 1 Cor. 15 : 21 — "by man came death, by man came also the resurrection of the dead "; 1 Tim. 2 : 5 — "one mediator also between God and men, himself man, Christ Jesus." Compare the genealogies in Mat. 1:1-17 and Luke 3 :23-38, the former of which proves Jesus to be in the royal line, and the latter of which proves him to be in the natural line, of succession from David ; the former tracing back his lineage to Abraham, and the latter to Adam. Christ is therefore the son of David, and of the stock of Israel. Compare also the phrase "Son of man," *e. g.*, in Mat. 20 : 28, which, however much it may mean in addition, certainly indicates the veritable humanity of Jesus. Compare, finally, the term "flesh" ' — human nature), applied to him in John 1 : 14 — "And the Word became flesh," and in 1 John 4 : 2 — "every spirit that confesseth that Jesus Christ is come in the flesh is of God."

" Jesus is the true Son of man whom he proclaimed himself to be. This implies that he is the representative of all humanity. Consider for a moment what is implied in your being a man. How many parents had you ? You answer, Two. How many grandparents ? You answer, Four. How many great-grandparents ? Eight. How many great-great-grandparents ? Sixteen. So the number of your ancestors increases as you go further back, and if you take in only twenty generations, you will have to reckon yourself as the outcome of more than a million progenitors. The name Smith or Jones, which you bear, represents only one strain of all those million; you might almost as well bear any other name; your existence is more an expression of the race at large than of any particular family or line. What is true of you, was true, on the human side, of the Lord Jesus. In him all the lines of our common humanity converged. He was the Son of man, far more than he was Son of Mary "; see A. H. Strong, Sermon before the London Baptist Congress.

(b) He possessed the essential elements of human nature as at present constituted — a material body and a rational soul.

Mat. 26 : 38 — "My soul is exceeding sorrowful"; John 11 : 33 — "he groaned in the spirit"; Mat. 26 : 26 — ' this is my body "; 28 — "this is my blood"; Luke 24 : 39 — "a spirit hath not flesh and bones, as ye behold me having "; Heb. 2 : 14 — "Since then the children are sharers in flesh and blood, he also himself in like manner partook of the same "; 1 John 1 : 1 — "that which we have heard, that which we have seen with our eyes, that which we beheld, and our hands handled, concerning the Word of life"; 4 : 2 — "every spirit that confesseth that Jesus Christ is come in the flesh is of God."

Yet Christ was not all men in one, and he did not illustrate the development of all human powers. Laughter, painting, literature, marriage — these provinces he did not invade. Yet we do not regard these as absent from the ideal man. The perfection of Jesus was the perfection of self-limiting love. For our sakes he sanctified himself (John 17 : 19), or separated himself from much that in an ordinary man would have been excellence and delight. He became an example to us, by doing God's will and reflecting God's character in his particular environment and in his particular mission — that of the world's Redeemer; see H. E. Robins, Ethics of the Christian Life, 259–303.

Moberly, Atonement and Personality, 86–105 — "Christ was not a man only amongst men. His relation to the human race is not that he was another specimen, differing, by being another, from every one but himself. His relation to the race was not a differentiating but a consummating relation. He was not generically but inclusively man. . . . . The only relation that can at all directly compare with it is that of Adam, who in a real sense was humanity. . . . . That complete indwelling and possessing of even one other, which the yearnings of man toward man imperfectly approach, is only possible, in any fulness of the words, to that spirit of man which is the Spirit of God : to the Spirit of God become, through incarnation, the spirit of man. . . . . If Christ's humanity were not the humanity of Deity, it could not stand in the wide, inclusive, consummating relation, in which it stands, in fact, to the humanity of all other men. . . . . Yet the centre of Christ's being as man was not in himself but in God. He was he expression, by willing reflection, of Another."

(c) He was moved by the instinctive principles, and he exercised the active powers, which belong to a normal and developed humanity (hunger, thirst, weariness, sleep, love, compassion, anger, anxiety, fear, groaning, weeping, prayer).

Mat. 4 : 2 — "he afterward hungered"; John 19 : 28 — "I thirst"; 4 : 6 — "Jesus therefore, being wearied with his journey, sat thus by the well"; Mat. 8 : 24 — "the boat was covered with the waves: but he was asleep"; Mark 10 : 21 — "Jesus looking upon him loved him"; Mat. 9 : 36 — "when he saw the multitudes, he was moved with compassion for them"; Mark 3 : 5 — "looked round about on them with anger, being grieved at the hardening of their heart "; Heb. 5 : 7 — "supplications with strong crying and tears unto him that was able to save him from death"; John 12 : 27 — "Now is my soul troubled; and what shall I say? Father, save me from this hour"; 11 : 33 — "he groaned in the spirit"; 35 — "Jesus wept"; Mat. 14 : 23 — "he went up into the mountain apart to pray." Heb. 2 : 16 — "For it is not doubtless angels whom he rescueth, but he rescueth the seed of Abraham" (Kendrick).

Prof. J. P. Silvernail, on The Elocution of Jesus, finds the following intimations as to his delivery. It was characterized by 1. Naturalness (sitting, as at Capernaum); 2. Deliberation (cultivates responsiveness in his hearers); 3. Circumspection (he looked at Peter); 4. Dramatic action (woman taken in adultery); 5. Self-control (authority, poise, no vociferation, denunciation of Scribes and Pharisees). All these are manifestations of truly human qualities and virtues. The epistle of James, the brother of our Lord, with its exaltation of a meek, quiet and holy life, may be an unconscious reflection of the character of Jesus, as it had appeared to James during the early days at Nazareth. So John the Baptist's exclamation, "I have need to be baptized of thee" (Mat. 3 : 14), may be an inference from his intercourse with Jesus in childhood and youth.

(*d*) He was subject to the ordinary laws of human development, both in body and soul (grew and waxed strong in spirit ; asked questions ; grew in wisdom and stature ; learned obedience ; suffered being tempted ; was made perfect through sufferings).

Luke 2 : 40 — "the child grew, and waxed strong, filled with wisdom "; 46 — " sitting in the midst of the teachers, both hearing them, and asking them questions " (here, at his twelfth year, he appears first to become fully conscious that he is the Sent of God, the Son of God ; 49 — "knew ye not that I must be in my Father's house ? " lit. 'in the things of my Father') ; '2 — "advanced in wisdom and stature "; Heb. 5 : 8 — "learned obedience by the things which he suffered " ; 2 : 18 — "in that he himself hath suffered being tempted, he is able to succor them that are tempted "; 10 — "it became him . . . . to make the author of their salvation perfect through sufferings."

Keble : " Was not our Lord a little child, Taught by degrees to pray ; By father dear and mother mild Instructed day by day ? " Adamson, The Mind in Christ : "To Henry Drummond Christianity was the crown of the evolution of the whole universe. Jesus' growth in stature and in favor with God and men is a picture in miniature of the age-long evolutionary process." Forrest, Christ of History and of Experience, 185 — The incarnation of the Son was not his one revelation of God, but the interpretation to sinful humanity of all his other revelations of God in nature and history and moral experience, which had been darkened by sin. . . . . The Logos, incarnate or not, is the τέλος as well as the ἀρχή of creation."

Andrew Murray, Spirit of Christ, 26, 27 — "Though now baptized himself, he cannot yet baptize others. He must first, in the power of his baptism, meet temptation and overcome it ; must learn obedience and suffer ; yea, through the eternal Spirit, offer himself a sacrifice to God and his Will ; then only could he afresh receive the Holy Spirit as the reward of obedience, with the power to baptize all who belong to him " ; see Acts 2 : 33 — " Being therefore by the right hand of God exalted, and having received of the Father the promise of the Holy Spirit, he hath poured forth this, which ye see and hear."

(*e*) He suffered and died (bloody sweat ; gave up his spirit ; his side pierced, and straightway there came out blood and water).

Luke 22 : 44 — "being in an agony he prayed more earnestly ; and his sweat became as it were great drops of blood falling down upon the ground " ; John 19 : 30 — "he bowed his head, and gave up his spirit "; 34 — "one of the soldiers with a spear pierced his side, and straightway there came out blood and water " — held by Stroud, Physical Cause of our Lord's Death, to be proof that Jesus died of a broken heart.

Anselm, Cur Deus Homo, 1 : 9-19 — " The Lord is said to have grown in wisdom and favor with God, not because it was so, but because he acted as if it were so. So he was exalted after death, as if this exaltation were on account of death." But we may reply : Resolve all signs of humanity into mere appearance, and you lose the divine nature as well as the human ; for God is truth and cannot act a lie. The babe, the child, even the man, in certain respects, was ignorant. Jesus, the boy, was not making crosses, as in Overbeck's picture, but rather yokes and plows, as Justin Martyr relates — serving a real apprenticeship in Joseph's workship : Mark 6 : 3 — "Is not this the carpenter, the son of Mary ? "

See Holman Hunt's picture, " The Shadow of the Cross " — in which not Jesus, but only Mary, sees the shadow of the cross upon the wall. He lived a life of faith, as well as of prayer (Heb. 12 : 2 — "Jesus the author [captain, prince] and perfecter of our faith "), dependent upon Scripture, which was much of it, as Ps. 16 and 118, and Is. 49, 50, 61, written for him, as well as about him. See Park, Discourses, 297-327 ; Deutsch, Remains, 131 — "The boldest transcendental flight of the Talmud is its saying : 'God prays.' " In Christ's humanity, united as it is to deity, we have the fact answering to this piece of Talmudic poetry.

B. Its Integrity. We here use the term 'integrity' to signify, not merely completeness, but perfection. That which is perfect is, *a fortiori*, complete in all its parts. Christ's human nature was :

(*a*) Supernaturally conceived ; since the denial of his supernatural conception involves either a denial of the purity of Mary, his mother, or a denial of the truthfulness of Matthew's and Luke's narratives.

Luke 1 : 34, 35 — "And Mary said unto the angel, How shall this be, seeing I know not a man ? And the angel answered and said unto her, The Holy Spirit shall come upon thee, and the power of the Most High shall overshadow thee "

The "seed of the woman" (Gen. 3 : 15) was one who had no earthly father. "Eve" = life, not only as being the source of physical life to the race, but also as bringing into the world him who was to be its spiritual life. Julius Müller, Proof-texts, 29 — Jesus Christ "had no earthly father; his birth was a creative act of God, breaking through the chain of human generation." Dorner, Glaubenslehre, 2 : 447 (Syst. Doct., 3 : 345) — "The new science recognizes manifold methods of propagation, and that too even in one and the same species."

Professor Loeb has found that the unfertilized egg of the sea-urchin may be made by chemical treatment to produce thrifty young, and he thinks it probable that the same effect may be produced among the mammalia. Thus parthenogenesis in the highest order of life is placed among the scientific possibilities. Romanes, even while he was an agnostic, affirmed that a virgin-birth even in the human race would be by no means out of the range of possibility; see his Darwin and After Darwin, 119, foot note — "Even if a virgin has ever conceived and borne a son, and even if such a fact in the human species has been unique, it would not betoken any breach of physiological continuity." Only a new impulse from the Creator could save the Redeemer from the long accruing fatalities of human generation. But the new creation of humanity in Christ is scientifically quite as possible as its first creation in Adam ; and in both cases there may have been no violation of natural law, but only a unique revelation of its possibilities. " Birth from a virgin made it clear that a new thing was taking place in the earth, and that One was coming into the world who was not simply man." A. B. Bruce : " Thoroughgoing naturalism excludes the virgin life as well as the virgin birth." See Griffith-Jones, Ascent through Christ, 254-270 ; A. H. Strong, Christ in Creation, 176.

Paul Lobstein, Incarnation of our Lord, 217 — " That which is unknown to the teachings of St. Peter and St. Paul, St. John and St. James, and our Lord himself, and is absent from the earliest and the latest gospels, cannot be so essential as many people have supposed." This argument from silence is sufficiently met by the considerations that Mark passes over thirty years of our Lord's life in silence ; that John presupposes the narratives of Matthew and of Luke; that Paul does not deal with the story of Jesus' life. The facts were known at first only to Mary and to Joseph; their very nature involved reticence until Jesus was demonstrated to be " the Son of God with power . . . . by the resurrection from the dead " (Rom. 1 : 4); meantime the natural development of Jesus and his refusal to set up an earthly kingdom may have made the miraculous events of thirty years ago seem to Mary like a wonderful dream ; so only gradually the marvellous tale of the mother of the Lord found its way into the gospel tradition and creeds of the church, and into the inmost hearts of Christians of all countries; see F. L. Anderson, in Baptist Review and Expositor, 1904 : 25-44, and Machen, on the N. T. Account of the Birth of Jesus, in Princeton Theol. Rev., Oct. 1905, and Jan. 1906.

Cooke, on The Virgin Birth of our Lord, in Methodist Rev., Nov. 1904 : 849-857 — " If there is a moral taint in the human race, if in the very blood and constitution of humanity there is an ineradicable tendency to sin, then it is utterly inconceivable that any one born in the race by natural means should escape the taint of that race. And, finally, if the virgin birth is not historical, then a difficulty greater than any that destructive criticism has yet evolved from documents, interpolations, psychological improbabilities and unconscious contradictions confronts the reason and upsets all the long results of scientific observation, — that a sinful and deliberately sinning and unmarried pair should have given life to the purest human being that ever lived or of whom the human race has ever dreamed, and that he, knowing and forgiving the sins of others, never knew the shame of his own origin." See also Gore, Dissertations, 1-68, on the Virgin Birth of our Lord, J. Armitage Robinson, Some Thoughts on the Incarnation, 42, both of whom show that without assuming the reality of the virgin birth we cannot account for the origin of the narratives of Matthew and of Luke, nor for the acceptance of the virgin birth by the early Christians. Per contra, see Hoben, in Am. Jour. Theol., 1902 : 473-506, 709-752. For both sides of the controversy, see Symposium by Bacon, Zenos, Rhees and Warfield, in Am. Jour. Theol., Jan. 1906 : 1-30 ; and especially Orr, Virgin Birth of Christ.

(b) Free, both from hereditary depravity, and from actual sin ; as is shown by his never offering sacrifice, never praying for forgiveness, teaching that all but he needed the new birth, challenging all to convict him of a single sin.

Jesus frequently went up to the temple, but he never offered sacrifice. He prayed :

"Father, forgive them " (Luke 23 : 34); but he never prayed : " Father, forgive *me*." He said : " he must be born anew" (John 3 : 7); but the words indicated that *he* had no such need. " At no moment in all that life could a single detail have been altered, except for the worse." He not only *yielded* to God's will when made known to him, but he *sought* it : " I seek not mine own will, but the will of him that sent me " (John 5 : 30). The anger which he showed was no passionate or selfish or vindictive anger, but the indignation of righteousness against hypocrisy and cruelty — an indignation accompanied with grief : " looked round about on them with anger, being grieved at the hardening of their heart " (Mark 3 : 5). F. W. H. Myers, St. Paul, 19, 53 — "Thou with strong prayer and very much entreating Willest be asked, and thou wilt answer then, Show the hid heart beneath creation beating, Smile with kind eyes and be a man with men. . . . . Yea, through life, death, through sorrow and through sinning, He shall suffice me, for he hath sufficed : Christ is the end, for Christ was the beginning, Christ the beginning, for the end is Christ." Not personal experience of sin, but resistance to it, fitted him to deliver us from it.

Luke 1 : 35 — "wherefore also the holy thing which is begotten shall be called the Son of God"; John 8 : 46 — "Which of you convicteth me of sin?" 14 : 30 — "the prince of the world cometh : and he hath nothing in me" = not the slightest evil inclination upon which his temptations can lay hold; Rom. 8 : 3 — "in the likeness of sinful flesh " = in flesh, but without the sin which in other men clings to the flesh; 2 Cor. 5 : 21 — "Him who knew no sin"; Heb. 4 : 15 — "in all points tempted like as we are, yet without sin"; 7 : 26 — "holy, guileless, undefiled, separated from sinners" — by the fact of his immaculate conception ; 9 : 14 — " through the eternal Spirit offered himself without blemish unto God " ; 1 Pet. 1 : 19 — "precious blood, as of a lamb without blemish and without spot, even the blood of Christ"; 2 : 22 — "who did no sin, neither was guile found in his mouth"; 1 John 3 : 5, 7 — "in him is no sin . . . . he is righteous."

Julius Müller, Proof-texts, 29 — "Had Christ been only human nature, he could not have been without sin. But *life* can draw out of the putrescent clod materials for its own living. Divine life appropriates the human." Dorner, Glaubenslehre, 2 : 446 (Syst. Doct., 3 : 344) — "What with us is regeneration, is with him the incarnation of God." In this origin of Jesus' sinlessness from his union with God, we see the absurdity, both doctrinally and practically, of speaking of an immaculate conception of the Virgin, and of making her sinlessness precede that of her Son. On the Roman Catholic doctrine of the immaculate conception of the Virgin, see H. B. Smith, System, 389–392; Mason, Faith of the Gospel, 129-131 — "It makes the regeneration of humanity begin, not with Christ, but with the Virgin. It breaks his connection with the race. Instead of springing sinless from the sinful race, he derives his humanity from something not like the rest of us." Thomas Aquinas and Liguori both call Mary the Queen of Mercy, as Jesus her Son is King of Justice; see Thomas, Præf. in Sept. Cath. Ep., Comment on Esther, 5 : 3, and Liguori, Glories of Mary, 1 : 80 (Dublin version of 1836). Bradford, Heredity, 289 — "The Roman church has almost apotheosized Mary; but it must not be forgotten that the process began with Jesus. From what he was, an inference was drawn concerning what his mother must have been."

"Christ took human nature in such a way that this nature, without sin, bore the consequences of sin." That portion of human nature which the Logos took into union with himself was, in the very instant and by the fact of his taking it, purged from all its inherent depravity. But if in Christ there was no sin, or tendency to sin, how could he be tempted? In the same way, we reply, that Adam was tempted. Christ was not omniscient : Mark 13 : 32 — "of that day or that hour knoweth no one, not even the angels in heaven, neither the Son, but the Father." Only at the close of the first temptation does Jesus recognize Satan as the adversary of souls : Mat. 4 : 10 — "Get thee hence, Satan." Jesus could be tempted, not only because he was not omniscient, but also because he had the keenest susceptibility to all the forms of innocent desire. To these desires temptation may appeal. Sin consists, not in these desires, but in the gratification of them out of God's order, and contrary to God's will. Meyer : "Lust is appetite run wild. There is no harm in any natural appetite, considered in itself. But appetite has been spoiled by the Fall." So Satan appealed (Mat. 4 : 1-11) to our Lord's desire for food, for applause, for power ; to "Ueberglaube, Aberglaube, Unglaube" (Kurtz); *cf.* Mat. 26 : 39; 27 : 42; 26 : 53. All temptation must be addressed either to desire or fear; so Christ "was in all points tempted like as we are" (Heb. 4 : 15). The first temptation, in the wilderness, was addressed to desire; the second, in the garden, was addressed to fear. Satan, after the first, "departed from him for a season" (Luke 4 : 13); but he returned, in Gethsemane — "the prince of the world cometh : and he hath nothing in me" (John 14 : 30) — if possible, to deter Jesus from his work, by rousing within him vast and agonizing fears of the suffering and death that lay before him. Yet, in spite of both the desire and the fear with which his holy soul was moved, he was "without sin" (Heb. 4 : 15). The tree on the edge of the precipice is fiercely blown by the winds; the strain upon the roots is tremendous, but the roots hold. Even in Gethsemane and on Calvary, Christ never prays for forgiveness, he only imparts it to others. See Ullman, Sinlessness of Jesus; Thomasius, Christi Person und Werk, 2 : 7–17, 126–136, esp. 135, 136; Schaff, Person of Christ, 51–72; Shedd, Dogm. Theol., 3 : 330–349.

(c) Ideal human nature, — furnishing the moral pattern which man is progressively to realize, although within limitations of knowledge and of activity required by his vocation as the world's Redeemer.

Psalm 8 : 4–8 — "thou hast made him but little lower than God, And crownest him with glory and honor. Thou madest him to have dominion over the works of thy hands; Thou hast put all things under his feet " — a description of the ideal man, which finds its realization only in Christ. Heb. 2 : 6–10 — " But now we see not yet all things subjected to him. But we behold him who hath been made a little lower than the angels, even Jesus, because of the suffering of death crowned with glory and honor." 1 Cor. 15 : 45 — " The first . . . . Adam . . . . The last Adam"— implies that the second Adam realized the full concept of humanity, which failed to be realized in the first Adam ; so verse 49 — " as we have borne the image of the earthly [man], we shall also bear the image of the heavenly " [man]. 2 Cor. 3 : 18 — " the glory of the Lord " is the pattern, into whose likeness we are to be changed. Phil. 3 : 21 — " who shall fashion anew the body of our humiliation, that may be conformed to the body of his glory "; Col. 1 : 18 — " that in all things he might have the pre-eminence "; 1 Pet. 2 : 21 — "suffered for you, leaving you an example, that ye should follow his steps "; 1 John 3 : 3 — " every one that hath is hope set on him purifieth himself, even as he is pure."

The phrase " Son of man " (John 5 : 27 ; cf. Dan. 7 : 13, Com. of Pusey, in loco, and Westcott, in Bible Com. on John, 32–35) seems to intimate that Christ answers to the perfect idea of humanity, as it at first existed in the mind of God. Not that he was surpassingly beautiful in physical form ; for the only way to reconcile the seemingly conflicting intimations is to suppose that in all outward respects he took our average humanity — at one time appearing without form or comeliness (Is. 52 : 2), and aged before his time (John 8 : 57 — "Thou art not yet fifty years old "), at another time revealing so much of his inward grace and glory that men were attracted and awed (Ps. 45 : 2 — "Thou art fairer than the children of men "; Luke 4 : 22 — "the words of grace which proceeded out of his mouth " ; Mark 10 : 32 —"Jesus was going before them: and they were amazed ; and they that followed were afraid "; Mat. 17 : 1–8 — the account of the transfiguration). Compare the Byzantine pictures of Christ with those of the Italian painters, — the former ascetic and emaciated, the latter types of physical well-being. Modern pictures make Jesus too exclusively a Jew. Yet there is a certain truth in the words of Mozoomdar : " Jesus was an Oriental, and we Orientals understand him. He spoke in figure. We understand him. He was a mystic. You take him literally : you make an Englishman of him." So Japanese Christians will not swallow the Western system of theology, because they say that this would be depriving the world of the Japanese view of Christ.

But in all spiritual respects Christ was perfect. In him are united all the excellences of both the sexes, of all temperaments and nationalities and characters. He possesses, not simply passive innocence, but positive and absolute holiness, triumphant through temptation. He includes in himself all objects and reasons for affection and worship ; so that, in loving him, "love can never love too much." Christ's human nature, there- fore, and not human nature as it is in us, is the true basis of ethics and theology. This absence of narrow individuality, this ideal, universal manhood, could not have been secured by merely natural laws of propagation,— it was secured by Christ's miraculous conception ; see Dorner, Glaubenslehre, 2 : 446 (Syst. Doct., 3 : 344). John G. Whittier, on the Birmingham philanthropist, Joseph Sturge : "Tender as woman, manliness and meekness In him were so allied, That they who judged him by his strength or weak- ness Saw but a single side."

Seth, Ethical Principles, 420 — " The secret of the power of the moral Ideal is the con- viction which it carries with it that it is no mere ideal, but the expression of the supreme Reality." Bowne, Theory of Thought and Knowledge, 364 — " The a priori only outlines a possible, and does not determine what shall be actual within the limits of the possible. If experience is to be possible, it must take on certain forms, but those forms are compatible with an infinite variety of experience." No a priori truths or ideals can guarantee Christianity. We want a historical basis, an actual Christ, a realization of the divine ideal. " Great men," says Amiel, "are the true men." Yes, we add, but only Christ, the greatest man, shows what the true man is. The heavenly perfection of Jesus discloses to us the greatness of our own possible being, while at the same time it reveals our infinite shortcoming and the source from which all restoration must come.

Gore, Incarnation, 168 — "Jesus Christ is the catholic man. In a sense, all the greatest men have overlapped the boundaries of their time. 'The truly great Have all one age, and from one visible space Shed influence. They, both in power and act Are permanent, and time is not with them, Save as it worketh for them, they in it.' But in a unique sense the manhood of Jesus is catholic; because it is exempt, not from the limitations which belong to manhood, but from the limitations which make our manhood narrow and isolated, merely local or national." Dale, Ephesians, 42 — "Christ is a servant and something more. There is an ease, a freedom, a grace, about his doing the will of God, which can belong only to a Son. . . . There is nothing constrained . . . he was born to it. . . . He does the will of God as a child does the will of its father, naturally, as a matter of course, almost without thought. . . . No irreverent familiarity about his communion with the Father, but also no trace of fear, or even of wonder. . . . . Prophets had fallen to the ground when the divine glory was revealed to them, but Christ stands calm and erect. A subject may lose his self-possession in the presence of his prince, but not a son."

Mason, Faith of the Gospel, 148 — "What once he had perceived, he thenceforth knew. He had no opinions, no conjectures; we are never told that he forgot, nor even that he remembered, which would imply a degree of forgetting; we are not told that he arrived at truths by the process of reasoning them out; but he reasons them out for others. It is not recorded that he took counsel or formed plans; but he desired, and he purposed, and he did one thing with a view to another." On Christ, as the ideal man, see Griffith-Jones, Ascent through Christ, 307–336; F. W. Robertson, Sermon on The Glory of the Divine Son, 2nd Series, Sermon XIX; Wilberforce, Incarnation, 22–99; Ebrard, Dogmatik, 2 : 25; Moorhouse, Nature and Revelation, 37; Tennyson, Introduction to In Memoriam; Farrar, Life of Christ, 1 : 148–154, and 2 : excursus iv; Bushnell, Nature and the Supernatural, 276–332; Thomas Hughes, The Manliness of Christ; Hopkins, Scriptural Idea of Man, 121–145; Tyler, in Bib. Sac., 22 : 51, 620; Dorner, Glaubenslehre, 2 : 451 sq.

(d) A human nature that found its personality only in union with the divine nature, — in other words, a human nature impersonal, in the sense that it had no personality separate from the divine nature, and prior to its union therewith.

By the impersonality of Christ's human nature, we mean only that it had no personality before Christ took it, no personality before its union with the divine. It was a human nature whose consciousness and will were developed only in union with the personality of the Logos. The Fathers therefore rejected the word ἀνυποστασία, and substituted the word ἐνυποστασία, — they favored not unpersonality but inpersonality. In still plainer terms, the Logos did not take into union with himself an already developed human person, such as James, Peter, or John, but human nature before it had become personal or was capable of receiving a name. It reached its personality only in union with his own divine nature. Therefore we see in Christ not two persons — a human person and a divine person — but one person, and that person possessed of a human nature as well as of a divine. For proof of this, see pages 683–700, also Shedd, Dogm. Theol., 2 : 289–308.

Mason, Faith of the Gospel, 136 — "We count it no defect in our bodies that they have no personal subsistence apart from ourselves, and that, if separated from ourselves, they are nothing. They share in a true personal life because we, whose bodies they are, are persons. What happens to them happens to us." In a similar manner the personality of the Logos furnished the organizing principle of Jesus' two-fold nature. As he looked backward he could see himself dwelling in eternity with God, so far as his divine nature was concerned. But as respects his humanity he could remember that it was not eternal, — it had had its beginnings in time. Yet this humanity had never had a separate personal existence, — its personality had been developed only in connection with the divine nature. Göschel, quoted in Dorner's Person of Christ, 5 : 170 — "Christ is humanity; we have it; he is it entirely; we participate therein. His personality precedes and lies at the basis of the personality of the race and its individuals. As idea, he is implanted in the whole of humanity; he lies at the basis of every human consciousness, without however attaining realization in an individual; for this is only possible in the entire race at the end of the times."

Emma Marie Caillard, on Man in the Light of Evolution, in Contemp. Rev., Dec. 1893: 873–881 — "Christ is not only the goal of the race which is to be conformed to him, but he is also the vital principle which moulds each individual of that race into its own similitude. The perfect type exists potentially through all the intermediate stages by which it is more and more nearly approached, and, if it did not exist, neither could they. There could be no development of an absent life. The goal of man's evolution, the perfect type of manhood, is Christ. He exists and always has existed potentially in the race and in the individual, equally before as after his visible incarnation, equally in the millions of those who do not, as in the far fewer millions of those who do, bear his name. In the strictest sense of the words, he is the life of man, and that in a far deeper and more intimate sense than he can be said to be the life of the universe." Dale, Christian Fellowship, 159 — "Christ's incarnation was not an isolated and abnormal wonder. It was God's witness to the true and ideal relation of all men to God." The incarnation was no detached event,—it was the issue of an eternal process of utterance on the part of the Word "whose goings forth are from of old, from everlasting" (Micah 5 : 2).

(*e*) A human nature germinal, and capable of self-communication, — so constituting him the spiritual head and beginning of a new race, the second Adam from whom fallen man individually and collectively derives new and holy life.

In Is. 9 : 6, Christ is called "Everlasting Father." In Is. 53 : 10, it is said that "he shall see his seed." In Rev. 22 : 16, he calls himself "the root" as well as "the offspring of David." See also John 5 : 21 — "the Son also giveth life to whom he will"; 15 : 1 — "I am the true vine" — whose roots are planted in heaven, not on earth; the vine-man, from whom as its stock the new life of humanity is to spring, and into whom the half-withered branches of the old humanity are to be grafted that they may have life divine. See Trench, Sermon on Christ, the True Vine, in Hulsean Lectures. John 17 : 2 — "thou gavest him authority over all flesh, that to all whom thou hast given him, he should give eternal life"; 1 Cor. 15 : 45 — "the last Adam became a life-giving spirit" — here "spirit" = not the Holy Spirit, nor Christ's divine nature, but "the ego of his total divine-human personality."

Eph. 5 : 23 — "Christ also is the head of the church " = the head to which all the members are united, and from which they derive life and power. Christ calls the disciples his "little children" (John 13 : 33); when he leaves them they are "orphans" (14 : 18 marg.). "He represents himself as a father of children, no less than as a brother" (20 : 17 — "my brethren"; *cf.* Heb. 2 : 11 — "brethren", and 13 — "Behold, I and the children whom God hath given me"; see Westcott, Com. on John 13 : 33). The new race is propagated after the analogy of the old; the first Adam the source of the physical, the second Adam of spiritual, life; the first Adam the source of corruption, the second of holiness. Hence John 12 : 24 — "if it die, it beareth much fruit"; Mat. 10 : 37 and Luke 14 : 26 — "He that loveth father or mother more than me is not worthy of me "= none is worthy of me, who prefers his old natural ancestry to his new spiritual descent and relationship. Thus Christ is not simply the noblest embodiment of the old humanity, but also the fountain-head and beginning of a new humanity, the new source of life for the race. *Cf.* 1 Tim. 2 : 15 — "she shall be saved through the child-bearing" — which brought Christ into the world. See Wilberforce, Incarnation, 227-241; Baird, Elohim Revealed, 638-664; Dorner, Glaubenslehre, 2 : 451 *sq.* (Syst. Doct., 3 : 349 *sq.*).

Lightfoot on Col. 1 : 1' — "who is the beginning, the first fruits from the dead " — " Here ἀρχή = 1. priority in time. Christ was first fruits of the dead (1 Cor. 15 : 20, 23); 2. originating power, not only *principium principiatum*, but also *principium principians* As he *is* first with respect to the universe, so he *becomes* first with respect to the church; *cf.* Heb. 7 : 15, 16 — 'another priest, who hath been made, not after the law of a carnal commandment, but after the power of an endless life'." Paul teaches that "the head of every man is Christ" (1 Cor. 11 : 3), and that "in him dwelleth all the fulness of the Godhead bodily" (Col. 2 : 9). Whiton, Gloria Patri, 88-92, remarks on Eph. 1 : 10, that God's purpose is "to sum up all things in Christ, the things in the heavens, and the things upon the earth " — to bring all things to a head (ἀνακεφαλαιώσασθαι). History is a perpetually increasing incarnation of life, whose climax and crown is the divine fulness of life in Christ. In him the before unconscious sonship of the world awakes to consciousness of the Father. He is worthiest to bear the name of *the* Son of God, in a preëminent, but not exclusive right. We agree with these words of Whiton, if they mean that Christ is the only giver of life to man as he is the only giver of life to the universe.

Hence Christ is the only ultimate authority in religion. He reveals himself in nature, in man, in history, in Scripture, but each of these is only a mirror which reflects *him* to us. In each case the mirror is more or less blurred and the image obscured, yet HE appears in the mirror notwithstanding. The mirror is useless unless there is an eye to look into it, and an object to be seen in it. The Holy Spirit gives the eyesight, while

Christ himself, living and present, furnishes the object (James 1:23-25; 2 Cor. 3:18; 1 Cor. 13:12). Over against mankind is Christ-kind; over against the fallen and sinful race is the new race created by Christ's indwelling. Therefore only when he ascended with his perfected manhood could he send the Holy Spirit, for the Holy Spirit which makes men children of God is the Spirit of Christ. Christ's humanity now, by virtue of its perfect union with Deity, has become universally communicable. It is as consonant with evo-lution to derive spiritual gifts from the second Adam, a solitary source, as it is to derive the natural man from the first Adam, a solitary source; see George Harris, Moral Evolution, 409; and A. H. Strong, Christ in Creation, 174.

Simon, Reconciliation, 308 — "Every man is in a true sense essentially of divine nature—even as Paul teaches, θεῖον γένος (Acts 17:29). . . . . At the centre, as it were, enswathed in fold after fold, after the manner of a bulb, we discern the living divine spark, impressing us qualitatively if not quantitatively, with the absoluteness of the great sun to which it belongs." The idea of truth, beauty, right, has in it an absolute and divine quality. It comes from God, yet from the depths of our own nature. It is the evidence that Christ, "the light that lighteth every man" (John 1:9), is present and is working within us.

Pfleiderer, Philos. of Religion, 1:272 — "That the divine idea of man as 'the son of his love' (Col. 1:13), and of humanity as the kingdom of this Son of God, is the immanent final cause of all existence and development even in the prior world of nature, this has been the fundamental thought of the Christian Gnosis since the apostolic age, and I think that no philosophy has yet been able to shake or to surpass this thought — the corner stone of an idealistic view of the world." But Mead, Ritschl's Place in the History of Doctrine, 10, says of Pfleiderer and Ritschl: "Both recognize Christ as morally perfect and as the head of the Christian Church. Both deny his pre-existence and his essential Deity. Both reject the traditional conception of Christ as an atoning Redeemer. Ritschl calls Christ God, though inconsistently; Pfleiderer declines to say one thing when he seems to mean another."

The passages here alluded to abundantly confute the Docetic denial of Christ's veritable human body, and the Apollinarian denial of Christ's veritable human soul. More than this, they establish the reality and integrity of Christ's human nature, as possessed of all the elements, faculties, and powers essential to humanity.

2. The Deity of Christ.

The reality and integrity of Christ's divine nature have been sufficiently proved in a former chapter (see pages 305–315). We need only refer to the evidence there given, that, during his earthly ministry, Christ:

(a) Possessed a knowledge of his own deity.

John 3:13 — "the Son of man, who is in heaven" — a passage with clearly indicates Christ's con-sciousness, at certain times in his earthly life at least, that he was not confined to earth but was also in heaven [here, however, Westcott and Hort, with א and B, omit ὁ ὢν ἐν τῷ οὐρανῷ; for advocacy of the common reading, see Broadus, in Hovey's Com. on John 3:13]; 8:58 — "Before Abraham was born, I am" — here Jesus declares that there is a respect in which the idea of birth and beginning does not apply to him, but in which he can apply to himself the name "I am" of the eternal God; 14:9, 10 — "Have I been so long time with you, and dost thou not know me, Philip? he that hath seen me hath seen the Father; how sayest thou, Show us the Father? Believest thou not that I am in the Father, and the Father in me?"

Adamson, The Mind in Christ, 24–49, gives the following instances of Jesus' super-natural knowledge: 1. Jesus' knowledge of Peter (John 1:42); 2. his finding of Philip (1:43); 3. his recognition of Nathanael (1:47-50); 4. of the woman of Samaria (4:17-19,39): 5. miraculous draughts of fishes (Luke 5:6-9; John 21:6); 6. death of Lazarus (John 11:14); 7. of the ass's colt (Mat. 21:2); 8. of the upper room (Mark 14:15); 9. of Peter's denial (Mat. 26:34); 10. of the manner of his own death (John 12:33; 18:32); 11. of the manner of Peter's death (John 21:19); 12. of the fall of Jerusalem (Mat. 24:2).

Jesus does not say "our Father" but "my Father" (John 20:17). Rejection of him is a greater sin than rejection of the prophets, because he is the "beloved Son" of God (Luke 20:13). He knows God's purposes better than the angels, because he is the Son of God (Mark 13:32). As Son of God, he alone knows, and he alone can reveal, the Father (Mat.

ii: 27). There is clearly something more in his Sonship than in that of his disciples (John 1:14 — "only begotten"; Heb. 1:6 — "first begotten"). See Chapman, Jesus Christ and the Present Age, 37; Denney, Studies in Theology, 33.

(b) Exercised divine powers and prerogatives.

John 2:24, 25 — "But Jesus did not trust himself unto them, for that he knew all men, and because he needed not that any one should bear witness concerning man; for he himself knew what was in man"; 18:4 — "Jesus therefore, knowing all the things that were coming upon him, went forth"; Mark 4:39 — "he awoke, and rebuked the wind, and said unto the sea, Peace, be still. And the wind ceased, and there was a great calm"; Mat. 9:6 — "But that ye may know that the Son of man hath authority on earth to forgive sins (then saith he to the sick of the palsy), Arise, and take up thy bed, and go unto thy house"; Mark 2:7 — "Why doth this man thus speak? he blasphemeth: who can forgive sins but one, even God?"

It is not enough to keep, like Alexander Severus, a bust of Christ, in a private chapel, along with Virgil, Orpheus, Abraham, Apollonius, and other persons of the same kind; see Gibbon, Decline and Fall, chap. xvi. "Christ is all in all. The prince in the Arabian story took from a walnut-shell a miniature tent, but that tent expanded so as to cover, first himself, then his palace, then his army, and at last his whole kingdom. So Christ's being and authority expand, as we reflect upon them, until they take in, not only our-selves, our homes and our country, but the whole world of sinning and suffering men, and the whole universe of God"; see A. H. Strong, Address at the Ecumenical Mission-ary Conference, April 23, 1900.

Matheson, Voices of the Spirit, 39 — "What is that law which I call gravitation, but the sign of the Son of man in heaven? It is the gospel of self-surrender in nature. It is the inability of any world to be its own centre, the necessity of every world to center in something else. . . . In the firmament as on the earth, the many are made one by giving the one for the many." "Subtlest thought shall fail and learning falter; Churches change, forms perish, systems go; But our human needs, they will not alter, Christ no after age will e'er outgrow. Yea, amen, O changeless One, thou only Art life's guide and spiritual goal; Thou the light across the dark vale lonely, Thou the eternal haven of the soul."

But this is to say, in other words, that there were, in Christ, a knowl-edge and a power such as belong only to God. The passages cited furnish a refutation of both the Ebionite denial of the reality, and the Arian denial of the integrity, of the divine nature in Christ.

Napoleon to Count Montholon (Bertrand's Memoirs): "I think I understand some-what of human nature, and I tell you all these [heroes of antiquity] were men, and I am a man; but not one is like him: Jesus Christ was more than man." See other testimonies in Schaff, Person of Christ. Even Spinoza, Tract. Theol.-Pol., cap. 1 (vol. 1:383), says that "Christ communed with God, mind to mind . . . . this spiritual close-ness is unique" (Martineau, Types, 1:254), and Channing speaks of Christ as more than a human being, — as having exhibited a spotless purity which is the highest distinction of heaven. F. W. Robertson has called attention to the fact that the phrase "Son of man" (John 5:27; cf. Dan. 7:13) itself implies that Christ was more than man; it would have been an impertinence for him to have proclaimed himself Son of man, unless he had claimed to be something more; could not every human being call himself the same? When one takes this for his characteristic designation, as Jesus did, he implies that there is something strange in his being Son of man; that this is not his original condition and dignity; in other words, that he is also Son of God.

It corroborates the argument from Scripture, to find that Christian experience instinctively recognizes Christ's Godhead, and that Christian history shows a new con-ception of the dignity of childhood and of womanhood, of the sacredness of human life, and of the value of a human soul, — all arising from the belief that, in Christ, the God-head honored human nature by taking it into perpetual union with itself, and by bearing its guilt and punishment, and by raising it up from the dishonors of the grave to the glory of heaven. We need both the humanity and the deity of Christ; the humanity, — for, as Michael Angelo's Last Judgment witnesses, the ages that neglect Christ's humanity must have some human advocate and Savior, and find a poor substitute for the ever-present Christ in Mariolatry, the invocation of the saints, and the 'real pres-ence' of the wafer and the mass; the deity, — for, unless Christ is God, he cannot offer an infinite atonement for us, nor bring about a real union between our souls and the

Father. Dorner, Glaubenslehre, 2: 325-327 (Syst. Doct., 3: 221-223)—"Mary and the saints took Christ's place as intercessors in heaven; transubstantiation furnished a present Christ on earth." It might almost be said that Mary was made a fourth person in the Godhead.

Harnack, Das Wesen des Christenthums: "It is no paradox, and neither is it rationalism, but the simple expression of the actual position as it lies before us in the gospels: Not the Son, but the Father alone, has a place in the gospel as Jesus proclaimed it"; *i. e.*, Jesus has no place, authority, supremacy, in the gospel,— the gospel is a Christianity without Christ; see Nicoll, The Church's One Foundation, 48. And this in the face of Jesus' own words: "Come unto me" (Mat. 11:28); "the Son of man . . . . shall sit on the throne of his glory: and before him shall be gathered all the nations" (Mat. 25:31, 32); "he that hath seen me hath seen the Father" (John 14:9); "he that obeyeth not the Son shall not see life, but the wrath of God abideth on him" (John 3:36). Loisy, The Gospel and the Church, advocates the nut-theory in distinction from the onion-theory of doctrine. Does the fourth gospel appear a second century production? What of it? There is an evolution of doctrine as to Christ. "Harnack does not conceive of Christianity as a seed, at first a plant in potentiality, then a real plant, identical from the beginning of its evolution to the final limit, and from the root to the summit of the stem. He conceives of it rather as a fruit ripe, or over ripe, that must be peeled to reach the incorruptible kernel, and he peels his fruit so thoroughly that little remains at the end." R. W. Gilder: "If Jesus is a man, And only a man, I say That of all mankind I will cleave to him, And will cleave alway. If Jesus Christ is a God, And the only God, I swear I will follow him through heaven and hell, The earth, the sea, and the air."

On Christ manifested in Nature, see Jonathan Edwards, Observations on Trinity, ed Smyth, 92-97—"He who, by his immediate influence, gives being every moment, and by his Spirit actuates the world, because he inclines to communicate himself and his excellencies, doth doubtless communicate his excellency to bodies, as far as there is any consent or analogy. And the beauty of face and sweet airs in men are not always the effect of the corresponding excellencies of the mind; yet the beauties of nature are really emanations or shadows of the excellencies of the Son of God. So that, when we are delighted with flowery meadows and gentle breezes of wind, we may consider that we see only the emanations of the sweet benevolence of Jesus Christ. When we behold the fragrant rose and lily, we see his love and purity. So the green trees and fields, and singing of birds, are the emanations of his infinite joy and benignity. The easiness and naturalness of trees and vines are shadows of his beauty and loveliness. The crystal rivers and murmuring streams are the footsteps of his favor, grace and beauty. When we behold the light and brightness of the sun, the golden edges of an evening cloud, or the beauteous bow, we behold the adumbrations of his glory and goodness, and in the blue sky, of his mildness and gentleness. There are also many things wherein we may behold his awful majesty: in the sun in his strength, in comets, in thunder, in the hovering thunder clouds, in ragged rocks and the brows of mountains. That beauteous light wherewith the world is filled in a clear day is a lively shadow of his spotless holiness, and happiness and delight in communicating himself. And doubtless this is a reason why Christ is compared so often to these things, and called by their names, as the Sun of Righteousness, the Morning Star, the Rose of Sharon, and Lily of the Valley, the apple tree among trees of the wood, a bundle of myrrh, a roe, or a young hart. By this we may discover the beauty of many of those metaphors and similes which to an unphilosophical person do seem so uncouth. In like manner, when we behold the beauty of man's body in its perfection, we still see like emanations of Christ's divine perfections, although they do not always flow from the mental excellencies of the person that has them. But we see the most proper image of the beauty of Christ when we see beauty in the human soul."

On the deity of Christ, see Shedd, History of Doctrine, 1:262, 351; Liddon, Our Lord's Divinity, 127, 207, 458; Thomasius, Christi Person und Werk, 1:61-64; Hovey, God with Us, 17-23; Bengel on John 10:30. On the two natures of Christ, see A. H. Strong, Philosophy and Religion, 201-212.

III. The Union of the two Natures in one Person.

Distinctly as the Scriptures represent Jesus Christ to have been possessed of a divine nature and of a human nature, each unaltered in essence and undivested of its normal attributes and powers, they with equal distinctness represent Jesus Christ as a single undivided personality in whom these two natures are vitally and inseparably united, so that he is properly, not God and man, but the God-man. The two natures are bound together, not by the moral tie of friendship, nor by the spiritual tie which links the believer to his Lord, but by a bond unique and inscrutable, which constitutes them one person with a single consciousness and will, — this consciousness and will including within their possible range both the human nature and the divine.

Whiton, Gloria Patri, 79–81, would give up speaking of the union of God *and* man; for this, he says, involves the fallacy of two natures. He would speak rather of the manifestation of God *in* man. The ordinary Unitarian insists that Christ was "a mere man." As if there could be such a thing as *mere* man, exclusive of aught above him and beyond him, self-centered and self-moved. We can sympathize with Whiton's objection to the phrase "God *and* man," because of its implication of an imperfect union. But we prefer the term "God-man" to the phrase "God *in* man," for the reason that this latter phrase might equally describe the union of Christ with every believer. Christ is "the only begotten," in a sense that every believer is not. Yet we can also sympathize with Dean Stanley, Life and Letters, 1 : 115 — "Alas that a Church that has so divine a service should keep its long list of Articles! I am strengthened more than ever in my opinion that there is only needed, that there only should be, one, *viz.*, 'I believe that Christ is both God and man.'"

1. *Proof of this Union.*

(*a*) Christ uniformly speaks of himself, and is spoken of, as a single person. There is no interchange of 'I' and 'thou' between the human and the divine natures, such as we find between the persons of the Trinity (John 17 : 23). Christ never uses the plural number in referring to himself, unless it be in John 3 : 11 — "we speak that we do know," — and even here "we" is more probably used as inclusive of the disciples. 1 John 4 : 2 — "is come in the flesh" — is supplemented by John 1 : 14 — "became flesh"; and these texts together assure us that Christ so came in human nature as to make that nature an element in his single personality.

John 17 : 23 — "I in them, and thou in me, that they may be perfected into one; that the world may know that thou didst send me, and lovedst them, even as thou lovedst me"; 3 . 11 — "We speak that which we know, and bear witness of that which we have seen; and ye receive not our witness"; 1 John 4 : 2 — "every spirit that confesseth that Jesus Christ is come in the flesh is of God"; John 1 : 14 — "And the Word became flesh, and dwelt among us" = he so came in human nature that human nature and himself formed, not two persons, but one person.

In the Trinity, the Father is objective to the Son, the Son to the Father, and both to the Spirit. But Christ's divinity is never objective to his humanity, nor his humanity to his divinity. Moberly, Atonement and Personality, 97 — "He is not so much God *and* man, as God *in*, and *through*, and *as* man. He is one indivisible personality throughout. . . . . We are to study the divine in and through the human. By looking for the divine side by side with the human, instead of discerning the divine within the human, we miss the significance of them both." We mistake when we say that certain words of Jesus with regard to his ignorance of the day of the end (Mark 13 : 32) were spoken by his human nature, while certain other words with regard to his being in heaven at the same time that he was on earth (John 3 : 13) were spoken by his divine nature. There was never any separation of the human from the divine, or of the divine from the human, —all Christ's words were spoken, and all Christ's deeds were done, by the one person, the God-man. See Forrest, The Authority of Christ, 49–100.

(*b*) The attributes and powers of both natures are ascribed to the one Christ, and conversely the works and dignities of the one Christ are ascribed to either of the natures, in a way inexplicable, except upon the principle that these two natures are organically and indissolubly united in a single person (examples of the former usage are Rom. 1 : 2 and 1 Pet.

3 : 18 ; of the latter, 1 Tim. 2 : 5 and Heb. 1 : 2, 3). Hence we can say, on the one hand, that the God-man existed before Abraham, yet was born in the reign of Augustus Cæsar, and that Jesus Christ wept, was weary, suffered, died, yet is the same yesterday, to-day, and forever ; on the other hand, that a divine Savior redeemed us upon the cross, and that the human Christ is present with his people even to the end of the world (Eph. 1 : 23 ; 4 : 10 ; Mat. 28 : 20).

Rom. 1 : 3 — " his Son, who was born of the seed of David according to the flesh " ; 1 Pet. 3 : 18 — "Christ also suffered for sins once . . . . being put to death in the flesh, but made alive in the spirit" ; 1 Tim. 2 : 5 — " one mediator also between God and men, himself man, Christ Jesus " ; Heb. 1 : 2, 3 — " his Son, whom he appointed heir of all things . . . . who being the effulgence of his glory . . . . when he had made purification of sins, sat down on the right hand of the Majesty on high " ; Eph. 1 : 22, 23 — " put all things in subjection under his feet, and gave him to be head over all things to the church, which is his body, the fulness of him that filleth all in all " ; 4 : 10 — "He that descended is the same also that ascended far above all the heavens, that he might fill all things " ; Mat. 28 : 20 — "lo, I am with you always, even unto the end of the world."

Mason, Faith of the Gospel, 142-145 — " Mary was Theotokos, but she was not the mother of Christ's Godhood, but of his humanity. We speak of the blood of God the Son, but it is not as God that he has blood. The hands of the babe Jesus made the worlds, only in the sense that he whose hands they were was the Agent in creation. . . . . Spirit and body in us are not merely put side by side, and insulated from each other. The spirit does not have the rheumatism, and the reverent body does not commune with God. The reason why they affect each other is because they are equally ours. . . . . Let us avoid sensuous, fondling, modes of addressing Christ — modes which dishonor him and enfeeble the soul of the worshiper. . . . . Let us also avoid, on the other hand, such phrases as ' the dying God ', which loses the manhood in the Godhead." Charles H. Spurgeon remarked that people who " dear " everybody reminded him of the woman who said she had been reading in " dear Hebrews."

(c) The constant Scriptural representations of the infinite value of Christ's atonement and of the union of the human race with God which has been secured in him are intelligible only when Christ is regarded, not as a man of God, but as the God-man, in whom the two natures are so united that what each does has the value of both.

1 John 2 : 2 — "he is the propitiation for our sins; and not for ours only, but also for the whole world," — as John in his gospel proves that Jesus is the Son of God, the Word, God, so in his first Epistle he proves that the Son of God, the Word, God, has become man ; Eph. 2 : 16-18 — " might reconcile them both [Jew and Gentile] in one body unto God through the cross, having slain the enmity thereby ; and he came and preached peace to you that were far off, and peace to them that were nigh : for through him we both have our access in one Spirit unto the Father " ; 21, 22 — " in whom each several building, fitly framed together, groweth into a holy temple in the Lord ; in whom ye also are builded together for a habitation of God in the Spirit " ; 2 Pet. 1 : 4 — "that through these [promises] ye may become partakers of the divine nature." John Caird, Fund. Ideas of Christianity, 2 : 107 — " We cannot separate Christ's divine from his human acts, without rending in twain the unity of his person and life."

(d) It corroborates this view to remember that the universal Christian consciousness recognizes in Christ a single and undivided personality, and expresses this recognition in its services of song and prayer.

The foregoing proof of the union of a perfect human nature and of a perfect divine nature in the single person of Jesus Christ suffices to refute both the Nestorian separation of the natures and the Eutychian confounding of them. Certain modern forms of stating the doctrine of this union, however — forms of statement into which there enter some of the misconceptions already noticed — need a brief examination, before we proceed to our own attempt at elucidation.

Dorner, Glaubenslehre, 2 : 403-411 (Syst. Doct., 3 : 300-308) — " Three ideas are included in incarnation : (1) assumption of human nature on the part of the Logos (Heb. 2 : 14 —

"partook of . . . . . flesh and blood'; 2 Cor. 5 : 19 —'God was in Christ'; Col. 2 : 9 —'in him dwelleth all the fulness of the Godhead bodily'); (2) new creation of the second Adam, by the Holy Ghost and power of the Highest (Rom. 5 : 14 — 'Adam's transgression, who is a figure of him that was to come' ; 1 Cor. 15 : 22 — 'as in Adam all die, so also in Christ shall all be made alive'; 15 : 45 — 'The first man Adam became a living soul. The last Adam became a life-giving Spirit'; Luke 1 : 35 —'the Holy Spirit shall come upon thee, and the power of the Most High shall overshadow thee'; Mat. 1 : 20 — 'that which is conceived in her is of the Holy Spirit'); (3) becoming flesh, without contraction of deity or humanity (1 Tim. 3 : 16 — 'who was manifested in the flesh'; 1 John 4 : 2 — 'Jesus Christ is come in the flesh'; John 6 : 41, 51 — 'I am the bread which came down out of heaven . . . . I am the living bread'; 2 John 7 —'Jesus Christ cometh in the flesh'; John 1 : 14 —'the Word became flesh '). This last text cannot mean : The Logos ceased to be what he was, and began to be only man. Nor can it be a mere theophany, in human form. The reality of the humanity is intimated, as well as the reality of the Logos."

The Lutherans hold to a communion of the natures, as well as to an impartation of their properties : (1) *genus idiomaticum* = impartation of attributes of both natures to the one person ; (2) *genus apotelesmaticum* (from ἀποτέλεσμα, 'that which is finished or completed,' *i. e.*, Jesus' work) = attributes of the one person imparted to each of the constituent natures. Hence Mary may be called " the mother of God," as the Chalcedon symbol declares, " as to his humanity," and what each nature did has the value of both ; (3) *genus majestaticum* = attributes of one nature imparted to the other, yet so that the divine nature imparts to the human, not the human to the divine. The Lutherans do not believe in a *genus tapeinoticon, i. e.*, that the human elements communicated themselves to the divine. The only communication of the human was to the person, not to the divine nature, of the God-man. Examples of this third *genus majestaticum* are found in John 3 : 13 — "no one hath ascended into heaven, but he that descended out of heaven, even the Son of man who is in heaven" [here, however, Westcott and Hort, with ℵ and B, omit ὁ ὢν ἐν τῷ οὐρανῷ]; 5 : 27 — "he gave him authority to execute judgment, because he is a son of man." Of the explanation that this is the figure of speech called " *allœosis*," Luther says : " *Allœosis* est larva quædam diaboli, secundum cujus rationes ego certe nolim esse Christianus."

The *genus majestaticum* is denied by the Reformed Church, on the ground that it does not permit a clear distinction of the natures. And this is one great difference between it and the Lutheran Church. So Hooker, in commenting upon the Son of man's "ascending up where he was before," says : " By the 'Son of man' must be meant the whole person of Christ, who, being man upon earth, filled heaven with his glorious presence ; but not according to that nature for which the title of man is given him." For the Lutheran view of this union and its results in the communion of natures, see Hase, Hutterus Redivivus, 11th ed., 195–197; Thomasius, Christi Person und Werk, 2 : 24, 25. For the Reformed view, see Turretin, loc. 13, quæst. 8; Hodge, Syst. Theol., 2 : 387-3 7, 407-418.

2. *Modern misrepresentations of this Union.*

A. Theory of an incomplete humanity.— Gess and Beecher hold that the immaterial part in Christ's humanity is only contracted and metamorphosed deity.

The advocates of this view maintain that the divine Logos reduced himself to the condition and limits of human nature, and thus literally became a human soul. The theory differs from Apollinarianism, in that it does not necessarily presuppose a trichotomous view of man's nature. While Apollinarianism, however, denied the human origin only of Christ's πνεῦμα, this theory extends the denial to his entire immaterial being,—his body alone being derived from the Virgin. It is held, in slightly varying forms, by the Germans, Hofmann and Ebrard, as well as by Gess ; and Henry Ward Beecher was its chief representative in America.

Gess holds that Christ gave up his eternal holiness and divine self-consciousness, to become man, so that he never during his earthly life thought, spoke, or wrought as God, but was at all times destitute of divine attributes. See Gess, Scripture Doctrine of the Person of Christ ; and synopsis of his view, by Reubelt, in Bib. Sac., 1870 : 1-32; Hofmann, Schriftbeweis, 1 : 234-241, and 2 : 20 ; Ebrard, Dogmatik, 2 : 144-151, and in Herzog, Encyclopädie, art. : Jesus Christ, der Gottmensch ; also Liebner, Christliche Dogmatik. Henry Ward Beecher, in his Life of Jesus the Christ, chap. 3, emphasizes the word "flesh," in John 1:14, and declares the passage to mean that the divine Spirit enveloped himself in a human body, and in that condition was subject to the indispensable limitations of material laws. All these advocates of the view hold that Deity was dormant, or paralyzed, in Christ during his earthly life. Its essence is there, but not its efficiency at any time.

Against this theory we urge the following objections :

(a) It rests upon a false interpretation of the passage John 1 : 14 — ὁ λόγος σὰρξ ἐγένετο. The word σάρξ here has its common New Testament meaning. It designates neither soul nor body alone, but human nature in its totality (cf. John 3 : 6 — τὸ γεγεννημένον ἐκ τῆς σαρκὸς σάρξ ἐστιν ; Rom. 7 : 18 — οὐκ οἰκεῖ ἐν ἐμοί, τοῦτ' ἐστιν ἐν τῇ σαρκί μου, ἀγαθόν). That ἐγένετο does not imply a transmutation of the λόγος into human nature, or into a human soul, is evident from ἐσκήνωσεν which follows — an allusion to the Shechinah of the Mosaic tabernacle ; and from the parallel passage 1 John 4 : 2 — ἐν σαρκὶ ἐληλυθότα — where we are taught not only the oneness of Christ's person, but the distinctness of the constituent natures.

John 1 : 14 — "the Word became flesh, and dwelt [tabernacled] among us, and we beheld his glory"; 3 : 6 — "That which is born of the flesh is flesh " ; Rom. 7 : 18 — "in me, that is, in my flesh, dwelleth no good thing "; 1 John 4 : 2 — "Jesus Christ is come in the flesh." Since "flesh," in Scriptural usage, denotes human nature in its entirety, there is as little reason to infer from these passages a change of the Logos into a human body, as a change of the Logos into a human soul. There is no curtailed humanity in Christ. One advantage of the monistic doctrine is that it avoids this error. Omnipresence is the presence of the whole of God in every place. Ps. 85:9 — "Surely his salvation is nigh them that fear him, That glory may dwell in our land " — was fulfilled when Christ, the true Shekinah, tabernacled in human flesh and men "beheld his glory, glory as of the only begotten from the Father, full of grace and truth " (John 1 : 14). And Paul can say in 2 Cor. 12 : 9 — " Most gladly therefore will I rather glory in my weaknesses, that the power of Christ may spread a tabernacle over me."

(b) It contradicts the two great classes of Scripture passages already referred to, which assert on the one hand the divine knowledge and power of Christ and his consciousness of oneness with the Father, and on the other hand the completeness of his human nature and its derivation from the stock of Israel and the seed of Abraham (Mat. 1 : 1–16 ; Heb. 2 : 16). Thus it denies both the true humanity, and the true deity, of Christ.

See the Scripture passages cited in proof of the Deity of Christ, pages 305-315. Gess himself acknowledges that, if the passages in which Jesus avers his divine knowledge and power and his consciousness of oneness with the Father refer to his earthly life, his theory is overthrown. "Apollinarianism had a certain sort of grotesque grandeur, in giving to the human body and soul of Christ an infinite, divine πνεῦμα. It maintained at least the divine side of Christ's person. But the theory before us denies both sides." While it so curtails deity that it is no proper deity, it takes away from humanity all that is valuable in humanity ; for a manhood that consists only in body is no proper manhood. Such manhood is like the "half length " portrait which depicted only the lower half of the man. Mat. 1 : 1-16, the genealogy of Jesus, and Heb. 2 : 16 — "taketh hold of the seed of Abraham " — intimate that Christ took all that belonged to human nature.

(c) It is inconsistent with the Scriptural representations of God's immutability, in maintaining that the Logos gives up the attributes of Godhead, and his place and office as second person of the Trinity, in order to contract himself into the limits of humanity. Since attributes and substance are correlative terms, it is impossible to hold that the substance of God is in Christ, so long as he does not possess divine attributes. As we shall see hereafter, however, the possession of divine attributes by Christ does not necessarily imply his constant exercise of them. His humiliation indeed consisted in his giving up their independent exercise.

See Dorner, Unveränderlichkeit Gottes, in Jahrbuch für deutsche Theologie, 1 : 361;
2 : 440; 3 : 579; esp. 1 : 390-412 — " Gess holds that, during the thirty-three years of Jesus'
earthly life, the Trinity was altered ; the Father no more poured his fulness into the
Son ; the Son no more, with the Father, sent forth the Holy Spirit; the world was
upheld and governed by Father and Spirit alone, without the mediation of the Son;
the Father ceased to beget the Son. He says the Father alone has aseity ; he is the only
Monas. The Trinity is a family, whose head is the Father, but whose number and condition is variable. To Gess, it is indifferent whether the Trinity consists of Father, Son,
and Holy Spirit, or (as during Jesus' life) of only one. But this is a Trinity in which
two members are accidental. A Trinity that can get along without one of its members
is not the Scriptural Trinity. The Father depends on the Son, and the Spirit depends
on the Son, as much as the Son depends on the Father. To take away the Son is to take
away the Father and the Spirit. This giving up of the actuality of his attributes, even
of his holiness, on the part of the Logos. is in order to make it possible for Christ to
sin. But can we ascribe the possibility of sin to a being who is really God? The reality
of temptation requires us to postulate a veritable human soul."

(d) It is destructive of the whole Scriptural scheme of salvation, in that
it renders impossible any experience of human nature on the part of the
divine,— for when God becomes man he ceases to be God ; in that it renders
impossible any sufficient atonement on the part of human nature,— for
mere humanity, even though its essence be a contracted and dormant deity,
is not capable of a suffering which shall have infinite value ; in that it
renders impossible any proper union of the human race with God in the
person of Jesus Christ,— for where true deity and true humanity are both
absent, there can be no union between the two.

See Dorner, Jahrbuch f. d. Theologie, 1 : 390 — " Upon this theory only an exhibitory
atonement can be maintained. There is no real humanity that, in the strength of divinity, can bring a sacrifice to God. Not substitution, therefore, but obedience, on this
view, reconciles us to God. Even if it is said that God's Spirit is the real soul in all men,
this will not help the matter ; for we should then have to make an essential distinction
between the indwelling of the Spirit in the unregenerate, the regenerate, and Christ,
respectively. But in that case we lose the likeness between Christ's nature and our
own,— Christ's being preëxistent, and ours not. Without this pantheistic doctrine,
Christ's unlikeness to us is yet greater ; for he is really a wandering God, clothed in a
human body, and cannot properly be called a human soul. We have then no middle-
point between the body and the Godhead ; and in the state of exaltation, we have no
manhood at all,— only the infinite Logos, in a glorified body as his garment."

Isaac Watts's theory of a preëxistent humanity in like manner implies that humanity
is originally in deity; it does not proceed from a human stock, but from a divine;
between the human and the divine there is no proper distinction; hence there can be
no proper redeeming of humanity; see Bib. Sac., 1875 : 421. A. A. Hodge, Pop. Lectures,
226 — " If Christ does not take a human πνεῦμα, he cannot be a high-priest who feels with
us in all our infirmities, having been tempted like us." Mason, Faith of the Gospel,
138 — " The conversion of the Godhead into flesh would have only added one more man
to the number of men — a sinless one, perhaps, among sinners — but it would have
effected no union of God and men." On the theory in general, see Hovey, God with
Us, 62–69 ; Hodge, Syst. Theol., 2 : 430–440 ; Philippi, Glaubenslehre, 4 : 386–408 ; Biedermann, Christliche Dogmatik, 356–359 ; Bruce, Humiliation of Christ, 187, 230 ; Schaff,
Christ and Christianity, 115–119.

B.   Theory of a gradual incarnation.— Dorner and Rothe hold that the
union between the divine and the human natures is not completed by the
incarnating act.

The advocates of this view maintain that the union between the two
natures is accomplished by a gradual communication of the fulness of the
divine Logos to the man Christ Jesus. This communication is mediated
by the human consciousness of Jesus. Before the human consciousness
begins, the personality of the Logos is not yet divine-human.   The per-

sonal union completes itself only gradually, as the human consciousness is sufficiently developed to appropriate the divine.

Dorner, Glaubenslehre, 2 : 660 (Syst. Doct., 4 : 125) — "In order that Christ might show his high-priestly love by suffering and death, the different sides of his personality yet stood to one another in relative separableness. The divine-human union in him, accordingly, was before his death not yet completely actualized, although its completion was from the beginning divinely assured." 2 : 431 (Syst. Doct., 3 : 328) — "In spite of this *becoming*, inside of the *Unio*, the Logos is from the beginning united with Jesus in the deepest foundation of his being, and Jesus' life has ever been a divine-human one, in that a present receptivity for the Godhead has never remained without its satisfaction. . . . . . Even the unconscious humanity of the babe turns receptively to the Logos, as the plant turns toward the light. The initial union makes Christ already the God-man, but not in such a way as to prevent a subsequent *becoming*; for surely he did become omniscient and incapable of death, as he was not at the beginning."

2 : 464 *sq.* (Syst. Doct., 3 : 363 *sq.*) — "The actual life of God, as the Logos, reaches beyond the beginnings of the divine-human life. For if the *Unio* is to complete itself by growth, the relation of impartation and reception must continue. In his personal consciousness, there was a distinction between duty and being. The will had to take up practically, and turn into action, each new revelation or perception of God's will on the part of intellect or conscience. He had to maintain, with his will, each revelation of his nature and work. In his twelfth year, he says: 'I must be about my Father's business.' To Satan's temptation: 'Art thou God's Son?' he must reply with an affirmation that suppresses all doubt, though he will not prove it by miracle. This moral growth, as it was the will of the Father, was his task. He hears from his Father, and obeys. In him, imperfect knowledge was never the same with false conception. In us, ignorance has error for its obverse side. But this was never the case with him, though he grew in knowledge unto the end." Dorner's view of the Person of Christ may be found in his Hist. Doct. Person Christ, 5 : 248-261; Glaubenslehre, 2 : 347-474 (Syst. Doct., 3 : 243-373).

A summary of his views is also given in Princeton Rev., 1873 : 71-87 — Dorner illustrates the relation between the humanity and the deity of Christ by the relation between God and man, in conscience, and in the witness of the Spirit. "So far as the human element was immature or incomplete, so far the Logos was not present. Knowledge advanced to unity with the Logos, and the human will afterwards confirmed the best and highest knowledge. A resignation of both the Logos and the human nature to the union is involved in the incarnation. The growth continues until the idea, and the reality, of divine humanity perfectly coincide. The assumption of unity was gradual, in the life of Christ. His exaltation began with the perfection of this development." Rothe's statement of the theory can be found in his Dogmatik, 2 : 49-182; and in Bib. Sac., 27 : 386.

It is objectionable for the following reasons :

(*a*) The Scripture plainly teaches that that which was born of Mary was as completely Son of God as Son of man (Luke 1 : 35); and that in the incarnating act, and not at his resurrection, Jesus Christ became the God-man (Phil. 2 : 7). But this theory virtually teaches the birth of a man who subsequently and gradually became the God-man, by consciously appropriating the Logos to whom he sustained ethical relations — relations with regard to which the Scripture is entirely silent. Its radical error is that of mistaking an incomplete consciousness of the union for an incomplete union.

In Luke 1 : 35 —"the holy thing which is begotten shall be called the Son of God "—and Phil. 2 : 7 —"emptied himself, taking the form of a servant, being made in the likeness of men "—we have evidence that Christ was both Son of God and Son of man from the very beginning of his earthly life. But, according to Dorner, before there was any human consciousness, the personality of Jesus Christ was not divine-human.

(*b*) Since consciousness and will belong to personality, as distinguished from nature, the hypothesis of a mutual, conscious, and voluntary appro-

44

priation of divinity by humanity and of humanity by divinity, during the earthly life of Christ, is but a more subtle form of the Nestorian doctrine of a double personality. It follows, moreover, that as these two personalities do not become absolutely one until the resurrection, the death of the man Jesus Christ, to whom the Logos has not yet fully united himself, cannot possess an infinite atoning efficacy.

Thomasius, Christi Person und Werk, 2:68-70, objects to Dorner's view, that it "leads us to a man who is in intimate communion with God,—a man of God, but not a man who *is* God." He maintains, against Dorner, that "the union between the divine and human in Christ exists before the consciousness of it." 193-195—Dorner's view "makes each element, the divine and the human, long for the other, and reach its truth and reality only in the other. This, so far as the divine is concerned, is very like pantheism. Two *willing* personalities are presupposed, with ethical relation to each other,—two persons, at least at the first. Says Dorner: 'So long as the manhood is yet unconscious, the person of the Logos is not yet the central *ego* of this man. At the beginning, the Logos does not impart himself, so far as he is person or self-consciousness. He keeps apart by himself, just in proportion as the manhood fails in power of perception.' At the beginning, then, this man is not yet the God-man; the Logos only works in him, and on him. 'The *unio personalis* grows and completes itself, — becomes ever more all-sided and complete. Till the resurrection, there is a relative separability still.' Thus Dorner. But the Scripture knows nothing of an ethical relation of the divine to the human in Christ's person. It knows only of one divine-human subject." See also Thomasius, 2:80-92.

(c) While this theory asserts a final complete union of God and man in Jesus Christ, it renders this union far more difficult to reason, by involving the merging of two persons in one, rather than the union of two natures in one person. We have seen, moreover, that the Scripture gives no countenance to the doctrine of a double personality during the earthly life of Christ. The God-man never says : "I and the Logos are one "; "he that hath seen me hath seen the Logos"; "the Logos is greater than I "; "I go to the Logos." In the absence of all Scripture evidence in favor of this theory, we must regard the rational and dogmatic arguments against it as conclusive.

Liebner, in Jahrbuch f. d. Theologie, 3:349-366, urges, against Dorner, that there is no sign in Scripture of such communion between the two natures of Christ as exists between the three persons of the Trinity. Philippi also objects to Dorner's view: (1) that it implies a pantheistic identity of essence in both God and man; (2) that it makes the resurrection, not the birth, the time when the Word became flesh; (3) that it does not explain how two personalities can become one; see Philippi, Glaubenslehre, 4:364-380. Philippi quotes Dorner as saying: "The unity of essence of God and man is the great discovery of this age." But that Dorner was no pantheist appears from the following quotations from his Hist. Doctrine of the Person of Christ, II, 3:5, 23, 69, 115— " Protestant philosophy has brought about the recognition of the essential connection and unity of the human and the divine. . . . . To the theology of the present day, the divine and human are not mutually exclusive but connected magnitudes, having an inward relation to each other and reciprocally confirming each other, by which view both separation and identification are set aside. . . . . And now the common task of carrying on the union of faculties and qualities to a union of essence was devolved on both. The difference between them is that only God has aseity. . . . . Were we to set our face against every view which represents the divine and human as intimately and essentially related, we should be wilfully throwing away the gains of centuries, and returning to a soil where a Christology is an absolute impossibility."

See also Dorner, System, 1:123—"Faith postulates a difference between the world and God, between whom religion seeks a union. Faith does not wish to be a mere relation to itself or to its own representations and thoughts. That would be a monologue; faith desires a dialogue. Therefore it does not consent with a monism which recognizes only God or the world (with the ego). The duality (not the dualism, which is opposed to such monism, but which has no desire to oppose the rational demand for unity) is in fact a condition of true and vital unity." The *unity* is the foundation of religion; the *difference* is the foundation of morality. Morality and religion are but different manifestations of the same principle. Man's moral endeavor is the working of God within him. God can be revealed only in the perfect character and life of Jesus Christ. See Jones, Robert Browning, 146.

Stalker, Imago Christi: "Christ was not half a God and half a man, but he was perfectly God and perfectly man." Moberly, Atonement and Personality, 95 — "The Incarnate did not oscillate between being God and being man. He was indeed *always* God, and yet never otherwise God than as expressed within the possibilities of human consciousness and character." He knew that he was something more than he was as incarnate. His miracles showed what humanity might become. John Caird, Fund. Ideas of Christianity, 14 — "The divinity of Christ was not that of a divine nature in local or mechanical juxtaposition with a human, but of a divine nature that suffused, blended, identified itself with the thoughts, feelings, volitions of a human individuality. Whatever of divinity could not organically unite itself with and breathe through a human spirit, was not and could not be present in one who, whatever else he was, was really and truly human." See also Biedermann, Dogmatik, 351-353; Hodge, Syst. Theol., 2 : 428-430.

3. *The real nature of this Union.*

(*a*) Its great importance. — While the Scriptures represent the person of Christ as the crowning mystery of the Christian scheme (Matt. 11 : 27 ; Col. 1 : 27 ; 2 : 2 ; 1 Tim. 3 : 16), they also incite us to its study (John 17 : 3 ; 20 : 27 ; Luke 24 : 39 ; Phil. 3 : 8, 10). This is the more needful, since Christ is not only the central point of Christianity, but is Christianity itself — the embodied reconciliation and union between man and God. The following remarks are offered, not as fully explaining, but only as in some respects relieving, the difficulties of the subject.

Matt. 11 : 27 — "no one knoweth the Son, save the Father; neither doth any know the Father, save the Son, and he to whomsoever the Son willeth to reveal him." Here it seems to be intimated that the mystery of the nature of the Son is even greater than that of the Father. Shedd, Hist. Doct., 1 : 408 — The Person of Christ is in some respects more baffling to reason than the Trinity. Yet there is a profane neglect, as well as a profane curiosity : Col. 1 : 27 — "the riches of the glory of this mystery . . . . which is Christ in you, the hope of glory"; 2 : 2, 3 — "the mystery of God, even Christ, in whom are all the treasures of wisdom and knowledge hidden"; 1 Tim. 3 : 16 — "great is the mystery of godliness; He who was manifested in the flesh " — here the Vulgate, the Latin Fathers, and Buttmann make μυστήριον the antecedent of ὅς, the relative taking the *natural* gender of its antecedent, and μυστήριον referring to Christ; Heb. 2 : 11 — "both he that sanctifieth and they that are sanctified are all of one [not father, but race, or substance]" (*cf.* Acts 17 : 26 — " he made of one every nation of men ") — an allusion to the solidarity of the race and Christ's participation in all that belongs to us.

John 17 : 3 — "this is life eternal, that they should know thee the only true God, and him who thou didst send, even Jesus Christ"; 20 : 27 — "Reach hither thy finger, and see my hands; and reach hither thy hand, and put it into my side : and be not faithless, but believing"; Luke 24 : 39 — "See my hands and my feet, that it is I myself: handle me, and see; for a spirit hath not flesh and bones, as ye behold me having"; Phil. 3 : 8, 10 — "I count all things to be loss for the excellency of the knowledge of Christ Jesus my Lord . . . . that I may know him"; 1 John 1 : 1 — "that which we have heard, that which we have seen with our eyes, that which we beheld, and our hands handled, concerning the Word of life."

Nash, Ethics and Revelation, 254, 255 — "Ranke said that Alexander was one of the few men in whom biography is identical with universal history. The words apply far better to Christ." Crane, Religion of To-morrow, 267 — "Religion being merely the personality of God, Christianity the personality of Christ." Pascal : "Jesus Christ is the centre of everything, and the object of everything, and he who does not know him knows nothing of the order of nature and nothing of himself." Goethe in his last years wrote : "Humanity cannot take a retrograde step, and we may say that the Christian religion, now that it has once appeared, can never again disappear; now that it has once found a divine embodiment, cannot again be dissolved." H. B. Smith, that man of clear and devout thought, put his whole doctrine into one sentence : "Let us come to Jesus, — the person of Christ is the centre of theology." Dean Stanley never tired of quoting as his own Confession of Faith the words of John Bunyan: "Blest Cross - blest Sepulchre — blest rather he — The man who there was put to shame _or me!" And Charles Wesley wrote on Catholic Love: "Weary of all this wordy strife, These motions, forms, and modes and names, To thee, the Way, the Truth, the Life, Whose love my simple heart inflames — Divinely taught, at last I fly, With thee and thine to live and die."

"We have two great lakes, named Erie and Ontario, and these are connected by the Niagara River through which Erie pours its waters into Ontario. The whole Christian Church throughout the ages has been called the overflow of Jesus Christ, who is infinitely greater than it. Let Lake Erie be the symbol of Christ, the pre-existent Logos, the Eternal Word, God revealed in the universe. Let Niagara River be a picture to us of this same Christ now confined to the narrow channel of His manifestation in the flesh, but within those limits showing the same eastward current and downward gravitation which men perceived so imperfectly before. The tremendous cataract, with its waters plunging into the abyss and shaking the very earth, is the suffering and death of the Son of God, which for the first time makes palpable to human hearts the forces of righteousness and love operative in the Divine nature from the beginning. The law of universal life has been made manifest; now it is seen that justice and judgment are the foundations of God's throne; that God's righteousness everywhere and always makes penalty to follow sin; that the love which creates and upholds sinners must itself be numbered with the transgressors, and must bear their iniquities. Niagara has demonstrated the gravitation of Lake Erie. And not in vain. For from Niagara there widens out another peaceful lake. Ontario is the offspring and likeness of Erie. So redeemed humanity is the overflow of Jesus Christ, but only of Jesus Christ after He has passed through the measureless self-abandonment of His earthly life and of His tragic death on Calvary. As the waters of Lake Ontario are ever fed by Niagara, so the Church draws its life from the cross. And Christ's purpose is, not that we should repeat Calvary, for that we can never do, but that we should reflect in ourselves the same onward movement and gravitation towards self-sacrifice which He has revealed as characterizing the very life of God" (A. H. Strong, Sermon before the Baptist World Congress, London, July 12, 1905).

(*b*) The chief problems. — These problems are the following : 1. one personality and two natures ; 2. human nature without personality ; 3. relation of the Logos to the humanity during the earthly life of Christ ; 4. relation of the humanity to the Logos during the heavenly life of Christ. We may throw light on 1, by the figure of two concentric circles ; on 2, by remembering that two earthly parents unite in producing a single child ; on 3, by the illustration of latent memory, which contains so much more than present recollection ; on 4, by the thought that body is the manifestation of spirit, and that Christ in his heavenly state is not confined to place.

Luther said that we should need "new tongues" before we could properly set forth this doctrine, — particularly a new language with regard to the nature of man. The further elucidation of the problems mentioned above will immediately occupy our attention. Our investigation should not be prejudiced by the fact that the divine element in Jesus Christ manifests itself within human limitations. This is the condition of all revelation. John 14:9 — "he that hath seen me hath seen the Father"; Col. 2:9 — "in him dwelleth all the fulness of the Godhead bodily" — up to the measure of human capacity to receive and to express the divine. Heb. 2:11 and Acts 17:26 both attribute to man a consubstantiality with Christ, and Christ is the manifested God. It is a law of hydrostatics that the smallest column of water will balance the largest. Lake Erie will be no higher than the water in the tube connected therewith. So the person of Christ reached the level of God, though limited in extent and environment. He was God manifest in the flesh.

Robert Browning, Death in the Desert: "I say, the acknowledgment of God in Christ Accepted by thy reason, solves for thee All questions in the earth and out of it, And has so far advanced thee to be wise"; Epilogue to Dramatis Personæ: "That one Face, far from vanish, rather grows, Or decomposes but to recompose, Become my Universe that feels and knows." "That face," said Browning to Mrs. Orr, as he finished reading the poem, "is the face of Christ. That is how I feel him." This is his answer to those victims of nineteenth century scepticism for whom incarnate Love has disappeared from the universe, carrying with it the belief in God. He thus attests the continued presence of God in Christ, both in nature and humanity. On Browning as a Christian Poet, see A. H. Strong, The Great Poets and their Theology, 373-447; S. Law Wilson, Theology of Modern Literature, 181-236.

(c) Reason for mystery.—The union of the two natures in Christ's person is necessarily inscrutable, because there are no analogies to it in our experience. Attempts to illustrate it on the one hand from the union and yet the distinctness of soul and body, of iron and heat, and on the other hand from the union and yet the distinctness of Christ and the believer, of the divine Son and the Father, are one-sided and become utterly misleading, if they are regarded as furnishing a rationale of the union and not simply a means of repelling objection. The first two illustrations mentioned above lack the essential element of two natures to make them complete : soul and body are not two natures, but one, nor are iron and heat two substances. The last two illustrations mentioned above lack the element of single personality : Christ and the believer are two persons, not one, even as the Son and the Father are not one person, but two.

The two illustrations most commonly employed are the union of soul and body, and the union of the believer with Christ. Each of these illustrates one side of the great doctrine, but each must be complemented by the other. The former, taken by itself, would be Eutychian ; the latter, taken by itself, would be Nestorian. Like the doctrine of the Trinity, the Person of Christ is an absolutely unique fact, for which we can find no complete analogies. But neither do we know how soul and body are united. See Blunt, Dict. Doct. and Hist. Theol., art. : Hypostasis ; Sartorius, Person and Work of Christ, 27-65 ; Wilberforce, Incarnation, 39-77 ; Luthardt, Fund. Truths, 281-334.

A. A. Hodge, Popular Lectures, 218, 230 — " Many people are Unitarians, not because of the difficulties of the Trinity, but because of the difficulties of the Person of Christ. . . . The union of the two natures is not mechanical, as between oxygen and nitrogen in our air ; nor chemical, as between oxygen and hydrogen in water ; nor organic, as between our hearts and our brains ; but personal. The best illustration is the union of body and soul in our own persons,— how perfectly joined they are in the great orator ! Yet here are not two natures, but one human nature. We need therefore to add the illustration of the union between the believer and Christ." And here too we must confess the imperfection of the analogy, for Christ and the believer are two persons, and not one. The person of the God-man is unique and without adequate parallel. But this constitutes its dignity and glory.

(d) Ground of possibility.— The possibility of the union of deity and humanity in one person is grounded in the original creation of man in the divine image. Man's kinship to God, in other words, his possession of a rational and spiritual nature, is the condition of incarnation. Brute-life is incapable of union with God. But human nature is capable of the divine, in the sense not only that it lives, moves, and has its being in God, but that God may unite himself indissolubly to it and endue it with divine powers, while yet it remains all the more truly human. Since the moral image of God in human nature has been lost by sin, Christ, the perfect image of God after which man was originally made, restores that lost image by uniting himself to humanity and filling it with his divine life and love.

2 Pet. 1 : 4 — "partakers of the divine nature." Creation and providence do not furnish the last limit of God's indwelling. Beyond these, there is the spiritual union between the believer and Christ, and even beyond this, there is the unity of God and man in the person of Jesus Christ. Dorner, Glaubenslehre, 2 : 283 (Syst. Doct., 3 : 180) — " Humanity in Christ is related to divinity, as woman to man in marriage. It is receptive, but it is exalted by receiving. Christ is the offspring of the [marriage] covenant between God and Israel."

Ib., 2 : 403–411 (Syst. Doct., 3 : 301–308) — "The question is: How can Christ be both Creator and creature? The Logos, as such, stands over against the creature as a distinct object. How can he become, and be, that which exists only as object of his activity and inworking? Can the cause become its own effect? The problem is solved, only by remembering that the divine and human, though distinct from each other, are not to be thought of as foreign to each other and mutually exclusive. The very thing that distinguishes them binds them together. Their essential distinction is that God has aseity, while man has simply dependence. 'Deep calleth unto deep' (Ps. 42 : 7) — the deep of the divine riches, and the deep of human poverty, call to each other. 'From me a cry,— from him reply.' God's infinite resources and man's infinite need, God's measureless supply and man's boundless receptivity, attract each other, until they unite in him in whom dwells all the fulness of the Godhead bodily. The mutual attraction is of an ethical sort, but the divine love has 'first loved' (1 John 4 : 19).

"The new second creation is therefore not merely, like the first creation, one that distinguishes from God,— it is one that unites with God. Nature is distinct from God, yet God moves and works in nature. Much more does human nature find its only true reality, or realization, in union with God. God's uniting act does not violate or unmake it, but rather first causes it to be what, in God's idea, it was meant to be." Incarnation is therefore the very fulfilment of the idea of humanity. The supernatural assumption of humanity is the most natural of all things. Man is not a mere tangent to God, but an empty vessel to be filled from the infinite fountain. Natura humana in Christo capax divinæ. See Talbot, in Bap. Quar., 1868 : 129 ; Martensen, Christian Dogmatics, 270.

God could not have become an angel, or a tree, or a stone. But he could become man, because man was made in his image. God in man, as Phillips Brooks held, is the absolutely natural. Channing said that "all minds are of one family." E. B. Andrews: "Divinity and humanity are not contradictory predicates. If this had been properly understood, there would have been no Unitarian movement. Man is in a true sense divine. This is also true of Christ. But he is infinitely further along in the divine nature than we are. If we say his divinity is a new kind, then the new kind arises out of the degree." "Were not the eye itself a sun, No light for it could ever shine : By nothing godlike could the soul be won, Were not the soul itself divine."

John Caird, Fund. Ideas of Christianity, 1 : 165 — "A smaller circle may represent a larger in respect of its circularity ; but a circle, small or large, cannot be the image of a square." . . . . 2 : 101 — "God would not be God without union with man, and man would not be man without union with God. Immanent in the spirits he has made. he shares their pains and sorrows. . . . Showing the infinite element in man, Christ attracts us toward his own moral excellence." Lyman Abbott, Theology of an Evolutionist, 190 — "Incarnation is the indwelling of God in his children, of which the type and pattern is seen in him who is at once the manifestation of God to man, and the revelation to men of what humanity is to be when God's work in the world is done — perfect God and perfect man, because God perfectly dwelling in a perfect man."

We have quoted these latter utterances, not because we regard them as admitting the full truth with regard to the union of the divine and human in Christ ; but because they recognize the essential likeness of the human to the divine, and so help our understanding of the union between the two. We go further than the writers quoted, in maintaining not merely an indwelling of God in Christ, but an organic and essential union. Christ moreover is not the God-man by virtue of his possessing a larger measure of the divine than we, but rather by being the original source of all life, both human and divine. We hold to his deity as well as to his divinity, as some of these authors apparently do not. See Heb. 7 : 15, 16 — "another priest, who hath been made . . . . after the power of an endless life " ; John 1 : 4 — "In him was life ; and the life was the light of men."

(*e*) **No double personality.**— This possession of two natures does not involve a double personality in the God-man, for the reason that the Logos takes into union with himself, not an individual man with already developed personality, but human nature which has had no separate existence before its union with the divine. Christ's human nature is impersonal, in the sense that it attains self-consciousness and self-determination only in the personality of the God-man. Here it is important to mark the distinction between nature and person. Nature is substance possessed in common; the persons of the Trinity have one nature; there is a common nature of mankind. Person is nature separately subsisting, with powers of consciousness and will. Since the human nature of Christ has not and never had a separate subsistence, it is impersonal, and in the God-man the Logos furnishes the principle of personality. It is equally important to observe that self-consciousness and self-determination do not belong to nature as such, but only to personality. For this reason, Christ has not two consciousnesses and two wills, but a single consciousness and a single will. This consciousness and will, moreover, is never simply human, but is always theanthropic — an activity of the one personality which unites in itself the human and the divine (Mark 13 : 32 ; Luke 22 : 42).

The human father and the human mother are distinct persons, and they each give something of their own peculiar nature to their child; yet the result is, not two persons in the child, but only one person, with one consciousness and one will. So the Fatherhood of God and the motherhood of Mary produced not a double personality in Christ, but a single personality. Dorner illustrates the union of human and divine in Jesus by the *Holy Spirit* in the Christian, — nothing foreign, nothing distinguishable from the human life into which it enters; and by the *moral sense*, which is the very presence and power of God in the human soul,— yet conscience does not break up the unity of the life; see C. C. Everett, Essays, 32. These illustrations help us to understand the interpenetration of the human by the divine in Jesus; but they are defective in suggesting that his relation to God was different from ours not in kind but only in degree. Only Jesus could say : "Before Abraham was born, I am" (John 8 : 58); "I and the Father are one" (John 10 : 30).

The theory of two consciousnesses and two wills, first elaborated by John of Damascus, was an unwarranted addition to the orthodox doctrine propounded at Chalcedon. Although the view of John of Damascus was sanctioned by the Council of Constantinople (681), " this Council has never been regarded by the Greek Church as œcumenical, and its composition and spirit deprive its decisions of all value as indicating the true sense of Scripture "; see Bruce, Humiliation of Christ, 90. *Nature* has consciousness and will, only as it is manifested in *person*. The one person has a single consciousness and will, which embraces within its scope at all times a human nature, and sometimes a divine. Notice that we do not say Christ's human nature had no will, but only that it had none before its union with the divine nature, and none separately from the one will which was made up of the human and the divine united; *versus* Current Discussions in Theology, 5 : 283.

Sartorius uses the illustration of two concentric circles: the one ego of personality in Christ is at the same time the centre of both circles, the human nature and the divine. Or, still better, illustrate by a smaller vessel of air inverted and sunk, sometimes below its centre, sometimes above, in a far larger vessel of water. See Mark 13 : 32 — " of that day or that hour knoweth no one, not even the angels in heaven, neither the Son "; Luke 22 : 42 — "Father, if thou be willing, remove this cup from me : nevertheless not my will, but thine, be done." To say that, although in his capacity as man he was ignorant, yet at that same moment in his capacity as God he was omniscient, is to accuse Christ of unveracity. Whenever Christ spoke, it was not one of the natures that spoke, but the person in whom both natures were united.

We subjoin various definitions of personality : Boëthius, quoted in Dorner, Glaubenslehre, 2 : 415 (Syst. Doct., 3 : 313) — " Persona est animæ rationalis individua substantia "; F. W. Robertson, Lect. on Gen., p. 3 — " Personality = self-consciousness, will, character "; Porter, Human Intellect, 626 — " Personality = distinct subsistence, either actually or latently self-conscious and self-determining"; Harris, Philos. Basis of Theism, 408 — " Person = being, conscious of self, subsisting in individuality and identity, and endowed with intuitive reason, rational sensibility, and free-will." Dr. E. G. Robinson defines "nature" as "that substratum or condition of being which determines the kind and attributes of the person, but which is clearly distinguishable from the person itself."

Lotze, Metaphysics, §244 — " The identity of the subject of inward experience is all that we require. So far as, and so long as, the soul knows itself as this identical subject, it is and is named, simply for that reason, substance." Illingworth, **Personality, Human** and Divine, 32 — "Our conception of substance is not derived from the physical, but from the mental, world. Substance is first of all that which underlies our mental affections and manifestations. Kant declared that the idea of freedom is the source of our idea of personality. Personality consists in the freedom of the whole soul from the mechanism of nature." On personality, see Windelband, Hist. Philos., 238. For the theory of two consciousnesses and two wills, see Philippi, Glaubenslehre, 4 : 129, 234; Kahnis, Dogmatik, 2 : 314; Ridgeley, Body of Divinity, 1 : 476; Hodge, Syst. Theol., 2 : 378–391; Shedd, Dogm. Theol., 2 : 289–308, esp. 328. *Per contra*, see Hovey, God with Us, 66; Schaff, Church Hist., 1 : 757, and 3 : 751; Calderwood, Moral Philosophy, 12–14; Wilberforce, Incarnation, 148–169; Van Oosterzee, Dogmatics, 512–518.

(*f*) Effect upon the human.—The union of the divine and the human natures makes the latter possessed of the powers belonging to the former; in other words, the attributes of the divine nature are imparted to the human without passing over into its essence,— so that the human Christ even on earth had power to be, to know, and to do, as God. That this power was latent, or was only rarely manifested, was the result of the self-chosen state of humiliation upon which the God-man had entered. In this state of humiliation, the communication of the contents of his divine nature to the human was mediated by the Holy Spirit. The God-man, in his servant-form, knew and taught and performed only what the Spirit permitted and directed (Mat. 3 : 16; John 3 : 34; Acts 1 : 2; 10 : 38; Heb. 9 : 14). But when thus permitted, he knew, taught, and performed, not, like the prophets, by power communicated from without, but by virtue of his own inner divine energy (Mat. 17 : 2; Mark 5 : 41; Luke 5 : 20, 21; 6 : 19; John 2 : 11, 24, 25; 3 : 13; 20 : 19).

Kahnis, Dogmatik, 2d ed., 2 : 77 — "Human nature does not become divine, but (as Chemnitz has said) only the medium of the divine; as the moon has not a light of her own, but only shines in the light of the sun. So human nature may derivatively exercise divine attributes, because it is united to the divine in one person." Mason, Faith of the Gospel, 151 — "Our souls spiritualize our bodies, and will one day give us the spiritual body, while yet the body does not become spirit. So the Godhead gives divine powers to the humanity in Christ, while yet the humanity does not cease to be humanity."

Philippi, Glaubenslehre, 4 : 131 — "The union exalts the human, as light brightens the air, heat gives glow to the iron, spirit exalts the body, the Holy Spirit hallows the believer by union with his soul. Fire gives to iron its own properties of lighting and burning; yet the iron does not become fire. Soul gives to body its life-energy; yet the body does not become soul. The Holy Spirit sanctifies the believer, but the believer does not become divine; for the divine principle is the determining one. We do not speak of airy light, of iron heat, or of a bodily soul. So human nature possesses the divine only derivatively. In this sense it is *our* destiny to become 'partakers of the divine nature' (2 Pet. 1 : 4)." Even in his earthly life, when he wished to be, or more correctly, when the Spirit permitted, he was omnipotent, omniscient, omnipresent, could walk the sea, or pass through closed doors. But, in his state of humiliation, he was subject to the Holy Spirit.

In Mat. 3 : 16, the anointing of the Spirit at his baptism was not the descent of a material dove ("as a dove"). The dove-like appearance was only the outward sign of the coming forth of the Holy Spirit from the depths of his being and pouring itself like a flood into his divine-human consciousness. John 3 : 34 — "for he giveth not the Spirit by measure"; Acts 1 : 2 — "after that he had given commandment through the Holy Spirit unto the apostles"; 10 : 38 — "Jesus of Nazareth, how God anointed him with the Holy Spirit and with power: who went about doing good, and healing all that were oppressed of the devil; for God was with him"; Heb. 9 : 14 — "the blood of Christ, who through the eternal Spirit offered himself without blemish unto God."

When permitted by the Holy Spirit, he knew, taught, and wrought as God: Mat. 17 : 2 — "he was transfigured before them"; Mark 5 : 41 — "Damsel, I say unto thee, Arise"; Luke 5 : 20, 21 — "Man, thy sins are forgiven thee . . . . Who can forgive sins, but God alone?" — Luke 6 : 19 — "power came forth from him, and healed them all"; John 2 : 11 — "This beginning of his signs did Jesus in Cana of Galilee, and manifested his glory"; 24, 25 — "he knew all men . . . . he himself knew what was in man"; 3 : 13 — "the Son of man, who is in heaven" [here, however, Westcott and Hort, with א and B, omit ὁ ὢν ἐν τῷ οὐρανῷ, — for advocacy of the common reading, see Broadus, in Hovey's Com., on John 3 : 13]; 20 : 19 — "when the doors were shut . . . . Jesus came and stood in the midst."

Christ is the "servant of Jehovah" (Is. 42 : 1-7; 49 : 1-12; 52 : 13; 53 : 11) and the meaning of παῖς (Acts 3 : 13, 26; 4 : 27, 30) is not "child" or "Son"; it is "servant," as in the Revised Version. But, in the state of exaltation, Christ is the "Lord of the Spirit" (2 Cor. 3 : 18 — Meyer), giving the Spirit (John 16 : 7 — "I will send him unto you"), present in the Spirit (John 14 : 18 — "I come unto you"; Mat. 28 : 20 — "I am with you always, even unto the the end of the world"), and working through the Spirit (1 Cor. 15 : 45 — "The last Adam became a life-giving spirit"); 2 Cor. 3 : 17 — "Now the Lord is the Spirit"). On Christ's relation to the Holy Spirit, see John Owen, Works, 282-297; Robins, in Bib. Sac., Oct. 1874 : 615; Wilberforce, Incarnation, 208-241.

Delitzsch : " The conception of the servant of Jehovah is, as it were, a pyramid, of which the base is the people of Israel as a whole; the central part, Israel according to the Spirit ; and the summit, the Mediator of Salvation who rises out of Israel." Cheyne on Isaiah, 2 : 253, agrees with this view of Delitzsch, which is also the view of Oehler. The O. T. is the life of a nation; the N. T. is the life of a man. The chief end of the nation was to produce the man; the chief end of the man was to save the world. Sabatier, Philos. Religion, 59 — "If humanity were not potentially and in some degree an Immanuel, God with us, there would never have issued from its bosom he who bore and revealed this blessed name." We would enlarge and amend this illustration of the pyramid, by making the base to be the Logos, as Creator and Upholder of all (Eph. 1 : 23; Col. 1 : 16); the stratum which rests next upon the Logos is universal humanity (Ps. 8 : 5, 6); then comes Israel as a whole (Mat. 2 : 15); spiritual Israel rests upon Israel after the flesh (Is. 42 : 1-7); as the acme and cap stone of all, Christ appears, to crown the pyramid, the true servant of Jehovah and Son of man (Is. 53 : 11; Mat. 20 : 28). We may go even further and represent Christ as forming the basis of another inverted pyramid of redeemed humanity ever growing and rising to heaven (Is. 9 : 6 — "Everlasting Father"; Is. 53 : 10 — "he shall see his seed"; Rev. 22 : 16 — "root and offspring of David"; Heb. 2 : 13 — "I and the children whom God hath given me."

(g) Effect upon the divine.—This communion of the natures was such that, although the divine nature in itself is incapable of ignorance, weakness, temptation, suffering, or death, the one person Jesus Christ was capable of these by virtue of the union of the divine nature with a human nature in him. As the human Savior can exercise divine attributes, not in virtue of his humanity alone, but derivatively, by virtue of his possession of a divine nature, so the divine Savior can suffer and be ignorant as man, not in his divine nature, but derivatively, by virtue of his possession of a human nature. We may illustrate this from the connection between body and soul. The soul suffers pain from its union with the body, of which apart from the body it would be incapable. So the God-man, although in his divine nature impassible, was capable, through his union with humanity, of absolutely infinite suffering.

Just as my soul could never suffer the pains of fire if it were only soul, but can suffer those pains in union with the body, so the otherwise impassible God can suffer mortal pangs through his union with humanity, which he never could suffer if he had not joined himself to my nature. The union between the humanity and the deity is so close, that deity itself is brought under the curse and penalty of the law. Because Christ was God, did he pass unscorched through the fires of Gethsemane and Calvary? Rather let us say, because Christ was God, he underwent a suffering that was absolutely infinite. Philippi, Glaubenslehre, 4 : 300 sq.; Lawrence, in Bib. Sac., 24 : 41; Schöberlein, in Jahrbuch für deutsche Theologie, 1871 : 459-501.

A. J. F. Behrends, in The Examiner, April 21, 1898 — " Jesus Christ is God in the form of man; as completely God as if he were not man; as completely man as if he were not God. He is always divine and always human. . . . . The infirmities and pains of his body pierced his divine nature. . . . . The demand of the law was not laid upon Christ from without, but proceeded from within. It is the righteousness in him which makes his death necessary."

(*h*) Necessity of the union.—The union of two natures in one person is necessary to constitute Jesus Christ a proper mediator between man and God. His two-fold nature gives him fellowship with both parties, since it involves an equal dignity with God, and at the same time a perfect sympathy with man (Heb. 2 : 17, 18 ; 4 : 15, 16). This two-fold nature, moreover, enables him to present to both God and man proper terms of reconciliation : being man, he can make atonement for man ; being God, his atonement has infinite value ; while both his divinity and his humanity combine to move the hearts of offenders and constrain them to submission and love (1 Tim. 2 : 5 ; Heb. 7 : 25).

Heb. 2 : 17, 18 — "Wherefore it behooved him in all things to be made like unto his brethren, that he might become a merciful and faithful high priest in things pertaining to God, to make propitiation for the sins of the people. For in that he himself hath suffered being tempted, he is able to succor them that are tempted " ; 4 : 15, 16 — "For we have not a high priest that cannot be touched with the feeling of our infirmities ; but one that hath been in all points tempted like as we are, yet without sin. Let us therefore draw near with boldness unto the throne of grace, that we may receive mercy, and may find grace to help us in time of need " ; 1 Tim. 2 : 5 — "one God, one mediator also between God and men, himself man, Christ Jesus " ; Heb. 7 : 25 — "Wherefore also he is able to save to the uttermost them that draw near unto God through him, seeing he ever liveth to make intercession for them."

Because Christ is man, he can make atonement for man and can sympathize with man. Because Christ is God, his atonement has infinite value, and the union which he effects with God is complete. A merely human Savior could never reconcile or reunite us to God. But a divine-human Savior meets all our needs. See Wilberforce, Incarnation, 170–208. As the high priest of old bore on his mitre the name Jehovah, and on his breastplate the names of the tribes of Israel, so Christ Jesus is God with us, and at the same time our propitiatory representative before God. In Virgil's Æneid, Dido says well : "Haud ignara mali, miseris succurrere disco " — "Myself not ignorant of woe, Compassion I have learned to show." And Terence uttered almost a Christian word when he wrote : "Homo sum, et humani nihil a me alienum puto "—"I am a man, and I count nothing human as foreign to me." Christ's experience and divinity made these words far more true of him than of any merely human being.

(*i*) The union eternal.—The union of humanity with deity in the person of Christ is indissoluble and eternal. Unlike the avatars of the East, the incarnation was a permanent assumption of human nature by the second person of the Trinity. In the ascension of Christ, glorified humanity has attained the throne of the universe. By his Spirit, this same divine-human Savior is omnipresent to secure the progress of his kingdom. The final subjection of the Son to the Father, alluded to in 1 Cor. 15 : 28, cannot be other than the complete return of the Son to his original relation to the Father ; since, according to John 17 : 5, Christ is again to possess the glory which he had with the Father before the world was (*cf.* Heb. 1 : 8 ; 7 : 24, 25).

1 Cor. 15 : 28 — "And when all things have been subjected unto him, then shall the Son also himself be subjected to him that did subject all things unto him, that God may be all in all " ; John 17 : 5 — "Father, glorify thou me with thine own self with the glory which I had with thee before the world was " ; Heb. 1 : 8 — "of the Son he saith, Thy throne, O God, is for ever and ever " ; 7 : 24 — "he, because he abideth forever, hath his priesthood unchangeable." Dorner, Glaubenslehre, 2 : 281–283 (Syst. Doct. 3 : 177–179), holds that there is a present and relative distinction between the Son's will, as Mediator, and that of the Father (Mat. 26 : 39 — " not as I will, but as thou wilt ")—a distinction which shall cease when Christ becomes Judge (John 16 : 26 — " In that day ye shall ask in my name : and I say not unto you, that I will pray the Father for you ") If Christ's *reign* ceased, he would be inferior to the saints, who are themselves to reign. But they are to reign only in and with Christ, their head.

The best illustration of the possible meaning of Christ's giving up the kingdom is found in the Governor of the East India Company giving up his authority to the Queen and merging it in that of the home government, he himself, however, at the same time becoming Secretary of State for India. So Christ will give up his vicegerency, but nor his mediatorship. Now he reigns by delegated authority; then he will reign in union with the Father. So Kendrick, in Bib. Sac., Jan. 1890 : 68–83. Wrightnour: "When the great remedy has wrought its perfect cure, the physician will no longer be looked upon as the physician. When the work of redemption is completed, the mediatorial office of the Son will cease." We may add that other offices of friendship and instruction will then begin.

Melanchthon: "Christ will finish his work as Mediator, and then will reign as God, immediately revealing to us the Deity." Quenstedt, quoted in Schmid, Dogmatik, 293, thinks the giving up of the kingdom will be only an exchange of outward administration for inward,—not a surrender of all power and authority, but only of one mode of exercising it. Hanna, on Resurrection, lect. 4—"It is not a giving up of his mediatorial authority,—that throne is to endure forever,—but it is a simple public recognition of the fact that God is all in all, that Christ is God's medium of accomplishing all." An. Par. Bible, on 1 Cor. 15 : 28—"Not his mediatorial relation to his own people shall be given up ; much less his personal relation to the Godhead, as the divine Word ; but only his mediatorial relation to the world at large." See also Edwards, Observations on the Trinity, 85 sq. Expositor's Greek Testament, on 1 Cor. 15 : 28, "affirms no other subjection than is involved in Sonship. . . . . This implies no inferiority of nature, no extrusion from power, but the free submission of love . . . . which is the essence of the filial spirit which actuated Christ from first to last. . . . . Whatsoever glory he gains is devoted to the glory and power of the Father, who glorifies him in turn."

Dorner, Glaubenslehre, 2 : 402 (Syst. Doct., 3 : 297–299)—"We are not to imagine incarnations of Christ in the angel-world, or in other spheres. This would make incarnation only the change of a garment, a passing theophany ; and Christ's relation to humanity would be a merely external one." Bishop of Salisbury, quoted in Swayne, Our Lord's Knowledge as Man, XX—"Are we permitted to believe that there is something parallel to the progress of our Lord's humanity in the state of humiliation, still going on even now, in the state of exaltation ? that it is, in fact, becoming more and more adequate to the divine nature ? See Col. 1 : 24—'fill up that which is lacking' ; Heb. 10 : 12, 13—'expecting till his enemies' ; 1 Cor. 15 : 28—'when all things have been subjected unto him.'" In our judgment such a conclusion is unwarranted, in view of the fact that the God-man in his exaltation has the glory of his preëxistent state (John 17 : 5) ; that all the heavenly powers are already subject to him (Eph. 1 : 21, 22) ; and that he is now omnipresent (Mat. 28 : 20).

(j) **Infinite and finite in Christ.**—Our investigation of the Scripture teaching with regard to the Person of Christ leads us to three important conclusions : 1. that deity and humanity, the infinite and the finite, in him are not mutually exclusive ; 2. that the humanity in Christ differs from his deity not merely in degree but also in kind ; and 3. that this difference in kind is the difference between the infinite original and the finite derivative, so that Christ is the source of life, both physical and spiritual, for all men.

Our doctrine excludes the view that Christ is only quantitatively different from other men in whom God's Spirit dwells. He is qualitatively different, in that he is the source of life, and they the recipients. Not only is it true that the fulness of the Godhead is in him alone,—it is also true that he is himself God, self-revealing and self-communicating, as men are not. Yet we cannot hold with E. H. Johnson, Outline of Syst. Theol., 176–178, that Christ's humanity was of one species with his deity, but not of one substance. We know of but one underlying substance and ground of being. This one substance is self-limiting, and so self-manifesting, in Jesus Christ. The determining element is not the human but the divine. The infinite Source has a finite manifestation ; but in the finite we see the Infinite ; 2 Cor. 5 : 19—"God was in Christ, reconciling the world unto himself" ; John 14 : 9—"he that hath seen me hath seen the Father." We can therefore agree with the following writers who regard all men as partakers of the life of God, while yet we deny that Christ is only a man, distinguished from his fellows by having a larger share in that life than they have.

J. M. Whiton: "How is the divine spirit which is manifest in the life of the man Christ Jesus to be distinguished, qua divine, from the same divine spirit as manifested in the life of humanity? I answer, that in him, the person Christ, dwelleth the fulness of the Godhead bodily. I emphasize fulness, and say : The God-head is alike in the race and in its spiritual head, but the fulness is in the head alone—a fulness of course not absolute, since circumscribed by a human organism, but a fulness to the limits of the organism. Essential deity cannot be ascribed to the human Christ, except as in common with the race created in the image of God. Life is one, and all life is divine." . . . . Gloria Patri, 88, 23 — " Every incarnation of life is *pro tanto* and in its measure an incarnation of God . . . . and God's way is a perpetually increasing incarnation of life whose climax and crown is the divine fulness of life in Christ. . . . . The *Homoousios* of the Nicene Creed was a great victory of the truth. But the Nicene Fathers builded better than they knew. The Unitarian Dr. Hedge praised them because they got at the truth, the logical conclusion of which was to come so long after, that God and man are of one substance." So Momerie, Inspiration, holds man's nature to be the same in kind with God's. See criticism of this view in Watts, New Apologetic, 133, 134. *Homoiousios* he regards as involving *homoousios ;* the divine nature capable of fission or segmentation, broken off in portions, and distributed among finite moral agents; the divine nature undergoing perpetual curtailment; every man therefore to some extent inspired, and evil as truly an inspiration of God as is good. Watts seems to us to lack the proper conception of the infinite as the ground of the finite, and so not excluding it.

Lyman Abbott affirms that Christ is, "not God *and* man, but God *in* man." Christ differs from other men only as the flower differs from the bulb. As the true man, he is genuinely divine. Deity and humanity are not two distinct natures, but one nature. The ethico-spiritual nature which is finite in man is identical with the nature which is infinite in God. Christ's distinction from other men is therefore in the degree in which he shared this nature and possessed a unique fulness of life — "anointed with the Holy Spirit and with power" (Acts 10 : 38). Phillips Brooks : " To this humanity of man as a part of God — to this I cling ; for I do love it, and I will know nothing else . . . . Man is, in virtue of his essential humanity, partaker of the life of the essential Word. . . . . Into every soul, just so far as it is possible for that soul to receive it, God beats his life and gives his help." Phillips Brooks believes in the redemptive indwelling of God in man, so that salvation is of man, for man, and by man. He does not scruple to say to every man : " You are a part of God."

While we shrink from the expressions which seem to imply a partition of the divine nature, we are compelled to recognize a truth which these writers are laboring to express, the truth namely of the essential oneness of all life, and of God in Christ as the source and giver of it. " Jesus quotes approvingly the words of Psalm 82 : 6 — 'I said, Ye are Gods.' Microscopic, indeed, but divine are we — sparks from the flame of deity. God is the Creator, but it is through Christ as the mediating and as the final Cause. 'And we through him' (1 Cor. 8 : 6) — we exist for him, for the realization of a divine humanity in solidarity with him. Christ is at once the end and the instrumental cause of the whole process." Samuel Harris, God the Creator and Lord of All, speaks of "the essentially human in God, and the essentially divine in man.'' The Son, or Word of God, "when manifested in the forms of a finite personality, is the essential Christ, revealing that in God which is essentially and eternally human."

Pfleiderer, Philos. Religion. 1 : 196 — " The whole of humanity is the object of the divine love ; it is an Immanuel and son of God ; its whole history is a continual incarnation of God ; as indeed it is said in Scripture that we are a divine offspring, and that we live and move and have our being in God. But what lies potentially *in* the human consciousness of God is not on that account also manifestly revealed *to* it from the beginning." Hatch, Hibbert Lectures, 175–180, on Stoic monism and Platonic dualism, tells us that the Stoics believed in a personal λόγος and an impersonal ὕλη, both of them modes of a single substance. Some regarded God as a mode of matter, *natura naturata :* " Jupiter est quodcunque vides, quodcunque moveris " (Lucan, Phars., 9 : 579) ; others conceived of him as the *natura naturans,* — this became the governing conception. . . . . The products are all divine, but not equally divine. . . . . Nearest of all to the pure essence of God is the human soul : it is an emanation or outflow from him, a sapling which is separate from and yet continues the life of the parent tree, a colony in which some members of the parent state have settled. Plato followed Anaxagoras in holding that mind is separate from matter and acts upon it. God is outside the world. He shapes it as a carpenter shapes wood. On the general subject of the union of deity and humanity in the person of Christ, see Herzog, Encyclopädie, art. : Christologie ; Barrows, in Bib. Sac., 10 : 765 ; 26 : 83 ; also, Bib. Sac., 17 : 535 ; John Owen, Person of Christ, in Works, 1 : 223 ; Hooker, Eccl. Polity, book v, chap. 51–56 : Boyce, in Bap. Quar., 1870 : 385 ; Shedd, Hist. Doct., 1 : 403 *sq.* ; Hovey, God with Us, 61–88 ; Plumptre, Christ and Christendom, appendix ; E. H. Johnson, The Idea of Law in Christology, in Bib. Sac., Oct. 1889 : 599–625.

SECTION III.—THE TWO STATES OF CHRIST.

I. THE STATE OF HUMILIATION.

1. *The nature of this humiliation.*

We may dismiss, as unworthy of serious notice, the views that it consisted essentially either in the union of the Logos with human nature,—for this union with human nature continues in the state of exaltation; or in the outward trials and privations of Christ's human life,—for this view casts reproach upon poverty, and ignores the power of the soul to rise superior to its outward circumstances.

E. G. Robinson, Christian Theology, 224—"The error of supposing it too humiliating to obey law was derived from the Roman treasury of merit and works of supererogation. Better was Frederick the Great's sentiment when his sturdy subject and neighbor, the miller, whose windmill he had attempted to remove, having beaten him in a lawsuit, the thwarted monarch exclaimed: 'Thank God, there is law in Prussia!'" Palmer, Theological Definition, 79—"God reveals himself in the rock, vegetable, animal, man. Must not the process go on? Must there not appear in the fulness of time a man who will reveal God as perfectly as is possible in human conditions—a man who is God under the limitations of humanity? Such incarnation is humiliation only in the eyes of men. To Christ it is lifting up, exaltation, glory; John 12 : 32—'And I, if I be lifted up from the earth, will draw all men unto myself.'" George Harris, Moral Evolution, 409—"The divinity of Christ is not obscured, but is more clearly seen, shining through his humanity."

We may devote more attention to the

A. Theory of Thomasius, Delitzsch, and Crosby, that the humiliation consisted in the surrender of the relative divine attributes.

This theory holds that the Logos, although retaining his divine self-consciousness and his immanent attributes of holiness, love, and truth, surrendered his relative attributes of omniscience, omnipotence, and omnipresence, in order to take to himself veritable human nature. According to this view, there are, indeed, two natures in Christ, but neither of these natures is infinite. Thomasius and Delitzsch are the chief advocates of this theory in Germany. Dr. Howard Crosby has maintained a similar view in America.

The theory of Thomasius, Delitzsch, and Crosby has been, though improperly, called the theory of the Kenosis (from ἐκένωσεν—"emptied himself"—in Phil. 2 : 7), and its advocates are often called Kenotic theologians. There is a Kenosis of the Logos, but it is of a different sort from that which this theory supposes. For statements of this theory, see Thomasius, Christi Person und Werk, 2 : 233–255, 542–550; Delitzsch, Biblische Psychologie, 32)–333; Howard Crosby, in Bap. Quar., 1870 : 350–363—a discourse subsequently published in a separate volume, with the title: The True Humanity of Christ, and reviewed by Shedd, in Presb. Rev., April, 1881 : 429–431. Crosby emphasizes the word "became," in John 1 : 14—"and the Word became flesh"—and gives the word "flesh" the sense of "man," or "human." Crosby, then, should logically deny, though he does not deny, that Christ's body was derived from the Virgin.

We object to this view that :

(*a*) It contradicts the Scriptures already referred to, in which Christ asserts his divine knowledge and power. Divinity, it is said, can give up its world-functions, for it existed without these before creation. But to give up divine attributes is to give up the substance of Godhead. Nor is it a sufficient reply to say that only the relative attributes are given up, while the immanent attributes, which chiefly characterize the Godhead, are retained ; for the immanent necessarily involve the relative, as the greater involve the less.

Liebner, Jahrbuch f. d. Theol., 3 : 349–356 — "Is the Logos here? But wherein does he show his presence, that it may be known?" Hase, Hutterus Redivivus, 11th ed., 217, note. John Caird, Fund. Ideas of Christianity, 2 : 125–146, criticises the theory of the Kenosis, but grants that, with all its self-contradictions, as he regards them, it is an attempt to render conceivable the profound truth of a sympathizing, self-sacrificing God.

(b) Since the Logos, in uniting himself to a human soul, reduces himself to the condition and limitations of a human soul, the theory is virtually a theory of the coëxistence of two human souls in Christ. But the union of two finite souls is more difficult to explain than the union of a finite and an infinite,—since there can be in the former case no intelligent guidance and control of the human element by the divine.

Dorner, Jahrbuch f. d. Theol., 1 : 397–408 — "The impossibility of making two finite souls into one finally drove Arianism to the denial of any human soul in Christ" (Apollinarianism). This statement of Dorner, which we have already quoted in our account of Apollinarianism, illustrates the similar impossibility, upon the theory of Thomasius, of constructing out of two finite souls the person of Christ. See also Hovey, God with Us, 68.

(c) This theory fails to secure its end, that of making comprehensible the human development of Jesus,— for even though divested of the relative attributes of Godhood, the Logos still retains his divine self-consciousness, together with his immanent attributes of holiness, love, and truth. This is as difficult to reconcile with a purely natural human development as the possession of the relative divine attributes would be. The theory logically leads to a further denial of the possession of any divine attributes, or of any divine consciousness at all, on the part of Christ, and merges itself in the view of Gess and Beecher, that the Godhead of the Logos is actually transformed into a human soul.

Kahnis, Dogmatik, 3 : 343 — "The old theology conceived of Christ as in full and unbroken use of the divine self-consciousness, the divine attributes, and the divine world-functions, from the conception until death. Though Jesus, as fœtus, child, boy, was not almighty and omnipresent according to his human nature, yet he was so, as to his divine nature, which constituted one *ego* with his human. Thomasius, however, declared that the Logos gave up his relative attributes, during his sojourn in flesh. Dorner's objection to this, on the ground of the divine unchangeableness, overshoots the mark, because it makes any *becoming* impossible.

" But some things in Thomasius' doctrine are still difficult : 1st, divinity can certainly give up its world-functions, for it has existed without these before the world was. In the nature of an absolute personality, however, lies an absolute knowing, willing, feeling, which it cannot give up. Hence Phil. 2 : 6–11 speaks of a giving-up of divine glory, but not of a giving-up of divine attributes or nature. 2d, little is gained by such an assumption of the giving-up of *relative* attributes, since the Logos, even while divested of a part of his attributes, still has full possession of his divine self-consciousness, which must make a purely human development no less difficult. 3d, the expressions of divine self-consciousness, the works of divine power, the words of divine wisdom, prove that Jesus was in possession of his divine self-consciousness and attributes.

" The essential thing which the Kenotics aim at, however, stands fast ; namely, that the divine personality of the Logos divested itself of its glory (John 17 : 5), riches (2 Cor. 8 : 6), divine form (Phil. 2 : 6). This divesting is the becoming man. The humiliation. then, was a giving up of the *use*, not of the possession, of the divine nature and attributes. That man can thus give up self-consciousness and powers. we see every day in sleep. But man does not thereby, cease to be man. So we maintain that the Logos, when he became man, did not divest himself of his divine person and nature, which was impossible; but only divested himself of the use and exercise of these— these being latent to him— in order to unfold themselves to use in the measure to which his human nature developed itself—a use which found its completion in the condition of exaltation." This statement of Kahnis, although approaching correctness, is still neither quite correct nor quite complete.

B. Theory that the humiliation consisted in the surrender of the independent exercise of the divine attributes.

This theory, which we regard as the most satisfactory of all, may be more fully set forth as follows. The humiliation, as the Scriptures seem to show, consisted :

(a) In that act of the preëxistent Logos by which he gave up his divine glory with the Father, in order to take a servant-form. In this act, he resigned not the possession, nor yet entirely the use, but rather the independent exercise, of the divine attributes.

John 17 : 5 —"glorify thou me with thine own self with the glory which I had with thee before the world was"; Phil. : 6, 7 — "who, existing in the form of God, counted not the being on an equality with God a thing to be grasped, but emptied himself, taking the form of a servant, being made in the likeness of men"; 2 Cor. 8 : 9 — "For ye know the grace of our Lord Jesus Christ, that, though he was rich, yet for your sakes he became poor, that ye through his poverty might become rich." Pompilia, in Robert Browning's The Ring and the Book : "Now I see how God is likest God in being born."

Omniscience gives up all knowledge but that of the child, the infant, the embryo, the infinitesimal germ of humanity. Omnipotence gives up all power but that of the unpregnated ovum in the womb of the Virgin. The Godhead narrows itself down to a point that is next to absolute extinction. Jesus washing his disciples' feet, in John 13: 1-20, is the symbol of his coming down from his throne of glory and taking the form of a servant, in order that he may purify us, by regeneration and sanctification, for the marriage-supper of the Lamb.

b) In the submission of the Logos to the control of the Holy Spirit and the limitations of his Messianic mission, in his communication of the divine fulness of the human nature which he had taken into union with himself.

Acts 1 : 2 — Jesus, "after that he had given commandment through the Holy Spirit unto the apostles whom he had chosen"; 10 : 38 — "Jesus of Nazareth, how God anointed him with the Holy Spirit and with power"; Heb. 9 : 14 — "the blood of Christ, who through the eternal Spirit offered himself without blemish unto God." A minor may have a great estate left to him, yet may have only such use of it as his guardian permits. In Homer's Iliad, when Andromache brings her infant son to part with Hector, the boy is terrified by the warlike plumes of his father's helmet, and Hector puts them off to embrace him. So God lays aside "That glorious form, that light unsufferable And that far-beaming blaze of majesty." Arthur H. Hallam, in John Brown's Rab and his Friends, 282, 283 — "Revelation is the voluntary approximation of the infinite Being to the ways and thoughts of finite humanity."

(c) In the continuous surrender, on the part of the God-man, so far as his human nature was concerned, of the exercise of those divine powers with which it was endowed by virtue of its union with the divine, and in the voluntary acceptance, which followed upon this, of temptation, suffering, and death.

Mat. 26 : 53 —"thinkest thou that I cannot beseech my Father, and he shall even now send me more than twelve legions of angels?" John 10 : 17, 18 — "Therefore doth the Father love me, because I lay down my life, that I may take it again. No one taketh it away from me, but I lay it down of myself. I have power to lay it down, and I have power to take it again"; Phil. 2 : 8 — "and being found in fashion as a man, he humbled himself, becoming obedient even unto death, yea, the death of the cross." Cf. Shakespeare, Merchant of Venice : "Such music is there in immortal souls, That while this muddy vesture of decay Doth close it in, we cannot see it."

Each of these elements of the doctrine has its own Scriptural support. We must therefore regard the humiliation of Christ, not as consisting in a single act, but as involving a continuous self-renunciation, which began with the Kenosis of the Logos in becoming man, and which culminated in the self-subjection of the God-man to the death of the cross.

Our doctrine of Christ's humiliation will be better understood if we put it midway between two pairs of erroneous views, making it the third of five. The list would be as follows: (1) Gess: The Logos gave up all divine attributes; (2) Thomasius: The Logos gave up relative attributes only; (3) True View: The Logos gave up the independent exercise of divine attributes; (4) Old Orthodoxy: Christ gave up the use of divine attributes; (5) Anselm: Christ acted as if he did not possess divine attributes. The full exposition of the classical passage with reference to the humiliation, namely, Phil. 2 : 5-8, we give below, under the next paragraph, pages 705, 706. Brentius illustrated Christ's humiliation by the king who travels incognito. But Mason, Faith of the Gospel, 158, says well that " to part in appearance with only the fruition of the divine attributes would be to impose upon us with a pretence of self-sacrifice; but to part with it in reality was to manifest most perfectly the true nature of God."

This same objection lies against the explanation given in the Church Quarterly Review, Oct. 1891 : 1-30, on Our Lord's Knowledge as Man: " If divine knowledge exists in a different form from human, and a translation into a different form is necessary before it can be available in the human sphere, our Lord might know the day of judgment as God, and yet be ignorant of it as man. This must have been the case if he did not *choose* to translate it into the human form. But it might also have been incapable of translation. The processes of divine knowledge may be far above our finite comprehension." This seems to us to be a virtual denial of the unity of Christ's person, and to make our Lord play fast and loose with the truth. He either knew, or he did not know; and his denial that he knew makes it impossible that he should have known in any sense.

2. *The stages of Christ's humiliation.*

We may distinguish : (*a*) That act of the preïncarnate Logos by which, in becoming man, he gave up the independent exercise of the divine attributes. (*b*) His submission to the common laws which regulate the origin of souls from a preëxisting sinful stock, in taking his human nature from the Virgin,—a human nature which only the miraculous conception rendered pure. (*c*) His subjection to the limitations involved in a human growth and development,—reaching the consciousness of his sonship at his twelfth year, and working no miracles till after the baptism. (*d*) The subordination of himself, in state, knowledge, teaching, and acts, to the control of the Holy Spirit,—so living, not independently, but as a servant. (*e*) His subjection, as connected with a sinful race, to temptation and suffering, and finally to the death which constituted the penalty of the law.

Peter Lombard asked whether God could know more than he was aware of ? It is only another way of putting the question whether, during the earthly life of Christ, the Logos existed outside of the flesh of Jesus. We must answer in the affirmative. Otherwise the number of the persons in the Trinity would be variable, and the universe could do without him who is ever "upholding all things by the word of his power " (Heb. 1 : 3), and in whom "all things consist " (Col. 1 : 17). Let us recall the nature of God's omnipresence (see pages 279-282). Omnipresence is nothing less than the presence of the whole of God in every place. From this it follows, that the whole Christ can be present in every believer as fully as if that believer were the only one to receive of his fulness, and that the whole Logos can be united to and be present in the man Christ Jesus, while at the same time he fills and governs the universe. By virtue of this omnipresence, therefore, the whole Logos can suffer on earth, while yet the whole Logos reigns in heaven. The Logos outside of Christ has the perpetual consciousness of his Godhead, while yet the Logos, as united to humanity in Christ, is subject to ignorance, weakness, and death. Shedd, Dogm. Theol., 1 : 153 — " Jehovah, though present in the form of the burning 'ush, was at the same time omnipresent also"; 2 : 265-284, esp. 282—"Because the sun is shining in and through a cloud, it does not follow that it cannot at the same time be shining through the remainder of universal space, unobstructed by any vapor whatever." Gordon, Ministry of the Spirit, 21—"Not with God, as with finite man, does arrival in one place necessitate withdrawal from another." John Calvin: "The whole Christ was there; but not all that was in Christ was there." See Adamson, The Mind of Christ.

How the independent exercise of the attributes of omnipotence, omniscience, and omnipresence can be surrendered, even for a time, would be inconceivable, if we were regarding the Logos as he is in himself, seated upon the throne of the universe. The matter is somewhat easier when we remember that it was not the Logos *per se*, but rather the God-man, Jesus Christ, in whom the Logos submitted to this humiliation. South, Sermons, 2 : 9—"Be the fountain never so full, yet if it communicate itself by a little pipe, the stream can be but small and inconsiderable, and equal to the measure of its conveyance." Sartorius, Person and Work of Christ, 39—"The human eye, when open, sees heaven and earth; but when shut, it sees little or nothing. Yet its inherent capacity does not change. So divinity does not change its nature, when it drops the curtain of humanity before the eyes of the God-man."

The divine in Christ, during most of his earthly life, is latent, or only now and then present to his consciousness or manifested to others. Illustrate from second childhood, where the mind itself exists, but is not capable of use; or from first childhood, where even a Newton or a Humboldt, if brought back to earth and made to occupy an infant body and brain, would develop as an infant, with infantile powers. There is more in memory than we can at this moment recall,—memory is greater than recollection. There is more of us at all times than we know,—only the sudden emergency reveals the largeness of our resources of mind and heart and will. The new nature, in the regenerate, is greater than it appears: "Beloved, now are we children of God, and it is not yet made manifest what we shall be. We know that, if he shall be manifested, we shall be like him" (1 John 3 : 2). So in Christ there was an ocean-like fulness of resource, of which only now and then the Spirit permitted the consciousness and the exercise.

Without denying (with Dorner) the completeness, even from the moment of the conception, of the union between the deity and the humanity, we may still say with Kahnis: "The human nature of Christ, according to the measure of its development, appropriates more and more to its conscious use the latent fulness of the divine nature." So we take the middle ground between two opposite extremes. On the one hand, the Kenosis was not the extinction of the Logos. Nor, on the other hand, did Christ hunger and sleep by miracle,—this is Docetism. We must not minimize Christ's humiliation, for this was his glory. There was no limit to his descent, except that arising from his sinlessness. His humiliation was not merely the giving-up of the appearance of Godhead. Baird, Elohim Revealed, 585—"Should any one aim to celebrate the condescension of the emperor Charles the Fifth, by dwelling on the fact that he laid aside the robes of royalty and assumed the style of a subject, and altogether ignore the more important matter that he actually became a private person, it would be very weak and absurd." *Cf.* 2 Cor. 8 : 9—"though he was rich, yet for your sakes he became poor " = he beggared himself. Mat. 27 : 46 —"My God, my God, why hast thou forsaken me ?" = non-exercise of divine omniscience.

Inasmuch, however, as the passage Phil. 2 : 6-8 is the chief basis and support of the doctrine of Christ's humiliation, we here subjoin a more detailed examination of it.

EXPOSITION OF PHILIPPIANS, 2 : 6-8. The passage reads : "who, existing in the form of God, counted not the being on an equality with God a thing to be grasped, but emptied himself, taking the form of a servant, being made in the likeness of men; and being found in fashion as a man, he humbled himself, becoming obedient even unto death, yea, the death of the cross."

The subject of the sentence is at first (verses 6, 7) Christ Jesus, regarded as the preëxistent Logos; subsequently (verse 8), this same Christ Jesus, regarded as incarnate. This change in the subject is indicated by the contrast between μορφῇ θεοῦ (verse 6) and μορφὴν δούλου (verse 7), as well as by the participles λάβών and γενόμενος (verse 7) and εὑρεθείς (verse 8) it is asserted, then, that the preëxisting Logos, "although subsisting in the form of God, did not regard his equality with God as a thing to be forcibly retained, but emptied himself by taking the form of a servant, (that is,) by being made in the likeness of men. And being found in outward condition as a man, he (the incarnate son of God, yet further) humbled himself, by becoming obedient unto death, even the death of the cross " (verse 8).

Here notice that what the Logos divested himself of, in becoming man, is not the substance of his Godhead, but the "form of God" in which this substance was manifested. This "form of God" can be only that independent exercise of the powers and prerogatives of Deity which constitutes his "equality with God." This he surrenders, in the act of 'taking the form of a servant"—or becoming subordinate, as man. (Here other Scriptures complete the view, by their representations of the controlling influence of the Holy Spirit in the earthly life of Christ.) The phrases "made in the likeness of men" and "found in fashion as a man"—are used to intimate, not that Jesus Christ was not really man, but that he was God as well as man, and therefore free from the sin which clings to man (cf. Rom. 8 : 3 — ἐν ὁμοιώματι σαρκὸς ἁμαρτίας —Meyer). Finally, this one person, now God and man united, submits himself, consciously and voluntarily, to the humiliation of an ignominious death.

See Lightfoot, on Phil. 2:8 —" Christ divested himself, not of his divine nature, for that was impossible, but of the glories and prerogatives of Deity. This he did by taking the form of a servant." Evans, in Presb. Rev., 1883 : 287 — " Two stages in Christ's humiliation, each represented by a finite verb defining the central act of the particular stage, accompanied by two modal participles. 1st stage indicated in v. 7. Its central act is : 'he emptied himself.' Its two modalities are : (1) 'taking the form of servant' ; (2) 'being made in the likeness of men.' Here we have the humiliation of the Kenosis,— that by which Christ became man. 2d stage, indicated in v. 8. Its central act is : 'he humbled himself.' Its two modalities are : (1) 'being found in fashion as a man' ; (2) 'becoming obedient unto death, yea, the death of the cross.' Here we have the humiliation of his obedience and death, — that by which, in humanity, he became a sacrifice for our sins."

Meyer refers Eph. 5:31 exclusively to Christ and the church, making the completed union future, however, i. e., at the time of the Parousia. " For this cause shall a man leave his father and mother" = " in the incarnation, Christ leaves father and mother (his seat at the right hand of God), and cleaves to his wife (the church), and then the two (the descended Christ and the church) become one flesh (one ethical person, as the married pair become one by physical union). The Fathers, however, (Jerome, Theodoret, Chrysostom), referred it to the incarnation." On the interpretation of Phil. 2 : 6-11, see Comm. of Neander, Meyer, Lange, Ellicott.

On the question whether Christ would have become man had there been no sin, theologians are divided. Dorner, Martensen, and Westcott answer in the affirmative ; Robinson, Watts, and Denney in the negative. See Dorner, Hist. Doct. Person of Christ, 5 : 236 ; Martensen, Christian Dogmatics, 327-329 ; Westcott, Com. on Hebrews, page 8 — " The Incarnation is in its essence independent of the Fall, though conditioned by it as to its circumstances." Per contra, see Robinson, Christ. Theol., 219, note — " It would be difficult to show that a like method of argument from a priori premises will not equally avail to prove sin to have been a necessary part of the scheme of creation." Denney, Studies in Theology, 101, objects to the doctrine of necessary incarnation irrespective of sin, that it tends to obliterate the distinction between nature and grace, to blur the definite outlines of the redemption wrought by Christ, as the supreme revelation of God and his love. See also Watts, New Apologetic, 198-202; Julius Müller, Dogmat. Abhandlungen, 66-126 ; Van Oosterzee, Dogmatics, 512-526, 543-548 ; Forrest, The Authority of Christ, 340-345. On the general subject of the Kenosis of the Logos, see Bruce, Humiliation of Christ; Robins, in Bib. Sac., Oct. 1874 : 615 ; Philippi, Glaubenslehre, 4 : 138-150, 386-475 ; Pope, Person of Christ, 23 ; Bodemeyer, Lehre von der Kenosis ; Hodge, Syst. Theol., 2 : 610-625.

II. The State of Exaltation.

1. The nature of this exaltation.

It consisted essentially in : (a) A resumption, on the part of the Logos, of his independent exercise of divine attributes. (b) The withdrawal, on the part of the Logos, of all limitations in his communication of the divine fulness to the human nature of Christ. (c) The corresponding exercise, on the part of the human nature, of those powers which belonged to it by virtue of its union with the divine.

The eighth Psalm, with its account of the glory of human nature, is at present fulfilled only in Christ (see Heb. 2 : 9 — "but we behold . . . . Jesus"). Heb. 2 : 7 — ἠλάττωσας αὐτον βραχύ τι παρ' ἀγγέλους — may be translated, as in the margin of the Rev. Vers.: "Thou madest him *for a little while* lower than the angels." Christ's human body was not necessarily subject to death; only by outward compulsion or voluntary surrender could he die. Hence resurrection was a natural necessity (Acts 2 : 24 — "whom God raised up, having loosed the pangs of death : because it was not possible that he should be holden of it "; 31 — "neither was he left unto Hades, nor did his flesh see corruption "). This exaltation, which then affected humanity only in its head, is to be the experience also of the members. Our bodies also are to be delivered from the bondage of corruption, and we are to sit with Christ upon his throne.

2. *The stages of Christ's exaltation.*

(a) The quickening and resurrection.

Both Lutherans and Romanists distinguish between these two, making the former precede, and the latter follow, Christ's "preaching to the spirits in prison." These views rest upon a misinterpretation of 1 Pet. 3 : 18-20. Lutherans teach that Christ descended into hell, to proclaim his triumph to evil spirits. But this is to give ἐκήρυξεν the unusual sense of proclaiming his triumph, instead of his gospel. Romanists teach that Christ entered the underworld to preach to Old Testament saints, that they might be saved. But the passage speaks only of the disobedient ; it can-not be pressed into the support of a sacramental theory of the salvation of Old Testament believers. The passage does not assert the descent of Christ into the world of spirits, but only a work of the preïncarnate Logos in offering salvation, through Noah, to the world then about to perish.

Augustine, Ad Euodiam, ep. 99 —"The spirits shut up in prison are the unbelievers who lived in the time of Noah, whose spirits or souls were shut up in the darkness of ignorance as in a prison ; Christ preached to them, not in the flesh, for he was not yet incarnate, but in the spirit, that is, in his divine nature." Calvin taught that Christ descended into the underworld and suffered the pains of the lost. But not all Calvinists hold with him here ; see Princeton Essays, 1 : 153. Meyer, on Rom. 10 : 7, regards the question — "Who shall descend into the abyss ? (that is, to bring Christ up from the dead)"—as an allusion to, and so indirectly a proof-text for, Christ's descent into the underworld. Mason, Faith of the Gospel, 211, favors a preaching to the dead : "During that time [the three days] he did not return to heaven and his Father." But though John 20 : 17 is referred to for proof, is not this statement true only of his body? So far as the soul is concerned, Christ can say : "Father, into thy hands I commend my spirit," and "To-day thou shalt be with me in Paradise" (Luke 23 : 43, 46).

Zahn and Dorner best represent the Lutheran view. Zahn, in Expositor, March, 1898 : 216-223 — "If Jesus was truly man, then his soul, after it left the body, entered into the fellowship of departed spirits. . . . If Jesus is he who lives forevermore and even his dying was his act, this tarrying in the realm of the dead cannot be thought of as a purely passive condition, but must have been known to those who dwelt there. . . . . If Jesus was the Redeemer of mankind, the generations of those who had passed away must have thus been brought into personal relation to him, his work and his kingdom, without waiting for the last day."

Dorner, Glaubenslehre, 2 : 662 (Syst. Doct., 4 : 127), thinks "Christ's descent into Hades marks a new era of his pneumatic life, in which he shows himself free from the limitations of time and space." He rejects "Luther's notion of a merely triumphal progress and proclamation of Christ. Before Christ," he says, "there was no abode peopled by the damned. The descent was an application of the benefit of the atonement (implied in κηρύσσειν). The work was prophetic, not high-priestly nor kingly. Going to the spirits in prison is spoken of as a spontaneous act, not one of physical necessity. No power of Hades led him over into Hades. Deliverance from the limitations of a mortal body is already an indication of a higher stage of existence. Christ's soul is bodiless for a time — πνεῦμα only — as the departed were.

"The ceasing of this preaching is neither recorded, nor reasonably to be supposed, — indeed the ancient church supposed it carried on through the apostles. It expresses the universal significance of Christ for former generations and for the entire kingdom of the dead. No physical power is a limit to him. The gates of hell, or Hades, shall not prevail over or against him. The intermediate state is one of blessedness for him, and he can admit the penitent thief into it. Even those who were not laid hold of by Christ's historic manifestation in this earthly life still must, and may, be brought into relation with him, in order to be able to accept or to reject him. And thus the universal relation of Christ to humanity and the absoluteness of the Christian religion are confirmed." So Dorner, for substance.

All this *versus* Strauss, who thought that the dying of vast masses of men, before and after Christ, who had not been brought into relation to Christ, proves that the Christian religion is not necessary to salvation, because not universal. For advocacy of Christ's preaching to the dead, see also Jahrbuch für d. Theol., 23 : 177-228 ; W. W. Patton, in N. Eng., July, 1882 : 400-478 ; John Miller, Problems Suggested by the Bible, part 1 : 93-98 ; part 2 : 38 ; Plumptre, The Spirits in Prison ; Kendrick, in Bap. Rev., Apl. 1888 ; Clemen, Niedergefahren zu den Toten.

For the opposite view, see " No Preaching to the Dead," in Princeton Rev., March. 1875 : 197 ; 1878 : 451-491 ; Hovey, in Bap. Quar., 4 : 486 *sq.*, and Bib. Eschatology, 97-107 ; Love, Christ's Preaching to the Spirits in Prison ; Cowles, in Bib. Sac., 1875 : 401 ; Hodge. Syst. Theol., 2 : 616-622 ; Salmond, in Popular Commentary ; and Johnstone, Com., *in loco.* So Augustine, Thomas Aquinas, and Bishop Pearson. See also E. D. Morris, Is There Salvation after Death ? and Wright, Relation of Death to Probation, 22 : 28 —" If Christ preached to spirits in Hades, it may have been to demonstrate the *hopelessness* of adding in the other world to the privileges enjoyed in this. We do not read that it had any favorable effect upon the hearers. If men will not hear Moses and the Prophets, then they will not hear one risen from the dead. ' To-day thou shalt be with me in Paradise ' (Luke 8 : 43) was not comforting, if Christ was going that day to the realm of lost spirits. The antediluvians, however, were specially favored with Noah's preaching, and were especially wicked."

For full statement of the view presented in the text, that the preaching referred to was the preaching of Christ as preëxisting Logos to the spirits, now in prison, when once they were disobedient in the days of Noah, see Bartlett, in New Englander, Oct. 1872 : 601 *sq.*, and in Bib. Sac., Apr. 1883 : 333-373. Before giving the substance of Bartlett's exposition, we transcribe in full the passage in question, 1 Pet. 3 : 18-20 — "Because Christ also suffered for sins once, the righteous for the unrighteous, that he might bring us to God ; being put to death in the flesh, but made alive in the spirit ; in which also he went and preached unto the spirits in prison, that aforetime were disobedient, when the longsuffering of God waited in the days of Noah."

Bartlett expounds as follows : " 'In which ' [πνεύματι, divine nature] ' he went and preached to the spirits in prison when once they disobeyed.' ἀπειθήσασιν is circumstantial aorist, indicating the time of the preaching as a definite past. It is an anarthrous dative, as in Luke 8 : 27 ; Mat. 8 : 23 ; Acts 15 : 25 ; 22 : 17. It is an appositive, or predicative, participle. [That the aorist participle does not necessarily describe an action preliminary to that of the principal verb appears from its use in verse 18 (θανατωθείς), in 1 Thess. 1 : 6 (δεξάμενοι), and in Col. 2 : 11, 13.] The connection of thought is : Peter exhorts his readers to endure suffering bravely, because Christ did so,—in his lower nature being put to death, in his higher nature enduring the opposition of sinners before the flood. Sinners of that time only are mentioned, because this permits an introduction of the subsequent reference to baptism. *Cf.* Gen. 6 : 3 ; 1 Pet. 1 : 10, 11 ; 2 Pet. 2 : 4, 5."

(*b*) The ascension and sitting at the right hand of God.

As the resurrection proclaimed Christ to men as the perfected and glorified man, the conqueror of sin and lord of death, the ascension proclaimed him to the universe as the reinstated God, the possessor of universal dominion, the omnipresent object of worship and hearer of prayer. *Dextra Dei ubique est.*

Mat. 28 : 18, 20 — "All authority hath been given unto me in heaven and on earth. . . . . lo, I am with you always, even unto the end of the world " ; Mark 16 : 19 — " So then the Lord Jesus, after he had spoken unto them, was received up into heaven, and sat down at the right hand of God" ; Acts 7 : 55 — "But he, being full of the Holy Spirit, looked up stedfastly into heaven, and saw the glory of God, and Jesus standing on the right hand of God " ; 2 Cor. 13 : 4 —"he was crucified through weakness, yet he liveth through the power of God" ; Eph. 1 : 22, 23 — "he put all things in subjection under his feet, and gave him to be head over all things to the church, which is his body, the fulness of him that filleth all in all " ; 4 : 10 — " He that descended is the same also that ascended far above all the heavens, that he might fill all things." Philippi, Glaubenslehre, 4 : 184-189 — " Before the resurrection, Christ was *the God-man ;* since the resurrection, he is the *God-man.* . . . . He ate with his disciples, not to show the *qualitu* but the *reality,* of his human body." Nicoll, Life of Christ:

"It was hard for Elijah to ascend"—it required chariot and horses of fire—"but it was easier for Christ to ascend than to descend,"—there was a gravitation upwards. Maclaren: "He has not left the world, though he has ascended to the Father, any more than he left the Father when he came into the world"; John 1 : 18 — "the only begotten Son, who is in the bosom of the Father"; 3 : 13 — "the Son of man, who is in heaven."

We are compelled here to consider the problem of the relation of the humanity to the Logos in the state of exaltation. The Lutherans maintain the ubiquity of Christ's human body, and they make it the basis of their doctrine of the sacraments. Dorner, Glaubenslehre, 2 : 674–676 (Syst. Doct., 4 : 133–142), holds to "a presence, not simply of the Logos, but of the whole God-man, with all his people, but not necessarily likewise a similar presence in the world ; in other words, his presence is morally conditioned by men's receptivity." The old theologians said that Christ is not in heaven, *quasi carcere*. Calvin, Institutes, 2 : 15 — he is "incarnate, but not incarcerated." He has gone into heaven, the place of spirits, and he manifests himself there ; but he has also gone far *above* all heavens, that he may fill all things. He is with his people alway. All power is given into his hand. The church is the fulness of him that filleth all in all. So the Acts of the Apostles speak constantly of the Son of man, of the man Jesus as God, ever present, the object of worship, seated at the right hand of God, having all the powers and prerogatives of Deity. See Westcott, Bible Com., on John 20 : 22 — "he breathed on them, and saith unto them, Receive ye the Holy Spirit"—"The characteristic effect of the Paschal gift was shown in the new faith by which the disciples were gathered into a living society ; the characteristic effect of the Pentecostal gift was shown in the exercise of supremacy potentially universal."

Who and what is this Christ who is present with his people when they pray? It is not enough to say, He is simply the Holy Spirit ; for the Holy Spirit is the "Spirit of Christ" (Rom. 8 : 9), and in having the Holy Spirit we have Christ himself (John 16 : 7 — "I will send him [the Comforter] unto you"; 14 : 18 —"I come unto you"). The Christ, who is thus present with us when we pray, is not simply the Logos, or the divine nature of Christ,—his humanity being separated from the divinity and being localized in heaven. This would be inconsistent with his promise, "Lo, I am with you," in which the "I" that spoke was not simply Deity, but Deity and humanity inseparably united ; and it would deny the real and indissoluble union of the two natures. The elder brother and sympathizing Savior who is with us when we pray is man, as well as God. This manhood is therefore ubiquitous by virtue of its union with the Godhead.

But this is not to say that Christ's human *body* is everywhere present. It would seem that body must exist in spatial relations, and be confined to place. We do not know that this is so with regard to soul. Heaven would seem to be a place, because Christ's body is there ; and a spiritual body is not a body which is spirit, but a body which is suited to the uses of the spirit. But even though Christ may manifest himself, in a glorified human body, only in heaven, his human soul, by virtue of its union with the divine nature, can at the same moment be with all his scattered people over the whole earth. As, in the days of his flesh, his humanity was confined to place, while as to his Deity he could speak of the Son of man who is in heaven, so now, although his human body may be confined to place, his human soul is ubiquitous. Humanity can exist without body ; for during the three days in the sepulchre, Christ's body was on earth, but his soul was in the other world ; and in like manner there is, during the intermediate state, a separation of the soul and the body of believers. But humanity cannot exist without soul ; and if the human Savior is with us, then his humanity, at least so far as respects its immaterial part, must be everywhere present. *Per contra*, see Shedd, Dogm. Theol., 2 : 326, 327. Since Christ's human nature has derivatively become possessed of divine attributes, there is no validity in the notion of a progressiveness in that nature, now that it has ascended to the right hand of God. See Philippi, Glaubenslehre, 4 : 131; Van Oosterzee, Dogmatics, 558, 576.

Shedd, Dogm. Theol., 2 : 327 — "Suppose the presence of the divine nature of Christ in the soul of a believer in London. This divine nature is at the same moment conjoined with, and present to, and modified by, the human nature of Christ, which is in heaven and not in London." So Hooker, Eccl. Pol., 54, 55, and E. G. Robinson : "Christ is in heaven at the right hand of the Father, interceding for us, while he is present in the church by his Spirit. We pray to the theanthropic Jesus. Possession of a human body does not now constitute a limitation. We know little of the nature of the present body." We add to this last excellent remark the expression of our own conviction that the modern conception of the merely relative nature of space, and the idealistic view of matter as only the expression of mind and will, have relieved this subject of many of

its former difficulties. If Christ is omnipresent and if his body is simply the manifestation of his soul, then every soul may feel the presence of his humanity even now and
"every eye" may "see him" at his second coming, even though believers may be separated
as far as is Boston from Pekin. The body from which his glory flashes forth may be
visible in ten thousand places at the same time; (Mat. 28 : 20; Rev. 1 : 7).

SECTION IV.—THE OFFICES OF CHRIST.

The Scriptures represent Christ's offices as three in number,—prophetic,
priestly, and kingly. Although these terms are derived from concrete
human relations, they express perfectly distinct ideas. The prophet, the
priest, and the king, of the Old Testament, were detached but designed
prefigurations of him who should combine all these various activities in
himself, and should furnish the ideal reality, of which they were the
imperfect symbols.

1 Cor. 1 : 30 —"of him are ye in Christ Jesus, who was made unto us wisdom from God, and righteousness and sanctification, and redemption." Here "wisdom" seems to indicate the prophetic, "righteousness" (or "justification") the priestly, and "sanctification and redemption" the kingly work of Christ. Denovan:
"Three offices are necessary. Christ must be a prophet, to save us from the ignorance
of sin; a priest, to save us from its guilt; a king, to save us from its dominion in our
flesh. Our faith cannot have firm basis in any one of these alone, any more than a stool
can stand on less than three legs." See Van Oosterzee, Dogmatics, 583-586; Archer
Butler, Sermons, 1 : 314.

A. A. Hodge, Popular Lectures, 235 —"For 'office,' there are two words in Latin:
munus = position (of Mediator), and *officia* = functions (of Prophet, Priest, and King).
They are not separate offices, as are those of President, Chief-Justice, and Senator.
They are not separate functions, capable of successive and isolated performance. They
are rather like the several functions of the one living human body — lungs, heart, brain
— functionally distinct, yet interdependent, and together constituting one life. So the
functions of Prophet, Priest, and King mutually imply one another: Christ is always a
prophetical Priest, and a priestly Prophet; and he is always a royal Priest, and a
priestly King; and together they accomplish one redemption, to which all are equally
essential. Christ is both μεσίτης and παράκλητος."

I. THE PROPHETIC OFFICE OF CHRIST.

1. *The nature of Christ's prophetic work.*

(*a*) Here we must avoid the narrow interpretation which would make
the prophet a mere foreteller of future events. He was rather an inspired
interpreter or revealer of the divine will, a medium of communication
between God and men (προφήτης = not foreteller, but forteller, or forth-
teller. *Cf.* Gen. 20 : 7,— of Abraham ; Ps. 105 : 15,— of the patriarchs ;
Mat. 11 : 9,—of John the Baptist ; 1 Cor. 12 : 28, Eph. 2 : 20, and 3 : 5,—
of N. T. expounders of Scripture).

Gen. 20 : 7 —"restore the man's wife; for he is a prophet" — spoken of Abraham ; Ps. 105:15 — "Touch not
mine anointed ones, And do my prophets no harm" — spoken of the patriarchs; Mat. 11 : 9 — "But wherefore
went ye out? to see a prophet? Yea, I say unto you, and much more than a prophet" — spoken of John the
Baptist, from whom we have no recorded predictions, and whose pointing to Jesus as
the "Lamb of God" (John 1 : 29) was apparently but an echo of Isaiah 53. 1 Cor. 12 : 28 —"first apostles,
secondly prophets"; Eph. 2 : 20 —"built upon the foundation of the apostles and prophets"; 3 : 5 — "revealed unto his
holy apostles and prophets in the Spirit" — all these latter texts speaking of New Testament
expounders of Scripture.

Any organ of divine revelation, or medium of divine communication, is a prophet.
"Hence," says Philippi, "the books of Joshua, Judges, Samuel, and Kings are called
'*prophetæ priores*,' or 'the earlier prophets.' Bernard's *Respice, Aspice, Prospice*

describes the work of the prophet; for the prophet might see and might disclose things in the past, things in the present, or things in the future. Daniel was a prophet, in telling Nebuchadnezzar what his dream had been, as well as in telling its interpretation (Dan. 2:28, 36). The woman of Samaria rightly called Christ a prophet, when he told her all things that ever she did (John 4:29)." On the work of the prophet, see Stanley, Jewish Church, 1 : 491.

(*b*) The prophet commonly united three methods of fulfilling his office, — those of teaching, predicting, and miracle-working. In all these respects, Jesus Christ did the work of a prophet (Deut. 18 : 15 ; *cf.* Acts 3 : 22 ; Mat. 13 : 57 ; Luke 13 : 33 ; John 6 : 14). He taught (Mat. 5–7), he uttered predictions (Mat. 24 and 25), he wrought miracles (Mat. 8 and 9), while in his person, his life, his work, and his death, he revealed the Father (John 8 : 26 ; 14 : 9 ; 17 : 8).

Deut. 18 : 15 — "Jehovah thy God will raise up unto thee a prophet, from the midst of thee, of thy brethren, like unto me; unto him shall ye hearken " ; *cf.* Acts 3 : 22 — where this prophecy is said to be fulfilled in Christ. Jesus calls himself a prophet in Mat. 13 : 57 —"A prophet is not without honor, save in his own country, and in his own house"; Luke 13 : 33 —"Nevertheless I must go on my way to-day and to-morrow and the day following : for it cannot be that a prophet perish out of Jerusalem." He was called a prophet : John 6 : 14—"When therefore the people saw the sign which he did, they said, This is of a truth the prophet that cometh into the world." John 8 : 26 —"the things which I heard from him [the Father], these speak I unto the world "; 14 : 9—"he that hath seen me hath seen the Father "; 17 : 8 — "the words which thou gavest me I have given unto them."

Denovan: " Christ teaches us by his word, his Spirit, his example." Christ's miracles were mainly miracles of healing. "Only sickness is contagious with us. But Christ was an example of perfect health, and his health was contagious. By its overflow he healed others. Only a 'touch' (Mat. 9:21) was necessary."

Edwin P. Parker, on Horace Bushnell: "The two fundamental elements of prophecy are insight and expression. Christian prophecy implies insight or discernment of spiritual things by divine illumination, and expression of them, by inspiration, in terms of Christian truth or in the tones and cadences of Christian testimony. We may define it, then, as the publication, under the impulse of inspiration, and for edification, of truths perceived by divine illumination, apprehended by faith, and assimilated by experience. . . . It requires a natural basis and rational preparation in the human mind, a suitable stock of natural gifts on which to graft the spiritual gift for support and nourishment. These gifts have had devout culture. They have been crowned by illuminations and inspirations. Because insight gives foresight, the prophet will be a seer of things as they are unfolding and becoming; will discern far-signalings and intimations of Providence; will forerun men to prepare the way for them, and them for the way of God's coming kingdom."

2. *The stages of Christ's prophetic work.*

These are four, namely:

(*a*) The preparatory work of the Logos, in enlightening mankind before the time of Christ's advent in the flesh. — All preliminary religious knowledge, whether within or without the bounds of the chosen people, is from Christ, the revealer of God.

Christ's prophetic work began before he came in the flesh. John 1: 9 — " There was the true light, even the light which lighteth every man, coming into the world " = all the natural light of conscience, science, philosophy, art, civilization, is the light of Christ. Tennyson: " Our little systems have their day, They have their day and cease to be ; They are but broken lights of thee, And thou, O Lord, art more than they." Heb. 12 : 25, 26 —"See that ye refuse not him that speaketh. . . . . whose voice then [at Sinai] shook the earth : but now he hath promised, saying, Yet once more will I make to tremble not the earth only, but also the heaven "; Luke 11 : 49 — " Therefore said the wisdom of God, I will send unto them prophets and apostles"; *cf.* Mat. 23 : 34 — "behold, I send unto you prophets, and wise men, and scribes : some of them shall ye kill and crucify" — which shows that Jesus was referring to his own teachings, as well as to those of the earlier prophets.

(*b*) The earthly ministry of Christ incarnate. — In his earthly ministry, Christ showed himself the prophet *par excellence*. While he submitted, like the Old Testament prophets, to the direction of the Holy Spirit, unlike them, he found the sources of all knowledge and power within himself. The word of God did not *come* to him, — he was *himself* the Word.

Luke 6 : 19 —"And all the multitude sought to touch him ; for power came forth from him, and healed them all "; John 2 : 11 — "This beginning of his signs did Jesus in Cana of Galilee, and manifested *his glory* " ; 8 : 38, 58 — "I speak the things which I have seen with my Father . . . . Before Abraham was born, I am "; *cf.* Jer. 2 : 1 — "the word of Jehovah came to me " : John 1 : 1 — "In the beginning was the Word." Mat. 26 : 53 — "twelve legions of angels "; John 10 : 18 — of his life : "I have power to lay it down, and I have power to take it again "; 34 — "Is it not written in your law, I said, Ye are gods ? If he called them gods, unto whom the word of God came . . . . say ye of him, whom the Father sanctified and sent into the world, Thou blasphemest, because I said, I am the Son of God ? " Martensen, Dogmatics, 295–301, says of Jesus' teaching that " its source was not inspiration, but incarnation." Jesus was not inspired, — he was the Inspirer. Therefore he is the true "Master of those who know." His disciples act in his name ; he acts in his own name.

(c) The guidance and teaching of his church on earth, since his ascension. — Christ's prophetic activity is continued through the preaching of his apostles and ministers, and by the enlightening influences of his Holy Spirit (John 16 : 12–14 ; Acts 1 : 1). The apostles unfolded the germs of doctrine put into their hands by Christ. The church is, in a derivative sense, a prophetic institution, established to teach the world by its preaching and its ordinances. But Christians are prophets, only as being proclaimers of Christ's teaching (Num. 11 : 29 ; Joel 2 : 28).

John 16 : 12–14 — "I have yet many things to say unto you, but ye cannot bear them now. Howbeit when he, the Spirit of truth, is come, he shall guide you into all the truth. . . . . He shall glorify me : for he shall take of mine and shall declare it unto you " ; Acts 1 : 1 — "The former treatise I made, O Theophilus, concerning all that Jesus began both to do and to teach " = Christ's prophetic work was only *begun*, during his earthly ministry ; it is continued since his ascension. The inspiration of the apostles, the illumination of all preachers and Christians to understand and to unfold the meaning of the word they wrote, the conviction of sinners, and the sanctification of believers,— all these are parts of Christ's prophetic work, performed through the Holy Spirit.

By virtue of their union with Christ and participation in Christ's Spirit, all Christians are made in a secondary sense prophets, as well as priests and kings. Num. 11 : 29 — " Would that all Jehovah's people were prophets, that Jehovah would put his Spirit upon them "; Joel 2 : 28 — "I will pour out my spirit upon all flesh ; and your sons and your daughters shall prophesy." All modern prophecy that is true, however, is but the republication of Christ's message — the proclamation and expounding of truth already revealed in Scripture. "All so-called new prophecy, from Montanus to Swedenborg, proves its own falsity by its lack of attesting miracles."

A. A. Hodge, Popular Lectures, 242 —" Every human prophet presupposes an infinite eternal divine Prophet from whom his knowledge is received, just as every stream presupposes a fountain from which it flows. . . . . As the telescope of highest power takes into its field the narrowest segment of the sky, so Christ the prophet sometimes gives the intensest insight into the glowing centre of the heavenly world to those whom this world regards as unlearned and foolish, and the church recognizes as only babes in Christ."

(d) Christ's final revelation of the Father to his saints in glory (John 16 : 25 ; 17 : 24, 26 ; *cf.* Is. 64 : 4 ; 1 Cor. 13 : 12). — Thus Christ's prophetic work will be an endless one, as the Father whom he reveals is infinite.

John 16 : 25 —. "the hour cometh, when I shall no more speak unto you in dark sayings, but shall tell you plainly of the Father "; 17 : 24 — "I desire that where I am, they also may be with me; that they may behold my glory, which thou hast given me "; 26 — "I made known unto them thy name, and will make it known." The revelation of his own glory will be the revelation of the Father, in the Son. Is. 64 : 4 — "For from of old men have not heard, nor perceived by the ear, neither hath the eye seen a God besides thee, who worketh for him that waiteth for him "; 1 Cor. 13 : 12 — "now we see in a mirror, darkly ; but then face to face : now I know in part; but then shall I know fully even as also I was fully known." Rev. 21 : 23 —"And the city hath no need of the sun, neither of the moon, to shine upon it : for the glory of God did lighten it, and the lamp thereof is the Lamb " — not light, but lamp. Light is something generally diffused ; one sees *by* it, but one cannot see *it.*

Lamp is the narrowing down, the concentrating, the focusing of light, so that the light becomes definite and visible. So in heaven Christ will be the visible God. We shall never see the Father separate from Christ. No man or angel has at any time seen God, "whom no man hath seen, nor can see." " The only begotten Son . . . . he hath declared him," and he will forever declare him (John 1 :18; 1 Tim. 6 : 16).

The ministers of the gospel in modern times, so far as they are joined to Christ and possessed by his spirit, have a right to call themselves prophets. The prophet is one—1. sent by God and conscious of his mission; 2. with a message from God which he is under compulsion to deliver; 3. a message grounded in the truth of the past, setting it in new lights for the present, and making new applications of it for the future. The word of the Lord must come to him; it must be *his* gospel; there must be things new as well as old. All mathematics are in the simplest axiom; but it needs divine illumination to discover them. All truth was in Jesus' words, nay, in the first prophecy uttered after the Fall, but only the apostles brought it out. The prophet's message must be 4. a message for the place and time — primarily for contemporaries and present needs; 5. a message of eternal significance and worldwide influence. As the prophet's word was for the whole world, so our word may be for other worlds, that " unto the principalities and the powers in the heavenly places might be made known through the church the manifold wisdom of God' {Eph. 3 : 10). It must be also 6. a message of the kingdom and triumph of Christ, which puts over against the distractions and calamities of the present time the glowing ideal and the perfect consummation to which God is leading his people: "Blessed be the glory of Jehovah from his place"; " Jehovah is in his holy temple: let all the earth keep silence before him" (Ex. 3 : 12; Hab 2 : 20). On the whole subject of Christ's prophetic office, see Philippi, Glaubenslehre, IV, 2 : 24-27; Bruce, Humiliation of Christ, 320-330; Shedd, Dogm. Theol., 2 : 366-370.

II. THE PRIESTLY OFFICE OF CHRIST.

The priest was a person divinely appointed to transact with God on man's behalf. He fulfilled his office, first by offering sacrifice, and secondly by making intercession. In both these respects Christ is priest.

Hebrews 7 : 24-28 — "he, because he abideth forever, hath his priesthood unchangeable. Wherefore also he is able to save to the uttermost them that draw near unto God through him, seeing he ever liveth to make intercession for them. For such a high priest became us, holy, guileless, undefiled, separated from sinners, and made higher than the heavens : who needeth not daily, like those high priests, to offer up sacrifices, first for his own sins, and then for the sins of the people : for this he did once for all, when he offered up himself. For the law appointeth men high priests, having infirmity; but the word of the oath, which was after the law, appointeth a Son, perfected for evermore." The whole race was shut out from God by its sin. But God chose the Israelites as a priestly nation, Levi as a priestly tribe, Aaron as a priestly family, the high priest out of this family as type of the great high priest, Jesus Christ. J. S. Candlish, in Bib. World, Feb. 1897 : 87-97, cites the following facts with regard to our Lord's sufferings as proofs of the doctrine of atonement : 1. Christ gave up his life by a perfectly free act; 2. out of regard to God his Father and obedience to his will; 3. the bitterest element of his suffering was that he endured it at the hand of God; 4. this divine appointment and infliction of suffering is inexplicable, except as Christ endured the divine judgment against the sin of the race.

1. *Christ's Sacrificial Work, or the Doctrine of the Atonement.*

The Scriptures teach that Christ obeyed and suffered in our stead, to satisfy an immanent demand of the divine holiness, and thus remove an obstacle in the divine mind to the pardon and restoration of the guilty. This statement may be expanded and explained in a preliminary way as follows : —

(a) The fundamental attribute of God is holiness, and holiness is not self-communicating love, but self-affirming righteousness. Holiness limits and conditions love, for love can will happiness only as happiness results from or consists with righteousness, that is, with conformity to God.

We have shown in our discussion of the divine attributes (vol. 1, pages 268-275) that holiness is neither self-love nor love, but self-affirming purity and right. Those who maintain that love is self-affirming as well as self-communicating, and therefore that holiness is God's love for himself, must still admit that this self-affirming love which is holiness conditions and furnishes the standard for the self-communicating love which is benevolence. But we hold that holiness is not identical with, nor a manifestation of, love. Since self-maintenance must precede self-impartation ; and since benevolence finds its object, motive, standard, and limit in righteousness, holiness, the self-affirming attribute, can in no way be resolved into love, the self-communicating. God must first maintain his own being before he can give to another ; and this self-maintenance must have its reason and motive in the worth of that which is maintained. Holiness cannot be love, because love is irrational and capricious except as it has a standard by which it is regulated, and this standard cannot be itself love, but must be holiness. To make holiness a form of love is really to deny its existence, and with this to deny that any atonement is necessary for man's salvation.

(b) The universe is a reflection of God, and Christ the Logos is its life. God has constituted the universe, and humanity as a part of it, so as to express his holiness, positively by connecting happiness with righteousness, negatively by attaching unhappiness or suffering to sin.

We have seen, in vol. I, pages 109, 309-311, 335-338, that since Christ is the Logos, the immanent God, God revealed in nature, in humanity, and in redemption, the universe must be recognized as created, upheld and governed by the same Being who in the course of history was manifest in human form and who made atonement for human sin by his death on Calvary. As all God's creative activity has been exercised through Christ (vol. I, page 310), so it is Christ in whom all things consist or are held together (vol. I, page 311). Providence, as well as preservation, is his work. He makes the universe to reflect God, and especially God's ethical nature. That pain or loss universally and inevitably follow sin is the proof that God is unalterably opposed to moral evil ; and the demands and reproaches of conscience witness that holiness is the fundamental attribute of God's being.

(c) Christ the Logos, as the Revealer of God in the universe and in humanity, must condemn sin by visiting upon it the suffering which is its penalty ; while at the same time, as the Life of humanity, he must endure the reaction of God's holiness against sin which constitutes that penalty.

Here is a double work of Christ which Paul distinctly declares in Rom. 8 : 3 — "For what the law could not do, in that it was weak through the flesh, God, sending his own Son in the likeness of sinful flesh and for sin, condemned sin in the flesh." The meaning is that God did through Christ what the law could not do, namely, accomplish deliverance for humanity ; and did this by sending his son in a nature which in us is identified with sin. In connection with sin (περὶ ἁμαρτίας), and as an offering for sin, God condemned sin, by condemning Christ. Expositor's Greek Testament, in loco : " When the question is asked, In what sense did God send his Son ' in connection with sin', there is only one answer possible. He sent him to expiate sin by his sacrificial death. This is the centre and foundation of Paul's gospel ; see Rom. 3 : 25 sq." But whatever God did in condemning sin he did through Christ ; "God was in Christ, reconciling the world unto himself" (2 Cor. 5 : 19) ; Christ was the condemner, as well as the condemned ; conscience in us, which unites the accuser and the accused, shows us how Christ could be both the Judge and the Sin-bearer.

(d) Our personality is not self-contained. We live, move, and have our being naturally in Christ the Logos. Our reason, affection, conscience, and will are complete only in him. He is generic humanity, of which we are the offshoots. When his righteousness condemns sin, and his love voluntarily endures the suffering which is sin's penalty, humanity ratifies the judgment of God, makes full propitiation for sin, and satisfies the demands of holiness.

My personal existence is grounded in God. I cannot perceive the world outside of me nor recognize the existence of my fellow men, except as he bridges the gulf between me and the universe. Complete self-consciousness would be impossible if we did not partake of the universal Reason. The smallest child makes assumptions and uses processes of logic which are all instinctive, but which indicate the working in him of an absolute and infinite Intelligence. True love is possible only as God's love flows into us and takes possession of us; so that the poet can truly say: "Our loves in higher love endure." No human will is truly free, unless God emancipates it; only he whom the Son of God makes free is free indeed; "work out your own salvation with fear and trembling; for it is God who worketh in you both to will and to work" (Phil. 2 : 12, 13). Our moral nature, even more than our intellectual nature, witnesses that we are not sufficient to ourselves, but are complete only in him in whom we live and move and have our being (Col. 2 : 10; Acts 17 : 28). No man can make a conscience for himself. There is a common conscience, over and above the finite and individual conscience. That common conscience is one in all moral beings. John Watson: "There is no consciousness of self apart from the consciousness of other selves and things, and no consciousness of the world apart from the consciousness of the single Reality presupposed in both." This single Reality is Jesus Christ, the manifested God, the Light that lighteth every man, and the Life of all that lives (John 1 : 4, 9). He can represent humanity before God, because his immanent Deity constitutes the very essence of humanity.

(e) While Christ's love explains his willingness to endure suffering for us, only his holiness furnishes the reason for that constitution of the universe and of human nature which makes this suffering necessary. As respects us, his sufferings are substitutionary, since his divinity and his sinlessness enable him to do for us what we could never do for ourselves. Yet this substitution is also a sharing — not the work of one external to us, but of one who is the life of humanity, the soul of our soul and the life of our life, and so responsible with us for the sins of the race.

Most of the recent treatises on the Atonement have been descriptions of the effects of the Atonement upon life and character, but have thrown no light upon the Atonement itself, if indeed they have not denied its existence. We must not emphasize the effects by ignoring the cause. Scripture declares the ultimate aim of the Atonement to be that God "might himself be just" (Rom. 3 : 26); and no theory of the atonement will meet the demands of reason or conscience that does not ground its necessity in God's righteousness, rather than in his love. We acknowledge that our conceptions of atonement have suffered some change. To our fathers the atonement was a mere historical fact, a sacrifice offered in a few brief hours upon the Cross. It was a literal substitution of Christ's suffering for ours, the payment of our debt by another, and upon the ground of that payment we are permitted to go free. Those sufferings were soon over, and the hymn, " Love's Redeeming Work is Done," expressed the believer's joy in a finished redemption. And all this is true. But it is only a part of the truth. The atonement, like every other doctrine of Christianity, is a fact of life; and such facts of life cannot be crowded into our definitions, because they are greater than any definitions that we can frame. We must add to the idea of substitution the idea of sharing. Christ's doing and suffering is not that of one external and foreign to us. He is bone of our bone, and flesh of our flesh; the bearer of our humanity; yes, the very life of the race.

(f) The historical work of the incarnate Christ is not itself the atonement, — it is rather the revelation of the atonement. The suffering of the incarnate Christ is the manifestation in space and time of the eternal suffering of God on account of human sin. Yet without the historical work which was finished on Calvary, the age-long suffering of God could never have been made comprehensible to men.

The life that Christ lived in Palestine and the death that he endured on Calvary were the revelation of a union with mankind which antedated the Fall. Being thus joined to us from the beginning, he has suffered in all human sin; "in all our affliction he has been afflicted " (Is. 63 : 9); so that the Psalmist can say : "Blessed be the Lord, who daily beareth our burden, even the God who is our salvation " (Ps. 68 : 19). The historical sacrifice was a burning-glass which focused the diffused rays of the Sun of righteousness and made them effective in the melting of human hearts. The sufferings of Christ take deepest hold upon us only when we see in them the two contrasted but complementary truths: that holiness must make penalty to follow sin, and that love must share that penalty with the transgressor. The Cross was the concrete exhibition of the holiness that required, and of the love that provided, man's redemption. Those six hours of pain could never have procured our salvation if they had not been a revelation of eternal facts in the being of God. The heart of God and the meaning of all previous history were then unveiled. The whole evolution of humanity was there depicted in its essential elements, on the one hand the sin and condemnation of the race, on the other hand the grace and suffering of him who was its life and salvation. As he who hung upon the cross was God, manifest in the flesh, so the suffering of the cross was God's suffering for sin, manifest in the flesh. The imputation of our sins to him is the result of his natural union with us. He has been our substitute from the beginning. We cannot quarrel with the doctrine of substitution when we see that this substitution is but the sharing of our griefs and sorrows by him whose very life pulsates in our veins. See A. H. Strong, Christ in Creation, 72-80, 177-180.

(*g*) The historical sacrifice of our Lord is not only the final revelation of the heart of God, but also the manifestation of the law of universal life — the law that sin brings suffering to all connected with it, and that we can overcome sin in ourselves and in the world only by entering into the fellowship of Christ's sufferings and Christ's victory, or, in other words, only by union with him through faith.

We too are subject to the same law of life. We who enter into fellowship with our Lord "fill up . . . . that which is lacking of the afflictions of Christ . . . . for his body's sake, which is the church" (Col. 1:24). The Christian Church can reign with Christ only as it partakes in his suffering. The atonement becomes a model and stimulus to self-sacrifice, and a test of Christian character. But it is easy to see how the subjective effect of Christ's sacrifice may absorb the attention, to the exclusion of its ground and cause. The moral influence of the atonement has taken deep hold upon our minds, and we are in danger of forgetting that it is the holiness of God, and not the salvation of men, that primarily requires it. When sharing excludes substitution; when reconciliation of man to God excludes reconciliation of God to man; when the only peace secured is peace in the sinner's heart and no thought is given to that peace with God which it is the first object of the atonement to secure; then the whole evangelical system is weakened, God's righteousness is ignored, and man is practically put in place of God. We must not go back to the old mechanical and arbitrary conceptions of the atonement,— we must go forward to a more vital apprehension of the relation of the race to Christ. A larger knowledge of Christ, the life of humanity, will enable us to hold fast the objective nature of the atonement, and its necessity as grounded in the holiness of God; while at the same time we appropriate all that is good in the modern view of the atonement, as the final demonstration of God's constraining love which moves men to repentance and submission. See A. H. Strong, Cleveland Address, 1904 : 16-18; Dinsmore, The Atonement in Literature and in Life, 213-250.

A. Scripture Methods of Representing the Atonement.

We may classify the Scripture representations according as they conform to moral, commercial, legal or sacrificial analogies.

(*a*) MORAL. — The atonement is described as

A *provision originating in God's love,* and manifesting this love to the universe; but also as an *example of disinterested love,* to secure our deliverance from selfishness.— In these latter passages, Christ's death is referred to as a source of moral stimulus to men.

A provision : John 3 : 16 —"For God so loved the world, that he gave his only begotten Son "; Rom. 5 : 8 — "God commendeth his own love toward us, in that, while we were yet sinners, Christ died for us "; 1 John 4 : 9 — "Herein was the love of God manifested in us, that God hath sent his only begotten Son into the world that we might live through him "; Heb. 2 : 9 — "Jesus, because of the suffering of death crowned with glory and honor, that by the grace of God he should taste of death for every man " —redemption originated in the love of the Father, as well as in that of the Son.— *An example :* Luke 9 : 22-24 — "The Son of man must suffer . . . and be killed. . . . If any man would come after me, let him . . . . take up his cross daily, and follow me . . . . whosoever shall lose his life for my sake, the same shall save it "; 2 Cor. 5 : 15 — "he died for all, that they that live should no longer live unto themselves "; Gal. 1 : 4 — "gave himself for our sins, that he might deliver us out of this present

evil world " ; Eph. 5 : 25-27 — "Christ also loved the church, and gave himself up for it; that he might sanctify it",
Col. 1 : 22 — "reconciled in the body of his flesh through death, to present you holy"; Titus 2 : 14 — "gave himself for
us, that he might redeem us from all iniquity, and purify"; 1 Pet. 2 : 21-24 — "Christ also suffered for you, leaving you
an example, that ye should follow his steps: who did no sin . . . . who his own self bare our sins in his body upon the
tree, that we, having died unto sins, might live unto righteousness." Mason, Faith of the Gospel, 181 —
"A pious cottager, on hearing the text, 'God so loved the world,' exclaimed: 'Ah, that *was*
love! I could have given myself, but I could never have given my son.'" There was
a wounding of the Father through the heart of the Son: "they shall look unto *me* whom they
have pierced; and they shall mourn for *him*, as one mourneth for his only son" (Zech. 12 : 10).

(b) COMMERCIAL. — The atonement is described as

A *ransom*, paid to free us from the bondage of sin (note in these passages the use of ἀντί, the preposition of price, bargain, exchange). — In
these passages, Christ's death is represented as the price of our deliverance
from sin and death.

Mat. 20 : 28, and Mark 10 : 45 — "to give his life a ransom for many" — λύτρον ἀντὶ πολλῶν. 1 Tim. 2 : 6 —
"who gave himself a ransom for all" — ἀντίλυτρον. 'Αντί ("for," in the sense of "instead of") is
never confounded with ὑπέρ ("for," in the sense of "in behalf of," "for the benefit of").
'Αντί is the preposition of price, bargain, exchange ; and this signification is traceable in
every passage where it occurs in the N. T. See Mat. 2 : 22 — "Archelaus was reigning over Judea in
the room of [ἀντί] his father Herod " ; Luke 11 : 11 — "shall his son ask . . . . a fish, and he for [ἀντί] a fish give
him a serpent ?" Heb. 12 : 2 — "Jesus the author and perfecter of our faith, who for [ἀντί = as the price of]
the joy that was set before him endured the cross"; 16 — "Esau, who for [ἀντί = in exchange for] one mess
of meat sold his own birthright." See also Mat. 16 : 26 —"what shall a man give in exchange for (ἀντάλλαγμα) his
life" — how shall he buy it back, when once he has lost it ? 'Αντίλυτρον — substitutionary
ransom. The connection in 1 Tim. 2 : 6 requires that ὑπέρ should mean "instead of." We
should interpret this ὑπέρ by the ἀντί in Mat. 20 : 28. "Something befell Christ, and by
reason of that, the same thing need not befall sinners " (E. Y. Mullins).
Meyer, on Mat. 20 : 28 — "to give his life a ransom for many "—" The ψυχή is conceived of as λύτρον,
a ransom, for, through the shedding of the blood, it becomes the τιμή (price) of redemption." See also 1 Cor. 6 : 20 ; 7 : 23 — "ye were bought with a price "; and 2 Pet. 2 : 1 — "denying even the
Master that bought them." The word "redemption," indeed, means simply "repurchase," or
"the state of being repurchased "— *i. e.*, delivered by the payment of a price. Rev. 5 : 9 —
"thou wast slain, and didst purchase unto God with thy blood men of every tribe." Winer, N. T. Grammar,
258 — "In Greek, ἀντί is the preposition of price." Buttmann, N. T. Grammar, 321 —
"In the signification of the preposition ἀντί (instead of, for), no deviation occurs from
ordinary usage." See Grimm's Wilke, Lexicon Græco-Lat.: " ἀντί, *in vicem, anstatt* ";
Thayer, Lexicon N. T. — " ἀντί, of that for which anything is given, received, endured ;
. . . . of the price of sale (or purchase) Mat. 20 : 28 "; also Cremer, N. T. Lex., on
ἀντάλλαγμα.
Pfleiderer, in New World, Sept. 1899, doubts whether Jesus ever really uttered the
words "give his life a ransom for many " (Mat. 20 : 28). He regards them as essentially Pauline,
and the result of later dogmatic reflection on the death of Jesus as a means of
redemption. So Paine, Evolution of Trinitarianism, 377-381. But these words occur
not in Luke, the Pauline gospel, but in Matthew, which is much earlier. They represent at any rate the apostolic conception of Jesus' teaching, a conception which Jesus
himself promised should be formed under the guidance of the Holy Spirit, who should
bring all things to the remembrance of his apostles and should guide them into all the
truth (John 14 : 26 ; 16 : 13). As will be seen below, Pfleiderer declares the Pauline doctrine
to be that of substitutionary suffering.

(c) LEGAL. — The atonement is described as

An act of *obedience* to the law which sinners had violated ; a *penalty*,
borne in order to rescue the guilty ; and an *exhibition* of God's righteousness, necessary to the vindication of his procedure in the pardon and restoration of sinners. — In these passages the death of Christ is represented
as demanded by God's law and government.

Obedience: Gal. 4 : 4, 5 — "born of a woman, born under the law, that he might redeem them that were under
the law": Mat. 3 : 15 — "thus it becometh us to fulfil all righteousness " — Christ's baptism prefigured

his death, and was a consecration to death ; cf. Mark 10 : 38 — "Are ye able to drink the cup that I drink ? or to be baptized with the baptism that I am baptized with ?" Luke 12 : 50 — "I have a baptism to be baptized with; and how am I straitened till it be accomplished !" Mat. 26 : 39 — "My Father, if it be possible, let this cup pass away from me: nevertheless, not as I will, but as thou wilt "; 5 : 17 — "Think not that I came to destroy the law or the prophets : I came not to destroy, but to fulfil "; Phil. 2 : 8 — "becoming obedient even unto death "; Rom. 5 : 19 — "through the obedience of the one shall the many be made righteous "; 10 : 4 — "Christ is the end of the law unto righteousness to every one that believeth." — Penalty : Rom. 4 : 25 — "who was delivered up for our trespasses, and was raised for our justification "; 8 : 3 — "God, sending his own Son in the likeness of sinful flesh and for sin, condemned sin in the flesh "; 2 Cor. 5 : 21 — " Him who knew no sin he made to be sin on our behalf " — here "sin "— a sinner, an accursed one (Meyer) ; Gal. 1 : 4 — " gave himself for our sins "; 3 : 13 — "Christ redeemed us from the curse of the law, having become a curse for us ; for it is written, Cursed is every one that hangeth on a tree "; cf. Deut. 21 : 23 — "he that is hanged is accursed of God." Heb. 9 : 28 — "Christ also, having been once offered to bear the sins of many "; cf. Lev. 5 : 17 —"if any one sin .... yet is he guilty, and shall bear his iniquity "; Num. 14 : 34 —"for every day a year, shall ye bear your iniquities, even forty years "; Lam. 5 : 7 — "Our fathers sinned and are not; And we have borne their iniquities." — Exhibition : Rom. 3 : 25, 26 — "whom God set forth to be a propitiation, through faith, in his blood, to show his righteousness because of the passing over of the sins done aforetime, in the forbearance of God "; cf. Heb. 9 : 15 — "a death having taken place for the redemption of the transgressions that were under the first covenant."

On these passages, see an excellent section in Pfleiderer, Die Ritschl'sche Theologie, 38–53. Pfleiderer severely criticizes Ritschl's evasion of their natural force and declares Paul's teaching to be that Christ has redeemed us from the curse of the law by suffering as a substitute the death threatened by the law against sinners. So Orelli Cone, Paul, 261. On the other hand, L. L. Paine, Evolution of Trinitarianism, 288-307, chapter on the New Christian Atonement, holds that Christ taught only reconciliation on condition of repentance. Paul added the idea of mediation drawn from the Platonic dualism of Philo. The Epistle to the Hebrews made Christ a sacrificial victim to propitiate God, so that the reconciliation became Godward instead of manward. But Professor Paine's view that Paul taught an Arian Mediatorship is incorrect. "God was in Christ" (2 Cor. 5 : 19) and God "manifested in the flesh " (1 Tim. 3 : 16) are the keynote of Paul's teaching, and this is identical with John's doctrine of the Logos: "the Word was God," and "the Word became flesh " (John 1 : 1, 14).

The Outlook, December 15, 1900, in criticizing Prof. Paine, states three postulates of the New Trinitarianism as : 1. The essential kinship of God and man,— in man there is an essential divineness, in God there is an essential humanness. 2. The divine immanence,— this universal presence gives nature its physical unity, and humanity its moral unity. This is not pantheism, any more than the presence of man's spirit in all he thinks and does proves that man's spirit is only the sum of his experiences. 3. God transcends all phenomena,— though in all, he is greater than all. He entered perfectly into one man, and through this indwelling in one man he is gradually entering into all men and filling all men with his fulness, so that Christ will be the first-born among many brethren. The defects of this view, which contains many elements of truth, are : 1. That it regards Christ as the product instead of the Producer, the divinely formed man instead of the humanly acting God, the head man among men instead of the Creator and Life of humanity ; 2. That it therefore renders impossible any divine bearing of the sins of all men by Jesus Christ, and substitutes for it such a histrionic exhibition of God's feeling and such a beauty of example as are possible within the limits of human nature, — in other words, there is no real Deity of Christ and no objective atonement.

(d) SACRIFICIAL. — The atonement is described as

A work of *priestly mediation*, which reconciles God to men, — notice here that the term ' reconciliation ' has its usual sense of removing enmity, not from the offending, but from the offended party ; — a *sin-offering*, presented on behalf of transgressors ; — a *propitiation*, which satisfies the demands of violated holiness ; — and a *substitution*, of Christ's obedience and sufferings for ours. — These passages, taken together, show that Christ's death is demanded by God's attribute of justice, or holiness, if sinners are to be saved.

Priestly mediation : Heb. 9 : 11 : 12 —"Christ having come a high priest, ... nor yet through the blood of goats and calves, but through his own blood, entered in once for all into the holy place, having obtained eternal redemption " ; Rom. 5 : 10 —"while we were enemies, we were reconciled to God through the death of his Son " ; 2 Cor. 5 : 18, 19 — "all things are of God, who reconciled us to himself through Christ . . . . God was in Christ reconciling the world unto himself, not reckoning unto them their trespasses " ; Eph. 2 : 16 — "might reconcile them both in one body unto God through the cross, having slain the enmity thereby " ; cf. 12, 13, 19 — "strangers from the covenants of the promise . . . . far off . . . . no more strangers and sojourners, but ye are fellow-citizens with the saints, and of the household of God " ; Col. 1 : 20 —"through him to reconcile all things unto himself, having made peace through the blood of his cross."

On all these passages, see Meyer, who shows the meaning of the apostle to be, that " we were 'enemies,' not actively, as hostile to God, but passively, as those with whom God was angry." The epistle to the Romans begins with the revelation of wrath against Gentile and Jew alike (Rom. 1 : 18). " While we were enemies " (Rom. 5 : 10) — " when God was hostile to us." "Reconciliation " is therefore the removal of God's wrath toward man. Meyer, on this last passage, says that Christ's death does not remove man's wrath toward God [this is not the work of Christ, but of the Holy Spirit]. The offender reconciles the person offended, not himself. See Denney, Com. on Rom. 5 : 9-11, in Expositor's Gk. Test.

Cf. Num. 25 : 13, where Phinehas, by slaying Zimri, is said to have "made atonement for the children of Israel." Surely, the "atonement " here cannot be a reconciliation of Israel. The action terminates, not on the subject, but on the object — God. So, 1 Sam. 29 : 4 —"wherewith should this fellow reconcile himself unto his lord ? should it not be with the heads of these men ? " Mat. 5 : 23, 24 — "If therefore thou art offering thy gift at the altar, and there rememberest that thy brother hath aught against thee, leave there thy gift before the altar, and go thy way, first be reconciled to thy brother [i. e., remove his enmity, not thine own], and then come and offer thy gift." See Shedd, Dogm. Theol., 2 : 387-398.

Pfleiderer, Die Ritschl'sche Theologie, 42 — " Ἐχθροὶ ὄντες (Rom. 5 : 10) — not the active disposition of enmity to God on our part, but our passive condition under the enmity or wrath of God." Paul was not the author of this doctrine,—he claims that he received it from Christ himself (Gal. 1 : 12). Simon, Reconciliation, 167 — " The idea that only man needs to be reconciled arises from a false conception of the unchangeableness of God. But God would be unjust, if his relation to man were the same after his sin as it was before." The old hymn expressed the truth. " My God is reconciled ; His pardoning voice I hear ; He owns me for his child ; I can no longer fear ; With filial trust I now draw nigh, And 'Father, Abba, Father' cry."

A sin-offering: John 1 : 29 — "Behold, the Lamb of God, that taketh away the sin of the world " — here αἴρων means to take away by taking or bearing ; to take, and so take away. It is an allusion to the sin-offering of Isaiah 53 : 6-12 — " when thou shalt make his soul an offering for sin . . . . as a lamb that is led to the slaughter . . . . Jehovah hath laid on him the iniquity of us all." Mat. 26 : 28 — "this is my blood of the covenant, which is poured out for many unto remission of sins " ; cf. Ps. 50 : 5 — "made a covenant with me by sacrifice." 1 John 1 : 7 — "the blood of Jesus his Son cleanseth us from all sin " — not sanctification, but justification ; 1 Cor. 5 : 7 — "our passover also hath been sacrificed, even Christ"; cf. Deut. 16 : 2-6 — "thou shalt sacrifice the passover unto Jehovah thy God." Eph. 5 : 2 — "gave himself up for us, an offering and a sacrifice to God for an odor of a sweet smell " (see Com. of Salmond, in Expositor's Greek Testament); Heb. 9 : 14 — "the blood of Christ, who through the eternal Spirit offered himself without blemish unto God " ; 22, 26 — "apart from shedding of blood there is no remission . . . . now once in the end of the ages hath he been manifested to put away sin by the sacrifice of himself" ; 1 Pet. 1 : 18, 19 — "redeemed . . . . with precious blood, as of a lamb without blemish and without spot, even the blood of Christ." See Expos. Gk. Test., on Eph. 1 : 7.

Lowrie, Doctrine of St. John, 35, points out that John 6 : 52-59 — " eateth my flesh and drinketh my blood " — is Christ's reference to his death in terms of sacrifice. So, as we shall see below, it is a propitiation (1 John 2 : 2). We therefore strongly object to the statement of Wilson, Gospel of Atonement, 64 —"Christ's death is a sacrifice, if sacrifice means the crowning instance of that suffering of the innocent for the guilty which springs from the solidarity of mankind ; but there is no thought of substitution or expiation." Wilson forgets that this necessity of suffering arises from God's righteousness ; that without this suffering man cannot be saved ; that Christ endures what we, on account of the insensibility of sin, cannot feel or endure ; that this suffering takes the place of ours, so that we are saved thereby. Wilson holds that the Incarnation constituted the Atonement, and that all thought of expiation may be eliminated. Henry B. Smith far better summed up the gospel in the words: "Incarnation in order to Atonement." We regard as still better the words: "Incarnation in order to reveal the Atonement."

A propitiation: Rom. 3 : 25, 26 — " whom God set forth to be a propitiation, . . . in his blood . . . that he might himself be just, and the justifier of him that hath faith in Jesus." A full and critical exposition of this passage will be found under the Ethical Theory of the Atonement, pages 750-760. Here it is sufficient to say that it shows: (1) that Christ's death is a propitiatory sacrifice: (2) that its first and main effect is upon God; (3) that the particular attribute in God which demands the atonement is his justice, or holiness; (4) that the satisfaction of this holiness is the necessary condition of God's justifying the believer.

Compare Luke 18 : 13, marg.—"God, be thou merciful unto me the sinner"; lit. : "God be propitiated toward me the sinner"—by the sacrifice, whose smoke was ascending before the publican, even while he prayed. Heb. 2 : 17—"a merciful and faithful high priest in things pertaining to God, to make propitiation for the sins of the people"; 1 John 2 : 2—"and he is the propitiation for our sins; and not for ours only, but also for the whole world"; 4 : 10—"Herein is love, not that we loved God, but that he loved us, and sent his Son to be the propitiation for our sins"; cf. Gen. 32 : 20, LXX.—" I will appease [ἐξιλάσομαι, 'propitiate'] him with the present that goeth before me"; Prov. 16 : 14, LXX.—"The wrath of a king is as messengers of death; but a wise man will pacify it" [ἐξιλάσεται, 'propitiate it'].

On propitiation, see Foster, Christian Life and Theology, 216—"Something was thereby done which rendered God inclined to pardon the sinner. God is made inclined to forgive sinners by the sacrifice, because his righteousness was exhibited by the infliction of the penalty of sin; but not because he needed to be inclined in heart to love the sinner or to exercise his mercy. In fact, it was he himself who 'set forth' Jesus as 'a propitiation' (Rom. 3 : 25, 26)." Paul never merges the objective atonement in its subjective effects, although no writer of the New Testament has more fully recognized these subjective effects. With him Christ *for* us upon the Cross is the necessary preparation for Christ *in* us by his Spirit. Gould, Bib. Theol. N. T., 74, 75, 89, 172, unwarrantably contrasts Paul's representation of Christ as priest with what he calls the representation of Christ as prophet in the Epistle to the Hebrews: " The priest says : Man's return to God is not enough,— there must be an expiation of man's sin. This is Paul's doctrine. The prophet says : There never was a divine provision for sacrifice. Man's return to God is the thing wanted. But this return must be completed. Jesus is the perfect prophet who gives us an example of restored obedience, and who comes in to perfect man's imperfect work. This is the doctrine of the Epistle to the Hebrews." This recognition of expiation in Paul's teaching, together with denial of its validity and interpretation of the Epistle to the Hebrews as prophetic rather than priestly, is a curiosity of modern exegesis.

Lyman Abbott, Theology of an Evolutionist, 107-127, goes still further and affirms : " In the N. T. God is never said to be propitiated, nor is it ever said that Jesus Christ propitiates God or satisfies God's wrath." Yet Dr. Abbott adds that in the N. T. God is represented as self-propitiated : " Christianity is distinguished from paganism by representing God as appeasing his own wrath and satisfying his own justice by the forth-putting of his own love." This self-propitiation however must not be thought of as a bearing of penalty : "Nowhere in the O. T. is the idea of a sacrifice coupled with the idea of penalty,— it is always coupled with purification—'with his stripes we are healed' (Is. 53 : 5). And in the N. T., 'the Lamb of God . . . taketh away the sin of the world' (John 1 : 29); 'the blood of Jesus . . . cleanseth' (1 John 1 : 7). . . . What humanity needs is not the removal of the penalty, but removal of the sin." This seems to us a distinct contradiction of both Paul and John, with whom propitiation is an essential of Christian doctrine (see Rom. 3 : 25; 1 John 2 : 2), while we grant that the propitiation is made, not by sinful man, but by God himself in the person of his Son. See George B. Gow, on The Place of Expiation in Human Redemption, Am. Jour. Theol., 1900 : 734-756.

A substitution : Luke 22 : 37—"he was reckoned with transgressors": cf. Lev. 16 : 21, 22—"and Aaron shall lay both his hands upon the head of the live goat, and confess over him all the iniquities of the children of Israel . . . . he shall put them upon the head of the goat . . . . and the goat shall bear upon him all their iniquities unto a solitary land "; Is. 53 : 5, 6—"he was wounded for our transgressions, he was bruised for our iniquities ; the chastisement of our peace was upon him; and with his stripes we are healed. All we like sheep have gone astray ; we have turned every one to his own way; and Jehovah hath laid on him the iniquity of us all." John 10 : 11—"the good shepherd layeth down his life for the sheep"; Rom. 5 : 6-8—" while we were yet weak, in due season Christ died for the ungodly. For scarcely for a righteous man will one die : for peradventure for the good man some one would even dare to die. But God commendeth his own love toward us, in that, while we were yet sinners, Christ died for us "; 1 Pet. 3 : 18—"Christ also suffered for sins once, the righteous for the unrighteous, that he might bring us to God."

To these texts we must add all those mentioned under (b) above, in which Christ's death is described as a ransom. Besides Meyer's comment, there quoted, on Mat. 20 : 28— "to give his life a ransom for many," λύτρον ἀντὶ πολλῶν—Meyer also says : " ἀντί denotes substitution. That which is given as a ransom takes the place of, is given instead of, those who are to be set free in consideration thereof. Ἀντί can only be understood in the sense of substitution in the act of which the ransom is presented as an equivalent, to secure the deliverance of those on whose behalf the ransom is paid, — a view which is only confirmed by the fact that, in other parts of the N. T., this ransom is usually spoken of as an expiatory sacrifice. That which they [those for whom the ransom is paid] are redeemed from, is the eternal ἀπώλεια in which, as having the wrath of God abiding upon them, they would remain imprisoned, as in a state of hopeless bondage, unless the guilt of their sins were expiated."

Cremer, N. T. Lex., says that "in both the N. T. texts, Mat. 16 : 26 and Mark 8 : 37, the word ἀντάλλαγμα, like λύτρον, is akin to the conception of atonement: *cf.* Is. 43 : 3, 4; 51 : 11; Amos 5 : 12. This is a confirmation of the fact that satisfaction and substitution essentially belong to the idea of atonement." Dorner, Glaubenslehre, 2 : 515 (Syst. Doct., 3 : 414)—" Mat. 20 : 28 contains the thought of a substitution. While the whole world is not of equal worth with the soul, and could not purchase it, Christ's death and work are so valuable, that they can serve as a ransom."

The sufferings of the righteous were recognized in Rabbinical Judaism as having a substitutionary significance for the sins of others; see Weber, Altsynagog. Palestin. Theologie, 314 ; Schürer, Geschichte des jüdischen Volkes, 2 : 466 (translation, div. II, vol. 2 : 186). But Wendt, Teaching of Jesus, 2 : 225–262, says this idea of vicarious satisfaction was an addition of Paul to the teaching of Jesus. Wendt grants that both Paul and John taught substitution, but he denies that Jesus did. He claims that ἀντί in Mat. 20 : 28 means simply that Jesus gave his life as a means whereby he obtains the deliverance of many. But this interpretation is a non-natural one, and violates linguistic usage. It holds that Paul and John misunderstood or misrepresented the words of our Lord. We prefer the frank acknowledgment by Pfleiderer that Jesus, as well as Paul and John, taught substitution, but that neither one of them was correct. Colestock, on Substitution as a Stage in Theological Thought, similarly holds that the idea of substitution must be abandoned. We grant that the idea of substitution needs to be supplemented by the idea of sharing, and so relieved of its external and mechanical implications, but that to abandon the conception itself is to abandon faith in the evangelists and in Jesus himself.

Dr. W. N. Clarke, in his Christian Theology, rejects the doctrine of retribution for sin, and denies the possibility of penal suffering for another. A proper view of penalty, and of Christ's vital connection with humanity, would make these rejected ideas not only credible but inevitable. Dr. Alvah Hovey reviews Dr. Clarke's Theology, Am. Jour. Theology, Jan. 1899 : 205—" If we do not import into the endurance of penalty some degree of sinful feeling or volition, there is no ground for denying that a holy being may bear it in place of a sinner. For nothing but wrong-doing, or approval of wrong-doing, is impossible to a holy being. Indeed, for one to bear for another the just penalty of his sin, provided that other may thereby be saved from it and made a friend of God, is perhaps the highest conceivable function of love or good-will." Denney, Studies, 126, 127, shows that "substitution means simply that man is dependent for his acceptance with God upon something which Christ has done for him, and which he could never have done and never needs to do for himself. . . . The forfeiting of his free life has freed our forfeited lives. This substitution can be preached, and it binds men to Christ by making them forever dependent on him. The condemnation of our sins in Christ upon his cross is the barb on the hook,— without it your bait will be taken, but you will not catch men; you will not annihilate pride, and make Christ the Alpha and Omega in man's redemption." On the Scripture proofs, see Crawford, Atonement, 1 : 1–193; Dale, Atonement, 65–256; Philippi, Glaubenslehre, iv. 2 : 243–342; Smeaton, Our Lord's and the Apostles' Doctrine of Atonement.

An examination of the passages referred to shows that, while the forms in which the atoning work of Christ is described are in part derived from moral, commercial, and legal relations, the prevailing language is that of sacrifice. A correct view of the atonement must therefore be grounded upon a proper interpretation of the institution of sacrifice, especially as found in the Mosaic system.

The question is sometimes asked: Why is there so little in Jesus' own words about atonement? Dr. R. W. Dale replies: Because Christ did not come to preach the gospel, —he came that there might be a gospel to preach. The Cross had to be endured, before it could be explained. Jesus came to *be* the sacrifice, not to *speak* about it. But his reticence is just what he told us we should find in his words. He proclaimed their incompleteness, and referred us to a subsequent Teacher — the Holy Spirit. The testimony of the Holy Spirit we have in the words of the apostles. We must remember that the gospels were supplementary to the epistles, not the epistles to the gospels.

722 CHRISTOLOGY, OR THE DOCTRINE OF REDEMPTION.

The gospels merely fill out our knowledge of Christ. It is not for the Redeemer to magnify the cost of salvation, but for the redeemed. "None of the ransomed ever knew." The doer of a great deed has the least to say about it.

Harnack: "There is an inner law which compels the sinner to look upon God as a wrathful Judge. . . . Yet no other feeling is possible." We regard this confession as a demonstration of the psychological correctness of Paul's doctrine of a vicarious atonement. Human nature has been so constituted by God that it reflects the demand of his holiness. That conscience needs to be appeased is proof that God needs to be appeased. When Whiton declares that propitiation is offered only to our conscience, which is the wrath of that which is of God within us, and that Christ bore our sins, not in substitution for us, but in fellowship with us, to rouse our consciences to hatred of them, he forgets that God is not only immanent in the conscience but also tran-scendent, and that the verdicts of conscience are only indications of the higher verdicts of God: 1 John 3 : 20 — "if our heart condemn us, God is greater than our heart, and knoweth all things." Lyman Abbott, Theology of an Evolutionist, 57 — " A people half emancipated from the pagan-ism that imagines that God must be placated by sacrifice before he can forgive sins gave to the sacrificial system that Israel had borrowed from paganism the same divine authority which they gave to those revolutionary elements in the system which were destined eventually to sweep it entirely out of existence." So Bowne, Atone-ment, 74 — "The essential moral fact is that, if God is to forgive unrighteous men, some way must be found of making them righteous. The difficulty is not forensic, but moral." Both Abbott and Bowne regard righteousness as a mere form of benevolence, and the atonement as only a means to a utilitarian end, namely, the restoration and happiness of the creature. A more correct view of God's righteousness as the funda-mental attribute of his being, as inwrought into the constitution of the universe, and as infallibly connecting suffering with sin, would have led these writers to see a divine wisdom and inspiration in the institution of sacrifice, and a divine necessity that God should suffer if man is to go free.

B. The Institution of Sacrifice, more especially as found in the Mosaic system.

(a) We may dismiss as untenable, on the one hand, the theory that sacrifice is essentially the presentation of a gift (Hofmann, Baring-Gould) or a feast (Spencer) to the Deity ; and on the other hand the theory that sacrifice is a symbol of renewed fellowship (Keil), or of the grateful offer-ing to God of the whole life and being of the worshiper (Bähr). Neither of these theories can explain the fact that the sacrifice is a bloody offering, involving the suffering and death of the victim, and brought, not by the simply grateful, but by the conscience-stricken soul.

For the views of sacrifice here mentioned, see Hofmann, Schriftbeweis, II, 1 : 214-294; Baring-Gould, Origin and Devel. of Relig. Belief, 368-390; Spencer, De Legibus Hebræ-orum ; Keil, Bib. Archäologie, sec. 43, 47 ; Bähr, Symbolik des Mosaischen Cultus, 2 : 196, 269 ; also synopsis of Bähr's view, in Bib. Sac., Oct. 1870 : 593 ; Jan. 1871 : 171. *Per contra*, see Crawford, Atonement, 228-240 ; Lange, Introd. to Com. on Exodus, 38 —"The heathen change God's symbols into myths (rationalism), as the Jews change God's sac-rifices into meritorious service (ritualism)." Westcott, Hebrews, 281-294, seems to hold with Spencer that sacrifice is essentially a feast made as an offering to God. So Philo : " God receives the faithful offerer to his own table, giving him back part of the sacrifice." Compare with this the ghosts in Homer's Odyssey, who receive strength from drinking the blood of the sacrifices. Bähr's view is only half of the truth. Reun-ion presupposes Expiation. Lyttleton, in Lux Mundi, 281 — " The sinner must first expiate his sin by suffering, — then only can he give to God the life thus purified by an expiatory death." Jahn, Bib. Archæology, sec. 373, 378 — " It is of the very idea of the sacrifice that the victim shall be presented directly to God, and in the presentation shall be destroyed." Bowne, Philos. of Theism, 253, speaks of the delicate feeling of the Biblical critic who, with his mouth full of beef or mutton, professes to be shocked at the cruelty to animals involved in the temple sacrifices. Lord Bacon : " Hiero-glyphics came before letters, and parables before arguments." " The old dispensation was God's great parable to man. The Theocracy was graven all over with divine hiero-glyphics. Does there exist the Rosetta stone by which we can read these hieroglyphics?

The shadows, that have been shortening up into definiteness of outline, pass away and vanish utterly under the full meridian splendor of the Sun of Righteousness." On Eph. 1 : 7 — "the blood of Christ," as an expiatory sacrifice which secures our justification, see Salmond, in Expositor's Greek Testament.

(*b*) The true import of the sacrifice, as is abundantly evident from both heathen and Jewish sources, embraced three elements,— first, that of satisfaction to offended Deity, or propitiation offered to violated holiness ; secondly, that of substitution of suffering and death on the part of the innocent, for the deserved punishment of the guilty ; and, thirdly, community of life between the offerer and the victim. Combining these three ideas, we have as the total import of the sacrifice : Satisfaction by substitution, and substitution by incorporation. The bloody sacrifice among the heathen expressed the consciousness that sin involves guilt ; that guilt exposes man to the righteous wrath of God ; that without expiation of that guilt there is no forgiveness ; and that through the suffering of another who shares his life the sinner may expiate his sin.

Luthardt, Compendium der Dogmatik, 170, quotes from Nägelsbach, Nachhomerische Theologie, 338 *sq.* — "The essence of punishment is retribution (Vergeltung), and retribution is a fundamental law of the world-order. In retribution lies the atoning power of punishment. This consciousness that the nature of sin demands retribution, in other words, this certainty that there is in Deity a righteousness that punishes sin, taken in connection with the consciousness of personal transgression, awakens the longing for atonement," — which is expressed in the sacrifice of a slaughtered beast. The Greeks recognized representative expiation, not only in the sacrifice of beasts, but in human sacrifices. See examples in Tyler, Theol. Gk. Poets, 196, 197, 245-253 ; see also Virgil, Æneid, 5 : 815 — " Unum pro multis dabitur caput " ; Ovid, Fasti, vi — " Cor pro corde, precor ; pro fibris sumite fibras. Hanc animam vobis pro meliore damus."

Stahl, Christliche Philosophie, 146 — " Every unperverted conscience declares the eternal law of righteousness that punishment shall follow inevitably on sin. In the moral realm, there is another way of satisfying righteousness — that of atonement. This differs from punishment in its effect, that is, reconciliation, — the moral authority asserting itself, not by the destruction of the offender, but by taking him up into itself and uniting itself to him. But the offender cannot offer his own sacrifice, — that must be done by the priest." In the Prometheus Bound, of Æschylus, Hermes says to Prometheus : " Hope not for an end to such oppression, until a god appears as thy substitute in torment, ready to descend for thee into the unillumined realm of Hades and the dark abyss of Tartarus." And this is done by Chiron, the wisest and most just of the Centaurs, the son of Chronos, sacrificing himself for Prometheus, while Hercules kills the eagle at his breast and so delivers him from torment. This legend of Æschylus is almost a prediction of the true Redeemer. See article on Sacrifice, by Paterson, in Hastings, Bible Dictionary.

Westcott, Hebrews, 282, maintains that the idea of expiatory offerings, answering to the consciousness of sin, does not belong to the early religion of Greece. We reply that Homer's Iliad, in its first book, describes just such an expiatory offering made to Phœbus Apollo, so turning away his wrath and causing the plague that wastes the Greeks to cease. E. G. Robinson held that there is " no evidence that the Jews had any idea of the efficacy of sacrifice for the expiation of moral guilt." But in approaching either the tabernacle or the temple the altar always presented itself before the laver. H. Clay Trumbull, S. S. Times, Nov. 30, 1901 : 801 — " The Passover was not a passing by of the houses of Israelites, but a passing over or crossing over by Jehovah to enter the homes of those who would welcome him and who had entered into covenant with him by sacrifice. The Oriental sovereign was accompanied by his executioner, who entered to smite the first-born of the house only when there was no covenanting at the door." We regard this explanation as substituting an incidental result and effect of sacrifice for the sacrifice itself. This always had in it the idea of reparation for wrong-doing by substitutionary suffering.

Curtis. Primitive Semitic Religion of To-day, on the Significance of Sacrifice, 218-237, tells us that he went to Palestine prepossessed by Robertson Smith's explanation that sacrifice was a feast symbolizing friendly communion between man and his God. He came to the conclusion that the sacrificial meal was not the primary element, but that there was a substitutionary value in the offering. Gift and feast are not excluded; but these are sequences and incidentals. Misfortune is evidence of sin; sin needs to be expiated; the anger of God needs to be removed. The sacrifice consisted principally in the shedding of the blood of the victim. The "bursting forth of the blood" satisfied and bought off the Deity. George Adam Smith on Isaiah 53 (2 : 364) — "Innocent as he is, he gives his life as a satisfaction to the divine law for the guilt of his people. His death was no mere martyrdom or miscarriage of human justice: in God's intent and purpose, but also by its own voluntary offering, it was an expiatory sacrifice. There is no exegete but agrees to this. 353 — The substitution of the servant of Jehovah for the guilty people and the redemptive force of that substitution are no arbitrary doctrine."

Satisfaction means simply that there is a principle in God's being which not simply refuses sin passively, but also opposes it actively. The judge, if he be upright, must repel a bribe with indignation, and the pure woman must flame out in anger against an infamous proposal. R. W. Emerson: "Your goodness must have some edge to it, — else it is none." But the judge and the woman do not enjoy this repelling, — they suffer rather. So God's satisfaction is no gloating over the pain or loss which he is compelled to inflict. God has a wrath which is calm, judicial, inevitable — the natural reaction of holiness against unholiness. Christ suffers both as one with the inflicter and as one with those on whom punishment is inflicted: "For Christ also pleased not himself; but, as it is written, The reproaches of them that reproached thee fell on me " (Rom. 15 : 3 ; *cf*. Ps. 69 : 9).

(*c*) In considering the exact purport and efficacy of the Mosaic sacrifices, we must distinguish between their theocratical, and their spiritual, offices. They were, on the one hand, the appointed means whereby the offender could be restored to the outward place and privileges, as member of the theocracy, which he had forfeited by neglect or transgression; and they accomplished this purpose irrespectively of the temper and spirit with which they were offered. On the other hand, they were symbolic of the vicarious sufferings and death of Christ, and obtained forgiveness and acceptance with God only as they were offered in true penitence, and with faith in God's method of salvation.

Heb. 9 : 13, 14 — "For if the blood of goats and bulls, and the ashes of a heifer sprinkling them that have been defiled, sanctify unto the cleanness of the flesh : how much more shall the blood of Christ, who through the eternal Spirit offered himself without blemish unto God, cleanse your conscience from dead works to serve the living God ? " 10 : 3, 4 — "But in those sacrifices there is a remembrance made of sins year by year. For it is impossible that the blood of bulls and goats should take away sins." Christ's death also, like the O. T. sacrifices, works temporal benefit even to those who have no faith ; see pages 771, 772.

Robertson, Early Religion of Israel, 441, 448, answers the contention of the higher critics that, in the days of Isaiah, Micah, Hosea, Jeremiah, no Levitical code existed — that these prophets expressed disapproval of the whole sacrificial system, as a thing of mere human device and destitute of divine sanction. But the Book of the Covenant surely existed in their day, with its command : "An altar of earth shalt thou make unto me, and shalt sacrifice thereon thy burnt-offerings" (Ex. 20 : 24). Or, if it is maintained that Isaiah condemned even that early piece of legislation, it proves too much, for it would make the prophet also condemn the Sabbath as a piece of will-worship, and even reject prayer as displeasing to God, since in the same connection he says : "new moon and Sabbath . . . . I cannot away with . . . . when ye spread forth your hands, I will hide mine eyes from you" (Is. 1 : 13–15). Isaiah was condemning simply *heartless* sacrifice ; else we make him condemn all that went on at the temple. Micah 6 : 8 — "what doth Jehovah require of thee, but to do justly?" This does not exclude the offering of sacrifice, for Micah anticipates the time when "the mountain of Jehovah's house shall be established on the top of the mountains, ... And many nations shall go and say, Come ye and let us go up to the mountain of Jehovah" (Micah 4 : 1, 2). Hos. 6 : 6 — "I desire goodness, and not sacrifice," is interpreted by what follows, "and the knowledge of God more than burnt-offerings." Compare Prov. 8 : 10 ; 17 : 12 ; and Samuel's words : "to obey is better than sacrifice" (1 Sam. 15 : 22). What was the altar from which Isaiah drew his description of God's theophany and from which was taken the live coal that touched his lips and prepared him to be a prophet ? (Is. 6 : 1-8). Jer. 7 : 22 — "I spake not . . . . concerning burnt-offerings or sacrifices . . . . but this thing . . . . Hearken unto my voice." Jeremiah insists only on the worthlessness of sacrifice where there is no heart.

(*d*) Thus the Old Testament sacrifices, when rightly offered, involved a consciousness of sin on the part of the worshiper, the bringing of a victim to atone for the sin, the laying of the hand of the offerer upon the victim's head, the confession of sin by the offerer, the slaying of the beast, the sprinkling or pouring-out of the blood upon the altar, and the consequent forgiveness of the sin and acceptance of the worshiper. The sin-offering and the scape-goat of the great day of atonement symbolized yet more distinctly the two elementary ideas of sacrifice, namely, satisfaction and substitution, together with the consequent removal of guilt from those on whose behalf the sacrifice was offered.

Lev. 1 : 4 — "And he shall lay his hand upon the head of the burnt-offering ; and it shall be accepted for him, to make atonement for him" ; 4 : 20 —"Thus shall he do with the bullock ; as he did with the bullock of the sin-offering, so shall he do with this ; and the priest shall make atonement for them, and they shall be forgiven" ; so 31 and 35 — 'and the priest shall make atonement for him as touching his sin that he hath sinned, and he shall be forgiven" ; so 5 : 10, 16 ; 6 : 7. Lev. 17 : 11 — "For the life of the flesh is in the blood ; and I have given it to you upon the altar to make atonement for your souls: for it is the blood that maketh atonement by reason of the life."

The patriarchal sacrifices were sin-offerings, as the sacrifice of Job for his friends witnesses : Job 42 : 7-9 — "My wrath is kindled against thee [Eliphaz] . . . . therefore, take unto you seven bullocks . . . . and offer up for yourselves a burnt-offering" ; *cf.* 33 : 24 — "Then God is gracious unto him, and saith, Deliver him from going down to the pit, I have found a ransom" ; 1 : 5 — Job offered burnt-offerings for his sons, for he said, "It may be that my sons have sinned, and renounced God in their hearts" ; Gen. 8 : 20 — Noah "offered burnt-offerings on the altar" ; 21 — "and Jehovah smelled the sweet savor ; and Jehovah said in his heart, I will not again curse the ground any more for man's sake."

That vicarious suffering is intended in all these sacrifices, is plain from Lev. 16 : 1-34 — the account of the sin-offering and the scape-goat of the great day of atonement, the full meaning of which we give below ; also from Gen. 22 : 13 — "Abraham went and took the ram, and offered him up for a burnt-offering in the stead of his son" ; Ex. 32 : 30-32 — where Moses says : "Ye have sinned a great sin : and now I will go up unto Jehovah ; peradventure I shall make atonement for your sin. And Moses returned unto Jehovah, and said, Oh, this people have sinned a great sin, and have made them gods of gold. Yet now, if thou wilt forgive their sin — ; and if not, blot me, I pray thee, out of thy book which thou hast written." See also Deut. 21 : 1-9 — the expiation of an uncertain murder, by the sacrifice of a heifer,— where Oehler, O. T. Theology, 1 : 389, says : "Evidently the punishment of death incurred by the manslayer is executed symbolically upon the heifer." In Is. 53 : 1-12 — "All we like sheep have gone astray ; we have turned every one to his own way ; and Jehovah hath laid on him the iniquity of us all . . . . stripes . . . . offering for sin " — the ideas of both satisfaction and substitution are still more plain.

Wallace, Representative Responsibility : "The animals offered in sacrifice must be animals brought into direct relation to man, subject to him, his property. They could not be spoils of the chase. They must bear the mark and impress of humanity. Upon the sacrifice human hands must be laid — the hands of the offerer and the hands of the priest. The offering is the substitute of the offerer. The priest is the substitute of the offerer. The priest and the sacrifice were *one symbol*. [Hence, in the new dispensation, the priest and the sacrifice are one — both are found in Christ.] The high priest must enter the holy of holies with his own finger dipped in blood : the blood must be in contact with his own person, — another indication of the identification of the two. Life is nourished and sustained by life. All life lower than man may be sacrificed for the good of man. The blood must be spilled on the ground. ' In the blood is the life.' The life is reserved by God. It is given *for* man, but not *to* him. Life for life is the law of the creation. So the life of Christ, also, for *our* life. — Adam was originally priest of the family and of the race. But he lost his representative character by the one act of disobedience, and his redemption was that of the individual, not that of the race. The race ceased to have a representative. The subjects of the divine government were henceforth to be, not the natural offspring of Adam as such, but the redeemed. That the body and the blood are both required, indicates the demand that the death should be by a violence that sheds blood. The sacrifices showed forth, not Christ himself [his character, his life], but Christ's death."

This following is a tentative scheme of the JEWISH SACRIFICES. The general reason for sacrifice is expressed in Lev. 17 : 11 (quoted above). I. *For the individual :* 1. The sin-offering = sacrifice to expiate sins of ignorance (thoughtlessness and plausible temptation) : Lev. 4 : 14. 20. 31. 2. The trespass-offering = sacrifice to expiate sins of omission : Lev. 5 : 5, 6. 3. The burnt-offering = sacrifice to expiate general sinfulness : **Lev. 1 : 3** (the offering of Mary, Luke 2 : 24). II. *For the family :* The Passover : **Ex. 12 : 27.** III. *For the people :* 1. The daily morning and evening sacrifice : **Ex. 29 : 38-46.** 2. The offering of the great day of atonement : **Lev. 16 : 6-10.** In this last, two victims were employed, one to represent the means — death, and the other to represent the result — forgiveness. One victim could not represent both the atonement — by shedding of blood, and the justification — by putting away sin.

Jesus died for our sins at the Passover feast and at the hour of daily sacrifice. McLaren, in S. S. Times, Nov. 30, 1901 : 801 — " Shedding of blood and consequent safety were only a part of the teaching of the Passover. There is a double identification of the person offering with his sacrifice : first, in that he offers it as his representative, laying his hand on its head, or otherwise transferring his personality, as it were, to it ; and secondly, in that, receiving it back again from God to whom he gave it, he feeds on it, so making it part of his life and nourishing himself thereby : 'My flesh . . . . which I will give . . . . for the life of the world . . . . he that eateth me, he also shall live because of me' (John 6 : 51, 57)."

Chambers, in Presb. and Ref. Rev., Jan. 1892 : 22-34 — On the great day of atonement " the double offering — one for Jehovah and the other for Azazel — typified not only the removing of the guilt of the people, but its transfer to the odious and detestable being who was the first cause of its existence," *i. e.,* Satan. Lidgett, Spir. Principle of the Atonement, 112, 113 — " It was not the punishment which the goat bore away into the wilderness, for the idea of punishment is not directly associated with the scape-goat. It bears the sin — the whole unfaithfulness of the community which had defiled the holy places — out from them, so that henceforth they may be pure. . . . . The sin-offering — representing the sinner by receiving the burden of his sin — makes expiation by yielding up and yielding back its life to God, under conditions which represent at once the wrath and the placability of God."

On the Jewish sacrifices, see Fairbairn, Typology, 1 : 209-223 ; Wünsche, Die Leiden des Messias ; Jukes, O. T. Sacrifices ; Smeaton, Apostle's Doctrine of Atonement, 25-53 ; Kurtz, Sacrificial Worship of O. T., 120 ; Bible Com., 1 : 502-508, and Introd. to Leviticus ; Candlish on Atonement, 123-142 ; Weber, Vom Zorne Gottes, 161-180. On passages in Leviticus, see Com. of Knobel, in Exeg. Handb. d. Alt. Test.

(*e*) It is not essential to this view to maintain that a formal divine institution of the rite of sacrifice, at man's expulsion from Eden, can be proved from Scripture. Like the family and the state, sacrifice may, without such formal inculcation, possess divine sanction, and be ordained of God. The well-nigh universal prevalence of sacrifice, however, together with the fact that its nature, as a bloody offering, seems to preclude man's own invention of it, combines with certain Scripture intimations to favor the view that it was a primitive divine appointment. From the time of Moses, there can be no question as to its divine authority.

Compare the origin of prayer and worship, for which we find no formal divine injunctions at the beginnings of history. Heb. 11 : 4 — " By faith Abel offered unto God a more excellent sacrifice than Cain, through which he had witness borne to him that he was righteous, God bearing witness in respect of his gifts — here it may be argued that since Abel's faith was not presumption, it must have had some injunction and promise of God to base itself upon. Gen. 4 : 3, 4 — " Cain brought of the fruit of the ground an offering unto Jehovah. And Abel, ne also brought of the firstlings of his flock and of the fat thereof. And Jehovah had respect unto Abel and to his offering : but unto Cain and to his offering he had not respect."

It has been urged, in corroboration of this view, that the previous existence of sacrifice is intimated in Gen. 3 : 21 — " And Jehovah God made for Adam and for his wife coats of skins, and clothed them." Since the killing of animals for food was not permitted until long afterwards (Gen. 9 : 3 — to Noah : " Every moving thing that liveth shall be food for you "), the inference has been drawn, that the skins with which God clothed our first parents were the skins of animals slain for sacrifice, — this clothing furnishing a type of the righteousness of Christ which secures our restoration to God's favor, as the death of the victims furnished a type of the suffering of Christ which secures for us remission of punishment. We must regard this, however, as a pleasing and possibly correct hypothesis, rather than as a demonstrated truth of Scripture. Since the unperverted instincts of human nature are an expression of God's will, Abel's faith may have consisted in trusting these, rather than the promptings of selfishness and self-righteousness. The death of animals in sacrifice, like the death of Christ which it signified, was only the hastening of what belonged to them because of their connection with human sin. Faith recognized this connection. On the divine appointment of sacrifice, see Park, in Bib. Sac., Jan. 1876 : 102–132. Westcott, Hebrews, 281 — "There is no reason to think that sacrifice was instituted in obedience to a direct revelation. . . . . It is mentioned in Scripture at first as natural and known. It was practically universal in prechristian times. . . . In due time the popular practice of sacrifice was regulated by revelation as disciplinary, and also used as a vehicle for typical teaching." We prefer to say that sacrifice probably originated in a fundamental instinct of humanity, and was therefore a divine ordinance as much as were marriage and government.

On Gen. 4: 3, 4, see C. H. M. — " The entire difference between Cain and Abel lay, not in their natures, but in their sacrifices. Cain brought to God the sin-stained fruit of a cursed earth. Here was no recognition of the fact that he was a sinner, condemned to death. All his toil could not satisfy God's holiness, or remove the penalty. But Abel recognized his sin, condemnation, helplessness, death, and brought the bloody sacrifice — the sacrifice of another — the sacrifice provided by God, to meet the claims of God. He found a substitute, and he presented it in faith — the faith that looks away from self to Christ, or God's appointed way of salvation. The difference was not in their persons, but in their gifts. Of Abel it is said, that God 'bore witness in respect of his gifts' (Heb. 11 : 4). To Cain it is said, ' if thou doest well (LXX. : ὀρθῶς προσενέγκῃς — if thou offerest correctly) shalt thou not be accepted ?' But Cain desired to get away from God and from God's way, and to lose himself in the world. This is 'the way of Cain ' (Jude 11)." Per contra, see Crawford, Atonement, 259 — " Both in Levitical and patriarchal times, we have no formal institution of sacrifice, but the regulation of sacrifice already existing. But Abel's faith may have had respect, not to a revelation with regard to sacrificial worship, but with regard to the promised Redeemer ; and his sacrifice may have expressed that faith. If so, God's acceptance of it gave a divine warrant to future sacrifices. It was not will-worship, because it was not substituted for some other worship which God had previously instituted. It is not necessary to suppose that God gave an expressed command. Abel may have been moved by some inward divine monition. Thus Adam said to Eve, ' This is now bone of my bones . . . .' (Gen. 2 : 23), before any divine command of marriage. No fruits were presented during the patriarchal dispensation. Heathen sacrifices were corruptions of primitive sacrifice." Von Lasaulx, Die Sühnopfer der Griechen und Römer, und ihr Verhältniss zu dem einen auf Golgotha, 1 — " The first word of the original man was probably a prayer, the first action of fallen man a sacrifice "; see translation in Bib. Sac., 1 : 368–408. Bishop Butler : " By the general prevalence of propitiatory sacrifices over the heathen world, the notion of repentance alone being sufficient to expiate guilt appears to be contrary to the general sense of mankind."

(f) The New Testament assumes and presupposes the Old Testament doctrine of sacrifice. The sacrificial language in which its descriptions of Christ's work are clothed cannot be explained as an accommodation to Jewish methods of thought, since this terminology was in large part in common use among the heathen, and Paul used it more than any other of the apostles in dealing with the Gentiles. To deny to it its Old Testament meaning, when used by New Testament writers to describe the work of Christ, is to deny any proper inspiration both in the Mosaic appointment of sacrifices and in the apostolic interpretations of them. We must therefore maintain, as the result of a simple induction of Scripture facts, that the death of Christ is a vicarious offering, provided by God's love for the purpose of satisfying an internal demand of the divine holiness, and of removing an obstacle in the divine mind to the renewal and pardon of sinners.

The epistle of James makes no allusion to sacrifice. But he would not have failed to allude to it, if he had held the moral view of the atonement ; for it would then have been an obvious help to his argument against merely formal service. Christ protested against washing hands and keeping Sabbath days. If sacrifice had been a piece of human formality, how indignantly would he have inveighed against it ! But instead of this he received from John the Baptist, without rebuke, the words : 'Behold, the Lamb of God, that taketh away the sin of the world' (John 1 : 29)."

A. A. Hodge, Popular Lectures, 247 — "The sacrifices of bulls and goats were like token-money, as our paper-promises to pay, accepted at their face-value till the day of settlement. But the sacrifice of Christ was the gold which absolutely extinguished all debt by its intrinsic value. Hence, when Christ died, the veil that separated man from God was rent from the bottom to the top by supernatural hands. When the real expiation was finished, the whole symbolical system representing it became *functum officio,* and was abolished. Soon after this, the temple was razed to the ground, and the ritual was rendered forever impossible."

For denial that Christ's death is to be interpreted by heathen or Jewish sacrifices, see Maurice on Sac., 154 — " The heathen signification of words, when applied to a Christian use, must be not merely modified, but inverted "; Jowett, Epistles of St. Paul, 2 : 479 — " The heathen and Jewish sacrifices rather show us what the sacrifice of Christ was not, than what it was." Bushnell and Young do not doubt the expiatory nature of heathen sacrifices. But the main terms which the N. T. uses to describe Christ's sacrifice are borrowed from the Greek sacrificial ritual, *e. g.*, θυσία, προσφορά, ἱλασμός, ἁγιάζω, καθαίρω, ἱλάσκομαι. To deny that these terms, when applied to Christ, imply expiation and substitution, is to deny the inspiration of those who used them. See Cave, Scripture Doctrine of Sacrifice ; art. on Sacrifice, in Smith's Bible Dictionary.

With all these indications of our dissent from the modern denial of expiatory sacrifice, we deem it desirable by way of contrast to present the clearest possible statement of the view from which we dissent. This may be found in Pfleiderer, Philosophy of Religion, 1 : 238, 260, 261 — " The gradual distinction of the moral from the ceremonial, the repression and ultimate replacement of ceremonial expiation by the moral purification of the sense and life, and consequently the transformation of the mystical conception of redemption into the corresponding ethical conception of education, may be designated as the kernel and the teleological principle of the development of the history of religion. . . . . But to Paul the question in what sense the death of the Cross could be the means of the Messianic redemption found its answer simply from the presuppositions of the Pharisaic theology, which beheld in the innocent suffering, and especially in the martyr-death, of the righteous, an expiatory means compensating for the sins of the whole people. What would be more natural than that Paul should contemplate the death on the Cross in the same way, as an expiatory means of salvation for the redemption of the sinful world ?

" We are thus led to see in this theory the symbolical presentment of the truth that the new man suffers, as it were, vicariously, for the old man ; for he takes upon himself the daily pain of self-subjugation, and bears guiltlessly in patience the evils which the old man could not but necessarily impute to himself as punishment. Therefore as Christ is the exemplification of the moral idea of man, so his death is the symbol of that moral process of painful self-subjugation in obedience and patience, in which the true inner redemption of man consists. . . . . In like manner Fichte said that the only proper means of salvation is the death of selfhood, death *with* Jesus, regeneration.

" The defect in the Kant-Fichtean doctrine of redemption consisted in this, that it limited the process of ethical transformation to the individual, and endeavored to explain it from his subjective reason and freedom alone. How could the individual deliver himself from his powerlessness and become free ? This question was unsolved. The Christian doctrine of redemption is that the moral liberation of the individual is not the effect of his own natural power, but the effect of the divine Spirit, who, from the beginning of human history, put forth his activity as the power educating to the good, and especially has created for himself in the Christian community a permanent organ for the education of the people and of individuals. It was the moral individualism of Kant which prevented him from finding in the historically realized common spirit of the good the real force available for the individual becoming good."

C. Theories of the Atonement.

1st. The Socinian, or Example Theory of the Atonement.

This theory holds that subjective sinfulness is the sole barrier between man and God. Not God, but only man, needs to be reconciled. The only method of reconciliation is to better man's moral condition. This can be effected by man's own will, through repentance and reformation. The death of Christ is but the death of a noble martyr. He redeems us, only as his human example of faithfulness to truth and duty has a powerful influence upon our moral improvement. This fact the apostles, either consciously or unconsciously, clothed in the language of the Greek and Jewish sacrifices. This theory was fully elaborated by Lælius Socinus and Faustus Socinus of Poland, in the 16th century. Its modern advocates are found in the Unitarian body.

The Socinian theory may be found stated, and advocated, in Bibliotheca Fratrum Polonorum, 1:566–600; Martineau, Studies of Christianity, 83–176; J. F. Clarke, Orthodoxy, Its Truths and Errors, 235–265; Ellis, Unitarianism and Orthodoxy; Sheldon, Sin and Redemption, 146–210. The text which at first sight most seems to favor this view is 1 Pet. 2:21 — "Christ also suffered for you, leaving you an example, that ye should follow his steps." But see under (e) below. When Correggio saw Raphael's picture of St. Cecilia, he exclaimed: "I too am a painter." So Socinus held that Christ's example roused our humanity to imitation. He regarded expiation as heathenish and impossible; every one must receive according to his deeds; God is ready to grant forgiveness on simple repentance.

E. G. Robinson, Christian Theology, 277 — "The theory first insists on the inviolability of moral sequences in the conduct of every moral agent; and then insists that, on a given condition, the consequences of transgression may be arrested by almighty fiat. . . . . Unitarianism errs in giving a transforming power to that which works beneficently only after the transformation has been wrought." In ascribing to human nature a power of self-reformation, it ignores man's need of regeneration by the Holy Spirit. But even this renewing work of the Holy Spirit presupposes the atoning work of Christ. "Ye must be born anew" (John 3:7) necessitates "Even so must the Son of man be lifted up" (John 3:14). It is only the Cross that satisfies man's instinct of reparation. Harnack, Das Wesen des Christenthums, 99 — "Those who regarded Christ's death soon ceased to bring any other bloody offering to God. This is true both in Judaism and in heathenism. Christ's death put an end to all bloody offerings in religious history. The impulse to sacrifice found its satisfaction in the Cross of Christ." We regard this as proof that the Cross is essentially a satisfaction to the divine justice, and not a mere example of faithfulness to duty. The Socinian theory is the first of six theories of the Atonement, which roughly correspond with our six previously treated theories of sin, and this first theory includes most of the false doctrine which appears in mitigated forms in several of the theories following.

To this theory we make the following objections:

(a) It is based upon false philosophical principles,—as, for example, that will is merely the faculty of volitions; that the foundation of virtue is in utility; that law is an expression of arbitrary will; that penalty is a means of reforming the offender; that righteousness, in either God or man, is only a manifestation of benevolence.

If the will is simply the faculty of volitions, and not also the fundamental determination of the being to an ultimate end, then man can, by a single volition, effect his own reformation and reconciliation to God. If the foundation of virtue is in utility, then there is nothing in the divine being that prevents pardon, the good of the creature, and not the demands of God's holiness, being the reason for Christ's suffering. If law is an expression of arbitrary will, instead of being a transcript of the divine nature, it may at any time be dispensed with, and the sinner may be pardoned on mere repentance. If penalty is merely a means of reforming the offender, then sin does not involve objective guilt, or obligation to suffer, and sin may be forgiven, at any moment, to all who forsake it,—indeed, must be forgiven, since punishment is out of place when the sinner is reformed. If righteousness is only a form or manifestation of benevolence, then God can show his benevolence as easily through pardon as through penalty, and Christ's death is only intended to attract us toward the good by the force of a noble example.

Wendt, Teaching of Jesus, 2:218–264, is essentially Socinian in his view of Jesus' death. Yet he ascribes to Jesus the idea that suffering is *necessary*, even for one who stands in perfect love and blessed fellowship with God, since earthly blessedness is not the true blessedness, and since a true piety is impossible without renunciation and stooping to minister to others. The earthly life-sacrifice of the Messiah was his necessary and greatest act, and was the culminating point of his teaching. Suffering made him a perfect example, and so ensured the success of his work. But why God should have made it necessary that the holiest must suffer, Wendt does not explain. This constitution of things we can understand only as a revelation of the holiness of God, and of his punitive relation to human sin. Simon, Reconciliation, 357, shows well that example might have sufficed for a race that merely needed leadership. But what the race needed most was energizing, the fulfilment of the conditions of restoration to God on their behalf by one of themselves, by one whose very essence they shared, who created them, in whom they consisted, and whose work was therefore their work. Christ condemned with the divine condemnation the thoughts and impulses arising from his subconscious life. Before the sin, which for the moment seemed to be his, could become his, he condemned it. He sympathized with, nay, he revealed, the very justice and sorrow of God. Hebrews 2 : 16-18 — "For verily not to angels doth he give help, but he giveth help to the seed of Abraham. Wherefore it behooved him in all things to be made like unto his brethren, that he might become a merciful and faithful high priest in things pertaining to God, to make propitiation for the sins of the people. For in that he himself hath suffered being tempted, he is able to succor them that are tempted."

(b) It is a natural outgrowth from the Pelagian view of sin, and logically necessitates a curtailment or surrender of every other characteristic doctrine of Christianity — inspiration, sin, the deity of Christ, justification, regeneration, and eternal retribution.

The Socinian theory requires a surrender of the doctrine of inspiration; for the idea of vicarious and expiatory sacrifice is woven into the very warp and woof of the Old and New Testaments. It requires an abandonment of the Scripture doctrine of sin; for in it all idea of sin as perversion of nature rendering the sinner unable to save himself, and as objective guilt demanding satisfaction to the divine holiness, is denied. It requires us to give up the deity of Christ; for if sin is a slight evil, and man can save himself from its penalty and power, then there is no longer need of either an infinite suffering or an infinite Savior, and a human Christ is as good as a divine. It requires us to give up the Scripture doctrine of justification, as God's act of declaring the sinner just in the eye of the law, solely on account of the righteousness and death of Christ to whom he is united by faith; for the Socinian theory cannot permit the counting to a man of any other righteousness than his own. It requires a denial of the doctrine of regeneration; for this is no longer the work of God, but the work of the sinner; it is no longer a change of the affections below consciousness, but a self-reforming volition of the sinner himself. It requires a denial of eternal retribution; for this is no longer appropriate to finite transgression of arbitrary law, and to superficial sinning that does not involve nature.

(c) It contradicts the Scripture teachings, that sin involves objective guilt as well as subjective defilement; that the holiness of God must punish sin; that the atonement was a bearing of the punishment of sin for men; and that this vicarious bearing of punishment was necessary, on the part of God, to make possible the showing of favor to the guilty.

The Scriptures do not make the main object of the atonement to be man's subjective moral improvement. It is to God that the sacrifice is offered, and the object of it is to satisfy the divine holiness, and to remove from the divine mind an obstacle to the showing of favor to the guilty. It was something external to man and his happiness or virtue, that required that Christ should suffer. What Emerson has said of the martyr is yet more true of Christ: "Though love repine, and reason chafe, There comes a voice without reply, 'T is man's perdition to be safe, When for the truth he ought to die." The truth for which Christ died was truth internal to the nature of God; not simply truth externalized and published among men. What the truth of God required, that Christ rendered — full satisfaction to violated justice. "Jesus paid it all"; and no obedience or righteousness of ours can be added to his work, as a ground of our salvation.

E. G. Robinson, Christian Theology, 276 — "This theory fails of a due recognition of that deep-seated, universal and innate sense of ill-desert, which in all times and everywhere has prompted men to aim at some expiation of their guilt. For this sense of guilt and its requirements the moral influence theory makes no adequate provision, either in Christ or in those whom Christ saves. Supposing Christ's redemptive work to consist merely in winning men to the practice of righteousness, it takes no account of penalty, either as the sanction of the law, as the reaction of the divine holiness against sin, or as the upbraiding of the individual conscience. . . . The Socinian theory overlooks the fact that there must be some objective manifestation of God's wrath and displeasure against sin."

(d) It furnishes no proper explanation of the sufferings and death of Christ. The unmartyrlike anguish cannot be accounted for, and the forsaking by the Father cannot be justified, upon the hypothesis that Christ died as a mere witness to truth. If Christ's sufferings were not propitiatory, they neither furnish us with a perfect example, nor constitute a manifestation of the love of God.

Compare Jesus' feeling, in view of death, with that of Paul: "having the desire to depart" (Phil. 1 : 23). Jesus was filled with anguish: "Now is my soul troubled; and what shall I say? Father, save me from this hour" (John 12 : 27). If Christ was simply a martyr, then he is not a perfect example; for many a martyr has shown greater courage in prospect of death, and in the final agony has been able to say that the fire that consumed him was "a bed of roses." Gethsemane, with its mental anguish, is apparently recorded in order to indicate that Christ's sufferings even on the cross were not mainly physical sufferings. The Roman Catholic Church unduly emphasizes the physical side of our Lord's passion, but loses sight of its spiritual element. The Christ of Rome indeed is either a babe or dead, and the crucifix presents to us not a risen and living Redeemer, but a mangled and lifeless body.

Stroud, in his Physical Cause of our Lord's Death, has made it probable that Jesus died of a broken heart, and that this alone explains John 19 : 34 — "one of the soldiers with a spear pierced his side, and straightway there came out blood and water" — i. e., the heart had already been ruptured by grief. That grief was grief at the forsaking of the Father (Mat. 27 : 46 — "My God, my God, why hast thou forsaken me?"), and the resulting death shows that that forsaking was no imaginary one. Did God make the holiest man of all to be the greatest sufferer of all the ages? This heart broken by the forsaking of the Father means more than martyrdom. If Christ's death is not propitiatory, it fills me with terror and despair; for it presents me not only with a very imperfect example in Christ, but with a proof of measureless injustice on the part of God. Luke 23 : 28 — "weep not for me, but weep for yourselves" = Jesus rejects all pity that forgets his suffering for others.

To the above view of Stroud, Westcott objects that blood does not readily flow from an ordinary corpse. The separation of the red corpuscles of the blood from the serum, or water, would be the beginning of decomposition, and would be inconsistent with the statement in Acts 2 : 31 — "neither did his flesh see corruption." But Dr. W. W. Keen of Philadelphia, in his article on The Bloody Sweat of our Lord (Bib. Sac., July, 1897 : 469-484) endorses Stroud's view as to the physical cause of our Lord's death. Christ's being forsaken by the Father was only the culmination of that relative withdrawal which constituted the source of Christ's loneliness through life. Through life he was a servant of the Spirit. On the cross the Spirit left him to the weakness of unassisted humanity, destitute of conscious divine resources. Compare the curious reading of Heb. 2 : 9 — "that he apart from God (χωρὶς Θεοῦ) should taste death for every man."

If Christ merely supposed himself to be deserted by God, "not only does Christ become an erring man, and, so far as the predicate deity is applicable to him, an erring God; but, if he cherished unfounded distrust of God, how can it be possible still to maintain that his will was in abiding, perfect agreement and identity with the will of God?" See Kant, Lotze, and Ritschl, by Stählin, 219. Charles C. Everett, Gospel of Paul, says Jesus was not crucified because he was accursed, but he was accursed because he was crucified, so that, in wreaking vengeance upon him, Jewish law abrogated itself. This interpretation however contradicts 2 Cor. 5 : 21 — "Him who knew no sin he made to be sin on our behalf"— where the divine identification of Christ with the race of sinners antedates and explains his sufferings. John 1 : 29 — "the Lamb of God, that taketh away the sin of the world"— does not refer to Jesus as a lamb for gentleness, but as a lamb for sacrifice. Maclaren: "How does Christ's death prove God's love? Only on one supposition, namely, that Christ is the incarnate Son of God, sent by the Father's love and being his express image"; and, we may add, suffering vicariously for us and removing the obstacle in God's mind to our pardon.

(e) The influence of Christ's example is neither declared in Scripture, nor found in Christian experience, to be the chief result secured by his death. Mere example is but a new preaching of the law, which repels and condemns. The cross has power to lead men to holiness, only as it first shows a satisfaction made for their sins. Accordingly, most of the passages which represent Christ as an example also contain references to his propitiatory work.

There is no virtue in simply setting an example. Christ did nothing, simply for the sake of example. Even his baptism was the symbol of his propitiatory death ; see pages 761, 762. The apostle's exhortation is not " abstain from all *appearance* of evil" (1 Thess. 5 : 22, A. Vers.), but "abstain from every *form* of evil" (Rev. Vers.). Christ's death is the payment of a real debt due to God ; and the convicted sinner needs first to see the debt which he owes to the divine justice paid by Christ, before he can think hopefully of reforming his life. The hymns of the church : " I lay my sins on Jesus," and " Not all the blood of beasts," represent the view of Christ's sufferings which Christians have derived from the Scriptures. When the sinner sees that the mortgage is cancelled, that the penalty has been borne, he can devote himself freely to the service of his Redeemer. Rev. 12 : 11 — "they overcame him [Satan] because of the blood of the Lamb " = as Christ overcame Satan by his propitiatory sacrifice, so we overcome by appropriating to ourselves Christ's atonement and his Spirit ; *cf*. 1 John 5 : 4 — "this is the victory that hath overcome the world, even our faith." The very text upon which Socinians most rely, when it is taken in connection with the context, proves their theory to be a misrepresentation of Scripture. 1 Pet. 2 : 21 — "Christ also suffered for you, leaving you an example, that ye should follow his steps " — is succeeded by verse 24 — "who his own self bare our sins in his body upon the tree, that we, having died unto sins, might live unto righteousness; by whose stripes ye were healed "— the latter words being a direct quotation from Isaiah's description of the substitutionary sufferings of the Messiah (Is. 53 : 5).

When a deeply convicted sinner was told that God could cleanse his heart and make him over anew, he replied with righteous impatience : "That is not what I want, — I have a debt to pay first ! " A. J. Gordon, Ministry of the Spirit, 28, 89 — " Nowhere in tabernacle or temple shall we ever find the laver placed before the altar. The altar is Calvary, and the laver is Pentecost, — one stands for the sacrificial blood, the other for the sanctifying Spirit. . . . So the oil which symbolized the sanctifying Spirit was always put 'upon the blood of the trespass-offering' (Lev. 14 : 17)." The extremity of Christ's suffering on the Cross was coincident with the extremest manifestation of the guilt of the race. The greatness of this he theoretically knew from the beginning of his ministry. His baptism was not intended merely to set an example. It was a recognition that sin deserved death ; that he was numbered with the transgressors ; that he was sent to die for the sin of the world. He was not so much a teacher, as he was the subject of all teaching. In him the great suffering of the holy God on account of sin is exhibited to the universe. The pain of a few brief hours saves a world, only because it sets forth an eternal fact in God's being and opens to us God's very heart.

Shakespeare, Henry V, 4 : 1 — "There is some soul of goodness in things evil, Would men observingly distil it out." It is well to preach on Christ as an example. Lyman Abbott says that Jesus' blood purchases our pardon and redeems us to God, just as a patriot's blood redeems his country from servitude and purchases its liberty. But even Ritschl, Just. and Recon., 2, goes beyond this, when he says : " Those who advocate the example theory should remember that Jesus withdraws himself from imitation when he sets himself over against his disciples as the Author of forgiveness. And they perceive that pardon must first be appropriated, before it is possible for them to imitate his piety and moral achievement." This is a partial recognition of the truth that the removal of objective guilt by Christ's atonement must precede the removal of subjective defilement by Christ's regenerating and sanctifying Spirit. Lidgett, Spir. Princ. of Atonement, 265-280, shows that there is a fatherly demand for satisfaction, which must be met by the filial response of the child. Thomas Chalmers at the beginning of his ministry urged on his people the reformation of their lives. But he confesses : " I never heard of any such reformations being effected amongst them." Only when he preached the alienation of men from God, and forgiveness through the blood of Christ, did he hear of their betterment.

Gordon, Christ of To-day, 129 - " The consciousness of sin is largely the creation of Christ." Men like Paul, Luther, and Edwards show this impressively. Foster, Christian life and Theology, 198–201 — " There is of course a sense in which the Christian must imitate Christ's death, for he is to 'take up his cross daily' (Luke 9 : 23) and follow his Master ; but in its highest meaning and fullest scope the death of Christ is no more an object set for our imitation than is the creation of the world. . . . Christ does for man in his sacrifice what man could not do for himself. We see in the Cross : 1. the magnitude of the guilt of sin ; 2. our own self-condemnation ; 3. the adequate remedy, — for the object of law is gained in the display of righteousness ; 4. the objective ground of forgiveness." Maclaren : " Christianity without a dying Christ is a dying Christianity."

(*f*) This theory contradicts the whole tenor of the New Testament, in making the life, and not the death, of Christ the most significant and important feature of his work. The constant allusions to the death of Christ as the source of our salvation, as well as the symbolism of the ordinances, cannot be explained upon a theory which regards Christ as a mere example, and considers his sufferings as incidents, rather than essentials, of his work.

Dr. H. B. Hackett frequently called attention to the fact that the recording in the gospels of only three years of Jesus' life, and the prominence given in the record to the closing scenes of that life, are evidence that not his life, but his death, was the great work of our Lord. Christ's death, and not his life, is the central truth of Christianity. The cross is *par excellence* the Christian symbol. In both the ordinances — in Baptism as well as in the Lord's Supper — it is the death of Christ that is primarily set forth. Neither Christ's example, nor his teaching, reveals God as does his death. It is the death of Christ that links together all Christian doctrines. The mark of Christ's blood is upon them all, as the scarlet thread running through every cord and rope of the British navy gives sign that it is the property of the crown.

Did Jesus' death have no other relation to our salvation than Paul's death had ? Paul was a martyr, but his death is not even recorded. Gould, Bib. Theol. N. T., 92 — " Paul does not dwell in any way upon the life or work of our Lord, except as they are involved in his death and resurrection." What did Jesus' words : "It is finished"(John 19 : 30) mean ? What was finished on the Socinian theory ? The Socinian salvation had not yet begun. Why did not Jesus make the ordinances of Baptism and the Lord's Supper to be memorials of his birth, rather than of his death ? Why was not the veil of the temple rent at his baptism, or at the Sermon on the Mount ? It was because only his death opened the way to God. In talking with Nicodemus, Jesus brushed aside the complimentary : " we know that thou art a teacher come from God " (John 3 : 2). Recognizing Jesus as teacher is not enough. There must be a renewal by the Spirit of God, so that one recognizes also the lifting up of the Son of man as atoning Savior (John 3 : 14, 15). And to Peter, Jesus said : "If I wash thee not, thou hast no part with me " (John 13 : 8). One cannot have part with Christ as Teacher, while one rejects him as Redeemer from sin. On the Socinian doctrine of the Atonement, see Crawford, Atonement, 279–296 ; Shedd, History of Doctrine, 2 : 376–386 ; Doctrines of the Early Socinians, in Princeton Essays, 1 : 194–211 ; Philippi, Glaubenslehre, IV, 2 : 156–180 ; Fock, Socinianismus.

2nd. **The Bushnellian, or Moral Influence Theory of the Atonement.**

This holds, like the Socinian, that there is no principle of the divine nature which is propitiated by Christ's death ; but that this death is a manifestation of the love of God, suffering in and with the sins of his creatures. Christ's atonement, therefore, is the merely natural consequence of his taking human nature upon him ; and is a suffering, not of penalty in man's stead, but of the combined woes and griefs which the living of a human life involves. This atonement has effect, not to satisfy divine justice, but so to reveal divine love as to soften human hearts and to lead them to repentance ; in other words, Christ's sufferings were necessary, not in order to remove an obstacle to the pardon of sinners which exists in the mind of God, but in order to convince sinners that there exists no such obstacle. This theory, for substance, has been advocated by Bushnell, in

America; by Robertson, Maurice, Campbell, and Young, in Great Britain; by Schleiermacher and Ritschl, in Germany.

Origen and Abelard are earlier representatives of this view. It may be found stated in Bushnell's Vicarious Sacrifice. Bushnell's later work, Forgiveness and Law, contains a modification of his earlier doctrine, to which he was driven by the criticisms upon his Vicarious Sacrifice. In the later work, he acknowledges what he had so strenuously denied in the earlier, namely, that Christ's death has effect upon God as well as upon man, and that God cannot forgive without thus "making cost to himself." He makes open confession of the impotence of his former teaching to convert sinners, and, as the only efficient homiletic, he recommends the preaching of the very doctrine of propitiatory sacrifice which he had written his book to supersede. Even in Forgiveness and Law, however, there is no recognition of the true principle and ground of the Atonement in God's punitive holiness. Since the original form of Bushnell's doctrine is the only one which has met with wide acceptance, we direct our objections mainly to this.

F. W. Robertson, Sermons, 1:163-178, holds that Christ's sufferings were the necessary result of the position in which he had placed himself of conflict or collision with the evil that is in the world. He came in contact with the whirling wheel, and was crushed by it; he planted his heel upon the cockatrice's den, and was pierced by its fang. Maurice, on Sacrifice, 209, and Theol. Essays, 141, 228, regards Christ's sufferings as an illustration, given by the ideal man, of the self-sacrifice due to God from the humanity of which he is the root and head, all men being redeemed in him, irrespective of their faith, and needing only to have brought to them the news of this redemption. Young, Life and Light of Men, holds a view essentially the same with Robertson's. Christ's death is the necessary result of his collision with evil, and his sufferings extirpate sin, simply by manifesting God's self-sacrificing love.

Campbell, Atonement, 129-191, quotes from Edwards, to show that infinite justice might be satisfied in either one of two ways: (1) by an infinite punishment; (2) by an adequate repentance. This last, which Edwards passed by as impracticable, Campbell declares to have been the real atonement offered by Christ, who stands as the great Penitent, confessing the sin of the world. Mason, Faith of the Gospel, 160-210, takes substantially the view of Campbell, denying substitution, and emphasizing Christ's oneness with the race and his confession of human sin. He grants indeed that our Lord bore penalty, but only in the sense that he realized how great was the condemnation and penalty of the race.

Schleiermacher denies any satisfaction to God by substitution. He puts in its place an influence of Christ's personality on men, so that they feel themselves reconciled and redeemed. The atonement is purely subjective. Yet it is the work of Christ, in that only Christ's oneness with God has taught men that they can be one with God. Christ's consciousness of his being in God and knowing God, and his power to impart this consciousness to others, make him a Mediator and Savior. The idea of reparation compensation, satisfaction, substitution, is wholly Jewish. He regarded it as possible only to a narrow-minded people. He tells us that he hates in religion that kind of historic relation. He had no such sense of the holiness of God, or of the guilt of man, as would make necessary any suffering of punishment or offering to God for human sin. He desires to replace external and historical Christianity by a Christianity that is internal and subjective. See Schleiermacher, Der Christliche Glaube, 2:94-161.

Ritschl however is the most recent and influential representative of the Moral Influence theory in Germany. His view is to be found in his Rechtfertigung und Versöhnung, or in English translation, Justification and Reconciliation. Ritschl is anti-Hegelian and libertarian, but like Schleiermacher he does not treat sin with seriousness; he regards the sense of guilt as an illusion which it is the part of Christ to dispel; there is an inadequate conception of Christ's person, a practical denial of his pre-existence and work of objective atonement; indeed, the work of Christ is hardly put into any precise relation to sin at all, see Denney Studies in Theology, 136-151. E. H. Johnson: "Many Ritschlians deny both the miraculous conception and the bodily resurrection of Jesus. Sin does not particularly concern God; Christ is Savior only as Buddha was, achieving lordship over the world by indifference to it; he is the Word of God, only as he reveals this divine indifference to things. All this does not agree with the N. T. teaching that Christ is the only begotten Son of God, that he was with the Father before the world was, that he made expiation of sins to God, and that sin is that abominable thing that God hates." For a general survey of the Ritschlian theology, see Orr, Ritschlian Theology, 231-271; Presb. and Ref. Rev., July, 1891 : 443-458 (art. by Zahn), and Jan. 1892: 1-21 (art. by C. M. Mead); Andover Review, July, 1893 : 440-461; Am. Jour. Theology, Jan. 1899 : 22-44 (art. by H. R. Mackintosh); Lidgett, Spir. Prin. of Atonement, 190-207; Foster, Christ. Life and Theology; and the work of Garvie on Ritschl. For statement and criticism of other forms of the Moral Influence theory, see Crawford, Atonement 297-366; Watts, New Apologetic, 210-247.

To this theory we object as follows :

(*a*) While it embraces a valuable element of truth, namely, the moral influence upon men of the sufferings of the God-man, it is false by defect, in that it substitutes a subordinate effect of the atonement for its chief aim, and yet unfairly appropriates the name 'vicarious,' which belongs only to the latter. Suffering *with* the sinner is by no means suffering *in his stead*.

Dale, Atonement, 137, illustrates Bushnell's view by the loyal wife, who suffers exile or imprisonment with her husband; by the philanthropist, who suffers the privations and hardships of a savage people, whom he can civilize only by enduring the miseries from which he would rescue them; by the Moravian missionary, who enters for life the lepers' enclosure, that he may convert its inmates. So Potwin says that suffering and death are the *cost* of the atonement, not the atonement *itself*.

But we reply that such sufferings as these do not make Christ's sacrifice *vicarious*. The word 'vicarious' (from *vicis*) implies substitution, which this theory denies. The vicar of a parish is not necessarily one who performs service with, and in sympathy with, the rector, — he is rather one who stands in the rector's place. A vice-president is one who acts in place of the president; ' A. B., appointed consul, *vice* C. D., resigned,' implies that A. B. is now to serve in the stead of C. D. If Christ is a ' vicarious sacrifice,' then he makes atonement to God *in the place and stead* of sinners. Christ's suffering *in and with* sinners, though it is a most important and affecting fact, is not the suffering in their stead in which the atonement consists. Though suffering in and with sinners may be in part the *medium* through which Christ was enabled to endure God's wrath against sin, it is not to be confounded with the *reason* why God lays this suffering upon him; nor should it blind us to the fact that this reason is his standing in the sinner's place to answer for sin to the retributive holiness of God.

(*b*) It rests upon false philosophical principles, — as, that righteousness is identical with benevolence, instead of conditioning it; that God is subject to an eternal law of love, instead of being himself the source of all law; that the aim of penalty is the reformation of the offender.

Hovey, God with Us, 181-271, has given one of the best replies to Bushnell. He shows that if God is subject to an eternal law of love, then God is necessarily a Savior; that he must have created man as soon as he could; that he makes men holy as fast as possible; that he does all the good he can; that he is no better than he should be. But this is to deny the transcendence of God, and reduce omnipotence to a mere nature-power. The conception of God as subject to law imperils God's self-sufficiency and freedom. For Bushnell's statements with regard to the identity of righteousness and love, and for criticisms upon them, see our treatment of the attribute of Holiness, vol. I, pages 268-275.

Watts, New Apologetic, 277-280, points out that, upon Bushnell's principles, there must be an atonement for fallen angels. God was bound to assume the angelic nature and to do for angels all that he has done for us. There is also no reason for restricting either the atonement or the offer of salvation to the present life. B. B. Warfield, in Princeton Review, 1903:81-92, shows well that all the forms of the Moral Influence theory rest upon the assumption that God is only love, and that all that is required as ground of the sinner's forgiveness is penitence, either Christ's, or his own, or both together.

Ignoring the divine holiness and minimizing the guilt of sin, many modern writers make atonement to be a mere incident of Christ's incarnation. Phillips Brooks, Life, 2: 350, 351 — " Atonement by suffering is the result of the Incarnation; atonement being the necessary, and suffering the incidental element of that result. But sacrifice is an essential element, for sacrifice truly signifies here the consecration of human nature to its highest use and utterance, and does not necessarily involve the thought of pain. It is not the destruction but the fulfilment of human life. Inasmuch as the human life thus consecrated and fulfilled is the same in us as in Jesus, and inasmuch as his consecration and fulfilment makes morally possible for us the same consecration and fulfilment of it which he achieved, thereio. : his atonement nd his sacrifice, and incidentally his suffering, become vicarious. _ ~ot that they aake unnecessary, but that they make possible and successful in us, the same processes which were perfect in him."

(c) The theory furnishes no proper reason for Christ's suffering. While it shows that the Savior necessarily suffers from his contact with human sin and sorrow, it gives no explanation of that constitution of the universe which makes suffering the consequence of sin, not only to the sinner, but also to the innocent being who comes into connection with sin. The holiness of God, which is manifested in this constitution cf things and which requires this atonement, is entirely ignored.

B. W. Lockhart, in a recent statement of the doctrine of the atonement, shows this defect of apprehension : " God in Christ reconciled the world to himself ; Christ did not reconcile God to man, but man to God. Christ did not enable God to save men : God enabled Christ to save men. The sufferings of Christ were vicarious as the highest illustration of that spiritual law by which the good soul is impelled to suffer that others may not suffer, to die that others may not die. The vicarious sufferings of Jesus were also the great revelation to man of the vicarious nature of God; a revelation of the cross as eternal in his nature ; that it is in the heart of God to bear the sin and sorrow of his creatures in his eternal love and pity ; a revelation moreover that the law which saves the lost through the vicarious labors of godlike souls prevails wherever the godlike and the lost soul can influence each other."

While there is much in the above statement with which we agree, we charge it with misapprehending the reason for Christ's suffering. That reason is to be found only in that holiness of God which expresses itself in the very constitution of the universe. Not love but holiness has made suffering invariably to follow sin, so that penalty falls not only upon the transgressor but upon him who is the life and sponsor of the transgressor. God's holiness brings suffering to God, and to Christ who manifests God. Love bears the suffering, but it is holiness that necessitates it. The statement of Lockhart above gives account of the effect — reconciliation ; but it fails to recognize the cause — propitiation. The words of E. G. Robinson furnish the needed complement : " The work of Christ has two sides, propitiatory and reconciling. Christ felt the pang of association with a guilty race. The divine displeasure rested on him as possessing the guilty nature. In his own person he redeems this nature by bearing its penalty. Propitiation must precede reconciliation. The Moral Influence theory recognizes the necessity of a subjective change in man, but makes no provision of an objective agency to secure it."

(d) It contradicts the plain teachings of Scripture, that the atonement is necessary, not simply to reveal God's love, but to satisfy his justice ; that Christ's sufferings are propitiatory and penal ; and that the human conscience needs to be propitiated by Christ's sacrifice, before it can feel the moral influence of his sufferings.

That the atonement is primarily an offering to God, and not to the sinner, appears from Eph. 5 : 2 —" gave himself up for us, an offering and a sacrifice to God "; Heb. 9 : 14 —" offered himself without blemish unto God." Conscience, the reflection of God's holiness, can be propitiated only by propitiating holiness itself. Mere love and sympathy are maudlin, and powerless to move, unless there is a background of righteousness. Spear : " An appeal to man, without anything back of it to emphasize and enforce the appeal, will never touch the heart. The mere appearance of an atonement has no moral influence." Crawford, Atonement, 358-367—" Instead of delivering us from penalty, in order to deliver us from sin, this theory makes Christ to deliver us from sin, in order that he may deliver us from penalty. But this reverses the order of Scripture. And Dr. Bushnell concedes, in the end, that the moral view of the atonement is morally powerless ; and that the objective view he condemns is, after all, indispensable to the salvation of sinners."

Some men are quite ready to forgive those whom they have offended. The Ritschlian school sees no guilt to be atoned for, and no propitiation to be necessary. Only man needs to be reconciled. Ritschlians are quite ready to forgive God. The only atonement is an atonement, made by repentance, to the human conscience. Shedd says well: "All that is requisite in order to satisfaction and peace of conscience in the sinful soul is also requisite in order to the satisfaction of God himself." Walter Besant: "It is not enough to be forgiven,— one has also to forgive one's self." The converse proposition is yet more true: It is not enough to forgive one's self,— one has also to be forgiven; indeed, one cannot rightly forgive one's self, unless one has been first forgiven; 1 John 3 : 20 — "if our heart condemn us, God is greater than our heart, and knoweth all things." A. J. Gordon, Ministry of the Spirit, 201 —"As the high priest carried the blood into the Holy of Holies under the old dispensation, so does the Spirit take the blood of Christ into the inner sanctuary of our spirit in the new dispensation, in order that he may 'cleanse your conscience from dead works to serve the living God' (Heb. 9 : 14)."

(e) It can be maintained, only by wresting from their obvious meaning those passages of Scripture which speak of Christ as suffering for our sins ; which represent his blood as accomplishing something for us in heaven, when presented there by our intercessor ; which declare forgiveness to be a remitting of past offences upon the ground of Christ's death ; and which describe justification as a pronouncing, not a making, just.

We have seen that the forms in which the Scriptures describe Christ's death are mainly drawn from sacrifice. Notice Bushnell's acknowledgment that these "altar-forms" are the most vivid and effective methods of presenting Christ's work, and that the preacher cannot dispense with them. Why he should not dispense with them, if the meaning has gone out of them, is not so clear.

In his later work, entitled Forgiveness and Law, Bushnell appears to recognize this inconsistency, and represents God as affected by the atonement, after all; in other words, the atonement has an objective as well as a subjective influence. God can forgive, only by "making cost to himself." He "works down his resentment, by suffering for us." This verges toward the true view, but it does not recognize the demand of divine holiness for satisfaction ; and it attributes passion, weakness, and imperfection to God. Dorner, Glaubenslehre, 2 : 591 (Syst. Doct., 4 : 59, 69), objects to this modified Moral Influence theory, that the love that can do good to an enemy is already forgiving love ; so that the benefit to the enemy cannot be, as Bushnell supposes, a condition of the forgiveness.

To Campbell's view, that Christ is the great Penitent, and that his atonement consists essentially in his confessing the sins of the world, we reply, that no confession or penitence is possible without responsibility. If Christ had no substitutionary office, the ordering of his sufferings on the part of God was manifest injustice   Such sufferings, moreover, are impossible upon grounds of mere sympathy. The Scripture explains them by declaring that he bore our curse, and became a ransom in our place. There was more therefore in the sufferings of Christ than "a perfect Amen in humanity to the judgment of God on the sin of man." Not Phinehas's zeal for God, but his execution of judgment, made an atonement (Ps. 106 : 30 —"executed judgment"— LXX.: ἐξιλάσατο, "made propitiation") and turned away the wrath of God. Observe here the contrast between the priestly atonement of Aaron, who stood between the living and the dead, and the judicial atonement of Phinehas, who executed righteous judgment, and so turned away wrath. In neither case did mere confession suffice to take away sin. On Campbell's view see further, on page 760.

Moberly, Atonement and Personality, 98, has the great merit of pointing out that Christ shares our sufferings in virtue of the fact that our personality has its ground in him ; but that this sharing of our penalty was necessitated by God's righteousness he has failed to indicate. He tells us that "Christ sanctified the present and cancels the past. He offers to God a living holiness in human conditions and character; he makes the awful sacrifice in humanity of a perfect contrition. The one is the offering of obedience, the other the offering of atonement ; the one the offering of the life, the other the offering of the death." This modification of Campbell's view can be rationally maintained only by   nnecting with it a prior declaration that the fundamental attribute of God is holi ss ; that holiness is self-affirming righteousness ; that this righteousness necessari   expresses itself in the punishment of sin ; that Christ's relation to the race as its upholder and life made him the bearer of its guilt and justly responsible for its sin. Scripture declares the ultimate aim of the atonement to be that God "migh¹ himself be just" (Rom. 3 : 26), and no theory of the atonement will meet the demands of either reason or conscience that does not ground its necessity in God's righteousness, rather than in his love.

E. Y. Mullins : "If Christ's union with humanity made it possible for him to be 'the representative Penitent,' and to be the Amen of humanity to God's just condemnation of sin, his union with God made it also possible for him to be the representative of the Judge, and to be the Amen of the divine nature to suffering, as the expression of condemnation." Denney, Studies in Theology, 102, 103 —"The serious element in sin is not man's dislike, suspicion, alienation from God, nor the debilitating, corrupting effects of vice in human nature, but rather God's condemnation of man. This Christ endured, and died that the condemnation might be removed. 'Bearing shame and scoffing rude, In my place condemned he stood ; Sealed my pardon with his blood ; Hallelujah !'" Bushnell regards Mat. 8 : 17 —"Himself took our infirmities, and bare our diseases "— as indicating the nature of Christ's atoning work. The meaning then would be, that he sympathized so fully with all human ills that he made them his own. Hovey, however, has given a more complete and correct explanation. The words mean rather: "His deep sympathy with these effects of sin so moved him, that it typified his final bearing of the sins themselves, or constituted a preliminary and partial endurance of the suffering which was to expiate the sins of men." His sighing when he cured the deaf man (Mark 7 : 34) and his weeping at the grave of Lazarus (John 11 : 35) were caused by the anticipatory realization that he was one with the humanity which was under the curse, and that he too had "become a curse for us " (Gal. 3 : 13). The great error of Bushnell is his denial of the objective necessity and effect of Jesus' death, and all Scripture which points to an influence of the atonement outside of us is a refutation of his theory.

(*f*) This theory confounds God's method of saving men with men's experience of being saved. It makes the atonement itself consist of its effects in the believer's union with Christ and the purifying influence of that union upon the character and life.

Stevens, in his Doctrine of Salvation, makes this mistake. He says : "The old forms of the doctrine of the atonement — that the suffering of Christ was necessary to appease the wrath of God and induce him to forgive; or to satisfy the law of God and enable him to forgive ; or to move upon man's heart to induce him to accept forgiveness; have all proved inadequate. Yet to reject the passion of Christ is to reject the chief element of power in Christianity. . . . To me the words 'eternal atonement' denote the dateless passion of God on account of sin ; they mean that God is, by his very nature, a sin-bearer — that sin grieves and wounds his heart, and that he sorrows and suffers in consequence of it. It results from the divine love — alike from its holiness and from its sympathy — that 'in our affliction he is afflicted.' Atonement on its 'Godward side' is a name for the grief and pain inflicted by sin upon the paternal heart of God. Of this divine sorrow for sin, the afflictions of Christ are a revelation. In the bitter grief and anguish which he experienced on account of sin we see reflected the pain and sorrow which sin brings to the divine love."

All this is well said, with the exception that holiness is regarded as a form of love, and the primary offence of sin is regarded as the grieving of the Father's heart. Dr. Stevens fails to consider that if love were supreme there would be nothing to prevent unholy tolerance of sin. Because holiness is supreme, love is conditioned thereby. It is holiness and not love that connects suffering with sin, and requires that the Redeemer should suffer. Dr. Stevens asserts that the theories hitherto current in Protestant churches and the theory for which he pleads are "forever irreconcilable"; they are "based on radically different conceptions of God." The British Weekly, Nov. 16, 1905 — "The doctrine of the atonement is not the doctrine that salvation is deliverance from sin, and that this deliverance is the work of God, a work the motive of which is God's love for men ; these are truths which every one who writes on the Atonement assumes. The doctrine of the Atonement has for its task to explain *how* this work is done. . . . . Dr. Stevens makes no contribution whatever to its fulfilment. He grants that we have in Paul 'the theory of a substitutionary expiation.' But he finds something else in Paul which he thinks a more adequate rendering of the apostle's Christian experience — the idea, namely, of dying with Christ and rising with him ; and on the strength of accepting this last he feels at liberty to drop the substitutionary expiation overboard as something to be explained from Paul's controversial position, or from his Pharisaic inheritance, something at all events which has no permanent value for the Christian mind. . . . The experience is dependent on the method. Paul did not die with Christ as an alternative to having Christ die with him ; he died with Christ wholly and solely because Christ died for him. It was the meaning carried by the last two words—the meaning unfolded in the theory of substitutionary expiation—which had the moral motive in .t to draw Paul into union with his Lord in life and death. . . . On Dr. Stevens' own showing, Paul held the two ideas side by side ; for him the mystical union with Christ was only possible through the acceptance of truths with which Dr. Stevens does not know what to do."

(g) This theory would confine the influence of the atonement to those who have heard of it,—thus excluding patriarchs and heathen. But the Scriptures represent Christ as being the Savior of all men, in the sense of securing them grace, which, but for his atoning work, could never have been bestowed consistently with the divine holiness.

Hovey : " The inward influence of the atonement is far more extensive than the moral influence of it." Christ is Advocate, not with the sinner, but with the Father. While the Spirit's work has moral influence over the hearts of men, the Son secures, through the presentation of his blood, in heaven, the pardon which can come only from God (1 John 2 : 1 — " we have an advocate with the Father, Jesus Christ the righteous : and he is the propitiation for our sins "). Hence 1 : 9 —" If we confess our sins, he [God] is faithful and righteous [faithful to his promise and righteous to Christ] to forgive us our sins." Hence the publican does not first pray for change of heart, but for mercy upon the ground of sacrifice (Luke 18 : 13, — "God, be thou merciful to me a sinner," but literally : "God be propitiated toward me the sinner "). See Balfour, in Brit. and For. Ev. Rev., Apr. 1884 : 230-254; Martin, Atonement, 216-237 ; Theol. Eclectic, 4 : 364-409.

Gravitation kept the universe stable, long before it was discovered by man. So the atonement of Christ was inuring to the salvation of men, long before they suspected its existence. The "Light of the world " (John 8 : 12) has many " X rays," beyond the visible spectrum, but able to impress the image of Christ upon patriarchs or heathen. This light has been shining through all the ages, but "the darkness apprehended it not " (John 1 : 5). Its rays register themselves only where there is a sensitive heart to receive them. Let them shine through a man, and how much unknown sin, and unknown possibilities of good, they reveal ! The Moral Influence theory does not take account of the pre-existent Christ and of his atoning work before his manifestation in the flesh. It therefore leads logically to belief in a second probation for the many imbeciles, outcasts, and heathen who in this world do not hear of Christ's atonement. The doctrine of Bushnell in this way undermines the doctrine of future retribution.

To Lyman Abbott, the atonement is the self-propitiation of God's love, and its influence is exerted through education. In his Theology of an Evolutionist, 118, 190, he maintains that the atonement is "a true reconciliation between God and man, making them at one through the incarnation and passion of Jesus Christ, who lived and suffered, not to redeem men from future torment, but to purify and perfect them in God's likeness by uniting them to God. . . . Sacrifice is not a penalty borne by an innocent sufferer for guilty men,—a doctrine for which there is no authority either in Scripture or in life (1 Peter 3 : 18?)—but a laying down of one's life in love, that another may receive life. . . . Redemption is not restoration to a lost state of innocence, impossible to be restored, but a culmination of the long process when man shall be presented before his Father 'not having spot or wrinkle or any such thing' (Eph. 5 : 27). . . . We believe not in the propitiation of an angry God by another suffering to appease the Father's wrath, but in the perpetual self-propitiation of the Father, whose mercy, going forth to redeem from sin, satisfies as nothing else could the divine indignation against sin, by abolishing it. . . . Mercy is hate pitying ; it is the pity of wrath. The pity conquers the hate only by lifting the sinner up from his degradation and restoring him to purity." And yet in all this there is no mention of the divine righteousness as the source of the indignation and the object of the propitiation !

It is interesting to note that some of the greatest advocates of the Moral Influence theory have reverted to the older faith when they came to die. In his dying moments, as L. W. Munhall tells us, Horace Bushnell said : " I fear what I have written and said upon the moral idea of the atonement is misleading and will do great harm ;" and, as he thought of it further, he cried : " Oh Lord Jesus, I trust for mercy only in the shed blood that thou didst offer on Calvary!" Schleiermacher, on his deathbed. assembled his family and a few friends, and himself administered the Lord's Supper. After praying and blessing the bread, and after pronouncing the words: "This is my body, broken for you," he added: "This is our foundation!" As he started to bless the cup, he cried: "Quick, quick, bring the cup! I am so happy!" Then he sank quietly back, and was no more; see life of Rothe, by Nippold, 2 : 53, 54. Ritschl, in his History of Pietism, 2 : 65, had severely criticized Paul Gerhardt's hymn: "O Haupt voll Blut und Wunden," as describing physical suffering; but he begged his son to repeat the two last verses of that hymn: "O sacred head now wounded!" when he came to die. And in general, the convicted sinner finds peace most quickly and surely when he is pointed to the Redeemer who died on the Cross and endured the penalty of sin in his stead.

3d. The Grotian, or Governmental Theory of the Atonement.

This theory holds that the atonement is a satisfaction, not to any internal principle of the divine nature, but to the necessities of government. God's government of the universe cannot be maintained, nor can the divine law preserve its authority over its subjects, unless the pardon of offenders is accompanied by some exhibition of the high estimate which God sets upon his law, and the heinous guilt of violating it. Such an exhibition of divine regard for the law is furnished in the sufferings and death of Christ. Christ does not suffer the precise penalty of the law, but God graciously accepts his suffering as a substitute for the penalty. This bearing of substituted suffering on the part of Christ gives the divine law such hold upon the consciences and hearts of men, that God can pardon the guilty upon their repentance, without detriment to the interests of his government. The author of this theory was Hugo Grotius, the Dutch jurist and theologian (1583–1645). The theory is characteristic of the New England theology, and is generally held by those who accept the New School view of sin.

Grotius was a precocious genius. He wrote good Latin verses at nine years of age; was ripe for the University at twelve; edited the encyclopædic work of Marcianus Capella at fifteen. Even thus early he went with an embassy to the court of France, where he spent a year. Returning home, he took the degree of doctor of laws. In literature he edited the remains of Aratus, and wrote three dramas in Latin. At twenty he was appointed historiographer of the United Provinces; then advocate-general of the fisc for Holland and Zealand. He wrote on international law; was appointed deputy to England; was imprisoned for his theological opinions; escaped to Paris; became ambassador of Sweden to France. He wrote commentaries on Scripture, also history, theology, and poetry. He was indifferent to dogma, a lover of peace, a compromiser, an unpartisan believer, dealing with doctrine more as a statesman than as a theologian. Of Grotius, Dr. E. G. Robinson used to say: "It is ordained of almighty God that the man who dips into everything never gets to the bottom of anything."

Grotius, the jurist, conceived of law as a mere matter of political expediency — a device to procure practical governmental results. The text most frequently quoted in support of his theory, is Is. 42 : 21 — "It pleased Jehovah, for his righteousness' sake, to magnify the law, and make it honorable." Strangely enough, the explanation is added: "even when its demands are unfulfilled." Park: "Christ satisfied the law, by making it desirable and consistent for God not to come up to the demands of the law. Christ suffers a divine chastisement in consequence of our sins. Christ was cursed for Adam's sin, just as the heavens and the earth were cursed for Adam's sin, — that is, he bore pains and sufferings on account of it."

Grotius used the word *acceptilatio*, by which he meant God's sovereign provision of a suffering which was not itself penalty, but which he had determined to accept as a substitute for penalty. Here we have a virtual denial that there is anything in God's nature that requires Christ to suffer; for if penalty may be remitted in part, it may be remitted in whole, and the reason why Christ suffers at all is to be found, not in any demand of God's holiness, but solely in the beneficial influence of these sufferings upon man; so that in principle this theory is allied to the Example theory and the Moral Influence theory, already mentioned.

Notice the difference between holding to a *substitute for penalty*, as Grotius did, and holding to an *equivalent substituted penalty*, as the Scriptures do. Grotius's own statement of his view may be found in his Defensio Fidei Catholicæ de Satisfactione (Works, 4 : 297-338). More modern statements of it are those of Wardlaw, in his Systematic Theology, 2 : 358-395, and of Albert Barnes, on the Atonement. The history of New England thought upon the subject is given in Discourses and Treatises on the Atonement, edited by Prof. Park, of Andover. President Woolsey: "Christ's suffering was due to a deep and awful sense of responsibility, a conception of the supreme importance to man of his standing firm at this crisis. He bore, not the wrath of God, but suffering, as the only way of redemption so far as men's own feeling of sin was concerned, and so far as the government of God was concerned." This unites the Governmental and the Moral Influence theories.

Foster, Christian Life and Theology, 226, 227 — "Grotius emphasized the idea of law rather than that of justice, and made the sufferings of Christ a legal example and the occasion of the relaxation of the law, and not the strict penalty demanded by justice. But this view, however it may have been considered and have served in the clarification of the thinking of the times, met with no general reception, and left little trace of itself among those theologians who maintained the line of evangelical theological descent."

To this theory we urge the following objections :

(*a*) While it contains a valuable element of truth, namely, that the suf-ferings and death of Christ secure the interests of God's government, it is false by defect, in substituting for the chief aim of the atonement one which is only subordinate and incidental.

In our discussion of Penalty (pages 655, 656), we have seen that the object of punishment is not primarily the security of government. It is not right to punish a man for the beneficial effect on society. Ill-desert must go before punishment, or the punishment can have no beneficial effect on society. No punishment can work good to society, that is not just and right in itself.

(*b*) It rests upon false philosophical principles, — as, that utility is the ground of moral obligation ; that law is an expression of the will, rather than of the nature, of God ; that the aim of penalty is to deter from the com-mission of offences ; and that righteousness is resolvable into benevolence.

Hodge, Syst. Theol., 2 : 573-581 ; 3 : 188, 189 — "For God to take that as satisfaction which is not really such, is to say that there is no truth in anything. God may take a part for the whole, error for truth, wrong for right. The theory really denies the necessity for the work of Christ. If every created thing offered to God is worth just so much as God accepts it for, then the blood of bulls and goats might take away sins, and Christ is dead in vain." Dorner, Glaubenslehre, 2 : 570, 571 (Syst. Doct., 4 : 38-40)— "*Acceptilatio* implies that nothing is good and right in itself. God is indifferent to good or evil. Man is bound by authority and force alone. There is no necessity of punishment or atonement. The doctrine of indulgences and of supererogation logically follows."

(*c*) It ignores and virtually denies that immanent holiness of God of which the law with its threatened penalties, and the human conscience with its demand for punishment, are only finite reflections. There is some-thing back of government ; if the atonement satisfies government, it must be by satisfying that justice of God of which government is an expression.

No deeply convicted sinner feels that his controversy is with government. Undone and polluted, he feels himself in antagonism to the purity of a personal God. Government is not greater than God, but less. What satisfies God must satisfy government. Hence the sinner prays: "Against thee, thee only, have I sinned " (Ps. 51 : 4) ; "God be propitiated toward me the sinner " (literal translation of Luke 18 : 13),—propitiated through God's own appointed sacrifice whose smoke is ascending in his behalf even while he prays.

In the divine government this theory recognizes no constitution, but only legislative enactment; even this legislative enactment is grounded in no necessity of God's nature, but only in expediency or in God's arbitrary will; law may be abrogated for merely economic reasons, if any incidental good may be gained thereby.   J. M. Campbell, Atonement, 81, 144 —" No awakened sinner, into whose spirit the terrors of the law have entered, ever thinks of rectoral justice, but of absolute justice, and of absolute justice only. . . . Rectoral justice so presupposes absolute justice, and so throws the mind back on that absolute justice, that the idea of an atonement that will satisfy the one, though it might not the other, is a delusion."

N. W. Taylor's Theology was entitled: " Moral Government," and C. G. Finney's Systematic Theology was a treatise on Moral Government, although it called itself by another name. But because New England ideas of government were not sufficiently grounded in God's holiness, but were rather based upon utility, expediency, or happiness, the very idea of government has dropped out of the New School theology, and its advocates with well-nigh one accord have gone over to the Moral Influence theory of the atonement, which is only a modified Socinianism. Both the Andover atonement and that of Oberlin have become purely subjective. For this reason the Grotian or Governmental theory has lost its hold upon the theological world and needs to have no large amount of space devoted to it.

(d) It makes that to be an exhibition of justice which is not an exercise of justice ; the atonement being, according to this theory, not an execution of law, but an exhibition of regard for law, which will make it safe to pardon the violators of law.   Such a merely scenic representation can inspire respect for law, only so long as the essential unreality of it is unsuspected.

To teach that sin will be punished, there must be punishment. Potwin: " How the exhibition of what sin deserves, but does not get, can satisfy justice, is hard to see." The Socinian view of Christ as an example of virtue is more intelligible than the Grotian view of Christ as an example of chastisement. Lyman Abbott: " If I thought that Jesus suffered and died to produce a moral impression on me, it would not produce a moral impression on me." William Ashmore: " A stage tragedian commits a mock murder in order to move people to tears. If Christ was in no sense a substitute, or if he was not co-responsible with the sinner he represents, then God and Christ are participants in a real tragedy the most awful that ever darkened human history, simply for the sake of its effect on men to move their callous sensibilities — a stage-trick for the same effect."

The mother pretends to cry in order to induce her child to obey. But the child will obey only while it thinks the mother's grief a reality, and the last state of that child is worse than the first. Christ's atonement is no passion-play. Hell cannot be cured by homœopathy. The sacrifice of Calvary is no dramatic exhibition of suffering for the purpose of producing a moral impression on awe-stricken spectators. It is an object-lesson, only because it is a reality. All God's justice and all God's love are focused in the Cross, so that it teaches more of God and his truth than all space and time beside. John Milton, Paradise Lost, book 5, speaks of " mist, the common gloss of theologians." Such mist is the legal fiction by which Christ's suffering is taken in place of legal penalty, while yet it is not the legal penalty itself. E. G. Robinson: " Atonement is not an arbitrary contrivance, so that if one person will endure a certain amount of suffering, a certain number of others may go scot-free." Mercy never cheats justice. Yet the New School theory of atonement admits that Christ cheated justice by a trick. It substituted the penalty of Christ for the penalty of the redeemed, and then substituted something else for the penalty of Christ.

(e) The intensity of Christ's sufferings in the garden and on the cross is inexplicable upon the theory that the atonement was a histrionic exhibition of God's regard for his government, and can be explained only upon the view that Christ actually endured the wrath of God against human sin.

Christ refused the " wine mingled with myrrh " (Mark 15 : 23), that he might to the last have full possession of his powers and speak no words but words of truth and soberness. His cry of agony : " My God, my God, why hast thou forsaken me ? " (Mat. 27 : 46), was not an ejaculation of thoughtless or delirious suffering. It expressed the deepest meaning of the crucifixion. The darkening of the heavens was only the outward symbol of the hiding of the countenance of God from him who was *"made to be sin on our behalf"* (2 Cor. 5 : 21). In the case of Christ, above that of all others, *finis coronat*, and dying words are undying words. "The tongues of dying men Enforce attention like deep harmony ; When words are scarce they 're seldom spent in vain, For they breathe truth that breathe their words in pain." *Versus* Park, Discourses, 328–355.

A pure woman needs to meet an infamous proposition with something more than a mild refusal. She must flame up and be angry. Ps. 97 : 10 — "O ye that love Jehovah, hate evil " ; Eph. 4 : 26 — "Be ye angry, and sin not." So it belongs to the holiness of God not to let sin go unchallenged. God not only *shows* anger, but he *is* angry. It is the wrath of God which sin must meet, and which Christ must meet when he is numbered with the transgressors. Death was the cup of which he was to drink (Mat. 20 : 22 ; John 18 : 11), and which he drained to the dregs. Mason, Faith of the Gospel, 196 — "Jesus alone of all men truly 'tasted death' (Heb. 2 : 9). Some men are too stolid and unimaginative to taste it. To Christians the bitterness of death is gone, just because Christ died and rose again But to Jesus its terrors were as yet undiminished. He resolutely set all his faculties to sound to the depths the dreadfulness of dying."

We therefore cannot agree with either Wendt or Johnson in the following quotations. Wendt, Teaching of Jesus, 2 : 249, 250 — "The forsaking of the Father was not an absolute one, since Jesus still called him 'My God' (Mat. 27 : 46). Jesus felt the failing of that energy of spirit which had hitherto upheld him, and he expresses simply his ardent desire and prayer that God would once more grant him his power and assistance." E. H. Johnson, The Holy Spirit, 143, 144 — "It is not even necessary to believe that God hid his face from Christ at the last moment. It is necessary only to admit that Christ no longer saw the Father's face. . . . He felt that it was so ; but it was not so." These explanations make Christ's sufferings and Christ's words unreal, and to our mind they are inconsistent with both his deity and his atonement.

(*f*) The actual power of the atonement over the human conscience and heart is due, not to its exhibiting God's regard for law, but to its exhibiting an actual execution of law, and an actual satisfaction of violated holiness made by Christ in the sinner's stead.

Whiton, Gloria Patri, 143, 144, claims that Christ is the propitiation for our sins only by bringing peace to the conscience and satisfying the divine demand that is felt therein. Whiton regards the atonement not as a governmental work outside of us, but as an educational work within. Aside from the objection that this view merges God's transcendence in his immanence, we urge the words of Matthew Henry : "Nothing can satisfy an offended conscience but that which satisfied an offended God." C. J. Baldwin : "The lake spread out has no moving power ; it turns the mill-wheel only when contracted into the narrow stream and pouring over the fall. So the wide love of God moves men, only when it is concentrated into the sacrifice of the cross."

(*g*) The theory contradicts all those passages of Scripture which represent the atonement as necessary ; as propitiating God himself ; as being a revelation of God's righteousness ; as being an execution of the penalty of the law ; as making salvation a matter of debt to the believer, on the ground of what Christ has done ; as actually purging our sins, instead of making that purging possible ; as not simply assuring the sinner that God may now pardon him on account of what Christ has done, but that Christ has actually wrought out a complete salvation, and will bestow it upon all who come to him.

John Bunyan, Pilgrim's Progress, chapter vi — "Upon that place stood a Cross, and a little below, in the bottom, a Sepulchre. So I saw in my dream, that just as Christian came up with the Cross, his burden loosed from off his shoulders, and fell from off his back, and began to tumble, and so continued to do, till it came to the mouth of the Sepulchre, where it fell in, and I saw it no more. Then was Christian glad and lightsome, and said with a merry heart, He hath given me rest by his sorrow, and life by his death. Then he stood still awhile to look and wonder ; for it was very surprising to him that the sight of the Cross should thus ease him of his burden."

John Bunyan's story is truer to Christian experience than is the Governmental theory. The sinner finds peace, not by coming to God with a distant respect to Christ, but by coming directly to the "Lamb of God, which taketh away the sin of the world" (John 1 : 29). Christ's words to every conscious sinner are simply : "Come unto me" (Mat. 11 : 28). Upon the ground of what Christ has done, salvation is a matter of debt to the believer. 1 John 1 : 9 —"If we confess our sins, he is faithful and righteous to forgive us our sins" — faithful to his promise, and righteous to Christ. The Governmental theory, on the other hand, tends to discourage the sinner's direct access to Christ, and to render the way to conscious acceptance with God more circuitous and less certain.

When The Outlook says : "Not even to the Son of God must we come instead of coming to God," we can see only plain denial of the validity of Christ's demands and promises, for he demands immediate submission when he bids the sinner follow him, and he promises immediate salvation when he assures all who come to him that he will not cast them out. The theory of Grotius is legal and speculative, but it is not Scriptural, nor does it answer the needs of human nature. For criticism of Albert Barnes's doctrine, see Watts, New Apologetic, 210–300. For criticism of the Grotian theory in general, see Shedd, Hist. Doctrine, 2 : 347–369 ; Crawford, Atonement, 367 ; Cunningham, Hist. Theology, 2 : 355 ; Princeton Essays, 1 : 259–292 ; Essay on Atonement, by Abp. Thomson, in Aids to Faith ; McIlvaine, Wisdom of Holy Scripture. 194–196 ; S. H. Tyng, Christian Pastor ; Charles Hodge, Essays, 129–184 ; Lidgett, Spir. Prin. of Atonement, 151–154.

4th. The Irvingian Theory, or Theory of Gradually Extirpated Depravity.

This holds that, in his incarnation, Christ took human nature as it was in Adam, not before the Fall, but after the Fall,—human nature, therefore, with its inborn corruption and predisposition to moral evil ; that, notwithstanding the possession of this tainted and depraved nature, Christ, through the power of the Holy Spirit, or of his divine nature, not only kept his human nature from manifesting itself in any actual or personal sin, but gradually purified it, through struggle and suffering, until in his death he completely extirpated its original depravity, and reunited it to God. This subjective purification of human nature in the person of Jesus Christ constitutes his atonement, and men are saved, not by any objective propitiation, but only by becoming through faith partakers of Christ's new humanity. This theory was elaborated by Edward Irving, of London (1792–1834), and it has been held, in substance, by Menken and Dippel in Germany.

Irving was in this preceded by Felix of Urgella, in Spain († 818), whom Alcuin opposed. Felix said that the Logos united with human nature, without sanctifying it beforehand. Edward Irving, in his early life colleague of Dr. Chalmers, at Glasgow, was in his later years a preacher, in London, of the National Church of Scotland. For his own statement of his view of the Atonement, see his Collected Works, 5 : 9–398. See also Life of Irving, by Mrs. Oliphant ; Menken, Schriften, 3 : 279–404 ; 6 : 351 sq. ; Guericke, in Studien und Kritiken, 1843 : Heft 2 ; David Brown, in Expositor, Oct. 1887 : 264 sq., and letter of Irving to Marcus Dods, in British Weekly, Mch. 25, 1887. For other references, see Hagenbach, Hist. Doct., 2 : 496–498.

Irving's followers differ in their representation of his views. Says Miller, Hist. and Doct. of Irvingism, 1 : 85—;"If indeed we made Christ a sinner, then indeed all creeds are at an end and we are worthy to die the death of blasphemers. . . . The miraculous conception depriveth him of human personality, and it also depriveth him of original sin and guilt needing to be atoned for by another, but it doth not deprive him of the substance of sinful flesh and blood, — that is, flesh and blood the same with the flesh and blood of his brethren." 2 : 14—Freer says : "So that, despite it was fallen flesh he had assumed, he was, through the Eternal Spirit, born into the world 'the Holy Thing'." 11–15, 282–305 — " Unfallen humanity needed not redemption, therefore, Jesus did not take it. He took fallen humanity, but purged it in the act of taking it. The nature of which he took part was sinful in the lump, but in his person most holy."

So, says an Irvingian tract, " Being part of the very nature that had incurred the penalty of sin, though in his person never having committed or even thought it, part of the common humanity could suffer that penalty, and did so suffer, to mal r atonement for that nature, though he who took it knew no sin." Dr. Curry, quoted in McClintock and Strong, Encyclopædia, 4 : 663, 664 — "The Godhead came into vital union with humanity fallen and under the law. The last thought carried, to Irving's realistic mode of thinking, the notion of Christ's participation in the fallen character of humanity, which he designated by terms that implied a real sinfulness in Christ. He attempted to get rid of the odiousness of that idea, by saying that this was overborne, and at length wholly expelled, by the indwelling Godhead."

We must regard the later expounders of Irvingian doctrine as having softened down, if they have not wholly expunged, its most characteristic feature, as the following quotation from Irving's own words will show: Works, 5 : 115 — "That Christ took our fallen nature, is most manifest, because there was no other in existence to take." 123 — "The human nature is thoroughly fallen ; the mere apprehension of it by the Son doth not make it holy." 123 — "His soul did mourn and grieve and pray to God continually, that it might be delivered from the mortality, corruption, and temptation which it felt in its fleshly tabernacle." 152 — "These sufferings came not by imputation merely, but by actual participation of the sinful ana cursed thing." Irving frequently quoted Heb. 2 : 10 — "make the author of their salvation perfect through sufferings."

Irving's followers deny Christ's sinfulness, only by assuming that inborn infirmity and congenital tendencies to evil are not sin, — in other words, that not native depravity, but only actual trangression, is to be denominated sin. Irving, in our judgment, was rightly charged with asserting the sinfulness of Christ's human nature, and it was upon this charge that he was deposed from the ministry by the Presbytery in Scotland.

Irving was of commanding stature, powerful voice, natural and graceful oratory. He loved the antique and the grand. For a time in London he was the great popular sensation. But shortly after the opening of his new church in Regent's Square in 1827, he found that fashion had taken its departure and that his church was no longer crowded. He concluded that the world was under the reign of Satan; he became a fanatical millennarian ; he gave himself wholly to the study of prophecy. In 1830 he thought the apostolic gifts were revived, and he held to the hope of a restoration of the primitive church, although he himself was relegated to a comparatively subordinate position. He exhausted his energies, and died at the age of forty-two. "If I had married Irving," said Mrs. Thomas Carlyle, "there would have been no tongues."

To this theory we offer the following objections :

(*a*) While it embraces an important element of truth, namely, the fact of a new humanity in Christ of which all believers become partakers, it is chargeable with serious error in denying the objective atonement which makes the subjective application possible.

Bruce, in his Humiliation of Christ, calls this a theory of "redemption by sample." It is a purely subjective atonement which Irving has in mind. Deliverance from sin, in order to deliverance from penalty, is an exact reversal of the Scripture order. Yet this deliverance from sin, in Irving's view, was to be secured in an external and mechanical way. He held that it was the Old Testament economy which should abide, while the New Testament economy should pass away. This is Sacramentarianism, or dependence upon the external rite, rather than upon the internal grace, as essential to salvation. The followers of Irving are Sacramentarians. The crucifix and candles, incense and gorgeous vestments, a highly complicated and symbolic ritual, they regard as a necessary accompaniment of religion. They feel the need of external authority, visible and permanent, but one that rests upon inspiration and continual supernatural help. They do not find this authority, as the Romanists do, in the Pope, — they find it in their new Apostles and Prophets. The church can never be renewed, as they think, except by the restoration of all the ministering orders mentioned in Eph. 4 : 11 — "apostles .... prophets .... evangelists .... pastors .... teachers." But the N. T. mark of an apostle is that Christ has appeared to him. Irving's apostles cannot stand this test. See Luthardt, Errinerungen aus vergangenen Tagen, 237.

(*b*) It rests upon false fundamental principles, — as, that law is identical with the natural order of the universe, and as such, is an exhaustive expression of the will and nature of God ; that sin is merely a power of moral evil within the soul, instead of also involving an objective guilt and desert of punishment ; that penalty is the mere reaction of law against the transgressor, instead of being also the revelation of a personal wrath against sin ; that the evil taint of human nature can be extirpated by suffering its natural consequences,—penalty in this way reforming the transgressor.

Dorner, Glaubenslehre, 2 : 463 (Syst. Doct., 3 : 361, 362)—" On Irving's theory, evil inclinations are not sinful. Sinfulness belongs only to evil acts. The loose connection between the Logos and humanity savors of Nestorianism. It is the work of the *person* to rid itself of something in the humanity which does not render it really sinful. If Jesus' sinfulness of nature did not render his person sinful, this must be true of us,—which is a Pelagian element, revealed also in the denial that for our redemption we need Christ as an atoning sacrifice. It is not necessary to a complete incarnation for Christ to take a *sinful* nature, unless sin is *essential* to human nature. In Irving's view, the death of Christ's body works the regeneration of his sinful nature. But this is to make sin a merely physical thing, and the body the only part of man needing redemption." Penalty would thus become a reformer, and death a Savior.

Irving held that there are two kinds of sin : 1. guiltless sin ; 2. guilty sin. Passive depravity is not guilty ; it is a part of man's sensual nature ; without it we would not be human. But the moment this fallen nature expresses itself in action, it becomes guilty. Irving near the close of his life claimed a sort of sinless perfection ; for so long as he could keep this sinful nature inactive, and be guided by the Holy Spirit, he was free from sin and guilt. Christ took this passive sin, that he might be like unto his brethren, and that he might be able to suffer.

(*c*) It contradicts the express and implicit representations of Scripture, with regard to Christ's freedom from all taint of hereditary depravity ; misrepresents his life as a growing consciousness of the underlying corruption of his human nature, which culminated at Gethsemane and Calvary ; and denies the truth of his own statements, when it declares that he must have died on account of his own depravity, even though none were to be saved thereby.

" I shall maintain until death," said Irving, " that the flesh of Christ was as rebellious as ours, as fallen as ours. . . . Human nature was corrupt to the core and black as hell, and this is the human nature the Son of God took upon himself and was clothed with.' The Rescuer must stand as deep in the mire as the one he rescues. There was no substitution. Christ waged war with the sin of his own flesh and he expelled it. His glory was not in saving others, but in saving himself, and so demonstrating the power of man through the Holy Spirit to cast out sin from his heart and life. Irving held that his theory was the only one taught in Scripture and held from the first by the church.

Nicoll, Life of Christ, 183 —" All others, as they grow in holiness, grow in their sense of sin. But when Christ is forsaken of the Father, he asks ' Why ?' well knowing that the reason is not in his sin. He never makes confession of sin. In his longest prayer, the preface is an assertion of righteousness : 'I glorified thee' (John 17 : 4). His last utterance from the cross is a quotation from Ps. 31 : 5 —' Father, into thy hands I commend my spirit (Luke 23 : 46), but he does not add, as the Psalm does, 'thou hast redeemed me, O Lord God of truth,' for he needed no redemption, being himself the Redeemer."

(*d*) It makes the active obedience of Christ, and the subjective purification of his human nature, to be the chief features of his work, while the Scriptures make his death and passive bearing of penalty the centre of all, and ever regard him as one who is personally pure and who vicariously bears the punishment of the guilty.

In Irving's theory there is no imputation, or representation, or substitution. His only idea of sacrifice is that sin itself shall be sacrificed, or annihilated. The many subjective theories of the atonement show that the offence of the cross has not ceased (Gal. 5 : 11 — "then hath the stumbling-block of the cross been done away "). Christ crucified is still a stumbling-block to modern speculation. Yet it is, as of old, "the power of God unto salvation" (Rom. 1 : 16 ; *cf.* 1 Cor. 1 : 23, 24 —" we preach Christ crucified, unto Jews a stumbling-block and unto Gentiles foolishness ; but unto them that are called, both Jews and Greeks, Christ the power of God, and the wisdom of God ").

As the ocean receives the impurities of the rivers and purges them, so Irving represented Christ as receiving into himself the impurities of humanity and purging the race
from its sin. Here is the sense of defilement, but no sense of guilt; subjective pollution, but no objective condemnation. We take precisely opposite ground from that of
Irving, namely, that Christ had, not hereditary depravity, but hereditary guilt; that he
was under obligation to suffer for the sins of the race to which he had historically
united himself, and of which he was the creator, the upholder, and the life. He was
"made to be sin on our behalf" (2 Cor. 5 : 21), not in the sense of one defiled, as Irving thought,
but in the sense of one condemned to bear our iniquities and to suffer their penal consequences. The test of a theory of the atonement, as the test of a religion, is its power
to "cleanse that red right hand" of Lady Macbeth; in other words, its power to satisfy
the divine justice of which our condemning conscience is only the reflection. The
theory of Irving has no such power. Dr. E. G. Robinson verged toward Irving's view,
when he claimed that "Christ took human nature as he found it."

(e) It necessitates the surrender of the doctrine of justification as a
merely declaratory act of God ; and requires such a view of the divine holiness, expressed only through the order of nature, as can be maintained
only upon principles of pantheism.

Thomas Aquinas inquired whether Christ was slain by himself, or by another. The
question suggests a larger one — whether God has constituted other forces than his
own, personal and impersonal, in the universe, over against which he stands in his
transcendence ; or whether all his activity is merged in, and identical with, the activity
of the creature. The theory of a merely subjective atonement is more consistent with
the latter view than the former. For criticism of Irvingian doctrine, see Studien und
Kritiken, 1845 : 319; 1877 : 354-374; Princeton Rev., April, 1863 : 207; Christian Rev., 28 :
234 sq.; Ullmann, Sinlessness of Jesus, 219-232.

5th. The Anselmic, or Commercial Theory of the Atonement.

This theory holds that sin is a violation of the divine honor or majesty,
and, as committed against an infinite being, deserves an infinite punishment; that the majesty of God requires him to execute punishment, while
the love of God pleads for the sparing of the guilty ; that this conflict of
divine attributes is eternally reconciled by the voluntary sacrifice of the
God-man, who bears in virtue of the dignity of his person the intensively
infinite punishment of sin, which must otherwise have been suffered extensively and eternally by sinners ; that this suffering of the God-man presents
to the divine majesty an exact equivalent for the deserved sufferings of the
elect ; and that, as the result of this satisfaction of the divine claims, the
elect sinners are pardoned and regenerated. This view was first broached
by Anselm of Canterbury (1033-1109) as a substitute for the earlier patristic view that Christ's death was a ransom paid to Satan, to deliver sinners
from his power. It is held by many Scotch theologians, and, in this
country, by the Princeton School.

The old patristic theory, which the Anselmic view superseded, has been called the
Military theory of the Atonement. Satan, as a captor in war, had a right to his captives, which could be bought off only by ransom. It was Justin Martyr who first propounded this view that Christ paid a ransom to Satan. Gregory of Nyssa added that
Christ's humanity was the bait with which Satan was attracted to the hidden hook of
Christ's deity, and so was caught by artifice. Peter Lombard, Sent., 3 : 19—"What did
the Reedemer to our captor? He held out to him his cross as a mouse-trap ; in it he
set, as a bait, his blood." Even Luther compares Satan to the crocodile which swallows
the ichneumon, only to find that the little animal eats its insides out.

These metaphors show this, at least, that no age of the church has believed in a
merely subjective atonement. Nor was this relation to Satan the only aspect in which
the atonement was regarded even by the early church. So early as the fourth century,
we find a great church Father maintaining that the death of Christ was required by the

truth and goodness of God. See Crippen, History of Christian Doctrine, 129 —" Atha-nasius (325-373) held that the death of Christ was the payment of a debt due to God. His argument is briefly this: God, having threatened death as the punishment of sin, would be untrue if he did not fulfil his threatening. But it would be equally unworthy of the divine goodness to permit rational beings, to whom he had imparted his own spirit, to incur this death in consequence of an imposition practiced on them by the devil. Seeing then that nothing but death could solve this dilemma, the Word, who could not die, assumed a mortal body, and, offering his human nature a sacrifice for all, fulfilled the law by his death." Gregory Nazianzen (390) " retained the figure of a ransom, but, clearly perceiving that the analogy was incomplete, he explained the death of Christ as an expedient to reconcile the divine attributes."

But, although many theologians had recognized a relation of atonement to God, none before Anselm had given any clear account of the nature of this relation. Anselm's acute, brief, and beautiful treatise entitled " Cur Deus Homo " constitutes the greatest single contribution to the discussion of this doctrine. He shows that " whatever man owes, he owes to God, not to the devil. . . . He who does not yield due honor to God, withholds from him what is his, and dishonors him; and this is sin. . . . It is necessary that either the stolen honor be restored, or that punishment follow." Man, because of original sin, cannot make satisfaction for the dishonor done to God,—" a sinner cannot justify a sinner." Neither could an angel make this satisfaction. None can make it but God. "If then none can make it but God, and none owes it but man, it must needs be wrought out by God, made man." The God-man, to make satisfaction for the sins of all mankind, must " give to God, of his own, something that is more valuable than all that is under God." Such a gift of infinite value was his death. The reward of his sacrifice turns to the advantage of man, and thus the justice and love of God are reconciled.

The foregoing synopsis is mainly taken from Crippen, Hist. Christ. Doct., 134, 135. The Cur Deus Homo of Anselm is translated in Bib. Sac., 11 : 729 ; 12 : 52. A synopsis of it is given in Lichtenberger's Encyclopédie des Sciences Religieuses, vol. 1, art.: Anselm. The treatises on the Atonement by Symington, Candlish, Martin, Smeaton, in Great Britain, advocate for substance the view of Anselm, as indeed it was held by Calvin before them. In America, the theory is represented by Nathanael Emmons, A. Alexander, and Charles Hodge (Syst. Theol., 2 : 470-540).

To this theory we make the following objections :

(a) While it contains a valuable element of truth, in its representation of the atonement as satisfying a principle of the divine nature, it conceives of this principle in too formal and external a manner, — making the idea of the divine honor or majesty more prominent than that of the divine holiness, in which the divine honor and majesty are grounded.

The theory has been called the " Criminal theory " of the Atonement, as the old patristic theory of a ransom paid to Satan has been called the " Military theory." It had its origin in a time when exaggerated ideas prevailed respecting the authority of popes and emperors, and when dishonor done to their majesty (crimen læsæ majestatis was the highest offence known to law. See article by Cramer, in Studien und Kritiken 1880 : 7, on Wurzeln des Anselm'schen Satisfactionsbegriffes.

Allen, Jonathan Edwards, 88, 89—" From the point of view of Sovereignty, there could be no necessity for atonement. In Mohammedanism, where sovereignty is the supreme and sole theological principle, no need is felt for satisfying the divine justice. God may pardon whom he will, on whatever grounds his sovereign will may dictate. It therefore constituted a great advance in Latin theology, as also an evidence of its immeasurable superiority to Mohammedanism, when Anselm for the first time, in a clear and emphatic manner, had asserted an inward necessity in the being of God that his justice should receive satisfaction for the affront which had been offered to it by human sinfulness."

Henry George, Progress and Poverty, 481—" In the days of feudalism, men thought of heaven as organized on a feudal basis, and ranked the first and second Persons of the Trinity as Suzerain and Tenant-in-Chief." William James, Varieties of Religious Experience, 329, 330—" The monarchical type of sovereignty was, for example, so ineradicably planted in the mind of our forefathers, that a dose of cruelty and arbitrariness in their Deity seems positively to have been required by their imagination. They called the cruelty 'retributive justice,' and a God without it would certainly not have struck them as sovereign enough. But to-day we abhor the very notion of eternal suffering inflicted; and that arbitrary dealing out of salvation and damnation to selected individuals, of which Jonathan Edwards could persuade himself that he had not only a conviction, but a 'delightful conviction,' as of a doctrine 'exceeding pleasant, bright, and sweet,' appears to us, if sovereignly anything, sovereignly irrational and mean.''

(b) In its eagerness to maintain the atoning efficacy of Christ's passive obedience, the active obedience, quite as clearly expressed in Scripture, is insufficiently emphasized and well nigh lost sight of.

Neither Christ's active obedience alone, nor Christ's obedient passion alone, can save us. As we shall see hereafter, in our examination of the doctrine of Justification, the latter was needed as the ground upon which our penalty could be remitted ; the former as the ground upon which we might be admitted to the divine favor. Calvin has reflected the passive element in Anselm's view, in the following passages of his Institutes : II, 17 : 3 — " God, to whom we were hateful through sin, was appeased by the death of his Son, and was made propitious to us." . . . II, 16:7—" It is necessary to consider how he substituted himself in order to pay the price of our redemption. Death held us under its yoke, but he, in our place, delivered himself into its power, that he might exempt us from it." . . . II, 16 : 2— " Christ interposed and bore what, by the just judgment of God, was impending over sinners ; with his own blood expiated the sin which rendered them hateful to God ; by this expiation satisfied and duly propitiated the Father ; by this interession appeased his anger ; on this basis founded peace between God and men ; and by this tie secured the divine benevolence toward them."

It has been said that Anselm regarded Christ's death not as a vicarious punishment, but as a voluntary sacrifice in compensation for which the guilty were released and justified. So Neander, Hist. Christ. Dogmas (Bohn), 2 : 517, understands Anselm to teach " the necessity of a satisfactio vicaria activa," and says: " We do not find in his writings the doctrine of a satisfactio passiva ; he nowhere says that Christ had endured the punishment of men.'' Shedd, Hist. Christ. Doctrine, 2 : 282, thinks this a misunderstanding of Anselm. The Encyclopædia Britannica takes the view of Shedd, when it speaks of Christ's sufferings as penalty : " The justice of man demands satisfaction, and as an insult to infinite honor is itself infinite, the satisfaction must be infinite, i. e., it must outweigh all that is not God. Such a penalty can only be paid by God himself, and, as a penalty for man, must be paid under the form of man. Satisfaction is only possible through the God-man. Now this God-man, as sinless, is exempt from the punishment of sin ; his passion is therefore voluntary, not given as due. The merit of it is therefore infinite ; God's justice is thus appeased, and his mercy may extend to man." The truth then appears to be that Anselm held Christ's obedience to be passive, in that he satisfied God's justice by enduring punishment which the sinner deserved ; but that he held this same obedience of Christ to be active, in that he endured this penalty voluntarily, when there was no obligation upon him so to do.

Shedd, Dogmatic Theology, 2 : 431, 461, 462 — " Christ not only suffered the penalty, but obeyed the precept, of the law. In this case law and justice get their whole dues. But when lost man only suffers the penalty, but does not obey the precept, the law is defrauded of a part of its dues. No law is completely obeyed, if only its penalty is endured. . . . Consequently, a sinner can never completely and exhaustively satisfy the divine law, however much or long he may suffer, because he cannot at one and the same time endure the penalty and obey the precept. He owes 'ten thousand talents' and has 'not wherewith to pay' (Mat. 18 : 24, 25). But Christ did both, and therefore he 'magnified the law and made it honorable' (Is. 42 : 21), in an infinitely higher degree than the whole human family would have done, had they all personally suffered for their sins." Cf. Edwards, Works, 1 : 406.

(c) It allows disproportionate weight to those passages of Scripture which represent the atonement under commercial analogies, as the payment of a debt or ransom, to the exclusion of those which describe it as an ethical fact, whose value is to be estimated not quantitatively, but qualitatively.

Milton, Paradise Lost, 3 : 209-212 — " Die he, or justice must, unless for him Some other. able and as willing. pay The rigid satisfaction, death for death.'' The main text relied upon by the advocates of the Commercial theory is Mat. 20 : 28 — "give his life a ransom for many." Pfleiderer, Philosophy of Religion, 1 : 257 — " The work of Christ, as Anselm construed it, was in fact nothing else than the prototype of the meritorious perform- ances and satisfactions of the ecclesiastical saints, and was therefore, from the point of view of the mediæval church, thought out quite logically. All the more remarkable is it that the churches of the Reformation could be satisfied with this theory, notwith- standing that it stood in complete contradiction to their deeper moral consciousness. If, according to Protestant principles generally, there are no supererogatory meritor- ious works, then one would suppose that such cannot be accepted even in the case of Jesus."

E. G. Robinson, Christian Theology, 258 — "The Anselmic theory was rejected by Abelard for grounding the atonement in justice instead of benevolence, and for taking insufficient account of the power of Christ's sufferings and death in procuring a sub- jective change in man." Encyc. Brit., 2 : 93 (art.: Anselm) — " This theory has exer- cised immense influence on the form of church doctrine. It is certainly an advance on the older patristic theory, in so far as it substitutes for a contest between God and Satan, a contest between the goodness and justice of God ; but it puts the whole rela- tion on a merely legal footing, gives it no ethical bearing, and neglects altogether the consciousness of the individual to be redeemed. In this respect it contrasts unfavor- ably with the later theory of Abelard."

(*d*) It represents the atonement as having reference only to the elect, and ignores the Scripture declarations that Christ died for all.

Anselm, like Augustine, limited the atonement to the elect. Yet Leo the Great, in 461, had affirmed that " so precious is the shedding of Christ's blood for the unjust, that if the whole universe of captives would believe in the Redeemer, no chain of the devil could hold them " (Crippen, 132). Bishop Gailor, of the Episcopal Church, heard General Booth-at Memphis say in 1903 : " Friends, Jesus shed his blood to pay the price, and he bought from God enough salvation to go round." The Bishop says : " I felt that his view of salvation was different from mine. Yet such teaching, partial as it is, lifts men by the thousand from the mire and vice of sin into the power and purity of a new life in Jesus Christ."

Foster, Christian Life and Theology, 221 — "Anselm does not clearly connect the death of Christ with the punishment of sin, since he makes it a supererogatory work volun- tarily done, in consequence of which it is ' fitting ' that forgiveness should be bestowed on sinners. . . . Yet his theory served to hand down to later theologians the great idea of the objective atonement."

(*e*) It is defective in holding to a merely external transfer of the merit of Christ's work, while it does not clearly state the internal ground of that transfer, in the union of the believer with Christ.

This needed supplement, namely, the doctrine of the Union of the Believer with Christ, was furnished by Thomas Aquinas, Summa, pars 3, quæs. 8. The Anselmic theory is Romanist in its tendency, as the theory next to be mentioned is Protestant in its tendency. P. S. Moxom asserts that salvation is not by substitution, but by incorpo- ration. We prefer to say that salvation is by substitution, but that the substitution is by incorporation. Incorporation involves substitution, and another's pain inures to my account. Christ being incorporate with humanity, all the exposures and liabilities of humanity fell upon him. Simon, Reconciliation by Incarnation, is an attempt to unite the two elements of the doctrine.

Lidgett, Spir. Prin. of Atonement, 132-189 — "As Anselm represents it, Christ's death is not ours in any such sense that we can enter into it. Bushnell justly charges that it leaves no moral dynamic in the Cross." For criticism of Anselm, see John Caird, Fund. Ideas of Christianity, 2 : 172-193 : Thomasius, Christi Person und Werk, III, 2 : 230-241 ; Philippi, Glaubenslehre, IV, 2 : 70 *sq.*; Baur, Dogmengeschichte, 2 : 416 *sq.*; Shedd, Hist. Doct., 2 : 273-286 ; Dale, Atonement, 279-292 ; McIlvaine, Wisdom of Holy Script- ure, 196-199 ; Kreibig, Versöhnungslehre, 176-178.

6th.   The Ethical Theory of the Atonement.

In propounding what we conceive to be the true theory of the atone- ment, it seems desirable to divide our treatment into two parts. No theory

can be satisfactory which does not furnish a solution of the two problems:
1. What did the atonement accomplish? or, in other words, what was the
object of Christ's death? The answer to this question must be a description of the atonement in its relation to holiness in God. 2. What were the
means used? or, in other words, how could Christ justly die? The answer
to this question must be a description of the atonement as arising from
Christ's relation to humanity. We take up these two parts of the subject
in order.

Edwards, Works, 1 : 609, says that two things make Christ's sufferings a satisfaction
for human guilt: (1) their equality or equivalence to the punishment that the sinner
deserves ; (2) the union between him and them, or the propriety of his being accepted,
in suffering, as the representative of the sinner. Christ bore God's wrath: (1) by the
sight of sin and punishment; (2) by enduring the effects of wrath ordered by God.
See also Edwards, Sermon on the Satisfaction of Christ. These statements of Edwards
suggest the two points of view from which we regard the atonement ; but they come
short of the Scriptural declarations, in that they do not distinctly assert Christ's endurance of penalty itself. Thus they leave the way open for the New School theories of
the atonement, propounded by the successors of Edwards.

Adolphe Monod said well : " Save first the holy law of my God, — after that you shall
save me." Edwards felt the first of these needs, for he says, in his Mysteries of Scripture, Works, 3 : 542 — " The necessity of Christ's satisfaction to divine justice is, as it
were, the centre and hinge of all doctrines of pure revelation. Other doctrines are
comparatively of little importance, except as they have respect to this." And in his
Work of Redemption, Works, 1 : 412 — "Christ was born to the end that he might die;
and therefore he did, as it were, begin to die as soon as he was born." See John 12 : 32 —
"And I, if I be lifted up from the earth, will draw all men unto myself. But this he said, signifying by what manner
of death he should die." Christ was "lifted up": 1. as a propitiation to the holiness of God,
which makes suffering to follow sin, so affording the only ground for pardon without
and peace within ; 2. as a power to purify the hearts and lives of men, Jesus being as
"the serpent lifted up in the wilderness " (John 3 : 14), and we overcoming "because of the blood of the Lamb'
(Rev. 12 : 11).

First, — the Atonement as related to Holiness in God.

The Ethical theory holds that the necessity of the atonement is grounded
in the holiness of God, of which conscience in man is a finite reflection.
There is an ethical principle in the divine nature, which demands that sin
shall be punished. Aside from its results, sin is essentially ill-deserving.
As we who are made in God's image mark our growth in purity by the
increasing quickness with which we detect impurity, and the increasing
hatred which we feel toward it, so infinite purity is a consuming fire to all
iniquity. As there is an ethical demand in our natures that not only
others' wickedness, but our own wickedness, be visited with punishment,
and a keen conscience cannot rest till it has made satisfaction to justice
for its misdeeds, so there is an ethical demand of God's nature that penalty
follow sin.

The holiness of God has conscience and penalty for its correlates and consequences.
Gordon, Christ of To-day, 216 — " In old Athens, the rock on whose top sat the Court of
the Areopagus, representing the highest reason and the best character of the Athenian state, had underneath it the Cave of the Furies." Shakespeare knew human
nature and he bears witness to its need of atonement. In his last Will and Testament
he writes : " First, I commend my soul into the hands of God, my Creator, hoping and
assuredly believing, through the only merits of Jesus Christ my Savior, to be made
partaker of life everlasting." Richard III, 1 : 4 — " I charge you, as you hope to have
redemption By Christ's dear blood shed for our grievous sins, That you depart and lay
no hands on me." Richard II, 4 : 1 — " The world's Ransom, blessed Mary's Son."
Henry VI, 2d part, 3 : 2 — "That dread King took our state upon him, To free us from

his Father's wrathful curse." Henry IV, 1st part, 1 : 1 —"Those holy fields, Over whose acres walked those blessed feet, Which fourteen hundred years ago were nailed For our advantage on the bitter Cross." Measure for Measure, 2 : 2 — " Why, all the souls that are were forfeit once ; And he that might the vantage best have took Found out the remedy." Henry VI, 2d part, 1 : 1 — " Now, by the death of him that died for all !" All's Well that Ends Well, 3 : 4 — " What angel shall Bless this unworthy husband ? He cannot thrive Unless her prayers, whom heaven delights to hear And loves to grant, reprieve him from the wrath Of greatest justice." See a good statement of the Ethical theory of the Atonement in its relation to God's holiness, in Denney, Studies in Theology, 100–124.

Punishment is the constitutional reaction of God's being against moral evil — the self-assertion of infinite holiness against its antagonist and would-be destroyer. In God this demand is devoid of all passion, and is consistent with infinite benevolence. It is a demand that cannot be evaded, since the holiness from which it springs is unchanging. The atonement is therefore a satisfaction of the ethical demand of the divine nature, by the substitution of Christ's penal sufferings for the punishment of the guilty.

John Wessel, a Reformer before the Reformation (1419–1489) : "Ipse deus, ipse sacerdos, ipse hostia, pro se, de se, sibi satisfecit" = " Himself being at the same time God, priest, and sacrificial victim, he made satisfaction to himself, for himself [i. e., for the sins of men to whom he had united himself], and by himself [by his own sinless sufferings]." Quarles's Emblems: " O groundless deeps ! O love beyond degree ! The Offended dies, to set the offender free ! "

Spurgeon, Autobiography, 1 : 98 —" When I was in the hand of the Holy Spirit, under conviction of sin, I had a clear and sharp sense of the justice of God. Sin, whatever it might be to other people, became to me an intolerable burden. It was not so much that I feared hell, as that I feared sin ; and all the while I had upon my mind a deep concern for the honor of God's name and the integrity of his moral government. I felt that it would not satisfy my conscience if I could be forgiven unjustly. But then there came the question : ' How could God be just, and yet justify me who had been so guilty ? ' .... The doctrine of the atonement is to my mind one of the surest proofs of the inspiration of Holy Scripture. Who would or could have thought of the just Ruler dying for the unjust rebel ? "

This substitution is unknown to mere law, and above and beyond the powers of law. It is an operation of grace. Grace, however, does not violate or suspend law, but takes it up into itself and fulfils it. The righteousness of law is maintained, in that the source of all law, the judge and punisher, himself voluntarily submits to bear the penalty, and bears it in the human nature that has sinned.

Matheson, Moments on the Mount, 221 — " In conscience, man condemns and is condemned. Christ was God in the flesh, both priest and sacrificial victim (Heb. 9 : 12). He is 'full of grace' — forgiving grace — but he is 'full of truth ' also, and so 'the only-begotten from the Father ' (John 1 : 14). Not forgiveness that ignores sin, not justice that has no mercy. He forgave the sinner, because he bore the sin." Kaftan, referring to some modern theologians who have returned to the old doctrine but who have said that the basis of the atonement is, not the juridical idea of punishment, but the ethical idea of propitiation, affirms as follows : " On the contrary the highest ethical idea of propitiation is just that of punishment. Take this away, and propitiation becomes nothing but the inferior and unworthy idea of appeasing the wrath of an incensed deity. Precisely the idea of the vicarious suffering of punishment is the idea which must in some way be brought to a full expression for the sake of the ethical consciousness.

" The conscience awakened by God can accept no forgiveness which is not experienced as at the same time a condemnation of sin. ... Jesus, though he was without sin and deserved no punishment, took upon himself all the evils which have come into the world as the consequence and punishment of sin, even to the shameful death on the Cross at the hand of sinners. ... Consequently for the good of man he bore all that which man had deserved, and thereby has man escaped the final eternal punishment and has become a child of God. . . . This is not merely a subjective conclusion upon the related facts, but it is as objective and real as anything which faith recognizes and knows."

Thus the atonement answers the ethical demand of the divine nature that sin be punished if the offender is to go free. The interests of the divine government are secured as a first subordinate result of this satisfaction to God himself, of whose nature the government is an expression; while, as a second subordinate result, provision is made for the needs of human nature, — on the one hand the need of an objective satisfaction to its ethical demand of punishment for sin, and on the other the need of a manifestation of divine love and mercy that will affect the heart and move it to repentance.

The great classical passage with reference to the atonement is Rom. 3 : 25, 26 — "whom God set forth to be a propit.at.on, through faith, in his blood, to show his righteousness because of the passing over of the sins done aforetime, in the forbearance of God; for the showing, I say, of his righteousness at this present season: that he might himself be just, and the justifier of him that hath faith in Jesus." Or, somewhat more freely translated, the passage would read:—"whom God hath set forth in his blood as a propitiatory sacr.fice, through faith, to show forth his righteousness on account of the pretermission of past offences in the forbearance of God; to declare his righteousness in the time now present, so that he may be just and yet may justify him who believeth in Jesus."

EXPOSITION OF ROM. 3:25, 26.— These verses are an expanded statement of the subject of the epistle—the revelation of the "righteousness of God" (= the righteousness which God provides and which God accepts)—which had been mentioned in 1:17, but which now has new light thrown upon it by the demonstration, in 1:18—3:20, that both Gentiles and Jews are under condemnation, and are alike shut up for salvation to some other method than that of works. We subjoin the substance of Meyer's comments upon this passage.

"Verse 25. 'God has set forth Christ as an effectual propitiatory offering, through faith, by means of his blood,' i. e., in that he caused him to shed his blood. ἐν τῷ αὐτοῦ αἵματι belongs to προέθετο, not to πίστεως. The purpose of this setting forth in his blood is εἰς ἔνδειξιν τῆς δικαιοσύνης αὐτοῦ, 'for the display of his [judicial and punitive] righteousness,' which received its satisfaction in the death of Christ as a propitiatory offering, and was thereby practically demonstrated and exhibited. 'On account of the passing-by of sins that had previously taken place,' i. e., because he had allowed the pre-Christian sins to go without punishment, whereby his righteousness had been lost sight of and obscured, and had come to need an ἔνδειξις, or exhibition to men. Omittance is not acquittance. πάρεσις, passing-by, is intermediate between pardon and punishment. 'In virtue of the forbearance of God' expresses the motive of the πάρεσις. Before Christ's sacrifice, God's administration was a scandal, — it needed vindication. The atonement is God's answer to the charge of freeing the guilty.

"Verse 26. εἰς τὸ εἶναι is not epexegetical of εἰς ἔνδειξιν, but presents the teleology of the ἱλαστήριον, the final aim of the whole affirmation from ὃν προέθετο to καιρῷ — namely, first, God's being just, and secondly, his appearing just in consequence of this. Justus et justificans, instead of justus et condemnans, this is the summum paradoxon evangelicum. Of this revelation of righteousness, not through condemnation, but through atonement, grace is the determining ground."

We repeat what was said on pages 719, 720, with regard to the teaching of the passage, namely, that it shows: (1) that Christ's death is a propitiatory sacrifice; (2) that its first and main effect is upon God; (3) that the particular attribute in God which demands the atonement is his justice, or holiness; (4) that the satisfaction of this holiness is the necessary condition of God's justifying the believer. It is only incidentally and subordinately that the atonement is a necessity to man; Paul speaks of it here mainly as a necessity to God. Christ suffers, indeed, that God may appear righteous; but behind the appearance lies the reality; the main object of Christ's suffering is that God may be righteous, while he pardons the believing sinner; in other words, the ground of the atonement is something internal to God himself. See Heb. 2:10—it "became" God = it was morally fitting in God, to make Christ suffer; cf. Zech. 6. 8—"they that go toward the north country have qui-ted my spirit in the north country" = the judgments inflicted on Babylon nave satisfied my justice.

48

Charnock: "He who once 'quenched the violence of fire' for those Hebrew children, has also quenched the fires of God's anger against the sinner, hotter than furnace heated seven times." The same God who is a God of holiness, and who in virtue of his holiness must punish human sin, is also a God of mercy, and in virtue of his mercy himself bears the punishment of human sin. Dorner, Gesch. prot. Theologie, 93 — "Christ is not only mediator between God and man, but between the just God and the merciful God " — cf. Ps. 85 : 10 — "Mercy and truth are met together; righteousness and peace have kissed each other.'; "Conscience demands vicariousness, for conscience declares that a gratuitous pardon would not be just"; see Knight, Colloquia Peripatetica, 88.

Lidgett, Spir. Principle of the Atonement, 219, 304 — "The Atonement 1. has Godward significance; 2. consists in our Lord's endurance of death on our behalf; 3. the spirit in which he endured death is of vital importance to the efficacy of his sacrifice, namely, obedience. . . . God gives repentance, yet requires it; he gives atonement, yet requires it. 'Thanks be to God for his unspeakable gift' (2 Cor. 9 : 15)." Simon, in Expositor, 6 : 321-334 (for substance) — "As in prayer we ask God to energize us and enable us to obey his law, and he answers by entering our hearts and obeying in us and for us; as we pray for strength in affliction, and find him helping us by putting his Spirit into us, and suffering in us and for us; so in atonement, Christ, the manifested God, obeys and suffers in our stead. Even the moral theory implies substitution also. God in us obeys his own law and bears the sorrows that sin has caused. Why can he not, in human nature, also endure the penalty of sin? The possibility of this cannot be consistently denied by any who believe in divine help granted in answer to prayer. The doctrine of the atonement and the doctrine of prayer stand or fall together."

See on the whole subject, Shedd, Discourses and Essays, 272-324, Philosophy of History, 65-69, and Dogmatic Theology, 2 : 401-463; Magee, Atonement and Sacrifice, 27, 53, 253; Edwards's Works, 4 : 140 sq.; Weber, Vom Zorne Gottes, 214-334; Owen, on Divine Justice, in Works, 10 : 500-512 ; Philippi, Glaubenslehre, IV, 2 : 27-114; Hopkins, Works, 1 : 319-363; Schöberlein, in Studien und Kritiken, 1845 : 267-318, and 1847 : 7-70, also in Herzog, Encyclopädie, art.: Versöhnung; Jahrbuch f. d. Theol., 3 : 713, and 8 : 213; Macdonnell, Atonement, 115-214; Luthardt, Saving Truths, 114-138; Baird, Elohim Revealed, 605-637; Lawrence, in Bib. Sac., 20 : 332-339; Kreibig, Versöhnungslehre; Waffle, in Bap. Rev., 1882 : 263-286; Dorner, Glaubenslehre, 2 : 641-662 (Syst. Doct., 4 : 107-124); Remensnyder, The Atonement and Modern Thought.

Secondly, — the Atonement as related to Humanity in Christ.

The Ethical theory of the atonement holds that Christ stands in such relation to humanity, that what God's holiness demands Christ is under obligation to pay, longs to pay, inevitably does pay, and pays so fully, in virtue of his two-fold nature, that every claim of justice is satisfied, and the sinner who accepts what Christ has done in his behalf is saved.

Dr. R. W. Dale, in his work on The Atonement, states the question before us: "What must be Christ's relation to men, in order to make it possible that he should die for them?" We would charge the form of the question, so that it should read: "What must be Christ's relation to men, in order to make it not only possible, but just and necessary, that he should die for them?" Dale replies, for substance, that Christ must have had an original and central relation to the human race and to every member of it; see Denney, Death of Christ, 318. In our treatment of Ethical Monism, of the Trinity, and of the Person of Christ, we have shown that Christ, as Logos, as the immanent God, is the Life of humanity, laden with responsibility for human sin, while yet he personally knows no sin. Of this race-responsibility and race-guilt which Christ assumed, and for which he suffered so soon as man had sinned, Christ's obedience and suffering in the flesh were the visible reflection and revelation. Only in Christ's organic union with the race can we find the vital relation which will make his vicarious sufferings either possible or just. Only when we regard Calvary as revealing eternal principles of the divine nature, can we see how the sufferings of those few hours upon the Cross could suffice to save the millions of mankind.

Dr. E. Y. Mullins has set forth the doctrine of the Atonement in five propositions: "1. In order to atonement Christ became vitally united to the human race. It was only by assuming the nature of those he would redeem that he could break the power of their captor. . . . The human race may be likened to many sparrows who had been caught in the snare of the fowler, and were hopelessly struggling against their fate.

A great eagle swoops down from the sky, becomes entangled with the sparrows in the net, and then spreading his mighty wings he soars upward bearing the snare and captives and breaking its meshes he delivers himself and them. . . . Christ the fountain head of life imparting his own vitality to the redeemed, and causing them to share in the experiences of Gethsemane and Calvary, breaking thus for them the power of sin and death — this is the atonement, by virtue of which sin is put away and man is united to God."

Dr. Mullins properly regards this view of atonement as too narrow, inasmuch as it disregards the differences between Christ and men arising from his sinlessness and his deity. He adds therefore that "2. Christ became the substitute for sinners; 3. became the representative of men before God; 4. gained power over human hearts to win them from sin and reconcile them to God; and 5. became a propitiation and satisfaction, rendering the remission of sins consistent with the divine holiness." If Christ's union with the race be one which begins with creation and antedates the Fall, all of the later points in the above scheme are only natural correlates and consequences of the first, — substitution, representation, reconciliation, propitiation, satisfaction, are only different aspects of the work which Christ does for us, by virtue of the fact that he is the immanent God, the Life of humanity, priest and victim, condemning and condemned, atoning and atoned.

We have seen how God can justly demand satisfaction; we now show how Christ can justly make it; or, in other words, how the innocent can justly suffer for the guilty. The solution of the problem lies in Christ's union with humanity. The first result of that union is obligation to suffer for men; since, being one with the race, Christ had a share in the responsibility of the race to the law and the justice of God. In him humanity was created; at every stage of its existence humanity was upheld by his power; as the immanent God he was the life of the race and of every member of it. Christ's sharing of man's life justly and inevitably subjected him to man's exposures and liabilities, and especially to God's condemnation on account of sin.

In the seventh chapter of Elsie Venner, Oliver Wendell Holmes makes the Reverend Mr. Honeywood lay aside an old sermon on Human Nature, and write one on The Obligations of an infinite Creator to a finite Creature. A. J. F. Behrends grounded our Lord's representative relation not in his human nature but in his divine nature. "He is our representative not because he was in the loins of Adam, but because we, Adam included, were in his loins. Personal created existence is grounded in the Logos, so that God must deal with him as well as with every individual sinner, and sin and guilt and punishment must smite the Logos as well as the sinner, and that, whether the sinner is saved or not. This is not, as is often charged, a denial of grace or of freedom in grace, for it is no denial of freedom or grace to show that they are eternally rational and conformable to eternal law. In the ideal sphere, necessity and freedom, law and grace, coalesce." J. C. C. Clarke, Man and his Divine Father, 337—"Vicarious atonement does not consist in any single act. . . . No one act embraces it all, and no one definition can compass it." In this sense we may adopt the words of Forsyth: "In the atonement the Holy Father dealt with a world's sin on (not in) a world-soul."

G. B. Foster, on Mat. 26 : 53, 54 —"Thinkest thou that I cannot beseech my Father, and he shall even now send me more than twelve legions of angels? How then should the Scriptures be fulfilled, that thus it must be?" "On this 'must be' the Scripture is based, not this 'must be' on the Scripture. The 'must be' was the ethical demand of his connection with the race. It would have been immoral for him to break away from the organism. The law of the organism is: From each according to ability; to each according to need. David in song, Aristotle in logic, Darwin in science, are under obligation to contribute to the organism the talent they have. Shall they be under obligation, and Jesus go scot-free? But Jesus can contribute atonement, and because he can, he must. Moreover, he is a member, not only of the whole, but of each part,— Rom. 12 : 5 — 'members one of another.' As membership of the whole makes him liable for the sin of the whole, so his being a member of the part makes him liable for the sin of that part."

Fairbairn, Place of Christ in Modern Theology, 483, 484 — "There is a sense in which the Patripassian theory is right; the Father did suffer; though it was not as the Son that he suffered, but in modes distinct and different. . . . Through his pity the misery of man became his sorrow. . . . There is a disclosure of his suffering in the surrender of the Son. This surrender represented the sacrifice and passion of the whole Godhead. Here degree and proportion are out of place; were it not, we might say that the Father suffered more in giving than the Son in being given. He who gave to duty had not the reward of him who rejoiced to do it. . . . One member of the Trinity could not suffer without all suffering. . . . The visible sacrifice was that of the Son; the invisible sacrifice was that of the Father." The Andover Theory, represented in Progressive Orthodoxy, 43–53, affirms not only the Moral Influence of the Atonement, but also that the whole race of mankind is naturally in Christ and was therefore punished in and by his suffering and death; quoted in Hovey, Manual of Christian Theology, 269; see Hovey's own view, 270–276, though he does not seem to recognize the atonement as existing before the incarnation.

Christ's share in the responsibility of the race to the law and justice of God was not destroyed by his incarnation, nor by his purification in the womb of the virgin. In virtue of the organic unity of the race, each member of the race since Adam has been born into the same state into which Adam fell. The consequences of Adam's sin, both to himself and to his posterity, are: (1) depravity, or the corruption of human nature; (2) guilt, or obligation to make satisfaction for sin to the divine holiness; (3) penalty, or actual endurance of loss or suffering visited by that holiness upon the guilty.

Moberly, Atonement and Personality, 117—"Christ had taken upon him, as the living expression of himself, a nature which was weighed down, not merely by present incapacities, but by present incapacities as part of the judicial necessary result of accepted and inherent sinfulness. Human nature was not only disabled but guilty, and the disabilities were themselves a consequence and aspect of the guilt"; see review of Moberly by Rashdall, in Jour. Theol. Studies, 3 : 198-211. Lidgett, Spir. Princ. of Atonement, 166-168, criticizes Dr. Dale for neglecting the fatherly purpose of the Atonement to serve the moral training of the child—punishment marking ill-desert in order to bring this ill-desert to the consciousness of the offender,—and for neglecting also the positive assertion in the atonement that the law is holy and just and good—something more than the negative expression of sin's ill-desert. See especially Lidgett's chapter on the relation of our Lord to the human race, 351-378, in which he grounds the atonement in the solidarity of mankind, its organic union with the Son of God, and Christ's immanence in humanity.

Bowne, The Atonement, 101—"Something like this work of grace was a moral necessity with God. It was an awful responsibility that was taken when our human race was launched with its fearful possibilities of good and evil. God thereby put himself under infinite obligation to care for his human family; and reflections upon his position as Creator and Ruler, instead of removing only make more manifest this obligation. So long as we conceive of God as sitting apart in supreme ease and self-satisfaction, he is not love at all, but only a reflex of our selfishness and vulgarity. So long as we conceive him as bestowing upon us out of his infinite fulness but at no real cost to himself, he sinks before the moral heroes of the race. There is ever a higher thought possible, until we see God taking the world upon his heart, entering into the fellowship of our sorrow, and becoming the supreme burdenbearer and leader in all self-sacrifice. Then only are the possibilities of grace and love and moral heroism and condescension filled up, so that nothing higher remains. And the work of Christ himself, so far as it was an historical event, must be viewed, not merely as a piece of history, but also as a manifestation of that Cross which was hidden in the divine love from the foundation of the world, and which is involved in the existence of the human world at all."

John Caird, Fund. Ideas of Christianity, 2 : 90, 91—"Conceive of the ideal of moral perfection incarnate in a human personality, and at the same time one who loves us with a love so absolute that he identifies himself with us and makes our good and evil his own—bring together these elements in a living, conscious human spirit, and you have in it a capacity of shame and anguish, a possibility of bearing the burden of human guilt and wretchedness, which lost and guilty humanity can never bear for itself."

If Christ had been born into the world by ordinary generation, he too would have had depravity, guilt, penalty. But he was not so born. In the womb of the Virgin, the human nature which he took was purged from its depravity. But this purging away of depravity did not take away guilt, or penalty. There was still left the just exposure to the penalty of violated law. Although Christ's nature was purified, his obligation to suffer yet remained. He might have declined to join himself to humanity, and then he need not have suffered. He might have sundered his connection with the race, and then he need not have suffered. But once born of the Virgin, once possessed of the human nature that was under the curse, he was bound to suffer. The whole mass and weight of God's displeasure against the race fell on him, when once he became a member of the race.

Because Christ is essential humanity, the universal man, the life of the race, he is the central brain to which and through which all ideas must pass. He is the central heart to which and through which all pains must be communicated. You cannot telephone to your friend across the town without first ringing up the central office. You cannot injure your neighbor without first injuring Christ. Each one of us can say of him: "Against thee, thee only, have I sinned" (Ps. 51 : 4). Because of his central and all-inclusive humanity, he must bear in his own person all the burdens of humanity, and must be "the Lamb of God, that" taketh, and so "taketh away, the sin of the world" (John 1 : 29). Simms Reeves, the great English tenor, said that the passion music was too much for him ; he was found completely overcome after singing the prophet's words in Lam. 1 : 12 — "Is it nothing to you, all ye that pass by ? Behold, and see if there be any sorrow like unto my sorrow, which is brought upon me, Wherewith Jehovah hath afflicted me in the day of his fierce anger."

Father Damien gave his life in ministry to the lepers' colony of the Hawaian Islands. Though free from the disease when he entered, he was at last himself stricken with the leprosy, and then wrote: " I must now stay with my own people." Once a leper, there was no release. When Christ once joined himself to humanity, all the exposures and liabilities of humanity fell upon him. Through himself personally without sin, he was made sin for us. Christ inherited guilt and penalty. Heb. 2 : 14, 15 — "Since then the children are sharers in flesh and blood, he also himself in like manner partook of the same; that through death he might bring to naught him that had the power of death, that is, the devil ; and might deliver all them who through fear of death were all their life-time subject to bondage."

Only God can forgive sin, because only God can feel it in its true heinousness and rate it at its true worth. Christ could forgive sin because he added to the divine feeling with regard to sin the anguish of a pure humanity on account of it. Shelley, Julian and Maddolo : " Me, whose heart a stranger's tear might wear, As water-drops the sandy fountain-stone ; Me, who am as a nerve o'er which do creep The Else unfelt oppressions of the earth." S. W. Culver : " We cannot be saved, as we are taught geometry, by lecture and diagram. No person ever yet saved another from drowning by standing coolly by and telling him the importance of rising to the surface and the necessity of respiration. No, he must plunge into the destructive element, and take upon himself the very condition of the drowning man, and by the exertion of his own strength, by the vigor of his own life, save him from the impending death. When your child is encompassed by the flames that consume your dwelling, you will not save him by calling to him from without. You must make your way through the devouring flame, till you come personally into the very conditions of his peril and danger, and, thence returning, bear him forth to freedom and safety."

Notice, however, that this guilt which Christ took upon himself by his union with humanity was: (1) not the guilt of personal sin — such guilt as belongs to every adult member of the race; (2) not even the guilt of inherited depravity — such guilt as belongs to infants, and to those who have not come to moral consciousness ; but (3) solely the guilt of Adam's sin, which belongs, prior to personal transgression, and apart from inherited depravity, to every member of the race who has derived his life from Adam. This original sin and inherited guilt, but without the depravity that ordinarily accompanies them, Christ takes, and so takes away. He can justly bear penalty, because he inherits guilt. And since this guilt is not his personal guilt, but the guilt of that one sin in which "all sinned"—the guilt of the common transgression of the race in Adam, the guilt of the root-sin from which all other sins have sprung—he who is personally pure can vicariously bear the penalty due to the sin of all.

Christ was conscious of innocence in his personal relations, but not in his race relations. He gathered into himself all the penalties of humanity, as Winkelried gathered into his own bosom at Sempach the pikes of the Austrians and so made a way for the victorious Swiss. Christ took to himself the shame of humanity, as the mother takes upon her the daughter's shame, repenting of it and suffering on account of it. But this could not be in the case of Christ unless there had been a tie uniting him to men far more vital, organic, and profound than that which unites mother and daughter. Christ is naturally the life of all men, before he becomes spiritually the life of true believers. Matheson, Spir. Devel. of St. Paul, 197-215, 244, speaks of Christ's secular priesthood, of an outer as well as an inner membership in the body of Christ. He is sacrificial head of the world as well as sacrificial head of the church. In Paul's latest letters, he declares of Christ that he is "the Savior of all men, specially of them that believe" (1 Tim. 4 : 10). There is a grace that "hath appeared, bringing salvation to all men" (Tit. 2 : 11). He "gave gifts unto men" (Eph. 4 : 8), "Yea, among the rebel'ious also, that Jehovah God might dwell with them" (Ps. 68 : 18). "Every creature of God is good, and nothing is to be rejected" (1 Tim. 4 : 4).

Royce, World and Individual, 2 : 408—"Our sorrows are identically God's own sorrows. . . . . I sorrow, but the sorrow is not only mine. This same sorrow, just as it is for me, is God's sorrow. . . . . The divine fulfilment can be won only through the sorrows of time. . . . Unless God knows sorrow, he knows not the highest good, which consists in the overcoming of sorrow." Godet, in The Atonement, 331-351—"Jesus condemned sin as God condemned it. When he felt forsaken on the Cross, he performed that act by which the offender himself condemns his sin, and by that condemnation, so far as it depends on himself, makes it to disappear. There is but one conscience in all moral beings. This echo in Christ of God's judgment against sin was to re-echo in all other human consciences. This has transformed God's love of compassion into a love of satisfaction. Holiness joins suffering to sin. But the element of reparation in the Cross was not in the suffering but in the submission. The child who revolts against its punishment has made no reparation at all. We appropriate Christ's work when we by faith ourselves condemn sin and accept him."

If it be asked whether this is not simply a suffering for his own sin, or rather for his own share of the sin of the race, we reply that his own share in the sin of the race is not the sole reason why he suffers ; it furnishes only the subjective reason and ground for the proper laying upon him of the sin of all. Christ's union with the race in his incarnation is only the outward and visible expression of a prior union with the race which began when he created the race. As "in him were all things created," and as "in him all things consist," or hold together (Col. 1 : 16, 17), it follows that he who is the life of humanity must, though personally pure, be involved in responsibility for all human sin, and "it was necessary that the Christ should suffer" (Acts 17 : 3). This suffering was an enduring of the reaction of the divine holiness against sin and so was a bearing of penalty (Is. 53 : 6 ; Gal. 3 : 13), but it was also the voluntary execution of a plan that antedated creation (Phil. 2 : 6, 7), and Christ's sacrifice in time showed what had been in the heart of God from eternity (Heb. 9 : 14 ; Rev. 13 : 8).

Our treatment is intended to meet the chief modern objection to the atonement. Greg, Creed of Christendom, 2 : 222, speaks of "the strangely inconsistent doctrine that God is so *just* that he could not let sin go unpunished, yet so *unjust* that he could punish it in the person of the innocent. . . . . It is for orthodox dialectics to explain how the divine justice can be *impugned* by pardoning the guilty, and yet *vindicated* by punishing the innocent " (quoted in Lias, Atonement, 16). In order to meet this difficulty, the following accounts of Christ's identification with humanity have been given:

1. That of Isaac Watts (see Bib. Sac., 1875 : 421). This holds that the humanity of Christ, both in body and soul, preëxisted before the incarnation, and was manifested to the patriarchs. We reply that Christ's human nature is declared to be derived from the Virgin.

2. That of R. W. Dale (Atonement, 265–440). This holds that Christ is responsible for human sin because, as the Upholder and Life of all, he is naturally one with all men, and is spiritually one with all believers (Acts 17 : 28 — "in him we live, and move, and have our being "; Col. 1 : 17—" in him all things consist " ; John 14 : 20 —"I am in my Father, and ye in me, and I in you "). If Christ's bearing our sins, however, is to be explained by the union of the believer with Christ the effect is made to explain the cause, and Christ could have died only for the elect (see a review of Dale, in Brit. Quar. Rev., Apr., 1876 : 221–225). The union of Christ with the race by creation — a union which recognizes Christ's purity and man's sin — still remains as a most valuable element of truth in the theory of Dr. Dale.

3. That of Edward Irving. Christ has a corrupted nature, an inborn infirmity and depravity, which he gradually overcomes. But the Scriptures, on the contrary, assert his holiness and separateness from sinners. (See references, on pages 744–747.)

4. That of John Miller, Theology, 114–128 ; also in his chapter: Was Christ in Adam ? in Questions Awakened by the Bible. Christ, as to his human nature, although created pure, was yet, as one of Adam's posterity, conceived of as a sinner in Adam. To him attached " the guilt of the act in which all men stood together in a federal relation. . . . He was decreed to be guilty for the sins of all mankind." Although there is a truth contained in this statement, it is vitiated by Miller's federalism and creatianism. Arbitrary imputation and legal fiction do not help us here. We need such an actual union of Christ with humanity, and such a derivation of the substance of his being, by natural generation from Adam, as will make him not simply the constructive heir, but the natural heir, of the guilt of the race. We come, therefore, to what we regard as the true view, namely :

5. That the humanity of Christ was not a new creation, but was derived from Adam, through Mary his mother; so that Christ, so far as his humanity was concerned, was in Adam just as we were, and had the same race-responsibility with ourselves. As Adam's descendant, he was responsible for Adam's sin, like every other member of the race; the chief difference being, that while we inherit from Adam both guilt and depravity, he whom the Holy Spirit purified, inherited not the depravity, but only the guilt. Christ took to himself, not sin (depravity), but the consequences of sin. In him there was abolition of sin, without abolition of obligation to suffer for sin; while in the believer, there is abolition of obligation to suffer, without abolition of sin itself.

The justice of Christ's sufferings has been imperfectly illustrated by the obligation of the silent partner of a business firm to pay debts of the firm which he did not personally contract; or by the obligation of the husband to pay the debts of his wife ; or by the obligation of a purchasing country to assume the debts of the province which it purchases (Wm. Ashmore). There have been men who have spent the strength of a lifetime in clearing off the indebtedness of an insolvent father, long since deceased. They recognized an organic unity of the family, which morally, if not legally, made their father's liabilities their own. So, it is said, Christ recognized the organic unity of the race, and saw that, having become one of that sinning race, he had involved himself in all its liabilities, even to the suffering of death, the great penalty of sin.

The fault of all the analogies just mentioned is that they are purely commercial. A transference of pecuniary obligation is easier to understand than a transference of criminal liability. I cannot justly bear another's penalty, unless I can in some way share his guilt. The theory we advocate shows how such a sharing of our guilt on the part of Christ was possible. All believers in substitution hold that Christ bore our guilt: "My soul looks back to see The burdens thou didst bear When hanging on the accursed tree, And hopes her guilt was there." But we claim that, by virtue of Christ's union with humanity, that guilt was not only an imputed, but also an imparted, guilt.

With Christ's obligation to suffer, there were connected two other, though minor, results of his assumption of humanity : first, the longing to suffer; and secondly, the inevitableness of his suffering. He felt the longing to suffer which perfect love to God must feel, in view of the demands upon the race, of that holiness of God which he loved more than he loved the race itself; which perfect love to man must feel, in view of the fact that bearing the penalty of man's sin was the only way to save him. Hence we see Christ pressing forward to the cross with such majestic determination that the disciples were amazed and afraid (Mark 10 : 32). Hence we hear him saying : "With desire have I desired to eat this passover" (Luke 23 : 15); "I have a baptism to be baptized with; and how am I straitened till is be accomplished!" (Luke 12 : 50).

Here is the truth in Campbell's theory of the atonement. Christ is the great Penitent before God, making confession of the sin of the race, which others of that race could neither see nor feel. But the view we present is a larger and completer one than that of Campbell, in that it makes this confession and reparation obligatory upon Christ, as Campbell's view does not, and recognizes the penal nature of Christ's sufferings, which Campbell's view denies. Lias, Atonement, 79 — "The head of a clan, himself intensely loyal to his king, finds that his clan have been involved in rebellion. The more intense and perfect his loyalty, the more thorough his nobleness of heart and affection for his people, the more inexcusable and flagrant the rebellion of those for whom he pleads, — the more acute would be his agony, as their representative and head. Nothing would be more true to human nature, in the best sense of those words, than that the conflict between loyalty to his king and affection for his vassals should induce him to offer his life for theirs, to ask that the punishment they deserved should be inflicted on him."

The second minor consequence of Christ's assumption of humanity was, that, being such as he was, he could not help suffering; in other words, the obligatory and the desired were also the inevitable. Since he was a being of perfect purity, contact with the sin of the race, of which he was a member, necessarily involved an actual suffering, of an intenser kind than we can conceive. Sin is self-isolating, but love and righteousness have in them the instinct of human unity. In Christ all the nerves and sensibilities of humanity met. He was the only healthy member of the race. When life returns to a frozen limb, there is pain. So Christ, as the only sensitive member of a benumbed and stupefied humanity, felt all the pangs of shame and suffering which rightfully belonged to sinners; but which they could not feel, simply because of the depth of their depravity. Because Christ was pure, yet had united himself to a sinful and guilty race, therefore "it must needs be that Christ should suffer" (A. V.) or, "it behooved the Christ to suffer" (Rev. Vers., Acts 17 : 3); see also John 3 : 14 — "so must the Son of man be lifted up" — "The Incarnation, under the actual circumstances of humanity, carried with it the necessity of the Passion" (Westcott, in Bib. Com., in loco).

Compare John Woolman's Journal, 4, 5 — "O Lord, my God, the amazing horrors of darkness were gathered about me, and covered me all over, and I saw no way to go forth; I felt the depth and extent of the misery of my fellow creatures, separated from the divine harmony, and it was greater than I could bear, and I was crushed down under it; I lifted up my head, I stretched out my arm, but there was none to help me; I looked round about, and was amazed. In the depths of misery, I remembered that thou art omnipotent and that I had called thee Father." He had vision of a "dull, gloomy mass," darkening half the heavens, and he was told that it was "human beings, in as great misery as they could be and live; and he was mixed with them, and henceforth he might not consider himself a distinct and separate being."

This suffering in and with the sins of men, which Dr. Bushnell emphasized so strongly, though it is not, as he thought, the principal element, is notwithstanding an indispensable element in the atonement of Christ. Suffering in and with the sinner is one way, though not the only way, in which Christ is enabled to bear the wrath of God which constitutes the real penalty of sin.

EXPOSITION OF 2 COR. 5 : 21. — It remains for us to adduce the Scriptural proof of this natural assumption of human guilt by Christ. We find it in 2 Cor. 5 : 21 — "Him who knew no sin he made to be sin on our behalf; that we might become the righteousness of God in him." "Righteousness" here cannot mean subjective purity, for then "made to be sin" would mean that God made Christ to be subjectively depraved. As Christ was not made unholy, the meaning cannot be that we are made holy persons in him. Meyer calls attention to this parallel between "righteousness" and "sin": — "That we might become the righteousness of God in him" = that we might become justified persons. Correspondingly, "made to be sin on our behalf" must = made to be a condemned person. "Him who knew no sin" = Christ had no experience of sin — this was the necessary postulate of his work of atonement. "Made sin for us," therefore, is the abstract for the concrete, and = made a sinner, in the sense that the penalty of sin fell upon him. So Meyer, for substance.

We must, however, regard this interpretation of Meyer's as coming short of the full meaning of the apostle. As justification is not simply remission of actual punishment, but is also deliverance from the obligation to suffer punishment, — in other words, as "righteousness" in the text = persons delivered from the guilt as well as from the penalty of sin, — so the contrasted term "sin," in the text, = a person not only *actually* punished, but also under *obligation* to suffer punishment ;— in other words, Christ is "made sin," not only in the sense of being put under *penalty*, but also in the sense of being put under *guilt*. (*Cf.* Symington, Atonement, 17.)

In a note to the last edition of Meyer, this is substantially granted. "It is to be noted," he says, "that ἁμαρτίαν, like κατάρα in Gal. 3 : 13, necessarily includes in itself the notion of guilt." Meyer adds, however : "The guilt of which Christ appears as bearer was not his own (μὴ γνόντα ἁμαρτίαν) ; hence the guilt of men was transferred to him ; consequently the justification of men is imputative." Here the implication that the guilt which Christ bears is his simply by imputation seems to us contrary to the analogy of faith. As Adam's sin is ours only because we are actually one with Adam, and as Christ's righteousness is imputed to us only as we are actually united to Christ, so our sins are imputed to Christ only as Christ is actually one with the race. He was "made sin " by being made one with the sinners ; he took our guilt by taking our nature. He who "knew no sin " came to be "sin for us " by being born of a sinful stock ; by inheritance the common guilt of the race became his. Guilt was not simply *imputed* to Christ ; it was *imparted* also.

This exposition may be made more clear by putting the two contrasted thoughts in parallel columns, as follows :

Made righteousness in him =	Made sin for us =
righteous persons ;	a sinful person ;
justified persons ;	a condemned person ;
freed from guilt, or obligation to suffer ;	put under guilt, or obligation to suffer ;
by spiritual union with Christ.	by natural union with the race.

For a good exposition of 2 Cor. 5 : 21, Gal. 3 : 13, and Rom. 3 : 25, 26, see Denney, Studies in Theology, 109–124.

The Atonement, then, on the part of God, has its ground (1) in the holiness of God, which must visit sin with condemnation, even though this condemnation brings death to his Son ; and (2) in the love of God, which itself provides the sacrifice, by suffering in and with his Son for the sins of men, but through that suffering opening a way and means of salvation.

The Atonement, on the part of man, is accomplished through (1) the solidarity of the race ; of which (2) Christ is the life, and so its representative and surety ; (3) justly yet voluntarily bearing its guilt and shame and condemnation as his own.

Melanchthon : " Christ was made sin for us, not only in respect to punishment, but primarily by being chargeable with guilt also (*culpæ et reatus*) " — quoted by Thomasius, Christi Person und Werk, 3 : 95, 102, 103, 107 ; also 1 : 307, 314 *sq.* Thomasius says that "Christ bore the guilt of the race by imputation ; but as in the case of the imputation of Adam's sin to us, imputation of our sins to Christ presupposes a real relationship. Christ appropriated our sin. He sank himself into our guilt." Dorner, Glaubenslehre, 2 : 442 (Syst. Doct., 3 : 350, 351), agrees with Thomasius, that "Christ entered into our natural mortality, which for us is a penal condition, and into the state of collective guilt, so far as it is an evil, a burden to be borne ; not that he had personal guilt, but rather that he entered into our guilt-laden common life, not as a stranger, but as one actually belonging to it — put under its law, according to the will of the Father and of his own love."

When, and how, did Christ take this guilt and this penalty upon him ? With regard to penalty, we have no difficulty in answering that, as his whole life of suffering was propitiatory, so penalty rested upon him from the very beginning of his life. This penalty was inherited, and was the consequence of Christ's taking human nature (Gal. 4 : 4, 5 — "born of a woman, born under the law "). But penalty and guilt are correlates ; if Christ inherited penalty, it must have been because he inherited guilt. This subjection to the common guilt of the race was intimated in Jesus' circumcision (Luke 2 : 21) ; in his ritual purification (Luke 2 : 22 — "their purification "— *i. e.*, the purification of Mary and the babe ; see Lange, Life of Christ ; Commentaries of Alford, Webster and Wilkinson ; and An. Par. Bible) ; in his legal redemption (Luke 2 : 23, 24 ; *cf.* Ex. 13 : 2, 13) ; and in his baptism (Mat. 3 : 15 — "thus it becometh us to fulfil all righteousness "). The baptized person went down into the water, as one laden with sin and guilt, in order that this sin and guilt might be buried forever, and that he might rise from the typical grave to a new and holy life. (Ebrard : " Baptism = death.") So Christ's submission to John's baptism of repentence was not only a consecration to death, but also a recognition and confession of his implication in that guilt of the race for which death was the appointed and inevitable penalty (*cf.* Mat. 10 : 38 ; Luke 12 : 50 ; Mat. 26 : 39) ; and, as his baptism was a prefiguration of his death, we may learn from his baptism something with regard to the meaning of his death. See further, under The Symbolism of Baptism.

As one who had had guilt, Christ was "justified in the spirit" (1 Tim. 3 : 16) ; and this justification appears to have taken place after he " was manifested in the flesh " (1 Tim. 3 : 16), and when " he was raised for our justification " (Rom. 4 : 25). Compare Rom. 1 : 4 — "declared to be the Son of God with power, according to the spirit of holiness, by the resurrection from the dead "; 6 : 7-10 — "he that hath died is justified from sin. But if we died with Christ, we believe that we shall also live with him ; knowing that Christ being raised from the dead dieth no more ; death no more hath dominion over him. For the death that he died, he died unto sin once : but the life that he liveth, he liveth unto God" — here all Christians are conceived of as ideally justified in the justification of Christ, when Christ died for our sins and rose again. 8 : 3 — "God, sending his own Son in the likeness of sinful flesh and for sin, condemned sin in the flesh" — here Meyer says : " The sending does not precede the condemnation ; but the condemnation is effected in and with the sending." John 16 : 10 — "of righteousness, because I go to the Father"; 19 : 30 — "It is finished." On 1 Tim. 3 : 16, see the Commentary of Bengel.

If it be asked whether Jesus, then, before his death, was an unjustified person, we answer that, while personally pure and well-pleasing to God (Mat. 3 : 17), he himself was conscious of a race-responsibility and a race-guilt which must be atoned for (John 12 : 27 — "Now is my soul troubled ; and what shall I say ? Father, save me from this hour. But for this cause came I unto this hour"); and that guilty human nature in him endured at the last the separation from God which constitutes the essence of death, sin's penalty (Mat. 27 : 46 — "My God, my God, why hast thou forsaken me ? "). We must remember that, as even the believer must "be judged according to men in the flesh " (1 Pet. 4 : 6), that is, must suffer the death which to unbelievers is the penalty of sin, although he "live according to God in the Spirit," so Christ, in order that we might be delivered from both guilt and penalty, was "put to death in the flesh, but made alive in the spirit" (3 : 18) ; — in other words, as Christ was man, the penalty due to human guilt belonged to him to bear ; but, as he was God, he could exhaust that penalty, and could be a proper substitute for others.

If it be asked whether he, who from the moment of the conception "sanctified himself" (John 17 : 19), did not from that moment also justify himself, we reply that although, through the retroactive efficacy of his atonement and upon the ground of it, human nature in him was purged of its depravity from the moment that he took that nature ; and although, upon the ground of that atonement, believers before his advent were both sanctified and justified ; yet his own justification could not have proceeded upon the ground of his atonement, and also his atonement have proceeded upon the ground of his justification. This would be a vicious circle ; somewhere we must have a beginning. That beginning was in the cross, where guilt was first purged (Heb. 1 : 3 — " when he had made purification of sins, sat down on the right hand of the Majesty on high "; Mat. 27 : 42 — "He saved others ; himself he cannot save "; *cf.* Rev. 13 : 8 — "the Lamb that hath been slain from the foundation of the world").

If it be said that guilt and depravity are practically inseparable, and that, if Christ had guilt, he must have had depravity also, we reply that in civil law we distinguish between them, — the conversion of a murderer would not remove his obligation to suffer upon the gallows ; and we reply further, that in justification we distinguish between them, — depravity still remaining, though guilt is removed. So we may say that Christ takes guilt without depravity, in order that we may have depravity without guilt. See page 645 ; also Bühl, Incarnation des göttlichen Wortes ; Pope, Higher Catechism, 118 ; A. H. Strong, on the Necessity of the Atonement, in Philosophy and Religion, 213-219. *Per contra*, see Shedd, Dogm. Theol., 2 : 59 note, 82.

Christ therefore, as incarnate, rather revealed the atonement than made it. The historical work of atonement was finished upon the Cross, but that historical work only revealed to men the atonement made both before and since by the extra-mundane Logos. The eternal Love of God suffering the necessary reaction of his own Holiness against the sin of his creatures and with a view to their salvation — this is the essence of the Atonement.

Nash, Ethics and Revelation, 252, 253 — " Christ, as God's atonement, is the revelation and discovery of the fact that sacrifice is as deep in God as his being. He is a holy Creator. . . . He must take upon himself the shame and pain of sin." The earthly tabernacle and its sacrifices were only the shadow of those in the heavens, and Moses was bidden to make the earthly after the pattern which he saw in the mount. So the historical atonement was but the shadowing forth to dull and finite minds of an infinite demand of the divine holiness and an infinite satisfaction rendered by the divine love. Godet, S. S. Times, Oct. 16, 1886 — " Christ so identified himself with the race he came to save, by sharing its life or its very blood, that when the race itself was redeemed from the curse of sin, his resurrection followed as the first fruits of that redemption " ; Rom. 4 : 25 — " delivered up for our trespasses . . . . . raised for our justification."

Simon, Redemption of Man, 322 — " If the Logos is generally the Mediator of the divine immanence in Creation, especially in man ; if men are differentiations of the effluent divine energy ; and if the Logos is the immanent controlling principle of all differentiation, *i. e.*, the principle of all *form* — must not the self-perversion of these human differentiations necessarily react on him who is their constitutive principle? 339 — Remember that men have not first to engraft themselves into Christ, the living whole. . . . They subsist naturally in him, and they have to separate themselves, cut themselves off from him, if they are to be separate. This is the mistake made in the ' Life in Christ ' theory. Men are treated as in some sense out of Christ, and as having to get into connection with Christ. . . . It is not that we have to create the relation, — we have simply to accept, to recognize, to ratify it. Rejecting Christ is not so much refusal to *become* one with Christ, as it is refusal to *remain* one with him, refusal to let him be our life."

A. H. Strong, Christ in Creation, 33, 172 — " When God breathed into man's nostrils the breath of life, he communicated freedom, and made possible the creature's self-chosen alienation from himself, the giver of that life. While man could never break the natural bond which united him to God, he could break the spiritual bond, and could introduce even into the life of God a principle of discord and evil. Tie a cord tightly about your finger ; you partially isolate the finger, diminish its nutrition, bring about atrophy and disease. Yet the life of the whole system rouses itself to put away the evil, to untie the cord, to free the diseased and suffering member. The illustration is far from adequate ; but it helps at a single point. There has been given to each intelligent and moral agent the power, spiritually, to isolate himself from God, while yet he is naturally joined to God, and is wholly dependent upon God for the removal of the sin which has so separated him from his Maker. Sin is the act of the creature, but salvation is the act of the Creator.

" If you could imagine a finger endowed with free will and trying to sunder its connection with the body by tying a string around itself, you would have a picture of man trying to sunder his connection with Christ. What is the result of such an attempt? Why, pain, decay ; possible, nay, incipient death, to the finger. By what law ? By the law of the organism, which is so constituted as to maintain itself against its own disruption by the revolt of the members. The pain and death of the finger is the reaction of the whole against the treason of the part. The finger suffers pain. But are there no results of pain to the body ? Does not the body feel pain also ? How plain it is that no such pain can be confined to the single part! The heart feels, aye, the whole organism feels, because all the parts are members one of another. It not only suffers, but that suffering tends to remedy the evil and to remove its cause. The body summons its forces, pours new tides of life into the dying member, strives to rid the finger of the ligature that binds it. So through all the course of history, Christ, the natural life of the race, has been afflicted in the affliction of humanity and has suffered for human sin. This suffering has been an atoning suffering, since it has been due to righteousness. If God had not been holy, if God had not made all nature express the holiness of his being, if God had not made pain and loss the necessary consequences of sin, then Christ would not have suffered. But since these things are sin's penalty and Christ is the life of the sinful race, it must needs be that Christ should suffer. There is nothing arbitrary in laying upon him the iniquities of us all. Original grace, like original sin, is only the ethical interpretation of biological facts." See also Ames, on Biological Aspects of the Atonement, in Methodist Review, Nov. 1905 : 943-953.

In favor of the Substitutionary or Ethical view of the atonement we may urge the following considerations :

(*a*) It rests upon correct philosophical principles with regard to the nature of will, law, sin, penalty, righteousness.

This theory holds that there are permanent states, as well as transient acts, of the will; and that the will is not simply the faculty of volitions, but also the fundamental determination of the being to an ultimate end. It regards law as having its basis, not in arbitrary will or in governmental expediency, but rather in the nature of God, and as being a necessary transcript of God's holiness. It considers sin to consist not simply in acts, but in permanent evil states of the affections and will. It makes the object of penalty to be, not the reformation of the offender, or the prevention of evil doing, but the vindication of justice, outraged by violation of law. It teaches that righteousness is not benevolence or a form of benevolence, but a distinct and separate attribute of the divine nature which demands that sin should be visited with punishment, apart from any consideration of the useful results that will flow therefrom.

(*b*) It combines in itself all the valuable elements in the theories before mentioned, while it avoids their inconsistencies, by showing the deeper principle upon which each of these elements is based.

The Ethical theory admits the indispensableness of Christ's example, advocated by the Socinian theory; the moral influence of his suffering, urged by the Bushnellian theory; the securing of the safety of government, insisted on by the Grotian theory; the participation of the believer in Christ's new humanity, taught by the Irvingian theory; the satisfaction to God's majesty for the elect, made so much of by the Anselmic theory. But the Ethical theory claims that all these other theories require, as a presupposition for their effective working, that ethical satisfaction to the holiness of God which is rendered in guilty human nature by the Son of God who took that nature to redeem it.

(*c*) It most fully meets the requirements of Scripture, by holding that the necessity of the atonement is absolute, since it rests upon the demands of immanent holiness, the fundamental attribute of God.

Acts 17:3 — "it behooved the Christ to suffer, and to rise again from the dead" — lit.: "it was necessary for the Christ to suffer"; Luke 24:26 — "Behooved it not the Christ to suffer these things, and to enter into his glory?" — lit.: "Was it not necessary that the Christ should suffer these things?" It is not enough to say that Christ must suffer in order that the prophecies might be fulfilled. Why was it prophesied that he should suffer? Why did God purpose that he should suffer? The ultimate necessity is a necessity in the nature of God.

Plato, Republic, 2:361 — "The righteous man who is thought to be unrighteous will be scourged, racked, bound; will have his eyes put out; and finally, having endured all sorts of evil, will be impaled." This means that, as human society is at present constituted, even a righteous person must suffer for the sins of the world. "Mors mortis Morti mortem n⸱s morte dedisset, Æternæ vitæ janua clausa foret" — "Had not the Death-of-death t Death his death-blow given, Forever closed were the gate, the gate of life and heav⸱ ⸱."

(*d*) It shows most satisfactorily how the demands of holiness are met; namely, by the propitiatory offering of one who is personally pure, but who by union with the human race has inherited its guilt and penalty.

"*Quo non ascendam?*"—"Whither shall I not rise?" exclaimed the greatest minister of modern kings, in a moment of intoxication. "Whither shall I not stoop?" says the Lord Jesus. King Humbert, during the scourge of cholera in Italy: "In Castellammare they make merry; in Naples they die: I go to Naples."

Wrightnour: "The illustration of Powhatan raising his club to slay John Smith, while Pocahontas flings herself between the uplifted club and the victim, is not a good one. God is not an angry being, bound to strike something, no matter what. If Powhatan could have taken the blow himself, out of a desire to spare the victim, it would be better. The Father and the Son are one. Bronson Alcott, in his school at Concord, when punishment was necessary, sometimes placed the rod in the hand of the offender and bade him strike his (Alcott's) hand, rather than that the law of the school should be broken without punishment following. The result was that very few rules were roken. So God in Christ bore the sins of the world, and endured the penalty for an's violation of his law."

(e) It furnishes the only proper explanation of the sacrificial language of the New Testament, and of the sacrificial rites of the Old, considered as prophetic of Christ's atoning work.

Foster, Christian Life and Theology, 207–211 — " The imposition of hands on the head of the victim is entirely unexplained, except in the account of the great day of Atonement, when by the same gesture and by distinct confession the sins of the people were ' put upon the head of the goat' (Lev. 16:21) to be borne away into the wilderness. The blood was sacred and was to be poured out before the Lord, evidently in place of the forfeited life of the sinner which should have been rendered up." Watts, New Apologetics, 205 — " The Lord will provide' was the truth taught when Abraham found a ram provided by God which he 'offered up as a burnt offering in the stead of his son' (Gen. 22:13, 14). As the ram was not Abraham's ram, the sacrifice of it could not teach that all Abraham had belonged to God, and should, with entire faith in his goodness, be devoted to him; but it did teach that 'apart from shedding of blood there is no remission' (Heb. 9:22)." 2 Chron. 29:27 — "when the ournt offering began, the song of Jehovah began also."

(f) It alone gives proper place to the death of Christ as the central feature of his work, — set forth in the ordinances, and of chief power in Christian experience.

Martin Luther, when he had realized the truth of the Atonement, was found sobbing before a crucifix and moaning: "Für mich! für mich!" — "For me! for me!' Elisha Kane, the Arctic explorer, while searching for signs of Sir John Franklin and his party, sent out eight or ten men to explore the surrounding region. After several days three returned, almost crazed with the cold — thermometer fifty degrees below zero — and reported that the other men were dying miles away. Dr. Kane organized a company of ten, and though suffering himself with an old heart-trouble, led them to the rescue. Three times he fainted during the eighteen hours of marching and suffering; but he found the men. " We knew you would come! we knew you would come, orother!" whispered one of them, hardly able to speak. Why was he sure Dr. Kane would come? Because he knew the stuff Dr. Kane was made of, and knew that he would risk his life for any one of them. It is a parable of Christ's relation to our salvation. He is our elder brother, bone of our bone and flesh of our flesh, and he not only risks death, but he endures death, in order to save us.

(g) It gives us the only means of understanding the sufferings of Christ in the garden and on the cross, or of reconciling them with the divine justice.

Kreibig, Versöhnungslehre: " Man has a guilt that demands the punitive sufferings of a mediator. Christ shows a suffering that cannot be justified except by reference to some other guilt than his own. Combine these two facts, and you have the problem of the atonement solved." J. G. Whittier: " Through all the depths of sin and loss Drops the plummet of the Cross; Never yet abyss was found Deeper than the Cross could sound." Alcestis purchased life for Admetus her husband by dying in his stead: Marcus Curtius saved Rome by leaping into the yawning chasm; the Russian servant threw himself to the wolves to rescue his master. Berdoe, Robert Browning, 47 — " To know God as the theist knows him may suffice for pure spirits, for those who have never sinned, suffered, nor felt the need of a Savior; but for fallen and sinful men the Christ of Christianity is an imperative necessity; and those who have never surrendered themselves to him have never known what it is to experience the rest he gives to the heavy-laden soul."

(h) As no other theory does, this view satisfies the ethical demand of human nature; pacifies the convicted conscience; assures the sinner that he may find instant salvation in Christ; and so makes possible a new life of holiness, while at the same time it furnishes the highest incentives to such a life.

Shedd: "The offended party (1) permits a substitution; (2) provides a substitute; (3) substitutes himself." George Eliot: "Justice is like the kingdom of God; it is not without us, as a fact: it is 'within us,' as a great yearning." But it is both without and within, and the inward is only the reflection of the outward; the subjective demands of conscience only reflect the objective demands of holiness.

And yet, while this view of the atonement exalts the holiness of God, it surpasses every other view in its moving exhibition of God's love — a love that is not satisfied with suffering in and with the sinner, or with making that suffering a demonstration of God's regard for law; but a love that sinks itself into the sinner's guilt and bears his penalty, — comes down so low as to make itself one with him in all but his depravity — makes every sacrifice but the sacrifice of God's holiness — a sacrifice which God could not make, without ceasing to be God; see 1 John 4:10 — "Herein is love, not that we loved God, but that he loved us, and sent his Son to be the propitiation for our sins."

The soldier who had been thought reprobate was moved to complete reform when he was once forgiven. William Huntington, in his Autobiography, says that one of his sharpest sensations of pain, after he had been quickened by divine grace, was that he felt such pity for God. Never was man abused as God has been. Rom. 2:4 — "the goodness of God leadeth thee to repentance"; 12:1 — "the mercies of God" lead you "to present your bodies a living sacrifice"; 2 Cor. 5:14, 15 — "the love of Christ constraineth us; because we thus judge, that one died for all, therefore all died; and he died for all, that they that live should no longer live unto themselves, but unto him who for their sakes died and rose again." The effect of Christ's atonement on Christian character and life may be illustrated from the proclamation of Garabaldi: "He that loves Italy, let him follow me! I promise him hardship, I promise him suffering, I promise him death. But he that loves Italy, let him follow me!"

D.   Objections to the Ethical Theory of the Atonement.

On the general subject of these objections, Philippi, Glaubenslehre, IV, 2:156-180, remarks: (1) that it rests with God alone to say whether he will pardon sin, and in what way he will pardon it; (2) that human instincts are a very unsafe standard by which to judge the procedure of the Governor of the universe; and (3) that one plain declaration of God, with regard to the plan of salvation, proves the fallacy and error of all reasonings against it. We must correct our watches and clocks by astronomic standards.

(a)   That a God who does not pardon sin without atonement must lack either omnipotence or love. — We answer, on the one hand, that God's omnipotence is the revelation of his nature, and not a matter of arbitrary will; and, on the other hand, that God's love is ever exercised consistently with his fundamental attribute of holiness, so that while holiness demands the sacrifice, love provides it. Mercy is shown, not by trampling upon the claims of justice, but by vicariously satisfying them.

Because man does not need to avenge personal wrongs, it does not follow that God must not. In fact, such avenging is forbidden to us upon the ground that it belongs to God; Rom. 12:19 — "Avenge not yourselves, beloved, but give place unto wrath: for it is written, Vengeance belongeth unto me; I will recompense, saith the Lord." But there are limits even to our passing over of offences. Even the father must sometimes chastise; and although this chastisement is not properly punishment, it becomes punishment, when the father becomes a teacher or a governor. Then, other than personal interests come in. "Because a father can forgive without atonement, it does not follow that the state can do the same" (Shedd). But God is more than Father, more than Teacher, more than Governor. In him, person and right are identical. For him to let sin go unpunished is to approve of it; which is the same as a denial of holiness.

Whatever pardon is granted, then, must be pardon through punishment. Mere repentance never expiates crime, even under civil government. The truly penitent man never feels that his repentance constitutes a ground of acceptance; the more he repents, the more he recognizes his need of reparation and expiation. Hence God meets the demand of man's conscience, as well as of his own holiness, when he provides a substituted punishment. God shows his love by meeting the demands of holiness, and by meeting them with the sacrifice of himself. See Mozley on Pedestination, 390.

The publican prays, not that God may be merciful without sacrifice, but: "God be propitiated toward me, the sinner!" (Luke 18:13); in other words, he asks for mercy only through and upon the ground of, sacrifice. We cannot atone to others for the wrong we have done them, nor can we even atone to our own souls. A third party, and an infinite being, must make atonement, as we cannot. It is only upon the ground that God himself has made provision for satisfying the claims of justice, that we are bidden to forgive others. Should Othello then forgive Iago? Yes, if Iago repents; Luke 17 : 3 – 'If thy brother sin, rebuke him ; and if he repent, forgive him." But if he does not repent? Yes, so far as Othello's own disposition is concerned. He must not hate Iago, but must wish him well ; Luke 6 : 27 — "Love your enemies, do good to them that hate you, bless them that curse you, pray for them that despitefully use you." But he cannot receive Iago to his fellowship till he repents. On the duty and ground of forgiving one another, see Martineau, Seat of Authority, 613, 614; Straffen, Hulsean Lectures on the Propitiation for Sin.

(*b*) That satisfaction and forgiveness are mutually exclusive. — We answer that, since it is not a third party, but the Judge himself, who makes satisfaction to his own violated holiness, forgiveness is still optional, and may be offered upon terms agreeable to himself. Christ's sacrifice is not a pecuniary, but a penal, satisfaction. The objection is valid against the merely commercial view of the atonement, not against the ethical view of it.

Forgiveness is something beyond the mere taking away of penalty. When a man bears the penalty of his crime, has the community no right to be indignant with him? There is a distinction between pecuniary and penal satisfaction. Pecuniary satisfaction has respect only to the thing due ; penal satisfaction has respect also to the person of the offender. If pardon is a matter of justice in God's government, it is so only as respects Christ. To the recipient it is only mercy. "Faithful and righteous to forgive us our sins" (1 John 1 : 9) = faithful to his promise, and righteous to Christ. Neither the atonement, nor the promise, gives the offender any personal claim.

Philemon must forgive Onesimus the pecuniary *debt*, when Paul pays it; not so with the personal *injury* Onesimus has done to Philemon ; there is no forgiveness of this, until Onesimus repents and asks pardon. An amnesty may be offered to all, but upon conditions. Instance Amos Lawrence's offering to the forger the forged paper he had bought up, upon condition that he would confess himself bankrupt, and put all his affairs into the hands of his benefactor. So the fact that Christ has paid our debts does not preclude his offering to us the benefit of what he has done, upon condition of our repentance and faith. The equivalent is not furnished by man, but by God. God may therefore offer the results of it upon his own terms. Did then the entire race fairly pay its penalty when one suffered, just as all incurred the penalty when one sinned? Yes, — all who receive their life from each — Adam on the one hand, and Christ on the other. See under Union with Christ — its Consequences ; see also Shedd, Discourses and Essays, 295 note, 321, and Dogm. Theol., 2 : 386–389 ; Dorner, Glauben-slehre, 2 : 614–615 (Syst. Doct., 4 : 82, 83). *Versus* Current Discussions in Theology, 5 : 281.

Hovey calls Christ's relation to human sin a vice-penal one. Just as vice-regal position carries with it all the responsibility, care, and anxiety of regal authority, so does a vice-penal relation to sin carry with it all the suffering and loss of the original punishment. The person on whom it falls is different, but his punishment is the same, at least in penal value. As vice-regal authority may be superseded by regal, so vice-penal suffering, if despised, may be superseded by the original penalty. Is there a waste of vice-penal suffering when any are lost for whom it was endured? On the same principle we might object to any suffering on the part of Christ for those who refuse to be saved by him. Such suffering may benefit others, if not those for whom it was in the first instance endured.

If compensation is made, it is said, there is nothing to forgive; if forgiveness is granted, no compensation can be required. This reminds us of Narvaez, who saw no reason for forgiving his enemies until he had shot them all. When the offended party furnishes the compensation, he can offer its benefits upon his own terms. Dr. Pentecost: "A prisoner in Scotland was brought before the Judge. As the culprit entered the box, he looked into the face of the Judge to see if he could discover mercy there. The Judge and the prisoner exchanged glances, and then there came a mutual recognition. The prisoner said to himself : 'It is all right this time,' for the Judge had been his classmate in Edinburgh University twenty-five years before. When sentence was pronounced, it was five pounds sterling, the limit of the law for the misdemeanor charged, and the culprit was sorely disappointed as he was led away to prison. But the Judge went at once and paid the fine, telling the clerk to write the man's discharge. This the Judge delivered in person, explaining that the demands of the law must be met, and having been met, the man was free."

(c) That there can be no real propitiation, since the judge and the sacrifice are one. — We answer that this objection ignores the existence of personal relations within the divine nature, and the fact that the God-man is distinguishable from God. The satisfaction is grounded in the distinction of persons in the Godhead ; while the love in which it originates belongs to the unity of the divine essence.

The satisfaction is not rendered to a *part* of the Godhead, for the whole Godhead is in the Father, in a certain manner ; as omnipresence = *totus in omni parte.* So the offering is perfect, because the whole Godhead is also in Christ (2 Cor. 5 : 19 — "God was in Christ reconciling the world unto himself"). Lyman Abbott says that the word "propitiate" is used in the New Testament only in the middle voice, to show that God propitiates himself. Lyttelton, in Lux Mundi, 302 — "The Atonement is undoubtedly a mystery, but all forgiveness is a mystery. It avails to lift the load of guilt that presses upon an offender. A change passes over him that can only be described as regenerative, life-giving ; and thus the assurance of pardon, however conveyed, may be said to obliterate in some degree the consequences of the past. 310 — Christ bore sufferings, not that we might be freed from them, for we have deserved them, but that we might be enabled to bear them, as he did, victoriously and in unbroken union with God."

(d) That the suffering of the innocent for the guilty is not an execution of justice, but an act of manifest injustice. — We answer, that this is true only upon the supposition that the Son bears the penalty of our sins, not voluntarily, but compulsorily ; or upon the supposition that one who is personally innocent can in no way become involved in the guilt and penalty of others, — both of them hypotheses contrary to Scripture and to fact.

The mystery of the atonement lies in the fact of unmerited sufferings on the part of Christ. Over against this stands the corresponding mystery of unmerited pardon to believers. We have attempted to show that, while Christ was personally innocent, he was so involved with others in the consequences of the Fall, that the guilt and penalty of the race belonged to him to bear. When we discuss the doctrine of Justification, we shall see that, by a similar union of the believer with Christ, Christ's justification becomes ours.

To one who believes in Christ as the immanent God, the life of humanity, the Creator and Upholder of mankind, the bearing by Christ of the just punishment of human sin seems inevitable. The very laws of nature are only the manifestation of his holiness, and he who thus reveals God is also subject to God's law. The historical process which culminated on Calvary was the manifestation of an age-long suffering endured by Christ on account of his connection with the race from the very first moment of their sin. A. H. Strong, Christ in Creation, 80-83 — "A God of love and holiness must be a God of suffering just so certainly as there is sin. Paul declares that he fills up "that which is lacking of the afflictions of Christ . . . . for his body's sake, which is the church " (Col. 1 : 24) ; in other words, Christ still suffers in the believers who are his body. The historical suffering indeed is ended ; the agony of Golgotha is finished ; the days when joy was swallowed up in sorrow are past ; death has no more dominion over our Lord. But sorrow for sin is not ended ; it still continues and will continue so long as sin exists. But it does not now militate against Christ's blessedness, because the sorrow is overbalanced and overborne by the infinite knowledge and glory of his divine nature. Bushnell and Beecher were right when they maintained that suffering for sin was the natural consequence of Christ's relation to the sinning creation. They were wrong in mistaking the nature of that suffering and in not seeing that the constitution of things which necessitates it, since it is the expression of God's holiness, gives that suffering a penal character and makes Christ a substitutionary offering for the sins of the world."

(e) That there can be no transfer of punishment or merit, since these are personal. — We answer that the idea of representation and suretyship is common in human society and government; and that such representation and suretyship are inevitable, wherever there is community of life between the innocent and the guilty. When Christ took our nature, he could not do otherwise than take our responsibilities also.

Christ became responsible for the humanity with which he was organically one. Both poets and historians have recognized the propriety of one member of a house, or a race, answering for another. Antigone expiates the crime of her house. Marcus Curtius holds himself ready to die for his nation. Louis XVI has been called a "sacrificial lamb," offered up for the crimes of his race. So Christ's sacrifice is of benefit to the whole family of man, because he is one with that family. But here is the limitation also. It does not extend to angels, because he took not on him the nature of angels (Heb. 2 : 16 — "For verily not of the angels doth he take hold, but he taketh hold of the seed of Abraham ")

"A strange thing happened recently in one of our courts of justice. A young man was asked why the extreme penalty should not be passed upon him. At that moment, a gray-haired man, his face furrowed with sorrow, stepped into the prisoner's box unhindered, placed his hand affectionately upon the culprit's shoulder, and said: 'Your honor, we have nothing to say. The verdict which has been found against us is just. We have only to ask for mercy.' 'We!' There was nothing against this old father. Yet, at that moment he lost himself. He identified his very being with that of his wayward boy. Do you not pity the criminal son because of your pity for his aged and sorrowing father? Because he has so suffered, is not your demand that the son suffer somewhat mitigated? Will not the judge modify his sentence on that account? Nature knows no forgiveness; but human nature does; and it is not nature, but human nature, that is made in the image of God"; see Prof. A. S. Coats, in The Examiner, Sept. 12, 1889.

(f) That remorse, as a part of the penalty of sin, could not have been suffered by Christ. — We answer, on the one hand, that it may not be essential to the idea of penalty that Christ should have borne the identical pangs which the lost would have endured; and, on the other hand, that we do not know how completely a perfectly holy being, possessed of superhuman knowledge and love, might have felt even the pangs of remorse for the condition of that humanity of which he was the central conscience and heart.

Instance the lawyer, mourning the fall of a star of his profession; the woman, filled with shame by the degradation of one of her own sex; the father, anguished by his daughter's waywardness; the Christian, crushed by the sins of the church and the world. The self-isolating spirit cannot conceive how perfectly love and holiness can make their own the sin of the race of which they are a part.

Simon, Reconciliation, 366 — "Inasmuch as the sin of the human race culminated in the crucifixion which crowned Christ's own sufferings, clearly the life of humanity entering him subconsciously must have been most completely laden with sin and with the fear of death which is its fruit, at the very moment when he himself was enduring death in its most terrible form. Of necessity therefore he felt as if he were the sinner of sinners, and cried out in agony: 'My God, my God, why hast thou forsaken me?' (Mat. 27 : 46)."

Christ could realize our penal condition. Beings who have a like spiritual nature can realize and bear the spiritual sufferings of one another. David's sorrow was not unjust, when he cried: "Would I had died for thee, O Absalom, my son, my son!" (2 Sam. 18 : 33). Moberly, Atonement and Personality, 117 — "Is penitence possible in the personally sinless? We answer that only one who is perfectly sinless can perfectly repent, and this identification of the sinless with the sinner is vital to the gospel." Lucy Larcom: "There be sad women, sick and poor, And those who walk in garments soiled; Their shame, their sorrow I endure; By their defeat my hope is foiled; The blot they bear is on my name; Who sins, and I am not to blame?"

(g) That the sufferings of Christ, as finite in time, do not constitute a satisfaction to the infinite demands of the law.—We answer that the infinite dignity of the sufferer constitutes his sufferings a full equivalent, in the eye of infinite justice. Substitution excludes identity of suffering; it does not exclude equivalence. Since justice aims its penalties not so much at the person as at the sin, it may admit equivalent suffering, when this is endured in the very nature that has sinned.

The sufferings of a dog, and of a man, have different values. Death is the wages of sin; and Christ, in suffering death, suffered our penalty. Eternity of suffering is unessential to the idea of penalty. A finite being cannot exhaust an infinite curse; but an infinite being can exhaust it, in a few brief hours. Shedd, Discourses and Essays, 307—"A golden eagle is worth a thousand copper cents. The penalty paid by Christ is strictly and literally *equivalent* to that which the sinner would have borne, although it is not *identical*. The vicarious bearing of it excludes the latter." Andrew Fuller thought Christ would have had to suffer just as much, if only one sinner were to have been saved thereby.

The atonement is a unique fact, only partially illustrated by debt and penalty. Yet the terms 'purchase' and 'ransom' are Scriptural, and mean simply that the justice of God punishes sin as it deserves; and that, having determined what is deserved, God cannot change. See Owen, quoted in Campbell on Atonement, 58, 59. Christ's sacrifice, since it is absolutely infinite, can have nothing added to it. If Christ's sacrifice satisfies the Judge of all, it may well satisfy us.

(*h*) That if Christ's passive obedience made satisfaction to the divine justice, then his active obedience was superfluous.—We answer that the active obedience and the passive obedience are inseparable. The latter is essential to the former; and both are needed to secure for the sinner, on the one hand, pardon, and, on the other hand, that which goes beyond pardon, namely, restoration to the divine favor. The objection holds only against a superficial and external view of the atonement.

For more full exposition of this point, see our treatment of Justification; and also, Owen, in Works, 5 : 175-204. Both the active and the passive obedience of Christ are insisted on by the apostle Paul. Opposition to the Pauline theology is opposition to the gospel of Christ. Charles Cuthbert Hall, Universal Elements of the Christian Religion, 140—"The effects of this are already appearing in the impoverished religious values of the sermons produced by the younger generation of preachers, and the deplorable decline of spiritual life and knowledge in many churches. Results open to observation show that the movement to simplify the Christian essence by discarding the theology of St. Paul easily carries the teaching of the Christian pulpit to a position where, for those who submit to that teaching, the characteristic experiences of the Christian life became practically impossible. The Christian sense of sin; Christian penitence at the foot of the Cross; Christian faith in an atoning Savior; Christian peace with God through the mediation of Jesus Christ — these and other experiences, which were the very life of apostles and apostolic souls, fade from the view of the ministry, have no meaning for the younger generation."

(*i*) That the doctrine is immoral in its practical tendencies, since Christ's obedience takes the place of ours, and renders ours unnecessary. — We answer that the objection ignores not only the method by which the benefits of the atonement are appropriated, namely, repentance and faith, but also the regenerating and sanctifying power bestowed upon all who believe. Faith in the atonement does not induce license, but "works by love" (Gal. 5 : 6) and "cleanses the heart" (Acts 15 : 9).

Water is of little use to a thirsty man, if he will not drink. The faith which accepts Christ ratifies all that Christ has done, and takes Christ as a new principle of life. Paul bids Philemon receive Onesimus as himself,— not the old Onesimus, but a new Onesimus into whom the spirit of Paul has entered (Philemon 17). So God receives us as new creatures in Christ. Though we cannot earn salvation, we must take it; and this taking it involves a surrender of heart and life which ensures union with Christ and moral progress.

What shall be done to the convicted murderer who tears up the pardon which his wife's prayers and tears have secured from the Governor? Nothing remains but to execute the sentence of the law. Hon. George F. Danforth, Justice of the New York State Court of Appeals, in a private letter says: "Although it may be stated in a general way that a pardon reaches both the punishment prescribed for the offence and the guilt of the offender, so that in the eye of the law he is as innocent as if he had never committed the offence, the pardon making him as it were a new man with a new credit and capacity, yet a delivery of the pardon is essential to its validity, and delivery is not complete without acceptance. It cannot be forced upon him. In that respect it is like a deed. The delivery may be in person to the offender or to his agent, and its acceptance may be proved by circumstances like any other fact."

(*j*) That if the atonement requires faith as its complement, then it does not in itself furnish a complete satisfaction to God's justice.—We answer that faith is not the ground of our acceptance with God, as the atonement is, and so is not a work at all; faith is only the medium of appropriation. We are saved not by faith, or on account of faith, but only through faith. It is not faith, but the atonement which faith accepts, that satisfies the justice of God.

Illustrate by the amnesty granted to a city, upon conditions to be accepted by each inhabitant. The acceptance is not the ground upon which the amnesty is granted; it is the medium through which the benefits of the amnesty are enjoyed. With regard to the difficulties connected with the atonement, we may say, in conclusion, with Bishop Butler: "If the Scripture has, as surely it has, left this matter of the satisfaction of Christ mysterious, left somewhat in it unrevealed, all conjectures about it must be, if not evidently absurd, yet at least uncertain. Nor has any one reason to complain for want of further information, unless he can show his claim to it." While we cannot say with President Stearns: "Christ's work removed the hindrances in the eternal justice of the universe to the pardon of the sinner, but *how* we cannot tell" — cannot say this, because we believe the main outlines of the plan of salvation to be revealed in Scripture — yet we grant that many questions remain unsolved. But, as bread nourishes even those who know nothing of its chemical constituents, or of the method of its digestion and assimilation, so the atonement of Christ saves those who accept it, even though they do not know *how* it saves them. Balfour, Foundations of Belief, 264–267 — "Heat was once thought to be a form of matter; now it is regarded as a mode of motion. We can get the good of it, whichever theory we adopt, or even if we have no theory. So we may get the good of reconciliation with God, even though we differ as to our theory of the Atonement." — "One of the Roman Emperors commanded his fleet to bring from Alexandria sand for the arena, although his people at Rome were visited with famine. But a certain shipmaster declared that, whatever the emperor commanded, his ship should bring wheat. So, whatever sand others may bring to starving human souls, let us bring to them the wheat of the gospel — the substitutionary atonement of Jesus Christ." For answers to objections, see Philippi, Glaubenslehre, IV, 2:156–189; Crawford, Atonement, 384–468; Hodge, Syst. Theol., 2:526–543 Baird, Elohim Revealed, 623 *sq.;* Wm. Thomson, The Atoning Work of Christ; Hopkins, Works, 1:321.

E. The Extent of the Atonement.

The Scriptures represent the atonement as having been made for all men, and as sufficient for the salvation of all. Not the *atonement* therefore is limited, but the *application* of the atonement through the work of the Holy Spirit.

Upon this principle of a universal atonement, but a special application of it to the elect, we must interpret such passages as Eph. 1:4, 7; 2 Tim. 1:9, 10; John 17:9, 20, 24—asserting a special efficacy of the atonement in the case of the elect; and also such passages as 2 Pet. 2:1; 1 John 2:2; Tim. 2:6; 4:10; Tit. 2:11—asserting that the death of Christ is for all.

Passages asserting special efficacy of the atonement, in the case of the elect, are the following: Eph. 1:4 — "chose us in him before the foundation of the world, that we should be holy and without blemish before him in love "; 7 — "in whom we have our redemption through his blood, the forgiveness of our trespasses, according to the riches of his grace ;" 2 Tim. 1 : 9, 10 — God "who saved us, and called us with a holy calling, not according to our works, but according to his own purpose and grace, which was given us in Christ Jesus before times eternal, but hath now been manifested by the appearing of our Savior Christ Jesus, who abolished death, and brought life and immortality to light through the gospel "; John 17 : 9 — "I pray for them : I pray not for the world, but for those whom thou hast given me "; 20 — "Neither for these only do I pray, but for them also that believe on me through their word "; 24 — "Father, that which thou hast given me, I desire that where I am, they also may be with me ; that they may behold my glory, which thou hast given me."

Passages asserting that the death of Christ is for all are the following : 2 Pet. 2 : 1 — "false teachers, who shall privily bring in destructive heresies, denying even the Master that bought them "; 1 John 2 : 2 — "and he is the propitiation for our sins; and not for ours only, but also for the whole world "; 1 Tim. 2 : 6 — Christ Jesus "who gave himself a ransom for all "; 4 : 10 — "the living God, who is the Savior of all men, specially of them that believe "; Tit. 2 : 11 — "For the grace of God hath appeared, bringing salvation to all men." Rom. 3 : 22 (A. V.)—"unto all and upon all them that believe "—has sometimes been interpreted as meaning "unto all men, and upon all believers " (εἰς = destination ; ἐπί = extent). But the Rev. Vers. omits the words "and upon all," and Meyer, who retains the words, remarks that τοὺς πιστεύοντας belongs to πάντας in both instances.

Unconscious participation in the atonement of Christ, by virtue of our common humanity in him, makes us the heirs of much temporal blessing. Conscious participation in the atonement of Christ, by virtue of our faith in him and his work for us, gives us justification and eternal life. Matthew Henry said that the Atonement is "sufficient for all ; effectual for many." J. M. Whiton, in The Outlook, Sept. 25, 1897 — "It was Samuel Hopkins of Rhode Island (1721–1803) who first declared that Christ had made atonement for all men, not for the elect part alone, as Calvinists affirmed." We should say "as some Calvinists affirmed " ; for, as we shall see, John Calvin himself declared that "Christ suffered for the sins of the whole world." Alfred Tennyson once asked an old Methodist woman what was the news. "Why, Mr. Tennyson, there 's only one piece of news that I know,— that Christ died for all men." And he said to her : "That is old news, and good news, and new news."

If it be asked in what sense Christ is the Savior of all men, we reply :

(*a*) That the atonement of Christ secures for all men a delay in the execution of the sentence against sin, and a space for repentance, together with a continuance of the common blessings of life which have been forfeited by transgression.

If strict justice had been executed, the race would have been cut off at the first sin. That man lives after sinning, is due wholly to the Cross. There is a pretermission, or "passing over of the sins done aforetime, in the forbearance of God " (Rom. 3 : 25), the justification of which is found only in the sacrifice of Calvary. This "passing over," however, is limited in its duration : see Acts 17 : 30, 31 — "The times of ignorance therefore God overlooked ; but now he commandeth men that they should all everywhere repent: inasmuch as he hath appointed a day in which he will judge the world in righteousness by the man whom he hath ordained."

One may get the benefit of the law of gravitation without understanding much about its nature, and patriarchs and heathen have doubtless been saved through Christ's atonement, although they have never heard his name, but have only cast themselves as helpless sinners upon the mercy of God. That mercy of God was Christ, though they did not know it. Our modern pious Jews will experience a strange surprise when they find that not only forgiveness of sin but every other blessing of life has come to them through the crucified Jesus. Matt. 8 : 11 — "many shall come from the east and the west, and shall sit down with Abraham, and Isaac, and Jacob, in the kingdom of heaven."

Dr. G. W. Northrup held that the work of Christ is universal in three respects : 1. It reconciled God to the whole race, apart from personal transgression ; 2. It secured the bestowment upon all of common grace, and the means of common grace ; 3. It rendered certain the bestowment of eternal life upon all who would so use common grace and the means of common grace as to make it morally possible for God as a wise and holy Governor to grant his special and renewing grace.

(*b*) That the atonement of Christ has made objective provision for the salvation of all, by removing from the divine mind every obstacle to the pardon and restoration of sinners, except their wilful opposition to God and refusal to turn to him.

Van Oosterzee, Dogmatics, 604—"On God's side, all is now taken away which could make a separation,—unless any should themselves choose to remain separated from him." The gospel message is not: God will forgive if you return; but rather: God *has* shown mercy; only believe, and it is your portion in Christ.

Ashmore, The New Trial of the Sinner, in Christian Review, 26 : 245–264—"The atonement has come to all men and upon all men. Its coëxtensiveness with the effects of Adam's sin is seen in that all creatures, such as infants and insane persons, incapable of refusing it, are saved without their consent, just as they were involved in the sin of Adam without their consent. The reason why others are not saved is because when the atonement comes to them and upon them, instead of consenting to be included in it, they reject it. If they are born under the curse, so likewise they are born under the atonement which is intended to remove that curse; they remain under its shelter till they are old enough to repudiate it; they shut out its influences as a man closes his window-blind to shut out the beams of the sun; they ward them off by direct opposition, as a man builds dykes around his field to keep out the streams which would otherwise flow in and fertilize the soil."

(*c*) That the atonement of Christ has procured for all men the powerful incentives to repentance presented in the Cross, and the combined agency of the Christian church and of the Holy Spirit, by which these incentives are brought to bear upon them.

Just as much sun and rain would be needed, if only one farmer on earth were to be benefited. Christ would not need to suffer more, if all were to be saved. His sufferings, as we have seen, were not the payment of a pecuniary debt. Having endured the penalty of the sinner, justice permits the sinner's discharge, but does not require it, except as the fulfilment of a promise to his substitute, and then only upon the appointed condition of repentance and faith. The *atonement* is unlimited,—the whole human race might be saved through it; the *application* of the atonement is limited,—only those who repent and believe are actually saved by it.

Robert G. Farley: "The prospective mother prepares a complete and beautiful outfit for her expected child. But the child is still-born. Yet the outfit was prepared just the same as if it had lived. And Christ's work is completed as much for one man as for another, as much for the unbeliever as for the believer."

Christ is specially the Savior of those who believe, in that he exerts a special power of his Spirit to procure their acceptance of his salvation. This is not, however, a part of his work of atonement; it is the application of the atonement, and as such is hereafter to be considered.

Among those who hold to a limited atonement is Owen. Campbell quotes him as saying : "Christ did not die for all the sins of all men; for if this were so, why are not all freed from the punishment of all their sins? You will say, 'Because of their unbelief,—they will not believe.' But this unbelief is a sin, and Christ was punished for it. Why then does this, more than other sins, hinder them from partaking of the fruits of his death?"

So also Turretin, loc. 4, quæs. 10 and 17; Symington, Atonement, 184–234; Candlish on the Atonement, Cunnningham, Hist. Theol., 2 : 323–370; Shedd, Dogm. Theol., 2 : 464–489. For the view presented in the text, see Andrew Fuller, Works, 2 : 373, 374; 689–698; 706–709; Wardlaw, Syst. Theol., 2 : 485–549; Jenkyn, Extent of the Atonement; E. P. Griffin, Extent of the Atonement; Woods, Works, 2 : 490–521; Richards, Lectures on Theology, 302–327.

2. *Christ's Intercessory Work.*

The Priesthood of Christ does not cease with his work of atonement, but continues forever. In the presence of God he fulfils the second office of the priest, namely that of intercession.

Heb. 7 : 23–25—"priests many in number, because that by death they are hindered from continuing: but he, because he abideth forever, hath his priesthood unchangeable. Wherefore also he is able to save to the uttermost them that draw near unto God through him, seeing he ever liveth to make intercession for them." C. H. M. on Ex. 17 : 12—"The hands of our great Intercessor never hang down, as Moses' did, nor does he need any one to hold them up. The same rod of God's power which was used by Moses to smite the rock (Atonement) was in Moses' hand on the hill (Intercession)."

Denney's Studies in Theology, 166 — "If we see nothing unnatural in the fact that Christ prayed for Peter on earth, we need not make any difficulty about his praying for us in heaven. The relation is the same ; the only difference is that Christ is now exalted, and prays, not with strong crying and tears, but in the sovereignty and prevailing power of one who has achieved eternal redemption for his people."

A. Nature of Christ's Intercession. — This is not to be conceived of either as an external and vocal petitioning, nor as a mere figure of speech for the natural and continuous influence of his sacrifice ; but rather as a special activity of Christ in securing, upon the ground of that sacrifice, whatever of blessing comes to men, whether that blessing be temporal or spiritual.

1 John 2 : 1 — "if any man sin, we have an Advocate with the Father, Jesus Christ the righteous" ; Rom. 8 : 34 — "It is Jesus Christ that died, yea rather, that was raised from the dead, who is at the right hand of God, who also maketh intercession for us" — here Meyer seems to favor the meaning of external and vocal petitioning, as of the glorified God-man : Heb. 7 : 25 — "ever liveth to make intercession for them." On the ground of this effectual intercession he can pronounce the true sacerdotal *benediction* ; and all the benedictions of his ministers and apostles are but fruits and emblems of this (see the Aaronic benediction in Num. 6 : 24-26, and the apostolic benedictions in 1 Cor. 1 : 3 and 2 Cor. 13 : 14).

B. Objects of Christ's Intercession. — We may distinguish (a) that general intercession which secures to all men certain temporal benefits of his atoning work, and (b) that special intercession which secures the divine acceptance of the persons of believers and the divine bestowment of all gifts needful for their salvation.

(a) General intercession for all men : Is. 53 : 12 — "he bare the sin of many, and made intercession for the transgressors" ; Luke 23 : 34 — "And Jesus said, Father, forgive them ; for they know not what they do" — a beginning of his priestly intercession, even while he was being nailed to the cross.

(b) Special intercession for his saints : Mat. 18 . 19, 20 — "if two of you shall agree on earth as touching anything that they shall ask, it shall be done for them of my Father which is in heaven. For where two or three are gathered together in my name, there am I in the midst of them" ; Luke 22 : 31, 32 — "Simon, Simon, behold, Satan asked to have you, that he might sift you as wheat : but I made supplication for thee, that thy faith fail not" ; John 14 : 16 — "I will pray the Father, and he shall give you another Comforter" ; 17 : 9 — "I pray for them ; I pray not for the world, but for those whom thou hast given me" ; Acts 2 : 33 — "Being therefore by the right hand of God exalted, and having received of the Father the promise of the Holy Spirit, he hath poured forth this, which ye see and hear" ; Eph. 1 : 6 — "the glory of his grace, which he freely bestowed on us in the Beloved" ; 2 : 18 — "through him we both have our access in one Spirit unto the Father" ; 3 : 12 — "in whom we have boldness and access in confidence through our faith in him" ; Heb. 2 : 17, 18 — "Wherefore it behooved him in all things to be made like unto his brethren, that he might become a merciful and faithful high priest in things pertaining to God, to make propitiation for the sins of the people. For in that he himself hath suffered being tempted, he is able to succor them that are tempted" ; 4 : 15, 16 — "For we have not a high priest that cannot be touched with the feeling of our infirmities ; but one that hath been in all points tempted like as we are, yet without sin. Let us therefore draw near with boldness unto the throne of grace, that we may receive mercy, and may find grace to help us in time of need" ; 1 Pet. 2 : 5 — "a holy priesthood, to offer up spiritual sacrifices, acceptable to God through Jesus Christ" ; Rev. 5 : 6 — "And I saw in the midst of the throne . . . . a Lamb standing, as though it had been slain, having seven horns, and seven eyes, which are the seven Spirits of God, sent forth into all the earth" ; 7 : 16, 17 — "They shall hunger no more, neither thirst any more ; neither shall the sun strike upon them, nor any heat : for the Lamb that is in the midst of the throne shall be their shepherd, and shall guide them unto fountains of waters of life : and God shall wipe away every tear from their eyes."

C. Relation of Christ's Intercession to that of the Holy Spirit. — The Holy Spirit is an advocate within us, teaching us how to pray as we ought ; Christ is an advocate in heaven, securing from the Father the answer of our prayers. Thus the work of Christ and of the Holy Spirit are complements to each other, and parts of one whole.

John 14 : 26 — "But the Comforter, even the Holy Spirit, whom the Father will send in my name, he shall teach you all things, and bring to your remembrance all that I said unto you" ; Rom. 8 : 26 — "And in like manner the Spirit also helpeth our infirmity : for we know not how to pray as we ought; but the Spirit himself maketh intercession for us with groanings which cannot be uttered "; 27 — " and he that searcheth the hearts knoweth what is the mind of the Spirit, because he maketh intercession for the saints according to the will of God."

The intercession of the Holy Spirit may be illustrated by the work of the mother, who teaches her child to pray by putting words into his mouth or by suggesting subjects for prayer. " The whole Trinity is present in the Christian's closet; the Father hears ; the Son advocates his cause at the Father's right hand ; the Holy Spirit intercedes in the heart of the believer." Therefore " When God inclines the heart to pray, He hath an ear to hear." The impulse to prayer, within our hearts, is evidence that Christ is urging our claims in heaven.

D. Relation of Christ's Intercession to that of saints. — All true intercession is either directly or indirectly the intercession of Christ. Christians are organs of Christ's Spirit. To suppose Christ in us to offer prayer to one of his saints, instead of directly to the Father, is to blaspheme Christ, and utterly misconceive the nature of prayer.

Saints on earth, by their union with Christ, the great high priest, are themselves constituted intercessors ; and as the high priest of old bore upon his bosom the breastplate engraven with the names of the tribes of Israel (Ex. 28 : 9-12), so the Christian is to bear upon his heart in prayer before God the interests of his family, the church, and the world (1 Tim. 2 : 1 — " I exhort therefore, first of all, that supplications, prayers, intercessions, thanksgivings be made for all men "). See Symington on Intercession, in Atonement and Intercession, 256-303 ; Milligan, Ascension and Heavenly Priesthood of our Lord.

Luckock, After Death, finds evidence of belief in the intercession of the saints in heaven as early as the second century. Invocation of the saints he regards as beginning not earlier than the fourth century. He approves the doctrine that the saints pray for us, but rejects the doctrine that we are to pray to them. Prayers for the dead he strongly advocates. Bramhall, Works, 1 : 57 — Invocation of the saints is " not necessary, for two reasons : first, no saint doth love us so well as Christ ; no saint hath given us such assurance of his love, or done so much for us as Christ ; no saint is so willing to help us as Christ ; and secondly, we have no command from God to invocate them." A. B. Cave : " The system of human mediation falls away in the advent to our souls of the living Christ. Who wants stars, or even the moon, after the sun is up ? "

III. The Kingly Office of Christ.

This is to be distinguished from the sovereignty which Christ originally possessed in virtue of his divine nature. Christ's kingship is the sovereignty of the divine-human Redeemer, which belonged to him of right from the moment of his birth, but which was fully exercised only from the time of his entrance upon the state of exaltation. By virtue of this kingly office, Christ rules all things in heaven and earth, for the glory of God and the execution of God's purpose of salvation.

(a) With respect to the universe at large, Christ's kingdom is a kingdom of power ; he upholds, governs, and judges the world.

Ps. 2 : 6-8 — " I have set my king .... Thou art my son .... uttermost parts of the earth for thy possession "; 8 : 6 — " madest him to have dominion over the works of thy hands ; Thou hast put all things under his feet "; cf. Heb. 2 : 8, 9 — " we see not yet all things subjected to him. But we behold .... Jesus .... crowned with glory and honor "; Mat. 25 : 31, 32 — " when the Son of man shall come in his glory .... then shall he sit on the throne of his glory : and before him shall be gathered all the nations "; 28 : 18 — " All authority hath been given unto me in heaven and on earth "; Heb. 1 : 3 — " upholding all things by the word of his power "; Rev. 19 : 15, 16 — " smite the nations .... rule them with a rod of iron .... King of Kings, and Lord of Lords."

Julius Müller, Proof-texts, 34, says incorrectly, as we think, that " the regnum naturæ of the old theology is unsupported, — there are only the regnum gratiæ and the regnum gloriæ." A. J. Gordon : " Christ is now creation's sceptre-bearer, as he was once creation's burden-bearer."

(b) With respect to his militant church, it is a kingdom of grace ; he rounds, legislates for, administers, defends, and augments his church on earth.

Luke 2 : 11 — "born to you . . . . a Savior, who is Christ the Lord " ; 19 : 38 — "Blessed is the King that cometh in the name of the Lord " ; John 18 : 36, 37 — "My kingdom is not of this world . . . . Thou sayest it, for I am a king . . . . Every one that is of the truth heareth my voice " ; Eph. 1 : 22 — "he put all things in subjection under his feet, and gave him to be head over all things to the church, which is his body, the fulness of him that filleth all in all", Heb. 1 : 8 — " of the Son he saith, Thy throne, O God, is for ever and ever."

Dorner, Glaubenslehre, 2 : 677 (Syst. Doct., 4 : 142, 143) — " All great men can be said to have an after-influence (*Nachwirkung*) after their death, but only of Christ can it be said that he has an after-activity (*Fortwirkung*). The sending of the Spirit is part of Christ's work as King." P. S. Moxom, Bap. Quar. Rev., Jan. 1886 : 25–36 — " Preëminence of Christ, as source of the church's being ; ground of the church's unity ; source of the church's law ; mould of the church's life." A. J. Gordon : " As the church endures hardness and humiliation as united to him who was on the cross, so she should exhibit something of supernatural energy as united with him who is on the throne." Luther : " We tell our Lord God, that if he will have his church, he must look after it himself. We cannot sustain it, and, if we could, we should become the proudest asses under heaven. . . . If it had been possible for pope, priest or minister to destroy the church of Jesus Christ, it would have been destroyed long ago." Luther, watching the proceedings of the Diet of Augsburg, made a noteworthy discovery. He saw the stars bestud the canopy of the sky, and though there were no pillars to hold them up they kept their place and the sky fell not. The business of holding up the sky and its stars has been on the minds of men in all ages. But we do not need to provide props to hold up the sky. God will look after his church and after Christian doctrine. For of Christ it has been written in 1 Cor. 15 : 25 — "For he must reign, till he hath put all his enemies under his feet."

" Thrice blessed is he to whom is given The instinct that can tell That God is in the field when he Is most invisible." Since Christ is King, it is a duty never to despair of church or of the world. Dr. E. G. Robinson declared that Christian character was never more complete than now, nor more nearly approaching the ideal man. We may add that modern education, modern commerce, modern invention, modern civilization, are to be regarded as the revelations of Christ, the Light of the world, and the Ruler of the nations. All progress of knowledge, government, society, is progress of his truth, and a prophecy of the complete establishment of his kingdom.

(c) With respect to his church triumphant, it is a kingdom of glory · he rewards his redeemed people with the full revelation of himself, upon the completion of his kingdom in the resurrection and the judgment.

John 17 : 24 — "Father, that which thou hast given me, I desire that where I am, they also may be with me, that they may behold my glory " ; 1 Pet. 3 : 21, 22 — "Jesus Christ ; who is on the right hand of God, having gone into heaven ; angels and authorities and powers being made subject unto him " ; 2 Pet. 1 : 11 — "thus shall be richly supplied unto you the entrance into the eternal kingdom of our Lord and Savior Jesus Christ." See Andrew Murray, With Christ in the School of Prayer, preface, vi — " Rev. 1 : 6 — 'made us to be a kingdom, to be priests unto his God and Father.' Both in the king and the priest, the chief thing is power, influence, blessing. In the king, it is the power coming downward ; in the priest, it is the power rising upward, prevailing with God. As in Christ, so in us, the kingly power is founded on the priestly : Heb. 7 : 25 — 'able to save to the uttermost, ... seeing he ever liveth to make intercession '."

Watts, New Apologetic, preface, ix — " We cannot have Christ as King without having him also as Priest. It is as the Lamb that he sits upon the throne in the Apocalypse ; as the Lamb that he conducts his conflict with the kings of the earth ; and it is from the throne of God on which the Lamb appears that the water of life flows forth that carries refreshing throughout the Paradise of God."

Luther : " Now Christ reigns, not in visible, public manner, but through the word, just as we see the sun through a cloud. We see the light, but not the sun itself. But when the clouds are gone, then we see at the same time both light and sun." We may close our consideration of Christ's Kingship with two practical remarks : 1. We never can think too much of the cross, but we may think too little of the throne. 2. We can not have Christ as our Prophet or our Priest, unless we take him also as our King. On Christ's Kingship, see Philippi, Glaubenslehre, iv, 2 : 342–351 ; Van Oosterzee, Dogmatics, 586 *sq.* ; Garbett, Christ as Prophet, Priest, and King, 2 : 243–438 ; J. M. Mason, Sermon on Messiah's Throne, in Works, 3 : 241–275.

SYSTEMATIC THEOLOGY.
VOLUME III.

CHAPTER II.

THE RECONCILIATION OF MAN TO GOD, OR THE APPLICATION OF REDEMPTION THROUGH THE WORK OF THE HOLY SPIRIT.

SECTION I.—THE APPLICATION OF CHRIST'S REDEMPTION IN ITS PREPARATION.

(*a*) In this Section we treat of Election and Calling ; Section Second being devoted to the Application of Christ's Redemption in its Actual Beginning,—namely, in Union with Christ, Regeneration, Conversion, and Justification ; while Section Third has for its subject the Application of Christ's Redemption in its Continuation,—namely, in Sanctification and Perseverance.

The arrangement of topics, in the treatment of the reconciliation of man to God, is taken from Julius Müller, Proof-texts, 35. "Revelation *to* us aims to bring about revelation *in* us. In any being absolutely perfect, God's intercourse with us by *faculty*, and by direct *teaching*, would absolutely coalesce, and the former be just as much God's voice as the latter " (Hutton, Essays).

(*b*) In treating Election and Calling as applications of Christ's redemption, we imply that they are, in God's decree, logically subsequent to that redemption. In this we hold the Sublapsarian view, as distinguished from the Supralapsarianism of Beza and other hyper-Calvinists, which regarded the decree of individual salvation as preceding, in the order of thought, the decree to permit the Fall. In this latter scheme, the order of decrees is as follows : 1. the decree to save certain, and to reprobate others ; 2. the decree to create both those who are to be saved and those who are to be reprobated ; 3. the decree to permit both the former and the latter to fall ; 4. the decree to provide salvation only for the former, that is, for the elect.

Richards, Theology, 302–307, shows that Calvin, while in his early work, the Institutes, he avoided definite statements of his position with regard to the extent of the atonement, yet in his latter works, the Commentaries, acceded to the theory of universal atonement. Supralapsarianism is therefore hyper-Calvinistic, rather than Calvinistic. Sublapsarianism was adopted by the Synod of Dort (1618, 1619). By Supralapsarian is meant that form of doctrine which holds the decree of individual salvation as preceding the decree to permit the Fall; Sublapsarian designates that form of doctrine which holds that the decree of individual salvation is subsequent to the decree to permit the Fall.

The progress in Calvin's thought may be seen by comparing some of his earlier with his later utterances. Institutes, 2:23:5—"I say, with Augustine, that the Lord created those who, as he certainly foreknew, were to go to destruction, and he did so because he so willed." But even then in the Institutes, 3:23:8, he affirms that "the perdition of the wicked depends upon the divine predestination in such a manner that the cause and matter of it are found in themselves. Man falls by the appointment of divine providence, but he falls by his own fault." God's blinding, hardening, turning the sinner he describes as the consequence of the divine *desertion*, not the divine *causation*. The relation of God to the origin of sin is not efficient, but permissive. In later days Calvin wrote in his Commentary on 1 John 2 : 2—"he is the propitiation for our sins; and not for ours only, but also for the whole world"—as follows: "Christ suffered for the sins of the whole world, and in the goodness of God is offered unto all men without distinction, his blood being shed not for a part of the world only, but for the whole human race; for although in the world nothing is found worthy of the favor of God, yet he holds out the propitiation to the whole world, since without exception he summons all to the faith of Christ, which is nothing else than the door unto hope."

Although other passages, such as Institutes, 3 : 21 : 5, and 3 : 23 : 1, assert the harsher view, we must give Calvin credit for modifying his doctrine with maturer reflection and advancing years. Much that is called Calvinism would have been repudiated by Calvin himself even at the beginning of his career, and is really the exaggeration of his teaching by more scholastic and less religious successors. Renan calls Calvin "the most Christian man of his generation." Dorner describes him as "equally great in intellect and character, lovely in social life, full of tender sympathy and faithfulness to his friends, yielding and forgiving toward personal offences." The device upon his seal is a flaming heart from which is stretched forth a helping hand.

Calvin's share in the burning of Servetus must be explained by his mistaken zeal for God's truth and by the universal belief of his time that this truth was to be defended by the civil power. The following is the inscription on the expiatory monument which European Calvinists raised to Servetus: "On October 27, 1553, died at the stake at Champel, Michael Servetus, of Villeneuve d'Aragon, born September 29, 1511. Reverent and grateful sons of Calvin, our great Reformer, but condemning an error which was that of his age, and steadfastly adhering to liberty of conscience according to the true principles of the Reformation and of the gospel, we have erected this expiatory monument, on the 27th of October, 1903."

John DeWitt, in Princeton Theol. Rev., Jan. 1904 : 95 — "Take John Calvin. That fruitful conception — more fruitful in church and state than any other conception which has held the English speaking world — of the absolute and universal sovereignty of the holy God, as a revolt from the conception then prevailing of the sovereignty of the human head of an earthly church, was historically the mediator and instaurator of his spiritual career." On Calvin's theological position, see Shedd, Dogm. Theol., 1 : 409, note.

(c) But the Scriptures teach that men as sinners, and not men irrespective of their sins, are the objects of God's saving grace in Christ (John 15 : 9 ; Rom. 11 : 5, 7 ; Eph. 1 : 4-6 ; 1 Pet. 1 : 2). Condemnation, moreover, is an act, not of sovereignty, but of justice, and is grounded in the guilt of the condemned (Rom. 2 : 6-11 ; 2 Thess. 1 : 5-10). The true order of the decrees is therefore as follows : 1. the decree to create ; 2. the decree to permit the Fall ; 3. the decree to provide a salvation in Christ sufficient for the needs of all ; 4. the decree to secure the actual acceptance of this salvation on the part of some,—or, in other words, the decree of Election.

That saving grace presupposes the Fall, and that men as sinners are the objects of it, appears from John 15 : 19 —"If ye were of the world, the world would love its own: but because ye are not of the world, but I chose you out of the world, therefore the world hateth you"; Rom. 11 : 5-7—"Even so then at this present time also there is a remnant according to the election of grace. But if it is by grace, it is no more of works: otherwise grace is no more grace. What then? That which Israel seeketh for, that he obtained not; but the election obtained it, and the rest were hardened." Eph. 1 : 4-6 —"even as he chose us in him before the foundation of the world, that we should be holy and without blemish before him in love: having foreordained us unto adoption as sons through Jesus Christ unto himself, according to the good pleasure of his will, to the praise of the glory of his grace, which he freely bestowed on us in the Beloved"; 1 Pet. 1 : 2 — elect, "according to the foreknowledge of God the Father, in sanctification of the Spirit unto obedience and sprinkling of the blood of Jesus: Grace to you and peace be multiplied."

That condemnation is not an act of sovereignty, but of justice, appears from Rom. 2: 6-9 —"who will render to every man according to his works . . . . wrath and indignation . . . . upon every soul of man that worketh evil": 2 Thess. 1: 6-9—"a righteous thing with God to recompense affliction to them that afflict you . . . . rendering vengeance to them that know not God and to them that obey not the gospel of our Lord Jesus: who shall suffer punishment." Particular persons are elected, not to have Christ die for them, but to have special influences of the Spirit bestowed upon them.

(*d*) Those Sublapsarians who hold to the Anselmic view of a limited Atonement, make the decrees 3. and 4., just mentioned, exchange places,— the decree of election thus preceding the decree to provide redemption. The Scriptural reasons for preferring the order here given have been already indicated in our treatment of the extent of the Atonement (pages 771-773).

When '3' and '4' thus change places, '3' should be made to read: "The decree to provide in Christ a salvation sufficient for the elect"; and '4' should read: "The decree that a certain number should be saved,— or, in other words, the decree of Election." Sublapsarianism of the first sort may be found in Turretin, loc. 4, quæs. 9; Cunningham, Hist. Theol., 416-439. A. J. F. Behrends: "The divine decree is our last word in theology, not our first word. It represents the *terminus ad quem*, not the *terminus a quo*. Whatever comes about in the exercise of human freedom and of divine grace—that God has decreed." Yet we must grant that Calvinism needs to be supplemented by a more express statement of God's love for the world. Herrick Johnson: "Across the Westminster Confession could justly be written: 'The Gospel for the elect only.' That Confession was written under the absolute dominion of one idea, the doctrine of predestination. It does not contain one of three truths: God's love for a lost world; Christ's compassion for a lost world, and the gospel universal for a lost world."

I. ELECTION.

Election is that eternal act of God, by which in his sovereign pleasure, and on account of no foreseen merit in them, he chooses certain out of the number of sinful men to be the recipients of the special grace of his Spirit, and so to be made voluntary partakers of Christ's salvation.

1. *Proof of the Doctrine of Election.*
A. From Scripture.

We here adopt the words of Dr. Hovey: "The Scriptures forbid us to find the reasons for election in the moral action of man before the new birth, and refer us merely to the sovereign will and mercy of God; that is, they teach the doctrine of personal election." Before advancing to the proof of the doctrine itself, we may claim Scriptural warrant for three preliminary statements (which we also quote from Dr. Hovey), namely:

First, that "God has a sovereign right to bestow more grace upon one subject than upon another,— grace being unmerited favor to sinners."

Mat. 20 : 12-15 —"These last have spent but one hour, and thou hast made them equal unto us . . . . Friend, I do thee no wrong . . . . Is it not lawful for me to do what I will with mine own?" Rom. 9 : 20, 21 — "Shall the thing formed say to him that formed it, Why didst thou make me thus? Or hath not the potter a right over the clay, from the same lump to make one part a vessel unto honor, and another unto dishonor?"

Secondly, that "God has been pleased to exercise this right in dealing with men."

Ps. 147 : 20 —"He hath not dealt so with any nation; And as for his ordinances, they have not known them". Rom. 3 : 1, 2 — "What advantage then hath the Jew? or what is the profit of circumcision? Much every way: first of all, that they were intrusted with the oracles of God"; John 15 : 16 —"Ye did not choose me, but I chose you, and appointed you, that ye should go and bear fruit"; Acts 9 : 15 —"he is a chosen vessel unto me, to bear my name before the Gentiles and kings, and the children of Israel."

Thirdly, that "God has some other reason than that of saving as many as possible for the way in which he distributes his grace."

Mat. 11 : 21 — Tyre and Sidon "would have repented," if they had had the grace bestowed upon Chorazin and Bethsaida ; Rom. 9 : 22–25 — " What if God, willing to show his wrath, and to make his power known, endured with much longsuffering vessels of wrath fitted unto destruction: and that he might make known the riches of his glory upon vessels of mercy, which he afore prepared unto glory ? "

The Scripture passages which directly or indirectly support the doctrine of a particular election of individual men to salvation may be arranged as follows :

(a) Direct statements of God's purpose to save certain individuals :

Jesus speaks of God's elect, as for example in Mark 13 : 27 —" then shall he send forth the angels, and shall gather together his elect "; Luke 18 : 7 — " shall not God avenge his elect, that cry to him day and night ? " Acts 13 : 48 —" as many as were ordained (τεταγμένοι) to eternal life believed "—here Whedon translates: " disposed unto eternal life," referring to κατηρτισμένα in verse 23, where " fitted "=" fitted themselves." The only instance, however, where τάσσω is used in a middle sense is in 1 Cor. 16:15—"set themselves"; but there the object, ἑαυτούς, is expressed. Here we must compare Rom. 13 : 1 —" the powers that be are ordained (τεταγμέναι) of God "; see also Acts 10 : 42 —" this is he who is ordained (ὡρισμένος) of God to be the Judge of the living and the dead."

Rom. 9 : 11–16 — " for the children being not yet born, neither having done anything good or bad, that the purpose of God according to election might stand, not of works, but of him that calleth . . . . I will have mercy upon whom I have mercy . . . . So then it is not of him that willeth, nor of him that runneth, but of God that hath mercy "; Eph. 1 : 4, 5, 9, 11 — " chose us in him before the foundation of the world, [not *because* we were, or were to be, holy, but] that we should be holy and without blemish before him in love: having foreordained us unto adoption as sons through Jesus Christ unto himself, according to the good pleasure of his will . . . . the mystery of his will, according to his good pleasure . . . . in whom also we were made a heritage, having been foreordained according to the purpose of him who worketh all things after the counsel of his will "; Col. 3 : 12 — "God's elect "; 2 Thess. 2 : 13 — " God chose you from the beginning unto salvation in sanctification of the Spirit and belief of the truth."

(b) In connection with the declaration of God's foreknowledge of these persons, or choice to make them objects of his special attention and care;

Rom. 8 : 27–30 — " called according to his purpose. For whom he foreknew, he also foreordained to be conformed to the image of his Son "; 1 Pet. 1 : 1, 2 — " elect . . . . according to the foreknowledge of God the Father, in sanctification of the Spirit, unto obedience and sprinkling of the blood of Jesus Christ." On the passage in Romans, Shedd, in his Commentary, remarks that "foreknew," in the Hebraistic use, " is more than simple prescience, and something more also than simply 'to fix the eye upon,' or to 'select.' It is this latter, but with the additional notion of a benignant and kindly feeling toward the object." In Rom. 8:27–30, Paul is emphasizing the divine sovereignty. The Christian life is considered from the side of the divine care and ordering, and not from the side of human choice and volition. Alexander, Theories of the Will, 87, 88 — " If Paul is here advocating indeterminism, it is strange that in chapter 9 he should be at pains to answer objections to determinism. The apostle's protest in chapter 9 is not against predestination and determination, but against the man who regards such a theory as impugning the righteousness of God."

That the word "know," in Scripture, frequently means not merely to " apprehend intellectually," but to " regard with favor," to " make an object of care," is evident from Gen. 18 : 19 — " I have known him, to the end that he may command his children and his household after him, that they may keep the way of Jehovah, to do righteousness and justice "; Ex. 2 : 25 — " And God saw the children of Israel, and God took knowledge of them "; *cf*. verse 24 — " God heard their groaning, and God remembered his covenant with Abraham, with Isaac, and with Jacob "; Ps. 1 : 6 — " For Jehovah knoweth the way of the righteous; But the way of the wicked shall perish "; 101 : 4, marg. — " I will know no evil person "; Hosea 13 : 5 — " I did know thee in the wilderness, in the land of great drought. According to their pasture, so were they filled "; Nahum 1 : 7 — "he knoweth them that take refuge in him "; Amos 3 : 2 — " You only have I known of all the families of the earth "; Mat. 7 : 23 — "then will I profess unto them, I never knew you "; Rom. 7 : 15 — " For that which I do I know not "; 1 Cor. 8 : 3 — "if any man loveth God, the same is known by him; Gal. 9 —"now that ye have come to know God, or rather, to be known by God "; 1 Thess. 5 : 12, 13 — "we beseech you, brethren, to know them that labor among you, and are over you in the Lord, and admonish you; and to esteem them exceeding highly in love for their work's sake." So the word foreknow " : Rom. 11 : 2 — " God did not cast off his people whom he foreknew "; 1 Pet. 1 : 20 — Christ, "who was foreknown indeed before the foundation of the world."

Broadus on Mat. 7 : 23 — " I never knew you " — says ; " Not in all the passages quoted above, nor elsewhere, is there occasion for the oft-repeated arbitrary notion, derived from the Fathers, that 'know' conveys the additional idea of approve or regard. It denotes acquaintance, with all its pleasures and advantages; 'knew,' *i. e.*, as mine, as my people."

But this last admission seems to grant what Broadus had before denied. See Thayer, Lex. N. T., on γινώσκω: "With acc. of person, to recognize as worthy of intimacy and love; so those whom God has judged worthy of the blessings of the gospel are said ὑπὸ τοῦ θεοῦ γινώσκεσθαι (1 Cor. 8:3; Gal. 4:9); negatively in the sentence of Christ: οὐδέποτε ἔγνων ὑμᾶς, "I never knew you," never had any acquaintance with you." On προγινώσκω, Rom. 8:29 — οὓς προέγνω, "whom he foreknew," see Denney, in Expositor's Greek Testament, in loco: "Those whom he foreknew — in what sense? as persons who would answer his love with love? This is at least irrelevant, and alien to Paul's general method of thought. That salvation begins with God, and begins in eternity, are fundamental ideas with him, which he here applies to Christians, without raising any of the problems involved in the relation of the human will to the divine. Yet we may be sure that προέγνω has the pregnant sense that γινώσκω often has in Scripture, e. g., in Ps. 1:6; Amos 3:2; hence we may render: 'those of whom God took knowledge from eternity (Eph. 1:4)."

In Rom. 8:28-30, quoted above, "foreknew" = elected — that is, made certain individuals, in the future, the objects of his love and care; "foreordained" describes God's designation of these same individuals to receive the special gift of salvation. In other words, "foreknowledge" is of persons: "foreordination" is of blessings to be bestowed upon them. Hooker, Eccl. Pol., appendix to book v, (vol. 2:751) — "'whom he did foreknow' (know before as his own, with determination to be forever merciful to them) 'he also predestinated to be conformed to the image of his Son' — predestinated, not to opportunity of conformation, but to conformation itself." So, for substance, Calvin, Rückert, DeWette, Stuart, Jowett, Vaughan. On 1 Pet. 1:1, 2, see Com. of Plumptre. The Arminian interpretation of "whom he foreknew" (Rom. 8:29) would require the phrase "as conformed to the image of his Son" to be conjoined with it. Paul, however, makes conformity to Christ to be the result, not the foreseen condition, of God's foreordination; see Commentaries of Hodge and Lange.

(c) With assertions that this choice is matter of grace, or unmerited favor, bestowed in eternity past :

Eph. 1:5-8 — "foreordained . . . . according to the good pleasure of his will, to the praise of the glory of his grace, which he freely bestowed on us in the Beloved . . . . according to the riches of his grace"; 2:8 — "by grace have ye been saved through faith; and that not of yourselves, it is the gift of God" — here "and that" (neuter τοῦτο, verse 8) refers, not to "faith" but to "salvation." But faith is elsewhere represented as having its source in God, — see page 782, (k). 2 Tim. 1:9 — "his own purpose and grace, which was given us in Christ Jesus before times eternal." Election is not because of our merit. McLaren: "God's own mercy, spontaneous, undeserved, condescending, moved him. God is his own motive. His love is not drawn out by our loveableness, but wells up, like an artesian spring, from the depths of his nature."

(d) That the Father has given certain persons to the Son, to be his peculiar possession :

John 6:37 — "All that which the Father giveth me shall come unto me"; 17:2 — "that whatsoever thou hast given him, to them he should give eternal life"; 6 — "I manifested thy name unto the men whom thou gavest me out of the world: thine they were, and thou gavest them to me"; 9 — "I pray not for the world, but for those whom thou hast given me"; Eph. 1:14 — "unto the redemption of God's own possession"; 1 Pet. 2:9 — "a people for God's own possession."

(e) That the fact of believers being united thus to Christ is due wholly to God :

John 6:44 — "No man can come to me, except the Father that sent me draw him"; 10:26 — "ye believe not, because ye are not of my sheep"; 1 Cor. 1:30 — "of him [God] are ye in Christ Jesus" == your being, as Christians, in union with Christ, is due wholly to God.

(f) That those who are written in the Lamb's book of life, and they only, shall be saved :

Phil. 4:3 — "the rest of my fellow-workers, whose names are in the book of life"; Rev. 20:15 — "And if any was not found written in the book of life, he was cast into the lake of fire"; 21:27 — "there shall in no wise enter into it anything unclean . . . but only they that are written in the Lamb's book of life" == God's decrees of electing grace in Christ.

(*g*)   That these are allotted, as disciples, to certain of God's servants :

Acts 17 : 4 — (literally) — " some of them were persuaded, and were allotted [by God] to Paul and Silas "— as disciples (so Meyer and Grimm) ; 18 : 9, 10 — " Be not afraid, but speak and hold not thy peace : for I am with thee, and no man shall set on thee to harm thee : for I have much people in this city."

(*h*)   Are made the recipients of a special call of God :

Rom. 8 : 28, 30 —" called according to his purpose . . . . . whom he foreordained, them he also called " ; 9 : 23, 24 — " vessels of mercy, which he afore prepared unto glory, even us, whom he also called, not from the Jews only, but also from the Gentiles " ; 11 : 29 — " for the gifts and the calling of God are not repented of " ; 1 Cor. 1 : 24-29 — " unto them that are called . . . . Christ the power of God, and the wisdom of God . . . . For behold your calling, brethren, ... the things that are despised, did God choose, yea and the things that are not, that he might bring to naught the things that are : that no flesh should glory before God " ; Gal. 1 : 15, 16 — " when it was the good pleasure of God, who separated me, even from my mother's womb, and called me through his grace, to reveal his Son in me " ; *cf.* James 2 : 23 — " and he [Abraham] was called [to be] the friend of God."

(*i*)   Are born into God's kingdom, not by virtue of man's will, but of God's will :

John 1 : 13 — " born, not of blood, nor of the will of the flesh, nor of the will of man, but of God " ; James 1 : 18 — " Of his own will he brought us forth by the word of truth " ; 1 John 4 : 10 — " Herein is love, not that we loved God, but that he loved us." S. S. Times, Oct. 14, 1899 — " The law of love is the expression of God's loving nature, and it is only by our participation of the divine nature that we are enabled to render it obedience. ' Loving God,' says Bushnell, ' is but letting God love us.' So John's great saying may be rendered in the present tense : ' not that we love God, but that he loves us.' Or, as Madame Guyon sings : ' I love my God, but with no love of mine, For I have none to give ; I love thee, Lord, but all the love is thine, For by thy life I live '."

(*j*)   Receiving repentance, as the gift of God :

Acts 5 : 31 — " Him did God exalt with his right hand to be a Prince and a Savior, to give repentance to Israel, and remission of sins " ; 11 : 18 — " Then to the Gentiles also hath God granted repentance unto life " ; 2 Tim. 2 : 25 — " correcting them that oppose themselves ; if peradventure God may give them repentance unto the knowledge of the truth." Of course it is true that God might give repentance simply by inducing man to repent by the agency of his word, his providence and his Spirit. But more than this seems to be meant when the Psalmist prays : " Create in me a clean heart, O God ; And renew a right spirit within me " (Ps. 51 : 10).

(*k*)   Faith, as the gift of God :

John 6 : 65 — " no man can come unto me, except it be given unto him of the Father " ; Acts 15 : 8, 9 — " God . . . . giving them the Holy Spirit . . . cleansing their hearts by faith " ; Rom. 12 : 3 — " according as God hath dealt to each man a measure of faith " ; 1 Cor. 12 : 9 — " to another faith, in the same Spirit " ; Gal. 5 : 22 —" the fruit of the Spirit s . . . faith " (A. V.) ; Phil. 2 : 13 — In all faith, " it is God who worketh in you both to will and to work, for his good pleasure " ; Eph. 6 : 23 — " Peace be to the brethren, and love with faith, from God the Father and the Lord Jesus Christ " ; John 3 : 8 — " The Spirit breatheth where he wills, and thou [as a consequence] hearest his voice " (so Bengel) ; see A. J. Gordon, Ministry of the Spirit, 166 ; 1 Cor. 12 : 3 —" No man can say, Jesus is Lord, but in the Holy Spirit " — but calling Jesus " Lord " is an essential part of faith,—faith therefore is the work of the Holy Spirit ; Tit. 1 : 1 — " the faith of God's elect "= election is not in consequence of faith, but faith is in consequence of election (Ellicott). If they get their faith of themselves, then salvation is not due to grace. If God gave the faith, then it was in his purpose, and this is election.

(*l*)   Holiness and good works, as the gift of God.

Eph. 1 : 4 — " chose us in him before the foundation of the world, that we should be holy " ; 2 : 9, 10 —" not of works, that no man should glory. For we are his workmanship, created in Christ Jesus for good works, which God afore prepared that we should walk in them " ; 1 Pet. 1 : 2 — elect " unto obedience." On Scripture testimony, see Hovey, Manual of Theol. and Ethics, 258-261 ; also art. on Predestination, by Warfield, in Hastings' Dictionary of the Bible.

These passages furnish an abundant and conclusive refutation, on the one hand, of the Lutheran view that election is simply God's determination from eternity to provide an objective salvation for universal humanity ;

and, on the other hand, of the Arminian view that election is God's determination from eternity to save certain individuals upon the ground of their foreseen faith.

Roughly stated, we may say that Schleiermacher elects all men subjectively; Lutherans all men objectively; Arminians all believers; Augustinians all foreknown as God's own. Schleiermacher held that decree logically precedes foreknowledge, and that election is individual, not national. But he made election to include all men, the only difference between them being that of earlier or of later conversion. Thus in his system Calvinism and Restorationism go hand in hand. Murray, in Hastings' Bible Dictionary, seems to take this view.

Lutheranism is the assertion that original grace preceded original sin, and that the *Quia Voluit* of Tertullian and of Calvin was based on wisdom, in Christ. The Lutheran holds that the believer is simply the non-resistant subject of common grace; while the Arminian holds that the believer is the coöperant subject of common grace. Lutheranism enters more fully than Calvinism into the nature of faith. It thinks more of the human agency, while Calvinism thinks more of the divine purpose. It thinks more of the church, while Calvinism thinks more of Scripture. The Arminian conception is that God has appointed men to salvation, just as he has appointed them to condemnation, in view of their dispositions and acts. As Justification is in view of *present* faith, so the Arminian regards Election as taking place in view of *future* faith. Arminianism must reject the doctrine of regeneration as well as that of election, and must in both cases make the act of man precede the act of God.

All varieties of view may be found upon this subject among theologians. John Milton, in his Christian Doctrine, holds that "there is no particular predestination or election, but only general. . . . There can be no reprobation of individuals from all eternity." Archbishop Sumner: "Election is predestination of communities and nations to external knowledge and to the privileges of the gospel." Archbishop Whately "Election is the choice of individual men to membership in the external church and the means of grace." Gore, in Lux Mundi, 320 — "The elect represent not the special purpose of God for a few, but the universal purpose which under the circumstances can only be realized through a few." R. V. Foster, a Cumberland Presbyterian, opposed to absolute predestination, says in his Systematic Theology that the divine decree "is unconditional in its origin and conditional in its application."

B. From Reason.

(*a*) What God does, he has eternally purposed to do. Since he bestows special regenerating grace on some, he must have eternally purposed to bestow it, — in other words, must have chosen them to eternal life. Thus the doctrine of election is only a special application of the doctrine of decrees.

The New Haven views are essentially Arminian. See Fitch, on Predestination and Election, in Christian Spectator, 3 : 622 — "God's foreknowledge of what would be the results of his present works of grace *preceded* in the order of nature the purpose to pursue those works, and presented the *grounds* of that purpose. Whom he foreknew — as the people who would be guided to his kingdom by his present works of grace, in which result lay the whole objective motive for undertaking those works — he did also, by resolving on those works, predestinate." Here God is very erroneously said to *foreknow* what is as yet included in a merely *possible* plan. As we have seen in our discussion of Decrees, there can be no foreknowledge, unless there is something fixed, in the future, to be foreknown; and this fixity can be due only to God's predetermination. So, in the present case, election must precede prescience.

The New Haven views are also given in N. W. Taylor, Revealed Theology, 373-444; for criticism upon them, see Tyler, Letters on New Haven Theology, 172-180. If God desired the salvation of Judas as much as of Peter, how was Peter elected in distinction from Judas? To the question, "Who made thee to differ?" the answer must be, "Not God, but my own will." See Finney, in Bib. Sac., 1877 : 711 — "God must have foreknown whom he *could* wisely save, prior in the order of nature to his determining to save them. But his knowing who *would* be saved, must have been, in the order of nature, subsequent to his election or determination to save them, and dependent upon that determination." Foster, Christian Life and Theology, 70 — "The doctrine of election is the consistent formulation, *sub specie eternitatis*, of prevenient grace..... 86 — With the doctrine of prevenient grace, the evangelical doctrine stands or falls."

(*b*) This purpose cannot be conditioned upon any merit or faith of those who are chosen, since there is no such merit, — faith itself being God's gift and foreordained by him. Since man's faith is foreseen only as the result of God's work of grace, election proceeds rather upon foreseen unbelief. Faith, as the effect of election, cannot at the same time be the cause of election.

There is an analogy between prayer and its answer, on the one hand, and faith and salvation on the other. God has decreed answer in connection with prayer, and salvation in connection with faith. But he does not change his mind when men pray, or when they believe. As he fulfils his purpose by inspiring true prayer, so he fulfils his purpose by giving faith. Augustine: " He chooses us, not because we believe, but that we may believe: lest we should say that we first chose him." (John 15 : 16 — " Ye did not choose me, but I chose you " ; Rom. 9 : 21 — "from the same lump " ; 16 — "not of him that willeth ").

Here see the valuable discussion of Wardlaw, Systematic Theol., 2 : 485-549 — "Election and salvation on the ground of works foreseen are not different in principle from election and salvation on the ground of works performed." *Cf.* Prov. 21 : 1 — "The king's heart is in the hand of Jehovah as the watercourses; He turneth it whithersoever he will " — as easily as the rivulets of the eastern fields are turned by the slightest motion of the hand or the foot of the husbandman ; Ps. 110 : 3 — "Thy people offer themselves willingly In the day of thy power."

(*c*) The depravity of the human will is such that, without this decree to bestow special divine influences upon some, all, without exception, would have rejected Christ's salvation after it was offered to them ; and so all, without exception, must have perished. Election, therefore, may be viewed as a necessary consequence of God's decree to provide an objective redemption, if that redemption is to have any subjective result in human salvation.

Before the prodigal son seeks the father, the father must first seek him, — a truth brought out in the preceding parables of the lost money and the lost sheep (Luke 15). Without election, all are lost. Newman Smyth, Orthodox Theology of To-day, 56 — "The worst doctrine of election, to-day, is taught by our natural science. The scientific doctrine of natural selection is the doctrine of election, robbed of all hope, and without a single touch of human pity in it."

Hodge, Syst. Theol., 2 : 335 — "Suppose the deistic view be true: God created men and left them ; surely no man could complain of the results. But now suppose God, foreseeing these very results of creation, should create. Would it make any difference, if God's purpose, as to the futurition of such a world, should precede it? Augustine supposes that God did purpose such a world as the deist supposes, with two exceptions : (1) he interposes to restrain evil ; (2) he intervenes, by providence, by Christ, and by the Holy Spirit, to save some from destruction." Election is simply God's determination that the sufferings of Christ shall not be in vain ; that all men shall not be lost ; that some shall be led to accept Christ ; that to this end special influences of his Spirit shall be given.

At first sight it might appear that God's appointing men to salvation was simply permissive, as was his appointment to condemnation (1 Pet. 2 : 8), and that this appointment was merely indirect by creating them with foresight of their faith or their disobedience. But the decree of salvation is not simply permissive, — it is efficient also. It is a decree to use special means for the salvation of some. A. A. Hodge, Popular Lectures, 143 — "The dead man cannot spontaneously originate his own quickening, nor the creature his own creating, nor the infant his own begetting. Whatever man may do after regeneration, the first quickening of the dead must originate with God."

Hovey, Manual of Theology, 287 — "Calvinism, reduced to its lowest terms, is election of believers, not on account of any foreseen conduct of theirs, either before or in the act of conversion, which would be spiritually better than that of others influenced by the same grace, but on account of their foreseen greater usefulness in manifesting the glory of God to moral beings and of their foreseen non-commission of the sin against the Holy Spirit." But even here we must attribute the greater usefulness and the abstention from fatal sin, not to man's unaided powers but to the divine decree: see Eph. 2:10 — "For we are his workmanship, created in Christ Jesus for good works, which God afore prepared that we should walk in them."

(d) The doctrine of election becomes more acceptable to reason when we remember : first, that God's decree is eternal, and in a certain sense is contemporaneous with man's belief in Christ ; secondly, that God's decree to create involves the decree of all that in the exercise of man's freedom will follow ; thirdly, that God's decree is the decree of him who is all in all, so that our willing and doing is at the same time the working of him who decrees our willing and doing. The whole question turns upon the initiative in human salvation : if this belongs to God, then in spite of difficulties we must accept the doctrine of election.

The timeless existence of God may be the source of many of our difficulties with regard to election, and with a proper view of God's eternity these difficulties might be removed. Mason, Faith of the Gospel, 349-351 — "Eternity is commonly thought of as if it were a state or series anterior to time and to be resumed again when time comes to an end. This, however, only reduces eternity to time again, and puts the life of God in the same line with our own, only coming from further back. . . . . At present we do not see how time and eternity meet."

Royce, World and Individual, 2:374 — "God does not temporally foreknow anything, except so far as he is expressed in us finite beings. The knowledge that exists in time is the knowledge that finite beings possess, in so far as they are finite. And no such foreknowledge can predict the special features of individual deeds precisely so far as they are unique. Foreknowledge in time is possible only of the general, and of the causally predetermined, and not of the unique and free. Hence neither God nor man can foreknow perfectly, at any temporal moment, what a free will agent is yet to do. On the other hand, the Absolute possesses a perfect knowledge at one glance of the whole of the temporal order, past, present and future. This knowledge is ill called foreknowledge. It is eternal knowledge. And as there is an eternal knowledge of all individuality and of all freedom, free acts are known as occurring, like the chords in the musical succession, precisely when and how they actually occur." While we see much truth in the preceding statement, we find in it no bar to our faith that God can translate his eternal knowledge into finite knowledge and can thus put it for special purposes in possession of his creatures.

E. H. Johnson, Theology, 2d ed., 250 — "Foreknowing what his creatures would do, God decreed their destiny when he decreed their creation ; and this would still be the case, although every man had the partial control over his destiny that Arminians aver, or even the complete control that Pelagians claim. The decree is as absolute as if there were no freedom, but it leaves them as free as if there were no decree." A. H. Strong, Christ in Creation, 40, 42 — "As the Logos or divine Reason, Christ dwells in humanity everywhere and constitutes the principle of its being. Humanity shares with Christ in the image of God. That image is never wholly lost. It is completely restored in sinners when the Spirit of Christ secures control of their wills and leads them to merge their life in his. . . . If Christ be the principle and life of all things, then divine sovereignty and human freedom, if they are not absolutely reconciled, at least lose their ancient antagonism, and we can rationally 'work out our own salvation,' for the very reason that 'it is God that worketh in us, both to will and to work, for his good pleasure' (Phil. 2:12, 13)."

2. *Objections to the Doctrine of Election.*

(a) It is unjust to those who are not included in this purpose of salvation.—Answer : Election deals, not simply with creatures, but with sinful, guilty, and condemned creatures. That any should be saved, is matter of pure grace, and those who are not included in this purpose of salvation suffer only the due reward of their deeds. There is, therefore, no injustice in God's election. We may better praise God that he saves any, than charge him with injustice because he saves so few.

50

God can say to all men, saved or unsaved, "Friend, I do thee no wrong . . . . Is it not lawful for me to do what I will with mine own?" (Mat. 20 : 13, 15). The question is not whether a father will treat his children alike, but whether a sovereign must treat condemned rebels alike. It is not true that, because the Governor pardons one convict from the penitentiary, he must therefore pardon all. When he pardons one, no injury is done to those who are left. But, in God's government, there is still less reason for objection; for God offers pardon to all. Nothing prevents men from being pardoned but their unwillingness to accept his pardon. Election is simply God's determination to make certain persons willing to accept it. Because justice cannot save all, shall it therefore save none?

Augustine, De Predest. Sanct., 8 —" Why does not God teach all? Because it is in mercy that he teaches all whom he does teach, while it is in judgment that he does not teach those whom he does not teach." In his Manual of Theology and Ethics, 260, Hovey remarks that Rom. 9 : 20 —"who art thou that repliest against God?"— teaches, not that might makes right, but that God is morally entitled to glorify either his righteousness or his mercy in disposing of a guilty race. It is not that he chooses to save only a few shipwrecked and drowning creatures, but that he chooses to save only a part of a great company who are bent on committing suicide. Prov. 8 : 36 —"he that sinneth against me wrongeth his own soul: All they that hate me love death." It is best for the universe at large that some should be permitted to have their own way and show how dreadful a thing is opposition to God. See Shedd, Dogm. Theol., 1 : 455.

(b) It represents God as partial in his dealings and a respecter of persons.—Answer : Since there is nothing in men that determines God's choice of one rather than another, the objection is invalid. It would equally apply to God's selection of certain nations, as Israel, and certain individuals, as Cyrus, to be recipients of special temporal gifts. If God is not to be regarded as partial in not providing a salvation for fallen angels, he cannot be regarded as partial in not providing regenerating influences of his Spirit for the whole race of fallen men.

Ps. 44 : 3 —"For they gat not the land in possession by their own sword, Neither did their own arm save them ; But thy right hand, and thine arm, and the light of thy countenance, Because thou wast favorable unto them "; Is. 45 : 1, 4, 5 —"Thus saith Jehovah to his anointed, to Cyrus, whose right hand I have holden, to subdue nations before him . . . . For Iacob my servant's sake, and Israel my chosen, I have called thee by thy name : I have surnamed thee, though thou hast not known me "; Luke 4 : 25-27 —"There were many widows in Israel . . . . and unto none of them was Elijah sent, but only to Zarephath, in the land of Sidon, unto a woman that was a widow. And there were many lepers in Israel . . . . and none of them was cleansed, but only Naaman the Syrian "; 1 Cor. 4 : 7 —"For who maketh thee to differ ? and what hast thou that thou didst not receive ? but if thou didst receive it, why dost thou glory, as if thou hadst not received it ? " 2 Pet. 2 : 4 —"God spared not angels when they sinned, but cast them down to hell "; Heb. 2 : 16 —"For verily not to angels doth he give help, but he giveth help to the seed of Abraham."

Is God partial, in choosing Israel, Cyrus, Naaman ? Is God partial, in bestowing upon some of his servants special ministerial gifts ? Is God partial, in not providing a salvation for fallen angels ? In God's providence, one man is born in a Christian land, the son of a noble family, is endowed with beauty of person, splendid talents, exalted opportunities, immense wealth. Another is born at the Five Points, or among the Hottentots, amid the degradation and depravity of actual, or practical, heathenism. We feel that it is irreverent to complain of God's dealings in providence. What right have sinners to complain of God's dealings in the distribution of his grace ? Hovey : " We have no reason to think that God treats all moral beings alike. We should be glad to hear that other races are treated better than we."

Divine election is only the ethical side and interpretation of natural selection. In the latter God chooses certain forms of the vegetable and animal kingdom without merit of theirs. They are preserved while others die. In the matter of individual health, talent, property, one is taken and the other left. If we call all this the result of system, the reply is that God chose the system, knowing precisely what would come of it. Bruce, Apologetics, 201 —" Election to distinction in philosophy or art is not incomprehensible, for these are not matters of vital concern ; but election to holiness on the part of some, and to unholiness on the part of others, would be inconsistent with God's own holiness." But there is no such election to unholiness except on the part of man himself. God's election secures only the good. See (c) below.

J. J. Murphy, Natural Selection and Spiritual Freedom, 73 —" The world is ordered on a basis of inequality ; in the organic world, as Darwin has shown, it is of inequality —

of favored races—that all progress comes; history shows the same to be true of the human and spiritual world. All human progress is due to elect human individuals, elect not only to be a blessing to themselves, but still more to be a blessing to multitudes of others. Any superiority, whether in the natural or in the mental and spiritual world, becomes a vantage-ground for gaining a greater superiority. . . . It is the method of the divine government, acting in the provinces both of nature and of grace, that all benefit should come to the many through the elect few."

(c) It represents God as arbitrary.—Answer : It represents God, not as arbitrary, but as exercising the free choice of a wise and sovereign will, in ways and for reasons which are inscrutable to us. To deny the possibility of such a choice is to deny God's personality. To deny that God has reasons for his choice is to deny his wisdom. The doctrine of election finds these reasons, not in men, but in God.

When a regiment is decimated for insubordination, the fact that every tenth man is chosen for death is for reasons; but the reasons are not in the men. In one case, the reason for God's choice seems revealed : 1 Tim. 1 : 16 —"howbeit for this cause I obtained mercy, that in me as chief might Jesus Christ show forth all his longsuffering, for an ensample of them that should thereafter believe on him unto eternal life"— here Paul indicates that the reason why God chose him was that he was so great a sinner : verse 15 — "Christ Jesus came into the world to save sinners ; of whom I am chief." Hovey remarks that "the uses to which God can put men, as vessels of grace, may determine his selection of them." But since the naturally weak are saved, as well as the naturally strong, we cannot draw any general conclusion, or discern any general rule, in God's dealings, unless it be this, that in election God seeks to illustrate the greatness and the variety of his grace,—the reasons lying, therefore, not in men, but in God. We must remember that God's sovreignty is the sovereignty of God — the infinitely wise, holy and loving God, in whose hands the destinies of men can be left more safely than in the hands of the wisest, most just, and most kind of his creatures.

We must believe in the grace of sovereignty as well as in the sovereignty of grace. Election and reprobation are not matters of arbitrary will. God saves all whom he can wisely save. He will show benevolence in the salvation of mankind just so far as he can without prejudice to holiness. No man can be saved without God, but it is also true that there is no man whom God is not willing to save. H. B. Smith, System, 511 — "It may be that many of the finally impenitent resist more light than many of the saved." Harris, Moral Evolution, 401 (for substance)—"Sovereignty is not lost in Fatherhood, but is recovered as the divine law of righteous love. Doubtless thou art our Father, though Augustine be ignorant of us, and Calvin acknowledge us not." Hooker, Eccl. Polity, 1 : 2 — "They err who think that of God's will there is no reason except his will." T. Erskine, The Brazen Serpent, 259 — Sovereignty is "just a name for what is unrevealed of God."

We do not know all of God's reasons for saving particular men, but we do know some of the reasons, for he has revealed them to us. These reasons are not men's merits or works. We have mentioned the first of these reasons: (1) Men's greater sin and need ; 1 Tim. 1 : 16 — "that in me as chief might Jesus Christ show forth all his longsuffering." We may add to this : (2) The fact that men have not sinned against the Holy Spirit and made themselves unreceptive to Christ's salvation ; 1 Tim. 1 : 13 — "I obtained mercy, because I did it ignorantly in unbelief"=the fact that Paul had not sinned with full knowledge of what he did was a reason why God could choose him. (3) Men's ability, by the help of Christ to be witnesses and martyrs for their Lord ; Acts 9 : 15, 16 —"he is a chosen vessel unto me, to bear my name before the Gentiles and kings, and the children of Israel : for I will show him how many things he must suffer for my name's sake." As Paul's mission to the Gentiles may have determined God's choice, so Augustine's mission to the sensual and abandoned may have had the same influence. But if Paul's sins, as foreseen, constituted one reason why God chose to save him, why might not his ability to serve the kingdom have constituted another reason ? We add therefore : (4) Men's foreseen ability to serve Christ's kingdom in bringing others to the knowledge of the truth ; John 15 : 16 —"I chose you and appointed you, that ye should go and bear fruit." Notice however that this is choice to service, and not simply choice on account of service. In all these cases the reasons do not lie in the men themselves, for what these men are and what they possess is due to God's providence and grace.

(d) It tends to immorality, by representing men's salvation as independent of their own obedience.—Answer : The objection ignores the fact that the salvation of believers is ordained only in connection with their regeneration and sanctification, as means ; and that the certainty of final triumph is the strongest incentive to strenuous conflict with sin.

Plutarch: "God is the brave man's hope, and not the coward's excuse." The purposes of God are an anchor to the storm-tossed spirit. But a ship needs engine, as well as anchor. God does not elect to save any without repentance and faith. Some hold the doctrine of election, but the doctrine of election does not hold them. Such should ponder 1 Pet. 1 : 2, in which Christians are said to be elect, "in sanctification of the Spirit, unto obedience and sprinkling of the blood of Jesus Christ."

Augustine: "He loved her [the church] foul, that he might make her fair." Dr. John Watson (Ian McLaren): "The greatest reinforcement religion could have in our time would be a return to the ancient belief in the sovereignty of God." This is because there is lack of a strong conviction of sin, guilt, and helplessness, still remaining pride and unwillingness to submit to God, imperfect faith in God's trustworthiness and goodness. We must not exclude Arminians from our fellowship — there are too many good Methodists for that. But we may maintain that they hold but half the truth, and that absence of the doctrine of election from their creed makes preaching less serious and character less secure.

(e) It inspires pride in those who think themselves elect.—Answer : This is possible only in the case of those who pervert the doctrine. On the contrary, its proper influence is to humble men. Those who exalt themselves above others, upon the ground that they are special favorites of God, have reason to question their election.

In the novel, there was great effectiveness in the lover's plea to the object of his affection, that he had loved since he had first set his eyes upon her in her childhood. But God's love for us is of longer standing than that. It dates back to a time before we were born,—aye, even to eternity past. It is a love which was fastened upon us, although God knew the worst of us. It is unchanging, because founded upon his infinite and eternal love to Christ. Jer. 31 : 3 — "Jehovah appeared of old unto me, saying, Yea, I have loved thee with an everlasting love: therefore with lovingkindness have I drawn thee "; Rom. 8 : 31-39 —"If God is for us, who is against us ? . . . . Who shall separate us from the love of Christ ?" And the answer is, that nothing "shall be able to separate us from the love of God, which is in Christ Jesus our Lord." This eternal love subdues and humbles : Ps. 115 : 1 —"Not unto us, O Jehovah, not unto us, But unto thy name give glory For thy lovingkindness, and for thy truth's sake."

Of the effect of the doctrine of election, Calvin, in his Institutes, 3 : 22 : 1, remarks that "when the human mind hears of it, its irritation breaks all restraint, and it discovers as serious and violent agitation as if alarmed by the sound of a martial trumpet." The cause of this agitation is the apprehension of the fact that one is an enemy of God and yet absolutely dependent upon his mercy. This apprehension leads normally to submission. But the conquered rebel can give no thanks to himself,—all thanks are due to God who has chosen and renewed him. The affections elicited are not those of pride and self-complacency, but of gratitude and love.

Christian hymnology witnesses to these effects. Isaac Watts (+ 1748): " Why was I made to hear thy voice And enter while there 's room, When thousands make a wretched choice, And rather starve than come. 'T was the same love that spread the feast That sweetly forced me in ; Else I had still refused to taste, And perished in my sin. Pity the nations, O our God! Constrain the earth to come; Send thy victorious word abroad, And bring the wanderers home." Josiah Conder (+ 1855): " 'T is not that I did choose thee, For, Lord, that could not be; This heart would still refuse thee; But thou hast chosen me;— Hast, from the sin that stained me, Washed me and set me free, And to this end ordained me That I should live to thee. 'T was sovereign mercy called me, And taught my opening mind ; The world had else enthralled me, To heavenly glories blind. My heart owns none above thee : For thy rich grace I thirst ; This knowing,— if I love thee, Thou must have loved me first."

(f) It discourages effort for the salvation of the impenitent, whether on their own part or on the part of others. — Answer : Since it is a secret decree, it cannot hinder or discourage such effort. On the other hand, it is a ground of encouragement, and so a stimulus to effort ; for, without election, it is certain that all would be lost (*cf.* Acts 18 : 10). While it humbles the sinner, so that he is willing to cry for mercy, it encourages him also by showing him that some will be saved, and (since election and faith are inseparably connected) that he will be saved, if he will only believe. While it makes the Christian feel entirely dependent on God's power, in his efforts for the impenitent, it leads him to say with Paul that he "endures all things for the elects' sake, that they also may attain the salvation that is in Christ Jesus with eternal glory " (2 Tim. 2 : 10).

God's decree that Paul's ship's company should be saved (Acts 27 : 24) did not obviate the necessity of their abiding in the ship (verse 31). In marriage, man's election does not exclude woman's ; so God's election does not exclude man's. There is just as much need of effort as if there were no election. Hence the question for the sinner is not, " Am I one of the elect ? " but rather " What shall I do to be saved ? " Milton represents the spirits of hell as debating foreknowledge and free will, in wandering mazes lost.

No man is saved until he ceases to debate, and begins to act. And yet no man will thus begin to act, unless God's Spirit moves him. The Lord encouraged Paul by saying to him : " I have much people in this city " (Acts 18 : 10) — people whom I will bring in through thy word. " Old Adam is too strong for young Melanchthon." If God does not regenerate, there is no hope of success in preaching : " God stands powerless before the majesty of man's lordly will. Sinners have the glory of their own salvation. To pray God to convert a man is absurd. God elects the man, because he foresees that the man will elect himself " (see S. R. Mason, Truth Unfolded, 298–307). The doctrine of election does indeed cut off the hopes of those who place confidence in themselves ; but it is best that such hopes should be destroyed, and that in place of them should be put a hope in the sovereign grace of God. The doctrine of election does teach man's absolute dependence upon God, and the impossibility of any disappointment or disarrangement of the divine plans arising from the disobedience of the sinner, and it humbles human pride until it is willing to take the place of a suppliant for mercy.

Rowland Hill was criticized for preaching election and yet exhorting sinners to repent, and was told that he should preach only to the elect. He replied that, if his critic would put a chalk-mark on all the elect, he would preach only to them. But this is not the whole truth. We are not only ignorant who God's elect are, but we are set to preach to both elect and non-elect (Ez. 2 : 7 — "thou shalt speak my words unto them, whether they will hear, or whether they will forbear "), with the certainty that to the former our preaching will make a higher heaven, to the latter a deeper hell (2 Cor. 2 : 15, 16 — " For we are a sweet savor of Christ unto God, in them that are saved, and in them that perish ; to the one a savor from death unto death ; to the other a savor from life unto life " ; *cf.* Luke 2 : 34 — "this child is set for the falling and the rising of many in Israel " = for the falling of some, and for the rising up of others).

Jesus' own thanksgiving in Mat. 11 : 25, 26 — "I thank thee, O Father, Lord of heaven and earth, that thou didst hide these things from the wise and understanding, and didst reveal them unto babes : yea, Father, for so it was well-pleasing in thy sight" — is immediately followed by his invitation in verse 28 — " Come unto me, all ye that labor and are heavy laden, and I will give you rest." There is no contradiction in his mind between sovereign grace and the free invitations of the gospel.

G. W. Northrup, in The Standard, Sept. 19, 1889 — "1. God will save every one of the human race whom he can save and remain God ; 2. Every member of the race has a full and fair probation, so that all might be saved and would be saved were they to use aright the light which they already have." .... (Private letter) : " Limitations of God in the bestowment of salvation : 1. In the power of God in relation to free will ; 2. In the benevolence of God which requires the greatest good of creation, or the greatest aggregate good of the greatest number ; 3. In the purpose of God to make the most perfect self-limitation ; 4. In the sovereignty of God, as a prerogative absolutely optional in its exercise ; 5. In the holiness of God, which involves immutable limitations on his part in dealing with moral agents. Nothing but some absolute impossibility, metaphysical or moral, could have prevented him ' whose nature and whose name is love ' from decreeing and securing the confirmation of all moral agents in holiness and blessedness forever."

(*g*) The decree of election implies a decree of reprobation. — Answer : The decree of reprobation is not a positive decree. like that of election, but a permissive decree to leave the sinner to his self-chosen rebellion and its natural consequences of punishment.

Election and sovereignty are only sources of good. Election is not a decree to destroy,—it is a decree only to save. When we elect a President, we do not need to hold a second election to determine that the remaining millions shall be non-Presidents. It is needless to apply contrivance or force. Sinners, like water, if simply let alone, will run down hill to ruin. The decree of reprobation is simply a decree to do nothing—a decree to leave the sinner to himself. The natural result of this judicial forsaking, on the part of God, is the hardening and destruction of the sinner. But it must not be forgotten that this hardening and destruction are not due to any positive efficiency of God,—they are a self-hardening and a self-destruction,—and God's judicial forsaking is only the just penalty of the sinner's guilty rejection of offered mercy.

See Hosea 11 : 8 — "How shall I give thee up, Ephraim? . . . . my heart is turned within me, my compassions are kindled together"; 4 : 17 — "Ephraim is joined to idols; let him alone"; Rom. 9 : 22, 23 — "What if God, willing to show his wrath, and to make his power known, endured with much longsuffering vessels of wrath fitted unto destruction : and that he might make known the riches of his glory upon vessels of mercy, which he afore prepared unto glory"— here notice that "which he afore prepared" declares a positive divine efficiency, in the case of the vessels of mercy, while "fitted unto destruction" intimates no such positive agency of God,—the vessels of wrath fitted themselves for destruction ; 2 Tim. 2 : 20 — "vessels . . . . some unto honor, and some unto dishonor"; 1 Pet. 2 : 8 — "they stumble at the word, being disobedient: whereunto also they were appointed"; Jude 4 — "who were of old set forth ['written of beforehand' — Am. Rev.] unto this condemnation"; Mat. 25 : 34, 41 — "the kingdom prepared for you . . . . the eternal fire which is prepared [not for you, nor for men, but] for the devil and his angels"= there is an election to life, but no reprobation to death ; a "book of life" (Rev. 21 : 27), but no book of death.

E. G. Robinson, Christian Theology, 313—"Reprobation, in the sense of absolute predestination to sin and eternal damnation, is neither a sequence of the doctrine of election, nor the teaching of the Scriptures." Men are not "appointed" to disobedience and stumbling in the same way that they are "appointed" to salvation. God uses positive means to save, but not to destroy. Henry Ward Beecher: "The elect are whosoever will ; the non-elect are whosoever won't." George A. Gordon, New Epoch for Faith, 44—"Election understood would have been the saving strength of Israel ; election misunderstood was its ruin. The nation felt that the election of it meant the rejection of other nations. . . . The Christian church has repeated Israel's mistake."

The Westminster Confession reads : "By the decree of God, for the manifestation of his glory, some men and angels are predestinated unto everlasting life, and others to everlasting death. These angels and men, thus predestinated and foreordained, are particularly and unchangeably designed ; and their number is so certain and definite that it cannot be either increased or diminished. The rest of mankind God was pleased, according to the unsearchable counsel of his own will, whereby he extendeth or withholdeth mercy as he pleaseth, for the glory of his sovereign power over his creatures, to pass by and to ordain them to dishonor and wrath for their sin, to the praise of his glorious justice." This reads as if both the saved and the lost were made originally for their respective final estates without respect to character. It is supralapsarianism. It is certain that the supralapsarians were in the majority in the Westminster Assembly, and that they determined the form of the statement, although there were many sublapsarians who objected that it was only on account of their foreseen wickedness that any were reprobated. In its later short statement of doctrine the Presbyterian body in America has made it plain that God's decree of reprobation is a permissive decree, and that it places no barrier in the way of any man's salvation.

On the general subject of Election, see Mozley, Predestination ; Payne, Divine Sovereignty ; Ridgeley, Works, 1 : 261-324, esp. 322 ; Edwards, Works, 2 : 527 sq. ; Van Oosterzee, Dogmatics, 446-458 ; Martensen, Dogmatics, 362-382 ; and especially Wardlaw, Systematic Theology, 485-549 : H. B. Smith, Syst. of Christian Theology, 502-514 ; Maule, Outlines of Christian Doctrine, 36-56 ; Peck, in Bapt. Quar. Rev., Oct. 1891 : 689-706. On objections to election, and Spurgeon's answers to them, see Williams, Reminiscences of Spurgeon, 189. On the homiletical uses of the doctrine of election, see Bib. Sac., Jan. 1896 : 79-92.

II. CALLING.

Calling is that act of God by which men are invited to accept, by faith, the salvation provided by Christ. — The Scriptures distinguish between :

(*a*) *The general, or external, call* to all men through God's providence, word, and Spirit.

Is. 45 : 22 — "Look unto me, and be ye saved, all the ends of the earth ; for I am God, and there is none else " ; 55 : 6 — "Seek ye Jehovah while he may be found ; call ye upon him while he is near " ; 65 : 12 — "when I called, ye did not answer ; when I spake, ye did not hear ; but ye did that which was evil in mine eyes, and chose that wherein I delighted not " ; Ez. 33 : 11 — " As I live, saith the Lord Jehovah, I have no pleasure in the death of the wicked ; but that the wicked turn from his way and live ; turn ye, turn ye from your evil ways ; for why will ye die, O house of Israel ? " Mat. 11 : 28 — " Come unto me, all ye that labor and are heavy laden, and I will give you rest " ; 22 : 3 — " sent forth his servants to call them that were bidden to the marriage feast : and they would not come " ; Mark 16 : 15 — " Go ye into all the world, and preach the gospel to the whole creation " ; John 12 : 32 — " And I, if I be lifted up from the earth, will draw all men unto myself " — draw, not drag ; Rev. 3 : 20 — " Behold, I stand at the door and knock : if any man hear my voice and open the door, I will come in to him, and will sup with him, and he with me."

(*b*) *The special, efficacious call* of the Holy Spirit to the elect.

Luke 14 : 23 — " Go out into the highways and hedges, and constrain them to come in, that my house may be filled " ; Rom. 1 : 7 — " to all that are in Rome, beloved of God, called to be saints : Grace to you and peace from God our Father and the Lord Jesus Christ " ; 8 : 30 — " whom he foreordained, them he also called : and whom he called, them he also justified " ; 11 : 29 — " For the gifts and the calling of God are not repented of " ; 1 Cor. 1 : 23, 24 — " but we preach Christ crucified, unto Jews a stumblingblock, and unto Gentiles foolishness ; but unto them that are called, both Jews and Greeks, Christ the power of God, and the wisdom of God " ; 26 — " For behold your calling, brethren, that not many wise after the flesh, not many mighty, not many noble, are called " ; Phil. 3 : 14 — " I press on toward the goal unto the prize of the high [marg. ' upward '] calling of God in Christ Jesus " ; Eph. 1 : 18 — " that ye may know what is the hope of his calling, what the riches of the glory of his inheritance in the saints " ; 1 Thess. 2 · 12 — " to the end that ye should walk worthily of God, who calleth you into his own kingdom and glory " ; 2 Thess. 2 : 14 — " whereunto he called you through our gospel, to the obtaining of the glory of our Lord Jesus Christ " , 2 Tim. 1 : 9 — " who saved us, and called us with a holy calling, not according to our works, but according to his own purpose and grace, which was given us in Christ Jesus before times eternal " ; Heb. 3 : 1 — " holy brethren, partakers of a heavenly calling " ; 2 Pet. 1 : 10 — " Wherefore, brethren, give the more diligence to make your calling and election sure."

Two questions only need special consideration :

A. Is God's general call sincere ?

This is denied, upon the ground that such sincerity is incompatible, first, with the inability of the sinner to obey ; and secondly, with the design of God to bestow only upon the elect the special grace without which they will not obey.

(*a*) To the first objection we reply that, since this inability is not a physical but a moral inability, consisting simply in the settled perversity of an evil will, there can be no insincerity in offering salvation to all, especially when the offer is in itself a proper motive to obedience.

God's call to all men to repent and to believe the gospel is no more insincere than his command to all men to love him with all the heart. There is no obstacle in the way of men's obedience to the gospel, that does not exist to prevent their obedience to the law. If it is proper to publish the commands of the law, it is proper to publish the invitations of the gospel. A human being may be perfectly sincere in giving an invitation which he knows will be refused. He may desire to have the invitation accepted, while yet he may, for certain reasons of justice or personal dignity, be unwilling to put forth special efforts, aside from the invitation itself, to secure the acceptance of it on the part of those to whom it is offered. So God's desires that certain men should be saved may not be accompanied by his will to exert special influences to save them.

These desires were meant by the phrase " revealed will " in the old theologians ; his purpose to bestow special grace, by the phrase " secret will." It is of the former that Paul speaks, in 1 Tim. 2 : 4 — " who would have all men to be saved." Here we have, not the active σῶσαι, but the passive σωθῆναι. The meaning is, not that God *purposes* to save all men, but that he *desires* all men to be saved through repenting and believing the gospel. Hence God's revealed will, or desire, that all men should be saved, is perfectly consistent with his secret will, or purpose, to bestow special grace only upon a certain number (see, on 1 Tim. 2 : 4, Fairbairn's Commentary on the Pastoral Epistles).

The sincerity of God's call is shown, not only in the fact that the only obstacle to compliance, on the sinner's part, is the sinner's own evil will, but also in the fact that

God has, at infinite cost, made a complete external provision, upon the ground of which "he that will" may "come" and "take the water of life freely" (Rev. 22:17); so that God can truly say: "What could have been done more to my vineyard, that I have not done in it?" (Is. 5:4). Broadus, Com. on Mat. 6:10 — "Thy will be done" — distinguishes between God's will of purpose, of desire, and of command. H. B. Smith, Syst. Theol., 521 — "Common grace passes over into effectual grace in proportion as the sinner yields to the divine influence. Effectual grace is that which effects what common grace tends to effect." See also Studien und Kritiken, 1887:7 sq.

(*b*) To the second, we reply that the objection, if true, would equally hold against God's foreknowledge. The sincerity of God's general call is no more inconsistent with his determination that some shall be permitted to reject it, than it is with foreknowledge that some will reject it.

Hodge, Syst. Theol., 2 : 643 — "Predestination concerns only the purpose of God to render effectual, in particular cases, a call addressed to all. A general amnesty, on certain conditions, may be offered by a sovereign to rebellious subjects, although he knows that through pride or malice many will refuse to accept it; and even though, for wise reasons, he should determine not to constrain their assent, supposing that such influence over their minds were within his power. It is evident, from the nature of the call, that it has nothing to do with the secret purpose of God to grant his effectual grace to some, and not to others. . . . According to the Augustinian scheme, the non-elect have all the advantages and opportunities of securing their salvation, which, according to any other scheme, are granted to mankind indiscriminately. . . . . God designed, in its adoption, to save his own people, but he consistently offers its benefits to all who are willing to receive them." See also H. B. Smith, System of Christian Theology, 515-521.

B.   Is God's special call irresistible ?

We prefer to say that this special call is efficacious,— that is, that it infallibly accomplishes its purpose of leading the sinner to the acceptance of salvation.   This implies two things:

(*a*) That the operation of God is not an outward constraint upon the human will, but that it accords with the laws of our mental constitution. We reject the term ' irresistible,' as implying a coercion and compulsion which is foreign to the nature of God's working in the soul.

Ps. 110 : 3 — "Thy people are freewill-offerings In the day of thy power: in holy array, Out of the womb of the morning Thou hast the dew of thy youth " — *i. e.*, youthful recruits to thy standard, as numberless and as bright as the drops of morning dew ; Phil. 2 : 12, 13 — "Work out your own salvation with fear and trembling ; for it is God who worketh in you both to will and to work, for his good pleasure " — *i. e.*, the result of God's working is our own working.   The Lutheran Formula of Concord properly condemns the view that, before, in, and after conversion, the will only resists the Holy Spirit: for this, it declares, is the very nature of conversion, that out of non-willing, God makes willing, persons (F. C., 60, 581, 582, 673).

Hos. 4 : 16 — "Israel hath behaved himself stubbornly, like a stubborn heifer," or " or as a heifer that slideth back " = when the sacrificial offering is brought forward to be slain, it holds back, settling on its haunches so that it has to be pushed and forced before it can be brought to the altar.   These are not "the sacrifices of God " which are "a broken spirit, a broken and a contrite heart" (Ps. 51:17).   E. H. Johnson, Theology, 2d ed., 250 — "The N. T. nowhere declares, or even intimates, ... that the general call of the Holy Spirit is insufficient.   And furthermore, it never states that the efficient call is irresistible.   Psychologically, to speak of irresistible influence upon the faculty of self-determination in man is express contradiction in terms.   No harm can come from acknowledging that we do not know God's unrevealed reasons for electing one individual rather than another to eternal life." Dr. Johnson goes on to argue that if, without disparagement to grace, faith can be a condition of justification, faith might also be a condition of election, and that inasmuch as salvation is *received* as a gift only on condition of faith exercised, it is in *purpose* a gift, even if only on condition of faith foreseen.   This seems to us to ignore the abundant Scripture testimony that faith itself is God's gift, and therefore the initiative must be wholly with God.

(*b*) That the operation of God is the originating cause of that new disposition of the affections, and that new activity of the will, by which the sinner accepts Christ. The cause is not in the response of the will to the presentation of motives by God, nor in any mere coöperation of the will of man with the will of God, but is an almighty act of God in the will of man, by which its freedom to choose God as its end is restored and rightly exercised (John 1 : 12, 13). For further discussion of the subject, see, in the next section, the remarks on Regeneration, with which this efficacious call is identical.

John 1 : 12, 13 — "But as many as received him, to them gave he the right to become children of God, even to them that believe on his name : who were born, not of blood, nor of the will of the flesh, nor of the will of man, but of God." God's saving grace and effectual calling are irresistible, not in the sense that they are never resisted, but in the sense that they are never successfully resisted. See Andrew Fuller, Works, 2 : 373, 513, and 3 : 807 ; Gill, Body of Divinity, 2 : 121–130 ; Robert Hall, Works, 3 : 75.

Matheson, Moments on the Mount, 128. 129 — "Thy love to Him is to his love to thee what the sunlight on the sea is to the sunshine in the sky — a reflex, a mirror, a diffusion ; thou art giving back the glory that has been cast upon the waters. In the attraction of thy life to him, in the cleaving of thy heart to him, in the soaring of thy spirit to him, thou art told that he is near thee, thou hearest the beating of his pulse for thee."

Upton, Hibbert Lectures, 302 — "In regard to our reason and to the essence of our ideals, there is no real dualism between man and God ; but in the case of the will which constitutes the essence of each man's individuality, there is a real dualism, and therefore a possible antagonism between the will of the dependent spirit, man, and the will of the absolute and universal spirit, God. Such *real* duality of will, and not the *appearance* of duality, as F. H. Bradley put it, is the essential condition of ethics and religion.

SECTION II. — THE APPLICATION OF CHRIST'S REDEMPTION IN ITS ACTUAL BEGINNING.

Under this head we treat of Union with Christ, Regeneration, Conversion (embracing Repentance and Faith), and Justification. Much confusion and error have arisen from conceiving these as occurring in chronological order. The order is logical, not chronological. As it is only "in Christ" that man is "a new creature" (2 Cor. 5 : 17) or is "justified" (Acts 13 : 39), union with Christ logically precedes both regeneration and justification ; and yet, chronologically, the moment of our union with Christ is also the moment when we are regenerated and justified. So, too, regeneration and conversion are but the divine and human sides or aspects of the same fact, although regeneration has logical precedence, and man turns only as God turns him.

Dorner, Glaubenslehre, 3 : 694 (Syst. Doct., 4 : 159), gives at this point an account of the work of the Holy Spirit in general. The Holy Spirit's work, he says, presupposes the historical work of Christ, and prepares the way for Christ's return. "As the Holy Spirit is the principle of union between the Father and the Son, so he is the principle of union between God and man. Only through the Holy Spirit does Christ secure for himself those who will love him as distinct and free personalities." Regeneration and conversion are not chronologically separate. Which of the spokes of a wheel starts first ? The ray of light and the ray of heat enter at the same moment. Sensation and perception are not separated in time, although the former is the cause of the latter.

"Suppose a non-elastic tube extending across the Atlantic. Suppose that the tube is completely filled with an incompressible fluid. Then there would be no interval of time between the impulse given to the fluid at this end of the tube, and the effect upon the fluid at the other end." See Hazard, Causation and Freedom in Willing, 33-38, who argues that cause and effect are always simultaneous; else, in the intervening time, there would be a cause that had no effect; that is, a cause that caused nothing; that is, a cause that that was not a cause. "A potential cause may exist for an unlimited period without producing any effect, and of course may precede its effect by any length of time. But actual, effective cause being the exercise of a sufficient power, its effect cannot be delayed; for, in that case, there would be the exercise of a sufficient power to produce the effect, without producing it,—involving the absurdity of its being both sufficient and insufficient at the same time.

"A difficulty may here be suggested in regard to the flow or progress of events in time, if they are all simultaneous with their causes. This difficulty cannot arise as to intelligent effort; for, in regard to it, periods of non-action may continually intervene; but if there are series of events and material phenomena, each of which is in turn effect and cause, it may be difficult to see how any time could elapse between the first and the last of the series. . . . . If, however, as I suppose, these series of events, or material changes, are always effected through the medium of motion, it need not trouble us, for there is precisely the same difficulty in regard to our conception of the motion of matter from point to point, there being no space or length between any two consecutive points, and yet the body in motion gets from one end of a long line to the other, and in this case this difficulty just neutralizes the other. . . . . So, even if we cannot conceive how motion involves the idea of time, we may perceive that, if it does so, it may be a means of conveying events, which depend upon it, through time also."

Martineau, Study, 1:148-150—"Simultaneity does not exclude duration,"—since each cause has duration and each effect has duration also. Bowne, Metaphysics, 106—"In the system, the complete ground of an event never lies in any one thing, but only in a complex of things. If a single thing were the sufficient ground of an effect, the effect would coëxist with the thing, and all effects would be instantaneously given. Hence all events in the system must be viewed as the result of the interaction of two or more things."

The first manifestation of life in an infant may be in the lungs or heart or brain, but that which makes any and all of these manifestations possible is the antecedent life. We may not be able to tell which comes first, but having the life we have all the rest. When the wheel goes, all the spokes will go. The soul that is born again will show it in faith and hope and love and holy living. Regeneration will involve repentance and faith and justification and sanctification. But the one life which makes regeneration and all these consequent blessings possible is the life of Christ who joins himself to us in order that we may join ourselves to him. Anne Reeve Aldrich, The Meaning: "I lost my life in losing love. This blurred my spring and killed its dove. Along my path the dying roses Fell, and disclosed the thorns thereof. I found my life in finding God. In ecstasy I kiss the rod; For who that wins the goal, but lightly Thinks of the thorns whereon he trod?"

See A. A. Hodge, on the Ordo Salutis, in Princeton Rev., March, 1888:304-321. Union with Christ, says Dr. Hodge, "is effected by the Holy Ghost in effectual calling. Of this calling the parts are two: (a) the offering of Christ to the sinner, externally by the gospel, and internally by the illumination of the Holy Ghost; (b) the reception of Christ, which on our part is both passive and active. The passive reception is that whereby a spiritual principle is ingenerated into the human will, whence issues the active reception, which is an act of faith with which repentance is always conjoined. The communion of benefits which results from this union involves: (a) a change of state or relation, called justification; and (b) a change of subjective moral character, commenced in regeneration and completed through sanctification." See also Dr. Hodge's Popular Lectures on Theological Themes, 340, and Outlines of Theology, 333-429.

H. B. Smith, however, in his System of Christian Theology, is more clear in the putting of Union with Christ before Regeneration. On page 502, he begins his treatment of the Application of Redemption with the title: "The Union between Christ and the individual believer as effected by the Holy Spirit. This embraces the subjects of Justification, Regeneration, and Sanctification, with the underlying topic which comes first to be considered. Election." He therefore treats Union with Christ (531-539) before Regeneration (553-569). He says Calvin defines regeneration as coming to us by participation in Christ, and apparently agrees with this view (559).

"This union [with Christ] is at the ground of regeneration and justification " (534). " The great difference of theological systems comes out here. Since Christianity is redemption through Christ, our mode of conceiving that will determine the character of our whole theological system " (536). " The union with Christ is mediated by his Spirit, whence we are both renewed and justified. The great fact of objective Christianity is incarnation in order to atonement ; the great fact of subjective Christianity is union with Christ, whereby we receive the atonement " (537). We may add that this union with Christ, in view of which God elects and to which God calls the sinner, is begun in regeneration, completed in conversion, declared in justification, and proved in sanctification and perseverance.

I. Union with Christ.

The Scriptures declare that, through the operation of God, there is constituted a union of the soul with Christ different in kind from God's natural and providential concursus with all spirits, as well as from all unions of mere association or sympathy, moral likeness, or moral influence, — a union of life, in which the human spirit, while then most truly possessing its own individuality and personal distinctness, is interpenetrated and energized by the Spirit of Christ, is made inscrutably but indissolubly one with him, and so becomes a member and partaker of that regenerated, believing, and justified humanity of which he is the head.

Union with Christ is not union with a system of doctrine, nor with external religious influences, nor with an organized church, nor with an ideal man,— but rather, with a personal, risen, living, omnipresent Lord (J. W. A. Stewart). Dr. J. W. Alexander well calls this doctrine of the Union of the Believer with Christ "the central truth of all theology and of all religion." Yet it receives little of formal recognition, either in dogmatic treatises or in common religious experience. Quenstedt, 886-912, has devoted a section to it ; A. A. Hodge gives to it a chapter, in his Outlines of Theology, 369 sq., to which we are indebted for valuable suggestions ; H. B. Smith treats of it, not however as a separate topic, but under the head of Justification (System, 531-539).

The majority of printed systems of doctrine, however, contain no chapter or section on Union with Christ, and the majority of Christians much more frequently think of Christ as a Savior outside of them, than as a Savior who dwells within. This comparative neglect of the doctrine is doubtless a reaction from the exaggerations of a false mysticism. But there is great need of rescuing the doctrine from neglect. For this we rely wholly upon Scripture. Doctrines which reason can neither discover nor prove need large support from the Bible. It is a mark of divine wisdom that the doctrine of the Trinity, for example, is so inwoven with the whole fabric of the New Testament, that the rejection of the former is the virtual rejection of the latter. The doctrine of Union with Christ, in like manner, is taught so variously and abundantly, that to deny it is to deny inspiration itself. See Kahnis, Luth. Dogmatik, 3 : 447-450.

1. *Scripture Representations of this Union.*

A. Figurative teaching. It is illustrated :

(a) From the union of a building and its foundation.

Eph. 2 : 20-22 — "being built upon the foundation of the apostles and prophets, Christ Jesus himself being the chief corner stone ; in whom each several building, fitly framed together, groweth into a holy temple in the Lord ; in whom ye also are builded together for a habitation of God in the Spirit "; Col. 2 : 7 — "builded up in him " — grounded in Christ as our foundation ; 1 Pet. 2 : 4, 5 — "unto whom coming, a living stone, rejected indeed of men, but with God elect, precious, ye also, as living stones, are built up a spiritual house " — each living stone in the Christian temple is kept in proper relation to every other, and is made to do its part in furnishing a habitation for God, only by being built upon and permanently connected with Christ, the chief corner-stone. *Cf.* Ps. 118 : 22 — "The stone which the builders rejected Is become the head of the corner "; Is. 28 : 16 — "Behold, I lay in Zion for a foundation a stone, a tried stone, a precious corner-stone of sure foundation : he that believeth shall not be in haste."

(b) From the union between husband and wife.

Rom. 7 : 4 — "ye also were made dead to the law through the body of Christ ; that ye should be joined to another, even to him who was raised from the dead, that we might bring forth fruit unto God " — here union with Christ is illustrated by the indissoluble bond that connects husband and wife, and makes them legally and organically one ; 2 Cor. 11 : 2 — "I am jealous over you with a godly jealousy : for I espoused you to one husband, that I might present you as a pure virgin to Christ" ; Eph. 5 : 31, 32 — "For this cause shall a man leave his father and mother, and shall cleave to his wife ; and the two shall become one flesh. This mystery is great : but I speak in regard of Christ and of the church " — Meyer refers verse 31 wholly to Christ, and says that Christ leaves father and mother (the right hand of God) and is joined to the church as his wife, the two constituting thenceforth one moral person. He makes the union future, however, — "For this cause *shall* a man leave his father and mother" — the consummation is at Christ's second coming. But the Fathers, as Chrysostom, Theodoret, and Jerome, referred it more properly to the incarnation.

Rev. 19 : 7 — "the marriage of the Lamb is come, and his wife hath made herself ready" ; 22 : 17 — "And the Spirit and the bride say, Come" ; *cf.* Is. 54 : 5 — "For thy Maker is thine husband" ; Jer. 3 : 20 — "Surely as a wife treacherously departeth from her husband, so have ye dealt treacherously with me, O house of Israel, saith Jehovah" ; Hos. 2 : 2-5 — "for their mother hath played the harlot"— departure from God is adultery ; the Song of Solomon, as Jewish interpreters have always maintained, is an allegorical poem describing, under the figure of marriage, the union between Jehovah and his people : Paul only adopts the Old Testament figure, and applies it more precisely to the union of God with the church in Jesus Christ.

(c) From the union between the vine and its branches.

John 15 : 1-10 — "I am the vine, ye are the branches : He that abideth in me, and I in him, the same beareth much fruit : for apart from me ye can do nothing " — as God's natural life is in the vine. that it may give life to its natural branches, so God's spiritual life is in the vine, Christ, that he may give life to his spiritual branches. The roots of this new vine are planted in heaven, not on earth ; and into it the half-withered branches of the old humanity are to be grafted, that they may have life divine. Yet our Lord does not say "I am the root." The branch is not something *outside*, which has to get nourishment *out of* the root,—it is rather a *part* of the vine. Rom. 6 : 5 — "if we have become united with him [σύμφυτοι — ' grown together ' — used of the man and horse in the Centaur, Xen., Cyrop., 4 : 3 : 18], in the likeness of his death, we shall be also in the likeness of his resurrection" ; 11 : 24 — "thou wast cut out of that which is by nature a wild olive tree, and wast grafted contrary to nature into a good olive tree" ; Col. 2 : 6, 7 — "As therefore ye received Christ Jesus the Lord, so walk in him, rooted and builded up in him " — not only grounded in Christ as our foundation, but thrusting down roots into him as the deep, rich, all-sustaining soil. This union with Christ is consistent with individuality : for the graft brings forth fruit after its kind, though modified by the tree into which it is grafted.

Bishop H. W. Warren, in S. S. Times, Oct. 17, 1891 — "The lessons of the vine are intimacy, likeness of nature, continuous impartation of life, fruit. Between friends there is intimacy by means of media, such as food, presents, care, words, soul looking from the eyes. The mother gives her liquid flesh to the babe, but such intimacy soon ceases. The mother is not rich enough in life continuously to feed the ever-enlarging nature of the growing man. Not so with the vine. It continuously feeds. Its rivers crowd all the banks. They burst out in leaf, blossom, clinging tendrils, and fruit, everywhere. In nature a thorn grafted on a pear tree bears only thorn. There is not pear-life enough to compel change of its nature. But a wild olive, typical of depraved nature, grafted on a good olive tree finds, contrary to nature, that there is force enough in the growing stock to change the nature of the wild scion."

(d) From the union between the members and the head of the body.

1 Cor. 6 : 15, 19 — "Know ye not that your bodies are members of Christ ? .... know ye not that your body is a temple of the Holy Spirit which is in you, which ye have from God ? " 12 : 12 — "For as the body is one, and hath many members, and all the members of the body, being many, are one body ; so also is Christ " — here Christ is identified with the church of which he is the head ; Eph. 1 : 22, 23 — "he put all things in subjection under his feet, and gave him to be head over all things to the church, which is his body, the fulness of him that filleth all in all " — as the members of the human body are united to the head, the source of their activity and the power that controls their movements, so all believers are members of an invisible body whose head is Christ. Shall we tie a string round the finger to keep for it its own blood ? No, for all the blood of the body is needed to nourish one finger. So Christ is "head over all things to [for the benefit of] the church " (Tyler, Theol. Greek Poets, preface, ii). "The church is the fulness (πλήρωμα) of Christ ; as it was not good for the first man, Adam, to be alone, no more was it good for the second man, Christ " (C. H. M.). Eph. 4 : 15, 16 — "grow up in all things into him, who is the head, even Christ ; from whom all the body .... maketh the increase of the body unto the building up of itself in love " ; 5 : 29, 30 — "for no man ever hated his own flesh ; but nourisheth and cherisheth it, even as Christ also the church ; because we are members of his body."

(e) From the union of the race with the source of its life in Adam.

Rom. 5 : 12, 21 — "as through one man sin entered into the world, and death through sin . . . . that, as sin reigned in death, even so might grace reign through righteousness unto eternal life through Jesus Christ our Lord " ; 1 Cor. 15 : 22, 45, 49 — "as in Adam all die, so also in Christ shall all be made alive . . . . The first man Adam became a living soul. The last Adam became a life-giving Spirit . . . . as we have borne the image of the earthy, we shall also bear the image of the heavenly " — as the whole race is one with the first man Adam, in whom it fell and from whom it has derived a corrupted and guilty nature, so the whole race of believers constitutes a new and restored humanity, whose justified and purified nature is derived from Christ, the second Adam. *Cf.* Gen. 2 : 23 — "This is now bone of my bones, and flesh of my flesh : she shall be called Woman, because she was taken out of Man " — here C. H. M. remarks that, as man is first created and then woman is viewed in and formed out of him, so it is with Christ and the church. "We are members of Christ's body, because in Christ we have the princi- ple of our origin ; from him our life arose, just as the life of Eve was derived from Adam . . . . The church is Christ's helpmeet, formed out of Christ in his deep sleep of death, as Eve out of Adam . . . . The church will be nearest to Christ, as Eve was to Adam." Because Christ is the source of all spiritual life for his people, he is called, in Is. 9 : 6, "Everlasting Father," and it is said, in Is. 53 : 10, that "he shall see his seed" (see page 680).

B. Direct statements.

(a) The believer is said to be in Christ.

Lest we should regard the figures mentioned above as merely Oriental metaphors, the fact of the believer's union with Christ is asserted in the most direct and prosaic manner. John 14 : 20 — "ye in me " Rom. 6 : 11 — "alive unto God in Christ Jesus" ; 8 : 1 — "no condemnation to them that are in Christ Jesus " ; 2 Cor. 5 : 17 — "if any man is in Christ, he is a new creature" ; Eph. 1 : 4 — "chose us in him before the foundation of the world" ; 2 : 13 — "now in Christ Jesus ye that once were far off are made nigh in the blood of Christ." Thus the believer is said to be "in Christ," as the element or atmosphere which surrounds him with its perpetual presence and which constitutes his vital breath ; in fact, this phrase "in Christ," always meaning "in union with Christ," is the very key to Paul's epistles, and to the whole New Testament. The fact that the believer is in Christ is symbolized in baptism : we are "baptized into Christ" (Gal. 3 : 27).

(b) Christ is said to be in the believer.

John 14 : 20 — "I in you" ; Rom. 8 : 9 — "ye are not in the flesh but in the Spirit, if so be that the Spirit of God dwelleth in you. But if any man hath not the Spirit of Christ, he is none of his " — that this Spirit of Christ is Christ himself, is shown from verse 10 — "And if Christ is in you, the body is dead because of sin ; but the spirit is life because of righteousness " ; Gal. 2 : 20 — "I have been crucified with Christ ; and it is no longer I that live, but Christ liveth in me " — here Christ is said to be in the believer, and so to live his life within the believer, that the latter can point to this as the dominating fact of his experience, — it is not so much he that lives, as it is Christ that lives in him. The fact that Christ is in the believer is symbolized in the Lord's supper : "The bread which we break, is it not a participation in the body of Christ ? " (1 Cor. 10 : 16).

(c) The Father and the Son dwell in the believer.

John 14 : 23 — "If a man love me, he will keep my word : and my Father will love him, and we will come unto him, and make our abode with him " ; *cf.* 10 — "Believest thou not that I am in the Father, and the Father in me ? the words that I say unto you I speak not from myself : but the Father abiding in me doeth his works " — the Father and the Son dwell in the believer ; for where the Son is, there always the Father must be also. If the union between the believer and Christ in John 14 : 23 is to be interpreted as one of mere moral influence, then the union of Christ and the Father in John 14 : 10 must also be interpreted as a union of mere moral influence. Eph. 3 : 17 — "that Christ may dwell in your hearts through faith " ; 1 John 4 : 16 — "he that abideth in love abideth in God, and God abideth in him."

(d) The believer has life by partaking of Christ, as Christ has life by partaking of the Father.

John 6 : 53, 56, 57 — "Except ye eat the flesh of the Son of man and drink his blood, ye have not life in yourselves . . . . He that eateth my flesh and drinketh my blood abideth in me, and I in him. As the living Father sent me and I live because of the Father, so he that eateth me, he also shall live because of me " — the believer has life by partaking of Christ in a way that may not inappropriately be compared with Christ's having life by partaking of the Father. 1 Cor. 10 : 16, 17 — "The cup of blessing which we bless, is it not a communion of the blood of Christ ? The bread which we break, is it not a communion of the body . Christ ? " — here it is intimated that the Lord's Supper sets forth, in the language of symbol, the soul's actual participation in the life of Christ; and the margin properly translates the word κοινωνία, not "communion," but "participation." *Cf.* 1 John 1:3 — "our fellowship (κοινωνία) is with the Father, and with his Son Jesus Christ." Foster, Christian Life and Theology, 216 — "In John 6, the phrases call to mind the ancient form of sacrifice, and the participation therein by the offerer at the sacrificial meal, — as at the Passover."

(*e*) All believers are one in Christ.

John 17 : 21-23 — "that they may all be one; even as thou, Father, art in me, and I in thee, that they also may be in us : that the world may believe that thou didst send me. And the glory which thou hast given me I have given unto them ; that they may be one, even as we are one ; I in them, and thou in me, that they may be perfected into one " — all believers are one in Christ, to whom they are severally and collectively united, as Christ himself is one with God.

(*f*) The believer is made partaker of the divine nature.

2 Pet. 1 : 4 — "that through these [promises] ye may become partakers of the divine nature" — not by having the essence of your humanity changed into the essence of divinity, but by having Christ the divine Savior continually dwelling within, and indissolubly joined to, your human souls.

(*g*) The believer is made one spirit with the Lord.

1 Cor. 6 : 17 — "he that is joined unto the Lord is one spirit " — human nature is so interpenetrated and energized by the divine, that the two move and act as one; *cf.* 19 — "know ye not that your body is a temple of the Holy Spirit which is in you, which ye have from God ?" Rom. 8 : 26 — "the Spirit also helpeth our infirmity : for we know not how to pray as we ought; but the Spirit himself maketh intercession for us with groanings which cannot be uttered " — the Spirit is so near to us, and so one with us, that our prayer is called his, or rather, his prayer becomes ours. Weiss, in his Life of Jesus, says that, in the view of Scripture, human greatness does not consist in a man's producing everything in a natural way out of himself, but in possessing perfect receptivity for God's greatest gift. Therefore God's Son receives the Spirit without measure; and we may add that the believer in like manner receives Christ.

2. *Nature of this Union.*

We have here to do not only with a fact of life, but with a unique relation between the finite and the infinite. Our descriptions must therefore be inadequate. Yet in many respects we know what this union is not; in certain respects we can positively characterize it.

It should not surprise us if we find it far more difficult to give a scientific definition of this union, than to determine the fact of its existence. It is a fact of life with which we have to deal ; and the secret of life, even in its lowest forms, no philosopher has ever yet discovered. The tiniest flower witnesses to two facts : first, that of its own relative independence, as an individual organism ; and secondly, that of its ultimate dependence upon a life and power not its own. So every human soul has its proper powers of intellect, affection, and will ; yet it lives, moves, and has its being in God (Acts 17 : 28).

Starting out from the truth of God's omnipresence, it might seem as if God's indwelling in the granite boulder was the last limit of his union with the finite. But we see the divine intelligence and goodness drawing nearer to us, by successive stages, in vegetable life, in the animal creation, and in the moral nature of man. And yet there are two stages beyond all these : first, in Christ's union with the believer ; and secondly, in God's union with Christ. If this union of God with the believer be only one of several approximations of God to his finite creation, the fact that it is, equally with the others, not wholly comprehensible to reason, should not blind us either to its truth or to its importance.

It is easier to-day than at any other previous period of history to believe in the union of the believer with Christ. That God is immanent in the universe, and that there is a divine element in man, is familiar to our generation. All men are naturally one with Christ, the immanent God, and this natural union prepares the way for that spiritual union in which Christ joins himself to our faith. Campbell, The Indwelling Christ, 131 — "In the immanence of Christ in nature we find the ground of his immanence in human nature. ... A man may be out of Christ, but Christ is never out of him. Those who banish him he does not abandon." John Caird, Fund. Ideas of Christianity, 2 : 233-

256 — "God is united with nature, in the atoms, in the trees, in the planets. Science is seeing nature full of the life of God. God is united to man in body and soul. The beating of his heart and the voice of conscience witness to God within. God sleeps in the stone, dreams in the animal, wakes in man."

A. Negatively. — It is not :

(*a*) A merely natural union, like that of God with all human spirits, — as held by rationalists.

In our physical life we are conscious of another life within us which is not subject to our wills: the heart beats involuntarily, whether we sleep or wake. But in our spiritual life we are still more conscious of a life within our life. Even the heathen said: "Est Deus in nobis; agitante calescimus illo," and the Egyptians held to the identification of the departed with Osiris (Renouf, Hibbert Lectures, 185). But Paul urges us to work out our salvation, upon the very ground that "it is God that worketh" in us, "both to will and to work, for his good pleasure" (Phil. 2:12, 13). This life of God in the soul is the life of Christ.

The movement of the electric car cannot be explained simply from the working of its own motor apparatus. The electric current throbbing through the wire, and the dynamo from which that energy proceeds, are needed to explain the result. In like manner we need a spiritual Christ to explain the spiritual activity of the Christian. A. H. Strong, Sermon before the Baptist World Congress in London, 1905 — "We had in America some years ago a steam engine all whose working parts were made of glass. The steam came from without, but, being hot enough to move machinery, this steam was itself invisible, and there was presented the curious spectacle of an engine, transparent, moving, and doing important work, while yet no cause for this activity was perceptible. So the church, humanity, the universe, are all in constant and progressive movement, but the Christ who moves them is invisible. Faith comes to believe where it cannot see. It joins itself to this invisible Christ, and knows him as its very life."

(*b*) A merely moral union, or union of love and sympathy, like that between teacher and scholar, friend and friend, — as held by Socinians and Arminians.

There is a moral union between different souls: 1 Sam. 18:1 — "the soul of Jonathan was knit with the soul of David, and Jonathan loved him as his own soul" — here the Vulgate has: "Anima Jonathæ agglutinata Davidi." Aristotle calls friends "one soul." So in a higher sense, in Acts 4:32, the early believers are said to have been "of one heart and soul." But in John 17:21, 26, Christ's union with his people is distinguished from any mere union of love and sympathy: "that they may all be one; even as thou, Father, art in me, and I in thee, that they also may be in us; . . . . that the love wherewith thou lovedst me may be in them, and I in them." Jesus' aim, in the whole of his last discourse, is to show that no mere union of love and sympathy will be sufficient: "apart from me," he says, "ye can do nothing" (John 15:5). That his disciples may be vitally joined to himself, is therefore the subject of his last prayer.

Dorner says well, that Arminianism (and with this doctrine Roman Catholics and the advocates of New School views substantially agree) makes man a mere tangent to the circle of the divine nature. It has no idea of the interpenetration of the one by the other. But the Lutheran Formula of Concord says much more correctly: "Damnamus sententiam quod non Deus ipse, sed dona Dei duntaxat, in credentibus habitent."

Ritschl presents to us a historical Christ, and Pfleiderer presents to us an ideal Christ, but neither one gives us the living Christ who is the present spiritual life of the believer. Wendt, in his Teaching of Jesus, 2:310, comes equally far short of a serious interpretation of our Lord's promise, when he says: "This union to his person, as to its contents, is nothing else than adherence to the message of the kingdom of God brought by him." It is not enough for me to be merely *in touch* with Christ. He must come to be "not so far as even to be near." Tennyson, The Higher Pantheism: "Closer is he than breathing, and nearer than hands or feet." William Watson, The Unknown God: "Yea, in my flesh his Spirit doth flow, Too near, too far, for me to know."

(*c*) A union of essence, which destroys the distinct personality and subsistence of either Christ or the human spirit, — as held by many of the mystics.

Many of the mystics, as Schwenkfeld, Weigel, Sebastian Frank, held to an *essential* union between Christ and the believer. One of Weigel's followers, therefore, could say to another : " I am Christ Jesus, the living Word of God ; I have redeemed thee by my sinless sufferings." We are ever to remember that the indwelling of Christ only puts the believer more completely in possession of himself, and makes him more conscious of his own personality and power. Union with Christ must be taken in connection with the other truth of the personality and activity of the Christian ; otherwise it tends to pantheism. Martineau, Study, 2 : 190— " In nature it is God's immanent life, in morals it is God's transcendent life, with which we commune."

Angelus Silesius, a German philosophical poet (1624–1677), audaciously wrote : " I know God cannot live an instant without me ; He must give up the ghost, if I should cease to be." Lowde, a disciple of Malebranche, used the phrase " Godded with God, and Christed with Christ," and Jonathan Edwards, in his Religious Affections, quotes 't with disapproval, saying that " the saints do not become actually partakers of the divine essence, as would be inferred from this abominable and blasphemous language of heretics " (Allen, Jonathan Edwards, 224). " Self is not a mode of the divine : it is a principle of isolation. In order to religion, I must have a will to surrender ....'Our wills are ours, to make them thine.'.... Though the self is, in *knowledge*, a principle of unification ; in *existence*, or metaphysically, it is a principle of isolation " (Seth).

Inge, Christian Mysticism, 30 — "Some of the mystics went astray by teaching a real *substitution* of the divine for human nature, thus depersonalizing man -- a fatal mistake, for without human personality we cannot conceive of divine personality." Lyman Abbott : " In Christ, God and man are united, not as the river is united with the sea, losing its personality therein, but as the child is united with the father, or the wife with the husband, whose personality and individuality are strengthened and increased by the union." Here Dr. Abbott's view comes as far short of the truth as that of the mystics goes beyond the truth. As we shall see, the union of the believer with Christ is a vital union, surpassing in its intimacy any union of souls that we know. The union of child with father, or of wife with husband, is only a pointer which hints very imperfectly at the interpenetrating and energizing of the human spirit by the divine.

(*d*) A union mediated and conditioned by participation of the sacraments of the church,—as held by Romanists, Lutherans, and High-Church Episcopalians.

Perhaps the most pernicious misinterpretation of the nature of this union is that which conceives of it as a physical and material one, and which rears upon this basis the fabric of a sacramental and external Christianity. It is sufficient here to say that this union cannot be mediated by sacraments, since sacraments presuppose it as already existing ; both Baptism and the Lord's Supper are designed only for believers. Only faith receives and retains Christ ; and faith is the act of the soul grasping what is purely invisible and supersensible : not the act of the body, submitting to Baptism or partaking of the Supper.

William Lincoln : " The only way for the believer, if he wants to go rightly, is to remember that truth is always two-sided. If there is any truth that the Holy Spirit has specially pressed upon your heart, if you do not want to push it to the extreme, ask what is the counter-truth, and lean a little of your weight upon that ; otherwise, if you bear so very much on one side of the truth, there is a danger of pushing it into a heresy. Heresy means selected truth ; it does not mean error ; heresy and error are very different things. Heresy is truth, but truth pushed into undue importance, to the disparagement of the truth upon the other side." Heresy (αἵρεσις) = an act of choice, the picking and choosing of a part, instead of comprehensively embracing the whole of truth. Sacramentarians substitute the symbol for the thing symbolized.

B.   Positively.—It is :

(*a*) An organic union,— in which we become members of Christ and partakers of his humanity.

Kant defines an organism, as that whose parts are reciprocally means and end. The body is an organism ; since the limbs exist for the heart, and the heart for the limbs. So each member of Christ's body lives for him who is the head ; and Christ the head equally lives for his members : Eph. 5 : 29, 30 — "no man ever hated his own flesh ; but nourisheth and cherisheth it, even as Christ also the church; because we are members of his body." The train-despatcher is a symbol of the concentration of energy; the switchmen and conductors who receive his orders are symbols of the localization of force; but it is all one organic system.

(*b*) **A vital union,—in which Christ's life becomes the dominating principle within us.**

This union is a vital one, in distinction from any union of mere juxtaposition or external influence. Christ does not work upon us from without, as one separated from us, but from within, as the very heart from which the life-blood of our spirits flows. See Gal. 2 : 20 — "it is no longer I that live, but Christ liveth in me: and that life which I now live in the flesh I live in faith, the faith which is in the Son of God, who loved me, and gave himself up for me;" Col. 3 : 3, 4 — "For ye died, and your life is hid with Christ in God. When Christ, who is our life, shall be manifested, then shall ye also with him be manifested in glory." Christ's life is not corrupted by the corruption of his members, any more than the ray of light is defiled by the filth with which it comes in contact. We may be unconscious of this union with Christ, as we often are of the circulation of the blood, yet it may be the very source and condition of our life.

(*c*) **A spiritual union,—that is, a union whose source and author is the Holy Spirit.**

By a spiritual union we mean a union not of body but of spirit, — a union, therefore, which only the Holy Spirit originates and maintains. Rom. 8 : 9, 10 — "ye are not in the flesh but in the Spirit, if so be that the Spirit of God dwelleth in you. But if any man hath not the Spirit of Christ, he is none of his. And if Christ is in you, the body is dead because of sin; but the spirit is life because of righteousness." The indwelling of Christ involves a continual exercise of efficient power. In Eph. 3 : 16, 17, "strengthened with power through his Spirit in the inward man" is immediately followed by "that Christ may dwell in your hearts through faith."

(*d*) **An indissoluble union,— that is, a union which, consistently with Christ's promise and grace, can never be dissolved.**

Mat. 28 : 20 — "lo, I am with you always, even unto the end of the world"; John 10 : 28 — "they shall never perish, and no one shall snatch them out of my hand"; Rom. 8 : 35, 39 — "Who shall separate us from the love of Christ? . . . . nor height, nor depth, nor any other creature, shall be able to separate us from the love of God, which is in Christ Jesus our Lord"; 1 Thess. 4 : 14, 17 — "them also that are fallen asleep in Jesus will God bring with him. . . . . then we that are alive, that are left, shall together with them be caught up in the clouds, to meet the Lord in the air: and so shall we ever be with the Lord."

Christ's omnipresence makes it possible for him to be united to, and to be present in, each believer, as perfectly and fully as if that believer were the only one to receive Christ's fulness. As Christ's omnipresence makes the whole Christ present in every place, each believer has the whole Christ with him, as his source of strength, purity, life; so that each may say: Christ gives all his time and wisdom and care to me. Such a union as this lacks every element of instability. Once formed, the union is indissoluble. Many of the ties of earth are rudely broken,—not so with our union with Christ,—that endures forever.

Since there is now an unchangeable and divine element in us, our salvation depends no longer upon our unstable wills, but upon Christ's purpose and power. By temporary declension from duty, or by our causeless unbelief, we may banish Christ to the barest and most remote room of the soul's house; but he does not suffer us wholly to exclude him; and when we are willing to unbar the doors, he is still there, ready to fill the whole mansion with his light and love.

(*e*) **An inscrutable union,—mystical, however, only in the sense of surpassing in its intimacy and value any other union of souls which we know.**

This union is inscrutable, indeed; but it is not mystical, in the sense of being unintelligible to the Christian or beyond the reach of his experience. If we call it mystical at all, it should be only because, in the intimacy of its communion and in the transforming power of its influence, it surpasses any other union of souls that we know, and so cannot be fully described or understood by earthly analogies. Eph. 5 : 32 — "This mystery is great: but I speak in regard of Christ and of the church"; Col. 1 : 27 — "the riches of the glory of this mystery among the Gentiles, which is Christ in you, the hope of glory."

See Diman, Theistic Argument, 380 — "As physical science has brought us to the conclusion that back of all the phenomena of the material universe there lies an invisible universe of forces, and that these forces may ultimately be reduced to one all-pervad-

51

ing force in which the unity of the physical universe consists; and as philosophy has advanced the rational conjecture that this ultimate all-pervading force is simply will-force; so the great Teacher holds up to us the spiritual universe as pervaded by one omnipotent life — a life which was revealed in him as its highest manifestation, but which is shared by all who by faith become partakers of his nature. He was Son of God: they too had power to become sons of God. The incarnation is wholly within the natural course and tendency of things. It was prepared for, it came, in the fulness of times. Christ's life is not something sporadic and individual, having its source in the personal conviction of each disciple; it implies a real connection with Christ, the head. Behind all nature there is one force; behind all varieties of Christian life and character there is one spiritual power. All nature is not inert matter,— it is pervaded by a living presence. So all the body of believers live by virtue of the all-working Spirit of Christ, the Holy Ghost." An epitaph at Silton, in Dorsetshire, reads: " Here lies a piece of Christ — a star in dust, A vein of gold, a china dish, that must Be used in heaven when God shall feed the just."

A. H. Strong, in Examiner, 1880: " Such is the nature of union with Christ,— such I mean, is the nature of every believer's union with Christ. For, whether he knows it or not, every Christian has entered into just such a partnership as this. It is this and this only which constitutes him a Christian, and which makes possible a Christian church. We may, indeed, be thus united to Christ, without being fully conscious of the real nature of our relation to him. We may actually possess the kernel, while as yet we have regard only to the shell; we may seem to ourselves to be united to Christ only by an external bond, while after all it is an inward and spiritual bond that makes us his. God often reveals to the Christian the mystery of the gospel, which is Christ *in* him the hope of glory, at the very time that he is seeking only some nearer access to a Redeemer outside of him. Trying to find a union of coöperation or of sympathy, he is amazed to learn that there is already established a union with Christ more glorious and blessed. namely, a union of life; and so, like the miners in the Rocky Mountains, while he is looking only for silver, he finds gold. Christ and the believer have the same life. They are not separate persons linked together by some temporary bond of friendship,— they are united by a tie as close and indissoluble as if the same blood ran in their veins. Yet the Christian may never have suspected how intimate a union he has with his Savior; and the first understanding of this truth may be the gateway through which he passes into a holier and happier stage of the Christian life."

So the Way leads, through the Truth, to the Life (John 14 : 6). Apprehension of an external Savior prepares for the reception and experience of the internal Savior. Christ is first the Door of the sheep, but in him, after they have once entered in, they find pasture (John 10 : 7-9). On the nature of this union, see H. B. Smith, System of Christian Theology, 531-539; Baird, Elohim Revealed, 601; Wilberforce, Incarnation, 208-272, and New Birth of Man's Nature, 1-30. *Per contra*, see Park, Discourses, 117-136.

3. Consequences of this Union as respects the Believer.

We have seen that Christ's union with humanity, at the incarnation, involved him in all the legal liabilities of the race to which he united himself, and enabled him so to assume the penalty of its sin as to make for all men a full satisfaction to the divine justice, and to remove all external obstacles to man's return to God. An internal obstacle, however, still remains — the evil affections and will, and the consequent guilt, of the individual soul. This last obstacle also Christ removes, in the case of all his people, by uniting himself to them in a closer and more perfect manner than that in which he is united to humanity at large. As Christ's union with the race secures the objective reconciliation of the race to God, so Christ's union with believers secures the subjective reconciliation of believers to God.

In Baird, Elohim Revealed, 607-610, in Owen, on Justification, chap. 8, in Boston, Covenant of Grace, chap. 2, and in Dale, Atonement, 265-440, the union of the believer with Christ is made to explain the bearing of our sins by Christ. As we have seen in our discussion of the Atonement, however (page 759), this explains the cause by the effect, and implies that Christ died only for the elect (see review of Dale, in Brit. Quar.

Rev., Apr. 1876 : 221-225). It is not the union of Christ with the believer, but the union of Christ with humanity at large, that explains his taking upon him human guilt and penalty.

Amnesty offered to a rebellious city may be complete, yet it may avail only for those who surrender. Pardon secured from a Governor, upon the ground of the services of an Advocate, may be effectual only when the convict accepts it,— there is no hope for him when he tears up the pardon. Dr. H. E. Robins: "The judicial declaration of acquittal on the ground of the death of Christ, which comes to all men (Rom. 5 : 18), and into the benefits of which they are introduced by natural birth, is inchoate justification, and will become perfected justification through the new birth of the Holy Spirit, unless the working of this divine agent is resisted by the personal moral action of those who are lost." What Dr. Robins calls " inchoate justification " we prefer to call " ideal justification " or "attainable justification." Humanity in Christ is justified, and every member of the race who joins himself to Christ by faith participates in Christ's justification. H. E. Dudley : " Adam's sin holds us all down just as gravity holds all, while Christ's righteousness, though secured for all and accessible to all, involves an effort of will in climbing and grasping which not all will make." Justification in Christ is the birthright of humanity ; but, in order to possess and enjoy it, each of us must claim and appropriate it by faith.

R. W. Dale, Fellowship with Christ, 7 — " When we were created in Christ, the fortunes of the human race for good or evil became his. The Incarnation revealed and fulfilled the relations which already existed between the Son of God and mankind. From the beginning Christ had entered into fellowship with us. When we sinned, he remained in fellowship with us still. Our miseries " [we would add : our guilt] " were his, by his own choice. . . . His fellowship with us is the foundation of our fellowship with him. . . . When I have discovered that by the very constitution of my nature I am to achieve perfection in the power of the life of Another — who is yet not Another, but the very ground of my being — it ceases to be incredible to me that Another — who is yet not Another — should be the Atonement for my sin, and that his relation to God should determine mine."

A tract entitled "The Seven Togethers" sums up the Scripture testimony with regard to the Consequences of the believer's Union with Christ: 1. Crucified together with Christ — Gal. 2 : 20 — συνεσταύρωμαι. 2. Died together with Christ — Col. 2 : 20 — ἀπεθάνετε. 3. Buried together with Christ — Rom. 6 : 4 — συνετάφημεν. 4. Quickened together with Christ — Eph. 2 : 5 — συνεζωοποίησεν. 5. Raised together with Christ — Col. 3 : 1 — συνηγέρθητε. 6. Sufferers together with Christ — Rom. 8 : 17 — συμπάσχομεν. 7. Glorified together with Christ — Rom. 8 : 17 — συνδοξασθῶμεν. Union with Christ results in common sonship, relation to God, character, influence, and destiny.

Imperfect apprehension of the believer's union with Christ works to the great injury of Christian doctrine. An experience of union with Christ first enables us to understand the death of sin and separation from God which has befallen the race sprung from the first Adam. The life and liberty of the children of God in Christ Jesus shows us by contrast how far astray we had gone. The vital and organic unity of the new race sprung from the second Adam reveals the depravity and disintegration which we had inherited from our first father. We see that as there is one source of spiritual life in Christ, so there was one source of corrupt life in Adam ; and that as we are justified by reason of our oneness with the justified Christ, so we are condemned by reason of our oneness with the condemned Adam.

A. H. Strong, Christ in Creation, 175 — " If it is consistent with evolution that the physical and natural life of the race should be derived from a single source, then it is equally consistent with evolution that the moral and spiritual life of the race should be derived from a single source. Scripture is stating only scientific fact when it sets the second Adam, the head of redeemed humanity, over against the first Adam, the head of fallen humanity. We are told that evolution should give us many Christs. We reply that evolution has not given us many Adams. Evolution, as it assigns to the natural head of the race a supreme and unique position, must be consistent with itself, and must assign a supreme and unique position to Jesus Christ, the spiritual head of the race. As there was but one Adam from whom all the natural life of the race was derived, so there can be but one Christ from whom all the spiritual life of the race is derived.'

The consequences of union with Christ may be summarily stated as follows :

(a) Union with Christ involves a change in the dominant affection of the soul. Christ's entrance into the soul makes it a new creature, in the sense that the ruling disposition, which before was sinful, now becomes holy. This change we call *Regeneration*.

Rom. 8 : 2 — "For the law of the Spirit of life in Christ Jesus made me free from the law of sin and of death" ; 2 Cor. 5 : 17 — "if any man is in Christ, he is a new creature" (marg. — "there is a new creation") ; Gal. 1 : 15, 16 — "it was the good pleasure of God . . . . to reveal his Son in me" ; Eph. 2 . 10 — "For we are his workmanship, created in Christ Jesus for good works." As we derive our old nature from the first man Adam, by birth, so we derive a new nature from the second man Christ, by the new birth. Union with Christ is the true "transfusion of blood." "The death-struck sinner, like the wan, anæmic, dying invalid, is saved by having poured into his veins the healthier blood of Christ" (Drummond, Nat. Law in the Spir. World). God regenerates the soul by uniting it to Jesus Christ.

In the Johnston Harvester Works at Batavia, when they paint their machinery, they do it by immersing part after part in a great tank of paint, — so the painting is instantaneous and complete. Our baptism into Christ is the outward picture of an inward immersion of the soul not only into his love and fellowship, but into his very life, so that in him we become new creatures (2 Cor. 5 : 17). As Miss Sullivan surrounded Helen Kellar with the influence of her strong personality, by intelligence and sympathy and determination striving to awaken the blind and dumb soul and give it light and love, so Jesus envelops us. But his Spirit is more encompassing and more penetrating than any human influence however powerful, because his life is the very ground and principle of our being.

Tennyson : "O for a man to arise in me, That the man that I am may cease to be !" Emerson : "Himself from God he could not free ; He builded better than he knew." Religion is not the adding of a new department of activity as an adjunct to our own life or the grafting of a new method of manifestation upon the old. It is rather the grafting of our souls into Christ, so that his life dominates and manifests itself in all our activities. The magnet which left to itself can lift only a three pound weight, will lift three hundred when it is attached to the electric dynamo. Expositor's Greek Testament on 1 Cor. 15 : 45, 46 — "The action of Jesus in 'breathing' upon his disciples while he said, 'Receive the Holy Spirit' (John 20 : 22 *sq.*) symbolized the vitalizing relationship which at this epoch he assumed towards mankind ; this act raised to a higher potency the original 'breathing' of God by which 'man became a living soul' (Gen. 2 : 7)."

(b) Union with Christ involves a new exercise of the soul's powers in repentance and faith ; faith, indeed, is the act of the soul by which, under the operation of God, Christ is received. This new exercise of the soul's powers we call *Conversion* (Repentance and Faith). It is the obverse or human side of Regeneration.

Eph. 3 : 17 — "that Christ may dwell in your hearts through faith" ; 2 Tim. 3 : 15 — "the sacred writings which are able to make thee wise unto salvation through faith which is in Christ Jesus." Faith is the soul's laying hold of Christ as its only source of life, pardon, and salvation. And so we see what true religion is. It is not a moral life ; it is not a determination to be religious ; it is not faith, if by faith we mean an external trust that somehow Christ will save us ; it is nothing less than the life of the soul in God, through Christ his Son. To Christ then we are to look for the origin, continuance and increase of our faith (Luke 17 : 5 — "said unto the Lord, Increase our faith"). Our faith is but a part of "his fulness" of which "we all received, and grace for grace" (John 1 : 16).

A. H. Strong, Sermon before the Baptist World Congress, London, 1905 — "Christianity is summed up in the two facts : Christ *for* us, and Christ *in* us — Christ *for* us upon the Cross, revealing the eternal opposition of holiness to sin, and yet, through God's eternal suffering for sin making objective atonement for us ; and Christ *in* us by his Spirit, renewing in us the lost image of God, and abiding in us as the all-sufficient source of purity and power. Here are the two foci of the Christian ellipse : Christ *for* us, who redeemed us from the curse of the law by being made a curse for us, and Christ *in* us, the hope of glory, whom the apostle calls the mystery of the gospel.

"We need Christ *in* us as well as Christ *for* us. How shall I, how shall society, find healing and purification within ? Let me answer by reminding you of what they did at Chicago. In all the world there was no river more stagnant and fetid than was Chicago River.

Its sluggish stream received the sweepings of the watercraft and the offal of the city, and there was no current to carry the detritus away. There it settled, and bred miasma and fever. At last it was suggested that, by cutting through the low ridge between the city and the Desplaines River, the current could be set running in the opposite direction, and drainage could be secured into the Illinois River and the great Mississippi. At a cost of fifteen millions of dollars the cut was made, and now all the water of Lake Michigan can be relied upon to cleanse that turbid stream. What Chicago River could never do for itself, the great lake now does for it. So no human soul can purge itself of its sin; and what the individual cannot do, humanity at large is powerless to accomplish. Sin has dominion over us, and we are foul to the very depths of our being, until with the help of God we break through the barrier of our self-will, and let the floods of Christ's purifying life flow into us. Then, in an hour, more is done to renew, than all our efforts for years had effected. Thus humanity is saved, individual by individual, not by philosophy, or philanthropy, or self-development, or self-reformation, but simply by joining itself to Jesus Christ, and by being filled in Him with all the fulness of God."

(c) Union with Christ gives to the believer the legal standing and rights of Christ. As Christ's union with the race involves atonement, so the believer's union with Christ involves *Justification.* The believer is entitled to take for his own all that Christ is, and all that Christ has done ; and this because he has within him that new life of humanity which suffered in Christ's death and rose from the grave in Christ's resurrection, — in other words, because he is virtually one person with the Redeemer. In Christ the believer is prophet, priest, and king.

Acts 13. 39 — "by him [lit. : 'in him' = in union with him] every one that believeth is justified " ; Rom. 6 : 7, 8 — "he that hath died is justified from sin . . . . we died with Christ" ; 7 : 4 — "dead to the law through the body of Christ" ; 8 : 1 — "no condemnation to them that are in Christ Jesus" ; 17 — "heirs of God, and joint-heirs with Christ" ; 1 Cor. 1 : 30 — "But of him ye are in Christ Jesus, who was made unto us wisdom from God, and righteousness [justification]" ; 3 : 21, 23 — "all things are yours . . . . and ye are Christ's" ; 6 : 11 — "ye were justified in the name of the Lord Jesus Christ, and in the Spirit of our God " ; 2 Cor. 5 : 14 — "we thus judge, that one died for all, therefore all died " ; 21 — "Him who knew no sin he made to be sin on our behalf ; that we might become the righteousness [justification] of God in him " = God's justified persons, in union with Christ (see pages 760, 761).

Gal. 2 : 20 — "I have been crucified with Christ ; and it is no longer I that live, but Christ liveth in me" ; Eph. 1 : 4, 6 — "chose us in him . . . . to the praise of the glory of his grace, which he freely bestowed on us in the Beloved " ; 2 : 5, 6 — "even when we were dead through our trespasses, made us alive together with Christ . . . . made us to sit with him in the heavenly places, in Christ Jesus " ; Phil. 3 : 8, 9 — "that I may gain Christ, and be found in him, not having a righteousness of mine own, even that which is of the law, but that which is through faith in Christ, the righteousness which is from God by faith " ; 2 Tim. 2 : 11 — "Faithful is the saying : For if we died with him, we shall also live with him." Prophet : Luke 12 : 12 — "the Holy Spirit shall teach you in that very hour what ye ought to say " ; 1 John 2 : 20 — "ye have an anointing from the Holy One, and ye know all things." Priest : 1 Pet. 2 : 5 — "a holy priesthood, to offer up spiritual sacrifices, acceptable to God through Jesus Christ" ; Rev. 20 : 6 — "they shall be priests of God and of Christ" ; 1 Pet. 2 : 9 — "a royal priesthood." King : Rev. 3 : 21 — "He that overcometh, I will give to him to sit down with me in my throne" ; 5 : 10 — "madest them to be unto our God a kingdom and priests." The connection of justification and union with Christ delivers the former from the charge of being a mechanical and arbitrary procedure. As Jonathan Edwards has said : "The justification of the believer is no other than his being admitted to communion in, or participation of, this head and surety of all believers."

(d) Union with Christ secures to the believer the continuously transforming, assimilating power of Christ's life, — first, for the soul ; secondly, for the body, — consecrating it in the present, and in the future raising it up in the likeness of Christ's glorified body. This continuous influence, so far as it is exerted in the present life, we call *Sanctification,* the human side or aspect of which is *Perseverance.*

For the soul : John 1 : 16 — "of his fulness we all received, and grace for grace " — successive and increasing measures of grace, corresponding to the soul's successive and increasing needs ; Rom. 8 : 10 — "if Christ is in you, the body is dead because of sin ; but the spirit is life because of righteousness " ; 1 Cor. 15 : 45 — "The last Adam became a life-giving spirit " ; Phil. 2 : 5 — "Have this mind in you, which was also in Chr.st Jesus " ; 1 John 3 : 2 — " if he shall be manifested, we shall be like him." "Can Christ let the believer fall out of his hands? No, for the believer is his hands."

For the body : 1 Cor. 6 : 17-20 — "he that is joined unto the Lord is one spirit . , . . know ye not that your body is a temple of the Holy Spirit which is in you . . . . glorify God therefore in your body " ; 1 Thess. 5 : 23 — "And the God of peace himself sanctify you wholly ; and may your spirit and soul and body be preserved entire, without blame at the coming of our Lord Jesus Christ " ; Rom. 8 : 11 — "shall give life also to your mortal bodies through his Spirit that dwelleth in you " ; 1 Cor. 15 : 49 — "as we have borne the image of the earthy [man], we shall also bear the image of the heavenly [man] " ; Phil. 3 : 20, 21 — "For our citizenship is in heaven ; from whence also we wait for a Savior, the Lord Jesus Christ : who shall fashion anew the body of our humiliation, that it may be conformed to the body of his glory, according to the working whereby he is able even to subject all things unto himself."

Is there a physical miracle wrought for the drunkard in his regeneration? Mr. Moody says, Yes ; Mr. Gough says, No. We prefer to say that the change is a spiritual one ; but that the " expulsive power of a new affection " indirectly affects the body, so that old appetites sometimes disappear in a moment ; and that often, in the course of years, great changes take place even in the believer's body. Tennyson, Idylls : " Have ye looked at Edyrn ? Have ye seen how nobly changed ? This work of his is great and wonderful ; His very face with change of heart is changed." "Christ in the soul fashions the germinal man into his own likeness, — this is the embryology of the new life. The cardinal error in religious life is the attempt to live without proper environment " (see Drummond, Natural Law in Spiritual World, 253-284). Human life from Adam does not stand the test, — only divine-human life in Christ can secure us from falling. This is the work of Christ, now that he has ascended and taken to himself his power, namely, to give his life more and more fully to the church, until it shall grow up in all things into him, the Head, and shall fitly express his glory to the world.

As the accomplished organist discloses unsuspected capabilities of his instrument, so Christ brings into activity all the latent powers of the human soul. " I was five years in the ministry," said an American preacher, " before I realized that my Savior is alive." Dr. R. W. Dale has left on record the almost unutterable feelings that stirred his soul when he first realized this truth ; see Walker, The Spirit and the Incarnation, preface, v. Many have struggled in vain against sin until they have admitted Christ to their hearts, — then they could say : "this is the victory that hath overcome the world, even our faith" (1 John 5 : 4). "Go out, God will go in ; Die thou, and let him live ; Be not, and he will be ; Wait, and he'll all things give." The best way to get air out of a vessel is to pour water in. Only in Christ can we find our pardon, peace, purity, and power. He is "made unto us wisdom from God, and justification and sanctification, and redemption" (1 Cor. 1 : 30). A medical man says : "The only radical remedy for dipsomania is religiomania" (quoted in William James, Varieties of Religious Experience, 268). It is easy to break into an empty house ; the spirit cast out returns, finds the house empty, brings seven others, and " the last state of that man becometh worse than the first" (Mat. 12 : 45). There is no safety in simply expelling sin ; we need also to bring in Christ ; in fact only he can enable us to expel not only actual sin but the love of it.

Alexander McLaren : " If we are 'in Christ,' we are like a diver in his crystal bell, and have a solid though invisible wall around us, which keeps all sea-monsters off us, and communicates with the upper air, whence we draw the breath of calm life and can work in security though in the ocean depths." John Caird, Fund. Ideas, 2 : 98 — " How do we know that the life of God has not departed from nature? Because every spring we witness the annual miracle of nature's revival, every summer and autumn the waving corn. How do we know that Christ has not departed from the world? Because he imparts to the soul that trusts him a power, a purity, a peace, which are beyond all that nature can give."

(e) Union with Christ brings about a fellowship of Christ with the believer, — Christ takes part in all the labors, temptations, and sufferings of his people ; a fellowship of the believer with Christ, — so that Christ's whole experience on earth is in some measure reproduced in him ; a fellowship of all believers with one another, — furnishing a basis for the spiritual unity of Christ's people on earth, and for the eternal communion of heaven. The doctrine of Union with Christ is therefore the indispensable preparation for *Ecclesiology*, and for *Eschatology*.

Fellowship of Christ with the believer: Phil. 4 : 13 —"I can do all things in him that strengtheneth me"; Heb. 4 : 15 —"For we have not a high priest that cannot be touched with the feeling of our infirmities"; cf. Is. 63 : 9 —"In all their affliction he was afflicted." Heb. 2 : 18 —"in that he himself hath suffered being tempted, he is able to succor them that are tempted "=are being tempted, are under temptation. Bp. Wordsworth : " By his *passion* he acquired *compassion.*" 2 Cor. 2 : 14 — "thanks be unto God, who always leadeth us in triumph in Christ " = Christ leads us in triumph, but his triumph is ours, even if it be a triumph over us. One with him, we participate in his joy and in his sovereignty. Rev. 3 :21 —"He that overcometh, I will give to him to sit down with me in my throne." W. F. Taylor on Rom. 8: 9 —"The Spirit of God dwelleth in you . . . . if any man hath not the Spirit of Christ, he is none of his "—"Christ dwells in us, says the apostle. But do we accept him as a resident, or as a ruler? England was first represented at King Thebau's court by her resident. This official could rebuke, and even threaten, but no more,— Thebau was sovereign. Burma knew no peace, till England ruled. So Christ does not consent to be represented by a mere resident. He must himself dwell within the soul, and he must reign." Christina Rossetti, Thee Only : " Lord, we are rivers running to thy sea, Our waves and ripples all derived from thee; A nothing we should have, a nothing be, Except for thee. Sweet are the waters of thy shoreless sea; Make sweet our waters that make haste to thee; Pour in thy sweetness, that ourselves may be Sweetness to thee ! "

Of the believer with Christ: Phil. 3 : 10 —"that I may know him, and the power of his resurrection, and the fellowship of his sufferings, becoming conformed unto his death "; Col. 1 : 24 —"fill up on my part that which is lacking of the afflictions of Christ in my flesh for his body's sake, which is the church "; 1 Pet. 4 : 13 —"partakers of Christ's sufferings." The Christian reproduces Christ's life in miniature, and, in a true sense, lives it over again. Only upon the principle of union with Christ can we explain how the Christian instinctively applies to himself the prophecies and promises which originally and primarily were uttered with reference to Christ : " thou wilt not leave my soul to Sheol ; Neither wilt thou suffer thy holy one to see corruption " (Ps. 16 : 10, '1). This fellowship is the ground of the promises made to believing prayer : John 14 :13 -"whatsoever ye shall ask in my name, that will I do"; Wescott, Bib. Com., *in loco:* "The meaning of the phrase ['in my name'] is 'as being one with me even as I am revealed to you.' Its two correlatives are 'in me' and the Pauline 'in Christ'." " All things are yours " (1 Cor. 3 : 21), because Christ is universal King, and all believers are exalted to fellowship with him. After the battle of Sedan, King William asked a wounded Prussian officer whether it were well with him. " All is well where your majesty leads!" was the reply. Phil. 1 : 21 —"For to me to live is Christ, and to die is gain." Paul indeed uses the words ' Christ ' and ' church ' as interchangeable terms : 1 Cor 12 : 12 —"as the body is one, and hath many members, ... so also is Christ." Denney, Studies in Theology, 171 —"There is not in the N. T. from beginning to end, in the record of the original and genuine Christian life, a single word of despondency or gloom. It is the most buoyant, exhilerating and joyful book in the world." This is due to the fact that the writers believe in a living and exalted Christ, and know themselves to be one with him. They descend crowned into the arena. In the Soudan, every morning for half an hour before General Gordon's tent there lay a white handkerchief. The most pressing message, even on matters of life and death, waited till that handkerchief was withdrawn. It was the signal that Christ and Gordon were in communion with each other.

Of all believers with one another: John 17 : 21 —"that they may all be one"; 1 Cor. 10 : 17—"we, who are many, are one bread, one body: for we all partake of the one bread "; Eph. 2 : 15 —"create in himself of the two one new man, so making peace "; 1 John 1 : 3 —"that ye also may have fellowship with us : yea, and our fellowship is with the Father, and with his Son Jesus Christ" — here the word κοινωνία is used. Fellowship with each other is the effect and result of the fellowship of each with God in Christ. Compare John 10 : 16 —"they shall become one flock, one shepherd"; Westcott, Bib. Com., *in loco:* "The bond of fellowship is shown to lie in the common relation to one Lord. . . . . Nothing is said of one 'fold' under the new dispensation." Here is a unity, not of external organization, but of common life. Of this the visible church is the consequence and expression. But this communion is not limited to earth,— it is perpetuated beyond death : 1 Thess. 4 : 17 —"so shall we ever be with the Lord "; Heb. 12 : 23 —"to the general assembly and church of the firstborn who are enrolled in heaven, and to God the Judge of all, and to the spirits of just men made perfect"; Rev. 21 and 22— the city of God, the new Jerusalem, is the image of perfect society, as well as of intensity and fulness of life in Christ. The ordinances express the essence of Ecclesiology — union with Christ — for Baptism symbolizes the incorporation of the believer in Christ, while the Lord's Supper symbolizes the incorporation of Christ in the believer. Christianity is a social matter, and the true Christian feels the need of being with and among his brethren. The Romans could not understand why "this new sect " must be holding meetings all the time — even daily meetings. Why could they not go singly, or in families, to the temples, and make offerings to their God, and then come away, as the pagans did ? It was this meeting together which exposed them to persecution and martyrdom. It was the natural and inevitable expression of their union with Christ and so of their union with one another.

The consciousness of union with Christ gives assurance of salvation. It is a great stimulus to believing prayer and to patient labor. It is a duty to "know what is the hope of his calling, what the riches of the glory of his inheritance in the saints, and what the exceeding greatness of his power to us-ward who believe" (Eph. 1 : 18, 19). Christ's command, "Abide in me, and I in you" (John 15 : 4), implies that we are both to realize and to confirm this union, by active exertion of our own wills. We are to abide in him by an entire consecration, and to let him abide in us by an appropriating faith. We are to give ourselves to Christ, and to take in return the Christ who gives himself to us,—in other words, we are to believe Christ's promises and to act upon them. All sin consists in the sundering of man's life from God, and most systems of falsehood in religion are attempts to save man without merging his life in God's once more. The only religion that can save mankind is the religion that fills the whole heart and the whole life with God, and that aims to interpenetrate universal humanity with that same living Christ who has already made himself one with the believer. This consciousness of union with Christ gives "boldness" (παρρησία — Acts 4 : 13 ; 1 John 5 : 14) toward men and toward God. The word belongs to the Greek democracies. Freemen are bold. Demosthenes boasts of his frankness. Christ frees us from the hidebound, introspective, self-conscious spirit. In him we become free, demonstrative, outspoken. So we find, in John's epistles, that boldness in prayer is spoken of as a virtue, and the author of the Epistle to the Hebrews urges us to "draw near with boldness unto the throne of grace " (Heb. 4 : 16). An engagement of marriage is not the same as marriage. The parties may be still distant from each other. Many Christians get just near enough to Christ to be engaged to him. This seems to be the experience of Christian in the Pilgrim's Progress. But our privilege is to have a present Christ, and to do our work not only *for* him, but *in* him. "Since Christ and we are one, Why should we doubt or fear ? " " We two are so joined, He 'll not be in heaven, And leave me behind."

We append a few statements with regard to this union and its consequences, from noted names in theology and the church. Luther: "By faith thou art so glued to Christ that of thee and him there becomes as it were one person, so that with confidence thou canst say : 'I am Christ,— that is, Christ's righteousness, victory, *etc.*, are mine; and Christ in turn can say : 'I am that sinner,— that is, his sins, his death, *etc.*, are mine, because he clings to me and I to him, for we have been joined through faith into one flesh and bone.'" Calvin: "I attribute the highest importance to the connection between the head and the members ; to the inhabitation of Christ in our hearts ; in a word, to the mystical union by which we enjoy him, so that, being made ours, he makes us partakers of the blessings with which he is furnished." John Bunyan: "The Lord led me into the knowledge of the mystery of union with Christ, that I was joined to him, that I was bone of his bone and flesh of his flesh. By this also my faith in him as my righteousness was the more confirmed ; for if he and I were one, then his righteousness was mine, his merits mine, his victory also mine. Now could I see myself in heaven and on earth at once — in heaven by my Christ, my risen head, my righteousness and life, though on earth by my body or person." Edwards: "Faith is the soul's active uniting with Christ. God sees fit that, in order to a union's being established between two intelligent active beings, there should be the mutual act of both, that each should receive the other, as entirely joining themselves to one another." Andrew Fuller: " I have no doubt that the imputation of Christ's righteousness presupposes a union with him ; since there is no preceivable fitness in bestowing benefits on one for another's sake, where there is no union or relation between."

See Luther, quoted, with other references, in Thomasius, Christi Person und Werk, 3 : 325. See also Calvin, Institutes, 1 : 660 ; Edwards, Works, 4 : 66, 69, 70; Andrew Fuller, Works, 2 : 685; Pascal, Thoughts, Eng. trans., 429; Hooker, Eccl. Polity, book 5, ch. 56 ; Tillotson, Sermons, 3 : 307 ; Trench, Studies in Gospels, 284, and Christ the True Vine, in Hulsean Lectures; Schöberlein, in Studien und Kritiken, 1847 : 7–69; Caird, on Union with God, in Scotch Sermons, sermon 2 ; Godet, on the Ultimate Design of Man, in Princeton Rev., Nov. 1880 — the design is "God in man, and man in God"; Baird, Elohim Revealed, 590–617; Upham, Divine Union, Interior Life, Life of Madame Guyon and Fénelon ; A. J. Gordon, In Christ; McDuff, In Christo ; J. Denham Smith, Lifetruths, 25–98 ; A. H. Strong, Philosophy and Religion, 220–225; Bishop Hall's Treatise on The Church Mystical ; Andrew Murray, Abide in Christ ; Stearns, Evidence of Christian Experience, 145, 174, 179 ; F. B. Meyer, Christian Living—essay on Appropriation of

Christ, *vs.* mere imitation of Christ; Sanday, Epistle to the Romans, supplementary essay on the Mystic Union; H. B. Smith, System of Theology, 531; J. M. Campbell, The Indwelling Christ.

II. REGENERATION.

Regeneration is that act of God by which the governing disposition of the soul is made holy, and by which, through the truth as a means, the first holy exercise of this disposition is secured.

Regeneration, or the new birth, is the divine side of that change of heart which, viewed from the human side, we call conversion. It is God's turning the soul to himself,— conversion being the soul's turning itself to God, of which God's turning it is both the accompaniment and cause. It will be observed from the above definition, that there are two aspects of regeneration, in the first of which the soul is passive, in the second of which the soul is active. God changes the governing disposition,— in this change the soul is simply acted upon. God secures the initial exercise of this disposition in view of the truth,— in this change the soul itself acts. Yet these two parts of God's operation are simultaneous. At the same moment that he makes the soul sensitive, he pours in the light of his truth and induces the exercise of the holy disposition he has imparted.

This distinction betweeen the passive and the active aspects of regeneration is necessitated, as we shall see, by the twofold method of representing the change in Scripture. In many passages the change is ascribed wholly to the power of God; the change is a change in the fundamental disposition of the soul; there is no use of means. In other passages we find truth referred to as an agency employed by the Holy Spirit, and the mind acts in view of this truth. The distinction between these two aspects of regeneration seems to be intimated in Eph. 2 : 5, 6 —"made us alive together with Christ," and "raised us up with him." Lazarus must first be made alive, and in this he could *not* coöperate; but he must also come forth from the tomb, and in this he *could* be active. In the old photography, the plate was first made sensitive, and in this the plate was passive; then it was exposed to the object, and now the plate actively seized upon the rays of light which the object emitted.

Availing ourselves of the illustration from photography, we may compare God's initial work in the soul to the sensitizing of the plate, his next work to the pouring in of the light and the production of the picture. The soul is first made receptive to the truth; then it is enabled actually to receive the truth. But the illustration fails in one respect,— it represents the two aspects of regeneration as successive. In regeneration there is no chronological succession. At the same instant that God makes the soul sensitive, he also draws out its new sensibility in view of the truth. Let us notice also that, as in photography the picture however perfect needs to be developed, and this development takes time, so regeneration is only the beginning of God's work; not all the dispositions, but only the governing disposition, is made holy; there is still need that sanctification should follow regeneration; and sanctification is a work of God which lasts for a whole lifetime. We may add that " heredity affects regeneration as the quality of the film affects photography, and environment affects regeneration as the focus affects photography " (W. T. Thayer).

Sacramentarianism has so obscured the doctrine of Scripture that many persons who gave no evidence of being regenerate are quite convinced that they are Christians. Uncle John Vassar therefore never asked : " Are you a Christian ? " but always : " Have you ever been born again ? " E. G. Robinson : " The doctrine of regeneration, aside from sacramentarianism, was not apprehended by Luther or the Reformers, was not indeed wrought out till Wesley taught that God instantaneously renewed the affections and the will." We get the doctrine of regeneration mainly from the apostle John, as we get the doctrine of justification mainly from the apostle Paul. Stevens, Johannine Theology, 366 —" Paul's great words are, justification, and righteousness ; John's are, birth from God, and life. But, for both Paul and John, faith is life-union with Christ.'

Stearns, Evidence of Christian Experience, 134 —" The sinful nature is not gone, but its power is broken ; sin no longer dominates the life ; it has been thrust from the centre to the circumference; it has the sentence of death in itself; the man is freed, at least in potency and promise. 218 — An activity may be immediate, yet not unmediated. God's action on the soul may be through the sense, yet still be immediate, as when finite spirits communicate with each other." Dubois, in Century Magazine, Dec. 1894: 233 — " Man has made his way up from physical conditions to the consciousness of spiritual needs. Heredity and environment fetter him. He needs spiritual help. God provides a spiritual environment in regeneration. As science is the verification of the ideal in nature, so religion is the verification of the spiritual in human life." Last sermon of Seth K. Mitchell on Rev. 21 : 5 — "Behold, I make all things new" — " God first makes a new man, then gives him a new heart, then a new commandment. He also gives a new body, a new name, a new robe, a new song, and a new home."

1. Scripture Representations.

(a) Regeneration is a change indispensable to the salvation of the sinner.

John 3 : 7 —" Ye must be born anew "; Gal. 6 : 15—"neither is circumcision anything, nor uncircumcision, but a new creature " (marg.—" creation ") ; cf. Heb. 12 : 14 —"the sanctification without which no man shall see the Lord " — regeneration, therefore, is yet more necessary to salvation ; Eph. 2 : 3—" by nature children of wrath, even as the rest "; Rom. 3 : 11 —"There is none that understandeth, There is none that seeketh after God "; John 6 : 44, 65 —"No man can come to me, except the Father that sent me draw him . . . . no man can come unto me, except it be given unto him of the Father "; Jer. 13 : 23 —"Can the Ethiopian change his skin, or the leopard his spots? then may ye also do good, that are accustomed to do evil."

(b) It is a change in the inmost principle of life.

John 3 : 3 —" Except one be born anew, he cannot see the kingdom of God "; 5 : 21 —"as the Father raiseth the dead and giveth them life, even so the Son also giveth life to whom he will "; Rom. 6 : 13 —"present yourselves unto God, as alive from the dead "; Eph. 2 : 1 —"And you did he make alive, when ye were dead through your trespasses and sins "; 5 :14 —" Awake, thou that sleepest, and arise from the dead, and Christ shall shine upon thee." In John 3 : 3 — " born anew "= not, " altered," " influenced," " reinvigorated," " reformed " ; but a new beginning, a new stamp or character, a new family likeness to God and to his children. " So is every one that is born of the Spirit " (John 3 : 8) == 1. secrecy of process ; 2. independence of the will of man ; 3. evidence given in results of conduct and life. It is a good thing to remove the means of gratifying an evil appetite ; but how much better it is to remove the appetite itself ! It is a good thing to save men from frequenting dangerous resorts by furnishing safe places of recreation and entertainment ; but far better is it to implant within the man such a love for all that is pure and good, that he will instinctively shun the impure and evil. Christianity aims to purify the springs of action.

(c) It is a change in the heart, or governing disposition.

Mat. 12 : 33, 35 —" Either make the tree good, and its fruit good ; or make the tree corrupt, and its fruit corrupt : for the tree is known by its fruit. . . . . The good man out of his good treasure bringeth forth good things : and the evil man out of his evil treasure bringeth forth evil things "; 15 :19 —" For out of the heart come forth evil thoughts, murders, adulteries, fornications, thefts, false witness, railings " ; Acts 16 : 14 —"And a certain woman named Lydia . . . . heard us : whose heart the Lord opened to give heed unto the things which were spoken by Paul "; Rom. 6 : 17 —"But thanks be to God, that, whereas ye were servants of sin, ye became obedient from the heart to that form of teaching whereunto ye were delivered "; 10 : 10 —"with the heart man believeth unto righteousness " ; cf. Ps. 51 : 10 —"Create in me a clean heart, O God ; And renew a right spirit within me "; Jer. 31 : 33 —"I will put my law in their inward parts, and in their hearts will I write it "; Ez. 11 : 19 —"And I will give them one heart, and I will put a new spirit within you ; and I will take the stony heart out of their flesh, and will give them a heart of flesh."

Horace Mann : " One former is worth a hundred reformers." It is often said that the redemption of society is as important as the regeneration of the individual. Yes, we reply ; but the regeneration of society can never be accomplished except through the regeneration of the individual. Reformers try in vain to construct a stable and happy community from persons who are selfish, weak, and miserable. The first cry of such reformers is : " Get your circumstances changed ! " Christ's first call is : " Get yourselves changed, and then the things around you will be changed." Many college settlements, and temperance societies, and self-reformations begin at the wrong end. They are like kindling a coal-fire by lighting kindlings at the top. The fire soon goes out. We need God's work at the very basis of character and not on the outer edge, at the very beginning, and not simply at the end. Mat. 6 : 33 —" seek ye first his kingdom, and his righteousness ; and all these things shall be added unto you."

(d) It is a change in the moral relations of the soul.

Eph. 2 : 5—"when we were dead through our trespasses, made us alive us together with Christ"; 4 : 23, 24 —"that ye be renewed in the spirit of your mind, and put on the new man, that after God hath been created in righteousness and holiness of truth"; Col. 1 : 13 —"who delivered us out of the power of darkness, and translated us into the kingdom of the Son of his love." William James, Varieties of Religious Experience, 508, finds the features belonging to all religions : 1. an uneasiness; and 2. its solution. 1. The uneasiness, reduced to its simplest terms, is a sense that there is *something wrong about us*, as we naturally stand. 2. The solution is a sense that we are *saved from the wrongness* by making proper connection with the higher powers.

(e) It is a change wrought in connection with the use of truth as a means.

James 1 : 18 —"Of his own will he brought us forth by the word of truth"— here in connection with the special agency of God (not of mere natural law) the truth is spoken of as a means; 1 Pet. 1 : 23 —"having been begotten again, not of corruptible seed, but of incorruptible, through the word of God, which liveth and abideth "; 2 Pet. 1 : 4 —"his precious and exceeding great promises; that through these ye may become partakers of the divine nature"; *cf.* Jer. 23 : 29 —"Is not my word like fire? saith Jehovah; and like a hammer that breaketh the rock in pieces? " John 15 : 3 —"Already ye are clean because of the word which I have spoken unto you "; Eph. 6 : 17 —"the sword of the Spirit, which is the word of God"; Heb. 4 : 12 —"For the word of God is living, and active, and sharper than any two-edged sword, and piercing even to the dividing of soul and spirit, of both joints and marrow, and quick to discern the thoughts and intents of the heart"; 1 Pet. 2 : 9 —"called you out of darkness into his marvellous light." An advertising sign reads : " For spaces and ideas, apply to Johnson and Smith." In regeneration, we need both the open mind and the truth to instruct it, and we may apply to God for both.

(f) It is a change instantaneous, secretly wrought, and known only in its results.

John 5 : 24 —"He that heareth my word, and believeth him that sent me, hath eternal life, and cometh not into judgment, but hath passed out of death into life"; *cf.* Mat. 6 : 24 —"No man can serve two masters: for either he will hate the one, and love the other ; or else he will hold to one, and despise the other." John 3 : 8 —"The wind bloweth where it will, and and thou hearest the voice thereof, but knowest not whence it cometh, and whither it goeth: so is every one that is born of the Spirit "; *cf.* Phil. 2 : 12, 13 — "work out your own salvation with fear and trembling ; for it is God who worketh in you both to will and to work, for his good pleasure " ; 2 Pet. 1 : 10 — "Wherefore, brethren give the more diligence to make your calling and election sure."

(g) It is a change wrought by God.

John 1 : 13 —"who were born, not of blood, nor of the will of the flesh, nor of the will of man, but of God "; 3 : 5 — "Except one be born of water and the Spirit, he cannot enter into the kingdom of God ;" 3 : 8, marg.—"The Spirit breatheth where it will"; Eph. 1 : 19, 20 —"the exceeding greatness of his power to us-ward who believe, according to that working of the strength of his might which he wrought in Christ, when he raised him from the dead, and made him to sit at his right hand in the heavenly places "; 2 : 10 —"For we are his workmanship, created in Christ Jesus for good works, which God afore prepared that we should walk in them "; 1 Pet. 1 : 3 —"Blessed be the God and Father of our Lord Jesus Christ, who according to his great mercy begat us again unto a living hope by the resurrection of Jesus Christ from the dead"; *cf.* 1 Cor. 3 : 6, 7 —"I planted, Apollos watered ; but God gave the increase. So then neither is he that planteth anything, neither he that watereth ; but God that giveth the increase."

We have seen that we are "begotten again . . . . through the word " (1 Pet. 1 : 23). In the revealed truth with regard to the person and work of Christ there is a divine adaptation to the work of renewing our hearts. But truth in itself is powerless to regenerate and sanctify, unless the Holy Spirit uses it —"the sword of the Spirit, which is the word of God " (Eph. 6 :17). Hence regeneration is ascribed preëminently to the Holy Spirit, and men are said to be "born of the Spirit" (John 3 : 8). When Robert Morrison started for China, an incredulous American said to him : " Mr. Morrison, do you think you can make any impression on the Chinese? " " No," was the reply; " but I think the Lord can."

(h) It is a change accomplished through the union of the soul with Christ.

Rom. 8 : 2 —"For the law of the Spirit of life in Christ Jesus made me free from the law of sin and death"; 2 Cor. 5 :17 —"if any man is in Christ, he is a new creature " (marg.—"there is a new creation"); Gal. 1 :15, 16 —"it was the good pleasure of God . . . . to reveal his Son in me "; Eph. 2 : 10 —"For we are his workmanship, created in Christ Jesus for good works." On the Scriptural representations, see E. D. Griffin, Divine Efficiency, 117–164 ; H. B. Smith, System of Theology, 553–569 —" Regeneration involves union with Christ, and not a change of heart without relation to him."

Eph. 3 : 14, 15 —"the Father, from whom every fatherhood in heaven and on earth is named." But even here God works through Christ, and Christ himself is called "Everlasting Father " (Is. 9 : 6). The real basis of our sonship and unity is in Christ, our Creator, and Upholder. Sin is repudiation of this filial relationship. Regeneration by the Spirit restores our sonship by joining us once more, ethically and spiritually, to Christ the Son, and so adopting us again into God's family. Hence the Holy Spirit does not reveal himself, but Christ. The Spirit is light, and light does not reveal itself, but all other things. I may know that the Holy Spirit is working within me whenever I more clearly perceive Christ. Sonship in Christ makes us not only individually children of God, but also members of a commonwealth. Ps. 87 : 4—"Yea, of Zion it shall be said, This one and that one was born in her"="the most glorious thing to be said about them is not something pertaining to their separate history, but that they have become members, by adoption, of the city of God" (Perowne). The Psalm speaks of the adoption of nations, but it is equally true of individuals.

2. *Necessity of Regeneration.*

That all men without exception need to be changed in moral character, is manifest, not only from Scripture passages already cited, but from the following rational considerations :

(a) Holiness, or conformity to the fundamental moral attribute of God, is the indispensable condition of securing the divine favor, of attaining peace of conscience, and of preparing the soul for the associations and employments of the blest.

Phillips Brooks seems to have taught that regeneration is merely a natural forward step in man's development. See his Life, 2 : 353 —"The entrance into this deeper consciousness of sonship to God and into the motive power which it exercises is Regeneration, the new birth, not merely with reference to time, but with reference also to profoundness. Because man has something sinful to cast away in order to enter this higher life, therefore regeneration must begin with repentance. But that is an incident. It is not essential to the idea. A man simply imperfect and not sinful would still have to be born again. The presentation of sin as guilt, of release as forgiveness, of consequence as punishment, have their true meaning as the most personal expressions of man's moral condition as always measured by, and man's moral changes as always dependent upon, God." Here imperfection seems to mean depraved condition as distinguished from conscious transgression ; it is not regarded as sinful ; it needs not to be repented of. Yet it does require regeneration. In Phillips Brooks's creed there is no article devoted to sin. Baptism he calls "the declaration of the universal fact of the sonship of man to God. The Lord's Supper is the declaration of the universal fact of man's dependence upon God for supply of life. It is associated with the death of Jesus, because in that the truth of God giving himself to man found its completest manifestation."

Others seem to teach regeneration by education. Here too there is no recognition of inborn sin or guilt. Man's imperfection of nature is innocent. He needs training in order to fit him for association with higher intelligences and with God. In the evolution of his powers there comes a natural crisis, like that of graduation of the scholar, and this crisis may be called conversion. This educational theory of regeneration is represented by Starbuck, Psychology of Religion, and by Coe, The Spiritual Life. What human nature needs however is not evolution, but involution and revolution — involution, the communication of a new life, and revolution, change of direction resulting from that life. Human nature, as we have seen in our treatment of sin, is not a green apple to be perfected by mere growth, but an apple with a worm at the core, which left to itself will surely rot and perish.

President G. Stanley Hall, in his essay on The Religious Affirmations of Psychology, says that the total depravity of man is an ascertained fact apart from the teachings of the Bible. There had come into his hands for inspection several thousands of letters written to a medical man who advertised that he would give confidential advice and treatment to all, secretly. On the strength of these letters Dr. Hall was prepared to say that John Calvin had not told the half of what is true. He declared that the necessity of regeneration in order to the development of character was clearly established from psychological investigation.

A. H. Strong, Cleveland Sermon, 1904—"Here is the danger of some modern theories of Christian education. They give us statistics, to show that the age of puberty is the age of strongest religious impressions; and the inference is drawn that conversion is nothing but a natural phenomenon, a regular stage of development. The free will, and the evil bent of that will, are forgotten, and the absolute dependence of perverse human nature upon the regenerating spirit of God. The age of puberty is the age of the strongest religious impressions? Yes, but it is also the age of the strongest artistic and social and sensuous impressions, and only a new birth from above can lead the soul to seek first the kingdom of God."

(b) The condition of universal humanity as by nature depraved, and, when arrived at moral consciousness, as guilty of actual transgression, is precisely the opposite of that holiness without which the soul cannot exist in normal relation to God, to self, or to holy beings.

Plutarch has a parable of a man who tried to make a dead body stand upright, but who finished his labors saying: "Deest aliquid intus"—"There's something lacking inside." Ribot, Diseases of the Will, 53—"In the vicious man the moral elements are lacking. If the idea of amendment arises, it is involuntary. . . . But if a first element is not given by nature, and with it a potential energy, nothing results. The theological dogma of grace as a free gift appears to us therefore founded upon a much more exact psychology than the contrary opinion." "Thou art chained to the wheel of the foe By links which a world cannot sever: With thy tyrant through storm and through calm thou shall go, And thy sentence is bondage forever."

Martensen, Christian Ethics: "When Kant treats of the radical evil of human nature, he makes the remarkable statement that, if a good will is to appear in us, this cannot happen through a partial improvement, nor through any reform, but only through a revolution, a total overturn within us, that is to be compared to a new creation." Those who hold that man may attain perfection by mere natural growth deny this radical evil of human nature, and assume that our nature is a good seed which needs only favorable external influences of moisture and sunshine to bring forth good fruit. But human nature is a damaged seed, and what comes of it will be aborted and stunted like itself. The doctrine of mere development denies God's holiness, man's sin, the need of Christ, the necessity of atonement, the work of the Holy Spirit, the justice of penalty. Kant's doctrine of the radical evil of human nature, like Aristotle's doctrine that man is born on an inclined plane and subject to a downward gravitation, is not matched by a corresponding doctrine of regeneration. Only the apostle Paul can tell us how we came to be in this dreadful predicament, and where is the power that can deliver us; see Stearns, Evidence of Christian Experience, 274.

Dean Swift's worthy sought many years for a method of extracting sunbeams from cucumbers. We cannot cure the barren tree by giving it new bark or new branches, —it must have new sap. Healing snakebites is not killing the snake. Poetry and music, the uplifting power of culture, the inherent nobility of man, the general mercy of God—no one of these will save the soul. Horace Bushnell: "The soul of all improvement is the improvement of the soul." Frost cannot be removed from a window pane simply by scratching it away,—you must raise the temperature of the room. It is as impossible to get regeneration out of reformation as to get a harvest out of a field by mere plowing. Reformation is plucking bitter apples from a tree, and in their place tying good apples on with a string (Dr. Pentecost). It is regeneration or degradation —the beginning of an upward movement by a power not man's own, or the continuance and increase of a downward movement that can end only in ruin.

Kidd, Social Evolution, shows that in humanity itself there resides no power of progress. The ocean steamship that has burned its last pound of coal may proceed on its course by virtue of its momentum, but it is only a question of the clock how soon it will cease to move, except as tossed about by the wind and the waves. Not only is there power lacking for the good, but apart from God's grace the evil tendencies constantly became more aggravated. The settled states of the affections and will practically dominate the life. Charles H. Spurgeon: "If a thief should get into heaven unchanged, he would begin by picking the angels' pockets." The land is full of examples of the descent of man, not *from* the brute, but *to* the brute. The tares are not degenerate wheat, which by cultivation will become good wheat,—they are not only useless but noxious, and they must be rooted out and burned. "Society never will be better than the individuals who compose it. A sound ship can never be made of rotten timber. Individual reformation must precede social reconstruction." Socialism will always be a failure until it becomes Christian. We must be born from above, as truly as we have been begotten by our fathers upon earth, or we cannot see the kingdom of God.

(c) A radical internal change is therefore requisite in every human soul —a change in that which constitutes its character. Holiness cannot be attained, as the pantheist claims, by a merely natural growth or development, since man's natural tendencies are wholly in the direction of selfishness. There must be a reversal of his inmost dispositions and principles of action, if he is to see the kingdom of God.

Men's good deeds and reformation may be illustrated by eddies in a stream whose general current is downward; by walking westward in a railway-car while the train is going east; by Capt. Parry's traveling north, while the ice-floe on which he walked was moving southward at a rate much more rapid than his walking. It is possible to be "ever learning, and never able to come to the knowledge of the truth" (2 Tim. 3:7). Better never have been born, than not be born again. But the necessity of regeneration implies its possibility : John 3:7— "Ye must be born anew" = ye may be born anew,— the text is not merely a warning and a command,— it is also a promise. Every sinner has the chance of making a new start and of beginning a new life.

J. D. Robertson, The Holy Spirit and Christian Service, 57 — "Emerson says that the gate of gifts closes at birth. After a man emerges from his mother's womb he can have no new endowments, no fresh increments of strength and wisdom, joy and grace within. The only grace is the grace of creation. But this view is deistic and not Christian." Emerson's saying is true of natural gifts, but not of spiritual gifts. He forgot Pentecost. He forgot the all-encompassing atmosphere of the divine personality and love, and its readiness to enter in at every chink and crevice of our voluntary being. The longing men have to turn over a new leaf in life's book, to break with the past, to assert their better selves, is a preliminary impulse of God's Spirit and an evidence of prevenient grace preparing the way for regeneration. Thus interpreted and yielded to, these impulses warrant unbounded hope for the future. "No star is ever lost we once have seen; We always may be what we might have been; The hopes that lost in some far distance seem May be the truer life, and this the dream."

The greatest minds feel, at least at times, their need of help from above. Although Cicero uses the term 'regeneration' to signify what we should call naturalization, yet he recognizes man's dependence upon God: "Nemo vir magnus, sine aliquo divino afflatu, unquam fuit." Seneca: "Bonus vir sine illo nemo est." Aristotle: "Wickedness perverts the judgment and makes men err with respect to practical principles, so that no man can be wise and judicious who is not good." Goethe: "Who ne'er his bread in sorrow ate, Who ne'er the mournful midnight hours Weeping upon his bed has sate, He knows you not, ye heavenly Powers." Shakespeare, King Lear: "Is there a reason in nature for these hard hearts?" Robert Browning, in Halbert and Hob, replies: "O Lear, That a reason out of nature must turn them soft, seems clear."

John Stuart Mill (see Autobiography, 132-142) knew that the feeling of interest in others' welfare would make him happy,— but the knowledge of this fact did not give him the feeling. The "enthusiasm of humanity"—unselfish love, of which we read in "Ecce Homo"—is easy to talk about; but how to produce it,—that is the question. Drummond, Natural Law in the Spiritual World, 61-94 — "There is no abiogenesis in the spiritual, more than in the natural, world. Can the stone grow more and more living until it enters the organic world ? No, Christianity is a new life,—it is Christ in you." As natural life comes to us mediately, through Adam, so spiritual life comes to us mediately, through Christ. See Bushnell, Nature and the Supernatural, 220-249; Anderson, Regeneration, 51-88; Bennet Tyler, Memoir and Lectures, 340-354.

3. *The Efficient Cause of Regeneration.*

Three views only need be considered, — all others are modifications of these. The first view puts the efficient cause of regeneration in the human will ; the second, in the truth considered as a system of motives; the third, in the immediate agency of the Holy Spirit.

John Stuart Mill regarded cause as embracing all the antecedents to an event. Hazard, Man a Creative First Cause, 12-15, shows that, as at any given instant the whole past is everywhere the same, the effects must, upon this view, at each instant be everywhere one and the same. "The theory that, of every successive event, the real cause is the whole of the antecedents, does not distinguish between the passive conditions acted upon and changed, and the active agencies which act upon and change them; does not distinguish what *produces*, from what merely *precedes*, change."

We prefer the definition given by Porter, Human Intellect, 592 — Cause is "the most conspicuous and prominent of the agencies, or conditions, that produce a result"; or that of Dr. Mark Hopkins: "Any exertion or manifestation of energy that produces a change is a cause, and nothing else is. We must distinguish cause from occasion, or material. Cause is not to be defined as 'everything without which the effect could not be realized.'" Better still, perhaps, may we say, that efficient cause is the competent producing power by which the effect is secured. James Martineau, Types, 1 : preface, xiii — "A cause is that which determines the indeterminate." Not the light, but the photographer, is the cause of the picture; light is but the photographer's servant. So the "word of God" is the "sword of the Spirit" (Eph. 6 : 17); the Spirit uses the word as his instrument; but the Spirit himself is the cause of regeneration.

A. The human will, as the efficient cause of regeneration.

This view takes two forms, according as the will is regarded as acting apart from, or in conjunction with, special influences of the truth applied by God. Pelagians hold the former; Arminians the latter.

(*a*) To the Pelagian view, that regeneration is solely the act of man, and is identical with self-reformation, we object that the sinner's depravity, since it consists in a fixed state of the affections which determines the settled character of the volitions, amounts to a moral inability. Without a renewal of the affections from which all moral action springs, man will not choose holiness nor accept salvation.

Man's volitions are practically the shadow of his affections. It is as useless to think of a man's volitions separating themselves from his affections, and drawing him towards God, as it is to think of a man's shadow separating itself from him, and leading him in the opposite direction to that in which he is going. Man's affections, to use Calvin's words, are like horses that have thrown off the charioteer and are running wildly, — they need a new hand to direct them. In disease, we must be helped by a physician. We do not stop a locomotive engine by applying force to the wheels, but by reversing the lever. So the change in man must be, not in the transient volitions, but in the deeper springs of action — the fundamental bent of the affections and will. See Henslow, Evolution, 134. Shakespeare, All's Well that Ends Well, 2 : 1 : 149 — "It is not so with Him that all things knows, As 'tis with us that square our guess with shows; But most it is presumption in us when The help of heaven we count the act of men."

Henry Clay said that he did not know for himself personally what the change of heart spoken of by Christians meant; but he had seen Kentucky family feuds of long standing healed by religious revivals, and that whatever could heal a Kentucky family feud was more than human. — Mr. Peter Harvey was a lifelong friend of Daniel Webster. He wrote a most interesting volume of reminiscenses of the great man. He tells how one John Colby married the oldest sister of Mr. Webster. Said Mr. Webster of John Colby: "Finally he went up to Andover, New Hampshire, and bought a farm, and the only recollection I have about him is that he was called the wickedest man in the neighborhood, so far as swearing and impiety went. I used to wonder how my sister could marry so profane a man as John Colby." Years afterwards news comes to Mr. Webster that a wonderful change has passed upon John Colby. Mr. Harvey and Mr. Webster take a journey together to visit John Colby. As Mr. Webster enters John Colby's house, he sees open before him a large-print Bible, which he has just been reading. When greetings have been interchanged, the first question John Colby asks of Mr. Webster is, "Are you a Christian?" And then, at John Colby's suggestion, the two men kneel and pray together. When the visit is done, this is what Mr. Webster says to Mr. Harvey as they ride away: "I should like to know what the enemies of religion would say to John Colby's conversion. There was a man as unlikely, humanly speaking, to become a Christian as any man I ever saw. He was reckless, heedless, impious, never attended church, never experienced the good influence of associating with religious people. And here he has been living on in that reckless way until he has got to be an old man, until a period of life when you naturally would not expect his habits to change. And yet he has been brought into the condition in which we have seen him to-day, — a penitent, trusting, humble believer." "Whatever people may say," added Mr. Webster, "nothing can convince me that anything short of the grace of Almighty God could make such a change as I, with my own eyes, have witnessed in the life of John Colby." When they got back to Franklin, New Hampshire, in the evening, they met another lifelong friend of Mr. Webster's, John Taylor, standing at his door. Mr. Webster called out: "Well, John Taylor, miracles happen in these latter days as well as in the days of old." "What now, Squire?" asked John Taylor. "Why," replied Mr. Webster, "John Colby has become a Christian. If that is not a miracle, what is?"

(*b*) To the Arminian view, that regeneration is the act of man, coöperating with divine influences applied through the truth (synergistic theory), we object that no beginning of holiness is in this way conceivable. For, so long as man's selfish and perverse affections are unchanged, no choosing God is possible but such as proceeds from supreme desire for one's own interest and happiness. But the man thus supremely bent on self-gratification cannot see in God, or his service, anything productive of happiness; or, if he could see in them anything of advantage, his choice of God and his service from such a motive would not be a holy choice, and therefore could not be a beginning of holiness.

Although Melanchthon (1497-1560) preceded Arminius (1560-1609), his view was substantially the same with that of the Dutch theologian. Melanchthon never experienced the throes and travails of a new spiritual life, as Luther did. His external and internal development was peculiarly placid and serene. This Præceptor Germaniæ had the modesty of the genuine scholar. He was not a dogmatist, and he never entered the ranks of the ministry. He never could be pursuaded to accept the degree of Doctor of Theology, though he lectured on theological subjects to audiences of thousands. Dorner says of Melanchthon: "He held at first that the Spirit of God is the primary, and the word of God the secondary, or instrumental, agency in conversion, while the human will allows their action and freely yields to it." Later, he held that " conversion is the result of the combined action (*copulatio*) of three causes, the truth of God, the Holy Spirit, and the will of man." This synergistic view in his last years involved the theologian of the German Reformation in serious trouble. Luthardt: "He made a *facultas* out of a mere *capacitas*." Dorner says again: "Man's causality is not to be coördinated with that of God, however small the influence ascribed to it. It is a purely *receptive*, not a productive, agency. The opposite is the fundamental Romanist error." Self-love will never induce a man to give up self-love. Selfishness will not throttle and cast out selfishness. " Such a choice from a selfish motive would be unholy, when judged by God's standard. It is absurd to make salvation depend upon the exercises of a wholly unspiritual power "; see Dorner, Glaubenslehre, 2 : 716-720 (Syst. Doct., 4 : 179-183). Shedd, Dogm. Theol., 2 : 505 — " Sin does not first stop, and then holiness come in place of sin ; but holiness positively expels sin. Darkness does not first cease, and then light enter ; but light drives out darkness." On the Arminian view, see Bib. Sac., 19 : 265, 266.

John Wesley's theology was a modified Arminianism, yet it was John Wesley who did most to establish the doctrine of regeneration. He asserted that the Holy Spirit acts through the truth, in distinction from the doctrine that the Holy Spirit works solely through the ministers and sacraments of the church. But in asserting the work of the Holy Spirit in the individual soul, he went too far to the oppo site extreme of emphasizing the ability of man to choose God's service, when without love to God there was nothing in God's service to attract. A. H. Bradford, Age of Faith: "It is as if Jesus had said: If a sailor will properly set his rudder the wind will fill his sails. The will is the rudder of the character; if it is turned in the right direction, all the winds of heaven will favor; if it is turned in the wrong direction, they will oppose." The question returns: What shall move the man to set his rudder aright, if he has no desire to reach the proper haven? Here is the need of divine power, not merely to coöperate with man, after man's will is set in the right direction, but to set it in the right direction in the first place. Phil. 2:13 — "it is God who worketh in you both to will and to work, for his good pleasure."

Still another modification of Arminian doctrine is found in the Revealed Theology of N. W. Taylor of New Haven, who maintained that, antecedently to regeneration, the *selfish* principle is suspended in the sinner's heart, and that then, prompted by *self-love*, he uses the means of regeneration from motives that are neither sinful nor holy. He held that all men, saints and sinners, have their own happiness for their ultimate end. Regeneration involves no change in this principle or motive, but only a change in the governing purpose to seek this happiness in God rather than in the world. Dr. Taylor said that man could turn to God, whatever the Spirit did or did not do. He could turn to God if he would; but he could also turn to God if he would n't. In other words, he maintained the power of contrary choice, while yet affirming the certainty that, without the Holy Spirit's influences, man would always choose wrongly. These doctrines caused a division in the Congregational body. Those who opposed Taylor withdrew their support from New Haven, and founded the East Windsor Seminary in 1834. For Taylor's view, see N. W. Taylor, Revealed Theology, 369–406, and in The Christian Spectator for 1829.

The chief opponent of Dr. Taylor was Dr. Bennet Tyler. He replied to Dr. Taylor that moral character has its seat, not in the purpose, but in the affections back of the purpose. Otherwise every Christian must be in a state of sinless perfection, for his governing purpose is to serve God. But we know that there are affections and desires not under control of this purpose — dispositions not in conformity with the predominant disposition. How, Dr. Tyler asked, can a sinner, completely selfish, from a selfish motive, resolve not to be selfish, and so suspend his selfishness? "Antecedently to regeneration, there can be no suspension of the selfish principle. It is said that, in suspending it, the sinner is actuated by self-love. But is it possible that the sinner, while destitute of love to God and every particle of genuine benevolence, should love himself at all and not love himself supremely? He loves nothing more than self. He does not regard God or the universe, except as they tend to promote his ultimate end, his own happiness. No sinner ever suspended this selfishness until subdued by divine grace. We can not become regenerate by preferring God to the world merely from regard to our own interest. There is no necessity of the Holy Spirit to renew the heart, if self-love prompts men to turn from the world to God. On the view thus combated, depravity consists simply in ignorance. All men need is enlightenment as to the best means of securing their own happiness. Regeneration by the Holy Spirit is, therefore, not necessary." See Bennet Tyler, Memoir and Lectures, 316–381, esp. 534, 370, 371; Letters on the New Haven Theology, 21–72, 143–163; review of Taylor and Fitch, by E. D. Griffin, Divine Efficiency, 13–54; Martineau, Study, 2:9 — "By making it a man's interest to be disinterested, do you cause him to forget himself and put any love into his heart? or do you only break him in and cause him to turn this way and that by the bit and lash of a driving necessity?" The sinner, apart from the grace of God, cannot see the truth. Wilberforce took Pitt to hear Cecil preach, but Pitt declared that he did not understand a word that Cecil said. Apart from the grace of God, the sinner, even when made to see the truth, resists it the more, the more clearly he sees it. Then the Holy Spirit overcomes his opposition and makes him willing in the day of God's power (Psalm 110 : 3).

B.   The truth, as the efficient cause of regeneration.

According to this view, the truth as a system of motives is the direct and immediate cause of the change from unholiness to holiness. This view is objectionable for two reasons :

(*a*) It erroneously regards motives as wholly external to the mind that is influenced by them. This is to conceive of them as mechanically constraining the will, and is indistinguishable from necessitarianism. On the contrary, motives are compounded of external presentations and internal dispositions. It is the soul's affections which render certain suggestions attractive and others repugnant to us. In brief, the heart makes the motive.

(*b*) Only as truth is loved, therefore, can it be a motive to holiness. But we have seen that the aversion of the sinner to God is such that the truth is hated instead of loved, and a thing that is hated, is hated more intensely, the more distinctly it is seen.   Hence no mere power of the truth can be regarded as the efficient cause of regeneration.   The contrary view implies that it is not the truth which the sinner hates, but rather some element of error which is mingled with it.

Lyman Beecher and Charles G. Finney held this view. The influence of the Holy Spirit differs from that of the preacher only in degree,— both use only moral suasion ; both do nothing more than to present the truth ; both work upon the soul from without. " Were I as eloquent as the Holy Ghost, I could convert sinners as well as he," said a popular preacher of this school (see Bennet Tyler, Letters on New Haven Theology, 164–171). On this view, it would be absurd to pray to God to regenerate, for that is more than he can do,— regeneration is simply the effect of truth.

Miley, in Meth. Quar., July, 1881 : 434-462, holds that " the will cannot rationally act without motive, but that it has always power to suspend action, or defer it, for the purpose of rational examination of the motive or end, and to consider the opposite motive or end. Putting the old end or motive out of view will temporarily break its power, and the new truth considered will furnish motive for right action. Thus, by using our faculty of suspending choice, and of fixing attention, we can realize the permanent eligibility of the good and choose it against the evil. This is, however, not the realization of a new spiritual life in regeneration, but the election of its attainment. Power to do this suspending is of grace [grace, however, given equally to all]. Without this power, life would be a spontaneous and irresponsible development of evil."

The view of Miley, thus substantially given, resembles that of Dr. Taylor, upon which we have already commented ; but, unlike that, it makes truth itself, apart from the affections, a determining agency in the change from sin to holiness. Our one reply is that, without a change in the affections, the truth can neither be known nor obeyed. Seeing cannot be the means of being born again, for one must first be born again in order to see the kingdom of God (John 3 : 3). The mind will not choose God, until God appears to be the greatest good.

Edwards, quoted by Griffin, Divine Efficiency, 64 —" Let the sinner apply his rational powers to the contemplation of divine things, and let his belief be speculatively correct ; still he is in such a state that those objects of contemplation will excite in him no holy affections." The Scriptures declare (Rom. 8 : 7) that "the mind of the flesh is enmity "— not against some error or mistaken notion of God — but "is enmity against God." It is God's holiness, mandatory and punitive, that is hated. A clearer view of that holiness will only increase the hatred. A woman's hatred of spiders will never be changed to love by bringing them close to her. Magnifying them with a compound oxy-hydrogen microscope will not help the matter. Tyler : "All the light of the last day will not subdue the sinner's heart." The mere presence of God, and seeing God face to face, will be hell to him, if his hatred be not first changed to love. See E. D. Griffin, Divine Efficiency, 105-116, 203–221 ; and review of Griffin, by S. R. Mason, Truth Unfolded, 383-407.

Bradford, Heredity and Christian Problems, 209 —"Christianity puts three motives before men : love, self-love, and fear." True, but the last two are only preliminary motives, not essentially Christian. The soul that is moved only by self-love or by fear has not yet entered into the Christian life at all. And any attention to the truth of God which originates in these motives has no absolute moral value, and cannot be regarded as even a beginning of salvation. Nothing but holiness and love are entitled to be called Christianity, and these the truth of itself cannot summon up. The Spirit of God must go with the truth to impart right desires and to make the truth effective. E. G. Robinson : " The glory of our salvation can no more be attributed to the word of God only, than the glory of a Praxiteles or a Canova can be ascribed to the chisel or the mallet with which he wrought into beauty his immortal creations."

C.   The immediate agency of the Holy Spirit, as the efficient cause of regeneration.

In ascribing to the Holy Spirit the authorship of regeneration, we do not affirm that the divine Spirit accomplishes his work without any accompanying instrumentality.   We simply assert that the power which regenerates is the power of God, and that although conjoined with the use of means, there is a direct operation of this power upon the sinner's heart which changes its moral character. We add two remarks by way of further explanation :

(*a*) The Scriptural assertions of the indwelling of the Holy Spirit and of his mighty power in the soul forbid us to regard the divine Spirit in regeneration as coming in contact, not with the soul, but only with the truth. The phrases, "to energize the truth," "to intensify the truth," "to illuminate the truth," have no proper meaning ; since even God cannot make the truth more true. If any change is wrought, it must be wrought, not in the truth, but in the soul.

The maxim, "Truth is mighty and will prevail," is very untrue, if God be left out of the account. Truth without God is an abstraction, and not a power. It is a mere instrument, useless without an agent. "The sword of the Spirit, which is the word of God" (Eph. 6 : 17), must be wielded by the Holy Spirit himself. And the Holy Spirit comes in contact, not simply with the instrument, but with the soul. To all moral, and especially to all religious truth, there is an inward unsusceptibility, arising from the perversity of the affections and the will. This blindness and hardness of heart must be removed, before the soul can perceive or be moved by the truth. Hence the Spirit must deal directly with the soul. Denovan : "Our natural hearts are hearts of stone. The word of God is good seed sown on the hard, trodden, macadamized highway, which the horses of passion, the asses of self-will, the wagons of imaginary treasure, have made impenetrable. Only the Holy Spirit can soften and pulverize this soil."

The Psalmist prays : "Incline my heart unto thy testimonies" (Ps. 119 : 36), while of Lydia it is said : "whose heart the Lord opened to give heed unto the things which were spoken by Paul" (Acts 16 : 14). We may say of the Holy Spirit : " He freezes and then melts the soil, He breaks the hard, cold stone, Kills out the rooted weeds so vile,—All this he does alone ; And every virtue we possess, And every victory won, And every thought of holiness, Are his, and his alone." Hence, in Ps. 90 : 16, 17, the Psalmist says, first : "Let *thy* work appear unto thy servants"; then "establish thou the work of *our* hands upon us"—God's work is first to appear,— then man's work, which is God's work carried out by human instruments. At Jericho, the force was not applied to the rams' horns, but to the walls. When Jesus healed the blind man, his power was applied, not to the spittle, but to the eyes. The impression is prepared, not by heating the seal, but by softening the wax. So God's power acts, not upon the truth, but upon the sinner.

Ps. 59 : 10 — "My God with his lovingkindness will meet me"; A. V.— "The God of my mercy shall prevent me," *i. e.,* go before me. Augustine urges this text as proof that the grace of God precedes all merit of man : "What didst thou find in me but only sins ? Before I do anything good, his mercy will go before me. What will unhappy Pelagius answer here ?" Calvin however says this may be a pious, but it is not a fair, use of the passage. The passage does teach dependence upon God ; but God's anticipation of our action, or in other words, the doctrine of prevenient grace, must be derived from other portions of Scripture, such as John 1 : 13, and Eph. 2 : 10. "The enthusiasm of humanity" to which J. R. Seeley, the author of Ecce Homo, exhorts us, is doubtless the secret of happiness and usefulness,— unfortunately he does not tell us whence it may come. John Stuart Mill felt the need of it, but he did not get it. Arthur Hugh Clough, Clergyman's First Tale : " Would I could wish my wishes all to rest, And know to wish the wish that were the best." Bradford, Heredity, 228 — "God is the environment of the soul, yet man has free will. Light fills the spaces, yet a man from ignorance may remain in a cave, or from choice may dwell in darkness." Man needs therefore a divine influence which will beget in him a disposition to use his opportunities aright.

We may illustrate the philosophy of revivals by the canal boat which lies before the gate of a lock. No power on earth can open the lock. But soon the lock begins to fill, and when the water has reached the proper level, the gate can be opened almost at a touch. Or, a steamer runs into a sandbar. Tugs fail to pull the vessel off. Her own engines cannot accomplish it. But when the tide comes in, she swings free without effort. So what we need in religion is an influx of spiritual influence which will make easy what before is difficult if not impossible. The Superintendent of a New York State Prison tells us that the common schools furnish 83 per cent., and the colleges and academies over 4 per cent., of the inmates of Auburn and Sing Sing. Truth without the Holy Spirit to apply it is like sunshine without the actinic ray which alone can give it vitalizing energy.

(*b*) Even if truth could be energized, intensified, illuminated, there would still be needed a change in the moral disposition, before the soul could recognize its beauty or be affected by it. No mere increase of light can enable a blind man to see; the disease of the eye must first be cured before external objects are visible. So God's work in regeneration must be performed within the soul itself. Over and above all influence of the truth, there must be a direct influence of the Holy Spirit upon the heart. Although wrought in conjunction with the presentation of truth to the intellect, regeneration differs from moral suasion in being an immediate act of God.

Before regeneration, man's knowledge of God is the blind man's knowledge of color. The Scriptures call such knowledge "ignorance" (Eph. 4 : 18). The heart does not appreciate God's mercy. Regeneration gives an experimental or heart knowledge; see Shedd, Dogm. Theol., 2 : 495. Is. 50 : 4 — God "wakeneth mine ear to hear." It is false to say that soul can come in contact with soul only through the influence of truth. In the intercourse of dear friends, or in the discourse of the orator, there is a personal influence, distinct from the word spoken, which persuades the heart and conquers the will. We sometimes call it "magnetism,"— but we mean simply that soul reaches soul, in ways apart from the use of physical intermediaries. Compare the facts, imperfectly known as yet, of second sight, mind-reading, clairvoyance. But whether these be accepted or not, it still is true that God has not made the human soul so that it is inaccessible to himself. The omnipresent Spirit penetrates and pervades all spirits that have been made by him. See Lotze, Outlines of Psychology (Ladd), 142, 143.

In the primary change of disposition, which is the most essential feature of regeneration, the Spirit of God acts directly upon the spirit of man. In the securing of the initial exercise of this new disposition — which constitutes the secondary feature of God's work of regeneration — the truth is used as a means. Hence, perhaps, in James 1 : 18, we read: "Of his own will he brought us forth by the word of truth" instead of "he begat us by the word of truth," — the reference being to the secondary, not to the primary, feature of regeneration. The advocates of the opposite view — the view that God works *only* through the truth as a means, and that his *only* influence upon the soul is a moral influence — very naturally deny the mystical union of the soul with Christ. Squier, for example, in his Autobiog., 343–378, esp. 360, on the Spirit's influences, quotes John 16 : 8 — he "will convict the world in respect of sin" — to show that God regenerates by applying truth to men's minds, so far as to convince them, by fair and sufficient arguments, that they are sinners.

Christ, opening blind eyes and unstopping deaf ears, illustrates the nature of God's operation in regeneration, — in the case of the blind, there is plenty of *light*, — what is wanted is *sight*. The negro convert said that his conversion was due to himself and God : he fought against God with all his might, and God did the rest. So our moral successes are due to ourselves and God, — we have done only the fighting against God, and God has done the rest. The sand of Sahara would not bring forth flowers and fruit, even if you turned into it a hundred rivers like the Nile. Man may hear sermons for a lifetime, and still be barren of all spiritual growths. The soil of the heart needs to be changed, and the good seed of the kingdom needs to be planted there.

For the view that truth is "energized" or "intensified" by the Holy Spirit, see Phelps, New Birth, 61, 121; Walker, Philosophy of Plan of Salvation, chap. 18. *Per contra*, see Wardlaw, Syst. Theol., 3 : 24, 25; E. D. Griffin, Divine Efficiency, 73–116; Anderson, Regeneration, 123–168; Edwards, Works, 2 : 547–597; Chalmers, Lectures on Romans, chap. 1; Payne, Divine Sovereignty, lect. 23 : 363–367; Hodge, Syst. Theol. 3 : 3–37, 466–485. On the whole subject of the Efficient Cause of Regeneration, see Hopkins, Works, 1 : 454; Dwight, Theology, 2 : 418–429; John Owen, Works, 3 : 282–297, 366–538; Robert Hall, Sermon on the Cause, Agent, and Purpose of Regeneration.

4. *The Instrumentality used in Regeneration.*

A. The Roman, English and Lutheran churches hold that regeneration is accomplished through the instrumentality of baptism. The Disciples, or followers of Alexander Campbell, make regeneration include baptism, as well as repentance and faith. To the view that baptism is a means of regeneration we urge the following objections:

(*a*) The Scriptures represent baptism to be not the means but only the sign of regeneration, and therefore to presuppose and follow regeneration. For this reason only believers — that is, persons giving credible evidence of being regenerated — were baptized (Acts 8 : 12). Not external baptism, but the conscientious turning of the soul to God which baptism symbolizes, saves us (1 Pet. 3 : 21 — συνειδήσεως ἀγαθῆς ἐπερώτημα). Texts like John 3 : 5, Acts 2 : 38, Col. 2 : 12, Tit. 3 : 5, are to be explained upon the principle that regeneration, the inward change, and baptism, the outward sign of that change, were regarded as only different sides or aspects of the same fact, and either side or aspect might therefore be described in terms derived from the other.

(*b*) Upon this view, there is a striking incongruity between the nature of the change to be wrought and the means employed to produce it. The change is a spiritual one, but the means are physical. It is far more rational to suppose that, in changing the character of intelligent beings, God uses means which have relation to their intelligence. The view we are considering is part and parcel of a general scheme of mechanical rather than moral salvation, and is more consistent with a materialistic than with a spiritual philosophy.

Acts 8 : 12 — " when they believed Philip preaching good tidings concerning the kingdom of God and the name of Jesus Christ, they were baptized " ; 1 Pet. 3 : 21 — " which also after a true likeness doth now save you, even baptism, not the putting away of the filth of the flesh, but the interrogation [marg.— 'inquiry', 'appeal'] of a good conscience toward God " — the inquiry of the soul after God, the conscientious turning of the soul to God.

Plumptre, however, makes ἐπερώτημα a forensic term equivalent to " examination," and including both question and answer. It means, then, the open answer of allegiance to Christ, given by the new convert to the constituted officers of the church. " That which is of the essence of the saving power of baptism is the confession and the profession which precede it. If this comes from a conscience that really renounces sin and believes on Christ, then baptism, as the channel through which the grace of the new birth is conveyed and the convert admitted into the church of Christ, ' saves us,' but not otherwise." We may adopt this statement from Plumptre's Commentary, with the alteration of the word " conveyed " into " symbolized " or " manifested." Plumptre's intepretation is, as he seems to admit, in its obvious meaning inconsistent with infant baptism; to us it seems equally inconsistent with any doctrine of baptismal regeneration.

Scriptural regeneration is God's (1) changing man's disposition, and (2) securing its first exercise. Regeneration, according to the Disciples, is man's (1) repentance and faith, and (2) submission to baptism. Alexander Campbell, Christianity Restored : " We plead that all the converting power of the Holy Spirit is exhibited in the divine Record." Address of Disciples to Ohio Baptist State Convention, 1871 : " With us regeneration includes all that is comprehended in faith, repentance, and baptism, and so far as it is expressive of birth, it belongs more properly to the last of these than to either of the former." But if baptism be the instrument of regeneration, it is difficult to see how the patriarchs, or the penitent thief, could have been regenerated. Luke 23 : 43 — " This day shalt thou be with me in Paradise." Bossuet : " ' This day ' — what promptitude ! ' With me ' — what companionship ! ' In Paradise ' — what rest ! " Bersier : " ' This day ' — what then ? no flames of Purgatory ? no long period of mournful expiation ? ' This day ' — pardon and heaven ! "

Baptism is a condition of being outwardly in the kingdom ; it is not a condition of being inwardly in the kingdom. The confounding of these two led many in the early church to dread dying unbaptized, rather than dying unsaved. Even Pascal, in later times, held that participation in outward ceremonies might lead to real conversion. He probably meant that an initial act of holy will would tend to draw others in its train. Similarly we urge unconverted people to take some step that will manifest religious interest. We hope that in taking this step a new decision of the will, inwrought by the Spirit of God. may reveal itself. But a religion which consists only in such outward performances is justly denominated a cutaneous religion, for it is only skin-deep. On John 3 : 5 — "Except one be born of water and the Spirit, he cannot enter into the kingdom of God"; Acts 2 : 38 — "Repent ye, and be baptized every one of you in the name of Jesus Christ unto the remission of your sins"; Col. 2 : 12 — "buried with him in baptism, wherein ye were also raised with him through faith"; Tit. 3 : 5 — "saved us, through the washing of regeneration and renewing of the Holy Spirit" — see further discussion and exposition in our chapter on the Ordinances. Adkins, Disciples and Baptists, a booklet published by the Am. Bap. Pub. Society, is the best statement of the Baptist position, as distinguished from that of the Disciples. It claims that Disciples overrate the externals of Christianity and underrate the work of the Holy Spirit. *Per contra*, see Gates, Disciples and Baptists.

B. The Scriptural view is that regeneration, so far as it secures an activity of man, is accomplished through the instrumentality of the truth. Although the Holy Spirit does not in any way illuminate the truth, he does illuminate the mind, so that it can perceive the truth. In conjunction with the change of man's inner disposition, there is an appeal to man's rational nature through the truth. Two inferences may be drawn:

(*a*) Man is not wholly passive at the time of his regeneration. He is passive only with respect to the change of his ruling disposition. With respect to the exercise of this disposition, he is active. Although the efficient power which secures this exercise of the new disposition is the power of God, yet man is not therefore unconscious, nor is he a mere machine worked by God's fingers. On the other hand, his whole moral nature under God's working is alive and active. We reject the "exercise-system," which regards God as the direct author of all man's thoughts, feelings, and volitions, not only in its general tenor, but in its special application to regeneration.

Shedd, Dogm. Theol., 2 : 503 — " A dead man cannot assist in his own resurrection." This is true so far as the giving of life is concerned. But once made alive, man can, like Lazarus, obey Christ's command and " come forth " (John 11 : 43). In fact, if he does not obey, there is no evidence that there is spiritual life. " In us is God; we burn but as he moves " — " Est deus in nobis; agitante calescimus illo." Wireless telegraphy requires an attuned receiver; regeneration attunes the soul so that it vibrates responsively to God and receives the communications of his truth. When a convert came to Rowland Hill and claimed that she had been converted in a dream, he replied: " We will see how you walk, now that you are awake."

Lord Bacon said he would open every one of Argus's hundred eyes, before he opened one of Briareus's hundred hands. If God did not renew men's hearts in connection with our preaching of the truth, we might well give up our ministry. E. G. Robinson: " The conversion of a soul is just as much according to law as the raising of a crop of turnips." Simon, Reconciliation, 377 — " Though the mere preaching of the gospel is not the *cause* of the conversion and revivification of men, it is a necessary *condition* — as necessary as the action of light and heat, or other physical agencies, are on a germ, if it is to develop, grow, and bear its proper fruit."

(*b*) The activity of man's mind in regeneration is activity in view of the truth. God secures the initial exercise of the new disposition which he has wrought in man's heart in connection with the use of truth as a means. Here we perceive the link between the efficiency of God and the activity of man. Only as the sinner's mind is brought into contact with the truth, does God complete his regenerating work. And as the change of inward disposition and the initial exercise of it are never, so far as we know, separated by any interval of time, we can say, in general, that Christian work is successful only as it commends the truth to every man's conscience in the sight of God (2 Cor. 4 : 2)

In Eph. 1:17, 18, there is recognized the divine illumination of the mind to behold the truth — "may give unto you a spirit of wisdom and revelation in the knowledge of him ; having the eyes of your heart enlightened, that ye may know what is the hope of his call ng." On truth as a means of regeneration, see Hovey, Outlines, 182, who quotes Cunningham, Historical Theology, 1 : 617 — "Regeneration may be taken in a limited sense as including only the first impartation of spiritual life . . . . or it may be taken in a wider sense as comprehending the whole of that process by which he is renewed or made over again in the whole man after the image of God, — *i. e.*, as including the production of saving faith and union to Christ. Only in the first sense did the Reformers maintain that man in the process was wholly passive and not active ; for they did not dispute that, before the process in the second and more enlarged sense was completed, man was spiritually alive and active, and continued so ever after during the whole process of his sanctification."

Dr. Hovey suggests an apt illustration of these two parts of the Holy Spirit's work and their union in regeneration : At the same time that God makes the photographic plate sensitive, he pours in the light of truth whereby the image of Christ is formed in the soul. Without the "sensitizing" of the plate, it would never fix the rays of light so as to retain the image. In the process of "sensitizing," the plate is passive ; under the influence of light, it is active. In both the "sensitizing" and the taking of the picture, the real agent is not the plate nor the light, but the photographer. The photographer cannot perform both operations at the same moment. God can. He gives the new affection, and at the same instant he secures its exercise in view of the truth.

For denial of the instrumentality of truth in regeneration, see Pierce, in Bap. Quar., Jan. 1872 : 52. *Per contra*, see Anderson, Regeneration, 89–122. H. B. Smith holds middle ground. He says : "In adults it [regeneration] is wrought most frequently by the word of God as the instrument. Believing that infants may be regenerated, we cannot assert that it is tied to the word of God absolutely." We prefer to say that, if infants are regenerated, they also are regenerated in conjunction with some influence of truth upon the mind, dim as the recognition of it may be. Otherwise we break the Scriptural connection between regeneration and conversion, and open the way for faith in a physical, magical, sacramental salvation. Squier, Autobiog., 368, says well, of the theory of regeneration which makes man purely passive, that it has a benumbing effect upon preaching : "The lack of expectation unnerves the efforts of the preacher ; an impres n of the fortuitous presence neutralizes his engagedness. This antinomian dependence on the Spirit extracts all vitality from the pulpit and sense of responsibility from the hearer, and makes preaching an *opus operatum*, like the baptismal regeneration of the formalist." Only of the first element in regeneration are Shedd's words true : "A dead man cannot assist in his own resurrection" (Dogm. Theol., 2:503).

Squier goes to the opposite extreme of regarding the truth alone as the cause of regeneration. His words are none the less a valuable protest against the view that regeneration is so entirely due to God that in no part of it is man active. It was with a better view that Luther cried : "O that we might multiply living books, that is, preachers!" And the preacher is successful only as he possesses and unfolds the truth. John took the little book from the Covenant-angel's hand and ate it (Rev. 10 : 8–11). So he who is to preach God's truth must feed upon it, until it has become his own : For the Exercise-system, see Emmons, Works, 4 : 339–411 ; Hagenbach, Hist. Doct., 2:439.

5. *The Nature of the Change wrought in Regeneration.*

A. It is a change in which the governing disposition is made holy. This implies that :

(*a*) It is not a change in the substance of either body or soul. Regeneration is not a physical change. There is no physical seed or germ implanted in man's nature. Regeneration does not add to, or subtract from, the number of man's intellectual, emotional or voluntary faculties. But regeneration is the giving of a new direction or tendency to powers of affection which man possessed before. Man had the faculty of love before, but his love was supremely set on self. In regeneration the direction of that faculty is changed, and his love is now set supremely upon God.

Eph. 2:10 — "created in Christ Jesus for good works" — does not imply that the old soul is annihilated, and a new soul created. The "old man" which is "crucified" — (Rom. 6:6) and "put away" (Eph. 4:22) is simply the sinful bent of the affections and will. When this direction of the dispositions is changed, and becomes holy, we can call the change a new birth of the old nature, because the same *faculties* that acted before are acting now, the only difference being that now these faculties are set toward God and purity. Or, regarding the change from another point of view, we may speak of man as having a "new nature," as "recreated," as being a "new creature," because this *direction* of "the affection and will, which ensures a different life from what was led before, is something totally new, and due wholly to the regenerating act of God. In 1 Pet. 1:23 — "begotten again, not of corruptible seed, but of incorruptible" — all materialistic inferences from the word "seed," as if it implied the implantation of a physical germ, are prevented by the following explanatory words : "through the word of God, which liveth and abideth."

So, too, when we describe regeneration as the communication of a new life to the soul, we should not conceive of this new life as a *substance* imparted or infused into us. The new life is rather a new direction and activity of our own affections and will. There is, indeed a union of the soul with Christ; Christ dwells in the renewed heart; Christ's entrance into the soul is the *cause* and *accompaniment* of its regeneration. But this entrance of Christ into the soul is not *itself* regeneration. We must distinguish the effect from the cause ; otherwise we shall be in danger of a pantheistic confounding of our own personality and life with the personality and life of Christ. Christ is indeed our life, in the sense of being the cause and supporter of our life, but he is not our life in the sense that, after our union with him, our individuality ceases. The effect of union with Christ is rather that our individuality is enlarged and exalted (John 10:10 — "I came that they may have life, and may have it abundantly." See page 799, (c).

We must therefore take with a grain of allowance the generally excellent words of A. J. Gordon, Twofold Life, 22 — "Regeneration is the communication of the divine nature to man by the operation of the Holy Spirit through the word (2 Pet. 1:4). . . . As Christ was made partaker of human nature by incarnation, that so he might enter into truest fellowship with us, we are made partakers of the divine nature, by regeneration, that we may enter into truest fellowship with God. Regeneration is not a change of nature, *i. e.*, a natural heart bettered. Eternal life is not natural life prolonged into endless duration. It is the divine life imparted to us, the very life of God communicated to the human soul, and bringing forth there its proper fruit." Dr. Gordon's view that regeneration adds a new substance or faculty to the soul is the result of literalizing the Scripture metaphors of creation and life. This turning of symbol into fact accounts for his tendency toward annihilation doctrine in the case of the unregenerate, toward faith cure and the belief that all physical evils can be removed by prayer. E. H. Johnson, The Holy Spirit: "Regeneration is a change, not in the quantity, but in the quality, of the soul." E. G. Robinson, Christian Theology, 320 — "Regeneration consists in a divinely wrought change in the moral affections."

So, too, we would criticize the doctrine of Drummond, Nat. Law in the Spir. World: "People forget the persistence of force. Instead of transforming energy, they try to create it. We must either depend on environment, or be self-sufficient. The 'cannot bear fruit of itself' (John 15:4) is the 'cannot' of natural law. Natural fruit flourishes with air and sunshine. The difference between the Christian and the non-Christian is the difference between the organic and the inorganic. The Christian has all the characteristics of life: assimilation, waste, reproduction, spontaneous action." See criticism of Drummond, by Murphy, in Brit. Quar., 1884:118-125 — "As in resurrection there is a physical connection with the old body, so in regeneration there is a natural connection with the old soul." Also, Brit. Quar., July, 1880, art.: Evolution Viewed in Relation to Theology — "The regenerating agency of the Spirit of God is symbolized, not by the vitalization of dead matter, but by the agency of the organizing intelligence which guides the evolution of living beings." Murphy's answer to Drummond is republished. Murphy's Natural Selection and Spiritual Freedom, 1-33 — "The will can no more create force, either muscular or mental, than it can create matter. And it is equally true that for our spiritual nourishment and spiritual force we are altogether dependent on our spiritual environment, which is God." In "dead matter" there is no sin.

Drummond would imply that, as matter has no promise or potency of life and is not responsible for being without life (or "dead," to use his misleading word), and if it ever is to live must wait for the life-giving influence to come unsought, so the human soul is not responsible for being spiritually dead, cannot seek for life, must passively wait for the Spirit. Plymouth Brethren generally hold the same view with

Drummond, that regeneration *adds* something — as *vitality* — to the substance of the soul. Christ is transsubstantiated into the soul's substance; or, the πνεῦμα is added. But we have given over talking of vitality, as if it were a substance or faculty. We regard it as merely a mode of action. Evolution, moreover, uses what already exists, so far as it will go, instead of creating new; as in the miracle of the loaves, and as in the original creation of man, so in his recreation or regeneration. Dr. Charles Hodge also makes the same mistake in calling regeneration an "origination of the principle of the spirit of life, just as literal and real a creation as the origination of the principle of natural life." This, too, literalizes Scripture metaphor, and ignores the fact that the change accomplished in regeneration is an exclusively moral one. There is indeed a new entrance of Christ into the soul, or a new exercise of his spiritual power within the soul. But the effect of Christ's working is not to add any new faculty or substance, but only to give new direction to already existing powers.

(*b*) Regeneration involves an enlightenment of the understanding and a rectification of the volitions. But it seems most consonant with Scripture and with a correct psychology to regard these changes as immediate and necessary consequences of the change of disposition already mentioned, rather than as the primary and central facts in regeneration. The taste for truth logically precedes perception of the truth, and love for God logically precedes obedience to God; indeed, without love no obedience is possible. Reverse the lever of affection, and this moral locomotive, without further change, will move away from sin, and toward truth and God.

Texts which seem to imply that a right taste, disposition, affection, logically precedes both knowledge of God and obedience to God, are the following : Ps. 34 : 8 — "Oh taste and see that Jehovah is good "; 119 : 36 — "Incline my heart unto thy testimonies"; Jer. 24 : 7 — "I will give them a heart to know me"; Mat. 5 : 8 — "Blessed are the pure in heart: for they shall see God "; John 7 : 17 — "If any man willeth to do his will, he shall know of the teaching, whether it is of God "; Acts 16 : 14 — of Lydia it is said : "whose heart the Lord opened to give heed unto the things which were spoken by Paul "; Eph. 1 : 18 — "having the eyes of your heart enlightened." " Change the centre of a circle and you change the place and direction of all its radii."

The text John 1 : 12, 13 — "But as many as received him, to them gave him the right to become children of God, even to them that believe on his name: who were born, not of blood, nor of the will of the flesh, nor of the will of man, but of God " — seems at first sight to imply that faith is the condition of regeneration, and therefore prior to it. " But if ἐξουσίαν here signifies the 'right' or 'privilege' of sonship, it is a right which may presuppose faith as the work of the Spirit in regeneration — a work apart from which no genuine faith exists in the soul. But it is possible that John means to say that, in the case of all who received Christ, their power to believe was *given* to them by him. In the original the emphasis is on 'gave,' and this is shown by the order of the words "; see Hovey, Manual of Theology, 345, and Com. on John 1 : 12, 13 — " The meaning would then be this : ' Many did not receive him ; but some did ; and as to all who received him, he *gave* them grace by which they were enabled to do this, and so to become God's children.' "

Ruskin : " The first and last and closest trial question to any living creature is, ' What do you like ? ' Go out into the street and ask the first man you meet what his taste is, and, if he answers candidly, you know him, body and soul. What we like determines what we are, and is the sign of what we are ; and to teach taste is inevitably to form character." If the taste here spoken of is moral and spiritual taste, the words of Ruskin are sober truth. Regeneration is essentially a changing of the fundamental taste of the soul. But by taste we mean the direction of man's love, the bent of his affections, the trend of his will. And to alter that taste is not to impart a new faculty, or to create a new substance, but simply to set toward God the affections which hitherto have been set upon self and sin. We may illustrate by the engineer who climbs over the cab into a runaway locomotive and who changes its course, not by adding any new rod or cog to the machine, but simply by reversing the lever. The engine slows up and soon moves in an opposite direction to that in which it has been going. Man needs no new faculty of love ; he needs only to have his love set in a new and holy direction ; this is virtually to give him a new birth, to make him a new creature, to impart to him a new life. But being born again, created anew, made alive from the dead, are physical metaphors, to be interpreted not literally but spiritually.

(c) It is objected, indeed, that we know only of mental substance and of mental acts, and that the new disposition or state just mentioned, since it is not an act, must be regarded as a new substance, and so lack all moral quality. But we reply that, besides substance and acts, there are habits, tendencies, proclivities, some of them native and some of them acquired. They are voluntary, and have moral character. If we can by repeated acts originate sinful tendencies, God can surely originate in us holy tendencies. Such holy tendencies formed a part of the nature of Adam, as he came from the hand of God. As the result of the Fall, we are born with tendencies toward evil for which we are responsible. Regeneration is a restoration of the original tendencies toward God which were lost by the Fall. Such holy tendencies (tastes, dispositions, affections) are not only not unmoral—they are the only possible springs of right moral action. Only in the restoration of them does man become truly free.

Mat. 12 : 33 — " Make the tree good, and its fruit good " ; Eph. 2 : 10 — " created in Christ Jesus for good works." The tree is first made good — the character renewed in its fundamental principle, love to God — in the certainty that when this is done the fruit will be good also. Good works are the necessary result of regeneration by union with Christ. Regeneration introduces a new force into humanity, the force of a new love. The work of the preacher is that of coöperation with God in the impartation of a new life — a work far more radical and more noble than that of moral reform, by as much as the origination of a new force is more radical and more noble than the guidance of that force after it has been originated. Does regeneration cure disease and remove physical ills ? Not primarily. Mat. 1 : 21 — " thou shalt call his name Jesus ; for it is he that shall save his people from their sins." Salvation from sin is Christ's first and main work. He performed physical healing only to illustrate and further the healing of the soul. Hence in the case of the paralytic, when he was expected to cure the body, he said first : " thy sins are forgiven " (Mat. 9 : 2) ; but, that they who stood by might not doubt his power to forgive, he added the raising up of the palsied man. And ultimately in every redeemed man the holy heart will bring in its train the perfected body : Rom. 8 : 23 — " we ourselves groan within ourselves, waiting for our adoption, to wit, the redemption of our body."

On holy affection as the spring of holy action, see especially Edwards, Religious Affections, in Works, 3 : 1–21. This treatise is Jonathan Edwards's Confessions, as much as if it were directly addressed to the Deity. Allen, his biographer, calls it " a work which will not suffer by comparison with the work of great teachers in theology, whether ancient or modern." President Timothy Dwight regarded it as most worthy of preservation next to the Bible. See also Hodge, Essays and Reviews, 1 : 48 ; Owen on the Holy Spirit, in Works, 3 : 297–336 ; Charnock on Regeneration ; Andrew Fuller, Works, 2 : 461–471, 512–560, and 3 : 796 ; Bellamy, Works, 2 : 502 ; Dwight, Works, 2 : 418 ; Woods, Works, 3 : 1–21 ; Anderson, Regeneration, 21–50.

B.   It is an instantaneous change, in a region of the soul below consciousness, and is therefore known only in its results.

(a) It is an instantaneous change. — Regeneration is not a gradual work. Although there may be a gradual work of God's providence and Spirit, preparing the change, and a gradual recognition of it after it has taken place, there must be an instant of time when, under the influence of God's Spirit, the disposition of the soul, just before hostile to God, is changed to love. Any other view assumes an intermediate state of indecision which has no moral character at all, and confounds regeneration either with conviction or with sanctification.

Conviction of sin is an ordinary, if not an invariable, antecedent of regeneration. It results from the contemplation of truth. It is often accompanied by fear, remorse, and cries for mercy. But these desires and fears are not signs of regeneration. They are selfish. They are quite consistent with manifest and dreadful enmity to God.

They have a hopeful aspect, simply because they are evidence that the Holy Spirit is striving with the soul. But this work of the Spirit is not yet regeneration; at most, it is preparation for regeneration. So far as the sinner is concerned, he is more of a sinner than ever before; because, under more light than has ever before been given him, he is still rejecting Christ and resisting the Spirit. The word of God and the Holy Spirit appeal to lower as well as to higher motives; most men's concern about religion is determined, at the outset, by hope or fear. See Shedd, Dogm. Theol., 2:512.

All these motives, though they are not the highest, are yet proper motives to influence the soul; it is right to seek God from motives of self-interest, and because we desire heaven. But the seeking which not only begins, but ends, upon this lower plane, is never successful. Until the soul gives itself to God from motives of love, it is never saved. And so long as these preliminary motives rule, regeneration has not yet taken place. Bible-reading, and prayers, and church-attendance, and partial reformations, are certainly better than apathy or outbreaking sin. They may be signs that God is working in the soul. But without complete surrender to God, they may be accompanied with the greatest guilt and the greatest danger; simply because, under such influences, the withholding of submission implies the most active hatred to God, and opposition to his will. Instance cases of outward reformation that preceded regeneration, — like that of John Bunyan, who left off swearing before his conversion. Park: "The soul is a monad, and must turn all at once. If we are standing on the line, we are yet unregenerate. We are regenerate only when we cross it." There is a prevenient grace as well as a regenerating grace. Wendelius indeed distinguished five kinds of grace, namely, prevenient, preparatory, operant, coöperant, and perfecting.

While in some cases God's preparatory work occupies a long time, there are many cases in which he cuts short his work in righteousness (Rom. 9:28). Some persons are regenerated in infancy or childhood, cannot remember a time when they did not love Christ, and yet take long to learn that they are regenerate. Others are convicted and converted suddenly in mature years. The best proof of regeneration is not the memory of a past experience, however vivid and startling, but rather a present inward love for Christ, his holiness, his servants, his work, and his word. Much sympathy should be given to those who have been early converted, but who, from timidity, self-distrust, or the faults of inconsistent church members, have been deterred from joining themselves with Christian people, and so have lost all hope and joy in their religious lives. Instance the man who, though converted in a revival of religion, was injured by a professed Christian, and became a recluse, but cherished the memory of his dead wife and child, kept the playthings of the one and the clothing of the other, and left directions to have them buried with him.

As there is danger of confounding regeneration with preparatory influences of God's Spirit, so there is danger of confounding regeneration with sanctification. Sanctification, as the development of the new affection, is gradual and progressive. But no *beginning* is progressive or gradual; and regeneration is a beginning of the new affection. We may gradually come to the *knowledge* that a new affection exists, but the knowledge of a beginning is one thing; the beginning itself is another thing. Luther had experienced a change of heart, long before he knew its meaning or could express his new feelings in scientific form. It is not in the sense of a gradual regeneration, but in the sense of a gradual recognition of the fact of regeneration, and a progressive enjoyment of its results, that "the path of the righteous" is said to be "as the dawning light"— the morning-dawn that begins in faintness, but— "that shineth more and more unto the perfect day" (Prov. 4:18). *Cf.* 2 Cor. 4:4 — "the god of this world hath blinded the minds of the unbelieving, that the light of the gospel of the glory of Christ, who is the image of God, should not dawn upon them." Here the recognition of God's work is described as gradual; that the work itself is instantaneous, appears from the following verse 6 — "Seeing it is God, that said, Light shall shine out of darkness, who shined in our hearts, to give the light of the knowledge of the glory of God in the face of Jesus Christ."

Illustrate by the unconscious crossing of the line which separates one State of the Federal Union from another. From this doctrine of instantaneous regeneration, we may infer the duty of reaping as well as of sowing: John 4:38 — "I sent you to reap." " It is a mistaken notion that it takes God a long time to give increase to the seed planted in a sinner's heart. This grows out of the idea that regeneration is a matter of *training*; that a soul must be *educated* from a lost state into a state of salvation. Let us remember that three thousand, whom in the morning Peter called murderers of Christ, were before night regenerated and baptized members of his church." Drummond, in his Nat. Law in the Spir. World, remarks upon the humaneness of sudden conversion. As self-limitation, self-mortification, suicide of the old nature, it is well to have it at once done and over with, and not to die by degrees.

(*b*) This change takes place in the region of the soul below consciousness. — It is by no means true that God's work in regeneration is always recognized by the subject of it. On the other hand, it is never directly perceived at all. The working of God in the human soul, since it contravenes no law of man's being, but rather puts him in the full and normal possession of his own powers, is secret and inscrutable. Although man is conscious, he is not conscious of God's regenerating agency.

We know our own natural existence only through the phenomena of thought and sense. So we know our own spiritual existence, as new creatures in Christ, only through the new feelings and experiences of the soul. "The will does not need to act solitarily, in order to act freely." God acts on the will, and the resulting holiness is true freedom. John 8 : 36 — "If therefore the Son shall make you free, ye shall be free indeed." We have the consciousness of freedom ; but the act of God in giving us this freedom is beyond or beneath our consciousness.

Both Luther and Calvin used the word regeneration in a loose way, confounding it with sanctification. After the Federalists made a distinct doctrine of it, Calvinists in general came to treat it separately. And John Wesley rescued it from identification with sacraments, by showing its connection with the truth. E. G. Robinson : "Regeneration is in one sense instantaneous, in another sense not. There is necessity of some sort of knowledge in regeneration. The doctrine of Christ crucified is the fit instrument. The object of religion is to produce a *sound* rather than an *emotional* experience. Revivals of religion are valuable in just the proportion in which they produce rational conviction and permanently righteous action." But none are left unaffected by them. "An arm of the magnetic needle must be attracted to the magnetic pole of the earth, or it must be repelled, — there is no such thing as indifference. Modern materialism, refusing to say that the fear of God is the beginning of wisdom, is led to declare that the hate of God is the beginning of wisdom" (Diesselhoff, Die klassische Poesie, 8).

(*c*) This change, however, is recognized indirectly in its results. — At the moment of regeneration, the soul is conscious only of the truth and of its own exercises with reference to it. That God is the author of its new affection is an inference from the new character of the exercises which it prompts. The human side or aspect of regeneration is Conversion. This, and the Sanctification which follows it (including the special gifts of the Holy Spirit), are the sole evidences in any particular case that regeneration is an accomplished fact.

Regeneration, though it is the birth of a perfect child, is still the birth of a child. The child is to grow, and the growth is sanctification ; in other words, sanctification, as we shall see, is simply the strengthening and development of the holy affection which begins its existence in regeneration. Hence the subject of the epistle to the Romans — salvation by faith — includes not only justification by faith (chapters 1-7), but sanctification by faith (chapters 8-16). On evidences of regeneration, see Anderson, Regeneration, 169-214, 227-295 ; Woods, Works, 44-55. The transition from justification by faith to sanctification by faith is in chapter 8 of the epistle to the Romans. That begins by declaring that there is *no condemnation* in Christ, and ends by declaring that there is *no separation* from Christ. The work of the Holy Spirit follows upon the work of Christ. See Godet on the epistle.

The doctrine of Alexander Campbell was a protest against laying an unscriptural emphasis on emotional states as evidences of regeneration — a protest which certain mystical and antinomian exaggerations of evangelical teaching very justly provoked. But Campbell went to the opposite extreme of practically excluding emotion from religion, and of confining the work of the Holy Spirit to the conscious influence of the truth. Disciples need to recognize a power of the Holy Spirit exerted below consciousness, in order to explain the conscious acceptance of Christ and of his salvation.

William James, Varieties of Religious Experience, 271 — " If we should conceive that the human mind, with its different possibilities of equilibrium, might be like a many sided solid with different surfaces on which it could lie flat, we might liken mental revolutions to the spatial revolutions of such a body. As it is pried up, say by a lever, from a position in which it lies on surface A, for instance, it will linger for a time unstably half way up, and if the lever cease to urge it, it will tumble back or relapse, under the continued pull of gravity. But if at last it rotate far enough for its centre of gravity to pass beyond the surface A altogether, the body will fall over, on surface B, say, and will abide there permanently. The pulls of gravity towards A have vanished, and may now be disregarded. The polyhedron has become immune against further attraction from this direction."

III. Conversion.

Conversion is that voluntary change in the mind of the sinner, in which he turns, on the one hand, from sin, and on the other hand, to Christ. The former or negative element in conversion, namely, the turning from sin, we denominate repentance. The latter or positive element in conversion, namely, the turning to Christ, we denominate faith.

For account of repentance and faith as elements of conversion, see Andrew Fuller, Works, 1: 666; Luthardt, Compendium der Dogmatik, 3d ed., 201–206. The two elements of conversion seem to be in the mind of Paul, when he writes in Rom. 6:11 — " reckon ye also yourselves to be dead unto sin, but alive unto God in Christ Jesus "; Col. 3:3 — "ye died, and your life is hid with Christ in God." *Cf.* ἀποστρέφω, in Acts 3 : 26 — "in turning away every one of you from your iniquities," with ἐπιστρέφω in Acts 11 : 21 — "believed" and "turned unto the Lord." A candidate for ordination was once asked which came first: regeneration or conversion. He replied very correctly: " Regeneration and conversion are like the cannon-ball and the hole — they both go through together." This is true however only as to their chronological relation. Logically the ball is first and causes the hole, not the hole first and causes the ball.

(*a*) Conversion is the human side or aspect of that fundamental spiritual change which, as viewed from the divine side, we call regeneration. It is simply man's turning. The Scriptures recognize the voluntary activity of the human soul in this change as distinctly as they recognize the causative agency of God. While God turns men to himself (Ps. 85 : 4 ; Song 1 : 4 ; Jer. 31 : 18 ; Lam. 5 : 21), men are exhorted to turn themselves to God (Prov. 1 : 23 ; Is. 31 : 6 ; 59 : 20 ; Ez. 14 : 6 ; 18 : 32 ; 33 : 9, 11 ; Joel 2 : 12–14). While God is represented as the author of the new heart and the new spirit (Ps. 51 : 10 ; Ez. 11 : 19 ; 36 : 26), men are commanded to make for themselves a new heart and a new spirit (Ez. 18 : 31 ; 2 Cor. 7 : 1 ; *cf.* Phil. 2 : 12, 13 ; Eph. 5 : 14).

Ps. 85 : 4 — "Turn us, O God of our salvation "; Song 1 : 4 — "Draw me, we will run after thee "; Jer. 31 : 18 — "turn thou me, and I shall be turned " ; Lam. 5 : 21 — "Turn thou us unto thee, O Jehovah, and we shall be turned." Prov. 1 : 23 — "Turn you at my reproof: Behold, I will pour out my spirit unto you "; Is. 31 : 6 — " Turn ye unto him from whom ye have deeply revolted, O children of Israel " ; 59 : 20 — "And a Redeemer will come to Zion, and unto them that turn from transgression in Jacob "; Ez. 14 : 6 — "Return ye, and turn yourselves from your idols "; 18 : 32 — "turn yourselves and live "; 33 : 9 — "if thou warn the wicked of his way to turn from it, and he turn not from his way, he shall die in his iniquity "; 11 — "turn ye, turn ye from your evil ways ; for why will ye die, O house of Israel ?" Joel 2 : 12–14 — "turn ye unto me with all your heart." Ps. 51 : 10 — "Create in me a clean heart, O God ; And renew a right spirit within me "; Ez. 11 : 19 — "And I will give them one heart, and I will put a new spirit within you ; and I will take the stony heart out of their flesh, and will give them a heart of flesh "; 36 : 26 — " A new heart also will I give you, and a new spirit will I put within you." Ez. 18 : 31 — "Cast away from you all your transgressions, wherein ye have transgressed ; and make you a new heart and a new spirit: for why will ye die, O house of Israel ?" 2 Cor. 7 : 1 — "Having therefore these promises, beloved, let us cleanse ourselves from all defilement of flesh and spirit, perfecting holiness in the fear of God "; *cf.* Phil. 2 : 12, 13 — " work out your own salvation with fear and trembling ; for it is God who worketh in you both to will and to work, for his good pleasure": Eph. 5 . 14 — "Awake, thou that sleepest, and arise from the dead, and Christ shall shine upon thee."

When asked the way to heaven, Bishop Wilberforce replied : "Take the first turn to the right, and go straight forward." Phillips Brooks's conversion is described by Professor Allen, Life, 1:206, as consisting in the resolve "to be true to himself, to renounce nothing which he knew to be good, and yet bring all things captive to the obedience of God, ... the absolute surrender of his will to God, in accordance with the example of Christ : 'Lo, I am come . . . . to do thy will, O God' (Heb. 10 : 7)."

(*b*) This twofold method of representation can be explained only when we remember that man's powers may be interpenetrated and quickened by the divine, not only without destroying man's freedom, but with the result of making man for the first time truly free. Since the relation between the divine and the human activity is not one of chronological succession, man is never to wait for God's working. If he is ever regenerated, it must be in and through a movement of his own will, in which he turns to God as unconstrainedly and with as little consciousness of God's operation upon him, as if no such operation of God were involved in the change. And in preaching, we are to press upon men the claims of God and their duty of immediate submission to Christ, with the certainty that they who do so submit will subsequently recognize this new and holy activity of their own wills as due to a working within them of divine power.

Ps. 110 : 3 — "Thy people offer themselves willingly in the day of thy power." The act of God is accompanied by an activity of man. Dorner : " God's act initiates action." There is indeed an original changing of man's tastes and affections, and in this man is passive. But this is only the first aspect of regeneration. In the second aspect of it — the rousing of man's powers — God's action is accompanied by man's activity, and regeneration is but the obverse side of conversion. Luther's word : "Man, in conversion, is purely passive," is true only of the first part of the change ; and here, by " conversion," Luther means "regeneration." Melanchthon said better : "Non est enim coāctio, ut voluntas non possit repugnare : trahit Deus, sed volentem trahit." See Meyer on Rom. 8 : 14 — "led by the Spirit of God " : " The expression," Meyer says, " is passive, though without prejudice to the human will, as verse 13 proves : 'by the Spirit ye put to death the deeds of the body.'"

As, by a well known principle of hydrostatics, the water contained in a little tube can balance the water of a whole ocean, so God's grace can be balanced by man's will. As sunshine on the sand produces nothing unless man sow the seed, and as a fair breeze does not propel the vessel unless man spread the sails, so the influences of God's Spirit require human agencies, and work through them. The Holy Spirit is sovereign, — he bloweth where he listeth. Even though there be uniform human conditions, there will not be uniform spiritual results. Results are often independent of human conditions as such. This is the truth emphasized by Andrew Fuller. But this does not prevent us from saying that, whenever God's Spirit works in regeneration, there is always accompanying it a voluntary change in man, which we call conversion, and that this change is as free, and as really man's own work, as if there were no divine influence upon him.

Jesus told the man with the withered hand to stretch forth his hand ; it was the man's duty to stretch it forth, not to wait for strength from God to do it. Jesus told the man sick of the palsy to take up his bed and walk. It was that man's duty to obey the command, not to pray for power to obey. Depend wholly upon God ? Yes, as you depend wholly upon wind when you sail, yet need to keep your sails properly set. "Work out your own salvation " comes first in the apostle's exhortation ; "for it is God who worketh in you" follows (Phil. 2 : 12, 13) ; which means that our first business is to use our wills in obedience ; then we shall find that God has gone before us to prepare us to obey.

Mat. 11 : 12 — " the kingdom of heaven suffereth violence, and men of violence take it by force." Conversion is like the invasion of a kingdom. Men are not to wait for God's time, but to act at once. Not bodily exercises are required, but impassioned earnestness of soul. Wendt, Teaching of Jesus, 2 : 49-56 — " Not injustice and violence, but energetic laying hold of a good to which they can make no claim. It is of no avail to wait idly, or to seek laboriously to earn it ; but it is of avail to lay hold of it and to retain it. It is ready as a gift of God for men, but men must direct their desire and will toward it. . . . . The man who put on the wedding garment did not earn his share of the feast thereby, yet he did show the disposition without which he was not permitted to partake of it."

James, Varieties of Religious Experience, 12 — " The two main phenomena of religion, they will say, are essentially phenomena of adolescence, and therefore synchronous with the development of sexual life. To which the retort is easy: Even were the asserted synchrony unrestrictedly true as a fact (which it is not), it is not only the sexual life, but the entire higher mental life, which awakens during adolescence. One might then as well set up the thesis that the interest in mechanics, physics, chemistry, logic, physiology and sociology, which springs up during adolescent years along with that in poetry and religion, is also a perversion of the sexual instinct, but this would be too absurd. Moreover, if the argument from synchrony is to decide, what is to be done with the fact that the religious age *par excellence* would seem to be old age, when the uproar of the sexual life is past? "

(c) From the fact that the word ' conversion ' means simply ' a turning,' every turning of the Christian from sin, subsequent to the first, may, in a subordinate sense, be denominated a conversion (Luke 22 : 32). Since regeneration is not complete sanctification, and the change of governing disposition is not identical with complete purification of the nature, such subsequent turnings from sin are necessary consequences and evidences of the first (*cf.* John 13 : 10). But they do not, like the first, imply a change of the governing disposition, — they are rather new manifestations of a disposition already changed. For this reason, conversion proper, like the regeneration of which it is the obverse side, can occur but once. The phrase ' second conversion,' even if it does not imply radical misconception of the nature of conversion, is misleading. We prefer, therefore, to describe these subsequent experiences, not by the term ' conversion,' but by such phrases as ' breaking off, forsaking, returning from, neglects or transgressions,' and ' coming back to Christ, trusting anew in him.' It is with repentance and faith, as elements in that first and radical change by which the soul enters upon a state of salvation, that we have now to do.

Luke 22 : 31, 32 — " Simon, Simon, behold, Satan asked to have you, that he might sift you as wheat: but I made supplication for thee, that thy faith fail not; and do thou, when once thou hast turned again [A. V.: 'art converted '], establish thy brethren "; John 13 : 10 — " He that is bathed [has taken a full bath] needeth not save to wash his feet, but is clean every whit [as a whole]." Notice that Jesus here announces that only one regeneration is needed, — what follows is not conversion but sanctification. Spurgeon said he believed in regeneration, but not in re-regeneration. Second blessing? Yes, and a forty-second. The stages in the Christian life are like ice, water, invisible vapor, steam, all successive and natural results of increasing temperature, seemingly different from one another, yet all forms of the same element.

On the relation between the divine and the human agencies, we quote a different view from another writer : " God decrees to employ means which in every case are sufficient, and which in certain cases it is foreseen will be effectual. Human action converts a sufficient means into an effectual means. The result is not always according to the varying use of means. The power is all of God. Man has power to resist only. There is a universal influence of the Spirit, but the influences of the Spirit vary in different cases, just as external opportunities do. The love of holiness is blunted, but it still lingers. The Holy Spirit quickens it. When this love is wholly lost, sin against the Holy Ghost results. Before regeneration there is a desire for holiness, an apprehension of its beauty, but this is overborne by a greater love for sin. If the man does not quickly grow worse, it is not because of positive action on his part, but only because negatively he does not resist as he might. ' Behold, I stand at the door and knock.' God leads at first by a resistible influence. When man yields, God leads by an irresistible influence. The second influence of the Holy Spirit confirms the Christian's choice. This second influence is called ' sealing.' There is no necessary interval of time between the two. Prevenient grace comes first ; conversion comes after."

To this view, we would reply that a partial love for holiness, and an ability to choose it before God works effectually upon the heart, seem to contradict those Scriptures which assert that " the mind of the flesh is enmity against God " (Rom. 8 : 7), and that all good works are the result of God's new creation (Eph. 2 : 10). Conversion does not precede regeneration, — it chronologically accompanies regeneration, though it logically follows it.

1. *Repentance.*

Repentance is that voluntary change in the mind of the sinner in which he turns from sin. Being essentially a change of mind, it involves a change of view, a change of feeling, and a change of purpose. We may therefore analyze repentance into three constituents, each succeeding term of which includes and implies the one preceding :

A. An intellectual element, — change of view — recognition of sin as involving personal guilt, defilement, and helplessness (Ps. 51 : 3, 7, 11). If unaccompanied by the following elements, this recognition may manifest itself in fear of punishment, although as yet there is no hatred of sin. This element is indicated in the Scripture phrase ἐπίγνωσις ἁμαρτίας (Rom. 3 : 20 ; *cf.* 1 : 32).

Ps. 51 : 3, 11 — "For I know my transgressions; And my sin is ever before me. . . . . . Cast me not away from thy presence, And take not thy Holy Spirit from me " ; Rom. 3 : 20 — "through the law cometh the knowledge of sin " ; *cf.* 1 : 32 — "who, knowing the ordinance of God, that they that practise such things are worthy of death, not only do the same, but also consent with them that practise them."

It is well to remember that God requires us to cherish no views or emotions that contradict the truth. He wants of us no false humility. Humility (*humus*) = groundness — a coming down to the hard-pan of facts — a facing of the truth. Repentance, therefore, is not a calling ourselves by hard names. It is not cringing, or exaggerated self-contempt. It is simple recognition of what we are. The " 'umble" Uriah Heep is the arrant hypocrite. If we see ourselves as God sees us, we shall say with Job 42 : 5, 6 — "I had heard of thee by the hearing of the ear ; But now mine eye seeth thee : Wherefore I abhor myself, And repent in dust and ashes."

Apart from God's working in the heart there is no proper recognition of sin, either in people of high or low degree. Lady Huntington invited the Duchess of Buckingham to come and hear Whitefield, when the Duchess answered : "It is monstrous to be told that you have a heart as sinful as the common wretches that crawl on the earth, — it is highly offensive and insulting." Mr. Moody, after preaching to the prisoners in the jail at Chicago, visited them in their cells. In the first cell he found two, playing cards. They said false witnesses had testified against them. In the second cell, the convict said that the guilty man had escaped, but that he, a mere accomplice, had been caught. In the last cell only Mr. Moody found a man crying over his sins. Henry Drummond, after hearing the confessions of inquirers, said : " I am sick of the sins of these men, — how can God bear it ? "

Experience of sin does not teach us to recognize sin. We do not learn to know chloroform by frequently inhaling it. The drunkard does not understand the degrading effects of drink so well as his miserable wife and children do. Even the natural conscience does not give the recognition of sin that is needed in true repentance. The confession "I have sinned " is made by hardened Pharaoh (Ex. 9 : 27), double minded Balaam (Num. 22 : 34), remorseful Achan (Josh. 7 : 20), insincere King Saul (1 Sam. 15 : 24), despairing Judas (Mat. 27 : 4) ; but in no one of these cases was there true repentance. True repentance takes God's part against ourselves, has sympathy with God, feels how unworthily the Ruler, Father, Friend of men has been treated. It does not ask, " What will my sin bring to me ? " but, " What does my sin mean to God ? " It involves, in addition to the mere recognition of sin :

B. An emotional element, — change of feeling — sorrow for sin as committed against goodness and justice, and therefore hateful to God, and hateful in itself (Ps. 51 : 1, 2, 10, 14). This element of repentance is indicated in the Scripture word μεταμέλομαι. If accompanied by the following element, it is a λύπη κατὰ Θεόν. If not so accompanied, it is a λύπη τοῦ κόσμου = remorse and despair (Mat. 27 : 3 ; Luke 18 : 23 ; 2 Cor. 7 : 9, 10).

Ps. 51 : 1, 2, 10, 14 — "Have mercy upon me . . . . blot out my transgressions. Wash me thoroughly from mine iniquity, And cleanse me from my sin. . . . . Create in me a clean heart, O God ; . . . . Deliver me from bloodguiltiness, O God " ; Mat. 27 : 3 — "Then Judas, who betrayed him, when he saw that he was condemned, repented himself, and brought back the thirty pieces of silver to the chief priests and elders, saying, I have sinned in that I betrayed innocent blood "; Luke 1R 23 — "when he heard these things, he became exceeding sorrowful; for he was very rich "; 2 Cor. 7:9. 10 — "I now rejoice, not that ye were made sorry, but that ye were made sorry unto repentance; for ye were made sorry after a godly sort . . . . For godly sorrow worketh repentance unto salvation, a repentance which bringeth no regret: but the sorrow of the world worketh death." We must distinguish sorrow for sin from shame on account of it and fear of its consequences. These last are selfish, while godly sorrow is disinterested. "A man may be angry with himself and may despise himself without any humble prostration before God or confession of his guilt " (Shedd, Dogm. Theol. 2:535, note).

True repentance, as illustrated in Ps. 51, does not think of 1. consequences, 2. other men, 3. heredity, as an excuse; but it sees sin as 1. transgression against God, 2. personal guilt, 3. defiling the inmost being. Perowne on Ps. 51:1 — "In all godly sorrow there is hope. Sorrow without hope may be remorse or despair, but it is not repentance." Much so-called repentance is illustrated by the little girl's prayer: "O God, make me good,—not real good, but just good enough so that I won't have to be whipped!" Shakespeare, Measure for Measure, 2:3 — "'T is meet so, daughter; but lest you do repent As that the sin hath brought you to this shame, Which sorrow is always towards ourselves, not heaven, Showing we would not spare heaven as we love it, But as we stand in fear. . . . . I do repent me as it is an evil, And take the shame with joy." Tempest, 3:3 —" For which foul deed, the Powers delaying, not forgetting, Have incensed the seas, and shores, yea, all the creatures, Against your peace. . . . . Whose wrath to guard you from . . . . is nothing but heart's sorrow And a clear life ensuing."

Simon, Reconciliation, 195, 379 — "At the very bottom it is God whose claims are advocated, whose part is taken, by that in us which, whilst most truly our own, yea, our very selves, is also most truly his, and of him. The divine energy and idea which constitutes us will not let its own root and source suffer wrong unatoned. God intends us to be givers as well as receivers, givers even to him. We share in his image that we may be creators and givers, not from compulsion, but in love." Such repentance as this is wrought only by the Holy Spirit. Conscience indeed is present in every human heart, but only the Holy Spirit convinces of sin. Why is the Holy Spirit needed? A. J. Gordon, Ministry of the Spirit, 189-201 — "Conscience is the witness to the law; the Spirit is the witness to grace. Conscience brings legal conviction; the Spirit brings evangelical conviction. The one begets a conviction unto despair; the other a conviction unto hope. Conscience convinces of sin committed, of righteousness impossible, of judgment impending; the Comforter convinces of sin committed, of righteousness imputed, of judgment accomplished — in Christ. God alone can reveal the divine view of sin, and enable man to understand it." But, however agonizing the sorrow, it will not constitute true repentance, unless it leads to, or is accompanied by:

C. A voluntary element,— change of purpose — inward turning from sin and disposition to seek pardon and cleansing (Ps. 51 : 5, 7, 10; Jer. 25 : 5). This includes and implies the two preceding elements, and is therefore the most important aspect of repentance. It is indicated in the Scripture term μετάνοια (Acts 2 : 38; Rom. 2 : 4).

Ps. 51:5, 7, 10 — "Behold, I was brought forth in iniquity; And in sin did my mother conceive me. . . . . Purge me with hyssop, and I shall be clean: Wash me, and I shall be whiter than snow. . . . . Create in me a clean heart, O God; And renew a right spirit within me"; Jer. 25:5 — "Return ye now every one from his evil way, and from the evil of your doings "; Acts 2:38 — "And Peter said unto them, Repent ye, and be baptized every one of you in the name of Jesus Christ "; Rom. 2:4 — "despisest thou the riches of his goodness and forbearance and longsuffering, not knowing that the goodness of God leadeth thee to repentance ? "

Walden, The Great Meaning of *Metanoia*, brings out well the fact that "repentance" is not the true translation of the word, but rather "change of mind"; indeed, he would give up the word "repentance" altogether in the N. T., except as the translation of μεταμέλεια. The idea of μετάνοια is abandonment of sin rather than sorrow for sin, — an act of the will rather than a state of the sensibility. Repentance is participation in Christ's revulsion from sin and suffering on account of it. It is repentance *from* sin, not *of* sin, nor *for* sin — always ἀπό and ἐκ, never περί or ἐπί. The true illustrations of repentance are found in Job (42:6 — "I abhor myself, And repent in dust and ashes "); in David (Ps. 51:10 — "Create in me a clean heart; And renew a right spirit within me "); in Peter (John 21:17 — "thou knowest that I love thee "); in the penitent thief (Luke 23 : 42 — " Jesus, remember me when thou comest in thy kingdom ") · in the prodigal son (Luke 15:18 — "I will arise and go to my Father ").

Repentance implies free will. Hence Spinoza, who knows nothing of free will, knows nothing of repentance. In book 4 of his Ethics, he says: "Repentance is not a virtue, that is, it does not spring from reason; on the contrary, the man who repents of what he has done is doubly wretched or impotent." Still he urges that for the good of society it is not desirable that vulgar minds should be enlightened as to this matter; see Upton, Hibbert Lectures, 315. Determinism also renders it irrational to feel righteous indignation either at the misconduct of other people or of ourselves. Moral admiration is similarly irrational in the determinist; see Balfour, Foundations of Belief, 24.

In broad distinction from the Scriptural doctrine, we find the Romanist view, which regards the three elements of repentance as the following: (1) contrition; (2) confession; (3) satisfaction. Of these, contrition is the only element properly belonging to repentance; yet from this contrition the Romanist excludes all sorrow for sin of nature. Confession is confession to the priest; and satisfaction is the sinner's own doing of outward penance, as a temporal and symbolic submission and reparation to violated law. This view is false and pernicious, in that it confounds repentance with its outward fruits, conceives of it as exercised rather toward the church than toward God, and regards it as a meritorious ground, instead of a mere condition, of pardon.

On the Romanist doctrine of Penance, Thornwell (Collected Writings, 1:423) remarks: "The *culpa* may be remitted, they say, while the *pœna* is to some extent retained." The priest absolves, not declaratively, but judicially. Denying the greatness of the sin, it makes man able to become his own Savior. Christ's satisfaction, for sins after baptism, is not sufficient; our satisfaction is sufficient. But performance of one duty, we object, cannot make satisfaction for the violation of another.

We are required to confess one to another, and specially to those whom we have wronged: James 5:16 — "Confess therefore your sins one to another, and pray one for another, that ye may be healed." This puts the hardest stress upon our natural pride. There are a hundred who will confess to a priest or to God, where there is one who will make frank and full confession to the aggrieved party. Confession to an official religious superior is not penitence nor a test of penitence. In the Confessional women expose their inmost desires to priests who are forbidden to marry. These priests are sometimes, though gradually, corrupted to the core, and at the same time they are taught in the Confessional precisely to what women to apply. In France many noble families will not permit their children to confess, and their women are not permitted to incur the danger.

Lord Salisbury in the House of Lords said of auricular confession: "It has been injurious to the moral independence and virility of the nation to an extent to which probably it has been given to no other institution to affect the character of mankind." See Walsh, Secret History of the Oxford Movement; A. J. Gordon, Ministry of the Spirit, 111 — "Asceticism is an absolute inversion of the divine order, since it seeks life through death, instead of finding death through life. No degree of mortification can ever bring us to sanctification." Penance can never effect true repentance, nor be other than a hindrance to the soul's abandonment of sin. Penance is something external to be done, and it diverts attention from the real inward need of the soul. The monk does penance by sleeping on an iron bed and by wearing a hair shirt. When Anselm of Canterbury died, his under garments were found alive with vermin which the saint had cultivated in order to mortify the flesh. Dr. Pusey always sat on a hard chair, traveled as uncomfortably as possible, looked down when he walked, and whenever he saw a coal-fire thought of hell. Thieves do penance by giving a part of their ill-gotten wealth to charity. In all these things there is no transformation of the inner life.

In further explanation of the Scripture representations, we remark:

(*a*) That repentance, in each and all of its aspects, is wholly an inward act, not to be confounded with the change of life which proceeds from it.

True repentance is indeed manifested and evidenced by confession of sin before God (Luke 18:13), and by reparation for wrongs done to men

[Luke 19 : 8). But these do not constitute repentance; they are rather fruits of repentance. Between 'repentance' and 'fruit worthy of repentance,' Scripture plainly distinguishes (Mat. 3 : 8).

Luke 18 : 13 — "But the publican, standing afar off, would not lift up so much as his eyes unto heaven, but smote his breast, saying, God, be thou merciful to me a sinner ['be propitiated to me the sinner']"; 19 : 8 — "And Zacchæus stood, and said unto the Lord, Behold, Lord, the half of my goods I give to the poor; and if I have wrongfully exacted aught of any man, I restore fourfold"; Mat. 3 : 8 — "Bring forth therefore fruit worthy of repentance." Fruit worthy of repentance, or fruits meet for repentance, are: 1. Confession of sin; 2. Surrender to Christ; 3. Turning from sin; 4. Reparation for wrong doing; 5. Right moral conduct; 6. Profession of Christian faith.

On Luke 17:3 — "if thy brother sin, rebuke him; and if he repent, forgive him" — Dr. B. H. Carroll remarks that the law is uniform which makes repentance indispensable to forgiveness. It applies to man's forgiveness of man, as well as to God's forgiveness of man, or the church's forgiveness of man. But I must be sure that I cherish toward the offender the spirit of love, whether he repents or not. Freedom from all malice toward him, however, and even loving prayerful labor to lead him to repentance, is not forgiveness. This I can grant only when he actually repents. If I do forgive him without repentance, then I impose my rule on God when I pray: "Forgive us our debts, as we also have forgiven our debtors" (Mat. 6 : 12).

On the question whether the requirement that we forgive without atonement implies that God does, see Brit. and For. Evang. Rev., Oct. 1881:678-691 — "Answer: 1. The present constitution of things is based upon atonement. Forgiveness on our part is required upon the ground of the Cross, without which the world would be hell. 2. God is Judge. We forgive, as brethren. When he forgives, it is as Judge of all the earth, of whom all earthly judges are representatives. If earthly judges may exact justice, much more God. The argument that would abolish atonement would abolish all civil government. 3. I should forgive my brother on the ground of God's love, and Christ's bearing of his sins. 4. God, who requires atonement, is the same being that provides it. This is 'handsome and generous.' But I can never provide atonement for my brother. I must, therefore, forgive freely, only upon the ground of what Christ has done for him."

(*b*) That repentance is only a negative condition, and not a positive means of salvation.

This is evident from the fact that repentance is no more than the sinner's present duty, and can furnish no offset to the claims of the law on account of past transgression. The truly penitent man feels that his repentance has no merit. Apart from the positive element of conversion, namely, faith in Christ, it would be only sorrow for guilt unremoved. This very sorrow, moreover, is not the mere product of human will, but is the gift of God.

Acts 5 : 31 — "Him did God exalt with his right hand to be a Prince and a Savior, to give repentance to Israel, and remission of sins"; 11 : 18 — "Then to the Gentiles also hath God granted repentance unto life"; 2 Tim. 2 : 25 — "if peradventure God may give them repentance unto the knowledge of the truth." The truly penitent man recognizes the fact that his sin deserves punishment. He never regards his penitence as offsetting the demands of law, and as making his punishment unjust. Whitefield: "Our repentance needeth to be repented of, and our very tears to be washed in the blood of Christ." Shakespeare, Henry V, 4:1— "More will I do: Though all that I can do is nothing worth, Since that my penitence comes after all, Imploring pardon" — imploring pardon both for the crime and for the imperfect repentance.

(*c*) That true repentance, however, never exists except in conjunction with faith.

Sorrow for sin, not simply on account of its evil consequences to the transgressor, but on account of its intrinsic hatefulness as opposed to divine holiness and love, is practically impossible without some confidence in God's mercy. It is the Cross which first makes us truly penitent (*cf.* John 12 : 32, 33). Hence all true preaching of repentance is implicitly a preaching of faith (Mat. 3 : 1–12 ; *cf.* Acts 19 : 4), and repentance toward God involves faith in the Lord Jesus Christ (Acts 20 : 21 ; Luke 15 : 10, 24 ; 19 : 8, 9 ; *cf.* Gal. 3 : 7).

John 12 : 32, 33 — "And I, if I be lifted up from the earth, will draw all men unto myself. But this he said, signifying by what manner of death he should die." Mat. 3 : 1–12 — John the Baptist's preaching of repentance was also a preaching of faith ; as is shown by Acts 19 : 4 — "John baptized with the baptism of repentance, saying unto the people that they should believe on him that should come after him, that is, on Jesus." Repentance involves faith : Acts 20 : 21 — "testifying both to Jews and to Greeks repentance toward God, and faith toward our Lord Jesus Christ" ; Luke 15 : 10, 24 — "there is joy in the presence of the angels of God over one sinner that repenteth. . . . . this my son was dead, and is alive again ; he was lost, and is found" ; 19 : 8, 9 — "the half of my goods I give to the poor ; and if I have wrongfully exacted aught of any man, I restore fourfold. And Jesus said unto him, To-day is salvation come to this house, forasmuch as he also is a son of Abraham" — the father of all believers ; *cf.* Gal. 3 : 6, 7 — "Even as Abraham believed God, and it was reckoned unto him for righteousness. Know therefore that they that are of faith, the same are sons of Abraham."

Luke 3 : 18 says of John the Baptist : "he preached the gospel unto the people," and the gospel message, the glad tidings, is more than the command to repent, — it is also the offer of salvation through Christ ; see Prof. Wm. Arnold Stevens, on John the Baptist and his Gospel, in Studies on the Gospel according to John. 2 Chron. 34 : 19 — "And it came to pass, when the king had heard the words of the law, that he rent his clothes." Moberly, Atonement and Personality, 44–46 — "Just in proportion as one sins, does he render it impossible for him truly to repent. Repentance must be the work of another in him. Is it not the Spirit of the Crucified which is the reality of the penitence of the truly penitent ?" If this be true, then it is plain that there is no true repentance which is not accompanied by the faith that unites us to Christ.

(*d*) That, conversely, wherever there is true faith, there is true repentance also.

Since repentance and faith are but different sides or aspects of the same act of turning, faith is as inseparable from repentance as repentance is from faith. That must be an unreal faith where there is no repentance, just as that must be an unreal repentance where there is no faith. Yet because the one aspect of his change is more prominent in the mind of the convert than the other, we are not hastily to conclude that the other is absent. Only that degree of conviction of sin is essential to salvation, which carries with it a forsaking of sin and a trustful surrender to Christ.

Bishop Hall : "Never will Christ enter into that soul where the herald of repentance hath not been before him." 2 Cor. 7 : 10 — "repentance unto salvation." In consciousness, sensation and perception are in inverse ratio to each other. Clear vision is hardly conscious of sensation, but inflamed eyes are hardly conscious of anything besides sensation. So repentance and faith are seldom equally prominent in the consciousness of the converted man ; but it is important to know that neither can exist without the other. The truly penitent man will, sooner or later, show that he has faith ; and the true believer will certainly show, in due season, that he hates and renounces sin.

The question, how much conviction a man needs to insure his salvation, may be answered by asking how much excitement one needs on a burning steamer. As, in the latter case, just enough to prompt persistent effort to escape ; so, in the former case, just enough remorseful feeling is needed, to induce the sinner to betake himself believingly to Christ.

On the general subject of Repentance, see Anderson, Regeneration, 279–288 ; Bp. Ossory, Nature and Effects of Faith, 40–48, 311–318 ; Woods, Works, 3 : 68–78 ; Philippi, Glaubenslehre, 5 : 1–10, 208–246 ; Luthardt, Compendium, 3d ed., 206–208 ; Hodge, Outlines of Theology, 3:5–381 ; Alexander, Evidences of Christianity, 47–60 ; Crawford, Atonement, 413–419.

2. *Faith.*

Faith is that voluntary change in the mind of the sinner in which he turns to Christ. Being essentially a change of mind, it involves a change of view, a change of feeling, and a change of purpose. We may therefore analyze faith also into three constituents, each succeeding term of which includes and implies the preceding :

A. An intellectual element (*notitia, credere Deum*), — recognition of the truth of God's revelation, or of the objective reality of the salvation provided by Christ. This includes not only a historical belief in the facts of the Scripture, but an intellectual belief in the doctrine taught therein as to man's sinfulness and dependence upon Christ.

John 2 : 23, 24 — "Now when he was in Jerusalem at the passover, during the feast, many believed on his name, beholding his signs which he did. But Jesus did not trust himself unto them, for that he knew all men " ; *cf.* 3 : 2 — Nicodemus has this external faith : "no one can do these signs that thou doest, except God be with him." 'ames 2 : 19 — "Thou believest that God is one ; thou doest well: the demons also believe, and shudder." Even this historical faith is not without its fruits. It is the spring of much philanthropic work. There were no hospitals in ancient Rome. Much of our modern progress is due to the leavening influence of Christianity, even in the case of those who have not personally accepted Christ.

McLaren, S. S. Times Feb. 22, 1902 : 107 — " Luke does not hesitate to say, in Acts 8 : 13, that 'Simon Magus also himself believed.' But he expects us to understand that Simon's belief was not faith that saved, but mere credence in the gospel narrative as true history. It had no ethical or spiritual worth. He was 'amazed,' as the Samaritans had been at his juggleries. It did not lead to repentance, or confession, or true trust. He was only 'amazed' at Philip's miracles, and there was no salvation in that." Merely historical faith, such as Disciples and Ritschlians hold to, lacks the element of affection, and besides this lacks the present reality of Christ himself. Faith that does not lay hold of a present Christ is not saving faith.

B. An emotional element (*assensus, credere Deo*), — assent to the revelation of God's power and grace in Jesus Christ, as applicable to the present needs of the soul. Those in whom this awakening of the sensibilities is unaccompanied by the fundamental decision of the will, which constitutes the next element of faith, may seem to themselves, and for a time may appear to others, to have accepted Christ.

Mat. 13 : 20, 21 — "he that was sown upon the rocky places, this is he that heareth the word, and straightway with joy receiveth it ; yet hath he not root in himself, but endureth for a while ; and when tribulation or persecution ariseth because of the word, straightway he stumbleth " ; *cf.* Ps. 106 : 12, 13 — "Then believed they his words ; they sang his praise. They soon forgat his works ; they waited not for his counsel " ; Ez. 33 : 31, 32 — " And they come unto thee as the people cometh, and they sit before thee as my people, and they hear thy words, but do them not ; for with their mouth they show much love, but their heart goeth after their gain. And, lo, thou art unto them as a very lovely song of one that hath a pleasant voice, and can play well on an instrument ; for they hear thy words, but they do them not " ; John 5 : 35 — Of John the Baptist : " He was the lamp that burneth and shineth ; and ye were willing to rejoice for a season in his light " ; 8 : 30, 31 — " As he spake these things, many believed on him (εἰς αὐτόν). Jesus therefore said to those Jews that had believed him (αὐτῷ), If ye abide in my word, then are ye truly my disciples." They believed *him*, but did not yet believe *on* him, that is, make him the foundation of their faith and life. Yet Jesus graciously recognizes this first faint foreshadowing of faith. It might lead to full and saving faith.

" Proselytes of the gate " were so called, because they contented themselves with sitting in the gate, as it were, without going into the holy city. " Proselytes of righteousness " were those who did their whole duty, by joining themselves fully to the people of God. Not *emotion*, but *devotion*, is the important thing. Temporary faith is as irrational and valueless as temporary repentance. It perhaps gained temporary blessing in the way of healing in the time of Christ, but, if not followed by complete surrender of the will, it might even aggravate one's sin ; see John 5 : 14 — "Behold, thou art made whole ; sin no more, lest a worse thing befall thee." The special faith of miracles was not a high, but a low, form of faith, and it is not to be sought in our day as indispensable to the progress of the kingdom. Miracles have ceased, not because of decline in faith, but because the Holy Spirit has changed the method of his manifestations, and has led the church to seek more spiritual gifts.

Saving faith, however, includes also :

C.   A voluntary element (*fiducia, credere in Deum*), — trust in Christ
is Lord and Savior ; or, in other words — to distinguish its two aspects :

(*a*)   Surrender of the soul, as guilty and defiled, to Christ's governance.

Mat. 11 : 28, 29 — "Come unto me, all ye that labor and are heavy laden, and I will give you rest. Take my yoke
upon you, and learn of me " ; John 8 : 12 — " I am the light of the world : he that followeth me shall not walk in the
darkness " ; 14 : 1 — "Let not your heart be troubled : believe in God, believe also in me " ; Acts 16 : 31 — "Believe on
the Lord Jesus, and thou shalt be saved." Instances of the use of πιστεύω, in the sense of trustful
commitance or surrender, are : John 2 : 24 — "But Jesus did not trust himself unto them, for that he knew
all men " ; Rom. 3 : 2 — "they were intrusted with the oracles of God " ; Gal. 2 : 7 — "when they saw that I had been
intrusted with the gospel of the uncircumcision." πίστις = " trustful self-surrender to God " (Meyer).

In this surrender of the soul to Christ's governance we have the guarantee that the
gospel salvation is not an unmoral trust which permits continuance in sin. Aside from
the fact that saving faith is only the obverse side of true repentance, the very nature
of faith, as submission to Christ, the embodied law of God and source of spiritual life,
makes a life of obedience and virtue to be its natural and necessary result. Faith is
not only a declaration of dependence, it is also a vow of allegiance. The sick man's
faith in his physician is shown not simply by trusting him, but by obeying him. Doing
what the doctor says is the very proof of trust. No physician will long care for a
patient who refuses to obey his orders. Faith is self-surrender to the great Physician,
and a leaving of our case in his hands. But it is also the taking of his prescriptions,
and the active following of his directions.

We need to emphasize this active element in saving faith, lest men get the notion
that mere indolent acquiescence in Christ's plan will save them. Faith is not simple
receptiveness. It gives itself, as well as receives Christ. It is not mere passivity, — it
is also self-committal. As all reception of knowledge is active, and there must be
attention if we would learn, so all reception of Christ is active, and there must be intelligent giving as well as taking. The Watchman, April 30, 1896 — " Faith is more than
belief and trust. It is the action of the soul going out toward its object. It is the
exercise of a spiritual faculty akin to that of sight ; it establishes a personal relation
between the one who exercises faith and the one who is its object. When the intellectual feature predominates, we call it belief ; when the emotional element predominates, we call it trust. This faith is at once ' An affirmation and an act Which bids
eternal truth be present fact.' "

There are great things received in faith, but nothing is received by the man who does
not first give himself to Christ. A conquered general came into the presence of his
conqueror and held out to him his hand : " Your sword first, sir ! " was the response.
But when General Lee *offered* his sword to General Grant at Appomattox, the latter
returned it, saying : " No, keep your sword, and go to your home.' Jacobi said that
" Faith is the reflection of the divine knowing and willing in the finite spirit of man."
G. B. Foster, in Indiana Baptist Outlook, June 19, 1902 — " Catholic orthodoxy is wrong
in holding that the authority for faith is the church ; for that would be an external
authority. Protestant orthodoxy is wrong in holding that the authority for faith is
the book ; for that would be an external authority. Liberalism is wrong in holding
that the reason is the authority for faith. The authority for faith is the revelation of
God." Faith in this revelation is faith in Christ the Revealer. It puts the soul in connection with the source of all knowledge and power. As the connection of a wire with
the reservoir of electric force makes it the channel of vast energies, so the smallest
measure of faith, any real connection of the soul with Christ, makes it the recipient of
divine resources.

While faith is the act of the whole man, and intellect, affection, and will are involved
in it, will is the all-inclusive and most important of its elements. No other exercise of
will is such a revelation of our being and so decisive of our destiny. The voluntary
element in faith is illustrated in marriage. Here one party pledges the future in permanent self-surrender, commits one's self to another person in confidence that this
future, with all its new revelations of character, will only justify the decision made.
Yet this is rational ; see Holland, in Lux Mundi, 46–48. To put one's hand into molten
iron, even though one knows of the " spheroidal state " that gives impunity, requires
an exertion of will ; and not all workmen in metals are courageous enough to make
the venture. The child who leaped into the dark cellar, in confidence that her father's
arms would be open to receive her, did not act irrationally, because she had heard her

father's command and trusted his promise. Though faith in Christ is a leap in the dark, and requires a mighty exercise of will, it is nevertheless the highest wisdom, because Christ's word is pledged that "him that cometh to me I will in no wise cast out" (John 6 : 37).

J. W. A. Stewart : " Faith is 1. a bond between persons, trust, confidence ; 2. it makes ventures, takes much for granted ; 3. its security is the character and power of him in whom we believe, — not our faith, but his fidelity, is the guarantee that our faith is rational." Kant said that nothing in the world is good but the good will which freely obeys the law of the good. Pfleiderer defines faith as the free surrender of the heart to the gracious will of God. Kaftan, Dogmatik, 21, declares that the Christian religion is essentially faith, and that this faith manifests itself as 1. doctrine ; 2. worship ; 3. morality.

(b) Reception and appropriation of Christ, as the source of pardon and spiritual life.

John 1 : 12 — " as many as received him, to them gave he the right to become children of God, even to them that bel'eve on his name " ; 4 : 14 — " whosoever drinketh of the water that I shall give him shall never thirst ; but the water that I shall give him shall become in him a well of water springing up unto eternal life " ; 6 : 53 — " Except ye eat the flesh of the Son of man and drink his blood, ye have not life in yourselves " ; 20 : 31 — " these are written, that ye may believe that Jesus is the Christ, the Son of God ; and that believing ye may have life in his name " ; Eph. 3 : 17 — " that Christ may dwell in your hearts through faith " ; Heb. 11 : 1 — " Now faith is assurance of things hoped for, a conviction of things not seen " ; Rev. 3 : 20 — " Behold, I stand at the door and knock : if any man hear my voice and open the door, I will come in to him, and will sup with him, and he with me."

The three constituents of faith may be illustrated from the thought, feeling, and action of a person who stands by a boat, upon a little island which the rising stream threatens to submerge. He first regards the boat from a purely intellectual point of view,— it is merely an *actually existing boat.* As the stream rises, he looks at it, secondly, with some accession of emotion,— his prospective danger awakens in him the conviction that it is a *good boat for a time of need,* though he is not yet ready to make use of it. But, thirdly, when he feels that the rushing tide must otherwise sweep him away, a volitional element is added,— he gets into the boat, trusts himself to it, accepts it as his *present, and only, means of safety.* Only this last faith in the boat is faith that saves, although this last includes both the preceding. It is equally clear that the getting into the boat may actually save a man, while at the same time he may be full of fears that the boat will never bring him to shore. These fears may be removed by the boatman's word. So saving faith is not necessarily assurance of faith ; but it becomes assurance of faith when the Holy Spirit "beareth witness with our spirit, that we are children of God " (Rom. 8 : 16). On the nature of this assurance, and on the distinction between it and saving faith, see pages 844-846.

" Coming to Christ," " looking to Christ," " receiving Christ," are all descriptions of faith, as are also the phrases : " surrender to Christ," " submission to Christ," " closing in with Christ." Paul refers to a confession of faith in Rom. 10 : 9 — " if thou shalt confess with thy mouth Jesus as Lord." Faith, then, is a taking of Christ as both Savior and Lord ; and it includes both appropriation of Christ, and consecration to Christ. The voluntary element in faith, however, is a giving as well as a taking. The giving, or surrender, is illustrated in baptism by submergence ; the taking, or reception, by emergence. See further on the Symbolism of Baptism. McCosh, Div. Government : " Saving faith is the consent of the will to the assent of the understanding, and commonly accompanied with emotion." Pres. Hopkins, in Princeton Rev., Sept. 1878 : 511-540 — " In its intellectual element, faith is receptive, and believes that God *is ;* in its affectional element, faith is assimilative, and believes that God is a *rewarder ;* in its voluntary element, faith is operative, and actually *comes* to God (Heb. 11 : 6)."

Where the element of surrender is emphasized and the element of reception is not understood, the result is a legalistic experience, with little hope or joy. Only as we *appropriate* Christ, in connection with our *consecration,* do we realize the full blessing of the gospel. Light requires two things : the sun to shine, and the eye to take in its shining. So we cannot be saved without Christ to save, and faith to take the Savior for ours. Faith is the act by which we receive Christ. The woman who touched the border of Jesus' garment received his healing power. It is better still to keep in touch with Christ so as to receive continually his grace and life. But best of all is taking him into our inmost being, to be the soul of our soul and the life of our life. This is the essence of faith, though many Christians do not yet realize it. Dr. Curry said well that faith can never be defined because it is a fact of life. It is a merging of our life in the life of Christ, and a reception of Christ's life to interpenetrate and energize ours. In faith we must take Christ as well as give ourselves. It is certainly true that surrender without trust will not make us possessors of God's peace. F. L. Anderson: "Faith is submissive reliance on Jesus Christ for salvation: 1. Reliance on Jesus Christ—not mere intellectual belief; 2. Reliance on him for salvation—we can never undo the past or atone for our sins; 3. Submissive reliance on Christ. Trust without surrender will never save."

The passages already referred to refute the view of the Romanist, that saving faith is simply implicit assent to the doctrines of the church; and the view of the Disciple or Campbellite, that faith is merely intellectual belief in the truth, on the presentation of evidence.

The Romanist says that faith can coëxist with mortal sin. The Disciple holds that faith may and must exist before regeneration,— regeneration being completed in baptism. With these erroneous views, compare the noble utterance of Luther, Com. on Galatians, 1:191, 247, quoted in Thomasius, III, 2:185 — "True faith," says Luther, "is that assured trust and firm assent of heart, by which Christ is laid hold of,—so that Christ is the object of faith. Yet he is not merely the object of faith; but in the very faith, so to speak, Christ is present. Faith lays hold of Christ, and grasps him as a present possession, just as the ring holds the jewel." Edwards, Works, 4:71-73; 2:601-641 — "Faith," says Edwards, "includes the whole act of unition to Christ as a Savior. The entire active uniting of the soul, or the whole of what is called coming to Christ, and receiving of him, is called faith in the Scripture." See also Belief, What Is It? 150-179, 290-298.

Hatch, Hibbert Lectures, 530—"Faith began by being: 1. a simple trust in God; then followed, 2. a simple expansion of that proposition into the assent to the proposition that God is good, and, 3. a simple acceptance of the proposition that Jesus Christ was his Son; then, 4. came in the definition of terms, and each definition of terms involved a new theory; finally, 5. the theories were gathered together into systems, and the martyrs and witnesses of Christ died for their faith, not outside but inside the Christian sphere; and instead of a world of religious belief which resembled the world of actual fact in the sublime unsymmetry of its foliage and the deep harmony of its discords, there prevailed the most fatal assumption of all, that the symmetry of a system is the test of its truth and the proof thereof." We regard this statement of Hatch as erroneous, in that it attributes to the earliest disciples no larger faith than that of their Jewish brethren. We claim that the earliest faith involved an implicit acknowledgement of Jesus as Savior and Lord, and that this faith of simple obedience and trust became explicit recognition of our Lord's deity and atonement just so soon as persecution and the Holy Spirit disclosed to them the real contents of their own consciousness.

An illustration of the simplicity and saving power of faith is furnished by Principal J. R. Andrews, of New London, Conn., Principal of the Bartlett Grammar School. When the steamer Atlantic was wrecked off Fisher's Island, though Mr. Andrews could not swim, he determined to make a desperate effort to save his life. Binding a life-preserver about him, he stood on the edge of the deck waiting his opportunity, and when he saw a wave moving shoreward, he jumped into the rough breakers and was borne safely to land. He was saved by faith. He accepted the conditions of salvation. Forty perished in a scene where he was saved. In one sense he saved himself; in another sense he depended upon God. It was a combination of personal activity and dependence upon God that resulted in his salvation. If he had not used the life-preserver, he would have perished; if he had not cast himself into the sea, he would have perished. So faith in Christ is reliance upon him for salvation; but it is also our own making of a new start in life and the showing of our trust by action. Tract 357, Am. Tract Society—"What is it to believe on Christ? It is: To feel your need of him; To believe that he is able and willing to save you, and to save you now; and To cast yourself unreservedly upon his mercy, and trust in him alone for salvation."

In further explanation of the Scripture representations, we remark:

(*a*) That faith is an act of the affections and will, as truly as it is an act of the intellect.

It has been claimed that faith and unbelief are purely intellectual states, which are necessarily determined by the facts at any given time presented to the mind; and that they are, for this reason, as destitute of moral quality and as far from being matters of obligation, as are our instinctive feelings of pleasure and pain. But this view unwarrantably isolates the intellect, and ignores the fact that, in all moral subjects, the state of the affections and will affects the judgment of the mind with regard to truth. In the intellectual act the whole moral nature expresses itself. Since the tastes determine the opinions, faith is a moral act, and men are responsible for not believing.

John 3 : 18–20 — "He that believeth on him is not judged: he that believeth not hath been judged already, because he hath not believed on the name of the only begotten Son of God. And this is the judgment, that the light is come into the world, and men loved the darkness rather than the light; for their works were evil. For every one that doeth evi. hateth the light, and cometh not to the light, lest his works should be reproved "; 5 : 40 — "ye will not come to me, that ye may have life"; 16 : 8, 9 — "And he, when he is come, will convict the world in respect of sin . . . . of sin, because they believe not on me"; Rev. 2 : 21 — "she willeth not to repent." Notice that the Revised Version very frequently substitutes the voluntary and active terms "disobedience" and "disobedient" for the "unbelief" and "unbelieving" of the Authorized Version,— as in Rom. 15 : 31; Heb 3 : 18; 4 : 6, 11; 11 : 31. See Park, Discourses, 45, 46.

Savages do not know that they are responsible for their physical appetites, or that there is any right and wrong in matters of sense, until they come under the influence of Christianity. In like manner, even men of science can declare that the intellectual sphere has no part in man's probation, and that we are no more responsible for our opinions and beliefs than we are for the color of our skin. But faith is not a merely intellectual act,— the affections and will give it quality. There is no moral quality in the belief that $2 + 2 = 4$, because we can not help that belief. But in believing on Christ there is moral quality, because there is the element of choice. Indeed it may be questioned, whether, in every judgment upon moral things, there is not an act of will.

Hence on John 7 : 17 —"If any man willeth to do his will, he shall know of the teaching, whether it is of God, or whether I speak from myself"— F. L. Patton calls attention to the two common errors: (1) that obedience will certify doctrine,— which is untrue, because obedience is the result of faith, not vice versa; (2) that personal experience is the ultimate test of faith,— which is untrue, because the Bible is the only rule of faith, and it is one thing to receive truth through the feelings, but quite another to test truth by the feelings. The text really means, that if any man is willing to do God's will, he shall know whether it be of God; and the two lessons to be drawn are: (1) the gospel needs no additional evidence; (2) the Holy Ghost is the hope of the world. On responsibility for opinions and beliefs, see Mozley, on Blanco White, in Essays Philos. and Historical, 2 : 142; T. T. Smith, Hulsean Lectures for 1839. Wilfrid Ward, The Wish to Believe, quotes Shakespeare: "Thy wish was father, Harry, to that thought"; and Thomas Arnold: "They dared not lightly believe what they so much wished to be true."

Pascal: "Faith is an act of the will." Emerson, Essay on Worship: "A man bears beliefs as a tree bears apples. Man's religious faith is the expression of what he is." Bain: "In its essential character, belief is a phase of our active nature, otherwise called the will." Nash, Ethics and Revelation, 257 — "Faith is the creative human answer to the creative divine offer. It is not the passive acceptance of a divine favor. . . . By faith man, laying hold of the personality of God in Christ, becomes a true person. And by the same faith he becomes, under God, a creator and founder of true society." Inge, Christian Mysticism, 52 —"Faith begins with an experiment and ends with an experience. But even the power to make the experiment is given from above. Eternal life is not $\gamma\nu\tilde{\omega}\sigma\iota\varsigma$, but the state of acquiring knowledge — $\tilde{\iota}\nu\alpha\ \gamma\iota\gamma\nu\tilde{\omega}\sigma\kappa\omega\sigma\iota\nu$. It is significant that John, who is so fond of the verb 'to know,' never uses the substantive $\gamma\nu\tilde{\omega}\sigma\iota\varsigma$." Crane, Religion of To-morrow, 148 — "'I will not obey, because I do not yet know'? But this is making the intellectual side the only side of faith, whereas the most important side is the will-side. Let a man follow what he does believe, and he shall be led on to larger faith. Faith is the reception of the personal influence of a living Lord, and a corresponding action."

William James, Will to Believe, 61 —"This life is worth living, since it is what we make it, from the moral point of view. . . . . Often enough our faith beforehand in an uncertified result is the only thing that makes the result come true. . . . . If your heart does not *want* a world of moral reality, your head will assuredly never make you believe in one. . . . . Freedom to believe covers only living options which the intellect cannot by itself resolve. . . . . We are not to put a stopper on our heart, and meantime act as if religion were not true"; Psychology, 2 : 282, 321 — " Belief is consent, willingness, turning of our disposition. It is the mental state or function of cognizing reality. We never disbelieve anything except for the reason that we believe something else which contradicts the first thing. We give higher reality to whatever things we select and emphasize and turn to with a will. . . . . We need only in cold blood *act* as if the thing in question were real, and keep acting as if it were real, and it will infallibly end by growing into such a connection with our life that it will become real. Those to whom God and duty are mere names, can make them much more than that, if they make a little sacrifice to them every day."

E. G. Robinson: " Campbellism makes intellectual belief to be saving faith. But saving faith is consent of the heart as well as assent of the intellect. On the one hand there is the intellectual element: faith is belief upon the ground of evidence; faith without evidence is credulity. But on the other hand faith has an element of affection; the element of love is always wrapped up in it. So Abraham's faith made Abraham like God; for we always become like that which we trust." Faith therefore is not chronologically subsequent to regeneration, but is its accompaniment. As the soul's appropriation of Christ and his salvation. it is not the result of an accomplished renewal, but rather the medium through which that renewal is effected. Otherwise it would follow that one who had not yet believed (*i. e.*, received Christ) might still be regenerate, whereas the Scripture represents the privilege of sonship as granted only to believers. See John 1 : 12, 13 — "But as many as received him, to them gave he the right to become children of God, even to them that believe on his name : who were born, not of blood, nor of the will of the flesh, nor of the will of man, but of God"; also 3 : 5, 6, 10–15 ; Gal. 3 : 26 ; 2 Pet. 1 : 3 ; *cf*. 1 John 5 : 1.

(*b*) That the object of saving faith is, in general, the whole truth of God, so far as it is objectively revealed or made known to the soul; but, in particular, the person and work of Jesus Christ, which constitutes the centre and substance of God's revelation (Acts 17 : 18; 1 Cor. 1 : 23; Col. 1 : 27; Rev. 19 : 10).

The patriarchs, though they had no knowledge of a personal Christ, were saved by believing in God so far as God had revealed himself to them; and whoever among the heathen are saved, must in like manner be saved by casting themselves as helpless sinners upon God's plan of mercy, dimly shadowed forth in nature and providence. But such faith, even among the patriarchs and heathen, is implicitly a faith in Christ, and would become explicit and conscious trust and submission, whenever Christ were made known to them (Mat. 8 : 11, 12; John 10 : 16; Acts 4 : 12; 10 : 31, 34, 35, 44; 16 : 31).

Acts 17 : 18 — "he preached Jesus and the resurrection " ; 1 Cor. 1 : 23 — "we preach Christ crucified "; Col. 1 : 27 — "this mystery among the Gentiles, which is Christ in you, the hope of glory: whom we proclaim "; Rev. 19 : 10 —"the testimony of Jesus is the spirit of prophecy." Saving faith is not belief in a dogma, but personal trust in a personal Christ. It is, therefore, possible to a child. Dorner: "The object of faith is the Christian revelation — God in Christ. . . . . Faith is union with objective Christianity — appropriation of the real contents of Christianity." Dr. Samuel Hopkins, the great uncle, defined faith as "an understanding, cordial receiving of the divine testimony concerning Jesus Christ and the way of salvation by him, in which the heart accords and conforms to the gospel." Dr. Mark Hopkins, the great nephew, defined it as "confidence in a personal being." Horace Bushnell: "Faith rests on a person. Faith is that act by which one person, a sinner, commits himself to another person, a Savior." In John 11 : 25 —"I am the resurrection and the life "— Martha is led to substitute belief in a person for belief in an abstract doctrine. Jesus is "the resurrection," because he is "the life." All doctrine and all miracle is significant and important only because it is the expression of the living Christ, the Revealer of God.

The object of faith is sometimes represented in the N. T., as being God the Father. John 5 : 24 —"He that heareth my word, and believeth him that sent me, hath eternal life " ; Rom. 4 : 5 — "to him that worketh not, but believeth on him that justifieth the ungodly, his faith is reckoned for righteousness." We can explain these passages only when we remember that Christ is God "manifested in the flesh (1 Tim. 3:16), and that "he that hath seen me hath seen the Father" (John 14:9). Man may receive a gift without knowing from whom it comes, or how much it has cost. So the heathen, who casts himself as a sinner upon God's mercy, may receive salvation from the Crucified One, without knowing who is the giver, or that the gift was purchased by agony and blood. Denney, Studies in Theology, 154—"No N. T. writer ever *remembered* Christ. They never thought of him as belonging to the past. Let us not preach about the *historical* Christ, but rather, about the *living* Christ; nay, let us preach *him*, present and omnipotent. Jesus could say: 'Whither I go, ye know the way' (John 14:4); for they knew *him*, and he was both the *end* and the *way*."

Dr. Charles Hodge unduly restricts the operations of grace to the preaching of the incarnate Christ: Syst. Theol., 2:648—"There is no faith where the gospel is not heard; and where there is no faith, there is no salvation. This is indeed an awful doctrine." And yet, in 2:668, he says most inconsistently: "As God is everywhere present in the material world, guiding its operations according to the laws of nature; so he is everywhere present with the minds of men, as the Spirit of truth and goodness, operating on them according to laws of their free moral agency, inclining them to good and restraining them from evil." This presence and revelation of God we hold to be through Christ, the eternal Word, and so we interpret the prophecy of Caiaphas as referring to the work of the personal Christ: John 11:51, 52—"he prophesied that Jesus should die for the nation; and not for the nation only, but that he might also gather together into one the children of God that are scattered abroad."

Since Christ is the Word of God and the Truth of God, he may be received even by those who have not heard of his manifestation in the flesh. A proud and self-righteous morality is inconsistent with saving faith; but a humble and penitent reliance upon God, as a Savior from sin and a guide of conduct, is an implicit faith in Christ; for such reliance casts itself upon God, so far as God has revealed himself,—and the only Revealer of God is Christ. We have, therefore, the hope that even among the heathen there may be some, like Socrates, who, under the guidance of the Holy Spirit working through the truth of nature and conscience, have found the way of life and salvation.

The number of such is so small as in no degree to weaken the claims of the missionary enterprise upon us. But that there are such seems to be intimated in Scripture: Mat. 8:11, 12—"many shall come from the east and the west, and shall sit down with Abraham, and Isaac, and Jacob, in the kingdom of heaven: but the sons of the kingdom shall be cast forth into the outer darkness"; John 10:16—"And other sheep I have, which are not of this fold: them also I must bring, and they shall hear my voice; and they shall become one flock, one shepherd"; Acts 4:12—"And in none other is there salvation: for neither is there any other name under heaven, that is given among men, wherein we must be saved"; 10:31, 34, 35, 44—"Cornelius, thy prayer is heard, and thine alms are had in remembrance in the sight of God. . . . . Of a truth I perceive that God is no respecter of persons: but in every nation he that feareth him, and worketh righteousness, is acceptable to him . . . . . While Peter yet spake these words, the Holy Spirit fell on all them that heard the word"; 16:31—"Believe on the Lord Jesus, and thou shalt be saved, thou and thy house."

And instances are found of apparently regenerated heathen; see in Godet on John 7:17, note (vol. 2:277), the account of the so-called "Chinese hermit," who accepted Christ, saying: "This is the only Buddha whom men ought to worship!" Edwards, Life of Brainard, 173-175, gives an account "of one who was a devout and zealous reformer, or rather restorer, of what he supposed was the ancient religion of the Indians." After a period of distress, he says that God "comforted his heart and showed him what he should do, and since that time he had known God and tried to serve him; and loved all men, be they who they would, so as he never did before." See art. by Dr. Lucius E. Smith, in Bib. Sac., Oct. 1881:622-645, on the question: "Is salvation possible without a knowledge of the gospel?" H. B. Smith, System, 323, note, rightly bases hope for the heathen, not on morality, but on sacrifice.

A chief of the Camaroons in S. W. Africa, fishing with many of his tribe long before the missionaries came, was overtaken by a storm, and while almost all the rest were drowned, he and a few others escaped. He gathered his people together afterwards and told the story of disaster. He said: "When the canoes upset and I found myself battling with the waves, I thought: To whom shall I cry for help? I knew that the god of the hills could not help me; I knew that the evil spirit would not help me. So I cried to the Great Father, Lord, save me! At that moment my feet touched the sand of the beach, and I was safe. Now let all my people honor the Great Father, and let no man speak a word against him, for he can help us." This chief afterwards used every effort to prevent strife and bloodshed, and was remembered by those who came after as a peace-maker. His son told this story to Alfred Saker, the missionary, saying

" Why did you not come sooner? My father longed to know what you have told us; he thirsted for the knowledge of God." Mr. Saker told this in England in 1879.

John Fiske appends to his book, The Idea of God, 168, 169, the following pathetic words of a Kafir, named Sekese, in conversation with a French traveler, M. Arbrouseille, on the subject of the Christian religion: "Your tidings," said this uncultured barbarian, "are what I want, and I was seeking before I knew you, as you shall hear and judge for yourself. Twelve years ago I went to feed my flocks; the weather was hazy. I sat down upon a rock, and asked myself sorrowful questions; yes, sorrowful, because I was unable to answer them. Who has touched the stars with his hands—on what pillars do they rest? I asked myself. The waters never weary, they know no other law than to flow without ceasing from morning till night and from night till morning; but where do they stop, and who makes them flow thus? The clouds also come and go, and burst in water over the earth. Whence come they—who sends them? The diviners certainly do not give us rain; for how could they do it? And why do I not see them with my own eyes, when they go up to heaven to fetch it? I cannot see the wind; but what is it? Who brings it, makes it blow and roar and terrify us? Do I know how the corn sprouts? Yesterday there was not a blade in my field; to-day I returned to my field and found some; who can have given to the earth the wisdom and the power to produce it? Then I buried my head in both hands."

On the question whether men are ever led to faith, without intercourse with living Christians or preachers, see Life of Judson, by his son, 84. The British and Foreign Bible Society publish a statement, made upon the authority of Sir Bartle Frere, that he met with "an instance, which was carefully investigated, in which all the inhabitants of a remote village in the Deccan had abjured idolatry and caste, removed from their temples the idols which had been worshiped there time out of mind, and agreed to profess a form of Christianity which they had deduced from the careful perusal of a single Gospel and a few tracts." Max Müller, Chips, 4 : 177-189, apparently proves that Buddha is the original of St. Josaphat, who has a day assigned to him in the calendar of both the Greek and the Roman churches. "Sancte Socrates, ora pro nobis."

The Missionary Review of the World, July, 1896 : 519-523, tells the story of Adiri, afterwards called John King, of Maripastoon in Dutch Guiana. The Holy Spirit wrought in him mightily years before he heard of the missionaries. He was a coal-black negro, a heathen and a fetish worshiper. He was convicted of sin and apparently converted through dreams and visions. Heaven and hell were revealed to him. He was sick unto death, and One appeared to him declaring himself to be the Mediator between God and man, and telling him to go to the missionaries for instruction. He was persecuted, but he won his tribe from heathenism and transformed them into a Christian community.

S. W. Hamblen, missionary to China, tells of a very earnest and consistent believer who lived at rather an obscure town of about 2800 people. The evangelist went to visit him and found that he was a worthy example to those around him. He had become a Christian before he had seen a single believer, by reading a Chinese New Testament. Although till the evangelist went to his house he had never met a Baptist and did not know that there were any Baptist churches in existence, yet by reading the New Testament he had become not only a Christian but a strong Baptist in belief, so strong that he could argue with the missionary on the subject of baptism.

The Rev. K. E. Malm, a pioneer Baptist preacher in Sweden, on a journey to the district as far north as Gestrikland, met a woman from Lapland who was on her way to Upsala in order to visit Dr. Fjellstedt and converse with him as to how she might obtain peace with God and get rid of her anxiety concerning her sins. She said she had traveled 60 (= 240 English) miles, and she had still far to go. Malm improved the opportunity to speak to her concerning the crucified Christ, and she found peace in believing on his atonement. She became so happy that she clapped her hands, and for joy could not sleep that night. She said later: "Now I will return home and tell the people what I have found." This she did, and did not care to continue her journey to Upsala, in order to get comfort from Dr. Fjellstedt.

(c) That the ground of faith is the external word of promise. The ground of assurance, on the other hand, is the inward witness of the Spirit that we fulfil the conditions of the promise (Rom. 4 : 20, 21 ; 8 : 16 ; Eph. 1 : 13 ; 1 John 4 : 13 ; 5 : 10). This witness of the Spirit is not a new revelation from God, but a strengthening of faith so that it becomes conscious and indubitable.

True faith is possible without assurance of salvation. But if Alexander's view were correct, that the object of saving faith is the proposition: "God, for Christ's sake, now looks with reconciling love on me, a sinner," no one could believe, without being at the same time assured that he was a saved person. Upon the true view, that the object of saving faith is not a proposition, but a person, we can perceive not only the simplicity of faith, but the possibility of faith even where the soul is destitute of assurance or of joy. Hence those who already believe are urged to seek for assurance (Heb. 6 : 11 ; 2 Peter 1 : 10).

Rom. 4 : 20, 21 — " looking unto the promise of God, he wavered not through unbelief, but waxed strong through faith, giving glory to God, and being fully assured that what he had promised, he was able also to perform " ; 8 : 16 — " The Spirit himself beareth witness with our spirit, that we are children of God " ; Eph. 1 : 13 — " in whom, having also believed, ye were sealed with the Holy Spirit of promise " ; 1 John 4 : 13 — " hereby we know that we abide in him, and he in us, because he hath given us of his Spirit " ; 5 : 10 — " He that believeth on the Son of God hath the witness in him." This assurance is not of the essence of faith, because believers are exhorted to attain to it : Heb. 6 : 11 — " And we desire that each one of you may show the same diligence unto the fulness of hope [marg. — 'full assurance'] even to the end " ; 2 Pet. 1 : 10 — " Wherefore, brethren, give the more diligence to make your calling and election sure." Cf. Prov. 14 : 14 — " a good man shall be satisfied from himself."

There is need to guard the doctrine of assurance from mysticism. The witness of the Spirit is not a new and direct revelation from God. It is a strengthening of previously existing faith until he who possesses this faith cannot any longer doubt that he possesses it. It is a general rule that all our emotions, when they become exceedingly strong, also become conscious. Instance affection between man and woman.

Edwards, Religious Affections, in Works, 3 : 83–91, says the witness of the Spirit is not a new word or suggestion from God, but an enlightening and sanctifying influence so that the heart is drawn forth to embrace the truth already revealed, and to perceive that it embraces it. " Bearing witness " is not in this case to declare and assert a thing to be true, but to hold forth evidence from which a thing may be proved to be true : God " beareth witness ...... by signs and wonders " (Heb. 2 : 4) So the " seal of the Spirit " is not a voice or suggestion, but a work or effect of the Spirit, left as a divine mark upon the soul, to be an evidence by which God's children may be known. Seals had engraved upon them the image or name of the persons to whom they belonged. The " seal of the Spirit, " the " earnest of the Spirit," the " witness of the Spirit, " are all one thing. The childlike spirit, given by the Holy Spirit, is the Holy Spirit's witness or evidence in us.

See also illustration of faith and assurance, in C. S. Robinson's Short Studies for S. S. Teachers, 179, 180. Faith should be distinguished not only from assurance, but also from feeling or joy. Instance Abraham's faith when he went to sacrifice Isaac ; and Madame Guyon's faith, when God's face seemed hid from her. See, on the witness of the Spirit, Short, Bampton Lectures for 1846 ; British and For. Evan. Rev., 1888 : 617–631. For the view which confounds faith with assurance, see Alexander, Discourses on Faith, 83–118.

It is important to distinguish saving faith from assurance of faith, for the reason that lack of assurance is taken by so many real Christians as evidence that they know nothing of the grace of God. To use once more a well-worn illustration : It is getting into the boat that saves us, and not our comfortable feelings about the boat. What saves us is faith in Christ, not faith in our faith, or faith in the faith. The astronomer does not turn his telescope to the reflection of the sun or moon in the water, when he can turn it to the sun or moon itself. Why obscure our faith, when we can look to Christ ?

The faith in a distant Redeemer was the faith of Christian, in Bunyan's Pilgrim's Progress. Only at the end of his journey does Christian have Christ's presence. This representation rests upon a wrong conception of faith as laying hold of a promise or a doctrine, rather than as laying hold of the living and present Christ. The old Scotch woman's direction to the inquirer to " grip the promise " is not so good as the direction to " grip Christ." Sir Francis Drake, the great English sailor, had for his crest an anchor with a cable running up into the sky. A poor boy, taught in a mission school in Ireland, when asked what was meant by saving faith, replied: "It is grasping God with the heart."

The view of Charles Hodge, like that of Alexander, puts doctrine before Christ, and makes the formal principle, the supremacy of Scripture, superior to the material principle, justification by faith. The Shorter Catechism is better: "Faith in Christ is a saving grace, whereby we receive and rest *on him alone* for salvation, as he is offered to us in the gospel." If this relation of faith to the personal Christ had been kept in mind, much religious despondency might have been avoided. Murphy, Natural Selection and Spiritual Freedom, 30, 31, tells us that Frances Ridley Havergal could never fix the date of her conversion. From the age of six to that of fourteen she suffered from religious fears, and did not venture to call herself a Christian. It was the result of confounding *being* at peace with God and being *conscious* of that peace. So the mother of Frederick Denison Maurice, an admirable and deeply religious woman, endured long and deep mental suffering from doubts as to her personal election.

There is a witness of the Spirit, with some sinners, that they are *not* children of God, and this witness is through the truth, though the sinner does not know that it is the Spirit who reveals it to him. We call this work of the Spirit conviction of sin. The witness of the Spirit that we are children of God, and the assurance of faith of which Scripture speaks, are one and the same thing, the former designation only emphasizing the source from which the assurance springs. False assurance is destitute of humility, but true assurance is so absorbed in Christ that self is forgotten. Self-consciousness, and desire to display one's faith, are not marks of true assurance. When we say: "That man has a great deal of assurance," we have in mind the false and self-centered assurance of the hypocrite or the self-deceiver.

Allen, Jonathan Edwards, 231 — "It has been said that any one who can read Edwards's Religious Affections, and still believe in his own conversion, may well have the highest assurance of its reality. But how few there were in Edwards's time who gained the assurance, may be inferred from the circumstance that Dr. Hopkins and Dr. Emmons, disciples of Edwards and religious leaders in New England, remained to the last uncertain of their conversion." He can attribute this only to the semi deistic spirit of the time, with its distant God and imperfect apprehension of the omnipresence and omnipotence of Christ. Nothing so clearly marks the practical progress of Christianity as the growing faith in Jesus, the only Revealer of God in nature and history as well as in the heart of the believer. As never before, faith comes directly to Christ, abides in him, and finds his promise true: "Lo, I am with you always, even unto the end of the world" (Mat. 28 : 20). "Nothing before, nothing behind; The steps of faith Fall on the seeming void and find The Rock beneath."

(*d*) That faith necessarily leads to good works, since it embraces the whole truth of God so far as made known, and appropriates Christ, not only as an external Savior, but as an internal sanctifying power (Heb. 7 : 15, 16 ; Gal. 5 : 6).

Good works are the proper evidence of faith. The faith which does not lead men to act upon the commands and promises of Christ, or, in other words, does not lead to obedience, is called in Scripture a "dead," that is, an unreal, faith. Such faith is not saving, since it lacks the voluntary element—actual appropriation of Christ (James 2 : 14-26).

Heb. 7 : 15, 16 — "another priest, who hath been made, not after the law of a carnal commandment, but after the power of an endless life " ; Gal. 5 : 6 — "For in Chr st Jesus neither circumcision availeth anything, nor uncircumcision ; but faith working through love " ; James 2 : 14, 26 — " What doth it profit, my brethren, if a man say he hath faith, but have not works ? Can that faith save him ? . . . . For as the body apart from the spirit is dead, even so faith apart from works is dead."

The best evidence that I believe a man's word is that I act upon it. Instance the bank-cashier's assurance to me that a sum of money is deposited with him to my account. If I am a millionaire, the communication may cause me no special joy. My faith in the cashier's word is tested by my going, or not going, for the money. So my faith in Christ is evidenced by my acting upon his commands and promises. We may illustrate also by the lifting of the trolley to the wire, and the resulting light and heat and motion to the car that before stood dark and cold and motionless upon the track.

Salvation by works is like getting to one's destination by pushing the car. True faith depends upon God for energy, but it results in activity of all our powers. Rom. 3 : 28 — "We reckon therefore that a man is justified by faith apart from the works of the law." We are saved only by faith, yet this faith will be sure to bring forth good works; see Gal. 5 : 6 — "faith working through love." Dead faith might be illustrated by Abraham Lincoln's Mississippi steamboat, whose whistle was so big that, when it sounded, the boat stopped. Confession exhausts the energy, so that none is left for action.

A. J. Gordon, The First Thing in the World, or The Primacy of Faith : "David Brainard speaks with a kind of suppressed astonishment of what he observed among the degraded North American Indians; how, preaching to them the good news of salvation through the atonement of Christ and persuading them to accept it by faith, and then hastening on in his rapid missionary tours, he found, on returning upon his track a year or two later, that the fruits of righteousness and sobriety and virtue and brotherly love were everywhere visible, though it had been possible to impart to them only the slightest moral or ethical teaching."

(e) That faith, as characteristically the inward act of reception, is not to be confounded with love or obedience, its fruit.

Faith is, in the Scriptures, called a work, only in the sense that man's active powers are engaged in it. It is a work which God requires, yet which God enables man to perform (John 6 : 29 — ἔργον τοῦ Θεοῦ. Cf. Rom. 1 : 17 — δικαιοσύνη Θεοῦ). As the gift of God and as the mere taking of undeserved mercy, it is expressly excluded from the category of works upon the basis of wh'ch man may claim salvation (Rom. 3 : 28; 4 : 4, 5, 16). It is not the act of the full soul bestowing, but the act of an empty soul receiving. Although this reception is prompted by a drawing of heart toward God inwrought by the Holy Spirit, this drawing of heart is not yet a conscious and developed love: such love is the result of faith (Gal. 5 : 6). What precedes faith is an unconscious and undeveloped tendency or disposition toward God. Conscious and developed affection toward God, or love proper, must always follow faith and be the product of faith. So, too, obedience can be rendered only after faith has laid hold of Christ, and with him has obtained the spirit of obedience (Rom. 1 : 5 — ὑπακοὴν πίστεως = "obedience resulting from faith"). Hence faith is not the procuring cause of salvation, but is only the instrumental cause. The procuring cause is the Christ, whom faith embraces.

John 6 : 29 — "This is the work of God, that ye believe on him whom he hath sent"; cf. Rom. 1 : 17 — "For therein is revealed a righteousness of God from faith unto faith : as it is written, But the righteous shall live by faith"; Rom. 3 : 23 — "We reckon therefore that a man is justified by faith apart from the works of the law"; 4 : 4, 5, 16 — "Now to him that worketh, the reward is not reckoned as of grace, but as of debt. But to him that worketh not, but believeth on h m that justifieth the ungodly, his faith is reckoned for righteousness. . . . . For this cause it is of faith, that it may be according to grace"; Gal. 5 : 6 — "For in Christ Jesus neither circumcision availeth anything, nor uncircumcision; but fa th working through love"; Rom. 1 : 5 — "through whom we received grace and apostleship, unto obedience of faith among all the nations."

Faith stands as an intermediate factor between the unconscious and undeveloped tendency or disposition toward God inwrought in the soul by God's regenerating act, on the one hand, and the conscious and developed affection toward God which is one of the fruits and evidences of conversion, on the other. Illustrate by the motherly instinct shown in a little girl's care for her doll,— a motherly instinct which becomes a developed mother's love, only when a child of her own is born. This new love of the Christian is an activity of his own soul, and yet it is a "fruit of the Sp.rit" (Gal. 5 . 22) To attribute it wholly to himself would be like calling the walking and leaping of the lame man (Acts 3 : 8) merely a healthy activity of his own. For illustration of the priority of faith to love, see Shedd, Dogm. Theol., 2 : 533, note; on the relation of faith to love, see Julius Müller, Doct. Sin, 1 : 116, 117.

The logical order is therefore : 1. Unconscious and undeveloped love; 2. Faith in Christ and his truth; 3. Conscious and developed love; 4. Assurance of faith. Faith and love act and react upon one another. Each advance in the one leads to a corresponding advance in the other. But the source of all is in God. God loves, and therefore he gives love to us as well as receives love from us. The unconscious and undeveloped love which he imparts in regeneration is the root of all Christian faith. The Roman Catholic is right in affirming the priority of love to faith, if he means by love only this unconscious and undeveloped affection. But the Protestant is also right in affirming the priority of faith to love, if he means by love a conscious and developed affection. Stevens, Johannine Theology, 368 —" Faith is not a mere passive receptivity. As the acceptance of a divine life, it involves the possession of a new moral energy. Faith works by love. In faith a new life-force is received, and new life-powers stir within the Christian man."

We must not confound repentance with fruits meet for repentance, nor faith with fruits meet for faith. A. J. Gordon, The First Thing in the World: " Love is the greatest thing in the world, but faith is the first. The tree is greater than the root, but let it not boast: 'if thou gloriest, it is not thou that bearest the root, but the root thee' (Rom. 11 : 18). Love has no power to branch out and bear fruit, except as, through faith, it is rooted in Christ and draws nourishment from him. 1 Pet. 1 : 5 —' who by the power of God are guarded through faith unto a salvation ready to be revealed in the last time '; 1 Cor. 13 : 13 —' now abideth faith, hope, love '; Heb. 10 : 19-25 — ' draw near . . . . in fulness of faith . . . . hold fast the confession of our hope . . . . provoke unto love and good works '; Rom. 5 : 1-5 —' justified by faith . . . . rejoice in hope . . . . love of God hath been shed abroad in our hearts '; 1 Thess. 1 : 1, 2 —' work of faith and labor of love and patience of hope.' Faith is the actinic ray, hope the luminiferous ray, love the calorific ray. But faith contains the principle of the divine likeness, as the life of the parent given to the child contains the principle of likeness to the father, and will insure moral and physical resemblance in due time."

A. J. Gordon, Ministry of the Spirit, 112 —" 'The love of the Spirit' (Rom. 15 : 30) is the love of the Spirit of Christ, and it is given us for overcoming the world. The divine life is the source of the divine love. Therefore the love of God is ' shed abroad in our hearts by the Holy Spirit who is given unto us ' (Rom. 5 : 5). Because we are by nature so wholly without heavenly affection, God, through the indwelling Spirit, gives us his own love with which to love himself." A. H. Strong, Christ in Creation, 286, 287, points out that in 2 Cor. 5 : 14 —" the love of Christ constraineth us " — the love of Christ is " not our love to Christ, for that is a very weak and uncertain thing; nor even Christ's love to us, for that is still something external to us. Each of these leaves a separation between Christ and us, and fails to act as a moving power within. . . . . Not simply our love to Christ, nor simply Christ's love to us, but rather Christ's love in us, is the love that constrains. This is the thought of the apostle." The first fruit of this love, in its still unconscious and undeveloped state, is faith.

(*f*) That faith is susceptible of increase.

This is evident, whether we consider it from the human or from the divine side. As an act of man, it has an intellectual, an emotional, and a voluntary element, each of which is capable of growth. . As a work of God in the soul of man, it can receive, through the presentation of the truth and the quickening agency of the Holy Spirit, continually new accessions of knowledge, sensibility, and active energy. Such increase of faith, therefore, we are to seek, both by resolute exercise of our own powers, and above all, by direct application to the source of faith in God (Luke 17 : 5).

Luke 17 : 5 —" And the apostles said unto the Lord, Increase our faith." The adult Christian has more faith than he had when a child,— evidently there has been increase. 1 Cor. 12 : 8, 9 —"For to one is given through the Spirit the word of wisdom . . . . to another faith, in the same Spirit." In this latter passage, it seems to be intimated that for special exigencies the Holy Spirit gives to his servants special faith, so that they are enabled to lay hold of the general promise of God and make special application of it. Rom. 8 : 26, 27 —" the Spirit also helpeth our infirmity . . . . maketh intercession for us . . . . maketh intercession for the saints according to the will of God " ; 1 John 5 : 14, 15 — "And this is the boldness which we have toward him, that, if we ask anything according to his will, he heareth us : and if we know that he heareth us whatsoever we ask, we know that we have the petitions which we have asked of him." Only when we begin to believe, do we appreciate our lack of faith, and the great need of its increase. The little beginning of light makes known the greatness of the surrounding darkness. Mark 9 : 24 —"I believe ; help thou mine unbelief"— was the utterance of one who recognized both the need of faith and the true source of supply.

On the general subject of Faith, see Köstlin, Die Lehre von dem Glauben, 13-85, 301.-341, and in Jahrbuch f. d. Theol., 4 : 177 *sq.* ; Romaine on Faith, 9-89 ; Bishop of Ossory Nature and Effects of Faith, 1-40; Venn, Characteristics of Belief, Introduction; Nitzsch, System of Christ. Doct., 294.

IV. Justification.

1. *Definition of Justification.*

By justification we mean that judicial act of God by which, on account of Christ, to whom the sinner is united by faith, he declares that sinner to be no longer exposed to the penalty of the law, but to be restored to his favor. Or, to give an alternative definition from which all metaphor is excluded : Justification is the reversal of God's attitude toward the sinner, because of the sinner's new relation to Christ. God did condemn ; he now acquits. He did repel ; he now admits to favor.

Justification, as thus defined, is therefore a declarative act, as distinguished from an efficient act ; an act of God external to the sinner, as distinguished from an act within the sinner's nature and changing that nature ; a judicial act, as distinguished from a sovereign act ; an act based upon and logically presupposing the sinner's union with Christ, as distinguished from an act which causes and is followed by that union with Christ.

The word 'declarative' does not imply a 'spoken' word on God's part,—much less that the sinner hears God speak. That justification is sovereign, is held by Arminians, and by those who advocate a governmental theory of the atonement. On any such theory, justification must be sovereign ; since Christ bore, not the penalty of the law, but a substituted suffering which God graciously and sovereignly accepts in place of our suffering and obedience.

Anselm, Archbishop of Canterbury, 1100, wrote a tract for the consolation of the dying, who were alarmed on account of sin. The following is an extract from it: "*Question.* Dost thou believe that the Lord Jesus died for thee? *Answer.* I believe it. *Qu.* Dost thou thank him for his passion and death? *Ans.* I do thank him. *Qu.* Dost thou believe that thou canst not be saved except by his death? *Ans.* I believe it." And then Anselm addresses the dying man : "Come then, while life remaineth in thee; in his death alone place thy whole trust ; in naught else place any trust ; to his death commit thyself wholly ; with this alone cover thyself wholly ; and if the Lord thy God will to judge thee, say, 'Lord, between thy judgment and me I present the death of our Lord Jesus Christ; no otherwise can I contend with thee.' And if he shall say that thou art a sinner, say thou : 'Lord, I interpose the death of our Lord Jesus Christ between my sins and thee.' If he say that thou hast deserved condemnation, say : 'Lord, I set the death of our Lord Jesus Christ between my evil deserts and thee, and his merits I offer for those which I ought to have and have not.' If he say that he is wroth with thee, say : 'Lord, I oppose the death of our Lord Jesus Christ between thy wrath and me.' And when thou hast completed this, say again : 'Lord, I set the death of our Lord Jesus Christ between thee and me.'" See Anselm, Opera (Migne), 1:686, 687. The above quotation gives us reason to believe that the New Testament doctrine of justification by faith was implicitly, if not explicitly, held by many pious souls through all the ages of papal darkness.

2. *Proof of the Doctrine of Justification.*

A. Scripture proofs of the doctrine as a whole are the following :

Rom. 1:17—"a righteousness of God from faith unto faith " ; 3 : 24-30—"being justified freely by his grace through the redemption that is in Christ Jesus . . . . the justifier of him that hath faith in Jesus. . . . . We reckon therefore that a man is justified by faith apart from the works of the law. . . . . justify the circumcision by faith, and the uncircumcision through faith " ; Gal. 3 : 11—"Now that no man is justified by the law before God, is evident: for, The righteous shall live by faith ; and the law is not of faith; but, He that doeth them shall live in them " ; Eph. i : 7—"in whom we have our redemption through his blood, the forgiveness of our trespasses, according to the riches of his grace " ;

Heb. 11 : 4, 7 — "By faith Abel offered unto God a more excellent sacrifice than Cain, through which he had witness borne to him that he was righteous. . . . . By faith Noah . . . . moved with godly fear, prepared an ark . . . . became heir of the righteousness which is according to faith "; *cf.* Gen. 15 : 6 —"And he believed in Jehovah; and he reckoned it to him for righteousness"; Is. 7 : 9 —"If ye will not believe, surely ye shall not be established"; 28 : 16 —"he that believeth shall not be in haste "; Hab. 2 : 4 —"the righteous shall live by his faith."

Ps. 85 : 8 — "He will speak peace unto his people."   God's great word of pardon includes all else Peace with him implies all the covenant privileges resulting therefrom. 1 Cor. 3 : 21-23 — "all things are yours," because "ye are Christ's; and Christ is God's."   This is not salvation by law, nor by ideals, nor by effort, nor by character; although obedience to law, and a loftier ideal, and unremitting effort, and a pure character, are consequences of justification. Justification is the change in God's attitude toward the sinner which makes all these consequences possible. The only condition of justification is the sinner's faith in Jesus, which merges the life of the sinner in the life of Christ. Paul expresses the truth in Gal. 2 : 16, 20 — "Knowing that a man is not justified by the works of the law but through faith in Jesus Christ, even we believed on Christ Jesus, that we might be justified by faith in Christ, and not by the works of the law . . . . . . I have been crucified with Christ; and it is no longer I that live, but Christ liveth in me: and that life which I now live in the flesh I live in faith, the faith which is in the Son of God, who loved me, and gave himself up for me."

With these observations and qualifications we may assent to much that is said by Whiton, Divine Satisfaction, 64, who distinguishes between forgiveness and remission : " Forgiveness is the righting of disturbed personal relations. Remission is removal of the consequences which in the natural order of things have resulted from our fault. God forgives all that is strictly personal, but remits nothing that is strictly natural in sin. He imparts to the sinner the power to bear his burden and work off his debt of consequences. Forgiveness is not remission. It is introductory to remission, just as conversion is not salvation, but introductory to salvation. The prodigal was received by his father, but he could not recover his lost patrimony. He could, however, have been led by penitence to work so hard that he earned more than he had lost.

" Here is an element in justification which Protestantism has ignored, and which Romanism has tried to retain. Debts must be paid to the uttermost farthing. The scars of past sins must remain forever. Forgiveness converts the persistent energy of past sin from a destructive to a constructive power. There is a transformation of energy into a new form. Genuine repentance spurs us up to do what we can to make up for time lost and for wrong done. The sinner is clothed anew with moral power. We are all to be judged by our works. That Paul had been a blasphemer was ever stimulating him to Christian endeavor. The faith which receives Christ is a peculiar spirit, a certain moral activity of love and obedience. It is not mere reliance on what Christ was and did, but active endeavor to become and to do like him. Human justice takes hold of *deeds*; divine righteousness deals with *character*. Justification by faith is justification by spirit and inward principle, apart from the merit of works or performances, but never without these. God's charity takes the will for the deed. This is not justification by outward conduct, as the Judaizers thought, but by the godly spirit." If this new spirit be the Spirit of Christ to whom faith has united the soul, we can accept the statement. There is danger however of conceiving this spirit as purely man's own, and justification as not external to the sinner nor as the work of God, but as the mere name for a subjective process by which man justifies himself.

B. Scripture use of the special words translated " justify " and " justification " in the Septuagint and in the New Testament.

(*a*) δικαιόω — uniformly, or with only a single exception, signifies, not to make righteous, but to declare just, or free from guilt and exposure to punishment. The only O. T. passage where this meaning is questionable is Dan. 12 : 3. But even here the proper translation is, in all probability, not 'they that turn many to righteousness,' but 'they that justify many,' *i. e.*, cause many to be justified. For the Hiphil force of the verb, see Girdlestone, O. T. Syn., 257, 258, and Delitzsch on Is. 53 : 11 ; *cf.* James 5 : 19, 20.

O. T. texts : Ex. 23 : 7 —"I will not justify the wicked "; Deut. 25 : 1 —"they [the judges] shall justify the righteous, and condemn the wicked "; Job 27 : 5 —"Far be it from me that I should justify you "; Ps. 143 : 2 —"in thy sight no man living is righteous "; Prov. 17 : 15 — "He that justifieth the wicked, and he that condemneth the righteous, both of them alike are an abomination to Jehovah "; Is. 5 : 23 — " that justify the wicked for a bribe, and take away the righteousness of the righteous from him "; 50 : 8 —"He is near that justifieth me "; 53 : 11 —"by the knowledge of himself shall my righteous servant justify many; and he shall bear their iniquities"; Dan. 12:3 — "and they that turn many to righteousness, as the stars for ever and ever" ('they that justify many,' *i. e.*, cause many to be justified); *cf.* James 5:19, 20 — "My brethren, if any among you err from the truth, and one convert him, let him know, that he who converteth a sinner from the error of his way shall save a soul from death, and shall cover a multitude of sins."

The Christian minister absolves from sin, only as he marries a couple: he does not join them, — he only declares them joined. So he declares men forgiven, if they have complied with the appointed divine conditions. Marriage may be invalid where these conditions are lacking, but the minister's absolution is of no account where there is no repentance of sin and faith in Christ; see G. D. Boardman, The Church, 178. We are ever to remember that the term justification is a forensic term which presents the change of God's attitude toward the sinner in a pictorial way derived from the procedure of earthly tribunals. The fact is larger and more vital than the figure used to describe it.

McConnell, Evolution of Immortality, 134, 135 — "Christ's terms are biological; those of many theologians are legal. It may be ages before we recover from the misfortune of having had the truth of Christ interpreted and fixed by jurists and logicians, instead of by naturalists and men of science. It is much as though the rationale of the circulation of the blood had been wrought out by Sir Matthew Hale, or the germ theory of disease interpreted by Blackstone, or the doctrine of evolution formulated by a legislative council. . . . . The Christ is intimately and vitally concerned with the eternal life of men, but the question involved is of their living or perishing, not of a system of judicial rewards and penalties." We must remember however that even biology gives us only one side of the truth. The forensic conception of justification furnishes its complement and has its rights also. The Scriptures represent both sides of the truth. Paul gives us the judicial aspect, John the vital aspect, of justification.

In Rom. 6:7 — ὁ γὰρ ἀποθανὼν δεδικαίωται ἀπὸ τῆς ἁμαρτίας = 'he that once died with Christ was acquitted from the service of sin considered as a penalty.' In 1 Cor. 4:4 — οὐδὲν γὰρ ἐμαυτῷ σύνοιδα. ἀλλ' οὐκ ἐν τούτῳ δεδικαίωμαι = 'I am conscious of no fault, but that does not in itself make certain God's acquittal as respects this particular charge.' The usage of the epistle of James does not contradict this; the doctrine of James is that we are justified only by such faith as makes us faithful and brings forth good works. "He uses the word exclusively in a judicial sense; he combats a mistaken view of πίστις, not a mistaken view of δικαιόω"; see James 2:21, 23, 24, and Cremer, N. T. Lexicon, Eng. trans., 182, 183. The only N. T. passage where this meaning is questionable is Rev. 22:11; but here Alford, with ℵ, A and B, reads δικαιοσύνην ποιησάτω.

N. T. texts: Mat. 12:37 — "For by thy words thou shalt be justified, and by thy words thou shalt be condemned"; Luke 7:29 — "And all the people . . . . justified God, being baptized with the baptism of John"; 10:29 — "But he, desiring to justify himself, said unto Jesus, And who is my neighbor?" 16:15 — "Ye are they that justify yourselves in the sight of men; but God knoweth your hearts"; 18:14 — "This man went down to his house justified rather than the other"; *cf.* 13 (lit.) "God, be thou propitiated toward me the sinner"; Rom. 4:6-8 — "Even as David also pronounceth blessing upon the man, unto whom God reckoneth righteousness apart from works, saying, Blessed are they whose iniquities are forgiven, And whose sins are covered. Blessed is the man to whom the Lord will not reckon sin"; *cf.* Ps. 32: 1, 2, — "Blessed is he whose transgression is forgiven, Whose sin is covered. Blessed is the man unto whom Jehovah imputeth not iniquity, And in whose spirit there is no guile."

Rom. 5:18, 19 — "So then as through one trespass the judgment came unto all men to condemnation; even so through one act of righteousness the free gift came unto all men to justification of life. For as through the one man's disobedience the many were made sinners, even so through the obedience of the one shall the many be made righteous"; 8:33, 34 — "Who shall lay anything to the charge of God's elect? It is God that justifieth; who is he that condemneth?" 2 Cor. 5: 19, 21 — "God was in Christ reconciling the world unto himself, not reckoning unto them their trespasses. . . . . Him who knew no sin he made to be sin on our behalf; that we might become the righteousness of God [God's justified persons] in him"; Rom. 6:7 — "he that hath died is justified from sin"; 1 Cor. 4:4 — "For I know nothing against myself; yet am I not hereby justified: but he that judgeth me is the Lord" (on this last text, see Expositor's Greek Testament, *in loco*).

James 2:21, 23, 24 — "Was not Abraham our father justified by works, in that he offered up Isaac his son upon the altar? . . . . Abraham believed God, and it was reckoned unto him for righteousness. . . . . Ye see that by works a man is justified, and not only by faith." James is denouncing a dead faith, while Paul is speaking of the necessity of a living faith; or, rather, James is describing the nature of faith, while Paul is describing the instrument of justification. "They are like two men beset by a couple of robbers. Back to back each strikes out against the robber opposite him, — each having a different enemy in his eye" (Wm. M. Taylor). Neander on James 2:14-26 — "James is denouncing mere adhesion to an external law, trust in intellectual possession of it. With him, law means an inward principle of life. Paul, contrasting law as he does with faith, commonly means by law mere external divine requisition . . . . James does not deny salvation to him who *has* faith, but only to him who falsely *professes* to have. When he says that 'by works a man is justified,' he takes into account the outward manifestation only, speaks from the point of view of human consciousness. In works only does faith show itself as genuine and complete." Rev. 22:11 — "he that is righteous, let him do righteousness still" — not, as the A. V. seemed to imply, "he that is just, let him be justified still " — *i. e.*, made subjectively holy.

Christ is the great Physician. The physician says: "If you wish to be cured, you must trust me." The patient replies: "I do trust you fully." But the physician continues: "If you wish to be cured, you must take my medicines and do as I direct." The patient objects: "But I thought I was to be cured by trust in you. Why lay such stress on what I do?" The physician answers: "You must show your trust in me by your action. Trust in me, without action in proof of trust, amounts to nothing" (S. S. Times). Doing without a physician is death; hence Paul says works cannot save. Trust in the physician implies obedience; hence James says faith without works is dead. Crane, Religion of To-morrow, 152-155 — "Paul insists on apple-tree righteousness, and warns us against Christmas-tree righteousness." Sagebeer, The Bible in Court, 77, 78 — "By works, Paul means works of law; James means by works, works of faith." Hovey, in The Watchman, Aug. 27, 1891 — "A difference of emphasis, occasioned chiefly by the different religious perils to which readers were at the time exposed."

(*b*) δικαίωσις — is the act, in process, of declaring a man just, — that is, acquitted from guilt and restored to the divine favor (Rom. 4:25 : 5·10 ·

Rom. 4:25 — "who was delivered up for our trespasses, and was raised for our justification . . . . . . — "unto all men to justification of life." Griffith-Jones, Ascent through Christ, 367, 368 — "Raised for our justification " — Christ's death made our justification possible, but it did not consummate it. Through his rising from the dead he was able to come into that relationship to the believer which restores the lost or interrupted sonship. In the church the fact of the resurrection is perpetuated, and the idea of the resurrection is realized.

(*c*) δικαίωμα — is the act, as already accomplished, of declaring a man just, — that is, no longer exposed to penalty, but restored to God's favor (Rom. 5:16, 18; *cf.* 1 Tim. 3:16). Hence, in other connections, δικαίωμα has the meaning of statute, legal decision, act of justice (Luke 1:6; Rom. 2:26; Heb. 9:1).

Rom. 5:16, 18 — "of many trespasses unto justification . . . . through one act of righteousness"; *cf.* 1 Tim. 3:16 — 'justified in the spirit." The distinction between δικαίωσις and δικαίωμα may be illustrated by the distinction between poesy and poem, — the former denoting something in process, an ever-working spirit; the latter denoting something fully accomplished, a completed work. Hence δικαίωμα is used in Luke 1:6 — "ordinances of the Lord "; Rom. 2:26 — "ordinances of the law "; Heb. 1:9 — "ordinances of divine service."

(*d*) δικαιοσύνη — is the state of one justified, or declared just (Rom. 8:10; 1 Cor. 1:30). In Rom. 10:3, Paul inveighs against τὴν ἰδίαν δικαιοσύνην as insufficient and false, and in its place would put τὴν τοῦ Θεοῦ δικαιοσύνην, — that is, a δικαιοσύνη which God not only requires, but provides ; which is not only acceptable to God, but proceeds from God, and is appropriated by faith, — hence called δικαιοσύνη πίστεως or ἐκ πίστεως. "The primary signification of the word, in Paul's writings, is therefore that state of the believer which is called forth by God's act of acquittal, — the state of the believer as justified," that is, freed from punishment and restored to the divine favor.

Rom. 8:10—"the spirit is life because of righteousness" 1 Cor. 1:30—"Christ Jesus, who was made unto us . . . . righteousness"; Rom. 10:3—"being ignorant of God's righteousness, and seeking to establish their own, they did not subject themselves to the righteousness of God." Shedd, Dogm. Theol., 2:542—"The 'righteousness of God' is the active and passive obedience of incarnate God." See, on δικαιοσύνη, Cremer, N. T. Lexicon, Eng. trans., 174; Meyer on Romans, trans., 68-70—"δικαιοσύνη Θεοῦ (gen. of origin, emanation from)=rightness which proceeds from God—the relation of being right into which man is put by God (by an act of God declaring him righteous)."

E. G. Robinson, Christian Theology, 304—"When Paul addressed those who trusted in their own righteousness, he presented salvation as attainable only through faith in another; when he addressed Gentiles who were conscious of their need of a helper, the forensic imagery is not employed. Scarce a trace of it appears in his discourses as recorded in the Acts, and it is noticeably absent from all the epistles except the Romans and the Galatians."

Since this state of acquittal is accompanied by changes in the character and conduct, δικαιοσύνη comes to mean, secondarily, the moral condition of the believer as resulting from this acquittal and inseparably connected with it (Rom. 14:17; 2 Cor. 5:21). This righteousness arising from justification becomes a principle of action (Mat. 3:15 ; Acts 10:35 ; Rom. 6:13, 18). The term, however, never loses its implication of a justifying act upon which this principle of action is based.

Rom. 14:17—"the kingdom of God is not eating and drinking, but righteousness and peace and joy in the Holy Spirit"; 2 Cor. 5:21—"that we might become the righteousness of God in him"; Mat. 3:15—"Suffer it now: for thus it becometh us to fulfil all righteousness"; Acts 10:35—"in every nation he that feareth him, and worketh righteousness, is acceptable to him"; Rom. 6:13—"present yourselves unto God, as alive from the dead, and your members as instruments of righteousness unto God." Meyer on Rom. 3:23—"Every mode of conception which refers redemption and the forgiveness of sins, not to a real atonement through the death of Christ, but subjectively to the dying and reviving with him guaranteed and produced by that death (Schleiermacher, Nitzsch, Hofmann), is opposed to the N. T.,—a mixing up of justification and sanctification."

On these Scripture terms, see Bp. of Ossory, Nature and Effects of Faith, 436-496; Lange, Com., on Romans 3:24; Buchanan on Justification, 226-249. Versus Moehler, Symbolism, 102—"The forgiveness of sins . . . . is undoubtedly a remission of the guilt and the punishment which Christ hath taken and borne upon himself; but it is likewise the transfusion of his Spirit into us"; Newman, Lectures on Justification, 68-143; Knox, Remains; N. W. Taylor, Revealed Theology, 310-372.

It is a great mistake in method to derive the meaning of δίκαιος from that of δικαιοσύνη, and not vice versa. Wm. Arnold Stevens, in Am. Jour. Theology, April, 1897—" δικαιοσύνη, righteousness, in all its meanings, whether ethical or forensic, has back of it the idea of law; also the idea of violated law; it derives its forensic sense from the verb δικαιόω and its cognate noun δικαίωσις; δικαιοσύνη therefore is legal acceptableness, the status before the law of a pardoned sinner."

Denney, in Expos. Gk. Test., 2:565—"In truth, 'sin,' 'the law,' ' the curse of the law,' 'death,' are names for something which belongs not to the Jewish but to the human conscience; and it is only because this is so that the gospel of Paul is also a gospel for us. Before Christ came and redeemed the world, all men were at bottom on the same footing: Pharisaism, legalism, moralism, or whatever it is called, is in the last resort the attempt to be good without God, to achieve a righteousness of our own, without an initial all-inclusive immeasurable debt to him; in other words, without submitting, as sinful men must submit, to be justified by faith apart from works of our own, and to find in that justification, and in that only, the spring and impulse of all good."

It is worthy of special observation that, in the passages cited above, the terms "justify" and "justification" are contrasted, not with the process of depraving or corrupting, but with the outward act of condemning ; and that the expressions used to explain and illustrate them are all derived, not from the inward operation of purifying the soul or infusing into it righteousness, but from the procedure of courts in their judgments, or of offended persons in their forgiveness of offenders. We conclude that these terms, wherever hey have reference to the sinner's relation to God, signify a declarative and udicial act of God, external to the sinner, and not an efficient and sovereign act of God changing the sinner's nature and making him subjectively righteous.

In the Canons and Decrees of the Council of Trent, session 6, chap. 9 is devoted to the refutation of the "inanis hæreticorum fiducia"; and Canon 12 of the session anathematizes those who say: "fidem justificantem nihil aliud esse quam fiduciam divinæ misericordiæ, peccata remittentis propter Christum"; or that "justifying faith is nothing but trust in the divine mercy which pardons sins for Christ's sake." The Roman Catholic doctrine on the contrary maintains that the ground of justification is not simply the faith by which the sinner appropriates Christ and his atoning work, but is also the new love and good works wrought within him by Christ's Spirit. This introduces a subjective element which is foreign to the Scripture doctrine of justification.

Dr. E. G. Robinson taught that justification consists of three elements: 1. Acquittal; 2. Restoration to favor; 3. Infusion of righteousness. In this he accepted a fundamental error of Romanism. He says: "Justification and sanctification are not to be distin. guished as chronologically and statically different. Justification and righteousness are the same thing from different points of view. Pardon is not a mere declaration of forgiveness — a merely arbitrary thing. Salvation introduces a new law into our sinful nature which annuls the law of sin and destroys its penal and destructive consequences. Forgiveness of sins must be in itself a gradual process. The final consequences of a man's sins are written indelibly upon his nature and remain forever. When Christ said: 'Thy sins are forgiven thee', it was an objective statement of a subjective fact. The person was already in a state of living relation to Christ. The gospel is damnation to the damnable, and invitation, love and mercy to those who feel their need of it. We are saved through the enforcement of law on every one of us. Forgiveness consists in the removal from consciousness of a sense of ill-desert. Justification, aside from its forensic use, is a transformation and a promotion. Sense of forgiveness is a sense of relief from a hated habit of mind." This seems to us dangerously near to a denial that justification is an act of God, and to an affirmation that it is simply a subjective change in man's condition.

E. H. Johnson: "If Dr. Robinson had been content to say that the divine fiat of justification had the manward effect of regeneration, he would have been correct; for the verdict would be empty without this manward efficacy. But unfortunately, he made the effect a part of the cause, identifying the divine justification with its human fruition, the clearance of the past with the provision for the future." We must grant that the words *inward* and *outward* are misleading, for God is not under the law of space, and the soul itself is not in space. Justification takes place just as much in man as outside of him. Justification and regeneration take place at the same moment, but logically God's act of renewing is the cause and God's act of approving is the effect. Or we may say that regeneration and justification are both of them effects of our union with Christ. Luke 1:37 —"For no word from God shall be void of power." Regeneration and justification may be different aspects of God's turning — his turning us, and his turning himself. But it still is true that justification is a change in God and not in the creature.

3. *Elements of Justification.*

These are two :

A. Remission of punishment.

(*a*) God acquits the ungodly who believe in Christ, and declares them just. This is not to declare them innocent,— that would be a judgment contrary to truth. It declares that the demands of the law have been satisfied with regard to them, and that they are now free from its condemnation.

Rom. 4:5 —"But to him that worketh not, but believeth on him that justifieth the ungodly, his faith is reckoned for righteousness"; *cf*. John 3:16 —"gave his only begotten Son, that whosoever believeth on him should not perish" see page 856, (*a*), and Shedd, Dogm. Theol., 2:549. Rom. 5:1 —"Being therefore justified by faith we have peace with God"—not subjective peace or quietness of mind, but objective peace or reconciliation, the opposite of the state of war, in which we are subject to the divine wrath. Dale, Ephesians, 67 —"Forgiveness may be defined: 1. in *personal* terms, as

a cessation of the anger or moral resentment of God against sin; 2. in *ethical* terms, as a release from the guilt of sin which oppresses the conscience; 3. in *legal* terms, as a remission of the punishment of sin, which is eternal death."

(*b*) This acquittal, in so far as it is the act of God as judge or executive, administering law, may be denominated pardon. In so far as it is the act of God as a father personally injured and grieved by sin, yet showing grace to the sinner, it is denominated forgiveness.

Micah 7 : 18 —" Who is a God like unto thee, that pardoneth iniquity, and passeth over the transgression of the remnant of his heritage?" Ps. 130 : 4 —" But there is forgiveness with thee, That thou mayst be feared." It is hard for us to understand God's feeling toward sin. Forgiveness seems easy to us, largely because we are indifferent toward sin. But to the holy One, to whom sin is the abominable thing which he hates, forgiveness involves a fundamental change of relation, and nothing but Christ's taking the penalty of sin upon him can make it possible. B. Fay Mills: "A tender spirited follower of Jesus Christ said to me, not long ago, that it had taken him twelve years to forgive an injury that had been committed against him." How much harder for God to forgive, since he can never become indifferent to the nature of the transgression!

(*c*) In an earthly tribunal, there is no acquittal for those who are proved to be transgessors,— for such there is only conviction and punishment. But in God's government there is remission of punishment for believers, even though they are confessedly offenders; and, in justification, God declares this remission.

There is no forgiveness in nature. F. W. Robertson preached this. But he ignored the *vis medicatrix* of the gospel, in which forgiveness is offered to all. The natural conscience says: "I must pay my debt." But the believer finds that "Jesus paid it all." Illustrate by the poor man, who on coming to pay his mortgage finds that the owner at death had ordered it to be burned, so that now there is nothing to pay. Ps. 34 : 22 — "Jehovah redeemeth the soul of his servants, And none of them that take refuge in him shall be condemned." A child disobeys his father and breaks his arm. His sin involves two penalties, the alienation from his father and the broken arm. The father, on repentance, may forgive his child. The personal relation is re-established, but the broken bone is not therefore at once reknit. The father's forgiveness, however, will assure the father's help toward complete healing. So justification does not ensure the immediate removal of all the natural consequences of our sins. It does ensure present reconciliation and future perfection. Clarke, Christian Theology, 364 —" Justification is not equivalent to acquittal, for acquittal declares that the man has not done wrong. Justification is rather the acceptance of a man, on sufficient grounds, although he has done wrong." As the Plymouth Brethren say : "It is not the *sin*-question, but the *Son*-question." "Their sins and their iniquities will I remember no more " (Heb. 10 : 17). The father did not allow the prodigal to complete the confession he had prepared to make, but interrupted him, and dwelt only upon his return home (Luke 15 : 22).

(*d*) The declaration that the sinner is no longer exposed to the penalty of law, has its ground, not in any satisfaction of the law's demand on the part of the sinner himself, but solely in the bearing of the penalty by Christ, to whom the sinner is united by faith. Justification, in its first element, is therefore that act by which God, for the sake of Christ, acquits the transgressor and suffers him to go free.

Acts 13 : 38, 39 —" Be it known unto you therefore, brethren, that through this man is proclaimed unto you remission of sins : and by him [lit. : 'in him'] every one that beleveth is justified from all things, from which ye could not be justified by the law of Moses" ; Rom. 3 : 24, 26 —" being justified freely by his grace through the redemption that is in Christ Jesus . . . . that he might himself e just, and the justifier of him that hath faith in Jesus" ; 1 Cor. 6 : 11 — "but ye were justified in the name of the Lord Jesus"; Eph. 1 : 7 — "in whom we have our redemption through his blood, the forgiveness of our trespasses, according to the riches of his grace."

This acquittal is not to be conceived of as the sovereign act of a Governor, but rather as a judicial procedure. Christ secures a new trial for those already condemned — a trial in which he appears for the guilty, and sets over against their sin his own righteousness, or rather shows them to be righteous in him.   C. H. M.: "When Balak seeks to curse the seed of Abraham, it is said of Jehovah: 'He hath not beheld iniquity in Jacob, Neither hath he seen perverseness in Israel' (Num. 23 : 21). When Satan stands forth to rebuke Joshua, the word is : 'Jehovah rebuke thee, O Satan . . . . is not this a brand plucked out of the fire?' (Zech. 3 : 2). Thus he ever puts himself between his people and every tongue that would accuse them. 'Touch not mine anointed ones,' he says, 'and do my prophets no harm' (Ps. 405 : 15). 'It is God that just.fieth; who is he that condemneth?' (Rom. 8 : 33, 34)." It is not sin, then, that condemns,—it is the failure to ask pardon for sin, through Christ. Illustrate by the ring presented by Queen Elizabeth to the Earl of Essex. Queen Elizabeth did not forgive the penitent Countess of Nottingham for withholding the ring of Essex which would have purchased his pardon. She shook the dying woman and cursed her, even while she was imploring forgiveness. There is no such failure of mercy in God's administration.

Kaftan, in Am. Jour. Theology, 4 : 698 — "The peculiar characteristic of Christian experience is the forgiveness of sins, or reconciliation — a forgiveness which is conceived as an unmerited gift of God, which is bestowed on man independently of his own moral worthiness. Other religions have some measure of revelation, but Christianity alone has the clear revelation of this forgiveness, and this is accepted by faith. And forgiveness leads to a better ethics than any religion of works can show."

B. Restoration to favor.

(a) Justification is more than remission or acquittal. These would leave the sinner simply in the position of a discharged criminal,—law requires a positive righteousness also. Besides deliverance from punishment, justification implies God's treatment of the sinner as if he were, and had been, personally righteous. The justified person receives not only remission of penalty, but the rewards promised to obedience.

Luke 15 : 22–24 — "Bring forth quickly the best robe, and put it on him; and put a ring on his hand, and shoes on his feet : and bring the fatted calf, and kill it, and let us eat, and make merry : for this my son was dead, and is alive again ; he was lost, and is found "; John 3 : 16 — "gave his only begotten Son, that whosoever believeth on him should . . . . have eternal life "; Rom. 5 : 1, 2 — "Being therefore justified by faith, we have peace with God through our Lord Jesus Christ ; through whom also we have had our access by faith into this grace wherein we stand ; and we rejoice in hope of the glory of God " — "this grace" being a permanent state of divine favor; 1 Cor. 1 : 30 — "But of him are ye in Christ Jesus, who was made unto us wisdom from God, and righteousness and sanctification, and redemption : that, according as it is written, He that glorieth, let him glory in the Lord "; 2 Cor. 5 : 21 — "that we might become the righteousness of God in him."

Gal. 3 : 6 — "Even as Abraham believed God, and it was reckoned unto him for righteousness "; Eph. 2 : 7 — "the exceeding riches of his grace in kindness toward us in Christ Jesus "; 3 : 12 — "in whom we have boldness and access in confidence through our faith in him "; Phil. 3 : 8, 9 — "I count all things to be loss for the excellency of the knowledge of Christ Jesus my Lord . . . . the righteousness which is from God by faith "; Col. 1 : 22 — "reconciled in the body of his flesh through death, to present you holy and without blemish and unreprovable before him "; Tit. 3 : 4, 7 — "the kindness of God our Savior . . . . that, being justified by his grace, we might be made heirs according to the hope of eternal life "; Rev. 19 : 8 — "And it was given unto her that she should array herself in fine linen, bright and pure : for the fine linen is the righteous acts of the saints."

Justification is setting one right before law. But law requires not merely freedom from offence negatively, but all manner of obedience and likeness to God positively. Since justification is in Christ and by virtue of the believer's union with Christ, it puts the believer on the same footing before the law that Christ is on, namely, not only acquittal but favor. 1 Tim. 3 : 16 — Christ was himself "justified in the spirit," and the believer partakes of his justification and of the whole of it, i. e., not only acquittal but favor. Acts 13 : 39 — "in him every one that believeth is justified " i. e., in Christ ; 1 Cor. 6 : 11 — "justified in the name of the Lord Jesus Christ " ; Gal. 4 : 5 — "that we m ght receive the adoption of sons " — a part of justification ; Rom. 5 : 11 — "through whom we have now received the reconciliation " — in justification ; 2 Cor. 5 : 21 — "that we might become the righteousness of God in him "; Phil. 3 : 9 — "the righteousnes which is from God by faith "; John 1 : 12 — "to them gave he the right to become children of God " — emphasis on "gave " — intimation that the "becoming children " is not subsequent to the justification, but is a part of it.

Ellicott on Tit. 3 : 7 — "δικαιωθέντες, 'justified,' in the usual and more strict theological sense ; not however as implying only a mere outward non-imputation of sin, but as involving a ' mutationem status,' an acceptance into new privileges, and an enjoyment of the benefits thereof (Waterland, Justif. vol. vi, p. 5) ; in the words of the same writer :

'Justification cannot be conceived without some work of the Spirit in conferring a title to salvation.'" The prisoner who has simply served out his term escapes without further punishment and that is all. But the pardoned man receives back in his pardon the full rights of citizenship, can again vote, serve on juries, testify in court, and exercise all his individual liberties, as the discharged convict cannot. The Society of Friends is so called, not because they are friends to one another, but because they regard themselves as friends of God. So, in the Middle Ages, Master Eckart, John Tauler, Henry Suso, called themselves the friends of God, after the pattern of Abraham; 2 Chron. 20:7 — "Abraham thy friend"; James 2:23 — "Abraham believed God, and it was reckoned unto him for righteousness; and he was called the friend of God", *i. e.*, one not merely acquitted from the charge of sin, but also admitted into favor and intimacy with God.

(*b*) This restoration to favor, viewed in its aspect as the renewal of a broken friendship, is denominated reconciliation ; viewed in its aspect as a renewal of the soul's true relation to God as a father, it is denominated adoption.

John 1:12 — "But as many as received him, to them gave he the right to become children of God, even to them that believe on his name"; Rom. 5:11 — "and not only so, but we also rejoice in God through our Lord Jesus Christ, through whom we have now received the reconciliation"; Gal. 4:4, 5 — "born under the law, that he might redeem them that were under the law, that we might receive the adoption of sons"; Eph. 1:5 — "having foreordained us unto adoption as sons through Jesus Christ unto himself"; *cf.* Rom. 8:23 — "even we ourselves groan within ourselves. waiting for our adoption, to wit, the redemption of our body" — that is, this adoption is completed, so far as the body is concerned, at the resurrection.

Luther called Psalms 32, 51, 130, 143, "the Pauline Psalms," because these declare forgiveness to be granted to the believer without law and without works. Ps. 130:3, 4 — "If thou, Jehovah, shouldst mark iniquities, O Lord, who could stand? But there is forgiveness with thee, That thou mayest be feared" is followed by verses 7, 8 — "O Israel, hope in Jehovah; For with Jehovah there is lovingkindness, And with him is plenteous redemption. And he will redeem Israel From all his iniquities." Whitefield was rebuked for declaring in a discourse that Christ would receive even the devil's castaways; but that very day, while at dinner at Lady Huntington's, he was called out to meet two women who were sinners, and to whose broken hearts and blasted lives that remark gave hope and healing.

(*c*) In an earthly pardon there are no special helps bestowed upon the pardoned. There are no penalties, but there are also no rewards ; law cannot claim anything of the discharged, but then they also can claim nothing of the law. But what, though greatly needed, is left unprovided by human government, God does provide. In justification, there is not only acquittal, but approval ; not only pardon, but promotion. Remission is never separated from restoration.

After serving a term in the penitentiary, the convict goes out with a stigma upon him and with no friends. His past conviction and disgrace follow him. He cannot obtain employment. He cannot vote. Want often leads him to commit crime again ; and then the old conviction is brought up as proof of bad character, and increases his punishment. Need of Friendly Inns and Refuges for discharged criminals. But the justified sinner is differently treated. He is not only delivered from God's wrath and eternal death, but he is admitted to God's favor and eternal life. The discovery of this is partly the cause of the convert's joy. Expecting pardon, at most, he is met with unmeasured favor. The prodigal finds the father's house and heart open to him, and more done for him than if he had never wandered. This overwhelms and subdues him. The two elements, acquittal and restoration to favor, are never separated. Like the expulsion of darkness and restoration of light, they always go together. No one can have, even if he would have, an incomplete justification. Christ's justification is ours ; and, as Jesus' own seamless tunic could not be divided, so the robe of righteousness which he provides cannot be cut in two.

Failure to apprehend this positive aspect of justification as restoration to favor is the reason why so many Christians have little joy and little enthusiasm in their religious lives. The preaching of the magnanimity and generosity of God makes the gospel "the power of God unto salvation" (Rom. 1:16). Edwin M. Stanton had ridden roughshod over Abraham Lincoln in the conduct of a case at law in which they had been joint counsel.

Stanton had become vindictive and even violent when Lincoln was made President. But Lincoln invited Stanton to be Secretary of War, and he sent the invitation by Harding, who knew of all this former trouble. When Stanton heard it, he said with streaming eyes: "Do you tell me, Harding, that Mr. Lincoln sent this message to me? Tell him that such magnanimity will make me work with him as man was never served before!"

(d) The declaration that the sinner is restored to God's favor, has its ground, not in the sinner's personal character or conduct, but solely in the obedience and righteousness of Christ, to whom the sinner is united by faith. Thus Christ's work is the procuring cause of our justification, in both its elements. As we are acquitted on account of Christ's suffering of the penalty of the law, so on account of Christ's obedience we receive the rewards of law.

All this comes to us in Christ. We participate in the rewards promised to his obedience: John 20:31 — "that believing ye may have life in his name"; 1 Cor. 3:21-23 — "For all things are yours; . . . . all are yours; and ye are Christ's; and Christ is God's." Denovan, Toronto Baptist, Dec. 1883, maintains that "grace operates in two ways: (1) for the *rebel* it provides a scheme of *justification*,— this is judicial, matter of debt; (2) for the *child* it provides pardon,— fatherly forgiveness on repentance." Heb. 7:19 — "the law made nothing perfect . . . . a bringing in thereupon of a better hope, through which we draw nigh unto God." This "better hope" is offered to us in Christ's death and resurrection. The veil of the temple was the symbol of separation from God. The rending of that veil was the symbol on the one hand that sin had been atoned for, and on the other hand that unrestricted access to God was now permitted us in Christ the great forerunner. Bonar's hymn, "Jesus, whom angel hosts adore," has for its concluding stanza: "'T is finished all: the veil is rent, The welcome sure, the access free :— Now then, we leave our banishment, O Father, to return to thee!" See pages 749 (b), 770 (h).

James Russell Lowell: "At the devil's booth all things are sold, Each ounce of dross costs its ounce of gold; For a cap and bells our lives we pay: Bubbles we buy with a whole soul's tasking; 'T is heaven alone that is given away, 'T is only God may be had for the asking." John G. Whittier: "The hour draws near, howe'er delayed and late, When at the Eternal Gate, We leave the words and works we call our own, And lift void hands alone For love to fill. Our nakedness of soul Brings to that gate no toll; Giftless we come to him who all things gives, And live because he lives."

H. B. Smith, System of Christian Doctrine, 523, 524 — "Justification and pardon are not the same in Scripture. We object to the view of Emmons (Works, vol. 5), that 'justification is no more nor less than pardon,' and that 'God rewards men for their own, and not Christ's, obedience,' for the reason that the words, as used in common life, relate to wholly different things. If a man is declared just by a human tribunal, he is not pardoned, he is acquitted; his own inherent righteousness, as respects the charge against him, is recognized and declared. The gospel proclaims both pardon and justification. There is no significance in the use of the word 'justify,' if pardon be all that is intended. . . .

"Justification involves what pardon does not, a righteousness which is the ground of the acquittal and favor; not the mere favor of the sovereign, but the merit of Christ, is at the basis — the righteousness which is of God. The ends of the law are so far satisfied by what Christ has done, that the sinner can be pardoned. The law is not merely set aside, but its great ends are answered by what Christ has done in our behalf. God might pardon as a sovereign, from mere benevolence (as regard to happiness); but in the gospel he does more,— he pardons in consistency with his holiness,— upholding that as the main end of all his dealings and works. Justification involves acquittal from all the penalty of the law, and the inheritance of all the blessings of the redeemed state. The penalty of the law — spiritual, temporal, eternal death — is all taken away; and the opposite blessings are conferred, in and through Christ — the resurrection to blessedness, the gift of the Spirit, and eternal life. . . .

"If justification is forgiveness simply, it applies only to the *past*. If it is also a title to life, it includes the future condition of the soul. The latter alone is consistent with the plan and decrees of God respecting redemption — his seeing the end from the beginning. The reason why justification has been taken as pardon is two-fold ; first, it *does* involve pardon,—this is its negative side, while it has a positive side also—the title to eternal life; secondly, the tendency to resolve the gospel into an ethical system. Only our acts of choice as meritorious could procure a title to favor, a positive reward. Christ might remove the obstacle, but the title to heaven is derived only from what we ourselves do.

"Justification is, therefore, not a merely governmental provision, as it must be on any scheme that denies that Christ's work has direct respect to the ends of the law· Views of the atonement determine the views on justification, if logical sequence is observed. We have to do here, not with views of natural justice, but with divine methods. If we regard the atonement simply as answering the ends of a governmental scheme, our view must be that justification merely removes an obstacle, and the end of it is only pardon, and not eternal life."

But upon the true view, that the atonement is a complete satisfaction to the holiness of God, justification embraces not merely pardon, or acquittal from the punishments of law, but also restoration to favor, or the rewards promised to actual obedience. See also Quenstedt, 3 : 524; Philippi, Active Obedience of Christ; Shedd, Dogm. Theol., 2 : 432, 433.

4. *Relation of Justification to God's Law and Holiness.*

A. Justification has been shown to be a forensic term. A man may, indeed, be conceived of as just, in either of two senses : (*a*) as just in moral character,— that is, absolutely holy in nature, disposition, and conduct; (*b*) as just in relation to law,— or as free from all obligation to suffer penalty, and as entitled to the rewards of obedience.

So, too, a man may be conceived of as justified, in either of two senses : (*a*) made just in moral character ; or, (*b*) made just in his relation to law. But the Scriptures declare that there does not exist on earth a just man, in the first of these senses (Eccl. 7 : 20). Even in those who are renewed in moral character and united to Christ, there is a remnant of moral depravity.

If, therefore, there be any such thing as a just man, he must be just, not in the sense of possessing an unspotted holiness, but in the sense of being delivered from the penalty of law, and made partaker of its rewards. If there be any such thing as justification, it must be, not an act of God which renders the sinner absolutely holy, but an act of God which declares the sinner to be free from legal penalties and entitled to legal rewards.

Justus is derived from *jus*, and suggests the idea of courts and legal procedures. The fact that ' justify ' is derived from *justus* and *facio*, and might therefore seem to imply the making of a man subjectively righteous, should not blind us to its forensic use. The phrases "sanctify the Holy One of Jacob" (Is. 29 : 23; *cf.* 1 Pet. 3 : 15—"sanctify in your hearts Christ as Lord ") and "glorify God" (1 Cor. 6 : 20) do not mean, to *make* God subjectively holy or glorious, for this he *is*, whatever we may do ; they mean rather, to *declare*, or *show*, him to be holy or glorious. So justification is not making a man righteous, or even pronouncing him righteous, for no man *is* subjectively righteous. It is rather to count him righteous so far as respects his relations to law, to treat him as righteous, or to declare that God will, for reasons assigned, so treat him (Payne). So long as any remnant of sin exists, no justification, in the sense of making holy, can be attributed to man : Eccl. 7 : 20—"Surely there is not a righteous man upon earth, that doeth good and sinneth not." If no man is just, in this sense, then God cannot pronounce him just, for God cannot lie. Justification, therefore, must signify a deliverance from legal penalties, and an assignment of legal rewards. O. F Gifford : There is no such thing as "salvation *by* character"; what men need is salva- tion *from* character. The only sense in which salvation by character is rational or Scriptural is that suggested by George Harris, Moral Evolution, 409—"Salvation by character is not self-righteousness, but Christ in us." But even here it must be remem- bered that Christ *in* us presupposes Christ *for* us. The objective atonement for sin must come before the subjective purification of our natures. And justification is upon the ground of that objective atonement, and not upon the ground of the subjective cleansing.

The Jews had a proverb that if only one man could perfectly keep the whole law even for one day, the kingdom of Messiah would at once come upon the earth. This is to state in another form the doctrine of Paul, in Rom. 7: 9 — "When the commandment came, sin revived, and I died." To recognize the impossibility of being justified by Pharisaic works was a preparation for the gospel; see Bruce, Apologetics, 419. The Germans speak of Werk-, Lehre-, Buchstaben-, Negations-, Parteigerechtigkeit; but all these are forms of self-righteousness. Berridge: "A man may steal some gems from the crown of Jesus and be guilty only of petty larceny, ... but the man who would justify himself by his own works steals the crown itself, puts it on his own head, and proclaims himself by his own conquests a king in Zion."

B. The difficult feature of justification is the declaration, on the part of God, that a sinner whose remaining sinfulness seems to necessitate the vindicative reaction of God's holiness against him, is yet free from such reaction of holiness as is expressed in the penalties of the law.

The fact is to be accepted on the testimony of Scripture. If this testimony be not accepted, there is no deliverance from the condemnation of law. But the difficulty of conceiving of God's declaring the sinner no longer exposed to legal penalty is relieved, if not removed, by the three-fold consideration:

(a) That Christ has endured the penalty of the law in the sinner's stead.

Gal. 3 : 13 — "Christ redeemed us from the curse of the law, having become a curse for us." Denovan: "We are justified by faith, instrumentally, in the same sense as a debt is paid by a good note or a check on a substantial account in a distant bank. It is only the intelligent and honest acceptance of justification already provided." Rom. 8 : 3 — "God, sending his own Son . . . . condemned sin in the flesh "= the believer's sins were judged and condemned on Calvary. The way of pardon through Christ honors God's justice as well as God's mercy ; cf. Rom. 3 : 26 — "that he might himself be just, and the justifier of him that hath faith in Jesus."

(b) That the sinner is so united to Christ, that Christ's life already constitutes the dominating principle within him.

Gal. 2 : 20 — "I have been crucified with Christ; and it is no longer I that live, but Christ liveth in me." God does not justify any man whom he does not foresee that he can and will sanctify. Some prophecies produce their own fulfilment. Tell a man he is brave, and you help him to become so. So declaratory justification, when published in the heart by the Holy Spirit, helps to make men just. Harris, God the Creator, 2 : 332 — "The objection to the doctrine of justification by faith insists that justification must be conditioned, not on faith, but on right character. But justification by faith is itself the doctrine of a justification conditioned on right character, because faith in God is the only possible beginning of right character, either in men or angels." Gould, Bib. Theol. N. T., 67-79, in a similar manner argues that Paul's emphasis is on the spiritual effect of the death of our Lord, rather than on its expiatory effect. The course of thought in the Epistle to the Romans seems to us to contradict this view. Sin and the objective atonement for sin are first treated ; only after justification comes the sanctification of the believer. Still it is true that justification is never the sole work of God in the soul. The same Christ in union with whom we are justified does at that same moment a work of regeneration which is followed by sanctification.

(c) That this life of Christ is a power in the soul which will gradually, but infallibly, extirpate all remaining depravity, until the whole physical and moral nature is perfectly conformed to the divine holiness.

Phil. 3 : 21 — "who shall fashion anew the body of our humiliation, that it may be conformed to the body of his glory, according to the working whereby he is able even to subject all things unto himself"; Col. 3 : 1-4 — ' If then ye were raised together with Christ, seek the things that are above, where Christ is, seated on the right hand of God. Set your mind on the things that are above, not on the things that are upon the earth. For ye died, and your life is hid with Christ in God. When Christ, who is our life, shall be manifested, then shall ye also with him be manifested in glory.'

Truth of fact, and ideal truth, are not opposed to each other. F. W. Robertson, Lectures and Addresses, 256 — "When the agriculturist sees a small, white, almond-like thing rising from the ground, he calls that an oak ; but this is not a truth of fact, it is an ideal truth. The oak is a large tree, with spreading branches and leaves and acorns: but that is only a thing an inch long, and imperceptible in all its development; yet the agriculturist sees in it the idea of what it shall be, and, if I may borrow a Scriptural phrase, he *imputes* to it the majesty, and excellence, and glory, that is to be hereafter." This method of representation is effective and unobjectionable, so long as we remember that the force which is to bring about this future development and perfection is not the force of unassisted human nature, but rather the force of Christ and his indwelling Spirit. See Philippi, Glaubenslehre, v, 1 : 201-208.

Gore, Incarnation, 224 — " ' Looking at the mother,' wrote George Eliot of Mrs. Garth in The Mill on the Floss, 'you might hope that the daughter would become like her— which is a prospective advantage equal to a dowry — the mother too often standing behind the daughter like a malignant prophecy: Such as I am, she will shortly be.' George Eliot imputes by anticipation to the daughter the merits of the mother, because her life is, so to speak, of the same piece. Now, by new birth and spiritual union, our life is of the same piece with the life of Jesus. Thus he, our elder brother, stands behind us, his people, as a prophecy of all good. Thus God accepts us, deals with us, 'in the Beloved,' rating us at something of his value, imputing to us his merits, because in fact, except we be reprobates, he himself is the most powerful and real force at work in us."

5. *Relation of Justification to Union with Christ and the Work of the Spirit.*

A. Since the sinner, at the moment of justification, is not yet completely transformed in character, we have seen that God can declare him just, not on account of what he is in himself, but only on account of what Christ is. The ground of justification is therefore not, (*a*) as the Romanists hold, a new righteousness and love infused into us, and now constituting our moral character ; nor, (*b*) as Osiander taught, the essential righteousness of Christ's divine nature, which has become ours by faith ; but (*c*) the satisfaction and obedience of Christ, as the head of a new humanity, and as embracing in himself all believers as his members.

Ritschl regarded justification as primarily an endowment of the church, in which the individual participated only so far as he belonged to the church; see Pfleiderer, Die Ritschl'sche Theologie, 70. Here Ritschl committed an error like that of the Romanist, — the church is the door to Christ, instead of Christ being the door to the church. Justification belongs primarily to Christ, then to all who join themselves to Christ by faith, and the church is the natural and voluntary aggregation of those who in Christ are thus justified. Hence the necessity for the resurrection and ascension of the Lord Jesus. " For as the ministry of Enoch was sealed by his reception into heaven, and as the ministry of Elijah was also abundantly proved by his translation, so also the righteousness and innocence of Christ. But it was necessary that the ascension of Christ should be more fully attested, because upon his righteousness, so fully proved by his ascension, we must depend for all our righteousness. For if God had not approved him after his resurrection, and he had not taken his seat at his right hand, we could by no means be accepted of God " (Cartwright).

A. J. Gordon, Ministry of the Spirit, 46, 193, 195, 206 — " Christ must be justified in the spirit and received up into glory, before he can be made righteousness to us and we can become the righteousness of God in him. Christ's coronation is the indispensable condition of our justification. . . . . Christ the High Priest has entered the Holy of Holies in heaven for us. Until he comes forth again at the second advent, how can we be assured that his sacrifice for us is accepted ? We reply : By the gift of the Holy Spirit. The presence of the Spirit in the church is the proof of the presence of Christ before the throne. . . . . The Holy Spirit convinces of righteousness, 'because I go unto the Father, and ye see me no more' (John 16 : 10). We can only know that ' we have a Paraclete with the Father, even Jesus Christ the Righteous ' (1 John 2 : 1), by that 'other Paraclete' sent forth from the Father, even the Holy Spirit (John 14 : 25, 26 ; 15 : 26). The church, having the Spirit, reflects Christ to the world. As Christ manifests the Father, so the church through the Spirit manifests Christ. So Christ gives to us his name, ' Christians,' as the husband gives his name to the wife."

As Adam's sin is imputed to us, not because Adam is in us, but because we were in Adam; so Christ's righteousness is imputed to us, not because Christ is in us, but because we are in Christ,—that is, joined by faith to one whose righteousness and life are infinitely greater than our power to appropriate or contain. In this sense, we may say that we are justified through a Christ outside of us, as we are sanctified through a Christ within us. Edwards: "The justification of the believer is no other than his being admitted to communion in, or participation of, this head and surety of all believers."

1 Tim. 1:14 —"faith and love which is in Christ Jesus"; 3:16 —"He who was manifested in the flesh, justified in the spirit"; Acts 13:39 —"and by him [lit. : 'in him'] every one that believeth is justified from all things, from which ye could not be justified by the law of Moses"; Rom. 4:25 —"who was delivered up for our trespasses, and was raised for our justification"; Eph. 1:6 —"accepted in the Beloved"—Rev. Vers.: "freely bestowed on us in the Beloved"; 1 Cor. 6:11 —"justified in the name of the Lord Jesus Christ." "We in Christ" is the formula of our justification; "Christ in us" is the formula of our sanctification. As the water which the shell contains is little compared with the great ocean which contains the shell, so the actual change wrought within us by God's sanctifying grace is slight compared with the boundless freedom from condemnation and the state of favor with God into which we are introduced by justification; Rom. 5:1, 2 —"Being therefore justified by faith, we have peace with God through our Lord Jesus Christ; through whom also we have had our access by faith into this grace wherein we stand; and we rejoice in hope of the glory of God."

Here we have the third instance of imputation. The first was the imputation of Adam's sin to us; and the second was the imputation of our sins to Christ. The third is now the imputation of Christ's righteousness to us. In each of the former cases, we have sought to show that the legal relation presupposes a natural relation. Adam's sin is imputed to us, because we are one with Adam; our sins are imputed to Christ, because Christ is one with humanity. So here, we must hold that Christ's righteousness is imputed to us, because we are one with Christ. Justification is not an arbitrary transfer to us of the merits of another with whom we have no real connection. This would make it merely a legal fiction; and there are no legal fictions in the divine government.

Instead of this external and mechanical method of conception, we should first set before us the fact of Christ's justification, after he had borne our sins and risen from the dead. In him, humanity, for the first time, is acquitted from punishment and restored to the divine favor. But Christ's new humanity is the germinal source of spiritual life for the race. He was justified, not simply as a private person, but as our representative and head. By becoming partakers of the new life in him, we share in all he is and all he has done; and, first of all, we share in his justification. So Luther gives us, for substance, the formula: "We in Christ = justification; Christ in us = sanctification." And in harmony with this formula is the statement quoted in the text above from Edwards, Works, 4:66.

See also H. B. Smith, Presb. Rev., July, 1881 —"Union with Adam and with Christ is the ground of imputation. But the parallelism is incomplete. While the sin of Adam is imputed to us because it is ours, the righteousness of Christ is imputed to us simply because of our union with him, not at all because of our personal righteousness. In the one case, character is taken into the account; in the other, it is not. In sin, our demerits are included; in justification, our merits are excluded." For further statements of Dr. Smith, see his System of Christian Theology, 524-552.

C. H. M. on Genesis, page 78 —"The question for every believer is not ' What am I?' but ' What is Christ?' Of Abel it is said : ' God testified of his gifts' (Heb. 11:4, A. V.). So God testifies, not of the believer, but of his gift,—and his gift is Christ. Yet Cain was angry because he was not received in his sins, while Abel was accepted in his gift. This was right, if Abel was justified in himself; it was wrong, because Abel was justified only in Christ." See also Hodge, Outlines of Theology, 384-388, 392; Baird, Elohim Revealed, 448.

B. The relation of justification to regeneration and sanctification, moreover, delivers it from the charges of externality and immorality. God does not justify ungodly men in their ungodliness. He pronounces them just only as they are united to Christ, who is absolutely just, and who, by his

Spirit, can make them just, not only in the eye of the law, but in moral character. The very faith by which the sinner receives Christ is an act in which he ratifies all that Christ has done, and accepts God's judgment against sin as his own (John 16 : 11).

John 16 : 11 — "of judgment, because the prince of this world hath been judged"— the Holy Spirit leads the believer to ratify God's judgment against sin and Satan. Accepting Christ, the believer accepts Christ's death for sin, and resurrection to life for his own. If it were otherwise, the first act of the believer, after his discharge, might be a repetition of his offences. Such a justification would offend against the fundamental principles of justice and the safety of government. It would also fail to satisfy the conscience. This clamors not only for pardon, but for renewal. Union with Christ has one legal fruit — justification; but it has also one moral fruit — sanctification.

A really guilty man, when acquitted by judge and jury, does not cease to be the victim of remorse and fear. Forgiveness of sin is not in itself a deliverance from sin. The outward acquittal needs to be accompanied by an inward change to be really effective. Pardon for sin without power to overcome sin would be a mockery of the criminal. Justification for Christ's sake therefore goes into effect through regeneration by the Holy Spirit; see E. H. Johnson, in Bib. Sac., July, 1892 : 362.

A Buddhist priest who had studied some years in England printed in Shanghai not long ago a pamphlet entitled "Justification by Faith the only true Basis of Morality." It argues that any other foundation is nothing but pure selfishness, but that morality, to have any merit, must be unselfish. Justification by faith supplies an unselfish motive—because we accept the work done for us by another, and we ourselves work from gratitude, which is not a selfish motive. After laying down this Christian foundation, the writer erects the structure of faith in the Amida incarnation of Buddha. Buddhism opposes to the Christian doctrine of a creative Person, only a creative process; sin has relation only to the man sinning, and has no relation to Amida Buddha or to the eternal law of causation; salvation by faith in Amida Buddha is faith in one who is the product of a process, and a product may perish. Tennyson: "They are but broken lights of Thee, And thou, O Christ, art more than they."

Justification is possible, therefore, because it is always accompanied by regeneration and union with Christ, and is followed by sanctification. But this is a very different thing from the Romanist confounding of justification and sanctification, as different stages of the same process of making the sinner actually holy. It holds fast to the Scripture distinction between justification as a declarative act of God, and regeneration and sanctification as those efficient acts of God by which justification is accompanied and followed.

Both history and our personal observation show that nothing can change the life and make men moral, like the gospel of free pardon in Jesus Christ. Mere preaching of morality will effect nothing of consequence. There never has been more insistence upon morality than in the most immoral times, like those of Seneca, and of the English deists. As to their moral fruits, we can safely compare Protestant with Roman Catholic systems and leaders and countries. We do not become right by doing right, for only those can do right who have become right. The prodigal son is forgiven before he actually confesses and amends (Luke 15 : 20, 21). Justification is always accompanied by regeneration, and is followed by sanctification ; and all three are results of the death of Christ. But the sin-offering must precede the thank-offering. We must first be accepted ourselves before we can offer gifts ; Heb. 11 : 4 — "By faith Abel offered unto God a more excellent sacrifice than Cain, through which he had witness borne to him that he was righteous, God bearing witness in respect of his gifts."

Hence we read in Eph. 5 : 25, 26 — "Christ also loved the church, and gave himself up for it; that he might sanctify it, having cleansed — [after he had cleansed] it by the washing of water with the word " [— regeneration]; 1 Pet. 1 : 1, 2 — "elect . . . . according to the foreknowledge of God the Father, in sanctification of the Spirit [regeneration], unto obedience [conversion] and sprinkling of the blood of Jesus Christ [justification]" ; 1 John 1 : 7 — "if we walk in the light, as he is in the light, we have fellowship one with another; and the blood of Jesus his Son cleanseth us from all sin " — here the ' cleansing ' refers primarily and mainly to justification, not to sanctification; for the apostle himself declares in verse 8 — "If we say that we have no sin, we deceive ourselves, and the truth is not in us."

Quenstedt says well, that "justification, since it is an act, outside of man, in God, cannot produce an intrinsic change in us." And yet, he says, "although faith alone justifies, yet faith is not alone." Melanchthon: "Sola fides justificat; sed fides non est sola." With faith go all manner of gifts of the Spirit and internal graces of character. But we should let go all the doctrinal gains of the Reformation if we did not insist that these gifts and graces are accompaniments and consequences of justification, instead of being a part or a ground of justification. See Girdlestone, O. T. Synonyms, 104, note — "Justification is God's declaration that the individual sinner, on account of the faith which unites him to Christ, is taken up into the relation which Christ holds to the Father, and has applied to him personally the objective work accomplished for humanity by Christ."

6.   *Relation of Justification to Faith.*

A. We are justified by faith, rather than by love or by any other grace: (*a*) not because faith is itself a work of obedience by which we merit justification,— for this would be a doctrine of justification by works; (*b*) nor because faith is accepted as an equivalent of obedience, — for there is no equivalent except the perfect obedience of Christ; (*c*) nor because faith is the germ from which obedience may spring hereafter,— for it is not the faith which accepts, but the Christ who is accepted, that renders such obedience possible; but (*d*) because faith, and not repentance, or love, or hope, is the medium or instrument by which we receive Christ and are united to him. Hence we are never said to be justified διὰ πίστιν, = on account of faith, but only διὰ πίστεως, = through faith, or ἐκ πίστεως, = by faith. Or, to express the same truth in other words, while the grace of God is the efficient cause of justification, and the obedience and sufferings of Christ are the meritorious or procuring cause, faith is the mediate or instrumental cause.

Edwards, Works, 4:69–73 — "Faith justifies, because faith includes the whole act of unition to Christ as a Savior. It is not the nature of any other graces or virtues directly to close with Christ as a mediator, any further than they enter into the constitution of justifying faith, and do belong to its nature"; Observations on Trinity 64–67 — "Salvation is not offered to us upon any condition, but freely and for nothing. We are to do nothing for it, — we are only to take it. This taking and receiving is faith." H. B. Smith, System, 524 — "An internal change is a *sine qua non* of justification, but not its meritorious ground." Give a man a gold mine. It is *his*. He has not to work *for* it; he has only to work *it*. Working *for* life is one thing; working *from* life is quite another. The marriage of a poor girl to a wealthy proprietor makes her possessor of his riches despite her former poverty. Yet her acceptance has not *purchased* wealth. It is hers, not because of what she is or has done, but because of what her husband is and has done. So faith is the condition of justification, only because through it Christ becomes ours, and with him his atonement and righteousness. Salvation comes not because our faith saves us, but because it links us to the Christ who saves; and believing is only the link. There is no more merit in it than in the beggar's stretching forth his hand to receive the offered purse, or the drowning man's grasping the rope that is thrown to him.

The Wesleyan scheme is inclined to make faith a work. See Dabney, Theology, 637. This is to make faith *the* cause and ground, or at least to add it to Christ's work as a *joint* cause and ground, of justification; as if justification were διὰ πίστιν, instead of διὰ πίστεως or ἐκ πίστεως. Since faith is never perfect, this is to go back to the Roman Catholic uncertainty of salvation. See Dorner, Glaubenslehre, 2:744, 745 (Syst. Doct. 4:206, 207). C. H. M. on Gen. 3:7 — "They made themselves aprons of fig-leaves, before God made them coats of skin. Man ever tries to clothe himself in garments of his own righteousness, before he will take the robe of Christ's. But Adam felt himself naked when God visited him, even though he had his fig-leaves on him."

We are justified efficiently by the grace of God, meritoriously by Christ, instrumentally by faith, evidentially by works. Faith justifies, as roots bring plant and soil together. Faith connects man with the source of life in Christ. "When the boatman with his hook grapples the rock, he does not pull the shore to the boat, but the boat to the shore; so, when we by faith lay hold on Christ, we do not pull Christ to us, but ourselves to him." Faith is a coupling; the train is drawn, not by the coupling, but by the locomotive; yet without the coupling it would not be drawn. Faith is the trolley that reaches up to the electric wire; when the connection is sundered, not only does the car cease to move, but the heat dies and the lights go out. Dr. John Duncan: "I have married the Merchant and all his wealth is mine!"

H. C. Trumbull: "If a man wants to cross the ocean, he can either try swimming, or he can trust the captain of a ship to carry him over in his vessel. By or through his faith in that captain, the man is carried safely to the other shore; yet it is the ship's captain, not the passenger's faith, which is to be praised for the carrying." So the sick man trusts his case in the hands of his physician, and his life is saved by the physician, — yet by or through the patient's faith. This faith is indeed an inward act of allegiance, and no mere outward performance. Whiton, Divine Satisfaction, 92 — "The Protestant Reformers saw that it was by an inward act, not by penances or sacraments that men were justified. But they halted in the crude notion of a legal court room process, a governmental procedure external to us, whereas it is an educational, inward process, the awakening through Christ of the filial spirit in us, which in the midst of imperfections strives for likeness more and more to the Son of God. Justification by principle apart from performance makes Christianity the religion of the spirit." We would add that such justification excludes education, and is an act rather than a process, an act external to the sinner rather than internal, an act of God rather than an act of man. The justified person can say to Christ, as Ruth said to Boaz: "Why have I found favor in thy sight, that thou shouldest take knowledge of me, seeing I am a foreigner?" (Ruth 2:10).

B. Since the ground of justification is only Christ, to whom we are united by faith, the justified person has peace. If it were anything in ourselves, our peace must needs be proportioned to our holiness. The practical effect of the Romanist mingling of works with faith, as a joint ground of justification, is to render all assurance of salvation impossible. (Council of Trent, 9th chap.: "Every man, by reason of his own weakness and defects, must be in fear and anxiety about his state of grace. Nor can any one know, with infallible certainty of faith, that he has received forgiveness of God."). But since justification is an instantaneous act of God, complete at the moment of the sinner's first believing, it has no degrees. Weak faith justifies as perfectly as strong faith; although, since justification is a secret act of God, weak faith does not give so strong assurance of salvation.

Foundations of our Faith, 216 — "The Catholic doctrine declares that justification is not dependent upon faith and the righteousness of Christ imputed and granted thereto, but on the actual condition of the man himself. But there remain in the man an undeniable amount of fleshly lusts or inclinations to sin, even though the man be regenerate. The Catholic doctrine is therefore constrained to assert that these lusts are not in themselves sinful, or objects of the divine displeasure. They are allowed to remain in the man, that he may struggle against them; and, as they say, Paul designates them as sinful, only because they are derived from sin, and incite to sin; but they only become sin by the positive concurrence of the human will. But is not internal lust displeasing to God? Can we draw the line between lust and will? The Catholic favors self here, and makes many things *lust*, which are really *will*. A Protestant is necessarily more earnest in the work of salvation, when he recognizes even the evil desire as sin, according to Christ's precept."

All systems of religion of merely human origin tend to make salvation, in larger or smaller degree, the effect of human works, but only with the result of leaving man in despair. See, in Ecclesiasticus 3:30, an Apocryphal declaration that alms make atonement for sin. So Romanism bids me doubt God's grace and the forgiveness of my

See Dorner, Gesch. prot. Theol., 228, 229, and his quotations from Luther. "But if the Romanist doctrine is true, that a man is justified only in such measure as he is sanctified, then: 1. Justification must be a matter of degrees, and so the Council of Trent declares it to be. The sacraments which sanctify are therefore essential, that one may be increasingly justified. 2. Since justification is a continuous process, the redeeming death of Christ, on which it depends, must be a continuous process also; hence its prolonged reiteration in the sacrifice by the Mass. 3. Since sanctification is obviously never completed in this life, no man ever dies completely justified; hence the doctrine of Purgatory." For the substance of Romanist doctrine, see Moehler, Symbolism, 79-190; Newman, Lectures on Justification, 253-345; Ritschl, Christian Doctrine of Justi. fication, 121-226.

A better doctrine is that of the Puritan divine: "It is not the quantity of thy faith that shall save thee. A drop of water is as true water as the whole ocean. So a little faith is as true faith as the greatest. It is not the measure of thy faith that saves thee,— it is the blood that it grips to that saves thee. The weak hand of the child, that leads the spoon to the mouth, will feed as well as the strong arm of a man; for it is not the hand that feeds, but the meat. So, if thou canst grip Christ ever so weakly, he will not let thee perish." I am troubled about the money I owe in New York, until I find that a friend has paid my debt there. When I find that the objective account against me is cancelled, then and only then do I have subjective peace.

A child may be heir to a vast estate, even while he does not know it; and a child of God may be an heir of glory, even while, through the weakness of his faith, he is oppressed with painful doubts and fears. No man is lost simply because of the greatness of his sins; however ill-deserving he may be, faith in Christ will save him. Luther's climbing the steps of St. John Lateran, and the voice of thunder: "The just shall live by faith," are not certain as historical facts; but they express the substance of Luther's experience. Not obeying, but receiving, is the substance of the gospel. A man cannot merit salvation; he cannot buy it; but one thing he must do,— he must take it. And the least faith makes salvation ours, because it makes Christ ours.

Augustine conceived of justification as a continuous process, proceeding until love and all Christian virtues fill the heart. There is his chief difference from Paul. Augustine believes in sin and grace. But he has not the freedom of the children of God, as Paul has. The influence of Augustine upon Roman Catholic theology has not been wholly salutary. The Roman Catholic, mixing man's subjective condition with God's grace as a ground of justification, continually wavers between self-righteousness and uncertainty of acceptance with God, each of these being fatal to a healthful and stable religious life. High-church Episcopalians, and Sacramentalists generally, are afflicted with this distemper of the Romanists. Dr. R. W. Dale remarks with regard to Dr. Pusey: "The absence of joy in his religious life was only the inevitable effect of his conception of God's method of saving men; in parting with the Lutheran truth concerning justification, he parted with the springs of gladness." Spurgeon said that a man might get from London to New York provided he took a steamer; but it made much difference in his comfort whether he had a first class or a second class ticket. A new realization of the meaning of justification in our churches would change much of our singing from the minor to the major key; would lead us to pray, not *for* the presence of Christ, but *from* the presence of Christ; would abolish the mournful upward inflections at the end of sentences which give such unreality to our preaching; and would replace the pessimistic element in our modern work and worship with the notes of praise and triumph. In the Pilgrim's Progress, the justification of the believer is symbolized by Christian's lodging in the Palace Beautiful whose window opened toward the sunrising.

Even Luther did not fully apprehend and apply his favorite doctrine of justification by faith. Harnack, Wesen des Christenthums, 168 sq., states the fundamental principles of Protestantism as: "1. The Christian religion is wholly given in the word of God and in the inner experience which answers to that word. 2. The assured belief that the Christian has a gracious God. 'Nun weisz und glaub' ich 's feste, Ich rühm 's auch ohne Scheu, Dasz Gott, der höchst' und beste, Mein Freund und Vater sei; Und dasz in allen Fällen Er mir zur Rechten steh', Und dampfe Sturm und Wellen, Und was mir bringet Weh'.' 3. Restoration of simple and believing worship, both public and private. But Luther took too much dogma into Christianity; insisted too much on the authority of the written word; cared too much for the *means* of grace, such as the Lord's Supper; identified the church too much with the organized body."

Yet Luther talked of beating the heads of the Wittenbergers with the Bible. so as to get the great doctrine of justification by faith into their brains. "Why do you teach your child the same thing twenty times?" he said. "Because I find that nineteer times is not sufficient."

C. Justification is instantaneous, complete, and final: instantaneous, since otherwise there would be an interval during which the soul was neither approved nor condemned by God (Mat. 6 : 24); complete, since the soul, united to Christ by faith, becomes partaker of his complete satisfaction to the demands of law (Col. 2 : 9, 10) ; and final, since the union with Christ is indissoluble (John 10 : 28, 29). As there are many acts of sin in the life of the Christian, so there are many acts of pardon following them. But all these acts of pardon are virtually implied in that first act by which he was finally and forever justified ; as also successive acts of repentance and faith, after such sins, are virtually implied in that first repentance and faith which logically preceded justification.

Mat. 6 : 24 — "No man can serve two masters" ; Col. 2 : 9, 10 — "in him dwelleth all the fulness of the Godhead bodily, and in him ye are made full, who is the head of all principality and power" ; John 10 : 28, 29 — "they shall never perish, and no one shall snatch them out of my hand. My Father, who hath given them unto me, is greater than all ; and no one is able to snatch them out of the Father's hand."

Plymouth Brethren say truly that the Christian has sin in him, but not on him, because Christ had sin on him, but not in him. The Christian has sin but not guilt, because Christ had guilt but not sin. All our sins are buried in the grave with Christ, and Christ's resurrection is our resurrection. Toplady: "From whence this fear and unbelief ? Hast thou, O Father, put to grief Thy spotless Son for me? And will the righteous Judge of men Condemn me for that debt of sin, Which, Lord, was laid on thee? If thou hast my discharge procured, And freely in my room endured The whole of wrath divine, Payment God cannot twice demand, First at my bleeding Surety's hand, And then again at mine. Complete atonement thou hast made, And to the utmost farthing paid Whate'er thy people owed ; How then can wrath on me take place, If sheltered in thy righteousness And sprinkled with thy blood ? Turn, then, my soul, unto thy rest ; The merits of thy great High-priest Speak peace and liberty ; Trust in his efficacious blood, Nor fear thy banishment from God, Since Jesus died for thee !"

Justification, however, is not eternal in the past. We are to repent unto the remis. sion of our sins (Act 2 : 38). Remission comes after repentance. Sin is not pardoned before it is committed. In justification God grants us actual pardon for past sin, but virtual pardon for future sin. Edwards, Works, 4 : 104 —" Future sins are respected, in that first justification, no otherwise than as future faith and repentance are respected in it ; and future faith and repentance are looked upon by him that justifies as virtually implied in that first repentance and faith, in the same manner that justification from future sins is implied in that first justification."

A man is not justified from his sins before he has committed them, nor is he saved before he is born. A remarkable illustration of the extreme to which hyper-Calvinism may go is found in Tobias Crisp, Sermons, 1 : 358 - "The Lord hath no more to lay to the charge of an elect person, yet in the height of iniquity, and in the excess of riot, and committing all the abomination that can be committed . . . . than he has to the charge of the saint triumphant in glory." A far better statement is found in Moberly, Atonement and Personality, 61—"As there is upon earth no consummated penitence, so neither is there any forgiveness consummated. . . . . Forgiveness is the recognition, by anticipation, of something which is to be, something toward which it is itself a mighty quickening of possibilities, but something which is not, or at least is not perfectly, yet.
. . . . Present forgiveness is inchoate, is educational. . . . . It reaches its final and perfect consummation only when the forgiven penitent has become at last personally and completely righteous. If the consummation is not reached but reversed, then forgiveness is forfeited (Mat. 18 : 32-35)." This last exception, however, as we shall see in our discussion of Perseverance, is only a hypothetical one. The truly forgiven do not finally fall away.

7. Advice to Inquirers demanded by a Scriptural View of Justification.

(*a*) Where conviction of sin is yet lacking, our aim should be to show the sinner that he is under God's condemnation for his past sins, and that no future obedience can ever secure his justification, since this obedience, even though perfect, could not atone for the past, and even if it could, he is unable, without God's help, to render it.

With the help of the Holy Spirit, conviction of sin may be roused by presentation of the claims of God's perfect law, and by drawing attention, first to particular overt transgressions, and then to the manifold omissions of duty, the general lack of supreme and all-pervading love to God, and the guilty rejection of Christ's offers and commands. " Even if the next page of the copy book had no blots or erasures, its cleanness would not alter the smudges and misshapen letters on the earlier pages." God takes no notice of the promise "Have patience with me, and I will pay thee " (Mat. 18:29), for he knows it can never be fulfilled.

(*b*) Where conviction of sin already exists, our aim should be, not, in the first instance, to secure the performance of external religious duties, such as prayer, or Scripture-reading, or uniting with the church, but to induce the sinner, as his first and all-inclusive duty, to accept Christ as his only and sufficient sacrifice and Savior, and, committing himself and the matter of his salvation entirely to the hands of Christ, to manifest this trust and submission by entering at once upon a life of obedience to Christ's commands.

A convicted sinner should be exhorted, not first to prayer and then to faith, but first to faith, and then to the immediate expression of that faith in prayer and Christian activity. He should pray, not *for* faith, but *in* faith. It should not be forgotten that the sinner never sins against so much light, and never is in so great danger, as when he is convicted but not converted, when he is moved to turn but yet refuses to turn. No such sinner should be allowed to think that he has the right to do any other thing whatever before accepting Christ. This accepting Christ is not an outward act, but an inward act of mind and heart and will, although believing is naturally evidenced by immediate outward action. To teach the sinner, however apparently well disposed, how to believe on Christ, is beyond the power of man. God is the only giver of faith. But Scripture instances of faith, and illustrations drawn from the child's taking the father at his word and acting upon it, have often been used by the Holy Spirit as means of leading men themselves to put faith in Christ.

Bengel: "Those who are secure Jesus refers to the law; those who are contrite he consoles with the gospel." A man left work and came home. His wife asked why. "Because I am a sinner." "Let me send for the preacher." "I am too far gone for preachers. If the Lord Jesus Christ does not save me I am lost." That man needed only to be pointed to the Cross. There he found reason for believing that there was salvation for him. In surrendering himself to Christ he was justified. On the general subject of Justification, see Edwards, Works, 4 : 64-132; Buchanan on Justification, 250-411; Owen on Justification, in Works, vol. 5; Bp. of Ossory, Nature and Effects of Faith, 48-152; Hodge, Syst. Theol., 3 : 114-212; Thomasius, Christi Person und Werk, 3 : 133-200; Herzog, Encyclopadie, art.: Rechtfertigung; Bushnell, Vicarious Sacrifice, 416-420, 435.

SECTION III.—THE APPLICATION OF CHRIST'S REDEMPTION IN ITS CONTINUATION.

Under this head we treat of Sanctification and of Perseverance. These two are but the divine and the human sides of the same fact, and they bear to each other a relation similar to that which exists between Regeneration and Conversion.

I. SANCTIFICATION.

1. *Definition of Sanctification.*

Sanctification is that continuous operation of the Holy Spirit, by which the holy disposition imparted in regeneration is maintained and strengthened.

Godet: "The work of Jesus in the world is twofold. It is a work accomplished *for us*, destined to effect *reconciliation* between God and man; it is a work accomplished *in us*, with the object of effecting our *sanctification*. By the one, a right *relation* is established between God and us; by the other, the *fruit* of the reëstablished order is secured. By the former, the condemned sinner is received into the state of grace; by the latter, the pardoned sinner is associated with the life of God. . . . . How many express themselves as if, when forgiveness with the peace which it procures has been once obtained, ail is finished and the work of salvation is complete! They seem to have no suspicion that salvation consists in the health of the soul, and that the health of the soul consists in holiness. Forgiveness is not the reëstablishment of health; it is the crisis of convalescence. If God thinks fit to declare the sinner righteous, it is in order that he may by that means restore him to holiness." O. P. Gifford: "The steamship whose machinery is broken may be brought into port and made fast to the dock. She is *safe*, but not *sound*. Repairs may last a long time. Christ designs to make us both safe and sound. Justification gives the first — safety; sanctification gives the second — soundness."

Bradford, Heredity and Christian Problems, 220 — "To be conscious that one is forgiven, and yet that at the same time he is so polluted that he cannot beget a child without handing on to that child a nature which will be as bad as if his father had never been forgiven, is not salvation in any *real* sense." We would say: Is not salvation in any *complete* sense. Justification needs sanctification to follow it. Man needs God to continue and preserve his spiritual life, just as much as he needed God to begin it at the first. Creation in the spiritual, as well as in the natural world, needs to be supplemented by preservation; see quotation from Jonathan Edwards, in Allen's biography of him, 371.

Regeneration is instantaneous, but sanctification takes time. The "developing" of the photographer's picture may illustrate God's process of sanctifying the regenerate soul. But it is development by new access of truth or light, while the photographer's picture is usually developed in the dark. This development cannot be accomplished in a moment. "We try in our religious lives to practise instantaneous photography. One minute for prayer will give us a vision of God, and we think that is enough. Our pictures are poor because our negatives are weak. We do not give God a long enough sitting to get a good likeness."

Salvation is something past, something present, and something future; a past fact, justification; a present process, sanctification; a future consummation, redemption and glory. David, in Ps. 51:1, 2, prays not only that God will blot out his transgressions (justification), but that God will wash him thoroughly from his iniquity (sanctification). E. G. Robinson: "Sanctification consists *negatively*, in the removal of the penal consequences of sin from the moral nature; *positively*, in the progressive implanting and growth of a new principle of life. . . . . The Christian church is a succession of copies of the character of Christ. Paul never says : 'be ye imitators of me' (1 Cor. 4:16), except when writing to those who had no copies of the New Testament or of the Gospels."

Clarke, Christian Theology, 366 — "Sanctification does not mean perfection reached, but the progress of the divine life toward perfection. Sanctification is the Christianizing of the Christian." It is not simply deliverance from the penalty of sin, but the development of a divine life that conquers sin. A. A. Hodge, Popular Lectures, 343 — "Any man who thinks he is a Christian, and that he has accepted Christ for justification, when he did not at the same time accept him for sanctification, is miserably deluded in that very experience."

This definition implies:

(*a*) That, although in regeneration the governing disposition of the soul is made holy, there still remain tendencies to evil which are unsubdued.

John 13:10 — "He that is bathed needeth not save to wash his feet, but is clean every whit [*i. e.*, as a whole]" ; Rom. 6 · 12 — "Let not sin therefore reign in your mortal body, that ye should obey the lusts thereof " — sin *dwells* in a believer, but it *reigns* in an unbeliever (C. H. M.). Subordinate volitions in the Christian are not always determined in character by the fundamental choice; eddies in the stream sometimes run counter to the general course of the current.

This doctrine is the opposite of that expressed in the phrase: "the essential divinity of the human." Not culture, but crucifixion, is what the Holy Spirit prescribes for the natural man. There are two natures in the Christian, as Paul shows in Romans 7. The one flourishes at the other's expense. The vine dresser has to cut the rank shoots from self, that all our force may be thrown into growing fruit. Deadwood must be cut out; living wood must be cut back (John 15:2). Sanctification is not a matter of course, which will go on whatever we do, or do not do. It requires a direct superintendence and surgery on the one hand, and, on the other hand a practical hatred of evil on our part that coöperates with the husbandry of God.

(*b*) That the existence in the believer of these two opposing principles gives rise to a conflict which lasts through life.

Gal. 5:17—"For the flesh lusteth against the Spirit, and the Spirit against the flesh; for these are contrary the one to the other; that ye may not do the things that ye would'—not, as the A. V. had it, 'so that ye cannot do the things that ye would'; the Spirit who dwells in believers is represented as enabling them successfully to resist those tendencies to evil which naturally exist within them; James 4:5 (the marginal and better reading)—"That spirit which he made to dwell in us yearneth for us even unto jealous envy"—*i. e.*, God's love, like all true love, longs to have its objects wholly for its own. The Christian is two men in one; but he is to "put away the old man" and "put on the new man" (Eph. 4:22, 23). Compare Ecclesiasticus 2:1—"My son, if thou dost set out to serve the Lord, prepare +hy soul for temptation."

1 Tim. 6:12—"Fight the good fight of the faith"—ἀγωνίζου τὸν καλὸν ἀγῶνα τῆς πίστεως = the beautiful, honorable, glorious fight; since it has a noble helper, incentive, and reward. It is the commonest of all struggles, but the issue determines our destiny. An Indian received as a gift some tobacco in which he found a half dollar hidden. He brought it back next day, saying that good Indian had fought all night with bad Indian, one telling him to keep, the other telling him to return.

(*c*) That in this conflict the Holy Spirit enables the Christian, through increasing faith, more fully and consciously to appropriate Christ, and thus progressively to make conquest of the remaining sinfulness of his nature.

Rom. 8:13, 14—"for if ye live after the flesh, ye must die; but if by the Spirit ye put to death the deeds of the body, ye shall live. For as many as are led by the Spirit of God, these are sons of God"; 1 Cor. 6:11—"but ye were washed, but ye were sanctified, but ye were justified in the name of the Lord Jesus Christ, and in the Spirit of our God"; James 1:26 —"If any man thinketh himself to be religious, while he bridleth not his tongue but deceiveth his heart, this man's religion is vain"—see Com. of Neander, *in loco*—"That religion is merely imaginary, seeming, unreal, which allows the continuance of the moral defects originally predominant in the character." The Christian is "crucified with Christ" (Gal. 2:20); but the crucified man does not die at once. Yet he is as good as dead. Even after the old man is crucified we are still to mortify him, or put him to death (Rom. 8:13; Col. 3:5). We are to cut down the old rosebush and cultivate only the new shoot that is grafted into it. Here is our probation as Christians. So "die Scene wird zum Tribunal"—the play of life becomes God's judgment.

Dr. Hastings: "When Bourdaloue was probing the conscience of Louis XIV, applying to him the words of St. Paul and intending to paraphrase them: 'For the good which I would, I do not, but the evil which I would not, that I do,' 'I find two men in me'—the King interrupted the great preacher with the memorable exclamation: 'Ah, these two men, I know them well!' Bourdaloue answered: 'It is already something to *know* them, Sire; but it is not enough,—one of the two must perish.'" And, in the genuine believer, the old does little by little die, and the new takes its place, as "David waxed stronger and stronger, but the house of Saul waxed weaker and weaker" (2 Sam. 3:1). As the Welsh minister found himself after awhile thinking and dreaming in English, so the language of Canaan becomes to the Christian his native and only speech.

2.   *Explanations and Scripture Proof.*

(*a*) Sanctification is the work of God.

1 Thess. 5:23—"And the God of peace himself sanctify you wholly." Much of our modern literature ignores man's dependence upon God, and some of it seems distinctly intended to teach

the opposite doctrine. Auerbach's "On the Heights," for example, teaches that man can make his own atonement; and "The Villa on the Rhine," by the same author, teaches that man can sanctify himself. The proper inscription for many modern French novels is: "Entertainment here for man and beast." The *Tendenznovelle* of Germany has its imitators in the sceptical novels of England. And no doctrine in these novels is so common as the doctrine that man needs no Savior but himself.

(*b*) It is a continuous process.

Phil. 1 : 6 —" being confident of this very thing, that he who began a good work in you will perfect it until the day of Jesus Christ "; 3 : 15 —" Let us therefore, as many as are perfect, be thus minded : and if in anything ye are otherwise minded, this also shall God reveal unto you "; Col. 3 : 9, 10 —" lie not one to another ; seeing that ye have put off the old man with his doings, and have put on the new man, that is being renewed unto knowledge after the image of him that created him "; *cf.* Acts 2 : 47 —" those that were being saved "; 1 Cor. 1 : 18 —" unto us who are being saved " ; 2 Cor. 2 : 15 —" in them that are being saved "; 1 Thess. 2 : 12 —" God, who calleth you into his own kingdom and glory."

C. H. Parkhurst : "The yeast does not strike through the whole lump of dough at a flash. We keep finding unsuspected lumps of meal that the yeast has not yet seized upon. We surrender to God in instalments. We may not mean to do it, but we do it. Conversion has got to be brought down to date." A student asked the President of Oberlin College whether he could not take a shorter course than the one prescribed. "Oh yes," replied the President, "but then it depends on what you want to make of yourself. When God wants to make an oak, he takes a hundred years, but when he wants to make a squash, he takes six months."

(*c*) It is distinguished from regeneration as growth from birth, or as the strengthening of a holy disposition from the original impartation of it.

Eph. 4 : 15 —" speaking the truth in love, may grow up in all things into him, who is the head, even Christ "; 1 Thess. 3 : 12 —" the Lord make you to increase and abound in love one toward another, and toward all men "; 2 Pet. 3 : 18 —" But grow in the grace and knowledge of our Lord and Savior Jesus Christ "; *cf.* 1 Pet. 1 : 23 —" begotten again, not of corruptible seed, but of incorruptible, through the word of God, which liveth and abideth " • 1 John 3 : 9 —" Whosoever is begotten of God doeth no sin, because his seed abideth in him : and he cannot sin, because he is begotten of God." Not sin only, but holiness also, is a germ whose nature is to grow. The new love in the believer's heart follows the law of all life, in developing and extending itself under God's husbandry. George Eliot : "The reward of one duty done is the power to do another." J. W. A. Stewart : "When the 21st of March has come, we say 'The back of the winter is broken.' There will still be alternations of frost, but the progress will be towards heat. The coming of summer is sure,—in germ the summer is already here." Regeneration is the crisis of a disease ; sanctification is the progress of convalescence. Yet growth is not a uniform thing in the tree or in the Christian. In some single months there is more growth than in all the year besides. During the rest of the year, however, there is solidification, without which the green timber would be useless. The period of rapid growth, when woody fibre is actually deposited between the bark and the trunk, occupies but four to six weeks in May, June, and July. 2 Pet. 1 : 5 —" adding on your part all diligence, in your faith supply virtue ; and in your virtue knowledge " = adding to the central grace all those that are complementary and subordinate, till they attain the harmony of a chorus (ἐπιχορηγήσατε).

(*d*) The operation of God reveals itself in, and is accompanied by, intelligent and voluntary activity of the believer in the discovery and mortification of sinful desires, and in the bringing of the whole being into obedience to Christ and conformity to the standards of his word.

John 17 : 17 —" Sanctify them in the truth : thy word is truth "; 2 Cor. 10 : 5 —" casting down imaginations, and every high thing that is exalted against the knowledge of God, and bringing every thought into captivity to the obedience of Christ "; Phil. 2 : 12, 13 —" work out your own salvation with fear and trembling ; for it is God who worketh in you both to will and to work, for his good pleasure "; 1 Pet. 2 : 2 —" as new-born babes, long for the spiritual milk which is without guile, that ye may grow thereby unto salvation." John 15 : 3 —" Already ye are clean because of the word which I have spoken unto you." Regeneration through the word is followed by sanctification through the word. Eph. 5 : 1 —" Be ye therefore imitators of God, as beloved children." Imitation is at first a painful effort of will, as in learning the piano ; afterwards it becomes pleasurable and ever unconscious. Children unconsciously imitate the handwriting of their parents. Charles Lamb sees in the mirror, as he is shaving, the apparition of his dead father. So our likeness to God comes out as we advance in years. Col. 3 : 4 —" When Christ who is our Life, shall be manifested, then shall ye also with him be manifested in glory."

Horace Bushnell said that, if the stars did not move, they would rot in the sky. The man wh rides the bicycle must either go on, or go off. A large part of sanctification consists in the formation of proper habits, such as the habit of Scripture reading, of secret prayer, of church going, of efforts to convert and benefit others. Baxter: " Every man must grow, as trees grow, downward and upward at once. The visible outward growth must be accompanied by an invisible inward growth." Drummond: "The spiritual man having passed from death to life, the natural man must pass from life to death." There must be increasing sense of sin : " My sins gave sharpness to the nails, And pointed every thorn." There must be a bringing of new and yet newer regions of thought, feeling, and action, under the sway of Christ and his truth. There is a grain of truth even in Macaulay's jest about " essentially Christian cookery."

A. J. Gordon, Ministry of the Spirit, 63, 109-111 —" The church is Christian no more than as it is the organ of the continuous passion of Christ. We must suffer with sinning and lost humanity, and so 'fill up . . . . that which is lacking of the afflictions of Christ' ' (Col. 1 : 24). Christ's crucifixion must be prolonged side by side with his resurrection. There are three deaths: 1. death in sin, our natural condition ; 2. death for sin, our judicial condition ; 3. death to sin, our sanctified condition. . . . . As the ascending sap in the tree crowds off the dead leaves which in spite of storm and frost cling to the branches al¹ the winter long, so does the Holy Spirit within us, when allowed full sway, subdue and expel the remnants of our sinful nature."

(*e*) The agency through which God effects the sanctification of the believer is the indwelling Spirit of Christ.

John 14:17, 18 —"the Spirit of truth . . . . he abideth with you, and shall be in you. I will not leave you desolate I come unto you " ; 15 : 3-5 —" Already ye are clean . . . . Abide in me . . . . apart from me ye can do nothing '' Rom. 8 : 9, 10 —"the Spirit of God dwelleth in you. But if any man hath not the Spirit of Christ, he is none of his. And if Christ is in you, the body is dead because of sin ; but the spirit is life because of righteousness " ; 1 Cor. 1 : 2, 30 — " sanctified in Christ Jesus . . . . Christ Jesus, who was made unto us . . . . sanctification " ; 6 : 19 —"know ye not that your body is a temple of the Holy Spirit which is in you, which ye have from God ? " Gal. 5 : 16 —" Walk by the Spirit, and ye shall not fulfil the lust of the flesh " ; Eph. 5 : 18 —" And be not drunken with wine, wherein is riot, but be filled with the Spirit " ; Col. 1 : 27-29 —" the riches of the glory of this mystery among the Gentiles, which is Christ in you, the hope of glory : whom we proclaim, admonishing every man and teaching every man in all wisdom, that we may present every man perfect in Christ ; whereunto I labor also, striving according to his working, which worketh in me mightily " ; 2 Tim. 1 : 14 —"That good thing which was committed unto thee guard through the Holy Spirit which dwelleth in us."

Christianity substitutes for the old sources of excitement the power of the Holy Spirit. Here is a source of comfort, energy, and joy, infinitely superior to any which the sinner knows. God does not leave the soul to fall back upon itself. The higher up we get in the scale of being, the more does the new life need nursing and tending,— compare the sapling and the babe. God gives to the Christian, therefore, an abiding presence and work of the Holy Spirit,— not only regeneration, but sanctification. C. E. Smith, Baptism of Fire : " The soul needs the latter as well as the former rain, the sealing as well as the renewing of the Spirit, the baptism of fire as well as the baptism of water. Sealing gives something additional to the document, an evidence plainer than the writing within, both to one's self and to others."

" Few flowers yield more honey than serves the bee for its daily food." So we must first live ourselves off from our spiritual diet ; only what is over can be given to nourish others. Thomas à Kempis, Imitation of Christ : " Have peace in thine own heart ; else thou wilt never be able to communicate peace to others." Godet : " Man is a vessel destined to receive God, a vessel which must be enlarged in proportion as it is filled, and filled in proportion as it is enlarged." Matthew Arnold, Morality : " We cannot kindle when we will The fire which in the heart resides ; The Spirit bloweth and is still ; In mystery our soul abides. But tasks in hours of insight willed Can be in hours of gloom fulfilled. With aching hands and bleeding feet, We dig and heap, lay stone on stone ; We bear the burden and the heat Of the long day, and wish 't were done. Not till the hours of light return All we have built do we discern."

(*f*) The mediate or instrumental cause of sanctification, as of justification, is faith.

Acts 15 : 9 —"cleansing their hearts by faith "; Rom. 1 : 17 —"For there'n is revealed a righteousness of God from faith unto faith : as it is written, But the righteous shall live from faith." The righteousness includes sanctification as well as justification; and the subject of the epistle to the Romans is not simply justification by faith, but rather righteousness by faith, or salvation by faith. Justification by faith is the subject of chapters 1-7; sanctification by faith is the subject of chapters 8-16. We are not sanctified by efforts of our own, any more than we are justified by efforts of our own.

God does not share with us the glory of sanctification, any more than he shares with us the glory of justification. He must do all, or nothing. William Law : " A root set in the finest soil, in the best climate, and blessed with all that sun and air and rain can do for it, is not in so sure a way of its growth to perfection, as every man may be whose spirit aspires after all that which God is ready and infinitely desirous to give him. For the sun meets not the springing bud that stretches toward him with half that certainty as God, the source of all good, communicates himself to the soul that longs to partake of him."

(*g*) The object of this faith is Christ himself, as the head of a new humanity and the source of truth and life to those united to him.

2 ˆr. 3 : 18 — " we all, with unveiled face, beholding as in a mirror the glory of the Lord, are transformed into the same image from glory to glory, even as from the Lord the Spirit "; Eph. 4 : 13 —"till we all attain unto the unity of the faith, and of the knowledge of the Son of God, unto a fullgrown man, unto the measure of the stature of the fulness of Christ." Faith here is of course much more than intellectual faith,—it is the reception of Christ himself. As Christianity furnishes a new source of life and energy—in the Holy Spirit : so it gives a new object of attention and regard—the Lord Jesus Christ. As we get air out of a vessel by pouring in water, so we can drive sin out only by bringing Christ in. See Chalmers' Sermon on The Expulsive Power of a New Affection. Drummond, Nat. Law in the Spir. World, 123-140—" Man does not grow by making efforts to grow, but by putting himself into the conditions of growth by living in Christ."

1 John 3 : 3 —" every one that hath this hope set on him (ἐπ' αὐτῷ) purifieth himself, even as he is pure." Sanctification does not begin from within. The objective Savior must come first. The hope based on him must give the motive and the standard of self-purification. Likeness comes from liking. We grow to be like that which we like. Hence we use the phrase " I like," as a synonym for " I love." We cannot remove frost from our window by rubbing the pane; we need to kindle a fire. Growth is not the product of effort, but of life. "Taking thought," or " being anxious " (Mat. 6 : 27), is not the way to grow. Only take the hindrances out of the way, and we grow without care, as the tree does. The moon makes no effort to shine, nor has it any power of its own to shine. It is only a burnt out cinder in the sky. It shines only as it reflects the light of the sun. So we can shine "as lights in the world " (Phil. 2 : 15), only as we reflect Christ, who is "the Sun of Righteousness" (Mal. 4 : 2) and "the Light of the world " (John 8 : 12).

(*h*) Though the weakest faith perfectly justifies, the degree of sanctification is measured by the strength of the Christian's faith, and the persistence with which he apprehends Christ in the various relations which the Scriptures declare him to sustain to us.

Mat. 9 : 29 —" According to your faith be it done unto you "; Luke 17 : 5 —"Lord, increase our faith "; Rom. 12: 2 —" be not fashioned according to this world: but be ye transformed by the renewing of your mind, that ye may prove what is the good and acceptable and perfect will of God "; 13 : 14 —" But put ye on the Lord Jesus Christ, and make not provision for the flesh, to fulfil the lusts thereof "; Eph. 4 : 24 —" put on the new man, that after God hath been created in righteousness and holiness of truth "; 1 Tim. 4 : 7 —" exercise thyself unto godliness." Leighton : " None of the children of God are born dumb." Milton : " Good, the more communicated, the more abundant grows." Faith can neither be stationary nor complete (Westcott, Bible Com. on John 15 : 8 —" so shall ye *become* my disciples"). Luther : " He who *is* a Christian is *no* Christian "; " Christianus non in esse, sed in fieri." In a Bible that belonged to Oliver Cromwell is this inscription : " O. C. 1644. Qui cessat esse melior cessat esse bonus "— " He who ceases to be better ceases to be good." Story, the sculptor, when asked which of his works he valued most, replied : " My next." The greatest work of the Holy Spirit is the perfecting of Christian character.

Col. 1 : 10 —" Increasing by the knowledge of God "— here the instrumental dative represents the knowledge of God as the dew or rain which nurtures the growth of the plant (Lightfoot). Mr. Gladstone had the habit of reading the Bible every Sunday afternoon to old women on his estate. Tholuck: "I have but one passion, and that is Christ." This is an echo of Paul's words: "to me to live is Christ" (Phil. 1:21). But Paul is far from thinking that he has already obtained, or is already made perfect. He prays "that I may gain Christ, . . . that I may know him " (Phil. 3 : 8, 10).

(*i*) From the lack of persistence in using the means appointed for Christian growth — such as the word of God, prayer, association with other believers, and personal effort for the conversion of the ungodly — sanctification does not always proceed in regular and unbroken course, and it is never completed in this life.

Phil. 3 : 12 —" Not that I have already obtained, or am already made perfect: but I press on, if so be that I may lay hold on that for which also I was laid hold on by Jesus Christ "; 1 John 1 : 8 —" If we say that we have no sin, we deceive ourselves, and the truth is not in us." Carlyle, in his Life of John Sterling, chap. 8, says of Coleridge, that " whenever natural obligation or voluntary undertaking made it his duty to do anything, the fact seemed a sufficient reason for his *not* doing it." A regular, advancing sanctification is marked, on the other hand, by a growing habit of instant and joyful obedience. The intermittent spring depends upon the reservoir in the mountain cave, — only when the rain fills the latter full, does the spring begin to flow. So to secure unbroken Christian activity, there must be constant reception of the word and Spirit of God.

Galen: "If diseases take hold of the body, there is nothing so certain to drive them out as diligent exercise." Williams, Principles of Medicine: "Want of exercise and sedentary habits not only predispose to, but actually cause, disease." The little girl who fell out of bed at night was asked how it happened. She replied that she went to sleep too near where she got in. Some Christians lose the joy of their religion by ceasing their Christian activities too soon after conversion. Yet others cultivate their spiritual lives from mere selfishness. Selfishness follows the line of least resistance. It is easier to pray in public and to attend meetings for prayer, than it is to go out into the unsympathetic world and engage in the work of winning souls. This is the fault of monasticism. These grow most who forget themselves in their work for others. The discipline of life is ordained in God's providence to correct tendencies to indolence. Even this discipline is often received in a rebellious spirit. The result is delay in the process of sanctification. Bengel: " Deus habet horas et moras "—" God has his hours and his delays." German proverb: " Gut Ding will Weile haben "—" A good thing requires time."

(*j*) Sanctification, both of the soul and of the body of the believer, is completed in the life to come, — that of the former at death, that of the latter at the resurrection.

Phil. 3 : 21 —" who shall fashion anew the body of our humiliation, that it may be conformed to the body of his glory, according to the working whereby he is able even to subject all things unto himself"; Col. 3 : 4 —" When Christ, who is our life, shall be manifested, then shall we also with him be manifested in glory "; Heb. 12 : 14, 23 — " Follow after peace with all men, and the sanctification without which no man shall see the Lord . . . . spirits of just men made perfect " ; 1 John 3 : 2 —" Beloved, now are we children of God, and it is not yet made manifest what we shall be. We know that, if he shall be manifested, we shall be like him ; for we shall see him even as he is "; Jude 24 —" able to guard you from stumbling, and to set you before the presence of his glory without blemish in exceeding joy " ; Rev. 14 : 5 —" And in their mouth was found no lie : they are without blemish."

A. J. Gordon, Ministry of the Spirit, 121, puts the completion of our sanctification, not at death, but at the appearing of the Lord "a second time, apart from sin, ... unto salvation " (Heb. 9 : 28 ; 1 Thess. 3 : 13 ; 5 : 23). When we shall see him as he is, instantaneous photographing of his image in our souls will take the place of the present slow progress from glory to glory (2 Cor. 3 : 18 ; 1 John 3 : 2). If by sanctification we mean, not a sloughing off of remaining depravity, but an ever increasing purity and perfection, then we may hold that the process of sanctification goes on forever. Our relation to Christ must always be that of the imperfect to the perfect, of the finite to the infinite ; and for finite spirits, progress must always be possible. Clarke, Christian Theology, 373—" Not even at death can sanctification end. . . . . The goal lies far beyond deliverance from sin. . . . . There is no such thing as bringing the divine life to such completion that no further progress is possible to it. . . . . Indeed. free and unhampered progress can scarcely begin until sin is left behind." "O snows so pure, O peaks so high! I shall not reach you till I die!"

As Jesus' resurrection was prepared by holiness of life, so the Christian's resurrection is prepared by sanctification. When our souls are freed from the last remains of sin, then it will not be possible for us to be holden by death (*cf.* Acts 2 : 24). See Gordon, The Twofold Life, or Christ's Work for us and in us; Brit. and For. Evang. Rev., April, 1884 : 205-229; Van Oosterzee, Christian Dogmatics, 657-662.

3. *Erroneous Views refuted by these Scripture Passages.*

A. The Antinomian, — which holds that, since Christ's obedience and sufferings have satisfied the demands of the law, the believer is free from obligation to observe it.

The Antinomian view rests upon a misinterpretation of Rom. 6 : 14 — "Ye are not under law, but under grace." Agricola and Amsdorf (1559) were representatives of this view. Amsdorf said that "good works are hurtful to salvation." But Melanchthon's words furnish the reply : " Sola fides justificat, sed fides non est sola." F. W. Robertson states it : " Faith alone justifies, but not the faith that is alone." And he illustrates : " Lightning alone strikes, but not the lightning which is without thunder; for that is summer lightning and harmless." See Browning's poem, Johannes Agricola in Meditation, in Dramatis Personæ, 300 — "I have God's warrant, Could I blend All hideous sins as in a cup, To drink the mingled venoms up, Secure my nature will convert The draught to blossoming gladness." Agricola said that Moses ought to be hanged. This is Sanctification without Perseverance.

Sandeman, the founder of the sect called Sandemanians, asserted as his fundamental principle the deadliness of all doings, the necessity for inactivity to let God do his work in the soul. See his essay, Theron and Aspasia, referred to by Allen, in his Life of Jonathan Edwards, 114. Anne Hutchinson was excommunicated and banished by the Puritans from Massachusetts, in 1637, for holding "two dangerous errors : 1. The Holy Spirit personally dwells in a justified person; 2. No sanctification can evidence to us our justification." Here the latter error almost destroyed the influence of the former truth. There is a little Antinomianism in the popular hymn : " Lay your deadly doings down, Down at Jesus' feet; Doing is a deadly thing; Doing ends in death." The colored preacher's poetry only presented the doctrine in the concrete : " You may rip and te-yar, You may cuss and swe-yar, But you 're jess as sure of heaven, 'S if you 'd done gone de-yar." Plain Andrew Fuller in England (1754-1815) did excellent service in overthrowing popular Antinomianism.

To this view we urge the following objections :

(*a*) That since the law is a transcript of the holiness of God, its demands as a moral rule are unchanging. Only as a system of penalty and a method of salvation is the law abolished in Christ's death.

Mat. 5 : 17-19 — "Think not that I came to destroy the law or the prophets: I came not to destroy, but to fulfil. For verily I say unto you, Till heaven and earth pass away, one jot or one tittle shall in no wise pass away from the law, till all things be accomplished. Whosoever therefore shall break one of these least commandments, and shall teach men so, shall be called least in the kingdom of heaven : but whosoever shall do and teach them, he shall be called great in the kingdom of heaven "; 48 — " Ye therefore shall be perfect, as your heavenly Father is perfect"; 1 Pet. 1 : 16 — "Ye shall be holy; for I am holy "; Rom. 10 : 4 — "For Christ is the end of the law unto righteousness to every one that believeth " ; Gal. 2 : 20 — "I have been crucified with Christ " ; 3 : 13 — " Christ redeemed us from the curse of the law, having become a curse for us " ; Col. 2 : 14 — " having blotted out the bond written in ordinances that was against us, which was contrary to us: and he hath taken it out of the way, nailing it to the cross "; Heb. 2 : 15 — " deliver all them who through fear of death were all their lifetime subject to bondage."

(*b*) That the union between Christ and the believer secures not only the bearing of the penalty of the law by Christ, but also the impartation of Christ's spirit of obedience to the believer, — in other words, brings him into communion with Christ's work, and leads him to ratify it in his own experience.

Rom. 8 : 9, 10, 15 — "ye are not in the flesh but in the Spirit, if so be that the Spirit of God dwelleth in you. But if any man hath not the Spirit of Christ, he is none of his. And if Christ is in you, the body is dead because of sin; but the spirit is life because of righteousness. . . . . For ye received not the spirit of bondage again unto fear; but ye received the spirit of adoption, whereby we cry, Abba, Father"; Gal. 5 : 22-25 — "But the fruit of the Spirit is love, joy, peace, longsuffering, kindness, goodness, faithfulness, meekness, self-control; against such there is no law. And they that are of Christ Jesus have crucified the flesh with the passions and the lusts thereof"; 1 John 1 : 6 — "If we say that we have fellowship with him and walk in the darkness, we lie, and do not the truth"; 3 : 6 — "Whosoever abideth in him sinneth not : whosoever sinneth hath not seen him, neither knoweth him."

(c) That the freedom from the law of which the Scriptures speak, is therefore simply that freedom from the constraint and bondage of the law, which characterizes those who have become one with Christ by faith.

Ps. 119 : 97 — "O how love I thy law ! it is my meditation all the day"; Rom. 3 : 8, 31 — "and why not (as we are slanderously reported, and as some affirm that we say), Let us do evil, that good may come ? whose condemnation is just. . . . . Do we then make the law of none effect through faith ? God forbid : nay, we establish the law"; 6 : 14, 15, 22 — "For sin shall not have dominion over you : for ye are not under law, but under grace. What then ? shall we sin, because we are not under law, but under grace ? God forbid . . . . now being made free from sin and become servants to God, ye have your fruit unto sanctification, and the end eternal life"; 7 : 6 — "But now we have been discharged from the law, having died to that wherein we were held; so that we serve in newness of the spirit, and not in oldness of the letter"; 8 : 4 — "that the ordinance of the law might be fulfilled in us, who walk not after the flesh, but after the Spirit"; 1 Cor. 7 : 22 — "he that was called in the Lord being a bondservant, is the Lord's freedman"; Gal. 5 : 1 — "For freedom did Christ set us free : stand fast therefore, and be not entangled again in a yoke of bondage"; 1 Tim. 1 : 9 — "law is not made for a righteous man, but for the lawless and unruly"; James 1 : 25 — "the perfect law, the law of liberty."

To sum up the doctrine of Christian freedom as opposed to Antinomianism, we may say that Christ does not free us, as the Antinomian believes, from the law as a rule of life. But he does free us (1) from the law as a system of curse and penalty ; this he does by bearing the curse and penalty himself. Christ frees us (2) from the law with its claims as a method of salvation ; this he does by making his obedience and merits ours. Christ frees us (3) from the law as an outward and foreign compulsion ; this he does by giving to us the spirit of obedience and sonship, by which the law is progressively realized within.

Christ, then, does not free us, as the Antinomian believes, from the law as a rule of life. But he does free us (1) from the law as a system of curse and penalty. This he does by bearing the curse and penalty himself. Just as law can do nothing with a man after it has executed its death-penalty upon him, so law can do nothing with us, now that its death-penalty has been executed upon Christ. There are some insects that expire in the act of planting their sting ; and so, when the law gathered itself up and planted its sting in the heart of Christ, it expended all its power as a judge and avenger over us who believe. In the Cross, the law as a system of curse and penalty exhausted itself ; so we were set free.

Christ frees us (2) from the law with its claims as a method of salvation : in other words, he frees us from the necessity of trusting our salvation to an impossible future obedience. As the sufferings of Christ, apart from any sufferings of ours, deliver us from eternal death, so the merits of Christ, apart from any merits of ours, give us a title to eternal life. By faith in what Christ has done and simple acceptance of his work for us, we secure a right to heaven. Obedience on our part is no longer rendered painfully, as if our salvation depended on it, but freely and gladly, in gratitude for what Christ has done for us. Illustrate by the English nobleman's invitation to his park, and the regulations he causes to be posted up.

Christ frees us (3) from the law as an outward and foreign compulsion. In putting an end to legalism, he provides against license. This he does by giving the spirit of obedience and sonship. He puts love in the place of fear ; and this secures an obedience more intelligent, more thorough, and more hearty, than could have been secured by mere law. So he frees us from the burden and compulsion of the law, by realizing the law within us by his Spirit. The freedom of the Christian is freedom in the law, such as the musician experiences when the scales and exercises have become easy, and work has turned to play. See John Owen, Works, 3 : 366-651 ; 6 : 1-313 ; Campbell, The Indwelling Christ, 73-81.

Gould, Bib. Theol. N. T., 195 — "The supremacy of those books which contain the words of Jesus himself [i. e., the Synoptic Gospels] is that they incorporate, with the other elements of the religious life, the regulative will. Here for instance [in John] is the gospel of the contemplative life, which, 'beholding as in a mirror the glory of the Lord is changed into the same image from glory to glory, as by the Spirit of the Lord ' (2 Cor. 3:18). The belief is that, with this beholding, life will take care of itself. Life will never take care of itself. Among other things, after the most perfect vision, it has to ask what aspirations, principles, affections, belong to life, and then to cultivate the will to embody these things. Here is the common defect of all religions. They fail to marry religion to the common life. Christ did not stop short of this final word ; but if we leave him for even the greatest of his disciples, we are in danger of missing it." This utterance of Gould is surprising in several ways. It attributes to John alone the contemplative attitude of mind, which the quotation given shows to belong also to Paul. It ignores the constant appeals in John to the will : "He that hath my commandments and keepeth them, he it is that loveth me " (John 14 : 21). It also forgets that "life" in John is the whole being, including intellect, affection, and will, and that to have Christ for one's life is absolutely to exclude Antinomianism.

B. The Perfectionist, — which holds that the Christian may, in this life, become perfectly free from sin. This view was held by John Wesley in England, and by Mahan and Finney in America.

Finney, Syst. Theol., 500, declares regeneration to be "an instantaneous change from entire sinfulness to entire holiness." The claims of Perfectionists, however, have been modified from "freedom from all sin," to "freedom from all known sin," then to "entire consecration," and finally to "Christian assurance." H. W. Webb-Peploe, in S. S. Times, June 25, 1898 — "The Keswick teaching is that no true Christian need wilfully or knowingly sin. Yet this is not sinless perfection. It is simply according to our faith that we receive, and faith only draws from God according to our present possibilities. These are limited by the presence of indwelling corruption ; and, while never needing to sin within the sphere of the light we possess, there are to the last hour of our life upon the earth powers of corruption within every man, which defile his best deeds and give to even his holiest efforts that ' nature of sin ' of which the 9th Article in the Church of England Prayerbook speaks so strongly." Yet it is evident that this corruption is not regarded as real sin, and is called ' nature of sin ' only in some non-natural sense.

Dr. George Peck says : "In the life of the most perfect Christian there is every day renewed occasion for self-abhorrence, for repentance, for renewed application of the blood of Christ, for application of the rekindling of the Holy Spirit." But why call this a state of perfection ? F. B. Meyer : " We never say that self is dead ; were we to do so, self would be laughing at us round the corner. The teaching of Romans 6 is, not that self is dead, but that the renewed will is dead to self, the man's will saying Yes to Christ, and No to self ; through the Spirit's grace it constantly repudiates and mortifies the power of the flesh." For statements of the Perfectionist view, see John Wesley's Christian Theology. edited by Thornley Smith, 265–273 ; Mahan, Christian Perfection, and art. in Bib. Repos. 2d Series, vol. IV, Oct. 1840 : 408–428 ; Finney, Systematic Theology, 586–766 ; Peck, Christian Perfection ; Ritschl, Bib. Sac., Oct. 1878 : 656 ; A. T. Pierson, The Keswick Movement.

In reply, it will be sufficient to observe :

(a) That the theory rests upon false conceptions : first, of the law, — as a sliding-scale of requirement graduated to the moral condition of creatures, instead of being the unchangeable reflection of God's holiness ; secondly, of sin, — as consisting only in voluntary acts instead of embracing also those dispositions and states of the soul which are not conformed to the divine holiness ; thirdly, of the human will, — as able to choose God supremely and persistently at every moment of life, and to fulfil at every moment the obligations resting upon it, instead of being corrupted and enslaved by the Fall.

This view reduces the debt to the debtor's ability to pay, — a short and easy method of discharging obligations. I can leap over a church steeple, if I am only permitted to make the church steeple low enough; and I can touch the stars, if the stars will only come down to my hand. The Philistines are quite equal to Samson, if they may only cut off Samson's locks. So I can obey God's law, if I may only make God's law what I want it to be. The fundamental error of perfectionism is its low view of God's law; the second is its narrow conception of sin. John Wesley: "I believe a person filled with love of God is still liable to involuntary transgressions. Such transgressions you may call sins, if you please; I do not." The third error of perfectionism is its exaggerated estimate of man's power of contrary choice. To say that, whatever may have been the habits of the past and whatever may be the evil affections of the present, a man is perfectly able at any moment to obey the whole law of God, is to deny that there are such things as character and depravity. Finney, Gospel Themes, 383, indeed, disclaimed "all expectations of attaining this state ourselves, and by our own independent, unaided efforts." On the Law of God, see pages 537-544.

Augustine: "Every lesser good has an essential element of sin." Anything less than the perfection that belongs normally to my present stage of development is a coming short of the law's demand. R. W. Dale, Fellowship with Christ, 359 — "For us and in this world, the divine is always the impossible. Give me a law for individual conduct which requires a perfection that is within my reach, and I am sure that the law does not represent the divine thought. 'Not that I have already obtained, or am already made perfect: but I press on, if so be that I may lay hold on that for which also I was laid hold on by Christ Jesus' (Phil. 3:12) — this, from the beginning, has been the confession of saints." The Perfectionist is apt to say that we must "take Christ twice, once for justification and once for sanctification." But no one can take Christ for justification without at the same time taking him for sanctification. Dr. A. A. Hodge calls this doctrine "Neonomianism," because it holds not to one unchanging, ideal, and perfect law of God, but to a second law given to human weakness when the first law has failed to secure obedience.

(1) The law of God demands perfection. It is a transcript of God's nature. Its object is to reveal God. Anything less than the demand of perfection would misrepresent God. God could not give a law which a sinner could obey. In the very nature of the case there can be no sinlessness in this life for those who have once sinned. Sin brings incapacity as well as guilt. All men have squandered a part of the talent intrusted to them by God, and therefore no man can come up to the demands of that law which requires all that God gave to humanity at its creation together with interest on the investment. (2) Even the best Christian comes short of perfection. Regeneration makes only the dominant disposition holy. Many affections still remain unholy and require to be cleansed. Only by lowering the demands of the law, making shallow our conceptions of sin, and mistaking temporary volition for permanent bent of the will, can we count ourselves to be perfect. (3) Absolute perfection is attained not in this world but in the world to come. The best Christians count themselves still sinners, strive most earnestly for holiness, have in puted but not inherent sanctification, are saved by hope.

(*b*) That the theory finds no support in, but rather is distinctly contradicted by, Scripture.

First, the Scriptures never assert or imply that the Christian may in this life live without sin; passages like 1 John 3 : 6, 9, if interpreted consistently with the context, set forth either the ideal standard of Christian living or the actual state of the believer so far as respects his new nature.

1 John 3 : 6 —"Whosoever abideth in him sinneth not: whosoever sinneth hath not seen him, neither knoweth him"; 9 —"Whosoever is begotten of God doeth no sin, because his seed abideth in him: and he cannot sin, because he is begotten of God." Ann. Par. Bible, *in loco* :—"John is contrasting the states in which sin and grace severally predominate, without reference to degrees in either, showing that all men are in one or the other." Neander: "John recognizes no intermediate state, no gradations. He seizes upon the radical point of difference. He contrasts the two states in their essential nature and principle. It is either love or hate, light or darkness, truth or a lie. The Christian life in its essential nature is the opposite of all sin. If there be sin, it must be the afterworking of the old nature." Yet all Christians are required in Scripture to advance, to confess sin, to ask forgiveness, to maintain warfare, to assume the attitude of ill desert in prayer, to receive chastisement for the removal of imperfections, to regard full salvation as matter of hope, not of present experience.

John paints only in black and white; there are no intermediate tints or colors. Take the words in 1 John 3 : 6 literally, and there never was and never can be a regenerate person. The words are hyperbolical, as Paul's words in Rom. 6 : 2 — "We who died to sin, how shall we any longer live therein"— are metaphorical; see E. H. Johnson, in Bib. Sac., 1892 : 375, note. The Emperor William refused the request for an audience prepared by a German-American, saying that Germans born in Germany but naturalized in America became Americans: "Ich kenne Amerikaner, Ich kenne Deutsche, aber Deutsch-Amerikaner kenne Ich nicht "—" I know Americans, I know Germans, but German-Americans I do not know."

Lowrie, Doctrine of St. John, 110 —" St. John uses the noun *sin* and the verb *to sin* in two senses: to denote the power or principle of sin, or to denote concrete acts of sin. The latter sense he generally expresses by the plural *sins*. . . . . The Christian is guilty of particular acts of sin for which confession and forgiveness are required, but as he has been freed from the bondage of sin he cannot habitually practise it nor abide in it, still less can he be guilty of sin in its superlative form, by denial of Christ."

Secondly, the apostolic admonitions to the Christians and Hebrews show that no such state of complete sanctification had been generally attained by the Christians of the first century.

Rom. 8 : 24 —" For in hope were we saved : but hope that is seen is not hope : for who hopeth for that which he seeth ?' The party feeling, selfishness, and immorality found among the members of the Corinthian church are evidence that they were far from a state of entire sanctification.

Thirdly, there is express record of sin committed by the most perfect characters of Scripture—as Noah, Abraham, Job, David, Peter.

We are urged by perfectionists "to keep up the standard." We do this, not by calling certain men perfect, but by calling Jesus Christ perfect. In proportion to our sanctification, we are absorbed in Christ, not in ourselves. Self-consciousness and display are a poor evidence of sanctification. The best characters of Scripture put their trust in a standard higher than they have ever realized in their own persons, even in the righteousness of God.

Fourthly, the word τέλειος, as applied to spiritual conditions already attained, can fairly be held to signify only a relative perfection, equivalent to sincere piety or maturity of Christian judgment.

1 Cor. 2 : 6 —" We speak wisdom, however, among the perfect," or, as the Am. Revisers have it, "among them that are fullgrown" ; Phil. 3 : 15 —"Let us therefore, as many as are perfect, be thus minded." Men are often called perfect, when free from any fault which strikes the eyes of the world. See Gen. 6 : 9 —" Noah was a righteous man, and perfect" ; Job 1 : 1 —" that man was perfect and upright." On τέλειος, see Trench, Syn. N. T., 1 : 110.

The τέλειοι are described in Heb. 5 : 14 —"Solid food is for the mature (τελείων) who on account of habit have their perceptions disciplined for the discriminating of good and evil " (Dr. Kendrick's translation). The same word "perfect" is used of Jacob in Gen. 25 : 27 —"Jacob was a quiet man, dwelling in tents " = a harmless man, exemplary and well-balanced, as a man of business. Genung, Epic of the Inner Life, 132 — " 'Perfect' in Job = Horace's 'integer vitae,' being the adjective of which 'integrity' is the substantive."

Fifthly, the Scriptures distinctly deny that any man on earth lives without sin.

1 K. 8 : 46 —" there is no man that sinneth not" ; Eccl. 7 : 20 —" Surely there is not a righteous man upon earth, that doeth good, and sinneth not"; James 3 : 2 —" For in many things we all stumble. If any stumbleth not in word, the same is a perfect man, able to bridle the whole body also " ; 1 John 1 : 8 —" If we say that we have no sin, we deceive ourselves, and the truth is not in us."

T. T. Eaton, Sanctification : " 1. Some mistake regeneration for sanctification. They have been unconverted church members. When led to faith in Christ, and finding peace and joy, they think they are sanctified, when they are simply converted. 2. Some mistake assurance of faith for sanctification. But joy is not sanctification. 3. Some mistake the baptism of the Holy Spirit for sanctification. But Peter sinned grievously at Antioch, after he had received that baptism. 4. Some think that doing the best one can is sanctification. But he who measures by inches, for feet, can measure up well.

5. Some regard sin as only a voluntary act, whereas the sinful nature is the fountain. Stripping off the leaves of the Upas tree does not answer. 6. Some mistake the power of the human will, and fancy that an act of will can free a man from sin. They ignore the settled bent of the will, which the act of will does not change."

Sixthly, the declaration : "ye were sanctified" (1 Cor. 6 : 11), and the designation : "saints" (1 Cor. 1 : 2), applied to early believers, are, as the whole epistle shows, expressive of a holiness existing in germ and anticipation ; the expressions deriving their meaning not so much from what these early believers were, as from what Christ was, to whom they were united by faith.

When N. T. believers are said to be "sanctified," we must remember the O. T. use of the word. 'Sanctify' may have either the meaning 'to make holy outwardly,' or 'to make holy inwardly.' The people of Israel and the vessels of the tabernacle were made holy in the former sense; their sanctification was a setting apart to the sacred use. Num. 8:17 —" all the firstborn among the children of Israel are mine . . . . I sanctified them for myself"; Deut. 33 : 3 —"Yea, he loveth the people; all his saints are in thy hand"; 2 Chron. 29:19 —"all the vessels . . . . have we prepared and sanctified." The vessels mentioned were first immersed, and then sprinkled from day to day according to need. So the Christian by his regeneration is set apart for God's service, and in this sense is a "saint" and "sanctified." More than this, he has in him the beginnings of purity,— he is "clean as a whole," though he yet needs "to wash his feet " (John 13 : 10) — that is, to be cleansed from the recurring defilements of his daily life. Shedd, Dogm. Theol., 2 : 551 —" The error of the Perfectionist is that of confounding *imputed* sanctification with *inherent* sanctification. It is the latter which is mentioned in 1 Cor. 1 : 30 —'Christ Jesus, who was made unto us . . . . sanctification.' "

Water from the Jordan is turbid, but it settles in the bottle and seems pure — until it is shaken. Some Christians seem very free from sin, until you shake them,— then they get "riled." Clarke, Christian Theology, 371 —" Is there not a higher Christian life ? Yes, and a higher life beyond it, and a higher still beyond. The Christian life is ever nigher and higher. It must pass through all stages between its beginning and its perfection." C. D. Case : "The great objection to [this theory of] complete sanctification is that, if possessed at all, it is not a development of our own character."

(*c*) That the theory is disapproved by the testimony of Christian experience.— In exact proportion to the soul's advance in holiness does it shrink from claiming that holiness has been already attained, and humble itself before God for its remaining apathy, ingratitude, and unbelief.

Phil. 3 : 12–14 —" Not that I have already obtained, or am already made perfect : but I press on, if so be that I may lay hold on that for which also I was laid hold on by Christ Jesus." Some of the greatest advocates of perfectionism have been furthest from claiming any such perfection ; although many of their less instructed followers claimed it for them, and even professed to have attained it themselves.

In Luke 7:1–10, the centurion does not think himself worthy to go to Jesus, or to have him come under his roof, yet the elders of the Jews say : " He is worthy that thou shouldest do this"; and Jesus himself says of him : "I have not found so great faith, no, not in Israel." "Holy to Jehovah" was inscribed upon the mitre of the high priest (Ex. 28 : 36). Others saw it, but he saw it not. Moses knew not that his face shone (Ex. 34 : 29). The truest holiness is that of which the possessor is least conscious; yet it is his real diadem and beauty (A. J. Gordon). "The nearer men are to being sinless, the less they talk about it " (Dwight L. Moody). "Always strive for perfection : never believe you have reached it" (Arnold of Rugby). Compare with this, Ernest Renan's declaration that he had nothing to alter in his life. "I have not sinned for some time," said a woman to Mr. Spurgeon. "Then you must be very proud of it," he replied. "Indeed I am!" said she. A pastor says : "No one can attain the 'Higher Life,' and escape making mischief." John Wesley lamented that not one in thirty retained the blessing.

Perfectionism is best met by proper statements of the nature of the law and of sin (Ps. 119 : 96). While we thus rebuke spiritual pride, however, we should be equally careful to point out the inseparable connection between justification and sanctification, and their equal importance as together mak-

ing up the Biblical idea of salvation. While we show no favor to those who would make sanctification a sudden and paroxysmal act of the human will, we should hold forth the holiness of God as the standard of attainment, and the faith in a Christ of infinite fulness as the medium through which that standard is to be gradually but certainly realized in us (2 Cor. 3 : 18).

We should imitate Lyman Beecher's method of opposing perfectionism — by searching expositions of God's law. When men know what the law is, they will say with the Psalmist: "I have seen an end of all perfection; thy commandment is exceeding broad" (Ps. 119: 96). And yet we are earnestly and hopefully to seek in Christ for a continually increasing measure of sanctification : 1 Cor. 1 : 30 — "Christ Jesus, who was made unto us . . . . sanctification" ; 2 Cor. 3 : 18 — "But we all, with unveiled face beholding as in a mirror the glory of the Lord, are transformed into the same image from glory to glory, even as from the Lord the Spirit." Arnold of Rugby : "Always expect to succeed, and never think you have succeeded."

Mr. Finney meant by entire sanctification only that it is possible for Christians in this life by the grace of God to consecrate themselves so unreservedly to his service as to live without conscious and wilful disobedience to the divine commands. He did not claim himself to have reached this point; he made at times very impressive confessions of his own sinfulness ; he did not encourage others to make for themselves the claim to have lived without conscious fault. He held however that such a state is attainable, and therefore that its pursuit is rational. He also admitted that such a state is one, not of absolute, but only of relative, sinlessness. His error was in calling it a state of entire sanctification. See A. H. Strong, Christ in Creation, 377-384.

A. J. Gordon, Ministry of the Spirit, 116 — "It is possible that one may experience a great crisis in his spiritual life, in which there is such a total surrender of self to God and such an infilling of the Holy Spirit, that he is freed from the bondage of sinful appetites and habits, and enabled to have constant victory over self instead of suffering constant defeat. . . . . If the doctrine of sinless perfection is a heresy, the doctrine of contentment with sinful imperfection is a greater heresy. . . . . It is not an edifying spectacle to see a Christian worldling throwing stones at a Christian perfectionist." Caird, Evolution of Religion, 1 : 138 — "If, according to the German proverb, it is provided that the trees shall not grow into the sky, it is equally provided that they shall always grow toward it ; and the sinking of the roots into the soil is inevitably accompanied by a further expansion of the branches."

See Hovey, Doctrine of the Higher Christian Life, Compared with Scripture , also Hovey, Higher Christian Life Examined, in Studies in Ethics and Theology, 344-427 ; Snodgrass, Scriptural Doctrine of Sanctification ; Princeton Essays, 1 : 335-365; Hodge, Syst. Theol., 3 : 213-258; Calvin, Institutes, III, 11 : 6; Bib. Repos., 2d Series, 1 : 44-58; 2 : 143-166; Woods, Works, 4 : 465-523; H. A. Boardman, The "Higher Life" Doctrine of Sanctification ; William Law, Practical Treatise on Christian Perfection ; E. H. Johnson, The Highest Life.

II. PERSEVERANCE.

The Scriptures declare that, in virtue of the original purpose and continuous operation of God, all who are united to Christ by faith will infallibly continue in a state of grace and will finally attain to everlasting life. This voluntary continuance, on the part of the Christian, in faith and well-doing we call perseverance. Perseverance is, therefore, the human side or aspect of that spiritual process which, as viewed from the divine side, we call sanctification. It is not a mere natural consequence of conversion, but involves a constant activity of the human will from the moment of conversion to the end of life.

Adam's holiness was mutable; God did not determine to keep him. It is otherwise with believers in Christ; God has determined to give them the kingdom (Luke 12: 32). Yet this keeping by God, which we call sanctification, is accompanied and followed by a keeping of himself on the part of the believer, which we call perseverance. The former is alluded to in John 17: 11, 12 — "keep them in thy name . . . . I kept them in thy name . . . . I guarded them and not one of them perished, but the son of perdition"; the latter is alluded to in 1 John 5: 18 — "he that was

56

begotten of God keepeth himself." Both are expressed in Jude 21, 24 — "Keep yourselves in the love of God
.... Now unto him that is able to guard you from stumbling ...."

A German treatise on Pastoral Theology is entitled: "Keep What Thou Hast"—an
allusion to 2 Tim. 1:14 — "That good thing which was committed unto thee guard through the Holy Spirit which
dwelleth in us." Not only the pastor, but every believer, has a charge to keep; and the
keeping of ourselves is as important a point of Christian doctrine as is the keeping of
God. Both are expressed in the motto: *Teneo, Teneor* — the motto on the front of the
Y. M. C. A. building in Boston, underneath a stone cross, firmly clasped by two hands.
The colored preacher said that "Perseverance means: 1. Take hold; 2. Hold on; 3.
Never let go."

Physically, intellectually, morally, spiritually, there is need that we persevere. Paul,
in 1 Cor. 9:27, declares that he smites his body under the eye and makes a slave of it, lest
after having preached to others he himself should be rejected; and in 2 Tim. 4:7, at the
end of his career, he rejoices that he has "kept the faith." A. J. Gordon, Ministry of the
Spirit, 115 — "The Christian is as 'a tree planted by the streams of water, that bringeth forth its fruit in its
season' (Ps. 1:3), but to conclude that his growth will be as irresistible as that of the tree,
coming as a matter of course simply because he has by regeneration been planted in
Christ, is a grave mistake. The disciple is required to be consciously and intelligently
active in his own growth, as the tree is not, 'to give all diligence to make his calling and election sure'
(2 Pet. 1:10) by surrendering himself to the divine action." Clarke, Christian Theology,
379 — "Man is able to fall, and God is able to keep him from falling; and through the
various experiences of life God will so save his child out of all evil that he will be
morally incapable of falling."

1. *Proof of the Doctrine of Perseverance.*

A. From Scripture.

John 10:28, 29 — "they shall never perish, and no one shall snatch them out of my hand. My Father, who hath
given them unto me, is greater than all; and no one is able to snatch them out of the Father's hand"; Rom. 11:29 —
"For the gifts and the calling of God are without repentance"; 1 Cor. 13:7 — "endureth all things"; *cf.* 13 — "But
now abideth faith, hope, love"; Phil. 1:6 — "being confident of this very thing, that he who began a good work in you
will perfect it until the day of Jesus Christ"; 2 Thess. 3:3 — "But the Lord is faithful, who shall establish you, and
guard you from the evil one"; 2 Tim. 1:12 — "I know him whom I have believed, and I am persuaded that he is able
to guard that which I have committed unto him against that day"; 1 Pet. 1:5 — "who by the power of God are
guarded through faith unto a salvation ready to be revealed in the last time"; Rev. 3:10 — "Because thou didst keep
the word of my patience, I also will keep thee from the hour of trial, that hour which is to come upon the whole world,
to try them that dwell upon the earth."

2 Tim. 1:12 — τὴν παραθήκην μου — Ellicott translates: "the trust committed to me," or "my deposit"
— the office of preaching the gospel, the stewardship entrusted to the apostle; *cf.* 1 Tim.
6:20 — "0 Timothy, keep thy deposit"—τὴν παραθήκην; and 2 Tim. 1:14—"Keep the good deposit"—where
the deposit seems to be the faith or doctrine delivered to him to preach. Nicoll, The
Church's One Foundation, 211 — "Some Christians waken each morning with a creed
of fewer articles, and those that remain they are ready to surrender to a process of
argument that convinces them. But it is a duty to *keep*. 'Ye have an anointing from the Holy
One, and ye know' (1 John 2:20) ..... Ezra gave to his men a treasure of gold and silver and
sacrificial vessels, and he charged them: 'Watch ye, and keep them, until ye weigh them .... in
thy chambers of the house of Jehovah' (Ezra 8:29)." See in the Autobiography of C. H. Spurgeon,
1:225, 256, the outline of a sermon on John 6:37 — "All that which the Father giveth me shall come unto
me; and him that cometh to me I will in no wise cast out." Mr. Spurgeon remarks that this text can
give us no comfort unless we see: 1. that God has given us his Holy Spirit; 2. that we
have given ourselves to him. Christ will not cast us out because of our great sins, our
long delays, our trying other saviors, our hardness of heart, our little faith, our poor
dull prayers, our unbelief, our inveterate corruptions, our frequent backslidings, nor
finally because every one else passes us by.

B. From Reason.

(*a*) It is a necessary inference from other doctrines, — such as election,
union with Christ, regeneration, justification, sanctification.

Election of certain individuals to salvation is election to bestow upon them such
influences of the Spirit as will lead them not only to accept Christ, but to persevere and
be saved. Union with Christ is indissoluble; regeneration is the beginning of a work of
new creation, which is declared in justification, and completed in sanctification. All

these doctrines are parts of a general scheme, which would come to naught if any single Christian were permitted to fall away.

(*b*) It accords with analogy,— God's preserving care being needed by, and being granted to, his spiritual, as well as his natural, creation.

As natural life cannot uphold itself, but we "live, and move, and have our being" in God (Acts 17 : 28), so spiritual life cannot uphold itself, and God maintains the faith, love, and holy activity which he has originated. If he preserves our natural life, much more may we expect him to preserve the spiritual. 1 Tim. 6 : 13 — "I charge thee before God who preserveth all things alive" (R. V. marg.) — ζωογονοῦντος τὰ πάντα = the great Preserver of all enables us to persist in our Christian course.

(*c*) It is implied in all assurance of salvation, — since this assurance is given by the Holy Spirit, and is based not upon the known strength of human resolution, but upon the purpose and operation of God.

S. R. Mason : "If Satan and Adam both fell away from perfect holiness, it is a million to one that, in a world full of temptations and with all appetites and habits against me, I shall fall away from imperfect holiness, unless God by his almighty power keep me." It is in the power and purpose of God, then, that the believer puts his trust. But since this trust is awakened by the Holy Spirit, it must be that there is a divine fact corresponding to it; namely, God's purpose to exert his power in such a way that the Christian shall persevere. See Wardlaw, Syst. Theol., 2 : 550-578 ; N. W. Taylor, Revealed Theology, 445-460.

Job 6 : 11 — "What is my strength, that I should wait? And what is mine end, that I should be patient?" "Here is a note of self-distrust. To be patient without any outlook, to endure without divine support — Job does not promise it, and he trembles at the prospect; but none the less he sets his feet on the toilsome way" (Genung). Dr. Lyman Beecher was asked whether he believed in the perseverance of the saints. He replied : "I do, except when the wind is from the East." But the value of the doctrine is that we can believe it even when the wind *is* from the East. It is well to hold on to God's hand, but it is better to have God's hand hold on to us. When we are weak, and forgetful and asleep, we need to be sure of God's care. Like the child who thought he was driving, but who found, after the trouble was over, that his father after all had been holding the reins, we too find when danger comes that behind our hands are the hands of God. The Perseverance of the Saints, looked at from the divine side, is the Preservation of the Saints, and the hymn that expresses the Christian's faith is the hymn : "How firm a foundation, ye saints of the Lord, Is laid for your faith in his excellent word!"

2.   *Objections to the Doctrine of Perseverance.*

These objections are urged chiefly by Arminians and by Romanists.

A.   That it is inconsistent with human freedom. — Answer : It is no more so than is the doctrine of Election or the doctrine of Decrees.

The doctrine is simply this, that God will bring to bear such influences upon all true believers, that they will freely persevere. Moule, Outlines of Christian Doctrine, 47 — "Is grace, in any sense of the word, ever finally withdrawn? Yes, if by grace is meant any free gift of God tending to salvation; or, more specially, any action of the Holy Spirit tending in its nature thither. . . . . But if by grace be meant the dwelling and working of Christ in the truly regenerate, there is no indication in Scripture of the withdrawal of it."

B.   That it tends to immorality. — Answer : This cannot be, since the doctrine declares that God will save men by securing their perseverance in holiness.

2 Tim. 2 : 19 — "Howbeit the firm foundation of God standeth, having this seal, The Lord knoweth them that are his; and, Let every one that nameth the name of the Lord depart from unrighteousness"; that is, the temple of Christian character has upon its foundation two significant inscriptions, the one declaring God's power, wisdom, and purpose of salvation; the other declaring the purity and holy activity, on the part of the believer, through which God's purpose is to be ful-

filled ; 1 Pet. 1 : 1, 2 — " elect . . . . according to the foreknowledge of God the Father, in sanctification of the Spirit unto obedience and sprinkling of the blood of Jesus Christ "; 2 Pet. 1 : 10, 11 —" Wherefore, brethren, give the more dili- gence to make your calling and election sure : for if ye do these things, ye shall never stumble : for thus shall be richly supplied unto you the entrance into the eternal kingdom of our Lord and Savior Jesus Christ."

C. That it leads to indolence. — Answer : This is a perversion of the doctrine, continuously possible only to the unregenerate ; since, to the regenerate, certainty of success is the strongest incentive to activity in the conflict with sin.

1 John 5 : 4 — "For whatsoever is begotten of God overcometh the world ; and this is the victory that hath overcome the world, even our faith." It is notoriously untrue that confidence of success inspires timid- ity or indolence. Thomas Fuller : " Your salvation is his business ; his service your business." The only prayers God will answer are those we ourselves cannot answer. For the very reason that " it is God who worketh in you both to will and to work, for his good pleasure," the apostle exhorts : " work out your own salvation with fear and trembling " (Phil. 2 : 12, 13).

D. That the Scripture commands to persevere and warnings against apostasy show that certain, even of the regenerate, will fall away. — Answer :

(a) They show that some, who are apparently regenerate, will fall away.

Mat. 18 : 7 — " Woe unto the world because of occasions of stumbling ! for it must needs be that the occasions come ; but woe to that man through whom the occasion cometh "; 1 Cor. 11 : 19 — "For there must be also factions [lit. 'heresies '] among you, that they that are approved may be made manifest among you "; 1 John 2 : 19 — " They went out from us, but they were not of us ; for if they had been of us, they would have continued with us : but they went out, that they might be made manifest that they all are not of us." Judas probably experienced strong emotions, and received strong impulses toward good, under the influence of Christ. The only falling from grace which is recognized in Scripture is not the falling of the regenerate, but the falling of the unregenerate, from influences tending to lead them to Christ. The Rabbins said that a drop of water will suffice to purify a man who has accidently touched a creeping thing, but an ocean will not suffice for his cleansing so long as he purposely keeps the creeping thing in his hand.

(b) They show that the truly regenerate, and those who are only appar- ently so, are not certainly distinguishable in this life.

Mal. 3 : 18 —"Then shall ye return and discern between the righteous and the wicked, between him that serveth God and him that serveth him not "; Mat. 13 : 25, 47 — " while men slept, his enemy came and sowed tares also among the wheat, and went away . . . . Again, the kingdom of heaven is like unto a net, that was cast into the sea, and gathered of every kind "; Rom. 9 : 6, 7 — " For they are not all Israel, that are of Israel : neither, because they are Abraham's seed, are they all children "; Rev. 3 : 1 — " I know thy works, that thou hast a name that thou livest, and thou art dead." The tares were never wheat, and the bad fish never were good, in spite of the fact that their true nature was not for a while recognized.

(c) They show the fearful consequences of rejecting Christ, to those who have enjoyed special divine influences, but who are only apparently regenerate.

Heb. 10 : 26–29 — " For if we sin wilfully after that we have received the knowledge of the truth, there remaineth no more a sacrifice for sins, but a certain fearful expectation of judgment, and a fierceness of fire which shall devour the adversaries. A man that hath set at nought Moses' law dieth without compassion on the word of two or three witnesses : of how much sorer punishment, think ye, shall he be judged worthy, who hath trodden under foot the Son of God, and hath counted the blood of the covenant wherewith he was sanctified an unholy thing, and hath done despite unto the Sp rit of grace ? " Here "sanctified " = external sanctification, like that of the ancient Israel- ites, by outward connection with God's people ; cf. 1 Cor. 7 : 14 — "the unbelieving husband is sanctified in the wife."

In considering these and the following Scripture passages, much will depend upon our view of inspiration. If we hold that Christ's promise was fulfilled and that his apostles were led into all the truth, we shall assume that there is unity in their teach- ing, and shall recognize in their variations only aspects and applications of the teach- ing of our Lord ; in other words, Christ's doctrine in John 10 : 28, 29 will be the norm for the

:nterpretation of seemingly diverse and at first sight inconsistent passages. There was a "faith which was once for all delivered unto the saints," and for this primitive faith we are exhorted "to contend earnestly " (Jude 3).

(*d*) They show what the fate of the truly regenerate would be, in case they should not persevere.

Heb. 6 : 4–6 — "For as touching those who were once enlightened and tasted of the heavenly gift, and were made partakers of the Holy Spirit, and tasted the good word of God, and the powers of the world to come, and then fell away, it is impossible to renew them again unto repentance ; seeing they crucify to themselves the Son of God afresh, and put him to an open shame." This is to be understood as a hypothetical case, — as is clear from verse 9 which follows : " But, beloved, we are persuaded better things of you, and things which accompany salvation, though we thus speak." Dr. A. C. Kendrick, Com. *in loco:* " In the phrase 'once enl'ghtened,' the 'once' is ἅπαξ = once for all. The text describes a condition subjectively possible, and therefore needing to be held up in earnest warning to the believer, while objectively and in the absolute purpose of God, it never occurs. . . . . If passages like this teach the possibility of falling from grace, they teach also the impossibility of restoration to it. The saint who once apostatizes has apostatized forever." So Ez. 18 : 24 — " when the righteous turneth away from his righteousness, and committeth iniquity . . . . in them shall he die " ; 2 Pet. 2 : 20 — " For if, after they have escaped the defilements of the world through the knowledge of the Lord and Savior Jesus Christ, they are again entangled therein and overcome, the last state is become worse with them than the first." So, in Mat. 5 : 13 — " if the salt have lost its savor, wherewith shall it be salted ? "— if this teaches that the regenerate may lose their religion, it also teaches that they can never recover it. It really shows only that Christians who do not perform their proper functions as Christians become harmful and contemptible (Broadus, *in loco*).

(*e*) They show that the perseverance of the truly regenerate may be secured by these very commands and warnings.

1 Cor. 9 : 27 — " I buffet my body, and bring it into bondage : lest by any means, after that I have preached to others, i myself should be rejected " — or, to bring out the meaning more fully : " I beat my body blue [or, ' strike it under the eye '], and make it a slave, lest after having been a herald to others, I myself should be rejected " (' unapproved,' ' counted unworthy of the prize ') ; 1C :12 — " Wherefore let h'm that thinketh he standeth take heed lest he fall." Quarles, Emblems : " The way to be safe is never to be secure." Wrightnour : " Warning a traveler to keep a certain path, and by this means keeping him in that path, is no evidence that he will ever fall into a pit by the side of the path simply because he is warned of it."

(*f*) They do not show that it is certain, or possible, that any truly regenerate person will fall away.

The Christian is like a man making his way up-hill, who occasionally slips back, yet always has his face set toward the summit. The unregenerate man has his face turneo downwards, and he is slipping all the way. C. H. Spurgeon : " The believer, like a man on shipboard, may fall again and again on the deck, but he will never fall overboard."

E.   That we have actual examples of such apostasy. — We answer :

(*a*)   Such are either men once outwardly reformed, like Judas and Ananias, but never renewed in heart ;

But, *per contra,* instance the experience of a man in typhoid fever, who apparently repented, but who never remembered it when he was restored to health. Sick-bed and death-bed conversions are not the best. There was one penitent thief, that none might despair ; there was but one penitent thief, that none might presume. The hypocrite is like the wire that gets a second-hand electricity from the live wire running parallel with it. This second-hand electricity is effective only within narrow limits, and its efficacy is soon exhausted. The live wire has connection with the source of power in the dynamo.

(*b*)   Or they are regenerate men, who, like David and Peter, have fallen into temporary sin, from which they will, before death, be reclaimed by God's discipline.

Instance the young profligate who, in a moment of apparent drowning, repented was then rescued, and afterward lived a long life as a Christian. If he had not been rescued, his repentance would never have been known, nor the answer to his mother's prayers. So, in the moment of a backslider's death, God can renew repentance and faith. Cromwell on his death-bed questioned his Chaplain as to the doctrine of final perseverance, and, on being assured that it was a certain truth, said : " Then I am happy, for I am sure that I was once in a state of grace." But reliance upon a past experience is like trusting in the value of a policy of life insurance upon which several years' premiums have been unpaid. If the policy has not lapsed, it is because of extreme grace. The only conclusive evidence of perseverance is a present experience of Christ's presence and indwelling, corroborated by active service and purity of life.

On the general subject, see Edwards, Works, 3 : 509-532, and 4 : 104; Ridgeley, Body of Divinity, 2 : 164-194 ; John Owen, Works, vol. 11 ; Woods, Works, 3 : 221-246 ; Van Oosterzee, Christian Dogmatics, 662-666.

PART VII.

ECCLESIOLOGY, OR THE DOCTRINE OF THE CHURCH.

CHAPTER I.

THE CONSTITUTION OF THE CHURCH. OR CHURCH POLITY.

I. DEFINITION OF THE CHURCH.

(*a*) The church of Christ, in its largest signification, is the whole company of regenerate persons in all times and ages, in heaven and on earth (Mat. 16:18 ; Eph. 1 : 22, 23 ; 3 :10 ; 5 :24, 25 ; Col. 1 :18 ; Heb. 12 :23). In this sense, the church is identical with the spiritual kingdom of God ; both signify that redeemed humanity in which God in Christ exercises actual spiritual dominion (John 3 : 3, 5).

Mat. 16 :18 — "thou art Peter, and upon this rock I will build my church ; and the gates of Hades shall not prevail against it " ; Eph. 1 : 22, 23 — "and he put all things in subjection under his feet, and gave him to be head over all things to the church, which is his body, the fulness of him that filleth all in all " ; 3 :10 — "to the intent that now unto the principalities and the powers in the heavenly places might be made known through the church the manifold wisdom of God " ; 5 : 24, 25 — " But as the church is subject to Christ, so let the wives also be to their husbands in everything. Husbands, love your wives, even as Christ also loved the church, and gave himself up for it " ; Col. 1 :18 — " And he is the head of the body, the church : who is the beginning, the firstborn from the dead ; that in all things he might have the preeminence " ; Heb. 12 :23 — "the general assembly and church of the firstborn who are enrolled in heaven " ; John 3: 3, 5 — " Except one be born anew, he cannot see the kingdom of God. . . . . Except one be born of water and the Spirit, he cannot enter into the kingdom of God."

Cicero's words apply here : " Una navis est jam bonorum omnium " — all good men are in one boat. Cicero speaks of the state, but it is still more true of the church invisible. Andrews, in Bib. Sac., Jan. 1883 :14, mentions the following differences between the church and kingdom, or, as we prefer to say, between the visible church and the invisible church : (1) the church began with Christ, — the kingdom began earlier ; (2) the church is confined to believers in the historic Christ, — the kingdom includes all God's children ; (3) the church belongs wholly to this world — not so the kingdom ; (4) the church is visible, — not so the kingdom ; (5) the church has *quasi* organic character, and leads out into local churches, — this is not so with the kingdom. On the universal or invisible church, see Cremer, Lexicon N. T., transl., 113, 114, 331 ; Jacob, Eccl. Polity of N. T., 12.

H. C. Vedder : " The church is a spiritual body, consisting only of those regenerated by the Spirit of God." Yet the Westminster Confession affirms that the church " consists of all those throughout the world that profess the true religion, together with their children." This definition includes in the church a multitude who not only give no evidence of regeneration, but who plainly show themselves to be unregenerate. In many lands it practically identifies the church with the world. Augustine indeed thought that "the field," in Mat. 13 :38, is the church, whereas Jesus says very distinctly that it "is the world." Augustine held that good and bad alike were to be permitted to

887

dwell together in the church, without attempt to separate them; see Broadus, Com. *in loco*. But the parable gives a reason, not why we should not try to put the wicked out of the church, but why God does not immediately put them out of the world, the tares being separated from the wheat only at the final judgment of mankind.

Yet the universal church includes all true believers. It fulfils the promise of God to Abraham in Gen. 15 : 5 — "Look now toward heaven, and number the stars, if thou be able to number them: and he said unto him, So shall thy seed be." The church shall be immortal, since it draws its life from Christ : Is. 65 : 22 — "as the days of a tree shall be the days of my people" ; Zech. 4 : 2, 3 — "a candlestick all of gold   . and two olive-trees by it." Dean Stanley, Life and Letters, 2 : 242, 243 — " A Spanish Roman Catholic, Cervantes, said : 'Many are the roads by which God carries his own to heaven.' Döllinger : 'Theology must become a science not, as heretofore, for making war, but for making peace, and thus bringing about that reconciliation of churches for which the whole civilized world is longing.' In their loftiest moods of inspiration, the Catholic Thomas à Kempis, the Puritan Milton, the Anglican Keble, rose above their peculiar tenets, and above the limits that divide denominations, into the higher regions of a common Christianity. It was the Baptist Bunyan who taught the world that there was 'a common ground of communion which no difference of external rites could efface.' It was the Moravian Gambold who wrote : 'The man That could surround the sum of things, and spy The heart of God and secrets of his empire, Would speak but love. With love, the bright result Would change the hue of intermediate things, And make one thing of all theology.' "

(*b*) The church, in this large sense, is nothing less than the body of Christ — the organism to which he gives spiritual life, and through which he manifests the fulness of his power and grace. The church therefore cannot be defined in merely human terms, as an aggregate of individuals associated for social, benevolent, or even spiritual purposes. There is a transcendent element in the church. It is the great company of persons whom Christ has saved, in whom he dwells, to whom and through whom he reveals God (Eph. 1 : 22, 23).

Eph. 1 : 22, 33 — "the church, which is his body, the fulness of him that filleth all in all." He who is the life of nature and of humanity reveals himself most fully in the great company of those who have joined themselves to him by faith. Union with Christ is the presupposition of the church. This alone transforms the sinner into a Christian, and this alone makes possible that vital and spiritual fellowship between individuals which constitutes the organizing principle of the church. The same divine life which ensures the pardon and the perseverance of the believer unites him to all other believers. The indwelling Christ makes the church superior to and more permanent than all humanitarian organizations; they die, but because Christ lives, the church lives also. Without a proper conception of this sublime relation of the church to Christ, we cannot properly appreciate our dignity as church members, or our high calling as shepherds of the flock. Not " ubi ecclesia, ibi Christus," but " ubi Christus, ibi ecclesia," should be our motto. Because Christ is omnipresent and omnipotent, " the same yesterday, and to-day, yea and forever " (Heb. 13 : 8), what Burke said of the nation is true of the church: It is " indeed a partnership, but a partnership not only between those who are living, but between those who are living, those who are dead, and those who are yet to be born."

McGiffert, Apostolic Church, 501 — " Paul's conception of the church as the body of Christ was first emphasized and developed by Ignatius. He reproduces in his writings the substance of all the Paulinism that the church at large made permanently its own : the preëxistence and deity of Christ, the union of the believer with Christ without which the Christian life is impossible, the importance of Christ's death, the church the body of Christ. Rome never fully recognized Paul's teachings, but her system rests upon his doctrine of the church the body of Christ. The modern doctrine however makes the kingdom to be not spiritual or future, but a reality of this world." The redemption of the body, the redemption of institutions, the redemption of nations, are indeed all purposed by Christ. Christians should not only strive to rescue individual men from the slough of vice, but they should devise measures for draining that slough and making that vice impossible; in other words, they should labor for the coming of the kingdom of God in society. But this is not to identify the church with politics, prohibition, libraries, athletics. The spiritual fellowship is to be the fountain

from which all these activities spring, while at the same time Christ's "kingdom is not of this world" (John 18 : 36).

A. J. Gordon, Ministry of the Spirit, 24, 25, 207 — "As Christ is the temple of God, so the church is the temple of the Holy Spirit. As God could be seen only through Christ, so the Holy Spirit can be seen only through the church. As Christ was the image of the invisible God, so the church is appointed to be the image of the invisible Christ, and the members of Christ, when they are glorified with him, shall be the express image of his person. . . . . The church and the kingdom are not identical terms, if we mean by the kingdom the visible reign and government of Jesus Christ on earth. In another sense they are identical. As is the king, so is the kingdom. The king is present now in the world, only invisibly and by the Holy Spirit ; so the kingdom is now present invisibly and spiritually in the hearts of believers. The king is to come again visibly and gloriously ; so shall the kingdom appear visibly and gloriously. In other words, the kingdom is already here in mystery : it is to be here in manifestation. Now the spiritual kingdom is administered by the Holy Spirit, and it extends from Pentecost to Parousia. At the Parousia — the appearing of the Son of man in glory — when he shall take unto himself his great power and reign (Rev. 11:17), when he who has now gone into a far country to be invested with a kingdom shall return and enter upon his government (Luke 19 : 15), then the invisible shall give way to the visible, the kingdom in mystery shall emerge into the kingdom in manifestation, and the Holy Spirit's administration shall yield to that of Christ."

(*c*) The Scriptures, however, distinguish between this invisible or universal church, and the individual church, in which the universal church takes local and temporal form, and in which the idea of the church as a whole is concretely exhibited.

Mat. 10 : 32 — "Every one therefore, who shall confess me before men, him will I also confess before my Father who is in heaven " ; 12 : 34, 35 — "out of the abundance of the heart the mouth speaketh. The good man out of his good treasure bringeth forth good things " ; Rom. 10 : 9, 10 — " if thou shalt confess with thy mouth Jesus as Lord, and shalt believe in thy heart that God raised him from the dead, thou shalt be saved : for with the heart man believeth unto righteousness ; and with the mouth confession is made unto salvation " ; James 1 : 18 — " Of his own will he brough t us forth by the word of truth, that we should be a kind of firstfruits of his creatures " — we were saved, not for ourselves only, but as parts and beginnings of an organic kingdom of God ; believers are called "firstfruits," because from them the blessing shall spread, until the whole world shall be pervaded with the new life ; Pentecost, as the feast of first-fruits, was but the beginning of a stream that shall continue to flow until the whole race of man is gathered in.

R. S. Storrs : "When any truth becomes central and vital, there comes the desire to utter it," — and we may add, not only in words, but in organization. So beliefs crystallize into institutions. But Christian faith is something more vital than the common beliefs of the world. Linking the soul to Christ, it brings Christians into living fellowship with one another before any bonds of outward organization exist ; outward organization, indeed, only expresses and symbolizes this inward union of spirit to Christ and to one another. Horatius Bonar : "Thou must be true thyself, If thou the truth wouldst teach ; Thy soul must overflow, if thou Another's soul wouldst reach ; It needs the overflow of heart To give the lips full speech. Think truly, and thy thoughts Shall the world's famine feed ; Speak truly, and each word of thine Shall be a fruitful seed ; Live truly, and thy life shall be A great and noble creed."

Contentio Veritatis, 128, 129 — "The kingdom of God is first a state of the individual soul, and then, secondly, a society made up of those who enjoy that state." Dr. F. L. Patton : "The best way for a man to serve the church at large is to serve the church to which he belongs." Herbert Stead : "The kingdom is not to be narrowed down to the church, nor the church evaporated into the kingdom." To do the first is to set up a monstrous ecclesiasticism ; to do the second is to destroy the organism through which the kingdom manifests itself and does its work in the world (W. R. Taylor). Prof. Dalman, in his work on The Words of Jesus in the Light of Postbiblical Writing and the Aramaic Language, contends that the Greek phrase translated "kingdom of God " should be rendered "the sovereignty of God." He thinks that it points to the reign of God, rather than to the realm over which he reigns. This rendering, if accepted, takes away entirely the support from the Ritschlian conception of the kingdom of God as an earthly and outward organization.

(*d*) The individual church may be defined as that smaller company of regenerate persons, who, in any given community, unite themselves voluntarily together, in accordance with Christ's laws, for the purpose of securing the complete establishment of his kingdom in themselves and in the world.

Mat. 18 : 17 —" And if he refuse to hear them, tell it unto the church : and if he refuse to hear the church also, let him be unto thee as the Gentile and the publican " ; Acts 14 : 23 —"appointed for them elders in every church " ; Rom. 16 : 5 —"salute the church that is in their house " ; 1 Cor. 1 : 2 —"the church of God which is at Corinth " ; 4 :17 — "even as I teach everywhere in every church " ; 1 Thess. 2 : 14 —"the churches of God which are in Judæa in Christ Jesus."

We do not define the church as a body of " baptized believers," because baptism is but one of " Christ's laws," in accordance with which believers unite themselves. Since these laws are the laws of church-organization contained in the New Testament, no Sunday School, Temperance Society, or Young Men's Christian Association, is properly a church. These organizations 1. lack the transcendent element — they are instituted and managed by man only ; 2. they are not confined to the regenerate, or to those alone who give credible evidence of regeneration ; 3. they presuppose and require no particular form of doctrine ; 4. they observe no ordinances ; 5. they are at best mere adjuncts and instruments of the church, but are not themselves churches ; 6. their decisions therefore are devoid of the divine authority and obligation which belong to the decisions of the church.

The laws of Christ, in accordance with which believers unite themselves into churches, may be summarized as follows : 1. the sufficiency and sole authority of Scripture as the rule both of doctrine and polity ; (2) credible evidence of regeneration and conversion as prerequisite to church-membership ; (3) immersion only, as answering to Christ's command of baptism, and to the symbolic meaning of the ordinance ; (4) the order of the ordinances, Baptism, and the Lord's Supper, as of divine appointment, as well as the ordinances themselves ; (5) the right of each member of the church to a voice in its government and discipline ; (6) each church, while holding fellowship with other churches, solely responsible to Christ ; (7) the freedom of the individual conscience, and the total independence of church and state. Hovey in his Restatement of Denominational Principles (Am. Bap. Pub. Society) gives these principles as follows : 1. the supreme authority of the Scriptures in matters of religion ; 2. personal accountability to God in religion ; 3. union with Christ essential to salvation ; 4. a new life the only evidence of that union ; 5. the new life one of unqualified obedience to Christ. The most concise statement of Baptist doctrine and history is that of Vedder, in Jackson's Dictionary of Religious Knowledge, 1 : 74-85.

With the lax views of Scripture which are becoming common among us there is a tendency in our day to lose sight of the transcendent element in the church. Let us remember that the church is not a humanitarian organization resting upon common human brotherhood, but a supernatural body, which traces its descent from the second, not the first, Adam, and which manifests the power of the divine Christ. Mazzini in Italy claimed Jesus, but repudiated his church. So modern socialists cry : " Liberty, Equality, Fraternity," and deny that there is need of anything more than human unity, development, and culture. But God has made the church to sit with Christ "in the heavenly places " (Eph. 2 : 6). It is the regeneration which comes about through union with Christ which constitutes the primary and most essential element in ecclesiology. " We do not stand, first of all, for restricted communion, nor for immersion as the only valid form of baptism, nor for any particular theory of Scripture, but rather for a regenerate church membership. The essence of the gospel is a new life in Christ, of which Christian experience is the outworking and Christian consciousness is the witness. Christian life is as important as conversion. Faith must show itself by works. We must seek the temporal as well as spiritual salvation of men, and the salvation of society also " (Leighton Williams).

E. G. Robinson : " Christ founded a church only proleptically. In Mat. 18 :17, ἐκκλησία is not used technically. The church is an outgrowth of the Jewish synagogue, though its method and economy are different. There was little or no organization at first Christ himself did not organize the church. This was the work of the apostles after Pentecost. The germ however existed before. Three persons may constitute a church, and may administer the ordinances. Councils have only advisory authority. Diocesan episcopacy is antiscriptural and antichristian."

The principles mentioned above are the essential principles of Baptist churches, although other bodies of Christians have come to recognize a portion of them. Bodies of Christians which refuse to accept these principles we may, in a somewhat loose and modified sense, call churches; but we cannot regard them as churches organized in all respects according to Christ's laws, or as completely answering to the New Testament model of church organization. We follow common usage when we address a Lieutenant Colonel as "Colonel," and a Lieutenant Governor as "Governor." It is only courtesy to speak of pedobaptist organizations as "churches," although we do not regard these churches as organized in full accordance with Christ's laws as they are indicated to us in the New Testament. To refuse thus to recognize them would be a discourtesy like that of the British Commander in Chief, when he addressed General Washington as "Mr. Washington."

As Luther, having found the doctrine of justification by faith, could not recognize that doctrine as Christian which taught justification by works, but denounced the church which held it as Antichrist, saying, "Here I stand; I cannot do otherwise, God help me," so we, in matters not indifferent, as feet-washing, but vitally affecting the existence of the church, as regenerate church-membership, must stand by the New Testament, and refuse to call any other body of Christians a regular church, that is not organized according to Christ's laws. The English word 'church' like the Scotch 'kirk' and the German 'Kirche,' is derived from the Greek κυριακή, and means 'belonging to the Lord.' The term itself should teach us to regard only Christ's laws as our rule of organization.

(e) Besides these two significations of the term 'church,' there are properly in the New Testament no others. The word ἐκκλησία is indeed used in Acts 7 : 38; 19 : 32, 39; Heb. 2 : 12, to designate a popular assembly; but since this is a secular use of the term, it does not here concern us. In certain passages, as for example Acts 9 : 31 (ἐκκλησία, sing., ℵ A B C), 1 Cor. 12 : 28, Phil. 3 : 6, and 1 Tim. 3 : 15, ἐκκλησία appears to be used either as a generic or as a collective term, to denote simply the body of independent local churches existing in a given region or at a given epoch. But since there is no evidence that these churches were bound together in any outward organization, this use of the term ἐκκλησία cannot be regarded as adding any new sense to those of 'the universal church' and 'the local church' already mentioned.

Acts 7 : 38 — "the church [marg. 'congregation'] in the wilderness"=the whole body of the people of Israel; 19 : 32 — "the assembly was in confusion"— the tumultuous mob in the theatre at Ephesus; 39 — "the regular assembly"; 9 : 31 — "So the church throughout all Judæa and Galilee and Samaria had peace, being edified"; 1 Cor. 12 : 28 — "And God hath set some in the church, first apostles, secondly prophets, thirdly teachers" Phil. 3 : 6 — "as touching zeal, persecuting the church"; 1 Tim. 3 : 15 — "that thou mayest know how men ought to behave themselves in the house of God, which is the church of the living God, the pillar and ground of the truth."

In the original use of the word ἐκκλησία, as a popular assembly, there was doubtless an allusion to the derivation from ἐκ and καλέω, to call out by herald. Some have held that the N. T. term contains an allusion to the fact that the members of Christ's church are called, chosen, elected by God. This, however, is more than doubtful. In common use, the term had lost its etymological meaning, and signified merely an assembly, however gathered or summoned. The church was never so large that it could not assemble. The church of Jerusalem gathered for the choice of deacons (Acts 6 : 2, 5), and the church of Antioch gathered to hear Paul's account of his missionary journey (Acts 14 : 27).

It is only by a common figure of rhetoric that many churches are spoken of together in the singular number, in such passages as Acts 9 : 31. We speak generically of man,' meaning the whole race of men; and of 'the horse,' meaning all horses. Gibbon, speaking of the successive tribes that swept down upon the Roman Empire, uses a noun in the singular number, and describes them as "the several detachments of that immense army of northern barbarians,"— yet he does not mean to intimate that these tribes had any common government. So we may speak of "the American college" or "the American theological seminary," but we do not thereby mean that the colleges or the seminaries are bound together by any tie of outward organization.

So Paul says that God has set in the church apostles, prophets, and teachers (1 Cor. 12 : 28), but the word 'church' is only a collective term for the many independent churches.

In this same sense, we may speak of "the Baptist church" of New York, or of America ; but it must be remembered that we use the term without any such implication of common government as is involved in the phrases 'the Presbyterian church,' or 'the Protestant Episcopal church,' or 'the Roman Catholic church' ; with us, in this connection, the term 'church' means simply 'churches.'

Broadus, in his Com. on Mat., page 359, suggests that the word ἐκκλησία in Acts 9 : 31 "denotes the original church at Jerusalem, whose members were by the persecution widely scattered throughout Judea and Galilee and Samaria, and held meetings wherever they were, but still belonged to the one original organization. . . . . When Paul wrote to the Galatians, nearly twenty years later, these separate meetings had been organized into distinct churches, and so he speaks (Gal. 1 : 22) in reference to that same period, of "the churches of Judæa which were in Christ." On the meaning of ἐκκλησία, see Cremer, Lex. N. T., 329 ; Trench, Syn. N. T., 1 : 18 ; Girdlestone, Syn. O. T., 367 ; Curtis, Progress of Baptist Principles, 301 ; Dexter, Congregationalism, 25 ; Dagg, Church Order, 100-120 ; Robinson, N. T. Lex., *sub voce.*

The prevailing usage of the N. T. gives to the term ἐκκλησία the second of these two significations. It is this local church only which has definite and temporal existence, and of this alone we henceforth treat. Our definition of the individual church implies the two following particulars :

A. *The church, like the family and the state, is an institution of divine appointment.* This is plain : (*a*) from its relation to the church universal, as its concrete embodiment ; (*b*) from the fact that its necessity is grounded in the social and religious nature of man ; (*c*) from the Scripture,—as for example, Christ's command in Mat. 18 : 17, and the designation 'church of God,' applied to individual churches (1 Cor. 1 : 2).

President Wayland : "The universal church comes before the particular church. The society which Christ has established is the foundation of every particular association calling itself a church of Christ." Andrews, in Bib. Sac., Jan. 1883 : 35-58, on the conception ἐκκλησία in the N. T., says that "the 'church' is the *prius* of all local 'churches.' ἐκκλησία in Acts 9 : 31 = the church, so far as represented in those provinces. It is ecumenical-local, as in 1 Cor. 10 : 33. The local church is a microcosm, a specialized localization of the universal body. קָהָל, in the O. T. and in the Targums, means the whole congregation of Israel, and then secondarily those local bodies which were parts and representations of the whole. Christ, using Aramaic, probably used קָהָל in Mat. 18 : 17. He took his idea of the church from it, not from the heathen use of the word ἐκκλησία, which expresses the notion of locality and state much more than קָהָל. The larger sense of ἐκκλησία is the primary. Local churches are points of consciousness and activity for the great all-inclusive unit, and they are not themselves the units for an ecclesiastical aggregate. They are faces, not parts of the one church."

Christ, in Mat. 18 : 17, delegates authority to the whole congregation of believers, and at the same time limits authority to the local church. The local church is not an end in itself, but exists for the sake of the kingdom. Unity is not to be that of merely local churches, but that of the kingdom, and that kingdom is internal, "cometh not with observation." (Luke 17 : 20), but consists in "righteousness and peace and joy in the Holy Spirit" (Rom. 14 : 17). The word church," in the universal sense, is not employed by any other N. T. writer before Paul. Paul was interested, not simply in individual conversions, but in the growth of the church of God, as the body of Christ. He held to the unity of all local churches with the mother church at Jerusalem. The church in a city or in a house is merely a local manifestation of the one universal church and derived its dignity therefrom. Teaching of the Twelve Apostles : "As this broken bread was scattered upon the mountains, and being gathered became one, so may thy church be gathered together from the ends of the earth into thy kingdom."

Sabatier, Philos. Religion, 92 —"The social action of religion springs from its very essence. Men of the same religion have no more imperious need than that of praying and worshiping together. State police have always failed to confine growing religious sects within the sanctuary or the home. . . . . God, it is said, is the place where spirits blend. In rising toward him, man necessarily passes beyond the limits of his own individuality. He feels instinctively that the principle of his being is the principle of the life of his brethren also, that that which gives him safety must give it to all." Rotne held that, as men reach the full development of their nature and appropriate the perfection of the Savior, the separation between the religious and the moral life will vanish, and the Christian state, as the highest sphere of human life representing all human functions, will displace the church. "In proportion as the Savior Christianizes the state by means of the church, must the progressive completion of the structure of the church prove the cause of its abolition. The decline of the church is not therefore to be deplored, but is to be recognized as the consequence of the independence and completeness of the religious life" (Encyc. Brit., 21 : 2). But it might equally be maintained that the state, as well as the church, will pass away, when the kingdom of God is fully come ; see John 4 : 21 —"the hour cometh, when neither in this mountain, nor in Jerusalem, shall ye worship the Father"; 1 Cor. 15 : 24 —"Then cometh the end, when he shall deliver up the kingdom to God, even the Father ; when he shall have abolished all rule and all authority and power "; Rev. 21 : 22 —"And I saw no temple therein : for the Lord God the Almighty, and the Lamb, are the temple thereof."

B. *The church, unlike the family and the state, is a voluntary society.* (*a*) This results from the fact that the local church is the outward expression of that rational and free life in Christ which characterizes the church as a whole. In this it differs from those other organizations of divine appointment, entrance into which is not optional. Membership in the church is not hereditary or compulsory. (*b*) The doctrine of the church, as thus defined, is a necessary outgrowth of the doctrine of regeneration. As this fundamental spiritual change is mediated not by outward appliances, but by inward and conscious reception of Christ and his truth, union with the church logically follows, not precedes, the soul's spiritual union with Christ.

We have seen that the church is the body of Christ. We now perceive that the church is, by the impartation to it of Christ's life, made a living body, with duties and powers of its own. A. J. Gordon, Ministry of the Spirit, 53, emphasizes the preliminary truth. He shows that the definition : The church a voluntary association of believers, united together for the purposes of worship and edification, is most inadequate, not to say incorrect. It is no more true than that hands and feet are voluntarily united in the human body for the purposes of locomotion and work. The church is formed from within. Christ, present by the Holy Ghost, regenerating men by the sovereign action of the Spirit, and organizing them into himself as the living centre, is the only principle that can explain the existence of the church. The Head and the body are therefore one — one in fact, and one in name. He whom God anointed and filled with the Holy Ghost is called "the Christ" (1 John 5 : 1 —"Whosoever believeth that Jesus is the Christ is begotten of God "); and the church which is his body and fulness is also called "the Christ" (1 Cor. 12 : 12 —"all the members of the body, being many, are one body ; so also is the Christ ").

Dorner includes under his doctrine of the church : (1) the genesis of the church, through the new birth of the Spirit, or Regeneration ; (2) the growth and persistence of the church through the continuous operation of the Spirit in the means of grace, or Ecclesiology proper, as others call it ; (3) the completion of the church, or Eschatology. While this scheme seems designed to favor a theory of baptismal regeneration, we must commend its recognition of the fact that the doctrine of the church grows out of the doctrine of regeneration and is determined in its nature by it. If regeneration has always conversion for its obverse side, and if conversion always includes faith in Christ, it is vain to speak of regeneration without faith. And if union with the church is but the outward expression of a preceding union with Christ which involves regeneration and conversion, then involuntary church-membership is an absurdity, and a misrepresentation of the whole method of salvation.

The value of compulsory religion may be illustrated from David Hume's experience. A godly matron of the Canongate, so runs the story, when Hume sank in the mud in her vicinity, and on account of his obesity could not get out, compelled the sceptic to say the Lord's Prayer before she would help him. Amos Kendall, on the other hand, concluded in his old age that he had not been acting on Christ's plan for saving the world, and so, of his own accord, connected himself with the church. Martineau, Study, 1 : 319 —" Till we come to the State and the Church, we do not reach the highest organism of human life, into the perfect working of which all the disinterested affections and moral enthusiasms and noble ambitions flow."

Socialism abolishes freedom, which the church cultivates and insists upon as the principle of its life. Tertullian: "Nec religionis est cogere religionem" — "It is not the business of religion to compel religion." Vedder, History of the Baptists: "The community of goods in the church at Jerusalem was a purely voluntary matter; see Acts 5 : 4 — 'While it remained, did it not remain thine own? and after it was sold, was it not in thy power?' The community of goods does not seem to have continued in the church at Jerusalem after the temporary stress had been relieved, and there is no reason to believe that any other church in the apostolic age practised anything of the kind." By abolishing freedom, socialism destroys all possibility of economical progress. The economical principle of socialism is that, relatively to the enjoyment of commodities, the individual shall be taken care of by the community, to the effect of his being relieved of the care of himself. The communism in the Acts was: 1. not for the community of mankind in general, but only for the church within itself; 2. not obligatory, but left to the discretion of individuals; 3. not permanent, but devised for a temporary crisis. On socialism, see James MacGregor, in Presb. and Ref. Rev., Jan. 1892 : 35–68.

Schurman, Agnosticism, 166 — "Few things are of more practical consequence for the future of religion in America than the duty of all good men to become identified with the visible church. Liberal thinkers have, as a rule, underestimated the value of the church. Their point of view is individualistic, 'as though a man were author of himself, and knew no other kin.' 'The old is for slaves,' they declare. But it is also true that the old is for freedmen who know its true uses. It is the bane of the religion of dogma that it has driven many of the choicest religious souls out of the churches. In its purification of the temple, it has lost sight of the object of the temple. The church, as an institution, is an organism and embodiment such as the religion of spirit necessarily creates. Spiritual religion is not the enemy, it is the essence, of institutional religion."

II. ORGANIZATION OF THE CHURCH.

1. *The fact of organization.*

Organization may exist without knowledge of writing, without written records, lists of members, or formal choice of officers. These last are the proofs, reminders, and helps of organization, but they are not essential to it. It is however not merely informal, but formal, organization in the church, to which the New Testament bears witness.

That there was such organization is abundantly shown from (*a*) its stated meetings, (*b*) elections, and (*c*) officers ; (*d*) from the designations of its ministers, together with (*e*) the recognized authority of the minister and of the church ; (*f*) from its discipline, (*g*) contributions, (*h*) letters of commendation, (*i*) registers of widows, (*j*) uniform customs, and (*k*) ordinances ; (*l*) from the order enjoined and observed, (*m*) the qualifications for membership, and (*n*) the common work of the whole body.

(*a*) Acts 20 : 7 — "upon the first day of the week, when we were gathered together to break bread, Paul discoursed with them"; Heb. 10 : 25 — "not forsaking our own assembling together, as the custom of some is, but exhorting one another."

(*b*) Acts 1 : 23–26 — the election of Matthias ; 6 : 5, 6 — the election of deacons.

(*c*) Phil. 1 : 1 — "the saints in Christ Jesus that are at Philippi, with the bishops and deacons."

(*d*) Acts 20 : 17, 28 — "the elders of the church . . . . the flock, in which the Holy Spirit hath made you bishops [marg. : 'overseers']."

(*e*) Mat. 18 : 17 — "And if he refuse to hear them, tell it unto the church : and if he refuse to hear the church also, let him be unto thee as the Gentile and the publican"; 1 Pet. 5 : 2 — "Tend the flock of God which is among you, exercising the oversight, not of constraint, but willingly, according to the will of God."

(*f*) 1 Cor. 5 : 4, 5, 13 — "in the name of our Lord Jesus, ye being gathered together, and my spirit, with the power of our Lord Jesus, to deliver such a one unto Satan for the destruction of the flesh, that the spirit may be saved in the day of the Lord Jesus, ... Put away the wicked man from among yourselves."

(*g*) Rom. 15 : 26 — "For it hath been the good pleasure of Macedonia and Achaia to make a certain contribution for the poor among the saints that are at Jerusalem" , 1 Cor. 16 : 1, 2 — "Now concerning the collection for the saints, as I gave order to the churches of Galatia, so also do ye. Upon the first day of the week let each one of you lay by him in store, as he may prosper, that no collection be made when I come."

(*h*) Acts 18 : 27 — "And when he was minded to pass over into Achaia, the brethren encouraged him, and wrote to the disciples to receive him " ; 2 Cor. 3 : 1 — "Are we beginning again to commend ourselves ? or need we, as do some epistles of commendation to you or from you ? "

(*i*) 1 Tim. 5 : 9 — "Let none be enrolled as a widow under threescore years old " ; *cf.* Acts 6 : 1 — "there arose a murmuring of the Grecian Jews against the Hebrews, because their widows were neglected in the daily ministration.'

(*j*) 1 Cor. 11 : 16 — "But if any man seemeth to be contentious, we have no such custom, neither the churches of God."

(*k*) Acts 2 : 41 — "They then that received his word were baptized " ; 1 Cor. 11 : 23-26 — "For I received of the Lord that which also I delivered unto you " — the institution of the Lord's Supper.

(*l*) 1 Cor. 14 : 40 — "let all things be done decently and in order " ; Col. 2 : 5 — " For though I am absent in the flesh, yet am I with you in the spirit, joying and beholding your order, and the stedfastness of your faith in Christ."

(*m*) Mat. 28 : 19 — "Go ye therefore, and make disciples of all the nations, baptizing them into the name of the Father and of the Son and of the Holy Spirit " ; Acts 2 : 47 — "And the Lord added to them day by day those that were being saved."

(*n*) Phil. 2 : 30 — "because for the work of Christ he came nigh unto death, hazarding his life to supply that which was lacking in your service toward me."

As indicative of a developed organization in the N. T. church, of which only the germ existed before Christ's death, it is important to notice the progress in names from the Gospels to the Epistles. In the Gospels, the word "disciples" is the common designation of Christ's followers, but it is not once found in the Epistles. In the Epistles, there are only "saints," "brethren," "churches." A consideration of the facts here referred to is sufficient to evince the unscriptural nature of two modern theories of the church :

A. The theory that the church is an exclusively spiritual body, destitute of all formal organization, and bound together only by the mutual relation of each believer to his indwelling Lord.

The church, upon this view, so far as outward bonds are concerned, is only an aggregation of isolated units. Those believers who chance to gather at a particular place, or to live at a particular time, constitute the church of that place or time. This view is held by the Friends and by the Plymouth Brethren. It ignores the tendencies to organization inherent in human nature; confounds the visible with the invisible church ; and is directly opposed to the Scripture representations of the visible church as comprehending some who are not true believers.

Acts 5 : 1-11 — Ananias and Sapphira show that the visible church comprehended some who were not true believers ; 1 Cor. 14 : 23 — "If therefore the whole church be assembled together and all speak with tongues, and there come in men unlearned or unbelieving, will they not say that ye are mad ? " — here, if the church had been an unorganized assembly, the unlearned visitors who came in would have formed a part of it ; Phil. 3 : 18 — "For many walk, of whom I told you often, and now tell you even weeping, that they are the enemies of the cross of Christ."

Some years ago a book was placed upon the Index, at Rome, entitled : "The Priesthood a Chronic Disorder of the Human Race." The Plymouth Brethren dislike church organizations, for fear they will become machines ; they dislike ordained ministers, for fear they will become bishops. They object to praying for the Holy Spirit, because he was given on Pentecost, ignoring the fact that the church after Pentecost so prayed : see Acts 4 : 31 — "And when they had prayed, the place was shaken wherein they were gathered together; and they were all filled with the Holy Spirit, and they spake the word of God with boldness." What we call a giving or descent of the Holy Spirit is, since the Holy Spirit is omnipresent, only a manifestation of the power of the Holy Spirit, and this certainly may be prayed for : see Luke 11 : 13 — "If ye then, being evil, know how to give good gifts unto your children, how much more shall your heavenly Father give the Holy Spirit to them that ask him ? "

The Plymouth Brethren would " unite Christendom by its dismemberment, and do away with all sects by the creation of a new sect, more narrow and bitter in its hostility to existing sects than any other." Yet the tendency to organize is so strong in human nature, that even Plymouth Brethren, when they meet regularly together, fall into an informal, if not a formal, organization ; certain teachers and leaders are tacitly recognized as officers of the body ; committees and rules are unconsciously used for facilitating business. Even one of their own writers, C. H. M., speaks of the "natural tendency to association without God, — as in the Shinar Association or Babel Confederacy of Gen. 11, which aimed at building up a name upon the earth. The Christian church is God's appointed association to take the place of all these. Hence God confounds the tongues in Gen. 11 (judgment) ; gives tongues in Acts 2 (grace) ; but only one tongue is spoken in Rev. 7 (glory)."

The Nation, Oct. 16, 1890 : 303 — "Every body of men must have one or more leaders. If these are not provided, they will make them for themselves. You cannot get fifty men together, at least of the Anglo-Saxon race, without their choosing a presiding officer and giving him power to enforce rules and order." Even socialists and anarchists have their leaders, who often exercise arbitrary power and oppress their followers. Lyman Abbott says nobly of the community of true believers : "The grandest river in the world has no banks ; it rises in the Gulf of Mexico ; it sweeps up through the Atlantic Ocean along our coast ; it crosses the Atlantic, and spreads out in great broad fanlike form along the coast of Europe ; and whatever land it kisses blooms and blossoms with the fruit of its love. The apricot and the fig are the witness of its fertilizing power. It is bound together by the warmth of its own particles, and by nothing else." This is a good illustration of the invisible church, and of its course through the world. But the visible church is bound to be distinguishable from unregenerate humanity, and its inner principle of association inevitably leads to organization.

Dr. Wm. Reid, Plymouth Brethrenism Unveiled, 79-143, attributes to the sect the following Church-principles : (1) the church did not exist before Pentecost ; (2) the visible and the invisible church identical ; (3) the one assembly of God ; (4) the presidency of the Holy Spirit ; (5) rejection of a one-man and man-made ministry ; (6) the church is without government. Also the following heresies : (1) Christ's heavenly humanity ; (2) denial of Christ's righteousness, as being obedience to law ; (3) denial that Christ's righteousness is imputed ; (4) justification in the risen Christ ; (5) Christ's non-atoning sufferings ; (6) denial of moral law as rule of life ; (7) the Lord's day is not the Sabbath ; (8) perfectionism ; (9) secret rapture of the saints, — caught up to be with Christ. To these we may add ; (10) premillenial advent of Christ.

On the Plymouth Brethern and their doctrine, see British Quar., Oct. 1873 : 202 ; Princeton Rev., 1872 : 48-77 ; H. M. King, in Baptist Review, 1881 : 438-465 ; Fish, Ecclesiology, 314-316 ; Dagg, Church Order, 80-83 ; R. H. Carson, The Brethren, 8-14 ; J. C. L. Carson, The Heresies of the Plymouth Brethren ; Croskery, Plymouth Brethrenism ; Teulon, Hist. and Teachings of Plymouth Brethren.

B. The theory that the form of church organization is not definitely prescribed in the New Testament, but is a matter of expediency, each body of believers being permitted to adopt that method of organization which best suits its circumstances and condition.

The view under consideration seems in some respects to be favored by Neander, and is often regarded as incidental to his larger conception of church history as a progressive development. But a proper theory of development does not exclude the idea of a church organization already complete in all essential particulars before the close of the inspired canon, so that the record of it may constitute a providential example of binding authority upon all subsequent ages. The view mentioned exaggerates the differences of practice among the N. T. churches ; underestimates the need of divine direction as to methods of church union ; and admits a principle of 'church powers,' which may be historically shown to be subversive of the very existence of the church as a spiritual body.

Dr. Galusha Anderson finds the theory of optional church government in Hooker's Ecclesiastical Polity, and says that not until Bishop Bancroft was there claimed a divine right of Episcopacy. Hunt, also, in his Religious Thought in England, 1 : 57, says that Hooker gives up the divine origin of Episcopacy. So Jacob, Eccl. Polity of the

N. T., and Hatch, Organization of Early Christian Churches, — both Jacob and Hatch belonging to the Church of England. Hooker identified the church with the nation ; see Eccl. Polity, book viii, chap. 1 : 7 ; 4 : 6 ; 8 : 9. He held that the state has committed itself to the church, and that therefore the church has no right to commit itself to the state. The assumption, however, that the state has committed itself to the church is entirely unwarranted; see Gore, Incarnation, 209, 210. Hooker declares that, even if the Episcopalian order were laid down in Scripture, which he denies, it would still not be unalterable, since neither "God's being the author of laws for the government of his church, nor his committing them unto Scripture, is any reason sufficient wherefore all churches should forever be bound to keep them without change."

T. M. Lindsay, in Contemp. Rev., Oct. 1895 : 548–563, asserts that there were at least five different forms of church government in apostolic times : 1. derived from the seven wise men of the Hebrew village community, representing the political side of the synagogue system ; 2. derived from the ἐπίσκοπος, the director of the religious or social club among the heathen Greeks; 3. derived from the patronate (προστάτης, προϊστάμενος) known among the Romans, the churches of Rome, Corinth, Thessalonica, being of this sort ; 4. derived from the personal preëminence of one man, nearest in family to our Lord, James being president of the church at Jerusalem ; 5. derived from temporary superintendents (ἡγούμενοι), or leaders of the band of missionaries, as in Crete and Ephesus. Between all these churches of different polities, there was intercommunication and fellowship. Lindsay holds that the unity was wholly spiritual. It seems to us that he has succeeded merely in proving five different varieties of one generic type — the generic type being only democratic, with two orders of officials, and two ordinances — in other words, in showing that the simple N. T. model adopts itself to many changing conditions, while the main outlines do not change. Upon any other theory, church polity is a matter of individual taste or of temporary fashion. Shall missionaries conform church order to the degraded ideas of the nations among which they labor? Shall church government be despotic in Turkey, a limited monarchy in England, a democracy in the United States of America, and two-headed in Japan? For the development theory of Neander, see his Church History, 1 : 179–190. On the general subject, see Hitchcock, in Am. Theol. Rev., 1860 : 28–54; Davidson, Eccl. Polity, 1–42 ; Harvey, The Church.

2. *The nature of this organization.*

The nature of any organization may be determined by asking, first : who constitute its members ? secondly : for what object has it been formed ? and, thirdly : what are the laws which regulate its operations ?

The three questions with which our treatment of the nature of this organization begins are furnished us by Pres. Wayland, in his Principles and Practices of Baptists.

A. They only can properly be members of the local church, who have previously become members of the church universal, — or, in other words, have become regenerate persons.

Only those who have been previously united to Christ are, in the New Testament, permitted to unite with his church. See Acts 2 : 47 — "And the Lord added to them day by day those that were being saved [Am. Rev. : 'those that were saved'] " ; 5 : 14 — "and believers were the more added to the Lord " ; 1 Cor. 1 : 2 — "the church of God which is at Corinth, even them that are sanctified in Christ Jesus, called to be saints, with all that call upon the name of our Lord Jesus Christ in every place, their Lord and ours."

From this limitation of membership to regenerate persons, certain results follow :

(*a*) Since each member bears supreme allegiance to Christ, the church as a body must recognize Christ as the only lawgiver. The relation of the individual Christian to the church does not supersede, but furthers and expresses, his relation to Christ.

1 John 2 : 20 — "And ye have an anointing from the Holy One, and ye know all things " — see Neander, Com., *in loco* — " No believer is at liberty to forego this maturity and personal independence, bestowed in that inward anointing [of the Holy Spirit], or to place himself in a dependent relation, inconsistent with this birthright, to any teacher whatever among men,

. . . . This inward anointing furnishes an element of resistance to such arrogated authority." Here we have reproved the tendency on the part of ministers to take the place of the church, in Christian work and worship, instead of leading it forward in work and worship of its own. The missionary who keeps his converts in prolonged and unnecessary tutelage is also untrue to the church organization of the New Testament and untrue to Christ whose aim in church training is to educate his followers to the bearing of responsibility and the use of liberty. Macaulay : "The only remedy for the evils of liberty is liberty." " Malo periculosam libertatem "—" Liberty is to be preferred with all its dangers." Edwin Burritt Smith : "There is one thing better than good government, and that is self-government." By their own mistakes, a self-governing people and a self-governing church will finally secure good government, whereas the "good government" which keeps them in perpetual tutelage will make good government forever impossible.

Ps. 144 : 12 — " our sons shall be as plants grown up in their youth." Archdeacon Hare : " If a gentleman is to grow up, it must be like a tree : there must be nothing between him and heaven." What is true of the gentleman is true of the Christian. There need to be encouraged and cultivated in him an independence of human authority and a sole dependence upon Christ. The most sacred duty of the minister is to make his church self-governing and self-supporting, and the best test of his success is the ability of the church to live and prosper after he has left it or after he is dead. Such ministerial work requires self-sacrifice and self-effacement. The natural tendency of every minister is to usurp authority and to become a bishop. He has in him an undeveloped pope. Dependence on his people for support curbs this arrogant spirit. A church establishment fosters it. The remedy both for slavishness and for arrogance lies in constant recognition of Christ as the only Lord.

(*b*) Since each regenerate man recognizes in every other a brother in Christ, the several members are upon a footing of absolute equality (Mat. 23 : 8-10).

Mat. 23 : 8-10 —"But be not ye called Rabbi : for one is your teacher, and all ye are brethren. And call no man your father on the earth : for one is your Father, even he who is in heaven "; John 15 : 5 —"I am the vine, ye are the branches"—no one branch of the vine outranks another; one may be more advantageously situated, more ample in size, more fruitful; but all are alike in kind, draw vitality from one source. Among the planets " one star differeth from another star in glory " (1 Cor. 15 : 41), yet all shine in the same heaven, and draw their light from the same sun. " The serving-man may know more of the mind of God than the scholar." Christianity has therefore been the foe to heathen castes. The Japanese noble objected to it, "because the brotherhood of man was incompatible with proper reverence for rank." There can be no rightful human lordship over God's heritage (1 Pet. 5 : 3 —" neither as lording it over the charge allotted to you, but making yourselves ensamples to the flock ").

Constantine thought more highly of his position as member of Christ's church than of his position as head of the Roman Empire. Neither the church nor its pastor should be dependent upon the unregenerate members of the congregation. Many a pastor is in the position of a lion tamer with his head in the lion's mouth. So long as he strokes the fur the right way, all goes well ; but, if by accident he strokes the wrong way, off goes his head. Dependence upon the spiritual body which he instructs is compatible with the pastor's dignity and faithfulness. But dependence upon those who are not Christians and who seek to manage the church with worldly motives and in a worldly way, may utterly destroy the spiritual effect of his ministry. The pastor is bound to be the impartial preacher of the truth, and to treat each member of his church as of equal importance with every other.

(*c*) Since each local church is directly subject to Christ, there is no jurisdiction of one church over another, but all are on an equal footing, and all are independent of interference or control by the civil power.

Mat. 22 : 21 —" Render therefore unto Cæsar the things that are Cæsar's; and unto God the things that are God's "; Acts 5 : 29 —"We must obey God rather than men." As each believer has personal dealings with Christ and for even the pastor to come between him and his Lord is treachery to Christ and harmful to his soul, so much more does the New Testament condemn any attempt to bring the church into subjection to any other church or combination of churches, or to make the church the creature of the state. Absolute liberty of conscience under

Christ has always been a distinguishing tenet of Baptists, as it is of the New Testament (*cf.* Rom. 14 : 4 —" Who art thou that judgest the servant of another ? to his own lord he standeth or falleth. Yea, he shall be made to stand; for the Lord hath power to make him stand "). John Locke, 100 years before American independence : " The Baptists were the first and only propounders of absolute liberty, just and true liberty, equal and impartial liberty." George Bancroft says of Roger Williams : " He was the first person in modern Christendom to assert the doctrine of liberty of conscience in religion. . . . . Freedom of conscience was from the first a trophy of the Baptists. . . . . Their history is written in blood."

On Roger Williams, see John Fiske, The Beginnings of New England : " Such views are to-day quite generally adopted by the more civilized portions of the Protestant world ; but it is needless to say that they were not the views of the sixteenth century, in Massachusetts or elsewhere." Cotton Mather said that Roger Williams " carried a windmill in his head," and even John Quincy Adams called him " conscientiously contentious." Cotton Mather's windmill was one that he remembered or had heard of in Holland. It had run so fast in a gale as to set itself and a whole town on fire. Leonard Bacon, Genesis of the New England Churches, vii, says of Baptist churches : " It has been claimed for these churches that from the age of the Reformation onward they have been always foremost and always consistent in maintaining the doctrine of religious liberty. Let me not be understood as calling in question their right to so great an honor."

Baptists hold that the province of the state is purely secular and civil,—religious matters are beyond its jurisdiction. Yet for economic reasons and to ensure its own preservation, it may guarantee to its citizens their religious rights, and may exempt all churches equally from burdens of taxation, in the same way in which it exempts schools and hospitals. The state has holidays, but no holy days. Hall Caine, in The Christian, calls the state, not the pillar of the church, but the caterpillar, that eats the vitals out of it. It is this, when it transcends its sphere and compels or forbids any particular form of religious teaching. On the charge that Roman Catholics were deprived of equal rights in Rhode Island, see Am. Cath. Quar. Rev., Jan. 1894 : 169-177. This restriction was not in the original law, but was a note added by revisers, to bring the state law into conformity with the law of the mother country. Ezra 8 : 22 — " I was ashamed to ask of the king a band of soldiers and horsemen . . . . because . . . . The hand of our God is upon all them that seek him, for good " — is a model for the churches of every age. The church as an organized body should be ashamed to depend for revenue upon the state, although its members as citizens may justly demand that the state protect them in their rights of worship. On State and Church in 1492 and 1892, see A. H. Strong, Christ in Creation, 209-246, esp. 239-241. On taxation of church property, and opposing it, see H. C. Vedder, in Magazine of Christian Literature, Feb. 1890 : 265-272.

B.   The sole object of the local church is the glory of God, in the complete establishment of his kingdom, both in the hearts of believers and in the world.   This object is to be promoted :

(*a*) By united worship,—including prayer and religious instruction ; (*b*) by mutual watchcare and exhortation ; (*c*) by common labors for the reclamation of the impenitent world.

(*a*) Heb. 10 : 25 — " not forsaking our own assembling together, as the custom of some is, but exhorting one another." One burning coal by itself will soon grow dull and go out, but a hundred together will give a fury of flame that will set fire to others. Notice the value of " the crowd " in politics and in religion. One may get an education without going to school or college, and may cultivate religion apart from the church ; but the number of such people will be small, and they do not choose the best way to become intelligent or religious.

(*b*) 1 Thess. 5 : 11 — "Wherefore exhort one another, and build each other up, even as also ye do "; Heb. 3 : 13 — "Exhort one another day by day, so long as it is called To-day ; lest any one of you be hardened by the deceitfulness of sin." Churches exist in order to : 1. create ideals ; 2. supply motives ; 3. direct energies. They are the leaven hidden in the three measures of meal. But there must be life in the leaven, or no good will come of it. There is no use of taking to China a lamp that will not burn in America. The light that shines the furthest shines brightest nearest home.

(*c*) Mat. 28 : 19 — " Go ye therefore, and make disciples of all the nations "; Acts 8 : 4 — " They therefore that were scattered abroad went about preaching the word "; 2 Cor. 8 : 5 — "and this, not as we had hoped, but first they gave their own selves to the Lord, and to us through the will of God "; Jude 23 — "And on some have mercy, who are in loubt; and some save, snatching them out of the fire." Inscribed upon a mural tablet of a Christian church, in Aneityum in the South Seas. to the memory of Dr. John Geddie, the pioneer missionary in that field, are the words: "When he came here, there were no Christians; when he went away, there were no heathen." Inscription over the grave of David Livingstone in Westminster Abbey: "For thirty years his life was spent in an unwearied effort to evangelize the native races, to explore the undiscovered secrets, to abolish the desolating slave trade of Central Africa, where with his last words he wrote: 'All I can add in my solitude is, May Heaven's richest blessing come down on everyone, American, English or Turk, who will help to heal this open sore of the world.'"

C. The law of the church is simply the will of Christ, as expressed in the Scriptures and interpreted by the Holy Spirit. This law respects:

(a) The qualifications for membership.—These are regeneration and baptism, i. e., spiritual new birth and ritual new birth ; the surrender of the inward and of the outward life to Christ; the spiritual entrance into communion with Christ's death and resurrection, and the formal profession of this to the world by being buried with Christ and rising with him in baptism.

(b) The duties imposed on members.—In discovering the will of Christ from the Scriptures, each member has the right of private judgment, being directly responsible to Christ for his use of the means of knowledge, and for his obedience to Christ's commands when these are known.

How far does the authority of the church extend? It certainly has no right to say what its members shall eat and drink; to what societies they shall belong; what alliances in marriage or in business they shall contract. It has no right, as an organized body, to suppress vice in the community, or to regenerate society by taking sides in a political canvass. The members of the church, as citizens, have duties in all these lines of activity. The function of the church is to give them religious preparation and stimulus for their work. In this sense, however, the church is to influence all human relations. It follows the model of the Jewish commonwealth rather than that of the Greek state. The Greek πόλις was limited, because it was the affirmation of only personal rights. The Jewish commonwealth was universal, because it was the embodiment of the one divine will. The Jewish state was the most comprehensive of the ancient world, admitting freely the incorporation of new members, and looking forward to a worldwide religious communion in one faith. So the Romans gave to conquered lands the protection and the rights of Rome. But the Christian church is the best example of incorporation in conquest. See Westcott, Hebrews, 386, 387 ; John Fiske, Beginnings of New England, 1-20 ; Dagg, Church Order, 74-99 ; Curtis on Communion, 1-61.

Abraham Lincoln: "This country cannot be half slave and half free "=the one part will pull the other over; there is an irrepressible conflict between them. So with the forces of Christ and of Antichrist in the world at large. Alexander Duff: "The church that ceases to be evangelistic will soon cease to be evangelical." We may add that the church that ceases to be evangelical will soon cease to exist. The Fathers of New England proposed "to advance the gospel in these remote parts of the world, even if they should be but as stepping-stones to those who were to follow them." They little foresaw how their faith and learning would give character to the great West. Church and school went together. Christ alone is the Savior of the world, but Christ alone cannot save the world. Zinzendorf called his society "The Mustard-seed Society " because it should remove mountains (Mat. 17 : 20). Hermann, Faith and Morals, 91, 238— "It is not by means of things that pretend to be imperishable that Christianity continues to live on ; but by the fact that there are always persons to be found who, by their contact with the Bible traditions, become witnesses to the personality of Jesus and follow him as their guide, and therefore acquire sufficient courage to sacrifice themselves for others."

3. *The genesis of this organization.*

(a) The church existed in germ before the day of Pentecost,—otherwise there would have been nothing to which those converted upon that day could have been "added" (Acts 2 : 47). Among the apostles, regenerate as they were, united to Christ by faith and in that faith baptized (Acts 19 : 4), under Christ's instruction and engaged in common work for him, there were already the beginnings of organization. There was a treasurer of the body (John 13 : 29), and as a body they celebrated for the first time the Lord's Supper (Mat. 26 : 26–29). To all intents and purposes they constituted a church, although the church was not yet fully equipped for its work by the outpouring of the Spirit (Acts 2), and by the appointment of pastors and deacons. The church existed without officers, as in the first days succeeding Pentecost.

Acts 2 : 47—"And the Lord added to them [marg.: 'together'] day by day those that were being saved"; 19 : 4 —"And Paul said, John baptized with the baptism of repentance, saying unto the people that they should believe on him that should come after him, that is, on Jesus"; John 13 : 29—"For some thought, because Judas had the bag, that Jesus said unto him, Buy what things we have need of for the feast; or, that he should give something to the poor"; Mat. 26 : 26–29—"And as they were eating, Jesus took bread . . . . and he gave to the disciples, and said, Take, eat . . . . And he took a cup, and gave thanks, and gave to them, saying, Drink ye all of it"; Acts 2—the Holy Spirit is poured out. It is to be remembered that Christ himself is the embodied union between God and man, the true temple of God's indwelling. So soon as the first believer joined himself to Christ, the church existed in miniature and germ.

A. J. Gordon, Ministry of the Spirit, 55, quotes Acts 2 : 41—"and there were added," not to them, or to the church, but, as in Acts 5 : 14, and 11 : 24—"to the Lord." This, Dr. Gordon declares, means not a mutual union of believers, but their divine couniting with Christ; not voluntary association of Christians, but their sovereign incorporation into the Head, and this incorporation effected by the Head, through the Holy Spirit. The old proverb, "Tres faciunt ecclesiam," is always true when one of the three is Jesus (Dr. Deems). Cyprian was wrong when he said that "he who has not the church for his mother, has not God for his Father"; for this could not account for the conversion of the first Christian, and it makes salvation dependent upon the church rather than upon Christ. The Cambridge Platform, 1648, chapter 6, makes officers essential, not to the being, but only to the well being, of churches, and declares that elders and deacons are the only ordinary officers; see Dexter, Congregationalism, 439.

Fish, Ecclesiology, 14–11, by a striking analogy, distinguishes three periods of the church's life: (1) the pre-natal period, in which the church is not separated from Christ's bodily presence; (2) the period of childhood, in which the church is under tutelage, preparing for an independent life; (3) the period of maturity, in which the church, equipped with doctrines and officers, is ready for self-government. The three periods may be likened to bud, blossom, and fruit. Before Christ's death, the church existed in bud only.

(b) That provision for these offices was made gradually as exigencies arose, is natural when we consider that the church immediately after Christ's ascension was under the tutelage of inspired apostles, and was to be prepared, by a process of education, for independence and self-government. As doctrine was communicated gradually yet infallibly, through the oral and written teaching of the apostles, so we are warranted in believing that the church was gradually but infallibly guided to the adoption of Christ's own plan of church organization and of Christian work. The same promise of the Spirit which renders the New Testament an unerring and sufficient rule of faith, renders it also an unerring and sufficient rule of practice, for the church in all places and times.

John 16 : 12–26 is to be interpreted as a promise of gradual leading by the Spirit into all the truth; 1 Cor. 14 : 37—"the things which I write unto you . . . . they are the commandments of the Lord." An examination of Paul's epistles in their chronological order shows a progress in definiteness of teaching with regard to church polity, as well as with regard to doctrine in general. In this matter, as in other matters, apostolic instruction was given as providential exigencies demanded it. In the earliest days of the church, attention was paid to preaching rather than to organization. Like Luther, Paul thought more of church order in his later days than at the beginning of his work. Yet even in his first epistle we find the germ which is afterwards continuously developed. See:

(1) 1 Thess. 5 : 12, 13 (A. D. 52) — "But we beseech you, brethren, to know them that labor among you, and are over you (προΐσταμένους) in the Lord, and admonish you ; and to esteem them exceeding highly in love for their work's sake."

(2) 1 Cor. 12 : 28 (A. D. 57) — "And God hath set some in the church, first apostles, secondly prophets, thirdly teachers, then miracles, then gifts of healings, helps [ἀντιλήψεις = gifts needed by deacons], governments [κυβερνήσεις = gifts needed by pastors], divers kinds of tongues."

(3) Rom. 12 : 6-8 (A. D. 58) — "And having gifts differing according to the grace that is given to us, whether prophecy, let us prophesy according to the proportion of our faith ; or ministry [διακονίαν], let us give ourselves to our ministry ; or he that teacheth, to his teaching ; or he that exhorteth, to his exhorting : he that giveth, let him do it with liberality ; he that ruleth [ὁ προΐστάμενος], with diligence ; he that showeth mercy, with cheerfulness."

(4) Phil. 1 : 1 (A. D. 62) — " Paul and Timothy, servants of Jesus Christ, to all the saints in Christ Jesus that are at Philippi, with the bishops [ἐπισκόποις, marg. : ' overseers '] and deacons [διακόνοις]."

(5) Eph. 4 : 11 (A. D. 63) — "And he gave some to be apostles ; and some, prophets ; and some, evangelists ; and some, pastors and teachers [ποιμένας καὶ διδασκάλους]."

(6) 1 Tim. 3 : 1, 2 (A. D. 66) — "If a man seeketh the office of a bishop, he desireth a good work. The bishop [τὸν ἐπίσκοπον] therefore must be without reproach." On this last passage, Huther in Meyer's Com remarks : " Paul in the beginning looked at the church in its unity, — only gradually does he make prominent its leaders. We must not infer that the churches in earlier time were without leadership, but only that in the later time circumstances were such as to require him to lay emphasis upon the pastor's office and work." See also Schaff, Teaching of the Twelve Apostles, 62-75.

McGiffert, in his Apostolic Church, puts the dates of Paul's Epistles considerably earlier, as for example : 1 Thess., circ. 48 ; 1 Cor., c. 51,52 ; Rom., 52, 53 ; Phil., 56-58 ; Eph., 52, 53, or 56-58 ; 1 Tim., 56-58. But even before the earliest Epistles of Paul comes James 5 : 14 — "Is any among you sick ? let him call for the elders of the church " — written about 48 A. D., and showing that within twenty years after the death of our Lord there had grown up a very definite form of church organization.

On the question how far our Lord and his apostles, in the organization of the church, availed themselves of the synagogue as a model, see Neander, Planting and Training, 28-34. The ministry of the church is without doubt an outgrowth and adaptation of the eldership of the synagogue. In the synagogue, there were elders who gave themselves to the study and expounding of the Scriptures. The synagogues held united prayer, and exercised discipline. They were democratic in government, and independent of each other. It has sometimes been said that election of officers by the membership of the church came from the Greek ἐκκλησία, or popular assembly. But Edersheim, Life and Times of Jesus the Messiah, 1 : 438, says of the elders of the synagogue that " their election depended on the choice of the congregation." Talmud, Berachob, 55 a : " No ruler is appointed over a congregation, unless the congregation is consulted."

(c) Any number of believers, therefore, may constitute themselves into a Christian church, by adopting for their rule of faith and practice Christ's law as laid down in the New Testament, and by associating themselves together, in accordance with it, for his worship and service. It is important, where practicable, that a council of churches be previously called, to advise the brethren proposing this union as to the desirableness of constituting a new and distinct local body ; and, if it be found desirable, to recognize them, after its formation, as being a church of Christ. But such action of a council, however valuable as affording ground for the fellowship of other churches, is not constitutive, but is simply declaratory ; and, without such action, the body of believers alluded to, if formed after the N. T. example, may notwithstanding be a true church of Christ. Still further, a band of converts, among the heathen or providentially precluded from access to existing churches, might rightfully appoint one of their number to baptize the rest, and then might organize, de novo, a New Testament church.

The church at Antioch was apparently self-created and self-directed. There is no evidence that any human authority, outside of the converts there, was invoked to constitute or to organize the church. As John Spillsbury put it about 1640 : "Where there is a beginning, some must be first." The initiative lies in the individual convert, and in his duty to obey the commands of Christ. No body of Christians can excuse itself for disobedience upon the plea that it has no officers. It can elect its own officers. Councils have no authority to constitute churches. Their work is simply that of recognizing the already existing organization and of pledging the fellowship of the churches which they represent. If God can of the stones raise up children unto Abraham, he can also raise up pastors and teachers from within the company of believers whom he has converted and saved.

Hagenbach, Hist. Doct., 2:294, quotes from Luther, as follows: "If a company of pious Christian laymen were captured and sent to a desert place, and had not among them an ordained priest, and were all agreed in the matter, and elected one and told him to baptize, administer the Mass, absolve, and preach, such a one would be as true a priest as if all the bishops and popes had ordained him." Dexter, Congregationalism, 51 — "Luther came near discovering and reproducing Congregationalism. Three things checked him : 1. he undervalued polity as compared with doctrine; 2. he reacted from Anabaptist fanaticisms ; 3. he thought Providence indicated that princes should lead and people should follow. So, while he and Zwingle alike held the Bible to teach that all ecclesiastical power inheres under Christ in the congregation of believers, the matter ended in an organization of superintendents and consistories, which gradually became fatally mixed up with the state."

III. GOVERNMENT OF THE CHURCH.

1. *Nature of this government in general.*

It is evident from the direct relation of each member of the church, and so of the church as a whole, to Christ as sovereign and lawgiver, that the government of the church, so far as regards the source of authority, is an absolute monarchy.

In ascertaining the will of Christ, however, and in applying his commands to providential exigencies, the Holy Spirit enlightens one member through the counsel of another, and as the result of combined deliberation, guides the whole body to right conclusions. This work of the Spirit is the foundation of the Scripture injunctions to unity. This unity, since it is a unity of the Spirit, is not an enforced, but an intelligent and willing, unity. While Christ is sole king, therefore, the government of the church, so far as regards the interpretation and execution of his will by the body, is an absolute democracy, in which the whole body of members is intrusted with the duty and responsibility of carrying out the laws of Christ as expressed in his word.

The seceders from the established church of Scotland, on the memorable 18th of May, 1843, embodied in their protest the following words: We go out "from an establishment which we loved and prized, through interference with conscience, the dishonor done to Christ's crown, and the rejection of his sole and supreme authority as King in his church." The church should be rightly ordered, since it is the representative and guardian of God's truth — its "pillar and ground" (1 Tim. 3 : 15) — the Holy Spirit working in and through it.

But it is this very relation of the church to Christ and his truth which renders it needful to insist upon the right of each member of the church to his private judgment as to the meaning of Scripture; in other words, absolute monarchy, in this case, requires for its complement an absolute democracy. President Wayland : "No individual Christian or number of individual Christians, no individual church or number of individual churches, has original authority, or has power over the whole. None can add to or subtract from the laws of Christ, or interfere with his direct and absolute sovereignty over the hearts and lives of his subjects." Each member, as equal to every other, has right to a voice in the decisions of the whole body; and no action of the majority can bind him against his conviction of duty to Christ.

John Cotton of Massachusetts Bay, 1643, Questions and Answers: "The royal government of the churches is in Christ, the stewardly or ministerial in the churches themselves." Cambridge Platform, 1648, 10th chapter—"So far as Christ is concerned, church government is a monarchy; so far as the brotherhood of the church is concerned, it resembles a democracy." Unfortunately the Platform goes further and declares that, in respect of the Presbytery and the Elders' power, it is also an aristocracy.

Herbert Spencer and John Stuart Mill, who held diverse views in philosophy, were once engaged in controversy. While the discussion was running through the press, Mr. Spencer, forced by lack of funds, announced that he would be obliged to discontinue the publication of his promised books on science and philosophy. Mr. Mill wrote him at once, saying that, while he could not agree with him in some things, he realized that Mr. Spencer's investigations on the whole made for the advance of truth, and so he himself would be glad to bear the expense of the remaining volumes. Here in the philosophical world is an example which may well be taken to heart by theologians. All Christians indeed are bound to respect in others the right of private judgment while stedfastly adhering themselves to the truth as Christ has made it known to them.

Loyola, founder of the Society of Jesus, dug for each neophyte a grave, and buried him all but the head, asking him: "Art thou dead?" When he said: "Yes!" the General added: "Rise then, and begin to serve, for I want only dead men to serve me." Jesus, on the other hand, wants only living men to serve him, for he gives life and gives it abundantly (John 10:10). The Salvation Army, in like manner, violates the principle of sole allegiance to Christ, and like the Jesuits puts the individual conscience and will under bonds to a human master. Good intentions may at first prevent evil results; but, since no man can be trusted with absolute power, the ultimate consequence, as in the case of the Jesuits, will be the enslavement of the subordinate members. Such autocracy does not find congenial soil in America,—hence the rebellion of Mr. and Mrs. Ballington Booth.

A. Proof that the government of the church is democratic or congregational.

(a) From the duty of the whole church to preserve unity in its action.

Rom. 12:16 — "Be of the same mind one toward another"; 1 Cor. 1:10 — "Now I beseech you .... that ye all speak the same thing, and that there be no divisions among you; but that ye be perfected together in the same mind and in the same judgment"; 2 Cor. 13:11 — "be of the same mind"; Eph. 4:3 — "giving diligence to keep the unity of the Spirit in the bond of peace"; Phil. 1:27 — "that ye stand fast in one spirit, with one soul striving for the faith of the gospel"; 1 Pet. 3:8 — "be ye all likeminded."

These exhortations to unity are not mere counsels to passive submission, such as might be given under a hierarchy, or to the members of a society of Jesuits; they are counsels to coöperation and to harmonious judgment. Each member, while forming his own opinions under the guidance of the Spirit, is to remember that the other members have the Spirit also, and that a final conclusion as to the will of God is to be reached only through comparison of views. The exhortation to unity is therefore an exhortation to be open-minded, docile, ready to subject our opinions to discussion, to welcome new light with regard to them, and to give up any opinion when we find it to be in the wrong. The church is in general to secure unanimity by moral suasion only; though, in case of wilful and perverse opposition to its decisions, it may be necessary to secure unity by excluding an obstructive member, for schism.

A quiet and peaceful unity is the result of the Holy Spirit's work in the hearts of Christians. New Testament church government proceeds upon the supposition that Christ dwells in all believers. Baptist polity is the best possible polity for good people. Christ has made no provision for an unregenerate church-membership, and for Satanic possession of Christians. It is best that a church in which Christ does not dwell should by dissension reveal its weakness, and fall to pieces; and any outward organization that conceals inward disintegration, and compels a merely formal union after the Holy Spirit has departed, is a hindrance instead of a help to true religion.

Congregationalism is not a strong government to look at. Neither is the solar system. Its enemies call it a rope of sand. It is rather a rope of iron filings held together by a magnetic current. Wordsworth: "Mightier far Than strength of nerve or sinew, or the sway Of magic portent over sun and star, Is love." President Wayland: "We do not need any hoops of iron or steel to hold us together." At high tide all the little pools along the sea shore are fused together. The unity produced by the inflowing of the Spirit of Christ is better than any mere external unity, whether of organization or of creed, whether of Romanism or of Protestantism. The times of the greatest external unity, as under Hildebrand, were times of the church's deepest moral corruption. A revival of religion is a better cure for church quarrels than any change in church organization could effect. In the early church, though there was no common government, unity was promoted by active intercourse. Hospitality, regular delegates, itin erant apostles and prophets, apostolic and other epistles, still later the gospels, perse cution, and even heresy, promoted unity — heresy compelling the exclusion of the unworthy and factious elements in the Christian community.

Dr. F. J. A. Hort, The Christian Ecclesia: " Not a word in the Epistle to the Ephesians exhibits the one *ecclesia* as made up of many *ecclesiæ*. . . . . The members which make up the one *ecclesia* are not communities, but individual men. . . . . The unity of the universal *ecclesia* . . . . is a truth of theology and religion, not a fact of what we call ecclesiastical politics. . . . . The *ecclesia* itself, *i. e.*, the sum of all its male members, is the primary body, and, it would seem, even the primary authority. . . . . Of officers higher than elders we find nothing that points to an institution or system, nothing like the Episcopal system of later times. . . . . The monarchical principle receives practical though limited recognition in the position ultimately held by St. James at Jerusalem, and in the temporary functions entrusted by St. Paul to Timothy and Titus." On this last statement Bartlett, in Contemp. Rev., July, 1897, says that James held an unique position as brother of our Lord, while Paul left the communities organized by Timothy and Titus to govern themselves, when once their organization was set agoing. There was no permanent diocesan episcopate, in which one man presided over many churches. The *ecclesiæ* had for their officers only bishops and deacons.

Should not the majority rule in a Baptist church? No, not a bare majority, when there are opposing convictions on the part of a large minority. What should rule is the mind of the Spirit. What indicates his mind is the gradual unification of conviction and opinion on the part of the whole body in support of some definite plan, so that the whole church moves together. The large church has the advantage over the small church in that the single crotchety member cannot do so much harm. One man in a small boat can easily upset it, but not so in the great ship. Patient waiting, persuasion, and prayer, will ordinarily win over the recalcitrant. It is not to be denied, however, that patience may have its limits, and that unity may sometimes need to be purchased by secession and the forming of a new local church whose members can work harmoniously together.

(*b*) From the responsibility of the whole church for maintaining pure doctrine and practice.

1 Tim. 3 : 15 — " the church of the living God, the pillar and ground of the truth " ; Jude 3 — " exhorting you to contend earnestly for the faith which was once for all delivered unto the saints " ; Rev. 2 and 3 — exhortations to the seven churches of Asia to maintain pure doctrine and practice. In all these passages, pastoral charges are given, not by a so-called bishop to his subordinate priests, but by an apostle to the whole church and to all its members.

In 1 Tim. 3 : 15, Dr. Hort would translate " a pillar and ground of the truth " — apparently refer ring to the local church as one of many. Eph. 3 : 18 — " strong to apprehend with all saints what is the breadth and length and height and depth." Edith Wharton, Vesalius in Zante, in N. A. Rev., Nov. 1892 — " Truth is many-tongued. What one man failed to speak, another finds Another word for. May not all converge, In some vast utterance of which you and I, Fallopius, were but the halting syllables? " Bruce, Training of the Twelve, shows that the Twelve probably knew the whole O. T. by heart. Pandita Ramabai, at Oxford, when visiting Max Müller, recited from the Rig Veda *passim*, and showed that she knew more of it by heart than the whole contents of the O. T.

(*c*) From the committing of the ordinances to the charge of the whole church to observe and guard. As the church expresses truth in her teaching, so she is to express it in symbol through the ordinances.

Mat. 28 : 19, 20 — " Go ye therefore, and make disciples of all the nations, baptizing them . . . . teaching them " ; *cf.* Luke 24 : 33 — " And they rose up that very hour . . . . found the eleven gathered together, and them that were with them "; Acts 1 : 15 — "And in these days Peter stood up in the midst of the brethren, and said (and there was a multitude of persons gathered together, about a hundred and twenty)"; 1 Cor. 15 : 6 — "then he appeared to above five hundred brethren at once " — these passages show that it was not to the eleven apostles alone that Jesus committed the ordinances.

1 Cor. 11 : 2 — "Now I praise you that ye remember me in all things, and hold fast the traditions, even as I delivered them to you "; *cf.* 23, 24 — "For I received of the Lord that which also I delivered unto you, that the Lord Jesus in the night in which he was betrayed took bread; and when he had given thanks, he brake it, and said, This is my body, which is for you: this do in remembrance of me " — here Paul commits the Lord's Supper into the charge, not of the body of officials, but of the whole church. Baptism and the Lord's Supper, therefore, are not to be administered at the discretion of the individual minister. He is simply the organ of the church; and pocket baptismal and communion services are without warrant. See Curtis, Progress of Baptist Principles, 299; Robinson, Harmony of Gospels, notes, § 170.

(*d*) From the election by the whole church, of its own officers and delegates. In Acts 14 : 23, the literal interpretation of χειροτονήσαντες is not to be pressed. In Titus 1 : 5, "when Paul empowers Titus to set presiding officers over the communities, this circumstance decides nothing as to the mode of choice, nor is a choice by the community itself thereby necessarily excluded."

Acts 1 : 23, 26 — "And they put forward two . . . . and they gave lots for them; and the lot fell upon Matthias; and he was numbered with the eleven apostles "; 6 : 3, 5 — "Look ye out therefore, brethren, from among you seven men of good report . . . . And the saying pleased the whole multitude: and they chose Stephen, ... and Philip, and Prochorus, and Nicanor, and Timon, and Parmenas, and Nicolaus " — as deacons; Acts 13 : 2, 3 — "And as they ministered to the Lord, and fasted, the Holy Spirit said, Separate me Barnabas and Saul for the work whereunto I have called them. Then, when they had fasted and prayed and laid their hands on them, they sent them away."

On this passage, see Meyer's comment: " 'Ministered' here expresses the act of celebrating divine service on the part of the whole church. To refer αὐτῶν to the 'prophets and teachers' is forbidden by the ἀφορίσατε — and by verse 3. This interpretation would confine this most important mission-act to five persons, of whom two were the missionaries sent; and the church would have had no part in it, even through its presbyters. This agrees, neither with the common possession of the Spirit in the apostolic church, nor with the concrete cases of the choice of an apostle (ch. 1) and of deacons (ch. 6). Compare 14:27, where the returned missionaries report to the church. The imposition of hands (verse 3) is by the presbyters, as representatives of the whole church. The subject in verses 2 and 3 is 'the church' — (represented by the presbyters in this case). The church sends the missionaries to the heathen, and consecrates them through its elders."

Acts 15 : 2, 4, 22, 30 — "the brethren appointed that Paul and Barnabas, and certain other of them, should go up to Jerusalem . . . . And when they were come to Jerusalem, they were received of the church and the apostles and the elders . . . . Then it seemed good to the apostles and the elders, with the whole church, to choose men out of their company, and send them to Antioch with Paul and Barnabas . . . . So they . . . . came down to Antioch; and having gathered the multitude together, they delivered the epistle "; 2 Cor. 8 : 19 — " who was also appointed by the churches to travel with us in the matter of this grace " — the contribution for the poor in Jerusalem; Acts 14 : 23 — "And when they had appointed (χειροτονήσαντες) for them elders in every church " — the apostles announced the election of the church, as a College President confers degrees, *i. e.*, by announcing degrees conferred by the Board of Trustees. To this same effect witnesses the newly discovered Teaching of the Twelve Apostles, chapter 15: "Appoint therefore for yourselves bishops and deacons."

The derivation of χειροτονήσαντες, holding up of hands, as in a popular vote, is not to be pressed, any more than is the derivation of ἐκκλησία from καλέω. The former had come to mean simply 'to appoint,' without reference to the manner of appointment, as the latter had come to mean an 'assembly,' without reference to the calling of its members by God. That the church at Antioch "separated" Paul and Barnabas, and that this was not done simply by the five persons mentioned, is shown by the fact that, when Paul and Barnabas returned from the missionary journey, they reported not to these five, but to the whole church. So when the church at Antioch sent delegates to Jerusalem, the letter of the Jerusalem church is thus addressed: "The apostles and the elders, brethren, unto the brethren who are of the Gentiles in Antioch and Syria and Cilicia" (Acts 15 : 23). The Twelve had only spiritual authority. They could advise, but they did not command. Hence they could not transmit government, since they had it not. They could demand obedience, only as they convinced their hearers that their word was truth. It was not they who commanded, but their Master.

Hackett, Com. on Acts — "" χειροτονησαντες is not to be pressed, since Paul and Barnabas constitute the persons ordaining. It may possibly indicate a concurrent appointment, in accordance with the usual practice of universal suffrage; but the burden of proof lies on those who would so modify the meaning of the verb. The word *is* frequently used in the sense of choosing, appointing, with reference to the formality of raising the hand." *Per contra*, see Meyer, *in loco:* "The church officers were elective. As appears from analogy of 6:2-6 (election of deacons), the word χειροτονήσαντες retains its etymological sense, and does not mean 'constituted' or 'created.' Their choice was a recognition of a gift already bestowed, — not the ground of the office and source authority, but merely the means by which the gift becomes [known, recognized, and an actual office in the church."

Baumgarten, Apostolic History, 1:456 — "They — the two apostles — allow presbyters to be chosen for the community by voting." Alexander, Com. on Acts — "The method of election here, as the expression χειροτονήσαντες indicates, was the same as that in Acts 6:5, 6, where the people chose the seven, and the twelve ordained them." Barnes, Com. on Acts: "The apostles presided in the assembly where the choice was made, — appointed them in the usual way by the suffrage of the people." Dexter, Congregationalism, 138 — "'Ordained' means here 'prompted and secured the election' of elders in every church." So in Titus 1:5 — "appoint elders in every city." Compare the Latin: "dictator consules creavit" = prompted and secured the election of consuls by the people. See Neander, Church History, 1:189; Guericke, Church History, 1:110; Meyer, on Acts 13:2.

The Watchman, Nov. 7, 1901 — "The root-difficulty with many schemes of statecraft is to be found in deep-seated distrust of the capacities and possibilities of men. Wendell Phillips once said that nothing so impressed him with the power of the gospel to solve our problems as the sight of a prince and a peasant kneeling side by side in a European Cathedral." Dr. W. R. Huntington makes the strong points of Congregationalism to be: 1. a lofty estimate of the value of trained intelligence in the Christian ministry; 2. a clear recognition of the duty of every lay member of a church to take an active interest in its affairs, temporal as well as spiritual. He regards the weaknesses of Congregationalism to be: 1. a certain incapacity for expansion beyond the territorial limits within which it is indigenous; 2. an undervaluation of the mystical or sacramental, as contrasted with the doctrinal and practical sides of religion. He argues fo the object-symbolism as well as the verbal-symbolism of the real presence and grace c our Lord Jesus Christ. Dread of idolatry, he thinks, should not make us indifferent to the value of sacraments. Baptists, we reply, may fairly claim that they escape both of these charges against ordinary Congregationalism, in that they have shown unlimited capacity of expansion, and in that they make very much of the symbolism of the ordinances.

(*e*) From the power of the whole church to exercise discipline. Passages which show the right of the whole body to exclude, show also the right of the whole body to admit, members.

Mat. 18:17 — "And if he refuse to hear them, tell it unto the church: and if he refuse to hear the church also, let him be unto thee as the Gentile and the publican. Verily I say unto you, What things soever ye shall bind on earth shall be bound in heaven; and what things soever ye shall loose on earth shall be loosed in heaven" — words often inscribed over Roman Catholic confessionals, but improperly, since they refer not to the decisions of a single priest, but to the decisions of the whole body of believers guided by the Holy Spirit. In Mat. 18:17, quoted above, we see that the church has authority, that it is bound to take cognizance of offences, and that its action is final. If there had been in the mind of our Lord any other than a democratic form of government, he would have referred the aggrieved party to pastor, priest, or presbytery, and, in case of a wrong decision by the church, would have mentioned some synod or assembly to which the aggrieved person might appeal. But he throws all the responsibility upon the whole body of believers. *Cf.* Num. 15:35 — "all the congregation shall stone him with stones" — the man who gathered sticks on the Sabbath day. Every Israelite was to have part in the execution of the penalty.

1 Co.. 5:4, 5, 13 — "ye being gathered together . . . . to deliver such a one unto Satan . . . . Put away the wicked man from among yourselves"; 2 Cor. 2:6, 7 — "Sufficient to such a one is this punishment which was inflicted by the many; so that contrariwise ye should rather forgive him and comfort him"; 7:11 — "For behold, this self-same thing . . . . what earnest care it wrought in you, yea, what clearing of yourselves . . . . In every thing ye approved yourselves to be pure in the matter"; 2 Thess. 3:6. 14. 15 — "withdraw yourselves from every brother that

walketh disorderly . . . . if any man obeyeth not our word by this epistle, note that man, that ye have no company with him, to the end that he may be ashamed. And yet count him not as an enemy, but admonish him as a brother." The evils in the church at Corinth were such as could exist only in a democratic body, and Paul does not enjoin upon the church a change of government, but a change of heart. Paul does not himself excommunicate the incestuous man, but he urges the church to excommunicate him.

The educational influence upon the whole church of this election of pastors and deacons, choosing of delegates, admission and exclusion of members, management of church finance and general conduct of business, carrying on of missionary operations and raising of contributions, together with responsibility for correct doctrine and practice, cannot be overestimated. The whole body can know those who apply for admission, better than pastors or elders can. To put the whole government of the church into the hands of a few is to deprive the membership of one great means of Christian training and progress. Hence the pastor's duty is to develop the self-government of the church. The missionary should not command, but advise. That minister is most successful who gets the whole *body* to move, and who renders the church independent of himself. The test of his work is not while he is with them, but after he leaves them. Then it can be seen whether he has taught them to follow him, or to follow Christ; whether he has led them to the formation of habits of independent Christian activity, or whether he has made them passively dependent upon himself.

It should be the ambition of the pastor not "to run the church," but to teach the church intelligently and Scripturally to manage its own affairs. The word "minister" means, not master, but servant. The true pastor inspires, but he does not drive. He is like the trusty mountain guide, who carries a load thrice as heavy as that of the man he serves, who leads in safe paths and points out dangers, but who neither shouts nor compels obedience. The individual Christian should be taught: 1. to realize the privilege of church membership; 2. to fit himself to use his privilege; 3. to exercise his rights as a church member; 4. to glory in the New Testament system of church government, and to defend and propagate it.

A Christian pastor can either rule, or he can have the reputation of ruling; but he can not do both. Real ruling involves a sinking of self, a working through others, a doing of nothing that some one else can be got to do. The reputation of ruling leads sooner or later to the loss of real influence, and to the decline of the activities of the church itself. See Coleman, Manual of Prelacy and Ritualism, 87-125; and on the advantages of Congregationalism over every other form of church-polity, see Dexter, Congregationalism, 236-296. Dexter, 290, note, quotes from Belcher's Religious Denominations of the U. S., 184, as follows : " Jefferson said that he considered Baptist church government the only form of pure democracy which then existed in the world, and had concluded that it would be the best plan of government for the American Colonies. This was eight or ten years before the American Revolution." On Baptist democracy, see Thomas Armitage, in N. Amer. Rev., March, 1887 : 232-243.

John Fiske, Beginnings of New England : " In a church based upon such a theology [that of Calvin], there was no room for prelacy. Each single church tended to become an independent congregation of worshipers, constituting one of the most effective schools that has ever existed for training men in local self-government." Schurman, Agnosticism, 160 — " The Baptists, who are nominally Calvinists, are now, as they were at the beginning of the century, second in numerical rank [in America]; but their fundamental principle — the Bible, the Bible only — taken in connection with their polity, has enabled them silently to drop the old theology and unconsciously to adjust themselves to the new spiritual environment." We prefer to say that Baptists have not dropped the old theology, but have given it new interpretation and application ; see A. H. Strong, Our Denominational Outlook, Sermon in Cleveland, 1904.

B. **Erroneous views as to church government refuted by the foregoing passages.**

(*a*) The world-church theory, or the Romanist view. — This holds that all local churches are subject to the supreme authority of the bishop of Rome, as the successor of Peter and the infallible vicegerent of Christ, and, as thus united, constitute the one and only church of Christ on earth. We reply :

First,—Christ gave no such supreme authority to Peter. Mat. 16 : 18, 19, simply refers to the personal position of Peter as first confessor of Christ and preacher of his name to Jews and Gentiles. Hence other apostles also constituted the foundation (Eph. 2 : 20 ; Rev. 21 : 14). On one occasion, the counsel of James was regarded as of equal weight with that of Peter (Acts 15 : 7-30), while on another occasion Peter was rebuked by Paul (Gal. 2 : 11), and Peter calls himself only a fellow-elder (1 Pet. 5 : 1).

Mat. 16 : 18, 19 — "And I also say unto thee, that thou art Peter, and upon this rock I will build my church; and the gates of Hades shall not prevail against it. I will give unto thee the keys of the kingdom of heaven : and whatsoever thou shalt bind on earth shall be bound in heaven; and whatsoever thou shall loose on earth shalt be loosed in heaven." Peter exercised this power of the keys for both Jews and Gentiles, by being the first to preach Christ to them, and so admit them to the kingdom of heaven. The "rock" is a confessing heart. The confession of Christ makes Peter a rock upon which the church can be built. Plumptre on Epistles of Peter, Introd., 14 — " He was a stone — one with that rock with which he was now joined by an indissoluble union." But others come to be associated with him : Eph. 2 : 20 — "built upon the foundation of the apostles and prophets, Christ Jesus himself being the chief corner stone"; Rev. 21 : 14 — "And the wall of the city had twelve foundations, and on them twelve names of the twelve apostles of the Lamb." Acts 15 : 7-30 — the Council of Jerusalem. Gal. 2 : 11 — "But when Cephas came to Antioch, I resisted him to the face, because he stood condemned"; 1 Pet. 5 : 1 — " The elders therefore among you I exhort, who am a fellow-elder."

Here it should be remembered that three things were necessary to constitute an apostle : (1) he must have seen Christ after his resurrection, so as to be a witness to the fact that Christ had risen from the dead ; (2) he must be a worker of miracles, to certify that he was Christ's messenger ; (3) he must be an inspired teacher of Christ's truth, so that his final utterances are the very word of God. In Rom. 16 : 7 — "Salute Andronicus and Junias, my kinsmen, and my fellow-prisoners, who are of note among the apostles" means simply : ' who are highly esteemed among, or by, the apostles.' Barnabas is called an apostle, in the etymological sense of a messenger : Acts 13 : 2, 3 — "Separate me Barnabas and Saul for the work whereunto I have called them. Then, when they had fasted and prayed and laid their hands on them, they sent them away"; Heb. 3 : 1 — "consider the Apostle and High Priest of our confession, even Jesus." In this latter sense. the number of the apostles was not limited to twelve.

Protestants err in denying the reference in Mat. 16 : 18 to Peter ; Christ recognizes Peter's *personality* in the founding of his kingdom. But Romanists equally err in ignoring Peter's *confession* as constituting him the "rock." Creeds and confessions alone will never convert the world ; they need to be embodied in living personalities in order to save ; this is the grain of correct doctrine in Romanism. On the other hand, men without a faith, which they are willing to confess at every cost, will never convert the world ; there must be a substance of doctrine with regard to sin, and with regard to Christ as the divine Savior from sin ; this is the just contention of Protestantism. Baptist doctrine combines the merits of both systems. It has both personality and confession. It is not hierarchical, but experiential. It insists, not upon abstractions, but upon life. Truth without a body is as powerless as a body without truth. A flag without an army is even worse than an army without a flag. Phillips Brooks: "The truth of God working through the personality of man has been the salvation of the world." Pascal : " Catholicism is a church without a religion ; Protestantism is a religion without a church." Yes, we reply, if church means hierarchy.

Secondly, — If Peter had such authority given him, there is no evidence that he had power to transmit it to others.

Fisher, Hist. Christian Church, 247 — "William of Occam (1280-1347) composed a treatise on the power of the pope. He went beyond his predecessors in arguing that the church, since it has its unity in Christ, is not under the necessity of being subject to a single primate. He placed the Emperor and the General Council above the pope, as his judges. In matters of faith he would not allow infallibility even to the General Councils. ' Only Holy Scripture and the beliefs of the universal church are of absolute validity.' " W. Rauschenbusch, in The Examiner, July 28, 1892 — " The age of an ecclesiastical organization, instead of being an argument in its favor, is presumptive evidence against it, because all bodies organized for moral or religious ends manifest such a frightful inclination to become corrupt. . . . . Marks of the true church are: present spiritual power, loyalty to Jesus, an unworldly morality, seeking and saving the lost, self-sacrifice and self-crucifixion."

Romanism holds to a transmitted infallibility. The pope is infallible: 1. when he speaks as pope ; 2. when he speaks for the whole church ; 3. when he defines doctrine, or passes a final judgment ; 4. when the doctrine thus defined is within the sphere of faith or morality ; see Brandis, in N. A. Rev., Dec. 1892 : 654. Schurman, Belief in God, 114 —" Like the Christian pope, Zeus is conceived in the Homeric poems to be fallible as an individual, but infallible as head of the sacred convocation. The other gods are only his representatives and executives." But, even if the primacy of the Roman pontiff were acknowledged, there would still be abundant proof that he is not infallible. The condemnation of the letters of Pope Honorius, acknowledging monothelism and ordering it to be preached, by Pope Martin I and the first Council of Lateran in 649, shows that both could not be right. Yet both were *ex cathedra* utterances, one denying what the other affirmed. Perrone concedes that only one error committed by a pope in an *ex cathedra* announcement would be fatal to the doctrine of papal infallibility.

Martineau, Seat of Authority, 139, 140, gives instances of papal inconsistencies and contradictions, and shows that Roman Catholicism does not answer to either one of its four notes or marks of a true church, *viz.*: 1. unity ; 2. sanctity ; 3. universality ; 4. apostolicity. Dean Stanley had an interview with Pope Pius IX, and came away saying that the infallible man had made more blunders in a twenty minutes' conversation than any person he had ever met. Dr. Fairbairn facetiously defines infallibility, as "inability to detect errors even where they are most manifest." He speaks of " the folly of the men who think they hold God in their custody, and distribute him to whomsoever they will." The Pope of Rome can no more trace his official descent from Peter than Alexander the Great could trace his personal descent from Jupiter.

Thirdly,—There is no conclusive evidence that Peter ever was at Rome, much less that he was bishop of Rome.

Clement of Rome refers to Peter as a martyr, but he makes no claim for Rome as the place of his martyrdom The tradition that Peter preached at Rome and founded a church there dates back only to Dionysius of Corinth and Irenæus of Lyons, who did not write earlier than the eighth decade of the second century, or more than a hundred years after Peter's death. Professor Lepsius of Jena submitted the Roman tradition to a searching examination, and came to the conclusion that Peter was never in Italy.

A. A. Hodge, in Princetoniana, 129 —" Three unproved assumptions : 1. that Peter was primate ; 2. that Peter was bishop of Rome ; 3. that Peter was primate *and* bishop of Rome. The last is not unimportant ; because Clement, for instance, might have succeeded to the bishopric of Rome without the primacy ; as Queen Victoria came to the crown of England, but not to that of Hanover. Or, to come nearer home, Ulysses S. Grant was president of the United States and husband of Mrs. Grant. Mr. Hayes succeeded him, but not in both capacities ! "

On the question whether Peter founded the Roman Church, see Meyer, Com. on Romans, transl., vol. 1 : 23 —" Paul followed the principle of not interfering with another apostle's field of labor. Hence Peter could not have been laboring at Rome, at the time when Paul wrote his epistle to the Romans from Ephesus ; *cf.* Acts 19 : 21 ; Rom. 15 : 20 ; 2 Cor. 10 : 16." Meyer thinks Peter was martyred at Rome, but that he did not found the Roman church, the origin of which is unknown. "The Epistle to the Romans," he says, "since Peter cannot have labored at Rome before it was written, is a fact destructive of the historical basis of the Papacy " (p. 28). See also Elliott, Horæ Apocalypticæ, 3 : 560.

Fourthly,—There is no evidence that he really did so appoint the bishops of Rome as his successors.

Denney, Studies in Theology, 191 —" The church was first the company of those united to Christ and living in Christ ; then it became a society based on creed ; finally a society based on clergy." A. J. Gordon, Ministry of the Spirit, 130 —" The Holy Spirit is the real ' Vicar of Christ.' Would any one desire to find the clue to the great apostasy whose dark eclipse now covers two thirds of nominal Christendom, here it is : The rule and authority of the Holy Spirit ignored in the church ; the servants of the house assuming mastery and encroaching more and more on the prerogatives of the Head, till at last one man sets himself up as the administrator of the church, and daringly usurps the name of the Vicar of Christ." See also R. V. Littledale, The Petrine Claims.

The secret of Baptist success and progress is in putting truth before unity. James 3:17 —"the wisdom that is from above is first pure, then peaceable." The substitution of external for internal unity, of which the apostolic succession, so called, is a sign and symbol, is of a piece with the whole sacramental scheme of salvation. Men cannot be brought into the kingdom of heaven, nor can they be made good ministers of Jesus Christ, by priestly manipulation. The Frankish wholesale conversion of races, the Jesuitical putting of obedience instead of life, the identification of the church with the nation, are all false methods ot diffusing Christianity. The claims f Rome need irrefragible proof, if they are to be accepted. But they have no warrar t in Scripture or in history. Methodist Review: " As long as the Bible is recognized to be authoritative, the church will face Romeward as little as Leo X will visit America to attend a Methodist campmeeting, or Justin D. Fulton be elected as his successor in the Papal chair." See Gore, Incarnation, 208, 209.

Fifthly,— If Peter did so appoint the bishops of Rome, the evidence of continuous succession since that time is lacking.

On the weakness of the argument for apostolic succession, see remarks with regard to the national church theory, below. Dexter, Congregationalism, 715—" To spiritualize and evangelize Romanism, or High Churchism, will be to Congregationalize it." If all the Roman Catholics who have come to America had remained Roman Catholics, there would be sixteen millions of them, whereas there are actually only eight millions. If it be said that the remainder have no religion, we reply that they have just as much religion as they had before. American democracy has freed them from the domination of the priest, but it has not deprived them of anything but external connection with a corrupt church. It has given them opportunity for the first time to come in contact with the church of the New Testament, and to accept the offer of salvation through simple faith in Jesus Christ.

" Romanism," says Dorner, " identifies the church and the kingdom of God. The professedly perfect hierarchy is itself the church, or its essence." Yet Moehler, the greatest modern advocate of the Romanist system, himself acknowledges that there were popes before the Reformation " whom hell has swallowed up "; see Dorner, Hist. Prot. Theol., Introd., ad finem. If the Romanist asks: " Where was your church before Luther ? " the Protestant may reply : " Where was your face this morning before it was washed ? " Disciples of Christ have sometimes kissed the feet of Antichrist, but it recalls an ancient story. When an Athenian noble thus, in old times, debased himself to the King of Persia, his fellow-citizens at Athens doomed him to death. See Coleman, Manual on Prelacy and Ritualism, 265-274; Park, in Bib. Sac., 2:451; Princeton Rev., Apr. 1876:265.

Sixthly,— There is abundant evidence that a hierarchical form of church government is corrupting to the church and dishonoring to Christ.

A. J. Gordon, Ministry of the Spirit, 131-140—" Catholic writers claim that the Pope, as the Vicar of Christ, is the only mouthpiece of the Holy Ghost. But the Spirit has been given to the church as a whole, that is, to the body of regenerated believers, and to every member of that body according to his measure. The sin of sacerdotalism is, that it arrogates for a usurping few that which belongs to every member of Christ's mystical body. It is a suggestive fact that the name κλῆρος, ' the charge allotted to you,' which Peter gives to the church as 'the flock of God' (1 Pet. 5:2), when warning the elders against being lords over God's heritage, now appears in ecclesiastical usage as 'the clergy,' with its orders of pontiff and prelates and lord bishops, whose appointed function it is to exercise lordship over Christ's flock. . . . . But committees and majorities may take the place of the Spirit, just as perfectly as a pope or a bishop. . . . . This is the reason why the light has been extinguished in many a candlestick. . . . . The body remains, but the breath is withdrawn. The Holy Spirit is the only Administrator."

Canon Melville: " Make peace if you will with Popery, receive it into your Senate, enshrine it in your chambers, plant it in your hearts. But be ye certain, as certain as there is a heaven above you and a God over you, that the Popery thus honored and embraced is the Popery that was loathed and degraded by the holiest of your fathers; and the same in haughtiness, the same in intolerance, which lorded it over kings, assumed the prerogative of Deity, crushed human liberty, and slew the saints of God." On the strength and weakness of Romanism, see Harnack, What is Christianity? 246-263

(*b*) The national-church theory, or the theory of provincial or national churches.—This holds that all members of the church in any province or nation are bound together in provincial or national organization, and that this organization has jurisdiction over the local churches. We reply:

First,—the theory has no support in the Scriptures. There is no evidence that the word ἐκκλησία in the New Testament ever means a national church organization. 1 Cor. 12 : 28, Phil. 3 : 6, and 1 Tim. 3 : 15, may be more naturally interpreted as referring to the generic church. In Acts 9 : 31, ἐκκλησία is a mere generalization for the local churches then and there existing, and implies no sort of organization among them.

1 Cor. 12 : 28 —"And God hath set some in the church, first apostles, secondly prophets, thirdly teachers, then miracles, then gifts of healings, helps, governments, divers kinds of tongues"; Phil. 3 : 6 —"as touching zeal, persecuting the church"; 1 Tim. 3 : 15 —"that thou mayest know how men ought to behave themselves in the house of God, which is the church of the living God, the pillar and ground of the truth"; Acts 9 : 31—"So the church throughout all Judæa and Galilee and Samaria had peace, being edified." For advocacy of the Presbyterian system, see Cunningham, Historical Theology, 2 : 514-556; McPherson, Presbyterianism. *Per contra,* see Jacob, Eccl. Polity of N. T., 9 —"There is no example of a national church in the New Testament. "

Secondly,— It is contradicted by the intercourse which the New Testament churches held with each other as independent bodies,— for example at the Council of Jerusalem (Acts. 15 : 1–35)

Acts 15 : 2, 6, 13, 19, 22 —"the brethren appointed that Paul and Barnabas, and certain other of them, should go up to Jerusalem unto the apostles and elders about this question. . . . . And the apostles and the elders were gathered together to consider of this matter. . . . . James answered . . . . my judgment is, that we trouble not them that from among the Gentiles turn to God. . . . . it seemed good to the apostles and the elders, with the whole church, to choose men out of their company, and send them to Antioch with Paul and Barnabas." McGiffert, Apostolic Church, 645 —"The steps of developing organization were : 1. Recognition of the teaching of the apostles as exclusive standard and norm of Christian truth ; 2. Confinement to a specific office, the Catholic office of bishop, of the power to determine what is the teaching of the apostles ; 3. Designation of a specific institution, the Catholic church, as the sole channel of divine grace. The Twelve, in the church of Jerusalem, had only a purely spiritual authority. They could advise, but they did not command. Hence they were not qualified to transmit authority to others. They had no absolute authority themselves."

Thirdly,— It has no practical advantages over the Congregational polity, but rather tends to formality, division, and the extinction of the principles of self-government and direct responsibility to Christ.

E. G. Robinson : "The Anglican schism is the most sectarian of all the sects." Principal Rainey thus describes the position of the Episcopal Church : "They will not recognize the church standing of those who recognize them ; and they only recognize the church standing of those, Greeks and Latins, who do not recognize them. Is not that an odd sort of Catholicity ? " "Every priestling hides a popeling." The elephant going through the jungle saw a brood of young partridges that had just lost their mother. Touched with sympathy he said : "I will be a mother to you," and so he sat down upon them, as he had seen their mother do. Hence we speak of the "incumbent " of such and such a parish.

There were no councils that claimed authority till the second century, and the independence of the churches was not given up until the third or fourth century. In Bp. Lightfoot's essay on the Christian Ministry, in the appendix to his Com. on Philippians, progress to episcopacy is thus described : "In the time of Ignatius, the bishop, then *primus inter pares*, was regarded only as a centre of unity ; in the time of Irenæus, as a depositary of primitive truth ; in the time of Cyprian, as absolute vicegerent of Christ in things spiritual." Nothing is plainer than the steady degeneration of church polity in the hands of the Fathers. Archibald Alexander : "A better name than Church Fathers for these men would be church babies. Their theology was infantile. " Luther : " Never mind the Scribes,— what saith the Scripture ? "

Fourthly,—It is inconsistent with itself, in binding a professedly spiritual church by formal and geographical lines.

Instance the evils of Presbyterianism in practice. Dr. Park says that "the split between the Old and the New School was due to an attempt on the part of the majority to impose their will on the minority. . . . . The Unitarian defection in New England would have ruined Presbyterian churches, but it did not ruin Congregational churches. A Presbyterian church may be deprived of the minister it has chosen, by the votes of neighboring churches, or by the few leading men who control them, or by one single vote in a close contest." We may illustrate by the advantage of the adjustable card-catalogue over the old method of keeping track of books in a library.

A. J. Gordon, Ministry of the Spirit, 137, note—" By the candlesticks in the Revelation being seven, instead of one as in the tabernacle, we are taught that whereas, in the Jewish dispensation, God's visible church was one, in the Gentile dispensation there are many visible churches, and that Christ himself recognizes them alike" (quoted from Garratt, Com. on Rev., 32). Bishop Moule, Veni Creator, 131, after speaking of the unity of the Spirit, goes on to say : " Blessed will it be for the church and for the world when these principles shall so vastly prevail as to find expression from within in a harmonious counterpart of order ; a far different thing from what is, I cannot but think, an illusory prospect—the attainment of such internal unity by a previous exaction of exterior governmental uniformity."

Fifthly,—It logically leads to the theory of Romanism. If two churches need a superior authority to control them and settle their differences, then two countries and two hemispheres need a common ecclesiastical government,—and a world-church, under one visible head, is Romanism.

Hatch, in his Bampton Lectures on Organization of Early Christian Churches, without discussing the evidence from the New Testament, proceeds to treat of the post-apostolic development of organization, as if the existence of a germinal Episcopacy very soon *after* the apostles proved such a system to be legitimate or obligatory. In reply, we would ask whether we are under moral obligation to conform to whatever succeeds in developing itself. If so, then the priests of Baal, as well as the priests of Rome, had just claims to human belief and obedience. Prof. Black : " We have no objection to antiquity, if they will only go back far enough. We wish to listen, not only to the fathers of the church, but also to the grandfathers."

Phillips Brooks speaks of "the fantastic absurdity of apostolic succession." And with reason, for in the Episcopal system, bishops qualified to ordain must be : (1) baptized persons ; (2) not scandalously immoral ; (3) not having obtained office by bribery ; (4) must not have been deposed. In view of these qualifications, Archbishop Whately pronounces the doctrine of apostolic succession untenable, and declares that " there is no Christian minister existing now, who can trace up with complete certainty his own ordination, through perfectly regular steps, to the time of the apostles." See Macaulay's Review of Gladstone on Church and State, in his Essays, 4 : 166-178. There are breaks in the line, and a chain is only as strong as its weakest part. See Presb. Rev., 1886 : 89-126. Mr. Flanders called Phillips Brooks "an Episcopalian with leanings toward Christianity." Bishop Brooks replied that he could not be angry with "such a dear old moth-eaten angel." On apostolic succession, see C. Anderson Scott, Evangelical Doctrine, 37-48, 267-288.

Apostolic succession has been called the pipe-line conception of divine grace. To change the figure, it may be compared to the monopoly of communication with Europe by the submarine cable. But we are not confined to the pipe-line or to the cable. There are wells of salvation in our private grounds, and wireless telegraphy practicable to every human soul, apart from any control of corporations.

We see leanings toward the world-church idea in Pananglican and Panpresbyterian Councils. Human nature ever tends to substitute the unity of external organization for the spiritual unity which belongs to all believers in Christ. There is no necessity for common government, whether Presbyterian or Episcopal ; since Christ's truth and Spirit are competent to govern all as easily as one. It is a remarkable fact, that the Baptist denomination, without external bonds, has maintained a greater unity in doctrine, and a closer general conformity to New Testament standards, than the churches which adopt the principle of episcopacy, or of provincial organization. With Abp. Whately, we find the true symbol of Christian unity in " the tree of life, bearing twelve manner of fruits " (Rev. 22 : 2).   *Cf.* John 10 : 16 — γενήσονται μία ποίμνη, εἰς ποιμήν —" they shall become one flock, one shepherd "=. not one fold, not external unity, but one flock in many folds.   See Jacob, Eccl. Polity of N. T., 130 ; Dexter, Congregationalism, 256 ; Coleman, Manual on Prelacy and Ritualism, 128-264 ; Albert Barnes, Apostolic Church.

As testimonies to the adequacy of Baptist polity to maintain sound doctrine, we quote from the Congregationalist, Dr. J. L. Withrow : " There is not a denomination of evangelical Christians that is throughout as sound theologically as the Baptist denomination.   There is not an evangelical denomination in America to-day that is as true to the simple plain gospel of God, as it is recorded in the word, as the Baptist denomination."   And the Presbyterian, Dr. W. G. T. Shedd, in a private letter dated Oct. 1, 1886, writes as follows : " Among the denominations, we all look to the Baptists for steady and firm adherence to sound doctrine.   You have never had any internal doctrinal conflicts, and from year to year you present an undivided front in defense of the Calvinistic faith.   Having no judicatures and regarding the local church as the unit, it is remarkable that you maintain such a unity and solidarity of belief.   If you could impart your secret to our Congregational brethren, I think that some of them at least would thank you."

A. H. Strong, Sermon in London before the Baptist World Congress, July, 1905 — " Coöperation with Christ involves the spiritual unity not only of all Baptists with one another, but of all Baptists with the whole company of true believers of every name. We cannot, indeed, be true to our convictions without organizing into one body those who agree with us in our interpretation of the Scriptures.   Our denominational divisions are at present necessities of nature.   But we regret these divisions, and, as we grow in grace and in the knowledge of the truth, we strive, at least in spirit, to rise above them. In America our farms are separated from one another by fences, and in the springtime, when the wheat and barley are just emerging from the earth, these fences are very distinguishable and unpleasing features of the landscape.   But later in the season, when the corn has grown and the time of harvest is near, the grain is so tall that the fences are entirely hidden, and for miles together you seem to see only a single field.   It is surely our duty to confess everywhere and always that we are first Christians and only secondly Baptists.   The tie which binds us to Christ is more important in our eyes than that which binds us to those of the same faith and order.   We live in hope that the Spirit of Christ in us, and in all other Christian bodies, may induce such growth of mind and heart that the sense of unity may not only overtop and hide the fences of division, but may ultimately do away with these fences altogether."

2. *Officers of the Church.*

A.   The number of offices in the church is two : — first, the office of bishop, presbyter, or pastor ; and, secondly, the office of deacon.

(*a*) That the appellations ' bishop,' ' presbyter,' and ' pastor ' designate the same office and order of persons, may be shown from Acts 20 : 28 — ἐπισκόπους ποιμαίνειν (*cf.* 17 — πρεσβυτέρους) ; Phil. 1 : 1 ; 1 Tim. 3 : 1, 8 ; Titus 1 : 5, 7 ; 1 Pet. 5 : 1, 2 — πρεσβυτέρους . . . . παρακαλῶ ὁ συμπρεσβύτερος . . . . ποιμάνατε ποίμνιον . . . . ἐπισκοποῦντες.   Conybeare and Howson : " The terms ' bishop ' and ' elder ' are used in the New Testament as equivalent, — the former denoting (as its meaning of overseer implies) the duties, the latter the rank, of the office."   See passages quoted in Gieseler, Church History, 1 : 90, note 1 — as, for example, Jerome : " Apud veteres iidem episcopi et presbyteri, quia illud nomen dignitatis est, hoc ætatis.   Idem est ergo presbyter qui episcopus."

Acts 20 : 28 — " Take heed unto yourselves, and to all the flock, in which the Holy Spirit hath made you bishops [marg. 'overseers'], to feed [lit. 'to shepherd,' 'be pastors of'] the church of the Lord which he purchased with his own blood " ; *cf.* 17 — " the elders of the church " are those whom Paul addresses as bishops or overseers, and whom he exhorts to be good pastors.   Phil. 1 : 1 — " bishops and deacons " ; 1 Tim. 3 : 1, 8 — " If a man seeketh the office of a bishop, he desireth a good work . . . . Deacons in like manner must be grave " ; Tit. 1 : 5, 7 — " appoint elders in every city . . . . For the bishop must be blameless " ; 1 Pet. 5 : 1, 2 — " The elders therefore among you I exhort, who am a fellow-elder . . . . Tend [lit. 'shepherd,' 'be pastors of'] the flock of God which is among you, exercising the oversight [acting as bishops], not of constraint, but willingly, according to the will of God." In this last passage, Westcott and Hort, with Tischendorf's 8th edition, follow אֲ and B in omitting ἐπισκοποῦντες. Tregelles and our Revised Version follow A and אc in retaining it. Rightly, we think; since it is easy to see how, in a growing ecclesiasticism, it should have been omitted, from the feeling that too much was here ascribed to a mere presbyter.

Lightfoot, Com. on Philippians, 95-99—"It is a fact now generally recognized by theologians of all shades of opinion that in the language of the N. T. the same officer in the church is called indifferently 'bishop' (ἐπίσκοπος) and 'elder' or 'presbyter' (πρεσβύτερος). .... To these special officers the priestly functions and privileges of the Christian people are never regarded as transferred or delegated. They are called stewards or messengers of God, servants or ministers of the church, and the like, but the sacerdotal is never once conferred upon them. The only priests under the gospel, designated as such in the N. T., are the saints, the members of the Christian brotherhood." On Titus 1:5, 7—"appoint elders .... For the bishop must be blameless"— Gould, Bib. Theol. N. T., 150, remarks: "Here the word 'for' is quite out of place unless bishops and elders are identical. All these officers, bishops as well as deacons, are confined to the local church in their jurisdiction. The charge of a bishop is not a diocese, but a church. The functions are mostly administrative, the teaching office being subordinate, and a distinction is made between teaching elders and others, implying that the teaching function is not common to them all."

Dexter, Congregationalism, 114, shows that bishop, elder, pastor are names for the same office: (1) from the significance of the words; (2) from the fact that one same qualifications are demanded from all; (3) from the fact that the same duties are assigned to all; (4) from the fact that the texts held to prove higher rank of the bishop do not support that claim. Plumptre, in Pop. Com., Pauline Epistles, 555, 556—"There cannot be a shadow of doubt that the two titles of Bishop and Presbyter were in the Apostolic Age interchangeable."

(*b*) The only plausible objection to the identity of the presbyter and the bishop is that first suggested by Calvin, on the ground of 1 Tim. 5 : 17. But this text only shows that the one office of presbyter or bishop involved two kinds of labor, and that certain presbyters or bishops were more successful in one kind than in the other. That gifts of teaching and ruling belonged to the same individual, is clear from Acts 20 : 28-31 ; Eph. 4 : 11 ; Heb. 13 : 7 ; 1 Tim. 3 : 2—ἐπίσκοπον διδακτικόν.

1 Tim. 5:17—"Let the elders that rule well be counted worthy of double honor, especially those who labor in the word and in teaching"; Wilson, Primitive Government of Christian Churches, concedes that this last text "expresses a diversity in the exercise of the Presbyterial office, but not in the office itself"; and although he was a Presbyterian, he very consistently refused to have any ruling elders in his church.

Acts 20:28, 31—"bishops, to feed the church of the Lord .... wherefore watch ye"; Eph. 4:11—"and some, pastors and teachers"—here Meyer remarks that the single article binds the two words together, and prevents us from supposing that separate offices are intended. Jerome: "Nemo .... pastoris sibi nomen assumere debet, nisi possit docere quos pascit." Heb. 13:7—"Remember them that had the rule over you, men that spake unto you the word of God"; 1 Tim. 3:2—"The bishop must be .... apt to teach." The great temptation to ambition in the Christian ministry is provided against by having no gradation of ranks. The pastor is a priest, only as every Christian is. See Jacob, Eccl. Polity of N. T., 56; Olshausen, on 1 Tim. 5:17; Hackett on Acts 14:23; Presb. Rev., 1886: 89-126.

Dexter, Congregationalism, 52—"Calvin was a natural aristocrat, not a man of the people like Luther. Taken out of his own family to be educated in a family of the nobility, he received an early bent toward exclusiveness. He believed in authority and loved to exercise it. He could easily have been a despot. He assumed all citizens to be Christians until proof to the contrary. He resolved church discipline into police control. He confessed that the eldership was an expedient to which he was driven by circumstances, though after creating it he naturally enough endeavored to procure Scriptural proof in its favor." On the question, The Christian Ministry, is it a Priesthood? see C. Anderson Scott, Evangelical Doctrine, 205-224.

(*c*) In certain of the N. T. churches there appears to have been a plurality of elders (Acts 20 :17 ; Phil. 1 :1 ; Tit. 1 :5). There is, however, no evidence that the number of elders was uniform, or that the plurality which frequently existed was due to any other cause than the size of the churches for which these elders cared. The N. T. example, while it permits the multiplication of assistant pastors according to need, does not require a plural eldership in every case; nor does it render this eldership, where it exists, of coördinate authority with the church. There are indications, moreover, that, at least in certain churches, the pastor was one, while the deacons were more than one, in number.

Acts 20 : 17 — "And from Miletus he sent to Ephesus, and called to him the elders of the church"; Phil. 1 : 1 — "Paul and Timothy, servants of Christ Jesus, to all the saints in Christ Jesus that are at Philippi, with the bishops and deacons"; Tit. 1 : 5 — "For this cause I left thee in Crete, that thou shouldest set in order the things that were wanting, and appoint elders in every city, as I gave thee charge." See, however, Acts 12 : 17 — "Tell these things unto James, and to the brethren"; 15 : 13 — "And after they had held their peace, James answered, saying, Brethren, hearken unto me"; 21 : 18 — "And the day following Paul went in with us unto James; and all the elders were present"; Gal. 1 : 19 — "But other of the apostles saw I none, save James the Lord's brother"; 2 : 12 — "certain came from James." These passages seem to indicate that James was the pastor or president of the church at Jerusalem, an intimation which tradition corroborates.

1 Tim. 3 : 2 — "The bishop therefore must be without reproach"; Tit. 1 : 7 — "For the bishop must be blameless, as God's steward"; cf. 1 Tim. 3 : 8, 10, 12 — "Deacons in like manner must be grave . . . . And let these also first be proved; then let them serve as deacons, if they be blameless . . . . Let deacons be husbands of one wife, ruling their children and their own houses well" — in all these passages the bishop is spoken of in the singular number, the deacons in the plural. So, too, in Rev. 2 : 1, 8, 12, 18 and 3 : 1, 7, 14, "the angel of the church" is best interpreted as meaning the pastor of the church; and, if this be correct, it is clear that each church had, not many pastors, but one.

It would, moreover, seem antecedently improbable that every church of Christ, however small, should be required to have a plural eldership, particularly since churches exist that have only a single male member. A plural eldership is natural and advantageous, only where the church is very numerous and the pastor needs assistants in his work: and only in such cases can we say that New Testament example favors it. For advocacy of the theory of plural eldership, see Fish, Ecclesiology, 229-249; Ladd, Principles of Church Polity, 22-29. On the whole subject of offices in the church, see Dexter, Congregationalism, 77-98; Dagg, Church Order, 241-266; Lightfoot on the Christian Ministry, appended to his Commentary on Philippians, and published in his Dissertations on the Apostolic Age.

B. The duties belonging to these offices.

(a) The pastor, bishop, or elder is :

First, — a spiritual teacher, in public and private ;

Acts 20 : 20, 21, 35 — "how I shrank not from declaring unto you anything that was profitable, and teaching you publicly, and from house to house, testifying both to Jews and to Greeks repentance toward God, and faith toward our Lord Jesus Christ . . . . In all things I gave you an example, that so laboring ye ought to help the weak, and to remember the words of the Lord Jesus, that he himself said, It is more blessed to give than to receive"; 1 Thess. 5 : 12 — "But we beseech you, brethren, to know them that labor among you, and are over you in the Lord, and admonish you"; Heb. 13 : 7, 17 — "Remember them that had the rule over you, men that spake unto you the word of God; and considering the issue of their life, imitate their faith. . . . . Obey them that have the rule over you, and submit to them: for they watch in behalf of your souls, as they that shall give account."

Here we should remember that the pastor's private work of religious conversation and prayer is equally important with his public ministrations; in this respect he is to be an example to his flock, and they are to learn from him the art of winning the unconverted and of caring for those who are already saved. A Jewish Rabbi once said : "God could not be every where, — therefore he made mothers." We may substitute, for the word 'mothers,' the word 'pastors.' Bishop Ken is said to have made a vow every morning, as he rose, that he would not be married that day. His own lines best express his mind : "A virgin priest the altar best attends; our Lord that state commands not, but commends."

Secondly, — administrator of the ordinances ;

Mat. 28 : 19, 20 — "Go ye therefore and make disciples of all the nations, baptizing them into the name of the Father and of the Son and of the Holy Spirit: teaching them to observe all things whatsoever I commanded"; 1 Cor. 1 : 16, 17 —

"And I baptized also the household of Stephanas : besides, i know not whether I baptized any other. For Christ sent me not to baptize, but to preach the gospel." Here it is evident that, although the pastor administers the ordinances, this is not his main work, nor is the church absolutely dependent upon him in the matter. He is not set, like an O. T. priest, to minister at the altar, but to preach the gospel. In an emergency any other member appointed by the church may administer them with equal propriety, the church always determining who are fit subjects of the ordinances, and constituting him their organ in administering them. Any other view is based on sacramental notions, and on ideas of apostolic succession. All Christians are "priests unto . . . . God" (Rev. 1 : 6). " This universal priesthood is a priesthood, not of expiation, but of worship, and is bound to no ritual, or order of times and places " (P. S. Moxom).

Thirdly, — superintendent of the discipline, as well as presiding officer at the meetings, of the church.

Superintendent of discipline : 1 Tim. 5 : 17 — " Let the elders that rule well be counted worthy of double honor, especially those who labor in the word and in teaching"; 3 : 5 — "if a man knoweth not how to rule his own house, how shall he take care of the church of God ?" Presiding officer at meetings of the church : 1 Cor. 12 : 28 — "governments" — here κυβερνήσεις, or "governments," indicating the duties of the pastor, are the counterpart of ἀντιλήψεις, or "helps," which designate the duties of the deacons ; 1 Pet. 5 : 2, 3 — "Tend the flock of God which is among you, exercising the oversight, not of constraint, but willingly, according to the will of God ; nor yet for filthy lucre, but of a ready mind ; neither as lording it over the charge allotted to you, but making yourselves ensamples to the flock."

In the old Congregational churches of New England, an authority was accorded to the pastor which exceeded the New Testament standard. " Dr. Bellamy could break in upon a festival which he deemed improper, and order the members of his parish to their homes." The congregation rose as the minister entered the church, and stood uncovered as he passed out of the porch. We must not hope or desire to restore the New England régime. The pastor is to take responsibility, to put himself forward when there is need, but he is to *rule* only by moral suasion, and that only by guiding, teaching, and carrying into effect the rules imposed by Christ and the decisions of the church in accordance with those rules.

Dexter, Congregationalism, 115, 155, 157 — " The Governor of New York suggests to the Legislature such and such enactments, and then executes such laws as they please to pass. He is chief ruler of the State, while the Legislature adopts or rejects what he proposes." So the pastor's functions are not legislative, but executive. Christ is the only lawgiver. In fulfilling this office, the manner and spirit of the pastor's work are of as great importance as are correctness of judgment and faithfulness to Christ's law. "The young man who cannot distinguish the wolves from the dogs should not think of becoming a shepherd." Gregory Nazianzen : " Either teach none, or let your life teach too." See Harvey, The Pastor; Wayland, Apostolic Ministry; Jacob, Eccl. Polity of N. T., 99 ; Samson, in Madison Avenue Lectures, 261-288.

(*b*) The deacon is helper to the pastor and the church, in both spiritual and temporal things.

First, — relieving the pastor of external labors, informing him of the condition and wants of the church, and forming a bond of union between pastor and people.

Acts 6 : 1-6 — " Now in these days, when the number of the disciples was multiplying, there arose a murmuring of the Grecian Jews against the Hebrews, because their widows were neglected in the daily ministration. And the twelve called the multitude of the disciples unto them, and said, It is not fit that we should forsake the word of God, and serve tables. Look ye out therefore, brethren, from among you seven men of good report, full of the Spirit and of wisdom, whom we may appoint over this business. But we will continue stedfastly in prayer, and in the ministry of the word. And the saying pleased the whole multitude : and they chose Stephen, a man full of faith and of the Holy Spirit, and Philip, and Prochorus, and Nicanor, and Timon, and Parmenas, and Nicolaus a proselyte of Antioch ; whom they set before the apostles : and when they had prayed, they laid their hands upon them "; *cf.* 8-20 — where Stephen shows power in disputation ; Rom. 12 : 7 — "or ministry [διακονίαν], let us give ourselves to our ministry " ; 1 Cor. 12 : 28 — "helps " — here ἀντιλήψεις, "helps," indicating the duties of deacons, are the counterpart of κυβερνήσεις, "governments," which designate the duties of the pastor Phil. 1 : 1 — "bishops and deacons."

Dr. E. G. Robinson did not regard the election of the seven, in Acts 6 : 1-4, as marking the origin of the diaconate, though he thought the diaconate grew out of this election.

The Autobiography of C. H. Spurgeon, 3:22, gives an account of the election of "elders" at the Metropolitan Tabernacle in London. These "elders" were to attend to the spiritual affairs of the church, as the deacons were to attend to the temporal affairs. These "elders" were chosen year by year, while the office of deacon was permanent.

Secondly, — helping the church, by relieving the poor and sick and ministering in an informal way to the church's spiritual needs, and by performing certain external duties connected with the service of the sanctuary.

Since deacons are to be helpers, it is not necessary in all cases that they should be old or rich; in fact, it is better that among the number of deacons the various differences in station, age, wealth, and opinion in the church should be represented. The qualifications for the diaconate mentioned in Acts 6:1-4 and 1 Tim. 3:8-13, are, in substance: wisdom, sympathy, and spirituality. There are advantages in electing deacons, not for life, but for a term of years. While there is no New Testament prescription in this matter, and each church may exercise its option, service for a term of years, with re-election where the office has been well discharged, would at least seem favored by 1 Tim. 3:10 — "Let these also first be proved; then let them serve as deacons, if they be blameless"; 13 — "For they that have served well as deacons gain to themselves a good standing, and great boldness in the faith which is in Christ Jesus."

Expositor's Greek Testament, on Acts 5:6, remarks that those who carried out and buried Ananias are called οἱ νεώτεροι — "the young men" — and in the case of Sapphira they were οἱ νεανίσκοι — meaning the same thing. "Upon the natural distinction between πρεσβύτεροι and νεώτεροι — elders and young men — it may well have been that official duties in the church were afterward based." Dr. Leonard Bacon thought that the apostles included the whole membership in the "we," when they said: "It is not fit that we should forsake the word of God, and serve tables." The deacons, on this interpretation, were chosen to help the whole church in temporal matters.

In Rom. 16:1, 2, we have apparent mention of a deaconess — "I commend unto you Phœbe our sister, who is a servant [marg.: 'deaconess'] of the church that is at Cenchreæ .... for she herself also hath been a helper of many, and of mine own self." See also 1 Tim. 3:11 — "Women in like manner must be grave, not slanderers, temperate, faithful in all things" — here Ellicott and Alford claim that the word "women" refers, not to deacons' wives, as our Auth. Vers. had it, but to deaconesses. Dexter, Congregationalism, 69, 132, maintains that the office of deaconess, though it once existed, has passed away, as belonging to a time when men could not, without suspicion, minister to women.

This view that there are temporary offices in the church does not, however, commend itself to us. It is more correct to say that there is yet doubt whether there was such an office as deaconess, even in the early church. Each church has a right in this matter to interpret Scripture for itself, and to act accordingly. An article in the Bap. Quar., 1869:40, denies the existence of any diaconal rank or office, for male or female. Fish, in his Ecclesiology, holds that Stephen was a deacon, but an elder also, and preached as elder, not as deacon, — Acts 6:1-4 being called the institution, not of the diaconate, but of the Christian ministry. The use of the phrase διακονεῖν τραπέζαις, and the distinction between the diaconate and the pastorate subsequently made in the Epistles, seem to refute this interpretation. On the fitness of women for the ministry of religion, see F. P. Cobbe, Peak of Darien, 199-262; F. E. Willard, Women in the Pulpit; B. T. Roberts, Ordaining Women. On the general subject, see Howell, The Deaconship; Williams, The Deaconship; Robinson, N. T. Lexicon, ἀντιλήψις. On the Claims of the Christian Ministry, and on Education for the Ministry, see A. H. Strong, Philosophy and Religion, 269-318, and Christ in Creation, 314-331.

C. Ordination of officers.

(a) What is ordination ?

Ordination is the setting apart of a person divinely called to a work of special ministration in the church. It does not involve the communication of power, — it is simply a recognition of powers previously conferred by God, and a consequent formal authorization, on the part of the church, to exercise the gifts already bestowed. This recognition and authorization should not only be expressed by the vote in which the candidate is approved by the church or the council which represents it, but should also be accompanied by a special service of admonition, prayer, and the laying-on of hands (Acts 6:5, 6 ; 13 :2, 3 ; 14 :23 ; 1 Tim. 4 :14 ; 5 :22).

Licensure simply commends a man to the churches as fitted to preach. Ordination recognizes him as set apart to the work of preaching and administering ordinances, in some particular church or in some designated field of labor, as representative of the church.

Of his call to the ministry, the candidate himself is to be first persuaded (1 Cor. 9 :16 ; 1 Tim. 1 :12) ; but, secondly, the church must be persuaded also, before he can have authority to minister among them (1 Tim. 3 :2-7 ; 4 :14 ; Titus 1 : 6-9.

The word ' ordain ' has come to have a technical signification not found in the New Testament. There it means simply to choose, appoint, set apart. In 1 Tim. 2:7 — "whereunto I was appointed | $\dot{\epsilon}\tau\dot{\epsilon}\theta\eta\nu$] a preacher and an apostle . . . . a teacher of the Gentiles in faith and truth " — it apparently denotes ordination of God. In the following passages we read of an ordination by the church: Acts 6:5, 6 — "And the saying pleased the whole multitude: and they chose Stephen . . . . and Philip, and Prochorus, and Nicanor, and Timon, and Parmenas, and Nicolaüs . . . . whom they set before the apostles: and when they had prayed, they laid their hands upon them " — the ordination of deacons; 13:2, 3 — " And as they ministered to tne Lord, and fasted, the Holy Spirit said, Separate me Barnabas and Saul for the work whereunto I have called them. Then, when they had fasted and prayed and laid their hands on them, they sent them away "; 14:23 — "And when they had appointed for them elders in every church, and had prayed with fasting, they commended them to the Lord, on whom they had believed "; 1 Tim. 4:14 — "Neglect not the gift that is in thee, which was given thee by prophecy, with the laying on of the hands of the presbytery "; 5:22 — "Lay hands hastily on no man, neither be partaker of other men's sins."

Cambridge Platform, 1648, chapter 9 — " Ordination is nothing else but the solemn putting of a man into his place and office in the church whereunto he had right before by election, being like the installing of a Magistrate in the Commonwealth." Ordination confers no authority — it only recognizes authority already conferred by God. Since it is only recognition, it can be repeated as often as a man changes his denominational relations. Leonard Bacon: " The action of a Council has no more authority than the reason on which it is based. The church calling the Council is a competent court of appeal from any decision of the Council."

Since ordination is simply choosing, appointing, setting apart, it seems plain that in the case of deacons, who sustain official relations only to the church that constitutes them, ordination requires no consultation with other churches. But in the ordination of a pastor, there are three natural stages : (1) the call of the church ; (2) the decision of a council (the council being virtually only the church advised by its brethren) ; (3) the publication of this decision by a public service of prayer and the laying-on of hands. The prior call to be pastor may be said, in the case of a man yet unordained, to be given by the church conditionally, and in anticipation of a ratification of its action by the subsequent judgment of the council. In a well-instructed church, the calling of a council is a regular method of appeal from the church unadvised to the church advised by its brethren ; and the vote of the council approving the candidate is only the essential completing of an ordination, of which the vote of the church calling the candidate to the pastorate was the preliminary stage.

This setting apart by the church, with the advice and assistance of the council, is all that is necessarily implied in the New Testament words which are translated " ordain " ; and such ordination, by simple vote of church and council, could not be counted invalid. But it would be irregular. New Testament precedent makes certain accompaniments not only appropriate, but obligatory. A formal publication of the decree of the council, by laying-on of hands, in connection with prayer, is the last of the duties of this advisory body, which serves as the organ and assistant of the church. The laying-on of hands is appointed to be the regular accompaniment of ordination, as baptism is appointed to be the regular accompaniment of regeneration ; while yet the laying-on of hands is no more the substance of ordination, than baptism is the substance of regeneration.

The imposition of hands is the natural symbo' of the communication, not of grace, but of authority. It does not make a man a minister of the gospel, any more than coronation makes Victoria a queen. What it does signify and publish, is formal recognition and authorization. Viewed in this light, there not only can be no objection to the imposition of hands upon the ground that it favors sacramentalism, but insistence upon it is the bounden duty of every council of ordination.

Mr. Spurgeon was never ordained. He began and ended his remarkable ministry as a lay preacher. He revolted from the sacramentalism of the Church of England, which seemed to hold that in the imposition of hands in ordination divine grace trickled down through a bishop's finger ends, and he felt moved to protest against it. In our judgment it would have been better to follow New Testament precedent, and at the same time to instruct the churches as to the real meaning of the laying-on of hands. The Lord's Supper had in a similar manner been interpreted as a physical communication of grace, but Mr. Spurgeon still continued to observe the Lord's Supper. His gifts enabled him to carry his people with him, when a man of smaller powers might by peculiar views have ruined his ministry. He was thankful that he was pastor of a large church, because he felt that he had not enough talent to be pastor of a small one. He said that when he wished to make a peculiar impression on his people he put himself into his cannon and fired himself at them. He refused the degree of Doctor of Divinity, and said that "D. D." often meant "Doubly Destitute." Dr. P. S. Henson suggests that the letters mean only "Fiddle Dee Dee." For Spurgeon's views on ordination, see his Autobiography, 1 : 355 *sq.*

John Wesley's three tests of a call to preach : " Inquire of applicants," he says, " 1. Do they know God as a pardoning God? Have they the love of God abiding in them ? Do they desire and see nothing but God ? And are they holy, in all manner of conversation ? 2. Have they gifts, as well as grace, for the work ? Have they a clear sound understanding ? Have they a right judgment in the things of God ? Have they a just conception of salvation by faith ? And has God given them any degree of utterance ? Do they speak justly, readily, clearly ? 3. Have they fruit ? Are any truly convinced of sin, and converted to God, by their preaching ? " The second of these qualifications seems to have been in the mind of the little girl who said that the bishop, in laying hands on the candidate, was feeling of his head to see whether he had brains enough to preach. There is some need of the preaching of a " trial sermon " by the candidate, as proof to the Council that he has the gifts requisite for a successful ministry. In this respect the Presbyteries of Scotland are in advance of us.

(b) Who are to ordain ?

Ordination is the act of the church, not the act of a privileged class in the church, as the eldership has sometimes wrongly been regarded, nor yet the act of other churches, assembled by their representatives in council. No ecclesiastical authority higher than that of the local church is recognized in the New Testament. This authority, however, has its limits ; and since the church has no authority outside of its own body, the candidate for ordination should be a member of the ordaining church.

Since each church is bound to recognize the presence of the Spirit in other rightly constituted churches, and its own decisions, in like manner, are to be recognized by others, it is desirable in ordination, as in all important steps affecting other churches, that advice be taken before the candidate is inducted into office, and that other churches be called to sit with it in council, and if thought best, assist in setting the candidate apart for the ministry.

Hands were laid on Paul and Barnabas at Antioch, not by their ecclesiastical superiors, as High Church doctrine would require, but by their equals or inferiors, as simple representatives of the church. Ordination was nothing more than the recognition of a divine appointment and the commending to God's care and blessing of those so appointed. The council of ordination is only the church advised by its brethren, or a committee with power, to act for the church after deliberation.

The council of ordination is not to be composed simply of ministers who have been themselves ordained. As the whole church is to preserve the ordinances and to maintain sound doctrine, and as the unordained church member is often a more sagacious judge of a candidate's Christian experience than his own pastor would be, there seems no warrant, either in Scripture or in reason, for the exclusion of lay delegates from ordaining councils. It was not merely the apostles and elders, but the whole church at Jerusalem, that passed upon the matters submitted to them at the council, and others than ministers appear to have been delegates. The theory that only ministers can ordain has in it the beginnings of a hierarchy. To make the ministry a close corporation is to recognize the principle of apostolic succession, to deny the validity of all our past ordinations, and to sell to an ecclesiastical caste the liberties of the church of God. Very great importance attaches to decorum and settled usage in matters of ordination. To secure these, the following suggestions are made with regard to

I. Preliminary Arrangements to be attended to by the candidate: 1. His letter of dismission should be received and acted upon by the church before the Council convenes. Since the church has no jurisdiction outside of its own membership, the candidate should be a member of the church which proposes to ordain him. 2. The church should vote to call the Council. 3. It should invite all the churches of its Association. 4. It should send printed invitations, asking written responses. 5. Should have printed copies of an Order of Procedure, subject to adoption by the Council. 6. The candidate may select one or two persons to officiate at the public service, subject to approval of the Council. 7. The clerk of the church should be instructed to be present with the records of the church and the minutes of the Association, so that he may call to order and ask responses from delegates. 8. Ushers should be appointed to ensure reserved seats for the Council. 9. Another room should be provided for the private session of the Council. 10. The choir should be instructed that one anthem, one hymn, and one doxology will suffice for the public service. 11. Entertainment of the delegates should be provided for. 12. A member of the church should be chosen to present the candidate to the Council. 13. The church should be urged on the previous Sunday to attend the examination of the candidate as well as the public service.

II. The Candidate at the Council: 1. His demeanor should be that of an applicant. Since he asks the favorable judgment of his brethren, a modest bearing and great patience in answering their questions, are becoming to his position. 2. Let him stand during his narration, and during questions, unless for reasons of ill health or fatigue he is specially excused. 3. It will be well to divide his narration into 15 minutes for his Christian experience, 10 minutes for his call to the ministry, and 35 minutes for his views of doctrine. 4. A *viva voce* statement of all these three is greatly preferable to an elaborate written account. 5. In the relation of his views of doctrine: (*a*) the more fully he states them, the less need there will be for questioning ; (*b*) his statement should be positive, not negative — not what he does *not* believe, but what he *does* believe ; (*c*) he is not required to tell the *reasons* for his belief, unless he is specially questioned with regard to these ; (*d*) he should elaborate the later and practical, not the earlier and theoretical, portions of his theological system ; (*e*) he may well conclude each point of his statement with a single text of Scripture proof.

III. The Duty of the Council: 1. It should not proceed to examine the candidate until proper credentials have been presented. 2. It should in every case give to the candidate a searching examination, in order that this may not seem invidious in other cases. 3. Its vote of approval should read: " We do now set apart," and " We will hold a public service expressive of this fact." 4. Strict decorum should be observed in every stage of the proceedings, remembering that the Council is acting for Christ the great head of the church and is transacting business for eternity. 5. The Council should do no other business than that for which the church has summoned it, and when that business is done, the Council should adjourn *sine die.*

It is always to be remembered, however, that the power to ordain rests with the church, and that the church may proceed without a Council, or even against the decision of the Council. Such ordination, of course, would give authority only within the bounds of the individual church. Where no immediate exception is taken to the decision of the Council, that decision is to be regarded as virtually the decision of the church by which it was called. The same rule applies to a Council's decision to depose from the ministry. In the absence of immediate protest from the church, the decision of the Council is rightly taken as virtually the decision of the church.

In so far as ordination is an act performed by the local church with the advice and assistance of other rightly constituted churches, it is justly regarded as giving formal permission to exercise gifts and administer ordinances within the bounds of such churches. Ordination is not, therefore, to be repeated upon the transfer of the minister's pastoral relation from one church to another. In every case, however, where a minister from a body of Christians not Scripturally constituted assumes the pastoral relation in a rightly organized church, there is peculiar propriety, not only in the examination, by a Council, of his Christian experience, call to the ministry, and views of doctrine, but also in that act of formal recognition and authorization which is called ordination.

The Council should be numerous and impartially constituted. The church calling the Council should be represented in it by a fair number of delegates. Neither the church, nor the Council, should permit a prejudgment of the case by the previous announcement of an ordination service. While the examination of the candidate should be public, all danger that the Council be unduly influenced by pressure from without should be obviated by its conducting its deliberations, and arriving at its decision, in private session. We subjoin the form of a letter missive, calling a Council of ordination; an order of procedure after the Council has assembled; and a programme of exercises for the public service.

LETTER MISSIVE. — The —— church of —— to the —— church of —— : *Dear Brethren:* By vote of this church, you are requested to send your pastor and two delegates to meet with us in accordance with the following resolutions, passed by us on the —— ——, 19 — : *Whereas,* brother ——, a member of this church, has offered himself to the work of the gospel ministry, and has been chosen by us as our pastor, therefore, *Resolved,* 1. That such neighboring churches, in fellowship with us, as shall be herein designated, be requested to send their pastor and two delegates each, to meet and counsel with this church, at — o'clock —. M., on ——, 19 ——, and if, after examination, he be approved, that brother —— be set apart, by vote of the Council, to the gospel ministry, and that a public service be held, expressive of this fact. *Resolved,* 2. That the Council, if it do so ordain, be requested to appoint two of its number to act with the candidate, in arranging the public services. *Resolved,* 3. That printed letters of invitation, embodying these resolutions, and signed by the clerk of this church, be sent to the following churches, —— —— —— —— ——, and that these churches be requested to furnish to their delegates an officially signed certificate of their appointment, to be presented at the organization of the Council. *Resolved,* 4. That Rev. ——, and brethren —— ——, be also invited by the clerk of the church to be present as members of the Council. *Resolved,* 5. That brethren ——, ——, and ——, be appointed as our delegates, to represent this church in the deliberations of the Council; and that brother —— be requested to present the candidate to the Council, with an expression of the high respect and warm attachment with which we have welcomed him and his labors among us. In behalf of the church, —— ——, Clerk. ——, 19 —.

ORDER OF PROCEDURE.— 1. Reading, by the clerk of the church, of the letter-missive, followed by a call, in their order, upon all churches and individuals invited, to present responses and names in writing; each delegate, as he presents his credentials, taking his seat in a portion of the house reserved for the Council. 2. Announcement, by the clerk of the church, that a Council has convened, and call for the nomination of a moderator, — the motion to be put by the clerk, — after which the moderator takes the chair. 3. Organization completed by election of a clerk of the Council, the offering of prayer, and an invitation to visiting brethren to sit with the Council, but not to vote. 4. Reading, on behalf of the church, by its clerk, of the records of the church concerning the call extended to the candidate, and his acceptance, together with documentary evidence of his licensure, of his present church membership, and of his standing in other respects, if coming from another denomination. 5. Vote, by the Council, that the proceedings of the church, and the standing of the candidate, warrant an examination of his claim to ordination. 6. Introduction of the candidate to the Council, by some representative of the church, with an expression of the church's feeling respecting him and his labors. 7. Vote to hear his Christian experience. Narration on the part of the candidate, followed by questions as to any features of it still needing elucidation. 8. Vote to hear the candidate's reasons for believing himself called to the ministry. Narration and questions. 9. Vote to hear the candidate's views of Christian doctrine. Narration and questions. 10. Vote to conclude the public examination, and to withdraw for private session. 11. In private session, after prayer, the Council determines, by three separate votes, in order to secure separate consideration of each question, whether it is satisfied with the candidate's Christian experience, call to the ministry, and views of Christian doctrine. 12. Vote that the candidate be hereby set apart to the gospel ministry, and that a public service be held, expressive of this fact; that for this purpose, a committee of two be appointed, to act with the candidate, in arranging such service of ordination, and to report before adjournment. 13. Reading of minutes, by clerk of Council, and correction of them, to prepare for presentation at the ordination service, and for preservation in the archives of the church. 14. Vote to give the candidate a certificate of ordination, signed by the moderator and clerk of the Council, and to publish an account of the proceedings in the journals of the denomination. 15. Adjourn to meet at the service of ordination.

PROGRAMME OF PUBLIC SERVICE (two hours in length).—1. Voluntary — five minutes. 2. Anthem — five. 3. Reading minutes of the Council, by the clerk of the Council — ten. 4. Prayer of invocation — five. 5. Reading of Scripture — five. 6. Sermon — twenty-five. 7. Prayer of ordination, with laying-on of hands — fifteen. 8. Hymn — ten. 9. Right hand of fellowship — five. 10. Charge to the candidate — fifteen. 11. Charge to the church — fifteen. 12. Doxology — five. 13. Benediction by the newly ordained pastor.

The tenor of the N. T. would seem to indicate that deacons should be ordained with prayer and the laying-on of hands, though not by council or public service. Evangelists, missionaries, ministers serving as secretaries of benevolent societies, should also be ordained, since they are organs of the church, set apart for special religious work on behalf of the churches. The same rule applies to those who are set to be teachers of the teachers, the professors of theological seminaries. Philip, baptizing the eunuch, is to be regarded as an organ of the church at Jerusalem. Both home missionaries and foreign missionaries are evangelists; and both, as organs of the home churches to which they belong, are not under obligation to take letters of dismission to the churches they gather. George Adam Smith, in his Life of Henry Drummond, 265, says that Drummond was ordained to his professorship by the laying-on of the hands of the Presbytery: " The rite is the same in the case whether of a minister or of a professor, for the church of Scotland recognizes no difference between her teachers and her pastors, but lays them under the same vows, and ordains them all as ministers of Christ's gospel and of his sacraments."

Rome teaches that ordination is a sacrament, and " once a priest, always a priest," but only when Rome confers the ordination. It is going a great deal further than Rome to maintain the indelibility of all orders — at least, of all orders conferred by an evangelical church. At Dover in England, a medical gentleman declined to pay his doctor's bill upon the ground that it was not the custom of his calling to pay one another for their services. It appeared however that he was a retired practitioner, and upon that ground he lost his case. Ordination, like vaccination, may run out. Retirement from the office of public teacher should work a forfeiture of the official character. The authorization granted by the Council was based upon a previous recognition of a divine call. When by reason of permanent withdrawal from the ministry, and devotion to wholly secular pursuits, there remains no longer any divine call to be recognized, all authority and standing as a Christian minister should cease also. We therefore repudiate the doctrine of the " indelibility of sacred orders," and the corresponding maxim : " Once ordained, always ordained "; although we do not, with the Cambridge Platform, confine the ministerial function to the pastoral relation. That Platform held that " the pastoral relation ceasing, the ministerial function ceases, and the pastor becomes a layman again, to be restored to the ministry only by a second ordination, called installation. This theory of the ministry proved so inadequate, that it was held scarcely more than a single generation. It was rejected by the Congregational churches of England ten years after it was formulated in New England."

" The National Council of Congregational Churches, in 1880, resolved that any man serving a church as minister can be dealt with and disciplined by any church, no matter what his relations may be in church membership, or ecclesiastical affiliations. If the church choosing him will not call a council, then any church can call one for that purpose "; see New Englander, July, 1883 : 461-491. This latter course, however, presupposes that the steps of fraternal labor and admonition, provided for in our next section on the Relation of Local Churches to one another, have been taken, and have been insufficient to induce proper action on the part of the church to which such minister belongs.

The authority of a Presbyterian church is limited to the bounds of its own denomination. It cannot ordain ministers for Baptist churches, any more than it can ordain them for Methodist churches or for Episcopal churches. When a Presbyterian minister becomes a Baptist, his motives for making the change and the conformity of his views to the New Testament standard need to be scrutinized by Baptists, before they can admit him to their Christian and church fellowship; in other words, he needs to be ordained by a Baptist church. Ordination is no more a discourtesy to the other denomination than Baptism is. Those who oppose reördination in such cases virtually hold to the Romish view of the sacredness of orders.

The Watchman, April 17, 1902—"The Christian ministry is not a priestly class which the laity is bound to support. If the minister cannot find a church ready to support him, there is nothing to prevent his entering another calling. Only ten per cent. of the men who start in independent business avoid failure, and a much smaller proportion achieve substantial success. They are not failures, for they do useful and valuable work. But they do not secure the prizes. It is not wonderful that the proportion of ministers securing prominent pulpits is small. Many men fail in the ministry. There is no sacred character imparted by ordination. They should go into some other avocation. 'Once a minister, always a minister' is a piece of Popery that Protestant churches should get rid of." See essay on Councils of Ordination, their Powers and Duties, by A. H. Strong, in Philosophy and Religion, 259–268; Wayland, Principles and Practices of Baptists, 114; Dexter, Congregationalism, 136, 145, 146, 150, 151. *Per contra*, see Fish, Ecclesiology, 365–399; Presb. Rev., 1886 : 89–126.

3. *Discipline of the Church.*

A. Kinds of discipline.—Discipline is of two sorts, according as offences are private or public. (*a*) Private offences are to be dealt with according to the rule in Mat. 5 : 23, 24; 18 : 15-17.

Mat. 5 : 23, 24—"If therefore thou art offering thy gift at the altar, and there rememberest that thy brother hath aught against thee, leave there thy gift before the altar, and go thy way, first be reconciled to thy brother, and then come and offer thy gift "—here is provision for self-discipline on the part of each offender ; 18 : 15-17—"And if thy brother sin against thee, go, show him his fault between thee and him alone : if he hear thee, thou hast gained thy brother. But if he hear thee not, take with thee one or two more, that at the mouth of two witnesses or three every word may be established. And if he refuse to hear them, tell it unto the church : and if he refuse to hear the church also, let him be unto thee as the Gentile and the publican "—here is, first, private discipline, one of another ; and then, only as a last resort, discipline by the church. Westcott and Hort, however omit the εἰς σέ—"against thee "—in Mat. 18 : 15, and so make each Christian responsible for bringing to repentance every brother whose sin he becomes cognizant of. This would abolish the distinction between private and public offences.

When a brother wrongs me, I am not to speak of the offence to others, nor to write to him a letter, but to go to him. If the brother is already penitent, he will start from his house to see me at the same time that I start from my house to see him, and we will meet just half way between the two. There would be little appeal to the church, and little cherishing of ancient grudges, if Christ's disciples would observe his simple rules. These rules impose a duty upon both the offending and the offended party. When a brother brings a personal matter before the church, he should always be asked whether he has obeyed Christ's command to labor privately with the offender. If he has not, he should be bidden to keep silence.

(*b*) Public offences are to be dealt with according to the rule in 1 Cor. 5 : 3-5, 13, and 2 Thess. 3 : 6.

1 Cor. 5 : 3-5, 13 — "For I verily, being absent in body but present in spirit, have already as though I were present judged him that hath so wrought this thing, in the name of the Lord Jesus, ye being gathered together, and my spirit, with the power of our Lord Jesus, to deliver such a one unto Satan for the destruction of the flesh, that the spirit may be saved in the day of the Lord Jesus. . . . . Put away the wicked man from among yourselves."

Notice here that Paul gave the incestuous person no opportunity to repent, confess, or avert sentence. The church can have no valid evidence of repentance immediately upon discovery and arraignment. At such a time the natural conscience always reacts in remorse and self-accusation, but whether the sin is hated because of its inherent wickedness, or only because of its unfortunate consequences, cannot be known at once. Only fruits meet for repentance can prove repentance real. But such fruits take time.

And the church has no time to wait. Its good repute in the community, and its influence over its own members, are at stake. These therefore demand the instant exclusion of the wrong-doer, as evidence that the church clears its skirts from all complicity with the wrong. In the case of gross public offences, labor with the offender is to come, not before, but after, his excommunication; *cf.* 2 Cor. 2 : 6–8 —"Sufficient to such a one is this punishment which was inflicted by the many ; . . . . forgive him and comfort him ; . . . . confirm your love toward him."

The church is not a Mutual Insurance Company, whose object is to protect and shield its individual members. It is a society whose end is to represent Christ in the world, and to establish his truth and righteousness. Christ commits his honor to its keeping. The offender who is only anxious to escape judgment, and who pleads to be forgiven without delay, often shows that he cares nothing for the cause of Christ which he has injured, but that he has at heart only his own selfish comfort and reputation. The truly penitent man will rather beg the church to exclude him, in order that it may free itself from the charge of harboring iniquity. He will accept exclusion with humility, will love the church that excludes him, will continue to attend its worship, will in due time seek and receive restoration. There is always a way back into the church for those who repent. But the Scriptural method of ensuring repentance is the method of immediate exclusion.

In 2 Cor. 2 : 6–8 —"inflicted by the many " might at first sight seem to imply that, although the offender was excommunicated, it was only by a majority vote, some members of the church dissenting. Some interpreters think he had not been excommunicated at all, but that only ordinary association with him had ceased. But, if Paul's command in the first epistle to "put away the wicked man from among yourselves" (1 Cor. 5 : 13) had been thus disobeyed, the apostle would certainly have mentioned and rebuked the disobedience. On the contrary he praises them that they had done as he had advised. The action of the church at Corinth was blessed by God to the quickening of conscience and the purification of life. In many a modern church the exclusion of unworthy members has in like manner given to Christians a new sense of their responsibility, while at the same time it has convinced worldly people that the church was in thorough earnest. The decisions of the church, indeed, when guided by the Holy Spirit, are nothing less than an anticipation of the judgments of the last day ; see Mat. 18 : 18 —" What things soever ye shall bind on earth shall be bound in heaven ; and what things soever ye shall loose on earth shall be loosed in heaven." In John 8 : 7, Jesus recognizes the sin and urges repentance, while he challenges the right of the mob to execute judgment, and does away with the traditional stoning. His gracious treatment of the sinning woman gave no hint as to the proper treatment of her case by the regular synagogue authorities.

2 Thess 3 : 6 —" Now we command you, brethren, in the name of our Lord Jesus Christ, that ye withdraw yourselves from every brother that walketh disorderly, and not after the tradition which they received of us." The mere "dropping" of names from the list of members seems altogether contrary to the spirit of the N. T. polity. That recognizes only three methods of exit from the local church : (1) exclusion ; (2) dismission ; (3) death. To provide for the case of members whose residence has long been unknown, it is well for the church to have a standing rule that all members residing at a distance shall report each year by letter or by contribution, and, in case of failure to report for two successive years, shall be subject to discipline. The action of the church, in such cases, should take the form of an adoption of preamble and resolution : " *Whereas* A. B. has been absent from the church for more than two years, and has failed to comply with the standing rule requiring a yearly report or contribution, therefore, *Resolved*, that the church withdraw from A. B. the hand of fellowship."

In *all* cases of exclusion, the resolution may uniformly read as above ; the preamble may indefinitely vary, and should always cite the exact nature of the offence. In this way, neglect of the church or breach of covenant obligations may be distinguished from offences against common morality, so that exclusion upon the former ground shall not be mistaken for exclusion upon the latter. As the persons excluded are not commonly present at the meeting of the church when they are excluded, a written copy of the preamble and resolution, signed by the Clerk of the Church, should always be immediately sent to them.

B. Relation of the pastor to discipline.— (*a*) He has no original authority; (*b*) but is the organ of the church, and (*c*) superintendent of its labors for its own purification and for the reclamation of offenders ; and therefore (d) may best do the work of discipline, not directly, by constituting himself a special policeman or detective, but indirectly, by securing proper labor on the part of the deacons or brethren of the church.

The pastor should regard himself as a judge, rather than as a prosecuting attorney. He should press upon the officers of his church their duty to investigate cases of immorality and to deal with them. But if he himself makes charges, he loses dignity, and puts it out of his power to help the offender. It is not well for him to be, or to have the reputation of being, a ferreter-out of misdemeanors among his church members. It is best for him in general to serve only as presiding officer in cases of discipline, instead of being a partisan or a counsel for the prosecution. For this reason it is well for him to secure the appointment by his church of a Prudential Committee, or Committee on Discipline, whose duty it shall be at a fixed time each year to look over the list of members, initiate labor in the case of delinquents, and, after the proper steps have been taken, present proper preambles and resolutions in cases where the church needs to take action. This regular yearly process renders discipline easy ; whereas the neglect of it for several successive years results in an accumulation of cases, in each of which the person exposed to discipline has friends, and these are tempted to obstruct the church's dealing with others from fear that the taking up of any other case may lead to the taking up of that one in which they are most nearly interested. The church which pays no regular attention to its discipline is like the farmer who milked his cow only once a year, in order to avoid too great a drain ; or like the small boy who did not see how any one could bear to comb his hair every day,—he combed his own only once in six weeks, and then it nearly killed him.

As the Prudential Committee, or Committee on Discipline, is simply the church itself preparing its own business, the church may well require all complaints to be made to it through the committee. In this way it may be made certain that the preliminary steps of labor have been taken, and the disquieting of the church by premature charges may be avoided. Where the committee, after proper representations made to it, fails to do its duty, the individual member may appeal directly to the assembled church ; and the difference between the New Testament order and that of a hierarchy is this, that according to the former all final action and responsibility is taken by the church itself in its collective capacity, whereas on the latter the minister, the session, or the bishop, so far as the individual church is concerned, determines the result. See Savage, Church Discipline, Formative and Corrective ; Dagg, Church Order, 268–274. On church discipline in cases of remarriage after divorce, see A. H. Strong, Philosophy and Religion, 431–442.

IV. Relation of Local Churches to One Another.

1. *The general nature of this relation is that of fellowship between equals.*—Notice here :

(a) The absolute equality of the churches.—No church or council of churches, no association or convention or society, can relieve any single church of its direct responsibility to Christ, or assume control of its action.

(b) The fraternal fellowship and coöperation of the churches.—No church can properly ignore, or disregard, the existence or work of other churches around it. Every other church is presumptively possessed of the Spirit, in equal measure with itself. There must therefore be sympathy and mutual furtherance of each other's welfare among churches, as among individual Christians. Upon this principle are based letters of dismission, recognition of the pastors of other churches, and all associational unions, or unions for common Christian work.

H. O. Rowlands, in Bap. Quar. Rev., Oct. 1891 : 669–677, urges the giving up of special Councils, and the turning of the Association into a Permanent Council, not to take original cognizance of what cases it pleases, but to consider and judge such questions as may be referred to it by the individual churches. It could then revise and rescind its action, whereas the present Council when once adjourned can never be called together again. This method would prevent the packing of a Council, and the Council when once constituted would have greater influence. We feel slow to sanction such a plan, not only for the reason that it seems destitute of New Testament authority and example, but because it tends toward a Presbyterian form of church government. All permanent bodies of this sort gradually arrogate to themselves power; indirectly if not directly they can assume original jurisdiction; their decisions have altogether too great influence, if they go further than personal persuasion. The independence of the individual church is a primary element of polity which must not be sacrificed or endangered for the mere sake of inter-ecclesiastical harmony. Permanent Councils of any sort are of doubtful validity. They need to be kept under constant watch and criticism, lest they undermine our Baptist church government, a fundamental principle of which is that there is no authority on earth above that of the local church.

2. *This fellowship involves the duty of special consultation with regard to matters affecting the common interest.*

(*a*) The duty of seeking advice.— Since the order and good repute of each is valuable to all the others, cases of grave importance and difficulty in internal discipline, as well as the question of ordaining members to the ministry, should be submitted to a council of churches called for the purpose.

(*b*) The duty of taking advice.— For the same reason, each church should show readiness to receive admonition from others. So long as this is in the nature of friendly reminder that the church is guilty of defects from the doctrine or practice enjoined by Christ, the mutual acceptance of whose commands is the basis of all church fellowship, no church can justly refuse to have such defects pointed out, or to consider the Scripturalness of its own proceeding. Such admonition or advice, however, whether coming from a single church or from a council of churches, is not itself of binding authority. It is simply in the nature of moral suasion. The church receiving it has still to compare it with Christ's laws. The ultimate decision rests entirely with the church so advised or asking advice.

Churches should observe comity, and should not draw away one another's members. Ministers should bring churches together, and should teach their members the larger unity of the whole church of God. The pastor should not confine his interest to his own church or even to his own Association. The State Convention, the Education Society, the National Anniversaries, should all claim his attention and that of his people. He should welcome new laborers and helpers, instead of regarding the ministry as a close corporation whose numbers are to be kept forever small. E. G. Robinson: "The spirit of sectarianism is devilish. It raises the church above Christ. Christ did not say: ' Blessed is the man who accepts the Westminster Confession or the Thirty-Nine Articles.' There is not the least shadow of churchism in Christ. Churchism is a revamped and whitewashed Judaism. It keeps up the middle wall of partition which Christ has broken down."

Dr. P. H. Mell, in his Manual of Parliamentary Practice, calls Church Councils "Committees of Help." President James C. Welling held that " We Baptists are not true to our democratic polity in the conduct of our collective evangelical operations. In these matters we are simply a bureaucracy, tempered by individual munificence." A. J. Gordon, Ministry of the Spirit, 149, 150, remarks on Mat. 18:19 — "If two of you shall agree"— συμφωνήσωσιν, from which our word 'symphony' comes: "If two shall 'accord,' or 'symphonize' in what they ask, they have the promise of being heard. But, as in tuning an organ, all the notes must be keyed to the standard pitch, else harmony were impossible, so in prayer. It is not enough that two disciples agree with each other,— they must agree with a Third — the righteous and holy Lord, before they can agree in intercession There may be agreement which is in most sinful conflict with the divine will: 'How is it that ye have agreed together'— συνεφωνήθη — the same word —'to try the Spirit of the Lord?' says Peter (Acts 5:9). Here is mutual accord, but guilty discord with the Holy Spirit."

3. *This fellowship may be broken by manifest departures from the faith or practice of the Scriptures, on the part of any church.*

In such case, duty to Christ requires the churches, whose labors to reclaim a sister church from error have proved unavailing, to withdraw their fellowship from it, until such time as the erring church shall return to the path of duty. In this regard, the law which applies to individuals applies to churches, and the polity of the New Testament is congregational rather than independent.

Independence is qualified by interdependence. While each church is, in the last resort thrown upon its own responsibility in ascertaining doctrine and duty, it is to acknowledge the indwelling of the Holy Spirit in other churches as well as in itself, and the value of the public opinion of the churches as an indication of the mind of the Spirit. The church in Antioch asked advice of the church in Jerusalem, although Paul himself was at Antioch. Although no church or union of churches had rightful jurisdiction over the single local body, yet the Council, when rightly called and constituted, has the power of moral influence. Its decision is an index to truth, which only the gravest reasons will justify the church in ignoring or refusing to follow.

Dexter, Congregationalism, 695 — "Barrowism gave all power into the hands of the elders, and it would have no Councils. Congregationalism is Brownism. It has two foci : Independence and Interdependence." Charles S. Scott, on Baptist Polity and the Pastorate, in Bap. Quar. Rev., July, 1890 : 291-297 — "The difference between the polity of Baptist and of Congregational churches is in the relative authority of the Ecclesiastical Council. Congregationalism is Councilism. Not only the ordination and first settlement of the minister must be with the advice and consent of a Council, but every subsequent unsettlement and settlement." Baptist churches have regarded this dependence upon Councils after the minister's ordination as extreme and unwarranted.

The fact that the church has always the right, for just cause, of going behind the decision of the Council, and of determining for itself whether it will ratify or reject that decision, shows conclusively that the church has parted with no particle of its original independence or authority. Yet, though the Council is simply a counsellor — an organ and helper of the church, — the neglect of its advice may involve such ecclesiastical or moral wrong as to justify the churches represented in it, as well as other churches, in withdrawing, from the church that called it, their denominational fellowship. The relation of churches to one another is analogous to the relation of private Christians to one another. No meddlesome spirit is to be allowed ; but in matters of grave moment, a church, as well as an individual, may be justified in giving advice unasked.

Lightfoot, in his new edition of Clemens Romanus, shows that the Epistle, instead of emanating from Clement as Bishop of Rome, is a letter of the church at Rome to the Corinthians, urging them to peace. No pope and no bishop existed, but the whole church congregationally addressed its counsels to its sister body of believers at Corinth. Congregationalism, in A. D. 95, considered it a duty to labor with a sister church that had in its judgment gone astray, or that was in danger of going astray. The only primacy was the primacy of the church, not of the bishop ; and this primacy was a primacy of goodness, backed up by metropolitan advantages. All this fraternal fellowship follows from the fundamental conception of the local church as the concrete embodiment of the universal church. Park: "Congregationalism recognizes a voluntary coöperation and communion of the churches, which Independency does not do. Independent churches ordain and depose pastors without asking advice from other churches."

In accordance with this general principle, in a case of serious disagreement between different portions of the same church, the council called to advise should be, if possible, a mutual, not an *ex parte*, council ; see Dexter, Congregationalism, 2, 3, 61-64. It is a more general application of the same principle, to say that the pastor should not shut himself in to his own church, but should cultivate friendly relations with other pastors and with other churches, should be present and active at the meetings of Associations and State Conventions, and at the Anniversaries of the National Societies of the denomination. His example of friendly interest in the welfare of others will affect his church. The strong should be taught to help the weak, after the example of Paul in raising contributions for the poor churches of Judea.

The principle of church independence is not only consistent with, but it absolutely requires under Christ, all manner of Christian coöperation with other churches; and Social and Mission Unions to unify the work of the denomination, to secure the starting of new enterprises, to prevent one church from trenching upon the territory or appropriating the members of another, are only natural outgrowths of the principle. President Wayland's remark, " He who is displeased with everybody and everything gives the best evidence that his own temper is defective and that he is a bad associate," applies to churches as well as to individuals. Each church is to remember that, though it is honored by the indwelling of the Lord, it constitutes only a part of that great body of which Christ is the head.

See Davidson, Eccl. Polity of the N. T.; Ladd, Principles of Church Polity; and on the general subject of the Church, Hodge, Essays, 201; Flint, Christ's Kingdom on Earth, 53-82; Hooker, Ecclesiastical Polity; The Church,— a collection of essays by Luthardt, Kahnis, *etc.*; Hiscox, Baptist Church Directory; Ripley, Church Polity; Harvey, The Church; Crowell, Church Members' Manual; R. W. Dale, Manual of Congregational Principles; Lightfoot, Com. on Philippians, excursus on the Christian Ministry; Ross, The Church-Kingdom — Lectures on Congregationalism; Dexter, Congregationalism, 681-716, as seen in its Literature; Allison, Baptist Councils in America. For a denial that there is any real apostolic authority for modern church polity, see O. J. Thatcher, Sketch of the History of the Apostolic Church.

CHAPTER II.

THE ORDINANCES OF THE CHURCH.

By the ordinances, we mean those outward rites which Christ has appointed to be administered in his church as visible signs of the saving truth of the gospel. They are signs, in that they vividly express this truth and confirm it to the believer.

In contrast with this characteristically Protestant view, the Romanist regards the ordinances as actually conferring grace and producing holiness. Instead of being the external manifestation of a preceding union with Christ, they are the physical means of constituting and maintaining this union. With the Romanist, in this particular, sacramentalists of every name substantially agree. The Papal Church holds to seven sacraments or ordinances:—ordination, confirmation, matrimony, extreme unction, penance, baptism, and the eucharist. The ordinances prescribed in the N. T., however, are two and only two, viz. :—Baptism and the Lord's Supper.

It will be well to distinguish from one another the three words: symbol, rite, and ordinance. 1. A *symbol* is the sign, or visible representation, of an invisible truth or idea; as for example, the lion is the symbol of strength and courage, the lamb is the symbol of gentleness, the olive branch of peace, the sceptre of dominion, the wedding ring of marriage, and the flag of country. Symbols may teach great lessons ; as Jesus' cursing the barren figtree taught the doom of unfruitful Judaism, and Jesus' washing of the disciples' feet taught his own coming down from heaven to purify and save, and the humble service required of his followers. 2. A *rite* is a symbol which is employed with regularity and sacred intent. Symbols became rites when thus used. Examples of authorized rites in the Christian Church are the laying on of hands in ordination, and the giving of the right hand of fellowship. 3. An *ordinance* is a symbolic rite which sets forth the central truths of the Christian faith, and which is of universal and perpetual obligation. Baptism and the Lord's Supper are rites which have become ordinances by the specific command of Christ and by their inner relation to the essential truths of his kingdom. No ordinance is a sacrament in the Romanist sense of conferring grace; but, as the *sacramentum* was the oath taken by the Roman soldier to obey his commander even unto death, so Baptism and the Lord's Supper are sacraments, in the sense of vows of allegiance to Christ our Master.

President H. G. Weston has recorded his objections to the observance of the so-called ' Christian Year,' in words that we quote, as showing the danger attending the Romanist multiplication of ordinances. "1. The 'Christian Year' is not Christian. It makes everything of actions, and nothing of relations. Make a day holy that God has not made holy, and you thereby make all other days unholy. 2. It limits the Christian's view of Christ to the scenes and events of his earthly life. Salvation comes through spiritual relations to a living Lord. The ' Christian Year' makes Christ only a memory, and not a living, present, personal power. Life, not death, is the typical word of the N. T. Paul craved, not a knowledge of the fact of the resurrection, but of the power of it. The New Testament records busy themselves most of all with what Christ is doing now. 3. The appointments of the ' Christian Year' are not in accord with the N. T. These appointments lack the reality of spiritual life, and are contrary to the essential spirit of Christianity." We may add that where the "Christian Year" is most generally and rigidly observed, there popular religion is most formal and destitute of spiritual power.

I. BAPTISM.

Christian Baptism is the immersion of a believer in water, in token of his previous entrance into the communion of Christ's death and resurrection,— or, in other words, in token of his regeneration through union with Christ.

1. *Baptism an Ordinance of Christ.*

A. Proof that Christ instituted an external rite called baptism.

(*a*) From the words of the great commission ; (*b*) from the injunctions of the apostles ; (*c*) from the fact that the members of the New Testament churches were baptized believers ; (*d*) from the universal practice of such a rite in Christian churches of subsequent times.

(*a*) Mat. 28 : 19 —"Go ye therefore, and make disciples of all the nations, baptizing them into the name of the Father and of the Son and of the Holy Spirit"; Mark 16 : 16 — "He that believeth and is baptized shall be saved '— we hold, with Westcott and Hort, that Mark 16 : 9-20 is of canonical authority, though probably not written by Mark himself. (*b*) Acts 2 : 38 —"And Peter said unto them, Repent ye, and be baptized every one of you in the name of Jesus Christ unto the remission of your sins "; (*c*) Rom. 6 : 3-5 —"Or are ye ignorant that all we who were baptized into Christ Jesus were baptized into his death ? We were buried therefore with him through baptism into death : that like as Christ was raised from the dead through the glory of the Father, so we also might walk in newness of life. For if we have become united with him in the likeness of his death, we shall be also in the likeness of h's resurrection "; Col. 2 : 11, 12 —"in whom ye were also circumcised with a circumcision not made with hands, in the putting off of the body of the flesh, in the circumcision of Christ ; having been buried with him in baptism, wherein ye were also raised with him through faith in the working of God, who raised him from the dead." (*d*) The only marked exceptions to the universal requisition of baptism are found in the Society of Friends, and in the Salvation Army. The Salvation Army does not regard the ordinance as having any more permanent obligation than feet-washing. General Booth : " We teach our soldiers that every time they break bread, they are to remember the broken body of the Lord, and every time they wash the body, they are to remind themselves of the cleansing power of the blood of Christ and of the indwelling Spirit." The Society of Friends regard Christ's commands as fulfilled, not by any outward baptism of water, but only by the inward baptism of the Spirit.

B. This external rite intended by Christ to be of universal and perpetual obligation.

(*a*) Christ recognized John the Baptist's commission to baptize as derived immediately from heaven.

Mat. 21 : 25 —"The baptism of John, whence was it ? from heaven or from men ? "— here Jesus clearly intimates that John's commission to baptize was derived directly from God ; *cf.* John 1 : 25 — the delegates sent to the Baptist by the Sanhedrin ask him : "Why then baptizest thou, if thou art not the Christ, neither Elijah, neither the prophet ? " thus indicating that John's baptism, either in its form or its application, was a new ordinance that required special divine authorization.

Broadus, in his American Com. on Mat. 3 : 6, claims that John's baptism was no modification of an existing rite. Proselyte baptism is not mentioned in the Mishna (A. D. 200); the first distinct account of it is in the Babylonian Talmud (Gemara) written in the fifth century ; it was not adopted from the Christians, but was one of the Jewish purifications which came to be regarded, after the destruction of the Temple, as a peculiar initiatory rite. There is no mention of it, as a Jewish rite, in the O. T., N. T., Apocrypha, Philo, or Josephus.

For the view that proselyte-baptism did not exist among the Jews before the time of John, see Schneckenburger, Ueber das Alter der jüdischen Proselytentaufe ; Stuart, in Bib. Repos., 1833 : 338-355 ; Toy, in Baptist Quarterly, 1872 : 301-332. Dr. Toy, however, in a private note to the author (1884), says : " I am disposed now to regard the Christian rite as borrowed from the Jewish, contrary to my view in 1872." So holds Edersheim, Life and Times of Jesus, 2 : 742-744 —" We have positive testimony that the baptism of proselytes existed in the times of Hillel and Shammai. For, whereas the school of Shammai is said to have allowed a proselyte who was circumcised on the eve of the Passover, to partake, after baptism, of the Passover, the school of Hillel forbade it. This controversy must be regarded as proving that at that time [previous to Christ] the baptism of proselytes was customary."

Porter, on Proselyte Baptism, Hastings' Bible Dict., 4 : 132—"If circumcision was the decisive step in the case of all male converts, there seems no longer room for serious question that a bath of purification must have followed, even though early mention of such proselyte baptism is not found. The law (Lev. 11–15; Num. 19) prescribed such baths in all cases of impurity, and one who came with the deep impurity of a heathen life behind him could not have entered the Jewish community without such cleansing." Plummer, on Baptism, Hastings' Bible Dict., 1 : 239—" What is wanted is direct evidence that, before John the Baptist made so remarkable a use of the rite, it was the custom to make all proselytes submit to baptism ; and such evidence is not forthcoming. Nevertheless the fact is not really doubtful. It is not credible that the baptizing of proselytes was instituted and made essential for their admission to Judaism at a period subsequent to the institution of Christian baptism ; and the supposition that it was borrowed from the rite enjoined by Christ is monstrous."

Although the O. T. and the Apocrypha, Josephus and Philo, are silent with regard to proselyte baptism, it is certain that it existed among the Jews in the early Christian centuries ; and it is almost equally certain that the Jews could not have adopted it from the Christians. It is probable, therefore, that the baptism of John was an application to Jews of an immersion which, before that time, was administered to proselytes from among the Gentiles ; and that it was this adaptation of the rite to a new class of subjects and with a new meaning, which excited the inquiry and criticism of the Sanhedrin. We must remember, however, that the Lord's Supper was likewise an adaptation of certain portions of the old Passover service to a new use and meaning. See also Kitto, Bib. Cyclop., 3 : 593.

(b) In his own submission to John's baptism, Christ gave testimony to the binding obligation of the ordinance (Mat. 3 : 13-17). John's baptism was essentially Christian baptism (Acts 19 : 4), although the full significance of it was not understood until after Jesus' death and resurrection (Mat. 20 : 17-23 ; Luke 12 : 50 ; Rom. 6 : 3-6).

Mat. 3 : 13-17 —"Suffer it now : for thus it becometh us to fulfil all righteousness" ; Acts 19 : 4 —"John baptized with the baptism of repentance, saying unto the people that they should believe on him that should come after him, that is, on Jesus" ; Mat. 20 : 18, 19, 22 —"the Son of man shall be delivered unto the chief priests and scribes ; and they shall condemn him to death, and shall deliver him unto the Gentiles to mock, and to scourge, and to crucify. . . . . Are ye able to drink the cup that I am about to drink ?" Luke 12 : 50 —"But I have a baptism to be baptized with ; and how am I straitened till it be accomplished !" Rom. 6 : 3, 4 —"Or are ye ignorant that all we who were baptized into Christ Jesus were baptized into his death ? We were buried therefore with him through baptism into death : that like as Christ was raised from the dead through the glory of the Father, so we also might walk in newness of life."

Robert Hall, Works, 1 : 367-399, denies that John's baptism was Christian baptism, and holds that there is not sufficient evidence that all the apostles were baptized. The fact that John's baptism was a baptism of faith in the coming Messiah, as well as a baptism of repentance for past and present sin, refutes this theory. The only difference between John's baptism, and the baptism of our time, is that John baptized upon profession of faith in a Savior yet to come ; baptism is now administered upon profession of faith in a Savior who has actually and already come. On John's baptism as presupposing faith in those who received it, see treatment of the Subjects of Baptism, page 950.

(c) In continuing the practice of baptism through his disciples (John 4 : 1, 2), and in enjoining it upon them as part of a work which was to last to the end of the world (Mat. 28 : 19, 20), Christ manifestly adopted and appointed baptism as the invariable law of his church.

John 4 : 1, 2 —"When therefore the Lord knew that the Pharisees had heard that Jesus was making and baptizing more disciples than John (although Jesus himself baptized not, but his disciples)" ; Mat. 28 : 19, 20 —"Go ye therefore, and make disciples of all the nations, baptizing them into the name of the Father and of the Son and of the Holy Spirit : teaching them to observe all things whatsoever I commanded you : and lo, I am with you always, even unto the end of the world."

(d) The analogy of the ordinance of the Lord's Supper also leads to the conclusion that baptism is to be observed as an authoritative memorial of Christ and his truth, until his second coming.

1 Cor. 11 : 26 —"For as often as ye eat this bread, and drink the cup, ye proclaim the Lord's death till he come." Baptism, like the Lord's Supper, is a teaching ordinance, and the two ordinances together furnish an indispensable witness to Christ's death and resurrection.

(e) There is no intimation whatever that the command of baptism is limited, or to be limited, in its application, — that it has been or ever is to be repealed; and, until some evidence of such limitation or repeal is produced, the statute must be regarded as universally binding.

On the proof that baptism is an ordinance of Christ, see Pepper, in Madison Avenue Lectures, 85-114; Dagg, Church Order, 9-21.

2. *The Mode of Baptism.*

This is immersion, and immersion only. This appears from the following considerations:

A. The command to baptize is a command to immerse.—We show this:

(a) From the meaning of the original word βαπτίζω. That this is to immerse, appears:

First,—from the usage of Greek writers—including the church Fathers, when they do not speak of the Christian rite, and the authors of the Greek version of the Old Testament.

Liddell and Scott, Greek Lexicon: "βαπτίζω, to dip in or under water; Lat. *immergere.*" Sophocles, Lexicon of Greek Usage in the Roman and Byzantine Periods, 140 B. C. to 1000 A. D.—"βαπτίζω, to dip, to immerse, to sink. . . . . There is no evidence that Luke and Paul and the other writers of the N. T. put upon this verb meanings not recognized by the Greeks." Thayer, N. T. Lexicon: "βαπτίζω, literally to dip, to dip repeatedly, to immerge, to submerge, ... metaphorically, to overwhelm. . . . . βάπτισμα, immersion, submersion . . . . a rite of sacred immersion commanded by Christ." Prof. Goodwin of Harvard University, Feb. 13, 1895, says: "The classical meaning of βαπτίζω, which seldom occurs, and of the more common βάπτω, is dip (literally or metaphorically), and I never heard of its having any other meaning anywhere. Certainly I never saw a lexicon which gives either sprinkle or pour, as meanings of either. I must be allowed to ask why I am so often asked this question, which seems to me to have but one perfectly plain answer."

In the International Critical Commentary, see Plummer on Luke, p. 86—"It is only when baptism is administered by immersion that its full significance is seen"; Abbott on Colossians, p. 251—"The figure was naturally suggested by the immersion in baptism"; see also Gould on Mark, p. 127; Sanday on Romans, p. 154-157. No one of these four Commentaries was written by a Baptist. The two latest English Bible Dictionaries agree upon this point. Hastings, Bib. Dict., art.: Baptism, p. 243 a—"The mode of using was commonly immersion. The symbolism of the ordinance required this"; Cheyne, Encyc. Biblica, 1 : 473, while arguing from the *Didache* that from a very early date "a triple pouring was admitted where a sufficiency of water could not be had," agrees that "such a method [as immersion] is presupposed as the ideal, at any rate, in Paul's words about death, burial and resurrection in baptism (Rom. 6:3-5)."

Conant, Appendix to Bible Union Version of Matthew, 1-64, has examples "drawn from writers in almost every department of literature and science; from poets, rhetoricians, philosophers, critics, historians, geographers; from writers on husbandry, on medicine, on natural history, on grammar, on theology; from almost every form and style of composition, romances, epistles, orations, fables, odes, epigrams, sermons, narratives: from writers of various nations and religions, Pagan, Jew, and Christian, belonging to many countries and through a long succession of ages. In all, the word has retained its ground-meaning without change. From the earliest age of Greek literature down to its close, a period of nearly two thousand years, not an example has been found in which the word has any other meaning. There is no instance in which it signifies to make a partial application of water by affusion or sprinkling, or to cleanse, to purify, apart from the literal act of immersion as the means of cleansing or purifying." See Stuart, in Bib. Repos., 1833:313; Broadus on Immersion. 57, note.

Dale, in his Classic, Judaic, Christic, and Patristic Baptism, maintains that βάπτω alone means 'to dip,' and that βαπτίζω never means 'to dip,' but only 'to put within,' giving no intimation that the object is to be taken out again. But see Review of Dale, by A. C. Kendrick, in Bap. Quarterly, 1869: 129, and by Harvey, in Bap. Review, 1879: 141-163. "Plutarch used the word βαπτίζω, when he describes the soldiers of Alexander on a riotous march as by the roadside dipping (lit.: baptizing) with cups from huge wine jars and mixing bowls, and drinking to one another. Here we have βαπτίζω used where Dr. Dale's theory would call for βάπτω. The truth is that βαπτίζω, the stronger word, came to be used in the same sense with the weaker; and the attempt to prove a broad and invariable difference of meaning between them breaks down. Of Dr. Dale's three meanings of βαπτίζω — (1) intusposition without influence (stone in water), (2) intusposition with influence (man drowned in water), (3) influence without intusposition, — the last is a figment of Dr. Dale's imagination. It would allow me to say that when I burned a piece of paper, I baptized it. The grand result is this: Beginning with the position that baptize means immerse, Dr. Dale ends by maintaining that immersion is not baptism. Because Christ speaks of drinking a cup, Dr. Dale infers that this is baptism." For a complete reply to Dale, see Ford, Studies on Baptism.

Secondly, — every passage where the word occurs in the New Testament either requires or allows the meaning 'immerse.'

Mat. 3: 6, 11 — "I indeed baptize you in water unto repentance . . . . he shall baptize you in the holy Spirit and in fire"; cf. 2 Kings 5: 14 — "Then went he [Naaman] down, and dipped himself [ἐβαπτίσατο] seven times in the Jordan"; Mark 1: 5, 9 — "they were baptized of him in the river Jordan, confessing their sins. . . . . Jesus came from Nazareth of Galilee, and was baptized of John into the Jordan"; 7: 4 — "and when they come from the market-place, except they bathe [lit. : 'baptize'] themselves, they eat not: and many other things there are, which they have received to hold, washings [lit. : 'baptizings'] of cups, and pots, and brasen vessels " — in this verse, Westcott and Hort, with א and B, read ῥαντίσωνται, instead of βαπτίσωνται; but it is easy to see how subsequent ignorance of Pharisaic scrupulousness might have changed βαπτίσωνται into ῥαντίσωνται; but not easy to see how ῥαντίσωνται should have been changed into βαπτίσωνται. On Mat. 15: 2 (and the parallel passage Mark 7: 4), see Broadus, Com. on Mat., pages 332, 333. Herodotus, 2: 47, says that if any Egyptian touches a swine in passing, with his clothes, he goes to the river and dips himself from it.

Meyer, Com. in loco — " ἐὰν μὴ βαπτίσωνται is not to be understood of washing the hands (Lightfoot, Wetstein), but of immersion, which the word in classic Greek and in the N. T. everywhere means; here, according to the context, to take a bath." The Revised Version omits the words "and couches," although Maimonides speaks of a Jewish immersion of couches; see quotation from Maimonides in Ingham, Handbook of Baptism, 373 — " Whenever in the law washing of the flesh or of the clothes is mentioned, it means nothing else than the dipping of the whole body in a laver; for if any man dip himself all over except the tip of his little finger, he is still in his uncleanness. . . . . A bed that is wholly defiled, if a man dip it part by part, it is pure." Watson, in Annotated Par. Bible, 1126.

Luke 11: 38 — " And when the Pharisee saw it, he marvelled that he had not first bathed [lit. : 'baptized'] himself before dinner"; cf. Ecclesiasticus 31: 25 — " He that washeth himself after the touching of a dead body " (βαπτιζόμενος ἀπὸ νεκροῦ); Judith 12: 7 — " washed herself [ἐβαπτίζετο] in a fountain of water by the camp"; Lev. 22: 4-6 — " Whoso toucheth anything that is unclean by the dead . . . . unclean until the even . . . . bathe his flesh in water." Acts 2: 41 — "They then that received his word were baptized: and there were added unto them in that day about three thousand souls." Although the water supply of Jerusalem is naturally poor, the artificial provision of aqueducts, cisterns, and tanks, made water abundant. During the siege of Titus, though thousands died of famine, we read of no suffering from lack of water. The following are the dimensions of pools in modern Jerusalem: King's Pool, 15 feet x 16 x 3; Siloam, 53 x 18 x 19; Hezekiah, 240 x 140 x 10; Bethesda (so-called), 360 x 130 x 75; Upper Gihon, 316 x 218 x 19 ; Lower Gihon, 592 x 260 x 18; see Robinson, Biblical Researches, 1: 323-348, and Samson, Water-supply of Jerusalem, pub. by Am. Bap. Pub. Soc. There was no difficulty in baptizing three thousand in one day; for, in the time of Chrysostom, when all candidates of the year were baptized in a single day, three thousand were once baptized; and, on July 3, 1878, 2222 Telugu Christians were baptized by two administrators in nine hours. These Telugu baptisms took place at Velumpilly, ten miles north of Ongole. The same two men did not baptize all the time. There were six men engaged in baptizing, but never more than two men at the same time.

Acts 16: 33 — " And he took them the same hour of the night, and washed their stripes ; and was baptized, he and all his, immediately " — the prison was doubtless, as are most large edifices in the East, whether

public or private, provided with tank and fountain. See Cremer, Lexicon of N. T
Greek, *sub voce* — "βαπτίζω, immersion *or submersion* for a religious purpose."' Grimm's
ed. of Wilke — "βαπτίζω, 1. Immerse, submerge; 2. Wash or bathe, by immersing or
submerging (Mark 7 : 4, also Naaman and Judith); 3. Figuratively, to overwhelm, as
with debts, misfortunes, *etc.*" In the N. T. rite, he says it denotes "an immersion in
water', intended as a sign of sins washed away, and received by those who wished to be
admitted to the benefits of Messiah's reign."

Döllinger, Kirche und Kirchen, 337 — "The Baptists are, however, from the Protes
tant point of view, unassailable, since for their demand of baptism by submersion they
have the clear Bible text; and the authority of the church and of her testimony is not
regarded by either party " — *i. e.*, by either Baptists or Protestants, generally. Prof.
Harnack, of Giessen, writes in the Independent, Feb. 19, 1885 — "1. *Baptizein* undoubtedly
signifies immersion (*eintauchen*). 2. No proof can be found that it signifies anything
else in the N. T. and in the most ancient Christian literature. The suggestion regarding a 'sacred sense ' is out of the question. 3. There is no passage in the N. T. which
suggests the supposition that any New Testament author attached to the word *baptizein* any other sense than *eintauchen = untertauchen* (immerse, submerge)." See
Com. of Meyer, and Cunningham, Croall Lectures.

Thirdly, — the absence of any use of the word in the passive voice with
'water' as its subject confirms our conclusion that its meaning is "to
immerse." Water is never said to be baptized upon a man.

(*b*) From the use of the verb βαπτίζω with prepositions :

First, — with εἰς (Mark 1 : 9 — where 'Ιορδάνην is the element into which
the person passes in the act of being baptized).

Mark 1 : 9, marg.— "'And it came to pass in those days, that Jesus came from Nazareth of Galilee, and was baptized of
John into the Jordan."

Secondly, — with ἐν (Mark 1 :5, 8 ; *cf.* Mat. 3 :11. John 1 : 26, 31, 33 ;
cf. Acts 2 : 2, 4). In these texts, ἐν is to be taken, not instrumentally, but
as indicating the element in which the immersion takes place.

Mark 1 : 5, 8 — "they were baptized of him in the river Jordan, confessing their sins . . . . I baptized you in water ;
but he shall baptize you in the Holy Spirit " — here see Meyer's Com. on Mat. 3 : 11 — " ἐν is in accordance with the meaning of βαπτίζω (immerse), not to be understood instrumentally, but
on the contrary, in the sense of the element in which the immersion takes place."
Those who pray for a ' baptism of the Holy Spirit ' pray for such a pouring out of the
Spirit as shall fill the place and permit them to be flooded or immersed in his abundant
presence and power; see C. E. Smith, Baptism of Fire, 1881 : 305–311. Plumptre : "The
baptism with the Holy Ghost would imply that the souls thus baptized would be
plunged, as it were, in that creative and informing Spirit, which was the source of
light and holiness and wisdom."

A. J. Gordon, Ministry of the Spirit, 67 — " The upper room became the Spirit's baptistery. His presence 'filled all the house where they were sitting ' (Acts 2 : 2). . . . . Baptism in the
Holy Spirit was given once for all on the day of Pentecost, when the Paraclete came in
person to make his abode in the church. It does not follow that every believer has
received this baptism. God's gift is one thing, — our appropriation of that gift is quite
another thing. Our relation to the second and to the third persons of the Godhead is
exactly parallel in this respect. 'God so loved the world, that he *gave* his only begotten Son ' (John 3 : 16).
'But as many as *received* him, to them gave he the right to become children of God, even to them that believe on
his name' (John 1 : 12). We are required to appropriate the Spirit as sons, in the same way
that we are required to appropriate Christ as sinners . . . . 'He breathed on them, and saith unto
them, Receive ye' — take ye, actively — 'the Holy Spirit' (John 20 : 22)."

(*c*) From circumstances attending the administration of the ordinance
(Mark 1 : 10 — ἀναβαίνων ἐκ τοῦ ὕδατος ; John 3 : 23 — ὕδατα πολλά ; Acts 8 : 38,
39 — κατέβησαν εἰς τὸ ὕδωρ . . . . ἀνέβησαν ἐκ τοῦ ὕδατος).

Mark 1 : 10 — "coming up out of the water "; John 3 : 23 — "And John also was baptizing in Ænon near to Salim,
because there was much water there " — a sufficient depth of water for baptizing ; see Prof. W. A.

Stevens, on Ænon near to Salim, in Journ. Soc. of Bib. Lit. and Exegesis, Dec. 1883. Acts 8 : 38, 39 — "and they both went down into the water, both Philip and the eunuch ; and he baptized him. And when they came up out of the water . . . . ." In the case of Philip and the eunuch, President Timothy Dwight, in S. S. Times, Aug. 27, 1892, says : "The baptism was apparently by immersion." The Editor adds that "practically scholars are agreed that the primitive meaning of the word ' baptize ' was to immerse."

(d) From figurative allusions to the ordinance.

Mark 10 : 38 — "Are ye able to drink the cup that I drink ? or to be baptized with the baptism that I am baptized with ?"— here the cup is the cup of suffering in Gethsemane ; *cf.* Luke 22 : 42 — "Father, if thou be willing, remove this cup from me "; and the baptism is the baptism of death on Calvary, and of the grave that was to follow ; *cf.* Luke 12 : 50 — "I have a baptism to be baptized with ; and how am I straitened till it be accomplished !" Death presented itself to the Savior's mind as a baptism, because it was a sinking under the floods of suffering. Rom. 6 : 4 — "We were buried therefore with him through baptism into death : that like as Christ was raised from the dead through the glory of the Father, so we also might walk in newness of life" — Conybeare and Howson, Life and Epistles of St. Paul, say, on this passage, that "it cannot be understood without remembering that the primitive method of baptism was by immersion." On Luke 12 : 49, marg.— "I came to cast fire upon the earth, and how would I that it were already kindled !" — see Wendt, Teaching of Jesus, 2 : 225 — " He knew that he was called to bring a new energy and movement into the world, which mightily seizes and draws everything towards it, as a hurled firebrand, which wherever it falls kindles a flame which expands into a vast sea of fire " — the baptism of fire, the baptism in the Holy Spirit ?

1 Cor. 10 : 1, 2 — "our fathers were all under the cloud, and all passed through the sea ; and were all baptized unto Moses in the cloud and in the sea" ; Col. 2 : 12 — "having been buried with him in baptism, wherein ye were also raised with him" ; Heb. 10 : 22 — "having our hearts sprinkled from an evil conscience, and having our body washed [λελουμένοι] with pure water" — here Trench, N. T. Synonyms, 216, 217, says that " λούω implies always, not the bathing of a part of of the body, but of the whole." 1 Pet. 3 : 20, 21 — "saved through water : which also after a true likeness doth now save you, even baptism, not the putting away of the filth of the flesh, but the interrogation of a good conscience toward God, through the resurrection of Jesus Christ " — as the ark whose sides were immersed in water saved Noah, so the immersion of believers typically saves them ; that is, the answer of a good conscience, the turning of the soul to God, which baptism symbolizes. "In the ritual of Moses and Aaron, three things were used : oil, blood, and water. The oil was poured, the blood was sprinkled, the water was used for complete ablution first of all, and subsequently for partial ablution to those to whom complete ablution had been previously administered " (Wm. Ashmore).

(e) From the testimony of church history as to the practice of the early church.

Tertullian, De Baptismo, chap. 12 — "Others make the suggestion (forced enough, clearly) that the apostles then served the turn of baptism when in their little ship they were sprinkled and covered with the waves ; that Peter himself also was immersed enough when he walked on the sea. It is however, as I think, one thing to be sprinkled or intercepted by the violence of the sea ; another thing to be baptized in obedience to the discipline of religion." Fisher, Beginnings of Christianity, 565 — "Baptism, it is now generally agreed among scholars, was commonly administered by immersion." Schaff, History of the Apostolic Church, 570 — "Respecting the form of baptism, the impartial historian is compelled by exegesis and history substantially to yield the point to the Baptists." Elsewhere Dr. Schaff says : "The baptism of Christ in the Jordan, and the illustrations of baptism used in the N. T., are all in favor of immersion, rather than of sprinkling, as is freely admitted by the best exegetes, Catholic and Protestant, English and German. Nothing can be gained by unnatural exegesis. The persistency and aggressiveness of Baptists have driven pedobaptists to opposite extremes."

Dean Stanley, in his address at Eton College, March, 1879, on Historical Aspects of American Churches, speaks of immersion as "the primitive, apostolical, and, till the 13th century, the universal, mode of baptism, which is still retained throughout the Eastern churches, and which is still in our own church as positively enjoined in theory as it is universally neglected in practice." The same writer, in the Nineteenth Century, Oct. 1879, says that "the change from immersion to sprinkling has set aside the larger part of the apostolic language regarding baptism, and has altered the very meaning of the word." Neander, Church Hist., 1 : 310 — "In respect to the form of baptism, it was, in conformity with the original institution and the original import of the symbol, performed by immersion, as a sign of entire baptism into the Holy Spirit, of being entirely penetrated by the same. . . . . It was only with the sick, where exigency required it, that any exception was made. Then it was administered by sprinkling; but many superstitious persons imagined such sprinkling to be not fully valid, and stigmatized those thus baptized as clinics."

Until recently, there has been no evidence that clinic baptism, *i. e.*, the baptism of a sick or dying person in bed by pouring water copiously around him, was practised earlier than the time of Novatian, in the third century; and in these cases there is good reason to believe that a regenerating efficacy was ascribed to the ordinance. We are now, however, compelled to recognize a departure from N. T. precedent somewhat further back. Important testimony is that of Prof. Harnack, of Giessen, in the Independent of Feb. 19, 1885 — " Up to the present moment we possess no certain proof from the period of the second century, in favor of the fact that baptism by aspersion was then even facultatively administered; for Tertullian (De Pœnit., 6, and De Baptismo, 12) is uncertain; and the age of those pictures upon which is represented a baptism by aspersion is not certain. The 'Teaching of the Twelve Apostles,' however, has now instructed us that already, in very early times, people in the church took no offence when aspersion was put in place of immersion, when any kind of outward circumstances might render immersion impossible or impracticable. . . . . But the rule was also certainly maintained that immersion was obligatory if the outward conditions of such a performance were at hand." This seems to show that, while the corruption of the N. T. rite began soon after the death of the apostles, baptism by any other form than immersion was even then a rare exception, which those who introduced the change sought to justify upon the plea of necessity. See Schaff, Teaching of the Twelve Apostles, 29–57, and other testimony in Coleman, Christian Antiquities, 275; Stuart, in Bib. Repos., 1883 : 355-363.

The 'Teaching of the Twelve Apostles,' section 7, reads as follows: " Baptize . . . . . in living water. And if thou have no living water, baptize in other water ; and if thou canst not in cold, then in warm. And if thou have neither, pour water upon the head thrice." Here it is evident that ' baptize ' means only 'immerse,' but if water be scarce pouring may be substituted for baptism. Dr. A. H. Newman, Antipedobaptism, 5, says that ' The Teaching of the Twelve Apostles ' may possibly belong to the second half of the second century, but in its present form is probably much later. It does not explicitly teach baptismal regeneration, but this view seems to be implied in the requirement, in case of an absolute lack of a sufficiency of water of any kind for baptism proper, that pouring water on the head three times be resorted to as a substitute. Catechetical instruction, repentance, fasting, and prayer, must precede the baptismal rite.

Dexter, in his True Story of John Smyth and Sebaptism, maintains that immersion was a new thing in England in 1641. But if so, it was new, as Congregationalism was new — a newly restored practice and ordinance of apostolic times. For reply to Dexter, see Long, in Bap. Rev., Jan. 1883 : 12, 13, who tells us, on the authority of Blunt's Ann. Book of Com. Prayer, that from 1085 to 1549, the 'Salisbury Use' was the accepted mode, and this provided for the child's trine immersion. " The Prayerbook of Edward VI succeeded to the Salisbury Use in 1549; but in this too immersion has the place of honor — affusion is only for the weak. The English church has never sanctioned sprinkling (Blunt, 226). In 1664, the Westminster Assembly said 'sprinkle or pour, ' thus annulling what Christ commanded 1600 years before. Queen Elizabeth was immersed in 1533. If in 1641 immersion had been so generally and so long disused that men saw it with wonder and regarded it as a novelty, then the more distinct, emphatic, and peculiarly their own was the work of the Baptists. They come before the world, with no partners, or rivals, or abettors, or sympathizers, as the restorers and preservers of Christian baptism."

(f) From the doctrine and practice of the Greek church.

De Stourdza, the greatest modern theologian of the Greek church, writes: " βαπτίζω signifies literally and always ' to plunge.' Baptism and immersion are therefore identical, and to say ' baptism by aspersion ' is as if one should say ' immersion by aspersion,' or any other absurdity of the same nature. The Greek church maintain that the Latin church, instead of a βαπτισμός, practice a mere ῥαντισμός, — instead of baptism, a mere sprinkling " — quoted in Conant on Mat., appendix, 99. See also Broadus on Immersion, 18.

The evidence that immersion is the original mode of baptism is well summed up by Dr. Marcus Dods, in his article on Baptism in Hastings' Dictionary of Christ and the Apostles. Dr. Dods defines baptism as "a rite wherein by immersion in water the participant symbolizes and signalizes his transition from an impure to a pure life, his death to a past he abandons, and his birth to a future he desires." As regards the "mode of baptism," he remarks: "That the normal mode was by immersion of the whole body may be inferred (a) from the meaning of *baptizo*, which is the intensive or frequentative form of *bapto*, 'I dip,' and denotes to *immerse* or *submerge* — the point is, that 'dip' or 'immerse' is the primary, 'wash' the secondary meaning of *bapto* or *baptizo*. (b) The same inference may be drawn from the law laid down regarding the baptism of proselytes: 'As soon as he grows whole of the wound of circumcision, they bring him to baptism, and being placed in the water, they again instruct him in some weightier and in some lighter commands of the Law, which being heard, he plunges himself and comes up, and behold, he is an Israelite in all things' (Lightfoot's Horæ Hebraicæ). To use Pauline language, his old man is dead and buried in water, and he rises from this cleansing grave a new man. The full significance of the rite would have been lost had immersion not been practised. Again, it was required in proselyte baptism that 'every person baptized must dip his whole body, now stripped and made naked, at one dipping. And wheresoever in the Law washing of the body or garments is mentioned, it means nothing else than the washing of the whole body.' (c) That immersion was the mode of baptism adopted by John is the natural conclusion from his choosing the neighborhood of the Jordan as the scene of his labors; and from the statement of John 3:23 that he was baptizing in Enon 'because there was much water there.' (d) That this form was continued in the Christian Church appears from the expression *Loutron palingenesias* (bath of regeneration, Titus 3:5), and from the use made by St. Paul in Romans 6 of the symbolism. This is well put by Bingham (Antiquities xi. 2)." The author quotes Bingham to the effect that "total immersion under water" was the universal practice during the early Christian centuries "except in some particular cases of exigence, wherein they allow of sprinkling, as in the case of a clinic baptism, or where there is a scarcity of water." Dr. Dods continues: "This statement exactly reflects the ideas of the Pauline Epistles and the '*Didache*'" (Teaching of the Twelve Apostles).

The prevailing usage of any word determines the sense it bears, when found in a command of Christ. We have seen, not only that the prevailing usage of the Greek language determines the meaning of the word 'baptize' to be 'immerse,' but that this is its fundamental, constant, and only meaning. The original command to baptize is therefore a command to immerse.

As evidence that quite diverse sections of the Christian world are coming to recognize the original form of baptism to be immersion, we may cite the fact that a memorial to the late Archbishop of Canterbury has recently been erected in the parish church of Lambeth, and that it is in the shape of a "font-grave," in which a believer can be buried with Christ in baptism; and also that the Rev. G. Campbell Morgan has had a baptistery constructed in the newly renovated Westminster Congregational Church in London.

Pfleiderer, Philos. Religion, 2:211—"As in the case of the Lord's Supper, so did Baptism also first receive its sacramental significance through Paul. As he saw in the immersing under water the symbolical repetition of the death and resurrection of Christ, baptism appeared to him as the act of spiritual dying and renovation, or regeneration, of incorporation into the mystical body of Christ, that 'new creation.' As for Paul the baptism of adults only was in question, faith in Christ is already of course presupposed by it, and baptism is just the act in which faith realizes the decisive resolution of giving one's self up actually as belonging to Christ and his community. Yet the outward act is not on that account a mere semblance of what is already present in faith, but according to the mysticism common to Paul with the whole ancient world, the symbolical act effectuates what it typifies, and therefore in this case the mortification of the carnal man and the animation of the spiritual man." For the view that sprinkling or pouring constitutes valid baptism, see Hall, Mode of Baptism. *Per contra*, see Hovey, in Baptist Quarterly, April, 1875; Wayland, Principles and Practices of Baptists, 85; Carson, Noel, Judson, and Pengilly, on Baptism; especially recent and valuable is Burrage, Act of Baptism.

B. No church has the right to modify or dispense with this command of Christ. This is plain :

(*a*) From the nature of the church. Notice:

First,—that, besides the local church, no other visible church of Christ is known to the New Testament. Secondly,—that the local church is not a legislative, but is simply an executive, body. Only the authority which originally imposed its laws can amend or abrogate them. Thirdly,—that the local church cannot delegate to any organization or council of churches any power which it does not itself rightfully possess. Fourthly,—that the opposite principle puts the church above the Scriptures and above Christ, and would sanction all the usurpations of Rome.

Mat. 5:19—"Whosoever therefore shall break one of these least commandments, and shall teach men so, shall be called least in the kingdom of heaven: but whosoever shall do and teach them, he shall be called great in the kingdom of heaven"; *cf*. 2 Sam. 6:7—"And the anger of Jehovah was kindled against Uzzah; and God smote him there for his error; and there he died by the ark of God." Shakespeare, Henry VI, Part I, 2:4—"Faith, I have been a truant in the law, And never yet could frame my will to it, And therefore frame the law unto my will." As at the Reformation believers rejoiced to restore communion in both kinds, so we should rejoice to restore baptism as to its subjects and as to its meaning. To administer it to a wailing and resisting infant, or to administer it in any other form than that prescribed by Jesus' command and example, is to desecrate and destroy the ordinance.

(*b*) From the nature of God's command :

First,—as forming a part, not only of the law, but of the fundamental law, of the church of Christ. The power claimed for a church to change it is not only legislative but constitutional. Secondly,—as expressing the wisdom of the Lawgiver. Power to change the command can be claimed for the church, only on the ground that Christ has failed to adapt the ordinance to changing circumstances, and has made obedience to it unnecessarily difficult and humiliating. Thirdly,—as providing in immersion the only adequate symbol of those saving truths of the gospel which both of the ordinances have it for their office to set forth, and without which they become empty ceremonies and forms. In other words, the church has no right to change the method of administering the ordinance, because such a change vacates the ordinance of its essential meaning. As this argument, however, is of such vital importance, we present it more fully in a special discussion of the Symbolism of Baptism.

Abraham Lincoln, in his debates with Douglas, ridiculed the idea that there could be any constitutional way of violating the Constitution. F. L. Anderson: "In human governments we change the constitution to conform to the will of the people; in the divine government we change the will of the people to conform to the Constitution." For advocacy of the church's right to modify the form of an ordinance, see Coleridge, Aids to Reflection, in Works, 1:333-348—"Where a ceremony answered, and was intended to answer, several purposes which at its first institution were blended in respect of the time, but which afterward, by change of circumstances, were necessarily disunited, then either the church hath no power or authority delegated to her, or she must be authorized to choose and determine to which of the several purposes the ceremony should be attached." Baptism, for example, at the first symbolized not only entrance into the church of Christ, but personal faith in him as Savior and Lord. It is assumed that entrance into the church and personal faith are now necessarily disunited. Since baptism is in charge of the church, she can attach baptism to the former, and not to the latter.

We of course deny that the separation of baptism from faith is ever necessary. We maintain, on the contrary, that thus to separate the two is to pervert the ordinance, and to make it teach the doctrine of hereditary church membership and salvation by outward manipulation apart from faith. We say with Dean Stanley (on Baptism, in the Nineteenth Century, Oct. 1879), though not, as he does, with approval, that the change in the method of administering the ordinance shows " how the spirit that lives and moves in human society can override the most sacred ordinances." We cannot with him call this spirit " the free spirit of Christianity,"— we regard it rather as an evil spirit of disobedience and unbelief. " Baptists are therefore pledged to prosecute the work of the Reformation until the church shall return to the simple forms it possessed under the apostles " (G. M. Stone). See Curtis, Progress of Baptist Principles, 234-245.

Objections: 1. Immersion is often impracticable.— We reply that, when really impracticable, it is no longer a duty. Where the will to obey is present, but providential circumstances render outward obedience impossible, Christ takes the will for the deed.

2. It is often dangerous to health and life.— We reply that, when it is really dangerous, it is no longer a duty. But then, we have no warrant for substituting another act for that which Christ has commanded. Duty demands simple delay until it can be administered with safety. It must be remembered that ardent feeling nerves even the body. " Brethren, if your hearts be warm, Ice and snow can do no harm." The cold climate of Russia does not prevent the universal practice of immersion by the Greek church of that country.

3. It is indecent.— We reply, that there is need of care to prevent exposure, but that with this care there is no indecency, more than in fashionable sea-bathing. The argument is valid only against a careless administration of the ordinance, not against immersion itself.

4. It is inconvenient.— We reply that, in a matter of obedience to Christ, we are not to consult convenience. The ordinance which symbolizes his sacrificial death, and our spiritual death with him, may naturally involve something of inconvenience, but joy in submitting to that inconvenience will be a test of the spirit of obedience. When the act is performed, it should be performed as Christ enjoined.

5. Other methods of administration have been blessed to those who submitted to them.— We reply that God has often condescended to human ignorance, and has given his Spirit to those who honestly sought to serve him, even by erroneous forms, such as the Mass. This, however, is not to be taken as a divine sanction of the error, much less as a warrant for the perpetuation of a false system on the part of those who know that it is a violation of Christ's commands. It is, in great part, the position of its advocates, as representatives of Christ and his church, that gives to this false system its power for evil.

3.   *The Symbolism of Baptism.*

Baptism symbolizes the previous entrance of the believer into the communion of Christ's death and resurrection,— or, in other words, regeneration through union with Christ.

A.   Expansion of this statement as to the symbolism of baptism. Baptism, more particularly, is a symbol:

(*a*) Of the death and resurrection of Christ.

Rom. 6:3 —"Or are ye ignorant that all we who were baptized into Christ Jesus were baptized into his death?" *cf.* Mat. 3:13 —"Then cometh Jesus from Galilee to the Jordan unto John, to be baptized of him"; Mark 10:38 — "Are ye able to drink the cup that I drink? or to be baptized with the baptism that I am baptized with?"; Luke 12 50 —"But I have a baptism to be baptized with; and how am I straitened till it be accomplished!" Col. 2:12 — "buried with him in baptism, wherein ye were also raised with him through faith in the working of God, who raised him from the dead." For the meaning of these passages, see note on the baptism of Jesus, under B. (*a*), pages 942, 943.

Denney, in Expositor's Greek Testament, on Rom. 6:3-5 —"The argumentative requirements of the passage . . . . demand the idea of an actual union to, or incorporation in Christ. . . . . We were buried with him [in the act of immersion] through that baptism into his death. . . . . If the baptism, *which is a similitude of Christ's death,* has had a reality answering to its obvious import, so that we have really died in it as Christ died, then we shall have a corresponding experience of resurrection. Baptism, inasmuch as one emerges from the water after being immersed, is a similitude of resurrection as well as of death."

(*b*) Of the purpose of that death and resurrection,—namely, to atone for sin, and to deliver sinners from its penalty and power.

Rom. 6:4 —"We were buried therefore with him through baptism into death: that like as Christ was raised from the dead through the glory of the Father, so we also might walk in newness of life"; *cf.* 7, 10, 11 —"for he that hath died is justified from sin. . . . . For the death that he died, he died unto sin once: but the life that he liveth, he liveth unto God. Even so reckon ye also yourselves to be dead unto sin, but alive unto God in Christ Jesus"; 2 Cor. 5:14 — "we thus judge, that one died for all, therefore all died." Baptism is therefore a confession of evangelical faith both as to sin, and as to the deity and atonement of Christ. No one is properly a Baptist who does not acknowledge these truths which baptism signifies.

T. W. Chambers, in Presb. and Ref. Rev., Jan. 1890:113-118, objects that this view of the symbolism of baptism is based on two texts, Rom. 6:4 and Col. 2:12, which are illustrative and not explanatory, while the great majority of passages make baptism only an act of purification. Yet Dr. Chambers concedes: "It is to be admitted that nearly all modern critical expositors (Meyer, Godet, Alford, Conybeare, Lightfoot, Beet) consider that there is a reference here [in Rom. 6:4] to the act of baptism, which, as the Bishop of Durham says, 'is the grave of the old man and the birth of the new — an image of the believer's participation both in the death and in the resurrection of Christ. . . . . As he sinks beneath the baptismal waters, the believer buries there all his corrupt affections and past sins; as he emerges thence, he rises regenerate, quickened to new hopes and a new life.' "

(*c*) Of the accomplishment of that purpose in the person baptized,— who thus professes his death to sin and resurrection to spiritual life.

Gal. 3:27 —"For as many of you as were baptized into Christ did put on Christ"; 1 Pet. 3:21 —"which [water] also after a true likeness doth now save you, even baptism, not the putting away of the filth of the flesh, but the interrogation of a good conscience toward God, through the resurrection of Jesus Christ"; *cf.* Gal. 2:19, 20 —"For I through the law died unto the law, that I might live unto God. I have been crucified with Christ; and it is no longer I that live, but Christ liveth in me: and that life which I now live in the flesh I live in faith, the faith which is in the Son of God, who loved me, and gave himself up for me''; Col. 3:3 — "For ye died, and your life is hid with Christ in God."

C. H. M.: "A truly baptized person is one who has passed from the old world into the new. . . . . The water rolls over his person, signifying that his place in nature is ignored, that his old nature is entirely set aside, in short, that he is a dead man, that the flesh with all that pertained thereto — its sins and its liabilities — is buried in the grave of Christ and can never come into God's sight again. . . . . When the believer rises up from the water, expression is given to the truth that he comes up as the possessor of a new life, even the resurrection life of Christ, to which divine righteousness inseparably attaches."

(*d*) Of the method in which that purpose is accomplished,— by union with Christ, receiving him and giving one's self to him by faith.

Rom. 6:5 —"For if we have become united [σύμφυτοι] with him in the likeness of his death, we shall be also in the likeness of his resurrection"— σύμφυτοι, or συμπεφυκώς, is used of the man and the horse as grown together in the Centaur, by Lucian, Dial. Mort., 16:4, and by Xenophon, Cyrop., 4:3:18. Col. 2:12 —"having been buried with him in baptism, wherein ye were also raised with him through faith in the working of God, who raised him from the dead." Dr. N. S. Burton: "The oneness of the believer and Christ is expressed by the fact that the one act of immersion sets forth the death and resurrection of both Christ and the believer." As the voluntary element in faith has two parts, a giving and a taking, so baptism illustrates both. Submergence = surrender to Christ; emergence = reception of Christ; see page 839, (*b*). "Putting on Christ" (Gal. 3:27) is the burying of the old life and the rising to a new. *Cf.* the active and the passive obedience of Christ (pages 749, 770), the two elements of justification (pages 854-859), the two aspects of formal worship (page 23), the two divisions of the Lord's Prayer.

William Ashmore holds that incorporation into Christ is the root idea of baptism, union with Christ's death and resurrection being only a part of it. We are "baptized into Christ" (Rom. 6:3), as the Israelites were "baptized into Moses" (1 Cor. 10:2). As baptism symbolizes the incorporation of the believer into Christ, so the Lord's Supper symbolizes the incorporation of Christ into the believer. We go down into the water, but the bread goes down into us. We are "in Christ," and Christ is "in us." The candidate does not baptize himself, but puts himself wholly into the hands of the administrator. This seems symbolic of his committing himself entirely to Christ, of whom the administrator is the representative. Similarly in the Lord's Supper, it is Christ who through his representative distributes the emblems of his death and life.

E. G. Robinson regarded baptism as implying: 1. death to sin; 2. resurrection to new life in Christ; 3. entire surrender of ourselves to the authority of the triune God. Baptism "into the name of the Father and of the Son and of the Holy Spirit" (Mat. 28:19) cannot imply supreme allegiance to the Father, and only subordinate allegiance to the Son. Baptism therefore is an assumption of supreme allegiance to Jesus Christ. N. E. Wood, in The Watchman, Dec. 3, 1896 15 —" Calvinism has its five points; but Baptists have also their own five points: the Trinity, the Atonement, Regeneration, Baptism, and an inspired Bible. All other doctrines gather round these."

(e) Of the consequent union of all believers in Christ.

Eph. 4 : 5 —" one Lord, one faith, one baptism "; 1 Cor. 12 : 13 —" For in one Spirit were we all baptized into one body, whether Jews or Greeks, whether bond or free; and were all made to drink of one Spirit"; cf. 10 : 3, 4 —"and did all eat the same spiritual food; and did all drink the same spiritual drink : for they drank of a spiritual rock that followed them: and the rock was Christ."

In Eph. 4 : 5, it is noticeable that, not the Lord's Supper, but baptism, is referred to as the symbol of Christian unity. A. H. Strong, Cleveland Sermon, 1904 —" Our fathers lived in a day when simple faith was subject to serious disabilities. The establishments frowned upon dissent and visited it with pains and penalties. It is no wonder that believers in the New Testament doctrine and polity felt that they must come out from what they regarded as an apostate church. They could have no sympathy with those who held back the truth in unrighteousness and persecuted the saints of God. But our doctrine has leavened all Christendom. Scholarship is on the side of immersion. Infant baptism is on the decline. The churches that once opposed us now compliment us on our stedfastness in the faith and on our missionary zeal. There is a growing spirituality in these churches, which prompts them to extend to us hands of fellowship. And there is a growing sense among us that the kingdom of Christ is wider than our own membership, and that loyalty to our Lord requires us to recognize his presence and blessing even in bodies which we do not regard as organized in complete accordance with the New Testament model. Faith in the larger Christ is bringing us out from our denominational isolation into an inspiring recognition of our oneness with the universal church of God throughout the world."

(f) Of the death and resurrection of the body,—which will complete the work of Christ in us, and which Christ's death and resurrection assure to all his members.

1 Cor. 15 · 12, 22 —"Now if Christ is preached that he hath been raised from the dead, how say some among you that there is no resurrection of the dead ? . . . . For in Adam all die, so also in Christ shall all be made alive." In the Scripture passages quoted above, we add to the argument from the meaning of the word βαπτίζω the argument from the meaning of the ordinance. Luther wrote, in his Babylonish Captivity of the Church, section 103 (English translation in Wace and Buchheim, First Principles of the Reformation, 192): " Baptism is a sign both of death and resurrection. Being moved by this reason, I would have those that are baptized to be altogether dipped into the water, as the word means and the mystery signifies." See Calvin on Acts 8 : 38; Conybeare and Howson on Rom. 6 : 4; Boardman, in Madison Avenue Lectures, 115-135.

B.   Inferences from the passages referred to :

(a) The central truth set forth by baptism is the death and resurrection of Christ,—and our own death and resurrection only as connected with that.

The baptism of Jesus in Jordan, equally with the subsequent baptism of his followers, was a symbol of his death. It was his death which he had in mind, when he said : " Are ye able to drink the cup that I drink ? or to be baptized with the baptism that I am baptized with ? " (Mark 10 : 38); "But I have a baptism to be baptized with; and how am I straitened till it be accomplished ! " (Luke 12 : 50). The being immersed and overwhelmed in waters is a frequent metaphor in all languages to express the rush of successive troubles; compare Ps. 69 : 2 —"I am come into deep waters, where the floods overflow me "; 42 : 7 —"All thy waves and thy billows are gone over me "; 124 : 4, 5 —"Then the waters had overwhelmed us, The stream had gone over our soul; Then the proud waters had gone over our soul."

So the suffering, death, and burial, which were before our Lord, presented themselves to his mind as a baptism, because the very idea of baptism was that of a complete submersion under the floods of waters. Death was not to be poured upon Christ,—it was no mere sprinkling of suffering which he was to endure, but a sinking into the mighty waters, and a being overwhelmed by them. It was the giving of himself to this, which he symbolized by his baptism in Jordan. That act was not arbitrary, or formal, or ritual. It was a public consecration, a consecration to death, to death for the sins of the world. It expressed the essential nature and meaning of his earthly work: the baptism of water at the beginning of his ministry consciously and designedly prefigured the baptism of death with which that ministry was to close.

Jesus' submission to John's baptism of repentance, the rite that belonged only to sinners, can be explained only upon the ground that he was "made to be sin on our behalf" (2 Cor. 5 : 21). He had taken our nature upon him, without its hereditary corruption indeed, but with all its hereditary guilt, that he might redeem that nature and reunite it to God. As one with humanity, he had in his unconscious childhood submitted to the rites of circumcision, purification, and legal redemption (Luke 2: 21–24; *cf.* Ex. 13 : 2, 13 see Lange, Alford, Webster and Wilkinson on Luke 2: 24) — all of them rites appointed for sinners. "Made in the likeness of men" (Phil. 2 : 7), " the likeness of sinful flesh " (Rom. 8 : 3), he was "t⁹ put away sin by the sacrifice of himself" (Heb. 9 : 26).

In his baptism, therefore, he could say, "Thus it becometh us to fulfil all righteousness " (Mat. 3 : 15) because only through the final baptism of suffering and death, which this baptism in water foreshadowed, could he "make an end of sins " and "bring in everlasting righteousness" (Dan 9:24) to the condemned and ruined world. He could not be "the Lord our Righteousness" (Jer. 23 : 6) except by first suffering the death due to the nature he had assumed, thereby delivering it from its guilt and perfecting it forever. All this was indicated in that act by which he was first "made manifest to Israel" (John 1 : 31). In his baptism in Jordan, he was buried in the likeness of his coming death, and raised in the likeness of his coming resurrection. 1 John 5 : 6 —"This is he that came by water and blood, even Jesus Christ; not in the water only but in the water and in the blood "=in the baptism of water at the beginning of his ministry, and in the baptism of blood with which that ministry was to close.

As that baptism pointed forward to Jesus' death, so our baptism points backward to the same, as the centre and substance of his redeeming work, the one death by which we live. We who are "baptized into Christ" are "baptized into his death" (Rom. 6 : 3), that is, into spiritual communion and participation in that death which he died for our salvation; in short, in baptism we declare in symbol that his death has become ours. On the Baptism of Jesus, see A. H. Strong, Philosophy and Religion, 226–237.

(*b*) The correlative truth of the believer's death and resurrection, set forth in baptism, implies, first,—confession of sin and humiliation on account of it, as deserving of death ; secondly,—declaration of Christ's death for sin, and of the believer's acceptance of Christ's substitutionary work ; thirdly,—acknowledgment that the soul has become partaker of Christ's life, and now lives only in and for him.

A false mode of administering the ordinance has so obscured the meaning of baptism that it has to multitudes lost all reference to the death of Christ, and the Lord's Supper is assumed to be the only ordinance which is intended to remind us of the atoning sacrifice to which we owe our salvation. For evidence of this, see the remarks of President Woolsey in the Sunday School Times : " Baptism it [the Christian religion] could share in with the doctrine of John the Baptist, and if a similar rite had existed under the Jewish law, it would have been regarded as appropriate to a religion which inculcated renunciation of sin and purity of heart and life. But [in the Lord's Supper] we go beyond the province of baptism to the very *penetrale* of the gospel, to the efficacy and meaning of Christ's death."

Baptism should be a public act. We cannot afford to relegate it to a corner, or to celebrate it in private, as some professedly Baptist churches of England are said to do. Like marriage, the essence of it is the joining of ourselves to another before the world. In baptism we merge ourselves in Christ, before God and angels and men. The Mohammedan stands five times a day, and prays with his face toward Mecca, caring not who sees him. Luke 12 : 8 —" Every one who shall confess me before men, him shall the Son of man also confess before the angels of God."

(c) Baptism symbolizes purification, but purification in a peculiar and divine way,—namely, through the death of Christ and the entrance of the soul into communion with that death. The radical defect of sprinkling or pouring as a mode of administering the ordinance, is that it does not point to Christ's death as the procuring cause of our purification.

It is a grievous thing to say by symbol, as those do say who practice sprinkling in place of immersion, that a man may regenerate himself, or, if not this, yet that his regeneration may take place without connection with Christ's death. Edward Beecher's chief argument against Baptist views is drawn from John 3 : 22-25 —" a questioning on the part of John's disciples with a Jew about purifying." Purification is made to be the essential meaning of baptism, and the conclusion is drawn that any form expressive of purification will answer the design of the ordinance. But if Christ's death is the procuring cause of our purification, we may expect it to be symbolized in the ordinance which declares that purification ; if Christ's death is the central fact of Christianity, we may expect it to be symbolized in the initiatory rite of Christianity.

(d) In baptism we show forth the Lord's death as the original source of holiness and life in our souls, just as in the Lord's Supper we show forth the Lord's death as the source of all nourishment and strength after this life of holiness has been once begun. As the Lord's Supper symbolizes the sanctifying power of Jesus' death, so baptism symbolizes its regenerating power.

The truth of Christ's death and resurrection is a precious jewel, and it is given us in these outward ordinances as in a casket. Let us care for the casket lest we lose the gem. As a scarlet thread runs through every rope and cord of the British navy, testifying that it is the property of the Crown, so through every doctrine and ordinance of Christianity runs the red line of Jesus' blood. It is their common reference to the death of Christ that binds the two ordinances together.

(e) There are two reasons, therefore, why nothing but immersion will satisfy the design of the ordinance : first,—because nothing else can symbolize the radical nature of the change effected in regeneration—a change from spiritual death to spiritual life ; secondly,—because nothing else can set forth the fact that this change is due to the entrance of the soul into communion with the death and resurrection of Christ.

Christian truth is an organism. Part is bound to part, and all together constitute one vitalized whole. To give up any single portion of that truth is like maiming the human body. Life may remain, but one manifestation of life has ceased. The whole body of Christian truth has lost its symmetry and a part of its power to save.

Pfleiderer, Philos. Religion, 2 : 212 —" In the Eleusinian mysteries, the act of reception was represented as a regeneration, and the hierophant appointed to the temple service had to take a sacramental bath, out of which he proceeded as a ' new man ' with a new name, which signifies that, as they were wont to say, ' the first one was forgotten,'— that is, the old man was put off at the same time with the old name. The parallel of this Eleusinian rite with the thoughts which Paul has written about Baptism in the Epistle to the Romans, and therefore from Corinth, is so striking that a connection between the two may well be conjectured ; and all the more that even in the case of the Lord's Supper, Paul has brought in the comparison with the heathen festivals, in order to give a basis for his mystical theory."

(f) To substitute for baptism anything which excludes all symbolic reference to the death of Christ, is to destroy the ordinance, just as substituting for the broken bread and poured out wine of the communion some form of administration which leaves out all reference to the death of Christ would be to destroy the Lord's Supper, and to celebrate an ordinance of human invention.

Baptism, like the Fourth of July, the Passover, the Lord's Supper, is a historical monument. It witnesses to the world that Jesus died and rose again. In celebrating it, we show forth the Lord's death as truly as in the celebration of the Supper. But it is more than a historical monument. It is also a pictorial expression of doctrine. Into it are woven all the essential truths of the Christian scheme. It tells of the nature and penalty of sin, of human nature delivered from sin in the person of a crucified and risen Savior, of salvation secured for each human soul that is united to Christ, of obedience to Christ as the way to life and glory. Thus baptism stands from age to age as a witness for God — a witness both to the facts and to the doctrine of Christianity. To change the form of administering the ordinance is therefore to strike a blow at Christianity and at Christ, and to defraud the world of a part of God's means of salvation. See Ebrard's view of Baptism, in Baptist Quarterly, 1869 : 257, and in Olshausen's Com. on N. T., 1 : 270, and 3 : 594. Also Lightfoot, Com. on Colossians 2 : 20, and 3 : 1.

Ebrard: "Baptism = Death." So Sanday, Com. on Rom. 6 — "Immersion=Death; Submersion=Burial (the ratification of death); Emergence=Resurrection (the ratification of life)." William Ashmore: "Solomon's Temple had two monumental pillars : *Jachin*, 'he shall establish,' and *Boaz*, 'in it is strength.' In Zechariah's vision were two olive trees on either side of the golden candlestick. In like manner, Christ has left two monumental witnesses to testify concerning himself — Baptism and the Lord's Supper." The lady in the street car, who had inadvertently stuck her parasol into a man's eye, very naturally begged his pardon. But he replied: "It is of no consequence, madame, I have still one eye left." Our friends who sprinkle or pour put out one eye of the gospel witness, break down one appointed monument of Christ's saving truth,—shall we be content to say that we have still one ordinance left? At the Rappahannock one of the Federal regiments, just because its standard was shot away, was mistaken by our own men for a regiment of Confederates, and was subjected to a murderous enfilading fire that decimated its ranks. Baptism and the Lord's Supper are the two flags of Christ's army,—we cannot afford to lose either one of them.

4. *The Subjects of Baptism.*

The proper subjects of baptism are those only who give credible evidence that they have been regenerated by the Holy Spirit,—or, in other words, have entered by faith into the communion of Christ's death and resurrection.

A. Proof that only persons giving evidence of being regenerated are proper subjects of baptism :

(a) From the command and example of Christ and his apostles, which show :

First, that those only are to be baptized who have previously been made disciples.

Mat. 28 : 19 —"Go ye therefore, and make disciples of all the nations, baptizing them into the name of the Father and of the Son and of the Holy Spirit "; Acts 2 : 41 —"They then that received his word were baptized."

Secondly, that those only are to be baptized who have previously repented and believed.

Mat. 3 : 2, 3, 6 —"Repent ye . . . . make ye ready the way of the Lord . . . . and they were baptized of him in the river Jordan, confessing their sins "; Acts 2 : 37, 38 —"Now when they heard this, they were pricked in their heart, and said unto Peter and the rest of the apostles, Brethren, what shall we do? And Peter said unto them, Repent ye, and be baptized every one of you "; 8 : 12 —"But when they believed Philip preaching good tidings concerning the kingdom of God and the name of Jesus Christ, they were baptized, both men and women "; 18 : 8 —"And Crispus, the ruler of the synagogue, believed in the Lord with all his house; and many of the Corinthians hearing believed, and were baptized "; 19 : 4 —"John baptized with the baptism of repentance, saying unto the people that they should believe on him that should come after him, that is, on Jesus."

(b) From the nature of the church — as a company of regenerate persons.

John 3 : 5 —"Except one be born of water and the Spirit, he cannot enter into the kingdom of God "; Rom. 6 : 13 — "neither present your members unto sin as instruments of unrighteousness; but present yourselves unto God, as alive from the dead, and your members as instruments of righteousness unto God."

(*c*) From the symbolism of the ordinance,—as declaring a previous spiritual change in him who submits to it.

Acts 10 : 47 —"Can any man forbid the water, that these should not be baptized, who have received the Holy Spirit as well as we ? " Rom. 6 : 2-5 —"We who died to sin, how shall we any longer live therein ? Or are ye ignorant that all we who were baptized into Christ Jesus were baptized into his death ? We were buried therefore with him through baptism into death : that like as Christ was raised from the dead through the glory of the Father, so we also might walk in newness of life. For if we have become united with him in the likeness of his death, we shall be also in the likeness of his resurrection " ; Gal. 3 : 26, 27 —"For ye are all sons of God, through faith, in Christ Jesus. For as many of you as were baptized into Christ did put on Christ."

As marriage should never be solemnized except between persons who are already joined in heart and with whom the outward ceremony is only the sign of an existing love, so baptism should never be administered except in the case of those who are already joined to Christ and who signify in the ordinance their union with him in his death and resurrection. See Dean Stanley on Baptism, 24 — " In the apostolic age and in the three centuries which followed, it is evident that, as a general rule, those who came to baptism came in full age, of their own deliberate choice. The liturgical service of baptism was framed for full-grown converts, and is only by considerable adaptation applied to the case of infants " ; Wayland, Principles and Practices of Baptists, 93 ; Robins, in Madison Avenue Lectures, 136-159.

B.   Inferences from the fact that only persons giving evidence of being regenerate are proper subjects of baptism :

(*a*) Since only those who give credible evidence of regeneration are proper subjects of baptism, baptism cannot be the means of regeneration. It is the appointed sign, but is never the condition, of the forgiveness of sins.

Passages like Mat. 3 : 11 ; Mark 1 : 4 ; 16 : 16 ; John 3 : 5 ; Acts 2 : 38 ; 22 : 16 ; Eph. 5 : 26 ; Titus 3 : 5 ; and Heb. 10 : 22, are to be explained as particular instances " of the general fact that, in Scripture language, a single part of a complex action, and even that part of it which is most obvious to the senses, is often mentioned for the whole of it, and thus, in this case, the whole of the solemn transaction is designated by the external symbol." In other words, the entire change, internal and external, spiritual and ritual, is referred to in language belonging strictly only to the outward aspect of it. So the other ordinance is referred to by simply naming the visible " breaking of bread," and the whole transaction of the ordination of ministers is termed the " imposition of hands " (*cf.* Acts 2 : 42 ; 1 Tim. 4 : 14).

Mat. 3 : 11 —"I indeed baptize you in water unto repentance" ; Mark 1 : 4 —"the baptism of repentance unto remission of sins " ; 16 : 16 —"He that believeth and is baptized shall be saved " ; John 3 : 5 —"Except one be born of water and the Spirit, he cannot enter into the kingdom of God "—here Nicodemus, who was familiar with John's baptism, and with the refusal of the Sanhedrin to recognize its claims, is told that the baptism of water, which he suspects may be obligatory, is indeed necessary to that complete change by which one enters outwardly, as well as inwardly, into the kingdom of God ; but he is taught also, that to "be born of water" is worthless unless it is the accompaniment and sign of a new birth of "the Spirit" ; and therefore, in the further statements of Christ, baptism is not alluded to ; see verses 6, 8 —"that which is born of the Spirit is spirit . . . . so is every one that is born of the Spirit."

Acts 2 : 38 —"Repent ye, and be baptized . . . . unto the remission of your sins "—on this passage see Hackett : "The phrase 'in order to the forgiveness of sins' we connect naturally with both the preceding verbs ('repent' and 'be baptized'). The clause states the motive or object which should induce them to repent and be baptized. It enforces the entire exhortation, not one part to the exclusion of the other"— *i. e.*, they were to repent for the remission of sins, quite as much as they were to be baptized for the remission of sins. Acts 22 : 16 —"arise, and be baptized, and wash away thy sins, calling on his name " ; Eph. 5 : 26 —"that he might sanctify it [the church], having cleansed it by the washing of water with the word " ; Tit. 3 : 5 —

"according to his mercy he saved us, through the washing of regeneration [baptism] and renewing of the Holy Spirit [the new birth]" ; Heb. 10 : 22 —"having our hearts sprinkled from an evil conscience [regeneration]: and having our body washed with pure water [baptism]"; *cf.* Acts 2:42 —"the breaking of bread"; 1 Tim. 4:¼ — "the laying on of the hands of the presbytery."

Dr. A. C. Kendrick : "Considering how inseparable they were in the Christian profession — believe and be baptized, and how imperative and absolute was the requisition upon the believer to testify his allegiance by baptism, it could not be deemed singular that the two should be thus united, as it were, in one complex conception. . . . . We have no more right to assume that the birth from water involves the birth from the Spirit and thus do away with the one, than to assume that the birth from the Spirit involves the birth from water, and thus do away with the other. We have got to have them both, each in its distinctness, in order to fulfil the conditions of membership in the kingdom of God." Without baptism, faith is like the works of a clock that has no dial or hands by which one can tell the time ; or like the political belief of a man who refuses to go to the polls and vote. Without baptism, discipleship is ineffective and incomplete. The inward change — regeneration by the Spirit — may have occurred, but the outward change — Christian profession — is yet lacking.

Campbellism, however, holds that instead of regeneration preceding baptism and expressing itself in baptism, it is completed only in baptism, so that baptism is a means of regeneration. Alexander Campbell: "I am bold to affirm that every one of them, who in the belief of what the apostle spoke was immersed, did, in the very instant in which he was put under water, receive the forgiveness of his sins and the gift of the Holy Spirit." But Peter commanded that men should be baptized because they had already received the Holy Spirit: Acts 10: 47 —"Can any man forbid the water, that these should not be baptized, who have received the Holy Spirit as well as we?" Baptists baptize Christians; Disciples baptize sinners, and in baptism think to make them Christians. With this form of sacramentalism, Baptists are necessarily less in sympathy than with pedobaptism or with sprinkling. The view of the Disciples confines the divine efficiency to the word (see quotation from Campbell on page 821). It was anticipated by Claude Pajon, the Reformed theologian, in 1673; see Dorner, Gesch. prot. Theologie, 448-450. That this was not the doctrine of John the Baptist would appear from Josephus, Ant., 18:5 :2, who in speaking of John's baptism says: "Baptism appears acceptable to God, not in order that those who were baptized might get free from certain sins, but in order that the body might be sanctified, because the soul beforehand had already been purified through righteousness."

Disciples acknowledge no formal creed, and they differ so greatly among themselves that we append the following statements of their founder and of later representatives. Alexander Campbell, Christianity Restored, 138 (in The Christian Baptist, 5:100): "In and by the act of immersion, as soon as our bodies are put under water, at that very instant our former or old sins are washed away. . . . . Immersion and regeneration are Bible names for the same act. . . . . It is not our faith in God's promise of remission, but our going down into the water, that obtains the remission of sins." W. E. Garrison, Alexander Campbell's Theology, 247-299 — "Baptism, like naturalization, is the formal oath of allegiance by which an alien becomes a citizen. In neither case does the form in itself effect any magical change in the subject's disposition. In both cases a change of opinion and of affections is presupposed, and the form is the culmination of a process. . . . . It is as easy for God to forgive our sins in the act of immersion as in any other way." All work of the Spirit is through the word, only through sensible means, emotions being no criterion. God is transcendent; all authority is external, enforced only by appeal to happiness -- a thoroughly utilitarian system.

Isaac Erret is perhaps the most able of recent Disciples. In his tract entitled "Our Position," published by the Christian Publishing Company, St. Louis, he says : "As to the *design* of baptism, we part company with Baptists, and find ourselves more at home on the other side of the house; yet we cannot say that our position is just the same with that of any of them. Baptists say they baptize believers *because they are forgiven,* and they insist that they shall have the evidence of pardon before they are baptized. But the language used in the Scriptures declaring what baptism is for, is so plain and unequivocal that the great majority of Protestants as well as the Roman Catholics admit it in their creeds to be, in some sense, for the remission of sins. The latter, however, and many of the former, attach to it the idea of regeneration, and insist that in baptism regeneration by the Holy Spirit is actually conferred. Even the Westminster Confession squints strongly in this direction, albeit its professed adherents of the present time attempt to explain away its meaning. We are as far from this ritualistic extreme as from the anti-ritualism into which the Baptists have been driven. With us, regeneration must be so far accomplished before baptism that the subject is changed in heart, and in faith and penitence must have yielded up his heart to Christ — otherwise baptism is nothing but an empty form. But *forgiveness is something distinct from regeneration*. Forgiveness is an act of the Sovereign — not a change of the sinner's heart ; and while it is extended in view of the sinner's faith and repentance, it needs to be offered in a sensible and tangible form, such that the sinner can seize it and appropriate it with unmistakable definiteness. In baptism he *appropriates God's promise of forgiveness*, relying on the divine testimonies : ' He that believeth and is baptized shall be saved ' ; ' Repent and be baptized, every one of you, in the name of Jesus Christ, for the remission of sins, and you shall receive the gift of the Holy Spirit.' He thus lays hold of the promise of Christ and appropriates it as his own. He does not *merit* it, nor *procure* it, nor *earn* it, in being baptized ; but he *appropriates* what the mercy of God has provided and offered in the gospel. We therefore teach all who are baptized that, if they bring to their baptism a heart that renounces sin and implicitly trusts the power of Christ to save, they should rely on the Savior's own promise — He that believeth and is baptized shall be saved.' "

All these utterances agree in making forgiveness chronologically distinct from regeneration, as the concluding point is distinct from the whole. Regeneration is not entirely the work of God, — it must be completed by man. It is not wholly a change of heart, it is also a change in outward action. We see in this system of thought the beginnings of sacramentalism, and we regard it as containing the same germs of error which are more fully developed in pedobaptist doctrine. Shakespeare represents this view in Henry V, 1 : 2 — " What you speak is in your conscience washed As pure as sin with baptism "; Othello, 2 : 3 — Desdemona could " Win the Moor — were ' t to renounce his baptism — All seals and symbols of redeemed sin."

Dr. G. W. Lasher, in the Journal and Messenger, holds that Mat. 3 : 11 — "I indeed baptize you in water unto (εἰς) repentance " — does not imply that baptism effects the repentance ; the baptism was *because of* the repentance, for John refused to baptize those who did not give evidence of repentance before baptism. Mat. 10 : 42 — " whosoever shall give . . . . a cup of cold water only, in (εἰς) the name of a disciple " — the cup of cold water does not put one into the name of a disciple, or make him a disciple. Mat. 12 : 41 — " The men of Nineveh . . . . repented at (εἰς) the preaching of Jonah " = because of. Dr. Lasher argues that, in all these cases, the meaning of εἰς is " in respect to," " with reference to." So he would translate Acts 2 : 38 — "Repent ye, and be baptized . . . . with respect to, in reference to, the remission of sins." This is also the view of Meyer. He maintains that βαπτίζειν εἰς always means " baptize with reference to (cf. Mat. 28 : 19 ; 1 Cor. 10 : 12 ; Gal. 3 : 27 ; Acts 2 : 38 ; 8 : 16 ; 19 : 5). We are brought through baptism, he would say, into fellowship with his death, so that we have a share ethically in his death, through the cessation of our life to sin.

The better parallel, however, in our judgment, is found in Rom. 10 : 10 — " with the heart man believeth unto (εἰς) righteousness ; and with the mouth confession is made unto (εἰς) salvation," — where evidently salvation is the end *to* which works the whole change and process, including both faith and confession. So Broadus makes John's 'baptism unto repentance ' mean baptism in order to repentance, repentance including both the purpose of the heart and the outward expression of it, or baptism in order to complete and thorough repentance. Expositor's Greek Testament, on Acts 2 : 38 — " unto the remission of your sins ": " εἰς, unto, signifying the aim." For the High Church view, see Sadler, Church Doctrine, 41-124. On F. W. Robertson's view of Baptismal Regeneration, see Gordon, in Bap. Quar., 1869 : 405. On the whole matter of baptism for the remission of sins, see Gates, Baptists and Disciples (advocating the Disciple view) ; Willmarth, in Bap. Quar., 1877 : 1-26 (verging toward the Disciple view) ; and *per contra*, Adkins, Disciples and Baptists, booklet pub. by Am. Bap. Pub. Society (the best brief statement of the Baptist position) ; Bap. Quar., 1877 : 476-489 ; 1872 : 214 ; Jacob, Eccl. Pol. of N. T., 255, 256.

(*b*) As the profession of a spiritual change already wrought, baptism is primarily the act, not of the administrator, but of the person baptized.

Upon the person newly regenerate the command of Christ first terminates ; only upon his giving evidence of the change within him does it become the duty of the church to see that he has opportunity to follow Christ in baptism. Since baptism is primarily the act of the convert, no lack of qualification on the part of the administrator invalidates the baptism, so long as the proper outward act is performed, with intent on the part of the person baptized to express the fact of a preceding spiritual renewal (Acts 2 : 37, 38).

Acts 2 : 37, 38 — "Brethren, what shall we do? . . . . Repent ye and be baptized." If baptism be primarily the act of the administrator or of the church, then invalidity in the administrator or the church renders the ordinance itself invalid. But if baptism be primarily the act of the person baptized — an act which it is the church's business simply to scrutinize and further, then nothing but the absence of immersion, or of an intent to profess faith in Christ, can invalidate the ordinance. It is the erroneous view that baptism is the act of the administrator which causes the anxiety of High Church Baptists to deduce their Baptist line ge from regularly baptized ministers all the way back to John the Baptist, and which induces many modern endeavors of pedobaptists to prove that the earliest Baptists of England and the Continent did not immerse. All these solicitudes are unnecessary. We have no need to prove a Baptist apostolic succession. If we can derive our doctrine and practice from the New Testament, it is all we require.

The Council of Trent was right in its Canon : " If any one saith that the baptism which is even given by heretics in the name of the Father and of the Son and of the Holy Ghost, with the intention of doing what the church doeth, is not true baptism, let him be anathema." Dr. Norman Fox : " It is no more important who baptizes a man than who leads him to Christ." John Spilsbury, first pastor of the church of Particular Baptists, holding to a limited atonement, in London, was newly baptized in 1633, on the ground that " baptizedness is not essential to the administrator," and he repudiated the demand for apostolic succession, as leading logically to the " popedom of Rome." In 1641, immersion followed, though two or three years before this, or in March, 1639, Roger Williams was baptized by Ezekiel Holliman in Rhode Island. Williams afterwards doubted its validity, thus clinging still to the notion of apostolic succession.

(c) As intrusted with the administration of the ordinances, however, the church is, on its part, to require of all candidates for baptism credible evidence of regeneration.

This follows from the nature of the church and its duty to maintain its own existence as an institution of Christ. The church which cannot restrict admission into its membership to such as are like itself in character and aims must soon cease to be a church by becoming indistinguishable from the world. The duty of the church to gain credible evidence of regeneration in the case of every person admitted into the body involves its right to require of candidates, in addition to a profession of faith with the lips, some satisfactory proof that this profession is accompanied by change in the conduct. The kind and amount of evidence which would have justified the reception of a candidate in times of persecution may not now constitute a sufficient proof of change of heart.

If an Odd Fellows' Lodge, in order to preserve its distinct existence, must have its own rules for admission to membership, much more is this true of the church. The church may make its own regulations with a view to secure credible evidence of regeneration. Yet it is bound to demand of the candidate no more than reasonable proof of his repentance and faith. Since the church is to be convinced of the candidate's fitness before it votes to receive him to its membership, it is generally best that the experience of the candidate should be related before the church. Yet in extreme cases, as of sickness, the church may hear this relation of experience through certain appointed representatives.

Baptism is sometimes figuratively described as " the door into the church." The phrase is unfortunate, since if by the church is meant the spiritual kingdom of God, then Christ is its only door ; if the local body of believers is meant, then the faith of the candidate, the credible evidence of regeneration which he gives, the vote of the church itself, are all, equally with baptism, the door through which he enters. The door, in this sense, is a double door, one part of which is his confession of faith, and the other his baptism.

(*d*) As the outward expression of the inward change by which the believer enters into the kingdom of God, baptism is the first, in point of time, of all outward duties.

Regeneration and baptism, although not holding to each other the relation of effect and cause, are both regarded in the New Testament as essential to the restoration of man's right relations to God and to his people. They properly constitute parts of one whole, and are not to be unnecessarily separated. Baptism should follow regeneration with the least possible delay, after the candidate and the church have gained evidence that a spiritual change has been accomplished within him. No other duty and no other ordinance can properly precede it.

Neither the pastor nor the church should encourage the convert to wait for others' company before being baptized. We should aim continually to deepen the sense of individual responsibility to Christ, and of personal duty to obey his command of baptism just so soon as a proper opportunity is afforded. That participation in the Lord's Supper cannot properly precede Baptism, will be shown hereafter.

(*e*) Since regeneration is a work accomplished once for all, the baptism which symbolizes this regeneration is not to be repeated.

Even where the persuasion exists, on the part of the candidate, that at the time of baptism he was mistaken in thinking himself regenerated, the ordinance is not to be administered again, so long as it has once been submitted to, with honest intent, as a profession of faith in Christ. We argue this from the absence of any reference to second baptisms in the New Testament, and from the grave practical difficulties attending the opposite view. In Acts 19 : 1-5, we have an instance, not of rebaptism, but of the baptism for the first time of certain persons who had been wrongly taught with regard to the nature of John the Baptist's doctrine, and so had ignorantly submitted to an outward rite which had in it no reference to Jesus Christ and expressed no faith in him as a Savior. This was not John's baptism, nor was it in any sense true baptism. For this reason Paul commanded them to be " baptized in the name of the Lord Jesus."

In the respect of not being repeated, Baptism is unlike the Lord's Supper, which symbolizes the continuous sustaining power of Christ's death, while baptism symbolizes its power to begin a new life within the soul. In Acts 19:1-5, Paul instructs the new disciples that the real baptism of John, to which they erroneously supposed they had submitted, was not only a baptism of repentance, but a baptism of faith in the coming Savior. "And when they heard this, they were baptized in the name of the Lord Jesus " — as they had not been before. Here there was no rebaptism, for the mere outward submersion in water to which they had previously submitted, with no thought of professing faith in Christ, was no baptism at all — whether Johannine or Christian. See Brooks, in Baptist Quarterly, April, 1867, art.: Rebaptism.

Whenever it is clear, as in many cases of Campbellite immersion, that the candidate has gone down into the water, not with intent to profess a previously existing faith, but in order to be regenerated, baptism is still to be administered if the person subsequently believes on Christ. But wherever it appears that there was intent to profess an already existing faith and regeneration, there should be no repetition of the immersion, even though the ordinance has been administered by the Campbellites.

To rebaptize whenever a Christian's faith and joy are rekindled so that he begins to doubt the reality of his early experiences, would, in the case of many fickle believers, require many repetitions of the ordinance. The presumption is that, when the profession of faith was made by baptism, there was an actual faith which needed to be professed, and therefore that the baptism, though followed by much unbelief and many wanderings, was a valid one. Rebaptism, in the case of unstable Christians, tends to bring reproach upon the ordinance itself.

(*f*) So long as the mode and the subjects are such as Christ has enjoined, mere accessories are matters of individual judgment.

The use of natural rather than of artificial baptisteries is not to be elevated into an essential. The formula of baptism prescribed by Christ is "into the name of the Father and of the Son and of the Holy Spirit."

Mat. 28:19 — "baptizing them into the name of the Father and of the Son and of the Holy Spirit"; *cf.* Acts 8:16 — "they had been baptized into the name of the Lord Jesus"; Rom. 6:3 — "Or are ye ignorant that all we who were baptized into Christ Jesus were baptized into his death?" Gal. 3:27 — "For as many of you as were baptized into Christ did put on Christ." Baptism is immersion into God, into the presence, communion, life of the Trinity; see Com. of Clark, and of Lange, on Mat. 28:19; also C. E. Smith, in Bap. Rev., 1881:305–311. President Wayland and the Revised Version read, "into the name." *Per contra*, see Meyer (transl., 1:281, note) on Rom. 6:3; *cf.* Mat. 10:41; 18:20; in all which passages, as well as in Mat. 28:19, he claims that εἰς τὸ ὄνομα signifies "with reference to the name." In Acts 2:38, and 10:48, we have "in the name." For the latter translation of Mat. 28:19, see Conant, Notes on Mat., 171. On the whole subject of this section, see Dagg, Church Order, 13–73; Ingham, Subjects of Baptism.

C. Infant Baptism.

This we reject and reprehend, for the following reasons:

(*a*) Infant baptism is without warrant, either express or implied, in the Scripture.

First,—there is no express command that infants should be baptized. Secondly,—there is no clear example of the baptism of infants. Thirdly,— the passages held to imply infant baptism contain, when fairly interpreted, no reference to such a practice. In Mat. 19:14, none would have 'forbidden,' if Jesus and his disciples had been in the habit of baptizing infants. From Acts 16:15, *cf.* 40, and Acts 16:33, *cf.* 34, Neander says that we cannot infer infant baptism. For 1 Cor. 16:15 shows that the whole family of Stephanas, baptized by Paul, were adults (1 Cor. 1:16). It is impossible to suppose a whole heathen household baptized upon the faith of its head. As to 1 Cor. 7:14, Jacobi calls this text "a sure testimony against infant baptism, since Paul would certainly have referred to the baptism of children as a proof of their holiness, if infant baptism had been practised." Moreover, this passage would in that case equally teach the baptism of the unconverted husband of a believing wife. It plainly proves that the children of Christian parents were no more baptized and had no closer connection with the Christian church, than the unbelieving partners of Christians.

Mat. 19:14 — "Suffer the little children, and forbid them not, to come unto me: for to such belongeth the kingdom of heaven"; Acts 16:15 — "And when she [Lydia] was baptized, and her household"; *cf.* 40 — "And they went out of the prison, and entered into the house of Lydia: and when they had seen the brethren, they comforted them, and departed." Acts 16:33 — The jailor "was baptized, he and all his, immediately"; *cf.* 34 — "And he brought them up into his house, and set food before them, and rejoiced greatly, with all his house, having believed in God"; 1 Cor. 16:15 — "ye know the house of Stephanas, that it is the firstfruits of Achaia, and that they have set themselves to minister unto the saints"; 1:16 — "And I baptized also the household of Stephanas"; 7:14 — "For the unbelieving husband is sanctified in the wife, and the unbelieving wife is sanctified in the brother: else were your children unclean; but now are they holy" — here the sanctity or holiness attributed to unbelieving members of the household is evidently that of external connection and privilege, like that of the O. T. Israel.

Broadus, Am. Com., on Mat. 19:14 — "No Greek Commentator mentions infant baptism in connection with this passage, though they all practised that rite." Schleiermacher, Glaubenslehre, 2:383 — "All the traces of infant baptism which it has been desired to find in the New Testament must first be put into it." Pfleiderer, Grundriss, 184–187 —

"Infant baptism cannot be proved from the N. T., and according to 1 Cor. 7 : 14 it is ante-cedently improbable ; yet it was the logical consequence of the command, Mat. 28 : 19 sq., in which the church consciousness of the 2d century prophetically expressed Christ's appointment that it should be the universal church of the nations. . . . . Infant baptism represents one side of the Biblical sacrament, the side of the divine grace ; but it needs to have the other side, appropriation of that grace by personal freedom, added in confirmation."

Dr. A. S. Crapsey, formerly an Episcopal rector in Rochester, made the following statement in the introduction to a sermon in defence of infant baptism : " Now in support of this custom of the church, we can bring no express command of the word of God, no certain warrant of holy Scripture, nor can we be at all sure that this usage prevailed during the apostolic age. From a few obscure hints we may conjecture that it did, but it is only conjecture after all. It is true St. Paul baptized the household of Stephanas, of Lydia, and of the jailor at Philippi, and in these households there may have been little children ; but we do not know that there were, and these inferences form but a poor foundation upon which to base any doctrine. Better say at once, and boldly, that infant baptism is not expressly taught in holy Scripture. Not only is the word of God silent on this subject, but those who have studied the subject tell us that Christian writers of the very first age say nothing about it. It is by no means sure that this custom obtained in the church earlier than in the middle of the second or the beginning of the third century." Dr. C. M. Mead, in a private letter, dated May 27, 1895 — " Though a Congregationalist, I cannot find any Scriptural author-ization of pedobaptism, and I admit also that immersion seems to have been the prev-alent, if not the universal, form of baptism at the first."

A review of the passages held by pedobaptists to support their views leads us to the conclusion expressed in the North British Review, Aug. 1852 : 211, that infant baptism is utterly unknown to Scripture. Jacob, Eccl. Polity of N. T., 270–275 — " Infant bap-tism is not mentioned in the N. T. No instance of it is recorded there ; no allusion is made to its effects ; no directions are given for its administration. . . . . It is not an apostolic ordinance." See also Neander's view, in Kitto, Bib. Cyclop., art. : Baptism ; Kendrick, in Christian Rev., April, 1863 ; Curtis, Progress of Baptist Principles, 96 ; Wayland, Principles and Practices of Baptists, 125 ; Cunningham, lect. on Baptism, in Croall Lectures for 1886.

(b) Infant baptism is expressly contradicted :

First, — by the Scriptural prerequisites of faith and repentance, as signs of regeneration. In the great commission, Matthew speaks of baptizing disciples, and Mark of baptizing believers ; but infants are neither of these. Secondly, — by the Scriptural symbolism of the ordinance. As we should not bury a person before his death, so we should not symbolically bury a person by baptism until he has in spirit died to sin. Thirdly, — by the Scriptural constitution of the church. The church is a company of persons whose union with one another presupposes and expresses a previous con-scious and voluntary union of each with Jesus Christ. But of this conscious and voluntary union with Christ infants are not capable. Fourthly, — by the Scriptural prerequisites for participation in the Lord's Supper. Parti-cipation in the Lord's Supper is the right only of those who can discern the Lord's body (1 Cor. 11 : 29). No reason can be assigned for restrict-ing to intelligent communicants the ordinance of the Supper, which would not equally restrict to intelligent believers the ordinance of Baptism.

Infant baptism has accordingly led in the Greek church to infant communion. This course seems logically consistent. If baptism is administered to unconscious babes, they should participate in the Lord's Supper also. But if confirmation or any intelli-gent profession of faith is thought necessary before communion, why should not such confirmation or profession be thought necessary before baptism ? On Jonathan Edwards and the Halfway Covenant, see New Englander, Sept. 1884 : 601–614 ; G. L. Walker, Aspects of Religious Life of New England, 61–82 ; Dexter, Congregationalism, 487, note — " It has been often intimated that President Edwards opposed and destroyed the Halfway Covenant. He did oppose Stoddardism, or the doctrine that the Lord's Supper is a converting ordinance, and that unconverted men, because they are such, should be encouraged to partake of it." The tendency of his system was adverse to it; but, for all that appears in his published writings, he could have approved and administered that form of the Halfway Covenant then current among the churches. John Fiske says of Jonathan Edwards's preaching: "The prominence he gave to spiritual conversion, or what was called 'change of heart,' brought about the overthrow of the doctrine of the Halfway Covenant. It also weakened the logical basis of infant baptism, and led to the winning of hosts of converts by the Baptists."

Other pedobaptist bodies than the Greek Church save part of the truth, at the expense of consistency, by denying participation in the Lord's Supper to those baptized in infancy until they have reached years of understanding and have made a public profession of faith. Dr. Charles E. Jefferson, at the International Congregational Council of Boston, September, 1899, urged that the children of believers are already church members, and that as such they are entitled, not only to baptism, but also to the Lord's Supper — "an assertion that started much thought"! Baptists may well commend Congregationalists to the teaching of their own Increase Mather, The Order of the Gospel (1700), 11 — "The Congregational Church discipline is not suited for a worldly interest or for a formal generation of professors. It will stand or fall as godliness in the power of it does prevail, or otherwise. . . . . If the begun Apostacy should proceed as fast the next thirty years as it has done these last, surely it will come that in New England (except the gospel itself depart with the order of it) that the most conscientious people therein will think themselves concerned *to gather churches out of churches.*"

How much of Judaistic externalism may linger among nominal Christians is shown by the fact that in the Armenian Church animal sacrifices survived, or were permitted to converted heathen priests, in order they might not lose their livelihood. These sacrifices continued in other regions of Christendom, particularly in the Greek church, and Pope Gregory the Great permitted them; see Conybeare, in Am. Jour. Theology, Jan. 1893: 62-90. In The Key of Truth, a manual of the Paulician Church of Armenia, whose date in its present form is between the seventh and the ninth centuries, we have the Adoptianist view of Christ's person, and of the subjects and the mode of baptism: "Thus also the Lord, having learned from the Father, proceeded to teach us to perform baptism and all other commandments at the age of full growth and at no other time. . . . . For some have broken and destroyed the holy and precious canons which by the Father Almighty were delivered to our Lord Jesus Christ, and have trodden them underfoot with their devilish teaching, ... baptizing those who are irrational, and communicating the unbelieving."

Minority is legally divided into three septennates: 1. From the first to the seventh year, the age of complete irresponsibility, in which the child cannot commit a crime; 2. from the seventh to the fourteenth year, the age of partial responsibility, in which intelligent consciousness of the consequences of actions is not assumed to exist, but may be proved in individual instances; 3. from the fourteenth to the twenty-first year, the age of discretion, in which the person is responsible for criminal action, may choose a guardian, make a will, marry with consent of parents, make business contracts not wholly void, but is not yet permitted fully to assume the free man's position in the State. The church however is not bound by these hard and fast rules. Wherever it has evidence of conversion and of Christian character, it may admit to baptism and church membership, even at a very tender age.

(c) The rise of infant baptism in the history of the church is due to sacramental conceptions of Christianity, so that all arguments in its favor from the writings of the first three centuries are equally arguments for baptismal regeneration.

Neander's view may be found in Kitto, Cyclopædia, 1:287 — "Infant baptism was established neither by Christ nor by his apostles. Even in later times Tertullian opposed it, the North African church holding to the old practice." The newly discovered Teaching of the Apostles, which Bryennios puts at 140-160 A. D., and Lightfoot at 80-110 A. D., seems to know nothing of infant baptism.

Professor A. H. Newman, in Bap. Rev., Jan. 1884 — "Infant baptism has always gone hand in hand with State churches. It is difficult to conceive how an ecclesiastical establishment could be maintained without infant baptism or its equivalent. We should think, if the facts did not show us so plainly the contrary, that the doctrine of justification by faith alone would displace infant baptism. But no. The *establishment* must be maintained. The rejection of infant baptism implies insistence upon a baptism of believers. Only the baptized are properly members of the church. Even adults would not all receive baptism on professed faith, unless they were actually compelled to do so. Infant baptism must therefore be retained as the necessary concomitant of a State church.

"But what becomes of the justification by faith? Baptism, if it symbolizes anything, symbolizes regeneration. It would be ridiculous to make the symbol to forerun the fact by a series of years. Luther saw the difficulty; but he was sufficient for the emergency. 'Yes,' said he, 'justification is by faith alone. No outward rite, apart from faith, has any efficacy.' Why, it was against *opera operata* that he was laying out all his strength. Yet baptism is the symbol of regeneration, and baptism must be administered to infants, or the State church falls. With an audacity truly sublime, the great reformer declares that infants are regenerated in connection with baptism, and that they are *simultaneously justified by personal faith*. An infant eight days old believe? 'Prove the contrary if you can!' triumphantly ejaculates Luther, and his point is gained. If this kind of personal faith is said to justify infants, is it wonderful that those of maturer years learned to take a somewhat superficial view of the faith that justifies?"

Yet Luther had written: "Whatever is without the word of God is by that very fact against God"; see his Briefe, ed. DeWette, II: 292; J. G. Walch, De Fide in Utero. There was great discordance between Luther as reformer, and Luther as conservative churchman. His Catholicism, only half overcome, broke into all his views of faith. In his early years, he stood for reason and Scripture; in his later years he fought reason and Scripture in the supposed interest of the church.

Mat. 18:10 — "See that ye despise not one of these little ones" — which refers not to little children but to childlike believers, Luther adduces as a proof of infant baptism, holding that the child is said to believe—"Little ones that believe on me" (verse 6) — because it has been circumcised and received into the number of the elect. "And so, through baptism, children become believers. How else could the children of Turks and Jews be distinguished from those of Christians?" Does this involve the notion that infants dying unbaptized are lost? To find the very apostle of justification by faith saying that a little child becomes a *believer* by being baptized, is humiliating and disheartening (so Broadus. Com. on Matthew, page 384, note).

Pfleiderer, Philos. Religion, 2:342-345, quotes from Lang as follows: "By mistaking and casting down the Protestant spirit which put forth its demands on the time in Carlstadt, Zwingle, and others, Luther made Protestantism lose its salt; he inflicted wounds upon it from which it has not yet recovered to-day; and the ecclesiastical struggle of the present is just a struggle of spiritual freedom against Lutherism." E. G. Robinson: "Infant baptism is a rag of Romanism. Since regeneration is always through the truth, baptismal regeneration is an absurdity." See Christian Review, Jan. 1851; Neander, Church History, 1:311, 313; Coleman, Christian Antiquities, 258-260; Arnold, in Bap. Quarterly, 1869:32; Hovey, in Bap. Quarterly, 1871:75.

(*d*) The reasoning by which it is supported is unscriptural, unsound, and dangerous in its tendency:

First,—in assuming the power of the church to modify or abrogate a command of Christ. This has been sufficiently answered above. Secondly, —in maintaining that infant baptism takes the place of circumcision under the Abrahamic covenant. To this we reply that the view contradicts the New Testament idea of the church, by making it a hereditary body, in which fleshly birth, and not the new birth, qualifies for membership. "As the national Israel typified the spiritual Israel, so the circumcision which immediately followed, not preceded, natural birth, bids us baptize children, not before, but after spiritual birth." Thirdly,—in declaring that baptism belongs to the infant because of an organic connection of the child with the parent, which permits the latter to stand for the former and to make profession of faith for it,—faith already existing germinally in the child by virtue of this organic union, and certain for the same reason to be developed as the child grows to maturity. "A law of organic connection as regards character subsisting between the parent and the child,—such a connection as induces the conviction that the character of the one is actually included in the character of the other, as the seed is formed in the capsule." We object to this view that it unwarrantably confounds the personality of the child with that of the parent; practically ignores the necessity of the Holy Spirit's regenerating influences in the case of children of Christian parents; and presumes in such children a gracious state which facts conclusively show not to exist.

What takes the place of circumcision is not baptism but regeneration. Paul defeated the attempt to fasten circumcision on the church, when he refused to have that rite performed on Titus. But later Judaizers succeeded in perpetuating circumcision under the form of infant baptism, and afterward of infant sprinkling (McGarvey, Com. on Acts). E. G. Robinson : " Circumcision is not a type of baptism : 1. It is purely a gra‑ tuitous assumption that it is so. There is not a word in Scripture to authorize it : 2. Circumcision was a national, a theocratic, and not a personal, religious rite; 3. If circumcision be a type, why did Paul circumcise Timothy ? Why did he not explain, on an occasion so naturally calling for it, that circumcision was replaced by baptism ?"

On the theory that baptism takes the place of circumcision, see Pepper, Baptist Quarterly, April, 1857; Palmer, in Baptist Quarterly, 1871 : 314. The Christian Church is either a natural, *hereditary* body, or it was merely *typified* by the Jewish people. In the former case, baptism belongs to all children of Christian parents, and the church is indistinguishable from the world. In the latter case, it belongs only to spiritual descendants, and therefore only to true believers. "That Jewish Christians, who of course had been circumcised, were also baptized, and that a large number of them insisted that Gentiles who had been baptized should also be circumcised, shows con‑ clusively that baptism did not take the place of circumcision. . . . . The notion that the family is the unit of society is a relic of barbarism. This appears in the Roman law, which was good for property but not for persons. It left none but a servile station to wife or son, thus degrading society at the fountain of family life. To gain freedom, the Roman wife had to accept a form of marriage which opened the way for unlimited liberty of divorce."

Hereditary church-membership is of the same piece with hereditary priesthood, and both are relics of Judaism. J. J. Murphy, Nat. Selection and Spir. Freedom, 81 — "The institution of hereditary priesthood, which was so deeply rooted in the religions of antiquity and was adopted into Judaism, has found no place in Christianity ; there is not, I believe, any church whatever calling itself by the name of Christ, in which the ministry is hereditary." Yet there is a growing disposition to find in infant baptism the guarantee of hereditary church membership. Washington Gladden, What is Left ? 252-254 — " Solidarity of the generations finds expression in infant baptism. Families ought to be Christian and not individuals only. In the Society of Friends every one born of parents belonging to the Society is a birthright member. Children of Christian parents are heirs of the kingdom. The State recognizes that our children are organi‑ cally connected with it. When parents are members of the State, children are not aliens. They are not called to perform duties of citizenship until a certain age, but the rights and privileges of citizenship are theirs from the moment of their birth. The State is the mother of her children ; shall the church be less motherly than the State ? . . . . Baptism does not make the child God's child ; it simply recognizes and declares the fact."

Another illustration of what we regard as a radically false view is found in the ser‑ mon of Bishop Grafton of Fond du Lac, at the consecration of Bishop Nicholson in Philadelphia : " Baptism is not like a function in the natural order, like the coronation of a king, an acknowledgment of what the child already is. The child, truly God's loved offspring by way of creation, is in baptism translated into the new creation and incorporated into the Incarnate One, and made his child." Yet, as the great majority of the inmates of our prisons and the denizens of the slums have received this ' bap‑ tism,' it appears that this ' loved offspring ' very early lost its ' new creation ' and got 'translated' in the wrong direction. We regard infant baptism as only an ancient example of the effort to bring in the kingdom of God by externals, the protest against which brought Jesus to the cross. Our modern methods of salvation by sociology and education and legislation are under the same indictment, as crucifying the Son of God afresh and putting him to open shame.

Prof. Moses Stuart urged that the form of baptism was immaterial, but that the temper of heart was the thing of moment. Francis Wayland, then a student of his, asked : " If such is the case, with what propriety can baptism be administered to those who cannot be supposed to exercise any temper of heart at all, and with whom the form must be everything ? " — The third theory of organic connection of the child with its parents is elaborated by Bushnell, in his Christian Nurture, 90-223. *Per contra*, see Bunsen, Hippolytus and his Times, 179, 211 ; Curtis, Progress of Baptist Principles, 262. Hezekiah's son Manasseh was not godly ; and it would be rash to say that all the drunkard's children are presumptively drunkards.

(*e*) The lack of agreement among pedobaptists as to the warrant for infant baptism and as to the relation of baptized infants to the church, together with the manifest decline of the practice itself, are arguments against it.

The propriety of infant baptism is variously argued, says Dr. Bushnell, upon the ground of "natural innocence, inherited depravity, and federal holiness ; because of the infant's own character, the parent's piety, and the church's faith ; for the reason that the child is an heir of salvation already, and in order to make it such. . . . . No settled opinion on infant baptism and on Christian nurture has ever been attained to."

Quot homines, tot sententiæ. The belated traveler in a thunderstorm prayed for a little more light and less noise. Bushnell, Christian Nurture, 9-89, denies original sin, denies that hereditary connection can make a child guilty. But he seems to teach transmitted righteousness, or that hereditary connection can make a child holy. He disparages "sensible experiences" and calls them "explosive conversions." But because we do not know the time of conversion, shall we say that there never was a time when the child experienced God's grace? See Bib. Sac., 1872:665. Bushnell said : "I don't know what right we have to say that a child can't be born again before he is born the first time." Did not John the Baptist preach Christ before he was born ? (Luke 1 :15, 41, 44). The answer to Bushnell is simply this, that regeneration is through the truth, and an unborn child cannot know the truth. To disjoin regeneration from the truth, is to make it a matter of external manipulation in which the soul is merely passive and the whole process irrational. There is a secret work of God in the soul, but it is always accompanied by an awakening of the soul to perceive the truth and to accept Christ.

Are baptized infants members of the Presbyterian Church? We answer by citing the following standards : 1. The Confession of Faith, 25 : 2 —"The visible church . . . . consists of all those throughout the world, that profess the true religion, together with their children." 2. The Larger Catechism, 62 — "The visible church is a society made up of all such as in all ages and places of the world do profess the true religion, and of their children." 166 — "Baptism is not to be administered to any that are not of the visible church . . . . till they profess their faith in Christ and obedience to him : but infants descending from parents either both or but one of them professing faith in Christ and obedience to him are in that respect within the covenant and are to be baptized." 3. The Shorter Catechism, 96 — "Baptism is not to be administered to any that are out of the visible church, till they profess their faith in Christ and obedience to him : but the infants of such as are members of the visible church are to be baptized." 4. Form of Government, 3 —"A particular church consists of a number of professing Christians, with their offspring." 5. Directory for Worship, 1 — "Children born within the pale of the visible church and dedicated to God in baptism are under the inspection and government of the church. . . . . When they come to years of discretion, if they be free from scandal, appear sober and steady, and to have sufficient knowledge to discern the Lord's body, they ought to be informed it is their duty and their privilege to come to the Lord's Supper."

The Maplewood Congregational Church of Malden, Mass., enrolls as members all children baptized by the church. The relation continues until they indicate a desire either to continue it or to dissolve it. The list of such members is kept distinct from that of the adults, but they are considered as members under the care of the church.

Dr. W. G. T. Shedd: "The infant of a believer is born into the church as the infant of a citizen is born into the State. A baptized child in adult years may renounce his baptism, become an infidel, and join the synagogue of Satan, but until he does this, he must be regarded as a member of the church of Christ."

On the Decline of Infant Baptism, see Vedder, in Baptist Review, April, 1882: 173–189, who shows that in fifty years past the proportion of infant baptisms to communicants in general has decreased from one in seven to one in eleven; among the Reformed, from one in twelve to one in twenty; among the Presbyterians, from one in fifteen to one in thirty-three; among the Methodists, from one in twenty-two to one in twenty-nine; among the Congregationalists, from one in fifty to one in seventy-seven.

(*f*) The evil effects of infant baptism are a strong argument against it:

First,—in forestalling the voluntary act of the child baptized, and thus practically preventing his personal obedience to Christ's commands.

The person baptized in infancy has never performed any act with intent to obey Christ's command to be baptized, never has put forth a single volition looking toward obedience to that command; see Wilkinson, The Baptist Principle, 40–46. Every man has the right to choose his own wife. So every man has the right to choose his own Savior.

Secondly,—in inducing superstitious confidence in an outward rite as possessed of regenerating efficacy.

French parents still regard infants before baptism as only animals (Stanley). The haste with which the minister is summoned to baptize the dying child shows that superstition still lingers in many an otherwise evangelical family in our own country. The English Prayerbook declares that in baptism the infant is "made a child of God and an inheritor of the kingdom of heaven." Even the Westminster Assembly's Catechism 28:6, holds that grace is actually conferred in baptism, though the efficacy of it is delayed till riper years. Mercersburg Review: "The objective medium or instrumental cause of regeneration is baptism. Men are not regenerated outside the church and then brought into it for preservation, but they are regenerated by being incorporated with or engrafted into the church through the sacrament of baptism." Catholic Review: "Unbaptized, these little ones go into darkness; but baptized, they rejoice in the presence of God forever."

Dr. Beebe of Hamilton went after a minister to baptize his sick child, but before he returned the child died. Reflection made him a Baptist, and the Editor of The Examiner. Baptists unhesitatingly permit converts to die unbaptized, showing plainly that they do not regard baptism as essential to salvation. Baptism no more makes one a Christian, than putting a crown on one's head makes him a king. Zwingle held to a symbolic interpretation of the Lord's Supper, but he clung to the sacramental conception of Baptism. E. H. Johnson, Uses and Abuses of Ordinances, 33, claims that, while baptism is not a justifying or regenerating ordinance, it is a sanctifying ordinance, — sanctifying, in the sense of setting apart. Yes, we reply, but only as church going and prayer are sanctifying; the efficacy is not in the outward act but in the spirit which accompanies it. To make it signify more is to admit the sacramental principle.

In the Roman Catholic Church the baptism of bells and of rosaries shows how infant baptism has induced the belief that grace can be communicated to irrational and even material things. In Mexico people bring caged birds, cats, rabbits, donkeys, and pigs, for baptism. The priest kneels before the altar in prayer, reads a few words in Latin, then sprinkles the creature with holy water. The sprinkling is supposed to drive out any evil spirit that may have vexed the bird or beast. In Key West, Florida, a town of 22,000 inhabitants, infant baptism has a stronger hold than anywhere else at the South. Baptist parents had sometimes gone to the Methodist preachers to have their children baptized. To prevent this, the Baptist pastors established the custom of laying their hands upon the heads of infants in the congregation, and 'blessing' them, *i. e.*, asking God's blessing to rest upon them. But this custom came to be confounded with christening, and was called such. Now the Baptist pastors are having a hard struggle to explain and limit the custom which they themselves have introduced. Perverse human nature will take advantage of even the slightest additions to N. T. prescriptions, and will bring out of the germs of false doctrine a fearful harvest of evil. Obsta principiis — "Resist beginnings."

Thirdly,—in obscuring and corrupting Christian truth with regard to the sufficiency of Scripture, the connection of the ordinances, and the inconsistency of an impenitent life with church-membership.

Infant baptism in England is followed by confirmation, as a matter of course, whether there has been any conscious abandonment of sin or not. In Germany, a man is always understood to be a Christian unless he expressly states to the contrary — in fact, he feels insulted if his Christianity is questioned. At the funerals even of infidels and debauchees the pall used may be inscribed with the words : " Blessed are the dead that die in the Lord." Confidence in one's Christianity and hopes of heaven based only on the fact of baptism in infancy, are a great obstacle to evangelical preaching and to the progress of true religion.

Wordsworth, The Excursion, 596, 602 (book 5) — " At the baptismal font. And when the pure And consecrating element hath cleansed The original stain, the child is thus received Into the second ark, Christ's church, with trust That he, from wrath redeemed therein shall float Over the billows of this troublesome world To the fair land of ever-lasting life. . . . . The holy rite That lovingly consigns the babe to the arms Of Jesus and his everlasting care." Infant baptism arose in the superstitious belief that there lay in the water itself a magical efficacy for the washing away of sin, and that apart from baptism there could be no salvation. This was and still remains the Roman Catholic position. Father Doyle, in Anno Domini, 2:182 — " Baptism regenerates. By means of it the child is born again into the newness of the supernatural life." Theo-dore Parker was baptized, but not till he was four years old, when his " Oh, don't ! " — in which his biographers have found prophetic intimation of his mature dislike for all conventional forms — was clearly the small boy's dislike of water on his face ; see Chadwick, Theodore Parker, 6, 7. " How do you know, my dear, that you have been christened ? " " Please, mum, 'cos I 've got the marks on my arm now, mum ! "

Fourthly,—in destroying the church as a spiritual body, by merging it in the nation and the world.

Ladd, Principles of Church Polity : " Unitarianism entered the Congregational churches of New England through the breach in one of their own avowed and most important tenets, namely, that of a regenerate church-membership. Formalism, indifferentism, neglect of moral reforms, and, as both cause and results of these, an abundance of unrenewed men and women, were the causes of their seeming disasters in that sad epoch." But we would add, that the serious and alarming decline of religion which culminated in the Unitarian movement in New England had its origin in infant baptism. This introduced into the church a multitude of unregenerate persons and permitted them to determine its doctrinal position.

W. B. Matteson : " No one practice of the church has done so much to lower the tone of its life and to debase its standards. The first New England churches were estab-lished by godly and regenerated men. They received into their churches, through infant baptism, children presumptively, but alas not actually, regenerated. The result is well known — swift, startling, seemingly irresistible decline. 'The body of the rising generation,' writes Increase Mother, 'is a poor perishing, inconverted, and, except the Lord pour out his Spirit, an undone generation.' The ' Halfway Covenant ' was at once a token of preceding, and a cause of further, decline. If God had not indeed poured out his Spirit in the great awakening under Edwards, New England might well, as some feared, ' be lost even to New England and buried in its own ruins.' It was the new emphasis on personal religion — an emphasis which the Baptists of that day largely contributed — that gave to the New England churches a larger life and a larger useful-ness. Infant baptism has never since held quite the same place in the polity of those churches. It has very generally declined. But it is still far from extinct, even among evangelical Protestants. The work of Baptists is not yet done. Baptists have always stood, but they need still to stand, for a believing and regenerated church-member-ship."

Fifthly,—in putting into the place of Christ's command a commandment of men, and so admitting the essential principle of all heresy, schism, and false religion.

There is therefore no logical halting-place between the Baptist and the Romanist positions. The Roman Catholic Archbishop Hughes of New York, said well to a Presbyterian minister: "We have no controversy with you. Our controversy is with the Baptists." Lange of Jena: "Would the Protestant church fulfil and attain to its final destiny, the baptism of infants must of necessity be abolished." The English Judge asked the witness what his religious belief was. Reply: "I haven't any." "Where do you attend church?" "Nowhere." "Put him down as belonging to the Church of England." The small child was asked where her mother was. Reply: "She has gone to a Christian and devil mee'ing." The child meant a Christian Endeavor meeting. Some systems of doctrine and ritual, however, answer her description, for they are a mixture of paganism and Christianity. The greatest work favoring the doctrine which we here condemn is Wall's History of Infant Baptism. For the Baptist side of the controversy see Arnold, in Madison Avenue Lectures, 160-182; Curtis, Progress of Baptist Principles, 274, 275; Dagg, Church Order, 144-202.

II. The Lord's Supper.

The Lord's Supper is that outward rite in which the assembled church eats bread broken and drinks wine poured forth by its appointed representative, in token of its constant dependence on the once crucified, now risen Savior, as source of its spiritual life; or, in other words, in token of that abiding communion of Christ's death and resurrection through which the life begun in regeneration is sustained and perfected.

Norman Fox, Christ in the Daily Meal, 31, 33, says that the Scripture nowhere speaks of the wine as "poured forth"; and in 1 Cor. 11 : 24 — "my body which is broken for you," the Revised Version omits the word "broken"; while on the other hand the Gospel according to John (19 : 36) calls especial attention to the fact that Christ's body was *not* broken. We reply that Jesus, in giving his disciples the cup, did speak of his blood as "poured out" (Mark 14 : 24); and it was not the body, but "a bone of him," which was not to be broken. Many ancient manuscripts add the word "broken" in 1 Cor. 11 : 24. On the Lord's Supper in general, see Weston, in Madison Avenue Lectures, 183-195; Dagg, Church Order, 203-214.

1. The Lord's Supper an ordinance instituted by Christ.

(a) Christ appointed an outward rite to be observed by his disciples in remembrance of his death. It was to be observed after his death; only after his death could it completely fulfil its purpose as a feast of commemoration.

Luke 22 : 19 — "And he took bread, and when he had given thanks, he brake it, and gave to them, saying, This is my body which is given for you : this do in remembrance of me. And the cup in like manner after supper, saying, This cup is the new covenant in my blood, even that which is poured out for you "; 1 Cor. 11 : 23-25 — "For I received of the Lord that which also I delivered unto you, that the Lord Jesus in the night in which he was betrayed took bread; and when he had given thanks, he brake it, and said, This is my body, which is for you : this do in remembrance of me. In like manner also the cup, after supper, saying, This cup is the new covenant in my blood : this do, as often as ye drink it, in remembrance of me." Observe that this communion was Christian communion before Christ's death, just as John's baptism was Christian baptism before Christ's death.

(b) From the apostolic injunction with regard to its celebration in the church until Christ's second coming, we infer that it was the original intention of our Lord to institute a rite of perpetual and universal obligation.

1 Cor. 11 : 26 — "For as often as ye eat this bread, and drink the cup, ye proclaim the Lord's death till he come "; *cf.* Mat. 26 : 29 — "But I say unto you, I shall not drink henceforth of this fruit of the vine, until that day when I drink it new with you in my Father's kingdom "; Mark 14 : 25 — "Verily I say unto you, I will no more drink of the fruit of the vine, until that day when I drink it new in the kingdom of God." As the paschal supper continued until Christ came the first time in the flesh, so the Lord's Supper is to continue until he comes the second time with all the power and glory of God.

(c) The uniform practice of the N. T. churches, and the celebration of such a rite in subsequent ages by almost all churches professing to be

Christian, is best explained upon the supposition that the Lord's Supper is an ordinance established by Christ himself.

Acts 2 : 42 —" And they continued stedfastly in the apostles' teaching and fellowship, in the breaking of bread and the prayers"; 46 —"And day by day, continuing stedfastly with one accord in the temple, and breaking bread at home, hey took their food with gladness and singleness of heart"—on the words here translated "at home" (κατ' οἶκον), but meaning, as Jacob maintains, "from one worship-room to another," see page 961. Acts 20 : 7 —"And upon the first day of the week, when we were gathered together to break bread, Paul discoursed with them"; 1 Cor. 10 : 16 —"The cup of blessing which we bless, is it not a communion of the blood of Christ? The bread which we break, is it not a communion of the body of Christ? seeing that we, who are many, are one bread, one body: for we all partake of the one bread."

2.   The Mode of administering the Lord's Supper.

(a)   The elements are bread and wine.

Although the bread which Jesus broke at the institution of the ordinance was doubtless the unleavened bread of the Passover, there is nothing in the symbolism of the Lord's Supper which necessitates the Romanist use of the wafer. Although the wine which Jesus poured out was doubtless the ordinary fermented juice of the grape, there is nothing in the symbolism of the ordinance which forbids the use of unfermented juice of the grape,—obedience to the command "This do in remembrance of me" (Luke 22 : 19) requires only that we should use the "fruit of the vine" (Mat. 26 : 29).

Huguenots and Roman Catholics, among Parkman's Pioneers of France in the New World, disputed whether the sacramental bread could be made of the meal of Indian corn. But it is only as food, that the bread is symbolic. Dried fish is used in Greenland. The bread only symbolizes Christ's life and the wine only symbolizes his death. Any food or drink may do the same. It therefore seems a very conscientious but unnecessary literalism, when Adoniram Judson (Life by his Son, 352) writes from Burma: " No wine to be procured in this place, on which account we are unable to meet with the other churches this day in partaking of the Lord's Supper." For proof that Bible wines, like all other wines, are fermented, see Presb. Rev., 1881 : 80-114 : 1882 : 78-108, 394-399, 586; Hovey, in Bap. Quar. Rev., April, 1887 : 152-180. Per contra, see Samson, Bible Wines. On the Scripture Law of Temperance, see Presb. Rev., 1882 : 287-324.

(b)   The communion is of both kinds,—that is, communicants are to partake both of the bread and of the wine.

The Roman Catholic Church withholds the wine from the laity, although it considers the whole Christ to be present under each of the forms. Christ, however, says: "Drink ye all of it" (Mat. 26 : 27). To withhold the wine from any believer is disobedience to Christ, and is too easily understood as teaching that the laity have only a portion of the benefits of Christ's death. Calvin: " As to the bread, he simply said 'Take, eat.' Why does he expressly bid them all drink? And why does Mark explicitly say that 'they all drank of it' (Mark 14 : 23)?" Bengel: Does not this suggest that, if communion in "one kind alone were sufficient, it is the cup which should be used? The Scripture thus speaks, foreseeing what Rome would do." See Expositor's Greek Testament on 1 Cor. 11 : 27. In the Greek Church the bread and wine are mingled and are administered to communicants, not to infants only but also to adults, with a spoon.

(c)   The partaking of these elements is of a festal nature.

The Passover was festal in its nature. Gloom and sadness are foreign to the spirit of the Lord's Supper. The wine is the symbol of the death of Christ, but of that death by which we live. It reminds us that he drank the cup of suffering in order that we might drink the wine of joy. As the bread is broken to sustain our physical life, so Christ's body was broken by thorns and nails and spear to nourish our spiritual life.

1 Cor. 11 : 29 —"For he that eateth and drinketh, eateth and drinketh judgment unto himself, if he discern not the body." Here the Authorized Version wrongly had " damnation" instead of "judgment." Not eternal condemnation, but penal judgment in general, is meant. He who partakes "in an unworthy manner" (verse 27), i. e., in hypocrisy, or merely to satisfy bodily appetites, and not discerning the body of Christ of which the bread is the symbol (verse 29), draws down upon him God's judicial sentence. Of this judgment, the frequent sickness and death in the church at Corinth was a token. See verses 30-34, and Meyer's Com.; also

Gould, in Am. Com. on 1 Cor. 11:27—"unworthily"—"This is not to be understood as referring to the unworthiness of the person himself to partake, but to the unworthy manner of partaking. . . . . The failure to recognize practically the symbolism of the elements, and hence the treatment of the Supper as a common meal, is just what the apostle has pointed out as the fault of the Corinthians, and it is what he characterizes as an unworthy eating and drinking." The Christian therefore should not be deterred from participation in the Lord's Supper by any feeling of his personal unworthiness, so long as he trusts Christ and aims to obey him, for "All the fitness he requireth Is to feel our need of him."

(*d*) The communion is a festival of commemoration,—not simply bringing Christ to our remembrance, but making proclamation of his death to the world.

1 Cor. 11:24, 26—"this do in remembrance of me. . . . . For as often as ye eat this bread and drink this cup, ye proclaim the Lord's death till he come." As the Passover commemorated the deliverance of Israel from Egypt, and as the Fourth of July commemorates our birth as a nation, so the Lord's Supper commemorates the birth of the church in Christ's death and resurrection. As a mother might bid her children meet over her grave and commemorate her, so Christ bids his people meet and remember him. But subjective remembrance is not its only aim. It is public proclamation also. Whether it brings perceptible blessing to us or not, it is to be observed as a means of confessing Christ, testifying our faith, and publishing the fact of his death to others.

(*e*) It is to be celebrated by the assembled church. It is not a solitary observance on the part of individuals. No "showing forth" is possible except in company.

Acts 20:7—"gathered together to break bread"; 1 Cor. 11:18, 20, 22, 33, 34—"when ye come together in the church . . . . assemble yourselves together . . . . have ye not houses to eat and to drink in? or despise ye the church of God, and put them to shame that have not? . . . . when ye come together to eat. . . . . If any man is hungry, let him eat at home; that your coming together be not unto judgment."

Jacob, Eccl. Polity of N. T., 191-194, claims that in Acts 2:46—"breaking bread at home"— where we have οἶκος, not οἰκία, οἶκος is not a private house, but a 'worship-room,' and that the phrase should be translated "breaking bread from one worship-room to another," or "in various worship-rooms." This meaning seems very apt in Acts 5:42— "And every day, in the temple and at home [rather, 'in various worship-rooms'], they ceased not to teach and to preach Jesus as the Christ"; 8:3—"But Saul laid waste the church, entering into every house [rather, 'every worship-room'] and dragging men and women committed them to prison"; Rom. 16:5—"salute the church that is in their house [rather, 'in their worship-room']"; Titus 1:11—"men who overthrow whole houses [rather 'whole worship-rooms'], teaching things which they ought not, for filthy lucre's sake." *Per contra*, however, see 1 Cor. 11:34—"let him eat at home," where οἶκος is contrasted with the place of meeting; so also 1 Cor. 14:35 and Acts 20:20, where οἶκος seems to mean a private house.

The celebration of the Lord's Supper in each family by itself is not recognized in the New Testament. Stanley, in Nineteenth Century, May, 1878, tells us that as infant communion is forbidden in the Western Church, and evening communion is forbidden by the Roman Church, so solitary communion is forbidden by the English Church, and death-bed communion by the Scottish Church. E. G. Robinson: "No single individual in the New Testament ever celebrates the Lord's Supper by himself." Mrs. Browning recognized the essentially social nature of the ordinance, when she said that truth was like the bread at the Sacrament—to be passed on. In this the Supper gives us a type of the proper treatment of all the goods of life, both temporal and spiritual.

Dr. Norman Fox, Christ in the Daily Meal, claims that the Lord's Supper is no more an exclusively church ordinance than is singing or prayer; that the command to observe it was addressed, not to an organized church, but only to individuals; that every meal in the home was to be a Lord's Supper, because Christ was remembered in it. But we reply that Paul's letter with regard to the abuses of the Lord's Supper was addressed, not to individuals, but to "the church of God which is at Corinth." (1 Cor. 1:2). Paul reproves the Corinthians because in the Lord's Supper each ate without thought of others: "What, have ye not houses to eat and to drink in? or despise ye the church of God, and put them to shame that have not?" (11:22). Each member having appeased his hunger at home, the members of the church "come together to eat" (11:30), as the spiritual body of Christ. All this shows that the celebration of the Lord's Supper was not an appendage to every ordinary meal.

In Acts 20:7 —"upon the first day of the week, when we were gathered together to break bread, Paul discoursed with them "— the natural inference is that the Lord's Supper was a sacred rite, observed apart from any ordinary meal, and accompanied by religious instruction. Dr. Fox would go back of these later observances to the original command of our Lord. He would eliminate all that we do not find in Mark, the earliest gospel. But this would deprive us of the Sermon on the Mount, the parable of the Prodigal Son, and the discourses of the fourth gospel. McGiffert gives A. D. 52, as the date of Paul's first letter to the Corinthians, and this ante-dates Mark's gospel by at least thirteen years. Paul's account of the Lord's Supper at Corinth is therefore an earlier authority than Mark.

(*f*) The responsibility of seeing that the ordinance is properly administered rests with the church as a body ; and the pastor is, in this matter, the proper representative and organ of the church. In cases of extreme exigency, however, as where the church has no pastor and no ordained minister can be secured, it is competent for the church to appoint one from its own number to administer the ordinance.

1 Cor. 11 : 2, 23 —"Now I praise you that ye remember me in all things, and hold fast the traditions, even as I delivered them to you . . . . For I received of the Lord that which also I delivered unto you, that the Lord Jesus in the night in which he was betrayed took bread." Here the responsibility of administering the Lord's Supper is laid upon the body of believers.

(*g*) The frequency with which the Lord's Supper is to be administered is not indicated either by the N. T. precept or by uniform N. T. example. We have instances both of its daily and of its weekly observance. With respect to this, as well as with respect to the accessories of the ordinance, the church is to exercise a sound discretion.

Acts 2 : 46 — "And day by day, continuing stedfastly with one accord in the temple, and breaking bread at home [or perhaps, 'in various worship-rooms']"; 20 : 7 — "And upon the first day of the week, when we were gathered together to break bread." In 1878, thirty-nine churches of the Establishment in London held daily communion ; in two churches it was held twice each day. A few churches of the Baptist faith in England and America celebrate the Lord's Supper on each Lord's day. Carlstadt would celebrate the Lord's Supper only in companies of twelve, and held also that every bishop must marry. Reclining on couches, and meeting in the evening, are not commanded ; and both, by their inconvenience, might in modern times counteract the design of the ordinance.

3.   *The Symbolism of the Lord's Supper.*

The Lord's Supper sets forth, in general, the death of Christ as the sustaining power of the believer's life.

A.   Expansion of this statement.

(*a*) It symbolizes the death of Christ for our sins.

1 Cor. 11 : 26 — "For as often as ye eat this bread, and drink the cup, ye proclaim the Lord's death till he come "; *cf.* Mark 14 : 24 — "This is my blood of the covenant, which is poured out for many "— the blood upon which the covenant between God and Christ, and so between God and us who are one with Christ, from eternity past was based. The Lord's Supper reminds us of the covenant which ensures our salvation, and of the atonement upon which the covenant was based ; *cf.* Heb. 13 : 20 — "blood of an eternal covenant."

Alex. McLaren : "The suggestion of a violent death, implied in the *doubling* of the symbols, by which the body is separated from that of the blood, and still further implied in the *breaking* of the bread, is made prominent in the words in reference to the cup. It symbolizes the blood of Jesus which is 'shed.' That shed blood is covenant blood. By it the New Covenant, of which Jeremiah had prophesied, one article of which was, "Their sins and iniquities I will remember no more," is sealed and ratified, not for Israel only but for an indefinite 'many,' which is really equivalent to all. Could words more plainly declare that Christ's death was a sacrifice? Can we understand it, according to his own interpretation of it, unless we see in his words here a reference to his previous words (Mat. 20 : 28) and recognize that in shedding his blood 'for many,' he 'gave his life a ransom for many'? The Lord's Supper is the standing witness, voiced by Jesus himself, that he regarded his death as the very centre of his work, and that he regarded it not merely as a martyrdom, but as a sacrifice by which he put away sins forever. Those who reject that view of that death are sorely puzzled what to make of the Lord's Supper."

(b) It symbolizes our personal appropriation of the benefits of that death.

1 Cor. 11:24 — "This is my body, which is for you"; cf. 1 Cor. 5 : 7 — "Christ our passover is sacrificed for us"; or R. V. — "our passover also hath been sacrificed, even Christ"; here it is evident not only that the showing forth of the Lord's death is the primary meaning of the ordinance, but that our partaking of the benefits of that death is as clearly taught as the Israelites' deliverance was symbolized in the paschal supper.

(c) It symbolizes the method of this appropriation, through union with Christ himself.

1 Cor. 10:16 — "The cup of blessing which we bless, is it not a communion of [marg. : ' participation in'] the blood of Christ? The bread which we break, is it not a communion of [marg. : ' participation in '] the body of Christ?" Here "is it not a participation " = ' does it not symbolize the participation?' So Mat. 26 : 26 — "this is my body'' = ' this symbolizes my body.'

(d) It symbolizes the continuous dependence of the believer for all spiritual life upon the once crucified, now living, Savior, to whom he is thus united.

Cf. John 6 : 53 — "Verily, verily, I say unto you, except ye eat the flesh of the Son of man and drink his blood, ye have not life in yourselves "—here is a statement, not with regard to the Lord's Supper, but with regard to spiritual union with Christ, which the Lord's Supper only symbolizes; see page 965, (a). Like Baptism, the Lord's Supper presupposes and implies evangelical faith, especially faith in the Deity of Christ; not that all who partake of it realize its full meaning, but that this participation logically implies the five great truths of Christ's preëxistence, his supernatural birth, his vicarious atonement, his literal resurrection, and his living presence with his followers. Because Ralph Waldo Emerson perceived that the Lord's Supper implied Christ's omnipresence and deity, he would no longer celebrate it, and so broke with his church and with the ministry.

(e) It symbolizes the sanctification of the Christian through a spiritual reproduction in him of the death and resurrection of the Lord.

Rom. 8 : 10 — "And if Christ is in you, the body is dead because of sin; but the spirit is life because of righteousness"; Phil. 3 : 10 — "that I may know him, and the power of his resurrection, and the fellowship of his sufferings, becoming conformed unto his death ; if by any means I may attain unto the resurrection from the dead." The bread of life nourishes ; but it transforms me, not I it.

(f) It symbolizes the consequent union of Christians in Christ, their head.

1 Cor. 10 : 17 — "seeing that we, who are many, are one bread, one body: for we all partake of the one bread." The Roman Catholic says that bread is the unity of many kernels, the wine the unity of many berries, and all are changed into the body of Christ. We can adopt the former part of the statement, without taking the latter. By being united to Christ, we become united to one another ; and the Lord's Supper, as it symbolizes our common partaking of Christ, symbolizes also the consequent oneness of all in whom Christ dwells. Teaching of the Twelve Apostles, ix.— "As this broken bread was scattered upon the mountains, and being gathered together became one, so may thy church be gathered together from the ends of the earth into thy kingdom."

(g) It symbolizes the coming joy and perfection of the kingdom of God.

Luke 22 : 18 — "for I say unto you, I shall not drink from henceforth of the fruit of the vine, until the kingdom of God shall come "; Mark 14: 25 — " Verily I say unto you, I will no more drink of the fruit of the vine, until that day when I drink it now in the kingdom of God "; Mat. 26 : 29 — " But I say unto you, I shall not drink henceforth of this fruit of the vine, until that day when I drink it new with you in my Father's kingdom."

Like Baptism, which points forward to the resurrection, the Lord's Supper is anticipatory also. It brings before us, not simply death, but life ; not simply past sacrifice, but future glory. It points forward to the great festival, "the marriage supper of the Lamb" (Rev. 19 : 9). Dorner: "Then Christ will keep the Supper anew with us, and the hours of highest solemnity in this life are but a weak foretaste of the powers of the world to come." See Madison Avenue Lectures, 176-216 ; The Lord's Supper, a Clerical Symposium, by Pressensé, Luthardt, and English Divines.

B. Inferences from this statement.

(a) The connection between the Lord's Supper and Baptism consists in this, that they both and equally are symbols of the death of Christ. In Baptism, we show forth the death of Christ as the procuring cause of our new birth into the kingdom of God. In the Lord's Supper, we show forth the death of Christ as the sustaining power of our spiritual life after it has once begun. In the one, we honor the sanctifying power of the death of Christ, as in the other we honor its regenerating power. Thus both are parts of one whole, — setting before us Christ's death for men in its two great purposes and results.

If baptism symbolized purification only, there would be no point of connection between the two ordinances. Their common reference to the death of Christ binds the two together.

(b) The Lord's Supper is to be often repeated, — as symbolizing Christ's constant nourishment of the soul, whose new birth was signified in Baptism.

Yet too frequent repetition may induce superstitious confidence in the value of communion as a mere outward form.

(c) The Lord's Supper, like Baptism, is the symbol of a previous state of grace. It has in itself no regenerating and no sanctifying power, but is the symbol by which the relation of the believer to Christ, his sanctifier, is vividly expressed and strongly confirmed.

We derive more help from the Lord's Supper than from private prayer, simply because it is an *external* rite, impressing the sense as well as the intellect, celebrated in company with other believers whose faith and devotion help our own, and bringing before us the profoundest truths of Christianity — the death of Christ, and our union with Christ in that death.

(d) The blessing received from participation is therefore dependent upon, and proportioned to, the faith of the communicant.

In observing the Lord's Supper, we need to discern the body of the Lord (1 Cor. 11 : 29) — that is, to recognize the spiritual meaning of the ordinance, and the presence of Christ, who through his deputed representatives gives to us the emblems, and who nourishes and quickens our souls as these material things nourish and quicken the body. The faith which thus discerns Christ is the gift of the Holy Spirit.

(e) The Lord's Supper expresses primarily the fellowship of the believer, not with his brethren, but with Christ, his Lord.

The Lord's Supper, like Baptism, symbolizes fellowship with the brethren only as consequent upon, and incidental to, fellowship with Christ. Just as we are all baptized 'into one body " (1 Cor. 12 : 13) only by being "baptized into Christ " (Rom. 6 : 3), so we commune with other believers in the Lord's Supper, only as we commune with Christ. Christ's words: "this do in remembrance of me " (1 Cor. 11 :24), bid us think, not of our brethren, but of the Lord. Baptism is not a test of personal worthiness. Nor is the Lord's Supper a test of personal worthiness, either our own or that of others. It is not primarily an expression of Christian fellowship. Nowhere in the New Testament is it called a communion of Christians with one another. But it is called a communion of the body and blood of Christ (1 Cor. 10 : 16) — or, in other words, a participation in him. Hence there is not a single cup, but many : "divide it among yourselves " (Luke 22 :17). Here is warrant for the individual communion-cup. Most churches use more than one cup: if more than one why not many?

1 Cor. 11 : 26 — "as often as ye eat . . . . ye proclaim the Lord's death " — the Lord's Supper is a teaching ordinance, and is to be observed, not simply for the good that comes to the communicant and to his brethren, but for the sake of the witness which it gives to the world that the Christ who died for its sins now lives for its salvation. A. H. Ballard, in The Standard, Aug. 18, 1900, on 1 Cor. 11 : 29 — "eateth and drinketh judgment unto himself, if he discern not the body " — "He who eats and drinks, and does not discern that he is redeemed by the offering of the body of Jesus Christ once for all, eats and drinks a double condemnation, because he does not discern the redemption which is symbolized by the things which he eats and drinks. To turn his thought away from that sacrificial body to the company of disciples assembled is a grievous error — the error of all those who exalt the idea of fellowship or communion in the celebration of the ordinance."

The offence of a Christian brother, therefore, even if committed against myself, should not prevent me from remembering Christ and communing with the Savior. I could not commune at all, if I had to vouch for the Christian character of all who sat with me. This does not excuse the church from effort to purge its membership from unworthy participants; it simply declares that the church's failure to do this does not absolve any single member of it from his obligation to observe the Lord's Supper. See Jacob, Eccl. Polity of N. T., 285.

4. *Erroneous views of the Lord's Supper.*

A. The Romanist view,—that the bread and wine are changed by priestly consecration into the very body and blood of Christ; that this consecration is a new offering of Christ's sacrifice; and that, by a physical partaking of the elements, the communicant receives saving grace from God. To this doctrine of "transubstantiation" we reply:

(*a*) It rests upon a false interpretation of Scripture. In Mat. 26 : 26, "this is my body" means: "this is a symbol of my body." Since Christ was with the disciples in visible form at the institution of the Supper, he could not have intended them to recognize the bread as being his literal body. "The body of Christ is present in the bread, just as it had been in the passover lamb, of which the bread took the place" (John 6 : 53 contains no reference to the Lord's Supper, although it describes that spiritual union with Christ which the Supper symbolizes; *cf.* 63. In 1 Cor. 10 : 16, 17, κοινωίαν τοῦ σώματος τοῦ Χριστοῦ is a figurative expression for the spiritual partaking of Christ. In Mark 8 : 33, we are not to infer that Peter was actually "Satan," nor does 1 Cor. 12 : 12 prove that we are all Christs. *Cf.* Gen. 41 : 26; 1 Cor. 10 : 4).

Mat. 26 : 28 —"This is my blood . . . . which is poured out," cannot be meant to be taken literally, since Christ's blood was not yet shed. Hence the Douay version (Roman Catholic), without warrant, changes the tense and reads, "which shall be shed." At the institution of the Supper, it is not conceivable that Christ should hold his body in his own hands, and then break it to the disciples. There were not two bodies there, Zwingle : " The words of institution are not the mandatory ' become ' : they are only an explanation of the sign." When I point to a picture and say : " This is George Washington," I do not mean that the veritable body and blood of George Washington are before me. So when a teacher points to a map and says : " This is New York," or when Jesus refers to John the Baptist, and says : " this is Elijah, that is to come " (Mat. 11 : 14). Jacob, The Lord's Supper, Historically Considered —" It originally marked, not a real presence, but a real absence, of Christ as the Son of God made man "— that is, a real absence of his *body*. Therefore the Supper, reminding us of his body, is to be observed in the church " till he come " (1 Cor. 11 : 26).

John 6 : 53 — " Except ye eat the flesh of the Son of man and drink his blood, ye have not life in yourselves " must be interpreted by verse 63 —"It is the spirit that giveth life ; the flesh profiteth nothing : the words that I have spoken unto you are spirit, and are life." 1 Cor. 10 : 16 —"The cup of blessing which we bless, is it not a communion: [marg. : 'participation in '] the blood of Christ ? The bread which we break, is it not a communion of [marg.

participation in'] the body of Christ?"—see Expositor's Greek Testament, *in loco*; Mark 8:3.—'But he turning about, and seeing his disciples, rebuked Peter, and saith, Get thee behind me, Satan"; 1 Cor. 12:12—"For as the body is one, and hath many members, and all the members of the body, being many, are one body; so also is Christ." *cf.* Ger. 41:26—"The seven good kine are seven years; and the seven good ears are seven years: the dream is one;" 1 Cor. 10:4—"they drank of a spiritual rock that followed them: and the rock was Christ.'

Queen Elizabeth: "Christ was the Word that spake it: He took the bread and brake it; And what that Word did make it, That I believe and take it." Yes, we say; but what *does* the Lord make it? Not his body, but only a symbol of his body. Sir Thomas More went back to the doctrine of transubstantiation which the wisdom of his age was almost unanimous in rejecting. In his Utopia, written in earlier years, he had made deism the ideal religion. Extreme Romanism was his reaction from this former extreme. Bread and wine are mere remembrancers, as were the lamb and bitter herbs at the Passover. The partaker is spiritually affected by the bread and wine, only as was the pious Israelite in receiving the paschal symbols; see Norman Fox, Christ in the Daily Meal, 25, 42.

E. G. Robinson: "The greatest power in Romanism is its power of visible representation. Ritualism is only elaborate symbolism. It is interesting to remember that this prostration of the priest before the consecrated wafer is no part of even original Roman Catholicism." Stanley, Life and Letters, 2:213—"The pope, when he celebrates the communion, always stands in exactly the opposite direction [to that of modern ritualists], not with his back but with his face to the people, no doubt following the primitive usage." So in Raphael's picture of the Miracle of Bolsina, the priest is at the north end of the table, in the very attitude of a Protestant clergyman. Pfleiderer, Philos. Religion, 2:211—"The unity of the bread, of which each enjoys a part, represents the unity of the body of Christ, which consists in the community of believers. If we are to speak of a presence of the body of Christ in the Lord's Supper, that can only be thought of, in the sense of Paul, as pertaining to the mystical body, *i. e.*, the Christian Community. Augustine and Zwingle, who have expressed most clearly this meaning of the Supper, have therefore caught quite correctly the sense of the Apostle."

Norman Fox, Christ in the Daily Meal, 40-53—"The phrase 'consecration of the elements' is unwarranted. The leaven and the mustard seed were in no way consecrated when Jesus pronounced them symbols of divine things. The bread and wine are not arbitrarily appointed remembrancers, they are remembrancers in their very nature. There is no change in them. So every other loaf is a symbol, as well as that used in the Supper. When St. Patrick held up the shamrock as the symbol of the Trinity, he meant that every such sprig was the same. Only the bread of the daily meal is Christ's body. Only the washing of dirty feet is the fulfilment of Christ's command. The loaf not eaten to satisfy hunger is not Christ's symbolic body at all." Here we must part company with Dr. Fox. We grant the natural fitness of the elements for which he contends. But we hold also to a divine appointment of the bread and wine for a special and sacred use, even as the "bow in the cloud" (Gen. 9:13), because it was a natural emblem, was consecrated to a special religious use.

(*b*) It contradicts the evidence of the senses, as well as of all scientific tests that can be applied. If we cannot trust our senses as to the unchanged material qualities of bread and wine, we cannot trust them when they report to us the words of Christ.

Gibbon was rejoiced at the discovery that, while the real presence is attested by only a single sense—our sight [as employed in reading the words of Christ]—the real presence is disproved by three of our senses, sight, touch, and taste. It is not well to purchase faith in this dogma at the price of absolute scepticism. Stanley, on Baptism, in his Christian Institutions, tells us that, in the third and fourth centuries, the belief that the water of baptism was changed into the blood of Christ was nearly as firmly and widely fixed as the belief that the bread and wine of the communion were changed into his flesh and blood. Döllinger; "When I am told that I must swear to the truth of these doctrines [of papal infallibility and apostolic succession], my feeling is just as if I were asked to swear that two and two make five, and not four." Teacher: "Why did Henry VIII quarrel with the pope?" Scholar: "Because the pope had commanded him to put away his wife on pain of transubstantiation." The transubstantiation of Henry VIII is quite as rational as the transubstantiation of the bread and wine in the Eucharist.

(c) It involves the denial of the completeness of Christ's past sacrifice, and the assumption that a human priest can repeat or add to the atonement made by Christ once for all (Heb. 9 : 28 — $\check{\alpha}\pi\alpha\xi$ $\pi\rho\sigma\varepsilon\nu\varepsilon\chi\vartheta\varepsilon\acute{\iota}\varsigma$). The Lord's Supper is never called a sacrifice, nor are altars, priests, or consecrations ever spoken of, in the New Testament. The priests of the old dispensation are expressly contrasted with the ministers of the new. The former "ministered about sacred things," i. e., performed sacred rites and waited at the altar; but the latter "preach the gospel" (1 Cor. 9 : 13, 14).

Heb. 9 : 28 — "so Christ also, having been once offered " — here $\check{\alpha}\pi\alpha\xi$ means ' once for all,' as in Jude 3 — "the faith which was once for all delivered unto the saints"; 1 Cor. 9 : 13, 14 — " Know ye not that they that minister about sacred things eat of the things of the temple, and they that wait upon the altar have their portion with the altar? Even so did the Lord ordain that they that proclaim the gospel should live of the gospel. " Romanism introduces a mediator between the soul and Christ, namely, bread and wine, — and the priest besides.

Dorner, Glaubensiehre, 2 : 630–687 (Syst. Doct., 4 : 146–163) — " Christ is thought of as at a distance, and as represented only by the priest who offers anew his sacrifice. But Protestant doctrine holds to a perfect Christ, applying the benefits of the work which he long ago and once for all completed upon the cross. " Chillingworth : " Romanists hold that the validity of every sacrament but baptism depends upon its administration by a priest ; and without priestly absolution there is no assurance of forgiveness. But the intention of the priest is essential in pronouncing absolution, and the intention of the bishop is essential in consecrating the priest. How can any human being know that these conditions are fulfilled ? " In the New Testament, on the other hand. Christ appears as the only priest, and each human soul has direct access to him.

Norman Fox, Christ in the Daily Meal, 22 — " The adherence of the first Christians to the Mosaic law makes it plain that they did not hold the doctrine of the modern Church of Rome that the bread of the Supper is a sacrifice, the table an altar, and the minister a priest. For the old altar, the old sacrifice, and the old priesthood still remained, and were still in their view appointed media of atonement with God. Of course they could not have believed in two altars, two priesthoods and two contemporaneous sets of sacrifices." Christ is the only priest. A. A. Hodge, Popular Lectures, 257 — " The three central dangerous errors of Romanism and Ritualism are: 1. the perpetuity of the apostolate ; 2. the priestly character and offices of Christian ministers ; 3. the sacramental principle, or the depending upon sacraments, as the essential, initial, and ordinary channels of grace." " Hierarchy," says another, " is an infraction of the divine order ; it imposes the weight of an outworn symbolism on the true vitalities of the gospel ; it is a remnant rent from the shroud of the dead past, to enwrap the limbs of the living present."

(d) It destroys Christianity by externalizing it. Romanists make all other service a mere appendage to the communion. Physical and magical salvation is not Christianity, but is essential paganism.

Council of Trent, Session VII, On Sacraments in General, Canon IV : " If any one saith that the sacraments of the New Testament are not necessary to salvation, but are superfluous, and that without them, and without the desire thereof, men attain of God, through faith alone, the grace of justification ; though all [the sacraments] are not indeed necessary for every individual : let him be anathema." On Baptism, Canon IV : " If any one saith that the baptism which is even given by heretics in the name of the Father, Son and Holy Ghost, with the intention of doing what the church doth. is not true baptism, let him be anathema." Baptism, in the Romanist system, is necessary to salvation : and baptism, even though administered by heretics, is an admission to the church. All baptized persons who, through no fault of their own, but from lack of knowledge or opportunity, are not connected outwardly with the true church. though they are apparently attached to some sect, yet in reality belong to the soul of the true church. Many belong merely to the body of the Catholic church, and are counted as its members. but do not belong to its soul. So says Archbishop Lynch, of Toronto ; and Pius IX extended the doctrine of invincible ignorance, so as to cover the case of every dissentient from the church whose life shows faith working by love.

Adoration of the Host (Latin *hostia*, victim) is a regular part of the service of the Mass. If the Romanist view were correct that the bread and wine were actually changed into the body and blood of Christ, we could not call this worship idolatry. Christ's body in the sepulchre could not have been a proper object of worship, but it was so after his resurrection, when it became animated with a new and divine life. The Romanist error is that of holding that the priest has power to transform the elements; the worship of them follows as a natural consequence, and is none the less idolatrous for being based upon the false assumption that the bread and wine are really Christ's body and blood.

The Roman Catholic system involves many absurdities, but the central absurdity is that of making religion a matter of machinery and outward manipulation. Dr. R. S. MacArthur calls sacramentalism " the pipe-line conception of grace." There is no patent Romanist plumbing. Dean Stanley said that John Henry Newman " made immortality the consequence of frequent participation of the Holy Communion." Even Faber made game of the notion, and declared that it " degraded celebrations to be so many breadfruit trees." It is this transformation of the Lord's Supper into the Mass that turns the church into " the Church of the Intonement." " Cardinal Gibbons," it was once said, " makes his own God — the wafer." His error is at the root of the super-sanctity and celibacy of the Romanist clergy, and President Garrett forgot this when he made out the pass on his railway for " Cardinal Gibbons and wife." Dr. C. H· Parkhurst : " There is no more place for an altar in a Christian church than there is for a golden calf." On the word " priest " in the N. T., see Gardiner, in O. T. Student, Nov. 1889 : 285-291 ; also Bowen, in Theol. Monthly, Nov. 1889 : 316-329. For the Romanist view, see Council of Trent, session XIII, canon III : *per contra*, see Calvin, Institutes, 2 : 585-602 ; C. Hebert, The Lord's Supper : History of Uninspired Teaching.

B.   The Lutheran and High Church view, — that the communicant, in partaking of the consecrated elements, eats the veritable body and drinks the veritable blood of Christ in and with the bread and wine, although the elements themselves do not cease to be material. To this doctrine of " consubstantiation " we object :

(*a*) That the view is not required by Scripture. — All the passages cited in its support may be better interpreted as referring to a partaking of the elements as symbols. If Christ's body be ubiquitous, as this theory holds, we partake of it at every meal, as really as at the Lord's Supper.

(*b*) That the view is inseparable from the general sacramental system of which it forms a part. — In imposing physical and material conditions of receiving Christ, it contradicts the doctrine of justification only by faith ; changes the ordinance from a sign, into a means, of salvation ; involves the necessity of a sacerdotal order for the sake of properly consecrating the elements ; and logically tends to the Romanist conclusions of ritualism and idolatry.

(*c*) That it holds each communicant to be a partaker of Christ's veritable body and blood, whether he be a believer or not, — the result, in the absence of faith, being condemnation instead of salvation. Thus the whole character of the ordinance is changed from a festival occasion to one of mystery and fear, and the whole gospel method of salvation is obscured.

Encyc. Britannica, art. : Luther, 15 : 81 — " Before the peasants' war, Luther regarded the sacrament as a secondary matter, compared with the right view of faith. In alarm at this war and at Carlstadt's mysticism, he determined to abide by the tradition of the church, and to alter as little as possible. He could not accept transubstantiation, and he sought a *via media*. Occam gave it to him. According to Occam, matter can be present in two ways, first, when it occupies a distinct place by itself, excluding every other body, as two stones mutually exclude each other ; and. secondly, when it occupies the same space as another body at the same time. Everything which is omnipresent must occupy the same space as other things, else it could not be ubiquitous. Hence consubstantiation involved no miracle. Christ's body was in the bread and wine naturally, and was not brought into the elements by the priest. It brought a blessing, not because of Christ's presence, but because of God's promise that this particular presence of the body of Christ should bring blessings to the faithful partaker." Broadus, Am. Com. on Mat., 529 — " Luther does not say how Christ is in the bread and wine, but his followers have compared his presence to that of heat or magnetism in iron. But how then could this presence be in the bread and wine separately ? "

For the view here combated, see Gerhard, x : 352 — " The bread, apart from the sacrament instituted by Christ, is not the body of Christ, and therefore it is ἀρτολατρία (bread-worship) to adore the bread in these solemn processions " (of the Roman Catholic church). 397 — " Faith does not belong to the substance of the Eucharist; hence it is not the faith of him who partakes that makes the bread a communication of the body of Christ; nor on account of unbelief in him who partakes does the bread cease to be a communication of the body of Christ." See also Sadler, Church Doctrine, 124–199; Pusey, Tract No. 90, of the Tractarian Series; Wilberforce, New Birth; Nevins, Mystical Presence.

Per contra, see Calvin, Institutes, 2 : 525–584; G. P. Fisher, in Independent, May 1, 1884 — " Calvin differed from Luther, in holding that Christ is received only by the believer. He differed from Zwingle, in holding that Christ is truly, though spiritually, received." See also E. G. Robinson, in Baptist Quarterly, 1869 : 85–109; Rogers, Priests and Sacraments. Consubstantiation accounts for the doctrine of apostolic succession and for the universal ritualism of the Lutheran Church. Bowing at the name of Jesus, however, is not, as has been sometimes maintained, a relic of the papal worship of the Real Presence, but is rather a reminiscence of the fourth century, when controversies about the person of Christ rendered orthodox Christians peculiarly anxious to recognize Christ's deity.

" There is no ' corner' in divine grace " (C. H. Parkhurst). " All notions of a needed 'priesthood,' to bring us into connection with Christ, must yield to the truth that Christ is ever with us " (E. G. Robinson). " The priest was the conservative, the prophet the progressive. Hence the conflict between them. Episcopalians like the idea of a priesthood, but do not know what to do with that of prophet." Dr. A. J. Gordon : " Ritualism, like eczema in the human body, is generally a symptom of a low state of the blood. As a rule, when the church becomes secularized, it becomes ritualized, while great revivals, pouring through the church, have almost always burst the liturgical bands and have restored it to the freedom of the Spirit."

Puseyism, as defined by Pusey himself, means : 1. high thoughts of the two sacraments; 2. high estimate of Episcopacy as God's ordinance; 3. high estimate of the visible church as the body wherein we are made and continue to be members of Christ; 4. regard for ordinances as directing our devotions and disciplining us, such as daily public prayers, fasts and feasts; 5. regard for the visible part of devotion, such as the decoration of the house of God, which acts insensibly on the mind; 6. reverence for and deference to the ancient church, instead of the reformers, as the ultimate expounder of the meaning of our church." Pusey declared that he and Maurice worshiped different Gods.

5. *Prerequisites to Participation in the Lord's Supper.*

A. There are prerequisites. This we argue from the fact :

(*a*) That Christ enjoined the celebration of the Supper, not upon the world at large, but only upon his disciples; (*b*) that the apostolic injunctions to Christians, to separate themselves from certain of their number, imply a limitation of the Lord's Supper to a narrower body, even among professed believers; (*c*) that the analogy of Baptism, as belonging only to a specified class of persons, leads us to believe that the same is true of the Lord's Supper.

The analogy of Baptism to the Lord's Supper suggests a general survey of the connections between the two ordinances : 1. Both ordinances symbolize primarily the death of Christ; then secondarily our spiritual death to sin because we are one with him; it being absurd, where there is no such union, to make our Baptism the symbol of his death. 2. We are merged in Christ first in Baptism; then in the Supper Christ is more and more taken into us; Baptism = we in Christ, the Supper = Christ in us.

3. As regeneration is instantaneous and sanctification continues in time, so Baptism should be for once, the Lord's Supper often; the first single, the second frequent. 4. If one ordinance, the Supper, requires discernment of the Lord's body, so does the other, the ordinance of Baptism; the subject of Baptism should know the meaning of his act. 5. The order of the ordinances teaches Christian doctrine, as the ordinances do; to partake of the Lord's Supper before being baptized is to say in symbol that one can be sanctified without being regenerated. 6. Both ordinances should be public, as both "show forth" the Lord's death and are teaching ordinances; no celebration of either one is to be permitted in private. 7. In both the administrator does not act at his own option, but is the organ of the church; Philip acts as organ of the church at Jerusalem when he baptizes the eunuch. 8. The ordinances stand by themselves, and are not to be made appendages of other meetings or celebrations; they belong, not to associations or conventions, but to the local church. 9. The Lord's Supper needs scrutiny of the communicant's qualifications as much as Baptism; and only the local church is the proper judge of these qualifications. 10. We may deny the Lord's Supper to one whom we know to be a Christian, when he walks disorderly or disseminates false doctrine, just as we may deny Baptism to such a person. 11. Fencing the tables, or warning the unqualified not to partake of the Supper, may, like instruction with regard to Baptism, best take place before the actual administration of the ordinance; and the pastor is not a special policeman or detective to ferret out offences. See Expositor's Greek Testament on 1 Cor. 10:1–6.

B. The prerequisites are those only which are expressly or implicitly laid down by Christ and his apostles.

(a) The church, as possessing executive but not legislative power, is charged with the duty, not of framing rules for the administering and guarding of the ordinance, but of discovering and applying the rules given it in the New Testament. No church has a right to establish any terms of communion; it is responsible only for making known the terms established by Christ and his apostles. (b) These terms, however, are to be ascertained not only from the injunctions, but also from the precedents, of the New Testament. Since the apostles were inspired, New Testament precedent is the "common law" of the church.

English law consists mainly of precedent, that is, past decisions of the courts. Immemorial customs may be as binding as are the formal enactments of a legislature. It is New Testament precedent that makes obligatory the observance of the first day, instead of the seventh day, of the week. The common law of the church consists, however, not of any and all customs, but only of the customs of the apostolic church interpreted in the light of its principles, or the customs universally binding because sanctioned by inspired apostles. Has New Testament precedent the authority of a divine command? Only so far, we reply, as it is an adequate, complete and final expression of the divine life in Christ. This we claim for the ordinances of Baptism and of the Lord's Supper, and for the order of these ordinances. See Proceedings of the Baptist Congress, 1896:23.

The Mennonites, thinking to reproduce even the incidental phases of N. T. action, have adopted: 1. the washing of feet; 2. the marriage only of members of the same faith; 3. non-resistance to violence; 4. the use of the ban, and the shunning of expelled persons; 5. refusal to take oaths; 6. the kiss of peace; 7. formal examination of the spiritual condition of each communicant before his participation in the Lord's Supper; 8. the choice of officials by lot. And they naturally break up into twelve sects, dividing upon such points as holding all things in common; plainness of dress, one sect repudiating buttons and using only hooks upon their clothing, whence their nickname of Hookers; the holding of services in private houses only; the asserted possession of the gift of prophecy (A. S. Carman).

C. On examining the New Testament, we find that the prerequisites to participation in the Lord's Supper are four, namely:

First,—Regeneration.

The Lord's Supper is the outward expression of a life in the believer, nourished and sustained by the life of Christ. It cannot therefore be partaken of by one who is "dead through . . . . trespasses and sins." We give no food to a corpse. The Lord's Supper was never offered by the apostles to unbelievers. On the contrary, the injunction that each communicant "examine himself" implies that faith which will enable the communicant to "discern the Lord's body" is a prerequisite to participation.

1 Cor. 11:27–29 — "Wherefore whosoever shall eat the bread or drink the cup of the Lord in an unworthy manner, shall be guilty of the body and the blood of the Lord. But let a man prove himself, and so let him eat of the bread, and drink of the cup. For he that eateth and drinketh, eateth and drinketh judgment unto himself, if he discern not the Lord's body." Schaff, in his Church History, 2:517, tells us that in the Greek Church, in the seventh and eighth centuries, the bread was dipped in the wine, and both elements were delivered in a spoon. See Edwards, on Qualifications for Full Communion, in Works, 1:81.

Secondly,—Baptism.

In proof that baptism is a prerequisite to the Lord's Supper, we urge the following considerations.

(a) The ordinance of baptism was instituted and administered long before the Supper.

Mat. 21:25 — "The baptism of John, whence was it? from heaven or from men?" — Christ here intimates that John's baptism had been instituted by God before his own.

(b) The apostles who first celebrated it had, in all probability, been baptized.

Acts 1:21, 22 — "Of the men therefore that have companied with us all the time that the Lord Jesus went in and went out among us, beginning from the baptism of John . . . . of these must one become a witness with us of his resurrection": 19:4 —"John baptized with the baptism of repentance, saying unto the people that they should believe on him that should come after him, that is, on Jesus." Several of the apostles were certainly disciples of John. If Christ was baptized, much more his disciples. Jesus recognized John's baptism as obligatory, and it is not probable that he would take his apostles from among those who had not submitted to it. John the Baptist himself, the first administrator of baptism, must have been himself unbaptized. But the twelve could fitly administer it, because they had themselves received it at John's hands. See Arnold, Terms of Communion, 17.

(c) The command of Christ fixes the place of baptism as first in order after discipleship.

Mat. 28:19, 20 — "Go ye therefore, and make disciples of all the nations, baptizing them into the name of the Father and of the Son and of the Holy Spirit: teaching them to observe all things whatsoever I commanded you " — here the first duty is to make disciples, the second to baptize, the third to instruct in right Christian living. Is it said that there is no formal command to admit only baptized persons to the Lord's Supper? We reply that there is no formal command to admit only regenerate persons to baptism. In both cases, the practice of the apostles and the general connections of Christian doctrine are sufficient to determine our duty.

(d) All the recorded cases show this to have been the order observed by the first Christians and sanctioned by the apostles.

Acts 2:41, 46 — "They then that received his word were baptized . . . . And day by day, continuing stedfastly with one accord in the temple, and breaking bread at home [rather, 'in various worship-rooms '] they took their food with gladness and singleness of heart "; 8:12 — "But when they believed Philip . . . . they were baptized "; 10:47, 48 — "Can any man forbid the water, that these should not be baptized, who have received the Holy Spirit as well as we? And he commanded them to be baptized in the name of Jesus Christ "; 22:16 — "And now why tarriest thou? arise, and be baptized, and wash away thy sins, calling on his name."

(e) The symbolism of the ordinances requires that baptism should precede the Lord's Supper. The order of the facts signified must be expressed in the order of the ordinances which signify them ; else the world is taught that sanctification may take place without regeneration. Birth must come before sustenance—'*nascimur, pascimur.*' To enjoy ceremonial privileges, there must be ceremonial qualifications. As none but the circumcised could eat the passover, so before eating with the Christian family must come adoption into the Christian family.

As one must be "born of the Spirit" before he can experience the sustaining influence of Christ, so he must be "born of water" before he can properly be nourished by the Lord's Supper. Neither the unborn nor the dead can eat bread or drink wine. Only when Christ had raised the daughter of the Jewish ruler to life, did he say : "Give her to eat." The ordinance which symbolizes regeneration, or the impartation of new life, must precede the ordinance which symbolizes the strengthening and perfecting of the life already begun. The Teaching of the Twelve Apostles, dating back to the second half of the second century, distinctly declares (9 : 5, 10)—"Let no one eat or drink of your Eucharist except those baptized into the name of the Lord ; for as regards this also the Lord has said : ' Give not that which is holy unto the dogs '. . . . . The Eucharist shall be given only to the baptized."

(*f*) The standards of all evangelical denominations, with unimportant exceptions, confirm the view that this is the natural interpretation of the Scripture requirements respecting the order of the ordinances.

"The only protest of note has been made by a portion of the English Baptists." To these should be added the comparatively small body of the Free Will Baptists in America. Pedobaptist churches in general refuse full membership, office-holding, and the ministry, to unbaptized persons. The Presbyterian church does not admit to the communion members of the Society of Friends. Not one of the great evangelical denominations accepts Robert Hall's maxim that the only terms of communion are terms of salvation. If individual ministers announce this principle and conform their practice to it, it is only because they transgress the standards of the churches to which they belong.

See Tyerman's Oxford Methodists, preface, page vi—"Even in Georgia, Wesley excluded dissenters from the Holy Communion, on the ground that they had not been properly baptized ; and he would himself baptize only by immersion, unless the child or person was in a weak state of health." Baptist Noel gave it as his reason for submitting to baptism, that to approach the Lord's Supper conscious of not being baptized would be to act contrary to all the precedents of Scripture. See Curtis, Progress of Baptist Principles, 304.

The dismission of Jonathan Edwards from his church at Northampton was due to his opposing the Halfway Covenant, which admitted unregenerate persons to the Lord's Supper as a step on the road to spiritual life. He objected to the doctrine that the Lord's Supper was "a converting ordinance." But these very unregenerate persons had been baptized, and he himself had baptized many of them. He should have objected to infant baptism, as well as to the Lord's Supper, in the case of the unregenerate.

(*g*) The practical results of the opposite view are convincing proof that the order here insisted on is the order of nature as well as of Scripture. The admission of unbaptized persons to the communion tends always to, and has frequently resulted in, the disuse of baptism itself, the obscuring of the truth which it symbolizes, the transformation of Scripturally constituted churches into bodies organized after methods of human invention, and the complete destruction of both church and ordinances as Christ originally constituted them.

Arnold, Terms of Communion, 76 — The steps of departure from Scriptural precedent have not unfrequently been the following : (1) administration of baptism on a weekday evening, to avoid giving offence ; (2) reception, without baptism, of persons renouncing belief in the baptism of their infancy ; (3) giving up of the Lord's Supper as non-essential,— to be observed or not observed by each individual, according as he finds it useful; (4) choice of a pastor who will not advocate Baptist views; (5) adoption of Congregational articles of faith; (6) discipline and exclusion of members for propagating Baptist doctrine. John Bunyan's church, once either an open communion church or a mixed church both of baptized and unbaptized believers, is now a regular Congregational body. Armitage, History of the Baptists, 482 *sq.*, claims that it was originally a Baptist church. Vedder, however, in Bap. Quar. Rev., 1886 : 289, says that "The church at Bedford is proved by indisputable documentary evidence never to have been a Baptist church in any strict sense." The results of the principle of open communion are certainly seen in the Regent's Park church in London, where some of the deacons have never been baptized. The doctrine that baptism is not essential to church membership is simply the logical result of the previous practice of admitting unbaptized persons to the communion table. If they are admitted to the Lord's Supper, then there is no bar to their admission to the church. See Proceedings of the Baptist Congress, Boston, November, 1902; Curtis, Progress of Baptist Principles, 296–298.

Thirdly,—Church membership.

(*a*) The Lord's Supper is a church ordinance, observed by churches of Christ as such. For this reason, membership in the church naturally precedes communion. Since communion is a family rite, the participant should first be a member of the family.

Acts 2 : 46   47 — "breaking bread at home [rather, 'in various worship-rooms']" (see Com. of Meyer); 20 : 7—"upon the first day of the week, when we were gathered together to break bread "; 1 Cor. 11 : 18, 22—"when ye come together in the church . . . have ye not houses to eat and to drink in ? or despise ye the church of God, and put them to shame that have not ? "

(*b*) The Lord's Supper is a symbol of church fellowship. Excommunication implies nothing, if it does not imply exclusion from the communion. If the Supper is simply communion of the individual with Christ, then the church has no right to exclude any from it.

1 Cor. 10 : 17 —"we, who are many, are one bread, one body: for we all partake of the one bread." Though the Lord's Supper primarily symbolizes fellowship with Christ, it symbolizes secondarily fellowship with the church of Christ. Not all believers in Christ were present at the first celebration of the Supper, but only those organized into a body — the apostles. I can invite proper persons to my tea-table, but that does not give them the right to come uninvited. Each church, therefore, should invite visiting members of sister churches to partake with it. The Lord's Supper is an ordinance by itself, and should not be celebrated at conventions and associations, simply to lend dignity to something else.

The Panpresbyterian Council at Philadelphia, in 1880, refused to observe the Lord's Supper together, upon the ground that the Supper is a church ordinance, to be observed only by those who are amenable to the discipline of the body, and therefore not to be observed by separate church organizations acting together. Substantially upon this ground, the Old School General Assembly long before, being invited to unite at the Lord's table with the New School body with whom they had dissolved ecclesiastical relations, declined to do so. See Curtis, Progress of Baptist Principles, 304; Arnold, Terms of Communion, 36.

Fourthly,—An orderly walk.

Disorderly walking designates a course of life in a church member which is contrary to the precepts of the gospel. It is a bar to participation in the Lord's Supper, the sign of church fellowship. With Arnold, we may class disorderly walking under four heads : —

(*a*) Immoral conduct.

1 Cor. 5 : 1-13 — Paul commands the Corinthian church to exclude the incestuous person: "I wrote unto you in my epistle to have no company with fornicators ; . . . . but now I write unto you not to keep company, if any man that is named a brother be a fornicator or covetous, or an idolater, or a reviler, or a drunkard, or

an extortioner; with such a one no, not to eat. . . . . Put away the wicked man from among yourselves." — Here it is evident that the most serious forms of disorderly walking require exclusion not only from church fellowship but from Christian fellowship as well.

(b) Disobedience to the commands of Christ.

1 Cor. 14 : 37 —"If any man thinketh himself to be a prophet, or spiritual, let him take knowledge of the things which I write unto you, that they are the commandments of the Lord "; 2 Thess. 3 : 6, 11, 15 —"Now we command you, brethren, ... that ye withdraw yourselves from every brother that walketh disorderly, and not after the tradition which they received of us. . . . . For we hear of some that walk among you disorderly, that work not at all, but are busybodies. . . . . And if any man obeyeth not our word by this epistle, note that man, that ye have no company with him, to the end that he may be ashamed. And yet count him not as an enemy, but admonish him as a brother." — Here is exclusion from church fellowship, and from the Lord's Supper its sign, while yet the offender is not excluded from Christian fellowship, but is still counted "a brother." *Versus* G. B. Stevens, in N. Englander, 1887 : 40-47.

In these passages Paul intimates that "not to walk after the tradition received from him, not to obey the word contained in his epistles, is the same as disobedience to the commands of Christ, and as such involves the forfeiture of church fellowship and its privileged tokens" (Arnold, Prerequisites to Communion, 68). Since Baptism is a command of Christ, it follows that we cannot properly commune with the unbaptized. To admit such to the Lord's Supper is to give the symbol of church fellowship to those who, in spite of the fact that they are Christian brethren, are, though perhaps unconsciously, violating the fundamental law of the church. To withhold protest against plain disobedience to Christ's commands is to that extent to countenance such disobedience. The same disobedience which in the church member we should denominate disorderly walking must *a fortiori* destroy all right to the Lord's Supper on the part of those who are not members of the church.

(c) Heresy, or the holding and teaching of false doctrine.

Titus 3 : 10 —"A man that is heretical [Am. Revisers : 'a factious man'] after a first and second admonition refuse " ; see Ellicott, Com., *in loco :* " αἱρετικὸς ἄνθρωπος = one who gives rise to divisions by erroneous teaching, not necessarily of a fundamentally heterodox nature, but of the kind just described in verse 9." *Cf.* Acts 20 : 30 —"from among your own selves shall men arise, speaking perverse things, to draw away the disciples after them "; 1 John 4 : 2, 3 — "Hereby know ye the Spirit of God : every spirit that confesseth that Jesus Christ is come in the flesh is of God : and every spirit that confesseth not Jesus is not of God : and this is the spirit of the antichrist." ג. B. Bosworth : "Heresy, in the N. T., does not necessarily mean the holding of erroneous opinions,— it may also mean the holding of correct opinions in an unbrotherly or divisive spirit." We grant that the word 'heretical' may also mean 'factious'; but we claim that false doctrine is the chief source of division, and is therefore in itself a disqualification for participation in the Lord's Supper. Factiousness is an additional bar, and we treat it under the next head of Schism.

The Panpresbyterian Council, mentioned above, refused to admit to their body the Cumberland Presbyterians, because, though the latter adhere to the Presbyterian form of church government, they are Arminian in their views of the doctrines of grace. As we have seen, on pages 940-942, that Baptism is a confession of evangelical faith, so here we see that the Lord's Supper also is a confession of evangelical faith, and that no one can properly participate in it who denies the doctrines of sin, of the deity, incarnation and atonement of Christ, and of justification by faith, which the Lord's Supper symbolizes. Such denial should exclude from all Christian fellowship as well.

There is heresy which involves exclusion only from church fellowship. Since pedobaptists hold and propagate false doctrine with regard to the church and its ordinances — doctrines which endanger the spirituality of the church, the sufficiency of the Scriptures, and the lordship of Christ — we cannot properly admit them to the Lord's Supper. To admit them or to partake with them, would be to treat falsehood as if it were truth. Arnold, Prerequisites to Communion, 72 —" Pedobaptists are guilty of teaching that the baptized are not members of the church, or that membership in the church is not voluntary; that there are two sorts of baptism, one of which is a profession of faith of the person baptized, and the other is profession of faith of another person; that regeneration is given in and by baptism, or that the church is composed in great part of persons who do not give, and were never supposed to give, any evidence of regeneration; that the church has a right to change essentially one of Christ's institutions, or that it is unessential whether it be observed as he ordained it or in some other manner, that baptism may be rightfully administered in a way which makes much of the language in which it is described in the Scriptures wholly unsuitable and inapplicable, and which does not at all represent the facts and doctrines which baptism is declared in the Scriptures to represent; that the Scriptures are not in all religious matters the sufficient and only binding rule of faith and practice."

(d) Schism, or the promotion of division and dissension in the church. — This also requires exclusion from church fellowship, and from the Lord's Supper which is its appointed sign.

Rom. 16:17 —"Now I beseech you, brethren, mark them that are causing the divisions and occasions of stumbling contrary to the doctrine which ye learned: and turn away from them." Since pedobaptists, by their teaching and practice, draw many away from Scripturally constituted churches,—thus dividing true believers from each other and weakening the bodies organized after the model of the New Testament,—it is imperative upon us to separate ourselves from them, so far as regards that communion at the Lord's table which is the sign of church fellowship. Mr. Spurgeon admits pedobaptists to commune with his church "for two or three months." Then they are kindly asked whether they are pleased with the church, its preaching, doctrine, form of government, etc. If they say they are pleased, they are asked if they are not disposed to be baptized and become members? If so inclined, all is well ; but if not, they are kindly told that it is not desirable for them to commune longer. Thus baptism is held to precede church membership and permanent communion, although temporary communion is permitted without it.

Arnold, Prerequisites to Communion, 80 —"It may perhaps be objected that the passages cited under the four preceding subdivisions refer to church fellowship in a general way, without any specific reference to the Lord's Supper. In reply to this objection, I would answer, in the first place, that having endeavored previously to establish the position that the Lord's Supper is an ordinance to be celebrated in the church, and expressive of church fellowship, I felt at liberty to use the passages that enjoin the withdrawal of that fellowship as constructively enjoining exclusion from the Communion, which is its chief token. I answer, secondly, that the principle here assumed seems to me to pervade the Scriptural teachings so thoroughly that it is next to impossible to lay down any Scriptural terms of communion at the Lord's table, except upon the admission that the ordinance is inseparably connected with church fellowship. To treat the subject otherwise, would be, as it appears to me, a violent putting asunder of what the Lord has joined together. The objection suggests an additional argument in favor of our position that the Lord's Supper is a church ordinance." "Who Christ's body doth divide, Wounds afresh the Crucified ; Who Christ's people doth perplex, Weakens faith and comfort wrecks ; Who Christ's order doth not see, Works in vain for unity ; Who Christ's word doth take for guide, With the Bridegroom loves the Bride."

D. The local church is the judge whether these prerequisites are fulfilled in the case of persons desiring to partake of the Lord's Supper.— This is evident from the following considerations :

(a) The command to observe the ordinance was given, not to individuals, but to a company.

(b) Obedience to this command is not an individual act, but is the joint act of many.

(c) The regular observance of the Lord's Supper cannot be secured, nor the qualifications of persons desiring to participate in it be scrutinized, unless some distinct organized body is charged with this responsibility.

(d) The only organized body known to the New Testament is the local church, and this is the only body, of any sort, competent to have charge of the ordinances. The invisible church has no officers.

(e) The New Testament accounts indicate that the Lord's Supper was observed only at regular appointed meetings of local churches, and was observed by these churches as regularly organized bodies.

(*f*) Since the duty of examining the qualifications of candidates for baptism and for membership is vested in the local church and is essential to its distinct existence, the analogy of the ordinances would lead us to believe that the scrutiny of qualifications for participation in the Lord's supper rests with the same body.

(*g*) This care that only proper persons are admitted to the ordinances should be shown, not by open or forcible debarring of the unworthy at the time of the celebration, but by previous public instruction of the congregation, and, if needful in the case of persistent offenders, by subsequent private and friendly admonition.

"What is everybody's business is nobody's business." If there be any power of effective scrutiny, it must be lodged in the local church. The minister is not to administer the ordinance of the Lord's Supper at his own option, any more than the ordinance of Baptism. He is simply the organ of the church. He is to follow the rules of the church as to invitations and as to the mode of celebrating the ordinance, of course instructing the church as to the order of the New Testament. In the case of sick members who desire to communicate, brethren may be deputed to hold a special meeting of the church at the private house or sick room, and then only may the pastor officiate. If an invitation to the Communion is given, it may well be in the following form : "Members in good standing of other churches of like faith and practice are cordially invited to partake with us." But since the comity of Baptist churches is universally acknowledged, and since Baptist views with regard to the ordinances are so generally understood, it should be taken for granted that all proper persons will be welcome even if no invitation of any sort is given.

Mr. Spurgeon, as we have seen, permitted unbaptized persons temporarily to partake of the Lord's Supper unchallenged, but if there appeared a disposition to make participation habitual, one of the deacons in a private interview explained Baptist doctrine and urged the duty of baptism. If this advice was not taken, participation in the Lord's Supper naturally ceased. Dr. P. S. Henson proposes a middle path between open and close communion, as follows ; "Preach and urge faith in Jesus and obedience to him. Leave choice with participants themselves. It is not wise to set up a judgment-seat at the Lord's table. Always preach the Scriptural order — 1. Faith in Jesus ; 2. Obedience in Baptism ; 3. Observance of the Lord's Supper." J. B. Thomas: "Objections to strict communion come with an ill grace from pedobaptists who withhold communion from their own baptized, whom they have forcibly made quasi-members in spite of the only protest they are capable of offering, and whom they have retained as subjects of discipline without their consent."

A. H. Strong, Cleveland Sermon on Our Denominational Outlook, May 19, 1904 — "If I am asked whether Baptists still hold to restricted communion, I answer that our principle has not changed, but that many of us apply the principle in a different manner from that of our fathers. We believe that Baptism logically precedes the Lord's Supper, as birth precedes the taking of nourishment, and regeneration precedes sanctification. We believe that the order of the ordinances is an important point of Christian doctrine, and itself teaches Christian doctrine. Hence we proclaim it and adhere to it, in our preaching and our practice. But we do not turn the Lord's Supper into a judgment-seat, or turn the officers of the church into detectives. We teach the truth, and expect that the truth will win its way. We are courteous to all who come among us ; and expect that they in turn will have the courtesy to respect our convictions and to act accordingly. But there is danger here that we may break from our moorings and drift into indifferentism with regard to the ordinances. The recent advocacy of open church-membership is but the logical consequence of a previous concession of open communion. I am persuaded that this new doctrine is confined to very few among us. The remedy for this false liberalism is to be found in that same Christ who solves for us all other problems. It is this Christ who sets the solitary in families, and who makes of one every nation that dwells on the face of the earth. Christian denominations are at least temporarily his appointment. Loyalty to the body which seems to us best to represent his truth is also loyalty to him. Love for Christ does not involve the surrender of the ties of family, or nation, or denomination, but only consecrates and ennobles them.

" Yet Christ is King in Zion. There is but one army of the living God, even though there are many divisions. We can emphasize our unity with other Christian bodies, rather than the differences between us. We can regard them as churches of the Lord Jesus, even though they are irregularly constituted. As a marriage ceremony may be valid, even though performed without a license and by an unqualified administrator; and as an ordination may be valid, even though the ordinary laying-on of hands be omitted; so the ordinance of the Lord's Supper as administered in pedobaptist churches may be valid, though irregular in its accompaniments and antecedents. Though we still protest against the modern perversions of the New Testament doctrine as to the subjects and mode of Baptism, we hold with regard to the Lord's Supper that irregularity is not invalidity, and that we may recognize as churches even those bodies which celebrate the Lord's Supper without having been baptized. Our faith in the larger Christ is bringing us out from our denominational isolation into an inspiring recognition of our oneness with the universal church of God throughout the world.' On the whole subject, see Madison Avenue Lectures, 217-260; and A. H. Strong, on Christian Truth and its Keepers, in Philosophy and Religion, 238-244.

E.   Special objections to open communion.

The advocates of this view claim that baptism, as not being an indispensable term of salvation, cannot properly be made an indispensable term of communion.

Robert Hall, Works, 1 : 285, held that there can be no proper terms of communion which are not also terms of salvation. He claims that " we are expressly commanded to tolerate in the church all those diversities of opinion which are not inconsistent with salvation." For the open communion view, see also John M. Mason, Works, 1 : 3:9; Princeton Review, Oct. 1850; Bib. Sac., 21 : 449 ; 24 : 482 ; 25 : 401 ; Spirit of the Pilgrims, 6 : 103, 142. But, as Curtis remarks, in his Progress of Baptist Principles, 292, this principle would utterly frustrate the very objects for which visible churches were founded — to be "the pillar and ground of the truth " (1 Tim. 3 : 15); for truth is set forth as forcibly in ordinances as in doctrine.

In addition to what has already been said, we reply :

(a) This view is contrary to the belief and practice of all but an insignificant fragment of organized Christendom.

A portion of the English Baptists, and the Free Will Baptists in America, are the only bodies which in their standards of faith accept and maintain the principles of open communion. As to the belief and practice of the Methodist Episcopal denomination, the New York Christian Advocate states the terms of communion as being : 1. Discipleship ; 2. Baptism ; 3. Consistent church life, as required in the " Discipline "; and F. G. Hibbard, Christian Baptism, 174, remarks that, " in one principle the Baptist and pedobaptist churches agree. They both agree in rejecting from the communion at the table of the Lord, and denying the rights of church fellowship to all who have not been baptized. Valid baptism, they consider, is essential to constitute visible church membership. This also we [Methodists] hold. . . . . The charge of close communion is no more applicable to the Baptists than to us."
The Interior states the Presbyterian position as follows : " The difference between our Baptist brethren and ourselves is an important difference. We agree with them, however, in saying that unbaptized persons should not partake of the Lord's Supper. Close communion, in our judgment, is a more defensible position than open communion." Dr. John Hall : " If I believed, with the Baptists, that none are baptized but those who are immersed on profession of faith, I should, with them, refuse to commune with any others."
As to the views of Congregationalists, we quote from Dwight, Systematic Theology, sermon 160 — " It is an indispensable qualification for this ordinance that the candidate for communion be a member of the visible church of Christ, in full standing. By this I intend that he should be a man of piety; that he should have made a public profession of religion ; and that he should have been baptized." The Independent : " We have never been disposed to charge the Baptist church with any special narrowness or bigotry in their rule of admission to the Lord's table. We do not see how it differs from that commonly admitted and established among Presbyterian churches."

The Episcopal standards and authorities are equally plain. The Book of Common Prayer, Order of Confirmation, declares: "There shall none be admitted to the holy communion, until such time as he be confirmed, or be ready and desirous to be confirmed"— confirmation always coming after baptism. Wall, History of Infant Baptism, part 2, chapter 9 — "No church ever gave the communion to any persons before they were baptized. Among all the absurdities that ever were held, none ever maintained that any person should partake of the communion before he was baptized."

(*b*) It assumes an unscriptural inequality between the two ordinances. The Lord's Supper holds no higher rank in Scripture than does Baptism. The obligation to commune is no more binding than the obligation to profess faith by being baptized. Open communion, however, treats baptism as if it were optional, while it insists upon communion as indispensable.

Robert Hall should rather have said : "No church has a right to establish terms of baptism which are not also terms of salvation," for baptism is most frequently in Scripture connected with the things that accompany salvation. We believe faith to be one prerequisite, but not the only one. We may hold a person to be a Christian, without thinking him entitled to commune unless he has been also baptized.

Ezra's reform in abolishing mixed marriages with the surrounding heathen was not narrow nor bigoted nor intolerant. Miss Willard said well that from the Gerizim of holy beatitudes there comes a voice: "Blessed are the inclusive, for they shall be included," and from Mount Ebal a voice, saying: "Sad are the exclusive, for they shall be excluded." True liberality is both Christian and wise. We should be just as liberal as Christ himself, and no more so. Even Miss Willard would not include rumsellers in the Christian Temperance Union, nor think that town blessed that did not say to saloon keepers: "Repent, or go." The choir is not narrow because it does not include those who can only make discords, nor is the sheepfold intolerant that refuses to include wolves, nor the medical society that excludes quacks, nor the church that does not invite the disobedient and schismatic to its communion.

(*c*) It tends to do away with baptism altogether. If the highest privilege of church membership may be enjoyed without baptism, baptism loses its place and importance as the initiatory ordinance of the church.

Robert Hall would admit to the Lord's Supper those who deny Baptism to be perpetually binding on the church. A foreigner may love this country, but he cannot vote at our elections unless he has been naturalized. Ceremonial rites imply ceremonial qualifications. Dr. Meredith in Brooklyn said to his great Bible Class that a man, though not a Christian, but who felt himself a sinner and needing Christ, could worthily partake of the Lord's Supper. This is the logic of open communion. The Supper is not limited to baptized persons, nor to church members, nor even to converted people, but belongs also to the unconverted world. This is not only to do away with Baptism, but to make the Lord's Supper a converting ordinance.

(*d*) It tends to do away with all discipline. When Christians offend, the church must withdraw its fellowship from them. But upon the principle of open communion, such withdrawal is impossible, since the Lord's Supper, the highest expression of church fellowship, is open to every person who regards himself as a Christian.

H. F. Colby : "Ought we to acknowledge that evangelical pedobaptists are qualified to partake of the Lord's Supper? We are ready to admit them on precisely the same terms on which we admit ourselves. Our communion bars come to be a protest, but from no plan of ours. They become a protest merely as every act of loyalty to truth becomes a protest against error." Constitutions of the Holy Apostles, book 2, section 7 (about 250 A. D.) — "But if they [those who have been convicted of wickedness] afterwards repent and turn from their error, then we receive them as we receive the heathen, when they wish to repent, into the church indeed to hear the word, but do not receive them to communion until they have received the seal of baptism and are made complete Christians."

(*e*) It tends to do away with the visible church altogether. For no visible church is possible, unless some sign of membership be required, in addition to the signs of membership in the invisible church. Open communion logically leads to open church membership, and a church membership open to all, without reference to the qualifications required in Scripture, or without examination on the part of the church as to the existence of these qualifications in those who unite with it, is virtually an identification of the church with the world, and, without protest from Scripturally constituted bodies, would finally result in its actual extinction.

Dr. Walcott Calkins, in Andover Review: "It has never been denied that the Puritan way of maintaining the purity and doctrinal soundness of the churches is to secure a soundly converted membership. There is one denomination of Puritans which has never deviated a hair's breadth from this way. The Baptists have always insisted that regenerate persons only ought to receive the sacraments of the church. And they have depended absolutely upon this provision for the purity and doctrinal soundness of their churches."

At the Free Will Baptist Convention at Providence, Oct., 1874, the question came up of admitting pedobaptists to membership. This was disposed of by resolving that "Christian baptism is a personal act of public consecration to Christ, and that believers' baptism and immersion alone, as baptism, are fundamental principles of the denomination." In other words, unimmersed believers would not be admitted to membership. But is not the Lord's church? Have we a right to exclude? Is this not bigotry? The Free Will Baptist answers: "No, it is only loyalty to truth."

We claim that, upon the same principle, he should go further, and refuse to admit to the communion those whom he refuses to admit to church membership. The reasons assigned for acting upon the opposite principle are sentimental rather than rational. See John Stuart Mill's definition of sentimentality, quoted in Martineau's Essays, 1:94 — "Sentimentality consists in setting the sympathetic aspect of things, or their loveableness, above their æsthetic aspect, their beauty; or above the moral aspect of them, their right or wrong."

OBJECTIONS TO STRICT COMMUNION, AND ANSWERS TO THEM (condensed from Arnold, Terms of Communion, 82):

"1st. *Primitive rules are not applicable now.* Reply: (1) The laws of Christ are unchangeable. (2) The primitive order ought to be restored.

"2d. *Baptism, as an external rite, is of less importance than love.* Reply: (1) It is not inconsistent with love, but the mark of love, to keep Christ's commandments. (2) Love for our brethren requires protest against their errors.

"3d. *Pedobaptists think themselves baptized.* Reply: (1) This is a reason why they should act as if they believed it, not a reason why we should act as if it were so. (2) We cannot submit our consciences to their views of truth without harming ourselves and them.

"4th. *Strict communion is a hindrance to union among Christians.* Reply: (1) Christ desires only union in the truth. (2) Baptists are not responsible for the separation. (3) Mixed communion is not a cure but a cause of disunion.

"5th. *The rule excludes from the communion baptized members of pedobaptist churches.* Reply: (1) These persons are walking disorderly, in promoting error. (2) The Lord's Supper is a symbol of church fellowship, not of fellowship for individuals, apart from their church relations.

"6th. *A plea for dispensing with the rule exists in extreme cases where persons must commune with us or not at all.* Reply: (1) It is hard to fix limits to these exceptions: they would be likely to encroach more and more, till the rule became merely nominal. (2) It is a greater privilege and means of grace, in such circumstances, to abstain from communing, than contrary to principle to participate. (3) It is not right to participate with others, where we cannot invite them reciprocally.

"7. *Alleged inconsistency of our practice.* — (*a*) Since we expect to commune in heaven. Reply: This confounds Christian fellowship with church fellowship. We do commune with pedobaptists spiritually, here as hereafter. We do not expect to partake of the Lord's Supper with them, or with others, in heaven. (*b*) Since we reject the better and receive the worse. Reply: We are not at liberty to refuse to apply Christ's outward rule, because we cannot equally apply his inward spiritual rule of character. Pedobaptists withold communion from those they regard as unbaptized, though they may be more spiritual than some in the church. (c) Since we recognize pedobaptists as brethren in union meetings, exchange of pulpits, *etc.* Reply: None of these acts of fraternal fellowship imply the church communion which admission to the Lord's table would imply. This last would recognize them as baptized: the former do not.

" 8th. *Alleged impolicy of our practice.* Reply: (1) This consideration would be pertinent, only if we were at liberty to change our practice when it was expedient, or was thought to be so. (2) Any particular truth will inspire respect in others in proportion as its advocates show that they respect it. In England our numbers have diminished, compared with the population, in the ratio of 33 per cent.; here we have increased 50 per cent. in proportion to the ratio of population.

" *Summary.* Open communion must be justified, if at all, on one of four grounds: First, that baptism is not prerequisite to communion. But this is opposed to the belief and practice of all churches. Secondly, that immersion on profession of faith is not essential to baptism. But this is renouncing Baptist principles altogether. Thirdly, that the individual, and not the church, is to be the judge of his qualifications for admission to the communion. But this is contrary to sound reason, and fatal to the ends for which the church is instituted. For, if the conscience of the individual is to be the rule of the action of the church in regard to his admission to the Lord's Supper, why not also with regard to his regeneration, his doctrinal belief, and his obedience to Christ's commands generally? Fourthly, that the church has no responsibility in regard to the qualifications of those who come to her communion. But this is abandoning the principle of the independence of the churches, and their accountableness to Christ, and it overthrows all church discipline."

See also▪Hovey, in Bib. Sac., 1862: 133; Pepper, in Bap. Quar., 1867: 216; Curtis on Communion, 292; Howell, Terms of Communion; Williams, The Lord's Supper; Theodosia Ernest, pub. by Am. Bap. Pub. Soc.; Wilkinson, The Baptist Principle. In concluding our treatment of Ecclesiology, we desire to call attention to the fact that Jacob, the English Churchman, in his Ecclesiastical Polity of the N. T., and Cunningham, the Scotch Presbyterian, in his Croall Lectures for 1886, have furnished Baptists with much valuable material for the defence of the New Testament doctrine of the Church and its Ordinances. In fact, a complete statement of the Baptist positions might easily be constructed from the concessions of their various opponents. See A. H. Strong, on Unconscious Assumptions of Communion Polemics, in Philosophy and Religion, 245-249.

PART VIII.

ESCHATOLOGY, OR THE DOCTRINE OF FINAL THINGS.

Neither the individual Christian character, nor the Christian church as a whole, attains its destined perfection in this life (Rom. 8 : 24). This perfection is reached in the world to come (1 Cor. 13 : 10). As preparing the way for the kingdom of God in its completeness, certain events are to take place, such as death, Christ's second coming, the resurrection of the body, the general judgment. As stages in the future condition of men, there is to be an intermediate and an ultimate state, both for the righteous and for the wicked. We discuss these events and states in what appears from Scripture to be the order of their occurrence.

Rom. 8:24 —"in hope were we saved : but hope that is seen is not hope : for who hopeth for that which he seeth ? " 1 Cor. 13:10 —"when that which is perfect is come, that which is in part shall be done away." Original sin is not wholly eradicated from the Christian, and the Holy Spirit is not yet sole ruler. So, too, the church is still in a state of conflict, and victory is hereafter. But as the Christian life attains its completeness only in the future, so with the life of sin. Death begins here, but culminates hereafter. James 1:15 —"the sin, when it is full grown, bringeth forth death." The wicked man here has only a foretaste of "the wrath to come" (Mat. 3·7). We may "lay up . . . . treasures in heaven " (Mat. 6 : 20), but we may also "treasure up for ourselves wrath " (Rom. 2 : 5), *i. e.*, lay up treasures in hell.

Dorner : " To the actuality of the consummation of the church belongs a cessation of reproduction through which there is constantly renewed a world which the church must subdue. . . . . The mutually external existence of spirit and nature must give way to a perfect internal existence. Their externality to each other is the ground of the mortality of the natural side, and of its being a means of temptation to the spiritual side. For in this externality the natural side has still too great independence and exerts a determining power over the personality. . . . . Art the beautiful, receives in the future state its special place ; for it is the way of art to delight in visible presentation, to achieve the classical and perfect with unfettered play of its powers. Every one morally perfect will thus wed the good to the beautiful. In the rest, there will be no inactivity ; and in the activity also, no unrest."

Schleiermacher : " Eschatology is essentially prophetic ; and is therefore vague and indefinite, like all unfulfilled prophecy." Schiller's Thekla : " Every thought of beautiful, trustful seeming Stands fulfilled in Heaven's eternal day ; Shrink not then from erring and from dreaming,— Lofty sense lies oft in childish play." Frances Power Cobbe, Peak of Darien, 265 —" Human nature is a ship with the tide out ; when the tide of eternity comes in, we shall see the purpose of the ship." Eschatology deals with the precursors of Christ's second coming, as well as with the second coming itself. We are to labor for the coming of the kingdom of God in society as well as in the individual and in the church, in the present life as well as in the life to come.

Kidd, in his Principles of Western Civilization, says that survives which helps the greatest number. But the greatest number is always in the future. The theatre has become too wide for the drama. Through the roof the eternal stars appear. The image of God in man implies the equality of all men. Political equality implies universal suffrage ; economic equality implies universal profit. Society has already transcended first, city isolation, and secondly, state isolation. The United States presents thus far the largest free trade area in history. The next step is the unity of the English speaking peoples. The days of separate nationalities are numbered. *Laissez faire* = surviving barbarism. There are signs of larger ideas in art, ethics, literature, philosophy, science, politics, economics, religion. Competition must be moralized, and must take into account the future as well as the present. See also Walter Rauschenbusch, Christianity and the Social Crisis.

George B. Stevens, in Am. Jour. Theology, Oct. 1902 : 666–684, asks : " Is there a self-constituted New Testament Eschatology ? " He answers, for substance, that only three things are sure : 1. The certain triumph of the kingdom — this being the kernel of truth in the doctrine of Christ's second coming ; 2. the victory of life over death — the truth in the doctrine of the resurrection ; 3. the principle of judgment — the truth at the basis of the belief in rewards and punishments in the world to come. This meagre and abstract residuum argues denial both of the unity and the sufficiency of Scripture. Our view of inspiration, while it does not assure us of minute details, does notwithstanding give us a broad general outline of the future consummation, and guarantees its trustworthiness by the word of Christ and his apostles.

Faith in that consummation is the main incitement to poetic utterance and to lofty achievement. Shairp, Province of Poetry, 28 — " If poetry be not a river fed from the clear wells that spring on the highest summits of humanity, but only a canal to drain off stagnant ditches from the flats, it may be a very useful sanitary contrivance, but has not, in Bacon's words, any ' participation of divineness.' " Shakespeare uses prose for ideas detached from emotion, such as the merrymaking of clowns or the maundering of fools. But lofty thought with him puts on poetry as its singing robe. Savage, Life beyond Death, 1–5 — " When Henry D. Thoreau lay dying at Concord, his friend Parker Pillsbury sat by his bedside. He leaned over, took him by the hand, and said : ' Henry, you are so near to the border now, can you see anything on the other side ? ' And Thoreau answered : ' One world at a time, Parker ! ' But I cannot help asking about that other world, and if I belong to a future world as well as to this, my life will be a very different one. " Jesus knew our need of certain information about the future, and therefore he said : " In my Father's house are many mansions ; if it were not so, I would have told you ; for I go to prepare a place for you " (John 14 : 2).

Hutton, Essays, 2 : 211 — " Imagination may be powerful without being fertile ; it may summon up past scenes and live in them without being able to create new ones. National unity and supernatural guidance were beliefs which kept Hebrew poetry from being fertile or original in its dealings with human story ; for national pride is conservative, not inventive, and believers in actual providence do not care to live in a world of invention. The Jew saw in history only the illustration of these two truths. He was never thoroughly stirred by mere individual emotion. The modern poet is a student of beauty ; the O. T. poet a student of God. To the latter all creation is a mere shadow ; the essence of its beauty and the sustaining power of its life are in the spiritual world. Go beyond the spiritual nature of man, and the sympathy of the Hebrew poet is dried up at once. His poetry was true and divine, but at the expense of variousness of insight and breadth of sympathy. It was heliocentric, rather than geocentric. Only Job, the latest, is a conscious effort of the imagination." Apocalyptic poetry for these reasons was most natural to the Hebrew mind.

Balfour, Foundations of Belief, 66 — " Somewhere and for some Being, there shines an unchanging splendor of beauty, of which in nature and in art we see, each of us from his own standpoint, only passing gleams and stray reflections, whose different aspects we cannot now coördinate, whose import we cannot fully comprehend, but which at least is something other than the chance play of subjective sensibility or the far-off echo of ancestral lusts." Dewey, Psychology, 200 — " All products of the creative imagination are unconscious testimonials to the unity of spirit which binds man to man, and man to nature, in one organic whole." Tennyson, Idylls of the King : " As from beyond the limit of the world, Like the last echo born of a great cry, Sounds, as if some fair city were one voice Around a king returning from his wars." See, on the whole subject of Eschatology, Luthardt, Lehre von den letzten Dingen, and Saving Truths of Christianity ; Hodge, Systematic Theology, 3 : 713–880 ; Hovey, Biblical Eschatology ; Heagle, That Blessed Hope.

1. Physical Death.

Physical death is the separation of the soul from the body. We distinguish it from spiritual death, or the separation of the soul from God ; and from the second death, or the banishment from God and final misery of the reünited soul and body of the wicked.

Spiritual death : Is. 59 : 2 —"but your iniquities have separated between you and your God, and your sins have hid his face from you, so that he will not hear"; Rom. 7 : 24 —"Wretched man that I am ! who shall deliver me out of the body of this death ?" Eph. 2 : 1 —"dead through your trespasses and sins." The second death : Rev. 2 : 11 —"He that overcometh shall not be hurt of the second death"; 20 : 14 —"And death and Hades were cast into the ake of fire. This is the second death, even the lake of fire"; 21 : 8 —"But for the fearful, and unbelieving, and abominable, and murderers, and fornicators, and sorcerers, and idolaters, and all liars, their part shall be in the lake that burneth with fire and brimstone; which is the second death."

Julius Müller, Doctrine of Sin, 2 : 303 —"Spiritual death, the inner discord and enslavement of the soul, and the misery resulting therefrom, to which belongs that other death, the second death, an outward condition corresponding to that inner slavery." Trench, Epistles to the Seven Churches, 151 —"This phrase ['second death'] is itself a solemn protest against the Sadduceeism and Epicureanism which would make natural death the be-all and the end-all of existence. As there is a life beyond the present life for the faithful, so there is death beyond that which falls under our eyes for the wicked." E. G. Robinson : "The second death is the continuance of spiritual death in another and timeless existence." Hudson, Scientific Demonstration of a Future Life, 222 —"If a man has a power that transcends the senses, it is at least presumptive evidence that it does not perish when the senses are extinguished. . . . . The activity of the subjective mind is in inverse proportion to that of the body, though the objective mind weakens with the body and perishes with the brain."

Prof. H. H. Bawden : "Consciousness is simply the growing of an organism, while the organism is just that which grows. Consciousness is a function, not a thing, not an order of existence at all. It is the universe coming to a focus, flowering so to speak in a finite centre. Society is an organism in the same sense that the human being is an organism. The spatial separation of the elements of the social organism is relatively no greater than the separation of the unit factors of the body. As the neurone cannot deny the consciousness which is the function of the body, so the individual member of society has no reason for denying the existence of a cosmic life of the organism which we call society."

Emma M. Caillard, on Man in the Light of Evolution, in Contemp. Rev., Dec. 1893 : 878 —"Man is nature risen into the consciousness of its relationship to the divine. There is no receding from this point. When ' that which drew from out the boundless deep turns again home,' the persistence of each personal life is necessitated. Human life, as it is, includes, though it transcends the lower forms through which it has developed. Human life, as it will be, must include though it may transcend its present manifestation, viz., personality." " Sometime, when all life's lessons have been learned, And suns and stars forevermore have set, And things which our weak judgments here have spurned, The things o'er which we grieved with lashes wet, Will flash before us through our life's dark night, As stars shine most in deepest tints of blue : And we shall see how all God's plans were right, And most that seemed reproof was love most true : And if sometimes commingled with life's wine We find the wormwood and rebel and shrink, Be sure a wiser hand than yours or mine Pours out this portion for our lips to drink. And if some friend we love is lying low, Where human kisses cannot reach his face, O do not blame the loving Father so, But wear your sorrow with obedient grace; And you shall shortly know that lengthened breath Is not the sweetest gift God sends his friend, And that sometimes the sable pall of death Conceals the fairest boon his love can send. If we could push ajar the gates of life, And stand within, and all God's working see, We could interpret all this doubt and strife, And for each mystery find a key."

Although physical death falls upon the unbeliever as the original penalty of sin, to all who are united in Christ it loses its aspect of penalty, and becomes a means of discipline and of entrance into eternal life.

To the Christian, physical death is not a penalty : see Ps. 116 : 15—"Precious in the sight of Jehovah Is the death of his saints"; Rom. 8 : 10—"And if Christ is in you, the body is dead because of sin ; but the spirit is life because of righteousness"; 14 : 8 —"For whether we live, we live unto the Lord ; or whether we die, we die unto the Lord : whether we live therefore, or die, we are the Lord's"; 1 Cor. 3 : 22 —"whether Paul, or Apollos, or Cephas, or the world, or life, or death, or things present, or things to come ; all are yours"; 15 : 55 —"O death, where is thy victory ? 0 death, where is thy sting ?" 1 Pet. 4 : 6 —"For unto this end was the gospel preached even to the dead, that they might be judged indeed according to men in the flesh, but live according to God in the spirit"; cf. Rom. 1 : 18 —"For the wrath of God is revealed from heaven against all ungodliness and unrighteousness of men, who hinder the truth in unrighteousness"; 8 : 1, 2 —"There is therefore now no condemnation to them that are in Christ Jesus. For the law of the Spirit of life in Christ Jesus made me free from the law of sin and of death", Heb. 12 : 6 —"For whom the Lord loveth he chasteneth."

Dr. Hovey says that "the present sufferings of believers are in the nature of discipline, with an aspect of retribution ; while the present sufferings of unbelievers are retributive, with a glance toward reformation." We prefer to say that all penalty has been borne by Christ, and that, for him who is justified in Christ, suffering of whatever kind is of the nature of fatherly chastening, never of judicial retribution ; see our discussion of the Penalty of Sin, pages 652–660.

" We see but dimly through the mists and vapors Amid these earthly damps ; What are to us but sad funereal tapers May be Heaven's distant lamps. There is no death,— what seems so is transition ; This life of mortal breath Is but a suburb of the life Elysian Whose portal men call death." " 'Tis meet that we should pause awhile, Ere we put off this mortal coil, And in the stillness of old age, Muse on our earthly pilgrimage." Shakespeare, Romeo and Juliet, 4 : 5 —" Heaven and yourself Had part in this fair maid ; now Heaven hath all, And all the better is it for the maid : Your part in her you could not keep from death, But Heaven keeps his part in eternal life. The most you sought was her promotion, For 't was your heaven she should be advanced ; And weep ye now, seeing she is advanced Above the clouds, as high as Heaven itself ? " Phœbe Cary's Answered : " I thought to find some healing clime For her I loved ; she found that shore, That city whose inhabitants Are sick and sorrowful no more. I asked for human love for her ; The Loving knew how best to still The infinite yearning of a heart Which but infinity could fill. Such sweet communion had been ours, I prayed that it might never end ; My prayer is more than answered ; now I have an angel for my friend. I wished for perfect peace to soothe The troubled anguish of her breast ; And numbered with the loved and called She entered on untroubled rest. Life was so fair a thing to her, I wept and pleaded for its stay ; My wish was granted me, for lo ! She hath eternal life to-day ! "

Victor Hugo: "The tomb is not a blind alley ; it is a thoroughfare. It closes with the twilight, to open with the dawn. . . . . . I feel that I have not said the thousandth part of what is in me. . . . . The thirst for infinity proves infinity." Shakespeare : " Nothing is here for tears ; nothing to wail, Or knock the breast ; no weakness, no contempt, Dispraise or blame ; nothing but well and fair." O. W. Holmes : "Build thee more stately mansions, O my soul, As the swift seasons roll ! Leave thy low-vaulted past ! Let each new temple, nobler than the last Shut thee from heaven with a dome more vast, Till thou at length art free, Leaving thine outgrown shell by life's unresting sea !" J. G. Whittier : " So when Time's veil shall fall asunder, The soul may know No fearful change or sudden wonder, Nor sink the weight of mystery under, But with the upward rise, and with the vastness grow."

To neither saint nor sinner is death a cessation of being. This we maintain, against the advocates of annihilation :

1. *Upon rational grounds.*

(*a*) The metaphysical argument. — The soul is simple, not compounded. Death, in matter, is the separation of parts. But in the soul there are no parts to be separated. The dissolution of the body, therefore, does not necessarily work a dissolution of the soul. But, since there is an immaterial principle in the brute, and this argument taken by itself might seem to prove the immortality of the animal creation equally with that of man, we pass to consider the next argument.

The Gnostics and the Manichæans held that beasts had knowledge and might pray. The immateriality of the brute mind was probably the consideration which led Leibnitz, Bishop Butler, Coleridge, John Wesley, Lord Shaftesbury, Mary Somerville, James Hogg, Toplady, Lamartine, and Louis Agassiz to encourage the belief in animal immortality. See Bp. Butler, Analogy, part i, chap. i (Bohn's ed., 81-91) ; Agassiz, Essay on Classification, 99 — " Most of the arguments for the immortality of man apply equally to the permanency of this principle in other living beings." Elsewhere Agassiz says of animals : "I cannot doubt of their immortality any more than I doubt of my own." Lord Shaftesbury in 1881 remarked : " I have ever believed in a happy future for animals ; I cannot say or conjecture how or where ; but sure I am that the love, so manifested by dogs especially, is an emanation from the divine essence, and as such it can, or rather, it will, never be extinguished." St. Francis of Assisi preached to birds, and called sun, moon, earth, fire, water, stones, flowers, crickets, and death, his brothers and sisters. "He knew not if the brotherhood His homily had understood; He only knew that to one ear The meaning of his words was clear" (Longfellow, The Sermon of St. Francis — to the birds). "If death dissipates the sagacity of the elephant, why not that of his captor?" See Buckner, Immortality of Animals; William Adams Brown, Christian Theology in Outline, 240.

Mansel, Metaphysics, 371, maintains that all this argument proves is that the objector cannot show the soul to be compound, and so cannot show that it is destructible. Calderwood, Moral Philosophy, 259 — "The facts which point toward the termination of our present state of existence are connected with our physical nature, not with our mortal." John Fiske, Destiny of the Creature, 110 — "With his illegitimate hypothesis of annihilation, the materialist transgresses the bounds of experience quite as widely as the poet who sings of the New Jerusalem, with its river of life and its streets of gold   Scientifically speaking, there is not a particle of evidence for either view." John Fiske, Life Everlasting, 80-85 — "How could immortal man have been produced through heredity from an ephemeral brute? We do not know. Nature's habit is to make prodigious leaps, but only after long preparation. Slowly rises the water in the tank, inch by inch through many a weary hour, until at length it overflows, and straightway vast systems of machinery are awakened into rumbling life. Slowly the ellipse becomes eccentric, until suddenly the finite ellipse becomes an infinite paraboloid."

Ladd, Philosophy of Mind, 206 — "The ideas of dividing up or splitting off are not applicable to mind. The argument for the indestructibility of mind as growing out of its indiscerptibility, and the argument by which Kant confuted it, are alike absurd within the realm of mental phenomena." Adeney, Christianity and Evolution, 127 — "Nature, this argument shows, has nothing to say against the immortality of that which is above the range of physical structure." Lotze: "Everything which has once originated will endure forever so soon as it possesses an unalterable value for the coherent system of the world; but it will, as a matter of course, in turn cease to be, if this is not the case." Bowne, Int. to Psych. Theory, 315-318 — "Of what use would brutes be hereafter? We may reply: Of what use are they here? . . . . Those things which have perennial significance for the universe will abide." Bixby, Crisis in Morals, 203 — "In living beings there is always a pressure toward larger and higher existence. . . . . The plant must grow, must bloom, must sow its seeds, or it withers away. . . . . The aim is to bring forth consciousness, and in greatest fulness. . . . . Beasts of prey and other enemies to the ascending path of life are to be swept out of the way."

But is not the brute a part of that Nature which has been subjected to vanity, which groans and travails in pain, and which waits to be redeemed? The answer seems to be that the brute is a mere appendage to man, has no independent value in the creation, is incapable of ethical life or of communion with God the source of life, and so has no guarantee of continuance. Man on the other hand is of independent value. But this is to anticipate the argument which follows. It is sufficient here to point out that there is no proof that consciousness is dependent upon the soul's connection with a physical organism. McLane, Evolution in Religion, 261 — "As the body may preserve its form and be to a degree made to act after the psychic element is lost by removal of the brain, so this psychic element may exist, and act according to its nature after the physical element ceases to exist." Hovey, Bib. Eschatology, 19 — "If I am in a house, I can look upon surrounding objects only through its windows; but open the door and let me go out of the house, and the windows are no longer of any use to me." Shaler, Interpretation of Nature, 295 — "To perpetuate mind after death is less surprising than to perpetuate or transmit mind here by inheritance." See also Martineau, Study, 2 : 332-337, 363-365.

William James, in his Essay on Human Immortality, argues that thought is not necessarily a *productive* function of the brain; it may rather be a permissive or *transmissive* function. Thought is not *made* in the brain, so that when the brain perishes the soul dies. The brain is only the organ for the *transmission* of thought, just as the lens transmits the light which it does not produce. There is a spiritual world behind and above the material world. Our brains are thin and half transparent places in the veil, through which knowledge comes in. Savage, Life after Death, 289 — "You may attach a dynamo for a time to some particular machine. When you have removed the machine, you have not destroyed the dynamo. You may attach it to some other machine and find that you have the old time power. So the soul may not be confined to one body." These analogies seem to us to come short of proving personal immortality. They belong to "psychology without a soul," and while they illustrate the persistence of some sort of life, they do not render more probable the continuance of my individual consciousness beyond the bounds of death. They are entirely consistent with the pantheistic theory of a remerging of the personal existence in the great whole of which it forms a part. Tennyson, In Memoriam : "That each, who seems a separate whole, Should move his rounds and, fusing all The skirts of self again, should fall Remerging in the general Soul, Is faith as vague as all unsweet." See Pfleiderer, Die Ritschl'sche Theologie, 12 ; Howison, Limits of Evolution, 279–312.

Seth, Hegelianism : "For Hegel, immortality is only the permanence of the Absolute, the abstract process. This is no more consoling than the continued existence of the chemical elements of our bodies in new transformations. Human self-consciousness is a spark struck in the dark, to die away on the darkness whence it has arisen." This is the only immortality of which George Eliot conceived in her poem, The Immortal Choir : "O may I join the choir invisible Of those immortal dead who live again In minds made better by their presence ; live In pulses stirred to generosity, In deeds of daring rectitude, in scorn For miserable aims that end in self, In thoughts sublime that pierce the night like stars, And with their mild persistence urge man's search To vaster issues." Those who hold to this unconscious immortality concede that death is not a separation of parts, but rather a cessation of consciousness ; and that therefore, while the substance of human nature may endure, mankind may ever develop into new forms, without individual immortality. To this we reply, that man's self-consciousness and self-determination are different in kind from the consciousness and determination of the brute. As man can direct his self-consciousness and self-determination to immortal ends, we have the right to believe this self-consciousness and self-determination to be immortal. This leads us to the next argument.

(*b*) The teleological argument. — Man, as an intellectual, moral, and religious being, does not attain the end of his existence on earth. His development is imperfect here. Divine wisdom will not leave its work incomplete. There must be a hereafter for the full growth of man's powers, and for the satisfaction of his aspirations. Created, unlike the brute, with infinite capacities for moral progress, there must be an immortal existence in which those capacities shall be brought into exercise. Though the wicked forfeit all claim to this future, we have here an argument from God's love and wisdom to the immortality of the righteous.

In reply to this argument, it has been said that many right wishes are vain. Mill, Essays on Religion, 294 — "Desire for food implies enough to eat, now and forever? hence an eternal supply of cabbage?" But our argument proceeds upon three presuppositions : (1) that a holy and benevolent God exists ; (2) that he has made man in his image ; (3) that man's true end is holiness and likeness to God. Therefore, what will answer the true end of man will be furnished ; but that is not cabbage — it is holiness and love, *i. e.*, God himself. See Martineau, Study, 2 : 370–381.

The argument, however, is valuable only in its application to the righteous. God will not treat the righteous as the tyrant of Florence treated Michael Angelo, when he bade him carve out of ice a statue, which would melt under the first rays of the sun. In the case of the wicked, the other law of retribution comes in — the taking away of "even that which he hath " (Mat. 25 : 29). Since we are all wicked, the argument is not satisfactory, unless we take into account the further facts of atonement and justification — facts of which we learn from revelation alone.

But while, taken by itself, this rational argument might be called defective, and could never prove that man may not attain his end in the continued existence of the race, rather than in that of the individual, the argument appears more valuable as a rational supplement to the facts already mentioned, and seems to render certain at least the immortality of those upon whom God has set his love, and in whom he has wrought the beginnings of righteousness.

Lord Erskine : "Inferior animals have no instincts or faculties which are not subservient to the ends and purposes of their being. Man's reason, and faculties endowed with power to reach the most distant worlds, would be useless if his existence were to terminate in the grave." There would be wastefulness in the extinction of great minds; see Jackson, James Martineau, 439. As water is implied by the organization of the fish, and air by that of the bird, so "the existence of spiritual power within us is likewise presumption that some fitting environment awaits the spirit when it shall be set free and perfected, and sex and death can be dispensed with " (Newman Smyth, Place of Death in Evolution, 106). Nägeli, the German botanist, says that Nature tends to perfection. Yet the mind hardly begins to awake, ere the bodily powers decline (George, Progress and Poverty, 505). "Character grows firmer and solider as the body ages and grows weaker. Can character be vitally implicated in the act of physical dissolution ? " (Upton, Hibbert Lectures, 353). If a rational and moral Deity has caused the gradual evolution in humanity of the ideas of right and wrong, and has added to it the faculty of creating ethical ideals, must he not have provided some satisfaction for the ethical needs which this development has thus called into existence ? (Balfour, Foundations of Belief, 351).

Royce, Conception of God, 50, quotes Le Conte as follows: "Nature is the womb *in* which, and evolution the process *by* which, are generated sons of God. Without immortality this whole process is balked — the whole process of cosmic evolution is futile. Shall God be so long and at so great pains to achieve a *spirit*, capable of communing with himself, and then allow it to lapse again into nothingness ? " John Fiske, Destiny of Man, 116, accepts the immortality of the soul by "a supreme act of faith in the reasonableness of God's work." If man is the end of the creative process and the object of God's care, then the soul's career cannot be completed with its present life upon the earth (Newman Smyth, Place of Death in Evolution, 92, 93). Bowne, Philosophy of Theism, 254—" Neither God nor the future life is needed to pay us for present virtue, but rather as the condition without which our nature falls into irreconcilable discord with itself, and passes on to pessimism and despair. High and continual effort is impossible without correspondingly high and abiding hopes. . . . . It is no more selfish to desire to live hereafter than it is to desire to live to-morrow." Dr. M. B. Anderson used to say that there must be a heaven for canal horses, washerwomen, and college presidents, because they do not get their deserts in this life.

Life is a series of commencements rather than of accomplished ends. Longfellow, on Charles Sumner: "Death takes us by surprise, And stays our hurrying feet; The great design unfinished lies, Our lives are incomplete. But in the dark unknown Perfect their circles seem, Even as a bridge's arch of stone Is rounded in the stream." Robert Browning, Abt Vogler: "There never shall be one lost good " ; Prospice: "No work begun shall ever pause for death "; "Pleasure must succeed to pleasure, else past pleasure turns to pain; And this first life claims a second, else I count its good no gain "; Old Pictures in Florence: "We are faulty — why not? We have time in store "; Grammarian's Funeral : "What 's time ? Leave Now for dogs and apes,— Man has Forever." Robert Browning wrote in his wife's Testament the following testimony of Dante : "Thus I believe, thus I affirm, thus I am certain it is, that from this life I shall pass to another better, there where that lady lives, of whom my soul was enamored." And Browning says in a letter: "It is a great thing — the greatest — that a human being should have passed the probation of life, and sum up its experience in a witness to the power and love of God. . . . . I see even more reason to hold by the same hope."

(c) The ethical argument.—Man is not, in this world, adequately punished for his evil deeds. Our sense of justice leads us to believe that God's moral administration will be vindicated in a life to come. Mere extinction of being would not be a sufficient penalty, nor would it permit degrees of punishment corresponding to degrees of guilt. This is therefore an argument from God's justice to the immortality of the wicked. The guilty conscience demands a state after death for punishment.

This is an argument from God's justice to the immortality of the wicked, as the preceding was an argument from God's love to the immortality of the righteous. "History defies our moral sense by giving a peaceful end to Sulla." Louis XV and Madame Pompadour died in their beds, after a life of extreme luxury. Louis XVI and his queen, though far more just and pure, perished by an appalling tragedy. The fates of these four cannot be explained by the wickedness of the latter pair and the virtue of the former. Alexander the Sixth, the worst of the popes, was apparently prosperous and happy in his iniquities. Though guilty of the most shameful crimes, he was serenely impenitent, and to the last of his days he defied both God and man. Since there is not an execution of justice here, we feel that there must be a "judgment to come," such as that which terrified Felix (Acts 24: 25). Martineau, Study, 2 : 383-388. Stopford A. Brooke, Justice : "Three men went out one summer night, No care had they or aim, And dined and drank. ' Ere we go home We'll have,' they said, ' a game.' Three girls began that summer night A life of endless shame, And went through drink, disease, and death As swift as racing flame. Lawless and homeless, foul, they died ; Rich, loved and praised, the men : But when they all shall meet with God, And Justice speaks,— what then ? " See John Caird, Fund. Ideas of Christianity, 2:255-297. G. F. Wilkin, Control in Evolution : " Belief in immortality is a practical necessity of evolution. If the decisions of to-day are to determine our eternal destiny, then it is vastly more important to choose and act aright, than it is to preserve our earthly life. The martyrs were right. Conscience is vindicated. We can live for the ideal of manhood. Immortality is a powerful reformatory instrument." Martineau, Study of Religion, 2 : 388 —" If Death gives a final discharge to the sinner and the saint alike, Conscience has told us more lies than it has ever called to their account." Shakespeare, Henry V, 4 : 2—"If [transgressors] have defeated the law and outrun native punishment, though they can outstrip men, they have no wings to fly from God"; Henry VI, 2d part, 5 : 2 —" Can we outrun the heavens ? " Addison, Cato : " It must be so,— Plato, thou reasonest well.— Else whence this pleasing hope, this fond desire, This longing after immortality ? Or whence this secret dread and inward horror Of falling into naught ? Why shrinks the soul Back on herself and startles at destruction ? 'T is the divinity that stirs within us, 'T is Heaven itself that points out a hereafter, And intimates eternity to man."

Gildersleeve, in The Independent, March 30, 1899 — " Plato in the Phædo argues for immortality from the alternation of opposites : life must follow death as death follows life. But alternation of opposites is not generation of opposites. He argues from reminiscence. But this involves pre-existence and a cycle of incarnations, not the immortality which we crave. The soul abides, as the idea abides, but there is no guarantee that it abides forever. He argues from the uncompounded nature of the soul. But we do not know the soul's nature, and at most this is an analogy : as soul is like God, invisible, it must like God abide. But this is analogy, and nothing more." William James, Will to Believe, 87 —" That our whole physical life may lie soaking in a spiritual atmosphere, a dimension of being which we at present have no organ for apprehending, is vividly suggested to us by the analogy of the life of our domestic animals. Our dogs, for example, are *in* our human life, but are not *of* it. They bite, but do not know what it means ; they submit to vivisection, and do not know the meaning of that."

George Eliot, walking with Frederic Myers in the Fellows' Garden at Trinity, Cambridge, "stirred somewhat beyond her wont, and taking as her text the three words which have been used so often as the inspiring trumpet-calls of men— the words God, Immortality, Duty — pronounced with terrible earnestness how inconceivable was the first, how unbelievable the second, and yet how peremptory and absolute the third." But this idea of the infinite nature of Duty is the creation of Christianity — the last infinite would never have attained its present range and intensity, had it not been indissolubly connected with the other two (Forrest, Christ of History and Experience, 16).

This ethical argument has probably more power over the minds of men than any other. Men believe in Minos and Rhadamanthus, if not in the Elysian Fields. But even here it may be replied that the judgment which conscience threatens may be, not immortality, but extinction of being. We shall see, however, in our discussion of the endlessness of future punishment, that mere annihilation cannot satisfy the moral instinct which lies at the basis of this argument. That demands a punishment proportioned in each case to the guilt incurred by transgression. Extinction of being would be the same to all. As it would not admit of degrees, so it would not, in any case, sufficiently vindicate God's righteousness. F. W. Newman : "If man be not immortal, God is not just."

But while this argument proves life and punishment for the wicked after death, it leaves us dependent on revelation for our knowledge how long that life and punishment will be. Kant's argument is that man strives equally for morality and for well-being ; but morality often requires the sacrifice of well-being ; hence there must be a future reconciliation of the two in the well-being or reward of virtue. To all of which it might be answered, first, that there is no virtue so perfect as to merit reward ; and secondly, that virtue is its *own* reward, and so *is* well-being.

(*d*) The historical argument.—The popular belief of all nations and ages shows that the idea of immortality is natural to the human mind. I; is not sufficient to say that this indicates only such desire for continued earthly existence as is necessary to self-preservation ; for multitudes expect a life beyond death without desiring it, and multitudes desire a heavenly life without caring for the earthly. This testimony of man's nature to immortality may be regarded as the testimony of the God who made the nature.

Testimonies to this popular belief are given in Bartlett, Life and Death Eternal, preface : The arrow-heads and earthen vessels laid by the side of the dead Indian ; the silver obolus put in the mouth of the dead Greek to pay Charon's passage money ; the furnishing of the Egyptian corpse with the Book of the Dead, the papyrus-roll containing the prayer he is to offer and the chart of his journey through the unseen world. The Gauls did not hesitate to lend money, on the sole condition that he to whom they lent it would return it to them in the other life, — so sure were they that they should get it again (Valerius Maximus, quoted in Boissier, La Religion Romaine, 1 : 264). The Laplanders bury flint and tinder with the dead, to furnish light for the dark journey. The Norsemen buried the horse and armor for the dead hero's triumphant ride. The Chinese scatter paper images of sedan porters over the grave, to help along in the sombre pilgrimage. The Greenlanders bury with the child a dog to guide him (George Dana Boardman, Sermon on Immortality).

Savage, Life after Death, 1–18 —" Candles at the head of the casket are the modern representatives of the primitive man's fire which was to light the way of the soul on its dark journey. . . . . Ulysses talks in the underworld with the shade of Hercules though the real Hercules, a demigod, had been transferred to Olympus, and was there living in companionship with the gods. . . . . The Brahman desired to escape being reborn. Socrates : ' To die and be released is better for me.' Here I am walking on a plank. It reaches out into the fog, and I have got to keep walking. I can see only ten feet ahead of me. I know that pretty soon I must walk over the end of that plank,— I haven't the slightest idea into what, and I don't believe anybody else knows. And I don't like it." Matthew Arnold : " Is there no other life ? Pitch this one high." But without positive revelation most men will say : "Let us eat and drink, for to-morrow we die" (1 Cor. 15 : 32).

" By passionately loving life, we make Loved life unlovely, hugging her to death." Theodore Parker : " The intuition of mortality is written in the heart of man by a Hand that writes no falsehoods. . . . . There is evidence of a summer yet to be, in the buds which lie folded through our northern winter — efflorescences in human nature unaccountable if the end of man is in the grave." But it may be replied that many universal popular impressions have proved false, such as belief in ghosts, and in the moving of the sun round the earth. While the mass of men have believed in immortality, some of the wisest have been doubters. Cyrus said : " I cannot imagine that the soul lives only while it remains in this mortal body." But the dying words of Socrates were : " We part ; I am going to die, and you to live : which of us goes the better way is known to God alone." Cicero declared : " Upon this subject I entertain no more than conjectures ; " and said that, when he was reading Plato's argument for immortality, he seemed to himself convinced, but when he laid down the book he found that all his doubts returned. Farrar, Darkness and Dawn, 134 —" Though Cicero wrote his Tusculan Disputations to prove the doctrine of immortality, he spoke of that doctrine in his letters and speeches as a mere pleasing speculation, which might be discussed with interest, but which no one practically held."

Aristotle, Nic. Ethics, 3 : 9, calls death " the most to be feared of all things . . . . for it appears to be the end of everything ; and for the deceased there appears to be no longer either any good or any evil. " Æschylus : " Of one once dead there is no resurrection. " Catullus : " When once our brief day has set, we must sleep one everlasting night." Tacitus : " If there is a place for the spirits of the pious ; if, as the wise suppose, great souls do not become extinct with their bodies." "In that *if*, " says Uhlhorn, " lies the whole torturing uncertainty of heathenism." Seneca, Ep. liv. —" Mors est non esse " —"Death is not to be " ; Troades, V, 393 —" Post mortem nihil est, ipsaque mors nihil " —" There is nothing after death, and death itself is nothing." Marcus Aurelius : " What springs from earth dissolves to earth again, and heavenborn things fly to their native seat." The Emperor Hadrian to his soul : " Animula, vagula, blandula, Hospes comesque corporis, Quæ nunc abibis in loca? Pallidula, rigida, nudula." Classic writers might have said of the soul at death : " We know not where is that Promethean torch That can its light relume."

Chadwick, 184 — " With the growth of all that is best in man of intelligence and affection, there goes the development of the hope of an immortal life. If the hope thus developed is not a valid one, then we have a radical contradiction in our moral nature. The survival of the fittest points in the same direction." Andrew Marvell (1621–1678)— " At my back I always hear Time's winged chariot hurrying near ; And yonder all before us lie Deserts of vast Eternity." Goethe in his last days came to be a profound believer in immortality. " You ask me what are my grounds for this belief ? The weightiest is this, that we cannot do without it." Huxley wrote in a letter to Morley : " It is a curious thing that I find my dislike to the thought of extinction increasing as I get older and nearer the goal. It flashes across me at all sorts of time that in 1900 I shall probably know no more of what is going on than I did in 1800. I had sooner be in hell, a great deal,— at any rate in one of the upper circles, where climate and the company are not too trying."

The book of Job shows how impossible it is for man to work out the problem of personal immortality from the point of view of merely natural religion. Shakespeare, in Measure for Measure, represents Claudio as saying to his sister Isabella : " Aye, but to die, and go we know not where ; To lie in cold obstruction and to rot ; This sensible warm motion to become A kneaded clod." Strauss, Glaubenslehre. 2 : 739 —" The other world is in all men the one enemy, in its aspect of a future world, however, the last enemy, which speculative criticism has to fight, and if possible to overcome." Omar Khayyám, Rubáiyát, Stanzas 28–35 —" I came like Water, and like Wind I go. . . . . Up from Earth's Centre through the seventh gate I rose, and on the throne of Saturn sate, And many a knot unravelled by the Road, But not the master-knot of human fate. There was the Door to which I found no Key ; There was the Veil through which I might not see : Some little talk awhile of *Me* and *Thee* There was,— And then no more of *Thee* and *Me*. Earth could not answer, nor the Seas that mourn, In flowing purple, of their Lord forlorn ; Nor rolling Heaven, with all his signs revealed, And hidden by the sleeve of Night and Morn. Then of the *Thee in Me*, who works behind The veil, I lifted up my hands to find A Lamp, amid the darkness ; and I heard As from without — ' The Me within Thee blind.' Then to the lip of this poor earthen Urn I leaned, the secret of my life to learn ; And Lip to Lip it murmur'd—' While you live, Drink !— for, once dead, you never shall return ! ' " So " The Phantom Caravan has reached The Nothing it set out from." It is a demonstration of the hopelessness and blindness and sensuality of man, when left without the revelation of God and of the life to come.

The most that can be claimed for this fourth argument from popular belief is that it indicates a general appetency for continued existence after death, and that the idea is congruous with our nature. W. E. Forster said to Harriet Martineau that he would rather be damned than annihilated ; see F. P. Cobbe, Peak of Darien, 44. But it may be replied that there is reason enough for this desire for life in the fact that it ensures the earthly existence of the race, which might commit universal suicide without it. There is reason enough in the present life for its existence, and we are not necessitated to infer a future life therefrom. This objection cannot be fully answered from reason alone. But if we take our argument in connection with the Scriptural revelation concerning God's making of man in his image, we may regard the testimony of man's nature as the testimony of the God who made it.

We conclude our statement of these rational proofs with the acknowledgment that they rest upon the presupposition that there exists a God of truth, wisdom, justice, and love, who has made man in his image, and who desires to commune with his creatures. We acknowledge, moreover, that these proofs give us, not an absolute demonstration, but only a balance of probability, in favor of man's immortality. We turn therefore to Scripture for the clear revelation of a fact of which reason furnishes us little more than a presumption.

Everett, Essays, 76, 77 —" In his Träume eines Geistersehers, Kant foreshadows the Method of his Kritik. He gives us a scheme of disembodied spirits, and calls it a bit of mystic (*geheimen*) philosophy ; then the opposite view, which he calls a bit of vulgar (*gemeimen*) philosophy. Then he says the scales of the understanding are not quite impartial, and the one that has the inscription ' Hope for the future ' has a mechanical advantage. He says he cannot rid himself of this unfairness. He suffers feeling to determine the result. Th is is intellectual agnosticism supplemented by religious faith." The following lines have been engraved upon the tomb of Professor Huxley : " And if there be no meeting past the grave, If all is darkness, silence, yet 't is rest. Be not afraid, ye waiting hearts that weep, For God still giveth his beloved sleep, And if an endless sleep he wills, so best." Contrast this consolation with : " Let not your heart be troubled: ye believe in God, believe also in me. In my Father's house are many mansions : if it were not so, I would have told you. I go to prepare a place for you. And if I go and prepare a place for you. I will come again, and receive you unto myself, that where I am, there ye may be also " (John 14 : 1-3.

Dorner: " There is no rational evidence which compels belief in immortality. Immortality has its pledge in God's making man in his image, and in God's will of love for communion with men." Luthardt, Compendium, 289—" The truth in these proofs from reason is the idea of human personality and its relation to God. Belief in God is the universal presupposition and foundation of the universal belief in immortality." When Strauss declared that this belief in immortality is the last enemy which is to be destroyed, he forgot that belief in God is more ineradicable still. Frances Power Cobbe Life, 92—" The doctrine of immortality is to me the indispensable corollary of that of the goodness of God."

Hadley, Essays, Philological and Critical, 392–379 —" The claim of immortality may be based on one or the other of two assumptions : (1) The same organism will be repro, duced hereafter, and the same functions, or part of them, again manifested in connec, tion with it, and accompanied with consciousness of continued identity ; or, (2) The same functions may be exercised and accompanied with consciousness of identity, though not connected with the same organism as before ; may in fact go on without interruption, without being even suspended by death, though no longer manifested to us." The conclusion is : " The light of nature, when all directed to this question, does furnish a presumption in favor of immortality, but not so strong a presumption as to exclude great and reasonable doubts upon the subject."

For an excellent synopsis of arguments and objections, see Hase, Hutterus Redivivus, 276. See also Bowen, Metaph. and Ethics, 417–441 ; A. M. Fairbairn, on Idea of Immortality, in Studies in Philos. of Religion and of History ; Wordsworth, Intimations of Immortality ; Tennyson, Two Voices ; Alger, Critical History of Doctrine of Future Life, with Appendix by Ezra Abbott, containing a Catalogue of Works relating to the Nature, Origin, and Destiny of the Soul ; Ingersoll Lectures on Immortality, by George A. Gordon, Josiah Royce, William James, Dr. Osler, John Fiske, B. I. Wheeler, Hyslop, Münsterberg, Crothars.

2. *Upon scriptural grounds.*

(*a*) The account of man's creation, and the subsequent allusions to it in Scripture, show that, while the body was made corruptible and subject to death, the soul was made in the image of God, incorruptible and immortal.

Gen. 1 : 26, 27 —" Let us make man in our image " ; 2 : 7 —" And Jehovah God formed man of the dust of the ground. and breathed into his nostrils the breath of life ; and man became a living soul "— here, as was shown in our treatment of Man's Original State, page 523, it is not the divine image, but the body, that is formed of dust ; and into this body the soul that possesses the divine image is breathed. In the Hebrew records, the animating soul is everywhere distinguished from the earthly body. Gen. 3 : 22, 23 —" Behold, the man is become as one of us, to know good and evil ; and now, lest he put forth his hand, and take also of the tree of life, and eat, and live for ever : therefore Jehovah God sent him forth from the garden of Eden " — man had immortality of soul, and now, lest to this he add immortality of body, he is expelled from the tree of life. Eccl. 12 : 7 —" the dust returneth to the earth as it was, and the spirit returneth unto God who gave it " ; Zech. 12 : 1 —" Jehovah, who stretcheth forth the heavens, and layeth the foundation of the earth, and formeth the spirit of man within him."

Mat. 10 : 28 —" And be not afraid of them that kill the body, but are not able to kill the soul : but rather fear him who is able to destroy both soul and body in hell " ; Acts 7 : 59 —" And they stoned Stephen, calling upon the Lord, and saying, Lord Jesus, receive my spirit " ; 2 Cor. 12 : 2 —" I know a man in Christ, fourteen years ago (whether in the body, I know not ; or whether out of the body, I know not ; God knoweth), such a one caught up even to the third heaven " ; 1 Cor. 15 : 45, 46 —" The first man Adam became a living soul The last Adam became a life-giving spirit Howbeit that is not first which is spiritual, but that which is natural : then that which is spiritual " — the first

Adam was made a being whose body was psychical and mortal—a body of flesh and blood, that could not inherit the kingdom of God. So Paul says the spiritual is not first, but the psychical; but there is no intimation that the soul was created mortal, and needed external appliances, like the tree of life, before it could enter upon immortality.

But it may be asked: Is not all this, in 1 Cor. 15, spoken of the regenerate—those to whom a new principle of life has been communicated? We answer, yes; but that does not prevent us from learning from the passage the natural immortality of the soul; for in regeneration the essence is not changed, no new substance is imparted, no new faculty or constitutive element is added, and no new principle of holiness is infused. The truth is simply that the spirit is morally readjusted. For substance of the above remarks, see Hovey, State of Impenitent Dead, 1-27.

Savage, Life after Death, 46, 53—"The word translated 'soul', in Gen. 2:7, is the same word which in other parts of the O. T. is used to denote the life-principle of animals. It does not follow that soul implies immortality, for then all animals would be immortal. . . . . The firmament of the Hebrews was the cover of a dinner-platter, solid, but with little windows to let the rain through. Above this firmament was heaven where God and angels abode, but no people went there. All went below. But growing moral sense held that the good could not be imprisoned in Hades. So came the idea of resurrection. . . . . If a *force*, a universe with God left out, can do all that has been done, I do not see why it cannot also continue my existence through what is called death."

Dr. H. Heath Bawden : " It is only the creature that is born that will die. Monera and Amœbæ are immortal, as Weismann tells us. They do not die, because they never are born. The death of the individual as a somatic individual is for the sake of the larger future life of the individual in its germinal immortality. So we live ourselves spiritually into our children, as well as physically. An organism is nothing but a centre or focus through which the world surges. What matter if the irrelevant somatic portion is lost in what we call death ! The only immortality possible is the immortality of function. My body has changed completely since I was a boy, but I have become a larger self thereby. Birth and death simply mark steps or stages in the growth of such an individual, which in its very nature does not exclude but rather includes within it the lives of all other individuals. The individual is more than a passive member, he is an active organ of a biological whole. The laws of his life are the social organism functioning in one of its organs. He lives and moves and has his being in the great spirit of the whole, which comes to a focus or flowers out in his conscious life."

(*b*) The account of the curse in Genesis, and the subsequent allusions to it in Scripture, show that, while the death then incurred includes the dissolution of the body, it does not include cessation of being on the part of the soul, but only designates that state of the soul which is the opposite of true life, *viz.*, a state of banishment from God, of unholiness, and of misery.

Gen. 2:17—"in the day that thou eatest thereof thou shalt surely die"; *cf.* 3 : 8 —"the man and his wife hid themselves from the presence of Jehovah God "; 16-19— the curse of pain and toil: 22-24 — banishment from the garden of Eden and from the tree of life. Mat. 8:22—"Follow me ; and leave the dead to bury their own dead "; 25 : 41, 46—" Depart from me, ye cursed, into the eternal fire. . . . . These shall go away into eternal punishment " ; Luke 15 : 32—" this thy brother was dead, and is alive again ; and was lost, and is found " ; John 5 : 24—"He that heareth my word, and believeth him that sent me, hath eternal life, and cometh not into judgment, but hath passed out of death into life "; 6 : 47, 53, 63—"He that believeth hath eternal life, ... Except ye eat the flesh of the Son of man and drink his blood, ye have not life in yourselves . . . . the words that I have spoken unto you are spirit, and are life " ; 8 : 51—"If a man keep my word, he shall never see death."

Rom. 5 : 21—"that, as sin reigned in death, even so might grace reign through righteousness unto eternal life " ; 8 : 13—"if ye live after the flesh, ye must die ; but if by the Spirit ye put to death the deeds of the body, ye shall live " ; Eph. 2 : 1—"dead through your trespasses and sins " ; 5 : 14—"Awake, thou that sleepest, and arise from the dead, and Christ shall shine upon thee " ; James 5 : 20—" he who converteth a sinner from the error of his way shall save a soul from death, and shall cover a multitude of sins "; 1 John 3 : 14—" We know that we have passed out of death into life, because we love the brethren " ; Rev. 3 : 1 —"I know thy works, that thou hast a name that thou livest, and thou art dead."

We are to interpret O. T. terms by the N. T. meaning put into them. We are to interpret the Hebrew by the Greek, not the Greek by the Hebrew. It never would do to interpret our missionaries' use of the Chinese words for "God", "spirit", "holiness", by the use of those words among the Chinese before the missionaries came. By the later usage of the N. T., the Holy Spirit shows us what he meant by the usage of the O. T.

(c) The Scriptural expressions, held by annihilationists to imply cessation of being on the part of the wicked, are used not only in connections where they cannot bear this meaning (Esther 4 :16), but in connections where they imply the opposite.

Esther 4 : 16 —"if I perish, I perish"; Gen. 6 :11 —" And the earth was corrupt before God" — here, in the LXX, the word ἐφθάρη, translated "was corrupt," is the same word which in other places is interpreted by annihilationists as meaning extinction of being. In Ps. 119:176, "I have gone astray like a lost sheep" cannot mean " I have gone astray like an annihilated sheep." Is. 49 :17 —"thy destroyers [annihilators ?] and they that made thee waste shall go forth from thee " ; 57:1, 2 —" The righteous perisheth [is annihilated ?] and no man layeth it to heart; and merciful men are taken away, none considering that the righteous is taken away from the evil to come. He entereth into peace ; they rest in their beds, each one that walketh in his uprightness "; Dan. 9 :26 —" And after the three score and two weeks shall the anointed one be cut off [annihilated ?]."

Mat. 10 : 6, 39, 42 —"the lost sheep of the house of Israel . . . . he that loseth his life for my sake shall find it . . . . he shall in no wise lose his reward" — in these verses we cannot substitute " annihilate " for " loss " ; Acts 13 : 41 —" Behold, ye despisers, and wonder, and perish "; cf. Mat. 6 :16 —" for they disfigure their faces " —where the same word ἀφανίζω is used. 1 Cor. 3 :17 —" If any man destroyeth [annihilates ?] the temple of God, him shall God destroy " ; 2 Cor. 7 :2 —" we corrupted no man " —where the same word φθείρω is used. 2 Thess. 1 :9 —" who shall suffer punishment, even eternal destruction from the face of the Lord and from the glory of his might " = the wicked shall be driven out from the presence of Christ. Destruction is not annihilation. "Destruction from" = separation ; (per contra, see Prof. W. A. Stevens, Com. in loco : "from" = the source from which the "destruction" proceeds). " A ship engulfed in quicksands is destroyed ; a temple broken down and deserted is destroyed"; see Lillie, Com. in loco. 2 Pet. 3 :7 —" day of judgment and destruction of ungodly men " — here the word " destruction " (ἀπωλείας) is the same with that used of the end of the present order of things, and translated " perished " (ἀπώλετο) in verse 6. " We cannot accordingly infer from it that the ungodly will cease to exist, but only that there will be a great and penal change in their condition " (Plumptre, Com. in loco).

(d) The passages held to prove the annihilation of the wicked at death cannot have this meaning, since the Scriptures foretell a resurrection of the unjust as well as of the just ; and a second death, or a misery of the reunited soul and body, in the case of the wicked.

Acts 24 :15 —"there shall be a resurrection both of the just and unjust "; Rev. 2 :11 —"He that overcometh shall not be hurt of the second death "; 20:14, 15 —"And death and Hades were cast into the lake of fire. This is the second death, even the lake of fire. And if any was not found written in the book of life, he was cast into the lake of fire "; 21 : 8 —" their part shall be in the lake that burneth with fire and brimstone ; which is the second death." The " second death " is the first death intensified. Having one's "part in the lake of fire " is not annihilation.

In a similar manner the word " life " is to be interpreted not as meaning continuance of being, but as meaning perfection of being. As death is the loss not of life, but of all that makes life desirable, so life is the possession of the highest good. 1 Tim. 5 :6 —"She that giveth herself to pleasure is dead while she liveth " — here the death is spiritual death, and it is implied that true life is spiritual life. John 10 :10 —" I came that they may have life, and may have it abundantly " — implies that " life " is not : 1. mere existence, for they had this before Christ came ; nor 2. mere motion, as squirrels go in a wheel, without making progress ; nor 3. mere possessions, " for a man's life consisteth not in the abundance of things which he possesseth " (Luke 12 :15). But life is : 1. right relation of our powers, or holiness ; 2. right use of our powers, or love ; 3. right number of our powers, or completeness ; 4. right intensity of our powers, or energy of will ; 5. right environment of our powers, or society ; 6. right source of our powers, or God.

(e) The words used in Scripture to denote the place of departed spirits have in them no implication of annihilation, and the allusions to the condition of the departed show that death, to the writers of the Old and the New

63

Testaments, although it was the termination of man's earthly existence, was not an extinction of his being or his consciousness.

On שְׁאוֹל Sheol, Gesenius, Lexicon, 10th ed., says that, though שְׁאוֹל is commonly explained as infinitive of שָׁאַל, to demand, it is undoubtedly allied to שָׁעַל (root שַׁל), 'to be sunk, and = sinking,' 'depth,' or 'the sunken, deep, place.' ῎Αιδης, Hades,—not 'hell,' but the 'unseen world,' conceived by the Greeks as a shadowy, but not as an unconscious, state of being. Genung, Epic of the Inner Life, on Job 7:9—"Sheol, the Hebrew word designating the unseen abode of the dead; a neutral word, presupposing neither misery nor happiness, and not infrequently used much as we use the word 'the grave', to denote the final undefined resting-place of all."

Gen. 25:8, 9—Abraham "was gathered to his people. And Isaac and Ishmael his sons buried him in the cave of Machpelah." "Yet Abraham's father was buried in Haran, and his more remote ancestors in Ur of the Chaldees. So Joshua's generation is said to be 'gathered to their fathers' though the generation that preceded them perished in the wilderness, and previous generations died in Egypt" (W. H. Green, in S. S. Times). So of Isaac in Gen. 35:29, and of Jacob in 19:29, 33,—all of whom were gathered to their fathers before they were buried. Num. 20:24—"Aaron shall be gathered unto his people"—here it is very plain that being "gathered unto his people" was something different from burial. Deut. 10:6—"There Aaron died, and there he was buried." Job 3:13, 18—"For now should I have lain down and been quiet; I should have slept; then had I been at rest. . . . . There the prisoners are at ease together; They hear not the voice of the taskmaster"; 7:9—"As the cloud is consumed and vanisheth away, So he that goeth down to Sheol shall come up no more"; 14:22—"But his flesh upon him hath pain, And his soul within him mourneth."

Ez. 32:21—"The strong among the mighty shall speak to him out of the midst of Sheol"; Luke 16:23—"And in Hades he lifted up his eyes, being in torments, and seeth Abraham afar off, and Lazarus in his bosom"; 23:43—"To-day shalt thou be with me in Paradise"; cf. 1 Sam. 28:19—Samuel said to Saul in the cave of Endor: "to-morrow shalt thou and thy sons be with me"—evidently not in an unconscious state. Many of these passages intimate a continuity of consciousness after death. Though Sheol is unknown to man, it is naked and open to God (Job 26:6); he can find men there to redeem them from thence (Ps. 49:15)—proof that death is not annihilation. See Girdlestone, O. T. Synonyms, 447.

(*f*) The terms and phrases which have been held to declare absolute cessation of existence at death are frequently metaphorical, and an examination of them in connection with the context and with other Scriptures is sufficient to show the untenableness of the literal interpretation put upon them by the annihilationists, and to prove that the language is merely the language of appearance.

Death is often designated as a "sleeping" or a "falling asleep"; see John 11:11, 14—"Our friend Lazarus is fallen asleep; but I go, that I may awake him out of sleep. . . . . Then Jesus therefore said unto them plainly, Lazarus is dead." Here the language of appearance is used; yet this language could not have been used, if the soul had not been conceived of as alive, though sundered from the body; see Meyer on 1 Cor. 1:18. So the language of appearance is used in Eccl. 9:10—"there is no work, nor device, nor knowledge, nor wisdom, in Sheol whither thou goest"—and in Ps. 146:4—"His breath goeth forth; he returneth to his earth; In that very day his thoughts perish."

See Mozley, Essays, 2:171—"These passages often describe the phenomena of death as it presents itself to our eyes, and so do not enter into the reality which takes place beneath it." Bartlett, Life and Death Eternal, 189-358—"Because the same Hebrew word is used for 'spirit' and 'breath,' shall we say that the spirit is only breath? 'Heart' in English might in like manner be made to mean only the material organ; and David's heart, panting, thirsting, melting within him, would have to be interpreted literally. So a man may be 'eaten up with avarice,' while yet his being is not only not extinct, but is in a state of frightful activity."

(*g*) The Jewish belief in a conscious existence after death is proof that the theory of annihilation rests upon a misinterpretation of Scripture. That such a belief in the immortality of the soul existed among the Jews is abundantly evident: from the knowledge of a future state possessed by the Egyptians (Acts 7:22); from the accounts of the translation of Enoch and of Elijah (Gen. 5 : 24 ; *cf.* Heb. 11 : 5. 2 K. 2 : 11); from the invocation of the dead which was practised, although forbidden by the law (1 Sam. 28 : 7-14 ; *cf.* Lev. 20 : 28 ; Deut. 18 : 10, 11) ; from allusions in the O. T. to resurrection, future retribution, and life beyond the grave (Job 19 : 25-27 ; Ps. 16 : 9-11; Is. 26 : 19 ; Ez. 37 : 1-14; Dan. 12 : 2, 3, 13) ; and from distinct declarations of such faith by Philo and Josephus, as well as by the writers of the N. T. (Mat. 22 : 31, 32 ; Acts 23 : 6 ; 26 : 6-8 ; Heb. 11 : 13-16).

The Egyptian coffin was called " the chest of the living." The Egyptians called their houses " hostelries," while their tombs they called their " eternal homes " (Butcher, Aspects of Greek Genius, 30). See the Book of the Dead, translated by Birch, in Bunsen's Egypt's Place, 123–333 : The principal ideas of the first part of the Book of the Dead are " living again after death, and being born again as the sun," which typified the Egyptian resurrection (138). " The deceased lived again after death " (134). " The Osiris lives after he dies, like the sun daily ; for as the sun died and was born yesterday, so the Osiris is born " (164). Yet the immortal part, in its continued existence, was dependent for its blessedness upon the preservation of the body ; and for this reason the body was embalmed. Immortality of the body is as important as the passage of the soul to the upper regions. Growth or natural reparation of the body is invoked as earnestly as the passage of the soul. " There is not a limb of him without a god ; Thoth is vivifying his limbs " (197).

Maspero, Recueil de Travaux, gives the following readings from the inner walls of pyramids twelve miles south of Cairo : " O Unas, thou hast gone away dead, but living " ; " Teti is the living dead " ; " Arise, O Teti, to die no more " ; " O Pepi, thou diest no more " ; — these inscriptions show that to the Egyptians there was life beyond death. " The life of Unas is duration ; his period is eternity " ; " They render thee happy throughout all eternity " ; " He who has given thee life and eternity is Ra " ; — here we see that the life beyond death was eternal. " Rising at his pleasure, gathering his members that are in the tomb, Unas goes forth " ; " Unas has his heart, his legs, his arms " ; this asserts reunion with the body. " Reunited to thy soul, thou takest thy place among the stars of heaven " ; " the soul is thine within thee " ; — there was reunion with the soul. " A god is born, it is Unas " ; " O Ra, thy son comes to thee, this Unas comes to thee " ; " O Father of Unas, grant that he may be included in the number of the perfect and wise gods " ; here it is taught that the reunited soul and body becomes a god and dwells with the gods.

Howard Osgood : " Osiris, the son of gods, came to live on earth. His life was a pattern for others. He was put to death by the god of evil, but regained his body, lived again, and became, in the other world, the judge of all men." Tiele, Egyptian Religion, 280 — " To become like god Osiris, a benefactor, a good being, persecuted but justified, judged but pronounced innocent, was looked upon as the ideal of every pious man, and as the condition on which alone eternal life could be obtained, and as the means by which it could be continued." Ebers, Études Archéologiques, 21 — " The texts in the pyramids show us that under the Pharaohs of the 5th dynasty (before 2500 B. C.) the doctrine that the deceased became god was not only extant, but was developed more thoroughly and with far higher flight of imagination than we could expect from the simple statements concerning the other world hitherto known to us as from that early time." Revillout, on Egyptian Ethics, in Bib. Sac., July, 1890 : 304 — " An almost absolute sinlessness was for the Egyptian the condition of becoming another Osiris and enjoying eternal happiness. Of the penitential side, so highly developed in the ancient Babylonians and Hebrews, which gave rise to so many admirable penitential psalms, we find only a trace among the Egyptians. Sinlessness is the rule, — the deceased vaunts himself as a hero of virtue." See Uarda, by Ebers ; Dr. Howard Osgood, on Resurrection among the Egyptians, in Hebrew Student, Feb. 1885. The Egyptians, however, recognized no transmigration of souls ; see Renouf, Hibbert Lectures, 181-184.

It is morally impossible that Moses should not have known the Egyptian doctrine of immortality : Acts 7 : 22 — " And Moses was instructed in all the wisdom of the Egyptians." That Moses did not make the doctrine more prominent in his teachings, may be for the reason that it was so connected with Egyptian superstitions with regard to Osiris. Yet the Jews believed in immortality : Gen. 5 : 24 — " and Enoch walked with God : and he was not ; for God took him " ;

cf. Heb. 11 : 5 — "By faith Enoch was translated that he should not see death"; 2 Kings 2 : 11 — "Elijah went up by a whirlwind into heaven"; 1 Sam. 28 : 7-14 — the invocation of Samuel by the woman of Endor; *cf.* Lev. 20 : 27 — "A man also or a woman that hath a familiar spirit, or that is a wizard, shall surely be put to death"; Deut. 18 : 10, 11 — "There shall not be found with thee . . . . a consulter with a familiar spirit, or a wizard, or a necromancer."

Job 19 : 25-27 — "I know that my Redeemer liveth, And at last he will stand up upon the earth : And after my skin, even this body, is destroyed, Then without my flesh shall I see God; Whom I, even I, shall see, on my side, And mine eyes shall behold, and not as a stranger. My heart is consumed within me"; Ps. 16 : 9-11 — "Therefore my heart is glad, and my glory rejoiceth : My flesh also shall dwell in safety. For thou wilt not leave my soul to Sheol; Neither wilt thou suffer thy holy one to see corruption. Thou wilt show me the path of life : In thy presence is fulness of joy; In thy right hand there are pleasures for evermore"; Is. 26 : 19 — "Thy dead shalt live; my dead bodies shall arise. Awake and sing, ye that dwell in the dust; for thy dew is as the dew of herbs, and the earth shall cast forth the dead"; Ez. 37 : 1-14 — the valley of dry bones — "I will open your graves, and cause you to come up out of your graves, O my people" — a prophecy of restoration based upon the idea of immortality and resurrection; Dan. 12 : 2, 3, 13 — "And many of them that sleep in the dust of the earth shall awake, some to everlasting life, and some to shame and everlasting contempt. And they that are wise shall shine as the brightness of the firmament, and they that turn many to righteousness as the stars for ever and ever. . . . . But go thou thy way till the end be : for thou shalt rest, and shalt stand in thy lot, at the end of the days."

Josephus, on the doctrine of the Pharisees, in Antiquities, XVIII : 1 : 3, and Wars of the Jews, II : 8 : 10-14 — "Souls have an immortal vigor. Under the earth are rewards and punishments. The wicked are detained in an everlasting prison. The righteous shall have power to revive and live again. Bodies are indeed corruptible, but souls remain exempt from death forever. But the doctrine of the Sadducees is that souls die with their bodies." Mat. 22 : 31, 32 — "But as touching the resurrection of the dead, have ye not read that which was spoken unto you by God, saying, I am the God of Abraham, and the God of Isaac, and the God of Jacob? God is not the God of the dead, but of the living."

Christ's argument, in the passage last quoted, rests upon the two implied assumptions : first, that love will never suffer the object of its affection to die; beings who have ever been the objects of God's love will be so forever; secondly, that body and soul belong normally together; if body and soul are temporarily separated, they shall be united; Abraham, Isaac, and Jacob are living, and therefore they shall rise again. It was only an application of the same principle, when Robert Hall gave up his early materialism as he looked down into his father's grave : he felt that this could not be the end; *cf.* Ps. 22 : 26 — "Your heart shall live forever." Acts 23 : 6 — "I am a Pharisee, a son of Pharisees : touching the hope and resurrection of the dead I am called in question"; 26 : 7, 8 — "And concerning this hope I am accused by the Jews, O king! Why is it judged incredible with you, if God doth raise the dead?" Heb. 11 : 13-16 — the present life was reckoned as a pilgrimage; the patriarchs sought "a better country, that is, a heavenly"; *cf.* Gen. 47 : 9. On Jesus' argument for the resurrection, see A. H. Strong, Christ in Creation, 406-421.

The argument for immortality itself presupposes, not only the existence of a God, but the existence of a truthful, wise, and benevolent God. We might almost say that God and immortality must be proved together, — like two pieces of a broken crock, when put together there is proof of both. And yet logically it is only the existence of God that is intuitively certain. Immortality is an inference therefrom. Henry More : " But souls that of his own good life partake He loves as his own self; dear as his eye They are to him : he 'll never them forsake; When they shall die, then God himself shall die; They live, they live in blest eternity." God could not let Christ die, and he cannot let us die. Southey : "They sin who tell us love can die. With life all other passions fly; All others are but vanity. In heaven ambition cannot dwell, Nor avarice in the vaults of hell; They perish where they had their birth; But love is indestructible."

Emerson, Threnody on the death of his beloved and gifted child : "What is excellent, As God lives, is permanent : Hearts are dust, hearts' loves remain; Heart's love will meet thee again." Whittier, Snowbound, 200 *sq.*— " Yet Love will dream, and Faith will trust (Since He who knows our need is just), That somehow, somewhere, meet we must. Alas for him who never sees The stars shine through his cypress trees ! Who hopeless lays his dead away, Nor looks to see the breaking day Across his mournful marbles play ! Who hath not learned, in hours of faith, The truth to flesh and sense unknown, That Life is ever lord of death, And Love can never lose its own." Robert Browning, Evelyn Hope : " For God above Is great to grant as mighty to make, And creates the love to reward the love; I claim you still for my own love's sake ! Delayed it may be for more lives yet, Through worlds I shall traverse not a few; Much is to learn and much to forget, Ere the time be come for taking you."

The river St. John in New Brunswick descends seventeen feet between the city and the sea, and ships cannot overcome the obstacle, but when the tide comes in, it turns the current the other way and bears vessels on mightily to the city. So the laws of nature bring death, but the tides of Christ's life counteract them, and bring life and immortality (Dr. J. W. A. Stewart). Mozley, Lectures, 26-59, and Essays, 2:169 — "True religion among the Jews had an evidence of immortality in its possession of God. Paganism was hopeless in its loss of friends, because affection never advanced beyond its earthly object, and therefore, in losing it, lost all. But religious love, which loves the creature in the Creator, has that on which to fall back, when its earthly object is removed."

(h) The most impressive and conclusive of all proofs of immortality, however, is afforded in the resurrection of Jesus Christ, — a work accomplished by his own power, and demonstrating that the spirit lived after its separation from the body (John 2 : 19, 21 ; 10 : 17, 18). By coming back from the tomb, he proves that death is not annihilation (2 Tim. 1 : 10).

John 2 : 19, 21 — "Jesus answered and said unto them, Destroy this temple, and in three days I will raise it up. . . . . But he spake of the temple of his body " ; 10 : 17, 18 — " Therefore doth the Father love me, because I lay down my life, that I may take it again. . . . . I have power to lay it down, and I have power to take it again " ; 2 Tim. 1 : 10 — "our Savior Christ Jesus, who abolished death, and brought life and immortality to light through the gospel " — that is, immortality had been a truth dimly recognized, suspected, longed for, before Christ came ; but it was he who first brought it out from obscurity and uncertainty into clear daylight and convincing power. Christ's resurrection, moreover, carries with it the resurrection of his people : " We two are so joined, He'll not be in glory and leave me behind."

Christ taught immortality : (1) By exhibiting himself the perfect conception of a human life. Who could believe that Christ could become forever extinct ? (2) By actually coming back from beyond the grave. There were many speculations about a trans-Atlantic continent before 1492, but these were of little worth compared with the actual word which Columbus brought of a new world beyond the sea. (3) By providing a way through which his own spiritual life and victory may be ours ; so that, though we pass through the valley of the shadow of death, we may fear no evil. (4) By thus gaining authority to teach us of the resurrection of the righteous and of the wicked, as he actually does. Christ's resurrection is not only the best proof of immortality, but we have no certain evidence of immortality without it. Hume held that the same logic which proved immortality from reason alone, would also prove preëxistence. "In reality," he said, "it is the Gospel, and the Gospel alone, that has brought immortality to light." It was truth, though possibly spoken in jest.

There was need of this revelation. The fear of death, even after Christ has come, shows how hopeless humanity is by nature. Krupp, the great German maker of cannon, would not have death mentioned in his establishment. He ran away from his own dying relatives. Yet he died. But to the Christian, death is an exodus, an unmooring, a home-coming. Here we are as ships on the stocks ; at death we are launched into our true element. Before Christ's resurrection, it was twilight ; it is sunrise now. Balfour : "Death is the fall of the curtain, not at the end of the piece, but at the end of the act." George Dana Boardman : "Christ is the resurrection and the life. Being himself the Son of man — the archetypal man, the representative of human nature, the head and epitome of mankind — mankind ideally, potentially, virtually rose, when the Son of man rose. He is the resurrection, because he is the life. The body does not give life to itself, but life takes on body and uses it."

George Adam Smith, Yale Lectures : "Some of the Psalmists have only a hope of corporate immortality. But this was found wanting. It did not satisfy Israel. It cannot satisfy men to-day. The O. T. is of use in reminding us that the hope of immortality is a secondary, subordinate, and dispensable element of religious experience. Men had better begin and work for God's sake, and not for future reward. The O. T. development of immortality is of use most of all because it deduces all immortality from God." Athanasius : "Man is, according to nature, mortal, as a being who has been made of things that are perishable. But on account of his likeness to God he can by piety ward off and escape from his natural mortality and remain indestructible if he retain the knowledge of God, or lose his incorruptibility if he lose his life in God" (quoted in McConnell, Evolution of Immortality, viii, 46-48). Justin Martyr, 1 Apol., 17, expects resurrection of both just and unjust ; but in Dial.

Tryph., 5, he expressly denounces and dismisses the Platonic doctrine that the soul is immortal. Athenagoras and Tertullian hold to native immortality, and from it argue to bodily resurrection. So Augustine. But Theophilus, Irenæus, Clemens Alexandrinus, with Athanasius, counted it a pagan error. For the annihilation theory, see Hudson, Debt and Grace, and Christ our Life; also Dobney, Future Punishment. *Per contra*, see Hovey, State of the Impenitent Dead, 1-27, and Manual of Theology and Ethics, 153-168; Luthardt, Compendium, 289-292; Delitzsch, Bib. Psych., 397-407; Herzog, Encyclop., art.: Tod; Splittgerber, Schlaf und Tod; Estes, Christian Doctrine of the Soul; Baptist Review, 1879: 411-439; Presb. Rev., Jan. 1882: 203.

II. THE INTERMEDIATE STATE.

The Scriptures affirm the conscious existence of both the righteous and the wicked, after death, and prior to the resurrection. In the intermediate state the soul is without a body, yet this state is for the righteous a state of conscious joy, and for the wicked a state of conscious suffering.

That the righteous do not receive the spiritual body at death, is plain from 1 Thess. 4 : 16, 17 and 1 Cor. 15 : 52, where an interval is intimated between Paul's time and the rising of those who slept. The rising was to occur in the future, "at the last trump." So the resurrection of the wicked had not yet occurred in any single case (2 Tim. 2 : 18 — it was an error to say that the resurrection was "past already") ; it was yet future (John 5 : 28-30 — "the hour cometh" — ἔρχεται ὥρα, not καὶ νῦν ἐστιν — "now is," as in verse 25 ; Acts 24 : 15 — " there shall be a resurrection " — ἀνάστασιν μέλλειν ἔσεσθαι). Christ was the firstfruits (1 Cor. 15 : 20, 23). If the saints had received the spiritual body at death, the patriarchs would have been raised before Christ.

1. *Of the righteous, it is declared :*

(*a*) That the soul of the believer, at its separation from the body, enters the presence of Christ.

2 Cor. 5 : 1-8 — "if the earthly house of our tabernacle be dissolved, we have a building from God, a house not made with hands, eternal in the heavens. For verily in this we groan, longing to be clothed upon with our habitation which is from heaven: if so be that being clothed we shall not be found naked. For indeed we that are in this tabernacle do groan, being burdened; not for that we would be unclothed, but that we would be clothed upon, that what is mortal may be swallowed up of life. . willing rather to be absent from the body, and to be at home with the Lord " — Paul hopes to escape the violent separation of soul and body — the being "unclothed" — by living till the coming of the Lord, and then putting on the heavenly body, as it were, over the present one (ἐπενδύσασθαι) ; yet whether he lived till Christ's coming or not, he knew that the soul, when it left the body, would be at home with the Lord.

Luke 23 : 43 — " To-day shalt thou be with me in Paradise " ; John 14 : 3 — "And if I go and prepare a place for you, I come again, and will receive you unto myself; that where I am, there ye may be also " ; 2 Tim. 4 : 18 — " The Lord will deliver me from every evil work, and will save me unto [or, 'into'] his heavenly kingdom " = will save me and put me into his heavenly kingdom (Ellicott), the characteristic of which is the visible presence of the King with his subjects. It is our privilege to be with Christ here and now. And nothing shall separate us from Christ and his love, " neither death, nor life . . . . nor things present, nor things to come " (Rom. 8 : 38) ; for he himself has said : " Lo, I am with you always, even unto the consummation of the age " (Mat. 28 : 20).

(*b*) That the spirits of departed believers are with God.

Heb. 12 : 23 — Ye are come "to the general assembly and church of the firstborn who are enrolled in heaven, and to God the Judge of all " ; *cf*. Eccl. 12 : 7 — "the dust returneth to the earth as it was, and the spirit returneth unto God who gave it " ; John 20 : 17 — " Touch me not ; for I am not yet ascended unto the Father " — probably means : "my body has not yet ascended." The soul had gone to God during the interval between death and the resurrection, as is evident from Luke 23 : 43, 46 — " with me in Paradise . . . . Father, into thy hands I commend my spirit."

(*c*) That believers at death enter paradise.

Luke 23 : 42, 43 — "And he said, Jesus, remember me when thou comest in thy kingdom. And he said unto him, Verily I say unto thee, To-day shalt thou be with me in Paradise"; *cf.* 2 Cor. 12 : 4 — "caught up into Paradise, and heard unspeakable words, which it is not lawful for a man to utter"; Rev. 2 : 7 — "To him that overcometh, to him will I give to eat of the tree of life, which is in the Paradise of God"; Gen. 2 : 8 — "And Jehovah God planted a garden eastward, in Eden; and there he put the man whom he had formed." Paradise is none other than the abode of God and the blessed, of which the primeval Eden was the type. If the penitent thief went to Purgatory, it was a Purgatory with Christ, which was better than a Heaven without Christ. Paradise is a place which Christ has gone to prepare, perhaps by taking our friends there before us.

(*d*) That their state, immediately after death, is greatly to be preferred to that of faithful and successful laborers for Christ here.

Phil. 1 : 23 — " I am in a strait betwixt the two, having the desire to depart and be with Christ; for it is very far better " — here Hackett says : " ἀναλῦσαι = departing, cutting loose, as if to put to sea, followed by σὺν Χριστῷ εἶναι, as if Paul regarded one event as immediately subsequent to the other." Paul, with his burning desire to preach Christ, would certainly have preferred to live and labor, even amid great suffering, rather than to die, if death to him had been a state of unconsciousness and inaction. See Edwards the younger, Works, 2 : 530, 531 ; Hovey, Impenitent Dead, 61.

(*e*) That departed saints are truly alive and conscious.

Mat. 22 : 32 —"God is not the God of the dead, but of the living "; Luke 16 : 22 — "carried away by the angels into Abraham's bosom"; 23 : 43 — "To-day shalt thou be with me in Paradise" — "with me " = in the same state, — unless Christ slept in unconsciousness, we cannot think that the penitent thief did ; John 11 : 26— "whosoever liveth and believeth on me shall never die "; 1 Thess. 5 : 10 — " who died for us, that, whether we wake or sleep, we should live together with him "; Rom. 8 : 10 — "And if Christ is in you, the body is dead because of sin; but the spirit is life because of righteousness." Life and consciousness clearly belong to the "souls under the altar" mentioned under the next head, for they cry : "How long ? " Phil. 1 : 6 — "he who began a good work in you will perfect it until the day of Jesus Christ " — seems to imply a progressive sanctification, through the Intermediate State, up to the time of Christ's second coming. This state is : 1. a conscious state ("God of the living ") ; 2. a fixed state (no "passing from thence") ; 3. an incomplete state ("not to be unclothed ").

(*f*) That they are at rest and blessed.

Rev. 6 : 9–11 —"I saw underneath the altar the souls of them that had been slain for the word of God, and for the testimony which they held ; and they cried with a great voice, saying, How long, O Master, the holy and true, dost thou not judge and avenge our blood on them that dwell on the earth ? And there was given them to each one a white robe; and it was said unto them, that they should rest yet for a little time, until their fellow-servants also and their brethren, who should be killed even as they were, should have fulfilled their course "; 14 : 13 —" Blessed are the dead who die in the Lord from henceforth : yea, saith the Spirit, that they may rest from their labors; for their works follow with them "; 20 : 14 —"And death and Hades were cast into the lake of fire " — see Evans, in Presb. Rev., 1883 : 303 —" The shadow of death lying upon Hades is the penumbra of Hell. Hence Hades is associated with death in the final doom. "

2. *Of the wicked, it is declared :*

(*a*) That they are in prison,—that is, are under constraint and guard (1 Peter 3 : 19 — φυλακή).

1 Pet. 3 : 19 —"In which [spirit] also he went and preached unto the spirits in prison " — there is no need of putting unconscious spirits under guard. Hovey : " Restraint implies power of action, and suffering implies consciousness."

(*b*) That they are in torment, or conscious suffering (Luke 16 : 23 — ἐν βασάνοις).

Luke 16 : 23 —"And in Hades he lifted up his eyes, being in torments, and seeth Abraham afar off, and Lazarus in his bosom. And he cried and said, Father Abraham, have mercy on me, and send Lazarus, that he may dip the tip of his finger in water, and cool my tongue; for I am in anguish in this flame."

Here many unanswerable questions may be asked : Had the rich man a body before the resurrection, or is this representation of a body only figurative ? Did the soul still feel the body from which it was temporarily separated, or have souls in the intermediate state temporary bodies ? However we may answer these questions, it is certain that the rich man suffers, while probation still lasts for his brethren on earth. Fire is here the source of suffering, but not of annihilation. Even though this be a parable, it proves conscious existence after death to have been the common view of the Jews, and to have been a view sanctioned by Christ.

(c) That they are under punishment (2 Pet. 2 : 9 — κολαζομένους).

2 Pet. 2 : 9 — "the Lord knoweth how to deliver the godly out of temptation, and to keep the unrighteous under punishment unto the day of judgment " — here " the unrighteous " = not only evil angels, but ungodly men ; cf. verse 4 — "For if God spared not angels when they sinned, but cast them down to hell, and committed them to pits of darkness, to be reserved unto judgment."

In the parable of the rich man and Lazarus, the body is buried, yet still the torments of the soul are described as physical. Jesus here accommodates his teaching to the conceptions of his time, or, better still, uses material figures to express spiritual realities. Surely he does not mean to say that the Rabbinic notion of Abraham's bosom is ultimate truth. "Parables, " for this reason among others, "may not be made primary sources and seats of doctrine. " Luckock, Intermediate State, 20 — "May the parable of the rich man and Lazarus be an anticipatory picture of the final state? But the rich man seems to assume that the judgment has not yet come, for he speaks of his brethren as still undergoing their earthly probation, and as capable of receiving a warning to avoid a fate similar to his own. "

The passages cited enable us properly to estimate two opposite errors.

A.   They refute, on the one hand, the view that the souls of both righteous and wicked sleep between death and the resurrection.

This view is based upon the assumption that the possession of a physical organism is indispensable to activity and consciousness — an assumption which the existence of a God who is pure spirit (John 4 : 24), and the existence of angels who are probably pure spirits (Heb. 1 : 14), show to be erroneous. Although the departed are characterized as 'spirits' (Eccl. 12 : 7 ; Acts 7 : 59 ; Heb. 12 : 23 ; 1 Pet. 3 : 19), there is nothing in this 'absence from the body ' (2 Cor. 5 : 8) inconsistent with the activity and consciousness ascribed to them in the Scriptures above referred to. When the dead are spoken of as 'sleeping' (Dan. 12 : 2 ; Mat. 9 : 24 ; John 11 : 11 ; 1 Cor. 11 : 30 ; 15 : 51 ; 1 Thess. 4 : 14 ; 5 : 10), we are to regard this as simply the language of appearance, and as literally applicable only to the body.

John 4 : 24 — "God is a Spirit [or rather, as margin, 'God is spirit'] " ; Heb. 1 : 14 — "Are they [angels] not all ministering spirits ? " ; Eccl. 12 : 7 — "the dust returneth to the earth as it was, and the spirit returneth unto God who gave it " ; Acts 7 : 59 — "And they stoned Stephen, calling upon the Lord, and saying, Lord Jesus, receive my spirit " ; Heb. 12 : 23 — "to God the Judge of all, and to the spirits of just men made perfect " ; 1 Pet. 3 : 19 — " in which also he went and preached unto the spirits in prison " ; 2 Cor. 5 : 8 — "we are of good courage, I say, and are willing rather to be absent from the body, and to be at home with the Lord " ; Dan. 12 : 2 — "many of them that sleep in the dust of the earth shall awake " ; Mat. 9 : 24 — "the damsel is not dead, but sleepeth " ; John 11 : 11 — "Our friend Lazarus is fallen asleep : but I go, that I may awake him out of sleep " ; 1 Cor. 11 : 30 — "For this cause many among you are weak and sickly, and not a few sleep " ; 1 Thess. 4 : 14 — "For if we believe that Jesus died and rose again, even so them also that are fallen asleep in Jesus will God bring with him " ; 5 : 10 — "who died for us, that, whether we wake or sleep, we should live together with him."

B.   The passages first cited refute, on the other hand, the view that the suffering of the intermediate state is purgatorial.

According to the doctrine of the Roman Catholic church, "all who die at peace with the church, but are not perfect, pass into purgatory." Here they make satisfaction for the sins committed after baptism by suffering a longer or shorter time, according to the degree of their guilt. The church on earth, however, has power, by prayers and the sacrifice of the Mass, to shorten these sufferings or to remit them altogether. But we urge, in reply, that the passages referring to suffering in the intermediate state give no indication that any true believer is subject to this suffering, or that the church has any power to relieve from the consequences of sin, either in this world or in the world to come. Only God can forgive, and the church is simply empowered to declare that, upon the fulfilment of the appointed conditions of repentance and faith, he does actually forgive. This theory, moreover, is inconsistent with any proper view of the completeness of Christ's satisfaction (Gal. 2 : 21 ; Heb. 9 : 28) ; of justification through faith alone (Rom. 3 : 28) ; and of the condition after death, of both righteous and wicked, as determined in this life (Eccl. 11 : 3 ; Mat. 25 : 10 ; Luke 16 : 26 ; Heb. 9 : 27 ; Rev. 22 : 11).

Against this doctrine we quote the following texts : Gal. 2 : 21 — "I do not make void the grace of God : for if righteousness is through the law, then Christ died for nought " ; Heb. 9 : 28 — "so Christ also, having been once [or, 'once for all'] offered to bear the sins of many, shall appear a second time, apart from sin, to them tha wait for him, unto salvation " ; Rom. 3 : 28 — " We reckon therefore that a man is justified by faith apart from the works of the law " ; Eccl. 11 : 3 — " if a tree fall toward the south or toward the north, in the place where the tree falleth there shall it be " ; Mat. 25 : 10 — "And while they went away to buy, the bridegroom came ; and they that were ready went in with him to the marriage feast : and the door was shut " ; Luke 16 : 26 — "And besides all this, between us and you there is a great gulf fixed, that they that would pass from hence to you may not be able, and that none may cross over from thence to us " ; Heb. 9 : 27 — "it is appointed unto men once to die, and after this cometh judgment " ; Rev. 22 : 11 — " He that is unrighteous, let him do unrighteousness still : and he that is filthy, let him be made filthy still : and he that is righteous, let him do righteousness still : and he that is holy, let him be made holy still. "

Rome teaches that the agonies of purgatory are intolerable. They differ from the pains of the damned only in this, that there is a limit to the one, not the other. Bellarmine, De Purgatorio, 2 : 14 — " The pains of purgatory are very severe, surpassing any endured in this life. " Since none but actual saints escape the pains of purgatory, this doctrine gives to the death and the funeral of the Roman Catholic a dreadful and repellent aspect. Death is not the coming of Christ to take his disciples home, but is rather the ushering of the shrinking soul into a place of unspeakable suffering. This suffering makes satisfaction for guilt. Having paid their allotted penalty, the souls of the purified pass into Heaven without awaiting the day of judgment. The doctrine of purgatory gives hope that men may be saved after death ; prayer for the dead has influence ; the priest is authorized to offer this prayer ; so the church sells salvation for money. Amory H. Bradford, Ascent of the Soul, 267-287, argues in favor of prayers for the dead. Such prayers, he says, help us to keep in mind the fact that they are living still. If the dead are free beings, they may still choose good or evil, and our prayers may help them to choose the good. We should be thankful, he believes, to the Roman Catholic Church, for keeping up such prayers. We reply that no doctrine of Rome has done so much to pervert the gospel and to enslave the world.

For the Romanist doctrine, see Perrone, Prælectiones Theologicæ, 2 : 391-420. *Per contra*, see Hodge, Systematic Theology, 3 : 743-770 ; Barrows, Purgatory. Augustine, Encheiridion, 69, suggests the possibility of purgatorial fire in the future for some believers. Whiton, Is Eternal Punishment Endless ? page 69, says that Tertullian held to a delay of resurrection in the case of faulty Christians ; Cyprian first stated the notion of a middle state of purification ; Augustine thought it " not incredible " ; Gregory the Great called it " worthy of belief " ; it is now one of the most potent doctrines of the Roman Catholic Church ; that church has been, from the third century, for all souls who accept her last consolations, practically restorationist. Gore, Incarnation, 18 — "In the Church of Rome, the ' peradventure ' of an Augustine as to purgatory for the imperfect after death — 'non redarguo', he says, ' quia forsitan verum est,' — has become a positive teaching about purgatory, full of exact information."

Elliott, Horæ Apocalypticæ, 1 : 410, adopts Hume's simile, and says that purgatory gave the Roman Catholic Church what Archimedes wanted, another world on which to fix its lever, that so fixed, the church might with it move this world. We must remember, however, that the Roman church teaches no radical change of character in purgatory, — purgatory is only a purifying process for believers. The true purgatory is only in this world, — for only here are sins purged away by God's sanctifying Spirit ; and in this process of purification, though God chastises, there is no element of penalty. On Dante's Purgatory, see A. H. Strong, Philosophy and Religion, 515-518.

Luckcck, After Death, is an argument, based upon the Fathers, against the Romanist doctrine. Yet he holds to progress in sanctification in the intermediate state, though the work done in that state will not affect the final judgment, which will be for the deeds done in the body. He urges prayer for the departed righteous. In his book entitled The Intermediate State, Luckock holds to mental and spiritual development in that state, to active ministry, mutual recognition, and renewed companionship. He does not believe in a second probation, but in a first real probation for those who have had no proper opportunities in this life. In their reaction against purgatory, the Westminister divines obliterated the Intermediate State. In that state there is gradual purification, and must be, since not all impurity and sinfulness are removed at death. The purging of the will requires time. White robes were given to them while they were waiting (Rev. 6:11). But there is no second probation for those who have thrown away their opportunities in this life. Robert Browning, The Ring and the Book, 232 (Pope, 2129), makes the Pope speak of following Guido "Into that sad, obscure, sequestered state Where God unmakes but to remake the soul He else made first in vain; which must not be." But the idea of hell as permitting essential change of character is foreign to Roman Catholic doctrine.

We close our discussion of this subject with a single, but an important, remark, — this, namely, that while the Scriptures represent the intermediate state to be one of conscious joy to the righteous, and of conscious pain to the wicked, they also represent this state to be one of incompleteness. The perfect joy of the saints, and the utter misery of the wicked, begin only with the resurrection and general judgment.

That the intermediate state is one of incompleteness, appears from the following passages: Mat. 8:29—"What have we to do with thee, thou Son of God? art thou come hither to torment us before the time?" 2 Cor. 5:3, 4—"if so be that being clothed we shall not be found naked. For indeed we that are in this tabernacle do groan, being burdened; not for that we would be unclothed, but that we would be clothed upon, that what is mortal may be swallowed up of life"; cf. Rom. 8:23—"And not only so, but ourselves also, who have the first-fruits of the Spirit, even we ourselves groan within ourselves, waiting for our adoption, to wit, the redemption of our body"; Phil. 3:11—"if by any means I may attain unto the resurrection from the dead"; 2 Pet. 2:9—"the Lord knoweth how to deliver the godly out of temptation, and to keep the unrighteous under punishment unto the day of judgment"; Rev. 6:10—"and they [the souls underneath the altar] cried with a great voice, saying, How long, O Master, the holy and true, dost thou not judge and avenge our blood on them that dwell on the earth?"

In opposition to Locke, Human Understanding, 2:1:10, who said that "the soul thinks not always"; and to Turner, Wish and Will, 48, who declares that "the soul need not always think, any more than the body always move; the essence of the soul is potentiality for activity"; Descartes, Kant, Jouffroy, Sir William Hamilton, all maintain that it belongs to mental existence continuously to think. Upon this view, the intermediate state would be necessarily a state of thought. As to the nature of that thought, Dorner remarks in his Eschatology that "in this relatively bodiless state, a still life begins, a sinking of the soul into itself and into the ground of its being, — what Steffens calls 'involution,' and Martensen 'self-brooding.' In this state, spiritual things are the only realities. In the unbelieving, their impurity, discord, alienation from God, are laid bare. If they still prefer sin, its form becomes more spiritual, more demoniacal, and so ripens for the judgment."

Even here, Dorner deals in speculation rather than in Scripture. But he goes further, and regards the intermediate state as one, not only of moral progress, but of elimination of evil; and holds the end of probation to be, not at death, but at the judgment, at least in the case of all non-believers who are not incorrigible. We must regard this as a practical revival of the Romanist theory of purgatory, and as contradicted not only by all the considerations already urged, but also by the general tenor of Scriptural representation that the decisions of this life are final, and that character is fixed here for eternity. This is the solemnity of preaching, that the gospel is "a savor from life unto life," or "a savor from death unto death" (2 Cor. 2·16).

Descartes: "As the light always shines and the heat always warms, so the soul always thinks." James, Psychology, 1:164-175, argues against unconscious mental states. The states were conscious at the time we had them; but they have been forgotten. In the Unitarian Review, Sept. 1884, Prof. James denies that eternity is given at a stroke to omniscience. Lotze, in his Metaphysics, 268, in opposition to Kant, contends for the transcendental validity of time. Green, on the contrary, in Prolegomena to Ethics, book 1, says that every act of knowledge in the case of man is a timeless act. In comparing the different aspects of the stream of successive phenomena, the mind must, he says, be itself out of time. Upton, Hibbert Lectures, 306, denies this timeless consciousness even to God, and apparently agrees with Martineau in maintaining that God does not foreknow free human acts.

De Quincey called the human brain a palimpsest. Each new writing seems to blot out all that went before. Yet in reality not one letter has ever been effaced. Loeb, Physiology of the Brain, 213, tells us that associative memory is imitated by machines like the phonograph. Traces left by speech can be reproduced in speech. Loeb calls memory a matter of physical chemistry. Stout, Manual of Psychology, 8 —" Consciousness includes not only awareness of our own states, but these states themselves whether we are aware of them or not. If a man is angry, that is a state of consciousness, even though he does not know that he is angry. If he does know that he is angry, that is another modification of consciousness, and not the same." On unconscious mental action, see Ladd, Philosophy of Mind, 378-382 —"Cerebration cannot be identified with psychical processes. If it could be, materialism would triumph. If the brain can do these things, why not do all the phenomena of consciousness? Consciousness becomes a mere *epiphenomenon*. Unconscious cerebration = wooden iron or unconscious consciousness. What then becomes of the soul in its intervals of unconsciousness? Answer: Unconscious finite minds exist only in the World-ground in which all minds and things have their existence."

On the whole subject, see Hovey, State of Man after Death ; Savage, Souls of the Righteous ; Julius Müller, Doct. Sin, 2 : 304-446 ; Neander, Planting and Training, 482-484 ; Delitzsch, Bib. Psychologie, 407-448 ; Bib. Sac., 13 : 153 ; Methodist Rev., 34 : 240 ; Christian Rev., 20 : 381 ; Herzog, Encyclop., art. : Hades ; Stuart, Essays on Future Punishment ; Whately, Future State ; Hovey, Biblical Eschatology, 79-144.

III. THE SECOND COMING OF CHRIST.

While the Scriptures represent great events in the history of the individual Christian, like death, and great events in the history of the church, like the outpouring of the Spirit at Pentecost and the destruction of Jerusalem, as comings of Christ for deliverance or judgment, they also declare that these partial and typical comings shall be concluded by a final, triumphant return of Christ, to punish the wicked and to complete the salvation of his people.

Temporal comings of Christ are indicated in : Mat. 24 : 23, 27, 34 —"Then if any man shall say unto you, Lo, here is the Christ, or, Here ; believe it not . . . . For as the lightning cometh forth from the east, and is seen even unto the west ; so shall be the coming of the Son of man. . . . . Verily I say unto you, This generation shall not pass away, till all these things be accomplished " ; 16 : 28 —"Verily I say unto you, There are some of them that stand here, who shall in no wise taste of death, till they see the Son of man coming in his kingdom " ; John 14 : 3, 18 —"And if I go and prepare a place for you, I come again, and will receive you unto myself ; that where I am, there ye may be also . . . . I will not leave you desolate : I come unto you " ; Rev. 3 : 20 — " Behold, I stand at the door and knock : if any man hear my voice and open the door, I will come in to him, and will sup with him, and he with me. So the Protestant Reformation, the modern missionary enterprise, the battle against papacy in Europe and against slavery in this country, the great revivals under Whitefield in England and under Edwards in America, were all preliminary and typical comings of Christ. It was a sceptical spirit which indited the words: "God's new Messiah, some great Cause " ; yet it is true that in every great movement of civilization we are to recognize a new coming of the one and only Messiah, "Jesus Christ, the same yesterday and to-day and forever " (Heb. 13 : 8). Schaff, Hist. Christ. Church, 1 : 840 —" The coming began with his ascension to heaven (*cf.* Mat. 26 : 64 —'henceforth [ἀπ' ἄρτι, *from now*] ye shall see the Son of man sitting at the right hand of Power, and coming on the clouds of heaven ')." Matheson, Spir. Devel. of St. Paul, 286 —" To Paul, in his later letters, this world is already the scene of the second advent. The secular is not to vanish away, but to be permanent, transfigured, pervaded by the divine life. Paul began with the Christ of the resurrection ; he ends with the Christ who already makes all things new. " See Metcalf Parousia vs. Second Advent, in Bib. Sac., Jan. 1907 : 61-65.

The final coming of Christ is referred to in : Mat. 24 : 30 — "they shall see the Son of man coming on the clouds of heaven with power and great glory. And he shall send forth his angels with a great sound of a grumpet, and they shall gather together his elect from the four winds, from one end of heaven to the other"; 25 : 31 — "But when the Son of man shall come in his glory, and all the angels with him, then shall he sit on the throne of his glory"; Acts 1 : 11 — "Ye men of Galilee, why stand ye looking into heaven? this Jesus, who was received up from you into heaven, shall so come in like manner as ye beheld him going into heaven"; 1 Thess. 4 : 16 — "For the Lord himself shall descend from heaven, with a shout, with the voice of the archangel, and with the trump of God"; 2 Thess. 1 : 7, 10 — "the revelation of the Lord Jesus from heaven with the angels of his power . . . . when he shall come to be glorified in his saints, and to be marvelled at in all them that believed"; Heb. 9 : 28 — "so Christ also, having been once offered to bear the sins of many, shall appear a second time, apart from sin, to them that wait for him, unto salvation"; Rev. 1 : 7 — "Behold, he cometh with the clouds; and every eye shall see him, and they that pierced him; and all the tribes of the earth shall mourn over him." Dr. A. C. Kendrick, Com. on Heb. 1 : 6 — "And when he shall conduct back again into the inhabited world the First-born, he saith, And let all the angels of God worship him" = in the glory of the second coming Christ's superiority to angels will be signally displayed — a contrast to the humiliation of his first coming.

The tendency of our day is to interpret this second class of passages in a purely metaphorical and spiritual way. But prophecy can have more than one fulfilment. Jesus' words are pregnant words. The present spiritual coming does not exhaust their meaning. His coming in the great movements of history does not preclude a final and literal coming, in which "every eye shall see him" (Rev. 1:7). With this proviso, we may assent to much of the following quotation from Gould, Bib. Theol. N. T., 44–56 —" The last things of which Jesus speaks are not the end of the world, but of the age — the end of the Jewish period in connection with the destruction of Jerusalem. . . . . After the entire statement is in, including both the destruction of Jerusalem and the coming of the Lord which is to follow it, it is distinctly said that that generation was not to pass away until all these things are accomplished. According to this, the coming of the Son of man must be something other than a visible coming. In O. T. prophecy any divine interference in human affairs is represented under the figure of God coming in the clouds of heaven. Mat. 26 : 64 says: 'From this time ye shall see the Son of man seated . . . . and coming in the clouds of heaven.' Coming and judgment are both continuous. The slow growth in the parables of the leaven and the mustard seed contradicts the idea of Christ's early coming. 'After a long time the Lord of these servants cometh' (Mat. 25 : 19). Christ came in one sense at the destruction of Jerusalem; in another sense all great crises in the history of the world are comings of the Son of man. These judgments of the nations are a part of the process for the final setting up of the kingdom. But this final act will not be a judgment process, but the final entire submission of the will of man to the will of God. The end is to be, not judgment, but salvation." We add to this statement the declaration that the final act here spoken of will not be purely subjective and spiritual, but will constitute an external manifestation of Christ comparable to that of his first coming in its appeal to the senses, but unspeakably more glorious than was the coming to the manger and the cross. The proof of this we now proceed to give.

1. *The nature of this coming.*

Although without doubt accompanied, in the case of the regenerate, by inward and invisible influences of the Holy Spirit, the second advent is to be outward and visible. This we argue:

(*a*) From the objects to be secured by Christ's return. These are partly external (Rom. 8 : 21, 23). Nature and the body are both to be glorified. These external changes may well be accompanied by a visible manifestation of him who 'makes all things new' (Rev. 21 : 5).

Rom. 8 : 10–23 —" in hope that the creation also shall be delivered from the bondage of corruption into the liberty of the glory of the children of God . . . . waiting for our adoption, to wit, the redemption of our body"; Rev. 21 : 5 — "Behold, I make all things new." A. J. Gordon, Ministry of the Spirit, 49 —" We must not confound the *Paraclete* and the *Parousia.* It has been argued that, because Christ came in the person of the Spirit, the Redeemer's advent in glory has already taken place. But in the Paraclete Christ comes spiritually and invisibly; in the Parousia he comes bodily and gloriously."

(*b*) From the Scriptural comparison of the manner of Christ's return with the manner of his departure (Acts 1 : 11) — see Commentary of

Hackett, *in loco :* — "ὃν τρόπον = visibly, and in the air. The expression is never employed to affirm merely the certainty of one event as compared with another. The assertion that the meaning is simply that, as Christ had departed, so also he would return, is contradicted by every passage in which the phrase occurs."

Acts 1 : 11 —"this Jesus, who was received up from you into heaven, shall so come in like manner as ye beheld him going into heaven"; *cf.* Acts 7 : 28 —"wouldest thou kill me, as [ὃν τρόπον] thou killedst the Egyptian yesterday ? " Mat. 23 : 37 —"how often would I have gathered thy children together, even as [ὃν τρόπον] a hen gathereth her chickens under her wings "; 2 Tim. 3 : 8 —"as [ὃν τρόπον] Jannes and Jambres withstood Moses, so do these also withstand the truth." Lyman Abbott refers to Mat. 23 : 37, and Luke 13 : 35, as showing that, in Acts 1 : 11, "in like *manner*" means only "in like *reality.*" So, he says, the Jews expected Elijah to return in *form,* according to Mal. 4 : 5, whereas he returned only in *spirit.* Jesus similarily returned at Pentecost in spirit, and has been coming again ever since. The remark of Dr. Hackett, quoted in the text above, is sufficient proof that this interpretation is wholly unexegetical.

(*c*) From the analogy of Christ's first coming. If this was a literal and visible coming, we may expect the second coming to be literal and visible also.

1 Thess. 4 : 16 —"For the Lord himself [= in his own person] shall descend from heaven, with a shout [something heard], with the voice of the archangel, and with the trump of God "— see Com. of Prof. W. A. Stevens : "So different from Luke 17 : 20, where 'the kingdom of God cometh not with observation." The 'shout' is not necessarily the voice of Christ himself (lit. 'in a shout,' or 'in shouting'). 'Voice of the archangel' and 'trump of God' are appositional, not additional." Rev. 1 : 7 —"every eye shall see him "; as every ear shall hear him : John 5 : 28, 29 —"all that are in the tombs shall hear his voice "; 2 Thess. 2 : 2 —"to the end that ye be not quickly shaken from your mind, nor yet be troubled . . . . as that the day of the Lord is now present "— they may have "thought that the first gathering of the saints to Christ was a quiet, invisible one — a stealthy advent, like a thief in the night " (Lillie). 2 John 7 —"For many deceivers are gone forth into the world, even they that confess not that Jesus Christ cometh in the flesh "— here denial of a future second coming of Christ is declared to be the mark of a deceiver.

Alford and Alexander, in their Commentaries on Acts 1 : 11, agree with the view of Hackett quoted above. Warren, Parousia, 61-65, 106-114, controverts this view and says that " an omnipresent divine being can *come,* only in the sense of *manifestation.*" He regards the parousia, or coming of Christ, as nothing but Christ's spiritual presence. A writer in the Presb. Review, 1883 : 221, replies that Warren's view is contradicted "by the fact that the apostles often spoke of the parousia as an event yet future, long after the promise of the Redeemer's spiritual presence with his church had begun to be fulfilled, and by the fact that Paul expressly cautions the Thessalonians against the belief that the parousia was just at hand." We do not know how all men at one time can see a bodily Christ ; but we also do not know the nature of Christ's body. The day exists undivided in many places at the same time. The telephone has made it possible for men widely separated to hear the same voice,—it is equally possible that all men may see the same Christ coming in the clouds.

2. *The time of Christ's coming.*

(*a*) Although Christ's prophecy of this event, in the twenty-fourth chapter of Matthew, so connects it with the destruction of Jerusalem that the apostles and the early Christians seem to have hoped for its occurrence during their life-time, yet neither Christ nor the apostles definitely taught when the end should be, but rather declared the knowledge of it to be reserved in the counsels of God, that men might ever recognize it as possibly at hand, and so might live in the attitude of constant expectation.

1 Cor. 15 : 51 —" We shall not all sleep, but we shall all be changed "; 1 Thess. 4 : 17 —" then we that are alive, that are left, shall together with them be caught up in the clouds, to meet the Lord in the air ; and so shall we ever be with the Lord "; 2 Tim. 4 : 8 —"henceforth there is laid up for me the crown of righteousness, which the Lord, the righteous judge, shall give to me at that day : and not only to me, but also to all them that have loved his appearing " ; James

5 : 7 —"Be patient therefore, brethren, until the coming of the Lord " ; 1 Pet. 4 : 7 —"But the end of all things is at hand: be ye therefore of sound mind, and be sober unto prayer " ; 1 John 2 : 18 —"Little children, it is the last hour: and as ye heard that antichrist cometh, even now have there risen many antichrists ; whereby we know that it is the last hour."

Phil. 4 : 5 — "The Lord is at hand (ἐγγύς). In nothing be anxious" — may mean "the Lord is near " (in space), without any reference to the second coming. The passages quoted above, expressing as they do the surmises of the apostles that Christ's coming was near, while yet abstaining from all definite fixing of the time, are at least sufficient proof that Christ's advent may not be near to our time. We should be no more warranted than they were, in inferring from these passages alone the immediate coming of the Lord.

Wendt, Teaching of Jesus, 2 : 349-350, maintains that Jesus expected his own speedy second coming and the end of the world. There was no mention of the death of his disciples, or the importance of readiness for it. No hard and fast organization of his disciples into a church was contemplated by him, — Mat. 16 : 18 and 18 : 17 are not authentic. No separation of his disciples from the fellowship of the Jewish religion was thought of. He thought of the destruction of Jerusalem as the final judgment. Yet his doctrine would spread through the earth, like leaven and mustard seed, though accompanied by suffering on the part of his disciples. This view of Wendt can be maintained only by an arbitrary throwing out of the testimony of the evangelist, upon the ground that Jesus' mention of a church does not befit so early a stage in the evolution of Christianity. Wendt's whole treatment is vitiated by the presupposition that there can be nothing in Jesus' words which is inexplicable upon the theory of natural development. That Jesus did not expect speedily to return to earth is shown in Mat. 25 : 19 —"After a long time the Lord of those servants cometh " ; and Paul, in 2 Thess., had to correct the mistake of those who interpreted him as having in his first Epistle declared an immediate coming of the Lord.

A. H. Strong, Cleveland Sermon, 1904 : 27 —" The faith in a second coming of Christ has lost its hold upon many Christians in our day. But it still serves to stimulate and admonish the great body, and we can never dispense with its solemn and mighty influence. Christ comes, it is true, in Pentecostal revivals and in destructions of Jerusalem, in Reformation movements and in political upheavals. But these are only precursors of another and literal and final return of Christ, to punish the wicked and to complete the salvation of his people. That day for which all other days are made will be a joyful day for those who have fought a good fight and have kept the faith. Let us look for and hasten the coming of the day of God. The Jacobites of Scotland never ceased their labors and sacrifices for their king's return. They never tasted wine, without pledging their absent prince ; they never joined in song, without renewing their oaths of allegiance. In many a prison cell and on many a battlefield they rang out the strain : ' Follow thee, follow thee, wha wadna follow thee ? Long hast thou lo'ed and trusted us fairly : Chairlie, Chairlie, wha wadna follow thee? King o' the Highland hearts, bonnie Prince Chairlie!' So they sang, so they invited him, until at last he came. But that longing for the day when Charles should come to his own again was faint and weak compared with the longing of true Christian hearts for the coming of their King. Charles came, only to suffer defeat, and to bring shame to his country. But Christ will come, to put an end to the world's long sorrow, to give triumph to the cause of truth, to bestow everlasting reward upon the faithful. ' Even so, Lord Jesus, come ! Hope of all our hopes the sum, Take thy waiting people home ! Long, so long, the groaning earth, Cursed with war and flood and dearth, Sighs for its redemption birth. Therefore come, we daily pray ; Bring the resurrection-day ; Wipe creation's curse away ! '"

(b) Hence we find, in immediate connection with many of these predictions of the end, a reference to intervening events and to the eternity of God, which shows that the prophecies themselves are expressed in a large way which befits the greatness of the divine plans.

Mat. 24 : 36 —"But of that day and hour knoweth no one, not even the angels of heaven, neither the Son, but the Father only " ; Mark 13 : 32 —"But of that day or that hour knoweth no one, not even the angels in heaven, neither the Son, but he Father. Take ye heed, watch and pray : for ye know not when the time is " ; Acts 1 : 7 —"And he said unto them, It is not for you to know times or seasons, which the Father hath set within his own authority" ; 1 Cor. 10 : 11 —"Now these things happened unto them by way of example ; and they were written for our admonition, upon whom the ends of the ages are come " ; 16 : 22 —"Marana tha [marg.: that is, O Lord, come !]" ; 2 Thess. 2 : 1-3 —"Now we beseech you, brethren, touching the coming of our Lord Jesus Christ, and our gathering together unto him ; to the end that ye be not quickly shaken from your mind, nor yet be troubled . . . . as that the day of the Lord is now present [Am. Rev. :

is just at hand '] ; let no man beguile you in any wise: for it will not be, except the falling away come first, and the man of sin be revealed, the son of perdition."

James 5:8, 9—"Be ye also patient; establish your hearts: for the coming of the Lord is at hand. Murmur not, brethren, one against another, that ye be not judged: behold, the judge standeth before the doors" : 2 Pet. 3:3-12—"in the last days mockers shall come . . . . saying, Where is the promise of his coming ? for, from the day that the fathers fell asleep, all things continue as they were from the beginning of the creation. For this they wilfully forget, that there were heavens from of old . . . . But forget not this one thing, beloved, that one day is with the Lord as a thousand years, and a thousand years as one day. The Lord is not slack concerning his promise . . . . But the day of the Lord will come as a thief . . . . what manner of persons ought ye to be in all holy living and godliness, looking for and earnestly desiring [marg.: 'hastening'] the coming of the day of God "—awaiting it, and hastening its coming by your prayer and labor.

Rev. 1:3—"Blessed is he that readeth, and they that hear the words of the prophecy, and keep the things that are written therein: for the time is at hand ": 22:12, 20—"Behold, I come quickly ; and my reward is with me, to render to each man according as his work is . . . . He who testifieth these things saith, Yea: I come quickly. Amen: come, Lord Jesus." From these passages it is evident that the apostles did not know the time of the end, and that it was hidden from Christ himself while here in the flesh. He, there-fore, who assumes to know, assumes to know more than Christ or his apostles—assumes to know the very thing which Christ declared it was not for us to know !

Gould, Bib. Theol. N. T., 152—"The expectation of our Lord's coming was one of the elements and *motifs* of that generation, and the delay of the event caused some ques-tioning. But there is never any indication that it may be indefinitely postponed. The early church never had to face the difficulty forced upon the church to-day, of belief in his second coming, founded upon a prophecy of his coming during the lifetime of a generation long since dead. And until this Epistle [2 Peter], we do not find any traces of this exegetical legerdemain as such a situation would require. But here we have it full-grown ; just such a specimen of harmonistic device as orthodox interpretation famil-iarizes us with. The definite statement that the advent is to be within that generation is met with the general principle that 'one day is with the Lord as a thousand years, and a thousand years as one day' (2 Pet. 3:8)." We must regard this comment of Dr. Gould as an unconscious fulfilment of the prediction that " in the last days mockers shall come with mockery " (2 Pet. 3:3). A better understanding of prophecy, as divinely pregnant utterance, would have enabled the critic to believe that the words of Christ might be partially fulfilled in the days of the apostles, but fully accomplished only at the end of the world.

(c) In this we discern a striking parallel between the predictions of Christ's first, and the predictions of his second, advent. In both cases the event was more distant and more grand than those imagined to whom the prophecies first came. Under both dispensations, patient waiting for Christ was intended to discipline the faith, and to enlarge the conceptions, of God's true servants. The fact that every age since Christ ascended has had its Chiliasts and Second Adventists should turn our thoughts away from curious and fruitless prying into the time of Christ's coming, and set us at immediate and constant endeavor to be ready, at whatsoever hour he may appear.

Gen. 4:1—"And the man knew Eve his wife; and she conceived, and bare Cain, and said, I have gotten a man with the help of Jehovah [lit.: 'I have gotten a man, even Jehovah'] "—an intimation that Eve fancied her first-born to be already the promised seed, the coming deliverer ; see MacWhorter, Jahveh Christ. Deut. 18:15—"Jehovah thy God will raise up unto thee a prophet from the midst of thee, of thy brethren, like unto me; unto him ye shall hearken"—here is a prophecy which Moses may have expected to be fulfilled in Joshua, but which God designed to be fulfilled only in Christ. Is. 7:14, 16—"Therefore the Lord himself will give you a sign: behold, a virgin shall conceive, and bear a son, and shall call his name Immanuel. . . . . For before the child shall know to refuse the evil, and choose the good, the land whose two kings thou abhorrest shall be forsaken"—a prophecy which the prophet may have expected to be fulfilled in his own time, and which was partly so fulfilled, but which God intended to be fulfilled ages thereafter. Luke 2:25—"Simeon; and this man was righteous and devout, looking for the consolation of Israel"—Simeon was the type of holy men, in every age of Jewish history, who were waiting for the ful-filment of God's promise, and for the coming of the deliverer. So under the Christian dispensation. Augustine held that Christ's reign of a thousand years, which occupies the last epoch of the world's history, did not still lie in the future, but began with the founding of the church (Ritschl, Just. and Reconc., 286). Luther, near the time of his death, said : "God forbid that the world should last fifty years longer ! Let him cut matters short with his last judgment ! " Melanchthon put the end less than two hundred years from his time. Calvin's motto was : " *Domine, quousque?* " — " O Lord, how long ? " Jonathan Edwards, before and during the great Awakening, indulged high expectations as to the probable extension of the movement until it should bring the world, even in his own lifetime, into the love and obedience of Christ (Life, by Allen, 234). Better than any one of these is the utterance of Dr. Broadus: " If I am always ready, I shall be ready when Jesus comes." On the whole subject, see Hovey, in Baptist Quarterly, Oct. 1877 : 416–432; Shedd, Dogm. Theol., 2 : 641–646 ; Stevens, in Am. Com. on Thessalonians, Excursus on The Parousia, and notes on 1 Thess. 4:13, 16 ; 5:11; 2 Thess. 2 : 3, 12 ; Goodspeed, Messiah's Second Advent; Heagle, That Blessed Hope.

3. *The precursors of Christ's coming.*

(*a*) Through the preaching of the gospel in all the world, the kingdom of Christ is steadily to enlarge its boundaries, until Jews and Gentiles alike become possessed of its blessings, and a millennial period is introduced in which Christianity generally prevails throughout the earth.

Dan. 2 : 44, 45 — "And in the days of those kings shall the God of heaven set up a kingdom which shall never be destroyed, nor shall the sovereignty thereof be left to another people ; but it shall break in pieces and consume all these kingdoms, and it shall stand forever. Forasmuch as thou sawest that a stone was cut out of the mountain without hands, and that it brake in pieces the iron, the brass, the clay, the silver, and the gold ; the great God hath made known to the king what shall come to pass hereafter : and the dream is certain, and the interpretation thereof sure."

Mat. 13 : 31, 32 — "The kingdom of heaven is like unto a grain of mustard seed . . . . which indeed is less than all seeds ; but when it is grown, it is greater than the herbs, and becometh a tree, so that the birds of heaven come and lodge in the branches thereof " — the parable of the leaven, which follows, apparently illustrates the intensive, as that of the mustard seed illustrates the extensive, development of the kingdom of God ; and it is as impossible to confine the reference of the leaven to the spread of evil as it is impossible to confine the reference of the mustard seed to the spread of good.

Mat. 24 : 14 — "And this gospel of the kingdom shall be preached in the whole world for a testimony unto all the nations ; and then shall the end come " ; Rom. 11 : 25, 26 — "a hardening in part hath befallen Israel, until the fulness of the Gentiles be come in ; and so all Israel shall be saved " ; Rev. 20 : 4–6 — "And I saw thrones, and they sat upon them, and judgment was given unto them : and I saw the souls of them that had been beheaded for the testimony of Jesus, and for the word of God, and such as worshipped not the beast, neither his image, and received not the mark upon their forehead and upon their hand ; and they lived, and reigned with Christ a thousand years."

Col. 1 : 23 — " the gospel which ye heard, which was preached in all creation under heaven " — Paul's phrase here and the apparent reference in Mat. 24 : 14 to A. D. 70 as the time of the end, should restrain theorizers from insisting that the second coming of Christ cannot occur until this text has been fulfilled with literal completeness (Broadus).

(*b*) There will be a corresponding development of evil, either extensive or intensive, whose true character shall be manifest not only in deceiving many professed followers of Christ and in persecuting true believers, but in constituting a personal Antichrist as its representative and object of worship. This rapid growth shall continue until the millennium, during which evil, in the person of its chief, shall be temporarily restrained.

Mat. 13 : 30, 38 — "Let both grow together until the harvest : and in the time of the harvest I will say to the reapers, Gather up first the tares, and bind them in bundles to burn them : but gather the wheat into my barn . . . . the field is the world ; and the good seed, these are the sons of the kingdom ; and the tares are the sons of the evil one " ; 24 : 5, 11, 12, 24 — "For many shall come in my name, saying, I am the Christ ; and shall lead many astray . . . . And many false prophets shall arise, and shall lead many astray. And because iniquity shall be multiplied, the love of the many shall wax cold . . . . For there shall arise false Christs, and false prophets, and shall show great signs and wonders ; so as to lead astray, if possible, even the elect."

Luke 21 : 12 — "But before all these things, they shall lay their hands on you, and shall persecute you, delivering you up to the synagogues and prisons, bringing you before kings and governors for my name's sake " ; 2 Thess. 2 : 3, 4, 7, 8, — "it will not be, except the falling away come first, and the man of sin be revealed, the son of perdition, he that opposeth and exalteth himself against all that is called God or that is worshipped ; so that he sitteth in the temple of God, setting himself forth as God. . . . . For the mystery of lawlessness doth already work : only there is one that restraineth new, until he be taken out of the way. And then shall be revealed the lawless one, whom the Lord Jesus shall slay with the breath of his mouth, and bring to nought by the manifestation of his coming."

Elliott, Horæ Apocalypticæ, 1:65, holds that "Antichrist means another Christ, a pro-Christ, a vice-Christ, a pretender to the name of Christ, and in that character, an usurper and adversary. The principle of Antichrist was already sown in the time of Paul. But a certain hindrance, i. e., the Roman Empire as then constituted, needed first to be removed out of the way, before room could be made for Antichrist's development." Antichrist, according to this view, is the hierarchical spirit, which found its final and most complete expression in the Papacy. Dante, Hell, 19: 106-117, speaks of the Papacy, or rather the temporal power of the Popes, as Antichrist: "To you St. John referred, O shepherds vile, When she who sits on many waters, had Been seen with kings her person to defile"; see A. H. Strong, Philosophy and Religion, 507.

It has been objected that a simultaneous growth both of evil and of good is inconceivable, and that the progress of the divine kingdom implies a diminution in the power of the adversary. Only a slight reflection however convinces us that, as the population of the world is always increasing, evil men may increase in numbers, even though there is increase in the numbers of the good. But we must also consider that evil grows in intensity just in proportion to the light which good throws upon it. "Wherever God erects a house of prayer, The devil always builds a chapel there." Every revival of religion stirs up the forces of wickedness to opposition. As Christ's first advent occasioned an unusual outburst of demoniac malignity, so Christ's second advent will be resisted by a final desperate effort of the evil one to overcome the forces of good. The great awakening in New England under Jonathan Edwards caused on the one hand a most remarkable increase in the number of Baptist believers, but also on the other hand the rise of modern Unitarianism. The optimistic Presbyterian pastor at Auburn argued with the pessimistic chaplain of the State's Prison that the world was certainly growing better, because his congregation was increasing; whereupon the chaplain replied that his own congregation was increasing also.

(c) At the close of this millennial period, evil will again be permitted to exert its utmost power in a final conflict with righteousness. This spiritual struggle, moreover, will be accompanied and symbolized by political convulsions, and by fearful indications of desolation in the natural world.

Mat. 24 : 29, 30 — "But immediately after the tribulation of those days the sun shall be darkened, and the moon shall not give her light, and the stars shall fall from heaven, and the powers of the heavens shall be shaken : and then shall appear the sign of the Son of man in heaven "; Luke 21 : 8-28 — false prophets ; wars and tumults ; earthquakes ; pestilences ; persecutions ; signs in the sun, moon, and stars ; "And then shall they see the Son of man coming in a cloud with power and great glory. But when these things begin to come to pass, look up, and lift up your heads ; because your redemption draweth nigh."

Interpretations of the book of Revelation are divided into three classes: (1) the *Præterist* (held by Grotius, Moses Stuart, and Warren), which regards the prophecy as mainly fulfilled in the age immediately succeeding the time of the apostles (666 = Neron Kaisar); (2) the *Continuous* (held by Isaac Newton, Vitringa, Bengel, Elliott, Kelly, and Cumming), which regards the whole as a continuous prophetical history, extending from the first age until the end of all things (666 = Lateinos); Hengstenberg and Alford hold substantially this view, though they regard the seven seals, trumpets, and vials as synchronological, each succeeding set going over the same ground and exhibiting it in some special aspect; (3) the *Futurist* (held by Maitland and Todd), which considers the book as describing events yet to occur, during the times immediately preceding and following the coming of the Lord.

Of all these interpretations, the most learned and exhaustive is that of Elliott, in his four volumes entitled Horæ Apocalypticæ. The basis of his interpretation is the "time and times and half a time" of Dan. 7: 25, which according to the year-day theory means 1260 years — the year, according to ancient reckoning, containing 360 days, and the "time" being therefore 360 years [360 + (2 × 360) + 180 = 1260]. This phrase we find recurring with regard to the woman nourished in the wilderness (Rev. 12: 14). The blasphemy of the beast for forty and two months (Rev. 13 : 5) seems to refer to the same period [42 × 30 = 1260, as before]. The two witnesses prophecy 1260 days (Rev. 11 : 3); and the woman's time in the wilderness is stated (Rev. 12: 6) as 1260 days. This period of 1260 years is regarded by Elliott as the time of the temporal power of the Papacy.

There is a twofold *terminus a quo*, and correspondingly a twofold *terminus ad quem*. The first commencement is A. D. 531, when in the edict of Justinian the dragon of the

Roman Empire gives its power to the beast of the Papacy, and resigns its throne to the rising Antichrist, giving opportunity for the rise of the ten horns as European kings (Rev. 13:1-3). The second commencement, adding the seventy-five supplementary years of Daniel 12:12 [1335 — 1260 = 75], is A. D. 606, when the Emperor Phocas acknowledges the primacy of Rome, and the ten horns, or kings, now diademed, submit to the Papacy (Rev. 17:12, 13). The first ending-point is A. D. 1791, when the French Revolution struck the first blow at the independence of the Pope [531 + 1260 = 1791]. The second ending-point is A. D. 1866, when the temporal power of the Pope was abolished at the unification of the kingdom of Italy [606 + 1260 = 1866]. Elliott regards the two-horned beast (Rev. 13:11) as representing the Papal Clergy, and the image of the beast (Rev. 13:14, 15) as representing the Papal Councils.

Unlike Hengstenberg and Alford, who consider the seals, trumpets, and vials as synchronological, Elliott makes the seven trumpets to be an unfolding of the seventh seal, and the seven vials to be an unfolding of the seventh trumpet. Like other advocates of the premillennial advent of Christ, Elliott regards the four chief signs of Christ's near approach as being: (1) the decay of the Turkish Empire (the drying up of the river Euphrates — Rev. 16:12); (2) the Pope's loss of temporal power (the destruction of Babylon — Rev. 17:19); (3) the conversion of the Jews and their return to their own land (Ez. 37; Rom. 11:12-15, 25-27 — but on this last, see Meyer); (4) the pouring out of the Holy Spirit and the conversion of the Gentiles (the way of the kings of the East — Rev. 16:12; the fulness of the Gentiles — Rom. 11:25).

Elliott's whole scheme, however, is vitiated by the fact that he wrongly assumes the book of Revelation to have been written under Domitian (94 or 96), instead of under Nero (67 or 68). His *terminus a quo* is therefore incorrect, and his interpretation of chapters 5-9 is rendered very precarious. The year 1866, moreover, should have been the time of the end, and so the *terminus ad quem* seems to be clearly misunderstood — unless indeed the seventy-five supplementary years of Daniel are to be added to 1866. We regard the failure of this most ingenious scheme of Apocalyptic interpretation as a practical demonstration that a clear understanding of the meaning of prophecy is, before the event, impossible, and we are confirmed in this view by the utterly untenable nature of the theory of the millennium which is commonly held by so-called Second Adventists, a theory which we now proceed to examine.

A long preparation may be followed by a sudden consummation. Drilling the rock for the blast is a slow process; firing the charge takes but a moment. The woodwork of the Windsor Hotel in New York was in a charred and superheated state before the electric wires that threaded it wore out their insulation, — then a slight increase of voltage turned heat into flame. The Outlook, March 30, 1895 — " An evolutionary conception of the Second Coming, as a progressive manifestation of the spiritual power and glory of Christ, may issue in a *dénouement* as unique as the first advent was which closed the preparatory ages."

Joseph Cook, on A. J. Gordon: "There is a wide distinction between the flash-light theory and the burning-glass theory of missions. The latter was Dr. Gordon's view. When a burning-glass is held over inflammable material, the concentrated rays of the sun rapidly produce in it discoloration, smoke, and sparks. At a certain instant, after the sparks have been sufficiently diffused, the whole material suddenly bursts into flame. There is then no longer any need of the burning-glass, for fire has itself fallen from on high and is able to do its own work. So the world is to be regarded as inflammable material to be set on fire from on high. Our Lord's life on earth is a burning-glass, concentrating rays of light and heat upon the souls of men. When the heating has gone on far enough, and the sparks of incipient conflagration have been sufficiently diffused, suddenly spiritual flame will burst up everywhere and will fill the earth. This is the second advent of him who kindled humanity to new life by his first advent. As I understand the premillenarian view of history, the date when the sparks shall kindle into flame is not known, but it is known that the duty of the church is to spread the sparks and to expect at any instant, after their wide diffusion, the victorious descent of millennial flame, that is, the beginning of our Lord's personal and visible reign over the whole earth." See article on Millenarianism, by G. P. Fisher, in McClintock and Strong's Cyclopædia; also by Semisch, in Schaff-Herzog, Cyclopædia; *cf.* Schaff, History of the Christian Church, 1:840.

4. *Relation of Christ's second coming to the millennium.*

The Scripture foretells a period, called in the language of prophecy " a thousand years," when Satan shall be restrained and the saints shall reign with Christ on the earth. A comparison of the passages bearing on this subject leads us to the conclusion that this millennial blessedness and dominion is prior to the second advent. One passage only seems at first sight to teach the contrary, *viz. :* Rev. 20 : 4-10. But this supports the theory of a premillennial advent only when the passage is interpreted with the barest literalness. A better view of its meaning will be gained by considering :

(*a*) That it constitutes a part, and confessedly an obscure part, of one of the most figurative books of Scripture, and therefore ought to be interpreted by the plainer statements of the other Scriptures.

We quote here the passage alluded to : Rev. 20 : 4-10 — "And I saw thrones, and they sat upon them, and judgment was given unto them : and I saw the souls of them that had been beheaded for the testimony of Jesus, and for the word of God, and such as worshipped not the beast, neither his image, and received not the mark upon their forehead and upon their hand ; and they lived, and reigned with Christ a thousand years. The rest of the dead lived not until the thousand years should be finished. This is the first resurrection. Blessed and holy is he that hath part in the first resurrection : over these the second death hath no power ; but they shall be priests of God and of Christ, and shall reign with him a thousand years."

Emerson and Parker met a Second Adventist who warned them that the end of the world was near. Parker replied : " My friend, that does not concern me ; I live in Boston." Emerson said : " Well, I think I can get along without it." A similarly cheerful view is taken by Denney, Studies in Theology, 232 — " Christ certainly comes, according to the picture in Revelation, before the millennium ; but the question of importance is, whether the conception of the millennium itself, related as it is to Ezekiel, is essential to faith. I cannot think that it is. The religious content of the passages — what they offer for faith to grasp — is, I should say, simply this : that *until* the end the conflict between the kingdom of God and the kingdom of the world must go on ; that as the end approaches it becomes ever more intense, progress in humanity not being a progress in goodness merely or in badness only, but in the antagonism between the two ; and that the necessity for conflict is sure to emerge even after the kingdom of God has won its greatest triumphs. I frankly confess that to seek more than this in such Scriptural indications seems to me trifling."

(*b*) That the other Scriptures contain nothing with regard to a resurrection of the righteous which is widely separated in time from that of the wicked, but rather declare distinctly that the second coming of Christ is immediately connected both with the resurrection of the just and the unjust and with the general judgment.

Mat. 16 : 27 — "For the Son of man shall come in the glory of his Father with his angels ; and then shall he render unto every man according to his deeds " ; 25 : 31-33 — "But when the Son of man shall come in his glory, and all the angels with him, then shall he sit on the throne of his glory : and before him shall be gathered all the nations : and he shall separate them one from another, as the shepherd separateth the sheep from the goats " ; John 5 : 28, 29 — "Marvel not at this : for the hour cometh, in which all that are in the tombs shall hear his voice, and shall come forth ; they that have done good, unto the resurrection of life ; and they that have done evil, unto the resurrection of judgment " ; 2 Cor. 5 : 10 — "For we must all be made manifest before the judgment seat of Christ ; that each one may receive the things done in the body, according to what he hath done, whether it be good or bad " ; 2 Thess. 1 : 6-10 — "if so be that it is a righteous thing with God to recompense affliction to them that afflict you, and to you that are afflicted rest with us, at the revelation of the Lord Jesus from heaven with the angels of his power in flaming fire, rendering vengeance to them that know not God, and to them that obey not the gospel of our Lord Jesus : who shall suffer punishment, even eternal destruction from the face of the Lord and from the glory of his might, when he shall come to be glorified in his saints, and to be marvelled at in all them that believed."

2 Pet. 3 : 7, 10 — "the day of judgment and destruction of ungodly men . . . . But the day of the Lord will come as a thief ; in the which the heavens shall pass away with a great noise, and the elements shall be dissolved with fervent heat, and the earth and the works that are therein shall be burned up " ; Rev. 20 : 11-15 — " And I saw a great white throne, and him that sat upon it, from whose face the earth and the heaven fled away ; and there was found no place for them. And I saw the dead, the great and the small, standing before the throne ; and books were opened : and another book was opened, which is the book of life : and the dead were judged out of the things that were written in the books, according to their works. And the sea gave up the dead that were in it ; and death and Hades gave up the dead that

were in them ; and they were judged every man according to their works. And death and Hades were cast into the lake of fire. This is the second death, even the lake of fire. And if any was not found written in the book of life, he was cast into the lake of fire."

Here is abundant evidence that there is no interval of a thousand years between the second coming of Christ and the resurrection, general judgment, and end of all things. All these events come together. The only answer of the premillennialists to this objection to their theory is, that the day of judgment and the millennium may be contemporaneous, — in other words, the day of judgment may be a thousand years long. Elliott holds to a conflagration, partial at the beginning of this period, complete at its close, — Peter's prophecy treating the two conflagrations as one, while the book of Revelation separates them ; so a nearer view resolves binary stars into two. But we reply that, if the judgment occupies the whole period of a thousand years, then the coming of Christ, the resurrection, and the final conflagration should all be a thousand years also. It is indeed possible that, in this case, as Peter says in connection with his prophecy of judgment, " one day is with the Lord as a thousand years, and a thousand years as one day " [2 Pet. 3:8). But if we make the word "day" so indefinite in connection with the judgment, why should we regard it as so definite, when we come to interpret the 1260 days ?

(c) That the literal interpretation of the passage — holding, as it does, to a resurrection of bodies of flesh and blood, and to a reign of the risen saints in the flesh, and in the world as at present constituted — is inconsistent with other Scriptural declarations with regard to the spiritual nature of the resurrection-body and of the coming reign of Christ.

1 Cor. 15 : 44, 50 — "it is sown a natural body ; it is raised a spiritual body. . . . . Now this I say, brethren, that flesh and blood cannot inherit the kingdom of God ; neither doth corruption inherit incorruption." These passages are inconsistent with the view that the resurrection is a physical resurrection at the beginning of the thousand years — a resurrection to be followed by a second life of the saints in bodies of flesh and blood. They are not, however, inconsistent with the true view, soon to be mentioned, that "the first resurrection" is simply the raising of the church to a new life and zeal. Westcott, Bib. Com. on John 14 : 18, 19 — " I will not leave you desolate [marg. : 'orphans'] : I come unto you. Yet a little while, and the world beholdeth me no more ; but ye behold me " : — " The words exclude the error of those who suppose that Christ will 'come' under the same conditions of earthly existence as those to which he submitted at his first coming." See Hovey, Bib. Eschatology, 66–78.

(d) That the literal interpretation is generally and naturally connected with the expectation of a gradual and necessary decline of Christ's kingdom upon earth, until Christ comes to bind Satan and to introduce the millennium. This view not only contradicts such passages as Dan. 2 :34, 35, and Mat. 13 : 31, 32, but it begets a passive and hopeless endurance of evil, whereas the Scriptures enjoin a constant and aggressive warfare against it, upon the very ground that God's power shall assure to the church a gradual but constant progress in the face of it, even to the time of the end.

Dan. 2 : 34, 35 — "Thou sawest till that a stone was cut out without hands, which smote the image upon its feet that were of iron and clay and brake them in pieces. Then was the iron, the clay, the brass, the silver, and the gold, broken in pieces together and became like the chaff of the summer threshing-floors ; and the wind carried them away, so that no place was found for them and the stone that smote the image became a great mountain, and filled the whole earth " ; Mat. 13 : 31, 32 — "The kingdom of heaven is like unto a grain of mustard seed, which a man took, and sowed in his field : which indeed is less than all seeds, but when it is grown, it is greater than the herbs, and becometh a tree, so that the birds of the heaven come and lodge in the branches thereof." In both these figures there is no sign of cessation or of backward movement, but rather every indication of continuous advance to complete victory and dominion. The premillennial theory supposes that for the principle of development under the dispensation of the Holy Spirit, God will substitute a reign of mere power and violence. J. B. Thomas : "The kingdom of heaven is like a grain of mustard seed, not like a can of nitro-glycerine." Leighton Williams : " The kingdom of God is to be realized on earth, not by a cataclysm, apart from effort and will, but through the universal dissemination of the gospel all but lost to the world." E. G. Robinson : "Second Adventism stultifies the system and scheme of Christianity." Dr. A. J. Gordon could not deny that the early disciples were mistaken in expecting the end of the world in their day. So we may be. Scripture does not declare that the end should come in the lifetime of the apostles, and no definite date is set. "After a long time" (Mat. 25 : 19) and "the falling away come first" (2 Thess. 2 : 3) are expressions which postpone indefinitely. Yet a just view of Christ's coming as ever possible in the immediate future may make us as faithful as were the original disciples.

The theory also divests Christ of all kingly power until the millennium, or, rather, maintains that the kingdom has not yet been given to him; see Elliott, Horæ Apocalypticæ, 1 : 94 — where Luke 19 : 12 — "A certain nobleman went into a far country, to receive for himself a kingdom, and to return " — is interpreted as follows: "Subordinate kings went to Rome to receive the investiture to their kingdoms from the Roman Emperor, and then returned to occupy them and reign. So Christ received from his Father, after his ascension, the investiture to his kingdom; but with the intention not to occupy it, till his return at his second coming. In token of this investiture he takes his seat as the Lamb on the divine throne " (Rev. 5 : 6-8). But this interpretation contradicts Mat. 28 : 18, 20 — "All authority hath been given unto me in heaven and on earth. . . . . lo, I am with you always, even unto the end of the world." See Presb. Rev., 1882 : 228. On the effects of the premillennial view in weakening Christian endeavor, see J. H. Seelye, Christian Missions, 94-127; *per contra*, see A. J. Gordon, in Independent, Feb. 1886.

(*e*) We may therefore best interpret Rev. 20 : 4-10 as teaching in highly figurative language, not a preliminary resurrection of the body, in the case of departed saints, but a period in the later days of the church militant when, under special influence of the Holy Ghost, the spirit of the martyrs shall appear again, true religion be greatly quickened and revived, and the members of Christ's churches become so conscious of their strength in Christ that they shall, to an extent unknown before, triumph over the powers of evil both within and without. So the spirit of Elijah appeared again in John the Baptist (Mal. 4 : 5; *cf.* Mat. 11 : 13, 14). The fact that only the spirit of sacrifice and faith is to be revived is figuratively indicated in the phrase: "The rest of the dead lived not again until the thousand years should be finished " = the spirit of persecution and unbelief shall be, as it were, laid to sleep. Since resurrection, like the coming of Christ and the judgment, is twofold, first, spiritual (the raising of the soul to spiritual life), and secondly, physical (the raising of the body from the grave), the words in Rev. 20 : 5 — "this is the first resurrection " — seen intended distinctly to preclude the literal interpretation we are combating. In short, we hold that Rev. 20 : 4-10 does not describe the events commonly called the second advent and resurrection, but rather describes great spiritual changes in the later history of the church, which are typical of, and preliminary to, the second advent and resurrection, and therefore, after the prophetic method, are foretold in language literally applicable only to those final events themselves (*cf.* Ez. 37 : 1-14; Luke 15 : 32).

Mal. 4 : 5 — "Behold, I will send you Elijah the prophet before the great and terrible day of Jehovah come "; *cf.* Mat. 11 : 13, 14 — " For all the prophets and the law prophesied until John. And if ye are willing to receive it, this is Elijah, that is to come "; Ez. 37 : 1-14 — the vision of the valley of dry bones = either the political or the religious resuscitation of the Jews; Luke 15 : 32 — "this thy brother was dead, and is alive again " — of the prodigal son. It will help us in our interpretation of Rev. 20 : 4-10 to notice that death, judgment, the coming of Christ, and the resurrection, are all of two kinds, the first spiritual, and the second literal:

(1) First, a spiritual death (Eph. 2 : 1 — "dead through your trespasses and sins "); and secondly, a physical and literal death, whose culmination is found in the second death (Rev. 20 : 14 — "And death and Hades were cast into the lake of fire. This is the second death, even the lake of fire ").

(2) First, a spiritual judgment (Is. 26 : 9 — "when thy judgments are in the earth "; John 12 : 31 — "Now is the judgment of this world: now shall the prince of this world be cast out "; 3 : 18 — "he that believeth not hath been judged already "); and secondly, an outward and literal judgment (Acts 17 : 31 — "hath appointed a day in which he will judge the world in righteousness by the man whom he hath ordained ").

(3) First, the spiritual and invisible coming of Christ (Mat. 16 : 28 — "shall in no wise taste of death, till they see the Son of man coming in his kingdom "— at the destruction of Jerusalem ; John 14 : 16 18 — "another Comforter .... I come unto you " — at Pentecost ; 14 : 3 — "And if I go and prepare a place for you I come again, and will receive you unto myself" — at death) ; and secondly, a visible literal coming (Mat. 25 : 31 — "the Son of man shall come in his glory, and all the angels with him ").

(4) First, a spiritual resurrection (John 5 : 25 — " The hour cometh, and now is, when the dead shall hear the voice of the Son of God ; and they that hear shall live ") ; and secondly, a physical and literal resurrection (John 5 : 28, 29 — " the hour cometh, in which all that are in the tombs shall hear his voice, and shall come forth ; they that have done good, unto the resurrection of life ; and they that have done evil, unto the resurrection of judgment "). The spiritual resurrection foreshadows the bodily resurrection.

This twofoldness of each of the four terms, death, judgment, coming of Christ, resurrection, is so obvious a teaching of Scripture, that the apostle's remark in Rev. 20 : 5 — "This is the first resurrection "— seems distinctly intended to warn the reader against drawing the premillenarian inference, and to make clear the fact that the resurrection spoken of is the first or spiritual resurrection, — an interpretation which is made indubitable by his proceeding, further on, to describe the outward and literal resurrection in verse 13 — "And the sea gave up the dead that were in it : and death and Hades gave up the dead that were in them." This physical resurrection takes place when " the thousand years " are "finished " (verse 5).

This interpretation suggests a possible way of reconciling the premillenarian and postmillenarian theories, without sacrificing any of the truth in either of them. Christ may come again, at the beginning of the millennium, in a spiritual way, and his saints may reign with him spiritually, in the wonderful advances of his kingdom ; while the visible, literal coming may take place at the end of the thousand years. Dorner's view is postmillennial, in this sense, that the visible coming of Christ will be after the thousand years. Hengstenberg curiously regards the millennium as having begun in the Middle Ages (800 — 1800 A. D.). This strange view of an able interpreter, as well as the extraordinary diversity of explanations given by others, convinces us that no exegete has yet found the key to the mysteries of the Apocalypse. Until we know whether the preaching of the gospel in the whole world (Mat. 24 : 14) is to be a preaching to nations as a whole, or to each individual in each nation, we cannot determine whether the millennium has already begun, or whether it is yet far in the future.

The millennium then is to be the culmination of the work of the Holy Spirit, a universal revival of religion, a nation born in a day, the kings of the earth bringing their glory and honor into the city of God. A. J. Gordon, Ministry of the Spirit, 211 — " After the present elective work of the Spirit has been completed, there will come a time of universal blessing, when the Spirit shall literally be poured out upon all flesh, when that which is perfect shall come and that which is in part shall be done away. . . . . The early rain of the Spirit was at Pentecost ; the latter rain will be at the Parousia."

A. H. Strong, Sermon before the Baptist World Congress, London, July 12, 1905 — " Let us expect the speedy spiritual coming of the Lord. I believe in an ultimate literal and visible coming of Christ in the clouds of heaven to raise the dead, to summon all men to the judgment, and to wind up the present dispensation. But I believe that this visible and literal coming of Christ must be preceded, and prepared for, by his invisible and spiritual coming and by a resurrection of faith and love in the hearts of his people. 'This is the first resurrection ' (Rev. 20 : 5). I read in Scripture of a spiritual second coming that precedes the literal, an inward revelation of Christ to his people, a restraining of the powers of darkness, a mighty augmentation of the forces of righteousness, a turning to the Lord of men and nations, such as the world has not yet seen. I believe in a long reign of Christ on earth, in which his saints shall in spirit be caught up with him, and shall sit with him upon his throne, even though this muddy vesture of decay com' passes them about, and the time of their complete glorification has not yet come. Let us hasten the coming of the day of God by our faith and prayer. ' When the Son of man cometh, shall he find faith on the earth ? ' (Luke 18 : 8). Let him find faith, at least in us. Our faith can certainly secure the coming of the Lord into our hearts. Let us expect that Christ will be revealed in us, as of old he was revealed in the Apostle Paul."

Our own interpretation of Rev. 20 : 1-10, was first given, for substance, by Whitby. He was followed by Vitringa and Faber. For a fuller elaboration of it, see Brown, Second Advent, 206-259 ; Hodge, Outlines of Theology, 447-453. For the postmillennial view generally, see Kendrick, in Bap. Quar., Jan. 1870 ; New Englander, 1874 : 356 ; 1879 : 47-49, 114-147 ; Pepper, in Bap. Rev., 1880 : 15 ; Princeton Review, March, 1879 : 415-434 ; Presb. Rev., 1883 : 221-252 ; Bib. Sac., 15 : 381, 625 ; 17 : 111 ; Harris, Kingdom of Christ, 220-237 ; Waldegrave, Bampton Lectures for 1854, on the Millennium ; Neander, Planting and Training, 526, 527 ; Cowles, Dissertation on Premillennial Advent, in Com. on Jeremiah and Ezekiel; Weiss, Premillennial Advent; Crosby, Second Advent; Fairbairn on Prophecy, 432-480; Woods, Works. 3:267; Abp. Whately, Essays on Future State. For the premillennial view, see Elliott, Horæ Apocalypticæ, 4:140-196; William Kelly, Advent of Christ Premillennial; Taylor, Voice of the Church on the Coming and Kingdom of the Redeemer; Litch, Christ Yet to Come.

IV. THE RESURRECTION.

While the Scriptures describe the impartation of new life to the soul in regeneration as a spiritual resurrection, they also declare that, at the second coming of Christ, there shall be a resurrection of the body, and a reunion of the body to the soul from which, during the intermediate state, it has been separated. Both the just and the unjust shall have part in the resurrection. To the just, it shall be a resurrection unto life; and the body shall be a body like Christ's — a body fitted for the uses of the sanctified spirit. To the unjust, it shall be a resurrection unto condemnation; and analogy would seem to indicate that, here also, the outward form will fitly represent the inward state of the soul — being corrupt and deformed as is the soul which inhabits it. Those who are living at Christ's coming shall receive spiritual bodies without passing through death. As the body after corruption and dissolution, so the outward world after destruction by fire, shall be rehabilitated and fitted for the abode of the saints.

Passages describing a spiritual resurrection are: John 5:24-27, especially 25 —"The hour cometh, and now is, when the dead shall hear the voice of the Son of God; and they that hear shall live"; Rom. 6:4, 5 — "as Christ was raised from the dead through the glory of the Father, so we also might walk in newness of life. For if we have become united with him by the likeness of his death, we shall be also by the likeness of his resurrection"; Eph. 2:1, 5, 6 —"And you did he make alive when ye were dead through your trespasses and sins .... even when we were dead through our trespasses, made us alive together with Christ .... and raised us up with him, and made us to sit with him in the heavenly places, in Christ Jesus"; 5:14 —"Awake, thou that sleepest, and arise from the dead, and Christ shall shine upon thee." Phil. 3:10 —"that I may know him, and the power of his resurrection"; Col. 2:12 '3 —"having been buried with him in baptism, wherein ye were also raised with him through faith in the working of God, who raised him from the dead. And you, being dead through your trespasses and the uncircumcision of your flesh, you, I say, did he make alive together with him"; cf. Is. 26:19 —"Thy dead shall live; my dead bodies shall arise. Awake and sing, ye that dwell in the dust; for thy dew is as the dew of herbs, and the earth shall cast forth the dead"; Ez. 37:1-14 — the valley of dry bones: "I will open your graves, and cause you to come up out of your graves, O my people; and I will bring you into the land of Israel."

Passages describing a literal and physical resurrection are: Job 14:12-15 —"So man lieth down and riseth not: Till the heavens be no more, they shall not awake, Nor be raised out of their sleep. Oh that thou wouldest hide me in Sheol, That thou wouldest keep me secret, until thy wrath be past, That thou wouldest appoint me a set time, and remember me! If a man die, shall he live again? All the days of my warfare would I wait, Till my release should come. Thou wouldest call, and I would answer thee: Thou wouldest have a desire to the work of thy hands"; John 5:28, 29 —"the hour cometh, in which all that are in the tombs shall hear his voice and shalt come forth: they that have done good, unto the resurrection of life; and they that have done evil, unto the resurrection of judgment."

Acts 24:15 —"having hope toward God .... that there shall be a resurrection both of the just and unjust"; 1 Cor. 15:13, 17, 22, 42, 51, 52 —"if there is no resurrection of the dead, neither hath Christ been raised .... and if Christ hath not been raised, your faith is vain; ye are yet in your sins .... as in Adam all die, so also in Christ shall all be made alive .... it is sown in corruption: it is raised in incorruption .... We shall not all sleep, but we shall all be changed, in a moment, in the twinkling of an eye, at the last trump: for the trumpet shall sound, and the dead shall be raised incorruptible"; Phil. 3:21 —"who shall fashion anew the body of our humiliation, that it may be conformed to the body of his glory, according to the working whereby he is able even to subject all things unto himself"; 1 Thess. 4:14-16 —"For if we believe that Jesus died and rose again, even so them also that are fallen asleep in Jesus will God bring with him. For this we say unto you by the word of the Lord, that we that are alive, that are left unto the coming of the Lord, shall in no wise precede them that are fallen asleep. For the Lord himself shall descend from heaven, with a shout, with the voice of the archangel, and with the trump of God: and the dead in Christ shall rise first."

2 Pet. 3:7, 10, 13 —"the heavens that now are, and the earth, by the same word have been stored up for fire. being reserved against the day of judgment and destruction of ungodly men .... But the day of the Lord will come as a thief: in the which the heavens shall pass away with a great noise, and the elements shall be dissolved with fervent heat, and the earth and the works that are therein shall be burned up .... But, according to his promise, we look for new heavens and a new earth, wherein dwelleth righteousness"; Rev. 20:13 —"And the sea gave up the dead that were

in it; and death and Hades gave up the dead that were in them"; 21:1, 5—"And I saw a new heaven and a new earth: for the first heaven and the first earth are passed away; and the sea is no more . . . . And he that sitteth on the throne said, Behold, I make all things new."

The smooth face of death with the lost youth restored, and the pure white glow of the marble statue with all passion gone and the lofty and heroic only visible, are indications of what is to be. Art, in its representations alike of the human form, and of an ideal earth and society in landscape and poem, is prophetic of the future, — it suggests the glorious possibilities of the resurrection-morning. Nicoll, Life of Christ : "The river runs through the lake and pursues its way beyond. So the life of faith passes through death and is only purified thereby. As to the body, all that is worth saving will be saved. Other resurrections [such as that of Lazarus] were resurrections to the old conditions of earthly life; the resurrection of Christ was the revelation of new life."

Stevens, Pauline Theology, 357 note—" If we could assume with confidence that the report of Paul's speech before Felix accurately reproduced his language in detail, the apostle's belief in a 'resurrection both of the just and of the unjust' (Acts 24:15) would be securely established : but, in view of the silence of his epistles, this assumption becomes a precarious one. Paul speaks afterwards of 'attaining to the resurrection from the dead' (Phil. 3 :11), as if this did not belong to all." The scepticism of Prof. Stevens seems to us entirely needless and unjustified. It is the blessed resurrection to which Paul would " attain, " and which he has in mind in Philippians, as in 1 Cor. 15 — a fact perfectly consistent with a resurrection of the wicked to "shame and everlasting contempt" (Daniel 12 : 2 ; John 5 : 29).

A. J. Gordon, Ministry of the Spirit, 205, 206 — " The rapture of the saints (1 Thess. 4:17) is the earthly Christ rising to meet the heavenly Christ; the elect church, gathered in the Spirit and named ὁ Χριστός (1 Cor. 12:12), taken up to be united in glory with Christ the head of the church, 'himself the Savior of the body ' (Eph. 5 : 23). It is not by acting upon the body of Christ from without, but by energizing it from within, that the Holy Ghost will effect its glorification. In a word, the Comforter, who on the day of Pentecost came down to form a body out of flesh, will at the Parousia return to heaven in that body, having fashioned it like unto the body of Christ (Phil. 3 : 31). . . . . Here then is where the lines of Christ's ministry terminate, — in sanctification, the perfection of the spirit's holiness; and in resurrection, the perfection of the body's health. "

E. G. Robinson : " Personality is the indestructible principle — not intelligence, else deny that infants have souls. Personality takes to itself a material organization. It is a divinely empowered second cause. This refutes materialism and annihilationism. No one pretends that the individual elements of the body will be raised. The individuality only, the personal identity, will be preserved. The soul is the organific power. Medical practice teaches that merely animal life is a mechanical process, but this is used by a personal power. Materialism, on the contrary, would make the soul the product of the body. Every man, in becoming a Christian, begins the process of resurrection. We do not know *but* resurrection begins at the moment of dissolution, yet we do not know *that* it does. But if Christ arose with identically the same body unchanged, how can his resurrection be a type of ours? Answer: The nature of Christ's resurrection body is an open question."

Upon the subject of the resurrection, our positive information is derived wholly from the word of God. Further discussion of it may be most naturally arranged in a series of answers to objections. The objections commonly urged against the doctrine, as above propounded, may be reduced to two :

1. *The exegetical objection,*— that it rests upon a literalizing of metaphorical language, and has no sufficient support in Scripture. To this we answer :

(a) That, though the phrase " resurrection of the body " does not occur in the New Testament, the passages which describe the event indicate a physical, as distinguished from a spiritual, change (John 5 :28, 29 ; Phil. 3 :21 ; 1 Thess. 4 :13-17). The phrase " spiritual body " (1 Cor. 15 : 44) is a contradiction in terms, if it be understood as signifying 'a body which is simple spirit.' It can only be interpreted as meaning a material organism, perfectly adapted to be the outward expression and vehicle of the purified soul. The purely spiritual interpretation is, moreover, expressly excluded by the apostolic denial that "the resurrection is past already" (2 Tim. 2 : 18), and by the fact that there is a resurrection of the unjust, as well as of the just (Acts 24 : 15).

John 5 : 28, 29 — "all that are in the tombs shall hear his voice, and shall come forth "; Phil. 3 : 21 — " who shall fashion anew the body of our humiliation " ; 1 Thess. 4 : 16, 17 — " For the Lord himself shall descend from heaven, with a shout, with the voice of the archangel, and with the trump of God; and the dead in Christ shall rise first " ; 1 Cor. 15 : 44 — " it is sown a natural [marg.: 'psychical'] body ; it is raised a spiritual body " ; 2 Tim. 2 : 17, 18 — "Hymenæus and Philetus ; men who concerning the truth have erred, saying that the resurrection is past already, and overthrow the faith of some " ; Acts 24 : 15 — " Having hope toward God . . . . that there shall be a resurrection both of the just and the unjust."

In 1 Cor. 15 : 44, the word ψυχικόν, translated "natural" or "psychical," is derived from the Greek word ψυχή, soul, just as the word πνευματικόν, translated "spiritual," is derived from the Greek word πνεῦμα, spirit. And as Paul could not mean to say that this earthly body is composed of soul, neither does he say that the resurrection body is composed of spirit. In other words, these adjectives "psychical" and "spiritual" do not define the material of the respective bodies, but describe those bodies in their relations and adaptations, in their powers and uses. The present body is adapted and designed for the use of the soul ; the resurrection body will be adapted and designed for the use of the spirit.

2 Tim. 2 : 18 — " saying that the resurrection is past already " = undue contempt for the body came to regard the resurrection as a purely spiritual thing (Ellicott). Dr. A. J. Gordon said that the " spiritual body " means " the body spiritualized." E. H. Johnson : " The phrase ' spiritual body ' describes not so much the nature of the body itself, as its relations to the spirit." Savage, Life after Death, 80 — " Resurrection does not mean the raising up of the body, and it does not mean the mere rising of the soul in the moment of death, but a rising again from the prison house of the dead, after going down at the moment of death." D. R. Goodwin, Journ. Soc. Bib. Exegesis, 1881 : 84 — "The spiritual body is body, and not spirit, and therefore must come under the definition of body. If it were to be mere spirit, then every man in the future state would have two spirits — the spirit that he has here and another spirit received at the resurrection."

(b) That the redemption of Christ is declared to include the body as well as the soul (Rom. 8 : 23 ; 1 Cor. 6 : 13-20). The indwelling of the Holy Spirit has put such honor upon the frail mortal tenement which he has made his temple, that God would not permit even this wholly to perish (Rom. 8 : 11 — διὰ τὸ ἐνοικοῦν αὐτοῦ πνεῦμα ἐν ὑμῖν, i. e., because of his indwelling Spirit, God will raise up the mortal body). It is this belief which forms the basis of Christian care for the dead (Phil. 3 : 21 ; cf. Mat. 22 : 32).

Rom. 8 : 23 — " waiting for our adoption, to wit, the redemption of our body " ; 1 Cor. 6 : 13-20 — "Meats for the belly and the belly for meats : but God shall bring to nought both it and them. But the body is not for fornication, but for the Lord ; and the Lord for the body : and God both raised the Lord, and will raise up us through his power . . . . But he that is joined unto the Lord is one spirit . . . . Or know ye not that your body is a temple of the Holy Spirit which is in you, which ye have from God ? . . . . glorify God therefore in your body " ; Rom. 8 : 11 — " But if the Spirit of him that raised up Jesus from the dead dwelleth in you, he that raised up Christ Jesus from the dead shall give life also to your mortal bodies through his Spirit that dwelleth in you " — here the Revised Version follows Tisch., 8th ed., and Westcott and Hort's reading of διὰ τοῦ ἐνοικοῦντος αὐτοῦ πνεύματος. Tregelles, Tisch., 7th ed., and Meyer, have διὰ τὸ ἐνοικοῦν αὐτοῦ πνεῦμα, and this reading we regard as, on the whole, the best supported. Phil. 3 : 21 — " shall fashion anew the body of our humiliation."

Dr. R. D. Hitchcock, in South Church Lectures, 338, says that " there is no Scripture declaration of the resurrection of the flesh, nor even of the resurrection of the body." While this is literally true, it conveys a false idea. The passages just cited foretell a quickening of our mortal bodies, a raising of them up, a changing of them into the likeness of Christ's body. Dorner, Eschatology : " The New Testament is not contented with a bodiless immortality. It is opposed to a naked spiritualism, and accords completely with a deeper philosophy which discerns in the body, not merely the sheath or garment of the soul, but a side of the person belonging to his full idea, his mirror and organ, of the greatest importance for his activity and history."

Christ's proof of the resurrection in Mat. 22 : 32 — "God is not the God of the dead, but of the living "— has for its basis this very assumption that soul and body belong normally together, and that, since they are temporally separated in the case of the saints who live with God, Abraham, Isaac, and Jacob shall rise again. The idealistic philosophy of thirty years ago led to a contempt of the body ; the recent materialism has done at least this service, that it has reasserted the claims of the body to be a proper part of man.

(c) That the nature of Christ's resurrection, as literal and physical, determines the nature of the resurrection in the case of believers (Luke 24 : 36 ; John 20 : 27). As, in the case of Christ, the same body that was laid in the tomb was raised again, although possessed of new and surprising powers, so the Scriptures intimate, not simply that the saints shall have bodies, but that these bodies shall be in some proper sense an outgrowth or transformation of the very bodies that slept in the dust (Dan. 12 : 2 ; 1 Cor. 15 : 53, 54). The denial of the resurrection of the body, in the case of believers, leads naturally to a denial of the reality of Christ's resurrection (1 Cor. 15 : 13).

Luke 24 : 39 — "See my hands and my feet, that it is I myself: handle me, and see ; for a spirit hath not flesh and bones, as ye behold me having " ; John 20 : 27 — "Then saith he to Thomas, Reach hither thy finger, and see my hands ; and reach hither thy hand, and put it into my side : and be not faithless, but believing " ; Dan. 12 : 2 — "And many of them that sleep in the dust of the earth shall awake, some to everlasting life, and some to shame and everlasting contempt " ; 1 Cor. 15 : 53, 54 — "For this corruptible must put on incorruption, and this mortal must put on immortality. But when this corruption shall have put on incorruption, and this mortal shall have put on immortality, then shall come to pass the saying that is written, Death is swallowed up in victory " ; 13 — "But if there is no resurrection of the dead, neither hath Christ been raised."

Sadducean materialism and Gnostic dualism, which last held matter to be evil, both denied the resurrection. Paul shows that to deny it is to deny that Christ rose ; since, if it were impossible in the case of his followers, it must have been impossible in his own case. As believers, we are vitally connected with him ; and his resurrection could not have taken place without drawing in its train the resurrection of all of us. Having denied that Christ rose, where is the proof that he is not still under the bond and curse of death ? Surely then our preaching is vain. Paul's epistle to the Corinthians was written before the Gospels ; and is therefore, as Hanna says, the earliest written account of the resurrection. Christ's transfiguration was a prophecy of his resurrection.

S. S. Times, March 22, 1902 : 161 — "The resurrection of Jesus was not a mere rising again, like that of Lazarus and the son of the widow of Nain. He came forth from the tomb so changed that he was not at once or easily recognized, and was possessed of such new and surprising powers that he seemed to be pure spirit, no longer subject to the conditions of his natural body. So he was the "first-fruits" of the resurrection-harvest (1 Cor. 15 : 20). Our resurrection, in like manner, is to involve a change from a corruptible body to an incorruptible, from a psychical to a spiritual."

(d) That the accompanying events, as the second coming and the judgment, since they are themselves literal, imply that the resurrection is also literal.

Rom. 8 : 19-23 — "For the earnest expectation of the creation waiteth for the revealing of the sons of God . . . . the whole creation groaneth and travaileth in pain together until now . . . . even we ourselves groan within ourselves, waiting for our adoption, to wit, the redemption of our body " — here man's body is regarded as a part of nature, or the "creation," and as partaking in Christ of its deliverance from the curse ; Rev. 21 : 4, 5 — "he shall wipe away every tear from their eyes ; and death shall be no more . . . . And he that sitteth on the throne said, Behold, I make all things new " — a declaration applicable to the body, the seat of pain and the avenue of temptation, as well as to outward nature. See Hanna, The Resurrection, 28 ; Fuller, Works, 3 : 291 ; Boston, Fourfold State, in Works, 8 : 271-289. On Olshausen's view of immortality as inseparable from body, see Aids to the Study of German Theology, 63. On resurrection of the flesh, see Jahrbuch f. d. Theol., 1 : 289-317.

2. *The scientific objection.*— This is threefold :

(a) That a resurrection of the particles which compose the body at death is impossible, since they enter into new combinations, and not unfrequently become parts of other bodies which the doctrine holds to be raised at the same time.

We reply that the Scripture not only does not compel us to hold, but it distinctly denies, that all the particles which exist in the body at death are present in the resurrection-body (1 Cor. 15 : 37 — οὐ τὸ σῶμα τὸ γενησόμενον : 50). The Scripture seems only to indicate a certain physical connection between the new and the old, although the nature of this connection is not revealed. So long as the physical connection is maintained, it is not necessary to suppose that even a germ or particle that belonged to the old body exists in the new.

1 Cor. 15 : 37, 38 — "that which thou sowest, thou sowest not the body that shall be, but a bare grain, it may chance of wheat, or of some other kind; but God giveth it a body even as it pleased him, and to each seed a body of its own." Jerome tells us that the risen saints "habent dentes, ventrem, genitalia, et tamen nec cibis nec uxoribus indigent." This view of the resurrection is exposed to the objection mentioned above. Pollok's Course of Time represented the day of resurrection as a day on which the limbs that had been torn asunder on earth hurtled through the air to join one another once more. The amputated arm that has been buried in China must traverse thousands of miles to meet the body of its former owner, as it rose from the place of its burial in England.

There are serious difficulties attending this view. The bodies of the dead fertilized the field of Waterloo. The wheat grown there has been ground and made into bread, and eaten by thousands of living men. Particles of one human body have become incorporated with the bodies of many others. " The Avon to the Severn runs, The Severn to the sea, And Wycliffe's dust shall spread abroad, Wide as the waters be." Through the clouds and the rain, particles of Wycliffe's body may have entered into the water which other men have drunk from their wells and fountains. There is a propagation of disease by contagion, or the transmission of infinitesimal germs from one body to another, sometimes by infection of the living from contact with the body of a friend just dead. In these various ways, the same particle might, in the course of history, enter into the constitution of a hundred living men. How can this one particle, at the resurrection, be in a hundred places at the same time? " Like the woman who had seven husbands, the same matter may belong in succession to many bodies, for ' they all had it ' " (Smyth). The cannibal and his victim cannot both possess the same body at the resurrection. The Providence Journal had an article entitled : " Who ate Roger Williams ? " When his remains were exhumed, it was found that one large root of an apple tree followed the spine, divided at the thighs, and turned up at the toes of Roger Williams. More than one person had eaten its apples. This root may be seen to-day in the cabinet of Brown University.

These considerations have led some, like Origen, to call the doctrine of a literal resurrection of the flesh " the foolishness of beggarly minds," and to say that resurrection may be only " the gathering round the spirit of new materials, and the vitalizing them into a new body by the spirit's God-given power " ; see Newman Smyth, Old Faiths in a New Light, 349-391; Porter, Human Intellect, 39. But this view seems as great an extreme as that from which it was a reaction. It gives up all idea of unity between the new and the old. If my body were this instant annihilated, and if then, an hour hence, God should create a second body, precisely like the present, I could not call it the same with the present body, even though it were animated by the same informing soul, and that soul had maintained an uninterrupted existence between the time of the annihilation of the first body and the creation of the second. So, if the body laid in the tomb were wholly dissipated among the elements, and God created at the end of the world a wholly new body, it would be impossible for Paul to say : "this corruptible must put on incorruption " (1 Cor. 15:53), or : "it is sown in dishonor; it is raised in glory " (verse 43). In short, there is a physical connection between the old and the new, which is intimated by Scripture, but which this theory denies.

Paul himself gives us an illustration which shows that his view was midway between the two extremes: "that which thou sowest, thou sowest not the body that shall be " (1 Cor. 15 : 37). On the one hand, the wheat that springs up does not contain the precise particles, perhaps does not contain any particles, that were in the seed. On the other hand, there has been a continous physical connection between the seed sown and the ripened grain at the harvest. If the seed had been annihilated, and then ripe grain created, we could not speak of identity between the one and the other. But, because there has been a constant flux, the old particles pressed out by new, and these new in their turn succeeded by others that take their places, we can say: "the wheat has come up." We bury grain in order to increase it. The resurrection-body will be the same with the body laid away in the earth, in the same sense as the living stalk of grain is identical with the seed from which it germinated. "This mortal must put on immortality" = not the immortal spirit put on an immortal body, but the mortal body put on immortality, the corruptible body put on incorruption (1 Cor. 15:53). "Ye know not the Scriptures, nor the power of God" (Mark 12:24), says our Lord; and Paul asks: "Why is it judged incredible with you, if God doth raise the dead?" (Acts 26:8).

Or, to use another illustration nearer to the thing we desire to illustrate: My body is the same that it was ten years ago, although physiologists declare that every particle of the body is changed, not simply once in seven years, but once in a single year. Life is preserved only by the constant throwing off of dead matter and the introduction of new. There is indeed a unity of consciousness and personality, without which I should not be able to say at intervals of years: "this body is the same; this body is mine." But a physical connection between the old and the new is necessary in addition.

The nails of the hands are renewed in less than four months, or about twenty-one times in seven years. They grow to full length, an average of seven twelfths of an inch, in from 121 to 138 days. Young people grow them more rapidly, old people more slowly. In a man of 21, it took 126 days; in a man of 67, it took 244; but the average was a third of a year. A Baptist pastor attempted to prove that he was a native of South Carolina though born in another state, upon the ground that the body he brought with him from Tennessee had exchanged its physical particles for matter taken from South Carolina. Two dentists, however, maintained that he still had the same teeth which he owned in Tennessee seven years before, there being no circulation in the enamel. Should we then say: Every particle of the body has changed, except the enamel of the teeth?

Pope's Martinus Scriblerus: "Sir John Cutler had a pair of black worsted stockings which his maid darned so often with silk that they became at last a pair of silk stockings." Adeney, in Christianity and Evolution, 122, 123—"Herod's temple was treated as identical with the temple that Haggai knew, because the rebuilding was gradual, and was carried on side by side with the demolition of the several parts of the old structure." The ocean wave travels around the world and is the same wave; but it is never in two consecutive seconds composed of the same particles of water.

The North River is the same to-day that it was when Hendrick Hudson first discovered it; yet not a particle of its current, nor the surface of the banks which that current touches now, is the same that it was then. Two things make the present river identical with the river of the past. The first is, that the same formative principle is at work,—the trend of the banks is the same, and there is the same general effect in the flow and direction of the waters drained from a large area of country. The second is, the fact that, ever since Hendrick Hudson's time, there has been a physical connection, old particles in continuous succession having been replaced by new.

So there are two things requisite to make our future bodies one with the bodies we now inhabit: first, that the same formative principle be at work in them; and secondly, that there be some sort of physical connection between the body that now is and the body that shall be. What that physical connection is, it is vain to speculate. We only teach that, though there may not be a single material particle in the new that was present in the old, there yet will be such a physical connection that it can be said: "the new has grown out of the old"; "that which was in the grave has come forth"; "this mortal has put on immortality."

(b) That a resurrection-body, having such a remote physical connection with the present body, cannot be recognized by the inhabiting soul or by other witnessing spirits as the same with that which was laid in the grave.

To this we reply that bodily identity does not consist in absolute sameness of particles during the whole history of the body, but in the organizing force, which, even in the flux and displacement of physical particles, makes the old the basis of the new, and binds both together in the unity of a single consciousness. In our recognition of friends, moreover, we are not wholly dependent, even in this world, upon our perception of bodily form;

and we have reason to believe that in the future state there may be methods of communication far more direct and intuitive than those with which we are familiar here.

Cf. Mat. 17 : 3, 4 — "And behold, there appeared unto them Moses and Elijah talking with him. And Peter answered, and said unto Jesus, Lord, it is good for us to be here : if thou wilt, I will make here three tabernacles ; one for thee, and one for Moses, and one for Elijah " — here there is no mention of information given to Peter as to the names of the celestial visitants ; it would seem that, in his state of exalted sensibility, he at once knew them. The recent proceedings of the English Society for Psychical Research seem to indicate the possibility of communication between two minds without physical intermediaries. Hudson, Scientific Demonstration of a Future Life, 294, 29ɔ, holds that telepathy is the means of communication in the future state.

G. S. Fullerton, Sameness and Identity, 6, 32, 67 — "Heracleitus of Ephesus declared it impossible to enter the same river twice. Cratylus replied that the same river could not be entered once. . . . . The kinds of sameness are : 1. Thing same *with itself* at any one instant ; 2. Same pain to-day I felt yesterday = a *like* pain ; 3. I see the same tree at different times = two or more percepts represent the same object ; 4. Two plants belonging to the same *class* are called the same ; 5. Memory gives us the same object that we formerly perceived ; but the object is not the past, it is the *memory-image* which represents it ; 6. Two men perceive the same object = they have like percepts, while both percepts are only representative of the same object ; 7. External thing same with its representative in consciousness, or with the substance or noumenon supposed to underlie it."

Ladd, Philosophy of Mind, 153, 255 — "What is called 'remaining the same,' in the case of all organic beings is just this,— remaining faithful to some immanent idea, while undergoing a great variety of changes in the pursuit, as it were, of the idea. . . . . Self-consciousness and memory are themselves processes of becoming. The mind that does not change, in the way of growth, has no claim to be called mind. One cannot be conscious of changes without also being conscious of being the very being that is changed When he loses this consciousness, we say that ' he has lost his mind.' Amid changes of its ideas the ego remains permanent because it is held within limits by the power of some immanent idea. . . . . Our bodies as such have only a formal existence. They are a stream in constant flow and are ever changing. My body is only a temporary loan from Nature, to be repaid at death."

With regard to the meaning of the term "identity," as applied to material things, see Porter, Human Intellect, 631 — "Here the substance is called the same, by a loose analogy taken from living agents and their gradual accretion and growth." The Euphrates is the same stream that flowed, "When high in Paradise By the four rivers the first roses blew," even though after that time the flood, or deluge, stopped its flow and obliterated all the natural features of the landscape. So this flowing organism which we call the body may be the same, after the deluge of death has passed away.

A different and less satisfactory view is presented in Dorner's Eschatology : "Identity involves : 1. Plastic form, which for the earthly body had its moulding principle in the soul. That principle could effect nothing permanent in the intermediate state ; but with the spiritual consummation of the soul, it attains the full power which can appropriate to itself the heavenly body, accompanied by a cosmical process, made like Christ. 2. Appropriation, from the world of elements, of what it needs. The elements into which everything bodily of earth is dissolved, are an essentially uniform mass, like an ocean ; and it is indifferent what parts of this are assigned to each individual man. The whole world of substance, which makes the constant change of substance possible, is made over to humanity as a common possession (Acts 4 : 32 —'not one of them said that aught of the things which he possessed was his own ; but they had all things common ')."

(*c*) That a material organism can only be regarded as a hindrance to the free activity of the spirit, and that the assumption of such an organism by the soul, which, during the intermediate state, had been separated from the body, would indicate a decline in dignity and power rather than a progress.

We reply that we cannot estimate the powers and capacities of matter, when brought by God into complete subjection to the spirit. The bodies of the saints may be more ethereal than the air, and capable of swifter motion than the light, and yet be material in their substance. That the soul, clothed with its spiritual body, will have more exalted powers and enjoy a more complete felicity than would be possible while it maintained a purely spiritual existence, is evident from the fact that Paul represents the culmination of the soul's blessedness as occurring, not at death, but at the resurrection of the body.

Rom. 8 : 23 —"waiting for our adoption, to wit, the redemption of our body "; 2 Cor. 5 : 4 —"not for that we would be unclothed, but that we would be clothed upon, that what is mortal may be swallowed up of life "; Phil. 3 : 11 —" if by any means I may attain unto the resurrection from the dead." Even Ps. 86 : 11 —"Unite my heart to fear thy name "—may mean the collecting of all the powers of the body as well as soul. In this respect for the body, as a normal part of man's being, Scripture is based upon the truest philosophy. Plotinus gave thanks that he was not tied to an immortal body, and refused to have his portrait taken, because the body was too contemptible a thing to have its image perpetuated. But this is not natural, nor is it probably anything more than a whim or affectation. Eph. 5 : 29 —" no man ever hated his own flesh ; but nourisheth and cherisheth it." What we desire is not the annihilation of the body, but its perfection.

Renouf, Hibbert Lectures, 188 —" In the Egyptian Book of the Dead, the soul reunites itself to the body, with the assurance that they shall never again be separated." McCosh, Intuitions, 213 —"The essential thing about the resurrection is the development, out of the dead body, of an organ for the communion and activity of the spiritual life." Ebrard, Dogmatik, 2 : 226-234, has interesting remarks upon the relation of the resurrection-body to the present body. The essential difference he considers to be this, that whereas, in the present body, matter is master of the spirit, in the resurrection-body spirit will be the master of matter, needing no reparation by food, and having control of material laws. Ebrard adds striking speculations with regard to the glorified body of Christ.

A. J. Gordon, Ministry of the Spirit, 126 —" *Now* the body bears the spirit, a slow chariot whose wheels are often disabled, and whose swiftest motion is but labored and tardy. *Then* the spirit will bear the body, carrying it as on wings of thought whithersoever it will. The Holy Ghost, by his divine inworking will, has completed in us the divine likeness, and perfected over us the divine dominion. The human body will now be in sovereign subjection to the human spirit, and the human spirit to the divine Spirit, and God will be all in all." Newman Smyth, Place of Death in Evolution, 112 —" Weismann maintains that the living germ not only persists and is potentially immortal, but also that under favorable conditions it seems capable of surrounding itself with a new body. If a vital germ can do this, why not a spiritual germ ?" Two martyrs were led to the stake. One was blind, the other lame. As the fires kindled, the latter exclaimed : " Courage, brother ! this fire will cure us both ! "

We may sum up our answers to objections, and may at the same time throw light upon the doctrine of the resurrection, by suggesting four principles which should govern our thinking with regard to the subject, — these namely : 1. Body is in continual flux ; 2. Since matter is but the manifestation of God's mind and will, body is plastic in God's hands ; 3. The soul in complete union with God may be endowed with the power of God ; 4. Soul determines body, and not body soul, as the materialist imagines.

Ice, the flowing stream, the waterfall with the rainbow upon it, steam with its power to draw the railway train or to burst the boiler of the locomotive, are all the same element in varied forms, and they are all *material.* Wundt regards physical development, not as the cause, but as the effect, of psychical development. Aristotle defines the soul as "the prime entelechy of the living body." Swedenborg regarded each soul here as fashioning its own spiritual body, either hideous or lovely. Spenser, A Hymne to Beautie : " For of the soul the body form doth take, For soul is form, and doth the body make." Wordsworth, Sonnet 36, Afterthought : " Far backward, Duddon, as I cast my eyes, I see what was, and is, and will abide ; Still glides the stream, and shall not cease to glide ; The Form remains, the Function never dies "; The Primrose of the Rock : " Sin-blighted as we are, we too, The reasoning sons of men, From one oblivious winter called, Shall rise and breathe again, And in eternal summer lose Our three-score years and ten. To humbleness of heart descends This prescience from on high, The faith that elevates the just Before and when they die, And makes each soul a separate heaven, A court for Deity." Robert Browning, Asolando: "One who never turned his back, but marched breastforward; Never doubted clouds would break; Never dreamed, though right were worsted, Wrong would triumph; Held we fall to rise, are baffled to fight better, Sleep to wake." Mrs. Browning: "God keeps a niche In heaven to hold our idols, and albeit He broke them to our faces and denied That our close kisses should impair their white, I know we shall behold them raised, complete, The dust shook off, their beauty glorified."

On the spiritual body as possibly evolved by will, see Harris, Philos. Basis of Theism, 386. On the nature of the resurrection-body, see Burnet, State of the Departed, chaps. 3 and 8 ; Cudworth, Intell. System, 3 : 310 *sq.* ; Splittgerber, Tod, Fortleben and Auferstehung. On the doctrine of the Resurrection among the Egyptians, see Dr. Howard Osgood, in Hebrew Student, Feb. 1885 ; among the Jews, see Gröbler, in Studien und Kritiken, 1879 : Heft 4 ; DeWünsche, in Jahrbuch f. prot. Theol., 1880 : Heft 2 and 4 ; Revue Théologique, 1881 : 1-17. For the view that the resurrection is wholly spiritual and takes place at death, see Willmarth, in Bap. Quar., October, 1868, and April, 1870 ; Ladd, in New Englander, April, 1874 ; Crosby, Second Advent.

On the whole subject, see Hase, Hutterus Redivivus, 280 ; Herzog, Encyclop., art.: Auferstehung ; Goulburn, Bampton Lectures for 1850, on the Resurrection ; Cox, The Resurrection ; Neander, Planting and Training, 479-487, 524-526 ; Naville, La Vie Éternelle, 253, 254 ; Delitzsch, Bib. Psychologie, 453-463 ; Moorhouse, Nature and Revelation, 87-112 ; Unseen Universe, 33 ; Hovey, in Baptist Quarterly, Oct. 1867 ; Westcott, Revelation of the Risen Lord, and in Contemporary Review, vol. 30 ; R. W. Macan, Resurrection of Christ ; Cremer, Beyond the Grave.

V. THE LAST JUDGMENT.

While the Scriptures represent all punishment of individual transgressors and all manifestations of God's vindicatory justice in the history of nations as acts or processes of judgment, they also intimate that these temporal judgments are only partial and imperfect, and that they are therefore to be concluded with a final and complete vindication of God's righteousness. This will be accomplished by making known to the universe the characters of all men, and by awarding to them corresponding destinies.

Passages describing temporal or spiritual judgment are : Ps. 9 : 7 —" He hath prepared his throne for judgment " ; Is. 26 : 9 —" when thy judgments are in the earth, the inhabitants of the world learn righteousness " Mat. 16 : 27, 28 —" For the Son of man shall come in the glory of his Father with his angels ; and then shall he render unto every man according to his deeds. Verily I say unto you, There be some of them that stand here, who shall in no wise taste of death, till they see the Son of man coming in his kingdom " ; John 3 : 18, 19 —" he that believeth not hath been judged already, because he hath not believed on the name of the only begotten Son of God. And this is the judgment, that the light is come into the world, and men loved the darkness rather than the light ; for their works were evil " ; 9 : 39 — 'For judgment came I into this world, that they that see not may see ; and that they that see may become blind ' ; 12 : 31 —" Now is the judgment of this world : now shall the prince of this world be cast out."

Passages describing the final judgment are : Mat. 25 : 31-46 —" But when the Son of man shall come in his glory, and all the angels with him, then shall he sit on the throne of his glory : and before him shall be gathered all the nations : and he shall separate them one from another, as the shepherd separateth the sheep from the goats . . . . " Acts 17 : 31 —" he hath appointed a day, in which he will judge the world in righteousness by the man whom he hath ordained ; whereof he hath given assurance unto all men, in that he hath raised him from the dead " ; Rom. 2 : 16 —" in the day when God shall judge the secrets of men, according to my gospel, by Jesus Christ " ; 2 Cor. 5 : 10 —" For we must all be made manifest before the judgment-seat of Christ ; that each one may receive the things done in the body, according to what he hath done, whether it be good or bad " ; Heb. 9 : 27, 28 —" And inasmuch as it is appointed unto men once to die, and after this cometh judgment ; so Christ also, having been once offered to bear the sins of many, shall appear a second time, apart from sin, to them that wait for him, unto salvation " ; Rev. 20 : 12 —" And I saw the dead, the great and the small, standing before the throne ; and books were opened : and another book was opened, which is the book of life : and the dead were judged out of the things which were written in the books, according to their works."

Delitzsch : " The fall of Jerusalem was the day of the Lord, the bloody and fiery dawn of the last great day — the day of days, the ending-day of all days, the settling day of all days, the day of the promotion of time into eternity, the day which for the church breaks through and breaks off the night of this present world." E. G. Robinson : " Judgment begins here. The callousing of conscience in this life is a penal infliction. Punishment begins in this life and is carried on in the next. We have no right to assert that there are no positive inflictions, but, if there are none, still every word of Scripture threatening would stand. There is no *day* of judgment or of resurrection all at one time. Judgment is an eternal process. The angels in 2 Pet. 2 : 4 — 'cast . . . . down to hell' — suffer the self-perpetuating consequences of transgression. . . . . Man is being judged every day. Every man honest with himself knows where he is going to. Those who are not honest with themselves are playing a trick, and, if they are not careful, they will get a trick played on them.''

1. *The nature of the final judgment.*

The final judgment is not a spiritual, invisible, endless process, identical with God's providence in history, but is an outward and visible event, occurring at a definite period in the future. This we argue from the following considerations :

(*a*) The judgment is something for which the evil are "reserved" (2 Peter 2 : 4, 9) ; something to be expected in the future (Acts 24 : 25 ; Heb. 10 : 27) ; something after death (Heb. 9 : 27) ; something for which the resurrection is a preparation (John 5 : 29).

2 Pet. 2 : 4, 9 — "God spared not angels when they sinned, but cast them down to hell . . . . reserved unto judgment . . . . the Lord knoweth how . . . . to keep the unrighteous unto punishment unto the day of judgment" ; Acts 24 : 25 — "as he reasoned of righteousness, and self-control, and the judgment to come, Felix was terrified" ; Heb. 10 : 27 — "a certain fearful expectation of judgment" ; 9 : 27 — "it is appointed unto men once to die, and after this cometh judgment" ; John 5 : 29 — "the resurrection of judgment."

(*b*) The accompaniments of the judgment, such as the second coming of Christ, the resurrection, and the outward changes of the earth, are events which have an outward and visible, as well as an inward and spiritual, aspect. We are compelled to interpret the predictions of the last judgment upon the same principle.

John 5 : 28, 29 — "Marvel not at this : for the hour cometh, in which all that are in the tombs shall hear his voice, and shall come forth ; they that have done good, unto the resurrection of life ; and they that have done evil, unto the resurrection of judgment" ; 2 Pet. 3 : 7, 10 — "the day of judgment . . . . the day of the Lord . . . . in the which the heavens shall pass away with a great noise, and the elements shall be dissolved with fervent heat" ; 2 Thess. 1 : 7, 8, 2 : 10 — "the revelation of the Lord Jesus from heaven with the angels of his power in flaming fire, rendering vengeance to them that know not God . . . . when he shall come . . . . in that day."

(*c*) God's justice, in the historical and imperfect work of judgment, needs a final outward judgment as its vindication. "A perfect justice must judge, not only moral units, but moral aggregates ; not only the particulars of life, but the life as a whole." The crime that is hidden and triumphant here, and the goodness that is here maligned and oppressed, must be brought to light and fitly recompensed. "Otherwise man is a Tantalus — longing but never satisfied" ; and God's justice, of which his outward administration is the expression, can only be regarded as approximate.

Renouf, Hibbert Lectures, 194 — "The Egyptian Book of the Dead represents the deceased person as standing in the presence of the goddess Maät, who is distinguished by the ostrich-feather on her head ; she holds the sceptre in one hand and the symbol of life in the other. The man's heart, which represents his entire moral nature, is being weighed in the balance in the presence of Osiris, seated upon his throne as judge of the dead." Rationalism believes in only present and temporal judgment ; and this it regards as but the reaction of natural law : "Die Weltgeschichte ist das Weltgericht, — the world's history is the world's judgment" (Schiller, Resignation). But there is an inner connection between present, temporal, spiritual judgments, and the final, outward, complete judgment of God. Nero's murder of his mother was not the only penalty of his murder of Germanicus.

Dorner : "With Christ's appearance, faith sees that the beginning of the judgment and of the end has come. Christians are a prophetic race. Without judgment, Christianity would involve a sort of dualism: evil and good would be of equal might and worth. Christianity cannot always remain a historic principle *alongside* of the contrary principle of evil. It is the only reality." God will show or make known his righteousness with regard to: (1) the disparity of lots among men; (2) the prosperity of the wicked; (3) the permission of moral evil in general; (4) the consistency of atonement with justice. "The συντέλεια τοῦ αἰῶνος ('end of the world,' Mat. 13:39) = stripping hostile powers of their usurped might, revelation of their falsity and impotence, consigning them to the past. Evil shall be utterly cut off, given over to its own nothingness, or made a subordinate element."

A great statesman said that what he dreaded for his country was not the day of judgment, but the day of no judgment. "Jove strikes the Titans down, Not when they first begin their mountain-piling, But when another rock would crown their work." R. W. Emerson: "God said: I am tired of kings, I suffer them no more; Up to my ears the morning brings The outrage of the poor." Royce, The World and the Individual, 2:384 *sq.* — "If God's life is given to free individual souls, then God's life can be given also to free nations and to a free race of men. There may be an apostasy of a family, nation, race, and a judgment of each according to their deeds."

The Expositor, March, 1898 — "It is claimed that we are being judged now, that laws execute themselves, that the system of the universe is automatic, that there is no need for future retribution. But all ages have agreed that there is not here and now any sufficient vindication of the principle of eternal justice. The mills of the gods grind slowly. Physical immorality is not proportionately punished. Deterioration is not an adequate penalty. Telling a second lie does not recompense the first. Punishment includes pain, and here is no pain. That there is not punishment here is due, not to law, but to grace."

Denney, Studies in Theology, 240, 241 — "The dualistic conception of an endless suspense, in which good and evil permanently balance each other and contest with each other the right to inherit the earth, is virtually atheistic, and the whole Bible is a protest against it. . . . It is impossible to overestimate the power of the final judgment, as a motive, in the primitive church. On almost every page of St. Paul, for instance, we see that he lives in the presence of it; he lets the awe of it descend into his heart to keep his conscience quick."

2. *The object of the final judgment.*

The object of the final judgment is not the ascertainment, but the manifestation, of character, and the assignment of outward condition corresponding to it.

(*a*) To the omniscient Judge, the condition of all moral creatures is already and fully known. The last day will be only "the *revelation* of the righteous judgment of God."

They are inwardly judged when they die, and before they die; they are outwardly judged at the last day: Rom. 2:5, 6 — "treasurest up for thyself wrath in the day of wrath and revelation of the righteous judgment of God; who will render to every man according to his works" — see Meyer on this passage; not "against the day of wrath," but "in the day of wrath" = wrath existing beforehand, but breaking out on that day. 1 Tim. 5:24, 25 — "Some men's sins are evident, going before unto judgment; and some men also they follow after. In like manner also there are good works that are evident; and such as are otherwise cannot be hid"; Rev. 14:13 — "for their works follow with them" — as close companions, into God's presence and judgment (Ann. Par. Bible).

Epitaph: "Hic jacet in expectatione diei supremi . . . . Qualis erat, dies iste indicabit" — "Here lies, in expectation of the last day. . . . . Of what sort he was, that day will show." Shakespeare, Hamlet, 3:3 — "In the corrupted currents of this world Offence's gilded hand may shove by justice. But 't is not so above. There is no shuffling, there the action lies In his true nature; and we ourselves compelled, Even to the teeth and forehead of our faults, To give in evidence"; King John, 4:2 — "Oh, when the last account 'twixt heaven and earth Is to be made, then shall this hand and seal [the warrant for the murder of Prince Arthur] Witness against us to damnation." "Not all your piety nor wit Can lure it [justice] back to cancel half a line, Nor all your tears wash out one word of it."

(5) In the nature of man, there are evidences and preparations for this final disclosure. Among these may be mentioned the law of memory, by which the soul preserves the records of its acts, both good and evil (Luke 16 : 25) ; the law of conscience, by which men involuntarily anticipate punishment for their own sins (Rom. 2 : 15, 16 ; Heb. 10 : 27) ; the law of character, by which every thought and deed makes indelible impress upon the moral nature (Heb. 3 : 8, 15).

The law of memory.—Luke 16 : 25 —"Son, remember!" See Maclaren, Sermons, 1 : 109–122 — Memory (1) will embrace all the events of the past life ; (2) will embrace them all at the same moment ; (3) will embrace them continuously and continually. Memory is a process of self-registry. As every business house keeps a copy of all letters sent or orders issued, so every man retains in memory the record of his sins. The mind is a palimpsest ; though the original writing has been erased, the ink has penetrated the whole thickness of the parchment, and God's chemistry is able to revive it. Hudson, Dem. of Future Life, 212, 213 —"Subjective memory is the retention of all ideas, however superficially they may have been impressed upon the objective mind, and it admits of no variation in different individuals. Recollection is the power of recalling ideas to the mind. This varies greatly. Sir William Hamilton calls the former ' mental latency.'"

The law of conscience.— Rom. 2 : 15, 16 —"they show the work of the law written in their hearts, their conscience bearing witness therewith, and their thoughts one with another accusing or else excusing them ; in the day when God shall judge the secrets of men, according to my gospel, by Jesus Christ" ; Heb. 10 : 27 —"a certain fearful expectation of judgment, and a fierceness of fire which shall devour the adversaries." Goethe said that his writings, taken together, constituted a great confession. Wordsworth, Excursion, III : 579 —" For, like a plague will memory break out, And, in the blank and solitude of things, Upon his spirit, with a fever's strength, Will conscience prey." A man who afterwards became a Methodist preacher was converted in Whitefield's time by a vision of the judgment, in which he saw all men gathered before the throne, and each one coming up to the book of God's law, tearing open his heart before it " as one would tear open the bosom of his shirt," comparing his heart with the things written in the book, and, according as they agreed or disagreed with that standard, either passing triumphant to the company of the blest, or going with howling to the company of the damned. No word was spoken ; the Judge sat silent ; the judgment was one of self-revelation and self-condemnation. See Autobiography of John Nelson (quoted in the Diary of Mrs. Kitty Trevylyan, 207, by Mrs. E. Charles, the author of The Schönberg-Cotta Family).

The law of character.— Heb. 3 : 8, 15 —"Harden not your hearts, as in the provocation, Like as in the day of the trial in the wilderness . . . . To-day, if ye shall hear his voice, Harden not your hearts, as in the provocation." Sin leaves its marks upon the soul ; men become "past feeling" (Eph. 4 : 19). In England, churchmen claim to tell a dissenter by his walk — not a bad sign by which to know a man. God needs only to hold up our characters to show what have been our lives. Sin leaves its scars upon the soul, as truly as lust and hatred leave their marks upon the body. So with the manifestation of the good —"the chivalry that does the right, and disregards The yea and nay of the world. . . . . Expect nor question nor reply At what we figure as God's judgment-bar" (Robert Browning, Ring and Book, 178, 202). Mr. Edison says : "In a few years the world will be just like one big ear ; it will be unsafe to speak in a house till one has examined the walls and the furniture for concealed phonographs." But the world even now is "one big ear", and we ourselves in our characters are writing the books of the judgment. Brooks, Foundations of Zoölogy, 134,135 —" Every part of the material universe contains a permanent record of every change that has taken place therein, and there is also no limit to the power of minds like ours to read and interpret the record."

Draper, Conflict of Science and Religion : " If on a cold polished metal, as a new razor, any object, such as a wafer, be laid, and the metal breathed upon, and when the moisture has had time to disappear, the wafer be thrown off, though now the most critical inspection of the polished surface can discern no trace of any form, if we breathe once more upon it, a spectral image of the wafer comes plainly into view ; and this may be done again and again. Nay, more ; if the polished metal be carefully put aside where nothing can injure its surface, and be kept so for many months, on breathing upon it again, the shadowy form emerges. A shadow never falls upon a wall without leaving thereon a permanent trace, a trace which might be made visible by resorting to proper processes. Upon the walls of our most private apartments, where we think the eye of intrusion is altogether shut out, and our retirement can never be profaned, there exist the vestiges of all our acts."

Babbage, Ninth Bridgewater Treatise, 113-115 —"If we had power to follow and detect the minutest effects of any disturbance, each particle of existing matter would furnish a register of all that has happened. The track of every canoe, of every vessel that has yet disturbed the surface of the ocean, whether impelled by manual force or elemental power, remains forever registered in the future movement of all succeeding particles which may occupy its place. The furrow which it left is indeed filled up by the closing waters, but they draw after them other and larger portions of the surrounding element, and these again, once moved, communicate motion to others in endless succession. The air itself is one vast library, in whose pages are forever written all that man has said or even whispered. There, in their mutable but unerring characters, mixed with the earliest as well as the latest sighs of mortality, stand forever recorded vows unredeemed, promises unfulfilled, perpetuating in the united movements of each particle the testimony of man's changeful will."

(c) Single acts and words, therefore, are to be brought into the judgment only as indications of the moral condition of the soul. This manifestation of all hearts will vindicate not only God's past dealings, but his determination of future destinies.

Mat. 12:36 —"And I say unto you, that every idle word that men shall speak, they shall give account thereof in the day of judgment"; Luke 12:2, 8, 9—"there is nothing covered up, that shall not be revealed; and hid, that shall not be known. . . . . Every one who shall confess me before men, him shall the Son of man also confess before the angels of God : but he that denieth me in the presence of men shall be denied in the presence of the angels of God "; John 3 :18 — "He that believeth on him is not judged: he that believeth not hath been judged already, because he hath not believed on the name of the only begotten Son of God "; 2 Cor. 5:10—"For we must all be made manifest [not : 'must all appear,' as in A. Vers.] before the judgment-seat of Christ."

Even the human judge, in passing sentence, commonly endeavors so to set forth the guilt of the criminal that he shall see his doom to be just. So God will awaken the consciences of the lost, and lead them to pass judgment on themselves. Each lost soul can say as Byron's Manfred said to the fiend that tortured his closing hour: "I have not been thy dupe, nor am thy prey, But was my own destroyer." Thus God's final judgment will be only the culmination of a process of natural selection, by which the unfit are eliminated, and the fit are caused to survive.

O. J. Smith, The Essential Verity of Religion : " Belief in the immortality of the soul and belief in the accountability of the soul are fundamental beliefs in all religion. The origin of the belief in immortality is found in the fact that justice can be established in human affairs only upon the theory that the soul of man is immortal, and the belief that man is accountable for his actions eternally is based upon the conviction that justice should and will be enforced. The central verity in religion therefore is eternal justice. The sense of justice makes us men. Religion has no miraculous origin, — it is born with the awakening of man's moral sense. Friendship and love are based on reciprocity, which is justice. 'Universal justice,' says Aristotle, 'includes all virtues.' " If by justice here is meant the divine justice, implied in the awakening of man's moral sense, we can agree with the above. As we have previously intimated, we regard the belief in immortality as an inference from the intuition of God's existence, and every new proof that God is just strengthens our conviction of immortality.

3. *The Judge in the final judgment.*

God, in the person of Jesus Christ, is to be the judge. Though God is the judge of all (Heb. 12 : 23), yet this judicial activity is exercised through Christ, at the last day, as well as in the present state (John 5 : 22, 27).

Heb. 12:23—"to God the judge of all "; John 5 : 22, 27 —"For neither doth the Father judge any man, but he hath given all judgment unto the Son . . . . and he gave him authority to execute judgment, because he is a son of man." Stevens, Johannine Theology, 349—" Jesus says that he judges no man (John 8:15). He does not personally judge men. His attitude toward men is solely that of Savior. It is rather his work, his word, his truth, which pronounces condemnation against them both here and hereafter. The judgment is that light is come; men's attitude toward the light involves their judgment; the light judges them, or, they judge themselves. . . . . The Savior does not come to judge but to save them ; but, by their rejection of salvation, they turn the saving message itself into a judgment."

This, for three reasons :

(a) Christ's human nature enables men to understand both the law and the love of God, and so makes intelligible the grounds on which judgment is passed.

Whoever says that God is too distant and great to be understood may be pointed to Christ, in whose human life the divine "law appears, drawn out in living characters," and the divine love is manifest, as suffering upon the cross to save men from their sins.

(b) The perfect human nature of Christ, united as it is to the divine, ensures all that is needful in true judgment, viz.: that it be both merciful and just.

Acts 17 : 31 — "he will judge the world in righteousness by the man whom he hath ordained ; whereof he hath given assurance unto all men, in that he hath raised him from the dead."

As F. W. Robertson has shown in his sermon on "The Sympathy of Christ (vol. 1: sermon vii), it is not sin that most sympathizes with sin. Sin blinds and hardens. Only the pure can appreciate the needs of the impure, and feel for them.

(c) Human nature, sitting upon the throne of judgment, will afford convincing proof that Christ has received the reward of his sufferings, and that humanity has been perfectly redeemed. The saints shall "judge the world " only as they are one with Christ.

The lowly Son of man shall sit upon the throne of judgment. And with himself he will join all believers. Mat. 19 : 28 — "ye who have followed me, in the regeneration when the Son of man shall sit on the throne of his glory, ye also shall sit upon twelve thrones, judging the twelve tribes of Israel " ; Luke 22 : 28–30 — " But ye are they that have continued with me in my temptations ; and I appoint unto you a kingdom, even as my Father appointed unto me, that ye may eat and drink at my table in my kingdom ; and ye shall sit on thrones judging the twelve tribes of Israel " ; 1 Cor. 6 : 2, 3 — "know ye not that the saints shall judge the world ? . . . Know ye not that we shall judge angels ? " Rev. 3 : 21 — " He that overcometh, I will give to him to sit down with me in my throne, as I also overcame, and sat down with my Father in his throne."

4: The subjects of the final judgment.

The persons upon whose characters and conduct this judgment shall be passed are of two great classes :

(a) All men — each possessed of body as well as soul, — the dead having been raised, and the living having been changed.

1 Cor. 15 : 51, 52 — "We all shall not sleep, but we shall all be changed, in a moment, in the twinkling of an eye, at the last trump : for the trumpet shall sound, and the dead shall be raised incorruptible, and we shall be changed " ; 1 Thess. 4 : 16, 17 — "For the Lord himself shall descend from heaven, with a shout, with the voice of an archangel, and with the trump of God : and the dead in Christ shall rise first ; then we that are alive, that are left, shall together with them be caught up in the clouds, to meet the Lord in the air : and so shall we ever be with the Lord."

(b) All evil angels, — good angels appearing only as attendants and ministers of the Judge.

Evil angels : 2 Pet. 2 : 4 — "For if God spared not angels when they sinned, but cast them down to hell, and committed them to pits of darkness, to be reserved unto judgment " ; Jude 6 — "And angels that kept not their own principality, but left their proper habitation, he hath kept in everlasting bonds under darkness unto the judgment of the great day " ; Good angels : Mat. 13 : 41, 42 — "The Son of man shall send forth his angels, and they shall gather out of his kingdom all things that cause stumbling, and them that do iniquity, and shall cast them into the furnace of fire : there shall be the weeping and the gnashing of teeth ' ; 25 : 31 — "But when the Son of man shall come in his glory, and all the angels with him, then shall he sit on the throne of his glory : and before him shall be gathered all the nations."

5. *The grounds of the final judgment.*

These will be two in number :

(*a*) The law of God, — as made known in conscience and in Scripture.

John 12 : 48 —"He that rejecteth me, and receiveth not my sayings, hath one that judgeth him: the word that I spake, the same shall judge him in the last day " ; Rom. 2 : 12 —"For as many as have sinned without the law shall also perish without the law : and as many as have sinned under the law shall be judged by the law." On the self-registry and disclosure of sin, see F. A. Noble, Our Redemption, 59-76. Dr. Noble quotes Daniel Webster in the Knapp case at Salem : " There is no refuge from confession but suicide, and suicide is confession." Thomas Carlyle said to Lord Houghton ; " Richard Milnes ! in the day of judgment, when the Lord asks you why you did not get that pension for Alfred Tennyson, it will not do to lay the blame on your constituents,— it is you that will be damned."

(*b*) The grace of Christ (Rev. 20 : 12),—those whose names are found " written in the book of life " being approved, simply because of their union with Christ and participation in his righteousness. Their good works shall be brought into judgment only as proofs of this relation to the Redeemer. Those not found " written in the book of life " will be judged by the law of God, as God has made it known to each individual.

Rev. 20 : 12 —" And I saw the dead, the great and the small, standing before the throne ; and books were opened : and another book was opened, which is the book of life : and the dead were judged out of the things which were written in the books, according to their works." The "book of life "= the book of justification, in which are written the names of those who are united to Christ by faith ; as the " book of death " would = the book of condemnation, in which are written the names of those who stand in their sins, as unrepentant and unforgiven transgressors of God's law.

Ferries, in Hastings' Bible Dictionary, 2 . 821 — " The judgment, in one aspect or stage of it, is a present act. For judgment Christ is come into this world (John 9 : 39). There is an actual separation of men in progress here and now. . . . This judgment which is in progress now, is destined to be perfected. . . . . In the last assize, Christ will be the Judge as before. . . . . It may be said that men will hereafter judge themselves. Those who are unlike Christ will find themselves as such to be separate from him. The two classes of people are parted because they have acquired distinct natures like the sheep and the goat. . . . . The character of each person is a 'book' or record, preserving, in moral and spiritual effects, all that he has been and done and loved, and in the judgment these books will be ' opened,' or each man's character will be manifested as the light of Christ's character falls upon it. . . . . The people of Christ themselves receive different rewards, according as their life has been."

Dr. H. E. Robins, in his Restatement, holds that only under the grace-system can the deeds done in the body be the ground of judgment. These deeds will be repentance and faith, not words of external morality. They will be fruits of the Spirit, such as spring from the broken and contrite heart. Christ, as head of the mediatorial kingdom, will fitly be the Judge. So Judgment will be an unmixed blessing to the righteous. To them the words " prepare to meet thy God " (Amos 4 : 12) should have no terror ; for to meet God is to meet their deliverance and their reward. " Teach me to live that I may dread The grave as little as my bed : Teach me to die, that so I may Rise glorious at the judgment day." On the whole subject, see Hodge, Outlines of Theology, 456, 457 ; Martensen, Christian Dogmatics, 465, 466 ; Neander, Planting and Training, 524-526 ; Jonathan Edwards, Works, 2 : 499, 500 ; 4 : 202-225 ; Fox, in Lutheran Rev., 1887 : 206-226.

VI. The Final States of the Righteous and of the Wicked.

1. *Of the righteous.*

The final state of the righteous is described as eternal life (Mat. 25 : 46), glory (2 Cor. 4 : 17), rest (Heb. 4 : 9), knowledge (1 Cor. 13 : 8-10), holiness (Rev. 21 : 27), service (Rev. 22 : 3), worship (Rev. 19 : 1), society (Heb. 12 : 23), communion with God (Rev. 21 : 3).

Mat. 25 : 46 —"And these shall go away into eternal punishment: but the righteous into eternal life"; 2 Cor. 4 : 17 — "For our light affliction, which is for the moment, worketh for us more and more exceedingly an eternal weight of glory"; Heb. 4 : 9 —"There remaineth therefore a sabbath rest for the people of God"; 1 Cor. 13 : 8–10 —"Love never faileth: but whether there be prophecies, they shall be done away; whether there be tongues, they shall cease; whether there be knowledge, it shall be done away. For we know in part, and we prophesy in part: but when that which is perfect is come, that which is in part shall be done away"; Rev. 21 : 27 —"and there shall in no wise enter into it anything unclean, or he that maketh an abomination and a lie: but only they that are written in the Lamb's book of life"; 22 : 3 —"and his servants shall serve him"; 19 : 1, 2 —"After these things I heard as it were a great voice of a great multitude in heaven, saying, Hallelujah; Salvation, and glory, and power, belong to our God; for true and righteous are his judgments"; Heb. 12 : 23 —"to the general assembly and church of the firstborn who are enrolled in heaven"; Rev. 21 : 3 —"And I heard a great voice out of the throne saying, Behold, the tabernacle of God is with men, and he shall dwell with them, and they shall be his peoples, and God himself shall be with them, and be their God."

Is. 35 : 7 —"The mirage shall become a pool" ═ aspiration shall become reality; Hos. 2 : 15 —"I will give her . . . . the valley of Achor [that is, Troubling] for a door of hope." Victor Hugo: "If you persuade Lazarus that there is no Abraham's bosom awaiting him, he will not lie at Dives' door, to be fed with his crumbs,— he will make his way into the house and fling Dives out of the window." It was the preaching of the Methodists that saved England from the general crash of the French Revolution. It brought the common people to look for the redress of the inequalities and injustices of this life in a future life — a world of less friction than this (S. S. Times). In the Alps one has no idea of the upper valleys until he enters them. He may long to ascend, but only actual ascending can show him their beauty. And then, "beyond the Alps lies Italy," and the revelation of heaven will be like the outburst of the sunny landscape after going through the darkness of the St. Gothard tunnel.

Robert Hall, who for years had suffered acute bodily pain, said to Wilberforce : "My chief conception of heaven is *rest*." "Mine," replied Wilberforce, "is *love* — love to God and to every bright inhabitant of that glorious place." Wilberforce enjoyed society. Heaven is not all rest. On the door is inscribed : " No admission except on business." 'His servants shall serve him' (Rev. 21 : 3). Butler, Things Old and New, 143 —" We know not; but if life be there The outcome and the crown of this : What else can make their perfect bliss Than in their Master's work to share ? Resting, but not in slumberous ease, Working, but not in wild unrest, Still ever blessing, ever blest, They see us as the Father sees." Tennyson, Crossing the Bar : " Sunset and evening star, And one clear call for me; And may there be no moaning of the bar When I put out to sea ! But such a tide as moving seems asleep, Too full for sound and foam, When that which drew from out the boundless deep Turns again home. Twilight and evening bell, And after that the dark ; And may there be no sadness of farewell, When I embark. For though from out our bourne of time and place The flood may bear me far, I hope to see my Pilot face to face, When I have crossed the bar."

Mat. 6 : 20 —"lay up for yourselves treasures in heaven" ═ there are no permanent investments except in heaven. A man at death is worth only what he has sent on before him. Christ prepares a place for us (John 14 : 3) by gathering our friends to himself. Louise Chandler Moulton: "Some day or other I shall surely come Where true hearts wait for me ; Then let me learn the language of that home, While here on earth I be; Lest my poor lips for want of words be dumb In that high company." Bronson Alcott: " Heaven will be to me a place where I can get a little conversation." Some of his friends thought it would be a place where he could hear himself talk. A pious Scotchman, when asked whether he ever expected to reach heaven, replied : " Why, mon, I live there noo ! "

Summing up all these, we may say that it is the fulness and perfection of holy life, in communion with God and with sanctified spirits. Although there will be degrees of blessedness and honor, proportioned to the capacity and fidelity of each soul (Luke 19 : 17, 19 ; 1 Cor. 3 : 14, 15), each will receive as great a measure of reward as it can contain (1 Cor. 2 : 9), and this final state, once entered upon, will be unchanging in kind and endless in duration (Rev. 3 : 12 ; 22 : 15).

Luke 19 : 17, 19 —"Well done, thou good servant: because thou wast found faithful in a very little, have thou authority over ten cities . . . Be thou also over five cities"; 1 Cor. 3 : 14, 15 —"If any man's work shall abide which he built thereon, he shall receive a reward. If any man's work shall be burned, he shall suffer loss : but he himself shall be saved ; yet so as through fire"; 2 : 9 —"Things which eye saw not, and ear heard not, And which entered not into the heart of man, Whatsoever things God prepared for them that love him"; Rev. 3 : 12 —" He that overcometh, I will make him a pillar in the temple of my God, and he shall go out thence no more " ; 22 : 15—"Without are the dogs, and the sorcerers, and the fornicators, and the murderers, and the idolaters, and every one that loveth and maketh a lie."

In the parable of the laborers (Mat. 20:1-16), each receives a penny. Rewards in heaven will be equal, in the sense that each saved soul will be filled with good. But rewards will vary, in the sense that the capacity of one will be greater than that of another; and this capacity will be in part the result of our improvement of God's gifts in the present life. The relative value of the penny may in this way vary from a single unit to a number indefinitely great, according to the work and spirit of the recipient. The penny is good only for what it will buy. For the eleventh hour man, who has done but little work, it will not buy so sweet rest as it buys for him who has "borne the burden of the day and the scorching heat." It will not buy appetite, nor will it buy joy of conscience.

E. G. Robinson : "Heaven is not to be compared to a grasshopper on a shingle floating down stream. Heaven is a place where men are taken up, as they leave this world, and are carried forward. No sinners will be there, though there may be incompleteness of character. There is no intimation in Scripture of that sudden transformation in the hour of dissolution which is often supposed." Ps. 84:7—"They go from strength to strength; Every one of them appeareth before God in Zion"—it is not possible that progress should cease with our entrance into heaven ; rather is it true that uninterrupted progress will then begin. 1 Cor. 13 :12—"now we see in a mirror, darkly ; but then face to face." There, progress is not towards, but within, the sphere of the infinite. In this world we are like men living in a cave, and priding themselves on the rushlights with which they explore it, unwilling to believe that there is a region of sunlight where rushlights are needless.

Heaven will involve deliverance from defective physical organization and surroundings, as well as from the remains of evil in our hearts. Rest, in heaven, will be consistent with service, an activity without weariness, a service which is perfect freedom. We shall be perfect when we enter heaven, in the sense of being free from sin ; but we shall grow to greater perfection thereafter, in the sense of a larger and completer being. The fruit tree shows perfection at each stage of its growth—the perfect bud, the perfect blossom, and finally the perfect fruit ; yet the bud and the blossom are preparatory and prophetic ; neither one is a finality. So "when that which is perfect is come, that which is in part shall be done away " (1 Cor 13 :10). A broadshouldered convert at the Rescue Mission said : "I'm the happiest man in the room to-night. I couldn't be any happier unless I were larger." A little pail can be as full of water as is a big tub, but the tub will hold much more than the pail. To be "filled unto all the fulness of God" (Eph. 3 :19) will mean much more in heaven than it means here, because we shall then "be strong to apprehend with all the saints what is the breadth and length and height and depth, and to know the love of Christ which passeth knowledge." In the book of Revelation, John seems to have mistaken an angel for the Lord himself, and to have fallen down to worship (Rev. 22 : 8). The time may come in eternity when we shall be equal to what we now conceive God to be (1 Cor. 2 : 9).

Plato's Republic and More's Utopia are only earthly adumbrations of St. John's City of God. The representation of heaven as a city seems intended to suggest security from every foe, provision for every want, intensity of life, variety of occupation, and closeness of relation to others; or, as Hastings' Bible Dictionary, 1:446, puts it: "Safety, Security, Service." Here, the greatest degradation and sin are found in the great cities. There, the life of the city will help holiness, as the life of the city here helps wickedness. Brotherly love in the next world implies knowing those we love, and loving those we know. We certainly shall not know less there than here. If we know our friends here, we shall know them there. And, as love to Christ here draws us nearer to each other, so there we shall love friends, not less but more, because of our greater nearness to Christ.

Zech. 8 : 5—"And the streets of the city shall be full of boys and girls playing in the streets thereof." Newman Smyth, Through Science to Faith, 125—"As of the higher animals, so even more of men and women it may be true, that those who play best may succeed best and thrive best." Horace Bushnell, in his essay, Work and Play, holds that ideal work is work performed so heartily and joyfully, and with such a surplus of energy, that it becomes play. This is the activity of heaven : John 10 :10—"I came that they may have life, and may have it abundantly." We enter into the life of God : John 5 :17—"My Father worketh even until now, and I work." A nurse who had been ill for sixteen years, said : "If I were well, I would be at the small-pox hospital. I'm not going to heaven to do nothing." Savage, Life after Death, 129, 292—"In Dante's universe, the only reason for any one's wanting to get to heaven is for the sake of getting out of the other place. There is nothing in heaven for him to do, nothing human for him to engage in. . . . . A good deacon in his depression thought he was going to hell; but when asked what he would do there, he replied that he would try to start a prayer meeting."

With regard to heaven, two questions present themselves, namely:

(*a*) Is heaven a place, as well as a state ?

We answer that this is probable, for the reason that the presence of Christ's human body is essential to heaven, and that this body must be confined to place. Since deity and humanity are indissolubly united in Christ's single person, we cannot regard Christ's human soul as limited to place without vacating his person of its divinity. But we cannot conceive of his human body as thus omnipresent. As the new bodies of the saints are confined to place, so, it would seem, must be the body of their Lord. But, though heaven be the place where Christ manifests his glory through the human body which he assumed in the incarnation, our ruling conception of heaven must be something higher even than this, namely, that of a state of holy communion with God.

John 14 : 2, 3 —"In my Father's house are many mansions ; if it were not so, I would have told you; for I go to prepare a place for you. And if I go and prepare a place for you, I come again, and will receive you unto myself; that where I am, there ye may be also " ; Heb. 12 : 14 —"Follow after peace with all men, and the sanctification without which no man shall see the Lord."

Although heaven is probably a place, we are by no means to allow this conception to become the preponderant one in our minds. Milton: "The mind is its own place, and in itself Can make a heaven of hell, a hell of heaven." As he goes through the gates of death, every Christian can say, as Cæsar said when he crossed the Rubicon: " Omnia mea mecum porto." The hymn " O sing to me of heaven, when I am called to die " is not true to Christian experience. In that hour the soul sings, not of heaven, but of Jesus and his cross. As houses on river-flats, accessible in time of flood by boats, keep safe only goods in the upper story, so only the treasure laid up above escapes the destroying floods of the last day. Dorner: "The soul will possess true freedom, in that it can no more become unfree; and that through the indestructible love-energy springing from union with God."

Milton: " What if earth be But the shadow of heaven, and things therein Each to the other like, more than on earth is thought?" Omar Khayyám, Rubáiyát, stanzas 66, 67 —" I sent my soul through the Invisible, Some letter of that After-life to spell: And by and by my soul returned to me, And answered ' I myself am Heaven and Hell '. . . . . Heaven but the vision of fulfilled desire, And Hell the shadow of a soul on fire." In other words, not the kind of place, but the kind of people in it, makes Heaven or Hell. Crane, Religion of To-morrow, 341 — " The earth is but a breeding-ground from which God intends to populate the whole universe. After death, the soul goes to that place which God has prepared as its home. In the resurrection they 'neither marry nor are given in marriage' (Mat. 22:30) = ours is the only generative planet. There is no reproduction hereafter. To incorporate himself into the race, the Father must come to the reproductive planet."

Dean Stanley: " *Till death us part !* So speaks the heart When each repeats to each the words of doom ; Through blessing and through curse, For better and for worse, We will be one till that dread hour shall come. Life, with its myriad grasp, Our yearning souls shall clasp, By ceaseless love and still expectant wonder, In bonds that shall endure, Indissolubly sure, Till God in death shall part our paths asunder. *Till death us join !* O voice yet more divine, That to the broken heart breathes hope sublime ; Through lonely hours and shattered powers, We still are one despite of change or time. Death, with his healing hand, Shall once more knit the band, Which needs but that one link which none may sever ; Till through the only Good, Heard, felt and understood, Our life in God shall make us one forever."

(*b*) Is this earth to be the heaven of the saints ? We answer:

First,— that the earth is to be purified by fire, and perhaps prepared to be the abode of the saints,—although this last is not rendered certain by the Scriptures.

Rom. 8 : 19-23 — "For the earnest expectation of the creation waiteth for the revealing of the sons of God. For the creation was subjected to vanity, not of its own will, but by reason of him who subjected it, in hope that the creation itself also shall be delivered from the bondage of corruption into the liberty of the glory of the children of God. For we know that the whole creation groaneth and travaileth in pain together until now. And not only so, but ourselves also, who have the first-fruits of the Spirit, even we ourselves groan within ourselves, waiting for our adoption, to wit, the redemption of our body " ; 2 Pet. 3 : 12, 13 — "looking for and earnestly desiring the coming of the day of God, by reason of which the heavens being on fire shall be dissolved, and the elements shall melt with fervent heat. But, according to his promise, we look for new heavens and a new earth, wherein dwelleth righteousness " ; Rev. 21 : 1 — "And I saw a new heaven and a new earth : for the first heaven and the first earth are passed away ; and the sea is no more." Dorner : " Without loss of substantiality, matter will have exchanged its darkness, hardness, heaviness, inertia, and impenetrableness, for clearness, radiance, elasticity, and transparency. A new stadium will begin — God's advance to new creations, with the coöperation of perfected mankind."

Is the earth a molten mass, with a thin solid crust ? Lord Kelvin says no, — it is more rigid and solid than steel. The interior may be intensely hot, yet pressure may render it solid to the very centre. The wrinkling of the surface may be due to contraction, or " solid flow," like the wrinkling in the skin of a baked apple that has cooled. See article on The Interior of the Earth, by G. F. Becker, in N. American Rev., April, 1893. Edward S. Holden, Director of the Lick Observatory, in The Forum, Oct. 1893 : 211-220, tells us that " the star Nova Aurigæ, which doubtless resembled our sun, within two days increased in brilliancy sixteen fold. Three months after its discovery it had become invisible. After four months again it reappeared and was comparatively bright. But it was no longer a star but a nebula. In other words it had developed changes of light and heat which, if repeated in the case of our own sun, would mean a quick end of the human race, and the utter annihilation of every vestige of animal and other life upon this earth. . . . . This catastrophe occured in December, 1891, or was announced to us by light which reached us then. But this light must have left the star twenty, perhaps fifty, years earlier."

Secondly, — that this fitting-up of the earth for man's abode, even if it were declared in Scripture, would not render it certain that the saints are to be confined to these narrow limits (John 14 : 2). It seems rather to be intimated that the effect of Christ's work will be to bring the redeemed into union and intercourse with other orders of intelligence, from communion with whom they are now shut out by sin (Eph. 1 : 20 ; Col. 1 : 20).

John 14 : 2 — " In my Father's house are many mansions " ; Eph. 1 : 10 — " unto a dispensation of the fulness of the times, to sum up all things in Christ, the things in the heavens, and the things upon the earth " ; Col. 1 : 20 — " through him to reconcile all things unto himself, having made peace through the blood of his cross ; through him, I say, whether things upon the earth, or things in the heavens. "

See Dr. A. C. Kendrick, in Bap. Quarterly, Jan. 1870. Dr. Kendrick thinks we need local associations. Earth may be our home, yet from this home we may set out on excursions through the universe, after a time returning again to our earthly abodes. So Chalmers, interpreting literally 2 Pet. 3. We certainly are in a prison here, and look out through the bars, as the Prisoner of Chillon looked over the lake to the green isle and the singing birds. Why are we shut out from intercourse with other worlds and other orders of intelligence ? Apparently it is the effect of sin. We are in an abnormal state of durance and probation. Earth is out of harmony with God. The great harp of the universe has one of its strings out of tune, and that one discordant string makes a jar through the whole. All things in heaven and earth shall be reconciled when this one jarring string is keyed right and set in tune by the hand of love and mercy. See Leitch, God's Glory in the Heavens, 327-330.

2. *Of the wicked.*

The final state of the wicked is described under the figures of eternal fire (Mat. 25 : 41) ; the pit of the abyss (Rev. 9 : 2, 11) ; outer darkness (Mat. 8 : 12) ; torment (Rev. 14 : 10, 11) ; eternal punishment (Mat. 25 : 46) ; wrath of God (Rom. 2 : 5) ; second death (Rev. 21 : 8) ; eternal destruction from the face of the Lord (2 Thess. 1 : 9) ; eternal sin (Mark 3 : 29).

Mat. 25 : 41 —"Depart from me, ye cursed, into the eternal fire which is prepared for the devil and his angels" ; Rev. 9 : 2, 11 —"And he opened the pit of the abyss ; and there went up a smoke out of the pit, as the smoke of a great furnace. . . . . They have over them as king the angel of the abyss : his name in Hebrew is Abaddon, and in the Greek tongue he hath the name Apollyon" ; Mat. 8 : 12 —"but the sons of the kingdom shall be cast forth into the outer darkness : there shall be the weeping and the gnashing of teeth " ; Rev. 14 : 10, 11 —"he also shall drink of the wine of the wrath of God, which is prepared unmixed in the cup of his anger ; and he shall be tormented with fire and brimstone in the presence of the holy angels, and in the presence of the Lamb : and the smoke of their torment goeth up for ever and ever " ; Mat. 25 : 46 —"And these shall go away into eternal punishment."

Rom. 2 : 5 —"after thy hardness and impenitent heart treasurest up for thyself wrath in the day of wrath and revelation of the righteous judgment of God" ; Rev. 21 : 8 —"But for the fearful, and unbelieving, and abominable, and murderers, and fornicators, and sorcerers, and idolaters, and all liars, their part shall be in the lake that burneth with fire and brimstone; which is the second death " : 2 Thess. 1 : 9 —" who shall suffer punishment, even eternal destruction from the face of the Lord and from the glory of his might " — here ἀπό, from,= not separation, but " proceeding from," and indicates that the everlasting presence of Christ, once realized, ensures everlasting destruction ; Mark 3 : 29 —"whosoever shall blaspheme against the Holy Spirit hath never forgiveness, but is guilty of an eternal sin" — a text which implies that (1) some will never cease to sin ; (2) this eternal sinning will involve eternal misery ; (3) this eternal misery, as the appointed vindication of the law, will be eternal punishment. As Uzziah, when smitten with leprosy, did not need to be thrust out of the temple, but "himself hasted also to go out " (2 Chron. 26 : 20), so Judas is said to go "to his own place" (Acts 1 : 25 ; cf. 4 : 23 — where Peter and John, " being let go, they came to their own company "). Cf. John 8 : 35 —" the bondservant abideth not in the house forever" = whatever be his outward connection with God, it can be only for a time ; 15 : 2 —" Every branch in me that beareth not fruit, he taketh it away" — at death ; the history of Abraham showed that one might have outward connection with God that was only temporary : Ishmael was cast out ; the promise belonged only to Isaac.

Wrightnour : " Gehenna was the place into which all the offal of the city of Jerusalem was swept. So hell is the penitentiary of the moral universe. The profligate is not happy in the prayer meeting, but in the saloon ; the swine is not at home in the parlor, but in the sty. Hell is the sinner's own place ; he had rather be there than in heaven ; he will not come to the house of God, the nearest thing to heaven ; why should we expect him to enter heaven itself ? "

Summing up all, we may say that it is the loss of all good, whether physical or spiritual, and the misery of an evil conscience banished from God and from the society of the holy, and dwelling under God's positive curse forever. Here we are to remember, as in the case of the final state of the righteous, that the decisive and controlling element is not the outward, but the inward. If hell be a place, it is only that the outward may correspond to the inward. If there be outward torments, it is only because these will be fit, though subordinate, accompaniments of the inward state of the soul.

Every living creature will have an environment suited to its character —"its own place." " I know of the future judgment, How dreadful so e'er it be, That to sit alone with my conscience Will be judgment enough for me." Calvin : " The wicked have the seeds of hell in their own hearts." Chrysostom, commenting on the words " Depart, ye cursed," says : " Their own works brought the punishment on them ; the fire was not prepared for them, but for Satan ; yet, since they cast themselves into it, ' Impute it to yourselves,' he says, ' that you are there.' " Milton, Par. Lost, 4 : 75 — Satan : " Which way I fly is hell ; myself am hell." Byron : "There is no power in holy men, Nor charm in prayer, nor purifying form Of penitence, nor outward look, nor fast, Nor agony, nor greater than all these, The innate torture of that deep despair Would make a hell of heaven, can exorcise From out the unbounded spirit the quick sense Of its own sins."

Phelps, English Style, 228, speaks of " a law of the divine government, by which the body symbolizes, in its experience, the moral condition of its spiritual inhabitant. The drift of sin is to physical suffering. Moral depravity tends always to a corrupt and tortured body. Certain diseases are the product of certain crimes. The whole catalogue of human pains, from a toothache to the angina pectoris, is but a witness to a state of sin expressed by an experience of suffering. Carry this law into the experience of eternal sin. The bodies of the wicked live again as well as those of the righteous. You have therefore a spiritual body, inhabited and used, and therefore tortured, by a guilty soul,—a body, perfected in its sensibilities, inclosing and expressing a soul matured in its depravity." Augustine, Confessions, 25—" Each man's sin is the instrument of his punishment, and his iniquity is turned into his torment." Lord Bacon: " Being, without well-being, is a curse, and the greater the being, the greater the curse."

In our treatment of the subject of eternal punishment we must remember that false doctrine is often a reaction from the unscriptural and repulsive over-statements of Christian apologists. We freely concede : 1. that future punishment does not necessarily consist of physical torments, — it may be wholly internal and spiritual ; 2. that the pain and suffering of the future are not necessarily due to positive inflictions of God, — they may result entirely from the soul's sense of loss, and from the accusations of conscience ; and 3. that eternal punishment does not necessarily involve endless successions of suffering,— as God's eternity is not mere endlessness, so we may not be forever subject to the law of time.

An over-literal interpretation of the Scripture symbols has had much to do with such utterances as that of Savage, Life after Death, 101—"If the doctrine of eternal punishment was clearly and unmistakably taught in every leaf of the Bible, and on every leaf of all the Bibles of all the world, I could not believe a word of it. I should appeal from these misconceptions of even the seers and the great men to the infinite and eternal Good, who only is God, and who only on such terms could be worshiped."

The figurative language of Scripture is a miniature representation of what cannot be fully described in words. The symbol is a symbol; yet it is less, not greater, than the thing symbolized. It is sometimes fancied that Jonathan Edwards, when, in his sermon on "Sinners in the Hands of an Angry God," he represented the sinner as a worm shriveling in the eternal fire, supposed that hell consists mainly of such physical torments. But this is a misinterpretation of Edwards. As he did not fancy heaven essentially to consist in streets of gold or pearly gates, but rather in holiness and communion with Christ, of which these are the symbols, so he did not regard hell as consisting in fire and brimstone, but rather in the unholiness and separation from God of a guilty and accusing conscience, of which the fire and brimstone are symbols. He used the material imagery, because he thought that this best answered to the methods of Scripture. He probably went beyond the simplicity of the Scripture statements, and did not sufficiently explain the spiritual meaning of the symbols he used; but we are persuaded that he neither understood them literally himself, nor meant them to be so understood by others.

Sin is self-isolating, unsocial, selfish. By virtue of natural laws the sinner reaps as he has sown, and sooner or later is repaid by desertion or contempt. Then the selfishness of one sinner is punished by the selfishness of another, the ambition of one by the ambition of another, the cruelty of one by the cruelty of another. The misery of the wicked hereafter will doubtless be due in part to the spirit of their companions. They dislike the good, whose presence and example is a continual reproof and reminder of the height from which they have fallen, and they shut themselves out of their company. The judgment will bring about a complete cessation of intercourse between the good and the bad. Julius Müller, Doctrine of Sin, 1 : 239 —" Beings whose relations to God are diametrically opposite, and persistently so, differ so greatly from each other that other ties of relationship became as nothing in comparison."

In order, however, to meet opposing views, and to forestall the common objections, we proceed to state the doctrine of future punishment in greater detail :

A. The future punishment of the wicked is not annihilation.—In our discussion of Physical Death, we have shown that, by virtue of its original creation in the image of God, the human soul is naturally immortal ; that neither for the righteous nor the wicked is death a cessation of being ; that on the contrary, the wicked enter at death upon a state of conscious suffering which the resurrection and the judgment only augment and render permanent. It is plain, moreover, that if annihilation took place at death, there could be no degrees in future punishment,— a conclusion itself at variance with express statements of Scripture.

The old annihilationism is represented by Hudson, Debt and Grace, and Christ our Life ; also by Dobney, Future Punishment. It maintains that κόλασις, "punishment" (in Mat. 25 : 46 —"eternal punishment "), means etymologically an everlasting " cutting-off." But we reply that the word had to a great degree lost its etymological significance, as is evident from the only other passage where it occurs in the New Testament, namely, 1 John 4 : 18 —"fear hath punishment" (A. V. : "fear hath torment"). For full answer to the old statements of the annihilation-theory, see under Physical Death, pages 991-998.

That there are degrees of punishment in God's administration is evident from Luke 12: 47, 48 —"And that servant, who knew his Lord's will, and made not ready, nor did according to his will, shall be beaten with many stripes ; but he that knew not, and did things worthy of stripes, shall be beaten with few stripes "; Rom. 2 : 5, 6 —"after thy hardness and impenitent heart treasurest up for thyself wrath in the day of wrath and revelation of the righteous judgment of God; who will render to every man according to his works" ; 2 Cor. 5 : 10 —"For we must all be made manifest before the judgment-seat of Christ ; that each one may receive the things done in the body, according to what he hath done, whether it be good or bad " ; 11 : 15 —"whose end shall be according to their works"; 2 Tim. 4 : 14 —"Alexander the coppersmith did me much evil : the Lord will render to him according to his works "; Rev. 2 : 23 —"I will give unto each one of you according to your works "; 18 : 5, 6 —"her sins have reached even unto heaven, and God hath remembered her iniquities. Render unto her even as she rendered, and double unto her the double according to her works : in the cup which she mingled, mingle unto her double."

A French Christian replied to the argument of his deistical friend : "Probably you are right ; probably you are not immortal; but I am." This was the doctrine of conditional immortality, the doctrine that only the good survive. We grant that the measure of our faith in immortality is the measure of our *fitness* for its blessings ; but it is not the measure of our *possession* of immortality. We are immortal beings, whether we believe it or not. The acorn is potentially an oak, but it may never come to its full development. There is a saltless salt, which, though it does not cease to exist, is cast out and trodden under foot of men. Denney, Studies in Theology, 256 —" Conditional immortality denies that man can exist after death without being united to Christ by faith. But the immortality of man cannot be something accidental, something appended to his nature, after he believes in Christ. It must be something, at the very lowest, for which his nature is constituted, even if apart from Christ it can never realize itself as it ought."

Broadus, Com. on Mat. 25: 46 (page 514) —" He who caused to exist could keep in existence. Mark 9 : 49 — 'Every one shall be salted with fire ' — has probably this meaning. Fire is usually destructive ; but this unquenchable fire will act like salt, preserving instead of destroying. So Keble, Christian Year, 5th Sunday in Lent, says of the Jews in their present condition : 'Salted with fire, they seem to show How spirits lost in endless woe May undecaying live. Oh, sickening thought ! Yet hold it fast Long as this glittering world shall last, Or sin at heart survive.' "

There are two forms of the annihilation theory which are more plausible, and which in recent times find a larger number of advocates, namely :

(a) That the powers of the wicked are gradually weakened, as the natural result of sin, so that they finally cease to be.—We reply, first, that moral evil does not, in this present life, seem to be incompatible with a constant growth of the intellectual powers, at least in certain directions, and we have no reason to believe the fact to be different in the world to come ; secondly, that if this theory were true, the greater the sin, the speedier would be the relief from punishment.

This form of the annihilation theory is suggested by Bushnell, in his Forgiveness and Law, 146, 147, and by Martineau, Study, 2 :107-8. Dorner also, in his Eschatology, seems to favor it as one of the possible methods of future punishment. He says : "To the ethical also pertains ontological significance. The 'second death' may be the dissolving of the soul itself into nothing. Estrangement from God, the source of life, ends in extinction of life. The orthodox talk about demented beings, raging in impotent fury, amounts to the same —annihilation of their human character. Evil is never the substance of the soul,— this remains metaphysically good." It is argued that even for saved sinners there is a loss. The prodigal regained his father's favor, but he could not regain his lost patrimony. We cannot get back the lost time, nor the lost growth. Much more, then, in the case of the wicked, will there be perpetual loss. Draper: "At every return to the sun, comets lose a portion of their size and brightness, stretching out until the nucleus loses control, the mass breaks up, and the greater portion navigates the sky, in the shape of disconnected meteorites."

To this argument it is often replied that certain minds grow in their powers, at least in certain directions, in spite of their sin. Napoleon's military genius, during all his early years, grew with experience. Sloane, in his Life of Napoleon, however, seems to show that the Emperor lost his grip as he went on. Success unbalanced his judgment; he gave way to physical indulgence; his body was not equal to the strain he put upon it; at Waterloo he lost precious moments of opportunity by vacillation and inability to keep awake. There was physical, mental, and moral deterioration. But may this not be the result of the soul's connection with a body? Satan's cunning and daring seem to be on the increase from the first mention of him in Scripture to its end. See Princeton Review, 1882: 673-694. Will not this very cunning and daring, however, work its own ruin, and lead Satan to his final and complete destruction? Does not sin blunt the intellect, unsettle one's sober standards of decision, lead one to prefer a trifling present triumph or pleasure to a permanent good?

Gladden, What is Left? 104, 105—"Evil is benumbing and deadening. Selfishness weakens a man's mental grasp, and narrows his range of vision. The schemer becomes less astute as he grows older; he is morally sure, before he dies, to make some stupendous blunder which even a tyro would have avoided. . . . . The devil, who has sinned longest, must be the greatest fool in the universe, and we need not be at all afraid of him." To the view that this weakening of powers leads to absolute extinction of being, we oppose the consideration that its award of retribution is glaringly unjust in making the greatest sinner the least sufferer; since to him relief, in the way of annihilation, comes the soonest.

(*b*) That there is for the wicked, certainly after death, and possibly between death and the judgment, a positive punishment proportioned to their deeds, but that this punishment issues in, or is followed by, annihilation.—We reply first, that upon this view, as upon any theory of annihilation, future punishment is a matter of grace as well as of justice — a notion for which Scripture affords no warrant; secondly, that Scripture not only gives no hint of the cessation of this punishment, but declares in the strongest terms its endlessness.

The second form of the annihilation theory seems to have been held by Justin Martyr (Trypho, Edinb. transl.)—" Some, who have appeared worthy of God, never die ; but others are punished so long as God wills them to exist and be punished." The soul exists because God wills, and no longer than he wills. " Whenever it is necessary that the soul should cease to exist, the spirit of life is removed from it, and there is no more soul, but it goes back to the place from which it was taken."

Schaff, Hist. Christ. Church, 2: 608, 609—" Justin Martyr teaches that the wicked or hopelessly impenitent will be raised at the judgment to receive an eternal punishment. He speaks of it in twelve passages : ' We believe that all who live wickedly and do not repent will be punished in eternal fire.' Such language is inconsistent with the annihilation theory for which Justin Martyr has been claimed. He does indeed reject the idea of the independent immortality of the soul, and hints at the *possible* final destruction of the wicked ; but he puts that possibility countless ages beyond the final judgment, so that it loses all practical significance."

A modern advocate of this view is White, in his Life in Christ. He favors a conditional immortality, belonging only to those who are joined to Christ by faith ; but he makes a retributive punishment and pain fall upon the godless, before their annihilation. The roots of this view lie in a false conception of holiness as a form or manifestation of benevolence, and of punishment as deterrent and preventive instead of vindicative of righteousness. To the minds of its advocates, extinction of being is a comparative blessing ; and they, for this reason, prefer it to the common view. See Whiton, Is Eternal Punishment Endless?

A view similar to that which we are opposing is found in Henry Drummond, Natural Law in the Spiritual World. Evil is punished by its own increase. Drummond, however, leaves no room for future life or for future judgment in the case of the unregenerate. See reviews of Drummond, in Watts, New Apologetic, 332 ; and in Murphy, Nat. Selection and Spir. Freedom, 19-21, 77-124. While Drummond is an annihilationist, Murphy is a restorationist. More rational and Scriptural than either of these is the saying of Tower : " Sin is God's foe. He does not annihilate it, but he makes it the means of displaying his holiness ; as the Romans did not slay their captured enemies, but made them their servants." The terms αἰών and αἰώνιος, which we have still to consider, afford additional Scripture testimony against annihilation. See also the argument from the divine justice, pages 1046-1051 ; article on the Doctrine of Extinction, in New Englander, March, 1879 : 201-224 ; Hovey, Manual of Theology and Ethics, 153-168 ; J. S. Barlow, Endless Being ; W. H. Robinson, on Conditional Immortality, in Report of Baptist Congress for 1886.

Since neither one of these two forms of the annihilation theory is Scriptural or rational, we avail ourselves of the evolutionary hypothesis as throwing light upon the problem. Death is not degeneracy ending in extinction, nor punishment ending in extinction, — it is atavism that returns, or tends to return, to the animal type. As moral development is from the brute to man, so abnormal development is from man to the brute.

Lord Byron : " All suffering doth destroy, or is destroyed." This is true, not of man's being, but of his well being. Ribot, Diseases of the Will, 115 —" Dissolution pursues a regressive course from the more voluntary and more complex to the less voluntary and more simple, that is to say, toward the automatic. One of the first signs of mental impairment is incapacity for sustained attention. Unity, stability, power, have ceased, and the end is extinction of the will." We prefer to say, loss of the freedom of the will. On the principle of evolution, abuse of freedom may result in reversion to the brute, annihilation not of existence but of higher manhood, punishment from within rather than from without, eternal penalty in the shape of eternal loss. Mat. 24 : 13 —" he that endureth to the end, the same shall be saved " — has for its parallel passage Luke 21 : 19 — " In your patience ye shall win your souls," i. e., shall by free will get possession of your own being. Losing one's soul is just the opposite, namely, losing one's free will, by disuse renouncing freedom, becoming a victim of habit, nature, circumstance, and this is the cutting off and annihilation of true manhood. " To be in hell is to drift ; to be in heaven is to steer " (Bernard Shaw).

In John 15 : 2 Christ says of all men — the natural branches of the vine — " Every branch in me that beareth not fruit, he taketh it away " ; Ps. 49 : 20 —" Man that is in honor, and understandeth not, Is like the beasts that perish " ; Rev. 22 : 15 —" Without are the dogs." In heathen fable men were turned into beasts, and even into trees. The story of Circe is a parable of human fate,— men may become apes, tigers, or swine. They may lose their higher powers of consciousness and will. By perpetual degradation they may suffer eternal punishment. All life that is worthy of the name may cease, while still existence of a low animal type is prolonged. We see precisely these results of sin in this world. We have reason to believe that the same laws of development will operate in the world to come.

McConnell, Evolution of Immortality, 85-95, 99, 124, 180 —" Immortality, or survival after death, depends upon man's freeing himself from the law which sweeps away the many, and becoming an individual (indivisible) that is fit to survive. The individual must become stronger than the species. By using will aright, he lays hold of the infinite Life, and becomes one who, like Christ, has 'life in himself' (John 5 : 26). Gravitation and chemical affinity had their way in the universe until they were arrested and turned about in the interest of life. Overproduction, death, and the survival of the fittest, had their ruthless sway until they were reversed in the interest of affection. The supremacy of the race at the expense of the individual we may expect to continue until something in the individual comes to be of more importance than that law, and no longer. . . . . Goodness can arrest and turn back for nations the primal law of growth, vigor, and decline. Is it too much to believe that it may do the same for an individual man ? . . . Life is a thing to be achieved. At every step there are a thousand candidates who fail, for one that attains. . . . . Until moral sensibility becomes self-conscious, all question of personal immortality becomes irrelevant, because there is, accurately speaking, no personality to be immortal. Up to that point the individual living creature, whether in human form or not, falls short of that essential personality for which eternal life can have any meaning." But how about children who never come to moral consciousness? McConnell appeals to heredity. The child of one who has himself achieved immortality may also prove to be immortal. But is there no chance for the children of sinners? The doctrine of McConnell leans toward the true solution, but it is vitiated by the belief that individuality is a transient gift which only goodness can make permanent. We hold on the other hand that this gift of God is "without repentance" (Rom. 11: 29), and that no human being can lose life, except in the sense of losing all that makes life desirable.

B. **Punishment after death excludes new probation and ultimate restora-** tion of the wicked. — Some have maintained the ultimate restoration of all human beings, by appeal to such passages as the following : Mat. 19 : 28 ; Acts 3 : 21 ; Eph. 1 : 9, 10.

Mat. 19 : 28 —"in the regeneration when the Son of man shall sit on the throne of his glory"; Acts 3 : 21 — Jesus, "whom the heaven must receive until the times of restoration of all things"; 1 Cor. 15 : 26 —"The last enemy that shall be abolished is death"; Eph. 1 : 9, 10 —"according to his good pleasure which he purposed in him unto a dispensation of the fulness of the times, to sum up all things in Christ, the things in the heavens, and the things upon the earth"; Phil. 2 : 10, 11 —"that in the name of Jesus every knee should bow, of things in heaven and things on earth and things under the earth, and that every tongue should confess that Jesus Christ is Lord, to the glory of God the Father"; 2 Pet. 3 : 9, 13 — "not wishing that any should perish, but that all should come to repentance. . . . . But, according to his promise, we look for new heavens and a new earth, wherein dwelleth righteousness."

Robert Browning : "That God, by God's own ways occult, May — doth, I will believe — bring back All wanderers to a single track." B. W. Lockhart : "I must believe that evil is essentially transient and mortal, or alter my predicates of God. And I must believe in the ultimate extinction of that personality whom the power of God cannot sometime win to goodness. The only alternative is the termination of a wicked life either through redemption or through extinction." Mulford, Republic of God, claims that the soul's state cannot be fixed by any event, such as death, outside of itself. If it could, the soul would exist, not under a moral government, but under fate, and God himself would be only another name for fate. The soul carries its fate, under God, in its power of choice ; and who dares to say that this power to choose the good ceases at death ?

For advocacy of a second probation for those who have not consciously rejected Christ in this life, see Newman Smyth's edition of Dorner's Eschatology. For the theory of restoration, see Farrar, Eternal Hope ; Birks, Victory of Divine Goodness ; Jukes, Restitution of All Things ; Delitzsch, Bib. Psychologie, 469-476 ; Robert Browning, Apparent Failure ; Tennyson, In Memoriam, § liv. *Per contra,* see Hovey, Bib. Eschatology, 95-144. See also, Griffith-Jones, Ascent through Christ, 406-440.

(a) These passages, as obscure, are to be interpreted in the light of those plainer ones which we have already cited. Thus interpreted, they foretell only the absolute triumph of the divine kingdom, and the subjection of all evil to God.

The true interpretation of the passages above mentioned is indicated in Meyer's note on Eph. 1 : 9, 10 — this namely, that "the allusion is not to the restoration of *fallen individuals,* but to the restoration of *universal harmony,* implying that the wicked are to be excluded from the kingdom of God." That there is no allusion to a probation after this life, is clear from Luke 16 : 19-31 — the parable of the rich man and Lazarus. Here penalty is inflicted for the sins done "in thy lifetime" (v. 25) ; this penalty is unchangeable —"there is a great gulf fixed" (v. 26) ; the rich man asks favors for his brethren who still live on the earth, but none for himself (v. 27, 28). John 5 : 25-29 —"The hour cometh, and now is, when the dead shall hear the voice of the Son of God ; and they that hear shall live. For as the Father hath life in himself, even so gave he to the Son also to have life in himself : and he gave him authority to execute judgment, because he is a son of man. Marvel not at this : for the hour cometh, in which all that are in the tombs shall hear his voice, and shall come forth ; they that have done good, unto the resurrection of life ; and they that have done evil, until the resurrection of judgment" — here it is declared that, while for those who have done good there is a resurrection of life, there is for those who have done ill only a resurrection of judgment. John. 8 : 21, 24 —"shall die in your sin : whither I go, ye cannot come . . . . except ye believe that I am he, ye shall die in your sins" — sayings which indicate finality in the decisions of this life.

Orr, Christian View of God and the World, 243 —"Scripture invariably represents the judgment as proceeding on the data of this life, and it concentrates every ray of appeal into the present." John 9 : 4 — "We must work the works of him that sent me, while it is day : the night cometh when no man can work " — intimates that there is no opportunity to secure salvation after death. The Christian hymn writer has caught the meaning of Scripture, when he says of those who have passed through the gate of death : " Fixed in an eternal state, They have done with all below ; We a little longer wait ; But how little, none can know."

(*b*) A second probation is not needed to vindicate the justice or the love of God, since Christ, the immanent God, is already in this world present with every human soul, quickening the conscience, giving to each man his opportunity, and making every decision between right and wrong a true probation. In choosing evil against their better judgment even the heathen unconsciously reject Christ. Infants and idiots, as they have not consciously sinned, are, as we may believe, saved at death by having Christ revealed to them and by the regenerating influence of his Spirit.

Rom. 1 : 18-28 — there is probation under the light of nature as well as under the gospel, and under the law of nature as well as under the gospel men may be given up "unto a reprobate mind " ; 2 : 6-16 — Gentiles shall be judged, not by the gospel, but by the law of nature, and shall "perish without the law . . . . in the day when God shall judge the secrets of men." 2 Cor. 5 : 10 — "For we must all be made manifest before the judgment-seat of Christ ; [not that each may have a new opportunity to secure salvation, but] that each one may recei the things done in the body, according to what he hath done, whether it be good or bad " ; Heb. 6 : 8 — "whose end is to be burned " — not to be quickened again ; 9 : 27 — "And inasmuch as it is appointed unto men once to die, and after this cometh [not a second probation, but] judgment." Luckock, Intermediate State, 22 — " In Heb. 9 : 27, the word 'judgment' has no article. The judgment alluded to is not the final or general judgment, but only that by which the place of the soul is determined in the Intermediate State."

Deuney, Studies in Theology, 243 — " In Mat. 25, our Lord gives a pictorial representation of the judgment of the heathen. All nations — all the Gentiles — are gathered before the King ; and their destiny is determined, not by their conscious acceptance or rejection of the historical Savior, but by their unconscious acceptance or rejection of him in the persons of those who needed services of love. . . . . This does not square with the idea of a future probation. It rather tells us plainly that men may do things of final and decisive import in this life, even if Christ is unknown to them. . . . . The real argument against future probation is that it depreciates the present life, and denies the infinite significance that, under all conditions, essentially and inevitably belongs to the actions of a self-conscious moral being. A type of will may be in process of formation, even in a heathen man, on which eternal issues depend. . . . Second probation lowers the moral tone of the spirit. The present life acquires a relative unimportance. I dare not say that if I forfeit the opportunity the present life gives me I shall ever have another, and therefore I dare not say so to another man."

For an able review of the Scripture testimony against a second probation, see G. F. Wright, Relation of Death to Probation, iv. Emerson, the most recent advocate of restorationism, in his Doctrine of Probation Examined, 42, is able to evade these latter passages only by assuming that they are to be spiritually interpreted, and that there is to be no literal outward day of judgment — an error which we have previously discussed and refuted, — see pages 1024, 1025.

(*c*) The advocates of universal restoration are commonly the most strenuous defenders of the inalienable freedom of the human will to make choices contrary to its past character and to all the motives which are or can be brought to bear upon it. As a matter of fact, we find in this world that men choose sin in spite of infinite motives to the contrary. Upon the theory of human freedom just mentioned, no motives which God can use will certainly accomplish the salvation of all moral creatures. The soul which resists Christ here may resist him forever.

Emerson, in the book just referred to, says : " The truth that sin is in its permanent essence a free choice, however for a time it may be held in mechanical combination with the notion of moral opportunity arbitrarily closed, can never mingle with it, and must in the logical outcome permanently cast it off. Scripture presumes and teaches the constant capability of souls to obey as well as to be disobedient." Emerson is correct. If the doctrine of the unlimited ability of the human will be a true one, then restoration in the future world is possible. Clement and Origen founded on this theory of will their denial of future punishment. If will be essentially the power of contrary choice, and if will may act independently of all character and motive, there can be no objective certainty that the lost will remain sinful. In short, there can be no finality, even to God's allotments, nor is any *last* judgment possible. Upon this view, regeneration and conversion are as possible at any time in the future as they are to-day.

But those who hold to this defective philosophy of the will should remember that unlimited freedom is unlimited freedom to sin, as well as unlimited freedom to turn to God. If restoration is possible, endless persistence in evil is possible also; and this last the Scripture predicts. Whittier: "What if thine eye refuse to see, Thine ear of heaven's free welcome fail, And thou a willing captive be, Thyself thine own dark jail?" Swedenborg says that the man who obstinately refuses the inheritance of the sons of God is allowed the pleasures of the beast, and enjoys in his own low way the hell to which he has confined himself. Every occupant of hell prefers it to heaven. Dante, Hell, iv — "All here together come from every clime, And to o'erpass the river are not loth, For so heaven's justice goads them on, that fear Is turned into desire. Hence never passed good spirit." The lost are *Heautoutimoroumenoi*, or self-tormentors, to adopt the title of Terence's play. See Whedon, in Meth. Quar. Rev., Jan. 1884; Robbins, in Bib. Sac., 1881 : 460-507.

Denney, Studies in Theology, 255 — "The very conception of human freedom involves the possibility of its permanent misuse, or of what our Lord himself calls 'eternal sin' (Mark 3:29). Shedd, Dogm. Theology, 2 : 699 — "Origen's restorationism grew naturally out of his view of human liberty " — the liberty of indifference — "endless alternations of falls and recoveries, of hells and heavens ; so that practically he taught nothing but a hell." J. C. Adams, The Leisure of God : " It is lame logic to maintain the inviolable freedom of the will, and at the same time insist that God can, through his ample power, through protracted punishment, bring the soul into a disposition which it does not wish to feel. There is no compulsory holiness possible. In our Civil War there was some talk of ' compelling men to volunteer,' but the idea was soon seen to involve a self-contradiction."

(*d*) Upon the more correct view of the will which we have advocated, the case is more hopeless still. Upon this view, the sinful soul, in its very sinning, gives to itself a sinful bent of intellect, affection, and will ; in other words, makes for itself a character, which, though it does not render necessary, yet does render certain, apart from divine grace, the continuance of sinful action. In itself it finds a self-formed motive to evil strong enough to prevail over all inducements to holiness which God sees it wise to bring to bear. It is in the next world, indeed, subjected to suffering. But suffering has in itself no reforming power. Unless accompanied by special renewing influences of the Holy Spirit, it only hardens and embitters the soul. We have no Scripture evidence that such influences of the Spirit are exerted, after death, upon the still impenitent ; but abundant evidence, on the contrary, that the moral condition in which death finds men is their condition forever.

See Bushnell's "One Trial Better than Many," in Sermons on Living Subjects ; also see his Forgiveness and Law, 146. 147. Bushnell argues that God would give us fifty trials, if that would do us good. But there is no possibility of such result. The first decision adverse to God renders it more difficult to make a right decision upon the next opportunity. Character tends to fixity, and each new opportunity may only harden the heart and increase its guilt and condemnation. We should have no better chance of salvation if our lives were lengthened to the term of the sinners before the flood. Mere suffering does not convert the soul ; see Martineau, Study, 2 : 100. A life of pain did not make Blanco White a believer : see Mozley, Hist. and Theol. Essays, vol. 2, essay 1.

Edward A. Lawrence, Does Everlasting Punishment Last Forever?—"If the deeds of the law do not justify here, how can the penalties of the law hereafter ? The pain from a broken limb does nothing to mend the break, and the suffering from disease does nothing to cure it. Penalty pays no debts,— it only shows the outstanding and unsettled accounts." If the will does not act without motive, then it is certain that without motives men will never repent. To an impenitent and rebellious sinner the motive must come, not from within, but from without. Such motives God presents by his Spirit in this life; but when this life ends and God's Spirit is withdrawn, no motives to repentance will be presented. The soul's dislike for God will issue only in complaint and resistance. Shakespeare, Hamlet, 3 : 4 —"Try what repentance can ? what can it not? Yet what can it, when one cannot repent ? " Marlowe, Faustus : " Hell hath no limits, nor is circumscribed In one self place; for where we are is hell, And where hell is, there we must ever be."

The pressure of the atmosphere without is counteracted by the resistance of the atmosphere within the body. So God's life within is the only thing that can enable us to bear God's afflictive dispensations without. Without God's Spirit to inspire repentance the wicked man in this world never feels sorrow for his deeds, except as he realizes their evil consequences. Physical anguish and punishment inspire hatred, not of sin, but of the effects of sin. The remorse of Judas induced confession, but not true repentance. So in the next world punishment will secure recognition of God and of his justice, on the part of the transgressor, but it will not regenerate or save. The penalties of the future life will be no more effectual to reform the sinner than were the invitations of Christ and the strivings of the Holy Spirit in the present life. The transientness of good resolves which are forced out of us by suffering is illustrated by the old couplet : " The devil was sick,— the devil a monk would be ; The devil got well,— the devil a monk was he."

Charles G. Sewall : " Paul Lester Ford, the novelist, was murdered by his brother Malcolm, because the father of the two brothers had disinherited the one who committed the crime. Has God the right to disinherit any one of his children ? We answer that God disinherits no one. Each man decides for himself whether he will accept the inheritance. It is a matter of character. A father cannot give his son an education. The son may play truant and throw away his opportunity. The prodigal son disinherited himself. Heaven is not a place,— it is a way of living, a condition of being. If you have a musical ear, I will admit you to a lovely concert. If you have not a musical ear, I may give you a reserved seat and you will hear no melody. Some men fail of salvation because they have no taste for it and will not have it."

The laws of God's universe are closing in upon the impenitent sinner, as the iron walls of the mediæval prison closed in night by night upon the victim,— each morning there was one window less, and the dungeon came to be a coffin. In Jean Ingelow's poem " Divided," two friends, parted by a little rivulet across which they could clasp hands, walk on in the direction in which the stream is flowing, till the rivulet becomes a brook, and the brook a river, and the river an arm of the sea across which no voice can be heard and there is no passing. By constant neglect to use our opportunity, we lose the power to cross from sin to righteousness, until between the soul and God " there is a great gulf fixed " (Luke 16 : 26).

John G. Whittier wrote within a twelvemonth of his death : " I do believe that we take with us into the next world the same freedom of will we have here, and that *there*, as *here*, he that turns to the Lord will find mercy ; that God never ceases to follow his creatures with love, and is always ready to hear the prayer of the penitent. But I also believe that *now* is the accepted time, and that he who dallies with sin may find the chains of evil habit too strong to break in this world or the other." And the following is the Quaker poet's verse : " Though God be good and free be heaven, Not force divine can love compel ; And though the song of sins forgiven Might sound through lowest hell, The sweet persuasion of his voice Respects the sanctity of will. He giveth day : thou hast thy choice To walk in darkness still."

Longfellow, Masque of Pandora : " Never by lapse of time The soul defaced by crime Into its former self returns again ; For every guilty deed Holds in itself the seed Of retribution and undying pain. Never shall be the loss Restored, till Helios Hath purified them with his heavenly fires ; Then what was lost is won, And the new life begun, Kindled with nobler passions and desires." Seth, Freedom as Ethical Postulate, 42 —" Faust's selling his soul to Mephistopheles, and signing the contract with his life's blood, is no single transaction, done deliberately, on one occasion ; rather, that is the lurid meaning of a life which consists of innumerable individual acts.— the life of evil means that." See John Caird, Fundamental Ideas of Christianity, 2 : 88 ; Crane, Religion of To-morrow, 315.

(e) The declaration as to Judas, in Mat. 26 : 24, could not be true upon the hypothesis of a final restoration. If at any time, even after the lapse of ages, Judas be redeemed, his subsequent infinite duration of blessedness must outweigh all the finite suffering through which he has passed. The Scripture statement that "good were it for that man if he had not been born" must be regarded as a refutation of the theory of universal restoration.

Mat. 26 : 24 —"The Son of man goeth, even as it is written of him : but woe unto that man through whom the Son of man is betrayed ! good were it for that man if he had not been born." G. F. Wright, Relation of Death to Probation : " As Christ of old healed only those who came or were brought to him, so now he waits for the coöperation of human agency. God has limited himself to an orderly method in human salvation. The consuming missionary zeal of the apostles and the early church shows that they believed the decisions of this life to be final decisions. The early church not only thought the heathen world would perish without the gospel, but they found a conscience in the heathen answering to this belief. The solicitude drawn out by this responsibility for our fellows may be one means of securing the moral stability of the future. What is bound on earth is bound in heaven ; else why not pray for the wicked dead ? " It is certainly a remarkable fact, if this theory be true, that we have in Scripture not a single instance of prayer for the dead.

The apocryphal 2 Maccabees 12 : 39 sq. gives an instance of Jewish prayer for the dead. Certain who were slain had concealed under their coats things consecrated to idols. Judas and his host therefore prayed that this sin might be forgiven to the slain, and they contributed 2,000 drachmas of silver to send a sin offering for them to Jerusalem. So modern Jews pray for the dead ; see Luckock, After Death, 54–66 — an argument for such prayer. John Wesley, Works, 9 : 55, maintains the legality of prayer for the dead. Still it is true that we have no instance of such prayer in canonical Scriptures. Ps. 132 : 1 —"Jehovah, remember for David All his affliction "— is not a prayer for the dead, but signifies : "Remember for David ", so as to fulfil thy promise to him, "all his anxious cares " — with regard to the building of the temple ; the psalm having been composed, in all probability, for the temple dedication. Paul prays that God will "grant mercy to the house of Onesiphorus " (2 Tim. 1 : 16). from which it has been unwarrantably inferred that Onesiphorus was dead at the time of the apostle's writing ; but Paul's further prayer in verse 18 —"the Lord grant unto him to find mercy of the Lord in that day " — seems rather to point to the death of Onesiphorus as yet in the future.

Shedd, Dogm. Theology, 2 : 715 note —" Many of the arguments constructed against the doctrine of endless punishment proceed upon the supposition that original sin, or man's evil inclination, is the work of God : that because man is born in sin (Ps. 51 · 5), he was created in sin. All the strength and plausibility of John Foster's celebrated letter lies in the assumption that the moral corruption and impotence of the sinner, whereby it is impossible to save himself from eternal death, is not self-originated and self-determined, but infused by his Maker. 'If,' says he, 'the very nature of man, as created by the Sovereign Power, be in such desperate disorder that there is no possibility of conversion or salvation except in instances where that Power interposes with a special and redeeming efficacy, how can we conceive that the main portion of the race, thus morally impotent (that is, really and absolutely impotent), will be eternally punished for the inevitable result of this moral impotence ? ' If this assumption of concreated depravity and impotence is correct, Foster's objection to eternal retribution is conclusive and fatal. . . . . Endless punishment supposes the freedom of the human will, and is impossible without it. Self-determination runs parallel with hell."

The theory of a second probation, as recently advocated, is not only a logical result of that defective view of the will already mentioned, but it is also in part a consequence of denying the old orthodox and Pauline doctrine of the organic unity of the race in Adam's first transgression. New School Theology has been inclined to deride the notion of a fair probation of humanity in our first father, and of a common sin and guilt of mankind in him. It cannot find what it regards as a fair probation for each individual since that first sin ; and the conclusion is easy that there must be such a fair probation for each individual in the world to come. But we may advise those who take this view to return to the old theology. Grant a fair probation for the whole race already passed, and the condition of mankind is no longer that of mere unfortunates unjustly circumstanced, but rather that of beings guilty and condemned, to whom present opportunity, and even present existence, is a matter of pure grace,— much more the general provision of a salvation, and the offer of it to any human soul. This world is already a place of second probation; and since the second probation is due wholly to God's mercy, no probation after death is needed to vindicate either the justice or the goodness of God. See Kellogg, in Presb. Rev., April, 1885:226-256; Cremer, Beyond the Grave, preface by A. A. Hodge, xxxvi *sq.*; E. D. Morris, Is There Salvation After Death? A. H. Strong, on The New Theology, in Bap. Quar. Rev., Jan. 1888,— reprinted in Philosophy and Religion, 164-179.

C. Scripture declares this future punishment of the wicked to be eternal. It does this by its use of the terms αἰών, αἰώνιος.— Some, however, maintain that these terms do not necessarily imply eternal duration. We reply :

(*a*) It must be conceded that these words do not *etymologically* necessitate the idea of eternity ; and that, as expressing the idea of " age-long," they are sometimes used in a limited or rhetorical sense.

2 Tim. 1:9 —"his own purpose and grace, which was given us in Christ Jesus before times eternal" — but the past duration of the world is limited; Heb. 9:26 —"now once at the end of the ages hath he been manifested" — here the αἰῶνες have an end; Tit. 1:2 —"eternal life .... promised before times eternal"; but here there may be a reference to the eternal covenant of the Father with the Son; Jer. 31:3 —"I have loved thee with an everlasting love" = a love which antedated time; Rom. 16:25, 26 —"the mystery which hath been kept in silence through times eternal .... according to the commandment of the eternal God" — here "eternal" is used in the same verse in two senses. It is argued that in Mat. 25:46 —"these shall go away into eternal punishment" — the word "eternal" may be used in the narrower sense.

Arthur Chambers, Our Life after Death, 222-236 —" In Mat. 13:39 — ' the harvest is the end of the αἰών,' and in 2 Tim. 4.10 —'Demas forsook me, having loved this present αἰών' — the word αἰών clearly implies limitation of time. Why not take the word αἰών in this sense in Mark 3:29—'hath never forgiveness, but is guilty of an eternal sin'? We must not translate αἰών by 'world,' and so express limitation, while we translate αἰώνιος by 'eternal,' and so express endlessness which excludes limitation; *cf.* Gen. 13:15—'all the land which thou seest, to thee will I give it, and to thy seed forever'; Num. 25:13 — 'it shall be unto him [Phinehas], and to his seed after him, the covenant of an everlasting priesthood'; Josh. 24:2 —'your fathers dwelt of old time [from eternity] beyond the River'; Deut. 23:3 —'An Ammonite or a Moabite shall not enter .... into the assembly of Jehovah for ever'; Ps. 24:7, 8 —'be ye lifted up, ye everlasting doors.'"

(*b*) They do, however, express the longest possible duration of which the subject to which they are attributed is capable ; so that, if the soul is immortal, its punishment must be without end.

Gen. 49:26 —"the everlasting hills"; 17:8, 13 —"I will give unto thee .... all the land of Canaan, for an everlasting possession .... my covenant [of circumcision] shall be in your flesh for an everlasting covenant"; Ex. 21:6 —"he [the slave] shall serve him [his master] for ever"; 2 Chron. 6:2 —"But I have built thee an house of habitation, and a place for thee to dwell in for ever"— of the temple at Jerusalem; Jude 6, 7 —"angels .... he hath kept in everlasting bonds under darkness unto the judgment of the great day. Even as Sodom and Gomorrah .... are set forth as an example, suffering the punishment of eternal fire"— here in Jude 6, bonds which endure only to the judgment day are called ἀΐδιοις (the same word which is used in Rom. 1:20 —"his everlasting power and divinity"), and fire which lasts only till Sodom and Gomorrah are consumed is called αἰωνίου. Shedd, Dogm. Theology, 2:687 —" To hold land forever is to hold it as long as grass grows and water runs, *i. e.*, as long as this world or æon endures."

In all the passages cited above, the condition denoted by αἰώνιος lasts as long as the object endures of which it is predicated. But we have seen (pages 982-998) that physical death is not the end of man's existence, and that the soul, made in the image of God, is immortal. A punishment, therefore, that lasts as long as the soul, must be an everlasting punishment. Another interpretation of the passages in Jude is, however, entirely possible. It is maintained by many that the "everlasting bonds" of the fallen angels do not cease at the judgment, and that Sodom and Gomorrah suffer "the punishment of eternal fire " in the sense that their condemnation at the judgment will be a continuation of that begun in the time of Lot (see Mat. 10 : 15 —" It shall be more tolerable for the land of Sodom and Gomorrah in the day of judgment, than for that city ").

(c) If, when used to describe the future punishment of the wicked, they do not declare the endlessness of that punishment, there are no words in the Greek language which could express that meaning.

C. F. Wright, Relation of Death to Probation : " The Bible writers speak of eternity in terms of time, and make the impression more vivid by reduplicating the longest time-words they had [e. g., εἰς τοὺς αἰῶνας τῶν αἰώνων ='unto the ages of the ages ']. Plato contrasts χρόνος and αἰών, as we do time and eternity, and Aristotle says that eternity [αἰών] belongs to God. . . . . The Scriptures have taught the doctrine of eternal punishment as clearly as their general style allows." The destiny of lost men is bound up with the destiny of evil angels in Mat. 25 : 41 —" Depart from me, ye cursed, into the eternal fire which is prepared for the devil and his angels." If the latter are hopelessly lost, then the former are hopelessly lost also.

(d) In the great majority of Scripture passages where they occur, they have unmistakably the signification " everlasting." They are used to express the eternal duration of God, the Father, Son, and Holy Spirit (Rom. 16 : 26 ; 1 Tim. 1 : 17 ; Heb. 9 : 14 ; Rev. 1 : 18) ; the abiding presence of the Holy Spirit with all true believers (John 14 : 17) ; and the endlessness of the future happiness of the saints (Mat. 19 : 29 ; John 6 : 54, 58 ; 2 Cor. 9 : 9).

Rom. 16 : 26 —" the commandment of the eternal God "; 1 Tim. 1 : 17 —" Now unto the King eternal, incorruptible, invisible, the only God, be honor and glory for ever and ever "; Heb. 9 : 14 —" the eternal Spirit "; Rev. 1 : 17, 18 —" I am the first and the last, and the Living one ; and I was dead, and behold, I am alive for evermore "; John 14 : 16, 17 —" And I will pray the Father, and he shall give you another Comforter, that he may be with you for ever, even the Spirit of truth "; Mat. 19 : 29 —" every one that hath left houses, or brethren, or sisters . . . . for my name's sake, shall receive a hundredfold, and shall inherit eternal life "; John 6 : 54, 58 —" He that eateth my flesh and drinketh my blood hath eternal life . . . . he that eateth this bread shall live for ever "; 2 Cor. 9 : 9 —" His righteousness abideth for ever "; cf. Dan. 7 : 18 —" But the saints of the Most High shall receive the kingdom, and possess the kingdom for ever, even for ever and ever."

Everlasting punishment is sometimes said to be the punishment which takes place in, and belongs to, an αἰών, with no reference to duration. But President Woolsey declares, on the other hand, that " αἰώνιος cannot denote ' pertaining to an αἰών, or world period.' " The punishment of the wicked cannot cease, any more than Christ can cease to live, or the Holy Spirit to abide with believers ; for all these are described in the same terms : " αἰώνιος is used in the N. T. 66 times,— 51 times of the happiness of the righteous, 2 times of the duration of God and his glory, 6 times where there is no doubt as to its meaning ' eternal,' 7 times of the punishment of the wicked ; αἰών is used 95 times,— 55 times of unlimited duration, 31 times of duration that has limits, 9 times to denote the duration of future punishment." See Joseph Angus, in Expositor, Oct. 1887 : 274–286.

(e) The fact that the same word is used in Mat. 25 : 46 to describe both the sufferings of the wicked and the happiness of the righteous shows that the misery of the lost is eternal, in the same sense as the life of God or the blessedness of the saved.

Mat. 25 : 46 —" And these shall go away into eternal punishment : but the righteous into eternal life." On this passage see Meyer : " The absolute idea of eternity, in respect to the punishments of hell, is not to be set aside, either by an appeal to the popular use of αἰώνιος, or by an appeal to the figurative term ' fire ' ; to the incompatibility of the idea of the eternal with that of moral evil and its punishment, or to the warning design of the representation ; but it stands fast exegetically, by means of the contrasted ζωὴν αἰώνιον, which signifies the endless Messianic life."

(f) Other descriptions of the condemnation and suffering of the lost, excluding, as they do, all hope of repentance or forgiveness, render it certain that αἰών and αἰώνιος, in the passages referred to, describe a punishment that is without end.

Mat. 12 : 31, 32 — "Every sin and blasphemy shall be forgiven unto men; but the blasphemy against the Spirit shall not be forgiven. . . . . it shall not be forgiven him, neither in this world, nor in that which is to come"; 25 :10 — "and the door was shut"; Mark 3 : 29 — "whosoever shall blaspheme against the Holy Spirit hath never forgiveness, but is guilty of an eternal sin"; 9 : 43, 48 — "to go into hell, into the unquenchable fire . . . . where their worm dieth not, and the fire is not quenched " — not the dying worm but the undying worm ; not the fire that is quenched, but the fire that is unquenchable; Luke 3 : 17 — "the chaff he will burn up with unquenchable fire "; 16 : 26 — "between us and you there is a great gulf fixed, that they that would pass from hence to you may not be able, and that none may cross over from thence to us " ; John 3 : 36 — "he that obeyeth not the Son shall not see life, but the wrath of God abideth on him."

Review of Farrar's Eternal Hope, in Bib. Sac., Oct. 1878: 782 — " The original meaning of the English word 'hell' and 'damn' was precisely that of the Greek words for which they stand. Their present meaning is widely different, but from what did it arise? It arose from the connotation imposed upon these words by the impression the Scriptures made on the popular mind. The present meaning of these words is involved in the Scripture, and cannot be removed by any mechanical process. Change the words, and in a few years ' judge ' will have in the Bible the same force that ' damn ' has at present. In fact, the words were not mistranslated, but the connotation of which Dr. Farrar complains has come upon them since, and that through the Scriptures. This proves what the general impression of Scripture upon the mind is, and shows how far Dr. Farrar has gone astray."

(*g*) While, therefore, we grant that we do not know the nature of eternity, or its relation to time, we maintain that the Scripture representations of future punishment forbid both the hypothesis of annihilation, and the hypothesis that suffering will end in restoration. Whatever eternity may be, Scripture renders it certain that after death there is no forgiveness.

We regard the argument against endless punishment drawn from αἰών and αἰώνιος as a purely verbal one which does not touch the heart of the question at issue. We append several utterances of its advocates. The Christian Union : " Eternal punishment is punishment in eternity, not throughout eternity ; as temporal punishment is punishment in time, not throughout time." Westcott : " Eternal life is not an endless duration of being in time, but being of which time is not a measure. We have indeed no powers to grasp the idea except through forms and images of sense. These must be used, but we must not transfer them to realities of another order."

Farrar holds that ἀίδιος, 'everlasting ', which occurs but twice in the N. T. (Rom. 1 : 20 and Jude 6), is not a synonym of αἰώνιος, 'eternal ', but the direct antithesis of it; the former being the unrealizable conception of endless time, and the latter referring to a state from which our imperfect human conception of time is absolutely excluded. Whiton, Gloria Patri, 145, claims that the perpetual immanence of God in conscience makes recovery possible after death ; yet he speaks of the possibility that in the incorrigible sinner conscience may become extinct. To all these views we may reply with Schaff, Ch. History, 2 : 66 — "After the general judgment we have nothing revealed but the boundless prospect of æonian life and æonian death. . . . . Everlasting punishment of the wicked always was and always will be the orthodox theory."

For the view that αἰών and αἰώνιος are used in a limited sense, see De Quincey, Theological Essays, 1 : 126-146 ; Maurice, Essays, 436 : Stanley, Life and Letters, 1 : 485-488 ; Farrar, Eternal Hope, 200 ; Smyth, Orthodox Theology of To-day, 118-123 ; Chambers, Life after Death; Whiton, Is Eternal Punishment Endless? For the common orthodox view, see Fisher and Tyler, in New Englander, March, 1878 ; Gould, in Bib. Sac., 1880 : 212-248 ; Princeton Review, 1873 : 620 ; Shedd, Doctrine of Endless Punishment, 12-117 ; Broadus, Com. on Mat. 25 : 45.

D. This everlasting punishment of the wicked is not inconsistent with God's justice, but is rather a revelation of that justice.

(*a*) We have seen in our discussion of Penalty (pages 652-656) that its object is neither reformatory nor deterrent, but simply vindicatory ; in other words, that it primarily aims, not at the good of the offender, nor at the welfare of society, but at the vindication of law. We have also seen (pages 269, 291) that justice is not a form of benevolence, but is the expression and manifestation of God's holiness. Punishment, therefore, as the inevitable and constant reaction of that holiness against its moral opposite, cannot come to an end until guilt and sin come to an end.

The fundamental error of Universalism is its denial that penalty is vindicatory, and that justice is distinct from benevolence. See article on Universalism, in Johnson's Cyclopædia : " The punishment of the wicked, however severe or terrible it may be, is but a means to a beneficent end ; not revengeful, but remedial ; not for its own sake, but for the good of those who suffer its infliction." With this agrees Rev. H. W. Beecher : " I believe that punishment exists, both here and hereafter ; but it will not continue after it ceases to do good. With a God who could give pain for pain's sake, this world would go out like a candle." But we reply that the doctrine of eternal punishment is not a doctrine of " pain for pain's sake," but of pain for holiness' sake. Punishment could have no beneficial effect upon the universe, or even upon the offender, unless it were just and right in itself. And if just and right in itself, then the reason for its continuance lies, not in any benefit to the universe, or to the sufferer, to accrue therefrom.

F. L. Patton, in Brit. and For. Ev. Rev., Jan. 1878 : 126-139, on the Philosophy of Punishment—" If the Universalist's position were true, we should expect to find some manifestations of love and pity and sympathy in the infliction of the dreadful punishments of the future. We look in vain for this, however. We read of God's anger, of his judgments, of his fury, of his taking vengeance ; but we get no hint, in any passage which describes the sufferings of the next world, that they are designed to work the redemption and recovery of the soul. If the punishments of the wicked were chastisements, we should expect to see some bright outlook in the Bible-picture of the place of doom. A gleam of light, one might suppose, might make its way from the celestial city to this dark abode. The sufferers would catch some sweet refrain of heavenly music which would be a promise and prophecy of a far-off but coming glory. But there is a finality about the Scripture statements as to the condition of the lost, which is simply terrible."

The reason for punishment lies not in the benevolence, but in the holiness, of God. That holiness reveals itself in the moral constitution of the universe. It makes itself felt in conscience — imperfectly here, fully hereafter. The wrong merits punishment. The right binds, not because it is the expedient, but because it is the very nature of God. " But the great ethical significance of this word *right* will not be known," (we quote again from Dr. Patton,) " its imperative claims, its sovereign behests, its holy and imperious sway over the moral creation will not be understood, until we witness, during the lapse of the judgment hours, the terrible retribution which measures the ill-desert of wrong." When Dr. Johnson seemed overfearful as to his future, Boswell said to him : " Think of the mercy of your Savior." " Sir," replied Johnson, " my Savior has said that he will place some on his right hand, and some on his left."

A Universalist during our Civil War announced his conversion to Calvinism, upon the ground that hell was a military necessity. " In Rom. 12 : 19, 'vengeance,' ἐκδίκησις, means primarily 'vindication.' God will show to the sinner and to the universe that the apparent prosperity of evil was a delusion and a snare " (Crane, Religion of To-morrow, 319 note). That strange book, Letters from Hell, shows how memory may increase our knowledge of past evil deeds, but may lose the knowledge of God's promises. Since we retain most perfectly that which has been the subject of most constant thought, retribution may come to us through the operation of the laws of our own nature.

Jackson, James Martineau, 193-195 —" Plato holds that the wise transgressor will seek not shun, his punishment. James Martineau painted a fearful picture of the possible lashing of conscience. He regarded suffering for sin, though dreadful, yet as altogether desirable, not to be asked reprieve from, but to be prayed for : 'Smite, Lord ; for thy mercy's sake, spare not !' The soul denied such suffering is not favored, but defrauded. It learns the truth of its condition, and the truth and the right of the universe are vindicated." The Connecticut preacher said : " My friends, some believe that all will be saved ; but we hope for better things. Chaff and wheat are not to be together always. One goes to the garner, and the other to the furnace."

Shedd, Dogm. Theology, 2:755 — "Luxurious ages and luxurious men recalcitrate at hell, and 'kick against the goad' (Acts 26:14). No theological doctrine is more important than eternal retribution to those modern nations which, like England, Germany and the United States, are growing rapidly in riches, luxury and earthly power. Without it, they will infallibly go down in that vortex of sensuality and wickedness that swallowed up Babylon and Rome. The bestial and shameless vice of the dissolute rich that has recently been uncovered in the commercial metropolis of the world is a powerful argument for the necessity and reality of 'the lake that burneth with fire and brimstone' (Rev. 21:8)." The conviction that after death there must be punishment for sin has greatly modified the older Universalism. There is little modern talk of all men, righteous and wicked alike, entering heaven the moment this life is ended. A purgatorial state must intervene. E. G. Robinson: "Universalism results from an exaggerated idea of the atonement. There is no genuine Universalism in our day. Restorationism has taken its place."

(*b*) But guilt, or ill-desert, is endless. However long the sinner may be punished, he never ceases to be ill-deserving. Justice, therefore, which gives to all according to their deserts, cannot cease to punish. Since the reason for punishment is endless, the punishment itself must be endless. Even past sins involve an endless guilt, to which endless punishment is simply the inevitable correlate.

For full statement of this argument that guilt, as never coming to an end, demands endless punishment, see Shedd, Doctrine of Endless Punishment, 118–163 — "Suffering that is penal can never come to an end, because guilt is the reason for its infliction, and guilt once incurred, never ceases to be. . . . . One sin makes guilt, and guilt makes hell." Man does not punish endlessly, because he does not take account of God. " Human punishment is only approximate and imperfect, not absolute and perfect like the divine. It is not adjusted exactly and precisely to the whole guilt of the offence, but is more or less modified, first, by not considering its relation to God's honor and majesty; secondly, by human ignorance of inward motives; and thirdly, by social expediency." But "hell is not a penitentiary. . . . . The Lamb of God is also Lion of the tribe of Judah. . . . . The human penalty that approaches nearest to the divine is capital punishment. This punishment has a kind of endlessness. Death is a finality. It forever separates the murderer from earthly society, even as future punishment separates forever from the society of God and heaven." See Martineau, Types, 2:65–69.

The lapse of time does not convert guilt into innocence. The verdict "Guilty for ten days" was Hibernian. Guilt is indivisible and untransferable. The whole of it rests upon the criminal at every moment. Richelieu: "All places are temples, and all seasons summer, for justice." George Eliot: "Conscience is harder than our enemies, knows more, accuses with more nicety." Shedd: "Sin is the only perpetual motion that has ever been discovered. A slip in youth, committed in a moment, entails lifelong suffering. The punishment nature inflicts is infinitely longer than the time consumed in the violation of law, yet the punishment is the legitimate outgrowth of the offence."

(*c*) Not only eternal guilt, but eternal sin, demands eternal punishment. So long as moral creatures are opposed to God, they deserve punishment. Since we cannot measure the power of the depraved will to resist God, we cannot deny the possibility of endless sinning. Sin tends evermore to reproduce itself. The Scriptures speak of an "eternal sin" (Mark 3:29). But it is just in God to visit endless sinning with endless punishment. Sin, moreover, is not only an act, but also a condition or state, of the soul; this state is impure and abnormal, involves misery; this misery, as appointed by God to vindicate law and holiness, is punishment; this punishment is the necessary manifestation of God's justice. Not the punishing, but the not-punishing, would impugn his justice; for if it is just to punish sin at all, it is just to punish it as long as it exists.

Mark 3:29 —"whosoever shall blaspheme against the Holy Spirit hath never forgiveness, but is guilty of an eternal sin "; Rev. 22:11 —"He that is unrighteous, let him do unrighteousness still; and he that is filthy, let him be made filthy still." Calvin: "God has the best reason for punishing everlasting sin everlastingly."

President Dwight: " Every sinner is condemned for his first sin, and for every sin that follows, though they continue forever." What Martineau (Study, 2 : 106) says of this life, we may apply to the next : " Sin being there, it would be simply monstrous that there should be no suffering."

But we must remember that men are finally condemned, not merely for *sins*, but for *sin*; they are punished, not simply for *acts* of disobedience, but for evil *character*. The judgment is essentially a remanding of men to their " own place " (Acts 1 : 25). The soul that is permanently unlike God cannot dwell with God. The consciences of the wicked will justify their doom, and they will themselves prefer hell to heaven. He who does not love God is at war with himself, as well as with God, and cannot be at peace. Even though there were no positive inflictions from God's hand, the impure soul that has banished itself from the presence of God and from the society of the holy has in its own evil conscience a source of torment.

And conscience gives us a pledge of the eternity of this suffering. Remorse has no tendency to exhaust itself. The memory of an evil deed grows not less but more keen with time, and self-reproach grows not less but more bitter. Ever renewed affirmation of its evil decision presents to the soul forever new occasion for conviction and shame. F. W. Robertson speaks of " the infinite maddening of remorse." And Dr. Shedd, in the book above quoted, remarks : " Though the will to resist sin may die out of a man, the conscience to condemn it never can. This remains eternally. And when the process is complete; when the responsible creature, in the abuse of free agency, has perfected his ruin; when his will to good is all gone; there remain these two in his immortal spirit — sin and conscience, ' brimstone and fire ' (Rev. 21 : 8)."

E. G. Robinson : " The fundamental argument for eternal punishment is the reproductive power of evil. In the divine law penalty enforces itself. Rom. 6 : 19 —' ye presented your members as servants . . . , to iniquity unto iniquity.' Wherever sin occurs, penalty is inevitable. No man of sense would now hold to eternal punishment as an objective judicial infliction, and the sooner we give this up the better. It can be defended only on the ground of the reactionary power of elective preference, the reduplicating power of moral evil. We have no right to say that there are no other consequences of sin but natural ones ; out, were this so, every word of threatening in Scripture would still stand. We shall never be as complete as if we never had sinned. We shall bear the scars of our sins forever. The eternal law of wrong-doing is that the wrong-doer is cursed thereby, and harpies and furies follow him into eternity. God does not need to send a policeman after the sinner ; the sinner carries the policeman inside. God does not need to set up a whipping post to punish the sinner ; the sinner finds a whipping post wherever he goes, and his own conscience applies the lash."

(*d*) The actual facts of human life and the tendencies of modern science show that this principle of retributive justice is inwrought into the elements and forces of the physical and moral universe. On the one hand, habit begets fixity of character, and in the spiritual world sinful acts, often repeated, produce a permanent state of sin, which the soul, unaided, cannot change. On the other hand, organism and environment are correlated to each other ; and in the spiritual world, the selfish and impure find surroundings corresponding to their nature, while the surroundings react upon them and confirm their evil character. These principles, if they act in the next life as they do in this, will ensure increasing and unending punishment.

Gal. 6 : 7, 8 —" Be not deceived ; God is not mocked : for whatsoever a man soweth, that shall he also reap. For he that soweth unto his own flesh shall of the flesh reap corruption "; Rev. 21 : 11 —" He that is unrighteous, let him do unrighteousness still: and he that is filthy, let him be made filthy still." Dr. Heman Lincoln, in an article on Future Retribution (Examiner, April 2, 1885) — speaks of two great laws of nature which confirm the Scripture doctrine of retribution. The first is that " the tendency of habit is towards a permanent state. The occasional drinker becomes a confirmed drunkard. One who indulges in oaths passes into a reckless blasphemer. The gambler who has wasted a fortune, and ruined his family, is a slave to the card-table. The Scripture doctrine of retribution is only an extension of this well-known law to the future life."

The second of these laws is thet "organism and environment must be in harmony. Through the vast domain of nature, every plant and tree and reptile and bird and mammal has organs and functions fitted to the climate and atmosphere ot its habitat. If a rudden change occur in climate, from torrid to temperate, or from temperate to arctic; .f the atmosphere change from dry to humid, or from carbonic vapors to pure oxygen, sudden death is certain to overtake the entire fauna and flora of the region affected, unless plastic nature changes the organism to conform to the new environment. The interpreters of the Bible find the same law ordained for the world to come. Surroundings must correspond to character. A soul in love with sin can find no place in a holy heaven. If the environment be holy, the character of the beings assigned to it must be holy also. Nature and Revelation are in perfect accord." See Drummond, Natural Law in the Spiritual World, chapters: Environment, Persistence of Type, and Degradation.

Hosea 13:9—"It is thy destruction, O Israel, that thou art against me, against thy help"= if men are destroyed, it is because they destroy themselves. Not God, but man himself, makes hell. Schurman: "External punishment is unthinkable of human sins." Jackson, James Martineau, 152—"Our light, such as we have, we carry with us; and he who in his soul knows not God is still in darkness though, like the angel in the Apocalypse, he were standing in the sun." Crane, Religion of To-morrow, 313—"To insure perpetual hunger deprive a man of nutritious food, and so long as he lives he will suffer; so pain will last so long as the soul is deprived of God, after the artificial stimulants of sin's pleasures have lost their effect. Death has nothing to do with it; for as long as the soul lives apart from God, whether on this or on another planet, it will be wretched. If the unrepentant sinner is immortal, his sufferings will be immortal." "Magnas inter opes, inops"—poverty-stricken amid great riches—his very nature compels him to suffer. Nor can he change his nature; for character, once set and hardened in this world, cannot be cast into the melting-pot and remoulded in the world to come. The hell of Robert G. Ingersoll is far more terrible than the orthodox hell. He declares that there is no forgiveness and no renewal. Natural law must have its way. Man is a Mazeppa bound to the wild horse of his passions; a Prometheus, into whose vitals remorse, like a vulture, is ever gnawing.

(e) As there are degrees of human guilt, so future punishment may admit of degrees, and yet in all those degrees be infinite in duration. The doctrine of everlasting punishment does not imply that, at each instant of the future existence of the lost, there is infinite pain. A line is infinite in length, but it is far from being infinite in breadth or thickness. "An infinite series may make only a finite sum; and infinite series may differ infinitely in their total amount." The Scriptures recognize such degrees in future punishment, while at the same time they declare it to be endless (Luke 12:47, 48; Rev. 20:12, 13).

Luke 12:47, 48—"And that servant, who knew his Lord's will, and made not ready, nor did according to his will shall be beaten with many stripes; but he that knew not, and did things worthy of stripes, shall be beaten with few stripes"; Rev. 20:12, 13—"And I saw the dead, the great and the small, standing before the throne; and books were opened: and another book was opened, which is the book of life: and the dead were judged out of the things which were written in the books, according to their works . . . . judged every man according to their works."

(f) We know the enormity of sin only by God's own declarations with regard to it, and by the sacrifice which he has made to redeem us from it. As committed against an infinite God, and as having in itself infinite possibilities of evil, it may itself be infinite, and may deserve infinite punishment. Hell, as well as the Cross, indicates God's estimate of sin.

Cf. Ez. 14:23—"ye shall know that I have not done without cause all that I have done in it, saith the Lord Jehovah." Valuable as the vine is for its fruit, it is fit only for fuel when it is barren. Every single sin, apart from the action of divine grace, is the sign of pervading and permanent apostasy. But there is no single sin. Sin is a germ of infinite expansion. The single sin, left to itself, would never cease in its effects of evil,—it would dethrone God. "The idea of disproportion between sin and its punishment grows out of a belittling of sin and its guilt. One who regards murder as a slight offence will think hanging an outrageous injustice. Theodore Parker hated the doctrine of eternal punishment, *because* he considered sin as only a provocation to virtue, a step toward triumph, a fall upwards, good in the making." But it is only when we regard its relation to God that we can estimate sin's ill desert. See Edwards the younger, Works, 1: 1-294.

Dr. Shedd maintains that the guilt of sin is infinite, because it is measured, not by the powers of the offender, but by the majesty of the God against whom it is committed; see his Dogm. Theology, 2: 740, 749 —" Crime depends upon the object against whom it is committed, as well as upon the subject who commits it. . . . . To strike is a voluntary act, but to strike a post or a stone is not a culpable act. . . . . Killing a dog is as bad as killing a man, if merely the subject who kills and not the object killed is considered. . . . . As God is infinite, offence against him is infinite in its culpability. . . . . Any man who, in penitent faith, avails himself of the vicarious method of setting himself right with the eternal Nemesis, will find that it succeeds ; but he who rejects it must through endless cycles grapple with the dread problem of human guilt in his own person, and alone."

Quite another view is taken by others, as for example E. G. Robinson, Christian Theology, 292 —" The notion that the qualities of a finite act can be infinite — that its qualities can be derived from the person to whom the act is directed rather than from the motives that prompt it, needs no refutation. The notion itself, one of the bastard thoughts of mediæval metaphysical theology, has maintained its position in respectable society solely by the services it has been regarded as capable of rendering." Simon. Reconciliation, 123 —" To represent sins as infinite, because God against whom they are committed is infinite, logically requires us to say that trust or reverence or love towards God are infinite, because God is infinite." We therefore regard it as more correct to say, that sin as a finite act demands finite punishment, but as endlessly persisted in demands an endless, and in that sense an infinite, punishment.

E.   This everlasting punishment of the wicked is not inconsistent with God's benevolence.—It is maintained, however, by many who object to eternal retribution, that benevolence requires God not to inflict punishment upon his creatures except as a means of attaining some higher good. We reply :

(*a*) God is not only benevolent but holy, and holiness is his ruling attribute. The vindication of God's holiness is the primary and sufficient object of punishment. This constitutes a good which fully justifies the infliction.

Even love has dignity, and rejected love may turn blessing into cursing. Love for holiness involves hatred of unholiness. The love of God is not a love without character. Dorner: "Love may not throw itself away. . . . . We have no right to say that punishment is just only when it is the means of amendment." We must remember that holiness conditions love (see pages 296–298). Robert Buchanan forgot God's holiness when he wrote: "If there is doom for one, Thou, Maker, art undone ! " Shakespeare, King John, 4 : 3 —" Beyond the infinite and boundless reach Of mercy, if thou didst this deed of death, Art thou damned, Hubert ! " Tennyson : " He that shuts Love out, in turn shall be Shut out from Love, and on the threshold lie How ling in utter darkness." Theodore Parker once tried to make peace between Wendell Phillips and Horace Mann, whom Phillips had criticized with his accustomed severity. Mann wrote to Parker: " What a good man you are ! I am sure nobody would be damned if you were at the head of the universe. But," he continued, " I will never treat a man with respect whom I do not respect, be the consequences what they may — so help me — Horace Mann ! " (Chadwick, Theodore Parker, 330). The spirit which animated Horace Mann may not have been the spirit of love, but we can imagine a case in which his words might be the utterance of love as well as of righteousness. For love is under law to righteousness, and only righteous love is true love.

(*b*) In this life, God's justice does involve certain of his creatures in sufferings which are of no advantage to the individuals who suffer ; as in the case of penalties which do not reform, and of afflictions which only harden and embitter. If this be a fact here, it may be a fact hereafter.

There are many sufferers on earth, in prisons and on sick-beds, whose suffering results in hardness of heart and enmity to God. The question is not a question of quantity, but of quality. It is a question whether any punishment at all is consistent with God's benevolence,—any punishment, that is to say, which does not result in good to the punished. This we maintain; and claim that God is bound to punish moral impurity, whether any good comes therefrom to the impure or not. Archbishop Whately says it is as difficult to change one atom of lead to silver as it is to change a whole mountain. If the punishment of *many* incorrigibly impenitent persons is consistent with God's benevolence, so is the punishment of *one* incorrigibly impenitent person; if the punishment of incorrigibly impenitent persons for eternity is inconsistent with God's benevolence, so is the punishment of such persons for a limited time, or for any time at all.

In one of his early stories William Black represents a sour-tempered Scotchman as protesting against the idea that a sinner he has in mind should be allowed to escape the consequences of his acts: " What's the good of being good," he asks, " if things are to turn out that way ? " The instinct of retribution is the strongest instinct of the human heart. It is bound up with our very intuition of God's existence, so that to deny its rightfulness is to deny that there is a God. There is "a certain fearful expectation of judgment" (Heb. 10:27) for ourselves and for others, in case of persistent transgression, without which the very love of God would cease to inspire respect. Since neither annihilation nor second probation is Scriptural, our only relief in contemplating the doctrine of eternal punishment must come from: 1. the fact that eternity is not endless *time*, but a state inconceivable to us; and 2. the fact that evolution suggests reversion to the brute as the necessary consequence of abusing freedom.

(c) The benevolence of God, as concerned for the general good of the universe, requires the execution of the full penalty of the law upon all who reject Christ's salvation. The Scriptures intimate that God's treatment of human sin is matter of instruction to all moral beings. The self-chosen ruin of the few may be the salvation of the many.

Dr. Joel Parker, Lectures on Universalism, speaks of the security of free creatures as attained through a gratitude for deliverance " kept alive by a constant example of some who are suffering the vengeance of eternal fire." Our own race may be the only race (of course the angels are not a " race ") that has fallen away from God. As through the church the manifold wisdom of God is made manifest "to principalities and powers in the heavenly places" (Eph. 3:10); so, through the punishment of the lost, God's holiness may be made known to a universe that without it might have no proof so striking, that sin is moral suicide and ruin, and that God's holiness is its irreconcilable antagonist.

With regard to the extent and scope of hell, we quote the words of Dr. Shedd, in the book already mentioned: " Hell is only a spot in the universe of God. Compared with heaven, hell is narrow and limited. The kingdom of Satan is insignificant, in contrast with the kingdom of Christ. In the immense range of God's dominion, good is the rule and evil is the exception. Sin is a speck upon the infinite azure of eternity; a spot on the sun. Hell is only a corner of the universe. The Gothic etymon denotes a covered-up hole. In Scripture, hell is a 'pit,' a 'lake'; not an ocean. It is 'bottomless,' not boundless. The Gnostic and Dualistic theories which make God, and Satan or the Demiurge, nearly equal in power and dominion, find no support in Revelation. The Bible teaches that there will always be some sin and death in the universe. Some angels and men will forever be the enemies of God. But their number, compared with that of unfallen angels and redeemed men, is small. They are not described in the glowing language and metaphors by which the immensity of the holy and blessed is delineated (Ps. 68:17; Deut. 32:2; Ps. 103:21; Mat. 6:13; 1 Cor. 15:25; Rev. 14:1; 21:16, 24, 25.) The number of the lost spirits is never thus emphasized and enlarged upon. The brief, stern statement is, that 'the fearful and unbelieving . . . . their part shall be in the lake that burneth with fire and brimstone' (Rev. 21:8). No metaphors and amplifications are added to make the impression of an immense multitude which no man can number.'" Dr. Hodge: " We have reason to believe that the lost will bear to the saved no greater proportion than the inmates of a prison do to the mass of a community."

The North American Review engaged Dr. Shedd to write an article vindicating eternal punishment, and also engaged Henry Ward Beecher to answer it. The proof sheets of Dr. Shedd's article were sent to Mr. Beecher, whereupon he telegraphed from Denver to the Review: "Cancel engagement, Shedd is too much for me. I half believe in eternal punishment now myself. Get somebody else." The article in reply was never written, and Dr. Shedd remained unanswered.

(*d*) The present existence of sin and punishment is commonly admitted to be in some way consistent with God's benevolence, in that it is made the means of revealing God's justice and mercy. If the temporary existence of sin and punishment lead to good, it is entirely possible that their eternal existence may lead to yet greater good.

A priori, we should have thought it impossible for God to permit moral evil,— heathenism, prostitution, the saloon, the African slave-trade. But sin is a fact. Who can say how long it will be a fact? Why not forever? The benevolence that permits it now may permit it through eternity. And yet, if permitted through eternity, it can be made harmless only by visiting it with eternal punishment. Lillie on Thessalonians, 457—"If the temporary existence of sin and punishment lead to good, how can we prove that their eternal existence may not lead to greater good?" We need not deny that it causes God real sorrow to banish the lost. Christ's weeping over Jerusalem expresses the feelings of God's heart: Mat. 23:37, 38— "O Jerusalem, Jerusalem, that killeth the prophets, and stoneth them that are sent unto her! how often would I have gathered thy children together, even as a hen gathered her chickens under her wings, and ye would not! Behold, your house is left unto you desolate"; *cf.* Hosea 11:8— "How shall I give thee up, Ephraim? how shall I cast thee off, Israel? how shall I make thee as Admah? how shall I set thee as Zeboiim? my heart is turned within me, my compassions are kindled together." Dante, Hell, iii—the inscription over the gate of Hell: "Justice the founder of my fabric moved; To rear me was the task of power divine, Supremest wisdom and primeval love."

A. H. Bradford, Age of Faith, 254, 267—"If one thinks of the Deity as an austere monarch, having a care for his own honor but none for those to whom he has given being, optimism is impossible. For what shall we say of our loved ones who have committed sins? That splendid boy who yielded to an inherited tendency—what has become of him? Those millions who with little light and mighty passions have gone wrong—what of them? Those countless myriads who peopled the earth in ages past and had no clear motive to righteousness, since their perception of God was dim--is this all that can be said of them: In torment they are exhibiting the glorious holiness of the Almighty in his hatred of sin? Some may believe that, but, thank God, the number is not large. . . . . No, penalty, remorse, despair, are only signs of the deep remedial force in the nature of things, which has always been at work and always will be, and which, unless counteracted, will result sometime in universal and immortal harmony. . . . . Retribution is a natural law; it is universal in its sweep; it is at the same time a manifestation of the beneficence that pervades the universe. This law must continue its operation so long as one free agent violates the moral order. Neither justice nor love would be honored if one soul were allowed to escape the action of that law. But the sting in retribution is ordained to be remedial and restorative rather than punitive and vengeful. . . . . Will any forever resist that discipline? We know not; but it is difficult to understand how any can be willing to do so, when the fulness of the divine glory is revealed."

(*e*) As benevolence in God seems in the beginning to have permitted moral evil, not because sin was desirable in itself, but only because it was incident to a system which provided for the highest possible freedom and holiness in the creature ; so benevolence in God may to the end permit the existence of sin and may continue to punish the sinner, undesirable as these things are in themselves, because they are incidents of a system which provides for the highest possible freedom and holiness in the creature through eternity.

But the condition of the lost is only made more hopeless by the difficulty with which God brings himself to this, his "strange work" of punishment (Is. 28:21). The sentence which the judge pronounces with tears is indicative of a tender and suffering heart, but it also indicates that there can be no recall. By the very exhibition of "eternal judgment" (Heb. 6:2), not only may a greater number be kept true to God, but a higher degree of holiness among that number be forever assured. The Endless Future, published by South. Meth. Pub. House, supposes the universe yet in its infancy, an eternal liability to rebellion, an ever-growing creation kept from sin by one example of punishment. Mat. 7:13, 14 — "few there be that find it" — "seems to have been intended to describe the conduct of men then living, rather than to foreshadow the two opposite currents of human life to the end of time"; see Hovey, Bib. Eschatology, 167. See Goulburn, Everlasting Punishment; Haley, The Hereafter of Sin.

A. H. Bradford, Age of Faith, 239, mentions as causes for the modification of view as to everlasting punishment: 1. Increased freedom in expression of convictions; 2. Interpretation of the word "eternal"; 3. The doctrine of the immanence of God,—if God is in every man, then he cannot everlastingly hate himself, even in the poor manifestation of himself in a human creature; 4. The influence of the poets, Burns, Browning, Tennyson, and Whittier. Whittier, Eternal Goodness: "The wrong that pains my soul below, I dare not throne above: I know not of his hate,— I know His goodness and his love." We regard Dr. Bradford as the most plausible advocate of restoration. But his view is vitiated by certain untenable theological presuppositions: 1. that righteousness is only a form of love; 2. that righteousness, apart from love, is passionate and vengeful; 3. that man's freedom is incapable of endless abuse; 4. that not all men here have a fair probation; 5. that the amount of light against which they sin is not taken into consideration by God; 6. that the immanence of God does not leave room for free human action; 7. that God's object in his administration is, not to reveal his whole character, and chiefly his holiness, but solely to reveal his love; 8. that the declarations of Scripture with regard to "an eternal sin" (Mark 3:29), "eternal punishment" (Mat. 25:46), "eternal destruction" (2 Thess. 1:9), still permit us to believe in the restoration of all men to holiness and likeness to God.

We regard as more Scriptural and more rational the view of Max Müller, the distinguished Oxford philologist: "I have always held that this would be a miserable universe without eternal punishment. Every act, good or evil, must carry its consequences, and the fact that our punishment will go on forever seems to me a proof of the everlasting love of God. For an evil deed to go unpunished would be to destroy the moral order of the universe." Max Müller simply expresses the ineradicable conviction of mankind that retribution must follow sin; that God must show his disapproval of sin by punishment; that the very laws of man's nature express in this way God's righteousness; that the abolition of this order would be the dethronement of God and the destruction of the universe.

F. The proper preaching of the doctrine of everlasting punishment is not a hindrance to the success of the gospel, but is one of its chief and indispensable auxiliaries. — It is maintained by some, however, that, because men are naturally repelled by it, it cannot be a part of the preacher's message. We reply :

(a) If the doctrine be true, and clearly taught in Scripture, no fear of consequences to ourselves or to others can absolve us from the duty of preaching it. The minister of Christ is under obligation to preach the whole truth of God ; if he does this, God will care for the results.

Ex. 2:7 — "And thou shalt speak my words unto them, whether they will hear, or whether they will forbear"; 3:10, 11, 18, 19 - - "Moreover he said unto me, Son of man, all my words that I shall speak unto thee receive in thine heart, and hear with thine ears. And go, get thee to them of the captivity, unto the children of thy people, and speak unto them, and tell them, Thus saith the Lord Jehovah; whether they will hear, or whether they will forbear. . . . . When I say unto the wicked, Thou shalt surely die; and thou givest him not warning, nor speakest to warn the wicked from his wicked way, to save his life; the same wicked man shall die in his iniquity; but his blood will I require at thy hand. Yet if thou warn the wicked, and he turn not from his wickedness, nor from his wicked way, he shall die in his iniquity; but thou hast delivered thy soul."

The old French Protestant church had as a coat of arms the device of an anvil, around which were many broken hammers, with this motto: "Hammer away, ye hostile bands; Your hammers break, God's anvil stands." St. Jerome: "If an offence come out of the truth, better is it that the offence come, than that the truth be concealed." Shedd, Dogm. Theology, 2:680 — "Jesus Christ is the Person responsible for the doctrine of eternal perdition." The most fearful utterances with regard to future punishment are those of Jesus himself, as for example, Mat. 23 : 33 — "Ye serpents, ye offspring of vipers how shall ye escape the judgment of hell?" Mark 3 : 29 — "whosoever shall blaspheme against the Holy Spirit hath never forgiveness, but is guilty of an eternal sin"; Mat. 10 : 28 — "be not afraid of them that kill the body, but are not able to kill the soul: but rather fear him who is able to destroy both soul and body in hell"; 25 : 46 — "these shall go away into eternal punishment."

(*b*) All preaching which ignores the doctrine of eternal punishment just so far lowers the holiness of God, of which eternal punishment is an expression, and degrades the work of Christ, which was needful to save us from it. The success of such preaching can be but temporary, and must be followed by a disastrous reaction toward rationalism and immorality.

Much apostasy from the faith begins with refusal to accept the doctrine of eternal punishment. Theodore Parker, while he acknowledged that the doctrine was taught in the New Testament, rejected it, and came at last to say of the whole theology which includes this idea of endless punishment, that it "sneers at common sense, spits upon reason, and makes God a devil."

But, if there be no eternal punishment, then man's danger was not great enough to require an infinite sacrifice ; and we are compelled to give up the doctrine of atonement. If there were no atonement, there was no need that man's Savior should himself be more than man ; and we are compelled to give up the doctrine of the deity of Christ, and with this that of the Trinity. If punishment be not eternal, then God's holiness is but another name for benevolence ; all proper foundation for morality is gone, and God's law ceases to inspire reverence and awe. If punishment be not eternal, then the Scripture writers who believed and taught this were fallible men who were not above the prejudices and errors of their times ; and we lose all evidence of the divine inspiration of the Bible. With this goes the doctrine of miracles ; God is identified with nature, and becomes the impersonal God of pantheism.

Theodore Parker passed through this process, and so did Francis W. Newman. Logically, every one who denies the everlasting punishment of the wicked ought to reach a like result ; and we need only a superficial observation of countries like India, where pantheism is rife, to see how deplorable is the result in the decline of public and of private virtue. Emory Storrs : " When hell drops out of religion, justice drops out of politics." The preacher who talks lightly of sin and punishment does a work strikingly analogous to that of Satan, when he told Eve : "Ye shall not surely die" (Gen. 3:4). Such a preacher lets men go on what Shakespeare calls "the primrose way to the everlasting bonfire " (Macbeth, 2 : 3).

Shedd, Dogm. Theology, 2 : 671 - " Vicarious atonement is incompatible with universal salvation. The latter doctrine implies that suffering for sin is remedial only, while the former implies that it is retribution. . . . . If the sinner himself is not obliged by justice to suffer in order to satisfy the law he has violated, then certainly no one needs suffer for him for this purpose." Sonnet by Michael Angelo : " Now hath my life across a stormy sea Like a frail bark reached that wide port where all Are bidden, ere the final reckoning fall Of good and evil for eternity. Now know I well how that fond fantasy, Which made my soul the worshiper and thrall Of earthly art, is vain ; how criminal Is that which all men seek unwillingly. Those amorous thoughts that were so lightly dressed — What are they when the double death is nigh ? The one I know for sure, the other dread. Painting nor sculpture now can lull to rest My soul that turns to his great Love on high, Whose arms, to clasp us, on the Cross were spread."

(*c*) The fear of future punishment, though not the highest motive, is yet a proper motive, for the renunciation of sin and the turning to Christ. It must therefore be appealed to, in the hope that the seeking of salvation which begins in fear of God's anger may end in the service of faith and love.

Luke 12 : 4, 5 — "And I say unto you my friends, Be not afraid of them that kill the body, and after that have no more that they can do. But I will warn you whom ye shall fear: Fear him, who after he hath killed hath power to cast into hell ; yea, I say unto you, Fear him "; Jude 23 — "and some save, snatching them out of the fire." It is noteworthy that the Old Testament, which is sometimes regarded, though incorrectly, as a teacher of fear, has no such revelations of hell as are found in the New. Only when God's mercy was displayed in the Cross were there opened to men's view the depths of the abyss from which the Cross was to save them. And, as we have already seen, it is not Peter or Paul, but our Lord himself, who gives the most fearful descriptions of the suffering of the lost, and the clearest assertions of its eternal duration.

Michael Angelo's picture of the Last Judgment is needed to prepare us for Raphael's picture of the Transfiguration. Shedd, Dogm. Theology, 2 : 752 — "What the human race needs is to go to the divine Confessional. . . . . Confession is the only way to light and peace. . . . . The denial of moral evil is the secret of the murmuring and melancholy with which so much of modern letters is filled." Matthew Arnold said to his critics: "Non me tua fervida terrent dicta; Dii me terrent et Jupiter hostis"—"I am not afraid of your violent judgments; I fear only God and his anger." Heb. 10 : 31 — "It is a fearful thing to fall into the hands of the living God." Daniel Webster said : "I want a minister to drive me into a corner of the pew, and make me feel that the devil is after me."

(d) In preaching this doctrine, while we grant that the material images used in Scripture to set forth the sufferings of the lost are to be spiritually and not literally interpreted, we should still insist that the misery of the soul which eternally hates God is greater than the physical pains which are used to symbolize it. Although a hard and mechanical statement of the truth may only awaken opposition, a solemn and feeling presentation of it upon proper occasions, and in its due relation to the work of Christ and the offers of the gospel, cannot fail to accomplish God's purpose in preaching, and to be the means of saving some who hear.

Acts 20 : 31 — "Wherefore watch ye, remembering that by the space of three years I ceased not to admonish every one night and day with tears"; 2 Cor. 2 : 14-17 — "But thanks be unto God, who always leadeth us in triumph in Christ, and maketh manifest through us the savor of his knowledge in every place. For we are a sweet savor of Christ unto God, in them that are being saved, and in them that are perishing ; to the one a savor from death unto death ; to the other a savor from life unto life. And who is sufficient for these things? For we are not as the many, corrupting the word of God : but as of sincerity, but as of God, in the sight of God, speak we in Christ "; 5 : 11 — "Knowing therefore the fear of the Lord, we persuade men, but we are made manifest unto God ; and I hope that we are made manifest also in your consciences"; 1 Tim. 4 : 16 — "Take heed to thyself and to thy teaching. Continue in these things ; for in doing this thou shalt save both thyself and them that hear thee."

"Omne simile claudicat" as well as "volat"—"Every simile halts as well as flies." No symbol expresses all the truth. Yet we need to use symbols, and the Holy Spirit honors our use of them. It is "God's good pleasure through the foolishness of the preaching to save them that believe" (1 Cor. 1 : 21). It was a deep sense of his responsibility for men's souls that moved Paul to say : "woe is unto me, if I preach not the gospel" (1 Cor. 9 : 16). And it was a deep sense of duty fulfilled that enabled George Fox, when he was dying, to say : "I am clear! I am clear!"

So Richard Baxter wrote : "I preached as never sure to preach again, And as a dying man to dying men." It was Robert M°Cheyne who said that the preacher ought never to speak of everlasting punishment without tears. McCheyne's tearful preaching of it prevailed upon many to break from their sins and to accept the pardon and renewal that are offered in Christ. Such preaching of judgment and punishment were never needed more than now, when lax and unscriptural views with regard to law and sin break the force of the preacher's appeals. Let there be such preaching, and then many a hearer will utter the thought, if not the words, of the Dies Iræ, 8-10 —"Rex tremendæ majestatis, Qui salvandos salvas gratis, Salva me, fons pietatis. Recordare, Jesu pie, Quod sum causa tuæ viæ : Ne me perdas illa die. Quærens me sedisti lassus, Redemisti crucem passus : Tantus labor non sit cassus." See Edwards, Works, 4 : 226-321 ; Hodge, Outlines of Theology, 459-468 ; Murphy, Scientific Bases of Faith, 310, 319, 464 ; Dexter, Verdict of Reason ; George, Universalism not of the Bible ; Angus, Future Punishment; Jackson, Bampton Lectures for 1875, on the Doctrine of Retribution; Shedd, Doctrine of Endless Punishment, preface, and Dogm. Theol., 2 : 667-754.

INDEXES

The author acknowledges his great indebtness to the Reverend Robert Kerr Eccles, M. D., of Lemoore, California, for the preparation of the exceedingly full and valuable Indexes which follow, and a similiar obligation to Mr. Herman K. Phinney, Assistant Librarian of the University of Rochester, for his care in the proof-reading of the whole work.

INDEX OF SUBJECTS.

Ability, gracious,---------------- 602, 640
  natural, of New School,----------640, 641
  not test of sin,----------------------- 558
  Pelagian, ------------------------------ 640
Abiogenesis, -------------------------------- 389
Absolute, its denotation,----------------- 9
  as applied to divine attributes,------ 249
  how related to finite,-----------58, 255
  Reason, an, the postulate of logical
    thought, ---------------------------- 60
Abydos, triad of,----------------------- 351
Acceptilatio, the Grotian,------------- 740
Acquittal of believing sinners, from
  punishment, --------------------------- 854
Action, divine, not in distantia,-------- 418
Acts, evil, God's concurrence with,---- 418
Ad aperturam libri,--------------------- 32
Adam, his original righteousness not
    immutable, --------------------------- 519
  had power of contrary choice,-------- 519
  not created undecided,---------------- 519
  his love, God-given,------------------ 519
  his exercise of holy will not merito-
    rious, ------------------------------- 520
  unfallen, according to Romish the-
    ologians, ---------------------------- 520
  his physical perfection,-------------- 523
  unfallen, according to Fathers and
    Scholastics, ------------------------- 523
  his relations to lower creation,------ 524
  his relations to God,----------------- 524
  his surroundings and society,-------- 525
  the test of his virtue,--------------- 526
  physical immortality possible to,---- 527
  his Fall, see Fall.
  his twofold death, resulting from
    Fall, -------------------------------- 590
  his communion with God interrup-
    ted, --------------------------------- 592
  his banishment from God,------------ 593
  imputation of his sin to his poster-
    ity, see Imputation.
  in him 'the natural,' had he con-
    tinued upright, might without
    death have obtained 'the spiritual,' 658
  was Christ in,------------------------ 759
  Christ, the Last,-------------------- 678
  Christ, the Second,------------------ 680
Adoption, what?------------------------ 857

Aequale temperamentum,--------------- 523
Affections, -----------------------------362, 815
  holy, authors on,--------------------- 826
Agency, free, and divine decrees,--359-362
Alexander, unifier of Greek East,------ 668
Allegorical arrangement in theology, 50
Alloeosis, ------------------------------ 686
Altruism, ------------------------------- 296
Ambition, what?------------------------ 569
American theology,-----------------48, 49
Anacoloutha, Paul's,------------------- 210
Analytical method, in theology,----45, 49
Ancestry of race, proofs of a common,
  --------------------------------------476-482
'Angel of the church, ----------------452, 916
'Angel of Jehovah,'-------------------- 319
Angelology of Scripture, not derived
    from Egyptian or Persian sources, 448
Angels' food,'-------------------------- 445
Angels, their class defined,------------ 443
  Scholastic subtleties regarding their
    influence, --------------------------443, 444
  Milton and Dante upon,-------------- 443
  their existence a scientific possibili-
    ty, ---------------------------------- 444
  faith in, enlarges conception of uni-
    verse, ------------------------------- 444
  list of authors upon,----------------- 444
  Scriptural statements and intima-
    tions concerning,----------------441-459
  are created beings,------------------- 444
  are incorporeal,--------------------- 445
  are personal,------------------------- 445
  possessed of superhuman intelli-
    gence, ------------------------------- 445
  distinct from and older than man,--- 445
  not personifications,----------------- 445
  numerous, ---------------------------- 447
  are a company, not a race,----------- 447
  were created holy,------------------- 450
  had a probation,--------------------- 450
  some preserved their integrity,------ 450
  some fell from innocence,------------ 450
  the good, confirmed in goodness,---- 450
  the evil, confirmed in evil,---------- 450
Angels, good, they stand worshiping
    God, -------------------------------- 451
  they rejoice in God's works,--------- 451
  they work in nature,----------------- 451

Angels, good, they guide nations,____ 451
  watch over interests of churches,___ 452
  assist individual believers,_____ 452
  punish God's enemies,_____ 452
  ministers of God's special provi-
    dences, _____ 452
  act within laws of spiritual and
    moral world,_____ 453
  their influence illustrated by psych-
    ic phenomena,_____453, 454
Angels, evil, oppose God,_____ 454
  hinder man's welfare,_____ 455
  tempt negatively and positively,____ 455
  their intercourse with Christ,_____ 456
  execute God's will,_____ 457
  their power not independent of hu-
    man will,_____ 457
  limited by permissive will of God, 458
  the doctrine of, not opposed to
    science, _____ 459
  not opposed to right views of space
    or spirit,_____ 459
  not impossible that, though wise,
    they should rebel,_____ 460
  the continuance and punishment of
    evil, not inconsistent with divine
    benevolence, _____ 461
  their organization, though sinful,
    not impossible,_____ 461
  the doctrine of evil, not hurtful,_461, 462
  the doctrine of evil, does not de-
    grade man,_____ 462
  good, the doctrine of, its uses,____ 462
  evil, the doctrine of, its uses,_____ 463
  fallen, if no redemption provided
    for, why?_____ 463
  created in Christ,_____ 464
  their salvation, Scripture silent up-
    on, _____ 464
Anger, sometimes a duty,_____ 294
Annihilation, of infants, held by Em-
    mons, _____ 609
  at death, inequitable,_____987, 1036
  disproved by Scripture,_____991-998
  terms which seemingly teach,_____ 993
  language adduced to prove, often
    metaphorical, _____ 994
  old view of,_____1036
  the theory that it is a result of the
    weakening of powers of soul by
    sin, considered,_____1036
  'second death' regarded as dissolu-
    tion of the soul,_____1036
  the theory that a positive punish-
    ment proportioned to guilt pre-
    cedes and ends in,_____1037
  the tenet of, rests on a defective
    view of holiness,_____1037
  a part of the 'conditional immor-
    tality' hypothesis,_____1037
  as connected with the principle,

'Evil is punished by its own in-
    crease,' _____1038
Annihilationists, _____ 487
'Answer (interrogation) of a good
    conscience,' phrase examined,_____ 821
Anthropological argument for God's
    existence, _____80-85
Anthropological method in theology,__ 50
Anthropology, a division of theology, 464
Anthropomorphism, _____122, 250
'Anthropomorphism inverse,'_____ 463
Antichrist, _____1009
'Anticipative consequences,'_____403, 658
Antinomianism, _____ 875
Antiquity of race, relation of Script-
    ure to,_____224-226
Apocalypse, its exegetic not yet
    found, _____1014
Apocrypha, _____115, 150, 865
Apollinarianism, _____487, 670, 671
Apostasy, man's state of,_____533-664
Apostasy of the believer, how treated
    in Scripture,_____884-886
A posteriori reasoning,_____66, 86
Apostles, _____199-201, 909, 971
Apotelesmaticum genus,_____ 686
A priori argument for God's exis-
    tence, the, see God.
  judgments, _____ 10
  reasons for expecting a divine rev-
    elation, _____111-114
Arbitrium, _____ 557
Argument ad hominem in Scripture,_ 230
  for existence of God, its value,____
    _____65-67, 71, 72, 87-89
Arianism, _____328-330, 670
Arminianism, _____362, 601-606
Arrangement of material in theology,
    _____2, 49, 50
Art, _____529, 1016
Aryan and Semitic languages, their
    connection, _____ 479
Ascension, Christ's,_____708-710
  Christ's humanity, how related to
    the Logos in,_____ 709
Aseity of God,_____256, 257
  not confined to Father,_____ 342
Assensus, an element in faith,_____ 837
Assurance of salvation,_____808, 845
'Asymptote of God,' man, the,_____ 565
Athanasian Creed,_____ 329
Atoms, _____96, 374
Atomism, _____600, 635
Atonement, facts in Christ's suffer-
    ings which prove, _____ 713
  defined, _____ 713
  satisfies holiness, the fundamental
    attribute of God,_____ 713
  meets the conditions of a universe
    in which happiness is connected
    with righteousness and suffering
    with sin_____ 714

Atonement, in it Christ as Logos, the Revealer of God in the universe, inflicts the penalty of sin, while, as Life of humanity, he endures the infliction, ---------------------- 714

humanity has made, when righteousness in Christ, as generic humanity, condemns sin, and love in Christ endures the penalty,-------- 714

substitutionary and sharing,-------- 715

in, Christ suffers as the very life of man, -------------------------------- 715

not made, but revealed, by Christ's historical sufferings,---------------- 715

the sacrifice of, the final revelation of the heart of God and of the law of universal life,-------------------- 716

a model of, and stimulus to, self-sacrifice, ---------------------------716

its subjective effects must not exclude consideration of its ground and cause,-------------------------- 716

Scripture methods of representing, --------------------------------716-722

originates in God's love and manifests it,------------------------------ 716

an example of disinterested love to secure our deliverance from selfishness, ----------------------716, 717

a ransom in which death is the price paid,-------------------------- 717

an act of obedience to law,--------- 717

an act of priestly mediation,------718-728

a sin-offering,-------------------- 719

a propitiation,--------------------- 719

a substitution,--------------------- 720

correct views of, grounded on proper interpretation of the institution of sacrifice,--------------------- 721

is it to be interpreted according to notions derived from Jewish or heathen sacrifices?-------------------- 728

theories of,---------------------728-766

Socinian (example) theory,------728, 729

objections to above,---------------735-740

Bushnellian (moral influence) theory, --------------------------733-735

objections to above,---------------735-740

Grotian (governmental) theory of, ---------------------------------740, 741

Irvingian (gradually extirpated depravity) theory of,-------------744, 745

objections to theory,---------------745-747

Anselmic (commercial) theory of,-- ---------------------------------747, 748

Military theory of,--------------------- 747

objections to,----------------------748-750

Criminal theory of,-------------------- 748

the Ethical theory of,-------------750-771

a true theory of, resolves two problems, -------------------------750, 751

grounded in holiness of God,-------- 751

Atonement, a satisfaction of an ethical demand of the divine nature, -----------------------751, 752, 753

substitution in, an operation of grace, ------------------------------- 753

the righteousness of law maintained in, ---------------------------------- 753

maintains, as a first subordinate result, the interests of the divine government, ----------------------- 753

provides, as a second subordinate result, for the needs of human nature, --------------------------------- 754

the classical passage with reference to, --------------------------------- 753

sets forth Christ as so related to humanity that he is under obligation to pay and does pay,--------- 754

explains how the innocent can suffer for the guilty in,-----755, 756, 757

Andover theory of,-------------------- 756

by one whose nature was purified, but his obligation to suffer undiminished, --------------------------- 757

the guilt resting on Christ in, what it was,---------------------645, 646, 757

as a member of the race, did he not suffer in, for his own sin?--------- 758

showed what had been in the heart of God from eternity,-------------- 758

explanations of Christ's identification with humanity as a reason why he made,--------------------759-761

exposition of 2 Cor. 5 : 21,------------ 760

grounded in the holiness and love of God,----------------------------- 761

is accomplished through the solidarity of the race, and Christ the common life, bearing guilt for men, 761

ground of, on the part of man,------- 761

rather revealed than made by incarnate Christ,-----------------762, 763

Ethical theory of, philosophically correct, --------------------------- 764

combines the valuable elements of other theories,--------------------- 764

shows most satisfactorily how demands of holiness are met,---------- 764

presents only explanation of sacrificial rites and language,---------- 765

alone gives proper place to death of Christ, ---------------------------- 765

is best explanation of sufferings of Christ, ---------------------------- 765

satisfies most completely the ethical demand of human nature,-----765, 766

objected to, as inconsistent with God's omnipotence or love,-------- 766

objected to, as presented ideas mutually exclusive,------------------- 767

objected to, as obviating real propitiation, ------------------------------ 768

Atonement, objected to, as an act of injustice, ---------------------------- 768
objected to, because transfer of punishment is impossible, ----------768, 769
objected to, because the remorse implied in it, was impossible to Christ, ---------------------------- 769
objected to, because sufferings finite in time cannot satisfy infinite demands of law, --------------------769, 770
objected to, that it renders Christ's active obedience superfluous, ------ 770
objected to, as immoral in tendency, 770
objected to, as requiring faith to complete a satisfaction which ought to be itself perfect, ---------- 771
extent of, --------------------------771–773
unlimited, --------------------------- 771
its application limited, --------------- 771
passages asserting its special efficacy, ---------------------------------- 771
passages asserting its sufficiency for all, ---------------------------------- 771
secures for all men delay in execution of sentence against sin, ------ 772
has made objective provision for all, --------------------------------772, 773
has procured for all incentives to repentance, ------------------------ 773
limited, advocates of, ---------------- 773
universal, advocates of, -------------- 773
Attributes, divine, see God.
mental, higher than those of matter, inference from, ----------------- 92
Aurignac Cave, its evidence doubtful, 532
Australian languages, their affinities, 479
Automatic, mental activity largely, -- 550
'Automatic excellence or badness,' ---- 611
Avarice, defined, ----------------------- 569
Avatars, Hindu, ----------------------- 187
Christ's incarnation unlike, ---------- 698
Ayat of Koran, --------------------- 213
Baalim, --------------------------------- 318
Balaam, inspired, yet unholy, --------- 207
Baptism and Lord's Supper, only accounted for as monuments, -------- 157
the formula of, correlates Christ's name with God's-------------------- 312
according to Romish church, -------- 522
of Jesus, its import, ----------761, 762, 942
Christian, definition of, -------------- 931
instituted by Christ, ----------------- 931
of universal and perpetual obligation, --------------------------------- 931
ignored by Salvation Army and Society of Friends, -------------------- 931
John's recognized by Christ, ----931, 922
John's, was it a modification of a previously existing rite?--------931, 932
proselyte, its existence discussed, ---------------------------931, 932

Baptism, John's, essentially Christian baptism, ----------------------- 732
made the law of the church, -------- 932
Christian, complementally related to Lord's Supper, is of equal permanency, ----------------------932, 933
its mode, immersion, ----------------- 933
meaning of its original word, according to Greek usage, --------933, 934
meaning of original word as determined by contextual relation, ------ 934
meaning of original word determined by voice used with 'water,' 935
meaning of original word determined by prepositional connections, ---------------------------------- 935
meaning of original word derived from circumstances, ----------------- 935
original meaning of word determined from figurative allusions, -- 936
original meaning of word determined by practice of early church, 936
occasional change in its mode permitted for seeming sufficient reason at an early date, --------------- 936
original meaning of word determined by usage of Greek church, ----------------------------------937, 938
Dr. Dods' statement as to its mode, 938
concession to its original method of observance in the introduction of baptisteries or 'fontgraves' into non-Baptist places of worship---- 938
the church, being only an executive body, cannot modify Christ's law concerning, ----------------------- 939
the law of, fundamental, and therefore unalterable save by Legislator himself, ------------------------ 939
any modification of, by church, implies unwisdom in Appointer of rite, ---------------------------------- 939
any change in mode vacates ordinance of its symbolic significance, 939
objections to its mode, immersion, -- 940
if its mode impracticable, ordinance not a duty, ------------------------ 940
when its mode dangerous, ordinance not to be performed, ----------------- 940
the mode of baptism decently impressive, ---------------------------- 940
the ordinance symbolizing suffering and death is consistently somewhat inconvenient, ----------------- 940
God's blessing on an irregular administration of, no sanction of irregularity, ------ ----------------- 940
its symbolism, ---- ----------------940–945
what it symbolizes in general, ------- 940
it symbolizes death and burial of Christ, ------------------------------- 940
it symbolizes union with Christ-- 941

Baptism, it symbolizes atonement and
redemption, -------------------------- 941
it symbolizes to the believer being
baptized his spiritual death and
resurrection, ------------------------- 941
it symbolizes union of believers with
each other,--------------------------- 942
it symbolizes the death and resurrection of the body,---------------- 942
the central truth, set forth by,------ 942
a correlative truth set forth by,----- 943
sets forth purification through communion with death of Christ,------ 944
symbolizes regenerating power of
Jesus' death,------------------------- 944
immersion in, alone symbolizes the
passage from death unto life in
regeneration and communion with
Christ in his death and rising,--- 944
the substituting for the correct mode
of, one which excludes all reference to Christ's death destroys
the ordinance,----------------------- 944
is a historical monument,------------ 945
is a pictorial expression of doctrine, 945
and Lord's Supper------------------- 945
subjects of,------------------------945-959
the proper subjects of,-------------- 945
those only to be baptized who have
first been made disciples,---------- 945
those only to be baptized who have
repented and believed,------------- 945
those only to be baptized who can
be members of the church,--------- 945
those only to be baptized for whom
the symbolism is valid,------------ 946
not a means of regeneration,-------- 946
the spiritual and the ritual so combined in, that the whole ordinance
may be designated by its outward
aspect, ----------------------------- 946
as a being 'born of water,'-------- 946
connected with repentance 'for the
remission of sins,'------------------ 946
without baptism, discipleship incomplete, and ineffective,-------------- 947
the teachings of Campbellism regarding, --------------------------947, 948
act of person baptized,-------------- 948
before it is administered, church
should require evidence that candidates are regenerated,----------- 949
incorrectly called 'door into the
church,' --------------------------- 949
as expressive of inward character
of candidate,----------------------- 950
as regeneration is once for all, baptism must not be repeated,-------- 950
as outward expression of inward
change, is the first of all duties,-- 950

Baptism should follow regeneration
with least possible delay,-------- 950
if an actual profession of faith, not
to be repeated,--------------------- 950
accessories to, matters of individual
judgment, -------------------------- 951
its formula,-------------------------- 951
Infant, -------------------------951-959
without warrant in Scripture,------- 951
has no express command,------------ 951
has no clear example,--------------- 951
passages held to imply it, have no
reference thereto,------------------- 951
expressly contradicted,-------------- 952
in it the prerequisites of faith and
repentance impossible,------------- 952
in it the symbolism of baptism has
lost significance,------------------- 952
its practice inconsistent with constitution of the church,----------- 952
is unharmonious with prerequisites
to the Lord's Supper,-------------- 952
has led in Greek Church to infant
communion, ------------------------ 953
denied by the Paulicians,----------- 953
the reasons of its rise and spread,-- 953
a necessary concomitant of a State
Church, --------------------------- 954
founded on unscriptural and dangerous reasonings,------------------ 954
it assumes power of church to tamper with Christ's commands,------ 954
contradicts New Testament ideas of
church, --------------------------- 954
assumes a connection of parent and
child closer and more influential
than facts of Scripture and experience will support,--------------954, 955
its propriety urged on various unsettled grounds,-------------------- 956
does it make its subjects members
of the church? --------------------- 956
its evil effects,------------------957-959
forestalls any voluntary act,------- 957
induces superstitious confidence,---- 957
has led to baptism of irrational and
material things,-------------------- 957
has obscured and corrupted Christian truth,------------------------- 958
is often an obstacle to evangelical
views, ---------------------------- 958
merges church in nation and world, 958
substitutes for Christ's command an
invention of men,-------------958, 959
literature concerning,--------------- 959
Baptismal Regeneration,--820-822, 946, 947
literature upon,--------------------- 948
Baptist Theology,--------------------- 47
Baptists, English,------------------972, 977
Free Will,--------------------972, 977, 979

Believers, and the 'old man,'_____ 870
  and the Intermediate State,_____998, 999
Bewusstsein, in Gottesbewusstsein,____ 63
Bible, see Scripture.
Bishop, office of, early made sole interpreter of apostles,_____ 912
  in his progress from primus inter
  pares to Christ's vicegerent,_____ 912
  ordaining, his qualifications in Episcopal church,_____ 913
  'presbyter' and 'pastor' designate
  same order,_____914, 915
  the duties of,_____916, 917
  ordination of,_____918–924
Blessedness, what?_____ 265
  contrasted with glory,_____ 265
Bodies, new, of saints, are confined to
  space, _____1032
Body, image of God, mediately or significative, _____ 523
  honorable, _____ 488
  suggestions as to reason why given, 488
  immortality of, sought by Egyptians, 995
  not indispensable to activity and
  consciousness, _____1000
  spiritual, what it imports,_1016, 1021–1023
  resurrection of, see Resurrection.
  same, though changed annually,____1020
  a 'flowing organism,'_____ 1021
  to regard it as a normal part of
  man's being, Scriptural and philosophical, _____1021, 1022
Bond-servant of sin,' what?____509, 510
Book may be called by name of chief
  author, _____ 239
Book of Mormon,_____ 141
  of Enoch,_____ 165
  of Judges,_____166, 171
  of the Law, its finding,_____ 167
Books of O. T. quoted by Jesus,____ 199
  of N. T. received and used, in 2d
  century, _____ 146
Brahma, _____ 181
Brahmanism, _____ 181
Bread, in Lord's Supper, its significance, _____ 963
  of life,_____ 963
Brethren, Plymouth,_____895, 896
Bride-catching, not primeval,_____ 528
'Brimstone and fire,' sin and conscience, _____1049
Brute, conscious but not self-conscious, _____252, 467
  cannot objectify self,_____252, 467
  is determined from without,____252, 468
  none ever thought 'I,'_____ 467
  has not apperception,_____ 467
  has no concepts,_____ 467
  has no language,_____ 467
  forms no judgments,_____ 467

Brute, does not associate ideas by
  similarity, _____- - 467
  cannot reason,_____ 467
  has no general ideas,_____ 463
  has no conscience,_____ 468
  has no religious nature,_____ 468
  man came not from the, but through
  the, _____ 467
Buddha,_____181, 182, 183
Buddhism, its grain of truth,_____ 181
  a missionary religion,_____ 181
  its universalism,_____ 181
  its altruism,_____ 181
  its atheism,_____ 182
  its fatalism,_____ 182
Buncombe,' _____ 17
Burial of food and weapons with the
  dead body, why practiced by some
  races, _____ 532
Burnt offering, its significance,_____ 726
Byzantine and Italian artists differ
  in their pictures of Jesus Christ, 678
Cæsar, writes in the third person,___ 151
  unifier of the Latin West,_____ 566
  his words on passing the Rubicon,_1032
'Caged-eagle theory' of man's life,____ 560
Caiaphas, inspired yet unholy,_____ 207
Cain, _____ 477
Calixtus, his analytic method in sys-
  tematic theology,_____45, 46
Call to ministry,_____ 919
Calling, efficacious,____777, 782, 790, 791,
  _____793, 794
  general or external,_____ 791
  is general, sincere?_____791, 792
Calvinism, in history,_____ 368
Calvinistic and Arminian views, their
  approximation, _____362, 368
Cambridge Platform,_____ 923
'Carnal mind,' its meaning,_____ 562
Carthage, Council of (397), and Epis-
  tle to the Hebrews,_____ 152
  Synod of (412), and Pelagius,_____ 597
Caste, what?_____ 181
  and Buddhism,_____ 181
  and Christianity,_____ 898
Casualism, _____427, 428
Casuistry, non-scriptural,_____ 648
Catacombs, _____ 191
Catechism, Roman, on originalis jus-
  titiæ donum additum,_____ 522
  Westminster Assembly's, on Infant
  Baptism, _____ 957
Causality, its law,_____ 73
  does not require a first cause,_____ 74
Cause and effect, simultaneity of,____ 793
Cause, equivalent to 'requisite,'____ 44
  formal, _____ 44
  material, _____ 44
  efficient, _____ 44

Cause, final,------------------------------ 44
  can an infinite, be inferred from a
    finite universe?----------------------- 79
  when the efficient, gives place to
    the final?----------------------------- 125
  various definitions of,--------------814, 815
Causes, Aristotle's four,----------------- 44
  an infinite series of, does not re-
    quire a cause of itself,-------------- 74
Celsus, derides the same religion for
  many peoples,------------------------- 192
Certainty not necessity,---------------- 362
Chalcedon (451) Symbol, on Mary as
  'mother of God,'----------------671, 686
  condemned Eutychianism,------------ 672
  promulgated orthodox doctrine as to
    the Person of Christ,--------------- 673
  its formula negative with a single
    exception, --------------------------- 673
Chance as a name for ignorance, term
  allowable, --------------------------- 423
  as implying absence of causal con-
    nection in phenomena, not allow-
    able, ------------------------------- 428
  as undesigning cause, insufficient,-- 428
Change, orderly, requires intelligent
  cause, ------------------------------- 75
Character, helped by systematic truth, 16
  changed rather than expressed by
    some actions,----------------------- 360
  what it is,----------------------506, 600
  how a man may change,-------------- 507
  extent of one's responsibility for,-- 605
  sinning makes,-----------------------1041
  sinful, renders certain continuance
    in sinful actions,-------------------1041
  dependent on habit,------------------1049
Chastisement, not punishment,----654, 766
Cherubim, ------------------------449, 593
Child, unborn, has promise and potency of spiritual manhood,-------- 644
  individuality of the,----------------- 492
  visited for sins of fathers,---------- 634
Chiliasts in all ages,-----------------1007
Chinese, their religion a survival of
  patriarchal family worship,-------- 180
  their history, its commencement,---- 225
  may have left primitive abodes while
    language still monosyllabic,-------- 478
Choice, of an ultimate end,---------- 504
  of means,---------------------------- 504
  decision in favor of one among sev-
    eral conflicting desires,---------505, 506
  not creation, our destiny,----------- 508
  New School idea of,----------------- 550
  first moral,--------------------------- 611
  evil, uniformity of, what it implies, 611
  contrary, possessed by Adam,-------- 519
  not essential to will,---------------- 600
  as at present possessed by man,----- 605
  God's, see Election.
Christ, his person and character must
  be historical,----------------------- 186

Christ, no source for conception of,
  other than himself,----------------- 187
  conception of, could not originate in
    human genius,---------------------- 187
  acceptance of the story of, a proof
    of his existence,------------------- 187
  some of the difficulties in which the
    assumption that the story of, is
    false, lands us,-------------------- 188
  if the story of, is true, Christianity
    is true,--------------------------- 188
  his testimony to himself, its sub-
    stance, -------------------------- 189
  his testimony to himself, not that of
    an intentional deceiver,----------- 189
  his testimony to himself, not that
    of insanity or vanity,------------- 189
  if neither mentally nor morally un-
    sound, his testimony concerning
    himself is true,------------------- 190
  in his sympathy and sorrow reveals
    God's feeling,--------------------- 266
  the whole Christ present in each be-
    liever, ---------------------------- 281
  his supreme regard for God,-------- 302
  recognized as God in certain pas-
    sages, ------------------------305-308
  some passages once relied on to
    prove his divinity now given up
    for textual reasons,--------------- 308
  Old Testament descriptions of God
    applied to him,-------------------- 309
  possesses attributes of God,-------- 309
  undelegated works of God are as-
    cribed to him,-------------------- 310
  receives honor and worship due only
    to God,------------------------- 311
  his name associated on equality with
    that of God,---------------------- 312
  equality with God expressly claimed
    for him,-------------------------- 312
  'si non Deus, non bonus,'---------- 313
  proofs of his divinity in certain
    phrases applied to him,----------- 313
  his divinity corroborated by Chris-
    tian experience,---------------313, 682
  his divinity exhibited in hymns and
    prayers of church,----------------- 313
  his divinity, passages which seem
    inconsistent with, how to be re-
    garded, ------------------------- 314
  as pre-incarnate Logos, Angel of Je-
    hovah, --------------------------- 319
  in pre-existent state, the Logos,----- 335
  in pre-existent state, the Image of
    God, ----------------------------- 335
  in pre-existent state, the Effulgence
    of God,--------------------------- 335
  the centrifugal action of Deity,----- 336
  and Spirit, how their work differs,-- 338
  his eternal Sonship,---------------- 340
  if not God, cannot reveal him,------- 349

Christ, orders of creation to be united
in, --------------------------------- 444
his human soul,----------------------- 493
his character convinces of sin,------- 539
he is the ideal and the way to it,-- 544
not law, 'the perfect Image' of God, 548
his holiness, in what it consisted,-- 572
in Gethsemane felt for the race,----- 635
with him believers have a connection of spiritual life,--------------- 636
human nature in, may have guilt
without depravity,-------------------- 645
educator of the race,----------------- 666
the Person of,--------------------669-700
the doctrine of his Person stated,--- 669
a brief historical survey of the doctrine of his Person,------------------ 669
views of the Ebionites concerning,-- 669
reality of his body denied by Docetæ, --------------------------------- 670
views of Arians concerning,--------- 670
views of Apollinarians ----------670, 671
views of Nestorians,-------------671, 672
views of Eutychians,----------------- 672
the two natures of, their integrity,-- 673
his humanity real,-------------------- 673
is expressly called 'a man,'--------- 673
his genealogies, --------------------- 673
had the essential elements of human nature,-------------------------- 674
had the same powers and principles
of normal humanity,------------------ 674
his elocution,------------------------- 674
subject to the laws of human development, ----------------------------- 675
in twelfth year seems to enter on
consciousness of his divine Sonship, -------------------------------- 675
suffered and died,-------------------- 675
dies (Stroud) of a broken heart,---- 675
lived a life of faith and prayer, and
study of Scripture,------------------ 675
the integrity of his humanity,---675-681
supernaturally conceived,------------ 675
free from hereditary depravity and
actual sin,--------------------------- 676
his ideal human nature,------------- 678
his human nature finds its personality in union with the divine,------- 679
his human nature germinal,--------- 680
the 'Everlasting Father,'---------- 680
the Vine-man,------------------------ 680
Docetic doctrine concerning, confuted, --------------------------------- 681
possessed a knowledge of his own
deity, ------------------------------- 681
exercised divine prerogatives,------- 682
in him divine knowledge and power, 682
union of two natures in his one person, -----------------------------683-700
possesses a perfect divine and human nature,----------------------683, 684
proof of this union of natures in,-- 684

Christ speaks of himself as a single
person, ----------------------------- 684
attributes of both his natures ascribed to one person,----------684, 685
Scriptural representation of infinite
value of atonement and union of
race with God prove him divine,-- 685
Lutheran view as to communion of
natures in,-------------------------- 686
four genera regarding the natures
of Christ,--------------------------- 686
union of natures in,------------------ 686
theory of his incomplete humanity, 686
objections to this theory,------687, 688
theory of his gradual incarnation,
---------------------------------688, 689
objections to this view,-----------689-691
real nature of union of persons in,
---------------------------------691-700
importance of correct views of the
person of,-----------------------691, 692
chief problems in the doctrine of the
person of,--------------------------- 692
why the union of the natures in the
person of Christ is inscrutable,-- 693
on what the possibility of the union
of deity and humanity in his person is grounded,----------------693, 694
no double personality in,----------694-696
union of natures in, its effect upon
his humanity,-------------------696, 697
union of natures in, its effect upon
the divine,-------------------------- 697
this union of natures in the person
of, necessary,----------------------- 698
the union of natures in, eternal, 698, 699
the infinite and finite in,---------699, 700
the two states of,----------------701-710
the nature of his humiliation,----701-706
not the union in him of Logos and
human nature,---------------------- 701
his humiliation did not consist in
the surrender of the relative divine attributes,---------------------- 701
objections to above view---------701-703
his humiliation consisted in the surrender of the independent exercise
of the Divine attributes,----------- 703
his humiliation consisted in the assumption by the pre-existent Logos of the servant-form,----------- 703
his humiliation consisted in the submission of the Logos to the Holy
Spirit, ------------------------------ 703
his humiliation consisted in the surrender as to his human nature of
all advantages accruing thereto
from union with deity,--------703, 704
the five stages of his humiliation,
------------------------------------704-706
his state of exaltation,------------706-710
the nature of his exaltation,------706, 707
the stages of his exaltation,------707-710

Christ, his quickening and resurrection, ---------------------------707, 708
his ascension,---------------------708-710
his offices,--------- ------------------710-776
his offices three,----------------------- 710
his Prophetic work,--------------710-713
prophet, its meaning as applied to him, --------------------------------- 710
three methods of fulfilling the prophet's office,---------------------- 711
his preparatory work as Logos,---- 711
his ministry as incarnate,--------711, 712
his ascended guidance and teaching of the church on earth,------------- 712
his final revelation of the Father to the saints in glory,----------712, 713
his Priestly office,------------------713-775
in what respects he was a priest,--- 713
his atoning work, see Atonement.
as immanent in the universe, see Logos.
bearer of our humanity, life of our race, --------------------------------- 715
his sufferings not atonement but revelation of atonement,----------- 715
his death a moral stimulus to men, 716
did he ever utter the words 'give his life a ransom for many'?---- 717
did not preach, but established the gospel, --------------------------------- 721
a noble martyr,----------------------- 729
his death the central truth of Christianity, ---------------------------733, 764
his death set forth by Baptism and Lord's Supper,----------------------- 733
the Great Penitent,----------734, 737, 760
the Savior of all men,---------------- 739
refused 'the wine mingled with myrrh,' ------------------------------- 742
never makes confession of sin,----- 746
a stumbling-block to modern speculation, --------------------------------- 746
had not hereditary depravity but guilt, ---------------------------747, 762
was he slain by himself or another? --------------------------------- 747
does he suffer intensively the infinite punishment of sin?----------- 747
his obedience, active and passive, needed in salvation,-------------749, 770
died for all,------------------------------ 750
incorporate with humanity, became our substitute,--------------------- 750
how 'lifted up,'---------------------- 751
mediator between the just God and the merciful God,-------------------- 754
in his organic union with the race is the vital relation which makes his vicarious sufferings either possible or just,------------------------- 754
as God immanent in humanity, is priest and victim, condemning and

condemned, atoning and atoned,--- 755
Christ created humanity, and as immanent God sustains it, while it sins, thus becoming responsible for its sin,---------------------755, 769
as Logos smitten by guilt and punishment, --------------------------- 755
the 'must be' of his sufferings, what? --------------------------------- 755
his race-responsibility not destroyed by incarnation, or purification in womb of Virgin,-------------------- 756
his sufferings reveal the cross hidden in the divine love from foundation of the world,------------756, 763
in womb of Virgin purged from depravity, guilt and penalty remaining, ---------------------------757, 759
the central brain of our race through which all ideas must pass, --------------------------------- 757
his guilt, what?----------------------- 757
innocent in personal, but not race relations, --------------------------- 758
his secular and church priesthood,--- 758
did he suffer only for his own share in sin of the race?----------------- 758
his incarnation an expression of a prior union with race beginning at creation, --------------------------- 758
various explanations of his identification with race,-------------------- 759
he longed to suffer,------------------- 759
he could not help suffering,--------- 760
all nerves and sensibilities of race meet in him,------------------------- 760
his place in 2 Cor. 5 : 21,---------760, 761
when and how did he take guilt and penalty on himself,----------------- 761
import of his submission to John's baptism, --------------------------- 762
was he unjustified till his death?--- 762
his guilt first purged on Cross,----- 762
as incarnate, revealed, rather than made, atonement,-------------------- 762
the personally unmerited sufferings of, the mystery of atonement,----- 763
may have felt remorse as central conscience of humanity,----------- 769
his sufferings, though temporal, met infinite demands of law,----------- 769
paid a penalty equivalent, though not identical,---------------------769, 770
how Savior of all men,--------------- 772
specially Savior of those who believe, ------------------------------- 773
his priesthood, everlasting,---------- 773
as Priest he is intercessor, see Intercession.
his Kingly office,----------------------- 775
his kingship defined,-------------------- 775
his kingdom of power,----------------- 775

Christ, his kingdom of grace,_____775, 776
  the only instance of *Fortwirkung*
  after death,_____ 776
  his kingdom of glory,_____ 776
  his kingdom, the antidote to despair concerning church,_____ 776
  his kingship, two practical remarks
  upon, _____ 776
  union with, see Union.
  ascended, communicates life to
  church, _____ 806
  heathen may receive salvation from
  Christ without knowing giver or
  how gift was purchased,_____ 843
  his sufferings secure acquittal from
  penalty of law,_____ 858
  his obedience secures reward of law, 858
  union with, secures his life as dominant principle in soul,_____ 860
  his life in believer will infallibly
  extirpate all depravity,_____ 860
  'we in,' Justification,_____ 862
  'in us,' Sanctification,_____ 862
  his twofold work in the world,_____ 869
  a new object of attention to the believer, _____ 873
  union with, secures impartation of
  spirit of obedience,_____ 875
  his commands must not be modified
  by any church,_____ 930
  submitted to rites appointed for
  sinners, _____ 943
  God's judicial activity exercised
  through, _____1027
  qualified by his two natures to act
  as judge,_____1027
  his body confined to space,_____1032
  his soul not limited to space,_____1032
Christianity, its triumph over paganism, the wonder of history,____191–193
  its influence on civilization,_____193, 194
  its influence on individuals,_____194, 195
  submits to judgment by only test of
  a religion, not ideals, but performances, _____ 195
  and pantheism,_____ 283
  circumstances favorable to its propagation, _____ 666
  Japanese objection to its doctrine
  of brotherhood,_____ 898
Christological method in theology,____ 50
Christology, _____665–776
Chronology, schemes of,_____224, 225
Church, its safety and aggressiveness
  dependent on sound doctrine,_____ 18
  its relation to truth,_____ 33
  polity and ordinances of, their purpose, _____ 546
  a prophetic institution,_____ 712
  doctrine of the,_____887–980
  constitution of the or its Polity,____
  _____887–929

Church, in its largest signification,___ 887
  and kingdom, difference between,____
  _____887, 889
  definition of, in Westminster Confession, _____ 887
  the universal, includes all believers, 888
  universal, the body of Christ,_____ 888
  a transcendent element in,_____ 888
  union with Christ, the presupposition of,_____ 888
  the indwelling Christ, its elevating
  privilege, _____ 888
  the universal or invisible distinguished from the local or visible, 889
  individual, defined,_____ 890
  the laws of Christ on which church
  gathered, _____ 890
  not a humanitarian organization,___ 890
  the term employed in a loose sense, 891
  significance of the term etymologically, _____ 891
  the secular use of its Greek form,__ 891
  used as a generic or collective term, 891
  the Greek term translated, its derivation, _____ 891
  applied by a figure of rhetoric to
  many churches,_____ 891
  the local, a divine appointment,____ 892
  the Hebrew terms for, its larger and
  narrower use,_____ 892
  Christ took his idea of, from Hebrew not heathen sources,_____ 892
  exists for sake of the kingdom,_____ 892
  will be displaced by a Christian
  state, _____ 893
  the decline of, not to be deplored,__ 893
  a voluntary society,_____ 893
  membership in, not hereditary or
  compulsory, _____ 893
  union with, logically follows union
  with Christ,_____ 893
  its doctrine, a necessary outgrowth
  of the doctrine of regeneration,___ 893
  highest organism of human life,_____ 894
  is an organism such as the religion
  of spirit necessarily creates,_____ 894
  its organization may be informal,__ 894
  its organization may be formal,_____ 894
  its organization in N. T. formal,____ 894
  its developed organization indicated
  by change of names from Gospels
  to Epistles,_____ 895
  not an exclusively spiritual organization, _____ 895
  doctrine of Plymouth Brethren concerning, _____895, 896
  organization of the, not definitely
  prescribed in N. T. and left to expediency ; an erroneous theory,____ 896
  government of, five alleged forms in
  N. T.,_____ 897
  regenerate persons only members of, 897

Church, Christ law-giver of,--------- 897
members on equality,----------------- 898
one member of, has no jurisdiction
over another,------------------------ 898
independent of civil power,---------- 899
local, its sole object,-------------- 899
local, united worship a duty of,----- 899
its law, the will of Christ,--------- 900
membership in, qualifications prescribed for,------------------------- 900
membership in, duties attached to, 900
its genesis,------------------------- 900
in germ before Pentecost,------------ 900
three periods in life of,------------ 901
officers elected as occasion demanded, --------------------------------- 901
Paul's teaching concerning, progressive, ------------------------------- 902
how far synagogue was model of,--- 902
a new, how constituted,-------------- 902
in formation of, a council not absolutely requisite,----------------902, 903
at Antioch, its independent career,- 903
its government,------------------903-926
its government, as to source of authority, an absolute monarchy,----- 903
its government, as to interpretation
and execution of Christ's law, an
absolute democracy,----------------- 903
should be united in action,---------- 904
union of, in action should be, not
passive submission, but intelligent
co-operation, ----------------------- 904
peaceful unity in, result of Spirit's
work, ------------------------------- 904
Baptist, law of majority-rule in,--- 904
as a whole responsible for doctrinal
and practical purity,--------------- 905
ordinances committed to custody of
whole, ------------------------------ 905
as a whole, elects its officers and
delegates, -------------------------- 906
as a whole, exercises discipline,---- 907
the self-government of, an educational influence,-------------------- 908
pastor's duty to,-------------------- 908
the world-church or Romanist theory of, considered,--------------908-911
Peter as foundation of, what meant
by the statement,---------------909-911
See also Peter.
the hierarchical government of, corrupting and dishonoring to Christ, 911
the theory of a national, considered,
------------------- ----------------912-914
Presbyterian system of the, authors
upon, ------------------------------- 912
independence of, when given up,----- 912
a spiritual, incapable of delimita-
tion, ------------------------------- 913
officers of the,-----------------914-924
offices in, two,-----------------914-916

Church, a plurality of eldership in the
primitive, occasional,-----------915, 916
the pastor, bishop or elder of the,
his three fold duty,-------------916, 917
the deacon, his duties,-----------917, 918
did women in the early church discharge diaconal functions?-------- 918
ordination of officers in,---------918-924
See Ordination.
local, highest ecclesiastical authority in N. T.,------------------------- 920
discipline of,------------------924-926
See Discipline.
relation of, to sister churches,---926-929
each, the equal of any other,-------- 926
each, directly responsible to Christ,
and with spiritual possibilities
equal to any other,----------------- 926
each, to maintain fraternity and co-
operation with other churches,----- 926
each, should seek and take advice
from other churches,---------------- 927
the fellowship of a, with another
church may be broken by departures from Scriptural faith and
practice, --------------------------- 928
independence of, qualified by interdependence, ------------------------- 928
what it ought to do if distressed by
serious internal disagreements,---- 928
its independence requires largest co-
operation with other churches,----- 929
list of authorities on general subject of the,------------------------- 929
ordinances of the,--------------930-980
See Ordinances, Baptism, and
Lord's Supper.
Circulatio, --------------------------- 332
Circumcision, of Christ, its import,-- 761
its law and that of baptism not the
same, ---------------------------954, 955
Circumincessio, ---------------------- 333
Civilization, can its arts be lost?---- 529
Coffin, called by Egyptians 'chest of
the living,'------------------------- 993
Cogito ergo Deus est,----------------- 61
Cogito ergo sum = cogito scilicet sum, 55
Cogito = cogitans sum, --------------- 55
Cognition of finiteness, dependence,
etc., the occasion of the direct
cognition of the Infinite, Absolute,
etc., ------------------------------- 52
Coming, second, of Christ,-------1003-1015
the doctrine of, stated,-------------1003
Scriptures describing,-----------1003, 1004
statements concerning, not all spiritual, ------------------------------1004
outward and visible,-----------------1004
the objects to be secured at,--------1004
said to be ' in like manner ' to his
ascension, ----------------------1004, 1005
analogous to his first,---------------1005

Coming, second, can all men at one
　time see Christ at the?_____1005
the time of, not definitely taught, 1005
predictions of, parallel those of his
　first, _____1007
patient waiting for, disciplinary,___1007
precursors of,_____1008–1010
a general prevalence of Christiani-
　ty, a precursor of,_____1008
a deep and wide spread develop-
　ment of evil, a precursor of,_____1008
a personal antichrist, a precursor
　of, _____1008
four signs of, according to some,____1010
millennium, prior to,_____1010, 1011
and millennium as pointed out in
　Rev. 20 : 4–10,_____1011
immediately connected with a gen-
　eral resurrection and judgment,___1011
of two kinds,_____1014
a reconciliation of pre-millenarian
　and post-millenarian theories sug-
　gested, _____1014
is the preaching which is to pre-
　cede, to nations as wholes, or to
　each individual in a nation?_____1014
the destiny of those living at,_____1015
Comings of Christ, partial and typi-
　cal, _____1003
Commenting, its progress,_____ 35
Commission, Christ's final, not con-
　fined to eleven,_____ 906
Commercial theory of Atonement,_____ 747
Common law of church, what?_____ 970
Communion, prerequisites to,_____969–980
limitation of, commanded by Christ
　and apostles,_____ 969
limitation of, implied in its analo-
　gy to Baptism,_____ 969
prerequisites to, laid down not by
　church, but by Christ and his
　apostles expressly or implicitly,___ 970
prerequisites to, are four,_____ 970
Regeneration, a prerequisite to,____ 971
Baptism, a prerequisite to,_____ 971
the apostles were baptized before,__ 971
the command of Christ places bap-
　tism before,_____ 971
in all cases recorded in N. T. bap-
　tism precedes,_____ 971
the symbolism of the ordinances re-
　quires baptism to precede,_____971, 972
standards of principal denomina-
　tions place baptism before,_____ 972
where baptism customarily does not
　precede, the results are unsatis-
　factory, _____ 972
church-membership, a prerequisite
　to, _____ 973
a church rite,_____ 973
a symbol of Christian fellowship,__ 973

Communion, an orderly walk, a pre-
　requisite to,_____ 973
immoral conduct, a bar to,_____973, 974
disobedience to the commands of
　Christ, a bar to,_____ 974
heresy, a bar to,_____ 974
schism, a bar to,_____ 975
restricted, the present attitude of
　Baptist churches to,_____ 976
local church under responsibility to
　see its, preserved from disorder,__
　_____ 975, 976
open, advocated because baptism
　cannot be a term of communion,
　not being a term of salvation,____ 977
open, contrary to the practice of
　organized Christianity,_____ 977
no more binding than baptism,_____ 978
open, tends to do away with bap-
　tism, _____ 978
open, destroys discipline,_____ 978
open, tends to do away with the
　visible church,_____ 979
strict, objections to, answered brief-
　ly, _____979, 980
open, its justification briefly con-
　sidered, _____ 980
a list of authors upon,_____ 980
Compact with Satan,_____ 458
Complex act, part may designate
　whole, _____ 946
Concept; not a mental image,_____ 7
in theology, may be distinguished
　by definition from all others,_____ 15
Concupiscence, what?_____ 522
Romish doctrine of,_____ 604
Concurrence in all operations at basis
　of preservation,_____ 411
divine efficiency in, does not de-
　stroy or absorb the efficiency as-
　sisted, _____ 418
God's, in evil acts only as they are
　natural acts,_____418, 419
Confession, Romanist view of,_____ 834
Conflagration, final,_____1012
Confucianism, _____180, 181
Confucius, _____180, 181
Connate ideas,_____53, 54
Conscience, what?_____82, 83
proves existence of a holy Lawgiver
　and Judge,_____ 82
its supremacy,_____ 82
warns of existence of law,_____ 82
speaks in imperative,_____ 82
represents to itself some other as
　judge, _____ 82
the will it expresses superior to
　ours, _____ 83
witness against pantheism,_____ 103
thirst of, assuaged by Christ's sac-
　rifice, _____ 297
its nature,_____ 498

Conscience, not a faculty, but a mode, 498
   intellectual element in,-------------- 498
   emotional element in,----------------- 498
   solely judicial,--------------------- 498
   discriminative, ---------------------- 498
   impulsive, --------------------------- 498
   other mental processes from which
     it is to be distinguished,----------- 499
   the moral judiciary of the soul,----- 500
   must be enlightened and cultivated, 500
   an echo of God's voice,--------------- 501
   in its relation to God as holy,------- 502
   the organ by which the human
     spirit finds God in itself, and itself
     in God,----------------------------- 503
   rendered less sensitive, but cannot
     be annulled, by sin,---------------- 647
   needs Christ's propitiation,---------- 736
   absolute liberty of, a distinguishing
     tenet of Baptists,---------------898, 899
Consciousness, Christian, not *norma*
   normans, but *norma normata,*------ 28
   defined, ----------------------------- 63
   not source of other knowledge,------- 63
   self, primarily a distinguishing of
     itself from itself,----------------- 104
   comes logically before consciousness
     of the world,----------------------- 104
   self-consciousness, what?------------ 252
Consubstantiation, ------------------- 968
Contrary choice, in Adam,------------- 519
   not essential to will,------------600, 605
   its present limits,------------------- 605
Contrition, Romish doctrine of,------- 834
Conversion, God's act in the will in,-- 793
   sudden, ------------------------------ 827
   defined, ----------------------------- 829
   relation to regeneration,------------- 829
   voluntary, --------------------------- 829
   man's relation to God in,------------- 830
   conversions other than the first,----- 831
   relations of the divine and human
     in, -------------------------------- 831
Cosmological argument, see God.
Covetousness, what?------------------- 569
Cranial capacity of man and apes,-- 473
Creatianism, its advocates,----------- 491
   its tenets,--------------------------- 491
   its untenability,----------------491-493
Creation, attributed to Christ,-------- 310
   attributed to Spirit,----------------- 316
   doctrine of,----------------------371-410
   definition of,-------------------371, 372
   by man of ideas and volitions and
     indirectly of brain-modifications, 371
   is change of energy into force,------ 371
   Lotzean, author's view of,---------- 372
   is not 'production out of nothing,' 372
   is not 'fashioning,'--------------372, 373
   not an emanation from divine sub-
     stance, --------------------------- 372

Creation, the divine in, the origination of substance,----------------- 373
   free act of a rational will, ---- 373
   externalization of God's thought,-- 373
   creation and 'generation' and 'pro-
     cession,' ------------------------- 373
   is God's voluntary limitation of
     himself, -------------------------- 373
   how an act of the triune God,------- 373
   not necessary to a trinitarian God, 373
   the doctrine of, proved only from
     Scripture, ------------------------ 374
   direct Scripture statements concern-
     ing, discussed,----------------374-375
   idea of, originates, when we think
     of things as originating in God
     immediately, ---------------------- 375
   Paul's idea of,--------------------- 376
   absolute, heathen had glimpses of, 376
   best expressed in Hebrew,----------- 376
   found among early Babylonians,---- 376
   found in pre-Zoroastrian, Vedic,
     and early Egyptian religions,---- 376
   in heathen systems,----------------- 377
   literature on,---------------------- 377
   'out of nothing,' its origin,-------- 377
   indirect evidence of, from Script-
     ure, -----------------------377, 378
   theories which oppose,----------378-391
   Dualism opposes, see Dualism.
   emanation opposes, see Emanation.
Creation from eternity, theory stated, 386
   not necessitated by God's omnipo-
     tence, --------------------------- 387
   contradictory in terms and irration-
     al, ------------------------------ 387
   another form of the see-saw philos-
     ophy, --------------------------- 387
   not necessitated by God's timeless-
     ness, ---------------------------- 387
   inconceivable, --------------------- 387
   not consistent with the conception
     of universe as an organism,------- 388
   not necessitated by God's immuta-
     bility, -------------------------- 388
   not necessitated by God's love,--388, 389
   inconsistent with God's independ-
     ence and personality,------------- 389
   outgrowth of Unitarian tendencies, 389
Creation, opposed by theory of spontaneous generation, see Generation, Spontaneous.
   Mosaic account of,----------------391-397
   asserts originating act of God in,-- 391
   makes God antedate and create mat-
     ter, ---------------------------- 391
   recognizes development,------------- 392
   lays the foundation for cosmogony, 392
   can be interpreted in harmony with
     mediate creation or evolution,---- 392
   not an allegory or myth,------------ 394

Creation, Mosaic account of, not the blending of inconsistent stories,__ 394
not to be interpreted in a hyperliteral way,------------------------------- 394
does not use 'day' for a period of twenty-four hours,------------------ 394
is not a precise geological record,__ 395
its scheme in detail,----------------395-397
literature upon,--------------------396, 397
Creation, God's end in,--------------397-402
God's end in, his own glory,---------- 398
God's chief end in, the manifestation of his glory,-------------------- 398
his glory most valuable end in,____ 399
his glory only end in, consistent with his independence and sovereignty, ----------------------------- 399
his glory the end in, which secures every interest of the universe,____ 400
his glory the end in, because it is the end proposed to his creatures, 401
its final value, its value for God,__ 402
the doctrine of, its relation to other doctrines, -----------------------402-410
its relation to the holiness and benevolence of God,------------------ 402
first, in what senses ' very good,'___ 402
pain and imperfection in, before moral evil, reasons for,------------- 402
sets forth wisdom and free-will of God, --------------------------------- 404
Christ, in the Revealer of God, and the remedy of pessimism,---------- 405
presents God in Providence and Redemption, --------------------------- 407
gives value to the Sabbath,---------- 408
Creation of man, exclusively a fact of Scripture, --------------------------- 465
Scripture declares it an act of God, 465
Scripture silent on method of,------- 465
Scripture does not exclude mediate creation of body, if this method probable from other sources,---465, 491
and theistic evolution,--------------- 466
his soul, its creation, though mediate, yet immediate,--------------466, 491
not from brute, but *from* God, *through* brute,----------------467, 469, 472
the last stage in the development of life, ----------------------------------- 469
unintelligible unless the immanent God is regarded as giving new impulses to the process,---------- 470
as to soul and body, in a sense immediate, ---------------------------- 470
natural selection, its relations to,___ 470
by laws of development, which are methods of the Creator,------------ 472
when finished presents, not a brute, but a man,------------------------- 472
constitutes him the offspring of God, and God his Father,-------- 474

Creation of man, as taking place through Christ, made its product a son of God by relationship to the Eternal Son,--------------------- 474
theory of its occurrence at several centres, ---------------------------- 481
and his new creation compared,__ 694
in it body made corruptible, soul incorruptible, ----------------------- 991
Creation, continuous, its doctrine,____ 415
its advocates,----------------------- 416
the element of truth in,------------- 416
its error,---------------- ---------------- 416
contradicts consciousness,----------- 416
exaggerates God's power at expense of other attributes,----------------- 417
renders personal identity inexplicable, ----------------------------------- 417
tends to pantheism,------------------ 417
Creatura, ----------------------------- 392
Credo quia impossibile est,------------- 34
Creeds, -----------------------------18, 42
Crime best prevented by conviction of its *desert* of punishment,----------- 655
Crimen læsæ majestatis,----------------- 748
Criminal theory,----------------------- 748
Criticism, higher,--------------------169-172
what it means,---------------------- 169
influenced by spirit in which conducted, -------------------------169, 170
its teachings on Pentateuch and Hexateuch, --------------------------- 170
reveals God's method in making up record of his revelation,---------- 172
literature upon,---------------------- 172
Cumulative arugment,------------------- 71
Cur Deus Homo, synopsis of,---------- 748
' Curse ' in Gal. 3 : 13,---------------- 760
' Custom, immemorial,' binding,------- 970
' Damn,' its present connotation acquired from impression made on popular mind by Scriptures,------1046
' Damnation ' in 1 Cor. 11 : 22, its meaning, ------------------------------- 960
Darwinism, its teaching,--------------- 470
its truth,----------------------------- 470
is not a complete explanation of the history of life----------------------- 470
fails to account for origin of substance and of variations,---------- 470
does not take account of sudden appearance in the geological record of important forms of life,-------- 470
leaves gap between highest anthropoid and lowest specimen of man unspanned, ------------------------- 471
fails to explain many important facts in heredity,------------------ 471
must admit that natural selection has not yet produced a species, as far as we know,----------------- 472
as its author understood it, was not opposed to the Christian faith, 473

Day in Gen. 1,----------------------------- 35
its meaning,--------------223, 224, 394, 395
Deacons, their duties,----------------917, 918
ordination of,------------------------- 919
Deaconesses, ----------------------------- 918
Dead, Christ's preaching to,--------707, 708
Dead, Egyptian Book of the,------------ 995
extracts from,------------------------- 995
resurrection in,-----------------------1022
judgment in,---------------------------1024
Deadly sins, the seven,' of Romanism, -------------------------------571, 572
Death, spiritual, a consequence of the
Fall, ------------------------------- 591
spiritual, in what it consists,------
-------------------------591, 659, 660, 982
physical, its nature,----------------656, 982
physical, a part of the penalty of
sin proved from Scripture,------656, 657
and sin complemental,---------------- 657
a natural law, on occasion of man's
sin, appointed to a moral use,----- 657
the liberator of souls,---------------- 658
the penalty of sin, proved from reason, ---------------------------------- 658
its universality how alone explained
consistently with idea of God's
justice, ----------------------------- 658
not a necessary law of organized being, --------------------------------- 658
higher being might have been attained without its intervention,---- 658
to Christian not penalty, but chastisement and privilege,-----659, 983, 984
eternal, what?------------------------- 660
second, -----------------648, 982, 983, 1013
not cessation of being,--_------------ 984
as dissolution, cannot affect indivisible soul,----------------------------- 984
as a cessation of consciousness preparatory to other development,
considered, ------------------------ 986
cannot terminate the development
for which man was made,---------- 986
cannot so extinguish being that no
future vindication of God's moral
government is possible,------------- 987
cannot, by annihilation, falsify the
testimony of man's nature to immortality, --------------------------- 989
man's body only made liable to,----- 991
as applied to soul, designates an unholy and unhappy state of being,-- 992
consciousness after, indicated in
many Scriptures,---------------993, 994
a 'sleep,'----------------------------- 994
of two kinds,-------------------------1013
its passionless and statuesque tran-
quility prophetic,------------------1016
Decree to act not the act,----------354, 359
Decree, the divine, permissive in case
of evil,------------------------354, 365

Decree, not a cause,------------------- 360
of end and means combined,--353, 363, 364
does not efficiently work evil choices
in men,----- ------------------------ 365
to permit sin, and the fact of the
permission of sin equally equitable, 365
to initiate a system in which sin
has a place, how consistent with
God's holiness?---------------------- 367
Decrees of God, the,--------------353-370
their definition,--------------------353-355
many to us, yet in nature one plan, 353
relations between, not chronological
but logical,------------------------- 353
without necessity,-------------------- 353
relate to things outside of God,----- 353
respect acts, both of God and free
creatures, ------------------------- 354
not addressed to creatures,---------- 354
all human acts covered by,---------- 354
none of them read 'you shall sin, -- 354
sinful acts of men, how related to, 354
how divided,-------------------------- 355
declared by Scripture to include all
things, ----------------------------- 355
declared by Scripture to deal with
special things and events,--------- 355
proved from divine foreknowledge, 356
respect foreseen results,------------- 356
provd from divine wisdom,---------- 358
proved from divine immutability,
-------------------------------358, 359
proved from the divine benevolence, 359
a ground of thanksgiving,---------- 359
not inconsistent with man's free
agency, ----------------------------- 359
do not remove motive for exertion, 363
and fate,----------------------------- 363
encourage effort,--------------------- 364
they do not make God the author of
sin, -------------------------------- 365
practical uses of the doctrine of,-- 368
the doctrine of, dear to matured understanding and deep experience, 368
how the doctrine should be preached, 369
Deism, defined,----------------------- 414
some of its advocates,--------------- 414
an exaggeration of God's transcendence, ------------------------------- 414
rests upon a false analogy,---------- 415
a system of anthropomorphism,----- 415
denies providential interference,---- 415
tends to atheism,-------------------- 415
'Delivering to Satan,'--------------- 457
Delphic oracle,---------------------- 136
Demons, see Angels, evil.
Depravity, explained by a personal
act in the previous timeless state
of being,---------------------------- 488
of nature, repented of by Christians, 555
Arminian theory of,-------------601, 602
New School theory of,---------606, 607

Depravity, Federal theory of,_____612, 613
 Augustinian theory of,_____619, 620
 defined, _____ 637
 total, its meaning,_____637-639
 is subjective pollution,_____645, 646
 Christ had no,_____645, 756-758
 of human will, requires special di-
    vine influence,_____ 784
 of all humanity,_____ 813
Determinatio est negatio,_____ 9
Determinism, _____362, 507-510
Deus nescit se quid est quia non est
    quid, _____ 244
Deuteronomy, _____167-169, 171, 239
Devil, _____454, 455
Dextra Dei ubique est,_____ 708
Diabolus nullus, nullus Redemptor,____ 462
Diatoms, and natural selection,_____ 471
Dichotomous and Dichotomy, see Man.
Dies Iræ, the,_____645, 1056
Dignity, the plural of,_____ 318
Disciples or Campbellites,_____821, 840, 947
Discrepancies, alleged, in Scripture,
    _____107, 108, 173, 174
Divorce, permitted by Moses,_____ 230
Docetæ, _____ 670
Doctor angelicus,_____ 44
Doctor subtilis,_____ 45
Doctrine,_____17, 33, 34
Documentary evidence,_____141, 142
Doddridge's dream,_____ 453
Dogmatic system implied in Script-
    ure, _____ 15
Dogmatism, _____ 42
Domine, quousque? Calvin's motto, 1008
Donum supernaturale,_____ 522
Dort, Synod of,_____614, 777
Douay version, Mat. 26 : 28 in,_____ 965
Dualism, two forms of,_____ 378
 a form of, holds two distinct and
    co-eternal principles,_____ 373
 a history of this form of,_____378-380
 this form of, presses the maxim ex
    nihilo nihil fit too far,_____ 380
 this form of, applies the test of in-
    conceivibility too rigidly,_____ 380
 this form of, unphilosophical,_____ 381
 this form of, limits God's power and
    blessedness, _____ 381
 this form of, fails to account for
    moral evil,_____ 381
 another form of, holds the exist-
    ence of two antagonistic spirits,
    _____381, 382
 this form of, at variance with the
    Scriptural representation of God, 382
 this form of, opposed to the Scrip-
    tural representation of the Prince
    of Evil,_____ 382
Ducit quemque voluptas,_____ 299
Duties, our, not all disclosed in rev-
    elation, _____ 545

Ebionism, _____ 669
Ebionites, _____669, 670
Ecclesiastes, _____ 240
Ecclesiology, _____887-980
Eden, adapted to infantile and inno-
    cent manhood,_____ 583
Education, by impersonal law, and by
    personal dependence,_____ 434
Efficacious call, its nature,_____792, 793
'Effulgence,' _____ 335
Ego, cognition of it logically pre-
    cedes that of non-ego,_____ 104
Egyptian language, old, its linguistic
    value, _____ 497
 idea of blessedness of future life de-
    pendent on preservation of body,__ 995
 idea of permanent union of soul
    and body,_____1022
 way of representing God,_____376, 377
 knowledge of future state,_____ 995
Einzige, der, every man is,_____ 353
Eldership, plural,_____915, 916
Election, its relation to God's de-
    crees, _____ 355
 logically subsequent to redemption 777
 not to share in atonement but to
    special influence of Spirit,_____ 779
 doctrine of,_____779-790
 definition, _____ 779
 proof from Scripture,_____779-782
 statement preliminary to proof,_____ 779
 asserted of certain individuals,_____ 780
 asserted in connection with divine
    foreknowledge, _____780, 781
 asserted to be a matter of grace,__ 781
 connected with a giving by Father
    to Son of certain persons,_____ 781
 connected with union with Christ, 781
 connected with entry in the Lamb's
    Book of Life,_____ 781
 conected with allotment as disciples
    to certain believers,_____ 782
 conected with a special call of God, 782
 connected with a birth by God's
    will, _____ 782
 connected with gift of repentance
    and faith, _____ 782
 connected with holiness and good
    works as a gift,_____ 782
 Lutheran view of,_____782, 783
 Arminian view of,_____ 783
 a group of views concerning,_____ 783
 proved from reason,_____783-785
 is the purpose or choice which pre-
    cedes gift of regenerating grace,__ 783
 is not conditioned on merit or faith
    in chosen, _____ 784
 needed by depravity of human will, 784
 other considerations which make it
    more acceptable to reason,_____ 785
 objections to, _____785-790
 is unjust, _____ 785

Election, is partial,------------------ 786
  the ethical side of natural selection, 786
  is arbitrary, --------------------- 787
  is immoral, --------------------787, 788
  fosters pride, --------------------- 788
  discourages effort, ------------788, 789
  implies reprobation,------------789, 790
  list of authors on,----------------- 790
Elijah, his translation, -------------- 995
  John the Baptist as,--------------1013
Elizabeth, Queen, immersed,--------- 937
Elohim, ------------------------318, 319
Emanation theory of origin of universe, ------------------------378-383
Empirical theory of morals, truth in, 501
  reconciled with intuitional theory, 501
Encratites, deny to woman 'the im-
  age of God,'------------------------ 524
Endor, woman of,-------------------- 966
'Enemies,' Rom. 5 : 10,-------------- 719
Energy, mental, life, ---------------- 252
  resisted, force, -------------------- 252
  universe derived from,-------------- 252
  its change into force is creation,--- 252
  dissipation of, -----------------374, 415
Enghis and Neanderthal crania,------ 471
Enmity to God, --------------569, 817, 818
Enoch, translation of, -------------658, 994
Environment, ---------------426, 1034, 1049
Eophyte and Eozoon,----------------- 395
Epicureanism, ------------------91, 184, 299
Error, systems of, suggest organizing
  superhuman intelligences, --------- 457
Errors in Scripture, alleged,--------222-236
Eschatology, ------------------981-1056
Esprit gelé (matter) Schelling's bon
  mot, ------------------------------ 386
Essenes, ---------------------------- 787
Esther, book of,------------------237, 309
'Eternal sin, an,'-----------------1034, 1048
Eternity, --------------------------- 276
Ethics, how conditioned,-------------- 3
  Christian and Christian faith insep-
  arable, ---------------------------- 636
Eucharist, see Supper, the Lord's.
Eutaxiology, ------------------------- 75
Eutychians (Monophysites) ---------- 672
Eve, ----------------------525, 526, 676
Evidence, principles of, ----------141-144
Evil, --------------------------354, 1053
Evolution, behind that of our own
  reason stands the Supreme Reason, 25
  and revelation constitute nature,--- 26
  an, of Scripture as of natural
  science, --------------------------- 35
  of ideas, not from sense to nonsense, ----------------------------- 64
  has given man the height from
  which he can discern stars of
  moral truth previously hidden below the horizon,-------------------- 65
  a process, not a power, ------------ 76

Evolution, only a method of God,---- 76
  spells purpose, -------------------- 76
  awake to ends within the universe,
  but not to the great end of the
  universe itself, ------------------- 76
  answers objections by showing the
  development of useful collocations
  from initial imperfections, ------- 78
  has reinforced the evidences of intelligence in the universe, -------- 79
  transfers cause to an immanent rational principle, ------------------ 79
  a materialized, logical process, ---- 84
  of universe inexplicable unless matter is moved from without,-------- 92
  extension and, being, having thought
  and will, reveals itself in,-------- 101
  only another name for Christ, ----- 109
  views nature as a progressive order consisting of higher levels and
  phenomena unknown before, ------ 121
  its principle, the Logos or Divine
  Reason, --------------------------- 123
  its continuity that of plan not of
  force, ----------------------------- 123
  depends on increments of force with
  persistency of plan,--------------- 123
  irreconcilable with Deism and its
  distant God, ---------------------- 123
  the basis and background of a Christianity which believes in a dynamical universe of which a personal and loving God is the inner
  source of energy, ----------------- 123
  implies not the *uniformity,* but *universality* of law, ----------------- 125
  has successive stages, with new laws
  coming in, and becoming dominant, ----------------------------- 125
  of Hegel, a fact but fatalistic,---- 176
  of human society not primarily intellectual, but religious, --------- 194
  is developing *reverence* with its
  allied qualities, ------------------- 194
  if not recognized in Scripture leads
  to a denial of its unity, --------- 217
  of ' Truth — evolvable from the
  whole, evolved at last painfully,'-- 218
  has given us a new Bible — a book
  which has grown, --------224, 230, 231
  in a progress in prophecy, doctrine
  and church-polity seen in Paul's
  epistles, -------------------------- 236
  not a tale of battle, but a love-
  story, ----------------------------- 264
  the object of nature, and altruism
  the object of evolution, ----------- 264
  explains the world as the return of
  the highest to itself,-------------- 266
  in the idea of holiness and love
  exhibited in the palæontological

struggle for life and for the life of others,------------------268, 393

Evolution, is God's omnipresence in time, ------------------------------ 282

of his own being, God not shut up to a necessary,-------------------- 287

working out a nobler and nobler justice is proof that God is just,-- 292

a method of Christ's operation,------ 311

in its next scientific form will maintain the divineness of man and exalt Jesus of Nazareth to an eminence secure and supreme,-------- 328

Father,' more than symbol of the cause of organic,--------------- 334

and gravitation, all the laws of, are the work and manifestation of the present Christ,--------------------- 337

the conception of God in, leads to a Trinitarian conception,---------- 349

theological, are the heathen trinities stages in?--------------------- 352

is a regress terminating in the necessity of a creator,------------------ 374

a self, of God, so Stoic monism regarded the world,---------------- 389

implies previous involution,--------- 390

assumes initial arrangements containing the possibilities of the order afterwards evolved,----------- 390

unable to create something out of nothing, -------------------------- 390

the attempt to comprehend the world of experience in terms of fundamental idealistic postulates,------- 390

that ignores freedom of God is pantheistic, -------------------------- 390

from the nebula to man, unfolds a Divine Self,---------------------- 390

but a habitual operation of God,----- 390

not an eternal or self-originated process, ---------------------------- 391

natural selection without teleological factors cannot account for biological, ------------------------- 391

and creation, no antagonism between, ---------------------------- 391

its limits,---------------------------- 392

Spencer's definition of, stated and criticized, ------------------------- 392

illustrated in progress from Orohippus to horse of the present,---- 392

of inorganic forces and materials, an, in this the source of animate species, yet the Mosaic account of creation not discredited,---------- 392

in all forms of energy, higher and lower, dependent directly on will of God,----------------------------- 393

the struggle for life in palæontological stages of, the beginning of the sense of right and justice, 268, 393

Evolution, the struggle for the life of others in palæontological stages of, the beginning of altruism,--268, 393

the science of, has strengthened teleology, ------------------------- 397

its flow constitutes the self-revalation of the Infinite One,----------- 412

process of, easier believed in as a divine self-evolution than as a mechanical proces,----------------- 459

of man, physical and psychical, no exception to process of, yet faith in God intact,--------------------- 465

cannot be explained without taking into account the originating agency of God,----------------------------- 465

does not make the idea of Creator superfluous, ----------------------- 466

theist must accept, if he keep his argument for existence of God from unity of design,--------------- 466

of music depends on power of transmitting intellectual achievements, 466

unintelligible except as immanent God gives new impulses to the process, --------------------------------- 470

according to Mivart, it can account neither for body or soul of man,-- 472

still incomplete, man is still on all fours, ---------------------------------- 472

an atheistic, a reversion to the savage view,------------------------------ 473

theistic, regards human nature as efflux and reflection of the Divine Personality, ----------------------- 473

atheistic, satirized,-------------------- 473

a superior intelligence has guided,-- 473

phylogenetic, in the creation of Eve, 525

normal, man's will may induce a counter-evolution to,--------------- 591

the goal of man's, is Christ,--------- 680

the derivation of spiritual gifts from the Second Adam consonant with, 681

of humanity, the whole, depicted in the Cross and Passion,------------- 716

the process by which sons of God are generated,---------------------- 967

Example, Christ did not simply set,-- 732

Exegesis based on trustworthiness of verbal vehicle of inspiration,------ 216

Exercise-system of Hopkins and Emmons,-----------45, 416, 417, 584, 607, 822

Existence of God, see God.

Ex nihilo nihil fit,--------------------- 380

Experience, --------------------28, 63-65

Expiation, representative, recognized among Greeks,----------------------- 723

Ezra, his relation to O. T.,----------- 167

Fact local, truth universal,----------- 240

Facts not to be neglected, because relations are obscure,--------------- 36

Faculties, mental, man's three,------- 487

Faith, a higher sort of knowledge,--- 3
physical science rests on,------------ 3
never opposed to reason,-------------- 3
conditioned by holy affection,------- 3
act of integral soul,----------------- 4
can alone furnish material for a
scientific theology,------------------ 4
not blind,---------------------------- 5
its *fiducia* includes *notitia*,---------- 5
its place in the Arminian system.
------------------------------------605, 864
in a truth, possible in spite of difficulties to us insoluble,------------ 629
does not save, but atonement which
it accepts,--------------------------- 771
saving, is the gift of God,----------- 782
an effect, not cause, of election,---- 784
involves repentance,----------------- 836
defined, ----------------------------- 8C6
analyzed, ---------------------------- 837
an intellectual element (*notitia,
credere Deum*) in,------------------ 837
must lay hold of a present Christ,-- 837
an emotional element (*assensus,
credere Deo*) in,------------------- 837
a voluntary element (*fiducia, credere in Deum*) in,------------------ 838
self-surrender to good physician,---- 838
the reflection of the Divine knowing and willing in man's finite
spirit, ------------------------------ 838
its most important element, will,--- 838
is a bond between persons,---------- 839
appropriates Christ as source of
pardon and life,--------------------- 839
its three elements illustrated,------- 839
phrases descriptive of,-------------- 839
no element in, must be exaggerated
at expense of the others,---------- 839
views refuted by a proper conception of,------------------------------ 840
an act of the affections and will,--- 840
not a purely intellectual state,------ 841
is a moral act, and involves responsibility, ----------------------------- 841
saving, its general and particular
objects, ----------------------------- 842
is believing in God as far as he has
revealed himself,-------------------- 842
is it ever produced 'without a
preacher'? ----------------------843, 844
its ground of faith, the external
word, -------------------------------- 844
its ground of assurance, the Spirit's
inward witness,---------------------- 844
it is possible without assurance?--- 845
necessarily leads to goods works,-- 846
is not to be confounded with love
or obedience,------------------------ 847
a work and yet excluded from the
category of works.------------------ 847
instrumental cause of salvation,---- 847

Faith, the intermediate factor between undeveloped tendency toward God and developed affection
for God,------------------------------ 847
must not be confounded with its
fruits, ------------------------------- 848
the actinic ray,---------------------- 848
is susceptible of increase,----------- 848
authors on the general subject of,-- 849
why justified by faith rather than
other graces?------------------------ 864
not with the work of Christ a joint
cause of justification,--------------- 864
its relation to justification,--------- 865
the mediate cause of sanctification, 872
secures righteousness (justification
plus sanctification),---------------- 873
Faithfulness, Divine, -------------288, 289
Fall, Scriptural account of temptation and,-------------------------582-585
if account of, mythical, yet inspired
and profitable,----------------------- 582
reasons for regarding account of,
as historical,--------------------582, 583
the stages of temptation that preceded, -----------------------------584, 585
how possible to a holy being?----585, 586
incorrect explanations of,----------- 585
God not its author,------------------ 586
was man's free act of revolt from
God, --------------------------------- 587
cannot be explained on grounds of
reason, ------------------------------ 587
was wilful resistance to the inworking God,------------------------ 587
was choice of supreme love to the
world and self rather than supreme devotion to God,------------ 587
cannot be explained psychologically, 587
is an ultimate fact,------------------- 587
an immanent preference which was
first a choice and then an affection, --------------------------------- 588
God's permission of the temptation
preceding, benevolent,-------------- 588
not Satanic, because not self-originated, ------------------------------- 588
its temptation objectified in an embodied seducer, an advantage,----- 588
presented no temptation having
tendency in itself to lead astray.
------------------------------------ 588, 589
the slightness of the command in,
the best test of obedience,--------- 589
the command in, was not arbitrary, 589
the greatness of the sanction incurred in, had been announced and
should have deterred,--------------- 590
the revelation of a will alienated
from God,---------------------------- 590
physical death a consequence of,---- 590
brought death at once,-------------- 590

Fall, mortal effects of the, counteracted by grace, --------------------- 590

death said by some not to be a consequence of the, ------------------ 591

spiritual death, a consequence of,-- 591

arrested the original tendency of man's whole nature to God, -------- 591

depraved man's moral and religious nature, ------------------------------ 591

left him with his will fundamentally inclined to evil, ------------------ 592

darkened the intuition of reason, ---- 592

rendered conscience perverse in its judgments, ------------------------- 592

terminated man's unrestrained intercourse with God, -------------592, 593

imposed banishment from the garden, -------------------------------- 593

constituted Adam's posterity sinful, see Imputation.

of human nature could only occur in Adam,----------------------------- 629

repented of, because apostasy of our common nature,---------------------- 629

all responsible for the one sin of the, as race-sin,----------------------- 630

has depraved human nature,---------- 637

has rendered human nature totally unable to do that which is good in God's sight,----------------------- 640

has brought the race under obligation to render satisfaction for self-determined violation of law,--- 644

Fallen condition of man, Romanist and Protestant views of,-------521, 522

Falsehood, what?----------------------- 569

Fatalism, -------------------------------- 427

Fate and the decrees of God,---------- 363

Father, God as, see Trinity.

'Father,' how applied to whole Trinity, ----------------------------------- 333

'our,' import,-------------------------- 334

Federal theology,----------45, 46, 50, 612-616

Feeling, ------------------------------17, 20, 21

Fellowship, Christian, not church,---- 979

Fetichism, --------------------------------56, 532

Fiction, the truest, has no heroes,---- 575

Final cause,--------------44, 52, 60, 62, 75-77

Final Things, doctrine of,---------981-1056

Finality, ----------------------------75, 76, 78, 79

Fishes, the earliest, ganoids large and advanced in type,-------------------- 470

Flesh, -------------------------------------1,562, 588, 673

'Fold,' none under New Dispensation, 807

Fons Trinitatis,------------------------- 341

Force, no mental image of,------------- 7

not the atom, the real ultimate,---- 91

a property of matter,--------------91, 96

behind all its forms, co-ordinating mind, ----------------------------- 95

atom a centre of,--------------------- 96

matter a manifestation of,--------96, 109

Force, expressed in vibrations foundation of all we know of extended world, ------------------------------ 96

the only, we know is that of our own wills,---------------------------- 96

real, lies in the Divine Being, as living, active will,------------------ 97

matter and mind as respectively external and internal centres of,-- 98

as a function of will,-----99, 109, 415, 416

all except that of men's free will, is the will of God,--------------------- 99

the product of will,-------------------- 109

in universe works in rational ways and must be product of spirit,---- 109

Christ, the principle of every manifestation of,------------------------ 109

is God with his moral attributes omitted, -------------------------- 259

is energy under resistance,----------- 371

is energy manifesting itself under self-conditioning or differential forms, -------------------------------- 371

identified with the Divine Will, theories in which,---------------------- 412

and will are one in God,-------------- 412

every natural, a generic volition of God, ---------------------------------- 413

a portion of God's, disjoined from him in the free-will of intelligent beings, --------------------------------- 414

super cuncta, subter cuncta,---------- 414

not always Divine will,--------------- 416

in its various differentiations adjusted by God,----------------------- 436

Foreknowledge of God of all future acts directly,------------------------- 284

acts of free will excepted by some, --------------------------------------284, 285

denial of the absolute, productive of dread, ------------------------------- 285

regarded by some as insoluble,------- 285

perhaps explicable by the possibility of an all-embracing present,--- 285

constant teaching of Scripture favors, ------------------------------- 285

mediate, what?------------------------- 285

immediate, what?--------------------- 285

if intuitive, difficulty removed,---- --------------------------- 285, 357, 362

rests on fore-ordination,------------- 356

preceded logically by decree,------356, 357

of undecreed actuals (*scientia media*), not possible,------------------- 357

two kinds of,----------------------------- 358

the middle knowledge of Molina,---- 358

of individuals,--------------------------- 781

distinguished from fore-ordination,-- 781

Forgiveness, not in nature but in grace, ------------------------------- 548

cannot be granted unconditionally by public bodies,------------------- 766

Forgiveness, more than the taking away of penalty,---------------- 767

optional with God since he makes satisfaction, ----------------- 767

human accorded without atonement, why not divine?---------------- 835

defined in personal, ethical and legal terms, --------------------854, 855

God's act as Father,----------------- 855

none in nature,---------------------- 855

does not ensure immediate removal of natural consequences of sin,--- 855

the peculiar characteristic of Christian experience,----------------- 856

Fore-ordination, its nature,--------355, 381

the basis of foreknowledge,---------- 356

distinguished from foreknowledge,-- 781

Forms of thought are facts of nature, 10

Fourth gospel, its genuineness,-------- 151

Free agency defined,------------------ 360

can predict its action,--------------- 360

Freedom, man's, consistent with the divine decrees,------------------359-362

four senses of word,----------------- 361

of indifference,---------------------- 362

of choice, which is not incompatible with the complete bondage of will, ----------------------------509, 510

remnants of, left to man,--------510, 640

Freundlos war der grosse Weltenmeister, ----------------------------- 386

Fürsehung and *Vorsehung* combined in 'Providence,'---------------------- 419

Future life, the evidence of Jewish belief in a,---------------------------- 994

Egyptian ideas about,---------------- 995

Moses instructed in Egyptian 'learning' concerning,------------------- 995

proof-texts for,---------------------- 996

doctrine of Pharisees supports,------- 996

Christ's argument for,--------------- 996

argument for, presupposes the existence of a truthful, wise and good creator, ----------------------------- 996

the most conclusive proof of, Christ's resurrection, ----------------------- 997

Christ taught the doctrine of,-------- 997

a revelation of, needed,-------------- 997

Futurist method of interpreting Revelation, ----------------------------1009

Galton's view of piety,---------------- 83

Ganoids, the first geologic fishes,------ 470

Gemachte, das, sin is,---------------- 566

Genealogies of Scripture,------------- 229

Generation, as applied to the Son, 340-343

spontaneous, ----------------------- 389

Genuineness of the Christian documents, ----------------------------143-154

of the books of O. T.,----------165-172

Genus apotelesmaticum,------------- 686

diomaticum, ----------------------- 686

majestaticum, ---------------------- 686

Genus tapeinoticon,------------------ 686

Gesetz, ------------------------------ 533

Gethsemane, ----------------------677, 731

Gewordene, das, is not sin,----------- 566

Glory, final state of righteous,--------1029

his own, why God's end in creation? ------------------------------397-402

Gnostic Ebionism, ----------------669, 670

Gnostics, --------------------20, 378, 383, 487

God, the subject of theology, though apprehended by faith, yet a subject of science,---------------------- 2

human mind can recognize God,------ 4

though not phenomenal, can be known, ----------------------------- 5

because of analogies between his nature and ours, can be known,--- 7

though no adequate image of, can be formed, yet may be known,------ 7

since all predicates of God are not negative, he may be known,------- 9

so limited and defined, that he may be known,-------------------------- 10

his laws of thought ours, and so he may be known,-------------------- 10

can reveal himself by external revelation, ----------------------------- 12

revealed in nature, history, conscience, Scripture,----------------- 14

Christ the only revealer of,---------- 14

the existence of,----------------52-110

definitions of the term,-------------- 52

his existence a first truth, or rational intuition,----------------------- 52

his existence conditions observation and reasoning,---------------------- 52

his existence rises into consciousness on reflection on phenomena of nature and mind,-------------- 52

knowledge of his existence, universal, ----------------------------56-58

knowledge of his existence, necessary, ----------------------------58, 59

knowledge of his existence, logically independent of and prior to, all other knowledge,------------------59-62

other suggested sources of our idea of, ----------------------------62-67

idea of, not from external revelation, ----------------------------62, 63

idea of, not from tradition,---------- 63

idea of, not from experience,------63-65

idea of, not from sense perception and reflection,--------------------63, 64

idea of, not from race-experience, 64, 65

idea of, not from actual contact of our sensitive nature with God, 65

rational intuition of, sometimes becomes presentative,---------------- 65

idea of, does not arise from reasoning, ----------------------------65, 66

God, faith in, not proportioned to strength of reasoning faculty,____ 65

we know more of, than reasoning can furnish,_____65, 66

idea of, not derived from inference,
_____66, 67

belief in, not a mere working hypothesis, _____ 67

intuition of, its contents,_____67-70

what he is, men to some extent know intuitively,_____ 67

a presentative intuition of, possible, 67

a presentative intuition of, perhaps normal experience,_____ 67

loss of love has weakened rational intuition of,_____ 67

the passage of the intuition of, into personal and presentative knowledge, ____ _____ 68

his existence not proved but assumed and declared in Scripture, 63

evidence of his existence inlaid in man's nature,_____ 68

knowledge of, though intuitive may be explicated and confirmed by argument, _____ 71

the intuition of, supported by arguments probable and cumulative,__ 71

the intuition of, explicated by reflection and reasoning,_____ 72

arguments for existence of, classified, _____ 72

Cosmological Argument for his existence, _____73-75

its proper statement,_____ 73

its defects,_____73, 74

its value,_____74, 75

Teleological Argument for his existence, _____75-80

its nature,_____75-78

its defects,_____78-80

its value,_____ 80

Anthropological Argument for his existence, _____80-85

its nature,_____80-83

its defects,_____ 84

its value,_____84, 85

Historical Argument for his existence, _____ 85

Biblical Argument for his existence, 85

Ontological Argument for his existence, _____85-89

its three forms,_____85, 86

its defects,_____ 87

its value,_____87-89

evidence of his existence from the intellectual starting-point,_____ 88

evidence of his existence from the religious starting-point,_____ 88

the nature, decrees and works of,
_____243-370

the attributes of,_____243-306

God, his acts and words arise from settled dispositions,_____ 243

his dispositions inhere in a spiritual substance, _____ 243

his attributes, definition of, _____ 244

relation of his attributes to his essence, _____244-246

his attributes have an objective existence, _____ 244

his attributes are distinguishable from his essence and from each other, _____ 244

regarded falsely as being of absolute simplicity,_____ 244

he is a being infinitely complex,_____ 245

nominalistic notion, its error,_____ 245

his attributes inhere in his essence,
_____245, 246

is not a compound of attributes,____ 245

extreme realism, its danger, _____ 245

attributes of, belong to his essence, 245

his attributes distinguished from personal distinctions in his Godhead, _____ 246

his attributes distinguished from his relations to the world,_____ 246

illustrated by intellect and will in man, _____ 246

his attributes essential to his being, 246

his attributes manifest his essence,_ 246

in knowing his attributes, we know the being to whom attributes belong, _____ 246

his attributes, methods of determining, _____246, 247

rational method of determining,_____ 247

three viæ of rational method of determining his attributes,_____ 247

Biblical method,_____ 247

his attributes, how classified, ____247-249

absolute or immanent,_____ 247

his relative or transitive attributes, 247

his attributes, a threefold division of the relative or transitive,_____ 248

his attributes, schedule of,_____ 248

order in which they present themselves to the mind,_____ 248

his moral perfection involves relation of himself to himself,_____ 249

his absolute or immanent attributes,
_____249-275

his spirituality,_____249-254

is not matter,_____ 249

is not dependent upon matter,_____ 249

the material universe, not his sensorium, _____ 250

his spirituality not denied by anthropomorphic Scriptures,_____ 250

pictures of him, degrading,_____ 250

desire for an incarnate God, satisfied in Christ,_____ 251

God, his spirituality involves life and personality, ---------------------251, 252
life as an attribute of,--------------- 251
life in, has a subject,------------------ 251
life in, not correspondence with environment, ------------------------ 251
life in, is mental energy, the source of universal being and activity,--- 252
personality, an attribute of,--------- 252
his personality, its content,---------- 252
his infinity, its meaning,-------------- 254
his infinity, a positive idea,---------- 254
does not involve identity with 'The All,' ------------------------------- 255
intensive rather than extensive,----- 255
his infinity enables him to love infinitely the single Christian,------ 256
his infinity qualifies his other attributes, ---------------------------- 256
what his infinity involves,--------256-260
his self-existence, what?-------------- 256
he is *causa sui*, ---------------------- 256
his aseity, what?---------------------- 256
exists by necessity of his own being, --------------------------------- 257
his immutability, what?-------------- 257
said to change, how explained,------- 257
his immutability secures his adaptation to the changing conditions of his children,----------------------- 258
his immutability consistent with the execution in time of his eternal purposes, --------------------------- 258
permits activity and freedom,-------- 258
his unity, what? --------------------- 259
notion of more than one, self-contradictory and unphilosophical,--- 259
his unity not inconsistent with Trinity, ---------------------------------- 259
his unity, its lessons,----------------- 259
his perfection, explanation of the term, ------------------------------- 260
involves moral attributes,--------260-275
himself, a sufficient object for his own activity,----------------------- 260
his truth, what?---------------------- 260
his immanent truth to be distinguished from veracity and faithfulness, ---------------------------- 260
he is truth, as the truth that is known, ----------------------------- 261
his truth, a guarantee of revelation, and ground of eternal divine self-contemplation, ---------------------- 262
his love, what?----------------------- 263
his immanent love to be distinguished from mercy and goodness, 263
his immanent love finds a personal object in his own perfection,------ 263
his immanent love, not his all-inclusive ethical attribute,--------------- 263

God, his immanent love, not a regard for mere being in general,-------- 263
his immanent love, not a mere emotional or utilitarian affection,---- 264
his immanent love, rational and voluntary, ----------------------------- 264
his immanent love subordinates its emotional element to truth and holiness, --------------------------- 265
his immanent love has its standard in his holiness, and a perfect object in the image of his own infinite perfections,-------------------- 265
his immanent love, a ground of his blessedness, ----------------------- 265
his immanent love involves the possibility of his suffering on account of sin, which suffering is atonement, ----------------------------- 266
is passible,---------------------------- 266
blessedness consistent with sorrow, 266
a suffering being, a N. T. thought,--- 267
his passibility, authors on,---------- 267
his holiness, self-affirming purity,--- 268
his holiness, not its expression, justice, ----------------------------------- 269
his holiness is not an aggregate of perfections, but simple and distinct, ----------------------------- 269
his holiness is not utilitarian self-love, ----------------------------------- 270
his holiness is neither love nor its manifestation, ---------------------- 271
his holiness is purity of substance,--- 273
his holiness is energy of will,-------- 273
his holiness is God's self-willing,---- 274
his holiness is purity willing itself, 274
his holiness, authors on,------------- 275
his relative or transitive attributes, -------------------------------------275-295
his eternity, defined,----------------- 275
his eternity, infinity in its relation to time,--------------------------- 276
regards existing time as an objective reality,---------------,------------ 277
in what sense the past, present and future are to him 'one eternal now,' --------------------------------- 277
his immensity, what?----------------- 278
not under law of space,--------------- 279
is not in space,----------------------- 279
space is in him,---------------------- 279
to him space has an objective reality, ------------------------------ 279
his omnipresence, what?------------- 279
his omnipresence not potential but essential, ---------------------------- 280
in what sense he 'dwells in Heaven,' ------------------------------- 280
his omnipresence mistaken by Socinian and Deist,------------------ 280

God, his whole essence present in every part of his universe at the same time, --------------------- 281

his omnipresence not necessary, but free, ---- ------------------------- 283

his omniscience, what? -------------- 283

his omniscience, from what deducible, ----------------------------- 283

its characteristics, as free from all imperfections, --------------------- 283

his knowledge direct, ----------------- 283

his omniscience, Egyptian symbol of, -------------------------------- 283

his intense scrutiny, ------------------ 283

knows things as they are, ----------- 284

foreknows motives and acts by immediate knowledge, ----------------- 284

his prescience not causative, -------- 286

his omniscience embraces the actual and the possible, ------------------- 286

his omniscience called in Scripture 'wisdom,' -------------------------- 286

his omnipotence, what? -------------- 286

his omnipotence does not extend to the self-contradictory or the contradictory to his own nature, -- 287

has power over his own power, ------ 287

can do all he will, not will do all he can, ---------------------------------- 287

has a will-power over his nature-power, ---------------------------- 287

his omnipotence implies power of self-limitation, ---------------------- 288

his omnipotence permits human freedom, -------------------------------- 288

his omnipotence humbles itself in the incarnation, --------------------- 288

his attributes which have relation to moral beings, -----------------288–295

his veracity and faithfulness, or transitive truth, --------------------- 288

his veracity secures the consistency of his revelations with himself, and with each other, ---------------- 288

his veracity secures the fulfilment of all promises expressed or implied, ---------------------------- 289

his mercy and goodness, or transitive love, ------------------------- 289

his mercy, what? --------------------- 289

his goodness, what? ------------------ 289

his love finds its object in his own nature, ----------------------------- 290

his love, men its subordinate objects 290

his justice and righteousness or transitive holiness, ----------------- 290

his righteousness, what? ------------- 291

his justice, what? --------------------- 291

his justice and righteousness not mere benevolence, nor so founded in the nature of things as to be apart from God, ------------------- 291

God, his justice and righteousness are revelations of his inmost nature, 292

do not bestow reward, ---------------- 293

are devoid of passion and caprice,- 294

revulsion of his nature from impurity and selfishness, ----------------- 294

his attributes, rank and relations,--
---------------------------------295–303

his attributes related, ---------------- 295

his moral attributes more jealously guarded than his natural, --------- 295

his fundamental attribute is holiness, --------------------------------- 296

may be merciful, but must be holy, 296

his holiness put most prominently in Scripture, ------------------------ 296

his holiness, its supremacy asserted by conscience, ---------------------- 296

his holiness conditions exercise of other attributes, ---------------------- 297

his holiness, a principle in his nature which must be satisfied before he can redeem, --------------------- 298

his holiness, the ground of moral obligation, -------------------------298–303

commands us to be holy on the ground of his own holiness, ------- 302

as holy, the object of the love that fulfils the law, ---------------------- 302

his holy will, Christ, our example, supremely devoted to, -------------- 302

the Doctrine of the Trinity in the One God, -------------------------304–352

see Trinity.

is causa sui, -------------------------- 338

is 'self-willing right,' --------------- 338

relations sustained by, in virtue of personal distinctions, ---------------- 343

unity and threeness equally essential to, ---------------------------------- 346

independence and blessedness of, require Trinity, ----------------------- 347

Doctrine of his Decrees, ------------353–370

definition of his decrees, itemized,--
------------------------------------353–355

evil acts, how objects of the decrees of, ------------------------------------ 354

his permissive, not conditional agency, ----------------------------------- 354

his decrees, how classified, ----------- 355

his decrees referred to in Scripture and supported by reason, ------355–359

can preserve from sin without violation of moral agency, ------------- 366

his works, or the execution of his decrees, ---------------------------371–464

not a demiurge working on eternal matter, ---------------------------- 391

his supreme end in creation, his own glory, --------------------------397–402

God, 'his own sake,' the fundamental reason of activity in,--------- 399

his self-expression not selfishness, but benevolence,------------------ 40c

the only Being who can rightly live for himself,------------------------ 401

that he will secure his end in creation, the great source of comfort,-- 401

his rest, a new exercise of power,--- 411

not 'the soul of the universe,' ---- 411

the physical universe in no sense independent of,------------------------- 413

has disjoined in the free will of intelligent beings a certain amount of force from himself,--------------- 414

the perpetual Observer,-------------- 415

does not work all, but all in all,---- 418

represented sometimes by Hebrew writers as doing what he only permits, --------------------------- 424

his agency, natural and moral, distinguished, ------------------------- 441

his Fatherhood,--------------------474-476

implied in man's divine sonship,---- 474

extends in a natural relation to all, 474

provides the atonement,------------- 474

special, towards those who believe,-- 474

secures the natural and physical sonship of all men,---------------- 474

this natural sonship preliminary in some to a spiritual sonship,---- 474

texts referring to, in a natural or common sense,---------------------- 474

in the larger sense, what it implies, 474

natural, mediated by Christ,------- 474

texts referring to, in a special sense, ---------------------------474, 475

to the race rudimental to the actual realization in Christ,--------------- 475

extends to those who are not his children, -------------------------- 475

controversy on the doctrine mere logomachy, ----------------------- 475

as anounced by Jesus, a relation of love and holiness,------------------ 475

if not true, then selfishness logical, 475

this relationship realized in a spiritual sense through atoning and regenerating grace,----------------- 475

logical outcome of the denial of,-- --------------------------------475, 476

universal ground for accepting,-- 476

authors upon,--------------------- 476

our knowledge of, conditioned by love, ---------------------------519, 520

'God prays' fulfilled in Christ,----- 675

reflected in universe,---------------- 714

the immanent, is Christ, the Logos, 714

exercises his creative, preserving and providential activity through Christ, ----------------------------- 714

the Revealer of, is Christ, the Logos, 714

God, personal existence grounded in him, -------------------------------- 714

all perceptions or recognitions of the objective through him,--------- 714

as Universal Reason, at the basis of our self-consciousness and thinking, ----------------------------714, 715

is the common conscience, over finite, individual consciences,------ 715

the eternal suffering of, on account of human sin, manifested in the historical sufferings of the incarnate Christ,------------------------- 715

the heart of, finally revealed in the historic sacrifice of Calvary,----- 716

dealings of repentant sinner with, rather than with government,--- 741

salvation of all, in which sense desired by,---------------------791, 792

Golden Age, classic references to,---- 526

Good deeds of an unregenerated man, how related to the tenor of his life, ---------------------------- 814

Goodness, defined,---------------------- 289

Goodness of God, witness to among heathen, ----------------------------- 113

Gospel, testimony of, conformable with experience,--------------------- 173

its initial successes, a proof of its divine origin,----------------------- 191

makes men moral,------------------- 863

Gospels, run counter to Jewish ideas, 156

superior in literary character to contemporary writings,------------- 158

their relation to a historical Christ, 159

coincidence of their statements with collateral circumstances,--------173, 174

Gottesbewusstsein, knowledge of God, 63

Government, common, not necessary in church of Christ,--------------- 913

Government, church,-------------903-926

Grace, supplements law as the expression of the whole nature of the lawgiver,----------------547, 548, 752

without works on the sinner's part, and without necessity on God's, 548

an expression of the heart of God, beyond law, and in Christ,------- 548

does not abrogate but reinforces and fulfils law,--------------------- 548

secures fulfilment of law by removing obstacles to pardon in the divine mind, and enabling man to obey, -------------------------------- 548

has its law which subsumes but transcends 'the law of sin and death,' ---------------------------- 548

has its place between the Pelagian and Rationalistic ideas of penalty, 548

a revelation partly of law, but chiefly of love,--------------------- 549

the Pelagian idea of,----------------- 598

Grace, universal, according to Wesley, 603
  what, from the Arminian point of
    view, ------------------------------- 605
  may afford sinners a better security
    for salvation than if they were
    Adams, ---------------------------- 635
  a kingdom of,----------------------- 775
  men as sinners, its objects,---------- 778
  certain sinful men chosen to be re-
    cipients of special,------------------ 779
  ' unmerited favor to sinners,'------- 779
  more may be equitably bestowed on
    one man than on another,----------- 779
Gracious Ability,-------------------602-604
Guilt, defined,---------------------614, 644
  how related to sin,----------------644, 645
  how incurred,----------------------- 644
  not mere liability to penalty,-------- 644
  constructive, has no place in divine
    government, ----------------------- 644
  to be distinguished from depravity,
    -------------------------------645, 762
  is obligation to satisfy outraged
    holiness of God,-------------------- 645
  of sin, how set forth in Scripture,-- 645
  how Christ may have, without de-
    pravity, --------------------------- 645
  and depravity, *reatus* and *macula*,-- 645
  of race, how Christ bears,--------646, 759
  not to be confounded with the con-
    sciousness of,---------------------- 647
  first a relation to God, then to con-
    science, --------------------------- 647
  administers its own anesthetics,----- 647
  degrees of,----------------------648-652
  degrees of, set forth in Mosaic rit-
    ual, ------------------------------ 648
  casuistical refinements upon, not
    to be regarded,-------------------- 648
  variety of award in Judgment ex-
    plained by degrees in,------------- 648
  measured by men's opportunities
    and powers,------------------------ 649
  measured by the energy of evil will, 649
  measured by degrees of unreceptive-
    ness in soul,---------------------- 650
  of race, shared in by Christ,-------- 759
  imparted and imputed to Christ,---- 759
Habit and character,-------------------1049
' Hands of the Living God,' what?-- 539
Hatred, what?------------------------- 569
Heart, its meaning in Scripture,------- 4
Heathen, the, their virtues, what?-- 570
  may be saved who have not heard
    the gospel,---------------------664, 843
  their religious systems corrupting, 666
  whatever good in their religions,
    God in,----------- ----------------- 666
  in proportion to their culture, be-
    come despairing,------------------- 666
  have an external revelation,-------- 666

Heathen, instances of apparently regenerated, ----------------------843, 844
Heathenism, a negative preparation
  for redemption,----------------665, 666
  partly a positive preparation for
    redemption, ----------------------- 665
  in it Christ as Logos or immanent
    God revealed himself in conscience
    and history,----------------------- 665
  had the starlight of religious knowl-
    edge, ----------------------------- 666
  their religions not the direct work
    of the devil,----------------------- 666
  authors on heathenism as an evan-
    gelical preparation,---------------- 666
Heaven, conception of,----------------1030
  elements of its happy perfection,--1031
  rewards in, equal yet various,-------1031
  is deliverance from defective physi-
    cal organization and circum-
    stances, --------------------------1031
  its rest,--------------------------1031
  how perfect on entering,------------1031
  a city,----------------------------1031
  its love,--------------------------1031
  its activities,---------------------1031
  is it a place as well as a state? 460, 1032
  probably a place,----------------460, 1032
  may be a state,-------------------- 460
  the essential presence of Christ's
    body would imply place,-----------1032
  is it on a purified and prepared
    earth? -----------------------1032, 1033
Hebrews, genuineness and authorship, 152
  anti-Ebionite, -------------------- 669
Hell, essentially an inward condition,
  -------------------------------460, 1034
  the outward corresponds with in-
    ward, ----------------------------1034
  the pains of, not necessarily posi-
    tive inflictions of God,------------1035
  is not an endless succession of suf-
    ferings, --------------------------1035
  its extent and scope,---------------1052
  compared with heaven, narrow and
    limited, --------------------------1052
  only a spot, a corner in the uni-
    verse, ---------------------------1052
Henotheism, what?------------------ 259
Heredity, none in the race to predetermine self-consciousness,------ 467
  some facts which heredity cannot
    explain, -------------------------- 471
  often presents a product differing
    from both the producing agents,-- 492
  its influence in fiction,------------- 492
  laws of, simply descriptions not ex-
    planations, ----------------------- 493
  illustrations of heredity,---------495, 496
  cause of variations in, discussed,---- 497
  Weismann's views of,-------466, 497, 631
  works for theology,-------------621, 632

Heredity, is God working in us,------ 624
   the law by which living beings tend
   to reproduce themselves in their
   descendants, ---------------------- 625
   the scientific attitude of mind in regard to,---------------------------- 632
   the opposing views of, illustrated, 632
   the conclusion best warranted by
   science in relation to,------------- 632
   when modifications are transmitted
   by, -------------------------------- 632
   may be intensified by individual action, ------------------------------ 632
   has given new currency to doctrine
   of 'Original Sin,'------------------ 636
Heresy, what?--------------------------- 800
Hingewandt zu, Dorner's translation
   of πρός in John 1 : 3,-------------- 337
Hipparion, the two-toed horse,------- 472
Holiness of God, see God.
Holy Spirit,-----------------------13, 337
   organ of internal revelation,----13, 337
   recognized as God,------------------ 315
   possession of,-------------------322, 343
   is a person,------------------------ 323
   his work other than that of Christ,
   --------------------------------338, 339
   sin against,---------------648, 650-652
   relation to Christ in his state of humiliation, ------------------669, 697, 703
   application of redemption through
   work of,------------------------777-886
Honestum and utile,-------------------- 300
Host, Romish adoration of,------------ 968
'Host,' Scriptural use of,------------- 448
Humanity, capable of religion,-------- 58
   full concept of, marred in First
   Adam, realized in Second,---------- 678
   its exaltation in Christ, the experience of his people,---------------- 707
   justified in Christ's justification,-- 862
Humanity of Christ,---------------673-681
   atonement as related to,---------754-763
   see Christ.
Humiliation of Christ,--------------701-706
   see Christ.
Humility, what?------------------. ,--- 832
Hyperphysical communication be-
   tween minds perhaps possible,---1021
'I Am,' as a Divine title,------------- 253
Idea of God, origin of our,----------52-70
   see God.
Ideal human nature in Christ,-------- 678
Idealism, its view of revelation,--11, 12
Idealism, Materialistic,-------------95-100
Ideas have decided fate of world,----- 426
Identity, Edwards's theory of,-------- 607
   what it consists in,-------------1020-1023
Idiomaticum genus,--------------------- 686
'Idle word,'--------------------------- 554
Idolatry, -----------7, 133, 251, 457, 532, 968
Ignorance, sins of,----------------554, 649

Ignorance, invincible,---------------- 967
Ignorantia legis neminem excusat,---- 358
Image, what it suggests,-----------335, 514
   and likeness,----------------------- 520
Image of God, in what it consisted,-- 514
   its natural element,---------------- 514
   its moral element,------------------ 514
   personality, an element in,--------- 51.
   holiness, an element in,---------515, 516
   its original righteousness,-------517, 518
   not confined to personality,------519, 520
   not consisting in a natural capacity
   for religion,-------------------520-523
   reflects itself in physical form,------ 523
   in soul proprie, in body significative, ------------------------------ 523
   subjects sensuous impulses to control of spirit,-----------------523, 524
   gives dominion over lower creation, 524
   secures communion with God,----524, 525
   had suitable surroundings and society, ------------------------------- 525
   furnished with tests of virtue,------ 526
   had associated with it, an opportunity of securing physical immortality, ------------------------------- 527
   combated by those who hold that
   civilization has proceeded from
   primitive savagery,-------------527-531
   combated by those who hold that religion begins in fetichism,------531, 532
Immortality, metaphysical argument
   for, ---------------------------984, 985
   teleological argument for,--------986, 987
   ethical argument for,------------987, 988
   historical argument,---------------- 989
   widespread belief in,------------989, 990
   a general appetency for,------------ 990
   idea of, congruous with our nature, 990
   authors for and against,------------ 991
   maintained on Scriptural grounds,
   -------------------------------991-998
   an inference from the intuition of
   the existence of God,-------------- 996
   the resurrection of Jesus Christ the
   most conclusive proof of,---------- 997
   Christ taught,---------------------- 997
Imprecatory Psalms,------------------- 231
Imputatio metaphysica,---- ---------- 615
Imputation of Adam's sin to his posterity, ------------------------593-637
   taught in Scripture,---------------- 593
   two questions demanding answer, 593
   the meaning of the phrase,--------- 354
   has a realistic basis in Scripture,-- 594
   two fundamental principles in,----- 595
   theories of New and Old Schools, 596, 597
   theories of,------------------597-637
   Pelagian theory of, considered,--597-601
   Arminian theory of, considered, 601-606
   New School theory of, considered,--
   -------------------------------606-612

Imputation, Federal theory of, con-
    sidered, ------------------------612–616
  Mediate theory of, ----------------616–619
  Augustinian theory of, considered,
    ----------------------------------619–637
  grounded on organic unity of man-
    kind, ------------------------------- 619
  tabular views,------------------------- 628
  objections to Augustinian theory,--
    ----------------------------------629–637
  authors on,--------------------------- 637
  of sin to Christ, grounded on a real
    union, ------------------------------- 758
  of Christ's righteousness to us,
    grounded on a real union,----805, 862
Indwelling of God,--------------------693, 798
Inexistentia, --------------------------- 333
Infant salvation,--------------------602, 609
  doctrine of,------------------------660–664
  is assured,--------------------------- 661
  its early advocates,------------------- 664
  leads to the conclusion that no one
    is lost solely for sin of nature,---- 664
Infanticide might have been encour-
    aged by too definite assurances of
    infant salvation,--------------------- 663
Infants, their death proves their sin-
    ful nature,-------------------------- 579
  are regarded by some as animals,
    ----------------------------579, 611, 957
  are unregenerate and in a state of
    sin, --------------------------------- 661
  relatively innocent,------------------- 661
  objects of special divine care,----661, 662
  chosen by Christ to eternal life,---- 662
  salvation assured to those who die
    prior to moral consciousness,----- 662
  in some way receive and are united
    to Christ,--------------------------- 662
  at final judgment among the saved, 662
  regeneration effected at soul's first
    view of Christ,---------------------- 663
Inference, its nature and kinds,------- 66
Infinite, ---------------------------9, 87, 254
Infinity of God,----------------------254–256
  see God.
Infirmity, sins of,--------------------649, 650
Innate or connate ideas, what?------- 54
Insitæ vel potius innatæ cogitationes, 53
Inspiration of Scripture,-----------196–242
  definition of,----------------------196–198
  defined by result,-------------------- 196
  may include revelation,-------------- 196
  may include illumination,----------- 196
  list of works on,--------------------- 198
  proof of,----------------------------- 198
  presumption in favor of,------------ 198
  of the O. T., vouched for by Jesus, 199
  promised by Jesus,---------------199, 200
  claimed by the apostles,----------200, 201
  attested by miracle or prophecy, 201

Inspiration of Scripture, chief proof
    of, internal characteristics,--------201
  theories of,----------------------202–222
  the Intuition-theory of,-------------- 202
  this theory of, its doctrinal connec-
    tions, ------------------------------- 202
  this theory of, uses only man's nat-
    ural insight,------------------------- 203
  this theory of, denies to man's in-
    sight, vitiated in matters of re-
    ligion and morals, an indispen-
    sable help,-------------------------- 203
  this theory of, is self-contradictory, 203
  is 'the growth of the Divine through
    the capacities of the human,'------ 204
  this theory of, makes moral and
    religious truth purely subjective,-- 204
  this theory of, practically denies a
    God who is Truth and its Reveal-
    er, --------------------------------- 204
  the Illumination-theory of,---------- 204
  this theory of, its doctrinal connec-
    tions, ------------------------------- 204
  this theory of, principal advocates
    of, --------------------------------- 205
  in some cases amounted only to il-
    lumination, ------------------------- 206
  more than an illumination, which
    cannot account for revelation of
    new truth,-------------------------- 206
  if illumination only, cannot secure
    writers from serious error,-------- 207
  as mere illumination can enlighten
    truth already imparted but not
    impart it,--------------------------- 207
  the Dictation-theory of,------------- 208
  this theory of, its doctrinal connec-
    tions, ------------------------------- 208
  this theory of, its principal advo-
    cates, ------------------------------- 208
  this theory of, post-reformation,---- 209
  this theory of, covers the few cases
    in which definite words were used
    with the command to write them
    down, ------------------------------- 209
  this theory of, rests on an imperfect
    induction of Scriptural facts,------- 210
  this theory of, fails to account for
    the human element in Scripture,-- 210
  this theory of, spendthrift in
    means, as dictating truth already
    known to recipient,----------------- 210
  this theory of, reduces man's high-
    est spiritual experience to mechan-
    ism, -------------------------------- 210
  the Dynamical theory of,--------211–222
  distinguished from other theories of, 211
  no theory of, necessary to Christian
    faith, ------------------------------- 211
  union of the Divine and human ele-
    ments in,-------------------------212–222

Inspiration of Scripture, its mystery, the union of the divine and human, ---------------------------------- 212

and hypnotic suggestion,------------- 212

the speaking and writing the words of God from within, in the conscious possession and exercise of intellect, emotion and will,-------- 212

pressed into service all the personal peculiarities, excellencies and defects of its subjects,----------------- 213

uses all normal methods of literary composition, ---------------------- 214

may use even myth and legend,------ 214

a gradual evolution,--------------214, 215

the divine side of what on its human side is discovery,-------------- 215

does not guarantee inerrancy in things not essential to its purpose, 215

in it God uses imperfect means,-- 215

is divine truth in historical and individually conditioned form,-------- 216

did not directly communicate the words which its subjects employed, 216

has permitted no form of words which would teach essential error, 216

verbal, refuted by two facts,-------- 216

constitutes its Scriptures an organic whole, ----------------------------- 217

develops a progressive system with Christ as centre,------------------ 217

furnishes, in the Bible as a whole, a sufficient guide to truth and salvation, ---------------------------- 218

overstatement of, has made sceptics, -------------------------------- 218

constitutes Scripture an authority, but subordinate to the ultimate authority, Christ,------------------- 219

three cardinal principles regarding, 220

three common questions regarding, ----------------------------------220, 221

objections to the doctrine of,----222-242

objected to, on the ground of errors in secular matters,----------------- 222

said to be erroneous in its science,-- 223

reply to above allegation against, ----------------------------------223-226

said to be erroneous in its history, 226

reply to above allegation against, ----------------------------------226-229

said to be erroneous in its morality, 230

reply to above allegation against, ----------------------------------230-232

said to be erroneous in its reasoning, -------------------------------- 232

reply to above allegation against, ----------------------------------232, 233

said to be erroneous in quotation and interpretation,----------------- 234

reply to above allegation against, ----------------------------------234, 235

Inspiration of Scripture, said to be erroneous in its prophecy,-------- 235

reply to above allegation against, ----------------------------------235, 236

admits books unworthy of a place as inspired,----------------------- 236

reply to above allegation against, ----------------------------------236-238

admits as authentic portions of books written by others than the persons to whom they are ascribed, --------------------------- 238

reply to above allegation against, ----------------------------------238-240

admits sceptical or fictitious narratives, ------------------------------ 240

reply to above allegation against, ----------------------------------240-242

acknowledges non-inspiration of its teachers and writers,-------------- 242

reply to above allegation against,-- 242

Intercession of Christ,-------------773-775 see Christ.

Intercessors, saints on earth are,----- 775

Intercommunicatio, -------------------- 333

Intercommunion of the Persons in the Trinity, ----------------------332-334

Intermediate State,----------------998-1003

of the righteous,----------------988, 999

of the wicked,-------------------999, 1000

not a sleep,----------------------------1000

not purgatorial,----------------------1000

one of incompleteness,----------------1002

a state of thought,--------------------1002

sin if preferred in this more spiritual state becomes demoniacal,----1002

some place the end of man's probation at the close of the,-------- 1002

Intuition,--------------52, 53, 67, 72, 125, 499

Intuition-theory of inspiration, see Inspiration.

Intuitional theory of morals,---------- 501

reconciled with the empirical theory, ----------------------------- 501

Intuitions, ---------------------52, 53, 67, 248

Isaiah, its composite character,------- 239

Islam, ---------------------------186, 427

James, the apostle, his position on Justification, ---------------------- 851

Jefferson, Thomas, on a Baptist church as the truest form of democracy, ------------------------- 903

Jehovah, ---------------------------256, 309

Jesus, bowing at the name of,--------- 969

Jews, the only forward-looking people, ----------------------------- 666

educated in three great truths, 666, 667

above truths presented by three agencies, -------------------667, 668

this education first of all by law,-- 667

this education by prophecy,-------- 667

this education by judgment,--------- 668

Jews, effects of the exile upon,---- 663
as propagators of the gospel,------ 668
authors on Judaism as a preparation for Christ,------------------ 668
Job, the book of, when written,------- 241
is a dramatic poem,-----------240, 241
John, gospel of, differs from synoptics
in its account of Jesus,------------ 143
its genuineness,------------------151, 152
compared with Revelation,------151, 152
does its characteristic Logos doctrine necessitate a later date? 320, 321
Judas, ----------------------------884, 1043
*Judex damnatur cum nocens absolvi-
tur,* ------------------------------- 293
Judge, Christ the final,----------1027, 1028
Judgment, the last, a final and complete vindication of God's righteousness, ------------------1023, 1024
its nature outward, visible, definite
in time,----------------------1024, 1025
its object, the manifestation of
character, and assignment of corresponding condition,----------1025, 1026
evidences of, and preparation for,
already in the nature of man,
----------------------------1026, 1027
single acts and words adduced in,
why? ------------------------1027, 1028
the judge in, see preceding item.
the subjects of, men and evil angels,
----------------------------1028, 1029
the grounds of, the law of God and
grace of Christ,-----------------1029
list of authors on,-------------------1029
Justice of God,------------------290–295
see God.
Justification, involved in union with
Christ, ----------------------------- 805
the doctrine of,-----------------849–868
defined, ----------------------------- 849
declarative and judicial,------------- 849
held as sovereign by Arminians,-849, 875
Scriptural proof of,---------------849, 850
its nature determined by Scriptural
use of 'justify' and its deriv-
atives, ------------------------850–854
James and Paul on,------------------ 851
includes remission of punishment,
----------------------------854–856
a declaration that the sinner is just
or free from condemnation of law, 854
is pardon or forgiveness as God is
regarded as judge or father,------- 855
is on the ground of union with
Christ who has borne the penalty, 855
includes restoration to favor,------- 856
since it treats the sinner as personally righteous it must give him
the rewards of obedience,---------- 856
is reconciliation or adoption as God
is regarded as friend or father,--- 857

Justification, this restoration rests
solely on the righteousness of
Christ to whom sinner is united
by faith, -------------------------- 858
its difficult feature stated,---------- 859
believed on testimony of Scripture, 860
the difficulty in, relieved by three
considerations, -------------------- 860
is granted to a sinner in whose
stead Christ has borne penalty,---- 860
is bestowed on one who is so united
to Christ as to have Christ's life
dominating his being,-------------- 860
is declared of one in whom the present Christ life will infallibly extirpate all remaining depravity,------ 860
its ground is not the infusion into
us of righteousness and love
(Romish view)--------------------- 861
its ground is not the essential
righteousness of Christ become
the sinner's by faith, (Osiander)-- 861
its ground is the satisfaction and
obedience of Christ the head of a
new humanity of which believers
are members,---------------------- 861
is ours, not because Christ is in us,
but because we are in Christ,----- 862
its relation to regeneration and
sanctification delivers it from externality and immorality,------862, 863
and sanctification, not different
stages of same process,------------ 863
a declarative, as distinguished from
the efficient acts of God's grace,
regeneration and sanctification,-- 863
gifts and graces accompaniments,
not consequences of,--------------- 864
why 'by faith' rather than other
graces? ---------------------------- 864
produced efficiently by grace, meritoriously by Christ, instrumentally by faith, evidentially by works, 865
as being complete at the moment of
believing, is the ground of peace, 865
is instantaneous, complete and final, 867
not eternal in the past,------------- 867
in, God grants actual pardon for
past sin, and virtual pardon for
future sin,------------------------- 867
cannot be secured by future obedience, ------------------------------ 868
must be secured by accepting Christ
and manifesting trust and submission by prompt obedience,------ 868
list of authors on,------------------- 868
Justitia civilis,---------------------- 639
Justus et justificans,--------------- 753
Kalpa, ------------------------------- 352
Karen tradition,---------------------- 116
Kenosis, -----------------701, 704, 705
Keri and Kethib,--------------------- 309

'Know,' its meaning in Scripture,-- 780
Knowledge includes faith as a higher
   sort of,------------------------3, 4, 5
   analogy to one's nature or exper-
     ience not necessary to,------------ 7
   is 'recognition and classification' 7
   mental image, not essential to,------- 7
   of whole not essential to partial,
     and of a part,---------------------- 8
   may be adequate though not ex-
     haustive, -------------------------- 8
   involves limitation or definition,---- 9
   relative to knowing agent,---------- 10
   is of the thing as it is,--------------- 10
   though imperfect, valuable,--------- 37
   requires pre-supposition of an Ab-
     solute Reason,---------------------- 61
   does not ensure right action,----111, 460
   aggravates, but is not essential to,
     sin, ------------------------------ 558
   two kinds of, and *scientia media*,--- 357
   sins of,---------------------------- 649
   final state of righteous one of,------1029
Koran, ---------------------------115, 186
Kung-fu-tse, see Confucius.
Language, difficulty of putting spiritual truths into,--------------------- 35
   dead only living,-------------------- 39
   not essential to thought,------------ 216
   defined, -------------------------- 467
   is the effect, not the cause of mind, 467
Law, cause and force known without
   mental image,---------------------- 7
   is method, not cause,--------------- 76
   the transcript of God's nature,------ 293
   in general,---------------------533-536
   its essential idea,------------------ 533
   its implications,-------------------- 533
   first used of voluntary agents,------ 533
   its use in physics implicitly con-
     fesses a Supreme Will,------------ 533
   its derivation in several languages, 523
   because of its ineradicable implica-
     tions, 'method' has been sug-
     gested as a substitute,------------ 533
   definitions of,------------------533, 534
   cannot reign,---------------------- 534
   its generality,--------------------- 534
   deals in general rules,-------------- 534
   implies power to enforce,--------534, 535
   without penalty is advice,----------- 535
   in the case of rational and free
     agents implies duty and sanctions, 535
   expresses and demands nature,----- 535
   formulates relations arising in na-
     ture, ----------------------------- 535
   of God in particular,-------------536-547
   elemental, --------------------536-544
   physical or natural,----------------- 536
   moral law,------------------------ 537
   moral law, its implications,--------- 537
   is discovered, not made,----------- 538

Law, not constituted, but tested, by
   utility, ---------------------------- 535
   of God, what?---------------------- 538
   the method of Christ,--------------- 539
   authors upon,---------------------- 539
   not arbitrary,---------------------- 539
   not temporary, or provisional,------- 540
   not merely negative,---------------- 540
   as seen in Decalogue,--------------- 540
   not addressed to one part of man's
     nature, --------------------------- 540
   not outwardly published,--------540, 541
   not limited by man's consciousness
     of it,----------------------------- 541
   not local,-------------------------- 541
   not modifiable,--------------------- 541
   not violated even in salvation,------- 541
   the ideal of human nature,---------- 542
   reveals love and mercy mandatorily,
     -----------------------------542, 549
   is all-comprehensive,--------------- 542
   is spiritual,------------------------ 543
   is a unit,-------------------------- 543
   is not now proposed as a method
     of salvation,---------------------- 543
   is a means of discovering and de-
     veloping sin,------------------543, 544
   reminds man of the heights from
     which he has fallen,-------------- 544
   as positive enactment,------------544-547
   as shown in general moral precepts, 545
   as shown in ceremonial or special
     injunctions, ---------------------- 545
   its positive form a re-enactment of
     its elemental principles,----------- 545
   the written, why imperfect?--------- 546
   the Puritan mistake in relation to,-- 546
   its relation to the grace of God,
     -----------------------------547-549
   is a general expression of God's
     will, ----------------------------- 547
   is a partial, not an exhaustive, ex-
     pression of God's nature,--------- 547
   pantheistic mistake in relation to,
     -----------------------------547, 548
   alone, leaves parts of God's nature
     to be expressed by gospel,-------- 548
   is not, Christ is, the perfect image
     of God,--------------------------- 548
   not abrogated by grace, but repub-
     lished and re-enforced,----------- 548
   of sin and death,------------------- 548
   in the manifestation of grace, com-
     bined with a view of the personal
     love of the Lawgiver,------------- 549
   its all-embracing requirement,------- 572
   identical with the constituent prin-
     ciples of being,------------------- 629
   all-comprehending demand of har-
     mony with God,------------------- 637
   the Mosaic, inspired hope of pardon
     and access to God,---------------- 667

Law, its basis in the nature of God, 764
    as a moral rule unchanging,_____ 875
    freedom from, what?_____ 876
    believer not free from obligation to
        observe, _____ 876
    as a system of penalty, believer
        free from,_____ 876
    as a method of salvation, believer
        free from,_____ 876
    as an outward and foreign compul-
        sion, believer free from,_____ 876
    not a sliding scale graduated to
        one's moral condition,_____ 877
    God's, as known in conscience and
        Scripture, a ground of final judg-
        ment, _____1029
Laws of knowing correspond to na-
    ture of things,_____ 10
    of theological thought, laws of God's
        thought, _____ 10
    of nature, not violated in miracle,__ 121
    of nature, act not merely singly,
        but in combination,_____434, 435
'Laying-on of hands,' its significance, 920
Letter-missive calling council of ordi-
    nation, _____ 922
Lex, its derivation,_____ 533
Licensure, its nature,_____ _____ 919
Life contains promise and potency of
    every form of matter,_____ 91
    not produced from matter,_____ 93
    as it ascends, it differentiates,_____ 240
    not definable,_____ 251
    not a mere process,_____ 251
    more than environmental corres-
        pondence, _____ 251
    ascribed to Christ,_____ 309
    ascribed to Holy Spirit,_____ 315
    animal, though propagated, not ma-
        terial, _____ 495
    has power to draw from the putres-
        cent material for its living,_____ 677
    its various relations honored by be-
        ing taken into union with Divinity
        in Christ,_____ 682
    man's physical, conscious of a life
        within not subject to will,_____ 799
    man's spiritual, conscious of life
        within its life,_____ 799
    man's natural, preserved by God,
        much more his spiritual,_____ 883
    Christian, attains completeness in
        future, _____ 981
    sinful, attains completeness in fu-
        ture, _____ 981
    book of,' the book of justification, 1029
Lineamenta extrema,_____ 614
Locutiones variæ, sed non con-
    trariæ; diversæ, sed non adversæ, 227
Logos, the whole, present in the man,
    Christ Jesus,___ _____ 281

Logos, John's doctrine of the radi-
    cally different from Philo's,__320, 321
    John's doctrine of the, related to
        the 'memra' doctrine,_____ 320
    doctrine of the, authorities on,_____ 321
    significance of term,_____ 335
    the pre-incarnate, granted to men
        a natural light of reason and con-
        science, _____ 603
    purged of depravity that portion of
        human nature which he assumed
        in Incarnation, in the very act of
        taking it,_____ 677
    during earthly life of Jesus existed
        outside of flesh,_____ 704
    the whole present in Christ, and yet
        present everywhere else,_____ 704
    can suffer on earth, and yet reign
        in heaven at same time,_____ 714
    his surrender of independent exer-
        cise of divine attributes, how best
        conceived, _____ 705
    his part in evangelical preparation, 711
'Lord of Hosts,' its significance,____ 448
Lord's Day,_____ 410
Lord's Supper,_____959–980
Lord's Supper and Baptism, historical
    monuments, _____ 151
Love, necessary to right use of reason
    with regard to God,_____3, 29, 519, 520
    its loss obscures rational intuitions
        of God,_____ 67
    God's, nature cannot prove it,_____ 84
    God's immanent, what?_____ 263
    not to be confounded with mercy
        and goodness,_____ 265
    God's, finds a personal object within
        the Trinity,_____ 285
    constitutes a ground of divine
        blessedness, _____ 285
    God's transitive, what?_____ 289
    God's transitive, is mercy and good-
        ness, _____ 289
    distinct from holiness,_____290, 567
    attributed to Christ,_____ 309
    attributed to Holy Spirit,_____ 316
    revealed in grace rather than in
        law, _____ 548
    defined, _____ 567
    to God, all-embracing requirement
        of law,_____ 572
    eternity of God's, an effective ele-
        ment in appeal,_____ 788
    God's, fixed on sinners of whom he
        knows the worst,_____ 788
    God's unchanging,_____ 788
    God's, has dignity,_____1051
    brotherly, in heaven implies knowl-
        edge, _____1031
Maat, the Egyptian goddess,_____1024
Maccabees, First, no direct mention
    of God in,_____ 306

Magister sententiarum,------------- 44
Magnetism, personal, what?--------- 820
Majestaticum genus,--------------- 686
Malice, what?---------------------- 569
Malum metaphysicum, what?--------- 424
Man, in what sense supernatural,------ 26
  furnishes highest type of intelli-
    gence and will in nature,---------- 79
  as to intellect and freedom, not eter-
    nal *a parte ante,*---------------- 81
  his intellectual and moral nature,
    implies an intellectual and moral
    author, --------------------------- 81
  his moral nature proves existence of
    a holy Lawgiver,------------------ 82
  his emotional and voluntary nature
    proves the existence of a Being
    who may be a satisfying object of
    human affection and end of human
    activity, -------------------------- 83
  recognizes in God, not his like, but
    his opposite,---------------------- 83
  mistakes as to his own nature lead
    him into mistakes as to the First
    Cause, ------------------------84, 253
  his consciousness, Royce's view,----- 99
  his will above nature,-------------- 121
  a concave glass towards God,------- 252
  can objectify self,----------------- 252
  is self-determining,---------------- 252
  not explicable from nature,--------- 411
  a spiritually reproductive agent, yet
    God begets,---------------------- 413
  a creation, and child of God,-- 465–476
  his creation a fact of Scripture,----- 465
  exists by creative acts of God,------- 465
  though result of evolution, yet or-
    iginating agency of God needed,-- 465
  whether mediately or immediately
    created Scripture does not ex-
    plicitly state,--------------------- 465
  the true doctrine of evolution con-
    sistent with the Scriptural doc-
    trine of creation,------------------ 466
  certain psychological human endow-
    ments cannot have come from the
    brute, ---------------------------- 466
  God's breathing into men was such a
    re-inforcement of the processes of
    life as turned the animal into
    man, ------------------------------ 467
  and brute, both created by the im-
    manent God, the former comes to
    his status not *from* but *through*
    the latter,------------------------- 467
  the beginnings of his conscious life, 467
  some simple distinctions between
    man and brute,-----------------467, 468
  if of brute ancestry, yet the off-
    spring of God,--------------------- 469
  Scripture teaches that man's nature
    is the creation of God,------------- 469

Man, his relations to animals, au-
    thors upon,----------------------- 469
  immediate creation of his body not
    forbidden by comparative physiol-
    ogy, ------------------------------- 470
  that his physical system is de-
    scended by natural generation
    from the simiæ, an irrational hy-
    pothesis, -------------------------- 470
  as his soul was an immediate crea-
    tion of God, so, in this sense, was
    his body also,---------------------- 470
  does not degenerate as we travel
    back in time,---------------------- 471
  no natural process accounts for his
    informing soul nor for the body
    informed by that soul,------------- 472
  the laws of development followed
    in man's origin from a brute an-
    cestry are but methods of God,
    and proofs of his creatorship,----- 47.
  comes upon the scene not as a brute
    but as a self-conscious, self-deter-
    mining being,---------------------- 472
  his original and new creation, both
    from within,----------------------- 472
  an emanation of that Divine Life
    of which the brute was a lower
    manifestation, --------------------- 472
  his nature not an undesigned result
    of atheous evolution but the
    efflux of the divine personality,-- 473
  natural selection may account for
    man's place *in* nature, but not for
    his place as a spiritual being
    above nature,---------------------- 473
  his intellectual and moral faculties
    have only an adequate cause in
    the world of spirits,--------------- 473
  apart from the controlling action of
    a higher intelligence, the laws of
    the material universe insufficient
    for his production,----------------- 473
  his brute ancestry, list of authors
    on, ---------------------------473, 474
  his racial unity,---------------476–483
  his racial unity, a fact of Scripture, 476
  his racial unity at foundation of
    certain Pauline doctrines,-------- 476
  his racial unity, the ground of natu-
    ral brotherhood,------------------- 476
  the pre-Adamite,-----------------476, 477
  his racial unity, sustained by his-
    tory, ------------------------------477, 478
  his racial unity, sustained by phi-
    lology, ---------------------------478, 479
  his racial unity, sustained by
    psychology, ----------------------- 479
  his racial unity, sustained by physi-
    ology, ----------------------------480, 483
  a single species under several vari-
    eties, ----------------------------- 480

Ian, unity of species of, argues unity
   of origin,---------------------------- 481
according to Agassiz from eight
   centres of origin,-------------------- 481
his racial unity, consistent with all
   existing physical varieties,----481, 482
physiological change in, illustrated, 482
his 'originally greater plasticity,'-- 482
his racial unity, authorities on, 482, 483
the essental elements of his nature,
   ----------------------------------483-488
the dichotomous theory of his nature, ---------------------------483, 484
the dichotomous theory of, supported by consciousness,----------------- 483
the dichotomous theory of, supported by Scripture,-----------------483, 484
the trichotomous theory of his nature, ----------------------------484-488
his ψυχή and πνεῦμα, ----------------- 484
his spirit and soul, texts on,------- 484
trichotomous theory of his nature,
   element of truth in,---------------- 484
the trichotomous theory of his nature untenable,-----------------485, 486
the true relation of πνεῦμα and ψυχή
   in his nature,-----------------486-488
is different in kind from the brute,
   though possessed of certain
   powers in common with it,-------- 486
since spirit is soul when in connection with the body, soul cannot
   be immortal unless with spiritual
   body, --------------------------- 486
the trichotomous theory of the nature of, untenable on psychological grounds,------------------------ 486
a true view of the spiritual nature
   of, refutes six errors,-----------486, 487
some who have held the trichoto-
   mous view of,---------------------- 487
his body, why honorable?------------ 488
has been provided with a fleshly
   body, for two suggested reasons, 488
origin of his soul,-----------------488-497
the theory of the pre-existence of
   his soul,----------------------488-491
the advocates, ancient and modern,
   of this theory of soul pre-existence, ------------------------488, 489
the truth at the basis of soul pre-
   existence, ------------------------ 488
the theory of soul pre-existence,
   founded on an illusion of memory, ----------------------------- 488
explanations of this illusion,-------- 488
the theory of the soul's pre-existence, without Scriptural warrant,
   ----------------------------489, 490
if his soul was conscious and personal in the pre-existent state,

why is recollection even of important decisions so defective?-- 490
Man, the pre-existence theory of the
   soul of, is of no theological assistance, --------------------------- 490
Müller's view of pre-existence stated and examined,---------------490, 491
the creatian theory of his soul, 491-493
its advocates,---------------------- 491
Scripture does not teach that God
   immediately creates his soul,------ 491
creatianism repulsively false as representing him as not father of his
   offspring's noblest part,----------- 492
his individuality, how best explained, --------------------------- 492
the creatian theory of his birth
   makes God the author of sin,----- 493
the creatian theory of his birth,
   certain mediating modifications of, 493
the traducian theory of his birth,
   -------------------------------- 493-497
the traducian theory, its advocates, 493
the traducian theory explained,----- 494
the traducian theory best accords
   with Scripture,--------------------- 494
the traducian theory is favored by
   the analogy of animal and vegetable life,------------------------- 495
the traducian theory supported by
   the transmission of physical, mental, and moral characteristics,
   ----------------------------495, 496
the traducian theory embraces the
   element of truth in the creatian
   theory in that it holds to a divine
   concurrence in the development of
   the human species,----------------- 497
his moral nature,------------------497-513
the powers which enter into his
   moral nature,---------------------- 497
his conscience defined,-------------- 498
has no separate ethical faculty,-- 498
his conscience discriminative and
   impulsive, ------------------------- 498
his conscience distinguished from
   related mental processes,---------- 499
his conscience the moral judiciary
   of the soul,------------------------ 500
his conscience an echo of God's
   voice, --------------------------- 501
has the authority of the personal
   God, of whose nature law is but
   a transcript,-------------------502-504
his will,------------------------504-513
his will defined,-----------------504, 505
his will and the other faculties,---- 505
his will and permanent states,--505, 506
his will and motives,-------------506, 507
his will and contrary choice,----507. 508
his will and his responsibility,--509, 510

Man, his responsibility for the inherited selfish preferences of his will, its Scriptural explanation,__ 510

his natural bent of will to evil so constant, inveterate, and powerful that only regeneration can save him from it,------------------------ 510

the hurtful nature of a deterministic theory of his will,----------511-513

and his will, authors upon,---------- 513

his original state,-------------------514-532

his original state described only in Scripture, ------------------------- 514

list of authors on his original state, 514

essentials of his original state,__514-523

made 'in the image of God,' what implied? --------------------------- 514

made in natural likeness to God or personality,----------------------- 514

made in moral likeness to God or holiness, --------------------------- 514

the elements in his original likeness to God, more clearly explicated, ---------------------------------514, 515

indwelt by the Logos or divine Reason, ---------------------------------- 515

never wholly loses 'the image of God,' ------------------------------------ 515

in a minor sense 'gods' and 'partakers of the divine nature,' -- 515

has 'a deeper depth' rooted and grounded in God,---------------------- 515

created a personal being with power to know and determine self,---------515

his natural likeness to God inalienable and the capacity that makes redemption possible,-------- 515

his personality further defined,------- 515

should reverence his humanity,__515, 516

originally possesssed such a direction of affections and will as constituted God the supreme end of his being, and himself a finite reflection of God's moral attributes, 517

his chief endowment, holiness,------- 517

his original righteousness as taught in Scripture,------------------------ 517

in what the dignity of his human nature consists,--------------------- 517

his original righteousness not the essence of his human nature,----- 518

his original righteousness not a gift from without and after creation, ---------------------------------- 518

his original righteousness a tendency of affections and will to God, 518

his original righteousness propagable to descendants,---------------- 518

his likeness to God, more than the perfect mutual adjustment of his spiritual powers,--------------------- 519

Man, his fall assigned by some to pre-existent state,---------------------------- 519

'the image of God' in, was, some say, merely the possibility (Anlage) of real likeness,------------ 519

his individual will will not the author of his condition of sin or of holiness, --------------------------------- 519

since he originally knew God, must have loved God,------------------519, 520

primal 'image of God,' not simply ability to be like God, but actual likeness, --------------------------- 520

if morally neutral, is a violator of God's law,-------------------------- 520

the original 'image of God' in, more than capacity for religion,__ 520

scholastics and the Romanist church distinguished between 'image' and 'likeness' as applied to his first estate,------------------- 520

his nature at creation, according to Romanism, received a donum superadditum of grace,---------------- 520

his progress from the state in puris naturalibus to the state spoliatus a nudo, as the Romish church teaches, pictorially stated,--------- 521

the Romish theory as to his original state considered in detail, ---------------------------------520-523

results of his original possession of the divine image,----------------533-525

his physical form reflects his original endowment,--------------------- 523

originally possessed an æquale temperamentum of body and spirit which, though physically perfect, was only provisional,-------------- 523

had dominion over the lower creation, --------------------------------- 524

enjoyed communion with God,__524, 525

concomitants of his possession of the divine image,----------------525-532

his surroundings and society fitted to afford happiness and help,__525, 526

his wife and her creation,---------- 525

was perhaps hermaphrodite,--------- 526

his garden, Eden,-------------------- 526

provisions for trying his virtue, 526, 527

opportunity for securing for himself physical immortality,-------- 527

the first, had he maintained his integrity, would have been developed and transformed without undergoing death,------------------------ 527

the Scriptural view of his original state opposed by those who hold a prehistoric development of the race from savagery to civilization, 527

the originally savage condition of, an ill-founded assumption,------527-531

Man, the Scriptural account of his original state opposed by those who hold the Positivist theory of the three consecutive conditions of knowledge, _____ 531

the assumption that he must hold fetichism, polytheism, and monotheism in successive steps, if he progresses religiously, contradicted by facts, _____531, 532

monotheistic before polytheistic, 531, 532

in some stocks never practiced fetichism, _____ 532

the earliest discovered sepulchral remains of, prove by presence of food and weapons an advance upon fetichism, _____ 532

his theologic thought not transient but rooted in his intuitions and desires, _____ 532

in what sense a law unto himself, __ 539

as finite needs law, _____ 542

as a free being needs moral law, __ 542

as a progressive being needs an ideal and infinite standard of attainment, _____ 542

according to Scripture responsible for more than his merely personal acts, _____ 634

not wholly a spontaneous development of inborn tendencies, _____ 649

the ideal, realized only in Christ, _____678, 679

his reconsiliation to God, _____777–885

his perfection reached only in the world to come, _____ 981

Manhood of Christ, ideal, _____678, 679

Manichæanism, _____382, 670

Moriolatry, invocation of saints, and transubstantiation, origin of, _____ 673

Marriage, a type of human and divine nature in Christ, _____ 693

Mary, mother of God,' _____671, 686

Material force as little observable as divine agency, _____ 8

organism, not necessarily a hindrance to activity of spirit, _____1021

Materialism, idealism, and pantheism, arise from desire after scientific unity, _____ 90

Materialism, what?, _____ 90

element of truth in, _____ 90

objection to, from intuition, _____ 92

objection to, from mind's attributes, _____92, 93

cannot explain the psychical from the physical, _____ 93

furnishes no sufficient cause for highest phenomena of universe, 94

furnishes no evidence of consciousness in others, _____94, 95

Materialism, Sadducean, denies resurrection of body, _____1018

recent, its services to proper views of body, _____1018

Materialistic Idealism, _____95–100

its definition, _____ 95

its development, _____95–97

defective in its definition of matter, 97

defective in its definition of mind, _____97, 98

opposed to the imperative assumptions of non-empirical, transcendent knowledge of things-in-themselves, _____ 98

however modified, cumbered with the difficulties of pure materialism, _____98, 99

a view of, held by many Christian thinkers, _____99, 100

Mathematics, a disclosure of the divine nature, _____ 261

crystallized, the heavens are, _____ 261

Matter, regarded as atoms which have force as a universal and inseparable property, _____90, 91

in its more modern aspect, a manifestation of force, _____ 91

the Tyndall and Crookes deliverances regarding, _____ 91

mind intuitively regarded as different from it in kind, and higher in rank, _____ 92

to be regarded as secondary and subordinate to mind, _____ 93

and mind, relations between, ____93, 94

does it provide 'the needful objectivity for God'?, _____ 347

its eternity not disprovable by reason, _____ 374

not stuff that emanated from God, 385

not stuff, but an activity of God, 385

according to Schelling, esprit gelé, 386

its continuance dependent on God, __ 413

made by God, and, therefore, pure, 560

its capacities, as subservient to spirit, inestimable, _____1021, 1022

Memory, its impeccability in the case of the apostles, secured by promised Spirit, _____ 207

a preparation for the final judgment, _____1026

of an evil deed, becomes keener with time, _____1029

Memra, relation to Johannine Logos, 320

Mendacium officiosum, _____ 262

Mennonites, _____ 970

Mens humana capax divinæ, _____ 212

Mens rea, essential to crime, _____ 554

Mercy. in the God of nature, some indications which point to, _____ 113

optional, _____271, 296, 297

defined, _____ 289

Mercy, divine, a matter of revelation, 296
election a matter of,_____ 779
Messiah, _____321, 667, 668
Metaphysical generation of the soul, 493
Military theory of atonement,_____ 747
Millennium, _____1008-1015
Mind, has no parts, yet divisible,_____ 9
its organizing instinct,_____15, 16
gives both final and efficient cause, 76
recognizes itself as another and
higher than the material organization it uses,_____ 92
its attributes and itself different in
kind and higher in rank than matter, _____92, 93
not transformed physical force,_____ 93
the only substantive thing in the
universe, all else is adjective,_____ 94
unsatisfactorily defined as a 'series
of feelings aware of itself,'_____ 97
Absolute, not conditioned as the finite mind,_____ 104
'carnal,' its meaning,_____ 592
Minister, his chief qualification,_____ 17
his relation to church work,_____ 898
forfeiture of his standing as, __923, 924
Miracle, a preliminary definition,_____ 117
modified definition suggested by
Babbage, _____117, 118
'signality' must be preserved in definition of,_____ 118
preferable definition,_____118, 119
never regarded in Scripture as an
infraction of law,_____ 119
natural processes may be in,_____ 119
the attitude of some theologians
towards, irrational,_____ 120
a number of opinions upon, presented, _____ 120
possibility of,_____121-123
not beyond the power of a God
dwelling in and controlling the
universe, shown in some observations, _____121-123
possibility of, doubly strong to those
who give the Logos or Divine Reason his place in his universe,__ 122
possible on Lotzean view of universe, _____ 123
possible because God is not far
away, _____ 123
possible because of the action and
reaction between the world and
the personal Absolute,_____ 123
a presumption against,_____ 124
presupposes, and derives its value
from, law,_____ 124
a uniformity of nature, inconsistent with miracle, non-existent,__ 124
no one is entitled to say a priori
that it is impossible (Huxley),__ 124

Miracle, but the higher stage as seen
from the lower,_____ 125
when the efficient cause gives place
to the final cause,_____ 125
exists because the uniformity of nature is of less importance in the
sight of God than the moral
growth of the human spirit,_____ 125
'the greatest I know, my conversion' (Vinet),_____ 125
our view of, determined by our belief in a moral or a non-moral
God, _____ 126
is extraordinary, never arbitrary,__ 126
not a question of power, but of rationality and love,_____ 126
implies self-restraint and self-unfolding, _____ 126
accompanied by a sacrifice of feeling on the part of Christ,_____ 126
probability of, greater from point
of view of ethical monism,_____ 126
a work in which God lovingly limits
himself, _____ 126
probability of, drawn from the concessions of Huxley,_____ 127
the amount of testimony necessary
to prove a,_____ 127
Hume's misrepresentation of the abnormality of,_____ 127
Hume's argument against, fallacious, _____ 127
evidential force of,_____128-131
accompanies and attests new communications from God,_____ 128
its distribution in history,_____128, 129
its cessation or continuance,_____
_____128, 132, 133
certifies directly not to the truth of
a doctrine, but of a teacher,____ 129
must be supported by purity of life
and doctrine,_____ 129
to see in all nature the working of
the living God removes prejudice
against, _____ 130
the revelation of God, not the proof
of that revelation,_____ 130
does not lose its value in the process of ages,_____ 130
of the resurrection sustains the authority of Christ as a teacher,__ 130
of Christ's resurrection, is it 'an
obsolete picture of an eternal
truth'?_____ 130
of Christ's resurrection, has complete historical attestation,____130, 131
of Christ's resurrection, not explicable by the swoon-theory of
Strauss, _____ 131
of Christ's resurrection, not explicable by the spirit-theory of Keim, 131

Miracle of Christ's resurrection, not explicable by the *vision-theory* of Renan,-------------------------- 131
of Christ's resurrection, its three lessons, --------------------------- 131
the counterfeit,---------------------- 132
only a direct act of God a,------- 132
the counterfeit, attests the true,-- 132
how the false, may be distinguished from the true,---------------132, 133
Miracles as attesting Divine Revelation, ---------------------------117-133
Mohammedanism, --------------186, 347, 427
Molecular movement and thought,-- 93
Molecules, manufactured articles,---- 77
Molluscs, their beauty inexplicable by 'natural selection,'----------------- 471
Monarchians, --------------------------- 327
Monism presents that deep force, in which effects, psychical and bodily, find common origin,----------..---- 69
there must be a basal,---------------- 80
Monism, Ethical, defined,-------------- 105
consistent with the teachings of Holy Writ,------------------------- 105
the faith of Augustine,-------------- 105
the faith of Anselm,-------------105, 106
embraces the one element of truth in pantheism,----------------------- 106
is entirely consistent with ethical fact, -------------------------------- 106
is Metaphysical Monism qualified by Psychological Monism,----.--------- 106
is supplanting Dualism in philosophic thought, -------------------- 106
it rejects the two main errors of pantheism, ----------------------107, 109
it regards the universe as a finite, partial, and progressive revelation of God, ----------------------107, 108
it regards matter as God's limitation under law of necessity,---- 107
it regards humanity as God's self-limitation under law of freedom, 107
it regards incarnation and atonement as God's self-limitation under law of grace,------------------ 107
regards universe as related to God as thought to the thinker,--------- 107
regards nature as the province of God's pledged and habitual causality, ----------------------------- 107
is the doctrine largely of the poets, ---------------------------------107, 108
guarantees individuality and rights of each portion of universe,------ 108
in moral realm estimates worth by the voluntary recognition and appropriation of the divine,-------- 108
does not, like pantheism, involve moral indifference to the variations observed in universe,------- 108

Monism, Ethical, does not regard saint and sensualist, men and mice as of equal value,------------- 108
it regards the universe as a graded and progressing manifestation of God's love for righteousness and opposition to wrong,----------------- 108
it recognizes the mysterious power of selfhood to oppose the divine law, ----------------------------- 108
it recognizes the protective and vindicatory reaction of the divine against evil,----------------------- 108
it gives ethical content to Spinoza's apophthegm, 'all things serve,'-- 108
it neither cancels moral distinctions, nor minifies retribution,----------- 108
recognizes Christ as the Logos of God in its universal acceptance, 109
recognizes as the Creator, Upholder, and Governor of the universe, Him who in history became incarnate and by death made atonement for human sin,-------------------------- 109
rests on Scriptural statements,-- 109
secures a Christian application of modern philosophical doctrine,---- 109
gives a more fruitful conception of matter, ------------------.------------ 109
considers nature as the omnipresent Christ, ----------------------------- 109
presents Christ as the unifying reality of physical, mental and moral phenomena,----.-------------- 109
its relation to pantheism and deism, --------------------------------- 109
furnishes a foundation for new interpretation in theology and philosophy, ---------------------------- 109
helps to acceptance of Trinitarianism, --.----------------------------- 109
teaches that while the natural bond uniting to God cannot be broken, the moral bond may,----------109, 110
how it interprets ' rejecting ' Christ, 110
enables us to understand the principle of the atonement,------------ 110
strengthens the probability of miracle, --------------------------------- 126
teaches that God is pure and perfect mind that passes beyond all phenomena and is their ground,-- 255
teaches that ' that which hath been made was life in him,' Christ,-- 311
teaches that in Christ all things ' consist,' hold together, as cosmos rather than chaos,----------------- 311
teaches that gravitation, evolution, and the laws of nature are Christ's habits, and nature but his constant will,------------------------- 311

Monism, Ethical, teaches that in Christ is the intellectual bond, the uniformity of law, the unity of truth, --------------------------- 311

teaches that Christ is the principle of induction, the medium of interaction, and the moral attraction of the universe, reconciling all things in heaven and earth,-- 311

teaches that God transcendent, the Father, is revealed by God immanent, the Son,------------------------ 314

teaches that Christ is the life of nature, ------------------------------- 337

teaches that creation is thought in expression, reason externalized,-- 381

teaches a dualism that holds to underground connections of life between man and man, man and nature, man and God,----------------- 386

teaches that the universe is a life and not a mechanism,-------------- 391

teaches that God personally present in the wheat makes it grow, and in the dough turns it into bread, ------------------------------ 411

teaches that every man lives, moves, and has his being in God, and that whatever has come into being, whether material or spiritual, has its life only in Christ,------------- 413

teaches that ' *Dei voluntas est rerum natura,*'--------------------------- 413

teaches that nothing finite is only finite, ---------------------------- 413

its further teaching concerning natural forces and personal beings, ---------------------------413, 414, 418, 419

allows of ' second cause,'------------- 416

Monogenism, modern science in favor of, --------------------------------- 480

Monophysites, --------------------------- 672
see Eutychians.

Monotheism, facts point to an original, ----------------------------56, 531

Hebrew, precedes polytheistic systems of antiquity,--------------531, 532

more and more evident in heathen religions as we trace them back, ----------------------------------531, 532

an original, authors on, -------531, 532

Montanists, ----------------------------- 304

Montanus, ------------------------------ 712

Moral argument for the existence of God, the designation criticized, 81

faculty, its deliverances, evidences of an intelligent cause,------------ 82

freedom, what?------------------------ 361

nature of man,----------------------497-512

likeness to himself, how restored by God, -------------------------------- 513

Moral law, what?------------------537-544

law, man's relations to, reach beyond consciousness,----------------- 594

government of God, recognizes race-responsibilities, --------------------- 594

union of human and divine in Christ, ------------------------------ 671

analogies of atonement,-------------- 716

evil, see Sin.

obligation, its grounds determined, ---------------------------------298-303

judgments, involve will,------------- 841

Morality, Christian, a fruit of doctrine, ------------------------------- 16

of N. T., ---------------------------177, 178

Christian, criticized by Mill, -------- 179

heathen systems of,--------- -----179-186

of Bible, progressive,------------------ 230

mere insistence on, cannot make men moral,--------- --------------- 863

' Morning stars,'----------------------- 445

' Mother of God,'----------------------- 681

Motive, not cause but occasion, 360, 506

man never acts without or contrary to,----------------------------- 360

a ground of prediction,-------------- 360

influences, without infringing on free agency, ---------------------- 360

the previously dominant, not always the impulsive,---------------- 360

Motives, man can choose between,-- 360

persuade but never compel,--362, 506, 649

not wholly external to mind influenced by them,----------------506, 817

lower, sometimes seemingly appealed to in Scripture,---------826, 827

Muratorian Canon,--------------------- 141

Music, reminiscent of possession lost, 526

Mystic, ----------------------------31, 81

Mysticism, true and false,------------ 32

Mystik and *Mysticismus,*--------------- 31

Myth, its nature,----------------------- 155

as distinguished from *saga* and legend, ------------------------------- 155

' the Divine Spirit can avail himself of ' (Sabatier),------------------- 155

' may be made the medium of revelation ' (Denney),----------------- 214

not a falsehood,--------------------155, 214

early part of Genesis may be of the nature of a,------------------------- 214

Myth-theory of the origin of the gospels (Strauss),--------------------155-157

described, ------------------------155, 156

objected to,----------------- --------156, 157

authors on,--------------------- -------- 157

Nachwirkung and *Fortwirkung,*------- 776

' Name, in my,'------------------------- 807

Names of God, the five Hebrew, Ewald on,--------------------- ------- 318

Nascimur, pascimur,------------------- 973

Natura, ... 392
Natura enim non nisi parendo vincitur, ... 541
Natura humana in Christo capax divinæ, ... 694
Natura naturans (Spinoza), ...244, 287
Natura naturata (Spinoza),...244, 287, 700
Naturæ minister et interpres, ... 2
Natural = psychical,................. 484
Natural insight as to source of religious knowledge,............ 203
Natural law, advantages of its general uniformity,................ 124
events aside from its general fixity to be expected if moral ends require, ... 125
life, God's gift of, foreshadows larger blessings,................ 289
realism, and location of mind in body, ... 280
revelation supplemented by Scripture, ... 27
Natural Selection, artificial after all, 93
its teaching,................................ 470
is partially true,................ 470
is not a complete explanation of the history of life,............ 470
gives no account of origin of substance or variations,................ 470
by the *survival* does not explain the *arrival* of the fittest,............ 470
does not explain the sudden and apparently independent appearance of important geologic forms,............ 470
certain entomological and anatomical facts are inexplicable upon the theory of,................ 471
fails to explain the beauty in lower forms of life,................ 471
no species has as yet been produced by either artificial or,............ 472
does not necessarily make the idea of Creator superfluous,............ 473
may account for man's place in, but not above, nature,............ 473
requires, according to Wallace, a superior intelligence to guide in definite direction or for special purpose, ... 473
a list of authors upon,............ 474
atheistically taught, is election with hope and pity left out,............ 784
Natural theology, what?................ 260
Nature, its usual sense,................26, 121
its proper sense,................26, 121
its witness to God, outward and inward,................ 26
argument for God's existence from change in,................73-75
argument for God's existence from useful collocation in,................75-80
Mill's indictment of,................ 78

Nature, apart from man, cannot be interpreted, ... 79
does not assure us of God's love and provision for the sinner,........113, 114
by itself furnishes a presumption against miracles,................ 124
as synonym of substance,................ 243
according to Schleiermacher,........ 287
its forces, dependent and independent, 414
the brute submerged in,................ 468
human, why it should be reverenced, 515
in what sense sin a,................ 518
as something inborn,........518, 577, 578
the race has a corrupted nature,...577-582
sinful acts and dispositions explained by a corrupt,................ 577
a corrupt, belongs to man from first moment of his being,................ 578
a corrupt, underlies man's consciousness, ... 578
a corrupt, which cannot be changed by a man's own power,................ 578
a corrupt, the common heritage of the race,................ 578
designates, not substance, but corruption of substance,................ 578
how responsible for a depraved, which one did not personally originate,.... 593
human, Pelagian view of,................ 598
human, semi-Pelagian view of,........ 598
human, Augustinian view of,........ 598
human, organic view of,................ 600
human, atomistic view of,................ 600
the whole human race once a personality in Adam,................ 629
human, can apostatize but once,........ 630
human, totally depraved,........ 637-639
man can to a certain extent modify his, ... 642
sin of, and personal transgression,.... 648
impersonal human, ... 694
and person,................ 694, 695
Robinson's definition of,................ 695
human, is it to develop into new forms? 986
'Nature of things, in the,' the phrase examined, ... 357
Nazarenes,................ 669
   see Ebionites.
Nebular hypothesis,................ 395
Necessitarian philosophy, correct for the brute, ... 468
Negation, involves affirmation, ... 9
Neron Kaisar, and '666',................1009
Nescience, divine,................ 286
   see God.
Nestorians,................ 671
Neutrality, moral, never created by God,................ 521
moral, a sin,................ 521
New England theology,................ 48, 49
New Haven theology,................ 49

New School theology,..............48, 49, 606
its definition of holiness,........... 271, 272
its definition of sin, how it differs from
   that of Old School,..................549, 550
ignores the unconscious and subconscious elements in human character, 550
its watchword as to sin,.................. 595
its theory of imputation, an evasion, 596
its theory of imputation explained,
   .... 606, 607
development of its theory of inspira-
   tion,.................................... 607, 608
modifications of view within,.......... 608
contradicts Scripture,.............. 608, 609
its advocates cannot understand Paul, 609
rests upon false philosophical principles, ...609, 610
impugns the justice of God,.......610, 611
inconsistent with facts,..............611, 612
its aim that of all the theories of
   imputation,................................ 612
Nihil in intellectu nisi quod ante fuerit
   in sensu, ... 63
Nineveh, winged creatures of,............ 449
Nirvana,.. 182
Noblesse oblige, ... 301
Nomina become *numina,*................... 245
Nominalism inconsistent with Script-
   ure,.. 244
Nominalist notion of God's nature,.... 244
Non apostolic writings recommended
   by apostles,............................... 201
Non-inspiration, seeming, of certain
   Scriptures,................................. 242
Non pleni nascimur,......................... 597
'Nothing, creation out of,' 372
Notitia, an element in faith,............. 837
Noumenon in external and internal
   phenomena, ... 6
Nullus in microcosmo spiritus, nullus in
   macrocosmo Deus,..................... 79
Obduracy, sins of, incomplete and final, 650
Obedience, Christ's active and passive,
   .... 749, 770
'Obey,' not the imperative of religion, 21
Obligation to obey law based on man's
   original ability,.......................... 541
Offences between men,.................... 766
   between church members,.........924, 925
Old School theology,..............49, 606, 607
Omission, sins of,....................554, 648
Omne virum e vivo (ex ovo),............. 389
Omnia mea mecum porto,...................1032
Omnipotence of God,.................286–288
   see God.
Omnipresence of God,................279–282
   see God.
Omnipresent, how God might cease to
   be,.. 282
Omniscience of God,.................282–286
   see God.
One eternal now,' how to be under-
   stood, ... 277

Ontological argument for existence of
   God,.....................................85–89
   see God.
Optimism, ... 404, 405
Oracles, ancient,........................... 135
Ordinances of the church,..........929–980
Ordination of church officers,.........918–929
Ordo salutis,................................. 794
Organic and organized substances,...... 98
Organic, the, and atomistic views of
   human nature,........................... 600
Original 'image of God' in man, its
   nature,................................514–523
Original natural likeness to God, or
   personality, ...515, 519, 520
moral likeness to God, man's, or holiness,.................................516–518
righteousness, what?.................517, 518
knowledge of God, man's, implied a
   direction of the affections and will
   toward God,............................. 519
sin, as held by Old School theologians, 49
two-fold problem of,..................... 593
its definition,...................... 594, 595
two principles fundamental to consideration of,.......................... 595
a correct view of race-responsibility
   essential to a correct view of,........ 595
some facts in connection with the
   guilt of,................................. 596
substance of Scriptural teaching concerning,.............................625–627
a misnomer, if applied to any theory
   but that of its author, Augustine,.. 636
no one finally condemned merely on
   account of,....................596, 663, 664
state of man,........................514–533
essentials of,.......................514–523
results of,.........................523–525
concomitants of,...................525–532
Romish and Protestant views of,...521, 522
Os sublime, manifestation of internal
   endowments, ... 523
Pain, physical, existed before entrance
   of moral evil into world,............. 402
this supralapsarian pain, how to be
   regarded, ... 402
due not to God, but to man,........... 402
verdicts declarative of the secondary
   place of,................................. 402
cannot explain its presence here by
   the good it may do,. 403
it is God's protest against sin,.......... 403
has its reason in the misconduct of
   man, ... 403
supralapsarian pain an 'anticipative
   consequence,' 403
God's frown upon sin, and warning
   against it,............................... 403
Palestine,...........................174, 421
Pantheism, Idealistic, defined........ 100
the elements of truth in,............... 100

Pantheism, Idealistic, its error,............ 100
denies real existence of the finite,..... 100
deprives the infinite of self-consciousness and freedom,...................... 100
in it the worshiped is the worshiper,.. 100
the later Brahmanism is,.............. 100
the fruit of absence of will and longing for rest as end of existence, as
among Hindus,.......................... 100
in Hegelianism, presents the alternative, no God or no man,.............. 100
of Hegel and Spinoza,..............100, 101
of Hegel, its different interpreters,... 101
of Hegel, as modified by Schopenhauer,................................... 101
its idea of God self-contradictory, 101, 102
its asserted unity of substance without proof,.............................. 102
it assigns no sufficient cause for
highest fact of universe, personal
intelligence............................ 102
it contradicts the affirmations of our
moral and religious nature,........ 103
antagonizes our intuitive conviction
of the absolute perfection of God, 104
its objection that in eternity there
was not not-self over against the
Infinite to call forth self-consciousness, without foundation,.......... 104
denies miracle,........................... 122
denies inspiration,........................ 204
anti-trinitarianism leads to,........... 347
involved in doctrine of emanation,... 383
assumes that law fully expresses God, 547
should worship Satan,................... 566
at basis of Docetism,................... 676
not involved in doctrine of Union
with Christ,.......................... 800
Parables,.............................240, 784
Paradise,...................... 403, 998, 999
Paradoxon summum evangelicum,....... 753
Pardon, limited by atonement, objections to, refuted,..................... 766
its conditions can of right be assigned
by God,................................ 767
the act of God as judge in justification,..................................... 855
and justification distinguished,.....858, 859
through Christ, honors God's justice
and mercy,..............+.............. 860
Parseeism,.............................. 185
Parsimony, law of,...................74, 87
Passion, the, necessitated by Christ's
incarnation,........................... 760
Passover,...................157, 723, 726, 960
Pastor,...................908, 914, 915, 917
'Pastors and teachers,'................. 915
Patripassians,............................ 327
Paul,......................210, 235, 851, 999
Peace,..................................... 865
Peccatum alienum,...................... 616

Pelagianism, a development of rationa-
ism,.................................... 89
its theory of imputation,.............597–601
its principal author and present advocates,................................. 597
its exposition,.......................... 597
its view of Romans 5 : 12,.............. 597
its seven points,....................... 597
its sinless men,........................ 597
its '*non pleni nascimur,*'............ 597
its misinterpretation of the divine influence in man,....................... 597
is deism applied to man's nature,..... 598
ignores his dignity and destiny,..... 598
unformulated and sporadic,........... 598
unscriptural,...................598, 598
a survival of paganism,............... 598
its key doctrine: *Homo libero arbitrio
emancipatus a Deo,*................. 598
its unscriptural tenets specified,..598, 599
regards sins as isolated volitions,... 599
its method contrasted with that of
Augustinianism,..................... 599
presents an Ebionitic view of Christ, 599
its principles false in philosophy,..... 600
ignores law by which acts produce
states,................................ 600
Penalty, what?.................294, 652, 653
Penalty,..............................652–660
its idea,................................ 652
more than natural consequences of
transgression,....................... 652
not essentially reformatory,........... 653
what essentially?...................... 653
not essentially to secure social or
governmental safety,..............653, 655
not essentially deterrent,............. 655
of sin, two-fold,....................... 656
of sin, is physical death,............656–659
of sin, is spiritual death,..........659, 666
Penitence,.............................. 766
Pentateuch (Hexateuch), its authorship,................................170–172
literature upon,........................ 172
Perfect, as applied to men,............ 574
Perfection, in God,..............9, 260–275
of Christian and church reached in
world to come,....................... 981
Perfectionism, its tenet,............... 877
its teachers,........................... 877
its modifications,...................... 877
authorities upon,...................... 877
its fundamental false conceptions, 877, 878
is contradicted by Scripture,......878–886
disproved by Christian experience,....886
how best met,.......................880, 881
Permanent states of the faculties,
......................506, 550, 551
Perseverance, human side of sanctification,.............................868, 881
definition,............................. 881
its proof from Scripture,.............. 882

Perseverance, its proof from reason, 882, 883
is not inconsistent with human free-
dom, ... 883
does not tend to immorality, ...883, 884
aoes not lead to indolence,.............. 884
the Scriptural warnings against apostasy do not oppose it, ...884, 885
apparent instances of apostasy do not
oppose it,.............................. 885, 886
list of authors on general subject of, 886
'Person' in doctrine of Trinity, only
approximately accurate,.............. 330
Persou, how communicated in different
measures,.............................. 324
Person and character of Christ, as proof
of revelation,.....................186–190
Person of Christ, the doctrine of,....669–700
historical survey of views regarding,
....669–673
the two natures in their reality and
integrity,.......................... 673–683
the union of the two natures in one,
...................................683–700
Personal identity,.....................92, 417
intelligences cannot be accounted for
by pantheism,........................ 102
influence, often distinct from word
spoken, ... 820
Personality, defined,......................
.... 82, 252, 253, 330, 335, 515, 695
of God, the conclusion of the anthropological argument,................... 84
of God, denied by pantheism, ... 100
the highest dependent on infiniteness, 104
self-conscious and self-determining,.. 253
triple, in Godhead, consistent with
essential unity,..................... 330
in man, inalienable,..................... 515
involves boundless possibilities,....... 515
foundation of mutual love among
men, ... 515
constitutes a capacity for redemption, 515
Pessimism,.........................404, 405
Peter, how he differed with Paul,........ 214
Romish assumptions regarding, 909
Peter, Second,.................147, 149. 153
Pharaoh, the hardening of his heart,.... 434
Phenomena,.............................. 6
Philemon and Onesimus, moralized, ... 767
Philosophy, defined, ... 42
Physico-theological argument, a term
of Kant's,.............................. 75
Physiology, comparative, favors unity
of race,.....................480–483
Pictures of Christ,...................... 251
Pie hoc potest dici, Deum esse Naturam, 107
Plasticity of species, greater toward
origin, ... 482
Plural quantitative,...................... 318
Pluralis majestaticus, ... 318
Poesy and poem,......................... 852
Poetry, ... 526

Polytheism, ...259, 347
Pools of modern Jerusalem,............ 934
Positive Philosophy,.........6, 9, 535, 545, 632
Possession by demons,.................. 456
Præterist interpreters of Revelation,... 1009
Prayer, relation of Providence to,....... 433
its effect, not solely reflex influence,.. 433
its answers not confined to spiritual
means, ... 433
not answered by suspension or breach
of the order of nature,.............. 434
has no direct influence on nature,.... 434
is answered by new combinations of
natural forces,...................... 434
as an appeal to a personal and present
God, it moves God,.................. 435
its answer, while an expression of God's
will, may come through the use of
appointed means,................... 435
God's immanency in nature helps to a
solution of the problem, how prayer
is answered,....................... 436
how the potency of prayer may be
tested,.........................437, 438
Prayer-book, English, Arminian,....... 46
on infant baptism,.................... 957
Prayer-book of Edward VI, mode of
baptism in,........................ 957
Preaching of doctrinal sermons,........ 19
of the decrees,...................... 369
of the organic unity of the race in
transgression, ... 634
larger part of, should consist in application of Divine law to personal
acts, ...648, 649
addressed to elect and non-elect,...... 789
must press immediate submission to
Christ, ... 830
of everlasting punishment an auxil-
iary to the gospel appeal,.......... 1053
Pre-Adamites,.......................... 476
Precedent, N. T., the 'common-law' of
the church,........................ 970
'Preconformity to future events,'...... 76
Predestination,.................355, 360, 781
Predicata, not attributes,.............. 245
Prediction, only a part of prophecy, 134, 710
'Pre-established harmony,'.............. 93
Pre-existence of soul,.............488–491
Preference, immanent,................. 514
'elective,'.............................. 557
Preparation, historical, for redemp-
tion,.........................665–668
Preraional instinct, ... 98
Prescience, Divine,..................... 286
Presentative intuition, ...52, 53, 67
Preservation,.........................410–419
definition of, positive and negative,
...............................410, 411
proofs of, from Scripture and reason.
...............................411–413

Preservation, deism, with its God withdrawn, denies,----------------------414, 415
continuous creation, with momently new universe, inconsistent with, 415-418
divine concurrence in, considered, 418, 419
Pretermission of sin,-------------------- 772
Preventive providence,----------------- 423
Pride, -------------------------------- 569
'Priest' and 'minister,'--------------915, 967
Priestly office of Christ,--------------713-775
Probability, ---------------------------- 71
Probation after death,----707, 1002, 1031-1044
in Adam,---------------------------- 629
Procession of the Holy Spirit, its true formula, ---------------------------- 823
consistent with his equality in Trinity, --------------------------------340, 341
Progress of early Christianity, what principally conduced to?----------- 187
Prolegomena,--------------------------- 1-15
Proof of Divine Revelation, principles of evidence applicable to, ----------41-44
Prophecy, as attesting a divine revelation,----------------------------134-141
defined in its narrow sense,--------134, 135
its relation to miracles,--------------- 135
requirements in,---------------------- 135
general features of Scriptural,----135, 136
Messianic in general,------------------ 136
as used by Christ,-----------------136-138
the double sense of,----------------138-140
evidential force of,------------------140, 141
alleged errors in,--------------------235, 236
Christians have gifts of,--------------- 712
modern, as far as true, what?--------- 712
Prophet, not always aware of meaning of his own prophecies,--------------- 139
later may elucidate earlier utterances, --------------------------------235, 236
his soul, is it rapt into God's timeless existence and vision?---------- 278
larger meaning of the word,-------- 710
Prophetæ priores,------------------------ 710
Prophetic office of Christ,----------710-713
see Christ.
its nature,------------------------710, 711
fulfilled in three ways,--------------- 711
its four stages,---------------------711-713
in his Logos-work,-------------------- 711
in his earthly ministry,-----------711, 712
in his guidance and teaching of the church since his ascension,-------- 712
in his revelations of the Father to the saints in glory,------------712, 713
will be eternal,----------------------- 712
Propitiation, ---------------------------719, 720
Proprietates, distinguished from attributes, -------------------------- 246
Proselyte-baptism, -----------------931, 932
Protevangelium, Scripture germinally, 175
Providence, doctrine of,-------------419-443
defined, ---------------------------- 419

Providence explains evolution and progress of universe,-----------419, 420
doctrine of, its proof from Scripture, ---------------------------421-425
a general providential control, 421, 422
a control extending to free actions of men in general,--------------422, 423
four sorts, preventive, permissive, directive, determinative,-------423-425
rational proof of,-----------------425-427
arguments *a priori,*----------------425, 426
arguments *a posteriori,*--------------- 426
opposed by theory of fatalism,------ 427
opposed by casualism,-------------427, 428
opposed by theory of a merely general providence,-----------------428-431
its relation to miracles and works of grace,-----------------------431-433
its relation to prayer,-------------433-439
its relation to Christian activity, --------------------------------439-441
to evil acts of free agents,--------441-443
'Providential miracles,'----------------- 432
Psychic phenomena,--------------------- 117
Punctiliousness, warning against,----- 428
Punishment, implied in man's moral nature, ---------------------------- 82
does not proceed from love,--------- 272
proceeds from justice,--------------- 293
its idea,----------------------------652, 752
what implied in its idea,---------652-656
has in it, beyond the natural consequences of transgression, a personal element,--------------------- 652
its object not the reformation of the sufferer,----------------------- 653
is the necessary reaction of divine holiness against sin,--------------- 653
is not esentially deterrent,--------- 655
of sin is physical death,----------656-659
of sin is spiritual death,----------659, 660
an ethical need of the divine nature, ---------------------------- 751
an ethical need in man's moral nature, ---------------------------- 751
of guilty, Christ's sufferings substituted for,----------------------- 752
is borne by the judge and punisher in the nature that has sinned,----- 752
as presented in atonement, what it secures,--------------------------- 753
endured by Christ righteously, because of his relation to the sinning race,-----------------------754, 755
remitted in justification,------------- 854
remitted on the ground of what Christ, to whom the sinner is united by faith, has done,------854, 858
the final, of the wicked described in Scriptural figures,----------1033, 1034
the final, of the wicked, summed up, --------------------------------1034

Punishment, future, some conces-sions regarding,------------------1035
of wicked, the future, not annihila-tion, ------------------------1035, 1036
not a weakening process ending in cessation of existence,--------1036, 1037
not an annihilating punishment after death,-----------------------1037
light from the evolutionary process thrown on,---------------------------1038
excludes new probation and ulti-mate restoration of the wicked,--1039
declared in Scripture to be eternal, 1044
is a revelation of God's justice,-----1046
as the reaction of holiness against sin must continue while sin con-tinues, -----------------------1046, 1047
is endless since guilt is endless,-- 1048
is eternal since sin is ' eternal,----1048
the facts of human life and ten-dencies of scientific thought point to the perpetuity of,---------------1049
may have degrees yet be eternal,-----1050
may be eternal as the desert of sin of infinite enormity,---------------1050
not inconsistent with God's benev-olence, -----------------------1051-1054
its proper preaching not a hin-drance to success of the gospel,--1054
if it is a fact, it ought to be preached, ------------------------1054
to ignore it in pulpit teaching lowers the holiness of God,------1055
the fear of, not the highest but a proper motive to seek salvation,--1055
in preaching it, the misery of the soul should have special emphas-is, -----------------------------1056
Purgatory,---------------659, 866, 1000-1002
Purification of Christ, the ritual,----
--------------------------761, 942, 943
Puritans, ----------------------------546, 557
Purpose of God includes many de-crees, ------------------------------ 353
in election, what?-------------------- 355
in reprobation, what?----------------- 355
to save individuals, passages which prove, ---------------------------780-783
to do what he does, eternal,---------- 783
to save, not conditioned upon merit or faith,---------------------------- 784
Quasi carcere, Christ not thus in Heaven, ----------------------------- 709
Quia voluit of Calvin, not final an-swer as to God's acts,----------- 404
Quickening, Christ's, distinguished from his resurrection,------------- 707
Quietism, ----------------------------439, 440
Quo non ascendam? not Christ's query, ------------------------------ 764
Race, Scripture teaches its descent from a single pair,----------------- 476

Race, its descent from a single pair a foundation truth of Paul's,------ 476
its descent from a single pair the foundation of brotherhood,-------- 476
its descent from a single pair cor-roborated by history,----------477, 478
its descent from a single pair corro-borated by language,-----------478, 479
its descent from a single pair cor-roborated by psychology,------479, 480
its descent from a single pair corro-borated by physiology,---------480-483
Race-responsibility, ----------------594-597
Rational intuition,------------------52, 67
Rationalism and Scripture,-------29, 30, 89
Readings, various,--------------------- 226
Realism, in relation to God,---------- 245
Reason, definition of,-----------------4, 29
its office,--------------------------- 29
says scio, not conscio,--------------- 500
moral, depraved,---------------------- 501
Reasoning, not reason,---------------- 29
not a source of the idea of God,---- 65
errors of, in Bible,--------------232, 233
Recognition, post-resurrectional, 1020, 1021
Recollection of things not before seen, the seeming, explained,------------- 488
memory greater than,----------------- 705
Reconciliation, removal of God's wrath, ----------------------------- 719
of man to God,-----------------777-886
objective, secured by Christ's union with race,-------------------------- 802
subjective, secured by Christ's union with believers,--------------- 802
Redemption and resurrection, what is secured by,----------------------- 527
wrought by Christ,---------------665-776
its meaning,-------------------------- 707
legal, of Christ, its import,-------- 761
its application,-----------------777-886
application of, in its preparation,777-793
application of, in its actual be-ginning, ----------------------793-868
application of, in its continuation,
--------------------------------868-886
Redi's maxim,------------------------- 389
Reformed theology,------------------44-46
Regenerate, some apparently such, will fall away,------------------ 884
the truly, not always distinguish-able in this life from the seem-ingly so,----------------------------- 884
their fate if they should not perse-vere described,---------------------- 883
these warnings secure their perse-verance, ----------------------------- 883
Regeneration, illustrative of inspira-tion, -------------------------------- 212
ascribed to Holy Spirit,------------- 316
its nature, according to Romanists, 522

Regeneration, the view that a child
   may be educated into,-------------- 606
   its place in the *ordo salutis,*-------- 793
   does a physical miracle attend?----- 806
   defined, ----------------------------- 809
   its active and passive aspects,------ 809
   how represented in Scripture,--810-812
   indispensable, ----------------------- 810
   a change in the inmost principle
      of life,---------------------------- 810
   a change in governing disposition,-- 810
   a change in moral relations,-----810, 811
   wrought through use of truth,------ 811
   is instantaneous,-------------------- 811
   wrought by God,-------------------- 811
   through union of soul with Christ,
      ----------------------------------811, 812
   its necessity,----------------------812-814
   its efficient cause,-----------------814-820
   the will not the efficient cause,--815-817
   is more than self-reformation,------ 815
   is not co-operation with divine in-
      fluence, which to the natural man
      is impossible,---------------------- 816
   the truth is not the efficient cause,
      ----------------------------------817, 818
   the Holy Spirit, the efficient cause
      of, -----------------------------818-820
   the Spirit in, operates not on the
      truth but on the soul,------------- 819
   the Spirit in, effects a change in the
      moral disposition,----------------- 820
   the instrumentality used in,------820-823
   baptism a sign of,-------------------- 821
   as a spiritual change cannot be
      effected by physical means,------- 821
   is accomplished through the instru-
      mentality of the truth,------------ 822
   man not wholly passive at time of
      his, -------------------------------- 822
   man's mind at time of, active in
      view of truth,---------------------- 822
   nature of the change wrought in,
      ----------------------------------823-820
   is a change by which governing dis-
      position is made holy,----------823-825
   does not affect the quantity but the
      quality of the soul,---------------- 821
   involves an enlightenment of the
      understanding and a rectification
      of the volitions,------------------- 825
   an origination of holy tendencies,-- 826
   an instantaneous change in soul, be-
      low consciousness and known only
      in results,------------------------826-829
   is an instantaneous change,------826, 827
   should not be confounded with pre-
      paratory stages,------------------- 827
   taken place in region of the soul
      below consciousness,--------------- 828
   is recognized indirectly in its re-
      sults, ------------------------------828, 829

Regeneration, the growth that follows, is sanctification,-------------- 829
Regna gloriæ, gratiæ (et naturæ),---- 775
Reign of sin, what?----------------553, 554
Religion and theology, how related,-- 19
   derivation of word,--------------19, 20
   false conceptions of it advocated
      by Hegel, Schleiermacher, and
      Kant, -------------------------20, 21
   its essential idea,-----------------21, 22
   there is but one,-------------------22, 23
   its content greater than that of
      theology, ------------------------- 23
   distinguished from formal worship,
      ----------------------------------23, 24
   conspectus of the systems of, in
      world, ----------------------179-186
Remorse, perhaps an element in
   Christ's suffering,----------------- 769
Reparative goodness of God in nature, 113
Repentance, more for sin than sins, 555
   the gift of God,--------------------- 782
   described, ------------------------- 832
   contains an intellectual element,--- 832
   contains an emotional element, 832, 833
   contains a voluntary element,--833, 834
   implies free-will,-------------------- 834
   Romish view,------------------------ 834
   wholly an inward act,-------------- 834
   manifested by fruits of repentance, 835
   a negative and not a positive means
      of salvation,----------------------- 835
   if true, is in conjunction with faith, 836
   accompanies true faith,-------------- 836
Reprobation, ------------------------- 355
Rerum natura Dei voluntas est,------ 119
Respice, aspice, prospice of Bernard
   applied to prophet's function,------ 710
Responsibility for whatever springs
   from will,-------------------------- 509
   for inherited moral evil, its ground, 509
   is special help of Spirit essential
      to? -----------------------------603, 604
   for a sinful nature which one did
      not personally originate, a fact,-- 629
   none for immediate heredities,------ 630
   for belief, authors on,--------------- 841
Restoration of all human beings,
      ----------------------------1039-1044
Resurrection, an event not within the
   realm of nature,-------------------- 118
   of Christ, the central and sufficient
      evidence of Christianity,--------- 138
   of Christ, dilemma for those who
      deny, ----------------------------- 130
   of Christ, Strauss fails to explain
      belief in,-------------------------- 157
   of Christ, attested by epistles re-
      garded as genuine by Baur,------ 160
   of Christ, Renan's view of,-----160, 161
   Christ's argument for, Matt. 22 : 32,
      --------------------------232, 996, 1013

Resurrection, attributed to Christ,____ 310
attributed to Holy Spirit,_____ 316
of Christ, angel present at,_____ 483
of Christ, gave proof that penalty
  of sin was exhausted,_____ 657
a stage in Christ's exaltation,_____ 707
proclaimed Christ as perfected and
  glorified man,_____ 708
of Christ, the time of his justification, _____ 762
secured to believer by union with
  Christ, _____805, 806, 867
relation to regeneration,_____ 824
sanctification completed at the,_____ 874
of Christ and of the believer, Baptism a symbol of,_____940-945
implied in symbolism of Lord's Supper, _____963, 964
Christ's body, an object that may be
  worshiped, _____ 968
an event preparing for the kingdom
  of God,_____ 981
allusions to, in O. T.,_____ 995
of Christ, the only certain proof of
  immortality, _____ 997
perfect joy or misery subsequent to, 1002
Scriptures describing a spiritual,__1015
Scriptures describing a physical,__1015
art and post-resurrection possibilities, _____1016
personality in, being indestructible,
  takes to itself a body,_____1016
Christ's body in, an open question, 1016
an exegetical objection to,_____1016
'of the body,' the phrase not in
  N. T.,_____1016
receive a 'spiritual body' in,__1016, 1017
the indwelling of the Holy Spirit
  secures preservation of body in,__1017
the believer's, as literal and physical as Christ's,_____1018
literal, to be suitable to events
  which accompany,_____1018
the physical connection between old
  and new body in, not unscientific, 1019
the oneness of the body in, and our
  present body, rests on two things, 1020
the body in, though not absolutely
  the same, will be identical with
  the present,_____1020, 1021
the spiritual body in, will complete
  rather than confine, the activities of spirit,_____1021, 1022
four principles should influence our
  thinking about,_____1022, 1923
authors on the subject in departments and entirety,_____1023
Revelation, of such a nature as to
  make scientific theology possible, 11-15
Revelation in nature requires supplementing, _____26, 27
God submits to limitations of,

which are largely those of theology, _____34-36
how regarded in 'period of criticism and speculation,'_____ 46
the Scriptures a, from God,_____111-242
reasons for expecting from God a,
  _____111-114
psychology shows that the intellectual and moral nature of man
  needs a,_____111, 112
history shows that man needs a,____ 112
what we know of God's nature
  leads to hope of a,_____112, 113
a priori reasons for expecting, 113, 114
marks of the expected,_____114-117
its substance,_____ 114
its method,_____114-116
will have due attestation,_____116, 117
attended by miracles,_____117-134
attested by prophecy,_____134-141
principles of historical evidence
  entering into proof of,_____141-144
a progress in the, of Scripture,____ 175
its connection with inspiration and
  illumination, _____196, 197
Revenge, what?_____ 569
'Reversion to type' never occurs in
  man, _____ 411
Rewards, earthly, appealed to in O. T., 230
proceed from goodness of God,___290, 293
not bestowed by justice or righteousness, _____ 293
goodness to creatures, righteousness
  to Christ,_____ 293
are motives, not sanctions,_____ 535
Right, abstract, not ground of moral
  obligations, _____ 299
God is self-willing,_____ 338
based on arbitrary will is not right, 338
based on passive nature, is not
  right, _____ 338
as being is Father,_____ 338
as willing is Son,_____ 338
Righteousness of God, what?_____ 290
holiness in its mandatory aspect,__ 291
its meaning in 2 Cor. 5: 21,_____ 760
demands punishment of sin,_____ 764
is justification and sanctification,__ 873
Romanism, and Scripture,_____33, 34
a mystical element in,_____ 33
it places church before the Bible,__ 33
would keep men in perpetual childhood, _____33, 3
Sabbath commemorates God's act of
  creation, _____ 406
made at creation applies to man
  always and everywhere,_____ 408
recognized in Assyria and Babylonia, as far back as Accadian
  times before Abraham,_____ 408
was not abrogated by our Lord or
  his apostles,_____ 409

opinions upon,---------------------- 409
Sabbath, Christ's example and apostolic sanction have transferred it
  from seventh to first day of week, 409
  Justin Martyr on,-------------------- 410
  authors on,-------------------------- 410
Sabellianism, ----------------------327, 328
Sacrifice, -------------------------722-728
  what it is not,--------------------722, 723
  its true import,-------------------723, 724
  pagan and Semitic, its implications,
  -----------------------------------723, 724
  in the legend of Æschylus,---------- 723
  of the Passover, H. C. Trumbull's
  views of,---------------------------- 723
  its theocratical and spiritual offices, ------------------------------ 724
  of O. T., when rightly offered, what
  implied in,-----------------------725, 726
  cannot present a formal divine institution, -------------------------- 726
  how Abel's differed from Cain's,---- 727
  the terminology of O. T. regarding,
  needful to correct interpretation
  of N. T. usage regarding atonement of Christ,-------------------- 727
  differing views as to significance of, 728
  sacrifices, Jewish, a tentative scheme
  of, -----------------------------725, 726
saints, prayer to,-------------------- 775
  how intercessors?------------------- 775
  as applied to believers,------------ 880
sanctification, related to regeneration and justification,----------862, 863
  definition of,----------------------- 869
  what implied in definition of,--869, 870
  explanations and Scripture proof of,
  -----------------------------------870-875
  a work of God,---------------------- 870
  a continuous process,---------------871
  distinguished from regeneration,--- 871
  shown in intelligent and voluntary
  activity of believer,------------871, 872
  the agency employed in, the indwelling Spirit of Christ,---------- 872
  its mediate or instrumental cause is
  faith, ----------------------------- 872
  the object of this instrumental
  faith is Christ himself,------------- 873
  measured by strength of faith,----- 873
  influenced by lack of persistency in
  using means of growth,----------- 874
  completed in life to come,---------- 874
  erroneous views of,--------------875-881
  the Antinomian view,------------875-877
  the Perfectionist view,-----------877-881
Sanctify, its twofold meaning,-------- 880
Satan, his personality,---------------- 447
  not a collective term for all evil
  beings, ---------------------------- 447
  various literary conceptions of,----- 447
  meaning of term,------------------- 454

Satan, opposed by Holy Spirit,-------- 454
  his temptations,---------------------- 455
  has access to human mind,---------- 455
  may influence through physical
  organism, ------------------------- 455
  ' delivering to,'---------------------- 457
  was specially active during earthly
  ministry of Christ,----------------- 458
  his power limited,------------------- 458
  the idea of his fall not self-contradictory, --------------------------- 460
  not irrational to suppose that by a
  single act he could change his
  nature, --------------------------- 460
  present passion may lead a wise being to enter on a foolish course,-- 460
  that God should create and uphold
  evil spirits no more inconsistent
  with benevolence than similar action towards evil men,------------- 461
  a ganglionic centre of an evil system, ------------------------------ 461
  the doctrine of, if given up, leads
  to laxity in administration of
  justice, --------------------------- 462
  as tool and slave of, humanity is
  indeed degraded, but was not always, nor needs to be,------------- 462
  the fall of, uncaused from without, 585
  like Adam, sins under the best circumstances, ----------------------- 588
  permitted to divide the guilt with
  man that man might not despair, 588
  grows in cunning and daring,-------1037
Satisfaction to an immanent demand
  of divine holiness rendered by
  Christ's obedience and suffering,
  -----------------------------------713, 723
  by substitution founded on incorporation, --------------------------- 723
  and forgiveness not mutually exclusive because the judge makes
  satisfaction to his own violated
  holiness, -------------------------- 767
  penal and pecuniary,---------------- 767
  sinner's own act, according to
  Romish view,---------------------- 834
Scholasticism and Scholastics,------
  ----------------------44, 45, 265, 268, 443
Science, defined,----------------------- 2
  its aim,----------------------------- 2
  on what its possibility is grounded, 2
  requires a knowledge of more than
  phenomena, ----------------------- 6
  existence of a personal God, its
  necessary datum,------------------ 60
Scientia media, simplicis intelligen-
* tiæ, visionis,*----------------------- 358
Scientific unity, desire for, its influence, --------------------------- 90
Scio and conscio,--------------------- 500
Scripture and nature,----------------- 26

Scripture and rationalism,------------29-31
contains nothing repugnant to a
properly conditioned and enlightened reason,------------------------ 29
and mysticism,---------------------31, 32
and Romanism,---------------------33, 34
knowledge of, incomplete,------------ 35
topics on which silent,--------------- 72
supernatural character of its teaching, ------------------------------- 175
its moral and religious ideas uncontradicted and unsuperseded,-- 175
its supernaturally secured unity,-- 176
Christ testifies to its supernatural
character, ------------------------- 180
result of its propagation, ---------- 191
how interpreted?------------------- 217
authors differ, divine mind one,----- 217
the Christian rule of faith and practice, ------------------------------- 218
contains no scientific untruth, ---- 224
not a code of practical action, but
an enunciation of principles,------- 545
Scriptures, the, a revelation from
God, -------------------------------111-242
work of one God, and so organically articulated (Scripture),-------- 217
why so many interpretations of?
----------------------------------223, 224
a rule in their interpretation,-------- 1011
'Sealing,'-----------------------------831, 872
Seals, in Revelation,------------------- 1010
Selection, natural, without teleological
factors, its inadequacy,------------- 391
is it in any sense the *cause* of the origin
of species?----------------------- 391
it has probably increased the rapidity
of development,----------------391, 392
or 'survival of the fittest,' how suggested?----------------------------- 403
defined, ---------------------------- 470
is partially true,----------------------- 470
it gives no account of the origin of
substance or variations,------------ 470
not the savior of the fittest, but the
destroyer of the failures,------------ 470
facts that it cannot explain,--------470, 471
nor artificial has produced a new
species,---------------------------- 471
Self-limitation, divine,-----------9, 126, 255
Selfishness, the essence of sin,----------- 567
cannot be resolved into simpler elements, ----------------------------- 568
forms in which it manifests itself, 568, 569
of unregenerate, the substitution of a
lower for a higher end,------------- 570
Sentimentality,----------------------- 979
'Signality,' in miracle,----------------- 118
Sin, God the author of free beings who
are the authors of,----------------- 365
the decree to permit not efficient,----- 365

Sin, its permission a difficulty of all
theistic systems,--------------------- 366
its permission, how not to be explained, ---------------------------- 366
its permission, how it may be partially
explained, ------------------------- 366
the problem of, one of four at present
not to be completely solved,-----366, 367
observations from many sources aiming to throw light on the existence
of moral evil,----------------------367, 368
man's, as suggested from without,
perhaps the mitigating circumstance that allows of his redemption, 462
in what sense a nature? --------------- 518
effect of first, not a weakening but a
perversion of human nature,-------- 521
the first did more than despoil man of
a special gift of grace,--------------- 521
or man's state of apostasy,---------533-664
its nature,----------------------------549-573
defined, ----------------------------- 549
Old and New School views regarding,
their difference and approximation,
----------------------------------549, 550
as a state, some psychological notes
explanatory of,-----------------550, 551
as a state is counteracted by an immanent divine power which leads
towards salvation------------------- 551
'total depravity' as descriptive of, an
out-grown phrase,------------------ 552
as act of transgression and disposition or state, proved from Scripture,-------------------------------- 552-554
the words which describe, applicable
to dispositions and states,---------- 552
N. T. descriptions of, give prominence
to states and dispositions,-------552, 553
and moral evil in the thoughts, affections, and heart,-------------------- 553
is name given to a state which originated wrong desires,---------------- 553
is represented as existing in soul prior
to consciousness of it,-------------- 553
a permanent power or reigning principle,------------------------------- 553
Mosaic sacrifices for sins other than
mere act,--------------------------- 554
universally attributed to disposition
or state, --------------------------- 554
attributed to outward act only when
such act is symptomatic of inward
state,------------------------------- 554
if it tend from act to a state, regarded
as correspondingly blameworthy,--- 554
in an individual condemned though
it cannot be traced back to a conscious originating act,-----------554, 555
when it becomes fixed and dominant
moral corruption, meets special disapprobation,------------------------ 555

Sin, regarded by the Christian as a manifestation of subconscious depravity of nature, ... 555

repented of, principally as a depravity of nature, ... 555

rather than 'sins' repented of by Christians advanced in spiritual culture ; a conspectus of quotations to prove this,...........................555-557

its definition as 'the voluntary transgression of known law' discussed, ...557-559

is not always a distinct and conscious volition, ... 557

intention aggravates, but is not essential to,.................................. 558

knowledge aggravates, but is not essential to,.............................. 558

ability to fulfil the law, not essential to,.. 558

definition of, ...558, 559

its essential principle,.................559-573

is not sensuousness,...................559-563

is not finiteness,.................... 563-566

is selfishness,..............................567-573

is universal,................................573-582

committed by every human being, arrived at maturity, ... 573

its universality set forth in Scripture, ...573, 574

its universality proved from history, 574

its universality proved from Christian experience,.......................... 576

the outcome of a corrupt nature possessed by every human being, ... 577

is act or disposition referred to a corrupt nature,.............................. 577

rests on men who are called in Scripture 'children of wrath,'.............. 578

its penalty, death, visits those who have never exercised personal or conscious choice,........................ 579

its universality proved from reason, ...579, 580

testimony of great thinkers regarding,.....................................580-582

its origin in the personal act of Adam, ...582-593

the origin of the sinful nature whence it comes is beyond the investigations of reason,........................ 582

Scriptural account of its origin,... 582-585

Adam's, its essential nature,............ 587

of Adam in resisting inworking God, 587

an immanent preference of the world,...................................... 587

not to be accounted for psychologically,.................................... 587

the external temptation to first sin a benevolent permission................ 588

self-originated, Satanic,................ 588

Sin, the first temptation to, had no tendency to lead astray, ... 589

the first, though in itself small, a revelation of will thoroughly alienated from God,.............................. 590

consequences of original, as respects Adam, ...590-593

physical death, a consequence of his first,.................. ....590, 591

spiritual death, a consequence of his first, ...591, 592

exclusion from God's presence, a consequence of his first,.................... 592

banishment from the Garden, a consequence of man's first,.............. 593

the, of our first parents constituted their posterity sinners,.............. 593

two insistent questions regarding the first, and the Scriptural answer,...... 593

imputation of, its true meaning,...... 594

original, its meaning,.................... 594

man's relations to moral law extend beyond conscious and actual,........ 595

God's moral government recognizes race-sin, ... 595

actual, more guilty than original...... 596

no man condemned for original, alone, ...596, 664

the only ground of responsibility for race-sin,.................................. 596

original, its correlate,.................... 596

imputation of Adam's,.............597-637

see Imputation.

Pelagian theory of the imputation of, ...597-601

Arminian theory of the imputation of,...................................601-606

New School theory of the imputation of,...................................606-612

Federal theory of the imputation of, ...612-616

Mediate theory of the imputation of, ...616-619

Augustinian theory of the imputation of,...................................619-637

table of theories of imputation of,... 628

apart from, and prior to, consciousness,...................................... 629

conscience and Scripture attest that we are responsible for our unborn tendency to, ... 629

as our nature, rightly punishable with resulting sin, ... 632

reproductive, each reproduction increasing guilt and punishment, ... 633

each man guilty of personal, which expresses more than original depravity of nature,.................... 633

is self-perpetuating, ... 633

is self-isolating,.......................... 634

the nature, and sins its expression,... 635

Sin, as Adam's, ruins, so Christ's obedience saves,................ 635
consequences of, to Adam's posterity,
..............................637-664
depravity a consequence of Adam's,
..............................637-640
in nature, as 'total depravity,' considered, ...637-640
total inability a consequence of
Adam's,........................640-644
guilt a consequence of Adam's,....644-652
penalty, a consequence of Adam's, 652-660
infants in a state of,................ 661
venial and mortal,................... 648
of nature and personal transgression,
..............................648, 649
of ignorance and of knowledge,....... 649
of infirmity and of presumption,..649, 650
of incomplete and final obduracy,..650-652
unto death, considered, ...650-652
against Holy Spirit, why unpardonable,........................651, 652
penalty of, considered,...........652-660
infants in a state of, ... 661
Christ free from hereditary and
actual, ...676-678
Christ responsible for human,......... 759
Christ responsible for Adam's,........ 759
Christ as great Penitent confesses
race-sin, ... 760
Christ, how made to be,.......... 760-763
a pretermission of, justified in cross,.. 772
does not condemn, but the failure to
ask pardon for it,.................. 856
judged and condemned on Calvary,... 860
future, the virtual pardon of,......... 867
'dwelling,' and 'reigning,'........869, 870
expelled by bringing in Christ,........ 873
does not most sympathize with sin,.. 1028
hinders intercourse with other worlds, 1033
'eternal,'............................ 1033
made the means of displaying God's
glory, ... 1038
chosen in spite of infinite motives to
the contrary,...................... 1040
Sinner, the incorrigible, glorifies God in
his destruction,................... 442
negatively described................637, 638
positively described,................. 639
what he can do,..................... 640
what he cannot do,.................. 640
under conviction, more of a sinner
than before,....................... 827
has no right to do anything before accepting Christ,.................. 868
'Six hundred sixty-six,'.............. 570
'Slope, the,'........................ 580
Society, atomistic theory of,.......... 623
Society, bellum omnium contra omnes
(Hobbes),....................... 461
Socinianism,..47, 328, 329, 524, 558, 597, 728-733
Solidarity, ... 624

Sola fides justificat, sed fides non est sola,.. 755
'Son,' its import in Trinity,............ 334
Son, the, a perfect object of will, knowledge and love to God,............275, 388
his eternal generation,............... 341
uncreate, ... 341
his essence not derived from essence
of the Father,.................... 341
his existence eternal,................ 341
exists by internal necessity of Divine
nature,.......................... 341
eternal generation of, a life movement of the Divine nature,....... 341
in person subordinate to person of
Father,.......................... 342
in essence equal with Father,......... 343
Son of man, connotes, among other
things, a veritable humanity,........ 673
Song of Solomon,...............233, 238
Sonship of Christ, eternal,.......... 340
metaphysical,...................... 340
authors on,....................... 343
Sorrow for sin,.................832, 833
Soteriology, ...665-894
Soul, what?........................ 92
dichotomous view of,............... 483
trichotomous view of,............... 484
distinguished from spirit,........... 484
its origin,......................... 488
its pre-existence, according to poets,.. 489
creatian theory of,................. 491
not something added from without,.... 492
introduced into body, sicut vinum in
vase acetoso,..................... 493
metaphysical generation of,.......... 493
traducian theory of,.............494-497
history of theory,...............493, 494
observations favorable to,.........494-497
image of God, proprie,............... 528
always active, though not always conscious,.......................... 550
may influence another soul apart from
physical intermediaries, ... 820
not inaccessible to God's direct operation, ... 820
as uncompounded cannot die,......... 984
see Immortality.
'Sovereign, the,' a title of Messiah,...... 321
Space,.........................278, 275
Space and time,..................85, 275
Space 'in God,'.................... 275
Species,.................392, 480-482, 494
Spirit, the Holy, his teaching, a necessity,............................ 27
hides himself,..................... 213
recognized as God,................. 315
divine characteristics and prerogatives ascribed to,................. 316
associated with God, ... 316
his deity supported by Christian experience,....................... 316
his deity, a doctrine of the church,... 314

Spirit, the Holy, his deity not disproved by O. T. limitations, ... 317
his deity, authors on, ... 317
is a person, ... 323
designations of personality given to him, ... 323
'the mother-principle' in the Godhead, 323
so mentioned with other persons as to imply personality, ...323, 324
performs acts of personality, ... 324
affected by acts of others, ... 324
posseses an emotional nature, ... 325
visibly appears as distinct from, yet connected with Father and Son, ... 325
ascription to him, of personal subsistence, ... 325
import of his presence in Trinity, ... 334
the centripetal movement of Deity, .. 336
and Christ, differences in their work, ...338–340
his nature and work, authors on, ... 340
his eternal procession, ...340–343
if not God, God could not be appropriated, ... 349
a work of completing belongs to, ... 343
applies Scriptural truth to present circumstances, ... 440
directs the God-man in his humiliation, ... 696
his intercession, ...774, 775
his intermediacy, ... 793
witness of, what? 844, 845
doctrine of 'sealing' distinguished from mysticism, ... 845
in believer, substitutes old excitements, ... 872
Spirit' and 'soul,' 843
Spirit, how applied to Christ, ... 333
Spirits, evil, tempt, ... 455
control natural phenomena, ... 455
execute God's plans, ... 457
not independent of human will, ... 457, 458
restrained by permissive will of God, 458
exist and act on sufferance, ... 459
their existence not inconsistent with benevolence of God, ... 461
are organized, ... 461
the doctrine of, not immoral, ...461, 462
doctrine of, not degrading, ... 462
their nature and actions illustrate the evil of sin, ... 463
knowledge of their existence inspires a salutary fear, ... 463
sense of their power drives to Christ, 463
contrasting their unsaved state with our spiritual advantages causes us to magnify grace of God, ... 463
'Spirits in prison,' 707, 708
Spiritual body, ...1018, 1017
Spiritualism, ...82, 132
Spontaneous generation, ... 389
Stoicism, ... 184

Style, ... 223
Sublapsarianism, ... 777
Subordinationism, ... 342
Substance, known, ... 5
its characteristics, ... 6
a direct knowledge of it as underlying phenomena, ... 97
Substances, the theory of two eternal, ...378–383
See Dualism.
Substantia una et unica, ... 86
Suffering, in itself not reformatory, ... 104
Suggestion, ...453, 454
'Sunday,' used by Justin Martyr, ... 148
Supererogation, works of, ... 522
Supper, the Lord's, a historical monument, ... 157
its ritual and import, ... 959
instituted by Christ, ...959, 960
its mode of administration, ...960–962
its elements, ... 960
its communion of both kinds, ... 960
is of a festal nature, ...960, 961
commemorative, ... 931
celebrated by assembled church, ... 961
responsibility of its proper observance rests with pastor as representative of church, ... 962
its frequency discretional, ... 962
it symbolizes personal appropriation of the benefits of Christ's death, ... 963
it symbolizes union with Christ, ... 963
it symbolizes dependence on Christ, ... 963
it symbolizes a reproduction of death and resurrection in believer, ... 963
it symbolizes union in Christ, ... 963
it symbolizes the coming joy and perfection of the kingdom of God, ... 963
its connection with baptism, ... 964
is to be often repeated, ... 964
implies a previous state of grace, ... 964
the blessing conveyed in communion depends on communicant, ... 964
expresses fellowship of believer, ... 964
the Romanist view of, ...965–968
the Lutheran and High Church view of, ...968, 969
there are prerequisites, ...969, 970
prerequisites laid down by Christ, ... 970
regeneration, a prerequisite to, ... 971
baptism, a prerequisite to, ...971–973
church membership, a prerequisite to, 973
an orderly walk, a prerequisite to, 973–975
the local church the judge as to the fulfilment of these prerequisites, 975–977
special objections to open communion presented, ...977–980
Supralapsarianism, ... 777
Symbol, derivation and meaning, ... 42
less than thing symbolized, ...1035
Symbolism, period of, ... 45
Symbolum Quicumque, ... 329

Synagogue,................................ 902
Synergism, ... 816
Synoptic gospels, date,................... 150
Synthetic idealization of our exist-
  ence,' 568
Synthetic method in theology,.......... 50
System of theology, a dissected map,
  some parts of which already put to-
  gether, ... 15
Systematic theologian, the first,........ 44
Systematic truth influences character, 16
Tabula rasa theory, of Locke,.......... 35
Talmud shows what the unaided genius
  for religion could produce,........... 115
Tapeinoticon genus, ... 686
'Teaching, the, of the Twelve Apostles,'
  ....159, 937, 953
Teleological argument for the existence
  of God,...............................75-80
  statement of argument,............... 75
  called also 'physico-theological,'..... 75
  divided by some into eutaxiology and
    teleology proper,.................... 75
  the major premise is a primitive and
    immovable conviction,.............. 75
  the minor premise, a working princi-
    ple of science,...................... 77
  it does not prove a personal God,....78, 79
  it does not prove unity, eternity, or
    infinity of God,...................79, 80
  adds intelligence and volition to the
    causative power already proved
    to exist,............................. 80
Telepathy,...............................1021
Temptation, prevented by God's providence,.................................. 423
  does not pervert, but confirms, the
    holy soul,.......................588, 589
  Adam's, Scriptural account of,....582, 583
  Adam's, its course and result,.....584, 585
  Adam's, contrasted with Christ's,..677, 678
  Christ's, as possible as that of Adam, 677
  aided by limitations of his human in-
    telligence, ... 677
  aided by his susceptibility to all forms
    of innocent gratification, ... 677
  in wilderness, addressed to desire,.... 677
  in Gethsemane. to fear,.............. 677
  Ueberglaube, Aberglaube, Unglaube,
    appealed to,......................... 677
  is always 'without sin,' 677
  authors upon, ... 678
  by Satan, negative and positive, ... 455
Tempter's promise, the,.................. 572
Tendency-theory of Baur,...........157-160
Tendency, undeveloped,.................. 847
Terminology, a, needed in progress of a
  science, ... 85
Testament New, genuineness of,.....146-165
  rationalistic theories to explain origin
    of its gospels,....................155-165
  its moral system,..................177-186

Testament New, its morality contrasted
  with that of heathenism,..........179-186
Testament, Old, in what sense its works
  are genuine,........................... 162
  how proved,.......................165-175
  alleged errors in quoting or inter-
    preting, ...234, 235
Testimony, science assumes faith in,..... 3
  amount of, necessary to prove miracle,
    ....127, 128
  in general, ...142-144
  statements in, may conflict without
    being false, ... 227
Tests, does God submit to ?.............. 437
Theologian, characteristics of,........38-41
Theological Encyclopædia,............... 42
Theology, its definition,..............1, 2
  its aim,................................. 2
  its possibility, ...2-15
  its necessity,.......................15-19
  its relation to religion,............19-24
  rests on God's self-revelation,........ 25
  rests on his revelation in nature,...... 26
  natural and Scriptural, how related, 26-29
  rests on Scripture and reason,......... 29
  rationalism hurtful to,...............30-31
  rests on Scripture and a true mysti-
    cism, ... 31
  avoids a false mysticism,............. 32
  accepts history of doctrine as ancil-
    lary,................................. 33
  declines the combination, Scripture
    and Romanism,...................33, 34
  its limitations, ...34-36
  a perfect system of, impossible,.....36, 37
  is progressive,........................ 37
  its method, ...38-51
  requisites to its study,.............38-41
  see Theologian.
  divisions of, ...41-44
  Biblical,.............................. 41
  historical,............................ 41
  systematic,.........................41, 42
  practical, ...42-44
Theology, Systematic, its history,....... 44
  in Eastern church,.................... 44
  in Western Church, ...44-46
  its period of scholasticism,.........44, 45
  its period of symbolism,...........45, 46
  its period of criticism and speculation, 46
  a list of authorities in, differing from
    Protestantism, ... 47
  British theology,...................47, 48
  Baptist theologians,.................. 47
  Puritan theologians,................47, 48
  Scotch Presbyterian theologians,..... 48
  Methodist theologians,............... 48
  Quaker theologians,.................. 48
  English Church theologians,.......... 48
  American theology,.................48, 49
  the Reformed system,..............48, 48
  the older Calvinism,................. 49

Theology, Systematic, order in which its
　　subjects may be treated,..........49, 50
　　analytic method in,................49, 50
　　synthetic method in,................ 50
　　text-books in,.................50, 51
Theonomy, ... 83
Theophany, Christ not a mere,......... 686
'Things,'..................95, 96, 254
Thought, does not go on in the brain, 93
　　possible without language,.......... 216
　　intermittent or continuous?.........1002
Three thousand baptized in one day in
　　time of Chrysostom,.............. 934
Thucydides never mentions Socrates,... 144
Time, its definition,................ 276
　　God not under law of,.............. 276
　　has objective reality to God,......... 276
　　his 'one eternal now,' how to be
　　understood,.................... 277
　　can the human spirit escape the con-
　　ditions of,.................... 278
　　authors on 'time' and 'eternity,'..... 278
Torments of wicked, outward, subordi-
　　nate results and accompaniments of
　　state of soul,....................1034
Tradition, and idea of God,.......... 63
　　cannot long be trusted to give cor-
　　rect evidence,.................. 142
　　of a 'golden age' and matters cog-
　　nate,....................480, 526
Traducianism, its advocates and teach-
　　ing,.......................493, 494
　　best accords with Scripture,.......494, 495
　　favored by analogy of vegetable and
　　animal life,.................... 496
　　heredities, mental, spiritual, and
　　moral, prove men's souls of human
　　ancestry,.................... 496
　　does not exclude divine concurrence
　　in the development of the human
　　species,.................... 496
　　Fathers, who held,.............. 620
Trafalgar, omitted in Napoleon's dis-
　　patches,.................... 143
Transcendence, divine, denied by pan-
　　theism,.................... 100
　　taught in Scripture,.............. 102
　　deism, an exaggeration of, ... 414
Transgression, a stab at heart of God,.. 541
　　not proper translation of 1 John 3:4,.. 452
　　its universality directly taught in
　　Scripture,.................... 573
　　its universality proved in universal
　　need of atonement, regeneration,
　　and repentance,.............. 573
　　its universality shown in condem-
　　nation that rests on all who do not
　　accept Christ,.................. 574
　　its universality, consistent with pas-
　　sages which ascribe a sort of good-
　　ness to some men,.............. 574

Transgression, its universality proved
　　by history, and individual experi-
　　ence and observation, ...574, 575
　　proved from Christian experience,.... 576
　　uniformity of actual transgression, a
　　proof that will is impotent, ... 611
　　all moral consequences flowing from,
　　are sanctions of law,.............. 637
Transubstantiation, what?.............. 965
　　rests on a false interpretation of Script-
　　ure, ... 965
　　contradicts the senses, ... 966
　　denies completeness of sacrifice of
　　Calvary,...................... 967
　　externalizes and destroys Christianity,
　　.............................967, 968
Trees of 'life' and 'knowledge,' 526, 527, 588
Trichotomous theory of man's nature,
　　.........................484-487
Trimurti, Brahman Trinity, ... 351
Trinitas dualitatem ad unitatem reducit, 338
Trinitatem, I ad Jordanem et videbis,... 325
Trinities, heathen,.................. 351
Trinity, renders possible an eternal
　　divine self-contemplation,.......... 262
　　the immanent love of God understood
　　only in light of, ... 265
　　the immanent holiness of God render-
　　ed intelligible by doctrine of,........ 274
　　has close relations to doctrine of im-
　　manent attributes,.............275, 336
　　doctrine of the,................304-352
　　a truth of revelation only, ... 304
　　intimated in O. T., made known in
　　N. T.,........................ 304
　　six main statements concerning,...... 304
　　the term ascribed to Tertullian,....... 304
　　a designation of four facts,.......... 304
　　held implicitly, or in solution, by the
　　apostles, ... 304
　　took shape in the Athanasian Creed
　　(8th or 9th century),.............. 305
　　usually connected with 'semi-trini-
　　tarian' Nicene Creed (325 A. D.),.... 305
　　references on doctrine of, ... 305
　　implies the recognition in Scripture of
　　three as God, ...305-322
　　presents proofs from N. T., ...305-317
　　presents Father as recognized as God, 305
　　presents Jesus Christ as recognized as
　　God,......................305-315
　　appeals to Christian experience as con-
　　firming the deity of Christ,......313, 314
　　explains certain passages apparently
　　inconsistent with Christ's deity, 314, 315
　　allows an order of office and operation
　　consistent with essential oneness
　　and equality, ...314, 342
　　doctrine of, how its construction
　　started, ... 314
　　presents the Holy Spirit recognized as
　　God,......................315-317

Trinity, intimations of, in the O. T., 317-322
seemingly alluded to in passages
which teach a plurality of some sort
in the Godhead,....................317-319
seemingly alluded to in passages relating to the Angel of Jehovah,......... 319
seemingly alluded to in descriptions
of Divine Wisdom and Word,....320, 321
owes nothing to foreign sources,...... 320
seemingly alluded to in descriptions of
the Messiah, ...321-322
O. T. contains germ of doctrine of,.... 322
its clear revelation, why delayed ? ... 322
insists that the three recognized as
God are presented in Scripture as
distinct persons,....................322-326
asserts that this tripersonality of the
divine nature is immanent and
eternal, ... 326
it alleges Scriptural proof that the
distinctions of personality are eternal,.................................... 326
the Sabellian heresy regarding,....327-328
the Arian heresy regarding, ...328-330
teaches a tripersonality which is not
tritheism, for while the persons are
three, the essence is one,............. 330
how the term 'person' is used in,..330, 331
the oneness of essence explained,...331-334
teaches an association which is more
than partnership,..................... 331
presents itself as the organism of the
deity,.................................. 331
permits intercommunion and mutual
immanency of persons,........... 332, 333
teaches equality of the three persons,
....................................334-343
teaches that the titles belong to the
persons, ...334, 335
employs the personal titles in a qualified sense,.........................335-340
presents to us life-movement in the
Godhead,............................336-338
teaches a 'generation' that is consistent with equality,..................... 340
teaches a 'procession' that is consistent with equality, ... 340
is inscrutable, ... 344
all analogies inadequate to represent
it, ... 344
illustrations of, their only use,........ 345
not self-contradictory,.................. 345
presents faculty and function at highest differentiation,.................... 346
its relations to other doctrines,........ 347
its acceptance essential to any proper
theism,................................ 347
its denial leads to pantheism,.......... 347
essential to any proper revelation,.... 349
evidence of, in prayer,................. 349
essential to any proper redemption. ... 350

Trinity, effects of its denial on religious
life, ...350, 351
essential to any proper model for
human life,............................ 351
sets law of love before us as eternal,.. 351
shows divine pattern of receptive life, 351
authors on the doctrine,................ 351
Trisagion, the,........................... 318
Tritheism, inconsistent with idea of God, 330
Trivialities in Scripture, their use,...... 217
Truth, God's, what?...................... 260
immanent,............................. 260
a matter of being, ... 261
foundation of truth among men, ... 261
the principle and guarantee of all revelation,............................... 262
not of God's will, but of his being,.... 262
God's transitive,.................... 288-290
see Veracity and Faithfulness.
attributed to Christ,................... 309
attributed to the Holy Spirit, ... 316
as the efficient cause of regeneration,
....................................817-820
hated by sinner,....................... 817
neither known nor obeyed without a
change of the affections, ... 818
even God cannot make it more true,.. 819
without God, an abstraction, not a
power, ... 819
Ubi caritas, ibi claritas,................. 520
Ubi Spiritus, ibi Christus,............... 333
Ubi tres medici, ibi duo athei,............ 39
Ubiquity of Christ's human body,....... 709
relation to Lord's Supper, ... 968
relation to views of heaven,...........1032
Ueberglaube, Aberglaube, Unglaube, the
chief avenues of temptation, ... 677
Uhlhorn, on the 'if's' of Tacitus,....... 989
Ullmann, on the derivation of sapientia, 4
Una navis est jam bonorum omnium,.... 881
Uncaused cause, the idea of, not from
logical inference, but intuitive be-
lief, ... 74
Unconditioned being, the presupposition of our knowing, ... 58
Unconscious mental action, ... 551, 555
Unconscious substance cannot produce
self-conscious and free beings,...... 102
Understanding, the servant of the will, 460
Unicus, as applied to the divine nature, 259
Uniformity of nature, a presumption
against miracles,...................... 124
not absolute and universal,............ 124
could only be asserted on the ground
of absolute and universal knowledge, ... 124
disproved by geology,.................. 124
breaks in, illustrated,.................. 125
final cause is beneath,................. 125
of volitional action rests on character, 509
of evil choice, implies tendency or
determination, ... 611

1114   INDEX OF SUBJECTS.

Uniformity of transgression, a demonstration of impotence of will, ... 611
Unio personalis, ... 689, 690
Union of the two natures in the one person of Christ, ... 683-700
moral, between different souls, ... 799
with Christ, believer's, and man's with Adam, compared, ... 627
with Christ, believer's, wholly due to God, ... 781
its relation to regeneration and conversion, ... 793
doctrine of, ... 795-808
reasons for its neglect, ... 795
Scripture representations of, ... 795-798
represented by building and foundation, ... 795
represented by marriage union, .. 795, 796
represented by vine and branch, ... 796
consistent with individuality, ... 796
represented by head and members, ... 796
represented by union of race with Adam, ... 797
believer is in Christ, ... 797
Christ is in believer, ... 797
Father and Son dwell in believer, ... 797
believer has life by Christ as Christ has life by union with the Father, ... 797
believers are one through, ... 797
believers made partakers of divine nature through, ... 798
by it believer made one spirit with the Lord, ... 798
nature of, ... 698-802
not a merely natural union, ... 799
not a merely moral union, ... 799
not a union of essence, ... 799, 800
in it believer most conscious of his personality and power, ... 800
not mediated by sacraments, ... 800
an organic union, ... 800
a vital union, ... 801
a spiritual union, ... 801
originated and sustained by Holy Spirit, ... 801
by virtue of omnipresence the whole Christ with each believer, ...281, 704, 801
inscrutable, ... 801
in what sense mystical, ... 801
authors on, ... 802
consequences of, to believer, ... 802-809
removes the internal obstacle to man's return to God, in the case of his people, ... 802
involves change in the dominant affection of the soul (Regeneration), ... 804
is the true 'transfusion of blood,' 804
involves a new exercise of soul's powers in Repentance and Faith (Conversion), ... 804
this phase of, illustrated by the depuration of Chicago River, ...804, 805

Union with Christ gives to believer legal standing and rights of Christ (Justification), ... 805
secures to the believer the transforming, assimilating power of Christ's life, for soul and body (Sanctification and Perseverance), ... 805
does it secure physical miracles in deliverance from fleshly besetments of those who experience it? 806
brings about a fellowship with Christ, and thus a fellowship of believers with one another here and hereafter (Ecclesiology and Eschatology), ... 806
secures among Christians the unity not of external organization, but of a common life, ... 807
gives assurance of salvation, ... 808
excerpts upon, from noted names in theology, ... 808
references upon, ... 808, 809
Unique, the, ... 244
Unitarianism, derivation of term, ... 330
its founders, ... 47
their relation to Arianism, ... 329
tends to pantheism, ... 347
fosters lax views of sin, ... 350
holds to Pelagian views of sin, ... 597
holds to Socinian views of atonement, ... 728, 729
Unity of Scripture, ... 175
Unity of God, ... 259, 304
consistent with a trinity, ... 259
Unity of human race, taught in Scripture, ... 476
lies at foundation of Pauline doctrine of sin and salvation, ... 476
ground of obligation of brotherhood among men, ... 476
various arguments for, ... 477-483
opposed by theorists who propound different centres of creation, ... 481
opposed on the ground that the physical diversities in the race are inconsistent with a common origin, ...481, 482
Universalia, ante and *post rem,* and *in re,* 621
Universalism, its error, ... 1047
Universality of transgression, ... 573-577
Universals, ... 621
Universe, regarded as thought, must have had an absolute thinker, ... 60
its substance cannot be shown to have had a beginning, ... 73
has its phenomena had a cause within itself (pantheism)? 73
mind in it, leads us to infer mind in maker, ... 73
if eternal, yet, as contingent and relative, it only requires an eternal creator, ... 74
since its infinity cannot be proved, why infer from its perhaps limited existence an infinite creator? 74

Universe, its order and useful collocation may be due to an impersonal intelligence (pantheism), ... 77

its present harmony proves a will and intelligence equal to its contrivance, ... 80

facts of, erroneous explanations of, 90-105

not necessary to divine blessedness, 265

'God's ceaseless conversation with his creatures,' 436

exists for moral and spiritual ends,... 436

a harp in which one string, our world, is out of tune, ... 451, 1033

Unus, as applied to divine nature, ... 259

Utopia, More's, an adumbration of St. John's City of God, ... 1031

Vacuum, ... 279

Vanity, what? 569

Variation, law of, ... 470, 491, 492

Variations, are in the divine operation, not in the divine plan, ... 258

Vedas, ... 56, 203, 222, 225

Veracity and faithfulness of God, the, his transitive truth, ... 288, 289

by virtue of, his revelations consist with his being and with each other, 288

by virtue of, he fulfils all his promises expressed or implied, ... 289

Vitæ, employed in determining the divine attributes, ... 247

Vice, can it be created? 520

Virgin-birth of Christ, ... 675-678

Virgin, the Immaculate Conception of, its absurdity, ... 677

Virtue, ... 298-303

see Moral obligation.

Vishnu, incarnations of, ... 351

Volition, the shadow of the affections,...815

executive, ... 504

a subordinate, not always determined by fundamental choice, ... 510, 870

'Voluntary' and 'volitional' contrasted, ... 557

'*Voluntas*' and '*arbitrium*' distinguished, ... 557

Vorsehung, an aspect of providence, ... 419

Vulgate, ... 226, 799

'Waters,' the best term in Hebrew to express 'fluid mass,' 395

Weltgeschichte, die, ist das Weltgericht, 1024

Wicked, in the intermediate state, 999, 1000

in intermediate state, under constraint and guard, ... 999

in intermediate state, in conscious suffering, ... 999

in intermediate state, under punishment, ... 1000

in intermediate state, their souls do not sleep, ... 1000

in the final state, ... 1033-1056

their final state, in Scriptural figures, 1033

Wicked, their final state, a summing up statement, ... 1034

their final state is not annihilation, ... 1035, 1036

their final state has in it no element of new probation or final restoration, ... 1039-1043

their final state, one of everlasting punishment, ... 1044-1046

their final state, a revelation of God's justice, ... 1046-1051

their final state, a revelation of a benevolence which permits the self-chosen ruin of a few to work for the salvation of the many, ... 1051-1054

their final state, should be preached with sympathy and solemnity, 1054-1056

Will, free, not under law of physical causation, ... 26

human, acts on nature without suspending its laws, ... 121

human, acts initially without means, 122

its power over body, ... 122

has not the freedom of indifference,... 363

an act of pure, unknown to human consciousness, ... 363, 507

and sensibility, two distinct powers,.. 363

Christianity gives us more, ... 440

Holy Spirit emancipates the, ... 440

defined, ... 504

determinism of, rejected, ... 504

and other faculties, ... 505

element in every act of soul, ... 505

man is chiefly, ... 504

the verb has no imperative, ... 505

and permanent state, ... 505, 506

slight decisions of, lead to fixation of character, ... 506

and motives, ... 506, 507

permanent states influence, ... 506

not compelled, but persuaded by motive, ... 506

in choosing between motives, chooses with a motive, namely the motive chosen, ... 507

and contrary choice, ... 507, 508

we know causality only as we know, 508

a power of originating action, limited by subjective and social conditions, 508

will, free, chooses between impulses, 508

and responsibility, ... 509, 510

naturally exercised with a bias, ... 509

free, gives existence to duty and morality, ... 510

is defeated in immorality, ... 511

deterministic theory of, objections to, 511

will does not create force, but directs it, ... 512

will as great a mystery as the Trinity, 512

references on, ... 513

evil, the man himself, ... 555

more than faculty of volitions, ... 600

Will, its impotence proved by uniformity of transgression,.................... 611
such a decision of, as will justify God
  in condemning men, when found, .. 612
a determination of the, prior to individual consciousness — a difficult but
  fruitful hypothesis,..................... 624
the cause of sin in holy beings,........ 629
not absolutely as a man's character, .. 633
character its surest but not its
  infallible index,..................... 633
man's, does more than express, it may
  curb, his nature,.................... 633
has permanent states, as well as transient acts,..................... 764
God's action, in conversion,.........792, 793
the depraved, has inconceivable
  power to resist God, ...1048
God's, not sole force in universe,....... 411
God's 'revealed' and 'secret,'........ 791
'Will' and 'shall,' as to man's actions,
  distinguished, ... 354
Wille and Wilkür,..................... 557
Wisdom, divine, its nature,............. 286

Wisdom, divine, in O. T., ... 320
  in Apocrypha,...................... 320
Witness of Spirit,.................844, 845
Word, divine, the medium and test of
  spiritual communications, ... 32
  divine, in O. T.,.................... 320
  Christ, the, ... 335
Works of God, ...371–464
World, final conflagration and rehabili-
  tation, ...1015
  may be part of the heaven of the
  saints, ...1032, 1033
Worship, defined, ... 23
  its relation to religion,................. 23
  depends on God's glory, ... 255
  final state of righteous one of,..1029, 1030
Wrong, must be punished whether good
  comes of it or not,.................. 655
'Yea, the' (2 Cor. 1:20) = objective
  certainty, ... 14
'Zechariah,' proper reading for 'Jeremiah,' in Mat. 27:9,................. 226
Zoroastrianism, Parseeism, ...185, 190, 382

INDEX OF AUTHORS.

Abbot, Ezra,_____148, 152, 159, 165, 180, 307
Abbott, A. E.,_____ 155
Abbott, F. E.,_____ _____ 621
Abbott, Lyman,___128, 201, 208, 379, 524, 589, 599, 694, 700, 720, 722, 732, 739, 768, 800, 896, 1005.
Abbott, T. K.,_____ 933
Abelard, Peter,_____1, 34, 44, 734
Ackermann, C.,_____ 666
Adams, J. C.,_____1041
Adams, John,_____ 228
Adams, John Quincy,_____ 899
Adams, Nehemiah,_____ 369
Adams, Thomas,_____ 48
Adamson, Thomas,_____133, 190, 314, 315, 439, 675, 681.
Addison, Joseph,_____649, 988
Adeney, W. F.,_____985, 1020
Adkins, F.,_____822, 948
Ælfric, _____ 505
Æschylus, _____111, 543, 723, 989
Æsop, _____ 369
Agassiz, Louis,_____396, 481, 984
Ahrens, Henri,_____ 536
"Aids to Faith,"_____139, 405
"Aids to Study of German Theology," _____ 74
Albertus Magnus,_____ 524
Alcuin, Flaccus,_____ 744
Alden, Joseph,_____ _____6, 11, 100
Aldrich, Anne Reeve,_____155, 794
Alexander, Archibald,_____51, 58, 101, 191, 301, 364, 488, 553, 557, 620, 644, 780, 912.
Alexander, J. A.,_____654, 907, 1005
Alexander, J. W.,_____795, 845, 846
Alexander, W. L.,_____117, 131, 135, 151, 155, 157, 177, 189.
Alford, Henry,___68, 150, 306, 377, 452, 1005
Alger, William R.,_____281, 493, 991
Allen, A. V. G.,_____25, 32, 36, 44, 147, 208, 341, 343, 361, 399, 620, 636, 748, 800, 846.
Allen, Grant, _____ 57
Allison, W. H.,_____ 929
Ambrose,_____25, 48, 297, 619, 620
American Theological Review,_____2, 15
Amiel, Henri F.,_____277, 280, 441, 599
Ammon, Christoph F.,_____ 46
Amos, Sheldon,_____534, 547
Amyraldus, Moses,_____ 46

Anderson, F. L.,_____840, 939
Anderson, Galusha,_____ 896
Anderson, Martin B.,_____11, 987
Andover Review,_____122, 133, 643
Andrews, E. A.,_____ 20
Andrews, E. B.,_____182, 694, 892
Andrews, J. N.,_____ 410
Andrews, J. R.,_____ 840
Andrews, Lancelot,_____ 340
Andrews, S. J.,_____ 229
Angelus Silesius,_____101, 800
Angus, Joseph,_____1045, 1056
Annotated Paragraph Bible,_____141, 226, 232, 307, 423, 457, 574, 578, 650, 699, 761, 878, 934, 1025.
Anselm,_____34, 44, 86, 87, 89, 105, 279, 447, 487, 613, 630, 631, 675, 701, 748, 834, 849.
Apollinaris, _____ 671
Apollos, _____ 152
Appleton, Jesse,_____ 426
Aquinas, Thomas,____45, 443, 569, 613, 630, 631, 747, 750.
Aratus, _____ 526
Argyll, Duke of,_____92, 99, 225, 389, 412, 435, 469, 474, 483, 528, 530, 536.
Aristotle,_____2, 33, 38, 40, 43, 44, 45, 58, 97, 120, 181, 184, 244, 252, 259, 262, 284, 378, 491, 516, 568, 579, 580, 581, 799, 814, 989, 1045.
Arius, _____ 328
Arminius, J.,_____47, 602
Armitage, Thomas,_____908, 973
Armour, J. M.,_____ 120
Armstrong, ———, _____ 283
Arnold, Albert N.,_____954, 959, 971, 972, 973, 974, 975, 979.
Arnold, Edwin,_____ 182
Arnold, Matthew,_____21, 23, 102, 118, 139, 155, 188, 191, 192, 207, 252, 253, 526, 575, 989, 1056.
Arnold, Thomas,_____139, 156, 207, 237, 294, 557, 841.
Arnot, William,_____ 659
Arthur, William,_____ 350
Ascham, Roger,_____ 576
Ashmore, William,_____292, 459, 636, 663, 759, 773, 936, 941, 945.
Askwith, E. H.,_____ 568
Asmus, P._____ 56

Athanasius,_____44, 388, 620, 748, 997
Athenagoras, _____ 998
Atwater, Lyman H.,_____97, 368, 637
Auber, H.,_____398, 593
Auberlen, C. A.,_____14, 131, 160
Auerbach, Berthold,_____ 871
Augustine,_____33, 44, 65, 83, 105, 119, 159,
  227, 234, 276, 317, 344, 395, 413, 428, 488,
  493, 518, 520, 521, 523, 537, 545, 557, 569, 570,
  585, 586, 598, 599, 612, 613, 619, 620, 630, 631,
  633, 707, 708, 784, 786, 788, 819, 887, 998,
  1001, 1035.
Austin, John,_____293, 533, 535
Baader, Franz von,_____ 25
Babbage, Charles,_____ 117
Babcock, Maltbie D.,_____ 208
Bacon, B. W.,_____147, 148, 149, 167
Bacon, Francis,_____36, 40, 43, 71, 138, 262,
  298, 514, 536, 541, 547, 583, 656, 722, 822, 982
Bacon, L. W., and G. B.,_____ 410
Bacon, Leonard,_____330, 899, 918
Bähr, K. C. W. F.,_____ 722
Baer, K. E. von,_____ 482
Bagehot, Walter,_____224, 658
Bailey, G. E.,_____ 249
Bain, Alexander,_____94, 96, 98
Baird, Samuel J.,_____49, 51, 404, 418, 494,
  544, 555, 571, 576, 585, 589, 606, 607, 610,
  611, 612, 615, 616, 619, 622, 630, 637, 640,
  644, 647, 660, 680, 705, 754, 771, 802, 808.
Baldwin, C. J.,____109, 332, 488, 511, 592, 743
Baldwin, J. Mark,_____ 43
Balfour, A. J.,_____3, 17, 18, 25, 43, 59,
  100, 122, 125, 215, 292, 512, 568, 771, 834,
  982, 987, 997.
Balfour, R. G.,_____ 739
Bancroft, Bishop,_____ 896
Bancroft, George,_____ 899
Baptist Magazine,_____ 396
Baptist Quarterly,_____658, 918, 948
Baptist Quarterly Review,_____ 410
Baptist Review,_____207, 575, 993
Barclay, Robert,_____ 48
Bardesanes, _____ 383
Barlow, J. L.,_____ 1038
Barlow, J. W.,_____ 405
Barnabas,_____147, 159, 235, 319
Barnes, Albert,_____741, 907, 914
Barnes, Stephen G.,_____ 272
Barrett, Elizabeth,_____ 571
Barrows, C. M.,_____ 69
Barrows, E. P.,_____ 700
Barrows, J. H.,_____ 27
Barrows, William,_____ 1001
Barry, Alfred,_____ 187
Bartlet, Vernon,_____ 905
Bartlett, S. C.,_____172, 201, 227, 532, 660,
  706, 989, 994.
Bascom, John,_____53, 55, 632
Basilides, _____151, 160, 378, 670
Bastian, H. C.,_____ 389
Baudissin, Count W. W.,_____275

Baumgarten, M.,_____ 907
Baur, F. C.,_____145, 155, 157, 158, 160, 328,
  382, 750.
Bawden, H. H.,_____28, 346, 525, 616, 983,
  992.
Baxter, Richard,_____47, 48, 205, 218, 294,
  872, 1056.
Bayle, Pierre,_____ 47
Bayne, Peter,_____100, 157
Beal, Samuel,_____ 183
Beale, Lionel,_____ 389
Beard, Charles,_____ 209
Beard, G. H.,_____ 405
Beck, ——,_____ 40
Beddoes, T. L.,_____ 380
Beebe, Alexander M.,_____ 957
Beecher, Edward,_____ 488
Beecher, H. W.,_____42, 76, 128, 147, 269,
  369, 406, 423, 790, 1047, 1052.
Beecher, Lyman,_____ 406
Beecher, Thomas K.,_____ 464
Beecher, Willis J.,_____ 141
Beet, J. A.,_____ 218
Behrends, A. J. F.,_____25, 39, 42, 102,
  367, 697, 755, 779.
Belcher, Joseph,_____ 908
Bellamy, Joseph,_____ 48
Bellarmine, R. P.,_____47, 522, 1001
Benedict, Wayland R.,_____ 80
Bengel, J. A.,_____132, 222, 661, 683, 762,
  782, 960, 1009.
Bennett, W. H.,_____ 321
Bentham, Jeremy,_____55, 439
Berdoe, Edward,_____162, 765
Berkeley, George,_____95, 96, 436
Bernard, St.,_____58, 710
Bernard, J. H.,_____120, 128, 129, 157
Bernard, T. D.,_____177, 221, 236
Bernhardt, Sarah,_____ 544
Bersier, Eugene,_____622, 821
Bertrand, H. G., Count de,_____ 682
Beryl, _____ 327
Besant, Walter,_____576, 737
Beyschlag, Willibald,_____213, 221, 310, 622,
  668.
Beza, Theodore,_____46, 777
Bible Commentary,_____238, 374, 375, 376,
  394, 396, 474, 583, 726.
Bible Dictionary, Hastings',_____118, 119,
  141, 148, 153, 165, 167, 479, 514, 933.
Bible Dictionary, Smith's,____118, 139, 147,
  153, 166, 167, 447, 449, 456, 479, 728.
Bibliotheca Fratrum Polonorum,__47, 729
Bibliotheca Sacra,_____6, 11, 12, 14, 20
  21, 29, 42, 53, 56, 62, 103, 127, 160, 162, 201,
  238, 528, 656, 790, 1046.
Bickersteth, Edward,_____ 437
Biedermann, A. Em.,_____68, 105, 119, 250
Binet, Alfred,_____ 454
Bingham, Joseph,_____ 933
Birch, Samuel,_____ 995
Birks, T. R.,_____174, 387, 488, 588, 615, 643

Bismarck, Otto von,--------------194, 401
Bissell, Edwin C.,-----166, 167, 170, 172, 309
Bittinger, J. B.,------------------------ 650
Bixby, J. T.,----65, 292, 300, 499, 530, 538, 985
Black, William,--------------------913, 1052
Blackie, John Stuart,------------------ 17
Blackstone, William,-------------------- 656
Bledsoe, Albert T.,--------------------367, 520
Bleek, Friedrich,---------------------- 149
Blount, Charles,---------------------- 414
Blunt, John H.,---------2, 86, 146, 153, 330,
383, 414, 937.
Blunt, John James,-------------------- 151
Boardman, George Dana,-----------19, 851,
942, 997.
Boardman, H. A.,--------------------- 881
Boardman, W. E.,--------------------- 344
Bodemeyer, J.,---------------------- 706
Böhl, Edward,------------------------ 762
Boehme, Jacob,------------------255, 264, 524
Boerne, Ludwig,---------------------- 561
Boethius,--------------------------253, 695
Boissier, M. L. Gaston,---------------- 989
Bolingbroke, Viscount,------------------ 414
Bonar, Horatius,-------------------650, 889
Bonnet, Charles,---------------------- 118
"Book of the Dead,"-------------------- 983
Booth, Ballington,--------------------- 904
Booth, William,----------------------- 750
Bose, see Dubose, W. P.
Bossuet, J. B.,--------------------47, 567, 821
Boston, Thomas,-----------48, 50, 802, 1018
Bowden, John,------------------------ 48
Bowen, Francis,------11, 29, 63, 68, 98, 99,
113, 121, 405, 412, 991.
Bowne, Borden P.,------6, 8, 10, 11, 43, 52,
54, 56, 60, 61, 64, 68, 71, 72, 73, 74, 76, 78,
96, 97, 99, 103, 108, 110, 125, 219, 244, 257,
261, 267, 273, 279, 280, 282, 285, 286, 294, 300,
381, 402, 405, 413, 416, 428, 493, 499, 507,
508, 536, 539, 559, 625, 655, 678, 722, 756,
794, 985, 987.
Boys, Thomas,------------------------ 133
Brace, C. L.,------------------------- 193
Bradford, A. H.,-------33, 60, 106, 406, 475,
516, 548, 594, 632, 635, 656, 677, 816, 818, 819,
1001, 1053.
Bradley, F. H.,-------------103, 276, 406, 505
Bramhall, John,---------------------- 775
Brandi, S. M.,----------------------- 910
Breckenridge, Robert J.,---------------- 49
"Bremen Lectures,"-------------------- 111
Brereton, C. H. S.,-------------------- 116
Bretschneider, K. G.,---------------46, 523
Brewer, Prof.,----------------------- 281
Bridgman, Laura,--------------------- 113
Briggs, C. A.,---------------140, 141, 489
Brinton, D. G.,----------------------- 476
British and Foreign Evangelical Review,
231, 347, 835, 845, 875.
British Quarterly,--------104, 116, 125, 152,
172, 300, 896.

British Weekly,----------------------- 738
Broadus, John A.,--------117, 138, 216, 227,
364, 452, 780, 888, 892, 931, 933, 934, 937,
948, 951, 954, 1008.
Bronson, J. M.,--------------------- 466
Brooke, Stopford A.,------------------- 988
Brooks, Kendall,-------------------434, 950
Brooks, Phillips,----------42, 122, 348, 436,
694, 700, 735, 812, 830, 909, 912.
Brooks, Thomas,---------------------- 463
Brooks, W. K.,---------64, 124, 497, 536, 673
Brougham, Henry,--------------------- 140
Brown, David,-----------------105, 744, 1014
Brown, J. Baldwin,-------------------- 131
Brown, John,------------------------ 368
Brown, T. B.,------------------------ 410
Brown, William Adams,------321, 348, 596,
612, 638.
Brown, W. R.,-----------------------83, 221
Browne, Sir Thomas,------------------- 143
Browning, Elizabeth Barrett,--------18, 59,
107, 441, 544, 571, 1023.
Browning, Robert,--------5, 38, 59, 62, 64,
107, 183, 193, 214, 218, 224, 252, 253, 262,
266, 273, 283, 298, 299, 312, 345, 366, 367, 369,
386, 398, 400, 403, 406, 420, 429, 439, 487,
489, 492, 496, 501, 506, 520, 544, 546, 549,
570, 581, 589, 642, 649, 651, 659, 692, 693,
703, 814, 987, 996, 1002, 1023, 1039.
Brownson, Orestes,-----------------37, 118
Bruce, A. Balmain,-------105, 131, 133, 139,
145, 156, 157, 160, 186, 187, 217, 237, 238,
274, 341, 414, 465, 666, 676, 745, 786, 905.
Bruch, J. F.,-----------------249, 293, 489, 497
Bryennios, Philotheos,----------------- 953
Buchanan, James,-------------------95, 857
Buchanan, Robert,-------------------- 1051
Buckle, H. T.,----------------------- 439
Buckley, J. M.,---------------------- 133
Buckner, E. D.,---------------------- 985
Büchner, Louis,----------------------- 91
Bückmann, R.,----------------------- 128
Buddeus, J. F.,--------------------46, 270
Bull, Bishop George,------------------ 217
Bulwer, Edward, Lord Lytton,---------- 645
Bunsen, J. C. C.,-------------447, 956, 995
Bunyan, John,----------40, 47, 221, 330, 462,
483, 544, 743. 827, 845, 888.
Burbank, Luther,--------------------- 632
Burgess, Ezenezer,-----------------157, 477
Burgesse, Anthony,-----------------630, 631
Burke, Edmund,---------------------- 135
Burnet, Gilbert,----------------------- 48
Burnet, Thomas,--------------------- 1023
Burnham, Sylvester,------------------- 582
Burns, Robert,----------------525, 560, 575
Burrage, Henry S.,-------------------- 938
Burroughs, John,--------------------- 469
Burton, E. D.,-------------158, 376, 571, 941
Burton, N. S.,----------------------549, 941
Bushnell, Horace,-------15, 26, 48, 103, 118,
133, 187, 245, 271, 294, 327, 335, 340, 369,

403, 433, 447, 502, 530, 541, 660, 668, 679, 728, 733, 734, 735, 736, 737, 738, 739, 813, 814, 956, 1036, 1041.

Butcher, S. H.,--------------------38, 115, 406

Butler, Joseph,----------30, 51, 71, 82, 114, 124, 232, 296, 300, 368, 417, 427, 668, 727, 771, 984.

Butler, William Archer,--------------- 317

Butterworth, H.,-----------------------437

Buttmann, Philip,---------------------- 717

Byrom, John,----------------------- 553

Byron, George Gordon, Lord,-------- 369 387, 404, 578.

C. H. M., see MacIntosh, C. H.

Cæsar, Julius,----------------------151, 1032

Caillard, Emma Marie,----------108, 470, 561, 679, 983.

Caine, T. H. Hall,------------------495, 899

Caird, Edward,-----------------6, 43, 58, 110

Caird, John,----------6, 21, 22, 29, 101, 103, 255, 258, 261, 277, 346, 352, 361, 386, 400, 415, 514, 542, 567, 571, 572, 577, 623, 638, 641, 647, 685, 691, 694, 702, 756, 798, 806, 988, 1043.

Cairns, John,-------------------------- 141

Calderwood, Henry,------5, 9, 10, 29, 34, 51, 58, 66, 67, 68, 74, 79, 85, 86, 87, 89, 93, 95, 101, 279, 302, 362, 437, 468, 500, 696, 985.

Calixtus, Georgius,------------------45, 49, 50

Calkins, P. W.,----------------------- 149

Calkins, Walcott,----------------------- 979

Calovius, Abraham,--------------------45, 52

Calthrop, Dr.,-------------------------- 348

Calvin, John,------28, 38, 45, 51, 53, 107, 140, 227, 234, 334, 344, 409, 419, 420, 514, 558, 569, 612, 613, 621, 644, 663, 664, 749, 772, 777, 781, 783, 788, 794, 808, 881, 942, 960, 969, 1008, 1034, 1048.

"Cambridge Platform,"------------904, 919

Campbell, Alexander,----------------821, 947

Campbell, George,--------------------- 128

Campbell, James M.,------------------- 798

Campbell, John M.,----------537, 548, 734, 737, 760.

Canaletto,--------------------------- 143

Candlish, James S.,-------------45, 340, 713

Candlish, Robert S.,--------476, 664, 726, 773

Canning, George,---------------------- 135

Canus, Melchior,----------------------- 47

Capes, J. M.,-------------------------- 185

Carey, H. C.,-------------------------- 536

Carlisle, Bishop of,--------------------- 1

Carlyle, Jane,------------------------- 745

Carlyle, Thomas,--------8, 40, 251, 277, 299, 309, 329, 406, 414, 469, 575.

Carman, A. S.,-------------- 358, 410, 416

Caro, E. M.,-------------------------- 101

Carpenter, W. B.,-----------------11, 156, 277

Carson, Alexander,--------------------- 938

Carson, J. C. L.,---------------------- 896

Carson, R. H.,------------------------ 896

Carter, Franklin,---------------------- 638

Carus, Paul,-------------------------- 349

Cary, Phœbe,------------------------- 987

Case, Mary E.,------------102, 276, 279, 530

Catechism, Larger,--------------------- 956

Racovian,-------------------------47, 524

Roman,----------------------------- 522

Shorter,--------------------------846, 956

Westminster,------------------52, 664, 957

Catholic Review,---------------------- 957

Cattell, J. M.,------------------------- 43

Catullus,----------------------------- 983

Cave, A. B.,-------------------------- 775

Cave, Arthur,------------------------- 205

Celsus,---------------------------192, 274

Chadbourne, P. A.,--------------------- 469

Chadwick, J. W.,---------------8, 126, 188, 198, 237, 304, 330, 473, 958, 990, 1051.

Chalmers, Thomas,--------48, 50, 124, 128, 141, 302, 394, 404, 415, 435, 616, 640, 820, 873, 1033.

Chamberlain, Jacob,----------------431, 575

Chamberlin, T. C.,------------------254, 510

Chambers, Arthur,--------------------- 1044

Chambers, T. W.,--------------17, 726, 941

Chamier, Daniel,----------------------- 46

Chandler, Arthur,------------------582, 590

Channing, William E.,----------12, 125, 694

Chapman, James,--------------------330, 474

Charles, Elizabeth,-------------------- 1026

Charles, R. H.,------------------------ 165

Charnock, Stephen,------244, 249, 259, 282, 283, 288, 362, 754, 826.

Charteris, A. H.,---------------------- 200

Chase, D. P.,------------------------- 580

Chase, F. H.,------------------------- 154

Chatham, Lord,----------------------- 190

Chaucer, Geoffrey,-------------------- 549

Chemnitz, Martin,--------------------- 45

Cheyne, T. K.,---------------137, 250, 697, 933

Chiba, Yugoro,----------------------- 180

Chillingworth, W.,---------------------- 20

Chitty, Joseph,------------------------ 38

Christian Review,-------------747, 954, 1003

Christian Union,---------------------- 1046

Christlieb, Theodor,------5, 53, 95, 105, 117, 131, 132, 157, 160, 162, 351, 414.

Chrysostom, John,----------39, 148, 796, 934

Church Quarterly Review,-------------- 704

Cicero,----------IV., 40, 53, 300, 425, 429, 516, 575, 589, 598, 647, 814, 887, 989.

Clark, G. W.,------------------------- 951

Clarke, Dorus,------------------------ 16

Clarke, J. C. C.,----------------246, 286, 755

Clarke, J. Freeman,--------58, 179, 186, 205, 329, 376, 394, 664, 729.

Clarke, Samuel,-------73, 85, 86, 279, 301, 330

Clarke, W. N.,------4, 22, 43, 63, 68, 76, 88, 116, 145, 205, 210, 221, 255, 264, 269, 271, 280, 284, 286, 295, 387, 721, 855.

Clay, Henry,-------------------------- 815

Clement of Alexandria,--------44, 154, 167, 225, 998, 1041.

Clement of Rome,_____149, 152, 153, 159, 312, 910, 928.
Clifford, W. K._____399, 511
Clough, A. H.,_____259, 819
Coats, A. S.,_____ 769
Cobbe, Frances Power,_____216, 404, 918, 981, 990, 991.
Cocceius, Johannes,_____46, 50, 612, 613
Cocker, B. F._____63, 414
Coe, E. B.,_____ 275
Coe, G. A.,_____599, 812
Colby, H. F.,_____ 978
Colegrove, F. W.,_____488, 489
Coleman, Lyman,_____908, 911, 914, 937, 954
Coleridge, Hartley,_____437, 495
Coleridge, Lord,_____ 345
Coleridge, Samuel T.,_____4, 18, 24, 30, 54, 72, 124, 203, 205, 252, 424, 488, 562, 581, 611, 939.
Colestock, H. T.,_____294, 721
Comte, Auguste,_____6, 11, 57, 531, 567
Conant, T. J.,_____224, 225, 933, 937, 951
Conder, Josiah,_____ 788
Condillac, E. B. de,_____ 91
Cone, Orello,_____ 610
Congdon, H. W.,_____ 449
Constantine,_____ 898
Constantinople, Council of,_____ 695
"Constitution of the Holy Apostles," 978
Contemporary Review,_____95, 97
Conybeare and Howson,_____668, 914, 936, 942.
Cook, Joseph,_____304, 344, 482, 537, 558, 1010.
Cooke, J. P.,_____34, 194, 436, 468, 676
Corelli, Marie,_____283, 542
Correggio, _____ 723
Cotterill, Henry,_____ 397
Cotton, John,_____ 904
Cousin, Victor,_____55, 61, 63, 97
Cowper, B. H.,_____ 159
Cox, Samuel,_____122, 156, 397, 437, 1023
Craig, Oscar,_____ 8
Cramer, H.,_____ 748
Cranch, C. P.,_____ 578
Crane, Frank,____21, 217, 230, 411, 425, 447, 599, 691, 841, 1047, 1050.
Crapsey, A. S.,_____ 952
Crawford, Thomas J.,_____476, 721, 722, 727, 733, 735, 736, 744, 771, 836.
Cremer, H.,_____221, 291, 484, 717, 721, 851, 887, 892, 935.
Crippen, T. G.,_____748, 750
Crooker, J. H.,_____217, 315
Crookes, William,_____ 252
Crooks and Hurst,_____ 42
Crosby, Alpheus,_____1015, 1023
Crosby, Fannie J.,_____ 515
Crosby, Howard,_____ 710
Croskery, Thomas,_____ 396
Crowell, William,_____ 929
Cudworth, Ralph,_____321, 376, 380, 1025

Culver, S. W.,_____ 757
Cumming, John,_____ 140
Cunningham, John,_____935, 952, 980
Cunningham, William,_____41, 368, 523, 614, 619, 640, 644, 744, 773, 779, 823, 912.
Curry, Daniel,_____285, 745
"Current Discussions in Theology," 626, 695, 767.
Curtis, E. L.,_____ 167
Curtis, T. F.,_____89, 157, 179, 723, 892, 900, 906, 940, 952, 956, 959, 972, 973, 977, 980
Curtiss, S. I.,_____ 538
Curtius, Georg,_____ 20
Cuvier, Georges,_____77, 444
Cyprian,_____33, 152, 620, 901, 1001
Cyril,_____ 342
Cyrus,_____ 989
Dabney, R. L.,_____49, 418, 497, 601, 603, 616, 864.
Dagg, J. L.,_____892, 896, 900, 926, 933, 951, 959.
Daggett, Dr.,_____ 518
Dale, J. W.,_____ 934
Dale, R. W.,_____42, 148, 238, 272, 369, 592, 632, 636, 654, 680, 721, 735, 750, 754, 759, 802, 803, 806, 854, 929.
Dalgairns, J. B.,_____ 8
Dalman, G. H.,_____313, 889
Damien, Peter,_____364, 757
Dana, James D.,_____224, 395, 396, 403, 473, 481.
Danforth, G. F.,_____ 771
Dannhauer, J. C.,_____45, 50
Dante Alighieri,_____45, 138, 256, 263, 271, 443, 447, 451, 492, 569, 653, 987, 1001, 1009, 1041, 1053.
D'Arcy, C. F.,_____35, 291, 332
Darwin, Charles,_____36, 57, 64, 468, 473, 480, 526, 534.
Darwin, G. H.,_____ 477
Daub, Carl,_____ 46
Davids, Rhys,_____ 182
Davidson, A. B.,_____134, 217, 667
Davidson, Samuel,_____897, 929
Davis, J. W.,_____ 652
Dawkins, W. Boyd,_____ 532
Dawson, J. W.,_____64, 412, 482, 525, 532
Day, H. N._____24, 213, 345, 504
Declaratory Act, Free Church of Scotland, _____ 641
DeCoverley, Sir Roger,_____ 649
Deems, C. F.,_____ 901
Defoe, Daniel,_____ 431
Delbœuf, Joseph,_____ 550
Delitzsch, Franz,_____137, 227, 477, 484, 487, 510, 520, 644, 647, 697, 701, 850, 998, 1003, 1023, 1039.
De Marchi, Joseph,_____ 191
Denney, James,_____18, 214, 237, 339, 590, 596, 633, 639, 640, 650, 721, 734, 738, 774, 781, 852, 853, 910, 940, 1011, 1025, 1040, 1041

Denovau, Joshua,_____339, 548, 710, 711, 819, 858, 800.

De Quincey, Thomas,_____128, 1003

Descartes, René,_____55, 262, 279, 299, 1002

Deutsch, Emanuel,_____ 675

DeWette, W. M. L.,_____15, 41, 46, 153, 517, 614, 661, 781.

Dewey, John, _____22, 40, 43, 51, 251, 252, 281, 300, 502, 505, 506, 982.

De Witt, John,_____43, 778

Dexter, Henry M.,_____892, 901, 903, 907, 911, 914, 916, 917, 918, 924, 928, 929, 937, 952, 1056.

Dick, John,_____48, 269, 353, 358

Dickens, Charles,_____223, 492

Dickey, F. O.,_____ 663

Dickson, W. P.,_____ 562

Didache,_____159, 311, 410, 892, 906, 937, 938.

Diestel, Ludwig,_____ 56

Dillmann, August,_____169, 268, 375, 377

Diman, J. L.,_____6, 66, 72, 76, 77, 79, 82, 84, 95, 104, 113, 129, 414, 433, 435, 438, 532, 535, 801.

Dinsmore, C. A.,_____ 646

Diognetus, _____147, 311

Dionysius, _____274, 910

Dippel, J. K., _____ 744

Disraeli, Benjamin,_____135, 447

Dix, Morgan,_____ 103

Dobney, H. H.,_____998, 1036

Doddridge, Philip,_____ 453

Dodge, Ebenezer,_____146, 448, 590

Dods, Marcus,_____158, 181, 321, 337, 394, 938.

Döederlein, L.,_____ 46

Döllinger, J. J. I.,_____888, 935

Dorner, A. J.,_____ 523

Dorner, I. A.,_____5, 13, 18, 21, 29, 30, 33, 34, 46, 51, 62, 69, 87, 104, 106, 118, 159, 187, 208, 238, 245, 253, 259, 265, 271, 274, 275, 278, 282, 296, 305, 309, 320, 324, 328, 331, 333, 337, 338, 344, 386, 388, 408, 411, 412, 413, 418, 439, 493, 523, 549, 550, 555, 565, 569, 596, 598, 599, 600, 604, 615, 620, 621, 631, 651, 654, 656, 669, 670, 671, 672, 673, 676, 677, 680, 683, 685, 688, 689, 693, 694, 695, 698, 699, 702, 707, 709, 721, 737, 741, 746, 754, 761, 767, 776, 793, 799, 816, 830, 842, 864, 866, 893, 911, 947, 964, 967, 981, 991, 1002, 1014, 1017, 1021, 1024, 1036, 1039, 1051.

Douglas, Frederick,_____ 439

Dove, Patrick E.,_____2, 3, 29, 39, 66, 71, 85, 86, 87, 103.

Doyle, Father,_____ 958

Dreiäuglein, _____ 253

Driver, S. R.,_____164, 166, 223

Drummond, Henry,_____26, 34, 224, 264, 266, 401, 441, 466, 528, 539, 804, 806, 814, 824, 827, 923.

Dubois, A. J.,_____60, 122, 810

Dubois, Eugene,_____ 471

Dubose, W. P.,_____ 18

Dudley, H. E.,_____ 803

Düsselfhoff,_____338, 828

Duff, Alexander,_____ 900

Duncan, G. M.,_____ 6f

Duncan, John,_____105, 21?

Dunn, Martha Baker,_____ 36

Duns Scotus, Johannes,_____45, 244, 26?, 299.

Du Prel, Karl,_____ 550

Duryea, Dr.,_____ 364

Dwight, Timothy,_____48, 300, 323, 573, 593, 608, 820, 826, 936, 977, 1049.

Dwinell, J. E.,_____ 550

Eaches, O. P.,_____ 222

Ebers, Georg,_____ 995

Ebrard, J. H. A.,_____21, 46, 52, 62, 72, 174, 217, 338, 449, 462, 477, 485, 493, 514, 679, 686, 762, 945, 1022.

Eccles, Robert Kerr,_____37, 84

Eddy, Mary Baker G.,_____ 573

Edersheim, Alfred,_____141, 172, 227, 902

Edison, Thomas A.,_____206

Edwards, Jonathan,_____19, 36, 48, 49, 50, 51, 208, 219, 263, 265, 270, 271, 278, 290, 299, 300, 333, 342, 362, 364, 365, 366, 399, 401, 402, 416, 417, 442, 461, 494, 504, 507, 518, 554, 555, 556, 557, 571, 577, 582, 585, 586, 593, 594, 595, 607, 612, 613, 619, 622, 637, 644, 668, 683, 699, 751, 754, 790, 800, 805, 808, 818, 820, 826, 840, 843, 845, 862, 864, 867, 868, 886, 952, 953, 971, 1008, 1029, 1035, 1056.

Edwards, Jonathan, Jr.,_____275, 278, 358, 362, 504, 999, 1051.

Eichhorn, Carl,_____105, 253

Elam, Charles,_____ 635

Elder, William,_____118, 121

Eliot, George,_____210, 492, 561, 575, 766, 988, 1048.

Ellicott, C. J.,_____35, 307, 318, 341, 450, 782, 856, 1017.

Elliott, E. B.,_____139, 151, 449, 910, 1001, 1009, 1010, 1013, 1015.

Ellis, George E.,_____308, 350, 598, 729

Emerson, G. H.,_____ 1040

Emerson, R. W.,_____4, 39, 97, 107, 119, 139, 151, 175, 203, 207, 256, 287, 296, 330, 406, 409, 416, 441, 496, 539, 567, 575, 609, 613, 643, 653, 724, 730, 804, 841, 1025, 1041.

Emmons, Nathanael, ____48, 359, 415, 416, 585, 606, 607, 608, 613, 823.

Empedocles, _____ 7

Encyclopædia Britannica,_____96, 149, 156, 191, 300, 411, 524, 586, 749, 750, 893.

" Endless Future, The,"_____ 1054

Epictetus, _____185, 425

Epicurus, _____184, 299

Epiphanius, _____319, 669

Episcoplus, Simon,_____47, 602

Erasmus,_____36, 3?

Erdmann, J. E.,_____ ?01

Ernesti, H. F. T. L.,----------------491, 563
Errett, Isaac,----------------------- 947
Erskine, Lord,----------------------- 986
Erskine, Thomas,--- ----------------351, 787
Estes, H. C.,------------------------ 998
Euripides, --------------------------- 582
Eusebius, --------------------------- 410
Evans, Christmas,-------------------- 245
Evans, L. J.,----------------229, 706, 999
Everett, C. C.,------------2, 6, 695, 731, 990
Ewald, J. L.,------------------------ 318
Expositor, -------------------------- 1025
Expositor's Greek Testament,----------135,
  699, 719, 948.
Faber, F. W.,------------------301, 334, 776
Faber, G. S.,------------------------ 1014
Fabri, Friedrich,------------------- 91
Fairbairn, A. M.,--------20, 59, 62, 63, 125,
  159, 186, 335, 354, 366, 403, 507, 536, 579, 755,
  910, 991.
Fairbairn, Patrick,------15, 135, 449, 668,
  726, 791, 1015.
Fairchild, James H.,----------300, 504, 559
"Faith and Free Thought,"---------- 232
"Faiths of the World,"-------------- 179
Farley, Robert G.,------------------- 773
Farrar, A. S.,--------53, 132, 135, 158, 403,
  420, 427, 433, 459.
Farrar, F. W.,------112, 124, 129, 132, 135,
  141, 157, 160, 179, 187, 193, 385, 428, 451, 456,
  479, 585, 666, 679, 989, 1039, 1046.
Farrer, J. A.,----------------------- 180
Faunce, D. W.,----------------------- 501
Faunce, W. H. P.--------------------- 221
Fechner, G. T.,---------------------- 281
Felix of Urgella,-------------------- 744
Ferguson, W. L.,--------------------- 152
Ferrier, J. F.,---------------------- 469
Feuerbach, L.,--------------------14, 83, 91
Fichte, J. G.,------------3, 40, 97, 407, 467,
  510, 616.
Fick, August,----------------------- 20
Finney, C. G.--------48, 238, 262, 278, 291,
  299, 300, 367, 546, 783, 818, 877.
Firmilianus, ------------------------ 153
Fischer, Kuno,---------------------- 512
Fish, E. J.,-------------896, 901, 916, 918, 924
Fisher, G. P.,------2, 4, 15, 21, 22, 34, 37,
  40, 41, 49, 51, 53, 58, 60, 65, 70, 71,
  72, 79, 87, 102, 115, 117, 121, 130, 131, 132,
  150, 152, 179, 189, 191, 202, 228, 231, 237, 305,
  424, 453, 456, 508, 532, 545, 580, 607. 608,
  613, 615, 616, 617, 664, 668, 936, 969, 1046.
Fiske, D. T.,----------------------- 358
Fiske, John,------97, 104, 369, 559, 844, 899,
  900, 908, 953, 985, 987.
Fitch, E. T.,----------------365, 554, 783
Fitzgerald, Prof.,------------------.. 416
Fleming, William,--------------6, 33, 53, 539
Flint, Austin,---------------------- 389
Flint, Robert--------6. 58, 63, 66, 73, 75, 79,
  80, 81, 85, 100. 112, 367. 404. 929.

Fock, Otto,------------------------- 733
Fonsegrive, G. L.,------------------- 512
Forbes, Archibald,------------------- 228
Forbes, G. M.,---------12, 43, 102, 291, 360
Forbes, John,----------------------- 360
Ford, David B.,--------------------- 934
Formula of Concord,------------------ 792
Formula of Consensus,---------------- 209
Forrest, D. W.,----------------180, 675, 988
Forrest, Edwin,--------------------- 577
Forster, W. E.,--------------------- 990
Forsyth, P. T.,--------------------26, 755
Foster, G. B.,--------120, 197, 201, 299, 305,
  311, 444, 720, 733, 741, 750, 755, 765, 798.
Foster, John,-----------------35, 128, 1047
Foster, R. V.,--------------------223, 783
"Foundations of our Faith,"----5, 79, 865
Fox, Caroline,---------------------- 461
Fox, George,--------------------48, 1056
Fox, L. A.,------------------------- 1029
Fox, Norman,--------------215, 663, 949, 959
Francis de Sales,------------------- 32
Francis of Assisi,----------------33, 984
Frank, F. H. R.,-------------------- 4
Frank, Sebastian,------------------- 800
Franklin, Benjamin,----------------363, 431
Fraser, A. C.,--------------------63, 417
Freer, G.,-------------------------- 744
French, Clara,---------------------- 261
Frere, B.,-------------------------- 844
Froschammer, J.,-------------491, 493, 494
Frothingham, A. L.,----------------- 380
Froude, James A.,--------------368, 438, 564
Fürst, Julius,---------------------- 669
Fuller, Andrew,------15, 47, 50, 51, 52, 368,
  773, 793, 808, 826, 829, 1018.
Fuller, Margaret,------------------- 369
Fuller, Thomas,----------------128, 290, 633
Fullerton, G. S.,-----------------255, 1021
Galton, Francis,------83, 439, 492, 495, 496,
  632.
Gambold, John,---------------------- 888
Gannett, W. C.,--------------------202, 290
Ganse, H. G.,----------------------- 351
Garbett, Edward,----------112, 177, 179, 193
Garbett, James,--------------------- 776
Gardiner, F.,--------------137, 139, 227, 322
Gardiner, H. N.,-------------------104, 137
Garibaldi, Giuseppe,---------------- 766
Garrison, W. E.,-------------------- 947
Garvie, A. E.,----------------------6, 270
Gassendi, Pierre,-----------------298, 373
Gates, Errett,---------------------- 948
Gaussen, L.,------------------------ 209
Gear, H. L.,------------------------ 344
Geddie, John,----------------------- 900
Geikie, Archibald,------------------ 225
Geikie, Cunningham,-------------156, 661
Gemara, ---------------------------- 931
Genung, J. F.,------------115, 300, 459, 994
George, Henry------------------530, 748
George, N. D.,--------------------- 1056

Gerhard, John,-------- ---4, 45, 244, 261, 969
Gerhardt, Paul,------------------------ 282
Gerhart, E. V.,------------------------ 290
Gesenius, William,--------------------- 944
Gess, W. F.,----------102, 686, 687, 688, 704
Geulinx, Arnold,----------------------- 94
Gibbon, Edward,-------47, 192, 204, 682, 966
Giesebrecht, Friedrich,---------------- 134
Gieseler, J. C. L.,------------------382, 914
Gifford, Lord,------------------------- 413
Gifford, O. P.,------------------------ 58
Gilbert, George H.,-------------------- 321
Gilder, R. W.,------------------------- 683
Gildersleeve, B. L.,------------------- 988
Gilfillan, George,--------------------- 410
Gill, John,------------------------47, 793
Gillespie, William H.,-----------62, 73, 85
Girdlestone, R. B.,--------------850, 864, 892
Gladden, Washington,-----56, 120, 122, 140,
   141, 237, 956.
Gladstone, W. E.,------44, 122, 223, 314, 396
Glennie, J. S. Stuart-,------------------ 527
Gloatz, Paul,-------------------------- 122
Godet, F.,----------21, 131, 150, 152, 158, 258,
   261, 309, 335, 337, 448, 487, 584, 758, 763.
Göschel, C. F.,----------------110, 484, 491
Goethe, J. W. von,------3, 20, 21, 24, 39,
   40, 60, 101, 117, 120, 188, 224, 309, 386, 444,
   455, 458, 511, 517, 520, 542, 558, 561, 562, 575,
   645, 691, 814, 990.
Goodwin, D. R.,----------------483, 485, 1017
Goodwin, Thomas,---------------------- 576
Goodwin, W. W.,----------------------- 933
Gordon, A. J.,------128, 133, 138, 140, 216,
   234, 274, 281, 285, 333, 359, 475, 529, 604,
   705, 732, 737, 775, 776, 782, 824, 834, 847, 848,
   889, 893, 901, 910, 911, 913, 927, 935, 948,
   1004, 1013, 1014, 1016, 1022.
Gordon, George A.,------17, 19, 28, 65, 188,
   346, 348, 397, 402, 405, 415, 492, 502, 542, 732,
   751, 790.
Gordon, H. A.,------------------------ 283
Gore, Charles,------12, 16, 25, 33, 112, 113,
   120, 121, 129, 164, 173, 187, 198, 214, 218,
   229, 240, 305, 321, 329, 333, 340, 351, 389, 414,
   500, 598, 671, 673, 679, 783, 911, 1001.
Gough, John B.,----------------------- 641
Goulbourn, E. M.,----------------1023, 1054
Gould, E. P.,--------------------720, 1046
Gould, S. Baring-,--------316, 326, 377, 457,
   562, 722, 733, 915, 933, 1004, 1007.
Grafton, Bishop,---------------------- 955
Grant, U. S.,-------------------------- 430
Gratry, ------,----------------------- 267
Grau, R. F.,--------------------------- 5
Gray, Asa,-----------------------470, 478
"Great Religions of the World,"----- 186
Green, J. R.,--------------------149, 557
Green, T. H.,-------------19, 43, 176, 505, 615
Green, W. H.,------167, 172, 225, 231, 375,
   477, 994.
Greenleaf, Simon,--------------------- 141

Greg, W. R.,--------------------135, 548, 758
Gregorovius, Ferdinand,--------------- 651
Gregory the Great,-------------------- 1001
Gregory, D. S.,----------------302, 447, 504
Gregory Nazianzen,---------------1, 748, 917
Gregory Nyssenus,---------44, 493, 620, 747
Gretillat, Augustin,------------------- 49
Grey, Lady Jane,---------------------- 33
Griffin, E. P.,------------------------ 733
Grimm, K. L. W.,---------------------- 782
Grimm-Wilke,---------------------717, 935
Grisi, Mme.,-------------------------- 650
Gröbler, Paul,------------------------ 1023
Grote, George,------------------156, 214
Grotius, Hugo,-------------47, 740, 741, 1009
Gubelmann, J. S.,--------------------- 317
Guericke, H. E. F.,-----330, 379, 382, 384,
   672, 744, 907.
Guizot, F.,---------------------193, 409
Gulick, J. T.,------------------------ 530
Gulliver, Julia H.,-------------------- 506
Gunsaulus, F. W.,----------------4, 122, 350
Guyon, Mme. de la Motte,----------32, 782
Guyot, Arnold,------------224, 374, 395, 477
Gwatkin, Henry,----------------------- 329
Hackett, H. B.,---------27, 113, 157, 452, 733,
   907, 915, 946, 999, 1005.
Hadley, James,----------------585, 586, 991
Hadrian, ------------------------------ 990
Haeckel, Ernst,----------------343, 471, 496
Hagenbach, K. P.,-----14, 36, 41, 44, 49, 50,
   51, 321, 323, 331, 382, 523, 601, 603, 607, 621,
   744, 833, 903.
Hahn, Aaron,-------------------------- 89
Hahn, G. L.,-------------------------- 483
Hales, William,----------------------- 224
Haley, John W.,-------------174, 228, 1054
Hall, Charles Cuthbert,---------------- 770
Hall, Edwin,-------------------------- 938
Hall, G. Stanley,---------------------- 812
Hall, James,-------------------------- 482
Hall, John,--------------------------589, 977
Hall, Joseph,------------------------- 836
Hall, Robert,-------47, 70, 74, 463, 793, 820,
   932, 972, 977, 978, 996.
Hallam, A. H.,--------115, 214, 303, 368, 437,
   703.
Haller, ------,----------------------- 229
Hamerton, P. G.,---------------------- 20
Hamilton, D. H.,----------------121, 437
Hamilton, Sir Wm.,------3, 7, 8, 9, 10, 34,
   39, 40, 66, 74, 96, 98, 121, 153, 516, 1002.
Hamlin, Cyrus,----------------------- 350
Hammond, W. A.,----------------281, 590
Hanna, W. T. C.,---------------------- 153
Hanna, William,-----------------699, 1018
Hanne, J. W.,-------------------105, 415
Hare, Julius Charles,-----------317, 556, 898
Harnack, A.,------46, 125, 130, 148, 152, 153,
   154, 158, 163, 208, 379, 433, 446, 456, 598.
   621, 683, 722, 729, 911, 935, 937.
Harnoch, G. A.,---------------------- 382

Harris, ———,_____ 467
Harris, George,_____26, 203, 293, 494, 571, 701, 787.
Harris, J. H.,_____103, 303
Harris, J. Rendel,_____ 151
Harris, Samuel,_____11, 51, 52, 60, 64, 65, 67, 69, 72, 92, 100, 133, 180, 204, 253, 255, 291, 468, 486, 499, 572, 600, 654, 695, 700, 1014, 1023.
Harris, W. T.,_____43, 62, 86
Harrison, Frederick,_____19, 57
Hart, A. S.,_____ 458
Hartmann, E. von,_____78, 80, 105, 404
Hartmann, Robert,_____ 473
Harvey, H.,_____42, 897, 917, 929, 934
Harvey, Lord,_____ 229
Hase, Karl,_____49, 50, 51, 158, 518, 558, 583, 621, 686, 702, 991, 1023.
Hastings' Bible Dictionary,_____118, 119, 141, 148, 153, 165, 167, 394, 479, 514, 933.
Hatch, Edwin,_____27, 44, 146, 255, 321, 389, 666, 700, 840, 897, 913.
Haug, Martin,_____ 382
Haven, Joseph,_____301, 437, 504
Hawthorne, Nathaniel,_____363, 400, 405, 496, 578, 645.
Hay, John,_____ 587
Hazard, R. G.,_____39, 279, 362, 504, 794, 814
Heagle, David,_____ 982
Heard, J. B.,_____ 484
Heber, Reginald,_____ 2
Hebert, C.,_____ 968
Hedge, F. H.,_____75, 377, 404
Hegel, G. W. F.,_____20, 27, 42, 55, 100, 101, 115, 176, 344, 378, 407, 550, 581, 653.
Heine, Heinrich,_____23, 104, 345, 562, 567
Helmholtz, H. L. F.,_____ 94
Hemphill, Samuel,_____148, 149, 151
Henderson, E.,_____128, 198, 199, 200, 204, 210, 216, 322, 614.
Hengstenberg, E. W.,_____319, 659, 668, 1009, 1010, 1014.
Henly, William Ernest,_____ 507
Henry VIII,_____ 26
Henry, Matthew,_____525, 743, 772
Henslow, George,_____469, 815
Henson, P. S.,_____122, 920
Heraclitus,_____222, 506
Herbert of Cherbury, Lord Edward,__ 37, 414.
Herbert, George_____15, 34, 37, 355, 414
Herbert, Thomas M.,_____11, 66, 94
Herder, J. G.,_____46, 230
Hermann, ———,_____46, 900
Hermas,_____ 159, 312
Herodotus,_____181, 250, 934
Herrick, C. L.,_____ 252
Herrick, Robert,_____ 362
Herron, G. D.,_____ 570
Herschel, J. F. W.,_____91, 99, 412
Hersey, H. E.,_____194, 436

Hershon, P. I.,_____ 501
Hervey, Arthur C.,_____ 229
Herzog, Encyclopædia,_____21, 33, 91, 158, 187, 368, 377, 382, 404, 444, 617, 670, 686, 700, 754, 868, 998, 1003, 1023.
Hesiod,_____391, 526
Hickok, L. P.,_____10, 43, 53, 301
Hicks, L. E.,_____75, 225, 403
Hilary (Hilarius)_____619, 620
Hildebrand,_____ 905
Hilgenfeld, A. B. C. C.,_____ 161
Hill, D. J.,_____8, 51, 58, 98, 120, 195, 319, 467, 586.
Hill, George,_____358, 368
Hill, Rowland,_____ 577, 78C
Hill, Thomas,_____ 92
Hillel,_____ 931
Hilprecht, H. V.,_____ 532
Hinton, James,_____5, 308
Hippolytus,_____ 159
Hiscox, Edward T.,_____ 929
Hitchcock, Edward,_____ 124
Hitchcock, R. D.,_____897, 1017
Hobbes, Thomas,_____40, 124, 298, 461, 567
Hodge, A. A.,_____49, 50, 121, 198, 323, 352, 362, 435, 486, 557, 586, 644, 688, 693, 710, 712, 728, 784, 794, 795, 836, 862, 910, 1014, 1029, 1044, 1056.
Hodge, Charles,_____1, 21, 27, 28, 30, 33, 49, 51, 52, 53, 100, 103, 132, 198, 213, 217, 272, 300, 328, 362, 397, 404, 413, 418, 420, 453, 480, 491, 514, 557, 559, 582, 587, 602, 612, 614, 616, 619, 622, 643, 655, 664, 686, 688, 601, 696, 706, 708, 741, 771, 781, 784, 792, 820, 825, 843, 846, 868, 881, 929, 982, 1001, 1052.
Hodge, C. W.,_____ 6
Hodgson, S. H.,_____5, 15, 100, 288, 512
Höffding, H.,_____458, 467
Hofmann, J. C. K. von,_____41, 68, 320, 519, 686, 722.
Hofmann, R. H.,_____ 503
Holbach, Baron Paul H. d',_____ 91
Holland, H. S.,_____22, 838
Holland, J. G.,_____91, 240
Hollaz, David,_____45, 261, 558. 615
Holliman, Ezekiel,_____ 949
Holmes, O. W.,_____369, 405, 496, 643, 755, 984.
Holzmann, ———,_____ 161
Homer,_____161, 404
Hood, Thomas,_____ 36
Hooker, Richard,_____48, 209, 218 518, 538, 548, 584, 686, 700, 781, 787, 808, 896, 897, 929.
Hopkins, Mark,_____4, 6, 25, 58, 77, 79, 93, 95, 120, 121, 122, 251, 270, 300, 301, 374, 380, 404, 405, 406, 416, 434, 435, 438, 450, 469, 503, 524, 525, 529, 537, 571, 679, 815, 839, 842.
Hopkins, Samuel,_____48, 271, 415, 416, 417, 467, 494, 518, 567, 593, 606, 607, 608, 613, 643, 754, 771, 772, 820. 842.

Horace,------------------124, 156, 190, 294, 581
Hort, F. J. A.,-----------------------154, 905
Hovey, Alvah,------5, 34, 45, 50, 102, 114,
  147, 153, 155, 197, 223, 227, 230, 255, 273,
  307, 316, 388, 404, 469, 486, 544, 567, 618, 624,
  629, 636, 662, 681, 688, 696, 697, 700, 702, 708,
  721, 735, 738, 739, 756, 779, 782, 784, 786, 787,
  823, 825, 852, 881, 890, 938, 954, 960, 980, 982,
  984, 985, 992, 998, 999, 1003, 1008, 1012, 102ა,
  1038, 1039, 1054.
Howard, George E.,-------------------- 530
Howe, John,----------47, 48, 52, 333, 334, 516
Howell, R. B. C., ------------------918, 980
Howland, S. W.,----------------------- 526
Howson, J. S.,------------------------- 160
Hudson, C. F.,-----------------------998, 1036
Hudson, Thomas J.,-------------------- 465
Hudson, Thompson J.,------281, 381, 454,
  458, 983.
Hughes, Archbishop,------------------- 959
Hughes, Thomas,------------------570, 679
Hugo, Victor,-------------------56, 453, 984
Humboldt, Alexander von,------1, 259, 412,
  480.
Hume, David,------43, 57, 73, 95, 121, 127,
  135, 175, 433, 893, 997, 1001.
Hunt, A. E.,-------------------------- 529
Hunt, John,-----------------------100, 896
Huntingdon, Wm.,------------------766, 907
Hurter, H.,---------------------------- 47
Huther, J. E.,-----------------------307, 902
Hutter, Leonhard,---------------------- 45
Hutton, R. H.,------27, 59, 67, 70, 82, 100,
  125, 131, 160, 162, 192, 204, 347, 351, 408, 440,
  511, 561, 564, 565, 571, 646, 667, 777, 982.
Huxley, Thomas,------57, 60, 76, 83, 94, 96,
  124, 127, 389, 392, 396, 466, 468, 470, 471,
  472, 480, 502, 575, 990.
Hyde, W. D.,-------------------------- 433
Hyslop, James H.,--------------------- 654
Iamblicus, -------------------------- 111
Ignatius,----------------44, 149, 159, 311, 312
Illingworth, J. R.,------4, 53, 72, 128, 253,
  346.
Immer, A.,--------------------------- 177
Independent, --------------------------- 977
Inge, W. R.,------31, 33, 237, 311, 800, 841
Ingelow, Jean,----------------------- 1042
Ingersoll, Robert G.,------38, 135, 159, 365,
  496, 570, 1050.
Ingham, Richard,-------------------934, 951
Interior, ----------------------------- 977
Ireland, W. W.,-------------------207, 281
Irenæus, ---------147, 152, 319, 620, 910, 998
Irving, Edward,--------132, 439, 744, 745,
  746, 747, 759.
Isocrates,-------------------------180, 222
Issel, Ernst,------------------------- 274
Iverach, James,----------------11, 79, 97
Jackson, A. V. W.,--------------------- 382
Jackson, A. W.,------103, 407, 501, 649, 1047

Jackson, William,---------------------- 105Ნ
Jacob, G. A.,--------887, 896, 912, 914, 915,
  917, 948, 952, 960, 961, 965, 980.
Jacobi, F. H.,-------14, 29, 46, 61, 81, 838, 951
Jahn, Johann,------------------------ 722
Jahrbuch für deutsche Theologie,---- 708,
  754, 1018.
James, William,------4, 33, 42, 55, 94, 96, 98,
  111, 122, 182, 274, 276, 281, 338, 403, 435,
  467, 468, 488, 504, 511, 536, 748, 806, 811,
  829, 831, 841, 985, 988, 1002.
Janet, Paul,------62, 75, 79, 91, 262, 401, 404,
  435, 504.
Janósik, ------,-----------------------.--- 525
Jansen, Cornelius,--------------------- 47
Jastrow, Morris, Jr.,------------------- 408
Jefferson, Charles E.,------------------ 953
Jellett, J. H.,-----------------------232, 437
Jenkyn, Thomas W.,------------------- 773
Jensen, ------,----------------------- 408
Jerome,----------148, 152, 159, 429, 491, 597,
  796, 914, 915.
Jerrold, Douglas,--------------------- 42
Jevons, W. S.,----------------------66, 124
John of Damascus,--------44, 344, 487, 671,
  673, 695.
John the Evangelist,------------------- 1
Johns, C. H. W.,----------------------- 169
Johnson, E. H.,------201, 281, 293, 297, 339,
  340, 347, 357, 376, 377, 383, 743, 785, 792, 824,
  854, 957, 1017.
Johnson, F. H.,-------------------25, 407, 470
Johnson, Franklin,-------------153, 235, 403
Johnson, Herrick,--------------------- 779
Johnson, Samuel,------36, 297, 525, 560, 575,
  1047.
Johnson's Cyclopædia,----------------- 1047
Johnstone, Robert,---------- -------- 708
Jones, E. Griffith-,---------119, 466, 528, 583,
  625, 657, 852.
Jones, Henry,--------101, 103, 108, 266, 291,
  406, 540.
Jonson, Ben,----------------------- 461
Josephus,--------144, 166, 226, 448, 947, 996
Jouffroy, T. S.,---------------------301, 1002
Journal of Christian Philosophy,------ 96
Jowett, Benjamin,-------------------728, 781
Judson, Adoniram,--------------194, 938, 960
Jukes, Andrew,--------------------726, 1039
Julian, ---------------------------- 598
Justin Martyr,------148, 152, 319, 410, 665,
  671, 675, 747, 997.
Juvenal, ---------------------------- 156
Kähler, Martin,---------------------- 503
Kaftan, J. W. M.,--------5, 14, 21, 25, 45, 46,
  207, 274, 520, 568, 569, 574, 649, 752, 839,
  856.
Kahnis, K. F. A.,------14, 20, 46, 52, 200,
  243, 247, 261, 49Ი, 493, 652, 696, 702, 705,
  795, 929.
Kane, Elisha Kent,-----------------40, 76ხ

Kant, Immanuel,------4, 6, 10, 21, 29, 43, 46, 53, 55, 61, 73, 75, 77, 79, 82, 85, 86, 87, 95, 401, 427, 488, 489, 498, 502, 504, 510, 536, 545, 581, 643, 655, 800, 813, 839, 988, 1002.

Keane, A. H.,------471, 477, 530

Keats, John,------120

Keble, John,------139, 526, 583, 675

Kedney, J. S.,------379

Keen, W. W.,------59, 731

Keil, J. K. F.,------477, 722

Keim, Theodor,------131

Keller, Helen,------66, 216, 478

Kellogg, S. H.,------182, 352, 1044

Kelly, William,------1009, 1015

Kelso, J. A.,------169

Kempis, Thomas à,------32, 556

Ken, Thomas,------916

Kendall, Amos,------893

Kendall, Henry,------622

Kendrick, A. C.,------152, 234, 316, 627, 661, 699, 708, 934, 947, 952, 1004, 1014, 1033.

Kennard, J. S.,------648

Kennedy, John,------131

Kenyon, F. G.,------141, 169

Kidd, Benjamin,------17, 194, 426, 567, 813, 981.

Kilpatrick, T. B.,------164

King, H. C.,------125, 328

King, H. M.,------427, 896

Kingsley, Charles,------183, 305, 421, 442, 473

Kipling, Rudyard,------420

Kirk, Dr.,------291

Kitto, John,------932

Kloppenburg, John,------614

Knapp, Georg Christian,------46

Knight, William A.,------43, 53, 59, 73, 104, 105, 327, 387, 434, 754.

Knobel, August,------726

Knox, Alexander,------853

Knox, John,------134

Köhler, H. O.,------621

Koran, ------420, 578

Krabbe, Otto,------660

Krauth, C. P.,------664

Kreibig, G.,------298, 403, 569, 633, 659, 750, 754, 765.

Krüger, Paul,------344

Külpe, Oswald,------43

Kuenen, A.,------134, 155, 170, 171, 199

Kurtz, J. H.,------51, 168, 172, 320, 394, 415, 660, 667, 668, 677.

Kuyper, Abraham,------338, 667

Lachelier, J. E. N.,------62

Lacouperie, A. Terrien de,------479

Lactantius, ------2, 20

Ladd, G. T.,------4, 10, 43, 55, 56, 61, 66, 70, 91, 106, 110, 121, 198, 205, 249, 263, 275, 361, 416, 459, 486, 495, 498, 499, 506, 509, 534, 537, 550, 916, 929, 958, 985, 1003, 1023.

Lamb, Charles,------312, 644

Lang, G. A.,------298, 531

Lange, F. A.,------91

Lange, J. L. F., ------20, 46, 273

Lange, J. P.,------51, 333, 382, 661, 722 761, 781, 853, 951.

Lanier, Sidney,------194

Lankester, E. Ray,------229, 528

Lao-tze, ------351

La Place, P. S. de,------250

Lardner, Nathaniel,------150

Lasaulx, Ernest von,------727

Lasher, G. W.,------948

Laurie, S. S.,------511

Law, William,------303, 557

Lawrence, E. A.,------697, 754, 1042

Lawrence, William,------133

Laycock, Thomas------95

Leathes, Stanley,------140, 168, 177, 221

LeBon, Gustave,------488

Lecky, W. E. H.,------294

LeConte, Joseph,------77, 110, 225, 250, 395, 396, 469, 474.

Lee, G. S.,------125, 237, 264, 362

LeFanu, Joseph S.,------575

Legge, James,------56, 180, 225, 531

Leibnitz, G. W.,------29, 43, 46, 63, 404, 405, 563.

Leighton, Robert,------401, 873

Leitch, William,------450, 1033

Lemme, Ludwig,------652

Lenormant, F.,------224, 225, 377

Leo the Great,------750

Lepsius, K. R.,------910

Lessing, G. E.,------30, 173, 510, 520

Letson, see LeBon, Gustave.

Lewes, G. H.,------64, 194, 251, 380, 533

Lewis, Mrs. A. S.,------151

Leydecker, Melchior,------46, 49, 50

Lias, J. J.,------759, 760

Lichtenberg, ------,------98

Lichtenberger, F.,------748

Liddell and Scott,------933

Liddon, Henry P.,------21, 51, 58, 190, 307, 309, 311, 314, 315, 321, 437, 491, 683.

Lidgett, J. S.,------295, 528, 726, 732, 750, 754, 756.

Liebner, Th. A.,------686, 690, 702

Life, ------512

Lightfoot, J. B.,------24, 35, 151, 160, 187, 311, 335, 341, 379, 379, 452, 485, 706, 912, 915, 916, 928, 929, 934, 938, 945, 953.

Lightfoot, John,------452

Lightwood, J. M.,------535

Lillie, Arthur,------183

Lillie, John,------294, 993, 1005, 1053

Lilly, W. S.,------112

Limborch, Philipp von,------47, 524, 602

Lincoln, Abraham,------231, 272, 516, 517, 596, 847, 900, 939.

Lincoln, Heman,------1049

Lincoln, William,------800

Lindsay, T. M.,------897

Lindsay, W. L.,------469

Lindsley, Philip,------39

Lipsius, Richard A.,------46, 380, 404

Lisle, W. M.,_____17, 486, 561
Litch, Josiah, _____ 1015
Litton, E. A.,_____ 48
Livingstone, David,_____ _____56, 900
Lobstein, Paul,_____ 676
Locke, John,_____43, 54, 63, 73, 81, 95, 213,
  444, 899, 1002.
Lockhart, B. W.,_____330, 560, 736
Lockhart, John G.,_____ 449
Lockyer, J. N.,_____ 229
Lodge, Oliver J.,_____416, 512
Loeb, Jacques,_____119, 525, 676, 1003
Loisy, Alfred,_____ 683
Lombard, Peter,_____44, 613, 704
Lombroso, Cesare,_____ 496
Long, J. C.,_____44, 937
Longfellow, H. W.,_____224, 400, 984, 985,
  987, 1042.
Lopp, W. T.,_____ 477
"Lord's Supper, The, A Clerical
  Symposium," _____ 964
Lorimer, James,_____ 536
Lorimer, P.,_____ 160
Lotz, Gulielmus,_____ 410
Lotze, Hermann,_____4, 6, 8, 12, 38, 53, 89,
  96, 99, 100, 104, 254, 273, 279, 282, 285, 332,
  385, 388, 416, 418, 495, 512, 513, 695, 820,
  985, 1002.
Louis XIV.,_____ 567
Louis, St., of France,_____ 192
Love, William D.,_____ 708
Lovelace, Richard,_____ 507
Lowde, ——,_____ 800
Lowell, James R.,_____13, 151, 407, 426,
  500, 503, 633.
Lowndes, R.,_____52, 67, 97, 279
Lowrie, Walter,_____159, 261, 310, 719
Loyola, Ignatius,_____33, 904
Lubbock, John,_____ 527
Lucan, _____ 700
Lucian, _____194, 941
Luckock, H. M.,_____659, 775,
  1000, 1002, 1043.
Lucretius,_____91, 255, 299, 380
Lünemann, G.,_____377, 485
Luthardt, C. E.,_____2, 14, 22, 30, 44, 46, 51,
  68, 84, 112, 222, 245, 249, 341, 404, 408, 530,
  559, 575, 668, 723, 754, 816, 829, 836, 929, 982,
  991, 998.
Luther, Martin,_____45, 156, 205, 209, 226,
  237, 240, 251, 329, 344, 364, 409, 437, 441,
  458, 487, 494, 556, 562, 569, 650, 654, 692,
  747, 776, 808, 823, 830, 840, 891, 902, 903,
  912, 942, 954, 969, 1008.
Lutheran Quarterly,_____ 300
Lyall, William,_____ 508
Lyell, Charles,_____65, 374, 532
Lynch, Archbishop,_____ 967
Lysias, Claudius,_____ 240
Lyttelton, Arthur,_____647, 722
Lytton, Edward Bulwer,_____ 645
M., C. H., see MacIntosh. C. H.

Macan, R. W.,_____ 1023
Macaulay, T. B.,_____40, 47, 406, 659, 872,
  898, 913.
McCabe, L. D.,_____285, 357, 358, 359
McCane, John Y.,_____ 577
McCheyne, Robert Murray,_____ 1056
McClintock and Strong,_____51, 603, 644
McConnell, S. D.,_____ 851
McCosh, James,_____6, 7, 8, 9, 10, 11, 43,
  54, 67, 70, 73, 77, 78, 87, 93, 94, 95, 102, 339,
  403, 427, 437, 839, 1022.
MacDonald, A.,_____ 2
MacDonald, G.,_____491, 569
Macdonnell, J. C.,_____ 754
McDuff, J. R.,_____ 808
McGarvey, J. W.,_____534, 955
McGiffert, A. C.,_____44, 888, 902
MacGregor, James,_____ 894
McIlvaine, C. P.,_____146, 150, 191
McIlvaine, J. H.,____193, 231, 394, 474, 583,
  644, 744, 750.
MacIntosh, C. H.,_____234, 410, 454, 548,
  583, 584, 727, 773, 796, 797, 856, 862, 864,
  870, 896, 941.
McKim, W. D.,_____ 656
Mackintock, Hugh R.,_____ 224
McLane, W. W.,_____ 985
McLeod, Norman,_____ 459
MacLaren, Alexander,_____29, 114, 139, 177,
  259, 319, 456, 458, 524, 544, 581, 726, 731,
  733, 781, 806, 837, 1026.
Maclaren, Ian, see Watson, John.
Macmillan, Hugh,_____ 145
McPherson, John,_____ 912
MacWhorter, A.,_____ 668
Magee, William,_____ 754
Mahaffy, J. P.,_____ 18
Mahan, Asa,_____ 877
Maimonides, Moses,_____ 934
Maine, Henry Sumner,_____ 535
Mair, Alexander,_____129, 154, 161
Maistre, Joseph de,_____ 576
Maitland, S. R.,_____ 1009
Malebranche, Nicolas de,_____100, 279
Malm, K. E.,_____ 844
Mani, _____ 382
Manly, Basil,_____198, 210
Mann, Horace,_____810, 1051
Manning, H. E.,_____ 317
Manning, J. M.,_____ 100
Mansel, Henry L.,_____7, 8, 9. 52, 54, 58,
  70, 121, 253, 254, 278. 379, 384, 385, 469,
  504, 546, 985.
Manton, Thomas,_____48, 458
Marchi, Joseph de,_____ 191
Marcion, _____147, 383, 385
Marck, Johann,_____ 614
Marcus Aurelius,_____185, 989
Margoliouth, Moses,_____ 450
Marheineke, P. C.,_____ 46
Marlowe, Christopher,_____449, 560, 1042
Marsh, W. H. H.,_____ 122

Martensen, H. L.,_____34, 49, 50, 245, 266, 274, 285, 289, 349, 380, 381, 386, 392, 445, 460, 474, 491, 556, 576, 593, 601, 622, 647, 668, 694, 712, 790, 813, 1002, 1003, 1029.

Martin, Hugh,_____ 739

Martin, W. A. P.,_____ 531

Martineau, Harriet,_____ 990

Martineau, James,_____6, 7, 8, 10, 11, 12, 14, 15, 21, 26, 37, 51, 53, 57, 59, 64, 66, 68, 72, 73, 76, 78, 81, 83, 85, 92, 94, 95, 97, 98, 99, 100, 102, 105, 107, 112, 114, 125, 141, 152, 159, 202, 230, 231, 245, 250, 279, 285, 293, 296, 298, 299, 301, 303, 347, 348, 359, 362, 365, 386, 399, 402, 403, 412, 413, 417, 426, 430, 437, 469, 485, 504, 512, 532, 534, 535, 536, 538, 542, 567, 571, 573, 647, 655, 658, 682, 729, 794, 800, 815, 817, 893, 979, 985, 986, 988, 1003, 1036, 1041, 1047, 1048, 1049.

Marvell, Andrew,_____ 990

Mason, J. M.,_____ 776

Mason, Otis T.,_____417, 529

Mason, S. R.,_____48, 259, 277, 316, 328, 337, 338, 348, 403, 406, 445, 446, 450, 451, 476, 492, 509, 588, 670, 672, 677, 679, 685, 688, 696, 704, 707, 717, 734, 743, 785, 789, 818, 883.

Maspero, G.,_____377, 995

Masson, David,_____385, 447

Mather, Cotton,_____ 899

Mather, Increase,_____953, 958

Matheson, George,_____8, 12, 23, 118, 180, 183, 185, 298, 338, 339, 382, 436, 452, 543, 584, 682, 752, 793, 1003.

Matteson, W. B.,_____ 958

Maudsley, Henry,_____416, 511, 554

Maupas, E.,_____494, 591

Maurice, F. D.,_____11, 410, 446, 594, 728, 734, 1046.

Maxwell, James Clerk,_____ 77

Mazzini, Giuseppe,_____ 890

Mead, C. M.,_____11, 14, 120, 263, 279, 475, 681, 952.

Meehan, Thomas,_____ 480

Melanchthon, Philip,_____45, 344, 414, 441, 558, 562, 613, 699, 761, 789, 816, 830, 864, 875, 1008.

Melito, _____ 150

Mell, P. H.,_____ 927

Melvill, Henry,_____ 911

Menken, Gottfried,_____ 744

Menzies, Allan,_____ 20

Mercersburgh Review,_____ 957

Meredith, ———,_____ 978

Methodist Quarterly Review,_____58, 75, 477, 911, 1003.

Meyer, F. B.,_____ 32

Meyer, H. A. W.,_____15, 51, 68, 138, 199, 210, 242, 306, 309, 335, 337, 340, 452, 456, 457, 474, 485, 487, 517, 562, 579, 633, 657, 658, 661, 706, 707, 717, 719, 720, 752, 760, 761, 782, 838, 853, 902, 906, 907, 910, 915, 934, 935, 948, 951, 960, 973, 994, 1010, 1039, 1045.

Meze, S. E.,_____ 277

Michael Angelo,_____986, 1055

Michaelis, J. D.,_____ 46

Miley, J.,_____ 818

Mill, James,_____114, 299

Mill, J. S.,_____11, 78, 80, 83, 85, 96, 127, 130, 131, 179, 188, 190, 299, 378, 379, 381, 402, 506, 532, 533, 814, 904, 979, 986.

Miller, Edward,_____ 744

Miller, G. C.,_____257, 270

Miller, Hugh,_____ 394

Miller, John,_____30, 53, 397, 708, 759

Millet, J. F.,_____ 256

Milligan, William,_____131, 151

Mills, B. Fay,_____ 855

Mills, L. H.,_____ 383

Milton, John,_____37, 237, 284, 286, 292, 329, 360, 385, 409, 443, 453, 494, 523, 560, 572, 583, 587, 589, 620, 647, 742, 749, 783, 789, 873, 1032, 1034.

Mind,_____468, 509

Minton, H. C.,_____6, 26, 348

Mishna, _____ 931

Mitchell, Arthur,_____ 529

Mitchell, E. C.,_____ 147

Mitchell, J. M.,_____182, 185

Mitchell, Seth K.,_____ 810

Mivart, St. George,_____9, 78, 97, 104, 283, 380, 468, 470, 472, 474, 528.

Moberly, R. C.,_____253, 260, 288, 291, 323, 328, 331, 333, 343, 345, 594, 654, 674, 684, 691, 737, 756, 769, 836.

Moehler, J. A.,_____47, 207, 518, 522, 853, 866, 911.

Moffat, Robert,_____ 56

Molina, Luis,_____ 358

Moltke, Count H. von,_____ 401

Momerie, A. W.,_____ 700

Monod, Adolphe,_____41, 541, 751

Monrad, D. G.,_____ 437

Montesquieu, S.,_____ 535

Moody, D. L.,_____188, 313, 506

Moore, A. L.,_____ 416

Moore, Aubrey,_____ 492

Moore, E. M.,_____ 481

Moorhouse, James,_____679, 1023

More, Sir Thomas,_____654, 1031

Morell, J. D.,_____4, 12, 20, 33, 88, 93, 202, 510.

Morgan, L. H.,_____527, 530

Morison, James,_____148, 149

Mormon, Book of,_____ 141

Morris, E. D.,_____45, 708, 1044

Morris, George S.,_____43, 253, 345

Morris, H. W.,_____ 483

Morrison, C. R.,_____ 131

Morton, S. G.,_____ 480

Mosheim, J. L. von,_____ 376

Moule, H. C. G.,_____48, 340, 485, 790, 913

Moulton, Richard G.,_____ 651

Moxom, P. S.,_____273, 302, 349, 495, 637, 750, 776.

Mozart, W. A.,_____ 276

Mozley, J. B.,------3, 75, 100, 117, 118, 124, 126, 129, 130, 132, 231, 432, 546, 570, 620, 622, 631, 766, 790, 841, 994, 997, 1041.
Mozoomdar, ----------------------------- 678
Müller, G. C.,--------------------------- 377
Müller, George,--------------------438, 439
Müller, Gustav A.,---------------------- 144
Müller, Julius, ------10, 21, 22, 31, 46, 51, 53, 74, 82, 105, 245, 257, 263, 278, 285, 341, 388, 418, 488, 489, 490, 507, 519, 544, 552, 557, 559, 562, 563, 566, 567, 569, 571, 577, 579, 582, 585, 600, 605, 606, 611, 612, 616, 618, 621, 634, 643, 644, 647, 651, 654, 657, 660, 661, 676, 677, 706, 775, 777, 847, 983, 1003.
Müller, F. Max,------20, 56, 101, 193, 225, 260, 309, 335, 469, 478, 479, 531, 668, 844.
Muir, William,---------------------157, 186
Mulford, Elisha,---------------------- 101
Mullins, E. Y.,--------------717, 738, 754, 755
Murphy, J. G.,-------------------------- 445
Murphy, J. J.,------4, 7, 8, 10, 11, 16, 71, 73, 76, 79, 80, 82, 99, 103, 121, 129, 276, 401, 412, 512, 538, 544, 548, 576, 606, 622, 786, 824, 846, 955, 1056.
Murray, Andrew,---------------------- 317
Murray, J. C.,-------------------------- 98
Murray, T. C.,----------------------172, 479
Murray, W. H. H.,--------------------- 447
Myers, F. W. H.,--------69, 120, 134, 206, 457, 677.
Myers, Frederic,---------------------- 205
Nägeli, C. von,----------------------- 987
Nägelsbach, C. F.,--------------------- 723
Nägelsbach, K. W. E.,------------------ 239
Nansen, F.---------------------------- 431
Napoleon, --------143, 349, 421, 512, 561, 682
Nash, H. S.,----------150, 157, 691, 763, 841
Nation, The,-------------------------- 896
Nature, ------------------------------ 471
Naville, Ernest,--------------508, 622, 1023
Neander, J. A. W.,------40, 41, 305, 335, 384, 487, 563, 587, 600, 621, 661, 670, 749, 852, 870, 878, 896, 897, 902, 907, 936, 951, 952, 953, 954, 1003, 1014, 1023, 1029.
Nelson, Horatio,---------------------- 577
Nelson, John,------------------------- 1026
Nestorius, ---------------------------- 671
Nevin, J. W.,-------------------------- 969
Nevius, J. L.,---------445, 453, 456, 457, 461
New Englander,------5, 6, 8, 38, 62, 74, 94, 98, 181, 185, 207, 278, 314, 413, 532, 616, 666, 923, 952, 1014, 1038.
New World,--------------------------- 507
Newman, A. H.,----------44, 379, 382, 385, 937, 953.
Newman, F. W.,-----12, 37, 202, 585, 988, 1055
Newman, J. H.,------5, 17, 33, 37, 114, 202, 208, 222, 451, 584, 586, 853, 866.
Newton, Sir Isaac,--------60, 139, 311, 1009
Newton, John,------------------------ 576
Newton, Thomas,---------------------- 135

Nicoll, W. R.,------130, 155, 161, 313, 659, 708, 746, 1016.
Niese, B.,---------------------------- 144
Nippold, Friedrich,------------------- 740
Nitzsch, Carl I.,------14, 20, 22, 31, 41, 46, 53, 59, 72, 269, 485, 519, 559, 583, 652, 849.
Noel, Baptist W.,-------------------938, 972
Noetus, ------------------------------ 327
Nordau, Max S.,----------------------- 40
Nordell, P. A.,------------------------ 290
North British Review,--------------363, 952
Northrup, G. W.--------255, 293, 474, 614, 640, 662, 772, 789.
Norton, Andrews,--------------------- 150
Norton, C. E.,------------------------ 138
Norton, John,------------------------- 539
Nott, J. C., and G. R. Gliddon, ------ 480
Novalis, ----------------------------43, 526
Novatian, ---------------------------- 937
Noyes, G. R.,------------------------- 548
Occam, William of,-----------45, 244, 298, 299, 909.
Œdipus,------------------------------ 469
Oehler, G. F.,----------137, 375, 376, 585, 725
Oetinger, F. C.,---------------------- 216
Oldenberg, Hermann,----------------- 183
Oliphant, Mrs. M. O. W.,-------------- 744
Olshausen, Hermann,----------------- 945
Omar Kháyyám,-----------407, 511, 542, 990
Oosterzee, J. J. Van, see Van Oosterzee, J. J.
Origen, ------15, 44, 53, 146, 153, 328, 386, 409, 451, 488, 489, 734, 1019, 1041.
Orr, James,--------------6, 30, 141, 172, 298
Osgood, Howard,------18, 172, 226, 995, 1023
Ossory, Bishop of,------836, 849, 853, 868
Outlook, The,----------305, 350, 650, 718, 744
Ovid,-----------------------416, 523, 575, 723
Owen, John,------47, 295, 297, 326, 340, 343, 613, 663, 697, 754, 770, 773, 802, 820, 826, 868, 876, 886.
Owen, Richard,------------77, 98, 389, 396, 480
Owen, Robert Dale,------------------- 506
Paine, L. L.,------44, 148, 262, 305, 308, 328, 500, 718.
Paine, Thomas,---------------------112, 564
Pajon, Claude,------------------------ 947
Paley, William,-----------174, 299, 409, 534
Palmer, Frederic,----------203, 342, 659, 701
Palmer, G. H.,------------------------ 182
Palmer, T. R.,------------------------ 955
Papias, --------------------------148, 149, 159
Park, E. A.,------197, 231, 271, 278, 290, 301, 304, 342, 354, 367, 401, 605, 608, 609, 637, 675, 727, 740, 743, 827, 911, 913, 928.
Parker, Edwin P.,--------------------- 711
Parker, Joel,------------------------- 1052
Parker, Joseph,----------------------- 317
Parker, Theodore,------12, 120, 186, 202, 446, 501, 958, 989, 1050, 1055.
Parkhurst, Charles H.,-----22, 242, 486, 584

Pascal, Blaise,_____4, 21, 38, 40, 47, 62, 120, 129, 205, 403, 469, 516, 581, 635, 691, 808, 821, 841, 909.

Paton, John G.,_____32, 76, 195, 423

Pattison, S. R.,_____ 225

Pattison, T. H.,_____24, 42, 200

Patton, F. L.,_____63, 70, 79, 172, 212, 297, 300, 368, 655, 841, 889, 1047.

Patton, W. W.,_____437, 708

Paulsen, Friedrich,_____ 281

Payne, B. H.,_____ 651

Payne, George,_____617, 790, 820

Peabody, A. P.,_____22, 29, 51, 60, 89. 112, 146, 157, 230, 503, 672.

Peabody, Ephraim,_____ 118

Pearson, John,_____48, 708

Pearson, Thomas,_____ 415

Peck, A. C.,_____ 790

Peck, George,_____ 877

Peirce, Benjamin,_____ 396

Pelagius, _____491, 597

Pengilly, R.,_____ 938

Penn, William,_____ 48

Pentecost, G. F.,_____767, 813

Pepper, G. D. B.,_____102, 124, 286, 353, 357, 425, 537, 629, 933, 955, 980, 1014.

Perowne, J. J. S.,_____172, 231, 403, 412, 451, 812, 833.

Perrone, J.,_____47, 523

Persius, _____330, 647

Peschel, O.,_____ 58

Petavius, Dionysius,_____ 47

Peter Lombard,_____44, 613, 704, 747

Peter Martyr,_____46, 524

Peters, ———,_____ 507

Peyrerius, _____ 476

Pezzi, D.,_____ 479

Pfleiderer, Otto,_____5, 8, 10, 12, 21, 54, 59, 60, 61, 63, 74, 87, 104, 111, 116, 120, 122, 134, 156, 158, 164, 182, 216, 237, 269, 328, 332, 365, 383, 386, 388, 406, 447, 466, 490, 492, 519, 530, 559, 571, 585, 586, 603, 608, 681, 700, 717, 718, 719, 721, 728, 750, 799, 839, 938, 951, 954.

Phelps, Austin,_____437, 496, 820, 1034

Philippi, F. A.,_____4, 20, 46, 51, 222, 257, 273, 287, 378, 418, 420, 442, 444, 462, 463, 491, 514, 516, 519, 520, 523, 539, 549, 563, 566, 571, 579, 585, 592, 606, 612, 622, 671, 673, 688, 690, 696, 697, 706, 708, 709, 710, 713, 721, 733, 750, 754, 766, 771, 776, 836, 859.

Phillips, Wendell,_____ 907

Philo,_____126, 166, 203, 244, 320, 321, 335, 340, 377, 488, 489, 722, 995.

Pickering, Charles,_____477, 480

Pictet, Benedict,_____ 46

Pierce, Nehemiah,_____ 823

Pierret, Paul,_____ 377

Pillsbury, Parker,_____ 982

Pinches, T. G.,_____ 531

Placeus, Joshua,_____46, 616, 617

Plato,_____16, 25, 29, 33, 67, 68, 111, 112, 143, 183, 203, 261, 262, 302, 310, 335, 364, 461, 488, 489, 516, 526, 560, 581, 647, 660, 700, 764, 989, 1031.

Pliny, _____191, 313

Plummer, A.,_____ 932

Plumptre, E. H.,_____153, 158, 700, 708, 821, 909, 915, 935, 993.

Plutarch,_____113, 429, 537, 575, 788, 813, 934

Polanus, A.,_____ 491

Pollok, Robert,_____ 1013

Polycarp, _____147, 149, 150

Pomeroy, John,_____ 536

Pond, Enoch,_____ 207

Pope, Alexander,_____77, 102, 404, 430, 1020

Pope, W. B.,_____48, 68, 394, 562, 578, 583, 602, 706, 762.

Porter, Frank C.,_____152, 934

Porter, Noah,_____6, 7, 8, 9, 10, 11, 14, 20, 43, 51, 52, 53, 54, 56, 60, 63, 66, 67, 73, 75, 78, 82, 86, 93, 96, 100, 125, 179, 253, 254, 257, 275, 278, 279, 280, 412, 417, 469, 486, 508, 516, 524, 695, 815, 1019, 1021.

Poteat, E. M.,_____ 108

Pott, A. F.,_____ 478

Potwin, Lemuel S.,_____ 735

Powell, Baden,_____434, 548

Praxeas, _____ 327

Prayer Book, English,_____46, 937, 957, 978

Prentiss, George L.,_____ 664

Presbyterian and Reformed Review,__ 26

Presbyterian Quarterly Review,_____5, 96, 132, 133, 182, 477, 614, 913, 915, 924, 960, 998, 1005, 1013, 1014.

"Present Day Tracts,"_____162, 177

Pressensé, E. D. de,_____130, 162, 187, 321, 666.

Prestwich, Joseph,_____ 226

Preyer, W. T.,_____ 43

Price, Richard,_____ 301

Prichard, J. C.,_____480, 483

Priestley, Joseph,_____198, 300

Prime, Samuel Irenæus,_____ 437

Princeton Essays,_____304, 330, 343, 359, 401, 555, 598, 600, 601, 611, 612, 613, 619, 644, 707, 733, 744, 881.

Princeton Review,_____5, 11, 78, 216, 469, 481, 622, 640, 708, 747, 896, 911, 977, 1014, 1037, 1046.

Proudhon, ———,_____ 1

Ptah-hotep, _____ 169

Pusey, E. B.,_____429, 518, 834, 969

Pym, John,_____ 419

Pythagoras,_____112, 183, 190, 386

Quarles, Francis,_____ 752

Quatrefages, A. de,_____474, 477, 480

Quenstedt, J. A.,_____45, 208, 244, 269, 444, 669, 795, 859, 864.

Racovian Catechism,_____47, 524

Rainy, Robert,_____12, 177, 221, 912

Ramabai, Pundita,_____161, 905

Ranke, Leopold von,_____ 369

Ratzel, Friedrich,_____ 530
Rauschenbusch, Augustus,_____ 410
Rauschenbusch, Walter,_____540, 909, 982
Rawlinson, George,_____56, 191, 225, 229, 351, 482, 483, 529, 531, 532.
Raymond, Miner,_____48, 53, 358, 362, 519, 602, 605, 606, 611, 621, 644.
Reade, Winwood,_____ 405
Records of the Past,_____ 377
Redford, R. A., _____ 141
Reid, Thomas,_____276, 279
Reid, William,_____ 896
Reinhard, F. V.,_____ 46
Renan, Ernest,_____57, 115, 131, 160, 161, 162, 174, 188, 666.
Renouf, P. Le Page,_____57; 58, 103, 351, 377, 397, 79, 482, 799, 995, 1022, 1024.
Renouvier, C. B.,_____ 512
Reubelt, John A.,_____ 686
Reusch, F. H.,_____ 397
Reuss, E.,_____41, 147, 579, 670
Réville, Jean,_____177, 321
Révillout, Eugène,_____226, 995
Revue Théologique,_____ 1023
Reynolds, Edward,_____ 622
Rhees, Rush,_____144, 190, 315
Ribot, Th.,_____497, 505, 625, 813
Rice, W. N.,_____ 120
Richards, James,_____ 555, 644, 773, 777
Richardson, J. H.,_____ 525
Richelieu, _____ 1048
Richter, Jean Paul,____105, 204, 467, 553, 641
Riddle, M. B.,_____152, 227
Rider, C. E.,_____173
Riggenbach, C. J.,_____ 485
Ridgeley, Thomas,___47, 48, 664, 696, 790, 886
Ripley, Henry J.,_____ 923
Ritchie, D. G.,_____12, 16, 60, 572, 615
Ritschl, Albrecht,_____5, 6, 11, 14, 21, 41, 46, 120, 245, 264, 291, 579, 622, 732, 734, 737, 799, 866, 877, 1008.
Ritter, Heinrich,_____ 79
Robbins, R. D. C.,_____ 1041
Roberts, B. T.,_____ 918
Roberts, W. Page-,_____ 496
Robertson, F. W.,_____39, 205, 253, 344, 346, 378, 379, 469, 548, 567, 570, 654, 656, 679, 682, 695, 734, 855, 860, 948, 1028, 1049.
Robertson, J. D.,_____ 814
Robertson, James,_____121, 143, 169, 668, 724.
Robie, Edward,_____351
Robin, C. P.,_____ 281
Robins, H. E.,_____647, 649, 663, 674, 697, 706, 803, 946.
Robinson, C. S.,_____ 845
Robinson, Edward,_____227, 862, 906, 918, 934.
Robinson, Ezekiel G.,_____3, 16, 18, 26, 31, 34, 39, 40, 42, 51, 68, 119, 129, 130, 156, 157, 162, 177, 205, 228, 231, 244, 268, 270, 273, 278, 287, 297, 299, 301, 302, 304, 314, 316, 319, 322,

326, 334, 342, 356, 357, 360, 367, 383, 398, 429, 432, 434, 436, 444, 458, 498, 499, 504, 512, 519, 536, 539, 540, 544, 550, 572, 586, 589, 594, 615, 638, 644, 662, 666, 667, 701, 709, 723, 729, 730, 736, 740, 747, 750, 776, 818, 822, 824, 828, 842, 853, 854, 890, 912, 917, 942, 954, 955, 969, 983, 1016, 1023, 1048, 1049, 1051.
Robinson, John,_____35, 222
Robinson, Willard H.,_____ 1038
Rogers, Henry,_____12, 115, 116, 156, 189, 204, 232, 282, 288.
Rogers, J. G.,_____969
Romaine, W.,_____437, 849
Romanes, G. J.,_____22, 69, 94, 250, 346, 466, 469, 470, 478, 510, 631, 676.
Roscelin, Jean,_____ 44
Ross, A. H.,_____ 929
Rossetti, Dante Gabriel,_____ 489
Rossetti, Maria F.,_____ 443
Rothe, Richard,_____50, 216, 244, 249, 285, 287, 416, 493, 559, 689, 740, 893.
Rousseau, J. J.,_____562, 576, 577
Row, C. A.,_____51, 121, 131, 152, 157, 160, 179, 187, 204, 233, 433.
Rowland, H. A.,_____ 60
Rowlands, H. O.,_____ 926
Rowley, F. H.,_____ 476
Royce, Josiah,_____16, 32, 54, 55, 56, 60, 69, 99, 110, 124, 261, 267, 276, 277, 283, 284, 286, 349, 357, 380, 405, 407, 442, 511, 558, 594, 615, 758, 785, 987, 1025.
Rückert, L. J.,_____517, 781
Ruskin, John,_____59, 415, 443, 482, 648, 825
Russell, John,_____ 287
Ryle, H. E.,_____ 168
Saarschmidt, see Schaarschmidt, Karl.
Sabatier, L. A.,_____21, 128, 137, 155, 205, 666, 697, 892.
Sabellius, _____ 327
Sadler, M. F.,_____948, 969
Sagebeer, J. E.,_____141, 153, 653, 852
Sainte-Beuve, C. A.,_____ 561
Saintine, X. B.,_____ 145
Saisset, Emil,_____86, 101
Saker, Alfred,_____ 843
Sakya-Mouni, _____ 161
Sale, George,_____ 143
Salisbury, Lord,_____ 834
Salmon, George,_____154, 160, 549
Salmond, S. D. F.,_____ 708
Salter, W. M.,_____300, 538, 541
Samson, G. W.,_____464, 917, 934, 960
Sanday, William,_____146, 152, 164, 165, 198, 203, 209, 228, 236, 307, 933, 945.
Sanders, F. W.,_____ 427
Sanderson, J. S. Burdon-,_____ 251
Santayana, George,_____269, 510
Sartorius, Ernest,_____693, 695, 705
Saturninus, _____ 385
Savage, Eleazer,_____ 926
Savage, M. J.,_____69, 432, 447, 985, 989, 992, 1017.
Savage, W. R.,_____ 1003

Savonarola, Girolamo,------------------ 135
Sayce, A. H.,-----------57, 376, 408, 478, 479
Schaarschmidt, Karl,------------------ 512
Schäfer, Bernhard,--------------------- 240
Schäffer, C. F.,----------------------- 323
Schaff, Philip,------44, 46, 50, 131, 189, 341,
  598, 599, 622, 637, 652, 668, 670, 678, 682, 696,
  902, 936, 937, 971, 1003.
Schelling, F. W. J. von,------101, 252, 386
Schenkel, Daniel,---------------------- 503
Scherer, E.,--------------------------- 460
Schiller, Friedrich,--------74, 303, 386, 633,
  644, 981.
Schleiermacher, F. E. D.,----14, 20, 34, 42,
  46, 244, 287, 314, 327, 461, 486, 503, 519, 559,
  563, 734, 740, 783, 951, 981.
Schliemann, H.,------------------------ 529
Schmid, C. F.,----------------------41, 68
Schmid, H.,---------------------------- 699
Schmid, Rudolph,--------------397, 479, 482
Schneckenburger, M.,------------------- 931
Schodde, George H.,-------------------- 165
Schöberlein, D. L.,------------637, 754, 808
Scholz, Paul,-------------------------- 56
Schopenhauer, A.,-----54, 78, 101, 105, 404
Schrader, Eberhard,-------------------- 408
Schürer, Emil,------------------------- 244
Schurman, J. G.,------8, 9, 19, 25, 55, 63, 67,
  94, 99, 129, 130, 254, 268, 332, 398, 439, 466,
  470, 615, 894, 908, 910, 1050.
Schwegler, A.,----------------------345, 504
Schweizer, A.,-----------------------42, 245
Schwenkfeld, Caspar------------------- 800
Scott, C. Anderson,---------------913, 915
Scott, C. S.,-------------------------- 928
Scott, Thomas,------------------------- 35
Scott, Pres. Walter,------------------- 444
Scott, Sir Walter,-----------177, 350, 489
Scotus Erigena, John,----------44, 244, 524
Scotus, Novanticus,-------------------- 511
Scribner, G. H.,----------------------- 478
Sears, E. H.,-------------------------- 227
Secrétan, Charles,--------------74, 621, 666
Seeley, J. R.,----------------295, 576, 819
Seelye, J. H.,----------------------528, 1013
Semler, J. S.,------------------------- 46
Seneca, M. Annæus,------83, 112, 177, 185,
  398, 404, 516, 575, 814, 863, 989.
Sennacherib, ------------------------- 143
Septuagint, --------------------------- 166
Serapion, ----------------------------- 150
Servetus, Michel,--------------------- 778
Seth, James,------61, 64, 97, 101, 104, 105,
  416, 418, 503, 505, 512, 536, 655, 678, 800, 986,
  1042.
Sewall, C. G.,------------------------- 1042
Shaftesbury, Lord,--------------------984
Shairp, J. C.,----------------------70, 982
Shakespeare, William,------17, 19, 23, 120,
  170, 288, 289, 369, 426, 439, 442, 450, 452,
  463, 472, 492, 502, 506, 511, 516, 526, 562,
  569, 572, 575, 581, 633, 638, 645, 647, 651, 703,

732, 751, 767, 814, 815, 833, 835, 841, 939,
  948, 984, 988, 990, 1042, 1051, 1055.
Shaler, N. S.,-------112, 119, 194, 225, 432,
  435, 468, 492, 529, 632.
Shammai, ----------------------------- 931
Shaw, Benjamin,----------------------- 78
Shedd, W. G. T.,-------5, 10, 16, 21, 26, 41,
  49, 51, 56, 57, 58, 69, 87, 95, 101, 105, 118,
  119, 125, 243, 246, 253, 255, 261, 262, 268,
  273, 277, 278, 290, 294, 296, 297, 298, 305, 314.
  315, 328, 332, 333, 334, 338, 341, 343, 345,
  348, 356, 367, 368, 373, 376, 380, 384, 400,
  408, 472, 474, 481, 494, 504, 517, 518, 522, 523,
  528, 537, 555, 557, 562, 564, 576, 578, 582, 585,
  586, 588, 592, 601, 602, 607, 619, 621, 622,
  625, 627, 630, 631, 635, 637, 640, 643, 645,
  647, 655, 671, 678, 679, 683, 696, 700, 704, 709,
  713, 719, 733, 737, 744, 749, 750, 754, 762, 766,
  767, 770, 773, 780, 786, 816, 820, 822, 823, 827,
  833, 847, 853, 880, 914, 957, 1041, 1043, 1044,
  1046, 1048, 1049, 1051, 1052, 1056.
Sheldon, D. N.,---------------------598, 729
Sheldon, H. C.,-----------------384, 603, 625
Shelley, P. B.,------------------57, 526, 757
Shipley, Orby,------------------------- 572
Short, Augustus,----------------------- 845
Sibbes, Richard,----------------------- 48
Sidgwick, Henry,-------------------64, 510
Siegfried, C.,------------------------- 321
Silvernail, J. P.,--------------------- 674
Simon, D. W.,----16, 110, 266, 285, 293, 295,
  346, 475, 541, 560, 625, 649, 671, 681, 719, 730,
  750, 754, 763, 769, 822, 833, 1051.
Small, A. W.,-------------------------- 106
Smalley, John,--------------------49, 608
Smeaton, George,----------------------- 726
Smith, Adam,--------------------------- 301
Smith, C. E.,-----------------340, 872, 935, 951
Smith, Edwin B.,----------------------- 898
Smith, George,------------------------- 377
Smith, George Adam,------122, 145, 203, 266,
  422, 582, 724, 923, 997.
Smith, Goldwin,-----------------303, 422, 429
Smith, H. B.,-------2, 3, 11, 42, 46, 49, 50,
  55, 62, 66, 87, 101, 117, 130, 157, 162, 251, 273,
  303, 350, 447, 503, 504, 513, 538, 546, 556, 570,
  578, 579, 581, 583, 587, 595, 604, 607, 609,
  612, 617, 621, 631, 634, 639, 656, 677, 691, 787,
  790, 792, 794, 795, 811, 823, 843, 858, 862, 864
Smith, H. P.,-------116, 172, 209, 228, 238, 240
Smith, J. A.,-------------------------- 368
Smith, J. Denham,--------------------- 808
Smith, J. Pye,-------------------------319, 394
Smith, Lucius E.,--------------------- 843
Smith, Philip,------------------------- 532
Smith, R. B.,-------------------------- 427
Smith, R. Payne,--------------135, 172, 239
Smith, R. T.,-------98, 113, 502, 503, 509, 642
Smith, T. T.,-------------------------- 841
Smith, Thornley,----------------------- 48
Smith, W. Robertson,----------134, 171, 221,
  275, 318.

Smith, William,--------------------118, 147
Smyth, Newman,------13, 30, 37, 62, 63, 65,
  122, 265, 271, 289, 291, 296, 302, 304, 335, 402,
  448, 591, 657, 784, 987, 1019, 1022, 1039, 1046
Smyth, Thomas,------------477, 479, 480, 483
Snodgrass, W. D.,------------------------ 881
Society of Biblical Archæology,------- 408
Socinus, Faustus,----------47, 284, 329, 729
Socinus, Laelius,----------------------47, 729
Socrates,----------111, 112, 143, 177, 183, 505,
  653, 989.
" Solar Hieroglyphics,"----------------- 344
Solly, Thomas,---------------------276, 545
Solon, ---------------------------------- 57
Sophocles,----------------57, 141, 144, 469, 540
Sophocles, E. A.,------------------------ 933
Smith, Robert,----------------128, 524, 705
Southall, James C.,--------------------- 529
Southampton, Bishop of,-------119, 130, 432
Southey, Robert,-----------------------32, 996
Spear, Samuel T.,--------------------------- 736
Spectator, London,-------------------170, 399
Spencer, Herbert,-------7, 8, 9, 10, 22, 29, 43,
  57, 63, 73, 74, 94, 96, 98, 187, 223, 245, 251,
  294, 301, 331, 416, 426, 438, 508, 528, 532, 566,
  722, 904.
Spencer, John,------------------------- 722
Spencer, Otto,--------------------------- 251
Spenser, Edmund,-----------------257, 463
Spilsbury, J.,----------------------------903, 949
Spinoza, Benedict de,-------9, 30, 43, 55, 86,
  94, 103, 244, 287, 415, 559, 563, 682, 834.
Splittgerber, F.,----------------------998, 1023
Spurgeon, Charles H.,------17, 27, 28, 247,
  364, 369, 458, 589, 752, 813, 918, 920, 975,
  976.
Squier, Miles P.,----------------------820, 823
Stählin, Leonhard,---------------------- 6
Staël, Madame de,---------------------- 23
Stahl, F. J.,-----------------------------636, 723
Stalker, James,--------------------------- 691
Stallo, J. B.,-----------------------------91, 397
Stanley, A. P.,---------35, 193, 227, 230, 239,
  242, 427, 691, 888, 910, 936, 940, 946, 957, 966
Stanley, Henry M.,------------------427, 430
Stanley, Hiram M.,--------------------- 278
Stapfer, J. F.,-------------------------20, 619
Starbuck, E. D.,-------------------------- 812
Starkie, Thomas,----------128, 141, 144, 174
Statement of Doctrine of Presbyte-
  rian Church in America, A Short, 790
Staupitz, Johann,---------------------- 556
Stead, Herbert,-------------------------- 889
Stearns, L. F.,-------5, 28, 33, 68, 125, 130,
  140, 635, 637, 771.
Steffens, H.,----------------------------- 1002
Stephen, J. F.,---------------------------- 656
Stephen, Leslie,----------------------114, 596
Sterrett, J. M.,-------20, 21, 23, 101, 407, 624
Steudel, J. C. F.,------------------------ 41
Stevens, G. B.,-------31, 270, 296, 525, 579,
  609, 623, 738, 848, 974, 982, 1016.

Stevens, W. A.,-------138, 149, 157, 294, 485,
  569, 572, 623, 836, 853, 936, 993, 1005, 1008.
Stevenson, R. L.,------------------------ 643
Stewart, Dugald,----------------285, 427, 571
Stewart, J. W. A.,--------21, 261, 339, 795,
  839, 997.
Stirling, J. H.,------------------100, 176, 389
Stirling, John,--------------------------- 40
Stone, G. M.,---------------------------- 940
Storr, G. C.,----------------------------- 46
Storrs, Emory,--------------------------- 1055
Storrs, R. S.,--------------------------19, 889
Story, W. W.,---------------------------- 36
Stourdza, A. de,------------------------- 937
Stout, G. F.,--------------------43, 295, 1003
Stowe, Calvin E.,------------------------ 205
Straffen, G. M.,-------------------------- 560
Strauss, D. F.,-------46, 57, 131, 135, 155, 156,
  349, 405, 407, 460, 523, 547, 708, 990.
Stoops, J. D.,--------------------------- 571
Strong, Augustus H.,-------3, 5, 10, 25, 29,
  35, 38, 39, 40, 45, 46, 53, 95, 97, 106, 110, 117,
  118, 123, 138, 140, 163, 164, 176, 193, 220, 221,
  252, 259, 262, 264, 268, 275, 277, 287, 294, 297,
  311, 340, 350, 356, 358, 362, 389, 440, 501, 504,
  520, 560, 569, 572, 596, 634, 644, 646, 651,
  674, 681, 683, 692, 693, 716, 762, 763, 768, 785,
  799, 802, 804, 808, 812, 848, 899, 908, 914,
  918, 924, 926, 942, 943, 977, 980, 1001, 1006,
  1009, 1044.
Strong, Charles A.,--------------97, 98, 281
Strong, John H.,------------------------- 472
Stroud, William,-------------------675, 731
Stuart, Moses,-------327, 328, 602, 615, 931,
  933, 937, 956, 1003, 1009.
Studien und Kritiken,-----------75, 747, 792
Sully, James,---------------------------- 488
Sumner, Charles,------------------------- 409
Sumner, J. B.,---------------------------- 783
Sunday School Times,--------122, 292, 301,
  468, 498, 502, 523, 549, 574, 589, 650, 782,
  852, 1018.
" Supernatural Religion,"----130, 151, 158
Swayne, W. S.,---------------------315, 699
Swedenborg, Emmanuel,-------32, 207, 251,
  383, 386, 1041.
Swift, Jonathan,------------------------- 405
Symington, William,----------761, 773, 775
Tacitus,---------191, 192, 442, 487, 569, 989
Taine, H. A.,----------------------------- 581
Talbot, Samson,-------39, 94, 98, 301, 302,
  508, 694.
Talleyrand, Prince de,-------------------- 176
Talmage, T. DeW.,------------------------ 464
Talmud,---------------------------------282, 902
Tatian, ---------------------------------151, 383
Taylor, Bayard,-------------------------- 525
Taylor, D. T.,---------------------------- 1015
Taylor, Father Edward T.,-------------- 453
Taylor, Herbert,------------------------- 403
Taylor, Isaac,----------------382, 422, 440, 526
Taylor, Jeremy,----------------------352, 651

Taylor, John,------------------416, 602
Taylor, John M.,---------------------- 396
Taylor, N. W.,------39, 48, 126, 295, 299, 351, 367, 420, 535, 567, 579, 607, 608, 783, 817, 853.
Taylor, W. M.,-------------------------852
Taylor, W. R.,---------------------- 889
"Teaching of the Twelve, The,"---- 159, 311, 410, 892, 906, 937, 938.
Temple, Frederick,--11, 59, 77, 115, 118, 474
Ten Broeke, James,---------------45, 184, 414
Tennyson, Alfred,------3, 8, 37, 57, 62, 65, 245, 252, 253, 256, 259, 276, 280, 284, 294, 301, 383, 400, 413, 424, 443, 444, 467, 489, 509, 515, 520, 525, 528, 571, 577, 581, 633, 653, 659, 679, 711, 772, 799, 804 806, 982, 986, 991, 1039, 1051.
Terence, ---------------------------- 698
Tertullian,--------34, 146, 150, 152, 159, 191, 493, 599, 619, 620, 665, 783, 894. 936, 937, 953, 998, 1001.
Teulon, J. S.,------------------------ 896
Thackeray, W. M.,-------------------151, 575
Thatcher, O. J.,---------------------- 929
Thayer, J. H.,------150, 152, 205, 228, 306, 717, 933.
"Theodosia Ernest,"------------------ 980
Theodoret, -----------------------319, 796
Theological Eclectic,---------------160, 739
Theophilus,-----------------------147, 319, 998
Thirlwall, Connop,---------------------- 205
Tholuck, F. A. G.,-------33, 46, 56, 68, 132, 205, 260, 275, 307, 379, 440, 485, 576, 578, 666.
Thomas à Kempis,-----------24. 32, 190, 556
Thomas, B. D.,---------------------- 36
Thomas, J. B.,---------------------- 653
Thomasius, G.,------46, 50, 51, 245, 249, 257, 261, 263, 270, 273, 274, 288, 297, 315, 328, 338, 342, 349, 487, 514, 527, 556, 579, 622, 647, 668, 678, 683, 690, 701, 750, 761, 808, 868.
Thompson, Chief Justice (Pennsylvania), -------------------------- 581
Thompson, Joseph D.,---------------340, 651
Thompson, R. A.,---------------------81, 87
Thompson, R. E.,-----------------237, 473
Thomson, J. Radford,------------------ 405
Thomson, Archbishop William,----66, 744
Thomson, William,---------------------- 771
Thomson, William, Lord Kelvin,----36, 473
Thoreau, H. D.,---------------------- 982
Thornton, W. S.,---------------128, 439, 654
Thornwell, James H.,----2, 49, 303, 600, 616, 618, 621, 631, 644, 647, 648, 834.
Thucydides, ---------------------- 144
Tiele, C. P.,------------------------ 995
Tillotson, John,---------------------- 808
Tindal, Matthew,---------------------- 414
Tischendorf, Constantinus,---------142, 915
Titchener, E. B.,---------------------- 43
Titcomb, J. H.,---------------------- 177
Todd, J. H.,---------------------------- 1009

Töllner, J. G.,---------------------- 576
Tophel, G.,---------------------- 571
Toplady, A. M.,---------------------- 369
Townsend, W. J.,---------------------- 45
Toy, C. H.,----------------------235, 931
Tract No. 357, American Tract Society, ---------------------------- 840
Tracy, Frederick,---------------------- 43
Treffrey, R.,---------------------- 343
Tregelles ,S. P.,-----------------147, 915
Trench, R. C.,------24, 120, 294, 432, 436, 447, 456, 462, 588, 680, 808, 892, 936, 983.
Trendelenburg, F. A.,-------------------- 62
Trent, Canons and Decrees of the Council of,----------------------521, 854
Trumbull, H. Clay,---------------------- 723
Tulloch, John,------6, 53, 77, 96, 379, 384, 405, 546, 563.
Turnbull, Robert,---------------------- 66
Turner, G. L.,----------------------126, 1002
Turner, J. M. W.,---------------------- 143
Turretin, F.,----------------46, 356, 491, 612, 613, 614, 644, 652, 686, 773, 779.
Twesten, A. D. C.,-------22, 28, 31, 46, 328, 338, 348, 350, 444.
Tyerman, L.,---------------------- 972
Tyler, Bennet,------358, 359, 360, 364, 367, 567, 579, 608, 644, 783, 796, 814, 817, 818.
Tyler, C. M.,---------------------- 57
Tyler, W. S.,------155, 276, 352, 442, 526, 679, 723, 796, 1046.
Tylor, E. B.,------58, 477, 480, 528, 529, 530
Tyndall, John,------14, 60, 83, 94, 96, 252, 311, 433.
Tyng, S. H.,---------------------- 744
Ueberweg, Friedrich,------------------ 36
Uhlhorn, Gerhard,----------------162, 989
Ullmann, K.,------------4, 189, 203, 678, 747
Ulpian, ---------------------------- 535
Ulrici, H.,----------------53, 58, 93, 368
"Unseen Universe, The,"----374, 379, 1023
Upham, L. C.,----------------32, 439, 808
Upton, C. B.,----22, 54, 73, 94, 385, 393, 413, 415, 435, 468, 505, 512, 834, 987.
Urban II.,------------------------ 192
Ursinus, Z.,---------------------- 50
Ussher, James,---------------------- 224
Valentinus, ----------------151, 160, 378, 670
Valerius Maximus,---------------------- 989
Van Dyke, Henry,---------------------- 236
Vaniçek, Alois,---------------------- 20
Van Oosterzee, J. J.,------5, 20, 22, 33, 42, 51, 66, 72, 311, 460, 462, 514, 523, 555, 556, 581, 593, 608, 651, 668, 696, 706, 709, 710, 773, 776, 790, 875, 886.
Vatke, J. K. W.,---------------------- 155
Vaughan, C. J.,---------------------- 781
Vaughan, Henry,-----------------276, 489
Vaughan, R. A.,-------------------33, 207
Vauvenargues, ---------------------- 46
Vedas, ---------------------------- 56

Vedder, H. C.,_____887, 890, 894, 899, 957, 973.
Veitch, John,_____97, 380
Venn, J.,_____849
Vincent, Marvin R.,_____133
Vinci, Leonardo da,_____190
Vinet, Alexander,_____38, 125, 267
Virchow, Rudolph,_____471
Virgil,_____57, 176, 400, 526, 615, 698, 723
Vischer, E.,_____152
Vitringa, Campegius,_____1009, 1014
Volkmar, Gustav,_____165
Voltaire,_____57, 77, 462
Vos, Geerhardus,_____263
Waffle, A. E.,_____407, 410, 754
Wagner, ———,_____480
Wagner, Richard,_____512
Walch, J. G.,_____954
Waldegrave, L.,_____1014
Walden, Treadwell,_____833
Walker, G. L.,_____952
Walker, J. B.,_____151, 317, 668, 820
Walker, W. L.,_____316, 349
Wall, William,_____959, 978
Wallace, A. R.,_____99, 402, 403, 412, 413, 470, 471, 473, 528, 632.
Wallace, Henry,_____725
Walton, Isaak,_____192
Ward, James,_____110, 124, 534
Ward, Clara E.,_____263
Ward, Mrs. Humphrey,_____568, 580, 633
Ward, Lydia A. Coonley,_____596
Ward, Wilfrid,_____841
Wardlaw, Ralph,_____1, 135, 269, 374, 741, 773, 784, 790, 820.
Warfield, B. B.,_____735, 782
Warner, Charles Dudley,_____229
Warren, H. W.,_____796
Warren, I. P.,_____1005, 1009
Warren, W. F.,_____532
Watchman, The,_____425, 907
Waterland, Daniel,_____856
Watkins, H. W.,_____34, 152
Watson, John,_____58
Watson, John (Ian McLaren),_____19, 42 237, 369, 439, 788.
Watson, Richard,_____48, 343, 350, 358, 404, 593, 602, 934.
Watson, William,_____35, 417, 420
Watts, Isaac,_____288, 688, 759
Watts, J. F.,_____508
Watts, Robert,_____170, 172, 216, 218, 229, 352, 735, 765, 776.
Vayland, Francis,_____301, 504, 533, 892, 897, 903, 905, 917, 924, 929, 938, 946, 951, 952, 956.
Webb, C. C. J.,_____104, 253
Weber, F. A.,_____294, 726
Webster, Daniel,_____815, 1056
Webster, H. E.,_____262
Webster, W.,_____761
Wedgwood, J.,_____42

Wegscheider, J. A. L.,_____46
Weigel, Valentine,_____800
Weismann, A.,_____229, 466, 470, 497, 530, 558, 590, 631, 650, 992.
Weiss, Bernhard,_____68, 149, 157, 160, 174, 343, 579, 798.
Weiss, ———,_____1015
Weisse, C. H.,_____660
Wellhausen, Julius,_____171, 526
Welling, J. C.,_____927
Wellington, Duke of,_____506
Wendelius,_____827
Wendt, H. H.,_____223, 262, 321, 379, 446, 448, 475, 517, 546, 661, 721, 729, 743, 799, 830, 936, 1006.
Wenley, R. M.,_____38
Wessel, John,_____752
Wesley, Charles,_____33, 363, 692
Wesley, John,_____33, 48, 368, 369, 443, 602, 603, 816, 877, 878, 920, 972, 984, 1043.
West, Nathaniel,_____131
Westcott, B. F.,_____21, 122, 133, 147, 149, 152, 153, 156, 160, 233, 256, 306, 311, 312, 320, 336, 341, 342, 424, 495, 678, 680, 709, 722, 723, 727, 731, 760, 807, 873, 900, 915, 924, 934, 1012, 1046.
Westermarck, E. A.,_____530
Westervelt, Z. F.,_____216
Westminster Catechism,_____52, 664, 957
Westminster Confession,_____145, 599, 613, 643, 779, 790, 887, 937.
Weston, Henry G.,_____930, 959
Wette, De, see De Wette, W. M. L.
Wetzer und Welte,_____572
Wharton, Edith,_____905
Wharton, Francis,_____656
Whately, Richard,_____39, 62, 66, 74, 128, 143, 174, 444, 528, 783, 913, 1003, 1015, 1052.
Whedon, D. D.,_____48, 262, 273, 286, 354, 362, 520, 559, 602, 603, 604, 606, 780, 1041.
Whewell, William,_____2, 74, 77, 500
Whitby, Daniel,_____602, 1014
White, Blanco,_____37, 570, 1041
White, Edward,_____1037
Whitefield, George,_____368, 835
Whitehouse, Owen C.,_____461
Whitman, Walt,_____567
Whitney, Adeline D. T.,_____439
Whitney, William D.,_____185, 217, 479
Whiton, J. M.,_____119, 208, 297, 305, 334, 336, 342, 343, 348, 413, 516, 542, 633, 680, 684, 699, 743, 772, 850, 1001, 1037, 1046.
Whittier, John G.,_____369, 678, 765, 984, 996, 1041, 1042.
Wicksteed, P. H.,_____277
Wieseler, Karl,_____144
Wiggers, G. F.,_____597, 644
Wilberforce, R. I.,_____671, 679, 680, 693, 696, 697, 698, 969.
Wilberforce, Samuel,_____472, 830
Wilder, Burt G.,_____470
Wilkin, G. F.,_____591, 988

Wilkinson, W. C.,------40, 182, 197, 294, 398, 641, 957, 980.

Wilkinson, W. F.,---------------------- 761

Wilkinson, W. F.,---------------------- 95

Willard, Frances E.,-----------------918, 978

William III,----------------------------- 512

William of Occam,------45, 244, 298, 299, 909

Williams, A. P.,---------------------- 980

Williams, ----------,--------------------- 918

Williams, Leighton,--------------208, 890

William, M. Monier,----------183, 352, 382

Williams, N. M.--------------------------- 577

Williams, Roger,--------------------369, 949

Williams, Rowland,--------------------- 100

Williams, W.,---------------------------- 790

Willis, N. P.,------------------------- 570

Willmarth, J. W.,-----------------948, 1023

Wilson, C. T.,--------------------------- 915

Wilson, J. M.,-------------------------- 719

Wilson, Woodrow,---------------------- 2

Winchell, Alexander,------------------ 476

Windelband, Wilhelm,------------------ 379

Winer, G. B.,--------------------523, 717

Winslow, Edward,--------------------- 227

Withrow, J. L.,------------------------- 914

Witsius, H.,----------------------46, 50

Wörter, Friedrich,--------------------- 598

Wollaston, William,------------------- 361

Wood, N. E.,--------------------------- 942

Wood, N. R.,--------------------------- 381

Wood, W. C.,-------------------------- 410

Woods, F. H.,------------------------- 171

Woods, Leonard,------48, 49, 268, 608, 773, 826, 828, 836, 881, 886, 1015.

Woolman, John,------------------------- 766

Woolsey, T. D.----------223, 741, 943, 1045

Wordsworth, C.,--------------68, 441, 458, 622

Wordsworth, William,------30, 39, 58, 59, 103, 252, 380, 406, 441, 489, 501, 568, 576, 599, 958, 991, 1022.

Wortman, J. L.,------------------------- 478

Wotton, Henry,------------------------- 523

Wright, Charles H. H.,--------167, 405, 476

Wright, Chauncey,--------------------76, 428

Wright, G. F.,------130, 154, 224, 225, 357, 432, 469, 471, 478, 708, 1040, 1043, 1045.

Wright, T. H.,--------------------120, 454, 456

Wrightnour, J. S.,--------214, 667, 699, 764

Wu Ting Fang,------------------------- 180

Wünsche, Aug. de,--------------------- 726

Wundt, Wilhelm,----------------43, 281, 505

Wuttke, Adolph,------62, 179, 182, 184, 185, 302, 516, 539, 581.

Wynne, F. H.,--------------------154, 159

Xenophon,--------------------143, 148, 941

Young, Edward,--------------------296, 557

Young, John,------189, 190, 367, 728, 734

Zahn, ----------,-------------------------- 278

Zahn, A.,-------------------------------- 735

Zahn, Th.,-------------------------707, 735

Zeller, Edward,----------------------38, 512

Zeno, -----------------------------------184

Zinzendorf, Count N. L.,--------------- 900

Zöckler, Otto,--------42, 225, 377, 397, 474, 478, 482, 514.

Zoroaster, ---------------------------- 382

Zwingle, Ulrich,--------45, 237, 621, 903, 957

INDEX OF SCRIPTURE TEXTS.

GENESIS.

CH. VERSE.	PAGE.
1 :	35.
1 : 1	309, 326, 333.
1 : 2	68, 134, 223, 287, 316, 318, 324, 326, 339, 378, 446.
1 : 1-3	286.
1 : 11	418.
1 : 24	465.
1 : 26,	318, 524.
1 : 26, 27	514, 991.
1 : 27	465.
1 : 27, 28	476, 494.
1 : 27-31	490.
1 : 31	450, 488, 514, 521.
2 : 2	412, 494.
2 : 3	408.
2 : 4	395.
2 : 7	197, 198, 340, 465, 469, 494, 523, 550, 991.
2 : 7, 22	476.
2 : 8	999.
2 : 9	526, 527.
2 : 16	524.
2 : 17	584, 590, 656, 660, 992.
2 : 19, 20	524.
2 : 23	797.
3 : 1	584.
3 : 1, 4	454.
3 : 1, 5	455.
3 : 1-7	582.
3 : 1-15	448.
3 : 3	584, 590.
3 : 4	461.
3 : 4, 5, 6	584.
3 : 5	572.
3 : 8	523, 524, 992.
3 : 9	592.
3 : 10	224.
3 : 12	566.
3 : 14	450.
3 : 15	175, 667, 676.
3 : 16-19	992.
3 : 17-19	658.
3 : 19	656.

CH. VERSE.	PAGE.
3 : 20	476, 477.
3 : 21	726.
3 : 22	523, 524, 585.
3 : 22, 23	991.
3 : 24	449.
4 : 1	494, 665.
4 : 3	408.
4 · 3, 4	593, 726.
4 : 14	476.
4 : 16	593.
4 : 17	476.
4 : 26	311.
5 : 3	494, 517.
5 : 6	225.
5 : 24	995.
6 : 1, 2	476.
6 : 2	445.
6 : 3	324, 604, 652.
6 : 6	258, 266.
7 : 19	223.
8 : 1	258.
8 : 10-12	408.
8 : 20, 21	725.
9 : 2, 3	524.
9 : 6	515.
9 : 13	396.
9 : 19	470.
9 : 20-27	230.
9 : 25	365.
10 : 6, 13, 15, 16	224.
11 :	896.
11 : 5	523.
11 : 7	318.
13 : 15	1044.
15 : 5	888.
15 : 6	850.
15 : 13	227.
15 : 16	638.
16 : 9-13	319.
16 : 13	283, 284.
17 : 1	286.
17 : 8-13	1044.
18 : 2	451.
18 : 2, 13	319.
18 : 8	443.
18 : 14	287.
18 : 15	523.
18 : 19	780.
18 : 25	290.

CH. VERSE.	PAGE.
19 : 24	318.
19 : 26	432.
19 : 30-38	230.
20 : 6	423.
20 : 7	710.
20 : 12	447.
20 : 13	318.
22 : 8-14	421.
22 : 11	464.
22 : 11-16	319.
22 : 13	725.
22 : 16	266.
24 : 9	51.
25 : 8, 9	994.
27 : 19-24	230.
28 :	134.
28 : 5	280.
28 : 12	463.
29 : 27, 28	408.
31 : 11, 13	319.
31 : 24	423.
32 : 1, 2	463.
32 : 2	448.
32 : 13, 14	765.
32 : 20	720.
32 : 24	463.
32 : 24-28	258.
35 : 1, 6, 9	259.
35 : 7	318.
35 : 18	483.
35 : 29	994.
39 : 19	318.
40 : 1	318.
41 : 8	483.
41 : 41-44	318.
46 : 26	494.
47 : 9	996.
47 : 31	234.
48 : 15, 16	319.
48 : 16	463.
49 :	134.
49 : 26	1044.
50 : 20	355, 365, 424

EXODUS.

CH. VERSE.	PAGE.
1 : 16	442.
2 : 24, 25	780.
3 : 2	451.

CH. VERSE.	PAGE.
3 : 2, 4, 5	319.
3 : 4	209.
3 : 5	319.
3 : 12	713.
3 : 14	253, 257, 275.
4 : 4–16	200.
4 : 16	307.
4 : 21	424.
6 : 3	257.
7 : 1	200, 307.
7 : 12	733.
7 : 13	424.
8 : 8, 15	424.
9 : 27	832.
10 : 28	459.
12 : 36	422.
12 : 40, 41	227.
13 : 2, 13	761.
14 : 14	241.
14 : 23	1050.
15 : 11	268.
16 : 5	408.
18 : 20	630, 644.
19 : 10–16	268.
20 : 1–17	545.
20 : 3	319.
20 : 8	408, 558.
20 : 12	230.
20 : 22	13.
20 : 23	169.
20 : 24	169.
20 : 25	545.
21 : 6	1044.
22 : 28	307.
23 : 7	850.
28 : 9–12	775.
28 : 22	653.
31 : 2, 3	197.
32 : 19	540.
32 : 24	418.
32 : 30, 32	725.
33 : 18	256.
33 : 18, 20	150.
33 : 31, 32	837.
34 : 10	337.
35 : 25	4.
36 : 21, 22	367, 397, 653.
39 : 7	397.

LEVITICUS.

CH. VERSE.	PAGE.
1 : 3	554
1 : 4	725.
4 : 14, 20, 31	554.
4 : 20, 31, 35	725
5 : 5, 6	554.
5 : 10–16	725.
5 : 11	554.
5 : 17	652, 647, 718.
6 : 7	725.
11 : 15	932.

CH. VERSE.	PAGE.
11 : 44	269.
12 : 8	554.
13 : 45	555.
14 : 17	732.
16 : 1–34	725.
16 : 8	448.
16 : 16, 21	552.
16 : 21	765.
16 : 21, 22	720.
17 : 12	725.
20 : 27	996.
20 : 28	995.
22 : 4–6	934.

NUMBERS.

CH. VERSE.	PAGE.
5 : 1	432.
6 : 24–26	318.
6 : 24, 26	774.
7 : 89	209.
8 : 1	209.
12 : 6–8	203.
14 : 34	718.
16 : 22	465, 484.
15 : 35	907.
16 : 29	656.
16 : 30	377.
19 : 29, 33	994.
23 : 5	197, 207.
23 : 19	258, 288.
23 : 21	454, 856.
25 : 9	227.
25 : 13	719, 1044.
25 : 28	552.
27 : 3	657.
27 : 16	465.
32 : 23	295.
33 : 2	169.

DEUTERONOMY.

CH. VERSE.	PAGE.
1 : 6, 7	549.
1 : 39	661.
4 : 19	448.
6 : 4	259.
8 : 2	423.
8 : 3	421.
10 : 6	994.
16 : 2, 6	719.
17 : 3	448.
18 : 10, 11	996.
18 : 15	139, 711.
21 : 1–8	725.
21 : 23	718.
23 : 3	1044.
25 : 1	850.
29 : 29	36, 364.
32 : 4	260. 290.
32 : 40	275.
33 : 2	447. 452.

JOSHUA.

CH. VERSE.	PAGE.
2 : 1–24	230.
2 : 18	234.
7 : 20	832.
10 : 12, 13	223.
24 : 2	1044.

JUDGES.

CH. VERSE.	PAGE.
4 : 17–22	230.
5 : 24	230.
5 : 30	231.
6 : 17, 36–40	116.
9 : 14, 15	241.
13 : 20–22	319.
13 : 24, 25	197.
14 : 12	408.
20 : 18	552.

1 SAMUEL.

CH. VERSE.	PAGE.
1 :	136.
1 : 11	448.
6 : 19	226.
9 : 27	199.
10 :	136.
15 : 11	258.
15 : 24	832.
15 : 29	258.
16 : 1	421.
18 : 1	799.
18 : 10	424.
23 : 12	282.
24 : 18	422.
28 : 7–14	995, 996.
28 : 19	994.
29 : 4	719.

2 SAMUEL.

CH. VERSE.	PAGE.
6 : 7	939.
11 : 1–4	230.
12 : 23	662.
14 : 20	445.
16 : 10	423.
18 : 33	769.
23 : 23	206.
24 : 1	423, 424.

1 KINGS.

CH. VERSE.	PAGE.
1 : 27	278.
8 : 27	105, 254, 281. 523.
8 : 46	573.
11 : 9	294.
12 : 15–24	355.
17 : 4, 9	443.
17 : 21	483.
18 : 36–38	116.
18 : 36–38	116. 431.

CH. VERSE.	PAGE.	CH. VERSE.	PAGE.	CH. VERSE.	PAGE.
18 : 42–45	433.	1 : 9	461.	8 : 4–8	678.
19 : 5	452.	1 : 9, 11	454.	8 : 5	515.
19 : 15	433.	1 : 11	459.	8 : 5–6	697.
22 :	136.	1 : 12	425.	8 : 5–8	524.
22 : 19	448.	1 : 12, 16, 19	455.	8 : 6	775.
22 : 23	457.	2 : 4, 5	454.	9 : 7	1023.
		2 : 5	459.	10 : 3	817.
2 KINGS.		2 : 6	425.	11 : 6	421.
		2 : 7	455.	11 : 10	63.
2 : 11	995, 996.	3 : 3	406.	14 : 1	217.
4 : 1–7	465.	3 : 13, 18	994.	16 :	675.
5 : 14	934.	4 : 18	445.	16 : 7	32.
5 : 26	13.	7 : 9	994.	16 : 9–11	995, 996
6 : 17	451, 459.	7 : 20	282, 412.	17 :	113.
17 : 6, 24, 26,		11 : 7	34.	17 : 13, 14	423.
28, 33	167.	11 : 7, 9	254.	18 : 24–26	290.
19 : 35	167.	12 : 23	421.	18 : 30	260.
22 : 8	167.	14 : 4	578, 661.	19 :	26.
23 : 2	167.	14 : 5	355.	19 : 1	27, 256.
		15 : 15	445.	19 : 1–6	26.
1 CHRONICLES.		19 : 25	667.	19 : 7	538.
		19 : 25, 27	995, 996.	19 : 12	553, 558, 578
21 : 1	448.	21 : 7	113.		647.
22 : 14	226.	23 : 10	431.	19 : 12, 13	650.
28 : 16	225.	23 : 13	252, 359.	19 : 13	423.
		23 : 13, 14	259.	22 : 20	458.
2 CHRONICLES.		24 : 1	113.	22 : 26	996.
		25 : 5	445.	22 : 28	421.
6 : 2	1044.	26 : 6	994.	23 : 2	364.
13 : 3, 17	226.	26 : 14	143, 287.	24 : 7, 8	1044.
16 : 12, 13	439.	27 : 3	483.	25 : 11	214, 401
17 : 14–19	226.	27 : 5	850.	25 : 14	40.
18 : 18	448.	27 : 5, 6	275.	26 : 9	1023.
29 : 27	765.	31 : 37	275.	29 : 1, 2	451.
32 : 31	423.	32 : 8	197, 198, 469,	29 : 3	424.
34 : 19	543, 836.		483.	31 : 5	746.
36 : 22	197	32 : 18	338.	32 :	431.
		33 : 4	484.	32 : 1	552.
EZRA.		34 : 14, 15	338.	32 : 1, 2	851.
		37 : 5, 10	421.	32 : 6	700.
1 : 2	27.	38 : 7	446, 451, 453.	32 : 8	440.
4 :	167.	42 : 5, 6	543, 832.	33 : 6	318, 326, 445
8 : 22	899.	42 : 6	833.	33 : 9	377.
9 : 6	634.	42 : 7–9	725.	33 : 13–15	282.
				33 : 14, 15	422.
NEHEMIAH.		**PSALMS.**		34 : 7	463.
				34 . 8	4, 825.
1 : 6	594, 634.	1 : 6	780, 781.	36 : 1	40.
8 : 12, 18	409.	2 : 1–4	541.	36 : 6	412.
9 : 6	412, 448.	2 : 6–8	775.	36 : 9	350.
		2 : 7	318, 322, 340.	37 :	113.
ESTHER.		2 : 7–8	356.	37 : 7	439.
		4 : 4	234.	40 : 5	283.
	309.	4 : 8	421.	40 : 6–8	234.
6 : 1	429.	5 : 5	290.	42 : 6	483.
		5 : 12	421.	42 : 7	694. 842
JOB.		7 : 9–12	290.	44 : 3	369, 786
		7 : 11	245, 258, 645.	45 : 2	678.
1 : 5	725.	7 : 12, 13	421.	45 : 6	318.
1 : 6	454.	8 :	706.	45 : 6, 7	322.
1 : 6–12	448.	8 : 3, 4	249.	49 :	113.

CH. VERSE.	PAGE.	CH. VERSE.	PAGE	CH. VERSE.	PAGE
49 : 15	994.	91 : 11	452.	139 : 16	421.
49 : 20	642.	93 : 1	223.	139 : 17, 18	284.
50 : 5	719.	94 : 9, 10	68.	140 : 5	377.
51 :	833.	94 : 10	666.	143 : 2	573, 850
51 : 1, 2, 10, 14	832.	96 : 10	403.	143 : 11	397.
51 : 2	552.	97 : 2	272, 292, 296.	144 : 12	898.
51 : 3. 7, 11	832.	97 : 7	306.	145 : 3	254.
51 : 4	573, 646, 757.	97 : 10	294, 646, 743.	145 : 5	292.
51 : 4–6	645.	97 : 11	667.	146 : 4	994.
51 : 5	578, 661, 1043.	99 : 4, 5, 9	296.	147 : 4	282.
51 : 6	555, 558, 578, 647.	101 : 4	780.	147 : 15–18	320.
		101 : 5, 6	294.	147 : 20	779.
51 : 6, 7	578.	102 : 13, 14	275.	148 : 2–5	444.
51 : 10	519, 782, 810, 829, 833.	102 : 27	257, 275.	149 : 6	646.
		103 : 11, 12, 17			
51 : 11	317.	103 : 19	421.		
51 : 17	792.	103 : 20	445, 451.	**PROVERBS.**	
56 : 8	282.	104 :	412.		
58 : 3	578.	104 : 4	451.	1 : 23	829.
59 : 10	364, 819.	104 : 14	421.	3 : 6	440.
63 : 8	421.	104 : 16	421.	3 : 19	320.
66 : 7	421.	104 : 21, 28	421.	4 : 18	827.
68 : 10	421.	104 : 24	282.	5 : 22	633, 652
68 : 17	447, 1052.	104 : 26	412.	8 : 1	320.
68 : 18	309, 758.	104 : 29, 30	412.	8 : 22, 30, 31	320.
69 : 2	942.	105 : 15	710, 856.	8 : 22–31	341.
69 : 9	724.	106 : 12, 13	837.	8 : 23	309, 378.
71 : 15	256.	106 : 13	440.	8 : 36	786.
72 : 6	518.	106 : 30	737.	14 : 9	649.
72 : 15	314.	107 : 20	320.	14 : 13	294.
72 : 18	445.	107 : 23, 23	431.	16 : 1	422.
73 :	113.	110 : 3	784, 792, 830.	16 : 4	397.
74 : 5	155.	113 : 4–6	256.	16 : 14	720.
75 : 6, 7	421.	113 : 5	105, 280.	16 : 32	288.
76 : 10	424.	113 : 5, 6	249, 255, 288.	16 : 33	421.
77 : 19, 20	119.	114 : 1	401, 788.	17 : 15	850.
78 : 25	443, 445.	115 : 3	122, 287.	19 : 21	423.
78 : 41	256.	116 : 1–8	437.	20 : 9	573.
78 : 49	457.	116 : 15	983.	20 : 24	423.
81 : 12, 13	423.	118 :	675.	20 : 27	22, 486.
82 : 1	307.	118 : 22	795.	21 : 1	423, 784.
82 : 6	380, 515.	118 : 22, 23	138.	30 : 4	318, 341.
82 : 6, 7	307.	119 : 18	35.	31 : 4	231.
82 : 7	614.	119 : 36	519, 819, 825.	31 : 6–7	231.
84 : 11	289, 336.	119 : 89	298, 320.		
85 : 4	829.	119 : 89–91	355.	**ECCLESIASTES.**	
85 : 8	850.	119 : 96	542.		
85 : 9	687.	121 : 3	421.	2 : 11	404.
85 : 10	298, 754.	123 : 1	280.	3 : 21	485.
85 : 10, 11	245.	124 : 2	425.	7 : 20	573.
86 : 11	346.	124 : 4, 5	942.	7 : 29	517.
87 : 4	812.	130 : 4	855.	9 : 10	994.
88 : 35	399.	132 : 1	1043.	11 : 3	1001.
89 : 2	256.	135 : 6, 7	421.	12 : 7	469, 483, 490, 991, 1000.
89 : 7	450.	138 : 2	288.		
90 : 2	275, 377.	139 : 2	282.		
90 : 7, 8	658.	139 : 6	282.	**SONG OF SOLOMON.**	
90 : 7–9	657.	139 : 7	105, 280, 316.		
90 : 8	577.	139 : 12	283.	1 : 4	829.
90 : 16, 17	819.	139 : 13, 14	491.		
		139 : 15, 16	495.		

ISAIAH.

1 : 1	239.
1 : 5	553.
4 : 5	377.
4 : 11	661.
5 : 4	404, 792.
5 : 13	135.
5 : 16	269.
5 : 18	650.
5 : 23	850.
6 : 1	309.
6 : 3	256, 268, 296, 318.
6 : 5	555, 634.
6 : 5, 7	268.
6 : 8	318.
7 :	136.
7 : 9	850.
7 : 10–13	437.
7 : 14–16	138, 1007.
8 :	136.
8 : 20	114, 440.
9 : 6	322, 680, 697, 797, 811.
9 : 6, 7	138, 310.
10 : 5	424.
10 : 5, 7	442.
13 : 16	136.
14 : 7	221.
14 : 12	518.
14 : 26, 27	355.
17 : 1	136.
24 : 22	139.
25 : 4	669.
25 : 7	666.
26 : 19	995, 996.
28 : 16	795, 850.
28 : 21	126, 1053.
31 : 6	829.
37 : 34–37	136.
38 : 17, 18	657.
40 : 3	309, 506.
40 : 18	119, 288.
40 : 15, 16	399.
40 : 66	239.
41 : 4	275.
41 : 8	136.
41 : 20	377.
41 : 21, 22	285.
41 : 23	135.
42 : 1	138, 485.
42 : 1–7	137, 697.
42 : 9	135.
42 : 16	426, 441.
42 : 19	649.
42 : 21	740, 749.
43 : 7	397.
44 : 6	259.
44 : 24	286.
44 : 28	136, 197, 282, 355.

CH. VERSE.	PAGE.
45 : 5	197, 421.
45 : 7, 8	377.
45 : 22	791.
46 : 9, 10	282.
46 : 10, 11	355.
48 : 11	397.
48 : 16	318.
48 : 18	284.
49 : 1–12	696, 697.
49 : 50, 61	675.
50 : 2	850.
52 : 2	678.
52 : 10	256.
53 :	137, 138.
53 : 1–12	725.
53 : 4, 10	423.
53 : 5	732.
53 : 5, 6	720.
53 : 6	265.
53 : 6–12	719.
53 : 10	680, 797.
53 : 10, 11	697.
53 : 11	850.
53 : 12	774.
54 : 5	796.
55 : 6	791.
57 : 2	439.
57 : 15	105, 280.
57 : 16	491.
57 : 19	377.
59 : 2	198, 983.
59 : 20	829.
60 : 21	397.
61 : 1	137.
61 : 3	397.
63 : 7, 10	318.
63 : 9	266.
63 : 10	324.
64 : 4	421.
65 : 12	791.
65 : 17	377.
65 : 22	888.
65 : 24	364.
66 : 1	254.
66 : 11	523.
66 : 13	323.

JEREMIAH.

1 : 4	27.
1 : 5	421.
3 : 15	16.
3 : 20	796.
3 : 25	394.
9 : 9	485.
9 : 23, 24	245.
9 : 24	3.
10 : 10	245, 251.
10 : 23	423.
10 : 24	272, 653.
13 : 21	578.

CH. VERSE.	PAGE.
13 : 23	810.
14 : 20	594.
17 : 9	553, 578.
18 : 8	136.
20 : 7	240.
23 : 6	943.
23 : 23, 24	105, 280.
23 : 29	811.
24 : 7	4, 825.
25 : 5	833.
26 : 13, 19	136.
31 : 3	788, 1044.
31 : 18	829.
31 : 22	377.
31 : 33	810.
32 : 18	634.
36 : 23	540.
44 : 4	295, 418, 652
45 : 5	410.
55 : 34, 44	241.

LAMENTATIONS.

1 : 12	757.
3 : 39–45	634.
5 : 7	718.
5 : 21	829.

EZEKIEL.

1 :	449.
1 : 5, 12	449.
2 : 7	789.
10 :	449.
11 : 19	810, 829.
14 : 6	829.
18 : 4	633.
18 : 31	829.
18 : 32	829.
20 : 5	630.
26 : 7–14	136.
28 : 14–19	450.
28 : 22	272.
29 : 17–20	136.
32 : 21	994.
33 : 9, 11	829.
33 : 11	791.
36 : 21, 22	272.
36 : 26	829.
37 : 1–14	995, 996.
37 : 6	449.
37 : 9–14	339.

DANIEL.

2 : 28, 36	711.
2 : 45	141.
3 : 18	426.
3 : 25, 28	319.
4 : 31	209.
4 : 35	355, 431.

CH. VERSE.	PAGE
6 : 22	452.
7 : 10	449.
7 : 13	141, 678, 682
9 : 27	141.
10 : 14	139.
10 : 19	445.
11 : 31	141.
11 : 36	138, 454.
12 : 1	141.
12 : 2	1000, 1018.
12 : 2, 3, 13	995, 996.
12 : 3	850.
12 : 8, 9	139

HOSEA.

1 : 7	318.
2 : 2–5	796.
2 : 6	423.
4 : 17	424, 652, 790.
4 : 18	792.
6 : 7	614.
8 : 1, 2	614.
11 : 1	138, 235.
11 : 8	790, 1053.
12 : 3, 4	463.
13 : 5	780.
13 : 9	1050.

JOEL.

2 : 12–14	829.
2 : 28	587.

AMOS.

1 :	136.
1 : 2	135.
2 :	136.
3 : 2	780, 781.
6 : 8	485.
9 : 9	136.
9 : 14	136.

JONAH.

2 : 9	137.
3 : 3	241.
3 : 4	136.
3 : 4, 10	258.
3 : 10	136.
4 : 11	661.

MICAH.

3 : 12	138.
5 : 2	322.
6 : 8	299.
7 : 3	650.
7 : 18	855.

NAHUM.

1 : 7	780.

HABAKKUK.

1 : 13	418
2 : 4	850.
3 : 4	143.
3 : 20	713.

HAGGAI

1 : 13	319.

ZECHARIAH.

3 : 1	454.
3 : 1–3	448.
3 : 2	454, 458, 856.
4 : 2, 3	888.
5 : 1	355.
6 : 8	753.
9 : 1–4	239.
12 : 1	469, 483, 491, 991.
12 : 10	717.

MALACHI.

1 : 6	638, 639.
2 : 10	474.
2 : 15	256.
3 : 1	322.
3 : 6	257, 259.
3 : 10	287, 438.
3 : 16	282.
4 : 4	114.

MATTHEW.

1 : 1	225.
1 : 1–16	687.
1 : 1–17	673.
1 : 12	826.
1 : 20	319, 686.
1 : 22, 23	138.
2 : 15	138, 235.
2 : 22	717.
3 : 1–12	836.
3 : 2, 3, 6	945.
3 : 3	309.
3 : 6	934.
3 : 6–11	934.
3 : 7	981.
3 : 8	835.
3 : 9	287.
3 : 11	287, 935.
3 : 13	940.
3 : 13, 17	932.
3 : 14	674.

CH. VERSE.	PAGE
3 : 15	717, 761, 853, 943.
3 : 16	696.
3 : 16, 17	325.
3 : 17	148, 209, 216, 341, 762.
4 : 1–11	677.
4 : 2	674.
4 : 3	461.
4 : 3, 6, 9	455.
4 : 4	16, 412.
4 : 4, 6, 7	199.
4 : 6, 7	217.
4 : 10	677.
4 : 11	452, 453.
5 : 1	227.
5 : 1–12	554.
5 : 3	669.
5 : 7	37.
5–8 :	545.
5 : 8	4, 67, 246, 524, 825.
5 : 10	230.
5–7 :	711.
5 : 17	718.
5 : 17, 18	545.
5 : 18	199, 288.
5 : 19	939.
5 : 21, 22	545, 645.
5 : 22	553.
5 : 27, 28	545.
5 : 23, 24	719, 924.
5 : 22, 28	545.
5 : 28	553.
5 : 32	242.
5 : 33, 34	545.
5 : 34	306.
5 : 38, 39	545.
5 : 39–42	546.
5 : 44	264.
5 : 44, 45	289, 475.
5 : 45	421.
5 : 48	260, 290, 302, 543, 545.
6 : 8	282, 421.
6 : 9, 10	272.
6 : 10	368, 434, 450, 792.
6 : 12	645, 835.
6 : 12–14	573.
6 : 13	256, 450.
6 : 16	288.
6 : 20	981.
6 : 22, 23	486, 501.
6 : 24	811.
6 : 26	421, 440.
6 : 30	421.
6 : 32, 33	421.
6 : 33	289, 401, 810.
7 : 11	578.
7 : 22	117, 780.

CH. VERSE.	PAGE.	CH. VERSE.	PAGE.	CH. VERSE.	PAGE.
7 : 23	780.	12 : 43, 45	458.	20 : 17–23	932.
8 : 11	772.	12 : 45	806.	20 : 22	743.
8 : 11, 12	842, 843.	13 : 5, 6	589.	20 : 28	483, 673, 697,
8 : 22	659, 902, 992.	13 : 19	27, 450, 506.		717, 750.
8 : 24	674.	13 : 20	281.	20 : 30	210, 227.
8 : 28	227, 446.	13 : 20, 21	837.	21 : 2	681.
8 : 29	457, 1002.	13 : 23	462.	21 : 21	437.
8 : 31	445.	13 : 24	310.	21 : 25	931.
9 : 2	826.	13 :24–30	354.	21 : 42	135.
9 : 4	310.	13 : 28	588.	22 : 3	791.
9 : 5	128.	13 : 30	234.	22 : 21	898.
9 : 6	682.	13 : 30, 38	1008.	22 : 23	131.
9 : 12	192.	13 : 31, 32	1008.	22 : 30	445, 447
9 : 12, 13	574.	13 : 33	234.	22 : 31, 32	995, 996.
9 : 24	1000.	13 : 38	592, 887.	22 : 32	999, 1017.
9 : 36	674.	13 : 39	454, 1044.	22 : 37	302.
9 : 56	129.	13 : 52	19, 41.	22 : 37–39	572.
10 : 1	201.	13 : 57	711.	22 : 37–40	545.
10 : 15	649, 1045.	14 : 19	465.	22 : 42	669.
10 : 17, 19, 20	207.	14 : 23	674.	22 : 43	314.
10 : 20	206.	15 : 2	934.	23 : 8, 10	898.
10 : 26	283.	15 : 13, 14	42.	23 : 23	638.
10 : 28	459, 483, 660,	15 : 18	506.	23 : 32	648.
	991, 1055.	15 : 19	553, 810.	23 : 33	1055.
10 : 29	282, 421, 851,	16 : 15	851.	23 : 35	315.
	991.	16 : 18	887.	23 : 37	1005.
10 : 30	282, 420, 421.	16 : 18, 19	909.	23 : 37, 38	1053.
10 : 32	645, 889.	16 : 25	642.	24 :	138.
10 : 38	718, 762.	16 : 26	717.	24 : 2	681.
10 : 40	516.	16 : 27	1011.	24 : 5, 11, 12, 24	1008.
10 : 41	951.	16 : 27, 28	1023.	24 : 14	1008.
10 : 42	948.	16 : 28	1003.	24 : 15	141.
11 : 3, 4, 5	156.	17 : 1–8	678.	24 : 23	1003.
11 : 9	710.	17 : 2	696.	24 : 29, 30	1009.
11 : 10	199.	17 : 5	210.	24 : 30	1003.
11 : 12	830.	17 : 8	234.	24 : 34	138.
11 : 19	320.	17 : 15, 18	456.	24 : 35	250.
11 : 21	780.	17 : 17	126.	24 : 36	445, 1006.
11 : 23	282.	17 : 20	900.	25 :	138.
11 : 24	638.	17 : 34	1021.	25 : 1–13	234.
11 : 25, 26	789.	18 : 5, 6, 10, 14	661.	25 : 10	1001, 1046.
11 : 27	163, 246, 334,	18 : 10	450, 451, 452,	25 : 19	1006.
	681, 691.		954.	25 : 24	293.
11 : 28	611, 683, 744,	18 : 14	662, 851.	25 : 27	540.
	791.	18 : 15–17	924.	25 : 29	986.
11 : 28, 29	838.	18 : 17	890, 892, 907.	25 : 31	138, 315, 453,
11 : 29	189.	18 : 18	925.		1004.
12 : 10–13	541.	18 : 19	927.	25 : 31, 32	310, 683, 775.
12 : 28	129, 316.	18 : 19, 20	774.	25 : 31–39	1011.
12 : 31	324.	18 : 20	951.	25 : 31, 46	1023.
12 : 31, 32	464, 650, 1046.	18 : 24, 25	749.	25 : 32	163.
12 : 32	652.	19 : 3–10	242.	25 : 34	790.
12 : 33	507, 826.	19 : 8	545.	25 : 41	448, 455, 457,
12 : 33–35	810.	19 : 14	648, 661, 951.		464, 660, 790.
12 : 34	578.	19 : 17	894.	25 : 41–46	992.
12 : 34, 35	889.	19 : 19	264.	25 : 45	648.
12 : 36	554.	19 : 26	287.	25 : 45, 46	662.
12 : 37	851.	19 : 29	1045.	25 : 46	293, 1044, 1045,
12 : 39	126, 137, 438.	20 : 3	489.		1055.
12 : 41	948.	20 : 12–15	779.	26 : 24	365, 1043.
12 : 43	445.	20 : 13, 15	786.	26 : 26. 28	674.

CH. VERSE.	PAGE.	CH. VERSE.	PAGE.	CH. VERSE.	PAGE.
26 : 26, 29	901.	7 : 14	738.	2 : 40, 46, 49, 52	675.
26 : 27	960.	7 : 15	546.	3 : 18	836.
26 : 28	210, 719.	7 : 34	126.	3 : 21, 22	325.
26 : 29	959, 960.	8 : 4	190.	3 : 22	216.
26 : 34	681.	8 : 27, 29	175.	3 : 23–38	673.
26 : 37	325.	8 : 36, 37	485.	3 : 38	474, 475.
26 : 38	674.	8 : 38	450.	4 : 4–12	199.
26 : 39	298, 438, 698, 718, 762.	9 : 24	848.	4 : 13	677.
26 : 39, 53	677.	9 : 25	456.	4 : 14	325.
26 : 53	448, 703.	9 : 29	458.	4 : 22	678.
26 : 53, 54	755.	9 : 43, 48	1046.	4 : 25–27	786.
26 : 60–75	230.	10 : 2	546.	4 : 34	445.
26 : 63–64	313.	10 : 5	545.	5 : 1	27.
26 : 64	141.	10 : 11	242.	5 : 6–9	681.
27 : 3, 4	832.	10 : 18	302.	5 : 8	296, 555.
27 : 9	226.	10 : 21	638, 674.	5 : 20, 21	696.
27 : 18	310.	10 : 21, 22	571.	6 : 17	227.
27 : 37	228.	10 : 23	269.	6 : 19	696.
27 : 42	677, 762.	10 : 32	678, 760.	6 : 43–45	578.
27 : 46	742, 743, 762.	10 : 38	940, 942.	7 : 13	130.
27 : 50	483.	10 : 39	936.	7 : 29	851.
28 : 1	410.	10 : 45	717.	7 : 35	320.
28 : 2	453.	11 : 24	433.	8 : 30, 31	456.
28 : 4	445.	12 : 29, 30	543.	9 : 22–24	716.
28 : 18	163, 775.	12 : 30	485.	9 : 24	943.
28 : 18–20	708.	12 : 30, 31	543.	10 : 17, 18	456.
28 : 19	219, 316, 895, 899, 931, 942, 945, 948, 951, 952.	13 : 19	578.	10 : 27	346.
		13 : 27	780.	10 : 30–37	574.
		13 : 32	314, 446, 677, 695, 1006.	10 : 31	428.
				11 : 11	717.
28 : 19, 20	905, 916, 932.	14 : 15	681.	11 : 13	573, 895.
28 : 20	163, 242, 310, 460, 685, 637, 699, 801, 846, 998.	14 : 23	960.	11 : 20	118.
		14 : 24	210, 959.	11 : 27	448.
		14 : 25	959.	11 : 27, 28	208.
		14 : 27	199.	11 : 29	131.
		15 : 23	742.	11 : 49	320.
28 : 29	324.	15 : 26	228.	12 : 4, 5	1055.
28 : 64	1003.	15 : 45	131.	12 : 12	324, 805.
		16 : 9–20	239, 573, 931.	12 : 14	241.
MARK.		16 : 15	604, 791.	12 : 47, 48	648, 649, 1050.
		16 : 16	573, 662, 931.	12 : 48	558.
1 : 5, 8	935.	16 : 19	708.	12 : 49	936.
1 : 5, 9	934.			12 : 50	645, 718, 762, 932, 936, 940, 942.
1 : 9, 10	935.	**LUKE.**			
1 : 41	118.	1 : 1–4	238.		
2 : 7	682.	1 : 6	852.	12 : 56	760.
2 : 27	409, 546.	1 : 34, 35	675.	13 : 2, 3	630.
3 : 5	674, 677.	1 : 35	309, 325, 339, 677, 686, 689.	13 : 4	645.
3 : 11, 12	456.			13 : 11, 16	455.
3 : 17	152.	1 : 37	854.	13 : 17	1046.
3 : 29	463, 650, 1041, 1046, 1048, 1053.	1 : 38	934.	13 : 23, 24	35.
		1 : 46	485.	13 : 33	711.
4 : 15	455.	1 : 52	421.	14 : 23	234, 791.
4 : 39	682.	2 : 11	776.	15 :	516, 784.
5 : 2, 4	456.	2 : 13	448, 453.	15 : 8	515.
5 : 9	455.	2 : 14	397.	15 : 10, 24	836.
5 : 19	190.	2 : 21	943.	15 : 11–32	241, 474.
5 : 39, 40	659.	2 : 21, 22, 23, 24	761.	15 : 12, 13	572.
5 : 41	696.	2 : 24	554, 943.	15 : 17	338, 558.
7 : 4	934.	2 : 25	1007.	15 : 18	833.
7 : 13	199.	2 : 34	709.	15 : 23, 24	856.

CH. VERSE.	PAGE	CH. VERSE.	PAGE.	CH. VERSE	PAGE.
15 : 32	659, 992.	1 : 4	309, 584, 694.	3 : 16	245, 264, 289,
16 : 1–8	241.	1 : 4, 9	715.		856, 935.
16 : 18	242.	1 : 5	603.	3 : 18	645.
16 : 22	452, 999.	1 : 9	68, 109, 134,	3 : 18, 19	1023.
16 : 23	994, 999.		197, 571, 603,	3 : 18–20	841.
16 : 23	994, 999.		666, 681, 744.	3 : 18–36	574, 645.
16 : 26	1001, 1042, 1046.	1 : 12	475, 839, 935.	3 : 21	5.
16 : 32	446.	1 : 12, 13	474, 793, 825,	3 : 23	935.
17 : 3	835.		842.	3 : 33	288.
17 : 5	804, 848.	1 : 13	495, 598, 642,	3 : 34	696.
17 : 7–10	293.		782, 811, 819.	3 : 36	645, 1046.
17 : 20	892.	1 : 14	109, 160, 234,	4 : 1	32.
18 : 7	780.		322, 341, 673,	4 : 1, 2	932.
18 : 13	556, 720, 741,		684, 686, 687.	4 : 6	314, 674.
	834.	1 : 15	310.	4 : 9	167.
18 : 23	832.	1 : 16	256, 804, 805.	4 : 10	239.
18 : 35	210, 227.	1 : 17	262, 548.	4 : 14	839.
19 : 8	835.	1 : 18	14, 246, 306,	4 : 17–19, 39	681.
19 : 8, 9	836.		322, 326, 337,	4 : 21	280, 893.
19 : 23	541.		338, 341, 349.	4 : 24,	250, 305, 335,
19 : 38	776.	1 : 19	109.		540, 1000.
20 : 13	681.	1 : 23	938.	4 : 29	176.
20 : 36	445, 447.	1 : 25	931.	4 : 38	827.
21 : 8–28	1009.	1 : 26	935.	4 : 39	711.
21 : 12	1008.	1 : 29	206, 554, 646,	4 : 48	117.
21 : 19	959.		647, 719, 728,	5 : 3, 4	239.
22 : 19	960.		744, 757.	5 : 14	837.
22 : 20	210.	1 : 31	935, 943.	5 : 17	253, 259, 412,
22 : 22	355.	1 : 33	935.		419, 426.
22 : 31	457.	1 : 41	137.	5 : 17, 19	333.
22 : 31, 32	774, 831.	1 : 42, 43	681.	5 : 18	313.
22 : 31, 40	458.	1 : 47–50	681.	5 : 19	302.
22 : 37	720.	1 : 50	256.	5 : 20–29	1024.
22 : 42	695, 936.	2 : 2	685, 771.	5 : 21	680, 810.
22 : 43	445, 453.	2 : 7–10	465.	5 : 22	333.
22 : 44	675.	2 : 11, 24, 25	696.	5 : 23	311.
23 : 15	760.	2 : 19	131.	5 : 24	659, 811, 842,
23 : 34	325, 462, 463,	2 : 19, 21	234.		992.
	649, 677, 774.	2 : 21	131.	5 : 26	245, 251, 309.
23 : 38	228.	2 : 23, 24	837.	5 : 27	678, 682.
23 : 42	833.	2 : 24	838.	5 : 27–29	310.
23 : 43	821, 994, 998.	2 : 24, 25	310, 682.	5 : 28	350.
23 : 43–46	998, 999.	3 : 2	837.	5 : 28, 29	1005, 1011, 1017
23 : 46	311, 746.	3 : 3	36, 810, 818,	5 : 28–30	998.
24 : 25	4.		887.	5 : 29	1042.
24 : 26	646, 764.	3 : 3–5	573.	5 : 30	302, 572, 677
24 : 27	114, 137.	3 : 5	642, 811, 821,	5 : 32–37	322.
24 : 33	905.		822, 887, 945.	5 : 35	837.
24 : 36	1018.	3 : 5, 6, 10–13	842.	5 : 39	19.
24 : 39	131, 674, 691.	3 : 6	495, 496, 578,	5 : 39, 40	20.
			599, 661, 687.	5 : 40	841.
JOHN.		3 : 7	677, 810, 814.	5 : 42	639.
		3 : 7, 14	729.	5 : 44	259.
1 : 1	2, 151, 305,	3 : 8	258, 287, 316,	5 : 46	239, 314.
	309, 335, 336,		324, 338, 340,	6 : 14	711.
	337, 378, 388.		732, 810, 811.	6 : 19	210.
1 : 1, 2	326.	3 : 11	684.	6 : 20	846.
1 : 1–4	109.	3 : 12	681.	6 : 27	293, 305.
1 : 1–18	320.	3 : 13	681, 686.	6 : 32	206.
1 : 3	275, 310, 326.	3 : 14	751, 760.	6 : 37	781, 839.
1 : 3, 4	311.	3 : 14, 15	733.	6 : 41, 51	686.

CH. VERSE. PAGE.

6 : 44 — 78, 642.
6 : 44, 65 — 810.
6 : 47, 52, 63 — 992.
6 : 50 — 573.
6 : 53 — 839.
6 : 53, 56, 57 — 797.
6 : 54, 58 — 1045.
6 : 55 — 297.
6 : 62 — 310.
6 : 64 — 315.
6 : 65 — 782.
6 : 69 — 309.
7 : 17 — 4, 20, 584, 825, 841.
7 : 18 — 552, 572.
7 : 39 — 317.
7 : 53 — 638.
8 : 1–11 — 239, 638.
8 : 7 — 925.
8 : 9 — 638.
8 : 12 — 838.
8 : 29 — 269.
8 : 30, 31 — 837.
8 : 31–36 — 509.
8 : 34 — 553, 642.
8 : 35 — 475.
8 : 36 — 509, 828.
8 : 40 — 673.
8 : 41–44 — 475.
8 : 44 — 450, 583, 657.
8 : 46 — 677.
8 : 51 — 659, 992.
8 : 57 — 348, 678.
8 : 58 — 163, 310, 326, 681, 695.
9 : 2, 3 — 630.
9 : 3 — 645.
9 : 30 — 1023.
10 : 3 — 364.
10 : 7 — 34.
10 : 7–9 — 802.
10 : 10 — 824.
10 : 11 — 720.
10 : 16 — 842, 843, 914.
10 : 17, 18 — 703.
10 : 18 — 131.
10 : 28 — 781, 801.
10 : 30 — 313, 695.
10 : 34–36 — 307, 515.
10 : 35 — 199.
10 : 36 — 294, 322, 669.
10 : 41 — 131, 156.
11 : 11 — 1000.
11 : 11–14 — 994.
11 : 14 — 681.
11 : 25 — 842.
11 : 26 — 660, 999.
11 : 33, 35 — 674.
11 : 35 — 738.
11 : 35, 43 — 130.
11 : 36 — 264.

11 : 43 — 822.
11 : 49–52 — 207.
11 : 51, 52 — 843.
12 : 24 — 680.
12 : 27 — 483, 731, 762.
12 : 31 — 1023.
12 : 32 — 311, 791.
12 : 32, 33 — 835.
12 : 33 — 315, 681.
12 : 41 — 309.
12 : 44 — 350.
12 : 47 — 241, 573.
13 : 1 — 315.
13 : 7 — 35.
13 : 8 — 571, 733.
13 : 10 — 831.
13 : 21 — 483.
13 : 27 — 424, 455, 674.
13 : 29 — 901.
13 : 33 — 680.
14 : 1 — 838.
14 : 1–3 — 991.
14 : 3 — 659, 998.
14 : 3–18 — 1003.
14 : 6 — 28, 251, 260, 309, 802.
14 : 9 — 14, 313, 333, 349, 699, 845.
14 : 9, 10 — 681.
14 : 10, 23 — 797.
14 : 11 — 117, 333.
14 : 12 — 120.
14 : 14 — 311.
14 : 16 — 774.
14 : 16, 17 — 323, 339.
14 : 16–18 — 323.
14 : 17 — 288, 604, 1045.
14 : 18 — 323, 333, 680.
14 : 20 — 759, 797.
14 : 21 — 256.
14 : 26 — 207, 323, 744.
14 : 28 — 314, 342.
14 : 30 — 448, 677.
15 : 1 — 516, 680, 796.
15 : 3 — 811.
15 : 4, 5 — 642.
15 : 4–6 — 110.
15 : 5 — 331, 898.
15 : 6 — 474, 475.
15 : 7 — 438.
15 : 9 — 778.
15 : 10 — 331.
15 : 15 — 21, 440, 737.
15 : 16 — 598, 779, 784, 787.
15 : 26 — 323, 333, 341.
15 : 26, 27 — 207.
16 : 2 — 192.
16 : 7 — 323, 604, 697.
16 : 8 — 316, 324, 339, 454, 856.

16 : 8, 9 — 841.
16 : 8–11 — 338.
16 : 9 — 350.
16 : 10 — 762.
16 : 11 — 448.
16 : 12 — 35.
16 : 12, 13 — 164.
16 : 12, 26 — 901.
16 : 13 — 31, 134, 137, 206, 207.
16 : 13, 14 — 316.
16 : 14 — 134, 323, 324, 326.
16 : 14, 15 — 317.
16 : 15 — 313, 349.
16 : 18 — 242.
16 : 26 — 698.
16 : 28, 30 — 310.
17 : 2 — 781.
17 : 3 — 3, 67, 259, 260, 261, 391.
17 : 4 — 324, 746.
17 : 4, 5 — 310.
17 : 5 — 256, 309, 314, 326, 378, 698, 699, 703.
17 : 6 — 787.
17 : 8 — 207.
17 : 9 — 774, 781.
17 : 9, 20, 24 — 771.
17 : 10 — 313.
17 : 11 — 272, 313.
17 : 12 — 430, 475.
17 : 19 — 674, 762.
17 : 21–23 — 798.
17 : 22 — 313.
17 : 22, 23 — 301.
17 : 23 — 245, 684.
17 : 24 — 263, 310, 326, 776.
17 : 25 — 274.
18 : 4 — 682.
18 : 8, 9 — 430.
18 : 11 — 743.
18 : 32 — 681.
18 : 36 — 889.
18 : 36, 37 — 776.
18 : 37 — 262, 633.
18 : 38 — 156.
19 : 11 — 648, 649.
19 : 19 — 228.
19 : 28 — 674.
19 : 30 — 733, 762.
19 : 30, 34 — 675.
19 : 36 — 959.
20 : 17 — 680, 681, 707, 998.
20 : 22 — 709, 935.
20 : 26 — 410.
20 : 27 — 691, 1018.
20 : 28 — 306, 311.

CH. VERSE.	PAGE.
20 : 31	839.
21 : 6	681.
21 : 17	833.
21 : 19	315, 355, 681.

ACTS.

CH. VERSE.	PAGE.
1 : 1	150, 164.
1 : 2	315, 316, 410, 696, 703.
1. 7	1006.
1 : 10	453.
1 : 11	1004.
1 : 15, 23, 26	906.
1 : 23–26	894.
1 : 24	310.
1 : 25	660, 1049.
2 :	896, 901.
2 : 2	287.
2 : 4	324.
2 : 22	117, 673.
2 : 23	258, 282, 355, 675.
2 : 24, 31	707.
2 : 31	131.
2 : 33	774.
2 : 37, 38	945, 949.
2 : 38	821, 822, 833, 931, 946, 948, 951.
2 : 41	934.
2 : 42	946, 959, 960.
2 : 46	959, 960.
2 : 47	895, 897, 901.
3 : 13, 26	697.
3 : 18	646.
3 : 22	137, 711.
3 : 26	829.
4 : 12	573, 842, 843.
4 : 27, 28	424.
4 : 27, 30	697.
4 : 31	895.
4 : 32	799.
5 : 3	455.
5 : 3, 4	315, 458.
5 : 3, 4, 9	324.
5 : 4	894.
5 : 6	918.
5 : 7–11	585.
5 : 9	927.
5 : 11	895.
5 : 14	897, 901.
5 : 29	898.
5 : 31	782, 835.
5 : 36	228.
6 : 1–4	918.
6 : 1–6	917.
6 : 2	891.
6 : 3, 5	906.
6 : 5	891.
5 : 5, 6	894, 919.

CH. VERSE.	PAGE.
6 : 8–20	917.
7 : 2	256.
7 : 6	127.
7 : 16	226.
7 : 22	169, 994, 995.
7 : 28	1004.
7 : 38	891.
7 : 39, 53	448.
7 : 42	448.
7 : 51	32.
7 : 53	452.
7 : 55	708.
7 : 59	311, 991, 1000.
7 : 60	595, 659.
8 : 4	899.
8 : 12	821, 945.
8 : 13	837.
8 : 16	948, 951.
8 : 25	27.
8 : 26	319.
8 : 29	324.
8 : 38, 39	935, 936.
9 : 5	209.
9 : 15	779.
9 : 15, 16	787.
9 : 31	891, 892, 912.
10 : 19, 20	324.
10 : 31–44	843.
10 : 34, 35	23.
10 : 35	574, 853.
10 : 38	315, 316, 325, 455, 696, 700, 703.
10 : 42	780.
10 : 43	137.
10 : 48	951.
11 : 18	782, 835.
11 : 21	829.
11 : 24	901.
11 : 28	137.
12 : 7	319.
12 : 15	452.
12 : 23	452.
13 : 2	324. 907.
13 : 2, 3	906, 909, 919.
13 : 33, 34, 35	340, 341.
13 : 38, 39	855.
13 : 39	793, 805.
13 : 48	780.
13 : 48, 49	27.
14 :	22.
14 : 15	23.
14 : 16	424.
14 : 16, 17	666.
14 : 17	26, 32, 113.
14 : 23	890, 906, 919.
14 : 27	891, 906.
15 : 1–35	912.
15 : 2, 4, 22, 30	906.
15 : 6–11	215.
15 : 7–30	909.

CH. VERSE.	PAGE.
15 : 8	282.
15 : 8, 9	782.
15 : 9	770.
15 : 18	282.
15 : 23	906.
15 : 28	324.
16 : 6, 7	324.
16 : 14	810, 819, 821.
16 : 15	951.
16 : 16	456.
16 : 31	843.
16 : 33	934.
16 : 33, 34, 40	951.
17 :	22.
17 : 3	110, 760, 764.
17 : 4	782.
17 : 18	842.
17 : 21–26	494.
17 : 22	23.
17 : 23	27.
17 : 25–27	113.
17 : 26	115, 355, 421, 476, 691, 692.
17 : 27	68.
17 : 27, 28	105, 280, 571.
17 : 28	254, 412, 474, 503, 715, 798.
17 : 29	759.
17 : 30	573, 649, 652.
17 : 31	333, 405.
18 : 8	945.
18 : 9, 10	782.
18 : 10	789.
18 : 14	152.
18 : 26	547.
18 : 27	895.
19 : 1–5	950.
19 : 4	836, 901, 932, 945.
19 : 5	948.
19 : 10, 20	27.
19 : 21	910.
19 : 32, 39	981.
20 : 7	410, 894, 960.
20 : 17	914.
20 : 20, 21	916.
20 : 21	836.
20 : 28	137, 894, 916.
20 : 28–31	915.
20 : 31	1056.
20 : 35	265, 916.
21 : 9	547.
21 : 10	137.
21 : 31–33	240.
22 : 16	946.
22 : 26–29	240.
23 : 5	242.
23 : 6	995, 996.
23 : 26–30	240.
24 : 15	998.
24 : 25	988, 1024.

CH. VERSE.	PAGE.	CH. VERSE.	PAGE.	CH. VERSE.	PAGE.
26 : 6–8	995.	3 : 24–30	849.	7 : 11, 13, 14, 17,	
26 : 7, 8	996.	3 : 25	112, 405, 423,	20	553.
26 : 9	500.		714.	7 : 14	540.
26 : 23	646.	3 : 25, 26	718, 719, 753.	7 : 15	780.
26 : 24, 25	31.	3 : 26	298, 846.	7 : 17	552.
27 : 10	137.	3 : 28	847, 1001.	7 : 18	562, 639, 642,
27 : 21–26	137.	3 : 31	548.		687.
27 : 22–24	364.	4 : 4–16	847.	7 : 23	581, 639, 646,
27 : 24	789.	4 : 5	842, 854.	7 : 24	555, 578, 642,
		4 : 6, 8	851.		983.
ROMANS.		4 : 17	287, 376, 377.	8 : 1	646, 647, 659,
		4 : 20, 21	844.	8 : 1–2	983.
1 : 3	684.	4 : 24, 25	15, 657.	8 : 1–17	805.
1 : 3, 4	340.	4 : 25	717, 763, 852.	8 : 2	316, 548, 590,
1 : 4	129, 676, 762.	5 : 1	854.		804, 811.
1 : 5	847.	5 : 1–2	856.	8 : 3	341, 677, 706,
1 : 7	791.	5 : 5	848.		714, 718, 762,
1 : 13	495.	5 : 6–8	720.		943.
1 : 16	746.	5 : 8	290, 726.	8 : 3, 10, 11	657.
1 : 17	847, 849.	5 : 10	544, 719.	8 : 4	548.
1 : 17–20	26.	5 : 11	856.	8 : 7	562, 571, 573,
1 : 18	266, 644, 983.	5 : 12	39, 210, 490,		580, 639, 818,
1 : 19	13.		495, 593, 604,		831.
1 : 19–21, 28, 32	68.		609, 610, 613,	8 : 7, 8	645.
1 : 19–25	319.		614, 620, 658.	8 : 9, 10	797, 801.
1 : 20	26, 32, 68,	5 : 12–14	579.	8 : 10	805, 852, 983,
	69, 1044, 1046.	5 : 12–17	657.		999.
1 : 23	256.	5 : 12–19	15, 476, 477,	8 : 11	316, 324, 339,
1 : 24	633.		603, 625.		488, 806, 1017.
1 : 24, 28	424.	5 : 12–21	622, 660, 797.	8 : 13	659, 992.
1 : 25	288.	5 : 13	594.	8 : 14	339, 441, 830.
1 : 28	68.	5 : 14	661, 662, 686.	8 : 14, 15	474.
1 : 32	26, 649, 832.	5 : 14, 18, 21	660.	8 : 16	502, 839, 844,
2 : 4	113, 289, 571,	5 : 15	673.	8 : 18–23	1018.
	776, 833.	5 : 16	593.	8 : 19	797.
2 : 5	981.	5 : 16–18	619, 852.	8 : 20, 21	402, 403.
2 : 5–6	662, 1025.	5 : 19	593, 614, 718.	8 : 20–23	658.
2 : 6	290, 648.	5 : 20	543.	8 : 21–23	1004.
2 : 6–11	778.	5 : 21	553, 992.	8 : 23	826, 1002, 1017,
2 : 7	917.	6 : 3	940, 941, 951.		1022.
2 : 12	558, 649.	6 : 3–5	931.	8 : 24	981.
2 : 14	574, 638.	6 : 3–6	932.	8 : 26	323, 324, 325,
2 : 14, 15	541.	6 : 4	936, 941.		338, 339, 439,
2 : 14, 19	538.	6 : 5	796, 941.		454, 798.
2 : 15	26, 68.	6 : 6	824.	8 : 26, 27	438, 774, 848.
2 : 10	1023.	6 : 7	851.	8 : 27	349.
2 : 26	617, 852.	6 : 7, 8	805.	8 : 27–30	780.
3 : 1, 2	779.	6 : 7–10	762.	8 : 28	353, 368, 421,
3 : 2	838.	6 : 9, 10	657.		443.
3 : 4	288.	6 :11	797, 829.	8 : 28, 29, 30	781.
3 : 9	574, 639.	6 : 12	553.	8 : 30	791.
3 : 10–12	573.	6 : 13	810, 945.	8 : 31–39	788.
3 : 11	810.	6 : 13, 18	853.	8 : 32	265, 266, 289,
3 : 12	115.	6 : 15–23	509.		341, 405.
3 : 15	68.	6 : 17	31, 810.	8 : 34	544, 774.
3 : 19	645.	6 : 19	633, 1049.	8 : 35–39	801.
3 : 19, 20, 23	573.	6 : 23	293, 645, 657.	8 : 38	998.
3 : 20	543, 832.	7 : 4	805.	8 : 39	278.
3 : 22	772.	7 : 7, 8	544.	9 :	780.
3 : 23	542, 610.	7 : 8, 9, 10	553.	9 : 1	502.
3 : 24–26	855.	7 : 10–11	941.	9 : 5	306.
3 : 25	**772.**				

CH. VERSE.	PAGE.	CH. VERSE.	PAGE.	CH. VERSE.	PAGE.
9 : 11	661.	15 : 31	841.	5 : 5	157.
9 : 11–16	780.	16 : 1, 2	918.	5 : 9	145, 150.
9 : 16	784.	16 : 5	890.	5 : 13	907, 924, 92
9 : 17	397.	16 : 7	909.	5 : 21	646, 747.
9 : 17, 18	424.	16 : 22	1006.	5 : 37, 38	426.
9 : 17, 22, 23	397.	16 : 25, 26	1044.	6 : 3	445, 446.
9 : 18	296.	16 : 26	1045.	6 : 11	805.
9 : 20	786.	19 : 23	662.	6 : 13–20	1017.
9 : 20, 21	779.	20 : 4–10	1011.	6 : 15, 19	796.
9 : 21	784.			6 : 17	798.
9 : 22, 23	790.	**1 CORINTHIANS.**		6 : 19	315, 488.
9 : 22–25	780.			6 : 20	717.
9 : 23	256.	1 : 2	201, 890, 892,	7 : 10, 12	242.
9 : 23, 24	782.		897.	7 : 14	597, 609, 661
9 : 28	827.	1 : 3	774.		951, 952.
10 : 3	852.	1 : 9	288.	7 : 17	201, 806.
10 : 4	544.	1 : 10	904.	7 : 23	717.
10 : 6–7	280.	1 : 16	210, 951.	7 : 40	242.
10 : 6–8	282.	1 : 16, 17	916.	8 : 3	520, 780, 781
10 : 7	707.	1 : 18	27.	8 : 4	259, 446, 457.
10 : 9	309, 839.	1 : 21	4, 1056.	8 : 6	15, 310, 378.
10 : 9, 10	889.	1 : 23	842.		419, 700.
10 : 9, 12	311.	1 : 23, 24	746.	8 : 12	501.
10 : 10	810, 948.	1 : 23, 24, 26	791.	9 : 16	919, 1056.
11 : 2	780.	1 : 24–29	782.	10 : 1–2	936.
11 : 5–7	778.	1 : 26	562.	10 : 2	941.
11 : 8	152.	1 : 28	377.	10 : 3, 4	942.
11 : 13	254.	1 : 30	710, 781, 805,	10 : 8	227.
11 : 16	397.		806, 852.	10 : 11	1006.
11 : 18	848.	1 : 31	152.	10 : 12	948.
11 : 25	668.	2 : 4	325.	10 : 13	425, 458.
11 : 25, 26	1008.	2 : 7	275, 356.	10 : 16, 17	797.
11 : 29	198, 782, 791	2 : 7–16	250.	10 : 20	457.
11 : 32	423.	2 : 9	36, 289.	10 : 31	401.
11 : 33	34, 282.	2 : 9–13	206.	10 : 33	892.
11 : 36	275, 337.	2 : 10	253, 316.	11 : 2	906.
11 : 38	378.	2 : 10–12	13, 324.	11 : 3	342, 515, 680
12 : 1	32, 776.	2 : 11	253, 316, 483.	11 : 5	547.
12 : 2	40, 260.	2 : 11, 12	40.	11 : 7	515.
12 : 3	782.	2 : 13	19, 35.	11 : 8	494.
12 : 5	755.	2 : 14	4, 484, 642.	11 : 10	452.
12 : 6–8	902.	2 : 14, 16	203.	11 : 11, 12	525.
12 : 15	615.	2 : 28	917.	11 : 16	895.
12 : 16	904.	3 : 1, 2	16.	11 : 23	200.
12 : 19	776.	3 : 6	574.	11 : 23, 24	906.
13 : 1	117, 780.	3 : 6, 7	811.	11 : 23–25	959.
13 : 5	780.	3 : 10	31, 338.	11 : 23–26	895.
13 : 8–10	572.	3 : 10–15	16.	11 : 24	959.
13 : 10	302.	3 : 16	315, 316.	11 : 24–25	311.
14 : 4	899.	3 : 21	40.	11 : 26	546, 933, 959.
14 : 7	572.	3 : 21, 23	805.	11 : 27	960.
14 : 8	983.	3 : 22	983.	11 : 29	952, 960.
14 : 14	241.	4 : 4	851.	11 : 30	1000.
14 : 17	853, 892	4 : 5	310, 894.	12 : 3	309, 782
14 : 23	32, 553.	4 : 7	604, 786.	12 : 4, 6	215.
15 : 2	265, 546, 568.	4 : 13	894.	12 : 4, 8, 11	325.
15 : 3	572, 724.	4 : 15	418.	12 : 6	418.
15 : 19	324, 325.	4 : 17	890.	12 : 8–11	324.
15 : 20	910.	5 : 3	483.	12 : 9	782.
15 : 26	894.	5 : 3–5	200, 924.	12 : 11	316.
15 : 30	263, 316, 324	5 : 4, 5	907.	12 : 12	796, 895.

N. VERSE.	PAGE.
12:13	942.
12:28	401, 710, 891, 902, 912, 917.
13:	35.
13:4	325.
13:10	981.
13:12	8, 35, 143, 219.
13:13	848.
14:23	895.
14:25	546.
14:37	901.
14:37,38	200.
14:40	895.
15:3,4	15.
15:6	906.
15:8	131.
15:12	942.
15:20,23	680, 998.
15:21	673.
15:21,22	476, 657.
15:22	495, 593, 603, 622, 942, 998.
15:22,45	686.
15:22,45,49	797.
15:24	893.
15:25	356, 776.
15:26	590.
15:28	314, 397, 698, 699.
15:32	989.
15:34	68.
15:37,38	1019.
15:38,40	563.
15:40	806.
15:40,45	678.
15:41	898.
15:42,50	658.
15:44	484, 488, 1016.
15:45	316, 333, 527, 697, 805.
15:45,46	802, 991.
15:46	524.
15:51	658, 1005.
15:53,54	1018.
15:54-57	659.
15:55	983.
16:1,2	894.
16:15	780, 951.
16:22	329, 1006.

2 CORINTHIANS.

CH. VERSE.	PAGE.
1:20	288.
1:24	205.
2:6,7	907.
2:6-8	925.
2:11	464.
2:14	431.
2:14-17	1056.
2:15,16	799

CH. VERSE.	PAGE.
2:16	1002.
3:1	895.
3:5	643.
3:6	35, 324.
3:15,16	5.
3:17,18	326, 333, 697.
3:18	219, 315, 663, 678.
4:2	822.
4:4	517, 518, 827.
4:6	286, 336, 337.
4:7	213.
4:17	256, 402.
5:1-8	998.
5:1-9	659.
5:3,4	1002.
5:4	235.
5:8	1000.
5:10	1011, 1023.
5:11	1056.
5:13	31.
5:14	622, 623, 805, 941.
5:14,15	766.
5:15	572, 662, 716.
5:17	793, 797, 804, 811.
5:18,19	719.
5:19	333, 686, 699, 714, 718, 768.
5:21	645, 677, 718, 731, 743, 760.
5:21	718, 731, 743, 805, 853, 856, 843.
6:17	474.
7:1	268, 639, 829.
7:9,10	832.
7:10	836.
7:11	294, 907.
8:5	899.
8:6	334.
8:9	703.
8:19	705, 906.
9:9	1045.
9:15	754.
10:5	543.
10:16	910.
11:1	210.
11:2	796.
11:14	450.
12:2	991.
12:4	35, 999.
12:7	438, 455.
12:8,9	848.
12:9	687.
12:10	10, 317.
13:4	708.
13:11	904.
13:12	201.
13:14	306, 324, 774.

GALATIANS.

1:2	200.
1:4	716, 718.
1:7	475.
1:12	200.
1:15,16	421, 782, 804, 811.
1:16	12.
1:22	892.
2:7	838.
2:10	715.
2:11	215, 909.
2:15	578.
2:16-20	850.
2:19-20	941.
2:20	514, 572, 643, 797, 801, 805.
2:21	1000.
3:6	856.
3:7	836.
3:10	152.
3:11	849.
3:11-13	242.
3:13	430, 657, 718, 728.
3:17	227.
3:19	448, 452, 453.
3:22	573.
3:24	544.
3:26	334, 474, 842.
3:26,27	946.
3:27	797, 941, 948, 951.
4:1-7	475.
4:3	665.
4:4	258, 322, 341, 388, 665.
4:4,5	761.
4:5	338, 717.
4:6	322, 323, 333, 334, 474.
4:9	780, 781.
4:19	13.
4:25	310.
4:28	577.
5:6	770, 846, 847.
5:11	746.
5:14	572.
5:19	554.
5:22	554, 782, 847.
6:1	650.
6:7,8	1049.
6:15	810.

EPHESIANS.

1:	355.
1:2,3	685.
1:3	592.
1:23	697.

CH. VERSE.	PAGE.
1 : 4	275, 309, 388, 781, 782, 797.
1 : 4–5	780.
1 : 4–6	778, 805.
1 : 4, 7	771.
1 : 5	334, 335.
1 : 5, 6	474.
1 : 5, 6, 9	397.
1 : 5–8	781.
1 : 6	774.
1 : 7	114, 849, 855.
1 : 9	253.
1 : 9–11	780.
1 : 10	444, 450, 680.
1 : 11	253, 287, 353, 355, 421.
1 : 13	844.
1 : 14	781.
1 : 17–18	823.
1 : 18	4, 69, 825, 791.
1 : 19	287.
1 : 19, 20	811.
1 : 21, 22	699.
1 : 22	776.
1 : 22, 23	109, 685, 708, 796, 887, 888.
1 : 23	163, 310, 418.
2 : 1	521, 643, 659, 810, 983, 992.
2 : 2	448, 451, 455, 642.
2 : 3	459, 475, 495, 578, 579, 593, 603, 609, 645, 661, 810.
2 : 5	811.
2 : 5, 6	805.
2 : 6	890.
2 : 8	781.
2 : 8–10	643.
2 : 10	355, 364, 423, 475, 521, 598, 782, 785, 804, 811, 819, 824, 826, 831.
2 : 12	68.
2 : 12, 16, 18, 19	719.
2 : 13	797.
2 : 15	545.
2 : 16–18, 21, 22	685.
2 : 18	774.
2 : 20	710, 909.
2 : 20–22	795.
2 : 28	338.
3 : 1	431.
3 : 5	710.
3 : 9	27, 113, 378.
3 : 10	282, 446, 450, 460, 713, 887, 1052.

CH. VERSE.	PAGE.
3 : 10, 11	356.
3 : 11	353.
3 : 12	774.
3 : 14, 15	334, 448, 474, 811.
3 : 16, 17	801.
3 : 17	797, 804, 339.
3 : 18	905.
3 : 19	8.
3 : 20	287.
4 : 3	904.
4 : 5	758, 941.
4 : 5, 6	259.
4 : 6	102, 333.
4 : 7–8	309.
4 : 8	340.
4 : 10	685, 708.
4 : 11	19, 745, 902, 915.
4 : 15, 16	796.
4 : 18	639, 820.
4 : 18, 19	647.
4 : 20	261.
4 : 22	824.
4 : 22–24	639.
4 : 23	484, 633.
4 : 23, 24	811.
4 : 24	514, 511.
4 : 26	234, 294, 743.
4 : 30	266, 316, 324, 325.
4 : 32	314.
5 : 1	543.
5 : 2	719, 736.
5 : 9	31.
5 : 10	32.
5 : 14	659, 810, 829, 992.
5 : 18	464.
5 : 21	311.
5 : 23	680.
5 : 24, 25	887.
5 : 25, 27	717.
5 : 26	946.
5 : 27	739.
5 : 29	1022.
5 : 29, 30	800.
5 : 31	706.
5 : 31, 32	796.
5 : 32	801.
6 : 11	458.
6 : 12	382, 445, 455.
6 : 16	458.
6 : 17	17, 32, 220, 811, 815, 819.
6 : 23	782.

PHILIPPIANS.

CH. VERSE.	PAGE.
1 : 1	894, 902, 914.
1 : 6	999.

CH. VERSE.	PAGE.
1 : 9	265, 297, 440.
1 : 19	333.
1 : 21, 23	659.
1 : 23	731, 999.
1 : 27	904.
2 : 5	806.
2 : 6	308, 313, 314, 326, 336, 703, 718.
2 : 6, 7	249, 703.
2 : 6–11	702, 706.
2 : 7	314, 572, 689, 943.
2 : 7, 8	288.
2 : 10	314.
2 : 10, 11	311.
2 : 12	829.
2 : 12, 13	258, 356, 364, 418, 641, 715, 785, 792, 799, 811, 830.
2 : 13	423, 782, 816.
2 : 16	33.
2 : 30	895.
3 : 6	891, 912.
3 : 8	706.
3 : 8, 9	544, 805.
3 : 8, 10	691.
3 : 9	856.
3 : 11	1002.
3 : 14	791.
3 : 15	574.
3 : 18	895.
3 : 20, 21	800.
3 : 21	678, 1015, 1017.
4 : 5	547, 781.
4 : 5	236, 1006.
4 : 13	512.
4 : 19	421.

COLOSSIANS.

CH. VERSE.	PAGE.
1 : 9, 10	440.
1 : 13	811.
1 : 15	313, 336, 340, 341, 515.
1 : 15, 17	326.
1 : 16	16, 310, 326, 378, 382, 397, 444, 445, 448, 474, 475, 679.
1 : 16, 17	109, 377, 464.
1 : 17	110, 310, 311, 378, 412, 759.
1 : 18	150, 678, 680, 887.
1 : 19	313.
1 : 20	169, 310, 388, 450, 719.
1 : 22	717.
1 : 23	1008.

CH. VERSE.	PAGE.	CH. VERSE.	PAGE.	CH. VERSE	PAGE.
1 : 24	716.	1 : 6–10	1011.	5 : 6	659.
1 : 27	19, 691, 801.	1 : 7	445.	5 : 9	895.
	842.	1 : 7, 10	1004.	5 : 17	915, 917.
1 : 28	260.	1 : 9	660.	5 : 21	447, 450, 452.
2 : 2	691.	2 : 1, 2	138, 140.	5 : 22	919.
3 : 2, 3	109.	2 : 1, 3	1006.	5 : 24	650.
2 : 3	28, 310.	2 : 2	150, 1005.	6 : 4	39.
2 : 5	895.	2 : 3	137, 138.	6 : 13	412.
2 : 7	795.	2 : 3, 4	572.	5 : 15	259, 445.
2 : 9	109, 308, 313,	2 : 3, 4, 7, 8	1008.	6 : 16	14, 246, 262,
	348, 680, 686,	2 : 3, 4, 9	454.		275, 444.
	692.	2 : 3–5	236.	6 : 20	39, 149.
2 : 9, 10	32, 253.	2 : 7	425, 587.		
2 : 10	444.	2 : 8	457.	**2 TIMOTHY.**	
2 : 11, 12	931.	2 : 9	132, 133, 457.		
2 : 12	821, 822, 936,	2 : 10	1024.	1 : 9	771, 781, 791,
	940, 941.	2 : 11, 12	423.		1044.
2 : 15	442, 459.	2 : 13	780.	1 : 10	131, 590.
2 : 18	446, 452, 453.	2 : 14	791.	1 : 12	67, 149.
2 : 20, 21, 22	217.	3 : 6	924, 925.	1 : 13	18.
2 : 21	216.	3 : 11	140.	1 : 14	149.
3 : 2	941.	3 : 14, 15	907.	1 : 16–18	1043.
3 : 3	829.			1 : 18	318.
3 : 3, 4	810.	**1 TIMOTHY.**		2 : 3	18.
3 : 10	514, 517.			2 : 10	789.
3 : 11	546.	1 : 3	787.	2 : 11	805.
3 : 12	780.	1 : 10	39.	2 : 15	19.
4 : 16	201.	1 : 11	245.	2 : 18	998, 1017.
		1 : 12	919.	2 : 20	790.
1 THESSALONIANS.		1 : 13, 15, 16	649.	2 : 25	17, 451, 782,
		1 : 15	556, 787.		835.
1 : 1, 2	848.	1 : 16	787.	2 : 26	445, 835.
1 : 6	294.	1 : 17	259, 275, 1045.	3 : 3	572, 639.
1 : 9	251.	1 : 20	457.	3 : 4	635.
2 : 10	294.	2 : 4	797.	3 : 7	814.
2 : 12	791.	2 : 5	308, 673, 685.	3 : 13	633, 638.
2 : 14	890.	2 : 5	308, 673, 685,	3 : 15	218, 804.
2 : 16	455.		698.	3 : 16	197, 200, 205.
3 : 5	455.	2 : 6	717, 771.	4 : 2	19.
3 : 13	268, 303.	2 : 11, 12	546.	4 : 6	236.
4 : 2, 8	200.	2 : 15	680.	4 : 8	1000, 1005.
4 : 7	268.	3 : 1	914.	4 : 13	217.
4 : 13–17	1017.	3 : 1, 2	902.	4 : 16	594.
4 : 14	1000.	3 : 2	19, 39, 915.	4 : 18	311, 998.
4 : 14–16	1015.	3 : 2–7	919.		
4 : 16	1004, 1005.	3 :	912.	**TITUS.**	
4 : 14, 17	801.	3 : 5	917.		
4 : 15–17	137, 235.	3 : 8	914.	1 : 1	782.
4 : 16	448, 998, 1004,	3 : 8–13	918.	1 : 2	288, 1044.
	1005.	3 : 11	918.	1 : 5	906, 914.
4 : 17	1005.	3 : 15	18, 33, 891,	1 : 6	919.
5 : 10	999, 1000.		903, 905, 977.	1 : 7	914.
5 : 11	899.	3 : 16	15, 686, 691,	1 : 9	19, 919.
5 : 12	916.		718, 762, 843,	1 : 12	165, 696.
5 : 12, 13	780, 902.		852, 856.	1 : 15	339.
5 : 22	732.	4 : 2	501.	2 : 10	333.
5 : 23	484, 485, 806.	4 : 4	758.	2 : 11	758, 771.
5 : 24	288.	4 : 10	758, 771.	2 : 13	307.
		4 : 14	919, 946	2 : 14	717.
2 THESSALONIANS.		4 : 16	1056.	3 : 4	290.
4 : 5–10	772.	5 : 3	464.		

CH. VERSE.	PAGE.
7 . 5	316, 821, 822, 946.

HEBREWS.

CH. VERSE.	PAGE.
1: 1	214, 221.
1: 2	160, 320, 326, 333, 378.
1: 2, 3	109, 412, 685.
1: 3	165, 256, 286, 310, 313, 320, 336, 419, 515, 762, 775.
1: 5, 6	340.
1: 6	307, 311, 1004.
1: 7	457.
1: 8	307, 318, 598, 776.
1: 9	266.
1:10	310, 326.
1:11	310.
1:14	445, 452, 1000.
2: 2	448, 452.
2: 2, 3	648.
2: 3	153.
2: 4	845.
2: 6	653.
2: 6-10	678.
2. 7	315, 706.
2: 8, 9	405, 775.
2: 9	716, 743.
2:10	675, 745.
2:11	476, 680, 692.
2:12	891.
2:13	697.
2:14	455, 459, 670, 685.
2:14, 15	757.
2:16	448, 453, 455, 464, 476, 687, 768, 786.
2:17	720.
2:17, 18	698, 774.
2:18	675.
3: 1	791, 909.
3: 3, 4	310.
3:12	553, 639.
3:13	899.
3:14, 16	674.
3:18	841.
4: 4	153.
4: 6, 11	841.
4: 5-9	410.
4:12	484, 485, 811.
4:13	282.
4:15	677.
4:15, 16	698, 774.
5: 7	674.
5: 8	675.
5:14	16.
6: 1, 3	15.

CH. VERSE.	PAGE.
6: 2	1053.
6:10	399.
6:11	844.
6:18	288.
6:18, 19	485.
7:10	494.
7:15, 16	680, 694, 846.
7:16	309.
7:23, 25	772.
7:24, 25	698.
7:25	639, 698, 774, 776.
7:26	309, 646, 677.
8: 2	260.
8: 5	152, 310.
8: 8, 9	614.
8:13	152.
9: 1	852.
9:11, 12	718.
9:13, 14	724.
9:14	298, 415, 316, 317, 326, 338, 341, 378, 677, 696, 703, 736, 1045.
9: 14, 22, 25	719.
9:15	718.
9:22	645, 766.
9:26	943, 1044.
9:27	1001, 1024.
9:27, 28	1023.
9:28	718, 1001, 1004.
10: 5-7	234.
10: 7	830.
10: 9	539.
10: 12	936.
10: 19-25	848.
10: 22	501, 946.
10: 25	894, 899.
10: 26, 29.	350.
10: 27	1052.
10: 28	350.
10: 31	539, 652, 660, 1056.
10: 38	485.
11: 1	839.
11: 2	675.
11: 3	377.
11: 4	726.
11: 4-7	850.
11: 5	995, 996.
11: 6	643.
11: 8	280, 441.
11: 12	234.
11: 13-16	995, 996.
11: 31	230, 841.
11: 34, 38	165.
12: 2	266.
12: 2, 16	717.
12: 6	272, 983.

CH. VERSE.	PAGE.
12: 9	465, 474, 483, 491, 495.
12:14	296.
12:19	209.
12:20	234.
12:22, 23	446.
12:23	333, 367, 483, 509, 887, 998, 1000.
12:29	268, 272, 653.
13: 7	915, 916.
13: 8	163, 309, 888, 1003.
13:17	916.
13:21	311.
13:22	680.

JAMES.

CH. VERSE.	PAGE.
1: 5	265, 440.
1: 13, 14	562.
1: 14, 15	562.
1: 15	573, 585, 633, 981.
1: 17	256, 257, 359.
1: 18	782, 811, 889.
1: 21	485.
1: 23, 24	543.
1: 23-25	219, 681.
1: 27	24.
2: 8	572.
2: 10	543.
2: 14-26	846.
2: 19	457, 837.
2: 21, 23, 24	851.
2: 23	782.
2: 25	230.
2: 26	483.
3: 2	573.
3: 9	515.
3: 17	297, 911.
4: 7	458.
4: 12	543.
4: 13-15	423.
4: 17	542, 553, 642.
5: 7	1006.
5: 8, 9	1007.
5: 9	236.
5: 11	241.
5: 14	902.
5: 16	834.
5: 19, 20	850.
5: 20	660, 992.

1 PETER.

CH. VERSE.	PAGE.
1: 1, 2	324, 450, 786, 781.
1: 2	305, 316, 324, 778, 782, 788.
1: 3	418, 811.

CH. VERSE.	PAGE.	CH. VERSE.	PAGE.	CH. VERSE.	PAGE.
1 : 5	848.	2 : 4	296, 382, 450,	5 : 7	261, 288.
1 : 10, 11	235.		464, 786.	5 : 10	200, 844.
1 : 11	134, 137, 197,	2 : 8, 9	1024.	5 : 14, 15	848.
	206.	2 : 9	1000, 1002.	5 : 16, 17	650.
1 : 11, 12	200.	2 : 11	445.	5 : 17	553.
1 : 12	445, 450.	3 : 2	200.	5 : 18, 19	450.
1 : 16	290, 296, 302,	3 : 3–12	1007.	5 : 19	574.
	543.	3 : 4	236.	5 : 20	260, 308.
1 : 18	719.	3 : 5	509, 558.		
1 : 19	677.	3 : 7, 10	1011, 1024.	2 JOHN.	
1 : 19, 20	266.	3 : 7, 10, 13	1015.		
1 : 20	780.	3 : 7–13	287.	7	686, 1005.
1 : 23	33, 811, 824.	3 : 15, 16	201.	6	293.
2 : 4, 5	795.	3 : 16	200.		
2 : 5	774.	3 : 18	16, 311.	3 JOHN.	
2 : 5, 6	805.				
2 : 8	355, 784, 790.	1 JOHN.		2	483.
2 : 9	401, 781, 811.	1 : 1	674.		
2 : 17	515.	1 : 3	797.	JUDE.	
2 : 21	678, 729, 732.	1 : 5	250, 269, 273,		
2 : 21, 24	717.		344.	3	42, 200, 202,
2 : 22	677.	1 : 7	719.		905.
3 : 1, 2	914.	1 : 7, 8	645.	4	790.
3 : 8	904.	1 : 8	573.	6	165, 450, 458.
3 : 15	311, 739.	1 : 9	289, 739.		1046.
3 : 16	501.	1 : 12	856.	6, 7	1044.
3 : 18	685, 720, 762.	2 : 1	322, 339, 739,	9	165, 448.
3 : 18. 20	707, 708.		774.	19	484, 485.
3 : 19	999, 1000.	2 : 1, 2	323.	21	324.
3 : 21	501, 776, 821,	2 : 2	720.	23	899.
	941.	2 : 7	40.	25	275, 388.
3 : 32	444.	2 : 7, 8	263.	28	1055.
4 : 6	657, 762, 983.	2 : 18	1006.		
4 : 7	236, 1006.	2 : 20	805, 897.	REVELATION.	
4 : 11	401, 641.	3 : 1, 2	474.		
4 : 14	256.	3 : 2	524, 663, 705,	1 : 1	140.
4 : 19	288.		806.	1 : 3	1007.
5 : 1	909.	3 : 3	678.	1 : 6	776, 917.
5 : 2	894, 911.	3 : 3–6	263.	1 : 7	460, 710, 1004,
5 : 2, 3	917.	3 : 4	552.		1005.
5 : 3	898.	3 : 5–7	677.	1 : 8	275, 310.
5 : 6	288.	3 : 8	459.	1 : 10	410.
5 : 8	454, 455.	3 : 9	418.	1 : 10, 11	209.
6 : 9	458.	3 : 14	660, 992.	1 : 18	1045.
		3 : 16	309.	1 : 20	452.
2 PETER.		3 : 20	647, 722.	2 :	905.
		4 : 1	440.	2 : 1	916.
		4 : 2	674, 684, 686.	2 : 6	310.
1 : 3	289, 842.	4 : 7	68, 152, 570.	2 : 7	999.
1 : 4	475, 515, 592,	4 : 7, 8	4.	2 : 8	916.
	685, 693, 797,	4 : 8	250, 263, 336,	2 : 11	983.
	811.		520.	2 : 12	916.
1 : 10	311, 791, 844.	4 : 9	716.	2 : 13	448.
1 : 11	776.	4 : 10	720, 776.	2 : 18	916.
1 : 16	157.	4 : 13	844.	2 : 21	841.
1 : 19	112.	4 : 16	797.	3 : 1	916, 992.
1 : 19, 20	139.	4 : 19	694.	3 : 7	309, 916.
1 : 21	137, 197, 200,	4 : 21	460.	3 : 14	310, 916.
	205, 317, 325,	5 : 1	893.	3 : 20	464, 791, 834,
	339.	5 : 4	732.		1008.
3 : 1	717, 771.	5 : 6	943.	3 : 21	805.

CH. VERSE.	PAGE.	CH. VERSE.	PAGE.	CH. VERSE.	PAGE.
4 : 3	272.	13 : 8	266, 285, 298,	20 : 12	1023.
4 : 6–8	449.		762.	20 : 12, 13	1023, 1050.
4 : 8	296.	14 : 10	464.	20 : 13	1015.
4 : 11	397, 406.	14 : 11	660.	20 : 14	983, 999.
5 : 1, 7, 9	356.	14 : 13	999.	20 : 15	781.
5 : 6	333, 774.	15 : 1–4	273, 653.	21 : 4, 5	1018.
5 : 9	449.	15 : 2	274.	21 : 5	209, 810, 1004
5 : 10	805.	15 : 8	275.	21 : 8	983, 1048.
5 : 11	447.	15 : 13	325.	21 : 9	1048.
5 : 12	140.	16 : 3	485.	21 : 10	310.
5 : 13, 14	311.	16 : 5	273, 653.	21 : 11	1049.
5 : 20	665.	16 : 10	448.	21 : 14	909.
6 : 9	483, 485.	17 : 17	355.	21 : 17	781.
6 : 9–11	999.	18 : 13	445, 516.	21 : 22	893.
6 : 10, 11	1002.	19 : 2	273, 653.	21 : 23	256, 712.
6 : 16	350.	19 : 5	653.	22 : 2	914.
7 :	896.	19 : 7	796.	21 : 27	790.
7 : 16	251.	19 : 9	209.	22 : 4	67.
7 : 16, 17	774.	19 : 10	842.	22 : 6	200, 465.
8 : 28, 29	782.	19 : 14	448.	22 : 8, 9	319, 453, 515.
10 : 6	278.	19 : 15, 16	775.	22 : 9	446.
10 : 8–11	823.	20 : 1–5	403, 1015.	22 : 11	851, 852, 1001,
11 : 11	251.	20 : 2	382, 455.		1048.
11 : 17	889.	20 : 2, 3	425.	22 : 12, 20	1007.
12 : 9–12	457.	20 : 2–10	445.	22 : 13, 14	326.
12 : 10	454.	20 : 4–6	1008.	22 : 14	527.
12 : 11	732. 751.	20 : 6	805.	22 : 16	630, 637.
12 : 12	445, 451,	20 : 10	382, 457, 464,	22 : 17	332, 547, 796
		20 : 11–15	1011.		

INDEX OF APOCRYPHAL TEXTS.

1 ESDRAS.

CH. VERSE.	PAGE.
1 : 28	166.
1 : 38	261.
4 : 35–38	320.
6 : 1	261.

2 ESDRAS.

3 : 7	626.
3 : 21	626.
5 : 55, 66	156.
7 : 11	626.
7 : 46	626.
7 : 48	626.
7 : 118	626.
9 : 19	626.

TOBIT.

4 : 15	181.

JUDITH.

12 : 71	934.

ESTHER, CONTINUATION OF.

CH. VERSE.	PAGE.
1 : 1	309.

WISDOM.

2 : 23, 24	626.
7 : 26	320.
7 : 28	320.
9 : 9, 10	320.
11 : 16	633.
11 : 17	377.

ECCLESIASTICUS, or SIRACH.

Prologue	166.
2 : 1	870.
2 : 30	865.
18 : 1	446.
24 : 23–27	166.
25 : 24	626.
31 : 25	934.
48 : 24	166.

BARUCH.

CH. VERSE.	PAGE.
2 : 21	166.

BEL AND THE DRAGON.

Book of	115.

1 MACCABEES.

Book of	165, 309.
12 : 9	166.

2 MACCABEES.

2 : 13–15	167.
6 : 26	166.
7 : 28	377.
12 : 39	1045.

BOOK OF ENOCH.

	165.

ASSUMPTION OF MOSES.

Book of	165.
v. 9	658.

INDEX OF GREEK WORDS.

ἃ οἶδεν, ... 67
ἀγαθῆς, ... 821
ἀγαθόν, ...562, 687
ἀγαπάω, ... 264
ἀγάπη, ...35, 342
ἀγάπην, τὴν, 1 John 3:16, — the personal
  Love, ... 309
ἀγγέλους, ... 706
ἁγιάζω, ... 728
ἀγνωσίαν Θεοῦ τινες ἔχουσιν, ... 68
ἀγῶνα, ... 870
ἀγωνίζου, ... 870
ἄγραφος νόμος, ... 541
ἀδικία, ... 552
ἄθεοι ἐν τῷ κόσμῳ, forsaken of God, ... 68
ἀθεράπευτον, ... 671
Ἅιδης, ... 994
ἀίδιος, ...1044, 1046
αἵματι, ... 753
αἱρετικὸς ἄνθρωπος, meaning in Titus 3:10, 974
αἵρων, its meaning in John 1:29, ... 719
αἴσθησις, spiritual discernment, Phil.
  1:9, ... 440
αἰών, ...1038, 1044, 1045, 1046
αἰῶνα, ... 307
αἰώνιος, ...1038, 1044, 1045, 1046
αἰώνος, ... 1025
αἰώνων, πρὸ τῶν, ... 275
ἀλήθεια, ... 204, 549
ἀληθής, the Veracious, ... 260
ἀληθινός, 1 John 5:20, ... 151, 260, 308
ἄλλο καὶ ἄλλο and the εἷς, ... 671
ἄλλος καὶ ἄλλος and the συνάφεια, ... 671
ἁμαρτάνειν, Rom. 5:12, 19, ... 626
ἁμαρτάνουσιν, ... 626
ἁμαρτία, ... 552, 657, 706, 714, 761, 832, 851
ἁμαρτωλοὶ κατεστάθησαν, ... 627
ἁμαρτωλὸν γίγνεσθαι, ... 626
ἀμνος, ... 151
ἀνά, ... 523
ἀναβαίνων, ... 935
ἀνακεφαλαιώσασθαι, ... 680
ἀναλῦσαι, ... 999
ἀνάστασιν μέλλειν, ἔσεσθαι, ... 998
ἀνδρός, ... 494
ἀνέβησαν, ... 935
ἀνήρ, ... 666
ἀνθρωπίνης σοφίας, ... 210

ἄνθρωπος, ...506, 523, 974
ἀνομία, the state of, ... 552
ἀντάλλαγμα, ...717, 721
ἀντί, ...717, 720
ἀντίληψεις, ...902, 917, 918
ἀντίλυτρον, ... 717
ἀνυποστασία, ...673, 679
ἄνω, ... 523
ἀπ' ἄρτι, ... 1003
ἅπαξ, once for all, ...200, 885, 967
ἅπαξ λεγόμενον, ... 222
ἀπαύγασμα, ... 336
ἀπεθάνετε, ... 803
ἀπειθήσασιν, 1 Pet. 3:20, ... 708
ἀπηλάθην, ... 233
ἀπηλγηκότες, ... 647
ἁπλῶς ἕν, τό, ... 245
ἀπό, ...833, 1034
ἀπὸ ὁ ὤν, ... 151
ἀποκαλύπτεται, ... 26
ἀποκάλυψις, ... 13
ἀπομνημονεύματα, ... 148
ἀποδώσει, ἀποδώῃ, ... 231
ἀποθανών, ... 851
ἀποστασία, ... 552, 1008
ἀποστρέφω, ... 829
ἀποτέλεσμα, genus apotelesmaticum, ... 686
ἀπρόσληπτον καὶ ἀθεράπευτον, τό, a patristic
  dictum, ... 671
ἀπώλεια, ... 721, 993
ἀπώλετο, ... 993
ἀρνίον, ... 151
ἄρτι, ... 1003
ἀρτολατρία, ... 969
ἀρχάγγελος, ... 320
ἀρχή, ... 310, 675
ἀρχῇ, ἐν, ... 309
ἀρχήν, ... 450
ἀρχιερεύς, ... 320
ἀσέβεια, ... 552
ἀττικίζων, ... 665
αὐτομάτη, ... 393
αὐτός, ... 310
αὐτῷ, ... 837
αὐτῶν, ... 906
ἀφανίζω, ... 993
ἀφορίσατε, ... 900
βαπτίζω, ... 923, 934, 935, 937, 938, 942, 943

βάπτισμα, 933
βαπτισμός, 937
βάπτω, 933, 934, 938
βάρβαροι, 579
βασάνοις, ἐν, 999
βασιλευόντων, 445
βασιλεὺς τῶν αἰώνων, 275
βδέλυγμα τῆς ἐρημώσεως, 151
βουλή, arbitrium, Willkür, 557
βραχύ τι, its translation in Heb. 2 : 7, 706
γέγονεν, 311
γέγραπται, 148
γενησόμενον, 1019
γενήσονται, 914
γενόμενος, 705
γένος, 681
γῆ, 393
γῆς ἐμῆς ἀπηλάθην, 233
γιγνώσκωσιν, 841
γινώσκεσθαι, 781
γινώσκω, 781
γνόντα, 761
γνώμη, 221
γνῶσις, 1 Tim. 6 : 20; cf. ἐπιγνωσις, 2 Pet.
    1 : 2, 31, 841
γνωστὸν τοῦ θεοῦ, 26, 68
γραφή, ἡ, singular denotes unity, 199
δαίμων, 506
δεδικαίωμαι, δεδικαίωται, 851
δεύτερος θεός, applied by Philo to his
    Logos, 320
δεξάμενοι, 1 Thess. 1 : 6, 708
διὰ πίστιν, justification not, but διὰ
    πίστεως or ἐκ πίστεως, 864
διὰ τὸ ἐνοικοῦν and διὰ τοῦ ἐνοικοῦντος,
    Rom. 8 : 11, 488, 1017
διὰ τοῦτο, Rom. 5 : 12, 39
διαθήκην, 614
διακονεῖν τραπέζαις, 918
διακονία, 902, 917
διάκονος, 902
διάβολος, 454
διδακτικόν, 915
διδακτοῖς, 210
διδάσκαλος, 902
διῆλθεν, 623
δίκαιοι κατασταθήσονται, 627
δίκαιος, 291
δικαιοσύνη, 852, 853
δικαιοσύνη Θεοῦ, that required and
    provided for by God, 847, 852, 853
δικαιοσύνην ποιησάτω, 851
δικαιοσύνην, τὴν ἰδίαν, repudiated by Paul, 852
δικαιοσύνη πίστεως, or ἐκ πίστεως, 852
δικαιοσύνης, 753
δικαιόω, 850, 851, 853
δικαιωθέντες, 856
δικαίωμα, 852
δικαίωσις, 852, 853
δίχα, 483
διψᾶν, 151
δοκῶ, 242, 670
δόξῃ, 307, 336

δουλεύω, 576
δοῦλοι, 579
δράκοντα, τόν, ὁ ὄφις, 151
δυνάμεις, 117
δύο, 345
ἑαυτόν, LXX, for Hebrew 'his soul,' 485
ἑαυτούς, 780
ἐγγύς, Phil. 4 : 5, 1006
ἐγένετο, 687
ἔγνων, 781
εἶδον ὄχλος πολύς, 151
εἰκών, 335
εἶναι, τὸ, 377, 753
εἶπεν αὐτῷ, 306
εἷς, 313, 627, 671
εἰς, 935, 948
εἰς and ἐπί, Rom. 3 : 22, 722
εἰς αὐτόν, 837
εἰς ὄνομα, 312
εἰς σέ, 924
εἰς τὸ ὄνομα, 951
εἰς τὸν κόλπον, John 1 : 18, 337
ἐκ, 833, 891
Ἔκδοσις ἀκριβὴς τῆς ὀρθοδόξου πίστεως,
    earliest work on Systematic The-
    ology, 44
ἐκεῖνος, applied to the Holy Spirit, 323
ἐκένωσεν, Phil. 2 : 7, 701
ἐκήρυξεν, 707
ἐκκλησία, 890, 891, 892, 905, 906, 912
ἐκκλησίαν, 308
ἐλευθερίας, 549
ἐληλυθότα, 687
ἐλλογᾶται, 594
ἔν, 313, 352
ἐν, its force with βαπτίζω, 935
ἐν ἀρχῇ, John 1 : 1, 309
ἐν σαρκὶ ἐληλυθότα, 687
ἔνδειξις, Rom. 3 : 25, 753
ἐνοικοῦν, ἐνοικοῦντος, 488, 1017
ἐνυπόστασια, 679
ἔνωσις, 671
ἕνωσις ὑποστατική, 673
ἐξ ἀμόρφου ὕλης, 377
ἐξακολουθέω, 157
ἐξηγήσατο, 349
ἐξιλάσομαι, 729, 737
ἐξ οὐκ ὄντων, ex nihilo, 2 Maccabees 7 : 28, 377
ἐξουσίαν, John 1 : 12, 825
ἐπ' αὐτῷ, 873
ἐπενδύσασθαι, 2 Cor. 5 : 2, 4, 235, 998
ἐπερώτημα, 821
ἐπί, 772, 833
ἐπίγνωσις, 2 Pet. 1 : 12; cf. γνῶσις, 1 Tim.
    6 : 20, 31, ἐπίγνωσις ἁμαρτίας, 832
ἐπιθυμία, state, 552
ἐπίσκοπος, 897, 902, 914, 915
ἐπισκοποῦντες, 914, 915
ἐπιστρέφω, 829
ἐπιταγὴ κυρίου, 221
ἐπιφάνεια, 307
ἐπιχορηγήσατε, 871
ἔργα, 117

ἔργον τοῦ Θεοῦ,........................... 847
ἔρχεται ὥρα, John 5 : 28-30, ... 998
ἐσκήνωσεν, John 1 : 14,............. 234, 687
ἐστίν,........................ 310, 562, 687
ἐτέθην, ... 919
εὐλογητός, Rom. 9 : 5,..................... 306
εὑρεθείς, Phil. 2 : 8, ... 705
ἐφ' ᾧ, Rom. 5 : 12,................... 39, 626
ἐφανερώθη,................................ 308
ἐφθάρη, Gen. 6 : 11, LXX, ... 993
ἔχθρα, state,............................. 552
ἐχθροί, ... 719
ζιζάνια, ... 149
ζωή, ... 311, 626, 1045
ζωογονοῦντος τὰ πάντα,................. 412, 883
ἡγούμενοι,................................ 897
ἦθος ἀνθρώπῳ δαίμων,...................... 506
ἡλάττωσας,............................... 106
ἥμαρτον,.............. 610, 622, 623, 625, 626
ἤν, ... 309, 310
ἠρεμία, rest, summit of Aristotle's"slope" 580
θάνατος,................................. 626
θανατωθείς,.............................. 708
θεῖα, ... 166
θεῖον,.... .... 57, 681
θεῖος ἀνήρ, ... 666
θέλημα, voluntas, Wille,................. 557
θεόπνευστος,......................... 197, 205
θεός,....57, 305, 306, 307, 308, 309, 321, 342, 517
θεοῦ,........................ 731, 781, 847
θηρίον, ... 151
θρήσκεια,................................. 24
θρόνος, ... 307
θυσία,................................... 728
ἱερώτατος,............................... 203
ἱλάσκομαι,............................... 728
ἱλασμός,................................. 728
ἱλαστήριον,.............................. 753
Ἰορδάνην, ... 935
Ἰσαάκ,................................... 517
καθαίρω,................................. 728
καθορᾶται, ... 63
καιρῷ,................................... 753
κακία,................................... 552
καλέω,.............................. 891, 896
καλόν,................................... 870
κανών,................................... 145
καρποφορεῖ, ... 393
κατ' οἶκον, Acts 2 : 46,.............. 960, 961
καταβολῆς κόσμου, πρό,..................... 275
κατάρα, ... 761
κατασταθήσονται,.......................... 627
κατεστάθησαν, ... 627
κατέβησαν, ... 935
κατηρτισμένα, Rom. 9 : 23, ... 780
κεντυρίων,................................ 151
κηρύσσειν, 1 Pet. 3 : 18-20, ... 707
κλῆρος,................................... 911
κοινωνία, 1 Cor. 10 : 16, 17; 1 John 1 : 3,
.... 798, 807, 965
κολαζομένους, 2 Pet. 2 : 9,............... 1000
κόλασις, Mat. 25 : 46; 1 John 4 : 18,.......1036
κόλπῳ,................................... 337

κόσμος, ... 568
κόσμος νοητός,............................ 320
κόσμου, ... 275
κτίσεως,................................. 341
κτίσις, creatura,........................ 392
κτίστης, οὐ τεχνίτης,................. 388
κυβερνήσεις, 1 Cor. 12 : 28,............ 902, 917
κυριακή, Kirche, kirk, church, ... 891
κυριευόντων,.. 445
Κύριος,............................... 306, 309
κυρίου,.................................. 308
Κυρίου Πνεύματος, 2 Cor. 3 : 18, ... 315
λαβών, Phil. 2 : 7,...................... 705
λελουμένοι,.............................. 936
λόγια,................................... 148
Λογίων κυριακῶν ἐξήγησις, ... 149
λογισθείη,............................... 594
λόγος, 2, 305, 306, 321, 335, 342, 549, 665,
.... 687, 700
Λόγος κατηχητικὸς ὁ μέγας, by Gregory of
Nyssa, ... 44
λόγος σπερματικός, ... 665
λόγος σοφίας,............................. 200
λόγος τέλειος, ... 549
λόγου Θείου τινός, ... 111
λούω, ... 936
λύπη κατὰ Θεόν, ... 832
λύπη τοῦ κόσμου,.......................... 832
λύτρον,.......................... 717, 720, 721
μέγας θεός, ὁ,........................... 57
μεσίτης,................................. 710
μεταβολή,................................ 672
μεταμέλεια, ... 833
μεταμέλομαι,............................. 832
μετάνοια,................................ 833
μὴ γνόντα ἁμαρτίαν,...................... 761
μὴ ὄντος, ... 37."
μόνη ἀρχή, ... 327
μονογενής,............................... 336
μονογενὴς Θεός, variant in John 1 : 18, 306, 341
μορφῇ Θεοῦ, Phil. 2 : 6,.................. 705
μορφὴν δούλου, ... 705
μύθοις,.................................. 157
μυστήριον,............................... 691
μύω,.................................... 31
Μωσῆς ἀττικίζων, ... 665
νεανίσκοι,............................... 918
νεκροῦ,.................................. 934
νέμω,.................................... 533
νεώτεροι,................................ 918
νόμος,.............................. 533, 541
νόμος τέλειος, Jas. 1 : 25,............... 549
νοσῶν,................................... 39
νοούμενα, Rom. 1 : 19-21, ... 68
νοῦς,.............. 33, 68, 352, 394, 670, 671
νῦν ἐστίν,............................... 998
ὁ, in John 1 : 1 and 4 : 24,.............. 305
ὁδηγεῖν, ... 151
οἱ πάντες, 2 Cor. 5 : 14,................. 623
οἱ πολλοί, Rom. 5 : 18, ... 627
οἶδεν, ... 67
οἰκεῖ, ... 562
οἰκία, ... 961

οἶκος, _____ 960, 961
ὁμοιούσιον and ὁμοούσιον, _____ 329, 336, 700
ὁμοιώματι σαρκὸς ἁμαρτίας, ἐν, _____ 706
ἐμοίως, _____ 626
ὃν τρόπον, Acts 1 : 11, _____1004
ὄνομα, _____ 951
ὀργή, Rom. 1 : 18, _____ 26
ὁρισθέντος, _____ 341
ὀρθῶς προσενέγκῃς, Gen. 4 : 7, _____ 727
ὅτι οἶδεν, _____ 67
οὐ τάξει, _____ 149
οὐδὲν ἐμαυτῷ σύνοιδα, _____ 851
οὐδέποτε, _____ 781
οὐρανός, _____ 309
οὐρανῷ, _____ 681, 686, 697
οὐσία, _____ 333, 578, 673
οὕτως, Rom. 5 : 12, _____ 626
παῖς, _____ 697
πᾶν, τό, _____ 102, 392
πάντα, τά, _____ 102
πάντα δι᾽ αὐτοῦ ἐγένετο, _____ 311
πάντας, _____ 772
πάντες ἥμαρτον, Rom. 5 : 12, _____ 622, 623, 626
παρά, _____ 337, 341
παραβαίνων, _____ 614
παραθήκην, _____ 149, 882
παρακαλῶ, _____ 914
παράκλητος, _____ 328, 339, 710
παρακοή, Rom. 5 : 19, _____ 627
πάρεσις, _____ 753
παρρησία, _____ 808
πατήρ, _____ 448
πατριά, _____ 334, 448
πεινᾶν, _____ 151
πεπίστευκας, _____ 306
περί, _____ 210, 714. 833
Περὶ Ἀρχῶν. of Origen, _____ 44, 489
Περὶ τοῦ Πυθαγορικοῦ βίου, of Iamblicus, 111
περιπατεῖν, _____ 151
περιχώρησις, _____ 333
Πέτρῳ, _____ 149
πεφυκός, _____ 580
πιστεύοντας, _____ 772
πιστεύω, _____ 838
πίστεως, _____ 753, 847, 864, 870
πίστις, _____ 838, 851
πλήρωμα, _____ 348, 796
πνεῦμα, 213, 323, 483-488, 490, 491, 562,
_____670, 671, 686, 687, 688, 707, 1017
πνεύματι, _____ 708
πνευματικόν, _____1017
πνεύματος, _____ 210
ποιεῖν, _____ 151
ποιήμασιν, τοῖς, _____ 68
ποιμαίνειν, _____ 151, 914
ποιμάνατε, _____ 914
ποιμένας, _____ 902
ποιμήν, εἰς, _____ 914
ποίμνη, μία, _____ 914
ποίμνιον, _____ 964
ποίνη, _____ 652
πόλις, _____ 337, 900
πολλοί, _____ 627

πολλούς, _____ 627
πολλῶν, _____ 717, 720
πολυμερῶς, _____ 221
πολυτροπῶς, _____ 214
πονηρία, _____ 552
πρασιαὶ πρασιαί, _____ 151
πρεσβύτερος, _____ 914, 915
προγινώσκω, _____ 781
προέγνω, _____ 781
προέθετο, _____ 753
προϊστάμενος, _____ 897, 902
πρός, John 1 : 1, _____ 337
προσενέγκῃς, _____ 727
προσενεχθείς, _____ 967
προστάτης, _____ 897
προσφορά, _____ 728
πρόσωπον, _____ 333, 673
προφήτης, _____ 710
πρωτότοκος, _____ 341
ῥαντίσωνται, variant in Mark 7 : 4, _____ 934
ῥαντισμός, _____ 937
σάρκα, _____ 307
σαρκί, _____ 562, 687
σαρκός, _____ 687, 706
σάρξ, _____ 552, 562, 563, 687
σέ, _____ 924
σεσοφισμένοις, _____ 157
σημεῖον, _____ 11;
σκηνοῦν ἐν, _____ 151
σοφίζειν, _____ 157
σπεκουλάτωρ, _____ 151
σπερματικός, _____ 665
σπερμάτων, _____ 233
σύγχυσις, _____ 672
συμβάλλειν, _____ 42
συμπάσκομεν, _____ 803
συμπεφυκώς, _____ 941
συμπρεσβύτερος, _____ 914
σύμφυτος, _____ 796, 941
συμφωνήθη, συμφωνήσωσιν, _____ 927
σὺν Χριστῷ εἶναι, _____ 999
συνάφεια, _____ 671
συνδοξασθῶμεν, _____ 803
συνεζωοποίησεν, _____ 803
συνειδήσεως ἀγαθῆς ἐπερώτημα, _____ 821
συνεσταύρωμαι, _____ 803
συνετάφημεν, _____ 803
συνηγέρθητε, _____ 803
συντέλεια, Mat. 13 : 39, _____1025
σχολή, _____ 38
σῶμα, _____ 484, 487, 671, 1019
σώματος τοῦ Χριστοῦ, _____ 965
σῶσαι and σωθῆναι, _____ 791
σωτῆρος ἡμῶν, _____ 307
σώφρων, 1 Tim. 3 : 2, _____ 39
τάξει, _____ 149
τάσσω, _____ 780
τέλειος, _____ 879
τέλος, _____ 675
τέμνω, _____ 483, 484
τέρατα, _____ 117
τεταγμένοι, Acts 13 : 48, _____ 780
τετραχηλισμένα, _____ 233

τεχνίτης, ... 388
τιμή, ... 717
τὸ γνωστὸν τοῦ Θεοῦ, ... 26
τὸ δὲ καθ᾽ εἷς, τὸ δὲ καθ᾽ ἕνα, ... 151
τοῦ διδόντος Θεοῦ, ... 265, 440
τοῦτο, ... 781
τραπέζαις, ... 918
τρίχα, ... 484
τρόπον, ...1005
ὕβρις, ... 569
ὑγιής, ... 39
ὕδατα, ὕδατος, ... 935
ὕδωρ, ... 935
υἱόν, ... 307
υἱοθεσία, ... 335
ὕλη, ... 321, 378, 700
ὑπακοή, ... 627
ὑπακοή πίστεως, ... 847
ὑπέρ, ... 210, 710
ὑπέρ and ἀντί, ... 717
ὑπερβάλλουσα τῆς γνώσεως, ... 31
ὑποστάσεως, ... 336
ὑπόστασις, ... 333, 673
ὑποστατική, ... 673
ὕστερον Πέτρῳ, ... 149

ὑστεροῦνται, ... 623
φανέρωσις, Rom. 1 : 19, 20, ... 13
φερόμενοι, 2 Pet. 1 : 21, ... 205
φθείρω, ... 993
φιλέω, ... 264
φυλακῇ, ἐν, ... 999
φύσις, natura, ... 392, 579
χαρακτήρ, Heb. 1 : 3, ... 336
χάριν ἀντὶ χάριτος, ... 256
χάρις and ὀργή, ... 26
χειροτονήσαντες, ... 906, 907
Χριστός, ...1016
Χριστοῦ, ... 965
χρόνος and αἰών, ...1045
χωρίς, ... 311, 731
ψυχαί, ... 485
ψυχή, 352, 385, 483-487, 490, 491, 671, 717, 1017
ψυχικοί, ... 485
ψυχικόν, ...1017
ὦν, ... 349, 681, 686, 697
ὥρα, ... 998
ὡρισμένος, Acts 10 : 42, ... 780
ὡς ἄνθρωπος, ... 614
ὤψ, ... 464

INDEX OF HEBREW WORDS.

א, Codex Sinaiticus,......306, 308, 449, 681, 686, 697, 851, 891, 915, 934.

אֶבְיוֹן, 'poor,' whence term 'Ebionite,'.. 669

אָדָם, Hos. 6:7, כְּאָדָם, ὡς ἄνθρωπος LXX, "like men that break a covenant," 614

אֲדֹנָי,... 309

אֶהְיֶה, Exod. 3:14, I am,..............252, 257

אֵל, a singular noun, might have been used instead of אֱלֹהִים,............. 318

אָלָה, to fear, to adore, root of אֱלֹהִים, 318

אֱלֹהִים,.............. 318
  employed with singular verb,....... 318
  applied to Son,........................ 318
  not a *pluralis majestaticus*,........... 318
  according to Oehler, "a quantitative plural,".............................. 318
  its derivation,........................ 318

בָּרָא, implies production of effect without natural antecedent,............. 375
  in Kal used only of God,............. 375
  never has accusative of material,... 375
  used, in Gen. 1 and 2, to mark introduction of world of matter, life, and spirit, ... 374
  distinguished from words signifying 'to make' and 'to form,'...... 375
  in Gen. 1:2, must mean 'calling into being,' 375
  the original signification 'to cut.' though retained in Piel, does not militate against a more spiritual sense in other species,............. 376
  the only word for absolute creation in Hebrew, ... 376
  the meaning 'creation by law' suggested,.................... 392

דְּמוּת, 'the likeness of God,' according to Moehler : 'the pious exercise of צֶלֶם, the religious faculty,'........ 52
  according to Romanist theologians, a product of man's obedience,.... 524
  a synonym of צֶלֶם,.................... 521

זֶרַע, "seed," Gen. 22:18, referred to in Gal. 3:16,.................... 231

חָטָא, ἁμαρτάνω, Hiphil, to make a miss, Judges 20:16,......................... 552

חֲטָאָה, ἁμαρτία, missing, failure, applicable not merely to act but likewise to state,.................... 552

יְהֹוָה,.............................. 30(

יוֹם, 'day,' Gen. 1, ... 38
  its hyperliteral interpretation,....... 394
  often used for a period of indefinite duration, ... 394
  theory that 'six days' indicates series merely,..................... 395
  a scheme harmonizing the Mosaic 'six days' creation with the order of the geologic record,......... 393–397

יָצַר,..................................... 371

כְּרוּבִים, Ez. 1, Ex. 37:6-9, Gen. 3:24,...... 449
  to be identified with the 'seraphim' and 'the living creatures,'.......... 449
  are temporary symbolic figures,.... 449
  symbols of human nature spiritualized and sanctified,.................. 449
  exalted to be the dwelling-place of God, ... 449
  symbols of mercy,..................... 449
  angels and cherubim never together,................................. 449

כְּרוּבִים (continued),

  in closing visions of Revelation no
    longer seen, ... 449
  some regard them as symbols of
    divine government, ... 449
  list of authorities on, ... 449

כְּתִיב, ... 309

מַלְאַךְ יְהֹוָה, identifies himself with Je-
    hovah, ... 319
  is so identified by others, ... 319
  accepts divine worship, ... 319
  with perhaps single exception in
    O. T., designates pre-incarnate Lo-
    gos, ... 319

עָוֹן, ἀδικία LXX, bending, perverseness,
    iniquity, referring to state as well
    as act, ... 552

עָשָׂה, ... 375

פָּקַד, judicial visitation, punishment, ... 657

פֶּשַׁע, ἀσέβεια LXX, separation from, re-
    bellion, indicative of state as well
    as act, ... 552

צֶלֶם, Gen. 1:26, according to Moehler,
    ' the religious faculty,' 522
  according to Bellarmine, 'ipsa natu-
    ra mentis et voluntatis' 522

צֶלֶם (continued),

  according to Scholastic and Roman-
    ist theologians, alone belonged to
    man's nature at its creation, ... 520
  required addition of supernatural
    grace that it might possess original
    righteousness, ... 520
  a synonym of דְּמוּת, ... 521

צָדַק, Hiphil form in Dan. 12:3, best ren-
    dered ' they that justify many,' ... 856

קָהָל, its meaning in O. T. and Targums, 892
  perhaps used by Christ in Mat. 18:17, 892
  how it differs from ἐκκλησία, ... 892

קְרִי, ... 309

רַע, bad, evil, ... 552

רָשָׁע, a wicked person, ... 552

שָׁאַל, an alleged root of Sheol, ... 994

שָׁעַל, a probable root of Sheol, ... 994

שֹׁל, ... 994

שְׁאוֹל, its derivation, ... 994
  its root-meaning, ... 994
  the soul is still conscious in, ... 994
  God can recover men from, ... 994

שְׂרָפִים, Is. 6:2, to be identified with the
    ' cherubim ' of Genesis, Exodus
    and Ezekiel, and with ' the living
    creatures ' of Revelation, ... 449